CW00548540

The ABC
Alphabetical Railway Guide
July 1923

The ABC
Alphabetical Railway Guide
July 1923

A new edition of the
July 1923 ABC Railway Guide
including a selection of advertisements
in hardback format

With introduction by
David St John Thomas

David & Charles
Newton Abbot   London   North Pomfret (Vt)

This is the first hardback edition
of an *ABC Alphabetical Railway Guide*
the issue for July 1923

This edition first published 1986

British Library Cataloguing in Publication Data

The ABC alphabetical railway guide, July 1923.
—New ed. . . . including a selection of
advertisements
1. Railroads—Great Britain—Time-tables
—History—20th century
I. The ABC or alphabetical railway guide
385'.2'0941   HE3014

ISBN 0-7153-8909-2

Introduction © David St John Thomas 1986

Printed in Great Britain
by Butler & Tanner Limited   Frome and London
for David & Charles Publishers plc
Brunel House   Newton Abbot   Devon

Published in the United States of America
by David & Charles Inc
North Pomfret   Vermont 05053   USA

INTRODUCTION

IMAGINE yourself a business with a penchant for exploration and an eye for a travel bargain when our railways were at their peak: you will quickly enjoy vicarious journeys with the aid of this reprint of one of the first issues of *The ABC Alphabetical Railway Guide* to be published after the 1923 'Grouping'. Although most of the references (mainly in advertisements) have been changed from the numerous old companies into the 'Big Four' that came into existence in January 1923, there had not yet been time to start eradicating some of the needless duplication. So Euston, Marylebone, St Pancras and King's Cross all offered services to many northern cities, including Manchester, the fare set by the shortest. You will, of course, discover that some of the alternatives were slow, not to mention inconvenient, but you will also be surprised on occasion. For example, if you left London at nine in the morning, you would get to Bridgwater in Somerset two minutes quicker from Waterloo via Templecombe than from Paddington . . . but then one of the purposes of reading the *ABC* is to remind ourselves of aspects of railway history, and Bridgwater rejoiced more when it received its second railway – competition was the theme of the age – than when the very first engine steamed in carrying man faster than the speed of a horse.

Devotees of that other timetable, *Bradshaw*, were apt to regard those who relied on the *ABC* – a relative upstart having only got going in 1853 – as somewhat lazy. Only the times to and from London are given, and though large numbers of journeys from one part of provincial Britain to another were inevitably through the capital, the *ABC* cheerfully ignored the rich variety of cross-country

services. It also posed almost more questions than it answered, and in a tight corner I would have to admit that it would not be my choice for a desert island. Yet it does wonderfully sharpen the railway historian's mind and study of its pages should do much to entertain and inform today's enthusiast who is not spoilt for choice of route.

The enjoyment of the *ABC* is not just about alternative routes, fascinating though the headings 'ANOTHER ROUTE' are. Great Western fans might note how very many destinations were served by some time-honoured trains from Paddington, such as the 7.30 in the morning which seemed to take people to pretty well everywhere in the southern half of its system – and even crops up in the London local timetables (always a valuable supplement of the *ABC*) since its first stop was at Ealing Broadway. Those interested in forgotten railways will note the excellent services that were provided to places such as Hunstanton, and it is not difficult to discover quicker 1923 services to or from London for many places that are still served by trains. Who would not be happier with Lowestoft's service then than that offered today? And those who look into the details in Scotland will discover that 'No through fares' from London still applied to some of the not-so-remote places as well as far-away ones.

The map and the advertisements, a selection of which are included in this facsimile reprint, show how confident our railways were in their prime, few of the scars of war showing here. The Southern Belle is claimed to be 'The most Luxurious Train in the World', almost all journeys to the Continent involve leaving London by train, while the Midland Grand Hotel at St Pancras beckons us with comfort, and we can travel by Salter's Pleasure Steamers from Oxford to Kingston for 15s (75p)! There are more uses for the *ABC* than first meet the eye; I have long used its population figures as a hand reference source, more convenient than the censuses themselves, for example, and in total the information given for each town or resort conjures up quite a portrait. Enjoy it!

DAVID ST JOHN THOMAS

No. 838.   JULY,   2s. net.
1923.

ESTABLISHED 1853.

THE
A B C
OR
ALPHABETICAL
RAILWAY GUIDE

DISTANCES FROM LONDON, FARES TO EVERY STATION
WHERE THROUGH TICKETS ARE ISSUED, AND POPULA-
TIONS REVISED AS FINAL CENSUS REPORTS ARE ISSUED.

SPECIAL NOTICE.

THIS ISSUE IS REVISED FROM
JULY 9th.

PARTICULARS OF OVER TWO THOUSAND PRINCIPAL HOTELS AND
BOARDING ESTABLISHMENTS IN ENGLAND, SCOTLAND, AND WALES.

THE PROPRIETORS DO NOT GUARANTEE THE ACCURACY OF THE INFORMATION CONTAINED IN
THIS GUIDE, OR UNDERTAKE ANY RESPONSIBILITY FOR ERRORS OR OMISSIONS OR THEIR
CONSEQUENCES. IT SHOULD ALSO BE UNDERSTOOD THAT THE SEVERAL COMPANIES DO NOT
GUARANTEE THE ARRIVAL OR DEPARTURE OF THE TRAINS OR BOATS AT THE TIMES STATED.

[Entered at Stationers' Hall.]

OFFICES: 15, FETTER LANE, FLEET STREET, LONDON, E.C. 4.
Telephone, Holborn 1125.   *Telegraphic Address,* "Absey Guide, London."

Via

NEWHAVEN, DIEPPE,

and the direct PONTOISE route to

PARIS and ALL PARTS of the CONTINENT

TWO EXPRESS SERVICES DAILY.

From LONDON.		1 & 2	1,2 &3	From PARIS.		1 & 2	1,2 &3
VICTORIA (L.B. & S.C.)	dep.	10. 0	20.20	PARIS (Lyon)	dep.	9.28	—
NEWHAVEN HAR.	,,	11.45*	22.15*	PARIS (St. Lazare)	,,	10.36	21.05
DIEPPE	arr.	14.55	2.15	DIEPPE	,,	13.30*	1.20*
PARIS (St. Lazare)	,,	17.58	6.00	NEWHAVEN HAR.	arr.	16.40	5. 0
PARIS (Lyon)	,,	19.20	—	VICTORIA (L.B. & S.C.)	,,	18.40†	7.25

* Up to 15 minutes earlier when possible.   † To July 8th Weekdays arrive 18.55.
The times given above are shown as Summer Time in England and France.

24-25-Knot Turbine Steamers. 1st and 2nd class Pullman Cars in England. Corridor Lavatory and Restaurant Cars Dieppe and Paris (St. Lazare), and Through Carriage Dieppe and Paris-Lyon (by Day) Couchette Compartments (by Night) in France. Through bookings from London to France, Switzerland, Italy, Spain, &c. Baggage booked through.

EXCURSIONS 1/15 day to Dieppe, Rouen, and Paris, July 12th, 13th and 14th (Passports required).

Every Friday and Saturday Week-ends to DIEPPE (without Passport)
(For particulars, see handbills.)

THE SOUTHERN RAILWAY

Now maintains the following Routes :—

DOVER–CALAIS	NEWHAVEN–DIEPPE
FOLKESTONE–BOULOGNE	SOUTHAMPTON–ST. MALO
DOVER–BOULOGNE	SOUTHAMPTON–CHERBOURG
DOVER–OSTEND	SOUTHAMPTON–HAVRE
GRAVESEND–ROTTERDAM	FOLKESTONE–FLUSHING

For full particulars, apply to :—
S.E. & C. SECTION.—Continental Traffic Department, Victoria Station (S.E. & C.), S.W.1.
BRIGHTON SECTION.—Continental Traffic Agent, Victoria Station (L.B. & S.C.), S.W.1.
SOUTH WESTERN SECTION.—Continental Enquiry Office, Waterloo Station, S.E. 1.

Printed for the Proprietors by WM. CLOWES AND SONS, Ltd., Duke Street, S.E.1.
All communications to be addressed THE A

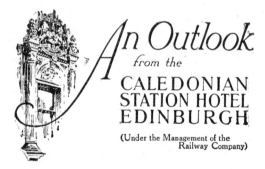

An Outlook
from the
CALEDONIAN
STATION HOTEL
EDINBURGH
(Under the Management of the
Railway Company)

*Showing the Castle, Princes St.
and Gardens*

Illustrated Souvenir on application to Hotel Manager

GLASGOW.

Sᴛ. ENOCH STATION
HOTEL

THIS HOTEL, one of the finest and largest Hotels in Scotland, **is within Cab Fare of all Railway and Steamboat termini in Glasgow,** and is conveniently situated for both business and the many delightful Tours to the Western Highlands, Ayr, Loch Lomond, &c. Particulars of these can be obtained from the Hall Porter. There are Passenger and Luggage Lifts, Electric Light, Lounge, Drawing, Writing, Billiard (four tables), and Smoking Rooms, &c. Suites of Rooms including Bath Room.

RESTAURANT AND GRILL ROOM

is on the Ground Floor, and is
open from noon to 9.0 p.m. daily.

J. H. THOMAS, *Manager.*

Sᴛ. Eɴᴏᴄʜ Hᴏᴛᴇʟ, Gʟᴀsɢᴏᴡ.

Telegrams: "SOUWESTERN, GLASGOW."

THE

A B C

OR

ALPHABETICAL RAILWAY GUIDE

JULY, 1923.

NOTE.—The Proprietors do not guarantee the accuracy of the information contained in this Guide, or undertake any responsibility for errors or omissions or their consequences. It should also be understood that the several Companies do not guarantee the arrival or departure of the trains or boats at the times stated.

REFERENCE NOTES.

a	signifies	First Class.
b	,,	Second Class.
c	,,	Third Class.
d	,,	On Saturdays only.
e	,,	Saturdays excepted.
f	,,	On Mondays only.
g	,,	Mondays excepted.
r	,,	Restaurant Car.
t	,,	Tea Car.
x	,,	Express.
R.T.	,,	Return Tickets.

All Trains in the Tables not otherwise marked carry Third Class Passengers.

ABBEY (Norfolk) from *Liverpool Street* 88¼ miles. No through fares. Departures *from* London as for Stoke Ferry. Departures *for* London about 4 times daily. *Map Square* 19.

ABBEYDORE (Hereford), from *Paddington*, 156¾ miles. Fares, 32/9*a*, 19/8*c*. R.T. for two months, 65/6*a*, 39/4*c*. Pop. 470. *Map Square* 17.

PAD.	A'DORE.	A'DORE.	PAD.
AM 1. 0*gl* 8.51	AM 8.19*hr*	2.3)
5.30*k* 1.36	11.40*k*	4.15
11.50*lr* 5.25	PM 4.20*l*	9.25
—	6.30*l*	3.30

Sunday Trains.

PM 9.15*l*	8.51	—	—

g Mondays excepted.
h Wednesdays only.
k Via Worcester.
l Via Newport.
r Restaurant Car.

ABBEY TOWN (Cumberland), 316¼ miles. No through fares. Departures *from* London as for Carlisle. Departures *for* London about 4 times daily. Pop. 793. *Map Square* 6.

ABBEY WOOD (London) from *Charing Cross*, 12½ miles. Fares, 2/6*a*, 2/0*b*, 1/6*c*. R. T. for two days, 5/0*a*, 3/11*b*, 3/0*c*. From *Cannon Street*. Fares, 2/3*a*, 1/9*b*, 1/4*c*. R. T. for two days, 4.6*a*, 3/6*b*, 2/8*c*. *See pp.* 547-551.

ABBOTSBURY (Dorset) from *Paddington*, 158¾ miles. Fares, 39/1*a*, 18/4*c*. R. T. for two months, 60/2*a*, 36/8*c*. Pop. 664. *Map Square* 27.

PAD.	AB'BURY	AB'BURY	PAD.
AM 1. 0*g* 10.54	AM 8.15	12.55
10.30 3.14	10.58	3.50
PM12.50*r* 5.14	PM 3.20	8.20
3.30 9.14	5.20	2.45
5. 5*d* 11.24	7.40*h*	2.45
—	—	—

No Sunday Trains.

d Saturdays only.
g Mondays excepted.
h Thursdays and Third Class only.
r Restaurant Car.

ABBOTTS RIPTON (Hunts) from *King's Cross*, 63¾ miles. Fares, 13/2*a*, 7/11*c*. R. T. for two months, 26/4*a*, 15/10*c*. Departures *from* London as for Holme. Departures *for* London about 4 times daily. Pop. 379. *Map Square* 18.

ABER (Carnarvon) from *Euston*, 233¾ miles. Fares, 48/7*a*, 29/2*c*. R.T. for two months, 97/2*a*, 58/4*c*. Departures *from* London as for Llanfairfechan. Departures *for* London about 4 times daily. Pop. 400. *Map Square* 11.

ABERAMAN (Glamorgan), 175 miles. Fares, 35/3*a*, 21/2*c*. R. T. for two months, 70.6*a*, 42/4*c*. Departures *from* London as for Mountain Ash. Departures *for* London about 4 times daily. Pop. 15,090. *Map Square* 21.

ABERANGELL (Merioneth), 217¾ miles. No through fares. Departures *from* London as for Dinas Mawddwy. Departures *for* London about 3 times daily.

ABERAVON (Sea Side) (Glamorgan), 186¾ miles. No through fares. Departures *from* London as for Port Talbot. Departures *for* London about 4 times daily. Pop. 15,370. *Map Square* 21.

ABERAYRON (Cardigan), 264 miles. Fares, 50/5*a*, 30/11*c*. R.T. for two months,100/10*a*,61/10*c*. Departures *from* London as for Lampeter. Departures *for* London about thrice daily. Pop. 1,313. *Map Square* 16.

ABERBEEG (Monmouth) from *Paddington*, 156 miles. Fares, 32/6*a*, 19/6*c*. R. T. for two months, 65/0*a*, 39/0*c*. *Map Square* 21.

PAD.	ABERB'G.	ABERB'G.	PAD.
AM 1. 0*g* 6.21	AM 6.27*r*	10.57
5.30 11.38	9.45*r*	1. 0
8.45*r* 12.48	10.41*r*	2.30
9. 0 2.57	11.46*r*	4.20
11.50*r* 4.42	PM 2.22*r*	6.15
PM 1.10*r* 6. 1	3.38*r*	8.35
3.35*r* 7.30	5.35*r*	9.25
5. 0*r* 9.25	9.26	3.30
6. 0*r* 10.32	—	—
6.30*r* 11.28	—	—
8. 0*d*11.59	—	—
9.15*e* 5.39	—	—

Sunday Trains.

AM 1. 0	10.16	AM 8. 7	3.35
9.10	2.44	PM 3.56*r*	8.25
PM12.30*r*	6.24	7.33	3.30
4.30	9.44	—	—
9.15	5.39	—	—

d Saturdays only.
e Saturdays excepted.
g Mondays excepted.
r Restaurant Car.

ABERBRAN (Brecon), 187¼ miles. Fares, 38/11*a*, 23/4*c*. R. T. for two months, 77.10*a*, 46/8*c*. Departures *from* London as for Brecon. Departures *for* London about twice daily. *Map Square* 16.

ABERCAIRNY (Perth), 447¼ miles. No through fares. Departures *from* London as for Perth. Departures *for* London about twice daily. Pop. 217. *Map Square* 37.

ABERCANAID (Glamorgan), 170¾ miles. Fares, 35/2*a*, 21/1*c*. R. T. for two months, 70/4*a*, 42/2*c*. Departures *from* London as for Merthyr (*via* Pontypool Road). Departures *for* London about 3 times daily.

ABERCARN (Monmouth) from *Paddington*, 151 miles. Fares, 31/6*a*, 18/11*c*. R. T. for two months, 63/0*a*, 37/10*c*. Departures *from* London as for Risca. Departures *for* London about 8 times daily. Pop. 20,123.
Map Square 21.

ABERCHALDER (Inverness), 535¾ miles. No through fares. Departures *from* London as for Fort William. Departures *for* London about twice daily.
Map Square 37.

ABERCRAVE (Brecon), 206½ miles. No through fares. Departures *from* London as for Neath or Brecon. Departures *for* London about 4 times daily.

ABERCYNON (Glamorgan), 168½ miles. Fares, 34/0*a*, 20/5*c*. R.T. for two months, 68/0*a*, 40/10*c*. Departures *from* London as for Pontypridd. Departures *for* London about 3 times daily. Pop. 9,109.
Map Square 21.

ABERDARE (Glamorgan) from *Paddington*, 176 miles. Fares, *via* Cardiff, 35/7*a*, 21/4*c*. R. T. for two months, 71/2*a*, 42/8*c*. Pop. 55,010.
Map Square 21.

	Pad.	Aberd.		Aberd.	Pad.
AM	1. 0*g*	8.58	AM	6.0*hr*	10.57
	5.30	12. 1		8.20*r*	1. 0
	8.45*r*	2.25		10.15*r*	4.20
	11.50*r*	4.14	PM	12.45*r*	6.15
PM	1.10*r*	6.54		3.50*r*	8.35
	3.35*r*	9. 5		4.35*hr*	9.25
	6. 0*r*	11. 0		9. 3	3.30
	9.15*eh*	6.54		—	—
	—	—		—	—

Sunday Trains.

AM	1. 0	9.27	AM	8.10	3.35
PM	12.30*r*	5.45		11.30*r*	8.25
	4.30	10. 8	PM	8.15	3.30
	9.15*h*	6.54		—	—

e Saturdays excepted.
g Mondays excepted.
h Passengers cross Cardiff at own expense.
r Restaurant Car.

ANOTHER ROUTE from *Paddington*, *via* Pontypool Road, 172 miles. Fares, 35/7*a*, 21/4*c*. R. T. for two months, 71/2*a*, 42/8*c*.

	Pad	Aberd.		Aberd.	Pad.
AM	1. 0*g*	8.54	AM	7.55*r*	1. 0
	5.30	12. 8		8.33*r*	2.30
	8.45*r*	2.38	PM	12. 5*r*	4.20
	9. 0	3.36		12.43*r*	6.15
	11.50*hr*	4.58		2.27*r*	8.35
	11.50*r*	6. 3		4.37*r*	9.25
PM	1.10*r*	7.42		6.58	3.30
	3.35*r*	8.52		10. 0*k*	7.10
	6. 0*kr*	10.52		—	—
	8. 0*dr*	9.29		—	—

Sunday Trains.

PM	12.30*r*	8. 4	AM	9.57	8.10
	9.15	8.54	PM	8.15	3.30

d Saturdays only.
g Mondays excepted.
h Fridays only.
k Thursdays and Saturdays only.
r Restaurant Car.

ABERDEEN from *King's Cross*, 522¾ miles. Fares, 100/0*a*, 60/0*c*. R. T. for two months, 200/0*a*, 120/0*c*. Pop. 158,963.
Map Square 38.

	King's +	Abrdn.		Abrdn.	King's +
AM	4.45	5.26	AM	6.15*r*	6.15
	10. 0*r*	10. 5		•9.50*r*	10. 0
PM	8.25*er*	7.30	PM	12.50	3.25
	11.25*dr*	11.11		3.40	6. 0
	11.25*er*	11.19		5.45	7. 5
	—	—		7.35	7.25
	—	—		—	—
	—	—		—	—
	—	—		—	—
	—	—		—	—

Sunday Trains.

PM	7.45*r*	7.30	PM	3.10	6. 0
	11.25	11.19		—	—

d Saturdays only.
e Saturdays excepted
r Restaurant Car.

ANOTHER ROUTE from *Euston*, 539¾ miles. Fares as above.

	Euston	Abrdn.		Abrdn.	Euston
AM	5. 0	9. 5	AM	6.50*r*	7.30*l*
	10. 0*r*	10.17		10. 5*r*	10.45*l*
PM	1.30*r*	3. 0*h*	PM	12.30*r*	5. 0*h*
	7.40*er*	7. 0		7.50	8. 0*h*
	11. 0*d*	11.50*h*		—	—
	11.35*e*	11.40*h*		—	—
	—	—		—	—
	—	—		—	—
	—	—		—	—
	—	—		—	—

Sunday Trains.

PM	7.50*r*	7.40*h*	PM	1.10	5. 0*h*
	11.35	11.40*h*		—	—
	—	—		—	—
	—	—		—	—
	—	—		—	—
	—	—		—	—

d Saturdays only.
e Saturdays excepted.
h A.M. *l* P.M.
r Restaurant Car.

Palace (Railway) Hotel. Patronised by Royal Family. Entrance from platform.
See advt. p. **25**.

Station Hotel. Central Heating. Lift. Garage. Moderate Terms.
See advt. p. **25**.

Grand Hotel. The Hotel de Luxe of the North. Easy access of Royal Deeside.
See advt. p. **25**.

ABERDOUR (Fife), 409¾ miles. Fares, 83/7*a*, 50/2*c*. R. T. for two months, 167/2*a*, 100/4*c*. *See* trains to Inverkeithing. Departures *for* London about 3 times daily. Pop. 3,063.
Map Square 41.

ABERDOVEY (Merioneth) 228¾ miles. Fares, 46/6*a*, 27/11*c*. R. T. for two months, 93/0*a*. Departures *from* London as for Machynlleth. Departures *for* London about 4 times daily. Pop. 1,253.
Map Square 16.

ABERDYLAIS (Glamorgan), 192½ miles. Fares, 39/9*a*, 23/10*c*. R. T., 79/6*a*, 47/8*c*. Departures *from* London as for Neath or Aberdare (*via* Pontypool Road). Departures *for* London about 6 times daily.

ABEREDW (Radnor), 181 miles. Fares from *Paddington*, 37/4*a*, 22/5*c*. R. T. for two months, 74/8*a*. Fares from *Euston*, 37/6*a*, 22/6*c*. R.T. for two months, 75/0*a*. Departures *from* London as for Builth Wells. Departures *for* London about twice daily. Pop. 211.
Map Square 16.

ABERERCH (Carnarvon), 268½ miles. Fares, 54/10*a*, 32/11*c*. R. T. for two months, 109/8*a*. Departures *from* London as for Pwllheli. Departures *for* London about 4 times daily. Pop. 1,102.
Map Square 11.

ABERFAN (Glamorgan), 167¾ miles. Fares, 34/7*a*, 20/9*c*. R. T. for two months, 69/2*a*, 41/6*c*. Departures *from* London as for Merthyr (*via* Pontypool Road). Departures *for* London about 3 times daily.

ABERFELDY (Perth), 482½ miles. Fares, 97/9*a*, 58/8*c*. R. T. for two months, 195/6*a*, 117/4*c*. Departures *from* London as for Dunkeld. Departures *for* London about 3 times daily. Pop. 1,560.
Map Square 37.

ABERFFRWD (Cardigan), 247 miles. No through fares. Departures *from* London as for Aberystwyth. Departures *for* London about 3 times daily.

ABERFOYLE (Perth), 437¾ miles. Fares, 87/8*a*, 52/7*c*. R. T. for two months, 175/4*a*, 105/2*c*. Departures *from* London as for Stirling. Departures *for* London about 3 times daily. Pop. 1,169.
Map Square 40.

ABERGAVENNY (Monmouth) from *Paddington*, 159½ miles. Fares, 33/2*a*, 19/11*c*. R. T. for two months, 66/4*a*, 39/10*c*. Pop. 9,008.
Map Square 22.

	Pad.	Ab'veny.		Ab'veny	Pad.
AM	1. 0*g*	8. 4	AM	9.15*r*	1. 0
	5.30	11.23		9.54*r*	2.30
	8.45*r*	12.15	PM	12.28*dr*	4.20
	9. 0	2.41		12.45*er*	4.20
	11.50*r*	3.20		1.55*r*	6.15
PM	1.10*r*	5.45		3.50*r*	8.35
	3.35*r*	7 22		5.25*r*	9.25
	6. 0*r*	9.52		6.25	2.45
	—	—		9. 1	3.30

Sunday Trains.

AM	1. 0	8.51	PM	9.15	3.30*l*
PM	12.30*r*	7. 0		—	—
	9.15	8. 4		—	—

d Saturdays only.
e Saturdays excepted.
g Mondays excepted.
l A.M.
r Restaurant Car.

Angel Hotel.—Telephone 7. First class. Centre of town. Central Heating, Public Restaurant. Trout and Salmon Fishing.
TRUST HOUSES, Ltd.

ABERGELE (Denbigh)

from *Euston*, 213½ miles. Fares, 44/5a, 26/8c. R.T. for two months, 88/10a, 53/4c. Pop. 2,632.
Map Square 11.

EUSTON	A'GELE.	A'GELE.	EUSTON.
AM 12.25	7.13	AM 7. 8cr12. 5
5. 0	11. 2	7. 8dr12.20
8.30er	2. 4	8. 7dr 1. 0
8.30dr	2.25	8.29er 1. 0
11.10dr	4.10	8.42r 1.45
11.10er	4.17	9.31r 2.20
11.50r	5.47	10.36r 4.15
12. 0nr	6.41	11.10r 5. 5
PM 2.35t	7.29	11.51lr 5. 5
4. 5r	9.15	PM12.38er 6.25
5.20r	10.19	2. 0dr 7.30
11.50d	11.24	2.21er 7.30
—	—	3.40r 9.20
—	—	4.52r 10.45
—	—	9.32 5. 0

Sunday Trains.

| PM12.10r | 7. 5 | AM 8. 7 | 4. 0 |
| — | — | PM 9.48 | 5. 0 |

d Saturdays only.
e Saturdays excepted.
h Fridays and Saturdays only.
n Noon.
r Restaurant Car.
t Tea Car.

ABERGWILI (Carmarthen)

from *Paddington*, 230 miles. Fares, 46/6a, 27/11c. R.T. for two months, 93/0a, 55/10c. Departures *from* London as for Carmarthen or Llandilo. Departures *for* London about 6 times daily. Pop. 1,452.
Map Square 21.

ABERGWYNFI (Glamorgan), 187 miles. Fares, 39/0a, 23/5c. R. T. for two months, 78/0a, 46/10c. Departures *from* London as for Maesteg. Departures *for* London about 5 times daily. Pop. 4,102.

Map Square 16.

ABERGYNOLWYN

(Merioneth), 239 miles. No through fares. Departures *from* London as for Machynlleth. Departures *for* London about 3 times daily.
Map Square 16.

ABERLADY (East Lothian),

379½ miles. Fares, 79/10a, 47/11c. R. T. for two months, 159/8a, 95/10c. Departures *from* London as for Dunbar. Departures *for* London about 4 times daily. Pop. 1,100.
Map Square 41.

ABERLLEFENI (Merioneth), 225½ miles. No through fares. Departures *from* London as for Machynlleth. Departures *for* London about 3 times daily.

Map Square 16.

ABERLOUR (Banff), 569½ miles. Fares, 106/3a, 63/9c. R.T. for two months, 212/6a, 127/6c. Departures *from* London as for Aviemore or Keith (*via* Aberdeen). Departures *for* London about twice daily. Pop. 2,518.

Map Square 35.

ABERMULE (Montgomery), 182 miles. Fares, 38/1a, 22/10c. R. T. for two months, 76/2a. Departures *from* London as for Montgomery. Departures *for* London about 5 times daily.

Map Square 16.

ABERNANT (Glamorgan),

173½ miles. Fares, 36/6a, 21/11c. R. T. for two months, 73/0a, 43/10c. Departures *from* London as for Merthyr. Departures *for* London about 4 times daily.
Map Square 21.

ABERNETHY (Perth),

441½ miles. No through fares. Departures *from* London as for Perth. Departures *for* London about 3 times daily. Pop. 1,282.
Map Square 38.

ABERSYCHAN (Monmouth), from *Paddington*, 152½ miles. Fares, 31/6a, 18/11c. R. T. for two months, 63/0.x, 37/10c. Pop. 27,989.

Map Square 22.

PAD.	AB'SCHN.	AB'SCHN.	PAD.
AM 1. 0g	7.66	AM 6.49r	10.57
5.30	11.24	8.50r	1. 0
8.45dr12.43		PM12. 4r	4.20
8.45r	1.15	1.54r	6.15
11.50r	3.37	3.29r	8.35
PM 1.10r	5.53	4.52r	9.25
3.35r	7.10	9.59	3.30
6. 0r 10.58		—	—
8. 0kr11.41		—	—
9.15e 5.30		—	—
—	—	—	—

Sunday Trains.

AM 1. 0	10. 8	AM 8. 0	3.35
9.10	2.41	PM 3.55r	8.25
PM12.30	6.24	7. 9	3.30
4.30	10. 1	—	—
9.15	5.30	—	—

d Saturdays only.
e Saturdays excepted.
g Mondays excepted.
k Thursdays and Saturdays only.
r Restaurant Car.

ABERTHAW (Glamorgan),

166½ miles. Fares, 34/9a, 20/10c. R. T. for two months, 69/6a, 41/8c. Departures *from* London as for Barry Docks. Departures *for* London about 4 times daily.

ABERTILLERY (Monmouth) from *Paddington*, 158 miles. Fares, 32/11a, 19/9c R.T. for two months, 65/10a, 39/6c. Departures *from* London as for Aberbeeg. Departures *for* London about 5 times daily. Pop. 38,805.

Map Square 21.

ABERTRIDWR (Glamorgan), 156 miles. Fares (*via* Cardiff), 34/0a, 20/5c. R. T. for two months, 68/0a, 40/10c. Departures *from* London as for Caerphilly or Cardiff. Departures *for* London about 4 times daily. Pop. 5,549.

ABERTYSSWG (Monmouth), 163½ miles. Fares, 34/0a, 20/5c. R. T. for two months, 68/0a, 40/10c. Departures *from* London as for Rhymney. Departures *for* London about 7 times daily. Pop. 2,124.

ABERYSTWYTH (Cardigan) from *Paddington*, *via* Welshpool, 239½ miles. Fares, 48/9a, 29/3c. R. T. for two months, 97/6a. Pop. 11,220.

Map Square 16.

PAD.	ABRYST.	ABRYST.	PAD.
AM 6.30	3.25	AM 7.50r	4.15
10.20r	4.15	10.15r	5. 0
10.40r	5.30	12. 0r	6.40
PM 2.10t	9. 0	PM 1. 0r	8. 5
12.15h	11.48	2.30d~10. 0	
12.15k	9.25	6. 0	3.30

No Sunday Trains.

d Saturdays only.
h Saturdays midnight excepted.
k Saturdays midnight only.
r Restaurant Car.
t Tea Car.

ABERYSTWYTH — continued.

ANOTHER ROUTE from *Euston*, 249½ miles. Fares as above.

EUSTON	ABRYST.	ABRYST.	EUSTON.
AM 5. 0	1.40	AM 7.50	3.10
10. 0r	5.30	10.15	6.15
10.40r	6.30	PM 1. 0dr	9.15
PM 1.15r	9. 0	1. 0er	9.20
9.30	6.32	6. 0	5. 0
11. 0d	9.25	—	—

Sunday Trains.

| PM 9:15 | 6.32 | PM 6.10h | 5. 0 |

d Saturdays only.
e Saturdays excepted.
h Via Crewe.
r Restaurant Car.

ANOTHER ROUTE from *Paddington*, *via* Carmarthen and Pencader, 284½ miles. Fares, 48/9a, 29 3c. R. T. for two months, 97/6a, 58/6c.

PAD.	ABRYST.	ABRYST.	PAD.
AM 1. 0g	12.50	AM 7. 0r	4.20
8.45r	3.57	10. 5r	6.15
11.50r	8.30	PM 1.15r	9.25
PM 9.15e	8.38	5. 0	3.30

Sunday Trains.

| PM 9.15 | 8.38 | — | — |

e Saturdays excepted.
g Mondays excepted.
r Restaurant Car.

Queen's Hotel. Leading Hotel. Excellent Cuisine and Wines. Reasonable Tariff. Telephone 93. MANAGER.
See advt. D. **26.**

ABINGDON (Berks) from *Paddington*, *via* Didcot, 61 miles. Fares, 12/9a, 7/8c. R. T. for two months, 25/6a, 15/4c. Fares, *via* Oxford, 13/2a, 7/11c. Pop. 7,167.

Map Square 23.

PAD.	ABING.	ABING.	PAD.
AM 5.30	7.35	AM 6.53	9. 0
6.30	9. 9	8.30	9.50
7.30	10. 7	9.28	12. 0
8.50	10.45	PM12.15	1.50
9. 0	11.53	1. 5	3.20
10.45	12.41	2.43	5. 6
11.20	1.32	4.45	7.20
PM 1.10r	3.32	5.55	8.20
3.18	5.23	6.50r	9.15
3.38	6.35	8.17	10.45
5.15	7.17	9.38	2.45
6. 5r	8. 5	—	—
6.55	9.14	—	—

Sunday Trains.

AM11.45	1.43	PM 4.33	6.20
PM 2. 0	5. 7	7.35	9.48
		8.40	11.38

r Restaurant Car.

Oxford and Kingston Steamers leave Abingdon Bridge for Henley at 11.0 a.m., and for Wallingford at 4.0 p.m. Up stream boats for Oxford at 11.30 a.m. and 5.15 p.m. every Week Day. *See advt.* facing first page of train service.

Queen's Hotel. First-class Residential and Family Hotel. A.A. and R.A.C. Best position. Garage for 13 Cars; Inspection Pit. Private Sitting-rooms. Smoking Lounge. Electric Light every room. Billiard Room. Phone 54. Proprietor—WILL A. WILKS.

For completion of Advertisements, see over.

ABINGDON—*continued.*

Lion Hotel. Principal Family and Commercial. (A.A. and Head-quarters R.A.C.) Renowned reputation. Spacious Coffee Room. Separate Tables. Excellent Cuisine. Lounge. Garage. Inspection pit. Electric light. Telephone 35.
B. S. MAYHEAD,
Resident Proprietor.

Crown and Thistle. Old established and most comfortable Family and Commercial Hotel. Within two minutes of river and station. Reasonable tariff. Garage. Under personal supervision.
V. J. HOEY.

ABINGTON (Lanark), 357 miles. Fares, 72/6*a*, 43/6*c*. R. T. for two months, 145/0*a*, 87/0*c*. Departures *from* London as for Lockerbie. Departures *for* London about 3 times daily.
Map Square 40.

ABOYNE (Aberdeen), 554 miles. Fares, 106/10*a*, 64/1*c*. R.T. for two months, 213/8*a*, 128/2*c*. Departures *from* London as for Ballater. Departures *for* London about 20 minutes later. Pop. 1,542.
Map Square 38.

ABY (Lincoln) 133¾ miles. Fares, 27/9*a*, 16/8*c*. R. T. for two months, 55/6*a*, 33/4*c*. Departures *from* London as for Willoughby. Departures *for* London about 5 times daily. Pop. 253.
Map Square 13.

ACCRINGTON (Lancs) from *Euston*, 208¾ miles. Fares, 43/2*a*, 25/11*c*. R.T. for two months, 86/4*a*, 51/10*c*. Pop. 43,610.
Map Square 12.

	Euston	Accring.		Accring.	Euston.
AM	12.25	6.27	AM	5.58*e*	12. 5
	2.35	9.38		5.58*d*	12.20
	5. 0	11.48		8.22*r*	1.15
	8.45*dr*	2.18		9.12*r*	3.10
	8.45*er*	3. 0		10.34*r*	3.55
	10.40*r*	3.57		11.40*e*	6. 0
	11.5)*er*	5. 5		11.45*dr*	6. 0
	11.50*dr*	5.42		11.55*dr*	6.15
	12. 0*nr*	7.31	PM	12.38*er*	6.15
PM	1.30*kr*	7.56		1.47*kr*	7.30
	2.50*t*	9.10		2.51*er*	9. 5
	4. 5*r*	10.18		2.51*dr*	9.15
	6. 5*r*	11.18		3.10*kr*	9.20
	11.50*d*	10.29		4.28*dr*	10. 0
	—	—		4.28*er*	10.10
	—	—		5. 0*kr*	10.45
	—	—		9.37*k*	5. 0
	—	—		9.57*e*	5.40
	—	—		9.57*d*	5.45

Sunday Trains.

PM	12.10*r*	6.28	AM	7.58	4.40
	12.30*r*	8.19		11. 9*r*	5.45
	—	—	PM	1.40*kr*	7.30
	—	—		8. 5	5. 0
	—	—		—	—
	—	—		—	—

d Saturdays only.
e Saturdays excepted.
k Via Preston.
n Noon.
r Restaurant Car.
t Tea Car.

ACHANALT (Ross), 607¾ miles. Fares, 110/8*a*, 66/5*c*. R.T. for two months, 221/4*a*, 132/10*c*. Departures *from* London as for Kyle of Lochalsh. Departures *for* London about 4 times daily.
Map Square 34.

ACH-NA-CLOICH (Argyle), 494¼ miles. Fares, 101/8*a*, 61/0*c*. R.T. for two months, 203/4*a*, 122/0*c*. Departures *from* London as for Crianlarich. Departures *for* London about 3 times daily.
Map Square 37.

ACHNASHEEN (Ross), 614¼ miles. Fares, 111/11*a*, 67/2*c*. R. T. for two months, 223/10*a*, 134/4*c*. Departures *from* London as for Kyle of Lochalsh. Departures *for* London about 3 times daily.
Map Square 34.

ACHNASHELLACH (Ross), 626¾ miles. Fares, 114/7*a*, 68/9*c*. R. T. for two months, 229/2*a*, 137/6*c*. Departures *from* London as for Kyle of Lochalsh. Departures *for* London about 3 times daily.
Map Square 34.

ACHTERNEED (Ross), 591 miles. Fares, 107/3*a*, 64/4*c*. R.T. for two months, 214/6*a*, 128/8*c*. Departures *from* London as for Kyle of Lochalsh. Departures *for* London about 3 times daily.

ACKLINGTON (Northumberland), 296½ miles. Fares, 62/6*a*, 37/6*c*. R. T. for two months, 125/0*a*, 75/0*c*. Departures *from* London as for Morpeth. Departures *for* London about 3 times daily. Pop. 230.
Map Square 3.

ACKWORTH (Yorks), from *St. Pancras*, 179 miles. Fares, 35/2*a*, 21/1*c*. R. T. for two months, 70/4*a*, 42/2*c*. Pop. 4,183.
Map Square 13.

	St. Pan.	Ackw'h.		Ackw'h.	St. Pan.
AM	2.25*g*	8.11	AM	8.19*r*	1.30
	4.25	10.27		11.37*r*	5.30
	9. 0*r*	2. 2	PM	1.56*r*	7.15
	9.50*dr*	3. 4		3.17*r*	7.55
PM	1.50*r*	6.26		4. 8*dr*	9. 5
	5. 0*r*	9.53		8.12	4.20
	—	—		—	—

No Sunday Trains.

d Saturdays only.
g Mondays excepted.
r Restaurant Car.

ACLE (Norfolk), 124½ miles. Fares, 25/3*a*, 15/2*c*. R. T. for two months, 50/6*a*, 30/4*c*. Departures *from* London as for Brundall. Departures *for* London about 6 times daily. Pop. 942.
Map Square 19.

ACOCK'S GREEN (Worcester) from *Paddington*, 106½ miles. Fares, 22/3*a*, 13/4*c*. R. T. for two months, 44/6*a*, 26/8*c*. Pop. 24,465.
Map Square 17.

	Pad.	Acks. G.		Acks. G.	Pad.
AM	5.30	10.18	AM	7.16*r*	10. 0
	6.30	11.52		8.23*r*	11. 0
	10.40	1.44		10.30*r*	1.25
PM	12.50*r*	4.27		11.33*r*	2. 5
	2.10	5.15	PM	1.30*er*	5. 0
	4.10*t*	6.44		1.45*dr*	5. 0
	6.10*r*	8.42		3.20*t*	5.55
	7.10*r*	9.40		5.25*r*	8. 5
	7.30	10.52		7. 4	10. 0
	12.15*k*	8.33		11.32	3.30
	12.15*l*	9.55		—	—

ACOCK'S GREEN—*con.*

Sunday Trains.

	Pad.	Acks. G.		Acks. G.	Pad.
AM	10.35	2.20	AM	10.46*r*	1.40
PM	6. 0	9. 4	PM	2. 1	6.20
	—	—		6.15*r*	9. 0
	—	—		—	—

d Saturdays only.
e Saturdays excepted.
k Saturdays midnight excepted.
l Saturdays midnight only.
r Restaurant Car.
t Tea Car.

ACREFAIR (Denbigh), 178¾ miles. Fares, 37/6*a*, 22/6*c*. R. T. for two months, 75/0*a*, 45/0*c*. Departures *from* London as for Llangollen. Departures *for* London about 4 times daily.
Map Square 12.

ACTON (Middlesex), 4¼ miles. Fares from *Paddington*, 0/10*a*, 0/6*c*. R. T. for two days, 1/6*a*, 0/9*c*. Pop. 61,299. *See* pp. 491-493.
Map Squares 23 *and* 58.

ANOTHER ROUTE from *Broad Street*, 12½ miles. Fares, 0/11½*a*, 0/7½*c*. R. T. for two days, 1/11*a*, 1/2*c*. *See* pp. 501-505.

ACTON EAST (Central London Tube). *See* back of Map.

ACTON SOUTH from *Broad Street*, 12½ miles. Fares, 0/11½*a*, 0/7½*c*. R. T. for two days, 1/11*a*, 1/2*c*. *See* pp. 501-505.
Map Square 67

ACTON TOWN from *Mansion House*, 9½ miles. Also to and from Ealing and Hounslow. *See* p. 489.
Map Square 58.

ACTON BRIDGE (Cheshire). From *Euston*, 172½ miles. Fares, 36/0*a*, 21/7*c*. R. T. for two months, 72/0*a*, 43/2*c*. Pop. 533.
Map Square 12.

	Euston	Acton B.		Acton B.	Euston.
AM	2.35	6.40	AM	8.28*er*	12. 5
	5. 0	9.49		8.28*dr*	12.20
	6.45	11.45		9. 2*r*	1. 0
	8.30*r*	12.33		10.39*r*	3.10
	11.50*r*	3.35	PM	1.53*r*	5.50
PM	1.30*r*	5.41		3.25*er*	7.30
	2.35*t*	6.15		5.24*er*	9. 5
	5.20*r*	9.26		5.24*dr*	9.15
	11.50*d*	8. 1		6.11*r*	10. 0
	—	—		8. 2*e*	5. 0
	—	—		10.43*d*	5. 0

Sunday Trains.

	—	—	AM	10.51	4. 0
	—	—		—	—
	—	—		—	—

d Saturdays only.
e Saturdays excepted.
r Restaurant Car.
t Tea Car.

ADDERBURY (Oxon), 65½ miles. Fares, 13/7*a*, 8/2*c*. R. T. for two months, 27/2*a*, 16/4*c*. Departures *from* London as for Chipping Norton. Departures *for* London about 5 times daily. Pop 334.
Map Square 18.

ADDERLEY (Salop) from *Paddington*, 162¾ miles. Fares, 32/11*a*, 19/9*c*. R. T. for two months, 65/10*a*, 39/6*c*. Departures *from* London as for Market Drayton. Departures *for* London about 4 times daily. Pop. 312.
Map Square 12.
Station closed on Sundays.

ADDERLEY PARK

Warwick), 111 miles. Fares, 23/1*a*, 13/10*c*. R. T. for two months, 46/2*a*, 27/8*c*. Departures *from* London as for Birmingham (New Street). Departures *for* London about 6 times daily.

ADDIEWELL (Midlothian),

394½ miles. No through fares. Departures *from* London as for Edinburgh or Wishaw (Central). Departures *for* London about 3 times daily. Pop. 3,041.
Map Square 40

ADDINGHAM (Yorks),

214½ miles. Fares, 42/4*a*, 25/5*c*. R.T. for two months, 84/8*a*, 50/10*c*. Departures *from* London as for Ilkley. Departures *for* London about 6 times daily. Pop. 1,987.
Map Square 7.

ADDISCOMBE ROAD.

See CROYDON (ADDISCOMBE ROAD).

ADDISON ROAD. *See*

KENSINGTON (ADDISON ROAD).

ADDLESTONE (Surrey)

from *Waterloo*, 21 miles. Fares, 4/5*a*, 2/8*c*. R. T. for two months, 8/10*a*, 5/3*c*. Pop. 8,098.
Map Square 23.

W'loo	Addlest.	Addlest.	W'loo
AM 4.50	5.54	AM 5.15	6.13
6.10	7. 7	6.48	7.41
7. 0	7.49	7.28	8.21
8.15	9.10	7.45	8.36
9.15	10.14	8.16	9. 5
10.20	11.14	8.44	9.31
11.20	12.14	8.52	9.36
PM12.15	1.14	9.51	10.45
12.54*d*	1.39	10.52	11.46
1.20	2.14	11.52	12.46
2.20	3.14	PM12.50	1.46
3.15	4.14	1.52	2.46
4.20	5.14	2.52	3.46
4.54*e*	5.37	3.50	4.46
5.20	6.14	4.52*e*	5.46
5.54*e*	6.37	4.54*d*	5.46
6.20	7.14	5.52*e*	6.46
7. 0*e*	7.44	5.55*d*	6.46
7.20	8.14	6.52	7.46
8.20	9.14	7.52	8.46
9.20	10.10	8.52	9.46
10.20	11. 9	9.55	10.46
11.40	12.29	10.52	12.16
—	—	—	—
—	—	—	—
—	—	—	—

Sunday Trains.

AM 8.20	9. 9	AM 8.31	9.45
9.45	10.44	10.28	11.16
10.20	11.16	11.45	12.41
11.20	12.19	PM 2.15	3.44
PM 1.50	2.39	3.54	5.41
3.20	4.19	5.37	6.46
5.20	6. 9	6.44	7.41
6.30	7.16	7.44	8.41
7.20	8.16	8.43	9.44
8.20	9.14	9.47	10.41
8.55	10. 7	—	—

d Saturdays only.
e Saturdays excepted.

ADISHAM (Kent) from

Victoria, Holborn Viaduct, and *St. Paul's,* 67¾ miles. Fares, 14/4*a*, 28/8*a*, 22/10*b*, 17/0*c*. Pop. 500.
Map Square 24.

	Vict. S.E. & C.	Leave Hol. V	St. Pl's.	Arr. at Adish
AM	—	3.50*n*	—	6.41
5. 5	4.57	5. 0	8.30
5.48*f*	5.40*f*	5.42*f*	8.29
—	7.30	7.33	10.40
10.40	—	—	12.44
11.40*d*	—	—	2. 7
11.40*e*	—	—	2.35
PM 2. 5*d*	—	—	4. 4
2. 8*e*	—	—	4.26
4.20	—	—	6.32
5.10*d*	5.10*e*	5.12*e*	7.18
5.30*e*	—	—	8.19
5.30*d*	—	—	8. 4
—	6.12*el*	—	8.19
8.30	—	—	10.30

Sunday Trains.

AM 8.15	8. 0		10.42
PM 3.30	—		6.39
8.25	—		10.43

Trains from Adisham.

Leave Adish.	St. Pl's.	Hol. V.	Arrive at Vict.
AM 7. 3*h*	—	—	9. 4*h*
7. 3	9.37	9.39	—
7.47*h*	—	—	9.52*h*
7.47	—	—	11. 2
10.12*e*	1. 0	1. 2	1.33
10.24*d*	—	—	1.22
PM12.12	—	—	2.43
2.21*e*	4.46	—	4.39
2.38*d*	—	—	4.55
3.19	—	—	5.26
d5.30*h*	—	—	8.20*h*
6.23	—	—	8.33
7.39*d*	—	—	10.25
8. 6*e*	—	—	10.25

Sunday Trains.

AM 9.24		11.58	11.51
PM 2.29		—	5.31
8.16		—	10.29

d Saturdays only.
e Saturdays excepted.
f Mondays only.
h Departs from or arrives at Cannon Street.
l Departs from Cannon Street.
n Third class only.

ADLESTROP (Gloucester)

from *Paddington*, 87 miles. Fares, 18/2*a*, 10/11*c*. R. T. for two months, 36/4*a*, 21/10*c*. Pop. 156.
Map Square 17.

Pad.	Adles.	Adles.	Pad.
AM 5.30	8.41	AM 7.32	9.50
9.45	12.35	11.45	2.12
PM 1.35*r*	4.40	PM 4.31	7.20
4.45*t*	6.58	8. 8	10.45
—	—	—	—

Sunday Trains.

AM10.35	12.58	AN11.51	2.40
PM 4.10	6.45	PM 7.13*r*	9.48

r Restaurant Car.
t Tea Car.

ADLINGTON (Cheshire)

from *Euston*, 170 miles. Fares, 35/3*a*, 21/2*c*. R. T. for two months, 70/6*a*, 42/4*c*. Departures *from* London as for Macclesfield. Departures *for* London about 5 times daily. Pop. 683.
Map Square 12.

ADLINGTON (Lancs.), 206

miles. No through fares. Departures *from* London as for Wigan or Bolton (*via* Manchester). Departures *for* London about 6 times daily. Pop. 4,393.
Map Square 12.

ADMASTON (Salop), 144½

miles. Fares, 30/0*a*, 18/0*c*. R. T. for two months, 60/0*a*, 36/0*c*. Departures *from* London as for Wellington (Salop). Departures *for* London about 5 times daily.
Map Square 17.

ADVIE (Elgin), 556½ miles.

Fares, 106/3*a*, 63/9*c*. R. T. for two months, 212/6*a*, 127/6*c*. Departures *from* London as for Aviemore or Keith (*via* Aberdeen). Departures *for* London about twice daily. Pop. 284.
Map Square 35.

AFON WEN (Carnarvon)

from *Euston*, 266 miles. Fares, 54/5*a*, 32/8*c*. R. T. for two months, 108/10*a*. Departures *from* London as for Criccieth. Departures *for* London about 4 times daily.
Map Square 11.

AINDERBY (Yorks), 220½

miles. Fares, 46/1*a*, 27/8*c*. R. T. for two months, 92/2*a*, 55/4*c*. Departures *from* London as for Leyburn. Departures *for* London about 6 times daily. Pop. 235.
Map Square 7.

AINSDALE (Lancs), 216½

miles. Fares, 43/9*a*, 26/3*c*. R. T. for two months, 87/6*a*, 52/6*c*. Departures *from* London as for Liverpool. Departures *for* London about 8 times daily. Pop. 2,100.
Map Square 12.

AINSDALE BEACH

(Ainsdale) (Lancs), 229½ miles. No through fares. Departures *from* London as for Warrington (Central). Departures *for* London about 8 times daily.
Map Square 12.

AINTREE (Lancs), 207½

miles. Fares, 41/6*a*, 24 11*c*. R. T. for two months, 83/0*a*, 49/10*c*. Departures *from* London as for Liverpool (Lime Street). Departures *for* London about 4 times daily. Pop. 298.
Map Square 12.

AIRDRIE (Lanark), 394½

miles. Fares, 80/3*a*, 48/2*c*. R. T. for two months, 160/6*a*, 96/4*c*. Departures *from* London as for Edinburgh (Waverley). Departures *for* London about 4 times daily. Pop. 25,093.
Map Square 40.

AIRTH (Stirling), 412¾ miles.

No through fares. Departures *from* London as for Larbert. Departures *for* London about twice daily. Pop. 1,777.
Map Square 40.

AKELD (Northumberland),

330 miles. Fares, 69/7*a*, 41/9*c*. R. T. for two months, 139/2*a*, 83/6*c*. Departures *from* London as for Alnwick. Departures *for* London about 4 times daily. Pop. 138.
Map Square 3.

AKEMAN STREET
(Bucks) from *Marylebone*, 48¾ miles.
Fares, 10/3a, 6/2c. R. T. for two
months, 20/6a, 11/10c.
Map Square 23.

M'BONE.	AK'NST.	AK'NST.	M'BONE.
AM 6.10	7.53	AM 8.18	9.55
PM 4.55	6.27	PM 8.22h	9.55

No Sunday Trains.

h Stops on notice being given at
the station.

ALBION (Stafford), 119
miles. Fares, 24/4a, 14/7c. R. T.
for two months, 48/8a, 29/2c. Departures *from* London as for Oldbury. Departures *for* London
about 6 times daily.
Map Square 17.

ALBRIGHTON (Salop)
from *Paddington*, 130¼ miles.
Fares, 27/3a, 16/4c. R. T. for two
months, 54/6a, 32/8c. Pop.1,076.
Map Square 17.

PAD.	ALBRIG.	ALBRIG.	PAD.
AM 9.10r	12.28	AM 8. 6r	11. 0
10.40dr	1.32	9.15	12.25
10.40r	2.25	10.50r	2. 5
10.45r	3.30	PM 1.37r	5. 0
PM 2.10t	6. 5	2.33t	5.55
4.10t	7. 8	4.32r	8. 5
6.10r	9.38	6. 6	10. 0
7.10r	10.12	9.10	3.30
12.15k	7.33	—	—
12.15h	8. 3	—	—

Sunday Trains.

PM12.50r	3.52	AM 9. 0r	1.40
6. 0r	8.53	PM 1. 5	6.20

d Saturdays only.
h Saturday midnights only.
k Saturday midnights excepted.
r Restaurant Car.
t Tea Car.

ALCESTER (Warwick)
from *Marylebone*, 103¼ miles.
No through fares. Pop. 2,168.
Map Square 17.

M'BONE	ALCESTER	ALCESTER	M'BONE
AM 6.45	11.13	AM10.56r	3. 0
PM12.15dr	7.55	PM 2.34r	8.55
12.15r	8.32	—	—
—	—	—	—

No Sunday Trains.
r Restaurant Car.

ALDEBURGH (Suffolk)
from *Liverpool Street*, 99¼ miles.
Fares, 21/0a, 12/7c. R. T. for two
months, 42/0a, 25/2c. Pop. 2,892.
Map Square 19.

L'POOL ST.	ALDB.	ALDB.	L'POOL ST.
AM 5. 0	8.32	AM 6.58r	10.30
8.15r	11.56	8.50r	11.30
10.20	1.56	10.22	1.20
PM 1. 0	3.47	PM12.50	3.42
3.18r	6.32	2.50	5.56
4.55r	7.52	4.11	7.51
—	—	5.25r	9.22
—	—	6.47r	10. 0

Sunday Trains.

PM 4.40	8.25	AM 7.42	11.38
—	—	PM 5.52r	9.10
—	—	7.20r	10.30

r Restaurant Car.

Wentworth Hotel. Comfort-
able, Clean, and excellent service.
Principal Hotel. Facing Sea.
The Golfers' Hotel. Telephone 12.
Telegrams: " Wentworth Hotel,
Aldeburgh."
GEORGE PRITT, Proprietor.

ALDEBURGH—*continued*.
Brudenell Hotel. Telephone
45. Within 30 yards of Sea and
300 yards from River. 'Bus to
Golf Links. Fishing, Wild Fowl-
ing and Yachting. Electric
Light. Ballroom.
TRUST HOUSES, Ltd.

Jay's Private Hotel. Old
Established. Finest position.
Facing Sea. Home Comforts.
Terms Moderate.
Mrs. S. JAY, Proprietress.

White Lion Hotel. First-class
family Hotel, facing sea. Fully
licensed. Open all year round.
Excellent Cuisine. Telephone
No. 20.
H. J. BEATTON, Proprietor.

The Esplanade Private
Hotel. Facing and close to Sea.
Separate Tables. Private Sitting
Room if required.
Proprietor, A. TABBENHAM.

House Agents and Auc-
tioneers. Complete *List* Furnished Houses or Properties for
Sale sent immediately. Woodcock
& Son, Aldeburgh. Telephone 46.

ALDEBY (Norfolk) from
Liverpool Street, 112½ miles. Fares,
23/7a, 14/2c. R. T. for two months,
47/2a, 28/4c. Departures *from*
London as for Beccles. Departures *for* London about 7 times
daily. Pop. 588.
Map Square 19.

ALDERLEY EDGE
(Cheshire) from *Euston*, 175½ miles.
Fares, 36/6a, 21/11c. R. T. for two
months, 73/0a, 43/10c. Pop. 3,072.
Map Square 12.

EUSTON	ALDER.	ALDER.	EUSTON
AM12.25	5.40	AM 8. 0cr	12. 5
2.35	7.23	8. 0dr	12.20
5. 0	10.31	8.46	1. 0
6.45	11.58	9.16r	1.45
8.30r	1.24	11. 7r	3 10
10.30r	2.18	11.47r	4.15
10.40r	2.55	PM12.28t	5.35
12. 0nr	4.47	1.12dr	5.50
PM 1.30r	5.24	1.52cr	6. 0
2.35t	6.41	2. 6dr	6. 0
4. 5r	8.22	2.48r	6.25
5.20r	9. 2	4. 3r	8.10
11.50d	5.30	5.16dr	9.15
—	—	5.23er	9. 5
—	—	6.12er	10.45
—	—	10. 8e	5. 0
—	—	11.35d	5. 0
—	—	—	—
—	—	—	—

Sunday Trains.

AM 9.15	3. 5	AM11.11	4. 0
PM12.10r	4.11	PM 1.32r	5.45
12.30r	5. 4	3.16	7.30
6. 0r	9.36	4.52r	8.55
—	—	7.17	5. 0

d Saturdays only.
e Saturdays excepted.
n Noon.
r Restaurant Car.
t Tea Car.

ALDERMASTON (Berks)
from *Paddington*, 44½ miles. Fares,
9/5a, 5/8c. R. T. for two months,
18/10a, 11/4c. Pop. 559.
Map Square 23.

PAD.	ALDER.	ALDER.	PAD.
AM 6.30	8.12	AM 8.17	9.30
8.45r	9.51	9.30	10.45
9.30	10.39	11.21	12.55
10.45	12.16	PM12.20	1.50
11.20	1.11	1.20	2.30
PM 1.10r	2.27	2.22	3.50
1.35r	3.22	3.20	4.35
3.18	4.57	5.29	7.20
4. 7	5.45	7.52	9.15
5. 5	6.19	8.35	10.25
5.40	6.57	9.23	10.45
8. 0	9. 4	—	—
10. 0f	11.17	—	—
—	—	—	—
—	—	—	—
—	—	—	—

Sunday Trains.

AM 9.10	10.33	AM 9.15	10.50
PM 5.15	6.52	PM 7.58	9.15

f Wednesdays and Saturdays only.
r Restaurant Car.

ALDERSGATE ST.
to and from *Mansion House,
Charing Cross, Victoria, South
Kensington, High Street, Praed
Street, Hammersmith, Baker St.,
King's Cross, Moorgate,* and in-
termediate Stations every few
minutes. Also to and from Ux-
bridge Road, Kensington (Addison
Road), about every 12 minutes
throughout the day. *See* back of
Map.
Map Square 61, *No.* 1

ALDERSHOT (Hants)
from *Waterloo*, 35¼ miles. Fares,
7/4a, 4/5c. R. T. for two months,
14/0a, 8/10c. Pop. 28,756.
Map Square 23.

W'LOO.	ALDER.	ALDER.	W'LOO.
AM 4.50	6.39	AM 6.33	7.46
5.50	7. 5	7.47	8.56
7. 0	8.29	8.39	9.41
7.50	9.20	8.53	10.11
9.20	10.28	9.38k	10.26
10.34	11.58	10.14	11.16
11.20	12.45	11.10	12.11
PM 1.10	2.14	11.38	12.40
1.20	2.45	PM12.39	1.40
3.15	4.20	1.15	2.46
4. 0	5. 4	2.33	3.36
5.10	6.13	3.16	4.46
5.18eh	6.58	4.20	5.46
5.50d	7. 3	4.56	6.16
6.10e	7.20	6. 5	7. 7
6.34k	7.31	7.26	8.46
6.40d	8. 7	7.49	9. 6
6.54e	8. 7	8.43	9.52
8. 0	9.18	9.49	11.10
9.50	11. 2	10.59	12.16
12. 5	1.10	—	—

ALDERSHOT (Hants) —*continued.*

Sunday Trains.

W'LOO.	ALDER.	ALDER.	W'LOO.
AM 8.45	10. 4	AM 9.54	11.16
11.15	12.31	11.30	12.52
PM12.18*h*	2.32	PM 1.57	3.13
1.50	3.12	3.34*h*	5.28
2.18*h*	5. 5	6. 8	7.41
4.18*h*	7. 5	8.38	9.37
6.20	7.30	9.26	10.47
6.30	8. 0	—	—
9.45	11.15	—	—
10.45	11.56	—	—
—	—	—	—
—	—	—	—

d Saturdays only.
e Saturdays excepted.
h Via Ascot.
k Does not stop at North Camp.

Victoria Hotel. — Telephone 178. Close to Station and convenient to Barracks. Good Garage. TRUST HOUSES, Ltd.

South Western Hotel. Old-established Family and Commercial (opposite station). Excellent cuisine. Motor-buses outside to all parts. Moderate Tariff. Telephone 179. Garage.
Proprietress, M. WELLS.

ALDERSHOT (North Camp) (Surrey), from *Waterloo*, 32¼ miles. Fares, 6/10*a*, 4/1*c*. R. T. for two months, 13/8*a*. Departures *from* London as for Aldershot. Departures *for* London about 18 times daily.
Map Square 23.

ALDERSHOT NORTH (Surrey) from *Charing Cross*, *Cannon Street*, and *London Bridge*, 52 miles. Fares, 6/10*a*, 5/5*b*, 4/1*c*. R. T. for two months, 13/1*a*, 8/9*b*. Departures *from* London as for Ash. Departures *for* London about 8 times daily.

ALDGATE. Trains to and from *Mansion House*, *Charing Cross*, *Victoria*, *South Kensington*, *High Street*, *Praed Street*, *Hammersmith*. *Baker Street*, *King's Cross*, *Moorgate Street*, and intermediate Stations every few minutes. Also to and from Uxbridge Road, Kensington (Addison Road), about every 12 minutes throughout the day *See* back of Map.
Map Square 61, *No.* 5.

Three Nuns Hotel. Adjoining Station. Centrally situated for Shipping Industry,
See advts. under London Hotels.

ALDGATE EAST from *Ealing*, *Hounslow*, *Richmond* and *Wimbledon*: *See* p. 489.
Map Square 61, *No.* 6.

ALDIN GRANGE (Durham), 253¾ miles. No through fares. Departures *from* London as for Durham. Departures *for* London about 5 times daily
Map Square 7.

ALDRIDGE (Stafford), 134¼ miles. Fares, 24/5*a*, 14/8*c*, R. T., double fare. Departures *from* London as for Water Orton. Departures *for* London about 4 times daily. Pop. 2,812.
Map Square 17.

ALDWYCH (Hammersmith and Finsbury Park Tube). *See* back of Map.

Station closed on Sundays.

ALEXANDRA PALACE from *King's Cross*, 6¾ miles. Fares, 1/2*a*, 0/11*b*, 0/8½*c*. R. T. for two days, 2/4*a*, 1/10*b*, 1/5*c*. From Moorgate Street and Broad Street, 1/3*a*, 1/0*b*, 0/9*c*. R. T. for two days, 2/6*a*, 2/0*b*, 1/6*c*. *See* pp. 518-522.
Map Square 51.

ALEXANDRIA (Dumbarton), 418¾ miles. Fares, 84/10*a*, 50/11*c*. R.T. for two months, 169/8*a*, 101/10*c*. Departures *from* London as for Dumbarton. Departures *for* London about 3 times daily. Pop. 10,359.
Map Square 40.

ALFORD (Aberdeen), 552¼ miles. Fares, 106/1*a*, 63/8*c*. R. T. for two months, 212/2*a*, 127/4*c*. Departures *from* London as for Aberdeen. Departures *for* London about twice daily. Pop. 1,408.
Map Square 35.

ALFORD (Lincoln), from *King's Cross*, 130¼ miles. Fares, 27/1*a*, 16/3*c*. R. T. for two months, 54/2*a*, 32/6*c*. Departures *from* London as for Willoughby. Departures *for* London about 5 times daily. Pop. 2,193.
Map Square 13.

ALFRETON (Derby) from *St. Pancras*, 136 miles. Fares, 27/6*a*, 16/6*c*. R. T. for two months, 55/0*a*, 33/0*c*. Pop. 20,485.
Map Square 13.

ST. PAN.	ALFRE.	ALFRE.	ST. PAN.
AM 2.25	9. 9	AM 7.48*r*	10.45
4.25	10.25	8.33*r*	1.20
9. 0*r*	12.48	11.57*r*	4.10
11. 0*r*	3.19	PM12.46*hr*	4.10
PM 1.50*r*	5.32	1.21*r*	5.30
3.30*r*	7. 5	3.32*r*	7.15
5. 0*r*	8.37	4.42*r*	9. 5
6.15*r*	9.45	8.32	4.20
—	—	—	—
—	—	—	—
—	—	—	—
—	—	—	—
—	—	—	—
—	—	—	—
—	—	—	—
—	—	—	—

Sunday Trains.

PM 3.15	6.53	AM10.39	5.27
—	—	PM 7.32	4.55
—	—	—	—
—	—	—	—
—	—	—	—
—	—	—	—

h Wednesdays and Saturdays only.
r Restaurant Car.

ALGARKIRK (Lincoln) from *King's Cross*, 100¾ miles. Fares, 21/0*a*, 12/7*c*. R. T. for two months, 42/0*a*, 25/2*c*. Departures *from* London as for Surfleet. Departures *for* London about 5 minutes earlier. Pop. 485.
Map Square 13.

ALLANFEARN (Inverness), 570¾ miles. No through fares. Departures *from* London as for Nairn. Departures *for* London about twice daily.
Map Square 34.

ALLANGRANGE (Ross), 586¼ miles. No through fares. Departures *from* London as for Inverness. Departures *for* London about twice daily.
Map Square 34.

ALLENDALE (Northumberland), 300¼ miles. Fares, 63/7*a*, 38/2*c*. R. T., for two months, 127/2*a*, 76/4*c*. Departures *from* London as for Hexham. Departures *for* London about 3 times daily. Pop. 2,185.
Map Square 3.

ALLERTON (Lancs), 195 miles. Fares, 40/5*a*, 24/3*c*. R. T. for two months, 80/10*a*, 48/6*c*. Departures *from* London as for Runcorn. Departures *for* London about 5 times daily. Pop. 1,312.

ALLERTON (Yorks), 200 miles. Fares, 41/8*a*, 25/0*c*. R. T. for two months, 83/4*a*, 50/0*c*. Departures *from* London as for York. Departures *for* London about 5 times daily. Pop. 209.
Map Square 8.

ALLOA (Clackmannan), 419¼ miles *via* Stirling. Fares, 85/0*a*, 51/0*c*. R. T. for two months, 170/0*a*, 102/0*c*. Departures *from* London as for Dunfermline or Stirling. Departures *for* London about 4 times daily. Pop. 18,450.
Map Square 40.

ALLOWAY (Ayr), 395¼ miles. Fares, 80/7*a*, 48/4*c*. R. T. for two months, 161/2*a*, 96/8*c*. Departures *from* London as for Turnberry. Departures *for* London about 4 times daily. Pop. 2,166.
Map Square 43.

ALMELEY (Hereford), 157 miles. Fares, 32/9*a*, 19/8*c*. R. T. for two months, 65/6*a*, 39/4*c*. Departures *from* London as for Titley. Departures *for* London about 3 times daily. Pop. 476.
Map Square 17.

ALMONDBANK (Perth), 453¾ miles. No through fares. Departures *from* London as for Perth. Departures *for* London about 3 times daily. Pop. 283.
Map Square 38.

ALNE (Yorks), 199 miles. Fares, 41/6*a*, 24/11*c*. R. T. for two months, 83/0*a*, 49/10*c*. Departures *from* London as for York. Departures *for* London about 8 times daily. Pop. 441.
Map Square 8.

ALNESS (Ross), 596¼ miles.
Fares, 106/3a, 63/9c. R. T. for two
months, 212/6a, 127/6c. Departures
from London as for Dingwall.
Departures *for* London about 3
times daily. Pop. 917.
Map Square 34.

ALNMOUTH (Northumberland), 302½ miles. Fares, 63/9a,
38/3c. R. T. for two months,
127/6a. Departures *from* London
as for Morpeth. Departures *for*
London about 3 times daily.
Pop. 542.
Map Square 3.

ALNWICK (Northumberland) from *King's Cross*, 305½ miles.
Fares, 64/5a, 38/8c. R. T. for two
months, 128/10a, 77/4c. Pop. 6,991.
Map Square 3.

King's +	Aln'wk.	Aln'w.	King's +
AM 4.45	1.32	AM 7.48g	3.15
10. 0r	5.10	8.35r	4.30
11.50r	6.55	10.35r	6.30
PM 1.50r	10.42	PM12.38r	9.25
11.25e	7.40	2.23r	10. 0
11.25d	7.50	5. 7	3.25
—	—	8.55e	5.40
—	—	9.37	6. 0

Sunday Trains.

AM11.30	8.29	AM 7. 0	5.15
PM11.40	7.40	PM 6.35	5.40
—	—	9.37	6. 0

d Saturdays only.
e Saturdays excepted.
g First and Third Class Pullman
Cars only.
r Restaurant Car.

ALPERTON (Middlesex)
from *Mansion House*, 12¼ miles.
Pop. 2,378. *See p.* 489.
Map Square 58.

ALRESFORD (Essex) from
Liverpool Street, 57¾ miles. Fares,
12/6a, 7/6c. R. T. for two months,
25/0a, 15/0c. Pop. 238.
Map Square 24.

L'pl.St.	Alres'fd.	Alres'fd.	L'pl.St.
AM 5. 0	6.53	AM 7.56	9.36
6.50	9.39	10. 0	11.42
8.46	11.30	PM12.13r	2. 3
11.26d	1.39	3. 1	5. 5
11.30e	1.39	4.55	6.32
PM 2.15	4.28	6.28	9.17
3.26	5.55	8.29	11.16
5.42	7.47	—	—
7.45r	9.37	—	—
8.45	10.21	—	—

Sunday Trains.

AM 9.20r	11.32	AM 9.29	11.38
PM 4.40	6.20	PM 6.26	8.25
—	—	7.15	10. 9

d Saturdays only.
e Saturdays excepted.
r Restaurant Car.

ALRESFORD (Hants)
from *Waterloo*, 57 miles. Fares,
11/11a, 7/2c. R. T. for two months,
23/10a, 14/4c. Pop. 2,272.
Map Square 23.

W'loo.	Alres'fd	Alres'fd.	W'loo.
AM 5.50	8. 7	AM 7.34	9.41
7. 0	9.30	8.27	10.26
9.20	11.29	10.33	12.40
PM 1.10	3.11	PM 1.27	3.36
4. 0	5.58	4.56	7. 7
6.34	8.30	7.36	9.52
—	—	—	—
—	—	—	—

Sunday Trains.

AM 8.45	11.21	AM 8.26	11.16
PM 6.20	8.34	PM 7.26	9.37

ALREWAS (Stafford), 120¾
miles. Fares, 24/5a, 14/8c. R. T.
for two months. 48/10a, 29/4c. Departures *from* London as for Lichfield. Departures *for* London
about 4 times daily. Pop. 1,461.
Map Square 17.

ALSAGER (Cheshire),
154½ miles. Fares, 34/2a, 20/6c.
R. T. for two months, 68/4a, 41/0c.
Departures *from* London as for
Crewe. Departures *for* London
about 5 times daily Pop. 2,693.
Map Square 12.

ALSOP-EN-LE-DALE
(Derby), 154 miles. Fares, 31/10a,
19/1c. R. T. for two months,
63/8a, 38/2c. Departures *from*
London as for Ashbourne. Departures *for* London about 5 times
daily. Pop. 69.
Map Square 12.

ALSTON (Cumberland),
316¼ miles. Fares, 63/7a, 38/2c.
R. T. for two months, 127/2a,
76/4c. Departures *from* London
as for Hexham or Carlisle. Departures *for* London about 4 times
daily. Pop. 3,075.
Map Square 7.

ALTCAR (Lancs), 224¼
miles. Fares, 42/6a, 25/6c. R. T.
for two months, 85/0a, 51/0c. Departures *from* London as for Warrington (Central). Departures *for*
London about 5 times daily. Pop.
488.
Map Square 12.

ALTHORNE (Essex) from
Liverpool Street, 40½ miles. Fares,
7/6a, 4/6c. R. T. for two months,
15/0a, 9/0c. Pop. 407.
Map Square 24.

Lpl. St.	Althne.	Althne	Lpl. St.
AM 5.26	7.24	AM 7.11	8.45
6.50	8.54	8.20	9.46
9. 1	10.44	9.36	11. 7
10.47d	12.26	11.26d	1.16
11.56	1.38	11.56e	1.25
PM 1.26d	2.37	PM 1.11d	3. 5
2.20e	4.27	2.51d	4.56
2.40d	4. 7	3. 2e	4.51
4.15e	5.25	5.11	6.52
4.18d	5.46	6.30	8.22
5.39	7. 0	8.12	9.56
6.26e	7.56	—	—
8. 2e	9.30	—	—
8.45d	10. 6	—	—

Sunday Trains.

AM 8.45	10.19	AM 7.43	10.25
9.30	11.19	PM 6.48	8.45
PM 6.42	8.29	7.55	9.52

d Saturdays only.
e Saturdays excepted.

ALTHORPE (Lincoln), 175½
miles. Fares, 36/0a, 21/7c. R. T.
for two months, 72/0a, 43/2c. Departures *from* London as for
Thorne. Departures *for* London
about 4 times daily. Pop. 643.
Map Square 13.

ALTHORP PARK (Northampton), 72 miles. Fares, 14/7a,
8/9c. R. T. for two months, 29/2a,
17/6c. Departures *from* London
as for Northampton (Castle). Departures *for* London about 5 times
daily. Pop. 48.
Map Square 18.

ALTNABREAC (Caithness), 701½ miles. Fares, 127/4a,
76/8c. R. T. for two months,
254/8a, 11/10c. Departures *from*
London as for Helmsdale. Departures *for* London about twice
daily.
Map Square 31.

ALTOFTS (Yorks), from
St. Pancras, 186½ miles. Fares,
36/10a, 22/1c. R. T. for two
months, 73/8a, 44/2c. Departures
from London as for Normanton.
Departures *for* London about 4
times daily. Pop. 5,050.
Map Square 12.

ALTON (Hants) from
Waterloo, 47 miles. Fares, 9/10a,
5/11c. R. T. for two months,
19/8a, 11/10c. Pop. 5,580.
Map Square 23.

W'loo.	Alton	Alton	W'loo.
AM 4.50	7. 6	AM 7.17	8.56
5.50	7.38	8. 9	9.41
7. 0	9. 1	9. 8	10.26
7.50	9.45	9.43	11.16
9.20	11. 2	10.42	12.11
10.34	12.23	11. 9	12.40
11.20	1.12	PM12. 9	1.40
PM 1.10	2.43	12.47	2.46
1.20	3.10	2. 1	3.36
3.15	4.48	2.47	4.46
4. 0	5.32	3.52	5.46
5.10	6.39	4.28	6.16
6.34	8. 4	5.34	7. 7
6.40d	8.33	7.20	9. 6
6.54e	8.33	8.12	9.52
8. 0	9.44	9.11	11.10
9.50	11.29	10.13	11.16
—	—	—	—

Sunday Trains.

AM 8.45	10.52	AM 9. 7	11.16
PM 6.20	8. 6	PM 8. 8	9.37
—	—	—	—

d Saturdays only.
e Saturdays excepted.

ALTON (Stafford), 143¼ miles.

Fares, 29/10a, 17/11c. R. T. for two months, 59/8a, 35/10c. Departures *from* London as for Uttoxeter. Departures *for* London about 5 times daily. Pop. 1,279.
Map Square 12.

ALTRINCHAM (Cheshire), from *Euston*, 191½ miles.

Fares, *via* Manchester, 40/2a, 24/1c. R. T. for two months, 80/4a, 48/2c. *Via* Northwich, 37/9a, 22/8c. R. T. for two months, 75/6a, 45/4c. Pop. 20,461.
Map Square 12.

Euston.	Alt'ch'm.	Alt'ch'm	Euston.
AM12.25	7. 0	AM 5.50dr	12. 5
2.35	8.49	5.50dr	12.20
5. 0	11. 3	7.47r	12.50
8.45dr	1.21	9. 0r	1.15
8.45er	1.30	9.15r	1.45
10.40r	3.10	9.25r	2.20
11.50r	4.40	9.45r	3.10
12. 0enr	6. 5	10.51hr	3.10
12. 0dnr	6.15	11. 0r	3.55
PM 2.35ht	6.50	11.45dr	5.50
2.50t	7.40	PM12.20r	6. 0
4. 5r	9. 0	1.25r	6.15
5.20hr	9.32	2. 0r	7.30
6. 5r	10.25	3.15r	8.10
11.55d	9. 5	3.45er	9. 5
—	—	3.45dr	9.15
—	—	5. 0dr	10. 0
—	—	5.15er	10.10
—	—	9.35	5. 0
—	—	10.25	5.40

Sunday Trains.

AM 9.15	5.25	AM 9.20r	5.45
PM12.30r	6.50	PM 1.50r	7.30
6. 0r	11.15	1.50r	8.55
—	—	9.30	5. 0
—	—	—	—
—	—	—	—
—	—	—	—
—	—	—	—

d Saturdays only.
e Saturdays excepted.
h *Via* Northwich.
n Noon.
r Restaurant Car.
t Tea Car.

ALVA (Clackmannan), 425 miles.

Fares, 85/8a, 51/5c. R. T. for two months, 171/4a, 102/10c. Departures *from* London as for Stirling. Departures *for* London about 4 times daily. Pop. 5,120.
Map Square 40.

ALVECHURCH (Worcester) 125¼ miles. Fares, 23/7a, 14/2c.

R. T. for two months, 47/2a, 28/4c. Departures *from* London as for Birmingham (New Street). Departures *for* London about 8 times daily. Pop. 2,207.
Map Square 17.

ALVERSTONE (Isle of Wight), 86½ miles. Fares, 19/2a, 11/9c.

R. T. for two months, 38/4a, 23/6c. Departures *from* London as for Sandown. Departures *for* London about 5 times daily.
Map Square 28.

ALVERTHORPE (Yorks), 177¼ miles. Fares, 36/10a, 22/1c.

R. T. for two months, 73/8a, 44/2c. Departures *from* London as for Dewsbury. Departures *for* London about 8 times daily. Pop. 1,349.
Map Square 12.

ALVES (Elgin), 576¼ miles.

Fares, 106/3a, 63/9c. R. T. for two months, 212/6a, 127/6c. Departures *from* London as for Elgin. Departures *for* London about 3 times daily. Pop. 957.
Map Square 35.

ALVESCOT (Oxon), from *Paddington*, 81 miles.

Fares, 16/10a, 10/1c. R.T. for two months, 33/8a, 20/2c. Departures *from* London as for Fairford. Departures *for* London about 4 times daily. Pop. 351.
Map Square 22.

ALYTH (Perth), 475¾ miles.

Fares, 95/8a, 57/5c. R.T. for two months, 191/4a, 114/10c. Departures *from* London as for Coupar Angus. Departures *for* London about 3 times daily. Pop. 2,837.
Map Square 38.

ALYTH JUNCTION (Forfar), 470½ miles.

Fares, 94/5a, 56/8c. R.T. for two months, 188/10a, 113/4c. Departures *from* London as for Coupar Angus. Departures *for* London about 4 times daily.
Map Square 38.

AMBERGATE (Derby), from *St. Pancras*, 138¼ miles.

Fares, 28/7a, 17/2c. R. T. for two months, 57/2a, 34/4c. Pop. 852.
Map Square 12.

St. Pan.	Amber.	Amber.	St. Pan.
AM 2.25	7. 0	AM 7.23r	11. 2
4.25	8.24	8. 9r	11.35
8.25r	12.53	10.20r	1.30
10.25r	1.40	11.19	3.25
PM12.25r	4.12	PM12.48r	4.20
2.25r	5.40	2. 4r	5.45
4.25r	7.38	3.17r	7.15
6.25r	10. 7	4. 9r	7.57
12. 0h	7.20	5. 0r	8.35
—	—	6.40r	10. 5
—	—	9.57	4.20

Sunday Trains.

PM 3.15	6.37	AM11.58r	5. 2
6.15r	9.55	PM 6.17r	9.52
—*	—	9.13	4.55

h Saturdays, midnight only.
r Restaurant Car.

AMBERLEY (Sussex), from *London Bridge*, *Victoria* and *Clapham Junction*, 54½ miles.

Fares, 11/5a, 6/10c. R. T. for two months, 22/10a, 13/8c. Pop. 541.
Map Square 28.

		Leave	Arr. at
Vict.	Clap. J.	Lon. B	Amber.
AM 6.18	6.25	6.35	8.18
7.23	7.29	7.25	10. 2
8.55	7.56	7.35	10.43
10.35	10.42	10.35	1.37
PM 1.40	1.47e	1.50	3.58
3.55	4. 2	4. 0	5.56
4.53	5. 0	5. 5	7. 4
7.20	7.28	7.15	9.19
—	—	—	—
—	—	—	—
—	—	—	—

Sunday Trains.

AM 8.18	8.25	8.25	10.30
PM 7. 0	7. 7	6.38	8.51

AMBERLEY—*continued*.

Trains from Amberley.

Leave Amber.	Lon. B.	Clap. J.	Vict.
AM 7. 9	9.10	9.31	9.19
8. 9	10.22	—	10.28
9.53	12. 8	—	12. 0
PM 1. 1	3.32	3.22	3.32
3.14	5.54	5. 4	5.12
5. 5	7.48	7.31	6.50
8.33	10.58	11.10	11.17
—	—	—	—
—	—	—	—

Sunday Trains.

AM 8.10	10.45	10.23	10.32
4. 5	7.56	7.25	7.33
PM 7.16	9.32	9.24	9.34

e Saturdays excepted.

AMBLE (Northumberland), 299¼ miles.

No through fares. Departures *from* London as for Morpeth. Departures *for* London about 4 times daily. Pop. 4,851.
Map Square 3.

AMERSHAM (Bucks) from *Marylebone*, 23½ miles.

Fares, 4/11a, 2/11c. R. T. for two months, 9/10a, 5/8½c. Pop. 3,392.
Map Square 23.

M'bone	Amers.	Amers.	M'bone
AM 6.45	7.30	AM 6.52	7.50
7.20	8.20	7.36	8.22
7.50	8.50	8. 2e	8.42
8.50	9.46	8. 2d	8.46
9.14	10. 6	8.29	9. 9
10. 5	10.59	9.10	9.46
11.15	12. 7	10.51	11.36
PM12.35d	1.42	PM12.14	12.59
1. 5d	1.52	1.14	2. 2
1.10e	2. 0	2. 7e	3.28
1.41d	2.33	3.15	3.59
1 55e	3.12	4. 6	4.56
2.15d	3.12	5. 9e	6.22
2.45d	4. 6	6.41	7.15
3.25	4.18	6.58	7.43
5. 4	5.55	7.26	8.11
5.24e	6.10	7.47	8.31
6. 0	6.52	9.57	10.41
6.25e	7. 2	10.18	11. 0
6.25d	7.10	—	—
6.31e	7.25	—	—
6.55e	8.11	—	—
7.30	8.24	—	—
8.20	9.11	—	—
9. 0	9.51	—	—
10.30	11.21	—	—
11.35	12.44	—	—
—	—	—	—
—	—	—	—
—	—	—	—

Sunday Trains.

AM 9.30	10.22	AM 9.25	10.13
11. 0	11.52	12. 0	12.46
PM 1. 0	1.52	PM 1.30	2.16
2.30	3.22	4.35	5.20
3.15	4.30	5.53	6.55
4.30	5.22	6.50	7.35
5.30	6.33	7.21	8.16
6.10	7.17	8.43	9.44
6.45	7.34	9.13	9.55
7.45	8.53	—	—
8.50	10.23	—	—

d Saturdays only.
e Saturdays excepted.

AMERSHAM—continued.
ANOTHER ROUTE from
Baker Street, 24 miles. Fares as above.

BAKER S.	AMERS.	AMERS.	BAKER S.
AM 6. 5	6.59	AM 6.52	7.41
6.30	7.30	7.36	8.35
7. 3	8.20	7.51	8.43
7.50	8.47	8. 2d	8.51
8.34	9.46	8. 2e	8.57
9. 1	10. 6	8.29	9.28
9.51e	10.38	8.55	9.39
9.51d	10.43	9.10	9.49
10.11d	11. 7	9.35	10.25
10.18e	11. 9	10.27	11. 5
11. 0	12. 7	10.51	11.50
PM12. 8	1. 6	11.43	12.35
12.50e	2. 0	PM12.14e	1.22
12.54d	1.42	12.14d	1.24
1.17d	2.14	1.14d	2.17
1.21d	2.33	1.14e	2.22
2.17e	3.12	2. 7	2.58
2.19d	3.14	2.37d	3.28
3.10	4.18	3. 5d	3.55
3.18d	4. 6	3.15	4.22
3.45e	4.41	4. 6	5.14
4.10d	5. 4	4.45	5.41
4.16e	5. 8	5. 9e	5.59
4.40d	5.55	5.46e	6.33
4.42e	5.55	5.49d	6.39
5. 7e	6. 9	6.41	7.32
5.45e	6.33	6.58	8. 0
5.46d	6.39	7.14	8. 8
5.49e	6.51	7.26	8.52
6.30	7.25	7.47	8.47
7.15e	8.11	8.43	9.37
7.15d	8.23	9. 8d	9.49
7.19e	8.23	9.37d	10.28
8. 5	9.11	9.37e	10.43
8.40	9.51	9.57	11. 2
9.25	10.18	10.18	11.18
10.10	11.21	10.51	11.40
11.50	12.44	—	—
—	—	—	—
—	—	—	—
—	—	—	—
—	—	—	—
—	—	—	—

Sunday Trains.

AM 8.47	9.44	AM 8.49	9.48
9.10	10.22	9.25	10.27
9.43	10.40	10.57	11.48
10.33	11.31	12. 0	1. 5
10.45	11.52	PM 1.30	2.35
11.11	12.11	2.19	3. 9
12. 0	12.54	3. 2	3.52
PM12.45	1.52	4.35	5.42
2. 0	2.56	5. 4	5.54
2.15	3.22	5.29	6.21
3.35	4.31	5.53	6.45
4. 2	4.56	6.50	7.57
4.15	5.22	7.21	8.12
5.37	6.34	7.59	8.51
6.24	7.17	8.22	9.12
6.30	7.34	8.43	9.31
7.59	8.54	9.13	10.20
9.29	10.24	10.23	11.14

d Saturdays only.
e Saturdays excepted.

Crown Hotel.—Telephone 60. Picturesque old house with modern comforts. Garage. TRUST HOUSES Ltd.

Ye Olde Griffin Hotel. An old-world Coaching House modernised. Oak-beamed Restaurant. Electric Light, Garage. 'Phone 75.

AMESBURY (Wilts) from
Waterloo, via Porton, 79¼ miles. Fares, *via* Grateley or Porton. 17/11a, 10/9c. R. T. for two months, 35/10a, 21/6c. *Via* Salisbury, 20/2a, 12/1c. R. T. for two months, 40/4a, 24/2c. Pop. 1,253.
Map Square 22.

W'LOO.	AMES.	AMES.	W'LOO.
AM 7.30h	10.48	AM 8.21	10.56
11. 0hr	1.14	11.17hr	1.56
PM 1. 0hr	3.38	PM 1.37hr	3.50
3. 0hr	5.18	3. 7hr	6. 0
5. 0	7.54	4.50h	7.40
6. 0r	9.38	5.57hr	8.30
—	—	8.22	11.28

Sunday Trains.

PM 6. 0	9. 3	—	—
—	—	—	—
—	—	—	—

h Via Salisbury.
r Restaurant Car.

George Hotel. Principal and nearest Hotel to Stonehenge (2 miles), Bulford, and other military camps. Highly recommended. M. WHISTLER, Proprietor.

The Avon Hotel. Unlicensed. Near Stonehenge, Larkhill. Open to non-residents. Garage, Stabling, Garden. Tel. 12. Tariff, Proprietresses, Misses FOWNES.

AMISFIELD (Dumfries),
335½ miles. Fares, 67/4a, 40/5c. R.T. for two months, 134/8a, 80/10c. Departures *from* London as for Lockerbie. Departures *for* London about 4 times daily. *Map Square 43.*

AMLWCH (Anglesey), from
Euston, 263 miles. Fares, 54/9a, 32/10c. R. T. for two months, 109/6a, 65/8c. Pop. 2,694. *Map Square 11.*

EUSTON	AMLW.	AMLW.	EUSTON
AM12.25	10. 8	AM 7. 0r	1.45
2.35	12.16	7.55r	4.15
5. 0h	1.57	9.15r	5. 5
8.30r	4.54	11.10er	7.30
11.10r	6.28	PM 1. 5r	9.20
PM 2.35t	9.51	2. 5hr	10.45
9.30e	6.38	7.10	5. 0

Sunday Trains.

PM 9.15	6.38	—	—

e Saturdays excepted.
h Thursdays excepted.
r Restaurant Car.
t Tea Car.

AMMANFORD (Carmarthen),299¾ miles. Fares,43/6a,26/1c. R. T. for two months, 87/0a, 52/2c. Departures *from* London as for Brynamman. Departures *for* London about 4 times daily. Pop. 6,984. *Map Square 21.*

AMOTHERBY (Yorks),
213¼ miles. No through fares. Departures *from* London as for Ampleforth. Departures *for* London about 4 times daily. Pop. 267. *Map Square 8.*

AMPLEFORTH (Yorks),
from *King's Cross*, 216¼ miles. Fares, *via* Pilmoor, 43/11a, 26/4c. R. T. for two months, 87/10a, 52/8c. Pop. 711.
Map Square 8.

King's+	A'FORTH	A'FORTH	King's+
AM 4.45	11. 6	AM 8.16r	1.15
10. 0r	3.59	10.50r	4.30
PM 1.50r	6.18	PM 6.46	3.25
11.25e	8.36	—	—

No Sunday Trains.
e Saturdays excepted.
r Restaurant Car.

AMPTHILL (Beds), from
St. Pancras, 41½ miles. Fares, 8/9a, 5/3c. R.T. for two months, 17/6a, 10/6c. Pop. 2,269.
Map Square 18.

ST. PAN.	AMPTH.	AMPTH.	ST. PAN
AM 6.25	8.12	AM 6.46	8.28
8.25r	9.37	7.48	9.13
9.25d	10.58	8.43	10. 5
11. 0r	12.27	10.54	12. 5
PM12.30	1.47	PM12. 5r	1.20
1.33d	2.59	1.36d	3.10
3.35	5. 2	2. 9	3.25
5. 5	6.15	3. 0d	5.10
5.40e	6.49	5. 2	6.30
6.35	7.56	6.41	8.20
7.50	9.16	8.43	10. 5
8.25d	10.49	10.18	11.45
10. 5	11.13	—	—

Sunday Trains.

AM 8. 0	9.49	AM 8.15	10.15
PM 4.35	6.24	PM 6.56	8.30

d Saturdays only.
e Saturdays excepted.
r Restaurant Car.

ANCASTER (Lincoln), from
King's Cross, 114¾ miles. Fares, 23/2a, 13/11c. R. T. for two months, 46/4a, 27/10c. Departures *from* London for Sleaford. Departures *for* London about 6 times daily. Pop. 536. *Map Square 13.*

ANDOVER (Hants), from
Waterloo, 67 miles. Fares, 14/2a, 8/6c. R.T. for two months, 28/4a, 17/0c. Departures *from* London as for Andover Junction. Departures *for* London about 4 times daily. Pop. 8,569. *Map Square 23.*

White Hart Hotel. Telephone 45. Old Established. First Class Hotel. Excellent Cuisine. Officially appointed by R.A.C. and A.A. Garage. Stabling. Moderate Charges. Motors for hire. Close to Town Station, Golf Links.

ANDOVER JUNCTION (Hants) from *Waterloo*, 66¼ miles. Fares, 13/11a, 8/4c. R. T. for two months, 27/10a, 16/8c. *Map Square 22.*

W'LOO	ANDOVER	ANDOVER	W'LOO.
AM 5.50	8.34	AM 7.55	9.56
7.50	9.14	9.17	10.56
9.30	11.40	10.56s	12.22
11.30r	1.41	PM12.15r	2.20
PM 1. 0r	2.30	1.11	2.36
1.30r	3.20	2. 3	4.20
3.50s	5.25	4. 8s	6.26
5. 0	6.36	5.58 -	7.40
6. 0r	7.26	7. 6r	8.30
7.50	9.25	9. 7	10.50
8. 0	10.28	9.25	11.28

ANDOVER JUNCTION
—continued.

Sunday Trains.

W'LOO.	ANDOVER.	ANDOVER	W'LOO.
AM 9. 0	11.33	AM 10.10	12.11
12. 0r	1.44	PM 7.42r	8.57
PM 6. 0	8. 3	—	—
—	—	—	—
—	—	—	—
—	—	—	—
—	—	—	—
—	—	—	—

r Restaurant Car.
s Refreshments served.

Star and Garter. First-class Family, Commercial. Principal Hotel, Central, convenient for Salisbury Plain. Table d'hôte. Billiards. Private Sitting-rooms. Garage. Motors for hire. R.A.C. & A.A. 'Phone 69. Telegrams: "Star."

ANDOVERSFORD
(Glo'ster) from *Paddington*, 101 miles. Fares, 42/2*a*, 12/8*c*. R. T. for two months, 42/2*a*, 25/4*c* Departures *from* London as for Bourton-on-Water. Departures *for* London about 4 times daily. Pop. 267.
Map Square 22.

ANERLEY
(London) from *London Bridge*, 7½ miles. Fares, 1/7*a*,0/11½*c*. R.T. for two days, 3/1*a*, 1/9*c*. *See* pp. 564, 565, 568-570.
Map Square 79.

ANOTHER ROUTE
from *Victoria* and *Clapham Junction*, 11½ miles. Fares, 1/11*a* 1/2*c*. R. T. for two days, 3/10*a*, 2/0*c*. *See* p. 580.

ANGEL, THE
(Islington) (City and South London Tube). *See* back of Map.

ANGEL ROAD
(Middlesex) for Edmonton from *Liverpool Street* 7½ miles. Fares, 1/0½*a*, 0/10*b*, 0/7½*c*. R. T. for two days, 2/1*a*, 1/8*b*, 1/2*c*. *See* pp. 526-527.

ANGERTON
(Northumberland), 292½ miles. Fares, 61/6*a*, 36/11*c*. R.T. for two months, 123/0*a*, 73/10*c*. Departures *from* London as for Morpeth. Departures *for* London about 3 times daily. Pop. 184.
Map Square 3.

ANGMERING
(Sussex), 64½ miles. Fares, 12/8*d*, 7/7*c*. R. T. for two months, 25/4*a*, 15/2*c*. Departures *from* London as for Worthing. Departures *for* London about 12 times daily. Pop. 1,026.
Map Square 28.

ANNAN
(Dumfries) from *St. Pancras*, 325¾ miles. Fares, 64/0*a*, 38/5*c*. R.T. for two months, 128/0*a*, 76/10*c*. Pop. 6,379.
Map Square 44.

ST. PAN	ANNAN	ANNAN	ST. PAN.
AM 4.25	1.21	AM 11.39*r*	6.35
9.50*r*	4.45*h*	PM 11.33*e*	7.25
PM 12.15*dr*	9.57	—	—
11.45*e*	6.35*h*	—	—
—	—	—	—
—	—	—	—
—	—	—	—

Sunday Trains.

PM 11.45	6.35*h*	PM 11.41	7.25
—	—	—	—
—	—	—	—
—	—	—	—

d Saturdays only.
e Saturdays excepted.
h Sets down on intimation to Travelling Ticket Examiner.
r Restaurant Car.

ANNBANK (Ayr), 387½ miles.
Fares, 78/11*a*, 47/4*c*. R. T. for two months, 157/10*a*, 94/8*c*. Departures *from* London as for Ayr. Departures *for* London about 4 times daily.
Map Square 40.

ANNESLEY
(Notts) from *St. Pancras*, 134¾ miles. Fares, 27/6*a*, 16/6*c*. R. T. for two months, 55/0*a*, 33/0*c*. Departures *from* London as for Hucknall. Departures *for* London about 12 times daily. Pop 1,183.
Map Square 13.

ANNFIELD PLAIN
(Durham), 269¼ miles. Fares, 59/10*a*, 35/11*c*. R. T. for two months, 119/8*a*, 71/10*c*. Departures *from* London as for Durham. Departures *for* London about 4 times daily. Pop. 16,524.
Map Square 3.

ANNITSFORD
(Northumberland) 275¾ miles. No through fares. Departures *from* London as for Newcastle-on-Tyne. Departures *for* London about 4 times daily.
Map Square 3.

ANSDELL
(Lancs), 224 miles. Fares, 46/6*a*, 27/11*c*. R. T. for two months, 93/0*a*, 55/10*c*. Departures *from* London as for Lytham. Departures *for* London about 8 times daily.
Map Square 12.

ANSTON
(Yorks) from *King's Cross*, 151½ miles. Fares, 31/6*a*, 18/11*c*. R.T. for two months, 63/0*a*, 37/10*c*. Departures *from* London as for Worksop. Departures *for* London about twice daily.
Pop. 2,184.

ANSTRUTHER
(Fife), 441¾ miles. Fares, 89/2*a*, 53/6*c*. R.T. for two months, 178/4*a*, 107/0*c*. Departures *from* London as for St. Andrews. Departures *for* London about 3 times daily. Pop. 1,535.
Map Square 41.

ANTWERP
(*via* Harwich) from *Liverpool Street*, 209 miles. Every weekday Express Trains and Geared Turbine Steamers. Single Fares, 53/0*a*, 31/0*b*.
See advt. p. **4.**

APPERLEY BRIDGE
(Yorks), 202¼ miles. Fares, 39/9*a*, 23/10*c*. R. T. for two months, 79/6*a*, 47/8*c*. Departures *from* London as for Calverley. Departures *for* London about 7 times daily.
Map Square 12.

APPIN
(Argyle), 511 miles. Fares, 102/6*a*, 61/6*c*. R. T. for two months, 205/0*a*, 123/0*c*. Departures *from* London as for Oban. Departures *for* London about twice daily. Pop. 564.
Map Square 37.

APPLEBY
(Lincoln), 175 miles. Fares, 54/5*a*, 20/8*c*. R. T. for two months, 68/10*a*, 41/4*c*. Departures *from* London as for Thorne or Barnetby. Departures *for* London 6 times daily. Pop. 609.
Map Square 13.

Station closed on Sundays.

APPLEBY
(Westmorland) from *St. Pancras*, 277¾ miles. Fares, 54/7*a*, 32/9*c*. R. T. for two months 109/2*a*, 65/6*c*. Pop. 1,786.
Map Square 3.

ST. PAN.	APPLB.	APPLB.	ST. PAN.
AM 4.25	12.20	AM 9.17*r*	5.30
9. 0*r*	3.15	11.45*r*	7.15
PM 12.15*r*	7. 0	PM 3.25*r*	9.15
11.50*e*	9.47	5.20	4.20
—	—	9.39*e*	7.25
—	—	—	—

Sunday Trains.

PM 11.45	9.47	—	—

e Saturdays excepted.
r Restaurant Car.

APPLEDORE
(Kent) from *Charing Cross, Cannon Street,* and *London Bridge*, 65 miles. Fares, 13/9*a*, 11/0*b*, 8/0*c*. R. T. for two months, 27/6*a*, 22/0*b*, 16/0*c*. Pop. 560.
Map Square 24.

	Leave		Arr. at
	CHAR. +	CAN. ST.	LON. B.	APPLE.
AM —	3.40*s*	3.43*s*	7. 9
—	5.20	5.25	8.27
9.15	—	9.23	11.10
11. 0	—	11. 7	1. 3
PM 1. 0	—	—	4.25
4.30*l*	—	4.37*l*	6.25
—	5. 0*k*	—	6.30
7.18	—	7.26	9.36

Sunday Trains.

AM 7.45	—	7.52	10. 3
9.35*h*	—	—	11.40
PM 5.15*h*	—	—	7.50
7.35	—	7.45	9.40

APPLEDORE—*continued.*

Trains from Appledore.

Leave Apple.	Arrive at Lon. B.	Can. St.	Char. +
AM 7.10	9.32	9.36	—
8.19	10. 0	10. 4	—
9.47	11.43	—	11.57
PM 1. 6	3.26	—	3.40
3.46	5.50	—	6. 3
6. 2	8.54	9. 1	—
8.12	10.22	—	10.35
—	—	—	—

Sunday Trains.

AM 7.18	10. 5	—	10.15
10.57*h*	—	1. 5*h*	—
PM 5.22	7. 9	—	7.17
8.22	10.16	—	10.26

e Saturdays excepted.
h Departs from or arrives at Victoria (S.E.&C.R.).
k Fridays only.
l Fridays excepted.
s Third Class only.

APPLETON (Lancs), 189¼

miles. Fares, 39/0*a*, 23/5*c*. R. T. for two months, 78/0*a*, 46/10*c*. Departures *from* London as for Warrington (Bank Quay). Departures *for* London about 6 times daily.
Map Square 12.

APPLEYBRIDGE (Lancs),

200½ miles. Fares, 41/5*a*, 24/10*c*. R. T. for two months, 82/10*a*, 49/8*c*. Departures *from* London as for Wigan. Departures *for* London about 6 times daily.
Map Square 12.

ARBIRLOT (Forfar), 468¼

miles. No through fares. Departures *from* London as for Dundee or Arbroath. Departures *for* London about twice daily. Pop. 789.
Map Square 38.

ARBROATH (Forfar) from

King's Cross, 468½ miles, *via* Forth and Tay Bridges. Fares, 93/9*a*, 56/3*c*. R. T. for two months, 187/6*a*, 112/6*c*. Pop. 21,385.
Map Square 38.

King's +	Arbro.	Arbro.	King's +
AM 4.45	3.57	AM 7.38*r*	6.15
10. 0*r*	8.39	11.16*r*	10. 0
PM 8.20*er*	6. 3	PM 2.21	3.25
11.25*dr*	9.40	5. 5	6. 0
11.25*er*	9.49	7.14*e*	6.50
—	—	7.56	7. 5
—	—	8.57	7.25

Sunday Trains.

PM 7.45*r*	6. 3	PM 4.37	6. 0
11.25	9.49	—	—
—	—	—	—

d Saturdays only.
e Saturdays excepted.
r Restaurant Car.

ANOTHER ROUTE from

Euston, 487½ miles. Fares as above.

Euston	Arbro.	Arbro.	Euston
AM 5. 0	8.10	AM 7.15*r*	7.30*l*
10. 0*r*	9.27	10.50*r*	10.45*l*
PM 7.50*er*	8.38*h*	PM 1.20*r*	5. 0*h*
11.35*e*	10.42	8.20	8. 0*h*
—	—	—	—
—	—	—	—

Sunday Trains.

PM 7.50*r*	8.38*h*	—	—
11.35	10.42	—	—
—	—	—	—

e Saturdays excepted
h A.M. *l* P.M.
r Restaurant Car.

ARDDLEEN (Montgomery),

173¾ miles. No through fares. Departures *from* London as for Buttington. Departures *for* London about once daily.

ARDINGLY (Sussex) from

London Bridge, Victoria, and *Clapham Junction, via* Hayward's Heath, 40½ miles. Fares, 8/4*a*, 5/0*c*. R. T. for two months, 16/8*a*, 10/0*c*. Pop. 1,332.
Map Square 23.

Leave Vict.	Clap. J.	Lon. B.	Arr. at Arding.
AM —	—	5.18	7.10
6.37	6.44	6.40	8.26
10. 5	10.11	9.50	11.36
12.45	—	12.10	2. 5
PM —	—	1.20*d*	2.30
2. 0	2. 7	2. 5	3.42
4.30	—	5. 5*d*	6. 7
—	—	5. 8*e*	6. 7
5.45*e*	—	5.55*e*	7. 0
6.50	6.57	7. 0	8.27
—	—	—	—

No Sunday Trains.

Trains from Ardingly.

Leave Arding.	Arrive at Lon. B	Clap. J.	Vict.
AM 7.46	8.53	9. 0	9. 8
8.41	9.58	—	—
8.59	10. 5	10. 5	10.12
11. 7	12.44	12.36	12.45
11.53	1.42	1.39	1.50
PM 2.45	4.32	4. 9	4.17
3.23*e*	5.54	5.47	5.55
3.30*d*	5.54	5.47	5.55
4.53	6.36	6.26	6.34
6.40	8.46	8.39	8.48
7.23*e*	10. 0	10. 2	10.10
8.57	10.25	10. 9	10.17
9.28	—	11.10	11.17

No Sunday Trains.

d Saturdays only.
e Saturdays excepted.

ANOTHER ROUTE from

Victoria, Cannon Street, and *London Bridge*, 38½ miles, *via* East Grinstead. Fares, 8/1*a*, 4/10*c*. R. T. for two months, 16/2*a*, 9/8*c*.

Vict.	Leave Can. St.	Lon. B.	Arr. at Arding.
AM 6.37	—	6.40	8.41
9.10	—	9. 6	11. 8
PM 1.20*e*	—	1.38*e*	3.23
1.25*d*	—	1.38*d*	3.30
—	—	2. 5*e*	4.53
2.25	—	2.25*d*	4 53
4. 0	—	4.10	6.40
6.50	—	7. 0	8.57
7.15	—	7.38	9.28

No Sunday Trains.

Trains from Ardingly.

Leave Arding.	Arrive at Lon. B.	Can. St.	Vict.
AM 6.50	8.37	—	8.40
7.10	9. 1*k*	9. 4	9. 8
8.26	10. 7	—	10.46
11.36	1.42	—	1.26
PM 2. 5	4.32	—	4.35
3.42	5.21	—	5.55
6. 7	8.46	—	8.27
8.27	10.25	—	11.17
—	—	—	—

No Sunday Trains.

d Saturdays only.
e Saturdays excepted.
k Departs from or arrives at London Bridge S.E. & C. Station.

ARDLEIGH (Essex) from

Liverpool Street, 56 miles. Fares, 11/11*a*, 7/2*c*. R. T. for two months, 23/10*a*, 14/4*c*. Pop. 1,440.
Map Square 19.

L'pool. St.	Ardl.	Ardl.	L'pool. St.
AM 5. 0	7.49	AM 7. 0	8.52
6.50	9.12	8.25*r*	9.53
10.20	11.52	9.35	11.16
11.30	1. 6	10.53	12.39
PM 1.33*d*	3.34	PM 1. 4	3.13
2.15	4. 2	1.42	3.36
3.23	4.59	3.57	5.48
3.26	5.30	6.28	7.51
5.42*d*	7.18	7.29*d*	9.36
5.42*e*	7.22	—	—
6.39*e*	8.11	—	—
8.45	10.21	—	—
8.54	11. 6	—	—
—	—	—	—

Sunday Trains.

AM 8.15	10.18	AM 10.12	12.40
PM 3.40	5.35	PM 6.56	8.58
7.40	9.22	8.13	10. 9
8.46	11. 0	—	—
—	—	—	—

d Saturdays only.
e Saturdays excepted.
r Restaurant Car.

ARDLER (Forfar), 468¼

miles. Fares 94/5*a*, 56/8*c*. R.T. for two months, 188/10*a*, 113/4*c*. Departures *from* London as for Coupar Angus. Departures *for* London about 3 times daily.
Map Square 38.

ARDLEY (Oxon), 57¼ miles.

Fares, 11/11*a*, 7/2*c*. R. T. for two months, 23/10*a*, 14/4*c*. Departures *from* London as for Bicester. Departures *for* London about 4 times daily. Pop. 162.
Map Square 18.

ARDLUI (Dumbarton), from

King's Cross, 485½ miles. Fares 89/5*a*, 53/8*c*. R. T. for two months, 178/10*a*, 107/4*c*. Departures *from* London as for Crianlarich. Departures *for* London about twice daily.
Map Square 40.

ARDROSSAN (Ayrshire)

from *St. Pancras*, 414¼ miles. Fares, 82/6*a*, 49/6*c*. R. T. for two months, 165/0*a*, 99/0*c*. Pop. 16,517.
Map Square 40.

St. Pan.	Ardsn.	Ardsn.	St. Pan.
AM 4.25	4. 0	AM 8.55*r*	6.35
9.50*r*	7.30	11.20*r*	9.15
PM 12.15*r*	9.47	PM 8.45*e*	7.25
9.30*e*	8. 2	10.30*d*	8.57
11.45	9.38	—	—
—	—	—	—
—	—	—	—

Sunday Trains.

PM 9.30	8. 2	PM 8.45*h*	7.25
11.45	9.38	—	—
—	—	—	—

d Saturdays only.
e Saturdays excepted.
h South Beach Station.
r Restaurant Car.

ARDROSSAN—*continued.*

ANOTHER ROUTE (*via* Carlisle) from *Euston*, 405¼ miles. Fares as above.

	Euston	Ardsn.		Ardsn.	Euston
AM	12.25*d*	2.25*l*	AM	8.55*r*	6.25
	2.35	4. 0		11.20*r*	10.30
	5. 0	5.33	PM	5. 7	5. 0*h*
	11.35*r*	9.47		8.10*d*	7.15
PM	8. 0*e*	6.53		8.45*e*	6.55
	9.20*e*	8. 2		—	—
	11. 0*d*	9.35		—	—
	11.35*e*	9.37		—	—
	11.45*e*	11. 7		—	—

Sunday Trains.

PM	8.30	6.53	PM	8.45	7.30
	11.35	9.38		—	—
	11.45	11. 7		—	—
	—	—		—	—

d Saturdays only.
e Saturdays excepted.
h A.M.
l P.M.
r Restaurant Car.

ARDSLEY (Yorks), 180 miles. Fares, 37/4*a*, 22/5*c*. R. T. for two months, 74/8*a*, 44/10*c*. Departures *from* London as for Wakefield (Westgate). Departures *for* London about 8 times daily. Pop. 7,058.
Map Square 12.

ARDWICK (Lancs), 183 miles. Fares, 38/7*a*, 23/2*c*. R.T. for two months, 77/2*a*, 46/4*c*. Departures *from* London as for Manchester. Departures *for* London about 6 times daily. Pop. 39,665.
Map Square 12.

ARENIG (Merioneth) from *Paddington*, 212¾ miles. Fares, 44/5*a*, 26/8*c*. R.T. for two months, 88/10*a*, 53/4*c*. Departures *from* London as for Blaenau Festiniog. Departures *for* London about 3 times daily.
Map Square 11.

ARGOED (Monmouth), 157¼ miles. Fares, 32/9*a*, 19/8*c*. R. T. for two months, 65/6*a*, 39/4*c*. Departures *from* London as for Tredegar. Departures *for* London about 4 times daily. Pop. 2,051.
Map Square 21.

ARISAIG (Inverness), 557¾ miles. Fares, 111/8*a*, 67/0*c*. R. T. for two months, 223/4*a*, 134/0*c*. Departures *from* London as for Fort William. Departures *for* London about twice daily. Pop. 1,375.
Map Square 36.

ARKHOLME (Lancs), 252¼ miles. Fares, 48/6*a*, 29/1*c*. R. T. for two months, 97/0*a*, 58/2*c*. Departures *from* London as for Giggleswick. Departures *for* London about 4 times daily. Pop. 319.
Map Square 7.

ARKSEY (Yorks), 158 miles. Fares, 32/9*a*, 19/8*c*. R. T. for two months, 65/6*a*, 39/4*c*. Departures *from* London as for Doncaster. Departures *for* London about 4 times daily. Pop. 6,497.
Map Square 13.

ARKWRIGHT TOWN (Derby), 151¼ miles. Fares, 30/3*a*, 18/2*c*. R.T. for two months, 60/6*a*, 36/4*c*. Departures *from* London as for Chesterfield (Central), or Edwinstowe. Departures *for* London about twice daily.
Map Square 13.

ARLESEY (Bedford) from *King's Cross*, 37 miles. Fares, 7/9*a*, 4/8*c*. R. T. for two months, 15/6*a*, 9/4*c*. Pop. 2,046.
Map Square 18.

	King's +	Arlsy.		Arlsy.	King's +
AM	5. 5	6.16	AM	7. 3	8.41
	7.45	8.55		8.46	9.56
	10.12	11.38	PM	12. 9	1.25
	11.30*d*	1. 1		2.44	3.50
PM	1.55	3. 8		5. 4	6.25
	3. 0	4.10		8.50	10.20
	5. 0*h*	5.58		—	—
	5.10	6.40		—	—
	6.15	7.25		—	—
	8.30	9.40		—	—

Sunday Trains.

AM	8.30	10. 0	PM	6.34	8. 8
PM	7.10	8.40		—	—
	—	—		—	—
	—	—		—	—

d Saturdays only.
h Mondays and Fridays only.

ARLEY (Warwick), 117¼ miles. Fares, 21/3*a*, 12/9*c*. R. T. for two months, 42/6*a*, 25/6*c*. Departures *from* London as for Water Orton. Departures *for* London about 5 times daily. Pop. 1,027.
Map Square 17.

ARLEY (Worcester) from *Paddington*, 133¾ miles. Fares, 27/1*a*, 16/3*c*. R.T. for two months, 54/2*a*, 32/6*c*. Departures *from* London as for Bewdley. Departures *for* London about 4 times daily. Pop. 634.
Map Square 17.

ARMADALE (Linlithgow), 413½ miles. No through fares. Departures *from* London as for Edinburgh (Waverley). Departures *for* London about 4 times daily. Pop. 4,927.
Map Square 40.

ARMATHWAITE (Cumberland) from *St. Pancras*, 298½ miles. Fares, 58/9*a*, 35/3*c*. R.T. for two months, 117/6*a*, 70/6*c*. Departures *from* London as for Lazonby. Departures *for* London about 4 times daily. Pop. 387.
Map Square 7.

ARMITAGE (Stafford) from *Euston*, 121 miles. Fares. 25/3*a*, 15/2*c*. R.T. for two months, 59/6*a*, 30/4*c*. Pop. 1,565.
Map Square 17.

	Euston	Armit.		Armit.	Euston
AM	5. 0	9.13	AM	7.59	11. 0
	8.45*r*	11.46		10.52*r*	2.20
	10.40*r*	2.15	PM	2.42*t*	6.15
	12.0*nr*	4. 0		4.54*r*	8.10
PM	2.50*t*	6.32		6.47*r*	10.45
	5.20*dr*	9.26		9.26	5. 0
	6.30*er*	9.26		—	—
	—	—		—	—

Sunday Trains.

	—	—	PM	1.16	5. 5
	—	—		—	—
	—	—		—	—

d Saturdays only.
e Saturdays excepted.
n Noon.
r Restaurant Car.
t Tea Car.

ARMLEY (Yorks), 185¼ miles. Fares, 38/7*a*, 23/2*c*. R.T. for two months, 77/2*a*, 46/4*c*. Departures *from* London as for Holbeck or Leeds (Wellington). Departures *for* London about 8 times daily. Pop. 37,419.
Map Square 12.

ARNAGE (Aberdeen), 546 miles. No through fares. Departures *from* London as for Fraserburgh or Peterhead. Departures *for* London about twice daily.
Map Square 35.

ARNSIDE (Westmorland), 242¼ miles. Fares, 50/5*a*, 30/3*c*. R.T. for two months, 100/10*a*, 60/6*c*. Departures *from* London as for Carnforth. Departures *for* London about 6 times daily. Pop. 1,090.
Map Square 7.

ARRAM (Yorks), 204¾ miles. No through fares. Departures *from* London as for Hull (Paragon) or Driffield. Departures *for* London about 4 times daily. Pop. 325.
Map Square 8.

ARROCHAR & TARBET (Dumbarton), 477½ miles. Fares, 87/9*a*, 52/8*c*. R. T. for two months, 175/6*a*, 105/4*c*. Pop. (Arrochar) 896.
Map Square 40.

	King's +	Ar'och'r		A'roch'r	King's +
AM	4.45	5. 6*k*	AM	10. 0*r*	10. 0*k*
PM	7.45*er*	7. 9*h*	PM	2.36	3.25
	8.25*e*	9.54*h*		7. 1	6.50*f*
	11.25*er*	12.18		—	—
	—	—		—	—

Sunday Trains.

PM	7.45*r*	7. 9		—	—
	8.25	9.54		—	—
	11.25	12.18*k*		—	—

d Saturdays only.
e Saturdays excepted.
f Arrives 7.5 A.M. Sundays.
h A.M.
k P.M.
r Restaurant Car.

ARTHINGTON (Yorks), 193¾ miles. Fares, 40/3*a*, 24/2*c*. R. T. for two months, 80/6*a*, 48/4*c*. Departures *from* London as for Leeds. Departures *for* London about 6 times daily. Pop. 413.
Map Square 7.

ARTHOG (Merioneth) 229 miles. Fares (*via* Dolgelley), 48/1*a*, 28/10*c*. R. T. for two months, 96/2*a*. (*Via* Welshpool), 48/4*a*, 29/0*c*. R. T. for two months, 96/8*a*. Departures *from* London as for Dolgelley or Barmouth. Departures *for* London about 5 times daily.
Map Square 16.

ARUNDEL (Sussex) from *London Bridge*, *Victoria*, and *Clapham Junction*, 58¼ miles. Fares, 12/1*a*, 7/3*c*. R.T. for two months, 24/2*a*, 14/6*c*. Pop. 2,741.
Map Square 28.

	Leave			Arr. at
	Vict	Clap. J.	Lond. B.	Arndl.
AM	6.18	6.25	6.35	8.26
	7.23	7.29	7.25	10.10
	8.55	—	—	10.27
	10.15	10.22	10.22	12. 7
	—	—	10.30	12.18
	10.35	10.42	10.35	1.46
PM	1.35	—	—	3. 0
	1.40	1.47*e*	1.50	3.31
	3.55	4. 2	4. 0	5.44
	—	—	4.50	6.16
	4.53	5. 0	—	6.37
	—	—	5. 5	7.14
	6.15	—	—	7.36
	7.20	7.27	7.15	9.27

Sunday Trains.

AM	8.35	8.42	—	10.10
	—	—	8.25	10.39
	9. 0	9. 7	8.55	10.51
PM	7. 0	7. 7	6.38	9. 0

ARUNDEL—*continued.*

Trains from Arundel.

Leave	Arrive at		
ARNDL.	LOND. B.	CLAP. J.	VICT.
AM 7. 1	9.10	9.31	9.19
8. 0	—	—	10.28
8.30	9.58	—	—
9. 1	10.45	10.45	10.53
9.32	10.55	—	—
10.28	12. 8	—	12. 0
PM12.54	3.32	3.22	3.32
2.26	4.15	—	—
2.49	4.27	4.26	4.34
3.33	5.54	4.52	5. 0
4.57	—	—	6.50
5.47	—·	7. 7	7.15
6. 0	7.48	7.31	7.39
8.19	10. 8	9.53	10. 1
8.25	10.58	11.10	11.17

Sunday Trains.

AM 8. 1	10.45	10.23	10.32
PM 3.57	7.56	7.25	7.33
6.18	—	7.41	7.49
6.59	8.50	8.33	8.42
7. 7	9.32	9.24	9.34

e Saturdays excepted.

Norfolk Hotel. Most Comfortable Family and Commercial in Sussex. Home Comforts. Garage. Repairs. Hire. Telephone 45. Telegrams, "Hare." Proprietor, G. W. HARE.

ASCOT (Berks) from

Waterloo, 29 miles. Fares, 5/5*a*, 3/3*c*. R.T. for two months, 10/10*a*, 6/6*c*. Pop. 2,351.
Map Square 23.

W'LOO.	ASCOT.	ASCOT.	W'LOO.
AM 5.10	6.46	AM 7.15	8.17
6.54	8.19	7.42	8.47
7.54	9.14	8.18	9.17
8.54	10. 7	8.55	9.47
9.54	11. 9	9.20	10.17
10.54	12.12	10.17	11.17
PM12.48	1.55	11.21	12.31
1.18*d*	2.21	PM12.21	1.27
1.48	2.54	1.21	2.27
2.18*d*	3.23	2.21	3.27
2.48	3.53	4.21	5.27
3.48*e*	4.54	5.21	6.27
3.48*d*	4.59	6.21	7.27
4.48*e*	5.46	7.21	8.27
4.48*d*	5.59	8.21	9.27
5.18*e*	6.20	9.28	10.37
5.48	6.50	10.50*e* 12. 5	
6.18*e*	7.20	10.50*d* 12. 8	
6.48	7.52	—	—
7.54	9. 9	—	—
9.24	10.37	—	—
10.24	11.39	—	—

Sunday Trains.

AM 8.18	9.39	AM 9. 5	10.30
9.18	10.19	11.17	12.43
PM12.18	1.36	PM12.52	2. 3
2.18	3.35	4.23	5.28
4.18	5.33	6.17	7.28
5.58	7.15	8.17	9.28
7.48	9. 3	9. 9	10.18
9.18	10.37	9.21	10.28

d Saturdays only.
e Saturdays excepted.

Berystede Hotel de Luxe. Enlarged and redecorated. Standing in its own lovely grounds of 30 acres. Tennis, croquet. Near Sunningdale Golf Course. Telephone, 154; Telegrams, "Berystede."

ASCOTTUnderWYCH-WOOD (Oxon) from *Paddington.*
72¾ miles. Fares, 16/10*a*,· 10/1*c*. R. T. for two months, 33/8*a*, 20/2*c*. Departures *from* London as for Charlbury. Departures *for* London about 4 times daily. Pop. 365.
Map Square 22.

ASFORDBY(Leicester)from
St.Pancras, 108 miles. Fares,21/8*a*, 13/0*c*. R.T. for two months, 43/4*a*, 26/0*c*. Pop. 1,336.
Map Square 18.

ST.PAN.	AS'F'DBY	AS'F'DBY	ST.PAN.
AM 2.25	7.11	AM 7. 6*r*	9.57
4.25	8.27	7.47*r*	11. 0
9.50*r*	12.27	9.31*r*	12.10
10.25*dr*	1.12	10. 5*r*	1.30
PM12.25*r*	3.57	PM 2. 6*r*	5.45
2.25*r*	5.39	6. 1*r*	8.35
3.30*r*	6.43	6.43*r*	9.15
4.25*r*	7.59	9. 3	4.20
6.25*r*	9.37	—	—

Sunday Trains.

PM 3.15	8.34	AM 8. 3	11.53
—	—	PM 6.31*r*	9.52

d Saturdays only.
r Restaurant Car.

ASH (Surrey) from *Charing*
Cross, Cannon Street, and *London Bridge.* 50 miles. Fares, 6/10*a*, 5/5*b*, 4/1*c*. R.T. for two months, 13/1*a*, 8/9*b*. Pop. 4,482.
Map Square 23.

	Leave		Arr. at
CHAR. +	CAN. ST.	LON. B.	ASH
AM —	4.44	5. 0	7. 8
—	—	7.50*l*	9.55
—	—	9.33*l*	11.34
10.55	—	11. 3	1.18
PM12.55	—	1. 4	3.15
2. 3*e*	2. 8*d*	2.10	4.11
—	—	2.22*dl*	4.18
3.15*d*	—	3.21*d*	5.26
3.15*e*	—	3.21*e*	5.28
4.22*d*	—	4.28*d*	6.27
—	4.44*e*	4.48*e*	6.26
—	5.24*e*	5.27*e*	7.15
5.42*d*	—	5.48*d*	7.44
—	6. 0*e*	6. 3*e*	7.58
6.34*d*	—	6.40*d*	8.41
—	6.56*e*	6.39*e*	8.40
7.24*d*	—	7.30*d*	9.35
8.28	—	8.36	10.43

Sunday Trains.

AM 6.25	—	6.32	8.45
10.20	—	10.28	12.27
PM 5.25	—	5.32	7.39
8.38	—	8.45	11.47

Trains from Ash.

Leave	Arrive at		
ASH	LON. B.	CAN. ST.	CHAR. +
AM 7. 6	8.56	—	—
8. 4	9.43	9.52	—
8.34	10.10	—	10.20
8.47*h*	10.31	—	10.43
9. 1	11. 0	—	—
10. 4	11.46	—	11.59
10.41	12.50	—	1. 0
PM12.34	2.38	—	2.46
2.48	5. 2	—	5.14
4. 2	5.56	—	—
5.13	7.20	—	7.29
7. 5	9. 2	—	9.15
8. 7	10. 3	—	10.13
10. 3	11.57	—	12.10

Sunday Trains.

AM 6.18	8.16	—	8.27
9.20	11.15	—	11.25
PM 5. 9	7.13	—	7.25
8.13	10.11	—	10.24

d Saturdays only.
e Saturdays excepted.
k Wednesdays only.
l Low Level platform.

ASH TOWN (Kent), 79½

miles. No through fares. Departures *from* London as for Wingham Colliery. Departures *for* London about 5 times daily. Pop. 2,049.

ASHBOURNE (Derby)

from *St. Pancras*, 151¾ miles. Fares, 30/3*a*, 18/2*c*. R.T. for two months, 60/6*a*, 36/4*c*. Pop. 4,147.
Map Square 12.

ST. PAN	ASHB'NE.	ASHB'NE.	ST. PAN.
AM 4.25	10.49	AM 9.10*r*	1.30
10.25*r*	3.28	11.40*r*	4.20
PM12.25*d*	5.27	PM 1.40*r*	6.15
1.25*er*	5.54	4.20*r*	8.35
1.25*dr*	6.19	9.15	4.20
2.25*r*	7. 1	—	—
4.25*r*	9. 9	—	—

Sunday Trains.

PM 3.15	7.58	AM10. 0*r*	5. 2
—	—	PM 6.10	4.55

d Saturdays only.
e Saturdays excepted.
r Restaurant Car.

ANOTHER ROUTE from
Euston, 146¾ miles. Fares as above.

EUSTON	ASHB'NE	ASHB'NE	EUSTON
AM 5. 0	10.49	AM 7.35*r*	2.20
6.45	1.14	10.40	5.35
8.45*r*	3.28	PM 1.40*r*	8.10
10.40*dr*	6.19	4.20*r*	10.45
12. 0*nr*	5.54	—	—
PM 2.50*t*	9 .9	—	—

No Sunday Trains.

d Saturdays only.
n Noon.
r Restaurant Car.
t Tea Car.

ASHBURTON (Devon)
from *Paddington*, 211½ miles. Fares, 43/7*a*, 26/2*c*. R. T. for two months, 87/2*a*, 52/4*c*. Pop. 2,362.
Map Square 26.

PAD.	ASHBTN.	ASHBTN	PAD.
AM 5.30	1.13	AM 7.45*r*	1.30
9.15*r*	3.38	11.45*r*	4.35
11.10*r*	4.43	PM 2.25*r*	9. 0
PM12. 5*r*	6. 8	5. 0	2.45
3.30*r*	8.48	6.25	7.10
12. 0*h*	9. 8	—	—

Sunday Trains.

PM10. 0	9. 8	—	—

h Saturdays midnight excepted.
r Restaurant Car.

ASHBURY (Devon) from
Waterloo, 206 miles. Fares, 42/11*a*, 25/9*c*. R. T. for two months, 85/10*a*, 51/6*c*. Pop. 58.
Map Square 26.

W'LOO.	ASHBURY	ASHBURY	W'LOO.
AM11. 0*r*	4.33	AM 8.20*r*	1.56
PM 1. 0*r*	6.43	10.44*r*	3.50
3. 0*r*	7.43	PM 2.49*r*	8.30
—	—	5. 2	10.50

No Sunday Trains.
r Restaurant Car.

ASHBURYS (Lancs), 204¼

miles. Fares, 38/6a, 23/1c. R. T., double fare. Departures *from* London as for Guide Bridge. Departures *for* London about 4 times daily.

ASHBY-DE-LA-ZOUCH

(Leicester) from *St. Pancras,* 117½ miles. Fares, 23/11a,14/4c. R. T., double fare. Pop. 4,983.
Map Square 17.

St. Pan.	Ashby	Ashby	St. Pan.
AM 2.25	7.54	AM 7.34*r*	11. 0
4.25	10.10	8.39*r*	11.35
10.25*r*	1.24	11.45	3.25
PM12.25*r*	3.41	PM 1.46*r*	5.45
2.25*r*	5.33	3.52*r*	6.35
3.30*r*	7. 9	6.12*r*	9.15
4.25*r*	7.35	9.18	4.20
6.25*r*	9. 7	—	—
—	—	—	—
—	—	—	—
—	—	—	—

Sunday Trains.

PM 6.15*r*	9.37	AM 7.43	11.53
;	—	PM 6.12*r*	9.52
—	—	—	—

r Restaurant Car.

ANOTHER ROUTE from

Euston, 119 miles. Fares as above.

Euston	Ashby	Ashby	Euston
AM 5. 0	8.50	AM 7. 3*r*	11. 0
10. 0	2.15	9. 1	12.50
PM 4.45*t*	3. 2	11.35*hr*	3.45
5.20*r*	9.31	11.35*r*	4.15
—	—	PM 3.55*r*	8.10
—	—	6. 8*r*	10.45
—	—	—	—
—	—	—	—
—	—	—	—

No Sunday Trains.

h Mondays and Saturdays only.
r Restaurant Car.
t Tea Car.

Midland Hotel. Close to Station. Tea Room. Tea Garden. Five Bedrooms. Stabling. Excellent Touring Centre. Parties catered for. Ample accommodation. P.R.H.A. House.

ASHBY MAGNA

(Leicester), 94 miles. Fares, 19/5a, 11/8c. R. T., double fare. Departures *from* London as for Lutterworth. Departures *for* London about 4 times daily. Pop. 262.
Map Square 18.

ASHCHURCH (Glo'ster),

117¾ miles. No through fares. Departures *from* London as for Evesham. Departures *for* London about 6 times daily. Pop. 786.
Map Square 17.

ASHCOTT (Somerset), 136¼

miles. Fares, 28/4a, 17/0c. R. T. for two months, 56/8a. Departures *from* London as for Glastonbury. Departures *for* London about 4 times daily. Pop. 612.
Map Square 22.

ASHEY (Isle of Wight),

82 miles. Fares, 18/4a, 11/3c. R.T. for two months, 36/8a, 22/6c. Departures *from* London as for Ryde. Departures *for* London about 4 times daily. Pop. 1,471.
Map Square 23.

ASHFORD (Middlesex)

from *Waterloo,* 17½ miles. Fares, 2/11a, 1 /9c R. T for eight days, 5/10a, 3/6c. Pop. 7,673.
Map Squares 23 and 74.

W'loo.	Ashford	Ashford	W'loo.
AM 5.10	6. 9	AM 6. 0	6.36
5.35	6.31	7. 0	7.36
6.54	7.34	7.30	8. 6
7.24	8. 4	7.45	8.17
7.54	8.34	8. 1	8.41
8.24	9. 5	8.13	8.47
8.54	9.34	8.33	9. 6
9.24	10. 5	9. 1	9.36
9.54	10.34	9.30	10. 6
10.24	11. 4	10.30	11. 6
10.54	11.37	10.48	11.17
11.24	12. 4	11.21	11.57
PM12.24	1. 4	11.51	12.31
12.54*d*	1.34	PM12.21	12.57
1.24	2. 4	12.51	1.27
1.54*d*	2.34	1.21	1.57
2.24	3. 4	1.51	2.27
3.24	4. 4	2.21	2.57
3.48*d*	4.24	2.51	3.27
4.24	5. 4	3.21	3.57
4.48*d*	5.24	4.21	4.57
4.58*e*	5.34	4.51	5.27
5.24	6. 4	5.21	5.57
5.54*e*	6.34	5.51	6.27
6.24	7. 4	6.21	6.57
6.54*e*	7.34	6.51	7.27
7.24	8. 4	7.21	7.57
7.54	8.34	7.51	8.27
8.24	9. 4	8.21	8.57
9.24	10. 4	8.51	9.27
10.24	11. 4	10. 0	10.37
11.44	12.23	11.20*e*	12. 5
—	—	11.20*d*	12. 8
—	—	—	—
—	—	—	—
—	—	—	—
—	—	—	—
—	—	—	—
—	—	—	—

Sunday Trains.

AM 8.18	9. 0	AM 8.48	9.28
8.48	9.28	9.39	10.30
9.18	9.52	11. 3	11.43
10.18	10.57	PM12. 3	12.43
11.18	11.57	1. 3	1.43
PM12.18	12.59	1.23	2. 3
1.18	1.57	3. 3	3.43
2.18	3. 0	4.52	5.28
3.18	3.57	5. 3	5.43
4.18	4.59	6. 3	6.43
5.18	5.57	6.48	7.28
5.58	6.38	7. 3	7.43
6.18	6.57	8. 3	8.43
7.18	7.57	8.48	9.28
7.48	8.27	9. 3	9.43
8.18	8.57	9.39	10.18
8.58	9.37	10. 3	10.43
9.18	9.59	11. 3	11.51
10.18	10.57	—	—
—	—	—	—

d Saturdays only.
e Saturdays excepted.

ASHFORD JUNCTION

(Kent) from *Charing Cross, Cannon Street,* and *London Bridge,* 56¾ miles. Fares, 11/11a, 9/7b, 6/11c. R. T. for two months, 23 10a, 19/2b. Pop. (Ashford) 14,355.
Map Square 24.

Char. +	Can. St	Lon. B.	Arr. at Ashf. J.
AM —	3.40*k*	3.43*k*	5.27
—	5.20	5.25	8. 5
—	6.45	6.50	9. 7
—	—	7.50*l*	9.46
9.15	—	9.23	10.43
9.25	—	9.33	11.18
—	—	(10. 3*v*	11.42
—	—	(10. 3*s*	11.45
11. 0	—	11. 7	12.38
—	,11.56	12. 0	1.47
PM12.40*d*	—	12.47*d*	2.33
1. 0	—	—	2. 5
3. 0	—	3. 8	4.27
4.30	—	4.37	5.47
—	4.36*e*	4.39*e*	6.19
—	5. 0*s*	—	6. 4
—	5.12*e*	—	6.28
5.15*e*	—	5.21*e*	6.57
5.20*d*	—	5.26*d*	7. 1
5.24*d*	—	5.34*d*	7.24
6. 0*e*	—	6. 5*e*	7.15
7.18	—	7.26	9.13
9.30	—	9.36	10.52
11.51*j*	—	—	1.22
—	—	—	—

Sunday Trains.

AM 7.45	—	7.52	9.39
10.10	—	10.18	11.36
PM 6.35	—	6.43	8.51
7.35	—	7.45	9.10
9.25	—	9.31	11.20

Trains from Ashford Junc.

	Leave	Arrive at	
Ashfd. J.	Lon. B.	Can. St.	Char. +
AM 6.40	8.40	8.44	—
7.44	9.32	9.36	—
8.36	10. 0	10. 4	—
8.43	10.28	10.32	—
9.24	10.54	—	11. 3
9.35	11.33	—	11.45
10.18	11.43	—	11.57
11.54	1.36	—	1.50
PM 2. 5	3.26	—	3.40
2.17*s*	4. 8	—	—
2.18*v*	4. 8	—	—
4.15	5.50	—	6. 3
5.54	—	—	7.49
6. 0	7.25	7.30	—
6.32	8.54	9. 1	—
8.51	10.22	—	10.35
9.52	11.34	—	11.43
11.31*k*	—	1.20	—
—	—	—	—

Sunday Trains.

AM 7.47	10.15	—	10.15
PM 5.53	7. 9	—	7.17
6.25	8.20	—	8.28
6.53	8.30	—	8.40
9. 2	10.16	—	10.26
11.31*k*	—	1.23	—
—	—	—	—
—	—	—	—
—	—	—	—

d Saturdays only.
e Saturdays excepted.
j Wednesdays only.
k Third Class only.
l Low Level platform.
s Fridays only.
v Mondays and Saturdays only.

ASHFORD JUNC.—cont.

ANOTHER ROUTE from *Victoria, Holborn Viaduct,* and *St. Paul's,* 59 miles. Fares as above.

S.E. & C.	Leave HOL. V.	S. PL.'s	Arr. at ASHF. J
AM —	6.40	6.42	9.16
9.45	—	—	11.23
11. 4	10.58	11. 0	1.38
PM —	1.24*d*	1.30*d*	3.24
2.12*e*	—	—	4.' 0
2.40*d*	—	—	5.10
2.50*e*	—	—	5.30
4.25*c*	—	—	6.14
7.22	—	—	9. 5
—	7.22*d*	7.24*d*	9.47
—	—	—	—
—	—	—	—
—	—	—	—
—	—	—	—

Sunday Trains.

AM —	8. 0	—	10.41
9.35	—	—	11.20
PM 5.15	—	—	7. 8
6.35	6.40	—	9. 4

Trains from Ashford Junc.

Leave ASHF. J.	S. PL.'s	Arrive at HOL. V.	VICT.
AM 7. 0	9.16	9.18	8.50
7.50	9.53	9.55	—
8.20*e*	10.21	10.23	10.16
8.27*d*	10.41	10.43	—
10.37	12.59	1. 2	12.49
PM12. 8	—	—	2.40
1.45	—	—	3.37
4. 0	—	—	5.42
4.30	6.58	7. 0	—
6.10	—	—	8.51
9.10	11.44	11.46	—

Sunday Trains.

AM 8.25	—	—	10.48
11.27	—	—	1. 5
PM 1.30	—	—	3.50
7. 0	—	9. 9	—
—	—	—	—

d Saturdays only.
e Saturdays excepted.

Fernley Hotel. Commercial, Family, Temperance. Well appointed Commercial, Dining, Coffee and Bedrooms. Large Garden. Every comfort. Phone 47. R. G. CAMPBELL, Proprietor.

Saracen's Head Hotel. Family and Commercial. Luncheons, 1 o'clock. Dinner, 7 o'clock. Stock Rooms. Garage, R.A.C. M.U. Bus meets all trains. New Management. Proprietor, W. MEADMORE.

Lee and Son. The leading House Furnishers, Auctioneers, Valuers, House and Estate Agents, Removal Contractors and Warehousemen, High Street. Tel. 88.

ASH GREEN (Surrey) from

Waterloo, 36 miles. Fares, 7/6*a*, 4/6*c*. R. T. for two months, 15/0*a*, 9/0*c*. Departures *from* London as for Wanborough. Departures *for* London about 5 minutes earlier.
Map Square 23.

ASHINGTON (Northumberland), 286½ miles. Fares, 60/7*a*, 36/4*c*. R. T., double fare. Departures *from* London as for Newcastle-on-Tyne. Departures *for* London about 6 times daily. Pop. 29,406.

ASHLEY (Cheshire), from

Euston, 182 miles. No through fares. Departures *from* London as for Knutsford. Departures *for* London about 5 times daily. Pop. 418.
Map Square 12.

ASHLEY & WESTON

(Northampton) from *Euston,* 88½ miles. Fares, 16/11*a*, 10/2*c*. R. T., double fare. Departures *from* London as for Market Harborough. Departures *for* London about 5 times daily. Pop. (Ashley) 191.
Map Square 18.

ASHLEY HILL (Glo'ster),

115 miles. Fares, 24/0*a*, 14/5*c*. R. T., double fare. Departures *from* London as for Bristol. Departures *for* London about 6 times daily.
Station Closed on Sundays.
Map Square 22.

ASHPERTON (Hereford),

128¾ miles. Fares, 27/9*a*, 16/8*c*. R. T., double fare. Departures *from* London as for Malvern. Departures *for* London about 6 times daily. Pop. 344.
Map Square 17.

ASHTEAD (Surrey) from

London Bridge, 19½ miles. Fares, 2/11*a*, 1/9*c*. R. T. for eight days, 5/10*a*, 3/6*c*. Pop. 3,226. *See pp.* 565, 566.
Map Square 23.

ANOTHER ROUTE from

Victoria, 18 miles. Fares as above. *See pp.* 571-574.

ANOTHER ROUTE from

Waterloo, 16½ miles. Fares as above. *See pp.* 583, 584.

ASHTON (Devon), 184½

miles. Fares, 38/1*a*, 22/10*c*. R. T., double fare. Departures *from* London as for Exeter (St. David's). Departures *for* London about 5 times daily. Pop. 176.
Map Square 26.

ASHTON (OLDHAM ROAD)

(Lancs) from *Euston* 184½ miles. Fares, 37/9*a*, 22/8*c*. R. T., double fare. Pop. 43,333.

EUSTON	ASHTON	ASHTON	EUSTON
AM 2.35	8.18	AM 7.42*er*12. 5	
5. 0	10.16	8. 9*r*	12.50
8.45*r*	12.54	9.18*r*	1.15
10.40*r*	2.46	10.20*r*	3.10
11.50*r*	3.49	11.52*r*	3.55
PM 1.30*er*	6.26	PM12.48*dr*	6. 0
2.50*t*	7. 5	1.39*r*	6.15
4. 5*r*	8.22	2.22*r*	7.30
4.45*r*	9.20	3.42*r*	8.10
6. 5*r*	10. 7	4.53*dr*10. 0	
11.50*d*	10. 7	5.44*er*10.15	
		10.10	5. 0

Sunday Trains.

PM12.10*r*	5.18	PM12.17*r*	5.45
12.30*r*	9.35	3.54*r*	8.55
—	—	9.47	5. 0

d Saturdays only.
e Saturdays excepted.
r Restaurant Car.
t Tea Car.

ANOTHER ROUTE (PARK PARADE) from *Marylebone,* 201¼ miles. Fares as above.

M'BONE.	ASHTON	ASHTON	M'BONE.
AM 2.32	9.11	AM 8.13*r*	1.13
8.45*r*	1.45	9.28*r*	3. 0
10. 0*r*	3.15*h*	PM 2.13*r*	6.38
PM12.15*er*	5.26	4.37*hr*	9.55
12.15*r*	6.55*h*	10.32*h*	3.57
3.20*r*	7.56	—	—
5. 0*r*	9.45*h*	—	—
6.20*dr*11.16*h*		—	—
10. 5*e*	5.22*h*	—	—

Sunday Trains.

AM11.15*r*	4.15*h*	PM12. 4*hr*	5.40
—	—	4.39*hr*10.24	

d Saturdays only.
e Saturdays excepted.
h Ashton (Oldham Road).
r Restaurant Car.

ANOTHER ROUTE (PARK PARADE) from *St. Pancras,* 184½ miles. No through fares.

ST. PAN.	ASHTON	ASHTON	ST. PAN.
AM 4.25	11.59	AM 6. 2*hr*11.35	
10.25*dr*	3.52	7. 9*r*	1.30
10.25*er*	5.26	9.28	3.25
PM 1.25*er*	6.35	PM12.18*r*	5.45
1.25*r*	8. 0*h*	2.13*r*	8.35
4.25*r*	9.45*h*	6.17*h*	4.20
12. 0*k*	10.55*h*	—	—

Sunday Trains.

PM 3.15	9. 5*h*	PM 1.53*hr*	9.52
—	—	—	—

d Saturdays only.
e Saturdays excepted.
h Oldham Road.
k Saturdays midnight only.
r Restaurant Car.

ASHTON-IN-MAKER-

FIELD (Lancs), 225½ miles. Fares, 40/0*a*, 24/0*c*. R. T., double fare. Departures *from* London as for St. Helens (Central). Departures *for* London about 5 times daily. Pop. 22,489.

ASHTON-UNDER-HILL (Gloucester), 112 miles. No through fares. Departures *from* London as for Evesham. Departures *for* London about 5 times daily. Pop. 350. *Map Square* 17.

ASHURST (Kent) from
London Bridge, Victoria, and Cannon Street, 32 miles. Fares 6/8*a*, 4/0*c*. R. T. for two months, 13/4*a*, 8/0*c*. Pop. 164. *Map Square* 24.

	Leave		Arr. at
VICT.	CAN. ST.	LON. B.	ASH'RST.
AM 5.30	—	5.18	6.54
6.37	—	6.40	8. 9
7.23	—	8. 7	9.31
9.10	—	9. 6	10.32
11. 5	—	10.35	12.53
12. 0*d*	12.16*d*	12.20*k*	1.36
PM 1.20*e*	—	1.38*e*	2.53
1.25*d*	—	1.38*d*	2.57
—	—	2. 5*e*	3.54
2.25	—	2.25*d*	3.54
3.45	—	—	4.37
4. 0*e*	4.16*e*	*e*4 20*k*	5.33
4.50	—	4.44*e*	6. 0
5. 5	—	5.21	6.34
6. 6	—	6. 8	7.28
6.50	—	7. 0	8.28
8. 5	—	8.10	9.23
9. 3*l*	—	9.12*l*	10.49
—	—	—	—
—	—	—	—
—	—	—	—
—	—	—	—

Sunday Trains.

AM 8.50	—	8.30	10. 3
PM 1.14	—	1.10	2.33
2.30	—	—	3.54
7. 5	—	6.46	8.20

Trains from Ashurst.

Leave	Arrive at		
ASHURST	LON. B.	CAN. ST.	VICT.
AM 6.49	8.15	—	8.24
7.23	8.37	—	8.40
7.57	9.15	—	9.19
8.49	10. 4	—	10.12
9.41	10.55	—	10.46
10. 8	—	—	11.35
10.59	12.13	—	12.17
11.51	1.42	—	1.26
PM 1.33	2.58	—	—
2.22	4. 0	—	3.45
5. 9	6.36	—	6.29
6.37	7.56	—	8.27
9. 4	10.25	—	10.10
—	—	—	—
—	—	—	—
—	—	—	—
—	—	—	—

Sunday Trains.

AM 8.46	10.18	—	10.20
PM12.13	—	—	1.40
5. 8	—	—	6.34
7.51	9.17	—	9. 0
8.54	—	—	9.47
—	—	—	—
—	—	—	—

d Saturdays only.
e Saturdays excepted.
k Departs.from or arrives at London Bridge (S.E. & C.) Station.
l Fridays only.

ASHWATER (Devon) from
Waterloo, 215 miles Fares, 44/10*a*, 26/11*c*. R. T. for two months, 89/8*a*, 53/10*c*. Departures *from* London as for Halwill Junction. Departures *for* London about 4 times daily. Pop. 679. *Map Square* 26.

ASHWELL (Herts) from
King's Cross, 41 miles. Fares, 8/7*a*, 5/2*c*. R. T., double fare. Departures *from* London as for Baldock. Departures *for* London about 8 times daily Pop. 1,163. *Map Square* 18.

ASHWELL (Rutland) from
St. Pancras, 97 miles. Fares, *via* Geddington, 19/5*a*, 11/8*c*. R. T., double fare. *Via* Leicester. 20/8*a*, 12/5*c*. R.T., double fare. Pop. 246. *Map Square* 18.

ST. PAN.	ASHWL.	ASHWL.	ST. PAN.
AM 2.25	7.13	AM 8. 2*r*	10.45
8.25*r*	11.33	9. 2*r*	12.10
9.50*r*	12.57	10. 2*r*	1.20
10.25*r*	1.51	PM12.57*r*	4.10
11.35	2.59	1.17*r*	4.20
PM12.25*r*	4.24	5.49	8.22
1. 0*r*	4.47	9.27	4.20
2.25*r*	5.48	—	—
3.30*r*	5.54	—	—
5.35*r*	8.22	—	—
6.25*r*	10. 5	—	—

Sunday Trains.

PM 3.15	9. 4	AM 7.33	11.53
—	—	PM 5.56*r*	9.52

r Restaurant Car.

ANOTHER ROUTE from
King's Cross, 105¼ miles, *via* Peterboro'. Fares, 19/5*a*, 11/8*c*. R. T., double fare.

KING's +	ASHWL.	ASHWL	KING's +
AM 5. 5	9. 2	AM 8. 2*r*	12.55
10.10*r*	1.17	10. 2	1. 5
PM 1.50*r*	4.47	PM 1.51*r*	4.45
3. 0	8.22	4.24*r*	7.10
5.45*r*	9.23	5.49*r*	9.25
—	—	10. 3	3.25
—	—	—	—
—	—	—	—

Sunday Trains.

12. 0*n*	5.56	AM10.25	3.45

n Noon.
r Restaurant Car.

ASHWELLTHORPE
(Norfolk), 107 miles. Fares, 22/6*a*, 13/6*c*. R. T., double fare. Departures *from* London as for Wymondham. Departures *for* London about 4 times daily. Pop. 351. *Map Square* 19.

ASKAM (Lancs), 263¼ miles.
Fares, 54/10*a*, 32/11*c*. R. T., double fare. Departures *from* London as for Barrow-in-Furness. Departures *for* London about 5 times daily. Pop. 484. *Map Square* 6.

ASKERN (Yorks) from
King's Cross, 162½ miles. Fares, 33/7*a*, 20/2*c*. R. T., double fare. Departures *from* London as for Knottingley. Departures *for* London about 10 minutes later. Pop. 988. *Map Square* 13.

ASKRIGG (Yorks), 247¼
miles. Fares, 51/1*a*, 30/8*c*. R. T., double fare. Departures *from* London as for Leyburn. Departures *for* London about 5 times daily. Pop. 470. *Map Square* 7.

ASLOCKTON (Notts),
117½ miles. Fares, 24/4*a*, 14/7*c*. R. T., double fare Departures *from* London as for Bottesford. Departures *for* London about 4 times daily. Pop. 359. *Map Square* 13.

ASPALL (Suffolk), 91¼ miles.
Fares, 19/3¼*a*, 11/7*c*. R. T., double fare. Departures *from* London as for Stradbroke. Departures *for* London about twice daily. Pop. 133. *Map Square* 19.

ASPATRIA (Cumberland),
319½ miles. Fares, 64/9*a*, 38/10*c*. R. T., double fare. Departures *from* London as for Maryport. Departures *for* London about 5 times daily. Pop. 3,525. *Map Square* 6.

ASTLEY(Lancs), 194½ miles.
Fares, 39/7*a*, 23/9*c*. R. T., double fare. Departures *from* London as for Kenyon. Departures *for* London about 5 times daily. Pop. 3,556.

ASTON (Warwick), 112
miles. Fares, 23/6*a*, 14/1*c*. R. T., double fare. Departures *from* London as for Birmingham (New Street). Departures *for* London about 7 times daily. Pop. 75,029. *Map Square* 17.

ASTON-BY-STONE
(Stafford) 137 miles. Fares, 28/7*a*, 17/2*c*. R. T., double fare. Departures *from* London as for Colwich. Departures *for* London about 3 times daily. Pop. 486. *Map Square* 12.

ASTON ROWANT
(Oxon) from *Paddington*, 41 miles. Fares, 7/8*a*, 4/11*c*. R. T., double fare. Departures *from* London as for Watlington. Departures *for* London about 3 times daily. Pop. 532. *Map Square* 23.

ASWARBY (Lincoln), 109
miles. Fares, 22/8*a*, 13/7*c*. R. T., double fare. Departures *from* London as for Bourne. Departures *for* London about 6 times daily. Pop. 108. *Map Square* 13.

ATHELNEY (Somerset),
135 miles. Fares, 28/2*a*, 16/11*c*. R. T., double fare. Departures *from* London as for Somerton. Departures *for* London about 4 times daily. *Map Square* 22.

ATHERSTONE (Warwick) from *Euston*, 102¼ miles. Fares, 21/3*a*, 12/9*c*. R. T. for two months, 42/6*a*, 25/6*c*. Pop. 5,607.
Map Square 17.

Euston	Ather.	Ather.	Euston
AM 5. 0	8.14	AM 6.50*r*	10. 0
6.45	9.25	8.45	11..0
8.45*r*	11. 4	11.35*r*	2.20
10.40*r*	1.31	PM12.42*r*	4.15
12. 0*nr*	3. 4	2.32*k*	5.35
PM 2.50*t*	5.39	3.33*t*	6.15
4.45*r*	7.15	5.48*r*	8.10
5.20*r*	8.31	7.48*r*	10.45
—	—	10. 9	5. 0
—	—	11.25*d*	5. 0
—	—	—	—

Sunday Trains.

AM 9.15	12.33	PM 1.57	5. 5
—	—	—	—

d Saturdays only.
k Tuesdays only.
n Noon.
r Restaurant Car.
t Tea Car.

ATHERTON (Lancs), 195 miles. Fares, 40/2*a*, 24/1*c*. R. T. for two months, 80/4*a*, 48/2*c*. Departures *from* London as for Kenyon. Departures *for* London about 6 times daily. Pop. 19,863.
Map Square 12.

ATTADALE (Ross), 634½ miles. Fares, 116/3*a*, 69/9*c*. R. T. for two months, 232/6*a*, 139/6*c*. Departures *from* London as for Kyle of Lochalsh. Departures *for* London about 3 times daily.
Map Square 34.

ATTENBORO' (Notts), 122 miles. Fares, *via* Trent, 25/0*a*, 15/0*c*. R. T. for two months, 50/0*a*, 30/0*c*. *Via* Nottingham, 25/8*a*, 15/5*c*. R. T. for two months, 51/4*a*, 30/10*c*. Departures *from* London as for Trent or Nottingham. Departures *for* London about 6 times daily. Pop. 2,218.
Map Square 13.

ATTERCLIFFE (Yorks), 161 miles. Fares, 32/9*a*, 19/8*c*. R. T. for two months, 65/6*a*, 39/4*c*. Departures *from* London as for Sheffield (Victoria). Departures *for* London about 4 times daily. Pop. 29,685.

ATTERCLIFFE ROAD (Yorks) from *St. Pancras*, 159½ miles. Fares, 32/9*a*, 19/8*c*. R. T. for two months, 65/6*a*, 39/4*c*. Departures *from* London as for Sheffield. Departures *for* London about 5 times daily.

ATTLEBOROUGH (Norfolk) from *Liverpool Street*, 108 miles. Fares, 22/3*a*, 13/4*c*. R. T. for two months, 44/6*a*, 26/8*c*. Pop. 2,513.
Map Square 19.

L'pl. St.	Attleb.	Attleb.	L'pl. St.
AM 5. 5	8.11	AM 7.11*r*	10.23
5.50	10. 0	8. 9	11.27
7.18*d*	11.18	9.24	12.40
8.30*r*	11.49	11. 5*r*	2.21
11.50*r*	3. 5	PM 1.53*r*	5.17
PM 2.34	5.29	5. 0*r*	8.22
5.49*r*	9. 2	5.31*r*	8.33
7.10*r*	10. 2	11. 2	2.50
10.12	1.25	—	—

Sunday Trains.

AM 9.25	1. 7	PM 3. 6	6.40
PM 3.25	6.59	6.47	9.40
9.12	1.22	11. 4	3. 0
—	—	—	—

d Saturdays only.
r Restaurant Car.

ATTLEBRIDGE (Norfolk) from *King's Cross*, 157 miles. Fares, 23/7*a*, 14/2*c*. R. T. for two months, 47/2*a*, 28/4*c*. Departures *from* London as for Guestwick. Departures *for* London about 3 times daily. Pop. 73.
Map Square 19.

AUCHENDINNY (Midlothian), 392½ miles. Fares, 80/5*a*, 48/3*c*. R. T. for two months, 160/10*a*, 96/6*c*. Departures *from* London as for Edinburgh (Waverley). Departures *for* London about 4 times daily. Pop. 311.

AUCHENGRAY (Lanark), 378½ miles. No through fares. Departures *from* London as for Carstairs. Departures *for* London about 4 times daily.
Map Square 40.

AUCHENHEATH (Lanark), 391 miles. No through fares. Departures *from* London as for Hamilton. Departures *for* London about 4 times daily.
Map Square 40.

AUCHENMADE (Ayr), 418¼ miles. No through fares. Departures *from* London as for Glasgow (Central). Departures *for* London about 3 times daily.
Map Square 40.

AUCHINCRUIVE (Ayr), 389½ miles. Fares, 79/4*a*, 47/7*c*. R. T. for two months, 158/8*a*, 95/2*c*. Departures *from* London as for Ayr. Departures *for* London about 4 times daily.
Map Square 40.

AUCHINDACHY (Banff), 579½ miles. No through fares. Departures *from* London as for Keith. Departures *for* London about twice daily.
Map Square 35.

AUCHINLECK (Ayr), 376½ miles. Fares, 76/6*a*, 45/11*c*. R. T. for two months, 153/0*a*, 91/10*c*. Departures *from* London as for Old Cumnock. Departures *for* London about 4 times daily. Pop. 7,178.
Map Square 40.

AUCHMACOY (Aberdeen) 545½ miles. No through fares. Departures *from* London as for Cruden Bay. Departures *for* London about twice daily.
Map Square 35.

AUCHNAGATT (Aberdeen), 549¾ miles. No through fares. Departures *from* London as for Fraserburgh or Peterhead. Departures *for* London about twice daily.
Map Square 35.

AUCHTERARDER (Perth), 436½ miles. Fares, 89/2*a*, 53/6*c*. R. T. for two months, 178/4*a*, 107/0*c*. Departures *from* London as for Dunblane. Departures *for* London about 4 times daily. Pop. 3,151.
Map Square 38.

AUCHTERHOUSE (Forfar), 463½ miles. No through fares. Departures *from* London as for Coupar Angus or Dundee (Tay Bridge). Departures *for* London about 3 times daily. Pop. 634.
Map Square 38.

AUCHTERLESS (Aberdeen), 557 miles. Fares, 106/3*a*, 63/9*c*. R. T. for two months, 212/6*a*, 127/6*c*. Departures *from* London as for Inverurie. Departures *for* London about twice daily. Pop. 1,496.
Map Square 35.

AUCHTERMUCHTY (Fife), 433½ miles. No through fares. Departures *from* London as for Cupar. Departures *for* London about twice daily. Pop. 1,763.
Map Square 41.

AUDLEM (Cheshire), 164¾ miles. Fares, 32/11*a*, 19/9*c*. R. T. for two months, 65/10*a*, 39/6*c*. Departures *from* London as for Market Drayton. Departures *for* London about 5 times daily. Pop. 1,480.
Map Square 12.

AUDLEY (Stafford), 155¾ miles. Fares, 32/9*a*, 19/8*c*. R. T. for two months, 65/6*a*, 39/4*c*. Departures *from* London as for Newcastle-under-Lyme. Departures *for* London about 6 times daily. Pop. 14,751.

AUDLEY END (Essex) from *Liverpool Street*, 41½ miles. Fares, 8/11*a*, 5/4*c*. R. T. for two months, 17/10*a*, 10/8*c*.
Map Square 19.

L'pl.St.	Audl'yE.	Audl'yE.	L'pl.St.
AM 5. 5	6.10	AM 1.19	2.50
5.50	7.32	7.12	8.57
7.18	9.16	8.10	9.27
8.30*r*	9.41	8.25	9.47
10. 5	11.20	9. 0	10.17
11.50*r*	12.58	10. 2	11.27
PM12.29*d*	1.50	PM12.25	2. 7
12.48*e*	2.42	1.43*d*	3.18
1.19*d*	2.56	2.41*h*	5. 9
2.34	3.41	2.56*k*	5. 9
2.48	4.33	3.41*r*	5.17
4.15	5.38	5. 5*r*	6.10
4.45	6. 1	6.10	7.58
5.49*r*	7.10	6.55*r*	8.22
6.30	7.45	9.29	10.30
7.10*r*	8.18	—	—
8.22	9.32	—	—
10.12	11.24	—	—

Sunday Trains.

AM 8.12	9.46	AM 1.19	3. 0
9.25	10.34	9.35	11.27
PM 1.50	3.56	PM 6. 1	7.26
9.12	11. 1	6.35	7.40
—	—	—	—

d Saturdays only.
e Saturdays excepted.
h Commencing July 23.
k Ceases to run after July 21.
r Restaurant Car.

AULDBAR ROAD (Forfar), 477½ miles. No through fares. Departures *from* London as for Forfar. Departures *for* London about 3 times daily.
Map Square 38.

AULDEARN (Nairn), 576½ miles. Fares, 106/3*a*, 63/9*c*. R. T. for two months, 212/6*a*, 127/6*c*. Departures *from* London as for Forres. Departures *for* London about twice daily. Pop. 1,213.
Map Square 34.

AULDGIRTH (Dumfries), 339¾ miles. Fares, 69/0*a*, 41/5*c*. R.T. for two months, 138/0*a*, 82/10*c*. Departures *from* London as for Dumfries. Departures *for* London about 3 times daily.
Map Square 43.

AUTHORPE (Lincoln), 135 miles. Fares, 28/1*a*, 16/10*c*. R. T. for two months, 56/2*a*, 33/8*c*. Departures *from* London as for Willoughby. Departures *for* London about 5 times daily. Pop. 130.
Map Square 13.

AVIEMORE (Inverness)

from Euston, 533¼ miles. Fares, 106/3a, 63/9c. R.T. for two months, 212/6a, 127/6c.
Map Square 37.

EUSTON	AVIEM.	AVIEM.	EUSTON
PM 1.30er	4.40h	AM12.50rz	7.30l
7.30ekr	7.25	9.44r	10.45
7.40er	7.48	11.55r	5. 0h
11.35e	2.24l	PM 5.45	7.40
—	—	—	—

Sunday Trains.

PM 7.50r	8.18l	—	—
11.35	2.24l	—	—

e Saturdays excepted.
h A.M.
k Commencing July 27.
l P.M.
r Restaurant Car.
z Sundays and Mondays excepted.

ANOTHER ROUTE from

King's Cross, 523½ miles. Fares as above.

KING'S+	AVIEM.	AVIEM.	KING'S+
AM 4.45	6.48h	AM12.50gr	6.30h
11.50er	4.40k	9.44r	10. 0h
PM 7.45er	7.48k	11.55	3.25k
11.25er	2.24h	PM 5.45	7. 5k

Sunday Trains.

PM 7.45r	8.18l	—	—
11.25	2.24l	—	—

e Saturdays excepted.
g Mondays excepted
h P.M.   k A.M.
r Restaurant Car.

AVOCH (Ross), 592 miles.

Fares, 106/3a, 63/9c. R. T. for two months, 212/6a, 127/6c. Departures from London as for Inverness. Departures for London about twice daily. Pop. 1,528.
Map Square 34.

AVONBRIDGE (Stirling),

416½ miles. No through fares. Departures from London as for Edinburgh (Waverley). Departures for London about 3 times daily.
Map Square 40.

AVONMOUTH DOCK

(Gloucester) from Paddington, 120¼ miles. Fares, 26/1a, 15/8c. R.T. for two months, 52/2a, 31/4c.
Map Square 22.

PAD.	A'M'THDK.	A'M'TH DK.	PAD.
AM 5.30	9. 9	AM 6.17r	10.15
7.30	11. 5	8.22	11.30
8.45	11.56	8.35	12.20
9. 0	12.46½	11.10r	2. 0
11.15r	2.33	PM 1. 2	4. 5
PM 1. 0r	4.15	2.22	6. 2
1.10r	5.30	3.40r	7. 0
2.45	6.31	4.32r	8.45
4.15r	7.16	5.12er	8.45
5. 0r	8. 1	6.40	10.25
6.30r	9.50	10.18	2.45
8. 0k	11.41	11. 5	7.10
12. 0h	5.39	—	—
12.30l	7.29	—	—
—	—	—	—

Sunday Trains.

AM 9.10	2.34	AM 7.45	3.35
10.35	3.54	PM 2.45r	7.55
PM12.30r	4.54	4. 5	8.10
4.30	9.24	5.10	10. 0
10. 0	5.39	9.35	3.15

e Saturdays excepted.
h Saturdays midnight excepted.
k Weds. and Sats. only.
l Saturdays midnight only.
r Restaurant Car.

Royal Hotel. Adjoining Docks. Opposite Railway Station. Comfortable Accommodation at Moderate charges. Special Terms for Board Residence. Telephone, 25 Avonmouth.

AVONWICK (Devon),

212 miles. Fares, 43/7a, 26/2c. R. T. for two months, 87/2a, 52/4c. Departures from London as for Kingsbridge. Departures for London about 5 times daily.
Map Square 26

AWRE (Gloucester) from

Paddington, 128½ miles. Fares (via Gloucester), 26/10a, 16/1c. R.T. for two months, 53/8a, 32/2c. Via Severn Tunnel, 31/6a, 18/11c. R.T. for two months, 63/0a, 37/10c.
Pop. 1,147.
Map Square 22.

PAD.	AWRE	AWRE	PAD.
AM 1. 0g	7.53	AM 8. 5	12.20
5.30	9.44	11. 5r	2.40
10.45	3.52	PM 3.15r	8.45
11.15kr	3.15	6.21	10.25
PM 1.30h	5.17	7.18	3.30
3.15t	7.54	—	—
6. 0dr	9.18	—	—

Sunday Trains.

AM 9.10k	4.21	PM 4.21	10. 0
PM 2. 0	8.46	—	—
9.15	7.53	—	—

d Saturdays only.
g Mondays excepted.
h Via Kingham.
k Via Severn Tunnel Junction.
r Restaurant Car.
t Tea Car.

AWSWORTH (Notts),

135½ miles. Fares, 26/10a, 15/7c. R.T. for two months, 52/0a, 31/2c. Departures from London as for Kimberley. Departures for London about 5 times daily. Pop.1,617.

AXBRIDGE (Somerset)

from Paddington, 130½ miles. Fares, via Witham, 27/1a, 16/3c. R. T. for two months, 54/2a, 32/6c. Via Yatton, 28/7a, 17/2c. R.T. for two months, 57/2a, 34/4c. Departures from London as for Winscombe. Departures for London about 8 times daily. Pop. 1,008.
Map Square 24.

AXMINSTER (Devon)

from Waterloo, 144½ miles. Fares, 30/3a, 18/2c. R. T. for two months, 60/6a, 36/4c. Pop. 2,049.
Map Square 27.

W'LOO.	AXMINS.	AXMINS.	W'LOO.
AM 7.30	11.42	AM 8. 5r	11.10
9. 0r	12.23	10. 1r	1.56
12. 0nr	3. 0	PM12. 7r	3. 8
PM 1. 0r	4.26	12.22r	3.50
3. 0r	6.14	2. 0r	6. 0
6. 0r	9.42	3.51	7.40
—	—	4.28r	8.30
—	—	6.40	10.60
—	—	8.47h	3.58

Sunday Trains.

AM 9. 0	2.40	PM 5.36r	8.57
12. 0nr	3.51	—	—

h Via Eastleigh.
n Noon.
r Restaurant Car.

AYCLIFFE (Durham),

237½ miles. Fares, 49/5a, 29/8c. R.T. for two months, 98/10a, 59/4c. Departures from London as for Darlington. Departures for London about 5 times daily. Pop. 750.
Map Square 7.

AYLESBURY (Bucks)

from Marylebone, 38 miles. Fares, 7/11a, 4/9c. R. T. for two months, 15/10a, 9/6c. Pop 12,114.
Map Square 3.

M'BONE.	AYLES.	AYLES.	M'BONE.
AM 6.25	7.37	AM 6.24	7.50
6.45	7.55	7. 5	8.22
7.20	8.43	7.30e	8.42
7.50	9.16	7.30d	8.46

AYLESBURY—continued.

M'BONE.	AYLES.	AYLES.	M'BONE.
AM 8.45	9.40	AM 8. 0	9. 9
8.50	10.11	8. 2	9.26
9. 5	10.48	8.42	9.46
10. 5	11.24	9.48	10.36
11.15	12.32	9.58	11.36
PM12.15	2. 6	11. 2	12. 2
1. 5d	2.18	11.45	12.59
1.10e	2.26	PM12.24	1.15
1.41d	2.59	12.42	2. 2
1.55e	3.38	2.12	3. 0
2.10	4.12	2.45	3.59
2.15d	3.38	3.37	4.56
2.45d	4.31	4.15e	6.22
3.25	4.44	6.21	7.15
5. 0	5.46	6.30	7.43
5. 4	6.20	6.42	8.11
5.24e	6.34	7.17	8.31
6.25e	7.28	8. 4	8.55
6.25d	7.35	9. 7	10.41
6.31e	7.50	9.49	11. 0
6.53e	8.36	—	—
7.30	8.49	—	—
9. 0	10.16	—	—
10. 0d	10.52	—	—
10. 5e	10.58	—	—
10.30	11.46	—	—
11.35	1. 8	—	—

Sunday Trains.

AM 9.30	10.47	AM 8.54	10.13
11. 0	12.18	11.30	12.46
PM 1. 0	2.18	PM 1. 0	2.16
2.30	3.47	4. 5	5.20
3.15	4.55	5.24	6.55
4.30	5.48	6.20	7.35
5.30	6.21	6.52	8 16
6.10	7.40	8.14	9.44
6.45	7.57	8.43	9.55
7.45	9.18	9.32	10.24
8.50	10.48	—	—

d Sats only.   Sats. excepted.

ANOTHER ROUTE from

Baker St., 38½ miles. Fares as above

BAKER ST.	AYLES.	AYLES.	BAKER St.
AM 6. 5	7.26	AM 6.24	7.41
6. 6	7.38	7. 5	8.35
6.30	7.55	7.20	8.42
7. 3	8.48	7.30d	8.51
7.50	9.16	7.30e	8.57
8.29	9.40	8. 0	9.28
8.34	10.11	8.24	9.39
9.51	11.24	8.42	9.49
10.11d	11.32	9. 5	10.25
10.18e	11.35	9.58	11. 5
11. 0	12.32	11. 2	12.22
PM12. 8	1.32	11.45e	1.22
12.50e	.2.26	11.45d	1.24
12.54d	2.18	PM12.42d	2.17
1.17d	2.40	12.42e	2.22
1.21d	2.59	1.37	2.58
2.17e	3.38	2.33d	3.55
2.19d	3.40	2.45	4.22
3.10	4.44	3.37	5.14
3.18d	4.32	4.15	5.41
4.10d	5.30	5. 0e	6.33
4.16e	6. 2	5.19d	6.39
4.40d	6.20	6.21	7.33
4.42e	6.20	6.30	8. 0
5. 7e	6.35	6.42	8. 8
5.45e	7. 0	7.17	8.47
5.46d	7. 5	8. 4	9.18
5.49e	7.28	8.10	9.36
6.30	7.50	9. 7d	10.28
7.15e	8.36	9. 7e	10.43
7.15d	8.48	9.49	11.18
7.19e	8.48	10.24	11.40
8.40	10.17	—	—
9.25	10.42	—	—
10.10	11.46	—	—
11.50	1. 8	—	—

AYLESBURY—*continued.*
Sunday Trains.

Baker St.	Ayles.	Ayles.	Baker St.
AM 8.47	10. 8	AM 8.14	9.48
9.10	10.47	8.54	10.27
9.47	11. 8	10.28	11.48
10.33	11.56	11.30	1. 5
10.45	12.18	PM 1. 0	2.35
11.11	12.36	1.50	3. 9
12. 0	1.20	2.33	3.52
PM 12.45	2.18	4. 5	5.42
2. 0	3.19	4.35	5.54
2.15	3.47	5.24	6.45
3.35	4.55	6.20	7.57
4.15	5.48	6.52	8.12
5.15	6.22	7.30	8.51
5.37	6.58	7.53	9.12
6.24	7.40	8.14	9.31
6.50	7.57	8.43	10.20
7.59	9.18	9.32	10.42
9.29	10.48	9.54	11.14

d Saturdays only.
e Saturdays excepted.

ANOTHER ROUTE from
Paddington, via Beaconsfield, 42 miles. Fares as above.

Pad.	Ayles.	Ayles.	Pad.
AM 7.33*h*	9.30	AM 7.10	8.34
9.10	10.15	7.45	9.20
9.20	11.28	8.52*r*	10. 0
PM 12.18	2. 5	10.50	12.32
1.25	2.50	11.38	1.18
2.23	4.12	PM 2. 7	3.50
3.40	5.25	3. 8	4.40
5.23	6.47	4.45	6.35
7.10	8.14	5.42	7.32
7.18	8.45	7. 8	9.18
9. 0	10.37	7.30	11. 4
—	—	9.20*d*	11.41

Sunday Trains.

AM 9.12	11. 2	AM 7.53	10.14
PM 2.35	4.32	10.15	2.26
4. 0	5.53	PM 6.35	8.25
—	—	7.42	9. 0

d Saturdays only.
h Not after July 27.
r Restaurant Car.

Bell Hotel.— Telephone 141. Enlarged and improved. Finest centre for district. Central Heating. Electric Light. Garage.
TRUST HOUSES, Ltd.

Bull's Head Hotel. First-class. Redecorated. Charming country for week-ends. Large Banquet Room. French Cuisine. Restaurant. Garages. Palm Lounge. Tel. 120.
Mr. & Mrs. GARGINI.

AYLESFORD (Kent) from
Charing Cross, Cannon Street, and *London Bridge,* 39½ miles. Fares, 8/4*a*, 6/8*b*, 5/0*c*. R. T. for two months, 16/8*a*, 13/4*b*. Pop. 3,113.
Map Square 24.

	Leave		Arr. at
Char. +	Can. St.	Lon. B.	Ayles.
AM —	—	3.22*h*	5.52
—	6.20	6.23	8. 5
—	7.16	7.19	8.46
—	7.44	7.47	9.19
8.10	—	8.17	9.52
9.32	—	9.41	11.12
11.55	—	12. 2	1.26
PM 12.30*d*	—	12.37*d*	1.54
1.20*e*	—	1.27*e*	3. 0
1.26*d*	—	1.34*d*	3. 0
—	1.48*d*	1.51*d*	3 28
2.45*e*	—	2.53*e*	4.33
3. 5*d*	—	3.12*d*	4.35
—	4.12*e*	4.15*e*	5.26
4.25*d*	—	4.31*d*	6. 9

AYLESFORD—*continued.*

	Leave		Arr. at
Char. +	Can. St.	Lon. B.	Ayles.
—	4.36*e*	4.39*e*	6. 9
4.35*d*	—	4.43*d*	6.41
—	5. 8*e*	5.11*e*	6.41
5.15*d*	—	5.22*d*	7. 7
—	5.56*e*	5.59*e*	7. 9
5.58*d*	—	6. 4*d*	7.32
—	6.20*e*	6.23*e*	7.37
6.22*e*	—	6.29*e*	8. 7
6.55*d*	—	7. 1*d*	8.53
—	7. 8*e*	7.11*e*	8.53
—	7.44	7.49	10. 3
—	9.35	9.38	11.19

Sunday Trains.

	Leave		Arr. at
Char. +	Can. St.	Lon. B.	Ayles.
AM 7.30	—	7.37	9.26
10.50	—	10.57	12.47
PM 1.15	—	1.22	3.12
4.50	—	4.57	6.40
7. 0	—	7. 7	8.44
8.42	—	8.49	10.26

Trains from Aylesford.

Leave		Arrive at	
Ayles.	Lon. B.	Can. St.	Char. +
AM 5. 6	7. 0	7. 4	—
7. 1	8.34	—	8.41
8. 3	9.34	—	9.43
8.34	9.54	—	10. 1
9.34	10.38	—	10.45
10.30	12. 3	—	12.14
11.56*d*	1.31	1.37	—
11.56*e*	1.36	—	1.45
PM 1.21*e*	2.54	—	3. 4
*d*1.1*h*	3.21	3.26	—
1.50*e*	3.26	—	3.36
2. 6*d*	3.58	—	4. 8
3. 8*e*	4.48	4.52	—
3.11*d*	4.57	—	5. 6
4. 8*e*	5.36	5.40	—
4. 8*d*	5.36	—	5.45
5.24	7.10	—	7.19
5.55	7.14	—	7.23
6.41	8.15	8.20	—
8. 5	9.36	—	9.46
9.17	10.51	—	10.59
10.26	12.35	—	12.45

Sunday Trains.

AM 7.14	9. 0	—	9. 9
8.33	10.16	—	10.24
11.19	1. 5	—	1.17
PM 2.22	4. 4	—	4.15
4.21	5.55	—	6. 4
7.47	9.46	—	9.55
9.28	11.15	—	11.23

d Saturdays only.
e Saturdays excepted.
h Third class only.

AYLSHAM (Norfolk) from
Liverpool Street, 131¼ miles, *via* Wroxham. Fares, 23/3*a*, 15/2*c*. R. T. for two months, 50/6*a*, 30/4*c*. Pop. 2,627.
Map Square 19.

L'pool. St.	Aylsh.	Aylsh.	L'pool. St.
AM 5. 5	10.28	AM 7.59*r*	11.22
5.50*h*	12.36	9.18	1.20
—	8.15*d*r	12.35	PM 12.36*r*	4.58
9.50*d*r	3.25	2.55*h*r	8.22
10.12	2.55	3.25*d*r	8.22
PM 12.33*r*	5.34	5.33*r*	9.22
5.18*e*r	9.16	7.58	2.50
5.18*d*r	9.48	—	—

No Sunday Trains.
d Saturdays only.
e Saturdays excepted.
h *Via* County School.
r Restaurant Car.

AYLSHAM TOWN
(Norfolk) from *King's Cross,* 156 miles. Fares as above.
Map Square 19.

King's +	Aylsh.	Aylsh.	King's +
AM 4.45	9.49	AM 8. 4	1. 5
7.15*r*	11. 1	9.51	3.50
10.10*r*	4.40	11.17*r*	4.30
PM 1.50*r*	6.49	PM 3.33	9. 0
3. 0	7.51	—	—

No Sunday Trains.
r Restaurant Car.

AYNHO (Northampton)
from *Paddington,* 80 miles. Fares (Aynho), 14/0*a*, 8/5*c*. R. T. for two months, 28/0*a*, 16/10*c*. (Aynho Park) 12/9*a*, 7/8*c*. R. T. for two months, 25/6*a*, 15/4*c*. Pop. 489.
Map Square 18.

	Pad.	Aynho.	Aynho Pk.
AM	5.30	8. 8	—
	5.45	—	8.49
	6.30	10.22	—
	9.10	—	12. 3
	9.45	12.35	—
PM 12.18	—	—	2.53
	1.35*r*	4.18	—
	4.10	—	5.37
	4.45*t*	7.16	—
	6.10	—	7.42
	7.10	—	8.49
	7.30	9.49	—

Sunday Trains.

PM 4.10	6.39	—	—

Trains from Aynho.

Aynho Pk.	Aynho.	Pad.
AM —	7.33	9.50
7.50	—	10. 0
—	9. 7	11.15
10.28	—	1.18
—	11.11	1.50
PM 2.10	—	4.40
—	3.20	5.50
3.33	—	6.35
6. 4	—	9.18
—	6.10*r*	9.15
—	8. 3	10.45

Sunday Trains.

—	7.19*r*	9.48

r Restaurant Car.
t Tea Car.

AYOT (Herts) from *King's Cross,* 22½ miles. Fares, 4/5*a*, 2/8*c*. R. T. for two months, 8/10*a*, 5/4*c*. Departures *from* London as for Welwyn Garden City. Departures *for* London about 10 times daily. Pop. 322.
Map Square 23.

AYR from *St. Pancras,* 401½ miles. Fares, 79/10*a*, 47/11*c*. R. T. for two months, 159/8*a*, 95/10*c*. Pop. 38,933.
Map Square 40.

St. Pan.	Ayr.	Ayr.	St. Pan.
AM 4.25	3.50	AM 9. 3*r*	6.35
9.50*r*	7.25	11.40*r*	9.15
PM 12.15*r*	9.38	PM 9. 0*e*	7.25
9.30*e*	7.45	10.5*h*	7.50
11.45*d*	9.15	10.55*d*	8.57
11.45*e*	9.24	—	—

Sunday Trains.

PM 9.30	7.45	PM 9. 0	7.25
11.45	9.24	—	—

d Saturdays only.
e Saturdays excepted.
h Wednesdays only.
r Restaurant Car.

AYR—*continued.*

ANOTHER ROUTE from
Euston, 392¼ miles. Fares as above.

Euston	Ayr	Ayr	Euston
AM12.25	2.50*l*	AM 9. 3*r*	6.25
2.35	3.50	11.40*r*	10. 0
5. 0	5. 0	PM 5.20	5. 0*h*
11.35*r*	9.38	8.45*d*	7.15
PM 8. 0*e*	6.25	9. 0*e*	6.55
9.20*e*	7.45	—	—
11. 0*d*	9.15	—	—
11.35*e*	9.27	—	—
11.45*e*	10.45	—	—

Sunday Trains.

PM 8.30	6.26	PM 9. 0	7.30
11.35	9.27	—	—
11.45	10.45	—	—
—	—	—	—

d Saturdays only.
e Saturdays excepted.
h A.M.
l P.M.

r Restaurant Car.

Station Hotel. Electric Light, Lift. Lounge. Splendid centre for tours in the beautiful Ayrshire District. Telegrams, Souwestern, Ayr.

AYSGARTH (Yorks), 242¾ miles. Fares, 50/8*a*, 30/5*c*. R. T. for two months, 101/4*a*, 60/10*c*. Departures *from* London as for Leyburn. Departures *from* London about 5 times daily. Pop. 279.
Map Square 7.

AYTON (Berwick), 342 miles. No through fares. Departures *from* London as for Berwick-on-Tweed. Departures *for* London about 3 times daily. Pop. 1,521.
Map Square 41.

REFERENCE NOTES.

a signifies First Class.
b   ,,   Second Class.
c   ,,   Third Class.
d   ,,   On Saturdays only.
e   ,,   Saturdays excepted.
f   ,,   On Mondays only.
g   ,,   Mondays excepted.
r   ,,   Restaurant Car.
t   ,,   Tea Car.
x   ,,   Express.
R.T.   ,,   Return Tickets.

⚇ Trains in the Tables not otherwise marked carry Third Class Passengers.

B

BACKWORTH (Northumberland), 274½ miles. Fares, 58 1*a*, 34 10*c*. R. T. for two months, 116/2*a*, 69 8*c*. Departures *from* London as for Newcastle-on-Tyne. Departures *for* London about 8 times daily. Pop. 2,235.
Map Square 3.

BACTON (Hereford), 157½ miles. Fares, 33/1*a*, 19/10*c*. R. T. for two months, 66/2*a*, 39/8*c*. Departures *from* London as for Abbeydore. Departures *for* London about 3 times daily. Pop. 109.
Map Square 17.

BACUP (Lancs) from *Euston*, 206½ miles, *via* Manchester. Fares, 41/10*a*, 25/1*c*. R. T. for two months, 83/8*a*, 50 2*c*. Pop. 21,256.
Map Square 12.

Euston	Bacup	Bacup	Euston
AM12.25	6.37	AM 5.22*dr*	12.20
2.35	9.49	6.58*r*	12.50
5. 0	11.59	7.40*r*	1.15
8.45*dr*	2.32	8.40*r*	2.20
8.45*er*	2.58	9. 0*r*	3.10
10.40*dr*	4. 0	10.20*r*	3.55
10.40*er*	4.25	11.30*er*	6. 0
11.50*r*	5.40	11.37*dr*	6. 0
12. 0*nr*	7.35	PM12.20*r*	6.15
PM 4. 5*r*	9.42	1.15*dr*	7.30
4.45*dr*	11. 2	2. 3*r*	8.10
6. 5*er*	11.27	2.55*er*	9. 5
6. 5*dr*	11.55	2.55*dr*	9.15
11.50*d*	11.42	3.57*er*	10. 0
—	—	4.30	10.10
—	—	7.50	5. 0
—	—	10. 5*e*	5.40
—	—	10. 5*d*	5.45

BACUP—*continued.*

Sunday Trains.

Euston	Bacup	Bacup	Euston
PM12.10*r*	6.29	AM 9.10*r*	5.45
12.30*r*	8.25	PM 2.30*r*	8.55
—	—	9.30	5. 0

d Saturdays only.
e Saturdays excepted.
r Restaurant Car.

BADMINTON (Glo'ster) from *Paddington*, 100 miles. Fares, 20/10*a*, 12/6*c*. R. T. for two months, 41/8*a*, 25/0*c*. Pop. 475.
Map Square 22.

Pad.	Badm'tn.	Badm'tn.	Pad.
AM 5.30	8 21	AM 7.17	10.45
9. 0	12. 6	9.44	12.20
10.45	2.25	PM12.35*r*	2.30
PM 1.10*r*	3.29	2.32*lr*	4.20
3.15*t*	6.11	3.38*r*	8.35
3.35*hr*	5.25	6.22*lr*	8.35
6. 0*kr*	8. 0	6.40	10.25
—	—	9. 5*d*	2.45

Sunday Trains.

PM12.30*r*	4.32	PM 6.22*r*	8.25
—	—	6.43	10. 0

d Saturdays only.
h Sets down 1st class passengers only.
k Stops to set down passengers on notice being given to the guard.
l Picks up 1st class passengers by request ; give notice at Station.
r Restaurant Car.
t Tea Car.

BAGG ROW (Cumberland), 321½ miles. No through fares. Departures *from* London as for Maryport. Departures *for* London about 4 times daily.
Map Square 6.

BAGILLT (Flint), 193¾ miles. Fares, 40/3*a*, 24/2*c*. R. T. for two months, 80/6*a*, 48/4*c*. Departures *from* London as for Chester. Departures *for* London about 5 times daily. Pop. 3,100.
Map Square 11.

BAGSHOT (Surrey) from *Waterloo, via* Ascot, 32½ miles. Fares, 6/1*a*, 3/8*c*. R. T for two months, 12/2*a*, 7/4*c*. Pop. 2,178.
Map Square 23.

W'loo.	Bagsh	Bagsh.	W'loo.
AM 5.10	8. 9	AM 6.59	8.17
6.54	8.32	7.29	8.47
7.54	9.37	8. 6	9.17
8.54	10.15	8.46	9.47
9.54	11.42	10. 5	11.17
10.54	12.22	10.53	12.31
PM12.48	2. 2	PM12.12	1.27
1.18*d*	2.28	1. 1	2.27
1.48	3.39	1.32	3.27
2.18*d*	3.29	3.53	5.27
2.48	4.32	5. 0	6.27
4.48*e*	6. 2	5.56*d*	7.27
4.48*d*	6. 7	6.43*e*	8.27
5.18*e*	6.28	8. 8	9.27
5.48	7.10	8.55	10.37
6.18*e*	7.28	—	—
6.48	8. 8	—	—
7.54	9.26	—	—

Sunday Trains.

AM 9.18	10.45	AM11. 3	12.43
PM12.18	2. 2	PM12. 3	2. 3
2.18	3.47	4. 3	5.28
4.18	5.47	6. 3	7.28
5.58	7.35	8. 5	9.28
7.48	9.10	9. 0	10.18

d Saturdays only.
e Saturdays excepted.

BAGSHOT—*continued.*

ANOTHER ROUTE from *Waterloo, via* Woking, 38¾ miles. Fares, 7/6*a*, 4/6*c*. R. T. for two months, 15/0*a*, 9/0*c*.

W'LOO.	BAGSH.	BAGSH.	W'LOO.
AM 5.40	6.59	AM 8. 9	9.26
5.50	7.29	8.32	10.11
8.15	10. 5	9.37	11.16
9.20	10.54	10.15	11.32
10.34	12.11	PM12.22	1.40
11.20	1. 1	1.40	3. 6
PM 1.20*d*	3.11	2. 3	3.36
1.20*d*	3.15	2.28*d*	4.46
2.20	3.53	3.29*d*	5.20
4.20*d*	5.55	3.39	5.46
5.30*e*	6.44	4.32	6.16
5.50*d*	7.38	7.10	8.46
6.10*z*	7.39	7.27*e*	9. 6
6.40*d*	8. 8	8. 8	9.46
6.54*e*	8. 8	9.26	10.50
7.20	8.54	—	—

Sunday Trains.

AM 8.20	10. 0	AM10.45	12·41
8.45 *a* 11. 3		PM12.35	2.44
10.20	12. 3	3.47	5.41
11.15*h*	1. 3	5.47	7.41
PM12.20	2. 3	7.35	9.12
1.50*h*	4. 3	9.10	10.47
3.20	5. 3	—	—
5.20	7. 3	—	—
6.20*h*	8. 5	—	—
7.20	9. 0	—	—

d Saturdays only.
e Saturdays excepted.
h Via North Camp.

BAGULEY (Cheshire) from
St. Pancras, 186½ miles. Fares, 37/9*a*, 22/8*c*. R. T. for two months, 75/6*a*, 45/4*c*. Departures *from* London as for Cheadle. Departures *for* London about 4 times daily. Pop. 970.

BAGWORTH (Leicester)
from *St. Pancras,* 109¾ miles. Fares, 22/9*a*, 13/8*c*. R. T. for two months, 45/6*a*, 27/4*c*. Pop. 1,419. *Map Square* 18.

ST. PAN.	BAGW.	BAGW.	ST. PAN.
AM 2.25	7.33	AM 7.11*r*	9.57
4.25	9.40	8. 6*r*	11. 0
9.50*dr*	12.45	9. 5*r*	11.35
10.25*r*	1. 0	PM12.14	3.25
PM12.25*r*	3.17	1.29*dr*	4.20
2.25*r*	5. 9	2.13*r*	5.45
3.30*r*	6.51	4.17*r*	6.35
4.25*r*	7. 8	6.41*r*	9.15
6.25*r*	8.55	9.49	4.20

Sunday Trains.

PM 6.15*r*	9.12	AM 8.14	11.53
—	—	PM 6.43	9.52

d Saturdays only.
r Restaurant Car.

BAILDON (Yorks), from
St. Pancras, 206¾ miles. Fares, 40/3*a*, 24/2*c*. R. T. for two months, 80/6*a*, 48/4*c*. Departures *from* London as for Ilkley. Departures *for* London about 5 times daily. Pop. 6,527. *Map Square* 12.

BAILEY GATE (Dorset),
117¾ miles. Fares, 24/5*a*, 14/8*c*. R. T. for two months, 48 10*a*, 29/4*c*. Departures *from* London as for Wimborne or Broadstone. Departures *for* London about 5 times daily. *Map Square* 27.

BAILLIESTON (Lanark),
396 miles. No through fares. Departures *from* London as for Coatbridge. Departures *for* London about 5 times daily. Pop. 13,390.

BAINTON (Yorks), 200
miles. Fares, 39/0*a*, 23/5*c*. R. T. for two months, 78/0*a*, 46/10*c*. Departures *from* London as for Market Weighton. Departures *for* London about 6 times daily. Pop. 337. *Map Square* 8.

BAKER STREET, to and
from *Mansion House, Charing Cross, Victoria, South Kensington, High Street, Praed Street, Hammersmith, King's Cross, Moorgate, Aldgate,* and intermediate stations every few minutes. Also to and from Uxbridge Road and Kensington (Addison Road) about every 12 minutes throughout the day. *See back of Map, Map Square* 60.

ANOTHER ROUTE (Bakerloo
Tube). *See back of Map.*

BAKEWELL (Derby) from
St. Pancras, 152¾ miles. Fares, 31/6*a*, 18/11*c*. R. T. for two months, 63/0*a*, 37/10*c*. Pop. 3,062. *Map Square* 12.

ST. PAN.	BAKWL.	BAKWL.	ST. PAN.
AM 2.25	8.27	AM 7.24*r*	11.35
4.25	10.35	9. 8*r*	1.30
10.25*r*	2.24	10.29	3.25
PM12.25*r*	5. 8	PM 1. 6*r*	5.45
2.25*r*	6.33	4.40*r*	8.35
4.25*r*	8.22	6. 2*r*	10. 5
6.25*r*	9.51	9. 1	4.20
12. 0*h*	8.25	—	—

Sunday Trains.

PM 3.15	7.12	AM11.19*r*	5. 2
—	—	PM 5.42*r*	9.52
—	—	8.25	4.55

h Saturdays midnight only.
r Restaurant Car.

Grand Hotel Hydro, Baslow,
nr. Bakewell. High Class. 150 rooms. Hotel Golf Links. Trains met by appointment. *See advt. p.* **26.**

BALA (Merioneth) from
Paddington, 205 miles. Fares, 42/11*a*, 25/9*c*. R. T. for two months, 85/10*a*, 51/6*c*. Pop. 1,408. *Map Square* 11.

PAD.	BALA	BALA	PAD.
AM10.40*r*	4. 2	AM 7.30*r*	1.25
PM12.50*r*	6.27	8.46*r*	2. 5
2.10*t*	7.50	11.10*r*	5. 0
12.15*h*	9. 5	PM 2.10*r*	8. 5
—	—	3.45*r*	10· 0
—	—	6.40	3.30

No Sunday Trains.

h Saturdays midnight excepted.
r Restaurant Car.
t Tea Car.

Plas Coch Hotel. Under
new management. Refurnished and redecorated. Every comfort combined with moderate charges. Fishing, golf, tennis. Telegrams, "Plascoch." 'Phone 9.
A. McFARLINE.

BALCOMBE (Sussex) from
London Bridge, Victoria, and *Clapham Junction,* 33⅓ miles. Fares, 7/1*a*, 4/3*c*. R. T. for two months, 14/2*a*, 8/6*c*. Pop. 1,221. *Map Square* 23.

		Leave		Arr. at
	VICT.	CLAP. J.	LON. B.	BALCM.
AM	—	—	5.18	6.48
7.23	7.29		7.25	8.56
9. 0	9. 8		9. 6·	10.13
10.35	10.42		10.35	11.50
12. 0	12. 7		12.10	1.19
PM 2. 0*e*	2. 7*e*		2. 5*e*	3.21
—	—		2. 8*d*	3.36
4.30	—		—	5.24
5. 5	5.12		5.10	6.23
5.45	—		—	6.33
6. 6	6.12		6. 8	7.36
7.15	7.22		7.20	8.39
10.30	10.38		10.35	11.55

Sunday Trains.

AM 6.55	7. 2	7. 2	8.37
8.50	8.57	8.55	10.20
PM 1.14	1.21	1.10	2.31
5.50	5.57	6. 0	7.21

Trains from Balcombe.

Leave		Arrive at	
BALCM.	LON. B.	CLAP. J.	VICT.
AM 6.48	8.15	8.15	8.24
8. 5	8.53	9. 0	9. 8
8.21	9.42	—	9.59
9.26	10.15	—	10.24
10.51	12.13	11.59	12. 7
PM12.16	1.42	1.39	1.50
1.16	2.22	2.13	2.22
4.25	5.54	5.47	5.55
5.58	7.42	7.37	7.45
7.17	8.46	8.39	8.48
9.31	10.58	11.10	11.17

Sunday Trains.

AM 9.19	10.45	10.42	10.50
PM 3.36	5. 3	5. 1	5.11
6.29	7.56	—	—
7.16	8.34	8.31	8.41

d Saturdays only.
e Saturdays excepted.

BALDERSBY (Yorks), 214½
miles. No through fares. Departures *from* London as for Ripon or Thirsk. Departures *for* London about 5 times daily. Pop. 236. *Map Square* 7.

BALDERTON (Cheshire),
191½ miles. Fares, 37/4*a*, 22/5*c*. R. T. for two months, 74/8*a*, 44/10*c*. Departures *from* London as for Rossett. Departures *for* London about 3 times daily. *Map Square* 12.

BALDOCK (Herts) from *King's Cross* 36¾ miles. Fares, 7/8*a*, 4/7*c*. R. T. for two months, 15/4*a*, 9/2*c*. Pop. 2,476.
Map Square 18.

King's+	Baldk.	Baldk.	King's+
AM 5. 5	6.36	AM 5.55	7.30
7. 0	8.47	7.15	8.41
8.45	9.56	7.50	8.55
10.12	11.41	8.25	9.34
11.30	12.57	8.44	9.56
PM12.40*d*	1.43	10. 8*h*	11.15
1.55	3.13	10. 8*k*	11.25
3. 0	3.59	PM12.15	1.25
4.15	5.30	2.25	3.50
5. 0	6. 3	3.25	5.45
5.10	6.13	4.54	6. 0
6.15	7.21	6.35	8. 5
7. 0	8.16	8.42	10.20
8.30	9.45	9.40	11. 0
9.10	10.30	—	—
10.55*l*	12. 6	—	—
—	—	—	—
—	—	—	—
—	—	—	—
—	—	—	—
—	—	—	—
—	—	—	—
—	—	—	—

Sunday Trains.

AM 8.30	10. 4	AM 8. 7	9.53
PM 7.10	8.31	PM 6.21	8. 8
—	—	9.16	10.20
—	—	—	—
—	—	—	—
—	—	—	—
—	—	—	—
—	—	—	—

d Saturdays only.
h Tuesdays only.
k Tuesdays excepted.
l Thursdays only.

BALDOVAN (Forfar), 458¼ miles. No through fares. Departures *from* London as for Coupar Angus or Dundee (Tay Bridge). Departures *for* London about 3 times daily.
Map Square 38.

BALDRAGON (Forfar), 459¼ miles. No through fares. Departures *from* London as for Coupar Angus or Dundee (Tay Bridge). Departures *for* London about 3 times daily.
Map Square 38.

BALERNO (Midlothian), 393¾ miles. No through fares. Departures *from* London as for Carstairs. Departures *for* London about 4 times daily. Pop. 701.
Map Square 41.

BALFRON (Stirling), 436¾ miles. Fares, 86/11*a*, 52/2*c*. R. T. for two months, 173/10*a*, 104/4*c*. Departures *from* London as for Stirling. Departures *for* London about twice daily. Pop. 1,190.
Map Square 40.

BALGOWAN (Perth), 449½ miles. No through fares. Departures *from* London as for Perth. Departures *for* London about 3 times daily.
Map Square 37.

BALHAM AND UPPER TOOTING (London) from *London Bridge*, 8¼ miles, or from *Victoria*, 4¼ miles. Fares from London Bridge, *via* Tulse Hill, 1/3*a*, 0/9*c*. R. T. for eight days, 2/6*a*, 1/4*c*. From Victoria, 0/10*a*, 0/6*c*. R. T. for two days, 1/5*a*, 0/10½*c*. Pop. (Balham) 50,888. *See* pp. 567, 568, 571–580.
Map Squares 23 *and* 78.

BALLACHULISH (Argyle) 525¼ miles. Fares, 105/3*a*, 63/2*c*. R. T. for two months, 210/6*a*, 126/4*c*. Departures *from* London as for Oban. Departures *for* London about twice daily. Pop. 1,202.
Map Square 37.

BALLATER (Aberdeen) from *King's Cross*, 565 miles. Fares, 109/0*a*, 65/5*c*. R. T. for two months, 218/0*a*, 130/10*c*. Pop. 1,542.
Map Square 37.

King's +	Ball.	Ball.	King's +
AM 4.45	7.48*k*	AM 8.30	10. 0*k*
PM 8.20*e*	9.45*h*	9.55	3.25*h*
11.25*e*	5. 0*k*	PM 5.55	7.25*h*
—	—	—	—
—	—	—	—
—	—	—	—
—	—	—	—

Sunday Trains.

PM 7.45	9.45*h*	—	—
—	—	—	—

e Saturdays excepted.
h A.M.
k P.M.
r Restaurant Car.

ANOTHER ROUTE from *Euston*, 581¾ miles. Fares as above.

Euston	Ball.	Ball.	Euston
PM 7.50*er*	9.45*h*	AM 8.30*r*	10.45*l*
11.35*e*	5. 0*l*	9.55*r*	5. 0*h*
—	—	PM 5.55	8. 0*h*
—	—	7.20	7.30*l*
—	—	—	—
—	—	—	—
—	—	—	—
—	—	—	—

Sunday Trains.

PM 7.50*r*	9.45*h*	—	—
11.35	5. 0*l*	—	—
—	—	—	—
—	—	—	—

e Saturdays excepted.
h A.M.
l P.M.
r Restaurant Car.

BALLINDALLOCH (Elgin), 559½ miles. Fares, 106/3*a*, 63/9*c*. R. T. for two months, 212/6*a*, 127/6*c*. Departures *from* London as for Aviemore or Keith (*via* Aberdeen). Departures *for* London about twice daily.
Map Square 35.

BALLINGHAM (Hereford) from *Paddington*, 137¼ miles. Fares, 28/7*a*, 17/2*c*. R. T. for two months, 57/2*a*, 34/4*c*. Departures *from* London as for Ross. Departures *for* London about 4 times daily. Pop. 152.
Map Square 17.

BALLINLUIG (Perth), 473¼ miles. Fares, 96/0*a*, 57/7*c*. R. T. for two months, 192/0*a*, 115/2*c*. Departures *from* London as for Dunkeld. Departures *for* London about 3 times daily.
Map Square 37.

BALLOCH (Dumbarton) from *King's Cross*, 455½ miles. Fares, 85/2*a*, 51/1*c*. R. T. for two months, 170/4*a*, 102/2*c*.
Map Square 40.

King's+	Balloch	Balloch	King's+
AM 4.45*e*	4.48	AM 7.16*r*	6.15
4.45*d*	4.11	10.40*r*	10. 0
10. 0*r*	9.37	PM 1.38*e*	3.25
11.50*r*	11.16	2.22*d*	3.25
PM 7.45*er*	7.42	4.41	6. 0*h*
8.25*e*	9.12	6.40	6.50*f*
11.25*e*	10.15	8.19*e*	7.25
—	—	8.40*d*	7.25
—	—	—	—
—	—	—	—
—	—	—	—
—	—	—	—

Sunday Trains.

PM 7.45*r*	7.42	—	—
8.25	9.12	—	—
11.25	10.15	—	—
—	—	—	—

d Saturdays only.
e Saturdays excepted.
f Arrives 7.5 Sundays.
h A.M.
r Restaurant Car.

BALMORE (Stirling), 440 miles. No through fares. Departures *from* London as for Glasgow. Departures *for* London about 3 times daily. Pop. 1,110.
Map Square 40.

BALNACOUL (Elgin), 590 miles. No through fares. Departures *from* London as for Keith or Elgin. Departures *for* London about twice daily.
Map Square 35.

BALNE (Yorks), 166 miles. Fares, 34/5*a*, 20/8*c*. R. T. for two months, 68/10*a*, 41/4*c*. Departures *from* London as for Doncaster. Departures *for* London about 5 times daily. Pop. 316.
Map Square 13.

BALQUHIDDER (Perth), 444½ miles. Fares, 90/10*a*, 54/6*c*. R. T. for two months, 181/8*a*, 109/0*c*. Departures *from* London as for Callander. Departures *for* London about twice daily. Pop. 875.
Map Square 37.

BALSHAW LANE AND EUXTON (Lancs), 202¼ miles.
Fares, 42/3a, 25/4c. R. T. for two months, 84/6a, 50/8c. Departures from London as for Wigan. Departures for London about 5 times daily. Map Square 12.

BAMBER BRIDGE (Lancs). 212 miles.
Fares, 43/7a, 26/2c. R. T. for two months, 87/2a, 52/4c. Departures from London as for Preston. Departures for London about 5 times daily. Pop. 8,110. Map Square 12.

BAMFORD (Derby), 162¼ miles.
Fares, 33/7a, 20/2c. R. T. for two months 67/2a, 40/4c. Departures from London as for Hathersage. Departures for London about 6 times daily. Pop. 989. Map Square 12.

BAMFURLONG (Lancs), 191¼ miles.
Fares, 39/10a, 23/11c. R. T. for two months, 79/8a, 47/10c. Departures from London as for Warrington (Bank Quay). Departures for London about 5 times daily. Pop. 2,276.

BAMPTON (Devon), 163¼ miles.
Fares, 35/0a, 21/0c. R. T. for two months, 70/0a, 42/0c. Departures from London as for Dulverton. Departures for London about 4 times daily. Pop. 1,467. Map Square 21.

BAMPTON (Oxon) from
Paddington, 78¼ miles. Fares, 16/5a, 9/10c. R. T. for two months, 32/10a, 19/8c. Departures from London as for Fairford. Departures for London about 4 times daily. Pop. 1,240. Map Square 22.

BANAVIE (Inverness), 526 miles.
Fares, 104/5a, 62/8c. R. T. for two months, 208/10a, 125/4c. Departures from London as for Fort William. Departures for London about twice daily. Map Square 37.

BANBURY (Oxon) from
Paddington, 67¼ miles. Fares, 14/0a, 8/5c. R. T. for two months, 28/0a, 16/10c. Pop. 13,347. Map Square 18.

PAD.	BANBURY	BANBURY	PAD.
AM 5.30	8.23	AM 1. 2g	3.30
6.30	9.11	7.16	9.50
9.10	10.24	8.35r	10. 0
9.45	12. 1	8.53	11.15
10.45	1.26	10. 6	12. 5
PM12. 8	2.42	11.15	12.25
2.10	3.24	11.39	1.50
4.10	5.50	12. 0	2.12
4.40	6.33	PM 1.27	3.50
6.10	7.21	2.20t	4.15
7.10	9. 2	3.50t	5. 0
7.30	9.23	5.11	7.20
12.15	2.36	7.12r	9.15
—	—	8.42	10.45
—	—	—	—
—	—	—	—

BANBURY—*continued.*
Sunday Trains.

PAD.	BANBURY	BANBURY	PAD.
AM10.35	12.48	AM 1. 2	3.30
11.45	4.10	2.55	10.14
PM 4.10	6.11	PM12.20	2.40
—	—	3.42	6.20
—	—	7.40r	9. 0
—	—	7.50r	9.48

g Mondays excepted.
r Restaurant Car.
t Tea Car.

ANOTHER ROUTE from
Marylebone, 76¾ miles. Fares as above.

M'BONE.	BANB.	BANB.	M'BONE.
AM 6.45	9.35	AM 8.25	10.36
8.45	10.47	9.45	12. 2
PM12.15	3. 3	PM 1.12	4.56
4.30	7.24	8.10	11. 0
4.55	8. 2	—	—

No Sunday Trains.

BANCHORY (Kincardine),
from *King's Cross*, 538¼ miles. Fares, 103/7a, 62/2c. R. T. for two months, 207/2a, 124/4c. Pop. 3,719. Map Square 38.

KING'S +	B'NC'RY	B'NC'RY	KING'S +
AM 4.45	6.15v	AM 8.45r	10. 0v
PM 8.20e	8.43l	10.52	3.25l
11.25e	12.48v	PM 6.46	7.25l
—	—	—	—
—	—	—	—
—	—	—	—

Sunday Trains.

PM 7.45	8.43l	—	—

e Saturdays excepted.
l A.M.
r Restaurant Car.
v P.M.

ANOTHER ROUTE from
Euston, 556 miles. Fares as above.

EUSTON	B'NC'RY	B'NC'RY	EUSTON
PM 7.50er	8.43h	AM 9.12r	10.45l
11.35k	2. 6l	10.52r	5. 0h
11.35e	3.58l	PM 6.46	5. 0h
—	—	8.17er	7.30l
—	—	—	—
—	—	—	—
—	—	—	—

Sunday Trains.

PM 7.50r	8.43h	—	—
11.35	3.58l	—	—
—	—	—	—
—	—	—	—

e Saturdays excepted.
h A.M.
k Friday nights only.
l P.M.
r Restaurant Car.

BANFF, 587¼ miles.
Fares, 106/3a, 63/9c. R. T. for two months, 212/6a, 127/6c. Departures from London as for Huntly. Departures for London about 3 times daily. Pop. 4,194. Map Square 35.

BANGOR (Carnarvon) from
Euston, 239 miles. Fares, 49/9a, 29/10c. R. T. for two months, 99/6a, 59/8c. Pop. 11,032. Map Square 11.

EUSTON	BANGOR	BANGOR	EUSTON
AM12.25	8.34	AM 7. 0dr	1. 0
2.35	10.56	7.12er	1. 0
5. 0	11.58	8.40r	1.45
8.30dr	2.33	9. 0dr	3.10
8.30er	3.19	9.20er	4.15
11.10r	4.10	11.57r	5. 5
11 50r	6.26	PM 1.10r	7.30
PM 2.35t	8.32	3.20r	9.20
4. 5r	10.33	3.47r	10.45
5.20r	11.25	9. 0	5. 0
6.30er12.27	—	—	
9.30c	4.26	—	—
11.50d	1.21	—	—

Sunday Trains.

PM12.10r	8.18	AM 7. 3	4. 0
9.15	4.26	PM 1. 5r	7.10
—	—	8.55	5. 0
—	—	—	—
—	—	—	—
—	—	—	—
—	—	—	—
—	—	—	—

d Saturdays only.
e Saturdays excepted.
r Restaurant Car.
t Tea Car.

BANGOR-ON-DEE (Denbigh), from *Euston*, 189¼ miles.
Fares, 37/4a, 22/5c. R. T. for two months, 74/8a. Departures from London as for Wrexham. Departures for London about 5 times daily. Pop. 574. Map Square 12.

BANK (City and South
London, Waterloo and City, and Central London Tubes). See back of Map.

BANKFOOT (Perth), 458
miles. No through fares. Departures from London as for Perth. Departures for London about 4 times daily. Pop. 713. Map Square 38.

BANKHEAD (Aberdeen),
527¼ miles. No through fares. Departures from London as for Aberdeen. Departures for London about twice daily. Map Square 35.

BANKHEAD (Lanark), 374¼
miles. No through fares. Departures from London as for Carstairs. Departures for London about 3 times daily. Map Square 40.

BANKNOCK (Stirling), 413
miles. No through fares. Departures from London as for Larbert. Departures for London about 3 times daily. Map Square 40.

BANKS (Lancs), 216½ miles.
Fares, 44/0a, 26/5c. R. T. for two months, 88/0a, 52/10c. Departures from London as for Wigan or Southport. Departures for London about 6 times daily. Map Square 12.

BANNOCKBURN (Stirling), 414½ miles. Fares, 84/7*a*, 50/9*c*. R. T. for two months, 169/2*a*, 101/6*c*. Departures *from* London as for Larbert. Departures *for* London about twice daily. Pop. 4,090.
Map Square 40.

BANSTEAD (Surrey) from *London Bridge, Victoria*, and *Clapham Junction*, 14½ miles. Fares from London Bridge or Victoria, 2/6*a*, 1/6*c*. R. T. for two days, 4/11*a*, 3/0*c*. Pop. 7,337. *See* pp. 582-583.

BARASSIE (Ayr), 395¼ miles. Fares, 81/1*a*, 48/8*c*. R. T. for two months, 162/2*a*, 97/4*c*. Departures *from* London as for Ayr or Kilmarnock. Departures *for* London about 4 times daily.
Map Square 40.

BARBERS BRIDGE (Glo'ster), 119¼ miles. Fares, 24/10*a*, 14/11*c*. R. T. for two months, 49/8*a*, 29/10*c*. Departures *from* London as for Ledbury. Departures *for* London about 5 times daily.
Map Square 22.

BARBON (Westmorland), from *Euston*, 268¾ miles. Fares, 51/11*a*, 31/2*c*. R. T. for two months, 103/10*a*, 62/4*c*. Departures *from* London as for Ingleton. Departures *for* London about 5 times daily. Pop. 274.
Map Square 7.

BARCOMBE (Sussex) from *London Bridge, Victoria*, and *Clapham Junction*, 46 miles. Fares *via* East Grinstead, 9/7*a*, 5/9*c*. R. T. for two months, 19/2*a*, 11/6*c*. Departures *from* London as for Sheffield Park. Departures *for* London about 15 minutes earlier Or *via* Lewes. Fares, 10/7*a*, 6/4*c*. R. T. for two months, 21/2*a*, 12/8*c*. Departures *from* London as for Sheffield Park or Lewes. Departures *for* London about 7 times daily. Pop. 1,277.
Map Square 23.

BARCOMBE MILLS (Sussex) from *London Bridge, Victoria*, and *Clapham Junction*, 50¾ miles. Fares, *via* Groombridge, 10/5*a*, 6/3*c*. R. T. for two months, 20/10*a*, 12/6*c*. *Via* Lewes, 10/7*a*, 6/4*c*. R. T. for two months, 21/2*a*, 12/8*c*. Departures *from* London as for Uckfield or Lewes. Departures *for* London about 6 times daily.
Map Square 23.

BARDNEY (Lincoln) from *King's Cross*, 129 miles. Fares, 26/10*a*, 16/1*c*. R. T. for two months, 53/8*a*, 32/2*c*. Pop. 1,302.
Map Square 13.

	King's+	Bard'ny.		Bard'ny.	King's+
AM	4.45	8.40	AM	8.43	1.55
	5. 5*s*	10.29		10.57	3.50
	7.15*r*	11.24		11.28*r*	4. 3
	8.45	1. 8	PM	4.15	9. 0
	11.30	4.12		4.20*r*	9.25
PM	3. 0	6.46		6.51	3.25
	—	—		—	—

Sunday Trains.

	12.0*nr*	3.58	PM	6.14*r*	10.20
	—	—		—	—
	—	—		—	—

n Noon.
r Restaurant Car.
s Fridays only.

BARDON HILL (Leices.) from *St. Pancras*, 111¼ miles. Fares, 22/11*a*, 13/9*c*. R. T. for two months, 45/10*a*, 27/6*c*. Departures *from* London as for Bagworth. Departures *for* London about 6 times daily. Pop. (Bardon) 554.
Map Square 18.

BARDON MILL (Northumberland), 298¾ miles. Fares, 60/10*a*, 36/6*c*. R.T. for two months, 121/8*a*, 73/0*c*. Departures *from* London as for Hexham. Departures *for* London about 6 times daily.
Map Square 3.

BARDOWIE (Stirling), 425¾ miles. No through fares. Departures *from* London as for Glasgow. Departures *for* London about 5 times daily.

BARDSEY (Yorks), 197¾ miles. No through fares. Departures *from* London as for Leeds or Wetherby. Departures *for* London about 4 times daily. Pop. 302.
Map Square 7.

BARE LANE (Lancs) from *Euston*, 232¼ miles. Fares, 48/7*a*, 29/2*c*. R. T. for two months, 97/2*a*, 58/4*c*. Departures *from* London as for Morecambe. Departures *for* London about 6 minutes later.
Map Square 7.

BARGEDDIE (Lanark), 429¼ miles. No through fares. Departures *from* London as for Edinburgh (Waverley). Departures *for* London about 4 times daily. Pop. 3,013.

BARGOED (Monmouth), from *Paddington* (*via* Newport), 160 miles. Fares, 33/4*a*, 20/0*c*. R. T. for two months, 66/8*a*, 40/0*c*. Pop. (Bargoed) 12,226.
Map Square 21.

	Pad.	B'goed.		B'goed.	Pad.
AM	1. 0*g*	9.26	AM	9.10*r*	1. 0
	5.30	11.50		10.22*r*	2.30
	8.45*r*	1. 0		11.27*r*	4.20
	11.50*r*	3.48	PM	1.45*r*	6.15
PM	1.10*r*	5.52		3.57*r*	8.35
	3.35*r*	7.41		5.31*r*	9.25
	6. 0*r*	10.18		7.45	3.30
	—	—		—	—
	—	—		—	—
	—	—		—	—
	—	—		—	—

Sunday Trains.

PM	9.15	9.26		—	—
	—	—		—	—
	—	—		—	—
	—	—		—	—
	—	—		—	—
	—	—		—	—

d Saturdays only.
e Saturdays excepted.
g Mondays excepted.
r Restaurant Car.

BARHAM (Kent) from *Charing Cross, Cannon Street*, and *London Bridge*, 77¼ miles. Fares, *Via* Canterbury, 14/5*a*, 11/7*b*, 8/8*c*. R. T. for two months, 28/10*a*, 23/2*b*. *Via* Shorncliffe, 14/7*a*, 11/8*b*, 8/9*c*. R. T. for two months, 29/2*a*, 23/4*b*. Departures *from* London as for Shorncliffe or Canterbury West. Departures *for* London about 5 times daily. Pop. 905.
Map Square 24.

Station closed on Sundays.

BARKING (Essex) from *Fenchurch Street*, 7½ miles. Fares, 1/5½*a*, 0/10½*c*. R. T. for two days, 2/11*a*, 1/9*c*. Pop. 35,523. *See* pp. 509, 510.

ANOTHER ROUTE from *Ealing, Hounslow, Richmond* and *Wimbledon via* District Railway. *See* p. 489.

ANOTHER ROUTE from *Moorgate Street* and *St. Pancras*, 13¾ miles. Fares from St. Pancras, 1/8*a*, 1/0*c*. R. T. for two months, 3/2½*a*, 1/9*c*. *See* pp. 506, 507.

BARKINGSIDE from *Liverpool Street* or *Fenchurch Street*, 9¾ miles. Fares, *via* Ilford, 1/5½*a*, 1/2*b*, 0/10½*c*. R. T. for two days, 2/11*a*, 2/4*b*, 1/7½*c*. See p. 536. Pop. 7,845.

BARKSTON (Lincoln), 109¾ miles. Fares, 22/9*a*, 13/8*c*. R. T. for two months, 45/6*a*, 27/4*c*. Departures *from* London as for Grantham. Departures *for* London about 3 times daily. Pop. 390.
Map Square 13.

BARLASTON (Stafford), 141¼ miles. Fares, 29/5*a*, 17/8*c*. R. T. for two months, 58/10*a*, 35/4*c*. Departures *from* London as for Stone. Departures *for* London about 5 times daily Pop. 790.
Map Square 12.

BARMBY (Yorks) from *St. Pancras*, 200½ miles. Fares, 35/0*a*, 21/0*c*. R. T. for two months, 70/0*a*, 42/0*c*. Departures *from* London as for Cudworth. Departures *for* London about 3 times daily. Pop. 344.
Map Square 13.

BARMING (Kent) from *Victoria, Holborn Viaduct*, and *St. Paul's*, 37½ miles. Fares, 8/1*a*, 6/5*b*, 4/9*c*. R. T. for two months, 16/2*a*, 12/10*b*. Departures *from* London as for Malling. Departures *for* London about 9 times daily. Pop. 1,112.
Map Square 24.

BARMOUTH (Merioneth)

from *Paddington* (via Ruabon), 234 miles. Fares, 48/7*a*, 29/2*c*. R. T. for two months, 97/2*a*. Pop. 3,559.

Map Square 16.

PAD.	BARM TH.	BARM'TH.	PAD.
AM 9.10*r*	3.39	AM 7.40*r*	2. 5
10.20*r*	4.58	10.15*r*	5. 0
10.40*r*	5. 5	11.33*r*	6.40
PM12.50*r*	7.31	PM 1.15*r*	8. 5
2.10*t*	8.53	2.35*r*	10. 0
12.15*k*	9.50	5.37	3.30
12.15*h*	10. 5	—	—
—	—	—	—

No Sunday Trains.

h Saturdays midnight excepted.
k Saturdays midnight only and *via* Oswestry.
r Restaurant Car.
t Tea Car.

ANOTHER ROUTE from *Euston*, 256¾ miles. Fares as above.

EUSTON	BARM'TH	BARM TH.	EUSTON
AM 5. 0	2.10	AM 7.35*r*	3.10
10. 0	5.40	9.32*r*	5.50
10.40*r*	7. 5	12. 0*dr*	9.15
PM 9.30*e*	7.13	12. 0*er*	9.20
11. 0*dh*	9.50	PM 5.37	5. 0
—	—	—	—
—	—	—	—
—	—	—	—
—	—	—	—
—	—	—	—

Sunday Trains.

PM 9.15	7.13	PM 5.45	5. 0
—	—	—	—
—	—	—	—
—	—	—	—
—	—	—	—

d Saturdays only.
e Saturdays excepted.
h *Via* Crewe.
r Restaurant Car.

Mount Argus Private Hotel. Superb position facing Sea. Beautiful grounds. Tennis. Billiards. Electric light. Garage. 'Phone 37. Illustrated Tariff—
PROPRIETOR.
See advt. p. **28.**

Marine Mansion. Best position Sea Front, accommodating over 100 visitors (in the house). First-class cuisine. Own poultry and vegetables. Excursions arranged. Evening entertainments. 2½ guineas to 4 guineas.
Mr. and Mrs. JACKSON.

Royal Hotel. Family and Commercial. Sea and mountain view. Central position. Billiards. C.T.C. Stock Room and Garage. Terms moderate. Apply—
PROPRIETRESS.

BARMOUTH—*continued.*

Hendre Hall. High-class Private Hotel and Board Residence. Beautiful grounds overlooking Bay. Separate tables.
Mrs. WILLIAMS.

Glencairn. The most Comfortable Private and Residential Hotel in N. Wales. Overlooking Sea. Luxuriously Furnished Lounge. Excellent Cuisine. Moderate inclusive Tariff (illustrated)..

BARNACK (Northampton), 95¾ miles. No through fares. Departures *from* London as for Stamford. Departures *for* London about 4 times daily. Pop. 608.
Map Square 18.

BARNARD CASTLE (Durham) from *King's Cross*, 248¾ miles. Fares, 51/10*a*, 31/1*c*. R. T. for two months, 103/8*a*, 62/2*c*. Pop. 4,737.
Map Square 7.

KING s+	B'CASTLE	B'CASTLE	KING's+
AM 4.45	1.18	AM 7.31*r*	1.30
10. 0*r*	3.39	9.19*r*	3.15
11.50*r*	5.43	PM12.21*r*	6.15
PM 1.50*r*	8.20	2.50*r*	9.25
11.25*e*	7.30	6.14	3.25
11.25*d*	9.29	9.36*e*	5.40
—	—	9.36*dr*	6. 0
—	—	—	—
—	—	—	—
—	—	—	—
—	—	—	—
—	—	—	—
—	—	—	—
—	—	—	—

Sunday Trains.

AM11.30*r*	8.55	AM 7.14	5.15
PM11.25	7.30	PM 6. 5	5.40

d Saturdays only.
e Saturdays excepted.
r Restaurant Car.

BARNBY DUN (Yorks),
160½ miles. Fares. 33/4*a*, 20/0*c*. R. T. for two months, 66/8*a*, 40/0*c*. Departures *from* London as for Doncaster. Departures *for* London about 3 times daily. Pop. 600.
Map Square 13.

BARNBY MOOR (Notts)
from *King's Cross*, 141½ miles. Fares, 29/5*a*, 17/8*c*. R. T., 58/10*a*, 35/4*c*. Departures *from* London as for Retford. Departures *for* London about 3 times daily. Pop. 260.
Map Square 13.

BARNEHURST (Kent)
from *Charing Cross, Cannon Street* and *London Bridge,* 14½ miles. Fares from Charing Cross, 2/11*a*, 2/4*b*, 1/9*c*. R. T. for eight days, 5/10*a*, 4/8*b*, 3/6*c*. From Cannon Street, 2/8*a*, 2/1*b*, 1/7*c*. R. T. for eight days, 5/4*a*, 4/2*b*, 3/2*c*. *See* pp. 555, 556.

BARNES (Surrey) from
Waterloo, 7 miles. Fares, 0/11½*a*, 0/7*c*. R. T. for two days, 1/9*a*, 1/2*c*. Pop. 34,281. *See* pp. 586-591.
Map Square 68.

BARNES BRIDGE
(Surrey), 7¼ miles. Fares, 0/11½*a*, 0/7*c*. R. T. for two days, 1/9*a*, 1/2*c*. *See* p. 586.
Map Square 68.

BARNETBY(Lincoln) from
Marylebone, 205 miles. Fares, 33/1*a*, 19/10*c*. R. T. for two months, 66/2*a*, 39/8*c*. Pop. 1,552.
Map Square 13.

M'BONE.	B'TBY.	B'TBY.	M'BONE.
AM 2.32	9.36	AM 6.58*r*	1.13
10. 0*r*	3.59	8.23*r*	3. 0
PM12.15*r*	6.29	PM 1.26*r*	6.38
3.20*r*	8.40	1.32*r*	8.55
10. 5*e*	4.54	4.37*r*	9.55
—	—	7.37	3.57
—	—	—	—
—	—	—	—
—	—	—	—

Sunday Trains.

AM11.15*r*	9.27	AM 9.31*r*	5.40

e Saturdays excepted.
r Restaurant Car.

BARNET HIGH (Herts)
from *King's Cross, Moorgate Street,* and *Broad Street,* 11⅛ miles. Fares, from King's Cross, 1/9½*a*, 1/5*b*, 1/1*c*. R.T. for two days, 3/7*a*, 2/10*b*, 2/2*c*. From Moorgate Street and Broad Street, 1/10½*a*, 1/6*b*, 1/1½*c*. R. T. for two days, 3/9*a*, 3/0*b*, 2/3*c*. Pop. (Barnet) 11,772. *See* pp. 518-522.
Map Square 23.

BARNET NEW (Herts)
from *King's Cross, Moorgate Street,* and *Broad Street,* 9½ miles. Fares from King's Cross, 1/9½*a*,1/5*b*, 1/1*c*. R. T. for two days, 3/7*a*, 2/10*b*, 2/2*c*. From Moorgate Street and Broad Street,1/10½*a*, 1/6*b*, 1/1½*c*. R. T. for two days, 3/9*a*, 3/0*b*, 2/3*c*. Pop. 4,790. *See* pp. 511-517.
Map Square 23.

BARNHAM (Suffolk), 86¾
miles. Fares, 18/4*a*, 11/0*c*. R. T. for two months, 36/8*a*, 22/0*c*. Departures *from* London as for Ingham. Departures *for* London about 3 times daily. Pop. 422.
Map Square 19.

BARNHAM (Sussex) from

London Bridge and *Victoria*, 63 miles. Fares, 13/2a, 7/11c. R.T. for two months, 26/4a, 15/10c. Pop. 299.
Map Square 28.

Leave VICTORIA.	Arrive at LONDON B.	BARNHAM.
AM 6.18	6.35	8.40
7.23	7.25	10.23
8.55	—	10.37
10.15	10.30	12.30
11.55k	11.50k	2.26
PM 1.40	1.50	3.41
1.55k	—	3.58
—	2.5k	4.55
3.55	4.0	5.54
—	4.50	6.26
4.53	—	6.47
—	5.5	7.33
—	5.8e	7.33
5.45e	5.55e	7.58
—	6.0k	8.7
6.15	—	7.47
7.20	7.15	9.40

Sunday Trains.

AM 6.55k	7.2k	10.33
8.18	8.25	10.52
9.0	8.55	11.2
PM 1.14k	1.10k	4.39
7.0	6.38	9.14

Trains from Barnham.

Leave BARNHAM.	Arrive at LONDON B.	VICTORIA.
AM 7.18f	—	9.22
7.26g	—	9.22
7.28k	9.50	—
7.44	—	10.28
8.19	9.58	—
8.46	10.45	10.53
8.54k	—	11.17
9.22	10.55	—
10.17	12.8	12.0
10.58	—	1.20
PM12.34	3.32	3.32
2.8	4.15	—
2.21d	4.58	4.45
2.21	—	4.50
3.23	—	5.'0
4.23	—	6.50
5.46	7.48	7.39
7.32d	10.0	9.45
8.5	10.8	10.1
8.18	—	11.17
9.48k	12.59	1.0

Sunday Trains.

AM 7.46	10.45	10.32
10.0k	—	1.0
11.4	—	1.35
PM 4.27k	—	7.0
6.48	8.50	8.42
6.54	9.32	9.34
8.15k	11.34	10.55

d Saturdays only.
e Saturdays excepted.
f Mondays only.
g Mondays excepted.
k Via Hove.

BARNHILL (Forfar), 456¼ miles. Fares, 82/6a, 49/6c. R.T. for two months, 165/0a, 99/0c. Departures *from* London as for Forfar. Departures *for* London about 3 times daily.
Map Square 38.

BARNOLDSWICK

(Yorks) from *St. Pancras*, 230¼ miles. Fares, 42/11a, 25/9c. R.T. for two months, 85/10a, 51/6c. Departures *from* London as for Colne. Departures *for* London about 7 times daily. Pop. 11,951.
Map Square 7.

BARNSBURY. See

CALEDONIAN ROAD AND BARNSBURY.

BARNSLEY (COURT HOUSE)

(Yorks) from *King's Cross*, 171¼ miles, via Doncaster. Fares,35/8a, 21/5c. R.T. for two months, 71/4a, 42/10c. Pop. 53,670.
Map Square 12.

KING'S+	BARNSL.	BARNSL.	KING'S+
AM 4.45	9.20	AM 7.44r	11.30
7.15r	12.1	9.35r	1.15
8.45	1.54	11.9	3.50
10.10dr	2.23	PM 1.25r	6.25
10.10er	3.49	2.30dr	7.10
PM 1.50r	6.37	5.6r	9.25
4.0r	9.9	10.40	3.25

Sunday Trains.

12.0nr 8.36	AM 9.4	3.45

d Saturdays only.
e Saturdays excepted.
n Noon.
r Restaurant Car.

ANOTHER ROUTE from

King's Cross, via Retford, 177 miles. Fares as above.

KING'S+	BARN'SL.	BARN'SL.	KING'S+
AM11.30	6.21	PM 2.40	9.0
PM 5.45r	11.2	10.40	3.25

Sunday Trains.

12.0nr 6.33	12.0n 5.55
PM 5.0r 10.7	—

n Noon.
r Restaurant Car.

ANOTHER ROUTE (COURT

HOUSE)from *St. Pancras,*174¾ miles. Fares as above.

ST. PAN.	BARNSL.	BARNSL.	ST. PAN.
AM 2.25g	8.27	AM 6.10r	10.45
4.25	10.1	7.55r	12.10
9.0r	1.46	8.32r	1.30
11.45r	4.11	10.4r	2.10
PM12.25r	6.3	11.4r	4.10
1.50r	6.11	11.50r	5.30
3.30r	8.5	PM 1.0r	5.45
5.0r	9.24	2.45r	7.15
6.16r	10.44	4.25r	9.5
11.50e	7.25	10.25	4.20
11.50d	8.22	—	—

Sunday Trains.

AM10.50r	4.30	PM12.20	5.27
PM 3.15	8.20	2.40r	9.43
—	—	9.55	4.55

d Saturdays only.
e Saturdays excepted.
g Mondays excepted.
r Restaurant Car.

BARNSLEY—continued.

ANOTHER ROUTE from

Marylebone, 180 miles. Fares as above.

M'BONE.	BARNSL.	BARNSL.	M'BONE.
AM 2.32	7.37	AM 5.54r	11.10
8.45r	1.23	8.20r	1.13
10.0r	3.37	9.30r	3.0
PM12.15r	5.4	PM 2.40r	6.38
3.20r	7.46	3.54r	8.55
5.0r	9.55	4.58r	9.55
6.20r	10.17	9.15e	3.57
—	—	9.38d	3.57

Sunday Trains.

AM11.15r	6.33
PM 5.30r	10.7

12. 0nr 5.40

d Saturdays only.
e Saturdays excepted.
n Noon
r Restaurant Car.

BARNSTAPLE (Devon)

from *Waterloo,* 211½ miles. Fares, 39/2a, 23/6c. R.T. for two months, 78/4a, 47/0c. Pop. 14,409.
Map Square 21.

Leave WATERLOO.	Arrive at B. JUNCT.	B. TOWN.
AM 9.0r	2.44	2.57
11.0r	3.50	4.2
PM 1.0r	6.36	6.48
3.0	7.38	7.50

No Sunday Trains.

Trains from Barnstaple.

Leave B. TOWN.	B. JUNCT.	Arrive at WATERLOO.
AM 8.34r	8.50r	1.56
10.48r	11.9r	3.50
PM12.43r	1.4r	6.0
1.27	1.37	7:40
2.2r	2.25r	8.30
3.42	4.0	10.50
5.4h	5.29h	3.58

No Sunday Trains.

h Via Eastleigh.
r Restaurant Car.

ANOTHER ROUTE from

Paddington, via Taunton, 187½ miles. Fares as above.

PAD.	BARNST.	BARNST.	PAD.
AM 5.30	1.16	AM 8.55r	1.30
9.15	2.15	10.35	4.5
PM12.5r	5.8	PM12.40t	5.30
2.0r	7.25	4.5r	9.0
3.30	7.39	6.0	2.45
4.15r	9.46	8.36	7.10
12.0h	9.57	—	—

Sunday Trains.

PM10.0	9.57r	—	—

h Saturdays midnight excepted.
r Restaurant Car.
t Tea Car.

Imperial Hotel.—Telephone 100. First-class Hotel. Unrivalled centre for North Devon. Gardens facing River. Garage.
TRUST HOUSES, Ltd.

BARNSTONE (Notts). 118¾ miles. Fares, 24/0a, 14/5c. R.T. for two months, 48/0a, 28/10c. Departures *from* London as for Halaton or Bottesford. Departures *for* London about 3 times daily. Pop. 453.
Map Square 13.

BARNT GREEN (Worcester), 123¼ miles. Fares, 23/7a, 14/2c. R.T. for two months, 47/2a, 28/4c. Departures *from* London as for Birmingham (New Street). Departures *for* London about 6 times daily.
Map Square 17.

BARNTON (Midlothian), 403 miles. Fares, 82/4a, 49.5c. R.T. for two months, 164/8a, 98/10c. Departures *from* London as for Edinburgh. Departures *for* London about 3 times daily.
Map Square 41.

BARNWELL (Cambs) from *Liverpool Street,* 57½ miles. Fares, 11/11a, 7/2c. R.T. for two months, 23/10a, 14/4c. Departures *from* London as for Mildenhall. Departures *for* London about 4 times daily.
Map Square 19.

BARNWELL (Northampton) from *Euston,* 93¼ miles. Fares, 15/0a, 9/0c. R.T. for two months, 30/0a, 18/0c. Departures *from* London as for Thrapston. Departures *for* London about 4 times daily. Pop. 334.
Map Square 18.

BARON'S COURT from *Mansion House,* 6 miles. Also to and from Ealing, Hounslow, and Richmond. Pop. 12,881. See p. 497.
Map Square 68.

ANOTHER ROUTE (Hammersmith and Finsbury Park Tube). See back of Map.

BARRAS (Westmorland), 265 miles. No through fares. Departures *from* London as for Barnard Castle. Departures *for* London about 4 times daily.
Map Square 7.

BARRASFORD (Northumberland), 294½ miles. No through fares. Departures *from* London as for Hexham or Carlisle. Departures *for* London about 4 times daily.
Map Square 3.

BARRHEAD (Renfrew), 407 miles. Fares, 82/6a, 49/6c. R.T. for two months, 165/0a, 99/0c. Departures *from* London as for Kilmarnock. Departures *for* London about 4 times daily. Pop. 11,466.
Map Square 40.

BARRHILL (Ayr), 417 miles. No through fares. Departures *from* London as for Girvan or Newton Stewart. Departures *for* London about twice daily. Pop. 946.
Map Square 43.

BARR MILL (Ayr), 403¼ miles. Fares, 81/11a, 49/2c. R.T. for two months, 163/10a, 98/4c. Departures *from* London as for Kilmarnock. Departures *for* London about 6 times daily.

BARROW (Cheshire), from Euston 184¾ miles. No through fares. Departures *from* London as for Northwich. Departures *for* London about 4 times daily. Pop. 699.
Map Square 12.

BARROW HAVEN (Lincoln), 172¼ miles. Fares. 35/3a, 21/2c. R. T. for two months, 70/6a, 42/4c. Departures *from* London as for New Holland. Departures *for* London about 6 times daily. Pop. 2,734.
Map Square 13.

BARROW-IN-FURNESS (Lancs) from *Euston,* 265 miles. Fares, 55/2a, 33/1c. R.T. for two months, 110/4c, 66/2c. Pop. 74,254.
Map Square 6.

EUSTON	BARROW		BARROW	EUSTON
AM12.25	9.35		AM 6.55r	3.10
2.35	11.5		8.35hr	3.45
5. 0	12.59		9.15r	4.15
6.45	2.42		10.50r	6. 0
11.35r	5.28		PM 1. 5r	7 30
11.50r	7.37		1.50er	9. 5
PM 1.30r	7.55		1.50dr	9.15
2.35t	10. 5		4.30r	10.45
5.20r	12. 5		8.35	5. 0
9.30e	7.25		—	—
11. 0d	8.52		—	—

Sunday Trains.

AM11.45r	6.45		12. 0nr	7.30
—	—		PM 8.10	5. 0

d Saturdays only.
e Saturdays excepted.
h Mondays and Saturdays only.
n Noon.
r Restaurant Car.
t Tea Car.

ANOTHER ROUTE from *St. Pancras,* 287¼ miles. Fares as above.

ST. PAN.	BARROW		BARROW	ST. PAN.
AM 4.25	2.42		AM 6.50r	4.10
9.50r	5.28		9.15r	5.30
PM12.15r	7.37		10.50hr	6.35
11.50e	11. 0		PM 1. 5r	9.15
11.50d	11.10		4.55	4.20

Sunday Trains.

AM10.50r	9.20		AM 7. 0	5.27
PM11.45	11. 0		PM 4.50	4.55

d Saturdays only.
e Saturdays excepted.
h Wednesdays and Thursdays excepted.
r Restaurant Car.

Furness Abbey Hotel. Inclusive Terms from 16/0 per day, for two or more days. 'Phone, 59 Barrow-in-Furness. Telegrams, Hotel, Furness Abbey Station.

Duke of Edinburgh. Family and Commercial. Directly opposite Station. Porter meets all Trains. Tel. 237.
T. EDW. EVANS, Manager.

BARROW-IN-FURNESS—*continued.*

Hotel Imperial, newly decorated and refurnished, nearest Post office, Docks and Vickers' Construction Works. 50 Rooms. Fully licensed.
FRED FORBES, Manager.

Victoria Park Hotel. First-class, modern. Headquarters Royal Automobile Club and Motor Union. 'Bus meets trains. For illustrated tariff apply
MANAGER.

BARROW-ON-SOAR (Leicester) from *St. Pancras,* 109 miles. Fares, 22/4a, 13/5c. R.T. for two months, 44/8a, 26/10c. Pop. 2,481.
Map Square 18.

ST. PAN.	BARROW		BARROW	ST. PAN.
AM 2.25	6.44		AM 6.43r	9.57
4.25	7.48		8.10r	11. 0
8.25r	11.18		8.57r	11.35
10.25r	12.56		10.52r	1.50
PM12.25r	3.12		11.47r	2.10
1.25r	4.13		PM 1.19r	4.20
2.25r	4.49		3. 9r	5.45
4.25r	7. 0		5.21r	7.55
6.25r	8.52		6.35r	9.15
—	—		10.23	4.20

Sunday Trains.

PM 6.15r	9. 5		AM 8.11	11.53
—	—		PM 6. 2r	9.52
—	—		9.42	4.55

r Restaurant Car.

BARRY DOCKS (Glamorgan) from *Paddington,* via Cardiff, 160¾ miles. Fares, 33/4a, 20/0c. R.T. for two months, 66/8a, 40/0c. Pop. 38,927.
Map Square 21.

PAD.	BARRY		BARRY	PAD.
AM 1. 0g	6.43		AM 4.54r	10.15
5.30	11. 7		7. 4r	10.57
8.45r	12.28		9.24r	1. 0
9. 0	2.36		10.21r	2.30
11.50r	3.19		PM12.47r	4.20
PM 1.10r	5. 3		2.36r	6.15
3.35r	7. 1		4.29r	8.35
5. 0r	9. 9		6. 3r	9.25
6. 0r	9.42		9.47	3.30
6.30r	10.51		—	—
8. 0r	11.21		—	—
9.15e	5.47		—	—

Sunday Trains.

AM 1. 0	9.32		AM10. 0	3.35
9.10	2.43		11.39	4. 5
PM12.30r	4.40		PM 4.25r	8.25
4.30	9.11		10. 5	3.30
9.15	5.47		—	—

e Saturdays excepted.
g Mondays excepted.
r Restaurant Car.

BARRY LINKS (Forfar),

460¾ miles. Fares, 92/4*a*, 55/5*c*. R. T. for two months, 184/8*a*, 110/10*c*. Departures *from London as for Dundee*. Departures *for London* about 3 times daily. Pop. 6,133.

Map Square 38.

BARTLOW (Cambs) from

Liverpool Street (via Saffron Waldon), 49 miles. Fares, 10/5*a*, 6/3*c*. R. T. for two months, 20/10*a*, 12/6*c*. Pop. 122.

Map Square 19.

L'PL. ST.	BARTLOW	BARTLOW	L'PL. ST.
AM 5.50	8.56	AM 7.41	9.27
8.30	10.29	9.14	11.27
11.50	1.24	10.42*l*	12.40
PM 2.48*h*	4.58	10.45	2. 7
2.48*k*	5. 9	PM12.44*dv*	3.18
5.49	7.34	12.44*y*	4. 2*s*
—	—	1.38	5. 9
—	—	5.37	7.58
—	—	7.55	10.30

No Sunday Trains.

d Saturdays only.
h Tuesdays excepted.
k Tuesdays only.
l Via Cambridge.
s Arrives at St. Pancras Station.
v Via Shelford.
y Will commence to run July 23.

BARTON (Lancs), from

Euston, 218¼ miles. No through fares. Departures *from London as for Southport*. Departures *for London* about 5 times daily. Pop. 432.

Map Square 12.

BARTON-ON-SEA

(Hants) Station at New Milton.

Map Square 27.

BARTON & BROUGH-

TON (Lancs), 213½ miles. Fares, 44/7*a*, 26/9*c*. R. T. for two months. 89/2*a*, 53/6*c*. Departures *from London as for Preston*. Departures *for London* about 6 times daily. Pop.(Barton) 432 ; (Broughton) 722.

Map Square 12.

BARTON & WALTON

(Stafford), 119½ miles. Fares, 24/9*a*, 14/10*c*. R. T., for two months, 49/6*a*, 29/8*c*. Departures *from London as for Burton-on-Trent*. Departures *for London* about 6 times daily. Pop. 1,554.

Map Square 17.

BARTON HILL (Yorks),

199¼ miles. Fares, 41/6*a*, 24/11*c*. R. T., for two months, 83/0*a*, 49/10*c*. Departures *from London as for York*. Departures *for London* about 4 times daily.

Map Square 8.

BARTON-LE-STREET

(Yorks), 215½ miles. No through fares. Departures *from London as for Amplerforth*. Departures *for London* about 3 times daily. Pop. 164.

Map Square 8.

BARTON MOSS (Lancs),

196¼ miles. Fares, 39/7*a*, 23/9*c*. R. T. for two months, 79/2*a*, 47/6*c*. Departures *from London as for Kenyon*. Departures *for London* about 5 times daily. Pop. 208.

BARTON - ON - HUM-

BER (Lincoln), 174½ miles. Fares, 35/8*a*, 21/5*c*. R. T. for two months, 71/4*a*, 42/10*c*. Departures *from London as for New Holland*. Departures *for London* about 5 times daily. Pop. 6,454.

Map Square 13.

BASCHURCH (Salop)

from *Paddington*, 160½ miles. Fares, 33/6*a*, 20/1*c*. R. T. for two months, 67/0*a*, 40/2*c*. Pop. 1,601

Map Square 17.

PAD.	BASCH.	BASCH.	PAD.
AM10.40*r*	2.29	AM 8.42	12.25
PM12.50*r*	5.10	9. 5*r*	1.25
2.10*t*	6.59	PM12.56*r*	5. 0
6.10*lr*	9.52	3.40*r*	8. 5
12.15*h*	8. 4	7.44	3.30
12.15*k*	9.32	—	—
—	—	—	—
—	—	—	—
—	—	—	—

Sunday Trains.

PM12.50	5.27	AM11.40	6.20
—	—	—	—
—	—	—	—
—	—	—	—

h Saturdays midnight excepted.
k Saturdays midnight only.
l Thursdays and Saturdays only.
r Restaurant Car.
t Tea Car.

BASFORD (Notts) from

St. Pancras, 127½ miles. Fares. 26/0*a*, 15/7*c*. R. T. for two months, 52/0*a*, 31/2*c*. Pop. 41,961.

Map Square 13.

ST.PAN.	BASFORD	BASFORD	ST.PAN.
AM 2.25	8.32	AM 6.28*r*	9.57
9. 0*r*	12.16	8. 0*r*	10.45
PM 1.50*r*	5. 8	8.40*r*	12.10
3.30*r*	6.36	10.44	3.25
5. 0*r*	8.26	PM12.29*dr*	4.10
6.15*r*	9.32	1.52*r*	5.30
—	—	3. 7*r*	6.35
—	—	4.55*r*	7.55
—	—	11.11	4.20

No Sunday Trains.

d Saturdays only.
r Restaurant Car.

BASFORD AND BUL-

WELL (Notts) from *King's Cross*, 131 miles. Fares. 26/0*a*, 15/7*c*. R. T. for two months, 52/0*a*, 31/2*c*.

Map Square 13.

KING'S+	BASFRD.	BASFRD.	KING'S+
AM 4.45	8.59	AM 7.31	10.40
7.15*r*	10.38	7.58*r*	11.30
8.45	12.55	9.11	1. 5
10.10*r*	1.28	10.16*r*	1.30
PM 1.50*r*	5.41	PM 2. 3	6.25
4. 0*r*	7.48	4.34	9. 0
5.35*r*	8.41	5.38*r*	9.25
5.45*er*10. 3		10. 2*e*	3.25
5.45*dr*10 28		10.22*d*	3.25
11.25*e*	6.19	—	—
—	—	—	—

Sunday Trains.

AM11.30*r*	3. 3	PM11.58	3.45
12. 0*r*	4.15	2. 8	5.55
11.25	6.19	—	—
—	—	—	—

d Saturdays only.
e Saturdays excepted.
r Restaurant Car.

BASINGSTOKE (Hants)

from *Waterloo*, 48 miles. Fares, 10/0*a*, 6/0*c*. R. T. for two months, 20/0*a*, 12/0*c*. Pop. 12,718.

Map Square 23.

W'LOO.	BASING.	BASING	W'LOO.
AM 5.40	6.50	AM 2.18	3.58
5.50	7.36	7.10	8.41
7.30	8.42	8. 3	9.26
8.34	10.10	8.43	9.56
9.30	10.40	9. 9	10.21
10.34	12.14	9.52	10.6
11.30*r*	12.28	11. 6	12. 0
PM12.40	2.16	11.28*s*	12.22
1.30*r*	2.28	11.40	1.20
2.34	4.18	PM 1.26*r*	2.20
3.30*s*	4.28	1.42	2.36
3.40	5.17	1.47	3.16
5. 0	6. 4	2 37	4. 6
5.30*r*	6.33	3.26	4.20
6. 0*r*	7.18	3.40	5.20
6.40*d*	8.16	4.40	6.16
6.54*e*	8.14	5.25	6.26
7.30	8.28	5.35	7. 7
8. 0	9.33	6.29	7.40
8.55	10.47	7.26*r*	8.20
10. 0	11.10	7.36*r*	8.30
—	—	7.40	9.26
—	—	9.38	10.50
—	—	10.17	11.28

. Sunday Trains.

AM 9. 0	10.35	AM 2.18	3.58
9.45	11.29	7.45	9.45
11.15	12.47	11.10	12.11
12. 0*r*	1.12	11.15	12.52
PM 5. 5	6.38	PM 4.45	6. 7
6. 0	7.10	7. 2	8.43
7.20	9. 3	7.37	9.12
8.15	9.25	9.18	10.52
9.28	11.15	—	—
—	—	—	—

d Saturdays only.
e Saturdays excepted.
r Restaurant Car.
s Refreshments served.

ANOTHER ROUTE from

Paddington, 51½ miles. Fares as above.

PAD.	BASING.	BASING.	PAD.
AM 7.30	9. 1	AM 7.55	9.30
9. 0	10.28	9. 5	10.45
9.45	11.48	9.35	11.35
11.20	12.49	10. 3	12. 0
PM12.30	2.23	11.20	12.55
1.10*dr*	2.51	PM12.18	1.50
1.35*r*	3.45	1.30	3.20
3.18	5.30	3. 3*d*	4.35
4. 8	5.55	3.30	5. 6
5.15	6.47	4.35	6. 2
6. 5	7.30	5.55	7.20
7.30	9. 9	6.42	8.20
9.15	10.48	9.17	10.45
10. 0*h*	11.35	11.30	2.45
—	—	—	—

Sunday Trains.

AM 9.10	11.10	AM10.10	1. 5
PM 4.45	7. 0	11.55	2.40
—	—	PM 7.50	9.48

d Saturdays only.
h Thursdays and Saturdays only.
r Restaurant Car.

Red Lion Hotel. Family and Commercial. Motor Garage. "Everything always ready." Charming country for week-ends. Telephone 187. Resident Propr.,
J. W. DALLIMORE,

BASONBRIDGE (Somerset), 144 miles. Fares, 29/9a, 17/10c. R. T. for two months, 59/6a, 35/8c. Departures *from* London as for Glastonbury. Departures *for* London about 4 times daily.
Map Square 22.

BASSALEG (Monmouth), 144 miles. Fares, 30/0a, 18/0c. R.T. for two months, 60/0a, 36/0c. Departures *from* London as for Bargoed. Departures *for* London about 8 times daily. Pop. 4,867.
Map Square 22.

BASSENTHWAITE LAKE (Cumberland) from *Euston*, 306¼ miles. Fares, 61/10a, 37/1c. R.T. for two months, 123/8a, 74/2c. Departures *from* London as for Keswick. Departures *for* London about 5 times daily. Pop. 428.
Map Square 6.

BATH (Somerset) from *Paddington*, 106¾ miles. Fares, 22/4a, 13/5c. R. T. for two months, 44/8a, 26/10c. Pop. 68,648.
Map Square 22.

PAD.	BATH	BATH	PAD.
AM 5.30	8. 5	AM12.33*f*	3.15
7.30	9.53	4.26	7.10
9. 0	11.39	8. 3*r*	10.15
11.15	1. 0	9.35	11.30
PM 1. 0	2.45	9.56	12.20
1.10*r*	3.52	11.29*r*	2.40
2.45	5.27	11.50	2.50
3.15*t*	6. 0	PM12.43	3.20
4.15*r*	6.12	2. 7	4. 5
5. 0*r*	7. 1	3.32	6. 2
5.15	8. 7	6.22*r*	8.45
6.30*r*	8.25	7.54	10.25
6.55	10.44	11.36	2.45
10. 0	12.35	—	—
12. 0*h*	2.47	—	—
12.30*k*	3.17	—	—
—	—	—	—
—	—	—	—
—	—	—	—
—	—	—	—
—	—	—	—

Sunday Trains.

AM 1. 0	5.26	AM 4.26	7. 5
9.10	11.51	PM12.53	3.35
10.35	2.19	1.34	6. 0
PM12.30*r*	3. 1	3.55	7.55
2. 0	7.55	5.53	8.10
10. 0	12.30	—	—
—	—	—	—
—	—	—	—
—	—	—	—
—	—	—	—

f Mondays only.
h Saturdays midnight excepted.
k Saturdays midnight only.
r Restaurant Car.
t Tea Car.

Empire Hotel, Bath. Finest in West of England. Close to Abbey and Baths. Magnificent Views. Orchestra. Special cuisine for invalids. Suites at moderate prices. Motor Bus meets all trains. Garage. Telephone, Bath 1227. Telegrams, "Empire, Bath." Photographic view of the hotel will be found on advt. p. **29.**

BATH—*continued.*
Grand Pump Room Hotel. Leading Family Hotel, most central position; inter-communication with Corporation Baths. Self-contained suites; bedrooms with private bathrooms; central heating. Excellent cuisine.
See advt. p. **30.**

The Spa Hotel. Old world grounds, 9 acres. Self-contained Suites. Perfect cuisine and appointments. Links 5 minutes. Orchestra. Entertainments. Garage. Motor Omnibus.
See advt. p. **31.**

York House Hotel. Good Class Family and Residential. Central. Quiet. Close to Pump Rooms. Garage. Inclusive Terms on application. R.A.C.A.A. Tel.59.
See advt. p. **28.**

Pratt's Hotel, South Parade. Close to Baths, Pump Room and Abbey.
See advt. p. **28.**

Pulteney Hotel. South aspect. Handsome public rooms. Lift. Electric light throughout. Billiards. Excellent cuisine. Near the Pump Room and Baths. Finest Hotel Garage in West of England. Telephone 1281.

Lansdown Grove Hotel. 400 feet above sea-level. Bracing air, due South. Extensive Garden on slopes of Lansdown. Motor 'Bus to and from Baths. Telegrams—"Lansdown Hotel." Telephone 1235.

Francis' Hotels, Queen Square and Bennett Street. High-class Residential Hotels. Centrally situated. Moderate Tariff. Electric Light. Garage. Motor-Bus.

Private Boarding House, 52, Pulteney Street. Home comforts. Smoke Room. On level and convenient for Baths.
Mrs. A. LAWRENCE.

Christopher, the oldest Family and Commercial Hotel, opposite Guildhall and Abbey. Close Baths and Station. Electric Light. Phone 302. Manageresses, The Misses ROBINSON.

Waldron's Private Hotel, Queen's Square. Is pleasantly and conveniently situated near the Mineral Baths, Park and County Club. Telephone 605.

BATH—*continued.*
Bromley House, Russell Street. High-class Private Hotel. Centrally situated, near Baths, Parks, etc. Recently considerably enlarged. Lounge. Smoke Room, Electric Light. Separate tables. Perfect sanitation. Highly recommended. 'Phone 117.
Mrs. SARGANT.

Southbourne Hotel. South Parade. Established 1897. Greatly enlarged. South aspect. Close to Baths, Pump Room, Abbey and Gardens. Table d'hôte 7 o'clock. Separate tables. Good catering, Telephone—Bath 606.

Donnybrook Private Hotel, Russell Street. Recently enlarged. Centrally situated on rising ground. Well-furnished, Comfortable Rooms. Lounge. Gas Fires in Bedrooms. Sanitation perfect. Telephone 835.
The Misses PARNABY.

Fernley Hotel, North Parade, has recently undergone extensive alterations and additions. New Lounge, Dining and Drawing Rooms, 55 Bedrooms. Inclusive Terms upon application. Telephone 680.
Proprietor, W. ADAMS.

Edgar Private Hotel, 2 and 3 Laura Place, Bath. Tel. 25. Quiet and Comfortable. Newly Decorated. Excellent cuisine. Certified Sanitation. A few minutes from Pump Room and Baths.
Proprietor, JOHN HOOPER.

Pendennis, Pierrepont Street. Refined Boarding Establishment. Two minutes Pump Rooms, Baths, Gardens, Band, G.W. Station. Excellent Cuisine.
PROPRIETRESS.

The Westbourne Hotel. Duke Street. Near Institution Gardens. Lovely view overlooking the Sham Castle. Close to Baths, Pump Room, and Abbey. Separate Tables. Gas Fires in all Bedrooms. Good Cuisine.
Proprietress, M. J. GITTINS.

The Grosvenor Hotel. Finest position in Bath, overlooking Institution Gardens. Lovely view. Baths, Pump Room and Abbey three minutes. Gas Fires in all Bedrooms. Separate Tables.

First-class Private Hotel. Electric Light. Gas Fires in Bedrooms. Close to Baths, Abbey. Central. BEARD, 7, Duke Street.

"Houses and Estates." FORTT, HATT, & BILLINGS, Auctioneers and Estate Agents. Register free on application. Offices, 3, Burton Street. Telephone 280.

BATHAMPTON (Somerset), 104½ miles. Fares, 21/10a, 13/1c. R. T. for two months, 43/8a, 26/2c ; (*via* Bath), 22/6a, 13/6c. R. T. for two months, 45/0a, 27/0c. Departures *from* London as *for* Box or Bath. Departures *for* London about 8 times daily. Pop. 427.
Map Square 22.

EMPIRE HOTEL, BATH.

BATHGATE (Linlithgow),

411 miles. Fares, 82/6*a*, 49/6*c*. R.T. for two months, 165/0*a*, 99/0*c*. Departures *from* London as *for* Edinburgh (Waverley). Departures *for* London about 3 times daily. Pop. 8,504.
Map Square 40.

BATLEY (Yorks) from

King's Cross, 183 miles. Fares, 37/9*a*, 22/8*c*. R. T. for two months, 75/6*a*, 45/4*c*. Pop. 36,151.
Map Square 12.

King's +	Batley	Batley	King's +
AM 4.45	9.24	AM 7.42*r*	11.30
7.15*r*	11.23	8.24	1. 5
10.10*r*	2.10	10. 9*r*	3.50
PM 1.30*r*	5.41	PM12.40*r*	5. 0
1.50*r*	6.26	1. 8	6.25
4. 0*r*	8.17	2.38*r*	7.10
5.45*r*	9.57	5. 7*r*	9.25
10.45*e*	5.50	9.57	3.25
—	—	—	—
—	—	—	—
—	—	—	—

Sunday Trains.

12. 0*nr*	5. 0	AM10.56*r*	3.45
PM 5. 0*r*	9.58	PM12.59	5.55
10.45	5.50	5.15*r*	10.20
—	—	—	—
—	—	—	—

e Saturdays excepted.
n Noon.
r Restaurant Car.

ANOTHER ROUTE from

Euston, 212¾ miles. Fares as above.

Euston	Batley	Batley	Euston
AM12.25	8.46	AM 6.11*r*	12.50
2.35	11. 7	8. 3*r*	1.15
5. 0	12.38	8.48*r*	3.10
8.45*r*	2.41	9.53*r*	3.55
10.40*r*	4.30	11. 6*dr*	5.50
11.50*r*	6. 1	PM12.40*er*	6. 0
12. 0*nr*	7.20	12.40*dr*	6.15
PM 1.30*r*	8.41	1.25*r*	7.30
4. 5*r*	10.18	1.48*r*	8.10
6. 5*r*	11.56	3.13*r*	10. 0
8. 0*e*	5.41	4.11*er*	10.10
11.50*d*	9.45	8.23	5. 0
—	—	9.51*e*	5.50
—	—	10.13*d*	5.50

Sunday Trains.

PM12.10*r*	6.56	AM 6.50	4. 0
12.30*r*	10.24	10.34*r*	5.45
7.50*r*	5.41	PM12.25*r*	7.30
—	—	5.19	5. 0
—	—	8.44	5.50

d Saturdays only.
e Saturdays excepted.
n Noon.
r Restaurant Car.

BATLEY CARR (Yorks),

182½ miles. Fares, 37/9*a*, 22/8*c*. R. T. for two months, 75/6*a*, 45/4*c*. Departures *from* London as for Dewsbury. Departures *for* London about 6 times daily. Pop. 5,167.

BATTERSBY (Yorks), 239½

miles. Fares, 50/0*a*, 30/0*c*. R. T. for two months, 100/0*a*, 60/0*c*. Departures *from* London as for Stockton-on-Tees. Departures *for* London about 5 times daily.
Map Square 8.

BATTERSEA (London).

From Clapham Junction, ¾ mile. Fares, 0/2½*a*, 0/1½*c*. R. T. for two days, 0/5*a*, 0/3*c*. Pop. 167,739. *See* p. 583.
Map Square 69.

From Kensington (Addison Road), 2½ miles. Fares, 0/7*a*, 0/4*c*. R. T. for two days, 1/0*a*, 0/7*c*. *See* p. 583.

BATTERSEA PARK

YORK ROAD) from *London Bridge*, 7¼ miles. Fares, *via* S. L. Line, 0/7*a*, 0/4½*c* R.T. for two days, 1/0*a*, 0/9*c*. From *Victoria*, 1¼ miles, 0/4½, 0/2½*c*. R. T. for two days, 0/9*a*, 0/5*c*. *See* pp. 570–574.
Map Square 69.

BATTLE (Sussex) from

Charing Cross, Cannon Street and *London Bridge*, 56¼ miles. Fares, 11/10*a*, 9/5*b*, 7/1*c*. R. T. for two months, 23/8*a*, 18/10*b*, 14/2*c*. Pop. 2,891.
Map Square 24.

Char. +	Leave Can. St.	Lon. B.	Arr at Battle
AM —	3.40*h*	3.43*h*	5.41
—	5.20	5.25	8.13
—	7.56	8. 0	10.27
9.25	—	9.33	11.33
10.40	—	10.46	12.14
PM12. 3	—	12.10	2. 6
2. 8	—	2.16	3.48
3.48*e*	—	—	5.39
5. 5*d*	—	—	6.58
—	5.12*e*	—	6.41
6. 3*e*	—	—	8. 3
—	6.16*e*	6.19*e*	7.39
7.30	—	—	9.29
9.30*y*	—	9.36*y*	11.11

Sunday Trains.

AM 7. 5	—	7.11	9.24
8.45	—	—	10.34
9.50	—	9.56	11.35
PM 7.35	—	7.45	9.50
—	—	—	—
—	—	—	—
—	—	—	—

Trains from Battle.

Leave Battle	Lon. B.	Arrive at Can. St.	Char. +
AM 7.25	—	9.15	—
8. 8	—	9.48	—
8.49*d*	10.29	—	10.39
9.21*e*	—	10.42	—
9.23*e*	11. 7	—	11.17
9.53*k*	11.31	—	11.38
10.33	—	—	12.49
PM12.33	3. 6	—	3.19
2. 4	4.15	—	4.25
3.48*d*	6.30	—	6.39
3.59*e*	6.44	—	6.54
5.57	8.26	—	8.35
8. 1	10.15	—	10.23
9.11	11.35	—	11.44

Sunday Trains.

AM 7.29	10. 5	—	10.15
9.27	11.23	—	11.34
PM 5.52	8.12	—	8.22
9. 1	11. 4	—	11.15
—	—	—	—
—	—	—	—
—	—	—	—

d Saturdays only.
e Saturdays excepted.
h Third Class only.
k Wednesdays only.
y Wednesdays and Saturdays only.

BATTLESBRIDGE

(Essex) from *Liverpool Street*, 31½ miles. Fares, 6/0*a*, 3/7*c*. R. T. for two months, 12/0*a*, 7/2*c*.
Map Square 24.

L'pool St	B'bdg.	B'bdg.	L'pool St
AM 5.26	7. 0	AM 7.32	8.45
6.50	8.28	8.44	9.46
9. 1	10.23	9.55	11. 7
10.47*d*	12. 6	11.46*d*	1.16
11.56	1.16	PM12.16*e*	1.25
PM 1.26*d*	2.17	1.31*d*	3. 5
2.20*e*	4. 2	3.12*d*	4.56
2.40*d*	3.47	3.22*e*	4.51
4.15*e*	5. 8	5.38	6.52
4.18*d*	5.26	6.56	8.23
5.39	6.39	8.35	9.56
6.26*e*	7.36	—	—
8. 2*e*	9.10	—	—
8.45*d*	9.46	—	—

Sunday Trains.

AM 8.45	9.59	AM 8. 6	10.25
9.30	11. 0	PM 7.14	8.45
PM 6.42	8. 6	8.19	9.32
—	—	—	—

d Saturdays only.
e Saturdays excepted.

BATTYEFORD (Yorks),

207¾ miles. Fares, 37/9*a*, 22/8*c*. R. T. for two months, 75/6*a*, 45/4*c*. Departures *from* London as for Huddersfield. Departures *for* London about 4 times daily. Pop. 3,587.

BAWTRY (Yorks) from

King's Cross, 147¾ miles. Fares, 30/8*a*, 18/5*c*. R. T. for two months, 61/4*a*, 36/10*c*. Pop. 1,098.
Map Square 13.

King's +	Bawtry	Bawtry	King's +
AM 4.45	8. 5	AM 8.11*r*	11.30
7.15*r*	10.37	9.11	1. 5
8.45	12.19	PM12.14	3.50
10.10*r*	1.46	2.27	6.25
11.30	3.37	2.36*r*	6.30
PM 1.50*r*	5.35	5. 5	9. 0
4. 0*r*	7.57	7.37	3.25
5.45*r*	9.12	—	—

Sunday Trains.

AM 8.30	1.51	PM 2.37	8. 8
PM 5. 0*r*	8.25	6.52*r*	10.20
—	—	—	—

r Restaurant Car.

BAXENDEN (Lancs), 206½

miles. Fares, 42/8*a*, 25/7*c*. R. T. for two months, 85/4*a*, 51/2*c*. Departures *from* London as for Haslingden. Departures *for* London 6 times daily. Pop. 1,671.
Map Square 12.

BAY HORSE (Lancs), 224¼

miles. Fares, 46/10*a*, 28/1*c*. R. T. for two months, 93/8*a*, 56/2*c*. Departures *from* London as for Preston. Departures *for* London about 4 times daily.
Map Square 7.

BAYNARDS (Surrey) from

Victoria, Clapham Junction and *London Bridge*, 46 miles. Fares, 8/1*a*, 4/10*c*. R. T. for two months, 16/2*a*, 9/8*c*. Departures *from* London as for Rudgwick. Departures *for* London about 7 times daily.
Map Square 23.

BEACONSFIELD

(Bucks) from *Paddington*, 21¾ miles. Fares 4/5*a*, 2/8*c*. R. T. for two months, 8/10*a*, 5/3*c*. Pop. 3,642.
Map Square 23

PAD	BEACFD	BEACFD.	PAD.
AM 5.45	6.59	AM 6.46	8.14
6.10	7 38	7.52	8.34
6.35	8. 3	8.11	9.14
7.33*h*	8.44	8.38	9.20
8.12	9. 7	10. 0	10.40
9. 5	10. 1	11.36	12.32
9.44*k*	11.28	PM12.35	1.18
PM12.18	1. 4	2.53	3.50
12.35	1.46	3. 5*d*	4.19*k*
1.25	2. 7	4. 1	4.40
2.23	3.17	5.44	6.35
3.40	4.23	6.39	7.32
4.40	5.16	7.17	9. 5
5.23	6. 3	8.23	9.18
6.25	7. 6	8.38	9.52
7.18	8. 3	9.48	11. 4
7.42	9.19	10.31	11.41
7.55*e*	9.19	—	—
9. 0	9.53	—	—
10.10	11.24	—	—

Sunday Trains.

AM 9.12	10. 8	AM 9.50	11. 4
9.35	11.13	PM12.58	2.26
11.15	12.12	2.29	3.27
PM 1.45	3. 6	3.33	4.45
2.28	3.23	6.49	7.47
3.15	4.26	7.29	8.25
4. 0	4.57	8. 7	9.35
6. 5	7.23	9.14	10. 7
7.20	8.12	10. 9	11. 0
8. 5	9.18	—	—
9.25	10.47	—	—

d Saturdays only.
e Saturdays excepted.
h Not after July 27.
k Departs from Bishop's Road Station.

ANOTHER ROUTE

from *Marylebone*, 23 miles. Fares as above.

M'BONE.	BEACFD.	BEACFD.	M'BONE.
AM 5.15	6. 1	AM 6.46	7.35
6.10	6.58	7.41	8.32
6.50	7.36	8.11	8.49
7.10	8. 3	8.53	9.26
8. 4	9. 7	9.17	9.55
9. 5	10. 1	11.36*d*	12.43
10.35	11.28	PM12.15	1. 5
PM12.55	1.46	12.35*d*	3.10
1.37*d*	2.19	2.33*d*	3.15
2.10	3. 1	2.33*e*	3.23
3. 5	3.56	3. 5*d*	3.53
4.55	5.35	3.38	4.28
5.38	6.13	4. 1	5.48
5.43	7. 6	5.11	6. 3
6.35*d*	7.24	5.44	7. 5
6.41*e*	7.18	7.17	8. 6
6.45*e*	8. 3	8.38	9.27
8.30	9.19	9.48	10.31
10.35	11.24	10.31	11.18
11.50	12.38	—	—
—	—	—	—

Sunday Trains.

AM 8.50	9.42	AM 9.50	10.43
10.20	11.13	PM12.58	1.48
11.50	12.41	1.53	2.43
PM 2.15	3. 5	3.33	4.23
3.35	4.26	5.33	6.23
6.30	7.24	8. 7	8.58
8.30	9.18	9.48	10.38
10. 0	10.47	—	—

d Saturdays only.
e Saturdays excepted.

Railway Hotel. A Good-Class Family and Residential Hotel at a very reasonable tariff. Most convenient for the Golf Links. 'Phone No. 15.
T. BORLASE, PROPRIETOR.

BEAL

(Northumberland), 326¾ miles. Fares, 68/9*a*, 41/3*c*. R. T. for two months, 137/6*a*, 82/6*c*. Departures *from* London as for Morpeth. Departures *for* London about 4 times daily.
Map Square 3.

BEALINGS

(Suffolk) from *Liverpool Street*, 76 miles. Fares, 16/1*a*, 9/8*c*. R. T. for two months, 32/2*a*, 19/4*c*. Pop. 610.
Map Square 19.

L'PL. ST	B'LINGS	B'LINGS	L'PL. ST.
AM 5. 0	7.23	AM 8.17*r*	10.30
8.15*r*	10.53	9.22*r*	11.22
10.20	12.44	10.30*h*	1.20
PM 1. 0	3. 6	11.57*r*	2. 3
3.18*r*	5.22	PM 1.33	3.42
5.18*r*	7.27	5.19	7.51
—	—	7.24*r*	9.22
—	—	8.24	11.16

Sunday Trains.

PM 4.40	6.52	AM 8.56	11.38
—	—	PM 7. 7*r*	9.10

h Tuesdays only.
r Restaurant Car.

BEAMISH

(Durham), 265 miles. Fares, 59/0*a*, 35/5*c*. R. T. for two months, 118/0*a*, 70/10*c*. Departures *from* London as for Durham. Departures *for* London about 6 times daily. Pop. 17,646.
Map Square 3.

BEARLEY

(Warwick) from *Paddington*, 98¼ miles. Fares, 20/7*a*, 12/4*c*. R. T. for two months, 41/2*a*, 24/8*c*. Pop. 211.
Map Square 17.

PAD.	BEARLEY	BEARLEY	PAD.
AM 9.10	11.16	AM 7.16*r*	10. 0
10.40	12.43	8.56*r*	11. 0
PM12.50*r*	3. 0	10.50*r*	1.25
2.10	4.41	11.57*r*	2. 5
4.10*t*	6.26	PM 2.38*r*	5. 0
6.10*r*	8.17	3.36*t*	5.55
7.30	10.40	5.31*r*	8. 5
12.15*h*	8.40	6.56	10. 0
12.15*l*	11.40	10. 2	3.30

Sunday Trains.

AM10.35	2.49	AM10.31*r*	1.40
PM 6. 0*r*	8.47	PM 2.16	6.20

h Saturdays midnight excepted.
l Saturdays midnight only.
r Restaurant Car.
t Tea Car.

BEARSDEN

(Dumbarton), 442¼ miles. No through fares. Departures *from* London as for Glasgow. Departures *for* London about 3 times daily. Pop. 2,929.
Map Square 40.

BEARSTEAD

(Kent) from *Victoria*, *Holborn Viaduct* and *St Paul's*, 42¾ miles. Fares, 9/2*a*, 7/4*b*, 5/5*c*. R. T. for two months, 18/4*a*, 14/8*b*. Pop. 924.
Map Square 24.

VICT. S.E. & C.	Leave HOL. V.	ST. PL.'S	Arr. at B'STEAD.
AM —	6.40	6.42	8.42
9.45	—	—	11.12
11. 4	10.58	11. 0	1. 3
PM —	1.24*d*	1.30*d*	2.50
2.12*e*	—	—	3.23
2.40*d*	—	—	4.30
2.50*e*	—	—	4.47
4.25*e*	—	—	5.38
*e*5.15*h*	—	*e*5.21*k*	6.42
*d*5.20*h*	—	*d*5.26*k*	6.42
7.22	—	—	8.32
—	7 22*d*	7.24*d*	9.12

Sunday Trains.

AM —	8. 0	—	10. 7
9.35	—	—	10.48
PM 5.15	—	—	6.30
6.35	6.40	—	8.30

BEARSTEAD—*continued.*

Trains from Bearstead.

Leave B'STEAD.	Arrive at ST. PL.'S	HOL. V.	VICT.
AM 7.36	—	—	8.50
8.24	9.52	9.55	—
8.58*e*	10.21	10.23	10.16
9. 5*d*	10.41	10.43	—
11.12	12.59	1. 2	12.49
PM12.42	—	—	2.40
2.26	—	—	3.37
5. 5	6.58	7. 0	—
6.49	—	—	8.51
9.47	11.43	11.45	—
—	—	—	—

Sunday Trains.

AM 9. 3	—	—	10.48
PM 2. 5	—	—	3.50
7.44	—	9. 9	—
—	—	—	—
—	—	—	—

d Saturdays only.
e Saturdays excepted.
h Departs from or arrives at Charing Cross (S.E. & C.R.).
k Departs from or arrives at London Bridge (S.E. & C.R.).

BEATTOCK

(Dumfries), 338¾ miles. Fares, 68/9*a*, 41/3*c*. R. T. for two months, 137/6*a*, 82/6*c*. Departures *from* London as for Lockerbie. Departures *for* London about 5 times daily.
Map Square 44.

BEAUCHIEF

(Derby), from *St. Pancras*, 155 miles. Fares, 32/3*a*, 19/4*c*. R.T. for two months, 64/6*a*, 38/8*c*. Departures *from* London as for Chesterfield. Departures *for* London about 4 times daily. Pop. 43.
Map Square 12.

BEAUFORT

(Monmouth), 171¼ miles. Fares, 33/9*a*, 20/3*c*. R. T. for two months, 67/6*a*, 40/6*c*. Departures *from* London as for Abergavenny. Departures *for* London about 4 times daily. Pop. 3,291.
Map Square 21.

BEAULIEU ROAD

(Hants) from *Waterloo*, 87¼ miles. Fares, 18/4*a*, 11/0*c*. R. T. for two months, 36/8*a*, 22/0*c*. Pop. 986.
Map Square 27.

W'LOO.	BEAU. R.	BEAU. R.	W'LOO.
AM 5.40	8.42	AM 7.28*r*	10. 6
5.50	9.38	8.43*s*	11. 0
8.30*s*	11.15	10.11*r*	12.50
10.30	12.48	11.41*r*	2.20
PM12.30*r*	2.57	PM 1.33	4.20
1.30*s*	4. 4	3.32*s*	6.26
2.30	4.52	4.38	6.58
3.30*s*	6. 2	5.30*r*	8.20
4.30*r*	6.48	6.30*r*	8.50
6.30*r*	8.41	8.16	11.28
7.30	10. 5	9.47	3.58

Sunday Trains.

AM11. 0*r*	1.46	AM 9.48*r*	2.27
PM 2. 0*r*	4.49	PM 5.11	8. 3
—	—	7. 3*r*	9.31
—	—	8.37	3.58

r Restaurant Car.
s Refreshments served.

BEAULY

(Inverness), 577¾ miles. Fares, 106/3*a*, 63/9*c*. R. T. for two months, 212/6*a*, 127/6*c*. Departures *from* London as for Inverness. Departures *for* London about 3 times daily. Pop. 805.
Map Square 34.

BEBINGTON

(Cheshire), 191¼ miles. Fares, 39/10*a*, 23/11*c*. R. T. for two months, 79/8*a*, 47/10*c*. Departures *from* London as for Hooton. Departures *for* London about 6 times daily. Pop. 16,460.
Map Square 12.

BEDFORD.—EMBANKMENT HOTEL. Beautifully Situated. Moderate Tariff. Inclusive Rates.

BEBSIDE (Northumberland), 282¼ miles. No through fares. Departures *from* London as for Newcastle-on-Tyne. Departures *for* London about 6 times daily. Pop. 58.
Map Square 3.

BECCLES (Suffolk) from *Liverpool Street*, 109½ miles. Fares, 22/11*a*, 13/9*c*. R.T. for two months, 45/10*a*, 27/6*c*. Pop. 7,077.
Map Square 19.

L'pl. St.	Beccles	Beccles	L'pl. St.
AM 5. 0	8.42	AM 6.58*r*	10.30
8.15*r*	11. 9	8. 2*r*	11.22
9.55	12.21	8.54*r*	11.30
10. 0	12.54	10.22	1.20
10.20	1.56	10.33*r*	2. 3
PM 1. 0	3.53	PM12.49	3.42
3.15	5.52	2.56	5.55
3.18*r*	6.46	4. 2	7.51
4.55*r*	7.43	6. 2*r*	9.22
5.18*dr*	8.39	6.56*r*	10. 0
5.18*er*	8.47	7. 7	11.16
—	—	—	—
—	—	—	—
—	—	—	—

Sunday Trains.

AM10. 5*r*	1.22	AM 7.33	11.38
11.30*r*	2. 0	PM 4. 9*r*	6.35
PM 4.40	8. 9	5.48*r*	9.10
—	—	7.30*r*	10.30
—	—	—	—

d Saturdays only.
e Saturdays excepted.
r Restaurant Car.

BECKENHAM HILL (Kent) from *Victoria*, *Holborn Viaduct*, *Ludgate Hill*, and *St. Paul's*, 9¼ miles. Fares, 1/6*a*, 1/2*b*, 0/10½*c*. R. T. for two days, 2/7*a*, 1/9*b*, 1/5*c*. *See* pp. 562-563.
Map Square 80.

BECKENHAM JUNC. (Kent) from *Charing Cross*, *Cannon Street*, and *London Bridge*, 10¾ miles. Fares, 1/8*a*, 1/4*b*, 1/0*c*. R. T. for two days, 3/4*a*, 2/8*b*, 2/0*c*. Pop. (Beckenham) 33,345. *See* pp. 544-547.
Map Square 80.

ANOTHER ROUTE from *Victoria*, *Holborn Viaduct*, and *Ludgate Hill*, 8¾ miles. Fares as above. *See* pp. 558-561.

BECKENHAM (NEW) (Kent) from *Charing Cross*, *Cannon Street*, and *London Bridge*, 10½ miles. Fares, 1/8*a*, 1/4*b*, 1/0*c*. R. T. for two days, 3/4*a*, 2/8*b*, 2/0*c*. *See* pp. 544-547.
Map Square 80.

BECKERMET (Cumberland), 294¼ miles. No through fares. Departures *from* London as for Sellafield. Departures *for* London about 3 times daily. Pop. 1,444.
Map Square 6.

BECKFORD (Gloucester), 114 miles. No through fares. Departures *from* London as for Evesham. Departures *for* London about 4 times daily. Pop. 456.
Map Square 17.

BECKINGHAM (Notts), 148¾ miles. Fares, 30/8*a*, 18/5*c*. R. T. for two months, 61/4*a*, 36/10*c*. Departures *from* London as for Gainsboro'. Departures *for* London about 5 times daily. Pop. 532.
Map Square 13.

BECKTON (Essex) from *Liverpool Street*, 9 miles, and *Fenchurch Street*, 8 miles. Fares, from Liverpool Street, 1/5½*a*, 1/2*b*, 0/10½*c*. R. T. for two days, 2/11*a*, 2/2½*b*, 1/7½*c*. Fenchurch Street, 1/3*a*, 1/0*b*, 0/9*c*. R. T. for two days, 2/6*a*, 2/0*b*, 1/5½*c*. Pop. 14,919. *See* pp. 537-540.

BEDALE (Yorks), 225¼ miles. Fares, 46/11*a*, 28/2*c*. R. T. for two months, 93/10*a*, 56/4*c*. Departures *from* London as for Leyburn. Departures *for* London about 6 times daily. Pop. 1,163.
Map Square 7.

BEDDINGTON LANE (Surrey) from *London Bridge* and *Victoria*, 11 miles. No through fares. Pop. (Beddington), 11,802. *See* p. 577.

BEDFORD from *St. Pancras*, 49¾ miles. Fares, 10/2*a*, 6/1*c*. R. T. for two months, 20/4*a*, 12/2*c*. Pop. 40,247.
Map Square 18.

St. Pan.	Bedfd.	Bedfd.	St. Pan.
AM 4.25	5.45	AM 3.10*g*	4.20
6.25	8.23	3.37*f*	4.55
7.50	9.10	3.40*g*	5. 5
8.25*r*	9.47	4.38*g*	6. 0
9.25	10.38	6.32	8.28
11. 0*r*	12.37	7.25	8.45
11.35	12.58	7.33	9.13
PM12.30	1.38	8.20	9.30
1. 0*r*	2.10	8.28	10. 5
1.33*d*	3. 9	9. 5	10.31
2.45	3.57	10.23	11.25
3.35	4.50	10.40	12. 5
4.30*r*	5.35	11.23	1. 3
4.40	6.15	PM12.15*r*	1.20
5. 5	6.25	2.15	3.25
5.35	6.35	3.58	5.20
5.40*e*	7. 0	4.48	6.30
6.30	7.37	5.50	7. 3
7.50	9.26	7.17	8.22
8.25	9.48	9. 1*r*	10. 5
10. 5	11.22	10. 3	11.45
11.50	1. 0	—	—
12. 0	1.17	—	—

Sunday Trains.

AM 8. 0	10. 7	AM 3.10	4.20
10.50*r*	12. 0	3.40	5. 5
11.15*r*	12.21	4.38	6. 0
PM 1.35	3. 5	7.50	8.57
4.35	6.35	8. 0	10.15
6.15*r*	7.20	10.40	11.53
8.25	9.48	11.27	1.30
9.30	10.30	PM 5. 2	6.27
11.55	1.17	6.37	8.30
—	—	8.38	9.43
—	—	9.43	11. 7
—	—	—	—

d Saturdays only.
e Saturdays excepted.
f Mondays only.
g Mondays excepted.
r Restaurant Car.

BEDFORD—*continued.*

ANOTHER ROUTE from *Euston*, 62¾ miles. Fares, 10/5*a*, 6/3*c*. R.T. for two months, 20/10*a*, 12/6*c*.

Euston	Bed.	Bed.	Euston
AM 6.45	8.49	AM 6.40	9. 5
7.35	10. 5	8.51	11.40
9.30	12.11	9.53	11.55
10.40	12.36	10.52*d*	12.20
12. 0*nr*	2.25	10.52*e*	12.32
PM12.15*e*	4. 5	11. 5	1.50
1.35*d*	4. 5	PM12.50*h*	2.45
2. 0	4.45	12.50*k*	4.15
3. 5	4.57	3. 6	5. 5
5.32	7.39	5.36	7.55
6.10*e*	8.20	5.45	8.35
7.15*d*	10. 0	7.57*e*	10.10
8. 0*e*	10. 0	7.57*d*	10.50
—	—	8.35	11.35
—	—	—	—
—	—	—	—
—	—	—	—
—	—	—	—

Sunday Trains.

AM 9.15	12.19	PM12.40	5. 5
PM12.30	2.39	7. 9	9.45
—	—	—	—

d Saturdays only.
e Saturdays excepted.
h Thursdays and Saturdays only.
k Thursdays and Saturdays excepted.
n Noon.
r Restaurant Car.

BEDLINGTON (Northumberland), 283½ miles. Fares, 59/10*a*, 35/11*c*. R. T. for two months, 119/8*a*, 71/10*c*. Departures *from* London as for Newcastle-on-Tyne. Departures *for* London about 6 times daily. Pop. 6,413.
Map Square 3.

BEDLINOG (Glamorgan), 166¾ miles. Fares, 34/0*a*, 20/5*c*. R. T. for two months, 68/0*a*, 40/10*c*. Departures *from* London as for Dowlais. Departures *for* London about 5 times daily. Pop. 4,820
Map Square 21.

BEDMINSTER (Somerset), 118¾ miles. Fares, 24/9*a*, 14/10*c*. R. T. for two months, 49/6*a*, 29/8*c*. Departures *from* London as for Bristol. Departures *for* London about 10 times daily. Pop. 42,181.
Map Square 22.

BEDWAS (Monmouth), 151¾ miles. Fares, 31/6*a*, 18/11*c*. R. T. for two months, 63/0*a*, 37/10*c*. Departures *from* London as for Bargoed. Departures *for* London about 4 times daily. Pop. 3,231.

BEDWELLTY PITS (Monmouth), 161½ miles. No through fares. Departures *from* London as for Tredegar. Departures *for* London about 3 times daily. Pop. 31,089.

BEDWORTH (Warwick), 100½ miles. Fares, 20/8*a*, 12/5*c*. R. T. for two months, 41/4*a*, 24/10*c*. Departures *from* London as for Nuneaton or Coventry. Departures *for* London about 6 times daily. Pop. 9,595.
Map Square 17.

BEDWYN (Wilts) from *Paddington* 66½ miles. Fares, 13/11*a*, 8/4*c*. R.T. for two months, 27/10*a*, 16/8*c*. Pop. 880
Map Square 22.

PAD.	BEDWYN	BEDWYN	PAD.
AM 7.30	9.22	AM 8.18	10. 0
8.45*r*	11. 5	10.27	12.55
10.45	12.44	PM 12.45	2.50
PM 12.30*r*	2.20	4.38	7.20
2.45	4.58	6.27	8.20
3.18	5.47	8.33	10.45
5. 5	6.45	—	—
5.55	7.30	—	—
6.30	8.12	—	—
—	—	—	—
—	—	—	—

Sunday Trains.

AM 9.10	11.22	AM 8.21	10.50
PM 5.15	7.41	PM 7. 3	9.15
—	—	—	—
—	—	—	—
—	—	—	—
—	—	—	—

r Restaurant Car.

BEECHBURN (Durham), 248¾ miles. No through fares. Departures *from* London as for Bishop Auckland. Departures *for* London about 4 times daily.
Map Square 7.

BEECHES HALT (Surrey) from *London Bridge* or *Victoria*, 13¾ miles. No through fares. *See* pp. 564, 565, 571–574.

BEESTON (Nottingham) from *St. Pancras*, 123¼ miles. Fares, *via* Trent, 25/3*a*, 15/2*c*. R.T. for two months, 50/6*a*, 30/4*c*. *Via* Nottingham, 25/8*a*, 15/5*c*. R. T. for two months, 51/4*a*, 30/10*c*. Departures *from* London as for Nottingham or Trent. Departures *for* London about 6 times daily. Pop. 12,468.
Map Square 13.

BEESTON (Yorks), 183¼ miles. Fares, 38/1*a*, 22/10*c*. Departures *from* London as for Wakefield (Westgate). Departures *for* London about 6 times daily. Pop. 7,392.
Map Square 12.

BEESTON CASTLE (Cheshire) from *Euston*, 168½ miles. Fares, 35/2*a*, 21/1*c*. R. T. for two months, 70/4*a*, 42/2*c*. Pop. 308.
Map Square 12.

EUSTON	BEES. C.	BEES. C.	EUSTON
AM 2.35	8.29	AM 8.32*er*	12. 5
5. 0	9.41	8.32*dr*	12.20
8.30*r*	12.16	8.59*r*	1. 0
10.30*r*	1.49	10.18*r*	1.45
11.50*r*	3.11	11.35*r*	3.10
12. 0*nr*	4.47	PM 12. 4*r*	4.15
PM 2.35*t*	6. 6	2.52*r*	6.25
4. 5*r*	7.50	5.37*er*	9. 5
5.20*r*	9. 8	5.37*dr*	9.15
11.50*d*	8.57	6.42*r*	10.45
—	—	10.24	5. 0
—	—	—	—

Sunday Trains.

PM 12.10*r*	4.23	AM 10.22	4. 0
—	—	PM 3.22*r*	7.10
—	—	8.14	5. 0
—	—	—	—

d Saturdays only.
e Saturdays excepted.
n Noon.
r Restaurant Car.
t Tea Car.

BEESTON TOR (Stafford), 165½ miles. No through fares. Departures *from* London as for Leek. Departures *for* London about 4 times daily.
Map Square 12.

BEIGHTON (Derby) from *Marylebone*, 158¼ miles. Fares, 32/1*a*, 19/3*c*. R. T. for two months, 64/2*a*, 38/6*c*. Pop. 4,748.
Map Square 13.

M'BONE.	B'TON.	B'TON.	M'BONE.
AM 2.32	8. 1	AM 5.25	10.36
10. 0*r*	3. 9	8.12*r*	1.13
PM 12.15*r*	4.56	10. 7*r*	3. 0
3.20*r*	7.49	PM 12. 7*r*	6.38
5. 0*r*	9.39	3.59*r*	8.55
—	—	5.25*r*	9.55
—	—	8.22	3.57

Sunday Trains.

PM 5.30*r*	10. 1	AM 10. 2*r*	5.40
—	—	—	—
—	—	—	—

r Restaurant Car.

BEITH (Ayr), 406¼ miles. Fares, 82/4*a*, 49/5*c*. R. T. for two months, 164/8*a*, 98/10*c*. Departures *from* London as for Kilmarnock. Departures *for* London about 4 times daily. Pop. 6,343.
Map Square 40.

BEKESBOURNE (Kent) from *Victoria*, *Holborn Viaduct*, and *St. Paul's*, 64¾ miles. Fares, 13/7*a*, 10/11*b*, 8/1*c*. R. T. for two months, 27/2*a*, 21/10*b*, 16/2*c*. Departures *from* London as for Adisham. Departures *for* London about 8 times daily. Pop. 332.
Map Square 21.

BELFAST from *Euston*, *via* Holyhead and Kingstown, 448 miles. Fares, 81/0 First and Saloon, 56/0 Third and Saloon, 48/6 Third and Steerage. R.T. for two months, 160/6 First and Saloon, 109/9 Third and Saloon, 96/0 Third and Steerage. Pop. 315,492.
Map Square 5.

EUSTON	B'FAST.	B'FAST.	EUSTON
AM 8.30*r*	9.10*l*	PM 5.30*e*	5.50*h*
PM 8.45*e*	9. 5	—	—
8.45*d*	1.35*l*	—	—
—	—	—	—
—	—	—	—

Sunday Trains.

PM 8.45	9. 5	PM 4.45	5.50*h*
—	—	—	—
—	—	—	—

d Saturdays only.
e Saturdays excepted.
h A.M. *l* P.M.
r Restaurant Car.

ANOTHER ROUTE, *via* Holyhead and Greenore, 415½ miles. Fares, 63/9 First and Saloon, 47/3 Third and Saloon, 35/3 Third and Steerage. R. T. for two months, 120/0 First and Saloon, 87/0 Third and Saloon, 70/6 Third and Steerage.

EUSTON	B'FAST.	B'FAST.	EUSTON
PM 6.30*e*	9.50*h*	PM 5.35	8. 0*h*
—	—	—	—
—	—	—	—

Sunday Trains.

PM 8.45	9.50*h*	—	—
—	—	—	—
—	—	—	—

e Saturdays excepted.
h A.M.

ANOTHER ROUTE from *Euston*, *via* Fleetwood, 350 miles. Fares, 63/9 First and Saloon, 47/3 Third and Saloon, 35/3 Third and Steerage. R. T. for two months, 120/0 First and Saloon, 87/0 Third and Saloon, 70/6 Third and Steerage.

EUSTON	B'FAST.	B'FAST.	EUSTON
PM 5.20*r*	6.30	PM 9.15*er*	11.10*h*
—	—	9.15*dr*	1.30*l*

No Sunday Service.

d Saturdays only.
e Saturdays excepted.
h A.M.
l P.M.
r Restaurant Car.

Irish Express Night Service.

BELFAST—*continued.*

ANOTHER ROUTE from Euston, 470 miles, *via* Stranraer and Larne. Fares, 71/3a, .42/9c. R.T. for two months, 142/6a, 85/6c.

Euston	B'fast.	B'fast.	Euston
AM10. 0r	11. 5l	AM 9. 5r	10. 0l
PM 8. 0e	9.30h	PM 6.25	7.15k
—	—	—	—

Sunday Trains.

PM 8.30	9.30h	—	—
—	—	—	—

e Saturdays excepted.
h A.M.
l P.M.
r Restaurant Car.

ANOTHER ROUTE from Euston via Liverpool, 336 miles. Fares, 63/9 First and Saloon, 47/3 Third and Saloon, 35/3 Third and Steerage. R.T. for two months, 120/0 First and Saloon, 87/0 Third and Saloon, 70/6 Third and Steerage.

Euston	B'fast.	B'fast.	Euston
PM 5.55r	7.30h	PM 9. 6k	12. 5
—	—	9. 0y	12.20
—	—	9. 0d	1.30l
—	—	—	—

No Sunday Service.
d Saturdays only.
h A.M.
k Fridays and Saturdays excepted.
l P.M. Sunday.
r Restaurant Car.
y Friday night only.

ANOTHER ROUTE from St. Pancras, *via* Heysham, 407 miles. Fares, 63/9 First and Saloon, 47/3 Third and Saloon, 35/3 Third and Steerage. R.T. for two months, 120/0 First and Saloon, 87/0 Third and Saloon, 70/6 Third and Steerage.

St. Pan.	Belfast	Belfast	St. Pan.
PM 5. 0r	8. 5h	PM 9. 0er	12.10
—	—	9. 0d	5.27
—	—	—	—

No Sunday Service.
d Saturdays only.
e Saturdays excepted.
h A.M.
r Restaurant Car.

Sailings to Belfast.
From Fleetwood, *see* page 596.
From Liverpool, *see* page 597.

Bank.—The National Bank, Ltd.

BELFORD (Northumberland),
319¼ miles. Fares, 67/4a, 40/5c. R.T. for two months, 134/8a, 80/10c. Departures *from* London as for Morpeth. Departures *for* London about 5 times daily. Pop. 743.
Map Square 3.

BELGRAVE (Leicester)
105½ miles. Fares, 20/8a, 12/5c. R. T. for two months, 41/4a, 24/10c. Departures *from* London as for Leicester (Central). Departures *for* London about 5 times daily. Pop. 13,053.
Map Square 18.

BELL BUSK (Yorks),
228 miles. Fares, 43/11a, 26/4c. R.T. for two months, 87/10a, 52/8c. Departures *from* London as for Skipton. Departures *for* London about 6 times daily.
Map Square 7.

BELLE VUE (Lancs),
183½ miles. Fares, 37/11a, 22/9c. R.T. for two months, 75/10a, 45/6c. Departures *from* London as for Marple or Guide Bridge. Departures *for* London about 6 times daily.

BELLINGHAM (Kent)
from *Victoria, Holborn Viaduct, Ludgate Hill,* and *St. Paul's,* 9 miles. Fares, 1/6a, 1/2b, 0/10½c. R.T. for two days, 2/7a, 1/9b, 1/5c. *See* pp. 562, 563.
Map Square 80.

BELLINGHAM (Northumberland),
304 miles. Fares, 64/5a, 38/8c. R. T. for two months, 128/10a, 77/4c. Departures *from* London as for Hexham. Departures *for* London about 3 times daily. Pop. 1,358.
Map Square 3.

BELLSHILL (Lanark),
391 miles. No through fares. Departures *from* London as for Edinburgh (Waverley). Departures *for* London about 3 times daily. Pop. 17,411.

BELMONT (Surrey)
from *London Bridge* and *Victoria,* 14½ miles. Fares, 2/6a, 1/6c. R. T. for two days, 4/11a, 3/0c. *See* pp. 582, 583.

BELPER (Derby)
from *St. Pancras.* 135½ miles. Fares, 28/1a, 16/10c. R.T. for two months. 56/2a, 33/8c. Pop. 12,125.
Map Square 12.

St. Pan.	Belper	Belper	St. Pan.
AM 2.25	6.51	AM 5.40	9.57
4.25	9. 8	7.32r	11. 2
8.25r	12.43	8.18r	11.35
10.25r	1.33	9.58r	1.30
PM12.25r	4. 2	11.27	3.25
2.25r	5.34	PM 1. 0r	4.20
4.25r	7.51	2.10r	5.45
6.25r	9.58	3.25r	7.15
12. 0h	7. 9	5.16r	8.35
—	—	6.45r	10. 5
—	—	10. 4	4.20

Sunday Trains.

PM 3.15	6.51	PM12. 3r	5. 2
6.15r	9.47	6.22r	9.52
—	—	9.18	4.55
—	—	—	—

h Saturdays midnight only.
r Restaurant Car.

BELSES (Roxburgh),
352½ miles. Fares, 71/8a, 43/0c. R. T. for two months, 143/4a, 86/0c. Departures *from* London as for Hawick. Departures *for* London about 4 times daily.
Map Square 41.

BELSIZE PARK (Hampstead Tube).
See back of Map.

BELTON (Lincoln),
179 miles. No through fares. Departures *from* London as for Goole or Gainsborough. Departures *for* London about 3 times daily. Pop. 1,531.
Map Square 13.

BELTON (Suffolk)
from *Liverpool Street,* 117¾ miles. Fares, 24/9a, 14/10c. R.T. for two months, 49/6a, 29/8c. Departures *from* London as for St. Olaves. Departures *for* London about 6 times daily. Pop. 850.
Map Square 19.

BELVEDERE (Kent) from
Charing Cross, Cannon Street, and *London Bridge,* 13½ miles. Fares, 2/11a, 2/4b, 1/9c. R. T. for eight days, 5/10a, 4/4b, 3/6c. From Cannon Street. Fares, 2/6a, 2/0b, 1/6c. R. T. for eight days, 5/0a, 3/11b, 3/0c. Pop. 9,288. *See* pp. 547-551.
Map Square 24.

BEMBRIDGE (Isle of
Wight) from *Waterloo,* 87 miles. Fares, 19/1a, 11/8c. R.T. for two months, 38/2a, 23/4c. Pop. 1,428.
Map Square 28.

W'loo.	B'bridge.	B'bridge.	W'loo.
AM 5.50	10.40	AM 8. 0	11.41
8.34r	12.42	10. 5r	1.52
9.50	1.40	PM 2. 5	5.56
10.50	3.57	3. 0	7.46
11.50d	3.57	4. 2r	7.56
PM12.50r	4.31	5. 2	10.46
1.50d	5.30	8.50	3.58
3.50s	7.30	—	—
5.50	9.15	—	—
—	—	—	—

Sunday Trains.

AM 9.15r	1.45	PM 2.23r	6.16
PM 1.50	6.57	4.17	8.52
—	—	5.50	10. 1
—	—	—	—

d Saturdays only.
r Restaurant Car.
s Refreshments served.

ANOTHER ROUTE from *Victoria* and *London Bridge,* 99¼ miles. Fares as above.

	Vict.	Leave Lon. B.	Arrive B'b'dge.
AM	8.55	—	12.42
	10.15	10.22	2.40
	11.35	—	3.27
PM	1.55	2. 5	7.30
	—	4.50	8.25
	—	—	—

Sunday Trains.

AM	9.55	—	1.45
PM	1.14	1.10	6.57

Trains from Bembridge.

	Leave B'b'dge.	Arrive Lon. B.	Vict.
AM	9. 5	—	1.10
PM	12. 5	4.27	4.34
	1. 5	—	5.12
	3. 0	7.48	6.50
	5. 2	—	8.33
	—	—	—

Sunday Trains.

PM	4.17	8.50	7.56
	—	—	—

BEMPTON (Yorks), 220½ miles. No through fares. Departures *from* London as for Bridlington. Departures *for* London about 4 times daily. Pop. 296.
Map Square 8.

BENDERLOCH (Argyle), 500½ miles. Fares, 100/3*a*, 60/2*c*. R.T. for two months, 200/6*a*, 120/4*c*. Departures *from* London as for Oban. Departures *for* London about twice daily.
Map Square 37.

BENFLEET (Essex) from *Fenchurch Street*, 29¼ miles. Fares, 4/10*a*, 2/11*c*. R.T. for two months, 9/8*a*, 5/10*c*. Pop. 2,209.
Map Square 24.

Fen. St.	B'fleet.	B'fleet.	Fen. St.
AM 5. 5	6.19	AM 5.41	6.43
5.37	7.35	6.14	7.34
6.52	8.35	7.17	8.15
7.42	8.45	8.14	9.10
7.53	9.13	8.51	9.53*h*
9.18	10.43	9.42	10.35
9.57*h*	11. 8	9.52	11.20
10.17	11.40	10.46	11.40
10.45	11.50	11.47*e*	1.22
11.57*d*	12.45	11.47*d*	1.27
PM 12. 9	1. 3	PM 12.46	1.56
1. 0*d*	1 49	2. 9	3.28
1.25*d*	2.18	2.26*d*	4.10
1.48*e*	3.30	3.31	5.18
2. 5*dk*	3.11	4.51	6.33
2.26*d*	3.19	5.22	6.45
2.30	3.49	5.37	7.24
3. 8*d*	4. 0	6.30*e*	7.29*h*
3.16*h*	4.26	6.39	7.51
3.25	5. 4	7.36	9.15
4.27	5.18	8.52	10. 8
5. 2*eh*	6.14	9.30	10.30
5.38*e*	6.30	9.48	11.23*h*
6.26	7.17	10.40	11.40
6.53*d*	8. 0	—	—
7.20	8.36	—	—
8. 0*e*	9.17	—	—
8.13	9.58	—	—
9.19*eh*	10.27	—	—
9.20*d*	10.27	—	—
10.15	11. 5	—	—
12.20	1.11	—	—

Sunday Trains.

AM 9.15	10.13	AM 8.31	10.18
9.45	11.13	10.32	11.35
10.40	11.45	PM 12.12	1.10
11.10	12.53	2.34	3.47
PM 2. 7	3.45	4.36	6. 0
2.45	4.11	5.44	7.16
4.30	6. 7	6. 0	7.45
5. 7*h*	6.25	7.27	8.32
6.10	7.26	7.35	8.59*h*
7.22	8.23	7.42	9.30
8.28	9.28	8.57	10. 9
8.45	10.27	9. 5	10.23
9.45	11. 3	9.18	11. 0
—	—	10.7	11.22*h*
—	—	—	—

d Saturdays only.
e Saturdays excepted.
h Departs from or arrives at Mark Lane Station.
k Departs from or arrives at Broad Street Station.

ANOTHER ROUTE from *St. Pancras*, 35½ miles. Fares as above.

St. Pan.	B'fleet	B'fleet	St. Pan.
AM 9.30	11. 8	AM 10.46	1.48
PM 12.20*d*	2.18	PM 6.22	7.45
12.20*e*	3.30	—	—
2.50	4.26	—	—
6.40	8. 0	—	—

Sunday Trains.

AM 10.10	11.46	PM 7.35	9.18

d Saturdays only.
e Saturdays excepted,

BENGEWORTH (Worcester), 108¼ miles. No through fares. Departures *from* London as for Evesham. Departures *for* London about 5 times daily. Pop. 2,872.
Map Square 17.

BENINGBROUGH (Yorks), 193¼ miles. Fares, 40/3*a*, 24/2*c*. R. T. for two months, 80/6*a*, 48/4*c*. Departures *from* London as for York. Departures *for* London about 5 times daily. Pop. 55.
Map Square 8.

BEN RHYDDING (Yorks), 202¾ miles. Fares, 41/6*a*, 24/11*c* R.T. for two months, 83/0*a*, 49/10*c*. Departures *from* London as for Ilkley. Departures *for* London about 4 times daily. Pop. 1,234.
Map Square 7

BENSHAM (Durham), 266¾ miles. Fares, 55/8*a*, 33/5*c*. R. T. for two, months, 111/4*a*, 66/10*c*. Departures *from* London as for Durham. Departures *for* London about 6 times daily. Pop. 7,993.
Map Square 3.

BENTHAM (Yorks), 246¼ miles. Fares, 47/9*a*, 28/8*c*. R. T. for two months, 95/6*a*, 57/4*c*. Departures *from* London as for Giggleswick. Departures *for* London about 5 times daily. Pop. 2,476.
Map Square 7.

BENTLEY (Hants) from *Waterloo*, 42 miles. Fares, 8/9*a*, 5/3*c*. R. T. for two months, 17/6*a*, 10/6*c*. Pop. 671.
Map Square 23.

W'loo.	Bentley	Bentley	W'loo.
AM 4.50	6.58	AM 7.26	8.56
5.50	7.26	8.19	9.41
7. 0	8.50	9.18	10.26
7.50	9.37	9.54	11.16
9.20	10.47	10.51	12.11
10.34	12.15	11.19	12.40
11.20	1. 4	PM 12.19	1.40
PM 1.10	2.31	12.56	2.46
1.20	3. 2	2.11	3.36
3.15	4.40	2.57	4.46
4. 0	5.22	4. 1	5.46
5.10	6.30	4.37	6.16
6.34	7.49	5.44	7. 7
6.40*d*	8.25	7.30	9. 6
6.54*e*	8.25	8.22	9.52
8. 0	9.36	9.29	11.10
9.50	11.21	10.22	12.16
—	—	—	—
—	—	—	—
—	—	—	—
—	—	—	—
—	—	—	—
—	—	—	—
—	—	—	—

Sunday Trains.

AM 8.45	10.22	AM 9.32	11.16
11.15	12.49	11.11	12.52
PM 1.50	3.28	PM 1.39	3.13
6.20	7.49	5.48	7.41
6.30	8.20	8.18	9.37
10.45	12.13	9. 8	10.47
—	—	—	—
—	—	—	—
—	—	—	—

d Saturdays only.
e Saturdays excepted.

BENTLEY (Suffolk) from *Liverpool Street*, 63¼ miles. Fares, 13/4*a*, 8/0*c*. R. T. for two months, 26/8*a*, 16/0*c*. Pop. 428.
Map Square 19.

L'pool.St.	Bent'y.	Bent'y.	L'pool.St.
AM 5. 0	8. 7	AM 8. 8*r*	9.53
6.50	9.31	9.18	11.16
8.46	10.56	PM 12.45	3.13
10.47	1.11	1.28*h*	3.36
11.30	1.25	3.39	5.48
PM 1.33*d*	3.54	6.10	7.51
2.15	4.20	7.12*d*	9.36
3.26	5.49	—	—
5.42*d*	7.36	—	—
5.42*e*	7.40	—	—
6.39*e*	8.29	—	—
8.54	11.24	—	—
—	—	—	—
—	—	—	—
—	—	—	—

Sunday Trains.

AM 8.15	10.38	AM 9.56	12.40
PM 3.40	5.54	PM 3.19	7.10
4.40	8. 1	6.36	8.58
8.46	11.18	—	—
—	—	—	—
—	—	—	—

d Saturdays only
e Saturdays excepted.
h Tuesdays only.
r Restaurant Car.

BENTLEY, GREAT (Essex) from *Liverpool Street*, 60¾ miles. Fares, 13/2*a*, 7/11*c*. R. T. for two months, 26/4*a*, 15/10*c*. Pop. 1,093.
Map Square 24.

L'pool.St.	G.Bent.	G.Bent.	L'pool.St.
AM 5. 0	7. 1	AM 7.48	9.36
6.50	9.47	9.52	11.42
8.46	11.58	PM 12. 5*r*	2. 3
11.26*d*	1.47	2.53	5. 5
11.30*e*	1.47	4.47	6.32
PM 2.15	4.36	6.20	9.17
3.26	6. 3	8.21	11.16
4.58*hr*	6.41	—	—
5.42	7.55	—	—
7.45*r*	9.45	—	—
8.45	10.29	—	—
—	—	—	—
—	—	—	—
—	—	—	—
—	—	—	—

Sunday Trains.

AM 9.20*r*	11.40	AM 9.21	11.38
PM 4.40	6.28	PM 6.18	8.25
—	—	7. 7	10. 9
—	—	—	—
—	—	—	—

d Saturdays only.
e Saturdays excepted.
h Tuesdays only.
r Restaurant Car.

BENTON (Northumberland), 272¾ miles. Fares, 57/6*a*, 34/6*c*. R.T. for two months, 115/0*a*, 69/0*c*. Departures *from* London as for Newcastle-on-Tyne. Departures *for* London about 5 times daily. Pop. 2,275.
Map Square 3.

BENTS (Linlithgow), 415½ miles. No through fares. Departures *from* London as for Edinburgh (Waverley). Departures *for* London about 3 times daily.
Map Square 40.

BERE ALSTON (Devon),

220¼ miles. Fares, 45/10a, 27/6c.
R.T. for two months, 91/8a, 55/0c.
Map Square 26.

W'loo.	B. Alston	B. Alston	W'loo.
AM 9. 0r	2.24	AM 8.29r	1.56
11. 0r	4.48	10.42r	3.50
PM 1. 0r	7.33	11.49r	6. 0
3. 0r	8.25	PM 2. 7r	8.30
—	—	3.36	10.50
—	—	5. 2h	3.58
—	—	—	—
—	—	—	—

Sunday Trains.

12. 0nr	6.42	PM 2.22r	8.57
—	—	—	—
—	—	—	—

h Via Eastleigh.
n Noon.
r Restaurant Car.

BERE FERRERS (Devon),

223 miles. Fares, 46/6a, 27/11c.
R.T. for two months, 93/0a, 55/0c.
Departures *from* London as for
Bere Alston. Departures *for*
London about 3 times daily.
Pop. 1,803.
Map Square 26.

BERKELEY (Glo'ster),

142 miles. Fares, 29/9a, 17/10c·
R.T. for two months, 59/6a, 35/8c.
Departures *from* London as for
Lydney. Departures *for* London
about 5 times daily. Pop. 826.
Map Square 22.

BERKELEY ROAD

(Gloucester), 144½ miles. Fares,
30/2a, 18/1c. R.T. for two months,
60/4a, 36/2c. Departures *from*
London as for Lydney. Departures
for London about 5 times
daily.
Map Square 22.

BERKHAMSTED

(Herts) from *Euston*, 28 miles.
Fares, from *Euston*, 5/8a, 3/5c.
R.T. for two months, 11/4a, 6/10c.
From *Broad Street*, 6/1a, 3/8c.
R. T. for two months 12/2a, 7/4c.
Pop. 7,295.
Map Square 23.

	Leave		Arr. at
	Euston	Broad St.	Berkh.
AM	5.25	—	6.47
	7.15	6.45	8.14
	7.35	7.10	8.37
	8.35	8.15	9.39
	9.40	9. 6	10.43
	10.50	10.17	11.49
PM	12.15	11.47	1.10
	12.50d	12.20d	1.40
	1. 3d	12.43d	2. 2
	1.10d	1.15d	2.23
	1.35d	1.18d	2.36
	1.35d	1.36e	3. 3
	2. 0	1.36e	3. 3
	2.40d	2. 6d	3.39
	4. 2	—	4.45
	4.10	3.47	5. 9
	4.55d	—	5.45
	4.55e	—	5.36
	5. 0e	4.50e	5.53
	5.20d	4.47d	6.20
	5.25	—	6.13
	—	5.24e	6.26
	5.45e	5.28e	6.43
	6.10e	—	6.51
	6.10d	5. 6d	6.58
	—	6. 0e	7. 2
	6.35	6.15e	7.24

BERKHAMSTED—

continued.

	Leave		Arr. at
	Euston	Broad St.	Berkh.
PM	—	6.40e	7.45
	—	6.47d	8.13
	7.15	6.52e	8.13
	8. 5	7.36	9. 0
	9. 5	8.17	10. 1
	9.55e	9.17e	10.54
	9.55d	9.17d	11. 0
	11.40	10.47	12.29

Sunday Trains.

AM	8.15	—	9.22
	9.23	8.55	10.37
	10.23	9.55	11.52
PM	12.53	12.25	2.22
	2.15	1.25	3. 9
	2.53	2.25	4. 5
	4.53	4.25	6. 7
	6.10	5.25	7. 7
	6.53	6.25	8. 5
	9.40	9.10	10.37

Trains from Berkhamsted.

	Leave	Arrive at	
	Berkh.	Broad St.	Euston
AM	5.52	7.15	7.18
	7.22	8.40	8.24
	7.47	—	8.58
	7.57	9. 0	8.58
	8.10	9.28d	9. 6
	8.20e	9.21	—
	8.29e	9.40	9.22
	8.49	—	9.40
	8.51	9.54	9.52e
	9.35	10.50	10.30
	10.40	12. 8	11.40
PM	12.47	2. 8	1.50
	2. 2	3.38	3. 5
	3.23	4.45	4.30
	4.12d	5.38	5.21
	5.11	6.36	6.15
	6. 7	7.38	7. 5
	6.47	8.15	7.55
	7.39	9. 8	8.35
	8.57	10.37	10.10
	9.45	11. 5	10.50
	10.54	11.48	11.35

Sunday Trains.

AM	8.15	10. 5	9.22
	11. 0	12.35	12.15
PM	12.53	2. 5	1.20
	1.32	3. 5	2.44
	2.47	4.20	4.14
	5.17	6.50	6.44
	6.32	8. 5	7.44
	7.17	8.50	8.15
	8.32	10. 5	—
	8.47	10.20	9.45
	9.42	11. 2	10.40

d Saturdays only.
e Saturdays excepted.

King's Arms Hotel.— Telephone 95. Electric Light. Billiards. First-class Restaurant accommodation. TRUST HOUSES, Ltd.

BERKSWELL (Warwick),

99½ miles. Fares, 20/8a, 12/5c. R. T.
for two months, 41/4a, 24/10c.
Departures *from* London as for
Coventry. Departures *for* London
about 5 times daily. Pop. 1,577.
Map Square 17.

BERMONDSEY

(SOUTH) from *London Bridge* and
Victoria, 1½ miles. Fares from
London Bridge, 0/5a, 0/3c. R. T.
for two days, 0/10a, 0/6c. Fares
from Victoria, 0/5a, 0/3c. R. T.
0/5½c. R. T. for two days, 1/2a,
0/9c. Pop. (Bermondsey) 76,126.
See p. 570.
Map Square 70.

BERNEY ARMS

(Norfolk), 121¾ miles. No through
fares. Departures *from* London as
for Reedham. Departures *for*
London about 4 times daily.

BERRINGTON (Salop),

152 miles. Fares, 31/11a, 19/2c.
R.T. for two months, 63/10a, 38/4c.
Departures *from* London as for
Iron Bridge or Shrewsbury. Departures *for* London about 4 times
daily. Pop. 1,083.
Map Square 17.

BERRINGTON (Hereford),

151¼ miles. Fares, 30/0a,
18/0c. R. T. for two months, 60/0a,
36/0c. Departures *from* London
as for Leominster. Departures
for London about 8 times daily.
Map Square 17.

BERRY BROW (Yorks),

185¼ miles. Fares, 37/9a, 22/8c.
R. T. for two months, 75/6a, 45/4c.
Departures *from* London as for
Penistone. Departures *for* London about 6 times daily.
Map Square 12.

BERVIE (Kincardine),

495¼ miles. No through fares.
Departures *from* London as for
Montrose. Departures *for* London
about 3 times daily. Pop. 2,153.
Map Square 38.

BERWICK (Sussex) from

Victoria and *London Bridge*, 57¼
miles. Fares, 11/8a, 7/0c. R. T.
for two months, 23/4a, 14/0c. Pop.
300.
Map Square 29.

	Leave		Arr. at
	Vict.	Lon. B.	Berwk.
	—	6.15	8.36
	9. 0	—	10.54
	10. 5	9.50	12.18
	12. 0	12.10	2.35
PM	—	12.50d	2.35
	1.20e	2. 0e	4. 7
	1.25d	2. 0d	4. 7
	3.20	—	4.50
	5.20	5. 5	7. 3
	6.50	7. 0	9.20

Sunday Trains.

AM 6.55	7.22	10.18
PM 12.15k	—	2.36
6.33	6.33	9.16
8.20	8. 0	10.24

Trains from Berwick.

	Leave	Arrive at	
	Berwick	Lon. B.	Vict.
AM	6.35	8.46	9. 8
	8. 4	9.50	10.24
	9.12	10.55	10.56
	10.22	12.44	12.45
	11. 9k	—	1.20
PM	12. 5	2.22	2.22
	2.12	4.32	4.35
	4. 1k	6.36	6.34
	4.56k	—	7.30
	7.46	10. 0	10.10
	9. 9	—	11.17

Sunday Trains.

AM 7.53	10.18	10.32
10.26k	—	1. 0
PM 5.57	7.56	7.37
8.26	10.50	10.19

d Saturdays only.
e Saturdays excepted.
k Via Brighton.

BERWICK-ON-TWEED

from *King's Cross*, 334¼ miles. Fares, 70/7*a*, 42/4*c*. R. T. for two months, 141/2*a*, 84/8*c*. Pop. 12,994.
Map Square 3

King's+	Berwk.	Berwk.	King's+
AM 4.45	2.17	AM12. 3*f*	7. 5
10. 0*r*	4.59	7.20*r*	4.30
11.50*r*	7. 6	11 26*r*	6.30
PM 1.15*r*	8.20	PM12. 7*r*	9.25
8.25	4.43	2.39*r*	10. 0
10.45*d*	8.32	6.32	3.25
10.45*e*	8.58	8. 5*e*	5.40
11.40*k*	6.28	9.10	6. 0
—		—	

Sunday Trains.

AM11.30	9.33	AM12. 3	7. 5
PM 8.25	4.47	6. 5	5.15
10.45	8.58	PM12.33*r*	8.15
11.40*k*	6.28	5.35	5.40
—		9.10	6. 0
—		—	
—		—	

d Saturdays only.
e Saturdays excepted.
f Mondays excepted.
k Stops when required.
r Restaurant Car.

BERWYN (Denbigh), 184¾

miles. Fares, 38/9*a*, 23/3*c*. R. T. for two months, 77/6*a*, 46/6*c*. Departures *from* London as for Llangollen. Departures *for* London about 5 times daily.
Map Square 11.

BESCAR LANE (Lancs),

208¾ miles. No through fares. Departures *from* London as for Wigan. Departures *for* London about 5 times daily.
Map Square 12.

BESCOT (Stafford), from

Euston, 118¾ miles. Fares, 24/5*a*, 14/8*c*. R.T. for two months, 48/10*a*, 29/4*c*.
Map Square 17.

Euston	Besc.	Besc.	Euston
AM 2.30	6.31	AM 6.51*t*	10. 0
5. 0	8.34	8. 0*r*	10.40
9.10*e*r11.32		9.24	12.40
9.15*d*r12.43		10.45*r*	1.25
9.15*e*r12.48		PM12.14*e*	3. 0
11.30*r*	2.51	1.39*t*	4.35
PM 1.15*r*	3.58	2.15*t*	5.35
2.20*t*	6.20	3.44*r*	6.50
4.35*r*	7. 8	5.54*r*	8.20
5.50*r*	9. 7	6.30*e*r10.20	
6.55*r* 10.18		10.35*e*	4. 0
7. 0	11. 8	10.35*d*	5. 0
—		—	
—		—	
—		—	
—		—	
—		—	

Sunday Trains.

PM 1. 0*r*	5.25	AM 9.57	1.45
5.10*r*	9.20	PM12.15	5. 5
—		4.34*r*	8.20
—		8.30	5. 0
—		—	
—		—	

d Saturdays only.
e Saturdays excepted.
r Restaurant Car.
t Tea Car.

BESTWOOD COL-

LIERY (Notts), 132¼ miles. Fares, 26/6*a*, 15/11*c*. R.T. for two months, 53/0*a*, 31/10*c*. Departures *from* London - as for Nottingham (Victoria). Departures *for* London about 5 times daily. Pop. 619.

BETCHWORTH (Surrey)

from *Charing Cross, Cannon Street*, and *London Bridge*, 28 miles. Fares, 5/0*a*, 4/0*b*, 3/0*c*. R.T. for two months, 10/0*a*, 7/10*b*, 5/8*c*. Pop. 1,908.
Map Square 23.

	Leave		Arr. at
Char. +	Can. St.	Lon. B.	Betch.
AM —	4.44	5. 0	6.11
—	—	7.50*l*	9. 3
—	—	9.33*l*	10.40
10.55	—	11. 3	12.22
PM —	12.55*d*	12.58*d*	1.48
12.55	—	1. 4	2.16
—	1.24*d*	1.27*d*	2.32
2. 3*e*	2. 8*d*	2.10	3.19
—	—	2.22*dl*	3.29
3.15	—	3.21	4.31
—	4.20*e*	4.23*e*	5. 7
4.22*d*	—	4.28*d*	5.31
—	5.24*e*	5.27*e*	6.19
5.42*d*	—	5.48*d*	6.49
—	6. 0*e*	6. 3*e*	6.56
5.27*e*	—	6.34*e*	7.29
6.34*d*	—	6.40*d*	7.43
—	6.36*e*	6.39*e*	7.41
7.24*d*	7.28*e*	7.30	8.38
8.28	—	8.36	9.46
10.17	—	10.23	11.24
11.27*h*	—	—	12.20

Sunday Trains.

AM 6.25	—	6.32	7.48
10. 5	—	10.11	11. 7
10.20	—	10.28	11.33
PM 1.30	—	1.37	2.38
5.25	—	5.32	6.41
8.38	—	8.45	9.54

Trains from Betchworth.

	Leave.		Arrive.	
Betch.	Lon B.	Can. St.	Char +
AM 7.29	8.24	8.28	—
8. 4	8.56	—	—
8.34	9.28	9.32	—
9. 4	9.49	9.52	—
9.35	10.27	10.32	—
10. 3	11. 0	—	—
11.42	12.50	—	1. 0
PM 1.34	2.38	—	2.46
2.43*d*	4. 8	—	—
3.46	5. 2	—	5.14
4.58	5.56	—	—
6.16	7.20	—	7.29
8. 3	9. 2	—	9.15
9. 4	10. 3	—	10.13
10.58	11.57	—	12.10

Sunday Trains.

AM 7.13	8.16	—	8.27
10.15	11.15	—	11.25
PM 3.36	4.33	—	4.42
6.10	7.13	—	7.25
8.55	9.52	—	—
9. 9	10.11	—	10.24

d Saturdays only.
e Saturdays excepted.
h Wednesdays and Saturdays only.
l Low Level Platform.

BETHESDA (Carnarvon),

242½ miles. Fares, 50/8*a*, 30/5*c*. R.T. for two months, 101/4*a*, 60/10*c*. Departures *from* London as for Bangor. Departures *for* London about 6 times daily. Pop. 4,154.
Map Square 11.

BETHNAL GREEN

from *Liverpool Street*, 1¼ miles. Fares, 0/2½*a*, 0/2*b*, 0/1½*c*. R. T. for two days, 0/5*a*, 0/4*b*, 0/3*c*. Pop. 117,238. See pp. 523, 524, 526-544
Map Square 61.

BETLEY ROAD (Che-

shire) from *Euston*, 153½ miles. Fares. 31/11*a*, 19/2*c*. R. T. for two months, 63/10*a*, 38/4*c*. Departures *from* London as for Madeley. Departures *for* London about 4 times daily. Pop. (Betley) 761.
Map Square 12.

BETTISFIELD (Flint)

177¼ miles. Fares, 35/3*a*, 21/2*c*. R.T. for two months, 70/6*a*. Departures *from* London as for Whitchurch (Salop). Departures *for* London about 6 times daily. Pop. 356.
Map Square 12.

BETTWS GARMON

(Carnarvon), 255½ miles. No through fares. Departures *from* London as for Carnarvon. Departures *for* London about thrice daily. Pop. 400.
Map Square 11.

BETTWS (LLANGE-

INOR) (Glamorgan), 181½ miles. No through fares. Departures *from* London as for Maesteg or Tondu. Departures *for* London about 4 times daily.
Map Square 21.

BETTWS-Y-COED (Car-

narvon) from *Euston*, 238 miles. Fares, 47/11*a*, 28/9*c*. R.T. for two months, 95/10*a*, 57/6*c*. Pop. 1,027.
Map Square 11.

Euston	Bettws	Bettws.	Euston
AN12.25	8.38	AM 6.55*dr*	1. 0
2.35	11.24	7. 5*er*	1. 0
5. 0	12.58	8.18*r*	1.45
10.30*r*	4.25	10.32*dr*	5. 5
10.40*r*	5.27	11. 5*er*	5. 5
11.50*r*	7.20	PM 1. 2*r*	7.30
PM 2.35*t*	8.30	2.28*r*	9.20
5.20*h*	11.31	8.32	5. 0
9.30*e*	5.27	—	

Sunday Trains.

PM 9.15	5.27	—	—

d Saturdays only.
e Saturdays excepted.
h Thursdays, Fridays and Saturdays only.
r Restaurant Car.
t Tea Car.

BEVERLEY (Yorks), 202¼

miles. Fares, 36/8a, 22/0c. R. T. for two months, 73/4a, 44/0c. Departures *from* London as for Hull (Paragon) or Driffield. Departures *for* London about 6 times daily. Pop. 13,469.
Map Square 13.

BEWDLEY (Worcester)

from *Paddington*, 137 miles. Fares, 26/8a, 15/9c. R. T. for two months, 52/6a, 31/6c. Pop. 2,758.
Map Square 17.

PAD.	BEWD.	BEWD.	PAD.
AM 5.30h	11.48	AM 6. 0h	r10. 0
9.10dh	12.50	7.33h	11. 0
9.45	1.50	7.50	11.15
10.40dh	1.48	7.55hv	11.15
10.40h	2. 3	8.35h	12.25
PM12.50hr	4.26	9.17	2.12
1.30r	4.46	9.58hr	1.25
1.35r	5.47	11. 0r	2.55
2.10ht	6. 8	PM 1. 0r	4.15
4.10ht	7.36	2.10	5.50
4.45t	7.58	3.19ht	6.40
6.10hr	9.15	4. 9hr	8. 5
12.15hk	7. 3	5. 0r	9.15
12.15hl	9.35	9.37h	3.30
—	—	—	—

Sunday Trains.

AM10.35r	4.26	AM 9.45	9.42
PM12.50qr	4.26	—	—
—	—	—	—

d Saturdays only.
h Via Kidderminster.
k Saturday midnights excepted.
l Saturday midnight only.
q Via Birmingham and Hartlebury.
r Restaurant Car.
t Tea Car.
v Thursdays only.

BEXHILL (CENTRAL)

(Sussex) from *London Bridge* and *Victoria*, 71½ miles. Fares, 12/6a, 7/6c. R. T. for two months, 25/0a, 15/0c. Pop. 20,363.
Map Square 29.

	Leave		Arr. at
VICT.	LON. B.	BEX.	
AM —	6.15	8.14	
6.37h	6.40h	9.57	
9. 0	—	11. 4	
10. 5	9.50	12.27	
11.55	—	1.47	
12. 0	12.10	2.30	
PM 1.20e	—	3.32	
1.25d	1.10d	3.32	
—	2. 0	3.56	
3.20	—	5. 2	
3.40	4. 5	6.10	
5.20	5. 5	7. 6	
5.45e	5.55e	8.13	
6.40	—	8.49	
6.50	7. 0	9.18	
10.30	10.35	1.11	

Sunday Trains.

AM 6.55	7.22	10. 4
9.30	9.30	11.43
11.15	—	2.10
PM12.15h	—	3. 8
6.33	6.33	9.40
9.25h	—	12. 3

BEXHILL (CENTRAL)—continued.

Trains from Bexhill.

	Leave	Arrive at	
BEXHILL	LON. B.		VICT.
AM 6. 0	8.46		—
6.55	8.53		9. 8
8. 2	10. 5		10.12
8.30	10.15		10.24
8.41	10.55		10.56
10.33	12.44		12.45
11. 6	—		1.15
11.58	2.22		2.22
PM 1.16	4. 0		4. 2
2.29	4.32		4.35
3.12h	6.36		6.34
4.20h	—		7.30
5.30	7.42		7.48
6.20h	—		8.48
7.45	10. 0		10.10
8.14	—		11.17
9.45h	12.59		1. 0

Sunday Trains.

AM 7. 1	10.18	10.32
9.31h	—	1. 0
PM 5. 0	7.56	7.37
6. 5	8.34	8.41
7.30	—	10.19
8.23	10.50	10.45
9.29h	12.27	

d Saturdays only.
e Saturdays excepted.
h Via Brighton.

ANOTHER ROUTE from

Charing Cross, Cannon Street and *London Bridge*, 62½ miles. Fares, 12/6a, 10/0b, 7/6c. R. T. for two months, 25/0a, 20/0b, 15/0c.

	Leave		Arr. at
CHAR. +	CAN. ST.	LON. B.	BEX.
AM —	5.20	5.25	8.40
—	7.56	8. 0	10.50
9.25	—	9.33	11.52
10.40	—	10.46	12.40
PM12. 3e	—	12.10e	3. 2
1. 5d	—	1.11d	3. 8
2. 0d	—	2. 5d	3.50
2. 8	—	2.16	4.21
3.48e	—	—	6. 2
5. 5d	—	—	6.48
—	5.12e	—	6.55
6. 3e	—	—	9.15
—	6.16e	6.19e	8. 0
7.30	—	—	9.15
9.30y	—	9.36y	11.34

Sunday Trains.

AM 7. 5	—	7.11	9.44
8.45	—	—	10.52
9.50	—	9.56	11.56
11.20	—	—	1. 1
PM 7.35	—	7.45	10.16

Trains from Bexhill.

	Leave	Arrive at		
BEXHILL	LON. B.	CAN. ST.	CHAR. +	
AM 6.55e	8.48	8.52		
7.36	—	9.15		
8.10	—	9.48		
9. 7e	—	10.42		
9.45	11.43	—	11.57	
11. 0	—	—	12.49	
PM12.12	3. 6	—	3.19	
2.30	4.15	—	4.25	
3.25d	6.30	—	6.39	
4.57	6.40	—	6.49	
6.15	8.26	—	8.35	
7.10	8.50	—	9. 0	
8.45	11.35	—	11.44	

BEXHILL—continued.

Sunday Trains.

	Leave	Arrive at		
BEXHILL	LON. B.	CAN. ST.	CHAR. +	
AM 7. 5	10. 5	—	10.15	
9. 5	11.23	—	11.34	
PM 5.20	—	—	7. 3	
g 5.20	8.12	—	8.22	
7.10	9. 4	—	9.14	
8.25	10. 8	—	10.16	

d Saturdays only.
e Saturdays excepted.
y Wednesdays and Saturdays only.

BEXHILL—*continued.*

Caple - ne - Ferne. Private Hotel, 18, Marine Mansions. Splendid position, facing Sea. Close to Golf Links. Every Comfort. Excellent Cuisine. Separate tables. PROPRIETRESS.

Nethercourt Private Hotel. Cantelupe Road. Sea view. Two minutes from Golf Links. Telephone No. 66.

The Anchorage, Bedford Avenue. Board Residence. Highly recommended. Minutes Sea and Golf Course. For Tariff write— PROPRIETRESS.

Hotel Metropole. First-class. Facing Sea. Special Weekend Terms. Close Golf Links. Garage. Telephone 132 Bexhill. Telegrams, "Metropole."

Staines & Co., 28, Devonshire Road, Bexhill, and at Cooden Beach. Furnished and Unfurnished Houses. Building Sites. Special Lists, Map and Guide gratis. Tel., Bexhill 349, Cooden 15.

House Agents (Oldest Est.). GORDON GREEN AND WEBBER, 3, Sea Road. Also 1. Terminus Road. Opposite both Railway Stations. Register, Map and Guide gratis. Telegrams and 'Phone, 410 Bexhill.

Stevens & Son, Sea Road, Bexhill, and Cooden Beach. PRINCIPAL AGENTS. All available Properties, Bexhill, Cooden, and District. Special Lists free on application. Tel. 409 Bexhill. 88 Cooden.

BEXLEY (Kent) from

Charing Cross, Cannon Street, and *London Bridge,* 14½ miles. Fares, 2/11*a,* 2/4*b,* 1/9*c.* R. T. From Cannon Street, 2/6*a,* 2/0*b,* 1/6*c.* R. T. for eight days, 5/10*a,* 4/8*b,* 3/6*c.* From Cannon Street, 2/6*a,* 2/0*b,* 1/6*c.* R. T. for eight days 5/0*a,* 4/0*b.* Pop. 21,457. *See* pp 552-554.
Map Square 24.

BEXLEY HEATH (Kent)

from *Charing Cross, Cannon Street,* and *London Bridge,* 13½ miles. Fares from Charing Cross, 2/9*a,* 2/3*b,* 1/8*c.* R. T. for eight days, 5/6*a,* 4/6*b,* 3/4*c.* From Cannon Street, 2/6*a,* 2/0*b,* 1/6*c.* R. T. for eight days, 5/0*a,* 4/0*b.* Pop. 9 504. *See* pp. 555-556.

BICESTER (Oxon) from

Euston, 65¾ miles. Fares, 11/1*a,* 6/8*c.* R. T. for two months, 22/2*a,* 13/4*c.* Pop. 2,918.
Map Square 23.

EUSTON	BICES.		BICES.	EUSTON
AM 6.45	9.29	AM 7.50*e*	9.52	
7.35	11. 3	7.50*d*	10. 0	
10.40	12.17	8.52	11.40	
12. 0*n*	2.12	9.39	11.55	
PM 3. 5	4.47	11. 7	1.50	
5.32*d*	8.28	PM 2.18	4.15	
6.10*e*	8.28	3.28	5.35	
7.15*d*	9.45	5. 3	7.55	
8. 0*k*	9.45	7.39*e*	10.10	
—	—	7.39*d*	10.50	
—	—	11.33*h*	5. 0	

Sunday Trains.

AM 8.15	11. 8	PM12.28	5. 5	
PM12.30	2.38	4.14	7.10	
3.50	6.28	7.52	10.10	

d Saturdays only.
e Saturdays excepted
h Thursdays and Saturdays only.
k Thursdays only.
n Noon.
r Restaurant Car.

BICESTER (Oxon)—*cont.*

ANOTHER ROUTE from *Paddington* 53¼ miles. Fares as above.

PAD.	BICES.		BICES.	PAD.
AM 5.45	8.28	AM 8.53	10. 0	
9.10	10.37	10.57	1.18	
PM12.18	2.30	PM 2.45	4.40	
2.23	4.40	4.15	6.35	
4.10	5.10	6.26	9.18	
4.40	6.10	—	—	
6.10	7.10	—	—	
7.10	8.31	—	—	

No Sunday Trains.

BICKERSHAW

(Lancs), from *King's Cross,* 222 mIles. Fares, 39/10*a,* 23/11*c.* R.T. for two months, 79/8*a,* 47/10*c.* Departures *from* London as for Wigan (Central). Departures *for* London about 5 times daily. Pop. 1,401.

BICKLEIGH (Devon) from

Paddington, 227 miles. Fares, 46/11*a,* 28/2*c.* R.T. for two months, 93/10*a,* 56/4*c.* Departures *from* London as for Tavistock. Departures *for* London about 4 times daily. Pop. 339.
Map Square 26.

BICKLEY (Kent) from

Victoria, Holborn Viaduct, Ludgate Hill, and *St. Paul's,* 12 miles. Fares, 2/6*a,* 2/0*b,* 1/6*c.* R. T. for two days, 5/0*a,* 4/0*b.* Pop. 6,154.
See pp. 558-561.
Map Square 23.

ANOTHER ROUTE from *Charing Cross, Cannon Street,* and *London Bridge,* 14 miles. Fares, from Charing Cross, 2/6*a,* 2/0*b,* 1/6*c.* R. T. for two days, 5/0*a,* 4/0*b.* From Cannon Street, 2/6*a,* 2/0*b,* 1/3*c.* R. T. for two days, 5/0*a,* 4/0*b.* *See* pp. 544-547.

BIDDENDEN (Kent), 49½

miles. No through fares. Departures *from* London as for Tenterden (*via* Headcorn). Departures *for* London about 4 times daily. Pop. 1,129.
Map Square 24.

BIDDULPH (Stafford), 155

miles. No through fares. Departures *from* London as for Stoke-on-Trent. Departures *for* London about 5 times daily. Pop. 7,936.
Map Square 12.

BIDEFORD (Devon) from

Waterloo, 220½ miles. Fares, 41/1*a,* 24/8*c.* R. T. for two months, 82/2*a,* 49/4*c.* Pop. 9,125.
Map Square 21.

W'LOO.	BIDE.		BIDE.	W'LOO.
AM 9. 0*r*	3. 7	AM 8.24*r*	1.56	
11. 0*r*	4.14	10.30*r*	3.50	
PM 1. 0*r*	6.59	PM12.34*r*	6. 0	
3. 0	8. 2	1.54*r*	8.30	
—	—	3.29	10.50	
—	—	4.54*h*	3.58	

No Sunday Trains.

h Via Eastleigh.
r Restaurant Car.

Golden Bay Hotel. For particulars see under Westward Ho! service.
See advt. p. 342.

Royal Hotel. The Leading Hotel. Best appointed. New Resident Proprietor.

BIDEFORD (Devon)—*cont.*

Tanton's Hotel, Family and Commercial. Moderate tariff. Boots and Bus meet all down trains. R.A.C., A.A. and M.U. Central for all most interesting parts of N. Devon. Established nearly a century. Tel. No. 94. H.O'D.VOSPER, Res. Proprietor.

BIDFORD - ON - AVON

(Warwick) from *Marylebone,* 99¼ miles. Fares, 22/4*a,* 13/5*c.* R. T. for two months, 44/8*a,* 26/10*c.* Departures *from* London as for Stratford-on-Avon. Departures *for* London about 4 times daily. Pop. 1,634.
Map Square 17.

BIDSTON (Cheshire), 204½

miles. No through fares. Departures *from* London as for Birkenhead or Liverpool. Departures *for* London about 4 times daily. Pop. 969.
Map Square 12.

BIELDSIDE (Aberdeen),

526¼ miles. No through fares. Departures *from* London as for Aberdeen. Departures *for* London about twice daily.
Map Square 38.

BIGGAR (Lanark) from

Euston, 369½ miles. Fares, 75/2*a,* 45/1*c.* R.T. for two months, 150/4*a,* 90/2*c.* Departures *from* London as for Peebles. Departures *for* London about 4 times daily. Pop. 1,489.
Map Square 41.

BIGGLESWADE (Beds)

from *King's Cross,* 41¼ miles. Fares, 8/7*a,* 5/2*c.* R. T. for two months, 17/2*a,* 10/4*c.* Pop. 5,396.
Map Square 18.

KING'S+	BIGGL'DE	BIGGL'DE	KING'S+
AM 5. 5	6.25	AM 6.55	8.41
7.45	9. 4	8.38	9.56
10.12	11.47	10.14	11.15
11.30	12.44	PM12. 1	1.25
PM 1.55	3.16	2.37	3.50
3. 0	4.18	5.16	6.25
4.15	5.28	7.56	9. 0
5.10	6.48	8.43	10.20
6.15	7.34	—	—
8.30	9.48	—	—

Sunday Trains.

AM 8.30	10. 8	PM 6.26	8. 8
PM 7.10	8.49	—	—

BILBSTER (Caithness), 724 miles.
No through fares. Departures *from* London as for Wick. Departures *for* London about twice daily.
Map Square 32.

BILLACOMBE (Devon),
226¼ miles. Fares, 47/0*a*, 28/4*c*. R. T. for two months, 73/11*a*, 56/8*c*. Departures *from* London as for Yealmpton. Departures *for* London about 6 times daily.
Map Square 26.

BILLERICAY (Essex) from
Liverpool Street, 24½ miles. Fares, 5/0*a*, 3/0*c*. R. T. for two months, 10/0*a*, 6/0*c*. Pop. 1,526.
Map Square 24.

L'PL. ST.	BILLER.	BILLER.	L'PL. ST.
AM 5.26	6.38	AM 6.53	7.35
6.50	8. 5	7.29	8.23
7.48	9.10	7.56	8.45
9. 1	10. 0	8.25	9.14
9. 6	10.20	9. 4	9.46
10. 3	10.51	10.26	11. 7
10.47*d*	11.51	10.52*h*	11.59
11.56	12.50	11. 2*k*	11.59
PM12.48*d*	1.29	PM12.13*e*	1.16
1.26*d*	2. 4	12.16*d*	1.16
1.50*d*	2.35	12.42*e*	1.25
2. 0*e*	2.55	1.57	5. 5
2.20*e*	3.27	3.56*e*	4.51
2.40*d*	3.33	4. 0*d*	4.56
2.58*d*	3.40	5.23	6. 8
3.26	4.25	6. 5	6.52
4.18	5. 6	7.26	8.22
4.48*e*	5.27	8.12	9.10
5.39	6.20	8.49	9.50
6. 5*e*	6.49	9.11	9.56
6.26*e*	7.16	10.36	11.30
6.26*d*	7.20	—	—
7.16*e*	8. 2	—	—
8. 2*d*	8.48	—	—
8. 2*e*	8.51	—	—
8.45	9.29	—	—
9.45*d*	10.26	—	—
9.45*e*	10.34	—	—
11. 0	11.56	—	—
12. 0*m*	12.43	—	—
—	—	—	—
—	—	—	—

Sunday Trains.

AM 8.45	9.44	AM 8.45	10.25
9.30	10.34	9.47	10.50
10.45	11.55	11. 5	12.40
PM 2.30	3.46	PM 2.15	3.15
6.42	7.45	4.23	5.15
8.46	9.52	6.49	7.44
10.10	11.10	7.48	8.45
—	—	8.39	9.32
—	—	8.50	9.48
—	—	9.19	10.45

d Saturdays only.
e Saturdays excepted.
h Fridays only.
k Fridays excepted.
m Midnight.

Crown Hotel. Family and Commercial. Central. Stabling and Loose Boxes for Hunters. Billiards. Garage. Minute from Station. Taxis. Telephone 35.

BILLING (Northampton)
from *Euston*, 70½ miles. Fares, 13/2*a*, 7/11*c*. R. T. for two months, 26/4*a*, 15/10*c*. Pop. 362.
Map Square 18.

EUSTON	BILLING	BILLING	EUSTON
AM 5. 0	7.27	AM 8.20	10.15
6.45	9.47	9.43	11.55
10.40	12.57	PM12. 4*h*	2.45
PM12.15*e*	2.57	12. 4*k*	4.15
12.15*d*	3. 2	1.18*d*	3.45
3. 5	5. 7	3.12	5.35
4.15	6.37	5.17	7.20
7. 0	8.52	8.47	11.35

No Sunday Trains.

d Saturdays only.
e Saturdays excepted.
h Thursdays and Saturdays only.
k Thursdays and Saturdays excepted.

BILLINGBORO (Lincoln),
104½ miles. Fares, 21/8*a*, 13/0*c*. R. T. for two months, 43/4*a*, 26/0*c*. Departures *from* London as for Bourne. Departures *for* London 5 times daily. Pop. 964.
Map Square 13.

BILLINGHAM (Durham),
239 miles. Fares, 49/10*a*, 29/11*c*. R. T. for two months, 99/8*a*, 59/10*c*. Departures *from* London as for Stockton-on-Tees. Departures *for* London about 6 times daily. Pop. 4,463.
Map Square 8.

BILLINGSHURST
(Sussex) from *London Bridge, Victoria,* and *Clapham Junction,* 44½ miles. Fares, 9/4*a*, 5/7*c*. R. T. for two months, 18/8*a*, 11/2*c*. Pop. 1,872.
Map Square 23.

	Leave		Arr. at
VICT.	CLAP. J.	LON. B.	BILLG.
AM 6.18	6.25	6.35	7.56
7.23	7.29	7.25	9.44
8.55	.7.56	7.35	10.23
10.35	10.42	10.35	1.16
11.55	—	11.50	1.45
PM 1.40	1.47*e*	1.50	3.31
3.55	4. 2	4. 0	5.37
4.53	5. 0	5. 5	6.44
6.15	—	—	7.32
7.20	7.27	7.15	8.57

Sunday Trains.

AM 6.55	7. 2	7. 2	9.18
8.18	8.25	8.25	10.10
PM 7. 0	7. 7	6.38	8.29
—	—	—	—
—	—	—	—

Trains from Billingshurst.

	Leave		Arrive at
BILLING.	LON. B.	CLAP. J.	VICT.
AM 7.33	9.10	9.31	9.19
8.23	9.58	—	—
8.33	10.22	—	10.28
10. 2	11.50	11.35	11.42
PM 1.25	3.32	3.22	3.32
1.36	3.40	3.37	3.45
3.36	5.54	5. 4	5.12
5.30	7.48	7.31	6.50
8. 4	10. 8	9.53	10. 1
8.56	10.58	11.10	11.17

Sunday Trains.

AM 7.37	10.11	10. 6	10.13
8.38	10.45	10.33	10.52
PM 5.47	7.56	7.25	7.33
7.41	9.32	9.24	9.34

e Saturdays excepted.

BILSTON (Stafford) from
Paddington, 120½ miles. Fares, 25/2*a*, 15/1*c*. R. T. for two months, 50/4*a*, 30/2*c*. Pop. 27,565.
Map Square 17.

PAD.	BILSTON	BILSTON	PAD.
AM 5.30	10.41	AM 6.57*r*	10. 0
9.10*er*	11.55	8.16*r*	11. 0
9.10*dr*	12.25	9.21	12.25
10.40*r*	1.51	10.42*r*	1.25
PM12.50*r*	3.18	11.21*r*	2. 5
2.10*t*	4.52	PM 1.49*r*	5. 0
4.10*t*	6.47	2.44*t*	5.55
6.10*r*	9. 6	3.38*t*	6.40
7.10*r*	9.38	4.59*r*	8. 5
7.30	11. 3	6.42	10. 0
12.15*k*	6. 6	11.12	3.30
12.15*h*	7.31	—	—
—	—	—	—
—	—	—	—

Sunday Trains.

AM10.35	2.53	AM11. 7*r*	1.40
PM12.50*r*	5.12	PM 1.44	6.20
4.10	8. 2	5.49*r*	9. 0
6. 0*r*	9. 2	—	—

d Saturdays only.
e Saturdays excepted.
h Saturday midnight only.
k Saturday midnight excepted.
r Restaurant Car.
t Tea Car.

BINEGAR (Somerset) from
Waterloo, 132½ miles. Fares, 24/0*a*, 14/5*c*. R. T. for two months, 48/0*a*, Departures *from* London as for Shepton Mallet. Departures *for* London about 4 times daily. Pop. 391.
Map Square 22.

BINGHAM (Notts), 119½ miles. Fares, 24/8*a*, 14/10*c*. R. T. for two months, 49/6*a*, 29/8*c*. Departures *from* London as for Bottesford. Departures *for* London about 6 times daily. Pop. 1,700.
Map Square 13.

BINGLEY (Yorks) from
St. Pancras, 209 miles. Fares, 40/0*a*, 24/0*c*. R. T. for two months, 80/0, 48/0*c*. Pop. 18,949.
Map Square 12.

ST. PAN.	BINGLEY	BINGLEY	ST. PAN.
AM 2.25*g*	10.10	AM 6.22*r*	12.10
4.25	11. 5	7.18*f*	12.10
9.50*r*	2.37	7.27*r*	1.30
PM12.15*er*	5. 2	8. 2*r*	1.45
1.50*r*	7.42	9. 0*r*	2.10
3.30*r*	8.30	10.17*r*	4.30
5. 0*dr*	10.20	11.52*r*	5.30
5. 0*r*	10. 8	PM 1.13*r*	6.35
6.15*r*	11.46	1.35*hr*	6.35
11.45*e*	4.33	1.47*r*	7.15
11.50*d*	7. 4	3. 7*r*	7.15
—	—	4.25*r*	9.15
—	—	9.20	4.20

Sunday Trains.

AM10.50*r*	5.32	AM11.18	6.25
PM11.45	4.33	PM12.56*r*	9.43
—	—	9.16	4.55
—	—	—	—
—	—	—	—

d Saturdays only.
e Saturdays excepted.
f Mondays only.
g Mondays excepted.
h Wednesdays and Thursdays excepted.
r Restaurant Car.

IDRIS GREEN GINGER WINE.

BINTON (Warwick) from
Marylebone, 96¾ miles. Fares, 21/11a, 13/2c. R. T. for two months, 43/10a, 26/4c. Departures *from London* as for Stratford-on-Avon. Departures *for London;* about 3 times daily. Pop. 245;
Map Square 17.

BIRCHINGTON (Kent)
from *Victoria, Holborn Viaduct,* and *St. Paul's,* 70¼ miles. Fares, 15/0a, 12/0b, 8/10c. R. T. for two months, 30/0a, 24/0b, 17/8c. Pop. 3,503.
Map Square 24.

VICT. (S.E.&C.)	Leave HOL. V.	St. PL.'s	Arr. at BIRCH.
AM	—	—	—
5. 5	3.50c	—	6.28
5.48f	4.57	5. 0	8.25
9. 0	5.40f	5.42f	8.14
9.20	—	—	10.51
10.40	—	—	11.25
11.30l	—	—	12 35
11.40e	—	—	1.17
PM 1.25d	—	—	2.47
2. 8e	—	—	3.38
3.20e	—	—	4.21
3.29d	—	—	5.14
4.15d	—	—	5.23
—	5.10e	5.12e	6.22
5.10d	—	—	7. 1
5.30d	—	—	7. 5
5.30e	—	—	8. 2
7. 0	—	—	8. 6
8.30	—	—	8.45
12. 0h	—	—	10.21
			1.55

Sunday Trains.

AM 7.20	—	—	9.49
9.10	—	—	10.58
10.25	—	—	12.11
10.40	—	—	12.33
PM 3.30	—	—	6.28
8.25	—	—	10.30

Trains from Birchington.

Leave BIRCH.	St. PL.'s	Arrive at HOL. V.	VICT.
AM 7. 6	9.37	9.39	—
8.12	—	—	11. 2
9.14	—	—	11.27
9.26h	—	—	11.23
10. 8	—	—	11.55
11.32d	—	—	1.40
PM12. 6d	—	—	2.15
12. 6	—	—	2.43
1.34	—	—	3.23
1.58l	—	—	4. 5
1.58e	4.46	—	4.39
2.50	—	—	5. 3
3.34	—	—	5.26
5.52	—	—	7.54
6.33	9.51	9.53	9.46
8. 2	—	—	10.25

Sunday Trains

AM 9.13	—	11.58	11.51
PM 3. 0	—	—	5.32
6.20	—	—	8.20
6.46	—	—	8.30
8. 1	—	—	10. 8
9.22	—	—	11. 5
—	—	—	—

d Saturdays only.
e Saturdays excepted.
f Mondays only.
h Wednesdays only.
k Third class only.
l Mondays, Fridays and Saturdays only.

BIRCHINGTON—*contd.*

ANOTHER ROUTE from
Charing Cross, Cannon Street, and *London Bridge, via* Strood, 69¼ miles. Fares as above.

	Leave CAN. ST.	LON. B.	Arr. at BIRCH.
CHAR. +			
AM —	—	3.57h	6.28
PM —	1.20d	1.23d	3. 3
—	4.12e	4.15e	6. 7
—	6.12e	—	8. 6
—	—	—	—
—	—	—	—
—	—	—	—
—	—	—	—

No Sunday Trains.

Trains from Birchington.

Leave BIRCH.	LON. B.	Arrive at CAN. ST.	CHAR. +
AM 7. 6	9. 0	9. 4	—
7.30	9.15	9.19	—
e8.12p	9.48	9.52.	—
8.12d	9.48	9.52	—
—	—	—	—
—	—	—	—
—	—	—	—

No Sunday Trains.

d Saturdays only.
e Saturdays excepted.
h Third class only.
p Pullman Car attached.

Bungalow Hotel. — Telephone 37.
Near Station and Sea. Tennis—three hard and five grass courts. Ballroom. Garden.
TRUST HOUSES, Ltd.

Principal House Agents
for Houses and Bungalows. Particulars gratis. Enquiries replied to per return post. 'Phone 15.
BENEFIELD & CORNFORD.

C. A. Edmonds.
Sole Agent for principal Bungalows and Houses. Largest and best selection, furnished, unfurnished and sale. Estab. 1891. 'Phone 50 Clyde House.

BIRCHVALE (Derby), 175
miles. Fares 36/1a, 21/8c. R. T. for two months, 72/2a, 43/4c. Departures *from London* as for Chinley. Departures *for London* about 6 times daily.
Map Square 12.

BIRDBROOK (Essex)
from *Liverpool Street,* 66 miles. Fares, 12/4a, 7/5c. R. T. for two months, 24/8a, 14/10c. Departures *from London* as for Halstead. Departures *for London* about 4 times daily. Pop. 428.
Map Square 19.

BIRDINGBURY (Warwick), 89¼ miles. Fares, 18/2a, 10/11c. R. T. for two months, 36/4a, 21/10c. Departures *from London* as for Rugby. Departures *for London* about 6 times daily. Pop. 209.
Map Square 18.

BIRDWELL (Yorks), 170
miles. Fares, 34/7a, 20/9c. R. T. for two months, 69/2a, 41/6c. Departures *from London* as for Barnsley. Departures *for London* about 6 times daily.
Map Square 12.

BIRKDALE (Lancs), Palace
Station, from *St. Pancras,* 232 miles. Fares, 44/0a, 26/5c. R. T. for two months, 88/0a, 52/10c. Departures *from London* as for Warrington (Central). Departures *for London* about 6 times daily. Pop. 18,000.
Map Square 12.

BIRKENHEAD (Cheshire)
Woodside, from *Paddington,* 209½ miles. Fares, 40/7a, 24/4c. R. T. for two months, 81/2a, 48/8c. Pop. 145,592.
Map Square 12.

PAD.	B'K HEAD	B'K'HEAD	PAD.
AM 9.10r	1.50	AM 7. 0	12.25
10.20r	2.50	8. 0r	1.25
10.40r	3.40	9. 5r	2. 5
PM12.50r	6.15	11.45r	5. 0
2.10t	6.55	PM 1. 5r	5.55
4.10t	9. 0	2. 5r	6.40
6.10r	11.10	2.40r	8. 5
12.15	7.17	4.35r	10. 0
—	—	7.15	3.30

Sunday Trains.

PM12.50r	6.23	AM 8.35	6.20
—	—	PM 2.55r	9. 0

r Restaurant Car.
t Tea Car.

ANOTHER ROUTE from
Euston, 194¾ miles. Fares as above.

EUSTON	B'K'HEAD	B'K'HEAD	EUSTON
AM12.25g	7.17	AM 7.35er	12. 5
12.25f	8.15	7.35d	r12.20
2.35	9.35	8.55r	1. 0
5. 0	10.35	9.18r	1.45
8.30r	12.58	9.35r	2.20
10.30r	2.43	10.45r	3.10
10.40r	3.40	PM 1.20r	5.50
11.50r	4. 5	2.20r	7.30
12. 0nr	6.15	3.40r	8.10
PM 2.35t	7. 0	4.35er	9. 5
4. 5r	8.44	4.35dr	9.15
5.20r	9.35	5.25r	10.45
6.30er	11.37	9.45	5. 0
8.45d	7.20	11. 3	5.50
9.30e	3.26	—	—
11.50d	11. 1	—	—

Sunday Trains.

PM12.10r	6.23	AM 8.35	4. 0
9.15	3.26	PM 2.15r	7.10
—	—	9.45	5. 0

d Saturdays only.
e Saturdays excepted.
f Mondays only.
g Mondays excepted.
n Noon.
r Restaurant Car.
t Tea Car.

BIRKENSHAW (Yorks),
187 miles. Fares, 38/9a, 23/3c. R. T. for two months, 77/6d, 46/6c. Departures *from London* as for Wakefield (Westgate). Departures *for London* about 6 times daily. Pop. 2,725.

BIRMINGHAM (New Street) (Warwick) from *Euston*,
113 miles. Fares, 23/1*a*, 13/10*c*.
R.T. for two months, 46/2*a*, 27/8*c*.
Pop. 919,438.
Map Square 17.

Euston	Birmg.	Birmg.	Euston
AM 2.30	4.35	AM12.15*g*	4. 0
5. 0	8. 7	12.15*f*	5. 0
6.45	10. 0	7.30*r*	10. 0
8.30*r*	10.50	8.40*r*	10.40
9.10*er*11.10		8.45	11.55
9.15*r*	11.33	10.10	12.40
10. 0	1.18	11.25*r*	1.25
11.30*r*	1.35	11.40*r*	2.20
12. 0*nr*	3. 5	PM 1. 0*er*	3. 0
PM 1.15*r*	3.15	2.30*r*	4.35
2.20*t*	4.20	3.25*t*	5.35
2.50*t*	6. 8	4.50*t*	6.50
4.35*t*	6.35	4.58*t*	7.20
4.45*t*	7.38	6.20*r*	8.20
5.50*r*	7.50	7. 5*dr*10.45	
6.55*r*	8.55	8.20*er*10.20	
7. 0*r*	9.38	—	—
9.30	12.25	—	—
11.50	2.53	—	—
—	—	—	—
—	—	—	—

Sunday Trains.
AM12.10	3.15	AM12.15	5. 0
9.15	1.30	8.40	12.25
PM 1. 0*r*	3.20	11.40*r*	1.45
5.10*r*	7.20	PM 1. 5	5. 5
9.15	12.30	5.15*r*	8.20
11.50	2.57	6.20*r*	8.35
—	—	—	—
—	—	—	—
—	—	—	—

d Saturdays only.
e Saturdays excepted.
f Mondays only.
g Mondays excepted.
n Noon.
r Restaurant Car.
t Tea Car.

ANOTHER ROUTE (Snow Hill) from *Paddington*, 110¾ miles.
Fares as above.

Pad.	Birmg.	Birmg.	Pad.
AM 5.30	10. 5	AM 7.30*r*	10. 0
6.30	10.28	9. 0*r*	11. 0
9.10*r*	11.10	10.20	12.25
10.20	12.20	11.25*r*	1.25
10.40*r*	12.40	PM12. 5*r*	2. 5
10.45*r*	2.24	12.45*r*	4.15
PM12.50*r*	2.50	2.55*r*	5. 0
2.10*t*	4.10	3.55*t*	5.55
4.10*t*	6.10	4.40*t*	6.40
6.10*r*	8.10	6. 0*r*	8. 5
7.10*r*	9.10	8. 0	10. 0
7.30	10.30	11.55	3.30
12.15*k*	3.49	—	—
12.15*l*	3.42	—	—

Sunday Trains.
AM10.35	2.15	AM11.40*r*	1.40
PM12.50*r*	2.50	PM 2. 0	6.20
4.10	7.25	6.30*r*	9. 0
6. 0*r*	8. 0		

k Saturdays midnight excepted.
l Saturdays midnight only.
r Restaurant Car.
t Tea Car.

Queen's Hotel. One of the finest and most spacious in the town. Adjoins New St. Station. Replete with every modern convenience. Tariff moderate.
See advt. p. 36.

The Grand Hotel. The best Hotel outside London. 300 rooms. Private Suites of Apartments, luxuriously furnished. Every Modern Improvement. 25 Stock Rooms. Passenger Lift Headquarters Automobile Club.
See advt. p. 37.

BIRMINGHAM—*contd.*
Imperial Hotel (Trust Houses, Ltd.), Excellent Public Restaurant. Telephone Central 6470.
See advt. p. 37.

Midland Hotel. Most central. Every modern convenience and luxury. Private suites. High-class cuisine. First-class restaurant. Two hundred bedrooms ; well-arranged stockrooms. Moderate tariff. Telegraphic address : "Nearest, Birmingham." Telephone : Midland, 2600 (8 lines); Manager, Midland, 2604.

Berkeley House. 119, Hagley Road, Edgbaston. High - class Boarding Establishment. Tennis and croquet lawns. Garage. 10 minutes city. Tel. 1067 Edgbaston

"Chad Hill," Edgbaston. Tel. 155. Single and Suites of rooms. Separate Tables. Wooded Grounds, Garages, Tennis. Billiards. High central position.

Lancashire and Cheshire Insurance Corporation Limited, 14, Temple St. Tel. Central 1335.
See advt. p. 3 of cover.

BIRSTALL, UPPER
(Yorks) from *Euston*, 215½ miles. No through fares. Pop. (Birstall) 7,086.
Map Square 12.

Euston	Birstall	Birstall	Euston
AM12.25	9. 2	AM 5.53*r* 12.50	
2.35	11. 7	7.28*r*	1.15
5. 0	1.29	8.16*r*	3.10
8.45*r*	3. 7	9.52*dr*	5.56
10.40*r*	4. 1	PM12. 2*er*	6. 0
11.50*r*	6.38	12. 2*dr*	6.15
12. 0*nr*	7.57	2.41*r*	8.10
PM 1.30*r*	9. 1	3.47*er*10.10	
4. 5*r*	11. 4	7.17	5. 0
8. 0*e*	6.19	10.25	5.50

Sunday Trains.
PM 7.50*r*	6.19	—	—

d Saturdays only.
e Saturdays excepted.
n Noon.
r Restaurant Car.

BIRSTWITH (Yorks), 205½ miles. Fares, 42/6*a*, 25/6*c*. R.T. for two months, 85/0*a*, 51/0*c*. Departures *from* London as for Pateley Bridge. Departures *for* London about 6 times daily. Pop. 490.
Map Square 7.

BIRTLEY (Durham), 262½ miles. Fares, 54/10*a*, 32/11*c*. R.T. for two months, 109/8*a*, 65/10*c*. Departures *from* London as for Durham. Departures *for* London about 6 times daily. Pop. 8,409.
Map Square 3.

BISHOP AUCKLAND
(Durham) from *King's Cross*, 244½ miles. Fares, 50/10*a*, 30/6*c*. R.T. for two months, 101/8*a*, 61/0*c*. Pop. 14,294.
Map Square 7.

King's+	B. Auck.	B. Auck.	King's+
AM 4.45	11.48	AM 7.52	1.30
8.45	3.38	9.24*r*	4.30
11.50*r*	5.44	9.24*g*	3.15
PM 1.15*r*	7.18	PM12.50*r*	6.15
1.50*r*	8.31	3.51*r*	10. 0
5.35*r*	11.11	7.32	3.25
11.25*e*	6. 9	11.25*e*	5.40
11.25*d*	9.26	11.25*d*	6. 0

BISHOP AUCKLAND
—*continued.*

Sunday Trains.
King's+	B. Auck.	B. Auck.	King's+
AM11.30*r*	8.55	AM 7.34	5.15
PM11.25	6. 9	PM 6.29	5.40

d Saturdays only.
e Saturdays excepted
g 1st and 3rd Class Pullman Cars only.
r Restaurant Car.

BISHOPBRIGGS (Lanark), 436¼ miles. No through fares. Departures *from* London as for Falkirk. Departures *for* London about 4 times daily. Pop. 5,258.
Map Square 24.

Station closed on Sundays.

BISHOP'S CASTLE
(Salop), 176¾ miles. No through fares. Departures *from* London as for Craven Arms. Departures *for* London about 3 times daily. Pop. 1,268.
Map Square 17.

BISHOP'S CLEEVE
(Gloucester), 112½ miles. Fares, 24/7*a*, 14/9*c*. R.T. for two months, 49/2*a*, 29/6*c*. Departures *from* London as for Winchcombe. Departures *for* London about 8 times daily. Pop. 657.
Map Square 17.

BISHOP'S LYDEARD
(Somerset) from *Paddington*, 148 miles. Fares, 31/0*a*, 18/7*c*. R.T. for two months, 62/0*a*, 37/2*c*. Pop. 1,895.
Map Square 21.

Pad.	B. Lyd'rd.	B. Lyd'rd.	Pad.
AM 5.30	11.20	AM10.27*r*	1.30
9.15	12.40	PM12.12	4. 5
PM12. 5	4.30	2.14*t*	5.30
3.30	6.30	2.37*r*	6.50
4.15*r*	8. 2	5.24	9. 0
12. 0*h*	7.35	8. 3	2.45
—	—	10.17	7.10

Sunday Trains.
PM10. 0	7.35	—	—

h Saturdays midnight excepted.
r Restaurant Car.
t Tea Car.

BISHOP'S NYMPTON
(Devon) from *Paddington*, 172½ miles. Fares, 36/1*a*, 21/8*c*. R.T. for two months, 72/2*a*, 43/4*c*. Departures *from* London as for Dulverton. Departures *for* London about 3 times daily. Pop. 870.
Map Square 21.

BISHOPSBOURNE
(Kent) from *Charing Cross, Cannon Street,* and *London Bridge,* 75 miles. Fares, *via* Canterbury, 14/2*a*, 11/4*b*, 8/6*c*. R. T. for two months, 28/4*a*, 22/8*b*, 17/0*c*. *Via* Shorncliffe, 14/7*a*, 11/8*b*, 8/9*c*. R. T. for two months, 29/2*a*, 23/4*b*. Departures *from* London as for Shorncliffe or Canterbury West. Departures *for* London about 5 times daily. Pop. 304.
Map Square 24.

BISHOP'S ROAD to and

from *Aldgate, Moorgate Street, King's Cross, Baker Street,* and all intermediate Stations every few minutes; also from Hammersmith, Uxbridge Road, and Kensington (Addison Road) at frequent intervals. Pop. (Paddington) 142,551.
See back of Map.
Map Square 60, *No.* 5.

BISHOP'S STORT-

FORD (Herts) from *Liverpool Street,* 30½ miles. Fares, 6/6a, 3/11c. R. T. for two months, 13/0a, 7/10c. Pop. 8,857.
Map Square 24.

L'PL. ST.	B. STORT.	B. STORT.	L'PL. ST.
AM 5. 5	5.47	AM 1.40	2.50
5.50	7. 2	6.56	8.18
7.18	8.44	7.29	8.49
8.30r	9.19	7.49	8.57
9.10	10.36	8.33	9.27
10. 5	10.56	8.54	9.46
10.34	12.26	9.27	10.17
11.50r	12.35	9.42r	10.23
PM 12.29d	1.21	9.49	10.59
12.40d	1.50	10.43	11.27
12.48e	2.13	10.51	12.15
1.19d	2.26	11.54	12.40
2. 0d	3. 8	PM 12.54	2. 7
2.34	3.18	1.40r	2.21
2.48	4. 2	2.13d	3.18
4.15	5. 4	3.40	5. 9
4.45	5.28	4.32r	5.17
5.10	6.18	5.26r	6.10
5.49r	6.35	5.43	7.19
6. 0e	7. 1	6.40	7.58
6.30	7.17	7.35r	8.22
7.10r	7.55	7.47	8.33
7.41d	8.49	8. 4	9.33
7.41e	8.52	9.48	10.30
8.22	9.10	9.59	11.12
9.17	10.39	—	—
10.12	10.57	—	—
11.50k	12.56	—	—
—	—	—	—

Sunday Trains.

AM 8.12	9.18	AM 1.40	3. 0
9.25	10.13	7.48	9.33
PM 1.50	3.27	10. 3	11.27
3.25	4.12	PM 5.58	6.40
4.50	6.18	6.32	7.26
7.15	8.24	6.57	7.40
9.12	10.35	7.48	9.10
—	—	9.18	10.40

d Saturdays only.
e Saturdays excepted.
k Wednesdays and Saturdays only.
r Restaurant Car.

Chequers Hotel. Family and Commercial. Highly recommended. Centre of Town. Moderate. No extras. Bus meets trains. Motor Carriages. Garage. Tel. 20. J. BRAZIER, Proprietor.

The George Hotel. Leading First Class Family and Commercial. Terms moderate. Omnibus meets all trains. Telephone 42. F. C. LITTLE, Proprietress.

BISHOP'S WALTHAM

(Hants) from *Waterloo,* 82½ miles. Fares, 16/3a, 9/9c. R. T. for two months, 32/6a, 19/6c. Pop. 2,488.
Map Square 23.

W'LOO.	B. WAL.	B. WAL.	W'LOO.
AM 5.40	8.30	AM 9.33	12. 0
5.50	9.28	11.45r	2.20
8.30s	11.10	PM 1.40	4.20
9.30	12.25	3. 5	6.16
11.30r	2.10	5.30r	8.20
PM 1.30s	3.50	7.28	10.50
3.30s	6.25	—	—
5.30r	8.10	—	—
—	—	—	—
—	—	—	—

Sunday Trains.

AM 11. 0r	5.50	AM 8.35	12.11
PM 2. 0	6.35	PM 5.15	8. 3
5. 5	8.10	7.30	10.52

r Restaurant Car.
s Refreshments served.

BISHOPTON (Renfrew),

411¾ miles. Fares, 83/6a, 50/1c. R. T. for two months, 167/0a, 100/2c. Departures as for Greenock (Central). Departures *for London* about 4 times daily. Pop. 560.
Map Square 40.

BISPHAM (Lancs), 225½

miles. Fares, 46/11a, 28/2c. R. T. for two months, 93/10a, 56/4c. Departures *from London* as for Kirkham. Departures *for London* about 4 times daily. Pop. 2,244.
Map Square 12.

BITTERNE (Hants)

from *Waterloo,* 77½ miles. Fares, 16/3a, 9/9c. R. T. for two months, 32/6a, 19/6c. Departures *from* London as for Netley. Departures *for London* about 8 times daily. Pop. 3,142.
Map Square 28.

BITTON (Glo'ster), 125½

miles. No through fares. Departures *from London* as for Bristol. Departures *for London* about 4 times daily. Pop. 3,244.
Map Square 22.

BLABY (Leicester), from

Euston, 110½ miles. Fares, 20/2a, 12·1c. R. T. for two months, 40/4a, 24/2c. Departures *from London* as for Hinckley. Departures *for London* about 9 times daily. Pop. 1,959.
Map Square 18.

BLACK BANK (Cambs),

75¼ miles. Fares, 15/10a, 9/6c. R. T. for two months, 31/8a, 19/0c. Departures *from London* as for March. Departures *for London* about 5 times daily.
Map Square 19.

BLACK BULL (Stafford),

152¼ miles. No through fares. Departures *from London* as for Stoke-on-Trent. Departures *for London* about 3 times daily.
Map Square 12.

BLACKBURN (Lancs).

from *Euston,* 212 miles. Fares, *via* Boar's Head or Manchester, 43/9a, 26/3c. R. T. for two months, 87/6a, 52/6c. *Via* Preston 43/9a, 26/3c. R. T. for two months, 87/6a, 52/6c. Pop. 126,630.
Map Square 12.

EUSTON	B'BURN.	B'BURN.	EUSTON
AM 12.25	6.49	AM 5.37er 12. 5
2.35	9.25	6.20r	12.50
5. 6	11.48	8. 3r	1.15
6.45	1.50	8.10r	1.45
8.45r	2.53	8.45r	3.10
10.40r	3.44	10.47r	3.55
11.35h	4.42	PM 12.36k	6. 0
11.50er	5.31	2. 4k	7.30
11.50dr	5.53	2.14	8.10
PM 1.30r	6.44	2.52dr	9.15
2.50t	8. 2	3.26r	9. 5
5.20r	10.27	4.43dr	10. 0
6. 5r	11. 5	4.43er	10.10
9.30	5.41	5.38kr	10.45
11.50d	8.56	9.55k	5. 0
—	—	—	—

Sunday Trains.

PM 12.10r	6.16	AM 8.40	4. 0
12.30r	8. 2	11.25r	5.45
9.15	5.41	PM 1.50r	7.30
—	—	2.20r	8.55
—	—	9.40	5. 0

d Saturdays only.
e Saturdays excepted.
h Tuesdays and Fridays only.
k *Via* Preston.
r Restaurant Car.
t Tea Car.

BLACKFORD (Perth), 432

miles. Fares, 88/2a, 52/11c. R. T. for two months, 176/4a, 105/10c. Departures *from* London as for Dunblane. Departures *for London* about 3 times daily. Pop. 1,593.
Map Square 40.

BLACKFRIARS

To and from *Mansion House, Charing Cross, Victoria, South Kensington, High Street, Praed Street, Baker Street, King's Cross, Moorgate Street,* and all intermediate Stations every few minutes. Also to and from *Ealing, Hounslow, Richmond* and *Wimbledon.* See p. 489.
Map Square 61, *No.* 11.

BLACKHEATH (Kent)

from *Charing Cross Cannon Street,* and *London Bridge,* 7½ miles. Fares from Charing Cross, 1/3a, 1/0b, 0/9c. R. T. for two days, 2/6a, 2/0b, 1/6c. From Cannon Street. Fares, 1/1a, 0/10b, 0/7½c. R. T. for two days, 2/2a, 1/8b, 1/3c. Pop. 7,018. See pp. 547-551, 555, 556.
Map Square 71.

BLACKHILL (Durham)

265¼ miles. Fares, 55/3a, 33/2c. R. T. for two months, 110/6a, 66/4c. Departures *from* London as for Bishop Auckland. Departures *for London* about 3 times daily. Pop. 5,141.
Map Square 3.

BLACKHORSE ROAD

(Essex) from *Moorgate Street* and *St. Pancras,* 7½ miles. Fares, 1/2a, 0/8½c. R. T. for two days, 2/2½a, 1/2c. See pp. 506, 507.
Map Square 53.

BLACK LANE (Lancs), 196
miles. No through fares. Departures *from* London as for Heywood. Departures *for* London about 6 times daily.
Map Square 12.

BLACK MILL (Glamorgan), 178¾ miles. Fares, 37/4*a*, 22/5*c*. R. T. for two months, 74/8*a*, 44/10*c*. Departures *from* London as for Tondu. Departures *for* London about 4 times daily.
Map Square 21.

BLACKMOOR (Devon),
201 miles. Fares, 41/8*a*, 25/0*c*. R.T. for two months, 83/4*a*, 50/0*c*. Departures *from* London as for Lynton. Departures *for* London about twice daily.
Map Square 21.

BLACKPOOL (Lancs)
(TALBOT ROAD) from *Euston*, 226¾ miles. Fares, 47/4*a*, 28/5*c*. R.T. for two months, 94/8*a*, 56/10*c*. Pop. 99,640.
Map Square 12.

EUSTON	B'POOL.	B'POOL.	EUSTON
AM12.25	8.11*h*	AM 7.47*hr* 1.45	
2.35	10.36	8.30*r* 3.10	
5. 0	11.56	9.55*hkr*3.45	
6.45*d*	1.13	10.10*dr* 3.45	
6.45*h*	1.31	10.10*hrv*4.15	
8.30	2. 3	12. 0*t* 5.50	
10.40*r*	3.57	PM12.10*eh* 6. 0	
11.35*r*	4.43	1. 5*dr* 6.25	
11.50*r*	6. 1*h*	2. 5*r* 7.30	
PM 1.30*r*	7.13*h*	2.45*r* 8.10	
2.35*t*	8.12*h*	3.25*er* 9. 5	
5.20*r*	10.42*h*	3.25*dr* 9.15	
9.30*d*	10. 0	5.10*r* 10.45	
11.50*d*	11.31	10. 0 5. 0	

Sunday Trains.

AM11	45*r*	5.40*h*	AM 7. 0*r*	1.30
—	—	—	PM 1.30*r*	7.30
—	—	—	8.50*h*	5. 0
—	—	—	—	—
—	—	—	—	—

d Saturdays only.
e Saturdays excepted.
h Arrives and departs from Central Station.
k Mondays and Saturdays only.
r Restaurant Car.
t Tea Car.
v Mondays and Saturdays excepted.

Hotel Metropole (Empire Hotels). Unique position in own grounds on Sea front, centre of Princess Parade. Tea and after Dinner Dances. Orchestra. Self-contained suites. Terms on application to Manager. Telephone, Blackpool 1040. Telegrams: "Metropole, Blackpool."
See advt. p. **38** .

Cliffs and Norbreck Hydro,
near Blackpool. 350 Rooms. Large Ball-Room. Dining-Room. Grounds. Tennis.
See advt. p. **37.**

Clifton Hotel. Blackpool's
Historic Guest House. Facing Sea. Moderate Tariff.

Park House, Claremont
Park (adjoining Imperial Hydro). Facing Sea. Best, most modern Residential Boarding House. Billiard and Smoking Rooms. Near Golf Links. Tel. 162. Apply, MANAGERESS.

BLACKROD (Lancs), 194
miles. No through fares. Departures *from* London as for Wigan or Bolton (*via* Manchester) Departures *for* London about 8 times daily. Pop. 3,868.
Map Square 12.

BLACKSBOAT (Elgin),
561½ miles. Fares, 106/3*a*, 63/9*c*. R.T. for two months, 212/6*a*, 127/6*c*. Departures *from* London as for Aviemore or Keith (*via* Aberdeen). Departures *for* London about twice daily.
Map Square 35.

BLACKSTON (Stirling),
415½ miles. No through fares. Departures *from* London as for Edinburgh (Waverley). Departures *for* London about twice daily.
Map Square 40.

BLACKTHORN (Oxon),
from *Paddington*, 50½ miles. Fares, 10/7*a*, 6/4*c*. R. T. for two months, 21/2*a*, 12/8*c*. Departures *from* London as for Brill and Ludgershall. Departures *for* London about 4 times daily. Pop. 249.

BLACKWALL (Middlesex)
from *Fenchurch Street*, 3½ miles. Fares, 0/5*a*, 0/4*b*, 0/3*c*. R. T. for two days, 0/10*a*, 0/7*b*, 0/5½*c*. See pp. 524, 525.
Map Square 62.

BLACKWATER (Hants)
from *Charing Cross, Cannon Street,* and *London Bridge,* 56¼ miles. Fares, 7/1*a*, 5/8*b*, 4/3*c*. R. T. for two months, 14/2*a*, 11/4*b*.
Map Square 23.

CHAR. +	CAN. ST.	LON. B.	Arr. at BLACK.
	Leave		
AM —	4.44	5. 0	7.27
—	—	7.50*l*	10.14
—	—	9.33*l*	11.54
10.55	—	11. 3	1.36
PM12.55	—	1. 4	3.35
2. 3*h*	—	2.10*h*	4.29
2. 3*k*	—	2.10*k*	4.43
—	2. 8*d*	—	4.43
—	—	2.22*dl*	4.36
3.15*d*	—	3.21*d*	5.43
3.15*e*	—	3.21*d*	5.49
4.22*d*	—	4.28*d*	6.44
—	4.44*e*	4.48*e*	6.44
—	5.24*e*	5.27*e*	7.30
5.42*d*	—	5.48*d*	8. 1
—	6. 0*e*	6. 3*e*	8.17
—	6.36*e*	6.39*e*	8.58
6.34*d*	—	6.40*d*	8.59
7.24*d*	—	7.30*d*	9.52
8.28	—	8.36	11. 0

Sunday Trains.

AM 6.25	—	6.32	9. 3
10.20	—	10.28	12.43
PM 5.25	—	5.32	7.56
8.38	—	8.45	11. 3
—	—	—	—
—	—	—	—
—	—	—	—

BLACKWATER—*contd.*
Trains from Blackwater.

Leave BLACK.	LON. B.	Arrive at CAN. ST.	CHAR. +
AM 6.49	8.56	—	—
8.18	10.10	—	10.20
8.31*y*	10.31	—	10.43
8.43	11. 0	—	—
9.46	11.46	—	11.59
10.24	12.50	—	1. 0
PM12.17	2.38	—	2.46
2.32	5. 2	—	5.14
3.46	5.56	—	—
4.56	7.20	—	7.29
6.47	9. 2	—	9.15
7.50	10. 3	—	10.13
9.47	11.57	—	12.10

Sunday Trains.

AM 6. 2	8.16	—	8.27
9. 4	11.15	—	11.25
PM 4.52	7.13	—	7.25
7.55	10.11	—	10.24
—	—	—	—

d Saturdays only.
e Saturdays excepted.
h Mondays, Fridays and Saturdays excepted.
k Mondays, Fridays and Saturdays only.
l Low Level Platform.
y Wednesdays only.

BLACKWATER (Isle of Wight), 90½ miles. Fares, 20/0*a*, 12/3*c*. R.T. for two months, 40/0*a*, 2/46*c*. Departures *from* London as for Newport (I. of W.). Departures *for* London about 4 times daily.
Map Square 28.

BLACKWELL (Worcester),
124½ miles. Fares, 23/9*a*, 14/3*c*. R. T. for two months, 47/6*a*, 28/6*c*. Departures *from* London as for Birmingham (New Street). Departures *for* London about 4 times daily.
Map Square 17.

BLACKWOOD (Lanark),
391½ miles. Fares, 80/5*a*, 48/3*c*. R.T. for two months, 160/10*a*, 96/6*c*. Departures *from* London as for Hamilton. Departures *for* London about 4 times daily.
Map Square 40.

BLACKWOOD (Monmouth), 155¼ miles. Fares, 32/4*a*, 19/5*c*. R.T. for two months, 64/8*a*, 38/10*c*. Departures *from* London as for Tredegar. Departures *for* London about 5 times daily. Pop. 4,221.

BLACON (Cheshire), 200¼
miles. No through fares. Departures *from* London as for Wrexham. Departures *for* London about 6 times daily. Pop. 267.

Station closed on Sundays.

BLAENAU FESTINIOG
(Merioneth) from *Euston*, 250¼ miles. Fares, 47/11*a*, 28/9*c*. R. T. for two months, 95/10*a*, 57/6*c*. Pop. 6,741.
Map Square 11.

EUSTON	BLAEN. F.	BLAEN. F.	EUSTON
AM12.25	9.20	AM 6.18*r*	1. 0
2. 35	12. 3	7.40*r*	1.45
5. 0	1.41	9.55*r*	5. 5
10.30*r*	5. 7	PM12.25*r*	7.30
10.40*r*	6.59	1.55*r*	9.20
PM 2.35*t*	9.12	7.40	5. 0
9.30*e*	6.12	—	—

Sunday Trains.

—	—	—	—
PM 9.15	6.12	—	—
—	—	—	—

e Saturdays excepted.
r Restaurant Car.
t Tea Car.

BLAENAU FESTINIOG —*continued.*

ANOTHER ROUTE from *Paddington*, 229¾ miles. Fares as above.

Pad.	Blaen. F.	Blaen. F.	Pad.
AM 10.40*r*	6.52	AM 7.40*r*	2. 5
12.15*h*	10.31	9.30*r*	5. 0
PM 2.10*kt*	9.48	PM 2.35*r*	10. 0
—	—	4.25*l*	3.30
—	—	—	—
—	—	—	—
—	—	—	—

No Sunday Trains.

h Saturdays midnight excepted.
k Thursdays and Saturdays only.
l Thursdays only.
r Restaurant Car.
t Tea Car.

BLAENAVON (Monmouth) from *Paddington*, 156¼ miles. Fares, 32/4*a*, 19/5*c*. R. T. for two months, 64/8*a*, 38/10*c*. Pop. 12,470.
Map Square 22.

Pad.	Blaen.	Blaen.	Pad.
AM 1. 0*g*	8.12	AM 6.35*r*	10.57
5.30	11.39	8.14*r*	1. 0
8.45*dr*	12.57	11.50*r*	4.20
8.45*r*	1.30	PM 1.40*r*	6.15
11.50*r*	3.52	3.15*r*	8.35
PM 1.10*r*	6. 8	4.38*r*	9.25
3.35*r*	7.25	9.45	3.30
6. 0*r*	10.53	—	—
8. 0*jr*	11.56	—	—
9.15*e*	5.45	—	—
—	—	—	—
—	—	—	—
—	—	—	—

Sunday Trains.

AM 1. 0	10.23	AM 7.45	3.35
9.10	2.56	PM 3.40*r*	8.25
PM 12.30*r*	6.40	6.55	3.30
4.30	10.15	—	—
9.15	5.45	—	—
—	—	—	—
—	—	—	—

d Saturdays only.
e Saturdays excepted.
g Mondays excepted.
j Thursdays and Saturdays only.
r Restaurant Car.

BLAENGARW (Glamorgan), 182¼ miles. Fares, 38/1*a*, 22/10*c*. R.T. for two months, 76/2*a*, 45/8*c*. Departures *from* London as for Tondu. Departures *for* London about 4 times daily. Pop. 4,362.

BLAENGWYNFY (Glamorgan), 186¾ miles. No through fares. Departures *from* London as for Treherbert. Departures *for* London about 5 times daily.

BLAEN-RHONDDA (Glamorgan), 189¾ miles. No through fares. Departures *from* London as for Treherbert. Departures *for* London about 5 times daily.
Map Square 21.

BLAGDON (Somerset), 137¾ miles. Fares, 28/7*a*, 17/2*c*. R. T. for two months, 57/2*a*, 34/4*c*. Departures *from* London as for Wrington. Departures *for* London about 4 times daily. Pop. 915.
Map Square 22.

BLAINA (Monmouth) from *Paddington*, 160½ miles. Fares, 33/6*a*, 20/1*c*. R. T. for two months, 67/0*a*, 40/2*c*. Departures *from* London as for Aberbeeg. Departures *for* London about 5 times daily.
Map Square 21.

BLAIRADAM (Kinross), 419¾ miles. Fares, 87/4*a*, 52/5*c*, R. T. for two months, 174/8*a*, 104/10*c*. Departures *from* London as for Dunfermline. Departures *for* London about 3 times daily.
Map Square 41.

BLAIR ATHOLL (Perth) from *Euston*, 485½ miles. Fares, 98/6*a*, 59/1*c*. R.T. for two months, 197/0*a*, 118/2*c*. Pop. 1,824.
Map Square 37.

Euston	B.Atholl	B.Atholl	Euston
AM 10. 0*r*	9.30	AM 7. 5*r*	7.30
PM 1.30*er*	2.50*h*	11. 8*r*	10.45
7.30*ekr*	5.59	PM 1.35*r*	5. 0*h*
7.40*er*	6.10	7.23	7.40
11.35	10.48	—	—
—	—	—	—
—	—	—	—
—	—	—	—
—	—	—	—

Sunday Trains.

PM 7.50*r*	7. 3	—	—
11.35	10.48	—	—
—	—	—	—
—	—	—	—

e Saturdays excepted.
h A.M.
k Commences July 27
l P.M
r Restaurant Car.

ANOTHER ROUTE from *King's Cross*, 465½ miles. Fares as above.

King's +	B.Athol'	B.Athol'	King's +
AM 4.45	4.57*k*	AM 7. 5*r*	6.30*h*
11.50*er*	2.50*k*	11. 8*r*	10. 0*h*
PM 7.45*er*	6.10*k*	PM 1.35	6 0*k*
11.25*e*	10.48*k*	7.23	7. 5*k*
—	—	—	—

Sunday Trains.

PM 7.45*r*	6.43	—	—
11.25	10.48*k*	—	—
—	—	—	—

e Saturdays excepted.
h P.M.
k A.M.
r Restaurant Car.

Atholl Arms Hotel. Magnificent Scenery. Unrivalled cuisine. Terms Moderate. *See* advt. p. **28**.

BLAIRGOWRIE (Perth) from *Euston*, 470½ miles. Fares, 95/3*a*, 57/2*c*. R.T. for two months, 190/6*a*, 114/4*c*. Pop. 4,319.
Map Square 38.

Euston	B'gwrie	B'gwrie	Euston
AM 5. 0	8.17	AM 7.35*r*	7.30*l*
10. 0*r*	8.52	9.40*r*	10.45*l*
PM 7.50*er*	8.12	PM 2.10*r*	5. 0*h*
11.35*e*	10. 2*h*	6.20	7.40
—	—	—	—
—	—	—	—

BLAIRGOWRIE—*contd.*

Sunday Trains.

Euston	B'gowrie	B'gowrie	Euston
PM 7.50*r*	8.12	—	—
11.35	10. 2*h*	—	—

d Saturdays only.
e Saturdays excepted.
h A.M.
l P.M.
r Restaurant Car.

BLAKE HALL (Essex) from *Fenchurch Street*, 21¼ miles, or from *Liverpool Street*, 20¼ miles. Fares, from Liverpool Street, 4/5*a*, 3/7*b*, 2/8*c*. R. T. for two months, 8/10*a*, 6/10½*b*, 4/11½*c*. From Fenchurch Street, 4/5*a*, 3/6*b*, 2/8*c*. R. T. for two months, 8/9*a*, 6/7*b*, 4/10*c*. *See* pp. 541-544.
Map Square 24.

BLAKENEY (Norfolk) Station at HOLT.

BLAKESLEY (Northampton) from *Euston*, 71¼ miles. Fares, 14/10*a*, 8/11*c*. R. T. for two months, 29/8*a*, 17/10*c*. Departures *from* London as for Towcester. Departures *for* London about 3 times daily. Pop. 423.
Map Square 18.

BLANDFORD (Dorset) from *Waterloo*, 123¾ miles, *via* Wimborne. Fares, 25/8*a*, 15/5*c*. R.T. for two months, 51/4*a*, 30/10*c*. Pop. 3,194.
Map Square 27.

W'loo.	Bland.	Bland.	W'loo.
AM 5.40*k*	10.13	AM 8.19*s*	12.22
5.50	11.44	10. 2*lr*	2.20
8.30*ks*	12.25	PM 12. 8*k*	4.20
10.30*k*	2.16	1. 5*l*	6.16
PM 12.30*lr*	4.11	2. 6	6.26
2.30*ls*	6.11	3. 5	6.58
3.30*ls*	7.31	5.35*kr*	8.50
—	—	5.46	10.50
—	—	6.58*k*	11.28
—	—	9.32*k*	3.55

No Sunday Trains.

k *Via* Bournemouth.
l *Via* Broadstone.
r Restaurant Car.
s Refreshments served.

ANOTHER ROUTE from *Waterloo*, 128¾ miles, *via* Templecombe. Fares as above.

W'loo.	Bland.	Bland	W'loo.
AM 9. 0*r*	1. 5	AM 7.37*r*	11.10
10. 0*r*	2. 6	10.38*r*	1.56
PM 1. 0*r*	5. 6	11.41*r*	3. 8
3. 0*r*	6.58	PM 12.55*r*	4.30
6. 0*r*	9.32	2.16*r*	6. 0
—	—	5. 0*r*	8.30
—	—	6.12	10.50
—	—	7.31*h*	3.58

No Sunday Trains.

h *Via* Eastleigh.
r Restaurant Car.

BLANEFIELD (Stirling), 443¾ miles. Fares, 85/0*a*, 51/0*c*, R. T. for two months, 170/0*a*, 102/0*c*. Departures *from* London as for Glasgow. Departures *for* London about twice daily.
Map Square 40.

BLANKNEY (Lincs), from *King's Cross,* 121¾ miles. Fares, 25/3*a*, 15/2*c*, R.T. for two months, 50/6*a*, 30/4*c*. Pop. 617. *Map Square* 13.

King's +	B'nkney	B'nkney	King's +
AM 4.45	8.40	AM 7.48	11.30
7.15*r*	12. 1	10.17	3.50
PM 1.15	5.12	PM 1.14	4.45
4. 0*r*	8. 3	4.30	9. 0
5.45*r*	10.17	6.29	3.25
—	—	—	—

No Sunday Trains.
d Saturdays only.
r Restaurant Car.

ANOTHER ROUTE from *Liverpool Street* 134¼ miles. Fares as above.

L'pool St.	B'nkney	B'nkney	L'pool St.
AM 5.50	12.4	AM 7.48	12.40
11.50	5.12	10.17*l r*	4. 2*h*
PM 2.34	8. 3	10.17	5. 9
4.45	10.17	PM 1.14	6.10
—	—	4.30	10.30

No Sunday Trains.
d Saturdays only.
e Saturdays excepted.
h Arrives at St. Pancras Station.
l Commencing July 23.

BLANTYRE (Lanark), 394¼ miles. Fares, 82/6*a*, 49/6*c*. R.T. for two months, 165/0*a*, 99/0*c*. Departures *from* London as for Hamilton. Departures *for* London about 4 times daily. Pop.18,154.

BLAYDON (Durham), 270½ miles. Fares, 57/4*a*, 34/5*c*. R.T. for two months, 114/8*a*, 68/10*c*. Departures *from* London as for Newcastle-on-Tyne. Departures *for* London about 8 times daily. Pop. 33,064. *Map Square* 3.

BLEADON (Somerset) from *Paddington*, 138 miles. Fares, 28/9*a*, 17/3*c*. R.T. for two months, 57/6*a*, 34/6*c*. Departures *from* London as for Yatton. Departures *for* London about 4 times daily. Pop. 603. *Map Square* 22.

BLEASBY (Notts), from *St. Pancras*, 134 miles. Fares, 25/0*a*, 15/0*c*. R.T. for two months, 50/0*a*, 30/0*c*. Departures *from* London as for Nottingham. Departures *for* London about 6 times daily. Pop.278. *Map Square* 13.

BLEDLOW (Bucks) from *Paddington*, 36¼ miles. Fares, 7/4*a*, 4/5*c*. R.T. for two months, 14/8*a*, 8/10*c*. Departures *from* London as for Thame. Departures *for* London about 4 times daily. Pop.954. *Map Square* 23.

BLENCOW (Cumberland), 284¼ miles. Fares, 57/3*a*, 34/4*c*. R.T. for two months, 114/6*a*, 68/8*c*. Departures *from* London for Keswick. Departures *for* London about 5 times daily. *Map Square* 7.

BLENHEIM (Oxon) from *Paddington*, 72¼ miles. Fares, 14/10*a*, 8/11*c*. R.T. for two months, 29/8*a*, 17/10*c*. Pop. 162.

Pad.	Blenh.	Blenhm.	Pad.
AM 5.30	8.32	AM 7.50	9.50
6.30	10. 0	9.23	11.15
9.45	12.18	11.22	1.50
PM 12. 8	2.41	PM 1. 7*r*	2.55
1.35*r*	4. 5	3.25	5.50
3.18	5.53	6.15*r*	9.15
4.45*t*	6.52	8.17	10.45
7.30	9.32	—	—

No Sunday Trains.
r Restaurant Car.
t Tea Car.

BLETCHINGTON(Oxon) from *Paddington*, 71 miles. Fares, 14/0*a*, 8/5*c*. R.T. for two months, 28/0*a*, 16/10*c*. Departures *from* London as for Kidlington. Departures *for* London about 4 times daily. Pop. 488.

BLETCHLEY (Bucks) from *Euston*, 46¾ miles. Fares, 9/9*a*, 5/10*c*. R.T. for two months, 19/6*a*, 11/8*c*. Pop. 5,532. *Map Square* 18.

Euston	Bletch.	Bletch.	Euston
AM 5.25	7.30	AM 3.45	5. 0
6.45	7.44	6.44	8.24
7.35	9.20	7.32	9. 6
8.35	10.25	7.52*e*	9.22
9.30	10.41	8.10	9.40
10.40	11.47	8.44*e*	9.52
10.50	12.30	9. 5	10. 0
12. 0*n r*	1. 2	10. 0	11.40
PM 12.15	1.53	10.52	11.55
12.50*d*	2.23	11.25*d*	12.20
1.35*d*	3.23	11.39*e*	12.32
2. 0	3.48	12. 0*n*	1.50
3. 5	4.12	PM 1.35*h*	2.45
4.15	5.11	3.18	4.15
4.55*d*	6.24	4. 3	5. 5
5. 0*e*	6.24	4.17	5.33
5.32	6.40	4.25	6.15
6.10*e*	7.25	6.38	7.55
6.10*d*	7.37	7. 0	8.35
6.15*e*	7.41	8.14	9.20
7.15	9. 3	9. 5*d*	10.50
7.50*e*	8.48	9.17*e*	10.10
8. 0*e*	9. 0	10. 4	11.35
9.55*e*	11.30	—	—
9.55*d*	11.37	—	—
12.10*d*m	1.17	—	—

Sunday Trains.

AM 8.15	10. 5	AM 3.45	5. 0
9.15	10.32	7.35	9.22
PM 12.30	1.28	11.20	12.25
2.15	3.50	11.38	1.20
3.50	5.22	PM 12.29	1.30
6.10	7.45	4. 0	5. 5
6.45	8. 2	4.22	5.50
7.50	8.47	6.11	7.10
9.15	10.14	6.40	8.15
9.40	11.15	8.10	9.45
—	—	8.53	10.10
—	—	9. 5	10.40

d Saturdays only.
e Saturdays excepted.
h Thursdays and Saturdays only.
m Midnight.
n Noon.
r Restaurant Car.

BLIDWORTH (Notts), 145 miles. Fares, 26/6*a*, 15/11*c*. R.T. for two months, 53/0*a*, 31/10*c*. Departures *from* London as for Mansfield or Southwell. Departures *for* London about 4 times daily. Pop. 1,184. *Map Square* 13.

BLISWORTH (Northampton) from *Euston*, 62¾ miles. Fares, 13/2*a*, 7/11*c*. R.T. for two months, 26/4*a*, 15/10*c*. Pop. 823. *Map Square* 18.

Euston	Blisw'h.	Blisw'h.	Euston.
AM 5. 0*h*	7.15	AM 1.28*gh*	5.40
6.45	8.35	7.18	9.40
9.15*r*	10.28	8.25*h*	10.15
9.30*h*	12. 0	9.14	11.40
12. 0*nr*	1.40	9.50*h*	11.55
PM 2. 0	4.35	10.46*d*	12.20
4.15*h*	6.10	11. 0*e*	12.32
5.32	7.25	PM 2.26	4.15
6.45*h*	8.30	3.15*h*	5.35
7.15*d h*	10.35	5.17	6.25
9.30	10.42	5.55	7.55
11.50	1.17	7.20*h*	9.20
—	—	8.21	10.50
—	—	8.35*h*	11.35

Sunday Trains.

AM 8.15	10.50	AM 10.51	1.20
—	—	PM 3.42	5.50

d Saturdays only.
e Saturdays excepted.
g Mondays excepted.
h Via Northampton
n Noon.
r Restaurant Car.

BLOCKLEY (Worcester) from *Paddington*, 94⅓ miles. Fares, 19/10*a*, 11/11*c*. R.T. for two months, 39/8*a*, 23/10*c*. Pop. 1,845. *Map Square* 17.

Pad.	Blockley	Blockley	Pad.
AM 5.30	9. 1	AM 7.15	9.50
9.45	12.54	9.10	12.5
PM 1.35*r*	4.58	11.27	2.12
4.45	6.52	PM 4.13	7.17
6.55	9.44	6.25*r*	9.15
—	—	7.48	10.45

Sunday Trains.

AM 10.35*r*	1.18	AM 11.33	2.40
PM 4.10	7. 3	PM 6.45*r*	9.48

r Restaurant Car.

BLODWELL (Salop), 179 miles. Fares, 36/6*a*, 21/11*c*. R.T. for two months, 73/0*a*. Departures *from* London as for Oswestry. Departures *for* London about 3 times daily. Pop. (Llanyblodwell) 840.

BLOWERS GREEN (Worcester), 121½ miles. Fares, 25/3*a*, 15/2*c*. R. T. for two months, 50/6*a*, 30/4*c*. Departures *from* London as for Stourbridge Junction. Departures *for* London about 6 times daily. Pop. 14,100.
Map Square 17.

BLOWICK (Lancs), 211½ miles. No through fares. Departures *from* London as for Wigan. Departures *for* London about 6 times daily.
Map Square 12.

BLOXHAM (Oxon), 68¼ miles. Fares (*via* Kingham), 19/7*a*, 12/5*c*. R. T. for two months, 39/2*a*, 24/10*c*. (*Via* Bicester), 15/6*a*, 9/6*c*. R. T. for two months, 31/0*a*, 19/0*c*. Departures *from* London as for Chipping Norton. Departures *for* London about 5 times daily. Pop. 1,335.
Map Square 18.

BLOXWICH (Stafford), 123 miles. Fares, 25/8*a*, 15/5*c*. R.T. for two months, 51/4*a*, 30/10*c*. Departures *from* London as for Walsall. Departures *for* London about 5 times daily. Pop. 8,411.
Map Square 17.

BLUE ANCHOR (Somerset), 164¼ miles. Fares, 34/4*a*, 20/7*c*. R. T. for two months, 68/8*a*, 41/2*c*. Departures *from* London as for Watchet. Departures *for* London about 4 times daily.
Map Square 21.

BLUNDELLSANDS & CROSBY (Lancs), 208 miles. Fares, 41/11*a*, 25/2*c*. R. T. for two months, 83/10*a*, 50/4*c*. Departures *from* London as for Liverpool. Departures *for* London about 4 times daily. Pop. 3,801.
Map Square 12.

BLUNHAM (Beds), from *Euston*, 69 miles. Fares, 10/5*a*, 6/3*c*. R.T. for two months, 20/10*a*, 12/6*c*. Departures *from* London as for Bedford. Departures *for* London about 5 times daily. Pop. 603.
Map Square 18.

BLUNTISHAM (Hunts) from *Liverpool Street*, 74¼ miles. Fares, 12/11*a*, 7/9*c*. R. T. for two months, 25/10*a*, 15/6*c*. Departures *from* London as for Haddenham. Departures *for* London about 4 times daily. Pop. 1,022.
Map Square 13.

BLYTH (Northumberland), 282½ miles. Fares, 60/3*a*, 36/2*c*. R.T. for two months, 120/6*a*, 72/4*c*. Departures *from* London as for Newcastle-on-Tyne. Departures *for* London about 6 times daily. Pop. 31,833.
Map Square 3.

BLYTHBURGH (Suffolk) from *Liverpool Street*, 105¼ miles. Fares, 22/3*a*, 13/4*c*. R. T. for two months, 44/6*a*, 26/8*c*. Departures *from* London as for Southwold. Departures *for* London about 4 times daily. Pop. 747.
Map Square 19.

BLYTHE BRIDGE (Stafford), 150¾ miles. Fares, 30/8*a*, 18/5*c*. R.T. for two months, 61/4*a*, 36/10*c*. Departures *from* London as for Longton. Departures *for* London about twice daily.
Map Square 12.

BLYTON (Lincoln), 153½ miles. Fares, 31/0*a*, 18/7*c*. R.T. for two months, 62/0*a*, 37/2*c*. Departures *from* London as for Gainsborough (*via* Retford). Departures *for* London about 4 times daily. Pop. 822.
Map Square 13.

BOARHILLS (Fife), 450¼ miles. No through fares. Departures *from* London as for St. Andrews. Departures *for* London about 3 times daily.
Map Square 41.

BOARSHEAD (Lancs), 196¼ miles. Fares, 40/10*a*, 24/6*c*. R. T. for two months, 81/8*a*, 49/0*c*. Departures *from* London as for Wigan. Departures *for* London about 6 times daily.
Map Square 12.

BOAT OF GARTEN (Inverness), 538½ miles. Fares, 106/3*a*, 63/9*c*. R. T. for two months, 212/6*a*, 127/6*c*. Departures *from* London as for Aviemore. Departures *for* London about 3 times daily. Pop. 322.
Map Square 34.

BODDAM (Aberdeen), 557½ miles. Fares, 107/4*a*, 64/5*c*. R. T. for two months, 214/8*a*, 128/10*c*. Departures *from* London as for Cruden Bay. Departures *for* London about 3 times daily.
Map Square 35.

BODFARI (Flint), 204¾ miles. Fares, 40/7*a*, 24/4*c*. R. T. for two months, 81/2*a*, 48/8*c*. Departures *from* London as for Mold. Departures *for* London about 4 times daily. Pop. 322.
Map Square 11.

BODIAM (Sussex), 54¾ miles. No through fares. Departures *from* London as for Tenterden (*via* Robertsbridge). Departures *for* London about 4 times daily. Pop. 239.
Map Square 24.

BODMIN (Cornwall) from *Waterloo*, 260½ miles. Fares, 52/1*a*. 31/3*c*. R. T. for two months, 104/2*a*, 62/6*c*. Pop. 5,527.
Map Square 25.

W'LOO.	BODM.	BODM.	W'LOO.
AM 10. 0*r*	5.10	AM 7.58*r*	3.50
11. 0*r*	6.44	9. 4*r*	4.30
—	—	11.28*r*	8.30
—	—	PM 1.55	10.50
—	—	—	—
—	—	—	—
—	—	—	—
—	—	—	—
—	—	—	—
—	—	—	—
—	—	—	—
—	—	—	—

No Sunday Trains.

r Restaurant Car.

BODMIN—*continued*.

ANOTHER ROUTE from *Paddington*, 256¼ miles. Fares, 52/1*a*, 31/3*c*. R.T. for two months, 104/2*a*, 62/6*c*.

PAD.	BODM.	BODM.	PAD.
AM 5.30	2.52	AM 10.15*r*	4.35
11.10*r*	5.10	PM 12.18*r*	6.50
PM 2. 0*r*	8.50	2. 5*r*	9. 0
12. 0*h*	9.14	7.55	7.10
—	—	—	—
—	—	—	—
—	—	—	—

Sunday Trains.

PM 10. 0	9.14	—	—
—	—	—	—

h Saturdays midnight excepted.
k Mondays and Fridays only.
r Restaurant Car.
s Fridays on y.

BODMIN ROAD (Cornwall) from *Paddington*, 252½ miles. Fares, 52/1*a*, 31/3*c*. R. T. for two months, 104/2*a*, 62/6*c*.
Map Square 25.

PAD.	BOD. RD.	BOD. RD.	PAD.
AM 5.30	1.23	AM 8.52*r*	3.55
11.10*r*	4.51	10.46*r*	4.35
PM 2. 0*r*	8.13	11. 2*kr*	4.45
12. 0*h*	8.56	PM 12.38*r*	6.50
12.30*l*	9.31	2.35*r*	9. 0
—	—	8.37	7.10
—	—	10.22*s*	7.10

Sunday Trains.

PM 10. 0	5.24	PM 12.45	7. 5
—	—	6.50	3.15

h Saturdays midnight excepted.
k Mondays and Fridays only.
l Saturdays midnight only.
r Restaurant Car.
s Fridays only.

BODORGAN (Anglesey), 251¾ miles. Fares, 52/4*a*, 31/5*c*. R. T. for two months, 104/8*a*, 62/10*c*. Departures *from* London as for Gaerwen. Departures *for* London about 3 times daily.
Map Square 11.

BOGNOR (Sussex) from *London Bridge*, *Victoria*, and *Clapham Junction*, 66¾ miles. Fares, 14/0*a*, 8/4*c*. R. T. for two months, 28/0*a*, 16/8*c*. Pop. 13,300.
Map Square 28.

Leave VICT.	Leave LON. B.	Arr. at BOGNOR.
AM 6.18	6.35	9. 3
7.23	7.25	10.35
8.55	—	10.47
10.15	10.30	12.38
11.55*k*	11.50*k*	2.42
PM 1.35	—	3.18
1.40	1.50	3.57
1.55*k*	—	4. 7
—	2. 5*k*	5. 7
3.55	4. 0	6. 7
—	4.50	6.37
4.53	—	7.12
—	5. 5	7.45
—	5. 8*e*	7.45
5.45*e*	5.55*e*	8. 6
—	6. 0*k*	8.19
6.15	—	7.55
7.20	7.15	10. 3

Sunday Trains.

AM 8.35	—	10.25
9. 0	8.55	11.12
PM 1.14*k*	1.10*k*	4.52
7. 0	6.38	9.27
—	—	—
—	—	—

BOGNOR—*continued.*

Trains from Bognor.

Leave Bognor	Arrive at Lon. B.	Vict.
AM 7.10*f*	—	9.22
7.19*g*	—	9.22
7.18*k*	9.50	—
8.10	9.58	—
8.30	10.45	10.53
8.45*k*	—	11.17
9.10	10.55	—
10. 0	12. 8	12. 0
10.50	—	1.20
PM12.25	3.32	3.32
2. 0	4.15	—
2. 7*d*	4.58	4.45
2. 7	—	4.50
3.15	—	5. 0
4.12	—	6.50
5.30	—	7.15
5.37	7.48	7.39
7.20*d*	10. 0	9.45
7.50	10. 8	10. 1
8.10	—	11.17
9.28*k*	12.59	1. 0

Sunday Trains.

AM 7.25	10.45	10.32
9.45*k*	—	1. 0
10.50	—	1.35
PM 4.15*k*	—	7. 0
6. 0	—	7.49
6.30	8.50	8.42
6.44	9.32	9.34
8. 0*k*	11.34	10.55

d Saturdays only.
e Saturdays excepted.
f Mondays only.
g Mondays excepted.
k Via Hove.

Royal Norfolk Hotel. Easy distance Goodwood and Arundel. Excellent Cuisine. *See* advt. p. **40.**

The Royal Hotel. Foremost First-class Hotel. Premier position on Marine Parade. West of Pier. Garage. Telephone 15. Telegrams: "Royal, Bognor." PROPRIETOR. *See* advt. p. **39.**

Clarence House Hotel for Children with their Governesses or Nurses. Facing Sea. Large Garden. Special Cuisine. Certified Sanitation. Telephone 24. *See* advt. p. **41.**

Sydney House Private Hotel. Sheltered Sea View. First-class accommodation. Tel. 103. *See* advt. p. **41.**

Beaulieu Private Hotel. Leading Private Hotel. Facing Sea. Open all the year round. Dances. Moderate Terms. *See* advt. p. **41.**

Rock Gardens Hotel. Overlooking Sea, Private Road and Lawns. Separate Tables. Forty Bedrooms. Garage. 'Phone 25. F. PULLIN.

Lansdowne Boarding House. Facing Pier. Late dinner. Smoking lounge. Cleanliness and every comfort. Personal supervision of Proprietress, Mrs. C. BRYAN. Cycle accommodation. Phone 12.

BOGNOR—*continued.*

Gothic House Boarding Establishment, The Steyne. Close to Esplanade and Sands. Central position. Good Catering. Personal supervision. Phone, 229. THE MISSES TODD.

Beach Hotel. Sea Front. Lounge, Bedrooms and Breakfasts only (two restaurants close by). Electric light. Telephone 161. Proprietor, ARTHUR TAYLOR.

Bellevue Private Hotel, Esplanade. Best position. Excellent Cuisine. Separate Tables. Heated throughout. Apartments if desired. Mrs. MARTIN. Residential Proprietress.

The Ascot Boarding House, Clarence Road. Minute Sea and Catholic Church. Electric Light. Separate Tables. Newly decorated. Personal supervision. L. GOOD.

Sussex Hotel. High-class Residential Hotel, near Golf Links and Sea. Electric Light. Tel.: 139 Bognor. Billiards. Garage. P. H. DARLING, Proprietor.

Sealands Boarding Establishment, Aldwick Road, West End. Excellent position, facing Sea. Good Cooking. Separate Tables. Address, PROPRIETRESS.

Alexandra Boarding Establishment, Clarence Road. Good sea view, central position, personal supervision. Proprietress, Mrs. BELL.

The Campo Private Hotel. West. Facing South. Good Cuisine. Spacious Dining Rooms and Lounge. Electric light throughout. Moderate terms. PROPRIETRESS.

Brantwood Boarding Establishment. Esplanade. High-class, central position. Sunny Balconies, facing sea. Smoke-room. 'Phone 199 Bognor. Proprietors, MISSES RAWSON & MARCH.

Victoria Hotel, West End. New Proprietorship. First-class Hotel. Lovely Gardens. Tennis. Garage. Electric Light. Moderate. Tel. 182. Proprietor, P. H. WEBBER.

Fairlight Boarding Establishment, Aldwick Road, West Bognor. Facing Sea, Good cooking. Moderate terms. Separate Tables. Cycle accommodation. PROPRIETRESS.

Knighton House. Private Hotel. West End. First-class. Spacious sunny rooms. Sea views. Electric light throughout. Excellent Cuisine. Smoking lounge. Garage adjacent. 'Phone 291. Mrs. ELLMORE.

Glencoe and Sealands, West Bognor. Boarding Establishment. Facing Sea. Excellent Cuisine. Separate Tables. Smoking Lounge. Near Tennis and Golf. Mrs. WHITE.

High-Class Apartments. Suites of Rooms in comfortable well-furnished house. Pleasant central position. Sea-views. Address, PROPRIETRESS, Portland House, Bognor.

BOGNOR—*continued.*

Hothamton Court. Private Hotel. Splendid position. Facing Sea. Private Tennis Court. First-class Cuisine and Attendance. Tel. 74. Proprietress, Mrs. N. S. DAVIDSON.

Marlborough Hotel. Facing Sea. Sunny Verandahs. Electric Light. Three Bathrooms. Excellent Cuisine. Also Furnished Suites without Board. Phone 232. PROPRIETRESS.

The Grafton Boarding Establishment. Sea Front. Sunny Balcony. Separate Tables. Excellent Cuisine. Special Winter Terms. Phone 321. Mrs. SYDNEY HEWETT.

Lopencroft Boarding House. 17, Waterloo Square. Pleasantly and centrally situated overlooking Sea. Half minute from Pier. Moderate Terms. Apply, PROPRIETRESS.

Albany House. Board Residence. Apartments May and June. Five minutes Sea. Two minutes Station. Tennis. Separate Tables. Home Comforts. Central Heating. PROPRIETRESS.

Carlton Private Hotel, Esplanade. Central position for all attractions. Separate Tables. Well Furnished. Electric Light. Recommended for Winter Apartments.

For Furnished Houses and Properties for sale apply to TREGEAR AND SONS, the leading House and Estate Agents. Selected lists free on application to 6 London Road, Bognor (Tel. 140), and Aldwick Road, West Bognor (Tel. 243). Telegrams—Tregear, Bognor.

Reynolds & Co., Auctioneers, House and Estate Agents. List of Furnished and Unfurnished Houses free. Telephone 162.

Dawson Siddall, Estate Agent. Opposite Station. All available Properties and Land for Sale, and Furnished Houses. Lists free. No Apartments. Telephone 204.

Bognor Furnished Houses. Write Whitehead's, House and Estate Agents. No apartments. 3, Station Road. Telephone Bognor 180.

BOGSIDE (Ayr), 399 miles. No through fares. Departures *from* London as for Irvine. Departures *for* London about 4 times daily. *Map Square* 40.

BOGSIDE (Fife), 419½ miles. No through fares. Departures *from* London as for Dunfermline. Departures *for* London about 3 times daily.

BOLLINGTON (Cheshire), 168 miles. Fares, 34/10*a*, 20/11*c*. R.T. for two months, 69/8*a*, 41/10*c*. Departures *from* London as for Macclesfield (Hibel Road). Departures *for* London about 6 times daily. Pop. 5,094. *Map Square* 12.

BOLSOVER (Derby) from *King's Cross*, 151½ miles. Fares, 30/2*t*, 18/1*c*. R. T. for two months, 60/4*a*, .36/9*c*. Departures *from* London as for Edwinstowe. Departures *for* London about twice daily. Pop. 11,481. *Map Square* 13.

BOGNOR.—ROCK GARDENS HOTEL (PRIVATE). Facing Sea. 'Phone 25. See advt. under trains.

BOLTON (Lancs) from

Euston, via Warrington, 200 miles. Fares, 40/5*a*, 24/3*c*. R. T. for two months, 80/10*a*, 48/6*c*. Pop.178,678. *Map Square* 12.

EUSTON	BOLTON	BOLTON	EUSTON
AM12.25	7.29	AM 6.45*er*12. 5	
2.35	9.26	6.45*dr*12.20	
5. 0	11.40	8.20*r*	1.45
6.45*d*	12.48	10.30*r*	4.15
6.45*e*	1.32	11.50*t*	5.50
8.30*r*	2.24	PM 1.50*r*	7.30
10.40*r*	5. 6	3.35*er*	9. 5
11.50*r*	5.58	3.35*dr*	9.15
PM 1.30*r*	6.26	8.35	5. 0
2.35*t*	7.38	—	—
5.20*r*	10.55	—	—
—	—	—	—

No Sunday Trains.

d Saturdays only.
e Saturdays excepted.
r Restaurant Car.
t Tea Car.

ANOTHER ROUTE from

Euston, via Manchester (Victoria) 196 miles. Fares as above.

EUSTON	BOLTON	BOLTON	EUSTON
AM12.25	5.47	AM6.45*dhr*12.20	
2.35	9.14	6.55*er*12. 5	
5. 0	11.15	7.20*r*	12.50
6.45*d*	12.48*h*	8.42*r*	1.15
6.45*e*	1.32	9. 0	1.45
8.45*r*	1.50	9. 6*r*	2.20
10.40*r*	3. 9	9.40*r*	3.10
11.50*r*	4.30	10.30*v*	3.45
PM 1.30*r*	6.26*h*	11.18*r*	3.55
2.50*t*	7.30	11.50*hr*	5.50
4. 5*r*	9.38	PM12. 6*et*	6. 0
6. 5*r*	10.30	12.39*dt*	6. 0
9.30*e*	5. 0	1. 3*er*	6.15
11.50*d*	8. 5	1.10*dr*	6.15
—	—	1.50*r*	7.30
—	—	3.13*r*	8.10
—	—	3.35*er*	9. 5
—	—	3.35*hr*	9.15
—	—	4.15*er*10. 0	
—	—	5.18*dr*10. 0	
—	—	5.18*er*10.10	
—	—	9.15	5. 0
—	—	9.49*d*	5. 0
—	—	10.38*e*	5.40
—	—	10.38*d*	5.45
—	—	—	—
—	—	—	—
—	—	—	—
—	—	—	—

Sunday Trains.

PM12.10*r*	5.40	AM 9.49	4. 0
12.30*r*	7.15	12. 0*nr*	5.45
9.15	5. 0	PM 1.27*r*	7.30
—	—	3. 5*r*	8.55
—	—	10.33	5. 0
—	—	—	—
—	—	—	—

d Saturdays only.
e Saturdays excepted.
h Great Moor Street Station.
n Noon.
r Restaurant Car.
t Tea Car.
v Mondays and Saturdays only.
Passengers cross Manchester at own expense.

BOLTON ABBEY

(Yorks), 216¼ miles. Fares, 42/9*a*, 25/8*c*. R. T. for two months, 85/6*a*, 51/4*c*. Departures *from* London as for Ilkley. Departures *for* London about 8 times daily. Pop. 191.
Map Square 7.

BOLTON-LE-SANDS

(Lancs), 234½ miles. Fares, 48/11*a*, 29/4*c*. R. T. for two months, 97/10*a*, 58/8*c*. Departures *from* London as for Lancaster (Castle). Departures *for* London about 6 times daily. Pop. 941.
Map Square 7.

BOLTON-PERCY

(Yorks), 195 miles. Fares, 40/8*a*, 24/5*c*. R. T. for two months, 81/4*a*, 48/10*c*. Departures *from* London as for York. Departures *for* London about five times daily. Pop. 246.
Map Square 8.

BOLTON-UPON-

DEARNE (Yorks), 169½ miles. Fares, 35/2*a*, 21/1*c*. R. T. for two months, 70/4*a*, 42/2*c*. Departures *from* London as for Swinton. Departures *for* London about 5 times daily. Pop. 11,957.
Map Square 13.

BONAR BRIDGE

(Sutherland), 625½ miles. Fares, 111/8*a*, 67/0*c*. R.T. for two months, 223/4*a*, 134/0*c*. Departures *from* London as for Tain. Departures *for* London about twice daily. Pop. 331.
Map Square 34.

BONCATH (Pembroke),

262½ miles. Fares, 53/4*a*, 32/0*c*. R.T. for two months 106/8*a*, 64/0*c*. Departures *from* London as for Cardigan. Departures *for* London about 4 times daily.
Map Square 16.

BOND STREET (Central

London Tube). *See* back of Map.

BO'NESS (Linlithgow), 416¾

miles. Fares, 81/11*a*, 49/2*c*. R. T. for two months, 163/10*a*, 98/4*c*. Departures *from* London as for Edinburgh(Waverley). Departures *for* London about 4 times daily.
Map Square 41.

BONNYBRIDGE (Stir-

ling), 406 miles. Fares, 82/6*a*, 49/6*c*. R. T. for two months, 165/0*a*, 99/0*c*. Departures *from* London as for Larbert. Departures *for* London about 4 times daily. Pop. 3,168.

BONNYRIGG (Mid-

lothian), 387¾ miles. No through fares. Departures *from* London as for Edinburgh (Waverley) or Peebles. Departures *for* London about 4 times daily. Pop. 3,146.

BONTNEWYDD (Meri-

oneth), from *Paddington*, 219 miles. Fares, 45/8*a*, 27/5*c*. R. T. for two months, 91/4*a*, 54/10*c*. Departures *from* London as for Corwen. Departures *for* London about 3 times daily.
Map Square 16.

BOOKHAM (Surrey) from

Waterloo, 20½ miles. Fares, 3/11*a*, 2/4*c*. R. T. for eight days, 7/10*a*, 4/8*c*. Pop. 1,938. *See* pp. 583-584.
Map Square 23.

BOOSBECK (Yorks), 251¼

miles. Fares, 52/4*a*, 31/5*c*. R.T. for two months, 104/8*a*, 62/10*c*. Departures *from* London as for Saltburn. Departures *for* London about 3 times daily. Pop. 1,055.
Map Square 8.

BOOTLE (Cumberland),

282 miles. Fares, 58/7*a*, 35/2*c*. R. T. for two months, 117/2*a*, 70/4*c*. Departures *from* London as for Millom. Departures *for* London about 4 times daily. Pop. 746.
Map Square 6.

BOOTLE (Lancs) from

Euston, 204½ miles. Fares, 41/3*a*, 24/9*c*. R. T. for two months, 82/6*a*, 49/6*c*. Departures *from* London as for Liverpool (Lime Street). Departures *for* London about 8 times daily. Pop. 76,508.
Map Square 12.

BORDESLEY (Warwick)

from *Paddington*,109½ miles. Fares, 22/9*a*, 13/8*c*. R.T. for two months, 45/6*a*, 27/4*c*. Departures *from* London as for Acock's Green. Departures *for* London about 6 times daily. Pop. 62,855.

BORDON (Hants) from

Waterloo, 46½ miles. Fares, 9/10*a*, 5/11*c*. R.T. for two months, 19/8*a*, 11/10*c*.
Map Square 23.

W'LOO.	BORDON	BORDON	W'LOO.
AM 5.50	8.39	AM 7.55	9.41
7.50	9.55	8.55	10.26
9.20	11.10	10.25	12.11
11.20	1.23	11.55	1.40·
PM 1.10	2.50	PM 1.47	3.36
3.15	4.58	4.15	6.16
4. 0	6. 1	5. 3	7. 7
5.10	6.50	7. 5	9. 6·
6.34	8. 8	9. 5	11.10
6.40*d*	8.55	—	—
6.54*e*	8.55	—	—
8. 0	9.57	—	—
9.50	11.39	—	—
—	—	—	—

Sunday Trains.

AM 8.45	10.37	AM 9.16	11.16
11.15	1. 3	10.55	12.52
PM 3.44	PM 1.23	3.13	
6.30	8.35	5.32	7.41
10.45	12.28	6.52	9.37
—	—	8.52	10.47
—	—	—	—

d Saturdays only.
e Saturdays excepted.

BOROUGH (City and South

London Tube). *See* back of Map.

BOROUGHBRIDGE

(Yorks), 208¼ miles. Fares, 43/9*a*, 26/3*c*. R. T. for two months, 87/6*a*, 52/6*c*. Departures *from* London as for Harrogate or York. Departures *for* London about 5 times daily. Pop. 842.
Map Square 8.

BORROWASH (Derby), 124¾ miles. Fares, 25/7a, 15/4c. R.T. for two months, 51/2a, 30/8c. Departures *from* London as for Trent. Departures *for* London about 6 times daily.
Map Square 13.

BORTH (Cardigan) 231 miles. Fares, 47/1a, 28/3c. R. T. for two months, 94/2a. Departures *from* London as for Machynlleth. Departures *for* London about 4 times daily.
Map Square 16.

BORWICK (Lancs), 256 miles. Fares, 49/2a, 29/6c. R. T. for two months, 98/4a, 59/0c. Departures *from* London as for Giggleswick. Departures *for* London about 4 time daily. Pop. 138.
Map Square 7.

BOSCOMBE (Hants) from *Waterloo*, 106 miles. Fares, 22/4a, 13/5c. R. T. for two months, 44/8a, 26/10c. Pop. 11,199.
Map Square 27.

W'loo.	Bosc.	Bosc.	W'loo.
AM 5.40	8.43	AM 7. 4r	10. 6
5.50	10.34	7.50s	11. 0
8.30s	12. 5	9.23s	12.22
9.30	12.30	10. 0r	12.50
10.30	1.39	11.26r	2.20
11.30r	2.13	PM12. 8	2.50
PM12.30r	3.24	1.25	4.20
1.30s	4.26	1.58	4.50
2.30	5.11	3.25s	6.26
3.30s	6.26	3.45	6.58
4.30r	7.42	5.25r	8.20
5.30r	8.26	7.10	10.50
6.30r	9.32	8. 2	11.28
7.30	10.53	9.19	3.58
—	—	—	—
—	—	—	—
—	—	—	—
—	—	—	—
—	—	—	—
—	—	—	—

Sunday Trains.

AM11. 0r	1.54	AM 8.54	12.11
PM 2. 0r	4.43	11.35r	2.27
7. 0r	9.53	PM 4.19	8. 3
—	—	6.16r	9.31
—	—	7.15	10.52
—	—	7.52	3.58
—	—	—	—
—	—	—	—
—	—	—	—

r Restaurant Car.
s Refreshments served.

The Hotel Burlington. 200 Rooms. Acres of sheltered pleasure grounds, sloping to pier. Winter garden 200 feet long. Magnificent Links quite close. Garage.
See advt. p. **55.**

The Salisbury Hotel, Boscombe. Central. Close to Pier. Links and Gardens. En Pension from £4 10s. Garage.
W. J. McCABE, Proprietor.
See advt. p. **64.**

The Chine Hotel, Boscombe. The Grandest Position on East Cliff.
Miss BARNETT, Manageress.
See advt. p. **67.**

Pier Hotel. Private. En pension. Facing Sea. South aspect. Heated throughout. Separate tables. Billiard room. Moderate Terms. Telephone 0981.
Apply PROPRIETRESS.

BOSCOMBE—*continued.*

Baronscourt, Horace Road. En pension. Near Pier, Cliff Gardens, Links, Tennis. South aspect. Separate tables. Smoking room. Moderate terms.
PROPRIETRESS.

Estate Agents. Hankinson & Son's illustrated Registers, post free. All available Properties, Boscombe and Bournemouth and district. 'Phone 1307 (3 lines).

BOSHAM (Sussex) from *London Bridge, Victoria* and *Clapham Junction*, 72½ miles. Fares, 13/11a, 8/4c. R. T. for two months, 27/10a, 16/8c. Pop. 1,477.
Map Square 28.

Leave Vict.	Clap. J.	Lon. B.	Arr. at Bosham
AM 6.18	6.25	6.35	9.46
8.55	—	—	12. 0
10.15	10.22	10.22	1.39
11.55h	—	11.50h	2.49
PM 1.40	1.47e	1.50	4.17
1.55h	e2. 2h	2. 5h	5.24
3.55	4. 2	4.50	6.45
4.53	5. 0	5. 5	7.57
—	—	5. 8e	7.57
5.45	—	6. 0k	8.27
7.20	7.27	7.15	10. 0
—	—	—	—
—	—	—	—
—	—	—	—
—	—	—	—
—	—	—	—
—	—	—	—

Sunday Trains.

AM 6.55h	7. 2h	7. 2h	11. 2
9. 0	9. 7	8.55	11.23
9.55	—	—	2. 7
PM 1.14h	1.21h	1.10h	5. 4
7. 0	7. 7	6.38	10. 2

Trains from Bosham.

Leave Bosham	Lon. B.	Arrive at Clap. J.	Vict.
AM 6.59g	9.50	—	9.22
7. 4f	9.50	—	—
7.48	9.58	10.44	10.52
8.52	10.55	—	—
9.28	12. 8	—	12. 0
11. 7	—	—	1.10
PM12. 6	3.32	3.22	3.32
1.57	4.27	4.26	4.34
4. 0	—	—	6.50
5.24	7.48	7.31	7.39
5.55	—	8.39	8.33
7. 9	10. 8	9.53	10. 1
7. 9d	10. 0	9.37	9.45
9.28h	12.59	12.50	1. 0
—	—	—	—
—	—	—	—
—	—	—	—

Sunday Trains.

AM 7.23	10.45	10.23	10.32
9.35h	—	12.49	1. 0
PM 4. 3h	—	—	7. 0
5.37	8.50	7.49	7.56
7.51h	11.34	10.41	10.55
—	—	—	—

e Saturdays excepted.
f Mondays only.
g Mondays excepted.
h *Via* Hove.
k First and third class Pullman Cars only.

BOSLEY (Cheshire), 161¾ miles. No through fares. Departures *from* London as for Leek. Departures *for* London about 4 times daily. Pop. 388.
Map Square 12.

BOSTON (Lincoln) from *King's Cross*, 107¼ miles. Fares, 22/4a, 13/5c. R.T. for two months, 44/8a, 26/10c. Pop. 16,100.
Map Square 13.

King's +	Boston	Boston	King's +
AM 4.45	7.46	AM 7.37	10.40
5. 5	8.58	7.40ry	11.30
7.15ry	10.35	10.34	1. 5
8.45	11.59	11.52	3.50
11.30	3.17	PM 1.45r	4.30
PM 1.15y	4.44	2.20lr	5. 0
1.50dr	4.39	2.45kr	6.30
3. 0	5.49	5.15	9. 0
4. 0r	6.33	6.55r	9.25
5.45r	8.27	9.37y	3.25
10.45e	3.58	—	—
—	—	—	—
—	—	—	—
—	—	—	—

Sunday Trains.

12. 0nr	3. 4	AM11.50r	3.45
PM10.45	3.58	PM 7.10r	10.20
—	—	—	—

d Saturdays only.
e Saturdays excepted.
k Wednesdays only *via* Grantham.
l Wednesdays only *via* Peterboro.
n Noon.
r Restaurant Car.
y *Via* Grantham.

BOSTON MANOR (Middlesex) from *Mansion House*, 11½ miles. *See* p. 489.
Map Square 67.

BOTHWELL (Lanark), 393 miles. Fares, 80/0a, 48/0c. R. T. for two months, 160/0a, 96/0c. Departures *from* London as for Motherwell. Departures *for* London about 4 times daily. Pop. 60,284.
Map Square 40.

BOTLEY (Hants) from *Waterloo*, 78¼ miles. Fares, 15/5a, 9/3c. R. T. for two months, 30/10a, 18/6c. Pop. 1,012.
Map Square 23.

W'loo.	Botley	Botley	W'loo.
AM 5.40	8.10	AM 6.47	9.26
5.50	9.17	9.48	12. 0
8.30s	10.40	PM12. 3r	2.20
9.30	12. 9	12.46	4. 6
11.30r	1.54	1.54	4.20
PM 1.30s	3.37	3.21	6.16
3.30s	5.45	6.11r	8.20
5.30r	7.43	7.50	10.50
7.30	9.42	8.58	11.28
8. 0	11.15	11.41	3.58
—	—	—	—
—	—	—	—
—	—	—	—
—	—	—	—

Sunday Trains.

AM11. 0r	1.12	AM 9.45	12.11
PM 2. 0	6.21	PM12.22r	2.27
5. 5	7.46	5.35	8. 3
7. 0r	9.18	7.56	10.52
9.28	12.21	11.13	3.58

r Restaurant Car.
s Refreshments served.

BOTTESFORD (Leicester) from King's Cross, 112¾ miles.

Fares, 23/4a, 14/0c. R. T. for two months, 46/8a, 28/0c. Pop. 1,174. Map Square 13.

KING'S +	BOTT.	BOTT.	KING'S +
AM 4.45	8. 0	AM 7.53	10.40
5. 5	9.15	10.21r	1. 5
7.15r	10. 3	PM12.24	3.50
8.45	11.49	2.55	6.25
10.10r	1.43	3.37r	6.30
PM 1.50r	4.30	5.30	9. 0
4. 0r	6.40	6.54r	9.25
5.45r	9. 5	11. 5e	3.25
—	—	11.15d	3.25
—	—	—	—
—	—	—	—
—	—	—	—
—	—	—	—

Sunday Trains.

AM11.30	2. 8	PM12.50	3.45
12. 0nr	3.23	3. 0	5.55
PM 5. 0r	8.25	—	—
—	—	—	—

n Noon.
r Restaurant Car.

BOTTISHAM (Cambs)

from Liverpool Street, 61¼ miles. Fares, 12/9a, 7/8c. R. T. for two months, 25/6a, 15/4c. Departures *from* London as for Mildenhall. Departures *for* London about 4 times daily. Pop. 704. Map Square 19.

BOUGHROOD (Radnor),

174 miles. Fares from *Paddington*, *via* Hereford, 36/0a, 21/7c. R. T. for two months, 72/0a. From *Euston, via* Shrewsbury, 37/6a, 22/5c. R. T. for two months, 75/0a. Departures *from* London as for Builth Wells. Departures *for* London about 3 times daily. Pop. 217. Map Square 16.

BOUGHTON (Notts) from

King's Cross, 136¼ miles. Fares, 28/1a, 16/10c. R. T. for two months, 56/2a, 33/8c. Departures *from* London as for Edwinstowe. Departures *for* London about 3 times daily. Pop. 269. Map Square 13.

BOULOGNE from Victoria

via Folkestone, 103 miles. Fares, 43/3a, 30/6b, 22/2c. R. T. for two months, 86/5a, 60/11b, 44/3c. Subject to exchange. Map Square 29.

Weekdays and Sundays.

Subject to special Passport regulations.

Leave Vict.	Arr. at B'logne.
AM 9.15	12.45
PM 8. 0	11.55
—	—
—	—

Liable to alteration.

BOULOGNE—*continued.*

Trains from Boulogne.

Leave B'logne.	Arrive at Vict.
PM 12. 0	3.45
7.25	11. 0
—	—
—	—

BOURNE (Lincoln) from

King's Cross, 95¼ miles. Fares, 19/10a, 11/11c. R.T.for two months, 39/8a, 23/10c. Pop. 4,317. Map Square 18.

KING'S+	BOURNE	BOURNE	KING'S +
AM 5. 5	8.50	AM 7.40	10.40
7.15r	10.38	9.25	12.25
8.45s	11.30	11. 0s	1.55
11.30	2.45	PM12.50s	3.50
PM 1.50ry	4.20	1. 0l	3.50
3. 0	5.35	3.28	6.25
5.45r	7.59	4.43r	7.10
—	—	5.58	9. 0
—	—	7.15	3.25
—	—	—	—
—	—	—	—
—	—	—	—

No Sunday Trains.

l Thursdays excepted.
r Restaurant Car.
s Thursdays only.
y Tuesdays and Fridays only.

ANOTHER ROUTE from

St. Pancras, 119¼ miles. No through fares.

ST. PAN.	BOURNE	BOURNE	ST. PAN.
AM 4.25	10.45	AM 8.55r	1.30
8.25r	12. 2	PM12.37r	4.20
10.25r	2.34	4.28	8.20
PM12.25r	4.35	6.28r	10. 5
4.25r	9. 3	—	—
—	—	—	—

No Sunday Trains.

r Restaurant Car.

Angel Hotel. Family and Commercial. Best Provisions. Comfort studied. All trains met. Officially appointed R.A.C., A.A., C.T.C. Good Fishing District. F. W. NASH, Proprietor.

BOURNE END (Bucks)

from *Paddington*, 28¼ miles. Fares, 5/3a, 3/2c. R. T. for two months, 10/6a, 6/4c. Map Square 23.

PAD.	BOURNE E.	BOURNE E.	PAD.
AM 5.45	7.16	AM 8. 8	8.56
6.30	8. 7	8.44	9.37
7.35	8.57	9.28	10.24
8.30	9.52	10. 2	11. 6
9.20	10.33	10.32	11.35
9.55	11. 6	11.18	12.15
11.25	12.26	PM 1.21	2.35
PM12.35e	2. 2	2.30d	3.38
1. 5d	2. 4	3.11	4.10
1.20d	2.24	4.22	5.37
2. 7	3. 7	5.43	6.55
3.38	4.34	6.42	7.45
4.50	5.45	7.50d	9.12
5.45	6.39	8.21	9.53
6.55	7.44	9.34	10.42
8.35	9.34	10.20	12. 0
10. 5	11. 3	—	—
12. 3h	1. 9	—	—
—	—	—	—

BOURNE END—*cont.*

Sunday Trains.

PAD.	BOURNE E.	BOURNE E.	PAD.
AM 8.20	9.44	AM 8.59	10.14
9.45	10.43	11.45	1. 5
10.25	11.17	PM 2.56	4.53
11.45	12.40	5.15	6.23
PM 2.35	3.38	7.38	8.45
5.15	6.18	7.48	9.17
6. 5	8.17	8.30	9.32
8.20	9.25	8.53	9.53
—	—	9.24	10.33
—	—	10. 4	11. 6

d Saturdays only.
e Saturdays excepted.
h Wednesdays and Saturdays only.

Salter's Steamers. Five minutes from station. Passengers ferry out from Townsend's. Up Stream, 11.30 A.M., 5.5 P.M. Down Stream, 11.20 A.M., 4.30 P.M. *See* advt. facing first page of train service.

Townsend Bros. Steam Launch and Boat Builders. Telephone 113. *See* advt. p. **41.**

Auctioneers and Estate Agents. All available houses furnished, unfurnished, or to be sold. Selected lists sent free to applicants stating requirements. HARVEY & CO. (E. S. Binge). 'Phone 66.

BOURNEMOUTH

(Hants) from *Waterloo*, 107½ miles. Fares, Central Station, 22/6a, 13/6c. R.T. for two months, 45/0a, 27/0c. West: Station (*via* Sway), 23/4a, 14/0c. R.T. for two months, 46/8a, 28/0c. *Via* Ringwood, 23/9a, 14/3c. R. T. for two months, 47/6a, 28/6c. Pop. 91,770. Map Square 27.

	Leave	Arrive at
WATERLOO.	B. CENTRAL	B. WEST.
AM 5.40	8.46	9.21
5.50	10.37	—·
8.30s	11.23	11.41
9.30	12.33	12.47
10.30	12.45	1. 3
11.30r	2.16	2.36
PM12.30r	2.45	3. 3
1.30s	4.29	4.43
2.30	4.45	5. 3
3.30s	6.29	6.43
4.30r	6.45	7. 3
5.30r	8.29	8.43
6.30r	8.45	9. 3
7.30	10.56	—
10. 0	2. 0	—
—	—	—

Sunday Trains.

AM11. 0r	1.57	2.10
PM 2. 0r	4.46	5.14
7. 0r	9.56	10.16
9.28	2. 0	—

BOURNEMOUTH—*cont.*

Trains from Bournemouth.

Leave		Arr. at
B. West.	B. Central	W'loo.
AM 7.23r	7.39r	10. 6
8.25s	8.46s	11. 0
9. 4s	9.18s	12.22
10.15r	10.35r	12.50
11. 8r	11.21r	2.20
PM12.15	12.35	2.50
1. 2	1.19	4.20
2.15	2.35	4.50
3. 3s	3.19s	6.26
4.15	4.35	6.58
5. 5r	5.19r	8.20
6.15r	6.35r	8.50
6.50r	7. 5r	10.50
7.35	7.57	11.28
—	11.38	3.58

Sunday Trains.

AM —	8.45	12.11
11. 5r	11.32r	2.27
PM 3.45r	4. 2r	6.24
—	4.15	8. 3
6.45r	7. 2r	9.31
—	7.10	10.52
—	11.38	3.58

n Noon.
r Restaurant Car.
s Refreshments served.

ANOTHER ROUTE (West)

from *Waterloo*, *via* Salisbury. 120 miles. Fares, 23/9a, 14/3c. R. T. for two months, 47/6a, 28/6c

W'loo.	B'm'th	W. W'loo.	B'm'th	W. W'loo.
AM 7.30	11.21	AM 6.30	10. 6
11. 0r	2.41	6.53h	10.56
PM 1. 0r	4.59	10.27r	1.56
3. 0r	6.46	PM 2.30r	6. 0
6. 0r	10.14	3.55r	8.30
—	—	—	—

Sunday Trains.

12. 0nr	5.25	PM 3.53	8.57
—	—	—	—
—	—	—	—
—	—	—	—

h Bournemouth Central Station.
n Noon.
r Restaurant Car.

The "Royal Bath."—
"Bournemouth's foremost Hotel. Unequalled site and a veritable palace by the sea. In its own grounds due south, overlooking Bournemouth's beautiful Bay and Pier." Tatler. En pension terms on application. Garage adjoining. Phone, No. 2873. (Management) Telegrams, "Luxuriate." *See advt.* p. **61.**

Linden Hall Hydro, East
Cliff. Same management 25 years. Position unique. Cuisine excellent. Terms, *see* illustrated advt. pp. **42** and **43.**

BOURNEMOUTH—*cont.*

Hotel Metropole. East Cliff.
Due South. Two hundred rooms. Magnificent Ball - Room. 'Buses meet all trains. Moderate inclusive terms. Fully licensed, and situated on the East Cliff. *See advt.* p. **44.**

Bournemouth Hydropathic.
Sun Lounge, faces Pines and Sea. N.B.—Turkish Baths, Sea Water Plunge, Billiards, Gymnasium and Spa Waters Free. Massage. Electric Baths. Terms moderate. Resident Physician. *See advt.* p. **45.**

Durley Dean Hydro. West
Cliff. Telephone No. 450. Telegrams, "Durley Dean, Bournemouth." Mr. and Mrs. W. J. EVANS. *See advt.* p. **46.**

Hotel Tollard Royal, Cliff
Top. 40 miles of Coast Scenery. Luxurious House. 100 Visitors. Lift.
JOHN A. BUTTERWORTH, Prop. *See advt.* p. **47.**

Bourne Hall Hotel, West
Cliff. A good-class Family Hotel at a reasonable Tariff. 100 Rooms. Lounge. Extensive Grounds. Book Bournemouth West Railway Station. *See advt.* p. **48.**

Priory. South aspect, central
position, near Golf and Tennis. Central Heating. Garage. Telegrams, "Sunny," Bournemouth. Tel. 1851.
Mrs. McDERMOTT, Proprietress. *See advt.* p. **49.**

Osborne. One minute pier
and Winter Gardens. Billiard and Recreation Rooms. Telegrams, "Osprey," Bournemouth. Telephone No. 81.
Mrs. McDERMOTT, Proprietress. *See advt.* p. **50.**

Prince's Hotel. First-class
Private Hotel. Most beautiful part of East Cliff. Enlarged. Redecorated. New Lounge. Electric Light everywhere. Many improvements. Private Garage. *See advt.* p **51.**

Branksome Tower Hotel.
Only Hotel with Grounds extending to Shore. Private Suites. Garage. Golf. *See advt.* p. **52.**

Hawthorns Hotel.—Family
Residential. West Cliff. Garage. 60 Cars. Table d'Hôte. Tel. 1911 (3 lines). Mrs. LANGLEY-TAYLOR, Resident Manager. *See advt.* p. **53.**

BOURNEMOUTH—*cont.*

New Savoy Hotel. Sea front-
age. 100 rooms, full South, and two acres of private gardens facing Bournemouth Bay. Lifts and Garage. Five minutes' walk from piers and the town. 'Phone 2150. *See advt.* p. **54.**

The Hotel Burlington. 200
Rooms. Acres of sheltered pleasure grounds, sloping to pier. Winter garden 200 feet long. Magnificent Links quite close. Garage. *See advt.* p. **55.**

Royal Exeter Hotel. Stands
in own beautiful grounds one minute from Pier, opposite Winter Gardens. Lift. Garage. Tel. 2274. Telegrams, "Excellent, Bournemouth." *See advt.* p. **56.**

Crag Hall. En Pension. West
Cliff; unique position. *See advt.* p. **57.**

Canford Cliffs Hotel. Sea
front, overlooking Bay and entrance to Poole Harbour. Sheltered from east wind by pines. Bracing. Bathing, boating, tennis, croquet. &c. Garage. *See advt.* p. **58.**

Norfolk Hotel. High-class,
luxuriously equipped. Standing in own beautiful grounds Close to Gardens, Pier. Nearly adjoining Links. *See advt.* p. **59.**

Earl's Court. East Cliff
(formerly residence of Earl Cairns). Charming bit of old Bournemouth. In pines. Close to sea. Tel. No. 322. *See advt.* p. **60.**

Meyrick Mansion Private
Residential Hotel de Luxe. Accommodating about 100 visitors. One minute from Pier. Dancing two evenings weekly. *See advt.* p. **62.**

Regina Court. Finest posi-
tion on Sea Front. Facing full South. Private Suites. Garage. Tennis. Central Heating.
C. ASHMAN CARTER. *See advt.* p. **63.**

The Salisbury Hotel. Bos-
combe. Central. Close to Pier, Links, and Gardens. Garage. En pension from £4 10s. per week.
W. J. McCABE, Proprietor. *See advt.* p. **64.**

Imperial Hotel, East Cliff.
Select position in own grounds. Modern Suites. Private Garage. Telegrams "Imperial." Telephone 1599. *See advt.* p. **65.**

Grand Hotel. Unrivalled cen-
tral position, beautiful grounds. Facing south. 200 rooms. Princes Hall for Banquets. Public Meetings. Tel. No. 2000–2001. Garage. *See advt.* p. **65.**

For completion of **Advertisements, see over.**

BOURNEMOUTH.—ROYAL BATH HOTEL. TARIFF: *À la Carte* or inclusive.

BOURNEMOUTH—*cont.*

Tralee. Boarding Establishment. Full South aspect. Fine Sea Views. Every modern convenience. Over fifty Bedrooms. Illustrated Tariff. Proprietress, Mrs. CLARIDGE SHARLAND. *See advt. p. 66.*

Vale Royal, Cliff Foot. Close Pier. Luxurious House. Lift. 100 Visitors. *See advt. p. 66.*

The Chine Hotel, Boscombe. The Grandest Position on East Cliff. Electric lift installed. Telephone 1738 Bournemouth. Manageress, Miss BARNETT. *See advt. p. 67.*

White Hall. Charming position overlooking Public Gardens. Pier one minute. *See advt. p. 67.*

Wimbledon Hall, East Cliff. Thoroughly comfortable Board-Residence. Terms, from 12/- per day. Billiards. Smoke Room. Separate Tables. Fine Lounge. *See advt. p. 68.*

Tarrazona Mansion. Private Residential Hotel. Highest and most bracing position. Inclusive terms. Proprietors, Mr. and Mrs. ERNEST WOOD. *See advt. p. 68.*

Grosvenor. First-class Private Hotel. Standing in own Grounds. *See advt. p. 69.*

Beacon Royal Hotel. West Cliff. First-class Private Hotel in own Grounds facing Sea. Full South. Phone 1186. Telegrams, "Beacon Royal." Proprietress, Miss WATSON, from Knowle Hotel, Sidmouth. *See advt. p. 69.*

Alexandra Private Hotel. Bath Road. Own grounds of one acre. Central for all amusements. Telephone 111. *See advt. p. 70.*

Connaught Court Hotel, West Cliff. Near Winter Gardens. Heated throughout. Miss J. SIEVERS. *See advt. p. 70.*

BOURNEMOUTH—*cont.*

Merton Boarding Establishment. On the East Cliff. Facing South, near Sea and Central Station. *See advt. p. 71.*

Towercliffe Private Hotel. Most comfortable. Close to edge of West Cliff, Gardens, and Pier. Separate tables. Billiards. Electric lift. Artificially warmed throughout. T. & M. WILLIAMS. *See advt. p. 71.*

Central Hotel, The Square. Close to all Places of Amusement. Business Centres, Principal Shops and Sea Front Fully Licensed. *See advt. p. 72.*

The Wharncliffe Private Hotel. East Cliff. Lounge. Billiards. Separate tables. Terms from 63s. Mr. & Mrs. HARRY JOHNSON. *See advt. p. 72.*

"Arnewood" Pension, West Cliff Road. Two minutes from Sea Front. Winter Gardens. Due South. *See advt. p. 73.*

Lammermoor, East Cliff. First-class en pension. Famous for cuisine. *See advt. p. 73.*

Westminster Hall Hotel. En pension or à la carte. Finest position West Cliff. Electric lift. Private suites with communicating Bathrooms. Tel. 1559. Tariff apply— Mrs. REID, Proprietress. *See advt. p. 74.*

The Carlton. High-class Residential Establishment on East Cliff. *See advt. p. 74.*

Meyrick Cliffs Hotel. High Class Pension. West Cliff, overlooking Sea. Tel. 1456. Telegrams, "Meyrick Cliffs, Bournemouth." Resident Proprietors— Mr. and Mrs. TOM MATTOCKS. *See advt. p. 75.*

BOURNEMOUTH—*cont.*

Weston Hall Hotel, West Cliff. 100 Rooms. Delightful Sun Lounge facing Garden and Sea. Tel. 278. Proprietors— R. LAMPLOUGH & SONS. *See advt. p. 75.*

East Anglia en Pension, Poole Road. Own Grounds. 30 Bedrooms. *See advt. p. 76.*

Glenroy Hall, West Cliff. One Minute Sea Front. Billiards. Hard Tennis Court. *See advt. p. 76.*

Solent Cliffs. The Private Hotel with the Premier Position on Sea Front. Proprietor, BRODIE CARPENTER. *See advt. p. 77.*

Oaklands, Private Hotel, West Hill Road. Near Winter Gardens. Gas fires in all bedrooms. Phone 2970. Miss H. E. KEAN. *See advt. p. 77.*

Southlea Private Hotel. Near Pier and Winter Gardens. Private Suites. *See advt. p. 78.*

Charborough Hall. Magnificent position. Every comfort. Renowned Cuisine. *See advt. p. 78.*

The Regent Private Hotel, South Cliff. Overlooking Sea and Pier. Luxuriously equipped. First class Chef. From 3½ Guineas. Tel. 3255. *See advt. p. 79.*

Devonshire House Hotel, Richmond Hill. Close Pier. Gardens, Links. Large Reception rooms. *See advt. p. 79.*

Hotel de Gresley, Southbourne. Family and Residential. Rebuilt. Ballroom. *See advt. p. 80.*

The Hall. 24, Poole Road. To be opened shortly. *See advt. p. 80.*

Pinehurst Private Hotel, West Cliff Gardens. Half minute Sea and Cliff Promenade. Good Table, Cooking and Service. Highly Recommended, Terms moderate. Mr. & Mrs. COOK. *See advt. p. 81.*

Ullswater Private Hotel. West Cliff Gardens. Separate tables. Excellent Cuisine. Gas Fires in all bedrooms. Phone 2364. GYLES. *See advt. p. 81.*

ROYAL BATH HOTEL. Magnificent Sea Frontage. Private Grounds. Due South. **BOURNEMOUTH**

BOURNEMOUTH—*cont.*

Tower House, Private Hotel, West Cliff Gardens. Facing south. Close Winter Gardens and Sea. Billiards. Chef. Also Bay View private suites.
Mr. and Mrs. A. B. LAW.
See advt. p. **81.**

"The Haven," Lansdowne Road. En Pension. Redecorated and refurnished. Conveniently situated for sea and golf. Terms from 3 Guineas. No extras. Tel. 1153. Resident Proprietors—
Mr. and Mrs. L. H. PETERS.
See advt. p. **81.**

Hotel Empress. Overlooks Sea and Pleasure Gardens. For special week-end offer *see* advt. p. **82.**

Woodleigh Tower Private Hotel, Exeter Road. Facing South. Sea View. Gas Fires in all Bedrooms. Terms from 3 guineas inclusive. PROPRIETORS—
Misses DIXON and CHAFFEY.
See advt. p. **82.**

The Beacon Private Hotel. Unique situation on West Cliff, overlooking Pier. Luxuriously Furnished. Tel.1970. Telegrams : "Ferrario, Beacon, Bournemouth."
Mr. and Mrs. FERRARIO.
(Ex-Chef Romano's Restaurant).
See advt. p. **82.**

Gordon Hotel, Southbourne, 2½ miles from Bournemouth. On the Cliffs. Frequent tram service. within 2 minutes of the Hotel.
See advt. p. **82.**

Abbeymount Private Hotel, Priory Road. Sea views. Smoking Lounge. Liberal table. Electric light. Garage.
Mrs. & Miss GREENHILL.
See advt. p. **83.**

Boscombe Spa Hotel. Overlooking Sea and Chine. Two minutes Pier. Moderate. Telegrams : "Spa, Boscombe." Tel. 1147.
See advt. p. **83.**

BOURNEMOUTH—*cont.*

Ottershaw Private Hotel, Priory Road. Full Sea Views. Tel. 280. Garage.
Proprietor, JNO. TAVERNER.
See advt. p. **83.**

Ellerslie Mansions Private Hotel. Central and convenient. Gas Fires in Bedrooms. Moderate.
See advt. p. **83.**

East Cliff House. Finest position on East Cliff. Sea front.
See advt. p. **84.**

Stranorlar, Bath Road, East Cliff. Four minutes from Sea. Garage. Terms from 3 Guineas.
Mr. & Mrs. PERCY DOWDALL.
See advt. p. **84.**

Elcombe Hall, Bath Road. Sea Front. Overlooking Pier. Thoroughly comfortable. From 3 guineas. New Resident Proprietor. Telephone 1543. Apply—
D. R. HARRISS.
See advt. p. **84.**

Karrakatta. En pension. Detached. Beautifully situated. East Cliff. From 3 guineas.
See advt. p. **84.**

Woodcroft Private Hotel. Tennis. Croquet. 2½ acres. Telephone 202.
See advt. p. **85.**

Ravello Hall, Lorne Park. Facing South. Terms from 52/6 per week.
See advt. p. **85.**

The Mansfield, West Cliff Gardens. Ideally situated, three minutes Sea, Pier, Winter Gardens. Central heating. From 3 Guineas. Tel. 2659.
E. CAESAR FLETCHER, Proprietor.
See advt. p. **85.**

Hanover House, St. Peter's Road, Bournemouth. Private Hotel. En Pension.
See advt. p. **85.**

The Paragon Private Boarding House, near the West Station. Beautifully situated on West Cliff; close to Sea. Full size Billiard Table. Terms moderate. (Phone 1075)—Address
Miss K. TOMKINS.

BOURNEMOUTH—*cont.*

Midland Family and Commercial Hotel. Opposite West Station. Midland and South-Western Railways. Special Boarding Terms. Home Comforts. Splendidly-appointed Public and Private Rooms. Apply Manageress.

Silver How Boarding Establishment. West Cliff Gardens. Near Cliff, Winter Gardens, Pier and Golf Links. Electric Light. Terms from 2 Guineas. Phone 976.
Mrs. HUME.

Ben Wyvis. First Class Family Boarding Establishment. The most charming position on West Cliff. Uninterrupted Sea Views. Good Dining and Drawing-Rooms. Lounge. 'Phone, 1877.
Miss BRIANT.

Sydney House, West Cliff. Well-established Boarding House. Unrivalled position, one minute Sea and Winter Gardens. Heated in Winter. Gas Fires in Bedrooms. Separate Tables. Terms moderate. Tel. 2219. Mrs. FREEMAN and Miss SHELLEY.

Staunton House. Facing Pier. Apartments. Good Cooking and Attendance. Lovely Views of Sea and Gardens. Close to Grand Pavilion and Great Pine Walk. Ten minutes from Golf Links. Exeter Park. PROPRIETRESS.

Para, Southern Road, West Southbourne. Board - Residence. Easy access Concerts, Theatre, Trams. Moderate charges.
Misses NEWLYN
(late Exeter Hotel, Bournemouth).

Boscombe Grange, Percy Road. Facing South. Near Links, Cliff Gardens, and Pier. Gas fires in bedrooms. Liberal table. From 3 guineas. Telephone 2131.
Miss RAYSON.

Beechwood, West Cliff. Favourite Boarding Establishment. Highest recommendations. Best position. Close Winter Gardens, Sea, and Pier. Delightful Garden. Splendid view. Moderate Terms. Gas Fires in Bedrooms. Phone 2354.
Mr. and Mrs. CUMBERLAND.

For completion of Advertisements, see over.

BOURNEMOUTH—*cont.*

The Braemar Royal. West Southbourne. One minute from sea. Tel: 111, Southbourne. Telegrams "Welfare" Bournemouth. THE MISSES WILLANS AND FARMER, Proprietors.

Loxley Grange. Landsdowne Road (Central). Electric Light. Billiard Room. Excellent Cuisine. Five minutes Sea. Terms from £3 3s. Phone, 2262. Apply— MANAGERESS.

South Cliff Towers. High-class Private Hotel. Specialises for visitors who appreciate comfort and good food. Moderate tariff. Separate Tables. Sea views. Special arrangements for families, also Winter months. Phone 1972. Miss ELKINGTON Proprietress.

Spa Hotel. Charmingly situated. Overlooking Sea and Chine. Sunny aspect. Near Pier, Shops, and Trams. Moderate charges. Telegrams, "Spa, Boscombe."

Southcliffe Hotel, West Cliff. Delightfully situated, Sea Front. First-class Chef. En Pension Terms. Garage. Phone 156.
Proprietors,
Mr. & Mrs. DUNCAN.

Chine Grange, Chine Crescent. Best part of West Cliff. In own grounds. Tennis Court. Near Sea, all Amusements, and West Station. Quiet at night. Excellent cuisine. Separate tables. Electric light. Under new and experienced management. Terms from 3 guineas. Telephone 3021.

The Grange, Florence Road, Boscombe. Board Residence. South aspect. Badminton. Large Garden. Separate Tables. Near Sea. Golf, Tennis. From 3 Guineas.

"Beauvoir," Marina, Boscombe. Board Residence. Choice position, facing Sea and Pier. Redecorated throughout. Home comforts. Satisfaction guaranteed. Terms moderate.
M. A. HARRIMAN.

House and Estate Agents. Hankinson & Son's illustrated Registers, post free. All available Properties, Bournemouth and Boscombe and district. Phone 1307 (3 lines).

BOURNEMOUTH—*cont.*

House and Estate Agents. Lists of Furnished and Unfurnished Houses for Sale or to Let, with map, sent free. 1, Arcade Chambers, Bournemouth. Telegrams, "Jolliffe, Bournemouth." Telephone, 36 and 199 (Trunk).
JOLLIFFE, FLINT & CROSS.

House and Estate Agents. Auctioneers, Valuers, Surveyors. Illustrated Lists of all available Furnished and Unfurnished Houses with map sent free. Specialists for sale of Hotels, Boarding and Apartment Houses and Businesses. Offices, The Square, Bournemouth. Telegrams: "Riddett & Ede, Auctioneers, Bournemouth." Telephone 127. Established 44 years. RIDDETT & EDE, F.A.I.

Rebbeck Brothers, Estate Agents, Valuers and Auctioneers, Gervis Place, Bournemouth, and County Gates, Westbourne. Phone 298 & 2203. Established 1845.

House and Estate Agents. LANE & SMITH (Established 1875), 81, Old Christchurch Road, Bournemouth. Full particulars by post gratis.

Messrs. Lawrences. Auctioneers and Estate Agents. West Southbourne (now the most popular part of Bournemouth). Map and list of Houses on application.

Leading Agents. Welch & Co., Bournemouth. Established 1893. Specialists for Sale of Boarding and Apartment Houses. Register gratis. Telephone 382.

Rumsey & Rumsey, Auctioneers, Estate Agents. Particulars of all properties free. Head Office, Bournemouth. Branch Offices, Bournemouth West, Canford Cliffs, and West Southbourne.

Fox & Sons, Auctioneers, House Agents and Valuers, 44 to 50, Old Christchurch Road, Bournemouth, and five branch offices.

BOURNVILLE (Worcester), 117½ miles. Fares, 23/11a, 14/4c. R. T. for two months, 47/10a, 28/8c. Departures *from* London as for Birmingham (New Street). Departures *for* London about 6 times daily.

BOURTON-ON-WATER
(Gloucester) from *Paddington*, 91¼ miles. Fares, 19/0a, 11/5c. R. T. for two months, 38/0a, 22/10c. Pop. 1,153.
Map Square 22.

	PAD.	BOURTON	BOURTON	PAD.
AM	5.30	8.55	AM 7.15	9.50
	9.45	1.29	11.21	2.12
PM	1.30	3.28	PM12.44r	2.55
	1.35r	5.20	3.56	7.20
	6. 5r	9. 5	7.46	10.45
	—	—	—	—
	—	—	—	—
	—	—	—	—
	—	—	—	—
	—	—	—	—
	—	—	—	—

No Sunday Trains.
r Restaurant Car.

BOVEY (Devon), 193 miles. Fares, *via* Newton Abbot, 41/1a, 24/8c. R. T. for two months, 82/2a, 49/4c, *via* Ide, 39/9a, 23/10c. R.T. for two months, 79/6a, 47/8c. Departures *from* London as for Moretonhampstead. Departures *for* London about 6 times daily. Pop. 2,809. *Map Square 26.*

BOW (Devon), 187¼ miles. Fares, 39/2a, 23/6c. R. T. for two months, 78/4a, 47/0c. Departures *from* London as for Yeoford. Departures *for* London about 6 times daily. Pop. 569. *Map Square 26.*

BOW from *Broad Street,* 5½ miles. Fares, 0/7½a, 0/6b, 0/4½c. R. T. for two days, 1/3a, 0/10½b, 0/7c. Pop. 40,217. *See* p. 500. *Map Square 62.*

BOWER (Caithness), 717¾ miles. No through fares. Departures *from* London as for Wick. Departures *for* London about twice daily. Pop. 1,172. *Map Square 32.*

BOWES (Yorks), 254¾ miles. Fares, 53/2a, 31/11c. R. T. for two months, 106/4a, 63/10c. Departures *from* London as for Barnard Castle. Departures *for* London about 4 times daily. Pop. 577. *Map Square 7.*

BOWES PARK from *King's Cross,* 5 miles. Fares, 1/0½a, 0/10b, 0/7½c. R. T. for two days, 1/2a, 1/8b, 1/3c. Fares from Moorgate Street and Broad Street, 1/2a, 0/11b, 0/8½c. R. T. for two days, 2/4a, 1/10b, 1/4½c. Pop. 8,013. *See* pp. 511-517.

BOWHOUSE (Stirling), 415¼ miles. No through fares. Departures *from* London as for Edinburgh (Waverley). Departures *for* London about twice daily. *Map Square 40.*

BOWLAND (Midlothian), 367¼ miles. No through fares. Departures *from* London as for Galashiels. Departures *for* London about twice daily. *Map Square 41.*

BOWLING (Dumbarton), 412 miles. Fares, 84/2a, 50/6c. R.T. for two months, 168/4a, 101/0c. Departures *from* London as for Dumbarton. Departures *for* London about 4 times daily. Pop. 1,617. *Map Square 40.*

BOW ROAD from *Fenchurch Street*, 3 miles. Fares, 0/2½a, 0/2b, 0/1½c. R. T. for two days, 0/5a, 0/4b. 0/3c. *See* pp. 528-534, 537-544. *Map Square 62.*

ANOTHER ROUTE
Ealing, Hounslow, Richmond, and *Wimbledon,* via District Railway. *See p. 489.*
Map Square 62, No. 2.

BOW STREET (Cardigan), 235 miles. Fares, 47/9a, 28/8c. R. T. for two months, 95/6a. Departures *from* London as for Machynlleth. Departures *for* London about 5 times daily. *Map Square 16.*

BOX (Wilts) from *Paddington,* 102 miles. Fares, 21/3a, 12/9c. R. T. for two months, 42/6a, 25/6c. Pop. 2,320. *Map Square 22.*

PAD.	BOX	BOX	PAD.
AM 5.30e	8.17	AM 7.20r	10.15
5.30	8.29	9. 3	12.20
7.30	10.14	11.43r	2.40
9. 0	12.14	PM 2.35	6. 2
10.45	2. 8	4.58r	8.35
PM 1.10r	4. 8	6.42	10.25
4.15	6.24	9. 2	2.45
6.30	9. 3	11.12d	2.45
6.55	10.33	—	—

Sunday Trains.

AM10.35	2. 9	PM 1.46	6. 0
PM 2. 0	7.46	—	—

d Saturdays only.
e Saturdays excepted.
r Restaurant Car.

BOXFORD (Berks) from *Paddington,* 57¼ miles. Fares, 12/1a, 7/3c. R. T. for two months, 24/2a, 14/6c. Departures *from* London as for Lambourn. Departures *for* London about 5 times daily. Pop. 516. *Map Square 24.*

BOX HILL (Burford Bridge) (Surrey) from *London Bridge* (L.B. & S.C.R.) 24½ miles. Fares, 4/7a, 2/9c. R. T. for two months, 9/0a, 5/5c. *Map Square 23.*

LON. B	BOX HILL	BOX HILL	LON. B.
AM 5.28	6.42	AM 7. 2	8.13
7.35	9. 7	7.34	8.41
9.22	10.35	7.59	9. 5
10.35	11.50	8.16	9.17
10.47	12.47	8.54	9.47
PM12.24	1.46	9.34	10.22
12.52d	1.54	PM12.16	1.28
1.53d	2.50	2.37	3.55
2. 0	3. 6	4. 4	5.18
3.10e	4.23	4.55e	6.25
3.15d	4.22	5.39	7.13
4. 9	5.15	7.26	8.41
5. 0	5.52	7.55	9.25
5.14	6.12	8.22	9.35
5.59	7. 9	8.52d	10. 8
6.30e	7.31	—	—
6.45d	7.56	—	—
7.30	8.38	—	—

Sunday Trains.

AM 6.55	8. 8	AM 8.43	10.11
9.10	10.29	9.47	11. 8
9.30	10.42	PM 1.32	2.44
10.35	12. 7	2.37	4. 3
PM12.45	2.17	4.27	5.54
1.25	2.48	6.34	8. 8
3.50	5. 8	7.29	8.46
5.40	7. 8	8.37	10. 1
8.27	9.45	8.50	10.22
—	—	9. 6	10.25
—	—	10. 2	11.15

d Saturdays only.
e Saturdays excepted.

BOX HILL (Burford Bridge)—*continued.*

ANOTHER ROUTE from *Victoria* (L.B. & S.C.R.), 23 miles. Fares as above.

VICT.	BOX HILL	BOX HILL	VICT.
AM 5.18	6.42	AM 7. 2	8.32
7.45	9. 7	7.34	8.53
8.58	10.35	7.59	9.12
10.30	11.50	8.16	9.34
11.40	12.47	8.54	9.59
PM12.35	1.46	9.10	10. 4
1.40e	3. 5	9.54	10.28
1.45d	2.50	11.39	12.45
3. 0d	4. 5	PM12.16	1.57
3. 0e	4.23	2.37	4. 0
4. 5	5.14	4. 4	6. 5
4.53	5.52	4.55	6. 8
6. 0	7. 9	5.39	6.45
6.30	7.24	7.12d	8.15
6.42d	7.56	7.26	8.55
7.20	8.38	7.55	9.30
—	—:	8.22e	9.42
—	—:	8.52d	9.57

Sunday Trains.

AM 9. 5	10.29	AM 8.43	10.15
9.10	10.42	9.47	11. 6
11. 3	12. 7	PM 1.32	2.53
PM 1.10	2.17	2.37	3.57
4. 5	5. 8	4.27	5.34
5.40	7. 7	6.34	7.33
8.10	9.45	7.29	8.37
—	—	8.50	9.50
—	—	9. 6	10.42
—	—	10. 2	11.52

d Saturdays only.
e Saturdays excepted.

BOXMOOR (Herts) from *Euston,* 24½ miles. Fares, Euston, 5/0a, 3/0c. R. T. for two months, 10/0a, 6/0c. From Broad Street, 5/5a, 3/3c. R. T. for two months, 10/10a, 6/6c. Pop. 6,540. *Map Square 23.*

	Leave		Arrive at
	EUSTON	BROAD ST.	BOXMOOR
AM 5.25	—	6.37
7.15	6.45	8. 5
7.35	7.10	8.28
8.35	8.15	9.29
9.40	9. 6	10.34
10.50	10.17	11.40
PM 12.15	11.47	1. 1
12.50d	12.20d	1.33
1. 3d	12.43d	1.54
1.10d	1.15d	2.15
1.35d	—	2.27
—	1.35d	2.52
2. 0	1.36e	2.52
2.40d	2. 6d	3.31
4. 2	—	4.37
4.10	3.47	5. 1
4.55e	—	5.29
4.55d	—	5.36
5. 0e	4.50e	5.45
5.20d	4.47d	6.12
5.25e	—	6. 4
5.45e	5.24e	6.19
—	5.22e	6.35
6.10e	—	6.43
6.10d	5. 6d	6.50
—	6. 0e	6.54
6.35	6.15e	7.16
—	6.40e	7.37
—	6.47d	8. 4
7.15	6.50e	8. 4
8. 5	7.36	8.52
9. 5	8.37	9.53
9.55e	9.17e	10.45
9.55d	9.17d	10.50
11.40	10.47	12.20

BOXMOOR—*continued.*
Sunday Trains.

Leave		Arrive at
EUSTON	BROAD ST.	BOXMOOR
AM 8.15	—	9.13
9.23	8.55	10.29
10.23	9.55	11.44
PM 12.53	12.25	2.14
2.15	1.25	3. 0
2.53	2.25	3.57
4.53	4.25	5.59
6.10	5.25	6.59
6.53	6.25	7.57
7.53	7.25	9.14
9.40	9.10	10.28

Trains from Boxmoor.

Leave		Arrive at
BOXMOOR	BROAD ST.	EUSTON
AM 5.59	7.15	7.18
7.30	8.40	8.24
7.54	—	8.38
8. 4	9. 0	8.58
8.17	9.28d	9. 5
8.27e	9.21	—
8.36e	9.40	9.22
8.56	—	9.40
8.58	9.54	9.52
9.42	10.50	10.30
10.48	12. 8	11.40
PM 12.55	2. 8	1.50
2.11	3.38	3. 5
3.32	4.45	4.30
4.20d	5.38	5.21
5.20	6.36	6.15
6.14	7.38	7. 5
6.55	8.15	7.55
7.46	9. 8	8.35
9. 5	10.37	10.10
9.53	11. 5	10.50
10.42	—	11.35

Sunday Trains.

AM 8.25	10. 5	9.22
11. 7	12.35	12.15
PM 12.23	2. 5	1.20
1.39	3. 5	2.44
2.54	4.20	4.14
5.24	6.50	6.44
6.39	8. 5	7.44
7.26	8.50	8.15
8.39	10. 5	—
8.55	10.20	9.45
9.25	10.47	—
9.50	11. 2	10.40

d Saturdays only.
e Saturdays excepted.

BRACEBORO' SPA (Lincoln), from *King's Cross,* 91 miles. Fares, 18/11a, 11/4c. R. T. for two months, 37/10a, 22/8c. Departures *from* London as for Bourne. Departures *for* London about 4 times daily. Pop. 169. *Map Square 18.*

BRACKENHILLS (Ayr), 418½ miles. No through fares. Departures *from* London as for Kilmarnock. Departures *for* London about 5 times daily.

BRACKLEY (Northampton) from *Marylebone*, 59¼ miles. Fares, 12/4a, 7/5c. R. T. for two months, 24/8a, 14/10c. Pop. 2,373. *Map Square* 18.

M'BONE.	BRACK'Y.	BRACK'Y.	M'BONE.
AM 6.45	8.48	AM 7.45	9.46
8.45r	10.10	9.20	10.36
11.15	1.23	10.26	12. 2
PM12.15r	1.37	11.58r	1.13
3.25	5.29	PM 1.47r	3. 0
4.30	5.53	2.51	4.56
4.55	6.52	5.45	7.15
6.20	7.40	7.59	.9.55
6.25e	8.16	9. 5	11. 0
6.25d	8.25	—	—
7.30	9.45	—	—
—	—	—	—

Sunday Trains.

AM 9.30	11.32	AM 7.52	10.13
PM 5.30r	6.50	PM 6.36	8.58
6.30	8.54	—	—
—	—	—	—

d Saturdays only.
e Saturdays excepted.
r Restaurant Car.

BRACKNELL (Berks) from *Waterloo*, 32½ miles. Fares, 6/1a, 3/8c. R. T. for two months, 12/2a, 7/4c. Pop. 2,508. *Map Square* 23.

W'LOO.	B'NELL.	B'NELL.	W'LOO.
AM 5.10	6.55	AM 7. 4	8.17
6.54	8.28	8. 7	9.17
7.54	9.22	8.44	9.47
9.54	11.17	9.11	10.17
10.54	12.22	10. 8	11.17
PM12.48	2. 3	11.12	12.31
1.48	3. 2	PM 1.12	2.27
2.48	4. 3	2.12	3.27
3.48e	5. 2	4.12	5.27
3.48d	5. 7	5.12	6.27
4.48e	5.54	6.12	7.27
4.48d	6. 7	7.12	8.27
5.48	7. 0	8.12	9.27
6.48	8. 0	9.20	10.37
7.54	9.17	10.41e	12. 5
10.24	11.47	10.41d	12. 8
—	—	—	—
—	—	—	—
—	—	—	—

Sunday Trains.

AM 8.18	9.47	AM 8.54	10.30
PM12.18	1.44	PM12.44	2; 3
4.18	5.41	6. 9	7.28
5.58	7.23	8. 9	9.28
9.18	10.45	9.13	10.28
—	—	—	—
—	—	—	—
—	—	—	—

d Saturdays only.
e Saturdays excepted.

BRADBURY (Durham), 242 miles. Fares, 50/7a, 30/4c. R. T. for two months, 101/2a, 60/8c. Departures *from* London as for Darlington. Departures *for* London about 4 times daily. Pop. 229. *Map Square* 7.

BRADFIELD (Essex) from *Liverpool Street*,62½ miles. Fares, 13/2a, 7/11c. R. T. for two months, 26/4a, 15/10c. Departures *from* London as for Mistley. Departures *for* London about 7 times daily. Pop. 787. *Map Square* 19.

BRADFORD (Yorkshire) from *King's Cross*, via Wakefield, 191½ miles. Fares, 39/9a, 23/10c. R. T. for two months, 79/6a, 47/8c. Pop. 285,979. *Map Square* 12.

KING'S+	BRDFD.	BRDFD.	KING'S+
AM 4.45	9.47	AM 7.25r	11.30
7.15r	11.45	8.40	1. 5
10.10r	2.12	9.50r	1.55
11.15k	3. 9	10.12kr	3.50
PM 1.30r	5.26	11.10k	3.15
1.50r	7. 0	11.10r	4.45
4. 0r	8.25	PM12.55r	5. 0
5.45r	9.55	1. 0hr	6.25
10.45e	3.35	3. 0r	7.10
—	—	5.10r	9.25
—	—	10. 5	3.25

Sunday Trains.

12. 0nr	4.52	AM10.35r	3.45
PM 5.0r	9.50	PM12.35	5.5ß
10.45	3.35	5.20r	10.20
—	—	—	—

e Saturdays excepted.
h Via Holbeck.
k First and Third Class Pullman Cars only.
n Noon.
r Restaurant Car.

ANOTHER ROUTE from *St. Pancras*, 208½ miles. Fares as above.

ST. PAN.	BRDFD.	BRDFD.	ST. PAN.
AM 4.25	10.54	AM 1.38	7.25
9. 0r	2.17	7.26r	12.10
9.50r	2.45	9.28r	2.10
PM12.15r	4.45	10.55hr	4.10
1.50r	6.45h	PM12.22r	5.30
3.30r	8.27	2. 2r	6.35
5. 0r	9.55	3.10r	7.57
6.15r	10.52h	4.32r	9.15
9.15d	2.28	8.55	4.20
9.30e	2.48	—	—
11.45e	4.30	—	—
11.45d	5. 0	—	—

Sunday Trains.

AM10.50r	5.50	AM11. 0	5.27
PM 3.15	8.38	PM 3.36	9.43
9.30	2.48	9.25	4.55
11.45	4.30	—	—
—	—	—	—

d Saturdays only.
e Saturdays excepted.
h Exchange Station.
r Restaurant Car.

ANOTHER ROUTE from *Euston*, 215½ miles. Fares as above.

EUSTON	BRDFD.	BRDFD.	EUSTON
AM12.25	8.21	AM 5.10e	12. 5
2.35	10.49	5.48r	12.50
5. 0	1.12	7.55r	1.15
8.45r	2.54	8.15r	1.45
10.40r	3.58	8.50r	3.10
11.50r	5.50	9.17dr	3.55
12. 0nr	7. 9	9.40er	3.55
PM 1.30r	8.41	10.42dt	5.50
2.50t	9. 6	11. 0dt	6. 0
4. 5r	9.29	PM12.40et	6. 0
6. 5r	11. 2	12.40dt	6.15
9.30e	6.38	12.45r	7.30
11.50d	10.41	2.36r	8.10
—	—	3.10r	10. 0
—	—	3.57er	10.10
—	—	7.32	5. 0
—	—	8.57	5.40
—	—	9.50	5.50
—	—	—	—
—	—	—	—
—	—	—	—

BRADFORD—*continued.*

Sunday Trains.

EUSTON	BRDFD.	BRDFD.	EUSTON
PM12.10r	6.36	AM11. 0r	5.45
12.30r	8.38	11.23r	7.30
9.15	6.38	PM 2.36r	8.55
—	—	7. 0	5. 0
—	—	9.10	5.50
—	—	—	—

d Saturdays only.
e Saturdays excepted.
n Noon.
r Restaurant Car.
t Tea Car.

ANOTHER ROUTE from *Marylebone*, 203½ miles. Fares as above.

M'BONE.	BRDFD.	BRDFD.	M'BONE.
AM 2.32	8.49	AM 7. 8r	1.13
10. 0r	2.55	10. 0r	3. 0
PM12.15r	6.26	PM 1.40r	6.38
3.20r	8.33	5. 0r	9.55
6.20r	11.17	9.15	3.57
—	—	—	—
—	—	—	—
—	—	—	—

Sunday Trains.

AM11.15r	9.49	PM 3.55r	10.24
PM 5.30r	11.10	—	—
—	—	—	—
—	—	—	—

r Restaurant Car.

Midland Hotel. Adjoining Midland Station. Convenient and comfortable Restaurant and Grill Room One 'of the "Midland Hotels.
ARTHUR TOWLE, Manager.
See advt. p. **86.**

Great Northern Victoria Hotel. This Hotel adjoins the Exchange Station. Re-decorated and re-furnished. Well appointed Restaurant and Grill Room, Stock Rooms and Billiard Room. Electric Lift. Excellent Cuisine. Telegraphic address: Northness, Bradford. Telephone: Local, Bradford 81; Trunk, 1356.

BRADFORD-ON-AVON (Wilts), from *Paddington*, 97½ miles. Fares, via Trowbridge, 20/7a, 12/4c. R. T. for two months, 41/2a,-24/8c. Pop. 4,621. *Map Square* 22.

PAD.	B.-ON-AVON	B.-ON-AVON	PAD.
AM 1. 0g	7.19	AM 6.48	10. 0
5.30	9. 9	10.11k	12.55
7.30	11.24	10.54r	2:40
10.30k	12.54	11.24	3.20
10.45	2.11	PM 2.12	6. 2
PM12. 5k	2.35	3. 6	6.50
12.30kr	3.43	5. 0k	8.20
2.45	5.54	6.59	10.25
3.30k	6.12	9.24	2.45
4.15t	7.15	—	—
5. 5k	8.26	—	—
6.30	9.50	—	—
—	—	—	—

Sunday Trains.

AM 9.10	1.18	AM10.52	3.35
PM12.30	4.29	PM 4.12kr	7.55
2.40k	6.29	—	—
—	—	—	—

g Mondays excepted.
k Via Westbury.
r Restaurant Car.
t Tea Car.

BRADFORD-ON-AVON —continued.

ANOTHER ROUTE from *Paddington, via Bath,* 116½ miles. Fares, 22/6a, 13/6c. R. T. for two months, 45/0a, 27/0c.

PAD.	B.-ON-AVON.	B.-ON-AVON.	PAD.
AM 5.30	9. 2	AM 7.19r	10.15
7.30	10.54	8.52	11.30
9. 0	12. 7	9. 9	12.20
11.15	1.29	10.30r	2.40
PM 1.10r	4.46	11.24	3.20
2.45	6.12	PM12.54	4. 5
4.15r	6.59	2.35	6. 2
5. 0r	8. 7	5.12r	8.45
6.30r	9.24	7.15	10.25
6.55	11.32	9.49	2.45
12. 0k	6.48	10.45l	2.45
12.30h	10.52	—	—

Sunday Trains.

PM12.30r	4.12	PM 1.18	7.55
10. 0	6.48	4.29	8.10
—	—	6.29	3.15

h Saturday midnight only.
k Saturday midnight excepted.
l Mondays and Saturdays only
r Restaurant Car.

BRADING (Isle of Wight),
83½ miles. Fares, 18/7a, 11/4c. R.T. for two months, 37/2a, 22/8c. Departures *from* London as for Ryde. Departures *for* London about 5 times daily. Pop. 1,563.
Map Square 28.

BRADLEY (Yorks), 206
miles. Fares, 37/9a, 22/8c. R. T. for two months, 75/6a, 45/4c. Departures *from* London as for Huddersfield. Departures *for* London about 8 times daily. Pop. 1,611.
Map Square 12.

BRADLEY FOLD (Lancs),
196½ miles. Fares, 40/7a, 24/4c. R. T. for two months, 81/2a, 48/8c. Departures *from* London as for Manchester. Departures *for* London about 5 times daily.

BRADNOP (Stafford), 155½
miles. No through fares. Departures *from* London as for Leek. Departures *for* London about 5 times daily. Pop. 432.
Map Square 12.

BRADWELL (Bucks), 53½
miles. Fares, 11/1a, 6/8c. R. T. for two months, 22/2a, 13/4c. Departures *from* London as for Newport Pagnell. Departures *for* London about 8 times daily. Pop. 3,938.
Map Square 18.

BRAEMAR (Aberdeen).
Station at Ballater, and thence by road motor about 18 miles. Pop. 502.
Map Square 38.

Braemar Fife Arms Hotel,
near Balmoral. Principal Hotel. Golf. Garage. Telephone No. 14, Braemar. Proprietor.

BRAFFERTON (Yorks),
206½ miles. Fares, 43/1a, 25/10c. R. T. for two months, 86/2a, 51/8c. Departures *from* London as for Harrogate or York. Departures *for* London about 3 times daily. Pop. 231.
Map Square 8.

BRAIDWOOD (Lanark),
379½ miles. Fares, 77/4a, 46/5c. R.T. for two months, 154/8a, 92/10c. Departures *from* London as for Carstairs. Departures *for* London about 3 times daily.
Map Square 40

BRAINTREE (Essex) from
Liverpool Street, via Witham, 45 miles. Fares, 9/7a, 5/9c. R. T. for two months, 19/2a, 11/6c. Pop. 6,980.
Map Square 19.

L'PL.ST.	BRAINT.	BRAINT.	L'PL.ST.
AM 5. 0	7. 2	AM 7.48	9.30
8.15	9.42	8.52	10.22
8.46	10.40	9.44	11.16
11.30	12.52	11.29	1.16
PM 2.15k	3.41	PM 1.25	3.13
2.15h	4.10	1.52h	3.36
3.26	5.11	4.16	5.48
4.58	6.20	5.30	7.40
6.39	8.11	7. 9	9.17
—	—	—	—

Sunday Trains.

AM 8.15	10. 9	AM 9. 5	11.15
10. 5	11.33	10.30	12.40
PM 3.40	5.19	PM 4.30	7.10
6.15	8.11	7. 5	8.58

h Fridays only.
k Fridays excepted.

ANOTHER ROUTE from
Liverpool Street, via Bishop's Stortford, 48¼ miles. Fares as above.

L'PL.ST.	BRAINT.	BRAINT.	L'PL.ST.
AM 7.18	9.40	AM 7.34	9.27
9.10	11.26	9.45	11.27
11.50h	1.42	11.41k	2. 7
PM12.29d	2.28	PM 2.24l	5. 9
2.34	4.12	2.30s	5. 9
4.45	6.23	4.14	6.10
6.30	8.15	6.24	8.22

No Sunday Trains.

d Saturdays only.
h Wednesdays and Thursdays only.
k Wednesdays, Thursdays and Saturdays only.
l Mondays and Tuesdays only.
s Mondays and Tuesdays excepted.

White Hart Hotel. — Telephone 48. In centre of town. Electric Light. Billiards. Garage. TRUST HOUSES, Ltd.

Horn Hotel. Family and Commercial. Trade Dinners and Banquets to any number. Motors and Carriages of every description for hire. Bus meets all trains. Under personal supervision of Oswald Trigg. Phone 37 Braintree. Manager, J. W. BARKWITH.

BRAITHWAITE (Cumberland), 301¼ miles. Fares, 60/8a, 36/5c. R.T. for two months, 121/4a, 72/10c. Departures *from* London as for Keswick. Departures *for* London about 5 times daily.
Map Square 6.

BRAMBER (Sussex), 53¾
miles. Fares from London Bridge or Victoria, 11/3a, 6/9c. R. T. for two months, 22/6a, 13/6c. Departures *from* London as for Henfield. Departures *for* London about 12 minutes earlier. Pop. 213.
Map Square 28.

BRAMFORD (Suffolk)
from *Liverpool Street,* 71½ miles. Fares, 15/0a, 9/0c. R. T. for two months, 30/0a, 18/0c. Pop. 1,281.
Map Square 19.

L'PL.ST	BRAM.	BRAM.	L'PL.ST.
AM 5. 0	9. 6	AM 8.32r	10.30
10.12	12.14	9.22r	11.22
PM12.33r	2.28	PM12. 9r	2. 3
1. 0	4.29	1. 1	3.36
1.33d	4.29	3.45	5.55
3.26	6.20	4.22	6.32
5.18r	7.16	5.34	7.51
5.42	8.21	6.28r	9.22
7.45r	9.58	8.42	11.16
—	—	—	—

Sunday Trains.

AM 9.20r	11.36	AM 9. 4	11.38
11.30r	2.31	PM 2.52	7.10
PM 4.40	6.32	7. 6r	9.10
—	—	8. 3	10.15

d Saturdays only.
r Restaurant Car.

BRAMHALL (Cheshire),
173½ miles. Fares, 36/1a, 21/8c. R. T. for two months, 72/2a 43/4c. Departures *from* London as for Cheadle Hulme or Macclesfield. Departures *for* London about 6 times daily. Pop. 2,337.
Map Square 12.

BRAMLEY (Hants) from
Paddington, 46½ miles. Fares, 9/9a, 5/10c. R. T. for two months, 19/6a, 11/8c. Pop. 417.
Map Square 23.

PAD.	BRAM.	BRAM.	PAD.
AM 7.30	8.49	AM 7.50	9. 0
9. 0	10.17	8. 9	9.30
9.45	11.36	9.16	10.45
11.20	12.38	9.48	11.35
PM12.30	2.12	11.34	12.55
1.10dr	2.39	PM12.31	1.50
1.35r	3.34	1.41	3.20
3.18	5.18	3.16d	4.35
4. 8	5.44	3.40	5. 6
5.15	6.37	4.47	6. 2
6. 5	7.18	6. 6	7.20
7.30	8.59	6.54	8.20
9.15k	10.40	9.28	10.45
10. 0h	11.25	11.41d	2.45
—	—	—	—

Sunday Trains.

AM 9.1C	11. 0	AM10.21	1. 5
PM 4.45	6.48	PM12. 6	2.40
—	—	8. 2	9.48

d Saturdays only.
h Thursdays and Saturdays only.
k Fridays and Saturdays only.
r Restaurant Car.

BRAMLEY (Surrey) from
Waterloo, 33½ miles. Fares, 7/1a, 4/3c. R. T. for two months, 14/2a. Departures *from* London as for Cranleigh. Departures *for* London about 6 times daily. Pop. 2,006.
Map Square 23.

BRAMLEY—*continued.*

ANOTHER ROUTE from *Victoria, Clapham Junction,* and *London Bridge, via* Horsham, 53¾ miles. Fares from London Bridge or Victoria 8/1*a*, 4/10*c*. R. T. for two months, 16/2*a*. Departures *from* London as for Cranleigh. Departures *for* London about 6 times daily.

Ye Olde Grantley Arms Hotel, Wonersh. Short distance from Bramley Station. Central heating. Moderate charges. 'Phone 51 Bramley.
CATERING HOUSES, LTD.

BRAMLEY (Yorks), 187¼ miles. Fares, 39/0*a*, 23/5*c*. R. T. for two months, 78/0*a*, 46/10*c*. Departures *from* London as for Holbeck. Departures *for* London about 8 times daily. Pop. 12,426.

BRAMPFORD SPEKE (Devon), 171 miles. Fares, 21/11*c*. R. T. for two months, 73/0*a*, 43/10*c*. Departures *from* London as for Exeter (St. Davids). Departures *for* London about 4 times daily. Pop. 296.
Map Square 26.

BRAMPTON (Suffolk), 104¾ miles. Fares, 21/11*a*, 13/2*c*. R. T. for two months, 43/10*a*, 26/4*c*. Departures *from* London as for Halesworth. Departures *for* London about 3 times daily. Pop. 315.
Map Square 19.

BRAMPTON JUNCT. (Cumberland), 310 miles. Fares, 60/10*a*, 36/6*c*. R. T. for two months, 121/8*a*, 73/0*c*. Departures *from* London as for Carlisle or Hexham. Departures *for* London about 7 times daily. Pop. 2,392.
Map Square 8.

BRANCEPETH (Durham), 261¼ miles. Fares, 53/11*a*, 32/4*c*. R. T. for two months, 107/10*a*, 64/8*c*. Departures *from* London as for Bishop Auckland. Departures *for* London about 5 times daily. Pop. 384.
Map Square 7.

BRANDON (Suffolk) from *Liverpool Street*, 86½ miles. Fares, 18/2*a*, 10/11*c*. R.T. for two months, 36/4*a*, 21/10*c*. Pop. 2,409.
Map Square 19.

L'PL. ST.	BRAND.	BRAND.	L'PL. ST
AM 5. 5	7.30	AM 7.53*r*	10.23
5.50	8.19	8.52	11.27
7.18*d*	10.42	10. 8	12.40
8.30*r*	11.14	11.48*r*	2.21
11.50*r*	2.16	PM 2.58*r*	5.17
PM 2.34	4.53	5.42*r*	8.22
5.49*r*	8.20	6. 8*r*	8.33
7.10*r*	9.27	11.51	2.50
10.12	12.45	—	—

Sunday Trains.

AM 9.25	12.26	PM 3.49	6.40
PM 3.25	6.16	7.24	9.40
9.12	12.43	11.51	3. 0

d Saturdays only.
r Restaurant Car.

BRANDON (Warwick) from

Euston, 89 miles. Fares, 18/7*a*, 11/2*c*. R. T. for two months, 37/2*a*, 22/4*c*. Pop. 398.
Map Square 18.

EUSTON	BRAND.	BRAND.	EUSTON
AM 5. 0	7. 6	AM 6.49*r*	10. 0
6.45	9.14	10.54*r*	1. 0
10. 0	12.14	PM12.50*d*	4.15
12. 0*nr*	2.24	2.45	5.35
PM 2.50*t*	5. 2	4.41*t*	7.20
4.45*r*	7.53	6.30*r*	9.20
12.10*dm*9. 6	7.53*dr*10.45		
—	—	8.56*er*10.45	
—	—	10.22*c*	4. 0
—	—	10.22*d*	5. 0

Sunday Trains.

AM 9.15	12.24	AM 9.45	12.25
PM 3.50	7. 6	PM 2.19	5. 5
—	—	6.19*r*	8.20
—	—	9.54	5. 0

d Saturdays only.
e Saturdays excepted.
m Midnight.
n Noon.
r Restaurant Car.
t Tea Car.

BRANKSOME (Dorset)

from *Waterloo, via* Southampton, 110 miles. Fares, *via* Sway, 23/1*a*, 13/10*c*. R. T. for two months, 46/2*a*, 27/8*c*. *Via* Ringwood, 23/9*a*, 14/3*c*. R. T. for two months, 47/6*a*, 28/6*c*. Pop. 5,774.

W'LOO.	BRANK.	BRANK.	W'LOO.
AM 5.40	9.28	AM 7.17*r*	10. 6
5.50	10.52	8.15*s*	11. 0
8.30*s*	12.23	8.22*s*	12.22
9.30	12.58	10. 5*r*	12.50
10.30	1.18	10.50*r*	2.20
PM12.30*r*	3. 7	PM12. 5	2.50
2.30*s*	5. 7	1. 0	4.20
3.30	6.33	2. 5	4.50
4.30*r*	7.11	2.44*s*	6.26
5.30	8.43	4. 4	6.58
6.30*r*	9..7	4.55*r*	8.20
—	—	6. 7*r*	8.50
—	—	6.42	10.50
—	—	7.29	11.28
—	—	10.26	3.58

Sunday Trains.

AM11. 0*r*	2.12	AM 8.32	12.11
PM 2. 0*r*	5. 4	11.13*r*	2.27
7. 0*r*	10.10	PM 3.42*r*	6.24
—	—	6.42*r*	9.31

r Restaurant Car.
s Refreshments served.

ANOTHER ROUTE from *Waterloo, via Salisbury,* 118¾ miles. Fares, 23/9*a*, 14/3*c*. R. T. for two months, 47/6*a*, 28/6*c*.

W'LOO.	BRANK.	BRANK.	W'LOO.
AM 7.30	11.17	AM 6.34	10.56
11. 0*r*	2.57	10.31*r*	1.56
PM 1. 0*r*	4.55	PM 2.34*r*	6. 0
3. 0*r*	6.42	3.59*r*	5.30
6. 0*r*	10.10	—	—

Sunday Trains.

12. 0*nr*	5.21	PM 3.57	8.57

n Noon.
r Restaurant Car.

BRANSFORD ROAD

(Worcester), 124½ miles. Fares, 24/7*a*, 14/9*c*. R. T. for two months, 49/2*a*, 29/6*c*. Departures *from* London as for Worcester. Departures *for* London about 8 times daily. Pop. (Bransford) 263.
Map Square 17.

BRANSTON (Lincoln),

127½ miles. Fares, 26/6*a*, 15/11*c*. R.T. for two months, 53/0*a*, 31/10*c*. Departures *from* London as for Blankney. Departures *for* London about 4 times daily. Pop. 1,324.
Map Square 13.

BRANSTON (Stafford),

127½ miles. Fares, 25/8*a*, 15/5*c*. R. T. for two months, 51/4*a*, 30/10*c*. Departures *from* London as for Burton-on-Trent. Departures *for* London about 4 times daily. Pop. 801.
Map Square 17

BRANTHWAITE (Cumberland),

310 miles. No through fares. Departures *from* London as for Moor Row or Cockermouth. Departures *for* London about 3 times daily.
Map Square 6.

BRASTED (Kent) from

Charing Cross, Cannon Street and *London Bridge,* 24⅜ miles. Fares, 4/10*a*, 3/11*b*, 2/11*c*. R. T. for two months, 9/8*a*, 7/10*b*. Pop. 1,327.
Map Square 24.

		Leave		Arrive
CHAR. +	CAN. ST.	LON. B.	BRASTED
AM —	5.20	5.25	6.48
—	6.45	6.50	8.26
—	7.56	8. 0	9. 8
9.38	—	9.45	11. 8
11.15	—	11.23	12.48
PM —	1.12*d*	1.15*d*	2. 8
2.17*d*	—	2.23*d*	3.23
3.50	—	3.57	5. 0
4.55*d*	—	5. 1*d*	6. 6
—	5. 4*e*	5. 7*e*	6. 6
5.35*d*	—	5.41*d*	6.40
—	5.44*e*	5.47*e*	6.53
6.34*e*	—	6.41*e*	7.24
7.18	—	7.26	8.24
9. 0	—	9. 6	10. 3
10.45*l*	—	10.51*l*	11.46
11.45*h*	—	—	12.38

Sunday Trains.

AM 8. 5	—	8.12	9.28
11.15	—	11.23	12.30
PM —	1. 7*k*	—	2.28
3. 5	—	3.13	4.18
6. 0	—	6. 6	7.18

BRASTED—*continued.*

Trains from Brasted.

Leave BRASTED	Arrive at		
	LON. B.	CAN. ST.	CHAR. +
AM 7.10	8. 9	—	8.19
7.45	8.40	8.44	—
8.44	9.40	9.44	—
9.43	10.28	10.32	—
10.43	11.32	—	11.44
PM12. 3	1.27	—	1.38
1.43	3. 7	—	3.19
3.53	4.40	—	4.53
5.15d	6.30	—	6.39
5.28e	6.44	—	6.54
7.48	8.54	9. 1	—
9.18	10.15	—	10.23
10.37l	11.34	—	11.44

Sunday Trains.

AM 8.51	10. 5	—	10.15
10.53	11.49	—	12. 0
PM12.50k	—	2.11k	—
5.23	6.27	—	6.41
7.53	9. 7	—	9.18
8.33	9.38	—	—
9.23k	—	10.54k	—
—	—	—	—

d Saturdays only.
e Saturdays excepted.
h Mondays and Thursdays only.
k Departs from or arrives at Victoria (S.E. & C.).
l Wednesdays only.

BRATTON FLEMING

(Devon), 197 miles. Fares, 40/10a, 24/6c. R. T. for two months, 81/8a, 49/0c. Departures *from* London as for Lynton. Departures *for* London about twice daily. Pop. 480.
Map Square 21.

BRAUGHING (Herts) from

Liverpool Street, 30½ miles. Fares, 6/6a, 3/11c. R. T. for two months, 13/0a, 7/10c. Departures *from* London as for Buntingford. Departures *for* London about 10 times daily. Pop. 928.
Map Square 18.

BRAUNSTON (North-

ampton) from *Euston*, 76½ miles. Fares, 16/0a, 9/7c. R. T. for two months, 32/0a, 19/2c. Pop. 1,059.
Map Square 18.

EUSTON	BRAUN.	BRAUN.	EUSTON
AM 6.45	9.28	AM 7.43	10.15
9.30	12.42	10. 2d	12.20
PM 2. 0	5.32	10. 2e	12.32
7. 0	9. 9	PM 3.42	6.25
—	—	7. 3c	10.10
—	—	7. 3d	10.50
—	—	11.17d	5.45

No Sunday Trains.

d Saturdays only.
e Saturdays excepted.

BRAUNSTON & WIL-

LOUGHBY (Northampton) from *Marylebone*, 78½ miles. Fares, 16/0a, 9/7c. R. T. for two months, 32/0a, 19/2c. Pop. 1,059.
Map Square 18.

M'BONE	BRAUN.	BRAUN.	M'BONE
AM 6.45	9.32	AM 5.57	9.46
PM12.15r	2.29	8.14	10.36
4.30	6.56	9.21	12. 2
6.25e	9. 2	PM 2. 8	4.56
6.25d	9.12	6. 0r	8.55
—	—	7.41r	9.55

BRAUNSTON & WIL-

LOUGHBY—*continued.*

Sunday Trains.

M'BONE	BRAUN.	BRAUN.	M'BONE
AM 9.30	12.15	AM 7. 5	10.13
PM 6.30	9.38	PM 5.50	8.58

d Saturdays only.
e Saturdays excepted.
r Restaurant Car.

BRAUNTON (Devon) from

Waterloo, 217½ miles. Fares, 40/3a, 24/2c. R. T. for two months, 80/6a. 48/4c. Pop. 2,328.
Map Square 21.

W'LOO.	BRAUN.	BRAUN.	W'LOO.
AM 9. 0r	3.10	AM 8.23r	1.56
11. 0r	4.18	10.35r	3.50
PM 1. 0r	7. 1	PM12.30r	6. 0
3. 0	8. 2	1.14	7.40
—	—	1.49r	8.30
—	—	3.29	10.50
—	—	4.50h	3.58

No Sunday Trains.

h Via Eastleigh.
r Restaurant Car.

ANOTHER ROUTE from

Paddington, via Taunton and Barnstaple, 194½ miles. Fares as above.

PAD.	BRAUN.	BRAUN.	PAD.
AM 5.30	1.52	AM 8.23r	1.30
9.15	2.45	9.55	4. 5
PM12. 5r	5.39	PM12.11t	5.30
2. 0r	8. 5	3.10r	9. 0
3.30	8.26	4.50	2.45
12. 0h	10.49	7.46	7.10

Sunday Trains.

PM10. 0	10.49	—	—

h Saturdays midnight excepted.
r Restaurant Car.
t Tea Car.

BRAYSTONES (Cumber-

land), 294½ miles. No through fares. Departures *from* London as for Sellafield. Departures *for* London about 3 times daily.
Map Square 6.

BRAYTON (Cumberland),

317½ miles. Fares, 64/4a, 38/7c. R. T. for two months, 128/8a, 77/2c. Departures *from* London as for Maryport. Departures *for* London about 6 times daily.
Map Square 6.

BREADSALL (Derby), 143½

miles. Fares, 26/6a, 15/11c. R. T. for two months, 53/0a, 31/10c. Departures *from* London as for Derby (Friar Gate). Departures *for* London about 5 times daily. Pop. 524.
Map Square 12.

BREAMORE (Hants) from

Waterloo, 93½ miles. Fares, 20/0a, 12/0c. R. T. for two months, 40/0a, 24/0c. Pop. 505.
Map Square 22.

W'LOO.	BREA.	BREA.	W'LOO.
AM 7.30	10. 7	AM 8.10	10.56
11. 0r	1.29	8.49r	11.10
PM 1. 0r	3.37	11.38r	1.56
3. 0r	5.20	PM 3.39r	6. 0
6. 0r	8.55	5.34r	8.30
—	—	—	—

Sunday Trains.

12. 0nr	3.25	PM 5.12	8.57

n Noon.
r Restaurant Car.

BRECHIN (Forfar) from

Euston, 496½ miles. Fares, 97/6a, 58/6c. R. T. for two months, 195/0a, 117/0c. Pop. 8,781.
Map Square 38.

EUSTON	BRECH.	BRECH.	EUSTON
AM 5. 0	8. 8	AM 7.10r	7.30l
10. 0r	9.26	10.35r	10.45l
PM 7.50er	6.53	PM 1.25r	5. 0h
11.35e	10.47	8.30	8. 0
—	—	—	—

Sunday Trains.

PM 7.50r	6.53	—	—
11.35	10.47	—	—

e Saturdays excepted.
h A.M.
l P.M.
r Restaurant Car.

BRECON (Brecknock) from

Paddington, via Hereford and L. M. & S. Rly., 182½ miles. Fares, 37/9a, 22/8c. R. T. for two months, 75/6a, 45/4c. Pop. 5,649.
Map Square 16.

PAD.	BRECON.	BRECON	PAD.
AM 1. 0g	11.10	AM 7. 0r	2.40
5.30	2.35	10.30hr	4.15
10.45	5.38	PM 1.10r	8.35
PM 4.45ht	10.18	6. 0	3.30
—	—	—	—

Sunday Trains.

PM 9.15	11.10	—	—

g Mondays excepted.
h Via Worcester.
r Restaurant Car.
t Tea Car.

ANOTHER ROUTE from

Paddington, via Newport, 201½ miles. Fares as above.

PAD.	BRECON	BRECON	PAD.
AM 1. 0g	11. 0	AM 7.35r	1. 0
5.30	1.40	12. 0r	6.15
11.50r	5.30	PM 2. 5r	8.35
PM 3.35r	9.15	6. 8	3.30
—	—	—	—

Sunday Trains.

PM 9.15	11. 0	—	—

g Mondays excepted.
r Restaurant Car.

ANOTHER ROUTE from

Euston, 247½ miles. Fares *via* Craven Arms, 37/9a, 22/8c. R. T. for two months, 75/6a. *Via* Whitchurch or Welshpool, 41/5a, 24/10c. R. T. for two months, 82/10a.

EUSTON BRECON		BRECON EUSTON	
AM 5. 0	2.25	AM 7.15hr	3.10
6.45	5.12	10.40ry	6.15
10.40r	6.28	PM 1.20dr	9.15
PM 1.15r	8.15	1.20er	9.20
9 20eh	7.40	5.10	5. 0l

Sunday Trains.

PM 9.15	7.40	—	—

e Saturdays excepted.
h Via Welshpool.
l A.M.
r Restaurant Car.
y Via Crewe.

BREDBURY (Cheshire) 179½ miles. Fares, 37/1*a*, 22/3*c*. R. T. for two months, 74/2*a*, 44/6*c*. Departures *from* London as for Marple. Departures *for* London about 6 times daily. Pop. 5,785.

BREDON (Worcester) from *Euston*, 149 miles. No through fares. Departures *from* London as for Worcester. Departures *for* London about 4 times daily. Pop. 1,059.
Map Square 17.

BREICH (Midlothian), 397¼ miles. No through fares. Departures *from* London as for Wishaw (Central). Departures *for* London about 3 times daily.
Map Square 40.

BRENT (Devon) from *Paddington*, 209½ miles. Fares, 43/2*a*, 25/11*c*. R.T. for two months, 86/4*a*, 51/10*c*. Pop. (South Brent) 1,624.
Map Square 26.

Pad.	Brent.	Brent.	Pad.
AM 5.30	11.50	AM 8.23*r*	1.30
9.15*r*	3.27	PM12.21*r*	4.35
11. 0*dr*	2.56	1.23*er*	6.50
11.10*r*	3.49	1.23*dr*	7. 5
PM12. 5*r*	5. 0	3.34*r*	9. 0
3.30*r*	8.16	5.15	2.45
12. 0*k*	8. 9	10. 5	7.10
12.30*h*	11.18	—	—
—	—	—	—
—	—	—	—
—	—	—	—
—	—	—	—
—	—	—	—
—	—	—	—
—	—	—	—

Sunday Trains.

AM10.30*r*	4.28	AM 7.42*r*	3.35
PM 2.40	8.59	PM 6.31	3.15
10. 0	8. 9	—	—
—	—	—	—
—	—	—	—
—	—	—	—
—	—	—	—
—	—	—	—

d Saturdays only.
e Saturdays excepted.
h Saturdays midnight only.
k Saturdays midnight excepted.
r Restaurant Car.

BRENTFORD (Middlesex) from *Waterloo*, 10¾ miles. Fares, *via* Barnes, 1/0*a*, 0/7*c*. R. T. for two days, 1/9*a*, 1/2*c*. Pop. 17,032. *See* p. 586.
Map Square 67.

ANOTHER ROUTE from *Paddington*, 12¾ miles. Fares, 1/10½*a*, 1/1½*c*. R. T. for two days, 3/9*a*, 2/3*c*. *See* pp. 491-493.

BRENTHAM (for North Ealing) from *Paddington*, 5½ miles. Fares, 0/7*c*. R. T. for two days, 1/0*c*. *See* pp. 490, 491.
Map Square 58.

BRENT-KNOLL (Somerset) from *Paddington*, 141¾ miles. Fares, 29/7*a*, 17/9*c*. R. T. for two months, 59/2*a*, 35/6*c*. Departures *from* London as for Yatton. Departures *for* London about 4 times daily. Pop. 803.
Map Square 22.

BRENTOR (Devon), 208¾ miles. Fares, 43/6*a*, 26/1*c*. R. T. for two months, 87/0*a*, 52/2*c*. Departures *from* London as for Lydford. Departures *for* London about 3 times daily. Pop. 507.
Map Square 23.

BRENTWOOD (Essex) from *Liverpool Street*, 18¼ miles. Fares, 3/9*a*, 3/0*b*, 2/3*c*. R. T. for two months, 7/6*a*, 6/0*b*, 4/6*c*. Pop. 6,870. *See* pp. 528-534.
Map Square 24.

BRETTELL LANE (Stafford), 124 miles. Fares, 25/3*a*, 15/2*c*. R. T. for two months, 50/6*a*, 30/4*c*. Departures *from* London as for Stourbridge Junction. Departures *for* London about 6 times daily.
Map Square 17.

BRICKETWOOD (Herts) from *Euston*, 20¾ miles. Fares, 4/0*a*, 2/5*c*. R. T. for two months, 8/0*a*, 4/8*c*. Departures *from* London as for St. Albans. Departures *for* London about 14 times daily.
Map Square 23.

BRIDESTOWE (Devon) 204¾ miles. Fares, 42/6*a*, 25/6*c*. R. T. for two months, 85/0*a*, 51/0*c*. Departures *from* London as for Okehampton. Departures *for* London about 4 times daily. Pop. 523.
Map Square 26.

BRIDGE (Kent) from *Charing Cross, Cannon Street*, and *London Bridge*, 73¾ miles. Fares, (*via* Canterbury), 13/9*a*, 11/0*b*, 8/3*c*. R. T. for two months, 27/6*a*, 22/0*b*. (*Via* Shorncliffe) 14/7*a*, 11/8*b*, 8/9*c*. R.T. for two months, 29/2*a*, 23/4*b*. Departures *from* London as for Shorncliffe or Canterbury West. Departures *for* London about 5 times daily. Pop. 699.
Map Square 24.

Station closed on Sundays.

BRIDGEND (Glamorganshire) from *Paddington*, 173 miles. Fares 36/1*a*, 21/8*c*. R. T. for two months, 72/2*a*, 43/4*c* Pop. 9,206.
Map Square 21.

Pad.	Bridg.	Bridg.	Pad.
AM 1. 0*g*	6.19	AM 9.22*r*	1. 0
5.30	10.58	10.45*r*	2.30
8.45*r*	12.56	PM12. 5*r*	4.20
11.50*r*	4.17	1.35*r*	6.15
PM 1.10*er*	5.48	4.30*r*	8.35
1.10*dr*	5.53	5.40*r*	9.25
3.35*r*	7. 8	10. 2	3.30
6. 0*r*	9.43	—	—
8. 0*r*	11.22	—	—
9.15	3.17	—	—
—	—	—	—
—	—	—	—
—	—	—	—

Sunday Trains.

AM 1. 0	7. 0	AM10. 8	3.35
9.10	3.18	11.35	4. 5
PM12.30*r*	4.58	PM 4. 6*r*	8.25
4.30	9.15	10. 2	3.30
9.15	3.17	—	—
—	—	—	—
—	—	—	—
—	—	—	—

d Saturdays only.
e Saturdays excepted.
g Mondays excepted.
r Restaurant Car.

BRIDGEFOOT (Cumberland), 313 miles. No through fares. Departures *from* London as for Cockermouth or Moor Row. Departures *for* London about 3 times daily
Map Square 6.

BRIDGE OF ALLAN (Stirling) from *Euston*, 419¾ miles. Fares, 85/0*a*, 51/0*c*. R. T. for two months, 170/0*a*, 102/0*c*. Pop. 3,579.
Map Square 40.

Euston	B. Allan	B. Allan	Euston
AM 5. 0	4.46	AM 9.36*r*	7.30
10. 0*r*	7.14	PM12.55*r*	10.45
PM 1.30*r*	12.20	3.59*r*	5. 0*h*
7.50*er*	5.45	9.29	7.40
11. 0*d*	8.51	—	—
11.35*e*	8.44	—	—
—	—	—	—
—	—	—	—
—	—	—	—
—	—	—	—

Sunday Trains.

PM 7.50*r*	5.45	PM 4.37*r*	5. 0*h*
11.35	8.44	—	—
—	—	—	—
—	—	—	—
—	—	—	—
—	—	—	—
—	—	—	—
—	—	—	—

d Saturdays only.
e Saturdays excepted.
h A.M.
r Restaurant Car.

The Allan Water Hotel. First-Class. Motoring. Golf. Fishing. *See* advt. p. **86**.

BRIDGE OF DEE (Kirkcudbright), 354¾ miles. Fares, 68/9*a*, 41/3*c*. R.T. for two months, 137/6*a*, 82/6*c*. Departures *from* London as for Kirkcudbright. Departures *for* London about 4 times daily.
Map Square 43.

BRIDGE OF DUN (Forfar), 497¼ miles. Fares, 97/1*a*, 58/3*c*. R. T. for two months, 194/2*a*, 116/6*c*. Departures *from* London as for Forfar. Departures *for* London about 3 times daily. Pop. (Dun) 463.
Map Square 38.

BRIDGE OF EARN (Perth), 436¼ miles. Fares, 90/3*a*, 54/2*c*. R. T. for two months, 180/6*a*, 108/4*c*. Departures *from* London as for Dunfermline. Departures *for* London about 3 times daily.
Map Square 38.

BRIDGE OF ORCHY (Argyle), 474½ miles. Fares, 94/0*a*, 56/5*c*. R. T. for two months, 188/0*a*, 112/10*c*. Departures *from* London as for Fort William. Departures *for* London about twice daily.
Map Square 37.

BRIDGE OF WEIR (Renfrew), 416 miles. Fares, 83/1*a*, 49/10*c*. R. T. for two months, 166/2*a*, 99/8*c*. Departures *from* London as for Greenock (Prince's Pier). Departures *for* London about 3 times daily. Pop. 1,914.
Map Square 40.

BRIDGNORTH (Salop)

from *Paddington*, 145¾ miles.
Fares, 29/0a, 17/5c. R. T. for two
months, 58/0a, 34/10c. Pop. 5,143.
Map Square 17.

PAD.	BRIDG'TH.	BRIDG'TH.	PAD.
AM10.40h	2.40	AM 7. 5fh11. 0	
PM 1.30r	5.27	9.20hr 1.25	
2.10ht	6.29	PM12.22r 4.15	
4.45t	8.48	2.45ht 6.40	
12.15hk	8.23	9. 5h 3.30	
12.15hl	10. 2	—	—
—	—	—	—
—	—	—	—
—	—	—	—
—	—	—	—
—	—	—	—

No Sunday Trains.

f Mondays only.
h Via Birmingham.
k Saturdays midnight excepted.
l Saturdays midnight only.
r Restaurant Car.
t Tea Car.

BRIDGWATER (Somerset)

from *Paddington*, 150¾ miles.
Fares, 30/8a, 18/5c. R. T. for two
months, 61/4a, 36/10c. Pop. 15,968.
Map Square 22.

PAD.	BRIDG'TR.	BRIDG'TR.	PAD.
AM 5.30	9.26	AM 5. 5	7.10
7.30	11.24	7.40	11.30
9. 0	1.51	10.16r	2. 0
11.15r	2.47	PM 1.47	6. 2
PM 1. 0r	5.18	2.50r	7. 0
1.10r	6.55	5.36	10.25
4.15	7.19	9.22	2.45
6.30r	10.23	—	—
8. 0d	12.19	—	—
12. 0h	7.16	—	—
12.30k	8. 5	—	—

Sunday Trains.

AM 9.10r	1.41	AM 3. 5	7. 5
PM12.30r	7. 3	10.45	3.35
10. 0	7.16	PM 4.10	8.10
—	—	11.15	3.15
—	—	←	—

d Saturdays only.
h Saturdays midnight excepted.
k Saturdays midnight only.
r Restaurant Car.

ANOTHER ROUTE from

Waterloo, via Templecombe 147¾
miles. Fares as above.

W'LOO	BRIDG'TR.	BRIDG'TR.	W'LOO
AM 9. 0r	1.49	AM 6.35r	11.10
12. 0r	4.34	9.40r	1.56
PM 1. 0r	5.54	11.35r	4.30
3. 0r	7.36	PM 5.10r	8.30
6. 0r	10. 9	5.10	10.50
—	—	6.30h	3.58
—	—	—	—
—	—	—	—
—	—	—	—
—	—	—	—

No Sunday Trains.
h Via Eastleigh.
r Restaurant Car.

BRIDLINGTON (Yorks)

from *King's Cross*, 217 miles.
Fares, *via* Goole or Selby, 41/5a,
24/10c. R. T. for two months,
82/10a, 49/8c. *Via* York, 50/8a,
30/5c. R. T. for two months,
101/4a, 60/10c. Pop. 22,768.
Map Square 8.

KING'S+	BRID'TN.	BRID'TN.	KING'S+
AM 4.45	11.26	AM 8.10r	1.15
7.15r	12.25	8.45r	1.30
8.45	3.10	9.15	3.50
10.10r	4. 2	10.55r	4.30
11.50r	6. 2	11.50r	4.45
PM 1.30r	6.16	PM12.16r	6.50
1.50r	7. 9	1.45dr	7.30
4. 0r	10. 2	3.34r	9.45
5.45fr	11.40	4. 7r	10. 0
10.45e	6.54	3.25	3.25
10.45d	8.19	- -	—
11.25e	8.27	—	—
11.25d	12.15	—	—
—	—	—	—
—	—	—	—

Sunday Trains.

PM10.45	6.54	PM 6.50	5.40
11.25	8.27	—	—
—	—	—	—

d Saturdays only.
e Saturdays excepted.
f Thursdays and Saturdays only.
r Restaurant Car.

BRIDPORT (Dorset) from

Paddington, 149½ miles. Fares,
30/3a, 18/2c. R. T. for two months,
60/6a, 36/4c. Pop. 5,910.
Map Square 27.

PAD	BRIDPT.	BRIDPT	PAD
AM 1. 0g	10. 1	AM 8.50	12.55
5.30	11.36	10.30	3.20
10.30	2.11	11.48	3.50
PM12.30r	4.21	PM 1.25t	5.30
2. 0	5.46	3. 5r	6.50
3.30	8.26	4.30	8.20
5. 5	9.27	7.10	2.45

Sunday Trains.

PM10. 0	10. 1	PM 3.20r	7.55

g Mondays excepted
r Restaurant Car.
t Tea Car

BRIERFIELD (Lancs)

from *Euston* or *St. Pancras*, 217
miles. Fares, 42/3a, 25/4c. R. T.
for two months, 84/6a, 50/8c. Departures *from* London as for Burnley.
Departures *for* London about 6
times daily. Pop. 8,343.
Map Square 12.

BRIERLEY HILL (Staf-

ford), 123¾ miles. Fares, 25/3a, 15/2c.
R. T. for two months, 50/6a, 30/4c.
Departures *from* London as for
Stourbridge Junction. Depar-
tures *for* London about 12 times
daily. Pop. 12,484.
Map Square 17.

BRIGG (Lincoln) from

King's Cross, 165¾ miles. Fares,
33/1a, 19/10c. R. T. for two months,
66/2a, 39/8c. Pop. 3,343.
Map Square 13.

KING'S+	BRIGG	BRIGG	KING'S+
AM 4.45	9.28	AM 6.46r	11.30
7.15r	11.24	9.12r	1. 5
10.10	3.51	PM 1.40	6.25
PM 1.50r	5.47	3.26	9. 0
4. 0r	8.33	7.45	3.25
8.25e	4.45	—	—

Sunday Trains.

PM 5. 0	9.19	AM 9.38r	3.45
8.25	4.45	PM 5.21r	10.20

e Saturdays excepted.
r Restaurant Car.

BRIGG—continued.

ANOTHER ROUTE from

Marylebone, 201¾ miles. Fares as
above.

M'BONE.	BRIGG	BRIGG	M'BONE.
AM 2.32	9.28	AM 6.46r	1.13
10. 0r	3.51	9.12r	3. 0
PM12.15r	5.47	11.52r	6.38
3.20r	8.33	PM 1.40r	8.55
10. 5e	4.44	4.44r	9.55
—	—	7.45	3.57

Sunday Trains.

AM11.15r	9.19	AM 9.38r	5.40

e Saturdays excepted.
r Restaurant Car.

BRIGHAM (Cumberland)

from *Euston* 313¾ miles. Fares,
63/4a, 38/0c. R. T. for two months,
126/8a, 76/0c. Departures *from*
London as for Cockermouth. Departures *for* London about 5 times
daily. Pop. 659.
Map Square 6

BRIGHOUSE (Yorks)

from *King's Cross*, *via* Horbury,
188½ miles. Fares, 38/7a, 23/2c.
R. T. for two months, 77/2a, 46/4c.
Pop. 20,277.

KING'S+	B'HOUSE	B'HOUSE	KING'S+
AM 4.45	11.14	AM 6.10	11.30
7.15r	12.33	8.12	1. 5
10.10r	2.59	9.36r	1.55
PM 1.30r	6.25	10.20	3.50
1.50r	7.57	11.14r	4.45
5.45r	10.52	PM12.10	5. 0
10.45e	8.40	2.40r	7.10
—	—	4.52r	9.25
—	—	9.29e	3.25

Sunday Trains.

12. 0hn6.44		PM10. 8r	3.45
—	—	PM12.18	5.55
—	—	3.29h	10.20

e Saturdays excepted.
h Passengers cross Wakefield at
own expense.
n Noon.
r Restaurant Car.

BRIGHTLINGSEA

(Essex) from *Liverpool Street*, 61¾
miles. Fares, 13/2a, 7/11c. R. T.
for two months, 26/4a, 15/10c. Pop.
4,495.
Map Square 24.

L'PL. ST.	BRIGHT.	BRIGHT.	L'PL.ST.
AM 5. 0	8.25	AM 7.39	9.36
6.50	9.58	8.37r	10.30
8.18	10.39	10.12	12.40
8.46	11.41	11.52r	2. 3
10.23	12.40	PM 1. 7	3.36
PM12.36	2.28	2.42	5. 5
3.23	5.15	5.27	7.40
4.58er	6.53	7.42	9.36
4.58dr	6.57	—	—
6.39	8.25	—	—
7.45r	9.53	—	—

Sunday Trains.

AM 9.20r	11.43	AM 9.12	11.38
PM 4.40	7.50	PM 6. 9	8.25
—	—	8. 8	10. 9

d Saturdays only.
e Saturdays excepted.
r Restaurant Car.

Royal Hotel, Family Commercial. Near Station. Garage.
Billiards. Good Cuisine. Large
room for Banquets, etc. 'Phone 18.
E. P. HELYAR.

BRIGHTON (Sussex) from

London Bridge and *Victoria*,
50½ miles. Fares, 10/6a, 6/4c.
R. T. for two months 21/0d, 12/8c.
Pop. 142,427.
Map Square 28.

Leave		Arr. at
VICT.	LON. B.	BRIGHT.
AM —	5.18	7.26
6.37	6.40	8.18
7.23	7.25	9.37
8.25	8. 7	10. 7
9. 0	—	10.29
—	9. 6	10.53
10. 5p	9.50	11.25
10.35	10.35	12.22
11. 0l	—	12. 0
11.40	—	12.45
—	11.40d	12.55
—	11.50	1.20
PM —	12.10	2.15
12.45p	—	1.57
—	1.15d	2.24
—	1.20d	2.45
1.48d	—	3. 0
1.55p	—	3. 5
2. 0d	—	3.44
2. 0e	—	4. 1
—	2. 5	3.30
—	2. 8d	4.30
3.10l	—	4.10
3.40p	—	4.50
—	4. 0	5.12
—	4. 5	5.52
4.30p	— 1	5.35
—	5. 0e	6. 0
—	5. 5d	6.31
—	5. 8e	6.31
—	5.10	6.53
5.35p	—	6.40
—	6. 0e	7.13
—	6. 0d	7.18
—	6. 8	8.17
6.35p	—	7.35
7.15p	7.20	8.42
8.35p	—	9.40
9. 3	9.12	10.47
10. 0p	—	11.10
10.30	10.35	12.30
12. 5p	—	1.10

Sunday Trains.

Leave		Arr. at
AM 6.55	7. 2	9.22
8.50	8.55	10.49
9.45k	—	10.54
11. 0h	—	12. 0
11. 5²	—	12.20
PM12.15p	—	1.30
1.10p	—	2.25
1.14	1.10	3.12
4.55k	—	6. 0
5.50	6. 0	8. 4
6.30h	—	7.30
8. 0	8. 0	10. 0
—	9.10	10.56
9.25p	—	10.35

Trains from Brighton.

Leave	Arrive at	
BRIGHTON	LON. B.	VICT.
AM 6.15	8.15	8.24
7.10	8.19	—
7.23	8.53	9. 8
8. 5p	—	9.15
8.10fp	—	9.22
8.15	9.26	—
8.48	9.50	—
8.57	—	10.24
9.20	10.33	—
9.45p	—	10.55

BRIGHTON—*continued.*

Leave BRIGHTON	Arrive at	
	LON. B.	VICT.
AM10. 0	11.10p	11.17
10. 8	12.13	12. 7
11. 0	12.19	12.17p
11.30	1.42	—
PM12.20p	—	1.20
12.28	2.22	2.22
1.20l	—	2.20
1.45	3.40	3.45
2.28	4.32	4.17
3.30d	4.58	4.45
3.40p	—	4.50
3.50	5.54	5.55
5. 5	6.36	6.34p
5.45l	—	6.45
6. 5	7.42	7.30p
6.30	8.46	—
7.30p	—	8.48
7.45	10. 0	10.10
8.30d	10. 0	9.45p
8.50	10.58	—
10. 0p	—	11.17
11.10	12.59	1. 0
—	—	—
—	—	—
—	—	—

Sunday Trains.

	Arrive at	
AM 8.30	10.45	—
9.30	11.15	10.50p
11.30k	—	12.35
11.40	—	1. 0
PM12.30	—	1.35
3.15	5. 3	5.11
5. 0h	—	6. 0
5.40p	—	7. 0
6.15	—	7.28
6.35k	7.56	7.44
7.35	9.17	9.13
9.30h	—	10.30
9.35p	—	10.55
9.40	11.34	11.42
10.40	12.27	—
—	—	—
—	—	—

d Saturdays only.
e Saturdays excepted.
f Mondays only.
h First Class Pullman Cars only.
k Third Class Pullman Cars only.
l First and Third Class Pullman Cars only.
p Pullman Car attached.

Hotel Metropole. Britain's leading Seaside Hotel. Appointments, Cuisine and Service unsurpassed. Music. Dancing. Tel. add. — " Metropole," Brighton." Telephone, No. 841 Brighton.
GORDON HOTELS, Ltd.
See advt. p. **87.**

Old Ship Hotel. An old Established Family Hotel. Facing Sea. Electric Light. Extensive Garage adjoins Hotel. Telegrams : "Old Ship, Brighton." Telephone, 4680 Brighton.
See advt. p. **88.**

Albemarle Hotel. Facing Palace Pier. New Lounge. Garage, R.A.C., A.A. Public rooms recently refurnished and enlarged. 'Phone 1468 P.O. Wires : "Albemarle."
See advt. p. **89.**

BRIGHTON—*continued.*

Queen's Hotel, King's Road. Spacious Public Rooms. Facing Sea. "Comfort, Cooking, Cleanliness." Terms from £4 10s. weekly. Sat. to Mon. from 30s. National Telephone: No. 368.
See advt. p. **91.**

Royal Crescent Hotel. Leading Family Hotel, situated upon King's Cliff, Marine Parade. Self-contained suites of apartments. Every modern improvement. Excellent cuisine.
See advt. p. **91.**

Bedford Hotel. Old-established, High-class. Centre of Sea Front. New Lounge. Phone 43. Manager, WALTER MERRETT.
See advt. p. **92.**

Silwood Hall Hotel. Old Established. Fully Licensed. First Class. Facing Sea. Own Grounds. Billiards. Garage. English Cooking. From 4½ Guineas. 'Phone : 860.
See advt. p. **93.**

Royal York Hotel. Views of the beautiful old Steyne Gardens and the English Channel. Now open, under management of H. I. PRESTON.
See advt. p. **94.**

Royal Albion Hotel. Best position. Charming sea views. Most comfortable Sea - front Lounge in Brighton. Illustrated Brochure and Tariff. Apply to MANAGER.
See advt. p. **94.**

Lion Mansion Hotel. Facing Sea. First Class.
See advt. p. **95.**

Portland House Private Hotel. Overlooking West Pier. Chef. Liberal Table. Dancing and Bridge. Phone 354.
See advt. p. **95.**

Palace Pier Mansions. High Class Private Hotel and Boarding Establishment.
See advt. p. **96.**

Norfolk Hotel. Reopens end July. Redecorated. Enlarged Dining Room, Lounge.
See advt. p. **96.**

Dudley Hotel, Lansdowne Place, Hove. Adjoining Hove Lawns. Terms inclusive or à la carte. National Telephone No. 2490 Hove.
See advt. p. **97.**

The King's Hotel. "On Brighton Front." Closed for reconstruction. Reopens end of summer.
See advt. p **97.**

Desmond Private Hotel, 2, 3, 4, and 5, Cannon Place. 75 Bedrooms. Lounge. Billiards. See advertisement for Terms.
BERNARD LETHER,
Proprietor.
See advt. p. **98.**

BRIGHTON—*continued.*

Berkeley Private Hotel, 154, King's Road. Finest position in Brighton. Moderate terms. Phone Brighton 5,137.
See advt. p. **98.**

New Ship Hotel. An old landmark which still combines comfort with economy. Telephone: 292 Brighton. Special inclusive Summer Terms.
Apply, NAT. J. VAUGHAN.
See advt. p. **99.**

Glenside, 65, 66, 67, and 69, Grand Parade. Sixty Bedrooms. Billiards. See advertisement for terms. ALFRED R. BAILLY, Proprietor (late Steward of Hailey-bury College).
See advt. p. **99.**

Marine Mansion Hotel (late Haxell's). Most reasonable First-class Hotel. Sea Front. Facing Pier. Excellent Cuisine. Inclusive Terms. Tel. 454, Kemp Town.
Apply MANAGERESS.
See advt. p. **100.**

Denbigh Private Hotel, 70-73, Grand Parade. Excellent Lounge. Accommodate 150 Guests. Separate Tables. Tel.: 6994 Kemp Town.
Mrs. F. MARKHAM, Proprietress.
See advt. p. **100.**

Hotel Alexandra, Hove. Directly overlooks Brunswick Lawns and Sea. Quiet. High-class. Family and Residential.
See advt. p. **101.**

Argyle Mansion Hotel. King's Road. Beautifully situated, facing Sea. Fully licenced.
Mr. and Mrs. R. J. HANNAH, Proprietors.
See advt. p. **101.**

Trory's Belvidere Mansions Hotel. Facing Sea, Lift. Billiards. Dancing. Reasonable Prices. Telephone 25. Telegrams, "Sunshine, Brighton."
See advt. p. **102.**

Court Royal Hotel, King's Cliff. Facing Sea. Entirely new management. Central heating. Nearest Links. Private Suites. Moderate inclusive terms. Tel. Post 106.
See advt. p. **102.**

Chatfield's Hotel, West Street. Two doors from Front. A house that makes Brighton Brighter.
See advt. p. **103.**

Hotel Bristol, King's Cliff. Self-contained Suites. Old Established. High Class.
See advt. p. **103.**

BRIGHTON—*continued.*

Arlington Hotel. Marine Parade. Overlooking Palace Pier. Liberal and excellent Table.
See advt. p. **104.**

The Brighton Hotel. Family and Commercial. Always best English catering. Phone, Kemp Town 6973. Proprietors, Mr. & Mrs. H. W. SMITH.
See advt. p. **104.**

Clarence Hotel. Family and Commercial. New Proprietors. Refurnished and Decorated. Tel. No. P.O. 910. Manageress—Mrs. PARTOON.
See advt. p. **105.**

Hotel Curzon, Ltd., near West Pier. Facing Sea. Handsome Lounge. Dining and Billiard rooms. Lift to all floors. Write for Tariff and en pension terms. Tel. P.O. 665.
See advt. p. **105.**

St. Alban's Private Hotel, 131, King's Road. Finest position, overlooking Sea. Central. Excellent table.
See advt. p **105.**

Wentworth Private Hotel, Marine Parade. Directly facing Sea. Lounge. Terms from 3 Guineas. Apply—
PROPRIETOR.
See advt. p. **106.**

The Belvedere, Bedford Square. Overlooking Sea and Lawns. Central. Amusements. Best English Catering. Terms from 3 gns. per week, 9s. 6d. per day. Telephone: Hove 2360.
See advt. p. **106.**

Regency House Private Hotel, Regency Square. Excellent Cuisine. Lounge. Electric Light. Under personal supervision of—Mr. & Mrs. GEO. BLAXLAND.
See advt. p. **106.**

Brighton House, Regency Square. Luxuriously furnished. Excellent Cuisine. Every comfort.
See advt. p. **106.**

Burleigh Hall Private Hotel, King's Road. Terms from 3½ gns. 'Phone 4581.
A. E. DAVIS.
See advt. p. **107.**

Speranza Private Hotel, Sillwood Place. Near Sea. Moderate inclusive terms.
Miss F. E. HAIGH.
See advt. p. **107.**

Marlborough House. Regency Square. Magnificent position. Exceptional Catering. Every comfort.
See advt. p. **107.**

BRIGHTON—*continued.*

Pier Hotel, Marine Parade. Facing Sea and Palace Pier. Tel. 1152 P.O. Proprietors—Mr. and Mrs. S. C. NELSON.
See advt. p. **107.**

Alexander Private Hotel, 18, Madeira Place. Central for amusements. 'Phone, Kemp Town, 1020.
See advt. p. **108.**

Steyne Gardens Private Hotel. Overlooking Sea. Well appointed. Personal supervision of Proprietress.
See advt. p. **108.**

Beacon Royal Private Hotel, Oriental Place. Few doors Sea Front. Terms from 2½ gns. Proprietress,
Mrs. B. L. STEWART.
See advt. p. **108.**

Stratheden Mansions Private Hotel, Regency Square. Facing West Pier. Bridge and Dance Room. Terms from 3½ guineas. Telephone 872.
See advt. p. **108.**

The Lawns Private Hotel. Facing Hove Lawns. Luxuriously appointed. Personal supervision of the Proprietors.
See ad. t. p. **86.**

Cavendish Mansions Private Hotel, Cavendish Place. Delightfully situated. Sea views. Near both Piers and Lawns. Electric light. Separate Tables. Inclusive moderate terms. Telegrams: "Meadmore, Brighton." Telephone 4553.
Apply, MANAGERESS.

Kingscliff Mansion, Private Hotel, 34, Marine Parade. Magnificent Sea View. Passenger lift to all floors, central heating. Terms 3 to 4½ gns. 'Phone, P.O. 973.
Proprietors, MR. & MRS. BANKS. (Late Miss Box.)

Blenheim Private Hotel, Marlboro' Place, Close to Royal Pavilion. High-class Central position, Spacious Reception and Billiard Rooms. Recreation Room. Dining-room. Cuisine excellent. Resident Proprietors. Telephone 119 National. Telegrams "Blenheim, Brighton."

Kingsville, 26, Regency Square. Facing Sea and West Pier. Re-decorated. Electric Light. Bathroom. Separate Tables. Telephone. P.O. 615 Brighton. The Misses RICE.

Saville House. High Class Boarding Establishment. Grand Parade. Celebrated for Home Comforts and Excellent Cuisine. Primest English-fed Meat. Terms Moderate.
Mrs. PRITCHARD.

For completion of **Advertisements, see over.**

D

BRIGHTON—*continued.*

Hockley's Private Hotel. Opposite West Pier. Finest position. Excellent Lounge. Inclusive Terms. Illustrated tariff. 'Phone, P.O. 134. Telegrams, "Front, Brighton." Apply PROPRIETOR.

Southleigh Boarding Establishment, Montpelier Road. Gas Fires in bedrooms. One minute Sea. Close to West Pier and Hove Lawns. Terms moderate. Central heating. Tel. 4785.

Sackville House Boarding Establishment, 64, Lansdowne Place, Hove. Central for all amusements, Close to Sea. Home Comforts. Separate Tables. Smoke Rooms. Moderate Terms Established 1891. Nat. Tel. 2359 Hove. Proprietress Miss MITCHELL.

Aynhoe, 50, The Drive, Hove. Superior Board Residence in Lady's well-appointed house. Few minutes from Sea. Entry to Private Tennis and Croquet Lawns. Near County Cricket Grounds. Miss BUTTERFIELD.

Langley House, Board Residence. Near Sea and St. Ann's Well Gardens. Lofty Rooms. Separate Tables. Moderate Terms. 118, Lansdowne Place, Hove. Tel. 2330 Hove.

Madeira Private Hotel. Sea Front. Charming position. Best catering in Brighton. From 3½ gns. Miss G. E. PEARMAN, Manageress.

Courtlands. The Drive, Hove. High-Class Private Hotel. Near sea and lawns. Separate tables. From 4 guineas. Tel. 2615 Hove.

Mutton's Restaurant and Hotel, King's Road. Comfortable bedrooms facing sea. Luncheons and Dinners at reasonable charges. Table d'Hôte, 3/0, 12.30 to 9 p.m.; and 4/0 from 6 to 9 p.m., separate tables. Choice Wines and Spirits. Established nearly a century. Refreshment Contractors in all branches.

Fairfax, 38, Bedford Square. Superior Boarding Establishment. Separate tables. Excellent cuisine. Moderate inclusive terms. Highly recommended. Tel. 5997. PROPRIETRESS.

Apartments in Square facing Sea. Three minutes Palace Pier and Aquarium. Overlooking private gardens. Good cooking. LOWSON, 12 New Steine.

23, New Steine. Board Residence. Fine Sea View close to all amusements and shops. Under personal supervision. Terms moderate. E. HEWETSON.

BRIGHTON—*continued.*

Sea View Private Hotel and Boarding Establishment, Black Lion Street. Facing Sea, between Piers. Separate Tables. English meat. Moderate. Reduction for Permanency. MRS. PEARSON.

Abbott's Private Hotel, 67 and 68, Regency Square. Thoroughly Up-to-date. Redecorated, Refurnished. Over 20 Bedrooms, 4 Bathrooms. Fine Public Rooms, overlooking West Pier and Tennis Courts. Excellent Cuisine. Terms from 3½ Guineas. Illustrated Tariff of Manageress. Telephone: "5879." Telegrams: "Abbott's Hotel."

Bank House Private Hotel, 112, Western Road, Hove. Close Sea, Lawns, Piers, St. Ann's Well Gardens. Separate Tables. Electric Light. Gas Fires in Bedrooms. From 3 Guineas. MRS. HARVEY FOSTER.

The Richmond Boarding Establishment, 22 and 23, Sillwood Place. Sea view from Lawn. 3 minutes from West Pier. Hove Lawns. Separate tables. Terms, from 45/- inclusive, Tel. 4894.

Ashdown House, 7, Cannon Place. Splendid position between the "Grand" and "Metropole" Hotels. Board-residence. Comfortable. Reasonable, Excellent cooking. Separate tables. F. E. STEVENSON.

Goodwins, 6 & 7, Clarence Square (minute West Pier). Board residence," good." Central shops and amusements. Highly recommended for excellent catering. Mid-day dinner. Bright rooms. Terms, from 45/-.

King's Road, 128, Suites Furnished. High-class. Good Cooking and Attendance. Facing Sea and West Pier. Tel. 1701. MRS. J. C. BUTLER. (And at Felixstowe).

Northumberland Hall Private Hotel, Marine Parade. Healthiest position. Spacious Reception and Bedrooms facing Sea. Billiards. Highly recommended by doctors. Liberal Menus. Separate Tables. Central for Amusements. Newly decorated throughout. Expert Management. Terms from 3 gns. each. Illustrated Tariff on application.

Highcliffe Private Hotel, Brighton, opposite Aquarium. Excellent Cuisine. Gas Fires in bedrooms, from 3½ Guineas weekly. Tel. Kemp Town 1061. MRS. CREEK.

Exeter Hotel, King's Road. Midway between Piers. Liberal catering. From 3½ Guineas. Tel. 4674. Telegrams, "Prospect, Brighton." Proprietor. "EDOUARD," Late of Hotel Metropole.

BRIGHTON—*continued.*

Wellington House, Oriental Place. Select Board Residence. Ideal position near Sea, Lawns, Shops. Home comforts. Moderate terms. Apply, Secretary.

Cremorne. Cavendish Place Superior Board Residence, opposite West Pier. Best part of Brighton. Moderate inclusive terms. Under personal supervision of Proprietress.

Talbot House, Regency Square. Facing Sea and West Pier. Excellent Catering. Separate Tables. From 3 Guineas. Reduction for Permanency.

Mr. and Mrs. Percy Hobbs, formerly of the Exeter Hotel, now at the Central Hotel, Old Steine, just ½ off sea front. Newly decorated. Gas fires all bedrooms. Telephone P.O. 1398.

Marina Private Hotel, New Steine. Marine Parade. High-class. Ideal position. Modern equipage. From 4 guineas. 'Phone Kemp Town 483. Miss JOHNSON.

Full Particulars of Furnished, Unfurnished and Freehold Houses in Brighton, Hove and Preston, on receipt of stamp and details of requirements. DUDENEY & SON, 74, St. James's Street, Brighton. Estab. 1850.

Auctioneers, House Agents, 56, Preston Street, Brighton. Selection of all available houses and flats to let (furnished or unfurnished) and for sale in Brighton and Hove. Telephone 313. Perrys, F.A.I.

Auctioneers, House Agents, 92, Goldstone Villas, Hove. Furnished and Unfurnished Houses and Flats To Let or For Sale in Brighton and Hove. Tel. 3075, Hove. H. FRANCIS & CO.

Messrs. Winkworths, F.A.I., 22, Preston Street, Brighton; 188, Church Road, Hove. The Leading House and Estate Agents, selected lists of the best Houses and Flats, furnished, unfurnished, or for sale, upon application. Telephones: Brighton 102, Hove 8915.

Reid & Co. Estab. 1800. Estate Agents, 15, Old Steine. Excellent selection of Houses for Sale, also Furnished and Unfurnished Flats to Let. Tel. Kemp Town 1452.

BRIGHTON ROAD (Worcester), 116½ miles. Fares, 23/6*a*, 14/1*c*. R. T. for two months, 47/0*a*, 28/2*c*. Departures *from* London as for Birmingham (New Street). Departures *for* London about 6 times daily.

BRIGHTSIDE (Yorks), from *St. Pancras,* 161½ miles. Fares, 32/9*a*, 19/8*c*. R. T. for two months, 65/6*a*, 39/4*c*. Departures *from* London as for Sheffield. Departures *for* London 4 times daily. Pop. 34,702. *Map Square* 12.

BRILL (Bucks), 50½ miles. Fares, 9/10*a*, 5/11*c*. R. T. for two months, 19/8*a*, 11/10*c*. Departures *from* London as for Waddesdon. Departures *for* London, about 4 times daily. Pop. 1,121. *Map Square* 23.

BRILL & LUDGERS-
HALL (Bucks) from *Paddington*.
47¾ miles. Fares, 9/10a, 5/11c. R. T.
for two months, 19/8a, 11/10c. Pop.,
Brill, 1,281; Ludgershall, 323.

Pad.	Brill	Brill	Pad.
AM 5.45	8.16	AM 8.36	10. 0
9.16	10.25	11.10	1.18
PM12.18	2.18	PM 2.58	4.40
2.23	4.25	4.28	6.35
4.40	6. 0	6.41	9.18
7.10	8.20	—	—
—	—	—	—

No Sunday Trains.

BRIMSCOMBE (Glos'ter)
from *Paddington*, 99½ miles. Fares,
20/8a, 12/5c. R. T. for two
months, 41/4a, 24/10c. Pop. 1,491.
Map Square 22.

Pad.	Brims.	Brims.	Pad.
AM 5.30	8.34	AM 8.12r	10.45
7.30	10. 4	9.26	12.20
9. 0	12. 4	PM12.42	3.20
PM 1.10r	3.59	2.36	5. 0
3.15t	5.54	5. 7hr	8.45
6. 0r	8.38	7.38	10.25
—	—	—	—

Sunday Trains.

PM12.30r	3.30	PM 7.19	10. 0
2. 0	7.22	—	—
—	—	—	—
—	—	—	—

h Fridays and Third Class only.
r Restaurant Car.
t Tea Car.

BRIMSDOWN (Middle-
sex) from *Liverpool Street*, 10½
miles. Fares, 1/8a, 1/4b, 1/0c.
R. T. for two days, 3/4a, 2/8b, 2/0c.
See pp. 526-527.

BRINKBURN (Northum-
berland), 306½ miles. No through
fares. Departures *from* London
as for Morpeth. Departures *for*
London about 3 times daily. Pop.
160.
Map Square 3.

BRINKLOW (Warwick)
from *Euston*. 88 miles. Fares,
18/4a, 11/0c. R. T. for two months,
36/8a, 22/0c. Pop. 667.
Map Square 18.

Euston	Brink.	Brink.	Euston
AM 5. 0	7.34	AM 7.36	10. 0
8.45r	10.34	9. 3r	11. 0
12. 0nr	2.24	PM12.11r	2.20
PM 2.50t	5. 4	4.15t	6.15
4. 5t	6. 1	6.29r	9.20
6.30er	8.34	—	—
7. 0dr	9 2	—	—
—	—	—	—

No Sunday Trains.

d Saturdays only.
e Saturdays excepted.
n Noon.
r Restaurant Car.
t Tea Car

BRINKWORTH (Wilts)
87 miles. Fares, 18/2a, 10/11c. R. T.
for two months, 36/4a, 21/10c. Departures *from* London as for Badminton. Departures *for* London
about 4 times daily. Pop. 1,031.
Map Square 22

BRINSCALL (Lancs),
206 miles. Fares, 43/1a, 25/10c.
R. T. for two months, 86/2a, 51 8c.
Departures *from* London as for
Chorley. Departures *for* London
about 6 times daily.
Map Square 12.

BRISLINGTON (Somer-
set), 118¾ miles. Fares, 25/0a,
15/0c. R. T. for two months, 50/0a,
30/0c. Departures *from* London as
Bristol. Departures *for* London for
about 6 times daily. Pop. 3,233.
Map Square 22.

BRISTOL (TEMPLE MEADS)
Gloucester, from *Paddington*, 117¾
miles. Fares, 24/5a, 14/8c. R. T.
for two months, 48/10a, 29/4c. Pop.
377,061.
Map Square 22.

Pad.	Bristol	Bristol	Pad.
AM 5.30	8.27	AM12.10f	3.15
7.30	10.15	4. 5	7.10
8.45	11. 3	7.45r	10.15
9. 0	12. 2	9.15	11.30
11.15r	1.15	9.35	12.20
PM 1. 0r	3. 0	12. 0r	2. 0
1.10r	4.15	PM12.20	3.20
2.45	5.49	1.45	4. 5
4.15r	6.32	3.10	6. 2
5. 0r	7.25h	5. 0r	7. 0
5. 0r	8.14	6. 0r	8.45
5.15	8.25	7.32	10.25
6.30r	8.47	11.10	2.45
8. 0	10.20	—	—
10. 0	12.57	—	—
12. 0k	3.15	—	—
12.30l	3.45	—	—
—	—	—	—

Sunday Trains.

AM 9.10	12.19	AM 4. 5	7. 5
10.35	2.41	PM12.30	3.35
PM12.30r	3.25	1.40r	4. 5
4.30	6.50	3.25	7.55
10. 0	12.53	5.30	8.10
—	—	5.55	10. 0
—	—	—	—
—	—	—	—

f Mondays only.
h Stapleton Road Station.
k Saturdays midnight excepted.
l Saturdays midnight only.
r Restaurant Car.

Royal Hotel, College Green.
First-class Family Hotel. Fitted
with every modern convenience.
Telegraphic address, "Banquet."
See advt. p. **109.**

Grand Hotel. The Finest
Family and Commercial Hotel in
the City. 200 rooms. Hotel Motor
'Bus meets trains. Telephone 2845.
Mrs. H. RAYMOND,
Manageress.
See advt. p. **109.**

Grand Spa Hotel. Beautifully
situated on Avon Gorge. Close
to Downs. Garage. Near Links.
See advt. p. **110.**

The Grosvenor Hotel.
Family and Commercial. Elec-
tric Grill till 10 p.m. Two
minutes Station. Moderate. Night
Porter. Telephone 1631.
J. LIDDELL, Proprietor.

BRISTOL—*continued.*

Hydro Hotel, College Green.
Hot water heating. Electric light.
Library, Billiards, Smoking and
Ladies' Drawing Rooms. First-
class cuisine. Terms from 9/6
per day. Illustrated Prospectus.
Phone 1851. Private Garage.
Miss BRACKSTONE, Manageress.

Cambridge House (En Pension); Royal York Crescent, Clifton. Pleasantly and conveniently
situated. Excellent cuisine. Personal supervision. Tariff application Proprietors. Telephone
2878 Bristol.

Pembroke Hall. Private
Hotel. Detached. South, near
College, Downs. Amusements.
Lofty Rooms. Electric Light
throughout. Garden. Excellent
cuisine. Separate tables. 'Phone
5550. PROPRIETRESS.

Rummer Hotel, Family and
Commercial Central. Bed and
Breakfast from 6/6. Not open for
Night Mails. Mrs. J. BAILEY,
Proprietress.

Fernhill Hotel, Pembroke
Road, Clifton. Central for every-
thing. Moderate Terms. Gas
Fires in all Bedrooms. Electric
Light throughout. Modern Bath
Rooms. Buses pass Hotel Tele-
grams, "Convenient, Bristol."
Phone, 630 Bristol.

Norwich Union Mutual, the
Outstanding British Life Office.
Reserves at 2½ per cent. 56 Corn
Street, Bristol.
See advt. cover, p. 6.

Bank.—The National Bank,
Limited, 27 Clare Street.

BRITHDIR (Glamorgan),
163½ miles. Fares *via* Cardiff,
35/8a, 21/5c. R. T. for two
months, 71/4a, 42/10c. Departures
from London as for Bargoed or
Cardiff. Departures *for* London
about 4 times daily.

BRITISH MUSEUM.
(Central London Tube.) *See* back
of Map.

BRITON FERRY (Gla-
morgan), 188½ miles. Fares, 39/4a,
23/7c. R. T. for two months, 78/8a,
47/2c. Departures *from* London
as for Port Talbot. Departures
for London about 4 times daily.
Pop. 9,176.
Map Square 21.

BRIXHAM (Devon), 206¼
miles. Fares, 42/8a, 25/7c. R. T.
for two months, 85/4a, 51/2c. Pop.
7,782.
Map Square 26.

Pad.	Brix.	Brix.	Pad.
AM 5.30	1. 2	AM 8.20r	1.30
9.15r	2.45	11.28r	3.45
12. 0r	4.12	PM 1.53er	8.50
PM12. 5r	5.17	1.53dr	7. 5
2. 0r	7.15	3.48r	9. 0
3.30r	8.22	4.45	2.45
4.15r	10.17	8.45	7.10
12. 0k	7.47	10.35h	7.10

Sunday Trains.

AM10.30r	3.55	PM 1.50r	7.45
PM 2.40	8. 0	7.20	3.15
10. 0	7.47	—	—

d Saturdays only.
e Saturdays excepted.
h Wednesdays, Fridays and
Saturdays only.
k Saturdays midnight excepted.
r Restaurant Car.

BRIXTON from *Victoria*
and *Ludgate Hill*, 3½ miles. Fares from Victoria, 0/7½a, 0/6b, 0/4½c. R. T. for two days, 1/2a, 1/0b, 0/9c. From Ludgate Hill,0/7a, 0/6b, 0/4½c. R. T. for two days, 1/0a, 0/10½b, 0/9c. Pop. 44,065. *See* pp. 558-561. *Map Square* 70.

BRIXTON EAST from
London Bridge, 5 miles, or from *Victoria*, 3½ miles, *via* South London Line. Fares from London Bridge, 0/7a, 0/4½c. R. T. for two days, 1/0a, 0/9c, or from Victoria, 0/5a, 0/3c. R. T. for two days, 0/10a, 0/6c. Pop. 6,985. *See* p. 570. *Map Square* 70.

BRIXTON ROAD
(Devon), 228 miles. Fares, 47/2a, 28/6c. R. T. for two months, 94/3a, 57/0c. Departures *from* London as for Yealmpton. Departures *for* London about 4 times daily. Pop. 674. *Map Square* 26.

BRIXWORTH (Northampton)
from *Euston*, 73 miles. Fares, 14/7a, 8/9c. R. T. for two months, 29/2a, 17/6c. Pop. 1,209. *Map Square* 18.

Euston	B'worth.	B'worth.	Euston
AM 5. 0	7.12	AM 8. 6	10.15
6.45	9.28	9.46	11.55
10.40	1.13	10.59	12.40
PM12.15	3.13	PM 1.11h	3.45
3. 5	5. 2	1.11k	4.15
4.15	6.18	3. 4	5.35
7. 0	8.40	5. 7	7.20
—	—	7.24e	9.20
—	—	8.14	11.35

No Sunday Trains.
e Saturdays excepted.
h Mondays and Saturdays only.
k Mondays and Saturdays excepted.

BROAD CLYST (Devon)
from *Waterloo*, 167 miles. Fares, 34/10a, 20/11c. R.T.for two months, 69/8a, 41/10c. Pop. 1,904. *Map Square* 26.

W'loo	Br.Clyst	Br. Clyst	W'loo
AM10. 0r	2.52	AM 9.11r	1.56
12. 0r	4.35	11. 5r	3. 8
PM 1. 0r	5.25	PM12.51r	6. 0
3. 0r	7. 7	1·55	7.40
6. 0r	10.52	3.36r	8.30
—	—	5.51	10.50
—	—	7.56h	3.58

Sunday Trains.

AM 9. 0	3.35	PM 3.41r	8.57
12. 0nr	5.22	—	—

h Via Eastleigh.
n Noon.
r Restaurant Car.

BROADFIELD (Lancs),177¼
miles. Fares, 40/7a, 24/4c. R. T. for two months, 81/2a, 48/8c. Departures *from* London as for Heywood. Departures *for* London 6 times daily. *Map Square* 12.

BROAD GREEN (Lancs)
198 miles. Fares, 41/5a, 24/10c. R. T.:for two months, 82/10a, 49/8c. Departures *from* London as for Liverpool (Lime Street), or Earlestown. Departures *for* London about 5 times daily.

BROADHEATH (Ch'shire),
18¼ miles. Fares, 37/9a, 22/8c. R. T. for two months, 75/6a, 45/4c. Departures *from* London as for Stockport. Departures *for* London about 5 times daily. Pop. 2,454.

BROADLEY (Lancs), 181
miles. Fares, 40/8a, 24/5c. R. T. for two months, 81/4a, 48/10c. Departures *from* London as for Rochdale. Departures *for* London about 6 times daily. *Map Square* 12.

BROADSTAIRS (Kent)
from *Victoria*, *Holborn Viaduct*, or *St. Paul's*, 77 miles. Fares, 15/5a, 12/4b, 9/3c. R. T. for two months, 30/10a, 24/8b. Pop. 15,465. *Map Square* 24.

	Leave			Arr. at
Vict. S.E. & C.	Hol. V.	S. Pl.'s		Broad
AM	—	3.50k	—	6.52
5. 5	4.57	—	5. 0	8.49
5.48f	5.40f	—	5.42f	8.49
8.25d	—	—	—	10.34
9. 0	—	—	—	10.47
9.20	—	—	—	11.49
10.10	—	—	—	12. 4
10.25d	—	—	—	12.27
10.40	—	—	—	1. 1
11.30l	—	—	—	1.42
PM12.30d	—	—	—	2.23
2.40d	—	—	—	2.36
11. 5d	—	—	—	3. 8
1.25d	—	—	—	4. 2
1.25e	—	—	—	3.17
2. 8e	—	—	—	4.44
2.20d	—	—	—	4.24
2.45d	—	—	—	4.52
3.15e	—	—	—	4.59
3.15d	—	—	—	5. 9
3.20e	—	—	—	5.38
3.29d	—	—	—	5.47
4.15d	—	—	—	6.47
		5. 5e		6.54
5.10d	—	—	—	7.29
		5.10e	5.12e	7.39
5.30	—	—	—	8.28
7. 0	—	—	—	9. 8
8.30	—	—	—	10.43
12. 0p	—	—	—	2.16
12. 5d	—	—	—	2. 6

Sunday Trains.

AM 7.20	—	—	10. 9
9. 0	—	—	10.45
9.10	—	—	11.17
10.15v	—	—	11.55
10.20	—	—	12. 6
10.40	—	—	12.54
PM 3.20	—	—	5.37
3.30	—	—	6.48
8.25	—	—	10.50

Trains from Broadstairs.

	Leave		Arrive at
	Broad.	S. Pl.'s	Hol. V.	Vict.
AM 6.42	9.37	9.39	—
8.52	—	—	10.40
9. 7h	—	—	11.23
9.48	—	—	11.55
10. 8	—	—	12. 7
11. 8d	—	—	1.40
11.43d	—	—	2.15
11.43	—	—	2.43
PM 1. 9	—	—	3.23
1.33e	4.46	—	4.39
2. 8l	—	—	4. 5
p3. 8l	—	—	5. 3
3. 8s	—	—	5. 3
5. 8	—	—	6.58
5.58	—	—	7.54
6.13	9.51	9.53	9.46
7.58	—	—	10.25

BROADSTAIRS—*contd.*
Sunday Trains.

	Leave		Arrive at
	Broad.	S. Pl.'s	Hol. V.	Vict.
AM 9.23	—	11.58	11.51
PM 2.23	—	—	4.42
2.38	—	—	5.32
4.24	—	—	6.24
5.14	—	—	7. 7
5.48	—	—	7.40
6.28	—	—	8.30
7.12v	—	—	8.50
7.28	—	—	9.27
9. 3	—	—	11. 5

d Saturdays only.
e Saturdays excepted.
f Mondays only.
h Wednesdays only.
k Third Class only.
l Mondays, Fridays and Saturdays only.
p Pullman Car attached.
s Mondays, Fridays and Saturdays excepted.
v First Class Pullman Cars only.

ANOTHER ROUTE from
Charing Cross, Cannon Street, and *London Bridge, via* Chatham, 76 miles. Fares as above.

		Leave	Arr. at
Char. +	Can. St.	Lon. B.	Broad.
AM —	—	3.57h	6.52
—	7.16	7.19	10.16
PM —	12.50d	12.53d	2.51
—	1.20d	1.23d	3.24
—	4.12e	4.15e	6.27
—	6.12e	—	8. 2

No Sunday Trains.

Trains from Broadstairs.

	Leave	Arrive at	
Broad.	Lon. B.	Can. St.	Char.+
AM 6.42	8.32	8.36	—
7.12	9.15	9.19	—
7.47g	9.28	9.32	—
7.47f	9.32	9.36	—

No Sunday Trains.
d Saturdays only.
e Saturdays excepted.
f Mondays only.
g Mondays excepted.
h Third Class only.

Taxi Cabs can be hired to meet any train at this station by letter, or telephone No. 48. Messrs. Chalk & Matthews, Station Garage.

BROADSTAIRS—contd.

Kingsgate Castle, near Broadstairs. Beautifully appointed Hotel between Broadstairs and Margate. See advt. p. 113.

The Nook Hotel. Facing Sea. Well Appointed. Best English Catering. See advt. p. 114.

Spero Boarding Establishment. High Class. Facing Sea and Bandstand. Lounge. Terms moderate. See advt. p. 110.

Railway Hotel, Family and Commercial. Minute from Station, five minutes Sea. Spacious Coffee, Billiard, and Smoking Rooms. Excellent Cuisine. Motor Accommodation. Terms moderate. Telephone 0130. L. W LUKEHURST, Proprietor.

Cholmeley Private Hotel, Granville Road Minute Sea. Bandstand. Separate Tables. Electric Light. Superior Catering. Moderate inclusive Tariff. 'Phone 423. PROPRIETRESS.

Warwick Private Hotel. Near Grand Hotel. Minute from Sea, Gardens, and Bandstand. Lounge. Garage. Separate tables. Under personal supervision. Moderate tariff. W. S. TYLER.

Lansdowne, Queen s Road. Close Sea, Gardens, and Bandstand. Smoking Lounge Hall. Liberal Table. Personal Supervision. Moderate Terms. PROPRIETRESS.

Willmot Private Hotel, Victoria Parade. Best position, Sea front, overlooking Band-stand. Table d'Hôte Meals. Separate Tables. Cuisine of the Highest Order. French Chef. Electric Light. Open all the year round. Telephone 139.

Glenmere, Chandos Square. Sea Front. Comfortable Boarding House. Midday Dinner. Liberal Table. Electric Light. From 3 guineas. Miss HARDY.

Locton Boarding House, Chandos Square. Good Catering. Late Dinner. Separate Tables. Moderate Terms, according to season. Mrs. BRENNAN, Proprietress.

Buckingham House, Granville Road. Board Residence. ModerateTerms. SeparateTables. Excellent Cuisine. Minute Sea. Electric Light. Open all the year.

Berkeley, Chandos Square. Adjoining Promenade. Finest position. Opposite Bandstand. Electric Light. Separate Tables. Excellent Cuisine. Late Dinner. Telegrams, "Berkeley."

"Woodberry" Boarding Establishment, "The Vale." Beautifully situated Minute Sea and Bandstand. Electric Light. Home comforts. Garage. Close Tennis. Terms moderate. PROPRIETRESS.

St. Michaels. A Charming Country House. Beautiful Garden. South aspect close to Sea, where invalids are received for rest, care, or convalescence. Accommodation for spinal cases. Excellent cooking. Moderate charges. Tel. 195, Broadstairs. Apply, Miss GERTRUDE FLETCHER, R.R.C.

BROADSTAIRS—contd.

Edencliffe, Eastern Esplanade. Facing Sea. Excellent cuisine and home comforts. Late dinner. Separate tables. Electric light.—Apply, Miss ALLEN.

Cleveland Private Hotel, Granville Road. Minute Sea, Bandstand. Cuisine a speciality. Electric Light. Tariff on application. Telephone 356. Miss WATSON.

Aralia, Stone Road. Minute from Sea. Board Residence. Newly Decorated. Electric Light. Geyser. Generous Table. Convenient Golf, Tennis. Mrs. ALLEN.

Stoneleigh, Granville Road. Comfortable Board Residence. Minute Bandstand and Sea. Separate Tables. Summer from 3 guineas; Winter from 2½ guineas. BAILEY.

Cockett, Henderson & Co., Auctioneers and Estate Agents. Register and Map of District, Station Gates, Broadstairs (Telephone 164), and 100, Jermyn St., London, S.W. 1.

Childs & Smith, House and Estate Agents, Offices facing Station Gates. Printed Map and selected lists sent on application. Telephone 127.

Ince, Howland & Miskin, House and Estate Agents. Lists of Furnished and Unfurnished Houses, free. Telegrams, "Ince, Broadstairs." Telephone 154, Broadstairs.

House Agent, B.J.Pearson, Station Gates, Broadstairs, for all available houses in Broadstairs and District. Lists free. Phone, 183. Telegrams, "Pearson"

BROADSTONE (Dorset)

from Waterloo, via Southampton and Wimborne, 115 miles. Fares, 24/2a, 14/6c. R.T. for two months, 48/4a, 29/0c. Pop. 1,309. Map Square 27.

W'LOO	B'STONE	B'STONE	W'LOO
AM 5.40	9.51	AM 6.53r	10. 6
9.30	1. 4	8.47s	12.22
11.30r	2.53	10.35r	2.20
PM12.30r	3.59	PM12.45	4.20
1.30s	4.59	1.48	6.16
3.50s	7. 3	2.16s	6.26
5.50r	8.53	4.48r	8.20
6.30r	10. 3	6.55r	11.28
—	—	10. 3h	3.58

Sunday Trains.

W'LOO	B'STONE	B'STONE	W'LOO
AM11. 0r	2.53	AM 8.39r	2.27
PM 2. 0r	6. 2	PM 3.54	8. 3
—	—	—	—
—	—	—	—

h Via Bournemouth. r Restaurant Car. s Refreshments served.

ANOTHER ROUTE from Waterloo, via Salisbury, 112 miles. Fares as above.

W'LOO	B'STONE	B'STONE	W'LOO
AM 7.30	10.56	AM 7.17	10.56
11. 0r	2.17	7.57r	11.10
PM 1. 0r	4.37	10.52r	1.56
3. 0r	6.20	PM 2.53r	6. 0
6. 0r	9.50	4.53r	8.30

Sunday Trains.

W'LOO	B'STONE	B'STONE	W'LOO
PM12. 0nr	4.58	PM 4.17	8.57
—	—	—	—

n Noon. r Restaurant Car.

BROADWAY (Worcester)

from Paddington. 106¾ miles. Fares, 22/3a, 13/4c. R. T. for two months, 44/6a, 26/8c. Pop. 1,793. Map Square 17.

PAD.	BROADWY.	BROADWY.	PAD.
AM 5.30	9.56	AM 9.15	12. 5
6.30k	11.26	10.41	2.12
9.45	1.36	PM12. 3r	2.55
PM 2.10k	5.55	4.36kr	8. 5
4.45	7.36	5.47r	9.15
—	—	7. 1	10.45

Sunday Trains.

PAD.	BROADWY.	BROADWY.	PAD.
PM 4.10	7.46	AM 8.34	2.40
—	—	M 5.56r	9.48
—	—	—	—
—	—	—	—

k Via Stratford-on-Avon. r Restaurant Car.

BROCK (Lancs), 216½ miles.

Fares, 45/2a, 27/1c. R. T. for two months, 90/4a, 54/2c. Departures from London as for Preston. Departures for London about 4 times daily. Map Square 12.

BROCKENHURST

(Hants) from Waterloo, 92 miles. Fares, 19/5a, 11/8c. R. T. for two months, 38/10a, 23/4c. Pop. 2,048. Map Square 27.

W'LOO.	BROCKN.	BROCKN.	W'LOO.
AM 5.40	8.17	AM 8. 2r	10. 6
5.50	9.45	8.35s	11. 0
8.30s	10.58	9.59s	12.22
9.30	11 58	10.29r	12.50
10.30	12.55	11.57r	2.20
11.30r	1.42	PM 1.57	4.20
PM12.30r	2.40	3. 0	6.16
1.30s	3.53	3.57s	6.26
2.30	4.41	5. 1	6.58
3.50s	5.53	5.57r	8.20
4.30r	6.55	6.22r	8.50
5.30r	7.53	7.40	10.50
6.30r	8.48	8.41	11.28
7.30	10.12	12.13m	3.58
10. 0	1.15	—	—

Sunday Trains.

W'LOO.	BROCKN.	BROCKN.	W'LOO.
AM11. 0r	1.23	AM 9.23	12.11
PM 2. 0r	4.17	12. 4r	2.27
7. 0r	9.22	PM 5. 2	3. 3
9.28	1.15	7.26r	9.31
—	—	7.43	10.52
—	—	12.13m	3.58

m Midnight. r Restaurant Car. s Refreshments served.

Balmer Lawn Hotel, ¾ mile Brockenhurst. First Class Family and Residential Hotel. Luxuriously Furnished. Garage. Stablery. Golf. See advt. p. 115.

Forest Park Hotel. In the heart of the New Forest. Telephone 8. Telegrams, "Foxhound." See advt. p. 114.

New Forest favourite village. Paying Guests. Excellent Cooking. Every convenience. Golf, Tennis, Hunting. Tel. 29. MASSEY, Forest Glen, Burley, Hants.

BROCKETSBRAE

(Lanark), 388½ miles. Fares, 80/8a, 48/5c. R. T. for two months, 161/4a, 96/10c. Departures from London as for Hamilton. Departures for London about 4 times daily. Map Square 40.

BROCKFORD (Suffolk), 89¼ miles. Fares, 18/9*a*, 11/3*c*. R.T. for two months, 37/6*a*, 22/6*c*. Departures *from* London as for Stradbroke. Departures *for* London about twice daily. Pop. 822.
Map Square 19.

BROCKHOLES (Yorks), 183¾ miles. Fares, 37/3*a*, 22/4*c*. R.T. for two months, 74/6*a*, 44/8*c*. Departures *from* London as for Penistone. Departures *for* London about 6 times daily.
Map Square 12.

BROCKLESBY (Lincoln) from *King's Cross*, 173¾ miles. Fares, 34/0*a*, 20/5*c*. R. T. for two months, 68/0*a*, 40/10*c*. Pop. 225.
Map Square 13.

King's +	Brock.	Brock.	King's +
AM 4.45	10.15	AM 6.23*r*	11.30
7.15*r*	11.42	8.13*r*	1. 5
10.10	4.12	PM 1. 5	6.25
PM 1.50*r*	6.40	3. 8	9. 0
4. 0*r*	8.54	7.24	3.25
8.25*e*	5.10	—	—
—	—	—	—
—	—	—	—
—	—	—	—

Sunday Trains.

PM 5. 0	9.37	AM 9.21*r*	3.45
8.25	5.10	PM 5. 5*r*	10.20
—	—	—	—

e Saturdays excepted.
r Restaurant Car.

ANOTHER ROUTE from *Marylebone*, 209¾ miles. Fares as above.

M'bone.	Brock.	Brock.	M'bone.
AM 2.32	10.15	AM 6.23*r*	1.13
10. 0*r*	4.13	8.13*r*	3. 0
PM12.15*r*	6.38	PM 1. 5*r*	6.38
3.20*r*	8.54	3.54*r*	9.55
10. 5*e*	5.10	7.24	3.57
—	—	—	—
—	—	—	—
—	—	—	—

Sunday Trains.

AM11.15*r*	9.37	AM 9.21*r*	5.40
—	—	—	—
—	—	—	—

e Saturdays excepted.
r Restaurant Car

BROCKLEY (Kent) from *London Bridge*, 3½ miles, or from *Victoria*, 12½ miles. Fares from London Bridge, 0/9½*a*, 0/5½*c*. R.T. for two days, 1/7*a*, 0/11*c*. From Victoria (Crystal Palace Line), 1/6*a*, 0/10½*c*. R. T. for eight days, 3/0*a*, 1/9*c*. *Via* Norwood Junction, 1/11*a*, 1/2*c*. R.T. for eight days, 3/10*a*, 2/0*c*. Pop. 16,926. *See* pp. 568-570, 580, 581.
Map Square 71.

BROCKLEY WHINS (Durham), 265¼ miles. Fares, 55/7*a*, 33/4*c*. R.T. for two months, 111/2*a*, 66/8*c*. Departures *from* London as for Newcastle-on-Tyne or Sunderland. Departures *for* London about 6 times daily.

BRODIE (Nairn), 572½ miles. Fares, 106/3*a*, 63/9*c*. R. T. for two months, 212/6*a*, 127/6*c*. Departures *from* London as for Forres. Departures *for* London about twice daily. Pop. 501.
Map Square 34.

BROMBOROUGH (Cheshire), 189 miles. Fares, 39/5*a*, 23/8*c*. R. T. for two months, 78/10*a*, 47/4*c*. Departures *from* London as for Hooton. Departures *for* London about 6 times daily. Pop. 2,650.
Map Square 12.

BROMFIELD (Salop), 160¾ miles. Fares, 31/11*a*, 19/2*c*. R. T. for two months, 63/10*a*, 38/4*c*. Departures *from* London as for Ludlow. Departures *for* London about 4 times daily. Pop. 539.
Map Square 17.

BROMLEY (Middlesex) from *Fenchurch Street*, 3¼ miles. Fares, 0/7½*a*, 0/4½*c*. R. T. for two days, 1/3*a*, 0/9*c*. Pop. 65,417. *See* pp. 510, 537-540.
Map Squares 23 and 62.

ANOTHER ROUTE from *Ealing, Hounslow, Richmond*, and *Wimbledon, via* District Railway. *See* p. 489.

BROMLEY CROSS (Lancs), 200¼ miles. Fares, 41/1*a*, 24/8*c*. R. T. for two months, 82/2*a*, 49/4*c*. Departures *from* London as for Bolton (*via* Manchester). Departures *for* London about 6 times daily. Pop. 1,586.

BROMLEY, NORTH (Kent) from *Charing Cross, Cannon Street*, and *London Bridge*, 11¼ miles. Fares from Charing Cross, 2/4*a*, 1/11*b*, 1/5*c*. R. T. for two days, 4/8*a*, 3/10*b*. From Cannon Street, 2/4*a*, 1/11*b*, 1/3*c*. R. T. for two days, 4/8*a*, 3/10*b*, 2/6*c*. Pop. 5,526. *See* pp. 556, 557.
Map Square 80.

BROMLEY, SOUTH (Kent) from *Victoria, Holborn Viaduct, Ludgate Hill*, and *St. Paul's*, 10¾ miles. Fares, 2/4*a*, 1/11*b*, 1/5*c*. R. T for two days, 4/8*a*, 3/10*b*. Pop. (Bromley) 35,052. See pp. 558-561.

ANOTHER ROUTE from *Charing Cross, Cannon Street*, and *London Bridge*, 13 miles, *via* Beckenham Junction. Fares as above. *See* pp. 544-547.

Bromley Hill Court. Ideal Country Hotel. Standing in twelve acres.
See advt. p. **23**.

BROMLEY SOUTH (Middlesex) from *Broad Street*, 6 miles. Fares, 0/7½*a*, 0/6*b*, 0/4½*c*. R. T. for two days, 1/3*a*, 0/10½*b*, 0/9*c*. *See* p. 500.
Map Square 62.

BROMPTON (Yorks), 220 miles. No through fares. Departures *from* London as for Stockton-on-Tees. Departures *for* London about 4 times daily. Pop. 1,487.
Map Square 7.

BROMPTON ROAD (Hammersmith and Finsbury Park Tube). *See* back of Map.

BROMPTON WEST from *Clapham Junction*, 2¼ miles. Fares, 0/7*a*, 0/4*c*. R.T. for two days, 1/2*a*, 0/7*c*. *See* p. 583. Pop. 5,772.
Map Square 68.

From *Kensington* (Addison Road), 1 mile. Fares, 0/2½*a*, 0/1½*c*. R.T. for two days, 0/5*a*, 0/3*c*. See p. 583.

From *Mansion House*, 5¼ miles. *See* p. 489.

BROMSGROVE (Worcester), from *Euston, via* Birmingham, 127 miles. Fares, 23/9*a*, 14/3*c*. R. T. for two months, 47/6*a*, 28/6*c*. Pop. 9,449.
Map Square 17.

Euston	B'msgr've	B'msgr've	Euston
AM 2.30	7.45	AM 3.35	10. 0
5. 0	9.27	7.42	10.40
6.45	11. 0	8.56	12.40
9.15*r*	12.57	10.29*r*	1.25
11.30*r*	2.33	PM 1. 0*t*	4.35
12. 0*nr*	3.52	3.40*r*	6.50
PM 2.20*t*	5.12	4.55*r*	8.20
2.50*t*	7. 0	6.15*dr*10.45	
4.35*r*	7.45	7.12*er*10.20	
6.55*r*	9.46	9.38*e*	4. 0
9.30	3.20	9.48*d*	5. 0
12.10*dm*	9.25	—	—
—	—	—	—
—	—	—	—
—	—	—	—
—	—	—	—

Sunday Trains.

AM 9.15	3.22	AM 3.35	12.25
PM 1. 0*r*	5.29	9.18*r*	1.45
5.10	9.24	11.31	5. 5
9.15	3.20	PM 9.38	5. 0
—	—	—	—
—	—	—	—
—	—	—	—

d Saturdays only.
e Saturdays excepted.
m Midnight.
n Noon.
r Restaurant Car.
t Tea Car.

BROMYARD (Hereford) from *Paddington*, 134¾ miles. Fares, 26/10*a*, 16/1*c*. R. T. for two months, 53/8*a*, 32/2*c*. Pop. 1,573.
Map Square 17.

Pad.	B'yard.	B'yard.	Pad.
AM 5.30	11. 9	AM 7.40	11.15
9.45	1.57	9.32	2.12
PM 1.35*r*	6.11	PM 1. 0*r*	4.15
4.45*t*	8. 9	4.55*r*	9.15
—	—	—	—
—	—	—	—
—	—	—	—
—	—	—	—

Sunday Trains.

AM10.35*r*	3.15	PM 3.25*r*	9.48

r Restaurant Car.
t Tea Car.

BRONDESBURY from *Broad Street*, 8¼ miles. Fares, 0/10*a*, 0/6*c*. R. T. for two days, 1/5½*a*, 0/10½*c*. Pop. 9,328. *See* pp. 501-505.
Map Square 59.

BRONDESBURY PARK from *Broad Street*, 9 miles. Fares, 0/11½*a*, 0/7½*c*. R.T. for two days, 1/11*a*, 1/2*c*. Pop. 9,430. *See* pp. 501-505.

BRONWYDD ARMS (Carmarthen), 231¼ miles. Fares 46/8*a*, 28/0*c*. R. T. for two months, 93/4*a*, 56/0*c*. Departures *from* London as for Carmarthen. Departures *for* London 5 times daily.
Map Square 16.

BROOKLAND (Kent) from *Charing Cross, Cannon Street*, and *London Bridge*, 67¾ miles. Fares, 14/2*a*, 11/4*b*, 8/6*c*. R.T. for two months, 28/4*a*, 22/8*b*. Departures *from* London as for Lydd. Departures *for* London about 5 times daily. Pop. 466.
Map Square 24.

BROOKLANDS (Ch'shire),

189½ miles. Fares, *via* Manchester, 39/10*a*,23/11*c*. R. T. for two months. 79/8*a*, 47/10*c*. Departures *from* London as for Manchester (London Road). Departures *for* London about 9 times daily.
Map Square 12.

Manchester. — Woodcourt

Private Hotel, Brooklands, Cheshire.
See advt. p. **246.**

BROOKSBY (Leicester),

108 miles. Fares, 21/8*a*, 13/0*c*. R. T. for two months, 43/4*a*, 26/0*c*. Departures *from* London as for Ashfordby. Departures *for* London about 6 times daily. Pop. 58.
Map Square 18.

BROOKWOOD (Surrey)

from *Waterloo*, 28 miles. Fares, 5/10*a*, 3/6*c*. R. T. for two months. 11/8*a*, 7/0*c*.
Map Square 23.

W'LOO	BROOKWD.	BROOKWD.	W'LOO.
AM 4.50	6.15	AM 6.49	7.46
5.40	6.51	7.49	8.41
5.50	6.45	8. 4	8.56
7. 0	8. 9	8.10	9. 8
7.30	8.26	8.35	9.26
7.50	9. 0	8.55	9.41
8.34	9.30	9. 9	10.11
9.20	10. 6	9.37	10.20
10.34	11.34	10.30	11.16
11.20	12.24	10.41	11.46
PM12.14*d*	1.11	11.26	12.11
12.40	1.36	11.54	12.40
1.10	1.54	PM12.20	1.20
1.15*d*	2.14	12.55	1.40
1.20	2.26	1.31	2.46
2.20	3.26	2. 6	3. 6
2.34	3.38	2.24	3.16
3.15	4. 0	2.49	3.36
3.40	4.37	3.16	4. 6
4. 0	4.45	3.33	4.46
4.20*d*	5.28	4.20	5.20
4.40	5.44	4.36	5.46
5.10	5.54	5.12	6.16
5.30*e*	6.17	6.21	7. 7
5.50*d*	6.44	7.42	8.46
6.10*e*	7. 1	8. 5	9. 6
6.40*d*	7.36	8.24	9.26
6.54*e*	7.41	8.35	9.46
7.20	8.28	8.59	9.52
8. 0	8.53	9.52	10.50
8.55	10. 3	10. 6	11.10
9.50	10.41	10.55	12.16
12. 5	12.51	—	—

Sunday Trains.

AM 8.20	9.34	AM 8.27	9.45
8.45	9.42	10.10	11.16
9. 0	9.53	11.10	12.41
9.45	10.50	11.55	12.52
10.20	11.37	PM 1. 0	2.44
11.15	12. 7	2.13	3.13
PM12.20	1.37	4.12	5.41
1.50	2.52	5.25	6. 7
3.20	4.37	6.25	7.41
5. 5	5.58	8.21	9.12
5.20	6.37	9.42	10.47
6. 0	6.54	—	—
6.20	7. 9	—	—
6.30	7.36	—	—
7.20	8.24	—	—
9.45	10.53	—	—
10.45	11.34	—	—

d Saturdays only.
e Saturdays excepted.

BROOM (Worcester), from

Marylebone, 100¾ miles. Fares, 22/8*a*, 13/7*c*. R. T. for two months, 45/4*a*, 27/2*c*. Departures *from* London as for Stratford-on-Avon. Departures *for* London about 4 times daily. Pop. 123.
Map Square 17.

BROOME (Salop), from

Euston, 185 miles. Fares, 32/6*a*, 19/6*c*. R. T. for two months, 65/0*a*, 39/0*c*. Departures *from* London as for Craven Arms. Departures *for* London about 4 times daily.
Map Square 17.

BROOMHILL (Inverness),

542½ miles. Fares, 106/3*a*, 63/9*c*. R. T. for two months, 212/6*a*, 127/6*c*. Departures *from* London as for Aviemore. Departures *for* London about twice daily.
Map Square 34.

BROOMHILL (Northumberland), 296¾ miles. No through

fares. Departures *from* London as for Morpeth. Departures *for* London about 4 times daily.
Map Square 34.

BROOMHOUSE (Lanark),

434¾ miles. No through fares. Departures *from* London as for Edinburgh (Waverley). Departures *for* London about 4 times daily.

BROOMIEKNOWE (Midlothian), 391½ miles. No through

fares. Departures *from* London as for Edinburgh (Waverley). Departures *for* London about 8 times daily.

BROOMLEE (Peebles), 398½

miles. No through fares. Departures *from* London as for Peebles. Departures *for* London about 3 times daily.
Map Square 41.

BRORA (Sutherland), 658

miles. Fares, 118/7*a*, 71/2*c*. R. T. for two months, 237/2*a*, 142/4*c*. Departures *from* London as for Golspie. Departures *for* London about 3 times daily. Pop. 1,210.
Map Square 34.

BROTTON (Yorks) from

King's Cross, 254 miles. Fares, 52/11*a*, 31/9*c*. R. T. for two months, 105/10*a*, 63/6*c*. Departures *from* London as for Saltburn or Sandsend. Departures *for* London about 4 times daily. Pop. 3,703.
Map Square 8.

BROUGH (Yorks). 186¼

miles. Fares 35/0*a*, 21/0*c*. R. T. for two months, 70/0*a*, 42/0*c*. Departures *from* London as for Goole. Departures *for* London about 6 times daily. Pop. 84.
Map Square 13.

BROUGHTON (Peebles),

from *Euston*, 374 miles. Fares, 76/1*a*, 45/8*c*. R. T. for two months, 152/2*a*, 91/4*c*. Departures *from* London as for Peebles. Departures *for* London about 4 times daily. Pop. 739.
Map Square 41.

BROUGHTON AND

BRETTON (Flint), 183½ miles. Fares, 38/2*a*, 22/11*c*. R. T. for two months, 76/4*a*, 45/10*c*. Departures *from* London as for Chester. Departures *for* London about 6 times daily.
Map Square 12.

BROUGHTON-AST-

LEY (Leicester) from *Euston*, 93½ miles. Fares, 19/5*a*, 11/8*c*. R. T. for two months, 38/10*a*, 23/4*c*. Pop. 1,339.
Map Square 18.

EUSTON	BROUG.	BROUG.	EUSTON
AM 5. 0	7.52	AM 6.40*er*	9.52
6.45	10.25	6.40*dr*10. 0	
10. 0	12.50	9. 7	11.55
12.*Gnr*	2.34	11.13*r*	2.20
PM 2.50*t*	5.32	PM 1.24*r*	4.15
5.20*r*	7.45	3.18*t*	5.50
12.10*d*	7.41	5.38*r*	9.20
—	—	8.17*er*10.45	
—	—	9.18*d*	5. 0
—	—	—	—
—	—	—	—

Sunday Trains.

AM12.10	7.41	AM 9.36	12.25
PM 3.50	7.20	PM 6. 5*r*	8.20
—	—	—	—
—	—	—	—

d Saturdays only.
e Saturdays excepted.
n Noon.
r Restaurant Car.
t Tea Car.

BROUGHTON CROSS

(Cumberland), 314½ miles. Fares, 63/11*a*, 38/4*c*. R. T. for two months, 127/10*a*, 76/8*c*. Departures *from* London as for Cockermouth. Departures *for* London about 3 times daily.
Map Square 6.

BROUGHTON-IN-FUR-

NESS (Lancs), 270½ miles. Fares, 56/3, 33/9*c*. R. T. for two months, 112/6*a*, 67/6*c*. Departures *from* London as for Coniston. Departures *for* London about 3 times daily. Pop. 1,073.
Map Square 6.

BROUGHTON LANE

(Yorks), 164½ miles. Fares 32/9*a*, 19/8*c*. R. T. for two months, 65/6*a*, 39/4*c*. Departures *from* London as for Sheffield (Victoria). Departures *for* London about 4 times daily.

BROUGHTON, UPPER

(Notts) from *St. Pancras*, 112½ miles. Fares, 23/2*a*, 13/11*c*. R. T. for two months, 46/4*a*,27/10*c*. Departures *from* London as for Melton Mowbray. Departures *for* London about 4 times daily. Pop. 323.
Map Square 18.

BROUGHTY FERRY

(Forfar), 455¾ miles. Fares, 91/11*a*, 55/2*c*. R. T. for two months,183/10*a*, 110/4*c*. Departures *from* London as for Dundee. Departures *for* London about 4 times daily.
Map Square 38.

BROWNHILLS (Stafford),

123¾ miles. Fares, 25/8*a*, 15/5*c*. R. T. for two months, 51/4*a*, 30/10*c*. Departures *from* London as for Lichfield. Departures *for* London about 6 times daily. Pop. 18,241
Map Square 17.

BROXBOURNE (Herts)

from *Liverpool Street*, 17½ miles. Fares, 3/9*a*, 3/0*b*, 2/3*c*. R. T. for two months, 7/6*a*, 6/0*b*, 4/4½*c*. Pop. 790. *See* pp. 526–527.
Map Square 23.

BROXTON (Cheshire), 180¼ miles. Fares, 36/8*a*, 22/0*c*. R. T. for two months, 73/4*a*, 44/0*c*. Departures *from* London as for Whitchurch or Chester. Departures *for* London about 6 times daily. Pop. 541.
Map Square 12.

BRUCE GROVE (Tottenham) from *Liverpool Street*, 6¼ miles. Fares, 0/10*a*, 0/8*b*, 0/6*c*. R. T. for two days, 1/8*a*, 1/4*b*, 0/10½*c*. *See* pp. 534-536.
Map Square 52.

BRUCKLAY (Aberdeen), 556 miles. No through fares. Departures *from* London as for Fraserburgh. Departures *for* London about twice daily.
Map Square 35.

BRUNDALL (Norfolk) from *Liverpool Street*, *via* Cambridge, 128¾ miles. Fares, 24/9*a*, 14/10*c*. R.T. for two months, 49/6*a*, 29/8*c*. Pop. 490.
Map Square 19.

L'pool St.	Brund.	Brund.	L'pool St.
AM 5. 5	9.14	AM 7.15	11.27
5.50	11. 5	8.18	12.40
8.30*r*	12.44	10 3*r*	2.21
11.50*r*	4. 4	PM 1.29*r*	5.17
PM 2.34	6.36	4. 1*dr*	8.22
5.49*r*	10. 0	4.34*r*	8.33
7.10*r*	10.59	9.55	2.50

Sunday Trains.

AM 9.25	2. 6	PM 1.58	6.40
PM 3.25	7.58	5.41	9.40
—	—	9.55	3. 0

r Restaurant Car.

ANOTHER ROUTE *via* Ipswich and Trowse, 119¾ miles. Fares as above.

L'pool St.	Brund.	Brund.	L'pool St.
AM 5. 0	9.14	AM 7.15*f*	10.36
8.15*r*	11.50	8.18*r*	11.22
9.50*r*	12.52	10. 3	1.20
10.12	2.32	PM 1.29*r*	4.58
PM12.33*r*	4. 4	2.42	6.32
3.10*r*	6.16	3.23	7.51
5.18*r*	8.55	6. 6*r*	9.22
—	—	6.45	11.16
—	—	—	—

Sunday Trains.

AM 9.20*r*	2. 5	PM 5.41*r*	9.10
PM 4.40	9.32	—	—

f Mondays only.
r Restaurant Car.

BRUSSELS. Air Route by Instone Air Line, Ltd. Cars from Hotel Metropole, London, to Aerodome daily at 10.00. Fares, £3 19s. 6*d*. R. T. £7 7s. 0*d*. Subject to Passport Regulations.

London	Brussels	Brussels	London
11.00	13.30	12.00	14.30

See also Cologne.

BRUTON (Somerset) from *Paddington*, 112 miles. Fares, 23/4*a*, 14/0*c*. R. T. for two months, 46/8*a*, 28/0*c*. Pop. 1,755.
Map Square 22.

Pad.	Bruton	Bruton	Pad.
AM 1. 0*g*	8. 0	AM 8. 7	10.52
5.30	10. 7	9.28	12.55
10.30	1.28	PM12.34	3.50
PM12.30*r*	3.22	3.29*r*	6.50
3.30	6. 7	5.24	8.20
5. 5	8.44	8.20	2.45
—	—	9.54*h*	2.45

BRUTON—*continued.*

Sunday Trains.

Pad.	Bruton	Bruton	Pad.
AM 9.10	1.59	AM11.21	3.35
PM 2.40	5.20	PM 3.42*r*	7.55
10. 0	8. 0	—	—

g Mondays excepted.
h Thursdays, and Third Class only.
r Restaurant Car.

BRYMBO (Denbigh), 185¾ miles. Fares, 37/9*a*, 22/10*c*. R. T. for two months, 75/6*a*, 45/8*c*. Departures *from* London as for Wrexham. Departures *for* London about 4 times daily. Pop. 505.
Map Square 12.

BRYN (Glamorgan), 190 miles. No through fares. Departures *from* London as for Maesteg or Tondu. Departures *for* London about 3 times daily.
Map Square 21.

BRYN (Lancs), 194½ miles. Fares, 40/8*a*, 24/5*c*. R. T. for two months, 81/4*a*, 48/10*c*. Departures *from* London as for Wigan or St. Helens. Departures *for* London about 5 times daily.
Map Square 12.

BRYNAMMAN (Carmarthen) from *Paddington*, 215½ miles. Fares, 44/2*a*, 26/6*c*. R. T. for two months, 88/4*a*, 53/0*c*. Pop. 5,072.
Map Square 21.

Pad.	Brnamn.	Brnamn.	Pad.
AM 1. 0*g*	10.50	AM 7.45*r*	2.30
8.45*r*	3.40	8.10*r*	4.20
11.50*r*	5.55	11.15*r*	6.15
PM 1.10*r*	8.25	PM12.30*r*	8.35
9.15*e*	6.30	2.12*r*	9.25
—	—	7.20	3.30
—	—	—	—
—	—	—	—

Sunday Trains.

PM 9.15	6.30	—	—
—	—	—	—
—	—	—	—
—	—	—	—

e Saturdays excepted.
g Mondays excepted.
r Restaurant Car.

BRYNGLAS (Merioneth), 235½ miles. No through fares. Departures *from* London as for Machynlleth. Departures *for* London about 3 times daily.
Map Square 16.

BRYNGWYN (Carnarvon), 255¼ miles. No through fares. Departures *from* London as for Carnarvon. Departures *for* London about 3 times daily.
Map Square 11.

BRYNGWYN (Montgomery), 183¼ miles. Fares, 37/5*a*, 22/6*c*. R. T. for two months, 75/0*a*. Departures *from* London as for Oswestry. Departures *for* London about 4 times daily.
Map Square 16.

BRYNKIR (Carnarvon), 260 miles. Fares, 54/2*a*, 32/6*c*. R. T. for two months, 108/4*a*, 65/0*c*. Departures *from* London as for Carnarvon. Departures *for* London about twice daily.
Map Square 11.

BRYNMAWR (Brecon), 162¾ miles. Fares, 33/2*a*, 19/11*c*. R. T. for two months, 66/4*a*, 39/10*c*. Departures *from* London as for Abersychan. Departures *for* London about 6 times daily. Pop. 8,062.
Map Square 21.

BRYNMENYN (Glamorgan), 176¾ miles. Fares, 36/11*a*, 22/2*c*. R. T. for two months, 73/10*a*, 44/4*c*. Departures *from* London as for Tondu. Departures *for* London about 4 times daily.

BRYN TEIFY (Carmarthen) from *Paddington*, 244¾ miles. Fares, 48/9*a*, 29/3*c*. R. T. for two months, 97/6*a*, 58/6*c*. Departures *from* London as for Lampeter. Departures *for* London about 4 times daily.
Map Square 16.

BUBWITH (Yorks), 180¾ miles. Fares, 36/5*a*, 21/10*c*. R. T. for two months, 72/10*a*, 43/8*c*. Departures *from* London as for Selby. Departures *for* London about 5 times daily. Pop. 460.
Map Square 13.

BUCHLYVIE (Stirling), 432½ miles. Fares, 87/8*a*, 52/7*c*. R.T. for two months, 175/4*a*, 105/2*c*. Departures *from* London as for Stirling. Departures *for* London about 4 times daily.

BUCKDEN (Hunts) from *St. Pancras*, 94¾ miles. Fares, 14/9*a*, 8/10*c*. R. T. for two months, 29/6*a*, 17/8*c*. Departures *from* London as for Kimbolton. Departures *for* London about 4 times daily. Pop. 995.
Map Square 18.

BUCKENHAM (Norfolk), 121¾ miles. Fares, 24/9*a*, 14/10*c*. R. T. for two months, 49/6*a*, 29/8*c*. Departures *from* London as for Brundall. Departures *for* London 8 minutes later. Pop. 77.
Map Square 19.

BUCKFASTLEIGH (Devon), 209 miles. Fares, 43/1*a*, 25/10*c*. R.T. for two months, 86/2*a*, 51/8*c*. Departures *from* London as for Ashburton. Departures *for* London about 5 times daily. Pop. 2,265.
Map Square 26.

BUCKHAVEN (Fife), 427 miles. No through fares. Departures *from* London as for Kirkcaldy. Departures *for* London about 3 times daily. Pop. 15,149.
Map Square 41.

BUCKHURST HILL (Essex) from *Fenchurch Street*, 10¾ miles, or from *Liverpool Street*, 10½ miles. Fares from Liverpool Street, 1/10½*a*, 1/6*b*, 1/1½*c*. R. T. for two days, 3/9*a*, 2/11*b*, 2/0½*c*. Fenchurch Street, 1/10½*a*, 1/6*b*, 1/1½*c*. R. T. for two days, 3/9*a*, 2/11*b*, 2/0½*c*. Pop. 5,008. *See* pp. 541-544.
Map Square 23.

BUCKIE (Banff), 595½ miles. Fares, 106/3*a*, 63/9*c*. R. T. for two months, 212/6*a*, 127/6*c*. Departures *from* London as for Huntly or Elgin (*via* Dunkeld). Departures *for* London about twice daily. Pop. 8,690.
Map Square 35.

BUCKINGHAM from
Euston, 60½ miles. Fares, 11/5a, 6/10c. R. T. for two months, 22/10a, 13/8c. Pop. 3,053.
Map Square 18.

EUSTON BUCKHM.		BUCKHM. EUSTON	
AM 6.45	8.54	AM 8.11	10. 0
7.35	10.57	9.45	11.55
10.40	1. 5	11.56h	2.45
12. 0nr	2.21	PM 1.15	4.15
PM 3. 5	5.26	3. 4	5.35
4.15	6. 4	5.32	7.55
5.32	7.25	7.26	9.20

Sunday Trains.

AM 9.15	12.20	fPM 3.35	5.50
PM 2.15	5.26	7.24	9.45

h Thursdays and Saturdays only.
n Noon.
r Restaurant Car.

Taxi Cabs can be hired to meet any train at this station by telegram, or telephone No. 21. Messrs. Phillips & Sons, Motor Works, Buckingham.

White Hart Hotel. Telephone 31. Comfortable and quiet. Excellent Garden. Good Stabling and Garage.
TRUST HOUSES, Ltd.

BUCKLEY (Flint), 191¼ miles. No through fares. Departures *from* London as for Wrexham. Departures *for* London about 4 times daily Pop. 6,734.
Map Square 12.

BUCKNALL (Stafford), 147½ miles. Fares, 30/10a, 18/6c. R.T. for two months, 61/8a, 37/0c. Departures *from* London as for Stoke-on-Trent. Departures *for* London about 6 times daily. Pop. 4,862.
Map Square 12.

BUCKNELL (Salop) from
Euston, 190½ miles. Fares, 33/7a, 20/2c. R.T. for two months, 67/2a, 40/4c. Departures *from* London as for Craven Arms. Departures *for* London about 4 times daily. Pop. 445.
Map Square 17.

BUCKSBURN (Aberdeen),
527 miles. No through fares. Departures *from* London as for Aberdeen. Departures *for* London about 3 times daily.
Map Square 35.

BUDE (Cornwall) from
Waterloo, 228½ miles. Fares, 47/8a, 28/7c. R.T. for two months, 95/4a, 57/2c. Pop. 2,219.
Map Square 26.

W'LOO	BUDE	BUDE	W'LOO
AM10. 0r	3.23	AM 7.20r	1.56
11. 0r	5.27	9.40r	3.50
PM 1. 0r	7.34	10.50r	4.30
3. 0r	8.36	PM 1.30r	8.30
—	—	3.37	10.50

No Sunday Trains.
r Restaurant Car.

Falcon Hotel. Largest, nearest Sea. Telephone No. 5. Telegrams: "Falcon."
See advt. p. **115.**

Erdiston Boarding Establishment. Highest Position. Adjoining Beach, Golf Links, and Tennis. Separate Tables. Smoking Lounge. Moderate terms.
Mrs. BANBURY.

BUDE—continued.

Norfolk Hotel, Family and Commercial (Unlicensed). Most central for Golf Links, Sea, or Station. Telegrams, "Norfolk, Bude."
Mrs. GILBERT, Proprietress.

The Edgcumbe Private Hotel, Summerleaze, adjoins Golf Links. Is considerably nearer the Sea than any hotel or boarding house in Bude. Telephone 43.

Grenville Hotel, Bude. Largest and only modern equipped Hotel. Facing Atlantic. Three minutes from N. Cornwall Golf Links. Lift. Central Heating. Fishing. R.A.C., A.A. Garage; all accessories. 'Phone 15 Bude. Telegrams: "Grenville, Bude."

BUDLEIGH EAST
(Devon), 169 miles. Fares, *via* Sidmouth Junct., 35/3a, 21/2c. R. T. for two months, 70/6a, 42/4c. *Via* Exeter, 39/7a, 23/9c. R. T. for two months, 79/2a, 47/6c. Departures *from* London as for Tipton St. Johns or Exeter. Departures *for* London about 4 times daily. Pop. 767.
Map Square 26.

BUDLEIGH SALTERTON (Devon) from *Waterloo, via* Tipton St. John's, 171 miles. Fares, 35/8a, 21/5c. R. T. for two months, 71/4a, 42.10c. Pop, 2,622.
Map Square 26.

W'LOO B. SALT'N	B. SALT'N W'LOO		
AM 9. 0r	1.11	AM 9.32r	1.56
10. 0r	3.10	10.29r	3. 8
12. 0nr	4.26	PM12.39r	6. 0
PM 1. 0r	6.11	2.31	7.40
3. 0r	8.11	5.31	10.50
—	—	7.31h	3.58

No Sunday Trains

h Via Eastleigh.
n Noon.
r Restaurant Car.

ANOTHER ROUTE, *via* Exeter and Exmouth, 184½ miles. Fares, 39/0a, 23/5c. R. T. for two months, 78/0a, 46/10c.

W'LOO B. SALT'N	B. SALT'N W'LOO		
AM10. 0r	2.31	AM 9.13r	1.56
11. 0r	4.27	11.25r	3.50
PM 1. 0r	6.31	PM 1.11r	6. 0
3. 0r	7.51	1.40	7.40
—	—	3.10r	8.30
—	—	5. 1	10.50
—	—	6.11h	3.58

No Sunday Trains.

h Via Eastleigh.
r Restaurant Car.

Rosemullion Hotel. Overlooking Sea. Near East Devon Golf Links. Tennis and Croquet Club. Good Cuisine. New Dining and Lounge. Central Heating. Electric light. Manageress—
ROSEMULLION HOTEL, LTD.

Otterbourne Hotel. Facing South. Two minutes Sea. Near Tennis, Croquet Club. Open for first time, July, 1922. New Equipment throughout. Write—
MANAGERESS.

BUGLE (Cornwall), 266¼ miles. Fares, 55/2a, 33/1c. R. T. for two months, 110/4a, 66/2c. Departures *from* London as for Newquay. Departures *for* London about 4 times daily.
Map Square 25.

BUGSWORTH (Derby)
from *St. Pancras,* 170½ miles. Fares, 35/3a, 21/2c. R. T. for two months, 70/6a, 42/4c. Pop. 1,761.
Map Square 12.

ST. PAN. B'SW'TH.	B'SW'TH. ST. PAN.		
AM 4.25	10. 3	AM 7.12r	11.35
8.25r	12.53	8.11r	1.30
10.25r	3.45	PM 3.54r	8.35
PM 1.25r	6.46	7.47	4.20
12. 0h	10. 3	—	—

Sunday Trains.

PM 3.15	9.16	AM 9.46r	5. 2
—	—	PM 7. 9	4.55

h Saturdays midnight only.
r Restaurant Car.

BUILDWAS (Salop) from
Paddington, 144 miles. Fares, 30/0a, 18/0c. R.T. for two months. 60/0a, 36/0c. Departures *from* London as for Ketley or Iron Bridge. Departures *for* London about 5 times daily. Pop. 294.
Map Square 17.

BUILTH ROAD (Radnor)
from *Euston,* 220 miles. Fares, *via* Craven Arms, 37/6a, 22/6c. R. T. for two months, 75/0a, 45/0c. *Via* Whitchurch or Welshpool, 41/5a, 24/10c. R. T. for two months, 82/10a.
Map Square 16.

EUSTON BUILTH		BUILTH EUSTON	
AM 5. 0	12.48	AM 8.40r	3.10
6.45h	1.41	PM12.22r	6.15
6.45	3.42	2.55dr	9.15
10.40r	4. 8	2.55er	9.20
PM 1.15r	7. 5	8.45y	5. 0
9.20ey	5.41		

Sunday Trains.

| PM 9.15 | 5.41 | | |

Saturdays excepted.
h Mondays and Fridays only.
r Restaurant Car
y Via Crewe.

BUILTH WELLS
(Radnor) from *Paddington, via* Hereford and L.M. & S. Rly., 185 miles. Fares, 37/9a, 22/8c. R. T. for two months, 75/6a. Pop. 1,776.
Map Square 16.

PAD. B. WELLS	B. WELLS PAD.		
AM 1. 0g	11.48	AM 6.36r	2.40
5.30	2.22	9.32h'r	4.15
10.45	6.13	PM 1.12r	8.45
4.45t	10.22	5.17	3.30

No Sunday Trains.

g Mondays excepted.
h Via Worcester.
r Restaurant Car.
t Tea Car.

BUILTH WELLS—*cont.*

ANOTHER ROUTE from *Euston*, 222½ miles. Fares, *via* Craven Arms 37/6*a*, 22/6*c*. R. T. for two months, 75/0*a*. *Via* Whitchurch or Welshpool, 41/5*a*, 24/10*c*. R. T. for two months, 82/10*a*.

Euston	B. Wells	B. Wells	Euston
AM 5. 0*k*	1. 9	AM 8.18*kr*	3.10
6.45*k*	4. 7	11.53*kr*	6.15
10.40*rv*	4.42	PM 2.25*kr*	9.20
10.40*r*	5.12	7.15	5. 0
PM 1.15*r*	7.14	—	—
9.20*eh*	6.33	—	—

Sunday Trains.

PM 9.15*y*	6.33	—	—
—	—	—	—
—	—	—	—

e Saturdays excepted.
h *Via* Welshpool.
k *Via* Craven Arms.
r Restaurant Car.
v Mondays and Saturdays only.
y *Via* Crewe.

BULFORD (Wilts) from

Waterloo, *via* Porton, 81¼ miles. Fares, *via* Porton, 18/2*a*, 10/11*c*. R.T. for two months, 36/4*a*, 21/10*c*. *Via* Salisbury, 20/5*a*, 12/3*c*. R. T. for two months, 40/10*a*, 24/6*c*. Pop. 3,232.
Map Square 22.

W'loo	B'lford.	B'lford.	W'loo.
AM 7.30*h*	10.55	AM 8.12	10.56
11. 0*hr*	1.21	11.10*hr*	1.56
PM 1. 0*hr*	3.45	PM 1.30*hr*	3.50
3. 0*hr*	5.25	3. 0*hr*	6. 0
5. 0	8. 1	4.43*h*	7.40
6. 0*r*	9.46	5.50*hr*	8.30
—	—	8.15	11.28
—	—	—	—
—	—	—	—
—	—	—	—

Sunday Trains.

PM 6. 0	9.12	—	—
—	—	—	—

h *Via* Salisbury.
r Restaurant Car.

BULKINGTON (Warwick)

from *Euston*, 93½ miles. Fares, 19/5*a*, 11/8*c*. R.T. for two months, 38/10*a*, 23/4*c* Pop. 2,219.
Map Square 18.

Euston	Bulktn.	Bulktn.	Euston
AM 5. 0	7.46	AM 7.20	10. 0
8.45*r*	11.31	8.47	11. 0
12. 0*nr*	2.36	11.57*r*	2.20
PM 2.50*t*	5.16	PM 4. 1*t*	6.15
6.30*er*	8.46	6.15*r*	9.20
7.0*dr*	9.14	—	—
—	—	—	—
—	—	—	—

No Sunday Trains.
d Saturdays only.
e Saturdays excepted.
n Noon.
r Restaurant Car.
t Tea Car.

BULLGILL (Cumberland),

322¾ miles. Fares, 65/0*a*, 39/0*c*. R. T. for two months, 130/0*a*, 78/0*c*. Departures *from* London as for Maryport. Departures *for* London about 5 times daily.
Map Square 6.

BULWELL (Notts) from

St. Pancras, 129 miles. Fares, 26/0*a*, 15/7*c*. R. T. for two months, 52/0*a*, 31/2*c*. Departures *from* London as for Hucknall. Departures *for* London about 6 times daily. Pop. 18,509.
Map Square 13.

BUNCHREW (Inverness),

571½ miles. No through fares. Departures *from* London as for Inverness. Departures *for* London about 3 times daily.
Map Square 34.

BUNGAY (Suffolk) from

Liverpool Street, *via* Beccles, 115¾ miles. Fares 23/9*a*, 14/3*c*. R. T. for two months, 47/6*a*, 28/6*c*. Pop. 3,106.
Map Square 19.

L'pl. St.	Bungay	Bungay	L'pl. St.
AM 5. 0	9.26	AM 8.19*r*	11.30
8.15*r*	12.40	10. 1*r*	2. 3
10.20	3.31	PM 2.16	5.55
PM 3.15*r*	6.23	3.30	7.51
3.18*r*	7.31	6.22*r*	10. 0
—	—	—	—
—	—	—	—

No Sunday Trains.
r Restaurant Car.

ANOTHER ROUTE *via* Tivetshall, 113¾ miles. Fares as above.

L'pl. St.	Bungay	Bungay	L'pl. St.
AM 5. 0	10. 1	AM 6.41*r*	10.30
10.12	2.16	9.26	1.20
PM12.33*r*	6.22	PM12.40*r*	4.58
5.18*ehr*	8.57	3.31	7.51
5.18*dr*	9. 2	6.23	11.16
—	—	—	—
—	—	—	—

No Sunday Trains.
d Saturdays only
e Saturdays excepted.
h *Via* Forncett.
r Restaurant Car.

BUNTINGFORD (Herts)

from *Liverpool Street*, 34 miles. Fares, 7/4*a*, 4/5*c*. R.T. for two months, 14/8*a*, 8/10*c*. Pop. 5,013.
Map Square 18.

L'pl. St.	Buntfd.	Buntfd.	L'pl. St.
AM 5.50	7.50	AM 7. 8	8.49
6.30	8.31	8.12	9.42
8.30	10. 7	8.47	10. 9
10.34	12.27	9.26	10.59
PM12.48*e*	2.55	11. 0	12.25
1.19*d*	2.50	PM 1.18*d*	3.21
2. 0	3.30	1.20*e*	3.16
3. 8*d*	5.53	3.12	5. 9
4.30*e*	5.57	5.12*d*	7. 0
5.10*e*	6.41	5.15*e*	7. 0
6. 0*e*	7.14	6.56*e*	9.26
6. 0*d*	7.23	8. 5*e*	10. 0
8.22	9.47	8.10*d*	10. 0
—	—	—	—
—	—	—	—

Sunday Trains.

AM 8.12	9.47	AM 7.35	9.33
10.12	11.46	10.10	12.57
PM 6.25	8.31	PM 6.56	8.40
—	—	—	—

d Saturdays only.
e Saturdays excepted.

Taxi Cabs can be hired to meet any train at this station by telegram or telephone No. 12. Mr. John Holmes, George Hotel, Buntingford.

BURDALE (Yorks), 215¾

miles. No through fares. Departures *from* London as for Malton or Driffield. Departures *for* London about 3 times daily. Pop. 80.
Map Square 8.

BURDETT ROAD from

Fenchurch Street, 2¼ miles. Fares, 0/2½*a*, 0/2*b*, 0/1½*c*. R. T. for two days, 0/5*a*, 0/4*b*, 0/3*c*. *See* pp. 510, 528-534, 537-544.
Map Square 62.

BURES (Suffolk) from

Liverpool Street, 53½ miles. Fares, 11/5*a*, 6/10*c*. R.T. for two months, 22/10*a*, 13/8*c*. Pop. 805.
Map Square 19.

L'pl. St.	Bures	Bures	L'pl. St.
AM 6.50	9.31	AM 8.24	9.53
10. 0	11.39	10.14	11.42
PM12.36	2.13	PM12.13*h*	2. 3
2.15	4.12	2.46*h*	5. 5
4.58	6.33	4.35*h*	6.32
5.42	7.21	6.56	9.17
—	—	—	—
—	—	—	—

Sunday Trains.

AM 9.20	11. 4	AM 9.29	12.40
PM 3.40	5.38	PM 4.49*h*	7.10
4.40*h*	8.25	6.47	8.58
—	—	—	—

h *Via* Colchester.

BURGESS HILL (Sussex)

from *London Bridge*, *Victoria*, and *Clapham Junction*, 41½ miles. Fares, 8/9*a*, 5/3*c*. R. T. for two months, 17/6*a*, 10/6*c*. Pop. 5,651.
Map Square 23.

Leave			Arr. at
Vict.	Clap. J.	Lon. B.	Bur. H.
AM —	—	5.18	7. 4
6.37	6.44	6.40	7.55
7.23	7.29	7.25	9.15
9. 0	9. 8	9. 6	10.32
10. 5	10.11	9.50	11.32
10.35	10.42	10.35	12.12
PM12.45	—	12.10	1.54
—	—	1.20*d*	2.34
2. 0	2. 7	2. 5	3.40
—	—	2. 8*d*	4. 8
3.40	—	—	4.46
—	—	4. 5	5.30
—	—	5. 5*d*	6. 9
4.30	—	5. 8*e*	6. 9
5.45	—	5.55*e*	7. 9
—	—	6. 0*d*	7. 9
6. 6	6.12	6. 8	7.55
7.15	7.22	7.20	8.56
8.35	—	—	9.45*l*
9. 3	9.10	9.12	10.43
10. 0	—	—	11.11
10.30	10.38	10.35	12.12
—	—	—	—
—	—	—	—

Sunday Trains.

AM 6.55	7. 2	7. 2	8.57
8.50	8.57	8.55	10.58
PM 1.14	1.21	1.10	2.48
5.50	5.57	6. 0	7.40
8. 0	8. 8	8. 0	9.37
—	—	—	—
—	—	—	—
—	—	—	—

BURGESS HILL—contd.

Trains from Burgess Hill.

Leave BUR. H.	LON. B	CLAP. J.	VICT.
AM 6.13	8.15	8.15	8.24
7.38	8.38	—	—
7.44	8.53	9. 0	9. 8
8.43	9.58	—	—
9.19	—	—	10.24
10.30	12.13	11.59	12. 7
11.54	1.42	1.39	1.50
PM 12.49	2.22	2.13	2.22
2. 3	3.40	3.37	3.45
2.49	4.32	4. 9	4.17
3.27	5.54	5.47	5.55
4.52	6.36	6.26	6.34
6. 9	7.42	7.21	7.30
6.55	8.46	8.39	8.48
8. 5	10. 0	10. 2	10.10
9.11	10.58	—	—
9.54	—	11.10	11.17
11.33	12.59	12.50	1. 0
—	—	—	—

Sunday Trains.

AM 8.54	10.45	10.42	10.50
PM 3.15	5. 3	5. 1	5.11
6. 8	7.56	8.31	8.41
10. 3	11.34	11.34	11.42
11. 4	12.27	—	—

d Saturdays only.
e Saturdays excepted.

BURGH (Cumberland), 305¼
miles. No through fares. Departures *from* London as for Carlisle. Departures *for* London about 3 times daily. Pop. 777.
Map Square 3.

BURGH (Lincoln) from
King's Cross, 124¼ miles. Fares, 25/10*a*, 15/6*c*. R.T. for two months, 51/8*a*, 31/0*c*. Departures *from* London as for Firsby. Departures *for* London about 4 times daily. Pop. 937.
Map Square 13.

BURGHCLERE (Hants)
from *Paddington*, 60¾ miles. Fares, 12/4*a*, 7/5*c*. R.T. for two months, 24/8*a*, 14/10*c*. Departures *from* London as for Highclere. Departures *for* London about 4 times daily. Pop. 816.
Map Square 23.

BURGHEAD (Elgin), 581¼
miles. Fares, 106/3*a*, 63/9*c*. R.T. for two months, 212/6*a*, 127/6*c*. Departures *from* London as for Forres. Departures *for* London about twice daily. Pop. 1,385.
Map Square 35.

BURLESCOMBE(Devon)
154½ miles. Fares, 32/4*a*, 19/5*c*. R. T. for two months, 64/8*a*, 38/10*c*. Departures *from* London as for Wellington (Somerset). Departures *for* London 4 times daily. Pop. 7,693.
Map Square 21.

BURLEY-IN-WHARFE-
DALE (Yorks) from *King's Cross* or *St. Pancras,* 199¾ miles. Fares, 41/1*a*, 24/8*c*. R.T. for two months, 82/2*a*, 49/4*c*. Departures *from* London as for Ilkley. Departures *for* London about 4 times daily. Pop. 3,808.
Map Square 7.

BURNAGE (Lancs), 183¼
miles. Fares, 37/11*a*, 22/9*c*. R.T. for two months, 75/10*a*, 45/6*c*. Departures *from* London as for Wilmslow. Departures *for* London about 6 times daily. Pop. 2,179.

BURNBANK (Lanark), 435
miles. Fares, 82/6*a*, 49/6*c*. R. T. for two months, 165/0*a*, 99/0*c*. Departures *from* London as for Edinburgh (Waverley). Departures *for* London about 4 times daily. Pop. 12,139.

BURNESIDE (Westmor-
land), 253¼ miles. Fares, 52/9*a*, 31/8*c*. R. T. for two months, 105/6*a*, 63/4*c*. Departures *from* London as for Kendal. Departures *for* London about 3 times daily. Pop. 1,145.
Map Square 7.

BURNGULLOW (Corn-
wall), 267½ miles. Fares, 55/3*a*, 33/2*c*. R. T. for two months, 110/6/*a*, 66/4*c*. Departures *from* London as for St. Austell. Departures *for* London about 4 times daily.
Map Square 25.

BURNHAM BEECHES
(Bucks) from *Paddington*, 21 miles. Fares, 4/4*a*, 2/7*c*. R. T. for two months, 8/8*a*, 5/2*c*. Pop. (Burnham) 3,941.
Map Square 23.

PAD.	B. B.	B. B.	PAD.
AM 5.45	6.51	AM 7.47	8.20
6.30	7.16	8. 9	8.49
6.35	7.43	8.39	9.25
7.35	8.36	9.21	10. 6
8.30	9. 9	9.42	10.55
9.55	10.38	10.16	11.18
10.55	11.40	10.58	11.35
PM 12. 8	1.26	PM 12.14	1.11
12.33*l*	1.26	12.52	1.4½
12.35*e*	1.36	1.52	2.35
1.20*d*	2. 2	2. 6	3.10
2. 7	2.41	2.59*d*	3.38
3.18	4.16	3.35	4.10
4.30	5. 6	4.14	5.17
5.18*e*	5.54	4.49	5.37
5.18*d*	6. 1	5.37	6.52
5.35*e*	6.24	6.10	6.55
5.40*d*	6.24	6.58	7.45
6.12*e*	6.56	7.27	8.10
6.35*d*	7.30	8.25*d*	9.12
7. 0	7.49	8.54	9.52
8. 5	8.38	—	—

Sunday Trains.

AM 8.20	9.19	AM 9.37	10.42
10. 5	10.44	PM 3.54	4.53
10.37	11.31	5.38	6.23
PM 2. 0	3. 0	6.55	7.37
2.35	3.31	8.14	9.17
4.45	5.43	—	—
6. 5	7. 6	—	—

d Saturdays only.
e Saturdays excepted.

BURNHAM MARKET
(Norfolk) from *Liverpool Street*, 124½ miles. Fares, 25/8*a*, 15/5*c*. R. T. for two months, 51/4*a*, 30/10*c*. Pop. 1,832.
Map Square 14.

L'PL ST.	BURN M.	BURN M.	L'PL ST.
AM 8.30*r*	12.25	AM 7.17	11.27
11.50*kr*	3.48	10.21*r*	2.21
11.50*hr*	4.24	PM 1.12*r*	6.10
PM 2.34*e*	6.43	5.29*e*	10.30
2.34*d*	7. 8	5.54*d*	10.30

No Sunday Trains.

d Saturdays only.
e Saturdays excepted.
h Tuesdays only.
k Tuesdays excepted.
r Restaurant Car.

BURNHAM - ON -
CROUCH (Essex), 43¼ miles. Fares, 8/2*a*, 4/11*c*. R. T. for two months, 16/4*a*, 9/10*c*. Pop. 3,433.
Map Square 24.

L'POOL ST.	BURN.C.	BURN.C.	L'POOL ST.
AM 5.26	7.31	AM 7. 5	8.45
6.50	9. 1	8.14	9.46
9. 1	10.51	9.30	11. 7
10.47*d*	12.33	11.20*d*	1.16
11.56	1.46	11.50*e*	1.25
PM 1.26*d*	2.43	PM 1. 5*d*	3. 5
2.20*e*	4.35	2.45*d*	4.56
2.40*d*	4.14	2.56*e*	4.51
4.15*e*	5.31	5. 4	6.52
4.18*d*	5.53	6.23	8.22
5.39	7. 5	8. 6	9.56
6.26*e*	8. 4	, —	—
3. 2*e*	9.36	—	—
8.45*d*	10.13	—	—

Sunday Trains.

AM 8.45	10.27	AM 7.36	10.25
9.30	11.27	PM 6.39	8.45
PM 6.42	8.36	7.47	9.32

d Saturdays only.
e Saturdays excepted.

White Hart Hotel. Principal Hotel for Yachtsmen and Visitors. Moderate Tariff. Billiards. Motor Garage. Telephone No. 6. ARTHUR J. NORRIS, Propr.

Anchor Hotel. Comfortable Family Hotel, facing River Crouch. Boating. Fishing. Wild Fowling Parties. Garage. 'Phone 17. A.A. & M.U. Proprietor, FRANK HUDSON.

Grand Hill Hotel (unlicensed). Old Country House. Beautiful Grounds. Tennis Courts. Extreme Comfort. Choice Cuisine. Garage. Telephone 26. Apply tariff.

BURNHAM-ON-SEA
(Somerset) from *Paddington*, 146¼ miles (*via* Highbridge). Fares, 30/7*a*, 18/4*c*. R T. for two months, 61/2*a*, 36/8*c*. Pop. 5,569.
Map Square 22.

PAD.	BURNHM.	BURNHM.	PAD.
AM 5.30	10.10	AM 7.35	11.30
7.30	12.40	10.20*r*	2. 0
8.45*d*	12.40	PM 1.15	6. 2
9. 0	1.52	2.20*r*	7. 0
11.15*r*	2.45	5.40	10.25
PM 1. 0*r*	5.15	9.25	2.45
1.10*r*	6.55	—	—
4.15*r*	8.20	—	—
6.30*r*	10.20	—	—
12. 0*h*	7.25	—	—

Sunday Trains.

PM 10. 0	7.25	—	—

d Saturdays only.
h Saturdays midnight excepted.
r Restaurant Car.

ANOTHER ROUTE from *Waterloo*, 147½ miles. Fares as above.

W'LOO	BURNHM.	BURNHM.	W'LOO.
AM 9. 0*r*	1.52	AM 9.25*r*	1.56
12. 0*r*	4.36	11.35*r*	4.30
PM 1. 0*r*	6. 0	PM 3. 0*r*	8.30
3. 0*r*	7.45	5. 5	10.50
6. 0*r*	10.20	6.30*h*	3.58

No Sunday Trains.
h *Via* Eastleigh.
r Restaurant Car.

Manor Hotel. Close to Sea and famous Golf Links. Central Heating. Every modern convenience. Excellent Cuisine. Illustrated Tariff. Tel. 11. Apply—
MANAGER

Burnham-on-Sea. Famous Golf Resort. Leading Hotel "The Queen and Golf." On Sea Front. Modernized. Redecorated. Excellent Cuisine. Adjoins County Club. Moderate Terms.
MANAGERESS.

BURNHILL (Durham), 260¼ miles. No through fares. Departures *from* London as for Bishop Auckland. Departures *for* London about 3 times daily.
Map Square 7.

BURNLEY (MANCHESTER ROAD), (Lancs) from *King's Cross*, *via* Horbury, 211¾ miles. Fares, 41/10*a*, 25/1*c*. R. T. for two months, 83/8*a*, 50/2*c*. Pop. 103,175.
Map Square 12.

KING'S+	BURNLEY	BURNLEY	KING'S+
AM 4.45	11.50	AM 6.41*r*	1. 5
7.15*dr*	1.55	8.33*r*	1.55
7.15*er*	3. 5	8.58	3.50
10.10*r*	4.54	10.10*r*	4.45
PM 1.50*r*	8.49	PM 12.42*r*	7.10
10.45*e*	10.10	3.29*r*	9.25
—	—	6.26*e*	3.25

Sunday Trains.

12. 0*hn*	8.12	AM 8.19*r*	3.45
—	—	10.13*r*	5.55
—	—	PM 2. 2*hr*	10.20

d Saturdays only.
e Saturdays excepted.
h Passengers cross Wakefield at own expense.
n Noon.
r Restaurant Car.

ANOTHER ROUTE (BANK TOP) from *Euston*, *via* Manchester 215 miles. Fares, 41/10*a*, 25/1*c*. R. T. for two months, 83/8*a*, 50/2*c*. *Via* Preston, 43/9*a*, 26/3*c*. R. T. for two months, 87/6*a*, 52/6*c*.

EUSTON	BURNLEY	BURNLEY	EUSTON
AM 12.25	6.57	AM 5.22*e*	12. 5
2.35	10. 0	7.55*r*	1.15
5. 0	12.14	8.45*r*	3.10
6.45*v*	2.36	10.14*r*	3.55
8.45*r*	3. 5*y*	11.50*y*	6. 0
10.40*r*	4.16	PM 12.14*er*	6.15
11.50*er*	5.17	1.25*kr*	7.30
11.50*dr*	6. 6	2.25*er*	9. 5
PM 1.30*kr*	7.28	2.42*ery*	9. 5
2.50*t*	9. 1*y*	2.42*dr*	9.15
4. 5*r*	10. 6	3.24*er*	10. 0
6. 5*r*	11.34	4. 7*dr*	10. 0
9.30*ek*	6.41*y*	4. 7*er*	10.10
11.50*d*	10. 6*y*	*y*4.54*kr*	10.45
—	—	9. 0	5. 0
—	—	9.28*ey*	5.40
—	—	9.28*dy*	5.45
—	—	—	—
—	—	—	—

Sunday Trains.

PM 12.10*r*	6.43	AM 7.20	4. 0
12.30*ry*	8.12	10.46*r*	5.45
9.15*ky*	6.41	PM 12.28*r*	7.30
—	—	2. 2*y*	8.55
—	—	7.46*y*	5. 0
—	—	—	—

d Saturdays only.
e Saturdays excepted.
k *Via* Preston.
r Restaurant Car.
t Tea Car.
v *Via* Wigan.
y Manchester Road Station.

BURNMOUTH (Berwick), 340¼ miles. No through fares. Departures *from* London as for Berwick-on-Tweed. Departures *for* London about 4 times daily. Pop. 802.
Map Square 41.

BURN NAZE (Lancs.), 226½ miles. Fares, 47/3*a*, 28/4*c*. R. T. for two months, 94/6*a*, 56/8*c*. Departures *from* London as for Kirkham. Departures *for* London about 8 times daily.
Map Square 7.

BURNTISLAND (Fife), 412½ miles. Fares, 83/7*a*, 50/2*c*. R. T. for two months, 167/2*a*, 100/4*c*. Departures *from* London as for Inverkeithing. Departures *for* London about 3 times daily. Pop. 6,567.
Map Square 40.

BURNT MILL (Essex) from *Liverpool Street*, 22¾ miles. Fares, 4/10*a*, 2/11*c*. R. T. for two months, 9/8*a*, 5/10*c*.
Map Square 23.

L'PL. ST.	B. MILL	B. MILL	L'PL. ST.
AM 5.50	6.42	AM 7.15	8.18
7.18	8.23	7.48	8.49
9.10	10.18	8. 3	8.57
10.34	12. 8	8.53	9.42
PM 12.40*d*	1.32	10. 8	10.59
12.48*e*	1.55	11.11	12.15
1.19*d*	2. 8	PM 1.13	2. 7
2. 0*d*	2.51	2.32*d*	3.18
2.48	3.44	3.59	5. 9
4.15	5. 0	6. 3	7.19
5.10	6. 0	6.59	7.58
6. 0*e*	6.44	8.23	9.33
6.30	7.14	10.18	11.12
7.41*d*	8.31	—	—
7.41*e*	8.34	—	—
9.17	10.21	—	—
11.50*k*	12.38	—	—

Sunday Trains.

AM 8.12	8.58	AM 8. 8	9.33
9.25	10.15	10.23	11.27
PM 1.50	3. 9	PM 8.11	9.10
4.50	6. 0	9.37	10.40
7.15	8. 6	—	—
9.12	10.14	—	—

d Saturdays only.
e Saturdays excepted.
k Wednesdays and Saturdays only.

BURRINGTON (Somerset), 136½ miles. Fares, 28/4*a*, 17/0*c*. R. T. for two months, 56/8*a*, 34/0*c*. Departures *from* London as for Wrington. Departures *for* London about 4 times daily. Pop. 411.
Map Square 22.

BURSCOUGH BRIDGE (Lancs) 205½ miles. Fares, 42/4*a*, 25/5*c*. R. T. for two months, 84/8*a*, 50/10*c*. Departures *from* London as for Wigan. Departures *for* London about 6 times daily. Pop. 4,390.
Map Square 12.

BURSLEDON (Hants) from *Waterloo*, *via* St. Denys, 81 miles. Fares, 17/6*a*, 10/6*c*. R. T. for two months, 35/0*a*, 21/0*c*. Pop. 1,018.
Map Square 28.

W'LOO	BURSLE.	BURSLE.	W'LOO
AM 5.40	8.55	AM 7. 0	10.20
5.50	9.31	8.16*s*	11. 0
8.30*s*	11.12	9.13	12. 0
9.30	12.23	10. 5*r*	12.50
11.30*r*	2.18	PM 1. 9	4.20
PM 1.30*s*	4.33	2. 4	6.16
2.30	5.31	5. 9*r*	8.20
3.30*s*	6.32	6.34*r*	8.50
5.30*r*	8.13	8. 6	11.28
7.30	10. 2	9.58	3.58
—	—	—	—
—	—	—	—

Sunday Trains.

12. 0*nr*	3.43	AM 9.23	12.11
PM 7. 0*hr*	9.45	9.59*r*	2.16
—	—	PM 4.23	8. 3
—	—	7. 0*hr*	10.52

h *Via* Southampton West.
n Noon.
r Restaurant Car.
s Refreshments served.

BURSLEM (Stafford) from *Euston*, 150 miles. Fares, 31/1*a*, 18/8*c*. R. T. for two months, 62/2*a*, 37/4*c*. Pop. 41,566.
Map Square 12.

EUSTON	BURSLM.	BURSLM.	EUSTON
AM 2.35	8.22	AM 5.52	11. 0
5. 0	9.46	8.21*er*	12. 5
8.45*r*	12. 7	8.21*dr*	12.20
10.40	2.47	9.17*r*	12.50
12. 0*nr*	4.33	10.20*r*	2.20
PM 2.50*t*	6. 4	11. 0*d*	3.10
4.45*r*	8.31	PM 12.42*r*	3.55
6.30*er*	10.38	2.36*t*	6.15
6.55*r*	11.17	4.46*r*	9.20
—	—	6.14*r*	10. 0
—	—	8.47	5. 0
—	—	—	—
—	—	—	—
—	—	—	—
—	—	—	—

No Sunday Trains.

d Saturdays only.
e Saturdays excepted.
n Noon.
r Restaurant Car.
t Tea Car.

BURSTON (Norfolk) from *Liverpool Street*, 97½ miles. Fares, 20/7*a*, 12/4*c*. R. T. for two months, 41/2*a*, 24/8*c*. Pop. 314.
Map Square 19.

L'PL. ST.	BURSTN.	BURSTN.	L'PL. ST.
AM 5. 0	7.56	AM 7.28*r*	10.30
10.12	1.17	11. 7*r*	2. 3
PM 12.33*r*	3.30	PM 1.40*r*	4.58
3.10*r*	5.58	4.30	7.51
5.18*dr*	8.15	5.24*dr*	9.22
5.18*er*	8.19	7.46	11.16
—	—	—	—
—	—	—	—
—	—	—	—
—	—	—	—

Sunday Trains.

AM 9.20*r*	12.38	AM 7.57	11.38
PM 4.40	7.31	PM 6.40	10.15

d Saturdays only.
e Saturdays excepted.
r Restaurant Car.
t Tea Car.

BURTONAGNES (Yorks), 211¾ miles. Fares, 40/3*a*, 24/2*c*. R. T. for two months, 80/6*a*, 48/4*c*. Departures *from* London as for Driffield. Departures *for* London about 5 times daily. Pop. 340.
Map Square 8.

BURTON & HOLME (Lancs), 240¾ miles. Fares, 50/3*a*, 30/2*c*. R. T. for two months, 100/6*a*, 60/4*c*. Departures *from* London as for Carnforth. Departures *for* London about 3 times daily. Pop. 661.
Map Square 7.

BURTON JOYCE (Notts) from *St. Pancras*, 128¼ miles. Fares, 26/1*a*, 15/8*c*. R. T. for two months, 52/2*a*, 31/4*c*. Departures *from* London as for Nottingham. Departures *for* London about 10 times daily. Pop. 963.
Map Square 13.

BURTON-ON-TRENT

(Stafford) from *St. Pancras*, 127½ miles Fares, 25/5*a*, 15/3*c*. R. T. for two months, 50/10*a*, 30/6*c*. Pop. 48,927.
Map Square 17.

St. Pan.	Burton	Burton	St. Pan.
AM 2.25	6.30	AM 2.45	7.25
4.25	8.32	5.10*g*	9.57
8.25*r*	12.15	6.50*r*	10.45
10.25*r*	1.45	7.37*r*	11. 0
11. 0*r*	2.59	8.15*r*	11.35
PM12.25*r*	3.24	10. 9*r*	1.30
1.25*r*	4.44	10.47*r*	1.45
2.25*r*	5.25	11. 3	3.25
4.25*r*	7.58	PM12.23*r*	4.10
6.25*r*	9.24	1.20*r*	4.20
9.15	12.58	2.38*r*	5.45
—	—	3.28*r*	6.35
—	—	5.10*r*	8.35
—	—	5.45*r*	9.15
—	—	6.43*r*	10. 5
—	—	11.55	4.20

Sunday Trains.

AM11.15*r*	3.14	AM 2.45	8. 5
PM 3.15	7.50	7.15	11.53
6.15*r*	10. 2	PM 1. 8*r*	5. 2
9.15	12.58	5.42*r*	9.52
—	—	11.55	4.55

g Mondays excepted.
r Restaurant Car.

ANOTHER ROUTE from

Euston, 122½ miles. Fares as above.

Euston	Burton	Burton	Euston
AM 5. 0	8.22	AM 6.50	11. 0
6.45	10.26	9.10*d*	12.20
8.45*r*	1. 1	9.10*er*	12.32
10.40*dr*	3.22	10.20*r*	2.20
12. 0*er*	3.55	PM 1.33	5.35
PM 2.50*t*	5.51	4.44*r*	8.10
4. 5*t*	7.29	6.28*r*	10.45
5.20*r*	8.23	8.14	5. 0
5.32*dr*	9.42	—	—
6.30*er*	9.42	—	—

No Sundays Trains.
d Saturdays only.
e Saturdays excepted
r Restaurant Car.
t Tea Car.

ANOTHER ROUTE from

King's Cross, 158½ miles. Fares as above.

King's +	Burton	Burton	King's +
AM 5. 5	11.33	AM 6.55*r*	11.30
10.10*r*	2.34	7.56*r*	1. 5
11.30	4.57	10.14	3.50
PM 1.50*er*	6.43	PM12.40	6.25
1.50*dr*	7.12	3.16	9. 0
5.35*r*	9.56	8.30*e*	3.25
11.25*e*	8.52	8.55*d*	3.25

Sunday Trains.

PM11.25	8.52	—	—
—	—	—	—
—	—	—	—

d Saturdays only.
e Saturdays excepted.
r Restaurant Car.

BURTON POINT

(Cheshire) 199½ miles. No through fares. Departures *from* London as for Wrexham. Departures *for* London about 5 times daily. Pop. (Burton) 264.
Map Square 12.

BURTON SALMON

(Yorks), 176¾ miles. Fares, 36/1*a*, 21/8*c*. R.T. for two months, 72/2*a*, 43/4*c*. Departures *from* London as for Ferrybridge. Departures *for* London about 4 times daily. Pop. 255.
Map Square 17.

BURWARTON (Salop),

152¼ miles. No through fares. Departures *from* London as for Cleobury Mortimer. Departures *for* London about twice daily. Pop.166.

BURWELL (Cambs) from

Liverpool Street, 65½ miles. Fares, 13/7*a*, 8/2*c*. R. T. for two months, 27/2*a*, 16/4*c*. Departures *from* London as for Mildenhall. Departures *for* London about 4 times daily. Pop. 2,144.
Map Square 19.

BURY (Lancs) from *Euston*,

196½ miles. Fares 40/7*a*, 24/4*c*. R. T. for two months, 81/2*a*, 48/8*c*. Pop. 56,426.
Map Square 12.

Euston	Bury	Bury	Euston
AM12.25	5.37	AM 6. 0*dr*	12.20
2.35	9. 3	6.40*er*	12. 5
5. 0	11.14	7.35*r*	12.50
8.45*r*	2.14	8.25	1.15
10.40*r*	3.14	9.20*r*	2.20
11.50*r*	4.54	9.45*r*	3.10
12. 0*nr*	6.49	11. 0*r*	3.55
PM 2.50*t*	8.14	11.27*dr*	5.0
4. 5*r*	8.54	PM12.14*er*	6. 0
4.45*r*	10.14	12.22*dr*	6. 0
6. 5*r*	10.43	1. 0*r*	6.15
11.50*d*	9.27	2. 0*r*	7.30
—	—	2.40*r*	8.10
—	—	3.40*er*	9. 5
—	—	3.40*dr*	9.15
—	—	4.40*dr*	10. 0
—	—	5.11*er*	10.10
—	—	8.40	5. 0
—	—	11. 0*e*	5.40
—	—	11. 0*d*	5.45
—	—	—	—
—	—	—	—
—	—	—	—

Sunday Trains.

PM12.10*r*	5.44	AM 7.59	4. 0
12.30*r*	7.35	10. 2*r*	5.45
—	—	PM 1.19*r*	7.30
—	—	3.20*r*	8.55
—	—	10.12	5. 0

d Saturdays only.
e Saturdays excepted.
r Restaurant Car.

BURY ST. EDMUNDS

(Suffolk) from *Liverpool Street*, via Cambridge, 85 miles. Fares, 16/3*a*, 9/9*c*. R.T. for two months, 32/6*a*, 19/6*c*. Pop. 15,941.
Map Square 19.

L'pl St.	B. St. Ed.	B. St. Ed.	L'pl St.
AM 5. 5	8.24	AM 7.34*r*	10.23
5.50	9.49	9. 4	11.27
8.30*r*	11. 2	9.52	12.40
10. 5*h*	1.18	11.20*r*	2.21
11.50*r*	2.49	PM 1.22*kl*	4. 2
PM 2.34	5.33	1.22	5. 9
4.45	7. 1	2.28*r*	5.17
5.49*r*	8.37	3.35*r*	6.10
7.10*r*	9.52	4. 6	7.58
8.22	10.57	5.43*r*	8.33
—	—	7.17	10.30

Sunday Trains.

AM 9.25	12.37	PM 3.30	6.40
PM 3.25	6.12	—	—
—	—	—	—
—	—	—	—

h Wednesdays only.
k Arrives at St. Pancras Station.
l Commencing July 23.
r Restaurant Car.

BURY ST. EDMUNDS

—*continued.*

ANOTHER ROUTE from

Liverpool Street(*via* Haughley), 95¼ miles. Fares as above.

L'pl. St.	B.St.Ed.	B.St.Ed.	L'pl.St.
AM 5. 0	8.28	AM 6.52*r*	10.30
8.15*r*	11. 7	8.30*r*	11.22
10.20	1.17	9.52	1.20
PM 1. 0	3.26	11. 6*r*	2. 3
3.10*r*	5.40	PM12.10	3.36
3.26	7.14	2. 0*r*	4.58
5.42	9.12	2.55	5.55
7.45*r*	10.50	3.32	6.32
—	—	4.10*h*	7.51
—	—	5.38*r*	9.22
—	—	7. 6*r*	10. 0
—	—	—	—

Sunday Trains.

AM 9.20*r*	12.38	AM 7.53	11.38
11.30*r*	3.22	PM 2. 0	7.10
PM 4.40	9.37	6.15*r*	9.10
—	—	7. 3	10.15
—	—	—	—

h Wednesdays only.
r Restaurant Car.

ANOTHER ROUTE from

Liverpool Street (*via* Mark's Tey), 78 miles. Fares as above.

L'pl. St.	B.St.Ed.	B.St.Ed.	L'pl.St.
AM 6.50	10.36	AM 7.26	9.53
10. 0	12.38	9.14	11.42
PM12.36	3.14	11.12*h*	2. 3
2.15	5. 9	PM 1.40*h*	5. 5
5.42	8.16	3.40*h*	6.32
—	—	5.50	9.17

No Sunday Trains.

d Saturdays only.
e Saturdays excepted.
h Via Colchester.

Suffolk Hotel. Family and Commercial Centrally situated. Dining and Commercial Rooms. Ladies' Drawing Room. Public and Private Billiard Rooms. Excellent Cuisine. Male Chef. Garage. Motor Bus. Appointed *c* * o A.A., R.A.C., A.C.U., C.T.C. Tel. 38.

Angel Hotel. County Hotel of West Suffolk. Telephone No. 23. Inspection Pit. Garage. Repairs. House of Dickens and Pickwick.

BUSBY (Lanark), 403 miles.

Fares, 82/6*a*, 49/6*c*. R. T. for two months, 165/0*a*, 99/0*c*. Departures *from* London as for Hamilton. Departures for London about 4 times daily. Pop. 692.
Map Square 40.

BUSHEY AND OXHEY

(Herts) from *Euston* and *Broad Street*, 16 miles. Fares from Euston, 3/1a, 1/10c. R. T. for two months, 6/2a, 3/4½c. Fares from Broad Street, 3/2a, 1/11c. R. T. for two months, 6/4a, 3/8c. Pop. 8,088.
See pp. 496-499.
Map Square 23.

BUSHEY (Bakerloo Tube).
See back of Map.

Bushey Hall Hotel. First Class. Fully Licensed. 80 Bedrooms. Golf Links. Moderate Tariff.
See advt. p. **116.**

BUSH HILL PARK (Middlesex) from *Liverpool Street*, 10 miles. Fares, 1/5½a, 0/10½c. R. T. for two days, 2/11a, 2/4b, 1/9c. Pop. 11,536. *See* pp. 534-536.

BUTLER'S HILL (Notts)
from *King's Cross*, 133¼ miles. Fares, 26/10a, 16/1c. R. T. for two months, 53/8a, 32/2c. Departures *from* London as for Nottingham (Victoria). Departures *for* London about 5 times daily.
Map Square 13.

BUTTERLEY (Derby),
139¾ miles. Fares (*via* Shipley Gate), 27/11a, 16/9c. R. T. for two months, 55/10a, 33/6c. *Via* Ambergate, 29/0a, 17/5c. R. T. for two months, 58/0a, 34/10c. Departures *from* London as for Langley Mill or Ambergate. Departures *for* London about 6 times daily. Pop. 109.
Map Square 13.

BUTTERMERE. Stations
at Keswick or Cockermouth, distance about 9 miles.

BUTTERTON (Stafford).
169 miles. No through fares. Departures *from* London as for Leek. Departures *for* London about 4 times daily. Pop. 279.
Map Square 12.

BUTTINGTON (Montgomery) from *Paddington*, 169¼ miles. Fares, 35/5a, 21/3c. R. T. for two months, 70/10a, 42/6c. Pop. 1,477.
Map Square 16.

PAD.	BUTGTN.	BUTGTN.	PAD.
AM10.40r	3.31	AM 9. 1r	2. 5
PM 2.10t	7.17	11.36r	5. 0
4.10t	8.17	PM 3.34r	8. 5
6.10r	10.18	6.16	3.30
12.15h	8.28	—	—

No Sunday Trains.

h Saturdays midnight excepted.
r Restaurant Car.
t Tea Car.

ANOTHER ROUTE from
Euston (*via* Shrewsbury), 179¼ miles. Fares as above.

EUSTON	BUTGTN.	BUTGTN.	EUSTON
AM 5. 0	11.11	AM 7.38r	1.45
10.40	3.31	9. 1r	2.20
PM 1.15r	7.16	10.35	5.35
2.20t	8.17	11.36r	6.15
4.45r	10.18	PM 3.34dr	9.15
9.20e	8.28	3.34er	9.20
—	—	4.35r	10.45
—	—	6.16	5. 0
—	—	8.45hy	5. 0

BUTTINGTON—*contd.*

Sunday Trains.

EUSTON-BUTGTN.	BUTGTN. EUSTON		
PM 9.15y	8.28	—	—
—	—	—	—
—	—	—	—

d Saturdays only.
e Saturdays excepted.
Mondays and Saturdays only.
r Restaurant Car.
t Tea Car.
y Via Crewe.

BUXTED (Sussex) from
London Bridge and *Victoria*, *via* Groombridge, 43¾ miles. Fares, 9/2a, 5/6c. R. T. for two months, 18/4a, 11/0c. Pop. 1,665.
Map Square 24.

	Leave		Arr. at
	VICT.	LON. B.	BUXTED
AM 5.30	5.18		7.37
7.23	8. 7		10.31
9.10	9. 6		10.59
11. 5	10.35		12.33
12. 0	11.50		2.33
12. 0d	d12.20k		2.33
PM 1.20e	1.38e		3.33
1.25d	1.38d		3.33
3.45	—		5. 3
—	4.44e		6. 4
4.50	—		6.30
5. 5	5.21		7.11
6. 6e	6. 8e		7.32
6. 6	6. 8		8. 7
8. 5	8.10		9.30
—	—		—
—	—		—
—	—		—

Sunday Trains.

AM 8.50	8.30		10.33
PM 1.14	1.10		4.13
2.30	—		5.20
7. 5	6.46		9.24
—	—		—
—	—		—
—	—		—

Trains from Buxted.

Leave	Arrive at	
BUXTED	LON. B.	VICT.
AM 7.45	9.32	9.40
8.37	10. 4	10.12
8.56	10.55	10.20
10.10	12.13	12.17
10.59	12.44	12.35
PM12.50	2.58	—
1.38	—	3.45
2.28	5.21	5.55
4.40	6.36	6.29
5.54	7.56	8.27
8.11	10.25	10.10
—	—	—
—	—	—
—	—	—

Sunday Trains.

AM10.31	—	1 40
PM 4.32	—	6.54
8. 5	—	9.47
—	—	—
—	—	—
—	—	—
—	—	—

d Saturdays only.
e Saturdays excepted.
k Departs from London Bridge S.E. & C. Station.

BUXTON (Derby) from
St. Pancras, 164¾ miles. Fares, 34/0a, 20/5c. R. T. for two months, 68/0a, 40/10c. Pop. 15,651.
Map Square 1.

ST. PAN.	BUXTON	BUXTON	ST. PAN
AM 4.25	9.25	AM 7.50r	11.35
8.25r	12.22	9.42r	1.30
10.25r	2.13	10.35	3.25
PM 1.25r	5.30	PM 2. 0r	5,45
2.25r	7. 0	4.10r	8.35
4.25hr	8.48	5.22r	10. 5
6.25r	10.17	8.15	4.20
12. 0k	9.10	—	—

Sunday Trains.

PM 3.15	7.50	AM10.35r	5. 2
—	—	PM 5.10r	9.52
—	—	7.10	4.55
—	—	—	—
—	—	—	—
—	—	—	—

h Via Chinley.
k Saturdays midnight only.
r Restaurant Car.

ANOTHER ROUTE from
Euston (*via* Stockport), 196½ miles. Fares, 37/9a, 22/8c. R. T. for two months, 75/6a, 45/4c.

EUSTON	BUXTON	BUXTON	EUSTON
AM12.25	8.45	AM 7.40r	12.50
2.35	10.23	9. 5r	1.15
5. 0e	11.55	9.30r	3.10
5. 0d	1.15	10.35r	3.55
8.45dr	1.48	11.25er	6. 0
8.45er	2.25	PM12.35dr	6. 0
10.40r	3.46	1.20er	6.15
11.50er	4.56	3.15r	8.10
11.50dr	5.16	4.25er	10. 0
12. 0enr	6.15	9.15	5. 0
12. 0dm	6.22	10.30d	5.45
PM 1.30dr	7.17		
1.30er	7.25		
2.50t	8.33		
4. 5r	10. 6		
6. 5r	11.33		
11.50d	9.45		

Sunday Trains.

PM12.30r	7.18	AM10.15r	5.45
—	—	PM 7.55	5. 0
—	—	—	—
—	—	—	—
—	—	—	—

d Saturdays only.
e Saturdays excepted.
n Noon.
r Restaurant Car.
t Tea Car.

Buxton. The most tonic Spa in the British Isles. Magnificent "Cure" Baths. Illustrated Booklet free.—H.L.B.PITT, Information Bureau, Buxton. See description on Map.

St. Ann's Hotel. Connected by covered Colonnade with Baths and Gardens.
See advt. p. **117.**

Buxton Hydro Hotel. 260 Rooms. Overlooking Gardens. Every description of Baths.
See advt. p. **117.**

BUXTON—*continued.*

Palace Hotel. Finest and Foremost Facing South. Over 200 Rooms. Golf. Tennis. Music. Mod. Tariff.
See advt. p. **118.**

George Hotel. First-class family. Close to Baths and Pump Room. W. F. MILL, Proprietor.
See advt. p. **118.**

The Crescent Hotel. The Premier Hotel of the Peak. Newly decorated and modernised. Telegrams: "Crescent, Buxton." Telephone : 20 Buxton. Proprietor, C. J. SMILTER.
See advt. p. **119.**

Savoy Hotel. Best position, adjoining Public Gardens and Baths. Lift. Lounge. Tel. 497. H. H. KIRK, Proprietor.
See advt. p. **119.**

Shakespeare Hotel. Excellent Cuisine. Restaurant. Garage. R.A. Club Listed Hotel. Tel. 480. Telegrams: "Shakespeare, Buxton."
W. P. RONAN, Manager.

Haddon Hall Hydro. Situated amidst charming scenery 1,200 Feet above Sea Level. Excellent Cuisine. Moderate Tariff. Electric Baths, etc. Tel. 4. Telegrams: "Haddon Hall," Buxton.

Lee Wood Hotel. Beautiful Situation. Moderate Tariff. National Telephone No. 2.

The Clarendon, near Mineral Baths, Wells and Pavilion Gardens. Central Heating. Moderate terms. Telephone 3.
Apply MANAGERESS.

Limehurst Boarding Establishment. New management. Redecorated. Charming situation. Garden. South - west aspect. Telephone 481.
Misses DOUGHTY,
(Late with Mrs. Lee "Balmoral.")

The Buckingham High Class Boarding and Residential Establishment. Corner of St. John's Road; opposite Gardens. Entrance on level. Electric light. Lounge. Terms moderate. Telephone 439. Mr. and Mrs.
CHARLES MARSHALL.

Southgate Private Hotel. Old established and comfortable. In quiet, central position. Enquiries as to terms, etc., invited.
Miss OWEN.

The Sandringham, Broad Walk. Hotel Pension. Ideal situation. Facing Pavilion Garden. Few minutes from Baths, Stations and Town. No dust, no hills. Fine lounge. Heated. Table d'Hote 7.0. Separate Tables. 'Phone 430. Mrs. STEWART.

BUXTON LAMAS (Norfolk), 128½ miles. Fares, 25/3*a*, 15/2*c*. R. T. for two months, 50/6*a*, 30/4*c*. Departures *from* London as for Aylsham. Departures *for* London about 4 times daily. Pop. (Buxton) 480.
Map Square 19.

BYERS GREEN (Durham), 247½ miles. No through fares. Departures *from* London as for Ferryhill. Departures *for* London about 6 times daily. Pop. 2,437.
Map Square 7.

BYFIELD (Northampton) from *Marylebone* 70¾ miles. Fares, 15/10*a*, 9/6*c*. R. T. for two months, 31/8*a*, 19/0*c*. Departures *from* London as for Kineton. Departures *for* London about 3 times daily. Pop. 809.
Map Square 18.

BYFLEET (Surrey) from *Waterloo*, 21¾ miles. Fares, 4/7*a*, 2/9*c*. R. T. for two months, 9/2*a*, 5/6*c* Pop. 4,173.
Map Square 23.

W'LOO.	BYFLEET	BYFLEET	W'LOO.
AM 4.50	5.51	AM 7.31	8.20
7. 0	7.43	7.47	8.36
7.50	8.36	8.29	9. 8
8.15	8.59	8.56	9.36
9.15	10. 5	9.28	10.11
10.20	11. 8	9.57	10.45
11.20	12. 5	10.58	11.46
PM12.14*d*	12.53	11.57	12.46
12.15	1. 5	PM12.57	1.46
1.15*d*	1.53	1.57	2.46
1.20	2. 3	2.57	3.46
1.44*d*	2.24	3.59	4.46
2.20	3. 6	4.57	5.46
3.15	4. 5	5.57	6.46
4.20	5. 6	6.57	7.46
4.40	5.23	7.57	8.46
5.15*e*	5.53	8.57	9.46
5.20	6. 8	9.57	10.46
6.15*e*	6.53	10.23	11.10
6.20	7. 8	11.18	12.16
7.20	8. 8	—	—
8.20	9. 8	—	—
9.20	10. 8	—	—
10.20	11. 8	—	—
11.15*e*	12. 1	—	—
11.40	12.27	—	—

Sunday Trains.

AM 8.20	9.10	AM 8.52	9.45
9.20	10.13	10.28	11.16
9.45	10.31	11.47	12.41
10.20	11.13	PM12.47	1.41
11.20	12.13	1.49	2.44
PM12.20	1.13	2.49	3.44
1.20	2.13	4.47	5.41
3.20	4.13	5.53	6.46
4.20	5. 6	6.47	7.41
5.20	6. 6	7.47	8.41
6.50	7.16	8.49	9.44
7.20	8. 6	9.46	10.41
8.20	9.13	10.47	11.43
9.45	10.33	—	—
—	—	—	—
—	—	—	—

d Saturdays only.
e Saturdays excepted.

Wheatsheaf Hotel. Facing Horsell Common. Lately rebuilt and refurnished. About ten minutes from Woking Station. Central for several Golf Courses. 'Phone Woking 173.
CATERING HOUSES, LTD.

BYKER (Northumberland), 269¼ miles. No through fares. Departures *from* London as for Newcastle-on-Tyne. Departures *for* London about 6 times daily. Pop. 48,709.

BYNEA (Carmarthen), 206¼ miles. Fares, 43/2*a*, 25/11*c*. R. T. for two months, 86/4*a*, 51/10*c*. Departures *from* London as for Llanelly. Departures *for* London about 5 times daily.
Map Square 21.

REFERENCE NOTES.

a signifies First Class.
b „ Second Class.
c „ Third Class.
d „ On Saturdays only.
e „ Saturdays excepted.
f „ On Mondays only.
g „ Mondays excepted.
r „ Restaurant Car.
t „ Tea Car.
x „ Express.
R.T. „ Return Tickets.

All Trains in the Tables not otherwise marked carry Third Class Passengers.

C

CADELEIGH (Devon), 167½ miles. Fares 35/0*a*. 21/0*c*. R. T. for two months, 70/0*a*, 42/0*c*. Departures *from* London as for Exeter (St. David's). Departures *for* London about 5 times daily. Pop. 189.
Map Square 26.

CADISHEAD (Lancs), 192¼ miles. Fares, 37/9*a*, 22/8*c*. R. T. for two months, 75/6*a*, 45/4*c*. Departures *from* London as for Timperley West. Departures *for* London about 8 times daily. Pop. 3,384.

CADOXTON (Glamorgan), 159½ miles. Fares, 33/2*a*, 19/11*c*. R.T. for two months, 66/4*a*, 39/10*c*. Departures *from* London as for Cardiff. Departures *for* London about 4 times daily. Pop. 5,844.
Map Square 21.

CAERAU (Glamorgan), 183¼ miles. Fares, 38/2*a*, 22/11*c*. R. T. for two months, 76/4*a*, 45/10*c*. Departures *from* London as for Maesteg. Departures *for* London about 5 times daily.

CAERGWRLE CASTLE (Flint), 187½ miles. No through fares. Departures *from* London as for Wrexham. Departures *for* London about 4 times daily.
Map Square 12.

CAERLEON (Monmouth), 142¾ miles. Fares, 29/10*a*, 17/11*c*. R. T. for two months, 59/8*a*. Departures *from* London as for Newport (Mon.). Departures *for* London about 6 times daily. Pop. 2,285.
Map Square 22.

CAERPHILLY Glamorgan) from *Paddington, via* Cardiff, 152¾ miles. Fares *via* Cardiff, 33/4*a*, 20/0*c*. R.T. for two months, 66/8*a*, 40/0*c*. *Via* Bassaleg, 31/11*a*, 19/2*c*. R.T. for two months, 63/10*a*, 38/4*c*. Pop. 36,893.
Map Square 21.

	Pad.	Caerpy		Caerpy.	Pad.
AM	1. 0*g*	7. 3	AM	7. 8*r*	10.57
	5.30	11. 1		8.55*r*	1. 0
	8.45*r*	12.18		10. 8*r*	2.30
	9. 0	2.28	PM	12.42*r*	4.20
	11.50*r*	3.17		2. 0*r*	6.15
PM	1.10*r*	5.26		4. 0*dr*	8.35
	3.35*r*	7.51		4.10*er*	8.35
	5. 0*r*	9.27		5.22*r*	9.25
	6. 0*r*	10.21		9.51	3.30
	6.30*dr*	11. 2		—	—
	6.30*r*	11.21		—	—
	9.15*e*	5.30		—	—
	—	—		—	—

Sunday Trains.

AM	1. 0	8.29	AM	10.59	4. 5
	9.10	3. 6	PM	3.30*r*	8.25
PM	12.30*r*	7. 4		9.19	3.30
	4.30*d*	9. 5		—	—
	9.15	5.30		—	—

d Saturdays only.
e Saturdays excepted.
g Mondays excepted.
r Restaurant Car.

CAERSWS (Montgomery), 191¼ miles. Fares, 40/0*a*, 24/0*c*. R. T. for two months, 80/0*a*. Departures *from* London as for Newtown. Departures *for* London about 4 times daily.
Map Square 16.

CAERWYS (Flint), 202¼ miles. Fares, 40/7*a*, 24/4*c*. R. T. for two months, 81/2*a*. Departures *from* London as for Mold. Departures *for* London about 4 times daily. Pop. 834.
Map Square 11.

CAIRNBULG (Aberdeen), 573¼ miles. No through fares. Departures *from* London as for Fraserburgh. Departures *for* London about 3 times daily.
Map Square 35.

CAIRNEYHILL (Fife), 412½ miles. Fares 86/6*a*, 51/11*c*. R. T. for two months, 173/0*a*, 103/10*c*. Departures *from* London as for Dunfermline. Departures *for* London about 4 times daily.
Map Square 41.

CAISTER (Norfolk) from *King's Cross*, 183½ miles. Fares, 25/3*a*, 15/2*c*. R. T. for two months, 50/6*a*, 30/4*c*. Departures *from* London as for North Walsham. Departures *for* London about 3 times daily. Pop. 1,938.
Map Square 19.

Manor House Hotel, Caister-on Sea. Close Golf Links. Yarmouth Station 20 minutes.
See advt. p **120.**

CALAIS from *Victoria*, 102 miles. Fares, 46/9*a*, 33/6*b*, 23/5*c*. R. T. for two months, 93/5*a*, 66/11*b*, 46/10*c*, subject to exchange.
Map Square 24.

Subject to special Passport Regulations.

Weekdays and Sundays.

	Vict.	Calais		Calais	Vict.
AM	11. 0*b*	2.10	AM	5.40	9.48
PM	2. 0	5.30	PM	4. 0	7.30
	—	—		—	—

CALBOURNE (Isle of Wight) from *Victoria, London Bridge* or *Waterloo, via* Portsmouth and Ryde, 93½ miles Fares, *via* Ryde, 20/10*a*, 12/9*c*. R.T. for two months, 41/8*a*, 25/6*c*. Departures *from* London as for Newport (I. of W.) Departures *for* London about 4 times daily. Pop. 720.
Map Square 28.

CALCOTS (Elgin), 574¾ miles. Fares, 106/3*a*, 63/9*c*. R.T. for two months, 212/6*a*, 127/6*c*. Departures *for* London as for Huntly or Elgin (*via* Dunkeld). Departures *for* London about 3 times daily.
Map Square 35.

CALDARVAN (Dumbarton), 443½ miles. Fares, 86/1*a*, 51/8*c*. R.T. for two months, 172/2*a*, 103/4*c*. Departures *from* London as for Stirling or Balloch. Departures *for* London about 3 times daily.
Map Square 40.

CALDER (Lanark), 394 miles. Fares, 80/3*a*, 18/2*c*. R. T. for two months, 160/6*a*, 96/4*c*. Departures *from* London as for Coatbridge. Departures *for* London about 4 times daily.

CALDERCRUIX (Lanark), 421¼ miles. No through fares. Departures *from* London as for Edinburgh (Waverley). Departures *for* London about 4 times daily. Pop. 1,303.
Map Square 40.

CALDWELL (Renfrew), 401½ miles. Fares, 81/11*a*, 49/2*c*. R. T. for two months, 163/10*a*, 98/4*c*. Departures *from* London as for Kilmarnock. Departures *for* London about 4 times daily.
Map Square 40.

CALDY (Cheshire), 197¾ miles. Fares, 41/1*a*, 24/8*c*. R. T. for two months, 82/2*a*. Departures *from* London as for Hooton. Departures *for* London about 6 times daily. Pop. 183.

CALEDONIAN ROAD (Hammersmith and Finsbury Park Tube). *See* back of Map.

CALEDONIAN ROAD AND BARNSBURY from *Broad Street*, 4 miles. Fares, 0/7½*a*, 0/4½*c*. R. T. for two days, 1/3*a*, 0/7*c*. Pop. (Barnsbury) 22,558. *See* pp. 501-505.
Map Square 61.

CALLANDER (Perth), 433

miles. Fares, 88/6*a*, 53/1*c*. R. T. for two months, 177/0*a*, 106/2*c*. Pop. 2,764.
Map Square 40.

Euston	C'lnder	C'lnder	Euston
AM 5. 0	5.36*l*	AM 8.31*r*	7.30*l*
10. 0*er*	7.50	PM12. 8*r*	10.45*l*
10. 0*dr*	9.46	2.55*r*	5. 0*h*
PM 1.30*er*	12.58*h*	8.20*e*	7.40
1.30*dr*	1. 4	—	—
7.50*er*	6.29*h*	—	—
11.35*e*	9.35*h*	—	—

Sunday Trains.

| PM 7.50*r* | 6.29*h* | — | — |
| 11.35 | 9.35*h* | — | — |

d Saturdays only.
e Saturdays excepted.
h A.M.
l P.M.
r Restaurant Car.

CALLERTON (North-

umberland), 275½ miles. No through fares. Departures *from* London as for Newcastle-on-Tyne. Departures *for* London about 6 times daily. Pop. 116.
Map Square 3.

CALLINGTON (Cornwall)

from *Waterloo*, 229½ miles. Fares, 48/4*a*, 29/0*c*. R. T. for two months, 96/8*a*, 58/0*c*. Departures *from* London as for Calstock. Departures *for* London about 3 times daily. Pop. 1,636.
Map Square 26.

CALLOWLAND (Herts)

from *Euston*, 18½ miles. Fares, 3/7*a*, 2/2*c*. R. T. for two months, 7/2*a*, 4/1*c*. Departures *from* London as for St. Albans. Departures *for* London about 14 times daily.

CALNE (Wilts) from *Pad-*

dington, 99 miles. Fares, 20/4*a*, 12/5*c*. R. T. for two months, 40/8*a*, 24/10*c*. Pop. 3,640.
Map Square 22.

Pad.	Calne	Calne	Pad.
AM 5.30	9.10	AM 7.35*r*	10.15
7.30	10.38	9.25	12.20
9. 0	11.55	10.45*r*	2.40
10.45	2.15	PM12.45	3.20
PM 1.10*r*	4.50	2.40	6. 2
4.15*r*	6.51	5.10*r*	8.35
6.30	8.45	7.10	10.25
12. 0*h*	6.40	9. 5	2.45
—	—	—	—

Sunday Trains.

| PM12.30*r* | 5.15 | PM 5.45 | 8.10 |
| — | — | — | — |

h Saturdays midnight excepted.
r Restaurant Car.

CALSTOCK (Cornwall)

from *Waterloo*, 222 miles. Fares, 46/8*a*, 28/0*c*. R.T. for two months, 93/4*a*, 56/0*c*. Pop. 4,880.
Map Square 26.

W'loo	C'stock'	C'stock	W'loo
AM 9. 0	2.36	AM 7.37*dr*	1.56
11. 0*er*	5.58	7.45*er*	1.53
11. 0*dr*	6. 6	10.26*r*	3.50
PM 1. 0*r*	8. 1	PM 1.13*r*	8.30
3. 0*dr*	10.11	—	—

No Sunday Trains.

d Saturdays only.
e Saturdays excepted.
r Restaurant Car

CALTHWAITE (Cumber-

land), 288½ miles. Fares, 58/2*a*, 34/11*c*. R.T. for two months, 116/4*a*, 69/10*c*. Departures *from* London as for Penrith. Departures *for* London about 4 times daily.
Map Square 7.

CALVELEY (Cheshire),166½

miles. Fares, 34/7*a*, 20/9*c*. R. T. for two months, 69/2*a*. Departures *from* London as for Crewe. Departures *for* London about 6 times daily. Pop. 316
Map Square 12.

CALVERLEY (Yorks) from

St. Pancras, 201 miles. Fares, 39/9*a*, 23/10*c*. R. T. for two months, 79/6*a*, 47/8*c*. Pop. 3,362.
Map Square 12.

St. Pan.	Calv.	Calv.	St. Pan.
AM 2.25*g*	9.40	AM 7.31	12.10
4.25	11.21	8.19*r*	1.45
9.50*r*	2.22	9.44*r*	2.10
PM12.15*er*	4.45	12. 3*r*	5.30
12.15*r*	4.55	PM 1.30*r*	6.35
1.50*r*	6.48	2.15*r*	7.15
3.30*r*	9. 0	4.45*r*	9.15
5. 0*r*	10.10	9.20	4.20
6.15*r*	11.18	—	—
11.45	6.15	—	—
11.50*d*	6.34	—	—
11.50*e*	6.58	—	—
—	—	—	—

Sunday Trains.

AM10.50*r*	5.55	AM11. 8	6.25
PM 3.15	11. 0	PM 1.23*r*	9.43
11.45	6.15	9.23	4.55
—	—	—	—

d Saturdays only.
e Saturdays excepted.
g Mondays excepted.
r Restaurant Car.

CALVERT (Bucks) from

Marylebone,46½ miles. Fares, 10/3*a*, 6/2*c*. R. T. for two months, 20/6*a*, 12/4*c*.
Map Square 18.

M'bone	Calvert	Calvert	M'bone
AM 6.45	8.28	AM 8.16	9.46
11.15	1. 4	10.42	12. 2
PM 3.25	5.12	PM 3.12	4.56
4.55	6.34	6. 1	7.15
6.25*e*	7.58	8.17	9.55
6.25*d*	8. 7	9.27	11. 0
7.30	9.21	—	—
—	—	—	—

Sunday Trains.

AM 8.50	10.45	AM 8.24	10.13
9.30	11.13	8.40	10.43
PM 6.30	8.30	11. 9	12.46
—	—	PM 6.57	8.58
—	—	—	—
—	—	—	—

d Saturdays only.
e Saturdays excepted.

CAM (Gloucester), 127¾ miles.

No through fares. Departures *from* London as for Gloucester. Departures *for* London about 4 times daily. Pop. 1,834.
Map Square 22.

CAMBERLEY (Surrey)

from *Waterloo* 35½ miles. Fares, *via* Woking, 7/4*a*, 4/5*c*. R.T. for two months, 14/8*a*, 8/10*c*.
Map Square 23.

W'loo	Camby	Camby	W'loo
AM 5.40	6.50	AM 8.19	9.26
5.50	7.26	8.41	10.11
8.15	9.55	9.47	11.16
9.20	10.45	10.55	11.32
10.34	12. 2	PM12.52	1.40
11.20	12.52	1.50	3. 6
PM 1.20*e*	3. 2	2.12	3.36
1.20*d*	3. 6	2.38*d*	4.46
2.20	3.44	3.38*d*	5.20
4.20*d*	5.47	3.48	5.46
5.30*e*	6.35	4.42	6.16
5.50*d*	7.20	7.19	8.46
6.10*e*	7.50	7.36*e*	9. 6
6.40*d*	7.59	8.18	9.46
6.54*e*	7.59	9.36	10.50
7.20	8.45	—	—

Sunday Trains.

AM 8.20	9.51	AM10.54	12.41
8.45	10.54	PM12.44	2.44
10.20	11.54	3.56	5.41
11.15*h*	12.54	5.56	7.41
PM12.20	1.54	7.44	9.12
1.50*h*	3.54	9.19	10.47
3.20	4.54	—	—
5.20	6.54	—	—
6.20*h*	7.56	—	—
7.20	8.51	—	—

d Saturdays only.
e Saturdays excepted.
h *Via* North Camp.

ANOTHER ROUTE from

Waterloo via Ascot, 35½ miles. Fares, 6/8*a*, 4/0*c*. R. T. for two months, 13/4*a*, 8/0*c*.

W'loo	Camby	Camby	W'loo
AM 5.10	8.19	AM 6.51	8.17
6.54	8.41	7.20	8.47
7.54	9.47	7.56	9.17
8.54	10.25	8.36	9.47
9.54	11.51	9.55	11.17
10.54	12.32	10.44	12.31
PM12.48	2.12	PM12. 3	1.27
1.18*d*	2.37	12.52	2.27
1.48	3.48	1.23	3.27
2.18*d*	3.38	3.44	5.27
2.48	4.42	4.51	6.27
4.48*e*	6.12	5.47*d*	7.27
4.48*d*	6.17	6.34*e*	8.27
5.18*e*	6.37	7.59	9.27
5.48	7.19	8.46	10.37
6.18*e*	7.36	—	—
6.48	8.19	—	—
7.54	9.36	—	—

Sunday Trains.

AM 9.18	10.54	AM10.54	12.43
PM12.18	2.11	11.54	2. 3
2.18	3.56	PM 3.54	5.28
4.18	5.56	5.54	7.28
5.58	7.44	7.56	9.28
7.48	9.19	8.51	10.18

d Saturdays only.
e Saturdays excepted.

CAMBERLEY—*continued.*

Estate Agents. For particulars of Residences and Building Sites, apply, SADLER & BAKER. Land Agents. Register on application. Established 1879.

House and Estate Agents. Illustrated Lists, with Map, sent free on application to HANKINSON & SON, 63, High Street. Camberley.

CAMBORNE (Cornwall)

from *Paddington,* 292 miles. Fares, 60/5a, 36/3c. R. T. for two months, 120/10a, 72/6c. Pop. 14,582.
Map Square 25.

PAD.	C'BORNE	C'BORNE	PAD.
AM 5.30	2.59	AM 8.41r	4.35
10.30r	5. 2	9.48r	4.45
11.10r	5.53	11.34r	6.50
PM 2. 0r	9.43	PM12.43r	9. 0
10. 0	6.58	9.19	7.10
12. 0k	10.49	—	—
12.30h	11.11	—	—
—	—	—	—

Sunday Trains.

AM10.30r	5.17	AM11.12r	7. 5
PM10. 0	6.58	PM12 52r	7.55
—	—	5.11	3.15

h Saturdays midnight only.
k Saturdays midnight excepted.
r Restaurant Car.

CAMBRIDGE from *Liverpool Street,* 55¾ miles. Fares, 11/6a, 6/11c. R. T. for two months, 23/0a. Pop. 59,262.
Map Square 18.

L'PL.ST.	CAMBDG.	CAMBDG.	L'PL.ST.
AM 5. 5	6.28	AM12.55	2.50
5.50	8. 1	6.42	8.57
7.18	9.45	7.47	9.27
8.30r	9.58	7.58	9.47
10. 5	11.38	8.35	10.17
h11.20lr	12.34	9. 5r	10.23
11.50r	1.17	10. 3	11.27
PM12.29d	2.18	11.14	12.40
12.48e	3.16	11.54	2. 7
1.19d	3.25	PM 1. 0r	2.21
2.54	3.58	1.12d	3.18
2.48	5. 3	2.10l	5. 9
4.15	5.50	2.25k	5. 9
4.45	6. 4	2.42lr	4. 2h
5.49r	7.14	3.52r	5.17
6.30	8.13	4.42r	6.10
7.10r	8.35	5.38	7.58
8.22	9.50	6.52r	8.22
10.12	11.42	7. 7r	8.33
—	—	9. 6	10.30

Sunday Trains.

AM 8.12	10.16	AM12.55	3. 0
9.25	10.55	9. 5	11.27
PM 1.50	4.29	PM 5.17	6.40
3.25	4.50	5.30	7.26
9.12	11.26	6.12	7.40
—	—	8.25	9.40

d Saturdays only.
e Saturdays excepted.
h Departs from or arrives at St. Pancras Station.
k Will cease to run after July 21.
l Commencing July 23.
r Restaurant Car.

CAMBRIDGE—*continued.*

ANOTHER ROUTE from *King's Cross,* 58 miles. Fares as above.

KING'S+	CAMBGE	CAMBGE	KING'S+
AM 7. 0	9.30	AM 7.35	9.34
8.45	10.41	8.27	9.56
11.30	1.42	9.18k	11.15
PM12.40d	2.14	10. 0	11.25
3. 0	4.43	11. 0	1.25
5. 0	6.25	PM 1.37	3.50
6.15	7.56	4. 5	6. 0
7. 0	8.59	6.20	8. 5
—	—	7.54	10.20
—	—	—	—
—	—	—	—
—	—	—	—
—	—	—	—

Sunday Trains.

AM 8.30	10.50	AM 7.20	9.53
—	—	PM 5.26	8. 8
—	—	—	—
—	—	—	—
—	—	—	—

d Saturdays only.
k Tuesdays only.

The Bull Hotel. Patronised by Royalty. Leading Family Hotel. Sixty rooms. Centre of principal Colleges. Terms moderate. Excellent Garage on the premises. Telephone No. 341.
See advt. p. **120.**

University Arms Hotel, First-class. For Families and Gentlemen. Electric Light. Close to Colleges. Suites of Rooms. Excellent Chef. Stabling. Motors on hire. Garage Pit. Standing for 50 Cars. Office telephone, 57. Visitors' telephone, 338.
Resident Proprietor,
M. D. BRADFORD.

Blue Boar Hotel. Opposite Trinity College. Recently enlarged and refurnished. Comfortable Lounge. Garage on premises. Telephone 303.

The Lion Hotel. Centre of town. Two minutes from Colleges, Town Hall. Table d'Hote. Luncheons and Dinners. Garage. Omnibus meets all trains. Telephone : 1391 (3 Lines).
A. A. MOYES, Proprietress.

Bath Commercial Hotel, Benet Street. Bed and Breakfast, 6/6. Near Colleges and Market. 'Phone 233.
Proprietor, H. C. MORTON.

CAMBRIDGE HEATH
from *Liverpool Street,* 1½ miles. Fares, 0/2½a, 0/2b, 0/1½c. R. T. for two days, 0/5a, 0/4b, 0/3c. *See* pp. 523, 524, 534-536.
Map Square 61.

CAMBUS (Clackmannan),
421¾ miles. No through fares. Departures *from* London as for Stirling. Departures *for* London about 4 times daily.
Map Square 40.

CAMBUSLANG (Lanark),
396¼ miles. Fares, 82/6a, 49/6c. R. T. for two months, 165/0a, 99/0c. Departures *from* London as for Motherwell. Departures *for* London about 4 times daily. Pop. 26,130.

CAMBUS O'MAY (Aberdeen),
561 miles. Fares, 108/2a, 64/11c. R. T. for two months, 216/4a, 129/10c. Departures *from* London as for Ballater. Departures *for* London about 3 times daily.
Map Square 38.

CAMDEN TOWN from
Broad Street, 5 miles. Fares, 0/7½a, 0/4½c. R. T. for two days, 1/3a, 0/9c. *See* pp. 501-505.
Map Square 60.

ANOTHER ROUTE (Hampstead Tube). *See back of Map.*

CAMELFORD (Cornwall)
from *Waterloo,* 240½ miles. Fares, 49/5a, 29/8c. R. T. for two months, 98/10a, 59/4c. Pop. 7,335.
Map Square 25.

W'LOO	CAMFD.	CAMFD.	W'LOO
AM10. 0r	3.38	AM 9. 9r	3.50
11. 0r	5.47	10.27r	4.30
PM 3. 0r	8.56	PM 1.25r	8.30
—	—	3.35	10.50
—	—	—	—
—	—	—	—
—	—	—	—
—	—	—	—
—	—	—	—
—	—	—	—

No Sunday Trains.
r Restaurant Car.

King Arthur's Castle Hotel. Ideal position on Cliffs. Links in Hotel grounds.
See advt p. **318.**

CAMERON BRIDGE
(Fife), 426¾ miles. Fares, 86/3a, 51/9c. R. T. for two months, 172/6a, 103/6c. Departures *from* London as for St. Andrews. Departures *for* London about 3 times daily. Pop. (Cameron) 621.

CAMERTON (Cumberland),
316½ miles. Fares, 63/11a, 38/4c. R. T. for two months, 127/10a, 76/8c. Departures *from* London as for Cockermouth. Departures *for* London about 4 times daily. Pop. 258.

CAMBRIDGE—UNIVERSITY ARMS HOTEL.
Leading Hotel.
See advt. above.

CAMERTON (Somerset)

108¾ miles. No through fares. Departures *from* London as for Limpley Stoke. Departures *for* London about 4 times daily.
Map Square 22.

CAMPDEN (Gloucester)

from *Paddington*, 96¾ miles. Fares 20/3*a*, 12/2*c*. R.T. for two months, 40/6*a*. Pop. 1,680.
Map Square 17.

Pad.	Campden	Campden.	Pad.
AM 5.30	9. 7	AM 7.10	9.50
9.45	1. 0	9. 4	12. 5
PM 1.35*r*	3.54	11.22	2.12
4.45	6.58	PM 4. 8	7.17
6.55	9.50	6.20*r*	9.15
—	—	7.42	10.45
—	—	—	—
—	—	—	—

Sunday Trains.

AM 10.35*r*	1.25	AM 11.27	2.40
PM 4.10	7. 9	PM 6.40*r*	9.48
—	—	—	—
—	—	—	—
—	—	—	—

r Restaurant Car.

CAMP HILL (Worcester),

150¾ miles. Fares, 23/4*a*, 14/0*c*. R.T. for two months, 46/8*a*. Departures *from* London as for Birmingham (New Street). Departures *for* London about 8 times daily.

CAMPSIE GLEN (Stirling),

439¼ miles. No through fares. Departures *from* London as for Glasgow. Departures *for* London about 4 times daily. Pop. (Campsie) 5,335.
Map Square 40.

CANNING TOWN

from *Liverpool Street*, 5¾ miles, and *Fenchurch Street*, 4¾ miles. Fares from Liverpool Street, 0/7½*a*, 0/6*b*, 0/4½*c*. R. T. for two days, 1/3*a*, 1/0*b*, 0/9*c*. Fenchurch Street, 0/7½*a*, 0/6*b*, 0/4½*c*. R. T. for two days, 1/3*a*, 0/10½*b*, 0/7*c*. Pop. 28,383. *See* pp. 537-540.
Map Square 62.

CANNOCK (Stafford),

128¼ miles. Fares, 26/3*a*, 15/9*c*. R. T. for two months, 52/6*a*. Departures *from* London as for Walsall. Departures *for* London about 8 times daily. Pop. 32,321.
Map Square 17.

CANNON STREET

from *Charing Cross*, 2 miles. Fares, 0/4½*a*, 0/3½*b*, 0/2½*c*. R. T. for two days, 0/9*a*, 0/6*b*, 0/4*c*. *See* pp. 544-557.
Map Square 61, *No.* 9.

ANOTHER ROUTE

to and from *Mansion House*, *Charing Cross*, *Victoria*, *South Kensington*, *High Street*, *Praed Street*, *Baker Street*, *King's Cross*, *Moorgate Street*, and all intermediate stations every few minutes. Also to and from Ealing, Hounslow, Richmond and Wimbledon. *See* p. 489.

CANONBIE (Dumfries),

314¼ miles. Fares, 63/11*a*, 38/4*c*. R.T. for two months, 127/10*a*, 76/8*c*. Departures *from* London as for Carlisle. Departures *for* London about twice daily. Pop. 1,756.
Map Square 44.

CANONBURY

from *Broad Street*, 3 miles. Fares, 0/5*a*, 0/3*c*. R. T. for two days, 0/10*a*, 0/5½*c*. Pop. 29,997. *See* pp. 501-505, 518-522.
Map Square 61.

CANTERBURY EAST

(Kent) from *Victoria*, *Holborn Viaduct*, and *St. Paul's*, 61¾ miles. Fares, 12/11*a*, 10/4*b*, 7/9*c*. R. T. for two months 25/10*a*, 20/8*b*. Pop. 23,738.
Map Square 24.

Vict. S.E. & C.	Leave Hol. V.	S. Pl.'s	Arr. at Canter.
AM —	3.50*l*	—	6.24
5. 5	4.57	5. 0	8.15
5.48*f*	5.40*f*	5.42*f*	8.15
—	7.30	7.33	10.26
9.20	—	—	11. 6
10.40	—	—	12.31
11.40*d*	—	—	1.55
11.40*e*	—	—	2.21
PM 2. 5*d*	—	—	3.51
2. 8*e*	—	—	4.12
4.20	—	—	6.18
—	5.10*e*	5.12*e*	7. 4
5.10*d*	—	—	7. 4
5.30*d*	—	—	7.50
5.30*e*	—	—	7.54
—	6.12*ey*	—	7.54
8.30	—	—	10.15

Sunday Trains.

AM 8.15	8. 0	—	10.28
10.40	—	—	12.24
PM 3.30	—	—	6.24
8.25	—	—	10.14
—	—	—	—
—	—	—	—

Trains from Canterbury.

Leave Canter.	S. Pl.'s	Arrive at Hol. V.	Vict.
AM 7.16*k*	—	—	9. 4*k*
7.16	9.37	9.39	—
8. 3*k*	—	—	9.52*k*
8. 3	—	—	11. 2
9.53	—	—	11.27
10.27*e*	1. 0	1. 2	1.33
10.39*d*	—	—	1.22
PM 12.29	—	—	2.43
2.37*e*	4.46	—	4.39
2.53*d*	—	—	4.55
3.49	—	—	5.26
*k*5.43*d*	—	—	8.20*k*
6.36	—	—	8.33
8.24	—	—	10.25

Sunday Trains.

AM 9.38	—	11.58	11.51
PM 2.45	—	—	5.31
7. 0	—	—	8.40
8.30	—	—	10.29
—	—	—	—

d Saturdays only.
e Saturdays excepted.
f Mondays only.
k Departs from or arrives at Cannon Street.
l Third class only.
y Departs from Cannon Street.

CANTERBURY SOUTH

(Kent), from *Charing Cross*, *Cannon Street*, and *London Bridge*, 71¼ miles. Fares, 13/4*a*, 10/8*b*, 8/0*c*. R. T. for two months, 26/8*a*, 21/4*b*. Departures *from* London as for Canterbury (West). Departures *for* London about 5 times daily.
Map Square 24.

Station closed on Sundays.

CANTERBURY WEST

(Kent), from *Charing Cross*, *Cannon Street*, and *London Bridge*, 71 miles. Fares, 12/11*a*, 10/4*b*, 7/9*c*. R. T. for two months, 25/10*a*, 20/8*b*.
Map Square 24.

Char. +	Leave Can. St.	Lon. B.	Arr. at Canter.
AM —	5.20	5.25	8.53
—	—	7.50*l*	10.15
9.15	—	9.23	11.21
—	—	*l*10. 3*h*	12.12
11. 0	—	11. 7	1.24
PM 1. 0*d*	—	—	2.33
1. 0	—	—	2.49
3. 0	—	3. 8	5. 4
4.30	—	4.37	6.31
5.15*e*	5.12*e*	5.21*e*	7.25
5.20*d*	—	5.20*d*	7.25
5.24*d*	—	5.34*d*	7.54
6. 0*e*	—	6. 5*e*	7.54
7.18	—	7.20	9.53
—	—	—	—
—	—	—	—

Sunday Trains.

AM 7.45	—	7.52	10.18
9.35*k*	—	—	11.52
PM 5.15*k*	—	—	7.50
7.35	—	7.45	9.50
9.25	—	9.31	12. 0
—	—	—	—
—	—	—	—

Trains from Canterbury W.

Leave Canter.	Lon. B.	Arrive at Can. St.	Char. +
AM 6.55	9.32	9.36	—
7.41	10. 0	10. 4	—
*e*7.41*k*	—	—	10.16*k*
8.49	10.54	—	11. 3
9.33	11.43	—	11.57
11. 4	1.36	—	1.50
PM 12.39	3.26	—	3.40
1.42*h*	4. 8	—	—
3.10*k*	—	—	5.42*k*
3.10	5.50	—	6. 3
5. 6	7.25	7.30	7.49
7.55	10.22	—	10.35
10.48*s*	—	1.20	—
—	—	—	—
—	—	—	—
—	—	—	—

Sunday Trains.

AM 7. 2	10. 5	—	10.15
9.16	—	—	1. 5*k*
PM 4.55	7. 9	—	7.17
6.17	8.30	—	8.40
8.10	10.16	—	10.26
10.42*s*	—	1.23	—
—	—	—	—
—	—	—	—

d Saturdays only.
e Saturdays excepted.
h Mondays, Fridays and Saturdays only.
k Departs from or arrives at Victoria (S. E. & C. R.).
l Low Level Platform.
s Third class only.

For completion of Advertisements, see over.

CANTERBURY WEST
—continued.

Baker's Family and Commercial Temperance Hotel. Erected 1643. Minute Cathedral. Home comforts. Moderate tariff. Bus all trains. 'Phone 177. Personal supervision.
C. G. SHEPPARD, Proprietor.

Royal Fountain Hotel. Oldest first-class Family Hotel in City. Re-organised and under new proprietorship. Close to Cathedral and Stations. Spacious Coffee Room and Lounge. Private Sitting Rooms. Re-decorated throughout. Lock-up Garage. Inspection pit. Electric light. Telephone 185.
F. C. LARGE, Proprietor.

St. George's Private Hotel (over National Provincial Bank). Three minutes Cathedral. Spacious Rooms. Well recommended. Reasonable Terms.
CHARLES WILSON, Proprietor.

Rose Hotel. First-class Family and Commercial. Nearest Cathedral. Up to date. Moderate tariff. Garage. Telephone 130. Proprietors—
Misses REDMAN & JEANS.

CANTLEY (Norfolk), 124
miles. Fares, 24/9a, 14/10c. R. T. for two months, 49/6a. Departures from London as for Brundall. Departures for London about 4 times daily. Pop. 259.
Map Square 19.

CAPEL (Suffolk) from Liverpool Street, 65½ miles. Fares 13/9a, 8/3c. R. T. for two months, 27/6a. Via Ipswich, 14/10a, 8/11c. R. T., 29/8a, 17/10c. Departures from London about 5 times daily. Pop. 516.
Map Square 19.

CAPEL BANGOR (Cardigan), 244 miles. No through fares. Departures from London as for Aberystwyth. Departures for London about 3 times daily.
Map Square 16

CAPENHURST
(Cheshire), 184½ miles. Fares, 38/6a, 23/1c. R. T. for two months, 77/0a. Departures from London as for Chester. Departures for London about 6 times daily. Pop. 146.
Map Square 12.

CARBIS BAY (Cornwall)
from *Paddington*, 302½ miles. Fares, 62/8a, 37/7c. R. T. for two months, 125/4a, 75/2c.
Map Square 25.

PAD.	CARBIS B.	CARBIS B.	PAD.
AM 5.30	3.41	AM 9.45r	4.45
10.30r	5. 6	10.30r	6.50
11.10r	6.46	11.55r	9. 0
PM 2. 0r	10.16	PM 8.40	7.10
10. 0e	7.40	—	—
10. 0d	10.11	—	—
12. 0k	11.36	—	—
12.30h	11.41	—	—

Sunday Trains.

AM 10.30r	5.46	AM 10.35	7. 5
PM 10. 0	7.40	PM 12. 5r	7.55
—	—	2.55	3.15
—	—	—	—

d Saturdays only.
e Saturdays excepted.
h Saturdays midnight only.
k Saturdays midnight excepted.
r Restaurant Car.

CARCROFT (Yorks), 160
miles. Fares, 33/2a, 19/11c. R. T., double fare. Departures from London as for Hemsworth. Departures for London about 6 times daily.
Map Square 13.

CARDENDEN (Fife), 419
miles. Fares 86/6a, 51/11c. R. T. for two months, 173/0a, 103/10c. Departures from London as for Dunfermline. Departures for London about 4 times daily.

CARDIFF (Glamorgan) from
Paddington. 153 miles. Fares, 31/11a, 19/2c. R. T. for two months, 63/10a. Pop. 200,262.
Map Square 21.

PAD.	CARDIFF	CARDIFF	PAD.
AM 1. 0g	5.31	AM 5.50r	10.15
5.30	10.12	7.45r	10.57
8.45r	11.33	8. 0	12.20
9. 0	1.42	10. 0r	1. 9
11.50r	2.42	10.10r	2. 0
PM 1.10r	4.54	11.20r	2.30
3.35r	6.30	PM 1.20r	4.20
5. 0r	8.29	3.15r	6.15
6. 0r	9. 5	5.10r	8.35
6.30r	10.15	6.35r	9.25
8. 0r	10.46	10.42	3.30
9.15	2.28	—	—

Sunday Trains.

AM 1. 0	5.55	AM 11. 0	3.35
9.10	2. 2	PM 12.30	4. 5
PM 12.30r	4.12	5. 0r	8.25
4.30	8.30	10.42	3.30
9.15	2.28	—	—

g Mondays excepted.
r Restaurant Car.

Park Hotel. Suites with Baths. Tea Lounge. Private Telephone Exchange connected to all Floors. Handsome Billiard Room, 5 Tables (Burroughs & Watts). Telephone 2566, 2567, 2568. Telegrams "Park Hotel."
See advt. p. 120.

Royal Hotel, Cardiff. The leading hotel of Wales. Family and Commercial. Most centrally situated, near G.W. Ry Station. All modern improvements. Restaurant and Grill Room. Large Stock Room accommodation. Omnibus and Porter meet trains.

Esplanade Hotel, Penarth. Within three miles of Cardiff. Overlooking the Bristol Channel. First-class Family Hotel. Recently entirely reconstructed, redecorated and refurnished. Every modern convenience. Excellent Cuisine.

CARDIFF—*continued.*

S. Hern, Pertwee, Farrell & Co., F.S.I., F.A.I., Auctioneers, Estate Agents and Surveyors, 93, St. Mary Street, Cardiff, and at Penarth. Proprietors of the South Wales Property Gazette. Sent free on application. Established 1849.

Bank.—The National Bank, Limited, 3, High Street, and 125, Bute Street.

CARDIGAN from *Paddington*, 268¼ miles. Fares, 54/9a, 32/10c. R. T. for two months, 109/6a, 65/8c. Pop. 3,452.
Map Square 16.

PAD.	CARD.	CARD.	PAD.
AM 1. 0g	1. 6	AM 7. 0r	4.20
8.45r	4. 0	9.50r	6.15
11.50r	7.55	PM 12.15r	9.25
PM 9.15e	7.48	5.35	3.30
—	—	—	—

Sunday Trains.

PM 9.15	7.48		

e Saturdays excepted.
g Mondays excepted.
r Restaurant Car.

CARDINGTON (Beds)
from *King's Cross*, 45½ miles. Fares, 9/5a, 5/8c. R. T., for two months, 18/10a, 11/4c. Departures from London as for Southill. Departures for London about 4 times daily. Pop. 423.
Map Square 18.

CARDONALD (Renfrew),
403½ miles. Fares. 82/6a, 49/6c. R. T. for two months, 165/0a, 99/0c. Departures from London as for Glasgow (Central). Departures for London about 4 times daily. Pop. 2,992.

CARDRONA (Peebles), 379
miles. Fares, 77/1a, 46/3c. R. T. for two months, 154/2a, 92/6c. Departures from London as for Galashiels. Departures for London about twice daily.
Map Square 41.

CARDROSS (Dumbarton), 454½ miles. Fares, 84/2*a*, 50/6*c*. R.T. for two months, 168/4*a*, 101/0*c*. Departures *from* London as for Arrochar and Tarbet. Departures *for* London about 3 times daily. Pop. 11,609.
Map Square 40

CARESTON (Forfar), 491¼ miles. Fares, 97/6*a*, 58/6*c*. R.T. for two months, 195/0*a*, 117/0*c*. Departures *from* London as for Brechin. Departures *for* London about 3 times daily. Pop. 197.
Map Square 38.

CARGILL (Perth), 461¼ miles. Fares, 93/4*a*, 56/0*c*. R. T. for two months, 186/8*a*, 112/0*c*. Departures *from* London as for Perth. Departures *for* London about 5 times daily. Pop. 1,385.
Map Square 38.

CARGO FLEET (Yorks), 239½ miles. Fares, 50/0*a*, 30/0*c*. R.T. for two months, 100/0*a*, 60/0*c*. Departures *from* London as for Middlesbrough. Departures *for* London about 5 times daily.
Map Square 8.

CARHAM (Northumberland), 346¼ miles. Fares, 73/1*a*, 43/10*c*. R.T. for two months, 146/2*a*, 87/8*c*. Departures *from* London as for Kelso. Departures *for* London about 4 times daily. Pop. 910.
Map Squares 3 *and* 41.

CARISBROKE (Isle of Wight), from *Victoria*, *London Bridge* or *Waterloo via* Portsmouth and Ryde, 89¼ miles. Fares, 20/0*a*, 12/3*c*. R.T. for two months, 40/0*a*, 24/6*c*. Departures *from* London as for Newport (I. of W.). Departures *for* London about 4 times daily.
Map Square 28.

CARK (Lancs), 249¾ miles. Fares, 51/11*a*, 31/2*c*. R.T. for two months, 103/10*a*, 62/4*c*. Departures *from* London as for Grange-over-Sands. Departures *for* London about 4 times daily.
Map Square 7.

CARLISLE (Cumberland) from *Euston*, 299 miles. Fares, 60/7*a*, 36/4*c*. R.T. for two months, 121/2*a*, 72/8*c*. Pop. 52,600.
Map Square 3.

EUSTON	CARL.	CARL.	EUSTON
AM12.25	10. 0	AM12. 5*d*	6.40
2.35*d*	11.45	12.13*g*	6.55
2.35*e*	12. 5	1.10	7.30
5. 0	1.13	1.20*g*	7.40
6.45*r*	3.24	1.45*g*	8. 0
10. 0*r*	3.50	1.57*y*	7.15
10.40*r*	6. 6	6.25*r*	3.10
11.35*r*	6.30	8.25*hr*	3.45
PM 1.30*r*	7.40	8.25*r*	4.15
7.30*ery*	1.25	9.45*r*	6. 0
7.40*er*	1.35	PM12.20	6.25
7.50*er*	2.14	1. 0*r*	7.30
8. 0*e*	2.29	1.25*er*	9. 5
9.20	4. 0	1.25*dr*	9.15
9.30*e*	4.52	3.51*r*	10. 0
9.30*d*	4.56	4. 8*r*	10.45
11. 0*d*	5.26	8.35	5. 0
11.35*e*	5.26	—	—
11.45*e*	6.40	—	—

Sunday Trains.

AM11.30*r*	6. 0	AM12.57	7.15
11.45*r*	8.56	1.10	7.30
PM 7.50*r*	2.15	1.20	7.40
9.30	4.46	1.45	8. 0
11 35	5.26	2. 5	1.30
11.45	6.40	PM12.45*r*	7.30
—	—	8.30	5. 0

d Saturdays only.
e Saturdays excepted.
g Mondays excepted.
h Mondays and Saturdays only.
r Restaurant Car.
y Commences July 27.

CARLISLE—*continued.*

ANOTHER ROUTE from *St. Pancras*, 308 miles. Fares as above.

ST. PAN.	CARL.	CARL.	ST. PAN.
AM 4.25	12.53	AM12.10	7.25
9. 0*r*	3.48	12.33	8. 3
9.50*r*	4.17	1.22	7.50
11.45*r*	6.22	8. 0*r*	5.30
PM12.15*r*	6.38	PM12.10*r*	6.35
9.15	4.15	12.24*r*	7.15
9.30	4.38	1.13*r*	7.57
11.45	6. 8	2.45*r*	9.15
—	—	4. 0	4.20

Sunday Trains.

PM 9.15	4.21	AM 1.57	8.57
9.30	4.38	—	—
11.45	6. 8	—	—
—	—	—	—

r Restaurant Car.

County and Station Hotel.
Adjoins Railway Station. New Restaurant Tea Room now open. Porter (scarlet coat) meets trains. Lift. Garage. Telephone, 119.
MORTON CHANCE, Manager.

Crown and Mitre Hotel.
First Class Family and Commercial. Moderate Tariff, Garage, 'Bus. Telegraphic Address, "Comfort." Telephone, 128.

CARLTON (Durham), 238¾ miles. No through fares. Departures *from* London as for Stockton-on-Tees. Departures *for* London about 4 times daily. Pop. 251.
Map Square 7.

CARLTON (Yorks), 196¾ miles. Fares, 35/0*a*, 21/0*c*. R. T. for two months, 70/0*a*. Departures *from* London as for Cudworth. Departures *for* London about 3 times daily. Pop. 2,289.
Map Square 13.

CARLTON (Notts), from *St. Pancras*, 126½ miles. Fares, 25/8*a*, 15/5*c*. R. T., double fare. Departures *from* London as for Nottingham. Departures *for* London about 6 times daily Pop. 18,511.

CARLTON COLVILLE (Suffolk), 115½ miles. Fares, 24/4*a*, 14/7*c*. R. T. for two months, 48/8*a*. Departures *from* London as for Lowestoft (*via* Ipswich). Departures *for* London about 5 times daily. Pop. 644.
Map Square 19.

CARLTON-ON-TRENT (Notts), from *King's Cross*, 136½ miles. Fares, 26/3*a*, 15/9*c*. R. T., double fare. Pop. 15,581.
Map Square 13.

KING'S +	CARLTON	CARLTON	KING'S +
AM 5. 5	9.19	AM 8.53*r*	11.30
10.10*r*	1. 0	10. 1	1. 5
PM 1.50*r*	4.50	PM12.22	3.50
4. 0*r*	7. 0	3.24*r*	6.30
5.45*r*	8.30	7.44*r*	10. 0

No Sunday Trains.
r Restaurant Car.

CARLUKE (Lanark), 381 miles. Fares, 77/6*a*, 46/6*c*. R.T. for two months, 155/0*a*, 93/0*c*. Departures *from* London as for Carstairs. Departures *for* London about 3 times daily. Pop. 10,178.

CARMARTHEN from *Paddington*, 228 miles. Fares 46/1*a*, 27/8*c*. R.T. for two months, 92/2*a*, 55/4*c*. Pop. 10,011.
Map Square 21.

PAD.	CARM.	CARM.	PAD.
AM 1. 0*g*	9.12	AM 7.10*r*	1. 0
5.30	1.14	8. 5*r*	2.30
8.45*r*	1.45	10.20*r*	4.20
11.50*r*	5. 6	PM12.42*r*	6.15
PM 1.10*r*	7.15	2.19*r*	8.45
3.35*r*	9.24	4. 6*r*	9.35
5. 0*hr*	10.27	8.10	3.30
9.15	5. 8	—	—
—	—	—	—
—	—	—	—

Sunday Trains.

PM12.30*r*	8.40	AM 7.49*h*	3.35
9.15	5. 8	PM 1.45*r*	8.25
—	—	8.10	3.30
—	—	—	—
—	—	—	—

g Mondays excepted.
h Arrives at and starts from Carmarthen Junction.
r Restaurant Car.

CARMONT (Kincardine), 501½ miles. No through fares. Departures *from* London as for Forfar. Departures *for* London about twice daily.
Map Square 38.

CARMYLE (Lanark), 396¾ miles. No through fares. Departures *from* London as for Motherwell or Hamilton. Departures *for* London about 4 times daily. Pop. 4,319.

CARMYLLIE (Forfar), 472¼ miles. No through fares. Departures *from* London as for Arbroath. Departures *for* London about twice daily. Pop. 805.
Map Square 38

CARNABY (Yorks), 214¾ miles. No through fares. Departures *from* London as for Driffield. Departures *for* London about 5 times daily. Pop. 189.
Map Square 8

CARNARVON from *Euston*, 247½ miles. Fares, 51/6*a*, 30/11*c*. R. T. for two months, 103/0*a*, 61/10*c*. Pop. 8,301.
Map Square 11.

EUSTON	CARN.	CARN.	EUSTON
AM12.25	9.22	AM 6.42*er*	1. 0
2.35	11.37	8. 2*r*	1.45
5. 0	12.36	8.48*e*	4.15
8.30*r*	2.55	11.33*r*	5. 5
11.10*r*	4.31	PM12. 8*dr*	7.30
11.50*r*	7.19	1.25*er*	7.30
PM 2.35*et*	9.20	2.50*r*	9.20
2.35*dt*	9.35	3.22*r*	10.45
4. 5*h*	11. 1	8.12	5. 0
5.20*r*	11.52	—	—
9.30*e*	5. 4	—	—
11.50*d*	7.52	—	—

Sunday Trains.

PM 9.15	5. 4	PM12.30*r*	7.10
—	—	8. 5	5. 0
—	—	—	—
—	—	—	—
—	—	—	—
—	—	—	—

d Saturdays only.
e Saturdays excepted.
h Thursdays and Saturdays only.
r Restaurant Car.
t Tea Car.

CARN BREA (Cornwall),

290½ miles. Fares 60/2*a*, 36/1*c*. R.T. for two months 120/4*a*, 72/2*c*. Departures *from* London as for Redruth. Departures *for* London about 6 times daily.
Map Square 25.

CARNFORTH (Lancs)

from *Euston*, 236¼ miles. Fares, 49/2*a*, 29/6*c*. R. T., double fare. Pop. 3,247.
Map Square 7.

Euston	Carnfth.	Carnfth.	Euston
AM 12.25	8. 2	AM 3.46*gr*	11.10
2.35	9.42	7.52*r*	1.45
5. 0	12. 0	8.41*r*	3.10
6.45	1.18	10. 0*hr*	3.45
10.40*r*	4. 5	10.28*r*	4.15
11.35*r*	4.23	12. 0*t*	6. 0
11.50*r*	6.12	PM 2. 5*r*	7.30
PM 1.30*r*	6.51	3.22*er*	6. 5
2.35*t*	8.23	3.22*dr*	9.15
5.20*r*	10.59	5.27*r*	10.45
9.30	3.20	10. 8	5. 0
11. 0*d*	4.20	—	—

Sunday Trains.

AM 11.45*r*	5.26	AM 4. 0*r*	1.30
PM 9.30	3. 9	PM 1.20*r*	7.30
—	—	10. 0	5. 0
—	—	—	—

d Saturdays only.
e Saturdays excepted.
g Mondays excepted.
h Mondays and Saturdays only.
r Restaurant Car.
t Tea Car.

ANOTHER ROUTE from

St. Pancras, 259 miles. Fares, as above.

St. Pan.	Carnfth.	Carnfth.	St. Pan.
AM 4.25	12.57	AM 8.30*r*	4.10
9.50*r*	4. 7	10.30*r*	5.30
PM 12.15*r*	6. 8	12. 0*hr*	6.35
11.50*e*	9.18	PM 2.30*r*	9.15
11.50*d*	9.42	7.10	4.20
—	—	—	—
—	—	—	—

Sunday Trains.

AM 10.50*r*	8. 0	AM 8.25	5.27
PM 11.45	9.18	PM 6.30	4.55
—	—	—	—

d Saturdays only.
e Saturdays excepted
h Mondays, Tuesdays, Fridays and Saturdays.
r Restaurant Car.

CARNO (Montgomery), 197½

miles. Fares, 41/1*a*, 24/8*c*. R. T. for two months, 82/2*a*. Departures *from* London as for Newtown. Departures *for* London about 4 times daily. Pop. 749.
Map Square 16.

CARNOUSTIE (Forfar),

462½ miles. Fares, 92/4*a*, 55/5*c*. R. T. for two months, 184/8*a*, 110/10*c*. Departures *from* London as for Dundee. Departures *for* London about 3 times daily. Pop. 5,957.
Map Square 38.

CARNTYNE (Lanark), 433½

miles. No through fares. Departures *from* London as for Edinburgh (Waverley). Departures *for* London about 4 times daily.

CARNWATH (Lanark),

374 miles. Fares, 76/1*a*, 45/8*c*. R. T. for two months, 152/2*a*, 91/4*c*. Departures *from* London as for Carstairs. Departures *for* London about 3 times daily. Pop. 6,547.
Map Square 40.

CARPENDERS PARK

(Herts) from *Euston* or *Broad Street*, 14¾ miles. Fares from Euston, 2/9*a*, 1/8*c*. R. T. for two months, 5/5*a*, 3/1*c*. From Broad Street, 3/1*a*, 1/10*c*. R. T. for two months, 5/8½*a*, 3/4½*c*. *See* pp. 496–499.

ANOTHER ROUTE (Bakerloo

Tube). *See* back of Map.

CARR BRIDGE (Inverness)

540 miles. Fares, 106/3*a*, 63/9*c*. R. T. for two months, 212/6*a*, 127/6*c*. Departures *from* London as for Aviemore. Departures *for* London about 3 times daily. Pop. 309.
Map Square 34.

CARRINGTON (Notts),

127½ miles. Fares 25/10*a*, 15/6*c*. R. T., double fare. Departures *from* London as for Nottingham (Victoria). Departures *for* London about 4 times daily. Pop. 11,014.
Map Square 13.

CARROG (Merioneth), 190½

miles. Fares, 40/0*a*, 24/0*c*. R. T. for two months, 80/0*a*, 48/0*c*. Departures *from* London as for Llangollen. Departures *for* London about 5 times daily.
Map Square 11.

CARRON (Elgin), 566½

miles. Fares, 106/3*a*, 63/9*c*. R. T. for two months, 212/6*a*, 127/6*c*. Departures *from* London as for Keith. Departures *for* London about twice daily.
Map Square 35.

CARRONBRIDGE (Dumfries),

349¾ miles. Fares, 71/0*a*, 42/7*c*. R. T. for two months, 142/0*a*, 85/2*c*. Departures *from* London as for Thornhill (Dumfries). Departures *for* London about 4 times daily.
Map Square 43.

CARSHALTON (Surrey)

from *Victoria*, *Clapham Junction*, and *London Bridge*, 10¾ miles. Fares from London Bridge or Victoria, 2/1*a*, 1/3*c*. R. T. for two days, 4/2*a*, 2/6*c*. Pop. 14,021.
See pp. 565, 566, 571–574.

CARSTAIRS (Lanark),

from *Euston*, 372¾ miles. Fares, 75/10*a*, 45/6*c*. R. T. for two months, 151/8*a*, 91/0*c*. Pop. 1,828.
Map Square 40.

Euston	C'stairs	C'stairs	Euston
AM 2.35	2.35	AM 8. 5	6.25
5. 0	3. 7	11.16*r*	7.30
6.45*r*	5.13	PM 2.28*r*	10.45
10. 0*r*	5.50	6.46*r*	5. 0
11.35*r*	8.27	10.20*e*	6.55
PM 1.30*r*	9.18	11.14	7.15
9.20	6. 1	11.24	7.30
11. 0*d*	7.27	11.32	7.40
11.35*e*	7. 6	—	—
11.45*e*	10.51	—	—
—	—	—	—
—	—	—	—

Sunday Trains.

AM 11.30*r*	7.50	AM 11. 0*r*	7.30*l*
PM 9.30	6.30	PM 6.32*r*	5. 0
11.35	7. 6	11.22	7.30
11.45	10.51	—	—
—	—	—	—
—	—	—	—

d Saturdays only.
e Saturdays excepted.
l P.M.
r Restaurant Car.

CARVILLE (Northumberland),

273¾ miles. Fares, 57/4*a*, 34/5*c*. R. T., double fare. Departures *from* London as for Newcastle-on-Tyne. Departures *for* London about 6 times daily.

CASSILLIS (Ayr), 395

miles. Fares, 81/1*a*, 48/8*c*. R. T. for two months, 162/2*a*, 97/4*c*. Departures *from* London as for Girvan or Ayr. Departures *for* London about 4 times daily.
Map Square 43.

CASTLE ASHBY (Northampton)

from *Euston*, 73½ miles. Fares, 13/2*a*, 7/11*c*. R. T., double fare. Departures *from* London as for Billing. Departures *for* London about 4 times daily. Pop. 232.
Map Square 18.

CASTLE BAR PARK

from *Paddington*, 7½ miles. Fares, 0/9*c*. R.T. for two days, 1/3*c*. *See* trains to Ealing West. Pop. 9,516.
Map Square 57.

CASTLE BROMWICH

(Warwick), 126½ miles. Fares, 23/1*a*, 13/10*c*. R.T. for two months, 46/2*a*. Departures *from* London as for Water Orton. Departures *for* London about 4 times daily. Pop. 953.
Map Square 17.

CASTLE BYTHAM

(Lincoln) from *St. Pancras*, 112½ miles. Fares, 21/11*a*, 13/2*c*. R. T., double fare. Departures *from* London as for Bourne. Departures *for* London about 4 times daily. Pop. 553.
Map Square 18.

CASTLE CAEREINION

(Montgomery), 177 miles. No through fares. Departures *from* London as for Welshpool. Departures *for* London about 4 times daily. Pop. 200.
Map Square 16.

CASTLE CARY (Somerset)

from *Paddington*, 115½ miles. Fares, 24/0*a*, 14/5*c*. R. T. for two months, 48/0*a*. Pop. 1,710.
Map Square 22.

Pad.	Castle C.	Castle C.	Pad.
AM 1. 0*g*	8. 9	AM 7.59	10.52
5.30	10.15	10. 5	12.55
10.30	1.36	PM 1.13	3.50
PM 12.30*r*	3.15	2.58*t*	5.30
3.30	6.15	3.20*r*	6.50
5. 5	8. 4	5.15	8.20
—	—	8.48	2.45
—	—	9.46*h*	2.45

Sunday Trains.

AM 9.10	2. 6	AM 11.12	3.35
PM 2.40	5.28	PM 5.11*r*	7.55
10. 0	8. 9	—	—

g Mondays excepted.
h Thursdays and 3rd Class only.
r Restaurant Car.
t Tea Car.

CASTLE DONINGTON

(Leicester), 123½ miles. Fares, 25/2*a*, 15/1*c*. R. T., double fare. Departures *from* London as for Trent. Departures *for* London about 4 times daily. Pop. 2,529.
Map Square 18.

CASTLE DOUGLAS

(Kirkcudbright) from *Euston*, 352 miles. Fares, 68/9*a*, 41/3*c*. R. T. for two months, 137/6*a*, 82/6*c*. Pop. 2,801.
Map Square 43.

EUSTON C.DOUG.		C.DOUG. EUSTON	
AM12.25	12.18	AM 7. 0*r*	6. 0
5. 0	3.28	10. 2*r*	6.25
10. 0*r*	6.24	PM 2. 0*r*	10. 0
11.35*r*	8.12	6. 0	5. 0
PM 8. 0*e*	4. 3	7.41*e*	6.55
9.20*e*	7.23	11.25	7.15
11. 0*d*	8. 0	—	—
11.45*e*	9.13	—	—
—	—	—	—

Sunday Trains.

PM 7.50*r*	4. 3	PM 9. 0	7.30
8.30	4.40	—	—
11.45	9.13	—	—
—	—	—	—

d Saturdays only.
e Saturdays excepted.
r Restaurant Car.

ANOTHER ROUTE from *St. Pancras*, 361 miles. Fares as above.

ST. PAN. C.DOUG.		C.DOUG. ST.PAN.	
AM 4.25	3.28	AM10. 2*r*	6.35
9.50*r*	6. 2	11.38*r*	9.15
PM12.15*r*	3.12	PM11.25*e*	7.50
9.30*e*	7.23	11.25*d*	8.57
11.45*d*	8. 0	—	—
11.45*e*	9.15	—	—
—	—	—	—
—	—	—	—

Sunday Trains.

PM 9.30	7.23	PM 9. 0	7.25
11.45	9.15	—	—
—	—	—	—

d Saturdays only.
e Saturdays excepted.
r Restaurant Car.

CASTLE EDEN (Durham), 248¾ miles. Fares, 52/3*a*, 31/4*c*. R. T. for two months,104/6*a*, 62/8*c*. Departures *from* London as for West Hartlepool. Departures *for* London about 4 times daily. Pop. 1,829.
Map Square 8.

CASTLEFORD (Yorks)

from *King's Cross*, 185 miles. Fares, 36/6*a*, 21/11*c*. R. T., double fare. Pop. 24,183.
Map Square 8.

KING'S+CAST'FD.		CAST'FD. KING'S+	
AM 7.15*r*	12.41	AM 6.50*r*	11.30
10.10*r*	2.48	8.27	1. 5
11.15	4.55	9.38*r*	1.55
PM 1.30*r*	5.41	PM 1. 3	6.25
1.50*r*	6.51	2.58*r*	7.10
4. 0	8.25	5. 7*r*	9.25
5.45*er*	9.55	8.38	3.25
5.45*dr*	10.36	—	—
10.45*e*	5.53	—	—

Sunday Trains.

12. 0*nr*	8.51	PM12. 5	5.55
—	—	3.38*r*	10.20
—	—	—	—

d Saturdays only.
e Saturdays excepted.
n Noon.
r Restaurant Car.

CASTLE HOWARD

(Yorks), 204 miles. Fares, 42/4*a*, 25/5*c*. R. T., double fare. Departures *from* London as for York. Departures *for* London about 4 times daily. Pop. 701.
Map Square 8.

CASTLE KENNEDY

(Wigtown), 402¾ miles. Fares, 68/9*a*, 41/3*c*. R. T. for two months, 137/6*a*. Departures *from* London as for Newton Stewart. Departures *for* London about 4 times daily.
Map Square 43.

CASTLETHORPE

(Bucks) from *Euston*, 54¾ miles. Fares, 11/6*a*, 6/11*c*. R. T. for two months, 23/0*a*. Pop. 514.
Map Square 18.

EUSTON C'THORPE		C'THORPE EUSTON	
AM 6.45	8.17	AM 7.36	9.40
7.35	10.25	9.34	11.40
9.30	11.18	PM 2.44	4.15
12. 0*nr*	1.32	6.12	7.55
PM12.15*d*	2.19	6.34	8.35
2. 0	4.16	8.38	10.50
4.15	5.43	9.52*d*	.5. 0
5.32	7. 8	—	—
6.10*e*	7.46	—	—
7.15*d*	9.34	—	—
7.50*e*	9.34	—	—

Sunday Trains.

AM 8.15	10.33	AM11.12	1.20
PM 6.45	8.27	PM 8.28	10.10

d Saturdays only.
e Saturdays excepted.
n Noon.
r Restaurant Car.

CASTLETON (Lancs), 195¾ miles. Fares, 40/2*a*, 24/1*c*. R. T. for two months, 80/4*a*. Departures *from* London as for Manchester. Departures *for* London about 8 times daily. Pop. 3,918.
Map Square 12.

CASTLETON (Yorks), 247 miles. Fares, 51/6*a*, 30/11*c*. R. T. for two months, 103/0*a*, 61/10*c*. Departures *from* London as for Whitby or Stockton-on-Tees. Departures *for* London about 4 times daily.
Map Square 8.

CASTOR (Northampton) from *King's Cross*, 80¾ miles. Fares, 15/10*a*, 9/6*c*. R. T., double fare. Departures *from* London as for Peterboro. Departures *for* London about 4 times daily. Pop. 586.
Map Square 18.

CATCLIFFE (Yorks) from *St. Pancras*, 159½ miles. Fares, 32/9*a*, 19/8*c*. R. T., double fare. Departures *from* London as for Sheffield. Departures *for* London about 4 times daily. Pop. 1,555.
Map Square 13.

CATERHAM (Surrey) from *Charing Cross, Cannon Street* and *London Bridge*, 20½ miles. Fares, 3/2*a*, 2/7*b*, 1/11*c*. R. T. for 8 days, 6/4*a*, 5/2*b*, 3/10*c*. Pop. 11,782.
Map Square 23.

	Leave		Arr. at
CHAR.+	CAN. ST.	LON. B.	CATER.
AM —	4.44	5. 0	6. 1
—	—	7.50*l*	9. 1
—	—	9.13*l*	9.58
—	10.12	10.15	11. 2
10.55	—	11. 3	11.57
—	11.40*d*	11.43*d*	12.32
11.48*e*	—	11.54*e*	12.41
PM —	12.40*d*	12.43*d*	1.27
—	—	12.45*el*	1.27
12.55*d*	—	1. 4*d*	1.54
—	1.20	1.23	2. 8
—	—	1.50*dl*	2.36
2. 3*e*	2. 8*d*	2.10	3. 2
—	—	2.22*dl*	3.13
2.46*d*	—	2.52*d*	3.40
3.15	—	3.21	4.13
—	—	4.20*dl*	5. 4
—	4.24*e*	4.28*e*	5.17
—	4.44*e*	4.48*e*	5.34
—	—	4.50*dl*	5.34
5. 6*e*	—	5.14*e*	6. 0
5.30*d*	—	5.36*d*	6.19
5.30*e*	—	5.37*e*	6.20
—	—	5.48*el*	6.36
—	6.20*e*	6.23*e*	7. 7
6.17*d*	—	6.23*d*	7. 8
6.46*e*	—	6.53*e*	7.40
7.24*d*	7.28*e*	7.30	8.21
8.28	—	8.36	9.27
9.25	—	9.31	10.19
10.17	—	10.23	11.14
11.42	—	—	12.29

Sunday Trains.

AM 6.25	—	6.32	7.27
9. 8	—	9.14	9.58
10.20	—	10.28	11.25
PM 1.30	—	1.37	2.27
5.25	—	5.32	6.22
6.50	—	6.56	7.42
7.45	—	7.52	8.37
8.38	—	8.45	9.35
9.40	—	9.47	10.37

Trains from Caterham.

	Leave		Arrive at
CATER.	LON. B.	CAN. ST.	CHAR.+
AM 7.19	7.58	—	8. 7
7.43	8.24	8.28	—
8. 1	8.40	8.44	—
8.24	9. 5	9. 9	—
8.35	9.22	—	9.30
8.57	9.39	9.43	—
9.11*h*	9.45	—	—
9.39	10.19	10.22	—
10.18	11. 0	—	—
10.40	11.24	—	11.33
11.46	12.26	—	—
PM 1.16	1.58	—	2. 5
1.54*e*	2.37	—	2.45
2.23	3. 4	3. 8*e*	—
3.13	3.52	—	—
4.12	5. 2	—	5.14
5.27	6.10	—	6.18
6.12	6.58	—	7. 5
7.36	8.23	—	8.31
8.20	9. 2	—	9.15
9.16	10. 3	—	10.13
11. 8	11.57	—	12.10
—	—	—	—

CATERHAM—*continued.*

Sunday Trains.

Leave Cater.	Lon. B.	Arrive at Can. St.	Char. +
AM 7.32	8.16	—	8.27
10.30	11.15	—	11.25
PM 3.45	4.33	—	4.42
5.40	6.25	—	6.34
6.29	7.13	—	7.25
8.15	9. 1	—	9. 9
9.46	10.25	—	10.32
—	—	—	—
—	—	—	—
—	—	—	—
—	—	—	—
—	—	—	—
—	—	—	—

d Saturdays only.
e Saturdays excepted.
h Does not stop at Warlingham.
l Low Level platform.

CATFIELD (Norfolk), from *King's Cross*, 170½ miles. Fares, 25/3*a*, 15/2*c*. R. T. for two months, 50/6*a*, 30/4*c*. Departures *from* London as for North Walsham. Departures *for* London about 3 times daily. Pop. 525.
Map Square 19.

CATFORD (Kent), from *Victoria, Holborn Viaduct, Ludgate Hill*, and *St. Paul's*, 8 miles. Fares, 1/6*a*, 1/2*b*, 0/10½*c*. R. T. for two days, 2/7*a*, 1/9*b*, 1/5*c*. Pop. 40,666. *See* pp. 562-563.
Map Square 80.

CATFORD BRIDGE (Kent), from *Charing Cross, Cannon Street*, and *London Bridge*, 8 miles. Fares, 1/6*a*, 1/2*b*, 0/10½*c*. R. T. for two days, 2/7*a*, 1/9*b*, 1/5*c*. *See* pp. 544-547.
Map Square 80.

CATON (Lancs), from *St. Pancras*, 256 miles. Fares, 47/11*a*, 28/9*c*. R. T. for two months, 95/10*a*, 57/6*c*. Departures *from* London as for Hornby. Departures *for* London about 4 times daily. Pop. 1,219.
Map Square 7.

CATRINE (Ayr), 380¼ miles. Fares, 77/6*a*, 46/6*c*. R. T. for two months, 155/0*a*, 93/0*c*. Departures *from* London as for Old Cumnock. Departures *for* London about 4 times daily. Pop. 2,274.

CATTAL (Yorks), 198 miles. Fares, 41/3*a*, 24/9*c*. R. T., double fare. Departures *from* London as for York. Departures *for* London about 5 times daily. Pop. 153.
Map Square 8.

CATTERICK BRIDGE (Yorks), 233 miles. Fares, 48/7*a*, 29/2*c*. R. T., double fare. Departures *from* London as for Richmond (Yorks). Departures *for* London about 4 times daily. Pop. (Catterick) 534.
Map Square 7.

CAULDCOTS (Forfar), 473¼ miles. Fares 94/9*a*, 56/10*c*. R. T. for two months, 189/6*a*, 113/8*c*. Departures *from* London as for Arbroath. Departures *for* London about 3 times daily.
Map Square 38.

CAUSELAND (Cornwall), 248¼ miles. No through fares. Departures *from* London as for Looe. Departures *for* London about 4 times daily.
Map Square 26.

CAUSEWAYEND (Stirling), 413¾ miles. No through fares. Departures *from* London as for Edinburgh (Waverley). Departures *for* London about 4 times daily.

CAUSEWAYHEAD (Stirling), 418 miles. Fares, 85/0*a*, 51/0*c*. R. T. for two months, 170/0*a*, 102/0*c*. Departures *from* London as for Stirling. Departures *for* London about 4 times daily. Pop. 690.
Map Square 40.

CAVENDISH (Suffolk) from *Liverpool Street*, 65 miles. Fares, 13/7*a*, 8/2*c*. R. T. for two months, 27/2*a*. Departures *from* London as for Long Melford or Clare (*via* Bishop's Stortford). Departures *for* London about 4 times daily. Pop. 873.
Map Square 19.

CAWOOD (Yorks), 179¼ miles. Fares, 36/1*a*, 21/8*c*. R. T., double fare. Departures *from* London as for Selby. Departures *for* London about 3 times daily. Pop. 955.
Map Square 13.

CAWSTON (Norfolk) from *Liverpool Street*, 136 miles. Fares, 24/0*a*, 14/5*c*. R. T. for two months, 48/0*a*. Departures *from* London as for Aylsham. Departures *for* London about 6 times daily. Pop. 1,023.
Map Square 19.

CAYTHORPE (Lincoln) from *King's Cross*, 115¼ miles. Fares, 23/9*a*, 14/3*c*. R. T., double fare. Departures *from* London as for Lincoln. Departures *for* London about 5 times daily. Pop. 867.
Map Square 13.

CAYTON (Yorks), 229¼ miles. No through fares. Departures *from* London as for Scarborough or Filey. Departures *for* London about 5 times daily. Pop. 601.
Map Square 8.

CEFN (Denbigh), 176¼ miles. Fares, 36/10*a*, 22/1*c*. R. T. for two months, 73/8*a*. Departures *from* London as for Chirk. Departures *for* London about 3 times daily. Pop. 7,150.
Map Square 12.

CEFN COED (Brecon) 178¼ miles. Fares, 35/2*a*, 21/1*c*. R. T. for two months, 70/4*a*, 42/2*c*. Departures *from* London as for Merthyr (*via* Newport). Departures *for* London about 5 times daily.

CEFN-Y-BEDD (Denbigh) 187 miles. No through fares. Departures *from* London as for Wrexham. Departures *for* London about 4 times daily.
Map Square 12.

CEMMAES (Montgomery), 215¼ miles. No through fares. Departures *from* London as for Dinas Mawddy. Departures *for* London about 3 times daily. Pop. 730.

CEMMES ROAD (Montgomery), 213¼ miles. Fares, 43/6*a*, 26/1*c*. R. T. for two months, 87/0*a*. Departures *from* London as for Newtown. Departures *for* London about 4 times daily.
Map Square 16.

CENTRAL STATION (ROYAL ALBERT DOCKS) (Essex) from *Liverpool Street* or *Fenchurch Street* 8 miles. Fares from *Liverpool Street*, 1/3*a*, 1/0*b*, 0/9*c*. R. T. for two days, 2/6*a*, 1/11*b*, 1/4*c*. From *Fenchurch Street*, 1/3½*a*, 0/10*b*, 0/7½*c*. R. T. for two days, 2/1*a*, 1/7½*b*, 1/2*c*. *See* pp. 537-540.

CERNEY (Gloucester), 111 miles. Fares, 19/0*a*, 11/5*c*. R.T. for two months, 38/0*a*. Departures *from* London as for Cricklade. Departures *for* London about 4 times daily. Pop. 1,469.
Map Square 22.

CHACEWATER (Cornwall) from *Paddington*, 284¼ miles. Fares, 58/2*a*, 34/11*c*. R. T. for two months, 116/4*a*, 69/10*c*. Pop. 1,410.
Map Square 25.

Pad.	C'water.	C'water.	Pad.
AM 5.30	2.35	AM 8.43*r*	4.35
10.30*r*	4.38	10. 9*r*	4.45
11.10*r*	5.48	11.28*r*	6.50
12. 5*r*	8.30	PM 1. 9*r*	9. 0
PM10. 0*e*	7.53	9.40	7.10
10. 0*d*	8.32	—	—
12. 0*l*	10.23	—	—
12.30*k*	10.48	—	—
—	—	—	—
—	—	—	—
—	—	—	—
—	—	—	—

Sunday Trains.

AM10.30*r*	5.52	AM11.30	7. 5
PM10. 0	7.53	PM 5.29	3.15
—	—	—	—
—	—	—	—
—	—	—	—
—	—	—	—
—	—	—	—

d Saturdays only.
e Saturdays excepted.
k Saturdays midnight only.
l Saturdays midnight excepted.
r Restaurant Car.

CHADWELL HEATH

(**Essex**) from *Liverpool Street* and *Fenchurch Street*, 10 miles. Fares, 1/8*a*, 1/4*b*, 1/0*c*. R. T. for two days; 3/4*a*, 2/7½*b*, 1/9*c*. From Fenchurch Street, 1/8*a*, 1/4*b*, 1/0*c*. R. T. for two days, 3/4*a*, 2/7½*b*, 1/9*c*. Pop. 6,429. *See* pp. 528–534. *Map Square* 24.

CHAILEY.   *See* NEWICK AND CHAILEY.

CHALDER (Sussex), 73

miles. No through fares. Departures *from* London as for Selsey. Departures *for* London about 5 times daily. *Map Square* 28.

CHALFONT & LATI-

MER (**Bucks**) from *Marylebone* or *Baker Street*, 21½ miles. Fares, 4/6*a*, 2/8*c*. R. T for two months, 9/0*a*, 5/3*c*. Pop. (Chalfont) 4,564. *See* pp. 494, 495. *Map Square* 29.

CHALFORD (Gloucester)

from *Paddington*, 98 miles. Fares, 20/3*a*, 12/2*c*. R T. for two months, 40/6*a*. Pop. 2,913. *Map Square* 22.

PAD.	CHAL.	CHAL.	PAD.
AM 5.30	8.29	AM 9.31	12.20
7.30	10. 0	PM12.47	3.20
9. 0	11.34	2.40	5. 0
PM 1.10*r*	3.55	5.12*hr*	8.45
3.15*t*	5.50	7.45	10.25
6. 0*r*	8.33	––	—
—	––	––	—
—	▼	—	—
—	—	—	—

Sunday Trains.

PM12.30*r*	3.24	PM 7.23	10. 0
2. 0	7.18	—	—
—	—	—	—
—	—	—	—
—	—	—	—

h Fridays and Third Class only.   *r* Restaurant Car.   *t* Tea Car.

CHALK FARM, from

Broad Street 5½ miles. Fares, 0/7½*a*, 0/4½*c*. R. T. for two days, 1/3*a*, 0/9*c*. *See* p. 496–499.

ANOTHER ROUTE (Hampstead Tube). *See* back of Map.

CHALLOW (Berks) from

Paddington, 64 miles. Fares, 13/4*a*, 8/0*c*. R. T. for two months, 26/8*a*. Pop. 699. *Map Square* 22.

PAD.	CHALLOW	CHALLOW	PAD.
AM 5.30	8.10	AM 7.17	9.30
7.30	10. 5	8.22*r*	10.15
9. 0	10.51	10. 1	12. 0
10.45	12.50	PM12.18	2.35
PM 1.35*r*	3.45	2.35	5. 6
3.38	6. 8	6.48	9.15
5.15	6.52	7.51	10.45
6.55	8.45	—	—
—	—	—	—
—	—	—	—

Sunday Trains.

AM10.35	12.33	PM 3.34	6. 0
PM 2. 0	6. 2	—	—
—	—	—	—
—	—	—	—

r Restaurant Car.

CHANCERY LANE

(Central London Tube). *See* back of Map.

CHANDLER'S FORD

(**Hants**) from *Waterloo*, 74½ miles. Fares, 15/10*a*, 9/6*c*. R. T. for two months, 31/8*a*, 19/0*c*. Pop. 1,641. *Map Square* 23.

W'LOO	CHAND.F.	CHAND.F.	W'LOO
AM 5.40	7.51	AM 7. 5*r*	10. 6
5.53	8.42	9.45	12. 0
8.30*s*	10.36	PM12.13*r*	2.20
9.30	12.21	1.25	4. 6
11.30*r*	1.26	2.10	4.20
PM 1.30*s*	3.44	3.15	6.16
3.30*s*	5.28	4.10*s*	6.26
3.40	6.33	5.24*r*	8.20
5.30*r*	7.28	6.45	9.52
6. 0	8.44	8. 5	10.50
7.30	9.36	8.59	11.28
8. 0*k*	11.27	10. 0	3.58
—	—	—	—
—	—	—	—

Sunday Trains.

AM11. 0*r*	12.53	AM 9.56	22.11
PM 2. 0	6.14	5.33	8. 3
6. 0	8.32	7.44	10.53
7. 0*r*	9.11	—	—
—	—	—	—
—	—	—	—

k Wednesdays and Saturdays only.   *r* Restaurant Car.   *s* Refreshments served.

CHANNEL ISLANDS.

See JERSEY and GUERNSEY.

CHAPEL-EN-LE-

FRITH (**Derby**), from *St. Pancras*, 167½ miles. Fares, 34/9*a*, 20/10*c*. R. T. for two months, 69/6*a*, 41/8*c*. Pop. 5,140. *Map Square* 12.

St. PAN.	C'FRITH.	C'FRITH.	St. PAN.
AM 4.25	9.50	AM 7.29*r*	11.35
10.25*r*	3. 7	8.25*r*	1.30
PM 1.25*r*	6. 7	9.56	3.25
4.25*r*	9. 9	PM12.28*r*	5.45
12. 0*h*	9.15	2.40*r*	8.35
—	—	5.23*r*	10. 5
—	—	8.12	4.20
—	—	—	—

Sunday Trains.

PM 3.15	9. 4	AM10.33*r*	5. 2
—	—	PM 7.38	4.55
—	—	—	—
—	—	—	—
—	—	—	—
—	—	—	—

h Saturdays midnight only.   *r* Restaurant Car.

CHAPEL LANE (Salop),

168 miles. No through fares. Departures *from* London as for Shrewsbury or Oswestry. Departures *for* London about 3 times daily.

CHAPELTON (Devon),

207½ miles. Fares, 38/9*a*, 23/3*c*. R. T. for two months, 77/6*a*, 46/6*c*. Departures *from* London as for Eggesford. Departures *for* London about 5 times daily.

CHAPELTOWN (Yorks)

from *St. Pancras*, 166 miles. Fares, 33/1*a*, 19/10*c*. R. T., double fare. Pop. 8,701. *Map Square* 12.

St.PAN.CHAPELTN.		CHAPELTN.St.PAN.	
AM 2.25*g*	8.27	AM 6.35*r*	10.45
4.25	10.14	8. 0*r*	12.10
8.25*r*	12.49	10.27*r*	2.10
9. 0*r*	1.43	PM12.15*r*	5.30
11.45*r*	3.44	3.11*r*	7.15
PM12.25*r*	5.34	4.50*r*	9. 5
1.50*r*	6.40	10.51	4.20
3.30*r*	7.39	··	··
5. 0*r*	8.58	—	—
6.15*r*	10.14	—	—
11.50*e*	6.58	—	—
12. 0*h*	9.28	—	—

Sunday Trains.

PM 3.15	9.13	AM10.36	5.27
—	—	PM10.19	4.55

e Saturdays excepted.   *g* Mondays excepted.   *h* Saturdays midnight only.   *r* Restaurant Car.

CHAPPEL (Essex) from

Liverpool St., 50½ miles. Fares, 10/7*a*, 6/4*c*. R. T. for two months, 21/2*a*. Pop. 357. *Map Square* 19.

L'PL.St.	CHAPPL.	CHAPPL.	L'PL.St.
AM 6.50	9.22	AM 8.35	9.53
10. 0	11.30	10.26	11.42
PM12.36	2. 4	PM12.23*h*	2. 3
2.15	4. 3	2.57*h*	5. 5
4.58	6.24	4.45*h*	6.52
5.42	7.12	7.12	9.17

Sunday Trains.

AM 9.20	10.55	AM 9.42	12.40
PM 3.40	5.29	PM 4.58*h*	7.10
4.40*h*	8.16	7. 0	8.58

h Via Colchester.

CHARD (JOINT) (Somerset)

from *Waterloo*, 142½ miles. Fares, 29/10*a*, 17/11*c*. R.T.for two months, 59/8*a*, 35/10*c*. Pop. 4,322. *Map Square* 27.

W'LOO	CHARD	CHARD	W'LOO
AM 7.30	11.59	AM 9.45*r*	1.56
12. 0*nr*	3.42	11.18*r*	3. 8
PM 1. 0*r*	5.26	PM 1.55*r*	6. 0
3. 0*r*	7. 9	3.15*r*	8.30
—	—	6.35	10.50
—	—	8.40*h*	3.58

No Sunday Trains.

h Via Eastleigh.   *n* Noon.   *r* Restaurant Car.

ANOTHER ROUTE from

Paddington 153½ miles. Fares, 29/10*a*, 17/11*c*. R.T. for two months, 59/8*a*, 35/10*c*.

PAD.	CHARD	CHARD	PAD.
AM 5.30	11.44	AM 6.35*f*	11.30
9.15*r*	2.30	9. 0*r*	1.30
PM12. 5*r*	4.56	PM12.10*r*	5.30
2. 0*r*	7.24	2.45*r*	6.50
6.30*dr*	11.26	5.15*r*	9. 0
10. 0*e*	3.50	7.50	2.45
12. 0*h*	8.37	9.40	7.10

Sunday Trains.

PM10. 0	3.50	—	—
—	—	—	—
—	—	—	—

d Saturdays only.   *e* Saturdays excepted.   *f* Mondays only.   *h* Saturdays midnight excepted.   *r* Restaurant Car.

CHARD JUNC. (Somerset)

from *Waterloo*, 139¾ miles. Fares, 29/2*a*, 17/6*c*. R. T. for two months, 58/4*a*, 35/0*c*.
Map Square 27.

	W'LOO	CHARD J.	CHARD J.	W'LOO
AM	7.30	11.32	AM 7.36*r*	11.10
	12. 0*n*r	3.30	10.12*r*	1.56
PM	1. 0*r*	5. 3	11.39*r*	3. 8
	3. 0*r*	6.51	PM 2.10*r*	6. 0
	6. 0*r*	9.53	4.39*r*	8.30
	—	—	6.51	10.50
	—	—	8.58*h*	3.58½
	—	—	—	—
	—	—	—	—

Sunday Trains.

AM	9. 0	2.30	PM 4.46*r*	8.57
	12. 0*n*r	4.21	—	—
	—	—	—	—

h Via Eastleigh.
n Noon.
r Restaurant Car.

CHARFIELD (Gloucester),

134 miles. No through fares. Departures *from* London as for Bristol or Gloucester. Departures *for* London about 4 times daily.
Pop. 607.
Map Square 22.

CHARING (Kent) from

Victoria, Holborn Viaduct, and *St. Paul's,* 53 miles. Fares, 11/3*a*, 9/0*b*, 6/9*c*. R. T. for two months, 22/6*a*, 18/0*b*, 13/6*c*. Pop. 1,297.
Map Square 24.

		Leave		Arr. at
VICT. S.E. & C.	HOL. V.	ST. PL.'s	CHAR'G
AM —	6.40	6.42	9. 4
9.45	—	—	11.39
11. 4	10.58	11. 0	1.26
PM —	1.24*d*	1.30*d*	3.12
2.12*e*	—	—	3.47
2.40*d*	—	—	4.58
2.50*e*	—	—	5.17
4.25*e*	—	—	6. 2
*e*5.15*h*	—	*e*5.21*k*	7. 4
*d*5.20*h*	—	*d*5.26*k*	7. 9
7.22	—	—	8.53
—	7.22*d*	7.24*d*	9.37

Sunday Trains.

AM —	8. 0	—	10.29
9.35	—	—	11.10
PM 5.15	—	—	6.56
6.35	6.40	—	8.52

Trains from Charing.

Leave		Arr. at	
CHARING	ST. PL.'s	HOL. V.	VICT.
AM 7.14	—	—	8.50
8. 4	9.52	9.55	—
8.38*e*	10.21	10.23	10.16
8.45*d*	10.41	10.43	—
10.51	12.59	1. 2	12.49
PM 12.22	—	—	2.40
2. 2	—	—	3.37
4.44	6.58	7. 0	—
6.25	—	—	8.51
9.25	11.42	11.44	—
—	—	—	—
—	—	—	—

Sunday Trains.

AM 8.39	—	—	10.48
PM 1.44	—	—	3.50
7.17	—	9. 9	—

d Saturdays only.
e Saturdays excepted.
h Departs from or arrives at Charing Cross (S.E. & C.R.).
k Departs from or arrives at London Bridge (S.E. & C.R.).

CHARING CROSS

from *Cannon Street* (S.E. & C.R.), 2 miles. Fares, 0/4½*a*, 0/3½*b*, 0/2½*c*. R. T. for two days, 0/9*a*, 0/6*b*, 0/4*c*.
See pp. 544-557.
Map Square 60.

ANOTHER ROUTE to and

from *Mansion House, Victoria, South Kensington, High Street, Praed Street, Baker Street, King's Cross, Moorgate Street,* and all intermediate Stations. Also to and from *Ealing, Hounslow, Richmond* and *Wimbledon See* p. 489.

ANOTHER ROUTE (Hampstead and Bakerloo Tube). *See* back of Map.

Hotel Cecil. Rehabilitated throughout. Few minutes Charing Cross.
See advt. under London Hotels.

Charing Cross Hotel, Strand.
Central. Most convenient for Families and Gentlemen for short periods.
See advt. amongst London Hotels.

For Messengers & Theatre
Tickets, apply, 4, Charing Cross, S.W. 1. Telephone No., Gerrard 3794.

CHARLBURY (Oxford)

from *Paddington*, 76¼ miles. Fares, 16/0*a*, 9/7*c*. R. T. for two months, 32/0*a*. Pop. 1,307.
Map Square 22.

	PAD.	CHARL.	CHARL.	PAD.
AM	5.30	8. 9	AM 8. 5	9.50
	9.45	12. 7	10.19	12. 5
	11.20*h*	2.16	PM 12.15	2.12
PM	1.35*r*	4.13	12.44*hr*	2.55
	4.45*t*	6.3½	5. 0	7.20
	6.55	9. 1	8.40	10.45
	—	—	—	—
	—	—	—	—
	—	—	—	—

Sunday Trains.

AM 10.35	12.32	PM 12.17	2 40
PM 4.10	6.20	7.43*r*	9.48
—	—	—	—
—	—	—	—
—	—	—	—

h Thursdays and Saturdays only.
r Restaurant Car.
t Tea Car.

CHARLESTOWN (Fife),

412½ miles. Fares, 86/6*a*, 51/11*c*. R. T. for two months, 173/0*a*, 103/10*c*. Departures *from* London as for Dunfermline. Departures *for* London about 3 times daily.

CHARLTON (Kent) from

Charing Cross, Cannon Street, and *London Bridge,* 8¼ miles. Fares, from Charing Cross, 1/8*a*, 1/4*b*, 1/0*c*. R. T. for two days, 3/4*a*, 2/8*b*, 1/11*c*. Fares, 1/5*a*, 1/1*b*, 0/10*c*. R. T. for two days, 2/10*a*, 2/2*b*, 1/8*c*. Pop. 21,978. *See* pp. 547-551.
Map Square 71.

CHARLTON KINGS

(Gloucester) from *Paddington*, 104¾ miles. Fares, 21/10*a*, 13/1*c*. R. T. for two months. 43/8*a*. Pop. 4,361.
Map Square 22.

	PAD.	CHARL. K.	CHARL. K.	PAD.
AM	5.30	9.27	AM 6.43	9.50
	9.45	2. 2	10.48	2.12
PM	1.30*h*	3.59	PM 12.16*kr*	2.55
	1.35*r*	5.52	3.23	7.20
	6. 5*r*	9.37	7. 9	10.45
	—	—	—	—
	—	—	—	—
	—	—	—	—

No Sunday Trains.

h Sets down passengers on notice to guard.
k Picks up passengers on notice at station.
r Restaurant Car.

CHARLTON MACKRELL (Somerset), 122½ miles.

Fares, 24/11*a*, 15/4*c*. R. T. for two months, 49/10*a*, 30/8*c*. Departures *from* London as for Somerton. Departures *for* London about 3 times daily. Pop. 146.
Map Square 22.

Station closed on Sundays.

CHARTHAM (Kent) from

Charing Cross, Cannon Street, and *London Bridge,* 67¼ miles. Fares, 12/11*a*, 10/4*b*, 7/9*c*. R. T. for two months, 25/10*a*, 20/8*b*. Pop. 2,959.
Map Square 24.

		Leave		Arr. at
CHAR. +	CAN. ST.	LON. B.	CHART.
AM —	5.20	5.25	8.44
9.15	—	9.23	11.13
11. 0	—	11. 7	1.17
PM 1. 0	—	—	2.42
3. 0	—	3. 8	4.57
4.30	—	4.37	6.24
5.24*d*	—	5.34*d*	8.11
6. 0*e*	—	6. 5*e*	8.11
7.18	—	7.26	9.46

Sunday Trains.

AM 7.45	—	7.52	10.12
n 9.35*h*	—	—	11.46
PM 5.15*h*	—	—	7.42
7.35	—	7.45	9.42

Trains from Chartham.

Leave		Arr. at	
CHART.	LON. B.	CAN. ST.	CHAR. +
AM 7. 4	9.32	9.36	—
7.51	10. 0	10. 4	—
*e*7.51*h*	—	—	10.16*h*
9.42	11.43	—	11.57
11.14	1.36	—	1.50
PM 12.48	3.26	—	3.40
3.20*h*	—	—	5.42*h*
3.20	5.50	—	6. 3
5.16	7.25	7.30	7.49
8. 4	10.22	—	10.35

Sunday Trains.

AM 7.12	10. 5	—	10.15
PM 5. 5	7. 9	—	7.17
8.20	10.16	—	10.26
9.52*v*	—	1.23*v*	—

d Saturdays only.
e Saturdays excepted.
h Departs from or arrives at Victoria (S.E. & C.R.).
v Third Class only.

CHARTLEY (Stafford)

141½ miles. Fares, 28/2*a*, 16/11*c*. R. T. for two months, 56/4*a*, 33/10*c*. Departures *from* London as for Stafford. Departures *for* London about 4 times daily. Pop. 49.
Map Square 17.

CHARWELTON (North-ampton) from *Marylebone*, 71¼ miles. Fares, 14/10a 8/11c. R. T., double fare. Pop.

Map Square 18.

M'BONE.	C'WELTON	C'WELTON	M'BONE
AM 6.45	9.20	AM 7.10	9.46
PM12.15r	2.18	8.27	10.36
4.30	6.45	9.34	12. 2
6.25e	8.51	PM 2.21	4.56
6.25d	9. 1	6.13r	8.55
—	—	7.54r	9.55

Sunday Trains.

AM 9.30	12. 4	AM 7.18	10.13
PM 6.30	9.26	PM 6. 3	8.58

d Saturdays only.

e Saturdays excepted.

r Restaurant Car.

CHATBURN (Lancs) from *Euston*, 224 miles. Fares (*via* Manchester or Wigan), 43/9a, 26/3c. R. T. for two months, 87/6a, 52/6c. *Via* Preston, 43/9a, 26/3c. R. T. for two months, 87/6a, 52/6c. Departures *from* London as for Clitheroe. Departures *for* London about 7 times daily. Pop. 861.

Map Square 7.

CHATHAM (Kent) from *Victoria, Holborn Viaduct,* and *St. Paul's,* 34¾ miles. Fares, 6/8a, 5/4b, 4/0c. R. T. for two months, 13/4a, 10/8b. Pop. 42,665.

Map Square 24.

VICT.	Leave		Arr. at
S.E. & C.	HOL. V.	S.PAUL'S	CHATM.
AM —	3.50h	—	4.56
5. 5	4.57	5. 0	6.41
5.48f	5.40f	5.42f	6.46
—	7.30	7.33	8.55
7.40f	—	—	8.30
9.20	—	—	10. 9
11.40d	—	—	12.47
11.40e	—	—	1. 8
11.55d	—	—	1.17
PM 1.23d	—	—	2.15
—	1.24d	1.27d	2.35
2. 5d	—	—	2.57
2. 8e	—	—	3. 1
—	3.22	3.25	4.58
3.40d	3.33d	3.36d	5.31
4.15d	—	—	5. 7
4.20	—	—	5.15
4.25e	—	—	5.31
5.30e	—	—	6.28
5.30d	—	—	6.30
—	—	5.33e	6.50
6.16	6.10e	6.13e	7.41
7. 5	7. 0	7. 3	8.15
7.50	—	—	8.44
9. 0e	8.57e	9. 0e	10.27
10.17	10.11	10.13	11.40
12. 0l	—	—	12.58

Sunday Trains.

AM 7.20	—	—	8.40
8.15	8. 0	—	9.16
10.30	10.25	—	12. 4
PM 3.20	—	—	4.13
3.30	—	—	4.57
6.35	—	—	7.57
7.50	—	—	8.46
8.25	—	—	9.16
—	10.12	—	11.48
10.25	—	—	11.26

CHATHAM—*continued.* Trains from Chatham.

CHATHAM	S.PAUL'S	HOL. V.	VICT.
AM 6.38	8. 8	8. 9	8.14
6.56	8.25	8.27	8.29
7.31	9.16	9.18	—
8.16	9.37	9.39	—
9.49	—	—	11. 2
10.35	—	—	11.27
11.32d	1. 0	1. 2	—
11.50e	12.59	1. 2	—
11.55e	—	—	1.33
11.58d	—	—	1.22
PM12.40d	—	—	1.40
1.23d	—	—	2.15
1.44	—	—	2.43
1.57	—	—	3.23
3.32e	—	—	4.39
3.45e	5.32	5.34	5.21
3.50d	—	—	4.55
4.47k	—	—	5.37
5. 3	—	—	5.56
5.16e	6.45	6.47	—
6.30d	8. 0	8. 2	—
7.37	—	—	8.33
8.15	9.50	9.54	9.46
9.27	—	—	10.25
9.58	11.21	11.23	—

Sunday Trains.

AM 7.51	—	9.40	9.31
9.45	—	11.27	11.23
10.50	—	11.58	11.51
11.25	—	1. 2	12.56
PM 3.47	—	—	4.42
4.30	—	—	5.31
4.45	—	—	6. 3
7.47	—	—	8.40
9.32	—	—	10.29
10.18	—	12. 0	11.44

d Saturdays only.

e Saturdays excepted.

f Mondays only.

h Third class only.

k Fridays only.

l Wednesdays only.

ANOTHER ROUTE from *Charing Cross, Cannon Street* and *London Bridge,* 33¼ miles. Fares as above.

	Leave		Arr. at
CHAR.+	CAN. ST.	LON. B	CHATM.
AM —	—	3.57h	4.56
—	6.20	6.23	7.51
—	7.16	7.19	8.43
—	7.44	7.47	9. 3
8.10	—	8.17	9.37
8.51	—	8.57	10.18
9.32	—	9.41	11. 7
—	10.58	11. 1	12.26
—	11. 8d	11.11d	12.58
11.55	—	12. 2	1.20
PM12.30d	—	12.37d	1.41
1.20e	—	1.27e	2.44
1.26d	—	1.34d	2.44
—	2.40e	2.43e	3.56
2.45e	—	2.53e	4.26
3. 5d	—	3.12d	4.28
3.16d	—	3.17d	4.48
—	4.12e	4.15e	5. 8
4.25d	—	4.31d	5.52
—	4.36e	4.39e	5.52
—	5. 8e	5.11e	6.25
5.15d	—	5.22d	6.52
5.17e	—	5.25e	6.40
5.21e	—	5.29e	6.54
5.58d	—	6. 4d	7.16
—	6.12e	—	6.59
6.22e	—	6.29e	7.47
6.55d	—	7. 1d	8.34
—	7. 8e	7.11e	8.34
7.34	—	7.41	9. 9
—	7.44d	7.47d	9.57
—	9.35	9.38	10.59
10.20	—	10.27	11.45
11.24	—	—	12.35

CHATHAM—*continued.* Sunday Trains.

	Leave		Arr. at
CHAR +	CAN. ST.	LON. B.	CHATM.
AM —	—	7.30	8.45
7.30	—	7.37	9. 9
9.46	—	9.52	11.20
10.50	—	10.57	12.31
PM 1.15	—	1.22	2.56
3.15	—	3.22	4.51
4.50	—	4.57	6.24
7. 0	—	7. 7	8.21
8.42	—	8.49	10. 9
10.30	—	10.38	12.23

Trains from Chatham.

Leave		Arrive at	
CHATHAM	LON. B.	CAN. ST.	CHAR. +
AM 4.20	5.47	5.51	—
5.29	7. 0	7. 4	—
6.27	8.13	8.17	—
7. 7	8.31	8.35	—
7.22	8.34	—	8.41
7.35	8.51	8.55	—
8.13	9. 0	9. 4	—
8.30	9.34	—	9.43
8.55	9.54	—	10. 1
9. 0	10.24	10.28	—
9.27	10.33	—	10.45
9.58	11.20	11.24	—
10.45	12. 3	—	12.14
PM12.12d	1.31	1.37	—
12.12e	1.36	—	1.45
12.59d	2. 1	2. 5	—
1.15d	2.44	—	2.54
1.35e	2.53	—	3. 4
2. 6e	3.26	—	3.36
2.24d	3.58	—	4. 8
3.22e	4.48	4.52	—
3.27d	4.57	—	5. 7
4. 6e	5.36	5.40	—
4. 6d	5.36	—	5.45
5. 8e	6.35	6.39	—
5.40	7.10	—	7.19
6.15	7.14	—	7.23
6.56	8.15	8.20	—
7.41	9. 6	9.11	—
8.27	9.36	—	9.46
9.32	10.51	—	10.59
10.50	12.35	—	12.45

Sunday Trains.

AM 7.30	9. 0	—	9. 9
8.52	10.16	—	10.24
11.35	1. 5	—	1.17
PM12.48	2.14	—	2.24
2.37	4. 4	—	4.15
4.39	5.55	—	6. 4
5.32	6.49	—	6.59
6.31	8. 1	—	8.10
8. 7	9.46	—	9.55
9.46	11.15	—	11.23
9.58	11.20	—	—

d Saturdays only.

e Saturdays excepted.

h Third class only.

CHATHAM—continued.

Bull Hotel, Rochester. Ten minutes from Chatham Station. First class. Phone 175. Resident Proprietors— Mr. and Mrs. W. H. OLIVER, formerly Hotel Metropole, Dublin.

CHATHILL (Northumber-

land), 313¾ miles. Fares, 66/1*a*, 39/8*c*. R. T., double fare. Departures *from* London as for Morpeth. Departures *for* London about 3 times daily. Pop. 58. *Map Square 3.*

CHATTERIS (Cambridge)

from *Liverpool Street*, 81¼ miles. Fares, 14/5*a*, 8/8*c*. R. T. for two months, 28/10*a*. Pop. 5,086. *Map Square 18.*

L'POOL ST.	CHAT.	CHAT.	L'POOL ST.
AM 5.50	9.13	AM 7.50*r*	10.23
8.30*r*	11.17	10.44	2. 7
11.50*r*	2.23	PM 1. 9*lr*	4. 2*k*
PM 2.34	5. 4	1. 9	5. 9
5.49*r*	8.16	3.23*r*	6.10
7.10*dr*	9.43	5.51*r*	8.33
—	—	8.31*d*	2.50
—	—	—	—
—	—	—	—

Sunday Trains.

PM 3.25	6. 9	PM 3.53	6.40
—	—	—	—
—	—	—	—

d Saturdays only.
k Arrives at St. Pancras Station.
l Commencing July 23.
r Restaurant Car.

CHATTERLEY (Stafford),

150¾ miles. Fares, 31/3*a*, 18/9*c*. R. T. for two months, 62/6*a*, 37/6*c*. Departures *from* London as for Stoke-on-Trent. Departures *for* London about 5 times daily. *Map Square 12.*

CHEADLE (Cheshire) from

King's Cross, 202¾ miles. Fares, 37/9*a*, 22/8*c*. R. T., double fare. Pop. 9,913. *Map Square 12.*

KING'S + CHEAD.		CHEAD. KING'S +	
AM 8.45	3.31	AM 9. 8	6.25
10.10*r*	6.16	PM 1.20	9. 0
PM 1.50*r*	9. 5	6.18	3.25

No Sunday Trains.
r Restaurant Car.

ANOTHER ROUTE from

St. Pancras, 182½ miles. Fares as above.

ST. PAN. CHEAD.		CHEAD. ST. PAN.	
AM 4.25	11.25	AM 11.14*r*	5.45
10.25*r*	6.16	PM 2.58*r*	8.35
PM 4.25*r*	9. 5	4.25*r*	10. 5
12. 0*h*	6.45	6.18	4.20
—	—	10. 0	6. 0
—	—	—	—

Sunday Trains.

PM 11.55	6.45	—	—
—	—	—	—
—	—	—	—

h Saturdays midnight excepted.
r Restaurant Car.

CHEADLE (Stafford),

156½ miles. Fares, 31/6*a*, 18/11*c*. R. T., 63/0*a*. Departures *from* London as for Longton. Departures *for* London about 5 times daily. Pop. 5,841. *Map Square 12.*

CHEADLE HEATH

(Cheshire) from *St. Pancras*, 181½ miles. Fares, 37/9*a*, 22/8*c*. R. T. double fare.

ST. PAN. CHEAD.		CHEAD. ST. PAN.	
AM 4.25	11.27	AM 9. 2*r*	1.30
10.25*r*	2.37	10.10	3.25
PM 12.25*r*	4.12	PM 12.30*r*	4.20
1.25*r*	6.32	1.45*r*	6.15
4.25*r*	8.30	5.55*r*	10. 5
6.25*r*	10.12	—	—

No Sunday Trains.
r Restaurant Car.

CHEADLE HULME

(Cheshire) from *Euston*, 180½ miles. Fares, 37/8*a*, 22/7*c*. R. T. for two months, 75/4*a*. Pop. 4,212.

EUSTON CHEAD.		CHEAD. EUSTON	
AM 12.25	7.14	AM 7.43*dr*	12.20
2.35	7.41	8.15*er*	12. 5
5. 0	10.48	9.50*r*	1.15
6.45	12.39	11.31*r*	4.15
10.30*r*	2.50	11.52	5.35
11.50*er*	4.44	PM 1.35*er*	6. 0
PM 1.40*r*	5.40	1.50*dr*	6. 0
2.35*t*	6.57	2.35*r*	6.25
4. 5*r*	8.37	3.48*r*	8.10
6. 5*r*	10.25	5. 0*dr*	9.15
11.50*d*	9.23	5. 8*er*	9. 5
—	—	5.48*er*	10. 0
—	—	9.52	5. 0
—	—	11.19*d*	5. 0

Sunday Trains.

PM 12.30*r*	8.56	AM 9.39	4. 0
6. 0*r*	10.12	PM 3. 0	7.30
—	—	7. 1	5. 0
—	—	—	—

d Saturdays only.
e Saturdays excepted.
r Restaurant Car.

CHEAM (Surrey) from

Victoria, Clapham Junction, and *London Bridge*, 13½ miles. Fares from London Bridge or Victoria, 2/4*a*, 1/5*c*. R.T. for two days, 4/8*a*, 2/10*c*. Pop. 7,849. *See* pp. 564-566, 571-574. *Map Square 23.*

CHECKER HOUSE

(Notts), 142¼ miles. Fares, 29/7*a*, 17/9*c*. R. T., double fare. Departures *from* London as for Worksop. Departures *for* London about 4 times daily. *Map Square 13.*

CHEDDAR (Somerset)

from *Paddington, via* Yatton, 139½ miles. Fares, 29/0*a*, 17/5*c*. R. T. for two months, 58/0*a*, 34/10*c*. Pop. 1,974. *Map Square 22.*

PAD. CHEDDAR		CHEDDAR PAD.	
AM 5.30	10.23	AM 7.36	11.30
7.30	11.57	10.11*r*	2. 0
11.15*r*	3.10	PM 12.55	6. 2
PM 1. 0*r*	4. 7	2.23*r*	7. 0
1.10*r*	6.46	5.16	10.25
4.15*r*	8.34	8.33	2.45
12. 0*h*	8.25	—	—
12.30*k*	12.59	—	—

Sunday Trains.

PM 10. 0	8.25	PM 7.15	3.15
—	—	—	—
—	—	—	—

h Saturdays midnight excepted.
k Saturdays midnight only.
r Restaurant Car.

CHEDDAR—continued.

ANOTHER ROUTE from

Paddington, via Witham, 128½ miles. Fares, 26/8*a*, 16/0*c*. R. T. for two months, 53/4*a*, 32/0*c*.

PAD. CHEDDAR		CHEDDAR PAD.	
AM 1. 0*g*	10.11	AM 8.25	12.55
7.30	12.55	10.23	3.50
10.30	2.23	11.57*r*	6.50
PM 12.30*r*	5.16	PM 3.10	8.20
3.30	8.33	6.24	2.40

Sunday Trains.

PM 2.40	7.15	PM 12.59*r*	7.55
—	—	—	—
—	—	—	—
—	—	—	—
—	—	—	—

g Mondays excepted.
r Restaurant Car.

CHEDDINGTON (Bucks)

from *Euston*, 36 miles. Fares, 7/4*a*, 4/5*c*. R. T. for two months, 14/8*a*, 8/10*c*. Pop. 547. *Map Square 23.*

EUSTON CHEDTN.		CHEDTN. EUSTON	
AM 5.25	7. 6	AM 7. 4	8.24
7.35	8.54	7.52	9. 6
8.35	9.59	8.12*e*	9.22
10.50	12. 7	8.31	9.40
PM 12.15	1.31	9. 3*e*	9.52
12.50*d*	2. 0	9.33	10.15
1.35*d*	2.57	10.21	11.40
2. 0	3.25	PM 12.25	1.50
4. 2	4.59	3. 3	4.30
4.10	5.28	4.48	6.15
4.55*d*	6. 4	7.20	8.35
5. 0*e*	6. 4	9.26	10.50
6.10*d*	7.14	—	—
6.10*e*	7. 4	—	—
6.15*e*	7.14	—	—
7.15	8.32	—	—

Sunday Trains.

AM 8.15	9.40	AM 7.54	9.22
PM 2.15	3.28	11.57	1.20
3.50	4.57	PM 4.42	5.50
6.10	7.24	6.59	8.15
—	—	8.29	9.45
—	—	9.24	10.40
—	—	—	—
—	—	—	—

d Saturdays only.
e Saturdays excepted.

CHEDDLETON (Staf-

ford), 152¾ miles. Fares, 31/6*a*, 18/11*c*. R. T. for two months, 63/0*a*. Departures *from* London as for Uttoxeter. Departures *for* London about 6 times daily. Pop. 3,221. *Map Square 12.*

CHEDWORTH (Glo'ster)

from *Waterloo*, 121½ miles. Fares, 20/5*a*, 12/3*c*. R.T. for two months, 40/10*a*. Departures *from* London as for Cirencester. Departures *for* London about 4 times daily. Pop. 710. *Map Square 22.*

CHELFHAM (Devon),

194 miles. Fares, 40/2*a*, 24/1*c*. R. T. for two months, 80/4*a*, 48/2*c*. Departures *from* London as for Lynton. Departures *for* London about twice daily. *Map Square 21.*

CHELFORD (Cheshire)

from *Euston*, 172¼ miles. Fares- 36/0*a*, 21/7*c*. R. T. for two months. 72/0*a*. Departures *from* London as for Sandbach. Departures *for* London about 6 times daily. Pop. 384.
Map Square 12.

CHELLASTON (Derby)

128¾ miles. Fares, 26/1*a*, 15/8*c*. R. T., double fare. Departures *from* London as for Trent or Derby. Departures *for* London about 4 times daily. Pop. 795.
Map Square 17.

CHELMSFORD (Essex)

from *Liverpool Street*, 29¾ miles. Fares, 6/5*a*, 3/10*c*. R. T. for two months, 12/10*a*. Pop. 20,761.
Map Square 24.

L'PL. ST.	CHELMS.	CHELMS.	L'PL. ST.
AM 5. 0	5.45	AM 2.29	3.50
5.10	6.28	6.46	8. 8
6.50	8. 7	8. 5r	8.52
7.28	8.46	8.10	9. 4
8.15r	9. 1	8.30	9.30
8.18	9.10	8.52	9.36
8.46	9.45	8.58	10.12
10.12	11. 0	9.39	10.22
10.20	11. 7	10. 9	10.58
10.23	11.20	10.33	11.16
10.47	11.52	11.57	12.40
11.26d	12.32	PM12.10	1.16
11.30	12.14	1.21lr	2. 3
PM12.36	1.22	1.47d	3. 5
1. 3d	2. 3	2.12	3.13
1.30dr	2.14	2.52	3.36
1.33d	2.30	3.35e	4.51
1.38e	2.52	3.35d	4.56
2. 3d	2.55	5. 4	5.48
2.15	3. 0	5.53	6.32
3.18r	4. 2	6. 5	7.29
3.23	4. 9	6.56	7.40
3.26	4.30	8. 7	9.17
4.18	5.12	8.57	9.36
4.58r	6. 0	9.16r	10. 0
5.18r	6. 0	9.38	10.52
5.42d	6.28	10.17	11.16
5.42e	6.32	—	—
6. 8	7. 8	—	—
6.39	7.24	—	—
7.16	8. 3	—	—
7.45r	8.26	—	—
8.45	9.30	—	—
8.54	10. 0	—	—
11. 0h	12. 0	—	—
12. 0d	12.54	—	—
12. 0k	12.57	—	—

Sunday Trains.

L'PL. ST.	CHELMS.	CHELMS.	L'PL. ST.
AM 7. 4	8.34	AM 2.29	3.50
8.15	9.18	8.50	10.25
9.20r	10.11	10. 3	11.15
10. 5r	10.53	10.40	11.38
10.45	11.55	11.20	12.40
PM 3.40	4.33	PM 2. 4	3.15
3.45	4.54	6.24	7.10
6.15	7.21	7.32	8.45
7.40	8.32	8. 1	8.58
8.46	9.55	9.15	10. 9
—	—	9.40r	10.30

d Saturdays only.
e Saturdays excepted.
h Wednesdays excepted.
k Wednesdays only.
l Fridays and Saturdays only.
r Restaurant Car.

CHELSEA & FULHAM

From *Clapham Junction*, 1¾ miles. Fares, 0/5*a*, 0/3*c*. R. T. for two days, 0/10*a*, 0/5½*c*. Pop. (Chelsea), 63,697. *See* p. 583.
Map Square 69.

From *Kensington* (Addison Road), 1½ miles. Fares, 0/4½*a*, 0/2½*c*. R. T. for two days, 0/7*a*, 0/5*c*. *See* p. 583.

CHELSFIELD (Kent) from

Charing Cross, Cannon Street and *London Bridge*, 16 miles. Fares, 3/4*a*, 2/8*b*, 2/0*c*. R. T. for eight days, 6/8*a*, 5/4*b* Pop. 2,108.
Map Square 24.

Leave			Arr. at
CHAR. +	CAN. ST.	LON. B.	CHEFD.
AM —	6.45	6.50	7.32
—	7.56	8. 0	8.42
9.58	—	9.45	10.23
11.15	—	11.23	12. 4
PM —	1.12d	1.15d	1.45
2.17d	—	2.23d	2.58
3.50	—	3.57	4.35
4.55d	—	5. 1d	5.41
—	5. 4e	5. 7e	5.40
5.35d	—	5.41d	6.17
—	5.44e	5.47e	6. 9
6.10e	—	6.17e	6.52
9. 0	—	9. 6	9.40
10. 0k	—	10. 6k	10.41
10.45k	—	10.51k	11.26

Sunday Trains.

CHAR. +	CAN. ST.	LON. B.	CHEFD.
AM 7. 5	—	7.11	7.57
8. 5	—	8.12	8.50
11.15	—	11.23	12. 6
PM —	1. 7h	—	2. 4
3. 5	—	3.13	3.55
6. 0	—	6. 6	6.49

Trains from Chelsfield.

Leave		Arrive at	
CHEFD.	LON. B.	CAN. ST.	CHAR +
AM 7.58	8.10	—	8.19
8.47	9.18	—	9.27
9. 7	9.40	9.44	—
11. 7	11.32	—	11.45
PM12.49	1.27	—	1.38
2.30	3. 7	—	3.19
5.45d	6.30	—	6.39
5.57e	6.44	—	6.54
9.41	10.15	—	10.23

Sunday Trains.

CHEFD.	LON. B.	CAN. ST.	CHAR +
AM 9.41	10.22	—	10.32
11.18	11.49	—	12. 0
PM 1.11h	—	2.11h	—
2.13	2.50	—	3. 0
5.50	6.27	—	6.41
9. 1	9.38	—	—
9.31h	—	10.28h	—

d Saturdays only.
e Saturdays excepted.
h Departs from or arrives at Victoria (S.E. & C.)
k Stops on notice being given to Guard.

CHELTENHAM (ST. JAMES's) (Gloucester)

from *Paddington*, via Gloucester, 121½ miles. Fares *via* Gloucester, 23/9*a*, 14/3*c*. R. T. for two months, 47/6*a*, 28/6*c*. Pop. 48,444.
Map Square 22.

	CHELT.	CHELT.	
PAD.	(S. JAMES)	(S. JAMES)	PAD.
AM 1. 0g	6.18	AM 7.15r	10.45
5.30	9.36	9.20	12.20
7.30	11. 1	11.40r	2.40
9. 0	12.36	PM 2.50	5. 0
10.45	2.20	5.30r	8.45
PM 1.10r	4.57	6.37	10.25
3.15t	6.17	10.40	3.30
6. 0r	8.55	—	—
9.15	1. 6	—	—

Sunday Trains.

PAD.	(S. JAMES)	(S. JAMES)	PAD.
AM 1. 0	4.38	PM 1. 0	4. 5
PM12.30r	4.29	6.20	10. 0
2. 0	8.33	10. 0	3.30

g Mondays excepted.
r Restaurant Car.
t Tea Car.

ANOTHER ROUTE via Bourton-on-Water,

108¾ miles. Fares, *via* Bourton-on-Water, 22/9*a*, 13/8*c*. R. T. for two months, 45/6*a*, 27/4*c*. *Via* Honeybourne, 24/7*a*, 14/8*c*. R.T. for two months, 49/2*a*, 29/6*c*.

	CHELT.	CHELT.	
PAD.	(S. JAMES)	(S. JAMES)	PAD.
AM 5.30	9.40	AM 6.30	9.50
6.30k	12.19	7.17h	12. 5
9.45	2.16	10.35	2.12
PM 1.30	4.12	12. 0r	2.55
1.35r	6. 5	PM 3.10	7.20
2.10k	6.55	3.40k	8. 5
4.45h	8. 6	5.10hr	9.15
6. 5r	9.50	6.55	10.45

Sunday Trains.

PAD.	(S. JAMES)	(S. JAMES)	PAD.
PM 4.10h	8.36	AM 7.40h	2.40
—	—	PM 4.53hr	9.48

h Via Honeybourne.
k Via Stratford-on-Avon.
r Restaurant Car.

ANOTHER ROUTE (LANSDOWNE) from Waterloo,

135 miles. Fares, 23/9*a*, 14/3*c*. R. T. for two months, 47/6*a*, 28/6*c*.

W'LOO	CHELT.	CHELT.	W'LOO
AM 7.30	1.15	AM10.28	2.36
PM 1. 0r	5.21	PM 1.35	6.26
3.30	8. 2	3. 0r	8.30

No Sunday Trains.
r Restaurant Car.

CHELTENHAM—contd.

Lansdown Hotel. Best first-class Hotel in town. Near Stations and Colleges. Luxurious Lounge. Hot and cold water to all bedrooms. Appointed A.A. & R.A.C. Garage. 'Phone 400. Mr. and Mrs. H. G. SWIFT, Proprietors. *See advt.* p. **121.**

Lilley Brook Hotel. A lovely country house. *See advt.* p. **122.**

Montpellier Spa Hotel. Modern Hotel with comfort of a private House. R.A.C., A.A. & M.U. Appointments. Central heating. Excellent cooking. Personal attention. Telephone 836. Miss BAYLIS, Manageress. *See advt.* p. **120.**

Tate's Private Hotel, 1, 2, & 3, Promenade Terrace. Facing Spa and Winter Gardens. Convenient for Colleges. Ladies' Drawing Room. Lounge. Bath Rooms. Personal Supervision. Tel. 949. Mrs. TATE, Proprietress.

Royal Hotel. Telephone 829. Situated in the busiest part of the town. Close to the famous promenade. Comfortable accommodation for business or holidays. Electric Light. Garage. TRUST HOUSES, Ltd.

Plough Hotel. Old Established First-class Family Hotel. Centrally situated. Large and complete Garage and Posting Yard—R.A.C. Tel. 899. For Tariff apply to— M. HOLMES, Manageress.

"Pyatt's" Hotel. Unique central position in own grounds. Three minutes G.W. Rly. Ladies' College one minute. Best food in West of England. Telephone 1069. Mr. and Mrs. DOUBLEDAY.

CHELTENHAM (South)

(Gloucester) from *Paddington,* 105¾ miles. Fares *via* Bourton-on-Water, 22/1*a,* 13/3*c.* R.T. for two months, 44/2*a,* 26/6*c.* *Via* Gloucester, 23/9*a,* 14/3*c.* R.T. for two months, 47/6*a,* 28/6*c.* Departures *from* London as for Charlton Kings. Departures *for* London about 4 times daily.

CHEPSTOW (Monmouth)

from *Paddington* 139 miles. Fares, *via* Severn Tunnel or Gloucester, 29/5*a,* 17/8*c.* R.T. for two months, 58/10*a,* 35/4*c.* *Via* Newport, 31/11*a,* 19/2*c.* R.T. for two months, 63/10*a,* 38/4*c.* Pop. 5,144. *Map Square* 22.

PAD.	CHEPS.	CHEPS.	PAD.
AM 1. 0g	6.10	AM 8.45	12.20
5.30	10.12	10.12kr	2. 0
8.45kr	1. 7	10.35r	2.40
9. 0	1.45	PM 1. 2	5. 0
10.45	2.59	1.45lr	6.15
11.15kr	2.45	4.56r	8.45
PM 1. 0kr	4.56	5.51	10.25
1.30h	5.52	5.50lr	9.25
3.15t	6.58	11.30	3.30
6. 0r	9.27	—	—
6.30kr	10.56	—	—
8. 0lr	11.30	—	—
9.15	1.33	—	—

CHEPSTOW—continued.

Sunday Trains.

PAD.	CHEPS.	CHEPS.	PAD.
AM 1. 0	5. 5	PM 3.52	10. 0
9.10k	3.52	11.30	3.30
PM 2. 0	9.20	—	—
4.30l	11.30	—	—
9.15	1.33	—	—

g Mondays excepted.
h Via Kingham.
k Via Severn Tunnel Junction.
l Via Newport.
r Restaurant Car.
t Tea Car.

CHEQUERBENT (Lancs),

197¼ miles. Fares, 40/5*a,* 24/3*c.* R.T. for two months, 80/10*a,* 48/6*c.* Departures *from* London as for Kenyon. Departures *for* London about 5 times daily. *Map Square* 12.

CHERRY BURTON

(Yorks), 206¼ miles. Fares, *via* Goole, 37/6*a,* 22/6*c.* R.T. for two months, 75/0*a,* 45/0*c.* Departures *from* London as for Hull (Paragon). Departures for London about 5 times daily. Pop. 366. *Map Square* 8.

CHERRY TREE (Lancs),

210¼ miles. Fares, 43/9*a,* 26/3*c.* R.T. for two months, 87/6*a,* 52/6*c.* Departures *from* London as for Chorley. Departures for London about 5 times daily. *Map Square* 12.

CHERTSEY (Surrey) from

Waterloo, 22½ miles. Fares, *via* Weybridge, 4/9*a,* 2/10*c.* R.T. for two months, 9/6*a,* 5/8*c.* Pop. 15,123. *Map Square* 23.

W'LOO	CHERTS.	CHERTS.	W'LOO
AM 4.50	5.59	AM 5.10	6.13
6.10	7.12	6.42	7.41
7. 0	7.55	7.22	8.21
8.15	9.15	7.40	8.56
9.15	10.19	8.10	9. 5
10.20	11.19	8.59	9.31
11.20	12.19	8.47	9.36
PM12.15	1.19	9.46	10.45
12.54d	1.47	10.47	11.46
1.20	2.19	11.47	12.46
2.20	3.19	PM12.45	1.46
3.15	4.19	1.47	2.46
4.20	5.19	2.47	3.46
4.54e	5.45	3.45	4.46
5.20	6.19	4.47e	5.46
5.54e	6.47	4.49d	5.46
6.20	7.19	5.47e	6.46
7. 0e	7.52	5.50d	6.46
7.20	8.19	6.47	7.46
8.20	9.19	7.47	8.46
9.20	10.15	8.47	9.46
10.20	11.14	9.50	10.46
11.40	12.34	10.47	12.16

CHERTSEY—continued.

Sunday Trains.

W'LOO.	CHERTS.	CHERTS.	W'LOO.
AM 8.20	9.14	AM 8.26	9.45
9.45	10.49	10.23	11.16
10.20	11.21	11.40	12.41
11.20	12.24	PM 2.10	3.44
PM 1.50	2.44	3.29	5.41
3.20	4.24	5.32	6.46
5.20	6.14	6.39	7.41
6.30	7.21	7.39	8.41
7.20	8.21	8.38	9.44
8.20	9.19	9.42	10.41
8.55	10.12	—	—

d Saturdays only.
e Saturdays excepted.

The Crown. Personally conducted. Comfortable. Moderate Hotel. Ten minutes Station, River, Golf. Billiards. Bowling Green, Garden, Garage. Tel. 59, Chertsey.

Station Hotel. Excellent cuisine. Central heating. Moderate charges. 'Phone No. 69 Chertsey. CATERING HOUSES, LTD.

Rendezvous. Private Hotel. Restaurant, Chertsey Bridge. Georgian house, Young Society. Home comforts. Tennis, Boating, Clock Golf, Billiards, Fishing. Phone 91. F. WHITE NILSSEN.

CHESHAM (Bucks) from

Marylebone or *Baker Street,* 25½ miles. Fares, 5/4*a,* 3/2*c.* R.T. for two months, 10/8*a,* 6/1½*c.* Pop. 8,584. *See* pp. 494, 495. *Map Square* 23.

CHESHUNT (Herts) from

Liverpool Street, 14 miles. Fares, 2/3½*a,* 1/10*b,* 1/4½*c.* R.T. for two months, 4/7*a,* 3/8*b,* 2/7½*c.* Pop. 13,628. *See* pp. 526-527. *Map Square* 23.

CHESTER from *Euston,*

179¼ miles. Fares, 37/4*a,* 22/5*c.* R.T. for two months, 74/8*a,* 44/10*c.* Pop. 40,794. *Map Square* 12.

EUSTON	CHESTER	CHESTER	EUSTON
AM12.25	5.36	AM 2. 5	5.50
2.35	8.56	4. 0g	8. 0
5. 0	9.58	8.17er	12. 5
8.30r	12.15	8.17dr	12.20
10.30r	2. 7	9.30r	1. 0
10.40r	3. 8	10. 5r	1.45
11.50r	3.29	10.32r	2.20
12. 0nr	5.25	11.20r	3.10
PM 2.35t	6.24	11.40r	4.15
4. 5t	8. 3	PM 2. 5r	5.50
5.20r	9. 1	2.25r	6.25
6.30er	10.53	3.17r	7.30
8.45	12.35	4.20r	8.10
9.30e	2.18	5.10er	9. 5
11.50d	9.20	5.10dr	9.15
—	—	6.17r	10.45
—	—	11. 5	5. 0

Sunday Trains.

EUSTON	CHESTER	CHESTER	EUSTON
PM12.10r	4.52	AM 2. 5	5.50
8.45	12.35	4. 0	8. C
9.15	2.18	9.50	4. 0
—	—	PM 3. 5r	7.10
—	—	11. 0	5. C

d Saturdays only.
e Saturdays excepted.
g Mondays excepted.
n Noon.
r Restaurant Car.
t Tea Car.

CHELTENHAM.—TATE'S PRIVATE HOTEL.

CHESTER—*continued.*

ANOTHER ROUTE from
Paddington 195¼ miles. Fares as above.

PAD.	CHESTER	CHESTER	PAD.
AM 9.10r	1.18	AM 7.40	12.25
10.20r	2.13	8.35r	1.25
10.40r	3. 0	9.41r	2. 5
PM12.50r	5.35	PM12.25r	5. 0
2.10t	6.19	1.38r	5.55
4.10t	8.20	2.40r	6.40
6.10r	10.32	3.12r	8. 5
12.15	6.30	5.10r	10. 0
—	—	8. 0	3.30

Sunday Trains.

PM12.50r	5.23	AM10. 0	6.20
—	—	PM 3.46r	9. 0

r Restaurant Car.
t Tea Car.

Queen Railway Hotel. First - class Family. Opposite Station, Tram Terminus. Residential Suites. Porters (scarlet liveries) meet all trains. Telegrams, "Queen," Chester. Telephone, 668.

Blossom's Hotel. First-class Family and Commercial Hotel. Opposite General Post Office. Stock Rooms. Garage. Omnibus meets trains. Telephone 186. Telegrams "Blossoms," Chester.

Grosvenor Hotel. The County Hotel, First Class. Centre of City. Garage. Night Porter. Telephones Nos. 795 and 706.

CHESTERFIELD
(Derby) from *St. Pancras*, 146 miles. Fares, 30/3a, 18/2c. R. T., double fare. Pop. 61,236.
Map Square 12.

ST. PAN.	CHESTFD.	CHESTFD.	ST.PAN.
AM 2.25g	6.27	AM12.10g	4.20
2.25f	7.35	12.10f	4.55
4.25	9.50	5.10r	9.57
9. 0r	12. 8	7.30r	10.45
9.50r	12.52	9.30r	1.20
11. 0r	2.29	9.57r	1.30
PM12.25r	4.10	10.19r	1.45
1.50r	5. 7	10.38	3.25
2.25r	6.10	PM12.44r	4.10
3.30r	6.44	1.53r	5.30
5. 0r	8. 8	2.15r	5.45
6.15r	9.12	4. 8r	7.15
6.25r	10.36	5.15r	8.35
9.15	1.18	5.53r	9. 5
11.50	3.52	—	—

Sunday Trains.

AM10.50r	2.45	AM12.10	4.20
PM 3.15	7.28	5.10	11.53
6.15r	10.18	PM 2. 6	5.27
9.15	1.18	5.44r	9.43

f Mondays only.
g Mondays excepted.
r Restaurant Car.

CHESTERFIELD—*contd.*

ANOTHER ROUTE (CENTRAL) from *Marylebone*, 152 miles. Fares as above.

M'BONE.	CHESTFD.	CHESTFD.	M'BONE.
AM 2.52	7.26	AM 6. 0	10.36
10. 0r	2.28	7.10r	11.10
PM12.15r	4.17	9.22r	1.13
3.20r	6.45	10.41r	3. 0
5. 0r	8.49	PM12.40r	6.38
6.20dr	10.42	5.31r	8.55
—	—	5.58r	9.55
—	—	9.10	3.57

Sunday Trains.

PM 5.30r	9.30	AM10.33r	5.40

d Saturdays only.
r Restaurant Car.

CHESTERFORD, GT.
(Essex) from *Liverpool Street*, 45¾ miles. Fares, 9/9a, 5/10c. R. T. for two months, 19/6a. Pop. 766.
Map Square 19.

L'PL.ST.	CHSTFD.	CHSTFD.	L'PL.ST.
AM 5.50	7.40	AM 7. 3	8.57
7.18	9.24	7.41	9.27
10. 5	11.43	8.16	9.47
11.50dr	1.23	9.49	11.27
PM12.29d	1.58	PM12.15	2. 7
12.48e	2.50	1.33d	3.18
1.19d	3. 4	2.31h	5. 9
2.48	4.41	2.46k	5. 9
4.15	5.29	4.21r	6.10
5.49r	7.17	5.59	7.58
6.30	7.53	8.59	10.30
8.22d	9.52	—	—
8.22e	10. 4	—	—

Sunday Trains.

AM 8.12	9.54	AM 9.26	11.27
PM 1.50	4. 4	PM 5.51	7.26
—	—	—	—

d Saturdays only.
e Saturdays excepted.
h Commencing July 23.
k Ceases to run after July 21.
r Restaurant Car.

CHESTER-LE-
STREET (Durham), 259½ miles. Fares, 54/0a, 32/5c. R. T., double fare. Departures *from* London as for Durham. Departures *for* London about 6 times daily. Pop. 15,594.
Map Square 3.

CHESTER ROAD (Warwick), 115 miles. Fares, 24/0a, 14/5c. R. T. for two months, 48/0a, 28/10c. Departures *from* London as for Birmingham (New Street). Departures *for* London about 6 times daily.
Map Square 17.

CHETTISHAM (Cambs).
73¼ miles. Fares, 15/7a, 9/4c. R. T. for two months, 31/2a. Departures *from* London as for March. Departures *for* London about 5 times daily. Pop. 173.
Map Square 19.

CHEVENING (Kent) from
Charing Cross, Cannon Street, and *London Bridge*, 22½ miles. No through fares. Departures *from* London as for Brasted. Departures *for* London about 7 minutes later. Pop. 1,031.

CHEVINGTON (Northumberland), 293½ miles. Fares, 61/11a, 37/2c. R. T., double fare. Departures *from* London as for Morpeth. Departures *for* London about 3 times daily. Pop. 4,359.
Map Square 3.

CHICHESTER (Sussex)
from *Victoria, Clapham Junction,* and *London Bridge*, 69¼ miles. Fares, 13/11a, 8/4c. R. T. for two months, 27/10a, 16/8c. Pop. 12,410.
Map Square 28.

	Leave		Arr. at
VICT.		LON. B.	CHICH.
AM 6.18		6.35	8.55
7.23		7.25	10.37
8.55		—	10.45
10.15		10.22	12.29
11.55k		11.50k	2.42
PM 1.40		1.50	3.56
1.55k		—	4.13
—		2. 5k	5.15
3.55		4. 0	6. 7
—		4.50	6.34
4.53		—	7. 0
—		5. 5	7.49
—		5. 8e	7.49
5.45k		6. 0k	8.20
7.20		7.15	9.53

Sunday Trains.

AM 6.55k		7. 2k	10.55
9. 0		8.55	11.16
9.55		—	11.38
PM 1.14k		1.10k	4.56
7. 0		6.38	9.27
—		—	—

Trains from Chichester.

	Leave	Arrive at	
	CHICH.	LON. B.	VICT.
AM 7. 8g		9.50	9.22
7.13f		9.50	—
7.29		—.	10.28
7.56		9.58	—
8.34		10.45	10.53
8.43k		—	11.17
9.11		10.55	—
10. 4		12. 8	12. 0
10.25k		1.42	—
11.28		—	1.10
PM12.15		3.32	3.32
2.28		4.27	4.34
2.40		—	5. 0
5.14		—	6.50
5.33		7.48	7.39
6.59		—	8.33
7.18d		—	9.45
7.52		10. 8	10. 1
9.36k		12.59	1. 0

Sunday Trains.

AM 7.33		10.45	10.32
9.45k		—	1. 0
PM 4.12k		—	7. 0
6.15		—	7.56
6.34		8.50	8.42
8. 0k		11.34	10.55

d Saturdays only.
e Saturdays excepted.
f Mondays only.
g Mondays excepted.
k Via Hove.

Anchor & Dolphin Hotel. Telephone 189. Two noted hotels now joined. Facing Cathedral. Headquarters of the County Club. Large Ballroom. Excellent quarters for Goodwood. Central Heating. Electric Light. Garage. TRUST HOUSES, Ltd.

CHICHESTER—*contd.*

North House Hotel. Close to Cathedral, St. Mary's Hospital, Priory, and Park. Exquisite Old English Garden. Excellent tariff. Garage. Phone, 118. Proprietors, Mr. & Mrs. BURR.

The Richmond Arms Hotel, Goodwood Park. Under new management. Thoroughly up-to-date. Catering a speciality. Ample accommodation. Stabling. P.R.H.A. Free House.

Globe Hotel and Restaurant. Family and Commercial. Adjoining Station. Phone 235 Chichester. CATERING HOUSES, LTD.

CHIGWELL (Essex) from

Liverpool Street or *Fenchurch Street*, 11¼ miles. Fares, from Liverpool Street, 2/1*a*, 1/8*b*, 1/3*c*. R. T. for two days, 4/2*a*, 3/2½*b*, 2/2½*c*. From Fenchurch Street, 2/1*a*, 1/8*b*, 1/3*c*. R. T. for two days, 4/2*a*, 3/1*b*, 2/2½*c*. Pop. 2,943. *See* p. 536
Map Square 23

CHIGWELL LANE

(Essex) from *Fenchurch Street*, 13¼ miles, or *Liverpool Street*, 13 miles. Fares from Liverpool Street, 2/9*a*, 2/3*b*, 1/8*c*. R. T. for two months, 5/6, 4/1*b*, 3/1*c*. Fares from Fenchurch Street, 2/9*a*, 2/2*b*, 1/8*c*. R. T. for two months, 5/6*a*, 3/9½*b*, 2/11*c*. *See* pp. 541-544.

CHILCOMPTON (Somerset)

from *Waterloo*, 134¾ miles. Fares, 24/0*a*, 14/5*c*. R. T. for two months, 48/0*a*. Departures *from* London as for Shepton Mallet. Departures *for* London about 4 times daily. Pop. 666.
Map Square 22.

CHILDWALL (Lancs), 212¼

miles. Fares, 41/1*a*, 24/8*c*. R. T. for two months, 82/2*a*, 49/4*c*. Departures *from* London as for Warrington (Central). Departures *for* London about 4 times daily. Pop. 198.
Map Square 12.

CHILHAM (Kent) from

Charing Cross, Cannon Street and *London Bridge*, 65¾ miles. Fares, 12/11*a*, 10/4*b*, 7/9*c*. R. T. for two months, 25/10*a*, 20/8*b*. Pop. 1,232.
Map Square 24.

Leave Char. +	Leave Can. St.	Leave Lon. B.	Arr. at Chil'm
AM —	5.20	5.25	8.38
9.15	—	9.23	11. 7
11. 0	—	11. 7	1.12
PM 1. 0	—	—	2.37
3. 0	—	3. 8	4.52
4.30	—	4.37	6.19
5.24*d*	—	5.34*d*	8. 6
6. 0*e*	—	6. 5*e*	8. 6
7.18	—	7.26	9.41
—	—	—	—
—	—	—	—
—	—	—	—

Sunday Trains.

AM 7.45	—	7.52	10. 7
9.35*h*	—	—	11.41
PM 5.15*h*	—	—	7.37
7.35	—	7.45	9.38
—	—	—	—

CHILHAM—*continued.*

Trains from Chilham.

Leave Chil'm	Arrive at Lon. B.	Arrive at Can. St.	Arrive at Char. +
AM 7. 9	9.32	9.36	—
*h*7.56*e*	—	—	10.16*h*
7.56	10. 0	10. 4	—
9.47	11.43	—	11.57
11.20	1.36	—	1.50
PM12.53	3.26	—	3.40
3.27*h*	—	—	5.42*h*
3.27	5.50	—	6. 3
5.22	7.25	7.30	7.49
8.11	10.22	—	10.35
*v*11. 5*d*	—	1.20	—
—	—	—	—
—	—	—	—
—	—	—	—
—	—	—	—
—	—	—	—
—	—	—	—
—	—	—	—
—	—	—	—

Sunday Trains.

AM 7.17	10. 5	—	10.15
PM 5.12	7. 9	—	7.17
6. 9	8. 9	—	8.21
8.25	10.16	—	10.26
9.57*v*	—	1.23*v*	—
—	—	—	—
—	—	—	—
—	—	—	—
—	—	—	—
—	—	—	—

d Saturdays only.
e Saturdays excepted.
h Departs from or arrives at Victoria (S.E.&C.R.)
v Third Class only.

CHILSWORTHY (Cornwall),

228¾ miles. No through fares. Departures *from* London as for Calstock. Departures *for* London about 4 times daily.

CHILTERN GREEN

(Beds) from *St. Pancras*, 27¼ miles. Fares, 5/8*a*, 3/5*c*. R. T., double fare.
Map Square 23.

St. Pan.	Chil. G.	Chil. G.	St. Pan.
AM 6. 0	7.13	AM 7. 5	8.15
7.30	8.46	8.29	9.13
9.55	11.12	PM 1.31	2.55
PM12.33	1.50	4. 1	5.10
3.35	4.28	7.17	8.42
5.45*e*	6.36	8.12	8.57
6.35	7.24	—	—
7.50	8.39	—	—
—	—	—	—
—	—	—	—
—	—	—	—
—	—	—	—
—	—	—	—
—	—	—	—
—	—	—	—
—	—	—	—

No Sunday Trains.
e Saturdays excepted.

CHILVERS COTON

(Warwick), 97¾ miles. Fares, 20/5*a*, 12/3*c*. R. T. for two months, 40/10*a*. Departures *from* London as for Nuneaton or Coventry. Departures *for* London about 5 times daily. Pop. 10,492.
Map Square 17.

CHILWORTH (Surrey)

from *Charing Cross, Cannon Street*, and *London Bridge*, 40 miles. Fares, 6/3*a*, 5/0*b*, 3/9*c*. R. T. for two months, 12/6*a*, 8/9*b*, 7/0*c* Pop. 240.
Map Square 23.

Leave Char. +	Leave Can. St.	Leave Lon. B.	Arr. at Chil.
AM —	4.44	5. 0	6.40
—	—	7.50*l*	9.28
—	—	9.33*l*	11. 7
10.55	—	11. 3	12.50
PM12.55	—	1. 4	2.43
2. 3*e*	2. 8*d*	2.10	3.44
3.15	—	3.21	4.59
4.22*d*	—	4.28*d*	6. 1
—	4.44*e*	4.48*e*	5.57
—	5.24*e*	5.27*e*	6.45
5.42*d*	—	5.48*d*	7.15
—	6. 0*e*	6. 3*e*	7.28
6.34*d*	—	6.40*d*	8.11
—	6.36*e*	6.39*e*	8.11
7.24*d*	—	7.30*d*	9. 9
8.28	—	8.36	10.14
—	—	—	—
—	—	—	—
—	—	—	—

Sunday Trains.

AM 6.25	—	6.32	8.16
10.20	—	10.28	12. 0
PM 5.25	—	5.32	7.10
8.38	—	8.45	10.21
—	—	—	—
—	—	—	—
—	—	—	—
—	—	—	—

Trains from Chilworth.

Leave Chil.	Arrive at Lon. B.	Arrive at Can. St.	Arrive at Char. +
AM 7.32	8.56	—	—
8.30	9.48	9.52	—
9. 1	10.10	—	10.20
9.31	11. 0	—	—
11.10	12.50	—	1. 0
PM 1. 3	2.38	—	2.46
3.16	5. 2	—	5.14
4.28	5.56	—	—
5.43	7.20	—	7.29
7.34	9. 2	—	9.15
8.35	10. 3	—	10.13
10.29	11.57	—	12.10
—	—	—	—
—	—	—	—
—	—	—	—

Sunday Trains.

AM 6.44	8.16	—	8.27
9.48	11.15	—	11.25
PM 5 39	7.13	—	7.25
8.41	10.11	—	10.24
—	—	—	—
—	—	—	—
—	—	—	—

d Saturdays only.
e Saturdays excepted.
l Low Level platform.

CHINGFORD (Essex)

from *Liverpool Street*, 10½ miles. Fares, 1/8*a*, 1/4*b*, 1/0*c*. R. T. for two days, 3/4*a*, 2/6*b*, 1/9*c*. Pop. 9,482. *See* pp. 523-524.
Map Square 23.

Royal Forest Hotel. Beautifully situated midst of Forest. Near Golf Links.

ROYAL FOREST HOTEL, Restaurant. 50 Bedrooms. **CHINGFORD.**

CHINLEY (Derby) from

St Pancras, 169¾ miles. Fares, 35/2*a*, 21/1*c*. R. T., double fare. Pop. 1,761.
Map Square 12.

St. Pan.	Chin.	Chin.	St. Pan.
AM 4.25	9.55	AM 7.20*r*	11.35
8.25*r*	12.25	9.43*r*	1.30
10.25*r*	2.16	10.38	3.25
PM 1.25*r*	5.32	PM12.20*r*	5.45
4.25*r*	8.10	2.25*r*	6.15
12. 0*h*	9.20	4. 5*r*	8.35
—	—	5.15*r*	10. 5
—	—	8. 4	4.20
—	—	—	—
—	—	—	—
—	—	—	—

Sunday Trains.

AM11.15*r*	3.35	PM12.50*r*	5. 2
PM 3.15	7.50	7.28	4.55
—	—	—	—

h Saturdays midnight only.
r Restaurant Car.

CHINNOR (Oxon) from

Paddington, 38½ miles. Fares, 7/5*a*, 4/7*c*. R. T. for two months, 14/10*a*, 9/2*c*. Departures *from* London as for Watlington. Departures *for* London about 3 times daily. Pop. 975.
Map Square 23.

CHIPPENHAM (Wilts)

from *Paddington*, 94 miles. Fares, 19/7*a* 11/9*c*. R. T. for two months, 39/2*a*. Pop. 7,713.
Map Square 22.

Pad.	Chiphm.	Chiphm.	Pad.
AM 5.30	7.42	AM12.57*f*	3.15
7.30	9.33	8.25*r*	10.15
9. 0	11.17	8.37	12. 0
10.45	1.25	10.20	12.20
PM 1.10*r*	3.30	PM12.25*r*	2.40
3.15*t*	5.32	1.10	3.20
4.15	5.57	3.13	6. 2
5.15	7.46	6. 3*r*	8.35
6.30	8. 9	8.20	10.25
6.55	10. 6	12. 2	2.45
12. 0*l*	2.23	—	—
12.30*l*	2.53	—	—

Sunday Trains.

AM10.35	1.39	PM12.45	3.35
PM12.30*r*	3.29	2.15	6. 0
2. 0	7.21	6.18	8.10
—	—	6.56	10. 0
—	—	—	—
—	—	—	—

f Mondays only.
k Saturdays midnight excepted.
l Saturdays midnight only.
r Restaurant Car.
t Tea Car.

Taxi Cabs can be hired to meet any train at this station by letter, or telephone No. 125. Messrs. Burridge's Motor Works, Station Hill.

Angel Hotel. Family and Commercial. Private Rooms. Luncheon daily. Motors. Garage. Repairs. Posting. Bus meets trains. Telephone 37.
W. M. BURRIDGE, Proprietor.

CHIPPING NORTON

(Oxon) from *Paddington*, 79¾ miles. Fares, *via* Bicester, 15/3*a*, 9/11*c*. R. T. for two months, 30/6*a*, 19/10*c*. *Via* Kingham, 18/6*a*, 11/1*c*. R. T. for two months, 37/0*a*, 22/2*c*. Pop. 3,522.
Map Square 17.

Pad.	C. Nor.	C. Nor.	Pad.
AM 5.30	9.12	AM 7.17	9.50
9.10*q*	11.27	8. 4*v*	11.15
9.45	12.48	9.50	12. 5
PM 1.30	3.28	11.29	2.12
2.10*q*	4.45	PM12.50*kr*	2.55
4.45*t*	7.23	12.53*lt*	4.15
6. 5*r*	8.38	2.55	5.50
6.10*q*	8.25	4.10	7.20
6.55	9.43	6.25*r*	9.15
12.15*hl*	7.12	7.40	10.45
—	—	9.55*q*	3.30
—	—	—	—
—	—	—	—
—	—	—	—
—	—	—	—

No Sunday Trains.

h Saturdays midnight excepted.
k Thursdays only.
l Via Oxford and Banbury.
q Via Bicester.
r Restaurant Car.
t Tea Car.
v Via King's Sutton.

CHIPPING SODBURY

(Gloucester) from *Paddington*, 104½ miles. Fares, 21/10*a*, 13/1*c*. R. T. for two months, 43/8*a*. Pop. 977.
Map Square 22.

Pad.	C.Sodby.	C.Sodby.	Pad.
AM 5.30	8.32	AM 7. 0	10.45
9. 0	12.17	9.33	12.20
10.45	2.37	11.17*r*	2.40
PM 3.15*t*	6.21	PM 3.27*r*	8.35
—	—	6.29	10.25
—	—	—	—

No Sunday Trains.

r Restaurant Car.
t Tea Car.

CHIPSTEAD (Surrey)

from *Charing Cross*, *Cannon Street*, and *London Bridge*, 19¼ miles. Fares, 2/11*a*, 2/4*b*, 1/9*c*. R. T. for eight days, 5/10*a*, 4/8*b*, 3/6*c*. Departures *from* London as for Kingswood. Departures *for* London about 16 times daily. Pop. 992.
Map Square 23.

CHIRK (Denbigh) from

Paddington, 174 miles. Fares, 36/3*a*, 21/9*c*. R. T. for two months, 72/6*a* 43/6*c*. Pop. 4,557.
Map Square 12.

Pad.	Chirk.	Chirk.	Pad.
AM 9.10*r*	1.54	AM 7.16	12.25
10.40*r*	3. 7	8.29*r*	1.25
PM 2.10*t*	6. 8	9.55*r*	2. 5
4.10*t*	9.12	PM12.20*r*	5. 0
6.10*r*	10. 8	1.21*t*	5.55
12.15*h*	8 44	2.53*r*	8. 5
12.15*k*	10.11	5.26	10. 0
—	—	8.20	3.30

Sunday Trains.

PM12.50*r*	6. 5	AM11. 2	6.20
—	—	—	—

h Saturdays midnight excepted.
k Saturdays midnight only.
r Restaurant Car.
t Tea Car.

CHIRNSIDE (Berwick),

350 miles. Fares, 73/7*a*, 44/2*c*. R. T. for two months, 147/2*a*. Departures *from* London as for Berwick-on-Tweed. Departures *for* London about 3 times daily. Pop. 1,402.
Map Square 41.

CHISLEDON (Wilts), 96

miles. Fares, 16/1*a*, 9/8*c*. R. T. for two months, 32/2*a*, 19/4*c*. Departures *from* London as for Marlborough. Departures *for* London about 3 times daily. Pop. 1,197.
Map Square 22.

CHISLEHURST (Kent)

from Charing Cross, Cannon Street, and *London Bridge*, 12 miles. Fares from Charing Cross, 2/6*a*, 2/0*b*, 1/6*c*. R. T. for two days, 5/0*a*, 4/0*b*. From Cannon Street, 2/6*a*, 2/0*b*, 1/3*c*. R. T. for two days, 5/0*a*, 4/0*b*. Pop. 8,981.
Map Square 23

	Leave		Arr. at
Char. +	Can. St.	Lon. B.	Chisle.
AM —	5.20	5.25	5.58
—	6.45	6.50	7.19
7.26	—	7.33	7.57
—	7.56	8. 0	8.28
—	9.36	9.39	10. 8
9.38	—	9.45	10. 9
11.15	—	11.23	11.53
11.42	—	11.49	12.20
PM —	12.48*d*	12.51*d*	1.21
12.50*e*	—	12.58*e*	1.33
1.34*d*	1.12*d*	1.15*d*	1.34
1.50*e*	—	1.41*d*	2. 7
2. 0*d*	—	1.58*e*	2.25
—	2. 4*d*	2. 5*d*	2.23
2.17*d*	—	2. 7*d*	2.32
2.30*e*	—	2.23*d*	2.47
2.50*d*	—	2.37*e*	3. 4
3.50	—	2.57*d*	3.23
—	—	3.57	4.20
4.44*e*	—	4.47*e*	5.16
4.55*d*	—	5. 1*d*	5.27
—	5. 4*e*	5. 7*e*	5.29
5.35*d*	—	5.41*d*	6. 5
—	5.40*e*	5.43*e*	6. 6
5.50*e*	—	5.57*e*	6.24
6.10*e*	—	6.17*e*	6.39
6.34*e*	—	6.41*e*	6.52
6.38*e*	—	6.45*e*	7.12
6.40*d*	—	6.48*d*	7.19
7. 6*e*	—	7.13*e*	7.41
8. 0	—	8. 8	8.27
9. 0	—	9. 6	9.28
10. 0	—	10. 6	10.29
10.43	—	10.51	11.15
11.45	—	—	12. 6
—	—	—	—
—	—	—	—
—	—	—	—
—	—	—	—

Sunday Trains.

AM 7. 5	—	7.11	7.42
3. 5	—	8.12	8.37
9.30	—	9.36	10. 2
11.15	—	11.23	11.53
PM 1. 0	—	1. 7	1.36
3. 5	—	3.13	3.41
6. 0	—	6. 6	6.34
7.10	—	7.20	7.45
9.25	—	9.31	9.55
10.35	—	10.43	11. 7
—	—	—	—
—	—	—	—
—	—	—	—

CHISLEHURST—*contd.*

Trains from Chislehurst.

Leave	Arrive at		
CHISLE.	LON. B.	CAN. ST.	CHAR. +
AM 6.40	7. 4	7. 8	—
7.19	7.42	—	7.49
7.49	8.10	—	8.19
8.18	8.40	8.44	—
8.30	8.56	9. 0	—
8.58	9.18	—	9.27
9. 3	9.24	9.28	—
9.18	9.40	9.44	—
9.37	9.58	—	10. 7
9.51	10.16	10.20	—
10.12	10 28	10.32	—
10.43	10.59	11. 3	—
PM12. 6*e*	12.35	12.40	—
12.21*d*	12.54	12.58	—
12.59	1.27	—	1.38
1.45*d*	2.12	—	2.20
1.46*e*	2.12	—	2.20
2.41	3. 7	—	3.19
4. 9	4.36	4.40*e*	4.45*d*
5. 1*e*	5.27	—	5.38
5.54*e*	6.22	6.28	—
5.58*d*	6.30	—	6.39
6. 12*e*	6.44	—	6.54
6.45*e*	7. 7	7.12	—
7. 5	7.25	7.30	—
8.26	8.54	9. 1	—
9.51	10.15	—	10.23
10.22	10.48	—	10.57
11. 8	11.34	—	11.43
—	—	—	—
—	—	—	—
—	—	—	—
—	—	—	—
—	—	—	—
—	—	—	—

Sunday Trains.

AM 8. 6	8.30	—	8.39
9.36	10. 5	—	10.15
9.52	10.22	—	10.32
10.40	11. 6	—	11.13
11.28	11.49	—	12. 0
PM12.50	1.20	—	1.29
2.25	2.50	—	3. 0
6. 1	6.27	—	6.41
7.51	8.12	—	8.22
7.59	8.20	—	8.28
8.10	8.30	—	8.40
8.43	9. 7	—	9.18
9.12	9.38	—	—
10.41	11. 4	—	11.15
—	—	—	—
—	—	—	—
—	—	—	—
—	—	—	—

d Saturdays only.
e Saturdays excepted.

CHISWICK (Middlesex)

from *Waterloo*, 8¾ miles. Fares, 0/11½*a*, 0/7*c*. R. T. for two days, 1/9*a*, 1/2*c*. Pop. 40,938. *See* p. 586.
Map Square 67.

CHISWICK PARK

(Middlesex) from *Mansion House*, 8½ miles. Also to and from Ealing and Hounslow. Pop. 9,105.
See p. 489.
Map Square 67.

CHOLLERTON (North-

umberland), 293½ miles. No through fares. Departures *from* London as for Hexham or Carlis'e. Departures *for* London about 3 times daily. Pop. 1,132.
Map Square 3.

CHOLSEY (Berks) from

Paddington, 48¾ miles. Fares, 10/2*a*, 6/1*c*. R. T. for two months, 20/4*a*. Pop. 2,248.
Map Square 23.

PAD.	CHOL.	CHOL.	PAD.
AM 5.30	7.24	AM 7.50	9. 0
6.30	8.34	8.12	9.30
7.30	9.14	8.42	10. 0
9. 0	10.28	9.19	10.45
9.45	11.14	10.23	12. 0
11.20	12.47	PM12.23	1.50
PM12.30	1.57	1.50	3.20
1.10*dr*	2.36	2.54	4.35
1.35*r*	2.57	3.41	5. 6
1.50*d*	3.41	4.39	6. 2
-3.18	5. 6	5.36	7.20
3.38	5.24	6.55	8.20
5. 0	6.17	7.50	9.15
5.40	7. 4	9. 6	10.45
6. 5	7.26	10. 3*h*	2.45
6.55	8.25	—	—
7.30	8.52	—	—
8. 5	9.47	—	—
10. 0*h*	11.36	—	—

Sunday Trains.

AM 9.10	10.44	AM 8.20	10.14
10.35	11.51	11.50	2.40
11. 0	12.37	PM 4.18	6. 0
PM 1.45	3.29	6.40	8.20
2. 0	4.11	7.40	9.15
4.10	5.59	8.19	9.48
5.15	7. 2	9.28	11.38
7.40	9.43	—	—

d Saturdays only.
h Wednesdays and Saturdays only.
r Restaurant Car.

CHOPPINGTON (North-

umberland),284⅜ miles. No through fares. Departures *from* London as for Morpeth. Departures *for* London about 4 times daily. Pop. 5,432.
Map Square 3.

CHORLEY (Lancs) from

Euston, 202¼ miles. Fares, 42/3*a*, 25/4*c*. R. T. for two months, 84/6*a*. Pop. 30,576.
Map Square 12.

EUSTON CHORLEY		CHORLEY EUSTON	
AM12.25	7.31	AM 5. 3*cr*12. 5	
2.35	9.39	5. 3*dr*12.20	
5. 0	11.16	8.3*8r* 1.45	
6.45	1.18	10.33*hr* 3.45	
8.30*r*	3.22	10.33*r* 4.15	
10.40*r*	4. 9	11.35*t* 5.50	
PM 1.30*r*	6.12	PM12.48*t* 6. 0	
2.35*t*	7.54	3.40*er* 9. 5	
5.20*r*	9.56	3.40*dr* 9.15	
—	—	9.15 5. 0	

Sunday Trains.

AM11.45	8.37	AM 8.43	4. 0
—	—	PM 8.45	5. 0

d Saturdays only.
e Saturdays excepted.
h Mondays and Saturdays only.
r Restaurant Car.
t Tea Car

CHORLEY WOOD

(Herts) from *Marylebone* or *Baker Street*, 19½ miles. Fares, 4/1*a*, 2/5*c*. R. T. for two months, 8/2*a*, 4/8*c*. Pop. 2,439. *See* pp. 494, 495.
Map Square 23.

Chorley Wood Hotel. Opposite Station. Residential. Excellent Cuisine. Lovely Garden. Near Golf Links. Telephone 5.
Proprietor, G. STEIB.

CHORLTON-CUM-

HARDY (Lancs), 180¼ miles. Fares, 38/7*a*, 23/2*c*. R. T., double fare. Departures *from* London as for Withington. Departures *for* London about 6 times daily. Pop. 24,977.

CHRISTCHURCH

(Hants) from *Waterloo*, 103¾ miles. Fares, *via* Sway, 21/10*a*, 13/1*c*. R. T. for two months, 43/8*a*, 26/2*c*. Pop. 6,991.
Map Square 27.

W'LOO.	CHRCH.	CHRCH.	W'LOO.
AM 5.40	8.56	AM 7.12*r*	10. 6
5.50	10.21	7.59*s*	11. 0
8.30*s*	11.55	9.31*s*	12.22
9.30	12.22	10. 8*r*	12.50
10.30	1.29	11.34*r*	2.20
11.30*r*	2. 5	PM12.15	2.50
PM12.30*r*	3.14	1.34	4.20
1.30*s*	4.17	2. 7	4.50
2.30	5. 3	3.34*s*	6.26
3.30*s*	6.17	3.54	6.58
4.30*r*	7.31	5.34*r*	8.20
5.30*r*	8.17	7.18	10.50
6.30*r*	9.22	8.11	11.28
7.30	10.45	11.48	3.58
10. 0	1.51	—	—
—	—	--	—

Sunday Trains.

AM11. 0*r*	1.45	AM 9. 2	12.11
PM 2. 0*r*	4.35	11.43	2.27
7. 0*r*	9.45	PM 4.30	8. 3
9.28	1.51	6.24*r*	9.51
—	—	7.22	10.52
—	—	11.48	3.58

r Restaurant Car.
s Refreshments served.

King's Arms Hotel. Splendidly situated. Lovely gardens. Private fishing. Garage. Telephone 9. Proprietor—
A. B. MARSHALL.

Gordon Hotel, Southbourne. Only Hotel on the Cliff, overlooking Needles, Poole, and Swanage Bays. Sheltered from East winds. Tel. 101 Southbourne.
See advt. p. **82.**

CHRIST'S HOSPITAL

(Sussex) from *Victoria, Clapham Junction* and *London Bridge*, 39¼ miles. Fares, 8/1*a*, 4/10*c*. R.T. for two months, 16/2*a*, 9/8*c*.
Map Square 23.

	Leave		Arr. at
VICT.	CLAP. J.	LON. B.	C. HOSP.
AM 5.18	5.28	5.28	7.25
6.18	6.25	6.35	7.57
7.23	7.29	7.25	9.34
8.55	7.56	7.35	10.12
10.15	10.22	10.30	11.50
10.35	10.42	10.35	1.10
11.55	—	11.50	1.42
PM 1.40	1.47*e*	1.50	3.17
2. 0	2. 7	2. 5	4.26
—	—	2. 8*d*	4.26
3.55	4. 2	4. 0	5.25
4.53	5. 0	5. 5	6.32
5. 5	5.12	5.14	6.52
6.15	—	6. 0	7.31
7.20	7.27	7.15	8.52
—	—	7.20*d*	9.24

Sunday Trains.

AM 6.55	7. 2	7. 2	9. 7
8.35	8.42	8.25	10. 0
PM 4. 5	4.13	3.50	6. 2
7. 0	7. 7	6.38	8.27

CHRIST'S HOSPITAL
— *continued.*

Trains from Christ's Hosp.

Leave C. Hosp.	Lon. B.	Clap. J.	Vict.
AM 7.43	9.10	9.31	9.19
9.11	10.45	10.40	10.48
10.12	11.50	11.35	11.42
10.43	12. 8	12.33	12. 0
11.13	1.28	—	1.10
PM 12.25	2.22	2.13	2.22
1.35	3.32	3.22	3.32
1.46	3.40	3.37	3.45
3. 5	4.27	4.27	4.33
3.46	5.54	5. 4	5.12
4.46	6.36	6.26	6.34
6. 0	7.48	7.31	7.39
8.30d	10. 8	9.53	10. 1
8.33e	10. 8	9.53	10. 1
9. 7	10.58	11.10	11.17
—	—	—	—

Sunday Trains.

AM 7.47	10.11	10. 6	10.13
8.34	10.45	10.23	10.32
PM 3.19	5.· 3	5. 1	5.11
5.58	—	7.25	7.33
7.18	8.50	8.33	8.42
7.51	9.32	9.24	9.34
—	—	—	—

a Saturdays only.
e Saturdays excepted.

CHRISTON BANK
(Northumberland). 311 miles. Fares, 65/7a, 39/4c. R. T., double fare. Departures *from* London as for Morpeth. Departures *for* London about 5 times daily. *Map Square 3.*

CHRISTOW (Devon), 183
miles. Fares, 37/9a, 22/8c. R. T. for two months, 75/6a, 45/4c. Departures *from* London as for Exeter (St. Davids). Departures *for* London about 4 times daily. Pop. 564. *Map Square 26.*

CHUDLEIGH (Devon), 188¼
miles. Fares, 38/9a, 23/3c. R. T. for two months, 77/6a, 46/6c. Departures *from* London as for Exeter (St. Davids). Departures *for* London about 4 times daily. Pop. 2,005. *Map Square 26.*

Clifford Arms Hotel.
An historic inn of the West Country. Ten miles beyond Exeter on the main Plymouth Road. Central Heating. Electric light. All home produce. Eighteen bedrooms. Fine Garage. R.A.C. A.A. Telephone 12.

CHURCH (Lancs), 209¾
miles. Fares, 43/4a, 26/0c. R. T. for two months, 86/8a, 52/0c. Departures *from* London as for Blackburn. Departures *for* London about 5 times daily. Pop. 6,751. *Map Square 12.*

CHURCH BRAMPTON
(Northampton), 69¾ miles. Fares, 14/0a, 8/5c. R. T. for two months, 28/0a, 16/10c. Departures *from* London as for Northampton (Castle). Departures *for* London about 5 times daily. Pop. 411.

CHURCHDOWN (Glo's-
ter), 110 miles. Fares, 23/9a, 14/3c. R. T. for two months, 47/6a. Departures *from* London as for Cheltenham (St. James). Departures *for* London about 8 times daily. Pop. 1,126. *Map Square 22.*

CHURCH FENTON
(Yorks) from *St. Pancras,* 192¼ miles. Fares, 37/4a, 22/5c. R. T., 74/8a, 44/10c. Pop. 581. *Map Square 13.*

St. Pan.	C. Fen.	C. Fen.	St. Pan.
AM 2.25g	8.47	AM 7.43r	1.30
9. 0r	2.42	10.27r	4.10
10.25r	3.43	PM 1.18r	7.15
PM 1.50r	7. 7	3.27r	7.55
5. 0r	10.21	7.37	4.20
—	—	—	—
—	—	—	—
—	—	—	—

No Sunday Trains.

g Mondays excepted.
r Restaurant Car.

ANOTHER ROUTE from
King's Cross, 180 miles. Fares, *via* Selby, 37/4a, 22/5c. R. T. for two months, 74/8a, 44/10c. *Via* York, 82/6a, 49/6c.

King's+.	C. Fen.	C. Fen.	King's+
AM 4.45h	10.11	AM 7.54r	1. 5
4.45	10.18	9.10r	1.30
7.15r	11.46	9.31hr	3.50
8.45	3.28	11. 7r	4.30
10.10hr	3.27	PM 2.39r	9.25
11.30hr	5.29	8.55	3.25
PM 1.40r	5.30	10.26	6. 0
1.50r	6.25	—	—
4. 0r	8.34	—	—
10.45e	7.18	—	—

Sunday Trains.

AM 11.30r	7.15	AM 8.43	5.15
PM 10.45	7.18	PM 7.46	6. 0

e Saturdays excepted.
h Via York.
r Restaurant Car.

CHURCHILL (Worcester),
126¼ miles. Fares, 25/3a, 15/2c. R. T. for two months, 50/6a. Departures *from* London as for Kidderminster. Departures *for* London about 4 times daily. Pop. 154. *Map Square 17.*

CHURCH ROAD (Mon-
mouth), 146½ miles. Fares, 30/8a, 18/5c. R. T. for two months, 61/4a, 36/10c. Departures *from* London as for Bargoed. Departures *for* London about 8 times daily. *Map Square 21.*

CHURCH STRETTON
(Salop) from *Euston,* 175 miles, *via* Shrewsbury. Fares, 31/11a, 19/2c. R. T. for two months, 63/10a, 38/4c. Pop. 1,671. *Map Square 17.*

Euston.	C. Stret.	C. Stret.	Euston.
AM 5. 0	10.44	AM 9. 0r	2.20
6.45k	12. 9	10.48r	3.10
6.45	1.34	PM 1.20r	6.15
10.40r	2.46	2.40r	9.20
PM 1.15r	5.50	9.20	5. 0
2.20t	8.38	—	—
4.45r	10. 9	—	—
9.20e	7. 3	—	—

Sunday Trains.

AM 9.15	5.49	AM 11. 5hr	5.45
PM 9.15h	7. 3	PM 9.16h	5. 0
—	—	—	—
—	—	—	—
—	—	—	—

e Saturdays excepted.
h Via Crewe.
k Mondays and Fridays only.
n Noon.
r Restaurant Car.

CHURCH STRETTON
— *continued.*

ANOTHER ROUTE from *Paddington, via* Shrewsbury, 165 miles. Fares as above.

Pad.	C. Stret.	C. Stret.	Pad.
AM 9.10r	1.34	AM 8.14	12.25
10.40r	2.46	9. 0r	1.25
10.45r	4.22	9.50r	2. 5
PM 12.50r	5.50	10.48r	4.15
2.10t	6.40	PM 1.20t	5.55
4.10t	8.38	2. 40r	8. 5
6.10r	10. 9	5.51	10. 0
12.15k	7. 3	9.20	3.30

Sunday Trains.

PM 12.50r	5.49	AM 11. 5r	6.20
—	—	—	—
—	—	—	—

k Saturdays midnight excepted.
r Restaurant Car.
t Tea Car.

ANOTHER ROUTE from *Paddington, via* Gloucester and Hereford, 182¼ miles. Fares as above.

Pad.	C. Stret.	C. Stret.	Pad.
AM 1. 0g	10.48	AM 7. 3r	2.40
5.30	1.20	10.44hr	4.15
10.45	5.51	PM 2.46r	8.45
PM 1.30hr	6.42	6.40	3.30
3.15t	9.20	—	—

Sunday Trains.

AM 10.35h	9.16	—	—
—	—	—	—

g Mondays excepted.
h Via Worcester.
r Restaurant Car.
t Tea Car.

Longmynd Hotel.
Principal Hotel. Highest in elevation. Finest position. Magnificent scenery. Golf, Croquet, Tennis. Central Heated. Electric Lift. Excellent Cuisine and Wines. Garage. Telephone 4. *See advt. p.* 123.

Denehurst Private Hotel.
New Management. Refurnished. Central Heating. Tel. 16. *See advt. p.* 123.

The Hotel.
First-class Hotel at base of Stretton Hills. Nearest Hotel to Golf Links. Every comfort. Large Garage. Appointed A.C. and M.U. Hotel. Telephone, Stretton." Telegrams, "Hotel, Church Stretton."

Sandford House Private
Hotel. Billiards. Tel. 20. A. Manageress.

CHURCHTOWN (Lancs),
214 miles. Fares, 44/0a, 26/5c. R. T. for two months, 88/0a, 52/10c. Departures *from* London as for Southport or Preston. Departures *for* London about 6 times daily. *Map Square 12.*

CHURCH VILLAGE
(Glamorgan), 165 miles. Fares, 34/0a, 20/5c. R.T. for two months, 68/0a, 40/10c. Departures *from* London as for Pontypridd. Departures *for* London about 4 times daily.

CHURSTON (Devon), 204¾

miles. Fares, 42/3*a*, 25/4*c*. R. T. for two months, 84/6*a*. Pop. 135.
Map Square 26.

PAD.	CHURS.	CHURS.	PAD.
AM 5.30	12. 6	AM 8.40*r*	1.30
9.15*r*	2.32	11.45*r*	3.45
12. 0*r*	4. 3	PM 2. 5e*r*	6.50
PM12. 5*r*	5. 7	2.35d*r*	7. 5
2. 0*r*	7. 5	4. 3*r*	9. 0
3.30*r*	8. 7	5. 6	2.45
4.15*r*	9.52	10.46	7.10
12. 0*k*	7.34	—	—
˙12.30*h*	9.11	—	—

Sunday Trains.

AM10.30*r*	3.41	AM10. 2*r*	4. 5
PM 2.40	7.50	PM 2. 5	7. 5
10. 0	7.34	8.31	3.15

h Saturdays midnight only.
k Saturdays midnight excepted.
r Restaurant Car.

CHURWELL (Yorks), 217¼

miles. Fares, 38/2*a*, 22/11*c*. R. T., double fare. Departures *from* London as for Batley. Departures *for* London about 6 times daily. Pop. 525.

CHWILOG (Carnarvon),

265 miles. Fares, 54/5*a*, 32/8*c*. R. T. for two months, 108/10*a*, 65/4*c*. Departures *from* London as for Criccieth. Departures *for* London about 4 times daily.
Map Square 11.

CILFREW (Glamorgan),

193¾ miles. No through fares. Departures *from* London as for Neath or Brecon. Departures *for* London about 4 times daily.

CILFYNYDD (Glamorgan),

161½ miles. No through fares. Departures *from* London as for Pontypridd. Departures *for* London about 4 times daily.

CILMERY (Brecon), 222

miles. Fares, 37/11*a*, 22/9*c*. R. T. for two months, 75/10*a*, 45/6*c*. Departures *from* London as for Builth Road. Departures *for* London about twice daily.
Map Square 16.

CINDERFORD (Glo'ster),

144½ miles. Fares, 30/0*a*, 18/0*c*. R. T. for two months, 60/0*a*, 36/0*c*. Departures *from* London as for Lydney. Departures *for* London about 4 times daily. Pop. 3,399.
Map Square 22.

CIRENCESTER (Glo'ster)

from *Paddington*, 95¼ miles. Fares, 19/2*a*, 11/6*c*. R.T. for two months, 38/4*a*, 23/0*c*. Pop. 7,408.
Map Square 22.

PAD.	CIREN.	CIREN.	PAD.
AM 5.30	8.50	AM 8. 0*r*	10.45
7.30	10. 5	10.10	12.20
9. 0	11.38	PM12.35*r*	2.40
10.45	1.30	2.40	5. 0
PM 1.10*r*	3.58	3.18	6. 2
3.15*t*	5.33	6.20*r*	8.45
4.15*t*	6.55	7.45	10.25
6. 0*r*	8.50	—	—

No Sunday Trains.

r Restaurant Car.
t Tea Car.

CIRENCESTER—*cont.*

ANOTHER ROUTE from

Waterloo, 114½ miles. Fares as above.

W'LOO.	CIREN.	CIREN.	W'LOO.
AM 7.30	12.39	AM11.12	2.36
PM 1. 0*r*	4.35	PM 2.17	6.26
3.30	7.22	3.56*r*	8.30

No Sunday Trains.

r Restaurant Car.

King's Head. First - class

Hunting Establishment. Convenient for V. W. H. (Lord Bathurst's and Mr. Butt Miller's), Duke of Beaufort's, Cotswold and other Packs. Every accommodation. Private Sitting Rooms, Billiard Room. Excellent Stabling. Garage. Terms moderate. Telephone 55. Proprietor, J. T. BROCKMAN.

CITY ROAD (City and

South London Tube). *See* back of Map.

CLACKMANNAN

AND KENNET, 423¼ miles. Fares, 85/0*a*, 51/0*c*. R. T. for two months, 170/0*a*, 102/0*c*. Departures *from* London as for Stirling or Dunfermline. Departures *for* London about 3 times daily. Pop. (Clackmannan) 2,373.
Map Square 40.

CLACTON (Essex) from

Liverpool Street, 69¾ miles. Fares, 15/0*a*, 9/0*c*. R. T. for two months, 30/0*a*, 18/0*c*. Pop. 17,049.
Map Square 24.

L'PL.ST.	CLACT.	CLACT.	L'PL.ST.
AM 5. 0	7.22	AM 6.58*r*	8.52
6.50	10.14	7.40	9.36
8.18	10.35	8. 8*r*	9.53
8.46	12. 2	9.53	11.42
10.23	12.38	11.40*r*	2. 3
10.26d*r*12.18		PM12.30*d*	2.23
11.26*d*	1.47	1.36	3.36
11.30	2. 8	2.55d*r*	4.32
PM12.36	2.37	3.12	5. 5
1.30d*r*	3.23	4.10d*r*	5.52
2. 3*d*	4. 4	4.22	6.32
2.15	4.59	5.42	7.40
3.23	5.22	5.55	9.17
3.26	6.23	7.40	9.36
4.58*r*	6.59	7.55	11.16
5.30*r*	7.10	—	—
5.42	8.17	—	—
6.39	8.32	—	—
7.45*r*	10. 7	—	—
8.45	10.51	—	—
12. 0*d*	1.56	—	—

Sunday Trains.

AM 9. 8	11. 0	AM 8.55	11.38
	9.20*r* 12. 2	PM 5.52	8.25
PM 4.40	6.53	8. 0	10. 9

d Saturdays only.
e Saturdays excepted.
r Restaurant Car.

Grand Hotel, Southcliff. 140

Rooms. Leading hotel. Facing Sea. Ballroom and Winter Garden added. Extensive Grounds. Croquet. Tennis. 18 Golf Course near. Tel. 86; Telegr. "Grand." F. F. CORRIGAN, Manager.
See advt. p. 124.

CLACTON—*continued.*

Grosvenor Court Private

Hotel. Facing Sea. Extensive Grounds. Magnificent Lounge. Two Tennis Courts. Billiard Room. Tel. 60. Mr. and Mrs. PERCY R. CLEMENTS, Proprietors.
See advt. p. 125.

Glengarry Boarding Es-

tablishment. Finest Position. Facing Sea. Marine Parade. Southcliff. Visitors' comfort studied. Separate tables. 'Phone and Electric Light. Proprietress, Mrs. POTTER.
See advt. p. 125.

Rosebank, Marine Parade.

Old-Established Boarding House. 'Phone 123. Proprietress— Mrs. F. M. COOPER.
See advt. p. 125.

The Bedford Private Hotel.

Every convenience and comfort for visitors.
See advt. p. 123.

Royal Hotel. Opposite Pier

and Bandstand. Redecorated. New and Comfortable Lounges. Central Heating throughout. Lock-up Garage. Billiards. Nearest Golf Links. Excellent Cuisine. Moderate Tariff. Week-end Terms. Telephone 15. Apply MANAGER.

Brunswick Hotel and Res-

taurant. Family and Commercial. Recently enlarged. Perfect sanitation. Central Sea View. Parties catered for. Tariff, &c., of ARTHUR SWANN, Proprietor.

Beaumont Hall Hotel.

Marine Parade. Facing South and Sea. Separate Tables. Billiards. Tennis. Croquet. Bow's. Electric Light. 'Phone 80. Tariff. C. L. BEAUMONT.

Ramsey Private Hotel,

Marine Parade, facing Sea, due South. Finest position. Smoking Lounge. Electric Light throughout. 'Phone 169. Tariff. Misses BELLAMY.

Glengariff Private Hotel.

Delightfully situated. Overlooking Sea and Links. Croquet Lawns. Billiards. Illustrated tariff. Telephone 156. Misses GRAY.

Central Hotel and Restau-

rant. 30 Bedrooms. Sea View. Electric Light. Large and small parties catered for. Tariff, &c. 'Phone 137. Proprietors, J. and E. WILSTON

Haroldene Boarding

Establishment, Southcliff. Splendid position. Close Pier. Shops, Amusements. Excellent Cuisine. Every comfort. Open all year. Telephone 218. Under Personal Supervision. Proprietress— Mrs. CLIVE PARSONS.

"Wellesley" Boarding Es-

tablishment, Marine Parade. Splendid position ; uninterrupted Sea View. ♦ Excellent Cuisine. Every Comfort. Separate Tables. Hot and Cold Bath. Moderate Terms. Under new management. E. NEWSON, Proprietor.

CLACTON—*continued.*

Shakespere Lodge, Carnarvon Road. Board residence. Two minutes Sea and Station. Late Dinners. Separate Tables. Excellent Cooking. 'Phone 27. Mrs. WESTAWAY, Proprietress.

"Mendip" Boarding Establishment, Carnarvon Road. Minute Sea, Bathing Châlet, and Station. Excellent Cooking. Late Dinners. Separate Tables. Only Establishment with Sea-water Bath. Proprietors—Mr. and Mrs. G. H. WATTS.

Wheatcroft Hotel. Private Residential. Three minutes sea and links. First-class cuisine. 'Phone 148. Proprietor—W. H. TUCKER. (Late Queen's, Frinton.)

"Hadleigh" Private Hotel and Boarding Establishment. Marine Parade. Facing Sea. Close Bandstand. Separate Tables. Excellent Cuisine. Moderate Tariff. Telephone 19.

"Sylvamere" Southcliff. Magnificent position; invigorating ozone; close Sea and Grand Hotel. Spacious Bedrooms. Extensive grounds; rose garden; tennis, croquet. Specialité Electric cuisine. Separate tables. Moderate Terms. Illustrated Tariff. Telephone 34.

Montague Private Hotel. Facing Sea, Pier and Bandstand. Separate Tables. Central Heating. Under New Management. 'Phone 48. Misses MAIN.

Harpsden Court, Carnarvon Road. First-class Boarding Establishment. Close to Pier and Amusements. Separate Tables. Smoking Lounge. Tariff—C. TAYLOR.

House Agent, Auctioneer, &c. Ernest Johnson, 42, Station Road. 20 years' local experience. Free Lists. Furnished and Unfurnished Houses, Land, Businesses, &c. Telephone 74.

House Agents. The oldest established firm of Auctioneers and House Agents in Clacton and Frinton. Lists of Furnished Houses and Properties to be Let or Sold. EDWIN J. GILDERS & CO.

CLANDON (Surrey)

from *Waterloo*, 25¼ miles. Fares, 5/5*a*, 3/3*c*. R.T. for two months, 10/10*a*, 6/6*c*. Pop. 759.
Map Square 23.

W'LOO.	CLANDON	CLANDON	W'LOO.
AM 6. 5	7. 4	AM 7. 6	8.19
7. 5	8. 5	7.27	8.30
8. 5	9. 4	7.49	8.48
9. 5	10. 4	8.21	9.21
10. 5	11. 7	9. 1	10. 0
11. 5	12. 4	9.39*e*	10.36
PM12. 5	1. 4	10. 9	11. 6
1. 5	2. 4	10.59	11.56
1.35*d*	2.34	PM12. 3	1. 0
2. 5	3. 4	1. 5	2. 2
3. 5	4. 4	2. 3	3. 0
4. 5	5. 4	3. 3	4. 0
5. 5	6. 4	4. 3	5. 0
5.37*e*	6.36	5.13	6.10
6. 5	7. 4	5.54	6.52
6.38*e*	7.36	7. 3	8. 0
7. 5	8. 4	8. 3	9. 0
8. 5	9.10	9. 3	10. 0
9. 5	10. 4	9.59	10.56
10. 5	11. 4	—	—
—	—	—	—
—	—	—	—

CLANDON—*continued.*

Sunday Trains.

W'LOO.	CLANDON.	CLANDON.	W'LOO.
AM 8.38	9.46	AM 9.54	10.55
10. 8	11.14	10.53	11.55
11. 8	12.14	11.53	12.55
PM12. 8	1.14	PM12.53	1.55
1. 8	2.14	1.53	2.55
2. 8	3.14	3.53	4.55
3. 8	4.14	5.53	6.55
5. 8	6.14	6.53	7.55
6. 8	7.14	8. 3	9. 5
7. 8	8.14	8.53	9.55
8. 8	9.14	9.53	10.55
9. 8	10.14	—	—
—	—	—	—

d Saturdays only.
e Saturdays excepted.

CLAPHAM (London)

from *London Bridge*, 6¼ miles, and *Victoria*, 2¼ miles, by L.B. & S.C.R. Fares from Victoria, 0/5*a*, 0/3*c*. R.T. for two days, 0/10*a*, 0/6*c*. Fares from London Bridge, 0/7*a*, 0/4½*c*. R. T. for two days, 1/0*a*, 0/9*c*. Pop. 60,540. *See* p. 570.
Map Square 69.

CLAPHAM COMMON

(City and South London Tube). *See* back of Map.

CLAPHAM JUNCTION

from *Victoria*, 2¾ miles. Fares, 0/5*a*, 0/3*c*. R. T. for two days, 0/10*a*, 0/6*c*. *See* pp. 571-580.
Map Squares 23 *and* 69.

From *Waterloo*, 4 miles. Fares, 0/5*a*, 0/3*c*. R.T. for two days, 0/10*a*, 0/6*c*. *See* pp. 583-595.

From *London Bridge*, *via* Tulse Hill, 10¼ miles. Fares, 1/3*a*, 0/9*c*. R. T. for two days, 2/6*a*, 1/4*c*; *via* Crystal Palace, 1/6*a*, 0/10½*c*. R. T. for eight days, 3/0*a*, 1/9*c*. *See* pp. 567, 568.

From *Kensington* (Addison Road), 3¼ miles. Fares, 0/9½*a*, 0/5½*c*. R.T. for two days, 1/5*a*, 0/9*c*. *See* p. 583.

CLAPHAM ROAD

(City and South London Tube). *See* back of Map.

CLAPHAM (Yorks)

242 miles. Fares, 46/11*a*, 28/2*c*. R.T., double fare. Departures *from* London as for Giggleswick. Departures *for* London about 5 times daily. Pop. 671.
Map Square 7.

CLAPTON

from *Liverpool Street*, 4 miles. Fares, 0/7½*a*, 0/6*c*, 0/4½*c*. R. T. for two days, 1/2*a*, 0/10½*b*, 0/7*c*. *See* pp. 523-524, 526-527.
Map Square 52.

CLARBESTON ROAD

(Pembroke), 253 miles. Fares, 50/0*a*, 30/0*c*. R.T. for two months, 100/0*a*. Departures *from* London as for Clynderwen. Departures *for* London about 3 times daily. Pop. 151.
Map Square 20.

CLARE (Suffolk)

from *Liverpool Street*, *via* Bishop's Stortford, 62½ miles. Fares, 13/2*a*, 7/11*c*. R.T. for two months, 26/4*a*. Pop. 1,483.
Map Square 19.

L'POOL ST.	CLARE	CLARE	L'POOL ST.
AM 5.50	9.37	AM 7. 8	9.27
8.30	11.35	10.10	12.40
11.50	2. 1	PM12.13*d*	3.18
PM 2.48	5.58	12.13*l*	4. 2*h*
5.49	8.17	12.13*e*	5. 9
—	—	4.46	7.58
—	—	7. 7	10.30

No Sunday Trains.
d Saturdays only.
e Saturdays excepted.
h Arrives at St. Pancras Station.
l Commencing July 23.

CLARE—(*continued.*)

ANOTHER ROUTE from *Liverpool Street*, *via* Marks Tey, 68 miles. Fares as above.

L'POOL ST.	CLARE	CLARE	L'POOL ST.
AM 6.50	10.10	AM 9.37	11.42
10. 0	12.13	11.35*h*	2. 3
PM 2.15	4.46	PM 2. 1*h*	5. 5
4.58	7. 6	5.58	9.17

No Sunday Trains.
h *Via* Colchester.

CLARKSTON (for Eaglesham)

(Lanark) from *Euston*, 424 miles. Fares, 82/6*a*, 49/6*c*. R. T. for two months, 165/0*a*, 99/0*c*. Departures *from* London as for Hamilton. Departures *for* London about 5 times daily. Pop. 5,383.
Map Square 40.

CLATFORD (Hants)

69 miles. Fares, 14/4*a*, 8/7*c*. R.T. for two months, 28/8*a*, 17/2*c*. Departures *from* London as for Andover Junction. Departures *for* London about 4 times daily.
Map Square 22.

CLAVERDON (Warwick)

95¾ miles. Fares, 19/10*a*, 11/11*c*. R. T. for two months, 39/8*a*, 23/10*c*. Departures *from* London as for Bearley. Departures *for* London about 6 times daily. Pop. 520.
Map Square 17.

CLAXBY (Lincoln)

147½ miles. Fares, 30/8*a*, 18/5*c*. R.T., double fare. Departures *from* London as for Lincoln. Departures *for* London about 4 times daily. Pop. 202.
Map Square 13.
Station closed on Sundays.

CLAYCROSS (Derby)

from *St. Pancras*, 142¼ miles. Fares, 29/4*a*, 17/7*c*. R.T., double fare. Departures *from* London as for Alfreton or Derby. Departures *for* London about 5 times daily. Pop. 8,685.
Map Square 13.

CLAYDON (Bucks)

from *Euston*, 57½ miles. Fares, 10/3*a*, 6/2*c*. R. T., double fare. Departures *from* London as for Verney. Departures *for* London about 5 times daily.
Map Square 18.

CLAYDON (Suffolk)

from *Liverpool Street*, 73¾ miles. Fares, 15/7*a*, 9/4*c*. R.T. for two months, 31/2*a*. Pop. 556.
Map Square 19.

L'PL ST.	CL'YD'N.	CL'YD'N.	L'P'L ST.
AM 5. 0	9.11	AM 8.27*r*	10.30
8.15*r*	10.24	9.17*r*	11.22
10.12	12.19	PM12. 4*r*	2. 3
PM12.33*r*	2.33	12.56	3.36
1. 0	4.34	3.40	5.56
1.33*d*	4.34	4.17	6.32
3.10*r*	4.59	5.29	7.51
3.26	6.25	6.23*r*	9.22
5.18*r*	7.21	8.37	11.16
5.42	8.26	—	—
7.45*r*	10. 3	—	—
—	—	—	—

Sunday Trains.

AM 9.20*r*	11.41	AM 8.59	11.38
11.30*r*	2.36	PM 2.46	7.10
PM 4.40	6.37	7. 1*r*	9.10
—	—	7.58	10.15

d Saturdays only.
r Restaurant Car.

"SUNNY CLACTON."—ROYAL HOTEL. See advertisement under Train Service.

CLAYGATE (Surrey)

from *Waterloo*, 15¼ miles. Fares, 2/9*a*, 1/8*c*. R. T. for eight days, 5/6*a*, 3/4*c*. Pop. 2,862.
Map Square 23.

W'LOO.	CLAYG.	CLAYG.	W'LOO.
AM 6. 5	6.34	AM 6.46	7.17
7. 5	7.34	7.57	8.30
8. 5	8.34	8.17	8.48
9. 5	9.34	8.51	9.21
10. 5	10.34	9.31	10. 0
11. 5	11.34	10. 7*e*	10.36
PM12. 5	12.34	10.37	11. 6
1. 5	1.34	11.27	11.56
1.35*d*	2. 4	PM12.31	1. 0
2. 5	2.34	1.33	2. 2
3. 5	3.34	2.31	3. 0
4. 5	4.34	3.31	4. 0
5. 5	5.34	4.31	5. 0
5.37*e*	6. 6	5.41	6.10
6. 5	6.34	6.23	6.52
6.38*e*	7. 6	7.31	8. 0
7. 5	7.34	8.31	9. 0
8. 5	8.35	9.31	10. 0
9. 5	9.34	10.27	10.56
10. 5	10.34	—	—
11.35	12. 4	—	—
—	—	—	—
—	—	—	—

Sunday Trains.

AM 8.38	9.16	AM10.21	10.55
10. 8	10.44	11.20	11.55
11. 8	11.44	PM12.20	12.55
PM12. 8	12.44	1.20	1.55
1. 8	1.44	2.20	2.55
2. 8	2.44	4.20	4.55
3. 8	3.44	6.20	6.55
5. 8	5.44	7.20	7.55
6. 8	6.44	8.30	9. 5
7. 8	7.44	9.20	9.55
8. 8	8.44	10.20	10.55
9. 8	9.44	—	—
—	—	—	—

d Saturdays only.
e Saturdays excepted.

CLAYPOLE (Lincoln)

from *King's Cross*, 115½ miles. Fares, 24/0*a*, 14/5*c*. R. T. double fare. Pop. 494.
Map Square 13.

KING'S+	CLAYPLE.	CLAYPLE.	KING'S+
AM 5. 5	8.58	AM 7.58	10.40
10.10*r*	12.40	10.23	1. 5
PM 1.50*r*	4.30	PM 3.44*r*	6.30
4. 0*r*	6.40	8. 4	3.25
—	—	—	—
—	—	—	—

Sunday Trains.

AM 8.30	12.43	PM 3.50	8. 8
—	—	—	—
—	—	—	—

r Restaurant Car.

CLAYTON (Yorks)

194¾ miles. Fares, 39/9*a*, 23/10*c*. R. T., double fare. Departures *from* London as for Bradford. Departures *for* London about 8 times daily. Pop. 5,040.
Map Square 12.

CLAYTON WEST

(Yorks), 186¾ miles. Fares, 37/9*a*, 22/8*c*. R.T., double fare. Departures *from* London as for Penistone. Departures *for* London about 6 times daily. Pop. 1,983.
Map Square 12.

CLEATOR MOOR

(Cumberland), 300¾ miles. Fares, 62/6*a*, 37/6*c*. R. T. for two months, 125/0*a*. Departures *from* London as for Moor Row. Departures *for* London about 6 times daily. Pop. 8,299.
Map Square 6.

CLECKHEATON (Yorks)

from *King's Cross*, *via* Horbury 187 miles. Fares 38/11*a*, 23/4*c*. R. T., double fare. Pop. 12,866.
Map Square 12.

KING'S+	CLECKTN.	CLECKTN	KING'S+
AM 4.45	11. 7	AM 6.10*r*	11.30
7.15*r*	12.54	8. 4*r*	1. 5
10.10*dr*	3.10	9.27*r*	1.55
10.10*er*	3.40	10. 7	3.50
PM 1.30*r*	6. 2	10.59*r*	4.45
1.50*r*	8.15	11.46	5. 0
5.45*r*	9.51	PM 1.51*r*	7.10
—	—	4.30*r*	9.25
—	—	8.40*e*	3.25

Sunday Trains.

12. 0/*n*	6.54	AM 9.26*r*	3.45
—	—	PM 2.17*h*	10.20
—	—	—	—
—	—	—	—

d Saturdays only.
e Saturdays excepted.
h Passengers cross Wakefield at own expense.
n Noon.
r Restaurant Car.

CLEETHORPES (Lincoln)

from *King's Cross*, 157¾ miles. Fares, 32/9*a*, 19/8*c*. R. T. for two months, 65/6*a*, 39/4*c*. Pop. 28,160.
Map Square 13.

KING'S+	CLEETH.	CLEETH.	KING'S+
AM 4.45	10.33	AM 5.30*r*	11.30
7.15*r*	12.15	8.32*r*	1. 5
10.10*r*	4.51	PM12.59	6.25
PM 1.50*r*	6.27	2.20	9. 0
4. 0*r*	9.31	6.45	3.25
8.25*e*	5.59	—	—
—	—	—	—

Sunday Trains.

PM 5. 0	10.15	AM 8.45*r*	3.45
8.25	5.59	PM 4.30*r*	10.20
—	—	—	—
—	—	—	—

e Saturdays excepted.
r Restaurant Car.

ANOTHER ROUTE

from *Marylebone*, 222¾ miles. Fares as above.

M'BONE.	CLEETH.	CLEETH	M'BONE.
AM 2.32	10.33	AM 5.30*r*	1.13
10. 0*r*	4.51	8.32*r*	3. 0
PM12.15*r*	6.27	PM12.39*r*	6.38
3.20*r*	9.31	4. 0*r*	9.55
10. 0*d*	6.26	6.45	3.57
10. 5*e*	5.59	—	—
—	—	—	—

Sunday Trains.

AM11.15*r*	10.15	AM 8.45*r*	5.40
—	—	—	—
—	—	—	—

d Saturdays only.
e Saturdays excepted.
r Restaurant Car.

CLEEVE (Gloucester)

121¼ miles. No through fares. Departures *from* London as for Evesham. Departures *for* London about 3 times daily. Pop. 260.
Map Square 17.

CLEGHORN (Lanark)

375¼ miles. No through fares. Departures *from* London as for Carstairs. Departures *for* London about twice daily.
Map Square 40.

CLELAND (Lanark)

388¾ miles. No through fares. Departures *from* London as for Wishaw (Central). Departures *for* London about 4 times daily.
Map Square 40.

CLENCHWARTON

(Norfolk) from *King's Cross*, 109¾ miles. Fares, 20/2*a*, 12/1*c*. R. T. for two months, 40/4*a*. Departures *from* London as for Terrington. Departures *for* London about 5 times daily. Pop. 628.
Map Square 19.

CLEOBURY MORTIMER

(Salop), from *Paddington*, 143½ miles. Fares, 27/6*a*, 16/6*c*. R. T. for two months, 55/0*a*. Pop. 1,531.
Map Square 17.

PAD.	CL. M.	CL. M.	PAD.
AM10.40*l*	2.29	AM 7.40*k*	11.15
PM 1.30*r*	5.10	9.17*lr*	1.25
2.10*lt*	6.31	PM12.38*r*	4.15
4.45*kt*	8.22	4.33*r*	9.15
12.15*hl*	9.16	7.25*l*	3.30
—	—	9.19*kl*	3.30
—	—	—	—
—	—	—	—

No Sunday Trains.

h Saturdays midnight excepted.
k Thursdays only.
l Via Birmingham.
r Restaurant Car.
t Tea Car.

CLEOBURY TOWN

(Salop), 145½ miles. No through fares. Departures *from* London as for Cleobury Mortimer. Departures *for* London about twice daily.

CLEVEDON (Somerset)

from *Paddington*, 133 miles. Fares, 27/9*a*, 16/8*c*. R. T. for two months, 55/6*a*, 33/4*c*. Pop. 6,726.
Map Square 22.

PAD.	CLEVE.	CLEVE.	PAD.
AM 5.30	10.20	AM 6.50*r*	10.15
7.30	10.56	7.50	11.30
8.45	11.55	8.48	12.20
9. 0	1.11	11.15*r*	2. 0
11.15*r*	2.20	PM12.35	4. 5
PM 1. 0*r*	4.13	2.27	6. 2
1.10*dr*	5.30	4.19*r*	7. 0
1.10*er*	5.43	5. 0*r*	8.45
2.45	6.53	6.25	10.25
4.15*r*	7.33	10. 5	2.45
5.15	9.18	—	—
6.30*r*	9.44	—	—
12. 0*k*	7.33	—	—
—	—	—	—

Sunday Trains.

PM12.30*r*	6.18	PM 7.50	3.15
10. 0	7.33	—	—

d Saturdays only.
e Saturdays excepted.
k Saturdays midnight excepted.
r Restaurant Car.

Tresco Boarding House, Albert Road. Highly recommended. Close Sea. Large airy rooms. Gas-fires in all bedrooms. Misses CULVERWELL.

CLEVEDON—continued.

Stancliff Boarding Establishment. Standing high. Overlooking Bristol Channel and Welsh hills. Special terms winter months. Telephone 4. Telegrams. Stancliffe. PROPRIETRESS.

"The Cliffe Hotel," Wellington Terrace. Delightfully situated in own grounds extending to the sea. New Proprietorship. Renovated and Reorganised. Near Golf Links. Illustrated Tariff. Telehone 101. MANAGERESS.

CLIBURN (Westmorland),
281¼ miles. No through fares. Departures *from* London as for Penrith. Departures *for* London about 4 times daily. Pop. 197. *Map Square* 7.

CLIFF COMMON
(Yorks), 177½ miles. Fares, 35/8*a*, 21/5*c*. R. T., double fare. Departures *from* London as for Selby. Departures *for* London about 5 times daily. *Map Square* 13.

CLIFFE (Kent) from *Charing Cross, Cannon Street,* and *London Bridge,* 30½ miles. Fares, 6/5*a*, 5/1*b*, 3/10*c*. R. T. for two months, 12/10*a*, 10/2*b*. Pop. 2,581. *Map Square* 24.

	Leave		Arr. at
Char. +	Can. St.	Lon. B.	Cliffe
AM 5.18	—	5.25	7.11
—	6.20	6.23	7.55
9.32	—	9.41	11. 2
PM 1.20*e*	—	1.27*e*	2.46
1.26*d*	—	1.34*d*	2.46
4.25*d*	—	4.31*d*	5.56
—	4.36*e*	4.39*e*	5.56
6.55*d*	—	7. 1*d*	8.25
—	7. 8*e*	7.11*e*	8.25
8.40*d*	—	8.48*d*	10.18
—	—	—	—
—	—	—	—
—	—	—	—

Sunday Trains.
AM 9.46	—	9.52	11.20
PM 1.15	—	1.22	2.55
4.50	—	4.57	6.26

Trains from Cliffe.
Leave		Arrive at	
Cliffe	Lon. B.	Can. St.	Char. +
AM 8.16	9.34	—	9.43
9.22	10.38	—	10.45
PM 1.37*e*	2.53	—	5. 4
*d*1.37*k*	3.21	3.26	—
4. 2*e*	5.36	5.40	—
4. 2*d*	5.37	—	5.44
6.17	7.14	—	7.23
7.16*d*	9. 6	9.11	—
9.34	10.51	—	10.59
10.50*d*	12.35	—	12.45
—	—	—	—
—	—	—	—

Sunday Trains.
AM 8.43	10.16	—	10.24
PM12.45	2.14	—	2.24
5.28	6.49	—	6.59
7.38	9.45	—	9.54
—	—	—	—

d Saturdays only.
e Saturdays excepted.
k Third class only.

CLIFFORD (Hereford),170¾
miles. Fares, 34/10*a*, 20/11*c*. R. T. for two months, 69/8*a*, 41/10*c*. Departures *from* London as for Abbeydore. Departures *for* London about 3 times daily. Pop. 436. *Map Square* 16.

CLIFTON (Derby), 145¾
miles. Fares, 30/3*a*, 18/2*c*. R. T. for two months, 60/6*a*, 36/4*c*. Departures *from* London as for Ashbourne. Departures *for* London about 4 minutes later. Pop. 570. *Map Square* 12.

CLIFTON (Westmorland),
278½ miles. No through fares. Departures *from* London as for Penrith. Departures *for* London about 4 times daily. Pop. 352. *Map Square* 7.

CLIFTON & LOWTHER (Westmorland), 277 miles. Fares, 55/8*a*, 33/5*c*. R. T. for two months, 111/4*a*, 66/10*c*. Departures *from* London as for Tebay. Departures *for* London about 4 times daily. Pop. (Lowther) 415. *Map Square* 7.

CLIFTON BRIDGE
(Somerset),120¼ miles. Fares, 25/3*a*, 15/2*c*. R. T. for two months, 50/6*a*. Departures *from* London as for Portishead. Departures *for* London about 6 times daily. *Map Square* 22.

CLIFTON DOWN (Gloster), 121 miles. Fares, 25/0*a*, 15/0*c*. R. T. for two months, 50/0*a*. Departures *from* London as for Avonmouth Docks. Departures *for* London about 8 times daily. Pop. 15,968. *Map Square* 22.

Royal Hotel, College Green, Bristol. First-class Family Hotel. Fitted with every modern convenience. Telegraphic address: "Banquet." *See advt. p.* 109.

Tudor Hall (En Pension), Pembroke Road. Detached Residence. Croquet and Tennis. Bathrooms. Electric light. Central. Terms moderate. Telephone 4265. PROPRIETRESS.

CLIFTON JUNCTION
(Lancs), 191½ miles. No through fares. Departures *from* London as for Manchester. Departures *for* London about 6 times daily. Pop. 2,743. *Map Square* 12.

CLIFTON MILL (Warwick) from *Euston,* 83½ miles. Fares, 17/4*a*, 10/5*c*. R. T. for two months, 34/8*a*. Departures *from* London as for Yelvertoft. Departures *for* London about 4 times daily. Pop. 627. *Map Square* 18.

CLIFTON-ON-TRENT
(Notts), 138 miles. Fares, 27/4*a*, 16/5*c*. R. T., double fare. Departures *from* London as for Lincoln or Edwinstowe. Departures *for* London about 4 times daily. Pop. 408. *Map Square* 13.

CLIPSTON(Northampton)
. from *Euston,* 80½ miles. Fares, 16/8*a*, 10/0*c*. R. T. for two months, 33/4*a*. Departures *from* London as for Lamport. Departures *for* London about 5 times daily. Pop. 497. *Map Square* 18.

CLITHEROE (Lancs)
from *Euston. Via* Manchester, 222 miles. Fares, *via* Boar's Head or Manchester, 43/9*a*, 26/3*c*. R. T. for two months, 87/6*a*, 52/6*c*. *Via* Preston, 43/9*a*, 26/3*c*. R. T. for two months, 87/6*a*, 52/6*c*. Pop. 12,204. *Map Square* 12.

Euston	Clith	Clith.	Euston
AM12.29	7.22	AM 7. 4	1.15
2.35*h*	10.11	7.30*r*	1.45
5. 0	12.53	8. 6*r*	3.10
6.45	2.39	9.53*r*	3.55
8.45*r*	3.27	11.33*ht*	6. 0
10.40*r*	4.17	PM 1.25*hr*	7.30
11.35*k*	5.15	2.30*er*	9. 5
11.50*er*	6. 6	2.30*dr*	9.15
PM 1.30*kr*	7.16	3.52*r*	10. 0
1.30*er*	7.37	5. 6*hr*	10.45
2.50*r*	9. 8	9.16*h*	5. 0
5.20*r*	11. 6	—	—
6. 5*r*	11.48	—	—
9.20*e*	6.32	—	—
11.55*d*	9.58	—	—
—	—	—	—

Sunday Trains.
PM12.10*r*	7. 7	AM 7.21*r*	4. 0
12.30*r*	8.59	PM 1.30*hr*	8.55
9.15	6.32	8.37	5. 0
—	—	—	—

d Saturdays only.
e Saturdays excepted.
h Via Preston.
k Tuesdays and Fridays only.
r Restaurant Car.
t Tea Car.

CLOCK FACE(Lancs),195½
miles. Fares, 39/7*a*, 23/9*c*. R. T. for two months, 79/2*a*, 47/6*c*. Departures *from* London as for Runcorn or Warrington (Bank Quay). Departures *for* London about 6 times daily. *Map Square* 12.

CLOCK HOUSE (Kent)
from *Charing Cross, Cannon Street,* and *London Bridge,* 11 miles. Fares, 1/8*a*, 1/4*b*, 1/0*c*. R. T. for two days, 3/4*a*, 2/8*b*, 2/0*c*. *See* pp. 544-55*c*. *Map Square* 79.

CLOCKSBRIGGS
(Forfar) 484½ miles. Fares, 96/8*a*, 58/0*c*. R. T. for two months, 193/4*a*, 116/0*c*. Departures *from* London as for Forfar. Departures *for* London about 3 times daily. *Map Square* 38.

CLOSEBURN (Dumfries),
343½ miles. Fares, 69/9*a*, 41/10*c*. R. T. for two months, 139/6*a*, 83/8*c*. Departures *from* London as for Dumfries. Departures *for* London about 3 times daily. Pop. 990. *Map Square* 43.

CLOUGH FOLD (Lancs), 205½ miles. Fares, 41/10*a*, 25/1*c*. R. T. for two months, 83/8*a*, 50/2*c*. Departures *from* London as for Bacup. Departures *for* London about 8 times daily. Pop. 3,110.
Map Square 12

CLOUGHTON (Yorks), 234½ miles. Fares, 49/0*a*, 29/5*c*. R. T. *for* two months 98/0*a*, 58/10*c*. Departures *from* London as for Ravenscar. Departures *for* London about 4 times daily. Pop. 541.
Map Square 8.

CLOVENFORDS (Selkirk), 367 miles. No through fares. Departures *from* London as for Galashiels. Departures *for* London about 3 times daily.
Map Square 41.

CLOWN (Derby), 152½ miles. Fares, 30/5*a*, 18/3*c*. R. T., double fare. Departures *from* London as for Mansfield. Departures *for* London about 4 times daily. Pop. 6,037.
Map Square 13.

CLUNES (Inverness), 575¼ miles. No through fares. Departures *from* London as for Inverness. Departures *for* London about twice daily.
Map Square 34.

CLUTTON (Somerset), from *Paddington* 113½ miles. Fares, 24/0*a*, 14/5*c*. R. T. for two months, 48/0*a*. Departures *from* London as for Midsomer Norton. Departures *for* London about 4 times daily. Pop. 1,341.
Map Square 22.

CLYDACH (Brecon), 167 miles. Fares, 33/9*a*, 20/3*c*. R. T. for two months, 67/6*a*, 40/6*c*. Departures *from* London as for Abergavenny. Departures *for* London about 4 times daily.
Map Square 21.

CLYDACH-ON-TAWE (Glamorgan), 204 miles. No through fares. Departures *from* London as for Swansea. Departures *for* London about 4 times daily. Pop. 7,707.

CLYNDERWEN (Carmarthen) from *Paddington*, 246½ miles. Fares, 50/0*a*, 30/0*c*. R. T. for two months, 100/0*a*.
Map Square 20.

PAD.	CLYND.	CLYND.	PAD.
AM 1. 0*g*	10.53	AM 8.16*r*	2.30
8.45*r*	2.37	8.58*r*	4.20
11.50*r*	6. 3	11.43*r*	6.15
PM 1.10*r*	8.31	PM 1.26*r*	8.35
5. 0*r*	10.56	3. 5*r*	9.25
9.15	6. 1	7.16	3.30

Sunday Trains.

PM 9.15	6. 1	PM 7.21	3.30
—	—	—	—

g Mondays excepted.
r Restaurant Car.

COALBROOKDALE (Salop), 143 miles. Fares, 29/10*a*, 17/11*c*. R. T. for two months, 59/8*a*. Departures *from* London as for Ketley. Departures *for* London about 6 times daily. Pop. 1,524.
Map Square 17.

COALBURN (Lanark), 389¼ miles. Fares, 81/5*a*, 48/10*c*. R. T. for two months, 162/10*a*, 97/8*c*. Departures *from* London as for Hamilton. Departures *for* London about 4 times daily.
Map Square 40.

COALEY JUNCTION (Gloucester), 126½ miles. No through fares. Departures *from* London as for Gloucester. Departures *for* London about 4 times daily. Pop. 673.
Map Square 22.

COALPIT HEATH (Gloucester), 108½ miles. Fares, 22/8*a*, 13/7*c*. R. T. for two months, 45/4*a*. Departures *from* London as for Chipping Sodbury. Departures *for* London about 4 times daily. Pop. 1,818.

COALPORT (Salop), 159 miles. Fares, 30/3*a*, 18/2*c*. R. T. for two months, 60/6*a*. Departures *from* London as for Bridgnorth. Departures *for* London about 4 times daily.
Map Square 17.

COALVILLE (Leicester) from *St. Pancras*, 113 miles. Fares, 22/11*a*, 13/9*c*. R. T., double fare. Pop. 20,468.
Map Square 13.

ST. PAN.	COAL.	COAL.	ST. PAN.
AM 2.25	7.45	AM 7. 0*r*	9.57
4.25	9.55	7.52*r*	11. 0
9.50*dr*	12.56	8.53*r*	11.35
10.25*r*	1.12	PM 12. 2	3.25
PM 12.25*r*	3.30	1.17*dr*	4.20
2.25*r*	5.21	2. 1*r*	5.45
3.30*r*	7. 2	4. 6*r*	6.35
4.25*r*	7.22	6.28*r*	9.15
6.25*r*	8.59	9.38	4.20
—	—	—	—

Sunday Trains.

PM 6.15*r*	9.25	AM 8. 0	11.53
—	—	PM 6.30*r*	9.52
—	—	—	—
—	—	—	—
—	—	—	—

d Saturdays only.
r Restaurant Car.

COANWOOD (Northumberland), 307½ miles. No through fares. Departures *from* London as for Hexham or Carlisle. Departures *for* London about 3 times daily. Pop. 94.
Map Square 3.

COATBRIDGE (Lanark) from *Euston*, 393½ miles. Fares, 80/3*a*, 48/2*c*. R. T. for two months, 160/6*a*, 96/4*c*.
Pop. 43,909.
Map Square 40.

EUSTON	COATBDGE	COATBDGE	EUSTON
AM 5. 0	3.49	AM 9.55*r*	6.25
10. 0*r*	6.25	10.36*r*	7.30
PM 1.30*r*	11. 6	PM 1.51*r*	10.45
11. 0*d*	8.10	5. 0*r*	5. 0
11.35*h*	7.47	10.48	7.40
11.35*e*	7.58	—	—
—	—	—	—
—	—	—	—

Sunday Trains.

PM 11.35*h*	7.47	—	—
11.35	7.58	—	—
—	—	—	—

d Saturdays only.
e Saturdays excepted.
h Calls to set down sleeping saloon passengers only.
r Restaurant Car.

COATDYKE (Lanark), 426¾ miles. No through fares. Departures *from* London as for Edinburgh (Waverley). Departures *for* London about 4 times daily. Pop. 6,119.

COBBINSHAW (Midlothian), 381½ miles. No through fares. Departures *from* London as for Carstairs. Departures *for* London about 3 times daily.

COBHAM (Surrey) from *Waterloo*, 19 miles. Fares, 4/0*a*, 2/5*c*. R. T. for eight days, 8/0*a*, 4/10*c*. Pop. 5,103.

W'LOO.	COBHAM	COBHAM	W'LOO.
AM 6. 5	6.45	AM 6.35	7.17
7. 5	7.46	7.46	8.30
8. 5	8.45	8. 6	8.43
9. 5	9.45	8.39	9.21
10. 5	10.47	9.19	10. 0
11. 5	11.45	9.56*e*	10.36
PM 12. 5	12.45	10.26	11. 6
1. 5	1.45	11.16	11.56
1.35*d*	2.15	PM 12.20	1. 0
2. 5	2.45	1.22	2. 2
3. 5	3.45	2.20	3. 0
4. 5	4.45	3.20	4. 0
5. 5	5.45	4.20	5. 0
5.37*e*	6.17	5.30	6.10
6. 5	6.45	6.11	6.52
6.38*e*	7.17	7.20	8. 0
7. 5	7.45	8.20	9. 0
8. 5	8.51	9.20	10. 0
9. 5	9.45	10.16	10.56
10. 5	10.45	—	—
11.35	12.15	—	—
—	—	—	—
—	—	—	—
—	—	—	—
—	—	—	—
—	—	—	—
—	—	—	—
—	—	—	—
—	—	—	—

Sunday Trains.

AM 8.38	9.27	AM 10.11	10.55
10. 8	10.55	11.10	11.55
11. 8	11.55	PM 12.10	12.55
PM 12. 8	12.55	1.10	1.55
1. 8	1.55	2.10	2.55
2. 8	2.55	4.10	4.55
3. 8	3.55	6.10	6.55
5. 8	5.55	7.10	7.55
6. 8	6.55	8.20	9. 5
7. 8	7.55	9.10	9.55
8. 8	8.55	10.10	10.55
9. 8	9.55	—	—
—	—	—	—

d Saturdays only.
e Saturdays excepted.

COBORN ROAD for
OLD FORD, from *Liverpool Street*,
2¼ miles. Fares, 0/2½a, 0/2b, 0/1¾c.
R. T. for two days, 0/5a, 0/4b, 0/3c.
See pp. 528-534, 541-544.
Map Square 62.

COBRIDGE (Stafford), 149¼
miles. Fares, 31/1a, 18/8c. R. T.
for two months,62/2a. Departures
from London as for Hanley.
Departures *for* London about 8
times daily. Pop. 10,711.

COCKBURNSPATH
(Berwick), 355¾ miles. No through
fares. Departures *from* London
as for Berwick-on-Tweed. Departures *for* London about 3 times
daily. Pop. 941.
Map Square 41.

COCKERMOUTH
(Cumberland) from *Euston*, 311½
miles. Fares, 62/9a, 37/8c. R. T.
for two months. 125/6a, 75/4c.
Pop. 4,845.
Map Square 6.

EUSTON	C'MOUTH	C'MOUTH	EUSTON
AM12.25	11.12	AM 7. 9hr	3.45
5. 0	2.35	7. 9½r	4.15
11.35r	7. 7	9.30r	6. 0
PM 1.30r	9.32	11.15r	7.30
11.45e	8.47	PM 2.37r	10.45
—	—	6. 0	5. 0
—	—	—	—
—	—	—	—
—	—	—	—
—	—	—	—
—	—	—	—

Sunday Trains.
PM11. 0	8.47	—	—
11.50	11.12	—	—
—	—	—	—
—	—	—	—
—	—	—	—
—	—	—	—

e Saturdays excepted.
h Mondays and Saturdays only.
k Mondays and Saturdays excepted.
r Restaurant Car.

COCKETT (Glamorgan)
from *Paddington*, 199½ miles.
Fares, 41/6a, 24/11c. R. T. for two
months, 83/0a, Departures *from*
London as for Landore. Departures *for* London about 5 times
daily. Pop. 8,488.
Map Square 21.

COCKFIELD (Durham),
250½ miles. Fares, 52/6a, 31/6c.
R.T. for two months, 105/0a, 63/0c.
Departures *from* London as for
Barnard Castle. Departures *for*
London about 5 times daily. Pop.
2,672.
Map Square 7.

COCKFIELD (Suffolk)
from *Liverpool Street*, 70 miles.
Fares, 14/1va, 8/11c. R. T. for two
months, 29/8a. Departures *from*
London as for Lavenham. Departures *for* London about 6 times
daily. Pop. 882.
Map Square 19.

COCKING (Sussex) from
Victoria and *London Bridge*, 63½
miles. Fares, *via* Midhurst, 13/2a,
7/11c. R. T. for two months, 26/4a,
15/10c. Departures *from* London
as for Singleton. Departures *for*
London about 6 times daily. Pop.
469.
Map Square 23.

CODFORD (Wilts) from
Paddington, 106½ miles. Fares,
via Theale, 20 0a, 12/0c. R.T. for
two months, 40/0a. *Via* Bath, 22/6a,
13/6c. R. T. for two months, 45/0a,
27/0c. Departures *from* London as
for Warminster. Departures *for*
London about 5 times daily. Pop.
542.
Map Square 22.

CODNOR PARK (Derby)
from *St. Pancras*,132½ miles. Fares,
26/11a, 16/2c. R. T., double fare.
Departures *from* London as for
Langley Mill or Newthorpe. Departures *for* London about 5
times daily. Pop. 788.
Map Square 13.

CODSALL (Stafford) from
Paddington, 127¾ miles. Fares,
26/8a, 16 0c. R. T. for two months,
53/4a. Pop. 1,634.
Map Square 17.

PAD.	CODSALL	CODSALL	PAD.
AM 9.10r	12.21	AM 8.15r	11. 0
10.40dr	1.25	9.24	12.25
10.40r	2.16	10.58r	2. 5
PM 2.10t	5.57	PM 1.45r	5. 0
4.10t	7. 2	2.41t	5.55
6.10r	9.31	4.40r	8. 5
7.10r	10. 5	6.15	10. 0
12.15k	7.25	9.18	3.30
12.15l	7.55	—	—
—	—	—	—
—	—	—	—

Sunday Trains.
PM12.50r	3.44	AM 9.10r	1.40
6. 0r	8.45	PM 1.15	6.20
—	—	—	—
—	—	—	—
—	—	—	—
—	—	—	—

d Saturdays only.
h Saturdays midnight only.
k Saturdays midnight excepted.
r Restaurant Car.
t Tea Car.

COED POETH(Denbigh),
188½ miles. Fares, 37/10a, 22/11c.
R. T. for two months, 75/8a, 45/10c.
Departures *from* London as for
Wrexham. Departures *for* Lon-
don about 4 times daily.
Map Square 11.

COED TALON (Flint), 192
miles. Fares, 40/2a, 24/1c. R. T.
for two months, 80/4a. Departures
from London as for Mold. Departures *for* London about 4 times
daily.
Map Square 11.

COGAN (Glamorgan), 155½
miles. Fares, 32/6a, 19/6c. R. T.
for two months, 65/0a, 39/0c. Departures *from* London as for
Cardiff. Departures *for* London
about 4 times daily.

COLBREN (Brecon), 202½
miles. No through fares. Departures *from* London as for
Neath or Brecon. Departures *for*
London about 4 times daily. Pop.
534.
Map Square 21.

COLCHESTER (Essex)
from *Liverpool Street*, 51¾ miles.
Fares, 11/0a, 6/7c. R. T. for two
months, 22/0a. Pop. 43,377.
Map Square 19.

L'PL. ST.	COLCH.	COLCH.	L'PL. ST.
AM 5. 0	6.19	AM 1.44	3.50
6.50	8.59	7.34r	8.52
8.15r	9.37	7.41	9.50
8.18	9.55	8.21	9.36
8.46	10.50	8.44r	9.53
10.12	11.31	9.16r	10.50
10.20	11.39	9.29f	10.35
10.23	11.53	9.34	10.58
10.47	12.44	9.45	11.16
11.30	12.54	10.51	11.42
PM12.33r	1.43	11. 5	12.40
12.36	1.56	PM12.53r	2. 3
1.30dr	2.44	1. 0d	2.23
1.33d	3.20	1.17	3.13
2. 3d	3.19	2.14	3.36
2.15	3.48	2.35	3.42
3.18r	4.31	3.54	5. 5
3.23	4.40	4. 9	5.47
3.26	5.18	5.22	6.32
4.58r	6.20	6.24	7.40
5.42d	7. 4	6.41	7.51
5.42e	7. 8	7. 8	9.17
6.39	7.54	8.24	9.36
7.16	8.45	8.43r	10. 0
7.45r	9.11	9.30	11.16
8.45	10. 0	—	—
8.54	10.51	—	—
12. 0d	1.25	—	—

Sunday Trains.
AM 8.15	10. 6	AM 1.44	3.50
9. 8	10.23	10. 6	11.38
9.20r	10.52	10.24	12.40
10. 5r	11.29	PM 5.47	7.10
PM 3.40	5.22	6.46	8.25
4.40	5.49	7. 9	8.58
7.40	9. 9	8.43	10. 9
8.46	10.47	8.53	10.15
—	—	9. 8r	10.30
—	—	—	—
—	—	—	—
—	—	—	—
—	—	—	—

d Saturdays only.
e Saturdays excepted.
f Mondays only.
r Restaurant Car.

COLCHESTER—*contd.*

Frank Cant & Co., Braiswick Rose Gardens, Colchester. Carefully note one mile from the Station, on the West Bergholt Rd.

Benjamin R. Cant & Sons, The Old Rose Gardens, Colchester. (Established 1765.) The Rose Gardens are half mile from the Station, on the Mile End Road, opposite Mile End Church.

COLDHAM (Cambs)

from *Liverpool Street*, 89¼ miles. Fares, 16/8*a*, 10/0*c*. R. T. for two months, 33/4*a*. Departures from London about 5 times daily. Pop. 383.
Map Square 18.

COLD NORTON (Essex)

from *Liverpool Street*, 37½ miles. Fares, 7/3*a*, 4/4*c*. R. T. for two months, 14/6*a*, 8/8*c*. Departures from London as for Maldon East (*via* Wickford). Departures for London about 5 times daily. Pop. 326.
Map Square 24.

COLDSTREAM (Berwick), 341 miles. Fares, 72/9*a*, 43/8*c*. R. T., double fare. Departures from London as for Alnwick. Departures for London about 3 times daily. Pop. 2,013.
Map Square 3.

COLE (Somerset) from

Waterloo, 120½ miles. Fares, 23/4*a*, 14/0*c*. R. T. for two months, 46/8*a*, 28/0*c*. Departures from London as for Wincanton. Departures for London about 6 times daily.
Map Square 22.

COLEFORD (Gloucester),

from *Paddington*, 142 miles. Fares, 29/7*a*, 17/9*c*. R. T. for two months, 59/2*a*, 35/6*c*. Pop. 2,781.
Map Square 22.

PAD.	COLE'FD	COLEF'D	PAD.
AM 1. 0*g*	7.50	AM 8. 5	12.20
5.30	12.47	8.50*r*	2.40
10.45	5.12	12. 0	5. 0
PM 3.15*t*	7.50	PM 4. 7*r*	8.45
—	—	6. 8	3.30
—	—	—	—
—	—	—	—
—	—	—	—
—	—	—	—

No Sunday Trains.

g Mondays excepted.
r Restaurant Car.
t Tea Car.

COLE GREEN (Herts),

from *King's Cross*, 24 miles. Fares, 5/0*a*, 3/0*c*. R. T., double fare. Departures from London as for Hertford. Departures for London about 8 times daily.
Map Square 23.

COLEHOUSE LANE

(Somerset), 136 miles. No through fares. Departures from London as for Clevedon. Departures for London about 3 times daily.
Map Square 22.

COLESHILL '(Warwick),

122¾ miles. Fares. 22/4*a*, 13/5*c*. R. T., double fare. Departures from London as for Water Orton. Departures for London about 4 times daily.
Map Square 17.

COLFIN (Wigtown), 409¼

miles. No through fares. Departures from London as for Stranraer. Departures for London about 3 times daily.

COLINTON (Midlothian),

397 miles. No through fares. Departures from London as for Carstairs. Departures for London about 4 times daily.
Map Square 41.

COLLESSIE (Fife), 434

miles. No through fares. Departures from London as for Leuchars. Departures for London about 4 times daily. Pop. 2,014.
Map Square 41.

COLLINGBOURNE

(Wilts) from *Waterloo*, 76¼ miles. Fares, 15/3*a*, 9/2*c*. R. T. for two months, 30/6*a*, 18/4*c*. Pop. 1,133.
Map Square 22.

W'LOO.	C'BOURNE	C'BOURNE	W'LOO.
PM 1. 0*r*	3. 6	AM 9.56	12.22
3.30	6. 0	PM 5.48*r*	8.30
6. 0*r*	8.16	—	—
—	—	—	—
—	—	—	—

Sunday Trains.

PM 6. 0	8.52	PM 5.43	8.57
—	—	—	—
—	—	—	—

r Restaurant Car.

COLLINGHAM (Notts)

from *St. Pancras*, 145 miles. Fares, 26/1*a*, 15/8*c*. R. T., double fare. Pop. 4,942.
Map Square 13.

ST. PAN.	COL'HAM	COL'HAN	ST. PAN.
AM 4.25	10. 0	AM 7. 8*r*	10.45
9. 0*r*	12.29	7.46*r*	12.10
11. 0*r*	2.51	9.44*r*	1.20
PM 1.50*r*	5. 8	11. 5	3.25
3.30*r*	8. 6	PM 1.20*r*	5.30
6.15*r*	9.56	3.40*r*	7.15
6.25*dr*	11.41	5.30*r*	9. 5
—	—	6.10*r*	10. 5
—	—	8.24	4.20
—	—	9.16*h*	4.20
—	—	—	—
—	—	—	—

Sunday Trains.

PM 3.15	9.23	PM12.35*r*	5. 2
—	—	5.25*r*	9.43
—	—	8.24	7.25

d Saturdays only.
h Thursdays and Saturdays only.
r Restaurant Car.

COLLINGHAM B'DGE

(Yorks), 193 miles. Fares, 40/3*a*, 24/2*c*. R. T., double fare. Departures from London as for Leeds or Wetherby. Departures for London about 4 times daily. Pop. (Collingham) 501.
Map Square 7.

COLLISTON (Forfar), 472

miles. Fares, 93/9*a*, 56/3*c*. R.T. for two months, 187/6*a*, 112/6*c*. Departures from London as for Arbroath. Departures for London about 3 times daily.
Map Square 38.

COLNBROOK (Bucks)

from *Paddington*, 16¼ miles. Fares, 2/11*a*, 1/9*c*. R. T. for two months, 5/10*a*, 3/4½*c*. Pop. 1,336.
Map Squares 23 *and* 64.

PAD.	COLNB'K.	COLNB'K	PAD.
AM 6.55*k*	7.31	AM 6.58*k*	7.55
7.55	8.17	7.59	8.28
8. 5	8.56	8.37*h*	9.24
9.20	9.58	9.22	10. 6
9.55	10.28	10.47	11.18
10.55	11.42	11.19*k*	11.55
PM12. 2*hk*	12.48	PM12.22	1.11
12.35*e*	1.23	1. 4*k*	2. 2
12.42*d*	1.23	1.43	2.35
1.15*e*	2.10	2.50	3.40
1.50*d*	2.29	3.52	5.17
2. 5*d*	2.53	4.48*d*	5.45
2.25	3.23	4.57*e*	5.52
2.33*d*	3.23	4.57	6. 3
3.45	4.17	5.52	6.52
4.50	5.26	7. 5	7.52
5.45*e*	6.18	7.49	8.40
5.45*d*	6.24	8.42*k*	9.33
7. 0	7.30	10.12*k*	11. 4
7.37*k*	8.12	—	—
8.35*k*	9.15	—	—
10. 5*k*	10.35	—	—

Sunday Trains.

AM 9.25*k*	10.14	AM 9.32*k*	10.14
10.37*k*	11.25	12. 0*k*	1. 5
11.35*k*	12.38	PM 2.10*k*	2.58
PM12.55*k*	1.46	2.47*k*	3.42
1.45*k*	2.30	3.57*k*	4.53
2.35*k*	3.13	5.42*k*	6.23
3.35*k*	4.28	6.17*k*	7.10
4.45*k*	5.59	7.17*k*	8.12
6. 5*k*	6.55	8.22*k*	9.17
8.20*k*	8.56	9.29*k*	10.22
9.25*k*	10. 2	—	—

d Saturdays only.
e Saturdays excepted.
h Departs from or arrives at Bishop's Road Station.
k These trains do not stop at Runemede Range.

COLNE (Lancs) from

Euston, 220½ miles. Fares, 42/6*a*, 25/6*c*. R. T., double fare. Pop. 24,755.
Map Square 12.

EUSTON	COLNE	COLNE	EUSTON
AM12.25	7.23	AM 7.40*r*	1.15
2.35	10.20	8.20*r*	3.10
5. 0	12.38	10. 0*r*	3.55
6.45	2.54	11.20*r*	6. 0
8.45*r*	5.47	12. 0*er*	6.15
10.40*r*	4.37	PM 1. 8*r*	7.30
11.50*er*	5.37	2.10*er*	9. 5
11.50*dr*	6.27	2.10*dr*	9.15
PM 1.30	7.52	3.10*er*	10. 0
2.50*t*	10.10	3.53*dr*	10. 0
4. 5*r*	11. 7	3.53*er*	10. 0
6. 5*r*	11.55	4.30*r*	10.45
11.50*d*	11.25	8.45	5. 0
—	—	9.15*e*	5.40
—	—	—	—

Sunday Trains.

PM12.10*r*	7. 3	AM 7. 0	4. 0
12.30*r*	9. 9	10.30*r*	5.45
—	—	11.55*r*	7.30
—	—	PM 7. 7	5. 0

d Saturdays only.
e Saturdays excepted.
r Restaurant Car.
t Tea Car.

COLNE—*continued.*
ANOTHER ROUTE from
St. Pancras, 223¼ miles. Fares as above.

St. Pan.	Colne	Colne	St. Pan.
AM 4.25	11.50	AM 7.50*r*	2.10
9.50*r*	4.20	8.55*r*	4.10
PM12.15*er*	6.49	10.26*r*	5.30
12.15*r*	7.15	PM12.25*r*	6.35
3.30*r*	9.50	1.43*dr*	7.57
5. 0*hr*10.44		2.23*r*	9.15
11.45*e*	7.30	6.53	4.20
11.50*d* 11.27		10.25*e*	7.25
—	—	10.25*d*	8. 5

Sunday Trains.
AM10.50*r*	7. 2	AM 9.30	5.27
—	—	PM 4.50	4.55
—	—	8.50	7.25

d Saturdays only.
e Saturdays excepted.
h Tuesdays, Fridays and Saturdays only.
r Restaurant Car.

COLOGNE. Air Route by
Instone Air Line, Ltd. Cars from Hotel Metropole, London to Aerodrome daily at 10.00. Fares, 119/6, R.T. 210/0. Subject to Passport Regulations.

Lond.	Cologne	Cologne	Lond.
11.00	15.30	10.00	14.30

See also Brussels.

COLTISHALL (Norfolk),
126 miles. Fares, 25/3*a*, 15/2*c*. R.T. for two months, 50/6*a*. Departures *from* London as for Wroxham. Departures *for* London about 5 times daily. Pop. 984.
Map Square 19.

COLWALL (Hereford),
131¾ miles. Fares, 26/1*a*, 15/8*c*. R. T. for two months, 52/2*a*, 31/4*c*. Departures *from* London as for Malvern. Departures *for* London about 4 times daily. Pop. 2,070.
Map Square 17.

COLWICH (Stafford) from
Euston, 127¾ miles. Fares, 26/6*a*, 15/11*c*. R.T. for two months, 53/0*a*. Pop. 1,527.
Map Square 17.

Euston	Colwh.	Colwh.	Euston
AM 5. 0	8.22	AM 5.44*r* 10. 0	
8.45*r* 12. 1		7.40	11. 0
10.40*r*	2.50	10.25*r*	2.20
12. 0*nr* 4.24		PM 2. 5*t*	6.15
PM 2.50*t*	6.49	4.39*r*	8.10
4. 5*et* 7.15		6.29*r* 10.45	
5.20*dr* 9.41		9. 5	5. 0
6.30*er* 9.41			

Sunday Trains.
AM 9.15	6.40	AM 8.40	5. 5

d Saturdays only.
e Saturdays excepted.
n Noon.
r Restaurant Car.
t Tea Car.

COLWYN BAY (Denbigh)
from *Euston*, 219¼ miles. Fares, 45/8*a*, 27/5*c*. R. T. for two months, 91/4*a*, 54/10*c*. Pop. 18,770.
Map Square 11.

Euston	Col. B.	Col. B.	Euston
AM12.25	7.35	AM 6.46*er*12. 5	
2.35	10.15	6.46*dr*12.20	
5. 0	11.15	7.56*dr* 1. 0	
8.30*er* 2.16		8.18*er* 1. 0	
8.30*dr* 2.37		8.21*r* 1.45	
10.30*r* 3.23		9.17*r* 2.20	
11.10*r* 3.45		10. 1*dr* 3.10	
11.50*e* 5.13		10.22*r* 4.15	
11.50*d* 5.47		PM12. 5*nr* 5. 5	
12. 0*nr* 6.52		12.42*r* 6.25	
PM 2.35*t* 7.39		2.42*r* 7.30	
4. 5*r* 9.12		2.50*hr* 8.10	
5.20*r* 10.35		3.27*r* 9.20	
9.30*e* 3.43		4.38*r* 10.45	
11.50*d* 11.39		9.43	5. 0

COLWYN BAY—*contd.*
Sunday Trains.

Euston	Col. B.	Col. B.	Euston
PM12.10*r*	7.21	AM 7.49	4. 0
9.15	3.43	PM 1.47*r*	7.10
—	—	9.35	5. 0

d Saturdays only.
e Saturdays excepted.
h Mondays and Saturdays only.
n Noon.
r Restaurant Car.
t Tea Car.

Colwyn Bay Hotel. First-class ; overlooks Bay. Private suites. Porters (in blue and scarlet livery) and Hotel Bus meet all trains. Garage.
See advt. p. **126.**

Pwllycrochan. First - class Family Hotel. Extensive grounds. Golf, Billiards. Excellent cuisine. Electric Light. Garage. Separate lock-ups. Lift. Telegrams; "Pwllycrochan, Colwyn Bay." Nat. Telephone 13.
See advt. p. **126.**

Rothesay Private Hotel and Winter Residence. Facing Sea. Lounge. 70 Bedrooms. Noted for good table. Garage. Near two Links. 'Phone 117.
See advt. p. **127.**

Capsthorne Towers Private Hotel. On Promenade. Close to Pier. High-class throughout, yet moderate. Miss GREENWOOD, Proprietress.
See advt. p. **127.**

Rhos Abbey Hotel, Rhos-on-Sea, Colwyn Bay. First-class. Standing in own grounds. Facing Pier. Nearest Hotel to Golf.

St. Winifreds, Rhôs-on-Sea. Private Hotel. Sea front. Opp. Pier. 43 Bedrooms. Sun Lounge. Billiards. Ballroom. Entertainments. Tel. 228 Colwyn Bay. Moderate Terms.

"Inishmore," Rhos-on-Sea, Private Hotel. Magnificent position, facing Sea and Pier. Close Golf Links. Excellent Cuisine. Electric Light. Winter Tariff. 'Phone, 161 Colwyn Bay.

Norfolk House. Private Hotel, Colwyn Bay. In own grounds. Facing Sea. West end of Bay. One minute Promenade. Electric Light. 'Phone 318. Telegrams, "Norfolk House, Colwyn Bay." HENRY WARNES.

The Towers. Private Hotel, Whitehall Road, Rhos-on-Sea. Sunny Position. Garage. Recreation Room. Private Sitting-Rooms. Tel. 233, Colwyn Bay.

COLWYN, OLD (Den-
bigh), from *Euston*, 218 miles. Fares, 45/5*a*, 27/3*c*. R. T. for two months, 90/10*a*, 54/6*c*. Departures *from* London as *for* Abergele. Departures *for* London about twice daily.
Map Square 11.

COLYFORD (Devon) from
Waterloo, 151 miles. Fares, 31/6*a*, 18/11*c*. R. T. for two months, 63/0*a*, 37/10*c*. Departures *from* London as for Seaton. Departures *for* London about 5 times daily.
Map Square 27.

COLYTON (Devon) from
Waterloo, 150 miles. Fares, 31/3*a*, 18/9*c*. R. T. for two months, 62/6*a*, 37/6*c*. Departures *from* London as for Seaton. Departures *for* London about 5 times daily. Pop. 1,948.
Map Square 27.

COMBPYNE (Devon)
from *Waterloo*, 149 miles. Fares, 31/1*a*, 18/8*c*. R.T. for two months, 62/2*a*, 37/4*c*. Departures *from* London as for Lyme Regis. Departures *for* London about 5 times daily. Pop. 104.
Map Square 27.

COMMONDALE (Yorks),
245½ miles. No through fares. Departures *from* London as for Whitby or Stockton-on-Tees. Departures *for* London about 4 times daily. Pop. 189.
Map Square 8.

COMMONDYKE (Ayr),
378½ miles. No through fares. Departures *from* London as for Old Cumnock. Departures *for* London about 4 times daily.
Map Square 40.

COMPTON (Berks), 61¼
miles. Fares, 12/9*a*, 7/8*c*. R. T. for two months, 25 6*d*. Departures *from* London as for Hampstead Norris. Departures *for* London about 3 times daily. Pop. 665.
Map Square 23.

COMRIE (Perth) from
Euston 449 miles. Fares, 91/11*a*, 55/2*c*. R.T. for two months,183/10*a*, 110/4*c*. Pop. 2,208.
Map Square 37.

Euston	Comrie	Comrie	Euston
AM 5. 0	6.13	AM 8.15*r*	7.30
10. 0*r*	9. 5	10.24*er*10.45	
PM 7.50*er* 7.15		11.45*dr*10.45	
11.35*e* 11. 0		PM 2. 7*r*	5. 0*h*
—	—	7.30	7.40

Sunday Trains.
PM 7.50*r*	7.15	—	—
11.35	11. 0	—	—

d Saturdays only.
e Saturdays excepted.
h A M.
r Restaurant Car.

CONDOVER (Salop), 156¾
miles. Fares, 31/11*a*, 19/2*c*. R.T. for two months, 63/10*a*. Departures *from* London as for Shrewsbury. Departures *for* London about 4 times daily. Pop. 1,765.
Map Square 17.

CONGLETON (Cheshire)

from *Euston*, 157¾ miles. Fares,
32/9*a*, 19/8*c*. R.T. for two months,
65/6*a*. Pop. 11,764.
Map Square 12.

EUSTON CONGLE.	CONGLE. EUSTON
AM 2.35 8.37	AM 8. 5*er*12. 5
5. 0 10. 2	8. 5*d*r12.20
8.45*r* 11.53	9.20*r* 12.50
10.40*r* 2.55	10.16*r* 2.20
12. 0*nr* 5.18	PM12. 2*r* 3.55
PM 2.50*t* 7.24	2. 2*t* 6.15
4.45*r* 8.20	4.29 9.20
6.53*er*11.10	6.13*r* 10. 0
*d*12.10*m*12. 8	8.29 5. 0

Sunday Trains.

PM12.10*r* 8.36	AM10.40 4. 0
— —	PM 1.18*r* 8.55
— —	7.56 5. 0

d Saturdays only.
e Saturdays excepted.
m Midnight.
n Noon.
r Restaurant Car.

CONGRESBURY (Somerset), 131½ miles. Fares, 27/4*a*, 16/5*c*. R.T. for two months, 54/8*a*. Departures *from* London as for Yatton. Departures *for* London about 6 times daily. Pop. 1,116.
Map Square 22.

CONINGSBY (Lincoln), .27¼ miles. Fares, 25/10*a*, 15/6*c*. R.T. for two months, 51/8*a*, 31/9*c*. Departures *from* London as for Midville. Departures *for* London about 4 times daily. Pop. 1,084.

CONISBOROUGH (Yorks), 160 miles. Fares, 33/4*a*, 20/0*c*. R.T., double fare. Departures *from* London as for Barnsley (*via* Doncaster). Departures *for* London about 8 times daily. Pop. 15,859.
Map Square 13.

CONISTON (Lancs) from *Euston*, 279 miles. Fares, 58/1*a*, 34/10*c*. R.T. for two months, 116/2*a*, 69/8*c*. Pop. 1,006.
Map Square 6.

EUSTON CONIST.	CONIST. EUSTON
AM 2.35 12.15	AM 7.15*hr* 3.45
5. 0 2. 0	7.15 4.15
6.45 3.45	11.10*r* 7.30
11.35*r* 6.23	PM 2.45*r* 10.45
PM 1.30*r* 8.50	6.30 5. 0
9.30 9.10	— —
11. 0*d* 10. 0	— —

Sunday Trains.

AM11.45*r* 8. 5	AM10.50*r* 7.30
— —	PM 6.45 5. 0

d Saturdays only.
h Mondays and Saturdays only.
r Restaurant Car.

ANOTHER ROUTE from *St. Pancras*, 301¼ miles. Fares as above.

ST. PAN. CONIST.	CONIST. ST. PAN.
AM 4.25 3.45	AM 7.15*r* 5.30
9.50*r* 6.23	11.10*r* 9.15
PM12.15*r* 8.50	PM 3.55 4.20
11.50*e* 12.15	
11.50*d* 3.22	— —

Sunday Trains.

PM11.45 12.15	AM10.50 4.55

d Saturdays only.
e Saturdays excepted.
r Restaurant Car.

CONNAH'S QUAY (Flint), 188 miles. Fares, 39/2*a*, 23/6*c*. R.T. for two months, 78/4*a*, 47/0*c*. Departures *from* London as for Chester. Departures *for* London about 5 times daily. Pop. 5,062.
Map Square 11.

CONNAUGHT ROAD (Royal Albert Docks) from *Fenchurch Street*, 6½ miles. Fares, 0/10*a*, 0/8*b*, 0/6*c*. R.T. for two days, 1/8*a*, 1/4*b*, 1/0*c*. See pp. 537-540.

CONNEL FERRY (Argyll), 497½ miles. Fares, 101/8*a*, 61/0*c*. R.T. for two months, 203/4*a*, 122/0*c*. Departures *from* London as for Crianlarich. Departures *for* London about 3 times daily. Pop. 458.
Map Square 37.

CONON (Ross) 584 miles. Fares, 106/3*a*, 63/9*c*. R.T. for two months, 212/6*a*, 127/6*c*. Departures *from* London as for Inverness. Departures *for* London about twice daily.
Map Square 34.

CONONLEY (Yorks) from *St. Pancras*, 218¾ miles. Fares, 42/1*a*, 25/3*c*. R.T., double fare. Departures *from* London as for Keighley. Departures *for* London about 5 times daily.
Map Square 7.

CONSALL (Stafford), 155 miles. Fares, 31/1*a*, 18/8*c*. R.T. for two months, 62/2*a*, 37/4*c*. Departures *from* London as for Uttoxeter. Departures *for* London about 5 times daily. Pop. 222.
Map Square 3.

CONSETT (Durham), 265½ miles. Fares, 60/8*a*, 36/5*c*. R.T., double fare. Departures *from* London as for Durham. Departures *for* London about 4 times daily. Pop. 12,151.
Map Square 3.

CONSTABLE BURTON (Yorks), 232¼ miles. Fares, 48/6*a*, 29/1*c*. R.T., double fare. Departures *from* London as for Leyburn. Departures *for* London about 8 times daily. Pop. 205.
Map Square 7.

CONWAY (Carnarvon) from *Euston*, 224½ miles. Fares, 46/10*a*, 28/1*c*. R.T. for two months, 93/8*a*, 56/2*c*. Pop. 6,506.
Map Square 11.

EUSTON CONWAY	CONWAY EUSTON
AM12.25 8. 1	AM 7.35*dr* 1. 0
2.35 11. 9	7.45*er* 1. 0
5. 0*e* 11.54	8.43*r* 1.45
5. 0*d* 12.32	9.51*dr* 3.10
8.30*dr* 2. 2	9.55*er* 4.15
8.30*er* 2.44	11.38*t* 5. 5
11.10*dr* 4.10	PM 1.42*r* 7.30
11.10*er* 4.20	3. 0*r* 9.20
11.50*r* 6.42	4.16*r* 10.45
PM 2.35*t* 7.58	9.20 5. 0
4. 5*r* 9.57	— —
5.20*r* 10.54	— —
11.50*d* 1. 0*l*	— —

Sunday Trains.

PM12.10*r* 7.46	AM 7.33 4. 0
— —	PM 1.27*r* 7.10
— —	9.15 5. 0

d Saturdays only.
e Saturdays excepted.
l P.M.
r Restaurant Car.
t Tea Car.

Oakwood Park Hotel.
Standing in 100 acres of grounds.
Most up-to-date in the district.
Golf, Tennis, etc.
See advt. p. 128.

Castle Hotel. Favourite
American resort. The most
famous Hotel in Wales.
See advt. p. 127.

CONWIL (Carmarthen), 234½ miles. Fares, 47/4*a*, 28/5*c*. R.T. for two months, 94/8*a*. Departures *from* London as for Carmarthen. Departures *for* London about 4 times daily. Pop. 1,276.
Map Square 16.

COOKHAM (Berks) from *Paddington*, 27½ miles. Fares, 5/3*a*, 3/2*c*. R.T. for two months, 10/6*a*, 6/4*c*. Pop. 4,915.
Map Square 23.

PAD. COOKM.	COOKM. PAD.
AM 5.45 7.10	AM 8.14 8.56
6.30 8. 1	8.51 9.37
7.35 8.46	9.34 10.24
8.30 9.47	10.10 11. 6
9.20 10.24	10.38 11.35
9.55 11. 1	11.24 12.15
11.25 12.19	PM 1.27 2.35
PM12.35*e* 1.55	2.36*d* 3.38
1. 5*d* 1.57	3.17 4.10
1.20*d* 2.19	4.29 5.37
2. 7 2.59	5.54 6.55
3.38 4.28	6.48 7.45
4.50 5.36	7.57*d* 9.12
5.45 6.31	8.27 9.33
6.55 7.38	9.40 10.42
8.35 9.28	10.24 12. 0
10. 5 10.58	— —
12. 3*h* 1. 2	— —
— —	— —

Sunday Trains.

AM 8.20 9.37	AM 9. 5 10.14
9.45 10.37	11.51 1. 5
10.25 11.12	PM 3. 2 4.53
11.45 12.34	5.21 6.23
PM 2.35 3.32	7.45 8.45
5.15 6.12	7.55 9.17
6. 5 8.12	8.37 9.32
8.20 9.19	8.59 9.53
— —	9.30 10.33
— —	10.10 11. 6

d Saturdays only.
e Saturdays excepted.
h Wednesdays and Saturdays only.

Crown Hotel. High-Class
Family Hotel. Fully Licensed.
Near River. Garage. Inspection
Pit. Officially Listed R.A.C.
Tel., Bourne End 163.
Capt. J. HUGHES,
Resident Proprietor.

Turk & Sons, Boat, Punt,
and Canoe Builders. Telephone
110, Bourne End.
See advt. p. 129.

Cookham Estate Offices.
Lists of all Properties for Sale
or Let, Furnished.
EDGAR S. BINGE, F.A.I. Cookham
Phone 42, Bourne End.

COOKSBRIDGE (Sussex)
from *London Bridge, Victoria,*
and *Clapham Junction*, 47½ miles.
Fares, from London Bridge or
Victoria, 10/0*a*, 6/0*c*. R.T. for two
months, 20/0*a*, 12/0*c*. Departures
from London as for Plumpton.
Departures *for* London about 6
times daily.
Map Square 28.

COOMBE (Cornwall), 245½ miles. No through fares. Departures *from* London as for Looe. Departures *for* London about 4 times daily.

Travel to South Ireland *via*

COOPER BRIDGE
(Yorks), 186¼ miles. Fares, 38/2*a*, 22/11*c*. R. T., double fare. Departures *from* London as for Huddersfield or Mirfield. Departures *for* London about 3 times daily.

COPGROVE (Yorks), 207¼
miles. Fares, 43/4*a*, 26/0*c*. R. T., double fare. Departures *from* London as for York or Harrogate. Departures *for* London about 5 times daily. Pop. 67.
Map Square 7.

COPLEY (Yorks), 194 miles.
Fares, 40/2*a*, 24/1*c*. R. T. for two months, 80/4*a*, 48/2*c*. Departures *from* London as for Sowerby Bridge. Departures *for* London about 5 times daily. Pop. 3,059.
Map Square 12.

COPMANTHORPE
(Yorks), 191 miles. Fares, 40/0*a*, 24/0*c*. R. T. for two months, 80/0*a*, 48/0*c*. Departures *from* London as for York. Departures *for* London about 5 times daily. Pop. 344.
Map Square 8.

COPPLESTONE
(Devon) from *Waterloo*, 186 miles. Fares, 36/11*a*, 22/2*c*. R. T. for two months, 73/10*a*, 44/4*c*. Departures *from* London as for Eggesford. Departures *for* London about 6 times daily.
Map Square 26.

COPPULL (Lancs), 199¾
miles. Fares, 41/6*a*, 24/11*c*. R. T. for two months, 83/0*a*. Departures *from* London as for Wigan. Departures *for* London about 4 times daily. Pop. 4,480.
Map Square 12.

CORBRIDGE (Northumberland),
284 miles. Fares, 60/3*a*, 36/2*c*. R. T., double fare. Departures *from* London as for Newcastle-on-Tyne. Departures *for* London about 4 times daily. Pop. 2,213.
Map Square 3.

CORBY (Lincoln) from
King's Cross, 97 miles. Fares, 20/3*a*, 12/2*c*. R. T., double fare. Pop. 710.
Map Square 18.

	King's +	Corby		Corby	King's +
AM	5. 5	8.16	AM	10. 1	12.25
	7.15*r*	10.13	PM	1. 9	3.50
	8.45	11.24		4.51*r*	7.10
	11.30	2.28		8.45	3.25
PM	3. 0	5.34		—	—
	5.45*r*	7.57		—	—
	—	—		—	—
	—	—		—	—

Sunday Trains.

AM	8.30	12. 1	PM	4.35	8. 8
	—	—		—	—
	—	—		—	—
	—	—		—	—

r Restaurant Car.

CORFE CASTLE
(Dorset) from *Waterloo*, 126¼ miles. Fares, 26/6*a*, 15/11*c*. R. T. for two months, 53/0*a*, 31/10*c*. Departures *from* London as for Swanage. Departures *for* London about 6 times daily. Pop. 1,406.
Map Square 27.

The Bankes Hotel. Situate close to Castle, and amidst historic surroundings. Tariff on application.

CORK from *Paddington, via*
Fishguard and Rosslare, 406 miles. Fares, First and Saloon, Third and Saloon, Third and Steerage. R. T. for two months, First and Saloon, Third and Saloon, Third and Steerage.
Pop. 76,632.

	Pad.	Cork		Cork	Pad.
PM	8. 0*er*	10. 0*l*	PM	7. 0*r*	9.10*l*
	8. 0*dr*	12. 0*n*		—	—
	—	—		—	—
	—	—		—	—
	—	—		—	—
	—	—		—	—

Service temporarily suspended.

d Saturdays only.
e Saturdays excepted.
l A.M.
n Noon.
r Restaurant Car.

ANOTHER ROUTE from
Paddington, via Fishguard and boat direct. 401½ miles. Fares, 56/11 First and Saloon, 32/8 Third and Steerage. R. T. for two months, 113/10 First and Saloon, 65/4 Third and Steerage.

	Pad.	Cork.		Cork.	Pad.
PM	5. 0*hr*	10. 0*l*	PM	6. 0*kr*	10.57*l*
	—	—		—	—
	—	—		—	—
	—	—		—	—
	—	—		—	—

h Tuesdays, Thursdays, and Saturdays only.
k Mondays, Wednesdays, and Fridays only.
l A.M.
r Restaurant Car.

For City of Cork Steam Packet Co. Service, *see* p. **598**.

Bank.—The National Bank, Ltd.

CORNFORTH WEST
(Durham), 246¾ miles. No through fares. Departures *from* London as for Ferryhill. Departures *for* London about 5 times daily. Pop. (Cornforth) 5,895.
Map Square 7.

CORNHILL (Banff), 579¼
miles. No through fares. Departures *from* London as for Huntly. Departures *for* London about twice daily.
Map Square 35.

CORNHOLME (Yorks),
206 miles. Fares, 40/7*a*, 24/4*c*. R. T. for two months, 81/2*a*. Departures *from* London as for Burnley (Manchester Road). Departures *for* London about 6 times daily.
Map Square 12.

CORNWOOD (Devon)
from *Paddington*, 217¼ miles. Fares, 44/10*a*, 26/11*c*. R. T. for two months, 89/8*a*. Departures *from* London as for Ivybridge. Departures *for* London about 5 times daily. Pop. 1,056.
Map Square 26.

CORPACH (Inverness),
527 miles. Fares, 105/3*a*, 63/2*c*. R. T. for two months, 210/6*a*, 126/4*c*. Departures *from* London as for Fort William. Departures *for* London about twice daily. Pop. 135.
Map Square 37.

CORPUSTY (Norfolk)
from *King's Cross*, 149½ miles. Fares, 25/3*a*, 15/2*c*. R. T. for two months, 50/6*a*. Departures *from* London as for Melton Constable. Departures *for* London about 3 times daily. Pop. 449.
Map Square 19.

CORRIS (Merioneth), 223¾
miles. No through fares. Departures *from* London as for Machynlleth. Departures *for* London about 3 times daily. Pop. 1,054.
Map Square 16.

CORSHAM (Wilts) from
Paddington, 98¼ miles. Fares, 20/7*a*, 12/4*c*, R. T. for two months, 41/2*a*. Pop. 4,209.
Map Square 22.

	Pad.	Corsh.		Corsh.	Pad.
AM	5.30*e*	8.10	AM	7.30*r*	10.15
	5.30	8.21		9.15	12.20
	7.30	10. 5		11.53*r*	2.40
	9. 0	12. 6	PM	2.45	6. 2
	10.45	2. 0		5. 8*r*	8.35
PM	1.10*r*	4. 0		6.54	10.25
	4.15	6.16		9.13	2.45
	6.30	8.55		11.24*d*	2.45
	6.55	10.25		—	—
	—	—		—	—

Sunday Trains.

AM	10.35	2. 0	PM	1.56	6. 0
PM	2. 0	7.37		—	—
	—	—		—	—

d Saturdays only.
e Saturdays excepted.
r Restaurant Car.

CORSTORPHINE (Midlothian),
396 miles. Fares, 81/8*a*, 49/0*c*. R.T. for two months, 163/4*a*, 98/0*c*. Departures *from* London as for Edinburgh (Waverley). Departures *for* London about 5 times daily.

CORTON (Suffolk), 120¼
miles. Fares, 25/5*a*, 15/3*c*. R. T. for two months, 50/10*a*, 30/6*c*. Departures *from* London as for Gorleston. Departures *for* London about 3 times daily. Pop. 546.
Map Square 19.

CORWEN (Merioneth) from
Paddington, 193½ miles. Fares, 40/7*a*, 24/4*c*. R. T. for two months, 81/2*a*, 48/8*c*. Pop. 2,856.
Map Square 11.

	Pad.	Corwen		Corwen	Pad.
AM	9.10*r*	2. 8	AM	8. 0*r*	1.25
	10.40*r*	3.25		9.21*r*	2. 5
PM	12.50*r*	5.51		11.50*r*	5. 0
	2.10*t*	7.11	PM	2.46*r*	8. 5
	4.10*t*	9.46		4.31*r*	10. 0
	12.15*h*	8.24		7.12	3.30

No Sunday Trains.

h Saturdays midnight excepted.
r Restaurant Car.
t Tea Car.

CORWEN—*continued.*

ANOTHER ROUTE from *Euston*, 227¼ miles. Fares, 40/7*a*, 24/4*c*. R. T. for two months, 81/2*a*, 48/8*c*.

EUSTON	CORWEN	CORWEN	EUSTON
AM 12.25	10. 5	AM 8. 5*r*	2.20
5. 0	12.57	10.55*hr*	5. 5
10.30*r*	4.21	PM 1.37*r*	8.10
11.10*hr*	6.12	7. 0	5. 0
PM 2.35*t*	8.55	—	—
—	—	—	—
—	—	—	—

No Sunday Trains.

e Saturdays excepted.
h Via Rhyl.
r Restaurant Car.
t Tea Car.

CORYTON (Devon), from

Paddington, 246¾ miles. Fares, 46/11*a*, 28/2*c*. R. T. for two months, 93/10*a*. Departures *from* London as for Launceston. Departures *for* London about 3 times daily. Pop. 159.
Map Square 26

COSHAM (Hants) from

Waterloo, via Eastleigh, 90 miles. Fares, 15/5*a*, 9/3*c*. R. T. for two months, 13/10*a*, 18/6*c*. Pop. 2,528.
Map Square 28.

W'LOO	COSH.	COSH.	W'LOO
AM 5.40	8.38	AM 6.19	9.26
5.50	10. 0	9.20	12. 0
8.30*s*	11. 2	11.34*r*	2.20
9.30	12.34	PM 12.17	4. 6
11.30*r*	2.21	12.39	4.20
PM 1.30*s*	4.30	2.25	6.16
3.30*s*	6.11	5.41*r*	8.20
5.30*r*	8. 8	7.19	10.50
7.30	10. 9	8.29	11.28
8. 0	11.41	11.14*f*	3.58
—	—	*m*12.28*g*	3.58

Sunday Trains.

AM 11. 0*r*	1.40	AM 12.28	3.58
PM 2. 0	6.49	9.11	12.11
5. 5	8.15	11.53*r*	2.27
7. 0*r*	9.48	PM 5. 5	8. 3
8.55	12.45	7.25	10.52
—	—	10.49	3.58

f Mondays only.
g Mondays excepted.
m Midnight.
r Restaurant Car.
s Refreshments served.

ANOTHER ROUTE from *Waterloo, via* Meon Valley, 78½ miles. Fares as above.

W'LOO	COSH'M	COSH'M	W'LOO
AM 4.50	8.38	AM 7.30	10.26
7. 0	10.23	9.20	12.11
9.20	12.34	PM 2.25	5.46
11.20	2.49	3.57	7. 7
PM 3. 4	6.11	7.39	11.10
6.34	9.35	—	—
—	—	—	—
—	—	—	—
—	—	—	—

Sunday Trains.

PM 6.20	9.30	PM 6.30	9.37
—	—	—	—

COSSINGTON (Somerset)

from *Waterloo*, 143½ miles. Fares, 29/10*a*, 17/11*c*. R. T. for two months, 59/8*a*, 35/10*c*. Departures *from* London as for Bridgwater. Departures *for* London about 4 times daily. Pop. 206.
Map Square 22.

COTEHILL (Cumberland)

from *St. Pancras*, 301¼ miles. Fares, 59/5*a*, 35/8*c*. R. T., double fare. Departures *from* London as for Lazonby. Departures *for* London about 4 times daily. Pop. 968.
Map Square 7.

COTHAM (Notts), 118

miles. Fares, 25/0*a*, 15/0*c*. R. T., double fare. Departures *from* London as for Newark or Bottesford. Departures *for* London about 3 times daily. Pop. 130.
Map Square 13.

COTHERSTONE (Yorks),

251½ miles. Fares, 52/4*a*, 31/5*c*. R. T., double fare. Departures *from* London as for Barnard Castle. Departures *for* London about 4 times daily. Pop. 644.
Map Square 7.

COTTAM (Notts), 146¾

miles. Fares, 29/4*a*, 17/7*c*. R. T., double fare. Departures *from* London as for Retford or Lincoln. Departures *for* London about 4 times daily. Pop. 102.
Map Square 13.

COTTINGHAM (Yorks),

198¼ miles. Fares, 35/10*a*, 21/6*c*. R. T. for two months, 71/8*a*. Departures *from* London as for Hull (Paragon) or Driffield. Departures *for* London about 5 times daily. Pop. 5,135.
Map Square 13.

COUGHTON (Warwick),

133¾ miles. Fares, 23/7*a*, 14/2*c*. R. T. for two months, 47/2*a*, 28/4*c*. Departures *from* London as for Studley. Departures *for* London about 4 times daily. Pop. 206.
Map Square 17.

COULSDON EAST

(Surrey) from *Charing Cross, Cannon Street,* and *London Bridge*, 17¾ miles. Fares, 2/11*a*, 2/4*b*, 1/9*c*. R. T. for eight days, 5/10*a*, 4/8*b*, 3/6*c*. Pop. 12,548.
Map Square 3.

CHAR. +	Leave CAN. ST.	LON. B.	Arr. at COULS. E
AM —	4.44	5. 0	5.36
—	—	7.50*l*	8.23
—	—	9.33*l*	10. 5
10.55	—	11. 3	11.42
PM —	12.55*d*	12.58*d*	1.24
12.55	—	1. 4	1.40
—	1.24*d*	1.27*d*	2. 4
—	—	1.30*el*	2. 3
2. 3*e*	2. 8*d*	2.10	2.47
—	—	2.22*dl*	2.58
2.35*d*	—	2.41*d*	3.10
3.15	—	3.21	3.58
4.22*d*	—	4.28*d*	5. 3
—	4.24*e*	4.28*e*	5. 1
—	5.24*e*	5.27*e*	5.53
5.42*d*	—	5.48*d*	6.16
—	6. 0*e*	6. 3*e*	6.30
6.27*e*	—	6.34*e*	7. 0
—	6.36*e*	6.39*e*	7.13
6.34*d*	—	6.40*d*	7.16
7.24*d*	7.28*e*	7.30	8. 6
8.28	—	8.36	9.12
9.25	—	9.31	10.10
10.17	—	10.23	10.58
11.27	—	—	11.54

Sunday Trains.

AM 6.25	—	6.32	7.13
10.20	—	10.28	11. 4
PM 1.30	—	1.37	2.11
5.25	—	5.32	6. 8
8.38	—	8.45	9.20

COULSDON EAST—*continued.*

Trains from Coulsdon East.

Leave COULS. E.	LON. B.	Arrive at CAN. ST.	CHAR. +
AM 6.48	7.18	—	7.30
7.56	8.24	8.28	—
8.32	8.56	—	—
9. 3	9.28	9.32	—
9.48	10.10	—	10.19
10. 1	10.27	10.32	—
10.32	11. 0	—	—
11.14	11.46	—	11.59
PM 12.17	12.50	—	1. 0
2. 7	2.38	—	2.46
2.58	3.28*e*	—	3.42*d*
3.35*h*	4. 8	—	—
4.26	5. 2	—	5.14
4.58*e*	5.28	—	—
5.28	5.56	—	—
6.50	7.20	—	7.29
8.32	9. 2	—	9.15
9.33	10. 3	—	10.13
11.27	11.57	—	12.10

Sunday Trains.

AM 7.45	8.16	—	8.27
10.43	11.15	—	11.25
PM 4. 3	4.33	—	4.42
6.43	7.13	—	7.25
9.38	10.11	—	10.24

d Saturdays only.
e Saturdays excepted.
h Mondays, Fridays and Saturdays only.
l Low Level platform.

COULSDON WEST

from *London Bridge* (L. B. & S. C. R.), 14¾ miles. Fares (First and Third) as above.

LON. B.	COULS. W.	COULS. W.	LON. B.
AM 5.18	6.38	AM 5.30	6.23
6.43	7.40	6.20	7.10
7. 7	7.57	7.19	7.55
8.17	9.11	8. 0	8.35
8.24	9.21	8.11	8.46
9.25	10.15	8.29	9. 1
9.50	10.46	8.42	9.26
10.20	11.14	8.59	9.35
10.40	11.32	9. 6	9.42
11.14	12. 7	9.28	10. 0
11.52	12.45	9.57	10.43
PM 12.30*d*	1.19	10.23	11.10
12.43*e*	1.45	10.57	11.57
1.10*d*	1.51	11.30	12.13
1.17	2.12	PM 12. 5	12.44
1.32*d*	2.18	12.55	1.43
1.38*e*	2.20	1.19*e*	2. 8
1.40*d*	2.34	1.32*d*	2.22
2. 5	3. 0	1.54*d*	2.46
2.10*d*	3. 0	1.58*e*	2.45
2.22*e*	3.15	2.30*e*	3.27
2.25*d*	3. 7	2.45*d*	3.42
2.38*d*	3.23	3. 1*d*	3.56
3. 0*e*	3.39	3. 5*e*	3.55
3.21*d*	4.10	3.20*e*	4. 7
3.30	4.22	4.14*e*	4.57
3.36	4.27	4.36	5.25
4.10	4.56	4.43*e*	5.31
4.23	5. 8	5. 8	5.54
4.35	5.27	5.27	6.15
5. 4	5.54	5.35	6.22
5.21	6. 3	6.22	7.16
5.41*e*	6.19	6.42	7.36
6.27*d*	7.16	7.22	7.56
6.30*e*	7.10	7.40	8.31
6.56	7.48	7.50	8.38
7.18*e*	8. 7	8.15	9. 3
7.40	8.28	8.43	9.42
8.10*e*	8.47	8.50	9.57
8.55	9.49	9.23	10.14
9.22	10.17	10.22	11.11
10.50*e*	11.41	—	—

COULSDON WEST—continued.

Sunday Trains.

Lon. B.	Couls.W.	Couls.W.	Lon. B.
AM 7.22	8.30	AM 8. 3	9. 9
7.50	8.55	8.42	9.29
8.35	9.30	9. 0	9.45
9.35	10.30	9.42	10.29
9.50	10.41	10.40	11.29
PM12.52	1.44	PM 3. 5	4. 3
1.10	1.53	4.49	5.39
1.45	2.53	5. 5	6. 5
2.40	3.55	6. 5	6.52
3.48	4.53	7. 2	7.56
4.43	5.53	8. 5	9.21
6. 0	6.53	9. 2	10. 1
6.46	7.53	9.55	10.46
8. 0	8.55	10.45	11.34
9.10	9.55	—	—
9.55	10.55	—	—

d Saturdays only.
e Saturdays excepted.

ANOTHER ROUTE from

Victoria (L. B. & S. C.R.), 15 miles. Fares (First and Third) as above.

Vict.	Couls.W.	Couls.W.	Vict.
AM 6.35	7.40	AM 5.30	6.23
7. 0	7.57	6.20	7.25
7.50	8.45	6.55	7.42
8.18	9.11	7.55	8.36
8.40	9.30	8.11	9. 2
9.25	10.14	8.29	9. 8
9.52	10.46	8.42	9.19
10.18	11.14	8.59	9.40
10.32	11.32	9. 6	9.44
11. 7	12. 7	9.34	10.12
11.54	12.45	10.23	11.14
PM12.24e	1.15	10.57	11.47
12.24d	1.19	11.30	12.19
12.42d	1.29	PM12. 5	12.45
12.53e	1.45	12.55	1.48
1.15d	1.56	1. 5	1.50
1.25e	2.20	1.19e	2.14
1.41d	2.34	1.32d	2.35
2. 8	3. 0	1.54d	2.51
2.25e	3.15	1.58e	2.49
2.28d	3.23	2.30e	3.20
2.37d	3.27	2.45d	3.35
3.10	4.10	3. 1d	3.51
3.20d	4.22	3. 5e	3.51
3.40	4.27	3.20e	4. 5
4.15	4.56	4.22	5.20
4.53	5.38	4.43d	5.33
4.58	5.54	5. 8	5.55
5.27	6 3	5.35	6.31
5.53	6.30	6.22	7.12
6.27	7. 2	6.42	7.33
6.40	7.35	7.22	8.10
7.15e	8. 7	7.40	8.37
7.38	8.28	8.15	9. 7
7.52e	8.47	8.50	9.38
8.30	9.19	9.23	10.18
9.22	10.17	10.22	11.13
9.55	10.42	—	—
11.15	12. 1	—	—
11.50h	12.21	—	—

Sunday Trains.

AM 7.40	8.30	AM 8. 3	8.53
8. 0	8.54	8.42	9.33
8.40	9.30	9. 0	10.13
9.40	10.30	9.42	10.33
12. 0	12.53	10. 8	10.50
PM 1. 0	1.53	10.40	11.33
2. 0	2.53	PM 1. 5	1.53
3. 0	3.55	2. 5	2.53
4. 0	4.33	2.30	3. 4
5. 0	5.53	3. 5	3.53
6. 0	6.53	4. 5	4.53
7. 0	7.53	5. 5	5.53
8. 0	8.55	6. 5	6.53
9. 5	9.55	7. 2	7.37
10. 0	10.55	8. 5	8.53

COULSDON WEST—continued.

Sunday Trains.

Vict.	Couls.W.	Couls.W.	Vict.
PM10.15	11. 1	PM 9. 2	9.53
10.50	11.32	9.12	10. 0
—	—	9.55	10.53
—	—	10.45	11.33

d Saturdays only.
e Saturdays excepted.
h Mondays and Thursdays only.

COULTER (Lanark) from

Euston, 368 miles. Fares, 74/9d, 44/10c. R.T. for two months. 149/6a, 89/8c. Departures *from* London as for Peebles. Departures *for* London about twice daily.
Map Square 40.

COUNDON (Durham), 245¾

miles. No through fares. Departures *from* London as for Ferryhill. Departures *for* London about 4 times daily. Pop. 6,912.
Map Square 7.

COUNDON ROAD

(Warwick), 95¼ miles. Fares,19/10a, 11/11c. R.T. for two months, 39/8a, 23/10c. Departures *from* London as for Coventry. Departures *for* London about 6 times daily. Pop. (Coundon) 346.
Map Square 17.

COUNTER DRAIN (Lincoln), 97¾ miles. Fares, 20/2a, 12/1c. R. T., double fare. Departures *from* London as for Spalding. Departures *for* London about 4 times daily.
Map Square 18.

COUNTESTHORPE

(Leicester) from *Euston*, 97 miles. Fares, 20/2a, 12/1c. R. T., double fare. Pop. 1,450.
Map Square 18.

Euston	Cnthpe.	Cnthpe.	Euston
AM 5. 0	8. 2	AM 6.29e	9.52
6.45	10.32	6.29dr10. 0	
10. 0	12.57	8.58	11.55
12. 0nr	2.41	11. 5r	2.20
PM 2.50t	5.39	PM 1.16r	4.15
5.20r	7.53	3. 8t	5.50
12.10d	7.51	5.30r	9.20
—	—	8. 7er10.45	
—	—	9. 8d	5. 0

Sunday Trains.

AM12.10	7.51	AM 9.28	12.25
PM 3.50	7.28	PM 5.56r	8.20

d Saturdays only.
e Saturdays excepted.
n Noon.
r Restaurant Car.
t Tea Car.

COUNTY SCHOOL

(Norfolk) from *Liverpool Street*, 128½ miles. Fares, 23/7a, 14/2c. R. T. for two months, 47/2a. Departures *from* London as for Dereham. Departures *for* London about 5 times daily.
Map Square 19.

COUPAR ANGUS

(Perth) from *Euston*, 465¾ miles. Fares, 94/4a, 56/7c. R. T. for two months, 188/8a, 113/2c. Pop. 2,531.
Map Square 38.

Euston	Coup.A.	Coup.A.	Euston
AM 5. 0k	7.11	AM 8.36r	7.30t
5. 0	7.48	10. 4r	10.45t
10. 0r	8.29	PM 2.34r	5. 0h
PM 7.50er	7.37	6.42	7.40
11. 0d	10. 1h	—	—
11.35e	9.42	—	—

COUPAR ANGUS—continued.

Sunday Trains.

Euston	Coup.A.	Coup.A.	Euston
PM 7.50r	7.37h	PM 3. 7	5. 0h
11.35	9.42	—	—

d Saturdays only.
e Saturdays excepted.
h A.M.
k Wednesdays only.
l P.M.
r Restaurant Car.

COURT SART (Glamorgan), 190 miles. No through fares. Departures *from* London as for Port Talbot. Departures *for* London about 5 times daily.

COVE BAY (Kincardine),

518 miles. No through fares. Departures *from* London as for Stonehaven. Departures *for* London about 3 times daily. *Map Square* 38.

COVENT GARDEN

(Hammersmith and Finsbury Park Tube). *See* back of Map.

COVENTRY (Warwick)

from *Euston*, 94 miles. Fares, 19/7a, 11/9c. R. T. for two months, 39/2a. Pop. 128,205.
Map Square 17.

Euston	Covent.	Covent.	Euston
AM 2.30	4. 9	AM 1. 0g	4. 0
5. 0	7.17	1. 0f	5. 0
6.45	9.24	6.40e	9.52
8.30r	10.26	8. 3r	10. 0
9.15r	11. 5	9.10	11. 0
10. 0	12.26	9.21	11.55
11.30r	1. 9	10.37	12.40
12. 0nr	2.35	11. 5r	1. 0
PM 1.15r	2.52	PM12.20r	2.20
1.30r	3.44	1.21er	3. 0
2.20t	3.57	2.55t	4.35
2.50t	5.15	3.49t	5.35
4. 5t	6. 2	5.19t	7.20
4.45	6.52	6.41r	8.20
5.50r	7.27	7.40dr10.45	
7. 0r	9. 2	8.41er10.20	
9.30	11.46	8.47er10.45	
11.50	2.21	—	—

Sunday Trains.

AM12.10	2.33	AM 1. 0	5. 0
9.15	12.34	9.35	12.25
PM 1. 0r	2.51	PM12. 4r	1.45
5.10r	6.53	2. 8	5. 5
9.15	11.52	6. 9r	8.20
11.50	2.23	6.48r	8.35

d Saturdays only.
e Saturdays excepted.
f Mondays only.
g Mondays excepted.
n Noon.
r Restaurant Car.
t Tea Car.

COWBIT (Lincoln), 96 miles.

Fares, 19/4a, 11/7c. R. T., double fare. Departures *from* London as for March. Departures *for* London about 4 times daily. Pop. 507.
Map Square 18.

COWBRIDGE (Glamorgan), 169¾ miles. Fares, 35/5a, 21/3c. R. T. for two months, 70/10d, 42/6c. Departures *from* London as for Llantrisant. Departures *for* London about 3 times daily. Pop. 1,159.
Map Square 21.

COWDEN (Kent) from *Victoria, Cannon Street* and *London Bridge,* 29¼ miles. Fares, 6/1a, 3/8c. R. T. for two months, 12/2a, 7/4c. Pop. 729.
Map Square 24.

Leave			Arr. at
Vict.	Can. St.	Lon. B.	Cowden
AM 5.30	—	5.18	6.48
6.37	—	6.40	8. 3
7.23	—	8. 7	9.25
9.10	—	9. 6	10.26
11. 5	—	10.35	12.47
12. 0d	12.16d	d12.20k	1.30
PM 1.20e	—	1.58e	2.47
1.25d	—	1.38d	2.51
—	—	2. 5e	3.48
2.25	—	2.25d	3.48
4. 0e	4.16e	e4.20k	5.27
4.50	—	4.44e	5.54
5. 5	—	5.21	6.28
5.48	—	—	7.14
6. 6e	—	6. 8e	7.14
6. 6	—	6. 8	7.22
6.50	—	7. 0	8.22
8. 5	—	8.10	9.17
9 3l	—	9.12l	10.43

Sunday Trains.

AM 8.50	—	8.30	9.57
PM 1.14	—	1.10	2.27
2.30	—	—	3.47
7. 5	—	6.46	8.14

Trains from Cowden.

Leave	Arrive at		
Cowden	Lon.B.	Can. St.	Vict.
AM 6.54	8.15	—	8.24
7.29	8.37	—	8.40
8. 4	9.15	—	9.19
8.21	9.32	—	9.40
8.56	10. 4	—	10.12
9.47	10.55	—	10.46
10.15	—	—	11.35
11. 5	12.13	—	12.17
11.53	1.42	—	1.26
PM 1.40	2.58	—	—
2.29	4. 0	—	3.45
5.17	6.36	—	6.29
6.44	7.56	—	8.27
9. 9	10.25	—	10.10

Sunday Trains.

AM 8.53	10.18	—	10.20
PM 12.19	—	—	1.40
5.15	—	—	6.34
7.57	9.17	—	9. 0
8.40	—	—	9.47

d Saturdays only.
e Saturdays excepted.
k Departs from or arrives at London Bridge (S.E. & C.) Station.
l Fridays only.

COWDENBEATH NEW (Fife), 414½ miles. Fares, 86/6a, 51/1c. R.T.for two months,173/0d, 103/10c. Departures *from* London as for Dunfermline. Departures *for* London about 5 times daily. Pop. 14,215.
Map Square 41.

COWES (Isle of Wight) from *Victoria* and *London Bridge,* 104¼ miles, *via* Ryde. Fares, 20/7a, 12/7c. R. T. for two months, 40/1a, 24/6c. Pop. 9,998.
Map Square 28.

Leave		Arr. at
Vict.	Lon. B.	Cowes
AM 6.18	6.35	11.34
8.55	—	1.34
10.15	10.22	3. 4
10.22	10.22	3.34
PM 1.35	—	5.34
1.40	1.50	6.34
1.55	2. 5	7.34
—	4.50	8.35

Sunday Trains.

AM 9.55	—	1.55
PM 1.14	1.10	7.18

Trains from Cowes.

Leave	Arrive at	
Cowes	Lon. B.	Vict.
AM 7.10	10.55	—
9.10	—	1.10
PM 12.10	4.27	4.34
1.10	—	5.12
3.10	7.48	6.50
4.10	—	8.33
5.10	10. 8	10. 1

Sunday Trains.

PM 3.55	8.50	7.56
—	—	—

h Via Sandown.
k Passengers cross Portsmouth at own expense.

ANOTHER ROUTE from *Waterloo, via* Southampton, 92¼ miles. Fares, 18/11a, 11/10c. R.T. for two months, 36/6a, 22/10c.

W'loo	Cowes	Cowes	W'loo
AM 5.40	9.20	AM 8. 0s	11. 0
8.30s	12.10	9.45r	12.50
PM12.30r	3.20	PM 1.30	4.50
1.30s	4.45	3.45	6.58
4.30r	7.20	6.25	10.50
6.30r	9.30	—	—

Sunday Trains.

AM11. 0r	3.45	AM 8.15	12.11
PM 2. 0r	6.20	10. 0r	2.27
—	—	PM 4. 0	8. 3
—	—	6.55	10.52

r Restaurant Car.
s Refreshments served.
Passengers cross Southampton at own expense.

COWES—*continued.*
ANOTHER ROUTE from *Waterloo, via* Ryde, 92½ miles. Fares, 20/7a, 12/7c. R. T. for two months, 40/1a, 24/6c.

W'LOO	COWES	COWES	W'LOO
AM 5.50	10.54	AM 7.10	11.32
9.50h	1.34	7.40	11.41
10.50	3.54	10.10r	1.52
PM12.50r	4.54	10.40d	3.20
1.50d	5.54	10.40e	4.16
3.50s	7.54	PM 2.10	5.56
5.50	9.42	4.10r	7.56
—	—	5.10	10.46
—	—	8.25kl	3.55

Sunday Trains.

AM 8. 0	12. 3	AM10.25	3.13
9.15r	1.55	PM 2. 0r	6.16
PM 1.50	7.18	3.55	8.52
—	—	5.43	10. 1

h Via Sandown.
k Via Eastleigh.
l Passengers cross Portsmouth at own expense.
r Restaurant Car.
s Refreshments served.

COWLEY (Middlesex) from *Paddington,* 14⅛ miles. Fares, 2/9a, 1/8c. R. T. for two months, 5/6a, 2/11c. Departures *from* London as for Uxbridge (Vine Street). Departures *for* London about 26 times daily. Pop. 1,106.
Map Square 23 and 55.

COWTON (Yorks), 225 miles. Fares, 46/11a, 28/2c. R. T., double fare. Departures *from* London as for Northallerton. Departures *for* London about 3 times daily. Pop. 347.
Map Square 7.

COXBENCH (Derby), 133 miles. Fares, 27/4a, 16/5c. R. T. double fare. Departures *from* London as for Ripley. Departures *for* London about 6 times daily.
Map Square 13.

COX GREEN (Durham), 259¼ miles. No through fares. Departures *from* London as for Ferryhill or Durham. Departures *for* London about 6 times daily.
Map Square 3.

COXHOE BRIDGE (Durham), 247¼ miles. Fares, 51/8*a*, 31/0*c*. R. T. for two months, 103/4*a*, 62/0*c*. Departures *from* London as for Ferryhill. Departures *for* London about 4 times daily. Pop. (Coxhoe) 3,833.
Map Square 7.

COXLODGE (Northumberland), 272¾ miles. No through fares. Departures *from* London as for Newcastle-on-Tyne. Departures *for* London about 6 times daily.

COXWOLD (Yorks), 207¾ miles. Fares, 43/4*a*, 26/0*c*. R. T. for two months, 86/8*a*, 52/0*c*. Departures *from* London as for Ampleforth. Departures *for* London about 5 times daily. Pop. 294.
Map Square 8.

CRADLEY HEATH (Stafford), 121½ miles. Fares, 25/0*a*, 15/0*c*. R. T. for two months, 50/0*a*. Departures *from* London as for Smethwick Junction. Departures *for* London about 4 times daily. Pop. 10,101.
Map Square 17.

CRADOC (Brecon), 185¼ miles. No through fares. Departures *from* London as for Brecon. Departures *for* London about twice daily.
Map Square 16.

CRAIGELLACHIE (Banff), 571¾ miles. Fares, 106/3*a*, 63/9*c*. R. T. for two months, 212/6*a*, 127/6*c*. Departures *from* London as for Aviemore or Keith (*via* Aberdeen). Departures *for* London about twice daily.
Map Square 35.

CRAIGENDORAN PIER (Dumbarton), 458 miles. Fares, 84/2*a*, 50/6*c*. R. T. for two months, 168/4*a*, 101/0*c*. Departures *from* London as for Arrochar and Tarbet. Departures *for* London about twice daily.
Map Square 40.

CRAIGLEITH (Midlothian), 400¼ miles. Fares, 81/8*a*, 49/0*c*. R. T. for two months, 163/4*a*, 98/0*c*. Departures *from* London as for Edinburgh. Departures *for* London about 6 times daily.

CRAIGO (Forfar), 487 miles. Fares, 98/4*a*, 59/0*c*. R. T. for two months, 196/8*a*, 118/0*c*. Departures *from* London as for Forfar. Departures *for* London about 3 times daily.
Map Square 38.

CRAIG-Y-NOS (Brecon), 201½ miles. Fares, 39/9*a*, 23/10*c*. R. T. for two months, 79/6*a*, 47/8*c*. Departures *from* London as for Brecon. Departures *for* London about twice daily.
Map Square 21.

CRAIL (Fife), 446 miles. Fares, 90/0*a*, 54/0*c*. R. T. for two months, 180/0*a*, 108/0*c*. Departures *from* London as for St. Andrews. Departures *for* London about twice daily. Pop. 2,017.
Map Square 41.

CRAKEHALL (Yorks), 227½ miles. No through fares. Departures *from* London as for Leyburn. Departures *for* London about 6 times daily. Pop. 420.
Map Square 7.

CRAMLINGTON (Northumberland), 277¼ miles. Fares, 58/7*a*, 35/2*c*. R. T., double fare. Departures *from* London as for Newcastle-on-Tyne. Departures *for* London about 4 times daily. Pop. 8,529.
Map Square 3.

CRANBROOK (Kent) from *Charing Cross, Cannon Street,* and *London Bridge,* 45½ miles. Fares, 9/7*a*, 7/8*b*, 5/9*c*. R. T. for two months, 19/2*a*, 15/4*b*, 11/6*c*. Departures *from* London as for Horsmonden. Departures *for* London about 4 times daily. Pop. 3,829.
Map Square 24.

CRANFORD (Northampton) from *St. Pancras* 74 miles. Fares, 14/9*a*, 8/10*c*. R. T., double fare. Departures *from* London as for Thrapston. Departures *for* London about 4 times daily. Pop. 423.
Map Square 18.

CRANK (Lancs), 194¼ miles. Fares, 40/5*a*, 24/3*c*. R. T. for two months, 80/10*a*. Departures *from* London as for St. Helens. Departures *for* London about 6 times daily.
Map Square 12.

CRANLEIGH (Surrey) from *Victoria, Clapham Junct.*, and *London Bridge*, 48½ miles. Fares, 8/1*a*, 4/10*c*. R.T. for two months, 16/2*a*. Pop. 3,746.
Map Square 23.

Leave Vict.	Clap. J.	Lon. B.	Arr. at Crangh.
AM 6.18	6.25	6.35	8.28
8.55	7.56	7.35	10.52
10.35	10.42	10.35	1.35
PM 1.40	1.47*e*	1.50	4. 5
3.55	4. 2	4. 0	5.55
5. 5	5.12	5.14	7.17
7.20*d*	7.27*d*	7.20*d*	9.48
—	—	—	—
—	—	—	—
—	—	—	—

Sunday Trains.

AM 8.35	8.42	8.25	10.34
PM 4. 5	4.13	3.50	6.23
—	—	—	—
—	—	—	—

CRANLEIGH—*continued.*

Trains from Cranleigh.

Leave Cranlgh.	Arrive at Lon. B.	Clap. J.	Vict.
AM 6.58*f*	9.10	9.31	9.19
8.30	10.45	10.40	10.48
9.33	11.50	11.35	11.42
10.49	1.28	—	1.10
11.58	2.22	2.13	2.22
PM 2.38	4.27	4.27	4.35
5.36	7.48	7.31	7.39
8. 6*d*	10. 8	9.53	10. 1
8. 9*e*	10. 8	9.53	10. 1

Sunday Trains.

AM 8. 1	10.45	10.23	10.32
PM 7.18	9.32	9.24	9.34
—	—	—	—
—	—	—	—

d Saturdays only.
e Saturdays excepted.
f Mondays only.

ANOTHER ROUTE from *Waterloo*, 38¼ miles. Fares, 8/1*a*, 4/10*c*. R. T. for two months, 16/2*a*.

W'loo.	Cranlgh.	Cranlgh.	W'loo.
AM 6.50	8.30	AM 8.28	9.44
7.50	9.33	9.52	11.32
9. 5	10.41	10.52	12.46
10.20	11.58	PM 1.35	3. 6
PM 12.50	2.38	4. 5	5.52
3.50*d*	5.36	5.55	7.46
4.15*e*	5.36	7.17	9. 6
5.50	7.15	9.48*d*	12.16
6.50*d*	8. 6	—	—
6.50*e*	8. 9	—	—
8.20*d*	10.32	—	—
9.50*d*	11.20	—	—

Sunday Trains.

AM 9.20	11.25	AM 7. 9	9.45
PM 5.20	7.18	10.34	12.41
—	—	PM 6.23	8.41

d Saturdays only.
e Saturdays excepted.

Railway Hotel and Garage. Cranleigh Common. Three minutes from station. Modern and comfortable. Phone 57 Cranleigh. Telegrams, Railway Hotel, Cranleigh.

CRANLEY GARDENS from *Moorgate Street, King's Cross* and *Broad Street,* 5¼ miles. Fares from King's Cross, 0/11½*a*, 0/9*b*, 0/7*c*. R.T. for two days, 1/11*a*, 1/6*b*, 1/2*c*. From Moorgate Street and Broad Street, 1/0½*a*, 0/10*b*, 0/7½*c*. R.T. for two days, 2/1*a*, 1/8*b*, 1/2½*c*. *See* pp. 518-522
Map Square 51.

CRANMORE (Somerset) from *Paddington,* 112¼ miles. Fares, 23/6*a*, 14/1*c*. R. T. for two months, 47/0*a*. Pop. 406.
Map Square 22.

Pad.	Cranre.	Cranre.	Pad.
AM 1. 0*g*	8.58	AM 9.44	12.55
7.30	11.28	PM 12.36	3.50
10.30	1. 9	1.27*t*	5.30
PM 12.30*r*	3.39	4.25	8.20
3.30	7.13	7.32	2.45
5. 5	9. 5	—	—

Sunday Trains.

PM 2.40	5.42	PM 3.16*r*	7.55
—	—	—	—

g Mondays excepted.
r Restaurant Car.
t Tea Car.

CRATHES (Kincardine)

535½ miles. Fares, 102/11a, 61/9c. R. T. for two months, 205/10a, 123/6c. Departures *from* London as for Banchory. Departures *for* London 3 times daily.
Map Square 38.

CRAVEN ARMS (Salop)

from *Euston, via* Shrewsbury, 182½ miles. Fares, 31/11a, 19/2c. R. T. for two months, 63/10a.
Map Square 17.

Euston	C. Arms	C. Arms	Euston
AM 5. 0	10.59	AM 8.43r	2.20
6.45k	12.19	10.55r	3.10
6.45	1.49	PM 1.39r	6.15
10.40r	2.48	4. 7r	9.20
PM 1.15r	5.42	9.56	5. 0
2.20t	8.53	—	—
4.45r	10.24	—	—
5.50d	4.18	—	—
9.20e	4. 6	—	—

Sunday Trains.

AM 9.15	6. 0	AM10.51hr	5.45
PM 9.15h	4. 6	PM 9. 1h	5. 0

d Saturdays only.
e Saturdays excepted.
h Via Crewe.
k Mondays and Fridays only.
n Noon.
r Restaurant Car.

ANOTHER ROUTE from

Paddington, via Shrewsbury, 172½ miles. Fares as above.

Pad.	C. Arms	C. Arms	Pad.
AM 9.10r	1.22	AM 7.57	12.25
10.40t	2.59	8.43r	1.25
10.45r	4.37	9.35r	2. 5
PM12.50r	5.43	10.32r	4.15
2.10t	6.52	11.45r	5. 0
4.10t	8.53	PM 1.39t	5.55
6.10r	10.24	2.24r	8. 5
12.15k	7.18	5.36	10. 0
—	—	9. 3	3.30

Sunday Trains.

PM12.50r	6. 0	AM10.51	6.20

k Saturdays midnight excepted.
r Restaurant Car.
t Tea Car.

ANOTHER ROUTE from

Paddington, via Gloucester and Hereford, 175½ miles. Fares as above.

Pad.	C. Arms	C. Arms	Pad.
AM 1. 0g	10.27	AM 7.20r	2.40
5.30	12.59	11. 0hr	4.15
10.45	5.34	PM 3. 2r	8.45
PM 1.30hr	6.25	6.55	3.30
3.15t	9. 1	—	—

Sunday Trains.

AM10.35h	8.57	—	—

g Mondays excepted.
h Via Worcester.
r Restaurant Car.
t Tea Car.

CRAWFORD (Lanark),

354½ miles. Fares, 71/11a, 43/2c. R.T. for two months, 143/10a, 86/4c. Departures *from* London for Lockerbie. Departures *for* London about 3 times daily. Pop. 2,041.
Map Square 40.

CRAWLEY (Sussex) from

London Bridge, Victoria and *Clapham Junc.,* 31 miles. Fares, 6/5a, 3/10c. R.T. for two months, 12/10a, 7/8c. Pop. 4,421.
Map Square 23.

	Leave		Arr. at
Vict.	Clap. J.	Lon. B.	Craly.
AM —	—	5.18	7.15
7.23	7.29	7.25	9.12
8.25	8.32	8. 7	9.55
9. 0	9. 8	9. 6	10.18
9.45	9.51	9.50	11.13
10.35	10.42	10.35	11.53
11.55	—	11.56	1. 9
PM 1.20e	1.27c	—	2.38
1.25d	—	1.10d	2.38
2. 0	2. 7	2. 5	3.45
—	—	2. 8d	3.45
4.30	4. 8	4. 5	5.22
—	—	5. 5	6. 4
5. 5	5.12	5.10	6.23
5.27	—	5.21	6.35
—	—	6. 0	7. 6
6. 6	6.12	6. 8	7.41
7.15	7.22	7.20	8.58
9. 3	9.10	9.12	10.24

Sunday Trains.

AM 6.55	7. 2	7. 2	8.39
8.18	8.25	8.25	9.58
PM 1.14	1.21	1.10	4. 9
6.33	6.40	6.33	7.52

Trains from Crawley.

Leave Craly.	Arrive at Lon. B.	Clap. J.	Vict.
AM 6.49	8.15	8.15	8.24
8.10	9.10	9.31	9.19
8.32	9.42	9.37	9.44
9.42	10.55	10.40	10.48
10.47	12.13	11.59	12. 7
PM12.15	1.42	1.39	1.50
12.50	2.22	2.13	2.22
2.11	3.39	3.37	3.45
3. 3	—	4. 9	4.17
3.28	4.32	4.27	4.35
4.31	5.54	5.47	5.57
5.33	6.36	6.26	6.34
7. 7	8.46	—	—
9.30	10.58	11.10	11.17

Sunday Trains.

AM 8.10	10.18	—	—
9.20	10.45	10.23	10.32
PM 3.41	5. 3	5. 1	5.11
6.31	7.56	—	7.50
8.15	9.32	9.24	9.34

d Saturdays only.
e Saturdays excepted.

George Hotel. Telephone 9. Fifteenth-century house. Central Heating. Electric Light. Tennis Court. Garden. Garage.
TRUST HOUSES, Ltd.

CRAY (Brecon), 194¾

miles. Fares, 39/9a, 23/10c. R. T. for two months, 79/6a, 47/8c. Departures *from* London as for Brecon. Departures *for* London about 3 times daily   Pop. 399.
Map Square 21.

CRAYFORD (Kent) from

Charing Cross, Cannon Street, and *London Bridge,* 16 miles. Fares, from Charing Cross, 3/4a, 2/8b, 2/0c. R. T. for eight days, 6/8a, 5/4b, 3/11c. Fares from Cannon Street, 3/2a, 2/4b, 1/9c. R. T. for eight days, 5/10a, 4/8b, 3/6c. Pop. 6,947.
See pp. 552-554.

CREAGAN (Argyll), 507½

miles. Fares, 101/10a, 61/1c. R. T. for two months, 203/8a, 122/2c. Departures *from* London as for Oban. Departures *for* London about twice daily.
Map Square 37.

CREDENHILL (Hereford),

146 miles. Fares, 30/10a, 18/6c. R. T. for two months, 61/8a, 37/0c. Departures *from* London as for Hay. Departures *for* London about 4 times daily. Pop. 372.
Map Square 17.

CREDITON (Devon) from

Waterloo, 179½ miles. Fares, 36/11a, 22/2c. R. T. for two months, 73/10a, 44/4c. Pop. 3,502.
Map Square 26.

W'loo.	Cred.	Cred.	W'loo.
AM 9. 0r	1.32	AM 9. 8r	1.56
11. 0r	3.15	11. 5r	3.50
PM 1. 0r	6. 2	PM 1.44r	6. 0
3. 0r	7.28	3.43r	8.30
—	—	5.20	10.50
—	—	6.50h	3.58

Sunday Trains.

12. 0nr	6.18	PM 3. 0r	8.57

h Via Eastleigh.
n Noon.
r Restaurant Car.

CREETOWN (Kirkcudbright), 375½

miles. Fares, 68/9a, 41/3c. R.T. for two months, 137/6a. Departures *from* London as for Castle Douglas. Departures *for* London about 3 times daily. Pop. 757.
Map Square 43.

CREIGIAU (Glamorgan),

161½ miles. Fares, 33/2a, 19/11c. R. T. for two months, 66/4a, 39/10c. Departures *from* London as for St. Fagans. Departures *for* London about 5 times daily

CRESSAGE (Salop), 148

miles. Fares, 30/10a, 18/6c. R. T. for two months, 61/8a. Departures *from* London as for Iron Bridge. Departures *for* London about 5 times daily. Pop. 328.
Map Square 17.

CRESSING (Essex), 43

miles. Fares, 9/2a, 5/6c. R. T. for two months, 18/4a. Departures *from* London as for Braintree (*via* Witham). Departures *for* London about 6 times daily. Pop. 612.
Map Square 24.

CRESSINGTON (Lancs),

221¼ miles. Fares,40/5a, 24/3c. R.T. for two months, 80/10a, 48.6c. Departures *from* London as for Warrington (Central). Departures *for* London about 4 times daily.

CRESSWELL (Stafford),

152½ miles. Fares, 35/8 *t*, 18/5c. R.T. for two months, 61/4 *a*. Departures *from* London as for Longton. Departures *for* London about 5 times daily. Pop. 46.
Map Square 12.

CREWE (Cheshire) from

Euston, 158 miles. Fares, 32/11a, 19/9c. R.T. for two months, 65/10a. Pop. 46,477.
Map Square 12.

EUSTON	CREWE	CREWE	EUSTON
AM12.25	3.23	AM12.50	5. 0
2.35	5.53	1. 5g	5.40
5. 0	9. 0	2.45	5.50
6.45	11. 5	3.20d	6.40
8.30r	11.36	3.43g	6.55
10. 0r	12.59	4. 5g	7.15
10.30r	1.25	4.20	7.30
10.40r	1.54	4.30g	7.40
11.50r	2.45	4.50g	8. 0
12. 0nr	4.12	9. 5er	12. 5
PM 1.30r	4.35	9. 5dr	12.20
2.35t	5.36	10. 0r	1. 0
4. 5r	7. 6	10.50r	1.45
5.20r	8.22	11. 7r	2.20
6.30er	10. 5	PM12. 9r	3.10
r7.30er	10.35	12.23g	3.45
7.40er	10.40	12.43r	4.15
7.50e	11. 9	1. 5	5.35
8. 0	11.22	2.40t	5.50
8.45	11.59	2.59t	6. 0
9.20	12.42	3.25t	6.25
9.30	1. 3	4.25r	7.30
11. 0d	1.55	5. 4r	8.10
11.35e	2.30	5.31r	9.20
11.45e	2.58	6.14er	9. 5
—	—	6.14dr	9.15
—	—	6.55r	10. 0
—	—	7.32r	10.45

Sunday Trains.

AM 9.15	2.16	AM12.50	5. 0
11.30r	2.41	1. 5	5.45
11.45r	3. 5	2.45	5.50
PM12.10r	3.54	4. 5	7.15
12.30r	3.57	4.20	7.30
3.50	8.43	4.30	7.40
6. 0r	9. 4	4.50	8. 0
7.50r	11. 9	10. 7r	1.30
9.15	1.27	11.55	4. 0
11.35	2.30	PM 2. 5r	5.45
—	—	3.55r	7.10
—	—	4.25r	7.30
—	—	5. 0r	8.20
—	—	5.25	8.55

d Saturdays only.
e Saturdays excepted,
g Mondays excepted,
h Via Birmingham.
n Noon.
r Restaurant Car.
t Tea Car.
v Commences July 27.
y Mondays and Saturdays only.

Crewe Arms Hotel. Under the management of the L. M. & S. Rly. Co. This Hotel adjoins Crewe Junction. Telegrams : " Bestotel, Crewe." Telephone No. 21.

CREWE GREEN (Mont-

gomery), 173½ miles. No through fares. Departures *from* London as for Shrewsbury or Oswestry. Departures *for* London about twice daily.

CREWKERNE (Somerset)

from *Waterloo*, 131¾ miles. Fares, 27/6 *t*, 16/6c. R.T. for two months, 55/0a, 33/0c Pop. 3,793.
Map Square 27.

W'LOO	CREWK.	CREWK.	W'LOO.
AM 7.30	11.19	AM 7.50r	11.10
12. 0r	3.17	10.26r	1.56
PM 1. 0r	4.50	11.53r	3. 8
3. 0r	6.38	PM 2.24r	6. 0
6. 0r	9.20	4.53r	8.30
—	—	7. 5	10.50
—	—	9.12h	3.58

Sunday Trains.

AM 9. 0	2.17	PM 5. 1r	8.57
12. 0nr	4. 7		

h Via Eastleigh.
n Noon.
r Restaurant Car.

CREWS HILL (Middlesex)

from *King's Cross, Moorgate Street* or *Broad Street*, 11½ miles. Fares from King's Cross, 2/2½a, 1/9b, 1/4c. R.T. for two days, 4/5a, 3/6b, 2/7½c. From Moorgate Street or Broad Street, 2/3½a, 1/10b, 1/4½c. R.T. for two days, 4/7a, 3/8b, 2/8c. *See* pp. 511-517.

CRIANLARICH (Perth)

from *Euston*, 462 miles. Fares, 91/6 *t*, 54/11c. R.T. for two months 183/0a, 109/10c.
Map Square 37.

EUSTON	CR'NL'CH.	CR'NL'CH.	EUSTON
AM 5. 0	7.53h	AM 7.15r	7.30t
PM 1.30er	2.34h	10.56r	10.45
1.30dr	2.45	PM 1.37r	5. 0h
7.50er	7.54h	7. 0	7.40h
11.35e	3. 0t	—	—

Sunday Trains.

PM 7.50r	7.54h	—	—
11.35	10.45h	—	—

d Saturdays only.
e Saturdays excepted.
h A.M.
l P.M.
r Restaurant Car.

ANOTHER ROUTE from

King's Cross, 494½ miles. Fares as above.

AM 4.45	5.44h	AM 2. 0	3.25h
PM 7.45er	7.44h	PM 6.24	6.50f
11.25ek	1.19	—	—

Sunday Trains.

PM 7.45r	7.44h	—	—
11.25	1.19k	—	—

e Saturdays excepted.
f Arrives 7.5 A.M. Sundays.
k P.M.

CRICCIETH (Carnarvon)

from *Paddington, via* Ruabon, 258 miles. Fares, 53/7a, 32/2c. R.T. for two months, 107/2a. Pop. 1,886.
Map Square 11.

PAD.	CRICC.	CRICC.	PAD.
AM 9.10r	4.42	AM 6.28r	2. 5
10.20r	5.34	9.12r	5. 0
10.40r	6. 5	10.32r	6.40
PM12.50r	8.55	PM12.12r	8. 5
2.10t	9.53	1.22r	10. 0
12.15h	1.23	4.21	3.30

No Sunday Trains.

h Saturday midnight excepted.
r Restaurant Car.
t Tea Car.

CRICCIETH—*continued.*

ANOTHER ROUTE from

Euston, 269¼ miles. Fares, *via* Shrewsbury or Whitchurch, 53/7a, 32/2c. R.T. for two months, 107/2a *Via* Carnarvon, 54/10a, 32/1c. R. T. for two months, 103/8a.

AM12.25	10.51	AM 6.50hr	1.45
2.35	1.22	10.10hr	5. 5
5. 0h	1.57	10.34dr	7.30
8.30hr	4.21	PM12.10er	7.30
11.10hr	5.36	1.23hr	9.20
11.50hr	8.53	2. 0hr	10.45
PM 9.30eh	6.28	6.45h	5. 0

Sunday Trains.

PM 9.15h	6.28	—	—

d Saturdays only.
e Saturdays excepted.
h Via Carnarvon.
r Restaurant Car.

CRICKLADE (Wilts) from

Waterloo, 107½ miles. Fares,18/2a, 10/11c. R.T. for two months, 36/4a. Pop. 1,521.
Map Square 22.

W'LOO.	CRICLDE.	CRICLDE	W'LOO.
PM 1. 0r	4.15	AM11.27	2.36
3.30	7. 6	PM 2.27d	6.26
—	—	4.15r	8.30

No Sunday Trains.

d Saturdays only.
r Restaurant Car.

CRICKLEWOOD (Mid-

dlesex) from *St. Pancras* and *Moorgate Street*, 5¼ miles. Fares, 1/0½a, 0/7½c. R.T. for two days, 2/0½a, 1/2c. *See* pp. 597, 508. Pop. 19,657.
Map Square 59.

CRIEFF (Perth) from *Eus-*

ton, 443 miles. Fares, 90/8a, 54/5c. R. T. for two months, 181/4a, 108/10c. Pop. 6,445.
Map Square 37.

EUSTON	CRIEFF	CRIEFF	EUSTON
AM 5. 0	5.45	AM 8.50r	7.30
10. 0r	8.46	PM12. 5r	10.45
PM 7.50er	6.55	2.28r	5. 0h
11.35e	9.45	7.47	7.40

Sunday Trains.

PM 7.50r	6.55	—	—
11.35	9.45	—	—

d Saturdays only.
e Saturdays excepted.
h A.M.
r Restaurant Car.

Drummond Arms Hotel. Situated on Great North Road. Recherché Cuisine. R.A.C. Garage adjoining. Telegrams : "Premier, Crieff." Telephone 87. *See* advt. p. **129**.

CRIGGION (Montgomery).

172 miles. No through fares. Departures *from* London as for Shrewsbury or Oswestry. Departures *for* London about twice daily. Pop. 136.
Map Square 17.

CRIGGLESTONE

(Yorks), 179¾ miles. Fares, 37/4*a*, 22/5*c*. R. T. for two months, 74/8*a*, 44/10*c*. Departures from London as for Wakefield. Departures *for* London about 8 times daily. Pop. 4,369.
Map Square 12.

CROFT (Leicester) from

Euston, 106½ miles. Fares, 20/2*a*, 12/1*c*. R. T., double fare. Departures *from* London as for Hinckley. Departures for London about 9 times daily. Pop. 742.
Map Square 18.

CROFTON (Yorks) from

King's Cross, 178¾ miles. Fares, 36/6*a*, 21/11*c*. R T., double fare. Departures *from* London as for Featherstone. Departures *for* London about 10 minutes earlier. Pop. 2,566.
Map Square 12.

CROFTON PARK

(Kent) from *Victoria, Holborn Viaduct, Ludgate Hill*, and *St. Paul's*, 7 miles. Fares, 1/3*a*, 1/0*b*, 0/9*c*. R. T. for two days, 2/0*a*, 1/4*b*, 1/0*c*. *See* pp. 562-563.
Map Square 71.

CROFT SPA (Yorks), 229¼

miles. Fares, 47/9*a*, 28/8*c*. R.T., double fare. Departures *from* London as for Northallerton. Departures *for* London about 5 times daily. Pop. 494.
Map Square 7.

CROMDALE (Elgin), 550¾

miles. Fares, 106/3*a*, 63/9*c*. R.T. for two months, 212/6*a*, 127/6*c*. Departures *from* London as for Aviemore or Keith (*via* Aberdeen). Departures *for* London about twice daily. Pop. 3,018.
Map Square 35.

CROMER (Norfolk) from

Liverpool Street, 138 miles. Fares, 26/3*a*, 15/9*c*. R.T. for two months, 52/6*a*, 31/6*c*. Pop. 5,435.
Map Square 13.

L'PL ST.	CROMER	CROMER	L'PL ST.
AM 5. 5	10.24	AM 6.32*f*	10.36
8.15*r*	12.19	7.45*r*	11.22
9.50*r*	1.35	9.10	1.20
PM12.25*r*	3.22	PM12.50*r*	3.50
12.33*r*	4.22	1. 0*r*	4.58
3.10*r*	6.45	2.20	6.32
5.18*r*	9.20	3.44*r*	8.33
—	—	5.30*r*	9.22
—	—	8.46	2.50

Sunday Trains.

AM 9.20*r*	3. 7	PM 1. 0	6.40
PM 4.40	10.8	5.40*r*	9.10
—	—	8. 0	3. 0

f Mondays only.
r Restaurant Car.

CROMER BEACH from

King's Cross, 159¼ miles. Fares as above.
Map Square 13.

KING'S +	CROM.B.	CROM.B.	KING'S+
AM 4.45	10.10	AM 7.55	1. 5
7.15*r*	1.22	9.30	3.50
10.10*r*	4.47	PM12.10	4.30
PM 1.50*r*	7.10	3. 5	9. 0
3. 0	7.29	—	—

No Sunday Trains.

r Restaurant Car.

CROMER—*continued.*

Royal Links Hotel. Near Golf Links. Excellent Cuisine. Spacious Garage. Telephone 120. *See advt.* p. **130.**

Hotel de Paris. Opposite Pier. Every modern luxury. Leading Cromer Hotel. Finest position.
See advt. p. **131.**

Tucker's Royal Hotel. Facing Sea. First-class. Comfortable, and moderate prices.
See advt. p. **131.**

Cliftonville Hotel. Beautifully situated, overlooking Sea. Ballroom. Billiards. Lift. Garage. Telephone No. 154. Apply PROPRIETOR *See advt.* p. **132.**

Parade Boarding Establishment. On Sea Front. Moderate.
See advt. p. **132.**

Southern Bungalow. First-class Private Hotel. In own grounds. *See advt.* p. **133.**

Craigside (Private and Residential). Excellent Cuisine. Private Tennis Lawn.
Apply, PROPRIETRESS.
See advt. p. **133.**

Sea View Private Hotel. Oldest-Established. First-class. Spacious rooms overlooking Cliffs and Sea. Illustrated Tariff. Proprietress, Mrs. NEWMAN.
See advt. p. **134.**

Grand Hotel. Finest position on West Cliff. Facing Sea. Redecorated throughout. Garage. Apply, MANAGER.
See advt. p. **134.**

Marlborough House Hotel. Facing Sea. Luxuriously Furnished. Garage for 30 Cars.
See advt. p. **135.**

Newhaven Court Guest House (Private Hotel). Standing in 10 acres of ground. Hard and Grass Courts. Dance Hall and Garage. Near Sea and Links.
See advt. p. **135.**

Elmhurst Private Hotel. Charming situation. 40 Bedrooms. Lounge. Electric light. Tel. 60. Tariff, apply—
Mrs. E. FARROW.
See advt. p. **135.**

West Cliff Hotel. Facing Pier. Fully licensed. Moderate terms. Old-established. Tel. 200.
See advt. p. **136.**

Brunswick House. Immediately overlooking Beach. Electric Light. Excellent Service. Moderate.
See advt. p. **136.**

Ye Olde Red Lion. First-class Family and Commercial Hotel. Garage. Facing Sea and Promenade. Telephone No. 43.
Proprietor, REILLY MEAD.

Westward Ho! Private Hotel. Ideal situation on Sea Front. Comfortable. Old-established. Billiards. 'Phone 23.
Proprietors—
Mr. & Mrs. ARTHUR VICARY.

Clifden Boarding House, East Runton, near Cromer. Facing Sea. Near Links. Good Bathing. Delightful walks. Open throughout the year. Propr'ess.—
Mrs. A. J. GREENHILL.

CROMER—*continued.*

Abbeville Boarding Establishment. Convenient, comfortable. Close Cliffs. Good sea view. Moderate tariff. Separate tables. Electric light, Proprietress—
Miss L. WILLIAMS.

Ship Hotel. Family and Commercial. Near Sea Front. Noted for Catering. Electric Light throughout. Moderate Charges. Garage. 'Phone 87.
F. W. FREEMAN.

Colne Guest House. Facing south, standing in picturesque grounds, over 3 acres. Five minutes Sea. Tennis. Near Links. Garage. Stabling. Separate tables. Moderate terms. Telephone 103. Proprietress,
A. M. DOWDING.

Glen Holme, Cabbell Road. Small First-class Boarding Establishment. One minute Sea and Promenade. Personal supervision throughout. Highest Testimonials. Mrs. PARKER.

Shrublands Boarding Establishment. Excellent position. Three minutes Sea. Separate Tables. Electric Light. Cooking and comfort thoroughly understood. Mrs. BARRINGER.

House Agents, Auctioneers, Valuers. Furnished Houses — Cromer, Sheringham, Overstrand, Mundesley. Please state requirements. Lists free. ALLMAN & GIBSON.
Tel. 63. Cromer.

Furnished Houses and all classes Property — Cromer, Sheringham, Overstrand, Mundesley and County. Register Free. LIMMERS, Cromer (Tel. 26), Sheringham (Tel. 4).

CROMFORD (Derby)

from *St. Pancras*, 143½ miles. Fares, 29/7*a*, 17/9*c*. R. T. for two months, 59/2*a*, 35/6*c*. Pop. 1,015.
Map Square 12.

ST. PAN.	CROMFD.	CROMFD.	ST. PAN.
AM 2.25	7.50	AM 7.55*r*	11.35
4.25	10.56	8.57*r*	1.20
8.25*r*	1. 6	11. 5	3.25
10.25*r*	1.53	PM 1.50*r*	5.45
PM12.25*r*	4.25	6.26*r*	10. 5
2.25*r*	6.34	9.33	4.20
4.25*r*	7.52	—	—
12. 0*h*	7.48	—	—

Sunday Trains.

PM 3.15	7.42	AM11.45*r*	5. 2
—	—	PM 8.58	4.55

h Saturdays midnight only.
r Restaurant Car.

Greyhound Hotel. Family and Commercial. Mile from Matlock. Motor Pit. Stabling. Near Golf and Fishing. Ample accommodation for Parties. P.R.H.A. House.

CRONBERRY (Ayr), 376¼

miles. No through fares. Departures *from* London as for Old Cumnock. Departures *for* London about 4 times daily.
Map Square 40.

CROOK (Durham), 250¼ miles. Fares, 52/1*a*, 31/3*c*. R.T. double fare. Departures *from* London as for Bishop Auckland. Departures *for* London about 5 times daily. Pop. 12,706.
Map Square 7.

CROOK OF DEVON (Kinross), 428 miles. No through fares. Departures *from* London as for Dunfermline or Stirling. Departures *for* London about 3 times daily.
Map Square 40.

CROOKSTON (Renfrew), 414½ miles. Fares, 82/6*a*, 49/6*c*. R.T. for two months, 165/0*a*, 99/0*c*. Departures *from* London as for Kilmarnock or Glasgow (St. Enoch). Departures *for* London about 4 times daily.

CROPREDY (Oxford) from *Paddington*, 71 miles. Fares, 14/10*a*, 8/11*c*. R.T. for two months, 29/8*a*. Departures *from* London as for Southam Road. Departures *for* London about 4 times daily. Pop. 405.
Map Square 18.

CROSBY GARRETT (Westmorland) from *St. Pancras*, 269¾ miles. Fares, 52/11*a*, 31/9*c*. R. T., double fare. Departures *from* London as for Kirkby Stephen. Departures *for* London about 3 times daily. Pop. 184.
Map Square 7.

CROSSENS (Lancs), 214¾ miles. Fares, 44/0*a*, 26/5*c*. R. T. for two months, 88/0*a*, 52/10*c*. Departures *from* London as for Southport or Preston. Departures *for* London about 6 times daily. Pop. 1,425.
Map Square 12.

CROSSFORD (Dumfries), 345¾ miles. No through fares. Departures *from* London as for Dumfries. Departures *for* London about twice daily.
Map Square 43.

CROSSGATES (Fife), 412¾ miles. No through fares. Departures *from* London as for Dunfermline. Departures *for* London about 3 times daily.
Map Square 41.

CROSS GATES (Yorks), 190½ miles. No through fares. Departures *from* London as for Selby or Leeds. Departures *for* London about 5 times daily.
Map Square 12.

CROSSHILL & CODNOR (Derby), 132½ miles. Fares, 26/11*a*, 16/2*c*. R.T. for two months, 53/10*a*, 32/4*c*. Departures *from* London as for Langley Mill. Departures *for* London about 4 times daily.

CROSSHOUSE (Ayr), 392½ miles. Fares, 79/10*a*, 47/11*c*. R.T. for two months, 159/8*a*, 95/10*c*. Departures *from* London as for Kilmarnock. Departures *for* London about 4 times daily. Pop. 2,424.

CROSS INN (Glamorgan), 163½ miles. Fares, 34/7*a*, 20/9*c*. R. T. for two months, 69/2*a*, 41/6*c*. Departures *from* London as for Pontypridd. Departures *for* London about 5 times daily.

CROSS KEYS (Monmouth) from *Paddington*, 148¾ miles. Fares, 31/1*a*, 18/8*c*. R. T. for two months, 62/2*a*. Departures *from* London as for Risca. Departures *for* London about 8 times daily.
Map Square 21.

CROSSMICHAEL (Kirkcudbright), 355½ miles. Fares, 68/9*a*, 41/3*c*. R.T. for two months, 137/6*a*, 82/6*c*. Departures *from* London as for Castle Douglas. Departures *for* London about 3 times daily. Pop. 1,231.
Map Square 43.

CROSSMYLOOF (Renfrew), 412½ miles. Fares, 82/6*a*, 49/6*c*. R. T. for two months, 165/0*a*, 99/0*c*. Departures *from* London as for Kilmarnock. Departures *for* London about 4 times daily.

CROSTON (Lancs), 216¼ miles. Fares 45/3*a*, 27/2*c*. R. T. for two months, 90/6*a*, 54/4*c*. Departures *from* London as for Preston. Departures *for* London about 4 times daily. Pop. 1,970.
Map Square 12.

CROUCH END (Middlesex) from *King's Cross*, *Moorgate Street*, and *Broad Street*, 3¼ miles. Fares from King's Cross, 0/7½*a*, 0/6*b*, 0/4½*c*. R.T. for two days, 1/3*a*, 1/0*b*, 0/9*c*. From Moorgate Street and Broad Street, 0/9*a*, 0/7*b*, 0/5½*c*. R. T. for two days, 1/6*a*, 1/2*b*, 0/10½*c*. Pop. 6,435. *See* pp. 518-522.
Map Square 51.

CROUCH HILL (London) from *Moorgate Street* and *St. Pancras*, 3¾ miles. Fares from St. Pancras, 0/9*a*, 0/5½*c*. R. T. for two days, 1/4*a*, 0/10½*c*. From Moorgate Street, 0/9*a*, 0/5½*c*. R. T. for two days 1/6*a*, 0/10½*c*. *See* pp. 506-507.
Map Square 51.

CROWBOROUGH (Sussex) from *London Bridge*, and *Victoria*, *via* Groombridge, 39 miles. Fares, 8/2*a*, 4/11*c*. R.T. for two months, 16/4*a*, 9/10*c*. Pop. 5,143.
Map Square 24.

	Leave Vict.	Leave Lon. B.	Arr. at Crobro'.
AM	5.30	5.18	7.27
	6.37	6.40	9.40
	7.23	8. 7	10.21
	9.10	9. 6	10.49
	11. 5	10.35	12.23
	12. 0	11.50	2.24
	12. 0*d*	12.20*dk*	2.24
PM	—	12.50*d*	2.55
	1.20*e*	1.38*e*	3.23
	1.25*d*	1.38*d*	3.23
	—	2. 5*e*	4.27
	2.25	2.25*d*	4.27
	3.45	—	4.52
	—	4.44*e*	5.54
	4.50	—	6.20
	5. 5	5.21	7. 1
	6. 6*e*	6. 8*e*	7.22
	6. 6	6. 8	7.57
	8. 5	8.10	9.20
	—	—	—
	—	—	—

Sunday Trains.

AM	8.50	8.30	10.22
PM	1.14	1.10	4. 3
	2.30	—	5. 8
	7. 5	6.46	9.14
	—	—	—

CROWBOROUGH—*cont.*

Trains from Crowborough.

	Leave Crobro'.	Arrive at Lon. B.	Arrive at Vict.
AM	7.59	9.32	9.40
	8.48	10. 4	10.12
	9.10	10.55	10.20
	10.23	12.13	12.17
	11.11	12.44	12.35
PM	1. 2	2.58	—
	1.50	—	3.45
	3. 5	5.21	5.55
	4.52	6.36	6.29
	6. 6	7.56	8.27
	8.24	10.25	10.10
	—	—	—

Sunday Trains.

AM	8.12	10.18	10.22
	10.43	—	1.41
PM	4.43	—	6.34
	8.18	—	9.47

d Saturdays only.
e Saturdays excepted.
k Depart from London Bridge S.E. & C. Station.

The Beacon Hotel. The Largest and Most Luxurious Country Hotel in the South. Magnificent grounds. Private Suites. Garage. Telephone No. 5. Apply MANAGER.
See advt. p **137**.

Crest Hotel. An Ideal Health Resort, 800 feet above sea-level. Near Golf Links. Spacious Public Rooms and Winter Garden. Electric Light. Large Grounds. Tennis, Croquet, and Billiards. Excellent cuisine. Comfort. Moderate Terms. Telegrams, "Crest, Crowborough." Telephone No. 94. For terms apply— MANAGER.

The Misses Wood, late of Ivy Hall, have transferred their First-class Boarding Establishment to the next house, "Strathmore." Tennis, Croquet. Home Comforts. THE MISSES WOOD. "Strathmore."

"The Rowans." Quiet Boarding House. Southern slope of Beacon. Ideal winter position. Facing Common and Golf Links. Uninterrupted views.

Ivy Hall. Most comfortable Private Hotel. Ideal position. 800 ft. above sea. Under owner's personal supervision. Tennis; Croquet. Seven minutes Golf. Telephone No. 26.

Craigmore House (Private and Residential). Beautifully situated. Extensive Grounds. Tennis, Croquet, Billiards, Garage. Near Links. Experienced supervision. 'Phone 252. MRS. ARTHUR CORNELL.

Moorside Dormy House. Splendid Position. Adjoining Golf House. Excellent Service and Cuisine. Tel. 251.

The Country House Hotel. Most comfortable Residential Hotel. Extensive Grounds. Central heating throughout. Billiards. Near Links and Village. Telephone 2.

CROWCOMBE (Somerset) from *Paddington*, 151¾ miles. Fares, 31/8*a*, 19/0*c*. R.T. for two months, 63/4*a*. Departures *from* London as for Bishop's Lydeard. Departures *for* London about 4 times daily. Pop. 408.
Map Square 21.

CROWBOROUGH.—CREST HOTEL. (See advt. above.)

CROWDEN (Derby), 185¼

miles. Fares. 37/6a, 22/6c. R. T., double fare. Departures *from* London as for Penistone. Departures *for* London about 3 times daily.
Map Square 12.

CROWHURST (Sussex)

from *Charing Cross, Cannon Street* and *London Bridge*, 58½ miles. Fares, 12/1a, 9/8b, 7/3c. R. T. for two months, 24/2a, 19/4b. Pop.451.
Map Square 29.

Leave			Arr. at
CHAR. +	CAN. ST	LON. B.	CROHST.
AM —	5.20	5.25	8.20
—	7.56	8. 0	10.33
9.25	—	9.33	11.11
10.40	—	10.46	12.19
PM 12. 3*c*	—	12.10*c*	2.35
1. 5*d*	—	1.11*d*	2.53
2. 0*d*	—	2. 5*d*	3.36
2. 8	—	2.16	4. 6
3.48*e*	—	—	5.44
5. 5*d*	—	—	6.33
—	5.12*e*	—	7. 2
6. 3*e*	—	—	8. 3
—	6.16*e*	6.19*e*	7.44
7.30	—	—	9. 0
9.30*y*	—	9.36*y*	11.23

Sunday Trains.

AM 7. 5	—	7.11	9.30
8.45	—	—	10.12
9.50	—	9.56	11.40
11.20	—	—	12.45
PM 7.35	—	7.45	9.58

Trains from Crowhurst.

Leave		Arrive at	
CROHST.	LON. B.	CAN. ST.	CHAR. +
AM 7. 9*e*	8.48	8.52	—
7.51	—	9.15	—
8.25	—	9.48	—
8.43*d*	10.29	—	10.39
9.20*e*	11. 7	—	11.17
10. 1	11.43	—	11.57
11.16	—	—	12.49
PM 12.26	3. 6	—	3.19
2.46	4.15	—	4.25
3.41*d*	6.30	—	6.39
5.12	6.40	—	6.49
6.32	8.26	—	8.35
7.24	8.50	—	9. 0
7.54	10.15	—	10.23
9. 4	11.35	—	11.44

Sunday Trains.

AM 7.21	10. 5	—	10.15
9.21	11.23	—	11.34
PM 5.35	—	—	7. 3
5.46	8.12	—	8.22
7.25	9. 4	—	9.14
8.39	10. 8	—	10.16
8.55	11. 4	—	11.15

d Saturdays only.
e Saturdays excepted.
y Wednesdays and Saturdays only.

CROWLE (Lincoln), 171¾

miles. Fares, 35/8a, 21/5c. R. T. for two months, 71/4a, 42/10c. Departures *from* London as for Thorne. Departures *for* London about twice daily. Pop. 3,010.
Map Square 13.

CROW PARK (Notts), 127½

miles. Fares, 26/6a, 15/11c. R. T., double fare. Departures *from* London as for Carlton-on-Trent. Departures *for* London about 4 times daily.
Map Square 13.

CROXALL (Stafford), 132½

miles. Fares, 24/2a, 14/6c. R.T. for two months, 48/4a, 29/0c. Departures *from* London as for Burton-on-Trent. Departures *for* London about 4 times daily. Pop. 218.
Map Square 17.

CROXDALE (Durham),

249¾ miles. Fares, 52/1a, 31/3c. R. T., double fare. Departures *from* London as for Ferryhill. Departures *for* London about 4 times daily.
Map Square 7.

CROXLEY GREEN

(Herts), 18 miles. Fares from Euston, 3/7a, 2/2c. R.T. for two months, 7/2a, 4/0½c. From Broad Street, 4/0a, 2/5c. R. T. for two months, 8/0a, 4/8c. Pop. 2,390.
See p. 500.

CROY (Dumbarton), 428

miles. Fares, 81/5a, 48/10c. R. T. for two months, 162/10a, 97/8c. Departures *from* London as for Falkirk. Departures *for* London about 4 times daily.
Map Square 40.

CROYDON (Addiscombe

Road) (Surrey)from *Charing Cross, Cannon Street,*and *London Bridge*, 13½ miles. Fares, 2/1a, 1/3b, 1/3c. R.T. for two days, 4/2a, 3/1b, 2/2c.
See pp. 546-547.

CROYDON EAST

(Surrey) from *London Bridge* (L.B. & S.C.R.), 10¼ miles. Fares, 2/1a, 1/3c. R.T. for two days, 4/2a, 2/2c. Pop. (Croydon) 190,684.
Map Square 23.

For extra trains to Local Station see pp. 568-570.

LON. B.	CROY. E.	CROY. E.	LON. B.
AM 5.18	5.50	AM 7.51	8.15
6.15	6.33	8. 1	8.19
6.40	6.58	8.20	8.37
7.25	7.57	8.29	8.46
8. 7	8.32	8.37	8.53
9. 6	9.25	8.44	9. 0
9.25	10. 3	8.52	9.10
9.50	10.12	8.58	9.15
10.35	11. 2	9. 8	9.25
11.40	11.58	9.14	9.32
PM 12.10	12.27	9.34	9.55
12.20*d*	12.41	10.21	10.38
12.50*d*	1. 8	10.37	10.55
1.38	1.58	10.53	11.10
2. 0	2.19	11. 3	11.20
2. 5	2.25	11.53	12.13
2.25*d*	2.42	PM 12. 2	12.19
2.57*d*	3.19	12.26	12.44
4. 5	4.22	1.20	1.42
4.10	4.30	2. 2	2.22

CROYDON EAST—*cont.*

LON. B.	CROY. E.	CROY. E.	LON. B.
PM 4.20	4.39	PM 2.40	2.58
4.44*c*	5. 2	3.14	3.40
5.10	5.30	3.43	4. 0
5.21	5.42	4.11	4.32*c*
5.41*c*	6. 2	4.30	4.57
6. 8	6.32	5. 2	5.21
7. 0	7.21	5.30	5.54
7.20	7.44	6.17	6.36
7.38	8. 0	7.19	7.42
8.10	8.33	7.38	7.56
9.12	9.30	8.21	8.46
10.35	10.54	8.59	9.42
10.50*e*	11.26	9.39	10. 0
—	—	10. 4	10.25
—	—	10.28	10.58
—	—	12.35	12.59
—	—	—	—
—	—	—	-. —

Sunday Trains.

AM 7. 2	7.39	AM 9.52	10.18
7.22	7.49	10.19	10.45
8.25	8.49	10.49	11.15
8.30	8.57	PM 4.39	5. 3
8.55	9.23	7.31	7.56
9.30	9.53	8. 9	8.34
PM 1.10	1.39	8.55	9.17
6. 0	6.30	9. 1	9.26
6.33	7. 0	9. 8	9.32
6.46	7.12	10.27	10.50
8. 0	8.34	11. 9	11.34
9.10	9.36	12. 3	12.27
—	—	—	—
—	—	—	—

d Saturdays only.
e Saturdays excepted.

ANOTHER ROUTE from

Victoria, 10 miles. Fares as above.
For extra trains to Local Station, see pp. 574-577.

VICT.	CROY. E.	CROY. E.	VICT.
AM 5.30	5.58	AM 7.55	8.24
6.37	7. 3	8.18	8.40
7.23	7.57	8.46	9. 8
8.25	8.49	9. 0	9.19
8.55	9.15	9.17	9.40
9. 0	9.23	9.37	9.58
9.10	9.38	9.52	10.12
9.45	10.12	10. 7	10.24
10. 5	10.29	10.15	10.36
10.35	11. 2	10 27	10.48
11. 5	11.28	10.34	10.56
11.15	11.33	10.59	11.17
12. 0	12.26	11.11	11.35
PM 1.20*e*	1.44	11.44	12. 7
2. 0	2.28	11.58	12.17
2.25	2.58	PM 12.13	12.55
4. 0	4.30	12.23	12.45
4.50	5.10	1. 6	1.26
5. 5	5.31	1.25	1.49
5.15*e*	6. 2	1.59	2.22
6. 6	6.35	3.23	3.45
6.50	7.14	3.40	4. 3
7.15	7.40	3.56	4.17
8. 5	8.31	4.14	4.35
8.20	8.38	4.25*d*	4.45
9. 3	9.31	4.39	5. 0
10. 0	10.18	5.34	5.55
10.30	10.55	6. 9	6.29
11.15	11.46	6.14	6.34
11.50*l*	12. 9	7. 7	7.30
—	—	7.23	7.45
—	—	7.32	7.50
—	—	7.56	8.27
—	—	8.25	8.48
—	—	9.24*d*	9.45
—	—	9.48	10.10
—	—	9.56	10.17
—	—	10.57	11.17
—	—	12.37	1. 0

CROYDON EAST—*cont.*
Sunday Trains.

VICT.	CROY. E.	CROY. E.	VICT.
AM 6.55	7.39	AM 9.46	10.20
8.18	8.46	10. 9	10.32
8.50	9.13	10.29	10.50
9.25	9.43	PM12.12	12.47
9.30	9.53	12.36	1. 0
10.20	10.58	1.18	1.35
11. 5	11.27	2.43	3. 5
11.15	11.37	4.42	5.11
PM12.15	12.37	6. 5	6.34
1.10	1.31	6.39	7. 0
1.14	1.40	7. 8	7.28
2.30	3.'1	7.16	7.37
4. 0	4.22	7.33	7.50
5.50	6.30	8.12	8.41
6.33	6.56	8.39	9. 0
7. 5	7.30	8.50	9.13
8. 0	8.28	9.11	9.34
8.20	8.38	9.27	9.47
9. 5	9.35	9.28	10. 0
9.25	9.43	9.58	10.19
—	—	10.24	10.45
—	—	10.32	10.55
—	—	10.37	10.59
—	—	11.12	11.42
—	—	—	—

e Saturdays excepted.
l Tuesdays and Fridays excepted.

ANOTHER ROUTE from
Charing Cross, Cannon Street, and *London Bridge,* 12¼ miles. Fares, 2/1*a*, 1/8*b*, 1/3*c*. R. T. for two days, 4/2*a*, 3/1*b*, 2/2*c*.

CHAR. +	CAN. ST.	LON. B.	CROY.E.
AM —	4.44	5. 0	5.19
—	—	*h*7.50	8. 8
—	—	*h*9.13	9.31
—	—	*h*9.33	9.51
—	—	*h*10. 3*l*	10.21
—	10.12	10.15	10.36
10.55	—	11. 3	11.24
—	11.40*d*	11.43*d*	12. 2
11.48*e*	—	11.54*e*	12.14
PM —	12.16*d*	12.19*d*	12.40
—	12.40*d*	12.45*d*	1. 2
—	—	*h*12.45*e*	1. 2
12.44*d*	—	12.51*d*	1.11
12.55	—	1. 4	1.25
—	1.20	1.23	1.41
—	1.24*d*	1.27*d*	1.51
—	—	*h*1.30*e*	1.48
—	—	*h*1.34*d*	1.54
—	—	*h*1.50*d*	2. 8
2. 3*e*	2. 8*d*	2.10	2.31
—	—	*h*2.22*d*	2.41
2.35*d*	—	2.41*d*	3. 0
2.46*d*	—	2.52*d*	3.11
3.15	—	3.21	3.43
—	4.16*e*	4.19*e*	4.38
—	—	*h*4.20*d*	4.38
4.22*d*	—	4.28*d*	4.49
—	4.24*e*	4.28*e*	4.48
—	—	*h*4.50*d*	5. 8
5. 6*e*	—	5.14*e*	5.36
—	—	*h*5.35*e*	5.51
5.30*e*	—	5.37*e*	5.56
5.30*d*	—	5.36*d*	5.55
—	—	*h*5.48*e*	6. 8
6.17*d*	—	6.23*d*	6.42
—	—	*h*6.27*e*	6.45
6.54*d*	—	6.40*d*	7. 1
—	6.36*e*	6.39*e*	6.58
6.46*e*	—	6.53*e*	7.12
7.24*d*	7.28*e*	7.30	7.50
8.28	—	8.36	8.56
9.25	—	9.31	9.51
10.17	—	10.23	10.42
11.42	—	—	12. 4
—	—	—	—

CROYDON EAST—*cont.*
Sunday Trains.

	Leave		Arr. at
CHAR. +	CAN. ST.	LON. B.	CROY.E.
AM 6.25	—	6.32	6.56
9. 8	—	9.14	9.32
10. 5	—	10.11	10.31
10.20	—	10.28	10.49
PM 1.30	—	1.37	1.57
5.25	—	5.32	5.52
6.50	—	6.56	7.15
7.45	—	7.52	8.12
8.38	—	8.45	9.12
9.40	—	9.47	10. 7
—	—	—	—

Trains from Croydon.

	Leave		Arrive at	
CROY.		LON. B.	CAN. ST.	CHAR. +
AM 7. 0		7.18	—	7.30
7.41		7.58	—	8. 7
8. 6		8.24	8.28	—
8.10		8.28	8.33	—
8.23		8.40	8.44	—
8.32		8.49	—	—
8.43		9. 0	9. 4	—
8.47		9. 4	9. 8	—
9. 3		9.21	—	9.30
9.19		9.39	9.43	—
9.27		9.45	—	—
10. 0		10.18	10.22	—
10. 9		10.27	10.32	—
10.43		11. 0	—	—
11. 7		11.24	—	11.33
11.27		11.46	—	11.59
PM12. 8		12.26	—	—
12.32		12.50	—	1. 0
1.38		1.58	—	2. 5
2.12		2.38	—	2.46
2.46		3. 4	3. 8*e*	—
3. 9		3.28*e*	—	3.42*d*
3.35		3.52	—	—
3.47*l*		4. 8	—	—
4.40		5. 2	—	5.14
5.10*e*		5.28	—	—
5.37		5.56	—	6.18
5.51		6.10	—	6.18
6.39		6.58	—	7. 5
7. 2		7.20	—	7.29
8. 4		8.23	—	8.31
8.44		9. 2	—	9.15
9.45		10. 3	—	10.13
11.39		11.57	—	12.10
12.59*k*		—	1.20	—

Sunday Trains.

AM 7.57		8.16	—	8.27
10.55		11.15	—	11.25
PM 4.15		4.33	—	4.42
6. 7		6.25	—	6.34
6.55		7.13	—	7.25
8.43		9. 1	—	9. 9
9.34		9.52	—	—
9.50		10.11	—	10.23
10. 7		10.25	—	10.32
1. 2		—	1.23	—

d Saturdays only.
e Saturdays excepted.
h Low Level Platform.
k Third Class only.
l Mondays, Fridays and Saturdays only.

CROYDON (South) (Surrey)
from *London Bridge,* 11¼ miles. Fares, 2/4*a*, 1/5*c*. R. T. for two days, 4/8*a*, 2/6*c*. *See* pp. 568-570.

ANOTHER ROUTE from
Victoria, 11½ miles. Fares as above. *See* pp. 574-577.

CROYDON (West) (Surrey)
from *London Bridge,* 10¼ miles. Fares, 2/1*a*, 1/3*c*. R. T. for two days, 4/2*a*, 2/2*c*. *See* pp. 564-565.

ANOTHER ROUTE from
Victoria, 10¼ miles. Fares as above. *See* pp. 571-574.

CRUCKTON (Salop), 158¼
miles. No through fares. Departures *from* London as for Shrewsbury. Departures *for* London about 3 times daily.

CRUDEN BAY (Aberdeen) from *King's Cross*, 552½ miles. Fares, 106/1*a*, 63/8*c*. R.T. for two months, 212/2*a*, 127/4*c*. Pop. 2,959.
Map Square 35.

King's +	Cr. B.	Cr. B.	King's +
AM 4.45	8.24*l*	AM 8.22*r*	10. 0*l*
4.45*k*	6.28*l*	10. 0*f*	3.25*h*
PM 8.20*e*	9.35*h*	PM 1. 3	6. 0*h*
11.25*e*	2. 8*l*	4. 3	7.25*h*
—	—	—	—

Sunday Trains.

PM 7.45	9.35*h*	—	—
—	—	—	—
—	—	—	—
—	—	—	—

e Saturdays excepted.
f 9.50*a* Mondays.
h A.M.
k Fridays only.
l P.M.
r Restaurant Car.

ANOTHER ROUTE from *Euston*, 569¾ miles. Fares as above.
Map Square 35.

Euston	Cr. B.	Cr. B.	Euston
PM 7.50*er*	9.35*h*	AM 8.22*r*	10.45*l*
11.35	2. 8*l*	9.50*fr*	5. 0*h*
—	—	10. 0*g*	5. 0*h*
—	—	PM 4. 3	8. 0*h*
—	—	—	—
—	—	—	—
—	—	—	—

Sunday Trains.

PM 7.50*r*	9.35	—	—
11.35	2. 8*l*	—	—
—	—	—	—
—	—	—	—
—	—	—	—

e Saturdays excepted.
f Mondays only.
g Mondays excepted.
h A.M.
l P.M.
r Restaurant Car.

Cruden Bay Hotel, Port Erroll. Splendidly Equipped. Joins Golf Course. See advt. p. **129**.

CRUDGINGTON (Salop) from *Paddington*, 147¼ miles. Fares, 30/8*a*, 18/5*c*. R. T. for two months, 61/4*a*. Departures *from* London as for Market Drayton. Departures *for* London 4 times daily.
Map Square 17.

CRUMLIN (Low Level) (Monmouth) from *Paddington*, 153¾ miles. Fares, 31/11*a*, 19/2*c*. R.T. for two months, 63/10*a*. Departures *from* London as for Risca. Departures *for* London about 8 times daily.
Map Square 21.

CRUMPSALL (Lancs), 189¾ miles. Fares, 39/0*a*, 23/5*c*. R. T. for two months, 78/0*a*, 46/10*c*. Departures *from* London as for Manchester. Departures *for* London about 6 times daily. Pop. 13,762.

CRYMMYCH ARMS (Pembroke), 257¾ miles. Fares, 52/4*a*, 31/5*c*. R. T. for two months, 104/8*a*, 62/10*c*. Departures *from* London as for Cardigan. Departures *for* London about 4 times daily.
Map Square 16.

CRYNANT (Glamorgan), 197¼ miles. No through fares. Departures *from* London as for Neath or Brecon. Departures *for* London about 4 times daily.
Map Square 21.

CRYSTAL PALACE (LOW LEVEL) from *London Bridge*, 7¼ miles. Fares, 1/6*a*, 0/10½*c*. R. T. for two days, 2/7*a*, 1/9*c*. See pp. 580-582.
Map Square 79.

From *Victoria*, L.B. & S.C. Rly., 8¾ miles. Fares as above. See pp. 578-579.

CRYSTAL PALACE (HIGH LEVEL) from *Victoria*, S. E. & C. Rly., 9¾ miles. Fares, 1/6*a*, 1/2*b*, 0/10½*c*. R. T., for two days, 2/7*a*, 2/0*b*, 1/9*c*.
Map Square 79.

Service suspended.

ANOTHER ROUTE from *Holborn Viaduct, Ludgate Hill* and *St. Paul's*, 9¾ miles. Fares, 1/6*a*, 1/2*b*, 0/10½*c*. R.T. for two days, 2/7*a*, 2/0*b*, 1/9*c*. See pp. 562, 563.

Queen's Hotel, Upper Norwood, First-class Residential Hotel. 7 Acres. 200 Rooms. See advt. p. **23**.

CUDDINGTON (Cheshire), 176 miles. No through fares. Departures *from* London as for Northwich. Departures *for* London about 6 times daily Pop. 503.

CUDWORTH (Yorks) from *St. Pancras*, 175 miles. Fares 35/8*a*, 21/5*c*. R. T., double fare. Pop. 7,608.
Map Square 12.

St. Pan.	C'worth.	C'worth	St. Pan.
AM 4.25	9.42	AM 3.46	7.50
9. 0*r*	1.14	8.12*r*	12.10
9.50*r*	2.31	8.51*r*	1.30
11.45*r*	4.54	9.31*r*	2.10
PM 1.50*r*	5.50	11.28*r*	4.10
3.30*r*	8.17	PM 1.16*r*	5.45
6.15*r*	10.15	2.42*r*	7.15
11.50	5. 4	3.53*r*	8.35
—	—	9.35	4.20
—	—	—	—
—	—	—	—
—	—	—	—
—	—	—	—
—	—	—	—
—	—	—	—

Sunday Trains.

AM10.50*r*	4. 5	AM 3.46	8.57
PM 3.15	8. 2	7.59*r*	5. 2
—	—	PM12.52	5.27
—	—	3. 0*r*	9.43
—	—	8. 1	4.55
—	—	—	—
—	—	—	—

r Restaurant Car.

CUFFLEY (Herts), from *King's Cross*, 13¼ miles. Fares, 2/6*a*, 2/0*b*, 1/6*c*. R. T. for two months, 5/0*a*, 4/0*b*, 3/0*c*, See pp. 511-517. Pop. 656.
Map Square 23.

CULCHETH (Lancs) from *Marylebone*. 220 miles. Fares, 39/2*a*, 23/6*c*. R.T. for two months, 78/4*a*. Departures *from* London as for Wigan (Central). Departures *for* London about 5 times daily. Pop. 2,765.
Map Square 12.

CULGAITH (Cumberland) from *St. Pancras*, 284¾ miles Fares, 55/8*a*, 33/5*c*. R. T., double fare. Departures *from* London as for Appleby. Departures *for* London about 4 times daily. Pop. 313.
Map Square 7.

CULHAM (Oxon) from *Paddington*, 56 miles. Fares. 11/8*a*, 7/0*c*. R. T. for two months, 23/4*a*. Pop. 450.
Map Square 23.

Pad.	Culham	Culham	Pad.
AM 5.30	6.59	AM 7.28	9. 0
6.30	8.17	8.17	10. 0
7.30	9.49	9. 2*r*	10.15
8.50	10.19	9.54	12. 0
9. 0	11.28	11.37	1.50
10.45	12.22	PM 1.25	3.20
11.20	1.15	3. 2	5. 6
PM 1.10*r*	3.15	5.54*h*	7.20
3.18	5. 5	6.19	8.20
3.38	6.19	7.12*r*	9.15
5.15	6.54	9.57	2.45
6. 5*r*	7.46	—	—
6.55	8.52	—	—
—	—	—	—
—	—	—	—
—	—	—	—
—	—	—	—

Sunday Trains.

AM 9.10	10.50	AM 7.57	10.14
11.45	1.24	10.11	2.40
PM 2. 0	4.47	PM 4.54	6.20
5.15	9.32	7.54	9.48
7.40	10. 2	8.59	11.38
—	—	9.57	3.15
—	—	—	—
—	—	—	—
—	—	—	—
—	—	—	—

h Stops on notice being given at Station before 5.10 p.m.
r Restaurant Car.

CULKERTON (Glo'ster), 95½ miles. Fares 19/10*a*, 11/11*c*. R. T. for two months, 39/8*a*. Departures *from* London as for Tetbury. Departures *for* London about 5 times daily.
Map Square 22.

CULLEN (Banff), 589½ miles. Fares, 106/3*a*, 63/9*c*. R. T. for two months, 212/6*a*, 127/6*c*. Departures *from* London as for Huntly. Departures *for* London about 3 times daily. Pop. 2,104.
Map Square 35.

CULLERCOATS (Northumberland), 277¾ miles. Fares, 58/4*a*, 35/0*c*. R. T. double fare. Departures *from* London as for Newcastle-on-Tyne. Departures *for* London about 8 times daily. Pop. 4,389.
Map Square 3.

CULLINGWORTH (Yorks), from *King's Cross*, 201 miles. Fares, 40/5*a*, 24/3*c*. R.T., double fare. Departures *from* London as for Keighley. Departures *for* London about 6 times daily. Pop. 1,895.
Map Square 12.

CULLODEN MOOR (Inverness), 561¼ miles. Fares, 106/3*a*, 63/9*c*. R.T. for two months, 212/6*a*, 127/6*c*. Departures *from* London as for Aviemore. Departures *for* London about twice daily.
Map Square 34.

CULLOMPTON (Devon) from *Paddington*, 161¼ miles. Fares, *via* Taunton, 33/7*a*, 20/2*c*. R. T. for two months, 67/2*a*; *via* Exeter, 36/11*a*, 22/2*c*. R. T. for two months, 73/10*a*. Pop. 2,923.
Map Square 26.

Pad.	Culltn.	Culltn.	Pad.
AM 5.30*h*	11.28	AM 9.38*r*	1.30
7.30	12.38	11.28	4. 5
11.15*r*	3.47	PM12.38*hr*	4.45
12. 0*hr*	4.10	1.27*r*	6.50
PM 2. 0*r*	6.20	4.10	10.25
4.15*r*	9. 2	7.45	2.45
12. 0*k*	7.56	9.48	7.10
12.30*l*	9.16	—	—
—	—	—	—

Sunday Trains.

PM10. 0	7.56	AM 9.46	3.35
—	—	—	—
—	—	—	—

h Via Exeter.
k Saturdays midnight excepted.
l Saturdays midnight only.
r Restaurant Car.

CULMSTOCK (Devon), 163¾ miles. Fares, 34/2*a*, 20/6*c*. R. T. for two months, 68/4*a*. Departures *from* London as for Uffculme. Departures for London about 4 times daily. Pop. 811.
Map Square 26.

CULRAIN (Ross), 628¼ miles. Fares, 112/4*a*, 67/5*c*. R. T. for two months, 224/8*a*. Departures *from* London as for Tain. Departures *for* London about 3 times daily.
Map Square 34.

CULROSS (Fife), 415½ miles. No through fares. Departures *from* London as for Dunfermline. Departures *for* London about 3 times daily. Pop. 3,261.
Map Square 40.

CULTER (Aberdeen), 529¾ miles. No through fares. Departures *from* London as for Banchory. Departures *for* London about twice daily. Pop. 5,744.
Map Square 38.

CULTS (Aberdeen), 525¾ miles. No through fares. Departures *from* London as for Aberdeen. Departures *for* London about 4 times daily.
Map Square 38.

CULWORTH (Northampton) from *Marylebone*, 66 miles. Fares, 13/9*a*, 8/3*c*. R. T., double fare. Pop. 453.
Map Square 18.

M'bone.	Culwth.	Culwth.	M'bone.
AM 6.45	9. 5	AM 7.25	9.46
11.15	2. 0	10.14*h*	12. 2
PM 4.55	7. 3	PM 2.36	4.56
6.20	7.55	8.47	11. 0
6.25*d*	8.41	—	—
7.30*d*	10. 3	—	—
—	—	—	—
—	—	—	—

Sunday Trains.

AM 9.30	11.48	AM 7.33	10.13
PM 6.30	9.10	PM 6.18	8.58
—	—	—	—
—	—	—	—
—	—	—	—

d Saturdays only.
h Stops on notice being given at Station.

CUMBERNAULD (Dumbarton), 399¾ miles. Fares, 81/5*a*, 48/10*c*. R.T. for two months, 162/10*a*, 97/8*c*. Departures *from* London as for Coatbridge. Departures *for* London about 3 times daily. Pop. 5,261.
Map Square 40.

CUMMERSDALE (Cumberland), 301¼ miles. No through fares. Departures *from* London as for Maryport. Departures *for* London about 4 times daily. Pop. 547.
Map Square 3

CUMMERTREES (Dumfries), 320 miles. Fares, 64/10*a*, 38/11*c*. R. T. for two months, 129/8*a*, 77/10*c*. Departures *from* London as for Annan. Departures *for* London about 3 times daily. Pop. 1,084.
Map Square 44.

CUMWHINTON (Cumberland) from *St. Pancras*, 304 miles. Fares, 60/0*a*, 36/0*c*. R. T., double fare. Departures *from* London as for Lazonby. Departures *for* London about 4 times daily.
Map Square 3.

CUNNINGHAMHEAD (Ayr), 394½ miles. Fares, 80/3*a*, 48/2*c*. R. T. for two months, 160/6*a*, 96/4*c*. Departures *from* London as for Kilmarnock. Departures *for* London about 3 times daily.
Map Square 40.

CUPAR (Fife) from *King's Cross*, 437 miles. Fares, 88/2*a*, 52/11*c*. R. T. for two months, 176/4*a*, 105/10*c*. Pop. 6,576.
Map Square 41.

King's +	Cupar	Cupar	King's +
AM 4.45	5. 0	AM 8.15	6.15
10. 0*r*	7.42	10.12*r*	10. 0
PM 8.25*e*	8.13	PM 3.35	3.25
11.25*r*	8.50	6. 4	6. 0
—	—	8.10*e*	6.50
—	—	9. 1	7. 5
—	—	—	—

Sunday Trains.

PM 8.25	8.13	PM 5.34	6. 0
11.25	8.50	—	—
—	—	—	—

e Saturdays excepted.
r Restaurant Car.

CURRIEHILL (Midlothian), 394¼ miles. Fares, 80/5*a*, 48/3*c*. R.T. for two months, 160/10*a*, 96/6*c*. Departures *from* London as for Carstairs. Departures *for* London about 3 times daily. Pop. (Currie) 2,660.
Map Square 41.

CURTHWAITE (Cumberland), 306¼ miles. Fares, 61/11*a*, 37/2*c*. R. T., double fare. Departures *from* London as for Maryport. Departures *for* London about 4 times daily.
Map Square 7.

CUSTOM HOUSE (Victoria Docks) (Essex) from *Fenchurch Street*, from *Liverpool Street*, 7 miles. Fares from Liverpool Street, 0/10*a*, 0/8*b*, 0/6*c*. R.T. for two days, 1/8*a*, 1/4*b*, 0/10½*c*. From Fenchurch Street, 0/7½*a*, 0/6*b*, 0/4½*c*. R. T. for two days, 1/3*a*, 1/0*b*, 0/9*c*. Pop. 32,030. *See* pp. 537-540.
Map Square 62.

CUTHLIE (Forfar), 469 miles. No through fares. Departures *from* London as for Arbroath. Departures *for* London about twice daily.
Map Square 38.

CUXTON (Kent) from *Charing Cross, Cannon Street*, and *London Bridge*, 34 miles. Fares, 7/1*a*, 5/8*b*, 4/3*c*. R. T. for two months, 14/2*a*, 11/4*b*, 8/6*c*. Departures *from* London as for Halling. Departures *for* London about 10 times daily. Pop. 652.
Map Square 24.

CWM (Monmouth) from *Paddington*, 159 miles. Fares, 33/2*a*, 19/11*c*. R.T. for two months, 66/4*a*. Departures *from* London as for Ebbw Vale. Departures *for* London about 7 times daily. Pop. 9,824.
Map Square 11.

CWMAVON (Monmouth) from *Paddington*, 154½ miles. Fares, 31/11*a*, 19/2*c*. R. T. for two months, 63/10*a*. Departures *from* London as for Blaenavon. Departures *for* London about 5 times daily.
Map Square 21.

CWM BARGOED (Glamorgan) from *Paddington*, 170 miles. Fares, 34/10*a*, 20/11*c*. R. T. for two months, 69/8*a*. Departures *from* London as for Dowlais. Departures *for* London about 4 times daily.
Map Square 21.

CWMBRAN (Monmouth) from *Paddington*, 146½ miles. Fares, 30/3*a*, 18/2*c*. R. T. for two months, 60/6*a*. Departures *from* London as for Newport (Mon.). Departures *for* London about 5 times daily.

CWMDU (Glamorgan), 184¼ miles. No through fares. Departures *from* London as for Maesteg or Tondu. Departures *for* London about 5 times daily. Pop. 12,597.
Map Square 21.

CWMMAWR (Carmar-
then), 224¼ miles. Fares, 46/10*a*,
28/1*c*. R. T. for two months,
93/8*a*, 56/2*c*. Departures *from*
London as for Pembrey. Departures *for* London about 3 times
daily.
Map Square 21.

CWM PRYSOR (Merio-
neth) from *Paddington*, 215¼ miles.
No through fares. Departures
from London as for Blaenau Festiniog. Departures *for* London
about 3 times daily.
Map Square 11.

CWMSYFIOG (Mon-
mouth), 161 miles. Fares, 33/4*a*,
20/0*c*. R. T. for two months, 66/8*a*,
40/0*c*. Departures *from* London as
for Rhymney. Departures *for*
London about 7 times daily. Pop.
3,485.

CWM-Y-GLO (Carnarvon),
254¼ miles. Fares, 52/11*a*, 31/9*c*.
R.T. for two months, 105/10*a*, 63/6*c*.
Departures *from* London as for
Carnarvon. Departures *for* London
about 4 times daily.
Map Square 11.

CYFRONYDD (Mont-
gomery), 179 miles. No through
fares. Departures *from* London
as for Welshpool. Departures *for*
London about 4 times daily.
Map Square 16.

CYMMER (Glamorgan),
184½ miles. Fares, 38/6*a*, 23/1*c*.
R. T. for two months, 77/0*a*. Departures *from* London as for
Maesteg. Departures *for* London
about 5 times daily. Pop. 2,521.
Map Square 21.

CYNGHORDY (Carmar-
then), 237¼ miles. Fares, 41/1*a*,
24/8*c*. R.T. for two months, 82/2*a*.
Departures *from* London as for
Llanwrtyd Wells. Departures *for*
London about twice daily.
Map Square 16.

CYNWYD (Merioneth),
195¼ miles. Fares, 41/6*a*, 24/7*c*.
R. T. for two months, 82/0*a*, 49/2*c*.
Departures *from* London as for
Corwen. Departures *for* London
about 3 times daily.
Map Square 11.

D

DACRE (Yorks), 209¼ miles.
Fares, 43/7*a*, 26/2*c*. R. T. for two
months, 87/2*a*, 52/4*c*. Departures
from London as for Pateley
Bridge. Departures *for* London
about 4 times daily. Pop. 563.
Map Square 7.

DAGENHAM (Essex) from
Fenchurch Street, 11¼ miles. Fares,
2/3½*a*, 1/4½*c*. R. T. for two days,
4/7*a*, 2/2*c*. Pop. 9,127. *See* p. 509.
Map Square 24.

ANOTHER ROUTE from
St. Pancras, 17 miles. Fares, 2/1*a*,
1/3*c*. R. T. for two months, 4/2*a*,
2/4*c*. *See* p. 508.

DAGENHAM DOCK
(Essex) from *Fenchurch Street*, 10¼
miles. Fares, 1/8*a*, 1/0*c*. R. T. for
two days, 3/4*a*, 2/0*c*. *See* p. 510.

DAGGONS ROAD (Dor-
set) from *Waterloo*, 97¼ miles.
Fares, 20/10*a*, 12/6*c*. R. T. for two
months, 41/8*a*, 25/0*c*. Departures
from London as for Fordingbridge.
Departures *for* London about 6
times daily.
Map Square 27.

DAILLY (Ayr), 405 miles.
Fares, 83/2*a*, 49/11*c*. R. T. for two
months, 166/4*a*, 99/10*c*. Departures *from* London as for Girvan.
Departures *for* London about 4
times daily. Pop. 1,895.
Map Square 43.

DAIRSIE (Fife), 440 miles.
No through fares. Departures
from London as for Cupar. Departures *for* London about twice
daily. Pop. 540.
Map Square 38.

DAISY BANK (Stafford),
125¼ miles. Fares, 25/7*a*, 15/4*c*.
R. T. for two months, 51/2*a*, 30/8*c*.
Departures *from* London as for
Dudley. Departures *for* London
about 3 times daily.
Map Square 17.

DAISYFIELD (Lancs), 212 miles. Fares, 43/9*a*, 26/3*c*. R. T. for two months, 87/6*a*, 52/6*c*. Departures *from* London as for Blackburn. Departures *for* London about 6 times daily.

DAISY HILL (Lancs), 200¼ miles. No through fares. Departures *from* London as for Manchester or Wigan. Departures *for* London about 10 times daily. Pop. 2,120.
Map Square 12.

DALBEATTIE (Kirkcudbright) from *Euston*, 347 miles. Fares, 68/9*a*, 41/3*c*. R. T. for two months, 137/6*a*, 82/6*c*. Pop. 2,998.
Map Square 43.

Euston	Dalb'tie	Dalb'tie	Euston
AM 12.25	12. 8	AM 7.12*r*	6. 0
5. 0	3.16	10.15*r*	6.25
10. 0*r*	6.14	PM 2.10	10. 0
11.35*r*	8. 2	6.11	5. 0
PM 8. 0	4.31	7.51*e*	6.55
9.20*e*	7. 8	7.51*d*	7.15
11. 0*d*	7.47	—	—
11.45*e*	9. 3	—	—
—	—	—	—
—	—	—	—
—	—	—	—
—	—	—	—
—	—	—	—
—	—	—	—

Sunday Trains.

PM 8.30	4.30	PM 9.20	7.30
11.45	9. 3	—	—
—	—	—	—
—	—	—	—
—	—	—	—
—	—	—	—
—	—	—	—

d Saturdays only.
e Saturdays excepted.
r Restaurant Car.

ANOTHER ROUTE from *St. Pancras*, 356 miles Fares as above.

St. Pan.	D'beat.	D'beat.	St. Pan.
AM 4.25	3.18	AM 10.15*r*	6.35
9.50*r*	5.52	11.50*r*	9.15
PM 12.15*r*	8. 2	PM 2.10	4.20
11.45*e*	9. 5	6.11	7.25
—	—	—	—
—	—	—	—
—	—	—	—
—	—	—	—

Sunday Trains.

PM 11.45	9. 5	PM 9.20	7.25
—	—	—	—
—	—	—	—
—	—	—	—
—	—	—	—

e Saturdays excepted.
r Restaurant Car.

DALCROSS (Inverness), 573½ miles. No through fares. Departures *from* London as for Nairn. Departures *for* London about twice daily. Pop. 949.

DALGUISE (Perth), 470½ miles. Fares, 95/3*a*, 57/2*c*. R. T. for two months, 190/6*a*, 114/4*c*. Departures *from* London as for Dunkeld. Departures *for* London about twice daily.
Map Square 37.

DALKEITH (Midlothian), 390 miles. No through fares. Departures *from* London as for Edinburgh (Waverley). Departures *for* London about 4 times daily Pop. 7,707.
Map Square 41.

DALMALLY (Argyle), 479¼ miles. Fares, 98/2*a*, 58/11*c*. R. T. for two months, 196/4*a*, 117/10*c*. Departures *from* London as for Crianlarich. Departures *for* London about twice daily.
Map Square 37.

DALMELLINGTON (Ayr), 394½ miles. Fares, 82/11*a*, 49/9*c*. R.T. for two months, 165/10*a*, 99/6*c*. Departures *from* London as for Ayr. Departures *for* London about 3 times daily. Pop. 6,155.
Map Square 43.

DALMENY (Linlithgow), 401¾ miles. Fares, 82/11*a*, 49/9*c*. R.T. for two months, 165/10*a*, 99/6*c*. Departures *from* London as for Edinburgh (Waverley). Departures *for* London about 4 times daily. Pop. 2,188.
Map Square 41.

DALMUIR (Dumbarton), 409 miles. Fares, 83/7*a*, 50/2*c*. R. T. for two months, 167/2*a*, 100/4*c*. Departures *from* London as for Dumbarton. Departures *for* London about 3 times daily. Pop. 11,500.
Map Square 40.

DALNASPIDAL (Perth), 491 miles. Fares, 101/8*a*, 61/0*c*. R.T. for two months, 203/4*a*, 122/0*c*. Departures *from* London as for Blair Atholl. Departures *for* London about 3 times daily.
Map Square 37.

DALREOCH (Dumbarton), 416 miles. Fares, 84/2*a*, 50/6*c*. R. T. for two months, 168/4*a*, 101/0*c*. Departures *from* London as for Dumbarton. Departures *for* London about twice daily. Pop. 4,960.
Map Square 40.

DALRY (Ayr), 401½ miles. Fares, 81/10*a*, 49/1*c*. R.T. for two months, 163/8*a*, 98/2*c*. Departures *from* London as for Kilmarnock. Departures *for* London about 3 times daily. Pop. 7,243.
Map Square 40.

DALRYMPLE (Ayr), 393 miles. Fares, 80/8*a*, 48/5*c*. R. T. for two months, 161/4*a*, 96/10*c*, Departures *from* London as for Girvan or Ayr. Departures *for* London about 4 times daily. Pop. 1,403.
Map Square 43.

DALSERF (Lanark), 394½ miles. Fares, 79/7*a*, 47/9*c*. R. T. for two months, 152/2*a*, 95/6*c*. Departures *from* London as for Hamilton. Departures *for* London about 3 times daily. Pop. 4,491.
Map Square 40.

DALSTON (Cumberland), 303¾ miles. No through fares. Departures *from* London as for Maryport. Departures *for* London about 5 times daily. Pop. 1,700.
Map Square 7.

DALSTON JUNC. from *Broad Street*, 2 miles. Fares, 0/4*a*, 0/3*b*, 0/2½*c*. R. T. for two days, 0/8*a*, 0/5½*b*, 0/3½*c*. *See* pp. 500, 501-505, 511-522.
Map Square 61.

DALTON (Lancs), 259¾ miles. Fares, 54/0*a*, 32/5*c*. R. T. for two months, 108/0*a*, 64/10*c*. Departures *from* London as for Ulverston. Departures *for* London about 4 times daily. Pop. 12,303.
Map Square 6.

DALWHINNIE (Inverness) 508½ miles. Fares, 103/2*a*, 61/11*c*. R. T. for two months, 206/4*a*, 123/10*c*. Departures *from* London as for Blair Atholl. Departures *for* London, about 3 times daily.
Map Square 37.

DAMEMS (Yorks), from *St. Pancras*, 214½ miles. Fares, 41/0*a*, 24/7*c*. R. T. double fare. Departures *from* London as for Keighley. Departures *for* London about 6 times daily.
Map Square 12.

DANBY (Yorks), 246¾ miles. Fares, 51/5*a*, 30/10*c*. R. T. for two months, 102/10*a*, 61/8*c*. Departures *from* London as for Whitby or Stockton-on-Tees. Departures *for* London about 4 times daily. Pop. 1,164.
Map Square 8.

DANBY WISKE (Yorks), 221½ miles. Fares, 46/3*a*, 27/9*c*. R. T. double fare. Departures *from* London as for Northallerton. Departures *for* London about 3 times daily. Pop. 300.
Map Square 7.

DANDALEITH (Elgin), 562¾ miles. Fares, 106/3*a*, 63/9*c*. R. T. for two months, 212/6*a*, 127/6*c*. Departures *from* London as for Aviemore or Keith (*via* Aberdeen). Departures *for* London about twice daily.
Map Square 35.

DANYGRAIG (Glamorgan), 195 miles. No through fares. Departures *from* London as for Swansea. Departures *for* London about 5 times daily.

DANZEY (Warwick), 105¾ miles. Fares, 21/11*a*, 13/2*c*. R. T. for two months, 43/10*a*. Departures *from* London as for Henley-in-Arden. Departures *for* London about 3 times daily.
Map Square 17.

DARCY LEVER (Lancs),

197¼ miles. No through fares. Departures *from* London as for Manchester. Departures *for* London about 6 times daily. Pop. 4,077.

Map Square 12.

DARESBURY (Cheshire),

181½ miles. Fares, 37/9*a*, 22/8*c*, R. T. for two months, 75/6*a*, 45/4*c*. Departures *from* London as for Chester. Departures *for* London about 6 times daily. Pop. 135.

Map Square 12.

DARFIELD (Yorks) from

St. Pancras, 171 miles. Fares, 34/9*a*, 20/10*c*. R. T., double fare. Pop. 5,566.

Map Square 13.

ST. PAN.	DARFLD.	DARFLD.	ST. PAN.
AM 2.25*g*	8. 2	AM 7.36*r*	12.10
4.25	9.59	9.41*r*	2.10
11.45*r*	4.47	1.43*r*	7.15
PM 3.30*r*	8.10	4. 5*r*	9. 5
6.15*r*	10.43	9.45	4.20

Sunday Trains.

PM 3.15	7.53	AM 8. 9*r*	5. 2
—	—	PM 3. 9*r*	9.43
—	—	8.10	4.55

g Mondays excepted.
r Restaurant Car.

DARLASTON (Stafford)

from *Euston,* 120½ miles. Fares, 25/0*a*, 15/0*c*. R. T. for two months, 50/0*a*. Departures *from* London as for Bescot. Departures *for* London about 4 minutes later. Pop. 18,218.

DARLEY (Yorks), 207¼ miles.

No through fares. Departures *from* London as for Pateley Bridge. Departures *for* London about 5 times daily. Pop. 580.

Map Square 7.

DARLEY DALE (Derby)

from *St. Pancras,* 147¼ miles. Fares, 30/5*a*, 18/3*c*. R. T. for two months, 60/10*a*, 36/6*c*. Pop. (North Darley), 4,005.

Map Square 12.

ST. PAN.	D'LYDALE	D'LYDALE	ST.PAN.
AM 2.25	8. 8	AM 7.40*r*	11.35
10.25*r*	2.10	9.23*r*	1.30
PM12.25*r*	4.41	10.50	3.25
2.25*r*	6.19	PM 1.30*r*	5.45
4.25*r*-	8. 7	4.52*r*	8.35
6.25*dr*	9.42	6.14*r*	10. 5
12. 0*h*	8. 6	9.16	4.20

Sunday Trains.

PM 3.15	8. 2	AM11.31*r*	5. 2
—	—	PM 5.54*r*	9.52
—	—	8.43	4.55

d Saturdays only.
h Saturdays midnight only.
r Restaurant Car.

DARLINGTON (Durham)

from *King's Cross,* 232 miles. Fares, 48/4*a*, 29/0*c*. R. T., double fare. Pop. 65,866.

Map Square 7.

KING'S +	DARLTN.	DARLTN.	KING'S +
AM 4.45	11. 5	AM12.13	6.50
7.15*r*	1.39	2. 5	6.50
10. 0*r*	2.50	2.21	7. 5
10.10*r*	3.53	6.27	1. 5
11.15*g*	4.10	7.25*r*	1.15
11.50*r*	4.32	8.54*r*	1.30
PM 1.15*r*	5.56	10.14*g*	3.15
1.50*r*	7.17	11.21*r*	4.30
5.30*r*	9.53	PM 1.32*r*	6.15
5.35*r*	10.36	3.43*r*	9.25
8.25	2. 3	5.16*r*	10. 0
11.25*d*	4.30	8.59	3.25
11.25*e*	4.18	11.55	5.40

Sunday Trains.

AM 8.30	4.32	AM12.13	6. 0
11.30*r*	7.39	2.21	7. 5
PM 5. 0*r*	10.57	11.20	5.15
8.25	2. 5	PM 3. 1*r*	8.15
11.25	4.18	11.55	5.40

d Saturdays only.
e Saturdays excepted.
g 1st and 3rd Class Pullman Cars only.
r Restaurant Car.

DARNALL (Yorks) from

Marylebone, 162¼ miles. Fares, 32/9*a*, 19/8*c*. R. T., double fare. Departures *from* London as for Worksop or Beighton. Departures *for* London about 10 minutes earlier. Pop. 33,196.

Map Square 12.

DARRAN (Glamorgan), 162

miles. Fares, 33/9*a*, 20/3*c*. R. T. for two months, 67/6*a*, 40/6*c*. Departures *from* London as for Bargoed. Departures *for* London about 4 times daily.

DARSHAM (Suffolk) from

Liverpool Street, 95½ miles. Fares, 20/2*a*, 12/1*c*. R. T. for two months, 40/4*a*. Pop. 342.

Map Square 19.

L'POOL ST.	D'SHAM	D'SHAM	L'POOLST.
AM 5. 0	8.10	AM 7.30*r*	10.30
8.15*r*	11.37	8.35*r*	11.22
10.20	1.29	11. 8*r*	2. 3
PM 1. 0	3.52	PM12.43	3.42
3.18*r*	6.12	3.25	5.55
5.18*dr*	8.10	4.34	7.51
5.18*er*	8.16	6.37*r*	9.22
—	—	7.38	11.16

Sunday Trains.

AM10. 5*r*	12.56	AM 8. 7	11.38
PM 4.40	7.39	PM 6.21*r*	9.10

d Saturdays only.
e Saturdays excepted.
r Restaurant Car.

DARTFORD (Kent) from

Charing Cross, Cannon Street, and *London Bridge.* 17¾ miles. Fares from Charing Cross, 3/9*a*, 3/0*b*, 2/3*c*. Fares from Cannon Street or London Bridge, 3/4*a*, 2/8*b*, 2/0*c*. R. T. for eight days, 6/8*a*, 5/4*b*, 4/0*c*. Pop. 26,005. *See* pp. 552-554.

Map Square 24.

DARTMOUTH (Devon)

from *Paddington,* 209 miles. Fares, 43/2*a*, 25/11*c*. R. T. for two months, 86/4*a*, 51/10*c*. Pop. 7,201.

Map Square 26.

PAD.	D'M'TH	D'M'TH	PAD.
AM 5.30	12.30	AM 8.10*r*	1.30
9.15*r*	2.55	11.10*r*	3.45
12. 0*r*	4.25	PM 1.30*er*	6.50
PM 2. 5*r*	5.30	2. 5*dr*	7. 5
2. 0*r*	7.30	3.35*r*	9. 0
3.30*r*	8.30	4.35	2.45
4.15*r*	10.15	10.25	7.10
12. 0*f*	7.55	—	—
12.30*h*	9.35	—	—

Sunday Trains.

AM10.30*r*	5. 5	AM 9.40*r*	4. 5
PM 2.40	8.15	PM12.45	7. 5
10. 0	7.55	8. 0	3.15

h Saturdays midnight only.
l Saturdays midnight excepted.
r Restaurant Car.

Royal Castle. The Principal Hotel. Old-fashioned and comfortable. Liberal table. Moderate Terms. Nearest to the Royal Naval College. Patronised by Royalty and Visitors to the Cadets. Electric Light. Carriages and Cars. 'Phone 25.
Address—PROPRIETOR.

Raleigh Hotel. Patronised by the Admiralty and Ladies and Gentlemen visiting H.M.S. Britannia. Electric Light. Terms moderate.

DARTON (Yorks), 182¼

miles. Fares, 38/2*a*, 22/11*c*. R. T. for two months, 76/4*a*, 45/10*c*. Departures *from* London as for Wakefield. Departures *for* London about 6 times daily. Pop. 11,266.

Map Square 12.

DARVEL (Ayr), 395½ miles.

Fares, 80/7*a*, 48/4*c*. R. T. for two months, 161/2*a*, 96/8*c*. Departures *from* London as for Kilmarnock. Departures *for* London about 4 times daily. Pop. 3,340.

Map Square 40.

DARWEN (Lancs) from

Euston, 207 miles. Fares, 42/4a, 25/5c. R. T. for two months, 84/8a, 50/10c. Pop. 37,913.
Map Square 12.

EUSTON	DARWEN	DARWEN	EUSTON
AM12.25	6.39	AM 5.48er	12. 5
2.35	10. 2	6.31r	12.50
5. 0	11.52	8.12r	1.15
8.45r	2.44	8.23r	1.45
10.40r	3.33	8.54	3.10
11.50er	5.21	10.56r	3.55
11.50dr	5.44	PM12.21r	6.15
12. 0nr	7.16	12.28dr	6.25
PM 2.50t	7.53	1.18r	7.30
4. 5r	10.13	2.25r	8.10
6. 5r	10.55	3. 0dr	9.15
9.30e	5.42	3.0er	9.20
11.50d	8.46	4.52dr	10. 0
—	—	4.52er	10.10
—	—	8.36	5. 0
—	—	9.59e	5.40
—	—	9.59d	5.45

Sunday Trains.

PM12.10r	6. 6	AM 8.51	4. 0
12.30r	7.51	11.34r	5.45
—	—	PM 2.31r	8.55
—	—	9.51	5. 0

d Saturdays only.
e Saturdays excepted.
n Noon.
r Restaurant Car.
t Tea Car.

DATCHET (Bucks) from

Waterloo, 24 miles. Fares, 4/4a, 2/7c. R. T. for two months, 8/8a, 5/2c. Pop. 2,056.
Map Squares 23 and 63.

W'LOO	DATCHET	DATCHET	W'LOO
AM 5.35	6.49	AM 5.42	6.36
7.24	8.22	6.42	7.36
8.24	9.23	7.12	8. 6
9.24	10.23	7.43	8.41
10.24	11.22	8.15	9. 6
11.24	12.22	8.40	9.36
PM12.24	1.22	9.12	10. 6
12.54d	1.52	10.12	11. 6
1.24	2.22	11. 3	11.57
1.54d	2.52	PM12. 3	12.57
2.24	3.22	1. 3	1.57
3.24	4.22	2. 3	2.57
4.24	5.22	3. 3	3.57
4.58e	5.52	4. 3	4.57
5.24	6.22	5. 3	5.57
5.54e	6.52	6. 3	6.57
6.24	7.22	7. 3	7.57
6.54e	7.52	8. 3	8.57
7.24	8.22	9.26	10.37
8.24	9.22	10.51e	12. 5
9.24	10.27	10.51d	12. 8
10.24	11.27	—	—
11.44	12.41	—	—

DATCHET—*continued.*

Sunday Trains.

W'LOO	DATCHET	DATCHET	W'LOO
AM 8.43	9.45	AM 8.31	9.28
10.18	11.13	10.45	11.43
11.18	12.13	11.45	12.43
PM12.18	1.31	PM12.45	1.43
1.18	2.13	2.45	3.43
2.18	3.22	3.45	5.28
3.18	4.13	4.45	5.43
4.18	5.22	5.45	6.43
5.18	6.13	6.45	7.43
6.18	7.13	7.45	8.43
7.18	8.13	8.45	9.43
8.18	9.17	9.45	10.43
8.58	9.53	10.45	11.51
10.18	11.13	—	—

d Saturdays only.
e Saturdays excepted.

DAUNTSEY (Wilts) from

Paddington, 87¼ miles. Fares, 18/2a, 10/11c. R. T. for two months, 36/4a, Pop. 634.
Map Square 22.

PAD.	DAUNT.	DAUNT.	PAD.
AM 5.30	7.56	AM 8. 5	10.45
7.30	9.40	10. 3	12.20
9. 0	11.28	PM12.36r	2.40
10.45	1.15	3.26	6. 2
PM 3.15t	5.22	6.18r	8.35
5.15	.7.36	9.38	2.45
6.55	9.53	—	—

Sunday Trains.

AM10.35	1.29	PM 2.27	6. 0
PM12.30r	3.19	7.14	10. 0
2. 0	7.11	—	—
10. 0	6.32	—	—

r Restaurant Car.
t Tea Car.

DAVA (Elgin), 554½ miles.

Fares, 106/3a, 63/9c. R. T. for two months, 212/6a, 127/6c. Departures from London as for Aviemore. Departures for London about twice daily.
Map Square 34.

DAVENPORT (Cheshire), 178¼ miles.

Fares, 37/9a, 22/8c. R. T., double fare. Departures from London as for Stockport. Departures for London about 8 times daily.

DAVENTRY (Northampton) from Euston, 73¾ miles.

Fares, 15/3a, 9/2c. R. T. for two months, 30/6a, 18/4c. Pop. 3,530.
Map Square 18.

EUSTON	DAVENT.	DAVENT.	EUSTON
AM 6.45	9.18	AM 7.54	10.15
9.30	12.31	10.20d	12.20
10.40	1.32	10.20e	12.32
12. 0nr	2.28	PM 1.45	4.15
PM12.13	4.50	2.45	5.35
2. 0	5.23	3.51	6.25
4.15	6.40	5. 0	7.55
7. 0	8.55	7.19e	10.10
—	—	7.19d	10.50
—	—	11.26d	5.45

No Sunday Trains.
d Saturdays only.
e Saturdays excepted.
n Noon.
r Restaurant Car.

DAVIDSON'S MAINS (Midlothian), 401¾ miles.

Fares, 82/4a, 49/5c. R. T. for two months, 164/8a, 98/10c. Departures from London as for Edinburgh. Departures for London about 6 times daily.

DAVIOT (Inverness), 557 miles.

Fares, 106/3a, 63/9c. R. T. for two months, 212/6a, 127/6c. Departures from London as for Aviemore. Departures for London about twice daily. Pop. 853.
Map Square 34.

DAWLEY (Salop), 155¼ miles.

Fares, 29/9a, 17/10c. R. T. for two months, 59/6a, 35/8c. Departures *from* London as for Wellington (Salop). Departures *for* London about 4 times daily. Pop. 177.
Map Square 17.

DAWLISH (Devon) from

Paddington, 185¼ miles. Fares, 38/2a, 22/11c. R.T. for two months, 76/4a, 45/10c. Pop. 4,672.
Map Square 26.

PAD.	DAWLISH	DAWLISH	PAD.
AM 5.30	11.43	AM 9.52r	1.30
7.30d	12.37	10.22	4. 5
7.30	12.55	PM12.48r	4.35
9.15r	1.20	1.48r	6.50
PM12. 5r	4. 2	4.30r	9. 0
2. 0r	5.53	6.21	2.45
3.30r	6.57	10.32	7.10
4.15r	8.40	—	—
6.30r	10.59	—	—
12. 0h	7.25	—	—
12.30k	9.45	—	—

Sunday Trains.

AM10.30r	2.46	AM 8.41r	3.35
PM 2.40	7.58	10.57r	4. 5
4.30r	9.25	PM 2.36	7. 5
10. 0	7.25	3.32r	7.55
—	—	9.46	3.15

d Saturdays only.
h Saturdays midnight excepted.
k Saturdays midnight only.
r Restaurant Car.

Grand Hotel.

High-Class Family. Overlooking Sea. Close to Beach and Station. Near Links. Good Bathing, Boating and Fishing. Garage on premises, free to Hotel Visitors, R.A.C., A A., and M.U. Terms strictly moderate. Proprietor,
FREDERICK HUGHES.

"Elmcroft," Private Hotel.

The Bartons. Sheltered position near Sea and Beautiful Country. Separate Tables. Billiards. From three guineas weekly.

Royal Hotel.

One minute from sea and station. Near Golf Links. Electric light throughout. Tariff. Telephone 37.
Proprietor, A. HATCHMAN.

Crows' Nest, Barton Terrace.

High-class Boarding Establishment. Electric Light. Gas Fires in Bedrooms. Hot and Cold Bath. Late Dinners. Separate Tables. Five minutes from Sea.
ARTHUR C. ATKINS.

DAWLISH WARREN (Devon), 184½ miles.

Fares, 38/1a, 22/10c. R. T. for two months, 76/2a, 45/8c. Departures *from* London for Starcross. Departures *for* London about 5 times daily.
Map Square 26.

DAYBROOK (Notts) from

King's Cross, 129 miles. Fares, 26/0a, 15/7c. R. T., double fare. Departures *from* London as for Basford and Bulwell. Departures *for* London about 3 minutes later. Pop. 4,648.
Map Square 13.

DDUALLT (Merioneth), 232¼ miles.

No through fares. Departures *from* London as for Blaenau-Festiniog. Departures *for* London about 4 times daily.
Map Square 11.

DEADWATER (Northumberland), 323½ miles.

No through fares. Departures *from* London as for Carlisle or Hexham. Departures *for* London about 4 times daily.
Map Square 3.

DEAL (Kent) from *Charing*

DEAL (Kent) from *Charing Cross, Cannon Street* and *London Bridge, via* Ashford and Minster Junction, 91¼ miles. Fares, 17/1d, 13/8b, 10/3c. R. T. for two months, 34/2a, 27/4b. Pop. 12,990. *Map Square* 24.

Leave			Arr. at
Char. +	Can. St.	Lon. B.	Deal
AM —	5.20	5.25	9.52
—	—	7.50*l*	10.59
9.15	—	9.23	12.38
11. 0	—	11. 7	2.28
PM 1. 0	—	—	3.41
3. 0	—	3. 8	5.57
5.15*e*	5.12*e*	5.21*e*	8. 1
5.20*d*	—	5.26*d*	8. 1
5.24*d*	—	5.34*d*	9.15
6. 0*e*	—	6. 5*e*	9.15
7.18	—	7.26	10.47

Sunday Trains.

AM 7.45	—	7.52	11.51
PM 7.35	—	7.45	10.49

Trains from Deal.

Leave	Arrive at		
Deal	Lon. B.	Can. St.	Char. +
AM 6. 6	9.32	9.36	—
8.15	10.54	—	11. 3
8.44	11.43	—	11.57
10.15	1.36	—	1.50
11.49	3.26	—	3.40
PM 2.18	5.50	—	6. 5
4.15	7.25	7.30	7.49
7. 5	10.22	—	10.35
10. 0*y*	—	1.20	—

Sunday Trains.

AM 6.15	10. 5	—	10.15
PM 4. 3	7. 9	—	7.17
5.35	8.30	—	8.40
7.30	10.16	—	10.26
10. 0*y*	—	1.23	—

d Saturdays only.
e Saturdays excepted.
l Low Level Platform.
y Third Class only.

ANOTHER ROUTE from

Charing Cross, Cannon Street, and *London Bridge, via* Dover, 86¾ miles. Fares as above.

	Leave		Arr. at
Char. +	Can. St.	Lon. B.	Deal
AM —	5.40*y*	5.43*y*	7.48
—	5.20	5.25	9.53
—	7.16*h*	7.19*h*	11.43
9.15	—	9.23	12.32
—	—	*l*10. 3*j*	12.51
11.15	—	—	1.25
PM 1. 0*p*	—	—	3. 6
1.50*d*	—	1.56*d*	3.54
4. 5	—	—	6. 1
4.30*l*	—	4.37*l*	6.54
—	5. 0*s*	—	6.59
—	5.12*e*	—	8. 8
6. 0*e*	—	6. 5*e*	8. 8
—	6.12*e*	—	8.56
7. 0	—	—	8.56
7.18	—	7.26	11.22
11.51*k*	—	—	2.33

Sunday Trains.

AM 9.35	—	—	11.35
10.15	—	—	12.26
PM 7.35	—	7.45	11.12

DEAL—continued.

Trains from Deal.

Leave	Arrive at		
Deal	Lon. B.	Can. St.	Char. +
AM *f*6. 0*h*	9. 4	9. 8	—
7.29*e*	9.36	9.40	—
7.25*d*	10. 0	10. 4	—
8.30	10.34	—	10.41
8.52	11.43	—	11.57
10.16	—	—	12.20
PM12.41	3.26	—	3.40
*d*12.41*p*	3.26	—	3.40
1.53	4. 2	—	4.10
2.20	5.50	—	6. 3
4.26	—	—	6.50
6.14	10.22	—	10.35
9.20*y*	—	1.20	—

Sunday Trains.

PM 4.25	—	—	6.30
6. 0	—	—	8.17
7.35	10.16	—	10.26
9. 0*y*	—	1.23	—

d Saturdays only.
e Saturdays excepted.
h Via Chatham.
j Mondays, Fridays and Saturdays only.
k Wednesdays only.
l Fridays excepted.
p Pullman Car attached.
s Fridays only.
y Third Class only.

ANOTHER ROUTE from

Victoria, Holborn Viaduct, and *St. Paul's, via* Chatham, 84¼ miles. Fares as above.

	Leave		Arr. at
S.E. & C.	Vict.	Hol. V.	St. Pl.'s	Deal
AM —	3.50*l*	—	—	7.48
5. 5	4.57	5. 0	—	9.25
5.48*f*	5.40*f*	5.42*f*	—	9.24
—	—	7.30	7.33	11.43
9.20	—	—	—	11.57
9.45	—	—	—	12.35
10.40	—	—	—	2.13
11.40*d*	—	—	—	3. 6
11.40*e*	—	—	—	4. 8
PM 2. 5*d*	—	—	—	4.43
2. 8*e*	—	—	—	5.25
5.10*d*	5.10*e*	5.12*e*	—	8.18
5.30*e*	—	—	—	8.56
5.30*d*	—	—	—	9.55
7.22*h*	—	—	—	10.47
8.50	—	—	—	11.22

Sunday Trains.

AM —	8. 0	—	12.26
9.35	—	—	12.43
10.40	—	—	3.57
PM 3.30	—	—	7.47
5.15	—	—	8.48
8.25	—	—	11.12

Trains from Deal.

Leave	Arrive at		
Deal	St. Pl.'s	Hol. V.	Vict.
AM 6. 0*f*	9.37	9.39	—
6. 6*h*	9.53	9.55	—
6.52	—	—	11. 2
8.52	—	—	11.27
9.10*d*	—	—	1.22
9.10*e*	1. 0	1. 2	1.33
11. 2	—	—	2.43
11.49*h*	—	—	3.36
PM 1.15*e*	4.46	—	4.39
1.53*d*	—	—	4.55
2.18*h*	—	—	5.42
2.20	—	—	5.26
5.20	—	—	8.33
6.59	—	—	10.25
7. 5*h*	11.44	11.46	—

DEAL—continued.

Sunday Trains.

Leave	Arrive at		
Deal	St. Pl.'s	Hol. V.	Vict.
AM 8.20	—	—	11.53	11.51
9.45*k*	—	—	1. 5
11.55*k*	—	—	3.50
PM 6. 0	—	—	8.40

d Saturdays only.
e Saturdays excepted.
f Mondays only.
h Via Minster Junction.
k Via Folkestone
l Third Class only.

DEAN (Hants) from *Waterloo*

DEAN (Hants) from *Waterloo,* 87¼ miles. Fares, 17/6a, 10/6c. R. T. for two months, 35/0a, 21/0c. Departures *from* London as for Salisbury or Romsey. Departures *for* London about 6 times daily. Pop. 126. *Map Square* 22.

DEAN LANE (Lancs), 189¾ miles. Fares, 38/7*a*, 23/2*c*. R. T. for two months, 77/2*a*, 46/4*c*. Departures *from* London as for Manchester. Departures *for* London about 6 times daily.

DEARHAM (Cumberland), 317¼ miles. No through fares. Departures *from* London as for Cockermouth or Carlisle. Departures *for* London about 5 times daily. Pop. 2,127.
Map Square 6.

DEARHAM BRIDGE (Cumberland), 324½ miles. No through fares. Departures *from* London as for Maryport. Departures *for* London about 5 times daily.
Map Square 6.

DEEPCAR (Yorks), 169½ miles. Fares, 34/4*a*, 20/7*c*. R. T. for two months, 68/8*a*, 41/2*c*. Departures *from* London as for Sheffield (Victoria). Departures *for* London about 6 times daily.
Map Square 12.

DEEPDALE (Lancs,) 210¼ miles. Fares, 43/11*a*, 26/4*c*. Departures *from* London as for Preston. Departures *for* London about 6 times daily.

DEEPDENE (Surrey) from *Charing Cross*, *Cannon Street*, and *London Bridge*, 30½ miles. Fares, 5/10*a*, 4/0*b*, 3/0*c*. R. T. for two months, 10/0*a*, 7/10*b*, 5/8*c*.

	Leave Char. +	Can. St.	Lon. B.	Arr. at Deep.
AM	—	4.44	5. 0	6.16
	—	—	7.50*l*	9. 9
	—	—	9.33*l*	10.45
	10.55	—	11. 3	12.28
PM	—	12.55*d*	12.58*d*	1.53
	12.55	—	1. 4	2.21
	—	1.24*d*	1.27*d*	2.38
	2. 3*e*	2. 8*d*	2.10	3.23
	—	—	2.22*dl*	3.33
	3.15	—	3.21	4.37
	—	4.20*e*	4.23*e*	5.13
	4.22*d*	—	4.28*d*	5.37
	—	5.24*e*	5.27*e*	6.25
	5.42*d*	—	5.48*d*	6.54
	—	6. 0*e*	6. 3*e*	7. 3
	6.27*e*	—	6.34*e*	7.35
	—	6.36*e*	6.39*e*	7.47
	6.34*d*	—	6.40*d*	7.48
	7.24*d*	7.28*e*	7.30	8.44
	8.28	—	8.36	9.51
	—	—	—	—
	—	—	—	—

Sunday Trains.

AM	6.25	—	6.32	7.54
	10. 5	—	10.11	11.13
	10.20	—	10.28	11.39
PM	1.30	—	1.37	2.44
	5.25	—	5.32	6.47
	8.38	—	8.45	9.59

Trains from Deepdene.

	Leave Deep.	Arrive at Lon. B.	Can. St.	Char. +
AM	7.22	8.24	8.28	—
	7.57	8.56	—	—
	8.27	9.28	9.32	—
	8.57	9.48	9.52	—
	9.29	10.27	10.32	—
	9.56	11. 0	—	—
	11.35	12.50	—	1. 0
PM	1.27	2.38	—	2.46
	2.37*d*	4. 8	—	—
	3.39	5. 2	—	5.14
	4.51	5.56	—	—
	6. 9	7.20	—	7.29
	7.56	9. 2	—	9.15
	8.57	10. 3	—	10.13
	10.51	11.57	—	12.10

DEEPDENE—*continued.*

Sunday Trains.

	Leave Deep.	Arrive at Lon. B.	Can. St.	Char. +
AM	7. 7	8.16	—	8.27
	10. 9	11.15	—	11.25
PM	3.30	4.33	—	4.42
	6. 4	7.13	—	7.25
	8.48	9.52	—	—
	9. 3	10.11	—	10.24

d Saturdays only.
e Saturdays excepted.
l Low Level Platform.

Star and Garter Hotel, Box Hill First-class accommodation, with moderate charges. Near Golf Course. 'Phone No. 20, Dorking.
CATERING HOUSES, LTD.

DEEPFIELDS (Stafford), 122½ miles. Fares, 25/2*a*, 15/1*c* R. T. for two months, 50/4*a*. Departures *from* London as for Oldbury. Departures *for* London about 6 times daily.
Map Square 17.

DEFFORD (Worcester), 122½ miles. No through fares. Departures *from* London as for Worcester. Departures *for* London about 4 times daily. Pop. 407.
Map Square 17.

DEGANWY (Carnarvon), 224¾ miles. Fares, 46/10*a*, 28/1*c*. R. T. for two months, 93/8*a*, 56/2*c*. Departures *from* London as for Llandudno. Departures *for* London about 4 times daily.
Map Square 11.

DEIGHTON (Yorks), 205¼ miles. Fares, 37/9*a*, 22/8*c*. R. T. double fare. Departures *from* London as for Huddersfield. Departures *for* London about 6 times daily.

DELABOLE (Cornwall) from *Waterloo*, 243¼ miles. Fares, 50/0*a*, 30/0*c*. R. T. for two months, 100/0*a*, 60/0*c*. Departures *from* London as for Camelford. Departures *for* London about 4 times daily.
Map Square 25.

DELAMERE (Cheshire), 179 miles. No through fares. Departures *from* London as for Northwich. Departures *for* London about 3 times daily. Pop. 666.
Map Square 12.

DELNY (Ross), 602½ miles. Fares, 106/11*a*, 64/2*c*. R. T. for two months, 213/10*a*, 128/4*c*. Departures *from* London as for Dingwall. Departures *for* London about twice daily.
Map Square 34.

DELPH (Yorks), 192½ miles. Fares, 37/9*a*, 22/8*c*. R. T., double fare. Departures *from* London as for Mossley. Departures *for* London about 6 times daily.
Map Square 12.

DENBIGH from *Euston*, 208½ miles. Fares, *via* Mold, 40/7*a*, 24/4*c*. R. T. for two months, 81/2*a*, 48/8*c*. Pop. 6,783.
Map Square 11.

	Euston	D'bigh		D'bigh	Euston
AM	12.25	7.55	AM	6.31*dr*	12. 5
	5. 0*h*	11.25		6.31*er*	12.20
	8.30*hr*	3.10		7.42*hr*	1. 0
	10.30*r*	3.23		8.35	1.45
	11.10*hr*	4.55		9. 6*r*	2.20
	11.50*r*	5.56		10. 0*hr*	4.15
	12. 0*nr*	7.25		12. 0*hr*	5. 5

DENBIGH—*continued.*

	Euston	D'bigh		D'bigh	Euston
PM	2.35*t*	7.55	PM	12. 5*r*	5.50
	4. 5*r*	9.32		1.24*hr*	7.30
	5.20*r*	10.42		2.35*r*	8.10
	—	—		3.20*er*	9. 5
	—	—		3.20*dr*	9.15
	—	—		4.58*r*	10.45
	—	—		9.12*h*	5. 0

No Sunday Trains.

d Saturdays only.
e Saturdays excepted.
h Via Rhyl.
n Noon.
r Restaurant Car.
t Tea Car.

DENBY (Derby), 135¾ miles. Fares, 27/4*a*, 16/5*c*. R. T., double fare. Departures *from* London as for Ripley. Departures *for* London about 6 times daily. Pop. 1,791.
Map Square 12.

DENBY DALE (Yorks), 178¾ miles. Fares, 36/1*a*, 21/8*c*. R. T. for two months, 72/2*a*. Departures *from* London as for Penistone. Departures *for* London about 8 times daily. Pop. 2,096.
Map Square 12.

DENHAM (Bucks) from *Paddington*, 14¾ miles. Fares, 2/9*a*, 1/8*c*. R. T. for two months, 5/6*a*, 2/11*c*. Pop. 1,290. *See* pp. 490–491.
Map Squares 23 *and* 46.

ANOTHER ROUTE from *Marylebone*, 16¼ miles. Fares as above. *See* pp. 495–496

DENHAM (Golf Club) (Bucks) from *Paddington* 15¾ miles. Fares, 2/11*a*, 1/9*c*. R.T. for two months, 5/10*a*, 3/2½*c*. *See* pp. 490–491.

ANOTHER ROUTE from *Marylebone*, 17 miles. Fares as above. *See* pp. 495–496.

DENHOLME (Yorks) from *King's Cross*, 198¾ miles. Fares, 40/0*a*, 24/0*c*. R. T. double fare. Departures *from* London as for Keighley. Departures *for* London about 6 times daily. Pop. 2,938.
Map Square 12.

DENMARK HILL (London) from *London Bridge* and *Victoria*, 4¼ miles. Fares from London Bridge, 0/7*a*, 0/4½*c*. R. T. for two days, 1/0*a*, 0/9*c*. From Victoria, 0/7½*a*, 0/4½*c*. R. T. for two days, 1/2*a*, 0/9*c*. *See* p. 570.
Map Square 70.

ANOTHER ROUTE from *Victoria*, *Ludgate Hill*, and *St. Paul's*, 4¼ miles. Fares from Victoria, 0/7½*a*, 0/6*b*, 0/4½*c*. R. T. for two days, 1/2*a*, 1/0*b*, 0/9*c*. From Ludgate Hill, 0/7*a*, 0/6*b*, 0/4½*c*. R. T. for two days, 1/0*a*, 0/10½*b*. *See* pp. 562, 563.

DENNY (Stirling), 410¾ miles. Fares, 83/11*a*, 50/4*c*. R. T. for two months, 167/10*a*, 100/8*c*. Departures *from* London as for Larbert. Departures *for* London about 4 times daily. Pop. 9,187.

DENNYLOANHEAD (Stirling), 411¾ miles. No through fares. Departures *from* London as for Larbert. Departures *for* London about 3 times daily.

DENSTONE (Stafford), 141 miles. Fares, 29/2*a*, 17/6*c*. R. T. for two months, 58/4*a*, 35/0*c*. Departures *from* London as for Uttoxeter. Departures *for* London about 4 times daily. Pop. 724.
Map Square 12

DEAL.—BEACH HOUSE HOTEL. FINEST POSITION ON FRONT. See Advt. opposite.

DENT (Yorks), 253½ miles.

Fares, 49/2*a*, 29/6*c*. R. T. for two months, 98/4*a*, 59/0*c*. Departures *from* London as for Settle. Departures *for* London about 6 times daily. Pop. 942.
Map Square 7.

DENTON (Lancs) from

Euston, 181¾ miles. Fares, 37/9*a*, 22/8*c*. R. T. for two months, 75/6*a*. Pop. 17,631
Map Square 12.

Euston	Denton	Denton	Euston
AM12.25	6.33	AM 7. 8*dr*	12.20
2.35	8.10	7.48*er*	12. 5
5. 0	10.10	8.18*r*	12.50
6.45*d*	12.32	9.27*r*	1.15
8.45*r*	12.42	9.40*r*	1.45
10.40*r*	2.38	10.28*r*	3.10
11.50*r*	3.42	11.59*r*	3.55
12. 0*er*	5.47	PM12.32*dr*	5.50
12. 0*dr*	5.54	12.32*er*	6. 0
PM 1.30*er*	6.19	12.55*dr*	6. 0
1.30*dr*	6.32	1.53*r*	6.15
2.50*t*	6.57	2.29*r*	7.30
4. 5*r*	8.14	3.56*r*	8.10
4.45*r*	9.13	4.59*dr*	10. 0
6. 5*r*	10. 0	5.50*er*	10.10
11.50*d*	7.44	10.20	5. 0
—	—	—	—

Sunday Trains.

PM12.10*r*	5.10	AM 9. 1	4. 0
12.30*r*	6.34	PM12.24*r*	5.45
—	—	2.30	7.30
—	—	4. 1*r*	8.55
—	—	9.54	5. 0

d Saturdays only.
e Saturdays excepted.
r Restaurant Car.
t Tea Car.

DENVER (Norfolk) from

Liverpool Street and *St. Pancras*, 84½ miles. No through fares. Departures *from* London as for Stoke Ferry. Departures *for* London about 4 times daily. Pop. 731.
Map Square 19.

DERBY from *St. Pancras*,

128½ miles. Fares, 26/6*a*, 15/11*c*. R. T., double fare. Pop. 129,836.
Map Square 12.

St. Pan.	Derby	Derby	St. Pan.
AM 2.25	5.22	AM 1.10*g*	4.20
4.25	8. 5	1.10*f*	4.55
8.25*r*	11.12	2.20*g*	6. 0
10.25*r*	12.55	3.18	7.25
11. 0*r*	2.30	6.36*r*	9.57
PM12.25*r*	2.54	7.25*r*	10.45
1.25*r*	4.13	8. 0*r*	11. 0
2.25*r*	4.54	8.55*r*	11.35
3.30*r*	6.56	10.47*r*	1.30
4.25*r*	7. 5	11.15*r*	1.45
6.15*r*	8.50	12. 0	3.25
6.25*r*	8.57	PM12.53*r*	4.10
8.25	12.10	1.54*r*	4.20
9.15	12.22	3. 4*r*	5.45
11.50	2.54	3.26*r*	6.15
12. 0	3.33	4.10*r*	7.15
—	—	4.33*r*	7.57
—	—	6. 4*r*	8.35
—	—	6.23*r*	9.15
—	—	7.22*r*	10. 5

Sunday Trains.

AM10.50*r*	2.11	AM 1.10	4.20
11.15*r*	2.18	2.20	6. 0
PM 3.15	6.10	3.18	8. 5
6.15*r*	9. 6	8. 8	11.53
8.25	12.10	PM 2. 0*r*	5. 2
9.15	12.25	2.31	5.27
11.55	3.33	7. 7*r*	9.52
—	—	—	—

f Mondays only.
g Mondays excepted.
r Restaurant Car.

DERBY—*continued.*

ANOTHER ROUTE (Friar Gate) from *King's Cross*, 145¼ miles. Fares as above.

King's +	Derby	Derby	King's +
AM 4.45	10.16	AM 5.35	10.40
5. 5	10.49	7.50*r*	11.30
8.45	1.30	8.30	1. 5
10.10*r*	2. 2	9.30*r*	1.30
11.30	4.16	10.50	3.50
PM 1.50*r*	5.59	PM 1.25	6.25
5.35*r*	9.17	3.57	9. 0
5.45*er*	10.40	5. 0*r*	9.25
5.45*dr*	11.11	9.25*e*	3.25
11.25*e*	6.56	9.45*d*	3.25
—	—	—	—

Sunday Trains.

AM11.30*r*	3.36	AM11.25	3.45
12. 0*r*	4.48	PM 1.35	5.55
PM 5. 0*r*	9.52	—	—
11.25	6.56	—	—
—	—	—	—

d Saturdays only.
e Saturdays excepted.
r Restaurant Car.

Royal Hotel. First-class. Central, convenient. Family and Commercial Headquarters of Motor Clubs. Garage. Stockrooms. Electric light. Tel. 246. Telegrams, Overflow, Derby.
A. O. FULLER.

Midland Hotel. Covered way from Midland Station. Excellent Cuisine. Garage 2 minutes. One of the "Midland Hotels."
ARTHUR TOWLE,
Manager.

DERBY ROAD (Suffolk),

74¾ miles. Fares, 15/8*a*, 9/5*c*. R. T. for two months, 31/4*a*. Departures *from* London as for Felixstowe. Departures *for* London about 6 times daily.
Map Square 19.

DEREHAM (Norfolk) from

Liverpool Street, 125¼ miles. Fares, 23/7*a*, 14/2*c*. R. T. for two months, 47/2*a*. Pop. 5,659.
Map Square 19.

L'pl St.	D'ham.	D'ham.	L'pl St.
AM 5. 5	9. 5	AM 7.14*f*	10.36
5.50	11.30	7.30*g*	11.27
9.50*r*	1.52	8.23	12.40
11.50*r*	4. 9	10.11*r*	2.21
PM12.33*dr*	4.42	11.18*d*	4.58
3.10*r*	7.29	PM 1.38*r*	5.17
5.18*r*	8.45	4.13*r*	8.22
—	—	4.50*h*	8.33
—	—	9.55	2.50
—	—	—	—
—	—	—	—

Sunday Trains.

PM 3.25	7.59	PM 5.46	9.40
—	—	—	—

d Saturdays only.
f Mondays only.
g Mondays excepted.
h Thursdays only.
r Restaurant Car.

DERRY ORMOND (Cardigan), 257¾ miles.

Fares, 48/9*a*, 29/3*c*. R. T. for two months, 97/6*a*. Departures *from* London as for Lampeter. Departures *for* London about 4 times daily.
Map Square 16.

DERSINGHAM (Norfolk)

from *Liverpool Street*, 104¾ miles. Fares, 22/1*a*, 13/3*c*. R. T. for two months, 44/2*a*, 26/6*c*. Departures *from* London as for Wolferton. Departures *for* London about 10 minutes later. Pop. 1,499.
Map Square 19.

DERWEN (Denbigh), 198¼

miles. Fares, 40/7*a*, 24/4*c*. R. T. for two months, 81/2*a*, 48/8*c*. Departures *from* London as for Corwen or Ruthin. Departures *for* London about 4 times daily. Pop. 437.
Map Square 11.

DERWYDD ROAD (Carmarthen),

220¾ miles. Fares, 43/2*a*, 25/11*c*. R. T. for two months, 86/4*a*. Departures *from* London as for Llandilo. Departures *for* London about 5 times daily.
Map Square 21.

DESBORO' (Northampton)

from *St. Pancras*, 78 miles. Fares, 16/1*a*, 9/8*c*. R. T., double fare. Pop. 4,108.
Map Square 18.

St. Pan.	Desboro	Desboro	St. Pan.
AM 4.25	7.31	AM 7.25*r*	9.57
8.25*r*	10.46	8.59*r*	11. 0
11.0*r*	12.55	11.22*r*	1.20
11.35	2.30	PM12.31*d*	3.25
PM 3.30*r*	5.17	1.57*r*	4.10
4.30*r*	6.40	4. 1	7. 3
6.25*r*	8. 7	5.46	8.22
6.30	9. 1	8.43	11.45
8.25*d*	11. 4	9.57*e*	5. 5
—	—	11.42*d*	5. 5

Sunday Trains.

AM 8. 0	11.30	AM 9.12	11.53
PM 6.15*r*	8.50	PM 5.16	8.30
—	—	8.50	11. 7
—	—	—	—
—	—	—	—

d Saturdays only.
e Saturdays excepted.
r Restaurant Car.

DESFORD (Leicester) from

St. Pancras, 104¼ miles. Fares, 21/10*a*, 13/1*c*. R. T. double fare. Pop. 1,118.
Map Square 18.

St. Pan.	Desf'd.	Desf'd.	St. Pan.
AM 2.25	7.21	AM 7.19*r*	9.57
4.25	9.28	8.15*r*	11. 0
9.50*dr*	12.35	9.13*r*	11.35
10.25*r*	12.49	PM12.22	3.25
PM12.25*r*	3. 5	1.37*dr*	4.20
2.25*r*	4.57	2.20*r*	5.45
3.30*r*	6.40	4.24*r*	6.35
4.25*r*	6.56	6.50*r*	9.15
6.25*r*	8.45	9.55	4.20
—	—	—	—

Sunday Trains.

PM 6.15*r*	8.59	AM 8.24	11.53
—	—	PM 6.53*r*	9.52
—	—	—	—
—	—	—	—

d Saturdays only.
r Restaurant Car.

DESS (Aberdeen), 551¼ miles.

Fares, 106/1a, 63/3c. R. T. for two months, 212/2a, 127/4c. Departures *from* London as for Ballater. Departures *for* London about 3 times daily.
Map Square 38.

DEVIL'S BRIDGE (Cardigan), 251¼ miles.

No through fares. Departures *from* London as for Aberystwyth. Departures *for* London about 3 times daily.
Map Square 16.

DEVIZES (Wilts) from Paddington, 86 miles.

Fares, via Theale, 17/9a, 10/8c. R. T. for two months, 35/6a. Via Chippenham, 19/10a, 11/11c. R. T. for two months, 39/8a. Pop. 6,022.
Map Square 22.

PAD.	DEVIZES	DEVIZES	PAD.
AM 1. 0g	7. 1	AM 7.40	10. 0
7.30	10. 3	8.50	10.52
8.45r	11.44	9.40	12 55
10.45	1.22	PM12.33	2.50
PM12.30r	3.15	1.24h	6. 2
2.45	4.41	3.5r	7.20
3.15ht	6.38	4.44h	8.20
4.15ht	7.28	6.43h	10.25
5.55	8. 1	7.37	10.45
6.30	9. 0	9.14h	2.45

Sunday Trains.

AM 9.10	12.26	AM 7.30	10.50
PM12.30h	6.12	PM12.28hr	7.55
5.15	8.22	6.16	9.15

g Mondays excepted.
h Via Trowbridge.
k Via Chippenham.
r Restaurant Car.
t Tea Car.

Bear Hotel. First - class Family and Commercial House. Principal Hotel in Town. Central and nearest Station. Convenient for Salisbury Plain and Stonehenge. Billiard, Smoking, and Private Sitting Rooms, with separate entrance. Cars for hire. Bus meets trains. Moderate.
Proprietor—
W. R. SUDWEEKS.

DEVONPORT (Devon) from Waterloo, 229¾ miles.

Fares, 46/8a, 28/0c. R. T. for two months, 93/4a, 56/0c. Pop. 81,678.
Map Square 26

W'LOO	D'PORT	D'PORT	W'LOO
AM 9. 0r	2.39	AM 8.45r	1.56
10. 0r	3.31	10.23r	3.50
11. 0r	4.28	PM12.19r	6. 0
PM 1. 0r	7. 5	2.32r	8.30
3. 0r	8. 7	4.17	10.50
6. 0r	11.42	4.30h	3.58

Sunday Trains.

12. 0nr	6.16	PM 3.18r	8.57

h Via Eastleigh.
n Noon.
r Restaurant Car.

DEVONPORT—contd.

ANOTHER ROUTE from Paddington, 227 miles.

Fares, 46/8a, 28/0c. R. T. for two months, 93/4a, 56/0c.

PAD.	D'PORT	D'PORT	PAD.
AM 5.30	12.30	AM 8.14r	1.30
7.30	2.50	11.37r	4.35
11.10r	3.50	11.52r	4.45
12. 5r	6.45	PM 1.28r	6.50
PM 2. 0r	7.22	1.36dr	7. 5
3.30r	8.50	3.37r	9. 0
4.15r	11.11	4. 4e	2.45
10. 0e	5.48	11.40	7.10
10. 0d	7.32	—	—
12. 0k	7.51	—	—
12.30h	8.27	—	—

Sunday Trains.

AM10.30r	3.55	AM 9.41r	4. 5
PM 2.40r	8.30	PM 1.42	7. 5
10. 0	5.48	7.55	3.15
—	—	10.41	7.10

d Saturdays only.
e Saturdays excepted.
h Saturdays midnight only.
k Saturdays midnight excepted.
r Restaurant Car.

DEVYNOCK (Brecon), 191¼ miles.

Fares, 39/7a, 23/9c. R.T. for two months, 79/2a, 47/6c. Departures *from* London as for Brecon. Departures *for* London about 3 times daily.
Map Square 16.

DEWSBURY (Yorks) from King's Cross, 182¼ miles.

Fares, 37/0d, 22/8c. R. T., double fare. Pop. 54,165.
Map Square 9.

KING'S+	DWSBY.	DEWSBY.	KING'S+
AM 4.45	9.20	AM 7.46r	11.30
7.15r	11.19	8.33	1. 5
10.10r	2. 5	10.13r	1.55
PM 1.30r	5.36	10.45	3.50
1.50r	6.21	PM12.46r	5. 0
4. 0r	8.12	1.14	6.25
5.45r	9.49	2.48r	7.10
10.45e	5.44	5.11r	9.25
—	—	10. 1	3.25

Sunday Trains.

12. 0nr	4.56	AM11. 0r	3.45
PM 5. 0r	9.54	PM 1. 3	6.15
10.45	5.44	5.21r	10.20

e Saturdays excepted.
n Noon.
r Restaurant Car.

DEWSBURY—continued.

ANOTHER ROUTE from Euston, 211¼ miles. Fares as above.

EUSTON	DEWSBY.	DEWSBY.	EUSTON
AM12.25	8.40	AM 6.16r	12.50
2.35	11. 0	8. 9r	1.15
5. 0	12.32	8.54r	3.10
8.45r	2.34	9.59r	3.55
10.40r	4.25	11.12dr	5.50
11.50r	5.55	PM12.47er	6. 0
12. 0nr	7.15	12.47dr	6.15
PM 1.30r	8.35	1.31r	7.30
4. 5r	10.12	1.55r	8.10
6. 5r	11.50	3.19r	10. 0
8. 0e	5.35	4.17er	10.10
11.50d	9.39	8.28	5. 0
—	—	9.57e	5.50
—	—	10.20d	5.50

Sunday Trains.

PM12.10r	6.50	AM 7. 0	4. 0
12.30r	10.18	10.40r	5.45
7.50r	5.35	PM12.31r	7.30
—	—	5.25	5. 0
—	—	8.50	5.50

d Saturdays only.
e Saturdays excepted.
n Noon.
r Restaurant Car.

DIDCOT (Berks) from Paddington, 53 miles.

Fares, 11/1a, 6/8c. R. T. for two months, 22/2a. Pop. 707.
Map Square 22.

PAD.	DIDCOT	DIDCOT	PAD.
AM 5.30	6.40	AM 1.17g	2.45
6.30	8. 4	2. 2f	3.15
7.30	9.23	2.20	3.30
8.50	10. 1	5.50	7.10
9. 0	10.15	7.39	9. 0
9.45	11.25	7.56	9.30
10.45	12. 2	8.29	10. 0
11.20	12.57	9.17r	10.15
PM12.30	2. 6	9.34	10.45
1.10r	2.21	10.43	12. 0
1.35r	3.11	PM12.12	1.50
1.50d	3.52	12.50	2.35
3.18	4.52	1.37	3.20
3.38	5.33	2.43	4.35
5.15	6.32	3.30	5. 6
5.40	7.15	4.54	6. 2
6. 5	7.35	5.25	7.20
6.55	8. 8	6.45	8.20
7.30	9. 6	7.39	9.15
8. 5	9.59	8.55	10.45
9.15	10.34	—	—
10. 0	11.10	—	—
12. 0h	1.15	—	—
12.30k	1.46	—	—

Sunday Trains.

AM 9.10	10.32	AM 1.17	2.45
10.35	12. 0	2.20	3.30
11. 0	12.46	5.50	7. 5
11.45	1.10	8. 9	10.14
PM12.30	1.35	PM 1.25	2.40
1.45	3.38	2.20	3.35
2. 0	4.20	4. 8	6. 0
4.10	6. 8	5. 5	6.20
5.15	7.11	6.30	8.20
7.40	9.52	7.30	9.15
9.15	10.36	8. 9	9.42
10. 0	11.10	8.51	10. 0
—	—	9.17	11.38

d Saturdays only.
f Mondays only.
g Mondays excepted.
h Saturdays midnight excepted.
k Saturdays midnight only.
r Restaurant Car.

DIDSBURY (Lancs), 183¼ miles. Fares, 37/11a, 22.9c. R. T. for two months, 75/10a, 45/6c. Departures *from* London as for Stockport (Tiviot Dale). Departures *for* London about 4 times daily. Pop. 14,798.
Map Square 12.

DIEPPE from *Victoria* (L.B. & S.C.), 190½ miles. Fares, 42/0a, 32/0b, 23/0c. R. T. for one month, 76/0a, 56/6b, 42/6c. Subject to exchange.
Map Square 29.

Subject to Special Passport Regulations.

Weekdays and Sundays.

VICT.	DIEPPE.
AM 10. 0b	2.55
PM 8.20	2.15

Trains from Dieppe.

DIEPPE.	VICT.
AM12.20	7.55
PM 1.30b	7.40

DIGBY (Lincoln), 117 miles. Fares, 24/5a, 14/8c. R. T. double fare. Departures *from* London as for Blankney. Departures *for* London about 4 times daily. Pop. 341.
Map Square 13.

DIGGLE (Yorks) from *Euston*, 192½ miles. Fares, 37/9a, 22/8c. R. T., double fare. Departures *from* London as for Saddleworth. Departures *for* London about 6 times daily.
Map Square 12.

DINAS (Carnarvon), 250½ miles. Fares, 52/3a, 31/4c. R. T. for two months, 104/6a, 62/8c. Departures *from* London as for Carnarvon. Departures *for* London about 5 times daily.
Map Square 11.

DINAS (Glamorgan), 169½ miles. Fares, 34/2a, 20/6c. R. T. for two months, 68/4a, 41/0c. Departures *from* London as for Treherbert. Departures *for* London about 4 times daily.

DINAS MAWDDY (Merioneth) from *Paddington*, 220½ miles. No through fares.
Map Square 16.

PAD.	MAWDDY	MAWDDY	PAD.
AM10.40r	6. 5	AM 8.20r	4.15
12.15h	11.15	PM12.40er	8. 5
—	—	3.45	3.30
—	—	—	—
—	—	—	—
—	—	—	—
—	—	—	—
—	—	—	—

No Sunday Trains.

e Saturdays excepted.
h Saturdays midnight excepted.
r Restaurant Car.

DINAS POWIS (Glamorgan), 157½ miles. Fares, 32/9a, 19/8c. R. T. for two months, 65/6a, 39/4c. Departures *from* London as for Cardiff. Departures *for* London about 4 times daily.
Map Square 21.

DINGESTOW (Monmouth), 148½ miles. Fares, 31/0a, 18/7c. R. T. for two months, 62/0a, 37/2c. Departures *from* London as for Monmouth. Departures *for* London about 4 times daily. Pop. 190.
Map Square 22.

DINGWALL (Ross) from *Euston*, 586½ miles. Fares, 106/3a, 63/9c. R. T. for two months, 212/6a. Pop. 2,551.
Map Square 34.

EUSTON	DINGW.	DINGW.	EUSTON
PM 1.30er	7.15h	AM 9.22r	5. 0h
7.40er	10.48h	PM 2. 0	7.40h
11.35v	4.10	8.27er	7.30l
11.35e	6.10l	—	—
—	—	—	—
—	—	—	—
—	—	—	—

Sunday Trains.

PM 7.50r	10.48h	—	—
11.35	6.10l	—	—
—	—	—	—
—	—	—	—
—	—	—	—

e Saturdays excepted.
h A.M.
l P.M.
r Restaurant Car.
v Thursday night.

ANOTHER ROUTE from *King's Cross*, 576½ miles. Fares as above.

KING'S +	DINGW.	DINGW.	KING'S+
AM11.50er	7.14k	AM 9. 22	3.25k
PM 7.45er	10.48k	PM 2. 0	7. 5k
11.25e	6.10f	8.27er	6.30k

Sunday Trains.

PM 7.45r	10.48k	—	—
11.25	6.10k	—	—

e Saturdays excepted.
f Arrives 4.10 on Fridays only.
h P.M.
k A.M.
r Restaurant Car.

DINMORE (Hereford), 151½ miles. Fares, 30/0a, 18/0c. R. T. for two months, 60/0a, 36/0c. Departures *from* London as for Hereford. Departures *for* London about 5 times daily. Pop. 25.
Map Square 17.

DINNET (Aberdeen), 558½ miles. Fares, 107/9a, 64/8c. R. T. for two months, 215/6a, 129/4c. Departures *from* London as for Ballater. Departures *for* London about twice daily.
Map Square 38.

DINNINGTON (Yorks), 166½ miles. Fares, 33/7a, 20/2c. R. T., double fare. Departures *from* London as for Doncaster. Departures *for* London about 4 times daily. Pop. 4,897.
Map Square 13.

DINSDALE (Durham), 235 miles. Fares, 49/2a, 29/6c. R. T., double fare. Departures *from* London as for Darlington. Departures *for* London about 4 times daily. Pop. 337.
Map Square 7.

DINTING. *See* GLOSSOP AND DINTING.

DINTON (Wilts) from *Waterloo*, 92 miles. Fares, 19/2a, 11/6c. R. T. for two months, 38/4a, 23/0c. Departures *from* London as for Wilton. Departures *for* London about 6 times daily. Pop. 449.
Map Square 22.

DINWOODIE (Dumfries), 330½ miles. No through fares. Departures *from* London as for Lockerbie. Departures *for* London about 3 times daily.
Map Square 44.

DIRLETON (East Lothian), 377 miles. No through fares. Departures *from* London as for North Berwick. Departures *for* London about 3 times daily. Pop. 2,623.
Map Square 41.

DISLEY (Cheshire), 174½ miles. Fares, *via* Macclesfield, 36/1a, 21/8c. R. T., double fare. *Via* Stockport, 72/2a, 43/4c. R. T., double fare. Departures *from* London as for Macclesfield or Stockport. Departures *for* London about 4 times daily. Pop. 2,958.
Map Square 12.

DISS (Norfolk) from *Liverpool Street*, 95 miles. Fares, 20/0a, 12/0c. R. T. for two months, 40/0a. Pop. 3,513.
Map Square 13.

L'POOL ST.	DISS	DISS	L'POOL ST.
AM 5. 0	7.50	AM 7.35r	10.30
8.15r	10.48	8.15f	10.36
9.50r	12. 5	9. 32	12.39
10.12	1.11	10.53	1.20
PM12.35r	3.24	11.14r	2. 3
3.10r	5.52	PM 2. 6r	4.58
5.18r	7.39	4. 4	6.32
—	—	4.38	7.51
—	—	7. 8r	9.22
—	—	7.53	11.16
—	—	—	—
—	—	—	—
—	—	—	—

Sunday Trains.

AM 9.20r	12.32	AM 8. 4	11.38
PM 4.40	7.25	PM 7.12	10.15
—	—	—	—
—	—	—	—

e Saturdays excepted.
f Mondays only.
r Restaurant Car.

DISTINGTON (Cumberland), 305½ miles. No through fares. Departures *from* London as for Whitehaven or Moor Row. Departures *for* London about twice daily. Pop. 2,159.
Map Square 6.

DITCHFORD (Northampton) from *Euston*, 79¾ miles. Fares, 13/2*a*, 7/11*c*. R. T., double fare. Departures *from* London as for Wellingborough. Departures *for* London about 4 times daily.
Map Square 18.

DITCHINGHAM (Norfolk) from *Liverpool Street*, *via* Beccles, 115 miles. Fares, 24/0*a*, 14/5*c*. R. T. for two months, 48/0*a*. Pop. 1,137.
Map Square 19.

L'pl. St.	Ditchm.	Ditchm.	L'pl. St.
AM 5. 0	9.20	AM 8.23*r*	11.30
8.15*r*	12.32	10. 6*r*	2. 3
10.20	3.26	PM 2.20	5.56
PM 3.15*r*	6.18	3.34	7.51
3.18*r*	7.25	6.26*r*	10. 0
—	—	—	—
—	—	—	—
—	—	—	—
—	—	—	—
—	—	—	—
—	—	—	—
—	—	—	—
—	—	—	—
—	—	—	—
—	—	—	—

No Sunday Trains.

r Restaurant Car.

ANOTHER ROUTE, *via* Tivetshall, 114½ miles. Fares as above.

L'pl. St.	Ditchm.	Ditchm.	L'pl. St.
AM 5. 0	10. 6	AM 6.37*r*	10.30
10.12	2.20	9.20	1.20
PM12.33*r*	6.26	PM12.32*r*	4.58
5.18*ehr*	9. 1	3.26	7.51
5.18*dr*	9. 6	6.18	11.16
—	—	—	—
—	—	—	—
—	—	—	—
—	—	—	—
—	—	—	—
—	—	—	—
—	—	—	—
—	—	—	—
—	—	—	—

No Sunday Trains.

d Saturdays only.
e Saturdays excepted.
h *Via* Forncett.
r Restaurant Car.

DITTON (Lancs), 190 miles. Fares, 39/5*a*, 23/8*c*. R. T. for two months, 78/10*a*. Departures *from* London as for Runcorn. Departures *for* London about 6 times daily. Pop. 2,900.
Map Square 12.

DITTON PRIORS (Salop), 155½ miles. No through fares. Departures *from* London as for Cleobury Mortimer. Departures *for* London about twice daily. Pop. 619.

DIXON FOLD (Lancs), 192¾ miles. No through fares. Departures *from* London as for Manchester. Departures *for* London about 8 times daily.

DOCKING (Norfolk) from *Liverpool Street*, 116 miles. Fares, 24/5*a*, 14/8*c*. R. T. for two months, 48/10*a*, 29/4*c*. Departures *from* London as for Burnham Market. Departures *for* London about 4 times daily. Pop. 1,237.
Map Square 14.

DODDINGTON (Lincoln), 136½ miles. Fares, 27/4*a*, 16/5*c*. R. T., double fare. Departures *from* London as for Lincoln or Edwinstowe. Departures *for* London about twice daily. Pop. 155.
Map Square 13.

DODWORTH (Yorks), 177¾ miles. Fares, 35/8*a*, 21/5*c*. R. T., double fare. Departures *from* London as for Barnsley. Departures *for* London about 3 times daily. Pop. 3,327.
Map Square 12.

DOE HILL (Derby), 138¾ miles. Fares, 28/2*a*, 16/11*c*. R. T., double fare. Departures *from* London as for Alfreton. Departures *for* London about 5 times daily.
Map Square 13.

DOGDYKE (Lincoln) from *King's Cross*, 118½ miles. Fares, 24/7*a*, 14/9*c*. R. T., double fare. Departures *from* London as for Kirkstead. Departures *for* London about 10 minutes later. Pop. 174.
Map Square 13.

DOLAU (Radnor), 207¼ miles. Fares, 37/3*a*, 22/4*c*. R. T. for two months, 74/6*a*, 44/8*c*. Departures *from* London as for Knighton. Departures *for* London about twice daily.
Map Square 16.

DOLDOWLOD (Radnor), 194½ miles. Fares, *via* Welshpool, 41/5*a*, 24/10*c*. R. T. for two months, 82/10*a*. Departures *from* London as for Llanidloes. Departures *for* London about 4 times daily.
Map Square 16.

DOLGARROG (Carnarvon), 231½ miles. Fares, 47/11*a*, 28/9*c*. R. T. for two months, 95/10*a*, 57/6*c*. Departures *from* London as for Llanwrst and Trefriw. Departures *for* London about 4 times daily. Pop. 107.
Map Square 11.

DOLGELLEY (Merioneth) from *Paddington*, 222¼ miles. Fares, 46/8*a*, 28/0*c*. R. T. for two months, 93/4*a*, 56/0*c*. Pop. 2,014.
Map Square 16.

Pad.	Dolg.	Dolg.	Pad.
AM 9.10*r*	3.13	AM 8.10*r*	2. 5
10.40*r*	4.35	10.40*r*	5. 0
PM12.50*r*	7. 0	PM 1.40*r*	8. 5
2.10*t*	8.25	3.15*r*	10. 0
12.15*k*	9.37	6. 7	3.30
—	—	—	—
—	—	—	—

No Sunday Trains.

k Saturdays midnight excepted.
r Restaurant Car.
t Tea Car.

ANOTHER ROUTE from *Euston*, 260½ miles. Fares, 48/4*a*, 29/0*c*. R.T. for two months, 96/8*a*.

Euston	Dolg.	Dolg.	Euston
AM 5. 0*h*	3. 3	AM 7. 0*r*	3.10
10. 0*r*	6.20	8.45*r*	6.15
PM 9.30*eh*	8. 5	11.46*dr*	9.15
—	—	11.46*er*	9.20*l*
—	—	PM 4.38	5. 0
—	—	—	—
—	—	—	—

Sunday Trains.

PM 9.15	8. 5	—	—
—	—	—	—
—	—	—	—

e Saturdays excepted.
h *Via* Crewe.
r Restaurant Car.

Golden Lion Hotel. The leading first-class Family Hotel. Remodelled, re-decorated, new lounge. Moderate tariff. *See* also Harlech, Llandudno, Rhyl.

DOLGOCH (Merioneth), 237¼ miles. No through fares. Departures *from* London as for Machynlleth. Departures *for* London about 4 times daily.
Map Square 16.

DOLLAR (Clackmannan), 431¼ miles. Fares, 86/1*a*, 51/8*c*. R. T. for two months, 172/2*a*, 103/4*c*. Departures *from* London as for Dunfermline or Stirling. Departures *for* London about 4 times daily. Pop. 1,954.
Map Square 40.

DOLLIS HILL from *Baker Street*, 4¾ miles. Fares, 0/11*a*, 0/6½*c*. R. T. for two days, 1/7½*a*, 1/0½*c*. *See* back of Map.
Map Square 59.

DOLPHINTON (Lanark), 383½ miles. Fares, 78/2*a*, 46/11*c*. R. T. for two months, 156/4*a*, 93/10*c*. Departures *from* London as for Carstairs. Departures *for* London about 3 times daily. Pop. 252.
Map Square 41.

DOLWEN (Montgomery),
195½ miles. Fares, 40/8a, 24/5c.
R. T. for two months, 81/4a. Departures *from* London as for
Llanidloes. Departures *for* London about 4 times daily.
Map Square 16.

DOLWYDDELEN
(Carnarvon), 243½ miles. Fares,
47/11a, 28/9c. R. T. for two months, 95/10a, 57/6c. Departures
from London as for Bettws-y-Coed. Departures *for* London
about 4 times daily. Pop. 1,004.
Map Square 11.

DOL-Y-GAER (Brecon),
176 miles. Fares, 36/0a, 21/7c.
R. T. for two months, 72/0a, 43/2c.
Departures *from* London as for
Bargoed. Departures *for* London
about 4 times daily.
Map Square 21.

DOLYHIR (Radnor), 165½
miles. Fares, 33/9a, 20/3c. R. T.
for two months 67/6a. Departures
from London as for Titley. Departures *for* London about 3 times
daily.
Map Square 16.

DONCASTER (Yorks)
from *King's Cross*, 156 miles.
Fares, 32/4a, 19/5c. R. T., double
fare. Pop. 54,052.
Map Square 13.

King's +	Donc.	Donc.	King's +
AM 4.45	8.17	AM 4.16g	7.25
7.15r	10.26	8.40r	11.30
8.45	12.31	9.50	1. 5
9.50r	12.50	10.18r	1.15
10.10r	1. 8	11. 4r	1.55
11.30	3.52	PM12. 2	3.50
PM 1.30r	4.24	1.11r	4.30
1.40r	4.50	1.35r	4.45
1.50r	5. 3	1.59r	5. 0
4. 0r	7.15	2.12	6.25
5.35r	8.33	2.25	6.30
5.45r	8.46	3.14r	6.15
8.25	12.10	4. 5r	7.10
10.45e	1.59	4.50	9. 0
—	—	6.21r	9.25
—	—	6.58r	10. 0
—	—	11.45	3.25

Sunday Trains.

AM 8.30	2. 9	AM 4.16	7.25
11.30r	2.50	PM12. 3r	3.45
12. 0r	3.35	1.42	5.15
PM 5. 0r	8.38	2.12r	5.55
8.25	12.10	2.20	8. 8
10.45	1.59	4.57r	8.15
—	—	6.38r	10.20

e Saturdays excepted.
g Mondays excepted.
r Restaurant Car.

Danum Hotel. R.A.C., A.A.,
A.C.U., and A.C. de France. 65
Bedrooms. Central Heating. Passenger Lift. First Class Family and
Commercial. Proprietors, The
Planet Trading Company (1920)
Ltd. Telegrams: "Danum," Doncaster. Phone 601-602. Resident
Manager— W. PROCTOR.

DONINGTON-ON-
BAIN (Lincoln), 142½ miles. Fares,
29/7a, 17/9c. R. T., double fare.
Departures *from* London as for
Wragby. Departures *for* London
about 4 times daily. Pop. 325.
Map Square 13.

DONINGTON ROAD
(Lincoln), 101½ miles. Fares, 21/1a,
12/8c. R. T., double fare. Departures *from* London as for Gosberton. Departures *for* London about
5 times daily. Pop. (Donington)
1,564.
Map Square 13.

DONISTHORPE
(Leicester), 114½ miles. Fares,
23/7a, 14/2c. R. T. for two
months, 47/2a. Departures *from*
London as for Shackerstone.
Departures *for* London about 5
times daily. Pop. 2,444.
Map Square 17.

DONNINGTON (Salop),
148½ miles. Fares, 29/9a, 17/10c.
R. T. for two months, 59/6a. Departures *from* London as for Newport
(Salop). Departures *for* London
about 3 times daily. Pop. 410.
Map Square 17.

DORCHESTER (Dorset)
from *Waterloo*, 135½ miles. Fares,
28/4a, 17/0c. R. T. for two months,
56/8a, 34/0c. Pop. 9,554.
Map Square 27.

W'loo.	Dorch.	Dorch.	W'loo.
AM 5.40	9.55	AM 7.56s	11. 0
5.50	11.59	9.39r	12.50
8.30s	12.16	11.39	2.50
10.30	1.38	11.57	4.20
PM12.30r	3.38	PM 1.39	4.50
2.30s	5.38	3.39	6.58
4.30r	7.38	5.41r	8.50
6.30r	9.38	7. 1	11.28
10. 0	3.19	10.15	3.58
—	—	—	—
—	—	—	—

Sunday Trains.

AM11. 0r	3.18	AM 7.25	12.11
PM 2. 0r	6.16	10.19r	2.27
7. 0r	11.20	PM 2.41r	6.24
9.28	3.19	5.41r	9.31
—	—	10.15	3.58

r Restaurant Car.
s Refreshments served.

ANOTHER ROUTE from
Paddington, 147 miles. Fares
as above.

Pad.	Dorch.	Dorch.	Pad.
AM 1. 0g	9.20	AM 7.11	10.52
5.30	11.59	9.11	12.55
10.30	1.38	10.47	3.20
PM12.30r	4. 8	PM12. 7	3.50
2. 0	5.28	2. 6t	5.50
3.30	6.29	3.26r	6.50
5. 5	9. 3	4.47	8.20
—	—	7.41	2.45
—	—	8.52h	2.45

Sunday Trains.

PM 2.40	6.40	AM 9.51	3.35
—	—	PM 3.54r	7.55
—	—	—	—
—	—	—	—

g Mondays excepted.
h Thursdays and Third Class only.
r Restaurant Car.
t Tea Car.

King's Arms Hotel. Family
and Commercial. Appointed
R.A.C. & M.U. Hotel. Phone 98.
Manager, W. G. WILLSON.

DORE (Derby) from *St. Pancras*, 154 miles. Fares, 31/11a, 19/2c.
R. T., double fare. Departures
from London as for Chesterfield.
Departures *for* London about 8
times daily. Pop. (Dore) 1,656.
Map Square 12.

DORKING NORTH
(Surrey) from *London Bridge*
(L.B. & S.O.R.), 25½ miles. Fares,
5/0a, 3/0c. R. T. for two months,
10/0a, 5/8c. Pop. 8,058.
Map Square 23.

Lon. B.	Dorking	Dorking	Lon. B.
AM 5.28	6.47	AM 7. 0	8.13
6.35	7.19	7.32	8.41
7.35	9.11	7.55	9. 5
9.22	10.44	8.12	9.17
10.22	11. 9	8.36	9.30
10.30	11.22	8.51	9.47
10.35	11.54	9.30	10.22
10.47	12.50	9.56	10.45
PM12.24	1.51	10.54	11.50
12.52d	1.57	PM12.13	1.28
1.53d	2.53	2.22	3.32
2. 0	3.10	2.34	3.56
3.10e	4.26	3.43	4.27
3.15d	4.25	4. 0	5.18
4. 0	5. 4	4.52e	6.25
4. 9	5.18	5.36	7.13
5. 0	5.57	6.54	7.48
5.14	6.15	7.22	8.41
5.44e	6.38	7.52	9.25
5.58d	6.51	8.20	9.35
5.59	7.16	8.50d	10. 8
6.30e	7.36	9.53	11.11
6.45d	8. 0	—	—
7.15	8.13	—	—
7.30	8.40	—	—
8.53	10. 6	—	—
10.30	12. 0	—	—

Sunday Trains.

AM 6.55	8.12	AM 8.39	10.11
8.55	9.58	9.44	11. 8
9.10	10.33	PM 1.30	2.44
9.30	10.46	2.35	4. 3
10.35	12.11	4.24	5.54
PM12.45	2.21	6.30	8. 8
1.25	2.51	7.26	8.46
3.50	5.15	8.35	10. 1
5.40	7.13	8.47	10.22
8.27	9.49	9. 2	10.25
9.35	11.11	10. 0	11.15

d Saturdays only.
e Saturdays excepted.

ANOTHER ROUTE from
Victoria (L.B. & S.C.R.) 23½ miles.
Fares as above.

Vict.	Dorking	Dorking	Vict.
AM 5.18	6.46	AM 7. 0	8.32
6.18	7.19	7.32	8.53
7.45	9.11	7.55	9.12
8.58	10.44	8.36	9.34
10.15	11. 9	8.51	9.59
10.30	11.54	9. 8	10. 4
11.40	12.50	9.30	10.28
PM12.35	1.51	9.56	10.53
1.40e	3. 9	10.54	11.42
1.45d	2.53	11.36	12.45
3. 0d	4. 9	PM12.13	1.57
3. 0e	4.26	2.22	3.32
4. 5	5. 4	2.34	4. 0
4.53	5.42	3.43	4.34
5.22e	6.38	4. 0	6. 5
6. 0	6.51	4.52	6. 8
6.30	7.27	5.36	6.45
6.42d	8. 0	6.54	7.39
7.20	8.13	7.10d	8.15
8.45d	10. 6	7.22	8.55
10.58	12. 0	7.52	9.30
—	—	8.20e	9.42
—	—	8.50d	9.57
—	—	9.53	11.20

DORKING NORTH —continued.

Sunday Trains.

VICT.	DORKING.	DORKING.	VICT.
AM 9. 0	9.58	AM 8.39	10.13
9. 5	10.33	9.44	11. 6
9.10	10.46	PM 1.30	2.53
11. 3	12.11	2.35	3.57
PM 1.10	2.21	4.24	5.34
4. 5	5.15	6.30	7.33
5.40	7.14	7.26	8.37
8.10	9.49	8.47	9.50
10. 5	11.11	9. 2	10.42
--	--	10. 0	11.52

d Saturdays only.
e Saturdays excepted.

DORKING TOWN from

Charing Cross, Cannon Street, and London Bridge, 31¼ miles. Fares, 5/0a, 4/0b, 3/0c. R. T. for two months, 10/0a, 7/10b, 5/8c.

	Leave		Arr. at
CHAR.+	CAN. ST.	LON. B.	DORK.
AM —	4.44	5. 0	6.19
—	—	7.50*l*	9.11
—	—	9.33*l*	10.48
10.55	—	11. 3	12.30
PM —	12.55d	12.58d	1.56
12.55	—	1. 4	2.24
—	1.24d	1.27d	2.41
2. 3e	2. 8d	2.10	3.26
—	—	d2.22*l*	3.36
3.15	—	3.21	4.40
—	4.20e	4.23e	5.16
4.22d	—	4.28d	5.40
—	4.44e	4.48e	5.39
—	5.20e	5.25e	6.13
—	5.24e	5.27e	6.28
5.42d	—	5.48d	6.57
—	6. 0e	6. 3e	7. 7
6.27e	—	6.34e	7.38
6.34d	—	6.40d	7.51
—	6.36e	6.39e	7.50
7.24d	7.28e	7.30	8.47
8.28	—	8.36	9.54
10.17	—	10.23	11.30
11.27h	—	—	12.27
12. 0k	—	—	12.57

Sunday Trains.

AM 6.25	—	6.32	7.57
10. 5	—	10.11	11.16
10.20	—	10.28	11.42
PM 1.30	—	1.37	2.47
5.25	—	5.32	6.50
8.38	—	8.45	10. 2

Trains from Dorking (Town.)

Leave		Arrive at	
DORK.	LON. B.	CAN. ST.	CHAR.+
AM 7.20	8.24	8.28	—
7.51	8.56	—	—
8.25	9.28	9.32	—
8.50	9.49	9.53	—
9.20	10.10	—	10.19
9.27	10.27	10.32	—
9.38k	10.31	—	10.43
9.52	11. 0	—	—
10.38	11.46	—	11.59
11.30	12.50	—	1. 0
PM 1.23	2.38	—	2.46
2.34d	4. 8	—	—
3.35	5. 2	—	5.14
4.47	5.56	—.	—
6. 4	7.20	—	7.29
7.52	9. 2	—	9.15
8.53	10. 3	—	10.13
10.47	11.57	—	12.10
—	—	—	—

DORKING TOWN—*cont.*

Sunday Trains.

Leave		Arrive at	
DORK.	LON. B.	CAN. ST.	CHAR.+
AM 7. 3	8.16	—	8.27
10. 6	11.15	—	11.25
PM 3.27	4.33	—	4.42
5.59	7.13	—	7.25
8.44	9.52	—	—
9. 0	10.11	—	10.24
—	—	—	—

d Saturdays only.
e Saturdays excepted.
h Wednesdays and Saturdays only.
k Wednesdays only.
l Low Level platform.

White Horse Hotel. Telephone 43. Fifteenth-century house with Dickens' associations. Comfortable Bedrooms and excellent Cuisine. Garage, and cars for hire. Quick train service from town. Lovely country. Electric Light.

TRUST HOUSES, Ltd.

Red Lion Hotel. Leading Family and Commercial. Refurnished and redecorated. Electric Light. Excellent Catering. Stock Room. Garage. Appointed A.A., M.U., R.A.C. Moderate. 'Phone 80. Proprietor, A. E. WINDER (late Prop. Black Horse, Horsham).

Star and Garter Hotel. First-class accommodation. Near Golf Course. Moderate Charges. Close to Box Hill Station, S.E. & C. Railway, and Dorking Station, L.B. & S.C. Railway. 'Phone No. 20 Dorking.

CATERING HOUSES, LTD.

Messrs. Crow, Estate Agents, Surveyors, Auctioneers and Valuers, 76, South Street. 'Phone 176 Dorking. Reports and Valuations. Extensive Property Register.

DORMANS (Surrey) from

Victoria, Cannon Street, and London Bridge, 27¾ miles. Fares, 5/10a, 3/6c. R. T. for two months, 11/8a, 7/0c.
Map Square 23.

	Leave		Arr. at
VICT.	CAN. ST.	LON. B.	DORMS.
AM 6.37	—	6.40	7.44
7.23	—	8. 7	9.16
9.10	—	9. 6	10.27
10.35	—	10.35*l*	11.45
12. 0	—	11.50	1.13
PM —	—	12.50d	1.50
1.20e	—	1.38e	2.46
1.25d	—	1.38d	2.51
—	—	2. 5e	3.52
2.25	—	2.25d	3.52
4. 0	—	4.10	5.14
4.50	—	4.44e	5.56
5: 5	—	5.21	6.27
5.48	—	5.41e	6.49
6.50	—	7. 0	8. 2
7.15	—	7.38	8.44
9. 3h	—	9.12h	10.11
—	—	—	—

Sunday Trains.

AM 8.18	—	8.30	9.39
PM 6.33	—	6.46	7.58
—	—	—	—

DORMANS—*continued.*

Trains from Dormans.

Leave		Arrive at	
DORMS.	LON. B.	CAN. ST.	VICT.
AM 7.20	8.37	—	8.40
7.59	9. 1k	9. 4	9. 8
8.19	9.32	—	9.40
8.52	9.55	—	9.58
9.19	10. 7	—	—
9.36	10.38	—	10.46
10.31	12.13	—	11.35
PM12.17	1.42	—	1.26
1.55	2.58	—	—
3. 2d	4.57	—	—
4.15	5.21	—	5.55
5.12	6.36	—	6.29
6.27	7.56	—	—
7. 7	8.46	—	8.27
9.20	10.25	—	11.17
—	—	—	—

Sunday Trains.

AM10. 3	11.15	—	—
PM 8.13	9.26*l*	—	9.34
—	—	—	—

d Saturdays only.
e Saturdays excepted.
h Wednesdays and Saturdays only.
k Departs from or arrives at London Bridge (S.E. & C.) Station

Dormans Park Hotel. Tennis, Croquet, Garage. Telephone 144 East Grinstead. See advt. p. 136.

DORNOCH (Sutherland),

656 miles. Fares, 118/2a, 70/11c. R. T. for two months, 236/4a. Departures from London as for Lairg. Departures for London about twice daily. Pop. 768. Map Square 34.

Station Hotel. Good food. Modern comfort. Overlooks first Green. Most fascinating Golf Links in Kingdom. H. H. WARD, L.M.S. Highland Hotels Manager, also Inverness, Kyle and Strathpeffer.

DORRINGTON (Salop),

158¾ miles. Fares,31/11a, 19/2c. R.T. for two months, 63/10a. Departures from London as for Shrewsbury. Departures for London about 4 times daily. Pop. 312. Map Square 17.

DORSTONE (Hereford),

164½ miles. Fares, 34/5a, 20/8c. R.T. for two months, 68/10a, 41/4c. Departures *from* London as for Abbeydore. Departures *for* London about 5 times daily. Pop. 388. *Map Square 17.*

DOUBLEBOIS (Cornwall),

246¾ miles. Fares, 51/1a, 30/8c. R.T. for two months, 102/2a. Departures *from* London as for Liskeard. Departures *for* London about 4 times daily. *Map Square 26.*

DOUGLAS (Isle of Man)

275¼ miles, from *Euston, via* Liverpool. Fares, 53/9 First and Saloon, 37/3 Third and Saloon, 32/3 Third and Steerage. R.T. for two months, 102/6 First and Saloon, 69/6 Third and Saloon, 62/0 Third and Steerage. *Map Square 6.*

ANOTHER ROUTE from

Paddington, via Liverpool, 286 miles. Fares as above.

Isle of Man Steam Packet

Service. *See advt. p. 133.*

Hotel Sefton, Douglas.

Manxland's brightest and best Hotel. Reasonable Tariff. *See advt. p. 138.*

The Savoy Private Hotel.

Central Promenade. Same ownership as the Windsor. Open all year round. Ideal situation. Every convenience and comfort. Proprietresses, The Misses LACE. *See advt. p. 139.*

The Hydro, Queen's Promenade.

Hotel and Boarding Establishment. 100 Apartments. *See advt. p. 139.*

DOUGLAS (Lanark), 383¼

miles. Fares, 77/11a, 46/9c. R.T. for two months, 155/10a, 93/6c. Departures *from* London as for Carstairs. Departures *for* London about 4 times daily. Pop. 3,120. *Map Square 40.*

DOUNE (Perth), 425¼ miles.

Fares, 86/11a, 52/2c. R.T. for two months, 173/10a, 104/4c. Departures *from* London as for Callander. Departures *for* London about 3 times daily. Pop. 865. *Map Square 40.*

DOUSLAND (Devon), 232

miles. Fares, 47/8a, 28/7c. R.T. for two months, 95/4a. Departures *from* London as for Princetown. Departures *for* London about 4 times daily. *Map Square 26.*

DOVECLIFFE (Yorks),

172½ miles. Fares, 35/.. ..1c. R.T., double fare. Departures *from* London as for Sheffield (Victoria). Departures *for* London about 5 times daily. *Map Square 12.*

DOVE HOLES (Derby),

184½ miles. Fares, *via* Macclesfield, 34/0a, 20/5c. R.T., double fare. *Via* Stockport, 3?/9a, 22/?c. R.T., double fare. Departures *from* London as for Macclesfield or Stockport. Departures *for* London about 4 times daily. *Map Square 12.*

DOVER (PRIORY) (Kent),

from *Charing Cross, Cannon Street,* and *London Bridge.* 7½ miles. Fares, 16/3a, 13/0b, 9/9c. R.T. for two months, 32/6a, 26/0b, 19/6c. Pop. 39,985. *Map Square 24.*

Leave CHAR. +	CAN. ST.	LON. B.	Arr. at DOVER
AM —	3.40y	3.45y	6.50
—	5.20	5.25	9.28
—	6.45	6.50	10.5s
9.15	—	9.23	11.16s
—	—	l10.3v	12.28
11.0	—	11.7	1.50
11.15	—	—	1.5
PM 1.0p	—	—	2.43
1.50d	—	1.56d	3.32
2.55d	—	3.1d	4.46s
3.0	—	3.8	5.25s
4.5	—	—	5.41
4.30j	—	4.37j	6.31
—	5.0h	—	6.36
—	5.12e	—	7.8k
5.24d	—	5.34d	8.25s
6.0e	—	6.5e	7.46
7.0	—	—	8.38
7.18	—	7.26	10.26
9.30	—	9.36	11.36
11.51	—	—	2.12

Sunday Trains.

AM10.10	—	10.18	12.23s
10.15	—	—	12.1
PM 7.35	—	7.45	10.25s
9.25	—	9.31	12.30

Trains from Dover.

Leave DOVER	LON. B.	CAN. ST.	CHAR. +
AM 6.41	9.0	9.4	—
7.45d	10.0	10.4	—
7.52e	9.36	9.40	—
8.56	10.34	—	10.41
9.16	11.43	—	11.57
10.42	—	—	12.20
10.46s	1.36	—	1.50
PM 1.9	3.26	—	3.40
dl. 9p	3.36	—	3.40
2.15	4.2	—	4.10
2.45	5.50	—	6.3
4.52	—	—	6.30
5.5s	7.25	7.30e	7.49
7.35	10.22	—	10.35
7.45s	10.22	—	10.35
9.15s	11.35	—	11.44
10.40y	—	1.20	—

Sunday Trains.

AM 6.45	10.5	—	10.15
PM 4.52	—	—	6.30
5.0	7.9	—	7.17
6.29	—	—	8.17
7.15s	10.16	—	10.26
8.0	10.16	—	10.26
10.40s	—	1.25	—

d Saturdays only.
e Saturdays excepted.
h Fridays only.
j Fridays excepted.
k Wednesdays only.
l Low Level Platform.
p Pullman Car attached.
s Marine Station.
v Mondays, Fridays and Saturdays only.
y Third Class only.

DOVER—*continued.*

ANOTHER ROUTE (PRIORY)

from *Victoria, Holborn Viaduct* and *St. Paul's (via Chatham),* 77¼ miles. Fares as above.

VICT. Leave	Hol. V.	ST. PL.'s	Arr. at DOVER
AM —	—	3.50k	7.8
5.5	4.57	5.0	9.1
5.48f	5.40f	5.42f	9.1
—	7.30	7.33	11.16
9.20	—	—	11.36
9.45	—	—	12.10
10.40	—	—	1.18
11.40d	—	—	2.29
11.40e	—	—	3.14
PM 2.5	—	—	4.30
2.8e	—	—	4.53
4.20	—	—	6.56
5.10d	5.10e	5.12e	7.51
5.30e	—	—	8.20
5.30d	—	—	8.37
8.30	—	—	11.4

Sunday Trains.

AM 8.15	8.0	—	11.14
10.40	—	—	12.56
PM 3.30	—	—	7.8
5.15	—	—	8.26
8.25	—	—	10.43

Trains from Dover.

Leave DOVER	ST. PL.'s	Hol. V.	VICT.
AM 6.41	9.37	9.39	—
7.16	—	—	11.2
9.20	—	—	11.27
9.42e	1.0	1.2	1.33
9.54d	—	—	1.22
11.41	—	—	2.43
PM 1.56e	4.46	—	4.39
2.16d	—	—	4.55
3.13	—	—	5.26
5.58	—	—	8.33
7.32e	—	—	10.25
7.52d	—	—	10.25

Sunday Trains.

AM 6.45	—	—	10.48
8.55	—	11.58	11.51
10.12h	—	—	1.5
PM12.30h	—	—	3.50
2.0	—	—	5.31
6.30	—	—	8.40
7.46	—	—	10.29

d Saturdays only.
e Saturdays excepted.
f Mondays only.
h Via Folkestone.
k Third Class only.

Lord Warden Hotel. The Leading Hotel. Facing Admiralty Pier. Appointments, Cuisine and Service unsurpassed. Telegrams: "Warden, Dover." Telephone No. 413. GORDON HOTELS, LTD. *See advt. p. 140.*

Hotel Burlington. Sheltered position facing Sea. Quiet stopping place for Continental travellers. Porter meets trains and Boats. Telegrams: "Burlington, Dover." Telephone: 155 Dover. FREDERICK HOTELS, Ltd. *See advt. p. 140.*

DOVER—*continued.*

Grand Hotel. Leading Family Hotel. High-class Cuisine. Private suites. Lift. Tel. 230.
N. BAVIN, Manager.

King's Head Hotel. Adjoining Admiralty Pier and Marine Station. Patronised by American, English, and Continental Families. Table d'Hote. "Rooms en Suite." On *y* parle Francais. Telephone 478.
J. BROMLEY, Proprietor.

Hotel de Paris. Close to both Railway Stations, Piers, Harbour, Granville Dock. No attendance charged. On parle Francais. 'Phone. 429.
T. WORSDELL, Proprietor

Station Temperance Hotel. 6, Stroud Street. Opposite Harbour Station. Five minutes Channel boats. Homely, comfortable. Excellent cooking. 'Phone, 80. Proprietress—
Mrs. FOWLE.

Esplanade Hotel. Only hotel on Sea Front. Three guineas weekly upwards. Boating, Fishing, Bathing. 'Phone, 442.
W. HAWKES, Manager.

House Agency Offices. Market Square, and at Folkestone. House Furnishers, Auctioneers, Estate Agents, &c. Removals and Storage. Undertakers.
FLASHMAN, & CO. (Ltd.).

DOVERCOURT BAY

(Essex) from *Liverpool Street*, 70¼ miles. Fares, 14/10*a*, 8/11*c*. R. T. for two months, 29/8*a*, 17/10*c*. Pop. 7,694.
Map Square 19.

L'POOL ST.	DOVCT.	DOVCT.	L'POOL ST.
AM 5. 0	7.31	AM 7. 8	9.36
6.50	10. 2	8.50	10.58
8.46	11.23	9.58	12.40
10.20	12.43	PM12.13	3.13
11.30	1.54	1.46	3.43
PM12.33*r*	2.31	3. 7	5.48
2.15	4.49	4.26	6.32
3.23	5.46	5.38	7.51
5.42	8. 5	7.43*r*	10. 0
7.16	9.29	8.33	11.16
8.40*r*	10.16	—	—
8.45	11. 6	—	—

Sunday Trains.

AM 9.20*r*	11.44	AM 9. 7	11.38
PM 4.40	6.41	PM 4.57	7.10
7.40	10. 3	6. 8	8.58
—	—	7.39	10. 9

r Restaurant Car.

Hotel Alexandra. Facing Sea. Comfort unequalled. Garage. Moderate terms. Close to Quay for Continent. G.E.R. week-end tickets. Proprietor—
C. ROSINSKY.
See advt. p. **141.**

Cliff Hotel. Central for Outdoor Sports. Excellent Cuisine.
See advt. p. **141.**

14, Cliff Road. Board Residence. Two minutes Sea. Five minutes Station. Good Cooking. Comfortable. Terms moderate.
A. GREEN.

DOVER STREET (Hammersmith and Finsbury Park Tube). *See back of Map.*

DOWLAIS (Glamorgan)

from *Paddington*, via Pontypool Road, 172½ miles. Fares, 34/10*a*, 20/11*c*. R. T. for two months, 69/8*a*. Pop. 18,112.
Map Square 21.

PAD.	DOWLAIS	DOWLAIS	PAD.
AM 1. 0*g*	10.29	AM 7.48*r*	1. 0
5.30*d*	1.31	11.48*r*	4.20
9. 0	4. 5	PM 1.55*dr*	8.35
11.50*r*	6.31	4.20*r*	9.25
PM 1.10*er*	8.11	6.40	3.30
3.35*dr*	9.31	9.40*d*	7.10
6. 0*dr*	12.12	—	—

Sunday Trains.

PM 9.15	10.29	—	—
—	—	—	—
—	—	—	—

d Saturdays only.
e Saturdays excepted.
g Mondays excepted.
r Restaurant Car.

DOWLAIS TOP (Glamorgan), 171 miles. Fares, 34/10*a*, 20/11*c*. R. T. for two months, 69/8*a*, 41/10*c*. Departures *from* London as for Bargoed. Departures *for* London about 4 times daily.
Map Square 21.

●

DOWNHAM (Norfolk)

from *Liverpool Street*, 86½ miles months, 36/4*a*. Pop. 2,343.
Map Square 19.

L'PL. ST.	DOWN'M.	DOWN'M.	L'PL. ST.
AM 5.50	9.13	AM 8. 4*r*	10.23
8.30*r*	11. 0	8.56	11.27
10. 5	12.59	10.48	2. 7
11.50*r*	2.18	11.59*r*	2.21
PM 2.34	4.51	PM 3.36*r*	6.10
4.45	6.59	3.59*h*	7.58
5.49*r*	8.15	5.53*r*	8.22
—	—	8. 1	10.30

Sunday Trains.

AM 9.25	12.30	PM 3.48	6.40
PM 3.25	6. 7	7.19	9.40

h Tuesdays only.
r Restaurant Car.

Castle Hotel. First-class Family and Commercial. Good Hunting, Shooting, and Fishing. Posting in all its branches. Bathroom. Motor-car kept. Garage. Omnibus meets trains.
J. H. RICHARDS, Proprietor.

DOWN STREET (Hammersmith and Finsbury Park Tube). *See back of Map.*

DOWNTON (Wilts) from

Waterloo, 90½ miles. Fares, 19/4*a*, 11/7*c*. R. T. for two months, 38/8*a*, 23/2*c*. Departures *from* London as for Breamore. Departures *for* London about 6 times daily. Pop. 1,933.
Map Square 22.

DRAX (Yorks), 198¼ miles.

Fares, 35/0*a*, 21/0*c*. R. T. for two months, 70/0*a*. Departures *from* London as for Cudworth. Departures *for* London about 3 times daily. Pop. 419.
Map Square 13.

DRAYCOTT (Derby), 122½

miles. Fares, 25/2*a*, 15/1*c*. R.T., double fare. Departures *from* London as for Trent. Departures *for* London about 4 times daily. Pop. 2,218.
Map Square 13.

DRAYCOTT (Somerset)

from *Paddington*, 126¾ miles. Fares, 29/5*a*, 17/8*c*. R. T. for two months, 58/10*a*, 35/4*c*. Departures *from* London as for Wells (Somerset). Departures *for* London about 4 times daily. Pop. 492.
Map Square 22.

DRAYTON (Norfolk) from

King's Cross, 161¾ miles. Fares, 23/1*a*, 14/2*c*. R. T. for two months, 47/2*a*, 28/4*c*. Departures *from* London as for Guestwick. Departures *for* London about 3 times daily. Pop. 514.
Map Square 19.

DRAYTON (Sussex) from

London Bridge, Victoria, and *Clapham Junction,* 67¼ miles. Fares, 13/11*a*, 8/4*c*. R. T. for two months, 27/10*a*, 16/8*c*. Departures *from* London as for Barnham Junction. Departures *for* London about 5 times daily.
Map Square 28.

DRAYTON GREEN

(Middlesex) from *Paddington*, 7 miles. Fares, 0/9*c*. R. T. for 2 days, 1/3*c*. See trains to Ealing West, and thence at frequent intervals. Pop. (Drayton) 7,535.
Map Square 58.

DRAYTON PARK

(Metropolitan Railway) (G.N. & City). *See back of Map.*

DREGHORN (Ayr), 395½

miles. Fares, 80/7*a*, 48/4*c*. R. T. for two months, 161/2*a*, 96/8*c*. Departures *from* London as for Irvine. Departures *for* London about 4 times daily. Pop. 4,523.
Map Square 40.

DREM (East Lothian), 374½

miles. Fares, 78/9*a*, 47/3*c*. R. T. for two months, 157/6*a*, 94/6*c*. Departures *from* London as for Dunbar. Departures *for* London about 4 times daily.
Map Square 41.

DRIFFIELD (Yorks), from

King's Cross, via Hull, 205½ miles. Fares, 39/0*a*, 23/5*c*. R. T. for two months, 78/0*a*. Pop. 5,674.
Map Square 8.

King's+	Dr'fld.	Dr'fld.	King's+
AM 4.45	11.43	AM 8.10*r*	1.30
7.15*dr*	1.19	9.33	3.40
7.15*er*	1.43	11.15*lr*	4.30
8.45*l*	2.52	PM12.38*r*	7.10
10.10*r*	3.44	4. 2*r*	9.25
PM 1.30*r*	6.44	8.43	3.25
1.50*r*	6.51	—	—
4. 0*r*	9.44	—	—
5.45*fr*	11.20	—	—
10.45*el*	6.23	—	—
10.45*dl*	7.47	—	—
—	—	—	—

Sunday Trains.

PM10.45*l*	6.23	PM 6.36	6. 0
—	—	—	—

d Saturdays only.
e Saturdays excepted.
f Thursdays and Saturdays only.
l Via Selby.
r Restaurant Car.

DRIGG (Cumberland), 288¼

miles. Fares, 60/2*a*, 36/1*c*. R. T. for two months, 120/4*a*, 72/2*c*. Departures *from* London as for Millom. Departures *for* London about 3 times daily. Pop. 447.
Map Square 6.

DRIGHLINGTON

(Yorks), 185¾ miles. Fares, 38/6*a*, 23/1*c*. R. T., double fare. Departures *from* London as for Wakefield (Westgate). Departures *for* London about 3 times daily. Pop. 4,092.

DROITWICH (Worcester)

from *Paddington*, 126 miles. Fares, 23/9*a*, 14/3*c*. R. T. for two months, 47/6*a*, 28/6*c*. Pop. 4,588.
Map Square 17.

Pad.	Droit.	Droit.	Pad.
AM 8.50	12. 0	AM 8.28	11.15
9.45	1. 4	9.53	2.12
PM 1.30*r*	4. 3	11.37*r*	2.55
1.35*r*	4.54	PM 1.41*r*	4.15
4.45*t*	7.26	2.40	5.50
6. 5*r*	9.11	5.37*r*	9.15
—	—	6.11	10.45
—	—	—	—

Sunday Trains.

AM10.35*r*	3. 3	AM 9.57	2.40
PM 4.10	8.35	PM 5.20*r*	9.48
—	—	—	—

r Restaurant Car.
t Tea Car.

ANOTHER ROUTE from

Euston, 133¾ miles. Fares, 23/9*a*, 14/3*c*. R. T. for two months, 47/6*a*, 28/6*c*.

Euston	Droit.	Droit.	Euston
AM 2.30	8. 3	AM 7.26	10.40
5. 0	9.42	8.37	12.40
6.45	11.14	10.13*r*	1.25
9.15*r*	1.13	PM12.44*t*	4.35
11.30*r*	3.20	3.25*r*	6.50
12. 0*nr*	4.10	4.38*r*	8.20
PM 2.20*t*	5.27	6.56*er*	10.20
2.50*t*	7.16	8.23*e*	4. 0
4.35*r*	7.57	8.23*d*	5. 0
6.55*r*	10. 2	—	—
*m*12.10*d*	9.42	—	—

DROITWICH—*continued.*

Sunday Trains.

Euston	Droit.	Droit.	Euston
AM 9.15	3.35	AM 8.56*r*	1.45
PM 1. 0*r*	5.45	11.15	5. 5
5.10	9.37	PM 8.28	5. 0
—	—	—	—
—	—	—	—
—	—	—	—
—	—	—	—

d Saturdays only
e Saturdays excepted.
m Midnight.
n Noon.
r Restaurant Car.
t Tea Car.

Droitwich Natural Brine Baths. Radio-Active; Radio-Emanative. Treatment obtainable only at the Droitwich Establishments. No substitute in any form. J. H. HOLLYER, Baths General Offices.
See advt. p. **5** of Cover.

Worcestershire Brine Baths Hotel. 150 Rooms. En pension terms.
T. CULLEY, Manager.
See advt. p. **141**.

The Raven Hotel. Oldest and most picturesque Hotel in Droitwich. Beautifully situated own grounds opposite the celebrated Brine Baths. Lock-up Garages. Moderate (daily and weekly) inclusive terms. Souvenir No. 201, with tariff, for stamp. Telephone No. 50. Proprietor, PERCY A. GEDDES, Ltd.

Ayrshire House. Superior Boarding Establishment in Corbett Avenue, 300 yards from St. Andrew's Baths. Telephone, 37. Miss REILLY, Proprietress.

The "Royal" Hotel. Situated in private grounds. Only one with covered entrance into Royal Brine Baths. Lounge. Lock-up Garages. Officially appointed by R.A.C. and A.A. Telephone 40.
H. B. FERRY, Proprietor.

Clarendon Private Hotel. Boarding Establishment. Near Baths. Every comfort. Croquet, Bowls, Billiards, etc. Moderate. Personal supervision.
Mr. and Mrs. J. YATES, Proprs.

Norbury House. Near Baths. Fine old house, beautiful garden. Modern comfort. Billiards. Own farm. Booklet. Telegrams. Telephone 53 Droitwich.

St. Andrews House. Best situation in fourteen acres of grounds. Only house with Electric Light. Central heating. H. & C. in Bedrooms. Vi-spring Box Mattresses. Garage, Private Lock-up. Telegrams. Telephone 56. Droitwich Booklet.

Merstowe Boarding Establishment. In best part of Droitwich. Home Comforts. Bedroom on Ground Floor. Terms moderate. Personal Supervision.
Mrs. LORD, Proprietress.

DRONFIELD (Derby)

from *St. Pancras*, 151½ miles. Fares, 31/3*a*. 18/9*c*. R. T., double fare. Departures *from* London as for Chesterfield Departures *for* London about 5 times daily. Pop. 4,435
Map Square 12.

DRONGAN (Ayr), 384 miles.

No through fares. Departures *from* London as for Ayr. Departures *for* London about 4 times daily.
Map Square 43.

DRONLEY (Forfar), 476¼

miles. No through fares. Departures *from* London as for Coupar Angus or Dundee (Tay Bridge). Departures *for* London about 3 times daily.
Map Square 38.

DROXFORD (Hants) from

Waterloo, 63¼ miles. Fares, 13/4*a*, 8/0*c*. R.T. for two months, 26/8*a*, 16/0*c*. Departures *from* London as for Tisted. Departures *for* London about 6 times daily. Pop. 572.
Map Square 23.

DROYLSDEN (Lancs), 184

miles. Fares, 38/7*a*, 23/2*c*. R. T., double fare Departures *from* London as for Manchester. Departures *for* London about 8 times daily. Pop. 13,877.

DRUM (Aberdeen), 531¼

miles. No through fares. Departures *from* London as for Banchory. Departures *for* London about 3 times daily.
Map Square 38.

DRUMBURGH (Cumberland),

308½ miles. No through fares. Departures *from* London as for Carlisle. Departures *for* London about 4 times daily.
Map Square 2.

DRUMCHAPEL (Dumbarton),

442½ miles. No through fares. Departures *from* London as for Dumbarton. Departures *for* London about 8 times daily. Pop. 423.

DRUMCLOG (Lanark),

404¼ miles. Fares, 49/0*c*. R.T. for two months, 98/0*c*. Departures *from* London as for Hamilton. Departures *for* London about 3 times daily.
Map Square 40.

DRUMLITHIE (Kincardine),

499½ miles. No through fares. Departures *from* London as for [illegible]. Departures *for* London about 3 times daily. Pop. 260.
Map Square 38.

DRUMMUIR (Banff), 582¼

miles. No through fares. Departures *from* London as for Keith. Departures *for* London about twice daily.
Map Square 35.

DRUMSHORELAND

(Linlithgow), 403¼ miles. Fares, 82/6*a*, 49/6*c*. R.T. for two months, 165/0*a*, 99/0*c*. Departures *from* London as for Edinburgh (Waverley). Departures *for* London about 3 times daily.

DRWS-Y-NANT (Merioneth) from *Paddington*, 215¼ miles. Fares, 45/2a, 27/1c. R. T. for two months, 90/4a, 54/2c. Departures *from* London as for Corwen. Departures *for* London about 3 times daily. *Map Square 16.*

DRYBRIDGE (Ayr), 395 miles. Fares, 80/7a, 48/4c. R. T. for two months, 161/2a, 96/8c. Departures *from* London as for Kilmarnock. Departures *for* London about 4 times daily. *Map Square 40.*

DRYBROOK ROAD (Gloucester), 153 miles. Fares, 29/9a, 17/1c R. T. for two months, 59/6a, 35/8c. Departures *from* London as for Lydney. Departures *for* London about 4 times daily. *Map Square 22.*

DRYMEN (Stirling), 440¼ miles. Fares, 86/8a, 52/3c. R. T. for two months, 173 a, 104/6c. Departures *from* London as for Balloch or Stirling. Departures *for* London about 3 times daily. Pop. 1,214. *Map Square 40.*

DRYSLLWYN (Carmarthen) from *Paddington*, 221 miles. No through fares Departures *from* London as for Llandilo or Carmarthen. Departures *for* London about 3 times daily. *Map Square 21.*

DUBLIN from *Euston, via* Holyhead, 334½ miles. Fares (Westland Row Station), 64/9 First and Saloon, 46/3 Third and Saloon, 38/9 Third and Steerage. R. T. for two months, 128/0 First and Saloon, 90/3 Third and Saloon, 76/6 Third and Steerage. (North Wall Station), 61/3 First and Saloon, 42/9 Third and Saloon, 36/9 Third and Steerage. R. T. for two months, 122/6 First and Saloon, 84/9 Third and Saloon, 73/6 Third and Steerage. Pop. 309,272. *Map Square 10.*

(Westland Row Station.)

Euston	Dub.	Dub.	Euston
AM 8.30r	6. 0	AM 8.25r	5.50
PM 8.45	6.35	PM 8.10	5.50
11.50d	6. 0l	—	—
—	—	—	—
—	—	—	—
—	—	—	—
—	—	—	—

(North Wall Station.)

—		—	
—		—	
—		—	
—		—	
—		—	
—		—	

DUBLIN—*continued.*

Sunday Trains.

Euston	Dub.	Dub.	Euston
PM 8.45	6.35	AM 8.25r	7.10
—	—	PM 8.10	5.50
—	—	—	—
—	—	—	—
—	—	—	—
—	—	—	—

d Saturdays only.
l P.M.
r Restaurant Car.

Shelbourne Hotel. The leading Dublin Hotel. Charmingly situated, overlooking Stephen's Green. First-class house. Elevator, Telephones. Free Garage. Moderate charges.

Royal Hibernian Hotel. First-class. Centrally situated. Excellent Wines and Cuisine. Moderate tariff. Free Garage. Telephone. Telegrams— "Hibernia," Dublin.

Edinburgh Hotel, Dublin, destroyed in recent disturbances. Notice of re-opening will be given in due course.

Bank.—The National Bank, Ltd.

DUBTON (Forfar), 500¼ miles. Fares, 97/6a, 58/6c R. T. for two months, 195/0a, 117/0c. Departures *from* London as for Forfar. Departures *for* London about 3 times daily. *Map Square 38.*

DUDBRIDGE (Gloucester), 125 miles. No through fares. Departures *from* London as for Stroud. Departures *for* London about 6 times daily. *Map Square 22.*

DUDLEY (Worcester) from *Euston,* 121½ miles. Fares, 24/10a, 14/11c. R. T. for two months, 49/8a. Pop. 55,908. *Map Square 17.*

Euston	Dudley	Dudley	Euston
AM 2.50	6. 8	AM 6.52r	10. 0
5. 0	9.22	8. 2r	10.40
8.30r	11.26	9.32	12.40
9.10er	11.49	10.52r	1.25
9.15r	12. 9	11. 4r	2.20
11.30r	2. 4	PM12.24er	3. 0
PM 1.15r	3.46	2. 0t	4.35
2.20t	4.50	2.36t	5.35
4.35t	7.24	4.17t	6.50
5.50r	8.21	5. 9r	8.20
6.55r	9.26	6.15dr	10.45
7. 0r	10.57	7. 9er	10.20
11.50e	6. 8	11. 0e	4. 0
—	—	11. 0d	5. 0

DUDLEY—*continued.*

Sunday Trains.

Euston	Dudley	Dudley	Euston
AM 9.15	2.15	AM10.59r	1.45
PM 1. 0r	3.54	11.59	5. 5
5.10r	7.56	PM 3.40r	8.20
11.50	6. 8	5.39r	8.35
—	—	9.49	5. 0
—	—	—	—

d Saturdays only.
e Saturdays excepted.
r Restaurant Car.
t Tea Car.

ANOTHER ROUTE from *Paddington, via* Birmingham, 122½ miles. Fares *via* Birmingham, 24 10a,14/11c. R.T. for two months, 49/8a, 29/10c. *Via* Worcester, 25/3a, 15/2c. R.T. for two months, 50/6a, 30/4c.

Pad.	Dudley	Dudley	Pad.
AM 5.30	10.51	AM 6.35r	10. 0
6.30	11.25	8.10r	11. 0
9.10r	12.35	9.38	12.25
10.40er	1.22	10.35r	1.25
10.40dr	1.37	11.15r	2. 5
PM12.50r	4. 5	PM12.22lr	4.15
2.10t	5. 5	1.20r	5. 0
4.10t	7.16	3.10t	5.55
4.45lt	8.41	5.15r	8. 5
6.10r	8.55	6.48	10. 0
7.16r	9.45	10.15	3.30
7.30	11.13	—	—
12.15k	6.32	—	—

Sunday Trains.

Pad.	Dudley	Dudley	Pad.
PM 6. 0r	9.43	AM 8.40	1.40
12.50r	4. 3	PM 4.20r	9. 0
—	—	—	—

d Saturdays only.
e Saturdays excepted.
k Saturdays midnight excepted.
l Via Worcester.
r Restaurant Car.
t Tea Car.

DUDLEY HILL (Yorks), 188¼ miles. Fares, 38 11a, 23/4c. R. T., double fare. Departures *from* London as for Wakefield (Westgate). Departures *for* London about 8 times daily. *Map Square 12.*

DUDLEYPORT(Stafford), 120½ miles. Fares, 24/5a, 14/8c R. T. for two months, 48/10a. Departures *from* London as for Oldbury. Departures *for* London about 8 times daily. Pop. 4,865. *Map Square 17.*

DUFFIELD (Derby) from *St. Pancras,* 133 miles. Fares, 27/6a, 16/6c. R. T., double fare. Pop. 2,136. *Map Square 12.*

St. Pan.	Duff.	Duff.	St. Pan.
AM 2.25	6.40	AM 5.50r	9.57
4.25	8.32	7.39r	11. 0
8.25r	12.24	8.26r	11.35
10.25r	1.27	10. 7r	1.30
PM12.25r	3.57	11.22	3.25
2.25r	5.19	PM 1.22r	4.20
4.25r	7.44	2.18r	5.45
6.25r	9.53	3.34r	7.15
12. 0h	7. 0	5.13r	8.35
—	—	6.52r	10. 5
—	—	10.12	4.20

DUFFIELD—*continued.*

Sunday Trains.

ST. PAN.	DUFF.	DUFF.	ST. PAN.
AM11.15r	4.28	PM12.12r	5. 2
PM 3.15	8.42	6.50r	9.52
6.15r	9.40	9.28	4.55

h Saturdays midnight only.
r Restaurant Car.

DUFFTOWN (Banff), 586¾
miles. Fares, 106/3a, 63/9c. R.T. for two months, 212/6a, 127/6c. Departures from London as for Keith. Departures for London about 3 times daily. Pop. 1,454.
Map Square 35.

DUIRINISH (Ross),
646 miles. No through fares. Departures from London as for Kyle of Lochalsh. Departures for London about once daily.
Map Square 33.

DUKERIES (Lincoln) from
King's Cross, 151¼ miles. Fares, 27/4a, 16/5c. R. T., double fare.
Map Square 13.

KING'S +	DUKER.	DUKER.	KING'S +
AM 5. 5	9.31	AM 9.49	1. 5
PM 1.50kr	5. 2	PM12.10k	3.50
4. 0r	7.12	3.13r	6.30
—	—	5.37	9. 0

No Sunday Trains.
k When required.
r Restaurant Car.

DUKINFIELD (Cheshire)
from *Euston*, 184¼ miles. Fares, 37/9a, 22/8c. R. T. for two months, 75/6a. Pop. 19,493.

EUSTON	DUKIN.	DUKIN.	EUSTON
AM12.25	6.44	AM 6.24dr	12.20
2.35	8.57	7.24er	12. 5
5. 0	10.49	7.59r	12.50
8.45r	12.51	9. 1r	1.15
10.40r	2.54	9.32r	1.45
12. 0nr	6. 5	10. 9r	3.10
PM 1.30r	6.42	PM12.24dr	5.50
2.50t	7.55	12.24er	6. 0
—	—	3.49r	8.10
—	—	4.44dr	10. 0
—	—	4.44er	10.10
—	—	9.14	5. 0

No Sunday Trains.

d Saturdays only.
e Saturdays excepted.
n Noon.
r Restaurant Car.
t Tea Car.

DULLATUR (Dumbarton),
426½ miles. Fares, 81/5a, 48/10c. R.T. for two months, 162/10a, 97/8c. Departures from London as for Falkirk. Departures for London about 4 times daily. Pop. 154.
Map Square 40.

DULLINGHAM (Cambridge) from *Liverpool Street*, 67 miles. Fares, 13/7a, 8/2c. R.T. for two months, 27/2a. Departures from London about 8 times daily. Pop. 765.
Map Square 19.

DULVERTON (Somerset)
from *Paddington*, 164 miles. Fares, 34/4a, 20/7c. R. T. for two months, 68/8a, 41/2c. Pop. 1,526.
Map Square 21.

PAD.	DULVERTON.	DULVTON.	PAD.
AM 5.30	12. 8	AM 9.53r	1.30
9.15	1.22	11.46	4. 5
PM12. 5r	4. 7	PM 1.45t	5.30
2. 0r	6.31	5. 5r	9. 0
3.30	6.53	7.21	2.45
4.15r	8.53	9.32	7.10
12. 0h	8.54	—	—

Sunday Trains.

PM10. 0	8.54	—	—

h Saturdays midnight excepted.
r Restaurant Car.
t Tea Car.

Carnarvon Arms Hotel. Midst meadows by Reserved Trout Fishing. Home farm dairy. Hunting. Hunters. Billiards. Phone 2. Wire, NELDER.
See advt. p 142.

The Green Hotel. In own Grounds. Free fishing to guests. Moderate. *See advt. p. 142.*

Red Lion Hotel. Oldest established. Trout fishing. Red Deer and Fox Hunting. Hunters Motors. Carriages. Telephone 4. Telegrams: "Lion."
F. W. DULLINGHAM.

Lamb Hotel. First-class Accommodation for Visitors. Stables. Hunters. Carriages. Garage. Motors. Inspection Pit. Billiards. Fishing. Telephone 9. Telegrams, "Stanbury."

DULWICH (London) from
Victoria, Ludgate Hill, and *Holborn Viaduct,* 5 miles. Fares, 1/1a, 0/10b, 0/7c. R. T. for two days, 1/9a, 1/5b, 1/2c. Pop. 16,043. *See* pp. 558-561.
Map Square 79.

DULWICH EAST (London) from *London Bridge* or from *Victoria,* 5¼ miles. Fares from London Bridge, 0/7¼a, 0/4½c. R.T. for two days, 1/3a, 0/9c. Fares from Victoria, via Tulse Hill, 1/3a, 0/9c. R. T. for two days, 2/6a, 1/6c. Via Peckham Rye, 0/10a, 0/6c. R. T. for two days, 1/8a, 1/0c. Pop. 45,237. *See* pp. 565-568, 570, 581, 582.
Map Square 70.

DULWICH NORTH
from *London Bridge* and *Victoria,* 8 miles. Fares from London Bridge, 0/10a, 0/6c. R. T. for two days, 1/4a, 0/10½c. Fares from Victoria, 1/0a, 0/7c. R. T. for two days, 2/0a, 1/2c. *See* pp. 565-568, 570, 581, 582.
Map Square 70.

DUMBARTON from
King's Cross, 451 miles. Fares, 84/2a, 50/6c. R.T. for two months, 168/4a, 101/0c. Pop. 17,428.
Map Square 40.

KING'S +	D'BARTON	D'BARTON	KING'S +
AM 4.45e	4.23f	AM 7.49r	6.15
10. 0r	8.17	11.17r	10. 0
11.50r	11. 2	PM 2.26	3.25
PM 7.45er	6.21	3. 8d	3.25
8.25e	8.28	4.58	6. 0h
11.25e	9.45	7.10	6.50l
—	—	9. 0	7.25

Sunday Trains.

PM 7.45r	6.21	—	—
8.25	8.28	—	—
11.25	9.45	—	—

d Saturdays only.
e Saturdays excepted.
f Arrives 3.59 on Saturdays.
h A.M.
l Arrives 7.5 on Sundays.
r Restaurant Car.

DUMFRIES from *St. Pancras,* 341 miles. Fares, 67/4a, 40/5c. R. T. for two months, 134/8a, 80/10c. Pop. 19,014.
Map Square 43.

ST. PAN.	DUMF.	DUMF.	ST. PAN.
AM 4.25	1.43	AM11.18r	6.35
9.50r	5. 7	PM 1.54r	9.15
PM12.15r	7.28	11.12e	7.25
9.30e	5.27	11.58h	7.50
11.45e	7. 0	—	—
11.45d	7. 5	—	—

Sunday Trains.

PM 9.30	5.27	AM 1. 4	8.57
11.45	7. 0	PM11.18	7.25

d Saturdays only.
e Saturdays excepted.
h Saturday midnight excepted.
r Restaurant Car.

ANOTHER ROUTE from
Euston, 332½ miles. Fares as above.

EUSTON	DUMF.	DUMF.	EUSTON
AM12.25	11.20	AM12. 5g	7.20
2.35	1.43	8. 5r	6. 0
5. 0	2.30	11.17r	6.28
6.45	4.49	PM 2.40r	10. 0
10. 0r	5.34	7.29	5. 0
11.35r	7.28	11. 0d	7.15
PM 1.30dr	10.22	11.12e	6.55
8. 0e	3.22	11.58	7.15
9.20e	5.27	—	—
11. 0d	7. 3	—	—
11.35e	6.59	—	—
11.45e	8. 5	—	—

DUMFRIES—continued.

Sunday Trains.

Euston	Dumf.	Dumf.	Euston
PM 7.50r	3.22	PM11.18	7.30
8.30	3.59	—	—
11.35	6.59	—	—
11.45	8.5	—	—

d Saturdays only.
e Saturdays excepted.
g Mondays excepted.
r Restaurant Car.

Station Hotel. Splendid centre for Tourists for Firth of Solway, and passengers resting between England and North of Ireland. Telegrams, "Souwestern, Dumfries."

DUMFRIES HOUSE
(Ayr), 377¼ miles. No through fares. Departures *from* London as for Ayr. Departures *for* London about 4 times daily. *Map Square* 43.

DUMGOYNE (Stirling),
446½ miles. Fares, 85/0a, 51/0c. R. T. for two months, 170/0a, 102/0c. Departures *from* London as for Glasgow. Departures *for* London about twice daily. *Map Square* 40.

DUNBALL (Somerset), 148¼
miles. Fares, 30/8a, 18/5c. R. T. for two months, 61/4a. Departures *from* London as for Highbridge. Departures *for* London about 4 times daily. *Map Square* 24.

No Sunday Trains.

DUNBAR (East Lothian)
from *King's Cross*, 363 miles. Fares, 76/5a, 45/10c. R. T. for two months, 152/10a. Pop. 5,311. *Map Square* 41.

King's +	Dunb.	Dunb.	King's +
AM 4.45	3.5	AM 8.7r	6.15
10.0r	6.55	PM 1.55h	10.0
11.50r	7.46	4.47	3.25
PM 8.25e	8.14	8.21	6.0
—	—	11.40h	7.25

Sunday Trains.

PM 8.25	8.14	PM 8.21	6.0
—	—	11.28h	7.5

e Saturdays excepted.
h Stops when required; passengers must give notice at station in good time.
r Restaurant Car.

Roxburghe Marine Hotel. First-class Family. On Golf Course and Beach. Hot and Cold Sea-water Baths. Garage. 'Phone 22.

DUNBLANE (Perth) from
Euston, 421¾ miles. Fares 86/1a, 51/8c. R. T for two months, 172/2a, 103/4c. Pop. 4,654. *Map Square* 40.

Euston	D'blane	D'blane	Euston
AM 5.0	4.51	AM 9.30r	7.30
10.0r	7.20	PM12.49r	10.45
PM 1.30r	12.29	4.9r	5.0h
7.50er	5.52	9.25	7.40
11.0d	8.55	—	—
11.35e	8.51	—	—

Sunday Trains.

PM 7.50r	5.52	PM 4.32r	5.0h
11.35	8.51	—	—

d Saturdays only.
e Saturdays excepted
h A.M.
r Restaurant Car.

Dunblane (Perthshire), Dunblane Hotel-Hydro. *See advt. p.* **142.**

DUNBRIDGE (Hants)
from *Waterloo*, 83½ miles. Fares, 17/6a, 10/6c. R. T. for two months, 35/0a, 21/0c. Departures *from* London as for Romsey. Departures *for* London about 6 times daily. *Map Square* 22.

DUNCHURCH (Warwick),
87 miles. Fares, 18/2a, 10 11c. R. T. for two months, 36/4a. Departures *from* London as for Rugby. Departures *for* London about 7 times daily. Pop. 935. *Map Square* 18.

DUNDEE (TAY BRIDGE)
(Forfar) from *King's Cross, via Berwick*, 451½ miles. Fares, 91 11a, 55 2c. R. T. for two months, 183/10a, 110/4c. Pop. 168,315. *Map Square* 38.

King's +	Dundee	Dundee	King's +
AM 4.45	3.29	AM 8.9r	6.15
10.0r	8.9	11.44r	10.0
PM 8.20er	5.34	PM 3.6	3.25
8.25e	8.44	5.36	6.0
11.25dr	9.10	7.42e	6.50
11.25er	9.17	8.33	7.5
—	—	9.25	7.25

Sunday Trains.

PM 7.45r	5.34	PM 5.9	6.0
8.25	8.44	—	—
11.25	9.17	—	—

d Saturdays only.
e Saturdays excepted.
r Restaurant Car.

DUNDEE—continued.

ANOTHER ROUTE (WEST)
from *Euston*, 470½ miles, *via* Carlisle. Fares as above.

Euston	Dundee	Dundee	Euston
AM 5.0	7.17	AM 3.25r	7.30
10.0r	8.45	11.30r	10.45
PM 7.50er	6.50	PM 2.25r	5.0
11.0d	10.17	7.25	7.40
11.35e	10.5	9.20	8.0

Sunday Trains.

PM 7.50r	6.50	PM 3.0r	5.0h
11.35	10.5	—	—

d Saturdays only.
e Saturdays excepted.
h A.M.
r Restaurant Car.

For Dundee, Perth and London Shipping Co., Ltd., service of steamers see page **597.**

DUNFERMLINE
(LOWER) (Fife) from *King's Cross*, 409½ miles. Fares, 86/6a, 51 11c. R.T. for two months,173/0a, 103/10c. Pop. 46,977. *Map Square* 41.

King's +	D'ferm.	D'ferm.	King's +
AM 4.45	2.17	AM 9.19r	6.15
9.50r	7.10	9.36r	6.30
10.0r	7.22	PM 1.8r	10.0
11.50r	9.27	4.26	3.25
PM 1.15dr	11.27	6.57	6.0
7.45er	6.39	9.34	7.5
8.25e	7.23	—	—
8.25d	9.9	—	—
11.25e	8.19	—	—
11.40e	8.46	—	—
11.40d	9.9	—	—

Sunday Trains.

PM 7.45	6.3+	AM10.0	8.15
8.25	7.23	PM 6.23	6.0
11.25	8.19	—	—
11.40	8.46	—	—

d Saturdays only.
e Saturdays excepted.
r Restaurant Car.

DUNFORD BRIDGE
(Yorks), 180½ miles. Fares, 36/0a, 21/1c. R. T., double fare. Departures *from* London as for Penistone. Departures *for* London about 4 times daily. *Map Square* 12.

DUNGENESS (Kent)
from *Charing Cross, Cannon Street,* and *London Bridge*, 76½ miles. Fares, 15 10a, 12/8b, 9/6c. R.T. for two months, 31/8a, 25/4b, 19/0c. Departures *from* London as for Lydd. Departures *for* London about twice daily. Pop. (Dymchurch) 548. *Map Square* 24.

DUNHAM (Norfolk) from
Liverpool Street, 114¾ miles. Fares, 23/4a, 14/2c. Departures *from* London as for Swaffham. Departures *for* London about 6 times daily. Pop. 596. *Map Square* 19.

DUNHAM HILL

(Cheshire), 183¾ miles. Fares, 37/9*a*, 22/8*c*. R.T. for two months, 75/6*a*. Departures *from* London as for Chester. Departures *for* London about 6 times daily. Pop. 284.
Map Square 12.

DUNHAM MASSEY

(Cheshire), 190 miles. Fares, 37/9*a*, 22/8*c*. R. T., double fare. Departures *from* London as for Lymm. Departures *for* London about 6 times daily. Pop. 2,928.
Map Square 12.

DUNKELD (Perth) from

Euston, 465½ miles. Fares, 94/4*a*, 56/7*c*. R. T. for two months, 188/8*a*, 113/2*c*. Pop. 1,049.
Map Square 37.

Euston	Dunkld.	Dunkld.	Euston
AM 10. 0*r*	8.47	AM 7.51	7.30
PM 1.30*er*	2. 4	10. 5*r*	10.45
7.40*er*	6.16	PM 1.10*r*	5. 0*h*
11.35*e*	10. 5	8. 0	7.40
—	—	—	—
—	—	—	—
—	—	—	—

Sunday Trains.

PM 7.50*r*	6.19	—	—
11.35	10. 5	—	—
—	—	—	—

e Saturdays excepted.
h A.M.
r Restaurant Car.

ANOTHER ROUTE from

King's Cross, 455¾ miles. Fares as above.

King's+	Dunkld.	Dunkld.	King's+
AM 4.45	4.38	AM 7.51*r*	6.30*h*
11.50*er*	2. 4*k*	10. 5*r*	10. 0*h*
PM 7.45*er*	6.16*k*	PM 1.10	3.25
11.25*e*	10. 5*k*	6. 0	7. 5
—	—	—	—
—	—	—	—

Sunday Trains.

PM 7.15*r*	6.19*k*	—	—
11.25	10. 5*k*	—	—

e Saturdays excepted.
h P.M. *k* A.M.
r Restaurant Car.

DUNKERTON (Somerset),

106 miles. No through fares. Departures *from* London as for Limpley Stoke. Departures *for* London about 4 times daily.
Map Square 22.

DUNLOP (Ayr), 398 miles.

Fares, 81/1*a*, 48/8*c*. R. T. for two months, 162/2*a*, 97/4*c*. Departures *from* London as for Kilmarnock. Departures *for* London about 4 times daily. Pop. 1,335.
Map Square 40.

DUNMOW (Essex) from

Liverpool Street, *via* Bishop's Stortford, 40 miles. Fares, 8/7*a*, 5/2*c*. R.T. for two months, 17/2*a*. Pop. 2,506.
Map Square 24.

L'pool St.	Dunm.	Dunm.	L'pool St.
AM 7.18	9.18	AM 8. 0	9.27
9.10	11. 7	10. 5	11.27
11.50*h*	1.21	PM 12. 4*k*	2. 7
PM 12.29*d*	2. 6	2.47*l*	5. 9
2.34	3.53	2.50*s*	5. 9
4.45	6. 1	4.37	6.10
6.30	7.53	6.47	8.22
—	—	—	—

No Sunday Trains.

d Saturdays only.
h Wednesdays and Thursdays only.
k Wednesdays, Thursdays and Saturdays only.
l Mondays and Tuesdays only
s Mondays and Tuesdays excepted.

DUNMOW—*continued.*

ANOTHER ROUTE from

Liverpool Street, *via* Witham, 53¼ miles. Fares as above.

L'pl. St.	Dunmow	Dunmow	L'pl. St.
AM 5. 0	8. 0	AM 9.18	11.16
8.15	10. 5	11. 7	1.16
8.46*l*	12. 4	PM 3.53	5.48
11.30*h*	2.47	6. 1	9.17
11.30*k*	2.50	—	—
PM 2.15	4.37	—	—
4.58	6.47	—	—
—	—	—	—
—	—	—	—
—	—	—	—

No Sunday Trains.

h Mondays and Tuesdays only.
k Mondays and Tuesdays excepted.
l Wednesdays, Thursdays and Saturdays only.

Saracen's Head Hotel. Telephone 20. Comfortable old house. Billiards. Stabling and Garage.
TRUST HOUSES, Ltd.

DUNNING (Perth), 440¼

miles. Fares, 89/10*a*, 53/11*c*. R. T. for two months, 179/8*a*, 107/10*c*. Departures *from* London as for Dunblane. Departures *for* London about 3 times daily. Pop. 1,136.
Map Square 40.

DUNOON (Argyle), 430

miles. No through fares. Departures *from* London as for Greenock, and thence by steamer at frequent intervals. Pop. 14,731.

DUNPHAIL (Elgin), 560¾

miles. Fares, 106/3*a*, 63/9*c*. R. T. for two months, 212/6*a*, 127/6*c*. Departures *from* London as for Forres. Departures *for* London about twice daily.
Map Square 34.

DUNRAGIT (Wigtown),

399¾ miles. Fares, 68/9*a*, 41/3*c*. R. T. for two months, 137/6*a*, 82/6*c*. Departures *from* London as for Newton Stewart. Departures *for* London about 4 times daily.
Map Square 43.

DUNS (Berwick), 354¾ miles

Fares, 75/0*a*, 45/0*c*. R. T. for two months, 150/0*a*. Departures *from* London as for Berwick-on-Tweed or St. Boswells. Departures *for* London about 3 times daily. Pop. 2,818.
Map Square 41.

DUNSCORE (Dumfries),

342¾ miles. Fares, 41/9*c*. R. T. for two months, 83/6*c*. Departures *from* London as for Dumfries. Departures *for* London about twice daily. Pop. 1,036.
Map Square 43.

DUNSLAND CROSS

(Devon) from *Waterloo*, 213¼ miles. Fares, 44/5*a*, 26/8*c*. R. T. for two months, 88/10*a*, 53/4*c*. Departures *from* London as for Holsworthy. Departures *for* London about 4 times daily.
Map Square 26.

DUNSTABLE (Beds) from

King's Cross, 37 miles. Fares, 7/1*a*, 4/3*c*. R. T. for two months, 14/2*a*. Pop. 8,894.
Map Square 23.

King's+	Dunsble.	Dunsble.	King's+
AM 7.45	9.17	AM 7.15	8.41
9.20	10.40	8.19	9.44
11.30	1.16	11. 9	12.45
PM 1. 8	2.53	PM 12.54	2.22
4.15	5.50	3.54	5.45
5.50	7.22	6.19	8. 5
7. 0	8.33	7.46	9.50
9.10*d*	10.53	—	—
—	—	—	—
—	—	—	—
—	—	—	—
—	—	—	—

Sunday Trains.

AM 8.30	10.10	AM 8. 6	9.53
PM 7.10	8.35	PM 5.50	7.40
—	—	8.10	9.48
—	—	—	—
—	—	—	—

d Saturdays only.

ANOTHER ROUTE from

Euston, 47 miles. Fares as above.

Euston	Dunsble.	Dunsble.	Euston
AM 5.25	8. 0	AM 6.50	9. 6
8.35	10.39	8.47	10.15
10.50	12.42	11.38	1.50
PM 12.15*e*	2.32	PM 1. 5*h*	2.45
12.50*d*	2.32	1. 5*k*	4.30
2. 0	5. 7	3.10	5.35
5.32	7.21	6. 0	7.55
7.15	9.41	8.12	10.50
—	—	—	—

No Sunday Trains.

d Saturdays only.
e Saturdays excepted.
h Thursdays and Saturdays only.
k Thursdays and Saturdays excepted.

DUNSTALL PARK

(Stafford) from *Paddington*, 124 miles. Fares, 25/10*a*, 15/6*c*. R. T. for two months, 51/8*a*, 31/0*c*. Departures *from* London as for Wolverhampton (Low Level). Departures *for* London about 4 times daily. Pop. 9,643.

DUNSTER (Somerset)

from *Paddington*, 166 miles. Fares, 34/9*a*, 20/10*c*. R T. for two months, 69/6*a*, 41/8*c*. Departures *from* London as for Watchet. Departures *for* London about 4 times daily. Pop. 1,380.
Map Square 21.

DUNSTON-ON-TYNE

(Durham), 268¾ miles. No through fares. Departures *from* London as for Newcastle-on-Tyne. Departures *for* London about 6 times daily. Pop. 9,272.

DUNSYRE (Lanark), 380¼

miles. No through fares. Departures *from* London as for Carstairs. Departures *for* London about 3 times daily. Pop. 161.
Map Square 41.

DUNTON GREEN (Kent)

from *Charing Cross, Cannon Street,* and *London Bridge,* 21¼ miles. Fares, 4/5*a*, 3/7*b*, 2/6*c*. R. T. for two months, 8/10*a*, 7/2*b*. Pop. 1,438.
Map Square 24.

Leave Char. +	Can. St.	Lon. B.	Arr. at Dun. G.
AM —	5.20	5.25	6.27
—	6.45	6.50	7.44
—	7.56	8. 0	8.54
9.38	—	9.45	10.34
11.15	—	11.23	12.16
PM —	1.12*d*	1.15*d*	1.57
2.17*d*	—	2.23*d*	3.10
3.50	—	3.57	4.47
4.55*d*	—	5. 1*d*	5.54
—	5. 4*e*	5. 7*e*	5.52
5.35*d*	—	5.41*d*	6.29
—	5.44*e*	5.47*e*	6.20
6.10*e*	—	6.17*e*	7. 4
6.34*e*	—	6.41*e*	7.13
7.18	—	7.26	8. 9
9. 0	—	9. 6	9.52
10. 0*l*	—	10. 6*l*	10.50
10.45	—	10.51	11.36
11.45*h*	—	—	12.25
—	—	—	—
—	—	—	—

Sunday Trains.

AM 7. 5	—	7.11	8. 8
8. 5	—	8.12	9. 1
11.15	—	11.23	12.17
PM —	1. 7*k*	—	2.15
3. 5	—	3.13	4. 7
6. 0	—	6. 6	7. 2

Trains from Dunton Green.

Leave Dun. G.	Arrive at Lon. B.	Can. St.	Char. +
AM 7.23	8.10	—	8.19
7.56	8.40	8.44	—
8.34	9.18	—	9.27
8.53	9.40	9.44	—
9.57	10.28	10.32	—
10.56	11.32	—	11.44
PM12.35	1.27	—	1.38
2.15	3. 7	—	3.19
4. 6	4.40	—	4.53
5.29*d*	6.30	—	6.39
5.41*e*	6.44	—	6.54
8. 4	8.54	9. 1	—
9.28	10.15	—	10.23
10.48	11.34	—	11.44
—	—	—	—
—	—	—	—

Sunday Trains.

AM 9.11	10. 5	—	10.15
9.28	10.22	—	10.32
11. 6	11.49	—	12. 0
PM12.57*k*	—	2.11*k*	—
2. 1	2.50	—	3. 0
5.35	6.27	—	6.41
8.21	9. 7	—	9.18
8.48	9.38	—	—
9.30*k*	—	10.54*k*	—
—	—	—	—

d Saturdays only.
e Saturdays excepted.
h Mondays and Thursdays only.
k Departs from and arrives at Victoria (S.E. & C.).
l Stops on notice being given to Guard.

DUNURE (Ayr), 399¾ miles.

Fares, 81/6*a*, 48/11*c*. R. T. for two months, 163/0*a*, 97/10*c*. Departures *from* London as for Turnberry. Departures *for* London about 4 times daily.
Map Square 43.

DUNVANT (Glamorgan),

204¾ miles. No through fares. Departures *from* London as for Swansea. Departures *for* London about 5 times daily.
Map Square 21.

DURHAM from *King's Cross*,

254 miles. Fares, 52/11*a*, 31/9*c*. R. T., double fare. Pop. 17,329.
Map Square 7.

King's +	Dur.	Dur.	King's +
AM 4.45	11.44	AM 8.23	1.30
7.15*r*	2.24	8.48*g*	3.15
10. 0*r*	4.36	10.42*r*	4.30
11.50*r*	5. 8	PM12.36*r*	6.15
PM 1.15*r*	7.24	2.29*r*	9.25
1.50*r*	7.54	4. 6*r*	10. 0
5.30*r*	10.25	7.43	3.25
5.35*r*	11.10	11.19*e*	5.40
11.25*d*	5.17	11.37	6. 0
11.25*e*	5.34	—	—

Sunday Trains.

AM11.30*r*	8.37	AM10.40	5.15
PM 5. 0*r*	11.29	PM11.19	5.40
11.25	5.34	11.37	6. 0
—	—	—	—

d Saturdays only.
e Saturdays excepted.
g First and Third Class Pullman Cars only.
r Restaurant Car.

Royal County Hotel, on Great North Road. First-class Family and Motorists'. New garage and stabling. Riverside landing stage. Telephone No. 136 Durham. Proprietors—
HOSTELRIES, Ltd.

DUROR (Argyle), 516½ miles.

Fares, 103/7*a*, 62/2*c*. R. T. for two months, 207/2*a*, 124/4*c*. Departures *from* London as for Oban. Departures *for* London about twice daily. Pop. 305.
Map Square 37.

DURSLEY (Glo'ster), 129

miles. No through fares. Departures *from* London as for Gloucester. Departures *for* London about 7 times daily. Pop. 2,601.
Map Square 22.

DURSTON (Somerset)

from *Paddington*, 137¼ miles. Fares, *via* Westbury and Somerton, 28/7*a*, 17/2*c*. R. T. for two months, 57/2*a*. *Via* Bristol and Bridgwater, 31/1*a*, 18/8*c*. R. T. for two months, 62/2*a*. Departures *from* London as for Somerton or Bridgwater. Departures *for* London about 7 times daily. Pop. 186.
Map Square 22.

DYCE (Aberdeen), 529 miles.

No through fares. Departures *from* London as for Aberdeen. Departures *for* London about 3 times daily. Pop. 1,319.
Map Square 35.

DYFFRYN (Merioneth),

239 miles. Fares, 49/9*a*, 29/10*c*. R. T. for two months, 99/6*a*. Departures *from* London as for Barmouth. Departures *for* London about 4 times daily.
Map Square 16.

DYMOCK (Glo'ster) from

Paddington, 128 miles. Fares, 26/8*a*, 16/0*c*. R. T. for two months, 53/4*a*. Departures *from* London as for Ledbury. Departures *for* London about 4 times daily. Pop. 1,297.
Map Square 17.

DYSART (Fife), 420¼ miles.

No through fares. Departures *from* London as for Kirkcaldy. Departures *for* London about 3 times daily. Pop. 4,579.
Map Square 41.

DYSERTH (Flint), 208¾

miles. No through fares. Departures *from* London as for Prestatyn. Departures *for* London about 6 times daily. Pop. 902.
Map Square 11.

IDRIS

SODA WATER
LEMONADE
DRY GINGER ALE
BREWED GINGER
BEER
GINGER ALE

To be obtained at all
Clubs, Hotels, Restaurants,
Grocers, Wine Merchants,
and Chemists.

REFERENCE NOTES.

a signifies First Class.
b ,, Second Class.
c ,, Third Class.
d ,, On Saturdays only.
e ,, Saturdays excepted.
f ,, On Mondays only.
g ,, Mondays excepted.
r ,, Restaurant Car.
t ,, Tea Car.
x ,, Express.
R.T. ,, Return Tickets.
All Trains in the Tables not
otherwise marked carry Third
Class Passengers.

E

EAGLESCLIFFE
(Durham), 232½ miles. Fares, 48/6a,
29/1c. R. T., double fare. Departures *from* London as for Stockton-on-Tees. Departures *for* London about 8 times daily. Pop. 1,383.
Map Square 7.

EALING (Broadway)
(Middlesex) from *Paddington*, 5½ miles. Fares, 1/0½a, 0/7c. R. T. for two days, 1/11a, 1/0c. Pop. 67,755. *See* pp. 491-493.
Map Squares 23 and 58.

ANOTHER ROUTE from
Mansion House, 10¾ miles. *See* p. 489.

ANOTHER ROUTE from
Liverpool Street (Central London Tube). *See* back of Map.

EALING COMMON
from *Mansion House*, 9¾ miles.
See p. 489
Map Square 58.

EALING (North) from
Mansion House, 10¼ miles. *See* p. 489.
Map Square 58.

EALING (South) from
Mansion House, 10¼ miles. *See* p. 489.
Map Square 67.

EALING WEST from
Paddington, 6½ miles. Fares, 1/2a, 0/8c. R. T. for two days, 2/3a, 1/1c. *See* pp. 491-493.
Map Square 58.

EARBY (Yorks), from *St. Pancras*, 228 miles. Fares, 42/6a, 25/6c. R. T., double fare. Departures *from* London as for Colne. Departures *for* London about 8 times daily. Pop. 5,898.
Map Square 7.

EARDINGTON (Salop)
from *Paddington*, 143½ miles. Fares, 28/6a, 17.1c. R. T. for two months, 57/0a. Departures *from* London as for Bewdley. Departures *for* London about 4 times daily. Pop. 330.
Map Square 17.

EARDISLEY (Hereford)
158¼ miles. Fares, 32/9a, 19/8c. R. T. for two months, 65/6a. Departures *from* London as for Hay or Titley. Departures *for* London about 5 times daily. Pop. 746.
Map Square 17.

EARITH BRIDGE
(Hunts), from *Liverpool Street*, 76½ miles. Fares, 13/4a, 8/0c. R. T. for two months, 26/8a. Departures *from* London as for Haddenham. Departures *for* London about 6 times daily.
Map Square 18.

EARLESTOWN (Lancs)
from *Euston*, 187 miles. Fares, 39/0a, 23/5c. R. T. for two months, 78/0a.

Euston	E'rlst'n.	E'rlst'n.	Euston
AM12.25f	5.50	AM 7.35er	12. 5
12.25g	6.24	7.35dr	12.20
2.35	7.30	9.16r	1.45
5. 0	10.39	11.25hr	3.45
6.45e	11.59	11.25r	4.15
6.45d	12. 6	PM 1. 7t	5.50
8.30dr	1.15	1.35t	6. 0
8.30er	1.36	3. 9r	7.30
10.40r	3.21	4.14er	9. 5
11.50er	5. 0	4.14dr	9.15
11.50dr	5.26	11. 5	5. 0
PM 1.30dr	5.56	—	—
1.30r	5.45	—	—
2.35t	6.48	—	—
5.20r	10. 1	—	—
11.40e	5.33	—	—
11.50d	8.30	—	—
—	—	—	—

Sunday Trains.

AM11.45r	6.10	AM 8.18r	1.30
PM 6. 0r	10.18	10.11	4. 0
11.45	5.33	PM 3. 6r	7.30
11.50	5.50	7.32	5. 0
—	—	—	—
—	—	—	—
—	—	—	—

d Saturdays only.
e Saturday excepted.
f Mondays only.
g Mondays excepted.
h Mondays and Saturdays only.
r Restaurant Car.
t Tea Car.

EARLEY (Berks) from

Waterloo, 40¼ miles. Fares, 7/6*a*, 4/6*c*. R. T. for two months, 15/0*a*, 9/0*c*. Pop. 456.
Map Square 23.

W'LOO	EARLEY	EARLEY	W'LOO
AM 5.10	7.12	AM 6.45	8.17
6.54	8.43	7.41	9.17
7.54	9.37	8.53	10.17
9.54	11.33	9.50	11.17
10.54	12.37	10.54	12.31
PM12.48	2.20	PM12.54	2.27
1.48	3.17	1.54	3.27
2.48	4.18	3.54	5.27
3.48*e*	5.17	4.54	6.27
3.48*d*	5.22	5.54	7.27
4.48*e*	6.9	6.54	8.27
4.48*d*	6.22	7.54	9.27
5.48	7.15	10.23*e*	12.5
6.48	8.16	10.23*d*	12.8
7.54	9.33	—	—
—	—	—	—
—	—	—	—

Sunday Trains.

AM 8.18	10.2	AM 8.28	10.30
PM12.18	1.59	PM12.26	2.3
4.18	5.56	5.51	7.28
5.58	7.38	7.47	9.28
9.18	11.0	8.55	10.28

d Saturdays only.
e Saturdays excepted.

EARLS COLNE (Essex)

from *Liverpool Street*, 54 miles. Fares, 11/3*a*, 6/9*c*. R. T. for two months, 22/6*a*. Departures *from* London as for Halstead. Departures *for* London about 4 times daily. Pop. 1,806.
Map Square 19.

EARLS COURT from

Mansion House, 5 miles. Also from Ealing, Hounslow, Richmond and Wimbledon. Pop.17,912.
See p. 489.
Map Square 68.

ANOTHER ROUTE from *Broad Street*, 14¼ miles. Fares, 1/2*a*, 0/8½*c*. R. T. for two days, 2/2½*a*, 1/4*c*. *See* pp. 591-595.

ANOTHER ROUTE (Hammersmith and Finsbury Park Tube). *See* back of Map.

EARLSFIELD (Surrey)

from *Waterloo*, 5¼ miles. Fares, 0/9*a*, 0/5½*c*. R. T. for two days, 1/6*a*, 0/11*c*. *See* pp. 583, 585, 591-594.
Map Square 77.

EARLSHEATON (Yorks)

from *King's Cross*, 181¼ miles. Fares, 37/4*a*, 22.5*c*. R.T., double fare. Departures *from* London as for Dewsbury. Departures *for* London about 5 minutes later.

EARLSTON (Berwick),

361¼ miles. No through fares. Departures *from* London as for St. Boswells. Departures *for* London about 3 times daily. Pop. 1,643.
Map Square 41.

EARLSWOOD (Surrey)

from *London Bridge, Victoria* and *Clapham Junction*, 21¼ miles. Fares, 4/5*a*, 2/8*c*. R. T. for two months, 8/10*a*, 5/1*c*.
Map Square 23.

	Leave		Arr. at
VICT.	CLAP. J.	LON. B.	EARLS.
AM —	—	5.18	6.18
7.23	7.29	7.25	8.25
9.0	9.8	—	9.44
9.45	9.51	9.50	10.45
10.35	10.42	10.35	11.25
PM 1.20*e*	1.27*e*	—	2.6
1.25*d*	—	1.10*d*	2.6
2.0*c*	2.7*e*	2.5*e*	2.55
—	—	2.8*d*	3.0
4.0	4.8	4.5	4.46
5.5	5.12	5.10	5.57
—	—	5.21	6.15
6.6	6.12	6.8	7.3
7.15	7.22	7.20	8.11
—	—	—	—
—	—	—	—

No Sunday Trains.

Trains from Earlswood.

Leave	Arrive at		
EARLS.	LON. B.	CLAP. J.	VICT.
AM 7.19	8.15	8.15	8.24
8.3	8.46	9.0	9.8
8.53	—	9.37	9.44
8.59	9.42	—	9.58
9.57	10.38	10.29	10.36
11.19	12.13	11.59	12.7
PM12.49	1.42	1.39	1.49
2.49	3.40	3.37	3.45
3.25	—	4-9	4.17
4.59	5.54	5.47	5.55
7.51	8.46	8.39	8.48

No Sunday Trains.

d Saturdays only.
e Saturdays excepted.

EARLSWOOD LAKES

(Warwick), 109½ miles. Fares, 22/9*a*, 13/8*c*. R.T. for two months, 45/6*a*, 27/4*c*. Departures *from* London as for Henley-in-Arden. Departures *for* London about 6 times daily.

EARSHAM (Norfolk)

from *Liverpool Street*, 112¾ miles. Fares, 23/7*a*, 14/2*c*. R. T. for two months, 47/2*a*. Departures *from* London as for Bungay or Harleston. Departures *for* London about 7 times daily. Pop. 603.
Map Square 8.

EARSWICK (Yorks), 190½

miles. Fares 39/9*a*, 23/10*c*. R.T. for two months, 79/6*a*, 47/8*c*. Departures *from* London as for York. Departures *for* London about 5 times daily. Pop. 135.
Map Square 8.

EASINGTON (Durham),

255¼ miles. No through fares. Departures *from* London as for West Hartlepool. Departures *for* London about 5 times daily. Pop. 2,711.

EASINGWOLD (Yorks),

201¼ miles. No through fares. Departures *from* London as for York. Departures *for* London about 8 times daily. Pop. 2,055.
Map Square 8.

EASSIE (Forfar), 474¼ miles.

Fares, 95/5*a*, 57/3*c*. R. T. for two months, 190/10*a*, 114/6*c*. Departures *from* London as for Coupar Angus. Departures *for* London about 3 times daily. Pop 504.
Map Square 38.

EAST ACTON. *See* ACTON, EAST.

EAST ANSTEY (Devon)

from *Paddington*,167¼ miles. Fares, 35/0*a*, 21/0*c*. R. T. for two months, 70/0*a*. Departures *from* London as for Dulverton. Departures *for* London about 3 times daily. Pop. 236.
Map Square 21.

EAST BARKWITH

(Lincoln), 138 miles. Fares 28/7*a*, 17/2*c*. R. T., double fare. Departures *from* London as for Wragby. Departures *for* London about 4 times daily. Pop. 308.
Map Square 13.

EAST BOLDON (Durham), 264½ miles. Fares, 55/3*a*,

33/2*c*. R. T., double fare. Departures *from* London as for Sunderland. Departures *for* London about 6 times daily. Pop. (Boldon) 2,982.
Map Square 3.

EASTBOURNE (Sussex)

from *London Bridge, Victoria* and *Clapham Junction*, 65¼ miles. Fares, 12/6*a*, 7/6*c*. R. T. for two months, 25/0*a*, 15/0*c*. Pop. 62,030
Map Square 29.

	Leave		Arr. at
	VICT.	LON. B.	E'TBNE.
AM —		6.15	8.4
6.37*k*		6.40*k*	10.4
9.0		—	10.53
9.45		—	11.30
10.5		9.50	12.25
11.15		—	12.52
11.55		—	1.35
12.0		12.10	2.25
PM 1.20*e*		—	3.17
1.25*d*		1.10*d*	3.17
—		2.0*e*	3.51
—		*p*2.0*d*	3.51
3.20*p*		—	4.49
3.40		4.5	5.55
4.30		—	6.20
—		*p*5.5*e*	6.30
—		5.5*d*	6.30
5.20		—	6.50
5.45*e*		5.55*e*	7.38
6.40		—	8.10
6.50		7.0	9.14
8.35		—	10.16
10.0		—	11.39
10.30		10.35	1.6

EASTBOURNE—*contd.*

Sunday Trains.

	Leave	Arr. at
	VICT.	LON. B.	E'TBNE.
AM 6.55	7.22	10. 1
9.25	—	11. 2
9.30	9.30	11.31
10.45*l*	—	12.15
11.15	—	1. 3
PM 12.15*k*	—	3. 1
6.33	6.33	9. 4
9.25*k*	—	11.59

Trains from Eastbourne.

Leave	Arrive at	
E'TBNE.	LON. B.	VICT.
AM 6. 5	8.46	—
7. 0	8.53	9. 8
7.30	9.10	9.19
7.46	9.50	—
8.33	10. 5*p*	10.12
8.50	10.55	10.56
9.30*p*	—	11. 5
10.40	12.44	12.45
11.45	—	1.15
PM 12. 5	2.22	2.22
2.25	4. 0	4. 3
4.30*l*	—	6. 0
5.30	7.42	7.45
6.15	7.56	7.50
7.50	10. 0	10.10
8.20	10.25	10.17
9.25	—	11.17
9.50*k*	12.59	1. 0

Sunday Trains.

AM 7. 8	10.18	10.32
8.40*k*	11.15	10.50
10. 4*k*	—	1. 0
PM 5.15*l*	—	6.45
5.55	7.56	7.37
6.10	8.34	8.41
8.40	—	10.19
8.50	10.50	10.45
9.30*k*	12.27	—

d Saturdays only.
e Saturdays excepted.
k Via Brighton.
l First and Third Class Pullman Cars only.
p First Class Pullman Car attached.

ANOTHER ROUTE from
London Bridge, Victoria, and *Clapham Junction, via Groom-bridge, 60¼ miles. Fares as above.*

	Leave	Arr. at
	VICT.	LON. B.	E'TBNE.
AM 5.30	5.18	8.39
6.37	6.40	10.42
9.10	9. 6	12.25
11. 5	10.35	1.30
12. 9	11.50	3.32
12. 0*d*	12.20*dk*	3.52
PM 3.45	—	6. 7
4.50	4.44*e*	7.28
5. 5	5.21	8.16
6. 6*e*	6. 8*e*	9. 3

Sunday Trains.

AM 8.50	8.30	11.51
PM 2.30	—	5.47
7. 5	6.46	9.50

EASTBOURNE—*contd.*

Trains from Eastbourne.

Leave	Arrive at	
E'TBNE.	LON. B.	VICT.
AM 6.38	9.32	9.40
7.53	10.55	10.20
9.52	12.44	12.35
PM 12.45	—	3.45
3.35	6.36	6.29
4.34	7.56	8.27
7.30	10.25	10.10

Sunday Trains.

AM 7. 8	10.18	10.22
10.20	—	1.40
PM 6.10	9.17	9. 0

d Saturdays only.
e Saturdays excepted.
k Departs from London Bridge (S.E. & C.R.) Station.

Grand Hotel. Eastbourne. Charming position. 300 Rooms. *See advt. p. 143.*

Queen's Hotel. First-class Family Hotel. Facing Sea. 200 Rooms. Lift to all floors. Self-contained suites (facing due south). Special London Dance Orchestra plays daily (Wednesdays excepted) for Dancing afternoon and evening. Moderate charges. Motor omnibus meets all trains. Garage. *See advt. p. 144.*

Cavendish Hotel. Situated in centre of Grand Parade, opposite Bandstand. Exquisite cuisine. Passenger lift to all floors. Moderate charges. *En pension* or *à la carte.* Tariff on application. Telephone, 1070 Eastbourne. *See advt. p. 145.*

Mostyn Private Hotel. Recently enlarged. Over 100 Bedrooms. Fine Lounges, Drawing-room, Card and Writing-rooms. Billiards (2 Tables). Tel. No. 1301 (3 lines). Telegrams, Mostyn Hotel. *See advt. p. 146.*

Kenilworth Court Private Hotel, Wilmington Square, Grand Parade. Finest position. Facing Sea. Electric Lift. Central Heating. Large Lounge, Billiards. Telephone, 657. Telegrams, Kenilworth court. Eastbourne. *See advt. p. 147.*

Chatsworth Hotel. Replete with every comfort. Catering a special feature. General tariff moderate. *See advt. p. 148.*

The Hydro Hotel, South Cliff, due South. 120 feet above Sea Level, facing Channel. Bowling Green. Croquet. Electric Light. Passenger Lift. High-class Cuisine; Table d'hote: separate Tables. Hydro 'Bus meets all principal Trains. *See advt. p. 149.*

EASTBOURNE—*contd.*

Burlington Hotel. Finest position on Grand Parade. First-class Family Hotel, renowned for comfort. Telegraphic address: Burlington, Eastbourne. Telephone, No. 28, Eastbourne. GORDON HOTELS, Ltd. *See advt. p. 150.*

Albion Hotel. Exactly opposite Sea. Fully licensed. The most charming and comfortable Hotel on South Coast. Special Week-end terms. Motor Garage. Telegrams: Albion, Eastbourne. Telephone : No. 1 Eastbourne. *See advt. p. 150.*

Alexandra Hotel, Grand Parade, facing Sea. First-class Family, fully licensed. Cuisine a special feature. Table d'hote open to non-residents. New Lounge. Telephone 132. W. E. WOOD, Proprietor. (late Trinity College, Cambridge). *See advt. p. 151.*

Bolton Hotel (Unlicensed), Burlington Place. One minute Sea Front and Park. Private Suites. Luxuriously furnished. Quite exceptional catering. Resident Proprietor. Telephone 486. *See advt. p. 151.*

St. Mildred's Court Private Hotel, Grand Parade. Every Room Faces Sea. Lounge, Dining Room, Separate Tables, Billiard Room. Verandah. Terms moderate. Telephone 578. *See advt. p. 152.*

Angles Private Hotel. Finest position facing sea. 26-31. Royal Parade. Central. Comfortable, Congenial. Commodious. Telephone No. 311. *See advt. p. 152.*

Queen's Court Private Hotel. Opposite Pier. Remodelled. New Lounge. Excellent Cuisine. Tel. 645. PROPRIETOR. *See advt. p. 153.*

Trinity Mansions Hotel. Finest position. Facing Sea. Excellent cuisine. From £4 14s. 6d. per week or 15/- per day. No extras. Lift to all floors. 'Phone No. 557. R. M. LENHAM, Proprietor. *See advt. p. 153.*

Sandhurst Private Hotel. Facing Sea. Over forty bedrooms. Full-size Billiard Table. Electric Light. Telegraphic address: "Sandhurst, Eastbourne." Telephone 797. *See advt. p. 154.*

Lansdowne Private Hotel, Grand Parade. Facing Sea and Lawns. Excellent cuisine. Moderate and inclusive terms. Telephone 636. *See advt. p. 154.*

EASTBOURNE—*contd.*

York House Private Hotel.
Sea Front ; 86 bedrooms. Billiard room ; Ball room ; central heating. Terms from 50/-. Tel. 918.
Proprietress -
Mrs. D. E. WILLIAMSON.
See advt. p. **155.**

West Rocks Private Hotel.
Facing sea. S.W. aspect. Central Heating. Terms from 3½ gns. per week. Telephone 421.
Miss HUGGETT.
See advt. p. **155.**

Imperial Hotel. Hotel Car (Wolseley 6 seater) meets trains and runs to Golf Courses (twice daily) ; also for Theatres and short or long distance journeys. Four new bathrooms. Billiard, Dance, and Cloak Rooms being enlarged. Wireless Installation being fixed.
See advt. p. **156.**

Southdown Hotel. First-class Family. Fully licensed. One door from Front. Close Devonshire Park and Links. Tel. 129. Miss GOLD,
See advt. p. **156.**

Royal Marine Private Hotel and Boarding Establishment, Royal Parade. Facing Sea, Pier, and Bandstand. Telephone 402. Proprietors.
See advt. p. **157.**

Haddon Hall Private Hotel, Devonshire Place. Overlooking Sea. 70 Bedrooms. 'el. No. 552,
HOWARD W. BANGS, Proprietor.
See advt. p. **157.**

Belgrave Private Hotel. Replete with every comfort. Over 50 bedrooms.
Proprietress, Miss J. WAKE.
See advt. p. **158.**

Glastonbury Private Hotel. Facing Sea. Oldest established on Royal Parade.
Proprietor, V. GREENFIELD.
See advt. p. **158.**

Wilmington Private Hotel, West End. One minute from Devonshire Park. Terms from 3½ guineas. Tel. 1219.
See advt. p. **159.**

Beachy Head Bungalow Hotel. Excellent Cuisine. Moderate Tariff. Apply MANAGER.
See advt. p. **159.**

San Remo. 39, 40 & 41. Royal Parade. Facing Sea. Excellent cuisine. Billiards and Dancing Room. Terms from 52/6.
Proprietresses, Mesdames DALE.
See advt. p. **160.**

Albemarle Hotel. Finest position nearest Sea. Central Heating. First-class cuisine. Appointed R.A.C. and A.A. Special week-end and Winter terms. 'Phone 665.
Apply MANAGER.
See advt. p. **160.**

Lascelles House Private Hotel. Established 1896. Smoking Lounge. Excellent Cooking. Central Heating. Views of Sea and Devonshire Park. 'Phone 633. Telegrams : "Lascelles."
Mrs. STOREY, Proprietress.
See advt. p. **161.**

EASTBOURNE—*contd.*

Royal Hotel. Family and Commercial. Central, near Station and Sea. English Cooking. Moderate Tariff. Tel. 153. Proprietor, Capt. W. J. PUGH, M.C.
See advt. p. **161.**

Araluen, Grand Parade. High-class Private Hotel Central. Lounge, Billiard, Reception Room and principal Bedrooms facing sea Terms upon application. Telephone 144.
Apply PROPRIETRESS.
See advt. p. **161.**

Howard House Hotel. Few yards Sea, Devonshire Park, Theatre. New Lounge, Drawing, and Smoking Rooms. Tel. 846.
Mr. & Mrs. HILL.
See advt. p. **161.**

Lathom House Private Hotel, Howard Square. Central. Terms from 3 guineas (except Season and Holidays). Telephone, 985.
Miss BRIDGE, Proprietress.
See advt. p. **162.**

Grampian Mansion Private Hotel, overlooking Sea, Devonshire Park. Moderate Terms.
See advt. p. **162.**

Blackwater Private Hotel. Opposite Pier. Unique position. Tel. No. 445. Resident Proprietors.
Mr. & Mrs. J. E. TICE.
See advt. p. **162.**

Claremont Private Hotel. Opposite Pier. All rooms facing Sea. Lounge. Moderate. Tel. 1417. Resident Proprietress.
Mrs. ANDREW SCOTT.
See advt. p. **162.**

Whitehall, Private Hotel, Howard Square. Finest situation. Well furnished. Cooking specially good. Separate tables. Telephone 492. The Misses HICKS.
See advt. p. **163.**

The Retreat Boarding Establishment, Pevensey Road. Excellent Catering. 'Phone 849.
See advt. p. **163.**

Sussex Hotel. First-class Family. Two minutes from Devonshire Park. Moderate charges. Telephone, 362.
WALTER P. JOHNS, Manager.

Croydon House, Wilmington Gardens. Old-established superior Private Hotel. Close to Sea, overlooks Devonshire Park. Separate tables. Moderate. Tennis. Special Winter Terms. Proprietresses,
Misses BRADSHAW.

Sandon, Marine Parade. Facing Sea. Close Pier. Board Residence or Private Apartments. 17 Bedrooms. Late Dinner. From 2¾ guineas.
Mrs. DUTTON and Miss SOUTAR.

EASTBOURNE—*contd.*

Clarendon House, 17, Hyde Gardens. Board Residence. Central. Highly recommended. En larged Bedroom Gas Fires. Smoke Room. Terms moderate. Telephone 1297. PROPRIETRESS.

Brentwood Boarding Establishment, Wilmington Gardens. Highly recommended, comfortable ; good table. Smoking Room. Opposite Devonshire Park. Sea one minute. Tennis lawn. Separate tables. Special winter terms
Mrs. HERBERT MILES.

Holyrood, Howard Square. Boarding Establishment. Excellent cooking. Separate Tables. Two minutes of Sea front and Park. Tel. 714.
Miss SARAH ANN REEVES.

Hartington Lawn. This High-class Pension is run on good private house lines, and specialises for Visitors who appreciate comfort, with thoroughly good food and cooking. Minute Front. Central for all Attractions. Large bright rooms. Separate tables. Electric Light. 'Phone 1468.
Mr. & Mrs. H. C. J. SMITH.

Medwyn, Carlisle Road. Finest position in Eastbourne. First-class Pension. Spacious Dining, Drawing, and Smoking Rooms, also Hall Lounge, replete with every comfort. Separate Tables. Extensive Lawns with free use of Tennis Courts. Close to Sea, Devonshire Park, and Theatre. Telephone 758.
Miss GODBER.

Clonsilla Private Hotel, 15 and 16, Wilmington Square. Overlooking Sea. Electric Light. Cuisine excellent. Separate tables. Recommended by Travel Editor of "Queen." Mrs. LEDGER.

Glendower Private Hotel, Burlington Place. Few doors Grand Parade. (centre) Devonshire Park. Theatre. Three spacious Public Rooms. 30 Bedrooms. Gas Fires. Winter 3 gns. Summer 4 gns. Telephone 489. No extras
Mrs. M. HAMILTON MOSS.

Morningside, Jevington Gardens. Well-appointed Boarding and Apartment House. Close to Sea, Devonshire Park. Tennis. Separate Tables. Smoking Room. Moderate terms.

Montague House, 26, Grand Parade. Private Pension. Facing Sea. Separate tables. Smoking room. Moderate terms. Telephone 1044. Apply—
Miss CLAXTON.

"Whinnyhall" Boarding Establishment, 15 Cavendish Place. Opposite Pier. Highly recommended. Good cooking. Thoroughly comfortable. Telegrams : "Whinnyhall," Eastbourne. PROPRIETRESS.

For completion of Advertisements, see over.

EASTBOURNE—*contd.*

Travancore Private Hotel, 7, Wilmington Gardens. Superior Position. Overlooking Sea, Devonshire Park and Downs. Electric light. Tennis. Terms moderate Proprietors—
Mr. & Mrs. W. ROBERTS.

21, Enys Road.   Paying guests received. Well appointed House. Every comfort. Gas-fires. Electric Light. Highest references.
Mrs. FRED. TOVEY.

Rosemullion, Meads. Close to Beachy Head, Golf and Sea. Excellent Cuisine. From four guineas in season.
The Misses ELLIOTT & HUDSON.

"Springhaven" Boarding Establishment, Jevington Gardens. Terms moderate. Every home comfort. Tennis. One minute sea and Devonshire Park.
DAKERS & SMITH.

Craigmuir, 7, Grand Parade, Board Residence. Facing Sea. Hot and cold water in bedrooms. Central heating. Terms moderate. Telephone 1249.

Good Class Apartments, near Devonshire Park. Close to Sea front. Comfortable. Electric Light. Mrs. WHITE, Anerley, 20, Jevington Gardens.

Kynance, 35, Royal Parade. Boarding Establishment. Facing Sea. Close to Pier. Tennis Court, and Bowling Green. Tariff on application.

Medlow, Lansdowne Terrace. Opposite Wish Tower. Sea front. Apartments. Board if desired. Constant Hot Water. Electric Light. Proprietress—
Mrs. CARR.

Berkeley, Meads.   Near Downs, Sea and Golf Links. Misses Elliott and Hudson. Terms on application.

Carlisle Private Hotel. Cent e Grand Parade. Every room sea view. Smoking room. Separate tables. Electric light. Close Devonshire Park.
PROPRIETRESS.

Maple Durham Private Hotel, West Cliff. Overlooks Sea and Downs. Excellent Cuisine. Good garden. Badminton, Croquet. Mrs. BACON & Mrs. DAFFARN.

House Agents. Oakden & Co. (Established 1879), 10, Cornfield Road. Auctioneers, Surveyors, and Valuers. Extensive selection of the principal residences for sale and to let. Monthly Register with map of town. Telephone 1234 Eastbourne.

EASTBOURNE—*contd.*

Maple & Co. (of London), House and Estate Agents, have the best selection of Furnished and Unfurnished Residences and Properties for Sale. Offices: opposite Railway Station. Telegraphic Address, "Elpam," Eastbourne.

House Agent, Auctioneer, etc. Furnished and Unfurnished Houses. Valuations. Established 1891. Telephone, 896.   8, Elms Buildings, Seaside Road.
R. W. H. HAMBLYN.

Eastbourne Houses of all kinds, shops, apartment houses. Auction Sales. Valuations, Surveys. 37 years' local experience. Telephone 1112.
Messrs. LAKE & CO.,
2A, Bolton Road.

Killick & Davies, Auctioneers, Estate Agents, Surveyors and Valuers. Illustrated Register with local information free. Terminus Road, Eastbourne. Telephone 229.

Peerless, Dennis & Co. (Telegrams, "Peerless Dennis, Eastbourne." 'Phone 1,597 for absolutely best selected List, self-contained Flats, Furnished and Unfurnished Houses, Owners of Estates. Sole Agents various Freehold Country Properties. 56, Grove Road, near Town Hall, Eastbourne.

EAST BRIXTON. *See* BRIXTON, EAST.

EAST BUDLEIGH. *See* BUDLEIGH, EAST.

EASTBURY (Berks) from
Paddington, 64¼ miles. Fares, 12/6*a*, 8/*c*. R. T. for two months, 25/0*a*, 16/0*c*. Departures *from* London as for Lambourn. Departures *for* London about 5 times daily. Pop. 295.
Map Square 22.

EASTCHURCH (Kent),
55 miles. Fares, 9/6*a*, 7/9*b*, 6/0*c*. R. T. for two months, 19/0*a*, 15/6*b*, 12/0*c*. Departures *from* London as for Queenborough. Departures *for* London about 5 times daily. Pop. 1,141.
Map Square 24.

EASTCOTE (Middlesex)
from *Baker Street*, 12½ miles. Fares, 2/3*4a*, 1/4½*c*. R. T. for two days, 3/8*a*, 2/6*c*. Departures *from* London as for Uxbridge. Departures *for* London about 10 minutes later. Pop. 1,268.
Map Square 48.

ANOTHER ROUTE from
Mansion House, 17½ miles. *via* Acton Town and South Harrow.
See p. 489.

EAST DULWICH. *See* DULWICH, EAST.

EASTERHOUSE (Lanark), 430½ miles. No through fares. Departures *from* London as for Edinburgh (Waverley). Departures *for* London about 3 times daily.

EAST FARLEIGH (Kent)
from *Charing Cross, Cannon St.,* and *London Bridge,* 43¼ miles. Fares, 8/6*a*, 6/9*b*, 5/1*c*. R. T. for two months, 17/0*a*, 13/6*b*. Pop. 1,564.
Map Square 24.

	Leave		Arr. at
CHAR. +	CAN. ST.	LON. B.	E. FAR.
AM —	5.20	5.25	7.44
—	6.45	6.50	8.57
—	7.56	8.0	10. 5
9.25	—	9.33	11.35
10.40*d*	—	10.46*d*	12.35
—.	11.56	12. 0	1.31
PM 2. 8	—	2.16	3.47
3. 0	—	3. 8	4.39
3.15	—	5.21	5.18
3.48*e*	—	—	5.18
3.50	—	3.57	6.14
—	4.36*e*	4.39*e*	6.14
5.35*d*	—	5.41*d*	7.43
6. 3*e*	—	6. 9*e*	7.38
8. 0	—	8. 8	9.52
—	—	—	—

Sunday Trains.

AM 8. 5	—	8.12	9.54
9.50	—	9.56	11.43
PM 7.10	—	7.20	8.58

Trains from East Farleigh.

	Leave	Arrive at		
	E. FAR.	LON. B.	CAN. ST.	CHAR. +
AM 6.12	8. 9	—	8.19
8. 0	9.32	9.36	—
9. 9	10.58	11. 2	—
10.12	11.43	—	11.57
11.51	1.36	—	1.50
PM 1.49	3.26	—	3.40
3.48	5.50	—	6. 3
4.56	7.25	7.30	—
6.37	8.26	—	8.35
8.16	10.22	—	10.35
*d*11. 5*s*	—	1.20	—
—	—	—	—

Sunday Trains.

AM 8.20	10.22	—	10.32
PM 6.36	8.12	—	8.22
7.16	9. 7	—	9.17

d Saturdays only.
e Saturdays excepted.
l Low Level Platform.
s Third Class only.

EAST FINCHLEY. *See* FINCHLEY, EAST.

EAST FORTUNE (East Lothian), 373¼ miles. Fares, 78/2*a*, 46/11*c*. R. T. for two months, 156/4*a*, 93/10*c*. Departures *from* London as for Dunbar. Departures *for* London about 3 times daily.
Map Square 41.

EAST GARSTON. *See* GARSTON, EAST.

EAST GATE (Durham), 263¼ miles. No through fares. Departures *from* London as for Bishop Auckland. Departures *for* London about 4 times daily. Pop. 342.
Map Square 7.

EAST GRANGE (Fife),

417¾ miles. No through fares. Departures *from* London as for Dunfermline. Departures *for* London about 3 times daily.

EAST GRINSTEAD

(Sussex) from *London Bridge*, *Victoria*, and *Cannon Street*, 30 miles. Fares, 6/3*a*, 3/9*c*. R. T. for two months, 12/6*a*, 7/6*c*. Pop. 7,319.

Map Square 23.

Leave Vict.	Leave Can. St.	Lon. B.	Arr. at E. Grin.
AM —	—	5.18	7.23
6.37	—	6.40	7.50
7.23	—	7.25	9.23
—	—	8. 7	9.24
9.10	—	9. 6	10.33
9.45	—	9.50	11.26
10.35	—	10.35	11.52
12. 0	—	11.50	1.20
PM —	—	12.50*d*	1.57
1.20*e*	—	1.38*e*	2.54
1.25*d*	—	1.38*d*	3. 0
—	—	2. 5*e*	3.59
2.25	—	2.25*d*	3 59
4. 0	—	4.10	5.21
4.50	—	4.44*e*	6. 4
—	—	5. 5	6.11
5. 5	—	5.21	6.34
5.48	—	5.41*e*	6.56
6. 6	—	6. 8	7.58
6.50	—	7. 0	8. 9
7.15	—	7.38	8.51
9. 3*h*	—	9.12*h*	10.18
—	—	—	—
—	—	—	—
—	—	—	—
—	—	—	—
—	—	—	—
—	—	—	—
—	—	—	—
—	—	—	—

Sunday Trains.

AM 8.18	—	8.30	9.46
PM 6.33	—	6.46	8. 5
—	—	—	—
—	—	—	—
—	—	—	—

Trains from East Grinstead.

Leave E. Grin.	Arrive at Lon. B.	Arrive at Can. St.	Arrive at Vict.
AM 6.38	8.15	—	8.24
7.14	8.37	—	8.40
7.53	9. 1*k*	9. 4	9. 8
7.57	9.10	—	9.19
8.14	9.32	—	9.40
8.47	9.55	—	9.58
9.15	10. 7	—	—
9.30	10.38	—	10.46
9.36	10.55	—	10.48
10.26	—	—	11.35
10.43	12.13	—	12. 7
PM12.12	1.42	—	1.26
1.50	2.58	—	—
3.20	4.32	—	4.35
4.10	5.21	—	5.55
5. 7	6.36	—	6.29
6.22	7.56	—	—
7. 2	8.46	—	8.27
9.15	10.25	—	11.17
—	—	—	—
—	—	—	—
—	—	—	—
—	—	—	—
—	—	—	—

EAST GRINSTEAD—*continued.*

Sunday Trains.

Leave E. Grin.	Arr. at Lon. B.	Arr. at Can. St.	Arr. at Vict.
AM 7.52	10.18	—	10.32
9.57	11.15	—	—
PM 6.22	7.56	—	8.41
8. 7	9.26	—	9.34
—	—	—	—
—	—	—	—

d Saturdays only.
e Saturdays excepted.
h Wednesdays and Saturdays only.
k Departs from or arrives at London Bridge S.E. & C. Station.

Taxi Cabs can be hired to meet any train at this station by telegram, or telephone No. 12 to Messrs. Nutt Bros., Station Road, East Grinstead.

Felbridge Hotel. An ideal old-world Residential and Motorist's Hotel. *See* advt. p. **163**.

Ye Dorset Arms Hotel. Established over 300 years. First class for Military, Families and Motorists. Main Eastbourne and Brighton roads. Hot luncheons and table d'hôte daily. Officially appointed A.A. and R.A.C. Best centre for beauty spots of Sussex and Surrey. Telephone No. 24.

Crown Hotel. Family and Commercial. Most centrally situated. Comfortable commercial dining and sitting rooms. Ordinary daily, 1 o'clock. Motors. Posting. Garage. Good Stabling. Billiards. Telephone 117.
Prop., STANLEY C. BALL.

EAST HAM (Essex) from

Fenchurch Street, 6½ miles. Fares, 1/0½*a*, 0/7½*c*. R.T. for two days, 1/9*a*, 1/0½*c*. Pop. 143,246. *See* pp. 509, 510.

Map Square 23.

ANOTHER ROUTE from

St. Pancras, 13¼ miles. Fares, 1/5½*a*, 0/10½*c*. R. T. for two days, 2/11*a*, 1/7½*c*. *See* pp. 506-507.

ANOTHER ROUTE from

Ealing, Hounslow, Richmond and *Wimbledon, via* District Railway *See* p. 489.

EASTHAVEN (Forfar),

464¼ miles. No through fares. Departures *from* London as for Dundee. Departures *for* London about 3 times daily.

Map Square 38.

EAST HORNDON (Essex)

from *Fenchurch Street*, 19½ miles. Fares, 3/4*a*, 2/0*c*. R. T. for two months, 6/8*a*, 3/6*c*. Pop. 414. *See* p. 509.

Map Square 24.

EAST KILBRIDE (Lanark),

398¾ miles. No through fares. Departures *from* London as for Hamilton. Departures *for* London about 6 times daily. Pop. 4,787.

Map Square 40.

EAST LANGTON

(Leicester), 86¾ miles. Fares, 17/8*a*, 10/7*c*. R. T., double fare. Departures *from* London as for Market Harborough. Departures *for* London about 5 times daily. Pop. 244.

Map Square 18.

EAST LEAKE (Notts) from

Marylebone, 117¼ miles. Fares, 23/11*a*, 14/4*c*. R. T., double fare. Departures *from* London as for Loughborough (Central). Departures *for* London about 5 times daily. Pop. 973.

Map Square 18.

EASTLEIGH (Hants) from

Waterloo, 73 miles. Fares, 15/5*a*, 9/3*c*. R. T. for two months, 30/10*a*, 18/6*c*. Pop. 15,617.

Map Square 23.

W'loo.	Eastl.	Eastl.	W'loo.
AM 5.40	7.35	AM 1.22	3.58
5.50	8.26	7. 6	9.26
7. 0	10. 5	8.20*r*	10. 6
7.30	10.13	10.10	12. 0
8.30*s*	10.19	10.40*s*	12.22
9.30	11.35	PM12.38*r*	2.20
11.30*r*	1.37	12.48	3.36
PM 1.30*s*	3.12	1.42	4. 6
3.30*s*	5.12	2.38	4.20
3.40	6.19	3.46	6.16
4. 0	6.33	4.38*s*	6.26
5. 0	6.59	6.38*r*	8.20
5.30*r*	7.14	6.58	9.52
6. 0	8.23	8.20	10.50
6.34	9. 4	9.25	11.28
7.30	9.11	—	—
8. 0	10.23	—	—
8.55	11.35	—	—
10. 0	12. 5	—	—

Sunday Trains.

AM 8.45	12. 0	AM 1.22	3.58
9.45	12.18	7.47	11.16
11. 0*r*	12.40	10.13	12.11
12. 0*nr*	2.10	PM12.50*r*	2.27
PM 2. 0*r*	3.33	3.51	6. 7
5. 5	7.24	6. 5	8. 3
6. 0	8.13	6.47	9.37
7. 0*r*	8.39	8.24	10.53
8.15	10. 7	—	—
9.28	12. 2	—	—
—	—	—	—

n Noon.
r Restaurant Car.
s Refreshments served.

EAST LINTON (East

Lothian), 368¾ miles. Fares, 77/8*a*, 46/7*c*. R. T. for two months, 155/4*a*, 93/2*c*. Departures *from* London as for Dunbar. Departures *for* London about 4 times daily. Pop. 761.

Map Square 41.

EAST NORTON. *See*

Norton, East.

EASTOFT (Lincs), 176¾

miles. Fares, 22/1*c*. R. T for two months, 44/2*c*. Departures *from* London as for Goole. Departures *for* London about 4 times daily. Pop. 502.

Map Square 13.

EASTON (Dorset), 149¾

miles. No through fares. Departures *from* London as for Portland. Departures *for* London about 4 times daily.

Map Square 27.

No Sunday Trains.

EASTON COURT

(Hereford), 151 miles. Fares, 30/0*a*, 18/0*c*. R.T. for two months, 60/0*a*. Departures *from* London as for Tenbury Wells. Departures *for* London about 4 times daily.

Map Square 17.

EASTON LODGE
(Essex) from *Liverpool Street* and *St. Pancras*, 38¼ miles. Fares, 8/2*a*, 4/11*c*. R.T. for two months, 16/4*a*, 9/10*c*. Departures *from* London as for Dunmow. Departures *for* London about 5 times daily. Pop. 909.
Map Square 24.

EAST PUTNEY. See
PUTNEY, EAST.

EASTRIGGS (Dumfries),
313¾ miles. Fares, 63/6*a*, 38/1*c*. R. T. for two months, 127/0*a*, 76/2*c*. Departures *from* London as for Carlisle. Departures *for* London about 4 times daily. Pop. 1,780.
Map Square 44.

EASTRINGTON
NORTH (Yorks), 182 miles. Fares, 35/0*a*, 21/0*c*. R.T. for two months, 70/0*a*, 42/0*c*. Departures *from* London as for Goole or Howden North. Departures *for* London about 6 times daily. Pop. 424.
Map Square 13.

EASTRINGTON
SOUTH (Yorks), 182 miles. Fares, 35/0*a*, 21/0*c*. R.T. for two months, 70/0*a*, 42/0*c*. Departures *from* London as for Cudworth. Departures *for* London about 3 times daily. Pop. 424.
Map Square 13.

EAST RUDHAM (Nor-
folk), 129½ miles. Fares, 23/6*a*, 14/1*c*. R.T. for two months, 47/0*a*, 28/2*c*. Departures *from* London as for Massingham. Departures *for* London about 6 minutes earlier. Pop. 691.
Map Square 19.

EASTRY (Kent) from *Victoria, Holborn Viaduct* and *St. Paul's*. 77¾ miles. No through fares. Pop. 1,457.

VICT. (S.E.&O.)	HOL. V.	ST. P'LS.	ARR. at EASTRY
AM —	3.50*h*	—	7.21
10.40	—	—	1.40
PM 2. 5*d*	—	—	5.46
2. 8*e*	—	—	5.31
4.20	5.10*e*	5.12*e*	8.24
5.10*d*	—	—	7.59

No Sunday Trains.

Trains from Eastry.

Leave EASTRY	ST. P'LS.	HOL. V.	Arrive at VICT. S.E.&C.
AM 9. 7	—	—	11.35
PM 2.22	—	—	5.56
6.25*e*	—	—	10.25
6.40*d*	—	—	10.25

No Sunday Trains.
d Saturdays only.
e Saturdays excepted.
h Third Class only.

EAST VILLE (Lincoln)
from *King's Cross*, 117 miles. Fares, 24/4*a*, 14/7*c*. R.T., double fare. Departures *from* London as for Old Leake. Departures *for* London about 15 minutes earlier. Pop. 290.
Map Square 13.

EAST WINCH (Norfolk)
from *Liverpool Street*, 101½ miles. Fares, 21/1*a* 12/8*c*. R.T. for two months, 42/2*a*. Departures *from* London as for Swaffham (*via* King's Lynn). Departures *for* London about 6 times daily. Pop. 528.
Map Square 19.

EASTWOOD (Notts)
from *King's Cross*, 137½ miles. Fares, 26/5*a*, 15/10*c*. R. T., double fare. Departures *from* London as for Newthorpe. Departures *for* London about 5 minutes earlier. Pop. 5,074.
Map Square 13.

EASTWOOD (Yorks),
201¾ miles. Fares, 40/10*a*, 24/6*c*. R.T. for two months, 81/8*a*, 49/0*c*. Departures *from* London as for Hebden Bridge. Departures *for* London about 8 times daily.
Map Square 12.

EATON (Salop), 172¼ miles.
No through fares. Departures *from* London as for Craven Arms. Departures *for* London about 3 times daily.
Map Square 17.

EBBERSTON (Yorks),
225½ miles. No through fares. Departures *from* London as for Malton. Departures *for* London about 4 times daily. Pop. 554.
Map Square 8.

EBBW VALE (Monmouth)
from *Paddington*, 162 miles. Fares, 33/9*a*, 20/3*c*. R. T. for two months, 67/6*a* Pop. 35,383.
Map Square 21.

	PAD.	EBBW		EBBW	PAD.
AM	1. 0*g*	8.10	AM	9.20*r*	1. 0
	5.30	12.10		10.15*r*	2.30
	8.45*r*	1.16		11.20*r*	4.20
	9. 0	3.30	PM	2. 0*r*	6.15
	11.50*r*	5.17		3.15*r*	8.35
PM	1.10*r*	6.31		5. 5*r*	9.25
	3.35*r*	8. 5		9. 0	3.30
	5. 0*r*	9.56		—	—
	6. 0*r*	11. 5		—	—
	6.30*r*	11.57		—	—
	9.15*c*	6.13		—	—

Sunday Trains.

AM 1. 0	10.45	AM 7.40	3.35
9.10	3.15	PM 3.30*r*	8.25
PM12.30*r*	6.55	7.10	3.30
4.30	10.15	—	—
9.15	6.13	—	—

e Saturdays excepted.
g Mondays excepted.
r Restaurant Car.

EBCHESTER (Durham),
268 miles. No through fares. Departures *from* London as for Durham or Bishop Auckland. Departures *for* London about 6 times daily. Pop. 510
Map Square 3.

ECCLEFECHAN (Dum-
fries), 319½ miles. Fares, 64/9*a*, 38/10*c*. R. T. for two months, 129/6*a*, 77/8*c*. Departures *from* London as for Carlisle. Departures *for* London about 4 times daily. Pop. 680.
Map Square 44.

ECCLES (Lancs), 187¾
miles. Fares, 39/0*a*, 23/5*c*. R. T. for two months 78/0*a*. Departures *from* London as for Manchester (London Road). Departures *for* London about 5 times daily. Pop. 44,237.
Map Square 12.

ECCLESALL. Station at
MILL HOUSES.

ECCLESFIELD (Yorks),
165½ miles. Fares, 33/7*a*, 20/2*c*. R. T., double fare. Departures *from* London as for Sheffield (Victoria). Departures *for* London about 6 times daily. Pop. 22,404.
Map Square 12.

ECCLESHILL (Yorks),
192½ miles. Fares, 39/9*a*, 23/10*c*. R. T., double fare. Departures *from* London as for Bradford. Departures *for* London about 8 times daily. Pop. 342.
Map Square 12.

ECCLES ROAD (Norfolk)
from *Liverpool Street*, 104½ miles. Fares, 21/5*a*, 12/10*c*. R.T. for two months, 42/10*a*. Pop. (Eccles) 198.
Map Square 19.

L'POOL ST.	ECCLES	ECCLES	L'POOL ST.
AM 5. 5	8. 4	AM 7.18*r*	10.23
5.50	9.53	8.16	11.27
11.50*r*	3.25	9.31	12.40
PM 2.34	6. 5	11.12*r*	2.21
5.49*r*	8.55	PM 2. 0*r*	5.17
—	—	5. 7*r*	8.22
—	—	11.10	2.50

Sunday Trains.

AM 9.25	1. 0	PM 3.14	6.40
PM 3.25	6.50	11.12	3. 0

r Restaurant Car.

ECCLESTON PARK
(Lancs), 194½ miles. Fares, 40/7*a*, 24/4*c*. R.T. for two months, 81/2*a*, 48/8*c*. Departures *from* London as for Earlestown. Departures *for* London about 4 times daily.

ECKINGTON(Worcester),
122½ miles. No through fares. Departures *from* London as for Worcester. Departures *for* London about 3 times daily. Pop. 689.
Map Square 17.

ECKINGTON AND
RENISHAW (Derby) from *St. Pancras*, 152½ miles. Fares, 31/3*a*, 18/9*c*. R.T., double fare. Departures *from* London as for Chesterfield. Departures *for* London about 8 times daily. Pop. 12,164.
Map Square 13.

ECTON(Stafford),169½miles.
No through fares. Departures *from* London as for Leek. Departures *for* London about 4 times daily.
Map Square 12.

EDALE (Derby)

from *St. Pancras*, 169½ miles. Fares, 35/10*a*, 21/6*c*. R.T. for two months, 71/8*a*, 43/0*c*. Departures *from* London as for Hathersage. Departures *for* London about 5 times daily. Pop. 451.
Map Square 12.

EDDERTON (Ross),

617¾ miles. Fares, 110/0*a*, 66/0*c*. R. T. for two months, 220/0*a*. Departures *from* London as for Tain. Departures *for* London about 3 times daily. Pop. 536.
Map Square 34.

EDDLESTON (Peebles),

386½ miles. No through fares. Departures *from* London as for Peebles. Departures *for* London about 3 times daily. Pop. 527.
Map Square 41.

EDENBRIDGE (Kent)

from *Charing Cross, Cannon Street,* and *London Bridge*, 28¾ miles. Fares, 5/3*a*, 4/3*b*, 3/2*c*. R. T. for two months, 10/6*a*, 8/6*b*, 6/4*c*. Pop. 2,890.
Map Square 23.

Char +	Leave Can. St.	Lon. B.	Arr. at Edenbg.
AM —	4.44	5. 0	6.15
—	—	9.33*l*	10.47
10.55	—	11 3	12.26
PM12.55	—	1. 4	2.23
—	—	1.34*dl*	2.34
2. 3*e*	2. 8*d*	2.10	3.27
3.15*d*	—	3.21*d*	5.17
—	4.20*e*	4.23*e*	5.17
—	5.20*e*	5.23*e*	6.23
5.42*d*	—	5.48*d*	6.54
—	6. 0*e*	6. 3*e*	7. 8
—	—	6.27*el*	7.25
7.24*d*	7.28*e*	7.30	8.42
8.28	—	8.36	9.51
—	—	—	—

Sunday Trains.

AM 6.25	—	6.32	8. 4
PM 5.25	—	5.32	6.57
8.38	—	8.45	9.57
—	—	—	—

Trains from Edenbridge.

Leave Edenbge.	Lon. B.	Arrive at Can. St.	Char. +
AM 7.13	8.24	8.28	—
7.52	8.49	—	—
8.25	9.28	9.32	—
9.21	10.27	10.32	—
10.32	11.46	—	11.59
11.36	12.50	—	1. 0
PM 1.25	2.38	—	2.46
2.23	3.28*e*	—	3.42*d*
3.44	5. 2	—	5.14
4.56	5.56	—	—
6. 8	7.20	—	7.29
7.48	9. 2	—	9.15
8.53	10. 3	—	10.13
10.46	11.57	—	12.10

Sunday Trains.

AM10. 4	11.15	—	11.25
PM 8.56	10.11	—	10.24
—	—	—	—

d Saturdays only.
e Saturdays excepted.
l Low Level platform.

EDENBRIDGE (TOWN)

from *Victoria, Cannon Street,* and *London Bridge*, 25½ miles. Fares, 5/3*a*, 3/2*c*. R. T. for two months, 10/6*a*, 6/4*c*.
Map Square 23.

Vict.	Leave Can. St.	Lon. B.	Arr. at Edb. Tn.
AM 5.30	—	5.18	6.38
6.37	—	6.40	7.54
7.23	—	8. 7	9.16
9.10	—	9. 6	10.16
11. 5	—	10.35	11.58
12. 0*d*	12.16*d*	*k*12.20*d*	1.21
PM 1.20*e*	—	1.38*e*	2.37
1.25*d*	—	1.38*d*	2.41
—	—	2. 5*e*	3.38
2.25	—	2.25*d*	3.58
4. 0*e*	4.16*e*	*k*4.20*e*	5.18
—	—	4.44*e*	5.30
4.50	—	—	5.45
5. 5	—	5.21	6.19
5.48	—	—	7. 5
6. 6*e*	—	6. 8*e*	6.56
6. 6	—	6. 8	7.13
6.50	—	7. 0	8.13
8. 5	—	8.10	8.57
9. 3*h*	—	9.12*h*	10. 6
—	—	—	—
—	—	—	—

Sunday Trains.

AM 8.50	—	8.30	9.48
PM 1.14	—	1.10	2.17
2.30	—	—	3.38
7. 5	—	6.46	8. 5
—	—	—	—
—	—	—	—
—	—	—	—

Trains from Edenbridge Town.

Leave Eden. Tn.	Lon. B.	Arrive at Can. St.	Vict.
AM 7. 3	8.15	—	8.24
7.39	8.37	—	8.40
8.14	9.15	—	9.19
8.32	9.32	—	9.40
9.13	10. 4	—	10.12
9.27	10.38	—	—
9.55	10.55	—	10.46
10.23	—	—	11.35
11.14	12.13	—	12.17
11.41	12.44	—	12.35
PM12. 6	1.42	—	1.26
1.49	2.58	—	—
2.40	4. 0	—	3.45
5.27	6.36	—	6.29
6.54	7.56	—	8.27
9.19	10.25	—	10.10
—	—	—	—
—	—	—	—
—	—	—	—

Sunday Trains.

AM 9. 4	10.18	—	10.20
PM12.29	—	—	1.40
5.25	—	—	6.34
8. 8	9.17	—	9. 0
8.51	—	—	9.47
—	—	—	—
—	—	—	—
—	—	—	—

d Saturdays only.
e Saturdays excepted.
h Tuesdays and Fridays only.
k Departs from or arrives at London Bridge (S.E. & C.) Station.

EDEN PARK (Kent)

from *Charing Cross, Cannon Street,* and *London Bridge*, 13 miles. Fares, 2/3*a*, 1/9*b*, 1/4*c*. R. T. for two days, 4/4*a*, 3/1*b*, 2/7*c*. Pop. 3,505. *See* pp. 544-547.

EDGEBOLD (Salop), 157¼

miles. No through fares. Departures *from* London as for Shrewsbury. Departures *for* London about 3 times daily.

EDGE HILL (Lancs), 199¼

miles. Fares, 41/3*a*, 24/9*c*. R. T. for two months, 82/6*a*, 49/6*c*. Departures *from* London as for Liverpool (Lime Street). Departures *for* London about 6 times daily. Pop. 31,493.
Map Square 12.

EDGWARE (Middlesex)

from *King's Cross, Moorgate Street,* and *Broad Street*, 11¼ miles. Fares, from King's Cross, 1/9½*a*, 1/5*b*, 1/1*c*. R. T. for two days, 3/7*a*, 2/10*b*, 2/2*c*. From Moorgate Street and Broad Street, 2/3½*a*, 1/10*b*, 1/4½*c*. R. T. for two days, 4/7*a*, 3/8*b*, 2/8*c*. Pop. 1,516. *See* pp. 518-522.
Map Square 23.

EDGWARE ROAD from

Mansion House, Charing Cross, Victoria, South Kensington, High Street, Praed Street, Baker Street, King's Cross, Moorgate Street, Aldgate, and all intermediate Stations. Also to and from Hammersmith, Uxbridge Road, and Kensington (Addison Road) about every 12 minutes throughout the day. *See* back of Map.
Map Square 60 *No.* 3.

ANOTHER ROUTE (Bakerloo

Tube). *See* back of Map.

EDINBURGH (WAVERLEY)

from *King's Cross*, 392¾ miles. Fares, 81/8*a*, 49/0*c*. R. T. for two months, 163/4*a*, 98/0*c*. Pop. 420,264.
Map Square 41.

King's +	Edin.	Edin.	King's +
AM 4.45	1.42	AM10. 0*r*	6.15
9.50*r*	6. 5	10.15*r*	6.30
10. 0*r*	6.15	PM 1.45*r*	10. 0
11.50*r*	8.25	5.15	3.25
PM 1.15*r*	9.40	7.40	6. 0
8.25	6. 6	10.35*e*	6.50
11.40	7.40	10.50	7. 5
—	—	—	—
—	—	—	—
—	—	—	—
—	—	—	—

Sunday Trains.

AM11.30*r*	8.30	AM11.15*r*	8.15
PM 8.25	6. 6	PM 7.40	6. 0
11.40	7.40	10.50	7. 5
—	—	—	—
—	—	—	—
—	—	—	—
—	—	—	—

r Restaurant Car.

EDINBURGH—continued.

ANOTHER ROUTE (PRINCE'S STREET) from *Euston*, 399¾ miles. Fares as above.

EUSTON	EDIN.	EDIN.	EUSTON
AM 2.35	3.20	AM10. 0r	6.25
5. 0	4. 0	10.10r	7.30
6.45r	6. 0	PM 1.30r	10. 0
10. 0r	6.15	5.35r	5. 0
11.35r	9.21	9.20e	6.55
PM 1.30r	10.10	10.30	7.15
11. 0d	8.10	—	—
11.35e	7.50	—	—
—	—	—	—

Sunday Trains.

AM11.30r	8.45	AM10. 0	7.30
PM11.35	7.50	PM 5.40r	5. 0
—	—	10.30	7.30

d Saturdays only.
e Saturdays excepted.
r Restaurant Car.

ANOTHER ROUTE (WAVERLEY) from *St. Pancras*, 406 miles. Fares as above.

ST. PAN.	EDIN.	EDIN.	ST. PAN.
AM 4.25	3.54	AM 9.45r	7.15
9. 0r	6.19	10.40r	7.55
11.45r	8.57	PM 9.50	8. 3
PM 9.15	7. 5	—	—
—	—	—	—

Sunday Trains.

PM 9.15	7. 5	PM 9.50	8. 3
—	—	—	—

r Restaurant Car.

The Royal Hotel, Princes Street. Leading Hotel. Officially appointed by the leading Automobile Club. Moderate Tariff. Telegrams: "Welcome, Edinburgh." Telephone No. 9304 Central (five lines). *See advt. p.* **164**.

North British Station Hotel. Owned and managed by the L. & N. E. Rly. Telegrams: "British, Edinburgh." For particulars apply to the MANAGER. *See advt. p.* **165**.

Caledonian Railway Company's Princes Street Station Hotel. Most modern in Edinburgh. Telegrams: "Luxury." Telephone 8702 (Private Branch Exchange). *See advt. p.* **166**.

Darling's Regent Hotel, 21, Waterloo Place. Family and Commercial Temperance Hotel. Personal Management of Miss DARLING. *See advt. p.* **167**.

Imperial (late Milne's) **Hotel,** Leith Street. Bed, Breakfast and Bath from 6/6. *See advt. p.* **163**.

The Cockburn Hotel (First-class Temperance). Adjoining Waverley Station. Overlooking Princes Street Gardens. The centre for business, pleasure, and convenience. Passenger Elevators. Electric Light. Proprietor, JAMES P. MACPHERSON.

EDINBURGH—continued.

Cranston's Waverley Temperance Hotel, Old Waverley, Princes Street. Recently entirely reconstructed and Refurnished. Elevator and Electric Light. Inclusive Charge for Bed, Breakfast, Attendance and Bath, 7/6. Established over half a century.

EDINGTON (Somerset),

140⅛ miles. Fares, 29/2a, 17/6c. R. T. for two months, 58/4a. Departures *from* London as for Glastonbury. Departures *for* London about 5 times daily. Pop. 415.
Map Square 22.

EDINGTON (Wilts) from

Paddington, 91½ miles. Fares, *via* Theale, 19/0a, 11/5c. R. T. for two months, 38/0a; *via* Westbury, 19/10a, 11/11c. R. T. for two months, 39/8a, 23/10c. Departures *from* London as for Lavington or Westbury (Wilts). Departures *for* London about 6 times daily. Pop. 726.
Map Square 22.

EDLINGHAM (Northumberland), 312½ miles. No through fares. Departures *from* London as for Alnwick. Departures *for* London about 4 times daily. Pop. 73.
Map Square 3.

EDMONTHORPE

(Leicester) from *St. Pancras*, 104 miles. Fares, 21/0a, 12/7c. R. T., double fare. Departures *from* London as for Bourne. Departures *for* London about 4 times daily. Pop. 207.
Map Square 18.

EDMONTON, LOWER

(Middlesex) from *Liverpool Street*, 8½ miles. Fares, 1/3a, 1/0b, 0/9c. R. T. for two days, 2/6a, 1/11b, 1/4c. Pop. (Edmonton) 66,807. *See* pp. 526, 527, 534-536.

EDROM (Berwick), 351½

miles. Fares, 75/0a, 45/0c. R. T. for two months, 150/0a, 90/0c. Departures *from* London as for Berwick-on-Tweed or St. Boswells. Departures *for* London about 3 times daily. Pop. 1,119.
Map Square 41.

EDWALTON (Notts) from

St. Pancras, 121 miles. Fares, 24/10a, 14/11c. R. T., double fare. Departures *from* London as for Melton Mowbray. Departures *for* London about 4 times daily. Pop. 205.
Map Square 13.

EDWINSTOWE (Notts)

from *King's Cross*, 140⅛ miles. Fares, 29/0a, 17/5c. R. T. double fare. Pop. 883.
Map Square 13.

KING's+	ED'STWE.	ED'STWE.	KING's+
AM 5. 5	10.27	AM 7.36r	1. 5
PM 1.50r	7. 5	10.59	3.50
—	—	PM 2.40h	6.30
—	—	4.44	9. 0

No Sunday Trains.

h Fridays only.
r Restaurant Car.

EDWINSTOWE—contd.

ANOTHER ROUTE from *St. Pancras*, 151½ miles. Fares as above.

ST. PAN.	ED'STWE.	ED'STWE.	ST. PAN.
AM 4.25	10.59	AM10.27r	4.10
11.45r	4.44	PM 1. 7r	9. 5
—	—	7. 5	4.20

No Sunday Trains.
r Restaurant Car.

ANOTHER ROUTE from *Marylebone*, 149½ miles. Fares as above.

M'BONE.	ED'STWE.	ED'STWE	M'BONE.
AM 2.32	7.36	AM 9.17r	1.13
8.45r	12.45	10.27r	3. 0
10. 0r	2.34	PM 3. 9r	6.38
PM12.15r	4.44	7.12	3.57
3.20r	6.39	10. 1d	3.57
6.20dr	9.45	—	—

No Sunday Trains.
d Saturdays only.
r Restaurant Car.

EDZELL (Forfar), 50¼ miles.

Fares, 98/11a, 59/4c. R. T. for two months, 197/10a, 118/8c. Departures *from* London as for Brechin. Departures *for* London about 3 times daily. Pop. 1,053.
Map Square 38.

Panmure Hotel. Every comfort. Spacious Lounge. Electric Light and Heating. Golf. Garage. *See advt.* p. **167**.

EFAIL ISAF (Glamorgan),

163½ miles. Fares, 33/2a, 19/11c. R. T. for two months, 66/4a, 39/10c. Departures *from* London as for St. Fagans. Departures *for* London about 5 times daily.

EFFINGHAM (Surrey) from

Waterloo, 21½ miles. Fares, 4/5a, 2/8c. R. T. for two months 8/10a, 5/4c. Pop. 605.
Map Square 23.

W'LOO.	EFFING.	EFFING.	W'LOO.
AM 6. 5	6.52	AM 7.18	8.19
6.45	7.45	7.39	8.30
7. 5	7.53	8. 1	8.48
7.45	8.42	8.54	9.21
8. 5	8.52	8.40	9.38
8.45	9.42	9.14	10. 0
9. 5	9.52	9.36	10.38
9.45	10.47	9.51e	10.36
10. 5	10.55	10.21	11. 6
10.45	11.44	10.36	11.38
11. 5	11.52	11.11	11.56
11.45	12.42	11.36	12.38
PM12.15	12.52	PM12.15	1. 0
12.45	1.42	12.36	1.38
1. 5	1.52	1.17	2. 2
1.35d	2.22	1.36	2.38
1.45	2.42	2.15	3. 0
2. 5	2.52	2.53	3.38
2.45	3.42	3.15	4. 0
3. 5	3.52	3.36	4.38
3.45	4.42	4.15	5. 0
4. 5	4.52	4.29	5.38
4.45	5.44	5.25	6.10
5. 5	5.52	5.36	6.38
5.37e	6.24	6. 6	6.52
5.45d	6.42	6.36	7.38
5.45e	6.58	7.15	8. 0
6. 5	6.52	7.36	8.38
6.38e	7.24	8.15	9. 0
6.45	7.42	8.36	9.38
7. 5	7.52	9.15	10. 0
7.45	8.50	9.36	10.38
8. 5	8.58	10.11	10.56
8.45	9.42	10.36	11.38
9. 5	9.52	—	—
9.45	10.45	—	—
10. 5	10.52	—	—

EFFINGHAM—continued.
Sunday Trains.

W'LOO	EFFING.	EFFING.	W'LOO.
AM 8.18	9.20	AM 10. 6	10.55
8.38	9.54	10.19	11.24
10. 8	11. 2	11. 5	11.55
10.38	11.40	AM 12. 5	12.55
11. 8	12. 2	12.19	1.24
11.38	12.40	1. 5	1.55
PM 12. 8	1. 2	1.19	2.24
12.38	1.42	2. 5	2.55
1. 8	2. 2	2.19	3.24
2. 8	3. 2	4. 5	4.55
2.38	3.40	4.19	5.24
3. 8	4. 2	6. 5*	6.55
4.38	5.40	6.19	7.24
5. 8	6. 2	7. 5	7.55
5.38	6.40	7.19	8.24
6. 8	7. 2	8.15	9. 5
6.38	7.40	8.22	9.24
7. 8	8. 2	9. 5	9.55
7.38	8.42	9.19	10.24
8. 8	9. 2	10. 5	10.55
8.38	9.40	10.19	11.24
9. 8	10. 2	—	—

d Saturdays only.
e Saturdays excepted.

EGGESFORD (Devon)
from *Waterloo*, 193¾ miles. Fares, 36/11a, 22/2c. R. T. for two months, 73/10a, 44/4c. Pop. 104.
Map Square 26.

W'LOO	E'FORD	E'FORD	W'LOO.
AM 9. 0r	2.10	AM 9.21r	1.56
11. 0r	4.59	10.27r	3.50
PM 1. 0r	6.38	PM 1.35r	6. 0
3. 0	8. 3	2. 7	7.40
—	—	3. 4r	8.30
—	—	4.37	10.50
—	—	6. 6h	3.58

No Sunday Trains.

h Via Eastleigh.
r Restaurant Car.

EGGINTON (Derby) from
King's Cross, 153¾ miles. Fares, 26/5a, 15/10c. R. T., double fare. Departures *from* London as for Derby (Friar Gate). Departures *for* London about 10 minutes later. Pop. 431.
Map Square 17.

EGHAM (Surrey) from
Waterloo, 21 miles. Fares, 3/9a, 2/3c. R. T. for eight days, 7/6a, 4/6c. Pop. 13,725.
Map Squares 23 and 73.

W'LOO	EGHAM	EGHAM	W'LOO.
AM 5.10	6.23	AM 7.33	8.17
6.54	7.46	8. 0	8.47
7.54	8.47	8.37	9.17
8.54	9.46	9.13	9.47
9.54	10.46	9.38	10.17
10.54	11.50	10.35	11.17
PM 12.48	1.30	11.39	12.31
1.18d	1.57	PM 12.39	1.27
1.48	2.28	1.39	2.27
2.18d	2.58	2.39	3.27
2.48	3.27	4.39	5.27
3.48e	4.28	5.39	6.27
3.48d	4.36	6.39	7.27
4.48e	5.23	7.39	8.27
4.48d	5.36	8.39	9.27
5.18e	5.57	9.47	10.37
5.48	6.27	11. 8e	12. 5
6.18e	6.57	11. 8d	12. 8
6.48	7.27	—	—
7.54	8.47	—	—
9.24	10.16	—	—
10.24	11.16	—	—

EGHAM—continued.
Sunday Trains.

W'LOO.	EGHAM	EGHAM	W'LOO.
AM 8.18	9.14	AM 9.24	10.30
9.18	10. 1	9.37	11.43
PM 12.18	1.13	11.35	12.43
2.18	3.14	PM 1.10	2. 3
4.18	5.10	4.41	5.28
5.58	6.52	6.35	7.28
7.48	8.39	8.36	9.28
9.18	10.12	9.27	10.18
—	—	9.40	10.28

d Saturdays only.
e Saturdays excepted.

EGLOSKERRY (Cornwall)
from *Waterloo*, 228 miles. Fares, 46/8a, 28/0c. R. T. for two months, 93/4a, 56/0c. Departures *from* London as for Launceston. Departures *for* London about 4 times daily. Pop. 366.
Map Square 26.

EGREMONT (Cumberland), 297½ miles. Fares, 61/10a, 37/1c. R. T. for two months, 123/8a. Departures *from* London as for Sellafield. Departures *for* London about 4 times daily. Pop. 6,584.
Map Square 6.

EGTON (Yorks) 239½ miles.
Fares, 49/10a, 29/11c. R. T. for two months, 99/8a, 59/10c. Departures *from* London as for Whitby. Departures *for* London about 3 times daily. Pop. 1,026.
Map Square 8.

ELBURTON CROSS
(Devon) from *Paddington*, 227½ miles. Fares, 47/1a, 28/5c. R. T. for two months, 94/2a, 56/10c. Departures *from* London as for Yealmpton. Departures *for* London about 4 times daily.
Map Square 6.

ELDERSLIE (Renfrew), 412 miles. Fares, 82/6a, 49/6c. R. T. for two months, 165/0a, 99/0c. Departures *from* London as for Kilmarnock. Departures *for* London about 4 times daily. Pop. 3,092.

ELEPHANT AND
CASTLE, from *Ludgate Hill, St. Paul's, Victoria*, and *Moorgate Street*, 5¼ miles. Fares from Victoria, 0/9d, 0/7b, 0/5½c. R. T. for two days, 1 2a, 1/0b, 0/9c. From Ludgate Hill, 0/4½a, 0/3½b, 0/2½c. R. T. for two days, 0/9a, 0/7b, 0/4c. See pp. 558-563.
Map Square 70.

ANOTHER ROUTE (City and South London and Bakerloo Tubes.) *See* back of Map.

ELFORD (Stafford), 134 miles. Fares, 23/9a, 14/3c. R.T., double fare. Departures *from* London as for Burton-on-Trent. Departures *for* London about 4 times daily. Pop. 38.
Map Square 17.

ELGIN from *King's Cross*,
via Aberdeen 603¼ miles. Fares, 106/3a, 63/9c. R. T. for two months, 212/6a, 127/6c. Pop. 9,376.
Map Square 35.

KING's +	ELGIN	ELGIN	KING's +
AM 4.45	9.22h	AM 6.40	10. 0h
PM 8.20e	9.56k	9.35	3.25k
11.25e	4.52h	PM 4.30	7.25k

Sunday Trains.

PM 7.45	9.56k	—	—
—	—	—	—

e Saturdays excepted.
h P.M.
k A.M.

ANOTHER ROUTE from
Euston, via Dunkeld, 581½ miles. Fares as above.

EUSTON	ELGIN	ELGIN	EUSTON
PM 1.30er	6.35h	AM 7.20r	10.45
7.30erv	9.20h	9.35r	5. 0h
7.40er	9.50h	PM 2.30	7.40
11.35e	4.20l	7.40kr	7.30l

Sunday Trains.

PM 7.50r	10.20h	—	—
11.35	4.20l	—	—

e Saturdays excepted.
h A.M.
k Via Inverness.
l P.M.
r Restaurant Car.
v Commences July 27.

ANOTHER ROUTE from
Euston, via Aberdeen, 620 miles. Fares as above.

EUSTON	ELGIN	ELGIN	EUSTON
PM 1.30er	8.30h	AM 6.40r	10.45l
7.50er	9.56h	9.32	5. 0h
11.35e	4.52l	PM 4.30	8. 0h

Sunday Trains.

PM 7.50r	9.56	—	—
11.35	4.52l	—	—

d Saturdays only.
e Saturdays excepted.
h A.M.
l P.M.
r Restaurant Car.

ELHAM (Kent), 74 miles. Fares, *via* Canterbury, 14/7*a*, 11/8*b*, 8/9*c*. R. T. for two months, 29/2*a*, 23/4*b*; *via* Shorncliffe, 14/7*a*, 11/8*b*, 8/9*c*. R. T. for two months, 29/2*a*, 23/4*b*. Departures *from* London as for Shorncliffe or Canterbury West. Departures *for* London about 5 times daily. Pop. 1,242.
Map Square 24.

Station closed on Sundays.

ELIE (Fife), 437 miles. Fares, 88/4*a*, 53/0*c*. R. T. for two months, 176/8*a*, 106/0*c*. Departures *from* London as for St. Andrews. Departures *for* London about 3 times daily. Pop. 2,448.
Map Square 41.

ELLAND (Yorks), 191 miles. Fares, 39/2*a*, 23/6*c*. R. T. for two months, 78/4*a*, 47/0*c*. Departures *from* London as for Brighouse. Departures *for* London about 8 times daily. Pop. 10,554.

ELLENBROOK (Lancs), 192 miles. Fares, 39/7*a*, 23/9*c*. R.T. for two months, 79/2*a*, 47/6*c*. Departures *from* London as for Manchester (London Road). Departures *for* London about 6 times daily.

ELLERBY (Yorks), 205½ miles. Fares, 37/1*a*, 22/3*c*. R. T. for two months, 74/2*a*, 44/6*c*. Departures *from* London as for Hull (Paragon). Departures *for* London about 8 times daily. Pop. 153.
Map Square 13.

ELLESMERE (Salop) from *Euston*, 181¾ miles. Fares, 35/3*a*, 21/2*c*. R.T. for two months, 70/6*a*, Pop. 1,831.
Map Square 12.

EUSTON	E'MERE	E'MERE	EUSTON
AM 2.35	8.40	AM 8.45	1.45
5. 0	10.23	11.40*t*	5.35
8.30*r*	1.40	PM 1. 4*r*	5.50
10. 0*r*	2.34	2.14*r*	7.30
11.50*r*	4.35	4.13*er*	9. 5
PM 2.35*t*	7.15	4.13*dr*	9.15
4. 5*r*	9.28	5.42*r*	10.45
11. 0*d*	3. 0	9.42	5. 0
9.30*e*	3. 7	—	—
—	—	—	—
—	—	—	—
—	—	—	—
—	—	—	—
—	—	—	—
—	—	—	—

Sunday Trains.

PM 9.15	3. 7	PM 9.40	5. 0
—	—	—	—
—	—	—	—
—	—	—	—
—	—	—	—

d Saturdays only.
e Saturdays excepted.
r Restaurant Car.
t Tea Car.

ELLESMERE PORT (Cheshire), 189¾ miles. Fares, 39/0*a*, 23/5*c*. R.T. for two months, 78/0*a*, 46/10*c*. Departures *from* London as for Hooton. Departures *for* London about 10 times daily. Pop 13,075.
Map Square 12.

ELLINGHAM (Norfolk), 113¼ miles. Fares, 23/9*a*, 14/3*c*. R. T. for two months, 47/6*a*. Departures *from* London as for Ditchingham (*via* Beccles). Departures *for* London about 7 times daily. Pop. 286.
Map Square 19.

ELLIOT (Forfar), 467¼ miles. No through fares. Departures *from* London as for Dundee or Forfar. Departures *for* London about 4 times daily.
Map Square 38.

ELLON (Aberdeen), 542¼ miles. Fares, 104/0*a*, 62/5*c*. R. T. for two months, 208/0*a*, 124/10*c*. Departures *from* London as for Fraserburgh or Peterhead. Departures *for* London about 3 times daily. Pop. 3,437.
Map Square 35.

ELMERS END (Kent) from *Charing Cross, Cannon Street*, and *London Bridge*, 11¼ miles. Fares, 1/11*a*, 1/7*b*, 1/2*c*. R. T. for two days, 3/10*a*, 2/11*b*, 2/2*c*. *See* pp. 544-547.

ELMESTHORPE (Leicester) from *Euston*, 104 miles. Fares, 20/2*a*, 12/1*c*. R. T., double fare. Departures *from* London as for Hinckley. Departures *for* London about 9 times daily. Pop. 84.
Map Square 18.

ELMSTEAD WOODS (Kent) from *Charing Cross, Cannon St.*, and *London Bridge*, 11 miles. Fares, 2/4*a*, 1/11*b*, 1/5*c*. R.T. for two days, 4/8*a*, 3/10*b*, 2/10*c*.

Leave CHAR. +	CAN. ST.	LON. B.	Arr. at ELMS'D
AM —	7.56	8. 0	8.24
—	9.36	9.39	10. 3
11.15	—	11.23	11.49
11.42	—	11.49	12.16
PM —	12.48*d*	12.51*d*	1.17
12.50*e*	—	12.58*e*	1.29
—	1.12*d*	1.15*d*	1.30
1.34*d*	—	1.41*d*	2. 3
1.50*e*	—	1.58*e*	2.21
—	2. 4*d*	2. 7*d*	2.28
2.17*d*	—	2.23*d*	2.43
2.30*e*	—	2.37*e*	3. 0
2.50*d*	—	2.57*d*	3.19
3.50	—	3.57	4.16
—	4.44*e*	4.47*e*	5.12
4.55*d*	—	5. 1*d*	5.23
—	5. 4*e*	5. 7*e*	5.25
5.35*d*	—	5.41*d*	6. 1
—	5.40*e*	5.43*e*	6. 3
5.50*e*	—	5.57*e*	6.19
6.10*e*	—	6.17*e*	6.36
6.38*e*	—	6.45*e*	7. 8
6.40*d*	—	6.48*d*	7.15
7. 6*e*	—	7.13*e*	7.37
9. 0	—	9. 6	9.24
10. 0	—	10. 6	10.25
10.43	—	10.51	11.11
—	—	—	—
—	—	—	—
—	—	—	—
—	—	—	—
—	—	—	—
—	—	—	—
—	—	—	—

Sunday Trains.

AM 7. 5	—	7.11	7.38
8. 5	—	8.12	8.33
9.30	—	9.36	9.58
11.15	—	11.23	11.49
PM 1. 0	—	1. 7	1.32
3. 5	—	3.13	3.37
6. 0	—	6. 6	6.30
—	—	—	—
—	—	—	—
—	—	—	—
—	—	—	—

ELMSTEAD WOODS —*continued.*

Trains from Elmstead Woods.

Leave ELMST'D.	LON. B.	Arrive at CAN. ST.	CHAR. +
AM 6.42	7. 4	7. 8	—
7.52	8.10	—	8.19
8.33	8.56	9. 0	—
9. 1	9.18	—	9.27
9.41	9.58	—	10. 7
9.54	10.16	10.20	—
11.19	11.32	—	11.45
PM 12.10*e*	12.35	12.40	—
12.25*d*	12.54	12.58	—
1. 4	1.27	—	1.38
1.49*d*	2.12	—	2.20
1.50*e*	2.12	—	2.20
2.45	3. 7	—	3.19
4.12	4.36	4.40*e*	4.45*d*
5. 5*e*	5.27	—	5.38
5.59*e*	6.22	6.28	—
6. 3*d*	6.30	—	6.39
6.17*e*	6.44	—	6.54
6.48*e*	7. 8	7.12	—
8.30	8.54	9. 1	—
9.55	10.15	—	10.23
10.26	10.48	—	10.57
11.11	11.34	—	11.44

Sunday Trains.

AM 9.57	10.22	—	10.32
10.44	11. 6	—	11.13
PM 12.54	1.20	—	1.29
2.28	2.50	—	3. 0
6. 5	6.27	—	6.41
8.47	9. 7	—	9.18
9.16	9.38	—	—

d Saturdays only.
e Saturdays excepted.

ELMSWELL (Suffolk) from *Liverpool Street, via* Haughley, 86½ miles. Fares, 18/1*a*, 10/10*c*. R. T. for two months, 36/2*a*. Pop. 853.
Map Square 19.

L'PL ST.	E'WELL	E'WELL	L'PL ST.
AM 5. 0	8.13	AM 7. 9*r*	10.30
8.15*r*	10.52	8.47*r*	11.22
10.20	1. 2	11.23*r*	2. 3
PM 12.33*r*	3.21	PM 12.27	3.36
3.10*r*	5.25	2.17*r*	4.58
3.26	6.59	3.12	5.55
5.42	8.57	3.49	6.32
7.45*r*	10.35	4.27*h*	7.51
—	—	5.55*r*	9.22
—	—	7.23*r*	10. 0
—	—	—	—

Sunday Trains.

AM 9.20*r*	12.23	AM 8.10	11.38
11.30	3. 7	PM 2.17	7.10
PM 4.40	9.22	6.32*r*	9.10

h Wednesdays only.
r Restaurant Car.

ANOTHER ROUTE *via* Cambridge, 93½ miles. Fares as above.

L'PL ST.	E'WELL	E'WELL	L'PL ST.
AM 5. 5	8.47	AM 8.13	11.27
8.30*r*	11.24	10.52*r*	2.21
10. 5*h*	2.17	PM 1. 2*lr*	4. 2*k*
11.50*r*	3.12	1. 2	5. 9
PM 2.34	5.55	3.19	7.58
4.45	7.23	5.25*r*	8.33
5.49*r*	8.59	6.59	10.30
—	—	—	—

Sunday Trains.

AM 9.25	2.17	PM 3. 7	6.40
PM 3.25	6.32	—	—
—	—	—	—

h Wednesdays only.
k Arrives at S . Pancras Station.
l Commences July 23.
r Restaurant Car.

ELMTON AND CRES-WELL(Derby), 149¼ miles. Fares, 29/10a, 17/11c. R. T., double fare. Departures *from* London as for Mansfield. Departures *for* London about 8 times daily. Pop. 5,361.
Map Square 13.

ELRINGTON (Northumberland), 293½ miles. No through fares. Departures *from* London as for Hexham. Departures *for* London about 4 times daily.
Map Square 3.

ELSECAR (Yorks), 169 miles. Fares, 34/7a, 20/9c. R. T., double fare. Departures *from* London as for Chapeltown. Departures *for* London about 6 times daily. Pop. 2,438.
Map Square 12.

ELSENHAM (Essex) from *Liverpool Street*, 35½ miles. Fares, 7/8a, 4/7c. R.T. for two months, 15/4a. Pop. 408.
Map Square 19.

	L'PL. ST.	ELSEN.		ELSEN.	L'PL. ST.
AM	5.50	7.18	AM	7.27	8.57
	7.18	9. 2		8. 5	9.27
	10. 5	11.20		8.41	9.46
PM	12.29d	1.36		9.15	10.17
	12.48e	2.28		10.17	11.27
	1.19d	2.42	PM	12.40	2. 7
	2.48	4.20		1.58d	3.18
	4.15	5.26		2.56h	5. 9
	4.45	5.49		3.11k	5. 9
	5.49r	6.56		3.56r	5.17
	6.30	7.32		4.46r	6.10
	8.22d	9.31		6.25	7.58
	8.22e	9.43		7.10r	8.22
	—	—		9.25	10.30

Sunday Trains.

AM	8.12	9.33	AM	9.50	11.27
PM	1.50	3.43	PM	6.16	7.26

d Saturdays only.
e Saturdays excepted.
h Commencing July 23.
k Ceases to run after July 21.
r Restaurant Car.

ELSHAM (Lincoln), 170½ miles. Fares, 33/6a, 20/1c. R. T., double fare. Departures *from* London as for Thorne or Barnetby. Departures *for* London about 6 times daily. Pop. 424.
Map Square 13.

ELSLACK (Yorks) from *St. Pancras*, 225 miles. Fares, 42/6a, 25/6c. R. T., double fare. Departures *from* London as for Colne. Departures *for* London about 8 times daily. Pop. 85.
Map Square 7.

ELSTED (Sussex) from *Waterloo*, 60¾ miles. Fares, 12/8a, 7/7c. R.T. for two months, 25/4a, 15/2c. Departures *from* London as for Rogate. Departures *for* London about 5 minutes later. Pop. 197.
Map Square 23.

ELSTREE (Herts) from *Moorgate Street, King's Cross* (Met.), and *St. Pancras*, 12¼ miles. Fares, 2/8a, 1/7c. R. T., double fare. From Moorgate Street, 2/9a, 1/8c. R. T. for two months, 5/6a, 3/4c. Pop. 2,238. See pp. 507, 508.
Map Square 23.

ELSWICK (Northumberland), 269½ miles. No through fares. See trains to Newcastle-on-Tyne, and thence at frequent intervals during the day. Pop. 58,352.
Map Square 3.

ELTHAM (Kent) from *Charing Cross, Cannon Street*, and *London Bridge* 10 miles. Fares from Charing Cross, 2/1a, 1/8b, 1/3c. R T. for two days, 4/2a, 3/4b, 2/6c. Fares from Cannon Street, 1/8a, 1/4b, 1/0c. R. T. for two days, 3/4a, 2/8b, 2/0c. Pop. 28,308. See pp. 552-554.
Map Square 23.

ELTHAM (NEW) (Kent) from *Charing Cross*, 11 miles. Fares, 2/3a, 1/9b, 1/4c. R. T. for two days, 4/6a, 3/6b, 2/8c. Fares from Cannon Street, 1/11a, 1/7b, 1/2c. R. T. for two days, 3/10a, 3/2b, 2/4c. See pp. 552-554.

ELTON (Hunts) from *Euston*, 100¼ miles. Fares, 15/10a, 9/6c. R. T. for two months, 31/8a. Departures *from* London as for Oundle. Departures *for* London about 4 times daily. Pop. 607.
Map Square 18.

ELTON (Notts), 115¼ miles. Fares, 23/11a, 14/4c. R. T., double fare. Departures *from* London as for Bottesford. Departures *for* London about 4 times daily. Pop. 58.
Map Square 13.

ELVANFOOT (Lanark), 351¼ miles. Fares, 71/6a, 42/11c. R.T. for two months, 143/0a, 85/10c. Departures *from* London as for Lockerbie. Departures *for* London about twice daily.
Map Square 43.

ELY (Cambridge) from *Liverpool Street*, 70½ miles. Fares, 14/10a, 8/11c. R. T. for two months 29/8a. Pop. 7,690.
Map Square 19.

	L'POOL ST.	ELY		ELY	L'POOL ST.
AM	5. 5	6.58	AM	12.23	2.50
	5.50	8.35		7.16	9.27
	7.18d	10.18		8.40r	10.23
	8.30r	10.25		9.34	11.27
	10. 5	12. 9		10.41	12.40
	11.50r	1.43		11.25	2. 7
PM	12.48e	3.54	PM	12.30r	2.21
	1.19d	3.54		1.36lr	4. 2h
	2.34	4.22		1.36	5. 9
	4.15	6.19		3.25r	5.17
	4.45	6.28		4.14r	6.10
	5.49r	7.41		5. 0	7.58
	7.10r	9. 1		6.26r	8.22
	10.12	12.10		6.39r	8.33
	—	—		8.39	10.30

Sunday Trains.

AM	8.12	10.46	AM	12.23	3. 0
	9.25	11.31		8.35	11.27
PM	1.50	5. 3	PM	4.32	6.40
	3.25	5.24		5.36	7.40
	9.12	12. 0		7.57	9.40
	—	—		—	—

d Saturdays only.
e Saturdays excepted.
h Arrives at St. Pancras Station.
l Commencing July 23.
r Restaurant Car.

Lamb Hotel. (Leading Family.) Headquarters Royal Automobile Club. Motors for hire. Garage. Omnibus meets trains. Telephone No 4.
Proprietor, KELSICK INMAN.

Bell Hotel. Principal Family and Commercial. Opposite the Cathedral. Garage and Inspection Pit. Cars for hire. Omnibus meets all trains. Hot Lunch daily, 1.15. Telephone 19. Telegrams, "Bell Hotel," Ely.
C. J. M. HOBSON, Proprietor.

ELY (Glamorgan) from *Paddington*, 155½ miles. Fares, 32/4a, 19/5c. R.T. for two months, 64/8a.
Map Square 21.

	PAD.	ELY		ELY	PAD.
AM	1. 0g	7.36	AM	9.35r	1. 0
	5.30	10.36		10.29r	2.30
	8.45r	1. 0		11.50r	4.20
	11.50r	3.10	PM	2.20r	6.15
PM	1.10r	5.27		3.45r	8.35
	3.35r	6.50		5.38r	9.25
	5. 0r	8.50		10.15	3.30
	6. 0r	9.51		—	—
	6.30r	10.50		—	—
	—	—		—	—

Sunday Trains.

AM	1. 0	10. 1	PM	1.55r	8.25
	9.10	2.36		9.22	3.30
PM	9.15	7.36		—	—

g Mondays excepted.
r Restaurant Car.

EMBLETON (Cumberland), 308¾ miles. Fares, 62/4a, 37/5c. R.T. for two months, 124/8a, 74/10c. Departures *from* London as for Keswick. Departures *for* London about 6 times daily. Pop. 377.
Map Square 6.

EMBO (Sutherland), 653¾ miles. No through fares. Departures *from* London as for Lairg. Departures *for* London about 3 times daily. Pop. 495.
Map Square 34.

EMBSAY (Yorks) from *St. Pancras*, 220¼ miles. Fares, 43/7a, 26/2c. R. T., double fare. Departures *from* London as for Skipton. Departures *for* London about 5 times daily. Pop. 845.
Map Square 7.

EMNETH (Norfolk) from *Liverpool Street*, 96 miles. Fares, 17/11a, 10/9c. R.T. for two months, 35/10a. Departures *from* London as for Wisbech. Departures *for* London about 4 times daily. Pop. 1,082.
Map Square 19.

EMSWORTH (Hants) from *London Bridge, Victoria*, and *Clapham Junction*, 76¼ miles. Fares, 13/11a, 8/4c. R. T. for two months, 27/10a, 16/8c. Pop. 2,303.
Map Square 28.

	Leave			Arr at
	VICT.	CLAP. J.	LON. B.	EMSW.
AM	6.18	6.25	6.35	9. 7
	8.55	7.56	—	11.40
	10.15	10.22	10.22	1.47
	11.55k	—	11.50k	2.57
PM	1.40	1.47e	1.50	4.29
	1.55k	e2. 2k	2. 5k	5.33
	3.55	4. 2	4.50	6.57
	4.53	5. 0	—	7.11
	—	—	5. 5	8. 5
	5.45k	—	6. 0k	8.35
	7.20	7.27	7.15	10. 8
	—	—	—	—
	—	—	—	—
	—	—	—	—

Sunday Trains.

AM	6.55k	7. 2k	7. 2k	11.11
	9. 0	9. 7	8.55	11.31
	9.55	—	—	2.19
PM	1.14k	1.21k	1.10k	5.12
	7. 0	7. 7	6.38	9.42
	—	—	—	—

ELY (Cambridge)—**LAMB HOTEL** Principal Hotel. *See advt. above.*

EMSWORTH—*continued.*

Trains from Emsworth.

Leave Emsw	Arrive at Lon. B.	Clap. J.	Vict.
AM 6.51*g*	9.50	—	9.22
6.56*f*	9.50	—	—
7.15	—	—	10.28
7.40	9.58	—	—
8.20	10.45	10.45	10.53
8.40	10.55	—	—
9.50	12. 8	—	12. 0
10.55	—	—	1.10
11.58	3.32	3.22	3.32
PM 1.48	4.27	4.26	4.34
3.52	—	—	6.50
5.16	7.48	7.31	7.39
5.43	—	8.39	8.33
7. 1*d*	10. 0	9.37	9.45
7.41	10. 8	9.53	10. 1
9.20*k*	12.59	12.50	1. 0

Sunday Trains.

AM 7.13	10.45	10.23	10.32
9.27*k*	—	12.49	1. 0
PM 3.54*k*	—	—	7. 0
5.25	—	7.49	7.56
6.18	8.50	8.33	8.42
7.42*k*	11.34	10.46	10.55

e Saturdays excepted.
f Mondays only.
g Mondays excepted.
k *Via* Hove.

ENDON (Stafford), 152¼ miles. Fares, 31/10*a*, 19/1*c*. R. T. for two months, 63/8*a* 38/2*c*. Departures *from* London as for Stoke-on-Trent. Departures *for* London about 5 times daily. Pop. 1,583.
Map Square 12.

ENFIELD (Middlesex) from *King's Cross*, 9 miles, *Moorgate Street*, and *Broad Street*. Fares from King's Cross, 1/9½*a*, 1/5*b*, 1/1*c*. R. T. for two days, 3/7*a*, 2/10*b*, 2/2*c*. From Moorgate Street and Broad Street, 1/10½*a*, 1/6*b*, 1/1½*c*. R. T. for two days, 3/9*a*, 3/0*b*, 2/3*c*. Pop. 60,738. *See* pp. 511-517.
Map Square 23.

ENFIELD LOCK for Enfield Highway (Middlesex), from *Liverpool Street*, 12 miles. Fares, 1/10½*a*, 1/6*b*, 1/1½*c*. R. T. for two days, 3/9*a*, 3/0*b*, 2/2½*c*. *See* pp. 526, 527.

ENFIELD TOWN (Middlesex) from *Liverpool Street*, 10¾ miles. Fares, 1/9½*a*, 1/5*b*, 1/1*c*. R. T. for two days, 3/7*a*, 2/10*b*, 2/2*c*. *See* pp. 534-536.

ENTHORPE (Yorks), 195½ miles. No through fares. Departures *from* London as for Market Weighton. Departures *for* London about 3 times daily.
Map Square 8.

ENTWISTLE (Lancs), 203¼ miles. No through fares. Departures *from* London as for Bolton (*via* Manchester). Departures *for* London about 6 times daily.
Map Square 12.

EPPING (Essex) from *Fenchurch Street* or *Liverpool Street*, 16½ miles. Fares, from Fenchurch Street, 3/7*a*, 2/10*b*, 2/2*c*. R.T. for two months, 7/0*a*, 5/3*b*, 3/9½*c*. From Liverpool Street, 3/7*a*, 2/11*b*, 2/2*c*. R. T. for two months, 7/2*a*, 5/6½*b*, 3/11½*c*. Pop. 4,197. *See* pp. 541-544.
Map Square 23.

EPSOM (Surrey) from *Waterloo*, 14¼ miles. Fares, 2/6*a*, 1/6*c*. R. T. for two days 4/11*a*, 3/0*c*. Pop. 18,804. *See* pp. 583, 584.

ANOTHER ROUTE from *London Bridge* and *Victoria*, 15¼ miles. Fares from London Bridge or Victoria, 2/6*a*, 1/6*c*. R. T. for two days, 4/11*a*, 3/0*c*. *See* pp. 564-566, 571-574.
Map Square 23.

Spread Eagle Hotel. Bed, Sitting, Smoking, Coffee Rooms. Hot Luncheon daily from 1 o'clock. Commercials on special terms. Telephone, 585 Epsom.
Mrs. L. KEEBLE, Proprietress.

King's Head Hotel and Assembly Rooms. First class. Luncheons, Dinners, Billiards, Garage, Stabling. Lawn. Bowls Tel.: 563 Epsom.
CHAS. TANTON, Proprietor.

EPSOM DOWNS (Surrey) from *London Bridge*, *Victoria*, and *Clapham Junction*, 16 miles. Fares from London Bridge or Victoria, 2/6*a*, 1/6*c*. R. T. for two days, 4/11*a*, 3/0*c*. *See* pp. 582, 583.
Map Square 23.

EPWORTH (Lincoln), 183 miles. No through fares. Departures *from* London as for Goole or Gainsborough. Departures *for* London about 3 times daily. Pop. 1,836.
Map Square 13.

ERDINGTON (Warwick), 114½ miles. Fares, 23/11*a*, 14/4*c*. R. T. for two months, 47/10*a*. Departures *from* London as for Birmingham (New Street). Departures *for* London about 8 times daily. Pop. 32,331.

ERIDGE (Sussex) from *London Bridge*, *Victoria*, and *Clapham Junction*, 35½ miles. Fares, 7/4*a*, 4/5*c*. R. T. for two months, 14/8*a*, 8/10*c*. Pop. (Eridge Green) 756.
Map Square 24.

Leave Vict.	Clap. J.	Lon. B.	Arr. at Eridge.
AM 5.30	5.37	5.18	7. 5
6.37	6.44	6.40	9.20
7.23	7.29	8. 7	10.12
9.10	9.17	9. 6	10.40
11. 5	11.12	10.35	12. 9
12. 0	12. 7	11.50	2. 6
12. 0*d*	12. 7*d*	*k*12.20*d*	2. 6
PM —	—	12.50*d*	2.47
1.20*e*	1.27*e*	1.38*e*	3.15
1.25*d*	—	1.38*d*	3.15
—	—	2. 5*e*	4.19
2.25	2.33	2.25*d*	4.19
3.45	—	—	4.38
4. 0*e*	4. 8*e*	4.44*e*	5.45
4.50	—	—	6. 8
5. 5	5.12	5.21	6.53
6. 6*e*	6.12*e*	6. 8*e*	7.13
6. 6	6.12	6. 8	7.49
8. 5	8.12	8.10	9.11
—	—	—	—

ERIDGE—*continued.*

Sunday Trains.

Leave Vict.	Clap. J.	Lon. B.	Arr. at Eridge.
AM 8.50	8.57	8.30	10.12
PM 1.14	1.21	1.10	3.54
2.30	2.37	—	4.24
7. 5	7.12	6.46	8.37
—	—	—	—

Trains from Eridge.

Leave Eridge	Arrive at Lon. B.	Clap. J.	Vict.
AM 8.14	9.32	9.31	9.40
8.56	10. 4	10. 5	10.12
9.22	—	—	10.20
9.25	10.55	10.39	10.46
10.31	12.13	—	12.17
11.23	12.44	12.26	12.35
PM 1.11	2.58	—	—
2. 7	—	3.37	3.45
3.12	5.21	5.47	5.55
5. 1	6.36	6.21	6.29
6.16	7.56	8.19	8.27
8.47	10.25	10. 2	10.10
—	—	—	—
—	—	—	—
—	—	—	—
—	—	—	—
—	—	—	—

Sunday Trains.

AM 8.26	10.18	10.13	10.22
11.37	—	1.32	1.40
PM 4.51	—	6.25	6.34
7.29	9.17	8.52	9. 0
8.26	—	9.39	9.47
—	—	—	—
—	—	—	—
—	—	—	—

d Saturdays only.
e Saturdays excepted.
k Departs from London Bridge S.E. & C. Station.

ERITH (Kent) from *Charing Cross*, 15 miles. Fares, 3/2*a*, 2/7*b*, 1/11*c*. R. T. for eight days, 6/4*a*, 4/10*b*, 3/10*c*. *Cannon Street.* Fares, 2/9*a*, 2/3*b*, 1/8*c*. R. T. for eight days, 5/6*a*, 4/4*b*, 3/4*c*. Pop. 31,558. *See* pp. 547 551, 555, 556.
Map Square 24.

ERROL (Perth), 460¼ miles. Fares, 91/11*a*, 55/2*c*. R. T. for two months, 183/10*a*, 110/4*c*. Departures *from* London as for Perth. Departures *for* London about 3 times daily. Pop. 2,059.
Map Square 38.

ERWOOD (Radnor), 178 miles. Fares, 36/11*a*, 22/2*c*. R. T. for two months, 73/10*a*. Departures *from* London as for Builth Wells. Departures *for* London about 5 times daily.
Map Square 16.

ESCRICK (Yorks), 181 miles. Fares, 37/8*a*, 22/7*c*. R. T., double fare. Departures *from* London as for Selby. Departures *for* London about 4 times daily. Pop. 597.
Map Square 8.

ESGAIRGEILIOG (Merioneth), 222¼ miles. No through fares. Departures *from* London as for Machynlleth. Departures *for* London about 3 times daily.
Map Square 16.

ESHER (Surrey) from *Water-loo*, 14½ miles. Fares, 2/6a, 1/6c. R. T. for two days, 5/0a, 3/0c. Pop. 2,883. *Map Square* 23.

W'LOO.	ESHER	ESHER	W'LOO.
AM 4.50	5.28	AM 3.24	3.58
6.10	6.50	5.32	6.13
7. 0	7.27	7. 7	7.41
7.50	8.17	7.52	8.20
8.15	8.41	8. 6	8.36
9.15	9.46	8.36	9. 5
10.20	10.48	9. 3	9.31
11.20	11.46	9.43	10.11
PM12.15	12.48	10.17	10.46
12.54d	1.21	11.17	11.46
1.20	1.48	PM12.17	12.46
2.20	2.48	1.17	1.46
3.15	3.46	2.17	2.46
4.20	4.48	3.17	3.46
4.54e	5.21	4.18	4.46
5.20	5.48	5.17	5.46
5.54e	6.21	6.17	6.46
6.20	3.48	7.17	7.46
7. 0e	7.26	8.17	8.46
7.20	7.48	9.17	9.46
8.20	8.48	10.17	10.46
8.55	9.28	10.42	11.10
9.20	9.48	11.41	12.16
10.20	10.48	—	—
11.15e	11.42	—	—
11.40	12. 6	—	—
—	—	—	—
—	—	—	—
—	—	—	—

Sunday Trains.

AM 8.20	8.51	AM 3.24	3.58
9.20	9.54	9.11	9.45
9.45	10.12	10.43	11.16
10.20	10.54	PM12. 6	12.41
11.20	11.54	1. 6	1.41
PM12.20	12.54	2. 9	2.44
1.20	1.54	3. 9	3.44
3.20	3.54	5. 6	5.41
4.20	4.47	6.12	6.46
5.20	5.47	7. 6	7.41
6.30	6.57	8. 6	8.41
7.20	7.47	9. 8	9.44
8.20	8.54	10. 4	10.41
9.28	10. 2	11. 7	11.43
9.45	10.15	—	—
10.15	10.47	—	—

d Saturdays only.
e Saturdays excepted.

ESHOLT (Yorks) from *St. Pancras*, 205½ miles. Fares, 40/3a, 24/2c. R. T., double fare. Departures *from* London as for Ilkley. Departures *for* London about 5 times daily. Pop. 355. *Map Square* 7.

ESKBANK (Midlothian), 387 miles. Fares, 79/5a, 47/8c. R. T. for two months, 158/10a, 95/4c. Departures *from* London as for Galashiels. Departures *for* London about 5 times daily.

ESKBRIDGE (Midlothian), 397 miles. No through fares. Departures *from* London as for Edinburgh (Waverley). Departures *for* London about 5 times daily.

ESKMEALS (Cumberland), 285 miles. Fares, 59/5a, 35/8c, R. T. for two months, 118/10a, 71/4c. Departures *from* London as for Millom. Departures *for* London about 3 times daily. *Map Square* 6.

ESSENDINE (Rutland) from *King's Cross*, 88¾ miles. Fares, 18/6a, 11/1c. R. T., double fare. Pop. 215. *Map Square* 18.

KING's+	ES'DINE.	ES'DINE.	KING's+
AM 4.45	6.34	AM 8.54	10.40
5. 5	7.57	10.15	12.25
7.15r	9.51	PM 1.25	3.50
8.45	11. 7	3.59	6.25
11.30	2. 0	5. 7r	7.10
PM 1.50lr	3.49	6.43	9. 0
3. 0	5.15	9. 1	3.25
4.15	6.48	—	—
5.45r	7.40	—	—
—	—	—	—
—	—	—	—

Sunday Trains.

AM 8.30	11.44	PM 4.52	8. 8
—	—	—	—
—	—	—	—
—	—	—	—

l Tuesdays and Fridays only.
r Restaurant Car.

ESSEX ROAD (Metropolitan Railway) (G.N. & City). *See* back of Map.

ESSLEMONT (Aberdeen), 540½ miles. No through fares. Departures *from* London as for Fraserburgh or Peterhead. Departures *for* London about 3 times daily. *Map Square* 35.

ESTON (Yorks), 243½ miles. No through fares. Departures *from* London as for Middlesbrough. Departures *for* London about 5 times daily. Pop. 30,634. *Map Square* 8.

ETCHINGHAM (Sussex) from *Charing Cross, Cannon Street,* and *London Bridge*, 48½ miles. Fares, 10/0a, 8/00, 6/0c. R.T. for two months, 20/9a, 16/0b. Pop. 1,015. *Map Square* 24.

	Leave		Arr. at
CHAR. +	CAN. ST.	LON. B.	ETCH'M
AM —	3.40h	3.43h	5.25
—	7.56	8. 0	10. 8
9.25	—	9.33	11.15
10.40	—	10.46	12.22
PM12. 3e	—	12.10e	2.11
12.40d	—	12.47d	2.12
1. 5d	—	1.11d	2.48
2. 8	—	2.16	3.44
3.48e	—	—	5.22
5. 5d	—	—	6.38
—	5.12e	—	6.40
6. 3e	6.16e	6.19e	7.45
7.30	—	—	9. 6

Sunday Trains.

AM 8.45	—	—	10.14
PM 7.35	—	7.45	9.27
—	—	—	—
—	—	—	—

ETCHINGHAM—*contd.*
Trains from Etchingham.

Leave		Arrive at	
ETCH'HM	LON. B.	CAN. ST.	CHAR. +
AM 7.45	—	9.15	—
8.23	—	9.48	—
9. 7d	10.29	—	10.39
9.46e	11. 7	—	11.17
PM12.51	—	—	12.49
—	3. 6	—	3.19
2.21	4.15	—	4.25
—	3.15d	5. 0	5. 8
4. 6d	6.30	—	6.39
4.16e	6.44	—	6.54
6.14	8.26	—	8.35
8.18	10.15	—	10.23
9.28	11.35	—	11 44
—	—	—	—
—	—	—	—
—	—	—	—

Sunday Trains.

AM 7.47	10. 5	—	10.15
9.46	11.23	—	11.34
PM 6.10	8.12	—	8.22
9.19	11. 4	—	11.15

d Saturdays only.
e Saturdays excepted.
h Third class only.

ETHERLEY (Durham), 246½ miles. Fares, 51/5a, 30/10c. R. T., double fare. Departures *from* London as for Bishop Auckland. Departures *for* London about 4 times daily. Pop. 1,812. *Map Square* 7.

ETRURIA (Stafford) from *Euston*, 147 miles. Fares, 30/8a, 18/5c. R. T. for two months, 61/4a. Departures *from* London as for Stoke-on-Trent. Departures *for* London about 5 times daily. *Map Square* 12.

ETTINGSHALL ROAD (Stafford), 124 miles. Fares, 25/3a, 15/2c. R. T. for two months, 50/6a. Departures *from* London as for Oldbury. Departures *for* London about 4 times daily. Pop. (Ettingshall) 5,486. *Map Square* 17.

ETTINGTON (Warwick) from *Marylebone*, 87½ miles. Fares, 20/0a, 12/0c. R. T. for two months, 40/0a. Departures *from* London as for Kineton. Departures *for* London about 3 times daily. Pop. (Ettington) 570. *Map Square* 17.

ETWALL (Derby) from *King's Cross*, 152 miles. Fares, 25/6a, 15/11c. R. T., double fare. Departures *from* London as for Derby (Friar Gate). Departures *for* London about 14 minutes later. Pop. 694. *Map Square* 17.

EUSTON (Hampstead and City and South London tubes).
See back of Map.
Map Squares 23 and 60.

EUSTON SQUARE to
and from *Mansion House, Charing Cross, Victoria, South Kensington, Kensington (High Street), Praed Street, Baker Street, Hammersmith, King's Cross, Moorgate, Aldgate,* and intermediate Stations every few minutes. Also to and from *Uxbridge Road, Kensington* (Addison Road), about every 12 minutes throughout the day.
See back of Map.
Map Square 60.

EVENWOOD (Durham),
248 miles. No through fares. Departures *from* London as for Bishop Auckland. Departures *for* London about 4 times daily. Pop. 4,987.
Map Square 7.

EVERCREECH (Somerset)
from *Waterloo,* 123 miles. Fares, 24/0*a*, 14/5*c*. R. T. for two months, 48 0*a*. Pop. 1,275.
Map Square 22.

W'LOO	E'CREECH	E'CREECH	W'LOO
AM 7.30	10.55	AM 8. 4*r*	11.10
9. 0*r*	12.15	10.49*r*	1.56
10. 0*r*	2.23	11.30*r*	3. 8
12. 0*r*	3.33	PM 1.30*r*	4.30
PM 1. 0*r*	3.54	2.32*r*	6. 0
3. 0*r*	6.34	3.50	7.40
6. 0*r*	9. 9	5. 5*r*	8.30
—	—	6.24	10.50
—	—	7.46*h*	3.58
—	—	—	—
—	—	—	—
—	—	—	—

No Sunday Trains.

h Via Eastleigh.
r Restaurant Car.

EVERCREECH, NEW
(Somerset), 124½ miles. Fares, 24/0*a*, 14/5*c*. R.T. for two months, 48/0*a*, 28/10*c*. Departures *from* London as for Evercreech. Departures *for* London about 5 times daily.
Map Square 22.

EVERINGHAM (Yorks),
188¼ miles. Fares, 37/11*a*, 22/9*c*. R. T., double fare. Departures *from* London as for Selby. Departures *for* London about 5 times daily. Pop. 236.
Map Square 13.

EVERSHOT (Dorset) from
Paddington, 135¼ miles. Fares, 27/8*a*, 16/7*c*. R.T. for two months, 55/4*a*. Departures *from* London as for Yetminster. Departures *for* London about 4 times daily. Pop. 325.
Map Square 27.

EVESHAM (Worcester)
from *Paddington,* 106½ miles. Fares, 22/1*a*, 13/3*c*. R. T. for two months, 44/2*a* Pop. 8,685.
Map Square 17.

PAD.	EVESHAM	EVESHAM	PAD.
AM 5.30	9.38	AM 6.53	9.50
8.50	11.21	7.48*h*	11. 0
9.45	12.24	9.24	12. 5
10.40*h*	2. 7	10.53	2.12
PM 1.35*r*	4. 9	PM12.25*r*	2.55
2.10*h*	5.40	1.50*hr*	5. 0
4.45	7.25	3.22	5.50
6. 5*r*	8.27	3.43	7.20
6.10*h*	9.20	4.36*hr*	8. 5
6.55	10.13	6.24*r*	9.15
—	—	7.15	10.45

Sunday Trains.

AM10.35*r*	1.45	AM11. 3	2.40
PM 4.10	7.31	PM 6.15*r*	9.48
—	—	—	—
—	—	—	—

h Via Stratford-on-Avon.
r Restaurant Car.

"The Mansion House."
High-class Boarding Establishment. Central heating. Spacious Lawns. Near River Avon. Boating. Fishing. 'Phone 215. Apply—
PROPRIETRESS.

EWELL EAST (Surrey)
from *London Bridge,* 16 miles. Fares, 2/4*a*, 1/5*c*. R. T. for two days, 4/8*a*, 2/10*c*. Pop. 4,187. *See* pp. 564-566.
Map Square 23.

From *Victoria,* 14¼ miles. Fares as above. *See* pp. 571-574.

EWELL WEST (Surrey)
from *Waterloo,* 13 miles. Fares, 2/4*a*, 1 5*c*. R. T. for two days, 4/8*a*, 2/10*c*. *See* pp. 583, 584.

EWESLEY (Northumberland), 301 miles. No through fares. Departures *from* London as for Morpeth Departures *for* London about 3 times daily. Pop. 13.
Map Square 3.

EWOOD BRIDGE
(Lancs), 203 miles. Fares, 41/10*a*, 25/1*c*. R.T. for two months, 83/8*a*, 50/2*c*. Departures *from* London as for Bacup. Departures *for* London about 4 times daily.

EXETER (QUEEN STREET)
(Devon) from *Waterloo* 171½ miles. Fares, 35/10*a*, 21/6*c*. R.T. for two months, 71/8*a*, 43/0*c* Pop. 59,608.

W'LOO	EXETER	EXETER	W'LOO
AM 7.30	12.33	AM 7.30*r*	11.10
9. 0*r*	12.49	10.30*r*	1.56
10. 0*r*	1.24	10.40*r*	3. 8
11. 0*r*	2.21	PM12.30*r*	3.50
12. 0*r*	4.47	1. 0*r*	4.30
PM 1. 0*r*	5.13	2.30*r*	6. 0
3. 0*r*	6.19	3. 0	7.40
6. 0*r*	9.57	4.30*r*	8.30
—	—	6.30	10.50
—	—	7.45*h*	3.58

Sunday Trains.

AM 9. 0	3.47	PM 5. 0*r*	8.57
12. 0*nr*	4.32	—	—
—	—	—	—

h Via Eastleigh.
n Noon.
r Restaurant Car.

EXETER—continued.

ANOTHER ROUTE (ST.
DAVID'S) from *Paddington,* 173¾ miles. Fares, 35/10*a*, 21/6*c*. R. T. for two months, 71/8*a*, 43/0*c*.
Map Square 26.

PAD.	EXETER	EXETER	PAD.
AM 5.30	10.37	AM 1.57	7.10
7.30*d*	12.12	6.20	11.30
7.30	12.27	10.15*r*	1.30
9.15*r*	12.53	11. 0	4. 5
11.10*r*	2.10	PM 1.25*r*	4.35
PM12. 5*r*	3.37	1.45*r*	4.45
2. 0*r*	5.28	3.27*r*	6.50
3.30*r*	6.30	5.42*r*	9. 0
4.15*r*	8.14	7.10	2.45
6.30*r*	10.35	—	—
10. 0	2.46	—	—
12. 0*h*	5.15	—	—
12.30*k*	5.45	—	—

Sunday Trains.

AM10.30*r*	1.45	AM 1.57	7. 5
PM 2.40	6.16	9.17	3.35
4.30*r*	8.35	11.50*r*	4. 5
10. 0	2.46	PM 3.55	7. 5
—	—	4.26*r*	7.55
—	—	10.10	3.15

d Saturdays only.
h Saturdays midnight excepted.
k Saturdays midnight only.
r Restaurant Car.

ANOTHER ROUTE (ST.
Thomas) from *Waterloo* 174½ miles. Fares, 36/0*a*, 21/7*c*. R.T. for two months, 72/0*a*, 43/2*c*. Departures *from* London as for Exeter (St. David's). Departures *for* London about 7 times daily.
Map Square 26.

Rougemont Hotel. R.A.C.
and A.A. Leading. Largest. Modern. Under Royal Patronage. The Hotel for Families and Tourists Electric Light. Electric Lift. Night Porter. Omnibus. A. MORGAN EDWARDS, Manager.
See advt. p. **167.**

Osborne Residential Hotel.
Close to both stations, City. Cathedral. Electric light. Every comfort. Moderate terms. 'Phone 522.
See advt. p. **168.**

Royal Clarence Hotel.
Facing Cathedral. Quiet and restful. An old-world Caravanserie. Every comfort. Excellent Cuisine. Telephone 244.

New London Hotel. First-
class. Most central. A charming 18th Century Hotel with every modern comfort. Heated by hot water radiators. Night Porter. Telegrams: New London, Exeter. Telephone 146.

Gt. Western Railway
Hotel. Telephone 480. Close to St. David's Station. Enlarged and modernised. First-class accommodation. Electric Light. Centre for South Devon.
TRUST HOUSES, Ltd.

EXETER—*continued.*

Globe Hotel. Quiet, comfortable, old-established Family and Commercial. Facing Cathedral, centrally situated. Electric light. Stock rooms.
Miss JEANS, Manageress.

Waverley Hotel. Family and Commercial. Facing General Post Office, High Street. Most Central. Comfortable, bright and quiet. Moderate Tariff. Electric light. Stock Rooms. Night Porter. Telephone 620.
Miss HART, Manageress.

EXMINSTER (Devon),
178¼ miles. Fares, 36/11*a*, 22/2*c*. R.T. for two months, 73/10*a*. Departures *from* London as for Exeter (St. Davids). Departures *for* London about 4 times daily. Pop. 2,711.
Map Square 26.

EXMOUTH (Devon) from
Waterloo, via Exeter, 180 miles. Fares, 38/1*a*, 22/10*c*. R. T. for two months, 76/2*a*, 45/8*c*. Pop. 13,614.
Map Square 26.

W'loo	Exmth.	W'loo		Exmth.	W'loo
AM10. 0*r*	2. 6		AM 6.35*r*	11.10
11. 0*r*	4. 7		9.35*r*	1.56
12. 0e*r*	5.36		11.45*r*	3.50
PM 1. 0*r*	6. 7		PM 1.35*r*	6. 0
3. 0*r*	7. 8		2.15	7.40
6. 0*r*	10.33		3.35*r*	8.36
—	—		5.37	10.50
—	—		6.37*dh*	3.58
—	—		7.10e*h*	3.58

Sunday Trains.

12. 0*nr*	5.41		PM 4.10*n*	8.57
—	—		—	—
—	—		—	—

d Saturdays only.
e Saturdays excepted.
h Via Eastleigh.
n Noon.
r Restaurant Car.

ANOTHER ROUTE *via* Budleigh Salterton, 176 miles. Fares, 36/8*a*, 22/0*c*. R.T. for two months, 73/4*a*, 44/0*c*.

W'loo	Exmth.		Exmth.	W'loo
AM 9. 0*r*	1. 28		AM 9.16*r*	1.56
10. 0*r*	3.26		10.15*r*	3. 8
12. 0*nr*	4.43		PM12.25*r*	6. 0
PM 1. 0*r*	6.28		2.17	7.40
3. 0*r*	8.28		5.17	10.50
—	—		7.17*h*	3.58

No Sunday Trains.

h Via Eastleigh.
n Noon.
r Restaurant Car.

Imperial Hotel. Principal First-class Family Hotel, in own grounds of seven acres. Charming Sea and Land Views. S.W. aspect. Moderate inclusive charges. Tel. 16 Exmouth.
See advt. p. **165.**

EXMOUTH—*continued.*

" Atlantic." The leading First-class Private Hotel. Centre of Promenade, facing Sea. Ten minutes from Railway Station and Pier.
S. BLACKMORE, Manager.

Dolforgan. Family and Residential Hotel. Recently enlarged. Charmingly situated, overlooking Sea. Tastefully decorated. Excellent Cuisine. Separate tables. Perfect sanitation. Moderate tariff. Telegrams, " Dolforgan, Exmouth." Telephone 5.
Proprietress, Miss BAKER.

Royal Beacon Hotel. Unrivalled position, commanding extensive views of land and sea. Close to Links. Special Winter Terms. Fully licensed. Telephone No. 41. Resident Proprietor.
A. W. BRADSHAW
(late Woolpack Hotel, Warwick).

London Hotel. Family and Commercial. Central position. New Management. Electric Light throughout. 'Phone 155. Garage. Boots meets trains.
PEARCE BROS., Proprietors.

Houses and Apartments. Full list from CREWS & SON, Oldest Established House Agents, Furnishers, Removers, Undertakers, 4 & 6, Rolle Street, Exmouth.

House and Estate Offices. Blackmore & Son, F.A.I., House Agents, Auctioneers, Furnishers, Removers. Printed register free. 36, Rolle Street, Exmouth.

EYARTH (Denbigh), 203¾
miles. Fares, 40/7*a*, 24/4*c*. R. T. for two months, 81/2*a*, 48/8*c*. Departures *from* London as for Corwen or Ruthin. Departures *for* London about 3 times daily.
Map Square 11.

EYE (Suffolk) from *Liverpool Street*, 94¼ miles. Fares, 19/10*a*, 11/11*c*. R.T. for two months, 39/8*a*. Pop. 1,781.
Map Square 19.

L'pl. St.	Eye		Eye	L'pl. St.
AM 5. 0	10.11		AM 9.21	12.39
8.15*hr*	11.41		11. 2*r*	2. 3
10.12*f*	1.19		PM12.45*fr*	4.58
PM12.33*r*	3.33		2.57*h*	6.32
3.10*r*	6. 1		4.29	7.51

No Sunday Trains.

f Mondays only.
h Via Diss.
r Restaurant Car.

White Lion Hotel. Telephone 14. Electric Light. Billiards. Stabling and Garage.
TRUST HOUSES, Ltd.

EYE GREEN (Northampton), 81½ miles. Fares, 16/8*a*, 10/0*c*. R. T., double fare. Departures *from* London as for Wisbech St. Mary. Departures *for* London about 4 times daily. Pop. 1,352.
Map Square 18.

EYEMOUTH (Berwick), 343¼ miles. No through fares. Departures *from* London as for Berwick-on-Tweed. Departures *for* London about 3 times daily. Pop. 2,5/3.
Map Square 41.

EYNSFORD (Kent) from *Victoria, Holborn Viaduct,* and *St. Paul's,* 20¼ miles. Fares, 4/5*a*, 3/7*b*, 2/7*c*. R. T. for two months, 8/10*a*, 7/2*b* Pop. 2,567.
Map Square 24.

Vict. S.E. & C.	Leave Holb.V.	St. Pl.'s	Arr. at Eyns.
AM —	6.40	6.42	7.40
8.32	8.20	8.23	9.33
11. 4	10.58	11. 0	12. 3
PM —	12.33*d*	12.36*d*	1.26
—	1.27*d*	1.30*d*	2.21
2. 9*d*	2.11*d*	2.14*d*	3.17
2.4*Cd*	—	—	3.32
2.50*e*	—	—	3.45
4.25*e*	—	—	5. 5
e5.15*h*	—	e5.21*k*	6. 1
d5.20*h*	—	d5.26*k*	6. 7
5.30*e*	—	5.33*e*	6.17
—	—	6.16*e*	6.55
6.40	6.34	6.37	7.31
7.22	7.22	7.24	8.14
8.55	—	—	9.39
10. 0	9.54	9.56	10.50

Sunday Trains.

AM —	8. 0	—	9.11
10.30	10.25	—	11.31
PM 2. 5	2. 3	—	3.12
6.35	6.40	—	7.33
10.15	10.12	—	11.12

Trains from Eynsford.

Leave Eyns.	St. Pl.'s	Arrive at Holb.V.	Vict.
AM 7.51	8.40	8.42	8.50
8.46	9.37	9.39	—
10.59	—	—	11.37
PM12. 9	12.59	1. 2	12.49
1.45	—	—	2.40
3.37	—	—	4.33
6.11	6.58	7. 0	—
6.51*d*	8. 0	8. 2	—
6.51*e*	8.18	8.20	8.10
7.48	—	—	8.51
9.14*d*	—	—	9.54
10.48	11.43	11.45	—

Sunday Trains.

AM10. 6	—	—	10.48
PM12.35	—	—	1.25
3. 3	—	—	3.50
5.20	—	6.20	6. 3
9.13	—	10.22	10. 5

d Saturdays only.
e Saturdays excepted.
h Departs from or arrives at Charing Cross (S.E. & C.R.).
k Departs from or arrives at London Bridge (S.E. & C.R.).

EYNSHAM (Oxon) from *Paddington*, 70½ miles. Fares, 14/7a, 8/9c. R. T. for two months, 29/2a. Departures *from* London as for Witney. Departures *for* London about 4 times daily. Pop. 1,683. *Map Square* 23.

EYTHORNE (Kent), 73¼ miles. No through fares. Departures *from* London as for Eastry. Departures *for* London about 5 times daily. Pop. 929.

IDRIS

SODA WATER
LEMONADE
DRY GINGER ALE
BREWED GINGER BEER
GINGER ALE

To be obtained at all Clubs, Hotels, Restaurants, Grocers, Wine Merchants, and Chemists.

REFERENCE NOTES.

a signifies First Class.
b   ,,   Second Class.
c   ,,   Third Class.
d   ,,   On Saturdays only.
e   ,,   Saturdays excepted.
f   ,,   On Mondays only.
g   ,,   Mondays excepted.
r   ,,   Restaurant Car.
t   ,,   Tea Car.
x   ,,   Express.
R.T. ,,   Return Tickets.

All Trains in the Tables not otherwise marked **carry Third Class Passengers.**

F

FACIT (Lancs), 200½ miles. Fares, 41/3a, 24/9c. R. T. for two months, 82 6a. Departures *from* London as for Rochdale. Departures *for* London about 8 times daily. Pop. 2,434. *Map Square* 12.

FAILSWORTH (Lancs), 190½ miles. Fares, 38/7a, 23/3c. R. T. for two months, 77 2a, 46/4c. Departures *from* London as for Manchester. Departures *for* London about 6 times daily. Pop. 16,972.

FAIRBOURNE (Merioneth) 241¼ miles. Fares, 48/4a, 29/0c. R. T. for two months, 96/8a. Departures *from* London as for Machynlleth. Departures *for* London about 3 times daily. *Map Square* 16.

FAIRFIELD (Lancs), from *Marylebone*, 202¼ miles. Fares, 37/11a, 22/9c. R. T., double fare. Departures *from* London as for Guide Bridge. Departures *for* London about 5 times daily. Pop. 22,740.

Station closed on Sundays.

FAIRFORD (Gloucester) from *Paddington*, 88¾ miles. Fares, 18/6a, 11/1c. R. T. for two months, 37/0a. Pop. 1,410. *Map Square* 22.

PAD.	FAIRFD.	FAIRFD.	PAD.
AM 6.30	10.28	AM 7. 3	9.50
9.45	12.50	9. 8	12. 5
PM 1.35r	5.20	10.55	1.50
4.45t	7.26	PM 2.30	5.50
7.30	10.10	6.30	10.45

Sunday Trains.

| AM11.45 | 5.58 | PM 6.30r | 9.48 |

r Restaurant Car.
t Tea Car.

FAIRLIE (Ayr), 413¼ miles. Fares, 84 4a, 50/7c. R. T. for two months, 168/8a, 101/2c. Departures *from* London as for Ardrossan. Departures *for* London about 4 times daily. Pop. 1,288. *Map Square* 40.

FAIRLOP from *Liverpool Street* or *Fenchurch Street*, 10½ miles. Fares from Liverpool St., *via* Ilford, 1/8a, 1/4b, 1/0c. R. T. for two days, 3/4a, 2/8b, 1/11c. *Via* Woodford, 2/1a, 1/8b, 1/3c. R. T. for two days, 4/2a, 3/2½b, 2/2½c. From Fenchurch St., *via* Ilford, 1/8a, 1/4b, 1/0c. R. T. for two days. 3/4a, 2/7½b, 1/11c. *Via* Woodford, 2/1a, 1/8b, 1/3c. R. T. for two days, 4/2a, 3/1b, 2/2½c. See p. 536. *Map Square* 23.

FAKENHAM (Norfolk)

from *Liverpool Street*, 134½ miles.
Fares, 23/7a, 14/2c. R. T. for two
months, 47/2a. Pop. 3,181.
Map Square 19

L'P L. ST.	FAKEN.	FAKEN.	L'P'L. ST.
AM 5. 5	9.37	AM 6.15f	10.36
5.50	12. 2	7.51	12.40
9.50er	2.24	9.36r	2.21
11.50er	4.46	PM 1.10r	5.17
PM12.33dr	5.12	3.40r	8.22
3.10r	8. 0	4.21h	8.33
5.18fr	9.16	6. 8e	2.50
—	—	6.18d	2.50
—	—	—	—
—	—	—	—
—	—	—	—
—	—	—	—
—	—	—	—

Sunday Trains.

PM 3.25	8.29	PM 5. 8	9.40
—	—	—	—
—	—	—	—
—	—	—	—

d Saturdays only.
e Saturdays excepted.
f Mondays only.
h Thursdays only.
r Restaurant Car.

FAKENHAM TOWN

from *King's Cross*, 135 miles.
Fares as above.

KING'S+	FAKN.T.	FAKN.T.	KING'S+
AM 4.45	8.57	AM 9. 5	1. 5
7.15r	12. 1	10.39	3.50
10.10r	3.12	PM 1. 9r	4.30
PM 1.50r	6.10	4.19	9. 0
3. 0	6.29	—	—
—	—	—	—
—	—	—	—
—	—	—	—
—	—	—	—

No Sunday Trains.

r Restaurant Car.

FALKIRK (HIGH) (Stirling)

from *King's Cross*, 417½ miles.
Fares, 82/6a, 49/6c. R. T. for two
months, 165/0a, 99/0c.
Pop. 42,762.
Map Square 40.

KING'S+	FALK.	FALK.	KING'S+
AM 4.45	4.42	AM 8.18r	6.30
10. 0r	7.33	PM12.12r	10. 0
PM 8.25e	7. 1	2.33	3.25
—	—	5.27	6. 0
—	—	9. 1	7.30
—	—	—	—
—	—	—	—
—	—	—	—

Sunday Trains.

—	—	AM10.26r	8.15
—	—	PM 9.56	7. 5
—	—	—	—
—	—	—	—

e Saturdays excepted.
r Restaurant Car.

Falkirk Temperance Hotel.

Finest of its kind in Scotland.
New Equipment throughout.
Near Golf Links. Moderate
charges. Write, MANAGER.

FALKLAND ROAD

(Fife), 428½ miles. Fares, 86/11a,
52/2c. R. T. for two months,
173/10a, 104/4c. Departures *from*
London as for Kirkcaldy. Departures *for* London about 3 times
daily. Pop. (Falkland) 2,332.
Map Square 41.

FALLOWFIELD (Lancs)

from *Marylebone*, 206½ miles.
Fares, 38/2a, 22/11c. R. T., double
fare, Pop. 3,316.

M'BONE	FAL'FD	FAL'FD	M'BONF
AM 8.45r	2. 5	AM 7.52r	1.13
PM12.15er	5.45	9.34r	3. 0
3.20r	7.35	PM 1.22r	6.38
—	—	4.42r	9.55
—	—	—	—
—	—	—	—

No Sunday Trains.
e Saturdays excepted.
r Restaurant Car.

FALMER (Sussex) from

Victoria, Clapham Junction, and
London Bridge, 53½ miles. Fares
from London Bridge or Victoria,
10/7a, 6/4c. R. T. for two months,
21/2a, 12/8c. Departures *from* London as for Lewes or Brighton.
Departures *for* London about 8
times daily. Pop. 450.
Map Square 28.

FALMOUTH (Cornwall)

from *Paddington*, 291¼ miles.
Fares, 60/3a, 36/2c. R. T. for two
months, 120/6a, 72/4c.
Pop. 13,318.
Map Square 25.

PAD.	FALM.	FALM.	PAD.
AM 5.30	3. 6	AM 9. 8r	4.35
10.30r	4.52	10.10r	4.45
11.10r	6. 7	11.20r	6.50
PM12. 5r	9. 5	PM12.25r	9. 0
2. 0r	10. 4	9.15	7.10
10. 0e	7.23	—	—
12. 0k	11. 4	—	—
12.30h	11.32	—	—
—	—	—	—

Sunday Trains.

AM10.30r	5.30	AM 9.45	7. 5
PM10. 0	7.23	PM12.30r	7.55
—	—	4. 0	3.15
—	—	—	—
—	—	—	—

e Saturdays excepted.
h Saturdays midnight only.
k Saturdays midnight excepted.
r Restaurant Car.

Falmouth Hydro Hotel.

Cliff Road. Every comfort.
Electric Light. Lift. Billiards.
Terms from 3½ guineas. Tele-
phone 180.
Miss ROW, Manageress.
See advt. p. **171.**

Falmouth Hotel. Own

grounds of four acres overlooking
Bay and Harbour and Pendennis
Castle. Certificated Sanitary
arrangements. Lift. Golf.
Moderate Tariff.
C. DUPLESSY, Manager.

FALMOUTH—*continued.*

Albion Hotel. Most con-
veniently situated. Magnificent
views. Close to Beaches, best
walks, and Pier for steamer trips.
Homelike. Excellent cooking.
Moderate en pension terms.
Tariff on application. Tel. 62.
W. C. THOMAS, Proprietor.

Gyllyngdune Hotel. Stand-
ing in its own Grounds,
directly facing Sea and close to
Station. Dining Room, Drawing
Room, Lounge, and Smoking
Room. Table d'Hôte. Separate
Tables. For Tariff and full
particulars, address
PROPRIETRESS.

The Bay Hotel. First-class
Family Hotel. Situated in own
grounds, overlooking the Bay and
Pendennis Castle.
Address, MANAGER.

Boscawen Private Hotel.
Magnificent position, centre Bay.
Overlooking Pendennis Point
and Lizard Coast. Table d'Hôte.
Separate Tables. Telegrams,
"Boscawen." 'Phone 141. Illus-
trated Tariff. PROPRIETORS.

Grandview, En Pension,
Home from Home. Situate on
water's edge. MagnificentScenery.
2 minutes town. Separate Tables.
Garage. Sailing and Rowing
Boats for hire. Telephone 86.

Private Boarding House.
Two minutes Beaches. Electric
light. Bath, hot and cold. Reason-
able terms. "Waratah," Melville
Road, Falmouth.
Misses RUSSELL.

House Agents and Auc-
tioneers, 19, Church Street.
Removal Contractors, Furnishers.
Also Truro, Newquay, and Pen-
zance.
JOHN JULIAN & CO., Ltd.

FALSTONE (North-

umberland), 312½ miles. No
through fares. Departures *from*
London as for Hexham. Departures *for* London about 3 times
daily. Pop. 872.
Map Square 3.

FAMBRIDGE (Essex) from

Liverpool Street, 37¼ miles. Fares,
7/1a, 4/3c. R. T. for two
months, 14/2a, 8/6c. Pop. 444.
Map Square 24.

L PL. ST.	FMBDGE.	FMBDGE.	L'PL. ST.
AM 5.26	7.18	AM 7.17	8.45
6.50	8.48	8.27	9.46
9. 1	10.38	9.42	11. 7
10.47d	12.20	11.32d	1.16
11.56	1.32	PM12. 2e	1.25
PM 1.26d	2.31	1.17d	3. 5
2.20e	4.20	2.57d	4.56
2.40d	4. 1	3. 8e	4.51
4.15e	5.19	5.20	6.52
4.18d	5.40	6.37	8.22
5.39	6.53	8.19	9.56
6.26e	7.50	—	—
8. 2e	9.24	—	—
8.45d	10. 0	—	—
—	—	—	—
—	—	—	—

FAMBRIDGE—*continued.*

Sunday Trains.

L'PL. ST.	FMBDGE.	FMBDGE.	L'PL. ST.
AM 8.45	10.13	AM 7.50	10.25
9.30	11.13	PM 6.57	8.45
PM 6.42	8.23	8. 2	9.32
—	—	—	—
—	—	—	—
—	—	—	—
—	—	—	—

d Saturdays only.
e Saturdays excepted.

FANGFOSS (Yorks), 200

miles. Fares, 41/8a, 25/0c. R. T., double fare. Departures *from* London as for York. Departures *for* London about 5 times daily. Pop. 144.

Map Square 8.

FAREHAM (Hants) from

Waterloo, via Eastleigh, 84½ miles. Fares, 15/5a, 9/3c. R. T. for two months, 30/10a, 18/6c. Pop. 10,066.

Map Square 28.

W'LOO	FAREH.	FAREH.	W'LOO
AM 5.40	8.21	AM 6.34	9.26
5 50	9.27	8. 0	10.56
8.30s	10.50	9.26	12. 0
9.30	12.19	11.51r	2.20
11.30r	2. 4	PM12.34	4. 6
PM 1.30s	3.49	1.42	4.20
3.30s	5.55	3. 7	6.16
5.30r	7.53	5.58r	8.20
7.30	9.52	7.36	10.50
8. 0	11.26	8.46	11.28
10. 0	1.50	11.30f	3.58
—	—	12.41mg	3.58

Sunday Trains.

AM11. Cr	1.22	AM12.41	3.58
PM 2. 0	6.31	9.30	12.11
5. 5	7.56	PM12.10r	2.27
7. 0r	9.30	5.23	8. 3
9.28	12.31	7.44	10.52
—	—	—	—
—	—	—	—
—	—	—	•—

f Mondays only.
g Mondays excepted.
m Midnight.
r Restaurant Car.
s Refreshments served.

ANOTHER ROUTE from

Waterloo, via Meon Valley, 72½ miles. Fares, 15/3a, 9/2c. R. T. for two months, 30/6a, 18/4c.

W'LOO	FAREH.	FAREH.	W'LOO
AM 4.50	8.16	AM 7.50	10.26
7. 0	10. 4	9.40	12.11
9.20	12. 9	11. 7	1.40
11.20	2.16	PM 2.50	5.46
PM 3.15	5.50	4.14	7. 7
6.34	9. 8	8. 5	11.10
—	—	—	—
—	—	—	—

Sunday Trains.

PM 6.20	9.12	PM 6.50	9.37

Red Lion Hotel. R.A.C., A.A. Under new and experienced Proprietorship. Unpretentious but Comfortable. Good Catering a speciality. Telephone 33 Fareham.

FARINGDON (Berks) from

Paddington, 70 miles. Fares, 14/7a, 8/9c. R. T. for two months, 29/2a, 17/6c. Pop. 3,079.

Map Square 22.

PAD.	FARDN.	FARDN.	PAD.
AM 5.30	8.31	AM 6.55	9.30
7.30	10.27	7.55r	10.15
9. 0	11.42	9.35	12. 0
10.45	1.19	11.55	2.35
PM 1.35r	4. 3	PM 2.15	5. 6
3.38	6.52	6.15	9.15
6.55	9. 4	7.30	10.45

No Sunday Trains.

r Restaurant Car.

FARINGTON (Lancs), 206¼

miles. Fares, 43/2a, 25/11c. R. T. for two months, 86/4a. Departures *from* London as for Leyland. Departures *for* London about 8 times daily. Pop. 2,321.

Map Square 12.

FARNBOROUGH (Hants)

from *Waterloo,* 33½ miles. Fares, 7/1a, 4/3c. R. T. for two months, 14/2a, 8/6c. Pop. 12,645.

Map Square 23.

W'LOO	FNBORO.	FNBORO.	W'LOO
AM 5.50	7. 4	AM 2.38	3.58
7.30	8.37	7.40	8.41
8.34	9.41	8. 0	9. 8
9.20	10.22	8.34	9.26
10.34	11.45	9.15	9.56
PM12.14d	1.20	9.28	10.21
12.40	1.47	10.13	10.56
1.15d	2.25	11.10	12.11
2.34	3.49	PM12.11	1.20
3.40	4.48	2.15	3.16
4.40	5.55	3. 7	4. 6
5.10e	6. 5	4.11	5.20
5.15e	6.16	5.11	6.16
5.20d	6.31	6. 7	7. 7
6. 0	6.44	8.15	9.26
6.40d	7.47	10.39	12.16
6.54e	7.45	—	—
8. 0	9. 5	—	—
8.55	10.15	—	—

Sunday Trains.

AM 9. 0	10. 4	AM 2.38	3.58
9.45	11. 0	8.18	9.45
11.15	12.18	10.43	12.41
PM 5. 5	6. 9	11.46	12.52
6. 0	7. 4	PM 5.16	6. 7
7.20	8.34	8.12	9.12
9.28	10.46	9.48	10.52
—	—	—	—
—	—	—	—
—	—	—	—
—	—	—	—
—	—	—	—

d Saturdays only.
e Saturdays excepted

Tumble-Down Dick Hotel. Family and Residential. Near Links. Garage. Stabling. Terms moderate. Near Station. Electric Light throughout. Telephone 58 North Farnborough.
R. RICHMOND.

FARNBOROUGH—*contd.*

Queen's Hotel (First-class Residential). Excellent Cuisine and Service. Reduced Terms for Officers and Families. Telephone 4 North Camp.

FARNCOMBE (Surrey)

from *Waterloo,* 33¾ miles. Fares, 7/1a, 4/3c. R. T. for two months, 14/2a, 8/6c.

Map Square 23.

W'LOO	F'COMBE	F'COMBE	W'LOO
AM 5.50	6.57	AM 6.56	8.20
6.50	8. 4	7.39	8.41
7.50	9.11	8.16	9.12
9.50	10.50	8.52	9.44
10.50	11.57	9.57	10.40
11.50d	12.50	10.31	11.32
PM12.20d	1.11	PM12.51r	1.52
12.50er	1.47	1.55	3. 6
1.50e	2.56	3.13	4.16
2. 0d	3. 6	4.48	5.52
2.34	3.53	6.24	7.46
3.50d	4.50	7.54	9. 6
4.15e	5. 6	8.24	9.46
5.24	6.14	9.22	10.46
5.50	6.52	10.43	12.16
6. 5e	7.24	—	—
6.50er	7.48	—	—
6.50dr	7.59	—	—
8. 0	9.15	—	—
9.50	10.54	—	—
—	—	—	—
—	—	—	—

No Sunday Trains.

d Saturdays only.
e Saturdays excepted.
r Restaurant Car.

FARNELL ROAD (For-

far), 494½ miles. Fares, 96/8a, 58/0c. R.T. for two months, 193/4a, 116/0c. Departures *from* London as for Forfar. Departures *for* London about 3 times daily. Pop. (Farnell) 500.

Map Square 38.

FARNHAM (Surrey) from

Waterloo, 38½ miles. Fares, 7/11a, 4/9c. R. T. for two months, 15/10a, 9/6c. Pop. 12,133.

Map Square 28.

W'LOO	FARNHAM	FARNHAM	W'LOO
AM 4.50	6.48	AM 6.24	7.46
5.50	7.15	7.36	8.56
7. 0	8.40	8.29	9.41
7.50	9.28	8.45	10.11
9.20	10.37	9.28	10.26
10.34	12. 6	10. 4	11.16
11.20	12.54	11. 1	12.11
PM 1.10	2.22	11.29	12.40
1.20	2.53	PM12.29	1.40
3.15	4.29	1. 6	2.40
4. 0	5.12	2.22	3.36
5.10	6.21	3. 7	4.46
5.18eh	7. 4	4.11	5.46
5.50d	7. 9	4.47	6.16
6.10e	7 26	5.55	7. 7
6.34	7.39	7.18	8.46
6.40d	8.15	7.40	9. 6
6.54e	8.15	8.33	9.52
8. 0	9.26	9.39	11.10
9.50	11.11	10.51	12.16
12. 5	1.16	—	—
—	—•.	—	—
—	—	—	—
—	—	—	—
—	—	—	—
—	—	—	—

FARNHAM—*continued.*

Sunday Trains.

W'LOO	FARNHAM	FARNHAM	W'LOO
AM 8.45	10.13	AM 9.42	11.16
11.15	12.39	11.21	12.52
PM12.18*h*	2.38	PM 1.48	3.13
1.50	3.20	3.25*h*	5.28
2.18*h*	5.11	5.58	7.41
4.18*h*	7.11	8.28	9.37
6.20	7.39	9.17	10.47
6.30	8. 8	—	—
9.45	11.22	—	—
10.45	12. 4	—	—

d Saturdays only.
e Saturdays excepted.
h Via Ascot.

Bush Hotel. For Families and Gentlemen. Standing in its own grounds with Southerly aspect. First-class Cuisine under an experienced Chef. Good Stabling and Motor garage. Table d'hote 7.30. Telephone No. 37, Farnham. Apply Manager,
W. H. FISHER.

FARNINGHAM ROAD

(Kent) from *Victoria, Holborn Viaduct,* and *St. Paul's*, 20¼ miles. Fares, 4/5*d*, 3/7*b*, 2/7*c*. R. T. for two months, 8/10*a*, 7/2*b*. Pop. (Farningham) 1,395.
Map Square 24.

VICT.	Leave		ARR. at
S.E. & C.	HOL. V.	ST. PL.'S	FAR.RD.
AM 5. 5	4.57	5. 0	6.10
—	5.57	5.59	7. 7
—	6.40	6.42	7.41
—	7.30	7.33	8.20
9.20	—	—	9.58
11.40*d*	—	—	12.34
11.40*e*	—	—	12.35
11.55*d*	—	—	12.45
PM —	1.24*d*	1.27*d*	2. 7
2. 9*d*	2. 4*d*	2. 7*d*	3.23
2.12*e*	2.13*e*	2.16*e*	3.16
—	3.22*e*	3.25*e*	4.24
—	3.22*d*	3.25*d*	4.26
3.40*d*	3.33*d*	3.36*d*	5. 2
3.56*e*	—	—	4.45
5.30*e*	—	5.35*e*	6.19
5.45*e*	5.31*e*	5.34*e*	6.35
5.45*d*	—	—	6.37
6.16	6.10*e*	6.13*e*	7. 8
7. 5	7. 0	7. 3	7.45
7.22	7.22	7.24	8.14
8.10*d*	8. 5*d*	8. 8*d*	9.19
9. 0*e*	8.57*e*	9. 0*e*	9.53
10.17	10.11	10.13	11. 7
—	—	—	—
—	—	—	—

Sunday Trains.

AM 7.20	—	—	8.10
8.25	—	—	9.24
10.30	10.25	—	11.31
11.30	—	—	12.25
PM 1. 7	1. 5	—	2.11
2. 5	2. 3	—	3.20
3.30	—	—	4.22
6.35	—	—	7.23
—	6.40	—	7.35
10.15	10.12	—	11.14
—	—	—	—
—	—	—	—
—	—	—	—
—	—	—	—

FARNINGHAM ROAD
—*continued.*

Trains from Farningham Road.

Leave			Arrive at
FAR. RD.	ST. PL.'S	HOL. V.	VICT.
AM 7.17	8. 8	8. 9	8.14
7.32	8.25	8.27	8.29
7.53	8.40	8.42	8.50
8.20	9.16	9.18	—
8.42	9.27	9.29	9.36
8.54	9.37	9.39	9.57
9.31	—	—	10.10
11.44	12.59	1. 2	12.49
PM12.12*d*	1. 0	1. 2	1.22
12.36*e*	—	—	1.32
1.30*d*	—	—	2.40
2.33	3.38	—	3.25
3. 5*d*	—	—	4.32
4.18*e*	5.32	5.34	5.21
5.56*e*	6.45	6.47	—
6.46*d*	7.54	—	—
7. 5*e*	8.17	8.20	8.10
7.10*d*	8. 0	8. 2	—
7.35	9.10	9.12	8.51
8.49	9.50	9.54	9.46
9. 4	10.29	10.31	10.22
10.34	11.21	11.23	11.35

Sunday Trains.

AM 8.27	—	9.40	9.31
10.22	—	11.27	11.23
PM12. 4	—	1. 2	12.56
1. 9	—	2.15	2.11
2.54	—	—	3.50
5.22	—	—	6. 3
9. 8	—	10.22	10. 5
10.55	—	12. 0	11.44

d Saturdays only.
e Saturdays excepted.

FARNLEY (Yorks), 218¾

miles. Fares, 38/7*a*, 23/2*c*. R. T., double fare. Departures from London as for Batley. Departures for London about 8 times daily. Pop. 4,298.

FARNSFIELD (Notts),

143½ miles. Fares, 26/0*a*, 15/7*c*. R. T., double fare. Departures from London as for Southwell. Departures for London about 3 times daily. Pop. 967.
Map Square 34.

FARNWORTH (Lancs),

205½ miles. Fares, 39/0*a*, 23/5*c*. R.T. for two months, 78/0*a*, 46/10*c*. Departures from London as for Warrington (Central). Departures for London about 4 times daily. Pop. 27,901.

FARNWORTH & BOLD

(Lancs), 194½ miles. Fares, 39/0*a*, 23/5*c*. R.T. for two months, 78/0*a*, 46/10*c*. Departures from London as for Warrington (Bank Quay). Departures for London about 6 times daily.
Map Square 12.

FARNWORTH & HAL-
SHAW MOOR (Lancs), 195½ miles. Fares, 40/3*a*, 24/2*c*. R. T. for two months, 80/6*a*, 48/4*c*. Departures from London as for Manchester. Departures for London about 8 times daily. Pop. 28,131.
Map Square 12.

FARRINGDON ST.

from *Hammersmith, Bishop's Road, Baker Street, King's Cross, Aldgate, Mansion House, Charing Cross, South Kensington, Victoria,* and intermediate Stations every few minutes. Also to and from Uxbridge Road and Kensington (Addison Road) about every 12 minutes throughout the day. *See back of Map.*
Map Square 61.

FARTHINGHOE (North-

ampton) from *Euston*, 73¼ miles. Fares, 14/0*a*, 8/5*c*. R. T. for two months, 28/0*a*. Departures from London as for Buckingham. Departures for London about 4 times daily. Pop. 266.
Map Square 18.

FAULDHOUSE (Linlith-

gow), 397½ miles. Fares 80/7*a*, 48/4*c*. R. T. for two months, 161/2*a*, 96/8*c*. Departures from London as for Edinburgh (Waverley) or Wishaw (Central). Departures for London about 4 times daily. Pop. 4,889.
Map Square 40.

FAVERSHAM (Kent)

from *Victoria, Holborn Viaduct,* and *St. Paul's,* 52 miles. Fares, 11/0*a*, 8/9*b*, 6/6*c*. R. T. for two months, 22/0*a*, 17/6*b*. Pop. 10,870.
Map Square 24.

VICT.	Leave		Arr. at
S.E.&C.	HOL. V.	S.PAUL'S	FAVER.
AM —	3.50*k*	—	5.46
5. 5	4.57	5. 0	7.37
5.48*f*	5.40*f*	5.42*f*	7.24
7.40*f*	—	—	9.20
—	7.30	7.33	9.46
9. 0	—	—	10.11
9.20	—	—	10.42
10.40	—	—	11.56
11.40*d*	—	—	1.32
11.40*e*	—	—	1.59
PM 1.23*d*	—	—	3. 0
2. 5*d*	—	—	3.25
2. 8*e*	—	—	3.40
3.20*e*	—	—	4.35
3.29*d*	—	—	4.44
4.15*d*	—	—	5.40
4.20	—	—	5.55
—	5.10*e*	5.12*e*	6.30
5.10*d*	—	—	6.27
5.30*e*	—	—	7.17
5.30*d*	—	—	7.20
6.16	6.10*e*	6.13*e*	8.45
7. 5	7. 0	7. 3	9.14
7.50	—	—	9.22
8.30	—	—	9.42
9. 0*e*	8.57*e*	9. 0*e*	11.45
12. 0*l*	—	—	1.20
—	—	—	—
—	—	—	—

Sunday Trains.

AM 8.15	8. 0	—	10. 2
9.10	—	—	10.22
10.40	—	—	11.56
PM 3.30	—	—	5.50
6.35	—	—	8.50
7.50	—	—	9.30
8.25	—	—	9.43
—	—	—	—
—	—	—	—
—	—	—	—
—	—	—	—

FAVERSHAM—*continued.*

Trains from Faversham.

Leave Faver.	S.Paul's	Hol. V.	Vict.
AM 5.49	8. 8	8. 9	8.14
6.39	9.16	9.18	—
7.39	9.37	9.39	—
8.55	—	—	11. 2
9.51	—	—	11.27
9.59l	—	—	11.23
10.54e	12.58	1. 2	1.33
11. 6d	—	—	1.22
PM12.46d	—	—	2.15
12.52	—	—	2.43
2.12	—	—	3.31
2.49v	—	—	4. 5
3. 0e	4.46	—	4.39
3.18d	—	—	4.55
4.12	—	—	5.26
4.18	—	—	5.56
6.40	—	—	7.54
6.58	—	—	8.32
8.48	—	—	10.25
9. 9	11.21	11.23	—

Sunday Trains.

AM 7. 4	—	9.40	9.31r
10.11	—	11.58	11.51
10.29	—	1. 2	12.56
PM 3.39	—	—	5.31
6.59	—	—	8.20
7.19	—	—	8.40
8.38	—	—	10. 8
8.57	—	—	10.29
9.25	—	12. 0	11.44

d Saturdays only.
e Saturdays excepted.
f Mondays only.
k Third class only.
l Wednesdays only.
v Mondays, Fridays and Saturdays only.

ANOTHER ROUTE from *Charing Cross, Cannon Street, and London Bridge, via* Strood, 51 miles. Fares as above.

Leave Char.+	Can. St.	Lon. B.	Arr. at Faver.
AM —	—	3.57h	5.46
—	7.16	7.19	9.20
—	10.58h	11. 1k	1.13
—	10.58l	11. 1l	1.23
PM 5.58d	—	6. 4d	8. 2
—	6.12e	—	7.23
6.22e	—	6.29e	8.45
6.55d	—	7. 1d	9.14
—	7. 8e	7.11e	9.14
—	9.35	9.38	11.45

Sunday Trains.

PM 7. 0	—	7. 7	9.10

Trains from Faversham.

Leave Faver.	Lon. B.	Can. St.	Char.+
AM 6.39	8.34	—	8.41
7.39	9. 0	9. 4	—
8.44	9.48	9.52	—
PM 4.59e	7.14	—	7.23
6. 5d	8.15	8.20	—

Sunday Trains.

PM 9.2	11.15	—	11.24

d Saturdays only.
e Saturdays excepted.
h Third class only.
k Wednesdays and Saturdays excepted.
l Wednesdays only.

Ship Hotel. Principal Family and Commercial. Tudor period. Modern appointments. Stockrooms, Stables, Garage. Large Garden. En-tout-cas Tennis Courts. Telephone 179.
PERCY ADAMS.

FAWKHAM (Kent) from

Victoria, Holborn Viaduct and St. Paul's, 23¾ miles. Fares, 5/0a, 4/0b, 3/0c. R. T. for two months, 10/0a, 8/0b. Pop. 302.
Map Square 24.

Leave S.E & C.	Hol. V.	S. Pl.'s	Arr. at Fawkh.
AM 5. 5	4.57	5. 0	6.17
—	7.30	7.33	8.27
9.20	—	—	10. 4
11.40e	—	—	12.41
11.55d	—	—	12.52
PM —	1.24d	1.27d	2.13
—	3.22	3.25	4.32
3.40d	3.33d	3.36d	5. 8
4.25e	—	—	5. 8
5.30e	—	5.33e	6.25
6.16	6.10e	6.13e	7.16
7. 5	7. 0	7. 3	7.52
9. 0e	8.57e	9. 0e	10. 0
10.17	10.11	10.13	11.14

Sunday Trains.

AM 7.20	—	—	8.17
10.30	10.25	—	11.38
PM 3.30	—	—	4.29
6.35	—	—	7.30
10.15	10.12	—	11.21

Trains from Fawkham.

Leave Fawkh.	S. Pl.'s	Hol. V.	Vict.
AM 7.10	8. 8	8. 9	8.14
7.26	8.25	8.27	8.29
8.14	9.16	9.18	—
8.48	9.37	9.39	—
10.20	—	—	11. 2
PM12. 4d	1. 0	1. 2	—
12.27e	—	—	1.32
2.27	—	—	3.23
4.11e	5.32	5.34	5.21
5.48e	6.45	6.47	—
7. 3d	8. 0	8. 2	—
8.42	9.50	9.54	9.46
10.28	11.21	11.23	—

Sunday Trains.

AM 8.21	—	9.39	9.31
10.15	—	11.27	11.23
11.57	—	1. 2	12.56
PM 5.16	—	—	6. 3
10.48	—	12. 0	11.44

d Saturdays only.
e Saturdays excepted.

FAWLEY (Hereford), from *Paddington,* 136½ miles. Fares, 28/4a, 17/0c. R. T. for two months for Ross. Departures for London about 4 times daily.
Map Square 17.

FAYGATE (Sussex) from *London Bridge, Victoria,* and *Clapham Junction,* 34¼ miles. Fares, 7/3a, 4/4c. R. T. for two months, 14/6a, 8/8c.
Map Square 23.

Leave Vict.	Clap. J.	Lon. B.	Arr. at Fayg.
AM —	—	5.18	7.23
7.23	7.29	7.25	9.20
8.25	8.32	8. 7	10. 5
9. 0	9. 8	9. 6	10.26
9.45	9.50	9.50	11.21
10.35	10.42	10.35	12. 3
11.55	—	11.50	1.17

FAYGATE—*continued.*

Leave Vict.	Clap. J.	Lon. B.	Arr. at Fayg.
PM 1.20e	1.27e	—	2.46
1.25d	—	1.10d	2.46
2. 0	2. 7	2. 5	3.55
—	—	2. 8d	3.55
4.30	4. 8	4. 5	5.30
—	—	5. 5	6.11
5. 5	5.12	5.10	6.33
—	—	6. 0	7.14
6. 6	6.12	6. 8	7.49
7.15	7.22	7.20	8.46
9. 3	9.10	9.12	10.32

Sunday Trains.

AM 6.55	7. 2	7. 2	8.47
8.18	8.25	8.25	9.46
PM 1.14	1.21	1.10	4.17
6.33	6.40	6.33	8. 2

Trains from Faygate.

Leave Faygate	Lon. B.	Clap. J.	Vict.
AM 6.42	8.15	8.15	8.24
8. 1	9.10	9.31	9.19
9.33	10.55	10.40	10.48
10.39	12.13	11.59	12. 7
PM12. 7	1.42	1.39	1.50
12.41	2.22	2.13	2.22
2. 3	3.39	3.37	3.45
2.54	—	4. 9	4.17
3.21	4.32	4.27	4.35
4.22	5.54	5.47	5.57
5.24	6.36	6.26	6.34
6.57	8.46	—	—
9.22	10.58	11.10	11.17

Sunday Trains.

AM 8. 2	10.18	—	—
9.11	10.45	10.23	10.32
PM 3.33	5. 3	5. 1	5.11
6.21	7.56	—	7.50
8. 7	9.32	9.24	9.34

d Saturdays only.
e Saturdays excepted.

FAZAKERLEY (Lancs), 209¼ miles. Fares, 41/3a, 24/9c. R. T., double fare. Departures *from* London as for Wigan or St. Helens. Departures *for* London about 5 times daily. Pop. 5,155.
Map Square 12.

FEARN (Ross), 608¼ miles. Fares, 108/2a, 64/11c. R. T. for two months, 216/4a. Departures *from* London as for Dingwall. Departures *for* London about 3 times daily. Pop. 1,680.
Map Square 34.

FEATHERSTONE (Yorks) from *King's Cross,* 175¾ miles. Fares, 36/3a, 21/9c. R. T. for two months, 72/6a. Pop. 14,839.
Map Square 13.

King's+	F'rst'ne	F'rst'ne	King's+
AM 4.45	9.48	AM 8.40r	1. 5
—	7.15r 11.52	9.14r	1.55
10.10r	2.34	11.12r	3.50
PM 1.50r	6.52	PM 1.58r	6.15
4. 0r	9.18	4.24	9.25
10.45e	8. 5	5.54	10. 0
—	—	8.24e	3.25
—	—	9.15d	3.25

Sunday Trains.

12. 0nr	5. 7	AM11.26	5.15
PM10.45	8. 5	—	—

d Saturdays only.
e Saturdays excepted.
n Noon.
r Restaurant Car.

FEATHERSTONE

PARK (Northumberland), 306½ miles. No through fares. Departures from London as for Hexham or Carlisle. Departures for London as 3 times daily. Pop. 9,167.
Map Square 3.

FELIN FACH (Cardigan),

262½ miles. Fares, 49/9a, 30/2c. R. T. for two months, 99/6a, 60/4c. Departures from London as for Lampeter. Departures for London about 3 times daily.
Map Square 16.

FELIN HEN (Carnarvon),

240½ miles. Fares, 50/3a, 30/2c. R. T. for two months, 100/6a, 60/4c. Departures from London as for Bangor. Departures for London about 6 times daily.
Map Square 11.

FELIXSTOWE (TOWN)

(Suffolk) from Liverpool Street. 84½ miles. Fares, 17/9a, 10/8c. R. T. for two months, 35/6a, 21/4c. Pop. 11,655.
Map Square 19.

L'POOL ST.	FELIX.	FELIX.	L'POOL ST.
AM 5. 0	7.35	AM 7. 7	9.53
8.15r	11. 4	7.57r	10.30
8.46	11.52	8.53fr	11.22
10.12	12.32	9.10gr	11.22
10.20	1. 2	9.22fr	11.30
10.47	2. 5	10.52	1.20
PM12.56r	3. 0	PM12.33	3.36
1. 0	3.20	1.52	3.56
1.33d	5. 0	2.20r	4.58
3.18r	5.45	3.39	5.55
4.55hr	6.55	4. 4	6.32
4.55r	7.10	5. 5	7.51
5.18r	7.43	6. 1r	9.22
5.42d	9.23	7.14r	10. 0
6.39e	9.23	8.12	11.16
7.45r	10.30	—	—

Sunday Trains.

AM10. 5r	12.46	AM 8.29	11.38
11.30	2.56	PM 4.41	7.10
PM 3.40	6.48	5.21	8.58
4.40	6.56	7.10r	9.10
—	—	7.35	10.15

d Saturdays only.
e Saturdays excepted.
f Mondays only.
g Mondays excepted.
h Fridays only.
r Restaurant Car.

Felix Hotel. Under the management of the London and North Eastern Railway. Facing Sea. Modern Hotel with charming grounds of 15 acres. 250 Rooms. Telephone 221.
See advt. p. 169.

The Cliff, late Quilter's. Facing Sea. Restaurant. Billiards.
See advt. p. 170.

Orwell Hotel. Near Sea. Tennis. Garage. Excellent Cuisine.
See advt. p. 170.

Grand Hotel. Facing Sea. Finest position on promenade. Telephone No. 84.
See advt. p. 171.

Spa Hotel. Small First-class Hotel. Beautifully situated. Terms moderate.
See advt. p. 171.

The Clifton Private Hotel and Boarding Establishment, on Cliffs. Good Sea Views. Separate tables. The Misses SURMAN.

FELIXSTOWE—contd.

Oakington House Boarding Establishment. Pleasantly situated on Cliff. Sea View. Separate tables. Well furnished. Comfort studied. Electric Light. Tennis Court. Moderate terms.
The Misses ROSE.

Marlborough Private Hotel. Best position. Sea front. Dancing and picnics. Farm produce. Garage, one minute. Phone 126.
Mr. and Mrs. DAWSON.

Chatsworth Private Hotel. First class. Sea front. Near tennis and all amusements. Manager. Under same Proprietorship as Marlborough Hotel. 'Phone 130.

Melrose Private Hotel. Facing Sea. Centre of Promenade. First-class Family Hotel. Finest Cuisine. Dancing. Bridge. Telephone 103.
Mrs. J. C. BUTLER.

Waverley (facing Sea); on Cliff. Private Hotel and Boarding House. Croquet. Own farm produce. Private Sitting-rooms. Telephone No. 67.
Mrs. EAGLE & DAUGHTERS.

Westcliff Boarding House, Leopold Road. Pleasantly situated on Cliffs. Near Sea and Shops. Misses WRIGHT.

Ordnance Hotel. A.A. (Family and Commercial.) Nearest Licensed Hotel to New Pier. Bandstand and Model Yacht Pond. Tennis Courts. Large Garage. Excellent Cuisine. Separate Tables. R.A.C. Telephone 83.
Proprietor, C. W. PACKE.

Pier Hotel. Adjoins Dock station. Twenty Bedrooms. Stabling. Motor Garage. Catering a speciality. Moderate Tariff. 'Phone 181.
P.R.H.A. House.

Restormel, Victoria Street. En Pension. Central Position. Minute Sea. Close Cliff Gardens and Pier. Well Furnished. Good Cuisine. Moderate.
Proprietor, S. R. HALL.

St. Edmundsbury Boarding Establishment. Sea Road. Facing Sea. Near Pier and all entertainments. Good table. Moderate terms. Miss M. O. NEAME.

"Sandbank," Sea Road. Board Residence. Facing Sea and Tennis Courts. Excellent cuisine. Under personal supervision of Mr. and Mrs. WOOD.

House Agent, Felixstowe and District. Illustrated Register Furnished Houses, reliable and precise, free, also Apartments. House Agent, Auctioneer.
R. J. GIRLING, F.S.I.

House Agents, Felixstowe. Established 50 years. Illustrated Register Furnished Houses, Apartments, Properties for Sale. Apply—
W. G. ARCHER & CO.

FELLING (Durham), 266¼ miles. Fares, 55/7a, 33/4c. R. T., double fare. Departures from London as for Newcastle-on-Tyne. Departures for London about 6 times daily. Pop. 26,152.
Map Square 3.

FELMINGHAM (Norfolk)

from King's Cross, 159½ miles. Fares, 25/3a, 15/2c. R. T. for two months, 50/6a, 30/4c. Departures from London as for Aylsham Town. Departures for London about 5 minutes earlier. Pop. 420.
Map Square 14.

FELSTEAD (Essex) from

Liverpool Street, via Bishop's Stortford, 42½ miles. Fares, 18/0a, 5/5c. R. T. for two months, 18/0a. Pop. 2,089.
Map Square 24.

L'POOL ST.	F'STEAD	F'STEAD	L'POOL ST.
AM 7.18	9.24	AM 7.53	9.27
9.10	11.13	9.58	11.27
11.50h	1.27	11.57k	2. 7
PM12.29d	2.12	PM 2.40l	5. 9
2.34	3.59	2.43s	5. 9
4.45	6. 7	4.30	6.10
6.30	7.59	6.40	8.22

No Sunday Trains.

d Saturdays only.
h Wednesdays and Thursdays only.
k Wednesdays, Thursdays and Saturdays only.
l Mondays and Tuesdays only.
s Mondays and Tuesdays excepted.

ANOTHER ROUTE from

Liverpool Street, via Witham, 51 miles. Fares as above.

L'POOL ST.	F'STEAD	F'STEAD	L'POOL ST.
AM 5. 0	7.53	AM 9.24	11.16
8.15	9.58	11.13	1.16
8.46l	11.57	PM 3.59	5.48
11.30h	2.40	6. 7	9.17
11.30k	2.45	—	—
PM 2.15	4.30	—	—
4.58	6.40	—	—

No Sunday Trains.

h Mondays and Tuesdays only.
k Mondays and Tuesdays excepted.
l Wednesdays, Thursdays and Saturdays only.

FELTHAM (Middlesex)

from Waterloo, 15 miles. Fares, 2/4a, 1/8c. R. T. for two days, 4/8a, 2/10c. Pop. 6,526.
Map Squares 23 and 74.

W'LOO	FELTHAM	FELTHAM	W'LOO
AM 5.10	6. 2	AM 6. 6	6.36
5.55	6.25	7. 6	7.36
6.54	7.27	7.36	8. 6
7.24	7.57	7.51	8.17
7.54	8.29	8. 7	8.41
8.24	8.58	8.19	8.47
8.54	9.27	8.39	9. 6
9.24	9.58	9. 8	9.36
9.54	10.27	9.36	10. 6
10.24	10.57	10.36	11. 6
10.54	11.30	11.27	11.57
11.24	11.57	11.57	12.31
PM12.24	12.57	PM12.27	12.57
12.54d	1.27	12.57	1.27
1.24	1.57	1.27	1.57
1.54d	2.27	1.57	2.27
2.24	2.57	2.27	2.57
3.24	3.57	2.57	3.27
3.48d	4.18	3.27	3.57
4.24	4.57	4.27	4.57
4.48d	5.18	4.57	5.27
4.58e	5.28	5.27	5.57
5.24	5.57	5.57	6.27
5.54e	6.27	6.27	6.57
6.24	6.57	6.57	7.27
6.54e	7.27	7.27	7.57
7.24	7.57	7.57	8.27
7.54	8.29	8.27	8.57
8.24	8.57	8.57	9.27
9.24	9.57	10. 6	10.37
10.24	10.57	11.26e	12. 5
11.44	12.17	11.26d	12. 8

FELTHAM—*continued.*

Sunday Trains.

W'LOO	FELTHAM	FELTHAM	W'LOO
AM 8.18	8.54	AM 8.54	9.28
8.48	9.22	9.45	10.30
10.18	10.50	11. 9	11.43
11.18	11.51	PM12. 9	12.43
PM12.18	12.53	1. 9	1.43
1.18	1.52	1.29	2. 3
2.18	2.54	3. 9	3.43
3.18	3.50	5. 9	5.43
4.18	4.52	6. 9	6.43
5.18	5.51	6.54	7.28
5.58	6.32	7. 9	7.43
6.18	6.51	8. 9	8.43
7.18	7.51	8.54	9.28
7.48	8.21	9. 9	9.43
8.18	8.50	9.45	10.18
8.58	9.31	10. 9	10.43
9.18	9.52	11. 9	11.51
10.18	10.50		

d Saturdays only.
e Saturdays excepted.

FENAY BRIDGE (Yorks),
208 miles. Fares, 37/9a, 22/8c. R. T., double fare. Departures from London as for Huddersfield. Departures for London about 6 times daily.

FENCEHOUSES (Durham),
256½ miles. Fares, 53/6a, 32/1c. R.T. double fare. Departures from London as for Ferryhill or Durham. Departures for London about 6 times daily.

FENCOTE (Hereford), 140
miles. Fares, 27/9a, 16/8c. R.T. for two months, 55/6a, 33/4c. Departures from London as for Bromyard. Departures for London about 4 times daily. *Map Square 17*

FENISCOWLES (Lancs),
209 miles. Fares, 43/7a, 26/2c. R.T. for two months, 87/2a, 52/4c. Departures from London as for Chorley. Departures for London about 6 times daily.

FENN'S BANK (Salop),
173¾ miles. Fares, 35/3a, 21/2c. R. T. for two months, 70/6a. Departures from London as for Whitchurch (Salop). Departures for London about 6 times daily. *Map Square 12.*

FENNY COMPTON
(Warwick) from *Paddington,* 76½ miles. Fares, 15/10a, 19/6c. R. T. for two months, 31/8½. Departures from London as for Southam Road or Kineton. Departures for London about 4 times daily. Pop. 510. *Map Square 18.*

FENNY STRATFORD
(Bucks) from *Euston,* 47¾ miles. Fares, 9/10a, 5/11c. R. T. for two months, 19/8a, 11/10c. Pop. 5,166. *Map Square 18.*

EUSTON	FENNY S.	FENNY S.	EUSTON
AM 6.45	8.18	AM 7.18	9. 5
7.35	10. 3	8.53	10. 0
10.40	12. 5	10.28	11.55
12. 0nr	1.38	11.51	1.50
PM 2. 0	3.58	PM 1.23h	2.45
3. 5	4.33	1.23k	4.15
5.32e	6.51	3.42	5. 5
5.32d	7. 8	6.11	7.55
6.10e	7.33	6.31	8.35
7.15d	9.28	7.13e	9.20
8. 0e	9.28	9.21	11.35

No Sunday Trains.

d Saturdays only.
e Saturdays excepted.
h Thursdays and Saturdays only.
k Thursdays and Saturdays excepted.
n Noon.
r Restaurant Car.

FENTON (Stafford), 146¼
miles. Fares, 30/7a, 18/4c. R. T. for two months, 61/2a. Departures from London as for Stoke-on-Trent. Departures for London about 6 times daily. Pop. 25,620. *Map Square 12.*

FERNDALE (Glamorgan),
167½ miles. Fares, 34/10a, 20/11c. R. T. for two months, 69/8a, 41/10c. Departures from London as for Pontypridd. Departures for London about 4 times daily. Pop. 18,144.

FERNHILL HEATH
(Worcester), 123 miles. Fares, 23/9a, 14/3c. R. T. for two months, 47/6a, 28/6c. Departures from London as for Worcester. Departures for London about 6 times daily. *Map Square 17.*

FERRIBY (Yorks), 189½
miles. Fares, 35/0a, 21/0c. R. T. for two months, 70/0a. Departures from London as for Goole. Departures for London about 6 times daily. Pop. 648. *Map Square 12.*

FERRY (Norfolk) from *King's*
Cross, 99 miles. Fares, 17/11a, 10/9c. R. T. for two months, 35/10a. Departures from London as for Wisbech. Departures for London about 4 times daily. *Map Square 18.*

FERRYBRIDGE (Yorks),
from *St. Pancras* 183½ miles. Fares, 35/8a, 21/5c. R. T., double fare.

ST. PAN.	F'BRIDGE	F'BRIDGE	ST. PAN.
AM 2.25g	8.25	AM 8. 4r	1.30
9. 0r	2.16	PM 1.38r	7.15
10.25r	3.26	3. 2r	7.55
PM 1.50r	6.42	7.53	4.26
5. 0r	10. 7		

No Sunday Trains.

e Saturdays excepted.
g Mondays excepted.
r Restaurant Car.

FERRY HILL (Durham)
from *King's Cross,* 244¼ miles. Fares, 51/1a, 30/8c. R. T., double fare. Pop. 10,133. *Map Square 7.*

KING'S+	FER. H.	FER. H.	KING'S+
AM 7.15r	2.23	AM10.25r	4.30
10. 0r	4.18	11.53r	6.15
11.50fr	5.10	PM 2.53r	9.25
PM 1.15r	7. 1	4.25r	10. 0
1.50dr	10. 1	8. 2	3.25
11.25d	5. 1		
11.25e	5.14		

Sunday Trains.

AM11.30r	8.36	AM 7.40	5.15
PM11.25	5.14	PM 6.39	5.40

d Saturdays only.
e Saturdays excepted.
f Mondays only.
r Restaurant Car.

FERRYSIDE (Carmarthen)
from *Paddington,* 221 miles. Fares, 46/1a, 27/8c. R.T. for two months, 92/2a, 55/4c. Departures from London as for Kidwelly. Departures for London about 5 times daily. *Map Square 21.*

FESTINIOG (Merioneth)
from *Paddington,* 226½ miles. Fares, 47/2a, 28/5c. R. T. for two months, 94/8a, 56/10c. Departures from London as for Blaenau Festiniog. Departures for London about 5 times daily. Pop. 8,143. *Map Square 11.*

FFAIRFACH (Carmarthen)
from *Paddington,* 216 miles. Fares, 43/2a, 25/11c. R. T. for two months, 86/4a. Departures from London as for Llandilo. Departures for London about 4 times daily. *Map Square 21.*

FFRIDD GATE (Merioneth), 219½ miles. No through fares.
Departures from London as for Machynlleth. Departures for London about 4 times daily. *Map Square 16.*

FFRITH (Denbigh), 194½
miles. Fares, 37/11a, 23/0c. R. T. for two months, 75/10a, 46/0c. Departures from London as for Wrexham. Departures for London about 5 times daily.

FIDLER'S FERRY
(Lancs), 185 miles. Fares, 38/4a, 23/0c. R. T. for two months, 76/8a 46/0c. Departures from London as for Widnes. Departures for London about 4 times daily.

FILEY (Yorks) from *King's Cross*, 230½ miles. Fares, 47/11*a*, 28/9*c*. R. T. *for* two months, 95/10*a*, 57/6*c*. Pop. 4,549.
Map Square 8.

King's +	Filey	Filey	King's +
AM 4.45	11.32	AM 7.36*r*	1.15
7.15*r*	1.50	7.56*r*	1.30
10. 0*er*	3.40	8.25	3.50
10.10*r*	4.35	10.16*r*	4.30
11.50*er*	4.53	10.42*r*	4.45
11.50*dr*	5.29	PM12.53*r*	6.30
PM 1.50*r*	8.17	1.58*er*	7.30
10.45*e*	7.34	2.24*dr*	7.30
10.45*d*	9. 0	2.52*r*	9.25
11.25*e*	7.53	4.39*r*	10. 0
11.25*d*	11.47	6.53*e*	3.25
—	—	8.21	5.40
—	—	—	—

Sunday Trains.

PM10.45	7.34	PM 7.21	5.40
11.25	7.53	—	—
—	—	—	—

d Saturdays only.
e Saturdays excepted.
r Restaurant Car.

Royal Crescent Hotel. Leading Hotel. Facing Sea. Lounge. Garage. 30 Private Lock-ups. Tennis. Central Heating. Telephone No. 60.
See advt. p. **172.**

FILLEIGH (Devon) from *Paddington*, 180½ miles. Fares, 37/9*a*, 22/8*c*. R.T. for two months, 75/6*a*, 45/4*c*. Departures *from* London as for Dulverton. Departures *for* London about 3 times daily. Pop. 288.
Map Square 21.

FILTON (Gloucester) from *Paddington*, 112¼ miles. Fares, 23/7*a*, 14/2*c*. R.T. for two months, 47/2*a*. Departures *from* London as for Bristol. Departures *for* London about 6 times daily. Pop. 658.
Map Square 22.

FINCHLEY (Church End) (Middlesex), from *King's Cross, Moorgate Street*, and *Broad Street*, 7¼ miles. Fares from King's Cross, 1/4½*a*, 1/1*b*, 0/10*c*. R. T. for two days, 2/7½*a*, 2/2*b*, 1/8*c*. From Moorgate Street and Broad Street, 1/5½*a*, 1/2*b*, 0/10½*c*. R. T. for two days, 2/11*a*, 2/4*b*, 1/9*c*. Pop. 46,716.
See pp. 518-522.
Map Square 23.

FINCHLEY, EAST (Middlesex) from *King's Cross, Moorgate Street* and *Broad Street*, 5¾ miles. Fares from King's Cross, 1/0½*a*, 0/10*b*, 0/7½*c*. R.T. for two days, 2/1*a*, 1/8*b*, 1/3*c*. From Moorgate Street and Broad Street, 1/2*a*, 0/11*b*, 0/8½*c*. R. T. for two days, 2/4*a*, 1/10*b*, 1/4½*c*. Pop. 13,499.
See pp. 518-522.
Map Square 51.

FINCHLEY ROAD from *Baker Street*, 2¼ miles. Fares, 0/5*a*, 0/3*c*. R. T. for two days, 0/10*a*, 0/6*c*. *See* back of Map.
Map Square 60.

Another Route from *Moorgate Street* and *St. Pancras*, 3½ miles. Fares from St. Pancras, 0/9*a*, 0/5½*c*. R. T. for two days, 1/5½*a*, 0/10½*c*. From Moorgate Street, 0/10*a*, 0/6*c*. R. T. for two days, 1/5½*a*, 0/10½*c*. *See* pp. 507, 508.
Map Square 60, No. 1.

FINCHLEY ROAD AND FROGNAL, from *Broad Street*, 7¾ miles. Fares, 0/10*a*, 0/6*c*. R. T. for two days, 1/5½*a*, 0/10½*c*. *See* pp. 501-505.
Map Square 60.

FINDOCHTY (Banff) 589¼ miles. No through fares. Departures *from* London as for Huntly or Elgin (*via* Dunkeld). Departures *for* London about twice daily. Pop. 1,646.
Map Square 35.

FINEDON (Northampton) 68¾ miles. Fares, 14/0*a*, 8/5*c*. R.T., double fare. Departures *from* London as for Wellingboro'. Departures *for* London about 6 times daily. Pop. 3,973.
Map Square 18.

FINGHALL LANE (Yorks), 231 miles. Fares, 48/2*a*, 28/11*c*. R.T., double fare. Departures *from* London as for Leyburn. Departures *for* London about 6 times daily. Pop. (Finghall) 81.
Map Square 7.

FINMERE (Oxford) from *Marylebone*, 54½ miles. Fares, 11/5*a*, 6/10*c*. R.T., double fare. Pop. 222.
Map Square 18.

M'bone	Finmere	Finmere	M'bone
AM 6.45	8.39	AM 7.57	9.46
8.45*r*	10. 2	9.27	10.36
11.15	1.15	10.34	12. 2
PM 3.25	5.21	PM 3. 2	4.56
4.30	5.45	5.53	7.15
4.55	6.43	8. 7	9.55
6.20	7.28	9.15	11. 0
6.25*e*	8. 7	—	—
6.25*d*	8.16	—	—
7.30	9.35	—	—
—	—	—	—

Sunday Trains.

AM 9.30	11.24	AM 8. 4	10.13
PM 6.30	8.43	PM 6.46	8.58
—	—	—	—
—	—	—	—
—	—	—	—

d Saturdays only.
e Saturdays excepted.
r Restaurant Car.

FINNINGHAM (Suffolk) from *Liverpool Street*, 86½ miles. Fares, 18/2*a*, 10/11*c*. R. T. for two months, 36/4*a*. Pop. 355
Map Square 19.

L'pl St.	Finhm.	Finhm.	L'pl St.
AM 5. 0	7.33	AM 7.53*r*	10.30
10.12	12.54	11.32*r*	2. 3
PM12.33*r*	3. 7	PM 2.24*r*	4.58
3.10*r*	5.35	4.57	7.51
5.18*dr*	7.53	5.49*dr*	9.22
5.18*er*	7.55	8.10	11.16
—	—	—	—
—	—	—	—
—	—	—	—
—	—	—	—
—	—	—	—

Sunday Trains.

AM 9.20*r*	12.16	AM 8.22	11.38
PM 4.40	7. 9	PM 7. 9	10.15
—	—	—	—
—	—	—	—

d Saturdays only.
e Saturdays excepted.
r Restaurant Car.

FINNINGLEY (Notts) 157¾ miles. Fares, 32/4*c*, 19/5*c*. R. T., double fare. Departures *from* London as for Gainsborough or Doncaster. Departures *for* London about 5 times daily. Pop. 337.
Map Square 1.

FINSBURY PARK from *King's Cross, Moorgate Street*, and *Broad Street*, 2¼ miles. Fares from King's Cross, 0/5*a*, 0/4*b*, 0/3*c*. R.T. for two days, 0/10*a*, 0/8*b*, 0/6*c*. From Moorgate Street and Broad Street, 0/5*a*, 0/4*b*, 0/3*c*. R. T. for two days, 0/10*a*, 0/8*b*, 0/6*c*. Pop. 7,319. *See* pp. 511-522.
Map Square 23 *and* 52.

Another Route (Hammersmith and Finsbury Park Tube and Metropolitan Railway (G.N. & City). *See* back of Map.

FIRSBY (Lincoln) from *King's Cross*, 122½ miles. Fares, 25/5*a*, 15/3*c*. R. T., double fare. Pop. 227.
Map Square 13.

King's +	Firsby	Firsby	King's +
AM 4.45	8.27	AM 6.57	10.40
7.15*r*	11. 0	10.10	1. 5
8.45	12.45	11. 5	3.50
11.30	4. 2	PM 1.20*r*	4.30
PM 4. 0*r*	6.58	3.59	9. 0
5.45*r*	8.55	6.17*r*	9.25
10.45*e*	4.23	9. 6	3.25
—	—	—	—
—	—	—	—

Sunday Trains.

12. 0*nr*	3.49	AM11.13*r*	3.45
PM10.45	4.23	—	—
—	—	—	—
—	—	—	—
—	—	—	—

e Saturdays excepted.
n Noon.
r Restaurant Car.

FISHGUARD HARBOUR (Pembroke) from *Paddington*, 269 miles. Fares, 50/0*a*, 30/0*c*. R. T. for two months, 100/0*a*, 60/0*c*. Pop. 2,999.

Pad.	F'guard	F'guard	Pad.
AM 1. 0*gk*	12. 9	AM 4.55*gr*	10.57
8.45*r*	2.50	7.50*r*	2.30
11.50*r*	7. 2	10.20*kr*	6.15
PM 1.10*dr*	9.28	PM12.25*kr*	8.35
5. 0*r*	11.30	2. 0*r*	9.25
9.15*ek*	10. 9	6.10	3.30
—	—	—	—
—	—	—	—

Sunday Trains.

PM 9.15*k*	10. 9	AM 6.20	3.35
—	—	—	—
—	—	—	—

d Saturdays only.
e Saturdays excepted.
g Mondays excepted.
k Fishguard and Goodwick.
r Restaurant Car.

Fishguard Bay Hotel. Entirely modern. Sub-tropical Gardens. Telephone: Fishguard 21.
See advt. p. **172.**

FISHPONDS (Gloucester),
120 miles. No through fares.
Departures *from* London as for
Bristol. Departures *for* London
about 6 times daily. Pop. 5,795.

FISKERTON (Notts) from
St. Pancras, 135¾ miles. Fares,
25/0a, 15/0c. R. T., double fare.
Departures *from* London as for
Nottingham. Departures *for* London about 6 times daily. Pop. 350.

FITTLEWORTH (Sussex)
from *London Bridge, Victoria,* and
Clapham Junction, 52¾ miles.
Fares, 11/0a, 6/7c. R. T. for two
months, 22/0a, 13/2c. Departures
from London as for Petworth.
Departures *for* London about 6
times daily. Pop. 648.
Map Square 23.

FIVE MILE HOUSE (Lincoln), 133 miles. Fares, 27/8a,
16/7c. R. T., double fare. Departures *from* London as for
Bardney. Departures *for* London
about 5 times daily.
Map Square 13.

FLADBURY (Worcester)
from *Paddington*, 109¾ miles. Fares.
22/9a, 13/8c. R. T. for two months,
45/6a. Departures *from* London
as for Evesham. Departures *for*
London about 5 times daily.
Pop. 468.
Map Square 17.

FLAMBOROUGH
(Yorks.) 219½ miles. Fares, 41/11a,
25/2c. R. T. for two months,
83/10a, 50/4c. Departures *from*
London as for Bridlington. Departures *for* London about 4 times
daily. Pop. 1,169.
Map Square 8.

FLAX BOURTON
(Somerset), 123½ miles. Fares,
25/8a, 15/5c. R. T. for two months,
51/4a. Departures *from* London
as for Bristol. Departures *for*
London about 8 times daily. Pop.
236.
Map Square 22.

FLAXTON (Yorks), 197¼
miles. Fares, 41/1a, 24/8c. R. T.,
double fare. Departures *from*
London as for York. Departures
for London about 6 times daily.
Pop. 320.
Map Square 8.

FLECKNOE (Northampton) from *Euston*, 79¾ miles. Fares,
16/6a, 9/11c. R.T. for two months,
33/0a. Departures *from* London
as for Braunston. Departures *for*
London about 4 times daily.
Map Square 18.

FLEDBOROUGH (Notts),
141½ miles. Fares, 27/4a, 16/5c.
R. T., double fare. Departures
from London as for Lincoln or
Edwinstowe. Departures *for* London about 3 times daily. Pop. 100.
Map Square 13.

FLEET (Hants) from *Waterloo*, 36½ miles. Fares, 7/8a, 4/7c.
R. T. for two months, 15/4a, 9/2c.
Pop. 3,689.
Map Square 23.

W'LOO	FLEET	FLEET	W'LOO
AM 5.50	7.15	AM 7.33	8.41
7.30	8.44	8.26	9.26
8.34	9.48	9. 7	9.56
9.20	10.31	9.57	10.56
10.34	11.52	11. 3	12.11
PM12.40	1.54	PM12. 3	1.20
1.15d	2.32	2. 8	3.16
2.34	3.56	3. 0	4. 6
3.40	4.55	4. 3	5.20
4.40	6. 2	5. 3	6.16
5.10e	6.12	5.59	7. 7
6. 0	6.56	8. 7	9.26
6.40d	7.54	10.52	12.16
6.54e	7.52	—	—
8. 0	9.12	—	—
8.55	10.23	—	—

Sunday Trains.

AM 9. 0	10.13	AM 8.10	9.45
9.45	11. 7	10.52	12.41
11.15	12.25	11.38	12.52
PM 5. 5	6.16	PM 5. 7	6. 7
6. 0	7.11	8. 2	9.12
7.20	8.41	9.41	10.52
9.28	10.53	—	—
—	—	—	—

d Saturdays only.
e Saturdays excepted.

FLEET (Lincoln) from
King's Cross, 102½ miles. Fares,
20/3a, 12.2c. R. T. for two months,
40/6a, 24/4c. Departures *from*
London as for Holbeach. Departures *for* London about 5 minutes earlier. Pop. 1,155.
Map Square 18.

FLEETWOOD (Lancs)
from *Euston*, 229¾ miles. Fares,
47/9a, 28/8c. R. T. for two months,
95/6a, 57/4c. Pop. 19,448.
Map Square 7.

EUSTON	FLWOOD.	FLWOOD.	EUSTON
AM12.25	8. 4	AM 6. 5gr11.10	
2.35	10. 4	7.47dr 1.45	
5. 0	12. 8	8. 2er 1.45	
8.30dr	2.39	8.20r 3.10	
10.40er	4.40	9.30r 4.15	
11.35	5.19	10.35t 5.50	
11.50r	6.33	10.50et 6. 0	
PM 1.30r	7.21	PM12. 5dt 6.25	
2.35t	8.51	1. 5r 7.30	
5.20r	10.25	1.20r 8.10	
9.30d	10.20	2.45er 9. 5	
11.50d	11.44	2.45dr 9.15	
—	—	4.50r 10.45	
—	—	9.25 5. 0	

Sunday Trains.

AM11.45r	9.59	AM 8. 5r	1.30
—	—	PM 1. 5r	7.30
—	—	7.15	5. 0

d Saturdays only.
e Saturdays excepted.
g Mondays excepted.
r Restaurant Car.
t Tea Car.

Sailings from Fleetwood
to Belfast daily. *See advt.* p. 596.
Map Square 7.

FLEMINGTON (Lanark),
387½ miles. Fares, 78/11a, 47/4c.
R. T.for two months 157/10a, 94/8c.
Departures *from* London as for
Carstairs. Departures *for* London about 3 times daily.

FLIMBY (Cumberland), 313¾
miles. No through fares. Departures *from* London as for Workington or Maryport. Departures
for London about 5 times daily.
Pop. 2,487.
Map Square 6.

FLINT, 191¼ miles. Fares,
39/10a, 23/11c. R. T. for two
months, 79/8a. Departures *from*
London as for Chester. Departures *for* London about 5 times
daily. Pop. 6,302.
Map Square 11.

FLITWICK (Beds) from
St. Pancras, 40 miles. Fares, 8/4a,
5/0c. R. T., double fare. Pop. 1,424.
Map Square 18.

ST. PAN.	FLITWK.	FLITWK.	ST.PAN.
AM 6.25	8. 4	AM 6.51	8.28
8.25r	9.33	7.54	9.13
9.25d	10.54	8.49	10. 5
11. 0r	12.23	10.59	12. 5
11.35d	12.52	PM12.10r	1.20
PM12.30	1.43	1.41d	3.10
1.35d	2.55	2.14	3.25
3.35	4.58	3. 5d	5.10
4.40	6. 6	5. 7	6.30
5.40e	6.45	6.46	8.20
6.35	7.53	8.48	10. 5
7.50	9.11	10.23	11.45
8.25d	10.46	—	—

Sunday Trains.

AM 8. 0	9.44	AM 8.21	10.15
PM 4.35	6.18	11.46	1.30
—	—	PM 7. 2	8.30
—	—	—	—
—	—	—	—

d Saturdays only.
e Saturdays excepted.
r Restaurant Car.

FLIXTON (Lancs), 195¼
miles. Fares, 39/10a, 23/11c. R. T.
for two months, 79/8a, 47/10c. Departures *from* London as for
Glazebrook. Departures *for* London about 6 times daily. Pop. 4,845.
Map Square 12.

FLORDON (Norfolk) from
Liverpool Street, 106¾ miles. Fares,
22/4a, 13/5c. R. T. for two months,
44/8a. Departures *from* London
as for Forncett. Departures *for*
London about 6 times daily. Pop.
190.
Map Square 19.

FLORISTON (Cumberland), 305¼ miles. No through
fares. Departures *from* London
as for Carlisle. Departures *for*
London about 4 times daily.
Map Square 3.

FLUSHDYKE (Yorks), 178¾

miles. Fares, 37/3a, 22/4c. R. T., double fare. Departures *from London* as for Dewsbury. Departures *for London* about 8 times daily.

FOCHABERS (Elgin), 591

miles. Fares, 106/3a, 63 9c. R. T. for two months, 212/6a, 127/6c. Departures *from London* as for Keith or Elgin. Departures *for London* about twice daily. Pop. 1,020.
Map Square 35.

FOCHRIW (Glamorgan),

167 miles. Fares, 34/5a, 20/8c. R.T. for two months, 68/10a, 41/4c. Departures *from London* as for Bargoed. Departures *for London* about 4 times daily. Pop. 3,994.

FOCKERBY (Lincoln), 179¼

miles. Fares, 22/5c. R. T., double fare. Departures *from London* as for Goole. Departures *for London* about 4 times daily. Pop. 74.

FOGGATHORPE

(Yorks), 183½ miles. No through fares. Departures *from London* as for Selby. Departures *for London* about 4 times daily. Pop. 128.
Map Square 13.

FOLESHILL (Warwick), 97

miles. Fares, 20/3a, 12/2c. R. T. for two months, 40/6a. Departures *from London* as for Coventry. Departures *for London* about 6 times daily. Pop. 7,781.
Map Square 17.

FOLKESTONE CENTRAL (Kent) from *Charing Cross, Cannon Street,* and *London Bridge*,

70¾ miles. Fares, 14/10a, 11/11b, 8/11c. R. T. for two months, 29/8a, 23/10b, 17/10c. Pop. 37 571.
Map Square 24.

	Leave		Arr. at
CHAR.+	CAN. ST.	LON. B.	FOLK. C.
AM —	3.40s	3.43s	6.12
—	5.20	5.25	8.58
—	6.45	6.50	9.44
—	—	7.50l	10. 8
9.15	—	9.23	11. 0
—	—	k10.30l	12. 6
11. 0	—	11. 7	1.20
11.15	—	—	12.48
PM1. 0p	—	—	2.20
1.50d	—	1.56d	3.16
2.55d	—	3. 1d	4.32
3. 0	—	3. 8	5. 0
4. 5	—	—	5.25
4.30	—	4.37	6.11
—	5. 0v	—	6.20
—	5.12e	—	6.47
5.15e	—	5.21e	7.20
5.24d	—	5.34d	8. 3
6. 0e	—	6. 5e	7.30
7. 0	—	—	8.20
7.18	—	7.26	10. 2
9.30	—	9.36	11.16
11.51h	—	—	1.48

Sunday Trains.

AM 7.45	—	7.52	10. 7
9 35	—	—	10.55
10.15	—	—	11.46
PM 7.35	—	7.45	10. 3

FOLKESTONE CENTRAL—*continued.*

Trains from Folkestone Central.

Leave		Arrive at	
FOLK. C.	LON. B.	CAN. ST.	CHAR.+
AM 7. 0	9.32	9.36	—
8. 8d	10. 0	10. 4	—
8.10e	9.36	9.40	—
9.15	10.34	—	10.41
9.37	11.43	—	11.57
10.50h	—	—	12.15
11. 0	—	—	12.20
11.15	1.36	—	1.50
PM 1.35	3.26	—	3.40
d1.35p	3.26	—	3.40
2.37	4. 1	—	4.10
3.17	5.50	—	6. 3
5.10	—	—	6.30
5.27	7.25	7.30e	7.49
8.10	10.22	—	10.35
11. 6s	—	1.20	—

Sunday Trains.

AM 7. 8	10. 5	—	10.15
PM 5.10	—	—	6.30
5.25	7. 9	—	7.17
6.48	—	—	8.17
8.35	10.16	—	10.26
11. 3s	—	1.23	—

d Saturdays only.
e Saturdays excepted.
h Wednesdays only.
k Mondays and Saturdays only.
l Low Level platform.
p Pullman car attached.
s Third class only.
v Fridays only.
y Wednesdays and Saturdays only.

ANOTHER ROUTE from

Victoria, 73 miles. Fares as above.

VICT.	Leave		Arrive
(S.E.&C.)	HOL. V.	ST. PLS.	FOLK. C.
AM —	6.40	6.42	9.44
—	—	—	11.48
9.45	—	—	2.13
11. 4d	10.58d	11. 0d	2.15
11. 4	10.58	11. 0	2.35
PM 2.12e	1.24d	1.30d	5. 0
2.50e	—	—	6.11
4.25e	—	—	6.47
7.22	—	—	10. 2
—	7.22d	7.24d	11.16
—	—	—	—

Sunday Trains.

AM 9.35	8. 0	—	12. 4
PM 5.15	—	—	7.50
6.35	6.40	—	10. 3

Trains from Folkestone Central.

Leave		Arrive	
FOLK. C.	ST. PLS.	HOL. V.	VICT.
AM 7. 0	9.53	9.55	—
10. 7	12.59	1. 2	12.49
11.15	—	—	2.40
PM12.50	—	—	3.37
3.17	—	—	5.42
5.27	—	—	8.51
8.10	11.43	11.45	—

Sunday Trains.

AM 7. 8	—	—	10.48
10.40	—	—	1. 5
PM 12.53	—	—	3.50
6.25	—	9. 9	—

d Saturdays only.
e Saturdays excepted.

FOLKESTONE JUNC.

(Kent) from *Charing Cross, Cannon Street,* and *London Bridge,* 71¾ miles. Fares, 15/0a, 12/0b, 9/0c. R. T. for two months, 30/0a, 24/0b, 18/0c.
Map Square 24.

	Leave		Arr. at
CHAR. +	CAN. ST.	LON. B.	FOLK. J.
AM —	3.40s	3.43s	6.21
—	5.20	5.25	9. 3
—	6.45	6.50	9.50
9.15	—	9.23	11.38
—	—	l10. 3j	12. 8
11. 0	—	11. 7	1.26
PM 1. 0	—	—	2.26
3. 0	—	3. 8	5. 7
—	5.12e	—	6.53
5.15e	—	5.21e	7.25
5.24d	—	5.34d	8.10
6. 0e	—	6. 5e	7.57
7. 0	—	—	8.33
7.18	—	7.26	10. 7
9.30	—	9.36	11.21
11.51	—	—	1.53

Sunday Trains.

AM 7.45	—	7.52	10.12
10.10	—	10.18	12. 9
PM 7.35	—	7.45	10. 9
9.25	—	9.31	12.10

Trains from Folkestone Junction.

Leave		Arrive at	
FOLK. J.	LON. B.	CAN. ST.	CHAR. +
AM 6.55	9.32	9.36	—
7.55e	10. 0	10. 4	—
8. 5d	10. 0	10. 4	—
8.52	10.54	—	11. 3
9.31	11.43	—	11.57
10.42k	—	—	12.15
11. 5	1.36	—	1.50
PM 1.25	3.26	—	3.40
1.41j	4. 8	—	—
3. 7	5.50	—	6. 3
5.20	7.25	7.30e	7.49
8. 0	10.22	—	10.35
9.27	11.35	—	11.44
10.56s	—	1.20	—

Sunday Trains.

AM 7. 0	10. 5	—	10.15
PM 5.17	7. 9	—	7.17
6.17	8.30	—	8.40
8.28	10.16	—	10.26
10.56s	—	1.23	—

d Saturdays only.
e Saturdays excepted.
h Wednesdays and Saturdays excepted.
j Fridays only.
k Wednesdays only.
l Low Level platform.
s Third Class only.

FOLKESTONE—*contd.*

Lyndhurst Private Hotel. Clifton Gardens. Elegantly appointed, overlooking the Leas. Perfect sea views. Lift. Tel. 101. *See advt.* p. **173.**

Royal Pavilion Hotel. Sole Caterers to S.E. & C. Railway. Continental Boats. Spacious Winter Garden; Garage. Telegrams: "Pavilion, Folkestone." Telephone : 86 Folkestone. FREDERICK HOTELS (Ltd.) *See advt.* p. **174.**

Hotel Metropole. The Leading Hotel. Finest position on Leas. Cuisine, Service and Appointments unsurpassed. Music. Dancing. Telegrams : "Metropole, Folkestone." Telephone : 446. GORDON HOTELS, Ltd. *See advt.* p. **175.**

The Burlington. Standing in own Grounds. Facing Sea. due South. Luxuriously furnished. Lift, Electric Light, Tennis. Telephone Nos. 33 and 413. *See advt.* p. **176.**

Hundert's Hotel Regina. 100 Apartments. Enlarged. Best position. Full South. Book for Central Station. Resident Proprietor. *See advt.* p. **176.**

Leas Hotel. Leading Family Hotel. Overlooking Leas and Gardens. The most reasonable Hotel in Folkestone. 100 Rooms. Fully licensed. Telephone, 45. Managing Director— T. H. VINNICOMBE. *See advt.* p **177.**

The Langhorne, Centre of Leas. Lounge and Recreation Room. Lift to all floors. 50 Bedrooms. Terms from 10/6 per day. Tel. 357. *See advt.* p. **177.**

Esplanade Hotel (late Bates). Overlooking Lawns, Sea View. Fully Licensed. Grill Room and Popular Café. Telephone 140. Apply Resident Proprietor, M. ROSÉNZ. *See advt.* p. **178.**

Moore's, Folkestone. On the Leas, facing Sea. South aspect. Certified Sanitation. 'Phone 254. Station. Central. *See advt.* p. **178.**

Hotel Majestic. Recently opened. Luxuriously furnished. 200 rooms. Sea views. Electric Lift. Orchestra. Garage. Telephone 286. Telegrams : "Majestic, Folkestone." *See advt.* p. **179.**

Hotel Wampach. Close to Sea. Links. Pleasure Grounds. Fully Licensed. Garage. Telephone 39. Telegrams : "Wampach, Folkestone." *See advt.* p. **179.**

Norfolk Hotel, 40 Rooms. Fine position, overlooking the Leas and Gardens. Recently modernized and redecorated. Under personal management of the Proprietor. Most reasonable tariff. Telephone 348. T. E SAINSBURY. *See advt.* p. **180.**

Clevedon, Longford Terrace. Sea View from every window. Moderate terms. Apply— Proprietress, Mrs. BRIX. *See advt.* p. **180.**

FOLKESTONE—*contd.*

Wynstead, Clifton Crescent. High-class Boarding Establishment. Tariff on application. *See advt.* p. **180.**

Sothoron Lodge Pension, West Leas. Best position. Sea views. *See advt.* p. **180.**

Pier Hotel, Sea Front, near Harbour. Terms moderate. Manager, RAYNER (formerly of Trust Houses). *See advt.* p. **181.**

Clifton Private Hotel, The Leas. Unique situation. Sea views from every window. Noted for Cuisine, Service, and Comfort. *See advt.* p. **181.**

The Belvedere, Trinity Crescent. Replete with every modern comfort. Tel. : 27. Telegrams : "Comfort." Manager, B. M. BARTLETT. *See advt.* p. **181.**

Bath Hotel. Sheltered position. Inclusive Terms from £3 3s. weekly. 'Phone 117. *See advt.* p. **181.**

The Cambridge. Latest up-to-date Private Hotel. Reasonable Terms. *See advt.* p. **182.**

Trevarra Private Hotel. Bouverie Road, West. Facing South. Central position. Near Sea, Leas and Links. Excellent Cuisine. Established 1900. Private Suites. Moderate. 'Phone 74. M. C. KEY. *See advt.* p. **182.**

Greystones, Clifton Crescent. Magnificent position on Leas. Gardens in front. Excellent Catering and attention. Separate Tables. Two Bath-rooms. Inclusive Terms. Mrs. W. E. THORPE. *See advt.* p. **182.**

Coman's Hotel. Castle Hill Avenue. Old established. Close to Leas, Theatre. Station. Terms from 3½ guineas. Tel. 241. *See advt.* p. **182.**

Whittall's Hotel. Clifton Gardens, Leas. Special Terms Winter and Spring. *See advt.* p. **183.**

Chatsworth Boarding Establishment, Marine Crescent. Facing Sea. Lounge. Liberal Table. Very Moderate Tariff. Tel. 360. Mrs. G. N. LESTER, Proprietress. *See advt.* p. **183.**

The Albany Private Hotel, Clifton Crescent. On Leas. Facing Sea. Near Bandstand, Pleasure Gardens. Tennis. Modern. Moderate. 'Phone 541. Mrs. McPHERSON, Proprietress. *See advt.* p. **183.**

Bouverie House Pension, 25 and 26, Bouverie Square. Private motor. Tennis. Home comforts. Central Station. F. W. POPE.

Cranbrook House, 59, Sandgate Road and Leas. Best position. Overlooking Private Gardens and Sea. Highly recommended Boarding House. Smoking Room. Tennis, Croquet. Central. PROPRIETRESS.

Central Hotel, opposite Central Station. Five minutes from Leas, Theatre, Town Hall. Newly Furnished. Sanitation perfect. Tel. 366 Folkestone. REMNANT & CO., Proprietors.

FOLKESTONE—*contd.*

Perth House, 11, Trinity Gardens. Comfortable Boarding House. Close to Leas and Bandstand. Misses JAMES, late of 6, Augusta Gardens.

Queen's Hotel. High-class Accommodation. Redecorated and partially Refurnished. By tariff or en pension. Table d'Hote (separate tables). Tel. No. 42.

Rose Hotel, Family and Commercial, close to Leas, now reopened. Hotel remodelled and refurnished, with latest improvements. Billiard Room, two tables. Coffee Room, open to non-residents. Tariff on application.

Edgecliffe. The Leas. High-class Pension. Sea views every window. Moderate terms. Apply, PROPRIETOR.

The Osborne. High-class Temperance Hotel, 10 Bouverie Road West. Near Sea, Theatre, Central Station. Every comfort. Moderate Tariff. Mrs. HOGBEN. Proprietress.

"Salisbury Private Hotel." Old-established, on Leas, due South, every window overlooking Sea. Luxurious lounge. Excellent cuisine. Perfect sanitation. Tennis. Croquet. Lift. Telephone 141. Station, Folkestone Central. Proprietress, Mrs. M. L. TURNER.

Casbon House, 14, Castle Hill Avenue, late of Trinity Crescent. High-class Pension. Home comforts studied. Separate tables. Miss CASBON.

"Blounts" Private Hotel. Clifton Gardens. Adjacent to Leas and Bandstand. Sea views. Large Private Pleasure Grounds. Tennis, etc. Cooking a special feature. Telephone 118. Moderate Tariff. Resident Proprietress. Mrs. PRATT.

Tressillian, Clifton Crescent (corner of Earl's Avenue). This comfortable Pension, liberally administered at its pre-war standard, offers good class accommodation from 4½ guineas weekly. Daily rate, 14/6. Winter, 12/6. Tel. 405. F. M. DELL, Proprietor.

Victoria Hotel, on Sea front. Near Cliff Gardens and Lift to Leas. Convenient for Continental passengers. Inclusive Terms. Telephone 64. RESIDENT PROPRIETRESS.

Parade House Boarding Establishment, The Parade. Overlooking Harbour. All rooms facing Sea and South. Finest views in Folkestone. Terms moderate. Every comfort. Well recommended. Apply— Miss FIELD.

Barrelle House, Marine Parade. Boarding Establishment. Facing sea. Newly decorated. Perfect sanitation. Personal supervision. From 2½ guineas. Mrs. WOLFE, Proprietress.

Lawnside Private Hotel, 23, Clifton Crescent, The Leas. Facing due South with full Sea Views, and situated in the most select part of Folkestone. This Hotel has been redecorated throughout, and is elegantly furnished. Excellent Cuisine. Telegrams, "Lawnside." Telephone 690.

FOLKESTONE—*contd.*

Rhodesia. The Leas. Standing in its own grounds. Overlooking Channel. Two minutes from Theatre and Bandstand. Special Winter Terms. 'Phone 712.
Proprietors—
Messrs. BARTON & DIXON.

Apartments. First - class position, overlooking Bandstand, Leas, and Sea. Comfortably furnished. Special Winter Terms. Resident Proprietors, Kingswood, Clifton Gardens, Folkestone.

The Carlton. The Leas. Best Central Position Sea Front: South Aspect. Excellent Cuisine. Separate Tables. Garden. Reasonable Inclusive Terms. 'Phone 290.

Beach House Hotel, Marine Parade. Facing Sea. Minute Cross-channel Steamers. Close to beautiful Under-cliff. Terms from 7/6 per day. No vexatious extras. 'Phone 671.

Lismore House, 5, Shorncliffe Road. Board Residence. Near Sea Golf Links and Station. The Misses MEDLEN.

San Remo Private Hotel, 19, Clifton Gardens. Charming residence in Private Gardens. Tennis Court. Board and Apartments. Terms from 8s. per day. Excellent cuisine. Tel. 730.

Holderness Private Hotel, Clifton Crescent, The Leas. Overlooking sea and private lawns. Ideal position. Well furnished. Excellent cuisine. Telegrams: "Holderness." Telephone 794.

Apartments. "Westbury," 38, Earls Avenue. Two minutes from Theatre, Leas, and Tennis Courts. Fine position. Excellent cooking. Terms moderate.

Sherwoods (Oldest Established), Auctioneers, House and Estate Agents, 100/2, Sandgate Road, Folkestone (opposite G.P.O.), and 112, High Street, Sandgate. Telephones, Folkestone 205, Sandgate 63. Telegrams, "Sherwoods, Folkestone."

Geo. Milne & Co., Auctioneers, House Agents, &c. Furnished and Unfurnished Houses. Businesses, Shops. Boarding and Apartment Houses for disposal. Printed register and map. 107, Sandgate Road. Tel. 619. Telegrams, "Milne, Folkestone."

Seager & Co., The Leas Estate Offices, specialize in Furnished and Unfurnished Residences, Shops, Lodging and Boarding Houses. Register with Map. Telephone 291.

House and Estate Agents, etc. Temple Barton & Co., 69, Sandgate Road. Lists of Houses to Let or for Sale. Telegrams: "Temple, Folkestone." Tel. 63.

House Agents, Auctioneers, Valuers. Kays, 108, Sandgate Road. Selected List of Properties and Map free. Personal attention. Telephone 508.

FORD (Devon), 228¾ miles.

Fares, 46/8*a*, 28/0*c*. R. T. for two months, 93/4*a*, 56/0*c*. Departures *from* London as for Tamerton Foliot. Departures *for* London about 6 times daily. Pop. 13,007.
Map Square 26.

FORD (Lancs), 206¾ miles.

No through fares. Departures *from* London as for Liverpool. Departures *for* London about 6 times daily. Pop. 400.

FORD (Salop) 160½ miles.

No through fares. Departures *from* London as for Shrewsbury. Departures *for* London about 3 times daily. Pop. 321.
Map Square 17.

FORD (Sussex) from *London Bridge, Victoria,* and *Clapham Junction,* 60¾ miles.

Fares, 12/8*a*, 7/7*c*. R. T. for two months, 25/4*a*, 15/2*c*. Pop. 99.
Map Square 28.

Leave Vict.	Leave Clap. J.	Leave Lon. B.	Arr. at Ford
AM 6.18	6.25	6.35	8.31
7.23	7.29	7.25	10.16
8.55	7.56	—	10.58
10.15	10.22	10.22	12.12
—	—	10.30	12.33
10.35	10.42	10.35	1.52
11.55*l*	—	11.50*l*	2.18
PM —	—	1.50	4.12
1.55*l*	*e*2. 2*l*	—	3.51
—	—	2. 5*l*	4.46
4.30*l*	—	—	6.29
4.53	5. 0	5. 5	7.20
*e*5.45*l*	—	*e*5.55*l*	7.51
—	—	6. 0*l*	8. 0
7.20	7.27	7.15	9.32
—	—	—	—

Sunday Trains.

AM 6.55*l*	7. 2*l*	7. 2*l*	10.27
8.18	8.25	8.25	10.45
PM 1.14*l*	1.21*l*	1.10*l*	4.31
7. 0	7. 7	6.38	9. 6

Trains from Ford.

Leave Ford	Arrive at Lon. B.	Arrive at Clap. J.	Arrive at Vict.
AM 5.49*l*	8.19	—	—
6. 5*l*	9.10	9.31	9.19
*f*7.24*l*	—	—	9.22
*g*7.33*l*	—	—	9.22
*f*7.35*l*	9.50	—	—
*g*7.38*l*	9.50	—	—
7.52	10.22	—	10.28
8.54	10.45	10.45	10.53
9. 6*l*	11.10	—	11.17
9.57*l*	12.19	—	12.17
PM 12.47	3.32	3.22	3.32
2.18	4.15	—	—
*d*2.30*l*	—	4.58	4.45
2.30*l*	—	4.42	4.50
2.57	5.54	4.52	5. 0
4.50	7.48	7. 7	7.15
5.19*l*	—	8.39	8.48
8.15	10. 8	9.53	10. 1
8.25*l*	—	11.10	11.17
9.57*l*	12.59	12.50	1. 0

Sunday Trains.

AM 7.54	10.45	10.23	10.32
10. 7*l*	—	12.49	1. 0
11.10*l*	—	—	1.35
PM 4.36*l*	—	—	7. 0
7. 2	9.32	9.24	9.34
8.23*l*	—	10.46	10.55

d Saturdays only.
e Saturdays excepted.
f Mondays only.
g Mondays excepted.
l *Via* Hove.

FORD BRIDGE (Hereford),

154¼ miles. Fares, 30/0*a*, 18/0*c*. R. T. for two months, 60/0*a*. Departures *from* London as for Hereford. Departures *for* London about 3 times daily. Pop. (Ford) 21.
Map Square 17.

FORDEN (Montgomery),

176¾ miles. Fares, 36/10*a*, 22/1*c*. R. T. for two months, 73/8*c*. Departures *from* London as for Welshpool. Departures *for* London about 6 times daily. Pop. 746.
Map Square 16.

FORD GREEN (Stafford),

150½ miles. No through fares. Departures *from* London as for Stoke-on-Trent. Departures *for* London about 4 times daily.

FORDHAM (Cambs) from

Liverpool Street, 69½ miles. Fares, 14/5*a*, 8/8*c*. R. T. for two months, 28/10*a*. Departures *from* London as for Mildenhall. Departures *for* London about 5 times daily. Pop. 1,410.
Map Square 19.

FORDINGBRIDGE

(Hants) from *Waterloo,* 96 miles. Fares, 20/5*a*, 12/3*c*. R. T. for two months, 40/10*a*, 24/6*c*. Pop. 3,456.
Map Square 27.

W'loo	F'bridge	F'bridge	W'loo
AM 7.30	10.14	AM 8. 1	10.56
11. 0*r*	1.36	8.42*r*	11.10
PM 1. 0*r*	3.47	11.30*r*	1.56
3. 0*r*	5.27	PM 3.31*r*	6. 0
6. 0*r*	9. 7	5.23*r*	8.30
—	—	—	—

Sunday Trains.

12. 0*nr*	3.37	PM 5. 5	8.57
—	—	—	—
—	—	—	—

n Noon.
r Restaurant Car.

FORDOUN (Kincardine),

495½ miles. Fares, 100/0*a*, 60/0*c*. R. T. for two months, 200/0*a*, 120/*c*. Departures *from* London as for Forfar. Departures *for* London about 3 times daily. Pop. 1,813.
Map Square 38.

FOREST GATE (Essex)

from *Liverpool Street* or from *Fenchurch Street,* 5½ miles. Fares from Liverpool Street, 0/10*a*, 0/8*b*, 0/6*c*. R. T. for two days, 1/8*a*, 1/4*b*, 0/10½*c*, From Fenchurch Street, 0/10*a*, 0/8*b*, 0/6*c*. R. T. for two days, 1/8*a*, 1/4*b*, 0/10½*c*. Pop. 19,445. *See* pp. 528-534.
Map Square 62.

FOREST HALL (Northumberland),

273 miles. Fares, 57/8*a*, 34/7*c*. R. T. for two months, 115/4*a*, 69/2*c*. Departures *from* London as for Newcastle-on-Tyne. Departures *for* London about 4 times daily.
Map Square 3.

FOREST HILL (London)

from *London Bridge,* 5½ miles. *Victoria,* 10¾ miles. Fares from London Bridge, 1/2*a*, 0/8½*c*. R. T. for two days, 2/4*a*, 1/4*c*. Fares from Victoria, *via* Norwood Junction, 1/11*a*, 1/2*c*. R. T. for eight days, 3/10*a*, 2/0*c*. *Via* Crystal Palace, 1/6*a*, 0/10½*c*. R. T. for two days, 3/0*a*, 1/9*c*. Pop. 22,594. *See* pp. 568-570, 580, 581.
Map Square 79.

FORESTMILL (Clackmannan),

422 miles. No through fares. Departures *from* London as for Dunfermline. Departures *for* London about 4 times daily.
Map Square 40.

FOREST ROW (Sussex)
from *Victoria, Cannon Street,* and *London Bridge,* 33½ miles, *via* East Grinstead. Fares, 6/8a, 4/0c. R. T. for two months, 13/4a, 8/0c. *Via* Groombridge, 7/8a, 4/6c. R. T. for two months, 15/0a, 9/0c. Pop. 3,035.
Map Square 23.

Leave			Arr. at
Vict.	Can. St	Lon. B.	F. Row
AM 5.30h	—	5.18h	7.59
—	—	5.18	7.53
6.37	—	6.40	8.23
7.23	—	8. 7	9.39
9.10	—	9. 6	10.47
12. 0	—	11.50	1.54
PM —	—	12.50d	2. 7
1.20e	—	—	3. 5
1.25d	—	1.10d	3. 5
—	—	d1.38h	3.45
—	—	2. 5e	4.16
2.25	—	2.25d	4.16
3.45h	—	—	5.16
4. 0	—	4.10	5.36
4.50	—	5. 5	6.20
5.48	—	5.41e	7. 6
6. 6	—	6. 8	8. 7
7.15	—	7.38	9. 7

Sunday Trains.

AM 8.18	—	8.30	10. 5
PM 2.30h	—	—	6.11
6.33	—	6.46	9. 8

Trains from Forest Row.

Leave		Arrive at	
F. Row	Lon. B.	Can. St.	Vict.
AM 7.59	9. 1k	9. 4	9. 8
8. 4	9.32	—	9.40
8.58	9.55	—	9.58
9. 0	10. 7	—	—
9.20	10.55	—	10.48
10.15	—	—	11.35
10.47h	12.44	—	12.35
11.45	1.42	—	1.26
PM 1.34h	4. 0	—	3.45
2.43	4.32	—	4.35
3.45	5.21	—	5.55
4.40	6.36	—	6.29
5.16	7.42	—	7.45
5.36h	7.56	—	—
6.37	8.46	—	8.27
8. 7h	—	—	10.10
8.50	10.25	—	11.17

Sunday Trains.

AM 7.41	10.18	—	10.32
10. 5h	—	—	1.40
PM 6.11	7.56	—	8.41

d Saturdays only.
e Saturdays excepted.
h *Via* Oxted.
k Departs from or arrives at London Bridge S.E. & C. Station.

Brambletye Hotel. Select Family and Residential. Delightful Garden. Tennis. Close Ashdown Forest Links. Motorists catered for. Telephone 5.
HORACE AYRES.

FORFAR from *Euston,*
482½ miles. Fares, 96/8a, 58/0c. R.T. for two months, 193/4a, 116/0c. Pop. 11,008.
Map Square 38.

Euston Forfar		Forfar Euston	
AM 5. 0	7.30l	AM 8.14r	7.30l
10. 0r	8.51	11.31r	10.45l
PM 1.30r	1.30	PM 2. 5r	5. 0h
7.50er	6.18	9.15	8. 0h
11. 0d	10.24	—	—
11.35e	10. 7	—	—

Sunday Trains.

PM 7.50r	6.18h	PM 2.38	5. 0h
11.35	10. 7	—	—

d Saturdays only.
e Saturdays excepted.
h A.M.
l P.M.
r Restaurant Car.

FORGANDENNY (Perth),
446 miles. Fares, 91/1a, 54/8c. R. T. for two months, 182/2a, 109/4c. Departures *from* London as for Dunblane. Departures *for* London about 3 times daily. Pop. 678.
Map Square 38.

FORGE VALLEY (Yorks),
230 miles. Fares, 48/2a, 28/11c. R.T. for two months, 96/4a, 57/10c. Departures *from* London as for Malton. Departures *for* London about 4 times daily.
Map Square 8.

FORMBY (Lancs), 212½
miles. Fares, 42/11a, 25/9c. R.T. for two months, 85/10a. Departures *from* London as for Liverpool. Departures *for* London about 8 times daily. Pop. 6,319
Map Square 12.

FORNCETT (Norfolk)
from *Liverpool Street,* 104 miles. Fares, 21/11a, 13/2c. R. T. for two months, 43/10a. Pop. 723.
Map Square 19.

L'FL.ST. Forncett		Forncett L'FL.ST.	
AM 5. 0	8.13	AM 7.11r	10.30
9.50r	12.19	7.58f	10.36
10.12	1.34	9.12	12.39
PM12.33r	3.47	10.57	1.20
3.10r	6.15	10.51r	2. 3
5.18r	7.55	PM 1.23	4.58
—	—	3.47	6.32
—	—	4.14	7.51
—	—	5.12dr	9.22
—	—	7.31	11.16

Sunday Trains.

AM 9.20r	12.55	AM 7.41	11.38
PM 4.40	7.47	PM 6.25	10.15

d Saturdays only.
e Saturdays excepted.
f Mondays only.
r Restaurant Car.

FORRES. (Elgin) from
Euston, 569½ miles. Fares, 106/3a, 63/9c. R. T. for two months, 212/6a. Pop. 4,669.
Map Square 34.

Euston Forres		Forres Euston	
AM 1.30er 6. 5h	AM 8. 5r 10.45		
7.30erv8.40	10.15r 5. 0h		
7.40er 9.10	PM 3. 5 7.40h		
11.35e 3.41l	8.12ekr7.50l		

Sunday Trains.

PM 7.50r 9.42h	— —		
11.35 3.41l	— —		

e Saturdays excepted.
h A.M.
k *Via* Inverness.
l P.M.
r Restaurant Car.
v Commences July 27.

ANOTHER ROUTE from
King's Cross, 559½ miles. Fares as above.

King's + Forres		Forres King's +	
AM 4.45 8. 8h	AM 8. 5 10. 0h		
11.50er 6. 5k	10.15 3.25k		
PM 7.45er 9.10k	PM 3. 5 7. 5k		
11.25e 3.41h	8.12er 6.30h		

Sunday Trains.

PM 7.45r 9.42k	— —		
11.25 3.41h	— —		

e Saturdays excepted.
h P.M.
k A.M.
r Restaurant Car.

Cluny Hill Hydro. Golf, Tennis, Croquet, Bowls. Electric, Turkish and Russian Baths. Telephone No. 4.

FORRESTFIELD
(Lanark), 419 miles. No through fares. Departures *from* London as for Edinburgh (Waverley). Departures *for* London about 4 times daily.

FORSINARD (Sutherland),
693½ miles. Fares, 125/10a, 75/6c. R. T. for two months, 251/8a. Departures *from* London as for Helmsdale. Departures *for* London about 3 times daily.
Map Square 31.

FORT AUGUSTUS
(Inverness), 539½ miles. Fares, 107/4a, 64/5c. R. T. for two months, 214/8a, 128/10c. Departures *from* London as for Fort William. Departures *for* London about twice daily. Pop. 1,030.
Map Square 37.

FORT BROCKHURST
(Hants) from *Waterloo,* via Eastleigh, 87½ miles. Fares, 15/5a, 9/3c. R. T. for two months, 30/10a, 18/6c.
Map Square 28.

W'loo F.B'hurst		F.B'hurst W'loo	
AM 5.40 8.47	AM 6.24 9.26		
5.50 9.47	9.22 12. 0		
8.30s 11.22	11.39r 2.20		
9.50 12.50	PM12.19 4. 6		
11.30r 2.47	1. 16 4.20		
PM 1.30s 3.59	2.49 6.16		
3.30s 6. 9	5.44r 8.20		
5.30r 8. 7	7.19 10.50		
7.30d 10.33	8.29 11.28		

No Sunday Trains.

d Saturdays only.
r Restaurant Car.
s Refreshments served.

IDRIS DRY GINGER ALE.

FORT BROCKHURST
—*continued.*

ANOTHER ROUTE from
Waterloo, via Meon Valley, 76½ miles. Fares as above.

W'loo	F.B'hurst	F.B'hurst	W'loo
AM 4.50	8.47	AM 7.39	10.26
7. 0	10.32	9.22	12.11
9.20	12.20	10.59	1.40
11.20	2.47	PM 2.31	5.46
PM 3.15	6. 9	4. 4	7. 7
6.34	9.33	7.42	11.10
—	—	—	—

No Sunday Trains.

FORTEVIOT (Perth), 443
miles. Fares, 90/7*a*, 54/4*c*. R. T. for two months, 181/2*a*, 108/8*c*. Departures *from* London as for Dunblane. Departures *for* London about 3 times daily. Pop. 532.
Map Square 38.

FORT GEORGE (Inverness), 577¾ miles. Fares, 106/3*a*, 63/9*c*. R. T. *from* two months, 212/6*a*, 127/6*c*. Departures *from* London as for Nairn. Departures *for* London about 4 times daily.
Map Square 34.

FORT MATILDA (Renfrew), 424¾ miles. Fares, 84/2*a*, 50/6*c*. R. T. for two months, 168/4*a*, 101/0*c*. Departures *from* London as for Greenock (Central). Departures *for* London about 6 times daily.

FORTROSE (Ross),
594¼ miles. Fares, 106/3*a*, 63/9*c*. R. T. for two months, 212/6*a*, 127/6*c*. Departures *from* London as for Inverness. Departures *for* London about 3 times daily. Pop. 983.
Map Square 34.

FORT WILLIAM (Inverness) from *Euston*, 525½ miles. Fares, 104/5*a*, 62/8*c*. R. T. for two months, 208/10*a*, 125/4*c*. Pop. 1,913.
Map Square 37.

Euston	FortWm.	FortWm.	Euston
PM 1.30*er*	10. 3*h*	AM 9.25	5. 0*h*
11.35*e*	8. 5*l*	PM 4. 5*e*	6.55*h*
—	—	4. 5*d*	7.30*h*

Sunday Trains.

PM 11.35	8.14*l*	—	—
—	—	—	—

d Saturdays only.
e Saturdays excepted.
h A.M.
l P.M.
r Restaurant Car.

FORT WILLIAM—*contd.*

ANOTHER ROUTE from
King's Cross, 557¼ miles. Fares as above.

King's+	Fort Wm.	Fort Wm.	King's+
AM 4.45	8. 5*l*	AM 11.40	3.25
PM 7.45*er*	10. 3*l*	PM 4. 5	6.50*fl*
11.25	3.39*k*	—	—

Sunday Trains.

PM 7.45*r*	10. 3*l*	—	—
11.25	3.39*k*	—	—

e Saturdays excepted.
f Arrives 7.5 A.M. Sundays.
k P.M.
l A.M.

Taxi Cabs can be hired to meet any train at this station by letter, or telegraphic address, Motors, Messrs. A. J. Macpherson, Gordon Square.

F O R Y D (Denbigh), 211
miles. Fares, 43/9*a*, 26/3*c*. R. T. for two months, 87/6*a*, 52/6*c*. Departures *for* London about twice daily.
Map Square 11.

FOSS CROSS (Glo'ster)
from *Waterloo*, 120½ miles. Fares, 20/5*a*, 12/3*c*. R. T. for two months, 40/10*a*. Departures *from* London as for Cirencester. Departures *for* London about 3 times daily.
Map Square 22.

FOULIS (Ross), 590½ miles.
Fares, 106/3*a*, 63/9*c*. R. T. for two months, 212/6*a*, 127/6*c*. Departures *from* London as for Dingwall. Departures *for* London about 3 times daily.
Map Square 34.

FOULRIDGE (Lancs) from
St. Pancras, 230½ miles. Fares, 42/6*a*, 25/6*c*. R. T., double fare. Departures *from* London as for Colne. Departures *for* London about 6 times daily. Pop. 1,399.
Map Square 7.

FOULSHAM (Norfolk),
132 miles. Fares, 23/7*a*, 14/2*c*. R. T. for two months, 47/2*a*. Departures *from* London as for Aylsham. Departures *for* London about 4 times daily. Pop. 922.
Map Square 19.

FOUNTAINHALL (Midlothian), 374½ miles. Fares, 76/5*a*, 45/10*c*. R. T. for two months, 152/10*a*, 91/8*c*. Departures *from* London as for Galashiels. Departures *for* London about 4 times daily.
Map Square 41.

FOUR ASHES (Stafford),
130 miles. Fares, 26/11*a*, 16/2*c*. R. T. for two months, 53/10*a*. Departures *from* London as for Wolverhampton (High Level). Departures *for* London about 5 times daily.
Map Square 17.

FOURCROSSES (Montgomery), 175 miles. Fares, 36/1*a*, 21/8*c*. R. T. for two months, 72/2*a*. Departures *from* London as for Buttington. Departures *for* London about 6 times daily.
Map Square 16.

FOUR OAKS (Warwick),
113½ miles. Fares, 24/4*a*, 14/7*c*. R. T. for two months, 48/8*a*. Departures *from* London as for Birmingham(New Street). Departures *for* London about 5 times daily.
Map Square 17.

FOUR STONES (Northumberland), 291 miles. Fares, 60/10*a*, 36/6*c*. R. T., double fare. Departures *from* London as for Hexham. Departures *for* London about 5 times daily.
Map Square 3.

FOWEY (Cornwall) from
Paddington, via Par, 265 miles. Fares, 54/2*a*, 32/6*c*. R. T. for two months, 108/4*a*, 65/0*c*. Pop. 2,168.
Map Square 25.

Pad.	Fowey	Fowey	Pad.
AM 5.30*h*	2.55	AM 9.55*hr*	4.35
11.10*hr*	5.20	11.50*er*	6.50
PM 12. 5*hr*	7.40	11.50*dr*	7. 5
2. 0*hr*	8.50	PM 2. 0*hr*	9. 0
10. 0*e*	6.52	9.10	7.10
12. 0*hl*	9.25	—	—

Sunday Trains.

PM 10. 0	6.52	—	—
—	—	—	—

d Saturdays only.
e Saturdays excepted.
h Via Lostwithiel.
l Saturdays midnight excepted.
r Restaurant Car.

The Fowey Hotel, overlooking picturesque Harbour of Fowey. Lighted throughout by Electricity and handsomely furnished. Spacious Lounge. Croquet and Tennis Lawns. Gardens and Grounds extend to the Foreshore. Private Landing Slip. Excellent Fishing. Golf Links within ten minutes.

St. Catherine's Hotel (Unlicensed). Best position on Esplanade. Uninterrupted views over Sea and Harbour. Cliff Garden with sheltered Summer Houses. Golf Course five minutes. Appointed A.A. Sea and river fishing. Telephone 4.
Apply, PROPRIETOR.

FOXFIELD (Lancs), 269
miles. Fares, 56/0*a*, 33/7*c*. R. T. for two months, 112/0*a*, 67/2*c*. Departures *from* London as for Barrow-in-Furness. Departures *for* London about 5 times daily.
Map Square 6.

FOXTON (Cambs) from
King's Cross, 51 miles. Fares, 10/8*a*, 6/5*c*. R. T., double fare. Departures *from* London as for Shepreth. Departures *for* London about 5 times daily. Pop. 481.
Map Square 18.

FRAMLINGHAM (Suffolk) from *Liverpool Street*, 91 miles. Fares, 19/2*a*, 11/6*c*. R. T. for two months, 38/4*a*. Pop. 2,400.
Map Square 19.

Lpl. St.	Framhm	Framhm.	L'pl. St.
AM 5. 0	8.19	AM 7.14*r*	10.30
8.15*dr*	12.14	8.30*r*	11.22
10.20	1.38	9.37*k*	1.20
PM 3.18	6.16	PM 12.34	3.42
4.55*r*	7.34	4.19	7.51
—	—	6.26*r*	9.22
—	—	—	—

No Sunday Trains.

d Saturdays only.
k Tuesdays only.
r Restaurant Car.

FRANKTON (Salop), 183¾
miles. Fares, 35/3*a*, 21/2*c*. R. T.
for two months, 70/6*a*. Departures
from London as for Ellesmere.
Departures *for* London about 6
times daily.
Map Square 12.

FRANSHAM (Norfolk)
from *Liverpool Street*, 116 miles.
Fares, 23/7*a*, 14/2*c*. R. T. for
two months, 47/2*a*. Departures
from London as for Swaffham.
Departures *for* London about 6
times daily. Pop. 286.
Map Square 19.

FRANT (Sussex) from
Charing Cross, Cannon Street, and
London Bridge, 37¼ miles. Fares,
7/11*a*, 6/4*b*, 4/6*c*. R. T. for two
months, 15/10*a*, 12/8*b*. Pop. 1,671.
Map Square 24.

	Leave		Arr. at
CHAR.+	CAN. ST.	LON. B.	FRANT
AM —	5.40*s*	5.43*s*	6. 6
—	5.20	5.25	7.31
—	6.45	6.50	8.46
—	7.56	8. 0	9.48
9.25	—	9.33	10.55
10.40	—	10.46	12. 1
PM12. 3*e*	—	12.10*e*	1.50
1. 5*d*	—	1.11*d*	2.26
2. 8*e*	—	2.16*e*	3.45
3. 0*d*	—	3. 8*d*	4.16
3.48*e*	—	—	4.59
3.50	—	3.57	5.35
5. 5*d*	—	—	6.15
—	5.12*e*	—	6.18¦
5.24*d*	—	5.34*d*	6.54
5.26*e*	—	5.33*e*	6.42
6. 3*e*	6.16*e*	6.19*e*	7.25
7.30	—	—	8.43
8. 0	—	8. 8	9.35

Sunday Trains.
AM 8.45	—	—	9.55
PM 7.35	—	7.45	9. 4

Trains from Frant.
Leave		Arrive at	
FRANT	LON. B.	CAN. ST.	CHAR.
AM 6.27	8.10	—	8.19
8.11	—	9.15	—
8.46	—	9.48	—
9. 5	10.28	10.32	—
9.33*d*	10.29	—	10.39
10.12*e*	11. 7	—	11.17
11.17	—	—	12.49
PM 1.19	3. 7	—	3.19
2.47	4.15	—	4.25
3 40*d*	5. 0	—	5. 8
4.10*e*	5.50	—	6. 3
4.54*d*	6.30	—	6.39
4.44*e*	6.44	—	6.54
5. 0*d*	6.40	—	6.48
5.55	7.25	7.30	—
6.41	8.26	—	8.35
8.43	10.15	—	10.23
9.53	11.34	—	11.44

Sunday Trains.
AM 8.14	10. 5	—	10.15
10.14	11.23	—	11.34
PM 6.58	8.12	—	8.22
7.40	9. 4	—	9.14
10.25*s*	—	1.23	—

d Saturdays only.
e Saturdays excepted.
s Third class only.

FRASERBURGH (Aberdeen) from *King's Cross*, 570¾ miles.
Fares, 109/10*a*, 65/11*c*. R. T. for two
months, 219/8*a*, 131/10*c*. Pop. 11,064.
Map Square 35.

KING'S +	FRASBH.	FRASBH.	KING'S +
AM 4.45	9.10*l*	AM 6.58*r*	10.10*l*
PM 8.20*e*	10. 5*h*	9.20	3.25*h*
11.25*e*	2.50*l*	PM12.33	6. 0*h*
—	—	3.30	7.30*h*

Sunday Trains.
PM 7.45	10. 5*h*	—	—

e Saturdays excepted.
h A.M.   *l* P.M.
r Restaurant Car.

ANOTHER ROUTE from
Euston, 587 miles. Fares as above.
Map Square 35.

EUSTON	FRASBGH.	FRASBGH.	EUSTON
PM 1.30*er*	8.56*h*	AM 6.58*r*	10.45*l*
7.50*er*	10. 5*h*	9.20	5. 0*h*
11.35*e*	2.50*l*	PM 3.30	8. 0*h*
—	—	6.58*e*	7.30*l*

Sunday Trains.
PM 7.50*r*	10. 5*h*	—	—
11.35	2.50*l*	—	—

e Saturdays excepted.
h A.M.   *l* P.M.
r Restaurant Car.

FRATTON (Hants) from
Waterloo, 72¼ miles. Fares, 15/3*a*,
9/2*c*. R.T. for two months, 30/6*a*,
18/4*c*. Pop. (Fratton) 10,645.
Map Square 28.

W'LOO	FRAT'N	FRAT'N	W'LOO
AM 5.50	8.32	AM 6.45	9.12
—	6.50	9.34	7.14*s*	9.44
8.34*r*	10.56	7.55*r*	9.52¦
9.50	11.42	8.15	10.50
10.50	1. 6	8.56	11.32
11.50*d*	1.56	9.50	11.41
PM12.50*r*	2.42	PM12. 2*r*	1.52
1.50*d*	3.42	12.20	3. 6
1.50*e*	4.27	1.23*d*	3.20
2. 0*d*	4.34	1.39	4.16
2.34	5.23	4. 2	5.52
3.50*s*	5.42	4.46	7.46
4.15*e*	6.40	6. 2*r*	7.56
4.50	7. 6	6.17	9. 6
5.50	7.46	7.45	10.46
6.50*r*	8.47	9.10	12.16
9.50	12.24	—	—

Sunday Trains.
AM 8. 0	10.18	AM 7.40	10.16
8.20	11.13	PM12.32	3.13
9.15*r*	11.37	4.18*r*	6.16
PM 1.50	4.28	6.13	8.52
4.20	7.29	7.32	10. 1
9.30	11.51	—	—

d Saturdays only.
r Restaurant Car.
s Refreshments served.

ANOTHER ROUTE from
Victoria, Clapham Junction, and
London Bridge, 84¼ miles. Fares
as above.

	Leave		Arr. at
VICT.	CLAP. J.	LON. B.	FRAT'N
AM 6.18	6.25	6.35	9.25
8.55	—	—	11. 8
10.15	10.22	10.22	12.55
11.35	—	—	2. 3
11.55*k*	—	11.50*k*	3.18
PM 1.35	—	—	3.25
1.40	1.47*e*	1.50	4.26
1.55*k*	*e*2. 2*k*	2. 5*k*	5.54
3.55	4. 2	4. 0	6.36
—	—	4.50	6.58
4.53	5. 0	—	7.29
—	—	5. 5	8.23
—	—	5. 8*e*	8.23
5.45*k*	—	6. 0*k*	8.51
7.20	7.27	7.15	10.24

FRATTON—*continued*.
Sunday Trains.
	Leave		Arr. at
VICT.	CLAP. J.	LON. B.	FRAT'N.
AM 6.55*k*	7. 2*k*	7. 2*k*	11.29
9. 0	9. 7	8.55	11.50
9.55	—	—	12. 5
PM 1.14*k*	1.21*k*	1.10*k*	5.34
7. 0	7. 7	6.38	10. 3

Trains from Fratton.
Leave		Arrive at	
FRAT'N	LON. B.	CLAP. J.	VICT.
AM 6.35*g*	9.50	—	9.22
6.38*f*	9.50	—	—
6.57	—	—	10.28
7.24	9.58	—	—
8. 3	10.45	10.45	10.53
8.47	10.55	—	—
9.33	12. 8	—	12. 0
10. 3	1.42	—	—
11. 3	—	—	1.10
11.40	3.32	3.22	3.32
PM 1.59	4.27	4.26	4.34
3. 3	—	5. 4	5.12
4.53	—	—	6.50
4.58	7.48	7.31	7.39
6.38	—	—	8.33
6.43*d*	10. 0	9.37	9.45
7.23	10. 8	9.53	10. 1
9. 3*k*	12.59	12.50	1. 0

Sunday Trains.
AM 6.52	10.45	10.23	10.32
9. 9*k*	—	12.49	1. 0
PM 3.35*k*	—	—	7. 0
5.53	—	7.49	7.56
5.59	8.50	8.33*	8.42
7.23*k*	11.34	10.46	10.55

d Saturdays only.
e Saturdays excepted.
f Mondays only.
g Mondays excepted.
k Via Hove.

Southsea, Royal Beach
Hotel. Facing South. Alight at
Fratton.
See advt. under SOUTHSEA.

FREMINGTON (Devon)
from *Waterloo*, 214¼ miles. Fares,
39/9*a*, 23/10*c*. R. T. for two months,
79/6*a*, 47/8*c*. Departures *from*
London as for Barnstaple. Departures *for* London about 6 times
daily. Pop. 1,200.
Map Square 21.

FRENCH DROVE
(Lincoln), 99¼ miles. Fares, 18/1*a*,
10/10*c*. R. T., double fare. Departures *from* London as for March.
Departures *for* London about 4
times daily.
Map Square 18.

FRESHFIELD (Lancs),
213½ miles. Fares, 43/4*a*, 26/0*c*.
R. T. for two months, 86/8*a*,
52/0*c*. Departures *from* London
as for Liverpool. Departures *for*
London about 8 times daily.
Map Square 12.

FRESHFORD (Somerset),
99¾ miles. Fares, 21/1*a*, 12/8*c*.
R. T. for two months, 42/2*a*. Departures *from* London as for Bradford-on-Avon. Departures *for*
London about 6 times daily.
Pop. 501.
Map Square 22.

FRESHWATER (Isle of Wight), from *Victoria* and *London Bridge*, 111¾ miles. Fares, 22/1a, 13/6c. R.T. for two months, 43/7a, 26/3c. Pop. 3,192. *Map Square 27.*

Leave Vict.	Lon. B.	Arr. at F'wat'r.
AM 6.18	6.35	12.12
8.55	—	1.47
11.35d	—	3.52
11.35e	—	5.14
PM 1.40	1.50	7.22
—	4.50d	9.17
—	—	—
—	—	—

No Sunday Trains.

Trains from Freshwater.

Leave F'water	Lon. B.	Vict.
AM 8. 5	—	1.10
9.40	4.27	4.34
PM12.20	—	5.12
2.20	7.48	6.50
4. 0d	10. 8	10. 1

No Sunday Trains.
d Saturdays only.
e Saturdays excepted.

ANOTHER ROUTE from *Waterloo, via Ryde*, 99¼ miles. Fares, 22/1a, 13/6c. R.T. for two months, 43/7a, 26/3c.

W'loo.	F'water	F'water	W'loo.
AM 5.50	12.12	AM 9.40	1.52
9.50d	3.52	PM 2.20r	7.56
PM12.50e	5.14	5.25e	10.46
12.50d	5.46	5.52d	10.46
1.50l	7.22	7.40hl	3.58
3.50ds	9.17	—	—

No Sunday Trains.
d Saturdays only.
e Saturdays excepted.
h Via Eastleigh.
l Passengers cross Portsmouth at own expense.
r Restaurant Car.
s Refreshments served.

ANOTHER ROUTE from *Waterloo, via Lymington and Yarmouth*, 104 miles. Fares 22/1a, 13/6c. R. T. for two months, 43/7a, 26/3c.

W'loo.	F'water	F'water	W'loo.
AM 5.40	10. 0	AM 6.50f	11. 0
9.30	1.35	8.30	12.50
11.30r	3.45	9.45r	2.20
PM 1.30s	6.25	PM12. 5	4.20
3.30s	7.35	2.55	6.58
4.30r	8.30	4. 5r	8.20
—	—	5.15	10.50

No Sunday Trains.
f Mondays only.
r Restaurant Car.
s Refreshments served.

FRESHWATER—*conta.*

ANOTHER ROUTE from *Waterloo, via Lymington, Yarmouth and coach*, 105 miles. Fares as above.

W'loo.	F'water	F'water	W'loo.
	about		
AM 5.40	10. 0	AM 6.50f	11. 0
9.30	1.35	8.30r	12.50
11.30r	3.45	9.45r	2.20
PM 1.30s	6.25	PM12. 5	4.20
3.30	7.35	2.55	6.58
4.30	8.30	4. 5r	8.20
—	—	5.15	10.50

No Sunday Service.
f Mondays only,
r Restaurant Car.
s Refreshments served.

FRICKLEY (Yorks), 172¼ miles. Fares, 35/2a, 21/1c. R. T. double fare. Departures *from* London as for Swinton. Departures *for* London about 5 times daily.
Map Square 13.

FRIMLEY (Surrey) from *Waterloo, via Woking*, 33¼ miles. Fares, 6/11a, 4/2c. R. T. for two months, 13/10a, 8/4c. Pop. 13,673. *Map Square 23.*

W'loo.	Frimley	Frimley	W'loo.
AM 5.40	6.42	AM 8.25	9.26
5.50	7.14	8.47	10.11
8.15	9.47	9.53	11.16
9.20	10.38	10.31	11.32
10.34	11.55	PM12.38	1.40
11.20	12.45	1.56	3. 6
PM 1.20e	2.56	2.18	3.36
1.20d	3. 0	2.44d	4.46
2.20	3.37	3.44d<	5.20
5.30d	5.49	3.54	5.40
5.30e	6.28	4.48	6.16
5.50d	7.23	7.25	8.46
6.10e	7.24	7.42e	9. 6
6.40d	7.52	8.25	9.46
6.54e	7.52	9.42	10.50
7.20	8.39	—	—

Sunday Trains.

W'loo.	Frimley	Frimley	W'loo.
AM 8.20	9.45	AM11. 0	12.41
8.45	10.48	PM12.50	2.44
10.20	11.48	4. 2	5.41
11.15h	12.48	6. 2	7.41
PM12.20	1.48	7.50	9.12
1.50h	3.48	9.25	10.47
3.20	4.48	—	—
5.20	6.48	—	—
6.20h	7.50	—	—
7.20	8.45	—	—

d Saturdays only.
e Saturdays excepted.
h Via North Camp.

ANOTHER ROUTE from *Waterloo, via Ascot*, 37¼ miles. Fares, 7/3a, 4/4c. R. T. for two months, 14/6a, 8/8c.

W'loo.	Frimley	Frimley	W'loo.
AM 5.10	8.25	AM 6.42	8.17
6.54	8.47	7.14	8.47
7.54	9.53	7.49	9.17
8.54	10.31	8.28	9.47
9.54	11.57	9.47	11.17
PM12.48	2.18	10.37	12.31
1.18d	2.44	11.56	1.27
1.48	3.54	PM12.45	2.27
2.18d	3.44	1.17	3.27
2.48	4.48	3.37	5.27
4.48e	6.18	5.40d	7.27
4.48d	6.23	6.28e	8.27
5.18e	6.45	7.52	9.27
5.48	7.25	8.39	10.37
6.18e	7.42	—	—
6.48	8.25	—	—
7.54	9.42	—	—

FRIMLEY—*continued.*

Sunday Trains.

W'loo.	Frimley	Frimley	W'loo.
AM 9.18	11. 0	AM10.48	12.43
PM12.18	2.17	11.48	2. 3
2.18	4. 2	PM 3.48	5.28
4.18	6. 2	5.48	7.28
5.58	7.50	7.50	9.28
7.48	9.25	8.45	10.18
—	—	—	—

d Saturdays only.
e Saturdays excepted.

FRINTON (Essex), from *Liverpool Street*, 69 miles. Fares, 14/10a, 8/11c. R. T. for two months, 29/8a, 17/10c. Pop. 3,037. *Map Square 24.*

L'pl. St.	Frinton	Frinton	L'pl St.
AM 5. 0	8.17	AM 6.57r	8.52
6.50	10.23	7.39	9.36
8.18	10.43	8. 7r	9.53
8.46	12. 9	9.54	11.42
10.23	12.44	11.38r	2. 3
11.26d	2.16	PM12.27d	2.23
11.30e	2.16	1.33	3.36
PM12.36	2.43	3.14	5. 5
1.30dr	3.24	4.20	6.32
2. 3d	4.10	5.41	7.40
2.15	5. 4	7.39	9.36
3.23	5.27	7.57	11·16
3.26	6.29	—	—
4.58r	7. 4	—	—
5.30r	7.14	—	—
5.42	8.23	—	—
6.39	8.37	—	—
7.45r	10.12	—	—
8.45	10.55	—	—
12. 0d	1.59	—	—

Sunday Trains.

L'pl. St.	Frinton	Frinton	L'pl St.
AM 9. 8	11. 5	AM 8.54	11.38
9.20r	12. 7	PM 5.48	8.25
PM 4.40	7.10	7.57	10. 9

d Saturdays only.
e Saturdays excepted.
r Restaurant Car.

FRINTON—*continued.*

Eastcliffe Private Hotel. Walton-on-Naze. 2 minutes rail Frinton. High-class. Select position, facing Sea. Six Hard Tennis Courts adjoining. Telephone 31.

Wm. Hayne, House and Estate Agent, Estate Offices, Connaught Avenue (Sea end). Branch Office opposite to Station. Full particulars of Furnished and Unfurnished Houses, Land, &c., free on application. Telephone, "Frinton," No. 9.

Tomkins, Homer, & Ley, House and Estate Agents, the Estate Office, Frinton. Furnished and Unfurnished Houses, Land, &c. Established 1895. Telephone, No. 19.

Gilbert, Brown & Roberts, Architects, Surveyors and Estate Agents. Furnished and Unfurnished Houses, Land. Telephone 147. Reserved Bus at Station for Clients.

Ratcliffe Bros. Garage. 100 Cars. The Reliable Motor Works. Private lock ups. R.A.C., A.A. Repairs four Star.

FRIOCKHEIM (Forfar),

475 miles. Fares, 93/9*a*, 56/3*c*. R. T. for two months, 187/6*a*, 112/6*c*. Departures *from* London as for Forfar or Arbroath. Departures *for* London about 4 times daily. Pop. 716.
Map Square 38.

FRISBY (Leicester), 110¼

miles. Fares, 21/8*a*, 13/0*c*. R. T., double fare. Departures *from* London as for Asfordby. Departures *for* London about 8 times daily. Pop. 385.
Map Square 18.

FRITTENDEN ROAD

(Kent), 48 miles. No through fares. Departures *from* London as for Tenterden (*via* Headcorn). Departures *for* London about 5 times daily. Pop. (Frittenden) 787.
Map Square 24.

FRITWELL (Oxon), from

Paddington, 77¾ miles. Fares, 14/0*a*, 8/5*c*. R. T. for two months, 28/0*a*. Departures *from* London as for Heyford. Departures *for* London about 4 times daily. Pop. 453.
Map Square 18.

FRIZINGHALL (Yorks),

206¾ miles. Fares, 39/9*a*, 23/10*c*. R. T., double fare. Departures *from* London as for Shipley Departures *for* London about 6 times daily. Pop. 4,052.

FRIZINGTON (Cumberland),

302 miles. Fares, 62/9*a*, 37/8*c*. R. T. for two months, 125/6*a*, 75/4*c*. Departures *from* London as for Moor Row. Departures *for* London about 3 times daily. Pop. 3,612.
Map Square 6.

FROCESTER (Glo'ster),

124¾ miles. No through fares. Departures *from* London as for Gloucester. Departures *for* London about 3 times daily. Pop. 217.
Map Square 22.

FRODINGHAM (Lincoln),

179¾ miles. Fares, 35/2*a*, 21/1*c*. R. T., double fare. Departures *from* London as for Thorne. Departures *for* London about 5 times daily. Pop. 1,734.
Map Square 13.

Crosby Hotel. Comfortable Commercial Hotel. Fine Coffee and Billiard Rooms. Bowling Green. Refreshment Hall. Excellent Bedrooms. P.R.H.A. 'Phone, Scunthorpe 12.

FRODSHAM (Cheshire),

188¾ miles. Fares, 37/9*a*, 22/8*c*. R. T. for two months, 75/6*a*. Departures *from* London as for Chester. Departures *for* London about 6 times daily. Pop. 3,049.
Map Square 12.

FROME (Somerset) from

Paddington, 101¼ miles. Fares, *via* Westbury, 21/1*a*, 12/8*c*. R. T. for two months, 42/2*a*. *Via* Bath, 22/6*a*, 13/6*c*. R. T. for two months, 45/0*a* Pop. 10,506.
Map Square 22.

PAD.	FROME	FROME	PAD.
AM 1. 0*g*	7 31	AM 6.40	10. 0
5.30	9.45	8.30	10.52
7.30	10.53	10.27	12.55
9.15	11.17	PM12. 3	3.20
10.30	12.21	1.34	3.50
PM12.30*r*	2.51	3.21*t*	5.30
2. 0	4.11	4.40*r*	6.50
3.30	5.24	6. 0	8.20
5. 5	7.42	6.33	10.45
6.30	10. 4	9.10	2.45
—	—	10.14*h*	2.45

Sunday Trains.

AM 9.10	1.33	AM11.50	3.35
PM 2.40	4.55	PM 5.34*r*	7.55
10. 0	7.31	—	—
—	—	—	—
—	—	—	—

g Mondays excepted.
h Thursdays only.
l Saturday midnight only.
r Restaurant Car.
t Tea Car.

FRONGOCH (Merioneth)

from *Paddington*, 207½ miles. Fares, 43/6*a*, 26/1*c*. R. T. for two months, 87/0*a*, 52/2*c*. Departures *from* London as for Blaenau Festiniog. Departures *for* London about 4 times daily.
Map Square 11.

FROSTERLEY (Durham),

258¾ miles. Fares, 53/9*a*, 32/3*c*. R. T., double fare. Departures *from* London as for Bishop Auckland. Departures *for* London about 4 times daily. Pop. 1,470.
Map Square 7.

FULBOURNE (Cambridge)

from *Liverpool Street*, 61 miles. Fares, 12/4*a*, 7/5*c*. R. T. for two months, 24/8*a*. Pop. 1,901.
Map Square 19.

L'P'L ST.	FULBNE.	FULBNE.	L'P'L ST.
AM 5. 5	7.23	AM 8.36*r*	10.23
5.50*h*	9.22	10.51	12.40
8.30*r*	11. 5	PM12.22*r*	2.21
11.50*r*	1.48	3.28*r*	5.17
PM 2.34	4.33	5. 3	7.58
4.45	6.50	6.43*r*	8.33
5.49*r*	7.39	8.15	10.30
7.10*r*	8.56	—	—
8.22	10. 8	—	—

FULBOURNE—*continued.*

Sunday Trains.

L'P'L ST.	FULBNE.	FULBNE.	L'P'L ST.
AM 9.25	11.40	PM 4.31	6.40
PM 3.25	5.15	8. 2	9.40
—	—	—	—
—	—	—	—
—	—	—	—

h Wednesdays only.
r Restaurant Car.

FULLERTON (Hants)

from *Waterloo*, *via* Andover Junction, 71¾ miles. Fares, 14/4*a*, 8/7*c*. R. T. for two months, 28/8*a*, 17/2*c*.
Map Square 23.

W'LOO	F'LTON	F'LTON	W'LOO
AM 7.30	9.36	AM 8.34	10.56
11.30*r*	2. 3	10. 6	12.22
PM 1.30*r*	4.28	PM 1.30	4.20
5. 0	6.56	4.31	7.40
6. 0	8.16	6.13*r*	8.30
—	—	8.19	10.50
—	—	—	—

Sunday Trains.

12. 0*nr*	2.32	PM 5.56*r*	8.57

n Noon.
r Restaurant Car.

ANOTHER ROUTE from

Waterloo, *via* Longparish, 68¾ miles. Fares as above.

W'LOO	F'LTON	F'LTON	W'LOO
AM 5.50	9.30	AM 7.29	9.56
PM 3.30	5.36	10.10	12.22
5. 0	7.13	PM 6.15	10.50
—	—	—	—
—	—	—	—

No Sunday Trains.

FULWELL (Bucks) from

Euston, 64¾ miles. Fares, 11/5*a*, 6/10*c*. R. T., double fare. Departures *from* London as for Buckingham. Departures *for* London about 5 times daily.
Map Square 18.

FULWELL (Middlesex)

from *Waterloo*, 13 miles. Fares, 1/11*a*, 1/2*c*. R. T. for two days, 3/10*a*, 2/4*c*. Pop. 3,318.
See p. 585.
Map Square 75.

FURNESS ABBEY

(Lancs) from *Euston* 261½ miles. Fares, 54/5*a*, 32/8*c*. R. T. for two months, 108/10*a*, 65/4*c*.
Map Square 6.

EUSTON	FURN. A.	FURN. A.	EUSTON
AM12.25	9.25	AM 7. 4*r*	3.10
2.35	10.56	8.45*hr*	3.45
5. 0	12.52	9.20	4.15
6.45	2.33	11. 0*t*	6. 0
11.35*r*	5.18	PM12.35*r*	7.30
11.50*r*	7.28	2. 0*er*	9. 5
PM 1.30*r*	7.48	2. 0*dr*	9.15
2.35*t*	9.56	3.15*r*	10.45
5.20*r*	11.56	7.50	5. 0
9.30*e*	8. 3	—	—
11. 0*d*	8.42	—	—

Sunday Trains.

AM11.45*r*	6.36	PM12.10*r*	7.30
—	—	8.20	5. 0
—	—	—	—

d Saturdays only.
e Saturdays excepted.
h Mondays and Saturdays only.
r Restaurant Car.
t Tea Car.

FURNESS ABBEY—
continued.

ANOTHER ROUTE from *St. Pancras,* 284 miles. Fares as above.

St. Pan.	Furn.A.	Furn.A.	St. Pan.
AM 4.25	2.33	AM 7. 0*r*	4.10
9.50*r*	5.20	9.20*hr*	5.30
PM12.15*r*	7.28	10.55*kr*	6.35
11.50*e*	10.56	PM12.35*r*	9.15
11.50*d*	11. 1	5. 3*e*	4.20
—	—	5.48*d*	4.20
—	—	—	—
—	—	—	—
—	—	—	—

Sunday Trains.

AM10.50*r*	9.11	AM 7.10	5.27
PM11.45	10.56	PM 5. 0	4.55
—	—	—	—
—	—	—	—

d Saturdays only.
e Saturdays excepted.
h Stops to take up.
k Wednesdays and Thursdays excepted.
r Restaurant Car.

Furness Abbey Hotel. *See* advt. under Barrow.

FURNESS VALE
(Cheshire), 177¼ miles. Fares, *via* Macclesfield, 35/8*a*, 21/5*c*. R. T., double fare; *via* Stockport, 37/9*a*, 22/8*c*. R. T., double fare. Departures *from* London as for Macclesfield or Stockport. Departures *for* London about 4 times daily.

FUSHIEBRIDGE (Midlothian), 384½ miles. No through fares. Departures *from* London as for Galashiels. Departures *for* London about 3 times daily. *Map Square* 41.

FYLING HALL (Yorks), 243 miles. Fares, 50/8*a*, 30/5*c*. R.T. for two months, 101/4*a*, 60/10*c*. Departures *from* London as for Ravenscar. Departures *for* London about 3 times daily. *Map Square* 8.

FYVIE (Aberdeen), 553¾ miles. Fares, 106/3*a*, 63/9*c*. R. T. for two months, 212/6*a*, 127/6*c*. Departures *from* London as for Inverurie. Departures *for* London about 3 times daily. Pop. 3,396. *Map Square* 35.

REFERENCE NOTES.

a signifies First Class.
b ,, Second Class.
c ,, Third Class.
d ,, On Saturdays only.
e ,, Saturdays excepted.
f ,, On Mondays only.
g ,, Mondays excepted.
r ,, Restaurant Car.
t ,, Tea Car.
x ,, Express.
R.T. ,, Return Tickets.

All Trains in the Tables not otherwise marked carry Third Class Passengers.

G

GAERWEN (Anglesey)
from *Euston,* 245½ miles. Fares, 51/1*a*, 30/8*c*. R. T. for two months, 102/2*a*, 61/4*c*. *Map Square* 11.

Euston	Gaern.	Gaern.	Euston
AM12.25	9. 8	AM 6.46*f*	1. 0
2.35	11.22	8.15*r*	1.45
5. 0	12.28	8.45*r*	4.15
8.30*r*	3. 2	10.17*er*	5. 5
11.10*dr*	5. 2	10.32*dr*	5. 5
11.50*r*	7.20	10.50*r*	5.50
PM 2.35*t*	8.53	PM 1.21*er*	7.30
9.30*e*	5. 4	1.56*r*	9.20
—	—	3. 6*r*	10.45
—	—	8.25	5. 0
—	—	—	—
—	—	—	—

Sunday Trains.

PM12.10*r*	8.45	PM 8.31	5. 0
9.15	5. 4	—	—
—	—	—	—
—	—	—	—
—	—	—	—

d Saturdays only.
e Saturdays excepted.
f Mondays only.
r Restaurant Car.
t Tea Car.

GAILES (Ayr), 397 miles. No through fares. Departures *from* London as for Ayr. Departures *for* London about 4 times daily. *Map Square* 40.

GAILEY (Stafford), 131½ miles. Fares, 27/3*a*, 16/4*c*. R. T. for two months, 54/6*a*. Departures *from* London as for Wolverhampton (High Level). Departures *for* London about 5 times daily. *Map Square* 17.

GAINFORD (Durham), 240¾ miles. Fares, 50/3*a*, 30/2*c*. R. T., double fare. Departures *from* London as for Barnard Castle. Departures *for* London about 5 times daily. Pop. 1,172. *Map Square* 7.

GAINSBORO' (Lincoln) from *King's Cross via* Grantham and Lincoln, 145¾ miles. Fares, 30/*a*, 18/0*c*. R. T., double fare. Pop. 19,694.
Map Square 13.

King's+	Gains.	Gains.	King's+
AM 4.45	10.15	AM 6.48	10.40
8.45	1. 6	9.39	1.30
11.30	4.50	PM12.15	6.25
PM 1.50*r*	6.17	3.12*r*	7.10
4. 0*r*	7.53	4.29*r*	9.25
5.45*r*	11.10	—	—
—	—	—	—

Sunday Trains.

AM12. 0*hr*	4.55	PM 5.16*hr*	10.20
—	—	—	—

h Via Peterborough and Boston.
r Restaurant Car.

ANOTHER ROUTE from *King's Cross*, 148¾ miles, *via* Retford. Fares as above.

King's+	Gains.	Gains.	King's+
AM 4.45	8.45	AM 7.22*r*	11.30
7.15*r*	10.48	9.35*r*	1. 5
10.10*r*	3.12	PM 2.17	6.25
PM 1.50*r*	5.22	3.59	9. 0
4. 0*r*	7.56	8.26	3.25
8.25*e*	4. 9	—	—
—	—	—	—
—	—	—	—

Sunday Trains.

PM 5. 0*r*	8.42	AM10.18*r*	3.45
8.25	4. 9	PM 6. 1*r*	10.20
—	—	—	—

e Saturdays excepted.
r Restaurant Car.

ANOTHER ROUTE from *Marylebone*, 185 miles. Fares as above.

M'bone	Gains.	Gains.	M'bone
AM 2.32	8.45	AM 7.22*r*	1.13
10. 0*r*	3.12	9.35*r*	3. 0
PM12.15*r*	5.21	PM 1.57*r*	6.38
3.20*r*	7.56	2.17*r*	8.55
10. 5*e*	4. 9	5. 9*r*	9.55
—	—	8.26	3.57
—	—	—	—

Sunday Trains.

AM11.15*r*	8.42	AM10.18*r*	5.40
—	—	—	—
—	—	—	—
—	—	—	—

e Saturdays excepted.
r Restaurant Car.

ANOTHER ROUTE from *Liverpool Street*, 159¾ miles. Fares as above.

L'pool St.	Gains.	Gains.	L'pool St.
AM 5.50	1. 4	AM 6.48	12.40
10. 5	2.56	8.37*lr*	4. 2*h*
11.50	6.15	8.37	5. 9
PM 2.34	8.52	11.46	5.17
4.45	11. 9	PM12.15	6.10
—	—	4.29	10.30
—	—	—	—
—	—	—	—

Sunday Trains.

AM 9.25	2. 4	PM 3. 6	7.40
—	—	—	—

h Arrives at St. Pancras Station.
l Commencing July 23.
r Restaurant Car.

GAIRLOCHY (Inverness), 519 miles. Fares, 103/2*a*, 61/11*c*. R. T. for two months, 206/4*a*, 123/10*c*. Departures *from* London as for Fort William. Departures *for* London about twice daily.
Map Square 37.

GAISGILL (Westmorland), 264½ miles. No through fares. Departures *from* London as for Tebay. Departures *for* London about 3 times daily.
Map Square 7.

GALASHIELS (Selkirk) from *St. Pancras*, 372¾ miles. Fares, 74/0*a*, 44/5*c*. R. T. for two months, 148/0*a*, 88/10*c*. Pop. 12,946.
Map Square 41.

St. Pan.	Galasls.	Galasls.	St. Pan.
AM 4.25	3. 3	AM10.39*r*	7.15
9. 0*r*	5.29	11.33*r*	7.55
11.45*r*	8. 8	PM10.47	8. 3
PM 9.15	6.12	—	—
—	—	—	—
—	—	—	—
—	—	—	—
—	—	—	—

Sunday Trains.

PM 9.15	6.12	PM10.47	8. 3
—	—	—	—
—	—	—	—
—	—	—	—
—	—	—	—
—	—	—	—

r Restaurant Car.

ANOTHER ROUTE from *Euston*, 363¾ miles. Fares as above.

Euston	Galasls.	Galasls.	Euston
AM 2.35	3. 3	AM 7.46*r*	6.25
5. 0	5.29	10.39*r*	7.30
10.40*r*	8.12	11.33*r*	9.20
PM 9.20*e*	6.12	PM 5.26	5. 0*h*
11.35*e*	10.35	6.56	6.55
—	—	10.47	7.30
—	—	—	—
—	—	—	—
—	—	—	—

Sunday Trains.

PM11.35	10.35	PM10.47	7.30
—	—	—	—
—	—	—	—
—	—	—	—
—	—	—	—

e Saturdays excepted.
h A.M.
r Restaurant Car.

GALGATE (Lancs), 225¾ miles. Fares, 46/11*a*, 28/2*c*. R.T. for two months, 93/10*a*, 56/4*c*. Departures *from* London as for Preston. Departures *for* London about 4 times daily.
Map Square 7.

GALLIONS (Royal Albert Docks) from *Fenchurch Street*, 8¼ miles. Fares, 1/0½*a*, 0/10*b*, 0/7½*c*. R. T. for two days, 2/1*a*, 1/7½*b*, 1/2*c*. See pp. 537-540.

GALSTON (Ayr), 392 miles. Fares, 79/9*a*, 47/10*c*. R. T. for two months, 159/6*a*, 95/8*c*. Departures *from* London as for Kilmarnock. Departures *for* London about 4 times daily. Pop. 6,821.
Map Square 40.

GAMLINGAY (Cambs) from *King's Cross*, 50 miles. Fares, 10/5*a*, 6/3*c*. R. T. for two months, 20/10*a*. Departures *from* London as for Sandy. Departures *for* London about 6 times daily. Pop. 1,797.
Map Square 18.

GANTON (Yorks), 222¼ miles. Fares, 46/3*a*, 27/9*c*. R. T., double fare. Departures *from* London as for Malton. Departures *for* London about 5 times daily. Pop. 398.
Map Square 8.

GARA BRIDGE (Devon) from *Paddington*, 214½ miles. Fares, 44/2*a*, 26/6*c*. R. T. for two months, 88/4*a*, 53/0*c*. Departures *from* London as for Kingsbridge. Departures *for* London about 5 times daily.
Map Square 26.

GARELOCHHEAD (Dumbarton), 471¾ miles. Fares, 85/8*a*, 51/5*c*. R. T. for two months, 171/4*a*, 102/10*c*. Departures *from* London as for Arrochar and Tarbet. Departures *for* London about twice daily. Pop. 1,535.
Map Square 40.

GARFORTH (Yorks), 193¾ miles. Fares, 40/2*a*, 24/1*c*. R. T. double fare. Departures *from* London as for Leeds. Departures *for* London about 5 times daily. Pop. 3,927.
Map Square 13.

GARGRAVE (Yorks), 225 miles. Fares, 43/4*a*, 26/0*c*. R. T., double fare. Departures *from* London as for Skipton. Departures *for* London about 6 times daily. Pop. 1,168.
Map Square 7.

GARGUNNOCK (Stirling), 420¾ miles. Fares, 86/3*a*, 51/9*c*. R.T. for two months, 172/6*a*, 103/6*c*. Departures *from* London as for Stirling. Departures *for* London about 3 times daily. Pop. 586.
Map Square 40.

GARMOUTH (Elgin), 580½ miles. Fares, 106/3*a*, 63/9*c*. R.T. for two months, 212/6*a*, 127/6*c*. Departures *from* London as for Huntly or Elgin (*via* Dunkeld). Departures *for* London about twice daily. Pop. 712.
Map Square 35.

GARNANT (Carmarthen), 213½ miles. Fares, 43/11*a*, 26/4*c*. R. T. for two months, 87/10*a*. Departures *from* London as for Brynamman. Departures *for* London about 5 times daily.
Map Square 21.

GARNEDDWEN (Merioneth), 224½ miles. No through fares. Departures *from* London as for Machynlleth. Departures *for* London about three times daily.
Map Square 16.

GARNKIRK (Lanark), 397¼ miles. No through fares. Departures *from* London as for Coatbridge. Departures *for* London about 5 times daily.
Map Square 40.

GARSTANG & CATTERALL (Lancs), 218¾ miles. Fares, 45/7*a*, 27/4*c*. R. T. for two months, 91/2*a*. Departures *from* London as for Preston. Departures *for* London about 4 times daily. Pop. 836.
Map Square 7.

GARSTON (Lancs), 195½ miles. Fares, 40/5*a*, 24/3*c*. R. T. for two months, 80/10*a*, 48/6*c*. Departure *from* London as for Warrington. Departures *for* London about 6 times daily. Pop. 14,359.
Map Square 12.

GARSTON, EAST (Berks), 63 miles. Fares, 12/4*a*, 7/11*c*. R. T. for two months, 24/8*a*, 15/10*c*. Departures *from* London as for Lambourn. Departures *for* London about 4 times daily. Pop. 408.
Map Square 23.

GARSWOOD (Lancs), 195½ miles. Fares, 40/8*a*, 24/5*c*. R. T. for two months, 81/4*a*, 48/10*c*. Departures *from* London as for Wigan or St. Helens. Departures *for* London about 3 times daily.
Map Square 12.

GARTCOSH (Lanark), 396 miles. No through fares. Departures *from* London as for Coatbridge. Departures *for* London about 3 times daily. Pop. 2,779.
Map Square 40.

GARTH (Brecknock), 225¼ miles. Fares, 38/7*a*, 23/2*c*. R. T. for two months, 77/2*a*. Departures *from* London as for Builth Road. Departures *for* London about 4 times daily.
Map Square 16.

GARTLY (Aberdeen), 558½ miles. Fares, 106/3*a*, 63/9*c*. R.T. for two months, 212/6*a*, 127/6*c*. Departures *from* London as for Inverurie. Departures *for* London about twice daily. Pop. 684.
Map Square 35.

GARTMORE (Perth), 436 miles. Fares, 87/8*a*, 52/7*c*. R. T. for two months, 175/4*a*, 105/2*c*. Departures *from* London as for Stirling. Departures *for* London about 3 times daily. Pop. 426.
Map Square 40.

GARTNESS (Stirling), 450¾ miles. Fares, 86/11*a*, 52/2*c*. R. T. for two months, 173/10*a*, 104/4*c*. Departures *from* London as for Stirling. Departures *for* London about 3 times daily.
Map Square 40.

GARTON (Yorks), 216¾ miles. Fares, 39/9*a*, 23/10*c*. R. T. for two months, 79/6*a*, 47/8*c*. Departures *from* London as for Driffield. Departures *for* London about 3 times daily. Pop. 414.
Map Square 8.

GARTSHERRIE (Lanark), 394½ miles. No through fares. Departures *from* London as for Coatbridge. Departures *for* London about 5 times daily. Pop. 15,674.
Map Square 40.

GARVE (Ross), 598¼ miles. Fares, 108/7*a*, 65/2*c*. R. T. for two months, 217/2*a*. Departures *from* London as for Kyle of Lochalsh. Departures *for* London about 3 times daily.
Map Square 34.

GATEACRE (Lancs) 211¼ miles. Fares, 40/10*a*, 24/6*c*. R.T. for two months, 81/8*a*, 49/0*c*. Departures *from* London as for Warrington (Central). Departures *for* London about 6 times daily. Pop. 1,289.
Map Square 12.

GATEHEAD (Ayr), 393 miles. Fares, 80/0*a*, 48/0*c*. R. T. for two months, 160/0*a*, 96/0*c*. Departures *from* London as for Kilmarnock. Departures *for* London about 4 times daily.
Map Square 40.

GATEHOUSE-OF-FLEET (Kirkcudbright). 371 miles. Fares, 68/9*a*, 41/3*c*. R. T. for two months, 137/6*a*, 82/6*c*. Departures *from* London as for Castle Douglas. Departures *for* London about 3 times daily. Pop. 893.
Map Square 43.

GATESHEAD (Durham), 267¾ miles. Fares, 55/10*a*, 33/6*c*. R. T., double fare. Departures *from* London as for Ferryhill or Newcastle-on-Tyne. Departures *for* London about 6 times daily. Pop. 124,514.
Map Square 3.

GATESIDE (Fife), 429¼ miles. No through fares. Departures *from* London as for Cupar. Departures *for* London about 3 times daily.
Map Square 41.

GATHURST (Lancs), 198½ miles. Fares, 41/0*a*, 24/7*c*. R. T. for two months, 82/0*a*, 49/2*c*. Departures *from* London as for Wigan. Departures *for* London about 6 times daily.
Map Square 12.

GATLEY (Cheshire), 181¾ miles. Fares, 37/11*a*, 22/9*c*. R.T., double fare. Departures *from* London as for Wilmslow. Departures *for* London about 6 times daily. Pop. 2,046.

GAVELL (Stirling), 438¼ miles. No through fares. Departures *from* London as for Glasgow Departures *for* London about 4 times daily.
Map Square 40.

GAYTON ROAD (Norfolk), 116½ miles. Fares, 20/10*a*, 12/6*c*. R. T. for two months, 41/8*a*, 25/0*c*. Departures *from* London as for Terrington. Departures *for* London about 4 times daily. Pop. (Gayton) 780.
Map Square 19.

GEDDINGTON (Northampton) from *St. Pancras*, 77 miles. Fares, 15/8*a*, 9/5*c*. R. T., double fare. Pop 1,009.
Map Square 18.

	St. Pan.	Geddtn.		Geddtn	St. Pan.
AM	2.25	6.26	AM	8.52*r*	11. 0
	8.25*r*	10.46		9.42	1. 3
	11.35	2.14	PM	1.46*r*	4.10
PM	3.30*r*	5. 8		6.56*r*	9. 5
	5.35*r*	7.32		—	—

No Sunday Trains.
r Restaurant Car.

GEDLING (Notts), 125¾ miles. Fares, 25/8*a*, 15/5*c*. R. T., double fare. Departures *from* London as for Basford and Bulwell. Departures *for* London about 5 times daily. Pop. 1,543.

GEDNEY (Lincoln) from *King's Cross*, 103¾ miles. Fares, 19/10*a*, 11/11*c*. R.T. for two months, 39/8*a*, 23/10*c*. Departures *from* London as for Holbeach. Departures *for* London about 5 minutes earlier. Pop. 1,834.
Map Square 18.

GELDESTON (Norfolk) from *Liverpool Street*, 111¾ miles. Fares, 23/6*a*, 14/1*c*. R. T. for two months, 47/0*a*. Departures *from* London as for Ditchingham *via* Beccles. Departures *for* London about 7 times daily. Pop. 295.
Map Square 19.

GEORGE LANE (Essex) from *Fenchurch Street* or *Liverpool Street*, 8 miles. Fares from Fenchurch St., 1/5½*a*, 1/2*b*, 0/10½*c*. R. T. for two days, 2/11*a*, 2/4*b*, 1/7½*c*. From Liverpool Street, 1/5½*a*, 1/2*b*, 0/10½*c*. R. T. for two days, 2/11*a*, 2/4*c*. 1/7½*c*. *See* pp. 541-544.
Map Squares 23 *and* 53.

GEORGEMAS (Caithness), 715 miles. Fares, 130/5*a*, 78/3*c*. R. T. for two months, 260/10*a*, 156/6*c*. Departures *from* London as for Helmsdale. Departures *for* London about twice daily.
Map Square 32.

GERRARD'S CROSS (Bucks) from *Paddington*, 17½ miles. Fares, 3/7*a*, 2/2*c*. R. T. for two months, 7/2*a*, 3/11½*c*. *See* pp. 490-491. Pop. 1,612.
Map Squares 23 *and* 45.

ANOTHER ROUTE from *Marylebone*, 18¾ miles. Fares as above. *See* pp. 495, 496.

Chalfont Park. First Class Family Hotel. Golf, Tennis. Telephone 37. Telegrams: "Chalpark." For tariff apply—
MANAGERESS.
See advt. p. **23.**

Francis Duck, House Agent. Particulars of Properties on application. Telephone 7 Gerrards Cross. Telegrams: Duck, Gerrards Cross. Surveys, Valuations, Auctions.

IDRIS GREEN GINGER WINE.

GIDEA PARK (Essex)

from *Liverpool Street*, 13¼ miles, or *Fenchurch Street*. Fares, 2/6a, 2/0b, 1/6c. R. T. for two months, 5/0a, 3/11½b, 2/7½c. *See* pp. 528-534.

GIFFEN (Ayr), 416¼ miles.

Fares, 83/2a, 49/11c. R. T. for two months, 166/4a, 99/10c. Departures *from* London as for Glasgow (Central). Departures *for* London about 3 times daily.
Map Square 40.

GIFFNOCK (Renfrew),

403¼ miles. Fares, 82/6a, 49/6c. R. T. for two months, 165/0a, 99/0c. Departures *from* London as for Hamilton. Departures *for* London about 4 times daily. Pop. 2,198.

GIFFORD (East Lothian),

401¼ miles. Fares, 81/8a, 49/0c. R. T. for two months, 163/4a, 98/0c. Departures *from* London as for Edinburgh (Waverley). Departures *for* London about twice daily. Pop. 345.
Map Square 41.

GIGGLESWICK (Yorks)

from *St. Pancras*, 236 miles. Fares, 45/8a, 27/5c. R. T., double fare. Pop. 994.
Map Square 7.

St. Pan.	Gigwk.	Gigwk.	St. Pan.
AM 2.25g	11.45	AM 7.48r	2.10
4.25	1.7	9.23r	4.10
9.50r	4.7	10.48r	5.30
PM12.15r	6.22	PM 2.0r	7.55
3.30r	9.47	8.13	4.20
11.50r	7.50	—	—
11.50d	8.30	—	—

Sunday Trains.

AM10.50r	6.50	AN 9.45	5.27
PM11.45	7.50	PM 7.45	4.55
—	—	—	—
—	—	—	—

d Saturdays only.
e Saturdays excepted.
g Mondays excepted.
r Restaurant Car.

GILDERSOME (Yorks),

184¼ miles. Fares, 38/2a, 22/11c. R. T., double fare. Departures *from* London as for Wakefield (Westgate). Departures *for* London about 8 times daily. Pop. 2,867.

GILESTON (Glamorgan),

168 miles. Fares, 35/0a, 21/0c. R. T. for two months, 70/0a, 42/0c. Departures *from* London as for Barry Docks. Departures *for* London about 7 times daily. Pop. 50.
Map Square 21.

GILFACH (Glamorgan),

183¼ miles. Fares, 38/2a, 22/11c. R. T. for two months, 76/4a, 45/10c. Departures *from* London as for Tondu. Departures *for* London about 4 times daily.
Map Square 21.

GILLESPIE ROAD.

(Hammersmith and Finsbury Park Tube.) *See* back of Map.

GILLING (Yorks), 212¾ miles.

Fares, 44/5a, 26/8c. R. T., double fare. Departures *from* London as for Ampleforth. Departures *for* London about 4 times daily. Pop. 208.
Map Square 8.

GILLINGHAM (Dorset)

from *Waterloo*, 105½ miles. Fares, 22/1a, 13/3c. R. T. for two months, 44/2a, 26/6c. Pop. 3,570.
Map Square 22.

W'loo.	G'l'ham.	G'l'ham.	W'loo.
AM 7.30	10.19	AM 7.50	10.56
10.0r	12.39	9.3r	11.10
12.0r	2.32	9.18	12.22
PM 1.0r	3.49	11.33r	1.56
3.0r	5.39	PM12.16r	3.8
5.0	7.50	3.21r	6.0
6.0r	8.53	4.20	7.40
10.0h	3.29	5.12r	8.30
—	—	7.22	10.50
—	—	10.13h	3.58

Sunday Trains.

AM 9.0	1.16	PM 6.39r	8.57
12.0nr	2.48		
PM 6.0	9.35		

h Via Eastleigh.
n Noon.
r Restaurant Car.

GILLINGHAM (Kent),

from *Victoria, Holborn Viaduct,* and *St. Paul's,* 36 miles. Fares, 6/8a, 5/4b, 4/0c. R. T. for two months, 13/4a, 10/8b. Pop. 54,038.
Map Square 24.

Vict. S. E. & C.	Leave Hol. V.	S.PL.'s.	Arr. at G'l'ham
AM —	3.50h	—	5.12
5.5	4.57	5.0	6.59
5.48f	5.40f	5.42f	6.52
7.40f	7.30	7.33	9.7
9.20	—	—	8.52
11.40d	—	—	10.17
11.40e	—	—	12.56
PM 1.23d	—	—	2.24
2.5d	—	—	4.39
2.8e	—	—	5.11
—	3.35d	3.36d	5.42
4.15d	—	—	5.18
4.20	—	—	5.25
4.25e	—	—	5.42
5.30e	—	—	6.36
5.30d	—	—	6.39
—	—	5.33e	6.56
6.16	6.10e	6.13e	8.1
7.5	7.0	7.3	8.22
7.50	—	—	8.55
9.0e	8.57e	9.0e	10.35
10.17	10.11	10.13	11.47

Sunday Trains.

AM 7.20	—	—	8.48
8.15	8.0	—	9.26
10.30	10.25	—	12.10
PM 3.20	—	—	4.31
3.30	—	—	5.10
6.35	—	—	8.9
7.50	—	—	8.58
—	10.12	—	11.55
10.25	—	—	11.35

GILLINGHAM—*contd.*

Trains from Gillingham.

Leave G'l'ham.	Arrive at St.P'l's	Hol. V.	Vict.
AM 6.32	8.8	8.9	8.14
6.50	8.25	8.27	8.29
7.16	9.16	9.18	—
8.7	9.37	9.39	—
9.34	—	—	11.2
10.20	—	—	11.27
11.56e	12.59	1.2	1.33
11.49d	—	—	1.22
PM 1.56	—	—	2.43
1.50	—	—	3.23
3.2e	4.46	—	4.39
3.13d	—	—	4.55
4.40k	—	—	5.37
4.57	—	—	5.56
7.28	—	—	8.33
8.2	9.50	9.54	9.46
9.19	—	—	10.25
9.49	11.21	11.23	—

Sunday Trains.

AM 7.45	—	9.40	9.31
9.30	—	11.27	11.23
10.42	—	11.58	11.51
11.14	—	1.2	12.56
PM 3.40	—	—	4.42
4.21	—	—	5.31
7.25	—	—	8.40
9.25	—	—	10.29
9.52	—	12.0	11.44

d Saturdays only.
e Saturdays excepted.
f Mondays only.
h Third class only.
k Fridays only.

ANOTHER ROUTE from *Charing Cross, Cannon Street,* and *London Bridge,* 35 miles. Fares as above.

Char. +	Leave Can. St.	Lon. B.	Arr. at G'l'ham
AM —	—	3.57h	5.12
—	6.20	6.23	7.58
—	7.16	7.19	8.52
—	7.44	7.47	9.12
8.10	—	8.17	10.4
8.51	—	8.57	10.26
9.32	—	9.41	11.13
—	10.58	11.1	12.34
11.55	—	12.2	1.33
PM12.50d	—	12.37d	2.5
1.20e	—	1.27e	2.55
1.26d	—	1.34d	2.55
2.45e	—	2.53e	4.39
3.5d	—	3.12d	4.39
3.10d	—	3.17d	4.55
—	4.12e	4.15e	5.16
4.25d	—	4.31d	6.2
—	4.36e	4.39e	6.2
—	5.8e	5.11e	6.36
5.15d	—	5.22d	7.0
5.17e	—	5.25e	6.46
5.21e	6.12e	5.29e	7.12
5.58d	—	6.4d	7.24
6.22e	—	6.29e	8.1
6.55d	—	7.1d	8.40
—	7.8e	7.11e	8.40
7.34	—	7.41	9.16
—	7.44d	7.47d	10.4
—	9.35	9.38	11.7
10.20	—	10.27	11.55
11.24	—	—	12.43

Sunday Trains.

AM —	—	7.30	8.54
7.30	—	7.37	9.26
9.46	—	9.52	11.42
10.50	—	10.57	12.40
PM 1.15	—	1.22	3.2
3.15	—	3.22	4.58
4.50	—	4.57	6.30
7.0	—	7.7	8.27
8.42	—	8.49	10.17
10.30	—	10.38	12.30

GILLINGHAM—*contd.*

Trains from Gillingham.

Leave G'L'HAM	Arrive at		
	LON. B.	CAN. ST	CHAR. +
AM 4.15	5.47	5.51	—
5.24	7. 0	7. 4	—
6.22	8.13	8.17	—
7. 2	8.31	8.35	—
7.16	8.34	—	8.41
7.30	8.51	8.55	—
8. 7	9. 0	9. 4	—
8.25	9.34	—	9.43
8.50	9.54	—	10. 1
8.54	10.24	10.28	—
9.22	10.38	—	10.45
9.50	11.20	11.24	—
10.20	12. 3	—	12.14
PM12. 5*d*	1.31	1.37	—
12. 5*e*	1.36	—	1.45
12.52*d*	2. 1	2. 5	—
1.10*d*	2.44	—	2.54
1.24*e*	2.53	—	3. 4
2. 0*e*	3.26	—	3.36
2.18*d*	3.58	—	4. 8
3. 2*e*	4.48	4.52	—
3.13*d*	4.57	—	5. 7
4. 0*e*	5.36	5.40	—
4. 0*d*	5.36	—	5.45
5. 3*e*	6.35	6.39	—
5.35	7.10	—	7.19
5.45	7.14	—	7.23
6.50	8.15	8.20	—
7.35	9. 6	9.11	—
9.25	10.51	—	10.59
10.42	12.35	—	12.45
—	—	—	—
—	—	—	—

Sunday Trains.

AM 7.20	9. 0	—	9. 9
8.40	10.16	—	10.24
11.14	1. 5	—	1.17
PM12.42	2.14	—	2.24
2.30	4. 4	—	4.15
4.33	5.55	—	6. 4
5.20	6.49	—	6.59
6.25	8. 1	—	8.10
7.25	9.46	—	9.55
9.40	11.15	—	11.23
9.52	11.20	—	—
—	—	—	—

d Saturdays only.
e Saturdays excepted.
h Third class only.

GILMERTON (Midlothian), 393½ miles. No through fares. Departures *from* London as for Edinburgh (Waverley). Departures *for* London about 3 times daily. *Map Square* 41.

GILNOCKIE (Dumfries), 316 miles. No through fares. Departures *from* London as for Carlisle. Departures *for* London about 3 times daily. *Map Square* 44.

GILSLAND (Cumberland), 308½ miles. Fares, 60/10*a*, 36/6*c*. R. T. for two months, 121/8*a*, 73/0*c*. Departures *from* London as for Hexham or Carlisle. Departures *for* London about 4 times daily. Pop. 370. *Map Square* 3.

GILWERN (Brecon), 165½ miles. Fares, 33/9*a*, 20/3*c*. R. T. for two months. 67/6*a*, 40/6*c*. Departures *from* London as for Abergavenny. Departures *for* London about 6 times daily. *Map Square* 21.

GIPSY HILL ·(London) from *London Bridge* and *Victoria*, 8 miles. Fares, ex London Bridge, 1/6*a*, 0/10½*c*. R. T. for two days, 2/7*a*, 1/9*c*. From Victoria, 1/3*a*, 0/9*c*. R. T. for two days, 2/6*a*, 1/5*c*. See pp. 578, 579, 581, 582. *Map Square* 79.

GIRVAN (Ayr) from *St. Pancras*, 419½ miles. Fares, 84/5*a*, 50/8*c*. R. T. for two months, 168/10*a*, 101/4*c*. Pop. 8,474. *Map Square* 43.

	ST. PAN.	GIRVAN	GIRVAN	ST. PAN.
AM 4.25	5. 0	AM 7.32*r*	6.35
	9.50*r*	8.55	9.45*r*	9.15
PM 9.30*e*	9.30	PM 7.20*e*	7.25
	11.45*e*	10.35	7.20*d*	8.57
—	—	—	—
—	—	—	—
—	—	—	—
—	—	—	—

Sunday Trains.

PM 9.30	9.30	—	—
11.45	10.35	—	—

d Saturdays only.
e Saturdays excepted.
r Restaurant Car.

GISBURN (Yorks), 230 miles. Fares, 43/9*a*, 26/3*c*. R. T. for two months, 87/6*a*, 52/6*c*. Departures *from* London as for Clitheroe. Departures *for* London about 3 times daily. Pop. 449. *Map Square* 7.

GLAIS (Glamorgan), 217½ miles. Fares, 41/5*a*, 24/10*c*. R. T. for two months, 82/10*a*, 49/8*c*. Departures *from* London as for Brecon (*via* Hereford). Departures *for* London about 3 times daily.

GLAISDALE (Yorks), 241 miles. Fares, 50/3*a*, 20/2*c*. R. T. for two months, 100/6*a*, 60/4*c*. Departures *from* London, as for Whitby or Stockton-on-Tees. Departures *for* London about 4 times daily. Pop. 968. *Map Square* 8.

GLAMIS (Perth), 476½ miles. Fares, 96/6*a*, 57/11*c*. R. T. for two months, 193/0*a*, 115/10*c*. Departures *from* London as for Coupar Angus. Departures *for* London about 3 times daily. Pop. 1,093. *Map Square* 38.

GLANAMMAN (Carmarthen), 212½ miles. Fares, 43/11*a*, 26/4*c*. R. T. for two months, 87/10*a*. Departures *from* London as for Brynamman. Departures *for* London about 6 times daily. *Map Square* 21.

GLAN CONWAY (Denbigh), 224½ miles. Fares, 46/11*a*, 28/2*c*. R. T. for two months, 93/10*a*, 56/4*c*. Departures *from* London as for Llanrwst and Trefriw. Departures *for* London about 5 times daily. *Map Square* 11.

GLANDYFI (Cardigan), 223½ miles. Fares, 45/5*a*, 27/3*c*. R. T. for two months, 90/10*a*. Departures *from* London as for Machynlleth. Departures *for* London about 4 times daily. *Map Square* 16.

GLANRAFON (Cardigan), 241½ miles. No through fares. Departures *from* London as for Aberystwyth. Departures *for* London about 3 times daily. *Map Square* 16.

GLANRHYD (Carmarthen), 221 miles. Fares, 43/2*a*, 25/11*c*. R. T. for two months, 86/4*a*. Departures *from* London as for Llandilo. Departures *for* London about 5 times daily. *Map Square* 16.

GLANTON (Northumberland), 317 miles. Fares, 66/11*a*, 40/2*c*. R. T., double fare. Departures *from* London as for Alnwick. Departures *for* London about 4 times daily. Pop. 447. *Map Square* 3.

GLAPWELL (Derby), 146 miles. Fares, 29/10*a*, 17/11*c*. R. T., double fare. Departures *from* London as for Mansfield. Departures *for* London about 4 times daily. Pop. 93. *Map Square* 13. ·

GLASBURY (Brecon), 169½ miles. Fares, 35/2*a*, 21/1*c*. R. T. for two months, 70/4*a*, 42/2*c*. Departures *from* London as for Hay. Departures *for* London about 3 times daily. Pop. 494. *Map Square* 3.

GLASGOW (CENTRAL) (Lanark) from *Euston*, *via* Carlisle, 401½ miles. Fares, 82/6*a*, 49/6*c*. R. T. for two months, 165/0*a*, 99/0*c*. Pop. 1,034,174. *Map Square* 40.

EUSTON	GLAS. (Central)	GLAS. (Central)	EUSTON
AM 2.35	3.20	AM10. 0*r*	6.25
5. 0	4.13	10.10*r*	7.30
6.45*r*	6. 5	PM 1.30*r*	10. 0
10. 0*r*	6.15	5.30*r*	5. 0
11.35*r*	9.20	9.30*e*	6.55
PM 1.30*r*	10. 0	10.30	7.30
9.20	6.55	—	—
11. 0*d*	8. 0	—	—
11.45*e*	9.35	—	—

Sunday Trains.

AM11.30*r*	8.45	AM10. 0*r*	7.30
PM 9.30	7.16	PM 5.30*r*	5. 0
11.45	9.35	10.30	7.30
—	—	—	—
—	—	—	—
—	—	—	—

d Saturdays only.
e Saturdays excepted.
r Restaurant Car.

GLASGOW—*contd.*

ANOTHER ROUTE from
St. Pancras, via Carlisle, 423½
miles. Fares as above.

St. Pan. Glasgow		Glasgow St. Pan.	
(St. Enoch)		(St. Enoch)	
AM 4.25	3.43	AM 9.20r	6.35
9.50r	7.11	12. 0r	9.15
PM12.15r	9.30	PM 9.15e	7.25
9.30e	7.35	10.45e	7.50
11.45e	9. 0	11.10d	8.57
11.45d	9. 7	—	—
—	—	—	—
—	—	—	—

Sunday Trains.

PM 9.30	7.35	PM 9.15	7.25
11.45	9. 0	10.45	7.50
—	—	—	—
—	—	—	—

d Saturdays only.
e Saturdays excepted.
r Restaurant Car.

ANOTHER ROUTE from
King's Cross, 438 miles. Fares as
above.

King's+Glasgow		Glasgow King's+	
(Queen St.)		(Queen St.)	
AM 4.45	3. 5h	AM 8.40r	6.15h
10. 0r	7.30h	PM12. 5	10. 0h
11.50r	9.39h	4. 0	3.25
PM 7.45er	5.30k	6. 0	6. 0k
8.25e	7.32k	8.25	6.50f
8.25d	9.35	9.45	7.25k
11.25e	8.55k	—	—
11.25d	9.35k	—	—

Sunday Trains.

AM11.30r	9.50h	AM 9.55r	8.15h
PM 7.45r	5.30k	PM 9.25	7. 5k
8.25	7.32k	—	—
11.25	8.55k	—	—

d Saturdays only.
e Saturdays excepted.
f Arrives 7.5 Sundays.
h P.M.   *k* A.M.
r Restaurant Car.

St. Enoch Station Hotel.
Provides every comfort. Best
centre for business and Tourists
West Highlands and Burns' Coun-
try. Telegrams, "Souwestern."
J. H. THOMAS, Manager.
See advt. p. **187.**

Central Station Hotel,
Glasgow. Largest and Most
Luxurious Hotel in Scotland.
Accommodation for 550 Guests.
Tariff Reasonable.
S. H. QUINCE.
See advt. p.-**188.**

Royal Hotel. First - class
Family and Commercial. Accom-
modation for 100 visitors. Hot
and cold water in each room.
Elevator.
See advt. p. **189.**

Wemyss Bay Hydro. Fifty
minutes from Glasgow. Finest
Scenery on Clyde. Russian,
Turkish, Sea - Water Baths.
Garage. Golf Course. Telegrams,
"Hydro, Skelmorlie."
See advt. p. **338.**

Cranston's Waverley Tem-
perance Hotel, 172, Sauchiehall
Street (only address in Glasgow).
Unsurpassed for comfort, catering.
Breakfast, 2s. and 3s. Tea, 2s.
and 3s. Bedroom, with attendance, 5s.

GLASGOW—*contd.*

More's Hotel, India Street,
Charing Cross. High - Class
Tourist and Residential Hotel.
Cuisine and service excellent.
Bedroom, Bath and Table d'Hote
Breakfast from 9/6. 'Phones 3297
and 3298 Central. Telegrams,
"Erom, Glasgow."

Norwich Union Mutual, the
Outstanding British Life Office.
Reserves at 2½ per cent. 125, St.
Vincent Street, Glasgow. ■
See advt. p. 6 of cover.

GLASSAUGH   (Banff),

586 miles. No through fares.
Departures *from* London as for
Huntly. Departures *for* London
about 3 times daily.
Map Square 35.

GLASSEL   (Aberdeen),

543 miles. No through fares. Departures *from* London as for Ballater. Departures *for* London
about 4 times daily.
Map Square 38.

GLASSFORD   (Lanark),

401¼ miles. No through fares.
Departures *from* London as for
Hamilton. Departures *for* Lon-
don about 4 times daily. Pop.
1,431.
Map Square 40.

GLASSON DOCK

(Lancs.), 235 miles. Fares, 49/0a,
29/5c. R.T. for two months, 98/0a,
58/10c. Departures *from* London
as for Lancaster (Castle). Departures *for* London about 4 times
daily.
Map Square 7.

GLASTERLAW   (Forfar,

491¾ miles. No through fares.
Departures *from* London as for
Forfar. Departures *for* London
about 3 times daily.
Map Square 38.

GLASTONBURY (Somer-

set) from *Waterloo*, 133½ miles.
Fares, 26/3a, 15/9c. R.T. for two
months, 52/6a, 31/6c. Pop. 4,326.
Map Square 22.

W'loo. Glastby.		Glastby. W'loo.	
AM 9. 0r	1.11	AM 7.14r	11.10
12. 0r	3.57	10.24r	1.56
PM 1. 0r	5. 8	PM12.25r	4.30
3. 0r	7. 5	3.59r	8.30
6. 0r	9.36	5.53	10.50
—	—	7.11h	3.58

✦ No Sunday Trains.

h Via Eastleigh.
r Restaurant Car.

GLAZEBROOK   (Lancs)

from *St. Pancras*, 193½ miles.
Fares, 37/9a, 22/8c. R.T. for
two months, 75/6a, 45/4c. Pop. 987.
Map Square 12.

St. Pan. G'brook		G'brook St. Pan.	
AM 2.25	7.35	AM 6. 5r	11.35
4.25	11.10	8.13r	1.30
8.25r	2. 0	8.45r	1.45
10.25r	3.58	9.18	3.25
PM12.25r	5.17	10.47r	5.45
2.25r	7. 8	PM 2.41r	8.55
4.25r	9.26	4.28r	10. 5
12. 0h	6.14	10.16	6. 0

GLAZEBROOK—*contd.*

Sunday Trains.

St. Pan.	G'brook	G'brook	St. Pan.
AM11.15	5.27	AM11.24r	5. 2
PM 3.15	9.27	PM 4.35r	9.52
11.55	6.21	9.56	4.55

h Saturdays midnight excepted.
r Restaurant Car.

GLEMSFORD   (Suffolk)

from *Liverpool Street*, 64 miles.
Fares, 13/7a, 8/2c. R. T. for two
months 27/2a. Departures *from*
London as for Long Melford. Departures *for* London about 6 times
daily. Pop. 1,444.
Map Square 19.

GLENBARRY (Banff), 575½

miles. No through fares. Departures *from* London as for Huntly.
Departures *for* London about
twice daily.
Map Square 35.

GLENBOIG (Lanark), 395½

miles. Fares, 80/7a, 48/4c. R. T.
for two months, 161/2a, 96/8c. Departures *from* London as for Coatbridge. Departures *for* London
about 3 times daily.
Map Square 40.

GLENBUCK (Ayr), 392½

miles. No through fares. Departures *from* London as for Carstairs.
Departures *for* London about 3
times daily. —Pop. 632.
Map Square 40.

GLENCARSE (Perth), 456½

miles. Fares, 91/11a, 55/2c. R. T.
for two months, 183/10a, 110/4c.
Departures *from* London as for
Perth. Departures *for* London
about 3 times daily.
Map Square 38.

GLENCORSE   (Mid

Lothian), 399 miles. Fares, 80/5a,
48/3c. R.T. for two months.160/10a,
96/6c. Departures *from* London
as for Edinburgh (Waverley).
Departures *for* London about 4
times daily. Pop. 1,385.
Map Square 41.

GLENDON (Northampton),

from *St. Pancras*, 74½ miles.
Fares, 15/7a, 9/4c. R. T., double
fare. Departures *from* London as
for Kettering. Departures *for*
London about 5 times daily. Pop.
48.
Map Square 18.

GLENEAGLES   (Perth),

434 miles. Fares, 88/7a, 53/2c.
R. T. for two months, 177/2a,
106/4c. Departures *from* London
as for Dunblane. Departures
for London about 4 times daily.
Pop. 486.
Map Square 40,

GLENFARG (Perth), 430

miles. No through fares. Departures *from* London as for Dum-
fermline. Departures *for* London
about 3 times daily. Pop. 409.
Map Square 41.

GLENFIELD   (Leicester),

107 miles. Fares, 22/8a, 13/7c.
R. T., double fare. Departures
from London as for Desford.
Departures *for* London about 3
times daily. Pop. 1,105.
Map Square 18.

GLENFINNAN (Inverness), 540 miles. Fares, 108/1*a*, 64/10*c*. R. T. for two months, 216/2*a*, 129/8*c*. Departures *from* London as for Fort William. Departures *for* London about twice daily.
Map Square 37.

GLENGARNOCK (Ayr), 403¼ miles. Fares, 82/4*a*, 49/5*c*. R. T. for two months, 164/8*a*, 98/10*c*. Departures *from* London as for Kilmarnock. Departures *for* London about 4 times daily.
Map Square 40.

GLENLUCE (Wigtown), 396½ miles. Fares, 68/9*a*, 41/3*c*. R.T. for two months, 137/6*a*, 82/6*c*. Departures *from* London as for Newton Stewart. Departures *for* London about 4 times daily. Pop. 2,171.
Map Square 43.

GLENSIDE (Ayr), 404½ miles. No through fares. Departures *from* London as for Turnberry. Departures *for* London about 4 times daily.
Map Square 43.

GLENWHILLY (Wigtown), 408½ miles. No through fares. Departures *from* London as for Newton Stewart or Girvan. Departures *for* London about 4 times daily.
Map Square 43.

GLOGUE (Pembroke) from *Paddington*, 255½ miles. Fares, 51/11*a*, 31/2*c*. R.T. for two months, 103/10*a*. Departures *from* London as for Cardigan. Departures *for* London about 4 times daily.
Map Square 16.

GLOSSOP (CENTRAL) (Derby) from *Marylebone*, 195 miles. Fares, 37/6*a*, 22/6*c*. R. T., double fare. Pop. 20,528.
Map Square 12.

M'BONE	GL'SOP.	GL'SOP.	M'BONE
AM 2.32	8.33	AM 5.53*r*	11.10
8.45*dr*	1.58	8.14*r*	1.13
10. 0*r*	2.49	9.45*r*	3. 0
PM12.15*r*	5. 5	10.50*dr*	6.58
3.20*r*	8. 7	PM12.40*er*	6.38
10. 5*e*	6.11	4.10*r*	9.55
—	—	6.55	3.57

Sunday Trains.

AM11.15*r*	4.21	AM11.14*r*	5.40
—	—	PM 4.24*r*	10.24

d Saturdays only.
e Saturdays excepted.
r Restaurant Car.

GLOSSOP AND DINTING (Derby), 191 miles.; Fares, 37/6*a*, 22/6*c*. R. T. for two months, 65/0*a*, 45/0*c*. Departures *from* London as for Penistone. Departures *for* London about 4 times daily. Pop. 3,292.
Map Square 12.

GLOUCESTER from *Paddington*, 114 miles. Fares, 23/9*a*, 14/3*c*. R. T. for two months, 47/6*a*. Pop. 51,330.
Map Square 22.

PAD.	GLO'STR	GLO'STR	PAD.
AM 1. 0*g*	3.55	AM12.25	3.30
5.30	9. 5	6. 0*k*	9.50
7.30	10.34	7.40*r*	10.45
9. 0	12.10	9.45	12.20
10.45	1.52	PM12. 5*r*	2.40
PM 1.10*r*	4.30	12.10	3.20
1.30*k*	4.35	2.40	5. 0
3.15*t*	5.57	6. 0*r*	8.45
4.45*h*	8.25	7. 5	10.25
6. 0*r*	8.33	—	—
9.15	12.25	—	—

Sunday Trains.

AM 1. 0	3.55	AM12.25	3.30
PM12.30*r*	4. 2	PM 1.25	4. 5
2. 0	7.54	6.45	10. 0
4.10*h*	9. 4	—	—
9.15	12.25	—	—

g Mondays excepted.
h Via Honeybourne.
k Via Kingham.
r Restaurant Car.
t Tea Car.

Bell Hotel. Centre of City, near Cathedral. Leading Hotel for Families and Gentlemen. Private Sitting Rooms, Drawing Room. Electric Light throughout. Excellent Stabling and Motor accommodation. Night Porter.
G. P. BEECHING, Manager.
Telephone 772.

Ram Hotel. Centre of City. Family and Commercial. Good Stock Rooms. Electric Light. Night Porter. Telephone 717.
Mrs. HUGHES, Manageress.

GLOUCESTER ROAD.
To and from *Mansion House, Charing Cross, Victoria, Kensington High Street, Praed Street, Baker Street, King's Cross, Moorgate Street, Aldgate,* and intermediate stations every few minutes. Also from Ealing, Hounslow, Richmond, and Wimbledon, about every 10 minutes. *See p. 489.*
Map Square 69.

ANOTHER ROUTE. (Hammersmith and Finsbury Park Tube.) *See back of Map.*

Bailey's Hotel, Gloucester Road, Kensington, S.W.7, opposite Gloucester Road Station and close to Hyde Park and Kensington Gardens. Splendid accommodation for Wedding Receptions. Most perfect cuisine. For terms apply to the Manager. Telephone: Kensington 3560. Telegrams: "Bailey's Hotel, London."
See advt. amongst London Hotels.

South Kensington Hotel, Queen's Gate Terrace, Kensington, S.W.7. Recommended for quiet and comfort. Two minutes from Kensington Gardens, three minutes from Gloucester Road Station, District Railway. Moderate inclusive terms on application to the Manager. Telephone: Kensington 3570. Telegrams: "Skenotel, Southkens, London."
See advt. amongst London Hotels.

GLYN ABBEY (Carmarthen), 217½ miles. Fares, 45/3*a*, 27/2*c*. R.T. for two months, 90/0*a*, 54/4*c*. Departures *from* London as for Pembrey. Departures *for* London about 3 times daily.

GLYNDE (Sussex) from *London Bridge,* and *Victoria,* 53 miles. Fares, 11/1*a*, 6/8*c*. R.T. for two months, 22/2*a*, 13/4*c*. Pop. 356.
Map Square 29.

	Leave		Arr. at
	VICT.	LON. B.	GLYNDE
AM	—	6.15	8.26
	9. 0	—	10.42
	10. 5	9.50	12. 8
	12. 0	12.10	2.26
PM	—	12.50*d*	2.26
	1.20*e*	2. 0*e*	3.55
	1.25*d*	2. 0*d*	3.55
	3.20	—	4.42
	*h*3.40	4. 5*h*	5.36
	4.30	—	5.58
	5.20	5. 5	6.53
	6.50	7. 0	9. 9
	—	—	—
	—	—	—

Sunday Trains.

AM	6.55	7.22	10. 5
PM	12.15*k*	—	2.24
	6.33	6.33	9. 6
	8.20	8. 0	10.13
	—	—	—
	—	—	—

Trains from Glynde.

	Leave	Arrive at	
	GLYNDE	LON. B.	VICT.
AM	6.44	8.46	9. 8
	8.12	9.50	10.24
	9.23	10.55	10.56
	10.32	12.44	12.45
	11.17*k*	—	1.20
PM	12.13	2.22	2.22
	2.21	4.32	4.35
	4.10*k*	6.36	6.34
	5. 7*k*	—	7.30
	7.56	10. 0	10.10
	9.17	—	11.17

Sunday Trains.

AM	8. 6	10.18	10.32
	10.34*k*	—	1. 0
PM	6. 5	7.56	7.37
	8.34	10.50	10.45
	—	—	—
	—	—	—
	—	—	—
	—	—	—

d Saturdays only.
e Saturdays excepted.
h Stops to set down first-class passengers only on notice being given to the guard.
k Via Brighton.

GLYNDYFRDWY (Merioneth), 188¼ miles. Fares, 39/7a, 23/6c. R. T. for two months, 79/2a, 47/6c. Departures *from* London as for Llangollen. Departures *for* London about 5 times daily. Pop. 170.
Map Square 11.

GLYN NEATH (Glamorgan), 182 miles. Fares, 37/11a, 22/9c. R. T. for two months, 75/10a. Departures *from* London as for Aberdare (*via* Pontypool Road). Departures *for* London about 5 times daily.
Map Square 21.

GNOSALL (Stafford), 139¼ miles. Fares, 29/2a, 17/6c. R. T. for two months, 58/4a. Departures *from* London as for Stafford. Departures *for* London about 8 times daily. Pop. 2,069.
Map Square 17.

GOATHLAND (Yorks), 234¾ miles. Fares, 48/11a, 29/4c. R. T. for two months, 97/10a, 58/8c. Departures *from* London as for Whitby. Departures *for* London about 3 times daily. Pop. 519.
Map Square 8.

GOBOWEN (Salop) from
Paddington, 171 miles. Fares, 35/8a, 21/5c. R. T. for two months, 71/4a.
Map Square 12.

PAD.	GOBOW.	GOBOW.	PAD.
AM 9.10r	1.15	AM 8.27	12.25
10.40r	2.50	8.42r	1.25
PM12.50r	5.33	10.28r	2. 5
2.10t	5.59	PM12.34r	5. 0
4.10t	8.11	1.31t	5.55
6.10r	9.50	4. 4r	8. 5
12.15h	8.25	5.59	10. 0
12.15k	5.35	8.46	3.30

Sunday Trains.
PM12.50r	4.40	AM11.15	6.20
—	—	PM 4.32r	9. 0

h Saturday midnight excepted.
k Saturday midnight only.
r Restaurant Car.
t Tea Car.

GODALMING (Surrey)
from *Waterloo*, 34½ miles. Fares, 7/3a, 4/4c. R. T. for two months, 14/6a, 8/8c. Pop. 9,193.
Map Square 23.

W'LOO	GODAL	GODAL.	W'LOO
AM 5.50	7. 2	AM 6.52	8.20
6.50	8. 9	7.35	8.41
7.50	9.16	8.13	9.12
8.34r	9.40	8.48s	9.44
9.50	10.55	9.22	10.15
10.50	11.53	9.53	10.50
11.50d	12.54	10.27	11.32
PM12.20d	1.51	PM12.47r	1.52
12.50er	1.51	1.51	3. 6
1.50e	3. 1	3. 9	4.16
2. 0d	3.10	4.44	5.52
2.34	3.57	6.20	7.46
3.50d	4.54	7.50	9. 6
4.15e	5.10	8.20	9.46
4.50	5.45	9.18	10.46
5.24	6.18	10.39	12.16
5.40	6.57	—	—
6.50er	7.53	—	—
6.50dr	8. 3	—	—
8. 0	9.20	—	—
9.50	11. 0	—	—
—	—	—	—

GODALMING—*continued.*

Sunday Trains.
W'LOO.	GODAL.	GODAL.	W'LOO.
AM 8. 0	9.12	AM 9.10	10.16
8.20	9.46	PM12.15	1.41
9.15r	10.19	2. 3	3.13
10.20	11.48	5. 3	6.17
PM 1.50	3. 3	7.10	8.41
4.20	5.42	8.47	10. 1
5.20	6.49	9.14	10.41
6.20	7.33	10.10	11.43
8.20	9.50	—	—
—	—	—	—

d Saturdays only.
e Saturdays excepted.
r Restaurant Car.
s Refreshments served.

King's Arms Royal Hotel.
First-class, for Military, Families and Visitors to Charterhouse. English chef; table d'hôte daily. Charming garden. Private sitting rooms, and large Garage. Officially appointed by A.A. and R.A.C. Best centre for Surrey's beauty spot. Telephone No. 60.

Angel Family & Commercial
Hotel. Every Comfort. Billiard Room; good Stabling; Posting Carriages of all descriptions; good Hunters. Telephone No. 13.
SYDNEY L. TAYLOR, Prop.

Bramley Grange Hotel.
Luxurious Country Hotel, suitable for visitors to Charterhouse School, 3 miles from Godalming Station. Hotel Car meets trains by arrangement. Excellent Luncheons and Dinners served to non-residents.
See advt. p. **194.**

GODLEY (Cheshire) from
King's Cross, 194¾ miles. Fares, 37/6a, 22/6c. R. T., double fare. Pop. 1,660.
Map Square 12.

KING'S +	GODLEY	GODLEY	KING'S +
AM 4.45	11. 6	AM 5.50r	11.50
7.15r	d12.31	8.57	3.50
8.45	2.50	10.30r	6.25
10.10r	5. 1	PM 7. 0	3.25
PM 1.50r	8.24	—	—
—	—	—	—

Sunday Trains.
12. 0nr	8.38	AM 7.12	3.45
—	—	10.54	5.55
—	—	PM 5.11r	10.20
—	—	—	—

d Saturdays only.
n Noon.
r Restaurant Car.

GODLEY—*continued.*

ANOTHER ROUTE from
Marylebone, 197¾ miles. Fares as above.

M'BONE.	GODLEY	GODLEY	M'BONE.
AM 2.32	8.51	AM 5.50r	11.10
10. 0r	2.50	8.57r	3. 0
PM12.15r	5. 1	10.30r	6.38
3.20r	8.24	PM 4.19r	9.55
6.20r	10.45	7. 0	3.57
10. 0d	2.41	—	—
10. 5e	3. 8	—	—
—	—	—	—

Sunday Trains.
AM11.15r	8.38	AM10.54r	5.40
PM 5.30r	10.43	PM 5.11r	10.24
—	—	—	—

d Saturdays only.
e Saturdays excepted.
r Restaurant Car.

GODMANCHESTER
(Hunts) from *King's Cross*, 59¼ miles. Fares, 12/3a, 7/4c. R. T., double fare. Pop. 2,034.
Map Square 18.

KING'S +	GODMTR.	GODMTR.	KING'S +
AM 5. 5	7.10	AM 7.37	9.56
8.45	10.41	8. 2	10.40
10.12	1.17	8.40f	10.40
11.30	2.50	9.10g	11.15
PM 1.55	4.27	11.16	1.25
5. 0	7.21	PM 2.16	3.50
6.15d	8.33	4. 5	6.25
6.15e	9. 8	7. 0	9. 0
—	—	—	—

No Sunday Trains.

d Saturdays only.
e Saturdays excepted.
f Mondays only.
g Mondays excepted.

ANOTHER ROUTE from
Liverpool Street, 75 miles. Fares as above.

L'F'L. ST	GODMTR.	GODMTR.	L'F'L.ST.
AM 5. 5	7.37	AM 8. 2r	10.23
5.50g	9.10	9.41	12.40
8.30r	11.16	10.41	2. 7
11.50r	2.16	11.40r	2.21
PM12.29d	3.23	PM 1.17lr	4. 2k
2.34	5.29	1.17	5. 9
4.45	7. 0	3.28r	6.10
5.49r	8.10	6. 1r	8.33
7.10d	9.35	7.21	10.30
—	—	—	—

No Sunday Trains.

d Saturdays only.
g Mondays excepted.
k Arrives at St. Pancras Station.
l Commencing July 23.
r Restaurant Car.

GODSHILL (Isle of Wight),
91½ miles. Fares, *via* Ryde, 20/3a, 12/5c. R. T. for two months, 40/6a, 24/10c. Departures *from* London as for Ventnor Town. Departures *for* London about 4 times daily. Pop. 964.
Map Square 28.

GODSTONE (Surrey) from

Charing Cross, Cannon Street, and London Bridge, 29 miles. Fares, 5/3a, 4/3b, 3/2c. R. T. for two months, 10/6a, 8/6b, 6/2c. Pop. 2,943.
Map Square 23.

CHAR. +	CAN. ST.	LON. B.	Arr. at G'DSTNE.
AM —	4.44	5. 0	6. 6
—	—	9.33l	10.39
10.55	—	11. 3	12.18
PM12.55	—	1. 4	2.15
2. 3e	2. 8d	2.10	3.19
3.15d	—	3.21d	5. 9
—	4.20e	4.23e	5. 9
—	5.20e	5.23e	6.15
5.42d	—	5.48d	6.46
—	6. 0e	6. 3e	7. 0
7.24d	7.28e	7.30	8.34
8.28	—	8.36	9.43

Sunday Trains.

AM 6.25	—	6.32	7.56
PM 5.25	—	5.32	6.49
8.38	—	8.45	9.49

Trains from Godstone.

Leave GODSTNE.	LON. B.	CAN. ST.	CHAR. +
AM 7.23	8.24	8.28	—
8. 1	8.56	—	—
8.34	9.28	9.32	—
9.30	10.27	10.32	—
10.41	11.46	—	11.59
11.44	12.50	—	1. 0
PM 1.33	2.38	—	2.46
2.31	3.28e	—	3.42d
3.52	5. 2	—	5.14
6.18	7.20	—	7.29
7.57	9. 2	—	9.15
9. 1	10. 3	—	10.13
10.54	11.57	—	12.10

Sunday Trains.

AM10.13	11.15	—	11.25
PM 9. 5	10.11	—	10.24

d Saturdays only.
e Saturdays excepted.
l Low Level Platform.

GOGAR (Midlothian), 397¾

miles, No through fares. Departures from London as for Edinburgh (Waverley). Departures for London about 6 times daily.

GOLANT (Cornwall), 259¾

miles. No through fares. Departures from London as for Fowey (via Lostwithiel). Departures for London about 3 times daily.
Map Square 25.

GOLBORNE (Lancs), 189

miles. Fares, 39/5a, 23/8c. R. T., double fare. Departures from London as for Warrington (Bank Quay). Departures for London about 8 times daily. Pop. 7,183.
Map Square 12.

GOLCAR (Yorks), 200¼

miles. Fares 37/9a, 22/8c. R. T., double fare. Departures from London as for Marsden. Departures for London about 8 times daily. Pop. 10,359.

GOLDEN GROVE (Carmarthen) from Paddington, 219

miles, via Llandilo, 43/7a, 26/2c. R. T. for two months, 37/2a, 52/4c. Via Carmarthen, 46/1a, 27/8c. R. T. for two months, 92/2a, 55/4c. Departures from London as for Llandilo or Carmarthen. Departures for London about 3 times daily.
Map Square 21.

GOLDERS GREEN.

(Hampstead Tube.) See back of Map.

Brent Bridge Hotel,

Hendon, N.W. 4. Five minutes from Golders Green.
See advt. p. 20.

GOLD HAWK ROAD

(Shepherd's Bush), from Aldgate, 8 miles. Trains run about every 6 minutes throughout the day.
See back of Map.

GOLDSBOROUGH

(Yorks), 201½ miles. Fares, 41/11a, 25/2c. R. T., double fare. Departures from London as for York. Departures for London about 5 times daily. Pop. 175.
Map Square 7.

GOLFA (Montgomery), 175

miles. No through fares. Departures from London as for Welshpool. Departures for London about 4 times daily.
Map Square 16.

GOLLANFIELD

(Elgin), 573½ miles. Fares, 106/3a, 63/9c. R. T. for two months, 212/6a, 127/6c. Departures from London as for Nairn. Departures for London about twice daily.
Map Square 34.

GOLSPIE (Sutherland)

from Euston, 652 miles. Fares, 117/4a, 70/5c. R. T. for two months, 234/8a. Pop. 1,518.
Map Square 34.

EUSTON	GOLSPIE	GOLSPIE	EUSTON
PM 1.30er	10.12l	AM 6. 7r	5. 0h
7.40er	1.40l	11.23	6.40h
11.35v	6.44h	PM 5.26er	7.30l

Sunday Trains.

PM 7.50r	1.40l	—	—

e Saturdays excepted.
h A.M.
l P.M.
r Restaurant Car.
v Thursdays only.

ANOTHER ROUTE from

King's Cross, 642½ miles, as above.

KING's+	GOLSPIE	GOLSPIE	KING's+
AM11.50er	10.12k	AM 6. 7	3.25k
PM 7.45er	1.40h	11.23	7. 5k
11.25s	6.44	PM 5.26er	6.30h

Sunday Trains.

PM 7.45r	1.40	—	—

e Saturdays excepted.
h P.M.
k A.M.
r Restaurant Car.
s Thursdays only.

GOMERSAL (Yorks).

214¼ miles. Fares, 38/11a, 23/4c. R. T., double fare. Departures from London as for Huddersfield. Departures for London about 6 times daily. Pop. 3,796.
Map Square 12.

GOMSHALL (Surrey) from

Charing Cross, Cannon Street, and London Bridge, 36 miles. Fares, 6/1a, 4/11b, 3/8c. R. T. for two months, 12/2a, 8/9b, 7/0c.
Map Square 23.

CHAR. +	CAN. ST.	LON. B.	Arr. at GOMSHL.
AM —	4.44	5. 0	6.32
—	—	7.50l	9.21
—	—	9.33l	11. 0
10.55	—	11. 3	12.42
PM —	12.55d	12.58d	2. 6
12.55	—	1. 4	2.35
2. 3e	2. 8d	2.10	3.37
3.15	—	3.21	4.51
—	4.20e	4.23e	5.26
—	—	4.28d	5.55
—	4.44e	4.48e	5.50
—	5.20e	5.23e	6.24
—	5.24e	5.27e	6.38
5.42d	—	5.48d	7. 8
—	6. 0e	6. 3e	7.19
6.27e	—	6.34e	7.49
6.34d	—	6.40d	8. 2
—	6.36e	6.39e	8. 2
7.24d	—	7.30d	9. 0
8.28	—	8.36	10. 5
11.27h	—	—	12.38
12. 0k	—	—	1. 8

Sunday Trains.

AM 6.25	—	6.32	8. 9
10. 5	—	10.11	11.27
10.20	—	10.28	11.54
PM 1.30	—	1.37	2.57
5.25	—	5.32	7. 4
8.38	—	8.45	10.14

Trains from Gomshall.

Leave GOMSHL.	LON. B.	CAN.ST.	CHAR. +
AM 7.41	8.56	—	—
8.40	9.49	9.53	—
9.10	10.10	—	10.20
9.28k	10.31	—	10.43
9.41	11. 0	—	—
11.19	12.50	—	1. 0
PM 1.12	2.38	—	2.46
2.25d	4. 8	—	—
3.25	5. 2	—	5.14
4.37	5.56	—	—
5.52	7.20	—	7.29
7.43	9. 2	—	9.15
8.44	10. 3	—	10.13
10.38	11.57	—	12.10

Sunday Trains.

AM 6.53	8.16	—	8.27
9.57	11.15	—	11.25
PM 3.18	4.33	—	4.42
5.48	7.13	—	7.25
8.35	9.52	—	—
8.50	10.11	—	10.24

d Saturdays only.
e Saturdays excepted.
h Wednesdays and Saturdays only.
k Wednesdays only.
l Low Level Platform.

Black Horse Hotel. Near

Station. New Proprietorship. Good centre for rambles. English cooking. Nice garden. 'Phone 51 Shere.

GOODGE STREET

(Hampstead Tube). *See* back of Map.

GOODMAYES (Essex)

from *Liverpool Street* and *Fenchurch Street*, 9¼ miles. Fares, 1/5½*a*, 1/2*b*, 0/10½*c*. R. T. for two days, 2/11*a*, 2/2½*b*, 1/5½*c*. *See* pp. 528-534.

GOOLE (Yorks) from *King's Cross*

173 miles. Fares, 35/0*a*, 21/0*c*. R.T., double fare. Pop. 19,118.
Map Square 13.

King's +	Goole	Goole	King's +
AM 4.45	9.22	AM 6.45*r*	11.30
7.15*r*	11.11	8.39*r*	1. 5
10.10*r*	1.46	9.42*r*	1.15
PM 1.30*r*	5.13	11.22	3.50
1.50*r*	7.43	PM12.33*r*	4.30
4. 0*r*	8. 0	12.42*r*	4.45
5.35*r*	9.11	3.23*r*	7.10
8.25	12.54	5.36*r*	9.25
10.45*e*	7.18	10.17	3.25

Sunday Trains.

PM10.45	7.18	—	—

e Saturdays excepted.
r Restaurant Car.

GOOSTREY (Cheshire),

168¼ miles. Fares, 35/2*a*, 21/1*c*. R. T. for two months, 70/4*a*. Departures *from* London as for Sandbach. Departures *for* London about 8 times daily. Pop. 644.
Map Square 12.

GORDON (Berwick), 366½

miles. Fares, 75/0*a*, 45/0*c*. R. T. for two months, 150/0*a*, 90/0*c*. Departures *from* London as for St. Boswells or Berwick-on-Tweed. Departures *for* London about 3 times daily. Pop. 719.
Map Square 41.

GORDON HILL (Middlesex)

from *King's Cross*, *Moorgate Street*, or *Broad Street*, 9¾ miles. Fares from King's Cross, 1/10½*a*, 1/6*b*, 1/1½*c*. R.T. for two days, 3/9*a*, 3/0*b*, 2/3*c*. From Moorgate Street or Broad Street, 2/0*a*, 1/7*b*, 1/2½*c*. R.T. for two days, 4/0*a*, 3/2*b*, 2/4*c*. *See* pp. 511-517.

GOREBRIDGE (Midlothian),

385½ miles. Fares, 78/7*a*, 47/2*a*. R.T. for two months, 157/2*a*, 94/4*c*. Departures *from* London as for Galashiels. Departures *for* London about 4 times daily. Pop. 1,495.
Map Square 41.

GORING (Oxford) from

Paddington, 44¾ miles. Fares, 9/5*a*, 5/8*c*. R. T. for two months, 18/10*a*. Pop. 1,785.
Map Square 23.

Pad.	Goring	Goring	Pad.
AM 5.30	7.14	AM 7.58	9. 0
6.30	8.22	8.21	9.30
7.30	9. 4	8.51	10. 0
9. 0	10.19	9.27	10.45
9.45	11. 5	10.32	12. 0
11.20	12.38	PM12.31	1.50
PM12.30	1.48	1.59	3.20
1.10*dr*	2.27	3. 2	4.35
1.35*r*	2.47	3.50	5. 6
1.50*d*	3.32	4.48	6. 2
3.18*h*	4.40	5.44	7.20
3.18	4.53	7. 3	8.20
3.38	5.15	7.58	9.15
5. 0	6.10	9.15	10.45
5.40	6.55	10.11*k*	2.45
6. 5	7.17	—	—
6.55	8.14	—	—
7.30	8.41	—	—
8. 5	9.38	—	—
10. 0*k*	11.26	—	—
12.15	1.28	—	—

Sunday Trains.

AM 9.10	10.35	AM 8.29	10.14
10.35	11.42	11.58	2.40
11. 0	12.28	PM 4.26	6. 0
PM 1.45	3.20	6.48	8.20
2. 0	4. 2	7.48	9.15
4.10	5.50	8.27	9.48
5.15	6.53	9.37	11.38
7.40	9.34	—	—

d Saturdays only.
h Fridays only.
k Wednesdays and Saturdays only.
r Restaurant Car.

Salter's Steamers (Goring Lock, 10 minutes from station). Up-stream, 12.40 P.M., 6.20 P.M. Down-stream, 10.0 A.M., 3.40 P.M. *See* advt. facing first page of train service.

Ye Miller of Mansfield. Large dining-room. The celebrated Sunday dinner in time for last up trains. Only hotel in Goring. Telegrams, "Miller, Goring, Reading." Telephone 29.

Bull Hotel, Streatley-on-Thames. The noted House in District. Excellent Cuisine, Wines, Spirits, &c. Stabling, Motor Garage. Billiards. Moderate Tariff. Telephone 57 Goring.
Proprietor, C. F. ROYLANCE.

GORING (Sussex), 62¼ miles.

Fares from London Bridge or Victoria, 12/8*a*, 7/7*c*. R.T. for two months, 25/4*a*, 15/2*c*. Departures *from* London as for Worthing. Departures *for* London about 9 times daily. Pop. 671.
Map Square 28.

GORLESTON (Suffolk)

from *Liverpool Street*, 124¼ miles. Fares, 25/7*a*, 15/4*c*. R. T. for two months 51/2*a*, 30/8*c*. Pop. 17,981.
Map Square 19.

L'pool St	Glstn.	Glstn.	L'pool St.
AM 5. 0	9.37	AM 8. 2*r*	11.30
8.15*r*	12.10	9. 2*h*	1.20
9.55	1.14	11.59	3.42
10. 0*h*	2.19	PM12.10*h*	3.56
10.20*h*	2.57	1.15*r*	4. 5
PM 1. 0*h*	5.34	3.52*r*	7.23
3.15*h*	7.24	6. 4*r*	10. 0
4.55*r*	8.38	—	—
5.18*hr*	9.51	—	—

No Sunday Trains.
h Via Lowestoft.
r Restaurant Car.

Cliff Hotel. The finest situation Norfolk Coast. Healthy. Overlooking Sea. Excellent Cuisine. Fully Licensed. Golf Links. Garage. 'Phone 77.
See advt. p. **189**.

St. Edmunds Private Hotel. Best position on Cliffs, facing Sea. One minute from Beach and Pier. Tariff on application. Tel. 119.
MANAGERESS.

Elmhurst Links Private Hotel. Boarding Establishment. Cliffs. Nearest Golf Links. Private grounds. Croquet, Tennis. Electric Light. Garage. Moderate. 'Phone 105. PROPRIETOR.

"Felix." Comfortable Boarding House. Facing South and Sea. Personal supervision. One minute Station, Beach and Trams. Near Links.
C. PARKER.

The Gables. Private Hotel. Charmingly situated on Cliffs. Facing the Sea. Excellent Cuisine. Tariff on application to—
MANAGERESS.

"Avondale" Boarding House Fine Sea View. Close Beach, Pier and Gardens. South aspect. Electric Light. Separate tables. Terms moderate.
Misses MILNER.

Pier Hotel. Finest position East Coast. Every room sea view. Foot pier and beach. Telephone 18. Tariff, apply—
H. LEE.

Gorleston-on-Sea and East Coast, Furnished Houses to Let, Coast or Country. Apply A. V. GEORGE, Gorleston and Gt. Yarmouth.

GORSEINON (Glamorgan),

207½ miles. No through fares. Departures *from* London as for Swansea (High Street). Departures *for* London about 3 times daily.

GORTON (Lancs), 200¼

miles. Fares, 38/2*a*, 22/11*c*. R.T., double fare. Departures *from* London as for Guide Bridge. Departures *for* London about 4 times daily. Pop. 40,578.

GOSBERTON (Lincoln) from *King's Cross*, 98 miles. Fares, 20/3*a*, 12/2*c*. R. T., double fare. Pop. 1,973.
Map Square 18.

King's +	Gosb'tn	Gosb'tn	King's +
AM 4.45	7.43	AM 8.41	1. 5
5. 5	10.55	11.13	3.50
11.30*e*	4.19	PM 2.14*k*	5. 0
PM 1.50*dr*	4.19	5.25	9. 0
5.45*r*	9.25	7.23	3.25
—	—	—	—

No Sunday Trains.
d Saturdays only.
e Saturdays excepted.
k Tuesdays and Wednesdays only.
r Restaurant Car.

GOSFORTH, SOUTH (Northumberland), 270¾ miles. Fares, 57/1*a*, 34/3*c*. R.T. for two months, 114/2*a*, 68/6*c*. Departures *from* London as for Newcastle-on-Tyne. Departures *for* London about 6 times daily. Pop. (Gosforth) 15,719.

GOSFORTH, WEST (Northumberland), 271¾ miles. No through fares. Departures *from* London as for Newcastle-on-Tyne. Departures *for* London about 6 times daily.
Map Square 4.

GOSPEL OAK from *Broad Street*, 6¼ miles. Fares, 0/7½*a*, 0/4½*c*. R. T. for two days, 1/3*a*, 0/9*c*.
See pp. 501-505.
Map Square 51.

GOSPORT (Hants) from *Waterloo, via* Eastleigh, 89¼ miles. Fares, 15/5*a*, 9/3*c*. R. T. for two months, 30/10*a*, 18/6*c*. Pop. 33,588.
Map Square 28.

W'loo	Gosport	Gosport	W'loo
AM 5.40	8.51	AM 6.20	9.26
5.50	9.51	9.18	12. 0
8.30*s*	11.26	11.35*r*	2.20
9.30	12.54	PM 12.15	4. 6
11.30*r*	2.51	1.12	4.20
PM 1.30*s*	4. 3	2.45	6.16
3.30*s*	6.13	5.40*r*	8.20
5.30*r*	8.11	7.15	10.50
7.30*d*	10.37	8.25	11.28

No Sunday Trains.
d Saturdays only.
r Restaurant Car.
s Refreshments served.

ANOTHER ROUTE from *Waterloo, via* Meon Valley 77¾ miles. Fares as above.

W'loo	Gosport	Gosport	W'loo
AM 4.50	8.51	AM 7.35	10.26
7. 0	10.36	9.18	12.11
9.20	12.24	10.55	1.40
11.20	2.51	PM 2.22	5.46
PM 3.15	6.13	4. 0	7. 7
6.34	9.37	7.38	11.10

No Sunday Trains.

GOSWICK (Northumberland) 328¾ miles. Fares, 69/4*a*, 41/7*c*. R. T., double fare. Departures *from* London as for Morpeth. Departures *for* London about 4 times daily.
Map Square

GOTHERINGTON (Gloucester), 117½ miles. Fares, 24/7*a*, 14/9*c*. R. T. for two months, 49/2*a*, 29/6*c*. Departures *from* London as for Winchcombe. Departures *for* London about 6 times daily. Pop. 369.
Map Square 17.

GOUDHURST (Kent) from *Charing Cross, Cannon Street,* and *London Bridge*, 42 miles. Fares, 8/9*a*, 7/0*b*, 5/3*c*. R. T. for two months, 17/6*a*, 14/0*b*. Departures *from* London as for Horsmonden. Departures *for* London about 4 times daily. Pop. 2,967.
Map Square 24.

GOURDON (Kincardine), 414 miles. No through fares. Departures *from* London as for Montrose. Departures *for* London about 3 times daily. Pop. 990.
Map Square 38.

GOUROCK (Renfrew), 425¾ miles. Fares, 84/2*a*, 50/6*c*. R. T. for two months, 168/4*a*, 101/0*c*. Departures *from* London as for Greenock (Central). Departures *for* London about 4 times daily. Pop. 10,128.
Map Square 40.

GOVILON (Monmouth), 164 miles. Fares, 33/9*a*, 20/3*c*. R. T. for two months, 67/6*a*, 40/6*c*. Departures *from* London as for Abergavenny. Departures *for* London about 3 times daily.
Map Square 22.

GOWERTON (Glamorgan), 202 miles. Fares from *Paddington*, 42/1*a*, 25/3*c*. R. T. for two months, 84/2*a*, 50/6*c*. From *Euston*, 42/11*a*, 25/9*c*, R. T. for two months, 85/10*a*, 51/6*c*. Departures *from* London as for Landore. Departures *for* London about 4 times daily. Pop. 2,748.
Map Square 21.

GOXHILL (Lincoln), 169 miles. Fares, 35/0*a*, 21/0*c*. R. T. for two months, 70/0*a*, 42/0*c*. Departures *from* London as for Brocklesby. Departures *for* London about 7 times daily. Pop. 1,181.
Map Square 13.

GRAFHAM (Hunts), 91½ miles. Fares, 14/9*a*, 8/10*c*. R. T., double fare. Departures *from* London as for Kimbolton. Departures *for* London about 4 times daily. Pop. 223.
Map Square 18.

GRAFTON (Wilts) from *Waterloo*, 80½ miles. Fares, 15/3*a*, 9/2*c*. R. T. for two months, 30/6*a*. Departures *from* London as for Collingbourne. Departures *for* London about 4 times daily. Pop. 684.
Map Square 22.

GRAMPOUND ROAD (Cornwall), 271¾ miles. Fares, 56/3*a*, 33/9*c*. R. T. for two months, 112/6*a*. Departures *from* London as for St. Austell. Departures *for* London about 4 times daily. Pop. (Grampound) 430.
Map Square 25.

GRANBOROUGH ROAD (Bucks) from *Baker Street* or *Marylebone*, 48 miles. Fares, 10/0*a* 6/0*c*. R. T. for two months, 20/0*a*, 11/11½*c*. Departures *from* London as for Verney. Departures *for* London about 9 times daily. Pop. 276.
Map Square 18.

GRANDTULLY (Perth), 477¾ miles. Fares, 96/11*a*, 58/2*c*. R. T. for two months, 193/10*a*, 116/4*c*. Departures *from* London as for Dunkeld. Departures *for* London about 3 times daily. Pop. 307.
Map Square 37.

GRANGE (Banff), 571¾ miles. No through fares. Departures *from* London as for Huntly. Departures *for* London about twice daily. Pop. 1,287.
Map Square 35.

GRANGE COURT (Gloucester) from *Paddington*. 121½ miles. Fares, 25/3*a*, 15/2*c*. R.T. for two months, 50/6*a*.
Map Square 22.

Pad.	Grange C.	Grange C.	Pad.
AM 1. 0*g*	7.33	AM 9.24	12.20
5.30	9.29	11.21*r*	2.40
7.30	11.20	PM 2. 6	5. 0
9. 0	12.50	5.33*r*	8.45
10.45	2.17	9.53	3.30
PM 1.30*k*	5. 3	—	—
3.15*t*	6.33	—	—
6. 0*r*	9. 2	—	—
—	—	—	—
—	—	—	—
—	—	—	—
—	—	—	—
—	—	—	—
—	—	—	—

Sunday Trains.

PM 2. 0	8.28	PM 4.39	10. 0
—	—	—	—
—	—	—	—
—	—	—	—
—	—	—	—
—	—	—	—
—	—	—	—

g Mondays excepted.
k *Via* Kingham.
r Restaurant Car.
t Tea Car.

GRANGE HILL from *Liverpool Street* or *Fenchurch Street*, 11¾ miles. Fares, from Liverpool Street *via* Ilford, 1/10½*a*, 1/6*b*, 1/1½*c*. R. T. for two days, 3/9*a*, 3/0*b*, 2/0½*c*. *Via* Woodford 2/1*a*, 1/8*b*, 1/3*c*. R. T. for two days, 4/2*a*, 3/2½*b*, 2/2½*c*. From Fenchurch Street *via* Ilford, 1/10½*a*, 1/6*b*, 1/1½*c*. R. T. for two days, 3/9*a*, 3/0*b*, 2/0½*c*. *Via* Woodford, 2/1*a*, 1/8*b*, 1/3*c*. R. T. for two days, 4/2*a*, 3/1*b*, 2/2½*c*. *See* p. 536.

GRANGE LANE (Yorks), 164¾ miles. Fares, 33/7*a*, 20/2*c*. R. T., double fare. Departures *from* London as for Sheffield (Victoria). Departures *for* London about 8 times daily.
Map Square 12.

GRANGEMOUTH (Stirling), 412¾ miles. Fares, 83/1*a*, 49/10*c*. R. T. for two months, 166/2*a*, 99/8*c*. Departures *from* London as for Larbert or Falkirk. Departures *for* London about 4 times daily. Pop. 18,798.
Map Square 40.

GRANGE-OVER-SANDS

SANDS (Lancs) from *St. Pancras*, 268 miles. Fares, 51/1*a*, 30/8*c*. R. T. for two months, 102/2*a*, 61/4*c*. Pop. 2,920.
Map Square 7.

St. Pan.	Grange	Grange	St. Pan.
AM 4.25	1.50	AM 7.43*r*	4.10
9.50*r*	4.51	9.58*r*	5.30
PM12.15*r*	6.45	11.27*hr*	6.35
11.50*e*	10.13	PM 1.20*r*	9.15
11.50*d*	10.22	5.41*e*	4.20
—	—	6.27*d*	4.20
—	—	—	—
—	—	—	—
—	—	—	—
—	—	—	—

Sunday Trains.

AM10.50*r*	8.32	AM 7.50	5.27
PM11.45	10.13	PM 5.40	4.55
—	—	—	—
—	—	—	—
—	—	—	—

d Saturdays only.
e Saturdays excepted.
h Wednesdays and Thursdays excepted.
r Restaurant Car.

ANOTHER ROUTE from

Euston, 245½ miles. Fares as above.

Euston	Grange	Grange	Euston
AM12.25	8.40	AM 7.45*r*	3.10
2.35	10.15	9.30*h*	3.45
5. 0	12.24	9.58*r*	4.15
6.45	1.52	11.27*r*	6. 0
11.35*r*	4.51	PM 1.20*r*	7.30
11.50*r*	6.47	2.45*er*	9. 5
PM 1.30*r*	7.16	2.45*dr*	9.15
2.35*t*	9.17	4. 0*r*	10.45
5.20*r*	11.25	9.13	5. 0
9.30*e*	7.23	—	—
11. 0*d*	8. 0	—	—

Sunday Trains.

AM11.45*r*	5.57	PM12.50*r*	7.30
		9. 0	5. 0
—	—	—	—
—	—	—	—
—	—	—	—
—	—	—	—

d Saturdays only.
e Saturdays excepted.
h Mondays and Saturdays only.
r Restaurant Car.
t Tea Car.

Grange-over-Sands. The
Golf Hotel (late Hazelwood Hydro). Electric Light throughout. R. H. DOORBAR.
See advt. p. 190.

Grange Hotel. Beautifully
situated. Overlooking Morecambe Bay.
See advt. p. 191.

GRANGE PARK (Middle-

sex) from *King's Cross, Moorgate Street, or Broad Street,* 8½ miles. Fares from King's Cross, 1/8*a*, 1/4*b*, 1/0*c*. R. T. for two days, 3/4*a*, 2/8*b*, 1/11½*c*. From Moorgate Street or Broad Street, 1/9½*a*, 1/5*b*, 1/1*c*. R. T. for two days, 3/7*a*, 2/10*b*, 2/0½*c*. *See pp. 511-517.*

GRANGE ROAD (Sussex)

from *London Bridge, Victoria,* and *Clapham Junction,* 33 miles. Fares, 6/3*a*, 3/9*c*. R. T. for two months, 12/6*a*, 7/6*c*.
Map Square 23.

	Leave			Arr. at
	Vict.	Clap. J.	Lon. B.	Gr. Rd.
AM —	—	—	5.18	7.17
7.23	7.29	7.25	9.16
9. 0	9. 8	9. 6	10.27
9.45	9.51	9.50	11.20
11.55	—	11.50	1.15
PM 1.20*e*	1.27*e*	—	2.47
1.25*d*	—	1.10*d*	2.47
2. 0	2. 7	2. 5*e*	3.55
—	—	2. 8*d*	3.55
4. 0	4. 8	4. 5	5.17
—	—	5. 5	6. 4
6. 6	6.12	6. 8	7.50
7.15	7.22	7.20	8.50
—	—	—	—
—	—	—	—
—	—	—	—

Sunday Trains.

AM 8.18	8.25	8.25	9.47
PM 6.33	6.40	6.33	8.48
—	—	—	—
—	—	—	—
—	—	—	—
—	—	—	—
—	—	—	—

Trains from Grange Road.

Leave		Arrive at		
Gr. Rd.	Lon. B.	Clap. J.	Vict.
AM 6.43	8.15	8.15	8.24
8. 4	9.10	—	9.19
9.43	10.55	10.40	10.48
10.48	12.13	11.59	12. 7
PM12.14	1.42	1.39	1.50
3.25	4.32	4.27	4.35
4.16	5.54	5.47	5.55
5.36	7.42	7.37	7.45
7. 6	8.46	8.39	8.48
9.11	10.58	11.10	11.17
—	—	—	—
—	—	—	—

Sunday Trains.

AM 7.59	10.18	10.23	10.32
PM 6.29	7.56	8.31	8.41
—	—	—	—
—	—	—	—
—	—	—	—
—	—	—	—

d Saturdays only.
e Saturdays excepted.

GRANGETOWN (Gla-

morgan), 154 miles. No through fares. Departures *from* London as for Cardiff. Departures *for* London about 8 times daily.
Map Square 21.

GRANGETOWN (Yorks),

242 miles. Fares, 50/7*a*, 30/4*c*. R. T. for two months, 101/2*a*, 60/8*c*. Departures *from* London as for Middlesbrough. Departures *for* London about 5 times daily.
Map Square 8.

GRANTHAM (Lincoln)

from *King's Cross,* 105½ miles. Fares, 21/11*a*, 13/2*c*. R. T., double fare. Pop. 18,902.
Map Square 13.

King's+	Grantm.	Grantm.	King's+
AM 4.45	6.59	AM 1. 1*g*	3.25
5. 5	8.33	3.14	5.40
7.15*r*	9.23	3.39	6. 0
8.45	11.17	4.46*g*	6.50
10. 0*r*	12. 0	5. 1	7. 5
10.10*r*	12.11	8.30*r*	10.40
11.30	2.25	9.36*r*	11.30
PM 1.15*r*	3.17	9.45	12.25
1.40*r*	3.45	11. 0	1. 5
1.50*r*	3.55	11.30*r*	1.20
4. 0*r*	6. 7	PM 1.18	3.50
4.15	7.13	2.41*r*	4.45
5.30*r*	7.27	3. 0*r*	5. 0
5.35*r*	7.35	3.33	6.25
5.45*r*	7.48	4.26*r*	6.30
7.45*er*	9.47	5. 9*r*	7.10
8.20*er*10.20	6.21	9. 0
8.25	10.52	7.21*r*	9.25
10.45	12.54	8. 1*r*	10. 0
11.25	1.25	—	—

Sunday Trains.

AM 8.30	12.17	AM 3.39	6. 0
11.30*r*	1.47	5. 1	7. 5
12. 0*r*	2.24	PM 1.22*r*	3.45
PM 5. 0	7.20	2.50	5.15
7.35*r*	9.47	3.31	5.55
8.25	10.52	4.18	8. 8
10.45	12.54	6. 5*r*	8.15
11.25	1.25	7.55*r*	10.20

e Saturdays excepted.
g Mondays excepted.
h Mondays and Fridays only.
k Mondays and Fridays excepted.
r Restaurant Car.

Angel Hotel. First-class
Family and Commercial. A.A., R.A.C. Special lock-up Garages. Stabling for Hunters. Cuisine a speciality. Terms inclusive by arrangement. Telephone 194.

The George Hotel. Family
and Commercial. A.A. and R.A.C. Electric light throughout. Table d'Hote Dinner and Lunch. Omnibuses meet trains. Bath Rooms. Modern sanitation. Extensive Garages. Loose boxes for Hunters. JOHN FILLINGHAM, Proprietor.

GRANTON (Midlothian),

394½ miles. Fares, 81/8*a*, 49/0*c*. R. T. for two months, 163/4*a*, 98/0*c*. Departures *from* London as for Edinburgh (Waverley). Departures *for* London about 5 times daily.
Map Square 41.

GRANTOWN-ON-SPEY

(Elgin), 545¾ miles. Fares, 106/3a, 63/9c. R. T. for two months, 212/6a, 127/6c. Departures from London as for Aviemore. Departures for London about 3 times daily. Pop. 1,622. Map Square 34.

Grant Arms Hotel. Famous Health Resort. Pine Woods. 12-miles Salmon, Trout fishing. Golf. Tennis. Bowls. Telephone No. 26.

GRANTSHOUSE

(Berwick), 351 miles. No through fares. Departures from London as for Berwick-on-Tweed. Departures for London about 3 times daily. Map Square 41.

GRASSINGTON

(Yorks), 229¼ miles. Fares, 44/9a, 26/10c. R. T. for two months, 89/6a, 53/8c. Departures from London as for Skipton. Departures for London about 6 times daily. Pop. 567. Map Square 7.

GRASSMOOR

(Derby), 149¾ miles. Fares, 30/2a, 18/1c. R. T., double fare. Departures from London as for Heath. Departures for London about 4 times daily. Map Square 13.

GRATELEY

(Hants) from Waterloo, 72¾ miles. Fares, 15/3a, 9/2c. R. T. for two months, 30/6a, 18/4c. Pop. 266. Map Square 22.

W'LOO	GRATELEY	GRATELEY	W'LOO
AM 5.50	8.48	AM 7.41	9.56
7.30	10.7	PM12.1r	2.20
9.30	11.53	12.54	2.36
11.30r	1.54	1.29	4.20
PM 1.30r	3.33	3.53s	6.26
3.30s	5.36	5.3	7.40
5.0	7.11	7.38	10.50
6.0r	8.22	9.12	11.28
7.30	9.36	—	—
8.0	10.41	—	—
—	—	—	—
—	—	—	—

Sunday Trains.

AM 9.0	11.46	AM 9.57	12.11
PM 6.0	8.18	PM 6.20	9.12

r Restaurant Car.
s Refreshments served.

GRAVELLY HILL

(Warwick), 113½ miles. Fares, 23/7a, 14/2c. R. T. for two months, 47/2a, 28/4c. Departures from London as for Birmingham (New Street). Departures for London about 12 times daily.

GRAVESEND (CENTRAL)

(Kent) from Charing Cross, Cannon Street, and London Bridge, 24½ miles. Fares, 5/0a, 4/0b, 3/0c. R. T. for two months, 7/10a, 6/1b, 5/3c. Pop. 31,137. Map Square 24.

	Leave		Arr. at
CHAR.+	CAN. ST.	LON. B.	GRAVES.
AM —	—	3.22k	4.18
5.18	—	5.25	6.54
—	6.20	6.23	7.20
—	6.28	6.31	7.45
—	7.16	7.19	8.8
—	7.44	7.47	8.39
8.10	—	8.17	9.12
8.51	—	8.57	10.0
9.32	—	9.41	10.36
—	10.58	11.1	11.54
—	k11.8d	k11.11d	12.37
11.55	—	12.2	12.49
PM12.30d	—	12.37d	1.18
—	1.2d	1.5d	2.4
1.20e	—	1.27e	2.15
1.26d	—	1.34d	2.19
—	1.23e	—	2.50
—	1.48d	1.51d	2.51
2.10d	—	2.17d	3.16
—	2.40	2.43	3.30
2.45e	—	2.53e	3.55
3.5d	—	3.12d	3.57
3.10d	—	3.17d	4.18
—	3.16e	3.19e	4.40
3.35d	—	3.42d	4.59
—	4.12e	4.15e	4.50
4.25d	—	4.31d	5.29
—	4.36e	4.39e	5.27
4.35d	—	4.43d	6.6
—	5.8e	5.11e	6.2
5.15d	—	5.22d	6.25
5.17e	—	5.25e	6.15
5.21e	—	5.29e	6.23
5.42e	—	—	6.52
—	5.56e	5.59e	6.40
5.58d	—	6.4d	6.54
—	6.20e	6.23e	7.3
6.22e	—	6.29e	7.20
—	6.40e	6.43e	7.52
6.55d	—	7.1d	8.3
—	7.8e	7.11e	8.4
—	7.8d	7.11d	8.33
7.34	—	7.41	8.43
—	7.44	7.47	9.2
8.40	—	8.48	10.0
—	9.35	9.38	10.28
10.20	—	10.27	11.18
11.24	—	—	12.14
11.33	—	—	12.32

Sunday Trains.

AM —	—	7.30	8.26
7.30	—	7.37	8.42
9.46	—	9.52	10.54
10.50	—	10.57	12.5
PM 1.15	—	1.22	2.30
3.15	—	3.22	4.23
4.50	—	4.57	6.1
7.0	—	7.7	7.55
8.42	—	8.49	9.36
10.30	—	10.38	11.55

GRAVESEND—continued.

Trains from Gravesend.

Leave		Arrive at	
GRAVES.	LON. B.	CAN. ST.	CHAR.+
AM 4.41	5.47	—	5.51
5.49	7.0	—	7.4
6.2	7.24	7.28	—
6.41	7.48	7.52	—
6.57	8.13	8.17	—
7.27	8.31	8.35	—
7.44	8.34	—	8.41
7.53	8.51	8.55	—
8.39	9.15	9.19	—
8.53	9.34	—	9.43
9.11	9.54	—	10.1
9.30	10.24	10.28	—
10.1	10.38	—	g10.45
10.21	11.20	11.24	—
11.12	12.3	—	12.14
11.44d	12.51	12.56	—
PM12.9	12.57	—	1.7
12.41d	1.31	1.37	—
12.41e	1.36	—	1.44
12.47d	2.18	2.22e	2.25d
1.19e	2.41	2.45	—
1.41d	2.44	—	2.54
d2.3k	3.21	3.26	—
2.4e	2.53	—	3.4
2.35e	3.26	—	3.36
2.54d	3.58	—	4.8
3.29e	4.30	4.36	—
3.53e	4.48	4.52	—
3.54d	4.57	—	5.7
4.46e	5.36	5.40	—
4.46d	5.37	—	5.44
5.14e	6.28	6.32	—
5.29e	6.35	6.39	—
6.6	7.10	—	7.19
6.38	7.14	—	7.23
6.54	8.8	8.14e	8.19d
7.24	8.15	8.20	—
7.31	8.50	—	8.58
8.2	9.6	9.11	—
8.54	9.38	—	9.47
9.6	10.47	10.51	—
9.57	10.51	—	10.59
10.26	12.26	—	12.33
11.19	12.35	—	12.45

Sunday Trains.

AM 7.59	8.59	—	9.8
9.17	10.16	—	10.24
11.58	1.5	—	1.17
PM 1.10	2.14	—	2.24
3.2	4.5	—	4.15
5.2	5.55	—	6.4
5.54	6.49	—	6.59
6.56	8.1	—	8.10
8.30	9.46	—	9.55
8.50	9.50	—	9.59
10.13	11.15	—	11.23
10.22	11.20	—	—

d Saturdays only.
e Saturdays excepted.
k Third class only.

GRAVESEND—*continued.*

ANOTHER ROUTE (WEST STREET) from *Victoria, Holborn Viaduct*, and *St. Paul's*, 27¼ miles. Fares as above.

Leave			Arr. at
Vict. S.E.&C.)	Hol. V.	St. Pl.'s	Graves.
AM —	5.57	5.59	7.25
—	6.40	6.42	8. 0
—	7.30	7.33	8.50
9.20	—	—	10.27
11.40d	—	—	12.53
11.40e	—	—	1. 0
PM —	1.24d	1.27d	2.33
2. 9d	2. 4d	2. 7d	3.42
2.12e	2.15e	2.16e	3.35
—	3.22d	3.25d	4.57
3.56e	—	—	5. 4
5. 3d	—	—	6.18
5. 8e	—	—	6.16
—	5.32e	5.35e	6.54
5.45	—	—	6.40
7.22	7.22	7.24	8.34
8.10d	8. 5d	8. 8d	9.37

Sunday Trains.

AM 7.20	—	—	8.50
8.25	—	—	9.43
11.30	—	—	12.44
PM 1. 7	1. 5	—	2.29
2. 5	2. 3	—	3.39
6.35	6.4C	—	7.55

Trains from Gravesend.

Leave	Arrive at		
Graves.	St. Pl.'s	Hol. V.	Vict.
AM 7.34	8.40	8.42	8.50
8.23	9.27	9.29	9.36
9.15	—	—	10.10
9.54	11.22	11.29	11. 9
11.25	1. 0	1. 2	12.49
PM 1.10d	3.38	—	3.23
2.46d	—	—	4.32
3.45e	—	—	5.20
5.15e	6.45	6.47	—
6.27d	7.54	—	—
6.44e	8.18	8.20	8.10
7.15	9.10	9.12	8.51
8.20	9.51	9.53	9.46
8.44	10.29	10.31	10.22
9.44d	11.21	11.23	11.35
—	—	—	—

Sunday Trains.

AM 9.50	—	11.27	11.23
PM12.52	—	2.15	2.11
2.37	—	—	3.50
4.50	—	—	6. 3
8.45	—	10.22	10. 5

d Saturdays only.
e Saturdays excepted.

ANOTHER ROUTE from *Fenchurch Street*, 23 miles. Fares, 2/11a, 1/9c. R.T. for two months, 5/3a, 3/1c.

Fen. St.	Graves.	Graves.	Fen. St.
AM 5.37	7. 1	AM 5.16	6.34
6.15	7.44	6. 6	7.22
6.52	8. 9	7. 8	8.24
7.30	8.49	7.35	8.48
8.11	9.32	8.52	9.34
9. 5	10.14	8.44	10. 4h
9.39	10.57	9. 8	10.22
10.17	11.15	9.36	10.50
11.13	12.12	10.13	11.20
11.35	12.52	10.54	12.16
11.42e	12.31	PM12. 8d	1.27
PM12.21	1.41	12.24e	1.22

GRAVESEND—*continued.*

Fen. St.	Graves.	Graves.	Fen. St.
PM 1.15d	2.17	PM12.48d	2.10
1.35d	2.45	1.20	2.34
1.48e	3. 4	2.21	3.18
2.15d	3.17	2.48	4.10
2.40	3.58	3.30	5. 4h
3.25	4.30	3.56	5.18
4.16	5.31	4.28e	5.42
4.46	5.51	4.53e	6.10
5.32	6.27	5.12	6.30
5.46e	6.53	5.38e	6.56
5.55e	7. 4	6. 8	7.24
6.17e	7.24	6.48	8. 4
6.38	7.49	7.58	9.15
6.55	8. 2	9. 2	10.23h
7.41e	8.51	10. 8	11.23h
8.13	9.30	10. 8	11.40
9.25	10.36	10.38	11.50
10.45	11.54	—	—
12. 0	1. 7	—	—

Sunday Trains.

AM 8.40	10. 1	AM 8.30	9.36
9.45	11.15	8.56	10.18
11.10	12.23	11.42	1. 1
PM 1. 6	2.16	PM 1.18	2.33
2. 7	3.21	2.46	4. 4
4.30	5.42	5.16	6.32
6.38	7.45	6.26	7.45
8.45	10. 3	7.53	9.11h
10.30	11.37	8. 6	9.30
—	—	9.43	11. 0

d Saturdays only.
e Saturdays excepted.
h Departs from or arrives at Mark Lane Station.

Clarendon Royal. Leading First Class Hotel, delightfully situated. Facing river. Terms moderate. Billiards. Garage. Tariff on application. Telephone, 950 Gravesend.

GRAYRIGG (Westmorland), 256¼ miles. Fares, 51/11a, 31/2c. R.T. double fare. Departures *from* London as for Oxenholme. Departures *for* London about 4 times daily. Pop. 197.
Map Square

GRAYS (Essex) from *Fenchurch Street*, 20 miles. Fares, 2/6a, 1/6c. R.T. for two months, 4/4½a, 2/7½c. Pop. 17,364.
Map Square 24.

Fen. St.	Grays	Grays	Fen. St.
AM 5.37	6.40	AM 5.39	6.34
6.15	7.27	6.27	7.22
6.52	7.51	7.30	8.24
7.30	8.27	·7.56	8.48
7.42	8.46	8.53	9.34
8.11	9.12	9. 3	10. 4h
9. 5	9.55	9.29	10.22
9.39	10.39	9.56	10.49
10.17	10.54	10.33	11.20
11.13	11.54	11.20	12.16
11.35	12.34	PM12.15d	1.10
11.42e	12.14	12.29d	1.27h
PM12.21	1.24	12.45e	1.22
1.15d	2. 1	1.11d	2.10
1.35d	2.28	1.41	2.34
1.48e	2.47	2.42	3.18
2.15d	3. 0	3.15	4.10
2.26d	3.13	3.51	5. 4h
2.40	3.39	4.17	5.18
3.25	4.12	4.48e	5.42
4.16	5. 9	4.56e	5.49

GRAYS—*continued.*

Fen. St.	Grays	Grays	Fen. St.
PM 4.46	5.34	PM 5.32	6.35
5.32	6. 9	5.59e	6.56
5.46e	6.34	6.23	7.24
5.55e	6.47	7. 4e	7.51
6.17e	7. 6	7.13	8. 4
6.38	7.32	8.19	9.15
6.53	7.45	9.23	10.23h
7.41e	8.32	10.28	11.23h
8.13	9.13	10.28	11.40
9.25	10.19	10.57	11.50
10.45	11.37	—	—
12. 0	12.49	—	—

Sunday Trains.

AM 8.40	9.43	AM 8.51	9.36
9.45	11. 0	9.17	10.18
11.10	12. 6	PM12. 1	1. 1
PM 1. 6	1.59	12.22	2. 2h
2. 7	3. 4	1.39	2.33
4.30	5.25	3. 8	4. 4
6.10	7.18	5.36	6.32
6.38	7.28	6.47	7.45
7.22	8.53	8.14	9.11h
8.45	9.44	8.28	9.30
10.30	11.20	10. 4	11. 0
—	—	10.19	11.22h

d Saturdays only.
e Saturdays excepted.
h Departs from or arrives at Mark Lane Station.

Queens Family and Commercial Hotel. Fully licensed. Two minutes Station. Redecorated and refurnished. Table d'hote. Banquets. Garage. R.A.C. Moderate Tariff.

GREAT ALNE (Warwick) from *Paddington*, 103 miles. Fares, 21/6a, 12/11c. R. T. for six months, 43/10a, 25/10c. Departures *from* London as for Bearley. Departures *for* London about five times daily. Pop.
Map Square 17.

GREAT AYTON (Yorks), 242¼ miles. Fares, 50/8a, 30/5c. R. T., double fare. Departures *from* London as for Middlesbrough. Departures *for* London about 4 times daily. Pop. 2,319.
Map Square 8.

GREAT BARR (Stafford), ·115¼ miles. Fares, 24/0a, 14/5c. R. T. for two months, 48/0a. Departures *from* London as for Birmingham (New Street). Departures *for* London about 9 times daily. Pop. 1,657.

GREAT BENTLEY (Essex). *See* BENTLEY, GREAT.

GREAT BRIDGE (Stafford), 122 miles. Fares, 24/5a, 14/8c. R. T. for two months, 48/10a. Departures *from* London as for Walsall. Departures *for* London about 8 times daily.

GREAT BRIDGEFORD (Stafford) from *Euston*, 136¾ miles. Fares, 28/7a, 17/2c. R. T. for two months, 57/2a. Departures *from* London as for Norton Bridge. Departures *for* London about 3 times daily.
Map Square 17.

GREAT CHESTERFORD. *See* CHESTERFORD, GREAT.

GREAT COATES (Lincoln), 157 miles. Fares, 32/8a, 19/7c. R. T., double fare. Departures *from* London as for Grimsby or Brocklesby. Departures *for* London about 3 times daily. Pop. 364.
Map Square 13.

GREAT DALBY (Leicester), from *Euston*, 103½ miles. Fares, 21/0*a*, 12/7*c*. R. T. for two months, 42/0*a*. Departures *from* London as for Hallaton. Departures *for* London about 6 times daily. Pop. 341.
Map Square 18.

GREAT GLEN (Leicester), 91½ miles. Fares, 18/7*a*, 11/2. R.T. for two months, 37/2*a*, 22/4*c*. Departures *from* London as for Kibworth. Departures *for* London about 4 times daily. Pop. 776.
Map Square 18.

GREATHAM (Durham), 242¾ miles. Fares, 50/8*a*, 30/5*c*. R. T., double fare. Departures *from* London as for Stockton. Departures *for* London about 6 times daily. Pop. 972.
Map Square 8.

GREAT HARWOOD (Lancs), 215¾ miles. Fares, 44/9*a*, 26/10*c*. R. T. for two months, 89/6*a*, 53/8*c*. Departures *from* London as for Blackburn. Departures *for* London about 8 times daily. Pop. 13,596.
Map Square 12.

GREAT HAYWOOD (Stafford), 128½ miles. Fares, 26/10*a*, 16/1*c*. R. T. for two months, 53/8*a*, 32/2*c*. Departures *from* London as for Colwich. Departures *for* London about 3 times daily. Pop. 571.
Map Square 17.

GREAT HORTON (Yorks), 193½ miles. Fares, 39/9*a*, 23/10*c*. R. T., double fare. Departures *from* London as for Bradford. Departures *for* London about 9 times daily. Pop. 23,415.
Map Square 12.

GREAT LINFORD (Bucks) from *Euston*, 55 miles. Fares, 11/6*a*, 6/11*c*. R. T. for two months, 23/0*a*. Departures *from* London as for Newport Pagnell. Departures *for* London about 8 times daily. Pop. 577.
Map Square 18.

GREAT LONGSTONE (Derby), 155½ miles. Fares, 31/11*a*, 19/2*c*. R. T., double fare. Departures *from* London as for Bakewell. Departures *for* London about 4 times daily. Pop. 627.
Map Square 12.

GREAT MISSENDEN. *See* Missenden, Great.

GREAT ORMESBY. *See* Ormesby, Great.

GREAT PONTON (Lincoln) from *King's Cross*, 102 miles. Fares, 21/1*a*, 12/8*c*. R. T., double fare. Departures *from* London as for Corby. Departures *for* London about 10 minutes earlier. Pop. 426.
Map Square 18.

GREAT PORTLAND STREET from *Aldgate, Moorgate, King's Cross, Mansion House, Charing Cross, Victoria, South Kensington, High Street, Praed Street, Hammersmith*, and intermediate stations every few minutes. Also to and from *Uxbridge Road* and *Kensington (Addison Road)* about every 12 minutes throughout the day. *See* back of Map.
Map Square 60, *No.* 4.

GREAT SHEFFORD. *See* Shefford, Great.

GREAT SOMERFORD. *See* Somerford, Great.

GREENFIELD (Yorks), 190¼ miles. Fares, 37/9*a*, 22/8*c*. R. T., double fare. Departures *from* London as for Mossley. Departures *for* London about 8 times daily. Pop. 1,403.
Map Square 2.

GREENFORD (Middlesex) from *Paddington*, 7¾ miles. Fares, 1/3*a*, 0/9*c*. R. T. for two days, 2/6*a*, 1/3*c*. Pop. 1,461. *See* pp. 490, 491.
Map Squares 23 *and* 57.

GREENHEAD (Northumberland), 306¾ miles. No through fares. Departures *from* London as for Hexham or Carlisle. Departures *for* London about 8 times daily.
Map Square 3.

GREENHILL (Stirling), 405¼ miles. Fares, 81/5*a*, 48/10*c*. R.T. for two months, 162/10*a*, 97/8*c*. Departures *from* London as for Coatbridge. Departures *for* London about 4 times daily.
Map Square 40.

GREENHITHE (Kent) from *Charing Cross, Cannon Street*, and *London Bridge*, 20½ miles. Fares, 4/4*a*, 3/5*b*, 2/7*c*. R. T. for two months, 7/10*a*, 6/1*b*, 4/11*c*. Pop. 2,761. *See* pp. 552, 554.
Map Square 24.

GREENLAW (Berwick), 362¼ miles. No through fares. Departures *from* London as for Berwick-on-Tweed or St. Boswells. Departures *for* London about 4 times daily. Pop. 909.
Map Square 41.

GREENLOANING (Perth), 427¾ miles. Fares, 87/4*a*, 52/5*c*. R. T. for two months, 174/8*a*, 104/10*c*. Departures *from* London as for Dunblane. Departures *for* London about 4 times daily.
Map Square 40.

GREENMOUNT (Lancs), 199½ miles. No through fares. Departures *from* London as for Bury. Departures *for* London about 6 times daily.
Map Square 12.

GREENOCK (Central) (Renfrew) from *Euston*, 422½ miles. Fares, 84/2*a*, 50/6*c*. R. T. for two months, 168/4*a*, 101/0*c*. Pop. 81,123.
Map Square 40.

Euston	Gr'ock.	Gr'ock.	Euston
AM 2.35*e*	4.38	AM 8.53*r*	6.25
5. 0	5.28	PM 12.30*r*	10. 0
10. 0*r*	7.25	4. 1*r*	5. 0
11.35*r*	10.37	8.16*e*	6.55
PM 1.30*ry*	11.35	9.10	7.30
1.30*hr*	11.42	—	—
9.20*e*	8.35	—	—
11. 0*d*	9.15	—	—
11.45*e*	10.30	—	—
—	—	—	—
—	—	—	—
—	—	—	—

Sunday Trains.

PM 9.30	8.35	PM 3.24*r*	5. 0
11.45	10.30	7.54	7.30
—	—	—	—
—	—	—	—
—	—	—	—
—	—	—	—
—	—	—	—

d Saturdays only.
e Saturdays excepted.
h Wednesdays and Saturdays only.
r Restaurant Car.
y Wednesdays and Saturdays excepted.

ANOTHER ROUTE from *St. Pancras*, 435¼ miles. Fares as above.

St. Pan.	Gr'ock	Gr'ock.	St. Pan.
AM 4.25	4.46	AM 8.18*r*	6.35
9.50*r*	8.35	10.15*r*	9.15
PM 12.15*r*	11.30	PM 7.15*e*	7.25
9.30*e*	8.47	9.30*e*	7.50
11.45*e*	10.27	10. 0*d*	8.57
—	—	—	—
—	—	—	—
—	—	—	—
—	—	—	—

Sunday Trains.

PM 9.30	8.47	—	—
11.45	10.27	—	—
—	—	—	—
—	—	—	—
—	—	—	—
—	—	—	—

d Saturdays only.
e Saturdays excepted.
r Restaurant Car.

GREENODD (Lancs), 255¼ miles. Fares, 53/2*a*, 31/11*c*. R. T. for two months, 106/4*a*, 63/10*c*. Departures *from* London as for Windermere (Lake Side). Departures *for* London about 4 times daily.
Map Square 7.

GREENORE (Louth) from *Euston*, 344¾ miles. Fares, 61/3, First and Saloon. 45/9, Third and Saloon. 33/9, Third and Steerage. R. T. for two months, 115/0, First and Saloon. 84/0, Third and Saloon. 67/6, Third and Steerage. *See* train service to Holyhead, and thence by boat. Pop. 289.

GREEN ROAD (Cumberland), 271 miles. Fares, 56/5*a*, 33/10*c*, R.T. for two months, 112/10*a*, 67/8*c*. Departures *from London as* for Barrow-in-Furness. Departures *for London* about 6 times daily. *Map Square* 6.

GREENWICH (Kent) from *Charing Cross, Cannon Street,* and *London Bridge,* 6¼ miles. Fares from Charing Cross, 1/3*a*, 1/0*b*, 0/8*c*. R.T. for two days, 2/6*a*, 2/0*b*, 1/4*c*. From Cannon Street, 1/0*a*, 0/9½*b*, 0/7*c*. R.T. for two days, 2/0*a*, 1/7*b*, 1/2*c*. Pop. 100,450. *See* pp. 547-551. *Map Square* 71.

GREENWICH NORTH from *Fenchurch Street,* 4½ miles. Fares, 0/9*a*, 0/7*b*, 0/5½*c*. R.T. for two days, 1/6*a*, 1/2*b*, 0/10½*c*. *See* pp. 524, 525. *Map Square* 71.

GREETLAND (Yorks) from *King's Cross,* 191¾ miles. Fares, 39/5*a*, 23/8*c*. R.T., double fare. Departures *from London as* for Brighouse. Departures *for London* about 20 minutes earlier. Pop. 4,357.

GRESFORD (Denbigh) from *Paddington,* 186¾ miles. Fares, 37/4*a*, 22/5*c*. R.T. for two months, 74/8*a*. Departures *from London as* for Wrexham. Departures *for London* about 4 times daily. Pop. 1,353. *Map Square* 12.

GRESLEY (Derby) from *St. Pancras,* 122¾ miles. Fares, 24/5*a*, 14/8*c*. R.T., double fare. Departures *from London as* for Moira. Departures *for London* about 10 minutes earlier. *Map Square* 17.

GRETNA (Dumfries), from *Euston,* 307¾ miles. Fares, 62/4*a*, 37/5*c*. R.T. for two months, 124/8*a*, 74/10*c*. Departures *from London as* for Carlisle. Departures *for London* about 4 times daily. Pop. 2,969. *Map Square* 3.

GRETNA GREEN (Dumfries), from *St. Pancras,* 317½ miles. Fares, 62/4*a*, 37/5*c*. R.T. for two months, 124/8*a*, 74/10*c*. Departures *from London as* for Carlisle. Departures *for London* about 4 times daily. *Map Square, 44.*

GRETTON (Northampton) from *St. Pancras,* 83 miles. Fares, 16/11*a*, 10/2*c*. R.T., double fare. Departures *from London as* for Weldon. Departures *for London* about 4 times daily. Pop. 771. *Map Square* 18.

GRIMOLDBY (Lincoln), 143 miles. Fares, 29/9*a*, 17/10*c*. R.T., double fare. Departures *from London as* for Louth. Departures *for London* about 6 times daily. Pop. 280. *Map Square* 13.

GRIMSARGH (Lancs), 214 miles. Fares, 44/7*a*, 26/9*c*. R.T. for two months, 89/2*a*, 53/6*c*. Departures *from London as* for Preston. Departures *for London* about 6 times daily. Pop. 494. *Map Square* 12.

GRIMSBY (Lincoln) from *King's Cross,* 155 miles. Fares, 32/3*a*, 19/4*c*. R.T. for two months, 64/6*a*, 38/8*c*. Pop. 82,329. *Map Square* 13.

KING'S +	GRIMS.	GRIMS.	KING'S +
AM 4.45	9.50	AM 5.50	10.40
7.15*kr*11.59		9. 5	1. 5
8.45	2. 1	PM12.20*r*	4.30
10.10*kr*	4.33	12.59*k*	6.25
11.30	5.31	2.30	9. 0
PM 1.50*kr*	6.12	2.52*k*	9. 0
4. 0*r*	7.54	4.50*r*	9.25
5.45*r*	9.50	8. 5	3.25
10.45*e*	5.20	—	—
—	—	—	—

Sunday Trains.

12. 0*nr*	5. 8	AM10. 0*r*	3.45
PM 5. 0*kr*10. 1		PM 4.45*kr*10.20	
10.45	5.20	—	—

e Saturdays excepted.
h Mondays and Fridays only.
k Via Retford.
n Noon.
r Restaurant Car.

ANOTHER ROUTE from *Marylebone,* 219¼ miles. Fares as above.

M'NONE	GRIMS.	GRIMS.	M'BONE.
AM 2.32	10.15	AM 5.52*r*	1.13
10. 0*r*	4.33	8.47*r*	3. 0
PM12.15*r*	6.12	PM12.59*r*	6.38
3.20*r*	9.17	4.15*r*	9.55
10. 0*d*	6. 1	7. 6	3.57
10. 5*e*	5.25	—	—

Sunday Trains.

AM11.15*r*	10. 1	AM 9. 5	5.40
—	—	—	—

d Saturdays only.
e Saturdays excepted.
r Restaurant Car.

Royal Hotel. Docks Station. First-class Family Hotel, under the London and North Eastern Company's direct management. Porter meets all trains. Telegrams, "Royal, Grimsby." Telephone 2030.

Yarboro' Hotel. Adjoining Town Station. Under the London and North Eastern Company's direct management. First-class Commercial Hotel. Porter meets all trains. Telephone 2016.

GRIMSTON (Leicester) from *St. Pancras,* 109½ miles. Fares, 22/4*a*, 13/5*c*. R.T., double fare. Departures *from London as* for Melton Mowbray. Departures *for London* about 6 times daily. Pop. 176. *Map Square* 18.

GRIMSTONE (Dorset), 143½ miles. Fares, 28/4*a*, 17/0*c*. R.T. for two months, 56/8*a*. Departures *from London as* for Maiden Newton. Departures *for* London about 4 times daily. *Map Square* 27.

GRIMSTON ROAD (Norfolk), 119½ miles. Fares, 21/5*a*, 12/10*c*. R.T. for two months, 42/10*a*. Departures *from London as* for Terrington. Departures *for London* about 4 times daily. Pop. (Grimston) 1,197. *Map Square* 19.

GRINDLEFORD (Derby) from *St. Pancras,* 158½ miles. Fares, 32/11*a*, 19/8*c*. R.T., double fare. Departures *from London* as for Hathersage. Departures *for London* about 5 times daily.

GRINDLEY (Stafford) 143¾ miles. Fares, 28/2*a*, 16/11*c*. R.T. for two months, 56/4*a*. Departures *from London as* for Stafford. Departures *for London* about 5 times daily. *Map Square* 17.

GRINDON (Stafford), 166 miles. No through fares. Departures *from London as* for Leek. Departures *for London* about 4 times daily. Pop. 354.

GRINKLE (Yorks), 259 miles. Fares, 54/0*a*, 32/5*c*. R.T., double fare. Departures *from* London as for Sandsend or Saltburn. Departures *for London* about 5 times daily. *Map Square* 8.

GRISTHORPE (Yorks), 231 miles. Fares, 48/2*a*, 28/11*c*. R.T., double fare. Departures *from London as* for Scarborough or Filey. Departures *for London* about 4 times daily. Pop. 208. *Map Square* 8.

GROESLON (Carnarvon), 252½ miles. Fares, 52/8*a*, 31/7*c*. R.T. for two months, 105/4*a*, 63/2*c*. Departures *from* London as for Carnarvon. Departures *for London* about 4 times daily. *Map Square* 11.

GROOMBRIDGE (Sussex) from *Victoria, Cannon Street,* and *London Bridge,* 34½ miles. Fares, 6/8*a*, 4/0*c*. R.T. for two months, 13/4*a*, 8/0*c*. Pop. 792. *Map Square* 24.

	Leave		
VICT.	CAN. ST.	LON. B.	ARR. at GR'BDGE
AM 5.30	—	5.18	7. 2
6.37	—	6.40	8.14
7.23	—	8. 7	9.36
9.10	—	9. 6	10.42
11. 5	—	10.35	12.58
12. 0	—	11.50	1.53
12. 0*d*	12.16*dk*12.20		1.44
PM —	—	12.50*d*	2.25
1.20*e*	—	1.38*e*	3. 0
1.25*d*	—	1.38*d*	3. 4
—	—	2. 5*e*	4. 1
2.25	—	2.25*d*	4. 1
3.45	—	—	4.44
4. 0	—	4.10	5.54
4. 0*e*	4.16*e*	4.20*e*	5.39
4.50	—	4.44*e*	6. 9
5. 5	—	5.21	6.41
5.48	—	5.41*e*	7.24
6. 6	—	6. 8	7.54
6.50	—··	7. 0	8.34
7.15	—	7.38	9.25
8. 5	—	8.10	9.30
9. 3*l*	—	9.12*l*	10.55
—	—	—	—
—	—	—	—
—	—	—	—

Sunday Trains.

AM 8.50	—	8.30	10.18
PM 1.14	—	1.10	2.41
2.50	—	—	4. 1
7. 5	—·	6.46	8.27

GROOMBRIDGE—contd.

Trains from Groombridge.

Leave Gr'bdge	Arrive at Lon. B.	Can. St.	Vict.
AM 6.42	8.15	—	8.24
7.16	8.37	—	8.40
7.21	9 1*k*	9. 4	9. 8
7.51	9.15	—	9.19
8.43	10. 4	—	10.12
9. 2	10.38	—	—
9.35	10.55	—	10.46
10. 2	—	—	11.35
10.52	12.13	—	12.17
11.12*h*	12.44	—	12.35
11.45	1.42	—	1.26
PM 1.27	2.58	—	—
2.14	4. 0	—	3.45
2.26	4.32	—	4.35
3.27	5.21	—	5.55
4.55	6.36	—	6.29
6.30	7.56	—	8.27
8.56	10.25	—	10.10
—	—	—	—
—	—	—	—

Sunday Trains.

AM 8.38	10.18	—	10.20
PM12. 6	—	—	1.40
5. 1	—	—	6.34
5.52	7.56	—	8.41
7.40	9.17	—	9. 0
—	—	—	—
—	—	—	—
—	—	—	—

d Saturdays only.
e Saturdays excepted.
k Departs from or arrives at London Bridge S.E. & C. Station.
l Fridays only.

GROSMONT (Yorks)

from *King's Cross*, 238 miles. Fares, 49/7*a*, 29/9*c*. R. T., double fare. Departures *from* London as for Whitby. Departures *for* London about 15 minutes later. *Map Square* 8.

GROTTON (Yorks), 190¼

miles. Fares, 38/7*a*, 23/2*c*. R. T., double fare. Departures *from* London as for Oldham (Clegg Street). Departures *for* London about 5 times daily. *Map Square* 12.

GROVE FERRY (Kent)

from *Charing Cross, Cannon Street*, and *London Bridge*, 77½ miles. Fares, 14/4*a*, 11/5*b*, 8/7*c*. R. T. for two months, 28/8*a*, 22/10*b*, 17/2*c*.

Map Square 24.

Char. +	Can. St.	Lon. B.	Arr. at Grov'F
AM —	5.20	5.25	9.13
9.15	—	9.23	11.38
11. 0	—	11. 7	1.40
PM 1. 0	—	—	3. 8
3. 0	—	3. 8	5.22
4.30	—	4.37	6.52
5.24*d*	—	5.34*d*	8.34
6. 0*e*	—	6. 5*e*	8.34
7.18	—	7.26	10.11
—	—	—	—
—	—	—	—
—	—	—	—

Sunday Trains.

AM 7.45	—	7.52	10.37
9.35*h*	—	—	12. 9
PM 7.35	—	7.45	10.11
—	—	—	—
—	—	—	—

GROVE FERRY—contd.

Trains from Grove Ferry.

Leave Grove F.	Arrive at Lon. B.	Can. St.	Char. +
AM 6.41	9.32	9.36	—
7.27	10. 0	10. 4	—
e7.27*h*	—	—	10.16*h*
9.16	11.43	—	11.57
10.50	1.36	—	1.50
PM12.25	3.26	—	3.40
2.55*h*	—	—	5.42*h*
2.55	5.50	—	6. 3
4.50	7.25	7.30	7.49
7.24	10.22	—	10.35
10.31*y*	—	1.20	—
—	—	—	—
—	—	—	—

Sunday Trains.

AM 6.47	10. 5	—	10.15
PM 4.41	7. 9	—	7.17
7.58	10.16	—	10.26
9.33*y*	—	1.23	—
—	—	—	—
—	—	—	—
—	—	—	—
—	—	—	—

d Saturdays only.
e Saturdays excepted.
h Departs from or arrives at Victoria (S. E. & C. R.).
y Third class only.

GROVE PARK (London)

from *Charing Cross, Cannon Street*, and *London Bridge*, 9½ miles. Fares from Charing Cross, 2/1*a*, 1/7*b*, 1/3*c*. R. T. for two days, 4/2*a*, 3/2*b*, 2/6*c*. From Cannon Street, 2/1*a*, 1/7*b*, 1/0*c*. R. T. for two days, 4/2*a*, 3/2*b*, 2/0*c*. *See* p. 556, 557.

Mop Squares 23 and 80.

GUARD BRIDGE (Fife),

446 miles. Fares, 90/3*a*, 54/2*c*. R. T. for two months, 180/6*a*, 108/4*c*. Departures *from* London as for Leuchars or St. Andrews. Departures *for* London about 5 times daily. Pop. 767. *Map Square* 38.

GUAY (Perth), 471¼ miles.

No through fares. Departures *from* London as for Dunkeld. Departures *for* London about 4 times daily. *Map Square* 37.

GUERNSEY from *Pad-*

dington, 227 miles (*via* Weymouth). Fares, 50/0, First and Saloon. 42/6, Third and Saloon. 30/0 Third and Second Cabin. R. T. for two months, 75/0, First and Saloon. 64/0, Third and Saloon. 45/0, Third and Second Cabin. Pop. 40,120.

Pad.	Guer.	Guer.	Pad.
AM 9.30	6. 0	AM10. 0*r*	7.35

r Restaurant Car.

ANOTHER ROUTE from

Waterloo, 199 miles. Fares, 50/0, First and Saloon. 42/6, Third and Saloon. 30/0, Third and Second Cabin. R. T. for two months, 75/0, First and Saloon. 64/0, Third and Second Cabin.

W'loo.	Guer.	Guer.	W'loo.
PM 9.30*r*	6.30	AM10. 0	7.20
—	—	—	—
—	—	—	—

No Sunday Service.

r Restaurant Car.

GUERNSEY—continued.

Royal Hotel. First-class. Oldest established, largest and best appointed. Lift. Omnibus meets Steamers. Telegrams, "Royal, Guernsey." Address—Manager.

See advt. p. **192.**

Gardner's Old Government House Hotel. Formerly the residence of Lieutenant-Governor. Every modern improvement. Telegraphic address, "Gov. Guernsey." *See advt.* p. **193.**

Victoria Hotel. Same direction as Royal. Family and Commercial. Omnibus meets Steamers. Telegrams, "Vic, Guernsey." Address—Manager. *See advt.* p. **192.**

The Richmond Hotel. Splendid Sea Views. Full Hotel Licence. No Bar. Billiard and Recreation Rooms. Illustrated Tariff.
Mrs. HART, Proprietress.

Lovell and Co., Complete House Furnishers, House Agents and Furniture Removers. Furnished and Unfurnished Houses to Let and for Sale. Particulars sent free.

GUESTWICK (Norfolk)

from *King's Cross*, 149 miles. Fares, 23/7*a*, 14/2*c*. R. T. for two months, 47/2*a*. Pop. 194. *Map Square* 19.

King's +	Guest.	Guest.	King's +
AM 4.45	9.56	AM 8.24	1.25
7.15*r*	12.54	11.52*r*	4.30
10.10*r*	3.53	PM 3.31	8.45
PM 3. 0	7.39	—	—
—	—	—	—

No Sunday Trains.
r Restaurant Car.

GUIDE BRIDGE (Lancs)

from *Marylebone*, 201 miles. Fares, 37/8*a*, 22/8*c*. R. T., double fare.

M'bone.	Guide B.	Guide B.	M'bone.
AM 2.32	8.59	AM 2. 0	10.36
8.45*r*	1.35	5.39*r*	11.10
10. 0*r*	3. 2	8.31*r*	1.13
PM12.15*r*	5. 7	10.14*r*	3. 0
3.20*r*	7.27	PM 2.26*r*	6.38
5. 0*r*	9.35	4. 1*r*	8.55
6.20*r*	10.52	5.11*r*	9.55
10. 0*d*	2.52	10.52	3.57
10. 5*e*	3.26		

Sunday Trains.

AM11.15*r*	3.59	PM12.36*r*	5.40
PM 5.30*r*	10.13	5. 1*r*	10.24
—	—	—	—

d Saturdays only.
e Saturdays excepted.
r Restaurant Car.

ANOTHER ROUTE from

King's Cross, 198 miles. Fares as above.

King's+	Guide B.	Guide B.	King's+
AM 4.45	10. 2	AM 5.39*r*	11.30
7.15*r*	11.54	10.14	3.50
8.45	3.37	11.40	6.25
10.10*r*	5. 8	PM12.51	6.30
11.30	6.40	2.26	9. 0
PM 1.50*r*	7. 4	7.41	3.25
4. 0*r*	9.35	—	—
5.45*r*	10.52	—	—

Sunday Trains.

12. 0*nr*	5.12	AM 6.58*r*	3.45
PM 5. 0	10.13	PM12.36	5.55
—	—	5. 1*r*	10.20

n Noon.
r Restaurant Car.

GUIDE BRIDGE—*contd.*

ANOTHER ROUTE from *Euston* (Hooley Hill), 183 miles. Fares as above.

EUSTON	GUIDE B.	GUIDE B.	EUSTON
AM12.25	6.39	AM 6.28*dr*12.20	
2.35	8.53	7.28*er*12. 5	
5. 0	10.45	8. 3*r* 12.50	
8.45*r*	12.46	9. 5*r* 1.15	
10.40*r*	2.49	9.36*r* 1.45	
12. 0*nr*	6. 0	10.13*r* 3.10	
PM 1.30*r*	6.37	PM12.28*dr* 5.50	
2.50*t*	7.50	12.28*er* 6. 0	
4.45*r*	9.33	1.48*r* 6.15	
11.50*d*	7.49	3.52*r* 8.10	
—	—	4.47*dr*10. 0	
—	—	4.47*er*10.10	
—	—	9.18 5. 0	

Sunday Trains.

PM12.30*r*	6.59	AM 8.57	4. 0
—	—	PM 2.25	7.30
—	—	7.22	5. 0

d Sats. only. *e* Sats. excepted.
n Noon.
r Restaurant Car.
t Tea Car.

GUILDFORD (Surrey)

from *Waterloo*, 30 miles. Fares, 6/3*a*, 3/9*c*. R. T. for two months, 12/6*a*, 7/6*c*. Pop. 24,927.
Map Square 23.

W'LOO	GUILD.	GUILD.	W'LOO
AM 5.50	6.44	AM 6.40	7.46
6. 5	7.15	6.52	8.19
6.50	7.52	7. 6	8.21
7. 5	8.16	7.13	8.30
7.50	8.59	7.24	8.56
8. 5	9.15	7.35	8.48
8.34	9.26	7.48	8.41
9. 0	9.59	8.28	9.12
9. 5	10.15	8.43	9.40
9.15	10.29	9. 1	9.44
9.50	10.33	9.32	10.15
10. 5	11.17	10. 8	10.50
10.20	11.32	10.42	11.32
10.50	11.38	11. 0	11.41
11. 5	12.15	11.30	12.46
11.20	12.34	11.49	1. 0
11.50*d*	12.33	PM 1.11	1.52
PM12. 5	1.15	1.30	2.46
12.15	1.29	1.49	3. 0
12.20*d*	1. 2	2. 4	3. 6
12.50	1.33	2.39*d*	3.20
1. 5	2.15	2.49	4. 0
1.35*d*	2.45	3.23	4.16
1.50*d*	2.31	3.34	4.46
1.50*e*	2.45	3.49	5. 0
2. 0*d*	2.55	4.21	5.46
2. 5	3.15	5.11	5.52
2.34	3.38	5.33	6.46
3. 5	4.15	5.40	6.52
3.15	4.29	6.34	7.46
3.50	4.33	6.49	8. 0
4. 5	5.15	7.13	7.56
4.15*e*	4.56	7.49	9. 0
4.20	.5.31	8. 4	9. 6
4.50	5.33	8.34	9.46
5. 0	5.53	8.49	10. 0
5.24	6. 5	9.32	10.46
5.37*e*	6.47	9.45	10.56
5.50	6.44	10.53	12.16
6. 5	7.15	—	—
6.10*e*	7. 0	—	—
6.50	7.31	—	—
6.54*e*	7.49	—	—
7. 5	8.15	—	—
8. 0	.9. 4	—	—
8. 5	9.20	—	—
8.20	9.34	—	—
9. 5	10.15	—	—
9.20*d*	10.28	—	—
9.50	10.41	—	—
10. 5	11.15	—	—
10.20	11.28	—	—
11.15*e*	12.21	—	—
11.35	12.39	—	—

GUILDFORD—*continued.*

Sunday Trains.

W'LOO	GUILD.	GUILD.	W'LOO
AM 8. 0	9. 0	AM 8.30	9.45
8.20	9.33	9.24	10.16
8.38	9.57	9.40	10.55
9.15	10. 2	10.40	11.55
9.20	10.36	11.25	12.41
10. 8	11.25	11.40	12.55
10.20	11.36	PM12.25	1.41
11. 8	12.25	12.40	1.55
11.20	12.33	1.25	2.44
PM12. 8	1.25	1.40	2.55
12.20	1.35	2.14	3.13
1. 8	2.25	2.25	3.44
1.50	2.50	3.40	4.55
2. 8	3.25	4.24	5.41
3. 8	4.25	5.30	6.17
3.20	4.33	5.40	6.55
4.20	5.26	6.24	7.41
5. 8	6.25	6.40	7.55
5.20	6.37	7.24	8.41
6.20	7.19	7.44	8.52
7. 8	8.25	7.50	9. 5
7.20	8.34	8.24	9.44
8. 8	9.25	8.40	9.55
8.20	9.37	8.58	10. 1
9.30	10.18	9.24	10 41
10.15	11.23	9.40	10.55
—	—	10.23	11.43

d Saturdays only.
e Saturdays excepted.

ANOTHER ROUTE (LONDON ROAD) from *Waterloo*, 28¼ miles. Fares, 6/0*a*, 3/7*c*. R. T. for two months, 12/0*a*, 7/2*c*.

W'LOO	GUILD.	GUILD	W'LOO
AM 6. 5	7.11	AM 6.58	8.19
7. 5	8.13	7.19	8.30
8. 5	9.11	7.41	8.48
9. 5	10.11	8.12	9.21
10. 5	11.14	8.52	10. 0
11. 5	12.11	9.31*d*	10.58
PM12. 5	1.11	10. 1	11. 6
1. 5	2.11	10.51	11.56
1.35*d*	2.41	11.55	1. 0
2. 5	3.11	PM12.57	2. 2
3. 5	4.11	1.55	3. 0
4. 5	5.11	2.55	4. 0
5. 5	6.11	3.55	5. 0
5.37*e*	6.42	5. 5	6.10
6. 5	7.11	5.46	6.52
6.38*e*	7.43	6.55	8. 0
7. 5	8.11	7.55	9. 0
8. 5	9.17	8.55	10. 0
9. 5	10.11	9.51	10.56
10. 5	11.11	—	—

Sunday Trains.

W'LOO	GUILD.	GUILD	W'LOO
AM 8.38	9.53	AM 9.45	10.55
10. 8	11.21	10.45	11.55
11. 8	12.21	11.45	12.55
PM12. 8	1.21	PM12.45	1.55
1. 8	2.21	1.45	2.55
2.38	3.21	3.45	4.55
3. 8	4.21	5.45	6.55
5. 8	6.21	6.45	7.55
6. 8	7.21	7.55	9. 5
7. 8	8.21	8.45	9.55
8. 8	9.21	9.45	10.55
9. 8	10.21	—	—

d Saturdays only.
e Saturdays excepted.

Lion Hotel. Most unique in Surrey. High Class Family and Commercial. Excellent cuisine. Officially appointed by R.A.C., A.A. and M.U. Garage; inspection pit. Stabling. Telephone 84.
MANAGERESS.
See advt. p. 193.

GUILDFORD—*continued.*

Shalford Park Hotel (unlicensed). Residential and Family. Three-quarter mile from Guildford.
See advt. p. 194.

Bramley Grange Hotel, Bramley, near Guildford (Station 100 yards). High Class, for Families and Golfers. Twenty acres beautiful ground. Telegrams: "Brassie, Guildford." Telephone: Bramley 5.
See advt. p. 194.

Ye Olde Grantley Arms Hotel, Wonersh. Short distance from Bramley Station. Central Heating. Moderate charges. 'Phone, No. 51 Bramley.
CATERING HOUSES, LTD.

Napoleon Hotel. Close to station. Family and Commercial. Central Heating. Moderate charges. 'Phone, No. 405 Guildford.
CATERING HOUSES, LTD.

House and Estate Agents. For available houses in Guildford and district, apply, Crowe, Bates and Weekes, Bridge Street, Opposite Station.

Estate Agents. Alex H. Turner & Co., incorporated with Alfred Savill & Sons. Station Approach. Telephone 57, and at Weybridge, Woking and London.

GUISBOROUGH (Yorks),

248¾ miles. Fares, 51/10*a*, 31/1*c*. R. T., double fare. Departures *from* London as for Middlesbrough. Departures *for* London about 5 times daily. Pop. 7,105.
Map Square 8.

GUISELEY (Yorks) from

St. Pancras, 205½ miles. Fares, 40/8*a*, 24/5*c*. R. T. double fare. Departures *from* London as for Ilkley. Departures *for* London about 6 times daily. Pop. 5,353.
Map Square 7.

GULLANE (East Lothian),

382½ miles. Fares, 79/10*a*, 47/11*c*. R. T. for two months, 159/8*a*, 95/10*c*. Departures *from* London as for Dunbar. Departures *for* London about 3 times daily. Pop. 1,354.
Map Square 48.

GUNNERSBURY (Middlesex) from *Broad Street*, 13 miles.

Fares, 0/11½*a*, 0/7½*c*. R. T. for two days, 1/11*a*, 1/3*c*. See pp. 501-505.
Map Square 67.
From *Mansion House*, 8¾ miles.
See p. 489.

GUNNISLAKE (Cornwall)

from *Waterloo*, 224¼ miles. Fares, 47/4*a*, 28/5*c*. R. T. for two months, 94/8*a*, 56/10*c*. Departures *from* London as for Calstock. Departures *for* London about 3 times daily.
Map Square 26.

GUNTON (Norfolk) from

Liverpool Street, 133½ miles. Fares, 26/0*a*, 15/7*c*. R. T. for two months, 52/0*a*, 31/2*c*. Departures *from* London as for North Walsham. Departures *for* London about 10 minutes earlier. Pop. 80.
Map Square 14.

GUTHRIE (Forfar), 489¼

miles. Fares, 96/11*a*, 58/2*c*. R. T. for two months, 193/10*a*, 116/4*c*. Departures *from* London as for Forfar. Departures *for* London about 3 times daily. Pop. 249.
Map Square 38.

GUYHIRNE (Cambs), 86¼

miles. Fares, 16/10*a*, 10/1*c*. R. T., double fare. Departures *from* London as for March. Departures *for* London about 4 times daily.
Map Square 18.

GWERSYLLT (Denbigh),

185 miles. No through fares. Departures *from* London as for Wrexham. Departures *for* London about 5 times daily. Pop. 4,594.

GWINEAR ROAD (Cornwall) from *Paddington*, 294½ miles.

Fares, 61/0a, 36/7c. R. T. for two months, 122/0a, 73/2c. Pop. (Gwinear) 1,327.
Map Square 25.

PAD.	GWIN. R.	GWIN. R.	PAD.
AM 5.30	5. 6	AM 8.54r	4.35
10.30r	4.36	10.30r	4.45
11.10r	6. 1	11. 3r	6.50
PM 2. 0r	9.48	PM12.56r	9. 0
10. 0e	7. 7	9.12	7.10
12. 0l	10.57	—	—
—	—	—	—
—	—	—	—

Sunday Trains.

PM10. 0	7. 7	—	—
—	—	—	—
—	—	—	—

e Saturdays excepted.
l Saturdays midnight excepted.
r Restaurant Car.

GWYDDELWERN

(Merioneth) from *Paddington*, 195¾ miles. Fares, 40/7a, 24/4c. R. T. for two months, 81/2a. Departures *from* London as for Corwen or Ruthin. Departures *for* London about 5 minutes earlier. Pop. 711.
Map Square 11.

GWYS (Brecon), 207¾ miles.

No through fares. Departures *from* London as for Swansea (High Street). Departures *for* London about 6 times daily.

IDRIS

SODA WATER
LEMONADE
DRY GINGER ALE
BREWED GINGER
BEER
GINGER ALE

To be obtained at all Clubs, Hotels, Restaurants, Grocers, Wine Merchants, and Chemists.

H

HABROUGH (Lincoln), 163

miles. Fares, 33/11a, 20/4c. R. T., double fare. Departures *from* London as for Brocklesby or Grimsby. Departures *for* London about 4 times daily. Pop. 396.
Map Square 13.

HACKBRIDGE (Surrey)

from *London Bridge* and *Victoria*, 10 miles. Fares, 1/11a, 1/2c. R. T. for two days, 3/10a, 2/4c. **See** pp. 565, 566, 571-574.

HACKNEY (London) from

Broad Street, 2¾ miles. Fares, 0/5x, 0/4b, 0/3c. R. T. for two days, 0/10a, 0/7b, 0/5½c. Pop. 222,142. **See** p. 500.
Map Square 61.

HACKNEY DOWNS

from *Liverpool Street*, 3 miles. Fares, 0/5x, 0/4b, 0/3c. R. T. for two days, 0/10a, 0/7b, 0/5½c. **See** pp. 523, 524, 526, 527, 534-536.
Map Square 61.

HADDENHAM (Bucks)

from *Marylebone*, 41¾ miles. Fares, 8/1a, 4/10c. R. T. for two months, 16/2a, 9/8c. Pop. 1,409.
Map Square 23.

M'BONE	HAD'HAM	HAD'HAM	M'BONE
AM 6.10	7.39	AM 8.35	9.55
8. 4	10.12	8.49d	12.43
PM12.15	2. 5	8.49	1. 5
2.10	4.10	11.23d	3.10
4.30	5.48	11.23e	3.23
4.55	6.12	PM 3.11	5.48
5.43	8. 7	4.41	7. 5
—	—	6.54	9.27
—	—	8.39	9.55

Sunday Trains.

AM 8.50	10.22	AM 9. 5	10.43
PM 6.30	8. 5	PM 7.22	8.58

d Saturdays only.
e Saturdays excepted.

ANOTHER ROUTE from

Paddington, 40¼ miles. Fares as above.

PAD.	HAD'HAM	HAD'HAM	PAD.
AM 5.45	7.39	AM 8.49	10. 0
9.10	10.12	11.23	1.18
PM12.18	2. 5	PM 3.11	4.40
2.23	4.10	4.41	6.35
4.40	5.48	6.54	9.18
7.10	8. 7	8.39	11. 4

Sunday Trains.

PM 6. 5	8. 5	AM 9. 5	11. 4
—	—	PM 7.22	9. 0

HADDENHAM (Cambs)

from *Liverpool Street*, via Ely, 74¾ miles. Fares, 14/7a, 8/9c. R. T. for two months, 29/2a. Pop. 1,678.
Map Square 18.

L FL. ST.	HAD'HAM	HAD'HAM	L'PL.ST.
AM 5.50	10.20	AM 8. 0	10.23
10. 5h	12.51	11.38h	2.21
11.50k	2.47	PM12.47l	5. 9s
PM 2.34	5. 0	1.12f	5. 9s
4.45	7. 5	3.43	6.10
—	—	5.52	8.22

No Sunday Trains.

f Mondays only.
h Mondays and Thursdays excepted.
k Mondays and Thursdays only.
l Thursdays only.
s From July 23 passengers can arrive at St. Pancras Station at 4.2 p.m.

ANOTHER ROUTE via

St. Ives, 82½ miles. Fares as above.

L'PL.ST.	HAD'HAM	HAD'HAM	L'PL.ST.
AM 5. 5	8. 0	AM10.20	2. 7
8.30h	12.38	PM12.51h	5. 9l
8.30k	12.47	7. 5	10.30
8.30f	1.12	—	—
11.50e	3.44	—	—
PM12.29d	3.44	—	—

No Sunday Trains.

d Saturdays only.
e Saturdays excepted.
f Mondays only.
h Mondays and Thursdays excepted.
k Thursdays only.
l From July 23 passengers can arrive at St. Pancras Station at 4.2 p.m.

HADDINGTON (East Lothian)

HADDINGTON (East Lothian), 388¾ miles. Fares, 80/8a, 48/5c. R. T. for two months, 161/4d, 96/10c. Departures from London as for Edinburgh (Waverley) or Dunbar. Departures for London about 3 times daily. Pop. 5,325. Map Square 41.

HADDISCOE (Norfolk)

HADDISCOE (Norfolk), 114¾ miles. Fares, 24/2a, 14/6c. R. T. for two months, 48/4d. Departures from London as for Beccles. Departures for London about 6 times daily. Pop. 439. Map Square 19.

HADFIELD (Derby)

HADFIELD (Derby), 187½ miles. Fares, 37/6a, 22/6c. R. T. double fare. Departures from London as for Penistone. Departures for London about 5 times daily. Pop. 6,731. Map Square 12.

HADHAM (Herts) from

Liverpool Street, 26 miles. Fares, 5/8a, 3/5c. R. T. for two months, 11/4a, 6/10c. Departures from London as for Buntingford. Departures for London about 10 times daily. Pop. 1,670. Map Square 23.

HADLEIGH (Suffolk) from

Liverpool Street, 70½ miles. Fares, 14/10a, 8/11c. R. T. for two months, 29/8a. Via Ipswich, 16/1a, 9/8c. R. T. for two months, 32/2a. Pop. 3,038. Map Square 19.

L'PL.ST.	HADL'GH	HADL'GH	L'PL.ST.
AM 5. 0	8.36	AM 7.32	9.53
6.50	10. 2	8.52	11.16
11.30	1.52	PM12.20	3.13
PM 3.26	6.43	5.17	7.51
5.42d	8. 8	6.55hr	10. 0
5.42e	8.12	—	—

No Sunday Trains.
d Saturdays only.
e Saturdays excepted.
h Via Ipswich.
r Restaurant Car.

HADLEY (Salop)

HADLEY (Salop), 151¼ miles. Fares, 29/9a, 17/10c. R. T. for two months, 59/6a Departures from London as for Newport (Salop). Departures for London about 6 times daily. Pop. 3,108. Map Square 17.

HADLEY WOOD (Middlesex) from

King's Cross, 10½ miles. Fares, 2/1a, 1/8b, 1/3c. R. T. for two days, 4/2a, 3/4b, 2/6c. See pp. 511-517. Map Square 23.

HADLOW ROAD (Cheshire)

HADLOW ROAD (Cheshire), 188½ miles. Fares, 39/4a, 23/7c. R. T. for two months, 78/8a, 47/2c. Departures from London as for Hooton. Departures for London about 4 times daily. Map Square 12.

HADNALL (Salop)

HADNALL (Salop), 167½ miles. Fares, 32/9a, 19/8c. R. T. for two months, 65/6a, 39/4c. Departures from London as for Shrewsbury. Departures for London about 6 times daily. Pop. 5,596. Map Square 17.

HAGGERSTON from

Broad Street, 1¼ miles. Fares, 0/5½a, 0/3½b, 0/2c. R. T. for two days, 0/9a, 0/5½b, 0/4c. Pop. 10,381. See pp. 499, 518-522. Map Square 61.

HAGLEY (Worcester) from

Paddington, 125 miles. Fares, 25/3a, 15/2c. R. T. for two months, 50/6a. Pop. 1,541. Map Square 17.

PAD.	HAGLEY	HAGLEY	PAD.
AM 6.30k	11.34	AM 6.23kr	10. 0
9.10kr	12.40	7.56kr	11. 0
10.40dk	1.40	7.56	11.15
10.40k	2. 8	9.13k	12.25
PM12.50kr	4. 5	10.32kr	1.25
1.30r	4.38	11. 5r	2.55
1.35r	5.31	PM12.57r	4.15
2.10kt	5.38	1.38kr	5. 0
4.10kt	7.16	2. 8	5.50
6.10kr	9.20	2.59kt	6.40
7.10kr	10.25	4.38dkr	8. 5
7.30kn	12.12	4.45ekr	8. 5
12.15kl	6.38	4.54r	9.15
12.15hk	9.25	6.31kr	10. 0
—	—	10. 8k	3.30

Sunday Trains.

AM10.35r	3.56	AM 9.25	2.40
PM12.50kr	3.50	11.46k	6.20
6. 0kr	9. 0	PM 3.56kr	9. 0
—	—	4.45r	9.48

d Saturdays only.
e Saturdays excepted.
h Sat. midnight only.
k Via Birmingham.
l Saturdays midnight excepted.
n Wednesdays and Saturdays only.
r Restaurant Car.
t Tea Car.

HAIGH (Yorks)

HAIGH (Yorks), 181½ miles. Fares, 37/9a, 22/8c. R. T. for two months, 75/6a, 45/4c. Departures from London as for Wakefield. Departures for London about 6 times daily. Map Square 12.

HAILSHAM (Sussex) from

London Bridge and Victoria, via Polegate, 64½ miles. Fares, 12/4a, 7/5c. R. T. for two months, 24/8a, 14/10c. Pop. 4,604. Map Square 29.

Leave VICT.	LON. B.	Arr. at HAIL.
AM —	6.15	8.16
6.37l	6.40l	10.16
9. 0	—	11.23
9.45	9.50	12.37
PM 1.20e	—	3.25
1.25d	1.10d	3.25
—	2. 0	3.55
3.20	—	5.12
—	4. 5	6.12
5.45e	5.55e	7.49
6.50	7. 0	9.42
8.35	—	10.53

Sunday Trains.

AM 6.55	7.22	10. 0
11.15h	—	2.19
PM 6.33	6.53	9.48
8.20	8. 0	10.43

HAILSHAM—continued.

Trains from Hailsham.

Leave HAIL.	Arrive at LON. B.	VICT.
AM 7..2	8.53	9. 8
8.19	10.55	10.56
10.21	12.44	12.45
PM12. 4	2.22	2.22
1.47h	4. 0	4. 2
3.37h	—	6. 0
5.25	7.42	7.45
7.52	10. 0	10.10
8.44h	—	11.17
l9.50s	12.59	1. 0

Sunday Trains.

AM 7.15	10.18	10.32
10. 6l	—	1. 0
PM 5.26	7.56	7.37
7.53	10.50	10.19
9.33l	12.27	—

d Saturdays only.
e Saturdays excepted.
h Via Eastbourne.
l Via Brighton.
s Wednesdays and Saturdays excepted.

ANOTHER ROUTE via

Groombridge, 53 miles. Fares, 11/1a, 6/8c. R. T. for two months, 22/2a, 13/4c.

Leave VICT.	LON. B.	Arr. at HAIL.
AM 5.30	5.18	8.19
6.37	6.40	10.14
9.10	9. 6	12. 4
11. 5	10.55	1.11
12. 0	11.50	3. 6
12. 0d	d12.20k	3. 6
PM 3.45	—	5.47
4.50	4.44e	7. 1
5. 5	5.21	7.52
6. 6e	6. 8e	8.44
8. 5	8.10	10.13

Sunday Trains.

AM 8.50	8.30	11.31
PM 2.30	—	5.26
7. 5	6.46	9.33

Trains from Hailsham.

Leave HAIL.	Arrive at LON. B.	VICT.
AM 6.58	9.32	9.40
8.16	10.55	10.20
10.16	12.44	12.35
PM 1.13	—	3.45
3.54	6.36	6.29
4.54	7.56	8.27
7.54	10.25	10.10

Sunday Trains.

AM 7.32	10.18	10.22
10.38	—	1.40
PM 6.30	9.17	9. 0

d Saturdays only.
e Saturdays excepted.
k Departs from London Bridge (S.E. & C.) Station.

HAIRMYRES (Lanark),

400¾ miles. No through fares. Departures *from* London as for Hamilton. Departures *for* London about 6 times daily.

HALBEATH (Fife), 411½

miles. No through fares. Departures *from* London as for Dunfermline. Departures *for* Londonabout 4 times daily.
Map Square 41.

HALE (Cheshire), 183¾ miles.

Fares, 37/9*a*, 22/8*c*. R. T., double fare. Departures *from* London as for Knutsford. Departures *for* London about 6 times daily. Pop. 9,285.
Map Square 12.

HALEBANK (Lancs), 191

miles. Fares, 39/10*a*, 23/11*c*. R. T. for two months, 79/8*a*, 47/10*c*. Departures *from* London as for Runcorn. Departures *for* London about 5 times daily.
Map Square 12.

HALESOWEN (Worcester), 120¼ miles.

Fares, 25/0*a*, 15/0*c*. R.T. for two months, 50/0*a*. Detures *from* London as for Smethwick Junction. Departures *for* London about 8 times daily. Pop. 4,121.
Map Square 17.

HALESWORTH (Suffolk)

from *Liverpool Street*, 100¾ miles. Fares, 21/1*a*, 12/8*c*. R. T. for two months, 42/2*a*. Pop. 2,059.
Map Square 19.

L'PL. ST.	H'WRTH.	H'WRTH.	L'PL. ST.
AM 5. 0	8.24	AM 7.19*r*	10.30
8.15*r*	11.49	8.24*r*	11.22
10. 0	12.39	10.41	1.20
10.20	1.41	10.56*r*	2. 3
PM 1. 0	3.38	PM 1. 9	3.42
3.18*r*	6.28	3.14	5.55
4.55*r*	7.28	4.23	7.51
5.18*dr*	8.21	6.26*r*	9.22
5.18*er*	8.29	7.27	11.16
—	—	—	—
—	—	—	—

Sunday Trains.

AM10. 5*r*	1. 9	AM 7.55	11.38
PM 4.40	7.50	PM 6. 9*r*	9.10
—	—	—	—
—	—	—	—
—	—	M'BONE	—

d Saturdays only.
e Saturdays excepted.
r Restaurant Car.

HALEWOOD (Lancs), 209

miles. Fares, 39/10*a*, 23/11*c*. R. T. for two months, 79/8*a*, 47/10*c*. Departures *from* London as for Warrington (Central). Departures *for* London about 4 times daily. Pop. 2,467.

HALIFAX (Yorks) from

King's Cross, *via* Wakefield (Westgate), 193⅝ miles. Fares, 39/9*a*, 23/10*c*. R. T., double fare. Pop. 99,129.
Map Square 12.

KING'S+	HALIFAX	HALIFAX.KING'S+	
AM 4.45*eh*	9.49	AM 6. 6*hr*11.30	
4.45*e*	10.36	7.52	1. 5
7.15*lr*12.29		9.35*rv*	1.55
10.10*dr*	2.50	10.10*g*	3.15
10.10*er*	2.25	10.26*h*	3.50
11.15*g*	4.10	11.27*ehr*4.45	
PM 1.30*r*	5.49	PM12. 5*hr*	6.25
1.50*hr*	7.48	2. 2*rv*	7.10
4. 0*r*	9. 0	4.29*hr*	9.25
5.45*rv*10. 7		9.10*v*	3.25
10.45*e*	4. 6	10. 7*r*	3.45
—	—	—	—

Sunday Trains.

12. 0*nr* 7.27	AM12. 0*n*	5.55
PM10.45	4. 6	PM 3.37*hr*10.20
—	—	—

d Saturdays only.
e Saturdays excepted.
g 1st and 3rd class Pullman Cars only.
h *Via* Holbeck.
l *Via* Bradford and L. M. & S. Line.
n Noon.
r Restaurant Car.
v *Via* Wakefield (Kirkgate).

ANOTHER ROUTE from

Euston, 214 miles. Fares as above.

EUSTON	HALIFAX	HALIFAX	EUSTON
AM12.25	7.51	AM 4.12*er*12.5	
2.35	10.24	4.12*dr*12.20	
5. 0	12.43	6.10*r*	12.50
8.45*r*	2.43	8.20*r*	1.15
10.40*r*	3.30	8.37*r*	1.45
11.50*r*	5.26	10.10*r*	3.55
12. 0*nr* 7. 6		10.32*dt*	5.50
PM 1.30*r*	8.12	11.34*dt*	6. 0
2.50*t*	8.38	PM 1. 5*et*	6. 0
4. 5*r*	9. 0	1. 5*dr*	6.15
6. 5*r*	10.47	1.13*r*	7.30
8. 0*e*	5.56	3. 5*r*	8.10
9.30	6. 3	4.28*er*10.10	
11.50*d*	9.56	8.18	5. 0
—	—	9.27	5.40
—	—	10.28	5.50

Sunday Trains.

PM12.10*r*	6. 5	AM11.35*r*	5.45
12.30*r*	8. 6	11.57*r*	7.30
7.50*r*	5.56	PM 3. 0*r*	8.55
9.15	6. 3	7.30	5. 0
—	—	9.48	5.50

d Saturdays only.
e Saturdays excepted.
n Noon.
r Restaurant Car.
t Tea Car.

ANOTHER ROUTE from

Marylebone, 202 miles. Fares as above.

M'BONE	HALIFAX	HALIFAX	M'BONE
AM 2.32	8.12	AM 7.45*r*	1.13
10. 0*r*	3. 7	9.43*r*	3. 0
PM12.15*r*	5.58	PM 1.13*r*	6.38
3.20*r*	8. 3	4.50*r*	9.55
6.20*r* 11.15		8.55	3.57

Sunday Trains.

AM11.15*r*	9.11	PM 4.23*r* 10.24
PM 5.30*r* 10.52		

r Restaurant Car.

White Swan Hotel. Cen-

trally situated. Grill. Coffee Rooms, Lounge, etc. Baths. Commodious Stock Rooms. Billiards. Garage.
H. A. POWELL, Manager.

HALKIRK (Caithness), 713¼

miles. Fares, 130/0*a*, 78/0*c*, R. T. for two months, 260/0*a*, 156/0*c* Departures *from* London as for Helmsdale. Departures *for* London about twice daily. Pop. 1,969.
Map Square 32.

HALLATON (Leicester)

from *Euston*, 90¾ miles. Fares, 18/2*a*, 10/11*c*. R. T. for two months, 36/4*a*. Pop. 566.
Map Square 18.

EUSTON.	HALTN.	HALTN.	EUSTON.
AM 5. 0	7.57	AM 8.33	11.55
6.45	10.12	10.25	12.40
10.40	2. 8	PM12.23*h*	3.45
PM12.15	4. 7	12.23*k*	4.15
4.15	7. 4	4.24	7.20
—	—	7.32	11.35
—	—	—	—
—	—	—	—

No Sunday Trains.

h Mondays and Saturdays only.
k Mondays and Saturdays excepted.

HALLATROW (Somerset)

from *Paddington*, 113½ miles. Fares, 23/9*a*, 14/3*c*. R. T. for two months, 47/6*a*. Departures *from* London as for Midsomer Norton. Departures *for* London about 5 times daily.
Map Square 22.

HALL GREEN (Warwick),

108 miles. Fares, 22/9*a*, 13/8*c*. R. T. for two months, 45/6*a*. Departures *from* London as for Henley-in-Arden. Departures *for* London about 3 times daily.

HALLING (Kent) from

Charing Cross, *Cannon Street*, and *London Bridge*, 35½ miles. Fares, 7/6*a*, 6/0*b*, 4/6*c*. R. T. for two months, 15/0*a*, 12/0*b*, 9/0*c*. Pop. 2,365.
Map Square 24.

	Leave		Arrive at
CHAR. +	CAN. ST.	LON. B.	HALLG.
AM —	—	3.22*h*	5.43
—	6.20	6.23	7.56
—	7.16	7.19	8.37
—	7.44	7.47	9.10
8.10	—	8.17	9.43
9.32	—	9.41	11. 3
11.55	—	12. 2	1.16
PM 1.20*e*	—	1.27*e*	2.51
1.26*d*	—	1.34*d*	2.51
—	1.48*d*	1.51*d*	3.19
2.45*e*	—	2.53*e*	4.24
3. 5*d*	—	3.12*d*	4.26
—	4.12*e*	4.15*e*	5.17
4.25*d*	—	4.31*d*	6. 0
—	4.36*e*	4.39*e*	6. 0
4.35*d*	—	4.43*d*	6.32
—	5. 8*e*	5.11*e*	6.32
5.15*d*	—	5.22*d*	6.58
5.58*d*	—	6. 4*d*	7.23
—	6.20*e*	6.23*e*	7.28
6.22*e*	—	6.29*e*	7.58
6.55*d*	—	7. 1*d*	8.44
—	7. 8*e*	7.11*e*	8.44
—	7.44	7.47	9.53
—	9.35	9.38	11.10

Sunday Trains.

AM 7.30	—	7.37	9.17
10.50	—	10.57	12.38
PM 1.15	—	1.22	3. 3
4.50	—	4.57	6.31
7. 0	—	7. 7	8.34
8.42	—	8.49	10.16
—	—	—	—
—	—	—	—

HALLING—*continued.*

Trains from Halling.

Leave HALLING	Arrive at LON. B.	CAN. ST.	CHAR. +
AM 5.15	7. 0	7. 4	—
7.11	8.34	—	8.41
8.12	9.34	—	9.43
8.44	9.54	—	10. 1
10.39	12. 3	—	12.14
PM12. 5*d*	1.31	1.37	—
12. 5*e*	1.36	—	1.45
*d*1.23*h*	3.21	3.26	—
1.30*e*	2.54	—	3. 4
1.59*e*	3.26	—	3.36
2.16*d*	3.58	—	4. 8
3.17*e*	4.48	4.52	—
3.20*d*	4.57	—	5. 6
4.17*e*	5.36	5.40	—
4.17*d*	5.38	—	5.45
5.33	7.10	—	7.19
6. 4	7.14	—	7.23
6.50	8.15	8.20	—
8.14	9.36	—	9.46
9.26	10.51	—	10.59
10.35	12.35	—	12.45
—	—	—	—
—	—	—	—

Sunday Trains.

AM 7.24	9. 0	—	9. 9
8.42	10.16	—	10.24
11.28	1. 5	—	1.17
PM 2.31	4. 4	—	4.15
4.31	5.55	—	6. 4
7.57	9.46	—	9.55
9.38	11.15	—	11.24
—	—	—	—
—	—	—	—
—	—	—	—
—	—	—	—
—	—	—	—
—	—	—	—
—	—	—	—

d Saturdays only.
e Saturdays excepted.
h Third class only.

HALLINGTON (Lincoln), 143¾ miles. Fares, 29/4*a*, 17/7*c*. R. T., double fare. Departures *from* London as for Wragby. Departures *for* London about 4 times daily. Pop. 85.
Map Square 13.

HALL ROAD (Lancs), 208¾ miles. Fares, 42/1*a*, 25/3*c*. R. T. for two months, 84/2*a*. Departures *from* London as for Liverpool. Departures *for* London about 8 times daily.
Map Square 12.

HALMEREND (Stafford), 154¾ miles. Fares, 32/3*a*, 19/4*c*. R. T. for two months, 64/6*a*, 38/8*c*. Departures *from* London as for Newcastle-under-Lyme. Departures *for* London about 4 times daily. Pop. 3,286.
Map Square 12.

HALSALL (Lancs), 217½ miles. No through fares. Departures *from* London as for Southport. Departures *for* London about 8 times daily. Pop. 1,426.
Map Square 12.

HALSTEAD (Essex), from *Liverpool Street*, 56½ miles. Fares, 11/10*a*, 7/1*c*. R. T. for two months, 23/8*a*, 14/2*c*. Pop. 5,916.
Map Square 19.

L'PL. ST.	HALST'D.	HALST'D.	L'PL. ST.
AM 6.50	9.43	AM 8.12	9.53
10. 0	11.50	10. 3	11.42
PM 2.15	4.22	PM 2.34*h*	5. 5
5.42	7.34	6.40	9.17
—	—	—	—
—	—	—	—
—	—	—	—
—	—	—	—
—	—	—	—

Sunday Trains.

AM 9.20	11.17	AM 9.18	12.40
PM 4.40*h*	9. 1	PM 6.34	8.58

h Via Colchester.

HALTON (Cheshire), 181½ miles. Fares, 37/9*a*, 22/8*c*. R. T. for two months, 75/6*a*, 45/4*c*. Departures *from* London as for Chester. Departures *for* London about 5 times daily. Pop. 1,294.
Map Square 12.

HALTON (Lancs), 257¾ miles. Fares, 47/11*a*, 28/9*c*. R. T., double fare. Departures *from* London as for Hornby. Departures *for* London about 5 times daily. Pop. 889.
Map Square 7.

HALTON, EAST (Lincs), from *Marylebone*, 217½ miles. Fares, 34/9*a*, 20/10*c*. R. T. for two months, 69/6*a*, 41/8*c*. Departures *from* London as for Brocklesby. Departures *for* London about 4 times daily. Pop. 567.
Map Square 13.

HALTON HOLGATE (Lincoln), 125 miles. Fares, 26/0*a*, 15/7*c*. R. T., double fare. Departures *from* London as for Spilsby. Departures *for* London about 6 times daily. Pop. 388.
Map Square 13.

HALTON, WEST (Lincoln), 184¼ miles. Fares, 21/10*c*. R. T., double fare. Departures *from* London as for Thorne or Barnetby. Departures *for* London about 3 times daily. Pop. 303.
Map Square 13.

HALTWHISTLE (Northumberland), 303½ miles. Fares, 60/10*a*, 36/6*c*. R. T., double fare. Departures *from* London as for Hexham or Carlisle. Departures *for* London about 4 times daily. Pop. 3,979.
Map Square 3.

HALWILL JUNCTION (Devon) from *Waterloo*, 210 miles. Fares, 43/9*a*, 26/3*c*. R. T. for two months, 87/6*a*, 52/6*c*. Pop. 410.
Map Square 26.

W'LOO.	H'WILL.	H'WILL.	W'LOO.
AM10. 0*r*	2.38	AM 8.11*r*	1.56
11. 0*r*	4.41	10.35*r*	3.50
PM 1. 0*r*	6.52	11.44*r*	4.30
3. 0*r*	7.51	PM 2.40*r*	8.30
—	—	4.53	10.50

No Sunday Trains.
r Restaurant Car.

HAMBLETON (Yorks), 178¾ miles. No through fares. Departures *from* London as for Selby. Departures *for* London about 6 times daily. Pop. 514.
Map Square 13.

HAMILTON (Lanark) from *Euston*, 392 miles. Fares, 82/6*a*, 49/6*c*. R. T. for two months, 165/0*a*, 99/0*c*. Pop. 39,420.
Map Square 40.

EUSTON	HAMILT'N	HAMILT'N	EUSTON
AM 5. 0*e*	4.23	AM 9.49*r*	6.25
5. 0*d*	5. 7	PM 4.10*dr*	5. 0
6.45	6. 5	4.54*er*	5. 0
10. 0*r*	6.37	9. 3*e*	6.55
11.35*r*	9.45	—	—
PM 9.20*e*	7.38	—	—
11.35*e*	8.28	—	—
11.45*y*	11.58	—	—
11.45*e*	12. 9*l*	—	—
—	—	—	—
—	—	—	—

Sunday Trains.

PM 9.30	7.38	—	—
11.35	8.28	—	—
11.45	12. 9*l*	—	—
—	—	—	—
—	—	—	—

d Saturdays only.
e Saturdays excepted.
l P.M.
r Restaurant Car.
y Friday night.

HAMMERSMITH from *Mansion House*, 6½ miles. Also to and from Ealing, Hounslow, and Richmond. Pop. 130,295. *See* p. 489.
Map Square 68.

ANOTHER ROUTE from *Aldgate*, 8½ miles. Trains run about every 12 minutes throughout the day. *See* back of Map.

ANOTHER ROUTE (Hammersmith and Finsbury Park Tube). *See* back of Map.

HAMMERTON (Yorks), 196½ miles. Fares, 41/1*a*, 24/8*c*. R. T., double fare. Departures *from* London as for York. Departures *for* London about 5 times daily. Pop. 371.
Map Square 8.

HAMMERWICH (Stafford), 121¼ miles. Fares, 25/2*a*, 15/1*c*. R. T. for two months, 50/4*a*. Departures *from* London as for Lichfield. Departures *for* London about 7 times daily. Pop. 1,611.
Map Square 17.

HAMPDEN PARK (Sussex), from *Victoria*, *Clapham Junction*, and *London Bridge*, 63¾ miles. Fares, 12/3*a*, 7/4*c*. R. T. for two months, 24/6*a*, 14/8*c*. Departures *from* London as for Polegate or Eastbourne. Departures *for* London about 8 times daily. Pop. 988.
Map Square 29.

HAMPOLE (Yorks), 162½ miles. Fares, 33/9*a*, 20/3*c*. R. T., double fare. Departures *from* London as for Hemsworth. Departures *for* London about twice daily. Pop. 154.
Map Square 13.

HAMPSTEAD

(Hampstead Tube). Pop. 86,153. *See* back of Map.

HAMPSTEAD HEATH

from *Broad Street*, 6¾ miles. Fares, 0/10*a*, 0/6*c*. R. T. for two days, 1/5½*a*, 0/10½*c*. Pop. (Hampstead) 85,495. *See* pp. 501-505.
Map Square 51.

HAMPSTEAD NORRIS

(Berks) from *Paddington*, 59¾ miles. Fares, *via* Didcot, 12/9*a*, 7/6*c*. R. T. for two months, 25/6*a*, *Via* Newbury, Fares, 12/6*a*, 7/6*c*. R. T. for two months, 25/0*a*. Pop. 1,217.
Map Square 23.

	Pad.	Hamp. N.		Hamp. N.	Pad.
AM	5.30*h*	8. 6	AM	8. 6*k*	10. 0
	7.30*k*	9.44		8.44*h*	10.15
	9. 0*h*	11.15		9.44*h*	12. 0
	10.45*h*	1. 0		11.15*k*	12.55
PM	12.30*kr*	2. 7	PM	1. 0*k*	2.50
	1.35*hr*	3.48		2. 7*h*	4.35
	2.45*k*	4.34		3.48*k*	5.50
	3.38*h*	6.21		4.34*h*	7.20
	5.15*h*	7.10		6.21*kr*	8.20
	5.55*k*	7.41		7.10*k*	9.15
	6.30*k*	8.29		7.41*h*	10.45
	—	—		—	—

No Sunday Trains.

h Via Didcot.
k Via Newbury.
r Restaurant Car.

HAMPSTEAD SOUTH

from *Euston* and *Broad Street*, 6¾ miles. Fares from Euston, 0/5*a*, 0/3*c*. R. T. for two days, 0/10*a*, 0/6*c*. From Broad Street, 0/10*a*, 0/6*c*. R.T. for two days, 1/5½*a*, 0/10½*c*. *See* pp. 496-499.
Map Square 60.

HAMPSTEAD WEST

from *St. Pancras* and *Moorgate Street*, 4 miles. Fares from St. Pancras, 0/9*a*, 0/5½*c*. R. T. for two days, 1/5½*a*, 0/10½*c*. From Moorgate Street, 0/10*a*, 0/6*c*. R. T. for two days, 1/5½*a*, 0/10½*c*. *See* pp. 507-508.
Map Square 59.

ANOTHER ROUTE from *Baker Street*, 2¼ miles. Fares, 0/6*a*, 0/3½*c*. R. T. for two days, 1/0*a*, 0/7*c*. *See* back of Map.
Map Square 59.

HAMPSTHWAITE

(Yorks), 204 miles. Fares, 42/6*a*, 25/6*c*. R. T. for two months, 85/0*a*, 51/0*c*. Departures *from* London as for Pateley Bridge. Departures *for* London about 5 times daily. Pop. 443.
Map Square 7.

HAMPTON

(Middlesex) from *Waterloo*, 14 miles. Fares, 2/3*a*, 1/4*c*. R. T. for two days, 4/6*a*, 2/8*c*. Pop. 10,675. *See* p. 585.
Map Square 76.

HAMPTON COURT

(Surrey) from *Waterloo*, 15 miles. Fares, 2/8*a*, 1/7*c*. R. T. for eight days, 4/10*a*, 3/2*c*. *See* pp. 594-595.

HAMPTON COURT—*continued.*

Salter's Steamers (Molesey Lock, 5 minutes from station). Up stream, 9.30 A.M., 3.0 P.M. Down stream, 1.0 P.M., 6.30 P.M. *See* advt. facing first page of train service.

Karsino Hotel and Restaurant. Dancing in Large Palm Court facing River. Catering a special feature. *See* advt. p. **195.**

Greyhound Hotel (Trust Houses, Ltd.). Three minutes from River.

Mitre Hotel. Old Established. Fine position on River Thames, overlooking the Palace. Close to Railway Station. Noted for excellent Luncheons and Dinners. Telephone, 849 P.O. Kingston.
SADLER BROS., Proprietors.

Harry Tagg's Thames Hotel. Modern improvements. Balconies overlook Palace and River. Adjoining Station. Excellent Cuisine. Commodious Motor Garage. Motor Cars and Launches for hire; also Steam Launches and Boats of every description and built to order. Coach leaves Metropole, London, daily for Thames Hotel. Telephone, 4 Molesey. HARRY TAGG, Proprietor.

Court Restaurant, Hampton Court Bridge. Non-residential. Finest position. Balconies overlooking River and Royal Palace. Spacious and well-appointed Saloons. Moderate Tariff. Excellent accommodation. Fully licensed. Telephone 760 Kingston. Proprietors, SAM ISAACS, Ltd.

HAMPTON-IN-ARDEN

(Warwick) from *Euston*, 102¾ miles. Fares, 21/6*a*, 12/11*c*. R. T. for two months, 43/0*a*. Pop. 1,084.
Map Square 17.

	Euston	Hamp'd'n		Hamp'd'n	Euston
AM	2.30	6.35	AM	7.24*r*	10. 0
	5. 0	7.36		7.58*r*	11. 0
	6.45	10. 7		9.19	12.40
	9.15*r*	12.29		10.50*r*	2.20
	10. 0*e*	12.53	PM	1.28*et*	4.35
	10. 0*d*	1.10		1.48*dt*	4.35
	11.30*r*	2.15		2.59*t*	5.35
PM	1.15*r*	3.35		4.29*t*	7.20
	2.20*t*	4.52		6. 5*r*	8.20
	2.50*t*	5.43		7. 2*dr*	10.45
	4.45*t*	7.15		7.46*er*	10.45
	5.50*r*	8. 6		11.11*e*	4. 0
	7. 0*r*	10.11		11.16*d*	5. 0
	12.10*dm*	9.52		—	—
	—	—		—	—
	—	—		—	—
	—	—		—	—

Sunday Trains.

AM	9.15	12.58	AM	9. 5	12.25
PM	1. 0*r*	5.35	PM	1.35	5. 5
	5.10*r*	7.37		5.37*r*	8.20
	—	—		9.14	5. 0
	—	—		—	—
	—	—		—	—
	—	—		—	—

d Saturdays only.
e Saturdays excepted.
m Midnight.
r Restaurant Car.
t Tea Car.

HAMPTON LOADE

(Salop) from *Paddington*, 141¼ miles. Fares, 28/2*a*, 16/11*c*. R. T. for two months, 56/4*a*. Departures *from* London as for Bewdley. Departures *for* London about 4 times daily.
Map Square 17.

HAMPTON WICK

(Middlesex) from *Waterloo*, 12¼ miles. Fares, 1/11*a*, 1/2*c*. R. T. for two days, 3/10*a*, 2/4*c*. Pop. 3,265. *See* pp. 584-585.
Map Square 76.

HAM STREET

(Kent) from *Charing Cross*, *Cannon Street* and *London Bridge*, 62½ miles. Fares, 13/1*a*, 10/5*b*, 7/10*c*. R. T. for two months, 26/2*a*, 20/10*b*. Departures *from* London as for Appledore (Kent). Departures *for* London about 5 times daily.
Map Square 24.

HAMWORTHY

(Dorset) from *Waterloo*, 115½ miles. Fares, 24/2*a*, 14/6*c*. R. T. for two months, 48/4*a*, 29/0*c*. Pop. 1,388.
Map Square 27.

	W'loo	Hmwy.		Hmwy.	W'loo
AM	5.40	9.57	AM	7.56*s*	11. 0
	5.50	11.13		8.38*s*	12.22
	10.30	1.26		9.45	12.50
PM	12.30*r*	3.27		11.47	2.50
	2.30*s*	5.27	PM	12.41	4.20
	4.30*r*	7.33		1.45	4.50
	6.30*r*	9.27		3.44*r*	6.58
	—	—		5.45*r*	8.50
	—	—		7.11	11.28
	—	—		10.56	3.58
	—	—		—	—

Sunday Trains.

AM	11. 0*r*	2.32	AM	8. 9	12.11
PM	2. 0*r*	5.29	PM	3.23*r*	6.24
	7. 0*r*	10.29		6.22*r*	9.31
	—	—		10.56	3.58
	—	—		—	—
	—	—		—	—

r Restaurant Car.
s Refreshments served.

HANDBORO'

(Oxford) from *Paddington*, 70¼ miles. Fares, 14/9*a*, 8/10*c*. R. T. for two months, 29/6*a*. Pop. 853.
Map Square 23.

	Pad.	H'boro'		H'boro'	Pad.
AM	5.30	7.57	AM	8.15	9.50
	9.45	11.56		10.30	12. 5
	11.20*h*	2. 6	PM	12.27	2.12
PM	1.35*r*	4. 2		12.56*hr*	2.55
	4.45*t*	6.20		5.11	7.20
	6.55	8.49		8.52	10.45
	—	—		—	—
	—	—		—	—

Sunday Trains.

AM	10.35	12.21	PM	12.28	2.40
PM	4.10	6. 8		7.55*r*	9.48
	—	—		—	—
	—	—		—	—

h Thursdays and Saturdays only.
r Restaurant Car.
t Tea Car.

HANDFORTH

(Cheshire) from *Euston*, 178¼ miles. Fares, 37/3*a*, 22/4*c*. R. T. for two months, 74/6*a*. Departures *from* London as for Wilmslow. Departures *for* London about 6 times daily. Pop. 904.
Map Square 12.

HAMPTON COURT.—GREYHOUND HOTEL. Telephone: 1878 Kingston TRUST HOUSES, Ltd.

HANDSWORTH AND SMETHWICK (Stafford)

from *Paddington*, 113¼ miles. Fares, 23/7*a*, 14/2*c*. R. T. for two months, 47/2*a*. Pop. 68,610.
Map Square 17.

PAD.	HANDSW'TH	HANDSW'TH	PAD.
AM 5.30	10.22	AM 7.10*r*	10. 0
6.30	10.46	8.37*r*	11. 0
9.10*er*	11.31	9.58	12.25
9.10*r*	11.57	11. 1*r*	1.25
10.20*d*	12.38	11.49*r*	2. 5
10.40*r*	1.16	PM 2.28*r*	5. 0
PM12.50*r*	3.22	3.30*t*	5.55
2.10*t*	4.31	3.49*t*	6.40
4.10*t*	6.28	5.40*r*	8. 5
6.10*r*	8.33	7.14	10. 0
7.10*r*	9.26	10.53	3.30
7.30	11.22	—	—
12.15*k*	5.45	—	—
12.15*h*	7.12	—	—
—	—	—	—
—	—	—	—

Sunday Trains.

AM12.50*r*	3. 7	AM 9.58*r*	1.40
PM 4.10	7.42	PM 2. 6	6.20
6. 0*r*	8.17	6.10*r*	9. 0
—	—	—	—
—	—	—	—

d Saturdays only.
e Saturdays excepted.
h Saturdays midnight only.
k Saturdays midnight excepted.
r Restaurant Car.
t Tea Car.

HANDSWORTH WOOD (Stafford)

114¾ miles. Fares, 23/6*a*, 14/1*c*. R. T. for two months, 47/0*a*, 28/2*c*.. Departures *from* London as for Birmingham (New Street). Departures *for* London about 8 times daily.

HANLEY (Stafford)

from *Euston*, 148¼ miles. Fares, 30/10*a*, 18/6*c*. R. T. for two months, 61/8*a*. Pop. 66,255.
Map Square 12.

EUSTON	HANLEY	HANLEY	EUSTON
AM 2.35	8.14	AM 6. 2	11. 0
5. 0	9.38	8.30*er*	12. 5
8.45*r*	11.59	8.30*dr*	12.20
10.40	2.39	9.25*r*	12.50
12. 0*nr*	4.40	10.30*r*	2.20
PM 2.50*t*	5.56	11.19*d*	3.10
4.45*r*	8.23	PM12.50*r*	3.55
6.30*er*	10.30	2.49*r*	6.15
6.55*r*	11. 9	4.56	9.20
—	—	6.24*r*	10. 0
—	—	8.55	5. 0
—	—	—	—
—	—	—	—
—	—	—	—
—	—	—	—
—	—	—	—

No Sunday Trains.

d Saturdays only.
e Saturdays excepted.
n Noon.
r Restaurant Car.
t Tea Car.

Grand Hotel. Telephone 1361. Commodious modern Hotel, opposite Station. Central Heating. Electric Light and Lifts. Garage. TRUST HOUSES, Ltd.

HANNINGTON (Wilts)

81 miles. Fares, 17/3*a*, 10/4*c*. R.T. for two months, 34/6*a*. Departures *from* London as for Stratton. Departures *for* London about 6 times daily. Pop. 239.
Map Square 22.

HANWELL AND ELTHORNE (Middlesex)

from *Paddington*, 7¼ miles. Fares, 1/3*a*, 0/9*c*. R. T. for two days, 2/6*a*, 1/3*c*. Pop. (Hanwell) 20,481. *See* pp. 491–493.
Map Square 57.

HANWOOD (Salop)

157¼ miles. Fares, 32/11*a*, 19/9*c*. R. T. for two months, 65/10*a*. Departures *from* London as for Buttington. Departures *for* London about 6 times daily. Pop. 358.
Map Square 17.

HAPTON (Lancs)

211¾ miles. Fares, 43/2*a*, 25/11*c*. R. T. for two months, 86/4*a*, 51/10*c*. Departures *from* London as for Accrington. Departures *for* London about 6 times daily. Pop. 2,137.
Map Square 12.

HARBORNE (Stafford)

116¾ miles. Fares, 23/9*a*, 14/3*c*. R. T. for two months, 47/6*a*. Departures *from* London as for Birmingham (New Street). Departures *for* London about 10 times daily. Pop. 14,876.

HARBURN (Midlothian)

384½ miles. No through fares. Departures *from* London as for Carstairs. Departures *for* London about 4 times daily.
Map Square 41.

HARBY (Leicester)

115 miles. Fares, 23/2*a*, 13/11*c*. R. T. for six months, 46/4*a*. Departures *from* London as for Hallaton or Bottesford. Departures *for* London about 6 times daily. Pop. 603.
Map Square 18.

HARDINGHAM (Norfolk)

from *Liverpool Street*, 116½ miles. Fares, 23/7*a*, 14/2*c*. R. T. for two months, 47/2*a*. Departures *from* London as for Dereham. Departures *for* London about 5 times daily. Pop. 438.
Map Square 19.

HARECASTLE (Stafford)

152 miles. Fares, 31/8*a*, 19/0*c*. R. T. for two months, 63/4*a*. Departures *from* London as for Stoke-on-Trent. Departures *for* London about 6 times daily.

HARE PARK (Yorks)

171¾ miles. Fares, 35/8*a*, 21/5*c*. R. T., double fare. Departures *from* London as for Hemsworth. Departures *for* London about 5 times daily.

HARESFIELD (Glo'ster)

119¾ miles. No through fares. Departures *from* London as for Gloucester. Departures *for* London about 4 times daily. Pop. 445.
Map Square 22.

HARKER (Cumberland)

303½ miles. No through fares. Departures *from* London as for Carlisle. Departures *for* London about 3 times daily.
Map Square 3.

HARLECH (Merioneth)

from *Paddington*, *via* Ruabon, 244½ miles. Fares, 50/10*a*, 30/6*c*. R. T. for two months, 101/8*a*. Pop. 1,006.
Map Square 16.

PAD.	HARLECH	HARLECH	PAD.
AM 9.10*r*	4. 5	AM 7. 5*r*	2. 5
10.20*r*	5. 1	9.45*r*	5. 0
10.40*r*	5.32	11. 6*r*	6.40
PM12.50*r*	8. 2	PM12.47*r*	8. 5
2.10*t*	9.23	1.59*r*	10. 0
12.15*h*	12.46	4.56	3.30
—	—	—	—
—	—	—	—

No Sunday Trains.

h Saturday midnight excepted.
r Restaurant Car.
t Tea Car.

ANOTHER ROUTE from *Euston*, 267 miles. Fares as above.

EUSTON	HARLECH	HARLECH	EUSTON
AM 5. 0*h*	2.51	AM 7. 5*r*	3.10
10. 0*r*	6. 4	8.58	5.50
10.40*r*	8. 2	11.26*dr*	9.15
PM 9.30	8. 6	11.26*er*	9.20
—	—	PM 4.56	5. 0
—	—	—	—
—	—	—	—

Sunday Trains.

PM 9.15	8. 6	—	—
—	—	—	—
—	—	—	—
—	—	—	—

d Saturdays only.
e Saturdays excepted.
h *Via* Crewe.
r Restaurant Car.

Castle Hotel. First-class Family Hotel. Overlooking celebrated Royal St. David's Golf Links. Moderate Tariff. *See* also Dolgelley, Llandudno, Rhyl.

HARLESDEN (Middlesex)

from *Euston*, 6 miles. Fares, 1/3*a*, 0/9*c*. R. T. for two days, 2/2½*a*, 1/5½*c*. From Broad Street, 1/2*a*, 0/8½*c*. R. T. for two days, 2/4*a*, 1/5*c*. Pop. 16,711. *See* pp. 496-499.

ANOTHER ROUTE (Bakerloo Tube). *See* back of Map.

HARLESTON (Norfolk)

from *Liverpool Street*, *via* Tivetshall, 107 miles. Fares, 22/4*a*, 13/5*c*. R. T. for two months, 44/8*a*. Pop. 209.
Map Square 19.

L'PL.ST.	HARLST'N	HARLST'N	L'PL.ST.
AM 5. 0	9.43	AM 6.57*r*	10.30
10.12	1.57	9.43	1.20
PM12.33*r*	6. 5	PM 1. 0*r*	4.58
5.18*ehr*	8.41	3.47	7.51
5.18*dr*	8.46	6.40	11.16
—	—	—	—
—	—	—	—
—	—	—	—

No Sunday Trains.

d Saturdays only.
e Saturdays excepted.
h *Via* Forncett.
r Restaurant Car.

HARLESTON—*contd.*

ANOTHER ROUTE *via* Beccles, 122½ miles. Fares as above.

L'pl.St.	Harlst'n	Harlst'n	L'pl.St.
AM 5. 0	9.44	AM 8. 3r	11.30
8.15r	1. 0	9.42r	2. 3
10.20	3.47	PM 1.57	5.55
PM 3.15r	6.40	3.12	7.51
3.18r	7.52	6. 5r	10. 0

No Sunday Trains.

r Restaurant Car.

HARLING ROAD

(Norfolk) from *Liverpool Street*, 101¼ miles. Fares, 20/8*a*, 12/5*c*. R. T. for two months, 41/4*a*. *Map Square* 19.

L'p'l.St.	Har. R.	Har. R.	L'p'l.St.
AM 5. 5	7.57	AM 7.25r	10.23
5.50	9.46	8.23	11.27
8.30hr	11.39	9.39	12.40
11.50r	3.18	11.19r	2.21
PM 2.34	5.58	PM 2. 7r	5.17
5.49r	8.48	5.14r	8.22
—	—	11.17	2.50

Sunday Trains.

AM 9.25	12.53	PM 3.21	6.40
PM 3.25	6.43	11.19	3. 0

h Tuesdays, Wednesdays and Saturdays only.

r Restaurant Car.

HARLINGTON

(Beds) from *St. Pancras*, 37 miles. Fares, 7/9*a*, 4/8*c*. R. T., double fare. Pop. 609. *Map Square* 18.

St. Pan.	Harling.	Harling.	St. Pan.
AM 6.25	7.57	AM 6.59	8.28
8.25	9.27	8. 1	9.13
9.25d	10.48	8.57	10. 5
11. 0r	12.16	PM12.18r	1.20
11.35d	12.46	2.21	3.25
PM12.30	1.38	3.13d	5.10
1.33d	2.49	5.15	6.30
3.35	4.52	6.53	8.20
4.40	5.58	8.55	10. 5
5.40e	6.39	10.30	11.45
6.35	7.47	—	—
7.50	9. 5	—	—
8.25d	10.40	—	—

Sunday Trains.

AM 8. 0	9.38	AM 8.28	10.15
PM 4.35	6. 9	PM 7.12	8.30

d Saturdays only.
e Saturdays excepted.
r Restaurant Car

HARLOW

(Essex), from *Liverpool Street*, 24½ miles. Fares, 5/3*a*, 3/2*c*. R. T. for two months, 10/6*a*. Pop. 2,962. *Map Square* 24.

L'p'l. St.	Harlow	Harlow	L'p'l. St.
AM 5.50	6.47	AM 1.54	2.50
7.18	8.28	7.10	8.18
9.10	10.23	7.43	8.49
10.34	12.13	7.56	8.57
PM12.29d	1. 8	8.48	9.42
12.40d	1.37	9.41	10.17
12.48e	2. 0	10. 3	10.59
1.19d	2.13	11. 6	12.15
2. 0d	2.56	PM 1. 8	2. 7
2.48	3.49	2.27d	3.18
4.15	4.55	3.54	5. 9
5.10	6. 5	5.57	7.19
6. 0e	6.49	6.54	7.58
6.30	7.19	8.18	9.33
7.41d	8.36	10.13	11.12
7.41e	8.39	—	—
9.17	10.26	—	—
11.50k	12.43	—	—

Sunday Trains.

AM 8.12	9. 4	AM 1.54	3. 0
9.25	10.20	8. 1	9.33
PM 1.50	3.14	10.18	11.27
4.50	6. 5	PM 8. 4	9.10
7.15	8.11	9.32	10.40
9.12	10.20	—	—

d Saturdays only.

e Saturdays excepted.

k Wednesdays and Saturdays only.

HARMSTON

(Lincoln), 124¼ miles. Fares, 25/8*a*, 15/5*c*. R. T., double fare. Departures *from* London as for Lincoln. Departures *for* London about 6 times daily. Pop. 277. *Map Square* 13.

HAROLD WOOD

(Essex) from *Liverpool Street*, 15 miles. Fares, 3/2*a*, 2/6*b*, 1/11*c*. R. T. for two months, 6/4*a*, 5/0*b*, 3/6*c*. Pop. 1,757. *See* pp. 528-534. *Map Square* 24.

HARPENDEN

(Herts) from *St. Pancras*, 24½ miles. Fares, 5/2*a*, 3/1*c*. R. T., double fare. Pop. 6,738. *Map Square* 23.

St.Pan.	Harp'd'n	Harp'd'n	St.Pan.
AM 4.25	5.30	AM 6.32	7.37
6. 0	7. 8	7.12	8.15
6.25	7.25	7.47	8.28
7.50	8.33	8.10	8.45
8. 0	8.52	8.36	9.13
8.50	9.50	8.48	9.32h
9.55	11. 7	9.10	9.50
11.35	12.22	9.27	10. 5
PM12.33	1.40	9.51	10.31
12.42d	1.25	11.27	12. 5
1. 8	1.50	PM12. 9	1. 3
1.33d	2.22	12.32d	1.55
2.15	3. 7	1.42	2.52
3.35	4.23	2.28	3.10

HARPENDEN—*contd.*

St.Pan.	Harp'd'n	Harp'd'n	St.Pan.
PM 4.40	5.32	PM 3.26	4.33
5. 5	5.51	4. 7	5.10
5.20e	6. 1	4.42	5.20
5.45e	6.30	5.44	6.30
6.35	7.18	6.24	7. 3
6.45e	7.35	7.25	8.42
7.50	8.35	8.18	8.57
8.25	9.10	9.47	10.48
10. 5	10.47	11. 0	11.45
10.35	11.34	—	—
12. 0	12.45	—	—

Sunday Trains.

AM 8. 0	9. 8	AM 9. 5	10.15
PM12.50	1.53	PM12.19	1.30
1.35	2.27	2.51	3.56
3. 0	4. 3	5.10	6.15
4.35	5.38	7.15	8.20
5.40	6.39	7.45	8.30
8.25	9.10	10.25	11. 7
11.55	12.39	—	—

d Saturdays only.
e Saturdays excepted.
h Arrives at King's Cross (Met. Station).

ANOTHER ROUTE from *King's Cross*, 27½ miles. Fares as above. Departures *from* London as for Wheathamstead. Departures *for* London about 6 times daily.

HARPERLEY

(Durham), 252¼ miles. No through fares. Departures *from* London as for Bishop Auckland. Departures *for* London about 5 times daily. *Map Square* 7.

HARRIETSHAM

(Kent) from *Victoria, Holborn Viaduct*, and *St. Paul's*, 47¼ miles. Fares, 10/2*a*, 8/1*b*, 6/0*c*. R. T. for two months, 20/4*a*, 16/2*b*. Departures *from* London as for Lenham. Departures *for* London about 7 times daily. Pop. 722. *Map Square* 24.

HARRINGAY

(Middlesex) from *King's Cross, Moorgate Street*, and *Broad Street*. 3½ miles. Fares from King's Cross, 0/7½*a*, 0/6*b*, 0/4½*c*. R. T. for two days, 1/3*a*, 1/0*b*, 0/9*c*. From Moorgate Street and Broad Street, 0/9*a*, 0/7*b*, 0/5½*c*. R. T. for two days, 1/6*a*, 1/2*b*, 0/10½*c*. Pop. 21,921. *See* pp. 511-517. *Map Square* 52.

HARRINGAY PARK

(Middlesex) from *Moorgate Street* and *St. Pancras*, 4½ miles. Fares, 0/10*a*, 0/6*c*. R.T. for two days, 1/8*a*, 0/10½*c*. *See* pp. 506-507. *Map Square* 52.

HARRINGTON

(Cumberland), 307¾ miles. Fares, 63/11*a*, 38/4*c*. R.T. for two months, 127/10*a*. Departures *from* London as for Whitehaven. Departures *for* London about 6 times daily. Pop. 4,373. *Map Square* 6.

HARRINGWORTH

(Northampton) from *St. Pancras*, 85 miles. Fares, 17/4*a*, 10/5*c*. R. T., double fare. Departures *from* London as for Weldon. Departures *for* London about 4 times daily. Pop. 257.
Map Square 18.

HARROGATE (Yorks)

from *King's Cross*, 198¼ miles *via* Holbeck. Fares, 41/3*a*, 24/9*c*. R.T. for two months, 82/6*a*, 49/6*c*. Pop. 38,938.
Map Square 7.

King's+	Har'g'te	Har'g'te	King's+
AM 4.45	10.44	AM 6.25*r*	11.30
7.15*r*	12. 5	7.55	1. 5
10.10*r*	2.45	8.25*kr*	1.15
11.15*g*	3.15	9.35*r*	1.55
11.30*k*	5.39	11.15*g*	3.15
PM 1.40*r*	6.10	PM12.30*r*	5. 0
1.50*kr*	7. 4	12.46*kr*	6.15
4. 0*r*	8.57	2.30*r*	7.10
5.45*r*	10.20	4.45*r*	9.25
10.45*e*	6.22	5. 2*kr*10. 0	
10.45*d*	8. 3	9.47	3.25
—	—	—	—

Sunday Trains.

12. 0*nr*	5:15	AM 8.10*k*	5.15
PM10.45	6.22	10.32	5.55
—	—	PM 9. 0*l*	5.40
—	—	—	—
—	—	—	—
—	—	—	—

d Saturdays only.
e Saturdays excepted.
g First and Third Class Pullman Cars only.
k Via York.
l Via York and Leeds (New Station).
n Noon.
r Restaurant Car.

ANOTHER ROUTE from *St. Pancras*, 210¼ miles. Fares as above.

St.Pan.	Har'g'te	Har'g'te	St.Pan.
AM 2.59*g*	10.10	AM 6.25*r*	12.10
4.25	10.58	7.25*r*	1.45
9. 0*r*	2.13	8.58*r*	2.10
9.50*r*	2.42	9.30*r*	4.10
11.45*r*	4.50	PM12. 3*r*	5.30
PM12.15*r*	5.10	12.47*r*	6.35
1.50*r*	7.55	3. 5*r*	7.57
3.30*r*	8.57	3.21*r*	9.15
5. 0*r*	10.13	9. 4	4.20
11.45*e*	6.22	9.47 .	7.25
11.50*d*	8. 3	—	—

Sunday Trains.

AM10.50*r*	6. 3	AM10.32	5.27
PM11.45	6.22	PM 9. 0	4.55
—	—	—	—
—	—	—	—
—	—	—	—

d Saturdays only.
e Saturdays excepted.
g Mondays excepted. ₄
r Restaurant Car.

Harrogate Handbook and List of Attractions, &c. Free from F. J. C. Broome, V.B.I. Dept., Harrogate.
See advt. on Map.

Queen Hotel. Standing in own grounds of five acres, facing Stray.
F. H. FOGG, Manager.
See advt. p. **196.**

HARROGATE—*continued.*

Hotel Majestic. Finest Spa Hotel in the world. Private grounds of ten acres. Cuisine and service par excellence. Commodious Garage. Telegrams: "Majestic, Harrogate." Telephone: 811 Harrogate.
FREDERICK HOTELS, LTD.
See advt. p. **197.**

The Harrogate (Swan) Hydropathic. 300 Guests. Five acres of ground.
See advt. p. **198.**

White Hart Hotel. Most Central. Near Wells, Baths, Royal Hall. Facing Stray. Magnificent Lounge. Telephone 435.
MANAGERESS.
See advt. p. **198.**

George Hotel. Family. 150 Rooms. Opposite Baths. Lift. Garage. Telephone 633. Moderate Tariff.
C. E. NORRIS ROBERTSON, Manager.
See advt. p. **199.**

Crown Hotel. Adjoining Pump Room and Royal Baths. Electric Light. Lift. Heated throughout. Tele. 1086. Full particulars sent on application to—
F. R. WHITTAKER, Manager.
See advt. p. **199.**

Cairn Hydro. Finest position. Accommodation 300. Ballroom with Spring Floor. Orchestra. Centrally heated. Telephone 58.
See advt. p. **200.**

Alexandra Hotel. Facing Stray. Three minutes from Pump Room. Lift. Telephone 426.
See advt. p. **200.**

Prospect Hotel. Finest position. Near Baths and Wells. 100 Rooms. Facing Stray. Private Suites. Restaurant Orchestra. Lift. Telephone 1035.
See advt. p. **201.**

Harlow Manor Hydro. In own grounds of seven acres. Healthiest situation. Garage. Lift. Ball Room Orchestra. Entertainments Motor Bus. Tel. 1203.
See advt. p. **201.**

Royal Hotel. Old-Established Family Hotel. Facing Stray. Noted for comfort and excellent cuisine. Very moderate terms.
J. CONNOR, Resident Proprietor.
See advt. p. **202.**

Wellington Hotel. Two minutes to Pump Room. Lift. Tennis. Telephone 257.
Mrs. STOKES, Manageress.
See advt. p. **202.**

Prince of Wales Hotel. Best position in Harrogate. Overlooking Stray. Facing South. Private Suites with Baths. Moderate Terms. Telegrams, "Elegance," Harrogate. Telephone No. 789.
For Tariff apply Manager.

HARROGATE—*continued.*

Stray Hotel, Harrogate. 200 yards from Baths, &c. Central position. Perfect cuisine. Tel. 943-944.
See advt. p. **195.**

Clarendon Hotel. Moderate Size. Facing Stray. Garage.
PROPRIETRESS.
See advt. p. **195.**

The Granby. First - class Residential Hotel, facing Stray. Tennis Ground adjoins Hotel, grass and red hard Courts. Three Golf Links within easy access. Terms moderate.
'Phone 626. Apply—
Mrs. HODGSON, Manageress.

The Cecil. Private Hotel. Overlooking Gardens. Near Pump Room and Baths. Recently enlarged and redecorated. 50 Bedrooms. All Public Rooms face the Gardens. Inclusive terms from 10/6 per day. Central heating throughout. 'Phone 438.
MANAGERESS.

St. Heliers Superior Boarding Establishment. Best position. Few minutes from Pump Room. Baths. Telephone 1132.

Spa Hydro. Central, overlooking Royal Hall Gardens. One minute Baths. Spacious public rooms. Terms from 10/0 per day inclusive.
PROPRIETRESS.

HARROW AND WEALD-

STONE (Middlesex) from *Euston*, 11¼ miles. Fares, 2/1*a*, 1/3*c*. R. T. for two days, 3/4½*a*, 2/0½*c*. Pop. (Wealdstone) 13,433. *See* pp. 496-499.
Map Squares 23 and 48.

ANOTHER ROUTE from *Broad Street, via* Willesden Junction, 15¼ miles. Fares, 2/3½*a*, 1/4½*c*. R. T. for two days, 3/9½*a*, 2/4*c*. *See* pp. 496-499.

ANOTHER ROUTE (Bakerloo Tube). *See* back of Map.

HARROW-ON-THE-HILL

from *Baker Street*, 9½ miles. Fares, 1/10½*a*, 1/1½*c*. R. T. for two days, 2/11*a*, 2/0½*c*. Pop. 19,469. *See* back of Map.

ANOTHER ROUTE from *Marylebone,* 9½ miles. Fares as from *Baker Street. See* pp. 494, 495.

HARROW NORTH from

Baker Street, 10½ miles. Fares, 2/2½*a*, 1/4*c*. R. T. for two days, 3/6*a*, 2/4*c*. *See* pp. 494, 495.

ANOTHER ROUTE from *Marylebone,* 10½ miles. Fares as from *Baker Street. See* pp. 494, 495.

HARROGATE.—PRINCE OF WALES HOTEL. *Overlooking Stray.* FACING SOUTH.

HARROW SOUTH from

Mansion House, 15¼ miles. See p. 489.
Map Square 48.

ANOTHER ROUTE from

Marylebone, 8¾ miles. Fares, 1/10½*a*, 1/1½*c*. R. T. for two days, 2/11*a*, 2/0½*c*. *See* pp. 495, 496.

HARROW WEST from

Baker Street, 10¼ miles. Fares, 2/0½*a*, 1/3*c*. R. T. for two days, 3/2½*a*. 2/2½*c*. Departures *from* London as for Uxbridge. Departures *for* London 15 minutes later.
Map Square 48.

HARSTON (Cambs) from

King's Cross, 52¾ miles. Fares, 11/0*a*, 6/7*c*. R. T. for two months, 22/0*a*. Pop. 671.
Map Square 18.

King's+	Harston	Harston	King's+
AM 7. 0	9.20	AM 7.44	9.34
8.45	10.31	9.27*k*	11.15
11.30	1.32	9.27*h*	11.25
PM 3. 0	4.33	11. 9	1.25
5. 0	6.37	PM 1.45	3.50
7. 0	8.49	4.14	6. 0
—	—	8. 3	10.20
—	—	—	—
—	—	—	—

Sunday Trains.

AM 8.30	10.40	AM 7.29	9.53
—	—	PM 5.35	8. 8
—	—	—	—
—	—	—	—
—	—	—	—

h Tuesdays excepted.
k Tuesdays only.

HART (Durham), 250¼ miles.

No through fares. Departures *from* London as for West Hartlepool. Departures *for* London about 5 times daily. Pop. 276.
Map Square 8.

HARTFIELD (Sussex) from

Victoria, Cannon Street, and *London Bridge*, 37 miles. Fares, 6/8*a*, 4/0*c*. R. T. for six months, 13/4*a*, 8/0*c*. Pop. 1,628.
Map Square 24.

Vict.	Leave Can. St.	Lon. B.	Arr. at Hartf'd
AM 5.30*h*	—	5.18*h*	7.31
6.37	—	6.40	8.31
7.23	—	8. 7	9.47
9.10	—	9. 6	10.55
12. 0	—	11.50	1.42
PM —	—	12.50*d*	2.15
1.20*e*	—	—	3.13
1.25*d*	—	1.10*d*	3.13
—	—	*d*1.38*h*	3.37
3.45*h*	—	—	5. 9
4. 0	—	4.10	5.44
4.50*h*	—	*e*4.44*h*	6.28
5.48	—	5.41*e*	7.14
6. 6	—	6. 8	8.15
7.15	—	7.38	9.15

Sunday Trains.

AM 8.18	—	8.30	10.13
PM 2.30*h*	—	—	6. 2
6.33	—	6.46	9.16
—	—	—	—
—	—	—	—
—	—	—	—

HARTFIELD—*continued.*

Trains from Hartfield.

Leave Hartf'd	Lon. B.	Arr. at Can. St.	Vict.
AM 7.31	9. 1*k*	9. 4	9. 8
7.56	9.32	—	9.40
8.51	10. 7	—	—
9.12	10.55	—	10.48
10. 6	—	—	11.35
10.55*h*	12.44	—	12.35
11.37	1.42	—	1.26
PM 1.42*h*	4. 0	—	3.45
2.36	4.32	—	4.35
3.37	5.21	—	5.55
5. 9	7.42	—	7.45
5.44*h*	7.56	—	—
6.28	8.46	—	8.27
8.15*h*	—	—	10.10
8.42	10.25	—	11.17
—	—	—	—

Sunday Trains.

AM 7.32	10.18	—	10.32
10.13*h*	—	—	1.40
PM 6. 2	7.56	—	8.41
—	—	—	—
—	—	—	—

d Saturdays only.
e Saturdays excepted.
h Via Groombridge.
k Departs from or arrives at London Bridge S.E. & C. station.

Taxi Cabs can be hired to meet any train at this station by letter, or telephone No. Coleman's Hatch 5, Messrs. Charles Elcock, Motor Works.

HARTFORD (Cheshire)

from *Euston*, 170 miles. Fares, 35/5*a*, 21/3*c*. R. T. for two months, 70/10*a*. Pop. 883.
Map Square 12.

Euston	Hartf'd	Hartf'd	Euston
AM 2.35	6.34	AM 8.41*er*	12. 5
5. 0	9.34	8.41*dr*	12.20
6.45	11.40	9. 8*r*	1. 0
8.30*r*	12.23	10. 3*r*	1.45
11.50*r*	3.29	11.11*r*	3.10
PM 1.30*r*	5.36	PM 1.59*r*	5.50
2.35*t*	6.10	3.29*er*	7.30
4. 5*r*	7.45	5.32*er*	9. 5
5.20*r*	9.21	5.32*dr*	9.15
11.50*d*	7.50	6.15*r*	10. 0
—	—	8. 7*e*	5. 0
—	—	10.48*d*	5. 0
—	—	—	—

Sunday Trains.

AM 9.15	2.47	AM 11. 1	4. 0
11.45*r*	3.33	PM 3.38*r*	7.30
PM 3.50	9.12	—	—
6. 0*r*	9.48	—	—
—	—	—	—
—	—	—	—

d Saturdays only.
e Saturdays excepted.
r Restaurant Car.
t Tea Car

HARTFORD AND GREENBANK (Cheshire), 173¼

miles. Fares, 35/5*a*, 21/3*c*. R. T. for two months, 70/10*a*, 42/6*c*. Departures *from* London as for Northwich. Departures *for* London about 3 times daily.
Map Square 12.

HARTINGTON (Derby),

158¾ miles from *Euston*. Fares, 32/9*a*, 19/8*c*. R. T. double fare. Departures *from* London as for Ashbourne. Departures *for* London about 4 times daily. Pop. 2,484.
Map Square 12.

HARTLEBURY (Worcester)

from *Paddington*, 131¼ miles. Fares, 25/3*a*, 15/2*c*. R. T. for two months, 50/6*a*. Pop. 2,514.
Map Square 17.

Pad.	Hartleb'y	Hartleb'y	Pad.
AM 9.45	1.17	AM 8.17	11.15
PM 1.30*r*	4.16	9.41	2.12
1.35*r*	5. 6	11.25*r*	2.55
4.45*t*	7.37	PM 1.30*r*	4.15
6. 5*r*	9.25	2.30	5.50
—	—	5.25*r*	9.15
—	—	6. 0	10.45
—	—	—	—

Sunday Trains.

AM 10.35*r*	3.14	AM 9.45	2.40
PM 4.10	8.47	PM 5. 8*r*	9.48

r Restaurant Car.
t Tea Car.

HARTLEPOOL (Durham).

See West Hartlepool.

HARTLEY (Northumberland),

279 miles. No through fares. Departures *from* London as for Newcastle-on-Tyne. Departures *for* London about 8 times daily. Pop. 1,688.
Map Square 3.

HARTON ROAD (Salop),

158¾ miles. Fares, 32/4*a*, 19/5*c*. R. T. for two months, 64/8*a*, 38/10*c*. Departures *from* London as for Much Wenlock or Craven Arms. Departures *for* London about 4 times daily.
Map Square 17.

HARTWOOD (Lanark),

392¾ miles. No through fares. Departures *from* London as for Wishaw (Central). Departures *for* London about 4 times daily.
Map Square 40.

HARVINGTON (Worcester),

110½ miles. No through fares. Departures *from* London as for Evesham. Departures *for* London about 4 times daily. Pop. 560.
Map Square 17.

HARWICH (Essex) from

Liverpool Street, 70¾ miles. Fares, 14/10*a*, 8/11*c*. R. T. for two months, 29/8*a*, 17/10*c*. Pop. 13,046.
Map Square 19.

L'pl.St.	Harwich	Harwich	L'pl.St.
AM 5. 0	7.33	AM 7. 5	9.36
6.50	10. 5	8.46	10.58
8.46	11.26	9.55	12.39
10.20	12.46	PM 12.10	3.13
11.30	1.57	1.40	3.43
PM 12.33*r*	2.34	3. 2	5.48
2.15	4.53	4.23	6.32
3.23	5.50	5.34	7.51
5.42	8. 8	7.40*r*	10. 0
7.16	9.32	8.30	11.16
8.40*r*	10.20	—	—
8.45	11. 9	—	—

Sunday Trains.

AM 9.20*r*	11.48	AM 9. 4	11.38
PM 4.40	6.44	PM 4.54	7.10
7.40	10. 7	6. 5	8.58
—	—	7.35	10. 9

r Restaurant Car.

The Great Eastern Hotel.
Under Management of London and North Eastern Railway. Facing Harbour. Fishing, Golf, Yachting. *See* advt. p. **203**.

HARROGATE.—PRINCE OF WALES HOTEL. Private Suites. *Moderate Tariff.*

HASLEMERE (Surrey)

from *Waterloo*, 42½ miles. Fares, 9/0a, 5/5c. R. T. for two months. 18/0a, 10/10c. Pop. 3,865.

Map Square 23.

W'LOO.	HASLE.	HASLE.	W'LOO.
AM 5.50	7.26	AM 6.32	8.20
6.50	8.34	7.15	8.41
7.50	9.41	7.54	9.12
8.34r	10. 0	8.28s	9.44
9.50	11.20	9. 6	10.15
10.50	12.13	9.32	10.50½
11.50d	1.19	10. 7	11.32¾
PM12.20d	1.39	PM12.26r	1.52½
12.50er	2.15	1.31	3. 6
1.50e	3.26	2.49	4.16½
2. 0d	3.35	4.23	5.52
2.34	4.22	5.59	7.46
3.50d	5.19	7.29	9. 6
4.15e	5.36	8.57	10.46
4.50	6. 5	10.19	12.16½
5.24	6.40	—	—
5.50	7. 0	—	—
6.50r	8. 3	—	—
8. 0	9.44	—	—
9.50	11.26	—	—
—	—	—	—

Sunday Trains.

AM 8. 0	9.30	AM 8.49	10.16
8.20	10.12	PM 1.43	3.13
9.15r	10.40	4.43	6.17
PM 1.50	3.29	7.18	8.52
4.20	6. 6	8.30	10. 1
6.20	8. 1	8.53	10.41
8.20	10.12	9.50	11.43
9.30	10.53	—	—
—	—	—	—

d Saturdays only.
e Saturdays excepted.
r Restaurant Car.
s Refreshments served.

The Hindhead Beacon. First-class Hotel (fully licensed). The choicest site on the beautiful Hindhead Hills. Large Lounge. Private Suites. Garage. Stabling. Telephone, 7 Hindhead. *See advt. p. 203.*

Hotel Moorlands. Facing main Portsmouth road, 800 feet above sea level. Finest views in the district. Billiards. Stables. Garage. Telegrams : "Moorlands, Hindhead." Telephone 10. W. BRUSA. *See advt. p. 204.*

Woodside Private Hotel. Facing South. Nearest Links. Tariff on application. Telephone : 68 Hindhead. *See advt. p. 204.*

Lake View Hotel (unlicensed). Close to Links. Telephone : Hindhead 59. *See advt. p. 205.*

Manor Hotel, Hindhead. Up-to-date. 'Phone 31. *See advt. p. 205.*

The Seven Thorns Hotel, Hindhead. Electric Light. Main Water. Latest modern Drainage. Guests and Catering. *See advt. p. 205.*

HASLEMERE—*contd.*

Georgian House Hotel. High-class residential. Recently opened. Newly decorated and furnished. Central Heating. Five minutes Station. 'Phone 268.

Thirlestane Hotel, Hindhead. 850 feet above Sea, overlooking Devil's Punch Bowl. Bracing air. splendid views over valleys. Near Links. Fully Licensed. Telephone: 5 Hindhead. Telegrams: "Crisp," Hindhead.

Thorshill Hotel (First-class Private). Highest residence in Surrey. On famous moorland. Well wooded grounds. Lift. Billiards, Tennis, Croquet. Near Golf Links. South Lounges. Excellent cuisine. Refurnished by Waring's. Central heating. Garage. Thorough comfort and repose. 'Phone 8, Hindhead.

High Croft, Hindhead. Well-appointed Boarding House. Near Links. Large sunny rooms. Lovely views. 'Phone 49 Hindhead. Proprietress, Miss BEALE.

Glen Lea Hotel, Hindhead. 700 feet above sea. Grounds. 5 acres. Home farm. Central heating. Under personal supervision of owner. Telephone 16, Grayshott.—PROPRIETOR.

Oaklands Private Hotel, Haslemere. Beautiful private grounds of over 3 acres. Tennis and Croquet Lawns. Separate Tables. Central Heating. Garage. Five minutes Station, Post and Church. Telephone 266. PROPRIETRESS.

Briarcombe. Lovely Situation, 700 feet. Near moors. Verandah and grounds. Croquet. 10 minutes station. Large Private Sitting Rooms. or Board from £2 12s. 6d. Garage. Electric Light. Central Heating. 'Phone No. 96. PROPRIETRESS.

Thorland's Private Hotel, Haslemere. 750 feet above sea level. South aspect. Near Moors. Beautiful grounds. Croquet. Electric Light. 15 minutes station. Telephone No. 97 Haslemere. Tariff, apply Proprietress— Mrs. BACKWELL.

Lingfield, Hindhead (Pension). Separate Tables. Fine sunny position, nearest Golf Course. Good cuisine. Tennis. Moderate Terms. 'Phone No. 51 Hindhead. Proprietors, Mr. & Mrs. LAURIE.

Grayshott, Fox and Pelican Hotel. Excellent accommodation. Main water supply. R.A.C. and A.C.U. Bracing air. Charming country. P.R.H.A. Free House.

Royal Huts Hotel (Fully Licensed). Excellent Cuisine. Most central position. 'Phone, No. 109 Hindhead. CATERING HOUSES, LTD.

Wilton Hindhead Pension. Charming Situation. Lovely Views. Electric Light. Close Links and Tennis Courts. Motor 'Bus from Haslemere passes door, conveying passengers and luggage. Telegrams: Wilton Hindhead. 'Phone : 111, Hindhead. Proprietress, Miss MANN.

HASLEMERE—*contd.*

Hindhead.—Barna Private Hotel. Open for winter months. Near to Golf Links and Church. 'Busses pass the gates. 'Phone 40 Hindhead. Telegrams : Barna, Hindhead. Proprietresses, Misses HAWKES.

Hindhead. — Brackenhurst, 850 feet above Sea Level. Lovely Gardens. Close Moors, Post Office, Library. Tennis, Garage. Tariff Moderate. Phone 30. PROPRIETRESS.

Hindhead. "Undershaw." Beautifully situated at the head of the lovely Nutcombe Valley. Attractively furnished and well appointed. 'Phone 47. Tariff and full particulars on application to PROPRIETRESS.

Nutcombe Height. Small Private Hotel. Within five minutes walk of Moors. Moderate terms. Telephone: Hindhead 76. Resident PROPRIETRESS.

HASLINGDEN (Lancs)

from *Euston*, 205 miles. Fares, 42/4a, 25/5c. R. T. for two months. 84/8a, 50/10c. Pop. 17,485.

Map Square 12.

EUSTON	HASLDN	HASLDN	EUSTON
AM12.25	6.11	AM 6.11e	12. 5
2.35	9.27	6.11d	12.20
5. 0	11.37	8.37r	1.15
8.45dr	2. 9	9.25r	3.10
8.45er	2.51	10.15er	3.55
10.40er	4. 7	11.58dr	6. 0
11.50r	5.33	11.53er	6. 0
12. 0nr	7.22	PM12.50er	6.15
PM 2.50½	9. 0	1.47r	8.10
4. 5r	10. 9	3. 4er	9. 5
6. 5	11.13	3. 4dr	9.15
11.50e	6.11	4.43dr 10. 0	
11.50d	10.19	4.43er 10.10	
—	—	8.54	5. 0
—	—	10.10e	5.40
—	—	10.10d	5.45

Sunday Trains.

PM12.30r	8. 9	AM 8.12	4. 0
—	—	10.44r	5.45
—	—	PM12.55r	7.30
—	—	8.20	5. 0
—	—	—	—

d Saturdays only.
e Saturdays excepted.
n Noon.
r Restaurant Car.
t Tea Car.

HASSALL GREEN

(Cheshire),156½ miles. No through fares. Departures *from London* as for Stoke-on-Trent. Departures *for London* about 5 times daily. Pop. (Hassall) 301.

HASSENDEAN (Roxburgh), 348¼ miles. Fares, 71/0a, 42/7c. R. T. for two months. 142/0a, 85/2c. Departures *from London* as for Hawick. Departures *for London* about twice daily.

Map Square 41.

HASSOCKS (Sussex)

from *London Bridge*, *Victoria*, and *Clapham Junction*, 43½ miles. Fares, 9/2a, 5/6c.   R. T. for two months, 18/4a, 11/0c.
Map Square 23.

	Leave		Arr. at
Vict.	Clap. J.	Lon. B.	Has'ks
AM —	—	5.18	7.10
6.37	6.44	6.40	8. 2
7.23	7.29	7.25	9.20
9. 0	9. 8	9. 6	10.37
10. 5	10.11	9.50	11.37
10.35	10.42	10.35	12.17
PM12.45	—	12.10	1.59
—	—	1.20d	2.38
2. 0	2. 7	2. 5	3.45
—	—	2. 8d	4.14
3.40	—	—	4.52
—	4. 5	4. 5	5.36
—	—	5. 5d	6.15
4.30	—	5. 8e	6.15
5.45	—	5.55e	7.16
—	—	6. 0d	7.16
6. 6	6.12	6. 8	8. 1
7.15	7.22	7.20	9. 2
8.35	—	—	9.51
9. 3	9.10	9.12	10.49
10. 0	—	—	11.17
10.30	10.38	10.35	12.17

Sunday Trains.

AM 6.55	7. 2	7. 2	9. 4
8.50	8.57	8.55	11. 4
PM 1.14	1.21	1.10	2.54
5.50	5.57	6. 0	7.47
8. 0	8. 8	8. 0	9.43
9. 5	9.13	9.10	10.58

Trains from Hassocks.

Leave	Arrive at		
Has'ks	Lon. B.	Clap. J.	Vict.
AM 6. 7	8.15	8.15	8.24
7.32	8.38	—	—
7.38	8.53	9. 0	9. 8
8.37	9.58	—	—
9.13	—	—	10.24
10.24	12.13	11.59	12. 7
11.47	1.42	1.39	1.50
PM12.44	2.22	2.13	2.22
1.57	3.40	3.37	3.45
2.43	4.32	4. 9	4.17
3.22	5.54	5.47	5.55
4.46	6.36	6.26	6.34
6. 4	7.42	7.21	7.30
6.47	8.46	8.39	8.48
8. 0	10. 0	10. 2	10.10
9. 6	10.58	—	—
9.49	—	11.10	11.17
11.27	12.59	12.50	1. 0

Sunday Trains.

AM 8 47	10.45	10.42	10.50
PM 3. 9	5. 3	5. 1	5.11
6. 1	7.56	8.31	8.41
9.57	11.34	11.34	11.42
10.58	12.27	—	—

d Saturdays only.
e Saturdays excepted.

HASSOP (Derby), 153¼

miles. Fares, 31/10a, 19/1c. R. T., double fare. Departures *from* London as for Bakewell. Departures *for* London about 5 times daily. Pop. 99.
Map Square 12.

HASTINGS (Sussex) from

Charing Cross, Cannon *Street*, and London Bridge, 63 miles. Fares, 12/8a, 10/1b, 7/7c. R. T. for two months, 25/4a, 20/2b. Pop. 66,496.
Map Square 29.

	Leave		Arr. at
	Char. +	Can. St.	Lon. B.	Hast.
AM —	3.40h	3.43h	6. 0
—	5.20	5.25	8.40
—	7.56	8. 0	10.50
8.30d	—	8.37d	10.20
9.25	—	9.33	11.28
10.40	—	10.46	12.34
PM12. 3	—	12.10	2.27
12.40d	—	12.47d	2.38
1. 5d	—	1.11d	3.10
2. 0d	—	2. 5d	3.56
2. 8	—	2.16	4. 4
2.40d	—	2.46d	4.37
3.40	—	—	5.10
3.48e	—	—	5.59
—	5. 4e	—	6.40
5. 5d	—	—	6.49
—	5.12e	—	7.16
6. 3e	—	—	8.22
—	6.16e	6.19e	7.59
7.30	—	—	9.15
9.30	—	9.36	11.25
12. 5y	—	—	1.48

Sunday Trains.

AM 7. 5	—	7.11	9.45
8.45	—	—	10.28
9.50	—	9.56	11.53
11.20	—	—	1. 0
PM 7.10	—	7.20	9.29
7.35	—	7.45	10.15

Trains from Hastings.

Leave		Arrive at	
Hastings	Lon. B.	Can. St.	Char. +
AM 6.55e	8.48	8.52	—
7.36	—	9.15	—
8.10	—	9.48	—
8.30d	10.29	—	10.39
8.55e	10.29	—	10.39
9. 2e	11. 7	—	11.17
9.35y	11.31	—	11.38
9.45	11.43	—	11.57
11. 0	—	—	12.49
PM12.10	3. 6	—	3.19
1.30d	3.19	—	3.27
2.30	4.15	—	4.25
3.15d	5. 0	—	5. 8
3.25d	6.30	—	6.39
4.57	6.40	—	6.49
6.15	8.26	—	8.35
7.10	8.50	—	9. 0
7.40	10.15	—	10.23
8.50	11.35	—	11.44

Sunday Trains.

AM 7. 5	10. 5	—	10.15
9. 5	11.23	—	11.34
PM 5.20	—	—	7. 3
5.30	8.12	—	8.22
7.10	9. 4	—	9.14
8.25	10. 8	—	10.16
8.40	11. 4	—	11.15

d Saturdays only.
e Saturdays excepted.
h Third class only.
y Wednesdays only.

HASTINGS—*continued.*

ANOTHER ROUTE from

London Bridge and *Victoria*, 70½ miles. Fares (First and Third) as above.

	Leave		Arr. at
Vict.	Lon. B.	Hastings
AM —	6.15	8.32
6.37h	6.40h	10.11
9. 0	—	11.20
10. 5	9.50	12.43
11.55	—	2. 2
12. 0	12.10	2.45
PM 1.20e	—	3.50
1.25d	1.10d	3.50
—	2. 0	4.13
3.20	—	5.20
3.40	4. 5	6.27
5.20	5. 5	7.23
5.45e	5.55e	8.30
6.40	—	9. 4
6.50	7. 0	9.34
10.50	10.35	1.27

Sunday Trains.

AM 6.55	7.22	10.20
9.30	9.30	12. 0
PM12.15h	—	3.24
6.33	6.33	10. 0
9.25h	—	12.19½

Trains from Hastings.

Leave	Arrive at	
Hastings.	Lon. B.	Vict.
AM 5.45	8 46	—
6.40	8.53	9. 8
7.45	10. 5	10.12
8.15	10.15	10.24
8.25	10.55	10.56
10.15	12.44	12.45
10.45	—	1.15
11.40	2.22	2.22
PM 1. 0	4. 0	4. 3
2.10	4.32	4.35
2.55h	6.36	6.34
4. 5h	—	7.30
5.12	7.42	7.48
6. 5h	—	8.48
7.30	10. 0	10.10
8. 0	—	11.17
9.30h	12.59	1. 0

Sunday Trains.

AM 6.45	10.18	10.32
9.15h	—	1. 0
PM 4.45	7.56	7.37
5.50	8.34	8.41
7.15	—	10.19
8. 8	10.50	10.45
9.15h	12.27	—

d Saturdays only.
e Saturdays excepted.
h Via Brighton.

ANOTHER ROUTE from

Victoria, *Holborn Viaduct* and *St. Paul's* (*via* Ashford), 63½ miles. Fares, 15/0a, 12/0b, 9/0c. R. T. for two months, 30/0a, 24/0b, 18/0c.

	Leave		Arr. at
	(S.E.&C.)		
Vict.	Hol. V	St. Pl.'s	Hast.
AM —	6.40	6.42	11.47
9.45	—	—	1.41
PM 2.12e	1.24d	1.30d	5. 4
2.40d	—	—	7.12
2.50e	—	—	7.12
2.50h	—	—	7.17
7.22	—	—	10.15

Sunday Trains.

AM 9.35	—	—	12.20
PM 5.15	—	—	8.32
6.35	6.40	—	10.18

HASTINGS.—ROBERTSON PRIVATE HOTEL.   FACING SEA.

HASTINGS—*continued.*

Trains from Hastings.

Leave HASTINGS	Arrive at		
	ST. PL.'s	HOL. V.	VICT.
AM 6.30	9.53	9.55	—
9.10	12.59	1. 2	12.49
PM 12.28	—	—	3.37
2.25	—	—	5.42
3.10	6.58	7. 0	—
7.30	11.43	11.45	—
—	—	—	—

Sunday Trains.

AM 6.40	—	—	10.48
10.20	—	—	1. 5
PM 4.45	—	9. 9	—
—	—	—	—

d Saturdays only.
e Saturdays excepted.
h Fridays only.
l Fridays and Saturdays excepted.

Albany Hotel, Hastings.
Finest situation, facing Gardens
and Sea. No noise from traffic.
First-class Hotel. London Phone,
Museum 3962.
See advt. p. 206.

Sussex Hotel. First-class.
Nearest links. Lift. Tennis.
Garage. Telephone 960 Hastings.
See advt. p. 207.

Royal Victoria Hotel. Leading Hotel. Facing Sea. Suites.
Garage. Terms from 5½ guineas
per week. Tel. 686 Hastings. Telegrams : "Victoria, St. Leonards."
See advt. p. 208.

Yelton Private Hotel. First
Class. Magnificent sea views.
Facing New Bandstand. Garage.
Billiards. Telephone : 614. Tele-
grams : Yelton.
Mr. and Mrs. F. S. BOUQUET
(*née* NOTLEY), Proprietors.
See advt. p. 209.

Robertson Private Hotel.
Central, sea front. Trams at
corner, but not passing hotel.
Full-size Billiard Table. Garage.
Eighty rooms. Personal Super-
vision. Telephone : 543. Tel-
grams : "Comfort."
Mr. & Mrs. H. A. SHIRLEY
(*née* BRUCE), Proprietors.
See advt. p. 211.

Queen's Hotel. Leading and
best. Facing sea. Magnificent
public rooms. Passenger lift and
Private Suites. En pension terms
by arrangement. Telephone 201.
See advt. p. 208.

Medlow. Private Hotel, Evers-
field Place. First Class. Facing
Sea. Perfect Cuisine. Electric
Light. Telephone : 127 Hastings.
See advt. p. 209.

Wilton Hotel, West
Marina. Extensive sea views from
every window. Close Golf and
Station. Terms from 3 guineas.
See advt. p. 210.

Eversfield Hotel, First-class.
Facing Sea. Telephone : 57
Hastings.
See advt. p. 210.

HASTINGS—*continued.*

Alexandra Hotel. First-
class Family. Facing Sea. South.
100 Rooms. Private Suites. A.A.
Inclusive Terms. Telephone :
603 Hastings.
See advt. p. 212.

Stafford Private Hotel.
Close to all amusements. Garage.
Excellent Cuisine. Refurnished.
See advt. p. 213.

St. Leonards-Adelphi
Hotel, Warrior Square. 80 rooms.
Ballroom. Billiards. Tennis.
Garage. Inclusive from 3½ guineas.
Tel. : 622. Telegrams : "Adelphi."
See advt. p. 212.

Cromwell Private Hotel.
Opposite St. Leonards pier. First
class residential hotel. Terms
from 3 guineas. Personal supervision. Telephone 807 Hastings.
Telegram, "Cromwell," St. Leonards-on-Sea.
See advt. p. 211.

Craig-y-Don. High-class
Private Hotel. Near Pier. In-
clusive Terms. Telephone and
Telegrams 448 Hastings.
See advt. p. 213.

Berwyn Private Hotel,
7 & 8, Eversfield Place. Facing
Sea, centre of Promenade. Re-
decorated. Refurnished. Electric
Light. Terms from £3 3s. Tel.
649. Resident Proprietors—
Mr. & Mrs. G. F. STONE.
See advt. p. 213.

Drayton House Hotel.
Centre of Promenade. Passenger
Lift. Bridge Club.
See advt. p. 214.

Priory Mount. Private
Hotel, Holmesdale Gardens.
Beautifully appointed mansion.
See advt. p. 214.

Chatsworth. (Sea Front.)
Private Residential Hotel, Carlisle Parade. Beautifully situated
off tram route. Public Rooms
command fine sea views. Every
comfort. Cuisine a speciality. Garage. Telegrams : Chatsworth
Hotel, Hastings. Telephone :
Hastings 454.
Mr. & Mrs. W. F. BLACKBURNE.

Edinburgh Hotel, Warrior
Square. Facing South and Sea.
Family Hotel. Electric Passenger
Lift. Balconies. Licensed. En
Pension Terms. Telephone 428.

Warrior House Hotel.
Family Hotel. Sunniest position.
South aspect. Balconies facing
Sea. Licensed. Telephone 390.

Carlton Private Hotel (Pension). 10, Warrior Square Terrace.
Best position between piers. Full
sea views. Private Tennis Court.
Sheltered. Electric light throughout. Excellent Cuisine. Modern
comfort. From £3 3s. 0d. per
week. MANAGERESS.

HASTINGS—*continued.*

Cornwallis House, 27-28,
Cornwallis Gardens. High-class
Boarding Establishment. Three
minutes from Station and Sea.
Billiards. Terms moderate.
Telephone 685.
Mrs. MORTLOCK.

Wilberforce Boarding Es-
tablishment. Central position on
sea front. Dining, Drawing and
Smoking Rooms. Facing Sea.
Good English Table. Terms from
2 guineas weekly. Permanent
winter Boarders. Under Personal
supervision of PROPRIETRESS.

Ferrari Bros., 28, Havelock
Road. The Leading Restaurant
of Hastings. Daily Table d'Hote,
Luncheons and Dinners. Also
service a la carte London style.
Fully Licensed. Large Room for
Beanfeast and other Parties.
Menu and prices on application.
'Phone 513.

Glenroyde, 1 and 2, Welling-
ton Square. First-class Board-
ing Establishment. Handsome
Lounge, Dining, Drawing Rooms.
Billiards. Terms from 2½ guineas.
'Phone 780.   Mrs. BOYES.

Grand Restaurant, Oppo-
site Pier. Band. Extension. Fully
Licensed. Spacious Buffet. Lounge.
Tea-Rooms. Luncheons, 2s. 6d.
Dinners, 4s. 6d. Orchestra.
'Phone 847.   R. M. KEY.

Priory Mount, Holmesdale
Gardens, close to Pier. Superb
mansion, with one acre beautiful
gardens. Tennis, Croquet. Newly
furnished. Excellent cuisine.
Personal supervision of Proprietress. From £4 4s. Telephone,
89 Hastings.

Charterhouse Private Ho-
tel, Warrior Square. Finest Sea
position between two Piers. Large
Rooms. Redecorated. Attractive
Amusements. Tennis, &c. Ex-
pert Catering. Best of everything.
Separate tables. Terms from
3 Guineas inclusive. Personal
Supervision. Resident Owners.
Telephone 1137.

H. J. Bohun, F.A.I. Houses
Furnished and Unfurnished.
Shops and businesses of all kinds,
to let and for sale. Selected Lists.
11, Havelock Road, Hastings.
Telephone 27x.

Thomas Bradford & Co.,
Hastings and St. Leonards Steam
Laundry, Bulverhythe Road, St.
Leonards-on-Sea. *See adv.* on Map.

HASWELL (Durham), 252
miles. Fares, 52/8a, 31/7c. R. T.,
double fare. Departures *from*
London as for West Hartlepool or
Sunderland. Departures *for* London about 6 times daily. Pop.
5,860.
Map Square 7.

HASTINGS. — CHATSWORTH.   PRIVATE HOTEL.
(See advt. above.)

HATCH (Somerset) from *Paddington*, 144½ miles. Fares, 29/10a, 17/11c. R.T. for two months, 59/8a. Departures *from* London as for Ilminster. Departures *for* London about 6 times daily. Pop. 356.
Map Square 22.

HATCH END (Middlesex) from *Euston* and *Broad Street*, 13½ miles. Fares from Euston, 2/6a, 1/6c. R. T. for two days, 4/8a, 2/7½c. Fares from Broad Street, 2/9a, 1/8c. R. T. for two days, 4/11½a, 3/1c. *See* pp. 496 409.

ANOTHER ROUTE (Bakerloo Tube). *See* back of Map.

HATFIELD (Herts) from *King's Cross*, 17¾ miles. Fares, 3/7a, 2/2c. R. T., double fare. Pop. 9,072. *See* pp. 511-517.
Map Square 23.

Red Lion Hotel. First Class. Lock-up Garage. Parties catered for. Redecorated throughout. Electric Light. Appointed R.A.C. Telephone: 53.
A. WARD.

HATFIELD PEVEREL (Essex) from *Liverpool Street*, 36 miles. Fares, 7/9a, 4/8c. R. T. for two months, 15/6a. Pop. 1,502.
Map Square 24.

	L'pl. St.	H.Pev.		H.Pev.	L'pl. St.
AM	5. 0	6. 5	AM	7.47	8.52
	6.50	8.21		8.19	9.30
	8.46	9.59		9.28	10.22
	10.47	12. 6		10.21	11.16
PM	1.33d	2.42		11.58	1.16
	2.15	3.13	PM	1.59	3.13
	3.26	4.42		2.22h	3.36
	4.18	5.24		4.38	5.47
	5.42d	6.50		6.15	7.40
	5.42e	6.54		7.55	9.17
	6.39	7.43		—	—
	7.16	8.15		—	—
	8.54	10.13		—	—

Sunday Trains.

AM	7. 4	8.49	AM	8.16	10.25
	10.45	12. 6		9.52	11.15
PM	3.40	4.46		11. 6	12.40
	3.45	5. 5	PM	1.52	3.15
	6.15	7.33		6.47	8.39
	7.40	8.43		8.40	10.22
	8.46	10. 8		—	—

d Saturdays only.
e Saturdays excepted.
h Fridays only.

HATHERN (Leicester) from *St. Pancras*, 114½ miles. Fares, 23/4a, 14/0c. R. T., double fare. Pop. 1,209.
Map Square 18.

	St. Pan.	Hath.		Hath.	St. Pan.
AM	2.25	7. 1	AM	6.30r	9.57
	4.25	8.11		7.55r	11. 0
	8.25r	11.33		9. 0r	11.35
	10.25r	1.10		10.39r	1.30
PM	12.25r	3.26		11.21r	2.10
	2.25r	5. 4	PM	1. 6r	4.20
	4.25r	7.15		2.58r	5.45
	6.25r	9. 7		5. 7r	7.55
	—	—		6.11r	9.15
	—	—		10. 9	4.20

Sunday Trains.

PM	1.35	5.18	AM	7.52	11.53
	6.15r	9.20	PM	5.46r	9.52
	—	—		9.28	4.55

r Restaurant Car.

HATHERSAGE (Derby) from *St. Pancras*, 161 miles. Fares, 33/4a, 20/0c. R. T. for two months, 66/8a, 40/0c. Pop. 1,624.
Map Square 12.

	St. Pan.	Hather.		Hather.	St. Pan.
AM	2.25	8.24	AM	8.11r	12.10
	4.25	11.17		9.12r	1.45
	9. 0r	1. 5		10.34r	4.10
	9.50kr	2.49	PM	1.17r	7.15
	9.50r	3. 2		2.37dr	7.15
PM	1.50r	6. 0		3.18r	7.55
	3.30r	7.38		3.32dr	7.55
	5. 0r	9.11		10.27	4.20
	6.15er	10.33		—	—
	6.15dr	11.11		—	—
	12. 0h	9.16		—	—

Sunday Trains.

AM	10.50r	6.47	AM	10.28	5.27
	—	—	PM	8.33	4.55

d Saturdays only
e Saturdays excepted.
h Saturday midnights only.
k Thursdays and Saturdays only.
r Restaurant Car.

HATTON (Aberdeen), 550½ miles. Fares, 105/8a, 63/5c. R. T. for two months, 211/4a, 126/10c. Departures *from* London as for Cruden Bay. Departures *for* London about 3 times daily. Pop. 299.
Map Square 35

HATTON (Warwick) from *Paddington*, 93½ miles. Fares, 19/5a, 11/8c. R. T. for two months, 38/10a. Pop. 1,524.
Map Square 17.

	Pad.	Hatton		Hatton	Pad.
AM	5.30	9.28	AM	7.30r	10. 0
	6.30	10.23		9. 8r	11. 0
	9.10	11. 3		11. 4r	1.25
	10.40	12.33	PM	12.11r	2. 5
PM	12.50r	2.46		2.52r	5. 0
	2.10	4.19		3.56t	5.55
	4.10t	6. 8		4.24	7.20
	6.10r	8. 3		5.52r	8. 5
	7.10r	9. 3		7.37	10. 0
	7.30	10. 8		10.22	3.30
	12.15k	7.30		—	—
	12.15l	9. 8		—	—

Sunday Trains.

AM	10.35	1.38	AM	11.24r	1.40
PM	6. 0r	8.29	PM	2.32	6.20
	—	—		5.57r	9. 0

k Saturdays midnight excepted.
l Saturdays midnight only.
r Restaurant Car.
t Tea Car.

HAUGHLEY (Suffolk) from *Liverpool Street*, 83 miles. Fares, 17/6a, 10/6c. R. T. for two months, 35/0a. Pop. 828.
Map Square 19.

	L'pl. St.	Haugh.		Haugh.	L'pl. St.
AM	5. 0	7.24	AM	8. 3r	10.30
	10.12	12.45		8.57r	11.22
	10.20	12.53		9.57	12.39
PM	12.33r	2.58		11.41r	2. 3
	3.10r	5.15	PM	12.36	3.36
	3.26	6.49		2.33r	4.58
	5.18r	7.44		3.20	5.55
	5.42	8.48		3.57	6.32
	7.45r	10.26		5. 7	7.51
	—	—		6. 3r	9.22
	—	—		7.33r	10. 0
	—	—		8.18	11.16

Sunday Trains.

AM	9.20r	12. 7	AM	8.30	11.38
	11.30r	2.58	PM	2.25	7.10
PM	4.40	7. 0		6.40r	9.10
	—	—		7.38	10.15

r Restaurant Car.

HAUGHTON (Stafford), 137½ miles. Fares, 28/7a, 17/2c. R. T. for two months, 57/2a, 34/4c. Departures *from* London as for Stafford. Departures *for* London about 3 times daily. Pop. 507.
Map Square 17.

HAVANT (Hants) from *London Bridge*, *Victoria*, and *Clapham Junction*, 77¾ miles. Fares, 13/11a, 8/4c. R. T. for two months, 27/10a, 16/8c. Pop. 4,405.
Map Square 28.

	Leave Vict.	Leave Clap. J.	Leave Lon. B.	Arr. at Havant
AM	6.18	6.25	6.35	9.13
	8.55	7.56	—	11.47
	10.15	10.22	10.22	12.43
	11.55k	—	11.50k	3. 5
PM	1.40	1.47e	1.50	4.11
	1.55k	2.2ek	2. 5k	5.42
	3.55	4. 2	4. 0	6.23
	—	—	4.50	6.47
	4.53	5. 0	—	7.17
	—	—	5. 5	8.11
	—	—	5. 8e	8.11
	5.45k	—	6. 0k	8.40
	7.20	7.27	7.15	10.13

Sunday Trains.

AM	6.55k	7. 2k	7. 2k	11.17
	9. 0	9. 7	8.55	11.38
	9.55	—	—	11.53
PM	1.14k	1.21k	1.10k	5.20
	7. 0	7. 7	6.38	9.48

YELTON PRIVATE HOTEL. (See advt. front of Guide), HASTINGS.

HAVANT—*continued.*

Trains from Havant.

Leave Havant	Lon. B.	Clap. J.	Vict.
AM 6.46g	9.50	—	9.22
6.51f	9.50	—	—
7. 9	—	—	10.28
7.35	9.58	—	—
8.15	10.45	10.45	10.53
8.58	10.55	—	—
9.45	12. 8	—	12. 0
11.15	—	—	1.10
11.53	3.32	3.22	3.32
PM 2.12	4.27	4.26	4.34
3.14	—	5. 4	5.12
3.47	—	—	6.50
5.10	7.48	7.31	7.39
5.56	—	8.39	8.33
6.56d	10. 0	9.37	9.45
7.35	10. 8	9.53	10. 1
9.15k	12.59	12.50	1. 0

Sunday Trains.

AM 7. 7	10.45	10.23	10.32
9.21k	—	12.49	1. 0
PM 3.48k	—	—	7. 0
5.18	—	7.49	7.56
6.12	8.50	8.33	8.42
7.36k	11.34	10.46	10.55

d Saturdays only.
e Saturdays excepted.
f Mondays only.
g Mondays excepted.
k Via Hove.
p First and Third Class Pullman Car only.

ANOTHER ROUTE from

Waterloo 66 miles. Fares, 13/11a, 8/4c. R.T. for two months, 27/10a, 16/8c.

W'loo.	Havant	Havant	W'loo.
AM 5.50	8.21	AM 6.57	9.12
6.50	9.25	7.27s	9.44
8.34r	10.45	8. 7r	9.52
9.50	12.10	8.28	10.50
10.50	12.55	9. 9	11.32
11.50d	2. 6	11.28r	1.52
PM 1.50e	4.16	PM12.32	3. 6
2. 0d	4.23	1.51	4.16
2.34	5.12	3.23	5.52
3.50d	6.13	4.58	7.46
4.15e	6.29	6.29	9. 6
4.50	6.55	7.57	10.46
5.50	7.35	9.22	12.16
6.50er	9. 8	—	—
6.50dr	9.20	—	—
9.50	12.13	—	—

Sunday Trains.

AM 8.20	11. 2	AM 7.52	10.16
9.15r	11.27	PM12.44	3.13
PM 1.50	4.17	3.40r	6.17
4.20	7.18	6.26	8.52
9.30	11.40	7.44	10. 1

d Saturdays only.
e Saturdays excepted.
r Restaurant Car.
s Refreshments served.

The Bear. Commercial and Family. First-class accommodation. Cabs and Carriages meet all trains. Posting and Stabling. Wines and Spirits. Wholesale and Retail. Motor Garage. National Telephone No. 050.
L. F. MORRIS, Proprietor.

HAVEN HOUSE (Lincoln) from *King's Cross*, 128¼ miles. Fares, 26/6a, 15/11c. R. T., double fare. Departures *from* London as for Skegness. Departures *for* London about 4 times daily.
Map Square 14.

HAVEN STREET (Isle of Wight), 83½ miles. Fares, 18/8a, 11/5c. R.T. for two months, 37/4a, 22/10c. Departures *from* London as for Ryde. Departures *for* London about 6 times daily.
Map Square 28.

HAVERFORDWEST (Pembroke) from *Paddington*, 258¼ miles. Fares, 52/6a, 31/6c. R.T. for two months, 105/0a, 63/0c. Pop. 5,750.
Map Square 20.

Pad.	Haverf'd	Haverf'd	Pad.
AM 1. 0g	11.20	AM 7.52r	2.30
8.45r	3. 2	8.29r	4.20
11.50r	6.28	11.16r	6.15
PM 1.10r	8.56	PM 1. 4r	8.35
5. 0hr	11.31	2.42r	9.25
9.15	6.24	6.53	3.30

Sunday Trains.

PM 9.15	6.24	PM 6.58	3.30

g Mondays excepted.
h Tuesdays, Thursdays and Saturdays only.
r Restaurant Car.

HAVERHILL (Suffolk) from *Liverpool Street*, 55¼ miles, *via* Bishop Stortford. Fares, 11/8a, 7/0c. R.T. for two months, 23/4a. Pop. 4,083.
Map Square 19.

L'pl.St.	Hav'hill	Hav'hill	L'pl.St.
AM 5.50	9.20	AM 7.26	9.27
8.30	11.19	10.28	12.40
11.50	1.44	PM12.32d	3.18
2.48	5.42	12.32l	4. 2h
5.49	8. 1	12.32e	5. 9
—	—	5. 5	7.58
—	—	7.25	10.50

No Sunday Trains.
d Saturdays only.
e Saturdays excepted.
h Arrives at St. Pancras Station.
l Commencing May 23.

ANOTHER ROUTE from

Liverpool Street, via Halstead, 69½ miles. Fares as above.

L'pl.St.	Hav'hill	Hav'hill	L'pl.St.
AM10. 0	12.21	AM 7.38f	9.53
PM 2.15	4.56	9.29	11.42
5.42	8. 8	PM 2. 0h	5. 5
—	—	6. 6	9.17

Sunday Trains.

AM 9.20	11.51	AM 8.44	12.40
PM 4.40h	9.35	PM 6. 0	8.58

f Mondays only.
h Via Colchester.

HAVERHILL—*continued.*

ANOTHER ROUTE *via* Sudbury, 75 miles. Fares as above.

L'pl.St.	Hav'hill	Hav'hill	L'pl.St.
AM 6.50	10.28	AM 9.20	11.42
10. 0	12.32	11.19h	2. 3
PM 2.15	5. 5	PM 1.45h	5. 5
4.58	7.24	5.42	9.17

No Sunday Trains.

h Via Colchester.

HAVERTHWAITE (Lancs), 258 miles. Fares, 53/7a, 32/2c. R.T. for two months, 107/2a, 64/4c. Departures *from* London as for Windermere (Lake Side). Departures *for* London about 6 times daily. Pop. 902.
Map Square 7.

HAVERTON HILL (Durham), 241½ miles. No through fares. Departures *from* London as for Stockton-on-Tees. Departures *for* London about 7 times daily. Pop. 4,243.
Map Square 8.

HAWARDEN (Flint) from Euston, 192½ miles. Fares, 39/0a, 23/5c. R. T. for two months, 78/0a. Departures *from* London as for Chester. Departures *for* London about 6 times daily. Pop. 6,490.
Map Square 12.

Glynne Arms Hotel (opposite Hawarden Park gates). Motor for Hire. Good Bedrooms, Billiards, Stabling, Catering. Large parties accommodated. P.R.H.A. House.

HAWES (Yorks), 251½ miles. Fares, 51/1a, 30/8c. R. T. for two months, 102/2a, 61/4c. Departures *from* London as for Leyburn. Departures *for* London about 5 times daily. Pop. 1,518.
Map Square 7.

HAWICK (Roxburgh) from *St. Pancras*, 353½ miles. Fares, 70/0a, 42/0c. R. T. for two months, 140/0a, 84/0c. Pop. 16,353.
Map Square 44.

St. Pan.	Hawick	Hawick	St. Pan.
AM 4.25	2.24	AM11.11r	7.15
9. 0r	5. 0	PM12. 3r	7.55
11.45r	7.36	11.20	8. 3
PM 9.15	5.36	—	—

Sunday Trains.

PM 9.15	5.36	PM11.20	8. 3

r Restaurant Car.

HAWICK—*continued.*

ANOTHER ROUTE from *Euston*, 344½ miles. Fares as above.

Euston	Hawick	Hawick	Euston
AM 2.35	2.24	AM 6. 0*r*	4.15
5. 0	5. 0	8.34*r*	6.25
10.40*r*	7.39	11.11*r*	7.30
PM 9.20*e*	5.36	PM12. 3*r*	9.20
11.35*e*	9.49	6.18	5. 0*k*
—	—	7.33	6.55
—	—	11.20	7.30
—	—	—	—

Sunday Trains.

PM11.35	9.49	PM11.20	7.30
—	—	—	—
—	—	—	—

e Saturdays excepted.
k A.M.
r Restaurant Car.

HAWKESBURY LANE

(Warwick), 99¾ miles. Fares, 20/8*a*, 12/5*c*. R. T. for two months, 41/4*a*, 24/10*c*. Departures *from* London as for Coventry. Departures *for* London about 5 times daily.

HAWKHURST (Kent)

from *Charing Cross, Cannon Street* and *London Bridge*, 47 miles. Fares, 9/10*a*, 7/11*b*, 5/11*c*. R. T. for two months, 19/8*a*, 15/10*b*. Pop. 3,120.
Map Square 24.

Leave Char. +	Leave Can. St.	Leave Lon. B.	Arr. at H'hurst
AM —	6.45	6.50	9. 0
9.25	—	9.33	11.35
—	11.56	12. 0	1.42
PM 3. 0	—	3. 8	4.55
3.50*d*	—	3.57*d*	6.21
—	4.36*e*	4.39*e*	6.21
5.35*d*	—	5.41*d*	7.54
6. 0*e*	—	6. 9*e*	7.49
—	—	—	—
—	—	—	—
—	—	—	—
—	—	—	—

No Sunday Trains.

Trains from Hawkhurst.

Leave H'hurst	Arrive at Lon. B	Arrive at Can. St.	Arrive at Char. +
AM 7.49	9.32	9.36	—
9.14	10.58	11. 2	—
11.44	1.36	—	1.50
PM 3.39	5.50	—	6. 3
4.57	7.25	7.30	—
6.29	8.26	—	8.35
8. 5	10.22	—	10.35
—	—	—	—
—	—	—	—

No Sunday Trains.

d Saturdays only.
e Saturdays excepted.

Queen's Hotel. Famous Health Resort replete with every comfort. Perfect Sanitary arrangements. Lovely grounds, bowls, billiards, carriages. Garage. Links near Hotel. Telephone No. 7. Mrs. CLEMENTS, Propr.

Tudor Hall Private Hotel. 300 feet above sea level. 4 acres of ground. Tennis. Home produce. Garage. Apply tariff. Telephone 54. Telegrams, Tudor, Hawkhurst.

HAWORTH (Yorks) from

St. Pancras, 216 miles. Fares, 41/5*a*, 24/10*c*. R. T., double fare. Departures *from* London as for Keighley. Departures *for* London about 8 times daily. Pop. 6,605.
Map Square 12.

HAWSKER (Yorks), 247¼

miles. No through fares. Departures *from* London as for Ravenscar. Departures *for* London about 5 times daily. Pop. 507.
Map Square 8.

HAWTHORNDEN (Mid-

lothian), 392 miles. No through fares. Departures *from* London as for Edinburgh (Waverley) or Peebles. Departures *for* London about 4 times daily.

HAXBY (Yorks), 192¾ miles.

Fares, 40/0*a*, 24/0*c*. R. T., double fare. Departures *from* London as for York. Departures *for* London about 6 times daily. Pop. 883.
Map Square 8.

HAXEY (Lincoln) from

King's Cross, 153¾ miles. Fares, 31/8*a*, 19/0*c*. R. T., double fare. Departures *from* London as for Gainsborough. Departures *for* London about 5 times daily. Pop. 2,035.
Map Square 13.

HAY (Brecknock) from

Paddington, via Gloucester, Hereford, and L. M. & S. Rly., 165½ miles. Fares, 34/4*a*, 20/7*c*. R. T. for two months, 68/8*a*. Pop. 1,533.
Map Square 16.

Pad.	Hay	Hay	Pad.
AM 1. 0*g*	10.11	AM 7.46*r*	2.40
5.30	1.35	11.25*hr*	4.15
10.45	4.47	PM 2. 7*r*	8.45
PM 4.45*ht*	9.35	6.43	3.30
—	—	—	—
—	—	—	—

Sunday Trains.

PM 9.15	10.11	—	—

g Mondays excepted.
h *Via* Worcester.
r Restaurant Car.
t Tea Car.

HAYBURNWYKE

(Yorks) 236½ miles. No through fares. Departures *from* London as for Ravenscar. Departures *for* London about 4 times daily.
Map Square 8.

HAYDOCK (Lancs), 227¼

miles. Fares, 40/0*a*, 24/0*c*. R. T. for two months, 80/0*a*, 48/0*c*. Departures *from* London as for St. Helens (Central). Departures *for* London about 5 times daily. Pop. 10,333.

HAYDON BRIDGE

(Northumberland), 294¾ miles. Fares, 60/10*a*, 36/6*c*. R. T., double fare. Departures *from* London as for Hexham. Departures *for* London about 6 times daily. Pop. (Haydon) 2,297.
Map Square 3.

HAYES (Kent) from

Charing Cross, Cannon Street, and *London Bridge*, 15 miles. Fares, 2/8*a*, 2/1*b*, 1/7*c*. R. T. for eight days, 5/4*a*, 4/1*b*, 3/2*c*. Pop. 1,010. *See* pp. 544-547.
Map Square 23.

HAYES (Middlesex) from

Paddington, 11 miles. Fares, 1/10½*a*, 1/1½*c*. R. T. for two days, 3/9*a*, 2/2½*c*. Pop. 6,303. *See* pp. 491-493.
Map Squares 23 and 56.

HAYFIELD (Derby), 176

miles. Fares, 36/5*a*, 21/10*c*. R. T., double fare. Departures *from* London as for Chinley. Departures *for* London about 5 times daily. Pop. 3,459.
Map Square 12.

HAYLE (Cornwall) from

Paddington, 298 miles. Fares, 61/8*a*, 37/0*c*. R. T. for two months, 123/4*a*, 74/0*c*. Pop. 1,026.
Map Square 25.

Pad.	Hayle	Hayle	Pad.
AM 5.30	3.13	AM 8.23*r*	4.35
10.30*r*	5.14	9.29*r*	4.45
11.10*r*	6. 9	10.52*r*	6.50
PM 2. 0*r*	9.55	PM12.23*r*	9. 0
10. 0*e*	7.15	9. 1	7.10
12. 0*k*	11. 5	—	—
12.30*h*	11.21	—	—

Sunday Trains.

AM10.30*r*	5.27	AM10.56	7. 5
PM10. 0	7.15	PM12.36*r*	7.55
—	—	4.55	3.15

e Saturdays excepted.
h Saturdays midnight only.
k Saturdays midnight excepted.
r Restaurant Car.

HAYLING ISLAND

(Hants) from *London Bridge, Victoria*, and *Clapham Junction*, 82½ miles. Fares, 14/10*a*, 8/11*c*. R. T. for two months, 29/8*a*, 17/10*c*. Pop. 1,844.
Map Square 28.

Leave Vict.	Leave Clap. J.	Leave Lon. B.	Arr. at Hayl'ng
AM 6.18	6.25	6.35	10. 3
8.55	7.56	—	12.15
10.15	10.22	10.22	1. 5
PM 1.40	1.47*e*	1.50	4.35
1.55*k*	*e*2. 2*k*	2. 5*k*	5.57
3.55	4. 2	4 0	6.45
4.53	5. 0	4.50	7.55
5.45*k*	—	6. 0*k*	9.33

Sunday Trains.

AM 9.55	—	—	12.15
PM 1.14*k*	1.21*k*	1.10*k*	6.45

Trains from Hayling.

Leave Hayling	Arrive at Lon. B.	Arrive at Clap. J.	Arrive at Vict.
AM 7.18	9.58	10.45	10.53
8.15	10.55	—	—
9.25	12. 8	—	12. 0
10.52	—	—	1.10
PM 1.20	4.27	4.26	4.34
2.50	—	5. 4	5.12
4.50	7.48	7.31	7.39
6. 5*d*	10. 0	9.37	9.45
6.55	10. 8	9.53	10. 1
8.15*k*	12.59	12.50	1. 0

Sunday Trains.

PM 3.15*k*	—	—	7. 0
5.40	8.50	8.33	8.42
7.10*k*	11.34	10.46	10.55

d Saturdays only.
e Saturdays excepted.
k *Via* Hove.

Royal Hotel. First-class Family. Facing Sea. Close to Golf Links and Southsea. Extended Lounge and Spacious Coffee Room. Excellent and Liberal Cuisine. Tennis. Large Garage. Private lock-ups. Telephone: Hayling 7.
Manageress, Miss HART.

HAYWARD'S HEATH

(Sussex) from *London Bridge, Victoria,* and *Clapham Junction,* 37¾ miles. Fares, 7/11a, 4/9c. R. T. for two months, 15/10a, 9/6c. Pop. 5,090

Map Square 23.

Leave			Arr. at
Vict.	Clap. J.	Lon. B.	Hay. H.
AM —	—	5.18	6.56
—	—	6.15	7.12
6.37	6.44	6.40	7.44
7.23	7.29	7.25	9. 5
8.25	8.32	8. 7	9.45
9. 0	9. 8	—	10. 6
—	—	9. 6	10.21
10. 5	10.11	9.50	11. 7
10.35	10.42	10.35	11.58
12. 0	12. 7	12.10	1.27
PM 12.45	—	—	1.36
—	—	1.20d	2.19
—	—	2. 5	3.10
—	—	—	3.23
2. 0d	2. 7d	—	3.29
2. 0e	2. 7e	—	3.29
—	—	2. 8d	3.45
3.40	—	—	4.35
—	—	4. 5	5. 3
4.30	—	—	5.30
—	—	5. 5d	5.53
—	—	5. 8e	5.57
5. 5	5.12	5.10	6.30
5.45	—	—	6.41
—	—	5.55e	6.49
—	—	6. 0d	6.58
6. 6	6.12	6. 8	7.44
6.40	—	—	7.31
6.50	6.57	7. 0	8.10
7.15	7.22	7.20	8.47
8.35	—	—	9.22
9. 3	9.10	9.12	10.25
10. 0	—	—	10.53
10.30	10.38	10.35	12. 3
12. 5k	—	—	12.52

Sunday Trains.

AM 6.55	7. 2	7. 2	8.45
—	7.22	7.22	8.49
8.50	8.57	8.55	10.28
11.15	11.22	—	12.19
PM 1.14	1.21	1.10	2.39
5.50	5.57	6. 0	7.29
6.33	6.40	6.33	7.54
8. 0	8. 8	8. 0	9.30
9. 5	9.13	9.10	10.28

Trains from Hayward's Heath.

Leave	Arrive at		
Hay. H.	Lon. B.	Clap. J.	Vict.
AM 6.39	8.15	8.15	8.24
7.35	8.46	—	—
7.57	8.53	9. 0	9. 8
8.32	9.42	—	9.59
8.52	9.58	—	—
9.15	10. 5	10. 5	10.12
9.29	—	—	10.24
9.40	10.33	—	—
10.10	—	—	11. 5
10.42	i2.13	11.59	12. 7
11.41	12.44	12.36	12.45
PM 12. 7	1.42	1.39	1.50
1. 7	2.22	2.13	2.22
2.13	3.40	3.37	3.45
3.10	4.32	4. 9	4.17
4.15	5.54	5.47	5.55
5.26	6.36	6.26	6.34
6.27	7.42	7.21	7.30
7. 7	8.46	8.39	8.48
8.59	10. 0	10. 2	10.10
9.11	10.25	10. 9	10.17
9.22	10.58	—	—
10.20	—	11 10	11.17
11.42	12.59	12.50	1. 0

HAYWARD'S HEATH—

continued.

Sunday Trains.

Leave		Arrive at	
Hay. H.	Lon. B.	Clap. J.	Vict.
AM 9. 1	10.18	10.23	10.32
9. 8	10.45	—	—
9.51	11.15	10.42	10.50
PM 5.38	5. 3	5. 1	5.11
6.19	7.56	—	—
7.16	8.34	8.31	8.41
7.58	9.17	9. 4	9.13
10.12	11.34	11.34	11.42
11.13	12.27	—	—

d Saturdays only.
e Saturdays excepted.
k Wednesdays and Saturdays only.

Birch Hotel. Standing in
own beautiful grounds, 130 acres. Own farm and garden produce. Billiards. Tennis. Stabling. Garage Hire. 'Phone 170.
                            MANAGERESS.

House and Estate Agent,
Auctioneer and Valuer. Offices close to station. For all available houses and estates in this beautiful health resort, apply—
                    SCOTT PITCHER.
No. 17 'Phone.

House and Estate Agents,
Auctioneers and Valuers. Market Place (opposite Railway Station). Telephone No. 7.
    T. BANNISTER & Co., F.S.I.

HAYWOOD (Lanark), 380
miles. No through fares. Departures *from* London as for Carstairs. Departures *for* London about 5 times daily. Pop. 838.
Map Square 40.

HAZEL GROVE (Cheshire), 179¾ miles. Fares, 36/6a, 21/11c. R. T., double fare. Departures *from* London as for Cheadle Heath. Departures *for* London about 8 times daily. Pop. 9,631.

HAZELWELL (Worcester),
118¼ miles. Fares, 23/7a, 14/2c. R.T. for two months. 47/2a, 28/4c. Departures *from* London as for Birmingham (New Street). Departures *for* London about 6 times daily.
Map Square 17.

HAZELWOOD (Derby),
135 miles. Fares, 27/11a, 16/9c. R.T., double fare. Departures *from* London as for Wirksworth. Departures *for* London about 5 times daily. Pop. 341.
Map Square 12.

HAZLEHEAD BRIDGE
(Yorks), 178¼ miles. Fares, 36/1a, 21/8c. R. T., double fare. Departures *from* London as for Penistone. Departures *for* London about 3 times daily.
Map Square 12.

HEACHAM (Norfolk)
from *Liverpool Street,* 109½ miles. Fares, 23/2c, 13/11c. R. T. for two months, 46/4a, 27/10c. Pop. 1,764.

Map Square 14.

L'pool St.	Heach.	Heach.	L'poolSt.
AM 5.50	10.48	AM 7. 7r	10.23
8.30r	11.54	7.56	11.27
10. 5	2.23	9. 7	2. 7
11.20klr	2. 4	11.12r	2.21
11.50r	3.16	PM 1.12lr	4. 2k
PM 2.34	5.47	2.40r	6.10
4.45	7.51	4.50r	8.22
5.49r	9.16	7.11	10.30
—	—	9.45	2.50

Sunday Trains.

AM 9.25	1.31	PM 6.26	9.40

k Departs from or arrives at
    St. Pancras Station.
l Commencing July 23.
r Restaurant Car.

HEADCORN (Kent) from
Charing Cross, Cannon Street, and *London Bridge,* 46 miles. Fares, 9/7a, 7/8b, 5/9c. R.T. for two months, 19/2a, 15/4b. Pop. 1,492.
Map Square 24.

	Leave		Arr. at
Char. †	Can. St.	Lon. B.	Headc'n
AM —	5.20	5.25	7.40
—	6.45	6.50	8.47
—	—	7.50l	9.30
9.25	—	9.33	10.57
—	11.56	12. 0	1.27
PM12.40d	—	12.47d	2.12
3. 0	—	3. 8	4.34
4.30	—	4.37	5.32
—	4.36e	4.39e	6. 0
5.24d	—	5.34d	7. 1
6. 0e	—	6. 5e	7.24
7.30	—	7.26	9.29
9.30	—	9.36	11. 0

Sunday Trains.

AM 7.45	—	7.52	9.17
PM 6.35	—	6.43	8.25

Trains from Headcorn.

Leave	Arrive at		
Headc'n	Lon. B.	Can. St.	Char. †
AM 6.58	8.40	8.44	—
8. 3	9.32	9.36	—
9. 1	10.28	10.32	—
9.54	11.35	—	11.45
11.43	1.36	—	1.50
PM 1.54	3.26	—	3.40
4.29	5.50	—	6. 3
4.59	7.25	7.30	—
6.51	8.54	9. 1	—
9.19	11.34	—	11.43

Sunday Trains.

AM 8. 7	10. 5	—	10.15
PM 6.44	8.20	—	8.28

d Saturdays only.
e Saturdays excepted.
l Low Level Platform.

HEADINGLEY (Yorks), 187½ miles. No through fares. Departures *from* London as for Leeds. Departures *for* London about 8 times daily. Pop. 48,302.

HEAD'S NOOK (Cumberland), 305 miles. Fares, 60/10*a*, 36/6*c*. R. T. for two months, 121/8*a*, 73/0*c*. Departures *from* London as for Carlisle or Hexham. Departures *for* London about 8 times daily.
Map Square 3.

HEADS OF AYR (Ayr), 398 miles. Fares, 81/1*a*, 48/8*c*. R. T. for two months, 162/2*a*, 97/4*c*. Departures *from* London as for Turnberry. Departures *for* London about 4 times daily.
Map Square 43.

HEADSTONE LANE (Middlesex), from *Euston*, 12¼ miles. Fares from Euston, 2/3½*a*, 1/4½*c*. R. T. for two days, 4/1*a*, 2/4*c*. From Broad Street, 2/9½*a*, 1/9*c*. R. T. for two days, 4/6½*a*, 2/7½*c*.
See p. 496–499.

ANOTHER ROUTE (Bakerloo Tube). *See* back of Map.

HEALD GREEN (Cheshire), 180¼ miles. Fares, 37/6*a*, 22/6*c*. R. T. for two months, 75/0*a*, 45/0*c*. Departures *from* London as for Wilmslow. Departures *for* London about 6 times daily.

HEALEY HOUSE (Yorks), 193 miles. Fares, 38/7*a*, 23/2*c*. R.T. for two months, 77/2*a*. Departures *from* London as for Lockwood. Departures *for* London about 4 times daily.
Map Square 12.

HEALING (Lincoln), 158¼ miles. Fares, 32/11*a*, 19/9*c*. R.T., double fare. Departures *from* London as for Brocklesby or Grimsby. Departures *for* London about 3 times daily. Pop. 514.
Map Square 13.

HEANOR (Derby), from *King's Cross*, 141 miles. Fares, 26/5*a*, 15/10*c*. R. T., double fare. Departures *from* London as for Ilkeston. Departures *for* London about 6 times daily. Pop. 21,438.

HEAPEY (Lancs), 204½ miles. Fares, 42/8*a*, 25/7*c*. R. T. for two months, 85/4*a*, 51/2*c*. Departures *from* London as for Chorley. Departures *for* London about 6 times daily. Pop. 606.
Map Square 12.

HEATH (Derby) from *Marylebone*, 146¾ miles. Fares, 29/9*a*, 17/10*c*. R. T., double fare. Pop. 2,132.
Map Square 13.

M'bone	Heath	Heath	M'bone
AM 2.32	7.15	AM 6.17	10.36
10. 0*r*	2.18	7.21*r*	11.10
PM 12.15*r*	4. 7	8.59*r*	1.13
3.20*r*	7. 8	10.57*r*	3. 0
5. 0*r*	8.39	PM 12.55*r*	6.38
6.20*dr*	10.32	4. 3*r*	8.55
—	—	6.13*r*	9.55
—	—	8. 5	3.57

Sunday Trains.

M'bone	Heath	Heath	M'bone
PM 5.30*r*	9.21	AM 10.48*r*	5.40

d Saturdays only.
r Restaurant Car.

HEATHER (Leicester), 110½ miles. Fares, 22/9*a*, 13/8*c*. R.T., double fare. Departures *from* London as for Shackerstone. Departures *for* London about 6 times daily. Pop. 702.
Map Square 18.

HEATHFIELD (Devon), 188¾ miles. Fares *via* Newton Abbot, 40/8*a*, 24/5*c*. R. T. for two months, 81/4*a*, 48/10*c*. *Via* Ide, 39/4*a*, 23/7*c*. R. T. for two months, 78/8*a*. Departures *from* London as for Moretonhampstead. Departures *for* London about 6 times daily.
Map Square 26.

HEATHFIELD (Sussex) from *Victoria* and *London Bridge*, *via* Groombridge, 45 miles. Fares, 9/5*a*, 5/8*c*. R. T. for two months, 18/10*a*, 11/4*c*. Pop. 3,150.
Map Square 24.

Leave Vict.	Leave Lon. B.	Arr. at Hhf'ld.
AM 5.30	5.18	7.49
6.37	6.40	9.50
9.10	9. 6	11.38
11. 5	10.35	12.48
12. 0	11.50	2.40
12. 0*d*	12.20*dk*	2.40
PM 3.45	—	5.22
4.50	4.44*e*	6.38
5. 5	5.21	7.28
6. 6*e*	6. 8*e*	7.47
8. 5	8.10	9.46
—	—	—

Sunday Trains.

Leave Vict.	Leave Lon. B.	Arr. at Hhf'ld.
AM 8.50	8.30	11. 5
PM 2.30	—	4.57
7. 5	6.46	9. 8
—	—	—
—	—	—

Trains from Heathfield.

Leave Hthf'ld.	Arrive at Lon. B.	Arrive at Vict.
AM 7.21	9.32	9.40
8.22	10. 4	10.12
8.44	10.55	10.20
10.43	12.44	12.35
PM 1.37	—	3.45
4.19	6.36	6.29
5.30	7.56	8.27
8.16	10.25	10.10
—	—	—
—	—	—
—	—	—

Sunday Trains.

Leave Hthf'ld.	Arrive at Lon. B.	Arrive at Vict.
AM 7.56	10.18	10.22
11. 5	—	1.40
PM 6.54	9.17	9. 0
—	—	—
—	—	—
—	—	—

d Saturdays only.
e Saturdays excepted.
k Departs from London Bridge (S.E. & C.) Station.

Tavistock Private Hotel, situated in 6 acres of grounds amidst pines and heather. Tennis, Croquet, Bowls, Billiards, Golf Links. Radiators and Electric light. Terms from 3½ Guineas.

Heathfield Hotel. Good accommodation. Private Families, Luncheons, Dinners. Garage. Tennis, Croquet. Golf. Own Cows and Poultry kept. Carriages and Motors on hire. Sole Agent L.B. & S.C.R. 'Phone 7 Heathfield Tower. Proprietress, Mrs. C. M. T. MACLAREN.

HEATLEY (Cheshire), 188¾ miles. Fares, 37/9*a*, 22/8*c*. R. T., double fare. Departures *from* London as for Lymm. Departures *for* London about 5 times daily.
Map Square 12.

HEATON (Northumberland), 269¼ miles. Fares, 56/11*a*, 34/2*c*. R. T., double fare. Departures *from* London as for Newcastle-on-Tyne. Departures *for* London about 6 times daily. Pop. 30,077.

HEATON CHAPEL (Lancs), 179 miles. Fares, 37/11*a*, 22/9*c*. R. T., double fare. Departures *from* London as for Stockport. Departures *for* London about 7 times daily. Pop. 3,001.

HEATON MERSEY (Lancs) from *St. Pancras* 182½ miles. Fares, 37/9*a*, 22/8*c*. R. T. for two months, 75/6*a*, 45/4*c*. Departures *from* London as for Stockport (Tiviot Dale). Departures *for* London about 7 times daily. Pop. 3,074.

HEATON NORRIS (Lancs), 178 miles. Fares, 37/9*a*, 22/8*c*. R. T., double fare. Departures *from* London as for Stockport. Departures *for* London about 8 times daily. Pop. 11,240.

HEBBURN (Northumberland), 266¾ miles. Fares, 55/8*a*, 33/5*c*. R. T., double fare. Departures *from* London as for Newcastle-on-Tyne. Departures *for* London about 8 times daily. Pop. 24,171.
Map Square 3.

HEBDEN BRIDGE (Yorks) from *King's Cross*, *via* Horbury, 199¾ miles. Fares, 40/10*a*, 24/6*c*. R. T. for two months, 81/8*a*. Pop. 6,459.
Map Square 12.

King's +	Heb. B.	Heb. B.	King's +
AM 4.45	11.37	AM 5.32	11.30
7.15*r*	1. 5	7.46*r*	1. 5
10.10*r*	4.18	9. 7*r*	1.55
PM 1.30*r*	6.50	9.57	3.50
1.50*r*	8.19	11.37	5. 0
10.45*e*	9.13	PM 1.58*r*	7.10
—	—	4. 9*r*	9.25
—	—	8.15*e*	3.25
—	—	—	—

Sunday Trains.

King's +	Heb. B.	Heb. B.	King's +
12. 0*hn*	7.23	AM 9.20*r*	3.45
—	—	11.41	5.55
—	—	PM 2.59*h*	10.20
—	—	—	—

e Saturdays excepted.
h Passengers cross Wakefield at own expense.
n Noon.
r Restaurant Car.

HECK (Yorks), 167¼ miles. No through fares. Departures *from* London as for Doncaster. Departures *for* London about 4 times daily. Pop. 202.
Map Square 13.

HECKINGTON (Lincoln), 118¼ miles. Fares, 23/2*a*, 13/11*c*. R. T., double fare. Departures *from* London as for Boston or Sleaford. Departures *for* London about 4 times daily. Pop. 1,666.
Map Square 13.

HECKMONDWIKE
(Yorks) from *King's Cross, via* Horbury, 184¼ miles. Fares, 38/4a, 23/0c. R. T., double fare. Pop. 9,008,
Map Square 12.

KING'S+	HECKWK	HECKWK	KING'S+
AM 4.45	10.59	AM 6.16r	11.30
7.15r	12.46	8.11r	1. 5
10.10dr	5. 0	9.33r	1.55
10.10er	3.32	10.13	3.50
PM 1.30r	5.54	11. 5r	4.45
1.50r	8. 6	11.52	5. 0
5.45r	9.43	PM 1.57r	7.10
—	—	4.37r	9.25
—	—	8.46e	3.25

Sunday Trains.
12. 0hn	6.46	AM 9.32r	3.45
—	—	PM 2.23h	10.20

d Saturdays only.
e Saturdays excepted.
h Passengers cross Wakefield at own expense.
n Noon.
r Restaurant Car.

HEDDON - ON - THE-
WALL (Northumberland), 277½ miles. Fares, 58/1a, 34/10c. R. T. for two months. 116/2a, 69/8c. Departures *from* London as for Newcastle-on-Tyne. Departures *for* London about 6 times daily.
Map Square 3.

HEDGELEY (Northumberland), 319 miles. Fares, 67/4a, 40/3c. R. T., double fare. Departures *from* London as for Alnwick. Departures *for* London about 3 times daily. Pop. 96.
Map Square 3.

HEDNESFORD (Stafford), 129 miles. Fares, 26/1a, 15/8c. R. T. for two months. 52/2a. Departures *from* London as for Rugeley. Departures *for* London about 6 times daily. Pop. 5,149.
Map Square 17.

HEDON (Yorks), 203¼ miles.
Fares, 36/8a, 22/0c. R. T. for two months, 73/4a, 44/0c. Departures *from* London as for Hull (Paragon). Departures *for* London about 5 times daily. Pop. 1,321.
Map Square 13.

HEELEY (Yorks) from *St.*
Pancras 157 miles. Fares, 32/4a, 19/5c. R. T., double fare. Departures *from* London as for Sheffield. Departures *for* London about 8 times daily. Pop. 33,938.
Map Square 12.

HEIGHINGTON (Durham), 237 miles. Fares, 49/7a, 29/9c. R. T., double fare. Departures *from* London as for Bishop Auckland. Departures *for* London about 6 times daily. Pop. 658.
Map Square 4.

HELE (Devon) from *Paddington,* 165½ miles. Fares, *via* Taunton, 34/5a, 20/8c. R. T. for two months, 68/10a. *Via* Exeter, 36/11a, 22/2c. R. T. for two months, 73/10a, 44/4c.
Map Square 26.

PAD.	HELE	HELE	PAD.
AM 5.30	11.19	AM 9.28r	1.30
7.30h	1. 6	11.18	4. 5
PM12. 5r	4.38	PM 1. 6r	5.30
2. 0hr	6. 8	4. 1e	9. 0
3.30	7.20	4.18d	9. 0
4.15r	9.11	7.32	2.45
12. 0k	8. 5	9.38	7.10

Sunday Trains.
PM10. 0	8. 5	—	—

d Saturdays only.
e Saturdays excepted.
h Via Exeter.
k Saturdays midnight excepted.

HELENSBURGH (Dumbarton) from *King's Cross, via* Dumbarton, 459½ miles. Fares, 84/2a, 50/6c. R. T. for two months, 168/4a, 101/0c. Pop. 9,703.
Map Square 40.

KING'S+	HELENS.	HELENS.	KING'S+
AM 4.45	4.41	AM 7.16r	6.15
10. 0r	8.38	10.40r	10. 0
11.50r	11.48	PM 2. 0	3.25
PM 7.45er	6.33h	2.45d	3.25
8.25e	8.49	4.28	6. 0
11.25e	10. 3	6.43	6.50l
—	—	7.43e	7.30
—	—	8.40	7.25

Sunday Trains.
PM 7.45r	6.33	—	—
8.25	8.49	—	—
11.25	10. 3	—	—

d Saturdays only.
e Saturdays excepted.
h A.M.
l Arrives 7.5 Sundays
r Restaurant Car.

HELLESDON (Norfolk)
from *King's Cross,* 163½ miles. Fares, 23/7a, 14/2c. R. T. for two months, 47/2a, 28/4c. Departures *from* London as for Guestwick. Departures *for* London about 3 times daily. Pop. 826.
Map Square 19.

HELLIFIELD (Yorks)
from *St. Pancras* 231½ miles. Fares, 44/7a, 26/9c. R. T., double fare. Pop. 952.
Map Square 7.

ST.PAN.	HELLIF.	HELLIF.	ST.PAN.
AM 4.25	11.15	AM 8. 5r	2.10
9.50r	2.45	9.35r	4.10
PM12.15r	5. 3	11.28r	5.30
5.30r	9.31	PM 2. 4r	7.15
5. 0r	10.30	2.55r	7.55
9.15	2.42	4.28r	9.15
9.30e	3. 5	8.33	4.20
11.50e	7.33	—	—
11.50d	8.15	—	—

Sunday Trains.
AM10.50r	6.30	AM10.10	6.25
PM 9.15	2.47	PM 8. 2	4.55
9.30	5. 5	—	—
11.45	7.33	—	—

d Saturdays only.
e Saturdays excepted.
r Restaurant Car.

HELLINGLY (Sussex) from
Victoria and *London Bridge,* 51½ miles. Fares, *via* Groombridge, 10/8a, 6/5c. R. T. for two months, 21/4a, 12/10c. Pop. 3,182.
Map Square 29.

	Leave		Arrive at
	VIC.	LON. B.	HEL'N'Y
AM	5 30	5.18	8. 9
	6.37	6.40	10. 8
	9.10	9. 6	11.59
	11. 5	10.35	1. 6
	12. 0	11.50	2.59
	12. 0d	d12.20k	2.59
PM	3.45	—	5.41
	4.50	4.44e	6.56
	5. 5	5.21	7.46
	6. 6e	6. 8s	8.37
	8. 5	8.10	10. 8

Sunday Trains.
AM	8.50	8.30	11.23
PM	2.30	—	5.19
	7. 5	6.46	9.28

HELLINGLY—*continued.*
Trains from Hellingly.

	Leave	Arrive at	
	HEL'N'LY	LON. B.	VIC.
AM	7. 3	9.32	9.40
	8.22	10.55	10.20
	10.22	12.44	12.35
PM	1.18	—	3.45
	3.59	6.36	6.29
	4.59	7.56	8.27
	7.59	10.25	10.10

Sunday Trains.
AM	7.38	10.18	10.22
	10.43	—	1.40
PM	6.35	9.17	9. 0

d Saturdays only.
e Saturdays excepted.
k Departs from London Bridge (S.E. & C.) Station.

HELMDON (Northampton), 62½ miles. Fares, 13/1a, 7/10c. R. T. for two months, 26/2a, 15/8c. Pop. 489.
Map Square 18.

M'BONE	H'LMD'N.	H'LMD'N.	M'BONE
AM 6.45	8.57	AM 7.34	9.46
11.15	1.53	10.19	12. 2
PM 6.20	7.48	2.43	4.56
6.25e	8.24	8.57	11. 0
6.25d	8.33	—	—
7.30	9.56	—	—

Sunday Trains.
AM 9.30	11.40	AM 7.42	10.13
PM 6.30	9. 2	PM 6.27	8.58

d Saturdays only.
e Saturdays excepted.

HELMSDALE (Sutherland) from *Euston,* 669 miles. Fares, 120/10a, 72/6c. R. T for two months, 241/8a. Pop. 691.
Map Square 31.

EUSTON	HELMS.	HELMS.	EUSTON
PM 1.30er	10.55h	AM 5.30r	5. 0h
7.40er	2.25l	10.45	7.40h
11.35v	7.25	PM 4.50er	7.30l

Sunday Trains.
PM 7.50r	2.25l	—	—

e Saturdays excepted.
h A.M.   *l* P.M.
r Restaurant Car.
v Thursdays only.

ANOTHER ROUTE from
King's Cross, 659½ miles. Fares as above.

KING'S+	HELMS.	HELMS.	KING'S+
AM11.50er	10.55	AM 5.30	3.25h
PM 7.45er	2.25	10.45	7. 5k
11.25es	7.25	PM 4.50er	6.30h

Sunday Trains.
PM 7.45r	2.25	—	—

d Saturdays only.
e Saturdays excepted.
h P.M.   *k* A.M.
r Restaurant Car.
s Fridays only.

HELMSHORE (Lancs), 203¾

miles. Fares, 41/11*a*, 25/2*c*. R. T. for two months, 83/10*a*, 50/4*c*. Departures *from* London as for Bury. Departures *for* London about 6 times daily.
Map Square 12.

HELMSLEY (Yorks), 219½

miles. Fares, 45/8*a*, 27/5*c*. R. T. for two months, 91/4*a*, 54/10*c*. Departures *from* London as for Ampleforth. Departures *for* London about 4 times daily. Pop. 1,393.
Map Square 8.

HELPRINGHAM (Lincoln), 108 miles. Fares, 22/3*a*, 13/4*c*. R. T., double fare. Departures *from* London as for Gosberton. Departures *for* London about 3 times daily. Pop. 732.
Map Square 13.

HELPSTON (Northampton), 81¾ miles. No through fares. Departures *from* London as for Peterborough. Departures *for* London about 4 times daily. Pop. 688.
Map Square 18.

HELSBY (Cheshire), 186

miles. Fares, 37/9*a*, 22/8*c*. R. T. for two months, 75/6*a*. Departures *from* London as for Chester. Departures *for* London about 8 times daily. Pop. 1,891.
Map Square 12.

HELSTON (Cornwall)

from *Paddington*, 303¼ miles. Fares, 62/9*a*, 37/8*c*. R. T. for two months, 125/6*a*, 75/4*c*. Pop. 2,616.
Map Square 25.

PAD	HELSTON	HELSTON	PAD.
AM10.30*r*	5.18	AM 7.55*r*	4.35
11.10*r*	6.35	9.45*r*	4.45
PM10. 0*e*	7.35	11.55*r*	9. 0
12. 0*k*	11.37	PM 8.35	7.10
—	—	—	—
—	—	—	—
—	—	—	—

Sunday Trains.

PM10. 0	7.35	—	—
—	—	—	—
—	—	—	—
—	—	—	—

e Saturdays excepted.
k Saturdays midnight excepted.
r Restaurant Car.

HEMEL HEMPSTED

(Herts) from *St. Pancras*, 32½ miles. Fares, 5/8*a*, 3/5*c*. R. T. for two months, 11/4*a*, 6/10*c*. Pop. 13,826.
Map Square 23.

ST. PAN.	H. HEM.	H. HEM.	ST. PAN.
AM 6. 0	7.38	AM 6.35	8.15
7.50	9.15	8. 0	9.13
11.35	12.52	PM 1. 6	2.52
PM 1. 8*d*	2.26	2.38*d*	4.33
3.35*e*	4.52	3.30*e*	5.10
5. 5	6.22	5. 0	6.30
6.35	7.52	6.40	8.42
7.50	9.10	8. 0	10.48
8.25*d*	10.25	9.18*d*	10.48
—	—	—	—

No Sunday Trains.

d Saturdays only.
e Saturdays excepted.

HEMINGBROUGH

(Yorks), 177¼ miles. Fares, 35/6*a*, 21/0*c*. R. T. for two months, 70/0*a*, 42/0*c*. Departures *from* London as for Howden. Departures *for* London about 5 times daily. Pop. 513.
Map Square 13.

HEMSBY (Norfolk) from

King's Cross, 179 miles. Fares, 25/3*a*, 15/2*c*. R. T. for two months, 50/6*a*, 30/4*c*. Departures *from* London as for North Walsham. Departures *for* London about 3 times daily. Pop. 713.
Map Square 19.

HEMSWORTH (Yorks)

from *King's Cross*, 167¾ miles. Fares, 34/2*a*, 20/6*c*. R. T., double fare. Pop. 11,235.
Map Square 13.

KING's+	HEMS'H.	HEMS'H.	KING's+
AM 4.45	9.29	AM 8. 0*r*	11.50
7.15*r*	11.45	10. 1	1. 5
10.10*r*	2.49	11.39	3.50
PM 1.30*r*	4.58	PM12.54*r*	4.45
1.50*r*	5.36	2.50	7.10
4. 0*r*	8.22	5.23*r*	9.25
5.45*r*	10.28	11.12	3.25
—	—	—	—
—	—	—	—
—	—	—	—
—	—	—	—
—	—	—	—
—	—	—	—
—	—	—	—

Sunday Trains.

12. 0*nr*	4.16	AM11.11	3.45
PM 5. 0*r*	9.21	PM 1.47	5.55
—	—	6.17*r*	10.20
—	—	—	—

n Noon.
r Restaurant Car.

HEMYOCK (Devon), 166¼

miles. Fares, 34/9*a*, 20/10*c*. R. T. for two months, 69/6*a*. Departures *from* London as for Uffculme. Departures *for* London about 4 times daily. Pop. 884.
Map Square 26.

HENBURY (Gloucester),

115½ miles. Fares, *via* Bristol, 25/10*a*, 15/6*c*. R. T. for two months, 51/8*a*. Departures *from* London as for Bristol. Departures *for* London about 6 times daily. Pop. 2,062.

HENDON (Middlesex) from

St. Pancras, 7 miles. Fares, 1/5½*a*, 0/10½*c*. R. T. for two days, 2/11*a*, 1/9*c*. From Moorgate Street, 1/8*a* 1/0*c*. R. T. for two days, 3/2½*a*, 1/9*c*. Pop. 56,013. *See* pp. 507-508.
Map Squares 23 *and* 50.

Brent Bridge Hotel. Beauti-

fully situated. Standing in own grounds, 15 acres. Luxuriously appointed. Hot and cold water in each bedroom. Cuisine and Service of first order. Garage. 'Phone 1374 Hendon. Tariff. Manager.
See advt. p. **20.**

HENDREFORGAN

(Glamorgan), 182¼ miles. Fares, 37/11*a*, 22/9*c*. R. T. for two months, 75/10*a*, 45/6*c*. Departures *from* London as for Tondu. Departures *for* London about 4 times daily.
Map Square 21.

HENFIELD (Sussex) from

London Bridge, Victoria and *Clapham Junction*, 49½ miles. Fares, 10/5*a*, 6/3*c*. R. T. for two months, 20/10*a*, 12/6*c*. Pop. 1,882.
Map Square 23.

	Leave		Arr. at
VICT.	CLAP.J.	LON. B.	HENFD.
AM 5.18	5.28	5.28	7.47
6.18	6.25	6.35	8.38
8.55	7.56	7.35	10.44
10.15	10.22	10.22	12. 6
11.55	—	11.50	2. 4
PM 1.40	1.47*e*	1.50	3.46
2. 0	2. 7	2. 5	4.49
—	—	2. 8*d*	4.49
4. 5	4.12	4. 0	6.10
5. 5	5.12	5.14	7.18
6.15	—	6. 0	7.55
7.20	7.27	7.15	9.15
—	—	—	—
—	—	—	—
—	—	—	—

Sunday Trains.

AM 6.55	7. 2	7. 2	9.36
PM 7. 0	7. 7	6.38	8.51
—	—	—	—
—	—	—	—

Trains from Henfield.

Leave	Arrive at		
HENFD.	LON.B.	CLAP.J.	VICT.
AM 7. 3	9.10	9.51	9.19
8.39	10.45	10.40	10.48
10.20	12. 8	12.33	12. 0
PM12.26	3.32	3.22	3.32
2.38	4.27	4.27	4.35
4.22	6.36	6.26	6.34
5.51	7.48	7.31	7.39
7.46	10. 8	9.53	10. 1
8.39	10.58	11.10	11.17
—	—	—	—
—	—	—	—

Sunday Trains.

AM 8. 4	10.45	10.23	10.32
PM 2.53	5. 3	5. 1	5.11
6.50	8.50	8.33	8.42
—	—	—	—

d Saturdays only.
e Saturdays excepted.

HENGOED (Glamorgan),

155 miles. Fares, *via* Pontypool Road, 33/2*a*, 19/11*c*. R. T. for two months, 66/4*a*, 39/10*c*. *Via* Cardiff, 34/9*a*, 20/10*c*. R. T. for two months, 69/6*a*, 41/8*c*. Departures *from* London as for Pontllanfraith or Cardiff. Departures *for* London about 6 times daily. Pop. 4,947.

HENIARTH (Montgomery),

180 miles. No through fares. Departures *from* London as for Welshpool. Departures *for* London about 4 times daily.
Map Square 16.

HENLEY-IN-ARDEN

(Warwick) from *Paddington*, 100 miles. Fares, 21/6a, 12/11c. R. T. for two months, 43/0a.
Pop. 1,062.
Map Square 17.

PAD.	H.-IN-A.	H.-IN-A.	PAD.
AM 9.10	11.56	AM 8.20r	11. 0
10.40d	2. 2	10.59r	2. 5
10.40	3. 0	PM12. 8rv	4.15
PM 2.10h	5. 5	2.10er	5. 0
4.10t	7.28	2.18dr	5. 0
6.10hr	8.41	3.21dr	8. 5
12.15kv	6.31	3.41er	8. 5
12.15lv	8. 0	6.30	10. 0
—	—	10. 5v	3.30

Sunday Trains.

AM10.35v	3.22	AM 8.55rv	1.40
PM12.50rv	4.25	11.55v	6.20
4.10v	8.25	PM 5.30rv	9. 0
6. 0rv	8.58		

d Saturdays only.
e Saturdays excepted.
h Via Wilmcote.
k Saturdays midnight excepted.
l Saturdays midnight only.
r Restaurant Car.
t Tea Car.
v Via Birmingham.

HENLEY-ON-THAMES

(Oxon) from *Paddington*, 35¼ miles. Fares, 7/4a, 4/5c. R. T. for two months, 14/8d. Pop. 6,841.
Map Square 23.

PAD.	HENLEY	HENLEY	PAD.
AM 6.30	7.45	AM 7. 8	8.20
7.35	9.32	7.27	8.28
9. 0	10. 2	7.50	8.56
9.20	10.50	8.50	9.43
9.55	11. 5	9.15	10.24
11.20	12.20	10. 0	11. 6
11.25	12.57	11.10	12.15
PM12. 8	1.26	11.30	1.11
12.33d	2.15	PM12.12	1.46
1.20d	2.30	1.14	2.35
1.50d	3. 0	2.23d	3.38
2. 7e	5.17	2.23e	4.10
2.18d	3.25	3.30	5.17
3.38	4.41	4.22	5.37
4. 7	5.20	5.45	6.55
5.15	6.12	6.45	8.10
5.18d	6.29	7.30d	9.12
5.40e	6.38	8. 5	9.33
5.40d	6.45	8.35	10.22
6.12e	7. 9	9.25	10.42
6.35	7.41	9.55	12. 0
6.55e	8. 7	—	—
6.55d	8.18	—	—
7.35	8.37	—	—
8. 5	9.20	—	—
9.15	10.12	—	—
12. 3	1.14	—	—

Sunday Trains.

AM 9.10	10.10	AM 8.50	10.14
10. 0	11. 5	9.35	10.50
10. 5	11.22	10.48	1. 5
10.45	11.46	PM 2.25	4.53
11. 0	12.12	4.47	6. 0
PM 1.45	3. 3	6.20	7.37
2. 0	3.45	7. 5	8.20
2.35	4.24	8.20	9.32
5.15	6.32	8.35	9.53
6. 5	7.42	9.15	10.33
7.40	9.15	10. 0	11. 6
8.30	9.57	—	—

d Saturdays only.
e Saturdays excepted.

Salter's Steamers (5 min. from station). Up-stream 9.10 a.m. and 2.45 p.m.; down-stream, 9.45 a.m. and 2.45 p.m. See advt. facing first page of train service.

HENLEY-ON-THAMES
—continued.

Red Lion Hotel. Moderate Tariff. Garage. Good Boats and Punts. Excellent Cuisine. Tel. 135.

Royal Hotel (facing river). Excellent Lounge. Garage. *See advt. p.* **217.**

Catherine Wheel Hotel. Old-established Family Hotel. Appointed R.A.C. and A.A. Excellent Cuisine. Garage. Telephone 100. MANAGERESS.

Little White Hart Hotel. Facing the River and Regatta Course. Largest Dining Room in Henley for Parties. Garage. Landing Stage. Telephone 168. MANAGERESS.

White Hart. Old Family and Commercial Hotel. Dining-room seats 100. Garage, stabling, C.T.C. Redecorated. Telephone, 103. PROPRIETOR.

Rivermead Hotel. Situate in Garden on River Bank. Close to Station, Garage, Boats, and Landing Stage. Electric Light. Telephone 109. L. GOHEGAN.

Boat Builders. Searle & Sons. By appointment to H.M. the King. Boats to let for any period. Reasonable prices. 'Phone 207.

HENLLAN (Cardigan) from

Paddington, 250½ miles (*via* Carmarthen). Fares, 50/8a, 30/5c. R. T. for two months, 101/4a, 60/10c. Departures *from* London as for Newcastle Emlyn. Departures *for* London about 4 times daily. Pop. 208.
Map Square 16.

HENLOW (Bedford), 36½

miles from *King's Cross*. Fares, 7/6a, 4/6c. R. T., double fare. Departures *from* London as for Shefford. Departures *for* London about 4 times daily. Pop. 914.
Map Square 18.

HENSALL (Yorks), 177

miles. No through fares. Departures *from* London as for Knottingley. Departures *for* London about 6 times daily. Pop. 350.
Map Square 13.

HENSTRIDGE (Somerset)

from *Waterloo*, 114¾ miles. Fares, 23/11a, 14/4c. R. T. for two months, 47/10a. Departures *from* London as for Templecombe. Departures *for* London about 6 times daily. Pop. 1,139.
Map Square 22.

HENWICK (Worcester),

121¼ miles. Fares, 24/0a, 14/5c. R. T. for two months, 48/0a. Departures *from* London as for Worcester. Departures *for* London about 6 times daily.
Map Square 22.

HEPSCOTT (North-

umberland), 286 miles. No through fares. Departures *from* London as for Morpeth. Departures *for* London about 5 times daily. Pop. 344.

HEREFORD from *Pad-*

dington, via Gloucester, 144½ miles. Fares, 30/0a, 18/0c. R. T. for two months, 60/0a, 36/0c. Pop. 23,324.
Map Square 17.

PAD.	HEREFD.	HEREFD.	PAD.
AM 1. 0g	8.40	AM 7.43	12.20
5.30	11. 0	10.17r	2.40
9. 0	1.52	PM 1.10	5. 0
10.45	3.19	4. 5r	8.45
PM 3.15t	7.42	4.40	10.25
6. 0r	10. 2	9. 0	3.30

Sunday Trains.

PM 9.15	8.40	—	—

g Mondays excepted.
r Restaurant Car.
t Tea Car.

ANOTHER ROUTE from *Paddington, via* Worcester, 149¼ miles. Fares as above.

PAD.	HEREFD.	HEREFD.	PAD.
AM 5.30	12.15	AM 7.25	11 15
8.50	1.36	8.20	2.12
9.45	2.17	10. 0r	2.55
PM 1.30	4.40	PM12.50r	4.15
1.35r	5.57	1. 0	5.50
4.45t	8.30	4.17r	9.15
6. 5r	10.21	4.40	10.45

Sunday Trains.

AM10.35r	3.33	PM 4.25r	9.48

r Restaurant Car.
t Tea Car.

ANOTHER ROUTE from *Euston, via* Shrewsbury, 213½ miles. Fares, 31/11a, 19/2c. R. T. for two months, 63/10a, 38/4c.

EUSTON	HEREFD.	HEREFD.	EUSTON
AM 5. 0	12.10	AM 2.10gy	8. 0
6.44h	1.45	7.30r	2.20
6.45	3. 9	9.15r	3.10
8.45r	3.20	11.40r	6.15
10.40r	4. 0	PM 1.12ry	7.30
12. 0nr	6. 4	1.20ry	8.10
PM 1.15r	7.35	4.10r	10. 0
2.20t	10.10	9.15	5. 0
4.45r	10.27	—	—
5.50dr	3.47	—	—
6.30r	3.47	—	—
9.20e	5.20	—	—

Sunday Trains.

AM 9.15	7. 8	AM 2.10y	8. 0
PM11. 0y	5.20	9.45y	5.45
—	—	PM 7.55y	5. 0

d Saturdays only.
e Saturdays excepted.
g Mondays excepted.
h Mondays and Saturdays only.
r Restaurant Car.
t Tea Car.
y Via Crewe.

Green Dragon Hotel. Close Cathedral, River Wye and principal shops. First-class Family Hotel. Lounge. Smoking and Billiard Rooms. Table d'Hote. Separate Tables. Garage in connection with Hotel. Telephone, 1028.

The Mitre Hotel. Centrally situated. Close to Cathedral and River. First-class Family Hotel. Excellent Cuisine. Table d'Hote. separate tables. Night Porter. Telephone No. 1147. Telegrams: "Mitre," Hereford.

Hoppole Hotel, Commercial Road. Good accommodation for large or small Parties. Excellent Bedrooms. Stabling. Catering. Good Centre Motoring. P.R.H.A. House.

HERIOT (Midlothian), 378¼ miles.

Fares, 77/1*a*, 46/3*c*. R. T. for two months, 154/2*a*, 92/6*c*. Departures *from* London as for Galashiels. Departures *for* London about 4 times daily. Pop. 414. *Map Square* 41.

HERMITAGE (Berks),

57 miles. Fares, 11/11*a*, 7/2*c*. R. T. for two months, 23/10*a*. Departures *from* London as for Hampstead Norris. Departures *for* London about 5 times daily. Pop. 460. *Map Square* 23.

HERNE BAY (Kent)

from *Victoria, Holborn Viaduct,* and *St. Paul's,* 62¼ miles. Fares, 13/2*a*, 10/7*b*, 7/10*c*. R. T. for two months, 26/4*a*, 21/2*b*. Pop. 11,872. *Map Square* 24.

Vict. (S.E.&C.)	Leave Hol V.	St. Pl.'s	Arr. at Hern.B.
AM —	3.50*k*	—	6.14
5. 5	4.57	5. 0	8.10
5.48*f*	5.40*f*	5.42*f*	8. 0
8.25*d*	—	—	10. 3
9. 0	—	—	10.37
9.20	—	—	11.11
10.25*d*	—	—	11.57
10.40	—	—	12.21
11.30*l*	—	—	1. 2
11.40*e*	—	—	2.33
PM 12.55*d*	—	—	2.31
1.23*d*	—	—	3.24
2. 8*e*	—	—	4. 7
2.45*d*	—	—	4.19
3.20*e*	—	—	5. 0
3.29*d*	—	—	5. 9
4.15*d*	—	—	6. 7
—	5.10*e*	5.12*e*	6.48
5.10*d*	—	—	6.51
5.30*e*	—	—	7.52
5.30*d*	—	—	7.46
7. 0	—	—	8.33
8.30	—	—	10. 7
12. 0*h*	—	—	1.42
12. 5*d*	—	—	1.37

Sunday Trains.

AM 7.20	—	—	9.36
9.10	—	—	10.45
10.25	—	—	11.58
10.40	—	—	12.19
PM 3.20	—	—	5. 7
3.30	—	—	6.14
8.25	—	—	10.15

Trains from Herne Bay.

Leave Hern B.	St. Pl.'s	Arrive at Hol. V.	Vict.
AM 7.18	9.37	9.39	—
8.23	—	—	11. 2
9.27	—	—	11.27
9.38*h*	—	—	11.23
10.20	—	—	11.55
11.46*d*	—	—	1.40
PM 12.20*d*	—	—	2.15
12.20	—	—*	2.43
1.48	—	—	3.23
2.12*l*	—	—	4. 5
2.12*e*	4.46	—	4.39
*p*3.37*l*	—	—	5. 3
3.57*s*	—	—	5. 3
3.48	—	—	5.26
6. 7	—	—	7.54
6.47	9.51	9.53	9.46
8.17	—	—	10.25

HERNE BAY—*continued.*

Sunday Trains.

Leave Hern B.	St. Pl.'s	Arrive at Hol. V.	Vict.
AM 9.31	—	11.58	11.51
PM 2.53	—	—	4.42
3.14	—	—	5.32
4.52	—	—	6.24
5.57	—	—	7.30
6.37	—	—	8.20
8.16	—	—	10. 8
9.34	—	—	11. 5

d Saturdays only.
e Saturdays excepted.
f Mondays only.
h Wednesdays only.
k Third Class only.
l Mondays, Fridays and Saturdays only.
p Pullman Car attached.
s Mondays, Fridays and Saturdays excepted.

ANOTHER ROUTE from

Charing Cross, Cannon Street, and *London Bridge,* 61¾ miles, *via* Strood. Fares as above.

Leave Char. +	Can. St.	Lon. B.	Arr. at Hern.B.
AM —	—	3.57*h*	6.14
—	7.16	7.19	9.47
PM —	12.50*d*	12.53*d*	2.22
—	1.20*d*	1.25*d*	2.49
—	4.12*e*	4.15*e*	5·54
—	6.12*e*	—	7.37

No Sunday Trains.

Trains from Herne Bay.

Leave Hern.B.	Lon. B	Arrive at Can. St	Char. +
AM 7. 6	8.32	8.36	—
7.18	9.10	9. 4	—
7.43	9.15	9.19	—
7.59*f*	9.28	9.32	—
*e*8.23*p*	9.48	9.52	—
8.23*d*	9.48	9.52	—

No Sunday Trains.

d Saturdays only.
e Saturdays excepted.
f Mondays only.
h Third Class only.
p Pullman Car attached.

Dolphin Hotel. Established 1834. The leading hotel on Sea Front. Opposite Pier. Electric light. Garage. Tel. No. 4. Proprietors Mr. & Mrs. J. TIERNAN *See advt.* p. 215.

Connaught Hotel. First-class Family Hotel. Large Garage. Moderate Tariff. Under entirely New Management. Telephone 25. Mrs. STANHOPE WILLIAMS, Manageress.
See advt. p. 215.

Grand Hotel. Most modern and best appointed. Tennis. Billiards. Garage. Stabling. Special terms, week-ends and golfers. Telephone : 39. Telegrams : Grand Hotel.
See advt. p. 216.

Norlands Private Hotel. Finest position on Downs, with extensive Gardens and Tennis Court.
See advt. p. 216.

Queen's Hotel. Near Sea and Golf Links. Personal supervision. Telephone 12, Herne Bay.
See advt. p. 216.

Sunnymede. Facing Sea, Downs, Bandstand. Excellent Cuisine. Separate Tables.
See advt. p. 217.

HERNE BAY—*continued.*

"St. Heliers," Telford Terrace. Old Established. Facing Sea and Band Stand. Separate Tables. Large Public Rooms. Moderate Charges.
Misses FOX.

Stanhope Boarding Establishment, Marine Parade. Established 25 years. Finest Position. Facing Sea. Near Downs, Bathing, Band-stands. Generous separate tables.
GRANT.

Fitzroy Private Hotel. On Downs. Facing Sea. Large Dining, Lounge and Smoke Room. Personal Supervision. Telephone 138.

Clarence House. Paying guests received. Large picturesque house. Shady old-fashioned garden. Tennis. One minute sea. Moderate terms.

Fairlawn Private Hotel and Boarding Establishment. High, healthy situation top of famous East Cliff. Close Sea, Band, Pavilion, &c. Specially recommended for comfort, cleanliness, and cuisine. Own tennis and croquet lawns. High-class accommodation at moderate charges. Booklet free. Telegrams : "Comfort," Herne Bay. DOUGLAS SMITH.

Favorita Boarding House, Canterbury Road. Close to Sea, Downs, King's Hall, Golf Links. Separate Tables, if desired. Moderate. Mrs. JOHNSON.

"Kroonstad," Canterbury Road. Old Established, under personal supervision. Cuisine a special feature. Separate Tables. Overlooking Sea and Downs. Telephone 229.

Highcroft Private Hotel, Beacon Hill. Finest Position on East Cliff. Facing Sea. Tennis Court. Garage. Home Comforts. Electric Light. Personal supervision. Moderate charges. Tariff on application. Telephone 169. Mrs. IVES.

Railway Hotel. Family and Commercial. Tea. Bed, Breakfast, 7/6. Daily 9/-. 'Phone 46. Proprietor, H. E. GLADDEN (late White Lion, Staines).

Bodelwyddan, Mickleburgh Hill. Board Residence. Three minutes Sea and Downs. South aspect. First Class Cooking and Service. Moderate.
PROPRIETOR.

House Agents and Auc-tioneers.—WILBEE AND SON, 107, Mortimer Street and Station Road. Furnished and Unfurnished Houses to rent or purchase. Telephone 10 and 10A.

House Agents, Auc-tioneers. — IGGULDEN AND SONS, Herne Bay. Register of property with vacant possession issued monthly. Telephone 4Y and 167.

HERNE HILL (Surrey)

from *Victoria, Holborn Viaduct,* and *Ludgate Hill,* 4 miles. Fares, 0/10*a*, 0/8*b*, 0/6*c*. R. T. for two days, 1/8*a*, 1/4*b*, 1/0*c*. *See* pp. 558-561.
Map Square 70.

HERTFORD from *Liverpool Street*, 24¾ miles. Fares, 5/0a, 4/0b, 3/0c. R. T. for two months. 10/0a, 8/0b. Pop. 10,712. Map Square 23.

L'PL.ST.	HERTF'D.	HERTF'D.	L'PL.ST.
AM 5.50	7.19	AM 5.58	7.25
6.30	7.53	7. 3	8.18
7.18	8.41	7.35	8.49
7.55	9.11	7.49	8.57
8.30	9.33	8.27	9.27
9.10	10.28	8.57	9.42
10. 5	11. 5	9.16	10. 9
10.34	11.57	9.53	10.59
11.20	12.48	10.50	12.15
PM12.40d	1.35	11.28	12.28
12.48e	2. 6	PM12. 5	1.23
1.19d	2.20	12.46	1.58
2. 0d	3. 0	2. 0d	3.21
2. 1e	3. 0	2. 5e	3.16
2.48	4. 1	2.45h	4.11
3. 5e	4.40	2.58k	4.11
3. 8d	4.40	3.45	5. 9
4.30e	5.24	4.35	5.47
5.10	6.11	5.48	7. 0
5.20	6.25	6.47	7.58
6. 0	6.54	7.52	9.26
6.30	7.30	8.43	10. 0
6.38e	7.38	9.35	11.12
7.41	8.42	10.26	11.35
7.48	8.58	—	—
8.22	9.17	—	—
9.17	10.30	—	—
10.40	11.51	—	—
12. 0	1. 8	—	—

Sunday Trains.

AM 8.12	9.10	AM 8. 4	9.33
8.50	10. 3	10. 9	11.27
10.12	11 31	11.39	12.57
10.42	11.58	PM 1.59	3.10
PM 1.50	3.19	4.59	6.10
3.42	4.54	6. 4	7.10
6.25	7.47	7.42	8.55
8.25	9.40	9.12	10.35
10.25	11.58	—	—

d Saturdays only.
e Saturdays excepted.
h Commencing July 23.
k Ceases to run after July 21.

ANOTHER ROUTE from *King's Cross*, 27¾ miles. Fares, first and third, as above.

KING'S+	HERTF'D.	HERTF'D.	KING'S+
AM 7.45	8.43	AM 7.42	8.41
8.45	9.44	8.50	9.44
9.20	10.16	9.25	10.22
11.30	12.51	11. 0	12. 3
PM 1. 8	2.16	11.35	12.45
2.30d	3.27	PM 1.15	2.22
4.15	5.26	4.10	5.45
5.10	6. 3	5.43	7. 5
5.50	6.53	7.10	8. 5
7. 0	8. 4	8.28	9.50
—	—	—	—

Sunday Trains.

AM 8.30	9.41	AM 8.25	9.53
—	—	PM 6.25	7.40

d Saturdays only.

Dimsdale Arms Hotel. Old
Established Family and Commercial Hotel. First Class Accommodation. Moderate charges. Stabling. Garage. Telephone 78. Mrs. A. E. MANLEY (Proprietress).

HERTINGFORDBURY (Herts) from *King's Cross*, 25¼ miles. Fares, 5/0a, 3/0c. R. T. for two months, 10/0a. Departures *from* London as for Hertford. Departures *for* London about 8 times daily. Pop. 756.

HESKETH BANK (Lancs), 216¾ miles. Fares, 44/0a, 26/5c. R. T. for two months, 88/0a, 52/10c. Departures *from* London as for Preston. Departures *for* London about 6 times daily. Map Square 12.

HESKETH PARK (Lancs), 213¼ miles. Fares, 44/0a, 26/5c. R. T. for two months, 88/0a, 52/10c. Departures *from* London as for Southport or Preston. Departures *for* London about 5 times daily.

HESLEDEN (Durham), 250 miles. No through fares. Departures *from* London as for West Hartlepool. Departures *for* London 5 times daily. Pop. (Monkhesleden) 2,093. Map Square 8.

HESLERTON (Yorks), 217¾ miles. Fares, 45/3a, 27/2c. R. T., double fare. Departures *from* London as for Malton. Departures *for* London about 6 times daily. Pop. 482. Map Square 8.

HESSAY (Yorks), 192¾ miles. No through fares. Departures *from* London as for York. Departures *for* London about 5 times daily. Pop. 103. Map Square 8.

HESSLE (Yorks), 192 miles. Fares, 35/0a, 21/0c. R. T. for two months, 70/0a, 42/0c. Departures *from* London as for Goole. Departures *for* London about 4 times daily. Pop. 6,107. Map Square 13.

HEST BANK (Lancs), 233¼ miles. Fares, 48/7a, 29/2c. R. T. for two months, 97/2a, 58/4c. Departures *from* London as for Lancaster (Castle). Departures *for* London about 6 times daily. Map Square 7.

HESTON-HOUNS-LOW (Middlesex) from *Mansion House*, 14 miles. Pop. (Heston) 6,822, (Hounslow) 23,606. *See* p. 489. Map Square 64.

HESWALL (Cheshire), 194 miles. Fares, 40/5a, 24/3c. R. T. for two months, 80/10a. Departures *from* London as for Hooton. Departures *for* London about 9 times daily. Pop. 3,616. Map Square 11.

HESWALL HILLS (Cheshire), 205 miles. No through fares. Departures *from* London as for Wrexham. Departures *for* London about 6 times daily. Map Square 11.

HETHERSETT (Norfolk), 117¾ miles. Fares, 23/7a, 14/2c. R. T. for two months, 47/2a. Departures *from* London as for Wymondham (*via* Cambridge). Departures *for* London about 6 times daily. Pop. 1,093. Map Square 19.

HETTON (Durham), 255¼ miles. Fares, 53/7a, 32/2c. R. T., double fare. Departures *from* London as for Durham or West Hartlepool. Departures *for* London about 6 times daily. Pop. 17,279. Map Square 7.

HEVER (Kent) from *Victoria, London Bridge,* and *Cannon Street*, 27¼ miles. Fares, 5/8a, 3/5c. R. T. for two months, 11/4a, 6/10c. Pop. 718. Map Square 24.

	VICT.	Leave CAN. ST.	LON. B.	Arr. at HEVER
AM	5.30	—	5.18	6.43
	6.37	—	6.40	7.58
	7.23	—	8. 7	9.20
	9.10	—	9. 6	10.20
	11. 5h	—	10.35h	12. 2
	11. 5	—	10.35	12.42
	12. 0d	12.16d	d12.20k	1.25
PM	1.20e	—	1.38c	2.42
	1.25d	—	1.38d	2.46
	—	—	2. 5e	3.42
	2.25	—	2.25d	3.42
	4. 0e	4.16e	e4.20k	5.22
	4.50	—	4.44e	5.49
	5. 5	—	5.21	6.23
	5.48	—	—	7. 9
	6. 6e	—	6. 8e	7. 9
	6. 6	—	6. 8	7.17
	6.50	—	7. 0	8.17
	8. 5	—	8.10	9.12
	9. 3l	—	9.12l	10. 38

Sunday Trains.

	VICT.		LON. B.	HEVER
AM	8.50	—	8.30	9.52
PM	1.14	—	1.10	2.21
	2.30	—	—	3.42
	7. 5	—	6.46	8. 9

Trains from Hever.

Leave HEVER	LON. B.	Arrive at CAN. ST.	VICT.
AM 6.59	8.15	—	8.24
7.34	8.37	—	8.40
8. 9	9.15	—	9.19
8.27	9.32	—	9.40
9. 3	10. 4	—	10.12
10.19	—	—	11.35
11.10	12.13	—	12.17
PM12. 2	1.42	—	1.26
1.45	2.58	—	—
2.35	4. 0	—	3.45
5.22	6.36	—	6.29
6.49	7.56	—	8.27
9.14	10.25	—	10.10
—	—	—	—
—	—	—	—

Sunday Trains.

AM 8.59	10.18	—	10.20
PM12.24	—	—	1.40
5.20	—	—	6.54
8. 3	9.17	—	9. 0
8.46	—	—	9.47

d Saturdays only.
e Saturdays excepted.
h Stops to set down first class passengers only.
k Departs from or arrives at London Bridge S. E. & C. Station.
l Fridays only.

HEVERSHAM

HEVERSHAM (Westmorland), 245¾ miles. Fares, 51/1a, 30/8c. R. T. for two months, 102/2a, 61/4c. Departures from London as for Carnforth. Departures for London about 4 times daily. Pop. 359.
Map Square 7.

HEXHAM

HEXHAM (Northumberland) from *King's Cross*, 287 miles. Fares, 60/10a, 36/6c. R. T., double fare. Pop. 8,849.
Map Square 3.

King's+	Hexham	Hexham	King's+
AM 4.45	12.38	AM 6.10r	1.30
7.15r	3.38	8.26g	3.15
9.50r	4.38	9.15r	4.30
10.10r	5.55	11.45r	6.25
11.15g	5.55	PM 1.0r	9.25
11.50r	6.43	3.24r	10.0
PM 1.15r	8.43	6.57	3.25
1.50r	9.21	9.0e	5.40
5.30hr	11.53	9.0d	6.0
11.40e	6.41	10.10d	6.0
11.40d	8.30	10.45	7.5

Sunday Trains.

AM 1.30r	6.52	AM 8.38	5.15
PM 11.40	6.41	PM 8.30	5.40

*d Saturdays only.
e Saturdays excepted.
g 1st and 3rd Class Pullman Cars only.
h Tuesdays and Saturdays only.
r Restaurant Car.*

HEYFORD

HEYFORD (Oxford) from *Paddington*, 75 miles. Fares 14/0a, 8/5c. R. T. for two months, 28/0a. Pop. 455.
Map Square 18.

Pad.	Heyfd.	Heyfd.	Pad.
AM 5.30	7.57	AM 7.48	9.50
6.30	10.7	9.20	11.15
9.45	12.21	11.24	1.50
PM 1.35r	4.5	PM 3.33	5.50
4.45t	6.56	6.23r	9.15
7.30	9.36	8.17	10.45

Sunday Trains.

AM 10.35	12.32	PM 3.58	6.20
PM 4.10	6.28	7.31r	9.48

*r Restaurant Car.
t Tea Car.*

HEYSHAM

HEYSHAM (Lancs) from *St. Pancras*, 267 miles. Fares, 49/4a, 29/7c. R. T. for two months, 98/8a. Pop. 5,024.
Map Square 7.

St Pan.	Heysh.	Heysh.	St. Pan.
AM 4.25	1.48	AM 5.45gr	12.10
9.50r	4.48	7.20r	2.10
PM 12.15er	7.3	8.47r	5.30
12.15dr	7.43	PM 12.8r	7.55
5.0r	11.30	1.53r	9.15
11.50e	9.23	5.45	4.20

HEYSHAM (Lancs)—*contd.*

Sunday Trains.

St. Pan.	Heysh.	Heysh.	St. Pan.
PM 11.45	9.23	AM 8.35	5.27

*d Saturdays only.
e Saturdays excepted.
g Mondays excepted.
r Restaurant Car.*

HEYTESBURY

HEYTESBURY (Wilts) from *Paddington*, 104 miles, *via* Newbury. Fares, 20/0a, 12/0c. R. T. for two months, 40/0a. *Via* Bath, 22/6a, 13/6c. R. T. for two months, 45/0a. Departures from London as for Warminster. Departures for London about 5 times daily. Pop. 553.
Map Square 22.

HEYWOOD

HEYWOOD (Lancs) from *Euston*, 196½ miles. Fares, 40/7a. 24/4c. R. T. for two months, 81/2a, 48/8c. Pop. 26,691.
Map Square 12.

Euston	Heywd.	Heywd.	Euston
AM 12.25	6.11	AM 5.22dr	12.20
2.35	9.7	6.51er	12.5
5.0	12.20	7.34r	12.50
8.45dr	1.37	8.34r	1.15
8.45er	2.1	9.6r	2.20
10.40r	3.44	9.26r	3.10
11.50r	5.24	11.4r	3.55
12.0nr	6.37	11.37dr	5.50
PM 2.50t	8.44	PM 12.9r	6.0
4.5r	9.42	1.13r	6.15
6.5er	10.42	2.55r	8.10
6.5dr	11.2	4.35dr	10.0
11.50d	9.20	4.35er	10.10
—	—	8.50	5.0
—	—	10.10e	5.40
—	—	10.10d	5.45

Sunday Trains.

PM 12.10r	5.34	AM 8.10	4.0
12.30r	7.20	10.24r	5.45
—	—	PM 1.35r	7.30
—	—	2.30r	8.55
—	—	10.23	5.0

*d Saturdays only.
e Saturdays excepted.
n Noon.
r Restaurant Car.*

HICKLETON

HICKLETON (Yorks), 167½ miles. No through fares. Departures from London as for Cudworth. Departures for London about 4 times daily. Pop. 139.
Map Square 13.

HIGHAM

HIGHAM (Kent) from *Charing Cross, Cannon Street,* and *London Bridge*, 29½ miles. Fares, 6/3a, 5/0b, 3/9c. R. T. for two months, 12/6a, 10/0b. Pop. 1,665.
Map Square 24.

Leave			Arr. at
Char. +	Can. St.	Lon. B.	Higham.
AM —	6.20	6.23	7.31
—	7.16	7.19	8.16
8.10	—	8.17	9.21
—	10.58	11.1	12.6
11.55	—	12.2	1.0

HIGHAM (Kent)—*continued.*

Leave			Arr. at
Char. +	Can. St.	Lon. B.	Highm.
PM —	1.2d	1.5d	2.14
1.20e	—	1.27e	2.26
—	1.48d	1.51d	3.1
2.10d	—	2.17d	3.26
2.45e	—	2.53e	4.5
3.5d	—	3.12d	4.7
3.10d	—	3.17d	4.30
4.25d	—	4.31d	5.39
—	4.36e	4.39e	5.37
5.15d	—	5.22d	6.37
5.17e	—	5.25e	6.25
5.21e	—	5.29e	6.34
6.22e	—	6.29e	7.30
6.55d	—	7.1d	8.12
—	7.8e	7.11e	8.15
7.34	—	7.41	8.54
—	7.44	7.47	9.15
—	9.35	9.38	10.39
10.20h	—	10.27h	11.25

Sunday Trains.

AM 7.30	—	7.37	8.53
9.46	—	9.52	11.4
10.50	—	10.57	12.15
PM 1.15	—	1.22	2.41
3.15	—	3.22	4.34
4.50	—	4.57	6.10
7.0	—	7.7	8.5
8.42	—	8.49	9.47
10.30	—	10.38	12.6

Trains from Higham.

Leave	Arrive at		
Higham	Lon. B.	Can. St.	Char +
AM 4.51	5.47	5.51	—
5.40	7.0	7.4	—
6.46	8.13	8.17	—
7.35	8.34	—	8.41'
8.43	9.34	—	9.43
9.19	10.24	10.28	—
10.12	11.20	11.24	—
11.2	12.3	—	12.14
PM 12.30d	1.31	1.37	—
12.30e	1.36	—	1.45
1.30d	2.44	—	2.54
k1.51d	3.21	3.26	—
1.53e	2.53	—	3.4
2.23e	3.26	—	3.36
2.43d	3.58	—	4.8
3.41e	4.48	4.52	—
3.44d	4.57	—	5.7
4.36e	5.36	5.40	—
4.36d	5.36	—	5.45
5.56	7.10	—	7.19
6.10	7.28	7.32	—
7.14	8.15	8.20	—
8.44	9.38	—	9.47
9.46	10.51	—	10.59
11.9	12.35	—	12.45

Sunday Trains.

AM 7.47	9.0	—	9.9
9.8	10.16	—	10.24
11.48	1.5	—	1.17
PM 2.51	4.4	—	4.15
4.53	5.55	—	6.4
5.45	6.49	—	6.59
6.46	8.1	—	8.10
8.20	9.46	—	9.55
10.3	11.15	—	11.24

*d Saturdays only.
e Saturdays excepted.
h Stops on Fridays only to set down First Class Passengers.
k Third Class only.*

HIGHAM. (Suffolk) from *Liverpool Street*, *via* Cambridge, 78¼ miles. Fares, 16/3*a*, 9/9*c*. R.T. for two months, 32/6*a*. Pop. 325.
Map Square 19.

L'POOL St.	HIGHAM	HIGHAM	L'POOL St.
AM 5. 5	8. 9	AM 7.50*r*	10.23
5.50*h*	10. 4	10. 8	12.40
8.30*r*	10.52	11.36*r*	2.21
11.50*r*	2.34	PM 2.44*r*	5.17
PM 2.34	5.18	4.22	7.58
4.45	7.35	5.59*r*	8.33
5.49*r*	8.22	7.33	10.30
7.10*r*	9.42	—	—
—	—	—	—
—	—	—	—
—	—	—	—

Sunday Trains.

AM 9.25	12.22	PM 3.45	6.40
PM 3.25	5.57	—	—
—	—	—	—
—	—	—	—

h Wednesdays only.
r Restaurant Car.

HIGHAM FERRERS (Northampton) from *St. Pancras*, 67 miles. Fares, 13/2*a*, 7/11*c*. R.T., double fare. Departures *from* London as for Rushden. Departures *for* London about 7 times daily. Pop. 2,851.
Map Square 18.

HIGHAM-ON-THE-HILL (Leicester), 100 miles. Fares, 20/8*a*, 12/5*c*. R.T., double fare. Departures *from* London as for Shackerstone. Departures *for* London about 6 times daily. Pop. 614.
Map Square 18.

HIGHAM'S PARK (Essex) from *Liverpool Street*, 8¼ miles. Fares, 1/3*a*, 1/0*b*, 0/9*c*. R.T. for two days, 2/6*a*, 1/11*b*, 1/4*c*. See pp. 523, 524.

HIGH BARNET. See BARNET, HIGH.

HIGH BLANTYRE (Lanark), 395¼ miles. No through fares. Departures *from* London as for Hamilton. Departures *for* London about 4 times daily.
Map Square 40.

HIGHBRIDGE (Somerset) from *Paddington*, 144½ miles. Fares, 30/2*a*, 18/1*c*. R.T. for two months, 60/4*a*. Pop. 2,478.
Map Square 22

PAD.	HIGHB.	HIGHB.	PAD.
AM 5.30	9.57	AM 7.55	11.30
7.30	11.54	10.45*r*	2. 0
8.45*d*	12.20	PM 2. 1	6. 2
9. 0	1.38	3. 8*r*	7. 0
11.15*r*	2.32	5.52	10.25
PM 1. 0*r*	5. 1	9.43	2.45
1.10*r*	6.42	—	—
4.15*r*	8. 6	—	—
6.30*r*	10.10	—	—
8. 0*d*	12. 9	—	—
12. 0*h*	7. 0	—	—
12.30*k*	7.48	—	—
—	—	—	—

HIGHBRIDGE—*continued.*

Sunday Trains.

PAD.	HIGHB.	HIGHB.	PAD.
AM 9.10*r*	3.29	AM 11. 0	3.35
PM 12.30*r*	6.50	PM 4.25	8.10
10. 0	7. 0	8.41	3.15
—	—	—	—
—	—	—	—
—	—	—	—

d Saturdays only.
h Saturdays midnight excepted.
k Saturdays midnight only.
r Restaurant Car.

HIGHBURY & ISLING-TON from *Broad Street*, 3½ miles. Fares, 0/5*a*, 0/3*c*. R.T. for two days 0/10*a*, 0/5½*c*. Pop. (Islington) 327,403. (Highbury) 33,417. See pp. 501-505.
Map Square 61.

ANOTHER ROUTE (Metropolitan Railway) (G. N. & City). See back of Map.

HIGHCLERE (Hants) from *Paddington*, 58¾ miles. Fares, 12/3*a*, 7/4*c*. R.T. for two months, 24/6*a*. Pop. 428.
Map Square 23.

PAD.	H'CLERE	H'CLERE	PAD.
AM 7.30	9.24	AM 8. 6	10. 0
9.30	12. 3	9. 7	10.52
PM 12.30*r*	2.13	11.17	12.55
2.45	4.25	PM 12.50	2.50
5.55	7.24	3.22	5.50
8. 0*d*	10.25	6.22*r*	8.20
—	—	—	—

No Sunday Trains.

d Saturdays only.
r Restaurant Car.

HIGH FIELD (Yorks), 181¾ miles. No through fares. Departures *from* London as for Selby. Departures *for* London about 4 times daily.
Map Square 13.

HIGHGATE (Middlesex) from *King's Cross, Moorgate Street,* and *Broad Street*, 4½ miles. Fares from King's Cross, 0/10*a*, 0/8*b*, 0/6*c*. R.T. for two days, 1/8*a*, 1/4*b*, 1/0*c*. From Moorgate Street and Broad Street, 0/11½*a*, 0/9*b*, 0/7*c*. R.T. for two days, 1/11*a*, 1/6*b*, 1/2*c*. Pop. 12,385. See pp.518-522.
Map Square 51.

ANOTHER ROUTE (Hampstead Tube). See back of Map.

HIGH HALDEN ROAD (Kent) from *Charing Cross, Cannon Street,* and *London Bridge,* 51¾ miles. No through fares. Departures *from* London as for Tenterden (*via* Headcorn). Departures *for* London about 4 times daily. Pop. 632.
Map Square 24.

HIGHLANDMAN (Perth), 441½ miles. No through fares. Departures *from* London as for Crieff. Departures *for* London about 3 times daily.
Map Square 37.

HIGH LANE (Cheshire), 173½ miles. Fares, 36/1*a*, 21/8*c*. R.T. for two months, 72/2*a*, 43/4*c*. Departures *from* London as for Macclesfield (Hibel Road). Departures *for* London about 5 times daily.

HIGHLEY (Salop) from *Paddington*, 139 miles. Fares, 27/6*a*, 16/6*c*. R.T. for two months, 55/0*a*. Departures *from* London as for Bewdley. Departures *for* London about 4 times daily. Pop. 1,489.
Map Square 17.

HIGH STREET, KEN-SINGTON. See KENSINGTON(HIGH STREET).

HIGHTOWN (Lancs), 210¾ miles. Fares, 42/6*a*, 25/6*c*. R.T. for two months, 85/0*a*. Departures *from* London as for Liverpool. Departures *for* London about 8 times daily.
Map Square 12.

HIGHWORTH (Wilts), 82 miles. Fares, 17/4*a*, 10/5*c*. R.T. for two months, 34/8*a*. Departures *from* London as for Stratton. Departures *for* London about 5 times daily. Pop. 2,153.
Map Square 22.

HIGH WYCOMBE. See WYCOMBE, HIGH.

HILDENBORO' (Kent) from *Charing Cross, Cannon Street* and *London Bridge*, 27¾ miles. Fares, 5/10*a*, 4/8*b*, 3/6*c*. R.T. for two months, 11/8*a*, 9/4*b*. Pop. 1,727.
Map Square 24.

	Leave		Arr. at
CHAR. +	CAN. St.	LON. B.	H'BORO'.
AM —	5.20	5.25	6.44
—	6.45	6.50	8. 1
—	7.56	8. 0	9. 9
9.38	—	9.45	10.49
—	11.56	12. 0	12.44
PM —	1.12*d*	1.15*d*	2.11
2.17*d*	—	2.23*d*	3.22
3.50	—	3.57	5. 0
—	4.36*e*	4.39*e*	5.22
5.24*d*	—	5.34*d*	6.14
5.26*e*	—	5.33*e*	6.14
5.35*d*	—	5.41*d*	6.44
6.34*e*	—	6.41*e*	7.26
8. 0	—	8. 8	9. 4
10. 0	—	10. 6	11. 2
11.45*h*	—	—	12.32
—	—	—	—

Sunday Trains.

AM 7. 5	—	7.11	8.23
8. 5	—	8.12	9.14
11.15	—	11.23	12.32
PM 3. 5	—	3.13	4.24
6.35	—	6.43	7.27
—	—	—	—

HILDENBORO'—*contd.*

Trains from Hildenboro'.

Leave H'boro'.	Lon. B.	Arrive at Can. St.	Char. +
AM 7. 6	8.10	—	8.19
8.16	9.18	—	9.27
8.49	9.32	9.36	—
9.22	10. 4	10. 8	—
10.40	11.32	—	11.44
PM12.17	1.27	—	1.38
12.47	1.36	—	1.50
1.56	3. 7	—	3.19
3.50	4.40	—	4.53
5.11*d*	6.30	—	6.39
5.20*e*	6.44	—	6.54
7.47	8.54	9. 1	—
10.31	11.34	—	11.44
—	—	—	—
—	—	—	—
—	—	—	—
—	—	—	—

Sunday Trains.

AM 8.52	10. 5	—	10.15
9.16	10.22	—	10.32
10.50	11.50	—	12. 0
PM 1.45	2.50	—	3. 0
5.16	6.27	—	6.41
8. 4	9. 7	—	9.18
—	—	—	—
—	—	—	—
—	—	—	—
—	—	—	—

d Saturdays only.
e Saturdays excepted.
h Tuesdays and Fridays only.

HILGAY (Norfolk), from
Liverpool Street, 81½ miles. Fares, 17/3*a*, 10/4*c*. R. T. for two months, 34/6*a*. Departures *from* London as for Littleport. Departures *for* London about 5 times daily. Pop. 1,590.
Map Square 19.

HILL END (Herts) from
King's Cross, 22 miles. Fares, 4/2*a*, 2/6*c*. R. T., double fare. Departures *from* London as for St. Albans. Departures *for* London about 3 minutes later.
Map Square 23.

HILLFOOT (Dumbarton),
443 miles. No through fares. Departures *from* London as for Glasgow. Departures *for* London about 4 times daily.

HILLINGTON (Norfolk)
from *King's Cross*, 121½ miles. Fares, 21/10*a*, 13/1*c*. R. T. for two months, 43/8*a*. Departures *from* London as for Terrington. Departures *for* London about 5 times daily. Pop. 262.
Map Square 19.

HILLSIDE (Forfar), 484½
miles. Fares, 97/6*a*, 58/6*c*. R. T. for two months, 195/0*a*, 117/0*c*. Departures *from* London as for Montrose. Departures *for* London about twice daily. Pop. 321.
Map Square 38.

HILTON HOUSE (Lancs),
200¾ miles. No through fares. Departures *from* London as for Wigan. Departures *for* London about 5 times daily.
Map Square 12.

HINCKLEY (Leicester)
from *St. Pancras*, 106¾ miles. Fares, 20/2*a*, 12/1*c*. R. T. for two months, 40/4*a*, 24/2*c*. Pop. 13,644.
Map Square 18.

St. Pan.	Hinck.	Hinck.	St. Pan.
AM 2.25	6.56	AM 8.20*r*	11. 0
4.25	8.47	10. 0*r*	1.20
8.25*r*	11.30	11.52	3.25
10.25*r*	1. 3	PM 2.41*r*	5.45
11.45*r*	2. 8	4.23*r*	7.57
PM12.15*r*	2.35	6.20*r*	9. 5
1.25*r*	4.28	7.16*er*	10. 5
2.25*r*	6. 6	11.45*d*	4.20
4.25*r*	7.46	—	—
6.25*dr*	8.53	—	—
—	—	—	—

Sunday Trains.

PM 3.15	8.30	AM 8. 7	11.53
—	—	PM 6.57*r*	9.52
—	—	—	—
—	—	—	—

d Saturdays only.
e Saturdays excepted.
r Restaurant Car.

ANOTHER ROUTE from
Euston, 101 miles. Fares as above.

Euston	Hinck.	Hinck.	Euston
AM 5. 0	7.36	AM 6.32	10. 0
6.45	9.37	8.36	11. 0
8.45*r*	11. 9	10.19	12.50
10. 0*dr*	12.58	PM12.45*r*	4.15
10. 0	1.25	1.49	5.35
12. 0*nr*	3.19	2.57*t*	6. 0
PM 2.50*t*	5.39	5.50*r*	8.10
4. 5*t*	6.42	6.36*r*	9.20
5.20*r*	7.40	7.34*r*	10.45
6.30*er*	9.20	11.45	5. 0
7. 0*dr*	9.20	—	—
9.30*e*	6. 9	—	—
—	—	—	—

Sunday Trains.

AM 9.15	2.39	PM 1.50	5. 5
PM 3.50	7.44	6.24*r*	8.55
9.15	6. 9	10. 3	5. 0
—	—	—	—
—	—	—	—
—	—	—	—

d Saturdays only.
e Saturdays excepted.
r Restaurant Car.
n Noon.
t Tea Car.

HINDERWELL (Yorks),
253¾ miles. Fares, 52/11*a*, 31/9*c*. R.T. for two months, 105/10*a*, 63/6*c*. Departures *from* London as for Sandsend. Departures *for* London about 4 times daily. Pop. 2,613.
Map Square 8.

HINDHEAD (Surrey).
Station at Haslemere.

HINDLEY (Lancs), 202
miles. Fares, 40/3*a*, 24/2*c*. R. T. for two months, 80/6*a*. Departures *from* London as for Manchester. Departures *for* London about 8 times daily. Pop. 23,574.
Map Square 12.

HINDLEY AND PLATT
BRIDGE (Lancs), 225¾ miles. Fares, 40/3*a*, 24/2*c*. R. T. for two months, 80/6*a*. Departures *from* London as for Wigan (Central). Departures *for* London about 5 times daily.

HINDLEY GREEN
(Lancs), 195½ miles. Fares, 40/10*a*, 24/6*c*. R. T. for two months, 81/8*a*. Departures *from* London as for Wigan. Departures *for* London about 4 times daily. Pop. 4,481.

HINDLOW (Derby), 168
miles. Fares, 34/0*a*, 20/5*c*. R. T., double fare. Departures *from* London as for Ashbourne. Departures *for* London 4 times daily.
Map Square 12.

HINDOLVESTONE
(Norfolk) from *King's Cross* 146½ miles. Fares, 23/7*a*, 14/2*c*. R. T. for two months, 47/2*a*. Departures *from* London as for Guestwick. Departures *for* London about 3 times daily. Pop. 630.
Map Square 19.

HINTON (Glo'ster), 110½
miles. No through fares. Departures *from* London as for Evesham. Departures *for* London about 5 times daily. Pop. 232.
Map Square 17.

HINTON ADMIRAL
(Hants) from *Waterloo*, 100½ miles. Fares, 21/1*a*, 12/8*c*. R. T. for two months, 42/2*a*, 25/4*c*. Departures *from* London as for New Milton. Departures *for* London about 5 times daily. Pop. 308.
Map Square 27.

HIPPERHOLME (Yorks),
192¾ miles. Fares, 39/9*a*, 23/10*c*. R. T., double fare. Departures *from* London as for Lowmoor. Departures *for* London about 5 times daily. Pop. 4,799.

HIRWAIN (Brecon), 175½
miles. Fares, *via* Pontypool Road, 36/6*a*, 21/11*c*. R.T. for two months, 73/0*a*. Departures *from* London as for Aberdare (*via* Pontypool Road). Departures *for* London about 5 times daily.
Map Square 21.

HISTON (Cambs), from
Liverpool Street, 60½ miles. Fares, 12/3*a*, 7/4*c*. R. T. for two months, 24/6*a*. Departures *from* London as for St. Ives (Hunts). Departures *for* London about 6 times daily. Pop. 1,385.
Map Square 18.

HITCHIN (Herts) from

King's Cross, 32 miles. Fares, 6/8*a*, 4/0*c*. R.T., double fare. Pop. 13,535.
Map Square 18.

King's +	Hitch.	Hitch.	King's +
AM 5. 5	6. 2	AM 6.15	7.30
7. 0	8.34	7.35	8.41
7.45	8.43	8. 2	8.55
8. 5	9.18	8.38	9.34
8.45	9.34	9.10	9.56
9.20*d*	10.21	9.15	10.22
10.12	11.21	10.29*h*	11.15
11.30	12.22	10.43	11.25
PM 12.40*d*	1.30	11. 0	12. 3
1. 8	2.23	PM 12.42	1.25
1.55	2.53	1. 0	2.32
2.30*d*	3.31	3. 5	3.50
3. 0	3.42	3.12	4.23
4.15	5.11	4.30	5.45
5. 0	5.42	5.10	6. 0
5.10	6. 1	5.40	6.25
5.50	6.50	5.55	7. 5
6.15	7. 8	7. 7	8. 5
6.30	7.28	8.15	9. 0
7. 0	8. 3	9. 5	10.20
8.30	9.28	10. 0	11. 0
9.10	10.15	—	—
10.55	11.53	—	—
11.45*k*	12.52	—	—
—	—	—	—
—	—	—	—

Sunday Trains.

AM 8.30	9.45	AM 8.22	9.53
10.30	11.30	PM 5.20	6.17
12. 0*n*	12.45	6.52	8. 8
PM 5. 0	5.43	9.33*r*	10.20
7.10	8.16	—	—
9.30	10.32	—	—

d Saturdays only. *h* Tuesdays only.
k Wednesdays only.
n Noon.

Taxi Cabs can be hired to meet any train at this station by letter, or telephone No. 91, Messrs. Ralph E. Sanders & Sons, Ltd., Motor Engineers.

Cock Hotel. Old-established Commercial and Posting House. Good Accommodation for Motors. Covered Yard. Carriages and Motors for Hire. Telephone No. 10. A. DOUGHTY, Proprietor.

The Sun Hotel. First-class Family and Commercial. Finest grounds north of London. Spacious Banqueting, Ball, and Coffee Rooms. Electric Light. Excellent Garage and Stabling. Covered Yard. Moderate tariff. Telephone 92. Telegrams, Sun, Hitchin. F. CARTWRIGHT and J. TIERNAN, Proprietors.

HITHER GREEN (London) from *Charing Cross, Cannon Street*, and *London Bridge*, 7¼ miles.

Fares from Charing Cross, 1/6*a*, 1/2*b*, 0/10½*c*. R.T. for two days, 3/0*a*, 2/4*b*, 1/9*c*. From Cannon Street, 1/3*a*, 1/0*b*, 0/9*c*. R.T. for two days, 2/6*a*, 2/0*b*. *See* pp. 552-554, 556, 557.
Map Square 80.

HIXON (Stafford), 130¾

miles. Fares, 27/1*a*, 16/3*c*. R. T. for two months, 54/2*a*, 32/6*c*. Departures *from* London as for Colwich. Departures *for* London about 3 times daily.
Map Square 17.

HOCKLEY (Essex), 36¼

miles. Fares, 5/5*a*, 3/3*c*. R. T. for two months, 10/10*a*. Departures *from* London as for Rayleigh. Departures *for* London about 9 times daily. Pop. 1,127.
Map Square 24.

HOCKLEY (Warwick), 111½

miles. Fares, 23/2*a*, 13/11*c*. R. T. for two months, 46/4*a*. Departures *from* London as for Birmingham (Snow Hill). Departures *for* London about 10 times daily.

HODNET (Salop) from

Paddington, 153¾ miles. Fares, 31/11*a*, 19/2*c*. R. T. for two months, 63/10*a*. Departures *from* London as for Market Drayton. Departures *for* London about 5 times daily. Pop. 1,524.
Map Square 17.

HOE STREET (Walthamstow) from *Liverpool Street*, 6¼

miles. Fares, 0/10*a*, 0/8*b*, 0/6*c*. R. T. for two days, 1/8*a*, 1/4*b*, 0/10½*c*. Pop. 23,895. *See* pp. 523-524.
Map Square 53.

HOGHTON (Lancs), 213¼

miles. Fares, 43/9*a*, 26/3*c*. R. T. for two months, 87/6*a*, 52/6*c*. Departures *from* London as for Preston. Departures *for* London about 5 times daily. Pop. 913.
Map Square 12.

HOLBEACH (Lincoln)

from *King's Cross*, 100¼ miles. Fares, 20/8*a*, 12/5*c*. R. T., double fare. Pop. 5,381.
Map Square 18.

King's +	Holb'h.	Holb'h.	King's +
AM 5. 5*e*	8.58	AM 7.39	10.40
5. 5*d*	9.25	11. 4	3.50
8.45	11.59	PM 1.22	4.30
11.30	3.45	4.50	9. 0
PM 3. 0	6. 9	6.47	9.25
5.45*r*	8.25	—	—
—	—	—	—
—	—	—	—
—	—	—	—
—	—	—	—
—	—	—	—

No Sunday Trains.

d Saturdays only.
e Saturdays excepted.
r Restaurant Car.

HOLBECK (Yorks), from

King's Cross, 185½ miles. Fares, 38/7*a*, 23/2*c*. R. T., double fare. Pop. 29,679.

King's +	H'beck.	H'beck.	King's +
AM 4.45	9.15	AM 7.53*r*	11.30
7.15*r*	11.16	9. 4	1. 5
10.10*r*	1.53	10.18*r*	1.55
PM 1.30*r*	5. 9	10.59	3.50
1.50*r*	6.26	PM 1.13*r*	5. 0
4. 0*r*	8. 1	1.21	6.25
5.45*r*	9.32	3.19*r*	7.10
10.45*e*	2.53	5.34*r*	9.25
—	—	10.28	3.25
—	—	—	—
—	—	—	—
—	—	—	—
—	—	—	—

Sunday Trains.

12. 0*nr*	4.25	AM 11. 4*r*	3.45
PM 5. 0*r*	9.38	PM 1.14	5.55
10.45	2.53	5.44*r*	10.20
—	—	—	—
—	—	—	—

e Saturdays excepted.
n Noon.
r Restaurant Car.

HOLBORN (Hammersmith and Finsbury Park Tube).

Pop. 43,192. *See* back of Map.

HOLCOMBE BROOK

(Lancs), 200½ miles. No through fares. Departures *from* London as for Bury. Departures *for* London about 6 times daily.
Map Square 12.

HOLKHAM (Norfolk) from

Liverpool Street, 125½ miles. Fares, 26/6*a*, 15/11*c*. R. T. for two months, 53/0*a*. Departures *from* London as for Burnham Market. Departures *for* London about 6 minutes later. Pop. 427.
Map Square 14.

HOLLAND ARMS

(Anglesey), 247½ miles. Fares, 51/6*a*, 30/11*c*. R.T. for two months, 103/*a*, 61/10*c*. Departures *from* London as for Gaerwen. Departures *for* London about 5 times daily.
Map Square 11.

HOLLAND PARK (Central London Tube).

See back of Map.

HOLLINGBOURNE

(Kent) from *Victoria, Holborn Viaduct*, and *St. Paul's*, 45 miles. Fares, 9/7*a*, 7/8*b*, 5/9*c*. R. T. for two months, 19/2*a*, 15/4*b*. Departures *from* London as for Lenham. Departures *for* London about 7 times daily. Pop. 754.
Map Square 24.

HOLLINWOOD (Lancs),

191¼ miles. Fares, 38/7*a*, 23/2*c*. R. T. for two months, 77/2*a*, 46/4*c*. Departures *from* London as for Manchester. Departures *for* London about 6 times daily.

HOLLOWAY ROAD

(Hammersmith and Finsbury Park Tube). *See* back of Map.

HOLLOWAY (UPPER)

from *Moorgate Street* and *St. Pancras*, 3 miles. Fares from St. Pancras, 0/7½*a*, 0/4½*c*. R. T. for two days, 1/3*a*, 0/9*c*. From Moorgate Street, 0/9*a*, 0/5½*c*. R. T. for two days, 1/6*a*, 0/10½*c*. Pop. 35,721. *See* pp. 506-507.
Map Square 5.

HOLLYBUSH (Ayrshire),

398 miles. Fares, 81/1*a*, 48/8*c*. R. T. for two months, 162/2*a*. Departures *from* London as for Ayr. Departures *for* London about 4 times daily.
Map Square 43.

HOLLY BUSH (Monmouth), 159¼ miles.
No through fares. Departures from London as for Tredegar. Departures for London about 6 times daily. Pop. 344.

HOLME (Hunts) from King's Cross, 69¼ miles.
Fares, 14/5a, 8/8c. R. T., double fare. Pop. 648. Map Square 18.

King's+	Holme	Holme	King's+
AM 5. 5	7.17	AM 7.30	9.56
7.45	10. 3	9.28	11.15
10.12	12.54	11. 8	1.25
PM 1.55	4.11	PM 1.28	3.50
5. 0	6.36	3.53	6.25
5.10	7.43	7.35	10.20

Sunday Trains.
AM 8.30	11. 2	PM 5.29	8. 8

HOLME (Lancs), 209 miles.
No through fares. Departures from London as for Burnley (Manchester Road). Departures for London about 5 times daily. Map Square 12.

HOLME (Yorks), 186¼ miles.
Fares, 37/6a, 22/6c. R. T. double fare. Departures from London as for Selby. Departures for London about five times daily. Map Square 13.

HOLME HALE (Norfolk) from Liverpool Street, 112 miles.
Fares, 22/11a, 13/9c. R. T. for two months, 45/10a. Departures from London as for Watton. Departures for London about 4 times daily. Pop. 301. Map Square 19.

HOLME LACY (Hereford) from Paddington, 140¼ miles.
Fares, 29/2a, 17/6c. R. T. for two months, 58/4a. Departures from London as for Ross. Departures for London about 4 times daily. Pop. 263. Map Square 17.

HOLMES (Yorks) from St. Pancras 162 miles.
Fares, 32/9a, 19/8c. R. T., double fare. Departures from London as for Sheffield. Departures for London about 9 times daily. Map Square 13.

HOLMES CHAPEL (Cheshire) from Euston, 166⅓ miles.
Fares, 34/9a, 20/10c. R. T. for two months, 69/6a. Departures from London as for Sandbach. Departures for London about 6 times daily. Map Square 12.

HOLMFIELD (Yorks), 196½ miles.
Fares, 39/9a, 23/10c. R. T., double fare. Departures from London as for Halifax. Departures for London about 10 times daily. Map Square 12.

HOLMFIRTH (Yorks) from King's Cross (via Horbury).
195½ miles. Fares, 37/9a, 22/8c. R. T. double fare. Pop.10,444. Map Square 12.

King's+	H'firth.	H'firth.	King's+
AM 4.45	12.32	AM 5.35	11.30
7.15r	1.47	7.15r	1. 5
10.10r	4.33	9.29	3.50
PM 1.30r	7.48	10.43	5. 0
1.50r	8.36	PM12.50r	7.10
—	—	3. 5r	9.25
—	—	7.57e	3.25

Sunday Trains.
12. 0hn	7.58	AM 9. 0r	3.45
—	—	11.10r	5.55

e Saturdays excepted.
h Passengers cross Wakefield at own expense.
n Noon.
r Restaurant Car.

ANOTHER ROUTE from Marylebone, 188¼ miles.
Fares, 37/8a, 22/7c. R. T. for two months, 75/4a, 45/2c.

M'bone.	H'firth.	H'firth.	M'bone.
AM 2.32	8. 8	AM 8.25r	1.13
10. 0r	2.55	9.29r	3. 0
PM12.15r	5.41	PM 1.55r	6.38
3.20r	7.48	4.42r	9.55
6.20r	10.58	8.50e	3.57
—	—	9.20d	3.57

Sunday Trains.
AM11.15r	7.58
PM 5.30r	10.39

d Saturdays only.
e Saturdays excepted.
r Restaurant Car.

HOLMSLEY (Hants) from Waterloo, 97¼ miles.
Fares, 20/5a, 12/3c. R. T. for two months, 40/10a, 24/6c. Map Square 27.

W'loo	Holmsley	Holmsley	W'loo
AM 5.40	9. 3	AM 7.39r	10. 6
5.50	10.11	9.28s	12.22
9.30	12.21	11.16r	2.20
11.30r	2.11	PM 1.30	4.20
PM12.30r	3.21	2.30	6.16
3.10s	4.18	3.27s	6.26
3.30s	6.23	5.31r	8.20
5.30r	8.14	7.53	11.28
6.30r	9.21	—	—

Sunday Trains.
AM11. 0r	2.13	AM 9.24r	2.27
PM 2. 0r	5.21	PM 4.38	8. 3

r Restaurant Car.
s Refreshments served.

HOLMWOOD (Surrey) from London Bridge(L.B.& S.C.R.), 30½ miles.
Fares, 6/1a, 3/8c. R. T. for two months, 12/2a, 7/4c. Map Square 23.

Lon. B.	H'wood	H'wood	Lon. B.
AM 5.28	6.58	AM 7.42	9. 5
7.35	9.22	8. 0	9.17
9.22	10.55	8.42	9.47
10.35	12. 4	9.17	10.22
PM12.24	2. 2	10.44	11.50
2. 0d	3.23	11.59	1.28
4. 0	5.15	PM 2.11	3.32
5. 0	6. 8	3.52d	5.18
5.38d	7. 2	4.41e	6.24
5.44e	7. 2	7.11	8.41
5.59	7.30	8.10e	9.35
6.30e	7.52	9.42	11.11
7.15	8.24	—	—

Sunday Trains.
AM 6.55	8.23	AM 8.27	10.11
9.30	10.57	9.33	11. 8
PM 5.40	7.25	PM 7.17	8.46
—	—	8.51	10.25

d Saturdays only.
e Saturdays excepted.

ANOTHER ROUTE from Victoria (L.B.& S.C.R.), 28¾ miles.
Fares as above.

Vict.	H'wood	H'wood	Vict.
AM 5.18	6.57	AM 7.42	9.12
7.45	9.22	8. 0	9.34
8.58	10.55	8.42	9.59
10.30	12. 5	9.17	10.28
PM12.35	2. 2	10.44	11.42
1.45d	3.23	11.27	12.45
4. 5	5.16	11.59	1.57
4.53	6. 8	PM 2.11	3.32
6. 0	7. 2	3.52d	6. 5
7.20	8.24	4. 0d	5.32
—	—	4.41	6. 8
—	—	7.11	8.55
—	—	8.10e	9.42
—	—	9.42	11.20

Sunday Trains.
AM 9.10	10.57	AM 8.27	10.13
PM 5.40	7.25	9.33	11. 6
—	—	PM 7.17	8.37
—	—	8.51	10.42

d Saturdays only.
e Saturdays excepted.

HOLSWORTHY (Devon) from Waterloo, 217¾ miles.
Fares, 45/5a, 27/3c. R. T. for two months, 90/10a, 54/6c. Pop. 1,417. Map Square 26.

W'loo	Holsw'thy	Holsw'thy	W'loo
AM10. 0r	3. 3	AM 7.41r	1.56
11. 0r	5. 7	10. 1r	3.50
PM 1. 0r	7.14	11. 9r	4.30
3. 0r	8.16	PM 1.52r	8.30
—	—	3.58	10.50

No Sunday Trains.
r Restaurant Car.

HOLT (Norfolk) from King's Cross, 149½ miles. Fares, 24/9a, 14/10c. R. T. for two months, 49/6a, 29/8c. Pop. 2,104.
Map Square 14.

KING'S +	HOLT	HOLT	KING'S +
AM 4.45	9.4l	AM 8.20	1.5
7.15r	12.56	9.59	3.50
10.10r	4.18	PM12.39r	4.30
PM 1.50r	6.43	3.35	9.0
3.0	7.5	—	—
—	—	—	—
—	—	—	—

No Sunday Trains.
r Restaurant Car.

Blakeney Hotel. 5¼ miles from Holt. Picturesque old-world seaside village. See advt. p. **39.**

HOLT (Wilts) from Paddington, 94 miles. Fares, via Chippenham, 19/7a, 11/9c. R. T. for two months, 39/2a. Via Westbury, 20/7a, 12/4c. R. T. for two months, 41/2a, 24/8c. Pop. 1,022.
Map Square 22.

PAD.	HOLT	HOLT	PAD.
AM 1.0g	6.52	AM 6.39	10.0
5.30	8.47	7.39r	10.15
7.30	10.25	8.9l	10.52
9.0	12.2	9.16	12.20
10.45	1.41	11.22r	2.40
PM12.30r	3.50	PM12.16	2.50
2.0s	4.43	2.38	6.2
2.45	5.2	3.32	7.20
3.15t	5.58	3.50rs	6.50
4.15r	6.43	5.5r	8.35
5.55	8.22	5.9rs	8.20
6.30	8.49	7.38	10.25
—	—	9.33s	2.45

Sunday Trains.

PM12.30r	3.52	PM 3.52rs	7.55
—	—	5.53	9.15

g Mondays excepted.
r Restaurant Car.
s Via Westbury.
t Tea Car.

HOLTBY (Yorks), 196 miles. Fares, 40/10a, 24/6c. R. T., double fare. Departures from London as for York. Departures for London about 6 times daily. Pop. 129.
Map Square 8.

HOLTON (Lincoln), 150½ miles. Fares, 31/1a, 18/8c. R. T., double fare. Departures from London as for Lincoln. Departures for London about 4 times daily. Pop. 175.
Map Square 13.

Station closed on Sundays.

HOLTON LE CLAY (Lincoln), 149½ miles. Fares, 31/1a, 18/8c. R. T., double fare. Departures from London as for Louth. Departures for London about 6 times daily. Pop. 276.
Map Square 13.

HOLYHEAD (Anglesey) from Euston, 263½ miles. Fares, 55/0a, 33/0c. R. T. for two months, 110/0a, 66/0c. Pop. 11,757.
Map Square 11.

EUSTON	HOLY'H'D.	HOLY'H'D.	EUSTON
AM12.25	9.54	AM12.13	5.50
5.0	1.20	2.10g	8.0
8.30r	2.5	6.5fr	1.0
11.10dr	5.42	7.25r	1.45
11.10er	6.15	9.30er	5.5
11.50r	8.4	9.45dr	5.5
PM 2.35t	9.39	PM12.13r	5.50
5.20dr	1.7	12.35er	7.30
6.30er	1.7	2.20r	10.45
8.45	2.25	7.30	5.0
9.30e	5.50	—	—
11.50d	1.59l	—	—

Sunday Trains.

PM12.10r	9.33	AM12.13	5.50
8.45	2.25	2.10	8.0
9.15	5.50	6.20	4.0
—	—	PM12.25r	7.10
—	—	7.50	5.0

d Saturdays only.
e Saturdays excepted.
f Mondays only.
g Monday excepted.
l P.M.
r Restaurant Car.
t Tea Car.

Station Hotel. Adjoins station platform and landing stage. Convenient for passengers crossing Irish Sea. See advt. p. **218.**

HOLYTOWN (Lanark), 389 miles. Fares, 79/5 t, 47/8c. R. T. for two months, 158/10a, 95/4c. Departures from London as for Wishaw (Central). Departures for London about 4 times daily. Pop. 11,095.
Map Square 40.

HOLYWELL JUNCTION (Flint), 196 miles. Fares, 40/8a, 24/5c. R. T. for two months, 81/4a, 48/10c. Departures from London as for Chester. Departures for London about 6 times daily. Pop. (Holywell) 2,907.
Map Square 11.

HOLYWOOD (Dumfries), 335½ miles. Fares, 68/1a, 40/10c. R. T. for two months, 136/2a, 81/8c. Departures from London as for Dumfries. Departures for London about 3 times daily. Pop. 947.
Map Square 43.

HOMERSFIELD (Suffolk) from Liverpool Street, 109½ miles. Fares, 23/1a, 13/10c. R. T. for two months, 46/2a. Departures from London as for Harleston or Bungay. Departures for London about 7 times daily. Pop. 144.
Map Square 19.

HOMERTON from Broad Street, 3¼ miles. Fares, 0/5a, 0/4b, 0/3c. R. T. for two days, 0/10a, 0/7b, 0/5½c. Pop. 35,478. See p. 500.
Map Square 62.

HONEYBOURNE (Gloucester) from Paddington, 101½ miles. Fares, via Stratford-on-Avon, 21/1a, 12/8c. R. T. for two months, 42/2a. Via Evesham, 22/6a, 13/6c. R. T. for two months, 45/0a.
Map Square 17.

PAD.	HONEYB'NE.	HONEYB'NE.	PAD.
AM 5.30	9.22	AM 8.1l	11.0
6.30l	11.4	9.34	12.5
9.45	12.14	9.50lr	1.25
10.40l	1.54	11.10	2.12
PM 1.35r	5.17	11.15lr	2.5
2.10l	5.25	PM12.36r	2.55
4.45	7.5	2.31r	5.0
6.10lr	9.5	3.55	7.17
6.55	10.3	4.55lr	8.5
—	—	6.7r	9.15
—	—	7.30	10.45

Sunday Trains.

AM10.35r	1.35	AM11.14	2.40
PM 4.10	7.20	PM 6.28r	9.48

l Via Stratford-on-Avon.
r Restaurant Car.

HONING (Norfolk) from King's Cross, 164½ miles. Fares, 25/3a, 15/2c. R. T. for two months, 50/6a, 30/4c. Departures from London as for North Walsham. Departures for London about 3 times daily. Pop. 325.
Map Square 19.

HONINGTON (Lincoln) from King's Cross, 111½ miles. Fares, 23/2a, 13/11c. R. T., double fare. Departures from London as for Lincoln or Sleaford. Departures for London about 5 times daily. Pop. 182.
Map Square 13.

HONITON (Devon) from Waterloo, 155 miles. Fares, 32/4a, 19/5c. R. T. for two months, 64/8a, 38/10c. Pop. 3,090.
Map Square 26.

W'LOO	HONITON	HONITON	W'LOO
AM 7.30	12.10	AM 7.5r	11.10
12.0r	4.10	9.39r	5.45
PM 1.0r	5.40	11.9r	3.8
3.0r	6.37	PM 1.40r	6.0
6.0r	10.10	3.31	7.40
—	—	4.6r	8.30
—	—	6.20	10.50
—	—	8.26h	3.58

Sunday Trains.

AM 9.0	3.10	PM 4.10r	8.57
12.0nr	4.56	—	—

h Via Eastleigh.
n Noon.
r Restaurant Car.

HONLEY (Yorks), 184¾

miles. Fares, 37/4*a*, 22/5*c*. R. T. for two months, 74/8*a*. Departures *from* London as for Penistone. Departures *for* London about 6 times daily. Pop. 4,700.
Map Square 12.

HONOR OAK (London)

from *Victoria* or *Ludgate Hill*, 7¼ miles. Fares, 1/3*a*, 1/0*b*, 0/9*c*. R. T. for two days, 2/4*a*, 1/9*b*, 1/4*c*. *See* pp. 562, 563.
Map Square 79.

HONOR OAK PARK

(London) from *London Bridge*, 4¾ miles, and *Victoria*, 11¼ miles. Fares from London Bridge, 1/0*a*, 0/7*c*. R. T. for two days, 2/0*a*, 1/2*c*. From Victoria, *via* Crystal Palace, 1/6*a*, 0/10½*c*. R. T. for two days, 3/0*a*, 1/9*c*. *See* pp. 568-570, 580, 581.
Map Square 79.

HOOK (Hants) from

Waterloo, 42¼ miles. Fares, 8/9*a*, 5/3*c*. R. T. for two months, 17/6*a*, 10/6*c*.
Map Square 23.

W'loo	Hook	Hook	W'loo
AM 5.50	7.27	AM 7.19	8.40
7.30	8.57	8.12	9.26
8.34	10. 1	8.53	9.56
9.20	10.44	9.43	10.56
10.34	12. 5	10.49	12.11
PM 12.40	2. 7	11.49	1.20
1.15*d*	2.45	PM 1.56	3.16
2.34	4. 9	2.46	4. 6
3.40	5. 8	3.49	5.20
4.40	6.15	4.49	6.16
5.10*e*	6.25	5.45	7. 7
6. 0	7. 9	7.51	9.26
6.40*d*	8. 7	10.18	12.16
6.54*e*	8. 5	—	—
8. 0	9.24	—	—
8.55	10.38	—	—
—	—	—	—
—	—	—	—
—	—	—	—

Sunday Trains.

AM 9. 0	10.26	AM 7.56	9.45
9.45	11.20	10.15	12.41
11.15	12.38	11.24	12.52
PM 5. 5	6.29	PM 4.54	6. 7
6. 0	7.24	7.47	9.12
7.20	8.54	9.27	10.52
9.28	11. 6	—	—
—	—	—	—
—	—	—	—
—	—	—	—

d Saturdays only.
e Saturdays excepted.

HOOKAGATE (Salop), 156

miles. No through fares. Departures *from* London as for Shrewsbury. Departures *for* London about 3 times daily.

HOOK NORTON (Oxon),

72¾ miles. Fares, *via* Bicester, 14/6*a*, 9/2*c*. R. T. for two months, 29/0*a*, 18/4*c*. *Via* Kingham, 19/1*a*, 11/11*c*. R. T. for two months, 38/2*a*, 23/10*c*. Departures *from* London as for Chipping Norton. Departures *for* London about 5 times daily. Pop. 1,349.
Map Square 17.

HOOK OF HOLLAND

from *Liverpool Street*, *via* Harwich, 190 miles, by special express trains and turbine steamers every weekday. Single Fares, 55/6*a*, 37/6*b*.
See advt. p. 3.

HOOLE (Lancs), 215¼ miles.

No through fares. Departures *from* London as for Preston. Departures *for* London about 6 times daily. Pop. 5,990.
Map Square 12.

HOOTON (Cheshire), from

Euston, 187¼ miles. Fares, 39/0*a*, 23/5*c*. R. T. for two months, 78/0*a*. Pop. 226.
Map Square 12.

Euston	Hooton	Hooton	Euston
AM 12.25*g*	6.57	AM 7.52*er*	12. 5
12.25*f*	7.40	7.52*dr*	12.20
2.35	9.42	9.11*r*	1. 0
5. 0	10.17	9.35*r*	1.45
8.30*r*	12.42	9.55*r*	2.20
10.30*r*	2.26	11. 1*r*	3.10
10.40*r*	3.21	PM 1.18*r*	5.50
11.50*r*	3.47	2.36*r*	7.30
12. 0*nr*	5.55	4. 0*r*	8.10
PM 2.35*t*	6.42	4.42*er*	9. 5
4. 5*r*	8.22	4.42*dr*	9.15
5.20*r*	9.18	5.41*r*	10.45
6.30*er*	11.20	10.13	5. 0
8.45*d*	6.58	11.29	5.50
11.50*d*	10.23	—	—
—	—	—	—

Sunday Trains.

PM 12.10*r*	5.55	AM 9. 2	4. 0
—	—	PM 2.41*r*	7.10
—	—	10.10	5. 0
—	—	—	—
—	—	—	—
—	—	—	—

d Saturdays only.
e Saturdays excepted.
f Mondays only.
g Mondays excepted.
n Noon.
r Restaurant Car.
t Tea Car.

ANOTHER ROUTE from

Paddington, 202¾ miles. Fares as above.

Pad.	Hooton	Hooton	Pad.
AM 9.10*r*	2.21	AM 7.20	12.25
10.20*r*	2.27	8.17*r*	1.25
10.40*r*	3.24	9.23*r*	2. 5
PM 12.50*r*	5.59	PM 12. 1*r*	5. 0
2.10*t*	6.38	1.21*r*	5.55
4.10*t*	8.45	2.36*r*	8. 5
6.10*r*	10.55	4.42*r*	10. 0
12.15	6.59	7.31	3.30
—	—	—	—
—	—	—	—
—	—	—	—

Sunday Trains.

PM 12.50*r*	5.58	AM 9. 2	6.20
—	—	PM 3.15*r*	9. 0
—	—	—	—
—	—	—	—
—	—	—	—

r Restaurant Car.
t Tea Car.

HOPE (Derby), 164 miles.

Fares, 34/0*a*, 20/5*c*. R. T., double fare. Departures *from* London as for Hathersage. Departures *for* London about 6 times daily. Pop. 579.
Map Square 12.

HOPE (Flint), 188¼ miles.

Fares, 39/2*a*, 23/6*c*. R. T. for two months, 78/4*a*. Departures *from* London as for Chester. Departures *for* London about 6 times daily. Pop. 4,806.
Map Square 12.

HOPEMAN (Elgin), 583¼

miles. Fares, 106/3*a*, 63/9*c*. R. T. for two months, 212/6*a*, 127/6*c*. Departures *from* London as for Forres. Departures *for* London about twice daily. Pop. 1,279.
Map Square 35.

HOPE VILLAGE (Flint),

188 miles. No through fares. Departures *from* London as for Wrexham. Departures *for* London about 5 times daily.
Map Square 12.

HOPTON (Suffolk), 122½

miles. Fares, 25/7*a*, 15/4*c*. R. T. for two months, 51/2*a*. Departures *from* London as for Gorleston. Departures *for* London about 4 times daily. Pop. 304.
Map Square 19.

HOPTON HEATH

(Salop), 177¾ miles. Fares, 33/1*a*, 19/10*c*. R. T. for two months, 66/2*a*, 39/8*c*. Departures *from* London as for Craven Arms. Departures *for* London about twice daily.
Map Square 17.

HORBURY (Yorks) from

King's Cross, 179 miles. Fares, 37/4*a*, 22/5*c*. R. T. for two months, 74/8*a*, 44/10*c*. Pop. 7,830.
Map Square 12.

King's +	Horb'y.	Horb'y.	King's +
AM 4.45	10.46	AM 6.39*r*	11.30
7.15*r*	12. 9	8.35*r*	1. 5
10.10*dr*	2.33	10. 2*r*	1.55
10.10*er*	3. 7	10.40	3.50
PM 1.30*r*	5.40	PM 12.32	5. 0
1.50*r*	7.28	3. 7*r*	7.10
5.45*r*	10.24	5.13*r*	9.25
—	—	9. 5*e*	3.25
—	—	—	—

Sunday Trains.

12. 0*hn*	6.13	AM 10.42	3.45
PM 10.45	5. 3*h*	PM 3.57*h*	10.20
—	—	—	—
—	—	—	—

d Saturdays only.
e Saturdays excepted.
h Passengers cross Wakefield at own expense.
n Noon.
r Restaurant Car.

HORBURY JUNC.

(Yorks), 177¼ miles. Fares, 37/1*a*, 22/3*c*. R. T. for two months, 74/2*a*, 44/6*c*. Departures *from* London as for Wakefield. Departures *for* London about 8 times daily.
Map Square 12.

HORDEN (Durham), 253¾

miles. Fares, 52/11*a*, 31/9*c*. R. T., double fare. Departures *from* London as for West Hartlepool. Departures *for* London about 5 times daily.
Map Square 8.

HORDERLEY (Salop), 169

miles. No through fares. Departures *from* London as for Craven Arms. Departures *for* London about 3 times daily.
Map Square 17.

HORHAM (Suffolk), 97 miles. Fares, 20/5*a*, 12/3*c*. R. T. for two months, 40/10*a*, 24/6*c*. Departures *from* London as for Stradbroke. Departures *for* London about twice daily. Pop. 290.
Map Square 19.

HORLEY (Surrey) from *London Bridge*, *Victoria*, and *Clapham Junction*, 25¾ miles. Fares, 5/5*a*, 3/3*c*. R. T. for two months, 10/10*a*, 6/6*c*. Pop. 6,100.
Map Square 23.

Vict.	Leave Clap. J.	Lon. B.	Arr. at Horley
AM —	—	5.18	6.27
7.23	7.29	7.25	8.34
8.25	8.32	8. 7	9.23
9.45	9.51	9.50	10.54
10.35	10.42	10.35	11.33
12. 0	12. 7	12.10	1. 0
PM —	—	1.20*d*	2. 0
—	—	2. 5	2.52
2. 0*d*	2. 7*d*	—	3. 1
2. 0*e*	2. 7*e*	—	3. 3
—	—	2. 8*d*	3.10
4. 0	4. 8	4. 5	4.54
—	—	5. 5	5.42
5. 5	5.12	5.10	6. 5
5.27	—	5.21	6.23
—	—	6. 0	6.39
6. 6	6.12	6. 8	7.11
6.50	6.57	7. 0	7.52
7.15	7.22	7.20	8.19
9. 3	9.10	9.12	10. 4
10.30	10.38	10.35	11.37
11.50*h*	—	—	12.34
—	—	—	—
—	—	—	—
—	—	—	—
—	—	—	—
—	—	—	—

Sunday Trains.

AM 6.55	7. 2	7. 2	8.15
—	—	7.22	8.25
8.18	8.25	8.25	9.19
8.50	8.57	8.55	9.59
9.30	9.37	9.30	10.25
PM 1.14	1.21	1.10	2.12
5.50	5.57	6. 0	7. 2
8. 0	8. 8	8. 0	9. 7
9. 5	9.13	9.10	10. 9
—	—	—	—
—	—	—	—
—	—	—	—
—	—	—	—
—	—	—	—

Trains from Horley.

Leave Horley	Lon. B.	Arrive at Clap. J.	Vict.
AM 7. 9	8.15	8.15	8.24
7.54	8.46	9. 0	9. 8
8.27	9.10	—	9.19
8.44	—	9.37	9.44
8.49	9.42	—	9.58
9.21	9.58	—	—
9.50	10.38	10.29	10.36
11.10	12.13	11.59	12. 7
PM12.40	1.42	1.39	1.49
2.40	3.40	3.37	3.45
3.17	—	4. 9	4.17
4.49	5.54	5.47	5.55
7.41	8.46	8.39	8.48
9.52	10.58	11.10	11.17
—	—	—	—
—	—	—	—
—	—	—	—

HORLEY—*continued.*

Sunday Trains.

Leave Horley	Lon. B.	Arrive at Clap. J.	Vict.
AM 9.41	10.45	10.42	10.50
PM 4. 3	5. 3	5. 1	5.11
6.57	7.56	8.31	8.41
8.30	9.32	9.24	9.34
10.37	11.34	11.34	11.42
—	—	—	—
—	—	—	—
—	—	—	—

d Saturdays only.
e Saturdays excepted.
h Wednesdays only.

House and Estate Agents.
For Furnished and Unfurnished Houses and Properties for Sale. Telephone No. 3.
BAKER & BAKER.

HORNBY (Lancs) from *St. Pancras*, 252 miles. Fares, 47/11*a*, 28/9*c*. R. T., double fare. Pop. 439.
Map Square 7.

St. Pan.	Hornby	Hornby	St. Pan.
AM 2.25*g*	12.24	AM 7. 8*r*	2.10
4.25	1.42	8.25*r*	4.10
9.50*r*	4.50	10. 6*r*	5.30
PM12.15*er*	6.37	11.35*hr*	6.35
12.15*dr*	8. 2	PM 1.20*r*	7.55
11.50*e*	8.30	7.12	4.20
11.50*d*	9.19	—	—
—	—	—	—

Sunday Trains.

AM10.50*r*	7.50	AM 8.53	5.27
PM11.45	8.30	PM 6.56	4.55
—	—	—	—
—	—	—	—
—	—	—	—
—	—	—	—

d Saturdays only.
e Saturdays excepted.
g Mondays excepted.
h Mondays, Tuesdays, Fridays and Saturdays only.
r Restaurant Car.

HORNCASTLE (Lincoln) from *King's Cross*, 130 miles. Fares, 27/1*a*, 16/3*c*. R. T., double fare. Pop. 3,461.
Map Square 13.

King's +	H'cas'e.	H'cas'e.	King's +
AM 4.45	8.55	AM 9.15	1. 5
7.15*r*	11.35	10.50	3.50
8.45	1.25	PM12.30	4.30
11.30	4.20	3.55	9. 0
PM 3. 0	7. 0	6. 5	3.25
4. 0	7.32	—	—
—	—	—	—
—	—	—	—
—	—	—	—
—	—	—	—

No Sunday Trains.

r Restaurant Car.

HORNCHURCH (Essex) from *Fenchurch Street*, 13 miles. Fares, 2/9*a*, 1/8*c*. R. T. for two months, 5/3*a*, 2/7½*c*. Pop. 10,891. *See* p. 509.
Map Square 24.

HORNCHURCH—*contd.*

ANOTHER ROUTE from *Moorgate Street* and *St. Pancras*, 19¾ miles. Fares from St. Pancras, 2/5*a*, 1/5½*c*. R. T. for two months, 4/10*a*, 2/9½*c*. *See* p. 508.

HORNINGLOW (Stafford), 123¾ miles. Fares, 25/5*a*, 15/3*c*. R. T., double fare. Departures *from* London as for Burton-on-Trent. Departures *for* London about 6 times daily. Pop. 6,538.
Map Square 17

HORNSEA (Yorks), 211 miles. Fares, 37/6*a*, 22/6*c*. R. T. for two months, 75/0*a*, 45/0*c*. Departures *from* London as for Hull (Paragon). Departures *for* London about 8 times daily. Pop. 4,278.
Map Square 8.

HORNSEY (Middlesex) from *King's Cross*, *Moorgate Street*, and *Broad Street*, 4 miles. Fares, from King's Cross, 0/9*a*, 0/7*b*, 0/5½*c*. R. T. for two days, 1/6*a*, 1/2*b*, 0/10½*c*. From Moorgate Street and Broad Street, 0/10*a*, 0/8*b*, 0/6*c*. R. T. for two days, 1/8*a*, 1/4*b*, 1/0*c*. Pop. 87,659. *See* pp. 511-517.
Map Squares 23 *and* 52.

HORNSEY ROAD from *Moorgate Street* and *St. Pancras*, 3¼ miles. Fares from St. Pancras, 0/9*a*, 0/5½*c*. R. T. for two days, 1/4*a*, 0/10½*c*. From Moorgate Street, 0/9*a*, 0/5½*c*. R. T. for two days, 1/6*a*, 0/10½*c*. *See* pp. 506, 507.
Map Square 51.

HORRABRIDGE (Devon) from *Paddington*, 232 miles. Fares, 46/11*a*, 28/2*c* R. T. for two months, 93/10*a*. Departures *from* London as for Tavistock. Departures *for* London about 8 times daily. Pop. 839.
Map Square 26.

HORRINGFORD (Isle of Wight), 93¾ miles. Fares, 19/9*a*, 12/1*c*. R. T. for two months, 39/6*a*, 24/2*c*. Departures *from* London as for Sandown. Departures *for* London about 4 times daily.
Map Square 28.

HORSE BRIDGE (Hants), 75 miles. Fares, 15/8*a*, 9/5*c*. R. T. for two months, 31/4*a*, 18/10*c*. Departures *from* London as for Longparish or Andover Junction. Departures *for* London about 6 times daily.
Map Square 22.

HORSEHAY (Salop), 144½ miles. Fares, 29/9*a*, 17/10*c*. R. T. for two months, 59/6*a*, 35/8*c*. Departures *from* London as for Ketley. Departures *for* London about 5 times daily.
Map Square 17.

HORSFORTH (Yorks), 190 miles. Fares, 39/7*a*, 23/9*c*. R. T. for two months, 79/2*a*, 47/6*c*. Departures *from* London as for Leeds. Departures *for* London about 6 times daily.
Map Square 12.

HORSHAM (Sussex) from

Victoria, Clapham Junction, and London Bridge, 37¼ miles. Fares, 7/11a, 4/9c. R.T. for two months, 15/10a, 9/6c. Pop. 11,413.
Map Square 23.

	Leave		Arr. at
VICT.	CLAP. J.	LON. B	HORS'M.
AM 5.18	5.28	5.28	7.17
6.18	6.25	6.35	7.39
7.23	7.29	7.25	9.27
7.45	7.56	7.35	9.43
8.55	—	—	9.59
—	8.32	8. 7	10.12
9. 0	9. 8	9. 6	10.34
—	—	9.22	11.13
9.45	9.51	9.50	11.28
10.15	10.22	10.22	11.31
—	—	10.30	11.43
10.35	10.42	10.35	12.14
11.55	—	11.50	1.29
PM12.35	12.42	12.24	2.22
1.20e	1.27e	—	2.53
1.25d	—	1.10d	2.53
1.40	1.47e	1.50	2.59
2. 0	2. 7	2. 5	4. 6
—	—	2. 8d	4. 6
3.55	4. 2	4. 0	5. 7
4. 5	4.12	—	5.34
4.30	—	4. 5	5.37
—	—	4.50	5.48
4.53	5. 0	—	6. 4
—	—	5. 5	6.19
5. 5	5.12	—	6.44
—	—	5.14	6.42
6. 0	—	—	7.17
—	—	6. 0	7.23
—	6.12	6. 8	7.56
6.15	—	—	7.10
7.20	7.27	7.15	8.40
—	—	7.20	8.53
9. 3	9.10	9.12	10.39

Sunday Trains.

	Leave		Arr. at
AM —	—	6.55	8.42
6.55	7. 2	7. 2	8.54
8.35	8.42	—	9.39
—	—	8.25	9.53
9. 0	9. 7	8.55	10.22
9.55	—	—	10.53
PM 4. 5	4.13	3.50	5.37
5.40	5.47	5.40	7.46
6.33	6.40	6.33	8. 9
7. 0	7. 7	6.38	8.12

Trains from Horsham.

Leave HORSHM.	LON. B.	Arrive at CLAP. J.	VICT.
AM 6.35	8.15	8.15	8.24
7.25	9. 4	9. 5	9.12
7.53	9.10	9.31	9.19
8.15	9.30	—	9.34
8.53	—	—	10.28
9. 1	9.58	—	—
9.25	—	10.40	10.48
9.33	10.45	10.44	10.53
10.24	11.50	11.35	11.42
10.32	12.13	11.59	12. 7
11. 5	12. 8	—	12. 0
11.10	—	12.33	12.42
11.35	1.28	—	—

HORSHAM—continued.

Leave HORSHM.	LON. B.	Arrive at CLAP. J.	VICT.
PM12.12	—	—	1.10
12.32	2.22	2.13	2.22
1.47	3.32	3.22	3.32
1.55	3.39	3.37	3.45
2.45	—	4. 9	4.17
2.57	4.15	—	—
3.20	4.27	4.27	4.35
4.10	—	5. 4	5.12
4.13	5.54	—	—
4.20	—	5.59	6. 8
5.15	6.36	6.26	6.34
5.57	—	—	6.50
6.32	7.48	7.31	7.39
6.48	8.41	8.46	8.55
6.50	8.46	—	—
8.55	10. 8	9.53	10. 1
9.14	10.58	11.10	11.17
9.20	11.11	11.12	11.20

Sunday Trains.

AM 8. 2	10.11	10. 6	10.13
9. 2	10.45	10.23	10.32
9.10	11. 8	10.59	11. 6
PM 3.25	5. 3	5. 1	5.11
6.10	—	7.25	7.33
6.13	7.56	—	—
7.34	8.50	8.33	8.42
7.59	9.32	9.24	9.34
8.25	10.25	10.32	10.42

d Saturdays only.
e Saturdays excepted.

f

Black Horse Hotel. Telephone 124. The leading Hotel. Ballroom and Masonic Temple. Central Heating. Electric Light. Enlarged and improved.
TRUST HOUSES, Ltd.

King's Head Hotel. "Leading and Oldest Established Hotel." Spacious Lounge, Coffee Rooms. Smoke and Billiard Rooms, Ball and Assembly Rooms. Excellent Cuisine. Moderate. Lock - up Garages, Inspection Pit, Loose Boxes for Hunters. Telephone 126. Proprietress, F. G. DRUCE.

Station Hotel (Family and Commercial), main entrance to Station. Electric Light. Perfect Sanitary arrangement. Sole Agents to the L.B. & S.C. Rly. Motors and Carriages meet all trains. Tel. No. 16. Proprietors, F. ROBERTS & SON.

HORSLEY (Surrey) from

Waterloo, 22¼ miles. Fares, 4/7a, 2/9c. R.T. for two months, 9/2a, 5/6c. Pop. 1,220.
Map Square 23.

W'LOO	HORSLEY	HORSLEY	W'LOO
AM 6. 5	6.57	AM 7.14	8.19
6.45	7.49	7.35	8.30
7. 5	7.58	7.57	8.48
7.45	8.46	8.30	9.21
8. 5	8.57	8.36	9.38
8.45	9.46	9.10	10. 0
9. 5	9.57	9.32	10.38
9.45	10.50	9.47e	10.36
10. 5	11. 0	10.17	11. 6
10.45	11.49	10.32	11.38
11. 5	11.57	11. 7	11.56
11.45	12.47	11.32	12.38
PM12. 5	12.57	PM12.11	1. 0
12.45	1.46	12.32	1.38
1. 5	1.57	1.13	2. 2
1.35d	2.27	1.32	2.38
1.45	2.46	2.11	3. 0
2. 5	2.57	2.32	3.38
2.45	3.46	3.11	4. 0
3. 5	3.57	3.32	4.38
3.45	4.47	4.11	5. 0
4. 5	4.57	4.25	5.38
4.45	5.49	5.21	6.10
5. 5	5.57	5.32	6.38
5.37e	6.29	6. 2	6.52
5.45d	6.46	6.32	7.38
5.45e	7. 3	7.11	8. 0
6. 5	6.57	7.32	8.38
6.38e	7.29	8.11	9. 0
6.45	7.47	8.32	9.38
7. 5	7.57	9.11	10. 0
7.45	8.53	9.32	10.38
8. 5	9. 3	10. 7	10.56
8.45	9.47	10.32	11.38
9. 5	9.57	—	—
9.45	10.48	—	—
10. 5	10.57	—	—
11.35	12.24	—	—

Sunday Trains.

AM 8.18	9.24	AM10. 2	10.55
8.38	9.39	10.15	11.24
10. 8	11. 7	11. 1	11.55
10.38	11.44	PM12. 1	12.55
11. 8	12. 7	12.15	1.24
11.38	12.44	1. 1	1.55
PM12. 8	1. 7	1.15	2.24
12.38	1.46	2. 1	2.55
1. 8	2. 7	2.15	3.24
2. 8	3. 7	4. 1	4.55
2.38	3.44	4.15	5.24
3. 8	4. 7	6. 1	6.55
4.38	5.44	6.15	7.24
5. 8	6. 7	7. 1	7.55
6. 8	7. 7	7.15	8.24
6.33	7.44	8.11	9. 5
7. 8	8. 7	9. 1	9.55
7.38	8.46	9.15	10.24
8. 8	9. 7	10. 1	10.55
8 38	9.44	10.15	11.24
9. 8	10. 7	—	—

d Saturdays only.
e Saturdays excepted.

HORSMONDEN (Kent)

from *Charing Cross, Cannon Street* and *London Bridge*, 40 miles. Fares, 8/4a, 6/8b, 5/0c. R. T. for two months, 16/8a, 13/4b. Pop. 1,446.
Map Square 24.

Leave			Arr. at
CHAR. +	CAN. ST.	LON. B.	HMNDN.
AM —	6.45	6.50	8.42
9.25	—	9.33	11.17
—	11.56	12. 0	1.24
PM 3. 0	—	3. 8	4.37
3.50d	—	3.57d	6. 3
—	4.36e	4.39e	6. 3
5.35d	—	5.41d	7.36
6. 0e	—	6. 9e	7.31

No Sunday Trains.

Trains from Horsmonden.

Leave		Arrive at	
HMNDN.	LON. B.	CAN. ST.	CHAR. +
AM 8. 6	9.32	9.36	—
9.31	10.58	11. 2	—
PM12. 4	1.36	—	1.50
3.56	5.50	—	6. 3
5.14	7.25	7.30	—
6.46	8.26	—	8.35
8.22	10.22	—	10.35

No Sunday Trains.

d Saturdays only.
e Saturdays excepted.
l Low Level Platform.

HORSTED KEYNES

(Sussex) from *London Bridge, Victoria,* and *Cannon Street,* 36¼ miles, *via* East Grinstead. Fares, 7/8a, 4/7c. R. T. for two months, 15/4a, 9/2c. Pop. 931.
Map Square 23.

Leave			Arr. at
VICT.	CAN. ST.	LON. B.	HORS.K.
AM 6.37	—	6.40	8.34
7.23	—	8. 7	9.53
9.10	—	9. 6	10.59
10.35	—	10.35	12.28
12. 0	—	11.50	1.45
PM 1.20e	—	1.38e	3.17
1.25d	—	1.38d	3.24
—	—	2. 5e	4.21
2.25	—	2.25d	4.21
4. 0	—	4.10	5.52
5.48	—	5.21	7.24
—	—	5.41e	7.24
6.50	—	7. 0	8.37
7.15	—	7.38	9.22

Sunday Trains.

Leave			Arr. at
VICT.	CAN. ST.	LON. B.	HORS.K.
AM 8.18	—	8.30	10.18
PM 6.33	—	6.46	8.33

HORSTED KEYNES—continued.

Trains from Horsted Keynes.

Leave	Arrive at		
HORS. K.	LON. B.	CAN. ST.	VICT.
AM 6.57	8.37	—	8.40
7.23	9. 1k	9. 4	9. 8
8.50	10. 7	—	10.46
9.57	12.13	—	11.35
11.44	1.42	—	1.26
PM 2.25	4.32	—	4.35
3.49	5.21	—	5.55
6.23	8.46	—	8.27
8.36	10.25	—	11.17

Sunday Trains.

Leave	Arrive at		
HORS. K.	LON. B.	CAN. ST.	VICT.
AM 9.32	11.15	—	—
PM 7.45	9.26	—	9.34

d Saturdays only.
e Saturdays excepted.
k Departs from or arrives at London Bridge S.E. & C. station.

ANOTHER ROUTE from

Victoria, Clapham Junction, and *London Bridge, via* Hayward's Heath, 42½ miles. Fares, 8/4a, 5/0c. R.T. for two months, 16/8a, 10/0c.

Leave			Arr. at
VICT.	CLAP. J.	LON. B.	HORS.K.
AM —	—	5.18	7.16
6.37	6.44	6.40	8.32
10. 5	10.11	9.50	11.42
12.45	—	12.10	2.11
PM 2. 0	2. 7	2. 5	3.48
4.30	—	5. 5d	6.13
—	—	5. 8e	6.13
5.45e	—	5.55e	7. 6
6.50	6.57	7. 0	8.34

No Sunday Trains.

Trains from Horsted Keynes.

Leave	Arrive at		
HORS. K.	LON.B.	CLAP. J.	VICT.
AM 7.40	8.53	9. 0	9. 8
8.36	9.58	—	—
8.54	10. 5	10. 5	10.12
11. 1	12.44	12.36	12.45
11.48	1.42	1.39	1.50
PM 3.18e	5.54	5.47	5.55
3.25d	5.54	5.47	5.55
4.48	6.36	6.26	6.34
6.35	8.46	8.39	8.48
7.18e	10. 0	10. 2	10.10
8.50	10.25	10. 9	10.17
9.22	—	11.10	11.17

No Sunday Trains.

d Saturdays only.
e Saturdays excepted.

HORTON (Yorks), 242¼

miles. Fares, 47/3a, 28/4c. R. T. for two months, 94/6a, 56/8c. Departures *from* London as for Settle. Departures *for* London about 5 times daily. Pop. 720.
Map Square 7.

HORTON PARK (Yorks),

193 miles. Fares, 39/9a, 23/10c. R. T., double fare. Departures *from* London as for Bradford. Departures *for* London about 8 times daily.
Map Square 12.

HORWICH (Lancs), 204¼

miles. Fares, 42/4a, 25/5c. R. T. for two months, 84/8a, 50/10c. Departures *from* London as for Bolton (*via* Manchester). Departures *for* London about 6 times daily. Pop. 15,616.
Map Square 12.

HOSCAR (Lancs), 204

miles. Fares, 42/1a, 25/3c. R. T. for two months, 84/2a, 50/6c. Departures *from* London as for Wigan. Departures *for* London about 6 times daily.
Map Square 12.

HOTHFIELD (Kent) from

Victoria, Holborn Viaduct, and *St. Paul's,* 55¼ miles. Fares, 11/8a, 9/4b, 7/0c. R. T. for two months, 23/4a, 18/8b. Departures *from* London as for Charing. Departures *for* London about 7 times daily. Pop. 315.
Map Square 24.

HOUGHAM (Lincoln)

from *King's Cross,* 111½ miles. Fares, 23/2a, 13/11c. R. T., double fare. Departures *from* London as for Claypole. Departures *for* London about 8 minutes later. Pop. 230.
Map Square 13.

HOUGH GREEN (Lancs),

207 miles. Fares, 39/5a, 23/8c. R.T. for two months, 78/10a, 47/4c. Departures *from* London as for Warrington (Central). Departures *for* London about 4 times daily.

HOUNSLOW (Middlesex)

from *Waterloo,* 13½ miles. Fares, *via* Barnes, 1/2a, 0/9c. R. T. for two days, 2/2a, 1/6c. Pop. 31,381.
See p. 586.

HOUNSLOW BAR-RACKS from *Mansion House,*

15 miles. *See p.* 489.
Map Square 66.

HOUNSLOW TOWN

from *Mansion House,* 13¾ miles. *See p.* 489.

HOUSTON (Renfrew), 414

miles. Fares, 32/9a, 49/8c. R. T. for two months, 165/6a, 99/4c. Departures *from* London as for Greenock. Departures *for* London about 4 times daily. Pop. 2,522.

HOVE (Sussex) from *London*

Bridge and *Victoria*, 50¾ miles.
Fares, 10/6*a*, 6/4*c*. R.T. for two
months, 21/0*a*, 12/8*c*. Pop. 46,519.
Map Square 28.

	Leave	Arr. at
VICT.	LON. B.	HOVE
AM		
—	5.18	7.44
6.37	6.40	8.36
7.23	7.25	9.57
8.25	8. 7	10.19
9. 0	—	10.44
—	9. 6	11. 4
10. 5	9.50	11.35
10.35	10.35	12.59
11. 0*l*	—	12.12
11.40	—	12.51
—	11.40*d*	1. 9
11.55	11.50	1.34
PM12.45	—	2. 1
—	1.20*d*	2.42
1.55	—	3.11
—	2. 5	3.48
2. 0*d*	—	3.59
2. 0*e*	—	4.24
—	2. 8*d*	4.54
3.10*l*	—	4.24
3.40*v*	—	5. 8
—	4. 0	5.27
4.30	—	5.49
—	5. 5*d*	6.15
—	5. 8*e*	6.13
5.45	—	7. 2
—	5.55*e*	7. 8
—	6. 0	7.29
—	6. 8	8.29
6.40	—	7.55
7.15	7.20	8.54
8.35	—	9.46
9. 3*d*	9.12*d*	11. 4
9. 3*e*	9.12*e*	11.14
10. 0	—	11 29

Sunday Trains.

AM 6.55	7. 2	9.34
8.50	8.55	11.14
9.45*k*	—	11.14
10.30*v*	—	11.43
11. 0*p*	—	12. 9
11. 5	—	12.34
PM12.15	—	1.49
1.10	—	2.44
1.14	1.10	3.29
4.55*k*	—	6.14
5.50	6. 0	8.44
6.30*p*	—	8.14
8. 0	8. 0	10.14
9.25	9.10	11.14

Trains from Hove.

Leave	Arrive at	
HOVE	LON. B.	VICT.
AM 6. 5	8.15	8.24
6.43	8.19	—
7.18	8.38	—
7.51	—	9.15
8. 0	9.25	—
8. 0*f*	—	9.22

HOVE—*continued.*

	Leave	Arrive at	
	HOVE	LON. B.	VICT.
AM 8. 9*g*	—	9.22
8.33*e*	9.50	—
8.38*d*	9.50	—
8.43*e*	—	10.24
8.51*e*	9.54	—
8.58*d*	10.33	—
9. 5*e*	10.33	—
9.34	—	10.55
9.47	11.10	—
10. 3	11.20	11.17
10.40	12.19	12.17
11. 5	1.42	—
PM12. 5	—	1.20
12.55*l*	—	2.20
1. 7*e*	2.23	—
1.22	3.40	3.45
2.47*v*	—	4.17
3.10*d*	4.58	4.45
3.10	—	4.50
3.36	5.54	5.55
4.45	6.36	6.34
5.33*l*	—	6.45
5.51	7.42	7.30
7.11	—	8.48
7.32	10.25	10.17
8.15*d*	10. 0	9.45
8.52	10.58	—
9.40	—	11.17
10.54	12.59	1. 0

Sunday Trains.

AM 7.51	10.45	—
9.18	11.15	10.50
11. 0	—	1. 0
PM12.18	—	1.35
2.55	5. 3	5.11
4.45*p*	—	6. 0
5.24	7.56	7. 0
5.58	—	7.28
6.39*v*	—	7.50
7.12	9.17	9.13
9.23	—	10.55
9.28	11.34	11.42
10.29	12.27	—

d Saturdays only.
e Saturdays excepted.
f Mondays only.
g Mondays excepted.
k Third class Pullman Cars only.
l First and third class Pullman
Car only.
p First class Pullman Cars only.
v Pullman Car attached.

Sussex Family Hotel. A.A.

Facing Sea, and close to Brine
Baths. Good English Fare.
Moderate terms. Telephone,
P.O. Brighton 890.

HOVINGHAM SPA

(Yorks), 216½ miles. Fares, 44/5*a*,
26/8*c*. R. T., double fare. Departures *from* London as for
Ampleforth. Departures *for* London about 5 times daily. Pop. 496.
Map Square 8.

HOWDEN (NORTH)

(Yorks) from *King's Cross*, via
Doncaster, 183 miles. Fares, 35/0*a*,
21/0*c*. R. T. for two months, 70/0*a*,
42/0*c*. Pop. 2,007.
Map Square 13.

KING'S +	HOWDEN	HOWDEN	KING'S +
AM 4.45*l*	10.32	AM 6.26*lr*	11.30
7.15*lr*	11.50	8.50*l*	3.50
8.45*l*	2.24	10.38*lr*	4.30
11.30*l*	5.47	PM 3.34*lr*	9.25
PM 4. 0*lr*	9.37	8.47*l*	3.25
5.45*lr*	11.25		
10.45*l*	4. 5	—	—

Sunday Trains.

AM11.30*lr*	8.26	AM 7.36*l*	5.15
PM10.45*l*	4. 5	PM 4. 2*lr*	8.15
		8.58*l*	6. 0

e Saturdays excepted.
l Via Selby.
r Restaurant Car.

HOWDEN (SOUTH) (Yorks),

203¼ miles. Fares, 35/0*a*, 21/0*c*.
R. T. for two months, 70/0*a*, 42/0*c*.
Departures *from* London as for
Cudworth. Departures *for* London
about 3 times daily. Pop. 2,007.
Map Square 13.

HOWDENCLOUGH

(Yorks), 185 miles. Fares, 37/9*a*,
22/8*c*. R. T., double fare. Departures *from* London as for
Batley. Departures *for* London
about 6 times daily.

HOWDON-ON-TYNE

(Northumberland), 273 miles.
Fares, 57/8*a*, 34/7*c*. R.T. double
fare. Departures *from* London
as for Newcastle-on-Tyne. Departures *for* London about 6 times
daily. Pop. 5,187.

HOW MILL (Cumberland),

306½ miles. No through fares. Departures *from* London as for Carlisle or Hexham. Departures *for*
London about 6 times daily.
Map Square 3.

HOWSHAM (Lincoln), 155

miles. Fares, 32/3*a*, 19/4*c*. R.T.,
double fare. Departures *from*
London as for Lincoln or Barnetby.
Departures *for* London about 4
times daily.
Map Square 13.

Station closed on Sundays.

HOWWOOD (Renfrew),

411 miles. Fares, 82/4*a*, 49/5*c*.
R. T. for two months, 164/8*a*,
98/10*c*. Departures *from* London
as for Kilmarnock. Departures
for London about 4 times daily.
Map Square 40.

HOY (Caithness), 716 miles.

No through fares. Departures
from London as for Thurso. Departures *for* London about three
times daily.
Map Square 32.

HOYLAKE (Cheshire), 200¾

miles. No through fares. Departures *from* London as for Hooton.
Departures *for* London about 6
times daily. Pop. 14,029.
Map Square 11.

HUBBERT'S BRIDGE

(Lincoln), 118¾ miles. Fares, 23/1*a*,
13/10*c*. R.T., double fare. Departures *from* London as for Boston.
Departures *for* London about 9
times daily.
Map Square 13.

HUCKNALL (Notts) from

St. Pancras, 131¼ miles. Fares, 26/10a, 16/1c. R.T., double fare. Pop, 16,835.
Map Square 13.

St. Pan.	Hcknl.	Hcknl.	St. Pan.
AM 2.25	8.47	AM 6.17r	9.57
4.25	9.53	7.48r	10.45
9. 0r	11.43	8.28r	12.10
9. 50r	1.45	9.54r	1.20
11.45r	3.24	11.25	3.25
PM 1.50r	5.20	PM12.26r	4.10
2.25r	6. 9	2.20r	5.30
3.30r	6.48	2.56r	6.35
5. 0r	7.47	4.43r	7.55
6.15r	9.45	5.35r	9. 5
6.25dr	10.54	11. 1	4.20
6.25er	11. 8	—	—

Sunday Trains.

AM10.50r	4.17	PM 1. 4r	5. 2
PM 3.15	9.20	8. 4	4.55

d Saturdays only.
e Saturdays excepted
r Restaurant Car.

ANOTHER ROUTE from

Marylebone, 132½ miles. Fares as above.

M'bone.	Huck.	Huck.	M'bone.
AM 2.32	6. 1	AM 7.28	10.36
8.45r	12. 4	8.23r	11.10
10. 0dr	1.26	9.59r	1.13
10. 0r	1.43	11.48r	3. 0
PM12.15r	3.54	PM 3.53r	6.38
3.20r	5.57	4.50r	8.55
5. 0r	7.46	6.46r	9.55
6.20r	9. 4	10.35e	3.57
—	—	10.43d	3.57

Sunday Trains.

AM11.15r	3.21	PM 1.35r	5.40
PM 5.30r	8.39	7.10r	10.24

d Saturdays only.
e Saturdays excepted.
r Restaurant Car.

HUDDERSFIELD

(Yorks) from *King's Cross*, via Horbury, 188 miles. Fares, 37/9a, 22/8c. R.T., double fare. Pop. 110,120.
Map Square 12.

King's +	Hudd'fd	Hudd'fd	King's +
AM 4.45	12.15	AM 6. 5	11.30
7.15r	12.47	8. 5r	1. 5
10.10r	3.15	9.30r	1.55
PM 1.30r	6.37	9.54r	3.50
1.50r	8. 0	10.45r	4.45
5.45r	10.56	11.18	5. 0
10.45e	8.53	PM 2.15r	7.10
—	—	4.30r	9.25
—	—	9.10e	3.25

Sunday Trains.

12. 0hn	7.10	AM10. 0r	3.45
—	—	PM12.10r	5.55
—	—	3.15	10.20

e Saturdays excepted.
h Passengers cross Wakefield at own expense.
n Noon.
r Restaurant Car.

HUDDERSFIELD—

continued.

ANOTHER ROUTE from

Marylebone, 191 miles. Fares as above.

M'bone.Hudd'fd.		Hudd'fd. M'bone.	
AM 2.32	7.39	AM 8.15r	1.13
8.45r	2. 1	10.31r	3. 0
10. 0r	2.23	PM 2.17r	6.38
PM12.15r	5.25	5.29r	9.55
3.20r	7.31	9.55	3.57
6.20r	10.33	—	—

Sunday Trains.

AM11.15r	8. 4	AM 7.40r	5.40
PM 5.30r	10.29	PM 4.55r	10.24

r Restaurant Car.

ANOTHER ROUTE from

Euston, via Stockport, 203¼ miles. Fares as above.

Euston Hudd'fd.		Hudd'fd. Euston	
AM12.25	8. 5	AM 6.15er	12. 5
2.35	10.13	6.50r	12.50
5. 0	12. 8	8.48r	1.15
8.45r	2.10	9.59r	3.10
10.40r	3. 0	10.25r	3.55
11.50r	5.20	11.34dr	5.50
12. 0nr	6.13	12. 0d	6. 0
PM 1.30r	8.11	PM 1.32et	6. 0
4. 5r	8.35	1.32dr	6.15
6. 5r	10.20	1.55r	7.30
8. 0c	1.51	3.30r	8.10
8.45d	1.51	3.59r	10. 0
11.50d	9.13	4.40er	10.10
—	—	9. 0	5. 0
—	—	11.24	5.50

Sunday Trains.

PM12.10r	5.31	AM 7.38	4. 0
12.30r	9.57	PM12.10r	5.45
7.50r	1.55	1. 5r	7.30
—	—	3.35r	8.55
—	—	5.55	5. 0
—	—	11.24	5.50

d Saturdays only.
e Saturdays excepted.
n Noon.
r Restaurant Car.
t Tea Car.

HUGGLESCOTE

(Leicester), 112½ miles. Fares, 22/11a. 13/7c. R.T., double fare. Departures *from London* for Shackerstone. Departures *for London* about 6 times daily. Pop. 5,659.
Map Square 18.

HULL (PARAGON) (Yorks)

from *King's Cross*, 196¾ miles. Fares, 35/0a, 21/0c. R.T. for two months, 70/0a, 42/0c. Pop. 287,013.
Map Square 13.

King's +	Hull	Hull	King's +
AM 4.45	9.55	AM 6. 5r	11.30
7.15r	12.0	9. 5r	1.15
10.10r	2.29	10.50	3.50
PM 1.30r	5.23	12. 0r	4.30
1.50r	7.57	PM 2.50r	7.10
4. 0r	8.51	5. 3r	9.25
5.35r	9.57	9.24	3.25
8.25	1.36	—	—
10.45	4.49	—	—

Sunday Trains.

AM11.30r	4.38	PM12.15	5.15
PM 5. 0r	11.22	3.20r	8.15
10.45	4.49	8. 5	6. 0

r Restaurant Car.

HULL—*continued.*

ANOTHER ROUTE (Cannon Street) from *St. Pancras*,

228 miles, *via* Cudworth. Fares as above.

St. Pan.	Hull	Hull	St. Pan.
AM 4.25	11.43	AM 6.50r	1.30
PM 1.50r	7.53	—	—

Sunday Trains.

AM10.50r	5.55	AM10.40	5.27

r Restaurant Car.

ANOTHER ROUTE (Paragon) from *St. Pancras*, 226¾ miles,

via Sheffield. Fares as above.

St. Pan.	Hull	Hull	St. Pan.
AM 2.25g	11. 6	AM 5.43r	1.30
4.25	1.33	9. 0r	4.10
9.50r	5.10	11. 5r	5.30
PM 1.50r	10.24	PM 1.55r	7.57
5. 0r	12. 1	8.40	4.20
9.15d	4.37	—	—
9.15e	4.47	—	—
11.50e	9.26	—	—
11.50d	10.15	—	—

Sunday Trains.

AM10.50r	9.13	AM 6.50	5.27
PM 9.15	4.47	11.30r	9.43
—	—	PM 8. 5	4.55

d Saturdays only.
e Saturdays excepted.
g Mondays excepted.
r Restaurant Car.

ANOTHER ROUTE (Paragon) from *Marylebone*, 221¾ miles.

Fares, *via* Goole, 35/0a, 21/0c. R.T. for two months, 70/0a, 42/0c. *Via* New Holland, 35/0a, 21/0c. R.T. for two months, 70/0a, 42/0c.

M'bone.	Hull	Hull	M'bone.
AM 2.32k	9.55	AM 5.25hr	1.13
8.45r	2.29	6. 5r	1.13
10. 0r	3.50	8.56r	3. 0
PM12.15r	7.57	11.45hr	6.38
12.15r	8. 0h	12. 0r	6.38
3.20r	8. 9	PM 2.50r	8.55
5. 0r	11.59	8.40k	3.57
6.20r	1.36	—	—
10. 5e	7.40h	—	—
10. 5e	8.12	—	—

Sunday Trains.

AM11.15r	10.30h	AM 8. 0hr	5.40
—	—	PM 3.20kr	10.24

e Saturdays excepted.
h Arrives at or departs from Corporation Pier Station.
k *Via* Selby.
r Restaurant Car.

Royal Station Hotel. Adjoins Paragon Station. Thoroughly up-to-date. Every Comfort. Owned and managed by London and North Eastern Railway Company. Grill Room and Tea Room on the platform
See advt. p. **217.**

HULLAVINGTON (Wilts) from *Paddington*, 94¼ miles. Fares, 19/9*a*, 11/10*c*. R. T. for two months, 39/6*a*. Departures *from* London as for Badminton. Departures *for* London about 5 times daily. Pop. 552.
Map Square 22.

HULME END (Stafford), 170¼ miles. No through fares. Departures *from* London as for Leek. Departures *for* London about 4 times daily.
Map Square 12.

HUMBERSTONE (Leicester), 107¾ miles. No through fares. Departures *from* London as for Hallaton or Bottesford. Departures *for* London about 3 times daily. Pop. 538.
Map Square 18.

HUMBERSTONE ROAD (Leicester), from *St. Pancras*, 99¾ miles. No through fares. Departures *from* London as for Leicester. Departures *for* London about 5 times daily.

HUMBIE (East Lothian), 397½ miles. No through fares. Departures *from* London as for Edinburgh (Waverley). Departures *for* London about twice daily. Pop. 652.
Map Square 41.

HUMSHAUGH (Northumberland), 292 miles. Fares, 62/1*a*, 37/3*c*. R. T. for two months, 124/2*a*, 74/6*c*. Departures *from* London as for Hexham or Carlisle. Departures *for* London about 3 times daily.
Map Square 3.

HUNCOAT (Lancs), 210¼ miles. Fares, 43/2*a*, 25/11*c*. R. T. for two months, 86/4*a*, 51/10*c*. Departures *from* London as for Accrington. Departures *for* London about 7 times daily. Pop. 1,494.
Map Square 12.

HUNDRED END (Lancs), 218¾ miles. No through fares. Departures *from* London as for Preston or Southport. Departures *for* London about 6 times daily.
Map Square 12.

HUNGERFORD (Berks) from *Paddington*, 61½ miles. Fares, 12/9*a*, 7/8*c*. R. T. for two months, 25/6*a*. Pop. 9,007.
Map Square 23.

	Pad.	Hungfd.		Hungfd.	Pad.
AM	7.30	9.12	AM	8.28	10. 0
	8.45*r*	10.50		9.34	10.52
	9.30	11.17		11.30	12.55
	10.45	12.34	PM	1.15	2.50
PM	12.30*r*	2.10		1.38	3.50
	1.10*r*	3. 5		3.50	5.50
	2.45	4.10		4.49	7.20
	3.18	5.37		6.37*r*	8.20
	5. 5	6.48		7.10	9.15
	5.55	7.20		8.44	10.45
	6.30	8. 2		10. 5	2.45
	8. 0	9.42		—	—
	—	—		—	—
	—	—		—	—

HUNGERFORD—*contd.*

Sunday Trains.

	Pad.	Hungfd.		Hungfd.	Pad.
AM	9.10	11.12	AM	8.32	10.50
PM	5.15	7.31	PM	7.14	9.15
	—	—		—	—
	—	—		—	—

r Restaurant Car.

Bear Hotel. High-class Family. Main Road, London. Bath. Fishing, River Kennet. Lounge. Garage. Billiards. Moderate Tariff. Phone 12.
PROPRIETRESS.

HUNMANBY (Yorks), 227¾ miles. Fares, 47/4*a*, 28/5*c*. R. T. for two months, 94/8*a*, 56/10*c*. Departures *from* London as for Bridlington. Departures *for* London about 4 times daily. Pop 1,370.
Map Square 8.

HUNNINGTON (Worcester), 122 miles. Fares, 25/5*a*, 15/3*c*. R.T. for two months, 50/10*a*, 30/6*c*. Departures *from* London as for Smethwick Junction. Departures *for* London about 4 times daily. Pop. 288.
Map Square 17.

HUNSLET (Yorks), 194¼ miles. Fares, 38/7*a*, 23/2*c*. R. T., double fare. Departures *from* London as for Woodlesford. Departures *for* London about 6 times daily. Pop. 69,795.
Map Square 12.

HUNSTANTON (Norfolk) from *Liverpool Street*, 111¾ miles. Fares, 23/7*a*, 14/2*c*. R. T. for two months, 47/2*a*, 28/4*c*. Pop. 4,282.
Map Square 14.

	L'pool..St.	Hunst.		Hunst.	L'pool.St.
AM	5.50	10.52	AM	7. 2*r*	10.23
	8.30*r*	11.58		7.50	11.27
	10. 5	2.28		9. 2	2. 7
	11.20*klr*	2. 8		11. 5*r*	2.21
	11.50*r*	3.20	PM	1. 5*lr*	4. 2*k*
PM	2.34	5.51		2.34*r*	6.10
	4.45	7.55		4.44*r*	8.22
	5.49*r*	9.20		7. 5	10.30
	—	—		9.40	2.50
	—	—		—	—

Sunday Trains.

AM	9.25	1.35	PM	6.20	9.40
	—	—		—	—
	—	—		—	—

k Departs from or arrives at St. Pancras Station.
l Commencing July 23.
r Restaurant Car.

Sandringham Hotel. Under the management of London and North Eastern Railway. Beautifully situated on Norfolk coast. Charming Suites of apartments. Adjoins Station. Telegrams, "Sands." Telephone, 21.
See advt. p. **218**.

Glebe Hotel. On the Cliffs. Garage. Telephone 35.
C. ERNEST GRAY, Proprietor.

Le Strange Arms and Golf Links Hotel. Overlooking Links and Sea. Suites containing Sitting Room and Bath Room. Splendid Golf all the year round. Garage. R.A.C. A.A. Telephone 10.
C. ERNEST GRAY, Proprietor.

HUNSTANTON—*contd.*

Golden Lion. Facing Pier. Open all the year. Large Garage, Stabling. Shady Garden. Telephone 18.
C. ERNEST GRAY, Proprietor.

Buckingham Palace Pri- vate Hotel. First Class. Splendid Sea View. Near Station. Links. (Excellent Cuisine guaranteed.) Personal supervision.
Proprietor.
CHARLES RANSHAW,

HUNSTON (Sussex), 71¼ miles. No through fares. Departures *from* London as for Selsey. Departures *for* London about 5 times daily. Pop. 304.
Map Square 28.

HUNTINGDON from *King's Cross*, 59 miles. Fares, 12/3*a*, 7/4*c*. R.T., double fare. Pop. 4,194.
Map Square 18.

	King's+	Huntdn.		Huntdn.	King's+
AM	5. 5	6.59	AM	7.52	9.56
	7.45	9.43		9.34	10.40
	8.45	10.12		9.45	11.15
	10.12	12.35		11.27	1.25
	11.30	1.14	PM	2.28	3.50
PM	1.55	3.53		4.46	6.25
	4.15	6. 1		7.29	9. 0
	5. 0	6.19		7.55	10.20
	5.10	7.23		—	—
	6.15	8.10		—	—
	8.30	10.21		—	—

Sunday Trains.

AM	8.30	10.43	PM	5.48	8. 8
PM	7.10	9.22		—	—
	—	—		—	—

ANOTHER ROUTE from *Liverpool Street*, 75¾ miles. Fares as above.

	L'p'l St.	Hunt'dn.		Hunt'dn.	L'p'l St.
AM	5. 5	7.39	AM	7.58*r*	10.23
	5.50*g*	9.12		9.36	12.40
	8.30*r*	11.18		10.38	2. 7
	11.50*r*	2.18		11.36*r*	2.21
PM	12.29*d*	3.26	PM	1.14*l*	4. 2*k*
	2.34	5.32		1.14	5. 9
	4.45	7. 2		3.22*r*	6.10
	5.49*r*	8.12		5.58*r*	8.33
	7.10*d*	9.37		7.18	10.30
	—	—		—	—

No Sunday Trains.

d Saturdays only.
g Mondays excepted.
k Arrives at St. Pancras Station.
l Commencing July 23.
r Restaurant Car.

Old Bridge Hotel. R.A.C. and A.A. Best appointed Touring Hotel for miles around. Central Heating. Cuisine a Speciality. Delightful Riverside Gardens. Boating, Fishing, Tennis, Croquet. Golf, Hunting, Loose Boxes. Garage. Telephone, 58. Telegrams, "Welcome," Huntingdon.
Resident Proprietor,
Captain H. C. ROBERTS.

George Hotel (appointed R.A.C., A.A., B.T.C.) The Old Coaching House. Patronised by King Charles I. Situate in midst of relics and surroundings of Cromwell. Boating, Fishing, Stabling, Posting, Garage. Telephone 96.

HUNSTANTON.—GLEBE HOTEL. On the Cliffs. *See advt. above.*

HUNTLY (Aberdeen)

from *King's Cross*, 563¾ miles. Fares, 106/3*a*, 63/9*c*. R. T. for two months, 212/6*a*, 127/6*c*. Pop. 4,544.

Map Square 35.

King's +	Huntly	Huntly	King's +
AM 4.45	7.32*l*	AM 8.18*r*	10. 0*l*
PM 8.20*e*	8.45*h*	11.20	3.25*h*
11.25*e*	3.36*l*	PM 1.28	6. 0*h*
—	—	5.58	7.25*h*
—	—	—	—

Sunday Trains.

PM 7.45	8.45*h*	—	—
—	—	—	—
—	—	—	—

e Saturdays excepted.
h A.M.
l P.M.
r Restaurant Car.

ANOTHER ROUTE

from *Euston*, 580¼ miles. Fares as above.

Euston	Huntly	Huntly	Euston
PM 1.30*er*	5.58*h*	AM 8.18*r*	10.45*l*
7.50*er*	9.17*h*	11.20*r*	5. 0*h*
11.35*e*	3.36*l*	PM 4. 0	8. 0*h*
—	—	9.11	7.30*l*
—	—	—	—
—	—	—	—
—	—	—	—

Sunday Trains.

PM 7.50*r*	9.17*h*	—	—
11.35	3.36*l*	—	—
—	—	—	—
—	—	—	—

d Saturdays only.
e Saturdays excepted.
h A.M.
l P.M.
r Restaurant Car.

HUNTS CROSS

(Lancs), 210¼ miles. Fares, 40/3*a*, 24/2*c*. R. T. for two months, 80/6*a*, 48/4*c*. Departures *from* London as for Warrington (Central). Departures *for* London about 4 times daily.

HUNWICK (Durham),

246¾ miles. No through fares. Departures *from* London as for Bishop Auckland. Departures *for* London about 6 times daily. Pop. 2,464.

Map Square 7.

HURDLOW (Derby), 162½

miles. Fares, 33/7*a*, 20/2*c*. R. T., double fare. Departures *from* London as for Ashbourne. Departures *for* London about 4 times daily.

Map Square 12.

HURLFORD (Ayr), 388½

miles. Fares, 79/0*a*, 47/5*c*. R. T. for two months, 158/0*a*, 94/10*c*. Departures *from* London as for Kilmarnock. Departures *for* London about 5 times daily. Pop. 3,730.

Map Square 40.

HURN (Hants) from *Waterloo*,

106½ miles. Fares, 22/11*a*, 13/9*c*. R. T. for two months, 45/10*a*, 27/6*c*. Departures *from* London as for Christchurch or Ringwood. Departures *for* London about 5 times daily. Pop. 922.

Map Square 27.

HURSTBOURNE

(Hants) from *Waterloo*, 61½ miles. Fares, 12/9*a*, 7/8*c*. R. T. for two months, 25/6*a*, 15/4*c*. Pop. 389.

Map Square 23.

W'loo.	H'brn.	H'brn.	W'loo.
AM 5.50	8.19	AM 8. 6	9.56
7.30	9.42	10.31*s*	12.22
9.30	11.28	PM12.26*r*	2.20
11.30*r*	1.29	2.14	4.20
PM 1.30*r*	3. 9	4.19*s*	6.26
3.30*s*	5.10	5.39	7.40
5. 0	6.45	8.12	10.50
6. 0*r*	7.56	9.36	11.28
7.30	9.10	—	—
8. 0	10.15	—	—

Sunday Trains.

AM 9. 0	11.18	AM10.21	12.11
PM 6. 0	7.51	PM 6.49	9.12
—	—	—	—
—	—	—	—
—	—	—	—

r Restaurant Car.
s Refreshments served.

HURWORTH BURN

(Durham), 245 miles. No through fares. Departures *from* London as for Stockton-on-Tees. Departures *for* London about 4 times daily.

Map Square 8.

HUSTHWAITE GATE

(Yorks), 206¼ miles. No through fares. Departures *from* London as for Ampleforth. Departures *for* London about 5 times daily. Pop. (Husthwaite) 431.

Map Square 8.

HUTTON & HOWICK

(Lancs), 212 miles. No through fares. Departures *from* London as for Preston. Departures *for* London about 6 times daily. Pop. (Hutton) 472, (Howick) 81.

Map Square 12.

HUTTON CRANSWICK

(Yorks), 210½ miles. Fares, 38/4*a*, 23/0*c*. R. T. for two months, 76/8*a*, 46/0*c*. Departures *from* London as for Hull (Paragon) or Driffield. Departures *for* London about 4 times daily. Pop. 967.

Map Square 8.

HUTTON GATE (Yorks),

247 miles. No through fares. Departures *from* London as for Middlesbrough. Departures *for* London about 5 times daily.

Map Square 8.

HUTTONS AMBO

(Yorks), 206½ miles. No through fares. Departures *from* London as for York. Departures *for* London about 5 times daily. Pop. 402.

Map Square 8.

HUYTON (Lancs), 196¼

miles. Fares, 40/10*a*, 24/6*c*. R.T. for two months, 81/8*a*. Departures *from* London as for Earlestown. Departures *for* London about 5 times daily. Pop. 5,171.

Map Square 12.

HYDE (Cheshire), from

St. Pancras, 181¼ miles. Fares, 37/6*a*, 22/6*c*. R.T., double fare. Pop. 33,437.

St. Pan.	Hyde	Hyde	St. Pan.
AM 4.25	11.11	AM 6.20*r*	11.35
8.25*r*	2.13	7.49*r*	1.30
10.25*dr*	3.21	9.46	3.25
10.25*r*	4.43	PM12.41*r*	5.45
PM 1.25*er*	6.13	2.50*r*	8.35
1.25*r*	7. 4	4.36*r*	10. 5
4.25*r*	9.10	6.46	4.20
12. 0*h*	10.25	—	—
—	—	—	—
—	—	—	—

Sunday Trains.

PM 3.15	8.44	AM 8.48*r*	5. 2
—	—	PM 2.14*r*	9.52
—	—	6.16	4.55
—	—	—	—
—	—	—	—
—	—	—	—

d Saturdays only.
e Saturdays excepted.
h Saturdays midnight only.
r Restaurant Car.

HYDE PARK CORNER

(Hammersmith and Finsbury Park Tube). *See* back of Map.

HYKEHAM (Lincoln), 152¾

miles. Fares, 26/11*a*, 16/2*c*. R.T., double fare. Departures *from* London as for Collingham. Departures *for* London about 5 times daily. Pop. 1,592.

Map Square 13.

HYLTON (Durham), 261¾

miles. Fares, 54/7*a*, 32/9*c*. R. T., double fare. Departures *from* London as for Ferryhill or Durham. Departures *for* London about 6 times daily. Pop. 3,038.

Map Square 3.

HYTHE (Essex) from *Liverpool Street*,

53¾ miles. Fares, 11/8*a*, 7/0*c*. R. T. for two months, 23/4*a*. Departures *from* London as for Colchester. Departures *for* London about 8 times daily.

Map Square 19.

HYTHE (Kent) from

Charing Cross, Cannon Street, and *London Bridge*, 67¾ miles. Fares, 14/2*a*, 11/4*b*, 8/6*c*. R. T. for two months, 28/4*a*, 22/8*b*. Pop. 7,764.

Map Square 24.

Char. +	Leave Can. St.	Lon. B.	Arr. at Hythe.
AM —	3.40*s*	3.43*s*	7.29
—	5.20	5.25	9.19
—	6.45	6.50	9 59
9.15	—	9.23	11.44
—	—	10. 3	12.14
11. 0	—	11. 7	1.17
11.15	—	—	12.49
PM 1. 0	—	—	2.34
2.55*d*	—	3. 1*d*	4.41
3. 0	—	3. 8	4.59
4.30*h*	—	4.37*h*	6.22
4.30*j*	—	4.37*j*	6.35
—	5.12*e*	—	6.51
5.15*e*	—	5.21*e*	7.17
5.20*d*	—	5.26*d*	7.17
5.24*d*	—	5.34*d*	7.57
6. 0*e*	—	6. 5*e*	7.49
7.18	—	7.26	9.59

Sunday Trains.

AM 7.45	—	7.52	10.15
10.10	—	10.18	12. 9

HYTHE—*continued.*

Trains from Hythe.

Leave HYTHE AM	Arrive at LON. B.	CAN. ST.	CHAR. +
7. 7	9.32	9.36	—
8. 3e	9.36	9.40	—
8.13d	10. 0	10. 4	—
8.59	10.54	—	11. 3
9.39	11.43	—	11.57
11.14	1.36	—	1.50
PM12.54	3.26	—	3.40
3.24	5.50	—	6. 3
5.14	7.25	7.30e	7.49
8.14	10.22	—	10.35
—	—	—	—

Sunday Trains.

PM			
5.12	7. 9	—	7.17
8. 4	10.16	—	10.26

d Saturdays only.
e Saturdays excepted.
h Fridays excepted.
j Fridays only.
k Mondays and Saturdays only.
l Low Level platform.
s Third class only.

ANOTHER ROUTE from *Victoria, Holborn Viaduct,* and *St. Paul's,* 70 miles. Fares us above.

VICT. (S.E.& C.) AM	Leave HOL. V.	ST. PL.'s	Arr. at HYTHE
—	6.40	6.42	9.59
9.45	—	—	11.44
11. 4d	10.58d	11. 0d	2.14
11. 4	10.58	11. 0	2.34
PM —	1.27d	1.30d	4.41
2.12e	—	—	4.41
2.40d	—	—	6.22
2.50e	—	—	6.22
2.50h	—	—	6.28
4.25e	3.22e	3.25e	6.51
7.22	—	—	9.59

Sunday Trains.

AM			
9.35	—	—	12. 9
PM 5.15	—	—	7.44

Trains from Hythe.

Leave HYTHE AM	Arrive at ST. PL.'s	HOL. V.	VICT.
7. 7	9.53	9.55	—
9.39	12.59	1. 2	12.49
11.14	—	—	2.40
PM12.54	—	—	3.37
3.24	—	—	5.42
3.42	6.58	7. 0	
5.14	—	—	8.51
8.14	11.43	11.45	—
—	—	—	—

Sunday Trains.

AM10.44	—	—	1. 5
PM12.54	—	—	3.50
5.12	—	9. 9	—

d Saturdays only.
e Saturdays excepted.
h Fridays only.
l Fridays and Saturdays excepted.

HYTHE—*continued.*

REFERENCE NOTES.

a	signifies	First Class.
b	,,	Second Class.
c	,,	Third Class.
d	,,	On Saturdays only.
e	,,	Saturdays excepted.
f	,,	On Mondays only.
g	,,	Mondays excepted.
r	,,	Restaurant Car.
t	,,	Tea Car.
x	,,	Express.
R.T.	,,	Return Tickets.

All Trains in the Tables not otherwise marked carry Third Class Passengers.

I

ICKENHAM from *Baker Street,* 14½ miles. Fares, 2/3½a, 1/4½c. R. T. for two days, 4/1a, 2/6c. Departures *from* London as for Uxbridge. Departures *for* London about 4 minutes later. Pop. 443.
Map Squares 23 and 47.

ANOTHER ROUTE from *Mansion House,* 19½ miles, *via* Acton Town and South Harrow.
See p. 489.

IDE (Devon), 177 miles. Fares, 36/6a, 21/11c. R. T. for two months, 73/0a. Departures *from* London as for Exeter (St. Davids). Departures *for* London about 5 times daily. Pop. 647.
Map Square 26.

IDLE (Yorks), from *King's*

Cross, 193¾ miles Fares, 39/9a. 23/10c. R. T., double fare. Departures *from* London as for Bradford. Departures *for* London about 8 times daily. Pop. 7,520. *Map Square 12.*

IDRIDGEHAY (Derby), 138

miles. Fares, 28/7a, 17/2c. R. T., double fare. Departures *from* London as for Wirksworth. Departures *for* London about 6 times daily. Pop. 297. *Map Square 12.*

ILDERTON (Northumber-

land), 324 miles. Fares, 68/4a. 41/0c. R. T., double fare. Departures *from* London as for Alnwick. Departures *for* London about 3 times daily. Pop. 88. *Map Square 3.*

ILFORD (Essex) from

Liverpool Street, or *Fenchurch Street*, 7¼ miles. Fares, 1/0½a, 0/10b, 0/7½c. R. T. for two days, 2/1a, 1/8b, 1/2c. Pop. 85,194. See pp. 528-534. 536. *Map Square 23.*

ILFRACOMBE (Devon)

from *Waterloo*, 226¼ miles. Fares, 42/1a, 25/3c. R. T. for two months, 84/2a, 50/6c. Pop. 11,779. *Map Square 21.*

W'LOO.	ILFRAC.	ILFRAC.	W'LOO.
AM 9. 0r	3.42	AM 8. 0r	1.56
11. 0r	4.50	10. 10r	3.50
PM 1. 0r	7.31	PM12. 5r	6. 0
3. 0	8.33	12.50	7.40
—	—	1.25r	8.30
—	—	3. 5	10.50
—	—	4.25h	3.58

No Sunday Trains.

h Via Eastleigh.
r Restaurant Car.

ANOTHER ROUTE from

Paddington, via Taunton and Barnstaple, 203¼ miles. Fares as above.

PAD.	ILFRAC.	ILFRAC.	PAD.
AM 5.30	2.21	AM 8. 0r	1.50
9.15	3.14	9.30	4. 5
PM12. 5r	6.10	11.45t	5.35
2. 0r	8.33	PM 2.45r	9. 0
3.30	8.55	4.25	2.45
12. 0h	11.18	7.23	7.10

Sunday Trains.

PM10. 0	11.18	—	—
—	—	—	—

h Saturdays midnight excepted.
r Restaurant Car.
t Tea Car.

Ilfracombe Hotel. Leading Hotel. Facing the Sea. *See advt.* p. **219.**

Cliffe Hydro Hotel. Facing Sea in extensive Grounds. Nearest Golf Links. Electric Light. Telegrams: "Hydro, Ilfracombe." Telephone No. 42. Apply G. K. WALLER, Resident Proprietor. *See advt.* p. **219.**

Runnacleave Hotel. 200 Rooms. Garage. Ball Room. Orchestra. Theatre. Moderate Tariff. The Ideal Holiday Hotel. 'Phone 36. L. I. HAND, Manager. *See advt.* p. **220.**

ILFRACOMBE—*contd.*

Imperial Private Hotel. Facing sea. En pension terms. Dancing. Telephone 22. *See advt.* p. **220.**

Woolacombe Bay Hotel (near Ilfracombe). Private grounds (6 acres). Golf Links adjoin. 200 apartments. Electric Light and Lift. Lock-up and open Garages. Apply MANAGER. *See advt.* p. **221.**

Atlantic Hotel. Facing Sea and Band Stand. Terms from 3 Guineas. *See advt.* p **221.**

Collingwood en Pension. Private Hotel. Facing Sea. 120 Bedrooms. Billiards. Lift. Garage. *See advt.* p. **221.**

Royal Clarence Hotel. (Re-modelled). Open throughout the year. Fully licensed. Terms from 15s. per day, inclusive. Bus meets all trains. Garage. Phone 126. *See advt.* p. **222.**

Grosvenor Private Hotel. Delightful situation. Minute Sea Parade. 50 Rooms. Lounge. Garage. Liberal table. First-class cuisine. Tel. 63. Miss A. PICKETT, Proprss. *See advt.* p. **222.**

Crescent Private Hotel. Most up-to-date and modern. Electric light. *See advt.* p. **222.**

Lee Bay Hotel, Lee, N. Devon, near Ilfracombe. Quiet, secluded. First Class. Own Farm. Bathing, Golf, Tennis, Fishing. DIGBY EASTON. *See advt.* p. **222.**

The Dudley Private Hotel. Excellent cuisine. Extensive sea views. PROPRIETRESS. *See advt.* p. **223.**

"Atlanta" for excellent Cuisine and Service. Glorious Sea Views. Moderate. *See advt.* p. **223.**

The Granville. Magnificent Sea Views. Good Cooking. Sociability. Comfort. Billiards. 42 Bedrooms. Electric Light. New lounge. 2,200 references. W. R. FOSTER.

The Gilbert. Charmingly situated. First-class Boarding establishment in Ilfracombe. Close to Sea, Capstone Parade. Pavilion and Pleasure Grounds. Drawing, Dining, Reading, Smoking Rooms. Billiards. 60 Bedrooms. Moderate. J. TRELEASE, Proprietor.

Kalwrose, 4, Hillsborough Terrace. Board Residence. Extensive Sea View. Excellent Cooking. Every Comfort. Mrs. PRICE (late Capstone Boarding House), Proprietress.

Royal Britannia Hotel, historic house, facing harbour, near Beaches. En pension terms. Garage. Spacious rooms. Sea views. TAMLYN, Proprietor.

ILFRACOMBE—*contd.*

The Grand. Private Hotel. Pleasantly situated on sea level. 'Phone 152. 40 Bedrooms. Separate Tables. Excellent cuisine. Miss CORMACK, Proprietress.

The Octagon. Opposite Wildersmouth Beach. Fine Balcony. Separate Tables. 18 Bedrooms. Electric Light. Dining, Lounge, Writing Rooms ground floor. PROPRIETRESS.

The Beacon. Private Hotel in own Grounds. Adjoining Tors Walk. Overlooking Sea. One of the finest positions in Ilfracombe. Telegrams : "Beacon, Ilfracombe." 'Phone 154. Proprietress, M. DARCH.

St. Petroc. Private Hotel. Centrally situated on level. Good Cooking. Home Comforts. 40 Bedrooms. Electric Light. Tariff. A. B. CHADDER.

ILKESTON (Derby) from

St. Pancras, 127½ miles. Fares, 26/0a, 15/7c. R. T., double fare. Pop. 32,269. *Map Square 13.*

ST. PAN.	ILKEST'N.	ILKEST'N.	ST. PAN.
AM 2.25e	7.52h	AM 7.16r	10.45
2.25	8.36	7.44r	11.35
4.25	9.16	8.27r	12.10
9. 0r	12. 9	9.20r	1.20
10.25r	2.15	PM12.30r	4.10
11. 0r	2.54h	12.52hr	4.20
PM12.25r	4.47	1. 9h1r4.10	
1.50r	4.54	2. 0r	5.30
3.30r	6.39	4. 7r	7.15
5. 0r	8.17	5.38r	9. 5
6.15r	9.23	9.32	4.20
12. 0k	10.30h	11.38h	4.20

Sunday Trains.

PM 3.15	6.29h	AM 7. 0h	11.53
—	—	PM 2.44h	5.27
—	—	7.58h	4.55

h Arrives at or departs from Ilkeston Junction.
k Saturdays midnight only.
l Wednesdays and Saturdays only.
r Restaurant Car.

ANOTHER ROUTE from

King's Cross, 137 miles. Fares as above.

KING'S+	ILKES'TN.	ILKES'TN.	KING'S+
AM 4.45	9.54	AM 7. 5	10.40
5. 5	10.24	8. 8r	11.30
8.45	1. 9	8.55	1. 5
10.10r	1.42	9.45r	1.30
11.30	3.56	11.11	3.50
PM 1.50r	5.39	PM 1.46	6.25
5.35r	8.57	4.18	9. 0
5.45er10.17		5.20r	9.25
5.45dr10.53		9.48e	3.25
11.25e	6.34	10. 8d	3.25
—	—	—	—

Sunday Trains.

AM11.30r	5.49h	PM11.44	3.45
12. 0r	4.29	1.54	5.55
PM 5. 0r	9.33	—	—
11.25	6.34	—	—

d Saturdays only.
e Saturdays excepted.
r Restaurant Car.

ILFRACOMBE HOTEL—The Best. **Moderate Tariff Inclusive Rates.**

ILKLEY (Yorks) from

King's Cross, 203 miles. Fares, 41/8*a*, 25/0*c*. R. T. for two months, 83/4*a*, 50/0*c*. Pop. 9,105.
Map Square 7.

KING'S +	ILKLEY	ILKLEY	KING'S +
AM 4.45	10.15	AM 6.14*r*	11.30
7.15*r*	12.42	8.12*r*	1.55
10.10*r*	3.39	10.37*r*	5. 0
PM 1.30*r*	6.18	PM 2.22*r*	7.10
4. 0*r*	9.55	4. 0*r*	9.25
5.45*fr*11.33	7.57*k*	3.25
10.45*er* 7.55	—	—

Sunday Trains.

12. 0*nr* 9.14	—	—
PM10.45 7.55	—	—

e Saturdays excepted.
f Wednesdays and Saturdays only.
k Via Holbeck and Leeds (New Station.)
n Noon.
r Restaurant Car.

ANOTHER ROUTE from

St. Pancras, 211½ miles. Fares as above.

ST. PAN.	ILKLEY	ILKLEY	ST. PAN.
AM 9.50*dr* 3.14	AM 7. 2*r*	12.10
9.50*r*	3.39	7.30*r*	1.30
PM12.15*er* 5.15	9.15*r*	2.10
12.15*dr* 5.42	9.24*r*	4.10
1.50*r* 7. 7	11.30*r*	5.30
5. 0*r* 10.32	PM 1.15*r*	6.35
6.15*r* 11.42	4.15*r*	9.15
11.45*e* 6.54	8.37	4.20
11.50*d* 9. 8	—	—

Sunday Trains.

AM10.50*r* 9.43	AM 9.24	6.25
PM11.45 4.00	PM 8.20	4.55

d Saturdays only.
e Saturdays excepted.
r Restaurant Car.

Ben Rhydding Hydro Hotel.

R.A.C. First Class. Free Golf.
See advt. p. **223.**

Highfield Residential Hotel

on Rombald's Moor. 850 feet above Sea Level. Beautiful situation commanding unrivalled views of Wharfedale. Telephone 222 Ilkley.

Middleton Hotel. Oldest established. Re-decorated throughout. Central heating. New Lounge. Golf, Tennis, Hunting, Fishing. Lovely scenery. Telephone 20. Telegrams: Comfort.

Stoney Lea Hydro, on edge of Rombold's Moor, 500 feet above. Excellent cuisine. Telephone 74. Mrs. ROBINSON, Miss EMMOTT, Proprietresses.

ILMINSTER (Somerset)

from *Paddington,* 149 miles. Fares, 29/10*a*, 17/11*c*. R.T. for two months, 59/8*a*. Pop. 2,367.
Map Square 27.

PAD.	ILMNS.	ILMNS.	PAD.
AM 5.30	11.55	AM 6.45*f*	11.30
9.15*r*	2.18	9.10*r*	1.30
PM12. 5*r*	4.47	PM12.20*r*	5.30
3.30	7.14	2.55*r*	6.50
6.30*dr*11.17	5.25*r*	9. 0
10. 0*e* 3.41	8. 2	2.45
12. 0*h* 8.28	9.51	7.10
—	—	—	—

Sunday Trains.

PM10. 0 3.41	—	—

d Saturdays only.
e Saturdays excepted.
f Mondays only.
h Saturdays midnight excepted.
r Restaurant Car.

IMMINGHAM (Lincoln),

from *Marylebone,* 221½ miles. Fares, 35/8*a*, 21/5*c*. R. T. for two months, 71/4*a*, 42/10*c*. Departures *from* London as for Brocklesby. Departures *for* London about 4 times daily. Pop. 2,031.
Map Square 13.

INCE (Lancs) 203½ miles.

Fares, 40/5*a*, 24/3*c*. R. T. for two months, 80/10*a*, 48/6*c*. Departures *from* London as for Manchester. Departures *for* London 7 times daily. Pop. 22,865.
Map Square 12.

INCE AND ELTON

(Cheshire), 188 miles. Fares, 39/0*a*, 23/5*c*. R. T. for two months, 78/0*a*, 46/10*c*. Departures *from* London as for Hooton. Departures *for* London about 4 times daily. Pop. 271.
Map Square 12.

INCHES (Lanark), 390 miles.

No through fares. Departures *from* London as for Carstairs. Departures *for* London about 3 times daily.
Map Square 40.

INCHTURE (Perth), 462½

miles. Fares, 91/11*a*, 55/2*c*. R. T. for two months, 183/10*a*, 110/4*c*. Departures *from* London as for Perth. Departures *for* London about 3 times daily. Pop. 490.
Map Square 38.

INGATESTONE (Essex)

from *Liverpool Street,* 23¾ miles. Fares, 5/2*a*, 3/1*c*. R. T. for two months, 10/4*a*. Pop. 2,013.
Map Square 24.

L'PL. ST.	INGATE.	INGATE.	L'PL. ST.
AM 5.10	6.19	AM 2.40	3.50
6.50	7.58	6.57	8. 8
7.28	8.37	8.21	9. 4
8.46	9.36	8.42	9.30
10.47	11.43	9.27	10.12
11.26*d*	12.37	9.50	10.22
PM12.42*e*	1.55	10.20	10.58
1. 3*d*	1.54	PM12.21	1.16
1.38*e*	2.43	1.58*d*	3. 5
2.15*d*	2.53	2.24	3.13
3.26	4.21	2.40*e*	3.59
4.18	5. 3	3.46*e*	4.51
5.42*e*	6.23	3.46*d*	4.56
5.42*d*	6.30	5.35	6.40
6. 8	7. 0	6.16	7.29
7.16	8. 6	8.18	9.17
8.54	9.52	9.49	10.52
11. 0*h*	11.51	—	—
12. 0*k*	12.48	—	—
—	—	—	—
—	—	—	—

Sunday Trains.

AM 7. 4	8.24	AM 2.40	3.50
8.15	9. 9	10.4	10.25
10.45	11.45	10.14	11.15
PM 3.40	4.24	11.33	12.40
3.45	4.44	PM 2.15	3.15
6.15	7.12	7.14	8.39
7.40	8.22	9. 3	10.22
8.46	9.45	—	—

d Saturdays only.
e Saturdays excepted.
h Wednesdays excepted.
k Wednesdays only.

INGERSBY (Leicester),

102½ miles. No through fares. Departures *from* London as for Hallaton or Bottesford. Departures *for* London about 3 times daily.
Map Square

INGESTRE (Stafford), 139¼

miles. Fares, 28/2*a*, 16.11*c*. R. T. for two months, 56/4*a*, 33 10*c*. Departures *from* London as for Stafford. Departures *for* London about 6 times daily. Pop. 134.
Map Square 17.

INGHAM (Suffolk) from

Liverpool Street, via Bury St. Edmunds, 81½ miles. Fares, 17/3*a*, 10/4*c*. R. T. for two months, 34/6*a*. Pop. 327.
Map Square 19.

L'POOL. ST.	INGH'M.	INGH'M.	L'POOL. ST.
AM 6.50	10.58	AM 9. 2	11.42
10.20	1.41	11.59	3.36
PM 1. 0	4.28	PM 3. 9	6.10
—	—	6.24	10. 0
—	—	—	—
—	—	—	—
—	—	—	—

No Sunday Trains.

ANOTHER ROUTE *via* Thetford, 102¾ miles. Fares as above.

L'POOL ST.	INGH'M.	INGH'M.	L'POOL ST.
AM 5. 5	9. 1	AM 8. 5	11.27
8.30	11.58	10.58	2.21
11.50	3. 8	PM 1.41	5.17
PM 2.34	6.23	4.28	8.22

No Sunday Trains.

INGLEBY (Yorks), 238¾

miles. Fares, 49/10*a*, 29/11*c*. R.T. for two months, 99/8*a*, 59/10*c*. Departures *from* London as for Stockton - on - Tees. Departures *for* London about 4 times daily. Pop. 394.
Map Square 8.

INGLETON (Yorks) from

St. Pancras, 246½ miles. Fares, 47/9*a*, 28/8*c*. R. T. for two months, 95/6*a*, 57/4*c*. Pop. 1,672.
Map Square 7.

ST. PAN.	INGLET'N.	INGLET'N.	ST. PAN.
AM 2.25*g* 12.20	AM 7.15*r*	2.10
4.25	2. 5	8.50*r*	4.10
9.50*r*	4.40	10.10*r*	5.30
PM12.15*r*	6.50	PM12.13*hr*	6.35
3.30*kr*10.20	1. 5*r*	7.55
11.50*e* 8.25	7.15	4.20
—	—	—	—
—	—	—	—
—	—	—	—

Sunday Trains.

PM11.45 8.25	—	—

e Saturdays excepted.
g Mondays excepted.
h Mondays, Tuesdays, Fridays and Saturdays only.
k Mondays, Wednesdays and Saturdays only.
r Restaurant Car.

INGLETON—*continued.*

ANOTHER ROUTE from *Euston,* 276¾ miles. Fares, 51/11*a*, 31/2*c*. R. T., double fare.

Euston	Ingle'tn.	Ingle'tn.	Euston
AM 12.25	9.45	AM 8.30*hr*	3.45
5. 0	2.35	8.30*kr*	4.15
11.35*r*	6.37	PM 12.30*er*	9.45
—	—	12.30*dr*	9.15
—	—	6.53	5. 0
—	—	—	—
—	—	—	—

Sunday Trains.

—	—	—	—
—	—	—	—
—	—	—	—

d Saturdays only.
e Saturdays excepted.
h Mondays and Saturdays only.
k Mondays and Saturdays excepted.
r Restaurant Car.

INGROW (Yorks) from
St. Pancras, 203¾ miles. Fares, 40/8*a*, 24/5*c*. R. T., double fare. Departures *from* London as for Keighley. Departures *for* London about 6 times daily. *Map Square* 12.

INNERLEITHEN
(Peebles), 376 miles. Fares, 76/6*a*, 45/11*c*. R. T. for two months, 153/0*a*, 91/10*c*. Departures *from* London as for Galashiels. Departures *for* London about 4 times daily. Pop. 3,855. *Map Square* 41.

INNERPEFFRAY (Perth),
445¾ miles. No through fares. Departures *from* London as for Perth. Departures *for* London about 3 times daily. *Map Square* 37.

INNERWICK (East
Lothian), 358½ miles. No through fares. Departures *from* London as for Berwick-on-Tweed. Departures *for* London about 3 times daily. Pop. 633. *Map Square* 41.

INSCH (Aberdeen), 550½
miles. Fares, 105/8*a*, 63/5*c*. R. T. for two months, 211/4*a*, 126/10*c*. Departures *from* London as for Inverurie. Departures *for* London about twice daily. Pop. 1,377. *Map Square* 35.

INSTOW (Devon) from
Waterloo, 218 miles. Fares, 40/5*a*, 24/3*c*. R. T. for two months, 80/10*a*. 48/6*c*. Departures *from* London as for Barnstaple. Departures *for* London 6 times daily. Pop. 648. *Map Square* 24.

INVERAMSAY (Aber-
deen), 543 miles. No through fares. Departures *from* London as for Inverurie. Departures *for* London about twice daily. *Map Square* 35.

INVERESK (Midlothian),
385½ miles. Fares, 81/1*a*, 48/8*c*. R. T. for two months, 162/2*a*, 97/4*c*. Departures *from* London as for Dunbar. Departures *for* London about 5 times daily. Pop. 21,220.

INVERGARRY (Inverness).
531¼ miles. Fares, 105/8*a*, 63/5*c*. R. T. for two months, 211/4*a*, 126/10*c*. Departures *from* London as for Fort William. Departures *for* London about twice daily. *Map Square* 37.

INVERGORDON (Ross),
599 miles. Fares, 106/3*a*, 63/9*c*. R.T. for two months, 212/6*a*, 127/6*c*. Departures *from* London as for Dingwall. Departures *for* London about 3 times daily. Pop. 1,384. *Map Square* 34.

INVERGOWRIE (Perth),
467 miles. Fares, 91/11*a*, 55/2*c*. R.T. for two months, 183/10*a*, 110/4*c*. Departures *from* London as for Perth. Departures *for* London about twice daily. Pop. 967. *Map Square* 38.

INVERKEILOR (Forfar),
474½ miles. Fares, 95/0*a*, 57/0*c*. R. T. for two months, 114/0*c*. Departures *from* London as for Arbroath. Departures *for* London about 3 times daily. Pop. 1,297. *Map Square* 38.

INVERKEITHING (Fife),
from *King's Cross*, 405½ miles. Fares, 83/7*a*, 50/2*c*. R. T. for two months, 167/2*a*, 100/4*c*. Pop. 5,464.

King's+	Inkthing	Inkthing	King's+
AM 4.45	2.51	AM 9.26*r*	6.15
9.50*r*	6.49	11.22	10. 0
10. 0*r*	6.59	PM 12.37*dr*	10. 0
11.50*r*	9.17	3.36	3.25
PM 1.15*dr*	11.16	6.51	6. 0
7.45*er*	6.27	9.52	7. 5
8.25*e*	7.13	—	—
8.25*d*	9. 1	—	—
11.40*e*	8.33	—	—
11.40*d*	9. 1	—	—

Sunday Trains.

PM 7.45	6.27	AM 10. 8	8.15
8.25	7.13	PM 6.31	6. 0
10.30	8.33	—	—
—	—	—	—

d Saturdays only.
e Saturdays excepted.
r Restaurant Car.

INVERKIP (Renfrew), 428½
miles. Fares, 85/3*a*, 51/2*c*. R. T. for two months, 170/6*a*, 102/4*c*. Departures *from* London as for Wemyss Bay. Departures *for* London about 3 times daily. Pop. 12,901. *Map Square* 40.

INVERNESS from *Euston,*
568 miles, *via* Dunkeld. Fares, 106/3*a*, 63/9*c*. R. T. for two months, 212/6*a*, 127/6*c*. Pop. 24,614.

Euston	Invern's.	Invern's.	Euston
PM 1.30*er*	6. 0*h*	AM 8.40*r*	10.45
7.40*er*	9.10	10.30*r*	5. 0*h*
11.35*e*	4.40*l*	PM 4.30	7.40
—	—	11.20*er*	7.30*l*
—	—	—	—

Sunday Trains.

PM 7.50*r*	9.35*h*	—	—
11.35	4.40*l*	—	—
—	—	—	—

e Saturdays excepted.
h A.M.
l P.M.
r Restaurant Car.

INVERNESS—*continued.*

ANOTHER ROUTE from *King's Cross,* 568 miles, *via* Dunkeld. Fares as above.

King's+	Invern's.	Invern's.	King's+
AM 4.45	8.12*h*	AM 8.40*r*	10. 0*h*
11.50*er*	6. 0*k*	10.30	3.25*k*
PM 7.45*er*	9.10*k*	PM 4.30	7. 5*k*
8.20*e*	11.20*k*	11.20*er*	6.30*h*
11.25*e*	4.40*h*	—	—

Sunday Trains.

| PM 7.45*r* | 9.35*k* | — | — |
| 11.25 | 4.40*h* | — | — |

e Saturdays excepted.
h P.M.   *k* A.M.
r Restaurant Car.

Caledonian Hotel. Largest in town. Opposite Station, overlooking Ness River. Scenery unsurpassed. Garage. Moderate charges. Tel. 246.
FRANK STEVEN, Proprietor.
See advt. p. **218**.

Royal Hotel. Telephone 244. Famous centre for the Highland meeting. Convenient to Station. Famous for its old furniture and china. Central Heating. Electric Light.
TRUST HOUSES, Ltd.

Station Hotel. Distinctly comfortable. Only hotel passenger lift. Night Porter. Suites. Private Bathrooms. H. H. WARD, L.M.S. Highland Hotels Manager. Also Kyle, Dornoch and Strathpeffer.

INVERSHIN (Sutherland),
629 miles. Fares, 112/4*a*, 67/5*c*. R. T. for two months, 224/8*a*, 134/10*c*. Departures *from* London as for Tain. Departures *for* London about twice daily. *Map Square* 34.

INVERUGIE (Aberdeen),
565 miles. No through fares. Departures *from* London as for Peterhead. Departures *for* London about twice daily. *Map Square* 35.

INVERURIE (Aberdeen),
from *King's Cross,* 539½ miles. Fares, 103/7*a*, 62/2*c*. R.T. for two months, 207/2*a*, 124/4*c*. Pop. 4,330 *Map Square* 35.

King's+	Inv'rur.	Inv'rur.	King's+
AM 4.45	6.35*l*	AM 9. 4*r*	10. 0*l*
PM 8.20*e*	8.31*h*	10. 7	3.25*h*
11.25*e*	2.10*l*	PM 2.25	6. 0*h*
—	—	6.12	7.25*h*

Sunday Trains.

PM 11.25	2.10*l*	—	—
—	—	—	—
—	—	—	—

e Saturdays excepted.
h A.M.
l P.M.
r Restaurant Car.

INVERURIE—*continued.*

ANOTHER ROUTE from *Euston*, 556½ miles. Fares as above.

EUSTON	INV'RUR.	INV'RUR.	EUSTON
PM 1.30*er*	5. 7*h*	AM 9. 4*r*	10.45*l*
7.50*er*	8.31*h*	10. 7*r*	5. 0*h*
11.35*e*	2.10*l*	PM 6.12	8. 0*h*
—	—	9.49	7.30*l*
—	—	—	—

Sunday Trains.

PM 7.50*r*	8.31	—	—
11.35	2.10*l*	—	—
—	—	—	—

d Saturdays only.
e Saturdays excepted.
h A.M.
l P.M.
r Restaurant Car.

INWORTH (Essex), 45¼
miles. No through fares. Departures *from* London as for Tolleshbury. Departures *for* London about 4 times daily. Pop. 804.
Map Square 24.

IPSTONES (Stafford), 158
miles. Fares, 33/2*a*, 19/11*c*. R. T. for two months, 66/4*a*, 39/10*c*. Departures *from* London as for Leek. Departures *for* London about 5 times daily. Pop. 1,482.
Map Square 12.

IPSWICH (Suffolk) from
Liverpool Street, 68¾ miles. Fares, 14/5*a*, 8/8*c*. R. T. for two months, 28/10*a*. Pop. 79,383.
Map Square 19.

L'PL. ST	IPSWICH	IPSWICH	L'PL. ST
AM 5. 0	6.45	AM 1. 5	3.50
6.50	9.41	6.35	8.52
8.15*r*	10. 2	7.30	9.36
8.46	11. 6	7.55*r*	9.53
9.50*er*	11.16	8.49*r*	10.30
10. 0	11.40	8.57*f*	10.36
10.12	11.58	9. 6	11.16
10.20	12.18	9.52*r*	11.22
10.47	1.21	10. 2*r*	11.30
11.30	1.35	10.27	12.39
PM12.33*r*	2.10	11.42	1.20
1. 0	2.31	PM12.23*r*	2. 3
1.33*d*	4. 4	12.32	3.13
2.15	4.30	1.16	3.36
3.10*r*	4.40	2. 5	3.42
3.15*r*	4.53	3.17*r*	4.58
3.18*r*	4.59	3.27	5.48
3.26	6. 0	4.24	5.56
4.55*r*	6.23	4.52	6.32
5.18*r*	6.53	5.58	7.51
5.42*d*	7.46	7.51*r*	9.22
5.42*e*	7.50	8. 4*r*	10. 0
6.39*e*	8.39	8.55	11.16
7.45*r*	9.45	—	—
8.45	10.45	—	—
8.54	11.34	—	—
—	—	—	—

Sunday Trains.

AM 8.15	10.48	AM 1. 5	3.50
9.20*r*	11.25	9.27	11.38
10. 5*r*	11.56	9.44	12.40
11.30*r*	12.59	PM 5.15	7.10
PM 3.40	6. 4	6.24	8.58
4.40	6.21	7.44*r*	9.10
7.40	9.46	8.20	10.15
8.46	11.28	8.37*r*	10.30
—	—	—	—

d Saturdays only.
e Saturdays excepted.
f Mondays only.
r Restaurant Car.

IPSWICH—*continued.*

Great White Horse Hotel. Telephone 584. Famous Dickens' house. Modern Restaurant. Central Heating. Electric Light. Garage. TRUST HOUSES, Ltd.

IRCHESTER (Northampton) from *St. Pancras*, 62½ miles.
Fares, 12/9*a*, 7/8*c*. R. T., double fare. Pop. 2,224.
Map Square 18.

ST. PAN.	IRCH'T'R.	IRCH'T'R.	ST. PAN.
AM 4.25	7.19	AM 7.48	9.30
6.25	9. 7	8.12	10.31
9.25	11.51	9.57	11.25
PM12.30	2. 9	10.47	1. 3
3.35	5.20	PM12.43	3.25
4.30*r*	6.28	3.22	5.20
5.35*r*	7.11	6.27	8.22
6.30	8.10	8.19*r*	10. 5
—	—	9.40	11.45
—	—	—	—
—	—	—	—
—	—	—	—

Sunday Trains.

AM 8. 0	10.39	AM10.55	1.30
PM 6.15*r*	8. 1	PM 6. 4	8.30

r Restaurant Car.

IRLAM (Lancs), 194 miles.
Fares, 40/3*a*, 24/2*c*. R. T. for two months, 80/6*a*, 48/4*c*. Departures *from* London as for Glazebrook. Departures *for* London about 6 times daily. Pop. 9,471.
Map Square 12.

IRLAMS-O'-TH'-HEIGHT (Lancs), 190½ miles.
Fares, 39/4*a*, 23/7*c*. R. T. for two months, 78/8*a*, 47/2*c*. Departures *from* London as for Manchester. Departures *for* London about 6 times daily.

IRON ACTON (Gloucester), 129½ miles. No through fares.
Departures *from* London as for Bristol. Departures *for* London about 4 times daily. Pop. 1,408.
Map Square 22.

IRON BRIDGE (Salop)
from *Paddington*, 145 miles. Fares, 30/7*a*, 18/4*c*. R. T. for two months, 61/2*a*. Pop. 2,695.
Map Square 17.

PAD.	IRON B.	IRON B.	PAD.
AM 9.10*r*	2.22	AM 8.57*hr*	1.25
10.40*h*	3. 5	12. 0*r*	4.15
PM 1.30*r*	5.54	PM 2.22*t*	6.40
2.10*ht*	6. 5	3. 5*r*	8. 5
4.10*t*	8.15	8.15*h*	5.30
12.15*hk*	8.47	—	—
—	—	—	—
—	—	—	—
—	—	—	—

No Sunday Trains.

h Via Birmingham.
k Saturday midnight excepted.
r Restaurant Car.
t Tea Car.

IRON GRAY (Dumfries),
337¼ miles. Fares, 41/1*c*. R.T. for two months, 82/2*c*. Departures *from* London as for Dumfries. Departures *for* London about twice daily.
Map Square 43.

IRTHLINGBOROUGH
(Northampton) from *Euston*, 82 miles. Fares, 13/2*a*, 7/11*c*. R. T., double fare. Departures *from* London as for Wellingboro'. Departures *for* London about 4 times daily. Pop. 4,809.
Map Square 18.

IRVINE (Ayr) from *St. Pancras*, 406¾ miles. Fares, 81/1*a*, 48/8*c*. R. T. for two months, 162/2*a*, 97/4*c*. Pop. 7,534.
Map Square 40.

ST. PAN.	IRVINE	IRVINE	ST. PAN.
AM 4.25	3.40	AM 9.16*r*	6.35
9.50*r*	7.10	11.41*r*	9.15
PM12.15*r*	9.27	PM 9. 7*e*	7.25
9.30*e*	7.40	10.53*d*	8.57
11.45*d*	9. 5	—	—
11.45*e*	9.15	—	—
—	—	—	—
—	—	—	—
—	—	—	—

Sunday Trains.

PM 9.30	7.40	PM 9.12	7.25
11.45	9.15	—	—
—	—	—	—

d Saturdays only.
e Saturdays excepted.
r Restaurant Car.

ISFIELD (Sussex), 48½ miles.
Fares from London Bridge or Victoria, *via* Groombridge, 10/3*a*, 6/2*c*. R. T. for two months, 20/6*a*, 12/4*c*. Fares *via* Lewes, 10/7*a*, 6/4*c*. R. T. for two months, 21/2*a*, 12/8*c*. Departures *from* London as for Uckfield or Lewes. Departures *for* London about 6 times daily. Pop. 470.
Map Square 24.

ISHAM (Northampton),
69¼ miles. Fares, 14/2*a*, 8/6*c*. R.T., double fare. Departures *from* London as for Wellingbro'. Departures *for* London about 4 times daily. Pop. 358.
Map Square 18.

ISLEHAM (Cambs) from
Liverpool Street, 72½ miles. Fares, 15/2*a*, 9/1*c*. R.T. for two months, 30/4*a*. Departures *from* London as for Mildenhall. Departures *for* London about 5 times daily. Pop. 1,643.
Map Square 19.

ISLEWORTH (Middlesex)
from *Waterloo*, 9¾ miles. Fares, *via* Barnes, 1/9*a*, 0/7½*c*. R. T. for two days, 1/9*a*, 1/3*c*. Pop. 16,236.
See p. 586.
Map Square 66.

ANOTHER ROUTE from *Whitechapel* and *Mansion House*. *See* OSTERLEY.

ISLIP (Oxford) from *Euston*,

71¾ miles.   Fares, 12/4*a*, 7/5*c*.
R.T. for two months, 24/8*a*. Departures *from* London as for Bicester.
Departures *for* London about 5
times daily.   Pop. 566.
Map Square 23.

ITCHIN ABBAS (Hants)

from *Waterloo*, 60¾ miles.   Fares,
12/8*a*, 7/7*c*.   R. T. for two months,
25/4*a*, 15/2*c*.   Departures *from*
London as for Alresford. Departures *for* London about 5 times
daily.   Pop. 232.
Map Square 23.

IVYBRIDGE (Devon) from

Paddington, 215 miles.   Fares,
44/4*a*, 26/7*c*.   R. T. for two months,
88/8*a*, 53/2*c*.   Pop. 1,574.
Map Square 26.

PAD.	IVYBRIDGE	IVYBRIDGE	PAD.
AM 5.30	1.14	AM 8. 6*r*	1.30
9.15*r*	3.42	11.46*r*	4.35
11. 0*dr*	3.42	PM 1. 9*er*	6.50
11.10*r*	3.59	1. 9*dr*	7. 5
PM12. 5*r*	5.16	3.16*r*	9. 0
3.30*r*	8.31	4.57	2.45
12. 0*l*	8.25	9.51	7.10
12.30*h*	11.33	—	—
—	—	—	—
—	—	—	—

Sunday Trains.

AM10.30*r*	4.40	AM 7.30*r*	3.35
PM 2.40	9.14	PM 8.35*k*	3.15
10. 0	8.25	—	—
—	—	—	—
—	—	—	—
—	—	—	—
—	—	—	—

d Saturdays only.
h Saturdays midnight only.
k Picks up by request—give notice
at Station before 7.0 p.m.
l Saturday midnight excepted.
r Restaurant Car.

REFERENCE NOTES.

a	signifies	First Class.
b	,,	Second Class.
c	,,	Third Class.
d	,,	On Saturdays only.
e	,,	Saturdays excepted.
f	,,	On Mondays only.
g	,,	Mondays excepted.
r	,,	Restaurant Car.
t	,,	Tea Car.
x	,,	Express.
R.T.	,,	Return Tickets.

All Trains in the Tables not
otherwise marked carry Third
Class Passengers.

J

JAMESTOWN (Dumbarton), 446¼ miles.   Fares, 85/7*a*,

51/4*c*.   R. T. for two months,
171/2*a*, 102/8*c*.   Departures *from*
London as for Balloch or Stirling.
Departures *for* London about 3
times daily.   Pop. 2,389.
Map Square 40.

JARROW (Durham), 268

miles.   Fares, 55/8*a*, 33/5*c*. R.T.,
double fare.   Departures *from*
London as for Newcastle-on-Tyne.
Departures *for* London about 10
times daily.   Pop. 35,590.
Map Square 3.

JEDBURGH (Roxburgh),

361 miles.   Fares, 76/0*a*, 45/7*c*.
R. T. for two months, 152/0*a*, 91/2*c*.
Departures *from* London as for
Kelso or St. Boswells.   Departures
for London about 4 times daily.
Pop. 3,533.
Map Square 41.

JEDFOOT (Roxburgh),

359¼ miles.   No through fares.
Departures *from* London as for
St. Boswells or Kelso.   Departures
for London about 3 times daily.
Map Square 41.

JERSEY from *Waterloo*, 229

miles.   Fares 50/0 First and Saloon,
42/6 Third and Saloon, 30/0 Third
and Second Cabin.   R.T. for two
months, 75/0 First and Saloon, 64/0
Third and Saloon, 45/0 Third and
Second Cabin.   Pop 49,494.

W'LOO	JERSEY	JERSEY	W'LOO
PM 9.10*k*	9.15	AM 7.30	7.20
9.30*hr*	9.15	—	—
—	—	—	—
—	—	—	—
—	—	—	—
—	—	—	—
—	—	—	—

No Sunday Service.

h Fridays excepted.
k Fridays only.
r Restaurant Car.

ANOTHER ROUTE from

Paddington, 241 miles.   Fares,
50/0 First and Saloon, 42/6 Third
and Saloon, 30/0 Third and Second
Cabin.   R.T. for two months, 75/0
First and Saloon, 64/0 Third and
Saloon, 45/0 Third and Second
Cabin.

PAD.	JERSEY	JERSEY	PAD.
AM 9.30	8.45	AM 7.30*r*	7.35
—	—	—	—
—	—	—	—

r Restaurant Car.

Grand Hotel.   The premier
Hotel of the Island.   Beautifully
situated.
See advt. p. **224.**

Pomme D'Or Hotel.   Nearest
to landing stages. Unrivalled Continental Cuisine.   MANAGER.
See advt. p. **224.**

JERSEY—*continued.*

The Sandringham, Colomberie. Near sea. Gardens. Young society. Dancing. Picnics. Liberal table. From 42s. weekly. Illustrated tariff. Bus meets boat.

The Somerville Hotel. Two acres terraced gardens overlooking Bay. Premier in the Channel Islands. Golf. Address— SOMERVILLE, St. Aubin's, Jersey.

Star Hotel. Near Railways, Boats, Post Office and Bathing Pools. Excellent cuisine and moderate tariff. Porter meets boats. RAYNOR SMITH, Proprietor.

Royal Yacht Hotel. Facing Sea. Close to Steamer Landing Stage. First-class in equipment, cuisine and comfort. Central for everywhere on Island. Moderate tariff. Porter meets Boats. T. C. SCUDDAN, Proprietor.

St. Cyres Hotel, Colomberie. High-class Board Residence. English Cuisine and Supervision. Open all the Year Round. Central Situation. Five minutes Harbour and Bathing Pool. Terms from Three Guineas.

St. Heliers. Ommaroo Hotel. Facing Sea. Unrivalled position. Excellent Cuisine and Service. Most convenient to Golf Links. Ideal for Anglo-Indians. Hard Tennis Courts. Moderate terms.

Amblève House, St. Aubins. Select Pension immediately facing sea. Prettiest spot in island. Highly recommended for excellent Cuisine and Comfort. Separate tables. Boating, Fishing. Near Golf Links. Moderate Tariff. Apply, M. E. BOSWELL.

House Agency. F. Le Gallais & Sons, Auctioneers and House Agents. Removal and Storage Contractors, Bath Street, Jersey.

James Gregory & Sons, Auctioneers, Valuers, Estate and House Agents, Beresford Auction Rooms, Jersey. Houses, Furnished or Unfurnished. Furniture Removers and Warehousemen. Established 1820.

Benest's House and Estate Agency. Principal Removers, Baggage and Storage Agents. Complete House Furnishers. Head Office—Queen Street, Jersey.

JERVAULX (Yorks), 229 miles. Fares, 47/9*a*, 28/8*c*. R. T., double fare. Departures *from* London as for Leyburn. Departures *for* London about 4 times daily. *Map Square* 7.

JESMOND (Northumberland), 269¼ miles. No through fares. Departures *from* London as *for* Newcastle-on-Tyne. Departures *for* London about 6 times daily. Pop. 21,367. *Map Square* 3.

JOHN O'GAUNT (Leicester), 100½ miles. Fares, 20/3*a*, 12/2*c*. R. T., double fare. Departures *from* London as for Hallaton. Departures *for* London about 6 times daily. *Map Square* 18.

JOHNSHAVEN (Kincardine), 490¾ miles. No through fares. Departures *from* London as for Montrose. Departures *for* London about 3 times daily. Pop. 777. *Map Square* 38.

JOHNSTON (Pembroke), 263¼ miles. Fares, 53/7*a*, 32/2*c*. R. T. for two months, 107/2*a*, 64/4*c*. Departures *from* London as for Haverfordwest. Departures *for* London about 6 times daily. Pop. 272. *Map Square* 20.

JOHNSTONE (Renfrew), 413 miles. Fares, 82/4*a*, 49/5*c*. R. T. for two months, 164/8*a*, 98/10*c*. Departures *from* London as for Kilmarnock. Departures *for* London about 5 times daily. Pop. 12,474. *Map Square* 40.

JOHNSTOWN (Denbigh) from *Paddington*, 179½ miles. Fares, 37/4*a*, 22/5*c*. R. T. for two months, 74/8*a*. Departures *from* London as for Ruabon. Departures *for* London 4 times daily. *Map Square* 12.

JORDANSTONE (Perth), 473¾ miles. Fares, 95/0*a*, 57/0*c*. R. T. for two months, 190/0*a*. 114/0*c*. Departures *from* London as for Coupar Angus. Departures *for* London about 4 times daily. *Map Square* 38.

JUNCTION ROAD (Holloway) from *Moorgate Street* and *St. Pancras*, 2¼ miles. Fares from St. Pancras, 0/6½*a*, 0/4*c*. R. T. for two days,1/1*a*, 0/8*c*. Fares from Moorgate Street, 0/9*a*, 0/5½*c*. R. T. for two days, 1/4*a*, 0/10½*c*. See pp. 506, 507. *Map Squares* 24 *and* 51.

JUNCTION ROAD (Sussex), 52½ miles. No through fares. Departures *from* London as for Tenterden (*via* Robertsbridge). Departures *for* London about 4 times daily. *Map Square* 24.

JUNIPER GREEN (Midlothian), 396 miles. No through fares. Departures *from* London as for Carstairs. Departures *for* London about 4 times daily.

JUSTINHAUGH (Forfar), 485¾ miles. Fares, 97/3*a*, 58/4*c*. R. T. for two months, 194/6*a*, 116/8*c*. Departures *from* London as for Brechin. Departures *for* London about 3 times daily. *Map Square* 38.

KEARSNEY (Kent),

75 miles, from *Victoria, Holborn Viaduct,* and *St. Paul's.* Fares, 15/10a, 12/8b, 9/5c. R. T. for two months, 31/8a, 25/4b.

Map Square 24.

VICT. (S.E.&C.)	Leave HOL V.	ST. PL.'s	Arr. at KEARS.
AM	3.50n	—	7. 5
5. 5	4.57	5. 0	8.53
5.48f	5.40f	5.42f	8.54
—	7.30	7.35	11. 5
9.20	—	—	11.28
10.40	—	—	1. 8
11.40d	—	—	2.22
11.40e	—	—	3. 2
PM 2. 5d	—	—	4.20
2. 8e	—	—	4.48
4.20	—	—	6.50
5.10d	5.10e	5.12e	7.42
5.30e	—	—	8.15
5.30d	—	—	8.27
—	e6.12l	—	8.15
8.30	—	—	10.54
—	—	—	—
—	—	—	—
—	—	—	—
—	—	—	—
—	—	—	—

Sunday Trains.

AM 8.15	8. 0	—	11. 6
10.40	—	—	12.50
PM 3.30	—	—	7. 5
8.25	—	—	11. 6
—	—	—	—
—	—	—	—
—	—	—	—

Trains from Kearsney.

Leave KEARS.	ST. PL.'s	Arrive at HOL.V.	VICT.
AM 6.48h	—	9. 4h	—
6.48	9.37	9.39	—
7.24h	—	9.52h	—
7.24	—	—	11. 2
9.28	—	—	11.27
9.48e	1. 0	1. 2	1.33
10 0d	—	—	1.22
11.49	—	—	2.43
PM 2. 4e	4.46	—	4.39
2.23d	—	—	4.55
3.22	—	—	5.26
d5. 6h	—	—	8.33
6. 5	—	—	8.20h
7.39e	—	—	10.25
8. 1d	—	—	10.25

Sunday Trains.

AM 9. 1	—	11.58	11.51
PM 2. 6	—	—	5.31
6.37	—	—	8.40
7.53	—	—	10.29
—	—	—	—
—	—	—	—

d Saturdays only.
e Saturdays excepted.
f Mondays only.
h Departs from or arrives at Cannon Street.
l Departs from Cannon Street.
n Third Class only.

REFERENCE NOTES.

a signifies	First Class.
b	,,	Second Class.
c	,,	Third Class.
d	,,	On Saturdays only.
e	,,	Saturdays excepted.
f	,,	On Mondays only.
g	,,	Mondays excepted.
r	,,	Restaurant Car.
t	,,	Tea Car.
x	,,	Express.
R.T.	,,	Return Tickets.

All Trains in the Tables not otherwise marked carry Third Class Passengers.

K

KEARSLEY (Lancs), 194½

miles. Fares, 40/3a, 24/2c. R. T. for two months, 80/6a, 48/4c. Departures *from* London as for Manchester. Departures *for* London about 8 times daily. Pop. 9,610.

Map Square 12.

KEELE (Stafford), 151¼ miles.

Fares, 31/6a, 18/11c. R. T. for two months, 63/0a, 37/10c. Departures *from* London as for Newcastle-under-Lyme. Departures *for* London about 8 times daily. Pop. 1,156.

Map Square 12.

KEGWORTH (Leicester)

from *St. Pancras,* 116 miles. Fares, 23/11a, 14/4c. R. T., double fare. Pop. 2,220.

Map Square 18.

ST. PAN.	KEGW'TH	KEGW'TH	ST. PAN.
AM 2.25	7. 7	AM 6.23r	9.57
4.25	8.20	8.20r	11. 0
8.25r	11.58	8.54r	11.35
10.25r	1.16	10.33r	1.30
PM12.25r	3.31	11.15r	2.10
2.25r	5.10	PM 1.49r	4.20
4.25r	7.20	2.52r	5.45
6.25r	9.12	5. 1r	7.55
—	—	6. 4r	9.15
—	—	7.13r	10. 5
—	—	10. 3	4.20

Sunday Trains.

PM 1.35	5.24	AM 7.42	11.53
6.15r	9.25	PM 5.38r	9.52
—	—	9.22	4.55
—	—	—	—
—	—	—	—

r Restaurant Car.

KEIGHLEY (Yorks) from

St. Pancras, 212 miles. Fares, 40/8a, 24/5c. R. T., double fare. Pop. 41,942.

Map Square 12.

ST. PAN.	KEIGHL'Y	KEIGHL'Y	ST. PAN.
AM 4.25	11.12	AM 2.12	7.25
9.50r	2.46	7.13r	12.10
PM12.15er	5. 8	7.20r	1.30
12.15dr	5.59	9.10r	2.10
1.50r	7.48	10. 8r	4.10
3.30r	8.38	PM12. 5r	5.30
5. 0r	9.58	1.39r	6.35
6.15r	11.52	2.58r	7.57
9.30e	2.35	4.15r	9.15
11.45d	4.18	9.11	4.20
11.45e	4.45	—	—
—	—	—	—

Sunday Trains.

AM10.50r	5.40	AM11. 5	6.25
PM 9.30	2.35	PM12.48r	9.43
11.45	4.45	9. 8	4.55
—	—	—	—

d Saturdays only.
e Saturdays excepted.
r Restaurant Car.

ANOTHER ROUTE from

King's Cross, 205 miles. Fares as above.

KING'S +	KEIGH.	KEIGH.	KING'S +
AM 4.45	10.57	AM 5.35r	11.30
7.15r	12.55	7.45	1. 5
10.10r	4. 8	8.58r	1.55
11.15k	4. 8	10. 3k	3.15
PM 1.30r	6.31	10. 3r	4.45
1.50r	8.19	11.50r	5. 0
[4. 0r	9.30	PM 1.38r	7.10
5.45r	10.47	4.18r	9.25
10.45e	6.39	8.35	3.25

Sunday Trains.

12. 0nr	6.28	AM 9.35	3.45
PM10.45	6.59	PM 3.54r	10.20
—	—	—	—

e Saturdays excepted.
k 1st and 3rd Class Pullman Cars only.
n Noon.
r Restaurant Car.

Queen's Hotel. Adjoining Midland Station. Comfortable and Convenient. Excellent cuisine. One of the "Midland Hotels." Telephone 128.

ARTHUR TOWLE, Manager.

KEINTON MANDE-VILLE (Somerset), 120 miles.
Fares, 24/8a, 15/0c. R. T. for two months, 49/4a, 30/0c. Departures *from* London as for Somerton. Departures *for* London about 4 times daily. Pop. 530.

KEITH (Banff) from
King's Cross, 576¼ miles, via Aberdeen. Fares, 106/3a, 63/9c. R. T. for two months, 212/6a, 127/6c. Pop. 5,972. *Map Square* 35.

King's +	Keith	Keith	King's +
AM 4.45	8.22h	AM 7.53r	10. 0h
PM 8.20e	k9. 4l	10.47	3.25k
11.25e	l3.58l	PM 1. 3	6. 0k
—	—	5.40	7.25k
—	—	—	—
—	—	—	—
—	—	—	—
—	—	—	—

Sunday Trains.
PM 7.45	9. 4k	—	—
—	—	—	—
—	—	—	—
—	—	—	—
—	—	—	—

e Saturdays excepted.
h P.M.
k A.M.
l Keith Town Station.
r Restaurant Car.

ANOTHER ROUTE from
Euston, 593 miles, via Aberdeen. Fares as above.

Euston	Keith	Keith	Euston
PM 1.30er	6.25h	AM 7.53	10.45l
7.50ehr9. 4v	10.47	5. 0h
11.35e	l3.58v	PM 5.40v	8. 0h
—	—	—	—
—	—	—	—
—	—	—	—

Sunday Trains.
PM 7.50r	h9. 4v	—	—
11.35	l3.58v	—	—
—	—	—	—
—	—	—	—

e Saturdays excepted.
h A.M.
l P.M.
r Restaurant Car.
v Town Station.

KELMARSH (Northampton) from *Euston*, 79 miles. Fares, 16/6a, 9/11c. R. T., double fare. Departures *from* London as for Lamport. Departures *for* London about 5 times daily. Pop. 152. *Map Square* 18.

KELMSCOTT (Oxford), 83 miles. Fares, 17/3a, 10/4c. R. T. for two months, 34/6a, 20/8c. Departures *from* London as for Fairford. Departures *for* London about 5 times daily. Pop. 159. *Map Square* 22.

KELSO (Roxburgh) from
King's Cross, 350¾ miles. Fares, 73/9a, 44/3c. R. T., double fare. Pop. 4,009. *Map Square* 41.

King's +	Kelso	Kelso	King's +
AM 4.45	5.10	AM 9.50r	6.30
10. 0r	6.32	PM 3.25r	3.25
PM11.25d	9.22	7.15d	6. 0
11.25e	9.33	7.15e	5.40
—	—	—	—
—	—	—	—

Sunday Trains.
PM11.25	9.33	AM 9.35r	8.15
—	—	PM 7.15	6. 0

d Saturdays only.
e Saturdays excepted.
r Restaurant Car.

ANOTHER ROUTE from
St. Pancras, 376¾ miles. Fares as above.

St. Pan.	Kelso.	Kelso.	St. Pan.
AM 4.25	3.57	AM 9.44r	7.15
9. 0r	6.25	PM 6.40	8. 3
PM 9.15e	7.12	8. 0e	8. 5

Sunday Trains.
PM 9.15	7.12	—	—

e Saturdays excepted.
r Restaurant Car.

KELSTON (Somerset), 128 miles. No through fares. Departures *from* London as for Bristol. Departures *for* London about 4 times daily. Pop. 179. *Map Square* 22.

KELTY (Fife), 417 miles. Fares, 86/11a, 52/2c. R. T. for two months, 173/10a, 104/4c. Departures *from* London as for Dunfermline. Departures *for* London about 4 times daily. Pop. 7,315. *Map Square* 41.

KELVEDON (Essex) from
Liverpool Street, 42½ miles. Fares, 9/0a, 5/5c. R. T. for two months, 18/0a. Pop. 1,547. *Map Square* 24.

L'pl. St.	Kelv'dn	Kelv'dn	L'pl.St.
AM 6.50	8.39	AM 2. 2	3.50
8.18	9.36	7.30	8.52
8.46	10.16	8. 1	9.30
10.47	12.22	9.11	10.22
PM 1.33d	2.58	10. 3	11.16
2.15	3.29	11.28	12.40
3.26	4.59	PM 1.40	3.13
4.18	5.39	4.33	5.47
5.42d	7. 5	5.50	7.40
5.42e	7. 9	7.35	9.17
6.39	7.59	9.51	11.16
7.45r	8.52	—	—
8.54	10.32	—	—

Sunday Trains.
AM 8.15	9.45	AM 2. 2	3.50
PM 3.40	5. 3	10.47	12.40
8.46	10.27	PM 7. 4	8 25
—	—	7.33	8.58

d Saturdays only.
e Saturdays excepted.
r Restaurant Car.

KEMBLE (Glos'ter) from
Paddington, 91 miles. Fares, 19/0a, 11/5c. R. T. for two months, 38/0a. Pop. 528. *Map Square* 22.

Pad.	Kemble	Kemble	Pad.
AM 1. 0g	3.10	AM 1.15	3.30
5.30	8. 7	8.32r	10.45
7.30	9.44	10.27	12.20
9. 0	11.19	PM12.53r	2.40
10.45	1. 7	1. 6	3.20
PM 1.10r	3.39	2.58	5. 0
3.15t	5.12	3.35	6. 2
4.15t	6.29	6.43r	8.45
6. 0r	8.14	8. 4	10.25
9.15	11.41	—	—

Sunday Trains.
AM 1. 0	3.10	AM 1.15	3.30
PM12.30r	3. 7	PM 2. 8	4. 5
2. 0	7. 1	7.42	10. 0
9.15	11.41	—	—

g Mondays excepted.
r Restaurant Car.
t Tea Car.

KEMNAY (Aberdeen), 540¼ miles. Fares, 103/9a, 62/3c. R. T., double fare. Departures *from* London as for Aberdeen. Departures *for* London about 3 times daily. Pop. 1,609. *Map Square* 35.

KEMSING (Kent) from
Victoria, Holborn Viaduct, and *St. Paul's*, 27 miles. Fares, 5/5a, 4/4b, 3/3c. R. T. for two months, 10/10a, 8/8b. Pop. 685. *Map Square* 24.

	Leave		Arr. at
Vict. (S E.& C.)	Hol. V.	St. Pl.'s	Kems.
AM —	6.40	6.42	7.59
8.32	8.20	8.23	9.54
11. 4	10.58	11. 0	12.22
PM —	12.33d	12.36d	1.42
—	1.27d	1.30d	2.37
2.40d	—	—	3.49
2.50e	—	—	4. 2
4.25e	—	—	5.21
e5.15h	—	e5.21k	6.18
d5.20h	—	d5.26k	6.24
5.30e	—	5.33e	6.33
—	—	6.16e	7.12
6.40	6.34	6.37	7.46
7.22	7.22	7.24	8.31
10. 0	9.54	9.56	11. 6

Sunday Trains.
AM —	8. 0	—	9.27
PM 2. 5	2. 3	—	3.30
6.35	6.40	—	7.51
10.15	10.12	—	11.23

KEMSING—continued.

Trains from Kemsing.

Leave KEMS.	ST. PL.'S	Arrive at HOL. V.	VICT.
AM 7.35	8.40	8.42	8.50
8.28	9.37	9.39	—
9. 4	9.52	9.55	—
9.50d	10.41	—	—
9.50	—	10.43	—
10.43	—	—	11.37
11.53	12.59	1. 2	12.49
PM 1.28	—	—	2.40
3.17	—	—	4.33
5.41	6.58	7. 0	—
6.35	7.36k	—	7.49h
6.35d	8. 0	8. 2	—
6.35e	8.18	8.20	8.10
7.31	—	—	8.51
8.57d	—	—	9.54
10.31	11.43	11.45	—

Sunday Trains.

AM 9.48	—	—	10.48
PM 2.46	—	—	3.50
5. 2	—	6.20	6. 3
8.56	—	10.22	10. 5

d Saturdays only.
e Saturdays excepted.
h Departs from or arrives at Charing Cross (S.E. & C.R.).
k Departs from or arrives at London Bridge (S.E. & C.R.).

KENDAL (Westmorland)
from *Euston*, 251¼ miles. Fares, 52/1a, 31/3c.   R. T. for two months, 104/2a, 62/6c. Pop. 14,149.
Map Square 7.

EUSTON	KENDAL		KENDAL	EUSTON
AM 12.25	8.35	AM	7.25r	1.45
2.35	10.25		7.41r	3.10
5. 0	12.37		9.31er	4.15
6.45	1.52		9.46hr	4.15
10.40dr	4.45		11.46t	6. 0
11.35r	5. 5	PM	2.36er	9. 5
11.50r	6.39		2.36dr	9.15
PM 1.30er	7. 1		4.50r	10.45
1.30dr	7.25		8.56	5. 0
2.35t	9. 5		—	—
5.20er	11.28		—	—
5.20dr	11.33		—	—
9.30	5. 5		—	—
11.45e	7.55		—	—

Sunday Trains.

AM 11.45r	7.15	PM 1.31	5. 0
PM 9.15	5. 5	—	—
11.45	7.55	—	—

d Saturdays only.
e Saturdays excepted.
h Mondays and Saturdays only.
r Restaurant Car.
t Tea Car.

KENFIG HILL (Glamorgan), 179¼ miles. Fares, 37/4a, 22/5c. R. T. for two months, 74/8a, 44/10c. Departures *from* London as for Pyle or Bridgend. Departures *for* London about 4 times daily. Pop. 301.
Map Square 21.

KENILWORTH (Warwick) (*via* Coventry), from *Euston*, 96¼ miles. Fares, 20/3a, 12/2c. R. T. for two months, 40/6a, 24/4c. Pop. 6,752.
Map Square 17.

EUSTON	KEN'TH.	KEN'TH.	EUSTON
AM 2.30	6.47	AM 7.34	10. 0
5. 0	8.39	8.38r	11. 0
6.45	9.42	8.40dk	12.20
9.15r	11.37	8.40ek	12.32
10. 0	12.48	9.20d	12.40
11.30d	1.30	10.56r	1. 0
11.30e	1.47	11.41r	2.20
12. 0nr	2.57	PM 12.47k	4.15
PM 2.20t	4.12	2. 2r	4.35
2.50t	5.50	3.22	5.35
4. 5r	6.17	4.51r	7.20
4.45r	7.25	5.53r	8.20
5.50r	8. 3	8. 1r	10.20
7. 0	9.32	10.33c	4. 0
—	—	10.33d	5. 0

Sunday Trains.

AM 9.15	2.28	AM 8.54	12.25
PM 1. 0r	3.17	11.42r	1.45
5.10	7.42	PM 12. 7t	5. 5
—	—	5.42r	8.20
—	—	8.37	5. 0

d Saturdays only.
e Saturdays excepted.
k *Via* Leamington.
n Noon.
r Restaurant Car.
t Tea Car.

The King's Arms Hotel.
Sir Walter Scott stayed here when writing his novel "Kenilworth," and his room contains all the original furniture. 'Phone 24. Garage. Officially appointed Hotel to the A.A. and M.U. also N.C.U.

KENLEY (Surrey) from
Charing Cross, Cannon Street, and *London Bridge* 17 miles. Fares, 2/9a, 2/3b, 1/8c. R. T. for eight days, 5/6a, 4/6b, 3/1c. Pop. 2,034.
Map Square 23.

	Leave CAN. ST.	LON. B.	Arr. at KENLEY
CHAR. +			
AM —	4.44	5. 0	5.47
—	—	7.50l	8.48
—	—	9.15l	9.45
—	10.12	10.15	10.49
10.55	—	11. 3	11.44
—	11.40d	11.43d	12.19
11.48e	—	11.54e	12.28
PM —	12.40d	12.43d	1.14
—	—	12.45le	1.14
12.55d	—	1. 4d	1.41
—	1.20	1.23	1.55
—	—	1.50dl	2.23
2. 3e	2. 8d	2.10	2.49
2.46d	—	2.52d	3. 0
3.15	—	3.21	4. 0
—	—	4.20dl	4.51
—	4.24e	4.28e	5. 4
—	4.44e	4.48e	5.21
—	—	4.50dl	5.21
5. 6e	—	5.14e	5.48
5.30d	—	5.36d	6. 7
5.30e	—	5.37e	6. 7
—	—	5.48el	6.23
—	6.20e	6.23e	6.52
6.17d	—	6.23d	6.53
—	—	6.53e	7.29
7.24d	7.28e	7.30	8. 8
8.28	—	8.36	9.14
9.25	—	9.31	10. 6
10.17	—	10.23	11. 1
11.42	—	—	12.16

KENLEY—continued.

Sunday Trains.

	Leave CAN. ST.	LON. B.	Arr. at KENLEY
CHAR. +			
AM 6.25	—	6.32	7.15
9. 8	—	9.14	9.46
10.20	—	10.28	11.13
PM 1.30	—	1.37	2.13
5.25	—	5.32	6.10
6.50	—	6.56	7.30
7.45	—	7.52	8.24
8.38	—	8.45	9.22
9.40	—	9.47	10.25

Trains from Kenley.

Leave KENLEY	LON. B.	Arrive at CAN. ST.	CHAR. +
AM 7.28	7.58	—	8. 7
7.53	8.24	8.28	—
8.11	8.40	8.44	—
8.34	9. 5	9. 9	—
8.45	9.22	—	9.30
9. 7	9.39	9.43	—
9.48	10.19	10.22	—
10.28	11. 0	—	—
10.50	11.24	—	11.33
11.56	12.26	—	—
PM 1.26	1.58	—	2. 5
2. 4e	2.37	—	2.45
2.35	3. 4	3. 8e	—
3.23	3.52	—	—
4.22	5. 2	—	5.14
5.37	6.10	—	6.18
6.22	6.58	—	7. 5
7.46	8.23	—	8.31
8.30	9. 2	—	9.15
9.26	10. 3	—	10.13
11.18	11.57	—	12.10

Sunday Trains.

AM 7.42	8.16	—	8.27
10.41	11.15	—	11.25
PM 3.56	4.33	—	4.42
5.50	6.25	—	6.34
6.39	7.13	—	7.25
8.25	9. 1	—	9. 9
9.56	10.25	—	10.32

d Saturdays only
e Saturdays excepted.
l Low Level Platform.

KENNET (Cambs) from
Liverpool Street, via Cambridge, 75½ miles. Fares, 15/8a, 9/5c. R. T. for two months, 31/4a. Pop. 182.
Map Square 19.

L'POOL ST.	KENNET		KENNET	L'POOL ST.
AM 5. 5	8. 2	AM	7.57r	10.23
5.50h	9.57		10.15	12.40
8.30r	11.43		11.43r	2.21
11.50r	2.27	PM	2.51r	5.17
PM 2.34	5.11		4.29	7.58
4.45	7.29		6. 6r	8.33
5.49r	8.15		7.40	10.30
7.10r	9.55		—	—

Sunday Trains.

AM 9.25	12.15	PM 3.52	6.40
PM 3.25	5.50	—	—

h Wednesdays only.
r Restaurant Car.

KENNETHMONT (Aberdeen), 555¾ miles. No through fares. Departures *from* London as for Inverurie. Departures *for* London about 3 times daily. Pop. 818.
Map Square 35.

KENNINGTON (City and South London Tube). *See* back of Map.

KENNISHEAD (Renfrew), 410 miles. Fares, 82/6*a*, 49/6*c*. R. T. for two months, 165/0*a*, 99/0*c*. Departures *from* London as for Kilmarnock. Departures *for* London about 5 times daily.

KENSAL GREEN from *Euston* or *Broad Street*, 4½ miles. Fares from *Euston*, 0/11½*a*, 0/7*c*. R.T. for two days, 1/9*a*, 1/2*c*. From *Broad Street*, 0/11½*a*, 0/7½*c*. R.T. for two days, 1/11*a*, 1/2*c*.

ANOTHER ROUTE (Bakerloo Tube). *See* back of Map.

KENSAL RISE (Middlesex) from *Broad Street*, 9¾ miles. Fares, 0/11½*a*, 0/7½*c*. R. T. for two days, 1/11*a*, 1/2*c*. Pop. 13,505. *See* pp. 501-505.
Map Square 59.

KENSINGTON (ADDISON ROAD) from *Earl's Court* in connection with trains from *Mansion House, Charing Cross, Victoria*, &c., 1 mile. Every 15 minutes during the day. Pop. 175,859, *See* pp. 502-505.
Map Square 68.

From *Clapham Junction*, 3¼ miles. Fares, 0/9½*a*, 0/5½*c*. R. T. for two days, 1/5*a*, 0/9*c*. *See* p. 583.

From *Broad Street*, 13¼ miles. Fares, 1/0½*a*, 0/7½*c*. R. T. for two days, 2/1*a*, 1/2*c*. *See* pp. 501-505.

From *Aldgate*, 8¼ miles. Trains run about every 12 minutes throughout the day. *See* back of Map.

KENSINGTON (HIGH STREET) to and from *Mansion House, Charing Cross, Victoria, South Kensington, Praed Street, Baker Street, King's Cross, Moorgate, Aldgate*, and all intermediate stations every few minutes. *See* back of Map
Map Square 68.

KENSINGTON (SOUTH), to and from *Mansion House, Charing Cross, Victoria, Kensington High Street, Praed Street, Baker Street, King's Cross, Moorgate, Aldgate*, and all intermediate stations every few minutes; also to and from Ealing, Hounslow, Richmond and Wimbledon. *See* p. 489.
Map Square 69.

ANOTHER ROUTE (Hammersmith and Finsbury Park Tube). *See* back of Map.

KENSINGTON WEST from *Mansion House*, 5½ miles. Also to and from Ealing, Hounslow and Richmond. *See* p. 489.
Map Square 68.

KENT HOUSE (Kent) from *Victoria, Holborn Viaduct*, and *St. Paul's*, 7¾ miles. Fares, 1/6*a*, 1/2*b*, 0/10½*c*. R. T. for two days, 3/0*a*, 2/4*b*, 1/9*c*. Pop. 6,483. *See* pp. 558-561.
Map Square 79.

KENTALLEN (Argyll), 520¼ miles. Fares, 104/5*a*, 62/8*c*. R. T. for two months, 208/10*a*, 125/4*c*. Departures *from* London as for Oban. Departures *for* London about 3 times daily.
Map Square 37.

KENTISH TOWN from *Broad Street*, 5½ miles. Fares, 0/7½*a*, 0/4½*c*. R T. for two days, 1/3*a*, 0/9*c*. *See* pp. 501-505.
Map Square 60, *No.* 2.

ANOTHER ROUTE from *St. Pancras*, 1½ miles. Fares, 0/4*a*, 0/2½*c*. R. T. for two days, 0/8*a*, 0/5*c*. And from *Moorgate Street*. Fares, 0/7½*a*, 0/4½*c*. R. T. for two days, 1/3*a*, 0/9*c*. *See* pp. 506-508.
Map Square 60.

ANOTHER ROUTE (Hampstead Tube). *See* back of Map.

KENTON (Middlesex) from *Euston*, 10½ miles. Fares, 1/9½*a*, 1/1*c*. R. T. for two days, 3/0½*a*, 1/9*c*. From *Broad Street*, 2/0*a*, 1/2½*c*. R. T. for two days, 3/5½*a*, 2/0½*c*. *See* pp. 496–499.

ANOTHER ROUTE (Bakerloo Tube). *See* back of Map.

KENTON (Northumberland), 274 miles. No through fares. Departures *from* London as for Newcastle-on-Tyne. Departures *for* London about 5 times daily. Pop. 462.
Map Square 3.

KENTON (Suffolk), 93 miles. Fares, 19/7*a*, 11/9*c*. R. T. for two months, 39/2*a*, 23/6*c*. Departures *from* London as for Stradbroke. Departures *for* London about twice daily. Pop. 209.
Map Square 19.

KENT'S BANK (Lancs), 247¼ miles. Fares, 51/6*a*, 30/11*c*. R. T. for two months, 103/0*a*, 61/10*c*. Departures *from* London as for Grange-over-Sands. Departures *for* London about 4 times daily.
Map Square 7.

KENYON (Lancs) from *Euston*, 191 miles. Fares, 39/7*a*, 23/9*c*. R. T., double fare. Pop. 327.
Map Square 12.

EUSTON	KENYON	KENYON	EUSTON
AM12.25	6.49	AM 7.15*er*	12. 5
2.35	7.55	7.15*dr*	12.20
5. 0	11.11	8.51*r*	1.45
6.45*d*	12.20	10.56*r*	4.15
6.45*e*	12.41	PM12.50*t*	5.50
8.30*dr*	1.40	2.34*r*	7.30
8.30*er*	1.55	4. 4*er*	9. 5
10.40*r*	3.34	4. 4*dr*	9.15
11.50*r*	5. 9	9.40	5. 0
PM 1.30*r*	5.57	—	—
2.35*t*	7. 6	—	—
5.20*r*	10.26	—	—
—	—	—	—
—	—	—	—

KENYON—*continued.*

Sunday Trains.

EUSTON	KENYON	KENYON	EUSTON
AM11.45	7.36	AM 8. 4*r*	1.30
—	—	10.17*r*	7.30
—	—	PM 6.57	5. 0
—	—	—	—
—	—	—	—
—	—	—	—
—	—	—	—

d Saturdays only.
e Saturdays excepted.
r Restaurant Car.
t Tea Car.

KERNE BRIDGE (Hereford) from *Paddington*, 136¼ miles. Fares, 28/4*a*, 17/0*c*. R. T. for two months, 56/8*a*.
Map Square 22.

PAD.	KERNE B.	KERNE B.	PAD.
AM 1. 0*g*	8.28	AM 7.48	12.20
5.30	11. 4	10. 6*r*	2.40
9. 0	1.56	PM12.59	5. 0
10.45	3.14	4. 6*r*	8.45
PM 3.15*t*	7.30	8.54	3.30
—	—	—	—
—	—	—	—

No Sunday Trains.

g Mondays excepted.
r Restaurant Car.
t Tea Car.

KERRY (Montgomery), 185¾ miles. Fare, 23/3*c*. Departures *from* London as for Montgomery. Departures *for* London about 5 times daily. Pop. 1,683.
Map Square 16.

KERSHOPE FOOT (Cumberland), 320¼ miles. No through fares. Departures *from* London as for Carlisle. Departures *for* London about 3 times daily.
Map Square 3.

KESWICK (Cumberland) from *Euston*, 298¾ miles. Fares, 60/3*a*, 36/2*c*. R. T. for two months, 120/6*a*, 72/4*c*. Pop. 5,559.
Map Square 6.

EUSTON	KESWICK	KESWICK	EUSTON
AM12.25	10.39	AM 7.40*gr*	4.15
5. 0	2. 2	8.15*fr*	3.45
11.35*r*	6.30	10.10*r*	6. 0
PM 1.30*r*	9. 1	11.50*r*	7.30
11.45*e*	8.14	PM 3.10*r*	10.45
—	—	6.31	5. 0
—	—	—	—
—	—	—	—
—	—	—	—
—	—	—	—

Sunday Trains.

PM11.45	8.14	—	—
—	—	—	—
—	—	—	—

e Saturdays excepted
f Mondays only.
g Mondays excepted.
r Restaurant Car.

Beautiful Buttermere. Victoria Family Hotel. Private and comfortable. *See* advt. p. **119**.

Keswick Hotel. Unrivalled position. Centre of English Lakes. Electric light and Lift. Golf. Garage.
A. B. WIVELL, Proprietor.

KETLEY (Salop) from Paddington, 142 miles. Fares, 29/9a, 17/10c. R. T. for two months, 59/6a, 35/8c. Pop. 2,204.
Map Square 17.

Pad.	Ketley	Ketley	Pad.
AM 9.10r	1.35	AM 6.45r	11. 0
10.40r	3. 5	7.43	12.25
PM12.50	4.35	9.20r	1.25
2.10t	5.30	PM12.37r	5. 0
4.10t	7.35	2.15t	5.55
12.15h	8.22	3.48r	8. 5
—	—	6.30	10. 0
—	—	—	—
—	—	—	—
—	—	—	—
—	—	—	—
—	—	—	—

No Sunday trains.

h Saturdays midnight excepted.
r Restaurant Car.
t Tea Car.

KETTERING (Northampton) from St. Pancras, 72 miles. Fares, 14/9a, 8/10c. R. T., double fare. Pop. 29,692.
Map Square 18.

St. Pan.	Ketter.	Ketter.	St. Pan.
AM 2.25	3.51	AM 2.58g	5. 5
4.25	6.28	6.38	8. 3
7.50	9.47	7.20	9.30
8.25r	9.57	8.29r	9.57
9.25	11.27	9.37r	11. 0
11. 0r	12.32	10.25	1. 3
11.35	2. 0	11.45r	1.20
PM12.30	2.35	PM 1.35	3.25
1. 0r	2.45	2.47r	4.10
2.45	4.37	3.22	5.20
3.30r	4.50	4. 8r	5.30
4.30r	6.12	5. 0	7. 3
5.35r	7. 8	6.42	8.22
6.25r	7.45	7.48r	9. 5
8.25	10.30	9. 0	11.45
12. 0	2. 0	—	—
—	—	—	—
—	—	—	—
—	—	—	—
—	—	—	—
—	—	—	—
—	—	—	—

Sunday Trains.

AM 8. 0	11.10	AM 2.58	5. 5
PM 1.15	3.50	6.38	8. 5
6.15r	8.30	10. 9	11.53
8.25	10.30	PM 4.30	6.27
11.55	2. 0	5.33	8.30
—	—	8. 5r	9.43
—	—	9. 3	11. 7
—	—	—	—
—	—	—	—
—	—	—	—

g Mondays excepted.
r Restaurant Car.

KETTLENESS (Yorks), 250¼ miles. No through fares. Departures *from* London as for Sandsend. Departures *for* London about 6 times daily.
Map Square 8.

KETTON (Rutland) from King's Cross, 91¾ miles. Fares, 17/3a, 10/4c. R. T., double fare. Pop. 992.
Map Square 18.

King's +	Ketton	Ketton	King's +
AM 5. 5	8.28	AM 8.45r	12.25
7.15r	9.47	10.33	1. 5
7.45	10.49	PM 2.23r	4.45
10.10r	12.41	4.54r	7.10
PM 1.50r	4.10	6.22r	9.25
3. 0	5.46	10.33	3.25
5.40r	8.53	—	—
—	—	—	—

Sunday Trains.

12. 0nr	5.21	AM10.57	3.45
—	—	—	—
—	—	—	—

n Noon.
r Restaurant Car.

ANOTHER ROUTE from St. Pancras, 97 miles. Fares as above.

St. Pan.	Ketton	Ketton	St. Pan.
AM 4.25	8.45	AM 8.28r	10.45
7.50	10.35	10.49r	1.20
10.25r	2.23	PM12.41r	4.10
PM12.25r	4.54	4.10r	7.55
3.30r	6.24	5.46	8.20
4.30r	7.35	8.53	4.20
6.25r	10.33	—	—
—	—	—	—

Sunday Trains.

PM 3.15	9.38	PM 5.21r	9.43
—	—	—	—
—	—	—	—

r Restaurant Car.

KEW BRIDGE (Middlesex) from Broad Street, 14¼ miles. Fares, 0/11½a, 0/7½c. R. T. for two days, 1/11a, 1/3c. See pp. 501-505.
Map Square 67.

From Waterloo, 9¼ miles. Fares, *via* Barnes, 0/11½a, 0/7c. R. T. for two days, 1/9a, 1/2c. See p. 586.

KEW GARDENS (Lancs), from Euston, 214 miles. Fares 44/5a, 26/8c. R. T. for two months, 88/10a, 53/4c. Departures *from* London as for Southport. Departures *for* London about 5 times daily.
Map Square 12.

KEW GARDENS (Surrey) from Broad Street, 15 miles. Fares, 1/2a, 0/9c. R. T. for two days, 2/4a, 1/6c. Pop. (Kew), 2,792. See pp. 501-505.
Map Square 67.

From Mansion House, 9¼ miles. See p. 489.

Kew Gardens Hotel, close to Royal Gardens and Kew Gardens Station. Spacious Dining and Private Rooms. Billiards. JOHN WARNER, Proprietor.

KEYHAM (Devon) from Paddington, 228 miles. Fares 46/8a, 28/0c. R. T. for two months, 93/4a. Pop. 11,172.
Map Square 26.

Pad.	Keyham	Keyham	Pad.
AM 5.30	1.16	AM 8. 8r	1.30
7.30	2.56	10.17r	4.35
11.10r	3.54	11.46r	4.45
PM12. 5r	6.52	PM 1.16r	6.50
2. 0r	7.39	3.12r	9. 0
3.30r	8.56	4. 1e	2.45
4.15r	11.15	10.37	7.10
10. 0e	6.55	11. 5d	7.10
10. 0d	7.35	—	—
12. 0k	7.56	—	—
12.30h	8.32	—	—

Sunday Trains.

AM10.30r	4. 1	AM 9.34r	4. 5
PM 2.40r	8.36	PM12.52	7. 5
10. 0	5.55	7. 9	3.15
—	—	10.36	7.10
—	—	—	—
—	—	—	—
—	—	—	—

d Saturdays only.
e Saturdays excepted.
h Saturdays midnight only.
k Saturdays midnight excepted.
r Restaurant Car.

KEYINGHAM (Yorks), 207¾ miles. No through fares Departures *from* London as for Hull (Paragon). Departures *for* London about 8 times daily. Pop. 547.
Map Square 13.

KEYNSHAM (Somerset) from Paddington, 113¾ miles. Fares, 23/7a, 14/2c. R. T. for two months, 47/2a. Pop. 3,720.
Map Square 22.

Pad.	Keynsh.	Keynsh.	Pad.
AM 5.30	8.36	AM 6.49r	10.15
7.30	10.24	8.44	11.30
9. 0	12.47	11.12r	2.40
11.15	1.34	PM12.58	4. 5
PM 1. 0	3.16	2.29	6. 2
1.10r	4.29	5.43r	8.45
4.15r	6.54	7.19	10.25
5. 0r	7.59	11. 0	2.45
6.30r	9.34	11.38	7.10
6.55	11. 2	—	—
12. 0k	6.30	—	—
12.30l	10.15	—	—

Sunday Trains.

AM 9.10	1.55	AM10.12	3.35
PM12.30r	5. 6	PM 1.17	6. 0
2. 0	8.20	3.37	7.55
10. 0	6.30	9.49	3.15
—	—	—	—
—	—	—	—
—	—	—	—

k Saturdays midnight excepted.
l Saturdays midnight only.
r Restaurant Car.

KIBWORTH (Leicester)

from *St. Pancras*, 89 miles. Fares, 18/2*a*, 10/11*c*. R. T., double fare. Pop. 1,807.
Map Square 18.

St. Pan.	Kibw'th.	Kibw'th.	St. Pan.
AM 4.25	7.55	AM 6.58*r*	9.57
8.25*r*	11.11	8.30*r*	11. 0
11. 0*r*	1.17	10.52*r*	1.20
11.35	2.55	PM12.51	3.25
PM 3.30*r*	5.42	1.28*r*	4.10
4.30*r*	7. 8	3.33	7. 3
6.25*r*	8.31	5.18	8.22
6.30	9.30	6.37*r*	9. 5
—	—	7.58*e*	11.45
—	—	9.29*e*	5. 5
—	—	11.14*d*	5. 5
—	—	—	—
—	—	—	—
—	—	—	—
—	—	—	—

Sunday Trains.

AM 8. 0	11.56	AM 8.40	11.53
PM 1.35	4.22	PM 4.45	8.30
6.15*r*	9.18	8.27	11. 7
—	—	—	—
—	—	—	—
—	—	—	—
—	—	—	—
—	—	—	—

d Saturdays only.
e Saturdays excepted.
r Restaurant Car.

KIDBROOKE (Kent)

from *Charing Cross, Cannon Street*, and *London Bridge*, 8¾ miles. Fares from Charing Cross, 1/6*a*, 1/2*b*, 0/10½*c*. R. T. for two days, 3/0*a*, 2/4*b*, 1/9*c*. Fares from Cannon Street, 1/3*a*, 1/0*b*, 0/9*c*. R.T. for two days, 2/6*a*, 2/0*b*. *See* pp. 555, 556.
Map Square 71.

KIDDERMINSTER

(Worcester) from *Paddington*, 129½ miles. Fares, 25/3*a*, 15/2*c*. R. T. for two months, 50/6*a*. Pop. 27,122.
Map Square 17.

Pad.	Kidder.	Kidder.	Pad.
AM 5.30	10.59	AM 6.10*hr*	10. 0
6.30*h*	11.49	7.45*h*	11. 0
8.50	12.17	8.10	11.15
9.10*hr*	12.21	9.24*h*	12.25
9.45	1.23	10.21*hr*	1.25
10.40*dh*	1.33	10.59*hr*	2. 5
10.40*eh*	1.41	11.17*r*	2.55
PM12.50*hr*	3.42	PM 1.19*r*	4.15
1.30*r*	4.25	1.25*hr*	5. 0
1.35*r*	5.18	2.22	5.50
2.10*ht*	5.40	3.47*ht*	6.40
4.10*t*	7.25	4.25*hr*	8. 5
4.45*t*	7.46	5.17*r*	9.15
6.10*hr*	9. 0	6.18*hr*	10. 0
*r*7.10*hq*	10.29	9.55*h*	3.30
7.10*hr*	10.34	—	—
7.30*hn*	12.22	—	—
12.15*hk*	6.47	—	—
12.15*hl*	8.47	—	—
—	—	—	—

Sunday Trains.

AM10.35*r*	3.23	AM 9.37	2.40
PM12.50*hr*	4. 2	11.33*h*	6.20
4.10	8.58	PM 4.10*hr*	9. 0
6. 0*r*	9.10	5. 0*r*	9.48
—	—	—	—
—	—	—	—

d Saturdays only.
e Saturdays excepted.
h Via Birmingham.
k Saturdays midnight excepted.
l Saturdays midnight only
n Wednesdays and Saturdays only.
q Thursdays and Saturdays only.
r Restaurant Car.
t Tea Car.

KIDLINGTON (Oxon)

from *Paddington*, 69 miles. Fares, 14/0*a*, 8/5*c*. R. T. for two months, 28/0*a*. Pop. 1,087.
Map Square 23.

Pad.	Kid'ingt'n	Kid'ingt'n	Pad.
AM 5.30	7.39	AM 8. 7	9.50
6.30	9.52	9.36	11.15
9.45	12. 7	11.40	1.50
PM12. 8	2.31	PM 1.17*r*	2.55
1.35*r*	3.50	3.48	5.50
3.18	5.42	6.38*r*	9.15
4.45*t*	6.39	8.33	10.45
7.30	9.22	—	—
—	—	—	—
—	—	—	—

Sunday Trains.

PM 4.10	6.11	PM 4.11	6.20
—	—	7.48*r*	9.48
—	—	—	—
—	—	—	—

r Restaurant Car.
t Tea Car.

KIDSGROVE (Staffs), 152½

miles. Fares, 32/1*a*, 19/3*c*. R. T. for two months, 64/2*a*, 38/6*c*. Departures *from* London as for Burslem. Departures *for* London about 8 times daily. Pop. 9,491.
Map Square 12.

KIDWELLY (Carmarthenshire)

from *Paddington*, 216¾ miles. Fares, 45/3*a*, 27/2*c*. R. T. for two months, 90/6*a*, 54/4*c*. Pop. 3,181.
Map Square 21.

Pad.	Kidwel.	Kidwel.	Pad.
AM 1. 0*g*	8.52	AM 7.30*r*	1. 0
8.45*r*	1.53	8.31*r*	2.30
11.50*r*	5.41	10.40*r*	4.20
PM 1.10*r*	6.55	PM12.21*r*	6.15
3.35*r*	9. 4	2.41*r*	8.35
5. 0*dr*	10.40	6.41	3.30
—	—	—	—
—	—	—	—
—	—	—	—

Sunday Trains.

PM12.30*r*	3.20	AM 8.16	3.35
9.15	8.52	PM 2. 5*r*	8.25
—	—	—	—
—	—	—	—
—	—	—	—

d Saturdays only.
g Mondays excepted.
r Restaurant Car.

KIELDER (Northumberland)

321 miles. No through fares. Departures *from* London as for Carlisle or Hexham. Departures *for* London about 3 times daily.
Map Square 3.

KILBAGIE (Clackmannan)

427½ miles. No through fares. Departures *from* London as for Stirling or Dunfermline. Departures *for* London about 4 times daily.
Map Square 40.

KILBARCHAN (Renfrew)

412¾ miles. Fares, 82/4*a*, 49/5*c*. R. T. for two months, 164/8*a*, 98/10*c*. Departures *from* London as for Kilmarnock. Departures *for* London about 3 times daily.
Map Square 40.

KILBIRNIE (Ayr), 405¼

miles. Fares, 82/4*a*, 49/5*c*. R. T for two months, 164/8*a*, 98/10*c*. *See* trains to Kilmarnock, and thence at frequent intervals. Pop. 8,032.
Map Square 40.

KILBOWIE (Dumbarton)

408 miles. Fares, 83/6*a*, 50/1*c*. R. T. for two months, 167/0*a*, 100/2*c*. Departures *from* London as for Dumbarton. Departures *for* London about 4 times daily.
Map Square 40.

KILBURN (Derby), 135

miles. Fares, 27/4*a*, 16/5*c*. R. T., double fare. Departures *from* London as for Ripley. Departures *for* London about 5 times daily. Pop. 1,672.
Map Square 12.

KILBURN (Middlesex)

from *Euston* or *Broad Street*, 3 miles. Fares from *Euston*, 0/7½*a*, 0/4½*c*. R. T. for two days, 1/3*a*, 0/9*c*. From *Broad Street* 0/10*a*, 0/6*c*. R. T. for two days, 1/5½*a*, 0/10½*c*. Pop. 15,699. *See* pp. 496-499.
Map Square 59.

KILBURN-BRONDESBURY

from *Baker Street*, 3¼ miles. Fares, 0/6*a*, 0/4*c*. R. T. for two days, 1/0*a*, 0/8*c*. *See* back of Map.
Map Square 59.

KILBURN PARK (Bakerloo Tube)

See back of Map.

KILCONQUHAR (Fife)

435½ miles. Fares, 88/2*a*, 52/11*c*. R. T. for two months 176/4*a*, 105/10*c*. Departures *from* London as for St. Andrews. Departures *for* London about 3 times daily. Pop. 1,319.
Map Square 41.

KILDALE (Yorks), 241¼

miles. Fares, 50/3*a*, 30/2*c*. R. T., double fare. Departures *from* London as for Stockton-on-Tees. Departures *for* London about 3 times daily. Pop. 220.
Map Square 8.

KILDARY (Ross), 604¼

miles. Fares, 107/4*a*, 64/5*c*. R.T. for two months, 214/8*a*. Departures *from* London as for Dingwall. Departures *for* London about 3 times daily.
Map Square 34.

KILDONAN (Sutherland)

678¼ miles. Fares, 122/9*a*, 73/8*c*. R. T. for two months, 245/6*a*. Departures *from* London as for Helmsdale. Departures *for* London about 3 times daily. Pop. 1,518.
Map Square 31.

KILDWICK (Yorks)

from *St. Pancras*, 217 miles. Fares, 41/6*a*, 24/11*c*. R. T., double fare. Departures *from* London as for Keighley. Departures *for* London about 6 times daily. Pop. 143.
Map Square 7.

KILGERRAN (Pembroke)

265¼ miles. Fares, 54/0*a*, 32/5*c*. R.T. for two months, 108/0*a*, 64/10*c*. Departures *from* London as for Cardigan. Departures *for* London about 4 times daily. Pop. 940.
Map Square 16.

KILGETTY (Pembroke)

252 miles. Fares, 51/3*a*, 30/9*c*. R. T. for two months, 102/6*a*. Departures *from* London as for Tenby. Departures *for* London about 5 times daily.
Map Square 20.

KILKERRAN (Ayr), 402¼ miles. Fares, 82/8*a*, 49/7*c*. R. T. for two months, 165/4*a*, 99/2*c*. Departures *from* London as for Girvan. Departures *for* London about 4 times daily.
Map Square 43.

KILLAMARSH (Derby), from *Marylebone*, 154½ miles. Fares, 31/8*a*, 19/0*c*. R. T., double fare. Departures *from* London as for Chesterfield (Central). Departures *for* London about 6 times daily. Pop. 4,544.
Map Square 13.

KILLAY (Glamorgan), 203½ miles. Fares, 41/5*a*, 24/10*c*. R. T. for two months, 82/10*a*, 49/8*c*. Departures *from* London as for Swansea (High Street). Departures *for* London about 4 times daily.
Map Square 21.

KILLEARN (Stirling), 448¼ miles. Fares, 85/0*a*, 51/0*c*. R. T. for two months, 170/0*a*, 102/0*c*. Departures *from* London as for Glasgow. Departures *for* London about twice daily. Pop. 1,054.
Map Square 40.

KILLIECRANKIE (Perth), 482 miles. Fares, 97/9*a*, 58/8*c*. R. T. for two months, 195/6*a*, 117/4*c*. Departures *from* London as for Pitlochry. Departures *for* London about 3 times daily.
Map Square 37.

KILLIN (Perth), 456½ miles. Fares, 92/8*a*, 55/7*c*. R. T. for two months, 185/4*a*, 111/2*c*. Departures *from* London as for Callander. Departures *for* London about 3 times daily. Pop. 1 502.
Map Square 37.

KILLIN JUNCTION (Perth), 452½ miles. No through fares. Departures *from* London as for Callander. Departures *for* London about 4 times daily.
Map Square 37.

KILLINGHOLME (Lincs) from *Marylebone*, 220 miles. Fares, 35/3*a*, 21/2*c*. R. T. for two months, 70/6*a*, 42/4*c*. Departures *from* London as for Brocklesby. Departures *for* London about 4 times daily. Pop. 1,232.
Map Square 13.

KILLINGWORTH (Northumberland), 276½ miles. Fares, 57/9*a*, 34/8*c*. R. T., double fare. Departures *from* London as for Newcastle-on-Tyne. Departures *for* London about 4 times daily. Pop. 10,601.
Map Square 3.

KILLOCHAN (Ayr), 407½ miles. Fares, 83/9*a*, 50/3*c*. R. T. for two months, 167/6*a*, 100/6*c*. Departures *from* London as for Girvan. Departures *for* London about 4 times daily.
Map Square 43.

KILLYWHAN (Kirkcudbright), 340½ miles. Fares, 68/9*a*, 41/3*c*. R.T. for two months, 137/6*a*, 82/6*c*. Departures *from* London as for Dumfries. Departures *for* London about 5 times daily.
Map Square 43.

KILMACOLM (Renfrew), 419¾ miles. Fares, 83/11*a*, 50/4*c*. R.T. for two months, 167/10*a*, 100/8*c*. Departures *from* London as for Greenock (Princes Pier). Departures *for* London about 4 times daily. Pop. 5,303.
Map Square 40.

KILMANY (Fife), 447½ miles. Fares, 91/3*a*, 54/9*c*. R. T. for two months, 182/6*a*, 109/6*c*. Departures *from* London as for Leuchars. Departures *for* London about twice daily. Pop. 514.
Map Square 38.

KILMARNOCK (Ayrshire) from *St. Pancras*. 399 miles. Fares, 79/5*a*, 47/8*c*. R. T. for two months, 158/10*a*, 95/4*c*. Pop. 34,625.
Map Square 40.

St. Pan.	K'mnk.	K'mnk.	St. Pan.
AM 4.25	3. 2	AM 9.57*r*	6.35
9.50*r*	6.28	PM 12.38*r*	9.15
PM 12.15*r*	8.47	9.52*e*	7.25
9.30*e*	6.50	11.22*e*	7.50
11.45*e*	8.17	11.47*d*	8.57
11.45*d*	8.22	—	—
—	—	—	—
—	—	—	—
—	—	—	—

Sunday Trains.

PM 9.30	6.50	PM 9.55	7.25
11.45	8.19	11.22	7.50
—	—	—	—
—	—	—	—

d Saturdays only.
e Saturdays excepted.
r Restaurant Car.

ANOTHER ROUTE from *Euston* 390¼ miles. Fares as above.

Euston	K'mnk.	K'mnk.	Euston
AM 12.25	1.32	AM 5.55*r*	6. 0
2.35	3. 2	9.57*r*	6.25
5. 0	4.40	PM 12.38*r*	10. 0
11.35*r*	8.47	6.10	5. 0*h*
PM 8. 0*e*	5.42	9. 0*d*	7.15
9.20*e*	6.50	9.52*e*	6.55
11. 0*d*	8.20	9.57*e*	6.55
11.35*e*	8.19	11.22*e*	8. 0
11.45*e*	10.18	—	—
—	—	—	—

Sunday Trains.

PM 8.30	5.42	PM 9.55	7.30
11.35	8.19	—	—
11.45	10.18	—	—
—	—	—	—
—	—	—	—

d Saturdays only.
e Saturdays excepted.
h A.M.
r Restaurant Car.

KILMAURS (Ayr), 392½ miles. Fares, 79/10*a*, 47/11*c*. R. T. for two months, 159/8*a*, 95/10*c*. Departures *from* London as for Kilmarnock. Departures *for* London about 4 times daily. Pop. 4,568.
Map Square 40.

KILNHURST (Yorks), from *St. Pancras*, 166 miles. Fares, 33/6*a*, 20/1*c*. R. T., double fare. Departures *from* London as for Rotherham (Masboro'). Departures *for* London about 4 times daily. Pop. 3,564.
Map Square 13.

KILPATRICK (Dumbarton), 446 miles. Fares 83/11*a*, 50/4*c*. R. T. for two months, 167/10*a*, 100/8*c*. Departures *from* London as for Dumbarton. Departures *for* London about 3 times daily. Pop. (Old Kilpatrick) 55,659.
Map Square 40.

KILSBY (Northampton), 81 miles. Fares, 16/6*a*, 9/11*c*. R. T. for two months, 33/0*a*. Departures *from* London as for Northampton (Castle). Departures *for* London about 5 times daily. Pop. 530.
Map Square 18.

KILSYTH (Stirling), 417 miles. Fares, 85/0*a*, 51/0*c*. R. T. for two months, 170/0*a*, 102/0*c*. Departures *from* London as for Larbert. Departures *for* London about 4 times daily. Pop. 10,364.
Map Square 40.

KILWINNING (Ayr), 401¼ miles. Fares, 81/10*a*, 49/1*c*. R. T. for two months, 163/8*a*, 98/2*c*. Departures *from* London as for Irvine. Departures *for* London about 4 times daily. Pop. 8,763.
Map Square 40.

KIMBERLEY (Norfolk) from *Liverpool Street*, 114¾ miles. Fares, 23/7*a*, 14/2*c*. R. T. for two months, 47/2*a*. Departures *from* London as for Dereham. Departures *for* London about 5 times daily. Pop. 155.
Map Square 19.

KIMBERLEY (Notts) from *King's Cross*, 134¼ miles. Fares, 26/0*a*, 15/7*c*. R. T., double fare. Pop. 5,174.

King's +	Kimb.	Kimb.	King's +
AM 4.45	9. 6	AM 7.25	10.40
5. 5	10.18	8.14*r*	11.30
7.15*r*	10.45	9. 5	1. 5
8.45	1. 0	10.10*r*	1.30
10.10*r*	1.35	11.21	3.50
11.30	3.51	PM 1.56	6.25
PM 1.50*r*	5.32	4.28*r*	9. 0
4. 0*r*	7.55	5.32*r*	9.25
5.35*r*	8.48	9.56*e*	3.25
5.45*er*	10.10	10.16*d*	3.25
5.45*dr*	10.45	—	—
11.25*e*	6.25	—	—
—	—	—	—
—	—	—	—
—	—	—	—
—	—	—	—

Sunday Trains.

AM 11.30*r*	3.10	AM 11.52	3.45
12. 0*nr*	4.22	PM 2. 2	5.55
PM 5. 0	9.25	—	—
11.25	6.25	—	—
—	—	—	—
—	—	—	—
—	—	—	—
—	—	—	—

d Saturdays only.
e Saturdays excepted.
n Noon.
r Restaurant Car.

KIMBOLTON (Hunts) from *St. Pancras*, 86¾ miles. Fares, 14/9*a*, 8/10*c*. R. T., double fare. Pop. 913.
Map Square 18.

St. Pan.	Kimbton.	Kimbton.	St. Pan.
AM 4.25	9.15	AM 8.32*r*	11. 0
8.25*r*	11.15	PM12.44	3.25
11.35	3. 0	3.51	7. 3
PM 6.25*r*	8.42	5.58	8.22
—	—	—	—
—	—	—	—
—	—	—	—
—	—	—	—

No Sunday Trains.

r Restaurant Car.

KINALDIE (Aberdeen), 533¼ miles. No through fares. Departures *from* London as for Aberdeen. Departures *for* London about 3 times daily.
Map Square 35.

KINBRACE (Sutherland), 685¾ miles. Fares, 124/4*a*, 74/7*c*. R. T. for two months. 248/8*a*, Departures *from* London as for Helmsdale. Departures *for* London about 3 times daily.
Map Square 31.

KINBUCK (Perth), 424½ miles. Fares, 86/8*a*, 52/0*c*. R. T. for two months, 173/4*a*, 104/0*c*. Departures *from* London as for Dunblane. Departures *for* London about 4 times daily.
Map Square 40.

KINCARDINE (Fife), 420¼ miles. No through fares. Departures *from* London as for Dunfermline or Stirling. Departures *for* London about 3 times daily.
Map Square 40.

KINCRAIG (Inverness), 527¼ miles. Fares, 106/3*a*, 63/9*c*. R. T. for two months, 212/6*a*, 127/6*c*. Departures *from* London as for Blair Atholl. Departures *for* London about 3 times daily.
Map Square 37.

KINETON (Warwick) from *Marylebone*, 84 miles. Fares 19/2*a*, 11/6*c*. R.T. for two months 38/4*a*, 23/0*c*. Pop. 1,018.
Map Square 17.

M'bone	Kineton	Kineton	M'bone
AM 6.45	10. 4	AM 8.20	10.36
PM12.15*r*	2.45	PM12.42*r*	3. 0
6.20	8.18	6.32*r*	8.55
—	—	—	—
—	—	—	—
—	—	—	—
—	—	—	—

No Sunday Trains.

r Restaurant Car.

KINFAUNS (Perth), 443¼ miles. Fares, 91/8*a*, 55/0*c*. R. T. for two months, 183/4*a*, 110/0*c*. Departures *from* London as for Perth. Departures *for* London about 3 times daily. Pop. 528.
Map Square 38.

KING EDWARD (Aberdeen), 568 miles. Fares, 106/3*a*, 63/9*c*. R. T. for two months, 212/6*a*, 127/6*c*. Departures *from* London as for Inverurie. Departures *for* London about 3 times daily. Pop. 2,125.
Map Square 35.

KINGENNIE (Forfar), 458½ miles. No through fares. Departures *from* London as for Forfar or Dundee (Tay Bridge). Departures *for* London about 3 times daily.

KINGHAM (Oxon) from *Paddington*, 84½ miles. Fares, 17/8*a*, 10/7*c*. R. T. for two months 35/4*a*. Pop. 876.
Map Square 22.

Pad.	Kinghm.	Kinghm.	Pad.
AM 5.30	8.35	AM 7.41	9.50
9.10*h*	11.39	7.50*v*	11.15
9.45	11.46	10. 6	12. 5
11.20*k*	2.34	11.54	2.12
PM 1.30	3. 2	PM 1.12*r*	2.55
1.35*r*	3.31	3.59	5.50
2.10*h*	4.59	4.40	7.20
4.45*t*	6.52	7. 6*r*	9.15
6. 5*r*	7.55	8.19	10.45
6.10*h*	8.44	9.30*h*	3.30
6.55	9.23	—	—
12.15*hl*	7.28	—	—

Sunday Trains.

AM10.35	12.50	AM11.59	2.40
PM 4.10	6.39	PM 7.23*r*	9.48
—	—	—	—
—	—	—	—
—	—	—	—
—	—	—	—

h Via Banbury.
k Thursdays and Saturdays only.
l Saturdays midnight excepted.
r Restaurant Car.
t Tea Car.
v Via King's Sutton.

KINGHORN (Fife), 415 miles. Fares, 83/7*a*, 50/2*c*. R. T. for two months, 167/2*a*, 100/4*c*. Departures *from* London as for Inverkeithing. Departures *for* London about 3 times daily. Pop. 3,212.
Map Square 41.

KINGSBARNS (Fife), 448¾ miles. No through fares. Departures *from* London as for St. Andrews. Departures *for* London about 3 times daily. Pop. 640.
Map Square 41.

KINGSBRIDGE (Devon) from *Paddington*, 222 miles. Fares, 45/8*a*, 27/5*c*. R. T. for two months, 91/4*a*, 54/10*c*. Pop. 2,945.
Map Square 26.

Pad.	Kingsb.	Kingsb.	Pad.
AM 5.30	1. 0	AM 7.25*r*	1.30
11. 0*dr*	3.46	11.25*r*	4.35
11.10*r*	4.40	PM 2.35*r*	9. 0
PM12. 5*r*	6.45	7. 5	7.10
3.30*r*	8.55	9.30*k*	7.10
12. 0*h*	9. 5	—	—
—	—	—	—
—	—	—	—
—	—	—	—

Sunday Trains.

PM10. 0	9. 5	—	—
—	—	—	—
—	—	—	—

d Saturdays only.
h Saturdays midnight excepted.
k Fridays only.
r Restaurant Car.

King's Arms Hotel. (First-class.) Officially appointed Royal Automobile Club. Horses and carriages of every description. Boots meets all trains. Telegrams: "Startup, Kingsbridge." Telephone No. 24.
G. E. STARTUP, Proprietor.

KINGSBRIDGE—*contd.*

Torcross Hotel, Kingsbridge, Devon. Fresh-water fishing: Pike, Perch, Rudd. Sea fishing. Tennis. Bathing, unique position on Sea Front. Garage.

Albion Hotel, Kingsbridge. Near Salcombe, S. Devon. First-class Family and Commercial. Excellent Cuisine. Radiated. Personal appointment A.A. and R.A.C. Charges moderate. Hard Courts. Fishing, Salmon and Trout. Rough Shooting in the neighbourhood. 18 hole Golf Course within reach. 'Phone 27. Telegrams: Albion, Kingsbridge.

Thurlestone Hotel, Thurlestone. The old-established, first class, residential hotel. Golf, Tennis, Fishing, Bathing, Billiards. Well sheltered gardens. Trains met by appointment. Garage. Telegrams: Thurlotel. Telephone 16 Kingsbridge.
PROPRIETRESS.

Links Hotel, Thurlestone, South Devon. High-class residential Hotel. Only Hotel on Sea Front. Adjoins Golf Course, 18 holes. Tennis. Croquet. Perfectly safe bathing. Luxurious Lounge and Public Rooms, Separate Tables. Central Heating. Electric Light. Garage. Phone 4. J. BOYD, Residential Proprietor.

KINGSBURY (Warwick), 124 miles. Fares, 22/8*a*, 13/7*c*. R. T., double fare. Departures *from* London as for Water Orton. Departures *for* London about 4 times daily. Pop. 3,331.
Map Square 17.

KINGSCLIFFE (Northampton), 87¼ miles. Fares, 17/4*a*, 10/5*c*. R. T. for two months, 34/8*a*. Departures *from* London as for Peterboro. Departures *for* London about 3 times daily. Pop. 1,086.
Map Square 18.

KINGSCOTE (Sussex) from *London Bridge, Victoria*, and *Clapham Junction*, 32½ miles. Fares, 6/8*a*, 4/0*c*. R. T. for two months, 13/4*a*, 8/0*c*. Departures *from* London as for West Hoathly. Departures *for* London about 7 times daily.
Map Square 23.

KING'S CROSS to and from *Aldgate, Moorgate, Mansion House, Charing Cross, Victoria, South Kensington, High Street, Praed Street, Hammersmith, Baker Street*, and intermediate Stations every few minutes. Also to and from *Uxbridge Road, Kensington (Addison Road)*, about every 10 minutes throughout the day. Pop. (St. Pancras) 211,366. *See* back of Map.
Map Squares 23 *and* 60.

ANOTHER ROUTE (City and South London and Hammersmith and Finsbury Park Tubes). *See* back of Map.

For Messengers & Theatre Tickets apply District Messenger Office, St. Pancras Station, N.

KING'S HEATH (Worcester). 117½ miles. Fares, 23/7*a*, 14/2*c*. R. T. for two months, 47/2*a*, 28/4*c*. Departures *from* London as for Birmingham (New Street). Departures *for* London about 6 times daily. Pop. 24,885.
Map Square 17.

KINGSKERSWELL

(Devon), 196½ miles. Fares, 40/3*a*, 24/2*c*. R. T. for two months, 80/6*a*. Departures *from* London as for Newton Abbot. Departures *for* London about 8 times daily. Pop. 989.
Map Square 26.

KINGSKETTLE (Fife),

430½ miles. No through fares. Departures *from* London as for Kirkcaldy. Departures *for* London about 5 times daily. Pop. (Kettle) 1,595.
Map Square 41.

KINGSKNOWE (Mid-

lothian), 396½ miles. No through fares. Departures *from* London as for Carstairs. Departures *for* London about 4 times daily.

KINGSLAND (Hereford),

144½ miles. Fares, 31/0*a*, 18/7*c*. R. T. for two months, 62/0*a*. Departures *from* London as for Titley. Departures *for* London about 5 times daily. Pop. 944.
Map Square 17.

KING'S LANGLEY

(Herts) from *Euston* and *Broad Street*, 21 miles. Fares from Euston, 4/0*a*, 2/5*c*. R. T. for two months, 8/0*a*, 4/10*c*. Fares from Broad Street, 4/4*a*, 2/7*c*. R. T. for two months, 8/8*a*, 5/1½*c*. Pop. 2,504.
Map Square 23.

Leave		Arrive at
EUSTON	BROAD ST.	KING'S L.
AM 5.25	—	6.29
7.15	6.45	7.58
7.35	7.10	8.21
8.35	8.15	9.22
9.40	9. 6	10.25
10.50	10.17	11.33
PM12.15	11.47	12.54
12.50*d*	12.20*d*	1.25
1. 3*d*	12.43*d*	1.46
1.10*d*	1.15*d*	2. 7
1.35*d*	1.18*d*	2.19
2. 0	1.36*e*	2.42
—	1.35*d*	2.42
2.40*d*	2. 6*d*	3.23
4. 2	—	4.30
4.10	3.47	4.54
4.55*d*	—	5.28
5. 0*e*	—	5.36
—	4.50*e*	5.38
5.20*d*	4.47*d*	6. 5
5.25*e*	—	5.57
—	5.24*e*	6.12
5.45*e*	5.23*e*	6.28
6.10*d*	—	6.43
6.15*e*	—	6.48
—	6. 0*e*	6.47
6.35	6.15*e*	7. 9
—	6.40*e*	7.29
—	6.38*d*	7.57
7.15	6.52*e*	7.57
8. 5	7.36	8.44
9. 5	8.17	9.45
9.55*e*	9.17*e*	10.38
9.55*d*	9.17*d*	10.41
11.40	10.47	12.13
—	—	—

Sunday Trains.

AM 8.15	—	9. 5
9.23	8.55	10.22
10.23	9.55	11.37
PM12.55	12.25	2. 7
2.15	1.25	2.52
2.53	2.25	3.50
4.53	4.25	5.52
6.10	5.25	6.52
6.53	6.25	7.50
7.53	7.25	9. 8
9.40	9.10	10.20

KING'S LANGLEY — *continued.*

Trains from King's Langley.

Leave	Arrive at	
KING'S L.	BROAD ST.	EUSTON
AM 6. 7	7.15	7.18
7.38	8.40	8.24
8. 1	—	8.38
8.11	9. 0	8.58
8.24	9.28	9. 5
8.54*e*	9.22	—
8.43*e*	9.40	9.22
9. 4	9.58	9.40
9. 5	9.54	9.52
9.49	10.50	10.30
10.56	12. 8	11.40
PM 1. 3	2. 8	1.50
2.19	3.38	3. 5
3.40	4.45	4.30
4.28*d*	5.38	5.21
5.28	6.36	6.15
6.21	7.38	7. 5
7. 3	8.15	7.55
7.54	9. 8	8.35
9.13	10.37	10.10
10. 1	11. 5	10.50
10.49	—	11.35
—	—	—

Sunday Trains.

AM 8.34	10. 5	9.22
11.14	12.35	12.15
PM12.31	2. 5	1.20
1.46	3. 5	2.44
3. 1	4.20	4.14
5.31	7. 5	6.44
6.46	8. 5	7.44
7.34	8.50	8.15
8.46	10. 5	—
9. 3	10.20	9.45
9.31	10.47	—
9.58	11. 2	10.40

d Saturdays only.
e Saturdays excepted.

KINGSLEY (Stafford), 148

miles. Fares, 30/8*a*, 18/5*c*. R. T. for two months, 61/4*a*, 36/10*c*. Departures *from* London as for Uttoxeter. Departures *for* London about 4 times daily. Pop. 1,905.
Map Square 12.

KING'S LYNN (Norfolk)

from *Liverpool Street*, 97 miles. Fares, 20/2*a*, 12/1*c*. R. T. for two months, 40/4*a*. Pop. 19,968.
Map Square 19.

L'POOLST.	K. LYNN	K. LYNN	L'POOLST.
AM 5.50	9.34	AM 7.41*r*	10.23
	8.30*r*	11.16	8.34	11.27
10. 5	1.22	8.45	12.40
	11.20*kl r*	1.33	10.25	2. 7
	11.50*r*	2.39	11.42*r*	2.21
PM 2.34	5.10	11.50	5. 9
4.45	7.15	PM 1. 41*l r*	4. 2*k*
	5.49*r*	8.40	3.12*r*	6.10
10.12	1.55	3.40*h*	7.58
—	—	5.30*r*	8.22
—	—	7.45	10.30
—	—	10.25	2.50

Sunday Trains.

AM 9.25	12.52	PM 3.25	6.40
PM 3.25	6.28	7. 2	9.40
—	—	—	—

h Tuesdays only.
k Departs from or arrives at St. Pancras Station.
l Commencing July 23.
r Restaurant Car.

KING'S LYNN—*contd.*

ANOTHER ROUTE from

King's Cross, 115 miles, via Peterborough. Fares as above.

KING'S +	K.LYNN	K.LYNN	KING'S +
AM 4.45	8. 9	AM 6.55	10.40
5. 5*e*	9.55	8.23	12.25
5. 5*d*	10.18	9.55	1. 5
7.15*r*	11.10	11.55	3.50
8.45	12.52	PM 1.28*r*	4.30
10.10*r*	2.29	2.10	6.25
PM 1.50*r*	4.55	4.50	9. 0
3. 0	6. 5	5.48*r*	9.25
5.45*r*	8.54	—	—
—	—	—	—
—	—	—	—
—	—	—	—
—	—	—	—
—	—	—	—
—	—	—	—

No Sunday Trains.

d Saturdays only.
e Saturdays excepted.
r Restaurant Car.

Duke's Head Hotel. Telephone 190. Famous old house facing the Market Square. Good Public Rooms. Convenient to Station. Central Heating. Electric Light. Billiards. Garage.
TRUST HOUSES, Ltd.

Globe Hotel. By Royal Appointment. Family and Commercial. Fully Licensed. Reading, Smoking and Billiard Rooms. Bowling Green. Garage. Telephone 179.

KINGSMUIR (Forfar), 485¼

miles. No through fares. Departures *from* London as for Forfar. Departures *for* London about 3 times daily.
Map Square 38.

KING'S NORTON

(Worcester), 118¼ miles. Fares, 23/7*a*, 14/2*c*. R.T. for two months, 47/2*a*, 28/4*c*. Departures *from* London as for Birmingham (New Street). Departures *for* London about 8 times daily. Pop. 81,153.

KING'S-SUTTON

(Northampton) from *Paddington*, 64 miles. Fares, *via* Bicester, 13/4*a*, 8/0*c*. R.T. for two months, 26/8*a*, 16/0*c*. *Via* Reading, 14/0*a*, 8/5*c*. R.T. for two months, 28/0*a*, 16/10*c*. Departures *from* London as for Aynho or Bicester. Departures *for* London about 8 times daily. Pop. 1,181.
Map Square 18.

KINGSTON (Surrey)

from *Waterloo*, 12½ miles. Fares, 1/11*a*, 1/2*c*. R.T. for two days, 3/10*a*, 2/4*c*. Pop. 39,479. *See* pp. 584-585.
Map Squares 23 *and* 7.

Salter's Steamers. (Sun Hotel. 10 minutes from Station.) 9 a.m. to Henley and 2.30 p.m. to Windsor. *See* advt. facing first page of train service.

KINGSTON—*continued.*

Bond's Sun Hotel and Restaurant. Private Sitting and Bed rooms. Coffee, Reading and Billiard rooms. The only Hotel in Kingston with Gardens extending to the River. Telephone 2449.
GEORGE C. SILCOCK, Propr.

Kingston Hotel. Opposite Station. Bed, Smoking and Coffee rooms. Luncheons, Dinners, etc. Very moderate terms. Telephone 744. Proprietor—
WILLIAM SMURTHWAITE.

KINGSTON ROAD

(Somerset), 137 miles. No through fares. Departures *from* London as for Clevedon. Departures *for* London about 3 times daily.
Map Square 22.

KINGSTOWN from

Euston, 330½ miles. Fares, 63/9 First and Saloon, 45/3 Third and Saloon, 38/3 Third and Steerage. R. T. for two months, 126/0 First and Saloon, 88/3 Third and Saloon 75/6 Third and Steerage. Departures *from* London as for Holyhead. Departures *for* London about twice daily.
Map Square 10.

Bank—The National Bank, Ltd.

KINGSWEAR (Devon) from

Paddington, 208½ miles. Fares, 42/11*a*, 25/9*c*. R.T. for two months, 85/10*a*. Pop. 819.
Map Square 26.

Pad.	Kingsw.	Kingsw.	Pad.
AM 5.30	12.16	AM 8.25*r*	1.30
9.15*r*	2.42	11.30*r*	3.45
12. 0*r*	4.13	PM 1.52*er*	6.50
PM 12. 5*r*	5.17	2.20*dr*	7. 5
2. 0*r*	7.15	3.50*r*	9. 0
3.30*r*	8.17	4.50	2.45
4.15*r*	9.42	10.35	7.10
12. 0*l*	7.44	—	—
12.30*h*	9.21	—	—
—	—	—	—
—	—	—	—
—	—	—	—

Sunday Trains.

AM 10.30*r*	4.53	AM 9.50*r*	4. 5
PM 2.40	8. 0	PM 1. 0	7. 5
10. 0	7.44	8.20	3.15
—	—	—	—
—	—	—	—
—	—	—	—
—	—	—	—
—	—	—	—

d Saturdays only.
e Saturdays excepted.
h Saturdays midnight only.
l Saturdays midnight excepted.
r Restaurant Car.

KINGSWOOD (Surrey)

from *Charing Cross, Cannon Street,* and *London Bridge,* 21¾ miles. Fares, 2/11*a*, 2/4*b*, 1/9*c*. R. T. for eight days, 5/10*a*, 4/8*b*, 3/6*c*. Pop. 1,140.
Map Square 23.

Leave Char.+	Can. St.	Lon. B.	Arr. at K'wood
AM —	4.44	5. 0	5.54
—	—	7.50*l*	8.43
—	—	9.13*l*	10. 1
—	10.12	10.15	11. 5
10.55	—	11. 5	11.58

KINGSWOOD—*contd.*

Leave Char.+	Can. St.	Lon. B.	Arr. at K'wood
AM —	11.40*d*	11.43*d*	12.29
11.48*e*	—	11.54*e*	12.44
PM —	—	12.45*el*	1.31
12.44*d*	—	12.51*d*	1.35
12.55*d*	—	1. 4*d*	1.55
—	1.20*d*	1.23*d*	2.11
—	—	1.50*dl*	2.31
2.46*d*	—	2.52*d*	3.35
3.15	—	3.21	4.16
—	—	4.20*dl*	5. 7
—	4.44*e*	4.48*e*	5.37
—	—	4.50*dl*	5.37
5. 6*e*	—	5.14*e*	6. 4
—	—	5.33*el*	6.15
5.30*d*	—	5.36*d*	6.23
—	—	5.48*el*	6.34
—	6.20*e*	6.23*e*	7. 8
6.17*d*	—	6.23*d*	7. 9
6.46*e*	—	6.53*e*	7.38
7.24*d*	7.28*e*	7.30	8.22
8.28	—	8.36	9.28
9.25	—	9.31	10.15
10.17	—	10.23	11.13
11.42	—	—	12.29
—	—	—	—
—	—	—	—

Sunday Trains.

AM 9. 8	—	9.14	9.54
10.20	—	10.28	11.27
PM 1.30	—	1.37	2.29
6.50	—	6.56	7.39
7.45	—	7.52	8.39
9.40	—	9.47	10.39
—	—	—	—
—	—	—	—

Trains from Kingswood.

Leave K'gswood	Arrive at Lon. B.	Can. St.	Char.+
AM 7.10	7.58	—	8. 7
7.53	8.40	8.44	—
8.16	9. 5	9. 9	—
8.37	9.22	—	9.30
8.58	9.45	—	—
9.31	10.19	10.22	—
10.43	11.24	—	11.33
11.39	12.26	—	—
PM 1. 9	1.58	—	2. 5
2.16	3. 4	3. 8*e*	—
3. 6	3.52	—	—
4. 6	5. 2	—	5.14
5.19	6.10	—	6.18
6.15	6.58	—	7. 5
7.39	8.23	—	8.31
8.14	9. 2	—	9.15
9.20	10. 3	—	10.13
11.13	11.57	—	12.10
—	—	—	—
—	—	—	—
—	—	—	—
—	—	—	—

Sunday Trains.

AM 10.24	11.15	—	11.25
PM 3.39	4.33	—	4.42
5.43	6.25	—	6.34
8.19	9. 1	—	9. 9
9.22	10.11	—	10.24
—	—	—	—
—	—	—	—
—	—	—	—
—	—	—	—

d Saturdays only.
e Saturdays excepted.
l Low Level platform.

KING'S WORTHY

(Hants), from *Paddington* 77¼ miles. Fares, 13/7*a*, 8/2*c*. R.T. for two months, 27/2*a*, 16/4*c*. Departures *from* London as for Whitchurch (Hants). Departures *for* London about 5 times daily. Pop. 464.
Map Square 23.

KINGTHORPE (Lincoln)

from *King's Cross,* 133 miles. Fares, 27/6*a*, 16/6*c*. R. T., double fare. Departures *from* London as for Wragby. Departures *for* London about 3 times daily.
Map Square 13.

KINGTON (Hereford),

161½ miles. Fares, 32/11*a*, 19/9*c*. R. T. for two months, 65/10*a*, 39/6*c*. Departures *from* London as for Titley. Departures *for* London about 5 times daily. Pop. 1,688.
Map Square 17.

KINGUSSIE (Inverness),

521½ miles. Fares, 106/0*a*, 63/7*c*. R. T. for two months, 212/0*a*, 127/2*c*. Departures *from* London as for Blair Atholl. Departures *for* London about 3 times daily. Pop. 2,718.
Map Square 37.

KINLOSS (Elgin), 572¼

miles. Fares, 106/3*a*, 63/9*c*. R.T. for two months, 212/6*a*, 127/6*c*. Departures *from* London as for Elgin. Departures *for* London about 3 times daily. Pop. 924.
Map Square 34.

KINNEIL (Linlithgow), 416

miles. No through fares. Departures *from* London as for Edinburgh (Waverley). Departures *for* London about 4 times daily.

KINNERLEY (Salop), 166¾

miles. No through fares. Departures *from* London as for Oswestry. Departures *for* London about 3 times daily.
Map Square 17.

KINNERSLEY (Hereford),

158¾ miles. Fares, 32/4*a*, 19/5*c*. R. T. for two months, 64/8*a*, 38/10*c*. Departures *from* London as for Hay. Departures *for* London about 4 times daily. Pop. 242.
Map Square 17.

KINNERTON (Flint), 185½

miles. Fares, 38/7*a*, 23/2*c*. R. T. for two months, 77/2*a*, 46/4*c*. Departures *from* London as for Chester. Departures *for* London about 5 times daily. Pop. 310.
Map Square 12.

KINROSS, 422¾ miles.

Fares, 87/9*a*, 52/8*c*. R. T. for two months, 175/6*a*, 105/4*c*. Departures *from* London as for Dunfermline. Departures *for* London about 3 times daily. Pop. 3,137.
Map Square 41.

KINTBURY (Berks) from *Paddington*, 58¾ miles. Fares, 12/3*a*, 7/4*c*. R. T. for two months, 24/6*a*. Pop. 1,737.

Map Square 23.

Pad.	Kintby.	Kintby.	Pad.
AM 7.30	9. 4	AM 8.35	10. 0
8.45*r*	10.47	10.46	12.55
9.30	11.11	PM 1.45	3.50
10.45	12.26	3.57	5.50
PM12.30*r*	2. 2	4.56	7.20
1.10*r*	2.59	6.44*r*	8.20
2.45	4.40	7.17	9.15
3.18	5.29	8.51	10.45
5. 5	6.42	10.11	2.45
5.55	7.12	—	—
6.30	7.55	—	—
8. 0	9.36	—	—
—	—	—	—
—	—	—	—

Sunday Trains.

AM 9.10	11. 5	AM 8.39	10.50
PM 5.15	7.23	PM 7.21	9.15
—	—	—	—

r Restaurant Car.

KINTORE (Aberdeen), 536¼ miles. No through fares. Departures *from* London as for Aberdeen. Departures *for* London about 3 times daily. Pop. 2,281.

Map Square 35.

KIPLING COTES (Yorks), 210¼ miles. Fares, 40/2*a*, 24/1*c*. R. T. for two months, 80/4*a*, 48/2*c*. Departures *from* London as for Hull (Paragon). Departures *for* London about 4 times daily.

Map Square 8.

KIPPAX (Yorks), 180¾ miles. No through fares. Departures *from* London as for Knottingley. Departures *for* London about 5 times daily. Pop. 4,075.

Map Square 13.

KIPPEN (Stirling), 426 miles. Fares, 86/6*a*, 51/11*c*. R. T. for two months, 173/0*a*, 103/10*c*. Departures *from* London as for Stirling. Departures *for* London about 3 times daily. Pop. 1,518.

Map Square 40.

KIRBY CROSS (Essex), 67¼ miles. Fares, 14/7*a*, 8/9*c*. R. T. for two months 29/2*a*. Departures *from* London as for Walton-on-the-Naze. Departures *for* London about 7 times daily. Pop. (Kirby-le-Soken) 1,094.

Map Square 24.

KIRBY MOORSIDE (Yorks), 224¾ miles. Fares, 46/11*a*, 28/2*c*. R.T. for two months, 93/10*a*, 56/4*c*. Departures *from* London as for Ampleforth. Departures *for* London about 4 times daily. Pop. 1,657.

Map Square 8.

KIRBY MUXLOE (Leicester), 102½ miles. Fares, 21/3*a*, 12/9*c*. R. T., double fare. Departures *from* London as for Leicester (London Road). Departures *for* London about 5 times daily. Pop. 1,063.

Map Square 18.

KIRBY PARK (Cheshire), 214 miles. Fares, 41/1*a*, 24/8*c*. R. T. for two months, 82/2*a*, 49/4*c*. Departures *from* London as for Hooton. Departures *for* London about 8 times daily.

Map Square 11.

KIRKANDREWS (Cumberland), 303¼ miles. No through fares. Departures *from* London as for Carlisle. Departures *for* London about 4 times daily. Pop. 132.

Map Square 3.

KIRKBANK (Roxburgh), 355½ miles. No through fares. Departures *from* London as for St. Boswells or Kelso. Departures *for* London about 4 times daily.

Map Square 41.

KIRKBRIDE (Cumberland), 311¾ miles. No through fares. Departures *from* London as for Carlisle. Departures *for* London about 3 times daily. Pop. 387.

Map Square 2.

KIRKBUDDO (Forfar), 467 miles. No through fares. Departures *from* London as for Forfar. Departures *for* London about 3 times daily.

Map Square 38.

KIRKBURTON (Yorks), 209½ miles. Fares, 37/9*a*, 22/8*c*. R. T., double fare. Departures *from* London as for Huddersfield. Departures *for* London about 8 times daily. Pop. 3,385.

Map Square 12.

KIRKBY (Lancs), 210¼ miles. Fares, 42/9*a*, 25/8*c*. R. T. for two months, 85/6*a*, 51/4*c*. Departures *from* London as for Liverpool. Departures *for* London about 6 times daily. Pop. 1,211.

Map Square 12.

KIRKBY & PINXTON (Notts) from *Marylebone*, 138½ miles. Fares, 27/4*a*, 16/5*c*. R.T., double fare.

M'bone	K. & P.	K. & P.	M'bone
AM 2.32	6.55	AM 6.37	10.36
10. 0*r*	1.59	7.40*r*	11.10
PM12.15*r*	3.48	9.18*r*	1.13
3.20*r*	6.49	11.17*r*	3. 0
5. 0*r*	8.20	PM 1.14*r*	6.38
6.20*dr*	10.13	4.22*r*	8.55
—	—	6.32*r*	9.55
—	—	9.33*h*	3.57
—	—	—	—
—	—	—	—
—	—	—	—
—	—	—	—
—	—	—	—
—	—	—	—
—	—	—	—

Sunday Trains.

PM 5.30*r*	9. 2	AM11. 7*r*	5.40
—	—	—	—
—	—	—	—
—	—	—	—
—	—	—	—

d Saturdays only.
h Stops on notice being given at Station.
r Restaurant Car.

KIRKBY-IN-ASHFIELD (Notts) from *St. Pancras*, 137 miles. Fares, 27/4*a*, 16/5*c*. R. T., double fare. Pop. 17,236.

Map Square 12.

St. Pan.	Kirkby	Kirkby	St. Pan.
AM 2.25	9.11	AM 6. 1*r*	9.57
4.25	10. 7	7.32*r*	10.45
9. 0*r*	11.57	8.12*r*	12.10
9.50*r*	2. 0	9.42*r*	1.20
11. 0*r*	2.24	11.14	3.25
11.45*r*	3.41	PM12.16*r*	4.10
PM 1.50*r*	5. 0	2. 7*r*	5.30
2.25*r*	6.24	2.39*r*	6.35
3.30*r*	7. 9	4.27*r*	7.55
5. 0*r*	8. 1	5.23*r*	9. 5
6.15*r*	10. 3	10.45	4.20
6.25*dr*	11.11	—	—
6.25*er*	11.22	—	—
—	—	—	—
—	—	—	—
—	—	—	—

Sunday Trains.

AM10.50*r*	4.31	PM12.53*r*	5. 2
PM 3.15	9.38	7.49	4.55
—	—	—	—
—	—	—	—
—	—	—	—
—	—	—	—
—	—	—	—

d Saturdays only.
e Saturdays excepted.
r Restaurant Car.

ANOTHER ROUTE from *Marylebone*, 138½ miles. Fares as above.

M'bone.	Kirkby	Kirkby.	M'bone.
AM 2.32	6.16	AM 7.18	10.36
8.45*r*	12.19	8.12*r*	11.10
10. 0*dr*	1.40	9.47*r*	1.13
10. 0*r*	2. 7	11.37*r*	3. 0
PM12.15*r*	3.55	PM 3.41*r*	6.38
3.20*r*	6.12	4.39*r*	8.55
5. 0*r*	7.58	6. 0*r*	9.55
6.20*r*	9.19	10.24*e*	3.57
—	—	10.32*d*	3.57
—	—	—	—
—	—	—	—
—	—	—	—
—	—	—	—
—	—	—	—
—	—	—	—
—	—	—	—

Sunday Trains.

AM11.15*r*	3.35	PM 1.24*r*	5.40
PM 5.30*r*	8.53	6.59*r*	10.24
—	—	—	—
—	—	—	—
—	—	—	—
—	—	—	—

d Saturdays only.
e Saturdays excepted.
r Restaurant Car.

KIRKBY-IN-FURNESS (Lancs), 266¾ miles. Fares, 55/7*a*, 33/4*c*. R. T. for two months, 111/2*a*, 66/8*c*. Departures *from* London as for Barrow-in-Furness. Departures *for* London about 5 times daily. Pop. 1,432.

Map Square 6.

KIRKBY LONSDALE (Westmorland) from *Euston*, 272 miles. Fares, 51/11*a*, 31/2*c*. R. T., for two months, 103/10*a*, 62/4*c*. Departures *from* London as for Ingleton. Departures *for* London about 5 times daily. Pop. 1,394.

Map Square 7.

KIRKBY STEPHEN

(Westmorland) from *St. Pancras*, 266¼ miles. Fares, 52/3*a*, 31/4*c*. R. T. for two months, 104/6*a*, 62/8*c*. Pop. 1,546.
Map Square 7.

St. Pan.	Kirkby	Kirkby	St. Pan.
AM 4.25	12.58	AM 9.44*r*	5.30
PM12.15*r*	6.58	PM12.13*r*	7.15
11.50*e*	9.24	5.47	4.20
—	—	—	—
—	—	—	—

Sunday Trains.

PM11.45	9.24	—	—
—	—	—	—

e Saturdays excepted.
r Restaurant Car.

KIRKBY THORE (West-

morland), 284¾ miles. Fares, 55/7*a*, 33/4*c*. R. T. for two months, 111/2*a*, 66/8*c*. Departures *from* London for Tebay. Departures *for* London about twice daily. Pop. 449.
Map Square 7.

KIRKCALDY (Fife)

from *King's Cross*, 418¼ miles. Fares, 83/7*a*, 50/2*c*. R. T. for two months, 167/2*a*, 100/4*c*. Pop. 45,915.
Map Square 41.

King's +	K'cldy	K'cldy	King's +
AM 4.45	3.22	AM 9. 3	6.15
10. 0*r*	7.14	PM12.42*r*	10. 0
11.50*r*	10.28	4.10	3.25
PM 1.15*dr*11.41		6.39	6. 0
8.25*e*	7.21	8.40*e*	6.50
11.25*r*	8.19	9.40	7. 5
11.40*e*	9.58	—	—
—	—	—	—
—	—	—	—

Sunday Trains.

PM 8.25	7.21	PM 6. 4	6. 0
11.25	8.19	—	—
11.40	9.58	—	—
—	—	—	—
—	—	—	—

d Saturdays only.
e Saturdays excepted.
r Restaurant Car.

KIRKCONNEL (Dum-

fries), 361¼ miles. Fares, 73/6*a*, 44/1*c*. R. T. for two months, 147/0*a*. Departures *from* London as for Thornhill (Dumfries). Departures *for* London about 4 times daily. Pop. 3,419.
Map Square 43.

KIRKCOWAN (Wigtown),

388 miles. Fares, 68/9*a*, 41/3*c*. R.T. for two months, 137/6*a*, 82/6*c*. Departures *from* London as for Newton Stewart. Departures *for* London about 4 times daily. Pop. 1,129.
Map Square 43.

KIRKCUDBRIGHT, 371¼

miles. Fares, 68/9*a*, 41/3*c*. R. T. for two months, 137/6*a*, 82/6*c*. Pop. 3,054.
Map Square 43.

St.Pan.Krkdbht.		Krkdbht.St.Pan.	
AM 4.25*e*	4. 5	AM 8.45*r*	6.35
4.25*d*	4.25	11. 0*r*	9.15
9.50*r*	6.52	PM 7.15*e*	7.25
PM12.15*r*	9. 0	—	—
9.30*e*	7.55	—	—
11.45*e*	10.35	—	—
—	—	—	—
—	—	—	—
—	—	—	—

Sunday Trains.

PM 9.30	7.55	—	—
11.45	10.35	—	—
—	—	—	—
—	—	—	—

d Saturdays only.
e Saturdays excepted.
r Restaurant Car.

KIRKGUNZEON (Kirk-

cudbright), 342½ miles. Fares, 68/9*a*, 41/3*c*. R. T. for two months, 137/6*a*, 82/6*c*. Departures *from* London as for Dumfries. Departures *for* London about 4 times daily. Pop. 548.
Map Square 43.

KIRKHAM (Lancs) from

Euston, 217 miles. Fares, 45/3*a*, 27/2*c*. R.T. for two months, 90/6*a*, 54/4*c*. Pop. 3,814.
Map Square 12.

Euston	Kirkh.	Kirkh.	Euston
AM12.25	7 30	AM 8.24*r*	1.45
2.35	10. 2	8.59*r*	3.10
5. 0	11.18	10.50*r*	4.15
6.45	1.19	11.41*dt*	6. 0
10.40*er*	4. 4	PM12.42*et*	6. 0
11.35*r*	4.38	2.22*r*	7.30
11.50*r*	5.54	5.34*r*	10.45
PM 1.50*r*	6.31	10.25	5. 0
2.35*t*	7.55	—	—
5.20*r*	10. 9	—	—
9.30*d*	9.47	—	—
11.50*d*	11. 8	—	—

Sunday Trains.

AM11.45*r*	6.28	AM 7.27*r*	1.30
—	—	PM 1.57	7.30
—	—	9.29	5. 0
—	—	—	—
—	—	—	—
—	—	—	—
—	—	—	—

d Saturdays only.
e Saturdays excepted.
r Restaurant Car.
t Tea Car.

KIRKHAM ABBEY

(Yorks), 203¾ miles. Fares, 42/3*a*, 25/4*c*. R. T., double fare. Departures *from* London as for York. Departures *for* London about 6 times daily. Pop. (Kirkham) 141.
Map Square 8.

KIRKHEATON (Yorks)

206¾ miles. Fares, 37/9*a*, 22/8*c*. R. T., double fare. Departures *from* London as for Huddersfield. Departures *for* London about 6 times daily. Pop. 2,704.
Map Square 12.

KIRKINNER (Wigtown),

391¼ miles. Fares, 70/8*a*, 42/5*c*. R. T. for two months, 141/4*a*, 84/10*c*. Departures *from* London as for Wigtown. Departures *for* London about 3 times daily. Pop. 1,156.
Map Square 43.

KIRKINTILLOCH (Dum-

barton), 435 miles. No through fares. Departures *from* London as for Glasgow. Departures *for* London about 4 times daily. Pop. 16,251.
Map Square 40.

KIRKLAND (Dumfries),

347½ miles. No through fares. Departures *from* London as for Dumfries. Departures *for* London about twice daily.
Map Square 43.

KIRKLINGTON (Notts),

141½ miles. Fares, 25/5*a*, 15/3*c*. R. T., double fare. Departures *from* London as for Southwell. Departures *for* London about 5 times daily. Pop. 218.
Map Square 13.

KIRKLISTON (Linlith-

gow), 402¾ miles. No through fares. Departures *from* London as for Edinburgh (Waverley). Departures *for* London about 4 times daily. Pop. 3,694.
Map Square 41.

KIRKNEWTON (North-

umberland), 333 miles. No through fares. Departures *from* London as for Alnwick. Departures *for* London about 4 times daily. Pop. 76.
Map Square 3.

KIRKPATRICK (Dum-

fries), 312 miles. No through fares. Departures *from* London as for Carlisle. Departures *for* London about 4 times daily. Pop. 1,152.
Map Square 44.

KIRKSMEATON (Yorks),

187½ miles. Fares, 35/9*a*, 21/6*c*. R.T. for two months, 70/6*a*, 42/0*c*. Departures *from* London as for Cudworth. Departures *for* London about twice daily. Pop. 337.
Map Square 13.

KIRKSTALL (Yorks), 198¼

miles. Fares, 39/4*a*, 23/7*c*. R. T. double fare. Departures *from* London as for Leeds (Wellington). Departures *for* London about 8 times daily. Pop. 5,400.
Map Square 12.

KIRKSTEAD. See Wood-

hall Junction.
Map Square 13.

KIRRIEMUIR (Forfar), 482¾ miles. Fares, 96/8a, 58/0c. R. T. for two months, 193/4a, 116/0c. Departures *from* London as for Forfar. Departures *for* London about 3 times daily. Pop. 5,074.
Map Square 38.

KIRTLEBRIDGE (Dumfries), 315¾ miles. Fares, 64/0a, 38/5c. R. T. for two months, 128/0a, 76/10c. Departures *from* London as for Carlisle. Departures *for* London about 3 times daily.
Map Square 44.

KIRTON (Lincoln) from King's Cross, 103¾ miles. Fares, 21/6a, 12/11c. R. T., double fare. Pop. 2,444.
Map Square 13.

King's +	Kirton	Kirton	King's +
AM 4.45	7.38	AM 7.45	10.40
5. 5	8.50	9.58	1. 5
7.15lr	10.17	12. 0	3.50
8.45	11.51	PM 1.53r	4.30
11.30	3. 9	2.28lr	5. 0
PM 1.50br	4.31	5.23	9. 0
3. 0	5.41	7.23e	3.25
5.45r	8.19	9.40d	3.25

Sunday Trains.

12. 0nr	2.56	AM11.58r	3.45
—	—	PM 7.18r	10.20

d Saturdays only.
e Saturdays excepted.
h Mondays and Fridays excepted.
k Mondays and Fridays only.
l Wednesdays only.
n Noon.
r Restaurant Car.

KIRTON LINDSEY (Lincoln), 159½ miles. Fares, 32/3a, 19/4c. R. T., double fare. Departures *from* London as for Gainsborough (*via* Retford). Departures *for* London about 5 times daily. Pop. 1,602.
Map Square 13.

KIVETON PARK (Yorks), 151½ miles. Fares, 31/6a, 18/11c. R. T., double fare. Departures *from* London as for Worksop or Sheffield (Victoria). Departures *for* London about 8 times daily.
Map Square 13.

KNAPTON (Yorks), 215¾ miles. No through fares. Departures *from* London as for Malton. Departures *for* London about 5 times daily. Pop. 235.
Map Square 8.

KNARESBOROUGH (Yorks) from King's Cross, 201¼ miles. Fares, 42/8a, 25/7c. R. T. for two months, 85/4a, 51/2c. Pop. 5,518.
Map Square 7.

King's +	Kn'boro.	Kn'boro.	King's +
AM 4.45	11. 6	AM 6. 8r	11.30
7.15r	12.56	7.25r	1. 5
10.10r	3.35	8.33r	1.15
11 15g	3.35	9. 2r	1.55
11.50r	5.29	10.41g	3.15
PM 1.30r	6.56	11.10r	4.30
1.50r	6.51	11.40	5. 0
4. 0r	9.30	PM12.56r	6.15
5.45r	10.35	2. 0r	7.10
10.45e	7. 0	4. 4r	9.25
11.25e	8. 1	5.12r	10. 0
—	—	9. 0e	3.25
—	—	9.17d	3.25

Sunday Trains.

King's +	Kn'boro.		
12. 0n	5.53	—	—
PM10.45	7. 0	—	—
11.25	8. 1	—	—

d Saturdays only.
e Saturdays excepted.
g First and Third Class Pullman Cars only.
n Noon.
r Restaurant Car.

KNEBWORTH (Herts) from King's Cross, 25 miles. Fares, 5/3a, 3/2c. R. T., double fare. Pop. 1,629.
Map Square 23.

King's +	Kneb'th.	Kneb'th.	King's +
AM 5. 5	5.50	AM 6.37	7.30
7. 0	8.22	7.52	8.41
8. 5	9. 6	8.16	8.55
9.20d	10. 9	8.54	9.34
10.12	11. 8	9.31	10.22
PM12.40d	1.17	11.14	12. 3
1. 8	2. 8	PM 1.15	2.22
1.55	2.40	3.27	4.23
2.30d	3.19	4.44	5.45
4.15	5.14	5.22	6. C
5.10	5.49	6. 9	7. 5
5.50	6.38	7.22	8. 5
6.30	7.15	9.19	10.20
7. 0	7.50	10.15	11. 0
8.30	9.15	—	—
9.10	10. 2	—	—
10.55	11.40	—	—
11.45h	12.39	—	—

Sunday Trains.

King's +	Kneb'th.	Kneb'th.	King's +
AM 8.30	9.33	AM 8.40	9.53
10.30	11.18	PM 5.35	6.17
PM 7.10	8. 2	7. 9	8. 8
9.50	10.19	—	—

d Saturdays only.
h Wednesdays only.
k Stops on notice being given at station.

KNIGHTON (Radnor), from Euston, 194½ miles. Fares, 34/5a, 20/8c. R. T. for two months, 68/10d, 41/4c. Pop. 1,701.
Map Square 17.

Euston	Knigh.	Knigh.	Euston
AM 5. 0	11.37	AM10.30r	3.10
6.45h	12.44	PM 1.15r	6.15
6.45	2.38	3.44dr	9.15
10.40r	3.12	3.44er	9.20
PM 1.15r	6. 8	9.32y	5. 0
9.20ey	4.34	—	—

Sunday Trains.

Euston	Knigh.		
PM 9.15	4.34	—	—
—	—	—	—
—	—	—	—

e Saturdays excepted.
h Mondays and Fridays only.
r Restaurant Car.
y Via Crewe.

KNIGHTSBRIDGE (Hammersmith and Finsbury Park Tube). See p. 489.

Royal Court Hotel, Sloane Square, S.W. 1. *See advt. under* London Hotels.

KNIGHTWICK (Worcester), 128½ miles. Fares, 25/7a, 15/4c. R. T. for two months, 51/2a. Departures *from* London as for Bromyard. Departures *for* London about 5 times daily. Pop. 172.
Map Square 17.

KNOCK (Banff), 574½ miles. No through fares. Departures *from* London as for Huntly. Departures *for* London about 3 times daily.
Map Square 35.

KNOCKANDO (Elgin), 563½ miles. Fares, 106/3a, 63/9c. R. T. for two months, 212/6a, 127 6c. Departures *from* London as for Aviemore or Keith (*via* Aberdeen). Departures *for* London about twice daily. Pop. 1,590.
Map Square 35.

KNOCKHOLT (Kent) from Charing Cross, Cannon St. and London Bridge, 17¼ miles. Fares, 3/9a, 3/0b, 2/3c. R. T. for eight days, 7/6a, 6/0b. Pop. 908.
Map Square 24.

| | Leave | | Arr. at |
Char. +	Can. St.	Lon. B.	K'holt.
AM —	5.20	5.25	6.20
—	6.45	6.50	7.36
—	7.56	8. 0	8.46
9.38	—	9.45	10.27
11.15	—	11.23	12. 8
PM —	1.12d	1.15d	1.49
2.17d	—	2.23d	3. 2
3.50	—	3.57	4.40
4.55d	—	5. 1d	5.46
—	5. 4e	5. 7e	5.45
5.35d	—	5.41d	6.22
—	5.44e	5.47e	6.14
6.10e	—	6.17e	6.57
8. 0	—	8. 8	8.45
9. 0	—	9. 6	9.45
10. 0	—	10. 6	10.43
10.45	—	10.51	11.29
11.45h	—	—	12.18

Sunday Trains.

Char. +	Can. St.	Lon. B.	K'holt.
AM 7. 5	—	7.11	8. 1
8. 5	—	8.12	8.54
11.15	—	11.23	12.10
PM —	1. 7k	—	2. 8
3. 5	—	3.13	3.59
6. 0	—	6. 6	6.53
9.25	—	9.31	10.10

KNOCKHOLT—*contd.*

Trains from Knockholt.

Leave K'HOLT.	Arrive at LON. B.	CAN. ST.	CHAR. +
AM 7.54	8.10	—	8.19
8. 6	8.40	8.44	—
8.43	9.18	—	9.27
9. 3	9.40	9.44	—
9.36	10. 0	10. 4	—
10.32	10.58	11. 2	—
PM12.45	1.27	—	1.38
2.26	3. 7	—	3.19
4.14	4.40	—	4.53
5.41*d*	6.30	—	6.39
5.53*e*	6.44	—	6.54
8.14	8.54	9. 1	—
9.37	10.15	—	10.23
10.57	11.34	—	11.44
—	—	—	—
—	—	—	—
—	—	—	—

Sunday Trains.

AM 9.38	10.22	—	10.32
11.15	11.49	—	12. 0
PM 1. 8*k*	—	2.11*h*	—
2.10	2.50	—	3. 0
5.46	6.27	—	6.41
7.39	8.12	—	8.22
8.30	9. 7	—	9.18
8.57	9.38	—	—
9.41*k*	—	10.54*k*	—

d Saturdays only.
e Saturdays excepted.
h Mondays and Thursdays only.
k Departs from or arrives at Victoria (S.E. & C.).

KNOTT END (Lancs), 229¾ miles. Fares, 47/9*a*, 28/8*c*. R. T. for two months, 95/6*a*, 57/4*c*. Departures *from* London as for Preston. Departures *for* London about 4 times daily
Map Square 7.

KNOTTINGLEY (Yorks) from *King's Cross*, 170¾ miles. Fares, 35/7*a*, 21/4*c*. R. T., double fare. Pop. 6,752.
Map Square 13.

KING'S +	KNOTLY.	KNOTLY.	KING'S +
AM 4.45	9.29	AM 9. 0	1. 5
7.15*r*	11.29	9.45	1.55
10.10*r*	2.14	11.37*r*	3.50
PM 1.50*r*	6.31	PM 2.15*r*	6.15
4. 0*r*	8.39	4.40*r*	9.25
5.45*dr*11.17		6.20	10. 0
10.45*e*	7.39	8.45*e*	3.25
—	—	9.30*d*	3.25
—	—	—	—
—	—	—	—
—	—	—	—
—	—	—	—
—	—	—	—

Sunday Trains.

12. 0*nr*	4.49	AM11.40	5.15
PM10.45	7.39		
—	—	—	—

d Saturdays only.
e Saturdays excepted.
n Noon.
r Restaurant Car.

KNOTT MILL (Lancs), 192 miles. Fares, 38/7*a*, 23/2*c*. R. T., double fare. Departures *from* London as for Manchester (London Road). Departures *for* London about 8 times daily.

KNOTTY ASH (Lancs), 214 miles. Fares, 41/3*a*, 24/9*c*. R. T., double fare. Departures *from* London as for Warrington (Central). Departures *for* London about 6 times daily.

KNOWESGATE (Northumberland), 299 miles. Fares, 63/1*a*, 37/10*c*. R. T. for two months, 196/2*a*, 75/8*c*. Departures *from* London as for Morpeth. Departures *for* London about twice daily.
Map Square 3.

KNOWESIDE (Ayr), 403 miles.. No through fares. Departures *from* London as for Turnberry. Departures *for* London about 5 times daily.
Map Square 43.

KNOWLE (Warwick) from *Paddington*, 100¼ miles. Fares, 21/0*a*, 12/7*c*. R. T. for two months, 42/0*a*. Pop. 2,357.
Map Square 17.

PAD.	KNOWLE	KNOWLE	PAD.
AM 5.30	9.45	AM 7.45*r*	10. 0
6.30	10.40	8.41*r*	11. 0
10.40	1.27	10.45*r*	1.25
PM12.50*r*	4.10	11.49*r*	2. 5
2.10	4.56	PM 2.29*r*	5. 0
4.10*t*	6.26	3.59*t*	5.55
6.10*r*	8.24	5.36*er*	8. 5
7.10*r*	9.24	5.39*dr*	8. 5
7.30	10.36	7.22	10. 0
12.15*k*	7.53	11.48	3.30
12.15*l*	9.38	—	—
—	—	—	—
—	—	—	—

Sunday Trains.

AM10.35	1.56	AM11. 7*r*	1.40
PM 6. 0*r*	8.48	PM 2.17	6.20
—	—	6.45*r*	9. 0
—	—	—	—
—	—	—	—

d Saturdays only.
e Saturdays excepted.
k Saturdays midnight excepted.
l Saturdays midnight only.
r Restaurant Car.
t Tea Car.

KNOWLTON (Kent), 75¼ miles. No through fares. Departures *from* London as for Eastry. Departures *for* London about 5 times daily. Pop. 41.

KNUCKLAS (Radnor), 197¼ miles. Fares, 35/0*a*, 21/0*c*. R. T. for two months, 70/0*a*, 42/0*c*. Departures *from* London as for Knighton. Departures *for* London about 3 times daily.
Map Square 16.

KNUTSFORD (Cheshire) from *Euston*, 177¾ miles. Fares 35/8*a*, 21/5*c*. R. T. double fare. Pop. 5,411.
Map Square 12.

EUSTON	KNUTSF'D.	KNUTSF'D.	EUSTON
AM 2.35	7.37	AM 7.53*r*	1. 0
5. 0	12. 6	10.54*dr*	4.15
8.30*er*	2. 4	11. 8*er*	3.10
10.40*r*	3.26	PM12.33*r*	5.50
PM 1.30*r*	5.51	2.11*er*	8.10
2.35*et*	6.32	3.22*dr*	8.10
2.35*dt*	7.36	4.17*dr*	9.15
5.20*r*	9.14	5. 2*er*	9. 5
—	—	5.55*r*	10.45
—	—	8.57	5. 0
—	—	—	—

No Sunday Trains.

d Saturdays only.
e Saturdays excepted.
r Restaurant Car.
t Tea Car.

KYLE OF LOCHALSH
(Ross) from *Euston*, 650 miles. Fares, 119/5*a*, 71/8*c*. R. T. for two months, 238/10*a*, 143/4*c*. Pop. 1,650.
Map Square 33.

EUSTON	LOCHALSH	LOCHALSH	EUSTON
PM 1.30*vr*10.58*h*		AM11. 0	7.40*h*
7.40*er*	2. 5*l*	PM 4.30*er*	7.30*l*
—	—	5.10*kr*	7.30*l*
—	—	—	—
—	—	—	—

Sunday Trains.

PM 7.50*r*	2. 5*l*	—	—
—	—	—	—

e Saturdays excepted.
h A.M.
k Wednesdays and Fridays only.
l P.M.
r Restaurant Car.
v Tuesdays and Thursdays only.

Station Hotel. Old fashioned, Comfortable. Looking across to Skye. H. H. WARD, L.M.S. Highland Hotels Manager. Also Inverness, Dornoch and Strathpeffer.

L

LADBROKE GROVE
from *Aldgate*, 6¾ miles. Fares, 0/9*a*, 0/6*c*. R. T. for two days, 1/6*a*, 1/0*c*. Trains run about every 12 minutes throughout the day. See back of Map.
Map Square 59.

LADYBANK (Fife), 431¼
miles. Fares, 87/6*a*, 52/6*c*. R. T. for two months, 175/0*a*, 105/0*c*. Departures *from* London as for Kirkcaldy. Departures *for* London about 3 times daily. Pop. 1,168.
Map Square 41.

LADYSBRIDGE (Banff),
584½ miles. No through fares. Departures *from* London as for Huntly. Departures *for* London about twice daily.
Map Square 35.

LADYWELL (London) from
Charing Cross and *Cannon Street*, 7¼ miles. Fares from Charing Cross, 1/6*a*, 1/2*b*, 0/10½*c*. R. T. for two days, 2/7*a*, 1/9*b*, 1/5*c*. From Cannon Street. Fares, 1/1*a*, 0/10*b*, 0/7½*c*. R. T. for two days, 2/2*a*, 1/8*b*, 1/3*c*. See pp. 544-547.
Map Square 71.

LAINDON (Essex) from
Fenchurch Street, 22½ miles. Fares, 4/0*a*, 2/5*c*. R. T. for two months, 8/0*a*, 4/4½*c*. Pop. 1,205. See p. 509.
Map Square 24.

LAIRG (Sutherland) from
Euston, 634½ miles. Fares, 113/7*a*, 68/2*c*. R. T. for two months, 227/2*a*. Pop. 1,046.
Map Square 34.

EUSTON	LAIRG	LAIRG	EUSTON
PM 1.30*er*	9.34*h*	AM 6.52*r*	5. 0*h*
7.40*er*	1. 0*l*	PM12. 7	7.40*h*
11.35*v*	6.30*h*	6.10*er*	7.30*l*
—	—	—	—
—	—	—	—
—	—	—	—
—	—	—	—
—	—	—	—

Sunday Trains.

PM 7.50*r*	1. 0*l*		—

e Saturdays excepted.
h A.M.
l P.M.
r Restaurant Car.
v Thursdays only.

ANOTHER ROUTE from
King's Cross, 624½ miles. Fares as above.

KING'S +	LAIRG	LAIRG	KING'S +
AM11.50*er*	9.34*k*	AM 6.52	3.25*k*
PM 7.45*er*	1. 0*h*	PM12. 7	7. 5*k*
11.25*es*	6. 5	6.10*er*	6.30*h*
—	—	—	—

No Sunday Trains.
e Saturdays excepted.
h P.M. *k* A.M.
r Restaurant Car.
s Fridays only when required.

LAISTER DYKE (Yorks)
from *King's Cross*, 190½ miles. Fares, 39/.. ../.. *c*. R. T., double fare. Departures *from* London as for Wakefield (Westgate). Departures *for* London about 5 minutes later. Pop. 18,516.

LAKENHEATH (Suffolk)
from *Liverpool Street*, 82¼ miles. Fares, 17/4*a*, 10/5*c*. R. T. for two months, 34/8*a*. Pop. 1,613.
Map Square 19.

L'POOL ST.	LKN'TH.	LKN'TH	L'POOL ST.
AM 5. 5	7.21	AM 8. 1*r*	10.23
5.50	9.10	9. 0	11.27
8.30*r*	11. 4	11.56*r*	2.21
11.50*r*	2.39	PM 2.43*r*	5.17
PM 2.34	5.21	5.52*r*	8.22
5.49*r*	8.11	9.12	2.50
—	—	—	—
—	—	—	—
—	—	—	—
—	—	—	—

Sunday Trains.

AM 9.25	12.17	PM 3.57	6.40
PM 3.25	6. 7	7.32	9.40
—	—	—	—
—	—	—	—
—	—	—	—
—	—	—	—

r Restaurant Car.

LAKE SIDE (Windermere).
See WINDERMERE (Lake Side).

LAMANCHA (Peebles),
394½ miles. No through fares. Departures *from* London as for Peebles. Departures *for* London about 3 times daily.
Map Square 41.

LAMBETH, NORTH
(Bakerloo Tube). Pop. (Lambeth) 302,868. See back of Map.

LAMBLEY (Northumberland), 308½ miles. No through fares. Departures *from* London as for Hexham or Carlisle. Departures *for* London about 4 times daily. Pop. 420.
Map Square 3.

LAMBOURN (Berks)
from *Paddington*, 65½ miles. Fares, 12/8*a*, 8/2*c*. R. T. for two months, 25/4*a*, 16/4*c*. Pop. 2,336.
Map Square 22.

PAD.	LAMB'N.	LAMB'N.	PAD.
AM 7.30	9.53	AM 7.45	10. 0
9.30	12.30	10.40	12.55
PM12.30*r*	2.45	PM12.42	2.50
2.45	5. 5	3.15	5.50
5.55	7.53	5.25*r*	8.20
—	—	—	—
—	—	—	—
—	—	—	—
—	—	—	—
—	—	—	—

No Sunday Trains.
r Restaurant Car.

REFERENCE NOTES.

a signifies First Class.
b „ Second Class.
c „ Third Class.
d „ On Saturdays only.
e „ Saturdays excepted.
f „ On Mondays only.
g „ Mondays excepted.
r „ Restaurant Car.
t „ Tea Car.
x „ Express.
R.T. „ Return Tickets.

All Trains in the Tables not otherwise marked carry Third Class Passengers.

LAMESLEY (Durham),

264 miles. Fares, 55/2*a*, 33/1*c*. R. T., double fare. Departures *from* London as for Durham. Departures *for* London about 6 times daily. Pop. 6,369.

Map Square 3.

LAMINGTON (Lanark),

362¼ miles. Fares, 73/7*a*, 44/2*c*. R. T. for two months, 147/2*a*, 88/4*c*. Departures *from* London as for Lockerbie. Departures *for* London about 3 times daily. Pop. 301.

Map Square 40.

LAMPETER (Cardigan)

from *Paddington*, 255¼ miles. Fares, 48/9*a*, 29/3*c*. R. T. for two months, 97/6*a*. Pop. 1,813.

Map Square 16.

PAD.	LAMP'T'R.	LAMP'T'R.	PAD.
AM 1. 0*g*	11.37	AM 8.16*r*	4.20
8.45*r*	2.52	11. 3*r*	6.15
11.50*r*	7.19	PM 2.34*r*	9.25
PM 9.15*e*	7.13	6.18	3.30
—	—	—	—
—	—	—	—
—	—	—	—

Sunday Trains.

PM 9.15	7.13	—	—
—	—	—	—
—	—	—	—
—	—	—	—

e Saturdays excepted.
g Mondays excepted.
r Restaurant Car.

LAMPHEY (Pembroke)

from *Paddington*, 265 miles. Fares, 53/11*a*, 32/4*c*. R. T. for two months, 107/10*a*, 64/8*c*. Departures *from* London as for Tenby. Departures *for* London about 4 times daily. Pop. 268.

Map Square 20.

LAMPLUGH (Cumber-

land), 307½ miles. Fares, 63/11*a*, 38/4*c*. R. T., double fare. Departures *from* London as for Moor Row or Cockermouth. Departures *for* London about 3 times daily. Pop. 1,089.

Map Square 6.

LAMPORT (Northamp-

ton) from *Euston*, 75½ miles. Fares, 15/5*a*, 9/3*c*. R. T. for two months, 30/10*a*. Pop. 175.

Map Square 18.

EUSTON	LAMP'RT.	LAMP'RT.	EUSTON
AM 5. 0	7.18	AM 8. 0	10.15
6.45	9.34	9.42	11.55
10.40	1.19	10.54	12.40
PM12.15	3.19	PM 1. 6*h*	3.45
3. 5	5. 8	1. 6*k*	4.15
4.15	6.24	2.59	5.35
7. 0	8.47	5. 2	7.20
		7.19*e*	9.20
		8. 8	11.35

No Sunday Trains.

e Saturdays excepted.
h Mondays and Saturdays only.
k Mondays and Saturdays excepted.

LANARK, 377½ miles.

Fares, 76/10*a*, 46/1*c*. R. T. for two months, 153/8*a*, 92/2*c*. Departures *from* London as for Carstairs. Departures *for* London about 3 times daily. Pop. 6,268.

Map Square 40.

LANCASTER (CAS-

TLE) from *Euston*, 230 miles. Fares, 47/9*a*, 28/8*c*. R. T. for two months, 95/6*a*, 57/4*c*. Pop. 40,226.

Map Square 7.

EUSTON	L'CAST'R	L'CAST'R	EUSTON
AM12.25	7.49	AM 4. 0*g*	11.10
2.35	9.26	8.11*r*	1.45
5. 0	11.46	8.55*r*	3.10
6.45	1. 2	10.25*hr*	3.45
10.40*r*	3.50	10.43*r*	4.15
11.35*r*	4. 9	PM12.31*t*	6. 0
11.50*er*	5.50	2.25*r*	7.30
11.50*dr*	5.59	3.37*er*	9. 5
PM 1.30*r*	6.12	3.37*dr*	9.15
2.35*t*	8. 1	5.50*r*	10.45
5.20*r*	10.38	9.53*e*	5. 0
9.30	4.10	9.57*d*	5. 0
11. 0*d*	3.35	—	—
11.50*d*	11.39	—	—

Sunday Trains.

AM11.45*r*	5.11	AM 7. 0*r*	1.30
PM 9.15	4.10	PM 1.40*r*	7.30
—	—	10.12	5. 0

d Saturdays only.
e Saturdays excepted.
g Mondays excepted.
h Mondays and Saturdays only.
r Restaurant Car.
t Tea Car.

ANOTHER ROUTE (GREEN

AYRE) from *St. Pancras*, 260 miles. Fares as above.

ST. PAN.	LANCAST.	LANCAST.	ST. PAN.
AM 2.25*g*	12.41	AM 7.56*r*	2.10
4.25	1. 5	9.45*r*	5.30
9.50*r*	4. 8	11.13*hr*	6.35
PM12.15*er*	6.55	PM12.58*r*	7.55
12.15*dr*	7. 2	2.48*r*	9.15
3.30*r*	10.27	6.50	4.20
5. 0*r*	11.12	—	—
11.50*e*	8.50	—	—
11.50*d*	9.38	—	—

Sunday Trains.

AM10.50*r*	8. 7	AM 9.10	5.27
PM11.45	8.50	PM 6.35	4.55

d Saturdays only.
e Saturdays excepted.
g Mondays excepted.
h Mondays, Tuesdays, Fridays and Saturdays only.
r Restaurant Car.

County Hotel. Tel. 125 Lancaster. Opp. L. & N.W. Railway Station. Porters attend all trains. Family. Commercial.
WALTER S. SPENCER,
Resident Proprietor.

LANCASTER GATE

(Central London Tube). See back of Map.

How's Private Residential Hotels. Lancaster Gate, W. *See* advt. amongst London Hotels.

LANCHESTER (Durham),

259¾ miles. No through fares. Departures *from* London as for Durham. Departures *for* London about 6 times daily. Pop. 5,208.

Map Square 7.

LANCING (Sussex) from

London Bridge and *Victoria*, 57½ miles. Fares, 12/1*a*, 7/3*c*. R. T. for two months, 24/2*a*, 14/6*c*. Pop. 2,022.

Map Square 28.

	Leave		Arr. at
	VICT.	LON. B.	LANCING
AM	—	5.18	8. 3
	6.37	6.40	8.54
	7.23	7.25	10.17
	9. 0	—	11. 4
	—•	9. 6	11.23
	10. 5	9.50	11.48
	11. 0*l*	—	12.40
	11.40	10.35	1.19

LANCING—*continued.*

	Leave		Arr. at
	VICT.	LON. B.	LANCING
AM	—	11.40*d*	1.30
	11.55	11.50	1.49
PM12.45	—	—	2.44
	—	1.20*d*	3.13
	1.55	—	3.38
	2. 0*d*	2. 5	4.24
	2. 0*e*	—	4.43
	—	2. 8*d*	5.13
	3.10*l*	—	4.43
	3.40	4. 0	5.44
	4.30	—	6.14
	—	5. 5*d*	6.38
	—	5. 8*e*	6.38
	5.45*e*	5.55*e*	7.22
	—	6. 0	7.55
	—	6. 8	8.48
	6.40	—	8. 7
	7.15	7.20	9.12
	8.35	—	10.24
	9. 3*d*	9.12*d*	11.33
	10. 0	9.12*e*	11.49

Sunday Trains.

AM 6.55	7. 2	9.54	
8.50	8.55	11.34	
9.45*k*	—	11.34	
11. 5	—	12.54	
PM12.55	—	2. 9	
1.10	—	3. 3	
1.14	1.10	3.49	
5.50	6. 0	9. 4	
6.30*p*	—	8.33	
8. 0	8. 0	10.34	

Trains from Lancing.

	Leave	Arrive at	
	LANCING	LON. B.	VICT.
AM 5.45	8.15	8.24	
6.21	8.19	—	
6.50	8.38	—	
7.30	9.25	9.15	
8. 8	9.50	—	
8.22*e*	9.54	10.24	
8.36*d*	10.33	—	
8.47*e*	10.33	—	
9.15	11.10	10.55	
10. 5	12.19	12.17	
10.37	1.42	—	
11.40	—	1.20	
PM12.32*l*	—	2.20	
12.42*e*	2.23	—	
1. 3	3.40	3.45	
1.55	—	4.17	
2.40*d*	4.58	4.45	
2.40	—	4.50	
3.15	5.54	5.55	
4.22	6.36	6.34	
5.14*l*	—	6.45	
5.39	7.42	7.30	
6.51	—	8.48	
7. 8	10.25	10.17	
7.38*d*	10. 0	9.45	
8.14	10.58	—	
9.19	—	11.17	
10.33	12.59	1. 0	

Sunday Trains.

AM 7.29	10.45	—	
8.59	11.15	10.50	
10.38	—	1. 0	
11.38	—	1.35	
PM 2.35	5. 3	5.11	
4.25*p*	—	6. 0	
4.55	7.56	7. 0	
5.35	—	7.28	
6.50	9.17	9.13	
9. 5	—	10.55	
10. 7	12.27	—	

d Sundays only.
e Saturdays excepted.
k Third class Pullman Cars only.
l First and Third class Pullman Cars only.
p First class Pullman Cars only.

LANDORE (HIGH LEVEL)

(Glamorgan) from *Paddington*, 197 miles.   Fares, 41/1*a*, 24/8*c*. R. T. for two months. 82/2*a*. Pop. 12,810.

PAD.	LANDORE	LANDORE	PAD.
AM 1. 0*g*	7.21	AM 6.40*r*	10.57
5.30	11.58	8.20*r*	1. 0
8.45*r*	12.38	9.52*r*	2.30
11.50*r*	4. 8	11. 6*r*	4.20
PM 1.10*r*	6.16	PM 1.46*r*	6.15
3.35*r*	9. 1	3.42*r*	8.35
5. 0*r*	9.36	3.55*r*	9.25
6. 0*hr*10.50		9.10	3.30
6. 0*dr*11. 2		—	—
9.15	4. 7	—	—

Sunday Trains.

AM 1. 0	8. 0	AM 9.12	3.35
PM12.30*r*	9.19	PM 9.10	3.30
9.15	4. 7	—	—

d Saturdays only.
g Mondays excepted.
h Thursdays only.
r Restaurant Car.

LANGBANK (Renfrew),

415¾ miles.   Fares, 84/2*a*, 50/6*c*. R. T. for two months, 168/4*a*, 101/0*c*.   Departures *from* London as for Greenock (Central).   Departures *for* London about 4 times daily.
Map Square 40.

LANGFORD (Essex) from

Liverpool Street, 43½ miles.   Fares, 8/2*a*, 4/11*c*.   R. T. for two months, 16/4*a*.   Departures *from* London as for Maldon East, *via* Witham. Departures *for* London about 7 times daily.   Pop. 182.
Map Square 24.

LANGFORD (Somerset),

135½ miles.   Fares, 28/2*a*, 16/11*c*. R. T. for two months, 56/4*a*. Departures *from* London as for Wrington.   Departures *for* London about 4 times daily.
Map Square 22.

LANGHO(Lancs), 216½ miles.

Fares, 43/9*a*, 26/3*c*.   R. T. for two months, 87/6*a*, 52/6*c*.   Departures *from* London as for Blackburn. Departures *for* London about 8 times daily.
Map Square 12.

LANGHOLM (Dumfries)

320 miles.   Fares, 65/0*a*, 39/0*c*. R. T. for two months, 130/0*a*, 78/0*c*. Departures *from* London as for Carlisle.   Departures *for* London about 3 times daily.   Pop. 2,981.
Map Square 44.

LANGLEY (Bucks) from

Paddington, 16¼ miles.   Fares, 3/4*a*, 2/0*c*.   R. T. for two months, 6/8*a*, 3/11½*c*.   Pop. 3,120.
Map Squares 23 and 53.

PAD.	LANGLEY	LANGLEY	PAD.
AM 5.45	6.30	AM 4.42	5.24
6.35	7.26	5.34	6.27
7.35	8.10	6.37	7.25
8. 5	8.43	7. 6	7.55
9.32	10.17	7.44	8.25*h*
10.27*h*	11.15	8.25	8.49
11.35	12.20	9. 1	9.25
PM12.33*d*	1. 0	10. 1	10.55
12.35*e*	1.21	11.25	11.55
12.42*d*	1.21	PM12.47	1.32
1.15	2. 0	2.21	3.10
1.50*d*	2.20	2.55	3.40
2.25	3.19	4.29	5.17
2.33*d*	3. 3	5. 9	6. 3
3.55	4.39	6. 5	6.52
4.35	5.24	6.44	7.29
5. 8*e*	5.52	7. 6*d*	7.52
5.32*d*	6.15	7.29	8.11
5.36*eh*	6.20	7.53	8.40

LANGLEY—*continued*.

PAD.	LANGLEY.	LANGLEY.	PAD.
PM 5.42*e*	6.35	PM 9. 9	9.52
6. 7*d*	6.53	9.40	10.22
6.20*e*	6.56	10.20	11. 4
6.38*d*	7.21	11. 9	12. 0
7. 0	7.25	—	—
7. 5*e*	7.49	—	—
7.42	8.25	—	—
8.40	9.23	—	—
9.30	10.14	—	—
10.40	11.23	—	—
11.33	12.16	—	—
12. 3	12.28	—	—

Sunday Trains.

AM 6.30	7.14	AM 6.56	7.40
8.20	9. 5	8.24	9. 8
9.25	10. 8	9.53	10.42
10.37	11.18	PM12.21	1. 5
11.35	12.18	2.14	2.58
PM12.55	1.38	2.57	3.42
2. 0	2.45	4. 8	4.53
3.35	4.18	5. 9	5.52
4.45	5.29	6.25	7.10
6. 5	6.48	7.27	8.12
7.40	8.23	8.29	9.17
10. 5	10.41	9.35	10.22
—	—	10.54	11.38

d Saturdays only.
e Saturdays excepted.
h Departs from or arrives at Bishop's Road Station.

LANGLEY (Northumber-

land), 296 miles.   No through fares. Departures *from* London as for Hexham.   Departures *for* London about 3 times daily.
Map Square 3.

LANGLEY GREEN

(Worcester), 116 miles.   Fares, 24/2*a*, 14/6*c*.   R.T. for two months, 48/4*a*, 29/0*c*.   Departures *from* London as for Smethwick Junction.   Departures *for* London about 8 times daily.
Map Square 17.

LANGLEY MILL (Derby)

from *St. Pancras*, 130 miles.   Fares, 26/5*a*, 15/10*c*.   R. T., double fare. Pop. 4,169.
Map Square 13.

ST.PAN.	L'LEY M.	L'LEY M.	ST.PAN.
AM 2.25	8.50	AM 7.14*r*	10.45
4.25	10. 7	8.12*r*	12.10
9. 0*r*	12.30	8.50*r*	1.20
11. 0*r*	3. 1	PM12.16*r*	4.10
PM 1.50*r*	5.14	1. 1*kr*	4.10
3.30*r*	6.45	1.38*r*	5.30
6. 0	8.19	3.49*r*	7.15
6.15*r*	9.27	5.12*r*	9. 5
12. 0*h*	10.41	8.48	4.20

Sunday Trains.

PM 3.15	6.38	AM 6.51	11.53
—	—	10.58	5.27
—	—	PM 7.50	4.55

h Saturdays midnight only.
k Wednesdays and Saturdays only.
r Restaurant Car.

LANGLOAN (Lanark), 393¼

miles.   No through fares.   Departures *from* London as for Coatbridge.   Departures *for* London about 5 times daily.

LANGPORT EAST

(Somerset), 130 miles.   Fares, 25/10*a*, 16/3*c*.   R. T. for two months, 51/8*a*, 32/6*c*.   Departures *from* London as for Somerton. Departures *for* London about 4 times daily.   Pop. (Langport) 773.
Map Square 22.

LANGPORT WEST

(Somerset), 155½ miles.   Fares, 30/5*a*, 18/3*c*.   R.T. for two months, 60/10*a*.   Departures *from* London as for Taunton.   Departures *for* London about 6 times daily.
Map Square 22.

LANGRICK (Lincoln) from

King's Cross, 112½ miles.   Fares, 23/4*a*, 14/0*c*.   R. T., double fare. Departures *from* London as for Kirkstead.   Departures *for* London about 5 times daily.
Map Square 13.

LANGSTON (Hants)

from *London Bridge*, *Victoria*, and *Clapham Junction*, 79 miles.   Fares, 14/2*a*, 8/6*c*.   R.T. for two months, 28/4*a*.   Departures *from* London as for Hayling Island.   Departures *for* London about 8 times daily.
Map Square 28.

LANGWATHBY (Cumber-

land) from *St. Pancras*, 288 miles. Fares, 56/9*a*, 34/1*c*.   R.T., double fare.   Departures *from* London as for Appleby.   Departures *for* London about 4 times daily.   Pop. 340.
Map Square 7.

LANGWITH (Derby), 147

miles.   Fares, 29/4*a*, 17/7*c*.   R. T., double fare.   Departures *from* London as for Mansfield.   Departures *for* London about 8 times daily.   Pop. 642.
Map Square 13.

LANGWORTH (Lincoln),

136 miles.   Fares, 28/2*a*, 16/11*c*. R. T., double fare.   Departures *from* London as for Lincoln.   Departures *for* London about 5 times daily.
Map Square 13.

Station closed on Sundays.

LAPFORD (Devon), 190

miles.   Fares, 36/11*a*, 22/2*c*.   R. T. for two months, 73/10*a*, 44/4*c*. Departures *from* London as for Eggesford.   Departures *for* London about 6 times daily.   Pop. 456.
Map Square 26.

LAPWORTH (Warwick)

from *Paddington*, 97¾ miles. Fares, 20/3*a*, 12/2*c*. R. T. for two months, 40/6*a*. Pop 853.

Map Square 17.

PAD.	LAPW'TH.	LAPW'TH.	PAD.
AM 5.30	9.38	AM 7.13*r*	10. 0
6.30	10.33	8.47*r*	11. 0
10.40	1.19	10.51*r*	1.25
PM12.50*r*	4. 3	11.56*r*	2. 5
2.10	4.49	PM 2.35*r*	5. 0
4.10*t*	6.19	3.45*t*	5.55
6.10*r*	8.17	5.42*er*	8. 5
7.10*r*	9.17	5.44*dr*	8. 5
7.30	10.29	7.28	10. 0
12.15*k*	7.44	11.54	3.30
12.15*l*	9.28	—	—

Sunday Trains.

AM10.35	1.49	AM11.14*r*	1.40
PM 6. 0*r*	8.40	PM 2.23	6.20
—	—	5.47*r*	9. 0

d Saturdays only.
e Saturdays excepted.
k Saturdays midnight excepted.
l Saturdays midnight only.
r Restaurant Car.
t Tea Car.

LARBERT (Stirling)

from *Euston*, 408¾ miles. Fares, 83/1*a*, 49/10*c*. R.T. for two months, 166/2*a*, 99/8*c*. Pop. 12,389.

Map Square 40.

EUSTON	L'BERT.	L'BERT.	EUSTON
AM 5. 0	4.16	AM10.11*r*	7.30
10. 0*r*	6.51	PM 1.29*r*	10.45
PM 1.30*r*	11.30	4.37*r*	5. 0
11.35*el*	8. 3	11. 8	8. 0
11.35*e*	8.21	—	—
11. 0*d*	8.32	—	—

Sunday Trains.

PM11.35*l*	8. 3	PM 5. 3*r*	5. 0*h*
11.35	8.21	—	—

d Saturdays only.
e Saturdays excepted.
h A.M.
l Sleeping Saloon passengers only.
r Restaurant Car.

LARGO (Fife), 431¾ miles.

Fares, 87/4*a*, 52/5*c*. R. T. for two months, 174/8*a*, 104/10*c*. Departures *from* London as for St. Andrews. Departures *for* London about 3 times daily. Pop. 3,215.

Map Square 41.

LARGS (Ayr), 416¼ miles.

Fares, 84/10*a*, 50/11*c*. R.T. for two months, 169/8*a*, 101/10*c*. Departures *from* London as for Ardrossan. Departures *for* London about 4 times daily. Pop. 12,637.

Map Square 40.

LARKHALL (Lanark), 393½ miles.

Fares, 79/5*a*, 47/8*c*. R. T. for two months, 158/10*a*, 95/4*c*. Departures *from* London as for Hamilton. Departures *for* London about 4 times daily. Pop. 14,974.

Map Square 40.

LARTINGTON (Yorks),

251 miles. Fares, 52/4*a*, 31/5*c*. R. T., double fare. Departures *from* London as for Barnard Castle. Departures *for* London about 3 times daily. Pop. 193.

Map Square 7.

LASSWADE (Midlothian),

390½ miles. No through fares. Departures *from* London as for Edinburgh (Waverley). Departures *for* London about 4 times daily. Pop. 10,349.

LATCHFORD (Cheshire),

183½ miles. Fares, 37/9*a*, 22/8*c*. R. T., double fare. Departures *from* London as for Lymm. Departures *for* London about 8 times daily. Pop. 755.

Map Square 12.

LATCHLEY (Cornwall),

226¾ miles. Fares, 47/11*a*, 28/9*c*. R. T. for two months, 95/10*a*. Departures *from* London as for Calstock. Departures *for* London about 4 times daily.

Map Square 26.

LATIMER ROAD

from *Aldgate* and *Moorgate Street*, 7 miles. Trains run about every 12 minutes throughout the day. *See* back of Map.

Map Square 59.

LAUDER (Berwick), 385

miles. Fares, 78/7*a*, 47/2*c*. R. T. for two months, 157/2*a*. Departures *from* London as for Galashiels. Departures *for* London about 3 times daily. Pop. 1,369.

Map Square 41.

LAUNCESTON (Cornwall)

from *Waterloo*, 223½ miles. Fares, 45/8*a*, 27/5*c*. R.T. for two months, 91/4*a*, 54/10*c*. Pop. 3,981.

Map Square 26.

W'LOO	LAUNCES.	LAUNCES.	W'LOO
AM10. 0*r*	3. 1	AM 7.40*r*	1.56
11. 0*r*	5.11	9.48*r*	3.50
PM 3. 0*r*	8.20	11. 7*r*	4.30
—	—	PM 2. 2*r*	8.30
—	—	4.12	10.50

No Sunday Trains.

r Restaurant Car.

ANOTHER ROUTE

from *Paddington*, 255 miles. Fares, 46/11*a*, 28/2*c*. R.T. for two months, 93/10*a*, 56/4*c*.

PAD.	LAUNCES.	LAUNCES.	PAD.
AM10.30*r*	4.56	AM 9.52*r*	4.35
PM12. 5*r*	8. 7	PM 2.15*r*	9. 0
12. 0*h*	9.21	6.25	7.10

LAUNCESTON—*contd.*

Sunday Trains.

PAD.	LAUNCES.	LAUNCES.	PAD.
PM10. 0	9.21	—	—

h Saturdays midnight excepted.
r Restaurant Car.

LAUNTON (Oxford)

from *Euston*, 63½ miles. Fares, 11/1*a*, 6/8*c*. R.T. for two months, 22/2*a*, 13/4*c*. Departures *from* London as for Verney. Departures *for* London about 5 times daily. Pop. 544.

Map Square 18.

LAURENCEKIRK (Kincardine),

492¼ miles. Fares, 99/5*a*, 59/8*c*. R. T. for two months, 198/10*a*, 119/4*c*. Departures *from* London as for Forfar. Departures *for* London about 3 times daily. Pop. 1,956.

Map Square 38.

LAURISTON (Kincardine),

488½ miles. No through fares. Departures *from* London as for Montrose. Departures *for* London about 3 times daily.

Map Square 38.

LAVANT (Sussex)

from *London Bridge*, *Victoria*, and *Clapham Junction*, 69½ miles. Fares *via* Midhurst or Chichester, 14/7*a*, 8/9*c*. R. T. for two months, 29/2*a*, 17/6*c*. Departures *from* London as for Singleton. Departures *for* London about 6 times daily. Pop. 736.

Map Square 28.

LAVENHAM (Suffolk)

from *Liverpool Street*, 66¾ miles. Fares, 14/0*a*, 8/5*c*. R. T. for two months, 28/0*a*. Pop. 1,963.

Map Square 19.

LP'L. ST.	LAV'HAM	LAV'HAM	L'PL. ST.
AM 6.50	10.14	AM 7.50	9.53
10. 0	12.16	9.36	11.42
PM12.36	2.52	11.34*h*	2. 3
2.15	4.47	PM 2. 2*h*	5. 5
5.42	7.54	4. 2*h*	6.32
—	—	6.13	9.17

No Sunday Trains.

h Via Colchester.

LAVERNOCK (Glamorgan),

158½ miles. No through fares. Departures *from* London as for Penarth. Departures *for* London about 5 times daily. Pop. 121.

Map Square 21.

LAVINGTON (Wilts)

from *Paddington*, 87 miles. Fares, *via* Theale, 18/2*a*, 10/11*c*. R. T. for two months, 36/4*a*. *Via* Westbury. Fares, 19/10*a*, 11/11*c*. R. T. for two months, 39/8*a*, 23/10*c*. Pop. 981.

Map Square 22.

PAD.	LAV'TON.	LAV'TON.	PAD.
AM 7.30	10.17	AM 7. 7	10. 0
10.45	2. 2	8.53*h*	10.52
PM12.30*r*	3.10	10.56	12.55
2. 0*l*	4.29	PM12.19	2.50
3.18	6.55	3.10*lr*	6.50
5. 5*h*	7.14	6. 0*hr*	8.20
6.30	8.55	7.22	10.45
—	—	8.55*l*	2.45
—	—	—	—

Sunday Trains.

PM 2.40*l*	5.31	PM 5.31	9.15
—	—	—	—
—	—	—	—
—	—	—	—
—	—	—	—

h Stops by request.
l Via Westbury.
r Restaurant Car.

LAW (Lanark), 383¼ miles.

Fares, 78/1*a*, 46/10*c*. R. T. for two months, 156/2*a*, 93/8*c*. Departures *from* London as for Carstairs. Departures *for* London about 3 times daily. Pop. 1,996.

Map Square 40.

LAWLEY BANK (Salop),

143¼ miles. Fares, 29/9*a*, 17/10*c*. R. T. for two months, 59/6*a*. Departures *from* London as for Ketley. Departures *for* London about 8 times daily.

Map Square 17.

LAWTON (Cheshire), 154

miles. No through fares. Departures *from* London as for Stoke-on-Trent. Departures *for* London about 4 times daily.

Map Square 12.

LAXFIELD (Suffolk), 102

miles. Fares, 21/6*a*, 12/11*c*. R.T. for two months, 43/0*a*, 25/10*c*. Departures *from* London as for Stradbroke. Departures *for* London about twice daily. Pop. 813.

Map Square 19.

LAZONBY (Cumberland)

from *St. Pancras*, 292¼ miles. Fares, 57/8*a*, 34/7*c*. R.T., double fare. Pop. 715.

Map Square 7.

ST. PAN.	LAZONBY	LAZONBY	ST. PAN.
AM 4.25	1.55	AM 8.37*r*	5.30
9. 0*r*	4.35	11. 5*r*	7.15
PM12.15*r*	7.44	PM 2.22*r*	9.15
11.50*e*	10.28	4.40	4.20
—	—	7.25*e*	7.25
—	—	—	—
—	—	—	—
—	—	—	—

Sunday Trains.

PM11.45	10.28	—	—
—	—	—	—

e Saturdays excepted.
r Restaurant Car.

LEA (Lincoln) from *King's Cross*,

143¼ miles. Fares, 29/7*a*, 17/9*c*. R. T., double fare. Departures *from* London as for Lincoln. Departures *for* London about 4 times daily. Pop. 184.

Map Square 13.

LEA BRIDGE (Essex)

from *Liverpool Street*, 5¼ miles. Fares, 0/10*a*, 0/8*b*, 0/6*c*. R. T. for two days, 1/8*a*, 1/4*b*, 0/10½*c*. Pop. 19,334. *See* pp. 526, 527.

Map Square 53.

LEADBURN (Midlothian),

391¾ miles. No through fares. Departures *from* London as for Peebles. Departures *for* London about 3 times daily.

Map Square 41.

LEADENHAM (Lincoln)

from *King's Cross*, 118 miles. Fares, 24/4*a*, 14/7*c*. R. T., double fare. Departures *from* London as for Lincoln. Departures *for* London about 5 times daily. Pop. 537.

Map Square 13.

LEADGATE (Durham), 266¾

miles. Fares, 56/1*a*, 33/8*c*. R. T., double fare. Departures *from* London as for Durham. Departures *for* London about 5 times daily. Pop. 5,163.

Map Square 3.

LEADHILLS (Lanark), 357¾

miles. No through fares. Departures *from* London as for Lockerbie. Departures *for* London about 3 times daily. Pop. 812.

Map Square 43.

LEAGRAVE (Beds) from

St. Pancras, 32¾ miles. Fares, 6/11*a*, 4/2*c*. R. T., double fare. Pop. 1,270.

Map Square 18.

ST. PAN	L'GRAVE	L'GRAVE	ST. PAN.
AM 6.25	7.48	AM 7. 8	8.28
8.25	9.19	8.16	9.13
9.25*d*	10.40	9. 7	10. 5
11. 0*r*	12. 7	PM12.27*r*	1.20
PM12.30	1.29	2.30	3.25
1.33*d*	2.41	3.22*d*	5.10
3.35	4.44	5.24	6.30
4.40	5.50	7. 2*r*	8.22
5.40*e*	6.32	9. 4	10. 5
6.35	7.39	10.39	11.45
7.50	8.57	—	—
8.25*d*	10.32	—	—
—	—	—	—
—	—	—	—
—	—	—	—

Sunday Trains.

AM 8. 0	9.28	AM 8.43	10.15
PM 4.35	5.58	PM 7.21	8.30
—	—	—	—
—	—	—	—
—	—	—	—
—	—	—	—
—	—	—	—

d Saturdays only.
e Saturdays excepted.
r Restaurant Car.

LEA GREEN (Lancs) 191¾

miles. Fares, 39/10*a*, 23/11*c*. R. T. for two months, 79/8*a*, 47/10*c*. Departures *from* London as for Earlestown. Departures *for* London about 4 times daily.

Map Square 12.

LEALHOLME (Yorks),

243¼ miles. No through fares. Departures *from* London as for Whitby or Stockton-on-Tees. Departures *for* London about 3 times daily.

Map Square 8.

LEAMINGTON SPA

(Warwick) from *Paddington*, 87½ miles. Fares, 18/2*a*, 10/11*c*. R. T. for two months, 36/4*a*, 21/10*c*. Pop. 28,946.

Map Square 17.

PAD.	LEAM'T'N.	LEAM'T'N.	PAD.
AM 5.30	9. 6	AM12.30*g*	3.30
6.30	9.43	6.30	9.50
9.10	10.44	8. 7*r*	10. 0
10.40	12.14	9.29*r*	11. 0
10.45	1.53	9.36	12. 5
PM12.50*r*	2.20	10.48	12.25
2.10	3.44	11.54*r*	1.25
4.10*t*	5.41	PM12.34*r*	2. 5
6.10*r*	7.41	1. 0	3.50
7.10*r*	8.40	1.17*r*	4.15
7.30	9.51	3.24*r*	5. 0
12.15	3.10	4.24*t*	5.55
—	—	4.41	7.20
—	—	6.31*r*	8. 5
—	—	6.40*r*	9.15
—	—	8.29	10. 0

Sunday Trains.

AM10.35	1.20	AM12.30	3.30
PM12.50*r*	2.21	PM12. 9*r*	1.40
4.10	6.44	3.10	6.20
6. 0*r*	7.31	7. 8*r*	9. 0

g Mondays excepted.
r Restaurant Car.
t Tea Car.

ANOTHER ROUTE from

Euston, 97½ miles. Fares as above.

EUSTON	LEAM'T'N.	LEAM'T'N.	EUSTON
AM 2.30	7. 2	AM 7.29*r*	10. 0
5. 0	8.51	8.52*r*	11. 0
6.45	9.55	9.10*d*	12.20
9.15*r*	11.50	9.25*e*	12.32
10. 0	12.51	9.25*dh*	12.40
11.30*dr*	1.43	10.47*r*	1. 0
11.30*er*	2. 0	11.30*r*	2.20
12. 0*nr*	3. 2	PM 1.20	4.15
PM 2.20*t*	4.24	1.50*t*	4.35
2.50*t*	4.55	3.24*t*	5.50
4. 5*t*	6.29	4.53*t*	7.20
4.45*r*	6.47	5.40*r*	8.20
5.50*r*	8.16	7.19*d*	11.35
7. 0*r*	9.45	7.47*er*	10.20
11.50*e*	3.49	10.20*e*	4. 0
—	—	10.20*d*	5. 0
—	—	—	—

Sunday Trains.

AM 9.15	2.42	AM 8.40	12.25
PM 1. 0*r*	3.32	11.30*r*	1.45
5.10*r*	7.55	11.55	5. 5
11.50	3.49	PM 5.30*r*	8.20
—	—	8.25	5. 0

d Saturdays only.
e Saturdays excepted.
h Via Northampton.
n Noon.
r Restaurant Car.
t Tea Car.

Taxi Cabs can be hired to meet any train at this station by letter, or Telephone No. 406, Messrs. Regent Garage, Parade.

LEAMINGTON SPA—continued.

Regent Hotel. Premier Hotel of the Midlands. Largest and best Family Hotel. Most centrally situated. Re-modelled. Lifts. Charming garden. Largest Garage in district. *See advt. p.* **225.**

The Clarendon. High-class Family Hotel. Near Pump Room. Lift. Garage. Tel. 663.—Apply MANAGERESS.

Manor House Hotel. High Class. Extensive Grounds facing Pump Room Gardens. Near Railway Stations. Lift. Proprietors. R. LAMPLOUGH & SONS.

Boarding House (High Class), Langton House, Leam Terrace. South aspect; near Parade and Gardens. Well-appointed. Bath and Smoking Room. Mrs. BROWN and Miss BRYAN.

LEAMSIDE (Durham), 254 miles. ...res, 52/11a, 31/9c. R.T., double fare. Departures *from* London as for Ferryhill or Durham. Departures *for* London about 10 times daily. *Map Square 7.*

LEA ROAD (Lancs), 212 miles. Fares, 44 2a, 26/6c. R.T. for two months, 88 4a. Departures *from* London as for Preston. Departures *for* London about 5 times daily. *Map Square 12.*

LEASOWE (Cheshire), 203¾ miles. No through fares. Departures *from* London as for Hooton. Departures *for* London about 4 times daily. *Map Square 11.*

LEATHERHEAD (Surrey) from *Victoria*, 19¼ miles, and *London Bridge*, 21¼ miles. Fares, 3/4a, 2/0c. R.T. for eight days, 6/8a, 4/0c. Pop. 5,821. *See pp.* 565, 566, 571-574. *Map Square 23.*

ANOTHER ROUTE from *Waterloo*, 18¼ miles. Fares as above. *See pp. 583, 584.*

Swan Hotel. Old-fashioned, with up-to-date management. Revised moderate prices. Carriages. Garage. Phone 92 Leatherhead. Write A. G. DOVEY for terms.

LEATON (Salop), 156¾ miles. Fares, 32/8a, 19/7c. R.T. for two months, 65/4a. Departures *from* London as for Shrewsbury. Departures *for* London about 5 times daily. Pop. 361. *Map Square 17.*

LECHLADE (Gloucester) from *Paddington*, 85¼ miles. Fares, 17/8a, 10/8c. R.T. for two months, 35/4a, 21/4c. Departures *from* London as for Fairford. Departures *for* London about 4 times daily. Pop. 1,167. *Map Square 22.*

LEDBURY (Hereford) from *Paddington*, via Gloucester, 133 miles. Fares, 26/11a, 16/2c. R.T. for two months, 53/10a. Pop. 3,152. *Map Square 17.*

PAD.	LEDB'Y.	LEDR'Y.	PAD.
AM 1. 0g	7.26	AM 8. 0h	11.15
5.30	10.14	8.10	12.20
9. 0	1.24	9.23h	2.12
9.45h	1.44	10.40r	2.40
10.45	4.45	PM 1.50	5. 0
PM 1.30hr	5. 5	4. 4hr	9.15
1.35hr	5.37	5.20	10.25
3.15t	7.45	8.20	3.30
4.45ht	7.58	—	—
6. 5hr	9.53	—	—
6.55hhk	11.46	—	—

Sunday Trains.

AM10.35hr 3.11		PM 4.53hr 9.48	
PM 9.15	7.26	—	—
—	—	—	—

g Mondays excepted.
h Via Worcester.
k Thursdays, Fridays and Saturdays only.
r Restaurant Car.
t Tea Car.

Feathers Hotel, Ledbury. Old established. First-class Hunting centre. Carriages, Cars, Garage. Bus meets trains. Telephone 6. Moderate Tariff.

LEDSHAM (Cheshire), 186 miles. Fares, 38/10a, 23/3c. R.T. for two months, 77/6a. Departures *from* London as for Chester. Departures *for* London about 8 times daily Pop 1,327. *Map Square 12.*

LEDSTON (Yorks), 179 miles. No through fares. Departures *from* London as for Castleford. Departures *for* London about 5 times daily. Pop. 250. *Map Square 13.*

LEE (London) from *Charing Cross*, 8¼ miles. Fares, 1/7a, 1/3b, 0/11½c. R.T. for two days, 3/2a, 2/6b, 1/11c. From *Cannon Street*, Fares, 1/5a, 1/1b, 0/10c. R.T. for two days, 2/10a, 2/2b, 1/8c. Pop. 26,915. *See pp. 552-554. Map Squares 23 and 80.*

LEEBOTWOOD (Salop), 161¾ miles. Fares, 31/11a, 19/2c. R.T. for two months, 63/10a, 38/4c. Departures *from* London as for Shrewsbury. Departures *for* London about 3 times daily. Pop. 189. *Map Square 17.*

LEEDS (CENTRAL) (Yorks) from *King's Cross*, 185½ miles. Fares, 38/7a, 23/2c. R.T., double fare. Pop. 458,320. *Map Square 12.*

KING'S +	LEEDS	LEEDS	KING'S +
AM 4.45	9.19	AM 7.50r	11.30
7.15r	11.20	9. 0	1. 5
10.10r	1.56	10.15r	1.55
11.15k	2.40	10.55	3.50
PM 1.30r	5.12	11.50k	3.15
1.50r	6.30	12. 0r	4.45
4. 0r	8. 5	PM 1.10r	5. 0
5.45r	9.35	1.17	6.25
10.45d	4.55l	3.15r	7.10
10.45e	2.57	5.30r	9.25
—	—	10.23	3.25
—	—	10.35el	5.40
—	—	10.35d	6. 0

Sunday Trains.

12. 0nr 4.30		AM11. 0r 3.45	
PM 5. 0	9.32	PM 1.10	5.55
10.45	2.57	5.40r	10.20
—	—	10.20l	5.40

d Saturdays only.
e Saturdays excepted.
k First and third Class Pullman Cars only.
l Leeds (New Station).
n Noon.
r Restaurant Car.

ANOTHER ROUTE (WELLINGTON) from *St. Pancras*, 196 miles. Fares as above.

ST. PAN.	LEEDS	LEEDS	ST. PAN.
AM 4.25	10.11	AM 2.43	7.25
9. 0r	1.22	3.48	7.50
9.50r	1.50	8. 0r	12.10
11.45r	4. 0	10. 0r	2.10
PM12.15r	4.10	10.50r	4.10
1.50r	6.12	PM 1. 0r	5.30
3.30r	7.58	2.35r	6.35
5. 0r	9.25	2.53r	7.15
6.15r	10.49	3.45r	7.57
9.15	1.43	5.15r	9.15
9.30e	2. 4	10. 0	4.20
11.45	3.45	—	—

Sunday Trains.

AM10.50r 4.52		AM 3. 6	8. 5
PM 3.15	8. 5	4.23	8.57
9.15	1.48	7. 5r	5. 2
9.30	2. 4	PM12.15	5.27
11.45	3.46	4.10r	9.43
—	—	10. 0	4.55

e Saturdays excepted.
r Restaurant Car.

LEEDS—*continued.*

ANOTHER ROUTE (NEW)
from *Euston*, 220¼ miles.   Fares as above.

EUSTON	LEEDS	LEEDS	EUSTON
AM12.25	8.45	AM 5.50*r*	12.50
2.35	11. 0	7.45*r*	1.15
5. 0	1. 8	9.22*r*	3.10
8.45*r*	3. 7	9.30*r*	3.55
10.40*r*	4.21	10.48*dr*	5.50
11.50*r*	5.57	PM12.15e*r*	6. 0
12. 0*nr*	6.50	12.15*dr*	6.15
PM 1.30*r*	9.10	1. 7*r*	7.30
4. 5*r*	10.45	2.23*r*	8.10
6. 5*r*	11.25	3.23*r*	10. 0
8. 0e	2.40	3.50e*r*10.10	
8.45*d*	2.40	8. 0	5. 0
11.50*d*	10.10	10.40	5.50

Sunday Trains.

PM12.10*r*	7.25	AM 6.30	4. 0
12.30*r*	10.50	10.15*r*	5.45
7.50*r*	2.40	PM12. 5*r*	7.30
—	—	5. 0	5. 0
—	—	10.40	5.50

d Saturdays only.
e Saturdays excepted.
n Noon.
r Restaurant Car.

Victory Hotel & Restaurant
(Trust Houses, Ltd.).   Best Restaurant in the North.   Telephone 20191.
See advt. p. **225.**

Queen's Hotel. Yorkshire's
Leading Hotel. Covered way from Station. Every modern convenience. One of the "Midland Hotels."
ARTHUR TOWLE, Manager.
See advt. p. **226.**

Golden Lion Hotel. Telephone 26911. Central position.
Stock rooms. Electric Light.
TRUST HOUSES, Ltd.

Great Northern Hotel,
adjoins Central Railway Station.
Handsome Lounge. Well appointed Restaurant and Grill Room, Stock Rooms, and Billiard Room. Elevator. Unrivalled Cuisine. Moderate Charges.
Telegraphic address. "Northness, Leeds." Telephone Nos. Local 20,579, Trunk 20,578.

Regent Court Residential
Club, Headingley, Leeds. Service Flats or single rooms, furnished or unfurnished. Smoke Room, Lounges, Dining-room. Extensive grounds. Three Tennis Courts. Dancing. 'Phone 349 Headingley.
Apply—   MANAGERESS.

Leeds—Cromer Hall
Residential Chambers Co. (Ltd.). Cromer Terrace, Mount Preston. For Ladies and Gentlemen. Five minutes from Town Hall. Hotel advantages. Rooms reserved for Visitors. Telephone, 25,921.
Apply—   LADY MANAGER.

Lancashire and Cheshire
Insurance Corporation, Limited. 26/27, Bond Street. Telephone 21778.
See advt. p. 3 of cover.

Norwich Union Mutual, the
outstanding British Life Office. Reserves at 2½ per cent. Savings Bank Chambers, Bond Street, Leeds.
See advt. p. 6 of cover.

Remington Typewriters.
Local branch, 29, Park Lane.
See advt. inside yellow cover, p. 2.

LEEGATE (Cumberland)
31¼ miles. No through fares. Departures *from* London as for Maryport. Departures *for* London about 5 times daily.
Map Square 6.

LEEK (Stafford) from *Euston*,
153¾ miles. Fares, 32/1*a*, 19/3*c*. R. T. for two months, 64/2*a*. Pop. 17,213.
Map Square 2.

EUSTON	LEEK	LEEK	EUSTON
AM 2.35	8.53	AM 7.42e*r*12. 5	
5. 0	10.42	7.42*dr*12.20	
8.45*r*	12.46	8.32*r*	12.50
10.40*r*	3.20	9.34*r*	2.20
12. 0e*nr*5.35		11.10*dr*	3.10
PM 2.50*t*	6.48	PM12.15e*r*	3.55
6.30*dr*11.43		12.30*dr*	3.55
7.55*lr*11.43		1.55*r*	6.15
—	—	3.40	9.20
—	—	5.50*dr*10. 0	
—	—	5.55e*r*10. 0	
—	—	8.10	5. 0
—	—	10.10*y*	5.40

Sunday Trains.

PM12.10*r*	5.40	AM10.15	4. 0
—	—	PM 7. 2	5. 0
—	—	—	—
—	—	—	—

d Saturdays only.
e Saturdays excepted.
h Wednesdays excepted.
k Wednesdays only.
l Thursdays only.
n Noon.
r Restaurant Car.
t Tea Car.
y Thursdays and Saturdays only.

LEEMING BAR (Yorks),
223¾ miles. Fares, 46/8*a*, 28/0*c*. R. T., double fare. Departures *from* London as for Leyburn. Departures *for* London about 6 times daily.
Map Square 7.

LEE-ON-SOLENT
(Hants) from *Waterloo*, via Eastleigh, 90¾ miles. Fares, 16/1*a*, 9/8*c*. R. T. for two months, 32/2*a*, 19/4*c*.
Map Square 28.

W'LOO	LEE-ON-S.	LEE-ON-S.	W'LOO
AM 5.40	9.25	AM11.20	2.20
9.30	1.10	PM 5.25*r*	8.20
11.30*r*	3.10	7. 0	10.50
PM 1.30*s*	4.22	8. 5	11.28
3.30*s*	6.30		

No Sunday Trains.

r Restaurant Car.
s Refreshments served.

ANOTHER ROUTE from
Waterloo, via Meon Valley, 79¾ miles. Fares as above.

W'LOO	LEE-ON-S.	LEE-ON-S.	W'LOO
AM 4.50	9.25	AM 9.40	1.40
7. 0	10.55	PM 1.20	5.46
9.20	1.10	3.43	7. 7
11.20	3.10	7. 0	11.10
PM 3.15	6.30		

No Sunday Trains.

Pier Hotel. Facing Sea.
Good Safe Bathing. Fishing. Golf. Telephone 51. Proprietor—
G. B. CUNDELL (late Royal Pier Hotel, Southampton).

LEES (Lancs), 190 miles.
Fares, 38/7*a*, 23/2*c*. R. T., double fare. Departures *from* London as for Oldham (Clegg Street). Departures *for* London about 5 times daily. Pop. 4,789.
Map Square 12.

LEGACY (Denbigh), 184
miles. No through fares. Departures *from* London as for Rhos. Departures *for* London about 4 times daily.

LEGBOURNE ROAD
(Lincoln), 138¾ miles. Fares, 28/9*a*, 17/3*c*. R. T. double fare. Departures *from* London as for Willoughby. Departures *for* London about 5 times daily. Pop. (Legbourne) 357.
Map Square 13.

LEICESTER (LONDON
ROAD) from *St. Pancras*, 99 miles. Fares, 20/2*a*, 12/1*c*. R. T., double fare. Pop. 234,190.
Map Square 18.

ST. PAN.	LEICES.	LEICES.	ST. PAN.
AM 2.25	4.30	AM 2. 0*g*	4.20
4.25	7.10	2.10*f*	4.55
8.25*r*	10.34	2.10*g*	5. 5
9.50*r*	11.39	3.10*g*	6. 0
10.25*r*	12.14	5.30	7.25
11.45*r*	1.59	7.52*r*	9.57
PM12.15*r*	2. 4	8.51*r*	11. 0
12.25*r*	2.14	9.36*r*	11.35
1.25*r*	3.32	10.23*r*	12.10*l*
2.25*r*	4.14	11.28*r*	1.30
3.30*r*	6. 4	11.55*r*	1.45
4.25*r*	6.24	PM12.23*r*	2.10
5.35*r*	7.48	12.49	3.25
6.25*r*	8.18	1. 5*r*	4.10
8.25	11.15	2.33*r*	4.20
11.45	1.34	2.38	5.20
11.50	2. 8	3.45*r*	5.45
12. 0	2.43	4.10*r*	6.15
—	—	4.48*r*	6.35
—	—	6. 7*r*	7.57
—	—	6.43*r*	8.35
—	—	7.28*r*	9.15
—	—	8. 0*r*	10. 5

Sunday Trains.

AM 8. 0	12.20	AM 2. 0	4.20
10.50*r*	1. 8	2.10	5. 5
11.15*r*	1.29	3.10	6. 0
PM 1.35	4.40	6.48	8.57
3.15	5.16	9.15	11.53
6.15*r*	8.25	PM 2.52*r*	5. 2
8.25	11.15	3.38	5.27
11.45	1.34	3.45	6.27
11.55	2.43	4.20	8.30
—	—	7.53*r*	9.52
—	—	8.10	11. 7

f Mondays only.
g Mondays excepted.
r Restaurant Car.

LEICESTER—continued.

ANOTHER ROUTE (CENTRAL) from *Marylebone*, 103 miles. Fares as above.

M'BONE.	LEICES.	LEICES.	M'BONE.
AM 2.52	4.26	AM 1.46g	3.57
6.45	10.19	6.10	9.46
8.45r	11. 4	8.18	10.36
10. 0r	12. 9	9.18r	11.10
PM12.15r	2.33	10.59r	1.13
3.20r	5. 9	PM12.49r	3. 0
5. 0r	6.52	1.20	4.56
6.20r	8.14	4.48r	6.38
6.25e	9.51	6.44r	8.55
6.25d	9.58	7.46r	9.55
7.30d	11.39	—	—
10. 0d	12.12	—	—
10. 5e	12.17	—	—

Sunday Trains.

AM 9.30	12.58	AM 1.46	3.57
11.15r	1.24	6.15	10.13
PM 5.30r	7.44	PM. 3.33r	5.40
6.30	10.31	5. 0	8.58
—	—	8.12r	10.24

d Saturdays only.
e Saturdays excepted.
g Mondays excepted.
r Restaurant Car.

ANOTHER ROUTE (LONDON ROAD) from *Euston, via Nuneaton*, 115¼ miles. Fares as above.

EUSTON	LEICES.	LEICES.	EUSTON
AM 5. 0	8.23	AM 5.50	10. 0
6.45	10.18	7.57	11. 0
8.45r	11.52	9.38	12.50
10. 0dr	1.45	PM12. 7r	4.15
10. 0	2. 8	1.10	5.35
12. 0nr	4. 0	2.15t	6. 0
PM 2.50t	6.19	5.10r	8.10
4. 5t	7.33	5.55r	9.20
5:20r	8.23	6.53r	10.45
6.30er10. 7		11. 0	5. 0
7. 0dr10. 7		—	—
9.30	3.45	—	—

Sunday Trains.

AM 9.15	3.20	PM 1.12	5. 5
PM 3.50	8.33	5.45r	8.55
9.15	3.45	9.30	5. 0

d Saturdays only.
e Saturdays excepted.
n Noon.
r Restaurant Car.
t Tea Car.

Bell Hotel. Telephone 2718-2719. Recently much enlarged and improved. New Grill Room and London Orchestra. Banqueting Hall. All-round first-class accommodation. Central Heating. Electric Light. Garage and Stabling. TRUST HOUSES, Ltd.

Grand Hotel. Magnificent First Class Family and Commercial Hotel of 100 Bedrooms in heart of City, close to Railway Stations, yet perfectly quiet. Beautifully appointed and luxuriously furnished. Spacious Stock and Public Rooms. Very moderate Tariff. Telephones, 4322-4323-4324. Apply, MANAGER.

LEICESTER SQUARE

(Hampstead and Hammersmith and Finsbury Park Tubes). See back of Map.

LEIGH (Essex) from Fenchurch Street, 33¾ miles.

Fares, 5/3a, 3/2c. R. T. for two months, 10/6a, 6/4c. Pop. 7,883.
Map Square 24.

FEN. ST.	LEIGH	LEIGH	FEN. ST.
AM 5. 5	6.27	AM 4.33	5.35
5.37	7.43	5.33	6.43
6.52	8.43	6.28	7.34
7.42	8.54	7. 0	8. 6
7.53	9.21	7. 9	8.15
9.18	10.51	7.23	8.22h
9.57h	11.16	7.39	8.44
10.13h	11.26	7.54	8.53
10.17	11.48	8. 6	9.10
10.45	11.59	8.31	9.30
11.57d	12.54	8.38	9.39
PM12. 9	1.11	8.44	9.54h
12.43d	1.40	8.54	9.49
12.55d	1.48	9.12	10. 1
1. 0e	1.51	9.22	10.18h
1. 0d	1.57	9.34	10.35
1. 0eh	2.10	9.55	10.57h
1. 5d	2. 4	10.38	11.40
1.11d	2.18	11.29e	12.22
1.25d	2.26	11.29d	12.38
1.48d	2.45	12. 0	1.11h
1.56d	2.52	PM12.58	1.56
2. 6	3. 0	2.28	3.28
2.26d	3.27	2.41d	3.51
2.30	3.57	3.40	4.54h
3. 8d	4. 8	4. 0d	5.12
3.16h	4.34	4.36	5.49
3.45d	4.43	4.43	6.33
4. 7	4.57	5.39	6.45
4.27	5.26	6.22e	7.29h
4.57e	5.47	6.31	7.51
5. 6e	5.58	7.16	8.30
5.16	6. 7	7.24	9.15
5.25e	6.29	8.12	9.17h
5.32	7. 6	8.44	10. 8
5.58e	6.37	9.10d	10.20
5.46e	6.46	9.22	10.30
6. 7e	6.59	9.40	11.23h
6.17e	7.12	10.32	11.40
6.26	7.25	—	—
6.53e	7.54	—	—
6.53d	8. 8	—	—
7.20	8.17	—	—
8. 0e	8.58	—	—
8.45	9.50	—	—
9.19eh10.35		—	—
9.20d	10.35	—	—
10.15	11.13	—	—
11.27e	12.31	—	—
11.27d	12.40	—	—
12.20	1.19	—	—

Sunday Trains.

AM 9.15	10.21	AM 7.59	9. 6
9.45	11.21	8.23	10.18
10.40	11.44	10.24	11.35
11. 8h	12.19	PM12.1	1.10
11.45	12.45	2.26	3.47
PM 2. 7	3.53	4.20	5.30
2.45	4.19	4.28	6. 0
4.30	6.15	5.36	7.16
5. 7h	6.33	5.52	7.45
6.10	7.34	7.18	8.32
7.22	8.31	7.49	8.59h
8.28	9.36	8.49	10. 9
8.45	10.35	8.57	10.23
9.45	11.11	9.50	10.48
10.36h	11.41	9.59	11.22

d Saturdays only.
e Saturdays excepted.
h Departs from or arrives at Mark Lane Station.

LEIGH—continued.

ANOTHER ROUTE from *St. Pancras*, 39½ miles. Fares, 5/0a, 3/0c. R. T. for two months, 10/0a, 6/0c.

ST PAN.	LEIGH	LEIGH	ST. PAN.
AM 9.30	11.16	AM 8.24	10.10
PM12.20	2.10	12. 0	1.48
2.50	4.54	PM 3.40	5.23
6.40	8. 8	6.14	7.45
—	—	—	—

Sunday Trains.

AM10.10	11.53	PM 7.26	9.18

Grand Hotel. Only fully licensed hotel in Leigh-on-Sea. Family and residential. Special terms for winter months. Billiard room and ball room. Write for tariff or Phone 150. Proprietor, S. J. TINNER.

Cliffs Hotel. Private and Residential. Finest position facing sea. Excellent table. Terms from 3 guineas. 10/6 per day. 'Phone 44. Proprietor, E. BEECROFT.

House Agent, WILBER L. BULLIVANT, 51, Broadway. Furnished and Unfurnished Houses, Land, Property Auctions. Valuations, Surveys. Map of town free. Telephone, 124 Leigh-on-Sea.

LEIGH (Lancs) from Euston, 193¾ miles.

Fares, 39/7a, 23/9c. R. T., double fare. Pop. (Leigh) 45,545.
Map Square 12.

EUSTON	LEIGH	LEIGH	EUSTON
AM12.25	7.33	AM 6.26er12. 5	
2.35	8.38	6.26dr12.20	
5. 0e	11.55	8. 0r	1.45
8.30r	2.18	10.15r	4.15
10.40r	3.43	11.40t	5.50
11.50r	5.45	PM 2.25r	7.30
PM 1.30dr	6.23	8.22e	5. 0
1.30er	6.38	9.22d	5. 0
2.35t	7.56	—	—
5.20r	11. 4	—	—

Sunday Trains.

AM11.45	7.47	AM10.10r	7.30
—	—	PM 6.50	5. 0

d Saturdays only.
e Saturdays excepted.
r Restaurant Car.
t Tea Car.

LEIGH (Stafford), 155¾ miles.

Fares, 31/6a,18/11c. R. T. for two months, 63/0a. Departures from London as for Longton. Departures for London about twice daily. Pop. 746.
Map Square 12.

LEIGH COURT (Worcester), 125¼ miles. Fares, 24/10*a*, 14/11*c*. R. T. for two months, 49/8*a*. Departures *from* London as for Bromyard. Departures *for* London about 5 times daily. Pop. (Leigh) 1,217.
Map Square 17.

LEIGHTON BUZZARD (Bedford) from *Euston*, 40¼ miles. Fares, 5/0*c*. R. T. for two months, 16/8*a*, 10/0*c*. Pop. 6,795.
Map Square 18.

EUSTON	LEIGH. B.	LEIGH. B.	EUSTON
AM 5.25	7.17	AM 6.55	8.24
7.35	9. 7	7.42	9. 6
8.35	10.10	8. 2*e*	9.22
9.30	10.30	8.22	9.40
10.50	12.17	8.55*e*	9.52
PM12.15	1.41	9.24	10.15
12.50*d*	2.10	10.11	11.40
1.35*d*	3. 7	PM12.13	1.50
2. 0	3.36	1.46*h*	2.45
4. 2	5. 6	2.53	4.30
4.10	5.36	4.28	5.35
4.55*l*	6.13	4.38	6.15
5. 0*e*	6.13	6.48	7.55
5.32	6.27	7.10	8.35
6.10*e*	7.13	8.16	10.50
6.10*d*	7.23	10.14	11.35
6.30*e*	7.20	—	—
7.15	8.45	—	—
9.55*e*	11.17	—	—
9.55*d*	11.24	—	—
11.50*f*	12.53	—	—
12.10*dm*1. 5	—	—	—

Sunday Trains.

AM 8.15	9·50	AM 7.45	9.22
PM 2.15	3.37	11.49	1.20
3.50	5. 9	PM 4.33	5.50
6.10	7.32	6.50	8.15
6.45	7·50	8.20	9.45
9.40	11. 0	9. 5	10.10
—	—	9.15	10.40

d Saturdays only.
e Saturdays excepted.
f Mondays only.
h Thursdays and Saturdays only.
m Midnight.

LEISTON (Suffolk) from *Liverpool Street*, 95 miles. Fares, 20/0*a*, 12/0*c*. R. T. for two months, 40/0*a*. Departures *from* London as for Aldeburgh. Departures *for* London about 7 times daily. Pop. 4,632.
Map Square 19.

LEITH (Central) (Midlothian), 392 miles. Fares, 81/8*a*, 49/0*c*. R. T. for two months, 163/4*a*, 98/0*c*. Departures *from* London as for Edinburgh (Waverley). Departures *for* London about 9 times daily.
Map Square 41.

LELANT (Cornwall) from *Paddington*, 300½ miles. Fares, 62/3*a*, 37/4*c*. R. T. for two months, 124/6*a*, 74/5*c*. Departures *from* London as for Carbis Bay. Departures *for* London about 5 times daily. Pop. 1,599.
Map Square 25.

LEMAN STREET from *Fenchurch Street*, ⅓ mile. Fares, 0/2½*a*, 0/2*b*, 0/1½*c*. R. T. for two days, 0/5*a*, 0/4*b*, 0/2½*c*. See pp. 524, 525.
Map Square 61.

LEMINGTON (Northumberland), 274¾ miles. Fares, 57/4*a*, 34/5*c*. R.T. for two months, 114/8*a*, 68/10*c*. Departures *from* London as for Newcastle-on-Tyne. Departures *for* London about 7 times daily.

LENHAM (Kent) from *Victoria*, *Holborn Viaduct*, and *St. Paul's*, 49 miles. Fares, 10/5*a*, 8/4*b*, 6/3*c*. R. T. for two months, 20/10*a*, 16/8*b*, 12/6*c*. Pop. 1,947.
Map Square 24.

VICT. (S.E.&C.)	Leave HOL. V.	ST. PL.'s	Arr. at LENHAM.
AM —	6.40	6.42	8.57
9.45	—	—	11.31
11. 4	10.58	11. 0	1.19
PM —	1.24*d*	1.30*d*	3. 5
2.12*e*	—	—	3.40
2.40*d*	—	—	4.51
2.50*e*	—	—	5. 8
4.25*e*	—	—	5.55
e5.15*h*	—	e5.21*k*	6.57
d5.20*h*	—	d5.26*k*	7. 2
7.22	—	—	8.46
—	7.22*d*	7.24*d*	9.30

Sunday Trains.

AM —	8. 0	—	10.22
9.35	—	—	11. 4
PM 5.15	—	—	6.49
6.35	6.40	—	8.45

Trains from Lenham.

Leave LENH.	St Pl.	Arrive at HOL. V.	VICT.
AM 7.22	—	—	8.50
8.11	9.52	9.55	—
8.45*e*	10.21	10.23	10.16
8.52*d*	10.41	10.43	—
10.58	12.59	1. 2	12.49
PM12.29	—	—	2.40
2.12	—	—	3.37
4.51	6.58	7. 0	—
6.35	—	—	8.51
9.35	11.43	11.45	—

Sunday Trains.

AM 8.48	—	—	10.48
PM 1.51	—	—	3.50
7.28	—	9. 9	—

d Saturdays only.
e Saturdays excepted.
h Departs from or arrives at Charing + (S.E. & C.R.).
k Departs from or arrives at London Bridge (S.E. & C.R.).

LENNOXTOWN (Stirling), 438½ miles. No through fares. Departures *from* London as for Glasgow. Departures *for* London about 4 times daily. Pop. 2,536.
Map Square 40.

LENTRAN (Inverness), 573½ miles. No through fares. Departures *from* London as for Inverness. Departures *for* London 3 times daily.
Map Square 34.

LENWADE (Norfolk) from *King's Cross*, 155½ miles. Fares, 23/7*a*, 14/2*c*. R. T. for two months, 47/2*a*. Departures *from* London as for Guestwick. Departures *for* London about 3 times daily.
Map Square 19.

LENZIE (Dumbarton), 433½ miles. Fares, 81/11*a*, 49/2*c*. R. T. for two months, 163/10*a*, 98/4*c*. See trains to Falkirk, and thence at frequent intervals. Pop. 1,159.
Map Square 40.

LEOMINSTER (Hereford) from *Paddington*, 147½ miles. Fares (*via* Bromyard), 29/5*a*, 17/8*c*. R. T. for two months, 58/10*a*. (*Via Hereford*), 30/0*a*, 18/0*c*. R. T. for two months, 60/0*a*, 36/0*c*. Pop. 5,539.
Map Square 17.

PAD.	LEOMIN.	LEOMIN.	PAD.
AM 1. 0*g*	9.42	AM 7. 0*h*	11.15
5.30*h*	11.45	8.50*h*	2.12
9.10*lr*	2.35	PM12.20*hr*	4.15
10.40*lr*	3.42	1.42*lr*	8. 5
10.45*r*	4.50	3.42*r*	8.45
PM 1.30*r*	5.40	4.15*hr*	9.15
2.10*lr*	7. 4	4.50*r*	10. 0
3.15*t*	8.23	8.23*l*	3.30
4.45*ht*	8.46	—	—
12.15*k*	8. 8	—	—

Sunday Trains.

PM12.50*lr*	6.42	AM10. 8*l*	6.20

g Mondays excepted.
h Via Bromyard and Worcester.
k Saturday midnight excepted.
l Via Shrewsbury.
r Restaurant Car.
t Tea Car.

ANOTHER ROUTE from *Euston*, 200½ miles. Fares, 31/11*a*, 19/2*c*. R. T. for two months, 63/10*a*.

EUSTON	LEOMIN.	LEOMIN.	EUSTON
AM 5. 0	11.49	AM 7.58*r*	2.20
6.45	2.35	9.42*r*	3.10
10.40*r*	3.42	PM12.12*r*	6.15
PM 1.15*r*	7. 4	1.42*r*	9.20
2.20*t*	9.36	8.23*h*	5. 0
5.50*dr*	5. 0	—	—
9.20*e*	4.55	—	—

Sunday Trains.

AM 9.15	6.42	AM10. 8*hr*	5.45
PM11. 0*h*	4.55	PM 8.23*h*	5. 0

d Saturdays only.
e Saturdays excepted.
h Via Crewe.
n Noon.
r Restaurant Car.
t Tea Car.

Royal Oak Hotel. (First-class.) Moderate Tariff. Posting. Omnibus. Motors, repairs, spares. Telegrams : "Oak, Leominster." Telephone : 10.
WM. BRADFORD, Proprietor.

LESLIE (Fife), 439¾ miles. Fares, 86/11*a*, 52/2*c*. R. T. for two months, 173/10*a*, 104/4*c*. Departures *from* London as for Kirkcaldy. Departures *for* London about 3 times daily. Pop. 3,660.

LESMAHAGOW(Lanark),

389 miles.   Fares, 80/8a, 48/5c, R. T. for two months, 161/4a, 96/10c.   Departures *from* London as for Hamilton.   Departures *for* London about 4 times daily. Pop. 12,931.
Map Square 40.

LETCHWORTH (Herts)

from *King's Cross*, 34½ miles. Fares, 7/3a, 4/4c. R. T., double fare. Pop. 10,313.
Map Square 18.

King's +	Letch.	Letch.	King's +
AM 5. 5	6.31	AM 6. 0	7.30
7. 0	8.42	7.21	8.41
8.45	9.50	7.55	8.55
10.12	11.36	8.30	9.34
11.30	12.52	9. 1	9.56
PM12.40d	1.38	10.14l	11.15
1.55	3. 8	10.54	11.25
3. 0	3.54	PM12.21	1.25
4.15	5.26	2.31	3.50
5. 0	5.51	3.31	5.45
5.19	6. 9	5. 1	6. 0
5.50	6.56	6.58	8. 5
6.15	7.16	8.49	10.20
7. 0	8.11	9.45	11. 0
8.30	9.40	—	—
9.10	10.26	—	—
10.55	12. 0	—	—
11.45h	12.58	—	—
—	—	—	—

Sunday Trains.

AM 8.30	9.59	AM 8.12	9.53
PM 7.10	8.26	PM 6.27	8. 8
9.30	10.39	9.21	10.20
—	—	—	—
—	—	—	—

d Saturdays only.
h Wednesdays only.
l Tuesdays only.

Letchworth Hall Hotel. The best Family and Golfing Hotel. Fine old manor house overlooking 18 hole links. Recommended by R.A.C. and A.A. Garage. Billiards. Telephone: 11 Letchworth. Telegrams: "Jacobean."

LETHAM GRANGE

(Forfar), 471½ miles. Fares, 94/4a, 56/7c.   R. T. for two months. 188/8a, 113/2c.   Departures *from* London as for Arbroath. Departures *for* London about 3 times daily.
Map Square 38.

LETHENTY (Aberdeen),

542 miles. No through fares. Departures *from* London as for Inverurie.   Departures *for* London about 4 times daily.
Map Square 35.

LETTERSTON (Pembroke), from *Paddington*, 263⅝ miles. Fares, 50/0a, 30/0c. R. T. for two months, 100/0a. Departures *from* London as for Clynderwen. Departures *for* London about 15 minutes later. Pop. 593.
Map Square 15.

LEUCHARS (Fife) from

King's Cross, 443½ miles. Fares, 90/0a, 54/0c.   R. T. for two months, 180/0a, 108/0c. Pop. 2,765.
Map Square 38.

King's +	Leuch.	Leuch.	King's +
AM 4.45	5.13	AM 8.26r	6.15
10. 0r	7.52	PM12. 1r	10. 0
PM 8.25e	8.25	3.23	3.25
11.25er	9. 0	5.53	6. 0
—	—	7.59e	6.50
—	—	8.50	7. 5

Sunday Trains.

PM 8.25	8.25	—	—
11.25	9. 0	—	—
—	—	—	—

e Saturdays excepted.
r Restaurant Car.

LEVEN (Fife), 429 miles.

Fares, 86/6a, 51/11c. R. T. for two months, 173/0a, 103/10c. Departures *from* London as for St. Andrews. Departures *for* London about 3 times daily. Pop. 7,180.
Map Square 41.

LEVENSHULME (Lancs),

180½ miles. Fares, 37/11a, 22/9c. R.T., double fare. Departures *from* London as for Stockport. Departures *for* London about 8 times daily. Pop. 19,527.

LEVERTON (Notts), 144

miles. Fares, 29/10a, 17/11c. R. T., double fare. Departures *from* London as for Retford or Lincoln. Departures *for* London about 6 times daily. Pop. 749.
Map Square 13.

LEVISHAM (Yorks), 226¼

miles. No through fares. Departures *from* London as for Whitby. Departures *for* London about 4 times daily. Pop. 103.
Map Square 8.

LEWES (Sussex) from *Victoria* and *London Bridge*, 50 miles. Fares 10/5a, 6/3c. R. T. for two months, 20/10a, 12/6c. Pop. 10,798.
Map Square 28.

Vict.	Lon. B.	Arr. at Lewes
AM —	6.15	7.33
6.37k	6.40k	9. 6
7.23	7.25	9.48
9. 0	—	10.22
9.45	—	11. 3
10. 5	9.50	11.46
11.15	—	12.27
11.55	—	1. 9
12. 0	12.10	1.49
PM —	12.50d	2. 9
1.20e	—	2.47
1.25d	1.10d	2.47
—	2. 0	3.16
2. 0	2. 5	4.12
3.20	—	4.24
3.40	4. 5	5.25
4.30	—	5.50
—	5. 5	6. 6
5.20	—	6.26
5.45e	5.55e	7.10
5.45d	6. 0d	7.37
6.40	—	7.46
6.50	7. 0	8.37
7.15k	7.20k	9.26
8.35	—	9.46
10. 0	—	11.14
10.30	10.55	12.29
—	—	—

LEWES—*continued.*

Sunday Trains.

	Vict.	Lon. B.	Arr at Lewes
AM	6.55	7.22	9.22
	9.25	—	10.37
	9.30	9.30	11. 1
	11.15	—	12.37
PM	12.15k	—	2.12
	1.14k	1.10k	3.46
	6.33	6.33	8.27
	8.20	8. 0	9.33
	9.25k	9.10k	11.24
	—	—	—
	—	—	—

Trains from Lewes.

	Leave Lewes	Lon. B.	Vict.
AM	6.58	8.46	—
	7.35	8.53	9. 8
	8.21k	9.50	—
	9. 2	10.15	10.24
	9. 8	10.33	—
	9.35	10.55	10.56
	11.17	12.44	12.45
	11.41k	—	1.20
PM	12.43	2.22	2.22
	1.14k	3.40	3.45
	1.50	—	4.17
	3. 5	4.32	4.35
	3. 8k	—	4.50
	4.23k	6.36	6.34
	5.16k	—	7.30
	6.12	7.42	7.45
	6.16	8.46	—
	6.39	7.56	7.50
	6.54k	—	8.48
	8.26	10. 0	10.10
	8.45	10.25	10.17
	9.51	—	11.17
	10.37k	12.59	1. 0
	—	—	—
	—	—	—
	—	—	—

Sunday Trains.

AM	8.22	10.18	10.32
	9. 4k	11.15	10.50
	10.57k	—	1. 0
	11.44k	—	1.35
PM	2.45k	5. 3	5.11
	5.16k	—	7.28
	6.21	7.56	7.37
	6.51	8.34	8.41
	9. 5	—	10.19
	9.17	10.50	10.45
	10.10k	12.27	—
	—	—	—
	—	—	—

d Saturdays only.
e Saturdays excepted.
k Via Brighton.

White Hart Hotel. First-class for Families and Gentlemen. Comfortable, convenient, moderate. Summer and Winter Gardens. Lounge. Centre of town. Opposite County Hall. Stabling. Garage. Telephone No. 94. H. W. WALTON Proprietor.

LEWISHAM JUNCT. (London) from *Charing Cross*, 6¾ miles. Fares, 1/2*a*, 0/11½*b*, 0/8½*c*. R.T. for two days, 2/4*a*, 1/9*b*, 1/4*c*. From *Cannon Street*. Fares, 0/10*a*, 0/8*b*, 0/6*c*. R.T. for two days, 1/8*a*, 1/4*b*, 1/0*c*. Pop. (Lewisham) 174,194. *See* pp. 544-551, 556.
Map Square 71.

LEYBURN (Yorks) from *King's Cross*, 235¼ miles. Fares, 49/0*a*, 29/5*c*. R. T. for two months, 98/0*a*, 58/10*c*. Pop. 832.
Map Square 7.

King's +	L'burn.	L'burn.	King's +
AM 4.45	11.32	AM 7.34*r*	1.15
7.15	2.29	11.38*r*	6.15
10. 0*r*	5. 1	PM 2. 5*r*	9.25
PM 1.50*r*	8. 3	7.32	3.25
11.25*e*	7.52	—	—

Sunday Trains.

PM11.25	7.52	—	—

e Saturdays excepted.
r Restaurant Car.

LEYCETT (Stafford), 152½ miles. No through fares. Departures *from* London as for Newcastle-under-Lyme. Departures *for* London about 5 times daily.
Map Square 12.

LEYLAND (Lancs), from *Euston*, 205 miles. Fares, 42/9*a*, 25/8*c*. R. T. for two months, 85/6*a*. Pop. 9,034.
Map Square 12.

Euston	Leyl'nd	Leyl'nd	Euston
AM12.25	6.51	AM 5.41*er*	12. 5
2.35	8.34	5.41*dr*	12.20
5. 0	12.12	8.25*r*	1.45
6.45	12.58	10.17*hr*	3.45
11.35*r*	4.45	10.17*r*	4.15
11.50*r*	5.46	PM12.30*t*	6. 0
PM 2.35*t*	7.15	1.45*dr*	7.30
5.20*er*	10.10	4.18*er*	9. 5
5.20*dr*	11.15	4.18*dr*	9.15
11.55*d*	10. 4	9.31	5. 0

Sunday Trains.

AM11.45*r*	4.56	AM 8.46	4. 0
—	—	PM 6.21	5. 0

d Saturdays only.
e Saturdays excepted.
h Mondays and Saturdays only.
r Restaurant Car.
t Tea Car.

LEYSDOWN (Kent), 58 miles. Fares, 9/11*a*, 8/2*b*, 6/5*c*, R. T. for two months, 19/10*a*, 16/4*b*, 12/10*c*. Departures *from* London as for Queenborough. Departures *for* London about 5 times daily. Pop. 221.
Map Square 24.

LEYSMILL (Forfar), 473½ miles. No through fares. Departures *from* London as for Forfar or Arbroath. Departures *for* London about 4 times daily.
Map Square 38.

LEYTON (Essex) from *Fenchurch Street*, 5¼ miles, and *Liverpool Street*, 5¾ miles. Fares, 0/10*a*, 0/8*b*, 0/6*c*. R. T. for two days, 1/8*a*, 1/4*b*, 1/0½*c*. Pop. 128,430. *See* pp. 541-544.
Map Square 53.

LEYTON—*continued.*

ANOTHER ROUTE from *Moorgate Street* and *St. Pancras*, 9 miles. Fares, 1/3*a*, 0/9*c*. R.T. for two days, 2/2½*a*, 1/2*c*. *See* pp. 506, 507.

LEYTONSTONE (Essex) from *Fenchurch Street* and *Liverpool Street*, 6½ miles. Fares, 1/0½*a*, 0/10*b*, 0/7½*c*. R. T. for two days, 2/0½*a*, 1/5½*b*, 1/0½*c*. Pop. 13,262. *See* pp. 541-544.
Map Square 53.

ANOTHER ROUTE from *Moorgate Street* and *St. Pancras*, 10 miles. Fares, 1/3*a*, 0/9*c*. R. T. for two days, 2/2½*a*, 1/2*c*. *See* pp. 506, 507.

LHANBRYDE (Elgin), 584¾ miles. Fares, 106/3*a*, 63/9*c*. R.T. for two months, 212/6*a*, 127/6*c*. Departures *from* London as for Elgin. Departures *for* London about 3 times daily. Pop. 1,150.
Map Square 35.

LICHFIELD (Trent Valley) (Stafford) from *Euston*, 116¼ miles. Fares, 24/4*a*, 14/7*c*. R. T., double fare. Pop. 8,394.
Map Square 17.

Euston	Lichfd.	Lichfd.	Euston
AM 5. 0	7.45	AM 6.17*r*	10. 0
6.45	9.54	8.10	11. 0
8.45*r*	11.34	10. 3*dr*	12.20
10.40*r*	2. 4	10.11*e*	12.32
12. 0*nr*	2.56	10.28*r*	12.50
PM 2.50*t*	5.18	11. 5*r*	2.20
4. 5*t*	6.47	PM12.18*r*	4.15
4.45*r*	7. 8	2. 8	5.35
5.20*dr*	9.14	3. 0*t*	6.15
6.30*er*	9. 6	5.10*r*	8.10
—	—	7.10*r*	10.45
—	—	9.37	5. 0

Sunday Trains.

AM 9.15	1. 0	PM 1.32	5. 5

d Saturdays only.
e Saturdays excepted.
n Noon
r Restaurant Car.
t Tea Car.

LIDLINGTON (Bedford) from *Euston*, 55¼ miles. Fares, 10/5*a*, 6/3*c*. R. T. for two months, 20/10*a*. Departures *from* London as for Woburn Sands. Departures *for* London about 6 times daily. Pop. 502.
Map Square 18.

LIFF (Forfar), 470¼ miles. No through fares. Departures *from* London as for Coupar Angus or Dundee. Departures *for* London about 4 times daily. Pop. 2,355.
Map Square 38.

LIFFORD (Worcester), 119¼ miles. Fares, 23/7*a*, 14/2*c*. R. T. for two months, 47/2*a*, 28/4*c*. Departures *from* London as for Birmingham (New Street). Departures *for* London about 8 times daily.
Map Square 17.

LIFTON (Devon) from *Paddington*, 250 miles. Fares, 46/11*a*, 28/2*c*. R.T. for two months, 93/10*a*, Departures *from* London as for Launceston. Departures *for* London about 4 times daily. Pop. 819.
Map Square 26.

LIGHTCLIFFE (Yorks), 191¾ miles. Fares, 39/9*a*, 23/10*c*. R. T., double fare. Departures *from* London as for Lowmoor. Departures *for* London about 8 times daily. Pop. 4,413.
Map Square 12.

LILBOURNE (Northamptonshire) from *Euston*, 86 miles. Fares, 17/6*a*, 10/6*c*. R. T. for two months, 35/0*a*. Departures *from* London as for Yelvertoft. Departures *for* London about 5 times daily. Pop. 198.
Map Square 18.

LIMEHOUSE from *Fenchurch Street*, 2¼ miles. Fares, 0/2½*a*, 0/2*b*, 0/1½*c*. R. T. for two days, 0/5*a*, 0/4*b*, 0/3*c*. Pop. 30,352. *See* pp. 524, 525.
Map Square 62.

LIMPLEY STOKE (Wilts) from *Paddington, via* Trowbridge, 100½ miles. Fares, 21/3*a*, 12/9*c*. R. T. for two months, 42/6*a*, 25/6*c*. Pop. 389.
Map Square 22.

Pad.	Limp. S.	Limp. S.	Pad.
AM 1. 0*g*	7.27	AM 6.37	10. 0
5.30	9.18	10. 0*h*	12.55
7.30	11.34	10.44*r*	2.40
10.30*h*	1. 4	PM 1.19	6. 2
10.45	2.18	2.50	6.50
PM12. 5*r*	2.45	4.51*hr*	8.20
12.30*h*	4.22	6.30	10.25
2.45	6. 5	7.55	2.45
4.15*t*	7.26	—	—
6.30	9.59	—	—

Sunday Trains.

AM 9.10	1.26	AM10.42	3.35
PM 2.40*h*	6.36	—	—

g Mondays excepted.
h Via Westbury.
r Restaurant Car.
t Tea Car.

ANOTHER ROUTE from *Paddington, via* Bath, 113¾ miles. Fares, 22/6*a*, 13/6*c*. R. T. for two months, 45/0*a*, 27/0*c*.

Pad.	Limp. S.	Limp. S.	Pad.
AM 5.30	8.51	AM 7.27*r*	10.15
7.30	10.44	9. 2	11.30
11.15	1.19	9.18	12.20
PM1.10*r*	4.36	11.34	3.20
2.45	6. 0	PM 1. 4	4. 5
5. 0*r*	7.55	2.45	6. 2
6.30*r*	10.25	4.26*r*	8.45
12. 0*h*	6.37	7.26	10.25
12.30*k*	10.42	9.59	2.45
—	—	10.51*l*	2.45

Sunday Trains.

PM12.30	7. 2	PM 1.26	7.55
10. 0	6.37	6.36	3.15

h Saturday midnight excepted.
k Saturday midnight only.
l Mondays and Saturdays only.
r Restaurant Car.

LINACRE ROAD (Lancs),

205¾ miles. No through fares.
Departures *from* London as for
Liverpool. Departures *for* London
about 6 times daily.

LINBY (Notts) from *St.*

Pancras, 133 miles. Fares, 26/11*a*,
16/2*c*. R. T., double fare. Departures *from* London as for Hucknall. Departures *for* London
about 9 times daily. Pop. 273.
Map Square 13.

LINCOLN from *King's*

Cross, 130 miles. Fares, 26/11*a*,
16/2*c*. R. T., double fare. Pop.
66,020.
Map Square 13.

King's+	Lincn.	Lincn.	King's+
AM 4.45	8. 5	AM 7.30	10.40
7.15*r*	10.26	8.25*r*	11.30
8.45	12.16	10.28*r*	1.30
11.30	3.40	PM12.40*r*	4.30
PM 1.50*r*	4.40	2.30	6.25
3. 0	7.13	3.20*r*	6.30
4. 0*r*	7. 5	4. 5*r*	7.10
5.45*r*	8.55	6.20*r*	9.25
—	—	—	—
—	—	—	—
—	—	—	—
—	—	—	—
—	—	—	—
—	—	—	—
—	—	—	—

Sunday Trains.

12. 0*nr*	4.21	PM 5.53*r*	10.20
—	—	—	—
—	—	—	—
—	—	—	—
—	—	—	—
—	—	—	—

n Noon.
r Restaurant Car.

ANOTHER ROUTE from

St. Pancras, 156 miles. Fares as
above.

St. Pan.	Lincn.	Lincn.	St. Pan.
AM 4.25	10.26	AM 6.50*r*	10.45
9. 0*r*	12.57	8.35*r*	12.10
9.50*kr*	2.43	9.25*r*	1.20
11. 0*r*	3.17	10.40	3.25
PM 1.50*r*	5.34	PM12.25*r*	4.10
3.30*r*	7.45	12.55*r*	5.30
6.15*r*	10.12	3.15*r*	7.15
6.25*dr*	12. 0	5.15*r*	9. 5
11.45	4.51	5.45*r*	10. 5
—	—	8. 7	4.20
—	—	8.50*k*	4.20
—	—	—	—
—	—	—	—
—	—	—	—
—	—	—	—

Sunday Trains.

PM 3.15	9.50	PM12.10*r*	5. 2
—	—	5. 0*r*	9.43
—	—	8. 7	7.25
—	—	—	—
—	—	—	—
—	—	—	—

d Saturdays only.
k Thursdays and Saturdays only.
r Restaurant Car.

LINCOLN—*continued.*

ANOTHER ROUTE from

Liverpool Street, 143¾ miles. Fares
as above.

L'pl. St.	Lincn.	Lincn.	L'pl. St.
AM 5.50	11.58	AM 7.26	12.40
10. 5	2.27	9.55*lr*	4. 2*h*
11.50	5.37	9.55	5. 9
PM 2.54	8.22	PM12.14	5.17
4.45	10.42	12.52	6.10
—	—	5.55	10.30
—	—	—	—
—	—	—	—
—	—	—	—
—	—	—	—

Sunday Trains.

AM 9.25	1.35	PM 3.37	7.40
—	—	—	—
—	—	—	—

d Saturdays only.
e Saturdays excepted.
h Arrives at St. Pancras Station.
l Commencing July 23.

White Hart Hotel. The

Leading Family Hotel. One
minute from Cathedral. Electric
Light. Telephone 27.
Proprietor, H. H. LEVEN.
See advt. p. **226.**

The Spread Eagle Hotel.

First - class Commercial Hotel.
Centre of city. 3 minutes Station.
Spacious stock rooms. Bus meets
trains. Garage. Telephone 349.
See advt. p. **226.**

Great Northern Railway

Hotel (Trust Houses, Ltd.). Opposite the Station. Excellent cuisine. Telephone 300.

Albion Hotel. Facing Great

Northern Station. Three minutes
from Midland. The most Comfortable Family Hotel in Lincoln.
Private Sitting Rooms. Telephone
297.
Miss E. MILLS, Proprietress.

LINDAL (Lancs), 258¼ miles.

Fares, 37/9*a*, 32/3*c*. R.T. for two
months, 107/6*a*, 64/6*c*. Departures
from London as for Ulverston. Departures *for* London about 4
times daily.
Map Square 6.

LINDEAN (Selkirk), 366

miles. No through fares. Departures *from* London as for Galashiels. Departures *for* London
about 5 times daily. Pop. 393.
Map Square 41.

LINDORES (Fife) 438¼

miles. Fares, 89/7*a*, 53/9*c*. R.T.
for two months, 179/2*a*, 107/6*c*.
Departures *from* London as for
Leuchars. Departures *for* London
about twice daily.
Map Square 38.

LINEFOOT JUNC.

(Cumberland) 316½ miles. No
through fares. Departures *from*
London as for Cockermouth or
Carlisle. Departures *for* London
about twice daily.

LINGFIELD (Surrey) from

Victoria, Cannon Street, and
London Bridge, 26¼ miles. Fares,
5/5*a*, 3/3*c*. R.T. for two months,
10/10*a*, 6/6*c*. Pop. 4,905.
Map Square 23.

		Leave		Arr. at
	Vict.	Can. St.	Lon. B.	L'field.
AM 6.37	—	6.40	7.39
7.23	—	8. 7	9.11
9.10	—	9. 6	10.22
10.35	—	10.35	11.39
12. 0	—	11.50	1. 8
PM —	—	12.50*d*	1.45
1.20*e*	—	1.38*e*	2.41
1.25*d*	—	1.38*d*	2.46
—	—	2. 5*e*	3.47
2.25	—	2.25*d*	3.47
4. 0	—	4.10	5. 9
4.50	—	4.44*e*	5.51
5. 5	—	5.21	6.22
5.48	—	5.41*e*	6.44
6.50	—	7. 0	7.57
7.15	—	7.38	8.39
9. 3*h*	—	9.12*h*	10. 6
—	—	—	—
—	—	—	—
—	—	—	—
—	—	—	—

Sunday Trains.

AM 8.18	—	8.30	9.34
PM 6.33	—	6.46	7.52
—	—	—	—
—	—	—	—

Trains from Lingfield.

Leave		Arrive at	
L'field.	Lon. B.	Can. St.	Vict.
AM 7.24	8.37	—	8.40
8. 4	9. 1*k*	9. 4	9. 8
8.25	9.32	—	9.40
8.56	9.55	—	9.58
9.23	10. 7	—	—
9.42	10.38	—	10.46
10.35	12.13	—	11.35
PM12.21	1.42	—	1.26
1.59	2.58	—	—
3. 6*d*	4.57	—	—
4.19	5.21	—	5.55
5.16	6.36	—	6.29
6.31	7.56	—	—
7.13	8.46	—	8.27
9.24	10.25	—	11.17

Sunday Trains.

AM10. 9	11.15	—	—
PM 8.20	9.26	—	9.34

d Saturdays only.
e Saturdays excepted.
h Wednesdays and Saturdays only.
k Departs from or arrives at London
Bridge (S.E. & C.) Station.

LINGWOOD (Norfolk),

122 miles. Fares, 25/3*a*, 15/2*c*.
R. T. for two months, 50/6*a*. Departures *from* London as for
Brundall. Departures *for* London
about 5 times daily. Pop. 495.
Map Square 19.

LINLEY (Salop) from *Pad-*

dington, 150 miles. Fares, 29/10*a*,
17/11*c*. R.T. for two months, 59/8*a*.
Departures *from* London as for
Bridgnorth. Departures *for* London about 4 times daily.
Map Square 17.

LINLITHGOW, 410 miles.

Fares, 82/6a, 49/6c. R. T. for two months, 165/0a, 99/0c. Departures *from* London as for Edinburgh (Waverley). Departures *for* London about 3 times daily. Pop. 3,880.
Map Square 40.

LINTON (Cambs) from

Liverpool Street, via Bishops Stortford, 51 miles. Fares, 10/10a, 6/6c. R. T. for two months, 21/8a. Pop. 1,501.
Map Square 19.

L'POOL. ST.	LINTON	LINTON	L'POOL. ST.
AM 5.50	9. 1	AM 7.44	10.17
8.30	11. 0	10.47	12.40
10. 5	1.26	PM12.49d	3.18
11.20hl	1.26	12.49l	4. 2h
PM 2.48	5.23	12.49e	5. 9
5.49	7.43	5.22	7.58
—	—	7.45	10.30

No Sunday Trains.
d Saturdays only.
e Saturdays excepted.
h Departs from or arrives at St. Pancras Station.
l Commencing July 23.

ANOTHER ROUTE, *via*

Mark's Tey, 83¼ miles. Fares as above.

L'POOL.ST.LINTON.		LINTON. L'POOL.ST.	
AM 6.50	10.47	AM 9. 1	11.42
10. 0	12.49	11. 0h	2. 3
PM 2.15	5.22	PM 1.26h	5. 5
4.58	7.44	5.23	9.17
—	—	—	—
—	—	—	—

No Sunday Trains.
h Via Colchester.

LINTZ GREEN (Durham),

271¼ miles. Fares, 56/6a, 33/11c. R. T., double fare. Departures *from* London as for Durham or Bishop Auckland. Departures *for* London about 6 times daily.
Map Square 3.

LIPHOOK (Hants) from

Waterloo, 46½ miles. Fares, 9/10a, 5/11c. R.T. for two months, 19/8a, 11/10c.
Map Square 23.

W'LOO.	LIPHOOK	LIPHOOK.	W'LOO.
AM 5.50	7.33	AM 7.45	9.12
6.50	8.41	8.18s	9.44
7.50	9.48	9.22	10.50
9.50	11.27	9.57	11.32
10.50	12.35	PM12.16r	1.52
11.50d	1.26	1.22	3. 6
PM12.20d	1.46	2.39	4.16
12.50er	2.21	4.13	5.52
1.50e	3.33	5.48	7.46
2. 0d	3.42	7.18	9. 6
2.34	4.29	8.47	10.46
3.50d	5.26	10.10	12.16
4.15e	5.43	—	—
4.50	6.12	—	—
5.50	7.14	—	—
6.50er	8.25	—	—
6.50dr	8.35	—	—
9.50	11.33	—	—

Sunday Trains.

AM 8.20	10.20	AM 8.39	10.16
PM 1.50	3.36	PM 1.33	3.13
4.20	6.13	4.33	6.17
6.20	8. 8	8.43	10.41
9.30	11. 0	9.41	11.43
—	—	—	—
—	—	—	—
—	—	—	—

d Saturdays only.
e Saturdays excepted.
r Restaurant Car.
s Refreshments served.

LIPHOOK—*continued*.

Wheatsheaf Hotel. An ideal Country House. Few minutes from Station. Central heating. Adjoining Golf Course (18 holes) and Club House. 'Phone No. 51 Liphook.
CATERING HOUSES, LTD.

LISCARD (Cheshire), 206

miles. No through fares. Departures *from* London as for Chester. Departures *for* London about 4 times daily. Pop. 38,659.
Map Square 12.

LISKEARD (Cornwall) from

Paddington, 243½ miles. Fares, 50/5a, 30/3c. R. T. for two months, 100/10a, 60/6c. Pop. 4,376.
Map Square 26.

PAD.	LISKEARD	LISKEARD	PAD.
AM 5.30	1. 7	AM 7.30r	1.50
11.10r	4.13	11. 6r	4.35
PM12. 5r	7. 0	11.22sr	4.45
2. 0r	7.56	PM 1.24r	6.50
4.15lr	11.55	1.52dr	7. 5
10. 0	5. 9	2.58r	9. 0
12. 0k	8.34	11. 9	7.10
12.30h	9.11	—	—
—	—	—	—
—	—	—	—

Sunday Trains.

PM 2.40r	9.30	AM 8.47r	4. 5
10. 0	5. 9	PM 1. 5	7. 5
—	—	7.14	3.15
—	—	9.40	7.10

d Saturdays only.
h Saturdays midnight only.
k Saturdays midnight excepted.
l Thursdays and Saturdays only.
r Restaurant Car.
s Mondays and Fridays only.

LISS (Hants) from *Waterloo,*

51¼ miles. Fares, 10/10a, 6/6c. R.T. for two months, 21/8a, 13/0c. Pop. 2,334.
Map Square 23.

W'LOO.	LISS	LISS	W'LOO.
AM 5.50	7.43	AM 7.32	9.12
6.50	8.50	8. 5s	9.44
7.50	9.57	9. 8	10.50
9.50	11.36	9.44	11.32
10.50	12.44	PM12. 3r	1.52
11.50d	1.35	1. 9	3. 6
PM12.20d	1.55	2.26	4.16
12.50er	2.30	4. 0	5.52
1.50e	3.40	5.35	7.46
2. 0d	3.49	7. 5	9. 6
2.34	4.38	8.34	10.46
3.50d	5.35	9.57	12.16
4.15e	5.52	—	—
4.50	6.21	—	—
5.50	7.23	—	—
6.50er	8.34	—	—
6.50dr	8.44	—	—
9.50	11.42	—	—

Sunday Trains.

AM 8.20	10.30	AM 8.26	10.16
PM 1.50	3.45	PM 1.20	3.13
4.20	6.22	4.20	6.17
6.20	8.18	8.25	10,41
9.30	11.10	9.28	11.43

d Saturdays only.
e Saturdays excepted.
r Restaurant Car.
s Refreshments served.

LITCHFIELD (Hants)

from *Paddington*, 63½ miles. Fares, 12/4a, 7/5c. R. T. for two months, 24/8a. Departures *from* London as for Highclere. Departures *for* London about 6 times daily. Pop. 116.
Map Square 23.

LITTLEBOROUGH

(Lancs), 198¾ miles. Fares, 40/0a, 24/0c. R. T. for two months, 80/0a. Departures *from* London as for Rochdale. Departures *for* London about 3 times daily. Pop. 11,488.
Map Square 12.

LITTLE BYTHAM

(Lincoln) from *King's Cross*, 92¾ miles. Fares, 19/2a, 11/6c. R. T., double fare. Departures *from* London as for Essendine. Departures *for* London about 4 times daily. Pop. 419.
Map Square 18.

LITTLE EATON (Derby),

131¼ miles. Fares, 27/3a, 16/4c. R. T., double fare. Departures *from* London as for Ripley. Departures *for* London about 6 times daily. Pop. 1,058.
Map Square 12.

LITTLEHAM (Devon), 174½

miles. Fares, *via* Sidmouth Junction, 36/5a, 21/10c. R. T. for two months, 72/10a, 43/8c. *Via* Exeter, 38/4a, 23/0c. R.T. for two months, 76/8a, 46/0c. Departures *from* London as for Budleigh Salterton (*via* Tipton St. John's) or Exeter (Queen St.) Departures *for* London about 4 times daily. Pop.6,053.
Map Square 26.

LITTLEHAMPTON

(Sussex) from *Victoria, Clapham Junction,* and *London Bridge*, 61¼ miles. Fares, 12/9a, 7/8c. R. T. for two months, 25/6a, 15/4c. Pop. 11,286.
Map Square 28.

VICT.	LON. B.	Arr. at L'HMTN.
AM	5.18k	8.38
6.18	6.35	8.46
8.55	—	10.42
9. 0	—	11.36
10.15	10.22	12.19
—	10.30	12.32
11.55k	11.50k	2.40
PM 1.35	—	3.17
1.40	1.50	3.47
1.55k	—	4. 0
—	2. 5k	5. 0
3.55	4. 0	5.59
—	4.50	6.28
4.53	—	6.52
—	5. 5	7.38
—	5. 8e	7.38
5.45e	5.55e	7.58
—	6. 0k	8.22
6.15	—	7.50
6.40	—	8.36
7.20	7.15	9.43

Sunday Trains.

AM 8.35	—	10.23
9. 0	8.55	11.12
PM 1.14k	1.10k	5. 2
7. 0	6.38	9.18
—	—	—
—	—	—

LITTLEHAMPTON—*continued.*

Trains from Littlehampton.

Leave L'HMTN.	Arrive at LON. B.	Arrive at VICT.
AM 5.40*k*	8.19	—
6.45	9.11	9.19
7.10*k*	9.50	9.22
7.35	—	10.28
8. 0*d*	9.50	—
8.15	9.58	—
8.44	10.45	10.53
8.52*k*	—	11.17
9.15	10.55	—
10.12	12. 8	12. 0
10.22	1.42	—
10.57	—	1.20
PM 12.25	3.32	3.32
2. 5	4.15	—
2.32	4.27	4.34
3.15	—	5. 0
4.35	—	6.50
5.30	—	7.15
7.10*d*	10. 0	9.45
8. 3	10. 8	10. 1
8. 6	—	11.17
9.48*k*	12.59	1. 0

Sunday Trains.

AM 7.45	10.45	10.32
9.55*k*	—	1. 0
PM 4. 5*k*	—	7. 0
6. 0	—	7.49
6.40	8.50	8.42
7.55*k*	11.34	10.55

e Saturdays excepted.
k *Via* Hove.
p First and Third Class Pullman Car only.

The Beach Hotel. The only First-class, Up-to-date, Fully Licensed Hotel. Situated in its own delightful grounds of several acres. Near the Links. Garage. Telephone 55, Littlehampton.
G. S. STACEY, Manager.
See advt. p. **228**.

Rustington Towers. First-class Private Hotel, facing Sea. Electric Light.
Apply MANAGER.
See advt. p. **229**.

Southlands Private Hotel. Premier position facing Sea. Renowned for comfort. Excellent Cuisine and Service. Reasonable inclusive terms. Telephone 42.
Miss WOOD, Manageress.

Norfolk Hotel. Family. Close to Golf Links. Inclusive Terms, from 4 Guineas. Electric Light. 'Phone 191.
T. A. HILL, Proprietor.

Dolphin Hotel. Family and Commercial. Central. Hot Luncheons daily. Garage.
T. R. HOLLISS, Proprietor.

Waldron's Private Hotel. South Terrace. Facing Sea. Sunny Rooms, Balconies. Separate Tables. Excellent Cuisine. Close to Golf Links. Moderate Terms. 'Phone, 11. Stamp.

Elim-Atta. Private Hotel. South Terrace. Facing Common and Sea. Under the personal supervision of proprietor—
R. H. PEACOCK. 'Phone 94.

LITTLEHAMPTON—*continued.*

New Inn, The. Beach. Family Hotel. Quiet, old-fashioned Comfort. Separate tables. Under personal supervision. Tel. 112.
GEO. RICE, Proprietor.

Principal House Agent. For Furnished Houses and Flats. Selection of all available Properties to be Let or Sold in Littlehampton and District sent free. LEGGETT, Station Approach, Littlehampton. 'Phone 64. Telegrams: "Leggett," Littlehampton. Established 1862.

T. Crunden. The Leading Estate Agent, Auctioneer, Surveyor and Valuer. Selected lists of all available properties in West Sussex free on application. Telephone 41. Telegrams: "Crunden," Littlehampton.

Lists of available Furnished Houses will be forwarded gratis on application to SPARKS & SON, Auctioneers, Littlehampton. Tel. No. 2. Telegrams: "Sparks."

LITTLE HULTON

(Lancs), 192¼ miles. Fares, 40/3*a*, 24/2*c*. R. T. for two months, 80/6*a*, 48/4*c*. Departures *from* London as for Manchester (London Road). Departures *for* London about 4 times daily. Pop. 7,911.

LITTLE KIMBLE (Bucks)

from *Paddington*, 37¾ miles. Fares, 7/6*a*, 4/6*c*. R. T. for two months, 15/0*a*, 9/0*c*. Departures *from* London as for Aylesbury. Departures *for* London about 12 times daily. Pop. 1,193.
Map Square 23.

LITTLE MILL (Monmouthshire)

151¾ miles. Fares, 31/11*a*, 19/2*c*. R. T. for two months, 63/10*a*. Departures *from* London as for Monmouth or Pontypool Road. Departures *for* London about 5 times daily.
Map Square 22.

LITTLE MILL (Northumberland)

307¼ miles. Fares, 64/10*a*, 38/11*c*. R. T., 129/8*a*, 77/10*c*. Departures *from* London as for Morpeth. Departures *for* London about 3 times daily.
Map Square 3.

LITTLEMORE (Oxon)

from *Paddington*, 52¼ miles. Fares (*via* Thame), 11/0*a*, 6/7*c*. R. T. for two months, 22/0*a*. (*Via* Oxford), 13/4*a*, 8/0*c*. R. T. for two months, 26/8*a*, 16/0*c*. Departures *from* London as for Wheatley or Oxford. Departures *for* London about 4 times daily. Pop. 1,909.
Map Square 23.

LITTLEPORT (Cambs)

from *Liverpool Street*, 76 miles. Fares, 16/1*a*, 9/8*c*. R. T. for two months, 32/2*a*. Pop. 4,477.
Map Square 19.

L'POOL ST.	L'PORT.	L'PORT.	L'POOL ST.
AM 5.50	8.53	AM 8.22*r*	10.23
10. 5	12.40	9.15	11.27
11.50*r*	1.58	11. 6	2. 7
PM 2.34	4.36	PM 12.14*r*	2.21
4.45	6.43	3.54*r*	6.10
5.49*r*	7.55	4.14*h*	7.56
—	—	6.11*r*	8.22
—	—	8.16	10.30

Sunday Trains.

AM 9.25	12.10	PM 4. 6	6.40
PM 3.25	5.50	7.35	9.40

h Tuesdays only.
r Restaurant Car.

LITTLE SALKELD

(Cumberland) from *St. Pancras*, 289½ miles. Fares, 56/11*a*, 34/2*c*. R. T., double fare. Departures *from* London as for Appleby Departures *for* London about 4 times daily. Pop. 96.
Map Square 7.

LITTLE SOMERFORD.

See SOMERFORD, LITTLE.

LITTLE STEEPING

(Lincoln) from *King's Cross*, 120¼ miles. Fares, 25/0*a*, 15/0*c*. R. T., double fare. Departures *from* London as for Old Leake. Departures *for* London about 3 times daily. Pop. 185.
Map Square 13.

LITTLESTONE (Kent).

See NEW ROMNEY.

Grand Hotel, Littlestone. First-class Family and Golf. Under entirely new management.

LITTLE SUTTON.

See SUTTON, LITTLE.

LITTLETON AND BADSEY

(Worcester), 104 miles. Fares, 21/8*a*, 13/0*c*. R. T. for two months, 43/4*a*, 26/0*c*. Departures *from* London as for Honeybourne. Departures *for* London about 4 times daily. Pop. 352.
Map Square 17.

LITTLE WEIGHTON

(Yorks) from *St. Pancras*, 218¾ miles. Fares, 35/0*a*, 21/0*c*. R. T. for two months, 70/0*a*. Departures *from* London as for Cudworth. Departures *for* London about 8 times daily.
Map Square 13.

LITTLEWORTH (Lincoln)

from *King's Cross*, 87¾ miles. Fares, 18/2*a*, 10/11*c*. R. T., double fare. Departures *from* London as for Peakirk. Departures *for* London about 6 times daily.
Map Square 18.

LIVERPOOL (LIME STREET) (Lancs)

from *Euston*, 200¾ miles. Fares, 41/3*a*, 24/9*c*. R. T., double fare. Pop. 803,118.
Map Square 12.

EUSTON	L'POOL	L'POOL	EUSTON
AM 12.25	4.45	AM 2.30*g*	6.55
2.35	6.50	8. 0*er*	12. 5
5. 0	10.24	8. 0*dr*	12.20
6.45	12.33	8. 5*r*	1. 0
8.30*er*	12.35	9.45*r*	1.45
8.30*dr*	12.39	10. 0*r*	2.20
10.30*r*	2.20	11. 5*r*	3.10
11.50*r*	3.45	12. 0*n*	5.35
12. 0*nr*	5.20	PM 1. 5*dr*	5.50
PM 2.35*t*	6.35	2. 0*r*	6. 0
4. 5*r*	8. 5	2.45*r*	7.30
5.55*r*	9.35	4. 5*r*	8.10
8.45	1. 5	5.20*er*	9. 5
11.35	3.45	5.20*dr*	9.15
11. 0*d*	3.45	5.30*r*	10. 0
11.50*d*	6.25	10. 0	5. 0
—	—	11.50	5.40

Sunday Trains.

AM 9.15	3.30	AM 8.40*r*	1.30
PM 12.30*r*	5. 0	10.40	4. 0
3.50	9.55	PM 1. 0*r*	5.45
6. 0*r*	10.15	3.55*r*	8.20
9.15	3.20	10.50	5. 0
—	—	—	—
—	—	—	—

d Saturdays only.
e Saturdays excepted.
g Mondays excepted.
n Noon.
r Restaurant Car.
t Tea Car.

LITTLEHAMPTON.—"SOUTHLANDS," - FIRST-CLASS - PRIVATE HOTEL.

LIVERPOOL—*continued.*

ANOTHER ROUTE (CENTRAL) from *St. Pancras,* 217½ miles. Fares as above.

ST. PAN.	L'POOL	L'POOL	ST. PAN
AM 2.25	8.33	AM 5. 5*r*	11.35
4.25	10.47	8.10*r*	1.30
8.25*r*	2.15	8.30*r*	1.45
10.25*r*	3.25	11.25*r*	4.20
PM12.25*r*	5. 5	PM12.55*r*	6.15
2.25*r*	7.15	3.30*r*	8.35
4.25*r*	9.30	5. 0*r*	10. 5
12. 0*h*	7. 0	6.30	4.20
12. 0*k*	9.49	10.45	6. 0

Sunday Trains.

AM11.15*r*	5.30	AM10.30*r*	5. 2
PM 3.15	10.30	PM 3.45*r*	9.52
11.55	7. 0	9.10	4.55

h Saturdays midnight excepted.
k Saturdays midnight only.
r Restaurant Car.

ANOTHER ROUTE (CENTRAL) from *Marylebone,* 240½ miles. Fares as above.

M'BONE	L'POOL	L'POOL	M'BONE
AM 2.32	10.47	AM 5. 5*r*	1.13
8.45*r*	3.25	8.30*r*	3. 0
10. 0*r*	4.26	PM12.30*k r*	5.58
PM12.15*r*	6.37	2.30*r*	8.55
3.20*r*	8.45	3.30*r*	9.55
5. 0*r*	11.27	9.30	3.57
10. 0*d*	4.35	—	—
10. 5*e*	5. 5	—	—

Sunday Trains.

AM11.15*r*	5.30	AM10.30*r*	5.40
—	—	PM 3.45*r*	10.24

d Saturdays only.
e Saturdays excepted.
k Passengers cross Manchester at own expense.
r Restaurant Car.

ANOTHER ROUTE (LANDING STAGE) from *Paddington,* 211 miles. Fares as above.

PAD.	L'POOL	L'POOL	PAD.
AM 9.10*r*	2. 7	AM 6.45	12.25
10.20*r*	3. 7	7.40*r*	1.25
10.40*r*	3.57	8.50*r*	2. 5
PM12.50*r*	6.27	11.30*r*	5. 0
2.10*t*	7. 7	PM12.50*r*	5.55
.4.10*t*	9.17	·1.50*r*	6.40
6.10*r*	11.22	2.20*r*	8. 5
12.15*h*	7.37	4.20*r*	10. 0
12.15*k*	7.52	7. 0	3.30

Sunday Trains.

PM12.50*r*	6.37	AM 8.20	6.20
—	—	PM 2.40*r*	9. 0

h Saturdays midnight excepted.
k Saturdays midnight only.
r Restaurant Car.
t Tea Car.

Midland Adelphi Hotel. The last word in Hotel construction. Telephone in every room. Post Office. One of the "Midland Hotels."
ARTHUR TOWLE, Manager.
See advt. p. **227.**

LIVERPOOL—*continued.*

Hotel St. George. Firstclass Family and Commercial. Opposite Lime Street Station. Electric Light. Lift. Lounge.
E. EATON, Manager.

Imperial Hotel, facing Lime Street Station. First-class Family and Commercial. Lift. Electric light. Fire escapes. Lounge. Night porter.

Limes Hotel, 51/53, Mount Pleasant. Centre of City. Established 25 years. Mrs. SAMUELS, Manageress. Bed and Breakfast 5/6. Telegrams, Limes Hotel, Liverpool.

Compton Hotel, Church Street. First-class Family and Commercial. Situated in the principal street. Recommended R.A.C. and A.A. Telegrams, Compton. Telephone, 3032 Royal.

Southport—Prince of Wales Hotel. "The leading Hotel." Excellent Cooking. Comfort. Moderate Terms. Home Farm. Great Golfing Centre. Motorists' Headquarters. Garage. Wires; "Prince, Southport." Phones, 1431.

Norwich Union Mutual, the outstanding British Life Office. Reserves at 2½ per cent. 10, Dale Street, Liverpool. *See* advt. p. 6 of cover.

Bank.—The National Bank, Ltd.

LIVERPOOL STREET

from *Mansion House, Charing Cross, Victoria, South Kensington, High Street, Praed Street, Hammersmith, Baker Street, King's Cross, Moorgate,* and intermediate stations every few minutes. Also to and from *Uxbridge Road* and *Kensington (Addison Road),* about every 12 minutes throughout the day. See back of Map. *Map Square* 23 and 61, *No.* 3.

ANOTHER ROUTE (Central London Tube). *See* back of Map.

LIVERSEDGE (Yorks)

from *King's Cross,* 185½ miles. Fares, 38/7*a,* 23/2*c.* R. T., double fare. Departures *from London* as for Heckmondwike. Departures *for London* about 10 times daily. Pop. 14,658.

LIVINGSTON (Linlithgow),

408 miles. No through fares. Departures *from London* as for Edinburgh (Waverley). Departures *for London* about 4 times daily. Pop. 2,015. *Map Square* 40.

LIZARD (Cornwall).

Station at HELSTON, distance about 10 miles. Pop. (Landewednack) 595. *Map Square* 25.

Housel Bay Hotel. First*c*lass. Most Southerly Hotel in England. Close to Sea and Bathing Beach. Magnificent Coast Scenery. Beautiful and bracing climate. Sheltered North and East. Terms very Moderate.
Apply MANAGERESS.

LLANARTHNEY (Carmarthen),

from *Paddington,* 223 miles. No through fares. Departures *from* London as for Carmarthen or Llandilo. Departures *for* London about 3 times daily. Pop. 3,022.
Map Square 21.

LLANBADARN (Cardigan),

240¾ miles. No through fares. Departures *from* London as for Aberystwyth. Departures *for* London about 3 times daily. Pop. 995.
Map Square 16.

LLANBEDR (Merioneth),

242 miles. Fares, 50/3*a,* 30/2*c.* R. T. for two months, 100/6*a.* Departures *from* London as for Barmouth. Departures *for* London about 4 times daily. Pop. 320.
Map Square 16.

LLANBERIS (Carnarvon),

256½ miles. Fares, 53/6*a,* 32/1*c.* R. T. for two months, 107/0*a,* 64/2*c.* Departures *from* London as for Carnarvon. Departures *for* London about 5 times daily. Pop. 2,912.
Map Square 16.

LLANBISTER ROAD

(Radnor), 204½ miles. Fares, 36/6*a,* 21/11*c.* R.T. for two months, 73/0*a.* Departures *from* London as for Knighton. Departures *for* London about 4 times daily. Pop. (Llanbister) 651.
Map Square 16.

LLANBRADACH (Glamorgan),

155½ miles. Fares (*via* Cardiff), 33/11*a,* 20/4*c.* R.T. for two months, 67/10*a,* 40/8*c.* Departures *from* London as for Cardiff. Departures *for* London about 5 times daily.

LLANBRYNMAIR (Montgomeryshire),

208½ miles. Fares, 42/4*a,* 25/5*c.* R. T. for two months, 84/8*a.* Departures *from* London as for Newtown. Departures *for* London about 4 times daily. Pop. 1,102.
Map Square 16.

LLANDAFF (Glamorgan),

158½ miles. Fares, 32/9*a,* 19/8*c.* R. T., 65/6*a.* Departures *from* London as for Cardiff. Departures *for* London about 4 times daily. Pop. 9,142.
Map Square 21.

LLANDDERFEL (Merioneth)

from *Paddington,* 201 miles. Fares, 42/1*a,* 25/3*c.* R. T. for two months, 84/2*a.* Departures *from* London as for Corwen. Departures *for* London about 4 times daily. Pop. 785.
Map Square 11.

LLANDEBIE (Carmarthen)

from *Paddington,* 211½ miles. Fares, 43/2*a,* 25/11*c.* R. T. for two months, 86/4*a.* Departures *from* London as for Llandilo. Departures *for* London about 4 times daily. Pop. 6,771.
Map Square 21.

LLANDENNY (Monmouth)

153½ miles. Fares, 31/11*a,* 19/2*c.* R.T. for two months, 63/10*a.* Departures *from* London as for Monmouth. Departures *for* London about 4 times daily. Pop. 362.
Map Square 22.

LLANDILO (Carmarthen)

from *Euston*, 253 miles. Fares,
42/11*a*, 25/9*c*. R.T. for two months,
85/10*a*. Pop. 2,102.
Map Square 21.

EUSTON	LL'DILO	LL'DILO	EUSTON
AM 5. 0	3.10	AM 7. 0*r*	3.10
6.45*k*	3.10	11.10*r*	6.15
10.40*r*	6.50	PM 1.38*dr*	9.15
PM 1.15*r*	8.21	1.38*er*	9.20
9.20*ey*	7. 0	7.29	5. 0*h*
—	—	—	—

Sunday Trains.
PM 9.15	7. 0	—	—
—	—	—	—

e Saturdays excepted.
h A.M.
k Mondays and Fridays only.
r Restaurant Car.
y Via Crewe.

ANOTHER ROUTE from
Paddington, 216¾ miles. Fares,
43/2*a*, 25/11*c*. R.T. for two months,
86/4*a*.

PAD.	LL'DILO	LL'DILO	PAD.
AM 1. 0*g*	11. 5	AM 7.40*r*	2.30
8.45*r*	3. 7	9. 2*r*	4.20
11.50*r*	5.52	11.14*r*	6.15
PM 1.10*r*	8.21	PM 2.40*r*	9.25
9.15*e*	6.28	7.21	3.30

Sunday Trains.
PM 9.15	6.28	—	—

e Saturdays excepted.
g Mondays excepted.
r Restaurant Car.

LLANDINAM (Montgomery),

192¾ miles. Fares, 40/3*a*,
24/2*c*. R.T. for two months, 80/6*a*.
Departures *from* London as for
Llanidloes. Departures *for* London about 4 times daily. Pop.
1,314.
Map Square 16.

LLANDOVERY (Carmarthen)

from *Euston*, 241¾ miles.
Fares, 42/1*a*, 25/3*c*. R.T. for two
months, 84/2*a*. Pop. 1,932.
Map Square 16.

EUSTON	L'DOVRY	L'DOVRY	EUSTON
AM 5. 0	2.40	AM 7.31*r*	3.10
6.45*k*	2.40	11.35*r*	6.15
6.45	4.48	PM 2. 3*dr*	9.20
10.40*r*	5.25	2.33*er*	9.20
PM 1.15*r*	7.54	7.57	5. 0*h*
9.20*ey*	6.31	—	—
—	—	—	—

Sunday Trains.
PM 9.15	6.31	—	—
—	—	—	—

d Saturdays only.
e Saturdays excepted.
h A.M.
k Mondays and Fridays only.
r Restaurant Car.
y Via Crewe.

ANOTHER ROUTE from
Paddington, 228 miles. Fares,
43/2*a*, 25/11*c*. R.T. for two months,
86/4*a*, 51/10*c*.

PAD.	L'DOVRY	L'DOVRY.	PAD.
AM 1. 0*g*	11.32	AM 6.34*r*	2.30
8.45*r*	3.38	8.20*r*	4.20
11.50*r*	6.24	10.40*r*	6.15
PM 1.10*r*	8.51	PM 2. 5*r*	9.35
9.15*e*	7.28	6.45	3.30

Sunday Trains.
PM 9.15	7.28	—	—
—	—	—	—

e Saturdays excepted.
g Mondays excepted.
r Restaurant Car.

LLANDRE (Cardigan), 233¾

miles. Fares, 47/6*a*, 28/6*c*. R. T.
for two months, 95/0*a*. Departures
from London as for Machynlleth.
Departures *for* London about 4
times daily. Pop. 1,741.
Map Square 16.

LLANDRILLO (Merioneth)

from *Paddington*, 198 miles.
Fares,41/6*a*, 24/11*c*. R. T. for two
months, 83/0*a*. Departures *from*
London as for Corwen. Departures
for London about 4 times daily.
Pop. 591.
Map Square 11.

LLANDRINDOD

WELLS (Radnor) from *Euston*,
214½ miles. Fares, 37/6*a*, 22/6*c*.
R. T. for two months, 75/0*a*,
45/9*c*. Pop. 4,605.
Map Square 16.

EUSTON	LL'DOD	LL'DOD	EUSTON
AM 5. 0	12.33	AM 9.54*r*	3.10
6.45*h*	1.25	PM 12.34*r*	6.15
6.45	3.26	3. 5*dr*	9.15
10.40*r*	3.53	3. 5*er*	9.20
PM 1.15*r*	6.47	8.57*y*	5. 0
9.20*ey*	5.25	—	—

Sunday Trains.
PM 9.15	5.25	—	—
—	—	—	—

e Saturdays excepted.
h Mondays and Fridays only.
r Restaurant Car.
y Via Crewe.

ANOTHER ROUTE from
Paddington, via Shrewsbury, 204¼
miles. Fares as above.

PAD.	LL'DOD.	LL'DOD.	PAD.
AM 5.30*h*	2.27	AM 8.53*hr*	4.15
9.10*r*	3.26	10.33*r*	5. 0
10.40*r*	4.22	PM 12.34*r*	5.55
PM 12.50*r*	6.47	1.27*hr*	8.45
2.10*r*	8.22	3. 5*r*	10. 0
12.15*k*	8.53	7.21	3.30

No Sunday Trains.

h Via Hereford.
k Saturdays midnight excepted.
r Restaurant Car.

Gwalia Hotel, Ltd. Beautiful outlook. Close to Mineral
Springs. Links. Tennis. Telephone 40.   MANAGER.
See advt. p. 229.

Ye Wells Hotel. The principal unlicensed Hotel. 120.
bedrooms. 2 Electric Lifts. Modern
comforts.
See advt. p. 230.

Hotel Plas Winton. Private
Hotel. Grounds of 3 acres. 60
Bedrooms. Tennis. Lift. Garage.
J. SHEEN, Proprietor.
See advt. p. 230.

Hotel Metropole. Luxuriously appointed. 150 Bedrooms.
Complete Bath Installation.
Lift. Garage. Tel. 32.
See advt. p. 231.

LLANDRINIO ROAD

(Montgomery), 171 miles. No
through fares. Departures *from*
London as for Shrewsbury or Oswestry. Departures *for* London
about twice daily. Pop. (Llandrinio) 713.
Map Square 17.

LLANDUDNO (Carnarvon)

from *Euston*, 226¾ miles. Fares,
47/3*a*, 28/4*c*. R. T. for two months,
94/6*a*. 56/8*c*. Pop. 19,290.
Map Square 11.

EUSTON	LL'D'NO	LL'D'NO	EUSTON
AM12.25	8.25	AM 6.20*er*12. 5	
2.35	10.48	6.20*dr*12.20	
5. 0	11.55	7.35*dr* 1. 0	
8.30*er*	2.45	8. 0*er* 1. 0	
8.50*dr*	3. 8	8.45*r* 1.45	
10.30*r*	3.55	9.40*dr* 3.10	
11.10*r*	4. 5	9.55*r* 4.15	
11.50*er*	5.40	11.40*r* 5. 5	
11.50*dr*	6. 5	PM12.10*r* 6.25	
12. 0*nr*	7.20	2.20*r* 7.30	
PM 2.35*t*	8.12	3. 5*r* 9.20	
4. 5*r*	9.36	3.25*dr*10.45	
5.20*r*	11. 7	4.15*er*10.45	
9.30*e*	4.45	9. 5 5. 0	
11.50*d*	1.10*l*	—	—

Sunday Trains.
PM12.10*r*	7.59	PM 1.15*r*	7.10
9.15	4.45	8.55	5. 0

d Saturdays only.
e Saturdays excepted.
l P.M.
n Noon.
r Restaurant Car.
t Tea Car.

Grand Hotel. Premier of
North Wales. Adjoins Pier, to
which visitors have free access.
Bus meets principal trains.
See advt. p. 231.

Clarence Hotel. Near Pier,
Pavilion, etc. Links close to
Hotel. Moderate Tariff. Telegrams: "Clarence, Llandudno."
See advt. p. 232.

Craigside Hydro. Magnificent position. Well appointed.
See advt. p. 232.

Imperial Hotel. Centrally
situated. Extensive Sea Frontage.
Lounge. 150 Rooms. Garage.
'Phone 391 (3 lines).
S. CHANTREY,
Managing Director.
See advt. p. 233.

Ormescliffe Private Hotel.
Facing Sea. Accommodation 250.
Ball Room. Dancing each evening. Imperial Jazz Band. Near
Golf Links. Wireless Concerts.
Mrs. A. B. SMITH.
See advt. p. 233.

St. George's Hotel. First-class. Premier Position. Covered
Terrace. Facing Sea and Grand
Promenade. Orchestra.
THOMAS P. DAVIES.

Chatsworth Hotel. Promenade, near Pier. First-class.
Moderate Tariff. Tel. 369.
See advt. p. 234.

Empire Hotel. One minute
Pier, Esplanade. Near 3 Golf
Links; Promenade. Garage.
Tel. 259. Tariff, apply—
Mrs. S. HALL, Proprietor.
See advt. p. 234.

Belmont Boarding Establishment. Finest position on
Promenade. Facing Pier.
H. & C. water in most bedrooms.
'Phone 368.
FRANK W. JEX, Proprietor.
See advt. p. 234.

"The Crescent" Boarding
House. Centre of Promenade.
Near Pier. *f* Free Tennis. Excellent cuisine. Tel. 274.
L. MORAN, Proprietor.
See advt. p. 234.

For completion of
Advertisements, see over.

LLANDUDNO—*continued*.

"The Hydro." Splendid Situation. Facing Sea. Recreation Room. Lift. Tennis. Turkish Baths. Moderate Tariff.

The Craig-y-Don Boarding House (Temperance). Facing Sea. New Electric Lift. Recreation Room.
Misses MIDDLETON & WOOD.

Royal Hotel. Two minutes from Pier. Stands in private grounds. Tennis and croquet lawns. All modern improvements. Moderate tariff. Private Garage. High-class cuisine. Telephone 263.
Apply MANAGER.

Brinkburn Boarding Establishment. Facing Sea. Near Pier. Liberal Table. Comfortable Lounges. Terms moderate.
LAWRENCE UNDERWOOD.

Queen's Hotel. First-class Family Hotel, centre of Parade. Lift. Moderate Tariff. Omnibus. Telephone 70. *See also* RHYL, HARLECH, DOLGELLEY.

Heath House Boarding Establishment. Neville Crescent. Centre of Bay. Facing Sea. Good Cuisine. Near Pier and Pavilion. Every comfort.
Misses LAWTON.

The Bryn Private Hotel, Craig-y-don. R.A.C. A.A. Facing South. Healthiest and sunniest position. Central Heating. New Lounge and Recreation Rooms. Separate Tables. Moderate. Telegrams: "Bryn Hotel, Llandudno." Telephone 262   Mrs. A. JONES.

Marine Hotel. 120 Rooms. Commercial Tariff. Stock Rooms. En Pension, Winter Months, 4½ guineas. For Tariff, apply—
MANAGER.

LLANDUDNO JUNCT.

from *Euston* 223½ miles. Fares, 46/6a, 27/11c. R.T. for two months, 90/0a, 55/10c.
Map Square 11.

EUSTON	LLAN.J.	LLAN.J	EUSTON
AM12.25	7.51	AM 6.35er	12. 5
2.35	10.26	6.35dr	12.20
5. 0	11.26	7.49dr	1. 0
8.30er	2.27	8.12er	1. 0
8.30dr	2.48	9. 5r	1.45
10.30r	3.35	9.10r	2.20
11.10r	3.56	9.54dr	3.10
11.50er	5.24	10.15r	4.15
11.50dr	5.47	11.58r	5. 5
12. 0nr	7. 2	PM12.35r	6.25
PM 2.35t	7.49	2.35r	7.30
4. 5r	9.37	3.20r	9.20
5.20r	10.46	4.31r	10.45
9.30e	3.55	9.36	5. 0
11.50d	11.50		

Sunday Trains.

PM12.10r	7.33	AM 7.42	4. 0
9.15	3.55	PM 1.40r	7.10
—	—	9.28	5. 0

d Saturdays only.
e Saturdays excepted.
n Noon.
r Restaurant Car.
t Tea Car.

LLANDULAS (Denbigh),
216 miles. Fares, 45/0a, 27/0c. R.T. for two months, 90/0a, 54/0c. Departures *from* London as for Abergele. Departures *for* London about 6 times daily.
Map Square 11.

LLANDYSSUL (Cardigan)
from *Paddington*, 246½ miles. Fares, 49/10a, 29/11c. R.T. for two months, 99/8a, 59/10c. Departures *from* London as for Newcastle Emlyn. Departures *for* London about 4 times daily. Pop. 7,984.
Map Square 16.

LLANELLY (Carmarthen)
from *Paddington*, 207½ miles. Fares, 43/2a, 25/11c. R.T. for two months, 86/4a. Pop. 36,504.
Map Square 21.

PAD.	LLANELLY.	LLANELLY.	PAD.
AM 1. 0g	8.30	AM 6.15gr	10.57
5.30	12.47	7.50r	1. 0
8.45r	1. 7	9.23r	2.30
11.50r	4.39	11.38r	4.20
PM 1.10r	6.36	PM 1.10r	6.15
3.35r	8.45	3. 2r	8.35
5. 0r	10. 2	4.44r	9.25
6. 0r	11.23	8.42	3.30
9.15	4.39	—	—

Sunday Trains.

AM 1. 0	3.55	AM 8.37	3.35
PM12.30r	8. 3	PM 2.24r	8.25
9.15	4.39	8.42	3.30

g Mondays excepted.
r Restaurant Car.

LLANERCHYMEDD
(Anglesey), 256½ miles. Fares, 53/4a, 32/0c. R.T. for two months, 106/8a, 64/0c. Departures *from* London as for Gaerwen. Departures *for* London about 5 times daily. Pop. 854.
Map Square 11.

LLANFAIR (Anglesey), 242½
miles. Fares, 50/5a, 30/3c. R.T. for two months, 100/10a, 60/6c. Departures *from* London as for Bangor. Departures *for* London about 4 times daily. Pop. 962.
Map Square 11.

LLANFAIR CAEREINION (Montgomery), 181½ miles.
No through fares. Departures *from* London as for Welshpool. Departures *for* London about 5 times daily. Pop. 1,806.
Map Square 16.

LLANFAIRFECHAN
(Carnarvon) from *Euston*, 231½ miles. Fares, 48/2a, 28/11c. R.T. for two months, 96/4a, 57/10c. Pop. 3,638.
Map Square 11.

EUSTON	L'FECHAN	L'FECHAN	EUSTON
AM12.25	8.17	AM 7.16dr	1. 0
2.35	11.27	7.28er	1. 0
5. 0e	12.11	8.26r	1.45
5. 0d	12.49	9.13dr	3.10
8.30dr	2.20	9.35er	4.15
8.30er	3. 1	11.20r	5. 5
11.10r	3.59	PM 1.23r	7.30
11.50r	7. 0	2.41r	9.20
PM 2.35t	8.15	5.39r	10.45
4. 5r	10.15	8.16	5. 0
5.20r	11.11	—	—

Sunday Trains.

PM12.10r	8. 3	AM 7.15	4. 0

d Saturdays only.
e Saturdays excepted.
r Restaurant Car.
t Tea Car.

LLANFALTEG (Carmarthen), 245 miles.
Fares, 49/9a, 29/10c. R.T. for two months, 99/6a. Departures *from* London as for Cardigan. Departures *for* London about 4 times daily. Pop. 315.
Map Square 21.

LLANFECHAIN (Montgomery), 184 miles.
Fares, 37/3a, 22/4c. R.T. for two months, 74/6a. Departures *from* London as for Oswestry. Departures *for* London about 4 times daily. Pop. 538.
Map Square 16.

LLANFYLLIN (Montgomery), 185½ miles.
Fares, 37/11a, 22/9c. R.T. for two months, 75/10a. Departures *from* London as for Oswestry. Departures *for* London about 4 times daily. Pop. 1,639.
Map Square 16.

LLANFYNYDD (Flint)
from *Paddington*, 188 miles. Fares, 38/1a, 23/2c. R.T. for two months, 76/2a, 46/4c. Departures *from* London as for Wrexham or Mold. Departures *for* London 4 times daily. Pop. 985.
Map Square 11.

LLANFYRNACH (Pembroke), 254 miles.
Fares, 51/6a, 30/11c. R.T. for two months, 103/0a. Departures *from* London as for Cardigan. Departures *for* London about 4 times daily. Pop. 925.
Map Square 16.

LLANDUDNO.—"THE HYDRO." CENTRE OF BAY.

LLANGADOCK (Carmarthen) from *Paddington*, 222½ miles.
Fares, 43/2a, 25/11c. R. T. for two months, 86/4a. Departures *from* London as for Llandilo. Departures *for* London about 4 times daily. Pop. 1,589.
Map Square 16.

LLANGAMMARCH
WELLS (Brecon) from *Euston*, 227 miles. Fares 39/0a, 23/5c. R.T. for two months 78/0a, 46/10c.
Map Square 16.

EUSTON	LLANG.W.	LLANG.W.	EUSTON
AM 5. 0	2. 2	AM 8. 4r	3.10
6.45k	2 .2	PM12. 6r	6.15
6.45	4. 4	2.36dr	9.15
10.40r	4.25	2.36er	9.20
PM 1.15r	7.21	8.25	5. 0
9.20e	9.40	—	—
—	—	—	—

Sunday Trains.

PM 9.15	9.40	—	—
—	—	—	—

d Saturdays only.
e Saturdays excepted.
k Mondays and Fridays only.
r Restaurant Car.

The Lake Hotel, Pump House and Baths. Celebrated Barium Springs. Good Private Trout Fishing. 18-hole Links. Tennis (hard and grass courts). Grounds 70 acres. Lovely Scenery. Booklet free.
MANAGER.

LLANGEDWYN (Denbigh), 183¾ miles. Fares, 37/8a, 22/7c. R.T. for two months, 75/4a. Departures *from* London as for Oswestry. Departures *for* London about 3 times daily. Pop. 254.
Map Square 16.

LLANGEFNI (Anglesey), 249¾ miles. Fares, 51/11a, 31/2c. R. T. for two months, 103/10a, 62/4c. Departures *from* London as for Gaerwen. Departures *for* London about 5 times daily. Pop. 1,691.
Map Square 11.

LLANGEINOR (Glamorgan).178¾ miles. Fares,37/4a, 22/5c. R.T. for two months, 74/8a, 44/10c. Departures *from* London as for Tondu. Departures *for* London about 4 times daily. Pop. 16,311.
Map Square 21.

LLANGENNECH (Carmarthen), 204 miles. Fares, 43/2a, 25/11c. R.T. for two months,86/4a. Departures *from* London as for Llanelly. Departures *for* London about 5 times daily. Pop. 2,618.
Map Square 21.

LLANGLYDWEN (Carmarthen), 250 miles. Fares, 50/8a, 30/5c. R.T. for two months, 101/4a, 60/10c. Departures *from* London as for Cardigan. Departures *for* London about 4 times daily. Pop. 229.
Map Square 16.

LLANGOLLEN (Denbigh) from *Paddington,* 183½ miles.
Fares, 38/6a, 23/1c. R.T. for two months, 77/0a, 46/2c.
Pop. 3,680.
Map Square 11.

PAD.	LLANGOLN.	LLANGOLN.	PAD.
AM 9.10r	1.50	AM 7.32	12.25
10.40r	3. 5	8.27r	1.25
PM12.50r	5.28	9.45r	2. 5
2.10t	6.48	PM12.15r	5. 0
4.10t	9.23	3. 7r	8. 5
12.15k	3.11l	4.58r	10. 0
12.15h	7.55	7.40	3.30

Sunday Trains.

PM12.50r	5.21	PM 3.55r	9. 0
—	—	—	—

h Saturday midnight excepted.
k Saturday midnight only.
l P.M. Sunday.
r Restaurant Car.
t Tea Car.

The Hand Hotel. One of the best in North Wales. Garage for 30 Cars attached to Hotel. Telephone 7. Resident Proprietor, JAMES S. SHAW.

LLANGONOYD (Glamorgan), 179½ miles. Fares, 37/4a, 22/5c. R.T. for two months, 74/8a. Departures *from* London as for Tondu. Departures *for* London about 4 times daily.
Map Square 21.

LLANGWYLLOG (Anglesey), 252½ miles. Fares, 52/6a, 31/6c. R.T. for two months, 105/0a, 63/0c. Departures *from* London as for Gaerwen. Departures *for* London about 4 times daily. Pop. 182.
Map Square 11.

LLANGYBI (Cardigan), 259 miles. Fares, 48/9a, 29/3c. R.T. for two months, 97/6a. Departures *from* London as for Lampeter. Departures *for* London about 4 times daily. Pop. 265.
Map Square 16.

LLANGYBI (Carnarvon), 263½ miles. Fares, 54/5a, 32/8c. R.T. for two months,108/10a, 65/4c. Departures *from* London as for Carnarvon. Departures *for* London about 5 times daily. Pop. 491.
Map Square 16.

LLANGYFELACH (Glamorgan), 198¾ miles. No through fares. Departures *from* London as for Swansea. Departures *for* London about 4 times daily.

LLANGYNOG (Montgomery), 192¾ miles. Fares, 39/5a, 23/8c. R.T. for two months, 78/10a. Departures *from* London as for Oswestry. Departures *for* London about 3 times daily. Pop. 518.
Map Square 16.

LLANHARAN (Glamorgan) from *Paddington,* 166½ miles. Fares, 34/9a, 20/10c. R. T. for two months, 69/6a. Pop. 1,504.
Map Square 21.

PAD.	LLANHN.	LLANHN.	PAD.
AM 1. 0g	8. 7	AM 9.10r	1. 0
5.30	11. 5	11.23r	4.20
8.45r	1.46	PM 1.51r	6.15
11.50r	3.59	3.17r	8.35
PM 1.10dr	5.38	5.11r	9.25
1.10r	6. 2	9. 5	3.30
3.35r	7.44	—	—
6. 0r	10.22	—	—

Sunday Trains.

AM 1. 0	10.28	PM 1.27r	8.25
9.10	3. 1	3.57	3.30
PM 9.15	8. 6	—	—

d Saturdays only.
g Mondays excepted.
r Restaurant Car.

LLANHARRY (Glamorgan), 165¼ miles. No through fares. Departures *from* London as for Llantrisant. Departures *for* London about 6 times daily. Pop. 369.
Map Square 21.

LLANHILLETH (Monmouth), 155½ miles. Fares, 32/4a, 19/5c. R.T. for two months, 64/8a. Departures *from* London as for Risca. Departures *for* London about 7 times daily. Pop. 9,652.

LLANIDLOES (Montgomery), from *Paddington,* 198¾ miles. Fares. 41/5a, 24/10c. R.T. for two months,82/10a. Pop.2,517.
Map Square 16.

PAD.	LL'LOES.	LL'LOES.	PAD.
AM 6.30h	2.32	AM 7.40r	2. 5
10.20r	3. 5	11.10r	5. 0
10.40r	4.12	PM12.50t	6.40
PM 2.10t	8.15	1.58r	8. 5
4.10t	9.38	3.22	10. 0
12.15k	10.17	7.22	3.30

No Sunday Trains.

h Mondays and Saturdays only.
k Saturdays midnight excepted.
r Restaurant Car.
t Tea Car.

ANOTHER ROUTE from *Euston* (via Welshpool), 208 miles. Fares as above.

EUSTON	LL'LOES.	LL'LOES.	EUSTON
AM 5. 0	1.23	AM 6.30hr	1.45
10. 0r	4.12	7.40r	2.20
12. 0nr	8.15	9.22r	3.10
PM 2.20t	9.38	11.10hr	5.50
9 .30eh	5.27	PM 1.58er	9.20
—	—	1.58dr	9.15
—	—	3.22hr	10.45
—	—	7.22	5. 0

Sunday Trains.

PM 9.15	5.27	—	—
—	—	—	—

e Saturdays excepted.
h Via Crewe.
n Noon.
r Restaurant Car.
t Tea Car.

LLANILAR (Cardigan), 245½ miles. Fares, 48/9a, 29/3c. R.T. for two months, 97/6a. Departures *from* London as for Lampeter. Departures *for* London about 4 times daily. Pop. 677.
Map Square 16.

LLANISHEN (Glamorgan), 156½ miles. Fares (via Cardiff), 32/8a. 19/7c. R.T. for two months, 65/4a, 39.2a. Departures *from* London as for Cardiff. Departures *for* London about 4 times daily. Pop. 1,733.
Map Square 21.

LLANMORLAIS (Glamorgan), 211 miles. No through fares. Departures *from* London as for Swansea. Departures *for* London about 4 times daily.
Map Square 21.

LLANPUMPSAINT (Carmarthen), 237¾ miles. Fares, 48/1a, 28/10c. R. T. for two months, 96/2a. Departures *from* London as for Carmarthen. Departures *for* London about 5 times daily. Pop. 705.
Map Square 16.

LLANRHAIADR (Denbigh), 211¼ miles. Fares, 40/7*a*, 24/4*c*. R.T. for two months, 81/2*a*. Departures *from* London as for Denbigh. Departures *for* London about 5 times daily. Pop. 304.
Map Square 11.

LLANRHAIADR MOCHNANT (Montgomery), 187¾ miles. Fares, 38/2*a*, 22/11*c*. R.T. for two months, 76/4*a*. Departures *from* London as for Oswestry. Departures *for* London about 3 times daily. Pop. 1,151.
Map Square 16.

LLANRHYSTYDROAD (Cardigan) from *Paddington*, 242½ miles. Fares, 48/9*a*, 29/3*c*. R.T. for two months, 97/6*a*. Departures *from* London as for Lampeter. Departures *for* London about 4 times daily. Pop. 1,079.
Map Square 16.

LLANRWST AND TREFRIW (Denbigh) from *Euston*, 234¼ miles. Fares, 47/11*a*, 28/9*c*. R.T. for two months, 95/10*a*, 57/6*c*. Pop. 2,368.
Map Square 11.

Euston	Ll'wst.	Ll'wst.	Euston.
AM12.25	8.28	AM 7. 3*dr*	1. 0
2.35	11.15	7.12*er*	1. 0
5. 0	12.49	8.27*r*	1.45
10.30*r*	4.16	10.39*r*	5. 5
10.40*r*	5.18	PM 1. 9*r*	7.30
11.50*r*	7.11	2.35*r*	9.20
PM 2.35*t*	8.22	8.39	5. 0
5.20*h*	11.22	—	—
9.30*e*	5.18	—	—
—	—	—	—
—	—	—	—
—	—	—	—
—	—	—	—

Sunday Trains.

PM 9.15	5.18	—	—
—	—	—	—
—	—	—	—
—	—	—	—
—	—	—	—

d Saturdays only.
e Saturdays excepted.
h Thursdays, Fridays and Saturdays only.
r Restaurant Car.
t Tea Car.

Hotel Belle Vue (Trefriw). Overlooking River Conway and beautiful Trefriw Valley. First class.
See advt. p. **333**.

LLANSAMLET (Glamorgan), 194½ miles. Fares, 40/8*a*, 24/5*c*. R. T. for two months, 81/4*a*. Departures *from* London as for Neath. Departures *for* London about 6 times daily. Pop. 7,411.
Map Square 21.

LLANSANTFFRAID (Montgomery), 182¾ miles. Fares, 36/10*a*, 22/1*c*. R.T. for two months, 73/8*a*. Departures *from* London as for Oswestry. Departures *for* London about 4 times daily. Pop. 1,149.
Map Square 16.

LLANSILIN ROAD (Montgomery), 182¾ miles. Fares, 37/3*a*, 22/4*c*. R.T. for two months, 74/6*a*. Departures *from* London as for Oswestry. Departures *for* London about 3 times daily. Pop. (Llansilin) 960.
Map Square 16.

LLANTARNAM (Monmouth), 145½ miles. Fares, 30/3*a*, 18/2*c*. R.T. for two months 60/6*a*. Departures *from* London as for Newport (Mon.). Departures *for* London about 6 times daily. Pop. 7,452.
Map Square 22.

LLANTRISANT (Glamorgan) from *Paddington*, 164 miles. Fares, 34/2*a*, 20/6*c*. R. T. for two months, 68/4*a*. Pop. 15,048.
Map Square 21.

Pad.	Llantrnt.	Llantrnt.	Pad.
AM 1. 0*g*	8. 0	AM 9.17*r*	1. 0
5.30	10.38	10.30*r*	2.30
8.45*r*	12.36	PM12.25*r*	4.20
11.50*r*	3.52	2. 0*r*	6.15
PM 1.10*r*	5.30	3.50*r*	8.35
3.35*r*	7.36	5.56*r*	9.25
6. 0*r*	10.10	9.15	3.30
8. 0*hr*	11.20	9.50*h*	3.30
—	—	—	—
—	—	—	—
—	—	—	—
—	—	—	—
—	—	—	—
—	—	—	—

Sunday Trains.

AM 1. 0	10.21	AM11.55	4. 5
9.10	2.54	PM 4.30*r*	8.25
PM12.30*r*	4.38	9. 5	3.30
4.30	8.55	—	—
9.15	7.59	—	—
—	—	—	—

g Mondays excepted.
h Thursdays and Saturdays only.
r Restaurant Car.

LLANTWIT (Glamorgan), 164½ miles. Fares, 34/2*a*, 20/6*c*. R.T. for two months, 68/4*a*. Departures *from* London as for Pontypridd. Departures *for* London about 4 times daily. Pop. 2,434.

LLANTWIT - MAJOR (Glamorgan), 171 miles. Fares, 35/8*a*, 21/5*c*. R.T. for two months, 71/4*a*. Departures *from* London as for Barry Docks. Departures *for* London about 5 times daily. Pop. 1,188.
Map Square 21.

LLANUWCHLLYN (Merioneth) from *Paddington*, 209½ miles. Fares, 44/0*a*, 26/5*c*. R. T. for two months, 88/0*a*, 52/10*c*. Departures *from* London as for Corwen. Departures *for* London about 3 times daily. Pop. 100.
Map Square 16.

LLANVIHANGEL (Monmouth), 161¾ miles. Fares, 33/2*a*, 19/11*c*. R. T. for two months, 66/4*a*. Departures *from* London as for Abergavenny. Departures *for* London about 6 times daily. Pop. 446.
Map Square 22.

LLANWERN (Monmouth) from *Paddington* 137¼ miles. Fares, 29/5*a*, 17/8*c*. R. T. for two months, 58/10*a*. *Via* Newport, 29/10*a*, 17/11*c*. R.T. for two months, 59/8*a*. Departures *from* London as for Severn Tunnel. Departures *for* London about 5 times daily. Pop. 92.
Map Square 22.

LLANWNDA (Carnarvon), 245¼ miles. Fares, 52/4*a*, 31/5*c*. R.T. for two months, 104/8*a*, 62/10*c*. Departures *from* London as for Carnarvon. Departures *for* London about 5 times daily. Pop. 2,054.
Map Square 11.

LLANWRDA (Carmarthen), 224¼ miles. Fares, 43/2*a*, 25/11*c*. R. T. for two months, 86/4*a*. Departures *from* London as for Llandilo. Departures *for* London about 5 times daily. Pop. 472.
Map Square 16.

LLANWRTYD WELLS (Brecon) from *Euston*, 230½ miles. Fares, 39/9*a*, 23/10*c*. R.T. for two months, 79/6*a*, 47/8*c*. Pop. 1,171.
Map Square 16.

Euston	Llan'tyd.	Llan'tyd.	Euston
AM 5. 0	2.10	AM 7.57*r*	3.10
6.45*k*	2.10	11.59*r*	6.15
6.45	4.12	PM 2.29*dr*	9.15
10.40*r*	4.35	2.29*er*	9.20
PM 1.15*r*	7.29	8.21	5. 0
9.20*e*	6. 7	—	—
—	—	—	—
—	—	—	—
—	—	—	—
—	—	—	—

Sunday Trains.

PM 9.15	6. 7	—	—
—	—	—	—
—	—	—	—
—	—	—	—
—	—	—	—
—	—	—	—

e Saturdays excepted.
k Mondays and Fridays only.
r Restaurant Car.

Abernant Lake Hotel. A High-class modern Hotel. Finest Sulphur Springs in the Kingdom. Private Golf Course. Shooting and Fishing. Electric Light. Illustrated Tariff on application.
See advt. p. **235**.

LLANYBLODWELL (Salop), 182¾ miles. Fares, 36/10*a*, 22/1*c*. R.T. for two months, 73/8*a*. Departures *from* London as for Oswestry. Departures *for* London about 3 times daily. Pop. 840.
Map Square 16.

LLANYBYTHER (Carmarthen) from *Paddington*, 250¼ miles. Fares, 48/9*a*, 29/3*c*. R.T. for two months, 97/6*a*. Departures *from* London as for Lampeter. Departures *for* London about 4 times daily. Pop. 1,171.
Map Square 16.

LLANYCEFN (Pembroke), 250¼ miles. Fares, 50/0*a*, 30/0*c*. R. T. for two months, 100/0*a*, 60/0*c*. Departures *from* London as for Clynderwen. Departures *for* London about twice daily. Pop. 292.
Map Square 20.

LLANYMYNECH (Salop), 179 miles. Fares, 36/1*a*, 21/8*c*. R. T. for two months, 72/2*a*. Departures *from* London as for Oswestry. Departures *for* London about 5 times daily. Pop. 577.
Map Square 16.

LLETTY BRONGU (Glamorgan), 183¾ miles. No through fares. Departures *from* London as for Maesteg or Tondu. Departures *for* London about 4 times daily.

LLWYDCOED (Glamorgan), 175 miles. Fares, 36/6*a*, 21/11*c*. R. T. for two months, 73/0*a*. Departures *from* London as for Merthyr (*via* Pontypool Road). Departures *for* London about 5 times daily.
Map Square 21.

LLWYNGWERN (Merioneth), 221 miles. No through fares. Departures *from* London as for Machynlleth Departures *for* London about twice daily.
Map Square 16.

LLWYNGWRIL (Merioneth), 239 miles. Fares, 48/4*a*, 29/0*c*. R.T. for two months, 96/8*a*. Departures *from* London as for Machynlleth. Departures *for* London about 5 times daily.
Map Square 16.

LLWYNYPIA (Glamorgan), 165½ miles. Fares, 34/5*a*, 20/8*c*. R. T. for two months, 68/10*a*, 41/4*c*. Departures *from* London as for Treherbert. Departures *for* London about 6 times daily. Pop. 18,718.

LLYNCLYS (Salop), 176¾ miles. Fares, 36/1*a*, 21/8*c*. R. T. for two months, 72/2*a*. Departures *from* London as for Oswestry. Departures *for* London about 5 times daily.
Map Square 17.

LLYSFAEN (Carnarvon), 217 miles. Fares, 45/3*a*, 27/2*c*. R. T. for two months, 90/6*a*, 54/4*c*. Departures *from* London as for Abergele. Departures *for* London about 6 times daily. Pop. 2,455.
Map Square 11.

LOANHEAD (Midlothian), 397¼ miles. No through fares. Departures *from* London as for Edinburgh (Waverley). Departures *for* London about 4 times daily. Pop. 3,441.
Map Square 41.

LOCHAILORT (Inverness), 549½ miles. Fares, 109/10*a*, 65/11*c*. R. T. for two months, 219/8*a*, 131/10*c*. Departures *from* London as for Fort William. Departures *for* London about twice daily.
Map Square 36.

LOCHANHEAD (Kirkcudbright), 338¼ miles. Fares, 68/7*a*, 41/2*c*. R. T. for two months, 137/2*a*, 82/4*c*. Departures *from* London as for Dumfries. Departures *for* London about 4 times daily.
Map Square 43.

LOCHARBRIGGS (Dumfries), 337 miles. Fares, 67/4*a*, 40/5*c*. R. T. for two months, 134/8*a*, 80/10*c*. Departures *from* London as for Lockerbie. Departures *for* London about 4 times daily.
Map Square 43.

LOCH-AWE (Argyle), 481¼ miles. Fares, 98/7*a*, 59/2*c*. R. T. for two months, 197/2*a*. Departures *from* London as for Crianlarich. Departures *for* London about 3 times daily
Map Square 37.

Loch Awe Hotel. Reached by Lift from Station. L.M. and S. First-class every respect.
See advt. p. **226**.

LOCHEE (Forfar), 472 miles. Fares, 91/11*a*, 55/2*c*. R.T. for two months, 183/10*a*, 110/4*c*. Departures *from* London as for Coupar Angus or Dundee. Departures *for* London about 3 times daily. Pop. 2,613.
Map Square 38.

LOCHEILSIDE (Inverness), 533¾ miles. Fares, 106/8*a*, 64/0*c*. R. T. for two months, 213/4*a*, 128/0*c*. Departures *from* London as for Fort William. Departures *for* London about twice daily.
Map Square 37.

LOCHGELLY (Fife), 416¾ miles. Fares, 86/6*a*, 51/11*c*. R. T. for two months, 173/0*a*, 103/10*c*. Departures *from* London as for Dunfermline. Departures *for* London about 4 times daily. Pop. 10,666.
Map Square 41.

LOCH LOMOND (Dumbarton). Station at Balloch.
Map Square 40.

Tarbet Hotel (de luxe). Excellent cuisine. Inclusive Tariff. Salmon and Trout Fishing. Golf. Boating. Garage. Petrol. Highlands touring centre. Telegraph.

LOCHLUICHART (Ross), 603½ miles. Fares, 109/10*a*, 65/11*c*. R. T. for two months, 219/8*a*, 131/10*c*. Departures *from* London as for Kyle of Lochalsh. Departures *for* London about 3 times daily.
Map Square 34.

LOCHMABEN (Dumfries), 329 miles. Fares, 66/10*a*, 40/1*c*. R.T. for two months, 133/8*a*, 80/2*c*. Departures *from* London as for Lockerbie. Departures *for* London about 4 times daily. Pop. 2,277.
Map Square 44.

LOCHSIDE (Renfrew), 418¼ miles. Fares, 82/4*a*, 49/5*c*. R.T. for two months, 164/8*a*, 98/10*c*. Departures *from* London as for Kilmarnock. Departures *for* London about 3 times daily.
Map Square 40.

LOCH TAY (Perth), 437¼ miles. Fares, 92/9*a*, 55/8*c*. R.T. for two months, 185/6*a*, 111/4*c*. Departures *from* London as for Callander. Departures *for* London about 3 times daily.
Map Square 37.

LOCHWINNOCH (Renfrew), 408½ miles. Fares, 82/4*a*, 49/5*c*. R. T. for two months, 164/8*a*, 98/10*c*. Departures *from* London as for Kilmarnock. Departures *for* London about 3 times daily. Pop. 4,224.
Map Square 40.

LOCKERBIE (Dumfries), from *Euston*, 325 miles. Fares, 65/10*a*, 39/6*c*. R.T. for two months, 131/8*a*, 79/0*c*. Pop. 2,344.
Map Square 44.

Euston	L'bie.	L'bie.	Euston
AM 2.35	1.23	AM 6.44*r*	4.15
5. 0	1.52	10. 1*r*	6.25
6.45	4. 1	PM 12.21*r*	7.30
10. 0*r*	4.27	1.21*r*	10. 0
11.35*r*	7.12	7.53*r*	5. 0
PM 1.30*r*	9. 5	11.24*e*	6.55
9.20	4.44	—	—
11. 0*dh*	6.26	—	—
11.45*e*	9. 3	—	—
—	—	—	—

Sunday Trains.

PM 9.30	5.20	AM 12.15	7.15
11.45	9. 3	12. 3*r*	7.30
—	—	7.45*r*	5. 0
—	—	—	—
—	—	—	—
—	—	—	—

d Saturdays only.
e Saturdays excepted.
h Sleeping Saloon passengers only.
r Restaurant Car.

LOCKINGTON (Yorks), 206½ miles. No through fares. Departures *from* London as for Hull (Paragon) or Driffield. Departures *for* London about 4 times daily. Pop. 471.
Map Square 8.

LOCKWOOD (Yorks) from *King's Cross*, *via* Horbury, 190½ miles. Fares, 37/9*a*, 22/8*c*. R. T., double fare. Pop. 16,641.
Map Square 12.

King's+	L'wood	L'wood	King's+
AM 4.45	12.13	AM 5.51	11.30
7.15*dr*	1. 9	7.54*r*	1. 5
7.15*r*	1.28	9.44	3.50
10.10*r*	3.39	10.26*r*	4.45
PM 1.30*r*	6.46	10.58	5. 0
1.50*r*	8.17	PM 1.54*r*	7.10
—	—	4.11*r*	9.25
—	—	8.56*e*	3.25
—	—	—	—
—	—	—	—
—	—	—	—
—	—	—	—

Sunday Trains.

12. 0*hn*	7.39	AM 9.15*r*	3.45
—	—	11.25*r*	5.55
—	—	—	—
—	—	—	—

d Saturdays only.
e Saturdays excepted.
h Passenger cross Wakefield at own expense.
n Noon.
r Restaurant Car.

LOCKWOOD—*continued.*

ANOTHER ROUTE from *Marylebone, via* Penistone. 189¾ miles. Fares, 37/9*a*, 22/8*c*. R. T. for two months, 75/6*a*, 45/4*c*.

M'BONE.	L'WOOD.	L'WOOD.	M'BONE.
AM 2.32	7.31	AM 8.20*r*	1.13
8.45*r*	1.54	10.16*r*	3. 0
10. 0*r*	2.53	PM 2.20*r*	6.38
PM12.15*r*	5.17	5. 2*r*	9.55
3.20*r*	8. 0	9.59	3.57
6.20*r*	10.27	—	—
—	—	—	—
—	—	—	—

Sunday Trains.

AM11.15*r*	7.54	PM 4.59*r*	10.24
PM 5.30*r*	10.19	—	—
—	—	—	—
—	—	—	—
—	—	—	—

r Restaurant Car.

LODDISWELL (Devon) from *Paddington*, 218½ miles. 45/0*a*, 27/0*c*. R.T. for two months, 90/0*a*. Departures *from* London as for Kingsbridge. Departures *for* London about 5 times daily. Pop. 678.
Map Square 26.

LODGE HILL (Somerset) from *Paddington*, 124¼ miles. Fares, *via* Witham, 25/8*a*, 15/5*c*. R. T. for two months, 51/4*a*. *Via* Yatton, 29/10*a*, 17/11*c*. R. T. for two months, 59/8*a*. Departures *from* London as for Wells (Somerset). Departures *for* London about 6 times daily.
Map Square 22.

LOFTHOUSE (Yorks), 178¾ miles. Fares, 37/1*a*, 22/3*c*. Departures *from* London as for Wakefield (Westgate). Departures *for* London about 8 times daily. Pop. 4,670.

LOFTHOUSE-IN-NIDDERDALE (Yorks), 219 miles. No through fares. Departures *from* London as for Pateley Bridge. Departures *for* London about 4 times daily.
Map Square 7.

LOFTUS (Yorks), 258¾ miles. Fares, 53/11*a*, 32/4*c*. R.T., double fare. Departures *from* London as for Saltburn or Sandsend. Departures *for* London about 6 times daily. Pop. 9,012.
Map Square 8.

LOGIERIEVE (Aberdeen), 539 miles. No through fares. Departures *from* London as for Fraserburgh or Peterhead. Departures *for* London about twice daily. Pop. 635.
Map Square 35.

LOGIN (Pembroke), 247½ miles. Fares, 50/3*a*, 30/2*c*. R. T. for two months, 100/6*a*, 60/4*c*. Departures *from* London as for Cardigan. Departures *for* London about 4 times daily.
Map Square 21.

LONDESBOROUGH (Yorks), 193¾ miles. No through fares. Departures *from* London as for Market Weighton. Departures *for* London about 6 times daily. Pop. 328.
Map Square 8.

LONDON BRIDGE from *Victoria*, 8¾ miles. Fares, *via* S. L. Line, 0/9*a*, 0/5½*c*. R. T. for two days, 1/2*a*, 0/9*c*. *Via* Norwood Junction, 1/11*a*, 1/2*c*. R. T. for two days, 3/10*a*, 2/0*c*. *See* p. 570.

From *Charing Cross*, 2¼ miles. Fares, 0/5*a*, 0/4*b*, 0/3*c*. R. T. for two days, 0/10*a*, 0/8*b*, 0/6*c*. *See* pp. 544-557.

From *Cannon Street*, ¾ mile. Fares, 0/2½*a*, 0/2*b*, 0/1½*c*. R. T. for two days, 0/5*a*, 0/4*b*, 0/3*c*. Every few minutes. *See* pp. 544-557.

City and South London Tube. *See* back of Map.
Map Square 61.

Argosy Hotels, 30 and 71, Borough, London Bridge. Two minutes from London Bridge Station. Phone, 1264 Hop.

London and Suburban HOTELS. *See* pp. **5-23.**

LONDON FIELDS from *Liverpool Street*, 2½ miles. Fares, 0/5*a*, 0/4*b*, 0/3*c*. R. T. for two days, 0/10*a*, 0/7*b*, 0/5½*c*. *See* pp. 523, 524, 534-536.
Map Square 61.

LONG BUCKBY (Northampton), 75½ miles. Fares, 15/3*a*, 9/2*c*. R. T. for two months, 30/6*a*. Departures *from* London as for Northampton (Castle). Departures *for* London about 6 times daily. Pop. 2,467.
Map Square 18.

LONG CLAWSON (Leicester), 112¾ miles. Fares, 22/8*a*, 13/7*c*. R. T. for two months, 45/4*a*. Departures *from* London as for Hallaton or Bottesford. Departures *for* London about 6 times daily. Pop. 735.
Map Square 18.

LONGDON ROAD (Gloucester), 98½ miles. Fares, 20/5*a*, 12/3*c*. R.T. for two months, 40/10*a*, 24/6*c*. Departures *from* London as for Shipston-on-Stour. Departures *for* London about 3 times daily.
Map Square 17.

LONGDOWN (Devon), 179½ miles. Fares, 36/11*a*, 22/2*c*. R. T. for two months, 73/10*a*. Departures *from* London as for Exeter (St. David's). Departures *for* London about 6 times daily.
Map Square 26.

LONG EATON (Derby) from *St. Pancras*, 120½ miles. Fares, 24/10*a*, 14/11*c*. R. T., double fare. Departures *from* London as for Trent. Departures *for* London about 12 times daily. Pop. 19,503.
Map Square 13.

LONGFORD (Warwick), 98¾ miles. Fares, 20/7*a*, 12/4*c*. R.T. for two months, 41/2*a*. Departures *from* London as for Coventry. Departures *for* London about 6 times daily. Pop. 4,236.
Map Square 17.

LONGFORGAN (Perth), 465 miles. Fares, 91/11*a*, 55/2*c*. R.T. for two months, 183/10*a*, 110/4*c*. Departures *from* London as for Perth. Departures *for* London about 3 times daily. Pop. 2,032.
Map Square 38.

LONGHAVEN (Aberdeen), 555¾ miles. No through fares. Departures *from* London as for Cruden Bay. Departures *for* London about twice daily.
Map Square 35.

LONGHIRST (Northumberland), 288 miles. Fares, 60/8*a*, 36/5*c*. R. T., double fare. Departures *from* London as for Morpeth. Departures *for* London about 6 times daily. Pop. 326.
Map Square 3.

LONGHOPE (Gloucester) from *Paddington*, 125¼ miles. Fares, 26/1*a*, 15/8*c*. R .T. for two months, 52/2*a*. Departures *from* London as for Ross. Departures *for* London about 6 times daily. Pop. 864.
Map Square 22.

LONGHOUGHTON (Northumberland), 305¼ miles. Fares, 64/5*a*, 38/8*c*. R. T., double fare. Departures *from* London as for Morpeth. Departures *for* London about 5 times daily. Pop. 589.
Map Square 3.

LONG-MARSTON (Gloucester) from *Paddington*, 104¾ miles. Fares, 21/1*a*, 12/8*c*. R. T. for two months, 42/2*a*. Departures *from* London as for Stratford-on-Avon. Departures *for* London about 4 times daily. Pop. 284.
Map Square 17.

LONG MARTON (Westmorland) from *St. Pancras*, 280 miles. Fares, 55/0*a*, 33/0*c*. R. T., double fare. Departures *from* London as for Appleby. Departures *for* London about 4 times daily. Pop. 587.
Map Square 7.

LONG MELFORD (Suffolk) from *Liverpool Street*, 61½ miles. Fares, 13/1*a*, 7/10*c*. R. T. for two months, 26/2*a*. Pop. 2,878.
Map Square 19.

L'PL.ST.	L'MELFD.	L'MELFD.	L'PL.ST.
AM 6.50	9.48	AM 8. 4	9.53
10. 0	11.55	9.56	11.42
PM12.36	2.36	11.56*h*	2. 3
2.15	4.28	PM 2.23*h*	5. 5
4.58	6.48	4.14*h*	6.32
5.42	7.38	6.31	9.17
—	—	—	—
—	—	—	—
—	—	—	—
—	—	—	—
—	—	—	—
—	—	—	—

No Sunday Trains.

h Via Colchester.

LONGMORN (Elgin), 571¾ miles. Fares, 106/3a, 63/9c. R. T. for two months, 212/6a, 127/6c. Departures *from* London as for Aviemore or Keith (*via* Aberdeen). Departures *for* London about twice daily.
Map Square 35.

LONGNIDDRY (East Lothian), 379 miles. Fares, 79/9a, 47/10c. R. T. for two months, 159/6a, 95/8c. Departures *from* London as for Dunbar. Departures *for* London about 4 times daily.
Map Square 41.

LONGPARISH (Hants) from *Waterloo*, 65½ miles. Fares, 13/9a, 8/3c. R. T. for two months, 27/6a, 16/6c. Pop. 729.
Map Square 23.

W'LOO	L'PARISH	L'PARISH	W'LOO
AM 5.50	9.20	AM 7.40	9.56
PM 3.30	5.26	10.19	12.22
5. 0	7. 3	PM 6.24	10.50
—	—	—	—
—	—	—	—

No Sunday Trains.

LONGPORT (Stafford) from *Euston*, 148¾ miles. Fares, 30/10a, 18/6c. R. T. for two months, 61/8a. Departures *from* London as for Stoke-on-Trent. Departures *for* London about 4 times daily.
Map Square 12.

LONG PRESTON (Yorks), 232¼ miles. Fares, 44/10a, 26/11c. R. T. for two months, 89/8a, 53/10c. Departures *from* London as for Hellifield. Departures *for* London about 4 times daily. Pop. 733.
Map Square 7.

LONGRIDGE (Lancs), 216½ miles. Fares, 45/0a, 27/0c, R. T. for two months, 90/0a, 54/0c. Departures *from* London as for Preston. Departures *for* London about 9 times daily. Pop. 4,303.
Map Square 12.

LONGRIGGEND (Lanark), 422½ miles. No through fares. Departures *from* London as for Edinburgh (Waverley). Departures *for* London about 4 times daily.
Map Square 40.

LONGSIDE (Aberdeen), 561¼ miles. Fares, 108/1a, 64/10c. R. T. for two months, 216/2a, 129/8c. Departures *from* London as for Peterhead. Departures *for* London about twice daily. Pop. 2,484.
Map Square 35.

LONGSIGHT (Lancs), 182 miles. Fares, 37/11a, 22/9c. R. T., double fare. Departures *from* London as for Stockport. Departures *for* London about 9 times daily. Pop. 19,488.

LONG STANTON (Cambridge) from *Liverpool Street*, 65 miles. Fares, 12/3a, 7/4c. R. T., double fare. Departures *from* London as for St. Ives (Hunts). Departures *for* London about 8 times daily. Pop. 412.
Map Square 18.

LONG SUTTON (Lincoln) from *King's Cross*, 105 miles. Fares, 19/9a, 11/10c. R. T. for two months, 39/6a. Departures *from* London as for Holbeach. Departures *for* London about 5 times daily. Pop. 3,192.
Map Square 18.

LONG SUTTON (Somerset), 128 miles. Fares, 25/7a, 16/0c. R. T. for two months, 51/2a, 32/0c. Departures *from* London as for Somerton. Departures *for* London about 4 times daily. Pop. 751.
Map Square 22.

LONGTON (Stafford) from *Euston*, 147½ miles. Fares, 30/8a, 18/5c. R. T. for two months, 61/4a. Pop. 37,479.
Map Square 12.

EUSTON	LONGTON	LONGTON	EUSTON
AM 2.35	8.12	AM 6.15	11. 0
5. 0	9.43	8.26er	12. 5
8.45r	12.12	8.26dr	12.20
10.40er	2.38	9.33r	12.50
10.40dr	2.58	10.40r	2.20
12. 0nr	4.46	11. 9d	3.10
PM 2.50t	5.52	PM12.45r	3.55
4.45r	8.18	2.48	6.15
6.30er	10.28	4.49r	9.20
6.55r	11.18	6.32r	10. 0
—	—	8.50	5. 0
—	—	10.48	5.40
—	—	11. 0d	5.45
—	—	—	—
—	—	—	—
—	—	—	—

Sunday Trains.

AM12.10	12. 8	AM10.35	4. 0
PM12.10r	4.18	PM 3.50	8.55
3.50	10.27	7.50	5. 0
—	—	—	—

d Saturdays only.
e Saturdays excepted.
n Noon.
r Restaurant Car.

LONGTON BRIDGE (Lancs), 214 miles. Fares, 44/5a, 26/8c. R. T. for two months, 88/10a. Departures *from* London as for Preston. Departures *for* London about 9 times daily.
Map Square 12.

LONGTOWN (Cumberland), 308¾ miles. Fares, 62/6a, 37/6c. R. T. for two months, 125/0a. Departures *from* London as for Carlisle. Departures *for* London about twice daily.
Map Square 3.

LONGVILLE (Salop), 154 miles. Fares, 32/1a, 19/3c. R. T. for two months, 64/2a, 38/6c. Departures *from* London as for Much Wenlock. Departures *for* London about 3 times daily.
Map Square 17.

LONGWITTON (Northumberland), 309½ miles. No through fares. Departures *from* London as for Morpeth. Departures *for* London about 3 times daily. Pop. 104.
Map Square 3.

LONGWOOD (Yorks), 201½ miles. Fares, 37/9a, 22/8c. R. T., double fare. Departures *from* London as for Marsden. Departures *for* London about 9 times daily. Pop. 5,837.
Map Square 12.

LONMAY (Aberdeen). 565 miles. No through fares. Departures *from* London as for Fraserburgh. Departures *for* London about twice daily. Pop. 1,884.
Map Square 35.

LOOE (Cornwall), 251¾ miles. Fares, 52/3a, 31/4c. R. T. for two months, 104/6a, 62/8c. Pop. 2,868.
Map Square 26.

PAD.	LOOE	LOOE	PAD.
AM 5.30	2.10	AM 6.35fr	1.30
11.10r	4.50	10.10r	4.35
PM 2. 0r	8.35	PM12.15r	6.50
10. 0e	7.52	7.15	7.10
12. 0h	9.55	8.50k	7.10
—	—	—	—
—	—	—	—
—	—	—	—

Sunday Trains.

PM10. 0	7.52	—	—
—	—	—	—
—	—	—	—

e Saturdays excepted.
f Mondays only.
h Saturdays midnight excepted.
k Wednesdays and Saturdays only.
r Restaurant Car.

LORD'S BRIDGE (Cambridge), from *King's Cross*, 59¾ miles. No through fares. Departures *from* London as for Sandy. Departures *for* London about 5 times daily.
Map Square 18.

LORDSHIP LANE from *Victoria* or *Holborn Viaduct*, 8¼ miles. Fares, 1/3a, 1/0b, 0/9c. R. T. for two days, 2/6a, 1/9b, 1/4c. See pp. 562, 563.
Map Square 79.

LOSSIEMOUTH (Elgin), 577¼ miles. Fares, 107/1a, 64/3c. R. T. for two months, 214/2a, 128/6c. Departures *from* London as for Elgin. Departures *for* London about 3 times daily. Pop. 4,166.
Map Square 35.

LOSTOCK (Lancs), 200¼ miles. Fares, 41/1a, 24/8c. R. T. for two months, 82/2a, 49/4c. Departures *from* London as for Bolton (*via* Manchester). Departures *for* London about 4 times daily.
Map Square 12.

LOSTOCK GRALAM

(Cheshire), 173 miles. Fares, 35/8*a*, 21/5*c*. R. T., double fare. Departures *from* London as for Northwich. Departures *for* London about 4 times daily. Pop. 2,196.
Map Square 12.

LOSTOCK HALL

(Lancs), 211¾ miles. No through fares. Departures *from* London as for Preston. Departures *for* London about 4 times daily.
Map Square 12.

LOSTWITHIEL

(Cornwall), 256 miles. Fares, 53/1*a*, 31/10*c*. R. T. for two months, 106/2*a*, 63/8*c*. Pop. 1,308.
Map Square 25.

PAD.	L'WITHL.	L'WITHL.	PAD.
AM 5.30	1.30	AM10.37*r*	4.35
11.10*r*	4.58	PM12.59*r*	6.50
PM12. 5*r*	7.21	1.27*dr*	7. 5
2. 0*r*	8.21	2.24*r*	9. 0
12. 0*h*	9. 5	10.44	7.10
12.30*k*	9.38	—	—
—	—	—	—

Sunday Trains.

PM10. 0	9 5	PM12.54	7. 5
—	—	6.40	3.15
—	—	—	—

d Saturdays only.
h Saturdays midnight excepted.
k Saturdays midnight only.
r Restaurant Car.

LOTH

(Sutherland), 663½ miles. No through fares. Departures *from* London as for Golspie. Departures *for* London about twice daily. Pop. 321.
Map Square 31.

LOUDOUN HILL

(Lanark), 398½ miles. No through fares. Departures *from* London as for Kilmarnock or Hamilton. Departures *for* London about 3 times daily.
Map Square 40.

LOUDWATER

(Bucks) from *Paddington*, 31½ miles. Fares, 5/3*a*, 3/2*c*. R. T. for two months, 10/6*a*, 6/4*c*. Pop. 1,513.
Map Square 23.

PAD.	LOUDWTR.	LOUDWTR.	PAD.
AM 5.45	7.26	AM 7.56	8.56
6.30	8.17	8.31	9.37
7.35	9. 9	9.36	11. 6
8.30	10. 2	10.20	11.35
9.20	10.44	11. 3	12.15
11.25	12.36	PM 1. 9	2.35
PM12.35*e*	2.12	2.58	4.10
1. 5*d*	2.14	4.11	5.37
2. 7	3.17	5.35	6.55
3.38	4.44	6.29	7.45
4.50	5.55	8. 9	9.33
5.45	6.49	9.21	10.42
6.55	7.54	10.11	12. 0
8.35	9.44	—	—
10. 5*h*	11.14	—	—
—	—	—	—
—	—	—	—

Sunday Trains.

AM 8.20	9.54	AM 8.47	10.14
9.45	10.53	11.32	1. 5
11.45	12.50	PM 2.46	4.53
PM 2.35	3.48	5. 2	6.22
5.15	6.28	7.35	9.17
8.20	9.35	8.42	9.53
—	—	—	—
—	—	—	—

d Saturdays only.
e Saturdays excepted.
h Wednesdays and Saturdays only.

LOUGHBOROUGH

(Leicester) from *St. Pancras*, 111½ miles. Fares, 22/11*a*, 13/9*c*. R. T., double fare. Pop. 25,874.
Map Square 18.

ST. PAN.	L'BORO'	L'BORO'	ST. PAN.
AM 2.25	4.58	AM 1.17*g*	4.20
4.25	7.40	1.36*f*	4.55
8.25*hr*	11. 0	7.30*r*	9.57
8.25*r*	11.26	8.29*r*	11. 0
9.50*r*	12.22	9. 6*r*	11.35
10.25*r*	12.43	10.45*r*	1.30
11.45*r*	2. 8	11.40*r*	2.10
PM12.25*r*	3. 3	PM12.27	3.25
1.25*r*	4. 1	2. 0*r*	4.20
2.25*r*	4.56	3. 4*r*	5.45
4.25*r*	7. 7	4. 9*r*	6.35
5.35*r*	8. 8	5.33*r*	7.55
6.25*r*	9. 0	6.48*r*	9.15
8.25	11.45	7.22*r*	10. 5
12. 0	3. 9	—	—
—	—	—	—
—	—	—	—

Sunday Trains.

AM10.50*r*	1.32	AM 1.17	4.20
PM 1.35	5.10	2.45	6. 0
3.15	5.53	8. 2	11.53
6.15*r*	9.13	PM 2.12*r*	5. 2
8.25	11.45	7.30*r*	9.52
11.55	3. 9	7.47	11. 7
—	—	—	—
—	—	—	—

f Mondays only.
g Mondays excepted.
h Mondays, Tuesdays and Fridays only.
r Restaurant Car.

ANOTHER ROUTE

(CENTRAL) from *Marylebone*, 113 miles. Fares as above.

M'BONE.	L'BORO'	L'BORO'	M'BONE.
AM 2.32	7. 3	AM 5.46	9.46
8.45*r*	11.22	8. 2	10.36
10. 0*r*	12.40	9. 2*r*	11.10
PM12.15*r*	2.51	10.18*r*	1.13
3.20*r*	5.41	PM12.32*r*	3. 0
5. 0*r*	7.10	12.54	4.56
6.20*r*	8.55	4. 3*r*	6.38
6.25	11. 2	6.27*r*	8.55
—	—	6.44*r*	9.55
—	—	10.42	3.57
—	—	—	—
—	—	—	—
—	—	—	—
—	—	—	—

Sunday Trains.

AM 9.30	1.27	PM 3.12*r*	5.40
11.15*r*	1.44	3.35	8.58
PM 5.30*r*	8.58	7.55*r*	10.24
—	—	—	—
—	—	—	—
—	—	—	—

r Restaurant Car.

ANOTHER ROUTE

(DERBY ROAD) from *Euston*, 123¾ miles. Fares as above.

EUSTON	L'BORO'	L'BORO'	EUSTON
AM 5. 0	8.42	AM 7. 0*r*	11. 0
10. 0	2.50	8.58	12.50
12. 0*nr*	4.40	11.10*hr*	3.45
PM 5.20*r*	8.50	11.10*r*	4.15
—	—	PM 1. 3	5.35
—	—	3.20*r*	8.10
—	—	6. 5*r*	10.45
—	—	—	—

No Sunday Trains.
h Mondays and Saturdays only.
n Noon.
r Restaurant Car.

LOUGHBORO'—*contd.*

King's Head Hotel. Telephone 510. Excellent Centre both for Hunting and Business. Electric Light. Billiards. Large Garage and Stabling.
TRUST HOUSES, Ltd.

LOUGHBOROUGH

JUNCTION, from *Victoria*, *Ludgate Hill*, and *St. Paul's*, 3¾ miles. Fares from Victoria, 0/7½*a*, 0/6*b*, 0/4½*c*. R. T. for two days, 1/2*a*, 1/0*b*, 0/9*c*. From Ludgate Hill, 0/7*a*, 0/6*b*, 0/4½*c*. R. T. for two days, 1/0*a*, 0/10½*b*. 0/9*c*. *See* pp. 558-563.
Map Square 70.

LOUGHOR

(Glamorgan) from *Paddington*, 204 miles. Fares, 42/6*a*, 25/6*c*. R. T. for two months, 85/0*a*. Pop. 4,118.
Map Square 21.

PAD.	LOUGHOR	LOUGHOR	PAD.
AM 1. 0*g*	8.21	AM 7.57*r*	1. 0
8.45*r*	1.26	9. 3*r*	2.30
11.50*r*	5.11	11. 7*r*	4.20
PM 1.10*r*	6.26	PM12.49*r*	6.15
3.35*r*	8.36	3. 9*r*	8.35
5. 0*dr*	10.14	4.17*r*	9.28
5. 0*hr*	10.54	7. 9	3.30
6. 0*r*	11.14	—	—
—	—	—	—

Sunday Trains.

PM 9.15	8.21	—	—
—	—	—	—
—	—	—	—

d Saturdays only.
g Mondays excepted.
h Tuesdays only.
r Restaurant Car.

LOUGHTON

(Essex) from *Fenchurch Street*, 11¾ miles, and *Liverpool Street*, 11½ miles. Fares, 2/1*a*, 1/8*b*, 1/3*c*. R. T. for two days, 4/2*a*, 3/4*b*, 2/4*c*. Pop. 5,749. *See* pp. 541-544.
Map Square 23.

LOUTH

(Lincoln) from *King's Cross*, 141 miles. Fares, 29/4*a*, 17/7*c*. R. T., double fare. Pop. 9,544.
Map Square 13.

KING'S +	LOUTH	LOUTH	KING'S +
AM 4.45	9.14	AM 6.19	10.40
8.45	1.35	9.32	1. 5
11.30	4.55	10.15	3.50
PM 4. 0*r*	7.33	PM12.45*r*	4.30
5.45*r*	9.25	3.10	9. 0
10.45*e*	4.56	5.28*r*	9.25
—	—	8.34	3.25
—	—	—	—
—	—	—	—
—	—	—	—
—	—	—	—
—	—	—	—
—	—	—	—

Sunday Trains.

12. 0*nr*	4.35	AM10.33*r*	3.45
PM10.45	4.56	—	—
—	—	—	—

e Saturdays excepted.
n Noon.
r Restaurant Car.

LOWDHAM (Notts), from
St. Pancras, 130½ miles. Fares, 26/1*a*, 15/8*c*. R. T., double fare. Departures *from* London as for Nottingham. Departures *for* London about 8 times daily. Pop. 982.
Map Square 13.

LOWER DARWEN
(Lancs), 209 miles. Fares, 43/2*a*, 25/11*c*. R. T. for two months, 86/4*a*, 51/10*c*. Departures *from* London as for Darwen. Departures *for* London about 8 times daily.
Map Square 12.

LOWER EDMONTON.
See EDMONTON (LOWER).

LOWERINCE (Lancs)
from *Marylebone*, 227¼ miles. Fares, 40/5*a*, 24/3*c*. R. T. for two months, 80/10*a*, 48/6*c*. Departures *from* London as for Wigan (Central). Departures *for* London about 4 times daily.

LOWER SYDENHAM.
See SYDENHAM (LOWER).

LOWESBY (Leicester), 99½
miles. No through fares. Departures *from* London as for Hallaton or Bottesford. Departures *for* London about 3 times daily. Pop. 147.
Map Square 18.

LOWESTOFT (CENTRAL)
(Suffolk) from *Liverpool Street, via* Ipswich, 117⅞ miles. Fares, 24/9*a*, 14/10*c*. R. T. for two months, 49/6*a*, 29/8*c*. Pop. 44,326.
Map Square 19.

L'PL. ST.	LOWES.	LOWES.	L'PL. ST.
AM 5. 0	9.13	AM 6.30r	10.30
8.15r	11.35	7.36r	11.22
9.55	12.48	8.25r	11.30
10. 0	1.20	9.55	1.20
10.20	2.22	PM12.20	3.42
PM12.56	3.36	1.15	3.56
1. 0	4.23	2.28	5.55
3.15	6.17	3.33	7.51
3.18r	7.15	4.28r	7.23
4.55r	8. 8	5.30r	9.22
5.18dr	9. 3	6.25r	10. 0
5.18er	9.12	—	—

Sunday Trains.

AM10½ 5r	1.48	AM 7. 5	11.38
11.30r	2.25	PM 3.40r	6.35
PM 4.40	8.35	5.20r	9.10
—	—	7. 0r	10.30

d Saturdays only.
e Saturdays excepted.
r Restaurant Car.

ANOTHER ROUTE (CENTRAL) from *Liverpool Street, via* Cambridge, 146¼ miles. Fares as above.

L'POOL ST.	L'TOFT.	L'TOFT.	L'POOL ST.
AM 5. 5	10. 7	AM 6.24	11.27
5.50	11.43	7.34	12.40
8.30r	1.38	8.54r	2.21
11.50r	4.10	PM12.35r	5.17
PM 2.34	7.20	2.39r	8.22
5.49r	10.48	3.43r	8.33
—	—	9. 0	2.50

Sunday Trains.

AM 9.25	3. 3	PM 1. 6	6.40
PM 3.25	8.43	9. 0	3. 0
—	—	—	—

r Restaurant Car.

Royal Hotel. First-class.
On Sea Front, facing Pier. Near Station. Two Tennis Courts. Ball Room. Orchestra. Inclusive Terms from 15/- per day. 'Phone 394, 395. Resident Proprietor,
J. B. WHALEY.
See advt. p. 236.

LOWESTOFT—*contd.*
Grand Hotel. Magnificent position near Links. 300 feet sea frontage. Standing in own grounds. Ballroom Orchestra. Garage. Tel. 190. Tariff—
MANAGER.
See advt. p. 237.

Kingswear Private Hotel.
Finest Position. Tennis. Sea Views. Tariff apply—
Mrs. L. MEADOWS.
Resident Proprietress.
See advt. p. 238.

The Clyffe. Private Hotel.
Facing sea, near Piers. Private Hard Tennis Court on Sea front. 10 mins. Golf Links. Moderate inclusive terms. Telegrams: "The Clyffe,"
Mrs. NEEVES.
See advt. p. 238.

Esplanade Hotel, High Class
Private Hotel. Lounge and Dining Room facing Sea. 'Phone 298. Mr. & Mrs. JENNER.
See advt. p. 239.

Sunnydene Private Hotel.
North Parade. Finest Position, overlooking Sea. Dancing. Tennis. Billiards.
Mrs. E. NORTON,
Resident Proprietress.
See advt. p. 235.

Hotel Victoria. First-class
Family Hotel. Spacious Rooms. Near Tennis Courts.
See advt. p. 235.

Banner House. Boarding
Establishment, South Lowestoft. Sea View. Modern Sanitation. Electric Light throughout. Spacious New Dining Hall. Separate Tables. Excellent and Liberal Cuisine. Moderate and Inclusive Terms. Apply—
Mrs. BLACKMORE.

Dagmar, Kirkley Cliff.
Facing Sea. Young Society. Dancing, Tennis, Picnics. Open all the Year. Boating. Personal Supervision. Stamp.
Mrs. FAIRCHILD.

Crown Hotel. Family and
Commercial. Thoroughly comfortable, and very moderate. Electric Light. Garage. Tel. 372.
J. B. STANSFIELD, Proprietor.

Hatfield House, The Esplanade. Best position on sea front.
Dining rooms open on to lawn and promenade. Excellent cuisine. All modern conveniences. Telephone 120. Mrs. HENDERSON.

LOWFELL (Durham), 265¼
miles. Fares, 55/3*a*, 33/2*c*. R. T. for two months, 110/6*a*, 66/4*c*. Departures *from* London for Durham. Departures *for* London about 6 times daily.
Map Square 3.

LOW GILL (Westmorland)
from *Euston*, 258 miles. Fares, 51/11*a*, 31/2*c*. R. T., double fare.
Map Square 7.

EUSTON	L. GILL.	L. GILL.	EUSTON
AM12.25	8.46	AM 7.55r	3.10
2.35	11.18	9.13hr	3.45
5. 0	1.34	9.13r	4.15
6.45	4. 9	11.1r	6. 0
11.35r	5.59	PM 1.34er	9. 5
PM 1.30r	7.49	1.34dr	9.15
—	—	7.21	5. 0

LOW GILL—*continued*
Sunday Trains.

EUSTON	L. GILL.	L. GILL	EUSTON
AM11.45	7.21	PM 5.32	5. 0

d Saturdays only.
e Saturdays excepted.
h Mondays and Saturdays only.
r Restaurant Car.

LOWMOOR (Yorks) from
King's Cross, via Horbury, 189½ miles. Fares, 39/5*a*, 23/8*c*. R. T. for two months, 78/10*a*, 47/4*c*. Pop. 2,138.
Map Square 12.

KING'S+	LOWMR.	LOWMR.	KING'S+
AM 4.45	11.13	AM 6. 4	11.30
7.15r	1. 0	7.58r	1. 5
10.10dr	3.16	9.21r	1.55
10.10er	3.46	10. 1r	3.50
PM 1.30r	6. 8	10.53r	4.45
1.50r	8.22	11.40	5. 0
5.45r	11.16	PM 1.45r	7.10
—	—	4.17r	9.25
—	—	8.34e	3.25

Sunday Trains.

12. 0hn 7. 0		AM 9.20r	3.45
—	—	PM 2.11½	10.20
—	—	—	—

d Saturdays only.
e Saturdays excepted.
h Passengers cross Wakefield at own expense.
n Noon.
r Restaurant Car.

ANOTHER ROUTE from
King's Cross, via Holbeck. 194½ miles. Fares as above.

KING'S+	LOWMR.	LOWMR.	KING'S+
AM 4.45	10.37	AM 6.25r	11.30
7.15r	12.14	8.12	1. 5
10.10	3.51	9.37r	1.55
PM 1.30r	5.34	10. 1	3.50
1.50r	7.56	11.40er	5. 0
4. 0r	9. 9	PM12.28	6.25
5.45r	10.54	2.17r	7.10
10.45e	5.10	4.40	9.25
—	—	8.57	3.25

Sunday Trains.

12. 0nr 7. 1		AM10.28r	3.45
—	—	PM12.30	5.55
—	—	4. 1r	10.20

e Saturdays excepted.
n Noon.
r Restaurant Car.

LOWROW (Cumberland),
313 miles. No through fares. Departures *from* London as for Hexham or Carlisle. Departures *for* London about 6 times daily.
Map Square 3.

LOW STREET (Essex)
from *Fenchurch Street*, 24 miles. Fares, 3/7*a*, 2/2*c*. R. T. for two months, 7/2*a*, 4/4*c*.
Map Square 24.

FEN. ST.	LOW ST	LOW ST.	FEN. ST.
AM 5.37	7. 4	AM 6. 9	7.22
6.52	8. 9	7.13	8.24
7.30	8.52	7.39	8.49
9. 5	10.17	8.33	9.34
10.17	11.12	10.16	11.20
11.13d	12.32	10.59	12.16
11.35	12.53	PM12.11e	1.22
11.42e	12.53	12.11d	1.27
PM 1.15d	2.22	1.21d	2.34
1.48e	3. 6	2.55	4.10
2.15d	3.18	3.57	5.18
3.25	4.32	5.15	6.33
4.16	5.34	6. 2	7.24
5.32	6.27	7.59	9.15
5.55e	7. 4	10.12	11.23h
6.38	7.50	10.12	11.40
7.41e	8.48	—	—
8.13	9.29	—	—
9.25	10.41	—	—

LOW STREET—*contd.*

Sunday Trains.

Fen. St	Low St.	Low St.	Fen. St.
AM 8.40	10. 5	AM 8.58	10.18
11.10	12.27	11.43	1. 1
PM 2. 7	3.21	PM 2.47	4. 4
4.30	5.43	6.27	7.45
7.22	9.12	7.54	9.11*h*
8.45	10. 3	8. 7	9.30
—	—	9.45	11. 0

d Saturdays only.
e Saturdays excepted.
h Arrives at Mark Lane Station.

LOWTHORPE (Yorks),

210 miles. No through fares. Departures *from* London as for Driffield. Departures *for* London about 4 times daily. Pop. 168.

Map Square 8.

LOWTON (Lancs), 188

miles. Fares, 39/2*a*, 23/6*c*. R. T. for two months, 78/4*a*. Departures *from* London as for Newton-le-Willows. Departures *for* London about 4 times daily. Pop. 3,429.

Map Square 12.

LOWTON ST. MARY'S

(Lancs), from Marylebone 222 miles. Fares, 39/2*a*, 23/6*c*. R. T. for two months, 78/4*a*, 47/0*c*. Departures *from* London as for Wigan (Central). Departures *for* London about 4 times daily. Pop. 1,684.

Map Square 12.

LUBENHAM (Leicester),

86½ miles. Fares, 17/6*a*, 10/6*c*. R. T. for two months, 35/0*a*. Departures *from* London as for Welford. Departures *for* London about 4 times daily. Pop. 661.

Map Square 18.

LUCKER (Northumberland),

317 miles. Fares, 66/11*a*, 40/2*c*. R. T. for two months, 133/10*a*, 80/4*c*. Departures *from* London as for Morpeth. Departures *for* London about 5 times daily. Pop. 184.

Map Square 3.

LUCKETT (Cornwall) from

Waterloo, 228 miles. Fares, 48/1*a*, 28/10*c*. R. T. for two months, 96/2*a*, 57/8*c*. Departures *from* London as for Calstock. Departures *for* London about 4 times daily.

Map Square 26.

LUDBOROUGH (Lincoln),

146¼ miles. Fares, 30/5*a*, 18/3*c*. R. T., double fare. Departures *from* London as for Louth. Departures *for* London about 5 times daily. Pop. 233.

Map Square 13.

LUDDENDENFOOT

(Yorks) from *King's Cross*, 196¼ miles. Fares, 40/3*a*, 24/2*c*. R. T. for two months, 80/6*a*. Departures *from* London as for Sowerby Bridge. Departures *for* London about 10 times daily. Pop. 2,821.

Map Square 12.

LUDDINGTON (Lincs),

178 miles. No through fares. Departures *from* London as for Goole. Departures *for* London about 3 times daily. Pop. 527.

Map Square 13.

LUDGERSHALL (Wilts)

from *Waterloo*, 73¾ miles. Fares, 15/3*a*, 9/2*c*. R. T. for two months, 30/6*a*, 18/4*c*. Pop. 1,117.

Map Square 22.

W'loo	L'shall.	L'shall.	W'loo.
AM 7.30	9.46	AM 8.54	10.56
9.30*d*	1.31	10. 5	12.22
PM 1. 0*r*	2.56	PM12.39	2.36
3.30	5.51	3.36	6.26
6. 0*r*	8. 6	5.39*e*	7.40
—	—	5.56*r*	8.30

Sunday Trains.

PM 6. 0	8.26	PM 5.51	8.57
—	—	—	—
—	—	—	—
—	—	—	—
—	—	—	—

d Saturdays only.
e Saturdays excepted.
r Restaurant Car.

LUDLOW (Salop) from

Paddington, 158¾ miles. Fares, 31/0*a*, 18/7*c*. R. T. for two months, 62/0*a*, 37/2*c*. Pop. 5,677.

Map Square 17.

Pad.	Ludlow	Ludlow	Pad.
AM 1. 0*l*	10.12	AM 7.35	12.25
5.30	12.39	9.13*r*	2. 5
9.10*r*	2.11	11.22*hr*	4.15
10.40*r*	3.13	PM12.39	5.55
PM 1.30*r*	6. 5	2. 4*r*	8. 5
2.10*t*	6.32	3.13*r*	8.45
3.15*t*	8.47	5.14	10. 0
4.10*t*	9.14	8.47	3.30
6.10*r*	10.39	—	—
12.15*k*	7.42	—	—
—	—	—	—
—	—	—	—
—	—	—	—

Sunday Trains.

PM12.50*r*	6.21	AM10.31*r*	6.20
—	—	—	—
—	—	—	—
—	—	—	—
—	—	—	—

h Via Leominster, Bromyard, and Worcester.
k Saturdays midnight excepted.
l Mondays excepted.
r Restaurant Car.
t Tea Car.

ANOTHER ROUTE from

Euston, 189¾ miles. Fares, 31/11*a*, 19/2*c*. R. T. for two months, 63/10*a*, 38/4*c*.

Euston	Ludlow	Ludlow	Euston
AM 5. 0	11.22	AM 8.24*r*	2.20
6.45	2.11	10.12*r*	3.10
10.40*r*	3.13	PM12.39*r*	6.15
PM 1.15*r*	6.32	2. 4*r*	9.20
2.20*t*	9.14	8.47	5. 0
4.45*r*	10.38	—	—
5.50*d*	4.35	—	—
9.20*e*	4.33	—	—
—	—	—	—
—	—	—	—
—	—	—	—
—	—	—	—
—	—	—	—

Sunday Trains.

AM 9.15	6.21	AM10.31*hr*	5.45
PM11. 0*h*	4.33	PM 8.47*h*	5. 0
—	—	—	—
—	—	—	—

d Saturdays only.
e Saturdays excepted.
h Via Crewe.
r Restaurant Car.
t Tea Car.

LUFFENHAM (Rutland)

from *King's Cross*, 94½ miles. Fares, 17/3*a*, 10/4*c*. R. T., double fare. Pop. 760.

Map Square 18.

King's +	Luff'm.	Luff'm.	King's +
AM 5. 5	8.36	AM 8.39*r*	12.25
7.15*r*	9.55	10.27	1. 5
7.45	10.57	PM 2.17*r*	4.45
10.10*r*	12.49	4.48*r*	7.10
PM 1.50*r*	4.18	6.16*r*	9.25
3. 0	5.54	10.27	3.25
5.45*r*	9. 1	—	—
—	—	—	—
—	—	—	—

Sunday Trains.

12. 0*nr*	5.29	AM10.51	3.45
—	—	—	—

n Noon.
r Restaurant Car.

ANOTHER ROUTE from *St.*

Pancras, 94½ miles. Fares as above.

St. Pan.	Luff'm.	Luff'm.	St. Pan.
AM 4.25	8.39	AM 8.36*r*	10.45
7.50	10.29	10.57*r*	1.20
10.25	2.17	PM12.49*r*	4.10
PM12.25	4.48	4.18*r*	7.55
3.30*r*	6.18	5.54	8.20
4.30*r*	7.29	9. 1	4.20
6.25*r*	10.27	—	—

Sunday Trains.

PM 3.15	9.30	PM 5.29*r*	9.43
—	—	—	—

r Restaurant Car.

LUGAR (Ayr), 377½ miles.

No through fares. Departures *from* London as for Old Cumnock. Departures *for* London about 4 times daily. Pop. 3,063.

Map Square 40.

LUGTON (Ayr), 400½ miles.

Fares, 81/6*a*, 48/11*c*. R. T. for two months, 163/0*a*, 97/10*c*. Departures *from* London as for Kilmarnock. Departures *for* London about 4 times daily.

Map Square 40.

LUIB (Perth), 455¾ miles.

Fares, 93/2*a*, 55/11*c*. R. T. for two months, 186/4*a*, 111/10*c*. Departures *from* London as for Callander. Departures *for* London about 3 times daily.

Map Square 37.

LUMPHANAN (Aberdeen),

548½ miles. No through fares. Departures *from* London as for Ballater. Departures *for* London about twice daily. Pop. 852.

Map Square 38.

LUNAN BAY (Forfar), 477½

miles. No through fares. Departures *from* London as for Arbroath. Departures *for* London about 4 times daily. Pop. 327.

Map Square 28.

LUNCARTY (Perth), 454

miles. Fares, 91/11*a*, 55/2*c*. R. T. for two months, 183/10*a*, 110/4*c*. Departures *from* London as for Perth. Departures *for* London about 3 times daily.

Map Square 38.

LUNDIN LINKS (Fife),

430¾ miles. Fares, 87/3a, 52/4c. R. T. for two months, 174/6a, 104/8c. Departures *from London* as for St. Andrews. Departures *for London* about 3 times daily.
Map Square 41.

LUSTLEIGH (Devon), 196

miles. Fares, *via* Newton Abbot, 41/8a, 25/6c. R. T. for two months, 83/4a, 50/0c, *via* Ide, 40/3a, 24/2c. Departures *from London* as for Moretonhampstead. Departures *for London* about 6 times daily. Pop. 434.
Map Square 26.

LUTHRIE (Fife), 443 miles.

Fares, 90/8a, 54/5c. R. T. for two months, 181/4a, 108/10c. Departures *from London* as for Leuchars. Departures *for London* about twice daily.
Map Square 38.

LUTON (Beds) from St.

Pancras, 30¼ miles. Fares, 6/1½a, 3/9c. R. T., double fare. Pop. 57,077.
Map Square 23.

ST. PAN.	LUTON	LUTON	ST. PAN.
AM 4.25	5.18	AM 4.10f	4.55
6. 0	7.20	4.14g	5. 0
6.25	7.36	5.13g	6. 0
7.50	8.45	6.22	7.37
8.25	9. 5	6.58	8.15
8.50	10. 0	7.36	8.28
9.25	10.14	7.57	8.45
9.55	11.18	8.22	9.13
11. 0	11.41	8.53	9.30
11.35	12.34	9.15	10. 5
PM12.30	1.15	9.40	10.31
1. 0	1.45	11. 0	11.35
1.33d	2.34	11.17	12. 5
2.15	3.17	11.57	1. 3
2.45	3.30	PM12.45	1.20
3.35	4.25	1.25	2.52
4.30	5.11	2.18	3.10
4.40	5.43	2.48	3.25
5. 5	6. 0	3.17	4.33
5.40e	6.25	3.55	5.10
5.45e	6.42	4.30	5.20
6.30	7.12	5.10	5.45
6.35	7.32	5.30	6.30
6.45e	7.44	6.23	7. 3
7.50	8.48	7.45	8.22
8.25	9.22	8. 5	8.57
10. 5	10.57	9.31	10. 5
10.35	11.42	9.37	10.48
11.50	12.35	10.47	11.45

Sunday Trains.

AM 8. 0	9.20	AM 4.14	5. 5
10.50	11.34	5.13	6. 0
PM12.50	2. 2	8.20	8.57
1.35	2.40	8.52	10.15
4.35	5.49	PM12. 7	1.30
8.25	9.22	2.40	3.56
11.55	12.51	5.36	6.27
—	—	7.30	8.30
—	—	10.15	11. 7

d Saturdays only.
e Saturdays excepted.
f Mondays only.
g Mondays excepted.

LUTON—*continued.*

ANOTHER ROUTE from

King's Cross, 32¾ miles. Fares as above.

KING'S+	LUTON	LUTON	KING'S+
AM 7.45	9. 2	AM 7.29	8.41
9.20	10.26	8.35	9.44
11.30	12.50	11.22	12.45
PM 1. 8	2.36	PM 1. 6	2.22
4.15	5.35	4. 7	5.45
5.50	7. 9	6.42	8. 5
7. 0	8.20	8.22	9.50
9.10d	10.27	—	—

Sunday Trains.

AM 8.30	9.56	AM 8.26	9.53
PM 7.10	8.22	PM 6. 5	7.40
—	—	8.24	9.48

d Saturdays only.

Red Lion Hotel. Telephone 628. In the centre of the town. Electric Light. Billiards. TRUST HOUSES, Ltd.

George Hotel. Principal and oldest established Family Commercial. First-class Cuisine, choicest wines. Central. Private Stock rooms. Garage. Moderate. Telephone 654 Luton. W. H. MILES, Resident Proprietor.

LUTON HOO (Beds) from

*King's Cross,*29¾ miles. Fares, 5/8a, 3/5c. R. T., double fare. Departures *from London* as for Wheathampstead. Departures *for London* about 9 times daily.
Map Square 23.

LUTTERWORTH

(Leicester) from *Marylebone,* 90 miles. Fares, 17/6a, 10/6c. R. T. for two months, 35/0a, 21/0c. Pop. 1,896.
Map Square 18.

M'BONE.	L'WORTH.	L'WORTH.	M'BONE.
AM 2.32	6.52	AM 6.37	9.46
6.45	9.57	8.35	10.36
10. 0rh	1. 6	8.59	12. 2
PM12.15r	2.48	11.43kr	3. 0
4.30	6.52	PM12.27dr	5. 0
6.25e	9.27	1.46	4.56
6.25d	9.34	6.58lr	8.55
—	—	7.19r	9.55

Sunday Trains.

AM 9.30	12.33	AM 6.44	10.13
PM 6.30	10. 4	PM 5.30	8.58
—	—	8.31r	10.24

d Saturdays only.
e Saturdays excepted.
h Wednesdays and Saturdays only.
k Wednesdays only.
l Stops on notice being given at Station.
r Restaurant Car.

LUXULYAN (Cornwall)

from *Paddington,*264½ miles. Fares, 54/9a, 32/10c. R. T. for two months, 109/6a, 65/8c. Departures *from London* as for Newquay. Departures *for London* about 4 times daily. Pop. 1,049.
Map Square 25.

LYBSTER (Caithness), 742¼

miles. Fares, 136/1a, 81/8c. R. T. for two months, 272/2a, 163/4c. Departures *from London* as for Wick. Departures *for London* about twice daily. Pop. 916.
Map Square 32.

LYDBROOK (Hereford),

137½ miles. Fares, 28/7a, 17/2c. R. T. for two months, 57/2a. Departures *from London* as for Kerne Bridge. Departures *for London* about 4 times daily. Pop. 2,388.
Map Square 22.

LYDD (Kent) from *Charing*

Cross, Cannon Street, and *London Bridge,* 72½ miles. Fares, 15/2a, 12/1b, 9/1c. R. T. for two months, 30/4a, 24/2b. Pop. 2,256.
Map Square 24.

	Leave			Arr. at
	CHAR.+	CAN.ST.	LON.B.	LYDD
AM	—	3.40s	3.43s	7.26
	—	5.20	5.25	10. 9
	9.15	—	9.23	11.30
	11. 0	—	11. 7	1.32
PM 1. 0	—	—		4.45
	4.30l	—	4.37l	6.50
	—	5. 0c	—	6.55
	7.18	—	7.26	9.56

No Sunday Trains.

Trains from *Lydd.*

	Leave	Arrive at		
	LYDD	LON.B.	CAN.ST.	CHAR.+
AM 8. 6	10. 0	10. 4	—	
9.25	11.43	—	11.57	
PM12.42	3.26	—	3.40	
3.22	5.50	—	6. 3	
5.38	8.54	9. 1	—	
7.47	10.22	—	10.35	

No Sunday Trains.

k Fridays only.
l Fridays excepted.
s Third Class only.

LYDFORD (Devon) from

Waterloo, 207¾ miles. Fares, 43/2a, 25/11c. R. T. for two months, 86/4a, 51/10c. Pop. 3,030.
Map Square 26.

W'LOO.	LYDFORD	LYDFORD	W'LOO.
AM11. 0r	4.24	AM 9. 0r	1.56
PM 1. 0r	6.59	10.29r	3.50
3. 0r	8. 1	PM12.19r	6. 0
—	—	4. 6	10.50
—	—	5.32h	3.58

Sunday Trains.

12. 0nr	7.30	PM12.17r	8.57

h Via Eastleigh.
n Noon.
r Restaurant Car.

Manor Hotel, five minutes from joint station; on edge of Dartmoor, in own grounds. Dairy and produce farm attached to hotel. Near three packs of hounds. Fishing (7 miles). Tennis, Croquet. Stabling. Garage. En pension from 4 guineas.
Mrs. A. E. MATHEWS.

LYDHAM HEATH

(Salop), 174¼ miles. No through fares. Departures from London as for Craven Arms. Departures for London about 4 times daily. Pop. (Lydham) 133. *Map Square* 17.

LYDIATE (Lancs), 223½

miles. Fares, 42/4a, 25/5c. R.T for two months, 84/8a, 50/10c. Departures *from* London as for Warrington (Central). Departures *for* London about 6 times daily. Pop. 1,046. *Map Square* 12.

LYDNEY (Glo'ster) from

Paddington, 133¾ miles. Fares, *via* Gloucester, 27/9a, 16/8c. R.T. for two months, 55/6a, 33/4c ; *via* Severn Tunnel, 30/7a, 18/4c. R.T. for two months, 61/2a, 36/8c. Pop. 3,776. *Map Square* 22.

PAD.	LYDNEY	LYDNEY	PAD.
AM 1. 0g	6.15	AM 9. 2	12.20
5.30	9.55	10.55r	2.40
9. 0	1.31	PM 1.19	5. 0
10.45	2.44	5.10r	8.45
11.15hr	3. 3	6.11	10.25
PM 1.30k	5.27	8. 4	3.30
3.15t	6.44	9.12h	3.30
6. 0r	9.12	—	—
9.15	1.18	—	—

Sunday Trains.

AM 1. 0	4.43	PM 4.10	10. 0
9.10h	4.10	—	—
PM 2. 0	8.57	—	—
9.15	1.18	—	—

g Mondays excepted.
h Via Severn Tunnel Junction.
k Via Kingham.
r Restaurant Car.
t Tea Car.

Feathers Hotel. Comfortable and well-furnished Hostelry. Nine Bedrooms. Modern Sanitation. Drawing, Coffee, Commercial, Reading, and Billiard Rooms. Under P.R.H.A. Management.

LYE (Worcester), 121½ miles.

Fares, 25/3a, 15/2c. R.T. for two months, 50/6a. Departures *from* London as for Smethwick Junction. Departures *for* London about 4 times daily. Pop. 7,636. *Map Square* 17.

LYME REGIS (Dorset)

from Waterloo, 151½ miles. Fares, 31/8a, 19/0c. R.T. for two months 63/4a, 38/0c. Pop. 2,883. *Map Square* 27.

W'LOO.	L.REGIS	L.REGIS	W'LOO.
AM 9. 0r	12.55	AM 9.30r	1.56
12. 0r	3.35	11.35r	3. 8
PM 1. 0r	4.58	PM 1.32r	6. 0
3. 0r	6.42	2.35	7.40
6. 0r	10.10	3.58r	8.30
—	—	5.20	10.50
—	—	8.20h	3.58

No Sunday Trains.

h Via Eastleigh.
r Restaurant Car.

LYME REGIS—*continued.*

Hotel Alexandra. Winter Resort, facing sea and south. In own grounds. Cuisine and service first class. Central Heating. Telegrams: "Alexandra." Telephone, Lyme Regis 10.
A. H. HINTON, Proprietor.

Stile House. Superior Board residence. In own grounds. Overlooking Sea. Facing South. Electric Light, Lounge, Separate Tables. Excellent Cuisine. Special terms for winter season.

Bow House Private Hotel. In own Grounds. Near Sea. High Situation. Beside Langmore Gardens. Splendid views Town, Cliffs and Sea. Comfortable Winter House. Separate Tables. Tariff. Mr. and Mrs. STOCKLEY.

Royal Lion Hotel. Close Sea. Modern comfort. Electric Light. Bus meets trains. Garage. R.A.C. Telegrams: "Royal." Phone, 14. Mrs. and Miss SLATER. Resident Proprietresses.

Victoria Hotel. Modern Family and Residential. Nearest Station and Golf Links. Extensive Land and Sea Views. Garage. Billiards. Separate Tables. Saddle Horses kept. Riding taught. Tariff from Proprietor, W. W. LLOYD-WORTH.

The Three Cups Hotel. Nearest Sea. Garage. Cars for Hire. Wires, "Cups." Phone 33. C. H. A. WHITE, Proprietor.

LYMINGE (Kent) from

Charing Cross, Cannon Street, and London Bridge, 72¼ miles. Fares, 14/7a, 11/8b, 8/9c. R. T. for two months, 29/2a, 23/4b. Departures *from* London as for Shorncliffe. Departures *for* London about 4 times daily. Pop. 1,398. *Map Square* 24.
Station closed on Sundays.

LYMINGTON (Town)

(Hants) from Waterloo, 97 miles. Fares, 20/5a, 12/3c. R.T. for two months, 40/10a, 24/6c. Pop. 4,598. *Map Square* 27.

W'LOO.	LYM'T'N.	LYM'T'N.	W'LOO.
AM 5.40	8.44	AM 7.45	10. 6
5.50	10.29	8.20s	11. 0
8.30s	11.19	9.33s	12.22
9.30	12.19	10. 9	12.50
10.30	1.15	11.35r	2.20
11.30r	2. 4	PM 1.35	4.20
PM12.30	3. 2	2.32	6.16
1.30s	4.15	3.35s	6.26
3.30s	6.15	4.35	6.58
4.30r	7.17	5.36r	8.20
5.30r	8.17	6.39	10.50
6.30r	9.14	8.24	11.28

No Sunday Trains.
r Restaurant Car.
s Refreshments served.

Hotel Victoria. Milford-on-Sea. On Cliff facing I. O. W. Motor centre for New Forest. Tel. 7, Milford-on-Sea. *See advt. p.* 267.

LYMM (Cheshire) from

Euston, via Warrington, 187 miles. Fares, 37/9a, 22/8c. R.T. double fare. Pop. 5,288. *Map Square* 12.

EUSTON	LYMM	LYMM	EUSTON
AM12.25	6.42	AM 7.38er	12. 5
2.35	8.10	7.38dr	12.20
5. 0	10.27	8.28r	1.45
6.45	12.30	9.53hr	3.45
8.30r	1.23	9.53r	4.15
10.40r	4.23	PM12.48t	5.50
11.50r	4.47	4.17er	9. 5
PM 1.30r	5.50	4.17dr	9.15
2.35t	6.56	9.44	5. 0
5.20r	10.13	—	—

Sunday Trains.

AM11.45	8.43	PM 2. 0r	7.30
—	—	7.15	5. 0

d Saturdays only.
e Saturdays excepted.
h Mondays and Saturdays only.
r Restaurant Car.
t Tea Car.

LYMPSTONE (Devon),

from Waterloo, 178 miles. Fares, 37/6a, 22/6c. R.T. for two months, 75/0a, 45/0c. Departures *from* London as for Exmouth (via Exeter). Departures *for* London about 7 times daily. Pop. 999. *Map Square* 26.

LYNDHURST ROAD

(Hants) from Waterloo, 84¾ miles. Fares, 17/11a, 10/9c. R.T. for two months, 35/10a, 21/6c. Pop. (Lyndhurst) 2,406. *Map Square* 27.

W'LOO.	LYND.R.	LYND.R.	W'LOO.
AM 4.30	8.35	AM 7.36r	10. 6
5.50	9.31	8.50s	11. 0
8.30s	11. 8	10.18r	12.50
10.30	12.40	11.48r	2.20
PM12.30r	2.50	PM 1.40	4.20
1.30s	3.57	3.12	6.16
2.30	4.45	3.38s	6.26
3.30s	5.55	4.44	6.58
4.30r	6.41	5.36r	8.20
6.30r	8.34	6.37r	8.50
7.30	9.58	8. 0	10.50
—	—	8.23	11.28
—	—	9.53	3.58

Sunday Trains.

AM11. 0r	1.39	PM12.16	2.27
PM 2. 0r	4.42	2.55r	6. 7
7. 0r	9.46	5.17	8. 3
—	—	7.10r	9.31
—	—	8.45	3.58

r Restaurant Car.
s Refreshments served.

Grand Hotel. Under entirely new management. Golf. Hunting. *See advt. p.* 239.

Crown Hotel. An old-established Family Hotel on high ground, Lyndhurst, the village capital of the New Forest. Sixty rooms, many of them having charming views over miles of the finest woodland scenery in Europe. Electric light throughout.

LYNE (Peebles), from *Euston* 382 miles. No through fares. Departures *from* London as for Peebles. Departures *for* London about 4 times daily. Pop. 78. *Map Square* 41.

LYNESIDE (Cumberland), 305¾ miles. No through fares. Departures *from* London as for Carlisle. Departures *for* London about three times daily. *Map Square* 3.

LYNN (SOUTH) (Norfolk),112¾ miles. Fares, 20/2*a*, 12/1*c*. R.T. for two months, 40/4*a*, 24/2*c*. Departures *from* London as for Terrington. Departures *for* London about 5 times daily. Pop. 6,571. *Map Square* 19.

LYNTON AND LYN-MOUTH (Devon) from *Waterloo*, 231½ miles. Fares, 43/4*a*, 26/0*c*. R. T. for two months, 86/8*a*, 52/0*c*. Pop. (Lynton) 2,649. *Map Square* 21.

W'loo.	Lyn.	Lyn.	W'loo.
AM11. 0*hr*	5.41	AM 9.10*r*	3.50
11. 0*kr*	6. 6	10.58*r*	6. 0
PM 1. 0*hr*	8.30	PM12.30*r*	8.30
—	—	—	—
—	—	—	—

No Sunday Trains.

h Commencing July 23.
k Will cease to run July 21.
r Restaurant Car.

ANOTHER ROUTE from *Paddington, via* Taunton and Barnstaple, 208½ miles. Fares as above.

Pad.	Lynton	Lynton	Pad.
AM 9.15	6. 6	AM 8. 3	4. 5
PM12. 5*h*	8.30	10.58	5.30
12. 0*k*	12. 6	PM12.30	9. 0
—	—	4.25*f*	2.45
—	—	6.20	7.10

Sunday Trains.

AM10. 0	11.59	—	—

f Fridays excepted.
h From July 23.
k Saturdays midnight excepted.

Valley of Rocks Hotel, largest and most famous Hotel in District, 600 feet above and overlooking Sea. Electric Light, Passenger Lift. Garage. For terms apply Manager. Telephone, Lynton 49. Telegrams: " Valrocks, Lynton." *See advt. p.* **240.**

Lee Abbey Hotel. Grounds reaching Sea. R.A.C. A.A. M.U. *See advt. p.* **241.**

Imperial Hotel. Magnificent position. Charming views. Excellent cuisine. *See advt. p.* **242.**

Royal Castle Hotel. Leading Family. Grounds (9 acres) facing Sea. Lounge. Garage. Minehead Motor Service daily throughout the year. See G.W.R. Time table. Telegrams: " Castle, Lynton." 'Phone, 48 Lynton. TOM JONES, Proprietor. *See advt. p.* **242.**

LYNTON AND LYN-MOUTH—*continued.*

The Tors Hotel. Finest position in Devon. Only Hotel on Sunny Side. Tennis. R.A.C. A.A. Telegrams: "Tors, Lynmouth." *See advt. p.* **243.**

Lynton Cottage Hotel. Situated in extensive grounds overlooking Sea. Proprietor, J. W. HOLMAN. *See advt. p.* **243.**

Crown Hotel. Family and Commercial. Hot and cold water in every room. *See advt* p. **243.**

Lyndale Hotel. Oldest-established. Beautifully situated. First-class Family. Electric Light throughout. Good Fishing. Garage. Telegrams : " Lyndale, Lynmouth." Telephone 45. Mrs. A. W. GAYDON, Proprietress.

"The Summer - house," Lynmouth. England's Switzerland, unrivalled scenery. Golf, Fishing, Bathing, Boating. Char-a-banc, Motor trips. Excellent cooking. Electric light. Tariff— ED. PETERS.

North Cliff Boarding Establishment. Ideal position on North Walk. Modern improvements. Excellent Cuisine. Electric Light throughout. Moderate Tariff. Telegrams :, " Northcliff."

Bevan's Lyn Valley Hotel. Excellent Cuisine. Sea and River Fishing. Moderate. Personal Supervision. Telephone, 46 Lynton. Telegrams : Bevan Hotel. Mrs. CECIL BEVAN, Proprietress.

Woody Bay Hotel. Most perfect spot in Devon. 700 ft. above sea. Modern sanitation. Baths. High Class Cooking STANLEY HOLMAN, Proprietor.

LYONSHALL (Hereford), 153¾ miles. Fares, 32/9*a*, 19/8*c*. R.T. for two months, 65/6*a*, 39/4*c*. Departures *from* London as for Titley. Departures *for* London about 3 times daily. Pop. 660. *Map Square* 17.

LYTHAM (Lancs) from *Euston*, 222¾ miles. Fares, 46/5*a*, 27/10*c*. R. T. for two months, 92/10*a*, 55/8*c*. Pop. 10,830. *Map Square* 12.

Euston	Lytham	Lytham	Euston
AM12.25	7.43	AM 8. 9*r*	1.45
2.35	10.53	8.42*r*	3.10
5. 0	11.53	10.22*hr*	3.45
6.45	1. 7	10.35*r*	4.15
11.35*r*	4.18	PM12.11*dt*	6. 0
11.50*r*	5.37	12.29*et*	6. 0
PM 1.30*r*	6.47	2.30*r*	7.30
2.35*t*	7.50	4.55*r*	10.45
5.20*r*	10.19	10. 5	5. 0
9.30*d*	9.32	—	—
11.50*d*	11.30	—	—

Sunday Trains.

AM11.45*r*	5.15	AM 6.55*r*	1.30
—	—	PM 1.28*r*	7.30
—	—	9.15	5. 0

d Saturdays only.
e Saturdays excepted.
h Mondays and Saturdays only.
r Restaurant Car.
t Tea Car.

LYNTON.—VALLEY OF ROCKS HOTEL.

M

MABLETHORPE (Lincoln)

from *King's Cross*, 137¾ miles. Fares, 28/7*a*, 17/2*c*. R. T. for two months, 57/2*a*, 34/4*c*. Pop. 2,852.
Map Square 14.

KING'S+	MAB'TH.	MAB'TH.	KING'S+
AM 4.45	9.10	AM 9.25	1. 5
7.15*r*	11.32	PM12. 5*r*	4.30
8.45	1.30	3.10	9. 0
11.30	5. 6	4.18*r*	9.25
PM 4. 0*r*	7.40	7.44	3.25
10.45*e*	8. 9	—	—
—	—	—	—

Sunday Trains.

PM10.45	8. 9	—	—

e Saturdays excepted.
r Restaurant Car.

MACBIE HILL (Peebles)

396 miles. No through fares. Departures *from* London as for Peebles. Departures *for* London about 4 times daily.
Map Square 41.

MACCLESFIELD (Hibel Road) (Cheshire)

from *Euston*, 165½ miles. Fares, 34/5*a*, 20/8*c*. R.T. for two months, 68/10*a*. Pop. 33,846.
Map Square 12.

EUSTON	M'FIELD	M'FIELD	EUSTON
AM12.25	6.22	AM 7*h*45*dr*	12.20
2.35	8.38	7*h*45*er*	12. 5
5. 0	10.20	9. 3*r*	12.50
8.45*r*	12. 7	10. 0*r*	2.20
10.40*r*	2.43	PM12.39*hr*	3.55
11.50*r*	4. 2	2.43*hr*	6.15
12. 0*nr*	5.32	3.20*r*	8.10
PM 2.50*t*	6.10*h*	4. 5*er*	9. 5
4.45*r*	8.34*h*	5.57*hr*	10. 0
6. 5*dr*	10.57	9.15*e*	5. 0
6. 5*er*	11.35	10. 8*e*	5.40
11.50*d*	9. 0	10.25*d*	5. 0
—	—	11. 0*d*	5.45
—	—	—	—

MACCLESFIELD—*con.*

Sunday Trains.

EUSTON	M'FIELD	M'FIELD	EUSTON
PM12.30*r*	6.18	AM 9.25	4. 0
—	—	PM12.45*r*	7.30
—	—	3.45*r*	8.55
—	—	10.20	5. 0
—	—	—	—

d Saturdays only.
e Saturdays excepted.
h *Via* Stoke.
n Noon.
r Restaurant Car.
t Tea Car.

MACDUFF (Banff)

573¼ miles. Fares, 106/3*a*, 63/9*c*. R. T. for two months, 212/6*a*, 127/6*c*. Departures *from* London as for Inverurie. Departures *for* London about twice daily. Pop. 3,344.
Map Square 34.

MACHEN (Monmouth)

148¾ miles. Fares, 31/1*a*, 18/8*c*, R. T. for two months, 62/2*a*. Departures *from* London as for Bargoed. Departures *for* London about 4 times daily. Pop. 1,705.
Map Square 21.

MACHYNLLETH (Montgomery)

from *Paddington*, 218¾ miles. Fares, 44/5*a*, 26/8*c*. R. T. for two months, 88/10*a* Pop. 1,870.
Map Square 16.

PAD.	MACH'LTH.	MACH'LTH.	PAD.
AM 6.30	2.28	AM 8.45*r*	4.15
10.20*r*	3.28	11. 8*t*	5. 0
10.40*r*	4.37	11.54*t*	6.40
PM 2.10*t*	7.54	PM 1.50*r*	8. 5
12.15*h*	10.43	3.28*d*	10. 0
12.15*k*	8.37	6.54	3.30

No Sunday Trains.

d Saturdays only.
h Saturdays midnight excepted.
k Saturdays midnight only.
r Restaurant Car.
t Tea Car.

ANOTHER ROUTE

from *Euston*, 228¾ miles. Fares as above.

EUSTON	MACHLTH.	MACHLTH.	EUSTON
AM 5. 0*h*	12.45	AM 8.45*r*	3.10
8.30*h*	4.15	10.45*hr*	5.50
10. 0	4.37	11. 8*r*	7.30
10.40*r*	5.36	PM 1.50*dr*	9.15
PM 1.15*r*	7.54	1.50*er*	9.20
9.30*eh*	5.41	6.54	5. 0
11. 0*d*	8.37	—	—

Sunday Trains.

PM 9.15	5.49	PM 7. 2	5. 0
—	—	—	—
—	—	—	—
—	—	—	—

d Saturdays only.
e Saturdays excepted.
h *Via* Crewe.
r Restaurant Car.

MACMERRY (East Lothian)

394½ miles. No through fares. Departures *from* London as for Edinburgh (Waverley). Departures *for* London about twice daily.
Map Square 41.

MADDERTY (Perth)

449½ miles. No through fares. Departures *from* London as for Perth. Departures *for* London about 4 times daily. Pop. 387.
Map Square 37.

MADELEY (Stafford)

from *Euston*, 150½ miles. Fares, 31/3*a*, 18/9*c*. R. T. for two months, 62/6*a*. Pop. 2,797.
Map Square 12.

EUSTON	MAD'L'Y	MAD'L'Y	EUSTON
AM 2.35	8.20	AM 6.42*er*	12. 5
5. 0	10. 5	6.42*dr*	12.20
10.40*r*	3.45	10. 0*r*	2.20
12. 0*nr*	5.59	PM 1.58*t*	6.15
PM 4. 5*t*	8.10	5.45*dr*	9.15
—	—	8.43	5. 0
—	—	—	—

No Sunday Trains.

d Saturdays only.
e Saturdays excepted.
n Noon.
r Restaurant Car.
t Tea Car.

MADELEY MARKET

(Salop), 157 miles. Fares, 29/9*a*, 17/10*c*. R.T. for two months, 59/6*a*, 35/8*c*. Departures *from* London as for Wellington (Salop). Departures *for* London about 3 times daily.
Map Square 17.

MADELEY ROAD

(Stafford), 154 miles. No through fares. Departures *from* London as for Newcastle-under-Lyme. Departures *for* London about 4 times daily.
Map Square 12.

MAENCLOCHOG (Pembroke)

253¼ miles. Fares, 50/0*a*, 30/0*c*. R. T. for two months, 100/0*a*, 60/0*c*. Departures *from* London as for Clynderwen. Departures *for* London about twice daily. Pop. 367.
Map Square 15.

MAENTWROG ROAD

(Merioneth) from *Paddington*, 220¼ miles. Fares, 46/11*a*, 28/2*c*. R. T. for two months, 93/10*a*, 56/4*c*. Departures *from* London as for Blaenau Festiniog. Departures *for* London about 3 times daily. Pop. 652.
Map Square 11.

MAERDY (Glamorgan)

175 miles. Fares, 35/3*a*, 21/2*c*. R. T. for two months, 70/6*a*, 42/4*c*. Departures *from* London as for Pontypridd. Departures *for* London about 4 times daily.
Map Square 21.

MAESBROOK (Salop)

169 miles. No through fares. Departures *from* London as for Oswestry. Departures *for* London about 3 times daily.
Map Square 17.

MAESTEG (Glamorgan)

from *Paddington*, 181½ miles. Fares, 37/9*a*, 22/8*c*. R. T. for two months, 75/6*a*. Pop. 28,960.
Map Square 21.

PAD.	MAESTEG	MAESTEG	PAD.
AM 1. 0*g*	9.28	AM 8.46*r*	1. 0
5.30	12. 3	10.23*r*	4.20
8.45*dr*	1.33	PM 1. 0*r*	6.15
8.45*r*	2.41	3.43*r*	8.35
11.50*r*	5.27	9. 1	3.30
PM 1.10*dr*	6.40	—	—
3.35*r*	8. 4	—	—
6. 0*r*	11.22	—	—

Sunday Trains.

PM 9.15	9.28	—	—

d Saturdays only.
g Mondays excepted.
r Restaurant Car.

MAES-Y-CRUGIAU (Carmarthen) from *Paddington*, 246½ miles. Fares, 48/9a, 29/3c. R.T. for two months, 97/6a. Departures *from* London as for Lampeter. Departures *for* London about 4 times daily. *Map Square* 16.

MAESYCWMMER (Monmouth), 156¼ miles. Fares, 32/4a, 19/5c. R.T. for two months, 64/8a, 38/10c. Departures *from* London as for Bargoed. Departures *for* London about 4 times daily.

MAGDALEN ROAD (Norfolk) from *Liverpool Street*, 91 miles. Fares, 19/2a, 11/6c. R.T. for two months, 38/4a. Departures *from* London as for King's Lynn. Departures *for* London about 10 minutes later. *Map Square* 19.

MAGHULL (Lancs), 210¼ miles. No through fares. Departures *from* London as for Liverpool (Lime Street). Departures *for* London about 3 times daily. Pop. 1,756. *Map Square* 12.

MAGOR (Monmouth), 133 miles. Fares, 29/5a, 17/8c. R.T. for two months, 58/10a. *Via* Newport, 30/3a, 18/2c. R.T. for two months, 60/6a. Departures *from* London as for Severn Tunnel. Departures *for* London about 3 times daily. Pop. 473. *Map Square* 22.

MAIDA VALE (BAKERLOO TUBE). *See* back of Map.

MAIDENHEAD (Berks) from *Paddington*, 24½ miles. Fares, 5/0a, 3/0c. R.T. for two months, 10/0a, 6/0c. Pop. 16,741. *Map Square* 23.

PAD.	MAID'H'D.	MAID'H'D.	PAD.
AM 5.45	7. 0	AM 6. 3	7.25
6.30	7.11	7.38	8.20
6.35	7.51	7.54	8.28
7.35	8.35	8. 0	8.49
8.30	9.17	8.23	8.56
9.20	10.14	8.30	9.25
9.55	10.40	8.54e	9.34
10.55	11.48	9. 1	9.37
11.25	12. 8	9.12	10. 6
PM12. 8	12.53	9.46	10.24
12.33d	1.36	10.27	11. 6
12.35e	1.44	10.49	11.35
1. 5d	1.47	11.36	12.15
1.20d	2.10	PM12. 4	1.11
1.50d	2.33	12.42	1.46
2. 7	2.50	1.43	2.35
2.18d	2.58	1.56	3.10
3.18	3.59	2.50d	3.38
3.38	4.13	3.26	4.10
4. 7	4.49	4. 5	5.17
4.30	5.14	4.54	5.37
4.50	5.27	6.11	6.55
5.18e	5.55	6.59	7.45
5.18d	6. 3	7.18	8.10
5.45	6.22	8.16d	9.12
6. 5	6.41	8.35	9.33
6.12e	7. 7	8.45	9.52
6.35	7.15	9.18	10.22
6.55	7.27	9.52	10.42
7. 0	7.57	9.57	11. 4
7.35	8. 9	10.45	12. 0
8. 5	8.47	—	—
8.35	9.18	—	—
10. 5	10.49	—	—
10.40	11.43	—	—
11.20	11.54	—	—
12. 3	12.48	—	—

MAIDENHEAD—*contd.*

Sunday Trains.

PAD.	MAID'H'D.	MAID'H'D.	PAD.
AM 8.20	9.27	AM 9.22	10.14
9.10	9.40	9.30	10.42
9.45	10.28	10. 3	10.50
10. 0	10.39	11.59	1. 5
10. 5	10.52	PM 3.45	4.53
10.25	11. 4	5.15	6. 0
10.45	11.23	5.29	6.23
11. 0	11.43	6.46	7.37
11.45	12.22	7.34	8.20
PM 1.45	2.35	7.54	8.45
2. 0	3.10	8. 5	9.17
2.35	3.23	8.46	9.32
4.45	5.51	9. 7	9.53
5.15	6. 1	9.12	10.22
6. 5	7.14	9.43	10.33
7.40	8.46	10.22	11. 6
8.20	9.10	10.31	11.38
8.30	9.23	—	—
10. 5	11. 2	—	—
11.15	12.10	—	—
—	—	—	—
—	—	—	—

d Saturdays only.
e Saturdays excepted.

Salter's Steamers (Boulter's Lock). 1½ miles, cabs available. Up stream, 10.45 a.m., 2.10 p.m. Down stream, 12.15 p.m., 5.30 p.m. *See advt.* facing first page of train service.

"Skindles." Principal and largest hotel. Unique position on river bank. Adjoining Maidenhead Bridge. Launches. Motor Cars. Telephone, No. 268 (4 lines). American Bar. JAS. D. HODGSON, Proprietor. *See advt. p.* 244.

Braymead Court Residential Hotel, Bray. Well appointed. Luncheons, dinners and teas. Central Heating. Fully licensed. *See advt. p.* 244.

Riviera Hotel. The Ideal River Hotel. American Bar. *See advt. p.* 245.

Thames Hotel. Principal Family. Best position. Inclusive terms. Noted for cuisine, wines, etc. Garage. Cars, Boats, Launches. Tennis. Telephone 109.

The Hermitage Hotel. Adjacent to River and Boathouse. Secluded Grounds. Two Tennis Lawns. Dining Room open to Non-residents. Tel. 388.

Hotel St. Ives. High and dry, on gravel soil. Five minutes Station, ten to River. Magnificent Reception Rooms. Billiards. Dances. Hard Tennis Courts. Ideal Winter Home for Families and Business Men. Cooking unsurpassed. 'Phone 188. Mrs. DRUMMOND, Proprietress.

New Swan Hotel and Restaurant. Five minutes from Station and River. Good catering. Moderate charges. Telephone 131. GEORGE RANDALL, Proprietor.

Bear Hotel. Old-Established Family and Commercial Hotel. Close to River. Large Parties catered for. Garage. Telephone 183. Proprietor— WILLIAM LEACH.

Elm Grove, Castle Hill. Small private hotel, highly recommended. Garth and Bucks District. Near Golf. Own Tennis, Croquet and Putting Lawns. Garage. Loose boxes. Central Heating. Maidenhead, 642. Mrs. SHAW.

MAIDENHEAD—*contd.*

Skindles Hotel Garage. Open day and night. Accommodation for 50 cars. Specialities; Repairs. Hire, open and closed Cars, any period. Tel. 289.

Andrews Boathouse, Ray Mead Road. Maidenhead, for Steam and Electric Launches, Boats, Punts, and Canoes. Terms reasonable. Telephone 56.

Auctioneers, House Agents. J. H. Humfrey & Co., Maidenhead. Largest Selection Residences, Furnished or unfurnished, on Thames. Lists free. Telephone, 132 Maidenhead.

MAIDEN NEWTON (Dorset) from *Paddington*, 140 miles. Fares, 28/4a, 17/0c. R.T. for two months, 56/8a. Pop. 600. *Map Square* 27.

PAD.	MAID.N.	MAID. N.	PAD.
AM 1. 0g	9. 2	AM 7.23	10.52
5.30	11. 3	9.25	12.55
10.30	1.21	11. 3	3.20
PM12.30r	3.53	PM12.21	3.50
2. 6	5.11	2.20t	5.30
3.30	7.40	3.41r	6.50
5. 5	8.49	5. 1	8.20
—	—	8. 0	2.45
—	—	9. 6h	2.45

Sunday Trains.

PM 2.40	6.24	AM10. 4	3.35
10. 0	9. 2	PM 4.11r	7.55

g Mondays excepted.
h Thursdays and Third Class only.
r Restaurant Car.
t Tea Car.

MAIDENS (Ayr), 407 miles. Fares, 83/1a, 49/10c. R.T. for two months, 166 2a, 99/8c. Departures *from* London as for Turnberry. Departures *for* London about 4 times daily. *Map Square* 4.

MAIDSTONE EAST (Kent) from *Victoria*, *Holborn Viaduct*, and *St. Paul's*, 40 miles. Fares, 8.6a, 6/9b, 5/1c. R.T. for two months, 17/9a, 13/6b. Pop. 37,448. *Map Square* 24.

VICT. (S.E.&C.)	Leave HOLB V.	ST. PL.'s	Arr. at MAIDST.
AM —	6.40	6.42	8.23
8.32	8.20	8.23	10.22
9.45	—	—	10.45
11. 4	10.58	11. 0	12.51
PM —	12.33d	12.36d	2. 9
—	1.24d	1.30d	2.40
—	1.27d	—	3. 4
2. 9d	2. 4d	2. 7d	3.25
2.12e	—	—	3.14
2.40d	—	—	4.16
2.50e	—	—	4.32
4.25e	—	—	5.25
5.30e	—	5.33e	7. 0
—	—	6.16e	7.37
6.40	6.34	6.37	8.13
7.22	—	—	8.23
—	7.22	7.24	9. 0
8.55	—	—	10.18
9.55	—	—	11. 2
10. 0	9.54	9.56	11.31

Sunday Trains.

AM —	8. 0	—	9.56
9.35	—	—	10.39
PM 2. 5	2. 3	—	3.58
5.15	—	—	6.18
6.35	6.40	—	8.20
10.15	10.12	—	11.53

MAIDSTONE EAST— continued.

Trains from Maidstone.

Leave MAIDST.	S. PL.'s	Arr. at HOL. V.	VICT.
AM 7. 5	8.40	8.42	—
7.45	—	—	8.50
7.55	9.37	9.39	—
8.34	9.52	9.55	—
9. 9e	10.21	10.23	10.16
9.20d	10.41	—	—
9.20	—	10.43	—
10.15	—	—	11.37
11.20	12.59	1. 2	12.49
PM12.55	—	—	2.40
2.36	—	—	3.37
2.42	—	—	4.33
4.34	—	—	5.42
5.15	6.58	7. 0	—
6.30d	8. 0	8. 2	—
6.30e	8.18	8.20	8.10
6.59	—	—	8.51
8.25d	—	—	9.54
9.57	11.43	11.45	—

Sunday Trains.

AM 9.14	—	—	10.48
11.30	—	—	12.37
PM 2.13	—	—	3.50
4.28	—	6.20	6. 3
8. 0	—	9. 9	—
8.20	—	10.22	10. 5
—	—	—	—
—	—	—	—
—	—	—	—

d Saturdays only.
e Saturdays excepted.

ANOTHER ROUTE from
Charing Cross, Cannon Street, and *London Bridge,* 39½ miles. Fares, 8/6*a*, 6/9*b*, 5/0*c*. R. T. for two months, 17/0*a*, 13/6*b*, 10/0*c*.

CHAR. +	Leave CAN. ST.	LON. B.	Arr. at MAIDS.
AM11. 0	—	11. 7	12. 5
PM 5.15e	—	5.21e	6.27
5.20d	—	5.26d	6.32
11.51l	—	—	12.49
—	—	—	—
—	—	—	—

No Sunday Trains.

Trains from Maidstone.

Leave MAIDST.	LON. B.	Arr. at CAN. ST.	CHAR.+
AM10. 0	10.54	—	11. 5
PM 6.30	7.36	—	7.49
—	—	—	—

Sunday Trains.

PM 7.27	8.30	—	8.40

d Saturdays only.
e Saturdays excepted.
l Wednesdays only.

Victoria Hotel. Family and Commercial, adjoining Maidstone East Station, opposite Kent Council Offices. Under same management twenty-one years. Mrs. SMITH, Proprietress.

MAIDSTONE WEST
from *Charing Cross, Cannon Street,* and *London Bridge,* via Strood, 43 miles. Fares as above. Map Square 24.

CHAR. +	Leave CAN. ST.	LON. B.	Arr. at MAIDST.
AM —	6.20	6.23	8.16
—	7.16	7.19	8.56
—	7.44	7.47	9.29
8.10	—	8.17	10. 2
9.32	—	9.41	11.22
11.55	—	12. 2	1.35
PM12.36d	—	12.37d	2. 4
1.20e	—	1.27e	3.11
1.26d	—	1.34d	3.11
—	1.48d	1.51d	3.38
—	2.40	2.43	4. 0
2.45e	—	2.53e	4.43
3. 5d	—	3.12d	4.45
—	4.12e	4.15e	5.37
4.25d	—	4.31d	6.19
—	4.36e	4.39e	6.19
4.35d	—	4.43d	6.51
5.15d	—	5.22d	7.17
—	5.56e	5.59e	7.19
—	6.20e	6.23e	7.43
6.22e	—	6.29e	8.17
6.55d	—	7. 1d	9. 3
—	7. 8e	7.11e	9. 3
—	7.44	7.47	10.13
—	9.35	9.38	11.29

Sunday Trains.

AM 7.30	—	7.37	9.37
10.50	—	10:57	12.58
PM 1.15	—	1.22	3.23
4.50	—	4.57	6.49
7. 0	—	7. 7	8.54
8.42	—	8.49	10.36

Trains from Maidstone.

Leave MAIDST.	LON. B.	Arr. at CAN. ST.	CHAR. +
AM 4.59	7. 0	7. 4	—
6.52	8.34	—	8.41
8.15	9.34	—	9.43
8.25	9.54	—	10. 1
9.25	10.38	—	10.45
10.21	12. 3	—	12.14
11.35	12.57	—	1. 7
11.47d	1.31	1.37	—
11.47e	1.36	—	1.45
PM 1.12e	2.54	—	3. 4
d1. 7h	3.21	3.26	—
1.41e	3.26	—	3.36
1.56d	3.58	—	4. 8
2.59e	4.48	4.52	—
3. 2d	4.57	—	5. 6
3.59e	5.36	5.40	—
3.59d	5.36	—	5.45
5.15	7.10	—	7.19
5.46	7.14	—	7.23
6.32	8.15	8.20	—
7.56	9.36	—	9.46
9. 8	10.51	—	10.59
10.17	12.35	—	12.45

Sunday Trains.

AM 7. 7	9. 0	—	9. 9
8.24	10.16	—	10.24
11.10	1. 5	—	1.17
PM 2.13	4. 4	—	4.15
4.11	5.55	—	6. 4
7.37	9.46	—	9.55
9.18	11.15	—	11.23
—	—	—	—
—	—	—	—

d Saturdays only.
e Saturdays excepted.
h Third Class only.

MAIDSTONE W.—contd.

ANOTHER ROUTE from
Charing Cross, Cannon Street, and *London Bridge* (via Paddock Wood), 45½ miles. Fares, 8/6*a*, 6/9*b*, 5/1*c*. R.T. for two months, 17/0*a*, 13/6*b*, 10/2*c*.

CHAR. +	Leave CAN. ST.	LON. B.	Arr. at MAIDST.
AM —	5.20	5.25	7.51
—	6.45	6.50	9. 4
—	7.56	8. 0	10.12
9.25	—	9.33	11.25
10.40d	—	10.46d	12.42
—	11.56	12. 0	1.38
PM 2. 8	—	2.16	3.55
3. 0	—	3. 8	4.46
3.15	—	3.21	5.25
3.48e	—	—	5.25
3.50	—	3.57	6.21
—	4.36e	4.39e	6.21
5.35d	—	5.41d	7.50
6. 3e	—	6. 9e	7.45
8. 0	—	8. 8	9.59

Sunday Trains.

AM 8. 5	—	8.12	10. 0
9.50	—	9.56	11.50
PM 7.10	—	7.20	9. 5

Trains from Maidstone via Paddock Wood.

Leave MAIDST.	LON. B.	Arrive at CAN. ST.	CHAR. +
AM 6. 5	8. 9	—	8.19
7.54	9.32	9.36	—
9.32	10.58	11. 2	—
10. 6	11.43	—	11.57
11.44	1.36	—	1.50
PM 1.42	3.26	—	3.40
4. 3	5.50	—	6. 3
4.49	7.25	7.30	—
6.31	8.26	—	8.35
8. 9	10.22	—	10.35
d10.59s	—	1.20	—

Sunday Trains.

AM 8.14	10.22	—	10.32
PM 5.29	8.12	—	8.22
7. 9	9. 7	—	9.17

d Saturdays only.
e Saturdays excepted.
s Third Class only.

Royal Star Hotel. New Proprietorship. Fifty additional bedrooms completed in modern style. Table d'hote Luncheons and Dinners. Garage, Lounge, Billiard and Sitting Rooms, best between London and Coast. Headquarters R.A.C., A.A., M.U., K.A.C. 'Phone, 291. Telegrams, "Star, Maidstone." N. S. JOHNSTONE, Manager.

Rose and Crown Hotel. Family and Commercial. Opposite G.P.O. Luncheons and Dinners. Garage. Telephone 350. Proprietor, C. D. BRISSENDEN.

New Inn Hotel. Family and Commercial. Opposite Maidstone East Station. Beds a speciality. Bathroom. Garage. Telephone 585. W. J. CLAPPERTON, Residential Proprietor.

MALDEN (Surrey) from *Waterloo,* 9½ miles. Fares, 1/8*a*, 1/0*c*. R. T. for two days, 3/4*a*, 2/0*c*. Pop. 12,642. See pp. 584, 585, 591-594. Map Square 77.

MALDON EAST (Essex)

From *Liverpool Street*, 44¼ miles, *via* Witham. Fares, 8/2*a*, 4/11*c*. R. T. for two months, 16/4*a*. Pop. (Maldon) 6,589.
Map Square 24.

L'PL. ST.	M'DON E.	M'DON E	L'PL. ST.
AM 5. 0	7.59	AM 7.17	8.52
8.15	9.40	8.54	10.22
8.46	10.35	9.47	11.16
11.30	12.54	11. 5*h*	12.39
PM 2.15	3.43	PM 1.25	3.13
3.26	5.13	4. 9	5.47
4.58	6.18	5.28	7.40
6.39	8.13	7.22	9.17
—	—	—	—

Sunday Trains.

AM 8.15	10. 2	AM 9.10	11.15
10. 5	11.35	10.35	12.40
PM 3.40	5.20	PM 4.25	7.10
6.15	8. 6	7.14	8.58

h Wednesdays excepted.

ANOTHER ROUTE from

Liverpool Street, via Wickford, 42¼ miles. Fares (East Station), 8/2*a*, 4/11*c*. R. T. for two months, 16/4*a*, 9/6*c*. (West Station), 7/11*a*, 4/9*c*. R.T. for two months, 15/10*a*, 9/6*c*.

Leave L'POOL ST.	Arrive at M'DON W.	M'DON E.
AM 6.50	9. 4	9. 7
9. 1	10.56	10.59
11.56*e*	1.48	1.51
PM 1.26*d*	2.47	2.50
4.15*e*	5.33	5.36
4.18*d*	5.56	5.59
5.39	7. 8	7.11
8. 2*e*	9.40	9.43
8.45*d*	10.16	10.19

No Sunday Trains.

Trains from Maldon.

Leave M'DON E.	M'DON W.	Arrive at L'POOL ST.
AM 8. 2	8. 6	9.47
9.19	9.23	11. 7
PM 12.57*d*	1. 1*d*	3. 5
12.57*e*	1. 1*e*	4.51
4.43*e*	4.47*e*	6.51
4.56*d*	5. 0*d*	6.51
6. 9	6.13	8.23
7.55	7.59	9.56

No Sunday Trains.
d Saturdays only.
e Saturdays excepted.

Blue Boar Hotel. A remarkably fine interior dating from 1370, carefully restored. Comfortable Bedrooms. First-class Cooking and Service. Electric Light. Billiards and Garage. Fishing and Shooting in locality. TRUST HOUSES, Ltd.

The King's Head Hotel. Leading Family and Commercial Hotel. Headquarters A.A. and M.U. Recently re-decorated throughout. Electric Light. Separate Tables. Commercial Room. Motor Bus meets all Trains. Moderate Tariff. Excellent Cuisine.—Apply, Manageress. Telephone 12. Proprietors— THE MALDON HOTELS, LTD.

MALINS' LEE (Salop)

154 miles. Fares, 29/9*a*, 17/10*c*. R.T. for two months, 59/6*a*, 35/8*c*. Departures *from* London as for Wellington (Salop). Departures *for* London about 3 times daily. Pop. 3,364.
Map Square 17.

MALLAIG (Inverness)

from *Euston*, 565¼ miles. Fares, 113/2*a*, 67/11*c*. R. T. for two months, 226/4*a*, 135/10*c*.
Map Square 36.

EUSTON	MLLIG.	MLLIG.	EUSTON
PM 1.30*er*	11.53*h*	AM 7.15	5. 0*h*
11.35*e*	5.58	PM 2. 0*e*	6.55*h*
—	—	2. 0*d*	7.30*h*

No Sunday Trains.
d Saturdays only.
e Saturdays excepted.
h A.M. *k* P.M.
r Restaurant Car.

ANOTHER ROUTE from

King's Cross, 597½ miles. Fares as above.

KING'S+	MLLIG.	MLLIG.	KING'S +
PM 7.45*er*	11.53*h*	AM 7.15	3.25*h*
11.25*e*	5.58*l*	PM 2. 0	*f*6.50*l*

Sunday Trains.

PM 7.45*r*	11.53*h*	—	—
11.25	5.58*l*	—	—

e Saturdays excepted.
f Arrives 7.5 a.m. Sunday.
h A.M. *l* P.M.
r Restaurant Car.

MALLING (Kent) from

Victoria, Holborn Viaduct, and *St. Paul's*, 34⅓ miles. Fares, 7/6*d*, 6/0*b*, 4/5*c*. R. T. for two months, 15/0*a*, 12/0*b*. Pop. 4,766.
Map Square 24.

	Leave (S.E.&C.)	HOL. V.	ST. PL.'s	Arr. at MAL'NG.
AM	—	6.40	6.42	8.15
	8.32	8.20	8.23	10. 9
	11. 4	10.58	11. 0	12.38
PM	—	12.33*d*	12.36*d*	1.56
	—	1.27*d*	1.30*d*	2.51
	2. 9*d*	2. 4*d*	2. 7*d*	3.16
	2.40*d*	—	—	4. 3
	2.50*e*	—	—	4.19
	4.25*e*	—	—	5.37
	*e*5.15*h*	—	*e*5.15*k*	6.17
	*d*5.20*h*	—	*d*5.26*k*	6.22
	5.30*e*	—	5.33*e*	6.48
	—	—	6.16*e*	7.27
	6.40	6.34	6.37	8. 2
	7.22	7.22	7.24	8.48
	8.55	—	—	10. 8
	9.55	—	—	10.52
	10. 0	9.54	8.56	11.21

Sunday Trains.

AM	—	8. 0	—	9.42
PM 2. 5	2. 3	—	3.45
6.35	6.40	—	8. 7
10.15	10.12	—	11.43

Trains from Malling.

Leave MALLING	ST. PL.'s	Arrive at HOLB V.	VICT.
AM 7.18	8.40	8.42	8.50
8. 9	9.37	9.39	—
8.47	9.52	9.55	—
9.33*d*	10.41	—	—
9.33	—	10.43	—
10.26	—	—	11.37
11.35	12.59	1. 2	12.49
PM 1.10	—	—	2.40
2.58	—	—	4.33
5.32	6.58	7. 0	—
6.20	7.36*k*	—	7.49*h*
6.20*d*	8. 0	8. 2	—
6.20*e*	8.18	8.20	8.10
7.14	—	—	8.51
8.40*d*	—	—	9.54
10.13	11.43	11.45	—

Sunday Trains.

AM 9.29	—	—	10.48
PM 2.28	—	—	3.50
4.43	—	6.20	6. 3
8.38	—	10.22	10. 5

d Saturdays only.
e Saturdays excepted.
h Departs from or arrives at Charing + (S.E. & C.A.)
k Departs from or arrives at London Bridge (S.E. & C.R.).

MALLWYD (Merioneth),

219½ miles. No through fares. Departures *from* London as for Dinas Mawddy. Departures *for* London about 3 times daily. Pop. 734.

MALMESBURY (Wilts)

from *Paddington*, 94½ miles. Fares, 19/9*a*, 11/10*c*. R. T. for two months, 39/6*a*. Pop. 2,405.
Map Square 22.

PAD.	MALMBY.	MALMBY.	PAD.
AM 5.30	8.33	AM 7.13	10.45
7.30	10.36	9.18	12.20
9. 0	11.56	PM 12.10*r*	2.40
10.45	2. 6	2.26	6. 2
PM 3.15*t*	6.36	4.53*r*	8.35
5.15	8. 3	7. 5	2.45

Sunday Trains.

PM 2. 0	7.38	PM 6.28	10. 0

r Restaurant Car.
t Tea Car.

MALPAS (Cheshire), 176¼

miles. Fares, 36/1*a*, 21/8*c*. R. T. for two months, 72/2*a*. Departures *from* London as for Whitchurch (Salop). Departures *for* London about 5 times daily. Pop. 1,166.
Map Square 17.

MALTBY (Yorks), 165¾

miles. Fares, 33/7*a*, 20/2*c*. R. T., double fare. Departures *from* London as for Doncaster. Departures *for* London about 4 times daily. Pop. 146.
Map Square 13.

MALTON (Yorks) from

King's Cross, 209½ miles. Fares, 43/7*a*, 26/2*c*. R. T. double fare. Pop. 4,438.
Map Square 8.

KING'S+	MALTON	MALTON	KING'S+
AM 4.45	10.18	AM 8.50*r*	1.15
7.15*r*	12.58	9.22	3.50
10. 0*r*	2.21	11.22*r*	4.30
10.10*r*	3. 9	PM12. 2*r*	4.45
11.30	5.31	1.57*r*	6.30
PM 1.50*r*	6.53	3.15*r*	7.30
5.35*er*	10. 1	5.29*r*	10. 0
5.35*dr*	11. 4	8.37	3.25
11.25*e*	5.25	10.28*e*	5.40
11.25*d*	9.17	10.28*d*	6. 0

Sunday Trains.

PM11.25	5.23	PM 8.28	5.40

d Saturdays only.
e Saturdays excepted.
r Restaurant Car.

MALVERN (Worcester)

from *Paddington*128½ miles. Fares, Link Station, *via* Worcester, 25/3*a*, 15/2*c*. R.T. for two months, 50/6*a*, 30/4*c*. *Via* Gloucester, 27/11*a*, 16/8*c*. R. T. for two months, 55/10*a*, 33/6*c*. Great Malvern, *via* Worcester, 25/7*a*, 15/4*c*. R. T. for two months, 51/2*a*, 30/8*c*. *Via* Gloucester, 27/11*a*, 16/9*c*. R.T. for two months, 55/10*a*, 33/6*c*. Malvern Wells, *via* Worcester, 25/8*a*, 15/5*c*. R.T. for two months, 51/4*a*, 30/10*c*. *Via* Gloucester, 27/11*a*, 16/9*c*. R. T. for two months, 55/10*a*, 33/6*c*. Pop. 17,809.
Map Square 17.

Leave PAD.	LINK.	Arrive at GT. MAL.	M.W'LLS
AM 5.30	10.42	10.44	10.50
8.50	11.58	12. 1	12. 6
9.45	1.17	1.20	1.26
PM 1.30*r*	4.26	4. 0	4.36
1.35*t*	5.10	5.13	5.50
4.45*t*	7.28	7.31	7.39
6. 5*r*	9. 5	9.10	—
6.55*k*	11.24	11.28	—
*h*1. 0*l*	8.30*h*	8.19*h*	8.17*h*

Sunday Trains.

AM10.35*r*	2.47	2.50	—
AM 4.10	8.26	8.29	—

MALVERN—continued.

Trains from Malvern.

	Leave		Arr. at
M. Wells	Gt. Mal.	Link.	Pad.
AM 8.17	8.25	3.30	11.15
9.38	9.41	9.45	2.12
h10.11r	10. 8hr	10. 2hr	2.40
10.56	11. 5r	11. 9	2.55
PM 1. 5r	1.34r	1.14r	4.15
1.26h	—	—	5. 0
1.58	2. 3	2. 9	5.50
5.15r	5.20r	5.25r	9.15
5.34	5.41	5.47	10.45
7.39h	7.35h	7.28h	3.30

Sunday Trains.

AM10. 0	10. 3	10. 8	2.40
PM —	5.12r	5.17r	9.48

d Saturdays only.
h Via Gloucester.
k Thursdays, Fridays and Saturdays only.
l Saturday midnight excepted.
t Tea Car.
r Restaurant Car.

Tudor Hotel. First-class: 500 feet above sea-level. Telephone 87. Telegrams, "Tudor Hotel, Malvern."
See advt. p. **245.**

Malvern Hydropathic. Excellent Cuisine. Lift. Prospectus on application to Assistant-Director.
See advt. p. **245.**

Portland Private Hotel. Delightfully situated. Close to Croquet and Tennis Courts.
See advt. p. **246.**

The Abbey Hotel. The leading Hotel. Elevator. Electric Light. Central Heating. Garage. Telephone 183.

Aldwyn Tower Boarding Establishment. Unrivalled situation, 600 ft. above sea-level. Balcony commanding magnificent views. Central heating. Reduced Winter terms. Electric Light. Telephone 304.
Mrs. FRED. J. SMITH.

Foley Arms Hotel. Centrally situated, commands beautiful views of surrounding country. Table d'hôte, separate tables. Telephone No. 197. Tariff on application to Proprietress.

Grosvenor Private Hotel. Centrally situated. South aspect. Magnificent views. Electric light. Lounge. Spacious open-air Balcony. Heated throughout. Private suites without board if desired. Telephone No. 155.
Mrs. WALWY YATES.

Gold Hill Private Hotel. Telephone No. 91. Every Home Comfort. Lounge. Electric Light throughout. Garden. Moderate Terms.
Mrs. BRAY HARTLAND.

Malvern House Hotel. Self-contained suites, Hot and cold water in every room. Lift. Central heating. Tennis and croquet lawns. 'Phone 338.

Hardwick Hotel. Unrivalled position. Every modern convenience. Nearest the College and Golf Links. Phone 246.
Proprietor, H. WILSON.

Montrose Hotel. High Class Family. In own grounds. Central heated. Near Colleges, Golf, and Tennis. 'Phone 355.

House Agents. Messrs. LEAR and Son, Church Street, Malvern, publish monthly "The Malvern Descriptive Property Register," with large map taken from Ordnance Survey. Free on application.

MALVERN LINK (see under MALVERN).
Pop. 5,218.
Map Square 17.

MALVERN WELLS
(see under MALVERN).
Pop. 1,699.

Hornyold Arms Hotel. Principal Hotel. Near Golf Course. Garage. Billiards. Winter Tennis. R.A.C. and A.A Hotel. 'Phone, Malvern 369.

MANCHESTER (LONDON ROAD) (Lancs) from *Euston*, 183¾ miles. Fares, 38/7a, 23/2c. R. T., double fare. Pop. 730,551.
Map Square 12.

Euston	Manch.	Manch.	Euston
AM12.25	4.40	AM 7.25dr	12.20
2.35	8. 7	8.10er	12. 5
5. 0	10. 2	8.30r	12.50
6.45	12.30	9.45r	1.15
8.45r	12.40	10. 0r	1.45
10. 0r	2. 5	10.15r	2.20
10.40r	2.20	10.40r	3.10
11.50r	3.40	PM12. 5r	3.55
12. 0nr	5.25	12.40dr	5.50
PM 2.50r	6.45	1.15er	6. 0
4. 5r	7.55	1.32dr	6. 0
4.45r	9.10	2.10r	6.15
6. 5r	9.35	2.15r	6.25
8. 0e	1.35	2.50r	7.30
8.45d	1.35	4.10r	8.10
9.30e	3.15	4.40dr	9.15
11. 0d	3.50	4.45er	9. 5
11.50d	6. 5	5.0dr10. 0	
—	—	6.15er10.10	
—	—	10.30e	5. 0
—	—	11. 0d	5. 0
—	—	12. 0gm	5.40

Sunday Trains.

AM 9.15	3.47	AM10.45	4. 0
PM12.10r	4.43	PM 1. 0r	5.45
12.30r	5.35	2.30r	7.30
6. 0r	10. 6	4.20r	8.55
7.50r	1.30	11.40	5. 0
9.15	3.15	—	—

d Saturdays only.
e Saturdays excepted.
g Mondays morning excepted.
m Midnight.
n Noon.
r Restaurant Car.

ANOTHER ROUTE (VICTORIA STATION), 186¾ miles. Fares as above.

Euston	Manch.	Manch.	Euston
AM10.40r	2.45	AM 9.20r	1.15
PM 2.50r	7. 2	11.40r	3.55
6. 5r	10. 5	5.45dr	10. 0
—	—	PM 5.50er	10.10

Sunday Trains.

PM12.10r	5.10	PM12.33r	5.45

d Saturdays only.
e Saturdays excepted.
r Restaurant Car.

ANOTHER ROUTE from
St. Pancras, 189¼ miles. Fares as above.

		MANCHESTER.	
St. Pan.	Cent.	Vict.	
AM 2.25	6.52	—	
4.25	9.52	—	
8.25r	12.53	—	
10.25r	2.25	3. 0	
PM 12.25r	4.25	—	
1.25r	—	6.15	
2.25r	6.25	—	
4.25r	8.45	—	
6.25r	10.25	—	
12. 0	5.15	6.27	

MANCHESTER—contd.

Sunday Trains.

		MANCHESTER.	
St. Pan.	Cent.	Vict.	
AM 11.15r	4.25	4.25	
PM 3.15	8.40	—	
6.15r	10.50	—	
11.55	5.45	—	

Trains from Manchester.

	MANCHESTER.		St. Pan.
	Vict.	Cent.	
AM —	—	7.20r	11.35
—	—	8.55r	1.30
—	—	9.45r	1.45
9.33	—	9.55	3.25
PM —	—	12.20r	4.20
1.15r	—	1.50r	5.45
—	—	4.35r	6.15
—	—	5.50r	8.35
—	—	7.25	10. 5
11.45	—	12. 0	4.20
			6. 0

Sunday Trains.

AM 11.35	12. 0r	5. 2	
PM —	5.20r	9.52	
—	10.40	4.55	

r Restaurant Car.

ANOTHER ROUTE (LONDON ROAD) from *King's Cross*, 203 miles. Fares as above.

King's+	Manch.	Manch.	King's+
AM 4.45	10.10	AM 5.25r	11.30
7.15r	12.14k	10. 3	3.50
8.45	3.17	11.20k	6.25
10.10r	5.19	PM12.40	6.30
11.30	6.52	3.18k	9. 0
PM 1.50r	7.15	7.20k	3.25
4. 0r	9.54k	—	—
5.45r	11. 2	—	—

Sunday Trains.

12. 0nr	5.32k	AM 6.40r	3.45
PM 5. 0r	10.23	PM12.15k	5.55
—	—	4.50r	10.20

k Central Station.
n Noon.
r Restaurant Car.

ANOTHER ROUTE (LONDON ROAD) from *Marylebone*, 206 miles. Fares as above.

M'bone.	Manch.	Manch.	M'bone.
AM 2.32	9.17	AM 1.50	10.56
8.45r	1.45	5.25r	11.10
10. 0r	3.17	8.20r	1.13
PM12.15r	5.18	10. 3r	3. 0
3.20r	7.45k	PM 2.15r	6.38
5. 0r	9.54k	3.50r	8.54
6.20r	11. 2	5. 0r	9.55
10. 0d	3. 5	10.30	3.57
10. 5e	3.40	10.30k	5.57

Sunday Trains.

AM11.15r	4.17k	PM12.15kr	5.40
PM 5.30r	10.23	5.35kr	10.24

d Saturdays only.
e Saturdays excepted.
k Arrives at or departs from Manchester (Central) Station.
r Restaurant Car.

Victoria Hotel (Empire Hotels). Most conveniently situated in centre of Manchester. Close to principal railway stations, Royal Exchange, Coal Exchange, Produce Exchange, and principal places of amusement. Inclusive terms arranged. Telegrams, Victoria Hotel. Telephone, Manchester City 5389.
See advt. p. **247.**

VICTORIA HOTEL, MANCHESTER.

MANCHESTER—*contd.*

"Woodcourt" Private Hotel, Brooklands, Cheshire. *See* advt. p. **246.**

"Beech Lawn." Private Residential Hotel, Dudley Road, Whalley Range. Billiards. Tennis. Electric light. Terms 10/6 per day. No. 11 Tram Car to terminus. 'Phone 437 Chorlton.

"Kenilworth" Residence, Dudley Road, Whalley Range. Comfort and refinement. Lounge. Hot and Cold Water in Bedrooms. Excellent Cuisine. Separate Tables. Terms from 10/6 per day. 'Phone 167 Chorlton.

The Victoria House, 254, Oxford Road. First-Class Commercial Hotel. Five minutes station. Cars 41 or 42. Alight at Burlington Street stage. 'Phone 6876 City. Terms from 7/-.

The Queen's Hotel, Piccadilly. One of the oldest and best Hotels in England. Redecorated throughout. Dancing and Music. Excellent Cuisine and choicest Wines. Magnificent New Restaurant. Telephone, 5612 Central. Under the direction of—JOSEPH, late Deputy Manager, Piccadilly Hotel, London.

Midland Hotel. Covered way from Central Station. Numerous private suites. French Restaurant. Trafford Restaurant. Grill Room. American Bar. Telephone in every room. Post Office. One of the "Midland Hotels." ARTHUR TOWLE, Manager.

Palace Hotel, Buxton. Easily accessible. Quick Train Service. Moderate Tariff. Excellent Cuisine.

Fir Hill Private Residential Hotel, East Downs Road, Bowdon, Cheshire. Near Golf Links and Station. Electric Light. Telephone. Garage. Tennis. Hot and Cold Water in all Bedrooms. Excellent Cooking. Terms Moderate.

Bank.—The National Bank, Ltd., Spring Gardens.

Lancashire and Cheshire Insurance Corporation, Ltd., Palatine Bank Buildings, 10, Norfolk Street. Tel. 7564 Central. *See* advt. p. 3 of cover.

Norwich Union Mutual, the outstanding British Life Office. Reserves at 2½ per cent. 73, King Street, Manchester. *See* advt. p. 6 of cover.

Remington Typewriters. Local Branch, 9, Victoria Street. *See* advt. inside Yellow Cover, p.2.

MANEA (Cambridge), 80¼
miles. Fares, 15/10*a*, 9/6*c*. R. T., double fare. Departures *from* London as for March. Departures *for* London about 5 times daily. Pop. 1,473.
Map Square 18.

MANGOTSFIELD
(Gloucester), 122 miles. No through fares. Departures *from* London as for Bristol. Departures *for* London about 6 times daily. Pop. 9,936.
Map Square 22.

MANNINGHAM (Yorks),
207½ miles. Fares, 39/9*a*, 23/10*c*. R. T., double fare. Departures *from* London as for Shipley. Departures *for* London about 5 times daily. Pop. 22,941.

MANNINGTREE (Essex)
from *Liverpool Street*, 59½ miles. Fares, 12/8*a*, 7/7*c*. R. T. for two months, 25/4*a*. Pop. 870.
Map Square 1.

L'pl. St.	Man.	Man.	L'pl. St.
AM 5. 0	6.55	AM 1.23	3.50
6.50	9.22	6.51	8.52
8.46	10.47	7.47	9.36
10.20	12. 3	8.16*r*	9.53
10.47	1. 2	9.19	10.58
11.30	1.16	9.26	11.16
PM12.33*r*	2. 4	10.44	12.39
1.33*d*	3.45	PM12.55	3.13
2.15	4.11	1.33	3.36
3.23	5. 6	3.48	5.47
3.26	5.40	4.50	6.32
5.42*d*	7.27	6.19	7.51
5.42*e*	7.31	7.20*d*	9.36
6.39*e*	8.20	8.25*r*	10. 0
7.16	9. 1	9.12	11.16
7.45*r*	9.30	—	—
8.45	10.30	—	—
8.54	11.15	—	—
Sunday Trains.			
AM 8.15	10.28	AM 1.23	3.50
9.20*r*	11.10	9.47	11.38
PM 3.40	5.44	10. 3	12.40
4.40	6. 6	PM 5.32	7.10
7.40	9.31	6.46	8.58
8.46	11. 9	8. 4	10. 9
—	—	—	—

d Saturdays only.
e Saturdays excepted.
r Restaurant Car.

MANOD (Merioneth) from
Paddington, 228½ miles. Fares, 47/9*a*, 28/8*c*. R. T. for two months, 95/6*a*, 57/4*c*. Departures *from* London as for Blaenau Festiniog. Departures *for* London about 3 times daily.
Map Square 11.

MANORBIER (Pembroke)
from *Paddington*, 261¼ miles. Fares, 53/2*a*, 31/11*c*. R. T. for two months, 106/4*a*, 63/10*c*. Departures *from* London as for Tenby. Departures *for* London about 4 times daily. Pop. 603.
Map Square 20.

MANOR PARK (Essex)
from *Liverpool Street*, *Fenchurch Street*, 6¼ miles. Fares from Liverpool Street, 1/0½*a*, 0/10*b*, 0/7½*c*. R. T. for two days, 1/11*a*, 1/5½*b*, 1/0½*c*. From Fenchurch Street, 1/0½*a*, 0/10*b*, 0/7½*c*. R. T. for two days, 1/9*a*, 1/4*b*, 1/0½*c*. Pop. 14,571.
See pp. 528-534.

MANOR WAY (Royal
Albert Docks), from *Fenchurch Street*, 7¾ miles. Fares, 1/0½*a*, 0/10*b*, 0/7½*c*. R. T. for two days, 2/1*a*, 1/7½*b*, 1/2*c*. *See* pp. 537-540.

MANSFIELD (Notts)
from *St. Pancras*, 141 miles. Fares, 28/2*a*, 16/11*c*. R. T., double fare. Pop. 44,418.
Map Square 13.

St. Pan.	Mans.	Mans.	St. Pan.
AM 2.25	9.24	AM 5.48*r*	9.57
4.25	10.17	7.20*r*	10.45
9. 0*r*	12. 6	8. 0*r*	12.10
9.50*r*	2.12	9.30*r*	1.20
11. 0*r*	2.34	11. 0	3.25
11.45*r*	3.51	PM12. 2*r*	4.10
PM 1.50*r*	5. 9	1.55*r*	5.30
2.25*r*	6.33	2.27*r*	6.35
3.30*r*	7.18	4. 7*r*	7.15
5. 0*r*	8.10	5.10*r*	9. 5
6.15*r*	10.16	10.32	4.20
6.25*dr*	11.24	—	—
6.25*er*	11.30	—	—
—	—	—	—

MANSFIELD—*continued.*

Sunday Trains.

St. Pan.	Mans.	Mans.	St. Pan.
AM10.50*r*	4.40	PM12.40*r*	5. 2
PM 3.15	9.50	7.36	4.55
—	—	—	—
—	—	—	—
—	—	—	—
—	—	—	—

d Saturdays only.
e Saturdays excepted.
r Restaurant Car.

ANOTHER ROUTE from
Marylebone, 142¾ miles. Fares as above.

M'bone.	Mans'fld.	Mansf'ld.	M'bone.
AM 2.32	6.27	AM 7. 5	10.36
8.45*r*	12.30	8. 0*r*	11.10
10. 0*dr*	1.51	9.33*r*	1.13
10. 0*r*	2.18	11.23*r*	3. 0
PM12.15*r*	4. 6	PM 3.27*r*	6.38
3.20*r*	6.22	4.25*r*	8.55
5. 0*r*	8. 9	5.45*r*	9.55
6.20*r*	9.30	10.10*e*	3.57
—	—	10.18*d*	3.57
—	—	—	—
—	—	—	—
—	—	—	—

Sunday Trains.

M'bone.	Mans'fld.	Mansf'ld.	M'bone.
AM11.15*r*	3.46	PM1.10*r*	5.40
PM 5.30*r*	9. 4	6.45*r*	10.24

d Saturdays only.
e Saturdays excepted.
r Restaurant Car.

MANSFIELD WOOD-
HOUSE (Notts), 142¼ miles. Fares 28/6*a*, 17/1*c*. R. T. for two months, 57/0*a*, 34/2*c*. Departures *from* London as for Mansfield. Departures *for* London about 6 times daily. Pop. 13,465.
Map Square 13.

MANSION HOUSE to
and from *Charing Cross*, *Victoria*, *South Kensington*, *High Street*, *Praed Street*, *Baker Street*, *King's Cross*, *Moorgate*, and all intermediate stations every few minutes. Also to and from *Ealing*, *Hounslow*, *Richmond*, and *Wimbledon*. *See* p. 489.
Map Square 61, *No.* 10.

MANTON (Rutland) from
St. Pancras, 90 miles. Fares, 18/1*a*, 10/10*c*. R. T., double fare. Pop. 291.
Map Square 18.

St. Pan.	Manton	Manton	St. Pan.
AM 2.25	6.56	AM 9. 6*r*	10.45
4.25	8.30	11.19*r*	1.20
7.50*r*	10.13	PM 1.15*r*	4.10
8.25*r*	11.15	6.18	8.20
9.50*r*	1.15	6.26*r*	9. 5
10.25*r*	2. 8	9. 9	4.20
11.35	2.43	—	—
PM12.25*r*	4.40	—	—
3.30*r*	5.38	—	—
4.30*r*	6.46	—	—
5.35*r*	8. 5	—	—
6.25*r*	10.18	—	—

Sunday Trains.

St. Pan.	Manton	Manton	St. Pan.
PM 3.15	9.21	AM 7.17	11.53
—	—	PM 7.37*r*	9.43
—	—	—	—
—	—	—	—

r Restaurant Car.

MANTON—*continued.*

ANOTHER ROUTE from *King's Cross*, 98¼ miles, *via* Peterborough. No through fares.

KING'S+	MANTON	MANTON	KING'S+
AM 5. 5	8.45	AM 8.30r	12.25
7.45	11. 6	10.18	1. 5
10.10r	1. 0	11.30	1.55
PM 1.50r	4.28	PM 2. 8r	4.45
3. 0	6. 3	4.40r	7.10
5.45r	9. 9	6. 8	9.25
—	—	10.18	3.25

Sunday Trains.

12. 0nr	5.38	AM10.42	3.45

n Noon.
r Restaurant Car.

MANUEL (Stirling), 412
miles. No through fares. Departures *from* London as for Edinburgh (Waverley). Departures *for* London about 4 times daily.
Map Square 40.

MARAZION (Cornwall),
303¼ miles. Fares, 62/9a, 37/8c. R.T. for two months, 125/6a, 75/4c. Departures *from* London as for St. Erth. Departures *for* London about 6 times daily. Pop. 1,237.
Map Square 25.

MARBLE ARCH. (Central London Tube.) *See* back of Map.

MARCH (Cambridge) from
Liverpool Street, 86 miles. Fares, 15/10a, 9/6c. R.T., double fare. Pop. 8,939.
Map Square 18.

L'POOL ST.	MARCH	MARCH	L'POOL ST.
AM 5.50	9.26	AM 6.43	9.27
8.30r	11.20	8. 7r	10.23
10. 5	12.56	9.52	12.40
11.50r	2.31	10.28	2. 7
PM12.48e	4.39	PM12.56lr	4. 2k
1.19d	4.39	12.56	5. 9
2.34	5.15	1.55r	5.17
4.45	6.56	3.30r	6.10
5.49r	8.34	4. 9r	7.58
7.10dr	9.59	5.37r	8.22
10.12	12.51	8.10	10.30
—	—	11.30	2.50

Sunday Trains.

AM 9.25	11.58	PM 3.37	6.40
PM 3.25	6.25	5. 6	7.40
9.12	12.51	11.30	3. 0

d Saturdays only.
e Saturdays excepted.
k Arrives at St. Pancras Station.
l Commencing July 23.
r Restaurant Car.

MARCHINGTON
(Stafford), 132¾ miles. Fares, 27/9a, 16/8c. R.T. for two months, 55/6a, 33/4c. Departures *from* London as for Tutbury. Departures *for* London about 5 times daily. Pop. 561.
Map Square 12.

MARCHMONT (Berwick),
358½ miles. No through fares. Departures *from* London as for Berwick-on-Tweed or St. Boswells. Departures *for* London about 3 times daily.
Map Square 41.

MARCHWIEL (Denbigh)
from Euston, 192 miles. Fares, 37/4a, 22/5c. R.T. for two months, 74/8a. Departures *from* London as for Wrexham. Departures *for* London about 5 times daily. Pop. 665
Map Square 12.

MARDEN (Kent) from
Charing Cross, Cannon Street, and *London Bridge,* 40 miles. Fares, 8/4a, 6/8b, 5/0c. R. T. for two months, 16/8a, 13/4b. Pop. 2,484.
Map Square 24.

	Leave		Arr. at
CHAR. +	CAN. ST.	LON. B.	MARDEN
AM —	5.20	5.25	7.23
—	6.45	6.50	8.52
9.25	—	9.33	10.45
—	11.56	12. 0	1.13
PM12.40d	—	12.47d	1.58
3. 0	—	3. 8	4.21
3.50d	—	3.57d	5.47
—	4.36d	4.39e	5.47
5.24d	—	5.34d	6.45
6. 0e	—	6. 5e	7. 9
7.30	—	7.26	9.15
9.30	—	9.36	10.47

Sunday Trains.

AM 7.45	—	7.52	9. 3
PM 6.35	—	6.43	8. 7
—	—	—	—
—	—	—	—

Trains from Marden.

Leave		Arrive at	
MARDEN	LON. B.	CAN. ST.	CHAR. +
AM 7.11	8.40	8.44	—
8.18	9.32	9.36	—
9.14	10.28	10.32	—
10.10	11.33	—	11.45
11.58	1.36	—	1.50
PM 2. 9	3.26	—	3.40
5.17	7.25	7.30	—
7. 6	8.54	9. 1	—
9.34	11.34	—	11.43
—	—	—	—

Sunday Trains.

AM 8.22	10. 5	—	10.15
PM 6.59	8.20	—	8.28

d Saturdays only.
e Saturdays excepted.

MARDOCK (Herts) from
Liverpool Street, 23 miles. Fares, 5/0a, 3/0c. R. T. for two months, 10/0a, 6/0c. Departures *from* London as for Buntingford. Departures *for* London about 10 times daily.
Map Square 23.

MARFLEET (Yorks), 200½
miles. No through fares. Departures *from* London as for Hull (Paragon). Departures *for* London about 6 times daily. Pop. 1,073.
Map Square 13.

MARGATE (WEST)
(Kent) from *Victoria, Holborn Viaduct,* and *St. Paul's,* 74 miles. Fares, 15/5a, 12/4b, 9/3c. R.T. for two months, 30/10a, 24/8b. Pop. 46,475.
Map Square 23.

	Leave		Arr. at
VICT. (S.E.&C.)	HOL. V.	ST. PL.'s	MARG.
AM —	3.50k	—	6.38
5. 5	4.57	5. 0	8.33
5.48f	5.40f	5.42f	8.23
8.25d	—	—	10.19
9. 0	—	—	10.35
9.20	—	—	11.35
10.10	—	—	11.48
10.25d	—	—	12.13
10.40	—	—	12.45
11.10d	—	—	12.50
11.50l	—	—	1.27
11.40e	—	—	2.56
PM12.30d	—	—	2.10
12.40d	—	—	2.20
12.55d	—	—	2.47
1. 5d	—	—	2.55
1.23d	—	—	3.48
1.25c	—	—	3. 4

MARGATE (WEST)—*continued.*

VICT. (S.E.&C.)	Leave		Arr. at
	HOL. V.	ST. PL.'s	MARG.
PM 2. 8e	—	—	4.31
2.20d	—	—	4.10
2.45d	—	—	4.39
3. 0d	—	—	4.45
3.15e	—	—	4.47
3.15d	—	—	4.56
3.20e	—	—	5.24
3.29d	—	—	5.33
4.15d	—	—	6.32
—	—	5. 5e	6.40
—	5.10e	5.12e	7.10
5.10d	—	—	7.15
5.30d	—	—	8.13
5.30e	—	—	8.15
7. 0	—	—	8.56
8.30	—	—	10.30
12. 0h	—	—	2. 4
12. 5d	—	—	1.55

Sunday Trains.

AM 7.20	—	—	9.58
9. 0	—	—	10.35
9.10	—	—	11. 7
10.15v	—	—	11.45
10.20	—	—	11.55
10.25	—	—	12.20
10.40	—	—	12.43
PM 3.20	—	—	5.25
3.30	—	—	6.37
8.25	—	—	10.40

Trains from Margate (West).

Leave		Arrive at	
MARGATE	ST. PL.'s	HOL. V.	VICT.
AM 6.56	9.37	9.39	—
9. 0	—	—	10.40
9. 4	—	—	11.27
9.16h	—	—	11.23
10. 0	—	—	11.55
10.15d	—	—	12. 3
10.20	—	—	12 .7
11.20d	—	—	1.40
11.55d	—	—	2.15
11.55	—	—	2.43
PM 1.22	—	—	3.23
1.45e	4.46	—	4.39
2.20l	—	—	4. 5
3.10d	—	—	4.58
l3.19p	—	—	5. 3
3.19s	—	—	5. 3
3.24	—	—	5.26
5.10d	—	—	6.56
5.20	—	—	6.58
6.10	—	—	7.54
6.23	9.51	9.53	9.46
7.50	—	—	10.25

Sunday Trains.

AM 9.35l	—	11.58	11.51
PM 2.35	—	—	4.42
2.49	—	—	5.52
4.35	—	—	6.24
5.25	—	—	7. 7
5.40	—	—	7.30
5.57	—	—	7.40
6. 8	—	—	8.20
6.38	—	—	8.30
7.20v	—	—	9.27
7.40	—	—	9.27
7.50	—	—	10. 8
9.12	—	—	11. 5

d Saturdays only.
e Saturdays excepted.
f Mondays only.
h Wednesdays only.
k Third class only.
l Mondays, Fridays and Saturdays only.
p Pullman Car attached.
s Mondays, Fridays and Saturdays excepted.
v First class Pullman Cars only.

MARGATE (WEST)—
continued.

ANOTHER ROUTE (West)
from *Charing Cross, Cannon Street*
and *London Bridge,* 73 miles.
Fares as above.

Leave			Arr. at
CHAR.✝	CAN. ST.	LON. B.	MARG.
AM —	—	3.57h	6.38
—	7.16	7.19	10. 3
PM —	12.50d	2.53d	2.38
—	1.20d	11.25d	3.12
—	4.12e	4.15e	6.17
—	6.12e	—	7.51

No Sunday Trains.

Trains from Margate
(*West*).

Leave			Arrive at
MARGATE	LON. B.	CAN. ST.	CHAR.✝
AM 6.50	8.32	8.36	—
6.56	9. 0	9. 4	—
7.20	9.15	9.19	—
7.43f	9.28	9.32	—
7.55g	9.28	9.32	—
7.55f	9.32	9.36	—
e8. 3p	9.48	9.52	—
8. 5d	9.48	9.52	—

No Sunday Trains.

d Saturdays only.
e Saturdays excepted.
f Mondays only.
g Mondays excepted.
h Third class only.
p Pullman car attached.

ANOTHER ROUTE *via*
Greenwich Pier, and North
Woolwich Pier by water ("Golden
Eagle"). Fares from *Fenchurch
Street,* 7/0a, 6/0c. R. T. for 15 days,
12/0a, 10/6c.

Leave			Arr. at
G. PIER	FEN. ST.	N.W.PIER	MARG.
AM 8.55	9.25	9.25	1.25

Service from Margate.

Leave	Arrive at		
MARG.	N.W.PIER	FEN. ST.	G. PIER
PM 3.10	7.30	7.36	7.45

Sunday Service.

20 minutes later at each point.
See advt. back of Map.

MARGATE (SANDS)
from *Charing Cross, Cannon Street*
and *London Bridge,* 90 miles.
Fares as above.

Leave			Arr. at
CHAR.✝	CAN. ST.	LON. B.	MARG.
AM —	5.20	5.25	9.48
—	—	7.50l	10.59
9.15	—	9.23	12.13
—	—	k10. 5l	12.52
11. 0	—	11. 7	2.18
PM 1. 0	—	—	3.43
1. 0d	—	—	3.11
3. 0	—	3. 8	5.55
4.30	—	4.36	7.25
5.15e	5.12e	5.21e	8. 8
5.20d	—	5.26d	8. 8
5.24d	—	5.34d	8.30
6. 0e	—	6. 5e	8.30
7.18	—	7.26	10.42

Sunday Trains.

AM 7.45	—	7.52	11.12
9.35h	—	—	12.43
PM 5.15h	—	—	9. 0
7.25	10.16	—	10.26
7.35	—	7.45	10.50

MARGATE (SANDS)—
continued.

Trains from Margate
(*Sands*).

Leave	Arrive at		
MARGATE	LON. B.	CAN. ST.	CHAR.✝
AM 6. 8	9.32	9.36	—
6.55	10. 0	10. 4	—
e6.55h	—	—	10.16h
8. 0	10.54	—	11. 3
8.40	11.43	—	11.57
10.15	1.36	—	1.50
11.50	3.26	—	3.40
PM 1. 5k	4. 8	—	—
2.20h	—	—	5.42h
2.20	5.50	—	6. 3
4.15	7.25	7.30	7.49
7.10	10.22	—	10.35
10. 0y	—	1.20	

Sunday Trains.

AM 6.15	10. 5	—	10.15
8.35	—	—	1. 5h
PM 4. 5	7. 9	—	7.17
5.32	8.30	—	8.40
10. 0y	—	1.23	

d Saturdays only.
e Saturdays excepted.
h Departs from or arrives at
Victoria (S.E. & C.R.).
k Mondays, Fridays and Saturdays
only.
l Low Level Platform.
y Third class only.

"Queen's Highcliffe," leading Hotel. Superb position in private grounds. Ballroom. Orchestra daily. Billiards. R.A.C. Telegrams, "Ozone," Telephone, 586 (4 lines).
See advt. p. **250.**

Hotel Florence, Cliftonville. Magnificent uninterrupted Sea Views. Recently erected. Grand Lounge. Electric lift to all floors. Mr. and Mrs. W. JAMIESON.
See advt. p. **248.**

St. George's Hotel. Recommended by the Automobile Association. Telephone No. is 360.
See advt. p. **249.**

Grand Hotel. Best position, facing Sea. Modern, up-to-date Hotel. Luxuriously furnished throughout. Garage. 'Phone 63. Telegrams, "Grand, Margate."
See advt. p. **251.**

Norfolk Hotel. Ideal position. Excellent Cuisine. Inclusive Tariff. Telephone 481.
See advt. p. **252.**

White Hart Hotel. Opposite Sea. High-class reputation. Moderate charges. Headquarters R.A.C. and A.A. Telephone 44. Telegrams, "White Hart." Apply W. E. BISHOP, Manager.
See advt. p. **253.**

Cliftonville Hotel. Unsurpassed position on Cliffs. Large private grounds between the hotel and the sea. Garage. Tel. Add.: Cliftonville, Margate. Telephone, No. 444, Margate (3 lines). Proprietors.
GORDON HOTELS, Ltd.
See advt. p. **254.**

Fort Paragon Hotel. Fully Licensed. Overlooking Sea and Winter Garden. New Dining Hall to accommodate 150 guests. Non-residents' meals a special feature. Coast Margate Phone 521. Apply MANAGERESS.
See advt. p. **255.**

Northdown Hall, Cliftonville. Splendid position. Near Sea and Flagstaff. High-class Catering. Best English and Scotch meat used. Dances weekly during Season.
See advt. p. **255.**

MARGATE—*continued.*

Fort Lodge Private Hotel. Licensed. Immediately opposite the Fort, Promenade and the new Pavilion and Winter Garden. Telegrams "Sea Breeze," Margate. Telephone No. 183.
See advt. p. **256.**

Endcliffe Hotel. Facing Sea and Oval. Spacious public rooms and full size billiard lounge. Every convenience on ground floor.
See advt. p. **256.**

Nayland Rock Hotel. (Trust Houses, Ltd.) On the Promenade. Excellent outlook. Telephone 46.
See advt. p. **257.**

Granville Court, Cliftonville. Finest position, near Bandstand. Excellent Cuisine. Moderate.
See advt. p. **257.**

Grosvenor Court. Exclusive and comfortable. Private Cars to Golf Links. Apply for Tariff to MANAGER.
See advt. p. **258.**

Cliftonville Court Hotel. High-class Family Hotel. Beautifully situated. On Sea Front. Excellent cuisine. Telephone 509.
See advt. p. **258.**:

Astor Hotel. Lewis Crescent, Cliftonville. Ideal Holiday Hotel. Specialities: Cuisine and Comfort. Telephone 461.
See advt. p. **259.**

Palm Bay Hotel. Finest position in Cliftonville. Facing Bathing Beach. Tennis Courts. Fully Licensed.
Mr. and Mrs. L. BURROWES.
Resident Proprietors.
See advt. p. **259.**

Durley Dean Private Hotel, Cliftonville. Splendidly situated, facing Sea. Near Pavilion. Private Suites during Winter months. Moderate and inclusive. Telephone ; 184.,
Proprietresses,
Mesdames HORSEY & ELLIS.
See advt. p. **260.**

Northdown Parade Hotel, Cliftonville. Splendid position. 30 Bedrooms. Telephone 402. Proprietors, E. T. FASHAM, Ltd.
See advt. p. **260.**

Albemarle Hotel, Cliftonville. First Class. Facing Sea. Good Cuisine. Separate tables. Telephone 117.
See advt. p. **261.**

Dalkeith, Cliftonville. High-class Private Hotel. Replete with every comfort. Facing Sea. Proprietress Mrs. E. FLASHOFF.
See advt. p. **261.**

Service Flats, Devonia Hall, Cliftonville. Self-contained suites. With Full Board, 25/- a day each person. 'Phone 111. Proprietor,
A. P. LEMON.
See advt. p. **261.**

Rathcoole Private Hotel, Norfolk Road. Close Promenade and Oval.
See advt. p. **261.**

For completion of
Advertisements, see over.

MARGATE.—CLIFTONVILLE HOTEL. The Leading Hotel.
GORDON HOTELS, Ltd.

MARGATE—*continued.*

Seaton Grange, Surrey Road, Cliftonville. Near Palm Bay. Best Quality Provisions; English Meat. Resident Proprietresses, Misses J. & A. MAYLE.
See advt. p. 262.

Balmoral Hotel, Cliftonville. Bijou. Pension. Facing Oval Bandstand. Every Comfort. Tel. 27. Telegrams, "Comfort, Margate."—Apply, PROPRIETRESS.
See advt. p. 262

Royston Private Hotel. Sea Views, Excellent English Cuisine.
See advt. p. 262.

The Gables Private Hotel, Cliftonville. Near Sea, Oval, Pavilion, and Bathing. 'Phone 232.
See advt. p. 262.

Surrey Hall Boarding Establishment, Cliftonville. Sea view. Moderate. Tel. 219. Proprietress,
Mrs. CURZON POOLE.
See advt. p. 263.

Carlton Private Hotel, Cliftonville. Splendidly situated, facing Sea and Oval. Excellent Cuisine. Moderate tariff. Telephone 315.
Mr. and Mrs. SAWARD.
See advt. p. 263.

First Avenue Hotel. Facing Oval Bandstand. Personal supervision. Proprietors.
Mr. and Mrs. DAWSON.
See advt. p. 263.

Walpole Bay Hotel. Newly erected Hotel, Overlooking Lawns. Every modern convenience.
Mrs. and Miss BUDGE.
See advt. p. 263.

The Leslie, 1 and 3, Surrey Road. Close to Oval and Palm Bay. Resident Proprietor—
A. H. BRUNTON.
See advt. p. 264.

Connaught Lodge, Harold Lodge, Cliftonville. Minute Sea. 50 Rooms. Tennis Court. Excellent Cuisine. Moderate Terms. 'Phone 400.
See advt. p. 264.

Clarence Private Hotel. Overlooking Sea and Oval Bandstand. 'Phone 38. Proprietress, H. FITZGIBBON.
See advt. p. 264.

Fort Road Private Hotel. Minute Jetty, Sea, Pavilion. Thoroughly Comfortable. Liberal Table. Terms from 2½ guineas. Proprietress Mrs. A. J. GATTRE.
See advt. p. 264.

Kingswear Boarding Establishment, Harold Road. Excellent Cuisine. 2 minutes Oval Bandstand. 40 Rooms. 'Phone 701.
Mrs. A. ASHFORD KING and Miss R. A. MUNNS.
See advt. p. 265.

Royal Albion Hotel and Restaurant. Facing Pier. Near Stations. English Cooking Grill. Lounge. Reduced Winter Tariff. Telephone 199.
FRANK FENNER, Proprietor.
See advt. p. 265.

Brackley Hotel, Ethelbert Crescent. Best Position, facing Sea and Lawns. Tennis. Separate Tables. 'Phone 349.
See advt. p. 265.

Thedden Grange Private Hotel, Norfolk Road, Cliftonville. Minute Sea, Oval, and Bathing. Dancing. From 3 guineas. Phone 479.
The MISSES DALE and MISS BAILEY, Proprietresses.
See advt. p. 265.

MARGATE—*continued.*

Stanmore Boarding House, 14, 16, Athelstan Road, Cliftonville. Sea View, near Fort, Promenade. Near Winter Gardens. Liberal table. Terms moderate. Stamp.
Mrs. LAWN. Proprietress.

Carisbrooke Private Hotel, Lewis Crescent, Cliftonville. Facing Sea. Well appointed and comfortable. Excellent Cuisine. Separate Tables. 'Phone 455. Apply—
PROPRIETRESS.

Hereward Boarding House, Cliftonville. 150 rooms. Lounge and Large Recreation and Ball Room. Half-minute Cliffs and Sands. Table d'hote, 6.30. Experienced Chef. Moderate. Telegrams: "Hereward, Margate." Telephone 244.
PROPRIETOR.

Kingsley Boarding House and Private Hotel, Cliftonville. 80 rooms. Handsome Lounge. Large Recreation and Ball Room. Three Tennis Courts. Table d'hote 6.30. Separate Tables. Experienced Chef. Telegrams: "Kingsley, Margate." Telephone : 579.

Lonsdale Boarding House, 28, Edgar Road, Cliftonville. Established 1904. Near Pavilion and Oval. Dinner 6.30. Terms moderate. Stamp.
PROPRIETRESS.

The Terrace Hotel, High Street and Marine Drive. Bed and breakfast from 5s. 6d. Accommodation for parties. Popular prices. Billiard Saloon, 8 tables. Proprietors,
S. H. MUNNS & SONS.

"Rosenburgh" Boarding House, Cliftonville. 110 rooms. Sea View. Minute to Sands and Concerts. Large Dining Hall, Recreation Room. Late Dinner. Moderate terms. 'Phone, 233. Proprietors. Mr. & Mrs. SHERRIN.

Apartments, Cliftonville. Very finest position. All Sea Views. Recommended. Good Cooking. Bath. Special attention to Convalescents.
PROPRIETRESS, "Raglan," Second Avenue.

Avenue House. Private Boarding House. All Sea Views. Excellent Cuisine. Separate Tables. Personal Supervision. Between Palm Bay and Oval Bathing.
PROPRIETRESS.

St. Cuthberts, Cliftonville. Superior Private Hotel. Finest position, facing Sea. Every comfort. Electric Light. Telephone 143.
Mrs. HENRY FLOWER.

Huntington, Surrey Road, Cliftonville. Superior Board Residence. Good English catering. Separate tables. Dinner 6.30. Situated between Palm Bay and Oval. Electric Light.
Proprietor. A. J. LIDWELL.

Beechwood Boarding House, Athelstan Road, Cliftonville. 40 Bedrooms. Minute Sea, Promenade, and Concert Parties. Redecorated. Electric Light. Hot Luncheon. Moderate Terms. Liberal Catering.
Mr. & Mrs. T. E. SHERRIN.

Ellison Private Hotel. Finest position Sea Front, Cliftonville. Adjoining Queen's Highcliffe annexe. Moderate terms. Separate tables. Apply—
PROPRIETRESS.

Lansdowne Lodge Board- ing Establishment, Cliftonville. Ideal position facing Sea. Well recommended. Families, Parties catered for. Separate Tables. Excellent Cuisine. Home Comforts. 'Phone 652.

MARGATE—*continued.*

Glaslyn Private Boarding House, Dalby Square, Cliftonville. Facing Sea and Tennis Courts. Good Cuisine. Separate Tables. Every comfort. Electric Light. Dances and Whist Drives arranged. Well recommended. Moderate inclusive Terms. Stamp Tariff. New Management. Telegrams: "Holidays." 'Phone 29.
Mrs. LEVETT.

Lilley's Hotel Arcadian. The Fort, facing Sea. Family and Commercial Wonderful good Stock room. Garage Telephone 190. Apply
PROPRIETOR.

Ellesmere, Eastern Esplanade, Cliftonville. Quiet Comfortable Board Residence. Facing Queen's Promenade. Lawns. Excellent Catering. Moderate Tariff. Personal Supervision.
PROPRIETRESSES.

The Dittons Private Hotel, Royal Crescent. Finest Position. Lawn to Sea. Bathing. Close to Tennis. Golf. Excellent Cuisine. Personal supervision.

Courtlands Private Hotel, Norfolk Road, Cliftonville. Modern Comforts. Best English Cuisine. Moderate inclusive Terms. 'Phone, 428. Telegrams, "Cosy." Illustrated Tariff, Apply
Mrs. B. LLOYD.

House Agents and Auc- tioneers. SCARLETT & GOLDSACK, Margate, Cliftonville, and at Ramsgate.

Furnished & Unfurnished Houses to Let and Properties for Sale. Estate Agents, Margate, and Cliftonville Chambers, Cliftonville; and at Broadstairs.
REEVE & BAYLY.

House Agents. PEARSON & COLE. 104, Northdown Road, Cliftonville, Margate. For all available houses, Lists free. 'Phone 676. And at Broadstairs.

Properties, Furnished and Unfurnished Residences. Selected list with map upon request. TAYLOR & PATTERSON, Auctioneers and Estate Agents, Cliftonville and Westbrook, Margate.

MARISHES ROAD

(Yorks), 216¼ miles. No through fares. Departures *from* London as for Whitby. Departures *for* London about 5 times daily. Pop. 244.
Map Square 8.

MARKET BOSWORTH

(Leicester) from *Euston*, 105½ miles. Fares, 21/8*a*, 13/0*c*. R. T., double fare. Departures *from* London as for Shackerstone. Departures *for* London about 6 times daily. Pop. 729.
Map Square 18.

MARKET DRAYTON

(Salop) from *Paddington*, 159¼ miles. Fares, 32/11*a*, 19/8*c*. R. T. for two months, 65/10*a*. Pop. 4,719.
Map Square 12.

	PAD.	M. DRAY.		M. DRAY.	PAD.
AM	6 50	12.19	AM	7.15	12.25
	9.10*r*	2.20		9.28*r*	1.25
	10 40*r*	4. 5		10.20*r*	2. 5
PM	12.50*r*	4.32	PM	1.40*t*	5.55
	2.10*t*	6.31		3.50*r*	8. 5
	6.10*r*	9.55		5.45	10. 0
	12.15*k*	8. 8		7.15	3.30
	12.15*c*	9.25		—	—

Sunday Trains.

PM	12.50*r*	6.23	AM	7.34*r*	1.40
	—	—		11.30	6.20
	—	—	PM	4.25*r*	9. 0

h Saturdays midnight excepted.
k Saturday midnight only.
r Restaurant Car.
t Tea Car.

MARKET HARBORO'

(Leicester) from *St. Pancras*, 83 miles. Fares, 16/11a, 10/2c. R. T., double fare. Pop. 8,577.
Map Square 18.

St.Pan.	Mark.H	Mark H.	St.Pan.
AM 4.25	7.40	AM 2.35*f*	4.55
8.25*r*	10.55	2.35*g*	5. 5
11. 0*r*	1. 4	3.40*g*	6. 0
11.35	2.39	7.12*r*	9.57
PM 3.30*r*	5.27	9.15*r*	11. 0
4.30*r*	6.52	11. 9*r*	1.20
5.35*r*	7.25	PM 1.13	3.25
6.25*r*	8.18	1.45*r*	4.10
6.30	9.13	3. 2	5.20
8.25	10.50	4.40	7. 3
12. 0	2.18	5.33	8.22
—	—	7.11*r*	9. 5
—	—	8.30	11.45

Sunday Trains.

AM 8. 0	11.40	AM 2.35	5. 5
PM 1.35	4.10	3.40	6. 0
6.15*r*	9. 0	9.40	11.53
8.25	10.50	PM 4. 8	6.27
11.55	2.18	5. 2	8.30
—	—	8.37	11. 7

f Mondays only.
g Mondays excepted.
r Restaurant Car.

ANOTHER ROUTE from

Euston, 83½ miles. Fares as above.

Euston	M.Har.	M. Har.	Euston
AM 2.35*h*	7.26	AM 6.25*eh*	9.52
5. 0	7.35	7.15*h*	10. 0
6.45	9.55	7.40	10.15
10.40	1.38	9.22	11.55
PM12.15	3.40	10.39	12.40
1.30*hr*	3.51	PM12.47*k*	3.45
3. 5	5.25	12.47*v*	4.15
4.15	6.45	2.40	5.35
4.45*h*	7.15	3.11*h*	5.50
7. 0	9. 4	4.43	7.20
11.50*eh*	3.44	7. 0*e*	9.20
12.10*dh*	3.44	7.45*h*r10.45	
—	—	7.48	11.35
—	—	8.58*eh*	4. 0
—	—	8.58*dh*	5. 0

Sunday Trains.

PM 6. 0*h*	8.33	PM 5.30*hr*	8.20

d Saturdays only.
e Saturdays excepted.
h Via Rugby.
r Restaurant Car.
v Mondays and Saturdays excepted.

MARKET RASEN (Lin-

coln), 144¾ miles. Fares, 30/0*a*, 18/0*c*. R. T., double fare. Departures *from* London as for Lincoln. Departures *for* London about 4 times daily. Pop. 2,177.
Map Square 13.
Station closed on Sundays.

MARKET WEIGHTON

(Yorks) from *King's Cross*, 191¾ miles. Fares, 38/7*a*, 23/2*c*. R. T., double fare. Pop. 1,770.
Map Square 8.

King's+	M.Wei.	M. Wei.	King's+
AM 7.15*r*	11.37	AM 9.5*r*	1.30
8.45	2.14	11.49*r*	4.30
11.30*e*	2.57	PM 4.21*r*	9.25
PM 1.50*r*	6.21	7.55	3.25
10.45*e*	9.11	—	—

Sunday Trains.

PM10.45	9.11	—	—

e Saturdays excepted.
r Restaurant Car.

MARKHAM VILLAGE

(Monmouth), 158¾ miles. Fares, 33/1*a*, 19/10*c*. R. T. for two months, 66/2*a*, 39/8*c*. Departures *from* London as for Tredegar. Departures *for* London about 6 times daily.

MARKINCH (Fife), 425¼

miles. Fares, 86/1*a*, 51/8*c*. R. T. for two months, 172/2*a*, 103/4*c*. Departures *from* London as for Kirkcaldy. Departures *for* London about 3 times daily. Pop. 8,685.
Map Square 41.

MARK LANE to and from

Mansion House, Charing Cross, Victoria, South Kensington, High Street, Praed Street, King's Cross, Moorgate, and all intermediate Stations every few minutes. Also from *Ealing, Hounslow, Richmond,* and *Wimbledon. See* p. 489.
Map Square 61, *No.* 7.

MARK'S TEY (Essex) from

Liverpool Street, 46¾ miles. Fares, 9/10*a*, 5/11*c*. R. T. for two months, 19/8*a*, 11/10*c*. Pop. 585.
Map Square 19.

L'pl. St.	M'ks.T.	M'ks.T.	L'pl.St.
AM 5. 0	6.10	AM 7.21	8.52
6.50	8.50	7.52	9.30
8.18	9.46	8.56*r*	9.53
10. 0	11. 9	9. 2	10.22
10.47	12.35	10.45	11.42
11.30	12.45	11.18	12.40
PM12.36	1.47	PM 1.30	3.13
1.33*d*	3.11	4.23	5.47
2.15	3.39	5.41	7.40
3.26	5. 9	7.24	9.17
4.18	5.47	9.42	11.16
4.58*r*	6.11	—	—
5.42*d*	6.55	—	—
5.42*e*	6.59	—	—
6.39	8.10	—	—
7.16	8.36	—	—
7.45*r*	9. 2	—	—
8.54	10.42	—	—

Sunday Trains.

AM 8.15	9.56	AM10.38	12.40
9.20*r*	10.43	PM 7.23	8.58
PM 3.40	5.13	—	—
8.46	10.36	—	—

d Saturdays only.
e Saturdays excepted.
r Restaurant Car.

MARLBOROUGH

(Wilts) from *Paddington*, 75¾ miles. Fares, 15/8*a*, 9/5*c*. R. T. for two months, 31/4*a*, 18/10*c*. Pop. 4,192.
Map Square 22.

Pad.	Marlboro'	Marlboro'	Pad.
AM 7.30	10. 0	AM 7.25	10. 0
8.45*r*	11.30	9. 5	10.52
10.45	1.22	PM12.20	2.50
PM12.36*r*	2.52	4.10	7.20
2.45	5.30	5.45	8.20
3.18	6.19	7.55	10.45
5. 5	7.20	—	—
6.30	8.42	—	—

No Sunday Trains.
r Restaurant Car.

ANOTHER ROUTE from

Waterloo, 88 miles. Fares as above.

W'loo.	Marlb.	Marlb.	W'loo.
AM 7.30	11.50	AM 9.50	12.22
PM 1. 0*r*	3.30	PM12.10	2.36
3.30	6.25	3.10	6.26
6. 0*r*	8.43	5. 7*r*	8.30

MARLBOROUGH—

continued.

Sunday Trains.

W'loo.	Marlb.	Marlb.	W'loo.
PM 6. 0	9.19	PM 5.17	8.57

r Restaurant Car.

Taxi Cabs can be hired to meet any train at this station by letter, or telephone No. 30. Messrs. James Duck, Marlborough, Wilts.

Ailesbury Arms Hotel. First class Residential. Close to Savernake Forest and College. Motor to order. Garage. Tel. No. 1. Tels. Ailesbury, Marlborough.

Castle and Ball. One of the Oldest Hotels between London and Bath. Garage, and Repairer by appointment to the Automobile Club, close to Hotel. Telephone No. 2. Proprietors, COUNTRY HOSTELS, LTD.

MARLBOROUGH

ROAD from *Baker Street*, 1½ miles. Fares, 0/2½*a*, 0/1½*c*. R. T. for two days, 0/5*a*, 0/3*c*. *See* back of Map.
Map Square 60.

MARLESFORD (Suffolk)

from *Liverpool Street*, 86¼ miles. Fares, 18/2*a*, 10/11*c*. R. T. for two months, 36/4*a*. Departures *from* London as for Framlingham. Departures *for* London about 7 times daily. Pop. 388.
Map Square 19.

MARLOW (Bucks) from

Paddington, 31¼ miles. Fares, 5/8*a*, 3/5*c*. R. T. for two months, 11/4*a*, 6/10*c*. Pop. 5,146.
Map Square 23.

Pad.	Marlow	Marlow	Pad.
AM 6.50	8.17	AM 7.58	8.56
7.35	9. 5	8.33	9.37
9.20	10.41	9.18	10.24
9.55	11.26	9.54	11. 6
11.25	12.35	10.20	11.35
PM12.35*e*	2.12	11. 8	12.15
1. 5*d*	2.12	PM 1. 5	2.35
1.20*d*	2.40	2.22*d*	3.38
2. 7	3.18	2.55	4.10
3.38	4.43	4.10	5.37
4.50	5.56	5.35	6.55
5.45	6.50	6.28	7.45
6.55	7.53	7.33*d*	9.12
8.35	9.44	8.10	9.33
10. 5	11.12	9.22	10.42
12. 3*h*	1.15	—	—

Sunday Trains.

AM 8.20	9.58	AM 8.47	10.14
9.45	10.51	11.33	1. 5
10.25	11.26	PM 2.47	4.53
11.45	12.50	5. 3	6.23
PM 2.35	3.46	7.27	8.45
5.15	6.27	8.18	9.52
6. 5	8.36	8.43	9.53
8.20	9.35	9.15	10.33
—	—	9.55	11. 6

d Saturdays only.
e Saturdays excepted.
h Wednesdays and Saturdays only.

Salter's Steamers (Marlow Lock, 10 minutes from station). Up stream, 12.5 P.M., 5.40 P.M. Down stream, 11.5 A.M., 4.15 P.M. *See* advt. facing first page of train service.

For completion of Advertisements, see over.

MARLOW—*continued.*

The Crown Hotel. Oldest Family. Near River, Station and Links. Nice Garden, Garage, Stabling. Private Sitting-rooms. Excellent Catering. Dancing and Music. Moderate. 'Phone 67.
Mrs. OLIVER P. TAYLOR, Proprietress.
See advt. p. **246**.

Compleat Angler Hotel. Old established Family Hotel. Own grounds of 5 acres. Finest position on river, adjoining Weir; overlooks Quarry Woods. Private sitting-rooms. Drawing Room. Lounge. 50 bedrooms. Electric Light throughout, Garage. Moderate. Telephone No. 15. A.A. Hotel.
ROBT. B. KILBY, Proprietor.

"The Chequers Hotel." Old-established Family and Commercial Hotel. Most central position. One minute River. Excellent cuisine and catering. Choice wines. Parties a speciality. Private sitting-rooms. Moderate. Phone 53.
LILIAN LONG, Proprietress.

George Kendall. House and Estate Agent. Opposite Railway Station and High Street. Furnished and Unfurnished Houses. Lists free. Telephone 44.

MARLPOOL (Derby) from

King's Cross, 139¾ miles. Fares, 26/5*a*, 15/10*c*. R. T., double fare. Departures *from* London as for Ilkeston. Departures *for* London about 6 times daily. Pop. 3,490.

MARPLE (Cheshire) from

St. Pancras, 176½ miles. Fares, 36/6*a*, 21/11*c*. R. T., double fare. Pop. 6,613
Map Square 12.

St. Pan.	Marple	Marple	St. Pan.
AM 4.25	10.20	AM12.45*g*	6. 0
8.25*r*	1.10	6.52*r*	11.35
10.25*r*	2.38	9.15*r*	1.30
PM 1.25*r*	5.48	10. 5	3.25
4.25*r*	8.33	PM 1.43*r*	5.45
12. 0*h*	9.40	3.33*r*	8.35
—	—	4.57*r*	10. 5
—	—	7.27	4.20
—	—	—	—
—	—	—	—
—	—	—	—
—	—	—	—
—	—	—	—
—	—	—	—

Sunday Trains.

AM11.15	4. 0	AM12.45	6. 0
PM 3.15	8. 7	PM12. 3*r*	5. 2
—	—	4.50*r*	9.52
—	—	6.48	4.55
—	—	—	—
—	—	—	—
—	—	—	—
—	—	—	—
—	—	—	—
—	—	—	—

g Mondays excepted.
h Saturdays midnight only.
r Restaurant Car.

MARSDEN (Yorks) from

Euston, 196½ miles. Fares, 37/9*a*, 22/8*c*. R. T., double fare. Pop. 5,962.
Map Square 12.

Euston	M'sden	M'sden	Euston
AM12.25	7.43	AM 6.37*er*	12. 5
2.35	9.55	7. 7*r*	12.50
5. 0	11.43	8.18*r*	1.15
8.45*r*	1.46	8.50*r*	1.45
10.40*r*	4. 2	9.49*r*	3.10
11.50*r*	5. 2	10.47*r*	3.55
12. 0*nr*	6.23	PM12.48*r*	6.15
PM 1.30*r*	7.47	1.43*r*	7.30
4. 5*r*	9.18	2.55*r*	8.10
6. 5*r*	10.10	4.55*er*	10.10
11.50*d*	8.48	9.22	5. 0
—	—	—	—

Sunday Trains.

PM12.10*r*	5.59	AM 8. 1	4. 0
12.30*r*	9.32	11.38*r*	5.45
—	—	PM 1.28*r*	7.30
—	—	6.18	5. 0

d Saturdays only.
e Saturdays excepted.
n Noon.
r Restaurant Car.

MARSH BROOK (Salop),

167¾ miles. Fares, 31/11*a*, 19/2*c*. R. T. for two months, 63/10*a*, 38/4*c*. Departures *from* London as for Church Stretton. Departures *for* London about 3 times daily.
Map Square 17.

MARSHFIELD (Monmouth),

146½ miles. Fares, 30/7*a*, 18/4*c*. R. T. for two months, 61/2*a*. Departures *from* London as for Newport (Mon.). Departures *for* London about 6 times daily. Pop. 592
Map Square 22.

MARSH GIBBON

(Bucks) from *Euston*, 61¾ miles. Fares, 11/1*a*, 6/8*c*. R. T. for two months, 22/2*a*. Departures *from* London as for Verney. Departures *for* London about 5 times daily. Pop. 587.
Map Square 18.

MARSH MILLS (Devon),

from *Paddington*, 223 miles. Fares, 46/11*a*, 28/2*c*. R.T. for two months, 93/10*a*. Departures *from* London as for Tavistock. Departures *for* London about 9 times daily.
Map Square 26.

MARSKE (Yorks), 249½

miles, Fares, 51/11*a*, 31/2*c*. R. T. for two months, 103/10*a*, 62/4*c*. Departures *from* London as for Redcar. Departures *for* London about 8 times daily. Pop. 2,955.
Map Square 8.

MARSTON GATE

(Herts) from *Euston*, 39 miles. Fares, 7/4*a*, 4/5*c*. R. T. for two months, 14/8*a*, 8/10*c*. Departures *from* London as for Cheddington. Departures *for* London about 9 times daily.
Map Square 23.

MARSTON GREEN

(Warwick) from *Euston*, 106½ miles. Fares, 22/3*a*, 13/4*c*. R. T. for two months, 44/6*a*. Departures *from* London as for Hampton-in-Arden. Departures *for* London about 6 times daily.
Map Square 17.

MARSTON MAGNA

(Somerset), 122¾ miles. Fares, 25/7*a*, 15/4*c*. R. T. for two months, 51/2*a*. Departures *from* London as for Castle Cary. Departures *for* London about 5 times daily. Pop. 311.
Map Square 22.

MARSTON MOOR

(Yorks), 193¾ miles. Fares, 40/5*a*, 24/3*c*. R. T., double fare. Departures *from* London as for York. Departures *for* London about 5 times daily.
Map Square 8.

MARTHAM (Norfolk) from

King's Cross, 176 miles. Fares, 25/3*a*, 15/2*c*. R. T. for two months, 50/6*a*, 30/4*c*. Departures *from* London as for North Walsham. Departures *for* London about 3 times daily. Pop. 1,260.
Map Square 19.

MARTIN MILL (Kent)

(for St. Margaret's Bay) from *Victoria*, *Holborn Viaduct* and *St. Paul's* (*via* Chatham), 79¾ miles. Fares, 16/8*a*, 13/4*b*, 10/0*c*. R. T. for two months, 33/4*a*, 26/8*b*.
Map Square 24.

Vict. (S.E.&C.)	Leave Hol. V.	St. Pl.'s	Arr. at M.Mill
AM —	3.50*l*	—	7.36
5. 5	4.57	5. 0	9.13
5.48*f*	5.40*f*	5.42*f*	9.12
—	7.30	7.33	11.31
9.20	—	—	11.45
9.45	—	—	12.23
10.40	—	—	2. 1
11.40*d*	—	—	2.54
11.40*e*	—	—	3.56
PM 2. 5*d*	—	—	4.36
2. 8*e*	—	—	5.13
5.10*d*	5.10*e*	5.12*e*	8. 6
5.30	—	—	9.43
8.30	—	—	11.10
—	—	—	—
—	—	—	—
—	—	—	—
—	—	—	—
—	—	—	—
—	—	—	—

Sunday Trains.

AM 8.15	8. 0	—	12.52
10.40	—	—	3.46
PM 3.30	—	—	7.36
5.15	—	—	8.37
8.25	—	—	11. 0

Trains from Martin Mill.

Leave M. Mill	St. Pl.'s	Arr. at Hol. V.	Vict.
AM 6.12*f*	9.37	9.39	—
7. 4	—	—	11. 2
9. 3	—	—	11.27
11.14	—	—	2.43
11.31*h*	—	—	3.36
PM 1.28*e*	4.46	—	4.39
1.28*d*	—	—	4.55
2. 1*h*	—	—	5.42
2.32	—	—	5.26
5.33	—	—	8.33
7.12	—	—	10.25
—	—	—	—
—	—	—	—
—	—	—	—

Sunday Trains.

AM 8.32	—	11.58	11.51
9.37*h*	—	—	1. 5
PM12. 7*h*	—	—	3.50
6.13	—	—	8.40

d Saturdays only.
e Saturdays excepted.
f Mondays only.
h Via Minster.
l Third Class only.

MARTIN MILL—*contd.*

ANOTHER ROUTE from *Charing Cross, Cannon Street* and *London Bridge, via* Dover 82¼ miles. Fares, 16/8*a*, 13/4*b*, 10/0*c*. R. T. for two months, 33/4*a*, 26/8*b*, 20/0*c*.

	Leave		Arr. at
CHAR. +	CAN. ST.	LON. B.	M. MILL
AM —	3.40*y*	3.43*y*	7.36
—	5.20	5.25	9.41
—	7.16*h*	7.19*h*	11.31
—	—	10. 3*l*	12.39
11.15	—	—	2. 1
PM 1. 0	—	—	2.54
1.50*d*	—	1.56*d*	3.56
4.30*j*	—	4.57*j*	6.42
—	5. 0*k*	—	6.47
—	6.12*e*	—	9.43
7. 0	—	—	9.43
7.18	—	7.26	11.10

Sunday Trains.

AM10.15	—	10.18	12.52
PM 7.35	—	7.45	11. 1

Trains from Martin Mill.

Leave		Arrive at	
M. MILL	LON. B.	CAN. ST.	CHAR. +
AM /6.12*h*	9. 0	9. 4	—
7. 4*e*	9.36	9.40	—
7. 4*d*	10. 0	10. 4	—
8.42	10.34	—	10.41
9. 3	11.43	—	11.57
10.29	—	—	12.20
PM12.54	3.26	—	3.40
1.28	4. 2	—	4.10
2.32	5.50	—	6. 3
4.39	—	—	6.30
6.27	10.22	—	10.35
9.32*y*	—	1.20	—

Sunday Trains.

PM 4.37	—	—	6.30
6.15	—	—	8.17
7.47	10.16	—	10.26
9.13*y*	—	1.23	—

d Saturdays only.
e Saturdays excepted.
f Mondays only.
h Via Chatham.
j Fridays excepted.
k Fridays only.
l Mondays, Fridays, and Saturdays only.
y Third class only.

ANOTHER ROUTE from *Charing Cross, Cannon Street* and *London Bridge, via* Minster, 83 miles. Fares, 17/1*a*, 13/8*b*, 10/3*c*. R.T. for two months, 34/2*a*, 27/4*b*, 20/6*c*.

	Leave		Arr. at
CHAR. +	CAN. ST.	LON. B	M. MILL
AM —	5.20	5.25	10. 9
—	—	7.50*l*	11.14
9.15	—	9.23	12.53
11. 0*d*	—	11. 7*d*	2.42
PM 1. 0	—	—	4. 0
3. 0	—	3. 8	6.27
5.15*e*	5.12*e*	5.21	8.17
5.24*d*	—	5.34*d*	9.32
6. 0*e*	—	6. 5*e*	9.32
7.18	—	7.26	11.13

Sunday Trains.

AM 7.45	—	7.52	12. 7

MARTIN MILL—*contd.*

Trains from Martin Mill.

Leave		Arrive at	
M. MILL	LON. B.	CAN. ST	CHAR. +
AM 7.36	10.54	—	11. 3
8.31	11.43	—	11.57
9.41	1.36	—	1.50
11.31	3.26	—	3.40
PM 2. 1	5.50	—	6. 3
3.56	7.25	7.30	7.49
6.42	10.22	—	10.35
9.43*y*	—	1.20	—

Sunday Trains.

PM 3.46	7. 9	—	7.17

d Saturdays only.
e Saturdays excepted.
l Low level platform.
y Third Class only.

St. Margaret's Bay.—GRANVILLE HOTEL—Standing on the Cliffs. Telephone 12, St. Margaret's-at-Cliffe. Station, Martin Mill. Under New Proprietorship.

MARTOCK (Somerset), 135 miles. Fares, 27/4*a*, 16/5*c*. R. T. for two months, 54/8*a*. Departures *from* London as for Yeovil (Pen Mill). Departures *for* London about 5 times daily. Pop. 2,035. *Map Square 22.*

MARTON (Warwick), 90¾ miles. Fares, 18/2*a*, 10/11*c*. R. T. for two months, 36/4*a*. Departures *from* London as for Rugby Departures *for* London about 6 times daily. Pop. 376. *Map Square 18.*

MARYKIRK (Kincardine), 489 miles. No through fares. Departures *from* London as for Forfar. Departures *for* London about 4 times daily. Pop. 1,285. *Map Square 38.*

MARYLAND POINT from *Liverpool Street* and *Fenchurch Street*, 4½ miles. Fares from Liverpool Street, 0/7½*a*, 0/6*b*, 0/4½*c*. R. T. for two days, 1/3*a*, 1/0*b*, 0/9*c*. Fenchurch Street, 0/7½*a*, 0/6*b*, 0/4½*c*. R. T. for two days, 1/2*a*, 0/10½*b*, 0/7*c*. *See* pp. 528-534. *Map Square 62.*

MARYLEBONE (Bakerloo Tube). Pop. 104,173. *See* back of Map.

MARYPORT (Cumberland), from *Euston* (*via* Carlisle), 326¾ miles. Fares, 65/0*a*, 39/0*c*. R. T., 130/0*a*, 78/0*c*. Pop. 10,895. *Map Square 6.*

EUSTON.	M'PORT.	M'PORT.	EUSTON.
AM 5. 0	2.50	AM 6.47*r*	4.15
10. 0*r*	5.15	8.25*t*	6. 0
10.40*dr*	7.36	10.50*r*	6.25
11.35*r*	7.56	PM 2. 8*r*	10. 0
PM 1.30*r*	10. 0	7.25	5. 0
11. 0*d*	9.15	10.12*e*	6.55
11.35*e*	6.30	10.12*d*	7.15
11.45*e*	9.20	—	—

Sunday Trains.

PM11.35	6.30	AM11.28*r*	7.30
11.45	9.20	PM 5.50	5. 0

d Saturdays only.
e Saturdays excepted.
r Restaurant Car.
t Tea Car.

MARYTAVY (Devon), from

Paddington, 239½ miles. Fares, 46/11*a*, 28/2*c*. R. T. for two months, 93/10*a*. Departures *from* London as for Launceston. Departures *for* London about 4 times daily. Pop. 725. *Map Square 26.*

MASBURY (Somerset) from *Waterloo*, 130¾ miles. Fares, 24/0*a*, 14/5*c*. R.T. for two months, 48/0*a*, 28/10*c*. Departures *from* London as for Shepton Mallet. Departures *for* London about 4 times daily. *Map Square 22.*

MASHAM (Yorks), 220¼ miles. Fares, 45/8*a*, 27/5*c*. R. T., double fare. Departures *from* London as for Ripon. Departures *for* London about 5 times daily. Pop. 2,047. *Map Square 7.*

MASSINGHAM (Norfolk) from *King's Cross*, 126 miles. Fares, 22/9*a*, 13/8*c*. R. T. for two months, 45/6*a*, 27/4*c*. Pop. 723. *Map Square 19.*

KING'S +	MASS.	MASS.	KING'S +
AM 4.45	8.38	AM 9.23	1. 5
7.15*r*	11.41	PM12.31*r*	4.30
10.10*r*	2.54	4. 6	9. 0
PM 3. 0	6.36	—	—

No Sunday Trains.
r Restaurant Car.

MATHRY (Pembroke) 262¾ miles. No through fares. Departures *from* London as for Clynderwen. Departures *for* London about 4 times daily. *Map Square 15.*

MATLOCK (Derby) from *St. Pancras*, 145 miles. Fares, 30/0*a*, 18/0*c*. R. T. for two months, 60/0*a*, 36/0*c* Pop. 7,055. *Map Square 12.*

ST. PAN.	MATL'K.	MATL'K.	ST. PAN.
AM 2.25	8. 0	AM 7.47*r*	11.35
4.25	8.40	9.30*r*	1.30
8.25*r*	11.42	11.22	3.25
10.25*r*	2. 4	PM 2.38*r*	5.45
PM 12.25*r*	4.35	4.57*r*	8.35
1.25*r*	4.48	6.19*r*	10. 5
2.25*r*	6.12	9.25	4.20
4.25*r*	8. 0	—	—
6.25*r*	9.37	—	—
12. 0*h*	4.23	—	—
12. 0*k*	7.59	—	—

Sunday Trains.

PM 3.15	6.54	AM11.36*r*	5. 2
11.55	4.23	PM 6. 0*r*	9.52
—	—	8.48	4.55

h Saturdays midnight excepted.
k Saturdays midnight only.
r Restaurant Car.

Rockside Hydropathic. High-class Health and Pleasure Resort. Pure mountain air. Complete installation of Baths. Near Golf (18 holes). Tel. 12. Book to Matlock Station. *See advt. p. 266.*

Royal Hotel. Ideal Position. Excellent Cuisine. *See advt. p. 266.*

Chatsworth Hydro, Matlock. Finest position, 800 ft. above sea level. Nearest to Golf Links. Bright social life. Electrical and other Baths. Excellent cuisine. Illustrated Booklet gratis. 'Phone 8. Apply—
MANAGERESS.

For completion of Advertisements, see over.

MATLOCK—*continued.*

The Lilybank Hydro. Extensive Pleasure Grounds. Tennis, Bowls. Croquet, Billiards. Excellent Cuisine. Electric Light. All Hydropathic Baths (free to Visitors). New Ballroom, Spring Floor. Garage, 6 lock-ups. Terms Moderate. Write for Booklet. 'Phone, 81.
Mr. & Mrs. JOHN KAY.

MATLOCK BATH

(Derby) from *St. Pancras*, 144 miles. Fares, 29/10*a*, 17/11*c*. R. T. for two months, 59/8*a*, 35/10*c*. Pop. 1,825.
Map Square 12.

St. Pan.	Mat. B.	Mat. B.	St. Pan.
AM 2.25	7.55	AM 7.51*r*	11.35
4.25	8.36	9.36*r*	1.30
8.25*r*	1.10	11. 2	3.25
10.25*r*	1.59	PM 1.47*r*	5.45
PM12.25*r*	4.30	5. 1*r*	8.35
1.25*r*	4.44	6.23*r*	10. 5
2.25*r*	6. 8	9.30	4.20
4.25*r*	7.56	—	—
6.25*r*	9.53	—	—
12. 0*h*	7.53	—	—
—	—	—	—

Sunday Trains.

PM 3.15	6.49	AM11.41*r*	5. 2
—	—	PM 6. 5*r*	9.52
—	—	8.53	4.55
—	—	—	—
—	—	—	—

h Saturdays midnight only.
r Restaurant Car.

MAUCHLINE (Ayr), 380¾

miles. Fares, 77/6*a*, 46/6*c*. R. T. for two months, 155/0*a*, 93/0*c*. Departures *from* London as for Old Cumnock. Departures *for* London about 4 times daily. Pop. 2,357.
Map Square 40.

MAUD (Aberdeen), 554

miles. Fares 106/6*a*, 63/11*c*. R. T. for two months, 213/0*a*, 127/10*c*. Departures *from* London as for Fraserburgh or Peterhead. Departures *for* London about 3 times daily.
Map Square 35.

MAULDETH ROAD

(Lancs), 184¾ miles. Fares, 37/11*a*, 22/9*c*. R. T., double fare. Departures *from* London as for Wilmslow. Departures *for* London about 6 times daily.

MAWCARSE (Kinross),

426½ miles. Fares, 88/9*a*, 53/3*c*. R. T. for two months, 177/6*a*, 106/6*c*. Departures *from* London as for Dunfermline. Departures *for* London about 3 times daily.
Map Square 41.

MAXTON (Roxburgh), 359

miles. No through fares. Departures *from* London as for St. Boswells. Departures *for* London about 3 times daily. Pop. 357.
Map Square 41.

MAXWELLTOWN (Kirkcudbright),

334 miles. Fares, 67/9*a*, 40/8*c*. R. T. for two months, 135/6*a*, 81/4*c*. Departures *from* London as for Dumfries. Departures *for* London about 5 times daily. Pop. 6,094.
Map Square 43.

MAYBOLE (Ayr), 397¾

miles. Fares, 81/10*a*, 49/1*c*. R. T. for two months, 163/8*a*, 98/2*c*. Departures *from* London as for Girvan. Departures *for* London about 4 times daily. Pop. 6,505.
Map Square 43.

MAYFIELD (Sussex) from

Victoria and *London Bridge*, 41½ miles. Fares, 8/9*a*, 5/3*c*. R. T. for two months, 17/6*a*, 10/6*c*. Departures *from* London as for Heathfield. Departures *for* London about 8 times daily. Pop. 2,803.
Map Square 24.

MAZE HILL (Kent) from

Charing Cross, Cannon Street, and *London Bridge*, 7 miles. Fares from Charing Cross, 1/6*a*, 1/2*b*, 0/10½*c*. R. T for two days, 3/0*a*, 2/4*b*, 1/7*c*. From Cannon Street, 1/1*a*, 0/10*b*, 0/7½*c*. R. T. for two days, 2/2*a*, 1/8*b*, 1/3*c*. *See* pp. 547-551.
Map Square 71.

MEALSGATE (Cumberland),

323½ miles. Fares, 64/2*a*, 38/6*c*. R. T. for two months, 128/4*a*, 77/0*c*. Departures *from* London as for Maryport. Departures *for* London about 4 times daily.
Map Square 6.

MEASHAM (Leicester)

from *Euston*, 112½ miles. Fares, 23/2*a*, 13/11*c*. R.T. for two months, 46/4*a*. Departures *from* London as for Shackerstone. Departures *for* London about 6 times daily. Pop. 2,303.
Map Square 17.

MEDGE HALL (Yorks),

169½ miles. Fares, 35/0*a*, 21/0*c*. R. T., double fare. Departures *from* London as for Thorne. Departures *for* London about 3 times daily.
Map Square 13.

MEDSTEAD (Hants) from

Waterloo, 51½ miles. Fares, 10/10*a*, 6/6*c*. R. T. for two months, 21/8*a*, 13/0*c*. Pop. 655.
Map Square 23.

W'loo.	Medst'd	Medst'd.	W'loo.
AM 5.50	7.56	AM 7.55	9.41
7. 0	9.15	8.52	10.26
9.20	11.16	10.52	12.40
PM 1.10	2.57	PM 1.46	3.36
4. 0	5.46	5.19	7. 7
6.34	8.18	7.55	9.52
—	—	—	—
—	—	—	—
—	—	—	—
—	—	—	—

Sunday Trains.

AM 8.45	11. 7	AM 8.49	11.16
PM 6.20	8.20	PM 7.49	9.37
—	—	—	—
—	—	—	—
—	—	—	—

MEIGLE (Perth), 471¾ miles.

Fares, 94/7*a*, 56/9*c*. R. T. for two months, 189/2*a*, 113/6*c*. Departures *from* London as for Coupar Angus. Departures *for* London about 3 times daily. Pop. 808.

MEIKLE EARNOCK

(Lanark), 398¾ miles. No through fares. Departures *from* London as for Hamilton. Departures *for* London about 4 times daily.
Map Square 40.

MEIR (Stafford), 149½ miles.

Fares, 31/1*a*, 18/8*c*. R. T. for two months, 62/2*a*, 37/4*c*. Departures *from* London as for Longton. Departures *for* London about 6 times daily.
Map Square 12.

MELBOURNE (Derby)

from *St. Pancras, via* Ashby, 127 miles. Fares, 26/3*a*, 15/9*c*. R. T., double fare. Pop. 3,722.
Map Square 18.

St. Pan.	Melb'n.	Melb'n.	St. Pan.
AM 2.25	8.26	AM10.39	3.25
4.25	11.38	PM 3. 5*r*	6.35
PM12.25*r*	4.24	7.52	4.20
3.30*r*	7.38	—	—
—	—	—	—

No Sunday Trains.
r Restaurant Car.

ANOTHER ROUTE from *St. Pancras*,

via Derby, 135½ miles. Fares, 27/9*a*, 16/8*c*. R.T., double fare.

St. Pan.	Melb'n.	Melb'n.	St. Pan.
AM 4.25	8.56	AM 7. 0*r*	10.45
10.25*r*	1.29	8.27*r*	11.35
11. 0*r*	3. 5	10. 0*r*	1.30
PM 2.25*r*	6.12	11.38	3.25
4.25*r*	7.52	PM 1.55*r*	5.45
6.25*d*	11. 3	4.24*r*	8.35
—	—	—	—

Sunday Trains.

AM11.15*r*	5.20	PM 5.55*h*	11. 7
—	—	—	—
—	—	—	—
—	—	—	—

d Saturdays only.
h Via Trent.
r Restaurant Car.

MELDON (Northumberland),

290½ miles. Fares, 61/1*a*, 36/8*c*. R. T. for two months, 122/2*a*, 73/4*c*. Departures *from* London as for Morpeth. Departures *for* London about 3 times daily. Pop. 128.
Map Square 3.

MELDRETH (Cambridge)

from *King's Cross*, 48 miles. Fares, 10/0*a*, 6/0*c*. R. T., double fare. Departures *from* London as for Royston. Departures *for* London about 5 times daily. Pop. 596.
Map Square 18.

MELIDEN (Flint), 207½

miles. No through fares. Departures *from* London as for Prestatyn. Departures *for* London about 6 times daily. Pop. 560.
Map Square 11.

MELKSHAM (Wilts) from

Paddington, 96½ miles. Fares, *via* Chippenham, 19/7*a*, 11/9*c*. R. T. for two months, 39/2*a*. *Via* Westbury, 21/1*a*, 12/8*c*. R. T. for two months, 42/2*a* Pop. 3,594.
Map Square 22.

Pad.	Melksh'm.	Melksh'm.	Pad.
AM 1. 0*g*	6.22	AM 7.50*r*	10.15
5.30	8.40	9.24	12.20
7.30	10.27	11.31*r*	2.40
9. 0	11.56	PM12.40	3.20
10.30*k*	12.40	2.50	6. 2
10.45	2.25	3.33*kr*	6.50
PM 2. 0*k*	4.49	5. 0*kr*	8.20
2.45*h*	5.14	5.45*r*	8.45
3.15*t*	5.52	7.46	10.25
4.15*r*	6.34	10.15	2.45
6.30	8.43	—	—
—	—	—	—

Sunday Trains.

PM12.30*r*	3.45	PM12.28	3.35
2.40*k*	6.44	3.45*kr*	7.55
10. 0	6.22	6.44	10. 0
—	—	—	—

g Mondays excepted.
h Via Holt.
k Via Westbury.
r Restaurant Car.
t Tea Car.

MELLING (Lancs) 251 miles.
Fares, 48/2a, 28/11c. R. T., double fare. Departures from London as for Giggleswick. Departures for London about 4 times daily. Pop. 187. Map Square 7.

MELLIS (Suffolk) from Liverpool Street, 91¼ miles.
Fares, 19/4a, 11/7c. R.T. for two months, 38/8a. Pop. 463. Map Square 19.

L'PL. ST.	MELLIS	MELLIS	L'PL. ST.
AM 5. 0	7.42	AM 7.44r	10.30
10.12	1. 3	9.41	12.59
PM12.33r	3.16	11.23r	2. 3
3.10r	5.44	PM 2.15r	4.58
5.18dr	8. 1	4.48	7.51
5.18er	8. 4	5.40dr	9.22
—	—	8. 1	11.16

Sunday Trains.

AM 9.20r	12.24	AM 8.12	11.38
PM 4.40	7.17	PM 7.20	10.15

d Saturdays only.
e Saturdays excepted.
r Restaurant Car.

MELLS ROAD (Somerset), 106¼ miles.
Fares, via Frome, 22/3a, 13/4c. R. T. for two months, 44/6a, 26/8c. Via Bristol, 25/5a, 15/3c. R.T. for two months, 50/10a, 30/6c. Departures from London as for Frome or Bristol. Departures for London about 5 times daily. Pop. (Mells) 836. Map Square 22.

MELMERBY (Yorks), 213 miles.
Fares, 44/4a, 26/7c. R.T., double fare. Departures from London as for Ripon. Departures for London about 5 times daily. Pop. 284. Map Square 7.

MELROSE (Roxburgh) from St. Pancras, 369 miles.
Fares, 73/4a, 44/0c. R. T. for two months, 146/8a, 88/0c. Pop. 2,155. Map Square 41.

ST. PAN.	MELROSE	MELROSE	ST. PAN.
AM 4.25	2.57	AM 9.49r	7.15
9. 0r	6. 2	11.40r	7.55
11.45r	8. 2	PM10.54	8. 5
PM 9.15e	7.23	—	—

Sunday Trains.

PM 9.15	7.23	PM10.54	8. 5

e Saturdays excepted.
r Restaurant Car.

ANOTHER ROUTE from Euston, 360 miles. Fares as above.

EUSTON	MELROSE	MELROSE	EUSTON
AM 2.35	2.57	AM 7.54r	6.25
10. 0r	6. 5	9.49	7.30
10.40r	8. 5	11.40r	9.20
PM 9.20e	7.24	PM 5.34	5. 0h
11.35e	10.28	7. 5	6.55
—	—	10.54	7.30

Sunday Trains.

PM11.35	10.28	PM10.54	7.30

e Saturdays excepted.
h A.M.
r Restaurant Car.

MELTHAM (Yorks), 190 miles.
Fares (via Penistone), 38/7a, 23/2c. R. T. for two months, 77/2a, 46/4c. Via Horbury, 38/7a, 23/2c. R. T. for two months, 77/2a, 46/4c. Departures from London as for Lockwood. Departures for London about 8 times daily. Pop. 5,058. Map Square 12.

MELTON (Suffolk) from Liverpool Street, 80½ miles.
Fares, 16/11a, 10/2c. R. T. for two months, 33/10a. Pop. 2,042. Map Square 19.

L'PL. ST.	MELTON	MELTON	L'PL. ST.
AM 5. 0	7.34	AM 8. 3r	10.30
8.15r	11. 4	9. 7r	11.22
10.20	12.55	10.18h	1.20
PM 1. 0	3.17	11.44r	2. 3
3.18r	5.33	PM 1.18	3.42
5.18dr	7.37	5. 6	7.51
5.18er	7.39	7.10r	9.22
—	—	8.10	11.16

Sunday Trains.

PM 4.40	7. 3	AM 8.43	11.38
—	—	PM 6.54r	9.10

d Saturdays only.
e Saturdays excepted.
h Tuesdays only.
r Restaurant Car.

MELTON CONSTABLE (Norfolk) from King's Cross, 144½ miles.
Fares, 23/7a, 14/2c. R. T. for two months, 47/2a, 28/4c. Pop. 1,157. Map Square 14.

KING'S+	ML.CON.	ML.CON.	KING'S+
AM 4.45	9.16	AM 8.46	1. 5
7.15r	12.21	10.24	3.50
10.10r	3.32	PM12.54r	4.30
PM 1.50r	6.25	4. 4	9. 0
3. 0	6.44	—	—

No Sunday Trains.
r Restaurant Car.

MELTON MOWBRAY (Leicester) from St. Pancras, 105 miles.
Fares, 21/8a, 13/0c. R. T., double fare. Pop. 9,187. Map Square 18.

ST. PAN.	MELT.M.	MELT. M.	ST. PAN.
AM 2.35	7.18	AM 7. 0r	9.57
4.25	8. 0	8.24r	10.45
7.50	10.40	9.25r	12.10
8.25r	11.10	10.58r	1.20
9.50r	12.34	11.32r	2.10
10.25dr	1.20	PM12.34r	4.10
10.25r	1.30	1.37r	4.20
11. 0r	1.12	3.23r	5.30
PM 1. 0	3.32	5. 7r	7.55
2.25r	5.28	5.52	8.22
3.50r	6.13	6.36r	9.15
4.30r	7.13	7.27r	10. 5
5.35	8.47	9.41	4.20
6.25r	9.41	—	—

Sunday Trains.

PM 3.15	8.42	AM 7.56	11.53
—	—	PM 7.11r	9.45

d Saturdays only.
r Restaurant Car.

MELTON MOWBRAY —continued.

ANOTHER ROUTE from King's Cross, 113¼ miles. Fares as above.

KING'S+	MELT.M.	MELT.M.	KING'S+
AM 5. 5	9.25	AM 8. 0r	12.25
7.15r	10.40	9.43	1. 5
7.45	11.32	10.58	1.55
10.10r	1.37	PM 1.30r	4.45
PM 1.50r	5. 7	4. 3r	7.10
3. 0	6.36	5.28r	9.25
5.45r	9.42	9. 41	3.25

Sunday Trains.

12. 0nr	6.23	AM10. 2	3.45

n Noon.
r Restaurant Car.

ANOTHER ROUTE from Euston, 107¼ miles. Fares as above.

EUSTON	MELT.M.	MELT.M.	EUSTON
AM 5. 0	8.31	AM 7.52	11.55
6.45	10.50	9.54	12.40
10.40	2.50	11.45k	3.45
PM12.15	4.58	11.45v	4.15
4.15	7.40	PM 3.46	7.20
—	—	6.50	11.35

No Sunday Trains.

h Via Rugby.
k Mondays and Saturdays only.
v Mondays and Saturdays excepted.

MELVERLEY (Salop), 168¾ miles.
No through fares. Departures from London as for Shrewsbury or Oswestry. Departures for London about twice daily. Pop. 177. Map Square 17.

MENAI BRIDGE (Carnarvon), 240¼ miles.
Fares, 50/0a, 30/0c. R.T. for two months 100/0a, 60/0c. Departures from London as for Bangor. Departures for London about 6 times daily. Pop. 1,767. Map Square 11.

MENDLESHAM (Suffolk), 87½ miles.
Fares, 18/5½a, 11/1c. R.T. for two months, 36/11a, 22/2c. Departures from London as for Stradbroke. Departures for London about twice daily. Pop. 927. Map Square 19.

MENHENIOT (Cornwall), 240½ miles.
Fares 49/9a 29/10c. R. T. for two months, 99/6a. Departures from London as for St. Germans. Departures for London about 4 times daily. Pop. 1,126. Map Square 26.

MENSTON (Yorks), from

St. Pancras, 206¾ miles. Fares, 41/1a, 24/8c. R. T., double fare. Departures from London as for Ilkley. Departures for London about 5 times daily. Pop. 3,537. *Map Square 7.*

MENSTRIE (Clackmannan),

423¼ miles. Fares, 85/8a, 51/5c. R. T. for two months, 171/4a, 102/10c. Departures from London as for Stirling. Departures for London about 4 times daily. Pop. 774. *Map Square 40.*

MENTHORPE GATE

(Yorks), 179¼ miles No through fares. Departures from London as for Selby. Departures for London about 5 times daily. Pop. (Menthorpe) 44. *Map Square 13.*

MÉOLE BRACE (Salop)

155 miles. No through fares. Departures from London as for Shrewsbury. Departures for London about 3 times daily.

MEOLS (Cheshire), 216¼

miles. No through fares. Departures from London as for Hooton. Departures for London about 4 times daily. *Map Square 11.*

MEOLS COP (Lancs),

213 miles. Fares, 44/0a, 26/5c. R.T. for two months, 88/0a, 52/10c. Departures from London as for Southport. Departures for London about 5 times daily.

MEOPHAM (Kent) from

Victoria, Holborn Viaduct, and St. Paul's, 26 miles. Fares, 5/7a, 4/5b, 3/3c. R. T. for two months, 11/2a, 8/10b, 6/6c. Pop. 1,464. *Map Square 24.*

VICT.	Leave		Arr. at
(S.E.&C.)	HOL. V.	ST. PL.'s	MEOPH.
AM 5. 5	4.57	5. 0	6.23
—	7.30	7.33	8.34
9.20	—	—	10.10
11.55d	—	—	12.59
11.40e	—	—	12.48
PM —	1.24d	1.27d	2.19
—	3.22	3.25	4.38
3.40d	3.33d	3.36d	5.14
4.25e	—	—	5.14
5.30e	—	5.33e	6.31
6.16	6.10e	6.13e	7.23
7. 5	7. 0	7. 3	7.59
9. 0e	8.57e	9. 0e	10. 7
10.17	10.11	10.13	11.21
—	—	—	—
—	—	—	—
—	—	—	—
—	—	—	—
—	—	—	—
—	—	—	—

Sunday Trains.

AM 7.20	—	—	8.23
10.30	10.25	—	11.45
PM 3.30	—	—	4.36
6.35	—	—	7.37
10.15	10.12	—	11.28
—	—	—	—
—	—	—	—
—	—	—	—

MEOPHAM—continued.

Trains from Meopham.

Leave		Arrive at	
MEOPH.	ST. PL.'s	HOL. V.	VICT.
AM 7. 3	8. 8	8. 9	8.14
7.19	8.25	8.27	8.29
8. 8	9.16	9.18	—
8.42	9.37	9.39	—
11.57d	1. 0	1. 2	—
PM12.19e	—	—	1.32
2.20	—	—	3.23
4. 5e	5.32	5.34	5.21
5.40e	6.45	6.47	—
6.56d	8. 0	8. 2	—
8.35	9.50	9.54	9.46
10.21	11.21	11.23	—

Sunday Trains.

AM 8.13	—	9.40	9.31
10. 8	—	11.27	11.23
11.50	—	1. 2	12.56
PM 5.10	—	—	6. 3
10.42	—	12. 0	11.44

d Saturdays only.
e Saturdays excepted.

MERSEY ROAD (Lancs),

213½ miles. Fares, 40/8a, 24/5c. R. T., double fare. Departures from London as for Warrington (Central). Departures for London about 4 times daily.

MERSTHAM (Surrey) from

Charing Cross, Cannon Street, and London Bridge, 21¼ miles. Fares, 3/9a, 3/0b, 2/3c. R. T. for eight days, 7/6a, 6 0b, 4/3c. Pop. 3,597. *Map Square 23.*

	Leave		Arr. at
CHAR. +	CAN. ST.	LON. B.	MERST.
AM —	4.44	5. 0	5.47
—	—	7.50l	8.32
—	—	9.33l	10.13
10.55	—	11. 3	11.53
PM —	12.55d	12.58d	1.32
12.55	—	1. 4	1.49
—	1.24d	1.27d	2.13
—	—	e1.30l	2.13
—	—	e1.48l	2.30
2. 3e	2. 8d	2.10	2.56
2.35d	—	d2.22l	3. 8
3.15·	—	2.41d	3.19
4.22d	—	3.21	4. 8
—	—	4.28d	5.12
—	4.24e	4.28e	5.10
—	5.24e	5.27e	6. 2
5.42d	—	5.48d	6.26
—	6. 0e	6. 3e	6.38
6.27e	—	6.34e	7.10
—	6.36e	6.39e	7.22
—	6.34d	6.40d	7.25
7.24d	7.28e	7.30	8.15
8.28	—	8.36	9.21
9.25	—	9.31	10.18
10.17	—	10.23	11. 7
11.27	—	—	12. 3

Sunday Trains.

AM 6.25	—	6.32	7.24
10.20	—	10.28	11.13
PM 1.30	—	1.37	2.21
5.25	—	5.32	6.18
8.58	—	8.45	9.29

MERSTHAM—continued.

Trains from Merstham.

Leave		Arrive at	
MERST.	LON. B.	CAN. ST.	CHAR.+
AM 6.40	7.18	—	7.30
7.47	8.24	8.28	—
8.23	8.56	—	—
8.54	9.28	9.52	—
9.53	10.27	10.52	—
11. 5	11.46	—	11.59
PM12. 6	12.50	—	1. 0
1.58	2.38	—	2.46
2.50	3.28e	—	3.42d
3.26h	4. 8	—	—
4.14	5. 2	—	5.14
4.49e	5.28	—	—
5.19	5.56	—	—
6.41	7.20	—	7.29
8.23	9. 2	—	9.15
9.24	10. 3	—	10.13
11.18	11.57	—	12.10

Sunday Trains.

AM 7.56	8.16	—	8.27
10.35	11.15	—	11.25
PM 3.54	4.33	—	4.42
6.34	7.13	—	7.25
9.29	10.11	—	10.24

d Saturdays only.
e Saturdays excepted.
h Mondays, Fridays and Saturdays only.
l Low Level Platform.

MERSTONE (Isle of

Wight) from London Bridge and Victoria, via Ryde, or from Waterloo, via Ryde, 90½ miles. Fares, 20/0a, 12/3c. R. T. for two months, 40/0a, 24/6c. Departures from London as for Sandown or Newport (I. of W.). Departures for London about 4 times daily. *Map Square 28.*

MERTHYR (Glamorgan)

from Paddington, via Cardiff, 177 miles. Fares, 35/8a, 21/5c. R. T. for two months, 71/4a. Pop. 80,161. *Map Square 21.*

PAD.	MERTHYR	MERTHYR	PAD.
AM 1. 0g	8.57	AM 6. 0hr	10.57
5.30	12. 0	8.25r	1. 0
8.45r	2.25	8.45r	2.30
11.50r	4.17	10.15r	4.20
PM 1.10r	6.55	PM12.45r	6.15
3.35r	9. 0	3.50r	8.35
6. 0r	11. 4	4.15r	9.25
6.30kr	12.15	9. 0	3.50
9.15eh	6.33	—	—

Sunday Trains.

AM 1. 0	9.33	AM 8.10	3.35
PM12.30r	5.50	11.30r	8.25
4.30	10.13	PM 8.15	3.50
9.15k	6.33	—	—

e Saturdays excepted
g Mondays excepted.
h Passengers cross Cardiff at own expense.
k Thursdays and Saturdays only.
r Restaurant Car.

MERTHYR—*continued.*

ANOTHER ROUTE from *Paddington*, 172½ miles. Fares, *via* Pontypool Road, 35/2*a*, 21/1*c*. R.T. for two months, 70/4*a*.

Pad.	Merthyr	Merthyr	Pad.
AM 1. 0*g*	9. 3	AM 8. 0*r*	1. 0
5.30	12.38	8.25*r*	2.30
8.45*r*	2.53	11.45*r*	4.20
9. 0	4.13	PM 12.45*r*	6.15
11.50*hr*	5.10	2.15*r*	8.35
11.50*r*	6.24	4.25*r*	9.25
PM 3.35*r*	9. 0	6.50	3.30
6. 0*kr*	11. 4	9. 0*l*	7.10
8. 0*dr*	9.33	10. 0*d*	7.10

Sunday Trains.

PM 12.30*r*	8. 7	AM 9.45	8.10
9.15	9. 3	PM 8.15	3.30
—	—	—	—

d Saturdays only.
g Mondays excepted.
h Fridays only.
k Thursdays and Saturdays only.
l Thursdays only.
r Restaurant Car.

MERTON PARK (Surrey)

9½ miles. No through Fares. *See* p. 577.
Map Square 77.

METHIL (Fife), 428½ miles.

Fares, 86/6*a*, 51/11*c*. R.T. for two months, 173/0*a*, 103/10*c*. Departures *from* London as for Kirkcaldy. Departures *for* London about 4 times daily. Pop. 384.
Map Square 41.

METHLEY (Yorks) from

St. Pancras, 188½ miles. Fares, 37/3*a*, 22/4*c*. R. T. double fare. Pop. 4,494.
Map Square 12.

St. Pan.	Methley	Methley	St. Pan.
AM 2.25*g*	8.44	AM 6.50*r*	12.10
9. 0*r*	2. 1	8.50*r*	2.10
PM 1.50*r*	6.28	PM 12.28*r*	5.45
3.30*r*	8.54	9.30	4.20
—	—	10.48*e*	7.50
—	—	11.20*d*	8. 5
—	—	—	—
—	—	—	—

Sunday Trains.

AM 11.15*r*	8.19	AM 7.23*r*	5. 2
PM 3.15	8.38	PM 2.17*r*	9.43
—	—	9.27	4.55
—	—	—	—

d Saturdays only.
e Saturdays excepted.
g Mondays excepted.
r Restaurant Car.

ANOTHER ROUTE from *King's Cross*, 183 miles. Fares as above.

King's +	Methley	Methley	King's +
AM 7.15*r*	12.37	AM 6.55*r*	11.30
10.10*r*	2.44	8.32	1. 5
11.15	4.50	9.43*r*	1.55
PM 1.30*r*	5.37	PM 1. 8	6.25
1.50*r*	6.47	3. 3*r*	7.10
4. 0	8.21	5.12*r*	9.25
5.45*er*	9.51	8.43	3.25
5.45*dr*	10.32	—	—
10.45*e*	5.49	—	—

Sunday Trains.

12. 0*nr*	8.47	PM 12.10	5.55
—	—	3.43*r*	10.20
—	—	—	—
—	—	—	—

d Saturdays only.
e Saturdays excepted.
n Noon.
r Restaurant Car.

METHVEN (Perth), 455¼ miles.

Fares, 92/8*a*, 55/7*c*. R. T. for two months, 185/4*a*, 111/2*c*. Departures *from* London as for Perth. Departures *for* London about 3 times daily. Pop. 1,772.
Map Square 37.

MEXBOROUGH (Yorks),

162½ miles. Fares, 33/9*a*, 20/3*c*. R. T., double fare. Departures *from* London as for Barnsley (*via* Doncaster) or Rotherham and Masboro'. Departures *for* London about 8 times daily. Pop. 15,410.
Map Square 13.

MICHELDEVER (Hants)

from *Waterloo*, 58¾ miles. Fares, 12/1*a*, 7/3*c*. R.T. for two months, 24/2*a*, 14/6*c*. Pop. 997.
Map Square 23.

W'loo	Michel.	Michel.	W'loo
AM 5.50	7.59	AM 1.57	3.58
7.30	9.45	7.43	9.26
9.30	11. 7	8.44	10.20
11.30*r*	1. 9	9.15	10.56
PM 1.30*s*	3. 5	10.46	12. 0
3.40	5.51	10.59*s*	12.22
5. 0	6.31	PM 12.58*r*	2.20
6. 0	7.54	2.18	4. 6
8. 0	9.55	2.58	4.20
—	—	4.20	6.16
—	—	6.23*r*	8.20
—	—	8.56	10.50
—	—	—	—
—	—	—	—
—	—	—	—

Sunday Trains.

AM 9.45	11.50	AM 1.57	3.58
12. 0*nr*	1.41	10.50	12.11
PM 6. 0	7.45	PM 6.42	8. 3
—	—	—	—
—	—	—	—
—	—	—	—

n Noon.
r Restaurant Car.
s Refreshments served.

MICKLEFIELD (Yorks),

185¼ miles. No through fares. Departures *from* London as for Selby or Leeds. Departures *for* London about 6 times daily. Pop. 1,539.
Map Square 13.

MICKLEOVER (Derby)

from *King's Cross*, 148½ miles. Fares, 26/6*a*, 15/11*c*. R. T., double fare. Departures *from* London as for Derby (Friar Gate). Departures *for* London about 8 times daily. Pop. 2,389.
Map Square 12.

MICKLETON (Yorks),

255¾ miles. No through fares. Departures *from* London as for Barnard Castle. Departures *for* London about 5 times daily. Pop. 566.
Map Square 7.

MICKLE TRAFFORD

(Cheshire), 181¼ miles. Fares, 37/9*a*, 22/8*c*. R. T. for two months, 75/6*a*, 45/4*c*. Departures *from* London as for Chester. Departures *for* London about 6 times daily. Pop. 274.
Map Square 12.

MIDCALDER (Midlothian),

389½ miles. Fares, 79/5*a*, 47/8*c*. R.T. for two months, 158/10*a*, 95/4*c*. Departures *from* London as for Carstairs. Departures *for* London about 3 times daily. Pop. 3,207.
Map Square 41.

MID CLYTH (Caithness),

738¼ miles. No through fares. Departures *from* London as for Wick. Departures *for* London twice daily.
Map Square 32.

MIDDLE DROVE (Norfolk)

from *Liverpool Street*, 95 miles. Fares, 18/7*a*, 11/2*c*. R. T. for two months, 37/2*a*. Departures *from* London as for Wisbech. Departures *for* London about 5 times daily.
Map Square 19.

MIDDLESBROUGH

(Yorks) from *King's Cross*, 238½ miles. Fares, 49/9*a*, 29/10*c*. R. T., double fare. Pop. 131,103.
Map Square 8.

King's +	Midd.	Midd.	King's +
AM 4.45	11.44	AM 5.47	1. 5
7.15*r*	2.36	7.50	1.15
10. 0*r*	3.27	9.12*g*	3.15
10.10*r*	4.35	9.48*r*	4.30
11.50*r*	5.10	PM 12.55*r*	6.15
PM 1.15*r*	6.35	2.53*r*	9.25
1.50*r*	8. 5	4.33*r*	10. 0
5.35*r*	10.49	8.13	3.25
11.25	5.45	11. 1*e*	5.40
—	—	11. 1*d*	6. 0
—	—	—	—
—	—	—	—
—	—	—	—

Sunday Trains.

AM 8.30	5.13	AM 9.52	5.15
11.30*r*	9. 2	PM 2.15*r*	8.15
PM 11.25	5.56	9.40	5.40
—	—	—	—
—	—	—	—

d Saturdays only.
e Saturdays excepted.
g First and Third Class Pullman Car only.
r Restaurant Car.

MIDDLETON (Lancs), 193¼

miles. Fares, 39/9*a*, 23/10*c*. R. T. for two months, 79/6*a*, 47/8*c*. Departures *from* London as for Manchester. Departures *for* London about 10 times daily. Pop. 28,309.
Map Square 12.

MIDDLETON (Norfolk)

from *Liverpool Street*, 99½ miles. Fares, 20/8*a*, 12/5*c*. R. T. for two months, 41/4*a*. Departures *from* London as for Swaffham (*via* King's Lynn). Departures *for* London about 7 times daily. Pop. 797.
Map Square 19.

MIDDLETON (Northumberland),

294½ miles. No through fares. Departures *from* London as for Morpeth. Departures *for* London about 3 times daily.
Map Square 3.

MIDDLETON (Westmorland),

265 miles. Fares, 51/11*a*, 31/2*c*. R. T., double fare. Departures *from* London as for Ingleton. Departures *for* London about 5 times daily. Pop. 222.
Map Square 7.

MIDDLETON-IN-TEESDALE (Durham), 257½ miles.

Fares, 53/7*a*, 32/2*c*. R. T., double fare. Departures *from* London as for Barnard Castle. Departures *for* London about 5 times daily. Pop. 1,863.
Map Square 7.

MIDDLETON-ON-

THE-WOLDS (Yorks), 198½ miles. Fares 39/0*a*, 23/5*c*. R. T. for two months, 78/0*a*. Departures *from* London as for Market Weighton. Departures · *for* London about 5 times daily. Pop. 646.
Map Square 8.

MIDDLETOWN HILLS

(Montgomery), 166½ miles. Fares, 34/10*a*, 20/11*c*. R.T. for two months, 69/8*a*. Departures *from* London as for Buttington. Departures *for* London about 4 times daily. Pop. 92.
Map Square 17.

MIDDLEWICH (Cheshire),

166½ miles. Fares, 36/1*a*, 21/8*c*. R. T. for two months, 72/2*a*, 43/4*c*. Departures *from* London as for Crewe. Departures *for* London about twice daily. Pop. 5,116.
Map Square 12.

MIDDLEWOOD (Cheshire),

172½ miles. Fares 37/9*a*, 22/8*c*. R. T. for two months, 75/6*a*, 45/4*c*. Departures *from* London as for Macclesfield (Hibel Road). Departures *for* London about 8 times daily.
Map Square 12.

MIDFORD (Somerset),

from *Waterloo*, 145 miles. Fares, 24/0*a*, 14/5*c*. R. T. for two months, 48/0*a*. Departures *from* London as for Radstock. Departures *for* London about 5 times daily.
Map Square 22.

MIDGE HALL (Lancs), 213½

miles. Fares, 44/9*a*, 26/10*c*. R. T. for two months, 89/6*a*, 53/8*c*. Departures *from* London as for Preston. Departures *for* London about 4 times daily.
Map Square 12.

MIDGHAM (Berks) from

Paddington, 46¾ miles. Fares, 9/9*a*, 5/10*c*. R. T. for two months, 19/6*a*. Pop. 308.
Map Square 23.

PAD.	MIDGHAM	MIDGHAM	PAD.
AM 6.30	8.18	AM 8.11	9.30
8.45*r*	9.57	8.57	10. 0
9.30	10.45	9.24	10.45
10.45	12.22	11.14	12.55
11.20	1.17	PM12.14	1.50
PM 1.10*r*	2.33	1.14	2.30
1.35*r*	3.28	2.16	3.50
3.18	5. 3	3.14	4.35
4. 7	5.51	4.23	5.50
5. 5	6.10	5.23	7.20
5.40	7. 3	7.46	9.15
8. 0	9.10	8.29	10.25
10. 0*f*	11.23	9.17	10.45
—	—	10.36	2.45
—	—	—	—
—	—	—	—
—	—	—	—

Sunday Trains.

AM 9.10	10.39	AM 9. 8	10.50
PM 5.15	6.58	PM 7.52	9.15
—	—	—	—
—	—	—	—
—	—	—	—

f Wednesdays and Saturdays only.
r Restaurant Car.

MIDHURST (Sussex) from

Waterloo, 63¾ miles. Fares, 12/8*a*, 7/7*c*. R. T. for two months, 25/4*a*, 15/2*c*. Pop. 1,894.
Map Square 23.

	W'LOO.	MIDH'RST	MIDH'RST	W'LOO.
AM	5.50	8.38	AM 7. 3*s*	9.44
	6.50	9.43	8. 2*r*	9.52
	8.34*r*	11. 0	8.53	11.32
	9.50	12.21	11.15*r*	1.52
	10.50	1.36	PM12.30	3. 6
PM	12.20*d*	3. 3	1.52	4.16
	12.50*er*	4.22	3.20	5.52
	2.34	5.24	4.55	7.46
	4.50	6.52	6. 0	9. 6
	5.50	7.53	8. 1	10.46
	6.50*er*	9.11	—	—
	6.50*dr*	9.16	—	—
	—	—	—	—
	—	—	—	—

Sunday Trains.

AM	9.15*r*	11.52	AM 7.30	10.16
PM	1.50	4.36	PM 3.20	6.46
	—	—	6.15	8.52
	—	—	—	—

d Saturdays only.
e Saturdays excepted.
r Restaurant Car.
s Refreshments served.

ANOTHER ROUTE from

Victoria, *London Bridge*, and *Clapham Junction*, 60¾ miles.
Fares as above.

	Leave			Arr. at
	VICT.	CLAP. J.	LON. B.	MIDHST.
AM	6.18	6.25	6.35	8.49
	8.55	7.56	7.35	11.15
	10.15	10.22	10.30	12.47
	11.55	—	11.50	2.25
PM	1.40	1.47*e*	1.50	4.15
	3.55	4. 2	4. 0	6. 9
	4.53	5. 0	5. 5	7.35
	7.20	7.27	7.15	9.43
	—	—	—	—

Sunday Trains.

AM	6.55	7. 2	7. 2	9.58
PM	7. 0	7. 7	6.38	9.40
	—	—	—	—

Trains from Midhurst.

	Leave	Arrive at		
	MIDHST.	LON. B.	CLAP. J.	VICT.
AM	7.25	9.58	—	10.28
	9.17	11.50	11.35	11.42
	10. 3	12. 8	12.33	12. 0
	11.20	3.32	3.22	3.32
PM	12.55	3.40	3.37	3.45
	2.47	5.54	5. 4	5.12
	4.35	7.48	7.31	6.50
	7.55	10. 8	9.53	10. 1
	—	—	—	—

Sunday Trains.

AM	6.50	10.11	10. 6	10.13
PM	4.55	7.56	7.25	7.33
	—	—	—	—

e Saturdays excepted.

Spread Eagle, 15th Century Inn. Oak panelling rooms, open fireplaces. Finest of its kind in England. Lounge, Private Sitting-rooms. Famous for good food, service and efficiency. Golf. Garage. 'Phone 10.
See advt. p. **273.**

The Angel. An old Coaching House. Now the Principal Hotel. Real comfort and good food especially studied. Farmhouse Milk, Butter, Eggs. Large quiet garden. Golf. South-down breezes. Phone 21 Midhurst.

MIDSOMER NORTON

(Somerset) from *Waterloo*, 136½ miles. Fares, 24/0*a*, 14/5*c*. R. T. for two months, 48/0*a*. Pop. 7,770.
Map Square 22.

	W'LOO.	MIDS.N.	MIDS.N.	W'LOO.
AM	9. 0*r*	12.59	AM 7.20*r*	11.10
	10. 0*r*	3.10	9. 5*r*	1.56
PM	1. 0*r*	5.28	PM12. 3*r*	4.30
	3. 0*r*	7.23	1.40*r*	6. 0
	6. 0*r*	9.49	5.23	10.50
	—	—	6.49*h*	3.58
	—	—	—	—

No Sunday Trains.

h Via Eastleigh.
r Restaurant Car.

ANOTHER ROUTE from

Paddington, via Frome, 110½ miles.
Fares, 23/2*a*, 13/11*c*. R. T. for two months, 46/4*a*.

	PAD.	MID.N.		MID.N.	PAD.
AM	1. 0*g*	8.50	AM	7.46	10.52
	5.30	11. 3		11.20	3.20
	10.30	1.11	PM	1.56*t*	5.30
PM	12.30*r*	3.51		3.34*r*	6.50
	2. 0	5.22		5.53	10.45
	3.30	6.46		8.28	2.45
	5. 5	8.42		—	—

Sunday Trains.

PM	2.40	7.16	AM10.18	3.35
	—	—	—	—

g Mondays excepted.
r Restaurant Car.
t Tea Car.

ANOTHER ROUTE from

Paddington, via Bristol, 132¼ miles. Fares, 25/5*a*, 15/3*c*. R.T. for two months, 50/10*a*.

	PAD.	MID.N		MID.N.	PAD.
AM	7.30	11.20	AM	8. 0	11.30
	9. 0	1.56		11. 3*r*	2. 0
	11.15*dr*	2.50	PM	1.11	6. 2
PM	1.10*r*	5.53		5.22	10.25
	2.45	7. 4		8.42	2.45
	4.15*r*	8.28		—	—
	6.30*r*	10.15		—	—
	12. 0*l*	7.46		—	—
	12.30*s*	10.18		—	—

Sunday Trains.

PM	12.30*r*	5.43	PM12.34*r*	4. 5
	10. 0	7.46	7.16	3.15
	—	—	—	—

d Saturdays only.
h Thursdays and Saturdays only.
l Saturdays midnight excepted.
r Restaurant Car.
s Saturdays midnight only.

MIDVILLE (Lincoln)

from *King's Cross, via* Little Steeping, 124½ miles. Fares, 25/3*a*, 15/2*c*. R. T. for two months, 50/6*a*, 30/4*c*. Pop. 205.
Map Square 13.

KINGS+	MIDVILLE	MIDVILLE	KINGS+
AM 4.45	9. 3	AM 9.20	1. 5
7.15*r*	12.15	PM12.15*r*	4.30
8.45	1. 8	3.35	9. 0
11.30	4.33	7.10	3.25
PM 3. 0	7.10	—	—

No Sunday Trains.

r Restaurant Car.

MILBORNE PORT

(Somerset) from *Waterloo*, 114½ miles. Fares, 23/11a, 14/4c. R.T. for two months, 47/10a, 28/8c. Pop. 1,630.
Map Square 22.

W'LOO	MIL.P.	MIL.P.	W'LOO
AM 9.0r	11.59	AM 7.29	10.56
10.0r	12.59	8.36r	11.10
12.0nr	2.36	11.7r	1.56
PM 1.0r	4.11	PM12.29r	3.8
3.0r	6.0	3.28r	6.0
5.0	8.12	4.51r	8.30
6.0r	9.14	6.57	10.50
—	—	9.51h	3.58

Sunday Trains.

AM 9.0	1.35	PM 5.44r	8.57

h Via Eastleigh.
n Noon.
r Restaurant Car.

MILCOTE (Warwick), from

Paddington, 106 miles. Fares, 21/1a, 12/8c. R.T. for two months, 42/2a. Departures *from* London as for Stratford-on-Avon. Departures *for* London about 4 times daily. Pop. 55.
Map Square 17.

MILDENHALL (Suffolk)

from *Liverpool Street*, 76½ miles. Fares, 16/0a, 9/7c. R.T. for two months, 32/0a. Pop. 3,645.
Map Square 19.

L'PL. ST.	MILD'HL	MILD'HL.	L'PL. ST.
AM 5.5	7.42	AM 7.51r	10.23
8.30r	11.29	11.36r	2.21
11.50hr	2.43	PM 3.7hr	6.10
PM 2.34	5.19	5.27r	8.22
5.49r	8.35	—	—

No Sunday Trains.
h Mondays and Saturdays only.
r Restaurant Car.

The "Bell" Hotel. The Old Original Commercial House. Homelike. Moderate Tariff. Same family 50 years. Shooting. Fishing. Golf.
Proprietors—
HARRY A. SMITH,
GRACE M. SMITH

MILDMAY PARK from

Broad Street, 2½ miles. Fares, 0/5a, 0/4b, 0/3c. R.T. for two days, 0/10a, 0/7b, 0/5½c. Pop. 25,433. See pp. 518-522.
Map Square 61.

MILE END from *Ealing*,

Hounslow, Richmond, and *Wimbledon.* See p. 489.
Map Square 62, No. 1.

MILES PLATTING

(Lancs), 187¼ miles. Fares, 38/7a, 23/2c. R.T. for two months, 77/2a. Departures *from* London as for Manchester. Departures *for* London about 8 times daily. Pop. 21,104.

MILFORD (Surrey) from

Waterloo. 36 miles. Fares, 7/8a, 4/7c. R.T. for two months, 15/4a, 9/2c. Pop. 1,858.
Map Square 23.

W'LOO	MILFORD	MILFORD	W'LOO
AM 5.50	7.8	AM 6.47	8.20
6.50	8.15	7.30	8.41
7.50	9.22	8.8	9.12
9.50	11.1	8.43s	9.44
10.50	12.8	9.47	10.50
11.50d	1.0	10.22	11.32
PM12.20d	1.20	PM12.41r	1.52
12.50er	1.57	1.46	3.6
1.50e	3.7	3.4	4.16
2.0d	3.16	4.38	5.52
2.34	4.3	6.14	7.46
3.50d	5.0	7.44	9.6
4.15e	5.16	9.12	10.46
5.24	6.23	10.34	12.16
5.40	7.3		
6.50er	7.59		
6.50dr	8.9		
8.0	9.26		
9.50	11.6		

Sunday Trains.

AM 8.20	9.53	AM 9.4	10.16
PM 1.50	3.9	PM 1.58	3.13
4.20	5.48	4.58	6.17
6.20	7.40	9.8	10.41
8.20	9.56	10.5	11.43

d Saturdays only.
e Saturdays excepted.
r Restaurant Car.
s Refreshments served.

MILFORD AND BROCTON

(Stafford), 129½ miles. Fares, 26/11a, 16/2c. R.T. for two months, 53/10a. Departures *from* London as for Colwich. Departures *for* London about 6 times daily.
Map Square 17.

MILFORD HAVEN

(Pembroke) from *Paddington*, 268 miles. Fares, 54/4a, 32/7c. R.T. for two months, 108/8a, 65/2c. Pop. 7,764.
Map Square 20.

PAD.	M.HAV.	M. HAV.	PAD.
AM 1.0g	11.50	AM 7.50r	4.20
8.45r	3.40	10.45r	6.15
11.50r	7.5	PM12.30r	8.35
PM 1.10r	9.35	6.15	3.30
5.0hr	12.0		
9.15e	7.0		

Sunday Trains.

PM 9.15	7.0	—	—

e Saturdays excepted.
g Mondays excepted.
h Tuesdays, Thursdays, and Saturdays only.
r Restaurant Car.

MILFORD - ON - SEA

(Hants). Stations at NEW MILTON or LYMINGTON, distance about 4 miles.

Hotel Victoria, Milford-on-Sea. On Cliff facing Isle of Wight. Motor centre for New Forest. Tel. 7 Milford-on-Sea.
See advt. p. 267.

MILFORD, SOUTH

(Yorks), 182 miles. Fares, 36/8a, 22/0c. R.T., double fare. Departures *from* London as for Selby. Departures *for* London about 6 times daily. Pop. 1,022.
Map Square 13.

MILKWALL (Gloster), 141

miles. Fares, 29/5a, 17/8c. R.T. for two months, 58/10r, 35/4c. Departures *from* London as for Lydney. Departures *for* London about 4 times daily.

MILLBROOK (Beds) from

Euston, 37 miles. Fares, 10/5a, 6/3c. R.T. for two months, 20/10a. Departures from London as for Woburn Sands. Departures *for* London about 5 times daily. Pop. 201.
Map Square 18.

MILLBROOK (Hants)

from *Waterloo*, 79½ miles. Fares, 16/8a, 10/0c. R.T. for two months, 33/4a, 20/0c. Pop. 9,171.
Map Square 28.

W'LOO	M'BROOK	M'BROOK	W'LOO
AM 5.40	8.17	AM 8.3r	10.6
5.50	9.12	9.7s	11.0
8.30s	10.52	10.0s	12.22
10.30	12.22	10.33r	12.50
11.30	1.50	PM12.3r	2.20
PM12.30r	2.33	12.57	2.50
1.30s	3.41	1.57	4.20
2.30	4.30	3.53s	6.26
3.30s	5.52	5.0	6.58
4.30r	6.24	5.52r	8.20
6.30r	8.19	6.53r	8.50
7.30r	9.42	8.16	10.50
8.0	10.56	8.39	11.28
—	—	10.8	3.58

Sunday Trains.

AM11.0r	1.22	AM 9.1	12.11
PM 2.0r	4.26	10.13r	2.27
—	—	PM 3.20r	6.7
—	—	5.33	8.3
—	—	7.25r	9.31
—	—	9.0	3.58

r Restaurant Car.
s Refreshments served.

MILLERHILL (Midlothian), 391 miles. Fares, 79/5a,

47/8c. R.T. for two months, 158/10a, 95/4c. Departures *from* London as for Galashiels. Departures *for* London about 4 times daily.

MILLER'S DALE

(Derby) from *St. Pancras*, 159 miles. Fares, 32/9a, 19/8c. R.T., double fare.
Map Square 12.

ST.PAN.	M.DALE	M. DALE	ST.PAN
AM 2.25	8.56	AM 8.14r	11.35
4.25	9.5	10.5r	1.30
8.25r	12.5	11.2	3.25
10.25r	1.57	PM 2.20r	5.45
PM 1.25r	5.11	4.28r	8.35
2.25r	6.48	5.45r	10.5
4.25r	8.45	8.40	4.20
6.25r	10.5	—	—
12.0h	8.46	—	—

Sunday Trains.

PM 3.15	7.27	AM11.0r	5.2
—	—	PM 5.31r	9.52
—	—	8.5	4.55

h Saturdays midnight only.
r Restaurant Car.

Bull's Head Hotel, Tideswell. Two miles from Station. Near Golf Links. Five Bedrooms. Ample accommodation for Parties. Posting. P.R.H.A. House.

MILLFIELD (Durham), 262¼ miles. Fares, 54/7*a*, 32/9*c*. R. T., double fare. Departures *from* London as for Sunderland. Departures *for* London about 6 times daily.
Map Square 3.

MILL HILL from *Moorgate Street* and *St. Pancras*, 9¼ miles. Fares from St. Pancras, 1/10½*a*, 1/1½*c*. R.T. for two days, 3/9*a*, 2/3*c*. From Moorgate Street, 2/1*a*, 1/3*c*. R. T. for two days, 4/2*a*, 2/6*c*. Pop. 6,118. *See* pp. 507, 508.
Map Square 23.

ANOTHER ROUTE from *King's Cross, Moorgate Street*, and *Broad Street*, 8¼ miles. Fares from King's Cross, 1/7*a*, 1/3*b*, 0/11½*c*. R. T. for two days, 3/2*a*, 2/6*b*, 1/11*c*. From Moorgate Street and Broad Street, 1/8*a*, 1/4*b*, 1/0*c*. R. T. for two days, 3/4*a*, 2/8*b*, 1/11½*c*. *See* pp. 518-522.

MILL HILL (Isle of Wight) from *Waterloo, London Bridge* and *Victoria, via* Ryde, 92 miles. Fares, 20/5*a*, 12/6*c*. R. T. for two months, 40/1*a*, 24/6*c*. Departures *from* London as for Newport (I. of W.). Departures *for* London about 4 times daily.
Map Square 28.

MILL HILL (Lancs), 211 miles. Fares, 43/9*a*, 26/3*c*. R. T. for two months, 87/6*a*, 52/6*c*. Departures *from* London as for Wigan. Departures *for* London about 6 times daily.

MILL HOUSES AND ECCLESALL (Yorks), from *St. Pancras*, 155¾ miles. Fares, 32/3*a*, 19/4*c*. R. T., double fare. Departures *from* London as for Chesterfield. Departures *for* London about 6 times daily.
Map Square 12.

MILLIKEN PARK (Renfrew) 412½ miles. Fares, 82/4*a*, 49/5*c*. R. T. for two months, 164/8*a*, 98/10*c*. Departures *from* London as for Kilmarnock. Departures *for* London about 4 times daily.
Map Square 40.

MILLISLE (Wigtown), 397 miles. Fares, 71/11*a*, 43/2*c*. R. T. for two months, 143/10*a*, 86/4*c*. Departures *from* London as for Wigtown. Departures *for* London about 3 times daily.
Map Square 43.

MILLOM (Cumberland) from *Euston*, 273½ miles. Fares, 56/11*a*, 34/2*c*. R. T. for two months, 113/10*a*. Pop. 8,709.
Map Square 6.

	Euston.	Millom.		Millom.	Euston.
AM	12.25*h*	10.20	AM	7.48*v*	3.45
	2.35	11.55		7.48*r*	4.15
	5. 0	1.45		10.29*t*	6. 0
	6.45	3.30	PM	12.30*r*	7.30
	11.35*r*	6.10		3.50*r*	10.45
	11.50*r*	8.22		8. 0	5. 0
PM	1.30*r*	8.35		—	—
	2.35*dt*	11.30		—	—
	9.30*e*	6.25		—	—
	11. 0*d*	9.39		—	—

Sunday Trains.

AM	11.45*r*	7.29	AM	11.11*r*	7.30
	—	—	PM	7.25	5. 0

d Saturdays only.
e Saturdays excepted.
h Thursdays only.
r Restaurant Car.
t Tea Car.
v Mondays and Saturdays only.

MILLTIMBER (Aberdeen), 528 miles. No through fares. Departures *from* London as for Aberdeen. Departures *for* London about 4 times daily.
Map Square 38.

MILLWALL DOCKS from *Fenchurch Street*, 3¾ miles. Fares, 0/9*a*, 0/7*b*, 0/5½*c*. R. T. for two days, 1/6*a*, 1/2*b*, 0/10½*c*. *See* pp. 524, 525.
Map Square 1.

MILLWALL JUNCTION, from *Fenchurch Street*, 3 miles. Fares, 0/4*a*, 0/3*b*, 0/2½*c*. R. T., double fare. *See* pp. 524, 525.
Map Square 62.

MILNATHORT (Kinross), 424 miles. Fares, 88/1*a*, 52/10*c*. R. T. for two months, 176/2*a*, 105/8*c*. Departures *from* London as for Dunfermline. Departures *for* London about 3 times daily. Pop. 1,207.
Map Square 41.

MILNGAVIE (Dumbarton), 444¾ miles. No through fares. Departures *from* London as for Edinburgh (Waverley). Departures *for* London about 4 times daily. Pop. 4,434.
Map Square 40.

MILNROW (Lancs), 194 miles. Fares, 39/10*a*, 23/11*c*. R. T. for two months, 79/8*a*, 47/10*c*. Departures *from* London as for Manchester. Departures *for* London about 6 times daily. Pop. 8,386.
Map Square 12.

MILNTHORPE (Westmorland), 243½ miles. Fares, 50/8*a*, 30/5*c*. R. T., double fare. Departures *from* London as for Carnforth. Departures *for* London about 5 times daily. Pop. 1,019.
Map Square 7.

MILTON (Stafford), 149½ miles. Fares, 31/3*a*, 18/9*c*. R. T. for two months, 62/6*a*, 37/6*c*. Departures *from* London as for Stoke-on-Trent. Departures *for* London about 5 tmes daily. Pop. 2,579.
Map Square 12.

MILTON OF CAMPSIE (Stirling), 436¾ miles. No through fares. Departures *from* London as for Glasgow. Departures *for* London about 3 times daily. Pop. 1,589.
Map Square 40.

MILTON ROAD (Somerset), 142 miles. No through fares. Departures *from* London as for Clevedon. Departures *for* London about 3 times daily.

MILVERTON (Somerset), 149½ miles. Fares, 31/3*a*, 18/9*c*. R. T. for two months, 62/6*a*. Departures *from* London as for Dulverton. Departures *for* London about 5 times daily. Pop. 1,437.
Map Square 26.

MINDRUM (Northumberland), 337½ miles. Fares, 71/1*a*, 42/8*c*. R. T., double fare. Departures *from* London as for Alnwick. Departures *for* London about 4 times daily.
Map Square 3.

MINEHEAD (Somerset) from *Paddington*, 167½ miles. Fares, 35/0*a*, 21/0*c*. R. T. for two months, 70/0*a*, 42/0*c*. Pop. 6,016.
Map Square 21.

	Pad.	Minhd.		Minhd.	Pad.
AM	5.30	12.18	AM	9.30*r*	1.30
	9.15	1.37		11.10	4. 5
PM	12. 5	4. 5	PM	1.15*t*	5.30
	3.30	7.24		2.30*r*	6.50
	4.15*r*	8.44		4.25*r*	9. 0
	12. 0*h*	8.29		7. 0	2.45
	—	—		9.20	7.10

Sunday Trains.

PM	10. 0	8.29		—	—

h Saturday midnight excepted.
r Restaurant Car.
t Tea Car.

Hotel Metropole. First-class Hotel, standing in grounds of four acres. Tennis and Croquet. Links (18 holes). Telephone, 11.
See advt. p. **268**.

Hopcott Hotel. High ground. Personal Management Proprietor and Wife. Garage. Phone 25.
See advt. p. **268**.

Beach Hotel, strictly reserved for families and gentlemen; facing the Sea. Nearest Hotel to the Station and Golf Links.
E. PERCIFULL, Proprietor.
See advt. p. **268**.

The Wellington Hotel. First-class. Under new ownership. Central for Hunting, Golf Links and Sea. Garage. Headquarters West Somerset Polo Club. Tel. 22.
R. G. SANDERSON, Proprietor.

The Avenue Private Hotel, nearest to Sands. Links. Overlooking Sea. Grounds of half an acre. Billiard Room Lounge. Telephone 171.
HENRY WESTACOTT, Proprietor.
(Late of Wellington Hotel).

Beaconwood. Private Residential Hotel. Highest, best position in Minehead. Standing in own grounds, facing South. Billiards. Tel. "Beaconwood, Minehead." PROPRIETOR.

Esplanade Private Hotel. Modern. Comfortable. Quiet. Near Golf Links and Station. Winter visitors specially catered for at very moderate terms. Telephone 17.

MINETY (Wilts) from *Paddington*, 85½ miles. Fares, 17/9*a*, 10/8*c*. R. T. for two months, 35/6*a*. Departures *from* London as for Purton. Departures *for* London about 4 times daily. Pop. 757.
Map Square 22.

MINFFORDD (Merioneth), 251 miles. Fares, *via* Welshpool or Dolgelley, 52/3*a*, 31/4*c*. R. T. for two months, 104/6*a*. *Via* Bangor, 54/10*a*, 32/11*c*. R.T. for two months, 109/8*a*. Departures *from* London as for Harlech or Portmadoc. Departures *for* London about 3 times daily.
Map Square 11.

MINEHEAD.—WELLINGTON HOTEL. (Central. High-Class. Moderate Tariff.)

MINSHULL VERNON

(Cheshire), 163 miles. Fares, 34/0*a*, 20/5*c*. R. T. for two months, 68/0*a*. Departures *from* London as for Crewe. Departures *for* London about 3 times daily. Pop. 288. *Map Square* 12.

MINSTER JUNCTION

(Kent) from *Charing Cross, Cannon Street,* and *London Bridge,* 82¼ miles. Fares, (*via Wye*), 15/5*a*, 12/4*b*, 9/3*c*. R. T. for two months, 30/10*a*, 24/8*b*, 18/6*c*. (*Via Deal*), 18/1*a*, 14/5*b*, 10/10*c*. R. T. for two months, 36/2*a*, 28/10*b*, 21/8*c*. Pop. (Minster) 2,915. *Map Square* 24.

	Leave		Arr. at
Char. +	Can. St.	Lon. B.	Mins. J.
AM —	5.20	5.25	9.22
—	—	7.50*l*	10.36
9.15	—	9.23	11.47
11. 0	—	11. 7	1.49
PM 1. 0	—	—	3.17
3. 0	—	3. 8	5.30
4.30	—	4.37	7. 0
5.15*e*	5.12*e*	5.21*e*	7.43
5.20*d*	—	5.26*d*	7.43
5.24*d*	—	5.34*d*	8.43
6. 0*e*	—	6. 5*e*	8.43
7.18	—	7.26	10.20

Sunday Trains.

AM 7.45	—	7.52	10.45
9.35*h*	—	—	12.16
PM 5.15*h*	—	—	8.37
7.35	—	7.45	10.19
9.25	—	9.31	12.23

Trains from Minster Junc.

Leave		Arrive at	
Minst. J.	Lon. B.	Can. St.	Char. +
AM 6.29	9.32	9.36	—
7.16	10. 0	10. 4	—
7.16*h*	—	—	10.20*h*
8.33	10.54	—	11. 3
9. 6	11.43	—	11.57
10.39	1.36	—	1.50
PM 12.14	3.26	—	3.40
2.45	5.50	—	6. 3
2.45*h*	—	—	5.42*h*
4.39	7.25	7.30	7.49
7.33	10.22	—	10.35
10.20*y*	—	1.20	—

Sunday Trains.

AM 6.37	10. 5	—	10.15
8.58	—	—	1. 5*h*
PM 4.31	7. 9	—	7.17
5.58	8.30	—	8.40
7.48	10.16	—	10.26
10.21*y*	—	1.23	—

d Saturdays only.
e Saturdays excepted.
h Departs from or arrives at Victoria (S.E. & C.R.).
l Low level platform.
y Third-class only.

MINSTER-ON-SEA

(Kent), 52½ miles. Fares, 9/3*a*, 7/6*b*, 5/9*c*. R.T. for two months, 18/6*a*, 15/0*b*, 11/6*c*. Departures *from* London as for Queenborough. Departures *for* London about 5 times daily. Pop. 3,059. *Map Square* 24.

MINSTERLEY (Salop).

162½ miles. Fares, 34/0*a*, 20/5*c*. R.T. for two months,68/0*a*. Departures *from* London as for Shrewsbury. Departures *for* London about 4 times daily. Pop. 747. *Map Square* 17.

MINTLAW (Aberdeen),

558 miles. Fares, 107/4*a*, 64/5*c*. R. T. for two months, 214/8*a*, 128/10*c*. Departures *from* London as for Peterhead. Departures *for* London about twice daily. Pop. 378. *Map Square* 35.

MIRFIELD (Yorks) from

King's Cross, via Horbury, 179¾ miles. Fares, 37/9*a*, 22/8*c*. R T., double fare. Pop. 12,133. *Map Square* 12.

King's +	Mirfd.	Mirfd.	King's +
AM 7.15*r*	12.21	AM 6.25	11.30
10.10*dr*	2.45	8.21*r*	1.5
10.10*er*	3.19	9.48*r*	1.55
PM 1.30*r*	6.34	10.30*r*	3.50
1.50*r*	7.42	11.21*r*	4.45
5.45*r*	10.58	PM 12.21	5. 0
—	—	2.54*r*	7.10
—	—	4.49*r*	9.25
—	—	8.52*e*	3.25

Sunday Trains.

12. 0*kn*	6.29	AM 10.23*r*	3.45
—	—	PM 3.44*k*	10.20

d Saturdays only.
e Saturdays excepted.
k Passengers cross Wakefield at own expense.
n Noon.
r Restaurant Car.

MISSENDEN, GREAT

(Bucks) from *Marylebone,* 28¼ miles. Fares, 6/1*a*, 3/8*c*. R.T. for two months, 12/2*a*, 7/2*c*. *Map Square* 23.

M'bone	Misdn.	Misdn.	M'bone
AM 6.25	7.23	AM 6.44	7.50
6.45	7.38	7.26	8.22
7.20	8.28	7.53*e*	8.42
7.50	8.58	7.53*d*	8.46
8.50	9.54	8.20	9. 9
9.14	10.13	9. 1	9.46
10. 5	11. 7	10.41	11.36
11.15	12.15	PM 12. 5	12.59
PM 1. 5*d*	2. 0	1. 5	2. 2
1.10*e*	2. 7	1.58*e*	3.28
1.41*d*	2.41	3. 6	3.59
1.55*e*	3.20	3.57	4.56
2.15*d*	3.20	4.36*e*	6.22
2.45*d*	4.14	5.40*d*	7.15
3.25	4.26	6.49	7.43
5. 4	6. 5	7. 5	8.11
5.24*e*	6.18	7.38	8.31
6.25*e*	7.10	9.48	10.41
6.25*d*	7.18	10. 9	11. 0
6.51*e*	7.35	—	—
6.53*e*	8.19	—	—
7.30	8.32	—	—
8.20	9.18	—	—
9. 0	10. 0	—	—
10.30	11.29	—	—
11.35	12.52	—	—

Sunday Trains.

AM 9.30	10.30	AM 9.15	10.13
11. 0	12. 0	11.51	12.46
PM 1. 0	2. 0	PM 1.21	2.16
2.30	3.30	4.26	5.20
3.15	4.38	5.44	6.55
4.30	5.30	6.41	7.35
5.30	6.41	7.12	8.16
6.10	7.25	8.34	9.44
6.45	7.42	9. 4	9.55
7.45	9. 1	—	—
8.50	10.31	—	—

d Saturdays only.
e Saturdays excepted.

MISSENDEN, GREAT

—continued.

ANOTHER ROUTE from *Baker Street,* 29 miles. Fares as above.

Baker St.	Misdn.	Misdn.	Baker St.
AM 6. 5	7. 7	AM 6.44	7.41
6. 6	7.23	7.26	8.35
6.30	7.38	7.42	8.42
7. 3	8.23	7.53*d*	8.51
7.50	8.58	7.53*e*	8.57
8.34	9.54	8.20	9.28
9. 1	10.13	8.46	9.39
9.51*e*	10.46	9. 1	9.49
9.51*d*	10.50	9.26	10.25
10.11*d*	11.15	10.18	11. 5
10.18*e*	11.17	10.41	11.50
11. 0	12.15	11.34	12.35
PM 12. 8	1.15	PM 12. 5*e*	1.22
12.50*e*	2. 8	12. 5*d*	1.24
12.54*d*	2. 0	1. 5*d*	2.17
1.17*d*	2.22	1. 5*e*	2.22
1.21*d*	2.41	1.58	2.58
2.17*e*	3.20	2.54*d*	3.55
2.19*d*	3.22	3. 6	4.22
3.10	4.26	3.57	5.14
3.18*d*	4.14	4.36	5.41
4.10*d*	5.12	5.37*e*	6.33
4.16*e*	5.16	5.40*d*	6.39
4.40*d*	6. 3	6.49	8. 0
4.42*e*	6. 3	7. 5	8. 8
5. 7*e*	6.17	7.38	8.47
5.45*e*	6.41	8.33	9.37
5.46*d*	6.47	9.28*d*	10.28
5.49*e*	7.10	9.28*e*	10.43
6.30	7.33	9.48	11. 2
7.15*e*	8.19	10. 9	11.18
7.15*d*	8.31	10.43	11.40
7.19*e*	8.31	—	—
8. 0	9.18	—	—
8.46	10. 0	—	—
9.25	10.26	—	—
10.16	11.29	—	—
11.50	12.52	—	—

Sunday Trains.

AM 8.47	9.52	AM 8.40	9.48
9.10	10.30	9.15	10.27
9.47	10.52	10.48	11.48
10.33	11.40	11.51	1. 5
10.45	12. 0	PM 1.21	2.35
11.11	12.19	2.10	3. 9
12. 0	1. 3	2.53	3.52
PM 12.45	2. 0	4.26	5.42
2. 0	3. 3	4.55	5.54
2.15	3.30	5.20	6.21
3.35	4.38	5.44	6.45
4. 2	5. 3	6.41	7.57
4.15	5.30	7.12	8.12
5.37	6.42	7.50	8.51
6.24	7.25	8.13	9.12
6.30	7.42	8.34	9.31
7.59	9. 2	9. 4	10.20
9.29	10.31	10.14	11.14

d Saturdays only.
e Saturdays excepted.

MISTERTON (Notts).

151½ miles. Fares, 31/3*a*, 18/9*c*. R. T., double fare. Departures *from* London as for Gainsboro'. Departures *for* London about 5 times daily. Pop. 1,694. *Map Square* 13.

MISTLEY (Essex) from

Liverpool Street, 61¼ miles. Fares, 12/11a, 7/9c. R.T. for two months, 25/10a. Pop. 1,991.
Map Square 19.

L'PL. ST.	MISTLEY	MISTLEY	L'PL. ST.
AM 5. 0	7. 4	AM 7.56	9.36
6.50	9.36	9.12	10.58
8.46	10.58	10.24	12.39
10.20	12.14	PM12.41	3.13
11.30	1.28	3.35	5.48
PM 2.15	4.22	6. 6	7.51
3.23	5.14	8. 9r	10. 0
5.42	7.41	8.58	11.16
7.16	9. 9	—	—
7.45r	10. 1	—	—
8.45	10.41	—	—

Sunday Trains.

AM 9.20r	11.21	AM 9.34	11.38
PM 4.40	6.18	PM 5.21	7.10
7.40	9.41	6.54	8.58
—	—	7.58	10. 9

r Restaurant Car.

MITCHAM (Surrey) from

London Bridge, 11 miles. From *Victoria*, 9½ miles. Fares, via Tulse Hill, 1/11a, 1/2c. R.T. for two days, 3/10a, 2/0c. Fares, via Croydon, 2/1a, 1/3c. R.T. for two days, 4/2a, 2/2c. Pop. 35,119.
See p. 577.

MITCHAM JUNCT.

(Surrey) from *London Bridge*, 10¼ miles. *Victoria*, 8½ miles, and *Clapham Junction*. Fares, via Croydon, 2/1a, 1/3c. R.T. for two days, 4/2a, 2/2c. Via Tulse Hill, 1/8a, 1/0c. R.T. for two days, 3/4a, 2/0c. *See* pp. 565, 566, 571-574, 577.

MITCHELDEAN ROAD

(Gloucester) 128 miles. Fares, 26/8a, 16/0c. R.T. for two months, 53/4a. Departures *from* London as for Ross. Departures *for* London about 5 times daily. Pop. (Mitcheldean) 626.
Map Square 22.

MOAT LANE (Montgomery), 190½ miles. Fares, 39/10a, 23/11c. R.T. for two months, 79/8a. Departures *from* London as for Newtown. Departures *for* London about 5 times daily.
Map Square 12.

MOBBERLEY (Cheshire), 180½ miles. Fares, 35/8a, 21/5c. R.T. double fare. Departures *from* London as for Knutsford. Departures *for* London about 6 times daily. Pop. 1,406.
Map Square 12.

MOCHDRE (Carnarvon), 221½ miles. Fares, 46/1a, 27/8c. R.T. for two months, 92/2a, 55/4c. Departures *from* London as for Colwyn Bay. Departures *for* London about 5 times daily.
Map Square 11.

MOFFAT (Dumfries) from

Euston, 340½ miles. Fares, 69/2a, 41/6c. R.T. for two months, 138/4a, 83/0c. Pop. 3,057.
Map Square 44.

EUSTON	MOFFAT	MOFFAT	EUSTON
AM 2.35	1.59	AM 5.55r	4.15
5. 0e	2.36	9. 5r	6.25
5. 0d	2.55	11.30r	7.30
6.45	4.40	PM12.35r	10. 0
10. 0r	5.10	7.15r	5. 0
11.35r	7.46	—	—
PM 9.20	5.46	—	—
11.45e	10.16	—	—

Sunday Trains.

PM11.45	10.16	—	—
—	—	—	—

d Saturdays only.
e Saturdays excepted.
r Restaurant Car.

MOIRA (Leicester) from St.

Pancras, 120 miles. Fares, 24/0a, 14/5c. R. T., double fare.
Map Square 17.

ST. PAN.	MOIRA	MOIRA	ST. PAN.
AM 2.25	8. 0	AM 7.25r	11. 0
4.25	10.17	8.32r	11.35
10.25r	1.31	11.38	3.25
PM12.25r	3.48	PM 1.40r	5.45
2.25r	5.39	3.45r	6.35
4.25r	7.40	6. 4r	9.15
6.25r	9.12	9.10	4.20

Sunday Trains.

PM 6.15r	9.43	AM 7.33	11.53
—	—	PM 6. 3r	9.52

r Restaurant Car.

MOLD (Flint) from *Euston*,

192½ miles. Fares, 40/2a, 24/1c. R.T. for two months, 80/4a, 48/2c. Pop. 4,659.
Map Square 11.

EUSTON	MOLD	MOLD	EUSTON
AM12.25	7.41	AM 7.14er	12. 5
5. 0	11. 2	7.14dr	12.20
8.30r	1.56	8.15r	1. 0
10.30r	2.41	9.14r	1.45
11.50r	5.13	9.46	2.20
12. 0nr	6.43	10.41r	4.15
PM 2.35t	7.20	PM 3. 2r	8.10
4. 5r	8.55	4. 2er	9. 5
5.20r	10. 5	4. 2dr	9.15
—	—	5.40r	10.45
—	—	8.52	5. 0

No Sunday Trains.

d Saturdays only.
e Saturdays excepted.
n Noon.
r Restaurant Car.
t Tea Car.

MOLLINGTON (Cheshire), 182 miles. Fares, 37/11a, 22/9c. R. T. for two months, 75/10a. Departures *from* London as for Chester. Departures *for* London about 6 times daily.
Map Square 12.

MOLYNEUX BROW

(Lancs), 192½ miles. No through fares. Departures *from* London as for Manchester. Departures *for* London about 6 times daily.

MONIAIVE (Dumfries), 349½

miles. Fares, 42/8c. R. T. for two months, 85/4c. Departures *from* London as for Dumfries. Departures *for* London about twice daily. Pop. 573.
Map Square 43.

MONIFIETH (Forfar), 458

miles. Fares, 92/4a, 55/5c. R. T. for two months, 184/8a, 110/10c. Departures *from* London as for Dundee. Departures *for* London about 4 times daily. Pop. 4,172.
Map Square 38.

MONIKIE (Forfar), 482½

miles. No through fares. Departures *from* London as for Forfar. Departures *for* London about 5 times daily. Pop. 1,155.
Map Square 38.

MONK BRETTON

(Yorks), 176 miles. No through fares. Departures *from* London as for Cudworth. Departures *for* London about 8 times daily. Pop. 5,139.

MONK FRYSTON

(Yorks), 178 miles. Fares, 36/6a, 21/11c. R.T. double fare. Departures *from* London as for Ferrybridge. Departures *for* London about 3 times daily. Pop. 522.
Map Square 13.

MONKSEATON (Northumberland) 277 miles. Fares, 58/4a, 35/0c. R. T., double fare. Departures *from* London as for Newcastle-on-Tyne. Departures *for* London about 8 times daily. Pop. 2,971.
Map Square 3.

MONKTON (Ayr), 391½

miles. Fares, 79/10a, 47/11c. R. T. for two months, 159/8a, 95/10c. Departures *from* London as for Ayr. Departures *for* London about 4 times daily. Pop. 9,432.
Map Square 40.

MONKTON COMBE

(Somerset), 102 miles. No through fares. Departures *from* London as for Limpley Stoke. Departures *for* London about 4 times daily.
Map Square 22.

MONKWEARMOUTH

(Durham), 261½ miles. Fares, 54/7a, 32/9c. R. T. double fare. Departures *from* London as for Sunderland. Departures *for* London about 6 times daily. Pop. 7,928.
Map Square 3.

MONMOUTH from *Paddington*, 144½ miles. Fares (May Hill), via Ross, 30/0a, 18/0c. R.T. for two months, 60/0a, 36/0c. *Via* Chepstow, 31/11a, 19/2c. R.T. for two months, 63/10a, 38/4c. (Troy), via Ross, 30/3a, 18/2c. R. T. for two months, 60/6a, 36/4c. *Via* Chepstow, 31/11a, 19/2c. R. T. for two months, 63/10a, 38/4c. Pop. 5,207.
Map Square 22.

PAD.	MAY HILL	TROY
AM 1. 0g	8.50	8.56
5.30	11.25	11.30
10.45	3.35	3.40
PM 1. 0hr	—	5.43
3.15t	7.52	7.58

Sunday Trains.

PM 9.15	8.52	8.57

MONMOUTH—contd.

Trains from Monmouth.

TROY	MAY HILL	PAD.
AM 9.5hr	—	2.0
9.42r	9.46r	2.40
PM12.35	12.39	5.0
3.42r	3.46r	8.45
4.0hr	—	8.45
8.30	8.34	5.30
—	—	—
—	—	—
—	—	—
—	—	—

No Sunday Trains.
g Mondays excepted.
h Via Chepstow.
r Restaurant Car.
t Tea Car.

King's Head Hotel. Telephone 17. Famous old inn in Agincourt Square. Garage. TRUST HOUSES, Ltd.

MONSAL DALE (Derby),
156¼ miles. Fares, 32/4a, 19/5c. R. T., double fare. Departures *from* London as for Bakewell. Departures *for* London about 5 times daily.
Map Square 12.

MONTACUTE (Somerset),
132¼ miles. Fares, 26/8a, 16/0c. R. T. for two months, 53/4a, 32 0c. Departures *from* London as for Yeovil (Pen Mill). Departures *for* London about 5 times daily. Pop. 713.
Map Square 22.

MONTGOMERY from
Paddington, 178¾ miles. Fares, 37/3a, 22/4c. R. T. for two months, 74/6a. Pop. 951.
Map Square 16.

PAD.	MONTG.	MONTG.	PAD.
AM 6.30	1.14	AM 8.31r	2.5
10.40r	4.5	10.12r	4.15
PM 2.10t	6.31	10.52t	5.0
4.10t	8.51	PM 1.5t	6.40
12.15k	9.18	3.2r	8.5
12.15h	7.26	4.11	10.0
—	—	8.22	5.30

No Sunday Trains.

h Saturdays midnight only.
k Saturdays midnight excepted.
r Restaurant Car.
t Tea Car.

ANOTHER ROUTE from
Euston, 188 miles. Fares as above.

EUSTON	MONTG.	MONTG.	EUSTON
AM 5.0	12.10	AM 7.15hr	1.45
10.40r	4.5	8.31r	2.20
PM 1.15r	6.31	10.12r	3.10
2.35	8.51	PM 3.2er	5.0
9.30eh	4.37	3.2dr	9.15
11.0dh	7.26	4.11hr	10.45
—	—	8.22	5.0

Sunday Trains.

PM 9.15	4.37	PM 8.21	5.0
—	—	—	—
—	—	—	—

d Saturdays only.
e Saturdays excepted.
h Via Crewe.
n Noon.
r Restaurant Car.
t Tea Car.

MONTGREENAN (Ayr),
396¼ miles. Fares, 80/8a, 48/5c. R. T. for two months, 161/4a, 96/10c. Departures *from* London as for Kilmarnock. Departures *for* London about 3 times daily.
Map Square 40.

MONTON GREEN
(Lancs), 189 miles. Fares, 39/7a, 23/9c. R. T. for two months, 79/2a, 47/6c. Departures *from* London as for Manchester (London Road). Departures *for* London about 6 times daily.

MONTPELIER (Gloucester),
120 miles. Fares, 24/10a, 14/11c. R. T. for two months, 49/8a. Departures *from* London as for Avonmouth Docks. Departures *for* London about 8 times daily. Pop. 6,127.

MONTROSE (Forfar)
from *King's Cross*, 482¼ miles. Fares, 97/6a 58/6c. R. T. for two months, 195/0a, 117/0c. Pop. 12,692.
Map Square 38.

KING'S+	M'TROSE	M'TROSE	KING'S+
AM 4.45	4.23	AM 7.15r	6.15
10.0r	9.4	10.52r	10.0
PM 8.20er	6.30	PM 1.56	3.25
11.25dr10.8		4.41	6.0
11.25er10.15		6.50e	6.50
—	—	7.32	7.5
—	—	8.35	7.25
—	—	—	—
—	—	—	—
—	—	—	—

Sunday Trains.

PM 7.45r	6.30	PM 4.12	6.0
11.25	10.15	—	—
—	—	—	—
—	—	—	—
—	—	—	—

d Saturdays only.
e Saturdays excepted.
r Restaurant Car.

ANOTHER ROUTE from
Euston, 503½ miles. Fares as above.

EUSTON	M'TROSE	M'TROSE	EUSTON
AM 5.0	8.17	AM 7.35r	7.30l
10.0r	9.35	10.55r	10.45l
PM 7.50er	7.5	PM 1.22r	5.0l
11.35e	10.54	8.27	8.0l
—	—	—	—
—	—	—	—

Sunday Trains.

PM 7.50r	7.5	—	—
11.35	10.54	—	—

d Saturdays only.
e Saturdays excepted.
h A.M.
l P.M.
r Restaurant Car.

MONUMENT (City).
Trains to and from *Mansion House, Charing Cross, Victoria, South Kensington, High Street, Praed Street, Baker Street, King's Cross, Moorgate,* and all intermediate Stations every few minutes. Also to and from *Ealing, Hounslow, Richmond* and *Wimbledon.* See p. 489.
Map Square 61, *No.* 3.

MONUMENT LANE
(Warwick), 1¾ miles. Fares, 23/9a, 13/11c. R. T. for two months, 46/4a. Departures *from* London as for Birmingham (New Street). Departures *for* London about 8 times daily.

MONYMUSK (Aberdeen),
543¾ miles. No through fares. Departures *from* London as for Aberdeen. Departures *for* London about 3 times daily. Pop. 968.
Map Square 35.

MOORE (Cheshire) from
Euston, 179¾ miles. Fares, 37/4a, 22/5c. R. T. for two months, 74/8a. Departures *from* London as for Acton Bridge. Departures *for* London about 6 times daily. Pop. 440.
Map Square 12.

MOORGATE STREET
from *Mansion House, Charing Cross, Victoria, South Kensington, High Street, Praed Street, Hammersmith, King's Cross,* and intermediate stations every few minutes. Also to and from *Uxbridge Road* and *Kensington (Addison Road)* about every 12 minutes throughout the day. See back of Map.
Map Square 61. *No.* 2.

ANOTHER ROUTE (City and
South London Tube and Metropolitan Railway, G.N and City).
See p. 489.

MOORHAMPTON
(Hereford), 153¾ miles. Fares, 31/10a, 19/1c. R. T. for two months, 63/8a, 38/2c. Departures *from* London as for Hay. Departures *for* London about 4 times daily.
Map Square 17.

MOORHOUSE (Yorks),
187 miles. No through fares. Departures *from* London as for Cudworth. Departures *for* London about 3 times daily.
Map Square 13.

MOOR ROW (Cumberland),
from *Euston,* 300 miles. Fares, 62/4a, 37/5c. R. T. for two months, 124/8a, 74/10c. Pop. 2,323.
Map Square 6.

EUSTON	M. ROW	M. ROW	EUSTON
AM 2.35	1.12	AM 6.28r	4.15
6.45	4.45	11.30r	7.30
11.35r	7.37	PM 2.30r	10.45
PM 1.30r	10.22	6.30	5.0
9.30e	8.55	—	—

No Sunday Trains.

d Saturdays only.
e Saturdays excepted.
r Restaurant Car.

MOORSIDE (Lancs), 192¼
miles. Fares, 39/7a, 23/9c. R. T. for two months, 79/2a, 47/6c. Departures *from* London as for Manchester. Departures *for* London about 6 times daily.

MOORTHORPE (Yorks),
174¾ miles. Fares, 34/2a, 20/6c. R. T., double fare. Departures *from* London as for Swinton (Yorks). Departures *for* London about 5 times daily.
Map Square 13.

MOORTOWN (Lincoln),
151½ miles. Fares, 31/6a, 18/11c. R.T., double fare. Departures *from* London as for Lincoln or Barnetby. Departures *for* London about 5 times daily.
Map Square 13.
Station closed on Sundays.

MORAR (Inverness), 562½
miles. Fares, 112/8a, 67/7c. R. T. for two months, 225/4a, 135/2c. Departures *from* London as for Fort William. Departures *for* London about twice daily.
Map Square 36.

MORCHARD ROAD
(Devon), 187½ miles. Fares, 36/11a, 22/2c. R. T. for two months, 73/10a, 44/4c. Departures *from* London as for Eggesford. Departures *for* London 5 times daily. Pop. 962.
Map Square 26.

MORCOTT (Rutland)
from *Euston*, 100 miles. Fares, 17/3a, 10/4c. R. T., double fare. Departures *from* London as for Seaton (Rutland). Departures *for* London about 5 times daily. Pop. 392.
Map Square 18.

MORDEN (Surrey) from
London Bridge, 12½ miles. From *Victoria*, 10½ miles. No through fares. Pop. 1,355. *See* p. 577.
Map Square 77.

MOREBATH (Devon)
from *Paddington*, 160¾ miles. Fares, 33/7a, 20/2c. R. T. for two months, 67/2a. Departures *from* London as for Dulverton. Departures *for* London about 4 times daily. Pop. 450.
Map Square 21.

MORECAMBE (Lancs)
from *Euston*, 233¾ miles. Fares, 48/7a, 29/2c. R. T. for two months, 97/2a, 58/4c. Pop. 19,182.
Map Square 7.

Euston	More'be	More'be	Euston
AM12.25	8.10	AM 8. 0*r*	1.45
2.35	9.50	8.30*r*	3.10
5. 0*d*	12.10	10.5*hr*	3.45
5. 0*e*	12.30	10.10*rv*	4.15
6.45	1.25	PM12. 0*t*	6. 0
11.35*r*	4.30	2. 0*r*	7.30
11.50*er*	6. 3	3.15*er*	9. 5
PM 1.30*r*	6.45	3.15*dr*	9.15
2.35*t*	8.25	5.20*r*	10.45
5.20*r*	11. 0	9.15*e*	5. 0
9.30*e*	7.30	9.35*d*	5. 0
11. 0*d*	9.20	—	—
11.50*d*	11.55	—	—

Sunday Trains.

AM11.45*r*	5.30	PM 1.15*r*	7.30
PM 9.15	7.30	9.30	5. 0
—	—	—	—

d Saturdays only.
e Saturdays excepted.
h Mondays and Saturdays only.
r Restaurant Car.
t Tea Car.
v Mondays and Saturdays excepted.

MORECAMBE—*contd.*
ANOTHER ROUTE from
St. Pancras, 263½ miles. Fares as above.

St. Pan.	More'be	More'be	St. Pan.
AM 4.25	1.15	AM 7.48*r*	2.10
9.50*r*	4.30	9.35*r*	5.30
PM12.15*er*	6.45	PM12.50*r*	7.55
12.15*dr*	7.10	2.40*r*	9.15
3.30*r*	10.38	6.40	4.20
5. 0*r*	11.25	—	—
11.50*e*	9. 2	—	—
11.50*d*	9.48	—	—
—	—	—	—
—	—	—	—
—	—	—	—

Sunday Trains.

AM10.50*r*	8.18	AM 8.58	5.27
PM11.45	9. 2	PM 6.25	4.55
—	—	—	—
—	—	—	—
—	—	—	—

d Saturdays only.
e Saturdays excepted.
r Restaurant Car.

Midland Hotel. Excellent family accommodation. Pension terms on application. Situated on foreshore. One of the "Midland Hotels."
ARTHUR TOWLE, Manager.

MORESBY PARKS
(Cumberland), 303½ miles. No through fares. Departures *from* London as for Whitehaven or Moor Row. Departures *for* London about twice daily. Pop. 1,086.
Map Square 6.

MORETON (Cheshire), 203½
miles. No through fares. Departures *from* London as for Hooton. Departures *for* London about 4 times daily. Pop. 970.
Map Square 11.

MORETON (Dorset) from
Waterloo, 129½ miles. Fares, 27/3a, 16/4c. R. T. for two months, 54/6a, 32/8c. Departures *from* London as for Wool. Departures *for* London about 7 times daily. Pop. 341.
Map Square 27.

MORETONHAMP-
STEAD (Devon) from *Paddington*, 199½ miles. Fares, *via* Newton Abbot, 42/6a, 25/6c. R. T. for two months, 85/0a, 51/0c. *Via* Ide, 41/1a, 24/8c. R. T. for two months, 82/2a, 49/4c. Pop. 1,561.
Map Square 26.

Pad.	M'rtnhad.	M'rtnhad.	Pad.
AM 5.30	1.19	AM 7.55*r*	1.30
11.10*r*	4. 2	12. 0*r*	4.35
12. 5*r*	6. 7	PM 1.35*er*	6.50
PM 2. 0*r*	7.25	1.35*dr*	7. 5
4.15*r*	9.52	4.20	9. 0
12. 0*h*	8.37	8.10	7.10
12.30*k*	10.51	—	—

Sunday Trains.

PM 2.40	7.58	AM11.10	7. 5
10. 0	8.37	PM 8.15	3.15
—	—	—	—
—	—	—	—

h Saturdays midnight excepted.
k Saturdays midnight only.
r Restaurant Car.

MORETON-IN-MARSH
(Gloucester) from *Paddington*, 91½ miles. Fares, 19/0a, 11/5c. R. T. for two months, 38/0a. Pop. 1,406.
Map Square 17.

Pad.	Moreton	Moreton	Pad.
AM 5.30	8.54	AM 7.23	9.50
8.50	11. 0	9.54	12. 5
9.45	11.59	11.36	2.12
PM 1.35*r*	3.44	PM12.56*r*	2.55
4.45	6.35	3.47	5.50
6. 5*r*	8. 7	4.22	7.20
6.55	9.38	6.54*r*	9.15
—	—	7.58	10.45
—	—	—	—
—	—	—	—
—	—	—	—

Sunday Trains.

AM10.35	1.11	AM11.42	2.40
PM 4.10	6.56	PM 6.59*r*	9.48
—	—	—	—
—	—	—	—
—	—	—	—

r Restaurant Car.

MORETON-ON-LUGG
(Hereford), 148½ miles. Fares, 30/0a, 18/0c. R. T. for two months, 60/0a, 36/0c. Departures *from* London as for Hereford. Departures *for* London about twice daily. Pop. 79.
Map Square 17.

MORLEY (Yorks), 182½
miles. Fares, 37/9a, 22/8c. R. T., double fare. Departures *from* London as for Wakefield (Westgate). Departures *for* London about 4 times daily. Pop. 23,935.
Map Square 12.

MORMOND (Aberdeen),
562½ miles. No through fares. Departures *from* London as for Fraserburgh. Departures *for* London about 3 times daily.
Map Square 35.

MORNINGTON CRES-
CENT (Hampstead Tube). *See* back of Map.

MORPETH (Northumberland) from *King's Cross*, 284½ miles. Fares, 60/0a, 36/0c. R. T. double fare. Pop. 7,580.
Map Square 3.

King's	+ Morp'h	Morp'h	King's +
AM 4.45	12.46	AM 6.56*r*	1.30
10. 0*r*	4.23	8.35*g*	3.15
11.50*r*	6.15	9.23*r*	4.30
PM 1.50*r*	9.42	11.33*r*	6.30
5.30*kr*	11.48	PM 1.46*r*	9.25
11.25*d*	6.57	3.23	10. 0
11.25*e*	6.54	6.44	3.25
—	—	9.38*e*	5.40
—	—	10.30	6. 0

Sunday Trains.

AM11.30	7.22	AM 8. 7	5.15
PM11.40	6.54	PM 8. 5	5.40
—	—	10.30	6. 0
—	—	—	—

d Saturdays only.
e Saturdays excepted.
g First and Third Class Pullman Cars only.
k Thursdays and Saturdays only.
r Restaurant Car.

MORRISTON (Glamorgan), 199½ miles. No through fares. Departures *from* London as for Swansea. Departures *for* London about 3 times daily. Pop. 10,844.
Map Square 21.

MORTEHOE (Devon)

from *Waterloo*, 223½ miles. Fares, 41/6*a*. 24/11*c*. R. T. for two months, 83/0*a*, 49/10*c*. Pop. 908.
Map Square 21.

W'loo	Mort'ho.	Mort'ho.	W'loo
AM 9. 0*r*	3.28	AM 8.10*r*	1.56
11. 0*r*	4.36	10.20*r*	3.50
PM 1. 0*r*	7.18	PM12.15*r*	6. 0
3. 0	8.20	1. 0	7.40
—	—	1.35*r*	8.30
—	—	3.15	10.50
—	—	4.35*h*	3.58

No Sunday Trains.
h Via Eastleigh
r Restaurant Car.

ANOTHER ROUTE

from *Paddington*, 200½ miles. Fares as above.

Pad.	Mort'ho.	Mort'ho.	Pad.
AM 5.30	2.11	AM 8.10*r*	1.30
9.15	3. 4	9.40	4. 5
PM12. 5*r*	6. 0	11.55*t*	5.30
2. 0*r*	8.23	PM 1.35	10.25
3.30	8.45	2.55*r*	9. 0
12. 0*h*	11. 8	4.35	2.45
—	—	7.33	7.10

Sunday Trains.

PM10. 0	11. 8	—	—
—	—	—	—

h Saturdays midnight excepted.
r Restaurant Car.
t Tea Car.

Woolacombe Bay Hotel (near Ilfracombe). Private grounds (6 acres). Golf Links adjoin. 200 apartments. Electric Light and Lift. Lock-up and open Garages. Apply Manager
See advt. p. **221**.

"Watersmeet" Private Hotel. Garden adjoining beach. Sunny, bracing. Highest reference. Own Car. Electric Light. 'Phone: 3 Woolacombe. Telegrams: "Watersmeet."
Proprietor, J. CHUGG.

Castle Rock. First-class Boarding Establishment. Table d'Hote. Good Winter Quarters. Golf. Private Sitting-rooms. Prospectuses on application to
Proprietor.

Melrose Private Hotel, Woolacombe. Sea Front twenty miles uninterrupted sea view. Spacious Rooms. Separate Tables Minute Sands (Mortehoe Station).
Proprietress.

MORTIMER (Berks)

from *Paddington*, 43¼ miles. Fares, 9/0*a*, 5/5*c*. R. T. for two months, 18/0*a*. Pop. 477.
Map Square 23.

Pad.	Mortim.	Mortim.	Pad.
AM 7.30	8.40	AM 7.57	9. 0
9. 0	10.10	8.20	9.30
9.45	11.27	9.23	10.45
11.20	12.31	9.57	11.35
PM12.30	2. 5	11.41	12.55
1.10*dr*	2.30	PM12.40	1.50
1.35*r*	3.27	1.48	3.20
3.18	5.10	3.25*d*	4.35
4. 8	5.37	3.47	5. 6
5.15	6.30	4.54	6. 2
6. 5	7.11	6.13	7.20
7.30	8.52	7. 3	8.20
9.15	10.33	9.35	10.45
10. 0*h*	11.18	—	—
—	—	—	—

Sunday Trains.

AM 9.10	10.52	AM10.28	1. 5
PM 4.45	6.37	PM12.12	2.40
—	—	8.10	9.48

d Saturdays only.
h Thursdays and Saturdays only.
r Restaurant Car.

MORTLAKE (Surrey)

from *Waterloo*, 8¾ miles. Fares, 1/2*a*, 0/8½*c*. R. T. for two days, 2/4*a*, 1/5*c*. Pop. 19,502. *See* pp. 587-591.
Map Square 67.

MORTON PINKNEY

(Northampton) from *Euston*, 74½ miles. Fares, 15/7*a*, 9/4*c*. R. T. for two months, 31/2*a*. Departures *from* London as for Towcester. Departures *for* London about 3 times daily.
Map Square 18.

MORTON ROAD (Lincoln)

98 miles. Fares, 20/3*a*, 12/2*c*. R. T. for two months, 40/6*a*. Departures *from* London as for Bourne. Departures *for* London about 6 times daily. Pop. (Morton) 839.
Map Square 18.

MOSELEY (Worcester)

116¾ miles. Fares, 23/7*a*, 14/2*c*. R. T. for two months, 47/2*a*, 28/4*c*. Departures *from* London as for Birmingham (New Street). Departures *for* London about 8 times daily. Pop. 24,885.
Map Square 17.

MOSES GATE (Lancs)

195¾ miles. Fares, 40/5*a*, 24/3*c*. R. T. for two months, 80/10*a*, 48/6*c*. Departures *from* London as for Manchester. Departures *for* London about 8 times daily.

MOSS (Denbigh)

185 miles. Fares, 37/7*a*, 22/8*c*. R. T. for two months, 75/2*a*, 45/4*c*. Departures *from* London as for Wrexham. Departures *for* London about 4 times daily.
Map Square 12.

MOSS (Yorks)

163 miles. Fares, 33/11*a*, 20/4*c*. R. T., double fare. Departures *from* London as for Doncaster. Departures *for* London about 5 times daily. Pop. 295.
Map Square 13.

MOSSBANK (Lancs)

193½ miles. No through fares. Departures *from* London as for St. Helens. Departures *for* London about 5 times daily.
Map Square 12.

MOSSEND (Lanark)

390 miles. Fares, 79/5*a*, 47/8*c*. R.T. for two months, 158/10*a*, 95/4*c*. Departures *from* London as for Wishaw (Central). Departures *for* London about 4 times daily.

MOSSLEY (Lancs)

from *Euston*, 188 miles. Fares, 37/9*a*, 22/8*c*. R. T., double fare. Pop. 12,705.
Map Square 12.

Euston	Mossley	Mossley	Euston
AM12.25	7.15	AM 5. 5*dr*	12.20
2.35	9.28	7. 0*er*	12. 5
5. 0	11.16	7.34*r*	12.50
8.45*r*	1.20	8.46*r*	1.15
10.40*r*	3.38	9.12*r*	1.45
12. 0*nr*	5.57	10.12*r*	3.10
PM 1.30*r*	7.19	11.10*r*	3.55
4. 5*r*	8.51	PM12. 7*dr*	5.50
6. 5*r*	10.36	12. 7*er*	6. 0
11.50*d*	8.21	1.12*r*	6.15
—	—	2. 6*r*	7.30
—	—	3.18*r*	8.10
—	—	9.49	5. 0
—	—	—	—
—	—	—	—
—	—	—	—

MOSSLEY—*continued.*

Sunday Trains.

Euston	Mossley	Mossley	Euston
PM12.10*r*	5.33	AM 8.30	4. 0
12.30*r*	9. 4	PM12. 3*r*	5.45
—	—	1.53*r*	7.30
—	—	6.46	5. 0

d Saturdays only.
e Saturdays excepted.
n Noon.
r Restaurant Car.

MOSSLEY HILL (Lancs)

196¾ miles. Fares, 40/10*a*, 24/6*c*. R. T. for two months, 81/8*a*. Departures *from* London as for Runcorn. Departures *for* London about 6 times daily.

MOSS SIDE (Lancs)

220¼ miles. No through fares. Departures *from* London as for Kirkham. Departures *for* London about 6 times daily.
Map Square 12.

MOSSTOWIE (Elgin)

578¼ miles. No through fares. Departures *from* London as for Elgin. Departures *for* London about 3 times daily.
Map Square 35.

MOSTON (Lancs)

191 miles. No through fares. Departures *from* London as for Manchester. Departures *for* London about 6 times daily. Pop. 4,080.
Map Square 12.

MOSTYN (Flint)

199¼ miles. Fares, 41/6*a*, 24/11*c*. R.T. for two months, 83/0*a*. Departures *from* London as for Chester. Departures *for* London about 6 times daily. Pop. 1,762.
Map Square 11.

MOTHERWELL (Lanark)

from *Euston*, 388½ miles. Fares, 79/0*a*, 47/5*c*. R. T. for two months, 158/0*a*, 94/10*c*. Pop. 68,869.
Map Square 40.

Euston.	M'well	M'well	Euston
AM 5. 0	3.37	AM10.19*r*	6.25
6.45	5.42	10.29*r*	7.30
10. 0*r*	5.52	PM 5.19*r*	5. 0
11.35*r*	8.57	9.49	6.55
PM 1.30*r*	10.55	10.50	7.30
9.20	6.31	—	—
11.35*e*	7.48	—	—
11. 0*d*	8. 0	—	—
11.45*e*	11.33	—	—
—	—	—	—

Sunday Trains.

AM11.30*r*	8.20	AM10.21	7.30*l*
PM 9.30	6.55	PM 5.51*r*	5. 0
11.35	7.48	10.50	7.30
11.45	11.34	—	—

d Saturdays only.
e Saturdays excepted.
l P.M.
r Restaurant Car.

MOTTISFONT (Hants)

77½ miles. Fares, 16/3*a*, 9/9*c*. R.T. for two months, 32/6*a*, 19/6*c*. Departures *from* London as for Longparish or Andover Junction. Departures *for* London about times daily. Pop. 559.
Map Square 22.

MOTTRAM (Cheshire), 193¼ miles. Fares, 37/6*a*, 22/6*c*. R. T., double fare. Departures *from* London as for Penistone. Departures *for* London about 5 times daily Pop. 2,882.
Map Square 12.

MOULDSWORTH (Cheshire) from *Euston*, 182 miles. No through fares. Departures *from* London as for Northwich. Departures *for* London about 5 times daily. Pop. 167.
Map Square 12.

MOULTON (Lincoln) from *King's Cross* 97 miles. Fares, 20/3*a*, 12/2*c*. R. T. double fare. Departures *from* London as for Holbeach. Departures *for* London about 5 times daily. Pop. 2,226.
Map Square 18.

MOULTON (Yorks), 229 miles. Fares 20/3*a*, 12/2*c*. R. T. for two months, 40/6*a*, 24/4*c*. Departures *from* London as for Richmond (Yorks). Departures *for* London about 6 times daily. Pop. 232.
Map Square 7.

MOUNTAIN ASH (Glamorgan) from *Paddington*, *via* Cardiff, 172½ miles. Fares, 34/9*a*, 20/10*c*. R. T. for two months, 69/6*a*, 41/8*c*. Pop. 43,292.
Map Square 21.

Pad.	M. Ash	M. Ash	Pad.
AM 1. 0*g*	8.46	AM 6. 9*hr*	10.57
5.30	11.49	8.31*r*	1. 0
8.45*r*	2.16	10.26*r*	4.20
11.50*r*	4. 4	PM12.56*r*	6.15
PM 1.10*r*	6.45	4. 1*r*	8.35
3.35*r*	8.53	4.46*hr*	9.25
6. 0*r*	10.50	9.13	3.30
9.15*eh*	6.44	—	—
—	—	—	—
—	—	—	—
—	—	—	—
—	—	—	—

Sunday Trains.

AM 1. 0	9.17	AM 8.20	3.35
PM12.30*r*	5.35	11.40*r*	8.25
4.30	9.58	PM 8.25	3.30
9.15*h*	6.44	—	—
—	—	—	—

e Saturdays excepted.
g Mondays excepted.
h Passengers cross Cardiff at own expense.
r Restaurant Car.

MOUNT MELVILLE (Fife), 449¾ miles. No through fares. Departures *from* London as for St. Andrews. Departures *for* London about 3 times daily.

MOUNT VERNON (Lanark), 397¼ miles. No through fares. Departures *from* London as for Coatbridge. Departures *for* London about 6 times daily. Pop. 5,014.

MOW COP (Stafford) from *Euston*, 154½ miles. Fares, 32/1*a*, 19/3*c*. R. T. for two months, 64/2*a*. Departures *from* London as for Stoke-on-Trent. Departures *for* London about 5 times daily.
Map Square 12.

MOY (Inverness), 553 miles. Fares, 106/3*a*, 63/9*c*. R. T. for two months, 212/6*a*, 127/6*c*. Departures *from* London as for Aviemore. Departures *for* London about twice daily. Pop. 723.
Map Square 34.

MUCHALLS (Kincardine), 511¼ miles. Fares, 100/0*a*, 60/0*c*. R. T. for two months, 200/0*a*, 120/0*c*. Departures *from* London as for Stonehaven. Departures *for* London about 3 times daily.
Map Square 38.

MUCH WENLOCK (Salop) from *Paddington*, 147½ miles. Fares, 30/8*a*, 18/5*c*. R. T. for two months, 61/4*a*, 36/10*c*. Pop. 13,712.
Map Square 17.

Pad.	M. Wen.	M. Wen.	Pad.
AM 9.10*r*	2.32	AM 7. 5	12.25
10.40*r*	3.45	8.30*r*	1.25
PM 2.10*t*	6.15	11.53*r*	5. 0
4.10*t*	8.27	PM 1.35*t*	5.55
12.15*k*	9.15	3. 0*r*	8. 5
—	—	5.40	10. 0
—	—	—	—
—	—	—	—
—	—	—	—
—	—	—	—
—	—	—	—
—	—	—	—
—	—	—	—

No Sunday Trains.

k Saturdays midnight excepted
r Restaurant Car.
t Tea Car.

MUIREND (Renfrew), 400¾ miles. Fares, 82/6*a*, 49/6*c*. R. T. for two months, 165/0*a*, 99/0*c*. Departures *from* London as for Glasgow (Central). Departures *for* London about 5 times daily.

MUIRKIRK (Ayr), 382¾ miles. Fares, 77/11*a*, 46/9*c*. R. T. for two months, 155/10*a*, 93/6*c*. Departures *from* London as for Old Cumnock. Departures *for* London about 4 times daily. Pop. 4,726.
Map Square 40.

MUIR-OF-ORD (Ross), 580¾ miles. Fares, 106/3*a*, 63/9*c*. R.T. for two months, 212/6*a*, 127/6*c*. Departures *from* London as for Inverness. Departures *for* London about twice daily. Pop. 1,036.
Map Square 34.

MULBEN (Elgin), 594½ miles. No through fares. Departures *from* London as for Keith or Elgin. Departures *for* London about 3 times daily.
Map Square 35.

MULLION (Cornwall). Station at Helston. Distance about 7 miles. Pop. 732.

Poldhu Hotel, Mullion. Largest in the district. Spacious lounge. Grand cliff scenery. Good bathing. Nearest to excellent Golf Links (18 holes). Manageress.

Mullion Cove Hotel. R.A.C.A.A. quarters. Fully Licensed. Electric Light. Excellent Golf. Sanitation perfect. Magnificent Views. Garage. Telephone 8. Manageress.

MUMBLES ROAD (Glamorgan), 201¾ miles. No through fares. Departures *from* London as for Swansea (High Street). Departures *for* London about 4 times daily.
Map Square 21.

MUMBY ROAD (Lincoln) from *King's Cross*, 131 miles. Fares, 27/1*a*, 16/3*c*. R. T., double fare. Departures *from* London as for Sutton-on-Sea. Departures *for* London about 4 times daily. Pop. 285.
Map Square 14.

MUNDESLEY (Norfolk) from *Liverpool Street*, 135¼ miles. Fares, 26/3*a*, 15/9*c*. R. T. for two months, 52/6*a*, 31/6*c*. Pop. 770.
Map Square 14.

L'pl St.	Mund'sy	Mund'sy	L'pl St.
AM 5. 5	10.23	AM 7.33*r*	11.22
8.15*r*	12.22	8.51	1.20
9.50*r*	1.34	PM12.40*r*	3.50
PM12.25*r*	3.24	2.15	6.32
12.33*r*	4.19	3.37*r*	8.33
3.10*r*	6.44	5.25*r*	9.22
5.18*r*	9.20	8.28	2.50
—	—	—	—
—	—	—	—
—	—	—	—

No Sunday Trains.
r Restaurant Car.

ANOTHER ROUTE from *King's Cross*. 166¾ miles. Fares as above.

King's +	Mun'sy	Mun'sy	Kings' +
AM 4.45	10.23	AM 7.33	1. 5
7.15*r*	2. 5	8.45	3.50
10.10*r*	5.24	11.33*r*	4.30
PM 1.50*r*	7.46	PM 2.30	9. 0
3. 0	8. 9	—	—
—	—	—	—
—	—	—	—

No Sunday Trains.
r Restaurant Car.

Grand Hotel. Leading. Finest position, with Sea and Country Views. Nearest Links. Hard Tennis Courts. Ballroom. Billiards. Garage.
See advt. p. **269**.

Clarence Hotel. Beautifully situated. Tennis. Croquet. Billiards. Garage. 'Phone 13.
See advt. p. **270**.

Manor Hotel. First-class. Central position, on cliff. Private Gangway to Beach. A.A. and R.A.C. Phone No. 9. Proprietor, A. J. BEESLEY.

MUNLOCHY (Ross), 588¾ miles. Fares, 106/3*a*, 63/9*c*. R. T. for two months, 212/6*a*, 127/6*c*. Departures *from* London as for Inverness. Departures *for* London about twice daily. Pop. 1,070.
Map Square 34.

MURROW (Cambs), 90¾ miles. Fares, 17/4*a*, 10/5*c*. R. T., double fare. Departures *from* London as for Wisbech St. Mary. Departures *for* London about 4 times daily.
Map Square 18.

MURTHLY (Perth), 460¼ miles. Fares, 93/2*a*, 55/11*c*. R. T. for two months, 186/4*a*, 111/10*c*. Departures *from* London as for Dunkeld. Departures *for* London about 3 times daily. Pop. 823.
Map Square 38.

MUNDESLEY.—MANOR HOTEL. **Phone: No. 9.**

MURTLE (Aberdeen), 527 miles. No through fares. Departures *from* London as for Aberdeen. Departures *for* London about twice daily.
Map Square 38.

MURTON (Durham), 254¼ miles. No through fares. Departures *from* London as for Sunderland or West Hartlepool. Departures *for* London about 6 times daily. Pop. 1,363.
Map Square 7.

MUSGRAVE (Westmorland), 275¼ miles. Fares, 53/1*a*, 31/10*c*. R. T., double fare. Departures *from* London as for Barnard Castle. Departures *for* London about 4 times daily. Pop. 205.
Map Square 7.

MUSSELBURGH (Midlothian), 389 miles. Fares, 81/8*a*, 49/0*c*. R. T. for two months, 163/4*a*, 98/0*c*. Departures *from* London as for Edinburgh (Waverley). Departures *for* London about 4 times daily. Pop. 17,110.
Map Square 41.

MUSWELL HILL from *Moorgate Street, King's Cross,* and *Broad Street* 6½ miles. Fares from King's Cross, 0/11½*a*, 0/9*b*, 0/7*c*. R. T. for two days, 1/11*a*, 1/6*b*, 1/2*c*. From Moorgate Street and Broad Street, 1/0*a*, 0/10*b*, 0/7½*c*. R. T. for two days, 2/1*a*, 1/8*b*, 1/2½*c*. Pop. 11,156. *See* pp. 518-522.
Map Square 50.

MUTHILL (Perth), 439 miles. Fares, 89/4*a*, 53/7*c*. R. T. for two months, 178/8*a*, 107/2*c*. Departures *from* London as for Crieff. Departures *for* London about 3 times daily. Pop. 1,287.
Map Square 37.

MUTLEY (Devon). *See* under PLYMOUTH.

MYTHOLMROYD (Yorks) from *King's Cross,* via Horbury, 198 miles. Fares, 40/10*a*, 24/6*c*. R. T. for two months, 81/8*a*. Pop. 4,159.
Map Square 12.

KING'S +	MYTH'D.	MYTH'D.	KING'S +
AM 4.45	12. 5	AM 5.56	11.30
7.15*r*	1. 1	7.30*r*	1. 5
10.10*r*	4.14	9. 0*r*	1.55
PM 1.30*r*	7.30	9.41	3.50
1.50*r*	9. 9	11.41	5. 0
—	—	PM 2. 2*r*	7.10
—	—	3.56*r*	9.25
—	—	8.46*e*	3.25

Sunday Trains.

12. 0*hn*	7.18	AM 9.25*r*	3.45
—	—	11.31	5.55

e Saturdays excepted.
h Passengers cross Wakefield at own expense.
n Noon.
r Restaurant Car.

IDRIS

SODA WATER
LEMONADE
DRY GINGER ALE
BREWED GINGER
BEER
GINGER ALE

To be obtained at all Clubs, Hotels, Restaurants, Grocers, Wine Merchants, and Chemists.

REFERENCE NOTES.

a	signifies	First Class.
b	,,	Second Class.
c	,,	Third Class.
d	,,	On Saturdays only.
e	,,	Saturdays excepted.
f	,,	On Mondays only.
g	,,	Mondays excepted.
r	,,	Restaurant Car.
t	,,	Tea Car.
x	,,	Express.
R.T.	,,	Return Tickets.

All Trains in the Tables not otherwise marked carry Third Class Passengers.

N

NABURN (Yorks), 184 miles. Fares, 38/2*a*, 22/11*c*. R. T., double fare. Departures *from* London as for Selby. Departures *for* London about 3 times daily. Pop. 541.
Map Square 8.

NAFFERTON (Yorks), 207¼ miles. Fares, 39/5*a*, 23/4*c*. R. T. for two months, 78/10*a*. Departures *from* London as for Driffield. Departures *for* London about 4 times daily. Pop. 1,207.
Map Square 8.

NAILSEA (Somerset), 125½ miles. Fares, 26/1*a*, 15/8*c*. R. T. for two months, 52/2*a*. Departures *from* London as for Bristol. Departures *for* London about 5 times daily. Pop. 1,866.
Map Square 22.

NAILSWORTH (Gloucester), 125½ miles. No through fares. Departures *from* London as for Stroud. Departures *for* London about 5 times daily. Pop. 3,148.
Map Square 22.

NAIRN from *Euston*, 578¾ miles. Fares, 106/3*a*, 63/9*c*. R. T. for two months, 212/6*a*, 127/6*c*. Pop. 5,622.
Map Square 34.

EUSTON	NAIRN	NAIRN	EUSTON
PM 1.30*ekr*	7. 5	AM 7.30*r*	10.45
7.30*erv*	9. 2*h*	9.42*r*	5. 0*h*
7.40*er*	9.42*h*	PM 2.32	7.40*h*
11.35*e*	4. 6*l*	8.34*ekr*	7.30*l*

Sunday Trains.

PM 7.50*r*	10.11*h*	—	—
11.35	4. 6*l*	—	—

e Saturdays excepted.
h A.M.
k Via Inverness.
l P.M.
r Restaurant Car.
v Commences July 27.

ANOTHER ROUTE from *King's Cross*, 568¾ miles. Fares as above.

KING'S +	NAIRN	NAIRN	KING'S +
AM 4.45	8.34*h*	AM 7.30*r*	10. 0*h*
11.50*er*	7. 5*k*	9.42	3.25*l*
PM 7.40*er*	9.42*k*	PM 2.32	7. 5*k*
11.25	4. 6*h*	8.34*er*	6.30*h*

Sunday Trains.

PM 7.45*r*	10.11	—	—
11.25	4. 6	—	—

e Saturdays excepted.
h P.M.   *k* A.M.
r Restaurant Car.

NANCEGOLLAN (Cornwall) from *Paddington*, 299½ miles. Fares, 61/11*a*, 37/2*c*. R. T. for two months, 123/10*a*, 74/4*c*. Departures *from* London as for Helston. Departures *for* London about 4 times daily.
Map Square 25.

NANNERCH (Flint), 198¾ miles. Fares, 40/7*a*, 24/4*c*. R. T. for two months, 81/2*a*, 48/8*c*. Departures *from* London as for Mold. Departures *for* London about 4 times daily. Pop. 300.
Map Square 11.

NANTCLWYD (Denbigh), 200½ miles. Fares, 40/7*a*, 24/4*c*. R.T. for two months, 81/2*a*, 48/8*c*. Departures *from* London as for Corwen or Ruthin. Departures *for* London about 3 times daily.
Map Square 11.

NANTGAREDIG (Carmarthen), from *Paddington*, 225½ miles. No through fares. Departures *from* London as for Carmarthen or Llandilo. Departures *for* London about 3 times daily.
Map Square 21.

NANTLLE (Flint), 255¾ miles. Fares, 53/2*a*, 31/11*c*. R.T. for two months, 106/4*a*, 63/10*c*. Departures *from* London as for Carnarvon. Departures *for* London about 4 times daily.
Map Square 11.

NANTWICH (Cheshire) from *Euston*, 161½ miles. Fares, 32/11*a*, 19/9*c*. R. T. for two months, 65/10*a*. Pop. 7,296.
Map Square 12.

Euston	Nantw'h.	Nantw'h.	Euston
AM 2.35	6.33	AM 8.40*er*	12. 5
5. 0	9.49	8.40*dr*	12.20
8.30*r*	12.21	10. 8*r*	1.45
10.30*dr*	1.52	10.52*r*	3.10
11.50*r*	3.25	11.58*h*	3.45
12. 0*nr*	4.37	11.58*r*	4.15
PM 1.30*r*	5.15	PM12.45*t*	5.35
2.35*t*	6. 2	1.11*er*	5.50
4. 5*r*	7.45	2.10*dr*	5.50
5.20*r*	9.14	2.50*r*	6.25
6.30*er*	10.27	3.31*r*	7.30
9.30	2.13	4.30*r*	8.10
11.50*d*	7. 9	5.28*er*	9. 5
—	—	5.28*dr*	9.15
—	—	7. 4*r*	10.45
—	—	10.46	5. 0
—	—	—	—
—	—	—	—
—	—	—	—
—	—	—	—
—	—	—	—
—	—	—	—

Sunday Trains.

PM 9.15	2.13	AM 7.35*r*	1.30
—	—	9.51	4. 0
—	—	PM 1.30*r*	5.45
—	—	10.37	5. 0
—	—	—	—
—	—	—	—
—	—	—	—
—	—	—	—
—	—	—	—
—	—	—	—

d Saturdays only.
e Saturdays excepted.
h Mondays and Saturdays only.
n Noon.
r Restaurant Car.
t Tea Car.

NANTYBWCH (Monmouth), 174 miles. Fares, 34/0*a*, 20/5*c*. R.T. for two months, 68/0*a*, 40/10*c*. Departures *from* London as for Abergavenny. Departures *for* London about 6 times daily.
Map Square 21.

NANTYDERRY (Monmouth), 154 miles. Fares, 32/1*a*, 19/3*c*. R. T. for two months, 64/2*a*, 38/6*c*. Departures *from* London as for Pontypool Road. Departures *for* London about 4 times daily.
Map Square 22.

NANTYFFYLLON (Glamorgan), 182¼ miles. Fares, 38/1*a*, 22/10*c*. R.T. for two months, 76/2*a*. Departures *from* London as for Maesteg. Departures *for* London about 4 times daily. Pop. 5,795.

NANTYGLO (Monmouth), from *Paddington*, 162 miles. Fares, 33/6*a*, 20/1*c*. R. T. for two months, 67/0*a*. Departures *from* London as for Aberbeeg. Departures *for* London about 7 times daily. Pop. 15,395.

NANTYMOEL (Glamorgan) 183¼ miles. Fares, 38/2*a*, 22/11*c*. R.T. for two months, 76/4*a*, 45/10*c*. Departures *from* London as for Tondu. Departures *for* London about 5 times daily. Pop. 5,498.

NANTYRONEN (Cardigan), 246 miles. No through fares. Departures *from* London as for Aberystwyth. Departures *for* London about 3 times daily.
Map Square 16.

NAPSBURY (Herts) from *St. Pancras*, 18 miles. Fares, 3/9*a*, 2/3*c*. R. T., double fare. *See* pp. 507, 508.
Map Square 23.

NAPTON (Warwick) from *Euston*, 83 miles. Fares, 16/11*a*, 10/2*c*. R. T. for two months, 33/10*a*. Departures *from* London as for Braunston. Departures *for* London about 4 times daily. Pop. 847.
Map Square 18.

NARBERTH (Pembroke), 246½ miles. Fares, 50/0*a*, 30/0*c*. R. T. for two months, 100/0*a*. Departures *from* London as for Tenby. Departures *for* London about 5 times daily. Pop. 1,140.
Map Square 20.

NARBOROUGH (Leicester) from *Euston*, 108¾ miles. Fares, 20/2*a*, 12/1*c*. R. T., double fare. Departures *from* London as for Hinckley. Departures *for* London about 9 times daily. Pop. 1,839.
Map Square 18.

NARBOROUGH (Norfolk) from *Liverpool Street*, 105 miles. Fares, 21/11*a*, 13/2*c*. R. T. for two months, 43/10*a*. Departures *from* London as for Swaffham (*via* Kings Lynn). Departures *for* London about 7 times daily. Pop. 336.
Map Square 19.

NASSINGTON (Northampton), 83½ miles. Fares, 17/4*a*, 10/5*c*. R. T. for two months, 34/8*a*, 20/10*c*. Departures *from* London as for Peterboro'. Departures *for* London about 3 times daily. Pop. 517.
Map Square 18.

NASTHYDE (Herts) from *King's Cross*, 19¾ miles. Fares, 4/0*a*, 2/5*c*. R. T. for two months, 8/0*a*, 4/10*c*. Departures *from* London as for St. Albans. Departures *for* London about 12 times daily.
Map Square 23.

NATEBY (Lancs), 222¼ miles. Fares, 46/5*a*, 27/10*c*. R.T. for two months, 92/10*a*, 55/8*c*. Departures *from* London as for Preston. Departures *for* London about 4 times daily. Pop. 292.
Map Square 7.

NAVENBY (Lincoln), 121¼ miles. Fares, 25/0*a*, 15/0*c*. R. T., double fare. Departures *from* London as for Lincoln. Departures *for* London about 5 times daily. Pop. 796.
Map Square 13.

NAWORTH (Cumberland), 311½ miles. Fares, 60/10*a*, 36/6*c*. R.T. for two months, 121/8*a*, 73/0*c*. Departures *from* London as for Hexham or Carlisle. Departures *for* London about 6 times daily.
Map Square 3.

NAWTON (Yorks), 222¼ miles. Fares, 46/5*a*, 27/10*c*. R.T., double fare. Departures *from* London as for Ampleforth. Departures *for* London about 4 times daily. Pop. 336.
Map Square 8.

NEASDEN KINGSBURY (Middlesex) from *Baker Street*, 5¾ miles. Fares, 0/11½*a*, 0/7*c*. R. T. for two days, 1/9*a*, 1/2*c*. Pop. 2,074 *See* back of Map.
Map Square 50.

NEATH (Glamorgan) from *Paddington*, 190¾ miles. Fares, 39/9*a*, 23/10*c*. R.T. for two months, 79/6*a*, 47/8*c*. Pop. 18,936.
Map Square 21.

Pad.	Neath	Neath	Pad.
AM 1. 0*g*	7. 4	AM 8.53*r*	1. 0
5.30	11.30	10. 7*r*	2.30
8.45*r*	1.38	PM12.20*r*	4.20
11.50*r*	3.55	2. 3*r*	6.15
PM 1.10*r*	5.59	3.57*r*	8.35
3.35*r*	7.39	5. 2*r*	9.25
6. 0*r*	10.23	9.26	3.30
8. 0*r*	11.54	—	—
9.15	3.52	—	—
—	—	—	—
—	—	—	—
—	—	—	—
—	—	—	—
—	—	—	—

Sunday Trains.

AM 1. 0	7.41	AM 9.28	3.35
PM12.30*r*	5.43	10.50	4. 5
4.30	9.57	PM 3.24*r*	8.25
9.15	3.52	9.26	3.30
—	—	—	—

g Mondays excepted.
r Restaurant Car.

NEEDHAM (Suffolk)

from *Liverpool Street*, 77¼ miles. Fares, 16/3*a*, 9/9*c*. R. T. for two months, 32/6*a*. Pop. 1,313.

Map Square 19.

L'PL. ST.	NEEDH'M	NEEDH'M	L'PL. ST.
AM 5. 0	7. 7	AM 8.17*r*	10.30
8.15*r*	10.32	9.10*r*	11.22
10.12	12.27	10.10	12.39
10.20	12.38	11.54*r*	2. 3
PM 12.33*r*	2.41	PM 12.49	3.36
1. 0	4.42	2.46*r*	4.58
1.33*d*	4.42	3.33	5.55
3.10*r*	5. 7	4.10	6.32
3.26	6.32	5.21	7.51
5.18*r*	7.29	6.16*r*	9.22
5.42	8.34	8.30	11.16
7.45*r*	10.11	—	—
—	—	—	—
—	—	—	—
—	—	—	—
—	—	—	—
—	—	—	—
—	—	—	—
—	—	—	—
—	—	—	—

Sunday Trains.

AM 9.20*r*	11.49	AM 8.48	11.38
11.30*r*	2.44	PM 2.39	7.10
PM 4.40	6.45	6.54*r*	9.10
—	—	7.51	10.15
—	—	—	—
—	—	—	—
—	—	—	—
—	—	—	—
—	—	—	—

d Saturdays only.
e Saturdays excepted.
r Restaurant Car.

NEEN SOLLARS (Salop)

143 miles. Fares, 28/4*a*, 17/0*c*. R. T. for two months, 56/8*a*, 34/0*c*. Departures *from* London as for Cleobury Mortimer. Departures *for* London about 5 times daily. Pop. 205.

Map Square 17.

NEEPSEND (Yorks)

163 miles. Fares, 32/11*a*, 19/9*c*. R. T., double fare. Departures *from* London as for Sheffield (Victoria). Departures *for* London about 4 times daily. Pop. 16,903.

Map Square 12.

NEILSTON (Renfrew)

405 miles. Fares, 82/6*a*, 49/6*c*. R. T. for two months, 165/0*a*, 99/0*c*. Departures *from* London as for Kilmarnock Departures *for* London about 4 times daily. Pop. 15,263.

Map Square 40.

NELSON (Glamorgan)

158¼ miles. No through fares. Departures *from* London as for Pontypridd. Departures *for* London about 7 times daily.

NELSON (Lancs)

218¼ miles. Fares, 42/4*a*, 25/5*c*. R. T. for two months, 84/8*a*. Departures *from* London as for Burnley or Colne. Departures *for* London about 6 times daily. Pop. 39,839.

Map Square 12.

NELSON AND LLANCAIACH (Glamorgan)

from *Paddington*, 162¾ miles, Fares, 33/7*a*, 20/2*c*. R. T. for two months, 67/2*a*, 40/4*c*.

Map Square 21.

PAD.	NELSON	NELSON	PAD.
AM 1. 0*g*	8.26	AM 8.35*r*	1. 0
5.30	11.39	9.10*r*	2.30
8.45*r*	2. 6	PM 12.30*r*	4.20
9. 0	3. 3	1.21*r*	6.15
11.50*hr*	4.25	2.56*r*	8.35
11.50*r*	5.34	5.11*r*	9.25
PM 1.10*r*	7. 4	7.26	3.30
3.35*r*	8.21	10.40*k*	7.10
6. 0*kr*	10.22	—	—
8. 0*dr*	8.57	—	—
—	—	—	—

Sunday Trains.

PM 12.30*r*	7.32	AM 10.28	8.10
9.15	8.26	PM 8.48	3.30
—	—	—	—
—	—	—	—

d Saturdays only.
g Mondays excepted.
h Fridays only.
k Thursdays and Saturdays only.
r Restaurant Car.

NESSCLIFF (Salop)

164½ miles. No through fares. Departures *from* London as for Oswestry. Departures *for* London about 3 times daily.

Map Square 17.

NESTON (Cheshire)

190¾ miles. Fares, 39/10*a*, 23/11*c*. R. T. for two months, 79/8*a*. Departures *from* London as for Hooton. Departures *for* London about 8 times daily.

Map Square 12.

NESTON AND PARKGATE (Cheshire)

202½ miles. No through fares. Departures *from* London as for Wrexham. Departures *for* London about 6 times daily. Pop. 5,191.

Map Square 12.

NETHERBURN (Lanark)

393¾ miles. No through fares. Departures *from* London as for Hamilton. Departures *for* London about 4 times daily.

Map Square 40.

NETHERCLEUGH

(Dumfries), 327½ miles. No through fares. Departures *from* London as for Lockerbie. Departures *for* London about 3 times daily.

Map Square 44.

NETHERFIELD (Notts)

from *King's Cross*, 125¼ miles. Fares, 25/8*a*, 15/5*c*. R. T. for two months, 51/4*a*, 30/10*c*. Departures *from* London as for Bottesford. Departures *for* London about 4 times daily. Pop. 6,386.

Map Square 13.

NETHERTON (Yorks)

188 miles. Fares, 38/2*a*, 22/11*c*. R. T. for two months, 76/4*a*, 45/10*c*. Departures *from* London as for Lockwood. Departures *for* London about 4 times daily.

NETHERTOWN (Cumberland)

296 miles. No through fares. Departures *from* London as for Sellafield. Departures *for* London about 4 times daily.

Map Square 6.

NETHY BRIDGE (Inverness)

543¼ miles. Fares, 106/3*a*, 63/9*c*. R. T. for two months, 212/6*a*, 127/6*c*. Departures *from* London as for Aviemore or Keith (*via* Aberdeen). Departures *for* London about twice daily. Pop. 329.

Map Square 34.

NETLEY (Hants)

from *Waterloo, via* St. Denys, 80¼ miles. Fares, 17/1*a*, 10/3*c*. R. T. for two months, 34/2*a*, 20/6*c*. Pop. 1,409.

Map Square 28.

W'LOO.	NETLEY	NETLEY	W'LOO.
AM 5.40	8.50	AM 7. 7	10.20
5.50	9.25	8.23*s*	11. 0
8.30*s*	11. 6	9.20	12. 0
9.30	12.17	10.34*r*	12.50
11.30*r*	2.13	PM 1.16	4.20
PM 12.30*r*	2.59	2.58	6.16
1.30*s*	4.28	5.17*r*	8.20
2.30	5.25	6.41*r*	8.50
3.30*s*	6.27	8.14	11.28
5.30*r*	8. 6	10. 5	3.58
6.30*r*	9. 5	—	—
7.30	9.56	—	—
—	—	—	—
—	—	—	—

Sunday Trains.

AM 11. 0*r*	1.52	AM 9.30	12.11
12. 0*nr*	3.37	10 6*r*	2.16
PM 7. 0*hr*	9.39	PM 2. 0*r*	6. 7
—	—	4.30	8. 3
—	—	7. 7*r*	10.52
—	—	—	—
—	—	—	—

h Via Southampton West.
n Noon.
r Restaurant Car.
s Refreshments served.

NEWARK (Notts)

from *King's Cross*, 120 miles. Fares, 25/0*a*, 15/0*c*. R. T., double fare. Pop. 16,957.

Map Square 13.

KING'S +	NEWARK	NEWARK	KING'S +
AM 4.45	7.21	AM 7.50	10.40
5. 5	9. 6	9. 3*r*	11.30
8.45	11.39	10.36	1. 5
10.10*r*	12.48	11.43*kr*	1.55
11.30	2.50	PM 12.54	3.50
PM 1.50*r*	4.38	3. 8	6.25
4. 0*r*	6.28	3.36*r*	6.30
5.45*r*	8.18	5.56*r*	9. 0
8.25	11.17	12.36	3.25
—	—	—	—
—	—	—	—
—	—	—	—
—	—	—	—
—	—	—	—
—	—	—	—
—	—	—	—
—	—	—	—
—	—	—	—
—	—	—	—

Sunday Trains.

AM 8.30	12.51	PM 12.56*r*	3.45
12. 0*r*	2.47	3. 5*r*	5.55
PM 5. 0*r*	7.43	3.41	8. 8
8.25	11.17	7.32*r*	10.20
—	—	—	—
—	—	—	—
—	—	—	—
—	—	—	—

k Wednesdays only.
r Restaurant Car.

NEW BASFORD (Notts)

from *Marylebone*, 128 miles. Fares, 26/9*a*, 15/7*c*. R. T., double fare. Pop. .
Map Square 13.

M'BONE.	N.B'FORD	N.B'FORD.	M'BONE
AM 2.32	5.50	AM 6.58	10.36
10. 0*r*	1.31	7.59*r*	11.10
PM12.15*r*	3.22	10. 8*r*	1.13
3.20*r*	6.23	11.44*r*	3. 0
5. 0*r*	7.55	PM 4. 2*r*	6.38
—	—	4.49*r*	8.55
—	—	6.56*r*	9.55
—	—	8. 6	3.57
—	—	—	—
—	—	—	—
—	—	—	—
—	—	—	—
—	—	—	—
—	—	—	—
—	—	—	—

Sunday Trains.

AM11.15*r*	3.10	PM 1.44*r*	5.40
—	—	7.19*r*	10.24
—	—	—	—
—	—	—	—
—	—	—	—

r Restaurant Car.

NEW BECKENHAM

(Kent). *See* BECKENHAM, NEW.

NEWBIGGIN (Northum-

berland), 289¼ miles. Fares, 61/1*a*, 36/8*c*. R. T. for two months, 122/2*a*, 73/4*c*. Departures *from* London as for Newcastle-on-Tyne. Departures *for* London about 6 times daily. Pop. 6,806.
Map Square 3.

NEW BIGGIN (Westmor-

land), from *St. Pancras*, 283½ miles. Fares, 55/8*a*, 33/5*c*. R. T., double fare. Departures *from* London as for Appleby. Departures *for* London about 5 times daily. Pop. 139.
Map Square 7.

NEWBIGGING (Lanark),

376½ miles. No through fares. Departures *from* London as for Carstairs. Departures *for* London about 3 times daily.
Map Square 40.

NEW BOLINGBROKE

(Lincoln), 129 miles. Fares, 26/3*a*, 15/9*c*. R. T. for two months, 52/6*a*, 31/6*c*. Departures *from* London as for Midville. Departures *for* London about 5 times daily. Pop. 337.
Map Square 13.

NEWBRIDGE (Mon-

mouth) from *Paddington*, 152½ miles. Fares, 31/10*a*, 19/1*c*. R. T. for two months, 63/8*a*. Departures *from* London s for Risca. Departures *for* London about 7 times daily.
Map Square 21.

NEWBRIDGE-ON-WYE

(Radnor), 190½ miles. Fares, *via* Welshpool, 41/5*a*, 24/10*c*. R. T. for two months, 82/10*a*. Departures *from* London as for Llanidloes. Departures *for* London about 3 times daily. Pop. 623.
Map Square 16.

NEW BRIGHTON

(Cheshire), 207½ miles. No through fares. Departures *from* London as for Birkenhead or Hooton. Departures *for* London about 8 times daily. Pop 7,871.
Map Square 12.

NEWBURGH (Fife), 439½

miles. Fares, 89/0*a*, 53/5*c*. R. T. for two months, 178/0*a*, 106/10*c*. Departures *from* London as for Leuchars. Departures *for* London about 3 times daily. Pop. 1,992.
Map Square 38.

NEWBURN (Northumber-

land), 276 miles. Fares, 57/9*a*, 34/8*c*. R. T., double fare. Departures *from* London as for Newcastle-on-Tyne. Departures *for* London about 6 times daily. Pop. 18,826.
Map Square 3.

NEWBURY (Berks) from

Paddington, 53 miles. Fares, 11/1*a*, 6/8*c*. R. T. for two months, 22/2*a*. Pop. 12,290.
Map Square 28.

PAD.	NEWB'Y	NEWB'Y.	PAD.
AM 6.30	8.31	AM 7.55	9.30
7.30	8.51	8.47	10. 0
8.45*r*	10.10	9.10	10.45
9.30	10.58	9.49	10.52
10.45	12.13	11.44	12.55
11.20	1.30	12. 0	1.50
PM12.30*r*	1.42	PM 1. 0	2.30
1.10*r*	2.46	1.32	2.50
1.35*r*	3.41	2. 2	3.50
2.45	3.54	3. 0	4.35*j*
3.18	5.16	4. 9	5.50
4. 7	6. 4	5. 9	7.20
5. 5	6.21	7.14*r*	8.20
5.55	6.58	7.31	9.15
6.30	7.39	8.15	10.25
8. 0	9.23	9. 3	10.45
10. 0*f*	11.36	10.22	2.45
—	—	—	—
—	—	—	—
—	—	—	—

Sunday Trains.

AM 9.10	10.52	AM 8.51	10.50
PM 5.15	7.11	PM 7.37	9.15
—	—	—	—
—	—	—	—

f Wednesdays and Saturdays only.
r Restaurant Car.

Taxi Cabs can be hired to meet any train at this Station by letter, or telephone No. 158. Messrs. Martin & Chillingworth, The Broadway, Newbury.

Chequer's Hotel. Telephone 267. Headquarters for Newbury Races and Hunting. Electric Light. Garage and Stabling. First-class hotel accommodation. TRUST HOUSES, Ltd.

Jack o' Newbury Hotel. First-class Family and Commercial. Oldest established in the county. R.A.C., A.A., and M.U. House Telephone 32. Telegrams: "Jack."

Queen's Hotel, Family and Commercial. Most Central Position. Stock Rooms. Under New Management. Garage. Stabling. 'Phone 47. Telegrams, Queen's Hotel.

NEWBURY PARK from

Liverpool Street, 9¼ miles, or from *Fenchurch Street*, 9¼ miles. Fares, *via* Ilford, from Liverpool Street, 1/3*a*, 1/0*b*, 0/9*c*. R.T. for two days, 2/6*a*. 1/11*b*, 1/4*c*. From Fenchurch Street, 1/3*a*, 1/1*b*, 0/9*c*. R. T. for two days, 2/6*a*, 1/11*b*, 1/4*c*. See p. 536.

NEWBY WISKE (Yorks),

229½ miles. No through fares. Departures *from* London as for Ripon. Departures *for* London about 3 times daily. Pop. 192.
Map Square 7.

NEWCASTLE EMLYN

(Carmarthen) from *Paddington*, 253 miles. Fares, 51/3*a*, 30/9*c*. R. T. for two months, 102/6*a*, 61/6*c*. Pop. 851.
Map Square 16.

PAD.	N. EM.	PAD.	N. EM.
AM 1. 0*g*	11.43	AM 8. 5*r*	4.20
8.45*r*	3.48	10.10*r*	6.15
11.50*r*	7.25	PM 2.20*r*	9.25
PM 9.15*e*	7.18	6. 0	3.30
—	—	—	—
—	—	—	—

Sunday Trains.

PM 9.15	7.18	—	—
—	—	—	—
—	—	—	—

e Saturdays excepted.
g Mondays excepted.
r Restaurant Car.

NEWCASTLE-ON-

TYNE (Northumberland) from *King's Cross*, 268 miles. Fares, 56/6*a*, 33/11*c*. R. T., double fare. Pop. 274,955.
Map Square 3.

KING'S+	NEWC.	NEWC.	KING'S+
AM 4.45	11.10	AM 1.14	6.50
7.15*r*	2.49	1.30	7. 5
9.50*r*	3.18	1.47*f*	7.25
10.10*r*	5.15	8. 0*r*	1.30
11.15*g*	5. 0	9.20*g*	3.15
11.50*r*	5.33	10.20*r*	4.30
PM 1.15*r*	6.50	PM12.10*r*	6.15
1.50*r*	8.20	12.54*r*	6.30
5.30*r*	10.50	2.45*r*	9.25
5.35*r*	11.37	4.24	10. 0
7.45*er*	1. 6	8. 3	3.25
8.20*e*	1.33	10.53*e*	5.40
8.25	3. 5	11.10	6. 0
10.45*e*	5.11	—	—
10.45*d*	5.53	—	—
11.25	4.43	—	—
11.40	4.59	—	—

Sunday Trains.

AM 8.30	5.32	AM 1.30	7. 5
11.30*r*	5.45	1.47	7.25
PM 5. 0*r*	11.55	10.10	5.15
7.45	1. 6	PM 2. 5*r*	8.15
8.25	3. 5	10.53	5.40
10.45	5.11	11.10	6. 0
11.25	4.43	—	—
11.40	4.59	—	—

d Saturdays only.
e Saturdays excepted.
f Mondays excepted.
g First and Third Class Pullman Cars only.
r Restaurant Car.

Central Station Hotel, adjoins Station. Thoroughly up-to-date. Every Comfort. Owned and managed by London and North Eastern Railway Company. Grill Room on the platform. *See* advt. p. 270.

NEWCASTLE-ON-TYNE— *continued.*

St. Margaret's Hotel,
Osborne Road. Pleasantly situated. In fashionable suburb of Newcastle. Garden. Billiards. Special Residential Terms. Telephone (Jesmond), 453. Take No. 7 car.

Imperial Hotel, Jesmond Road, Newcastle. Cars to and from Central Station every few minutes. Nat. Tel. 343. Residential Terms on application.

Lancashire and Cheshire Insurance Corporation, Ltd., 2 and 4, Grey Street. Tel. 1550 Central. *See* advt. p. 3 cover.

Norwich Union Mutual, the Outstanding British Life Office. Reserves at 2½ per cent. 1, Mosley Street, Newcastle. *See* advt. cover p. 6.

NEWCASTLETON
(Roxburgh), 323¾ miles. Fares, 65/8a, 39/5c. R. T. for two months, 131/4a. Departures *from* London as for Carlisle. Departures *for* London about 3 times daily. Pop. 867.
Map Square 44.

NEWCASTLE-UNDER-LYME (Stafford) from *Euston,* 147¾ miles. Fares, 30/8a, 18/5c. R. T. for two months, 61/4a. Pop. 20,418.
Map Square 12.

Euston	Newc.		Newc.	Euston
AM 2.35	8. 7	AM	6.25	11. 0
5. 0	10. 8		8.27er	12. 5
8.45r	12. 5		8.27d	12.20
10.40dr	2.47		9.22r	12.50
10.40er	3.13		10.45r	2.20
12. 0nr	4.36		11.25dr	3.10
PM 2.50t	5.54	PM	12.56r	3.55
4.45r	8.16		2.54er	6.15
6.30er	10.23		5. 2r	9.20
6.55r	11.16		6.19	10. 0
—	—		9. 2er	5. 0
—	—		10.40d	5.45
—	—		11.23e	5.40
—	—		—	—
—	—		—	—

Sunday Trains.

AM12.10	11.11	AM	11. 0	4. 0
PM12.10r	7.31	PM	2.26	8.55
—	—		8.12	5. 0
—	—		—	—

d Saturdays only.
e Saturdays excepted.
n Noon.
r Restaurant Car.

NEWCHAPEL (Stafford),
152 miles. Fares, 31/6a, 18/11c. R. T. for two months, 63/0a, 37/10c. Departures *from* London as for Burslem. Departures *for* London about 6 times daily. Pop. 3,911.
Map Square 12.

NEWCHURCH (Isle of Wight), 87¼ miles. Fares, 19/7a, 12/0c. R. T. for two months, 39/2a, 24/0c. Departures *from* London as for Sandown. Departures *for* London about 4 times daily. Pop. 751.
Map Square 28.

NEW CLEE (Lincoln), 156¼ miles. Fares, 32/6a, 19/6c. R. T., double fare. Departures *from* London as for Cleethorpes. Departures *for* London about 4 times daily. Pop. 14,489.
Map Square 13.

NEW CROSS (S. E. & C.R.) from *Charing Cross, Cannon Street,* and *London Bridge,* 5½ miles. Fares, from Charing Cross, 1/0a, 0/9½b, 0/7c. R. T. for two days, 2/0a, 1/4b, 1/2c. From Cannon Street, 0/7½a, 0/6b, 0/4½c. R. T. for two days, 1/3a, 1/0b, 0/9c. *See* pp. 544-557.

NEW CROSS GATE (London) (L.B. & S.C.R.) from *London Bridge,* 2½ miles. Fares, 0/7½a, 0/4½c. R. T. for two days, 1/3a, 0/9c. Fares from Victoria (Crystal Palace line), 1/6d, 0/10½c. R. T. for two days, 3/0a, 1/9c. *Via* Norwood Junction, 1/11a, 1/2c. R. T. for eight days, 3/10a, 2/0c. *Via* South London Line, 0/10a, 0/6c. R. T. for two days, 1/8a, 0/10½c. *See* pp. 568-570, 580, 581.
Map Square 71.

ANOTHER ROUTE (L.B. & S.C.R. or S.E. & C.R.), from *Hammersmith, Paddington (Bishop's Road), Baker Street, King's Cross* and *Liverpool Street (Met.),* 12¾ miles. Fares from Hammersmith, 1/3a, 0/9c. R. T., 2/4a, 1/5½c. From Paddington, 1/3a, 0/9c. R. T., 2/2½a, 1/5½c. From Baker Street, 1/1a, 0/8c. R. T., 2/2a, 1/4c. From King's Cross, 0/11½a, 0/7c. R. T., 1/11a, 1/2c. From Liverpool Street, 0/8a, 0/5c. R. T., 1/4a, 0/10c. *See* back of Map.

NEW CUMNOCK
(Ayr), 365 miles. Fares, 75/2a, 45/1c. R. T. for two months, 150/4a, 90/2c. Departures *from* London as for Thornhill (Dumfries). Departures *for* London about 4 times daily. Pop. 6,281.
Map Square 43.

NEWENT (Glo'ster), 124 miles. Fares, 25/10a, 15/6c. R. T. for two months, 51/8a. Departures *from* London as for Ledbury. Departures *for* London about 5 times daily. Pop. 2,485.
Map Square 17.

NEW GALLOWAY
(Kirkcudbright), 361 miles. Fares, 68/9a, 41/3c. R.T. for two months, 137/6a, 82/6c. Departures *from* London as for Castle Douglas. Departures *for* London about 3 times daily. Pop. 348.
Map Square 43.

NEW HAILES (Midlothian), 387½ miles. No through fares. Departures *from* London as for Dunbar. Departures *for* London about 6 times daily.

NEWHAM (Northumberland), 315 miles. No through fares. Departures *from* London as for Morpeth. Departures *for* London about 5 times daily. Pop. 158.
Map Square 3.

NEWHAVEN (Sussex)
from *London Bridge,* and *Victoria,* 56 miles. Fares (Town), 11/8a, 7/0c. R.T. for two months, 23/4a, 14/0c. Harbour, 11/10a, 7/1c. R.T. for two months, 23/8a, 14/2c. Pop. 6,496.
Map Square 28.

	Leave		Arr. at
	Vict.	Lon. B.	Town.	Harb'r
AM —	6.15	8. 6	8. 8
6.37k	6.40k	9.34	9.36
7.23	7.25	10. 8	10.10
9. 0	—	11. 0	11. 2
9.45	—	11.41	11.43
10. 5	9.50	12. 8	12.10
11.15	—	12.59	1. 1
11.55	—	1.34	1.36
12. 0	12.10	2. 9	2.11
PM 1.20e	2. 0e	3.35	3.37
1.25d	2. 0d	3.35	3.37
2. 0	2. 5	4.36	4.38
3.20	—	4.59	5. 1
3.40k	4. 5	5.45	5.47
4.30	5. 5	6.24	6.26
5.20	—	6.46	6.48
5.35k	—	7.29	7.31
5.45e	5.55e	7.29	7.31
6.40	6. 0d	8. 6	8. 8
6.50	7. 0	9.14	9.16
8.35	—	10. 6	10. 8
10. 0	—	11.54	—
—	—	—	—

Sunday Trains.

AM 6.55	7.22	10.11	10.13
9.30	9.30	11.29	11.31
11.15	—	1. 1	1. 3
PM12.15k	—	2.51	2.53
1.14k	1.10k	3.58	4. 0
6.33	6.33	9. 6	9. 8
8.20	8. 0	—	9.45

Trains from Newhaven.

	Leave		Arrive at
	Harb'ur.	Town.	Lon. B.	Vict.
AM 6.31	6.33	8.46	—
7.11	7.13	8.53	9. 8
8.38	8.40	10.15	10.24
8.53	8.55	10.55	10.56
10.36	10.38	12.44	12.45
11.21k	11.23k	—	1.20
PM12.16	12.18	2.22	2.22
12.33k	12.35k	3.40	3.45
1.26	1.28	—	4.17
2.36	2.38	4.32	4.35
4. 1k	4. 3k	6.36	6.34
4.56k	4.58k	—	7.30
5.41	5.43	7.42	7.45
6.17	6.19	7.56	7.50
8.15	8.17	10.25	10.17
9. 4	9. 6	—	11.17
10. 7k	10. 9k	12.59	1. 0

Sunday Trains.

AM 7.46	7.48	10.18	10.32
10.34k	10.36k	—	1. 0
PM 1.56k	1.58k	5. 3	5.11
5. 1	5. 3	—	7.28
5.57	5.59	7.56	7.37
8.43	8.45	—	10.19
9.35k	9.37k	12.27	—

d Saturdays only.
e Saturdays excepted.
k *Via* Brighton.

Taxi Cabs can be hired to meet any train at this Station by letter, or telephone No. 56 and 77. Messrs. Hughes, Motor and Engineering Works, Bridge Street.

For Advertisement list,
see over.

NEW HAVEN—*continued*.

Sheffield Hotel, Facing Harbour, opposite Continental Steamers. Large Bedrooms. Private Sitting Room. Good Fishing. Alight Town Station. Telephone 50.
C. H. FOWLER, Proprietor.

London and Paris Hotel, Adjoining Landing Stage and Newhaven Harbour Station. Residential and Commercial(50 rooms). High Class Cuisine. Tel. Newhaven, 72.
BERTRAM & CO., LTD.

NEW HEY (Lancs), 198¾ miles. Fares, 39/7*a*, 23/9*c*. R. T. for two months, 79/2*a*, 47/6*c*. Departures *from* London as for Manchester. Departures *for* London about 4 times daily. Pop. 3,219.
Map Square 12.

NEW HOLLAND (Lincoln) from *King's Cross*, 170½ miles. Fares, 35/0*a*, 21/0*c*. R. T. for two months, 70/0*a*, 42/0*c*.
Map Square 13.

KING'S+	N. HOL.	N. HOL.	KING'S+
AM 4.45	10.50	AM 5.55*r*	11.30
7.15*r*	12.23	7. 5*r*	1. 5
10.10*r*	5.42	PM12.20	6.25
PM 1.50*r*	7. 5	1.45	9. 0
4. 0*r*	10.18	6. 0	3.25
8.25*c*	7.12	—	—

Sunday Trains.

PM 5. 0*r*	10. 2	AM 8.30*r*	3.45
8.25	7.12	PM 4.35*r*	10.20

c Saturdays excepted.
r Restaurant Car.

NEWHOUSE (Lanark), 390½ miles. No through fares. Departures *from* London as for Wishaw (Central). Departures *for* London about 5 times daily.
Map Square 40.

NEWICK AND CHAILEY (Sussex) from *London Bridge, Victoria,* and *Clapham Junction,* 42½ miles. Fares, *via* East Grinstead, 8/11*a*, 5/4*c*. R. T. for two months, 17/10*a*, 10/8*c*. Departures *from* London as for Sheffield Park. Departures *for* London about 7 times daily. Pop. 887.
Map Square 23.

NEWINGTON (Kent) from *Victoria, Holborn Viaduct,* and *Ludgate Hill,* 41½ miles. Fares, 8/9*a*, 7/0*b*, 5/3*c*. R. T. for two months, 17/6*a*, 14/0*b*. Departures *from* London as for Rainham. Departures *for* London about 8 times daily. Pop. 1,127.
Map Square 24.

NEWLAY (Yorks), 199¾ miles. Fares, 39/7*a*, 23/9*c*. R. T., double fare. Departures *from* London as for Leeds (Wellington). Departures *for* London about 6 times daily.
Map Square 12.

NEW LUCE (Wigtown), 404¼ miles. No through fares. Departures *from* London as for Girvan or Newton Stewart. Departures *for* London about 4 times daily. Pop. 429.
Map Square 43.

NEWMACHAR (Aberdeen), 534½ miles. No through fares. Departures *from* London as for Fraserburgh or Peterhead. Departures *for* London about 3 times daily. Pop. 1,961.
Map Square 35.

NEWMAINS (Lanark), 386¼ miles. No through fares. Departures *from* London as for Wishaw (Central). Departures *for* London about 4 times daily. Pop. 6,718.
Map Square 40.

NEWMARKET (Suffolk) from *Liverpool Street,* 70½ miles. Fares, 14/9*a*, 8/10*c*. R. T. for two months, 29/6*a*. Pop. 9,753.
Map Square 19.

L'POOL ST.	N'WM'K.	N'WM'K.	L'POOL ST.
AM 5. 5	7. 8	AM 8.14*r*	10.23
5.50	9.25	9.29	11.27
8.30*r*	10.34	10.28	12.40
10. 5*h*	12.51	PM12. 0*r*	2.21
11.50*r*	2. 9	1.48*lr*	4. 2*k*
PM 2.34	4.54	1.48	5. 9
4.45	6.35	3. 6*r*	5.17
5.49*r*	8. 0	4. 1*r*	6.10
7.10*r*	9.17	4.41	7.58
8.22	10.29	6.20*r*	8.33
—	—	7.53	10.30

Sunday Trains.

AM 9.25	12. 1	PM 4. 9	6.40
PM 3.25	5.36	7.40	9.40

h Wednesdays only.
k Arrives at St. Pancras Station.
l Commencing July 23.
r Restaurant Car.

Rutland Arms Hotel. The Best and Leading Hotel. Motorists' Headquarters. Garage. Petrol and Oils. Telegrams, "Rutland." Telephone 16.
J. TAYLOR, Proprietress.

NEW MILLS (Derby), 173¾ miles. Fares, 35/10*a*, 21/6*c*. R. T., double fare. Departures *from* London as for Bugsworth. Departures *for* London about 5 times daily. Pop. 8,492.
Map Square 12.

NEWMILNS (Ayr), 393¾ miles. Fares, 80/2*a*, 48/1*c*. R. T. for two months, 160/4*a*, 96/2*c*. Departures *from* London as for Kilmarnock. Departures *for* London about 4 times daily. Pop. 4,519.
Map Square 40.

NEW MILTON (Hants) from *Waterloo*, 97¾ miles. Fares, 20/7*a*, 12/4*c*. R. T. for two months, 41/2*a*, 24/8*c*. Pop. 2,741.
Map Square 27.

W'LOO	MILTON	MILTON	W'LOO
AM 5.40	8.42	AM 7.26*r*	10. 6
5.50	10. 7	8.13*s*	11. 0
8.30*s*	11.40	9.46	12.22
10.30	1.15	11.18*r*	2.20
PM12.30*r*	2.59	PM 1. 9	4.20
2.30*s*	5.17	3. 9*s*	6.26
4.30*r*	7.16	4. 8	6.58
6.30*r*	9. 7	5. 7*r*	8.20
7.30	10.30	7.15	10.50
—	—	8.25	11.28
—	—	9.22	3.58
—	—	—	—

Sunday Trains.

AM11. 0*r*	2.14	AM 8.59	12.11
PM 2. 0*r*	5.15	PM 4.45	8. 3
7. 0*r*	10.16	6.38*r*	9.31
—	—	8.14	3.58

r Restaurant Car.
s Refreshments served.

Hotel Victoria. Milford-on-Sea. On Cliff facing I.O.W. Motor centre for New Forest. Tel. 7, Milford-on-Sea.
See advt. p. **267.**

Grand Marine Hotel, Barton-on-Sea, New Milton. First-class Family. Due South. Facing Isle of Wight. Lift. Tennis. Croquet. Golf. Garage. Tel. 25 New Milton.
M. FERRANTE, Manageress.
See advt. p. **27.**

NEWNHAM (Gloucester), from *Paddington*, 125 miles. Fares (*via* Gloucester) 26/1*a*, 15/8*c*. R. T. for two months, 52/2*a*, 31/4*c*; *via* Severn Tunnel, 32/4*a*, 19/5*c*. R. T. for two months, 64/8*a*, 38/10*c*. Pop. 1,181.
Map Square 22.

PAD.	NEWN.	NEWN.	PAD.
AM 1. 0*g*	5.58	AM 9.17	12.20
5.30	9.37	11.13*r*	2.40
7.30	11.27	PM 1.35	5. 0
9. 0	1.17	5.26*r*	8.45
10.45	2.28	6.30	10.25
11.15*hr*	3.22	7.26	3.30
PM 1.30*l*	5.11	8.52*k*	5.30
3.15*t*	6.28	8.58*h*	3.30
6. 0*r*	8.58	—	—
—	—	—	—

Sunday Trains.

AM 9.10*h*	4.30	PM 4.30	10. 0
PM 2. 0	8.36	—	—
9.15	5.58	—	—

g Mondays excepted.
h Via Severn Tunnel Junction.
k Thursdays and Saturdays only.
l Via Kingham.
r Restaurant Car.
t Tea Car.

NEWNHAM BRIDGE (Worcester), 145½ miles. Fares, 28/9*a*, 17/3*c*. R.T. for two months, 57/6*a*, 34/6*c*. Departures *from* London as for Cleobury Mortimer. Departures *for* London about 3 times daily.
Map Square 17.

NEWPARK (Midlothian),

391 miles. No through fares. Departures *from* London as for Edinburgh or Wishaw (Central). Departures *for* London about 4 times daily.

NEWPORT (Essex) from

Liverpool Street, 40 miles. Fares, 8/7a, 5/2c. R. T. for two months, 17/2a. Pop. 914. *Map Square* 19.

L'POOL ST.	NEWP'T.	NEWP'T.	L'POOL ST.
AM 5.50	7.26	AM 7.17	8.57
7.18	9.10	8.15	9.27
10. 5	11.28	8.30	9.46
PM12.29d	1.44	9. 5	10.17
12.48e	2.36	10. 7	11.27
1.19d	2.50	PM12.30	2. 7
2.48	4.27	1.48d	3.18
4.15	5.34	2.46h	5. 9
4.45	5.57	3. 1k	5. 9
5.49r	7. 4	3.46r	5.17
6.30	7.40	4.36r	6.10
8.22d	9.39	6.15	7.58
8.22e	9.51	7. 0r	8.22
—	—	9.15	10.30

Sunday Trains.

AM 8.12	9.41	AM 9.40	11.27
PM 1.50	3.51	PM 6. 6	7.26

d Saturdays only.
e Saturdays excepted.
h Commencing July 23.
k Ceases to run after July 22.
r Restaurant Car.

NEWPORT (Isle of Wight)

from *Victoria* and *London Bridge*, 100 miles. Fares, via Ryde, 19/7a, 12/0c. R. T. for two months, 39/2a, 24/0c. Pop. 11,036. *Map Square* 28.

Leave VICT.	LON. B.	Arr. at NEWPT.
AM 6.18	6.35	11.20
8.55	—	1.20
10.15	10.22	2.20
11.35	—	3.20
PM 1.35	—	5.20
1.40	1.50	6.20
1.55	2. 5	7.20
—	4.50	8.22

Sunday Trains.

AM 9.55		1.40
PM 1.14	1.10	7. 5

Trains from Newport.

Leave NEWPT.	Arrive at LON. B.	VICT.
AM 7.23	10.55	—
9.25	—	1.10
12.25	4.27	4.34
PM 1.25	—	5.12
3.25	7.48	6.50
4.25	—	8.33
5.25	10. 8	10. 1

Sunday Trains.

PM 4.13	8.50	7.56

NEWPORT—*continued.*

ANOTHER ROUTE from

Waterloo, via Ryde, 88 miles. Fares, 19/7a, 12/0c. R. T. for two months, 39/2a, 24/0c.

W'LOO.	NEWPT.	NEWPT.	W'LOO.
AM 5.50	11.20	AM 7.23	11.32
9.50h	1.20	7.55	11.41
10.50	3.20	10.25r	1.52
PM12.50r	4.20	11.25d	3.20
1.50d	5.20	11.25e	4.16
3.50s	7.20	PM 2.25	5.56
5 50	9.26	4.25r	7.56
—	—	5.25	10.46
—	—	8.42kl	3.53

Sunday Trains.

AM 8. 0	11.50	AM10.40	3.13
9.15r	1.40	PM 2.15r	6.16
PM 1.50	7. 5	4.13	8.52
—	—	5.56	10. 1

d Saturdays only.
e Saturdays excepted.
h Via Sandown.
k Via Eastleigh.
l Passengers cross Portsmouth at own expense.
r Restaurant Car.
s Refreshments served.

ANOTHER ROUTE from

Waterloo, via Southampton, 96¾ miles. Fares, 19/11a, 12/5c. R. T. for two months, 38/6a, 24/0c.

W'LOO.	NEWPT.	NEWPT.	W'LOO.
AM 5.40	9.50	AM 7.22s	11. 0
8.30s	12.50	9.22r	12.50
PM12.30r	3.50	PM12.54	4.50
1.30s	5.20	3.24	6.58
4.30r	7.50	5.54	10.50
6.30r	10. 0	—	—

Sunday Trains.

AM11. 0r	4. 5	AM 9.40r	2.27
PM 2. 0r	6.55	PM 3.35	8. 3
—	—	6.25	10.52

r Restaurant Car.
s Refreshments served.
Passengers cross Southampton at own expense.

Wheat Sheaf Commercial

and Family Hotel. Oldest established Commercial Hotel in the Island. Boots meets all trains. 'Phone 53.
READ, Proprietor.

Warburton's. The High-

Class Commercial and Family Hotel of Newport. Two minutes station. Boots meet all trains. 'Phone 55.
G. S. RICHARDSON, Proprietor.

NEWPORT—*continued.*

Bugle Hotel. First-class Family and Commercial. Re-decorated. Best situated. Stabling and Motor accommodation. Telephone 128.
H. T. READ, Proprietor.

NEWPORT (Monmouth)

from *Paddington*, 141 miles. Fares, 29/5a, 17/8c. R. T. for two months, 58/10a. Pop. 92,369. *Map Square* 22.

PAD.	NEWPORT	NEWPORT	PAD.
AM 1. 0g	5. 6	AM 6.12r	10.15
5.30	9.50	8. 5r	10.57
8.45r	11.14	8.22	12.20
9. 0	1.20	10.22r	1. 0
11.50r	2.20	10.31r	2. 0
PM 1.10r	4.15	11.41r	2.30
3.35r	6. 8	PM 1.42r	4.20
5. 0r	8. 8	3.37r	6.15
6. 0r	8.44	5.31r	8.35
6.30r	9.53	6.55r	9.25
8. 0r	10.27	11. 4	3.30
9.15	1.58	—	—

Sunday Trains.

AM 1. 0	5.31	AM11.30	3.35
9.10	1.38	PM12.52	4. 5
PM12.30r	3.49	5.23r	8.25
4.30	8. 5	11. 4	3.30
9.15	1.58	—	—

g Mondays excepted.
r Restaurant Car.

Westgate Hotel. (Trust Houses, Ltd.) The best Hotel in South Wales. Re-decorated and reconstructed throughout. Fully Licensed. Telephone 2407. *See advt. p.* **270.**

King's Head Hotel. Close to Station, Post Office, and Exchange. Coffee, Commercial, and Smoking Rooms, Private Sitting Rooms, well-furnished Bedrooms, large Rooms for Public Meetings, commodious Stock Rooms with Daylight. Night Porter. Tel. Hotel 3405.

Queen's Hotel. Near Station. Free from noise of traffic. Grill, Coffee, and Commercial Rooms. Private Sitting and good Stock Rooms Hotel Porters meet all trains. Night Porter. Telephone No. 2171—two lines.

Bank.—The National Bank, Ltd.

NEWPORT (Salop) from

Euston, 145 miles. Fares, 29/9*a*, 17/10*c.* R. T. for two months, 59/6*a.* Pop. 3,056.
Map Square 17.

EUSTON	N'PORT	N'PORT	EUSTON
AM 2.35	7.56	AM 8.41*e*r12. 5	
5. 0	9.12	8.41*d*r12.20	
6.45*h*	10.46	10.50*r*	2.20
6.45	12.14	PM12. 8*r*	3.10
8.45*r*	1.10	12.55*t*	5.35
10.40*r*	2.36	2.58*t*	6.15
12. 0*nr*	4. 2	3.43*r*	8.10
PM 1.15*r*	5.46	5.29*dr*	9.15
2.20*t*	6.32	5.29*er*	9.20
4.45*r*	8.10	6.32*r*	10. 0
5.50*dr*10.37		11.20	5. 0
6.30*er*10.37		—	—
9.20*e*	2.20	—	—

Sunday Trains.

AM 9.15	2.43	PM 4.43*r*	8.55
—	—	—	—

d Saturdays only.
e Saturdays excepted.
h Mondays and Fridays only.
n Noon.
r Restaurant Car.
t Tea Car.

NEWPORT (Yorks), 237¼

miles. No through fares. Departures *from London* as for Thornaby. Departures *for London* about 5 times daily. Pop. 11,593.
Map Square 8.
Station temporarily closed.
Nearest station Middlesbrough.

NEWPORT EAST (Fife),

451¼ miles. Fares, 91/5*a*, 54/10*c.* R. T. for two months, 182/10*a*, 109/8*c.* Departures *from London* as for Leuchars. Departures *for London* about 6 times daily. Pop. 3,295.
Map Square 38.

NEWPORT PAGNELL

(Bucks) from *Euston,* 56½ miles. Fares, 11/8*a*, 7/0*c.* R. T. for two months, 23/4*a.* Pop. 4,142
Map Square 18.

EUSTON	NEWP. P.	NEWP. P.	EUSTON
AM 6.45	8.28	AM 7.25	9.40
7.35	10. 2	8.45	10.15
9.30*e*	11.30	9.28	11.40
9.30*d*	12.33	10.40*d*	12.20
12. 0*n*	1.46	10.40*e*	12.32
PM12.15	3.13	PM 1. 0*h*	2.45
2. 0	4.28	1.52*d*	4.15
4.15	6. 3	2.25*e*	4.15
5.32	7.15	5.20	7.55
6.10*e*	7.58	6.20	8.35
7.15*d*	10.13	8. 5*e*	10.10
8. 0*e*	10. 3	8. 5*d*	10.50
—	—	9.10	11.35

No Sunday Trains.

d Saturdays only.
e Saturdays excepted.
h Thursdays and Saturdays only.
n Noon.

NEWQUAY (Cornwall)

from *Paddington,* 281½ miles. Fares, 58/2*a*, 34/11*c.* R. T. for two months, 116/4*a*, 69/10*c.* Pop. 6,633.
Map Square 25.

PAD.	N'QUAY	N'QUAY	PAD.
AM 5.30	3.28	AM 9. 0*r*	4.35
10.30*r*	5. 6	9.30*s*r	4.45
11. 0*dr*	5.30	11.40*er*	6.50
11.10*er*	5.48	PM12.15*dr*	7 5
PM12. 5*r*	8.32	12.45*r*	9. 0
10. 0*e*	7.25	7.23	7.10
10. 0*dk*	9.27	—	—
12. 0*h*	10.28	—	—
12.30*kl*12.37		—	—

NEWQUAY—*continued.*

Sunday Trains.

PAD.	N'QUAY	N'QUAY	PAD.
AM10.30*rk*	6.47	AM 9.40*kr*	7. 5
PM10. 0	7.23	PM 3.35*k*	3.15

d Saturdays only.
e Saturdays excepted.
h Saturdays midnight excepted.
k Via Chacewater.
l Saturday midnight only.
r Restaurant Car.
s Mondays and Fridays only.

Headland Hotel. Under new and entirely British management. The largest and most comfortable hotel in West of England. Grounds of 10 acres adjoin Golf Links. Garage. R.A.C. Open all Winter.
See advt. p 271.

Atlantic Hotel. First-class Family Hotel. Sea View from every window. Lift to all floors. Nearest hotel to Golf Pavilion. Excellent Garage. Private lockups. Telephone 6. Telegrams: "Atlantic, Newquay."
See advt. p.272.

Watergate Bay Hotel. R.A.C. (appointed). 60 Rooms always open. Glorious position on Atlantic Ocean facing South. "Cliff sheltered" East and North. Three miles from Newquay. Golf. Heated and Comfortable. Excellent Cuisine.
See advt. p. 272.

Hotel Victoria. Directly facing Sea. Passenger lift from every floor to bathing beaches. Garage pit. Officially appointed R.A.C., A.A. and M.U. Billiards.

Beachcroft Private Hotel. Beautifully situated in grounds of 2½ acres. On cliff-edge, facing Atlantic Ocean. Tennis, Croquet. Telegrams: "Beachcroft, Newquay, Cornwall." Telephone 22. Proprietor (late Manager, Atlantic Hotel).—B. LANGLER.

Tremont. En Pension. Unique Position. Grand Atlantic Views. Separate Tables. Excellent Cuisine. Garage. Moderate Inclusive Terms. Adjoining Golf Links. Special facilities for Golfers. Telephone 148.
Misses BUCKINGHAM.

Moirah Private Hotel. Well situated. Good sea views. Smoking Lounge. Central for Golf. Tennis adjoining. Electric Light.
Proprietress—Miss GREENWOOD.

Ocean View, Pentire. Facing Sea and River. Adjoining Beach. Golf Links. Good Cooking. Home Comforts. Terms moderate.
PROPRIETRESS.

St. Rumon's Boarding House. Close to Beach. Adjoining Golf Links. Moderate terms. Telephone 78. Apply—
Mrs. JOHNS.

Penolver Private Hotel, facing Atlantic Ocean. Near Links. Tennis. Bowls. Ideal Winter Residence. Electric Light and every Home Comfort.
PROPRIETOR.

Penhallow Residential Hotel. Ideal position on Cliff. Extensive Sea Views. Balconies. Smoking Lounge. Every Comfort. Proprietress, Mrs. PENHALL.

NEWQUAY—*continued.*

Tregwella Private Hotel. Situated Mount Wise. Extensive Sea View. Near Golf and Tennis. Excellent Cuisine. Separate Tables. Electric Light. Moderate inclusive terms. Under personal supervision of Proprietress,
Miss CHALMERS.

"Trecarn." Board Residence. Island Estate. Charming position with uninterrupted Sea Views. Apartments during winter season if desired. Electric. Every convenience and comfort. Moderate Terms.
Mr. and Mrs. LANDER.

House Agents and Auctioneers, 4, Victoria Parade. Removal Contractors. Furnishers. Also at Truro, Falmouth, and Penzance.
JOHN JULIAN & CO., Ltd.

NEW RADNOR (Radnor),

168 miles. Fares, 34/4*a*, 20/7*c.* R. T. for two months, 68/8*a*, 41/2*c.* Departures *from London* as for Titley. Departures *for London* about 4 times daily. Pop. 386.
Map Square 16.

NEW ROMNEY AND

LITTLESTONE (Kent) from *Charing Cross, Cannon Street,* and *London Bridge,* 76¼ miles. Fares, 15/10*a*, 12/8*b*, 9/6*c.* R. T. for two months, 31/8*a*, 25/4*b.* Pop. 1,605.
Map Square 24.

	Leave		Arr. at
CHAR. +	CAN. ST.	LON. B.	ROMNEY
AM —	3.40*s*	3.43*s*	7.42
—	5.20	5.25	10.19
9.15	—	9.23	11.41
11. 0	—	11. 7	1.52
PM 1. 0	—	—	4.54
4.30*j*	—	4.37*j*	7. 0
—	5. 0*v*	—	7. 5
7.18*l*	—	7.26*l*	10. 5

No Sunday Trains.

Trains from Romney.

Leave		Arrive at	
ROMNEY	LON. B.	CAN. ST.	CHAR. +
AM 7.58	10. 0	10. 4	—
9.15	11.43	—	11.57
PM12.30	3.36	—	3.40
3.12	5.50	—	6. 3
5.20	8.54	9. 1	—
7.33	10.22	—	10.35

No Sunday Trains.

e Saturdays excepted,
j Fridays excepted.
l Wednesdays and Fridays only.
s Third Class only.
v Fridays only.

Grand Hotel, Littlestone. Entirely under new management. First-class Family and Golfers'. For terms, apply MANAGER.

NEWSEAT (Aberdeen),

563½ miles. No through fares. Departures *from London* as for Peterhead. Departures *for London* about 4 times daily.
Map Square 35.

NEWSHAM (Northumber-

land), 280½ miles. Fares, 59/4*a*, 35/7*c.* R. T. double fare. Departures *from London* as for Newcastle-on-Tyne. Departures *for London* about 6 times daily. Pop. 6,985.
Map Square 3.

NEWSHOLME (Yorks)
231 miles. No through fares. Departures *from London* as for Clitheroe. Departures *for London* about 6 times daily. Pop. 49.
Map Square 7.

NEW SOUTHGATE.
See SOUTHGATE, NEW.

NEWSTEAD (Notts) from
St. Pancras, 134¼ miles. Fares, 26/11a, 16/2c. R. T., double fare. Departures *from London* as for Hucknall. Departures *for London* about 6 times daily. Pop. 961.
Map Square 13.

NEWTHORPE (Notts)
from *King's Cross*, 136½ miles. Fares, 26/1a, 15/8c. R. T., double fare.

KING'S +	NEWTHP	NEWTHP	KING'S +
AM 4.45	9.12	AM 7.18	10.40
7.15	10.52	8.14	1. 5
8.45	1.37	10. 3r	1.30
11.30	4.14	PM 1.35r	6.25
PM 1.50r	5.55	4. 4	9. 0
4. 0r	8. 2	5.25r	9.25
5.35dr	9.17	8.58	3.25
5.45dr	10.42	—	—
11.25e	7. 7	—	—
—	—	—	—

Sunday Trains.

PM 11.25	7. 7	—	—
—	—	—	—

d Saturdays only.
e Saturdays excepted.
r Restaurant Car.

NEWTON (Cheshire)
195½ miles. Fares, 37/6a, 22/6c. R. T., double fare. Departures *from London* as for Godley. Departures *for London* about 5 times daily. Pop. 7,723.
Map Square 12.

NEWTON ABBOT
(Devon) from *Paddington*, 193½ miles. Fares, 39/10a, 23/11c. R. T. for two months, 79/8a, 47/10c. Pop. 13,837.
Map Square 26.

PAD.	NEWTON A.	NEWTON A.	PAD.
AM 5.30	11.11	AM 1.23	7.10
7.30	1.13	9.31r	1.30
9.15r	1.38	PM 12.50r	4.35
11.10r	3. 7	2.55er	6.50
PM 12. 5r	4.20	3.25dr	7. 5
2. 0r	6.11	5. 8r	9. 0
3.30r	7.15	6. 0	2.45
4.15r	8.58	—	—
6.30r	11.17	—	—
10. 0	3.23	—	—
12. 0h	6. 1	—	—
12.30k	6.31	—	—
—	—	—	—

Sunday Trains.

AM 10.30r	2.20	AM 1.23	7. 5
PM 2.40	6.51	8.20r	3.35
4.30r	9. 9	11.15r	4. 5
10. 0	3.23	PM 2.59	7. 5
—	—	3.10r	7.55
—	—	9.20	3.15
—	—	—	—
—	—	—	—

d Saturdays only.
e Saturdays excepted.
h Saturdays midnight excepted.
k Saturdays midnight only.
r Restaurant Car.

Taxi Cabs can be hired to meet any train at this Station by telegram or telephone No. 37, Messrs. Balls, Ltd., 60/61, Queen Street.

NEWTONAIRDS (Dumfries), 339½ miles. Fares. 41/5c. R. T. for two months, 82/10c. Departures *from London* as for Dumfries. Departures *for London* about twice daily.
Map Square 43.

NEWTONGRANGE
(Midlothian), 387½ miles. No through fares. Departures *from London* as for Galashiels. Departures *for London* about 4 times daily. Pop. 4,471.

NEWTON HEATH
(Lancs), 189¼ miles. Fares, 38/7a, 23/2c. R. T. for two months, 77/2a. Departures *from London* as for Manchester. Departures *for London* about 5 times daily. Pop. 20,010.

NEWTONHILL (Kincardine), 512½ miles. No through fares. Departures *from London* as for Stonehaven. Departures *for London* about 4 times daily.
Map Square 38.

NEWTON KYME (Yorks), 186½ miles. Fares, 38/9a, 23/3c. R. T., double fare. Departures *from London* as for Wetherby. Departures *for London* about 6 times daily. Pop. 226.
Map Square 8.

NEWTON-LE-WIL-
LOWS (Lancs) from *Euston*, 188 miles. Fares, 39/2a, 23/6c. R. T. for two months, 78/4a. Pop. 18,776.

EUSTON	NEWTON	NEWTON	EUSTON
AM 12.25	6.28	AM 7.30er	12. 5
2.35	7.35	7.30dr	12.20
5. 0	10.50	9. 6r	1.45
6.45e	12. 4	11.12hr	3.45
6.45d	12.13	11.12r	4.15
8.30dr	1.34	PM 1. 4t	5.50
8.30er	1.41	1.25dt	6. 0
10.40r	3.29	3. 5r	7.30
11.50er	5. 3	4.10dr	9.15
11.50dr	5.29	4.10er	9. 5
PM 1.30r	5.47	10.51	5. 0
2.35t	6.58	—	—
5.20r	10. 8	—	—
9.30e	3. 8	—	—
11.40e	5.40	—	—
11.50d	8.34	—	—
—	—	—	—

Sunday Trains.

AM 11.45r	4.18	AM 8.12r	1.30
PM 6. 0r	10.21	10. 7	4. 0
9.15	3. 8	PM 3. 2r	7.30
11.45	5.40	11. 5	5. 0
—	—	—	—
—	—	—	—
—	—	—	—

d Saturdays only.
e Saturdays excepted.
h Mondays and Saturdays only.
r Restaurant Car.
t Tea Car.

NEWTONMORE (Inverness), 518¾ miles. Fares, 105/3a, 63/2c. R. T. for two months, 210/6a, 126/4c. Departures *from London* as for Blair Atholl. Departures *for London* about 3 times daily. Pop. 644.
Map Square 37.

NEWTON-ON-AYR
(Ayr), 391¾ miles. Fares, 79/10a, 47/11c. R. T. for two months, 159/8a, 95/10c. Departures *from London* as for Ayr. Departures *for London* about 4 times daily. Pop. 9,757.
Map Square 40.

NEWTON POPPLE-
FORD (Devon) from *Waterloo*, 166 miles. Fares, 34/7a, 20/9c. R. T. for two months, 69/2a, 41/6c. Departures *from London* as for Tipton St. Johns. Departures *for London* about 5 times daily. Pop. 450.
Map Square 26.

NEWTON ROAD
(Stafford), 116¾ miles. Fares, 24/5a, 14/8c. R. T. for two months, 48/10a. Departures *from London* as for Birmingham (New Street). Departures *for London* about 6 times daily.

NEWTON ST. CYRES
(Devon), 176¾ miles. Fares, 36/10a, 22/1c. R. T. for two months, 73/8a, 44/2c. Departures *from London* as for Exeter (Queen Street). Departures *for London* about 5 times daily. Pop. 677.
Map Square 26.

NEWTON STEWART
(Wigtown) from *St. Pancras*, 390¾ miles. Fares, 68/9a, 41/3c. R. T. for two months, 137/6a, 82/6c. Pop. 1,831.
Map Square 43.

ST. PAN.	N.ST'RT	N. ST'RT.	ST.PAN.
AM 4.25	4.40	AM 8.42r	6.35
9.50r	7. 0	10.31r	9.15
PM 12.15r	9.15	PM 10.30e	7.50
11.45e	10.25	10.30d	8.57
—	—	—	—
—	—	—	—
—	—	—	—

Sunday Trains.

—	—	—	—
PM 11.45	10.25	—	—
—	—	—	—

d Saturdays only.
e Saturdays excepted.
r Restaurant Car.

ANOTHER ROUTE from
Euston, 382 miles. Fares as above.

EUSTON	N.ST'RT	N.ST'RT	EUSTON
AM 5. 0	4.42	AM 8.42r	6.25
10. 0r	7. 0	PM 1. 3r	10. 0
11.35r	9 15	4.45	5. 0h
PM 8. 0e	4.58	10.30	7.15
11.45e	10.24	—	—

Sunday Trains.

PM 7.50r	4.58	—	—
8.50	10.35	—	—
11.45	10.24	—	—
—	—	—	—

e Saturdays excepted.
h A.M.
r Restaurant Car.

Crown Hotel. First-class Family and Commercial. Salmon and Trout Fishing. Motors. Garage. A.A. and M.U. Telephone 27.

NEWTON TONY
(Wilts) from *Waterloo*, 76½ miles. Fares, *via* Grateley, 17/1a, 10/3c. R.T. for two months, 34/2a, 20/6c. *Via* Salisbury, 19/5a, 11/8c. R.T. for two months, 28/10a, 23/4c. Departures *from London* as for Amesbury. Departures *for London* about 7 times daily. Pop. 306.

ROMNEY.—GRAND HOTEL, LITTLESTONE (New Romney.) See Opposite page.

NEWTOWN (Montgomery)

from *Paddington*, 186 miles. Fares, 38/9*a*, 23/3*c*. R. T. for two months, 77/6*a*. Pop. 5,670.

Map Square 16.

Pad.	Newtown	Newtown	Pad.
AM 6.30	1.29	AM 8.13*r*	2. 5
10.20*r*	3.17	9.53*r*	4.15
10.40*r*	3.40	PM12. 3*t*	5. 0
PM 2.10*t*	6.47	12.48*t*	6.40
4.10*t*	9. 8	2.46*r*	8. 5
12.15*h*	7.41	3.53	10. 0
12.15*k*	9.35	8. 6	3.30
—	—	—	—
—	—	—	—

No Sunday Trains.

h Saturdays midnight only.
k Saturday midnight excepted.
r Restaurant Car.
t Tea Car.

ANOTHER ROUTE

from *Euston*, 195¾ miles. Fares as above.

Euston	N'town	N'town	Euston
AM 5. 0*h*	11.50	AM 6.56*hr*	1.45
10. 0*r*	3.40	8.13*r*	2.20
10.40*r*	4.28	9.53*r*	3.10
PM 1.15*r*	6.47	11.43*r*	5.50
2.20*t*	9. 8	PM12. 3*r*	7.30
9.30*eh*	4.40	2.46*er*	9. 5
11. 0*dh*	7.41	2.46*dr*	9.15
—	—	3.53*hr*	10.45
—	—	8. 6	5. 0

Sunday Trains.

PM 9.15	4.42	PM 8. 5*h*	5. 0
—	—	—	—
—	—	—	—
—	—	—	—
—	—	—	—

d Saturdays only.
e Saturdays excepted.
h *Via* Crewe.
n Noon.
r Restaurant Car.
t Tea Car.

NEW TREDEGAR (Monmouth)

162¼ miles. Fares, 33/7*a*, 20/2*c*. R. T. for two months, 67/2*a*. Departures *from* London as for Rhymney. Departures *for* London about 7 times daily. Pop. 4,727.

Map Square 21.

NEWTYLE (Forfar)

471 miles. Fares, 94/5*a*, 56/8*c*. R. T. for two months 188/10*a*, 113/4*c*. Departures *from* London as for Coupar Angus. Departures *for* London about 3 times daily. Pop. 883.

Map Square 38.

NEYLAND (Pembroke)

from *Paddington*, 267¾ miles. Fares, 54/4*a*, 32/7*c*. R. T. for two months, 108/8*a*, 65/2*c*. Pop. 2,715.

Map Square 20.

Pad.	Neyland	Neyland	Pad.
AM 1. 0*g*	11.45	AM 7.30*r*	2.30
8.45*r*	3.25	8. 0*r*	4.20
11.50*r*	6.53	10.50*r*	6.15
PM 1.10*r*	9.20	PM12.40*r*	8.35
5. 0*hr*	11.55	2.20*r*	9.25
9.15	6.48	6.30	3.30

Sunday Trains.

PM 9.15	6.48	PM 6.35	3.30
—	—	—	—

g Mondays excepted.
h Tuesdays, Thursdays, and Saturdays only.
r Restaurant Car.

NIDD BRIDGE (Yorks)

202 miles. Fares, 41/11*a*, 25/2*c*. R. T., double fare. Departures *from* London as for Harrogate. Departures *for* London about 6 times daily. Pop. (Nidd) 205.

Map Square 7.

NIGG (Ross)

607 miles. Fares, 107/9*a*, 64/8*c*. R. T. for two months, 215/6*a*, 129/4*c*. Departures *from* London as for Dingwall. Departures *for* London about 3 times daily. Pop. 867.

Map Square 34.

NINE MILE POINT

(Monmouth), 149¾ miles. Fares, 31/1*a*, 18/8*c*. R. T. for two months, 62/2*a*, 37/4*c*. Departures *from* London as for Tredegar. Departures *for* London about 4 times daily.

Map Square 21.

NINGWOOD (Isle of Wight)

from *Victoria*, *London Bridge*, or *Waterloo*, *via* Ryde, 94¾ miles. Fares, *via* Ryde, 21/1*a*, 12/11*c*. R. T. for two months, 41/10*a*, 25/10*c*. Departures *from* London as for Newport (I. of W.). Departures *for* London about 4 times daily.

Map Square 28.

NISBET (Roxburgh)

358 miles. No through fares. Departures *from* London as for Kelso or St. Boswells. Departures *for* London about 4 times daily.

Map Square 41.

NITSHILL (Renfrew)

408¾ miles. Fares, 82/6*a*, 49/6*c*. R.T. for two months, 165/0*a*, 99/0*c*. Departures *from* London as for Kilmarnock. Departures *for* London about 4 times daily.

Map Square 40.

NOCTON (Lincoln)

123½ miles. Fares, 25/8*a*, 15/5*c*. R. T., double fare. Departures *from* London as for Blankney. Departures *for* London about 4 times daily. Pop. 566.

Map Square 13.

NOEL PARK (Wood Green) (Middlesex)

from *Liverpool Street*, 7½ miles. Fares, 0/10*a*, 0/8*b*, 0/6*c*. R. T. for two days, 1/8*a*, 1/4*b*, 0/10½*c*. Pop. 13,366. *See* pp. 534-536.

Map Square 52.

NORBITON (Surrey)

from *Waterloo*, 11½ miles. Fares, *via* Malden, 1/10*a*, 1/1*c*. R. T. for two days, 3/8*a*, 2/2*c*. *Via* Kingston, 2/1*a*, 1/3*c*. R. T. for two days, 4/2*a*, 2/6*c*. Pop. 12,652. *See* pp. 584, 585.

Map Square 76.

NORBURY (Derby)

142½ miles. Fares, 29/7*a*, 17/9*c*. R. T. for two months, 59/2*a*, 35/6*c*. Departures *from* London as for Ashbourne. Departures *for* London about 5 times daily. Pop. 350.

Map Square 12.

NORBURY (Surrey)

from *Victoria* and *London Bridge*, 7½ miles. Fares from Victoria, 1/6*a*, 0/10½*c*. R.T. for two days, 2/11*a*, 1/9*c*. From London Bridge, 1/11*a*, 1/2*c*. R.T. for two days, 3/10*a*, 2/0*c*. *See* pp. 567, 570-577.

Map Square 78.

NORHAM (Northumberland)

340½ miles. Fares, 71/8*a*, 43/0*c*. R. T., double fare. Departures *from* London as for Berwick-on-Tweed. Departures *for* London about 4 times daily. Pop. 757.

Map Square 3.

NORMACOT (Stafford)

148½ miles. Fares, 31/0*a*, 18/7*c*. R. T. for two months, 62/0*a*, 37/2*c*. Departures *from* London as for Longton. Departures *for* London about 6 times daily.

Map Square 12.

NORMANTON (Yorks)

from *St. Pancras*, 185½ miles. Fares, 36/6*a*, 21/11*c*. R. T., double fare. Pop. 15,858.

Map Square 12.

St. Pan.	Norm'n	Norm'n	St. Pan.
AM 4.25	10.32	AM 3.30	7.50
9. 0*r*	1.53	7. 2*r*	12.10
9.50*r*	2.48	8.33*r*	1.30
11.45*r*	5.27	9. 5*r*	2.10
PM 1.50*r*	5.54	11.10*r*	4.10
2.25*r*	7.33	PM12.38*r*	5.45
3.30*r*	8.42	3.30*r*	8.35
6.15*r*	10.33	10.18	4.20
9.15	2.54	—	—
11.50	5.28	—	—
—	—	—	—
—	—	—	—
—	—	—	—

Sunday Trains.

AM10.50*r*	4.30	AM 3.30	8.57
PM 3.15	7.45	7.32*r*	5. 2
9.15	2.54	PM12.33	5.27
—	—	4.27*r*	9.43
—	—	10.18	4.55
—	—	—	—
—	—	—	—
—	—	—	—

Restaurant Car.

NORTHALLERTON

(Yorks) from *King's Cross*, 217¾ miles. Fares, 45/5*a*, 27/3*c*. R.T., double fare. Pop. 4,791.

Map Square 7.

King's +	Northl.	Northl.	King's +
AM 4.45	10.41	AM 7. 4	1. 5
7.15*r*	1. 5	8.39*r*	1.15
10. 0*r*	3.26	8.57	3.50
11.50*r*	5.18	10.56*r*	4.30
PM 1.50*r*	6.57	PM 1.33*r*	6.15
5.35*r*	10.16	4. 5*r*	9.25
11.25*d*	4. 0	8.50	3.25
11.25*e*	4.26	—	—
—	—	—	—
—	—	—	—
—	—	—	—
—	—	—	—
—	—	—	—

Sunday Trains.

AM11.30*r*	6.50	AM11.35	5.15
PM11.25	4.26	PM 8.34	5.40
—	—	—	—
—	—	—	—
—	—	—	—
—	—	—	—
—	—	—	—
—	—	—	—

d Saturdays only.
e Saturdays excepted.
r Restaurant Car.

NORTHAM (Hants) from *Waterloo*, 77¾ miles. Fares, 16/5*a*, 9/10*c*. R. T. for two months, 32/10*a*, 19/8*c*. Departures *from* London as for St. Denys. Departures *for* London 5 times daily. Pop. 11,597.

NORTHAMPTON (CASTLE) from *Euston*, 65¾ miles. Fares, 13/2*a*, 7/11*c*. R. T., double fare. Pop. 90,923.
Map Square 18.

EUSTON	NORTHAM.	NORTHAM.	EUSTON
AM 5. 0	6.18	AM 4. 3*g*	5.40
6.45	8.15	7. 5	9.40
7.35	10. 8	8.10*e*	9.52
9.15*r*	10.46	8.45	10.15
9.30	11.12	8.50	11.40
10.40	12.18	10.21	11.55
12. 0*nr*	1.34	10.39*d*	12.20
PM12.15*e*	2.31	10.39*e*	12.32
12.15*d*	2.40	11.22	12.40
1.35*dy*	3. 5	PM 1. 0*h*	2.45
3. 5	4.41	2.10	4.15
4.15*r*	5.40	2.26*k*	3.45
5.32	7.16	3.44	5.35
6.10*e*	8 .7	5. 0*t*	6.25
7. 0*r*	8.16	6. 2*t*	7.20
7.15*d*	9.58	6.12	8.35
8. 0*e*	9.58	7.46	9.20
9.30	11. 5	9.20	11.35
11.50	1.38	—	—
—	—	—	—
—	—	—	—
—	—	—	—

Sunday Trains.

AM 9.15	11.10	AM 4. 3	5.45
PM 3.50	5.54	10.38	12.25
6.45	8.48	PM 2.30	4. 0
9.15	10.49	3.25	5 5
11.50	1.21	4.12	5.45
—	—	8. 7	10.10
—	—	—	—
—	—	—	—

d Saturdays only.
e Saturdays excepted.
g Mondays excepted.
h Thursdays and Saturdays only.
k Mondays and Saturdays only.
n Noon.
r Restaurant Car.
t Tea Car.
y Change at Willesden.

ANOTHER ROUTE from *St. Pancras*, 71¾ miles. Fares as above.

ST. PAN.	N'MPTON	N'MPTON	ST. PAN.
AM 4.25	7. 1	AM 7.10	9.30
6.25	9.21	7.38	10. 5
7.50	10.33	9.20	11.25
9.25	12.16	9.55	1. 3
11.35	2.19	11.37*r*	1.30
PM12.30	2.53	PM 1.20	3.25
1.25*r*	3.10	2.35	5.20
3.35	5.44	4.45	7. 3
4.30*r*	6.51	6. 3	8.22
6.30	8.42	7.30*r*	10. 5
—	—	9. 8	11.45
—	—	—	—
—	—	—	—

Sunday Trains.

AM 8. 0	11.35*h*	AM 9.40*h*	11.53
PM 1.35	4.21*h*	PM 5.20*h*	8.30
6.15*r*	9.45*h*	7.30*h*	11. 7
—	—	—	—

h Castle Station.
r Restaurant Car.

The Plough, Northampton. First-class Family and Commercial Hotel. Private suites: choice Wines, and moderate charges. Apply to MANAGER.

NORTH BERWICK (East Lothian) from *King's Cross*, 379½ miles. Fares, 79/10*a*, 47/11*c*. R. T. for two months, 159/8*a*, 95/10*c*. Pop. 5,217.
Map Square 41.

KING'S +	N. BER.	N. BER.	KING'S +
AM 4.45*e*	5.33	AM 7.15*r*	6.15
4.45*d*	6.24	PM 1.21*r*	10. 0
10. 0*r*	7.46	4. 8	3.25
PM 1.15*r*	9.37	6.30	6. 0
8.25*e*	9.25	—	—
11.40*e*	7.57	—	—
—	—	—	—

Sunday Trains.

PM 8.25	9.25 *f*	—	—
—	—	—	—

d Saturdays only.
e Saturdays excepted.
r Restaurant Car.

Marine Hotel. Leading Seaside Hotel in Scotland. Renowned Golfing Centre. Electric Light. Elevator. Spacious Lounge. New Garage. Telephone No. 110.
H. T. WESTON, Manager.

NORTH CAMP (Aldershot). *See* ALDERSHOT.
Map Square 23.

NORTH CAVE (Yorks), 213½ miles. Fares, 35/0*a*, 21/0*c*. R. T. for two months, 70/0*a*. Departures *from* London as for Cudworth. Departures *for* London about 5 times daily. Pop. 1,033.
Map Square 13.

NORTH CONNEL (Argyll), 498¾ miles. No through fares. Departures *from* London as for Oban. Departures *for* London about 3 times daily.
Map Square 37.

NORTH DROVE (Lincoln), 95½ miles. Fares, 19/10*a*, 11/11*c*. R. T., double fare. Departures *from* London as for Spalding. Departures *for* London about 3 times daily.
Map Square 18.

NORTH DULWICH. *See* DULWICH, NORTH.

NORTH EALING. *See* EALING, NORTH.

NORTH EASTRINGTON. *See* EASTRINGTON, NORTH.

NORTH ELMHAM (Norfolk) from *Liverpool Street*, 126¾ miles. Fares, 23/7*a*, 14/2*c*. R. T. for two months, 47/2*a*. Departures *from* London as for Dereham. Departures *for* London about 9 times daily. Pop. 919.
Map Square 19.

NORTHENDEN (Cheshire), 184¼ miles. Fares, 37/9*a*, 22/8*c*. R. T. for two months, 75/6*a*. Departures *from* London as for Cheadle. Departures *for* London about 4 times daily. Pop. 3,097.

NORTHFIELD (Worcester), 119 miles. Fares, 23/7*a*, 14/2*c*. R. T for two months, 47/2*a*. Departures *from* London as for Birmingham (New Street). Departures *for* London about 5 times daily. Pop. 31,395.
Map Square 17.

NORTHFIELDS (Middlesex), from *Mansion House*, 11 miles. *See* p. 489.
Map Square 67.

NORTHFLEET (Kent) from *Charing Cross*, *Cannon Street*, and *London Bridge*, 22½ miles. Fares from Charing Cross, 4/9*a*, 3/9*b*, 2/10*c*. R. T. for two months, 7/10*a*, 6/1*b*, 5/3*c*. From Cannon Street, 4/4*a*, 3/5*b*, 2/7*c*. R. T. for two months, 7/10*a*, 6/1*b*, 5/2*c*. Pop. 15,719. *See* pp. 552-554.
Map Square 24.

NORTH GREENWICH. *See* GREENWICH, NORTH.

NORTH GRIMSTON (Yorks), 214 miles. Fares, 44/7*a*, 26/9*c*. R. T., double fare. Departures *from* London as for Malton. Departures *for* London about 3 times daily. Pop. 157.
Map Square 8.

NORTH HARROW. *See* HARROW, NORTH.

NORTH HOWDEN. *See* HOWDEN, NORTH.

NORTHIAM (Sussex), 57¼ miles. No through fares. Departures *from* London as for Tenterden (*via* Robertsbridge). Departures *for* London about 4 times daily. Pop. 1,085.
Map Square 24.

NORTH KELSEY (Lincoln), 153¼ miles. Fares, 31/10*a*, 19/1*c*. R. T., double fare. Departures *from* London as for Lincoln or Barnetby. Departures *for* London about 3 times daily. Pop. 819.
Map Square 13.
Station closed on Sundays.

NORTHOLT (Middlesex) from *Paddington*, 8¾ miles. Fares, 0/10½*c*. R. T. for two days, 1/6*c*. Pop. 904. *See* pp. 490, 491.
Map Square 57.

NORTHOLT JUNCT. from *Paddington* or *Marylebone*, 10¼ miles. Fares, 2/0*a*, 1/2½*c*. R. T. for two days, 4/0*a*, 2/4*c*. *See* pp. 490, 491, 495, 496.
Map Square 48.

NORTHORPE (Lincoln), 156½ miles. Fares, 31/6*a*, 18/11*c*. R. T., double fare. Departures *from* London as for Gainsboro' (*via* Retford). Departures *for* London about 4 times daily. Pop. 169.
Map Square 13.

NORTHORPE (Yorks), from *Euston*, 209 miles. Fares, 37/9*a*, 22/8*c*. R. T., double fare. Departures *from* London as for Huddersfield. Departures *for* London about 4 times daily.

NORTH QUEENSFERRY

(Fife), 403¾ miles. Fares 83/7*a*, 50/2*c*. R. T. for two months, 167/2*a*, 100/4*c*. Departures *from* London as for Edinburgh (Waverley). Departures *for* London about 3 times daily.

NORTH RODE

(Cheshire), 160¾ miles. Fares 33/6*a*, 20/1*c*. R. T. for two months, 67/0*a*. Departures *from* London as for Congleton. Departures *for* London about twice daily. Pop. 274.
Map Square 12.

NORTH SEATON

(Northumberland), 285½ miles. Fares, 60/3*a*, 36/2*c*. R. T., for two months, 120/6*a*, 72/4*c*. Departures *from* London as for Newcastle-on-Tyne. Departures *for* London about 6 times daily. Pop. 1,904.
Map Square 3.

NORTH SKELTON

(Yorks), 252¾ miles. Fares, 52/9*a*, 31/8*c*. R. T., 105/6*a*, 63/4*c*. Departures *from* London as for Saltburn or Sandsend. Departures *for* London about 6 times daily. Pop. 1,877.
Map Square 8.

NORTH SUNDERLAND

(Northumberland), 320¼ miles. No through fares. Departures *from* London as for Morpeth. Departures *for* London about 4 times daily. Pop. 1,069.
Map Square 3.

NORTH TAWTON

(Devon) from *Waterloo*, 191 miles. Fares, 39/10*a*, 23/11*c*. R.T. for two months, 79/8*a*, 47/10*c*. Departures *from* London as for Yeoford. Departures *for* London about 5 times daily. Pop. 1,455.
Map Square 26.

NORTH THORESBY

(Lincoln) from *King's Cross*, 148 miles. Fares, 30/8*a*, 18/5*c*. R. T., double fare. Departures *from* London as for Louth. Departures *for* London about 5 times daily. Pop. 595.
Map Square 13.

NORTH WALSHAM

(Norfolk) from *Liverpool Street*, 130 miles. Fares, 25/3*a*, 15/2*c*. R. T. for two months, 50/6*a*. Pop. 4,156.
Map Square 19.

L'poolSt.	N.Wal.	N.Wal.	L'poolSt.
AM 5. 5	10. 3	AM 6.50*f*	10.36
8.15*r*	11.57	8. 4*r*	11.22
9.50*r*	1.14	9.29	1.20
PM12.25*r*	3. 4	PM 1. 8*r*	3.50
12.33*r*	3.59	1.20*r*	4.58
3.10	6.23	2.39	6.32
5.18*r*	8.59	4. 2*r*	8.33
—	—	5.49*r*	9.22
—	—	9. 4	2.50
—	—	—	—

Sunday Trains.

AM 9.20*r*	2.48	PM 1.17	6.40
PM 4.40	9.48	5.56*r*	9.10
—	—	8.18	3. 0
—	—	—	—

f Mondays only.
r Restaurant Car.

NORTH WALSHAM—*continued.*

ANOTHER ROUTE

from *King's Cross*, 161¾ miles. Fares as above.

King's +	N.Wal.	N.Wal.	King's +
AM 4.45	10. 3	AM 7.53	1. 5
7.15*r*	1.13	9.37	3.50
10.10*r*	4.33	11.49*r*	4.30
PM 1.50*r*	7. 2	PM 3.23	9. 0
3. 0	8. 3	—	—

No Sunday Trains.
r Restaurant Car.

NORTH WEALD

(Essex) from *Fenchurch Street*, 19½ miles, or from *Liverpool Street*, 19 miles. Fares, from Liverpool Street, 4/2*a*, 3/4*b*, 2/6*c*. R. T. for two months, 8/4*a*, 6/5*b*, 4/6½*c*. From Fenchurch Street, 4/0*a*, 3/2*b*, 2/5*c*. R. T. for two months, 7/10½*a*, 6/1½*b*, 4/4½*c*. Pop. 1,146. *See* pp. 541-544.
Map Square 24.

NORTH WEMBLEY.

See Wembley, North.

NORTHWICH

(Cheshire), from *Euston*, 171½ miles. Fares, 35/8*a*, 21/5*c*. R. T., double fare. Pop. 18,385.
Map Square 12.

Euston	N'thw'ch	N'thw'ch	Euston
AM12.25	6.24	AM 6.30*er*	12. 5
2.35	6.54	6.30*dr*	12.20
5. 0	11.45	8.40*r*	1. 0
8.30*r*	1.25	11.22*er*	3.10
10.40*r*	3. 7	11.55*r*	4.15
PM 1.30*r*	5.21	PM 1. 0*r*	5.50
2.35*t*	6.21	4. 3*r*	8.10
5.20*r*	9. 3	5.38*er*	9. 5
—	—	5.38*dr*	9.15
—	—	6.37*r*	10.45
—	—	9.40*e*	5. 0
—	—	10. 0*d*	5. 0

No Sunday Trains.
d Saturdays only.
e Saturdays excepted.
r Restaurant Car.
t Tea Car.

NORTHWICK PARK

AND KENTON (Middlesex) from *Baker Street*, 8½ miles. Fares, 1/9*a*, 1/0*c*. R.T. for two days, 2/11*a*, 1/9*c*. *See* back of Map.
Map Square 49.

NORTHWOOD

(Middlesex) from *Marylebone* and *Baker St.*, 13¾ miles. Fares, 2/10*a*, 1/8*c*. R. T. for two months, 5/8*a*, 3/2½*c*. Pop. 5,236. *See* pp 494, 495.
Map Square 23.

Eastbury House Hotel. First-class Residential. Golf, Tennis, Badminton, Billiards. 27 acres, glorious views. Inclusive Terms, Manageress. 'Phone, Northwood 21.

NORTH WOOLWICH

(Essex). *See* Woolwich, North.

NORTH WOOTTON.

See Wootton, North.

NORTON

(Cheshire), 183½ miles. Fares, 37/9*a*, 22/8*c*. R. T. for two months, 75/6*a*. Departures *from* London as for Chester. Departures *for* London about 5 times daily. Pop. 277.
Map Square 12.

NORTON

(Worcester), 117¼ miles. Fares, 23/9*a*, 14/3*c*. R. T. for two months, 47/6*a*. Departures *from* London as for Pershore. Departures *for* London about 4 times daily. Pop. 999.
Map Square 17.

NORTON

(Yorks) from *King's Cross*, 164 miles. Fares, 34/2*a*, 20/6*c*. Departures *from* London as for Knottingley. Departures *for* London about 5 times daily. Pop. 516.
Map Square 13.

NORTON BRIDGE

(Stafford) from *Euston*, 139 miles. Fares, 29/0*a*, 17/5*c*. R. T. for two months, 58/0*a*.
Map Square 17.

Euston	Nor. B.	Nor. B.	Euston
AM 2.35	7.31	AM 7. 5	11. 0
5. 0	9. 3	8.24*er*	12. 5
6.45	11. 0	8.24*dr*	12.20
10.40*r*	1.51	10.30*r*	2.20
12. 0*nr*	3.51	PM12.11*dr*	3.10
PM 4. 5*t*	7.43	1.10	5.35
4.45*r*	7.50	3. 9*t*	6.15
6.55*r*	10.28	5.43	9.20
—	—	6.12*dr*	9.15
—	—	7. 6*r*	10. 0
—	—	9.38	5. 0

Sunday Trains.

AM12.10	10.33	PM12. 3	4. 0
PM12.10*r*	3.38	5.34*r*	8.55
3.50	9.48	9. 6	5. 0

d Saturdays only.
e Saturdays excepted.
n Noon.
r Restaurant Car.
t Tea Car.

NORTON EAST

(Leicester) from *Euston*, 93 miles. Fares, 18/9*a*, 11/3*c*. R.T. for two months, 37/6*a*, 22/6*c*. Departures *from* London as for Hallaton. Departures *for* London about 3 times daily. Pop. 120.
Map Square 18.

NORTON FITZWARREN

(Somerset) from *Paddington*, 145 miles. Fares, 30/3*a*, 18/2*c*. R. T. for two months, 60/6*a*, Departures *from* London as for Taunton. Departures *for* London about 5 times daily. Pop. 630.
Map Square 21.

NORTON-IN-HALES

(Salop), 159½ miles. Fares, 32/11*a*, 19/9*c*. R. T. for two months, 65/10*a*. Departures *from* London as for Newcastle-under-Lyme. Departures *for* London about 4 times daily. Pop. 376.
Map Square 12.

NORTON-ON-TEES

(Durham), 238 miles. Fares, 49/9*a*, 29/10*c*. R. T., double fare. Departures *from* London as for Stockton-on-Tees. Departures *for* London about 4 times daily. Pop. 6,109.
Map Square 8.

NORWICH

(Norfolk) (Thorpe Station) *via* Colchester, from *Liverpool Street*, 115 miles. Fares, 23/7*a*, 14/2*c*. R. T. for two months, 47/2*a*, 28/4*c*. Pop. 120,653.
Map Square 19.

Leave L'pool St.	Arrive at Trowse.	Arrive at N'rw'ch.
AM 5. 0	8.35	8.43
8.15*r*	—	11.17
9.50*r*	—	12.37
10.12	1.56	2. 0
PM12.33*r*	—	3.15
3.10*r*	—	5.44
5.18*r*	8.11	8.15
—	—	—
—	—	—
—	—	—

Sunday Trains.

AM 9.20*r*	—	1.20
PM 4.40	—	8.10
—	—	—
—	—	—

NORWICH—*continued.*

Trains from Norwich.

Leave N'RW'CH.	TROWSE.	Arr at L'POOL ST.
AM 6.43*r*	6.48*r*	10.30
7.37*f*	7.42*f*	10.36
8.44*r*	—	11.22
8.50	8.55	12.39
10.17	—	1.20
10.22*r*	10.27*r*	2. 3
PM 2. 9	—	4.58
3.23	3.28	6.32
3.43	3.49	7.51
6.35*r*	6.40*r*	9.22
7. 2	7. 7	11.16

Sunday Trains.

AM 7.14	—	11.38
PM 6.29*r*	—	9.10

d Saturdays only.
e Saturdays excepted.
f Mondays only.
r Restaurant Car.

ANOTHER ROUTE (THORPE STATION) from *Liverpool Street*, *via* Cambridge, 124 miles. Fares as above.

Leave L'POOL ST.	TROWSE	Arrive at N'RW'CH.
AM 5. 5	8.43	8.50
5.50	10.32	10.38
8.30*r*	12.18	12.22
11.50*r*	—	3.19
PM 2.34	5.56	6. 3
5.49*r*	9.31	9.36
7.10*r*	—	10.29
10.12	1.54	1.58

Sunday Trains.

AM 9.25	—	1.38
PM 3.25	—	7.36
9.12	—	1.55

Trains from Norwich.

Leave N'RW'CH.	TROWSE.	Arr. at L'POOL ST.
AM 6.32*r*	6.37*r*	10.23
7.34	—	11.27
8.47	8.52	12.40
10.30*r*	10.35*r*	2.21
PM 1.57*r*	—	5.17
4.21*r*	4.26*r*	8.22
4.59*r*	—	8.33
10.24	10.30	2.50

Sunday Trains.

PM 2.24	—	6.40
6.15	—	9.40
10.24	—	3. 0

r Restaurant Car.

ANOTHER ROUTE (City) from *King's Cross*, 165¼ miles. Fares as above.

KING'S+	NORWH.	NORWH.	KING'S+
AM 4.45	10.23	AM 7.43	1. 5
7.15*r*	1.21	9.35	3.50
10.10*r*	4.34	11.43*r*	4.30
PM 1.50*r*	7.13	PM 3.15	9. 0
3. 0	8.19	—	—

No Sunday Trains.

r Restaurant Car.

NORWICH—*continued.*

Bell Hotel. Telephone 131. First-class Hotel in the centre of the City. Close to Market and business interests, Castle and Cathedral. An excellent centre for business or holidays. Modern comforts, Electric Light and Garage.

TRUST HOUSES, Ltd.

Royal Hotel. First - class Family and Commercial Hotel. Finest appointed Hotel in East Anglia. Excellent Lounges. Stockrooms, and Billiard Room. Moderate Tariff. Lift. Night Porter. Omnibus. Telegrams, "Primus, Norwich." Telephone 1411.
Address, MANAGERESS.

Maid's Head Hotel. Most unique hotel in England, combining comforts of 15th century hostelry with every up-to-date modern luxury. Electric light and sanitary certificate in every room. Perfect bath rooms. First-class chef. Omnibus meets trains. National Telephone 85.
Address, MANAGERESS.

NORWOOD JUNCT.
(London) from *London Bridge*, 8¾ miles. Fares, 1/8*a*, 1/9*c*. R. T. for two days, 3/4*a*, 2/0*c*. Pop. (Norwood) 31,773. *See* pp. 564, 565, 568-570.
Map Square 23.

From *Victoria*, 10¼ miles. Fares, *via* Crystal Palace, 1/8*a*, 1/0*c*. R. T. for two days, 3/4*a*, 2/0*c*. *Via* Selhurst, 1/11*a*, 1/2*c*. R. T. for two days 3/8*a*, 2/0*c*. *See* pp. 574-577.

Thomas Bradford & Co., Upper Norwood Steam Laundry. Church Road, Upper Norwood. *See advt. on Map.*

NORWOOD (WEST)
from *London Bridge* or *Victoria*, 7 miles. Fares, from London Bridge, *via* Tulse Hill, 1/3*a*, 0/9*c*. R. T. for two days, 2/4*a*, 1/4*c*. *Via* Crystal Palace, 0/10½*c*. R. T. for two days, 2/7*a*, 1/9*c*. From Victoria, 1/2*a*, 0/8½*c*. R. T. for two days, 2/4*a*, 1/4*c*. Pop. 36,294. *See* pp. 578, 579, 581, 582.
Map Square 79.

NOSTELL (Yorks),
170½ miles. Fares, 35/5*a*, 21/3*c*. R. T., double fare. Departures *from* London as for Hemsworth. Departures *for* London about 8 times daily. Pop. 540.
Map Square 13.

NOTGROVE (Gloucester),
96½ miles. Fares, 20/2*a*, 12/1*c*. R. T. for two months, 40/4*a*. Departures *from* London as for Bourton - on - Water. Departures *for* London about 3 times daily. Pop. 156.
Map Square 22.

NOTTINGHAM from
St. Pancras, 123¼ miles. Fares, 25/8*a*, 15/5*c*. R. T. double fare. Pop. 262,658.
Map Square 13.

ST. PAN.	NOT'H'M	NOT'H'M	ST. PAN.
AM 2.25	7.40	AM 12.30*g*	4.20
4.25	8.53	4.30	7.25
7.50	11. 5	5.30	8. 3
9. 0*r*	11.15	7. 0*r*	9.57
9.50*r*	12.49	8.23*r*	10.45
11. 0*r*	1.35	10.30*r*	1.20
11.45*r*	2.30	11.50	3.25
PM 1. 0*r*	3.58	PM 1.40*r*	4.10
1.50*r*	4. 5	2.57*r*	5.30
3.30*r*	5.50	3.45*r*	6.35
5. 0*r*	7.15	5. 0*r*	7.15
5.35*r*	8.34	5.25	8.20
6.15*r*	8.48	6.45*r*	9. 5
9.15	11.42	—	—
9.30*e*	12. 3	—	—
11.45	2.26	—	—

Sunday Trains.

AM 10.50*r*	2.20	AM 5.30	8. 5
PM 3.15	6.12	8. 5	11.53
6.15*r*	9.53	PM 1.50*r*	5. 2
9.15	11.42	2. 0	5.27
9.30	11.58	6.45*r*	9.43
11.45	2.26	8.42	4.55

e Saturdays excepted.
g Mondays excepted.
r Restaurant Car.

ANOTHER ROUTE (Victoria) from *Marylebone*,126½ miles. Fares as above.

M'BONE	NOT'H'M	NOT'H'M	M'BONE
AM 2.32	5. 0	AM 1. 7*g*	3.57
8.45*r*	11.58	5.20	9.46
10. 0*r*	12.39	7.40	10.36
PM 12.15*r*	3. 7	8.43*r*	11.10
3.20*r*	5.36	10.28*r*	1.13
5. 0*r*	7.26	PM 12.14*r*	3. 0
6.20*r*	8.44	12.36	4.56
6.25	11.20	4.18*r*	6.38
7.30*d*	12.16	6. 9*r*	8.55
10. 0*d*	12.44	7.14*r*	9.55
10. 5*e*	12.52	—	—

Sunday Trains.

AM 9.30	1.54	AM 1. 7	3.57
11.15*r*	2. 2	PM 2.53*r*	5.40
PM 5.30*r*	8.15	3. 5	8.58
—	—	7.37*r*	10.24

d Saturdays only.
e Saturdays excepted.
g Mondays excepted.
r Restaurant Car.

NOTTINGHAM—contd.

ANOTHER ROUTE (Victoria) from *King's Cross*, 128¾ miles. Fares as above.

KING'S +	NOT'H'M	NOT'H'M	KING'S +
AM 4. 45	8.42	AM 7.15	10.40
5. 5	9.54	8.30r	11.30
7.15r	10.19	9.40	1. 5
8.45	12.30	10.42r	1.30
10.10r	1. 7	11.43	3.50
11.30	3.34	PM 2.18	6.25
PM 1.50r	5. 9	2.57r	6.30
4. 0r	7.19	5. 0	9. 0
5.35r	8.29	6.16r	9.25
5.45r	9.44	10.25c	3.25
8.25	11.46	10.35d	3.25
11.25e	5.57	—	—
—	—	—	—
—	—	—	—

Sunday Trains.

AM 11.30r	2.43	PM 12.15r	3.45
12. 0r	3.5S	2.25	5.55
PM 5. 0r	9. 0	—	—
11.25	5.57	—	—
—	—	—	—
—	—	—	—
—	—	—	—
—	—	—	—

d Saturdays only.
e Saturdays excepted.
r Restaurant Car.

Flying Horse Hotel (Trust Houses Ltd.). Excellent Public Restaurant. Telephone 4164. *See advt. p.* **273.**

Victoria Station Hotel, adjoining G. N. & G. C. Ry. Leading Hotel in Midlands. Headquarters of Automobile Club.

High Peak Hotel. Adjacent to the Forest, Arboretum and Forest Road. Garage (50 cars). Telephone 1979.

Black Boy Hotel. First-class Family and Commercial. Every Comfort. Centre of Town in Great Market Place. Pleasant Coffee and Sitting Rooms. Large and Airy Stockrooms, connected with Hotel by telephone. Three minutes from Victoria Station. Telephone 3030, 3931. Garage. I. P. Petrol. Headquarters of the Nottingham Automobile Club.

George Hotel. First-class Family and Commercial. Re-decorated. Refurnished. Officially appointed Royal Automobile Club. Telephone : 2445. Telegrams : "George Hotel, Nottingham."

Lancashire and Cheshire Insurance Corporation, Ltd., 4, Low Pavement. Tel. 4142. *See advt. p. 3 cover.*

NOTTING HILL GATE

to and from *Charing Cross, Victoria, South Kensington, Praed Street, Baker Street, King's Cross, Moorgate, Aldgate,* and all intermediate Stations every few minutes. *See back of Map.*

Map Square 59.

NOTTING HILL GATE

(Central London Tube). *See back* of Map.

NOTTON (Yorks), 180¼

miles. Fares, 36/1a, 21/8c. R. T., double fare. Departures *from* London as for Barnsley. Departures *for* London about 5 times daily. Pop. 288.

NOVAR (Ross), 592¼ miles.

Fares, 106/3a, 63/9c. R. T. for two months, 212/6a, 127/6c. Departures *from* London as for Dingwall. Departures *for* London about 3 times daily.

Map Square 34.

NUNBURNHOLME

(Yorks), 195½ miles. Fares, 42/11a, 25/9c. R. T., double fare. Departures *from* London as for York. Departures *for* London about 6 times daily. Pop. 190.

Map Square 8.

NUNEATON (Warwick)

from *Euston,* 97 miles. Fares, 20/2a, 12/1c. R. T., double fare. Pop. 41,894.

Map Square 17.

EUSTON	NUN'TON	NUN'TON	EUSTON
AM 5. 0	7.13	AM 2.26	5. 0
6.45	9.12	7.13r	10. 0
8.45r	10.51	9. 8	11. 0
10. 0	12.54	10.54r	12.50
10.40r	1.14	11.49r	2.20
12. 0nr	2.28	PM 1.10r	4.15
PM 2.50t	4.50	2.43	5.35
4. 5t	6.14	3.55t	6.15
4.45r	6.41	6.20r	8.10
5.20r	7.24	6.53r	9.20
6.30er	8.37	8.49r	10.45
7. 0dr	9.23	—	—
9.30	11.37	—	—
—	—	—	—
—	—	—	—
—	—	—	—
—	—	—	—
—	—	—	—
—	—	—	—

Sunday Trains.

AM 9.15	12.16	AM 2.26	5. 0
PM 3.50	6.55	6. 7	8. 0
9.15	11.49	PM 2.19	5. 5
—	—	6.49	8.55
—	—	—	—
—	—	—	—
—	—	—	—
—	—	—	—
—	—	—	—
—	—	—	—

d Saturdays only,
e Saturdays excepted.
n Noon.
r Restaurant Car.
t Tea Car.

NUNEATON—continued.

ANOTHER ROUTE (Abbey Street) from *St. Pancras,* 111¼ miles. Fares as above.

ST. PAN.	NUN'TON	NUN'TON	ST. PAN.
AM 2.25	7. 8	AM 8. 9r	11. 0
4.25	9. 1	9.48r	1.20
8.25r	11.42	11.41	3.25
10.25r	1.15	PM 12.24r	4.10
11.45r	2.18	2.30r	5.45
PM 12.15r	2.46	4.11r	7.57
1.25r	4.42	6. 8r	9. 5
2.25r	6.20	7. 3er	10. 5
4.25r	8. 2	11.32d	4.20
6.25dr	9. 5	—	—
—	—	—	—
—	—	—	—
—	—	—	—

Sunday Trains.

PM 3.15	8.42	AM 7.54	11.53
—	—	PM 6.44r	9.52
—	—	—	—
—	—	—	—
—	—	—	—
—	—	—	—

d Saturdays only.
e Saturdays excepted.
r Restaurant Car.

NUNEHAM COURTENAY (Oxon). Station at Littlemore.

NUNHEAD (London) from

Victoria, Ludgate Hill, and *St. Paul's,* 6 miles. Fares from Victoria, 1/1a, 0/10b, 07/½c. R. T. for two days, 1/11a, 1/4b, 1/0c. From Ludgate Hill, 0/10a, 0/8b, 0/6c. R. T. for two days, 1/8a, 1/4b, 0/10½c. Pop. 14,025. *See pp.* 562-563.

NUNNINGTON (Yorks),

215¾ miles. No through fares. Departures *from* London as for Ampleforth. Departures *for* London about 5 times daily. Pop. 312.

Map Square 8.

NUNTHORPE (Yorks),

243 miles. Fares, 50/8a, 30/5c. R. T., double fare. Departures *from* London as for Middlesbrough. Departures *for* London about 4 times daily. Pop. 289.

Map Square 8.

NURSLING (Hants),

83 miles. Fares, 17/6a, 10/6c. R. T. for two months, 35/0a, 21/0c. Departures *from* London as for Romsey or Redbridge. Departures *for* London about 4 times daily. Pop. 661.

Map Square 23.

NUTFIELD (Surrey)

from *Charing Cross, Cannon Street,* and *London Bridge.* 25¼ miles. Fares, 4/.a, 3/8b, 2/9c. R. T. for two months, 8/2a, 7/4b, 5/3c. Departures *from* London as for Godstone. Departures *for* London about 9 times daily. Pop. 1,828.

Map Square 23.

Station Hotel. Adjoining Station. Beautifully situated on Surrey Hills. Ideal for quiet week-end. Every convenience. Moderate charges.

NOTTINGHAM (See Announcement above) **VICTORIA STATION HOTEL.**

OAKHAM (Rutland) from *St. Pancras*, 93¾ miles. Fares, 18/9*a*, 11/3*c*. R. T., double fare. Pop. 3,327. *Map Square 18.*

St. Pan.	Oakham	Oakham	St. Pan.
AM 2.25	7. 5	AM 8.43*r*	10.45
4.25	8.21	11. 5*r*	1.20
7.50*r*	10.22	11.15*r*	2.10
8.25*r*	11.25	PM 1. 5*r*	4.10
9.50*r*	1. 5	1. 9*r*	4.20
10.25*r*	1.58	6. 9	8.20
11.35	2.51	9.20	4.20
PM 1. 0*r*	3.16	—	—
3.30*r*	5.46	—	—
4.30*r*	6.55	—	—
5.35*r*	8.14	—	—
6.25*r*	10.11	—	—

Sunday Trains.

PM 3.15	9.12	AM 7.25	11.53
—	—	PM 7.28*r*	9.43
—	—	—	—

r Restaurant Car.

ANOTHER ROUTE from *King's Cross*, 102 miles. Fares as above.

King's +	Oakh'm	Oakh'm	King's +
AM 5. 5	8.54	AM 8.21*r*	12.25
7.15*r*	10. 8	10.10	1. 5
7.45	11.15	11. 5*r*	1.55
10.10*r*	1. 9	PM 1.58*r*	4.45
PM 1.50*r*	4.40	4.30*r*	7.10
3. 0	6.13	5.57*r*	9.25
5.45*r*	9.20	10.10*r*	3.25

Sunday Trains.

12. 0*nr* 5.47	AM10.32	3.45
—	—	—

n Noon.
r Restaurant Car.

OAKINGTON (Cambs) from *Liverpool Street*, 62½ miles. Fares, 12/3*a*, 7/4*c*. R. T., double fare. Departures *from London* as for St. Ives (Hunts). Departures *for London* about 8 times daily. Pop. 447. *Map Square 18.*

OAKLEIGH PARK (Herts) from *King's Cross, Moorgate Street*, and *Broad Street*, 8½ miles. Fares from King's Cross, 1/7*a*, 1/3*b*, 0/11½*c*. R. T. for two days, 3/2*a*, 2/6*b*, 1/11*c*. From Moorgate Street and Broad Street, 1/8*a*, 1/4*b*, 1/0*c*. R. T. for two days, 3/4*a*, 2/8*b*, 1/11½*c*. *See* pp. 511-517.

OAKLE STREET (Gloucester), 119½ miles. Fares, 24/10*a*, 14/11*c*. R.T. for two months, 49/8*a*, 29/10*c*. Departures *from London* as for Gloucester. Departures *for London* about 5 times daily. *Map Square 22.*

OAKLEY (Beds) from *St. Pancras*, 53 miles. Fares, 10/8*a*, 6/5*c*. R. T., double fare. Pop. 330. *Map Square 18*

St. Pan.	Oakley	Oakley	St. Pan.
AM 4 25	6.57	AM 8. 8	9.30
6.25	8.35	8.35	10.31
9.25	11.29	10.15	11.25
PM12.30	1.48	PM 1. 2	3.25
3.35	4.58	3.41	5.20
4.30*r*	6. 6	6.48	8.22
5.35*r*	6.49	—	—
6.30	7.47	—	—

Sunday Trains.

AM 8. 0	10.17	AM11.17	1.30
PM 6.15*r*	7.39	PM 6.24	8.50
—	—	—	—

r Restaurant Car.

O

OAKAMOOR (Stafford), 145¼ miles. Fares, 30/0*a*, 18/0*c*. R. T. for two months, 60/0*a*. Departures *from London* for Uttoxeter. Departures *for London* about 3 times daily. Pop. 993. *Map Square 12.*

OAKENGATES (Salop) from *Paddington*, 139¾ miles. Fares, 29/0*a*, 17/5*c*. R. T. for two months, 58/0*a*. Pop. 11,349. *Map Square 17.*

Pad.	Oaken.	Oaken.	Pad.
AM 9.10*r*	12.47	AM 7.43*r*	11. 0
10.40*r*	2.42	8.51	12.25
10.45*r*	3.49	10.29*r*	2. 5
PM 2.10*t*	6.25	PM 1.18*r*	5. 0
4.10*t*	7.15	2.38*t*	6.55
6.10*r*	9.59	4.13*r*	8. 5
7.10*r*	10.32	5.46	10. 0
12.15*h*	7. 5	8.49	3.30
12.15*h*	8.23	—	—
—	—	—	—
—	—	—	—

Sunday Trains.

PM12.50*r*	4.12	AM 8.42*r*	1.40
6. 0*r*	9.13	PM12.45	6.20
—	—	—	—
—	—	—	—

h Saturday midnight only.
k Saturday midnight excepted.
r Restaurant Car.
t Tea Car.

REFERENCE NOTES.

a signifies First Class.
b „ Second Class.
c „ Third Class.
d „ On Saturdays only.
e „ Saturdays excepted.
f „ On Mondays only.
g „ Mondays excepted.
r „ Restaurant Car.
t „ Tea Car.
x „ Express.
R.T. „ Return Tickets.

All Trains in the Tables not otherwise marked carry Third Class Passengers.

MILNERS' SAFES.

IDRIS

SODA WATER
LEMONADE
DRY GINGER ALE
BREWED GINGER BEER
GINGER ALE

To be obtained at all Clubs, Hotels, Restaurants, Grocers, Wine Merchants, and Chemists.

OAKLEY (Fife) 416 miles. Fares, 86/6a, 51/11c. R.T. for two months, 173/0a, 103/10c. Departures *from* London as for Dunfermline, Departures *for* London about 3 times daily. Pop. 2,486.

OAKLEY (Hants) from *Waterloo*, 52½ miles. Fares, 11/0a, 6/7c. R. T. for two months, 22/0a, 13/2c. Pop. 214.
Map Square 23.

W'loo	Oakley	Oakley	W'loo
AM 5.50	7.56	AM 8.29	9.56
7.30	9.23	11.5s	12.22
9.30	11.8	PM12.49r	2.20
11.30r	1.8	2.56	4.20
PM 1.30r	2.49	4.43s	6.26
3.30s	4.49	6.6	7.40
5.0	6.25	8.38	10.50
6.0r	7.35	9.57	11.23
7.30	8.49	—	—
8.0	9.56	—	—

Sunday Trains.

AM 9.0	10.54	AM 10.44	12.11
PM 6.0	7.28	PM 7.16	9.12

r Restaurant Car.
s Refreshments served.

OAKWORTH (Yorks), from *St. Pancras*, 215 miles. Fares, 42/8a, 25/7c. R.T., double fare. Departures *from* London as for Keighley. Departures *for* London about 6 times daily. Pop. 4,171.
Map Square 12.

OATLANDS (Cumberland), 309 miles. No through fares. Departures *from* London as for Whitehaven or Moor Row. Departures *for* London about twice daily.

OBAN (Argyll) from *Euston*, 503¼ miles. Fares, 102/4a, 61/5c. R. T. for two months, 204/8a, 122/10c. Pop. 6 344.
Map Square 37.

Euston	Oban	Oban	Euston
AM 5.0	9.40l	AM 5.40r	7.30l
PM 1.30er	4.50h	9.10r	10.45l
1.30dr	5.4	11.50r	5.0h
7.50er	9.50h	PM 5.15	7.40h
11.35e	12.33l	—	—

Sunday Trains.

PM 7.50r	9.50h	—	—
11.35	12.33l	—	—

d Saturdays only.
e Saturdays excepted.
h A.M.
l P.M.
r Restaurant Car.

Marine Hotel, Esplanade. Largest and Leading Unlicensed Hotel. Moderate Tariff.
See advt. p. 274.

Great Western Hotel. Largest and Leading Hotel in West Highlands.
See advt. p. 274.

OCCUMSTER (Caithness), 741 miles. No through fares. Departures *from* London as for Wick. Departures *for* London about twice daily.
Map Square 32.

OCHILTREE (Ayr), 379¼ miles. No through fares. Departures *from* London as for Ayr. Departures *for* London about 4 times daily. Pop. 2,102.
Map Square 43.

OCKENDON (Essex) from *Fenchurch Street, via Upminster*, 18½ miles. Fares, 3/4a, 2/0c. R. T. for two months, 6/8a, 3/6c. Pop. 1,758.
Map Square 24.

Fen. St.	Ock'don	Ock'don	Fen. St.
AM 6.13k	7.16	AM 6.31	7.34
6.36hk	8.5	7.15h	8.24
7.42	8.35	8.5	8.53k
8.11h	9.38	8.35h	9.34
9.18	10.20	9.39	10.22
10.17h	11.10	10.20h	11.20
10.45	12.10	11.10e	12.22
11.35h	12.52	11.10d	12.41
PM 1.0e	1.47	PM12.10eh	1.22
1.5d	1.47	12.10dh	1.27
1.15dh	2.15	12.50	1.56
2.26d	3.4	1.47h	3.18
2.40h	4.3	2.15	3.28
4.27	5.16	3.4h	4.10
4.46h	5.45	4.1	4.54k
5.36dk	6.56	5.10h	6.33
5.46e	8.24	5.45	6.45
4.17e	6.56	6.56h	8.4
6.53	7.35	7.35h	9.15
7.20d	8.40	7.53	10.8
8.0e	8.40	9.36	10.30
8.13h	9.36	—	—

Sunday Trains.

AM 8.40h	9.58	AM 9.4h	10.18
9.45	10.48	9.58	11.35
11.10h	12.32	10.48h	12.59
PM 1.6	2.46	PM12.32	2.2k
2.7h	3.25	2.46h	4.4
6.10	7.8	7.55	8.59k
6.30h	7.56	9.19h	11.0
8.28	9.19	10.29	11.22k
8.45h	9.58	—	—

d Saturdays only.
e Saturdays excepted.
h Via Grays.
k Departs from or arrives at Mark Lane Station.

OCKLEY (Surrey) from *London Bridge, Victoria*, and *Clapham Junction*, 31 miles. Fares, 6/6a, 3/11c. R. T. for two months, 13/0a, 7/10c. Pop. 625.
Map Square 23.

	Leave		Arr. at
Vict.	Clap. J.	Lon. B.	Ockley
AM 5.18	5.23	5.28	7.3
7.45	7.56	7.35	9.28
8.58	—	9.22	11.0
10.30	10.38	10.35	12.9
PM12.35	12.42	12.24	2.8
4.5	4.12	—	5.22
—	—	5.14	6.28
6.0	—	—	7.8
—	—	5.59	7.36
7.20	7.27	7.15	8.30

Sunday Trains.

AM	—	6.55	8.29
9.0	9.7	8.55	10.11
PM 5.40	5.47	5.40	7.33

Trains from Ockley.

Leave Ockley	Lon. B.	Arrive at Clap. J.	Vict.
AM 7.37	9.5	9.5	9.12
7.55	9.17	—	9.34
9.10	10.22	—	10.28
10.38	11.50	11.35	11.42
11.52	1.28	1.48	1.57
PM 2.5	3.32	3.22	3.32
4.35	—	5.59	6.8
7.5	8.41	8.46	8.55
9.36	11.11	11.12	11.20

Sunday Trains.

AM 8.21	10.11	10.6	10.13
9.27	11.8	10.59	11.6
PM 8.45	10.25	10.32	10.42

OFFORD (Hunts) from *King's Cross*, 56 miles. Fares, 11/6a, 6/11c. R. T., double fare. Pop. 579.
Map Square 18.

King's +	Offord	Offord	King's +
AM 5.5	6.53	AM 7.59	9.56
7.45	9.35	9.47	11.15
10.12	12.27	11.33	1.25
PM 1.55	3.46	PM 1.54	3.50
4.15	5.54	4.25	6.25
5.10	7.16	8.1	10.20
6.15	8.4	—	—
8.30	10.16	—	—

Sunday Trains.

AM 8.30	10.35	PM 5.54	8.8

OGBOURNE (Wilts) from *Waterloo*, 92½ miles. Fares, 16/1a, 9/8c. R. T. for two months, 32/2a. Departures *from* London as for Marlborough. Departures *for* London about 4 times daily. Pop. 910.
Map Square 22.

OGMORE VALE (Glamorgan), 181¾ miles. Fares, 37/9a 22/8c. R. T. for two months 75/6a, 45/4c. Departures *from* London as for Tondu. Departures *for* London about 4 times daily. Pop. 30,178.

OKEHAMPTON (Devon) from *Waterloo*, 197¼ miles. Fares, 41/3a, 24/9c. R. T. for two months, 82/6a, 49/6c. Pop. 3,456.
Map Square 26.

W'LOO.	OKEH'TON	OKEH'TON	W'LOO.
AM 9. 0r	1.39	AM 9.42r	1.56
10. 0r	2.40	11.29r	3.50
11. 0r	3.33	PM 1.19r	6. 0
PM 1. 0r	6. 7	3.34r	8.30
3. 0r	7.12	5.34	10.50
6. 0r	10.50	5.58h	3.58
—	—	—	—

Sunday Trains.

12. 0rn	5.24	PM 4.14r	8.57
—	—	—	—
—	—	—	—

h Via Eastleigh.
n Noon.
r Restaurant Car.

OLDBURY (Worcester) from *Euston*, 118¼ miles. Fares, 24/4a, 14/7c. R. T. for two months, 48/8a. Pop. 36,908.
Map Square 17.

EUSTON	OLDB'Y	OLDB'Y	EUSTON
AM 2.30	5.50	AM 6.21r	10. 0
5. 0	8.59	7.53r	10.40
6.45	11.26	9.21	12.40
9.15r	12.46	10. 4r	1.25
11.30r	2.53	11.38e	3. 0
PM 1.15r	4.15	11.38d	4.15
2.20t	5.23	PM 1.15t	4.35
4.35t	7.31	2.22t	5.35
5.50r	8.45	4. 2r	6.50
6.55r	9.36	5.24r	8.20
7. 0	10.40	5.58dr	10.45
11.50d	8.49	7.37e	10.2C
—	—	11.17e	4. 0
—	—	11.17d	5. 0
—	—	—	—

Sunday Trains.

AM 9.15	2.23	AM 9.51r	1.45
PM 1. 0r	7. 9	PM12.18	5. 5
5.10r	9.51	4. 7r	8.20
—	—	10. 6	5. 0
—	—	—	—

d Saturdays only.
e Saturdays excepted.
r Restaurant Car.
t Tea Car.

OLD CUMNOCK (Ayr), from *St. Pancras*, 383½ miles. Fares, 76/1a, 45/8c. R. T. for two months, 152/2a, 91/4c. Pop. 5,491.
Map Square 40.

ST. PAN.	CUMNK.	CUMNK.	ST. PAN.
AM 4.25	4. 7	AM 8.44r	6.35
9.50r	7.10	11. 5r	9.15
PM12.15dr	9.13	PM 9.37e	7.25
9.30e	8.10	9.37d	8.57
11.45e	9.44	—	—

Sunday Trains.

PM 9.30	8.10	—	—
11.45	9.44	—	—

d Saturdays only.
e Saturdays excepted.
r Restaurant Car.

OLD DALBY (Leicester) from *St. Pancras*, 111¼ miles. Fares, 22/11a, 13/9c. R. T., double fare. Departures *from* London as for Melton Mowbray. Departures *for* London about 6 times daily. Pop. 368.
Map Square 18.

OLD FORD from *Broad Street*, 4¾ miles. Fares, 0/7½a, 0/6b, 0/4½c. R. T. for two days, 1/3a, 0/10½b, 0/7c. *See* p. 500.
Map Square 62.

OLDHAM (CLEGG STREET) (Lancs) from *Euston*, 188¾ miles. Fares, 38/7a, 23/2c. R. T. for two months, 77/2a Pop. 145,001.
Map Square 12

EUSTON	OLDHAM	OLDHAM	EUSTON
AM12.25	5.51	AM 6. 7dr	12.20
2.35	8.28	7.35er	12. 5
5. 0	10.30	8. 2r	12.50
8.45r	1. 5	9.12r	1.15
10.40r	2.59	10.12	3.10
11.50r	4. 0	11.45r	3.55
PM 1.30er	6.36	PM12.10er	6. 0
2.50t	7.15	12.38dr	6. 0
4. 5r	8.34	1.30r	6.15
4.45r	9.33	2.15r	7.30
6. 5r	10.19	3.32r	8.10
11.50d	10.18	3.48er	9. 5
—	—	3.48dr	9.15
—	—	4.45er	10. 0
—	—	4.59dr	10. 0
—	—	5.35er	10.10
—	—	10. 0	5. 0
—	—	11. 0	5.40

Sunday Trains.

PM12.10r	5.27	AM 8.30	4. 0
12.30r	6.30	PM12.10r	5.45
—	—	3.47r	8.55
—	—	10.37	5. 0

d Saturdays only.
e Saturdays excepted.
r Restaurant Car.
t Tea Car.

ANOTHER ROUTE (CLEGG STREET) from *Marylebone*, 206¼ miles. Fares as above.

M'BONE.	OLDHAM	OLDHAM	M'BONE.
AM 2.32	10.38	AM 8. 6r	1.13
10. 0r	3.28	9.17r	3. 0
PM12.15r	5.55	PM 2. 2r	6.38
3.20r	8.10	4.27r	9.55
5 0r	9.55	10.22	3.57
6.20dr	11.26	—	—
10. 5e	5.32	—	—

Sunday Trains.

AM11.15r	4.24	PM11.55r	5.40
—	—	4.30r	10.24

d Saturdays only.
e Saturdays excepted.
r Restaurant Car.

OLD HILL (Stafford), 118¾ miles. Fares, 24/9a 14/10c. R. T. for two months, 49/6a. Departures *from* London as for Smethwick Junction. Departures *for* London about 5 times daily. Pop. 11,600.

OLD LEAKE (Lincoln) from *King's Cross*, 113¾ miles. Fares, 23/7a, 14/2c. R.T., double fare. Pop. 1,[illegible]40.
Map Square 13.

KING'S+	O.LEAK.	O.LEAK.	KING'S+
AM 4.45	8. 8	AM 7.16	10.40
8.45	12.28	11.25	3.50
11.30	3.43	PM 4.19r	9. 0
PM 4. 0r	7. 8	6.33r	9.25
—	—	—	—

Sunday Trains.

12. 0nr	3.29	AM11.32	3.45

n Noon.
r Restaurant Car.

OLD MELDRUM (Aberdeen), 545 miles. No through fares. Departures *from* London as for Inverurie. Departures *for* London about 3 times daily. Pop. 1,681.
Map Square 35.

OLD NORTH ROAD (Cambs) from *King's Cross*, 54½ miles. No through fares. Departures *from* London as for Sandy. Departures *for* London about six times daily.
Map Square 18.

OLD OAK LANE from *Paddington*, 3½ miles. Fares, 0/4½c. R. T. for two days, 0/9c. *See* pp. 490, 491.
Map Square 59.

OLD STREET. (City and South London Tube and Metropolitan Railway (G.N. & City). *See* back of Map.

OLDTRAFFORD (Lancs), 185¾ miles. Fares, 39/4a, 23/7c. R.T. for two months, 78/8a, 47/2c. Departures *from* London as for Manchester (London Road). Departures *for* London about 8 times daily. Pop. 12,651.
Map Square 12.

OLLERTON (Notts), 138¾ miles. Fares, 28/7a, 17/2c. R. T., double fare. Departures *from* London as for Edwinstowe. Departures *for* London about twice daily. Pop. 711.

OLNEY (Bucks) from *St. Pancras*, 60¼ miles. Fares, 11/11a, 7/2c. R. T., double fare. Pop. 2,871.
Map Square 18.

ST. PAN.	OLNEY	OLNEY	ST. PAN.
AM 4.25	6.43	AM 8. 3	10. 5
6.25	9. 0	9.45	11.25
9.25	11.54	PM 1. 1	3.25
PM12.30	2.31	2.59	5.20
3.35	5.21	6.27	8.22
6.30	8.20	9.32	11.45
—	—	—	—
—	—	—	—

No Sunday Trains.

OLTON (Warwick) from *Paddington*, 105½ miles. Fares, 21/11a, 13/2c. R.T. for two months, 43/10a. Departures *from* London as for Solihull. Departures *for* London about 6 times daily. Pop. 2,411.
Map Square 17.

OMOA (Lanark), 389¼ miles. No through fares. Departures *from* London as for Wishaw (Central). Departures *for* London about 6 times daily.

ONGAR (Essex) from *Fenchurch Street*, 23 miles, or from *Liverpool Street*, 22¾ miles. Fares from Fenchurch Street, 4/10a, 3/10b, 2/11c. R. T. for two months, 9/7½a, 7/0b, 5/3c. Fares from Liverpool Street, 4/10a, 3/11b, 2/11c. R. T. for two months, 9/8a, 7/3½b, 5/5c. Pop. 1,176. *See* pp. 541-544
Map Square 24.

ONIBURY (Salop), 163¼ miles. Fares, 31/11*a*, 19/2*c*. R. T. for two months, 63/10*a*, 38/4*c*. Departures *from* London as for Craven Arms or Hereford. Departures *for* London about 3 times daily. Pop. 451.
Map Square 17.

ONLLWYN (Brecon), 205½ miles. Fares, 39/9*a*, 23/10*c*. R. T. for two months, 79/6*a*, 47/8*c*. Departures *from* London as for Brecon. Departures *for* London about 3 times daily.
Map Square 21.

ORBLISTON (Elgin), 587¾ miles. Fares, 106/3*a*, 63/9*c*. R. T. for two months, 212/6*a*, 127/6*c*. Departures *from* London as for Elgin. Departures *for* London about 3 times daily.
Map Square 35.

ORDSALL LANE (Lancs), 185 miles. Fares, 38/7*a*, 23/2*c*. R. T., double fare. Departures *from* London as for Manchester (London Road) Departures *for* London about 8 times daily. Pop. 6,773.

ORE (Sussex) from *Charing Cross, Cannon Street,* and *London Bridge,* 64 miles. Fares. *via* Hastings, 12/11*a*, 10/4*b*, 7/9*c*. R. T. for two months, 25/10*a*, 20/8*b*. 81½ miles, *via* Ashford, 15/0*a*, 12/0*b*, 9/0*c*. R.T. for two months, 30/0*a*, 24/0*b*. Departures *from* London as for Winchelsea. Departures *for* London about 5 times daily. Pop. 379.
Map Square 24.

ORESTON (Devon) from *Waterloo*, 235¼ miles. Fares, 47/1*a*. 28/3*c*. R. T. for two months, 94/2*a*, 56/6*c*. Departures *from* London as for Plymouth (North Road). Departures *for* London about 6 times daily.

ORMESBY (Yorks), 241½ miles. Fares, 50/3*a*, 30/2*c*. R. T., double fare. Departures *from* London as for Middlesbrough. Departures *for* London about 6 times daily. Pop. 14,582.
Map Square 8.

ORMESBY, GREAT (Norfolk) from *King's Cross*, 180½ miles. Fares, 25/3*a*, 15/2*c*. R. T. for two months, 50/6*a*, 30/4*c*. Departures *from* London as for North Walsham. Departures *for* London about 3 times daily. Pop. 1,232.
Map Square 19.

ORMISTON (East Lothian) 392¾ miles. No through fares. Departures *from* London as for Edinburgh (Waverley). Departures *for* London about twice daily. Pop. 1,841.
Map Square 41.

ORMSIDE (Westmorland), 274¾ miles. Fares, 54/1*a*, 32/6*c*. R. T., double fare. Departures *from* London as for Kirkby Stephen. Departures *for* London about 3 times daily. Pop. 148.
Map Square 7.

ORMSKIRK (Lancs), 208¾ miles. Fares, 43/2*a*. 25/11*c*. R. T. for two months, 86/4*a*. Departures *from* London as for St. Helens, Liverpool (Lime Street) or Wigan. Departures *for* London about 6 times daily. Pop. 7,407.
Map Square 12.

ORPINGTON (Kent) from *Charing Cross, Cannon Street,* and *London Bridge,* 14½ miles. Fares, 3/1*a*, 2/5*b*, 1/10*c*. R.T. for eight days, 6/2*a*, 4/10*b*. Pop. 7,047.
Map Square 23.

Leave Char. +	Leave Can. St.	Leave Lon. B.	Arr. at Orping.
AM —	5.20	5.25	6. 7
—	6.45	6.50	7.27
7.26	—	7.33	8. 4
—	7.56	8. 0	8.36
—	9.36	9.39	10.15
9.38	—	9.45	10.17
11.15	—	11.23	11.59
11.42	—	11.49	12.26
PM 12. 3	—	12.10	12.46
—	12.48*d*	12.51*d*	1.28
12.50*e*	—	12.58*e*	1.39
—	1.12*d*	1.15*d*	1.40
1.34*d*	—	1.41*d*	2.14
1.50*e*	—	1.58*e*	2.33
—	2. 4*d*	2. 7*d*	2.39
2.17*d*	—	2.23*d*	2.54
2.30*e*	—	2.37*e*	3.11
2.50*d*	—	2.57*d*	3.31
3.30*e*	—	3.37*e*	4.17
3.50	—	3.57	4.28
4.26*e*	—	4.33*e*	5. 9
—	4.44*e*	4.47*e*	5.22
4.55*d*	—	5. 1*d*	5.34
—	5. 4*e*	5. 7*e*	5.35
5.35*d*	—	5.41*d*	6.12
—	5.40*e*	5.43*e*	6.14
5.45*d*	—	5.51*d*	6.28
5.50*e*	—	5.57*e*	6.31
6.10*e*	—	6.17*e*	6.46
6.38*e*	—	6.45*e*	7.18
6.40*d*	—	6.48*d*	7.26
7. 6*e*	—	7.13*e*	7.48
7.18	—	7.26	7.55
8. 0	—	8. 8	8.34
9. 0	—	9. 6	9.35
10. 0	—	10. 6	10.36
10.43	—	10.51	11.22
11.30	—	—	12. 9
—	—	—	—
—	—	—	—
—	—	—	—

Sunday Trains.

Leave Char. +	Leave Can. St.	Leave Lon. B.	Arr. at Orping.
AM 7. 5	—	7.11	7.50
8. 5	—	8.12	8.44
9.30	—	9.36	10. 8
11.15	—	11.23	12. 0
PM 1. 0	—	1. 7	1.43
3. 5	—	3.13	3.48
6. 0	—	6. 6	6.42
9.25	—	9.31	10. 1
10.35	—	10.43	11.15

Trains from Orpington.

Leave Orping.	Arrive at Lon B.	Arrive at Can. St.	Arrive at Char. +
AM 6.35	7. 4	7. 8	—
7.13	7.42	—	7.49
7.42	8.10	—	8.19
8.11	8.40	8.44	—
8.25	8.56	9. 0	—
8.51	9.18	—	9.27
8.58	9.24	9.28	—
9.11	9.40	9.44	—
9.32	9.58	—	10. 7
9.46	10.16	10.20	—
10.38	10.58	11. 2	—
11.11	11.32	—	11.44
12. 0*e*	12.35	12.40	—
PM 12. 5*e*	12.38	—	12.47
12.15*d*	12.54	12.58	—
12.52	1.27	—	1.38
1.15	1.36	—	1.50
1.23	—	—	2. 2
1.39*d*	2.12	—	2.20
1.40*e*	2.12	—	2.20

ORPINGTON—*continued.*

Leave Orping.	Arrive at Lon. B.	Arrive at Can. St.	Arrive at Char. +
PM 2.15*e*	2.50	—	2.59
2.34	3. 7	—	3.19
4. 4	4.36	4.40*e*	4.45*d*
4.20	4.40	—	4.53
4.55*e*	5.27	—	5.38
5.20*e*	5.46	—	5.54
5.49*e*	6.22	6.28	—
5.49*d*	6.30	—	6.39
6. 1*e*	6.44	—	6.54
6.40*e*	7. 7	7.12	—
6.46	—	—	7.25
7.48	8.26	—	8.35
8.19	8.54	9. 1	—
9.45	10.15	—	10.23
10. 2	10.22	—	10.35
10.17	10.48	—	10.57
11. 2	11.34	—	11.44
—	—	—	—
—	—	—	—
—	—	—	—

Sunday Trains.

Leave Orping.	Arrive at Lon. B.	Arrive at Can. St.	Arrive at Char. +
AM 8. 0	8.30	—	8.39
9.27	10. 5	—	10.15
9.45	10.22	—	10.32
10.35	11. 6	—	11.13
11.22	11.49	—	12. 0
PM 12.45	1.20	—	1.29
2.17	2.50	—	3. 0
5.54	6.27	—	6.41
7.45	8.12	—	8.22
7.52	8.20	—	8.28
8.36	9. 7	—	9.18
9. 5	9.38	—	—
10.34	11. 4	—	11.15
—	—	—	—
—	—	—	—

d Saturdays only.
e Saturdays excepted.

ANOTHER ROUTE from *Victoria, Holborn Viaduct,* and *St. Paul's,* 15 miles. Fares as above. *See* pp. 558-561.

ORRELL (Lancs), 199¾ miles. No through fares. Departures *from* London as for Wigan. Departures *for* London about 6 times daily. Pop. 6,775.
Map Square 12.

ORTON (Elgin), 591 miles. Fares, 106/3*a*, 63/9*c*. R. T. for two months, 212/6*a*, 127/6*c*. Departures *from* London as for Elgin. Departures *for* London about 3 times daily.
Map Square 35.

ORTON WATERVILLE (Hunts) from *King's Cross*, 78 miles. Fares, 15/10*a*, 9/6*c*. Departures *from* London as for Peterborough. Departures *for* London about 3 times daily.
Map Square 18.

ORWELL (Suffolk), 78 miles. Fares, 16/6*a*, 9/11*c*. R. T. for two months, 33/0*a*. Departures *from* London as for Felixstowe. Departures *for* London about 6 times daily.
Map Square 19.

OSSETT (Yorks), 179½ miles. Fares, 37/4*a*, 22/5*c*. R. T., double fare. Departures *from* London as for Dewsbury. Departures *for* London about 8 times daily. Pop. 14,802.
Map Square 12.

OSTEND from *Victoria*, *via* Dover, 138 miles. Fares, 38/10*a*, 27/1*b*, 17/11*c*. R.T. for 60 days, 77/2*a*, 53/7*b*, 35/3*c*. Subject to exchange.

Weekdays and Sundays.

Subject to special Passport regulations.

Vict.	Ost'd.	Ost'd.	Vict.
AM 8.55	3. 0	AM10.30	4.30
PM 2. 0	8. 0	PM 2.15	8.25
—	—	—	—

OSTERLEY from *Mansion House*, 12¾ miles. *See* p. 489. *Map Square* 66.

OSWESTRY (Salop) from *Paddington*, 173 miles. Fares, 36/1*a*, 21/8*c*. R. T. for two months, 72/2*a*. Pop. 9,790. *Map Square* 16.

Pad.	Oswestry	Oswestry	Pad.
AM 9.10*r*	1.40	AM 8. 3	12.25
10.40*r*	3. 1	8.25*r*	1.25
PM12.50*r*	5.46	10.14*r*	2. 5
2.10*t*	6.11	PM12.20*r*	5. 0
4.10*t*	8.22	1.18*t*	5.55
6.10*r*	10. 3	3.48*r*	8. 5
12.15*h*	8.41	5.35	10. 0
12.15*k*	6.10	8.35	3.30
—	—	—	—

No Sunday Trains.
h Saturday midnight excepted.
k Saturday midnight only.
r Restaurant Car.
t Tea Car.

ANOTHER ROUTE from *Euston*, 189 miles. Fares as above.

Euston	Oswes.	Oswes.	Euston
AM 2.35	9. 5	AM 8.22*r*	1.45
5. 0	10.43	PM 1. 5*r*	5.50
8.30*r*	2. 2	1.50*r*	7.30
10. 0*r*	2.28	3.57*r*	9.10
11.50*r*	4.57	5.20*r*	10.45
PM 2.35*t*	7.38	9.21	5. 0
4. 5*r*	9.57	—	—
9.30*e*	3.22	—	—
11. 0*d*	3.20	—	—
—	—	—	—

Sunday Trains.

—	—	PM 9.23	5. 0
—	—	—	—
—	—	—	—

d Saturdays only.
e Saturdays excepted.
r Restaurant Car.
t Tea Car.

Wynnstay Hotel. Telephone 38. Convenient to Stations. Billiards. Garage. Stabling. Electric Light. Large Garden.
TRUST HOUSES, Ltd.

OTFORD (Kent) from *Victoria, Holborn Viaduct,* and *St. Paul's*, 24 miles. Fares, 4/10*a*, 3/11*b*, 2/11*c*. R. T. for two months, 9/8*a*, 7/10*b*, 5/10*c*. Pop. 857. *Map Square* 24.

Vict. (S.E.&C.)	Leave Hol.V.	St. Pl.'s	Arr. at Otford.
AM —	6.40	6.42	7.51
—	7.30	7.33	8.44
8.32	8.20	8.23	9.47
11. 4	10.58	11. 0	12.14
PM —	12.33*d*	12.36*d*	1.36
—	1.27*d*	1.30*d*	2.31
2. 9*d*	2. 4*d*	2. 7*d*	2.58
—	2.11*d*	2.14*d*	3.26
2.40*d*	—	—	3.43
2.50*e*	—	—	3.56
4.25*e*	—	—	5.15
*e*5.15*h*	—	*e*5.21*k*	6.12
*d*5.20*h*	—	*d*5.26*k*	6.18

OTFORD—*continued.*

Vict. (S.E.&C.)	Leave Hol. V.	St. Pl.'s	Arr. at Otford.
5.30*e*	—	5.33*e*	6.28
—	—	6.16*e*	7. 5
6.40	6.34	6.37	7.41
7.22	7.22	7.24	8.25
8.55	—	—	9.49
10. 0	9.54	9.56	11. 0

Sunday Trains.

AM —	8. 0	—	9.21
10.30	10.25	—	11.40
PM 2. 5	2. 3	—	3.22
6.35	6.40	—	7.45
10.15	10.12	—	11.22

Trains from Otford.

Leave Otford	Arrive at St. Pl.'s	Hol. V.	Vict.
AM 7.41	8.40	8.42	8.50
8.36	9.37	9.39	—
9.10	9.52	9.55	—
9.35*e*	10.21	10.23	10.16
9.56*d*	10.41	—	—
9.56	—	10.43	—
10.49	—	—	11.57
11.59	12.59	1. 2	12.49
PM 1.35	—	—	2.40
3.24	—	—	4.33
5.59	6.58	7. 0	—
6.41*d*	8. 0	8. 2	—
6.41*e*	8.18	8.20	8.10
7.38	—	—	8.51
9. 3*d*	—	—	9.54
10.38	11.43	11.45	—

Sunday Trains.

AM 9.54	—	—	10.48
PM12.25	—	—	1.25
2.53	—	—	3.50
5.10	—	6.20	6. 3
9. 3	—	10.22	10. 5

d Saturdays only.
e Saturdays excepted.
h Departs from or arrives at Charing + (S.E. & C.R.).
k Departs from or arrives at London Bridge (S.E. & C.R.)

OTLEY (Yorks), 197 miles. Fares, 41/0*a*, 24/7*c*. R. T., double fare. Departures *from* London as for Ilkley. Departures *for* London about 6 times daily. Pop. 9,536. *Map Square* 7.

OTTERHAM (Cornwall) from *Waterloo*, 236½ miles. Fares, 48/6*a*, 29/1*c*. R. T. for two months, 97/0*a*, 58/2*c*. Departures *from* London as for Launceston. Departures *for* London about 4 times daily. Pop. 209. *Map Square* 26.

OTTERINGTON (Yorks), 214½ miles. Fares, 44/9*a*, 26/10*c*. R. T., double fare. Departures *from* London as for Thirsk. Departures *for* London about 6 times daily. Pop. 149. *Map Square* 7.

OTTERSPOOL (Lancs), 214 miles. Fares, 40/8*a*, 24/5*c*. R. T., double fare. Departures *from* London as for Warrington. Departures *for* London about 5 times daily. *Map Square* 12.

OTTERY ST. MARY (Devon) from *Waterloo*, 162½ miles. Fares, 33/11*a*, 20/4*c*. R. T. for two months, 67/10*a*, 40/8*c*. Pop. 3,538. *Map Square* 26.

W'loo.	Ottery.	Ottery.	W'loo.
AM 9. 0*r*	12.47	AM10.27*r*	1.56
10. 0*r*	1.43	11.14*r*	3. 8
12. 0*r*	3.56	PM 1. 4*r*	6. 0
PM 1. 0*r*	5.10	2.57	7.40
3. 0*r*	6.56	5.56	10.50
—	—	7.59*h*	3.58

No Sunday Trains.
h Via Eastleigh.
r Restaurant Car.

OTTRINGHAM (Yorks), 209¾ miles. No through fares. Departures *from* London as for Hull (Paragon). Departures *for* London about 4 times daily. Pop. 474. *Map Square* 13.

OUGHTY BRIDGE (Yorks), 167½ miles. Fares, 33/9*a*, 20/3*c*. R. T., 67/6*a*, 40/6*c*. Departures *from* London as for Sheffield (Victoria). Departures *for* London about 6 times daily. Pop. 2,600. *Map Square* 12.

OULTON BROAD (Suffolk), 116½ miles. Fares, 24/9*a*, 14/10*c*. R. T. for two months, 49/6*a*. Departures *from* London as for Lowestoft (*via* Cambridge). Departures *for* London about 4 times daily. Pop. 4,109. *Map Square* 19.

OUNDLE (Northampton) from *Euston*, 96 miles. Fares, 15/3*a*, 9/2*c*. R. T. for two months, 30/6*a*. Pop. 2,655. *Map Square* 18.

Euston	Oundle	Oundle	Euston
AM 5. 0	8.25	AM 7.16	10.15
6.45	10.50	8.36	11.55
9.30*d*	12.25	10.10	12.40
10.40	1.37	11. 4*h*	2.45
PM12.15*e*	4. 0	11. 4*k*	4.15
12.15*d*	4. 5	PM12.22*d*	3.45
3. 5	6. 5	2.10	5.35
4.15	7.40	4.14	7.20
7. 0	9.55	6.45	9.20
—	—	7.42	11.35

No Sunday Trains.
d Saturdays only.
e Saturdays excepted.
h Thursdays and Saturdays only.
k Thursdays and Saturdays excepted.

OVAL (Kennington). (City and South London Tube.) *See* back of Map.

OVENDEN (Yorks), 195¼ miles. Fares, 39/9*a*, 23/10*c*. R. T., double fare. Departures *from* London as for Halifax. Departures *for* London about 8 times daily. Pop. 6,604. *Map Square* 12.

OVER (Cheshire), 167¾ miles. Fares, 35/0*a*, 21/0*c*. R. T. for two months, 70/0*a*, 42/0*c*. Departures *from* London as for Hartford. Departures *for* London about 6 times daily. Pop. 7,300. *Map Square* 12.

OVERSTRAND (Norfolk) from *Liverpool Street*, 139½ miles. Fares, 26/3*a*, 15/9*c*. R. T. for two months, 52/6*a*, 31/6*c*. Pop. 429. *Map Square* 14.

L'pl.St.	O'strand	O'strand.	L'pl. St.
AM 5. 5	10.36	AM 7.21*r*	11.22
8.15*r*	12.43	8.25	1.20
9.50*r*	2.42	PM12.19*r*	3.50
PM12.25*r*	3.49	1.54	6.32
12.33*r*	4.32	3.25*r*	8.33
3.10*r*	7. 0	5.13*r*	9.22
5.18*r*	9.35	7.58	2.50

No Sunday Trains.
r Restaurant Car.

ANOTHER ROUTE from *King's Cross*, 161¾ miles. Fares as above.

King's+	O'strand	O'strand.	King's+
AM 4.45	10.36	AM 7.21	1. 5
7.15*r*	1.54	8.57	3.50
10.10*r*	5.13	11.45*r*	4.30
PM 1.50*r*	7.35	PM 2.42	9. 0
3. 0	7.58	—	—

No Sunday Trains.
r Restaurant Car.

OVERTON (Hants) from

Waterloo, 55¾ miles.　Fares, 11/8a,
7/0c.　R. T. for two months, 23/4a,
14/0c.　Pop. 1,616.
Map Square 23.

W'LOO.	OVERT'N.	OVERT'N	W'LOO.
AM 5.50	8. 4	AM 8.21	9.56
7.30	9.30	10.57s	12.22
9.30	11.15	PM12.41r	2.20
11.30r	1.15	2.28	4.20
PM 1.30r	2.56	4.34s	6.26
3.30s	4.57	5.56	7.40
5. 0	6.32	8.29	10.50
6. 0r	7.43	9.50	11.28
7.30	8.57	—	—
8. 0	10. 3	—	—
—	—	—	—
—	—	—	—
—	—	—	—

Sunday Trains.

AM 9. 0	11. 3	AM10.36	12.11
PM 6. 0	7.36	PM 7. 7	9.12
—	—	—	—

r Restaurant Car.
s Refreshments served.

OVERTON - ON - DEE

(Flint) from *Euston*, 186 miles.
Fares, 36/6a, 21/11c.　R.,T. for two
months, 73/0a.　Departures *from*
London as for Wrexham.　Departures *for* London about 4 times
daily.　Pop. 1,196.
Map Square 12.

OVERTOWN (Lanark),

384¾ miles.　No through fares.
Departures *from* London as for
Carstairs.　Departures *for* London
about 6 times daily.　Pop. 5,525.

OXENHOLME (Westmor-

land) from *Euston*, 249½ miles.
Fares, 51/11a, 31/2c.　R. T., double
fare.
Map Square 7.

EUSTON	OXENH.	OXENH.	EUSTON
AM12.25	8.24	AM 7.34r	1.45
2.35	10.11	8.15r	3.10
5. 0	12.30	10. 3r	4.15
6.45	1.43	PM12. 2t	6. 0
10.40r	4.30	3. 2er	9. 5
11.35r	4.47	3. 2dr	9.15
11.50r	6.33	5. 2r	10.45
PM 1.30r	7.13	9.11	5. 0
2.35t	8.57	—	—
5.20er11.22		—	—
5.20dr11.28		—	—
9.30	5. 5	—	—
11. 0d	4. 9	—	—
11.45e	5.21	—	—

Sunday Trains.

AM11.45r	7. 2	PM 5.57	5. 0
PM 9.30	5. 5		
11.45	5.20	—	—
—	—	—	—

d Saturdays only.
e Saturdays excepted.
r Restaurant Car.
t Tea Car.

OXENHOPE (Yorks), from

St. Pancras, 217¾ miles.　Fares,
41/6a, 24/11c.　R. T., double fare.
Departures *from* London as for
Keighley.　Departures *for* London
about 8 times daily.　Pop. 2,349.
Map Square 12.

OXFORD from Paddington,

63¾ miles.　Fares,13/2a, 7/11c.　R.T.
for two months, 26/4a.　Pop. 57,052.
Map Square 23.

PAD.	OXFORD	OXFORD	PAD.
AM 5.30	7.16	AM 1.45g	3.30
6.30	8.33	7.10	9. 0
7.30	10. 5	8.33	9.50
8.50	10.18	8.45r	10.15
9.45	11. 8	9.10	10.45
10.45	12.38	10. 5	11.15
11.20	1.31	10.50	12. 5
PM12. 8	1.55	11.12v	1.18
1.35r	2.57	PM12.20	1.50
2.23v	4.45	1. 0	2.12
3.18	5.21	1.45r	2.55
4.45t	5.55	2.12	3.50
5.15	7.11	3. 7t	4.15
6. 5r	7.23	4.30	5.50
6.55	8.27	5.48	7.20
7.30	8.47	6. 2	8.20
10. 0	11.41	7.50r	9.15
12.15	1.53	9.22	10.45
—	—	9.40	2.45

Sunday Trains.

AM 9.10	11. 5	AM 1.45	3.30
10.35	11.56	7.40	10.14
11.45	1.39	PM 1. 0	2.40
PM 2. 0	5. 5	4.37	6.20
4.10	5.36	5.55v	8.25
5.15	9.47	8.25r	9.48
7.40	10.17	8.42	11.38
10. 0	11.41	9.40	3.15
—	—	—	—

g Mondays excepted.
r Restaurant Car.
t Tea Car.
v Via Beaconsfield.

ANOTHER ROUTE from

Euston, 77¾ miles.　Fares as above.

EUSTON	OXFORD	OXFORD	EUSTON
AM 6.45	9.55	AM 7.25e	9.52
7.35	11.29	7.25d	10. 0
10.40	12.35	8.35	11.40
12. 0nr	2.38	9.15	11.55
PM 3. 5	5. 5	10.50	1.50
5.32d	8.57	11.30h	2.45
6.10e	8.57	PM 1.55	4.15
7.15d	10.13	3.10	5.35
8. 0y	10.13	4.40	7.55
—	—	7.15e	10.10
—	—	7.15d	10.50
—	—	10.10h	5. 0

Sunday Trains.

AM 8.15	11.33	PM12. 5	5. 5
PM12.30	3. 4	3.50	7.10
3.50	6.53	7.30	10.10

d Saturdays only.
e Saturdays excepted.
h Thursdays and Saturdays only.
n Noon.
r Restaurant Car.
y Thursdays only.

Salter's Steamers (Folly
Bridge) for Wallingford, Henley,
etc., 9.30 a.m., 2.30 p.m.　*See advt.*
facing first page of train service.

Clarendon Hotel (Trust
Houses, Ltd.).　Convenient for
places of interest.　Telephone
285.
See advt. p. 274.

Randolph Hotel.　First-class.
Only Modern Hotel.　Electric
Light.　Lift.　Night Porter.
'Phone 290.
Address, MANAGER.

OXFORD—continued.

Roebuck Hotel.　Old-estab-
lished Family Hotel.　Close
Colleges, River.　Central for
Business.　Garage.　Night Porter.
Telephone, 344.
W. BEAZLEY, Proprietor.

The Isis.　Private Hotel.
47–53, Iffley Road.　Pleasantly
situated, overlooking Christ
Church Cricket Ground.　Few
minutes from Magdalen Bridge,
where boats can be hired.　Garage.
Terms Moderate.　Telephone 776.
Miss BAKER, Proprietress.

Oxenford Hall, Private Hotel.
En pension.　13–17, Magdalen St.,
opposite Martyrs' Memorial.　Cen-
tral for Colleges.　Moderate tariff.
Telephone 748.
Miss WATSON, Proprietress.

Golden Cross Hotel.　Established 1860.　Family and Commercial.　Popular with visitors.
Few minutes Station, River and
Colleges.　Moderate charges.　Com-
pletely furnished.　Electric light.
'Phone 391.　Appointed R.A.C.
and C.T.C.　Mrs. BALL, Proprietress.

King's Arms Family Hotel.
Centre of Colleges.　Facing
Sheldonian Theatre.　Moderate
Tariff.　Electric Light through-
out.　Telephone 369.
Proprietor, R. J. HANNAH.

Mitre Hotel.　First - class.
Only Hotel in the famous High
Street.　Established 1400.　Electric
Light.　Night Porter.　'Phone 335.
C. J. VERT.

Wilberforce Hotel (unlicensed).　Family and Commercial Hotel.　Central for
pleasure and business.　Station
trams pass.　Electric light.
Moderate.　Phone 857.
W. BEAZLEY, Proprietor.

The Eastgate Hotel.　Situated in the High Street overlooking Magdalen College.　Close
to the Rivers Cherwell and Isis.
Electric Light.　Telephone 694.
Special terms on application.
Proprietress, MRS. COOMBES.

Castle Hotel.　Premier un-
licensed hotel in the City.　Facing
G. W. and L. & N. W. stations.
Garage, 100 cars.　Telephone 844.
Proprietor, A. TRUSCOTT.

House Agents.　HERBERT
DULAKE & Co., 11, Corn Market
Street, Oxford, send free a printed
Register of Properties for Sale or
Let.

OXFORD CIRCUS.
(Bakerloo and Central London
Tubes.)　*See back of Map.*

OXSHOTT (Surrey) from

Waterloo, 17 miles. Fares, 3/7a, 2/2c. R. T. for eight days, 7/2a, 4/4c.
Map Square 23.

W'LOO.	OXSHOTT	OXSHOTT	W'LOO.
AM 6. 5	6.40	AM 6.41	7.17
7. 5	7.40	7.52	8.30
8. 5	8.40	8.12	8.48
9. 5	9.40	8.46	9.21
10. 5	10.41	9.26	10. 0
11. 5	11.40	10. 2e	10.36
PM12. 5	12.40	10.32	11. 6
1. 5	1.40	11.22	11.56
1.35d	2.10	PM12.26	1. 0
2. 5	2.40	1.28	2. 2
3. 5	3.40	2.26	3. 0
4. 5	4.40	3.26	4. 0
5. 5	5.40	4.26	5. 0
5.37e	6.12	5.36	6.10
6. 5	6.40	6.17	6.52
6.38e	7.12	7.26	8. 0
7. 5	7.40	8.26	9. 0
8. 5	8.42	9.26	10. 0
9. 5	9.40	10.22	10.56
10. 5	10.40	—	—
11.35	12.10	—	—

Sunday Trains.

AM 8.38	9.22	AM10.16	10.55
10. 8	10.50	11.15	11.55
11. 8	11 50	PM12.15	12.55
PM12. 8	12.50	1.15	1.55
1. 8	1.50	2.15	2.55
2. 8	2.50	4.15	4.55
3. 8	3.50	6.15	6.55
5. 8	5.50	7.15	7.55
6. 8	6.50	8.25	9. 5
7. 8	7.50	9.15	9.55
8. 8	8.50	10.15	10.55
9. 8	9.50	—	—

d Saturdays only.
e Saturdays excepted.

OXTED (Surrey) from

Victoria, Cannon Street, and London Bridge. 20½ miles. Fares, 4/2a, 2/6c. R. T. for eight days, 8/4a, 4/11c. Pop. 3,284.
Map Square 23.

	Leave		Arr. at
VICT.	CAN. ST.	LON. B.	OXTED
AM 5.30	—	5.18	6.25
6.37	—	6.40	7.27
7.23	—	8. 7	9. 0
9.10	—	9. 6	10. 5
10.35	—	10.35	11.29
11. 5	—	—	11.47
12. 0	—	11.50	12.56
PM —	12.16d	d12.20h	1.11
—	—	12.50d	1.34
1.20e	—	1.38e	2.24
1.25d	—	1.38d	2.29
—	—	2. 5e	3.27
2.25	—	2.25d	3.27
—	—	2.57d	3.47
4. 0	—	4.10	4.57
—	4.16e	e4.20h	5. 7
—	—	4.44e	5.20
4.50	—	—	5.34
5. 5	—	5.10	6. 0
—	—	5.21	6. 9
5.48	—	5.41e	6.33
6. 6	—	6. 8	7. 4
6.50	—	7. 0	7.46
7.15	—	7.38	8.29
8. 5	—	8.10	8.48
9. 3	—	9.12	9.56
10.30	—	10.35	11.25
11.50h	—	—	12.38

OXTED—continued.

Sunday Trains.

	Leave		Arr. at
VICT.	CAN. ST.	LON. B.	OXTED
AM 8.18	—	8.30	9.23
8.50	—	—	9.36
10.20	—	—	11.25
PM 1.14	—	1.10	2. 6
2.30	—	—	3.28
6.33	—	6.46	7.39
7. 5	—	—	7.55
9. 5	—	9.10	10. 2

· Trains from Oxted.

Leave	Arrive at		
OXTED	LON. B.	CAN. ST.	VICT.
AM 7.16	8.15	—	8.24
7.52	8.37	—	8.40
8.16	9. 1k	9. 4	9. 8
8.27	9.15	—	9.19
8.46	9.32	—	9.40
9. 7	9.55	—	9.58
9.26	10. 5	—	10.12
9.56	10.38	—	—
10. 8	10.55	—	10.46
10.47	—	—	11.35
11.26	12.13	—	12.17
11.54	12.44	—	12.35
PM12.33	1.42	—	1.26
2.11	2.58	—	—
2.53	4. 0	—	3.45
4. 3d	4.57	—	—
4.32	5.21	—	5.55
5.41	6.36	—	6.29
7. 7	7.56	—	—
7.26	8.46	—	8.27
9.30	—	—	10.10
9.36	10.25	—	11.17

Sunday Trains.

AM 9.17	10.18	—	10.20
10.21	11.15	—	—
11.45	—	—	12.47
PM12.41	—	—	1.40
5.37	—	—	6.34
8.21	9.17	—	9. 0
8.33	9.26	—	9.34
9. 5	—	—	9.47
10.10	—	—	10.59

d Saturdays only.
e Saturdays excepted.
h Wednesdays only.
k Departs from or arrives at London Bridge (S.E. & C. station).

Hoskin's Arms Hotel.

Beautifully situated. Charming Scenery. Large Garden. Bowls Tennis. Minute Station. Moderate. Public and Private Sitting-rooms. Billiards. Garage. Stabling. Telephone: No. 11 New Oxted. Proprietor. ALBERT J. TAYLOR.

OXTON (Berwick), 381

miles. No through fares. Departures from London as for Gala-shiels. Departures for London about three times daily. Pop. 188.
Map Square 41.

OYNE (Aberdeen), 547½

miles. Fares, 105/2a, 63/1c. R. T. for two months, 210/4a, 126/2c. Departures from London as for Inverurie. Departures for London about 3 times daily. Pop. 700.
Map Square 35.

OYSTERMOUTH (Glamorgan), 203½ miles.

No through fares. Departures from London as for Swansea. Departures for London about twice daily. Pop. 6,098.
Map Square 21.

REFERENCE NOTES.

a signifies First Class.
b ,, Second Class.
c ,, Third Class.
d ,, On Saturdays only.
e ,, Saturdays excepted.
f ,, On Mondays only.
g ,, Mondays excepted.
r ,, Restaurant Car.
t ,, Tea Car.
x ,, Express.
R.T. ,, Return Tickets.

All Trains in the Tables not otherwise marked carry Third Class Passengers.

P

PADBURY (Bucks), 58¼ miles. Fares, 11/5a, 6/10c. R.T., double fare. Departures *from* London as for Buckingham. Departures *for* London about 5 times daily. Pop. 442.
Map Square 18.

PADDINGTON (Bakerloo Tube). Pop. 144,261. *See back of Map.*

PADDINGTON (Praed Street), from *Aldgate, Moorgate, King's Cross, Mansion House, Charing Cross, Victoria, South Kensington, High Street,* and all intermediate Stations, **every few minutes.** *See back of Map.*
Map Square 60.

PADDOCK WOOD
(Kent) from *Charing Cross, Cannon Street,* and *London Bridge,* 35¼ miles. Fares, 7/6a, 6/0b, 4/6c. R.T. for two months, 15/0a, 12/0b.
Map Square 24.

	Leave		Arr. at
CHAR. +	CAN. ST.	LON. B.	PAD. W.
AM —	**3.40**s	**3.45**s	4.48
—	5.20	5.25	7. 4
—	6.45	6.50	8.20
—	7.56	8. 0	9.39
9.25	—	9.33	10.37
10.40d	—	10.46d	12.14
—	11.56	12. 0	1. 4
PM12.40d	—	12.47d	1.51
2. 8	—	2.16	3.27
3. 0	—	3. 8	4.12
3.15	—	3.21	4.58
3.48e	—	—	4.58
3.50	—	3.57	5.38
—	4.36e	4.39e	5.39
5.24d	—	5.34d	6.35
5.35d	—	5.41d	7.24
—	5.44e	5.47e	7. 0
6. 3e	—	6. 9e	7.19
7.30	—	7.26	8.42
8. 0	—	8. 8	9.27
9.30	—	9.36	10.39

Sunday Trains.

AM 7.45	—	7.52	8.54
8. 5	—	8.12	9.34
9.50	—	9.56	11.19
PM 6.35	—	6.43	7.54
7.10	—	7.20	8.34
7.35	—	7.45	8.42

Trains from Paddock Wood.

Leave		Arrive at	
PAD. W.	LON. B.	CAN. ST.	CHAR. +
AM 6.33	8.10	—	8.19
7.22	8.40	8.44	—
8.29	9.32	9.36	—
9. 2	10. 0	10. 4	—
9.57	10.58	11. 2	—
10.22	11.32	—	11.44
10.45	11.43	—	11.57
PM12.27	1.36	—	1.50
2.20	3.26	—	3.40
4.47	5.50	—	6. 3
5.29	7.25	7.30	—
7. 2	8.26	—	8.35
7.22	8.55	9. 1	—
9.20	10.22	—	10.35
9.43	11.34	—	11.43
d11.29s	—	1.20	—

Sunday Trains.

AM 8.34	10. 5	—	10.15
8.46	10.22	—	10.32
PM. 7. 1	8.12	—	8.22
7.12	8.20	—	8.28
7.45	9. 7	—	9.18

d Saturdays only.
e Saturdays excepted.
s Third Class only.

PADESWOOD (Flint), 190 miles. Fares, 39/5a, 23/8c. R.T. for two months, 78/10a. Departures *from* London as for Mold. Departures *for* London about 4 times daily.
Map Square 11.

PADGATE (Lancs), 197½ miles. Fares, 37/9a, 22/8c. R.T for two months, 75/6a, 45/4c. Departures *from* London as for Glazebrook. Departures *for* London about 5 times daily. Pop. 1,961.
Map Square 12.

PADIHAM (Lancs), 214½ miles. Fares, 44/4a, 26/7c. R.T. for two months, 88/8a, 53/2c. Departures *from* London as for Blackburn. Departures *for* London about 5 times daily. Pop. 12,474.
Map Square 1

PADSTOW (Cornwall)
from *Waterloo,* 259½ miles. Fares, 53/4a, 32/0c. R.T. for two months, 106/8a, 64/0c. Pop. 1,737.
Map Square 25.

W'LOO.	PADSTOW	PADSTOW	W'LOO.
AM10. 0r	4.22	AM 8.20r	3.50
11. 0r	6.32	9.35r	4.30
PM 3. 0r	9.39	PM12.35r	8.30
—	—	2.45	10.50
—	—	—	—

No Sunday Trains.

r Restaurant Car.

Padstow. Cornish Riviera. Hotel Metropole. By the Sea. Modern. Comfortable.
See advt. p. 275.

PAIGNTON (Devon) from
Paddington, 201½ miles. Fares, 41/6a, 24/11c. R.T. for two months, 83/0a, 49/10c. Pop. 14,443.
Map Square 26.

PAD.	PAIGNTN.	PAIGNTN.	PAD.
AM 5.30	11.55	AM12.45g	7.10
7.30d	1.25	8.51r	1.30
7.30e	1.50	11.57r	3.45
9.15r	2.20	PM12.10r	4.35
11.10r	3.24	2.15er	6.50
12. 0r	3.51	2.45dr	7. 5
PM12. 5r	4.57	4.14r	9. 0
2. 0r	6.55	5.17	2.45
3.30r	7.55	—	—
4.15r	9.41	—	—
6.30r	11.48	—	—
12. 0k	7.22	—	—
12.30h	7.25	—	—

Sunday Trains.

AM10.30r	2.55	AM12.45	7. 5
PM 2.40	7.40	7.45r	3.35
4.30r	9.49	10.40r	4. 5
10. 0	7.22	PM 2.15	7. 5
—	—	8.40	3.15
—	—	10.30	7.10
—	—	—	—
—	—	—	—

d Saturdays only.
e Saturdays excepted.
g Mondays excepted.
h Saturdays midnight only.
k Saturdays midnight excepted.
r Restaurant Car.

Redcliffe Hotel. First-class Hotel, occupying finest position in Torbay. Large secluded gardens reach the sea. 100 Rooms. 'Phone 133. Under new Management.
J. R. GOFF, Manager.
See advt. p. 275.

Hotel Esplanade. First Class Family Hotel. On Sea Front facing Pier. Lovely Grounds. Perfect winter resort ; warm, yet bracing. Apply Illustrated Tariff. 'Phone 89.
See advt. p. 276.

For completion of Advertisements, see **over**.

PAIGNTON—*continued.*

Goodrington House Private Hotel. Electric Light throughout Own garden produce. *See* advt. p. **276**.

Balholm Private Hotel. Centre Esplanade. Spacious Lounge facing Sea. Gas Fires in all bedrooms. Central Heating. Electric Light. Illustrated Tariff. 'Phone 74. Misses SLATER.

Ramleh Private Hotel. First class. Unequalled situation. Centre sea front. Three minutes station. Glorious panoramic views from Sheltered Balconies overlooking Torquay Bay. Separate tables. Electric Light. Bathing tents. Gas Fires in Bedrooms. Telephone 114.
Mrs. WILSHERE.

House Agents. Kenwrick's Offices, 3 and 4 Seaway, Preston, Paignton. Register of Furnished and Unfurnished Houses available in Paignton, Preston and Torquay.

PAISLEY (GILMOUR STREET)

(Renfrew), 422¾ miles. Fares, 82/6*a*, 49/6*c*. R. T. for two months, 165/0*a*, 99/0*c*. Pop. 84,837.
Map Square 40.

ST. PAN.	PAISLEY	PAISLEY	ST PAN.
AM 4.25	4.16	AM 8.47*r*	6.35
9.50*r*	7.52	10.58*r*	9.15
PM12.15*r*	10.47	PM 8.17*e*	7.25
9.30*e*	8.18	10.11*e*	7.50
11.45*e*	9.41	10.42*d*	8.57
—	—	—	—
—	—	—	—

Sunday Trains.

PM 9.30	8.18	—	—
11.45	9.41	—	—
—	—	—	—

d Saturdays only.
e Saturdays excepted.
r Restaurant Car.

PALACE GATES (Wood Green)

from *Liverpool Street*, 8¼ miles. Fares, 0/11½*a*, 0/9*b*, 0/7*c*. R. T. for two days, 1/11*a*, 1/6*b*, 1/2*c*. *See* pp. 534-536.

PALLION (Durham), 263

miles. Fares, 54/7*a*, 32/9*c*. R. T., double fare. Departures *from* London as for Sunderland. Departures *for* London about 3 times daily. Pop. 9,145
Map Square 3.

PALMER'S GREEN

(Middlesex) from *King's Cross, Moorgate Street*, and *Broad Street*, 6¾ miles. Fares from King's Cross, 1/3*a*, 1/0*b*, 0/9*c*. R. T. for two days, 2/6*a*, 2/0*b*, 1/6*c*. From Moorgate Street and Broad Street, 1/4½*a*, 1/1*b*, 0/10*c*. R. T. for two days, 2/9*a*, 2/2*b*, 1/8*c*. *See* pp. 511-517.

PALNURE (Kirkcudbright),

378¾ miles. Fares, 68/9*a*, 41/3*c*. R.T. for two months, 137/6*a*. Departures *from* London as for Castle Douglas. Departures *for* London about 3 times daily.
Map Square 43.

PALTERTON (Derby), 148

miles. Fares, 30/2*a*, 18/1*c*. R. T., double fare. Departures *from* London as for Mansfield. Departures *for* London about 4 times daily.
Map Square 13.

PAMPISFORD (Cambs)

from *Liverpool Street*, 53¾ miles. Fares, 11/5*a*, 6/10*c*. R. T. for two months, 22/10*a*. Departures *from* London as for Linton. Departures *for* London about 12 times daily. Pop. 243.
Map Square 19.

PANDY (Monmouth), 159½

miles. Fares, 33/2*a*, 19/11*c*. R. T. for two months, 66/4*a*. 39/10*c*. Departures *from* London as for Abergavenny. Departures *for* London about 5 times daily.
Map Square 22.

PANGBOURNE (Berks)

from *Paddington*, 41½ miles. Fares, 8/7*a*, 5/2*c*. R. T. for two months, 17/2*a*. Pop. 1,677.
Map Square 23.

PAD.	PANGB'NE	PANGB'NE	PAD.
AM 5.30	7. 6	AM 8. 5	9. 0
6.30	8.15	8.29	9.30
7.30	8.56	8.59	10. 0
9. 0	10.12	9.34	10.45
9.45	10.58	10.39	12. 0
11.20	12.30	PM12.38	1.50
PM12.30	1.41	2. 6	3.20
1.10*dr*	2.20	3. 9	4.35
1.35*r*	2.39	3.57	5. 6
1.50*d*	3.24	4.57	6. 2
3.18	4.45	5.51	7.20
3.38	5. 8	7.10	8.20
5. 0	6. 2	8. 5	9.15
5.40	6.47	9.22	10.45
6. 5	7. 9	10.18*h*	2.45
6.55	8. 5	—	—
7.30	8.33	—	—
8. 5	9.31	—	—
10. 0*h*	11.18	—	—
—	—	—	—
—	—	—	—

Sunday Trains.

AM 9.10	10.28	AM 8.36	10.14
10.35	11.35	PM12. 5	2.40
11. 0	12.21	4.33	6. 0
PM 1.45	3.13	6.55	8.20
2. 0	3.55	7.55	9.15
4.10	5.43	8.34	9.48
5.15	6.46	9.45	11.38
7.40	9.27	—	—

d Saturdays only.
h Wednesdays and Saturdays only.
r Restaurant Car.

Salters' Steamers (Whitchurch Lock, 10 minutes from Station). Passengers ferry out from Swan Hotel. Up-stream, 12.0 noon, 5.40 p.m. Down-stream, 10.40 a.m., 4.20 p.m. *See* advt. facing first page of train service.

George Hotel. Adjacent River and Station. Electric Light. English Fare. Lounge. Garage. R.A.C. and A.A. 'Phone 37. Proprietor,
A. LINDSAY.

PANNAL (Yorks), 199¾ miles.

Fares, 41/3*a*. 24/9*c*. R. T., double fare. Departures *from* London as for Leeds. Departures *for* London about 6 times daily. Pop. 1,963.
Map Square 7.

PANT (Glamorgan), 172¾

miles. Fares, 34/10*a* 20/11*c*. R. T. for two months, 69/8*a*, 41/10*c*. Departures *from* London as for Bargoed. Departures *for* London about 4 times daily.
Map Square 21.

PANT (Salop), 178 miles.

Fares 36/1*a*, 21/8*c*. R. T. for two months, 72/2*a*. Departures *from* London as for Oswestry. Departures *for* London about 6 times daily.
Map Square 17.

PANTEG (Monmouth) from

Paddington, 149¼ miles. Fares, 30/10*a*, 18/6*c*. R. T. for two months, 61/8*a*. Departures *from* London as for Newport (Mon). Departures *for* London about 8 times daily. Pop. 10,984.

PANT GLAS (Carnarvon),

258 miles. Fares, 53/9*a*, 32/3*c*. R.T. for two months, 107/6*a*, 64/6*c*. Departures *from* London as for Carnarvon. Departures *for* London about 4 times daily.
Map Square 11.

PANTYDWR (Radnor),

205½ miles. Fares, 41/5*a*, 24/10*c*. R.T. for two months, 82/10*a*. Departures *from* London as for Llanidloes. Departures *for* London about 3 times daily.
Map Square 16.

PANTYFFYNNON (Carmarthen),

208¾ miles. Fares, 43/2*a*, 25/11*c*. R. T. for two months, 86/4*a*, 51/10*c*. Departures *from* London as for Llanelly. Departures *for* London about 4 times daily.
Map Square 21.

PANTYSCALLOG

(Glamorgan), 178¾ miles. No through fares. Departures *from* London as for Abergavenny Departures *for* London about 4 times daily.

PAR (Cornwall) from *Paddington*,

260½ miles. Fares, 53/11*a*, 32/4*c*. R. T. for two months, 107/10*a*, 64/8*c*. Pop. 1,934.
Map Square 25.

PAD.	PAR	PAR	PAD.
AM 5.30	1.43	AM10.25*r*	4.35
10.30*r*	4. 8	10.44*hr*	4.45
11. 0*dr*	4.32	PM12.47*er*	6.50
11.10*r*	4.42	1.15*dr*	7. 5
PM12. 5*r*	7.36	2.12*r*	9. 0
2. 0*r*	8.33	10.33	7.10
10. 0	5.40	—	—
12. 0*l*	9.18	—	—
12.30*k*	9.50	—	—

Sunday Trains.

PM10. 0	5.40	PM12.23	7. 5
—	—	2. 0*r*	7.55
—	—	6.28	3.15

d Saturdays only.
e Saturdays excepted.
h Mondays and Fridays only.
k Saturdays midnight only.
l Saturdays midnight excepted.
r Restaurant Car.

PARBOLD (Lancs), 202¼ miles. Fares, 41/10*a*, 25/1*c*. R. T. for two months, 83/8*a*, 50/2*c*. Departures *from* London as for Wigan. Departures *for* London about 4 times daily. Pop. 711.
Map Square 12.

PARHAM (Suffolk) from *Liverpool Street*, 88¾ miles. Fares, 18/7*a*, 11/2*c*. R. T. for two months, 37/2*a*. Departures *from* London as for Framlingham. Departures *for* London about 7 times daily. Pop. 338.
Map Square 19.

PARIS. From *Victoria*, 262 miles, *via* Boulogne. Fares, 59/2*a*, 41/2*b*, 29/3*c*. R. T. for one month, 110/1*a*, 77/8*b*, 55/2*c*. Subject to exchange.

Weekdays and Sundays.

Subject to Special Passport Regulations.

Vict.	Paris (Nord).
AM 9.15	4.40
PM 8. 0	5.15
—	—

Trains from Paris (Nord).

Paris (Nord).	Vict.
AM 8.30*b*	3.45
PM 4. 0*b*	11. 0
—	—

ANOTHER ROUTE from *Victoria, via* Calais 287 miles. Fares, 65/3*a*, 45/11*b*, 31/7*c*. R. T. for one month, 119/1*a*, 85/2*b*, 58/7*c*. Subject to exchange.

Subject to Special Passport Regulations.

Weekdays and Sundays.

Vict.	Paris (Nord)	Paris (Nord)	Vict.
AM11. 0*b*	6.30	12. 0*bn*	7.30
PM 2. 0*b*	9.40	PM11.45	9.48
—	—	—	—

n Noon.

ANOTHER ROUTE from *Victoria* (L. B. & S.C.), *via* Dieppe, 224¼ miles. Fares, 48/0*a*, 33/1*b*, 24/4*c*. R. T. for one month, 87/3*a*, 59/10*b*, 45/7*c*. Subject to exchange.

Subject to special Passport regulations.

Weekdays and Sundays.

Vict.	Paris (St. Lazare)
AM10. 0*b*	5.58
PM 8.20	6. 0
—	—

Trains from Paris.

Paris (St. Lazare)	Vict.
AM10.36*b*	6.40
PM 9. 5	7.25
—	—

PARIS—*continued.*

ANOTHER ROUTE from *Waterloo, via* Havre, 340 miles. Fares, 48/0 First and Saloon, 33/1 Third London to Southampton and Second beyond. R. T. for one month, 87/3 First and Saloon, 59/10 Second to Southampton and Third Southampton to London. Subject to exchange.

Subject to special Passport regulations.

W'loo	Paris. (St.Lazare)	Paris (St.Lazare)	W'loo.
PM 9.30*r*	11.33*k*	PM 7.40*r*	9.15*k*

No Sunday Service.

k A.M. (following day).
r Restaurant Car.

PARK (Aberdeen), 532¼ miles. No through fares. Departures *from* London as for Banchory. Departures *for* London about 3 times daily.
Map Square 38.

PARK (Lancs), 186½ miles. No through fares. Departures *from* London as for Manchester. Departures *for* London about 7 times daily.
Map Square 12.

PARK (Middlesex) from *Liverpool Street* 7 miles. Fares, 0/10*a*, 0/8*b*, 0/6*c*. R.T. for two days, 1/8*a*, 1/4*b*, 0/10½*c*. *See* pp. 526, 527.
Map Square 52.

PARK BRIDGE (Lancs), from *Euston* 186½ miles. Fares, 38/7*a*, 23/2*c*. R. T. for two months, 77/2*a*, 46/4*c*. Departures *from* London as for Ashton. Departures *for* London about 3 times daily.

PARK DRAIN (Notts), 156¼ miles. Fares, 32/4*a*, 19/5*c*. R. T. for two months, 64/8*a*. Departures *from* London as for Gainsborough. Departures *for* London about 5 times daily.
Map Square 13.

PARKEND (Gloucester), 137¾ miles. Fares, 28/7*a*, 17/2*c*. R. T. for two months, 57/2*a*. Departures *from* London as for Lydney. Departures *for* London about 5 times daily.
Map Square 22.

PARKESTON QUAY (Essex) from *Liverpool Street*, 69 miles. Fares, 14/7*a*, 8/9*c*. R.T. for two months, 29/2*a*, 17/6*c*. Departures *from* London as for Harwich. Departures *for* London about 9 times daily.
Map Square 19.

The Great Eastern Hotel, under Management of London and North Eastern Railway. Facing Quay. Most convenient for Continental passengers. *See* advt. p. **277.**

PARKGATE (Cheshire), 191¾ miles. Fares, 40/0*a*, 24/0*c*. R. T. for two months, 80/0*a*. Departures *from* London as for Hooton. Departures *for* London about 8 times daily.

PARKGATE AND ALDWARKE (Yorks), from *King's Cross*, 166¾ miles Fares, 32/11*a*, 19/9*c*. R. T., double fare. Departures *from* London as for Rotherham and Masboro'. Departures *for* London about 4 times daily.

PARKGATE AND RAWMARSH (Yorks), from *St. Pancras* 164 miles. Fares, 32/11*a*, 19/9*c*. R. T., double fare. Departures *from* London as for Rotherham (Masboro'). Departures *for* London about 6 times daily.
Map Square 13.

PARKHILL (Aberdeen), 530½ miles. No through fares. Departures *from* London as for Fraserburgh or Peterhead. Departures *for* London about 3 times daily.
Map Square 35.

PARK ROYAL from *Paddington*, 4¼ miles. Fares, 0/6*c*. R. T. for two days, 1/0*c*. *See* pp. 490, 491.
Map Square 58.

PARK ROYAL AND TWYFORD ABBEY from *Mansion House*, 11½ miles. Fares, 0/6*c*, R. T. for two days, 1/0*c*. Pop. (Twyford Abbey) 126. *See* p. 489.
Map Square 58.

PARKSTONE (Dorset) from *Waterloo, via* Southampton. 111¼ miles. Fares, *via* Sway, 23/4*a*, 14/0*c*. R. T. for two months, 46/8*a*, 28/0*c*. *Via* Ringwood, 23/9*a*, 14/3*c*. R. T. for two months, 47/6*a*, 28/6*c*. Pop. 9,892.
Map Square 27.

W'loo	P'stne.	P'stne.	W'loo.
AM 5.40	9.32	AM 7.11*r*	10. 6
5.50	10.57	8.10*s*	11. 0
8.30*s*	12.27	8.17*s*	12.22
9.30	1. 2	10. 0*r*	12.50
10.30	1.22	10.45*r*	2.20
PM12.30*r*	3.10	PM12. 0	2.50
2.30*s*	5.10	12.55	4.20
3.30	6.37	2. 0	4.50
4.30*r*	7.17	2.39*s*	6.26
5.30	8.47	3.59	6.58
6.30*r*	9.10	4.50*r*	8.20
10. 0	2.18	6. 2*r*	8.50
—	—	6.35	10.50
—	—	7.24	11.28
—	—	11.21	3.58

Sunday Trains.

AM11. 0*r*	2.16	AM 8.25	12.11
PM 2. 0*r*	5. 8	11. 8*r*	2.27
7. 0*r*	10.14	PM 3.37*r*	6.24
9.28	2.21	6.37*r*	9.31
—	—	11.21	3.58

r Restaurant Car.
s Refreshments served.

ANOTHER ROUTE from *Waterloo, via* Salisbury, 117¾ miles. Fares, 23/9*a*, 14/3*c*. R. T. for two months, 47/6*a*, 28/6*c*.

W'loo.	P'stne.	P'stne.	W'loo.
AM 7.30	11.12	AM 7. 3	10.56
11. 0*r*	2.32	10.36*r*	1.56
PM 1. 0*r*	4.50	PM 2.38*r*	6. 0
3. 0*r*	6.35	4. 3*r*	8.30
6. 0*r*	10. 5	—	—

Sunday Trains.

12. 0*nr*	5.15	PM 4. 1	8.57
—	—	—	—

n Noon.
r Restaurant Car.

PARKSTONE—*contd.*

Rumsey & Rumsey, Auctioneers, Estate Agents. Particulars of all properties free. Offices, Parkstone, Bournemouth, West Canford Cliffs Broadstone and West Southbourne.

James & Sons, F.A.I. Estate Agents, Auctioneers. Lists available properties surrounding District, free. Offices Parkstone, Poole Hill, Bournemouth. Established 1879.

PARK STREET (Herts)

from *Euston*, 22¼ miles. Fares, 4/2*a*, 2/6*c*. R. T. for two months, 8/4*a*, 5/0*c*. Departures *from* London as for St. Albans. Departures *for* London about 14 times daily.

PARSLEY HAY (Derby),

160½ miles. Fares, 33/2*a*, 19/11*c*. R. T., double fare. Departures *from* London as for Ashbourne. Departures *for* London about 4 times daily.
Map Square 12.

PARSONS GREEN from

Mansion House, 6½ miles. See p. 489.
Map Square 68.

PARTINGTON (Cheshire),

191¾ miles. Fares, 37/9*a*, 22/8*c*. R. T. for two months, 75/6*a*, 45/4*c*. Departures *from* London as for Timperley West. Departures *for* London about 3 times daily. Pop. 758.
Map Square 12.

PARTON (Cumberland),

304½ miles. No through fares. Departures *from* London as for Whitehaven. Departures *for* London about 6 times daily. Pop. 1,595.
Map Square 6.

PARTON (Kirkcudbright),

358¾ miles. Fares, 68/9*a*, 41/3*c*. R. T. for two months, 137/6*a*, 82/6*c*. Departures *from* London as for Castle Douglas. Departures *for* London about 3 times daily. Pop. 597.
Map Square 43.

PARTRIDGE GREEN

(Sussex) from *London Bridge, Victoria*, or *Clapham Junction*, 47¼ miles. Fares, 10/0*a*, 6/0*c*. R. T. for two months, 20/0*a*, 12/0*c*. Departures *from* London as for West Grinstead. Departures *for* London about 9 times daily.
Map Square 23.

PASTON (Norfolk) from

King's Cross, 168½ miles. Fares, 26/0*a*, 15/7*c*. R. T. for two months, 52/0*a*. Departures *from* London as for Mundesley. Departures *for* London about 8 times daily. Pop. 280.
Map Square 14.

PATCHWAY (Gloucester)

113 miles. Fares, 23/9*a*, 14/3*c*. R. T. for two months, 47/6*a*. Departures *from* London as for Bristol. Departures *for* London about 5 times daily.
Map Square 22.

PATELEY BRIDGE

(Yorks), from *King's Cross*, 213 miles. Fares, 44/2*a*, 26/6*c*. R. T. for two months, 88/4*a*, 53/0*c*. Pop. 2,492.
Map Square 7.

King's+	PtleyB.	PtleyB.	King's+
AM 4.45	11.32	AM 7.25*r*	1.55
7.15*r*	1. 8	10.10*g*	3.15
10.10*r*	4.37	11.47*r*	5. 0
11.15*g*	4.37	PM 1.25*r*	7.10
PM 4. 0*r*	10. 1	3.15	9.25
10.45*e*	9.54	7.20*e*	3 25
—	—	8. 0*d*	3.25

Sunday Trains.

PM10.45	9.54	—	—

d Saturdays only.
e Saturdays excepted.
g First and Third Class Pullman Cars only.
r Restaurant Car.

PATNA (Ayr), 389½ miles.

Fares, 81/11*a*, 49/2*c*. R. T. for two months, 163/10*a*, 98/4*c*. Departures *from* London as for Ayr. Departures *for* London about 4 times daily. Pop. 1,093.
Map Square 43.

PATNEY (Wilts) from

Paddington, 81 miles. Fares, 16/11*a*, 10/2*c*. R. T. for two months, 33/10*a*. Pop. 108.
Map Square 22.

Pad.	Patney	Patney	Pad.
AM 7.30	9.55	AM 7.21	10. 0
8.45*r*	11.36	9. 5	10.52
10.45	1.14	9.51	12.55
PM12.30*r*	3. 0	PM12.45	2.50
2. 0*h*	4.42	1.14*h*	6. 2
2.45	5.30	3. 5*hr*	6.50
3.18	6.41	4. 6	7.20
6.30	8.44	4.42	8.20
—	—	7.50	10.45

Sunday Trains.

AM 9.10	12.17	AM 7.41	10.50
PM 2.40*h*	5.41	PM 6.28	9.15
5.15	8.14	—	—

h Via Westbury.
r Restaurant Car.

PATRICROFT (Lancs),

188¾ miles. Fares, 39/0*a*, 23/5*c*. R. T. for two months, 78/0*a*. Departures *from* London as for Manchester (London Road). Departures *for* London about 5 times daily. Pop. 17,923.
Map Square 12.

PATRINGTON (Yorks),

212½ miles. Fares, 37/6*a*, 22/6*c*. R. T. for two months, 75/0*a*, 45/0*c*. Departures *from* London as for Hull (Paragon). Departures *for* London about 3 times daily. Pop. 1,147.
Map Square 13.

PATTERTON (Renfrew),

403¾ miles. Fares, 82/6*a*, 49/6*c*. R. T. for two months, 165/0*a*, 99/0*c*. Departures *from* London as for Glasgow (Central). Departures *for* London about 6 times daily.
Map Square 40.

PEACEHAVEN (Sussex),

53 miles from *Victoria* and *London Bridge*. Fares to Newhaven Town, from either Station, 11/8*a*, 7/0*c*. R. T. for two months, double fare. Fares to Brighton, 10/6*a*, 6/4*c*. R. T. for two months, double fare. Pop. 1,500.
Map Square 28.

Hotel Peacehaven. Charmingly situated on the Sussex Downs, close to the Sea. All modern conveniences. Central Heating. Fully Licensed. Beautiful sunken Gardens. Telephone, Newhaven 43. 'Buses from Brighton and Newhaven stop at door.
See advt. p. **277**.

PEAK FOREST (Derby),

163¾ miles. Fares, 34/0*a*, 20/5*c*. R. T., double fare. Departures *from* London as for Miller's Dale. Departures *for* London about 3 times daily. Pop. 433.
Map Square 12.

PEAKIRK (Northampton)

from *King's Cross*, 81¾ miles. Fares, 16/11*a*, 10/2*c*. R. T., double fare. Pop. 244.
Map Square 18.

King's+	Peakirk	Peakirk	King's+
AM 4.45	6.55	AM 8.32	10.40
5. 5	8. 6	10.47	1. 5
7.15*lr*	9.41	PM12.47	3.50
8.45	11. 0	3.12*kr*	5. 0
11.30	2.21	6. 9	9. 0
PM 1.50*dr*	3.36	8.12	3.25
3. 0	4.50	—	—
5.45*r*	7.33	—	—
—	—	—	—

Sunday Trains.

12. 0*nr*	2.15	PM 8. 3*r*	10.20
—	—	—	—
—	—	—	—

d Saturdays only.
k Tuesdays and Wednesdays only.
l Tuesdays only.
n Noon.
r Restaurant Car.

PEAR TREE (Derby), 129½

miles. Fares, 26/10*a*, 16/1*c*. R. T., double fare. Departures *from* London as for Derby. Departures *for* London about 3 times daily. Pop. 9,528.
Map Square 12.

PECKHAM RYE from

London Bridge, 3½ miles. Fares, 0/7*a*, 0/4½*c*. R. T. for two days, 1/0*a*, 0/9*c*, or from *Victoria*, *via* South London Line, 5¼ miles. Fares, 0/7½*a*, 0/4½*c*. R. T. for two days, 1/2*a*, 0/9*c*. *See* pp. 565-568, 570, 581, 582.
Map Square 70.

ANOTHER ROUTE from

Victoria, Ludgate Hill, and *St. Paul's*, 5¼ miles. Fares, from Victoria, 0/7½*a*, 0/6*b*, 0/4½*c*. R. T. for two days, 1/2*a*, 1/0*b*, 0/9*c*. From Ludgate Hill, 0/7*a*, 0/6*b*, 0/4½*c*. R. T. for two days, 1/0*a*, 0/10½*b*, 0/9*c*. *See* pp. 562-563.

PEDAIR FFORDD (Montgomery),

188¾ miles. No through fares. Departures *from* London as for Oswestry. Departures *for* London about 3 times daily.
Map Square 16.

PEEBLES from *Euston*,

385 miles. Fares, 77/11*a*, 46/9*c*. R. T. for two months, 155/10*a*, 93/6*c*. Pop. 6,107.
Map Square 41.

Euston	Peebles	Peebles	Euston
AM 2.35*e*	3.47	AM 7.40*r*	6.25
2.35*d*	4. 8	9.45*r*	7.30
5. 0*d*	6.15	PM 1. 5*dr*	10. 0
10. 0*er*	6.39	1.25*er*	10. 0
10. 0*dr*	7.50	3.20*d*	5. 0
PM11.35*e*	9.25	4.10*e*	5. 0
11.45*e*	11.20	7. 5*d*	7.40
—	—	7.20*e*	6.55

Sunday Trains.

PM11.35	9.25	—	—
11.45	11.20	—	—
—	—	—	—

d Saturdays only.
e Saturdays excepted.
r Restaurant Car.

PEEBLES—*continued.*

ANOTHER ROUTE from *St. Pancras*, 391¼ miles. Fares as above.

St. Pan.	Peebles	Peebles	St. Pan.
AM 4.25	5.21	AM 8.24*r*	7.15
9. 0*r*	7.51	10.43*r*	7.55
11.45*dr*	9.40	PM 9. 9	8. 5
PM 9.15*e*	7.35	—	—

Sunday Trains.

PM 9.15	7.35	—	—

d Saturdays only.
e Saturdays excepted.
r Restaurant Car.

Peebles Hotel Hydro. Baths and Electrical Treatment. Lovely Scenery. *See* advt. p. **278.**

PEGSWOOD (Northumberland), 286½ miles. No through fares. Departures *from* London as for Morpeth. Departures *for* London about 5 times daily Pop. 2,559.
Map Square 3.

PELAW (Durham), 265 miles. Fares, 55/3*a*, 33/2*c*. R. T., double fare. Departures *from* London as for Ferryhill or Newcastle-on-Tyne. Departures *for* London about 8 times daily.
Map Square 3.

PELSALL (Stafford), 123½ miles. Fares, 25/8*a*, 15/5*c*. R. T. for two months, 51/4*a*. Departures *from* London as for Lichfield. Departures *for* London about 8 times daily. Pop. 3,491.
Map Square 17.

PELTON (Durham), 263 miles. No through fares. Departures *from* London as for Durham. Departures *for* London about 5 times daily. Pop. 8,118.
Map Square 3.

PEMBERTON (Lancs), 197¾ miles. No through fares. Departures *from* London as for Wigan. Departures *for* London about 8 times daily Pop. 23,642.
Map Square 12.

PEMBREY (Carmarthen) from *Paddington*, 211½ miles. Fares, 44/0*a*, 26/5*c*. R. T. for two months, 88/0*a*. Pop. 4,549.
Map Square 21.

Pad.	Pemb'ry	Pemb'ry	Pad.
AM 1. 0*g*	8.39	AM 7.40*r*	1. 0
8.45*r*	1.44	8.45*r*	2.30
11.50*dr*	5.12	10.50*r*	4.20
11.50*r*	5.29	12.32*r*	6.15
PM 1.10*r*	6.45	PM 2.51*r*	8.35
3.35*r*	8.54	4.33*r*	9.25
5. 0*dr*11.52		6.51	3.30
5. 0*hr*11.10		—	—
6. 0*r* 11.30		—	—

Sunday Trains.

PM12.30*r*	8.11	PM 2.14*r*	8.25
9.15	8.39	—	—

d Saturdays only.
g Mondays excepted.
h Tuesdays only.
r Restaurant Car.

PEMBRIDGE (Hereford) from *Paddington*, 155½ miles. Fares, 31/8*a*, 19/0*c*. R. T. for two months, 63/4*a*. Departures *from* London as for Titley. Departures *for* London about 4 times daily. Pop. 995.
Map Square 17.

PEMBROKE from *Paddington*, 266½ miles. Fares (Pembroke), 54/2*a*, 32/6*c*. R. T. for two months, 108/4*a*, 65/0*c*. (Pembroke Dock), 54/4*a*, 32/7*c*. R. T. for two months, 108/8*a*, 65/2*c*. Pop. 15,481.
Map Square 20.

Pad.	Pemb'k.	Pemb'k D'k.
AM 1. 0*g*	12. 7	12.14
8.45*r*	3.24	3.31
11.50*r*	7.24	7.30
PM 1.10*r*	9.34	9.40
9.15*e*	7. 7	7.13
—	—	—

Sunday Trains.

PM 9.15	7. 7	7.13

Trains from Pembroke.

Pemb'k D'k.	Pemb'k.	Pad.
AM 9.25*r*	9.32*r*	4.20
10.15*r*	10.24*r*	6.15
11. 0*r*	11. 9*r*	8.35
PM 2. 0*r*	2.10*r*	9.25
6. 0	6. 9	3.30

No Sunday Trains.

e Saturdays excepted.
g Mondays excepted.
r Restaurant Car.

PENALLY (Pembroke), 258½ miles. Fares, 52/6*a*, 31/6*c*. R. T. for two months, 105/0*a*. Departures *from* London as for Tenby. Departures *for* London about 6 times daily. Pop. 466.
Map Square 20.

PENARTH (Town) (Glamorgan) from *Paddington*, via Cardiff, 156½ miles. Fares, 32/6*a*, 19/6*c*. R. T. for two months, 65/0*a*. Pop. 17,097.
Map Square 21.

Pad.	Penarth	Penarth	Pad.
AM 1. 0*g*	5.58	AM 5.22*r*	10.15
5.30	10.53	7.25*r*	10.57
8.45*r*	12.11	7.33	12.20
9. 0	2.17	9.28*r*	1. 0
11.50*r*	3.27	9.49*r*	2. 0
PM 1.10*r*	5.11	10.35*r*	2.30
3.35*r*	6.47	PM12.35*r*	4.20
5. 0*r*	8.51	2.50*r*	6.15
6. 0*r*	9.23	4.34*r*	8.35
6.30*r* 10.48		6.13*r*	9.25
8. 0*r* 11.15		10.13	3.30
—	—	—	—
—	—	—	—

Sunday Trains.

AM 1. 0	9.51	AM 7.45	3.35
9.10	3. 5	11.15	4. 5
PM12.30*r*	5.56	PM 4.25*r*	8.25
4.30	9.58	10.10	3.30
9.15	5.58	—	—

g Mondays excepted.
r Restaurant Car.

Esplanade Hotel. Within three miles of Cardiff. Overlooking the Bristol Channel. First-class Family Hotel. Recently entirely re-constructed, re-decorated and re-furnished. Every modern convenience. Excellent Cuisine.

PENCADER (Carmarthen) from *Paddington*, 242½ miles. Fares, 48/9*a*, 29/3*c*. R. T. for two months, 97/6*a*. Departures *from* London as for Lampeter. Departures *for* London about 4 times daily.
Map Square 16.

PENCAITLAND (Eastlothian) 393½ miles. No through fares. Departures *from* London as for Edinburgh (Waverley). Departures *for* London about 4 times daily. Pop. 1,366.
Map Square 41.

PENCLAWDD (Glamorgan), 209½ miles. No through fares. Departures *from* London as for Swansea. Departures *for* London about 4 times daily.,
Map Square 21.

PENCOED (Glamorgan), 269½ miles. Fares, 35/3*a*, 21/2*c*. R. T. for two months, 70/6*a*. Departures *from* London as for Llanharan. Departures *for* London about 4 times daily. Pop. 1,894.
Map Square 21.

PENDLEBURY (Lancs), 191½ miles. Fares, 39/5*a*, 23/8*c*. R. T. for two months, 78/10*a*, 47/4*c*. Departures *from* London as for Manchester. Departures *for* London about 6 times daily. Pop. 9,966.
Map Square 12.

PENDLETON (Lancs), 189½ miles. Fares, 39/0*a*, 23/5*c*. R. T. for two months, 78/0*a*. Departures *from* London as for Manchester. Departures *for* London about 6 times daily. Pop. 202.
Map Square 12.

PENGAM (Monmouth), 158½ miles. Fares (*via* Bassaleg), 32/11*a*, 19/9*c*. R. T. for two months. 65/10*a*, 39/6*c*. *Via* Cardiff 35/0*a*, 21/0*c*. R. T. for two months, 70/0*a*, 42/0*c*. Departures *from* London as for Bargoed or Cardiff. Departures *for* London about 4 times daily. Pop. 3,012.

PENGE EAST (Kent) from *Victoria*, *Holborn Viaduct*, and *Ludgate Hill*, 7½ miles. Fares, 1/3*a*, 1/0*b*, 0/9*c*. R. T. for two days, 2/6*a*, 1/9*b*, 1/5*c*. *See* pp. 558-561.

PENGE WEST (Kent) from *London Bridge*, 7 miles. Fares, 1/6*a*, 0/10½*c*. R. T. for two days, 2/7*a*, 1/7*c*. Pop. 26,284. *See* pp. **564, 565,** 568-570.
Map Square 79.

From *Victoria*, 12 miles. Fares, 1/11*a*, 1/2*c*. R. T. for two days, 3/10*a*, 2/0*c*. *See* p. 580.

PENICUIK (Midlothian) 394½ miles. Fares, 80/3*a*, 48/2*c*. R. T. for two months, 160/6*a*, 96/4*c*. Departures *from* London as for Edinburgh (Waverley). Departures *for* London about 4 times daily. Pop. 5,176.
Map Square 41.

PENISTONE (Yorks) from

King's Cross, 174¾ miles. Fares,
35/3*a*, 21/2*c*. R. T., double fare.
Pop. 3,791.
Map Square 12.

KING'S + PENIST.		PENIST. KING'S +	
AM 4.45	9.27	AM 6.55*r*	11.30
7.15*r*	11.16	7.55	1. 5
8.45	2. 9	10.51	3.50
10.10*r*	4.29	PM12.19	6.25
11.30	5.59	1.29	6.30
PM 1.50*r*	6.53	3.22	9. 0
4. 0*r*	8.58	8.35	3.25
5.45*r*	10.14		

Sunday Trains.

12. 0*nr*	4.37	AM 8.27	3.45
PM 5. 0*r*	9.35	PM 1.18	5.55
		5.46*r*	10.20

n Noon.

r Restaurant Car.

ANOTHER ROUTE from

Marylebone 177¾ miles. Fares as
above.

M'BONE PENIST.		PENIST. M'BONE.	
AM 2.32	6.34	AM 6.55*r*	11.10
8.45*r*	12.59	9.14*r*	1.13
10. 0*r*	1.59	10.51*r*	3. 0
PM12.15*r*	4.29	PM 3. 5*r*	6.38
3.20*r*	6.53	4.30*r*	8.55
5. 0*r*	8.58	5.59*r*	9.55
6.20*r*	9.58	11.36	3.57

Sunday Trains.

AM11.15*r*	3.23	PM 1.18*r*	5.40
PM 5.30*r*	9.35	5.46*r*	10.24
—	—	—	—

r Restaurant Car.

PENKRIDGE (Stafford),

133¾ miles. Fares, 27/9*a*, 16/8*c*.
R. T. for two months. 55/6*a*.
Departures *from* London as for
Stafford or Wolverhampton (High
Level). Departures *for* London
about 6 times daily. Pop. 1,200.
Map Square 17.

PENMAENMAWR (Car-

narvon) from *Euston,* 229 miles.
Fares, 47/9*a*, 28/8*c*. R. T. for two
months, 95/6*a*, 57/4*c*. Pop. 4,480.
Map Square 11.

EUSTON PENM'WR		PENM'WR. EUSTON	
AM12.25	8.11	AM 7.22*dr*	1. 0
2.35	11.20	7.34*er*	1. 0
5. 0*e*	12. 5	8.32*r*	1.45
5. 0*d*	12.43	9.20*dr*	3.10
8.30*dr*	2.14	9.43*er*	4.15
8.30*er*	2.55	11.27*r*	5. 5
·11.10*r*	3.52	PM 1.31*r*	7.30
11.50*r*	6.31	2.49*r*	9.20
PM 2.35*t*	8. 9	4. 6*r*	10.45
4. 5*r*	10. 8	8.22	5. 0
5.20*r*	11. 5	—	—

Sunday Trains.

PM 12.10*r*	7.57	AM 7.22	4. 0
—	—	—	—

d Saturdays only.
e Saturdays excepted.
r Restaurant Car.
t Tea Car.

Grand Hotel. Overlooking
sands and sea. Golfing. Fishing.
Mountaineering. Glorious
scenery. Garage.
See advt. p. **278.**

PEN MAEN POOL

(Merioneth) from *Euston,* 258
miles. Fares, 48/4*a*, 29/0*c*. R. T.
for two months, 96/8*a*. Departures *from* London as for Dolgelley.
Departures *for* London about 3
times daily.
Map Square 16.

ANOTHER ROUTE from

Paddington, 224½ miles. Fares,
47/1*a*, 28/8*c*. R.T. for two months,
94/2*a*. Departures *from* London
as for Dolgelley. Departures *for*
London about 3 times daily.

PENNINGTON (Lancs).

192½ miles. Fares, 39/7*a*, 23/9*c*.
R. T. for two months, 79/2*a*. Departures *from* London as for Kenyon. Departures *for* London about
6 times daily. Pop. 1,361.

PENNS (Warwick),

from *Euston,* 121½ miles. Fares,
24/5*a*, 14/8*c*. R.T. for two months,
48/10*a*, 29/4*c*. Departures *from*
London as for Birmingham (New
Street). Departures *for* London
about 8 times daily.
Map Square 17.

PENPERGWM (Mon-

mouth), 156¾ miles. Fares, 32/6*a*,
19/6*c*. R.T. for two months, 65/0*a*.
Departures *from* London as for
Pontypool Road. Departures *for*
London about 5 times daily.
Map Square 22.

PENRHIWCEIBER

(Glamorgan) from *Paddington,*
166¾ miles. Fares *via* Pontypool
Road, 34/5*a*, 20/8*c*. R. T. for two
months, 68/10*a*. Pop. 3,816.

PAD. PENRH'BR		PENRH'BR PAD.	
AM 1. 0*g*	8.41	AM 8. 8*r*	1. 0
5.30	11.55	8.49*r*	2.30
8.45*r*	2.25	10.42*r*	4.20
9. 0	3.20	PM 1. 0*r*	6. 5
11.50*hr*	4.44	2.40*r*	8.35
11.50*r*	5.50	4.51*r*	9.25
PM 1.10*r*	7.29	7.10	3.30
3.35*r*	8.38	10.24*k*	7.10
6. 0*kr*	10.39	—	—
8. 0*dr*	9.16	—	—

Sunday Trains.

PM12.30*r*	7.51	AM10.10	8.10
9.15	8.41	PM 8.30	3.30
—	—	—	—

d Saturdays only.
g Mondays excepted.
h Fridays only.
k Thursdays and Saturdays only.
r Restaurant Car.

PENRHYNDEUDRA-

ETH (Merioneth), 262½ miles.
Fares, 51/11*a*, 31/2*c*. R. T. for
two months, 103/10*a*. Departures
from London as for Harlech.
Departures *for* London about 4
times daily. Pop. 1,988.
Map Square 11.

PENRITH (Cumberland)

from *Euston,* 281¼ miles. Fares,
56/6*a*, 33/11*c*. R. T. for two
months, 113/0*a*, 67/10*c*. Pop. 8,342.
Map Square 7.

EUSTON PENRITH		PENRITH EUSTON	
AM12.25	9.35	AM 2.41*g*	11.10
2.35	11.18	7. 8*r*	3.10
5. 0	12.44	9. 0*hr*	3.41
10.40*r*	5.37	9. 0*r*	4.15
11.35*r*	5.49	10.52*r*	6. 0
PM 1.30*r*	8. 2	PM 1.37*r*	7.30
9.30*d*	4.32	2.0*er*	9. 5
11. 0*d*	5. 1	2. 0*dr*	9.15
11.45*e*	6.16	4.42*r*	10.45
		7.40	5. 0

PENRITH—*continued*.

Sunday Trains.

EUSTON PENRITH		PENRITH EUSTON	
AM11.45*r*	8. 8	AM 2.41*r*	1.30
PM11.45	6.16	PM 4.43	5. 0
—	—	—	—

d Saturdays only.
e Saturdays excepted.
g Mondays excepted.
h Mondays and Saturdays only.
r Restaurant Car.

Armstrong's George Hotel.
Leading County and Family.
Handsome Lounge. Covered
Garage. Pit. Resident Engineer.
Motors on Hire.
See advt. p. **278.**

PENRUDDOCK (Cumber-

land), 288¾ miles. Fares, 58/1*a*,
34/10*c*. R.T. for two months, 116/2*a*,
69/8*c*. Departures *from* London as
for Keswick. Departures *for* London about 5 times daily.
Map Square 7.

PENRYN (Cornwall) from

Paddington, 287¾ miles. Fares,
59/7*a*, 35/9*c*. R. T. for two months,
119/2*a*, 71/6*c*. Departures *from*
London as for Falmouth. Departures *for* London about 6 times
daily. Pop. 3,151.
Map Square 25.

PENSFORD (Somerset),

from *Paddington* 118½ miles. Fares,
via Frome, 24/10*a*, 14/11*c*; R.T. for
two months, 49/8*a*, 29/10*c*. *Via*
Bristol, 25/0*a*, 15/0*c*; R. T. for two
months, 50/0*a*. Departures *from*
London as for Midsomer Norton
or Bristol. Departures *for* London
about 5 times daily.
Map Square 22.

PENSHAW (Durham), 258¼

miles. Fares, 54/0*a*, 32/5*c*. R. T.
for two months, 108/0*a*, 64/10*c*. Departures *from* London as for
Ferryhill or Durham. Departures
for London about 6 times daily.
Map Square 3.

PENSHURST (Kent)

from *Charing Cross, Cannon Street,*
and *London Bridge,* 33½ miles.
Fares, 6/3*a*, 5/0*b*, 3/9*c*. R. T. for
two months, 12/6*a*, 10/0*b*, 7/6*c*.
Pop. 1,531.
Map Square 24.

		Leave			Arr. at
	CHAR. +	CAN.ST.	LON. B.		PENSRT.
AM —		4.44	5. 0		6.24
			9.33*l*		10.57
10.55		—	11. 3		12.34
PM12.55		—	1. 4		2.32
2. 3*e*		2. 8*d*	2.10		3.35
3.15*d*		—	3.21*d*		5.26
		4.20*e*	4.23*e*		5.26
		5.20*e*	5.23*e*		6.31
5.42*d*		—	5.48*d*		7. 2
		6. 0*e*	6. 3*e*		7.16
		—	6.27*el*		7.35
7.24*d*		7.28*e*	7.30		8.50
8.28		—	8.36		9.59
—		—	—		—
—		—	—		—
—		—	—		—
—		—	—		—

Sunday Trains.

AM 6.25		—	6.32		8.13
5.25		—	5.32		7. 5
8.38		—	8.45		10. 5

PENSHURST—*continued.*

Trains from Penshurst.

Leave PENS'RST.	LON. B.	Arrive at CAN. ST.	CHAR. +
AM 7. 5	8.24	8.28	—
7.44	8.49	—	—
8.17	9.28	9.32	—
9.12	10.27	10.52	—
10.24	11.46	—	11.59
11.28	12.50	—	1. 0
PM 1.17	2.38	—	2.46
2.15	3.28e	—	3.42d
3.56	5. 2	—	5.14
4.48	5.56	—	—
6. 0	7.20	—	7.29
7.40	9. 2	—	9.15
8.45	10. 3	—	10.13
10.38	11.57	—	12.10
—	—	—	—
—	—	—	—
—	—	—	—

Sunday Trains.

AM 9.55	11.15	—	11.25
PM 8.48	10.11	—	10.24
—	—	—	—
—	—	—	—
—	—	—	—

d Saturdays only.
e Saturdays excepted.
l Low Level platform.

PENTON (Roxburgh), 315¾ miles. Fares, 64/0a, 38/5c. R. T. for two months, 128/0a, 76/10c. Departures *from* London as for Carlisle. Departures *for* London about 3 times daily. *Map Square* 3.

PENTRAETH (Anglesey), 252¼ miles. Fares, 52/8a, 31/7c. R. T. for two months, 105/4a, 63/2c. Departures *from* London as for Gaerwen. Departures *for* London about 5 times daily. Pop. 768. *Map Square* 11.

PENTREBACH (Glamorgan), 169¼ miles. Fares, 35/3a, 21/2c. R. T. for two months, 70/6a, 42/4c. Departures *from* London as for Pontypridd. Departures *for* London about 6 times daily.

PENYBONT (Radnor), 210¾ miles. Fares, 37/6a, 22/6c. R. T. for two months, 75/0a, 45/0c. Departures *from* London as for Knighton. Departures *for* London about 3 times daily. *Map Square* 16.

PENYBONTFAWR (Montgomery), 190 miles. Fares, 38/11a, 23/4c. R. T. for two months, 77/10a. Departures *from* London as for Oswestry. Departures *for* London about 3 times daily. *Map Square* 16.

PEN-Y-FFORD (Flint), 190 miles. No through fares. Departures *from* London as for Wrexham. Departures *for* London about 4 times daily. *Map Square* 12.

PENYGRAIG (Glamorgan) from *Paddington*, 171¼ miles. Fares, 34/5a, 20/6c. R. T. for two months, 68/10a. Departures *from* London as for Llantrisant. Departures *for* London about 7 times daily. *Map Square* 21.

PENYGROES (Carnarvon), 254¼ miles. Fares, 52/11a, 31/9c. R.T. for two months, 105/10a, 63/6c. Departures *from* London as for Carnarvon. Departures *for* London about 5 times daily. *Map Square* 11.

PENYRHEOL (Glamorgan), 154¼ miles. Fares (*via* Cardiff) 33/7a, 20/2c. R.T. for two months, 67/2a, 40/4c. Departures *from* London as for Caerphilly or Cardiff. Departures *for* London about 4 times daily.

PENZANCE (Cornwall) from *Paddington*, 305¼ miles. Fares, 63/2a, 37/11c. R. T. for two months, 126/4a, 75/10c. Pop. 12,096. *Map Square* 25.

	PAD.	PENZ.		PENZ.	PAD.
AM	5.30	3.55	AM	10. 0r	4.45
	10.30r	5. 0		11. 0r	6.50
	11.10r	6.30		12. 0r	9. 0
PM	2. 0r	10.15	PM	8.40	7.10
	10. 0d	7.26		—	—
	10. 0e	7.40		—	—
	12. 0k	11.32		—	—
	12.30h	11.42		—	—
	—	—		—	—

Sunday Trains.

AM	10.30r	5.47	AM	10.35	7. 5
PM	10. 0	7.40	PM	12.15r	7.55
	—	—		4.35	3.15

d Saturdays only.
e Saturdays excepted.
h Saturdays midnight only.
k Saturdays midnight excepted.
r Restaurant Car.

Taxi Cabs can be hired to meet any train at this Station by telegram, or telephone No. 198. Messrs. Taylor's Garage, Ltd., Coinage Hall Street.

Queen's Family Hotel. Patronised by Royalty. Over 100 handsomely furnished rooms. Frontage of 250 feet facing the Sea. Excellent Garage. Electric Light throughout. Under same proprietorship as Bull Hotel, Cambridge.
Apply to MANAGER.
See advt. p. **279.**

Regent Hotel. Beautifully situated. Special Terms by Day or Week. Telephone 146. ROBERT THOMAS, Proprietor.
See advt. p. **279.**

Mount's Bay Hotel, Esplanade, Penzance. Facing Sea. First-class Family. Moderate Terms. Under New Management. Telegrams: "Hotel," Penzance. Telephone 18.

Marine Private Hotel. On the Esplanade, Facing Mounts Bay. View unequalled. Garage near House. MANN.

Beachfield Private Hotel, Penzance. On Esplanade. South aspect, with complete view of Mounts Bay. Close to Bathing Beach. Phone 67. Weekly terms from 3½ guineas. Mrs. ROLLESTON, Proprietress.

PEPLOW (Salop), 151¼ miles. Fares, 31/6a, 18/11c. R. T. for two months, 63/0a. Departures *from* London as for Market Drayton. Departures *for* London about 6 times daily. *Map Square* 17.

PERCY MAIN (Northumberland), 274 miles. Fares, 57/9a, 34/8c. R. T., double fare. Departures *from* London as for Newcastle-on-Tyne. Departures *for* London about 6 times daily.

PERIVALE (Middlesex) from *Paddington*, 7 miles. Fare, 0/7½c. R. T. for two days, 1/3c. Pop. 114. *See* pp. 490, 491. *Map Square* 58.

PERRANPORTH (Cornwall) from *Paddington*, 292 miles. Fares 58/2a, 34/11c. R. T. for two months, 116/4a, 69/10c. Pop. 2,366. *Map Square* 25.

	PAD.	PERRAN'TH.		PERRAN'TH.	PAD.
AM	5.30	3.52	AM	9.28r	4.45
	10.30r	5.13		10.38hr	6.50
	11.10r	6.43		11.44r	9. 0
PM	10. 0e	8.18	PM	8.11	7.10
	10. 0d	8.57		—	—
	12. 0k	11.43		—	—
	12.30l	12. 7		—	—

Sunday Trains.

AM	10.30r	6.17	AM	10.11r	7. 5
PM	10. 0	8.18	PM	4. 5	3.15

d Saturdays only.
e Saturdays excepted.
h *Via* Newquay.
k Saturdays midnight excepted.
l Saturdays midnight only.
r Restaurant Car.

Droskyn Castle. Comfortable Private Residential Hotel. Unique position on Cliffs, overlooking Sea, with magnificent views.
Apply to MANAGER.

PERRANWELL (Cornwall) from *Paddington*, 283¼ miles. Fares, 58/9a, 35/3c. R. T. for two months, 117/6a, 70/6c. Departures *from* London as for Falmouth. Departures *for* London about 6 times daily. *Map Square* 25.

PERRY BARR (Stafford), 113¾ miles. Fares, 23/6a, 14/1c. R. T. for two months, 47/0a. Departures *from* London as for Birmingham (New Street). Departures *for* London about 8 times daily. Pop. 2,701.

PERSHORE (Worcester) from *Paddington*, 112¼ miles. Fares, 23/6a, 14/1c. R. T. for two months, 47/0a. Pop. 3,462. *Map Square* 17.

	PAD.	PERSH'RE		PERSH'RE.	PAD.
AM	5.30	9.52	AM	6.42	9.50
	9.45	12.48		7.32h	11. 0
	10.40h	2.53		9.14	12. 5
PM	1.55r	4.21		10.38	2.12
	4.45	7.40	PM	12.14r	2.55
	6.10h	9.43		1.37hr	5. 0
	6.55	10.29		3.28	7.20
	—	—		4.57r	9.15
	—	—		7. 0	10.45

Sunday Trains.

AM	10.35r	2. 0	AM	10.48	2.40
PM	4.10	7.46	PM	6. 2r	9.48

h *Via* Stratford-on-Avon.
r Restaurant Car.

PERSLEY (Aberdeen),

526 miles. No through fares. Departures *from London as for* Aberdeen. Departures *for* London about 4 times daily.
Map Square 35.

PERTH from *Euston,* 450

miles. Fares, 91/1a, 54/8c. R. T. for two months, 182/2a, 109/4c. Pop. 33,208.
Map Square 38.

Euston	Perth	Perth	Euston
AM 5. 0	6. 3	AM 9. 7r	7.30
10. 0r	8. 0	PM12.22r	10.45
PM 1.30r	12.35	3.25r	5. 0h
7.40er	4.52	9.10	7.40
7.50er	5.33	10. 5	8. 0
11. 0d	9.32	—	—
11.35e	9.12	—	—

Sunday Trains.

PM 7.50r	5.35	PM 3.50r	5. 0h
11.35	9.12	—	—

d Saturdays only.
e Saturdays excepted.
h A.M.
r Restaurant Car.

ANOTHER ROUTE from

King's Cross. 440 miles. Fares as above.

King's +	Perth	Perth	King's +
AM 4.45	3.10	AM 6.25r	6.15
10. 0r	7.55	8.40r	6.30
11.50r	10.45	PM12.15r	10. 0
PM 7.45er	4.57	3.35	3.25
8.25e	8.39	5.28	6. 0
11.25e	8.55	8. 5e	6.50
—	—	9.20	7. 5

Sunday Trains.

PM 7.45	5.28	—	—
11.25	8.55	—	—

e Saturdays excepted.
r Restaurant Car.

For Dundee, Perth, and London Shipping Co., Ltd., service of Steamers, *see* p. 597.

Station Hotel (the property of the North British, Caledonian, and Highland Railways). First-class. Moderate Tariff. Entrance adjoins Station platform.

PETERBOROUGH

(Northampton) from *King's Cross,* 76¼ miles. Fares, 13/10a, 9/6c. R. T., double fare. Pop. 35,533.
Map Square 18.

King's +	P'boro	P'boro	King's +
AM 4.45	6.12	AM 1.45g	3.25
5. 5	7.31	4.25	6. 0
7.15r	8.42	5.55g	7.25
7.45	10.17	7.15	9.56
8.45	10.34	9.12r	10.40
10.10r	11.32	9.15r	11.15
10.12	1.22	10.40	12.25
11.30	1.35	11.38	1. 6
PM 1.30r	2.53	11.52	1.15
1.40r	3. 3	PM12.33r	1.55
1.50r	3.13	2. 4	3.50
1.55	4.25	2.53r	4.30
3. 0	4.35	3.19r	4.45
4. 0r	5.27	3.37r	5. 0
4.15	6.24	4.21	6.25
5. 0	6.45	5.46r	7.10
5.45r	7. 9	7. 5	9. 0
8.25	10. 2	8. 0	9.25
10.45	12.12	—	—
—	—	—	—

PETERBOROUGH—*con.*

Sunday Trains.

King's +	P'boro.	P'boro.	King's +
AM 8.30	11.14	AM 4.25	6. 0
11.30r	1. 0	5.55	7.25
12. 0nr	1.39	PM 2. 3r	3.45
PM 5. 0	6.35	3.33	5.15
7.10	9.45	4.13	5.55
8.25	10. 2	5.18	8. 8
10.45	12.12	6.45r	8.15
—	—	8.35r	10.20
—	—	—	—
—	—	—	—
—	—	—	—
—	—	—	—

g Mondays excepted.
n Noon.
r Restaurant Car.

ANOTHER ROUTE from

Liverpool Street, via Ely, 100 miles. Fares as above.

L'pool St.	P'boro.	P'boro.	L'pool St.
AM 5.50	10. 4	AM 6.17	9.27
8.30r	11.47	7. 5r	10.23
10. 5	1.26	9.24	12.40
11.50r	3.18	PM12.24lr	4. 2k
PM12.48e	5.12	12.24	5. 9
1.19d	5.12	1.10r	5.17
2.34	5.56	2.33r	6.10
4.45	7.25	3.34	7.58
5.49r	9. 4	5. 5r	8.22
10.12	1.17	7.15	10.30
—	—	11. 0	2.50
—	—	—	—
—	—	—	—
—	—	—	—
—	—	—	—

Sunday Trains.

AM 9.25	12.30	PM 3.10	6.40
PM 3.25	6.54	4.35	7.40
9.12	1.17	11. 0	3. 0

d Saturdays only.
e Saturdays excepted.
k Arrives at St. Pancras Station.
l Commencing July 23.
r Restaurant Car.

Great Northern Station
Hotel. Comfortable Family Hotel. Night Porter. Stabling, Garage. Officially appointed R.A.C., M.U. Near the Cathedral. Hunting, Fishing, Boating, and Golf in district. Telegraphic address, "Northness." Telephone, No. 176.

Angel Hotel. Central, near Cathedral. Family, Commercial, and Posting. Headquarters Automobile Club. Electric Light. "Decorated Hall" for Banquets, &c. Telephone 11.
J. CLIFTON, Proprietor.

Bull Hotel. Family and Commercial, Westgate. Central, near Cattle Market and Horse Repository. Stabling. Garage. Phone 194. Moderate Tariff.
MANAGER.

PETERCHURCH (Here-

ford), 162 miles. Fares, 34/0a, 20/5c. R. T. for two months, 68/0a, 40/10c. Departures *from* London as for Abbeydore. Departures *for* London about 3 times daily. Pop. 565.
Map Square 17.

PETERHEAD (Aberdeen)

from *King's Cross,* 567 miles. Fares, 109/2a, 65/6c. R. T. for two months, 218/4a, 131/0c. Pop. 16,144.
Map Square 35.

King's +	P'head.	P'head.	King's +
AM 4.45	9. 0l	AM 7.10r	10.10l
PM 8.20e	9.58h	9.30	3.25h
11.25e	2.40l	PM12.45	6. 0h
—	—	3.35	7.30h

Sunday Trains.

PM 8.20	9.58h	—	—

e Saturdays excepted.
h A.M.
l P.M.
r Restaurant Car.

ANOTHER ROUTE from

Euston, 584 miles. Fares as above.
Map Square 35.

Euston.	P'head.	P'head.	Euston.
PM 1.30er	8.46h	AM 7.10r	10.45l
7.50er	9.58h	9.30	5. 0h
11.35e	2.40l	PM 3.35	8. 0h
—	—	7. 0e	7.30l

Sunday Trains.

PM 7.50r	9.58h	—	—
11.35	2.40l	—	—

e Saturdays excepted.
h A.M.
l P.M.
r Restaurant Car.

PETERSFIELD (Hants)

from *Waterloo,* 54½ miles. Fares, 11/6a, 6/11c. R. T. for two months, 23/0a, 13/10c. Pop. 3,883.
Map Square 23.

W'loo	Petfld.	Petfld.	W'loo
AM 5.50	7.49	AM 7.24	9.12
6.50	8.56	7.57s	9.44
7.50	10. 3	8.32r	9.52
8.34r	10.17	9. 0	10.50
9.50	11.42	9.36	11.32
10.50	12.30	11.55r	1.52
11.50d	1.41	PM 1. 1	3. 6
PM12.20d	2. 1	2.18	4.16
12.50er	2.36	3.51	5.52
1.50e	3.46	5.27	7.46
2. 0d	3.55	6.57	9. 6
2.34	4.44	8.26	10.46
3.50d	5.41	9.49	12.16
4.15e	5.58	—	—
4.50	6.27	—	—
5.50	7.29	—	—
6.50er	8.40	—	—
6.50dr	8.50	—	—
9.50	11.48	—	—

Sunday Trains.

AM 8. 0	9.46	AM 8.18	10.16
8.20	10.36	PM 1.12	3.13
9.15r	10.57	4.51	6.17
PM 1.50	3.51	6.56	8.52
4.20	6.28	8. 9	10. 1
6.20	8.24	8.16	10.41
9.30	11.16	9.20	11.43
—	—	—	—
—	—	—	—
—	—	—	—
—	—	—	—

d Saturdays only.
e Saturdays excepted.
r Restaurant Car.
s Refreshments served.

Red Lion Hotel. First-class Family and Commercial. Billiards, Golf, Loose Boxes, Garage. Appointed Hotel to R.A.C., A.A., and M.U. Saddle Horses for Hire. Telephone and Telegrams, 25 Petersfield.
GERALD WOODS, Proprietor.

PETERSTON (Glamorgan)

from *Paddington*, 159½ miles. Fares, 33/2*a*, 19/11*c*. R. T. for two months, 66/4*a*. Departures *from* London as for St. Fagans. Departures *for* London about 7 times daily. Pop. 389.
Map Square 21.

PETWORTH (Sussex)

from *London Bridge*, *Victoria*, and *Clapham Junction*, 54¾ miles. Fares, 11/6*a*, 6/11*c*. R. T. for two months, 23/0*a*, 13/10*c*. Pop. 2,489.
Map Square 23.

	Leave		Arr. at
Vict.	Clap. J.	Lon. B.	Petwh.
AM 6.18	6.25	6.35	8.35
8.55	7.56	7.35	11. 2
10.15	10.22	10.30	12.33
11.55	—	11.50	2.11
PM 1.40	1.47*e*	1.50	4. 1
3.55	4. 2	4. 0	5.54
4.53	5. 0	5. 5	7.20
7.20	7.27	7.15	9.28
—	—	—	—

Sunday Trains.

AM 6.55	7. 2	7. 2	9.43
PM 7. 0	7. 7	6.38	9.22
—	—	—	—
—	—	—	—

Trains from Petworth.

Leave		Arr. at	
Petwth.	Lon. B.	Clap. J.	Vict.
AM 7.41	9.58	—	10.28
9.32	11.50	11.35	11.42
10.17	12. 8	12.33	12. 0
11.32	3.32	3.22	3.32
PM 1. 8	3.40	3.37	3.45
3. 2	5.54	5. 4	5.12
4.53	7.48	7.31	6.50
8. 8	10. 8	9.53	10. 1
—	—	—	—

Sunday Trains.

AM 7. 8	10.11	10. 6	10.13
PM 5.13	7.56	7.25	7.33
—	—	—	—
—	—	—	—

e Saturdays excepted.

Swan Hotel. Telephone 2. Excellent tourist centre for Sussex. Electric Light. Garage.
TRUST HOUSES, Ltd.

PEVENSEY (Sussex)

from *London Bridge*, *Victoria*, and *Clapham Junction*, 64¾ miles. Fares, 12/6*a*, 7/6*c*. R. T. for two months, 25/0*a*, 15/0*c*. Departures *from* London as for Polegate or Eastbourne. Departures *for* London about 10 times daily. Pop. 522.
Map Square 29.

PEWSEY (Wilts)

from *Paddington*, 75¼ miles. Fares, 15/8*a*, 9/5*c*. R. T. for two months, 31/4*a*. Pop. 1,731.
Map Square 22.

Pad.	Pewsey	Pewsey	Pad.
AM 7.30	9.40	AM 8. 1	10. 0
8.45*r*	11.22	10. 6	12.55
10.45	1. 1	PM 12.26	2.50
PM 12.30*r*	2.39	4.20	7.20
2.45	5.16	4.56	8.20
3.18	6.27	8.10	10.45
6.30	8.30	—	—
—	—	—	—
—	—	—	—
—	—	—	—
—	—	—	—

Sunday Trains.

AM 9.10	12. 3	AM 8. 0	10.50
PM 5.15	7.59	PM 6.43	9.15
—	—	—	—
—	—	—	—
—	—	—	—
—	—	—	—

r Restaurant Car.

PHILPSTOUN (Linlithgow)

406¾ miles. No through fares. Departures *from* London as for Edinburgh (Waverley). Departures *for* London about 4 times daily.
Map Square 41.

PICCADILLY CIRCUS

(Bakerloo and Hammersmith and Finsbury Park Tubes). *See* back of Map.

The Hôtel Washington, 6, Curzon Street, Mayfair.
See advt. under London Hotels.

PICKERING (Yorks)

220¼ miles. Fares, 45/10*a*, 27/6*c*. R. T. for two months, 91/8*a*, 55/0*c*. Departures *from* London as for Whitby. Departures *for* London about 6 times daily. Pop. 3,504.
Map Square 8.

PICKHILL Yorks)

217 miles. No through fares. Departures *from* London as for Ripon. Departures *for* London about twice daily. Pop. 588.
Map Square 7.

PICTON (Yorks)

227¾ miles. Fares, 47/4*a*, 28/5*c*. R. T., double fare. Departures *from* London as for Stockton-on-Tees. Departures *for* London about 4 times daily. Pop. 155.
Map Square 8.

PIDDINGTON (Northampton)

from *St. Pancras*, 65½ miles. Fares, 13/1*a*, 7/10*c*. R. T., double fare. Departures *from* London as for Olney. Departures *for* London about 5 times daily. Pop. 377.
Map Square 18.

PIEL (Lancs)

266¾ miles. No through fares. Departures *from* London as for Barrow-in-Furness. Departures *for* London about 5 times daily.
Map Square 6.

PIERCEBRIDGE (Durham)

238¼ miles. Fares, 49/9*a*, 29/10*c*. R. T., double fare. Departures *from* London as for Barnard Castle. Departures *for* London about 4 times daily. Pop. 209.
Map Square 7.

PILL (Somerset)

from *Paddington*, 125 miles. Fares, 26/1*a*, 15/8*c*. R. T. for two months, 52/2*a*. Departures *from* London as for Portishead. Departures *for* London about 6 times daily. Pop. 1,750.
Map Square 22.

PILLING (Lancs)

225¼ miles. Fares, 46/11*a*, 28/2*c*. R.T. for two months, 93/10*a*, 56/4*c*. Departures *from* London as for Preston. Departures *for* London about 3 times daily. Pop. 1,390.
Map Square 7.

PILMOOR (Yorks)

203¾ miles. No through fares. Departures *from* London as for York. Departures *for* London about 4 times daily.
Map Square 8.

PILNING (Glo'ster)

116¾ miles. Fares, 26/1*a*, 15/8*c*. R. T. for two months, 52/2*a*. Departures *from* London as for Bristol. Departures *for* London about 5 times daily. Pop. 929.
Map Square 22.

PILSLEY (Derby)

144½ miles. Fares, 18/2*a*, 16/11*c*. R. T., double fare. Departures *from* London as for Kirkby and Pinxton. Departures *for* London about 5 times daily. Pop. 2,746.

PINCHBECK (Lincoln)

95 miles. Fares, 19/9*a*, 11/10*c*. R. T., double fare. Departures *from* London as for Spalding Departures *for* London about 4 times daily. Pop. 2,836.
Map Square 18.

PINCHINGTHORPE

(Yorks), 246 miles. Fares, 51/5*a*, 30/10*c*. R. T. for two months, 102/10*a*, 61/8*c*. Departures *from* London as for Middlesbrough. Departures *for* London about 6 times daily. Pop. 65.
Map Square 8.

PINHOE (Devon)

169 miles. Fares, 35/3*a*, 21/2*c*. R. T. for two months, 70/6*a*, 42/4*c*. Departures *from* London as for Broad Clyst. Departures *for* London about 6 times daily. Pop. 1,009.
Map Square 26.

PINKHILL (Midlothian)

395½ miles. Fares, 81/8*a*, 49/0*c*, R.T. for two months, 163/4*a*, 98/0*c*. Departures *from* London as for Edinburgh (Waverley). Departures *for* London about 5 times daily.

PINMORE (Ayr), 415 miles. No through fares. Departures *from* London as for Girvan or Newton Stewart. Departures *for* London about 4 times daily.
Map Square 43.

PINNER (Middlesex) from *Marylebone* and *Baker Street*, 11¼ miles. Fares, 2/5*a*, 1/5½*c*. R. T. for two days, 4/8*a*, 2/7½*c*. Pop. 9,462. *See* pp. 494, 495.
Map Squares 23 *and* 48.

PINWHERRY (Ayr), 418¼ miles. No through fares. Departures *from* London as for Girvan or Newton Stewart. Departures *for* London about 3 times daily.
Map Square 43.

PINXTON (Derby) from *King's Cross*, 142½ miles. Fares, 27/8*a*, 16/5*c*. R. T., double fare. Departures *from* London as for Newthorpe. Departures *for* London about 9 times daily. Pop. 5,105.
Map Square 13.

PIPE GATE (Stafford), 157 miles. Fares, 32/9*a*, 19/8*c*. R. T. for two months, 65/6*a*. Departures *from* London as for Newcastle-under-Lyme. Departures *for* London about 4 times daily.
Map Square 12.

PITCAPLE (Aberdeen), 544¼ miles. No through fares. Departures *from* London as for Inverurie. Departures *for* London about 3 times daily.
Map Square 35.

PITFODELS (Aberdeen), 524¾ miles. No through fares. Departures *from* London as for Aberdeen. Departures *for* London about 4 times daily.
Map Square 38.

PITLOCHRY (Perth) from *Euston*, 478¼ miles. Fares, 96/11*a*, 58/2*c*. R. T. for two months, 193/10*a*, 116/4*c*. Pop. 2,241.
Map Square 37.

Euston	P'lchry	P'lchry	Euston
AM 10. 0*r*	9.15	AM 7.22*r*	7.30
PM 1.30*er*	2.33	9.31*r*	10.45
7.40*er*	6.45	PM 12.37*r*	5. 0*h*
11.35*e*	10.34	7.38	7.40
—	—	—	—
—	—	—	—
—	—	—	—
—	—	—	—
—	—	—	—
—	—	—	—

Sunday Trains.

PM 7.50*r*	6.48	—	—
11.35	10.34	—	—
—	—	—	—
—	—	—	—

e Saturdays excepted
h A.M.
r Restaurant Car.

ANOTHER ROUTE from *King's Cross*, 468½ miles. Fares as above.

King's+	P'lchry	P'lchry	King's+
AM 4.45	4.40*h*	AM 7.22*r*	6.30*h*
11.50*er*	2.33*k*	9.31*r*	10. 0*h*
PM 7.45*er*	6.45*k*	PM 12.37	3.25*k*
11.25*e*	10.34*k*	7.38	7. 5*k*
—	—	—	—

PITLOCHRY—*continued.*

Sunday Trains.

King's+	P'lchry	P'lchry	King's+
PM 7.45	6.48	—	—
11.25	10.34	—	—

e Saturdays excepted.
h P.M. *k* A.M.
r Restaurant Car.

The Pitlochry Hydro-Hotel. "The Switzerland of Scotland." See advt. p **279**.

Fisher's Hotel. Standing in its own beautiful garden. Motor Garage. See advt. p. **280**.

Atholl Palace Hotel. Finest Hotel in Scotland. Garage for forty Cars. Forty-six acres of grounds. See advt. p. **280**.

PITLURG (Aberdeen), 547¾ miles. No through fares. Departures *from* London as for Cruden Bay. Departures *for* London about 3 times daily.
Map Square 35.

PITMEDDEN (Aberdeen), 531 miles. No through fares. Departures *from* London as for Aberdeen. Departures *for* London about 3 times daily.
Map Square 35.

PITSEA (Essex) from *Fenchurch Street*, 26½ miles. Fares, 4/5*a*, 2/8*c*. R. T. for two months, 8/10*a*, 5/4*c*. Pop. 1,129.
Map Square 24.

Fen. St	Pitsea	Pitsea	Fen. St.
AM 5. 5	6.12	AM 5.48	6.43
6.15	7.25	5.52	7.22
6.52	8.29	6.21	7.34
7.53	9. 5	6.45	7.58
9.18	10.36	6.56	8.24
10.17	11.33	7.20	8.49
11.13*d*	12.48	7.56	8.53
11.35	1.10	8.10	9.34
11.42*e*	1.10	9.59	11.20
PM 12. 9	1.16	10.23	11.40
1.25*d*	2.24	10.39	12.16
1.48*e*	3.23	11.54*e*	1.22
2.15*d*	3.34	11.54*d*	1.27
2.26*d*	3.28	PM 12.53	1.56
2.30	3.42	1. 2*d*	2.34
3.25	4.56	2.16	3.28
4.27	5.27	2.37	4.10
5. 2*eh*	6. 7	3.59	5.18
5.32	6.53	4.58	6.33
5.55*e*	7.21	5.29	6.45
6.26	7.30	5.45	7.24
6.38	8.12	6.46	7.51
7.20	8.29	7.40	9.15
7.41*e*	9. 5	8.59	10. 8
8. 0*e*	9.10	9.55	11.23*h*
8.13	9.51	9.55	11.40
9.19*eh*	10.20	—	—
9.20*d*	10.20	—	—
9.25	11. 6	—	—
10.15	11.17	—	—
11.27*dh*	12.29	—	—

Sunday Trains.

AM 8.40	10.28	AM 8.38	10.18
9.45	11. 6	8.56	11.35
11.10	12.46	11.25	1. 1
PM 2. 7	3.38	PM 2.41	3.47
2.45	4. 4	4.43	6. 0
4.30	6. 0	5.51	7.16
6.10	7.19	6. 8	7.45
7.22	9.33	7.35	9.11*h*
8.45	10.20	7.49	9.30
9.45	10.56	9.12	10.23
—	—	9.27	11. 0

d Saturdays only.
e Saturdays excepted.
h Departs from or arrives at Mark Lane Station.

PITSFORD (Northampton) from *Euston* 69¾ miles. Fares, 14/0*a*, 8/5*c*, R. T., double fare. Departures *from* London as for Brixworth. Departures *for* London about 5 times daily. Pop. 464.
Map Square 18.

PITTENWEEM (Fife), 440 miles. Fares, 89/2*a*, 53/6*c*. R.T. for two months, 178/4*a*, 107/0*c*. Departures *from* London as for St. Andrews. Departures *for* London about 3 times daily. Pop. 1,774.
Map Square 41.

PITTINGTON (Durham), 253¼ miles. No through fares. Departures *from* London as for Durham or West Hartlepool. Departures *for* London about 6 times daily. Pop. 2,130.
Map Square 7.

PITTS HILL (Stafford), 151 miles. Fares, 31/6*a*, 18/11*c*. R. T. for two months, 63/0*a*, 37/10*c*. Departures *from* London as for Burslem. Departures *for* London about 6 times daily.
Map Square 12.

PLAIDY (Aberdeen), 565¾ miles. No through fares. Departures *from* London as for Inverurie. Departures *for* London about 3 times daily.
Map Square 35.

PLAISTOW (Essex) from *Fenchurch Street*, 4½ miles. Fares, 0/10*a*, 0/6*c*. R. T. for two days, 1/7½*a*, 0/10½*c*. Pop. 35,913. *See* p. 510.
Map Square 62.

ANOTHER ROUTE from *Ealing, Hounslow, Richmond*, and *Wimbledon, via* District Railway. *See* p. 489.

PLASHETTS (Northumberland), 317½ miles. Fares, 67/4*a*, 40/5*c*, R. T. for two months, 134/8*a*, 80/10*c*. Departures *from* London as for Carlisle or Hexham. Departures *for* London about 3 times daily. Pop. 597.
Map Square 3.

PLAS MARL (Glamorgan), 198½ miles. No through fares. Departures *from* London as for Swansea. Departures *for* London about 3 times daily.

PLAS POWER (Denbigh), 184½ miles. Fares, 37/7*a*, 22/8*c*. R. T. for two months, 75/2*a*, 45/4*c*. Departures *from* London as for Wrexham. Departures *for* London about 6 times daily.
Map Square 12.

PLATT BRIDGE (Lancs), 197 miles. Fares, 40/10*a*, 24/6*c*. R. T. for two months, 81/8*a*, 49/0*c*. Departures *from* London as for Wigan. Departures *for* London about 3 times daily.

PLAWSWORTH (Durham), 257¾ miles. No through fares. Departures *from* London as for Durham. Departures *for* London about 4 times daily. Pop. 1,333.
Map Square 7.

PLEALEY ROAD (Salop), 159¾ miles. Fares, 33/4*a*, 20/0*c*. R. T. for two months, 66/8*a*. Departures *from* London as for Shrewsbury. Departures *for* London about 4 times daily.

Map Square 17.

PLEAN (Stirling), 412¾ miles. Fares, 84/0*a*, 50/5*c*. R.T. for two days, 168/0*a*, 100/10*c*. Departures *from* London as for Larbert. Departures *for* London about 4 times daily. Pop. 4,963.

Map Square 40.

PLEASINGTON (Lancs), 211 miles. Fares, 43/9*a*, 26/3*c*. R. T. for two months, 87/6*a*, 52/6*c*. Departures *from* London as for Preston. Departures *for* London about 5 times daily. Pop. 475.

Map Square 12.

PLEASLEY (Derby), from *St. Pancras*, 145½ miles. Fares, 28/2*a*, 16/11*c*. R. T., double fare. Departures *from* London as for Mansfield. Departures *for* London about 4 times daily. Pop. 2,416.

Map Square 13.

PLESSEY (Northumberland), 279½ miles. Fares, 59/0*a*, 35/5*c*. R. T., double fare. Departures *from* London as for Newcastle-on-Tyne. Departures *for* London about 6 times daily.

Map Square 3.

PLOCKTON (Ross), 644½ miles. Fares, 118/4*a*, 71/0*c*. R. T. for two months, 236/8*a*, 142/0*c*. Departures *from* London as for Kyle of Lochalsh. Departures *for* London about 3 times daily.

Map Square 34.

PLODDER LANE (Lancs), 194 miles. Fares, 40/5*a*, 24/3*c*. R.T. for two months, 80/10*a*, 48/6*c*. Departures *from* London as for Manchester (London Road). Departures *for* London about 8 times daily.

PLOWDEN (Salop), 171 miles. No through fares. Departures *from* London as from Craven Arms. Departures *for* London about 3 times daily.

Map Square 17.

PLUCKLEY (Kent) from *Charing Cross*, *Cannon Street*, and *London Bridge*, 51½ miles. Fares, 10/8*a*, 8/7*b*, 6/5*c*. R. T. for two months, 21/4*a*, 17/2*b*. Pop. 900.

Map Square 24.

Char. +	Leave Can. St.	Lon. B.	Arr. at Pluck'y
AM —	5.20	5.25	7.52
—	6.45	6.50	8.57
9.25	—	9.33	11. 7
—	11.56	12. 0	1.37
PM12.40*d*	—	12.47*d*	2.21
3. 0	—	3. 8	4.43
4.30*d*	—	4.37*d*	6. 9
—	4.36*e*	4.39*e*	6. 9
5.24*d*	—	5.34*d*	7.11
6. 0*e*	—	6. 5*e*	7.33
7.30	—	7.26	9.39
9.30	—	9.36	11. 91

Sunday Trains.

AM 7.45	—	7.52	9.28
PM 6.35	—	6.43	8.38
—	—	—	—

PLUCKLEY—*continued.*

Trains from Pluckley.

Leave Pluck'y.	Lon. B.	Arrive at Can. St.	Char. +
AM 6.49	8.40	8.44	—
7.53	9.32	9.36	—
8.52	10.28	10.32	—
9.44	11.33	—	11.45
11.33	1.36	—	1.50
PM 1.44	3.26	—	3.40
4.49	7.25	7.30	—
6.41	8.54	9. 1	—
9. 9	11.34	—	11.43
—	—	—	—
—	—	—	—
—	—	—	—
—	—	—	—
—	—	—	—

Sunday Trains.

AM 7.57	10. 5	—	10.15
PM 6.34	8.20	—	8.28
—	—	—	—
—	—	—	—

d Saturdays only.
e Saturdays excepted.

PLUMBLEY (Lancs), 175 miles. Fares, 35/8*a*, 21/5*c*. R.T. for two months, 71/4*a*, 42/10*c*. Departures *from* London as for Northwich. Departures *for* London about 4 times daily. Pop. 359.

Map Square 12.

PLUMPTON (Cumberland), 286 miles. Fares, 57/9*a*, 34/8*c*. R.T. for two months, 115/6*a*, 69/4*c*. Departures *from* London as for Penrith. Departures *for* London about 4 times daily. Pop. (Plumpton Wall) 301.

Map Square 7.

PLUMPTON (Sussex) from *Victoria*, *Clapham Junction*, and *London Bridge*, 44½ miles. Fares, 9/4*a*, 5/7*c*. R. T. for two months, 18/8*a*, 11/2*c*. Pop. 709.

Map Square 23.

Vict.	Leave Clap. J.	Lon. B.	Arr. at Plump'n
AM —	—	6.15	7.33
7.23	7.29	7.25	9.34
9. 0	9. 8	—	10.30
10. 5	10.11	9.50	11.31
12. 0	12. 7	12.10	1.54
PM —	—	12.50*d*	1.54
2. 0	2. 7	2. 5	3.58
3.40	—	4. 5	5.26
5.45	—	5.55*e*	7.22
—	—	6. 0*d*	7.22
6.50	6.57	7. 0	8.24
—	—	—	—
—	—	—	—
—	—	—	—
—	—	—	—
—	—	—	—

Sunday Trains.

AM 6.55	7. 2	7.22	9. 8
PM 6.33	6.40	6.33	8.12
—	—	—	—
—	—	—	—
—	—	—	—
—	—	—	—

PLUMPTON—*continued.*

Trains from Plumpton.

Leave Plump'n.	Lon. B.	Arrive at Clap. J.	Vict.
AM 7.17	8.46	9. 0	9. 8
9.22	10.33	—	—
11.12	12.44	12.36	12.45
PM12.35	2.22	2.13	2.22
2. 4	4.32	4. 9	4.17
4. 4	6.36	6.26	6.34
5.13	7.42	7.21	7.30
6.31	8.46	8.39	8.48
8.42	10. 0	10. 2	10.10
10.15	12.59	12.50	1. 0
—	—	—	—
—	—	—	—
—	—	—	—

Sunday Trains.

AM 8.40	10.18	10.23	10.32
PM 6.50	8.34	8.31	8.41
—	—	—	—
—	—	—	—
—	—	—	—

d Saturdays only.
e Saturdays excepted.

PLUMSTEAD (London) from *Charing Cross*, 10¾ miles. Fares, 2/1*a*, 1/8*b*, 1/3*c*. R. T. for two days, 4/2*a*, 3/4*b*, 2/4*c*. From *Cannon Street*. Fares, 1/11*a*, 1/7*b*, 1/2*c*. R. T. for two days, 3/10*a*, 3/2*b*, 2/4*c*. Pop. 75,902. See pp. 547-551.

Map Square 24.

PLUMTREE (Notts) from *St. Pancras*, 118½ miles. Fares, 24/4*a*, 14/7*c*. R. T., double fare. Departures *from* London as for Melton Mowbray. Departures *for* London about 4 times daily. Pop. 244.

Map Square 13.

PLYMOUTH (Devon), from *Paddington*, 226½ miles. Fares, North Road or Millbay, 46/8*a*, 28/0*c*. R. T. for two months, 93/4*a*, 56/0*c*. Mutley, 46/6*a*, 27/11*c*. R. T. for two months, 93/0*a*, 55/10*c*. Pop. 209,857.

Map Square 26.

Leave Pad.	Mutl'y.	Arrive at N. Rd.	Millb'y.
AM 5.30	—	12.16	—
7.30	—	2.15	2.32
10.30*r*	—	2.37	—
*d*11. 0*r*	—	3.22	—
11.10*r*	—	3.33	—
12. 0*r*	—	4.48	—
PM 2. 0*r*	—	7. 6	7.38
3.30*r*	—	8. 7	8.15
4.15*r*	—	10. 0	10. 8
6.30*r*	—	12.18	12.28
10. 0	—	4.25	4.55
12. 0*h*	—	7.11	7.20
12.30*k*	7.40	7.43	7.53
—	—	—	—
—	—	—	—
—	—	—	—
—	—	—	—

Sunday Trains.

AM10.30*r*	—	3.15	—
PM 2.40*r*	—	7.50	7.58
4.30*r*	—	10. 5	10.13
10. 0	—	4.25	4.55
—	—	—	—
—	—	—	—

ROYAL HOTEL, PLYMOUTH. Most Central Position.

PLYMOUTH—*continued.*

Trains from Plymouth.

	Leave		Arr. at
Millb'y.	N. Rd.	Mutl'y.	Pad.
AM12.15	—	—	7.10
8.30r	—	8.36r	1.30
11.16r	11.50r	—	4.35
PM12.10r	12.30r	—	4.45
—	2. 0r	—	6.50
d2.15r	d2.30r	—	7. 5
—	4.10r	—	9. 0
4.20	4.26	4.29	2.45
—	—	—	—
—	—	—	—

Sunday Trains.

AM12.15	—	—	7. 5
7. 0r	—	7. 5r	3.35
10.10r	—	10.16r	4. 5
PM —	2. 0	—	7. 5
—	3.10r	—	7.55
7.50	8.15	—	3.15

d Saturdays only.
h Saturdays midnight excepted.
k Saturdays midnight only.
r Restaurant Car.

ANOTHER ROUTE from *Waterloo.* 231 miles. Fares, 46/8*a*, 28/0*c.* R. T. for two months, 93/4*a*, 56/0*c.*

Leave	Arrive at		Pl'm'th
W'loo.	N. Rd.	Mutl'y.	Friary.
AM 9. 0r	2.46	2.51	2.59
10. 0r	3.36	3.40	3.48
11. 0r	4.34	4.38	4.46
PM 1. 0r	7.12	7.16	7.24
3. 0r	8.15	8.19	8.27
6. 0r	11.47	11.50	11.58
—	—	—	—

Sunday Trains.

n12. 0r	6.23	6.27	6.35
—	—	—	—

Trains from Plymouth.

Pl'm'th	Leave		Arr. at
Friary.	Mutl'y.	N. Rd.	W'loo.
AM 8.30r	8.38r	8.40r	1.56
10. 0r	10. 9r	10.14r	3.50
n12. 0r	12. 9r	12 13r	6. 0
PM 2.12r	2.21r	2.25r	8.30
4. 0	4. 8	4.11	10.50
4.12h	4.20h	4.24h	3.58
—	—	—	—
—	—	—	—
—	—	—	—

Sunday Trains.

AM 3. 0r	3. 8r	3.12r	8.57

h Via Eastleigh.
n Noon.
r Restaurant Car.

Albion and Continental
Hotel (Trust Houses, Ltd.).
Adjoining Millbay Station. Near town and docks. Telephone 1423.
See advt. p. **280.**

PLYMOUTH—*continued.*

Grand Hotel. First-class Family Hotel. Due South. Facing Sea. On the glorious Hoe. Private Suites. Passenger Lift. Moderate charges. Motor Garage. Telegrams —"Grand, Plymouth." Telephone 1430.

Royal Hotel. Most central. Three minutes from Hoe. Lift. Grill Room Orchestra. Garage. Palm Court. Telephone 722.

Duke of Cornwall Hotel. Leading and largest hotel, centrally situated, opposite Millbay Station, near Sea front. Recognised hotel for Ocean passengers. Garage. Electric Light, Lift. Hotel Omnibus meets all trains "R. A. C." "A. A." Telegrams— "Dukotel," Plymouth.

The Hoe.—Roslyn Pension. 11, Leigham Terrace. Central position. Two minutes station. Redecorated. Separate Tables. Moderate Terms. Special Winter Terms. 'Phone 819.

Central Hotel. First Class Family and Commercial. The most central position. Close to Hoe. Theatre and Guildhall. Fully licensed. Excellent cuisine. Officially appointed by R.A.C. and A.A. Moderate tariff. Telephone 636.

Farley Hotel. Family and Commercial, Central Position, opposite G. W. R. Station. Moderate Tariff. 'Phone 1283.
Manageress, C. PROCTOR.

Hoe Mansions Hotel. First Class Residential. Sea View. Private Suites. Central Heating. Moderate Tariff. Telephone 533. Telegrams—"Hoe Mansion," Plymouth.

PLYMPTON (Devon).

221½ miles. Fares, 45/8*a*, 27/5*c.* R. T. for two months, 91/4*c.* Departures *from* London as for Ivybridge. Departures *for* London about 8 times daily. Pop. 3,940.
Map Square 26.

PLYMSTOCK (Devon),

225½ miles. Fares, 46/11*a*, 28/2*c.* R. T. for two months, 93/10*a.* Departures *from* London as for Plymouth. Departures *for* London about 8 times daily. Pop. 3,857.
Map Square 26.

POCKLINGTON (Yorks),

198 miles. Fares, 42/4*a*, 25/5*c.* R. T., double fare. Departures *from* London as for York. Departures *for* London about 6 times daily. Pop. 2,642.
Map Square 8.

POKESDOWN (Hants),

from *Waterloo,* 105½ miles. Fares, *via* Sway, 22/1*a*, 13/3*c.* R. T. for two months, 44/2*a*, 26/6*c.* Pop. 14,024.
Map Square 27.

W'loo.	Pokesdn.	Pokesdn.	W'loo.
AM 5.40	9. 2	AM 7. 7r	10. 6
5.50	10.27	7.53s	11. 0
8.30s	12. 1	9.18s	12.22
9.30h	1. 7	10.58r	2.20
10.30	1.35	11.38	2.50
PM12.30r	3.20	PM12.59	4.20
2.30s	5.37	2. 0	4.50
3.30s	7.16	2.48s	6.26
4.30r	7.37	3.48	6.58
6.30r	9.28	4.47r	8.20
—	—	6.52	10.50
—	—	8. 5	11.28
—	—	9.22	3.58
—	—	—	—
—	—	—	—

Sunday Trains.

AM11. 0r	2.34	AM 8.38	12.11
PM 2. 0r	5.31	PM 4.24	8. 3
7. 0r	10.36	6.19r	9.31
—	—	7.55	3.58
—	—	—	—

h Via Ringwood.
r Restaurant Car.
s Refreshments served.

POLEGATE (Sussex) from

London Bridge and *Victoria,* 61½ miles. Fares, 11/8*a*, 7/0*c.* R. T. for two months, 23/4*a*, 14/0*c.*
Map Square 29.

	Leave		Arr. at
AM	Vict.	Lon. B.	Polegate.
	—	6.15	7.55
	6.37h	6.40h	9.55
	9. 0	—	10.43
	10. 5	9.50	12. 7
	11.55	—	1.28
	12. 0	12.10	2.12
PM	—	12.50d	2.43
	1.20c	—	3. 8
	1.25d	1.10d	3. 8
	—	2. 0	3.38
	3.20	—	4.46
	3.40	4. 5	5.49
	5.20	5. 5	6.46
	5.45e	5.55e	7.29
	6.50	7. 0	8.59
	8.35	—	10. 5
	10.30	10.35	12.52
	—	—	—
	—	—	—
	—	—	—
	—	—	—

Sunday Trains.

AM 6.55	7.22	9.44
9.30	9.30	11.21
PM12.15h	—	2.45
6.33	6.33	8.53
8.20	8. 0	10.32
9.25h	—	11.46
—	—	—
—	—	—

POLEGATE—*continued.*

Trains from Polegate.

Leave POLEGATE.	Arrive at LON. B.	VICT.
AM 6.24	8.46	—
7.15	8.53	9. 8
7.56	9.50	10.24
9. 2	10.55	10.56
10.55	12.44	12.45
11. 0*h*	—	1.20
PM 12.22	2.22	2.22
2.48	4.32	4.35
3.51*h*	6.36	6.34
4.45*h*	—	7.30
5.50	7.42	7.45
6.37*h*	—	8.48
8. 7	10. 0	10.10
8.59	—	11.17
10. 7*h*	12.59	1. 0
—	—	—
—	—	—
—	—	—
—	—	—

Sunday Trains.

AM 7.40	10.18	10.32
10.16*h*	—	1. 0
11.14*h*	—	1.35
PM 5.47	7.56	7.37
6.30	8.34	8.41
8.16	10.50	10.19
9.50*h*	12.27	—

d Saturdays only.
e Saturdays excepted.
h Via Brighton.
l Stops to set down 1st class passengers only on notice being given to the Guard.

POLESWORTH (Warwick) from *Euston,* 106 miles. Fares, 22/1*a*, 13/3*c*. R. T. for two months, 44/2*a*. Pop. 5,619.

Map Square 17.

EUSTON	POLES'TH	POLES'TH	EUSTON
AM 5. 0	8.25	AM 6.38*r*	10. 0
8.45*r*	11.14	8.33	11. 0
10.40*r*	1.42	11.26*r*	2.20
12. 0*n*r	3.16	PM 3.23*t*	6.15
PM 2.50*t*	5.49	5.38*r*	8.10
5.20*r*	8.43	7.38*r*	10.45
—	—	9.59	5. 0

No Sunday Trains.
n Noon.
r Restaurant Car.
t Tea Car.

POLMONT (Stirling), 414¾ miles. Fares, 82/6*a*, 49/6*c*. R. T. for two months, 165/0*a*, 99/0*c*. Departures *from* London as for Edinburgh (Waverley). Departures *for* London about 4 times daily. Pop. 1,088.

POLSHAM (Somerset), 136¾ miles. Fares, 25/2*a*, 15/1*c*. R. T. for two months, 50/4*a*. Departures *from* London as for Glastonbury. Departures *for* London about 5 times daily.

Map Square 22.

POLTON (Midlothian), 391¾ miles. No through fares. Departures *from* London as for Edinburgh (Waverley). Departures *for* London about 6 times daily.

Map Square 41.

POMATHORN (Midlothian), 394¾ miles. No through fares. Departures *from* London as for Edinburgh (Waverley) or Peebles. Departures *for* London about 4 times daily.

PONDER'S END (Middlesex) from *Liverpool Street,* 10 miles. Fares, 1/7*a*, 1/3*b*, 0/11½*c*. R. T. for two days, 3/2*a*, 2/6*b*, 1/9*c*. Pop. 12,756. *See* pp. 526-527.

Map Square 23.

PONFEIGH (Lanark), 381¾ miles. No through fares. Departures *from* London as for Carstairs. Departures *for* London about 4 times daily.

Map Square 40.

PONTARDAWE (Glamorgan), 215 miles. Fares, 41/5*a*, 24/10*c*. R.T. for two months, 82/10*a*, 49/8*c*. Departures *from* London as for Brecon (*via* Hereford). Departures *for* London about 3 times daily. Pop. 31,498.

Map Square 21.

PONTARDULAIS (Glamorgan), 204 miles. Fares, 43/2*a*, 25/11*c*. R.T.for two months, 86/4*a*, 51/10*c*. Departures *from* London as for Llanelly. Departures *for* London about 4 times daily.

Map Square 21.

PONTDOLGOCH (Montgomery), 193¾ miles. Fares, 40/3*a*, 24/2*c*. R.T. for two months, 80/6*a*. Departures *from* London as for Newtown. Departures *for* London about 5 times daily.

Map Square 16.

PONTEFRACT (MONK-HILL) (Yorks) from *King's Cross,* 172¾ miles. Fares 35/8*a*, 21/5*c*. R. T., double fare. Pop. 16,763.

KING'S+	PONT'F'T	PONT'F'T	KING'S+
AM 4.45	9.40	AM 8.48	1. 5
7.15*r*	11.43	9.22*r*	1.55
10.10*r*	2.25	11.20*r*	3.50
PM 1.50*r*	6.43	PM 2. 6*r*	6.15
4. 0*r*	9.10	4.32	9.25
10.46*c*	7.58	6. 2	10. 0
—	—	8.32*c*	3.25
—	—	9.24*d*	3.25

Sunday Trains.

12. 0*m*r	4.58	AM 11.35	5.15
PM 10.45	7.58	—	—

d Saturdays only.
e Saturdays excepted.
n Noon.
r Restaurant Car.

ANOTHER ROUTE (BAG-HILL) from *St. Pancras,* 181½ miles.

St. Pan. as above.

ST. PAN.	PONT'F'T	PONT'F'T	ST. PAN.
AM 2.25*g*	8.18	AM 8.11*r*	1.30
4.25	10.33	10.46*r*	4.10
9. 0*r*	2.10	11.30*r*	5.30
9.50*r*	2.39	PM 1.46*r*	7.15
10.25*r*	3.20	3. 9*r*	7.55
PM 12.25*r*	5.38	4. 0*dr*	9. 5
1.50*r*	6.35	10. 5	4.20
5. 0*r*	10. 1	—	—

Sunday Trains.

—	—	PM 10. 5	4.55

d Saturdays only.
e Saturdays excepted.
g Mondays excepted.
r Restaurant Car.

PONTELAND (Northumberland), 277¾ miles. No through fares. Departures *from* London as for Newcastle-on-Tyne. Departures *for* London about 5 times daily. Pop. 1,029.

Map Square 3.

PONTESBURY (Salop), 161 miles. Fares, 33/7*a*, 20/2*c*. R. T. for two months, 67/2*a*. Departures *from* London as for Shrewsbury. Departures *for* London about 4 times daily. Pop. 2,690.

Map Square 17.

PONTHENRY (Carmarthen), 220 miles. Fares, 46/0*a*, 27/7*c*. R. T. for two months, 92/0*a*, 55/2*c*. Departures *from* London as for Pembrey. Departures *for* London about 4 times daily.

Map Square 21.

PONTHIR (Monmouth), 144¾ miles. Fares, 30/3*a*, 18/2*c*. R. T. for two months, 60/6*a*. Departures *from* London as for Newport (Mon.). Departures *for* London about 8 times daily.

Map Square 22.

PONT LAWRENCE (Monmouth), 150½ miles. Fares, 31/5*a*, 18/10*c*. R. T. for two months, 62/10*a*, 37/8*c*. Departures *from* London as for Tredegar. Departures *for* London about 4 times daily.

PONTLLANFRAITH (Monmouth) from *Paddington,* 158½ miles. Fares, *via* Pontypool Road, 32/9*a*, 19/8*c*. R. T. for two months, 65/6*a*. Pop. 2,318.

Map Square 22.

PAD.	PONTL'N'TH	PONTL'N'TH	PAD.
AM 1. 0*g*	8.14	AM 8.51*r*	1. 0
5.30	11.24	9.29*r*	2.30
8.45*r*	1.54	11.15*r*	4.20
9. 0	2.47	PM 1.36*r*	6.15
11.50*h*r	4.12	3. 9*r*	8.35
11.50*r*	5.22	5.26*r*	9.25
PM 1.10*r*	6.48	7.41	3.50
3.35*r*	8. 6	10.54*k*	7.10
6. 0*h*r	10. 9	—	—
8. 0*dr*	8.45	—	—

Sunday Trains.

PM 12.30*r*	7.20	AM 10.42	8.10
9.15	8.14	PM 9. 1	3.30

d Saturdays only
g Mondays excepted.
h Fridays only.
k Thursdays and Saturdays only.
r Restaurant Car.

PONT-LLANIO (Cardigan) from *Paddington,* 262¾ miles. Fares, 48/9*a*, 29/3*c*. R.T. for two months, 97/6*a*. Departures *from* London as for Lampeter. Departures *for* London about 4 times daily.

Map Square 16.

PONT-LLIW (Glamorgan), 201 miles. No through fares. Departures *from* London as for Swansea. Departures *for* London about 4 times daily.

PONTLOTTYN (Glamorgan), 167½ miles. Fares (*via* Bassaleg), 34/0*a*, 20/5*c*. R. T. for two months, 68/0*a*, 40/10*c*. *Via* Cardiff, 36/5*a*, 21/10*c*. R.T. for two months, 72/10*a*, 43/8*c*. Departures *from* London as for Bargoed or Cardiff. Departures *for* London about 4 times daily. Pop. 4,891.

PONTNEWYDD (Monmouth), 147½ miles. Fares 30/5*a*, 18/3*c*. R.T. for two months 60/10*a*, 36/6*c*. Departures *from* London as for Newport (Mon.). Departures *for* London about 6 times daily.

Map Square 22.

PONTNEWYNYDD (Monmouth), 151½ miles. Fares, 31/3*a*, 18/9*c*. R. T. for two months, 62/6*a*, 37/6*c*. Departures *from* London as for Abersychan. Departures *for* London about 7 times daily.

PONTRHYDYFEN (Glamorgan), 189 miles. No through fares. Departures *from* London as for Treherbert. Departures *for* London about 5 times daily.

PONTRHYTHALLT (Carnarvon), 253¼ miles. Fares, 52/8*d*, 31/8*c*. R. T. for two months, 105/6*a*, 63/4*c*. Departures *from* London as for Carnarvon. Departures *for* London about 4 times daily. *Map Square* 11.

PONTRILAS (Hereford), 154¼ miles. Fares, 32/4*a*, 19/5*c*. R.T. for two months, 64/8*a*. Departures *from* London as for Hereford. Departures *for* London about 5 times daily. *Map Square* 17.

PONT RUG (Carnarvon), 250½ miles. Fares, 52/3*a*, 31/4*c*. R. T. for two months, 104/6*a*, 62/8*c*. Departures *from* London as for Carnarvon. Departures *for* London about 4 times daily. *Map Square* 11.

PONTSARN (Glamorgan), 176½ miles. Fares, 35/2*a*, 21/1*c*. R.T. for two months, 70/4*a*, 42/2*c*. Departures *from* London as for Merthyr (*via* Newport). Departures *for* London about 4 times daily. *Map Square* 21.

PONTSTICILL (Glamorgan), 174¼ miles. Fares, 35/2*a*, 21/1*c*. R. T. for two months, 70/4*a*, 42/2*c*. Departures *from* London as for Bargoed. Departures *for* London about 4 times daily. *Map Square* 21.

PONTYATES (Carmarthen), 219 miles. Fares, 45/8*a*, 27/5*c*. R. T. for two months, 91/4*a*, 54/10*c*. Departures *from* London as for Pembrey. Departures *for* London about 3 times daily. *Map Square* 21.

PONTYBEREM (Carmarthen), 222½ miles. Fares, 46/5*a*, 27/10*c*. R. T. for two months, 92/10*a*, 55/8*c*. Departures *from* London as for Pembrey. Departures *for* London about 3 times daily. *Map Square* 21.

PONTYCYMMER (Glamorgan), 181½ miles. Fares, 37/9*a*, 22/8*c*. R.T. for two months, 75/6*a*, 45/4*c*. Departures *from* London as for Tondu. Departures *for* London about 4 times daily. Pop. 5,870.

PONTYPANT (Carnarvon), 242½ miles. Fares, 47/11*a*, 28/9*c*. R. T. for two months, 95/10*a*, 57/6*c*. Departures *for* London as for Bettws-y-Coed. Departures *for* London about 4 times daily. *Map Square* 11.

PONTYPOOL (CRANE STREET) (Monmouth), from *Paddington*, 150½ miles. Fares, 31/3*a*, 18/9*c*. R.T. for two months, 62/6*a*. Pop. 6,883. *Map Square* 22.

PAD.	P'POOL.	P'POOL.	PAD.
AM 1. 0*g*	7.36	AM 7. 0*r*	10.57
5.30	11.14	9.24*r*	1. 0
8.45*r*	12.55	PM12.14*r*	4.20
11.50*r*	3.28	2.15*r*	6.15
PM 1.10*r*	5.44	3.45*r*	8.35
3.35*r*	7. 2	5. 3*r*	9.25
6. 0*r*	9.33	10. 8	3.30
8. 0*kr*11.31	—	—
9.15*e*	5.20	—	—

Sunday Trains.

AM 1. 0	9.58	AM 8.11	3.35
9.10	2.32	PM 4. 6*r*	8.25
PM12.30*r*	6.15	7.20	3.30
4.30	9.52	—	—
9.15	5.20	—	—

e Saturdays excepted.
g Mondays excepted.
k Thursdays and Saturdays only.
r Restaurant Car.

PONTYPOOL ROAD (Monmouth) from *Paddington*, 150 miles. Fares, 31/3*a*, 18/9*c*. R. T. for two months, 62/6*a*. *Map Square* 22.

PAD.	P'POOL RD.	P'POOL RD.	PAD
AM 1. 0*g*	7.32	AM 4.24*gr*10.15
5.30	10.36	4.42*fr*10.15
8.45*r*	11.50	9.40*r*	1. 0
9. 0	1.25	10.43*r*	2.30
11.50*dr*	2.45	PM 1.18*r*	4.20
11.50*er*	2.57	2.50*r*	6.15
PM 1.10*r*	4.56	4.40*r*	8.35
3.35*r*	6.54	6. 5*r*	9.25
4.15*r*	8.11	7. 6	2.45
6. 0*r*	9.29	9.28	3.30
8. 0*r*	11.15	11.30	7.10
—	—	—	—

Sunday Trains.

AM 1. 0	8.32	PM 3. 8*r*	8.25
9.10	1.33	9.35	3.30
PM12.30*r*	6.25	—	—
4.30	1. 0	—	—
9.15	7.32	—	—

d Saturdays only.
e Saturdays excepted.
f Mondays only.
g Mondays excepted.
r Restaurant Car.

PONTYPRIDD (Glamorgan), from *Paddington*, *via* Cardiff, 165¾ miles. Fares, 33/2*a*, 19/11*c*. R. T. for two months, 66/4*a*, 39/10*c*. Pop. 47,171. *Map Square* 21.

PAD.	P'PRIDD	P'PRIDD	PAD.
AM 1. 0*gh* 6.59	AM 6.59*hr*10.57
5.30	11.10	9. 4*r*	1. 0
8.45*r*	12.31	9.54*r*	2.30
11.50*r*	3.34	PM12.30*r*	4.20
PM 1.10*r*	6.12	2. 5*hr*	6.15
3.35*r*	7.59	4.29*r*	8.35
6. 0*r*	9.50	5.27*hr*	9.25
6.30*r*	11.19	9.43	3.30
9.15*eh* 5.31	—	—

Sunday Trains.

AM 1. 0	8.45	AM 8.55	3.35
PM12.30*r*	5. 4	PM12.11*r*	8.25
4.30	9.25	9. 0	3.30
9.15*h*	5.31	—	—

e Saturdays excepted.
g Mondays excepted.
h Passengers cross Cardiff at own expense.
r Restaurant Car.

PONTYRHYLL (Glamorgan), 180 miles. Fares, 37/6*a*, 22/6*c*. R. T. for two months, 75/0*a*, 45/0*c*. Departures *from* London as for Tondu. Departures *for* London about 4 times daily.

POOL (Yorks), 194¼ miles. Fares, 40/7*a*, 24/4*c*. R. T., double fare. Departures *from* London as for Ilkley. Departures *for* London about 4 times daily. Pop. 753. *Map Square* 7.

POOLE (Dorset) from *Waterloo*, *via* Southampton, 113 miles. Fares, *via* Sway, 23/9*a*, 14/3*c*. R. T. for two months, 47/6*a*, 28/6*c*. Pop. 43,661. *Map Square* 27.

W'LOO	POOLE	POOLE	W'LOO.
AM 5.40	9.37	AM 7. 5*r*	10. 6
5.50	10.53	8.28*s*	11. 0
8.30*s*	11.53	10.17*r*	12.50
9.30	1. 0	10.39*r*	2.20
10.30	1.28	11.54	2.50
PM12.30*r*	3.16	PM12.32	4.20
2.30*s*	5. 0	2.17	4.50
3.30	6.43	2.55*s*	6.26
4.30*r*	7. 0	4.17	6.58
5.30	8.52	4.44*r*	8.20
6.30*r*	9. 0	6. 3*r*	8.50
10. 0	2.25	6.29	10.50
—	—	7.18	11.28
—	—	11.13	3.58
—	—	—	—
—	—	—	—
—	—	—	—

Sunday Trains.

AM11. 0*r*	2.21	AM 8.18	12.11
PM 2. 0*r*	5.14	11. 2	2.27
7. 0*r*	10.22	PM 3.31*r*	6.24
9.28	2.37	6.31	9.31
—	—	11.13	3.58

r Restaurant Car.
s Refreshments served.

ANOTHER ROUTE from *Waterloo*, *via* Salisbury, 115½ miles. Fares, 23/9*a*, 14/3*c*. R. T. for two months, 47/6*a*, 28/6*c*.

W'LOO	POOLE	POOLE	W'LOO.
AM 7.30	11. 2	AM 7. 8	10.56
11. 0*r*	2.23	10.43*r*	1.56
PM 1. 0*r*	4.44	PM 2.44*r*	6. 0
3. 0*r*	6.26	4. 7*r*	8.30
6. 0*r*	9.56	—	—
—	—	—	—
—	—	—	—

Sunday Trains.

12. 0*nr* 5. 4	PM 4. 8	8.57
—	—	—
—	—	—

n Noon.
r Restaurant Car.

Antelope Hotel. Family and Yachting House. Situated close to the Harbour. Good Motor Garage and Stabling. Billiards. E. ABLITT, Proprietress.

POOL QUAY (Montgomery), 171½ miles. Fares, 35/10*a*, 21/6*c*. R.T. for two months, 71/8*a*. Departures *from* London as for Buttington. Departures *for* London about 5 times daily. *Map Square* 16.

POPLAR (London)
from *Fenchurch Street*, 3¼ miles. Fares, 0/5*a*, 0/4*b*, 0/3*c*. R. T. for two days, 0/10*a*, 0/7*b*, 0/5½*c*. Pop. 162,578. *See* pp. 524-525.
Map Square 62.

ANOTHER ROUTE
from *Broad Street*, 6½ miles. Fares, 0/7½*a*, 0/6*b*, 0/4½*c*. R. T. for two days, 1/3*a*, 0/10½*b*, 0/9*c*. *See* p. 500.

POPPLETON (Yorks),
190½ miles. Fares, 39/10*a*, 23/11*c*. R. T., double fare. Departures *from* London as for York. Departures *for* London about 5 times daily. Pop. 758.
Map Square 8.

PORTBURY (Somerset),
126¾ miles. Fares, 26/6*a*, 15/11*c*. R. T. for two months, 53/0*a*. Departures *from* London as for Portishead. Departures *for* London about 6 times daily. Pop. 471.
Map Square 22.

PORT CARLISLE (Cumberland),
311¼ miles. No through fares. Departures *from* London as for Carlisle. Departures *for* London about 4 times daily.
Map Square 2.

PORTCHESTER (Hants)
from *Waterloo*, *via* Eastleigh, 87¼ miles. Fares, 15/5*a*, 9/3*c*. R.T. for two months, 30/10*a*, 18/6*c*. Pop. 901.
Map Square 28.

W'LOO.	PORTCHTR.	PORTCHTR.	W'LOO.
AM 5.40	8.32	AM 9.27	12. 0
5.50	9.54	11.41*r*	2.20
8.30*s*	11.34	PM12.24	4. 6
9.30	12.46	12.46	4.20
11.30*r*	2.13	2.32	6.16
PM 1.30*s*	4.24	5.48*r*	8.20
3.30*s*	6. 5	7.26	10.50
5.30*r*	8. 2	8.36	11.28
7.30	10. 1	11.21	3.58

Sunday Trains.

AM11. 0*r*	1.32	AM 9.18	12.11
PM 2. 0	6.40	12. 0*nr*	2.27
5. 5	8. 6	PM 5.12	8. 3
7. 0*r*	9.40	7.32	10.52
—	—	10.11	3.58
—	—	—	—

n Noon.
r Restaurant Car.
s Refreshments served.

ANOTHER ROUTE
from *Waterloo*, *via* Meon Valley, 76 miles. Fares as above.

W'LOO.	PORTCHTR.	PORTCHTR.	W'LOO.
AM 4.50	8.32	AM 7.37	10.26
7. 0	10.17	9.27	12.11
9.20	12.46	PM 2.32	5.46
11.20	2.42	4. 4	7. 7
PM 3.15	6. 5	7.26	11.10
6.34	9.28	—	—

Sunday Trains.

PM 6.20	9.22	PM 6.37	9.37

PORT CLARENCE
(Durham), 242½ miles. No through fares. Departures *from* London as for Stockton-on-Tees. Departures *for* London about 5 times daily.
Map Square 8.

PORT DINORWIC (Carnarvon),
243½ miles. Fares, 50/8*a*, 30/5*c*. R.T. for two months, 101/4*a*, 60/10*c*. Departures *from* London as for Bangor. Departures *for* London about 6 times daily.
Map Square 11.

PORTESHAM (Dorset)
from *Paddington* 157 miles. Fares, 29/11*a*, 18/2*c*. R. T. for two months, 59/10*a*, 36/4*c*. Departures *from* London as for Abbotsbury. Departures *for* London about 4 times daily. Pop. 550.
Map Square 27.

PORTESSIE (Banff), 587¼
miles. Fares, 106/3*a*, 63/9*c*. R. T. for two months, 212/6*a*, 127/6*c*. Departures *from* London as for Huntly or Elgin (*via* Dunkeld). Departures *for* London about 3 times daily.
Map Square 35.

PORT GLASGOW (Renfrew),
420 miles. Fares, 84/2*a*, 50/6*c*. R.T. for two months, 168/4*a*, 101/0*c*. Departures *from* London as for Greenock (Central). Departures *for* London about 5 times daily. Pop. 21,023.
Map Square 40.

PORTGORDON (Banff),
587 miles. No through fares. Departures *from* London as for Huntly or Elgin (*via* Dunkeld). Departures *for* London about twice daily. Pop. 1,280.
Map Square 35.

PORTH (Glamorgan), 168¼
miles. Fares, 33/11*a*, 20/4*c*. R. T. for two months, 67/10*a*. Departures *from* London as for Treherbert. Departures *for* London about 5 times daily.
Map Square 21.

PORTHCAWL (Glamorgan)
from *Paddington*, 181¾ miles. Fares, 37/11*a*, 22/9*c*. R. T. for two months, 75/10*a*, 45/6*c*. Pop. 6,642.
Map Square 21.

PAD.	P'CAWL.	P'CAWL.	PAD.
AM 1. 0*g*	7.56	AM 8.15*r*	1. 0
5.30	12. 3	9.25*r*	2.30
8.45*r*	1.36	11.18*r*	4.20
11.50*r*	4.59	PM12.54*r*	6.15
PM 1.10*r*	6.10	2.32*r*	8.35
3.35*r*	8.36	5.10*r*	9.25
6. 0*r*	10.13	9.28	3.30

Sunday Trains.

AM 1. 0	11.10	PM12.45*r*	8.25
9.10	3.42	8.15	3.30
PM12.30*r*	6.51	—	—
9.15*r*	9. 1	—	—

g Mondays excepted
r Restaurant Car.

Esplanade Hotel, 100 rooms. Special terms for Permanent Residents.
See advt. p. **282**.

PORTHYWAEN (Salop),
177¾ miles. No through fares. Departures *from* London as for Oswestry. Departures *for* London about 3 times daily.

PORT ISAAC ROAD
(Cornwall) from *Waterloo*. 247¼ miles. Fares, 50/10*a*, 30/6*c*. R. T. for two months, 101/8*a*, 61/0*c*.
Map Square 25.

W'LOO.	P. I. RD.	P. I. RD.	W'LOO
AM10. 0*r*	3.57	AM 8.52*r*	3.50
11. 0*r*	6. 2	10. 6*r*	4.30
PM 3. 0*r*	9.11	PM 1. 7*r*	8.30
—	—	3.16	10.50

No Sunday Trains.
r Restaurant Car.

PORTISHEAD (Somerset)
from *Paddington*, 128¾ miles. Fares, 26/11*a*, 16/2*c*. R.T. for two months, 53/10*a* Pop. 3,817.
Map Square 22.

PAD.	PORTISH'D	PORTISH'D	PAD.
AM 5.30	9.32	AM 6.50*r*	10.15
7.30	11.36	8.33	11.30
9. 0	12.46	10.54*r*	2. 0
11.15*r*	2.25	11.56	4. 5
PM 1.10*r*	4.57	PM 1.16	6. 2
2.45	7. 1	3.12*r*	7. 0
4.15*r*	8.23	5.20*r*	8.45
6.30*r*	10. 2	6.18	10.25
8. 0	10.57	10.15	2.45
12. 0*k*	7.37	—	—

Sunday Trains.

AM 9.10	3.19	PM 3.35	8.10
PM12.30*r*	6.19	9.35	3.15
4.30	9.19	—	—

k Saturdays midnight excepted.
r Restaurant Car.

PORTKNOCKIE (Banff),
591½ miles. No through fares. Departures *from* London as for Huntly or Elgin (*via* Dunkeld). Departures *for* London about twice daily. Pop. 1,664.
Map Square 35.

PORTLAND (Dorset),
from *Waterloo*, 146 miles. Fares, 30/5*a*, 18/3*c*. R. T. for two months, 60/10*a*. Pop. 12,434.
Map Square 27.

W'LOO.	P'TLAND.	P'TLAND.	W'LOO.
AM 5.40	11. 1	AM 6.50*s*	11. 0
8.30*s*	1.20	8.30*r*	12.50
10.30	2.20	9.45	2.50
PM12.30*r*	4.52	PM12.30	4.50
2.30*s*	6.29	2.30	6.58
4.30*r*	8.26	4.32*r*	8.50
6.30*r*	10.23	6. 8	11.28
—	—	9.28	3.58

Sunday Trains.

AM11. 0*r*	4.21	PM 1.30*r*	6.24
PM 2. 0*r*	7.26	4.30*r*	9.31
—	—	8.30	3.58

r Restaurant Car.
s Refreshments served.

ANOTHER ROUTE
from *Paddington*. 158½ miles. Fares as above.

PAD.	P'TLAND.	P'TLAND.	PAD.
AM 1. 0*g*	11 1	AM 8.30	12.55
5.30	12.20	9.45	3.20
9.30	1.20	11.15	3.50
10.30	2.20	PM12.30*t*	5.30
PM12.30*r*	4.52	2.30*r*	6.50
2. 0	6.38	3.35	8.20
3.30	7.48	6.15	2.45
5. 5	10.23	7.25*h*	2.45

Sunday Trains.

PM 2.40	7.26	PM 2.30*r*	7.55
—	—	—	—

g Mondays excepted.
h Thursdays and Third Class only.
r Restaurant Car.
t Tea Car.

PORTLETHEN (Kincardine), 514¾ miles. No through fares. Departures *from* London as for Stonehaven. Departures *for* London about 3 times daily. Pop. 873.
Map Square 38.

PORTMADOC (Carnarvon), from *Paddington, via* Ruabon, 253½ miles. Fares, 52/9*a*, 31/8*c*. R. T. for two months, 105/6*a*. Pop. 4,185.
Map Square 11.

PAD.	P'MADOC	P'MADOC	PAD.
AM 9.10*r*	4.27	AM 6.44*r*	2. 5
10.20*r*	5.22	9.26*r*	5. 0
10.40*r*	5.52	10.47*r*	6.40
PM12.50*r*	8.22	PM12.27*r*	8. 5
2.10*t*	9.42	1.37*r*	10. 0
12.15*h*	1.11	4.36	3.30
—	—	—	—
—	—	—	—
—	—	—	—

No Sunday Trains.

h Saturdays midnight excepted.
r Restaurant Car.
t Tea Car.

ANOTHER ROUTE from
Euston, 274½ miles. Fares, *via* Carnarvon, 54/10*a*, 32/11*c*. R. T. for two months, 109/8*a* ; *via* Shrewsbury or Whitchurch, 52/9*a*, 31/8*c*. R. T. for two months, 105/6*a*.

EUSTON	P'MADOC	P'MADOC	EUSTON
AM12.25	11. 3	AM 6.40*hr*	1.45
2.35	1.35	10. 0*r*	5. 5
5. 0*h*	2.10	10.25*dr*	7.30
8.30*hr*	4.31	12. 0*er*	7.30
11.10*hr*	5.50	PM 1.14*hr*	9.20
11.50*hr*	9. 5	1.50*hr*	10.45
PM 9.30*eh*	6.39	6.30*h*	5. 0
—	—	—	—
—	—	—	—
—	—	—	—
—	—	—	—
—	—	—	—

Sunday Trains.

PM 9.15*h*	6.39	—	—
—	—	—	—

d Saturdays only.
e Saturdays excepted.
h Via Carnarvon
r Restaurant Car.

PORT OF MENTEITH
(Perth), 429¾ miles. Fares, 87/4*a*, 52/5*c*. R. T. for two months, 174/8*a*, 104/10*c*. Departures *from* London as for Stirling. Departures *for* London about 4 times daily. Pop. 1,019.
Map Square 40.

PORTON (Wilts) from
Waterloo, 78½ miles. Fares, 16/5*a*, 9/10*c*. R. T. for two months, 32/10*a*, 19/8*c*. Departures *from* London as for Grateley. Departures *for* London about 6 times daily.
Map Square 22.

PORTPATRICK (Wigtown), 412¾ miles. Fares, 68/9*a*, 41/3*c*. R. T. for two months, 137/6*a*, 82/6*c*. Departures *from* London as for Stranraer. Departures *for* London about 3 times daily. Pop. 1,495.
Map Square 43.

PORTREE (Isle of Skye), from *Euston,* Fares, 126/1*a*, 75/0*c*. R. T. for two months, 250/4*a*, 148/1*c*. Departures *from* London as for Kyle of Lochalsh. Departures *for* London about twice daily. Pop. 2,120.
Map Square 33.

PORTSKEWETT (Monmouth) from *Paddington,* 134½ miles. Fares, 29/5*a*, 17/8*c*. R. T. for two months,58/10*a*. Departures *from* London as for Chepstow. Departures *for* London about 6 times daily. Pop. 958.
Map Square 22.

PORTSLADE (Sussex)
from *London Bridge* and *Victoria,* 52¼ miles. Fares, 10/10*a*, 6/6*c*. R. T. for two months, 21/8*a*, 13/0*c*. Pop. 7,696.
Map Square 28.

	Leave		Arr. at
	VICT.	LON. B.	PORT'DE
AM	—	5.18	7.48
	6.37	6.40	8.40
	7.23	7.25	10. 1
	9. 0	—	10.49
	—	9. 6	11. 8
	11.40	10.35	1. 4
	—	11.40*d*	1.13
	11.55	11.50	2. 9
	PM12.45	—	2.29
	—	1.20*d*	2.58
	1.55	—	3.23
	—	2. 5	3.52
	2. 0*d*	—	4. 9
	2. 0*e*	—	4.23
	—	2. 8*d*	4.58
	3.10*l*	—	4.28
	3.40	—	5 19
	4.30	4. 0	5.59
	—	5. 5*d*	6.51
	—	5. 8*e*	6.23
	5.45	5.55*e*	7.18
	—	6. 0	7.39
	—	6. 8	8.33
	6.40	—	8. 8
	7.15	7.20	8.59
	8.35	—	10. 8
	9. 3*d*	9.12*d*	11. 8
	9. 3*e*	9.12*e*	11.18
	10. 0	—	11.34
	—	—	—
	—	—	—
	—	—	—

Sunday Trains.

AM 6.55	7. 2	9.39	
8.50	8.55	11.19	
9.45*k*	—	11.19	
11. 5	—	12.39	
PM12.15	—	1.54	
1.10	—	2.48	
1.14	1.10	3.34	
4.55*k*	—	6.18	
5.50	6. 0	8.49	
6.30*p*	—	8.18	
8. 0	8. 0	10.19	
9.25	9.10	11.17	
—	—	---	
—	—	—	
—	—	—	
—	—	—	

PORTSLADE—*contd.*
Trains from Portslade.

	Leave	Arrive at	
	PORT'SDE	LON. B.	VICT.
AM 5.59	8.15	8.24	
6.38	8.19	—	
7. 6	8.38	—	
7.46	9.25	9.15	
8.29	9.50	—	
8.38*e*	9.54	10.24	
8.53*d*	10.33	—	
9. 1*e*	10.33	—	
9.30	11.10	10.55	
10.20	12.19	12.17	
10.53	1.42	—	
11.59	—	1.20	
PM12.49*l*	—	2.20	
12.49*e*	2.23	—	
1.16	3.40	3.45	
2.33	—	4.17	
2.56*d*	4.58	4.45	
2.56	—	4.50	
3.30	5.54	5.55	
4.40	6.36	6.34	
5.29*l*	—	6.45	
5.43	7.42	7.30	
7. 6	—	8.48	
7.27	10.25	10.17	
7.55*d*	10. 0	9.45	
8.27	10.58	—	
9.35	—	11.17	
10.49	12.59	.1. 0	

Sunday Trains.

AM 7.47	10.45	—	
9.14	11.15	10.50	
10.55	—	1. 0	
PM12.14	—	1.35	
2.50	5. 3	5.11	
4.40*p*	—	6. 0	
5.10	7.56	7. 0	
5.53	—	7.28	
7. 7	9.17	9.13	
9.19	—	10.55	
9.22	11.34	11.42	
10.24	12.27	—	

d Saturdays only.
e Saturdays excepted.
k Third class Pullman cars only.
l First and third class Pullman cars only.
p First class Pullman cars only.

PORTSMOUTH (Hants)
from *London Bridge* and *Victoria,* 85½ miles. Fares, TOWN STATION, 15/5*a*, 9/3*c*. R. T. for two months, 30/10*a*, 18/6*c*. HARBOUR STATION, 15/7*a*, 9/4*c*. R. T. for two months, 31/2*a*, 18/8*c*. Pop. 247,343.
Map Square 28.

	Leave		Arrive at	
	VICT.	LON. B.	TOWN.	HARB'R.
AM 6.18	6.35	9.31	9.37	
8.55	—	11.11	11.16	
10.15	10.22	12.58	1. 4	
11.35*p*	—	1.31	1.36	
11.55*k*	11.50*k*	3.23	3.28	
PM 1.35	—	3.30	3.35	
1.40	1.50	4.30	4.34	
1.55*k*	2. 5*k*	5.58	6. 5	
3.55	4. 0	6.39	6.44	
—	4.50	7. 1	7. 5	
4.53	—	7.32	7.37	
—	5. 5	8.26	—	
—	5. 8*e*	8.26	—	
5.45*k*	6. 0*k*	8.55	—	
7.20	7.15	10.28	—	

Sunday Trains.

AM 6.55*k*	7. 2*k*	11.33	—	
9. 0	8.55	11.55	12. 0	
9.55	—	12. 9	12.14	
PM 1.13*k*	1.10*k*	5.38	5.44	
7. 0	6.38	10. 7	—	

PORTSMOUTH.—KEPPEL'S HEAD HOTEL. C. SCULLARD, Proprietor.

PORTSMOUTH—*contd.*
Trains from Portsmouth.

	Leave	Arrive at	
HARBOUR.	TOWN.	LON. B.	VICT.
AM —	6.30*g*	9.50	9.22
—	6.35*f*	9.50	—
—	6.54	—	10.28
—	7.20	9.58	—
7.55	8. 0	10.45	10.53
8.40	8.45	10.55	—
9.25	9.30	12. 8	12. 0
—	10. 0	1.42	—
10.55	11. 0	—	1.10
11.30	11.37	3.32	3.32
ᵞM 1.50	1.56	4.27	4.34
2.55*p*	3. 0*p*	—	5.12
4.45*p*	4.50*p*	—	6.50
4.50	4.55	7.48	7.59
6.30	6.35	—	8.33
6.35*d*	6.40*d*	10. 0	9.45
7.15	7.20	10. 8	10. 1
—	9. 0*k*	12.59	1. 0

Sunday Trains.

AM —	6.48	10.45	10.32
—	9. 5*k*	—	1. 0
PM —	3.30*k*	—	7. 0
5.45	5.50	—	7.56
5.50	5.55	8.50	8.42
—	7.20*k*	11.34	10.55

d Saturdays only.
e Saturdays excepted.
f Mondays only.
g Mondays excepted.
k Via Hove.
p Pullman Car attached.

ANOTHER ROUTE from
Waterloo, via Godalming, 73¾ miles. Fares, Town Station, 15/5*a*, 9/3*c*. R. T. for two months, 30/10*a*, 18/6*c*. Harbour Station, 15/7*a*, 9/4*c*. R. T. for two months, 31/2*a*, 18/8*c*.

W'LOO.	TOWN.	HARBOUR.
AM 5.50	8.42	8.47
6.50	9.41	—
8.34*r*	11. 1	11. 7
9.50	11.48	11.54
10.50	1.11	1.17
11.50*d*	2. 1	2. 7
PM12.50*r*	2.48	2.54
1.50*d*	3.47	3.53
1.50*e*	4.32	—
2. 0*d*	4.39	—
2.34	5.28	5.34
3.50*s*	5.48	5.54
4.15*e*	6.45	—
4.50	7.11	—
5.50*r*	7.51	7.56
6.50*r*	8.52	8.58
9.50	12.29	—

Sunday Trains.

AM 8. 0	10.23	10.28
8.20	11.18	—
9.15*r*	11.44	11.53
PM 1.50	4.33	4.40
4.20	7.38	—
9.30	11.56	—

Trains from Portsmouth.

HARBOUR.	TOWN.	W'LOO.
AM —	6.40	9.12
7. 2*s*	7.10*s*	9.44
7.45*r*	7.52*r*	9.52
—	8.10	10.50
8.45	8.53	11.32
9.40	9.46	11.41
11.50*r*	11.56*r*	1.52
PM —	12.15	3. 6
1.10*d*	1.19*d*	3.20
1.30	1.36	4.16
3.50	3.58	5.52
4.34	4.42	7.46
5.50*r*	5.58*r*	7.56
—	6.13	9. 6
7.35	7.42	10.46
—	9. 5	12.16

PORTSMOUTH—*contd.*
Sunday Trains.

HARBOUR.	TOWN.	W'LOO.
AM —	7.35	10.16
PM12.20	12.28	3.13
4. 5*r*	4.14*r*	6.16
6. 0	6. 8	8.52
7.20	7.28	10. 1

d Saturdays only.
e Saturdays excepted.
r Restaurant Car.
s Refreshments served.

ANOTHER ROUTE from
Waterloo, via Eastleigh, 94½ miles. Fares as above.

W'LOO.	TOWN.	HARBOUR.
AM 5.40	8.52	8.58
5.50	10.14	—
8.30*s*	11.18	—
9.30	12.51	—
11.30*r*	2.36	—
PM 1.30*s*	4.43	—
3.30*s*	6.26	—
5.30*r*	8.23	—
7.30	10.22	—
8. 0	11.55	—
10. 0	2.14	—

Sunday Trains.

AM11. 0*r*	1.54	1.20
PM 2. 0	7. 5	—
5. 5	8.33	—
7. 0*r*	10. 4	—
9.28	1. 0	—

Trains from Portsmouth.

HARBOUR.	TOWN.	W'LOO.
AM —	6. 5	9.26
—	9. 5	12. 0
9.35*s*	9.40*s*	12.22
—	11.20*r*	2.20
PM —	12. 2	4. 6
—	12.55	4.20
2.33	2.41	6.16
—	5.25*r*	8.20
—	7. 3	10.50
—	8.15	11.28
—	11. 0*f*	3.58
—	*m*12.15*g*	3.58

Sunday Trains.

AM —	12.15	3.58
—	8.55	12.11
—	11.35*r*	2.27
PM —	4.50	8. 3
—	7.10	10.52

f Mondays only.
g Mondays excepted.
m Midnight.
r Restaurant Car.
s Refreshments served.

ANOTHER ROUTE from
Waterloo; via Meon Valley, 83 miles. Fares as above.

W'LOO.	TOWN.	HARBOUR.
AM 4.50	8.52	8.58
7. 0	10.36	—
9.20	12.51	—
11.20	3. 4	—
PM 3.15	6.26	—
6.34	9.50	—
—	—	—

Sunday Trains.

PM 6.20	9.44	—

PORTSMOUTH—*contd.*
Trains from Portsmouth.

HARBOUR.	TOWN.	W'LOO.
AM —	7.15	10.26
—	9. 5	12.11
—	9.50	1.40
PM —	2.10	5.46
—	3.40	7. 7
—	7.25	11.10
—	—	—

Sunday Trains.

PM —	6.15	9.37
—	—	—

PORTSMOUTH—*contd.*

Café Royal. Phone 5018. 78, Palmerston Road, Southsea. Table D'hote, Luncheons and Dinners, Grill and à la Carte. Licensed. Parties catered for.
C. FERRARI.

PORTSMOUTH (Yorks),

206¾ miles. Fares, 40/8*a*, 24/5*c*. R. T. for two months, 81/4*a*. Departures *from* London as for Burnley (Manchester Road). Departures *for* London about 6 times daily.
Map Square 12.

PORTSMOUTH ARMS

(Devon), 200¾ miles. Fares, 37/6*a*, 22/6*c*. R.T. for two months, 75/0*a*, 45/0*c*. Departures *from* London as for Eggesford. Departures *for* London about 6 times daily.
Map Square 21.

PORTSOY (Banff), 583¾

miles. Fares, 106/3*a*, 63/9*c*. R. T. for two months, 212/6*a*, 127/6*c*. Departures *from* London as for Huntley. Departures *for* London about twice daily. Pop. 1,723.
Map Square 35.

PORT TALBOT (Glamorgan)

from *Paddington*, 185¼ miles. Fares, 38/7*a*, 23/2*c*. R. T. for two months, 77/2*a*. Pop. 14,002.
Map Square 21.

	Pad.	Port T.		Port T.	Pad.
AM	1. 0*g*	6.44	AM	9. 4*r*	1. 0
	5.30	11.18		10.23*r*	2.30
	8.45*r*	1.22		11.32*r*	4.20
	11.50*r*	3.42	PM	2.17*r*	6.15
PM	1.10*r*	5.26		4. 9*r*	8.35
	3.35*r*	7.27		5.17*r*	9.25
	6. 0*r*	10. 6		9.37	3.30
	8. 0*r*	11.42		—	—
	9.15	3.37		—	—

Sunday Trains.

AM	1. 0	7.23	AM	9.46	3.35
PM	12.30*r*	5.22		11. 6	4. 5
	4.30	9.40	PM	3.40*r*	8.25
	9.15	3.37		9.37	3.30

g Mondays excepted.
r Restaurant Car.

Bank.—The National Bank Limited, Station Street.

PORT VICTORIA

(Kent) from *Charing Cross*, *Cannon Street*, and *London Bridge*, 40¼ miles. Fares, 8/4*a*, 6/8*b*, 5/0*c*. R. T. for two months, 16/8*a*, 13/4*b*.
Map Square 24.

	Leave Char. +	Leave Can. St.	Lon. B.	Arr. at P. Vict.
AM	5.18	—	5.25	7.36
	—	6.20	6.23	8.25
	9.32	—	9.41	11.28
PM	1.20*e*	—	1.27*e*	3.14
	1.26*d*	—	1.34*d*	3.14
	4.25*d*	—	4.31*d*	6.24
	—	4.36*e*	4.39*e*	6.24
	6.55*d*	—	7. 1*d*	8.51
	—	7. 8*e*	7.11*e*	8.51
	—	—	—	—
	—	—	—	—
	—	—	—	—
	—	—	—	—
	—	—	—	—
	—	—	—	—
	—	—	—	—

Sunday Trains.

AM	9.46	—	9.52	11.45
PM	1.15	—	1.22	3.20
	4.50	—	4.57	6.51

PORT VICTORIA—*cont.*

Trains from Port Victoria.

	Leave P. Vict.	Arrive at Lon. B.	Can. St.	Char. +
AM	7.48	9.34	—	9.43
	8.55	10.38	—	10.45
PM	*d*1. 5*k*	3.21	3.26	—
	1.10*e*	2.53	—	3. 4
	3.34*e*	5.36	5.40	—
	3.34*d*	5.37	—	5.44
	5.47	7.14	—	7.23
	6.45*d*	9. 6	9.11	—
	9. 6	10.51	—	10.59
	—	—	—	—
	—	—	—	—
	—	—	—	—
	—	—	—	—
	—	—	—	—

Sunday Trains.

AM	8.18	10.16	—	10.24
PM	12.15	2.14	—	2.24
	5. 0	6.49	—	6.59
	7.10	9.45	—	9.54

d Saturdays only.
e Saturdays excepted.
k Third Class only.

POSTLAND (Lincoln),

99¾ miles. Fares, 18/7*a*, 11/2*c*. R.T., double fare. Departures *from* London as for March. Departures *for* London about 4 times daily.
Map Square 18.

POST OFFICE. (Central

London Tube.) *See* back of Map.

POTTER HANWORTH

(Lincoln), 125½ miles. Fares, 26/1*a*, 15/8*c*. R. T., double fare. Departures *from* London as for Blankney. Departures *for* London about 4 times daily. Pop. 434.
Map Square 13.

POTTER HEIGHAM

(Norfolk) from *King's Cross*, 173¼ miles. Fares, 25/3*a*, 15/2*c*. R. T. for two months, 50/6*a*. Departures *from* London as for North Walsham. Departures *for* London about 3 times daily. Pop. 411.
Map Square 19.

POTTER'S BAR (Middlesex)

from *King's Cross*, 12¾ miles. Fares, 2/6*a*, 2/0*b*, 1/6*c*. R.T. for two months, 5/0*a*, 4/0*b*, 3/0*c*. *See* pp. 511-517.
Map Square 23.

POTTO (Yorks), 231½ miles.

Fares, 48/6*a*, 29/1*c*. R. T., double fare. Departures *from* London as for Stockton-on-Tees. Departures *for* London about 5 times daily. Pop. 170.
Map Square 8.

POTTON (Bedford) from

King's Cross, 47¼ miles. Fares, 9/10*a*, 5/11*c*. R.T. for two months, 19/8*a*, 11/10*c*. Departures *from* London as for Sandy. Departures *for* London about 5 times daily. Pop. 2,156.
Map Square 18.

POULTON (Lancs), 223½

miles. Fares, 46/6*a*, 27/11*c*. R. T. for two months, 93/0*a*, 55/10*c*. Departures *from* London as for Kirkham. Departures *for* London about 8 times daily. Pop. 2,732.
Map Square 12.

POWERSTOCK (Dorset)

from *Paddington*, 145¾ miles. Fares, 29/7*a*, 17/9*c*. R. T. for two months, 59/2*a*. Pop. 668.
Map Square 27.

	Pad	Powerst'k		Powerst'k	Pad.
AM	1. 0*g*	9.54	AM	8.59	12.55
	5.30	11.29		10.39	3.20
	10.30	2. 4		11.57	3.50
PM	12.30*r*	4.14	PM	1.34*t*	5.30
	2. 0	5.39		3.14*r*	6.50
	3.30	8.19		4.39	8.20
	5. 5	9.18		7.19	2.45

Sunday Trains.

PM	10. 0	9.54	PM	3.29*r*	7.55

g Mondays excepted.
r Restaurant Car.
t Tea Car.

POYNTON (Cheshire), 172¼

miles. Fares, 35/8*a*, 21/5*c*. R. T. for two months, 71/4*a*. Departures *from* London as for Macclesfield (Hibel Road) or Cheadle Hulme. Departures *for* London about 6 times daily. Pop. 2,793.
Map Square 12.

PRAED STREET. *See* Paddington (Praed Street).

Map Square 60.

PRAZE (Cornwall) from

Paddington, 297¼ miles. Fares, 61/6*a*, 36/11*c*. R.T. for two months, 123/0*a*, 73/10*c*. Departures *from* London as for Helston. Departures *for* London about 4 times daily.
Map Square 25.

PREES (Salop) 175¾, miles.

Fares, 34/7*a*, 20/9*c*. R. T. for two months, 69/2*a*. Departures *from* London as for Whitchurch. Departures *for* London about 6 times daily. Pop. 1,866.
Map Square 12.

PREESALL (Lancs), 228½

miles. Fares, 47/8*a*, 28/7*c*. R. T. for two months, 95/4*a*, 57/2*c*. Departures *from* London as for Preston. Departures *for* London about 4 times daily. Pop. 1,865.
Map Square 7.

PREESGWEENE (Salop),

172¾ miles. Fares, 36/0*a*, 21/7*c*. R. T. for two months, 72/0*a*, 43/2*c*. Departures *from* London as for Gobowen. Departures *for* London about 3 times daily.
Map Square 12.

PRESCOT (Lancs), 195½

miles. Fares, 40/8*a*, 24/5*c*. R. T. for two months, 81/4*a*, 48/10*c*. Departures *from* London as for Earlestown. Departures *for* London about 3 times daily. Pop. 9,043.

PRESTATYN (Flint), from

Euston, 205½ miles. Fares, 42/9*a*, 25/8*c*. R. T for two months, 85/6*a*, 51/4*c*. Pop. 4,085.
Map Square 11.

	Euston	P'tatyn.		P'tatyn.	Euston
PM	12.25	6.51	AM	7.27*er*	12. 5
	2.35	9.43		7.27*dr*	12.20
	5. 0*h*	10.59		8.26*dr*	1. 0
	5. 0*e*	11.38		8.46*er*	1. 0
	8.30*er*	1.37		9. 6*r*	1.45
	8.30*dr*	2. 3		9.50*r*	2.20
	10.30*r*	2.54		9.51*er*	3.10
	11.10*r*	3. 9		10.31*dr*	3.10
	11.50*e*	4.42		10.56*r*	4.15
	11.50*d*	5.20	PM	12.47*r*	5. 5
	12. 0*nr*	6.23		1.13*r*	6.25
PM	2.35*t*	7. 9		3.12*r*	7.30
	4. 5*r*	8.44		4.53*r*	10.45
	5.20*r*	9.58		8.25*e*	5. 0
	11.50*d*	11. 2		9. 5*d*	5. 0

SOUTHSEA.—ROYAL BEACH HOTEL. See advert. under Southsea.

PRESTATYN—*contd.*

Sunday Trains.

Euston	P'tatyn.	P'tatyn.	Euston
PM12.10*r*	6.43	AM 8.27	4. 0
—	—	PM 2. 5*r*	7.10
—	—	5.27	5. 0

d Saturdays only.
e Saturdays excepted.
h Mondays and Saturdays only.
n Noon.
r Restaurant Car.
t Tea Car.

Nant Hall Hotel. First-class. Billiards. Golf. Tennis. Bathing. Garage. Stabling. R.A.C. Telephone 199. Wires: "Nant Hall, Prestatyn."
M. DANE, Proprietress.

PRESTBURY (Cheshire),

168½ miles. Fares, 34/10*a*, 20/11*c*. R. T. for two months, 69/8*a*. Departures *from* London as for Macclesfield. Departures *for* London about 6 times daily. Pop. 314.
Map Square 12.

PRESTEIGN (Radnor),

165½ miles. Fares, 33/7*a*, 20/2*c*. R.T. for two months, 67/2*a*, 40/4*c*. Departures *from* London as for Titley. Departures *for* London about 4 times daily. Pop. 1,172.
Map Square 17.

PRESTHOPE (Salop),

150½ miles. Fares, 31/3*a*, 18/9*c*. R. T. for two months, 62/6*a*, 37/6*c*. Departures *from* London as for Much Wenlock. Departures *for* London about 5 times daily.
Map Square 17.

PRESTON (Lancs) from

Euston, 209 miles. Fares, 43/7*a*, 26/2*c*. R. T. for two months, 87/2*a*. Pop. 117,426.
Map Square 12.

Euston	Preston	Preston	Euston
AM12.25	7. 0	AM 5.30*g*	11.10
2.35	8.45	5.30*fr*	12. 5
5. 0	10.57	8.57*r*	1.45
6.45	12.28	9.29*r*	3.10
10.40*r*	3.15	10.58*hr*	3.45
11.35*r*	3.50	11.18*r*	4.15
11.50*r*	5. 7	PM 1. 9*t*	6. 0
PM 1.30*r*	6. 8	3.16*r*	7.30
2.35*t*	7.24	4.10*er*	9. 5
5.20*r*	9.48	4.10*dr*	9.15
9.30	2.37	6.23*r*	10.45
11.50*d*	10.15	10.52	5. 0

Sunday Trains.

AM11.45*r*	4.35	AM 8.40*r*	1.30
PM 6. 0*r*	11. 3	PM 2.25*r*	7.30
9.30	2.28	10.47	5. 0
—	—	—	—

d Saturdays only.
e Saturdays excepted.
f Mondays only.
g Mondays excepted.
h Mondays and Saturdays only.
r Restaurant Car.
t Tea Car.

Park Hotel. Covered way from Station. Commercial Tariff. Private access to Park.
See advt. p. **282**.

PRESTON BROOK

(Cheshire) from *Euston*, 177 miles. Fares, 36/10*a*, 22/1*c*. R.T. for two months, 73/8*a*. Departures *from* London as for Acton Bridge. Departures *for* London about 6 times daily. Pop. 440.
Map Square 12.

PRESTONPANS (East-

lothian), 382¾ miles. Fares, 80/7*a*, 48/4*c*. R. T. for two months, 161/2*a*, 96/8*c*. Departures *from* London as for Dunbar. Departures *for* London about 3 times daily. Pop. 5,154.
Map Square 41.

PRESTON PARK

(Sussex) from *Victoria, Clapham Junction*, and *London Bridge*, 49½ miles. Fares, 10/3*a*, 6/2*c*. R. T. for two months, 20/6*a*, 12/4*c*.
Map Square 28.

Leave Vict.	Leave Clap. J.	Leave Lon. B.	Arr. at Pr. Pk.
AM —	—	5.18	7.22
6.37	6.44	6.40	8.13
7.23	7.29	7.25	9.32
9. 0	9. 8	9. 6	10.48
10. 5	10.11	9.50	11.24
10.35	10.42	10.35	12.17
11.40	—	—	12.43
—	—	11.50	1.15
PM12.45	—	—	1.53
—	—	12.10	2.10
		1.20*d*	2.40
1.55	2. 2*e*	—	3. 4
2. 0	2. 7	2. 5	3.56
—	—	2. 8*d*	4.25
3.40	—	—	5. 3
—	—	4. 5	5.47
4.30	—	5. 5*d*	6.10
—	—	5. 8*e*	6. 9
5. 5	5.12	5.10	6.48
5.45	—	—	6.58
—	—	5.55*e*	7. 2
—	—	6. 0*d*	7.27
6. 6	6.12	6. 8	8.12
7.15	7.22	7.20	8.37
8.35	—	—	9.39
9. 3	9.10	9.12	11. 0
10. 0	—	—	11.28

Sunday Trains.

AM 6.55	7. 2	7. 2	9.17
8.50	8.57	8.55	10.45
PM 1.14	1.21	1.10	3. 7
5.50	5.57	6. 0	7.59
8. 0	8. 8	8. 0	9.55
9. 5	9.13	9.10	10.51

Trains from Preston Park.

Leave Pr. Pk.	Arrive at Lon. B.	Arrive at Clap. J.	Arrive at Vict.
AM 5.54	8.15	8.16	8.24
6.49	8.38	—	—
7.27	8.53	9. 0	9. 8
8.26	9.58	—	—
9. 1	—	—	10.24
10.12	12.13	11.59	12. 7
11.34	1.42	1.39	1.50
PM12.32	2.22	2.13	2.22
1.29	3.40	3.37	3.45
2.32	4.32	4. 9	4.17
3.11	5.54	5.47	5.55
4.34	6.36	6.26	6.34
5.52	7.42	7.21	7.30
6.34	8.46	8.39	8.48
7.49	10. 0	10. 2	10.10
8.54	10.58	—	—
9.37	—	11.10	11.17
11.14	12.59	12.50	1. 0
—	—	—	—

Sunday Trains.

AM 8.34	10.45	10.42	10.50
PM 2.56	5. 3	5. 1	5.11
5.49	7.56	8.31	8.41
9.44	11.34	11.34	11.42
10.44	12.27	—	—

d Saturdays only.
e Saturdays excepted.

PRESTON ROAD

(Lancs), 211 miles. Fares, 41/3*a*, 24/9*c*. R. T., double fare. Departures *from* London as for Wigan or St. Helens. Departures *for* London about 8 times daily.

PRESTON ROAD

(Middlesex) from *Baker Street*, 7¼ miles. Fares, 1/7*a*, 0/11½*c*. R.T. for two days, 2/7½*a*, 1/9*c*. *See* back of Map.
Map Square 49.

PRESTWICH (Lancs), 191¼

miles. Fares, 39/5*a*, 23/8*c*. R.T. for two months, 78/10*a*, 47/4*c*. Departures *from* London as for Manchester. Departures *for* London about 8 times daily. Pop. 18,750.
Map Square 12.

PRESTWICK (Ayr), 391¾

miles. Fares, 79/10*a*, 47/11*c*. R. T. for two months, 159/8*a*, 95/10*c*. Departures *from* London as for Ayr. Departures *for* London about 4 times daily. Pop. 8,516.
Map Square 40.

PRIESTFIELD (Stafford),

121¼ miles. Fares, 25/3*a*, 15/2*c*. R.T. for two months, 50/6*a*. Departures *from* London as for Bilston. Departures *for* London about 4 times daily.

PRINCES END (Stafford),

from *Paddington*, 122¼ miles. Fares, 25/3*a*, 15/2*c*. R.T. for two months, 50/6*a*, 30/4*c*. Departures *from* London as for Dudley. Departures *for* London about 4 times daily.
Map Square 17.
Station closed on Sundays.

PRINCE'S RISBOROUGH

(Bucks) from *Paddington*, 34¾ miles. Fares, 6/11*a*, 4/2*c*. R. T. for two months, 13/10*a*, 8/4*c*. Pop. 2,322.
Map Square 23.

Pad.	Prin. R.	Prin. R.	Pad.
AM 5.45	7.26	AM 7.26	8.34
7.33*h*	9.14	8. 6	9.20
8.12	9.38	9.17*r*	10. 0
9.10	9.52	9.31	10.40
9.20	11.10	11. 7	12.32
11.25	1. 6	PM12. 7	1.18
PM12.18	1.41	2.24	3.50
1.25	2.34	3.32	4.40
2.23	3.46	5. 3	6.35
3.40	5. 8	6. 3	7.32
4.40	5.38	6.50	9. 5
5.23	6.29	7.40	9.18
6.25	7.34	8.51	11. 4
7.10	7.53	9.44*d*	11.41
7.18	8.29	—	—
9. 0	10.20	—	—

Sunday Trains.

AM 9.12	10.37	AM 8.17	10.14
9.35	11.39	9.21	11. 4
PM 2.35	4.13	PM12.30	2.26
4. 0	5.26	6.59	8.25
6. 5	7.51	8.18	9. 0
—	—	—	—

d Saturdays only.
h Not after July 27th.
r Restaurant Car.

ANOTHER ROUTE from

Marylebone, 36 miles. Fares as above.

M'bone.	Prin. R.	Prin. R.	M'bone.
AM 6.10	7.25	AM 7.26	8.49
7.10	9.14	8.20	9.26
8. 4	9.38	8.48	9.55
9. 5	10.31	11. 7*d*	12.43
10. 0	11.10	11. 7	1. 5
PM12.15	1. 7	PM12. 7*d*	3.10
12.55	2.35	12. 7*e*	3.23
2.10	3.46	2.24*d*	3.53
3. 5	5. 8	2.24	4.28
4.30	5.20	3.32	5.48
4.55	6. 0	3.55	6. 3
5.38	6.37	5. 3	7. 5
5.43	7.34	6.50	8. 6
6.35*d*	8.29	7.40	9.27
6.45*e*	8.29	8.51	9.55
8.30	10.20	9.44*d*	11.18
—	—	—	—

PRINCE'S RISBORO'—continued.

Sunday Trains.

M'BONE.	PRIN. R.	PRIN. R.	M'BONE.
AM 8.50	10. 9	AM 9.21	10.43
10.20	11.39	PM12.30	1.48
PM 2.15	4.14	7.38	8.58
3.35	5.26	7.59	10.38
6.30	7.51	—	—

d Saturdays only.
e Saturdays excepted.

PRINCETOWN (Devon),
from *Paddington*, 241 miles. Fares, 47/8*a*, 28/7*c*. R.T. for two months, 95/4*a*, 57/2*c*.
Map Square 26.

PAD.	P'TOWN	P'TOWN.	PAD.
AM 5.50	3.30	AM10.15*r*	4.35
10.30*r*	5.33	PM12.25*kr*	6.50
PM12. 5*r*	7.38	5.50	7.10
3.30*kr*	9.38	7.50*kr*	7.10
12. 0*h*	9.28	—	—
—	—	—	—

Sunday Trains.

PM10. 0	9.28		

h Saturdays midnight excepted.
k Wednesdays and Saturdays only.
r Restaurant Car.

Duchy Hotel. Centre of Dartmoor. First-class accommodation for families. 1,400 feet above sea. Good fishing centre. Telephone 2.

GEO.' J. ROWE.

PRITTLEWELL (Essex)
from *Liverpool Street*, 41 miles. Fares, 5/5*a*, 3/3*c*. R.T. for two months, 10/10*a*. Pop. 59,980.
Map Square 24.

L'PL.ST.	P'TWLL.	P'TWLL.	L'PL.ST.
AM 5.10	6.22	AM 6.19	7.35
5.26	7.15	7.13	8.23
6.50	8.42	7.40	8.45
7.48	9.50	7.50	9.14
9. 6	10.54	8.14	9.17
10. 3	11.18	8.43	9.50
10.30	12. 4	9.19	10.16
11.56	1. 6	9.51	11. 7
PM12.48*d*	1.51	10.45	11.59
1.20*d*	2.26	11.38*e*	1.16
1.50*d*	2.49	11.41*d*	1.16
2. 0*e*	3.11	PM12. 7*e*	1.25
2.20*e*	4. 3	1.48	3. 5
2.30*d*	3.29	3.20*e*	4.51
2.58*d*	4. 2	3.24*d*	4.56
3.26	5. 1	4.47	6. 8
4.15	5.12	5.30	6.52
4.18	5.41	6.52	8.22
4.48*e*	6. 0	7.22	8.42
5.22*e*	6.20	7.34	9.10
5.39	6.54	8.13	9.50
6. 5*e*	7. 3	8.33	9.56
6.26*e*	7.33	9.14	10.32
6.26*d*	7.55	10.22	11.30
7.10*e*	8. 7	—	—
7.16*e*	8.35	—	—
8. 2*e*	9. 4	—	—
8. 2*d*	9.21	—	—
8.45	10. 2	—	—
9.45*e*	10.43	—	—
9.45*d*	10.58	—	—
11. 0	12.29	—	—
12. 0*m*	1. 5	—	—

PRITTLEWELL—contd.

Sunday Trains.

L'PL.ST.	P'TWLL.	P'TWLL.	L'PL.ST.
AM 8.30	9.54	AM 8.52	10.25
8.45	10.34	9.12	10.50
9.30	11.11	10.28	12.40
10.30	11.52	PM 1.30	3.15
10.45	12.31	3.48	5.15
11.35	12.56	6. 8	7.44
PM 2.30	4.21	6.35	7.58
6. 0	7.25	7. 7	8.45
6.42	8.21	8.13	9.48
8.46	10.26	9.36	10.45
10.10	11.42	—	—

d Saturdays only.
e Saturdays excepted.
m Midnight.

PRIVETT (Hants) from
Waterloo, 55½ miles. Fares, 11/8*a*, 7/0*c*. R.T. for two months, 23/4*a*, 14/0*c*. Departures *from* London as for Tisted. Departures *for* London about 6 times daily. Pop. 225.
Map Square 23.

PROBUS (Cornwall), 274½
miles. Fares, 56/10*a*, 34/1*c*. R.T. for two months, 113/8*a*, 68/2*c*. Departures *from* London as for St. Austell. Departures *for* London about 4 times daily. Pop. 1,259.
Map Square 25.

PRUDHOE (Northumberland), 277 miles. Fares, 58/9*a*, 35/3*c*. R. T., double fare. Departures *from* London as for Newcastle-on-Tyne. Departures *for* London about 8 times daily. Pop. 8,921.
Map Square 3.

PUDSEY (GREENSIDE)
(Yorks), 189½ miles. Fares, 39/5*a*, 23/8*c*. R. T., double fare. Departures *from* London as for Holbeck. Departures *for* London about 8 times daily. Pop. 14,315.
Map Square 12.

PULBOROUGH (Sussex)
from *London Bridge*, *Victoria*, and *Clapham Junction*, 49¼ miles. Fares, 10/5*a*, 6/3*c*. R. T. for two months, 20/10*a*, 12/6*c*. Pop. 1,969.
Map Square 23.

Leave / **Arr. at**

VICT.	CLAP. J.	LON. B.	PULB'RO
AM 6.18	6.25	6.35	8. 8
7.23	7.29	7.25	9.54
8.55	7.56	7.35	10.34
10.15	10.22	10.22	11.52
—	—	10.30	12. 5
10.35	10.42	10.35	1.28
11.55	—	11.50	1.55
PM 1.40	1.47*e*	1.50	3.41
3.55	4. 2	4. 0	5.29
4.53	5. 0	4.50	6.23
—	—	5. 5	6.55
6.15	—	—	7.42
7.20	7.27	7.15	9. 9

Sunday Trains.

AM 6.55	7. 2	7. 2	9.29
8.18	8.25	8.25	10.21
PM 7. 0	7. 7	6.38	8.41

Trains from Pulborough.

Leave / **Arrive at**

PULBORO	LON. B.	CLAP. J.	VICT.
AM 7.21	9.14	9.31	9.19
8. 8	9.58	—	—
8.20	10.22	—	—
9.50	11.50	11.35	11.42
10.43	12. 8	—	12. 0
PM 1.13	3.32	3.22	3.32
1.26	3.40	3.37	3.45
3.25	5.54	5. 4	5.12
5.16	7.48	7.31	6.50
8.33	10. 8	9.53	10. 1
8.44	10.58	11.10	11.17

PULBOROUGH—contd.

Sunday Trains.

Leave / **Arrive at**

PULBORO	LON. B.	CLAP. J.	VICT.
AM 7.26	10.11	10. 6	10.13
8.22	10.45	10.23	10.32
PM 5.32	7.56	7.25	7.33
7.27	9.32	9.24	9.34

e Saturdays excepted.

PULHAM MARKET
(Norfolk), 103½ miles. Fares, 21/8*a*, 13/0*c*. R.T. for two months, 43/4*a*, 26/0*c*. Departures *from* London as for Pulham St. Mary (via Tivetshall). Departures *for* London about 9 times daily.
Map Square 19.

PULHAM ST. MARY
(Norfolk) from *Liverpool Street*, via Tivetshall, 104½ miles. Fares, 21/11*a*, 13/2*c*. R.T. for two months, 43/10*a*. Pop. 1,739.
Map Square 19.

L'PL.ST.	P'HM S.M.	P'HM S.M.	L'PL.ST.
AM 5. 0	9.34	AM 7. 3*r*	10.30
10.12	1.47	9.49*h*	1.20
PM12.33*r*	5.56	PM 1. 6*r*	4.58
5.18*ehr*	8.33	3.53	7.51
5.18*dr*	8.38	6.46	11.16

No Sunday Trains.

d Saturdays only.
e Saturdays excepted.
h Via Forncett.
r Restaurant Car.

ANOTHER ROUTE *via*
Beccles, 125 miles. Fares as above.

L'PL.ST.	P'HM S.M.	P'HM S.M.	L'PL.ST.
AM 5. 0	9.49	AM 7.56*r*	11.30
8.15*r*	1. 6	9.34*r*	2. 3
10.20	3.53	PM 1.47	5.55
PM 3.15*r*	6.46	3. 6	7.51
3.18*r*	8. 0	5.56*r*	10. 0

No Sunday Trains.

r Restaurant Car.

PUNCHESTON (Pembroke), 259 miles. Fares, 50/0*a*, 30/0*c*. R.T. for two months, 100/0*a*, 60/0*c*. Departures *from* London as for Clynderwen. Departures *for* London about 3 times daily. Pop. 203.
Map Square 15.

PURFLEET (Essex) from
Fenchurch Street, 15¼ miles. Fares, 2/3½*a*, 1/4½*c*. R.T. for two months, 4/7*a*, 2/9*c*.
Map Square 24.

FEN. ST.	PURFLT.	PURFLT.	FEN. ST.
AM 5.37	6.30	AM 5.47	6.34
6.52	7.42	6.35	7.22
7.30	8.18	7.38	8.24
8.11	9. 3	8. 4	8.48
9. 5	9.45	9.12	10. 4*h*
9.39	10.30	10. 4	10.49
11.35	12.25	11.28	12.16
PM12.21	1.15	PM12.37*d*	1.27
1.35*d*	2.20	12.37*e*	1.33
1.48*e*	2.37	1.19*d*	2.10
2.40	3.29	1.49	2.34
4.16	4.59	3.23	4.10
4.46	5.24	4.25	5.18
5.32*d*	6.22	5. 4*e*	5.49
5.55*e*	6.39	5.40	6.33
6.38	7.24	6. 7*e*	6.56
7.41*e*	8.23	6.36	7.24
8.13	9. 4	7.21	8. 4
9.25	10.11	8.27	9.15
10.45	11.29	9.31	10.23*h*
12. 0	12.40	10.36	11.23*h*
		10.36	11.40
		11. 4	11.50

PURFLEET—*continued.*
Sunday Trains.

FEN.ST.	PURFLT.	PURFLT.	FEN.ST.
AM 8.40	9.53	AM 9.25	10.18
11.10	11.58	PM12. 9	1. 1
PM 1. 6	1.51	1.47	2.33
2. 7	2.56	3.16	4. 4
4.30	5.17	5.44	6.32
6.38	7.20	6.55	7.45
7.22	8.45	8.22	9.11h
8.45	9.36	8.36	9.30
10.30	11.12	10.12	11. 0

d Saturdays only.
e Saturdays excepted.
h Departs from or arrives at Mark Lane Station.

PURLEY (Surrey) from
London Bridge (L. B. & S. C. R.),
13¼ miles. Fares, 2/9a, 1/8c. R.T.
for eight days, 5/6a, 3/1c. Pop.5,566.
Map Square 23.

LON.B.	PURLEY	PURLEY	LON.B.
AM 5.18	5.58	AM 5.35	6.23
6.43	7.34	6.23	7.10
7. 7	7.52	7.22	7.55
7.25	8. 4	7.39	8.16
8.17	9. 7	8. 3	8.35
8.24	9.15	8.20	8.46
9.25	10.11	8.32	9. 1
9.50	10.23	8.45	9.26
10.20	11.10	9. 2	9.35
10.40	11.28	9.10	9.42
11.14	12. 2	9.31	10. 0
11.52	12.41	10. 0	10.43
PM12.30d	1.15	10.25	11.10
12.43e	1.41	10.59	11.57
12.50d	1.26	11.33	12.13
1.10d	1.47	PM12. 8	12.44
1.17	2. 8	1. 9	1.42
1.32d	2.14	1.21e	2. 8
1.38e	2.16	1.34d	2.22
1.40d	2.30	1.57d	2.46
2. 5	2.36	2. 0e	2.45
2. 8d	2.44	2.32e	3.27
2.10d	2.56	3. 4	3.40
2.22e	3.11	3. 7e	3.56
2.25d	3. 2	3.22e	4. 7
2.38d	3.18	4.17e	4.57
3. 0e	3.34	4.39	5.25
3.21d	4. 6	4.45e	5.31
3.30	4.17	5.19	5.54
3.36	4.22	5.30	6.15
4.10	4.51	5.37	6.22
4.23	5. 4	6.24	7.16
4.35	5.22	6.44	7.36
5.10	5.40	7.24	7.56
5.21	5.58	7.42	8.31
5.41e	6.18	7.53	8.38
6. 8	6.42	8.12	8.46
6.27d	7.12	8.17	9. 3
6.30e	7. 5	8.46	9.42
6.56	7.43	8.53	9.57
7.20	7.54	9.25	10.14
7.40	8.24	10.18	10.58
8.10e	8.42	10.24	11.11
8.55	9.44	—	—
9.22	10.13	—	—
10.35	11. 8	—	—
10.50e	11.36	—	—

Sunday Trains.

AM 7. 2	7.49	AM 8. 5	9. 9
7.22	8.26	8.44	9.29
7.50	8.52	9. 2	9.45
8.35	9.26	9.44	10.29
8.55	9.34	10. 8	10.45
9.35	10.26	10.42	11.29
9.50	10.36	PM 3. 7	4. 3
PM12.52	1.39	4.29	5. 3
1.10	1.46	4.52	5.39
1.45	2.50	5. 7	6. 5
2.40	3.51	6. 7	6.52
3.48	4.49	7.22	7.56
4.43	5.50	8. 7	9.21
6. 0	6.37	8.57	9.32
6.46	7.50	9. 4	10. 1

PURLEY—*continued.*

LON.B.	PURLEY	PURLEY	LON.B.
PM 8. 0	8.51	PM 9.58	10.46
9.10	9.52	10.47	11.34
9.55	10.51	—	—

d Saturdays only.
e Saturdays excepted.

ANOTHER ROUTE from
Victoria (L. B. & S. C. R.), 13½ miles.
Fares as above.

VICT.	PURLEY	PURLEY	VICT.
AM 6.37	7.34	AM 5.35	6.23
7. 0	7.52	6.23	7.25
7.23	8. 4	6.57	7.42
7.50	8.40	7.39	8.24
8.25	9. 7	7.58	8.36
8.40	9.23	8. 3	8.40
9.10	10.11	8.13	9. 2
9.45	10.23	8.32	9. 8
10. 5	10.42	8.45	9.19
10.18	11.10	9. 2	9.40
10.32	11.28	9.10	9.44
11. 7	12. 2	9.26	9.58
12. 0	12.41	9.37	10.12
PM12.24e	1.11	10.25	11.14
12.24d	1.15	10.59	11.34
12.42d	1.24	11.36	12. 7
12.53e	1.41	11.57	12.35
1.15d	1.52	PM12. 8	12.45
1.20e	2. 8	12.57	1.48
1.25e	2.16	1. 9	1.50
1.41d	2.30	1.21e	2.17
2. 0	2.36	1.34d	2.35
2. 8	2.56	1.57d	2.51
2.25e	3.11	2. 0e	2.49
2.28d	3.18	2.32e	3.20
2.37d	3.22	2.47d	3.35
3.10	4. 7	3. 4	3.45
3.20d	4.17	3. 7e	3.51
3.40	4.22	3.22e	4. 2
4.15	4.51	4.24	5. 0
4.50	5.22	4.45d	5.33
4.53	5.34	5.19	5.55
5. 5	5.40	5.37	6.31
5.27	5.58	6.24e	7.12
5.53	6.25	6.24d	7.23
6. 6	6.42	6.44	7.30
6.27	6.57	7.24	8.10
6.50	7.30	7.42	8.27
7.15	7.53	8.12	8.48
7.38	8.24	8.53	9.38
8. 5e	8.42	9.25	10.10
8.30	9.14	10.24	11.13
9. 3	9.44	—	—
9.22	10.13	—	—
10. 0	10.37	—	—
10.30	11. 8	—	—
11.15	11.56	—	—
11.50l	12.17	—	—

Sunday Trains.

AM 6.55	7.49	AM 8. 5	8.53
7.40	8.26	8.44	9.33
8. 0	8.52	9. 2	10.13
8.40	9.26	9.44	10.33
9.40	10.26	10.11	10.50
PM12. 0	12.49	10.42	11.33
1.14	1.46	PM 1. 7	1.53
2. 0	2.50	2. 7	2.53
3. 0	3.50	2.33	3. 4
4. 0	4.29	3. 7	3.53
5. 0	5.50	4. 7	4.53
5.50	6.37	4.29	5.11
6. 0	6.49	5. 7	5.53
7. 0	7.50	6. 7	6.53
8. 0	8.51	7. 4	7.37
9. 5	9.52	8. 7	8.53
10. 0	10.52	8.57	9.34
10.15	10.56	9. 4	9.53
10.50	11.27	9.15	10. 0
—	—	9.58	10.53
—	—	10.47	11.33

d Saturdays only.
e Saturdays excepted.
l Mondays and Thursdays only.

PURLEY—*continued.*
ANOTHER ROUTE from
Charing Cross, Cannon Street, and London Bridge, 16 miles. Fares, 2/9a, 2/3b, 1/8c. R.T. for eight days, 5/6a, 4/4b, 3/1c.

CHAR.	Leave CAN.ST.	LON.B.	Arr. at PURLEY
AM —	4.44	5. 0	5.29
—	—	7.50l	8.16
—	—	9.13l	9.39
—	—	9.33l	9.59
—	—	10. 3lh	10.31
—	10.12	10.15	10.44
10.55	—	11. 3	11.34
—	11.40d	11.43d	12.10
11.48e	—	11.54e	12.23
PM —	12.40d	12.43d	1. 9
—	—	12.45l	1. 9
12.44d	—	12.51d	1.18
12.55	—	1. 4	1.33
—	1.20d	1.23d	1.49
—	—	1.30el	1.56
—	—	1.50dl	2.15
2. 3e	2. 8d	2.10	2.40
—	—	2.22dl	2.51
2.46d	—	2.52d	3.18
3.15	—	3.21	3.51
—	—	4.20dl	4.46
4.22d	—	4.28d	4.55
—	4.24e	4.28e	4.55
—	4.44e	4.48e	5.14
—	—	4.50dl	5.16
5. 6e	—	5.14e	5.44
—	—	5.33el	5.58
5.30e	—	5.37e	6. 2
5.30d	—	5.36d	6. 2
—	—	5.48el	6.16
—	6.20e	6.23e	6.47
6.17d	—	6.23d	6.49
—	6.36e	6.39e	7. 6
6.34d	—	6.40d	7. 9
6.46e	—	6.53e	7.20
7.24d	7.28e	7.30	7.58
8.28	—	8.36	9. 4
9.25	—	9.31	9.58
10.17	—	10.23	10.51
11.42	—	—	12.11

Sunday Trains.

AM 6.25	—	6.32	7. 5
9. 8	—	9.14	9.39
10. 5	—	10.11	10.39
10.20	—	10.28	10.57
PM 1.30	—	1.37	2. 4
5.25	—	5.32	6. 1
6.50	—	6.56	7.22
7.45	—	7.52	8.19
8.38	—	8.45	9.13
9.40	—	—	10.16

Trains from Purley.

Leave PURLEY	Arrive at LON.B.	CAN.ST.	CHAR.
AM 6.53	7.18	—	7.30
7.54	7.58	—	8. 7
8. 0	8.24	8.28	—
8.17	8.40	8.44	—
8.40	9. 4	9. 8	—
8.57	9.21	—	9.30
9.11	9.39	9.43	—
9.21	9.45	—	—
9.55	10.18	10.22	—
10.37	11. 0	—	—
11. 2	11.24	—	11.33
11.20	11.46	—	11.59
PM12. 3	12.26	—	—
12.23	12.50	—	1. 0
1.32	1.58	—	2. 5
2.12	2.38	—	2.46
2.40	3. 4	3. 8e	—
3. 3	3.28e	—	3.42d
3.30	3.52	—	—
3.40h	4. 8	—	—

PURLEY—*continued.*

Trains from Purley.—*ctd.*

Leave PURLEY	Arrive at		
	LON. B.	CAN. ST.	CHAR. +
PM 4.33	5. 2	—	5.14
5. 3*e*	5.28	—	—
5.42	6.10	—	6.18
6.33	6.58	—	7. 5
6.55	7.20	—	7.29
7.57	8.23	—	8.31
8.37	9. 2	—	9.15
9.38	10. 3	—	10.13
11.32	11.57	—	12.10

Sunday Trains.

Leave PURLEY	Arrive at		
	LON. B.	CAN. ST.	CHAR. +
AM 7.50	8.16	—	8.27
10.48	11.15	—	11.25
PM 4. 9	4.33	—	4.42
6. 2	6.25	—	6.34
6.48	7.13	—	7.25
8.38	9. 1	—	9. 9
9.27	9.52	—	—
9.43	10.11	—	10.24
10. 2	10.25	—	10.32

d Saturdays only.
e Saturdays excepted.
h Mondays, Fridays and Saturdays only.
l Low Level Platform.

Auctioneers, House and Estate Agents, SLADE & CHURCH, 2, The Exchange, Purley. Oldest Estate Agents in District. Telephone Purley 7.

PURLEY OAKS (Surrey)

from *London Bridge, Victoria*, or *Clapham Junction*, 12¼ miles. Fares, 2/6*a*, 1/6*c*. R. T. for two days, 5/0*a*, 2/9*c*. Departures *from* London as for Coulsdon. Departures *for* London about 5 minutes later.

PURTON (Wilts)

from *Paddington*, 81¼ miles. Fares, 16/11*a*, 10/2*c*. R. T. for two months, 33/10*a*. Pop. 2,578.
Map Square 22.

PAD.	PURTON		PURTON	PAD.
AM 5.30	7.49	AM	8.22*r*	10.45
7.30	9.26		10.10	12.20
9. 0*d*	12.24	PM	12.55*dr*	2.40
10.45	1.55		1.24	3.20
PM 1.10*r*	3.21		3.17	5. 0
3.15*t*	5.15		3.54	6. 2
4.15*t*	6. 4		6.22*dr*	8.35
6. 0*r*	7.56		8.22	10.25
9.15*d*	11.39		—	—

Sunday Trains.

PM 12.30*r*	2.49	PM	7. 0	10. 0
2. 0	7.38		—	—

d Saturdays only.
r Restaurant Car.
t Tea Car.

PUTNEY (London) from

Waterloo, 6 miles. Fares, 0/10*a*, 0/6*c*. R. T. for two days, 1/8*a*, 1/0*c*. Pop. 28,558. *See pp. 586-591.*
Map Square 68.

PUTNEY BRIDGE

(Fulham) from *Mansion House*, 7 miles. *See p.* 489.
Map Square 68.

PUTNEY EAST

from *Mansion House*, 7¼ miles. *See p.* 489.
Map Square 68.

ANOTHER ROUTE from

Waterloo, 5¼ miles. Fares, 0/10*a*, 0/6*c*. R. T. for two days, 1/8*a*, 1/0*c*. *See p.* 595.

PUXTON (Somerset) from

Paddington, 133½ miles. Fares, 27/9*a*, 16/8*c*. R. T. for two months 55/6*a*. Departures *from* London as for Yatton. Departures *for* London about 6 times daily. Pop. 166.
Map Square 22.

PWLLHELI (Carnarvon)

from *Paddington*, via Ruabon, 266¼ miles. Fares, 55/3*a*, 33/2*c*. R.T. for two months. 110/6*a*. Pop. 3,811.
Map Square 11.

PAD.	PWLL'I.	PWLL'I.	PAD.
AM 9.10*r*	5. 0	AM 6. 5*r*	2. 5
10.20*r*	5.55	8.55*r*	5. 0
10.40*r*	6.23	10.15*r*	6.40
PM12.50*r*	9. 2	11.55*r*	8. 5
2.10*t*	10.10	PM 1. 0*r*	10. 0
12.15*h*	1.57	4. 0	3.30

No Sunday Trains.
h Saturday midnights excepted.
r Restaurant Car.
t Tea Car.

ANOTHER ROUTE from

Euston, 270¼ miles. Fares as above.

EUSTON	PWLL'I	PWLL'I	EUSTON
AM 12.25	11. 2	AM 6.45*hr*	1.45
2.35	1.25	10.25*r*	5. 5
5. 0*h*	1.58	PM12.10*er*	7.30
8.30*hr*	4.25	1.30*hr*	9.20
11.10*hr*	5.40	2. 0*hr*	10.45
11.50*hr*	8.51	6.40*h*	5. 0
PM 9.30*eh*	6.35	—	—

Sunday Trains.

PM 9.15*h*	6.35	—	—
—	—	—	—

e Saturdays excepted.
h Via Carnarvon.
r Restaurant Car.

South Beach Hotel. Facing South and Harbour. Charming Views. Re-furnished.
See advt. p. **282.**

PYE BRIDGE (Notts), 133½

miles. Fares, 26/11*a*, 16/2*c*. R. T., double fare. Departures *from* London as for Langley Mill. Departures *for* London about 6 times daily.

PYE HILL (Notts) from

King's Cross, 141½ miles. Fares, 26/11*a*, 16/2*c*. R.T., double fare. Departures *from* London as for Newthorpe. Departures *for* London about 9 times daily.
Map Square 13.

PYLE (Glamorgan) from

Paddington, 178½ miles. Fares, 37/3*a*, 22/4*c*. R. T. for two months, 74/6*a*. Pop. 2,708.
Map Square 21.

PAD.	PYLE		PYLE	PAD.
AM 1. 0*g*	6.30	AM	8.27*r*	1. 0
5.30	11.35		9.50*r*	2.30
8.45*r*	1.10		11.49*r*	4.20
11.50*r*	4.30	PM	1.20*r*	6.15
PM 1.10*r*	5.59		2.48*r*	8.35
3.35*r*	8.17		5.29*r*	9.25
6. 0*r*	9.55		9.38	3.30
—	—		—	—

Sunday Trains.

AM 1. 0	10.59	AM11.22	4. 5
9.10	3.31	PM 1.48*r*	8.25
PM12.30*r*	9.26	8.28	3.30
4.30	9.29	—	—
9.15	8.40	—	—

g Mondays excepted.
r Restaurant Car.

PYLLE (Somerset) from

Waterloo, 125 miles. Fares, 24/5*a*, 14/8*c*. R.T. for two months, 48/10*a*. Departures *from* London as for Glastonbury. Departures *for* London about 5 times daily. Pop. 201.
Map Square 22.

REFERENCE NOTES.

a signifies First Class.
b ,, Second Class.
c ,, Third Class.
d ,, On Saturdays only.
e ,, Saturdays excepted.
f ,, On Mondays only.
g ,, Mondays excepted.
r ,, Restaurant Car.
t ,, Tea Car.
x ,, Express.
R.T. ,, Return Tickets.

All Trains in the Tables not otherwise marked carry Third Class Passengers.

QUEENBOROUGH — continued.

Trains from Queenboro'.

Leave Qu'boro	Arrive at St. Pl.'s	Hol. V.	Vict.
AM 5.31	8. 8	8. 9	8.14
7.17	9.37	9.39	—
8.11	—	—	11. 2
9. 2	—	—	11.27
9.54	—	—	12. 7
10.39d	—	—	1.22
10.39e	12.59	1. 2	1.33
PM12.22j	—	←	2.15
12.22	—	—	2.43
2. 2e	4.46	—	4.39
2.12d	—	—	4.55
3 42	—	—	5.56
6.12	—	—	8.33
7. 2	9.50	9.54	9.46
8.22	—	—	10.25

Sunday Trains.

AM 6.35	—	9.40	9.31
9. 5	—	11.58	11.50
PM 1.50	—	—	4.42
3 25	—	—	5.31
8.13	—	—	10.29

d Saturdays only.
e Saturdays excepted.
f Mondays only.
h Third Class only.

QUEENSBURY (Yorks),

196 miles. Fares, 39/9a, 23/10c. R. T., double fare. Departures from London as for Bradford. Departures for London about 8 times daily. Pop. 5,870.
Map Square 12.

QUEEN'S PARK

(Kilburn) from *Euston*, 3¼ miles. Fares, 0/7½a, 0/4½c, R. T. for two days, 1/3a, 0/9c. See pp. 496-499.
Map Square 59.

ANOTHER ROUTE from

Broad Street, 8 miles. Fares, 0/11½a, 0/7½c. R. T. for two days, 1/11a, 1/2c. See pp. 496-499.

ANOTHER ROUTE (Bakerloo Tube). See back of Map.

QUEEN'S ROAD (Battersea) from *Waterloo*, 2¼ miles. Fares, 0/4a, 0/2c, R. T. for two days, 0/8a, 0/4c. See pp. 586-591, 595.
Map Square 69.

QUEEN'S ROAD (Bayswater) from *Aldgate, Moorgate, King's Cross, Mansion House, Charing Cross, Victoria, South Kensington, High Street*, and all intermediate Stations every few minutes. See back of Map.

ANOTHER ROUTE (Central London Tube). See back of Map.

QUEEN'S ROAD (Peckham), from *London Bridge*, 2¾ miles. Fares, 0/5a, 0/3c. R. T. for two days, 0/10a, 0/6c. From *Victoria*, 6 miles. Fares, 0/9a, 0/5½c. R. T. for two days, 1/2a, 0/9c. See pp. 567, 568, 570, 581, 582.
Map Square 70.

QUELLYN LAKE (Carnarvon), 258 miles. No through fares. Departures from London as for Carnarvon. Departures for London about 4 times daily.
Map Square 11.

Q

QUAINTON ROAD

(Bucks). 44½ miles. Fares, 9/2a, 5/6c. R.T. for two months, 18/4a, 10/11½c. Departures from London as for Waddesdon Manor. Departures for London about 11 times daily. Pop. 895.
Map Square 23.

QUAKER'S YARD (Glamorgan), 165¼ miles. Fares, via Pontypool Road, 34/2a, 20/6c. R. T. for two months, 68/4a, 41/0c. Departures from London as for Nelson and Llancaich. Departures for London about 4 times daily.
Map Square 21.

QUARTER (Lanark), 399½ miles. No through fares. Departures from London as for Hamilton. Departures for London about 4 times daily. Pop. 2,022.

QUEENBOROUGH

(Kent), 49¼ miles from *Charing Cross, Cannon Street, London Bridge, Victoria* and *Holborn Viaduct*. Fares, 8/9a, 7/0b, 5/3c. R. T. for two months, 17/6a, 14/0b. Pop. 3,073.
Map Square 24.

Leave Vict.	Hol. V.	St. Pl.'s	Arr. at Qu'boro
AM —	3.50h	—	6.12
5. 5	4.57	5. 0	7.48
5.48f	5.40f	5.42f	7.48
7.40f	7.30	7.33	10.17
9.20	—	—	11.10
11.40d	—	—	1.50
11.40e	—	—	2.23
PM 1.23d	—	—	3.20
2. 8e	—	—	4. 5
3.20e	—	—	4.50
3.29d	—	—	5. 0
4.20	—	—	6.30
5.30	—	—	7.35
7. 5	7. 0	7. 3	9.40
7.50	—	—	10.20

Sunday Trains.

AM 7.20	—	—	9.45
8.15	8. 0	—	11.20
10.30	10.25	—	3. 5
PM 3.30	—	—	6.15
7.50	—	—	9.50

QUORN (Leicester) from *Marylebone*, 111 miles. Fares, 22/4x, 13/5c. R. T., double fare. Departures from London as for Rothley. Departures for London about 8 times daily.
Map Square 18.

QUY (Cambs) from *Liverpool Street*, 60½ miles. Fares, 12/6a, 7/6c. R.T. for two months, 25/0a. Departures from London as for Mildenhall. Departures for London about 5 times daily. Pop. 327.
Map Square 19.

REFERENCE NOTES.

a signifies First Class.
b   „   Second Class.
c   „   Third Class.
d   „   On Saturdays only.
e   „   Saturdays excepted.
f   „   On Mondays only.
g   „   Mondays excepted.
r   „   Restaurant Car.
t   „   Tea Car.
x   „   Express.
R.T. „   Return Tickets.

All Trains in the Tables not otherwise marked carry Third Class Passengers.

R

RACKS (Dumfries), 328¼ miles. Fares, 66/6*a*, 39/11*c*. R. T. for two months, 133/0*a*, 79/10*c*. Departures *from* London as for Annan. Departures *for* London about 3 times daily.
Map Square 44.

RADCLIFFE (Lancs), 194 miles. Fares, 40/2*a*, 24/1*c*. R. T. for two months, 80/4*a*, 48/2*c*. Departures *from* London as for Manchester. Departures *for* London about 8 times daily. Pop. 24,677.
Map Square 12.

RADCLIFFE BRIDGE (Lancs), 194¾ miles. Fares, 40/2*a*, 24/1*c*. R.T. for two months, 80/4*a*, 48/2*c*. Departures *from* London as for Manchester. Departures *for* London about 6 times daily.

RADCLIFFE-ON-TRENT (Notts) from *King's Cross*, 123 miles. Fares, 25/5*a*, 15/3*c*. R. T., double fare. Departures *from* London as for Bottesford. Departures *for* London about 4 times daily. Pop. 2,735.

RADFORD (Notts) from *St. Pancras*, 125¾ miles. Fares, 26/0*a*, 15/7*c*. R. T., double fare.
Map Square 13.

St. Pan.	Radf'd	Radf'd	St. Pan.
AM 2.25	8.26	AM 6.33*r*	9.57
9. 0*r*	12.11	10.49	3.25
PM 1.50*r*	5. 4	PM12.35*dr*	4.10
3.30*r*	6.31	3.12*r*	6.35
5. 0*r*	8.21	—	—
—	—	—	—

No Sunday Trains.
d Saturdays only.
r Restaurant Car.

RADLETT (Herts), 15¼ miles. Fares from *St. Pancras*, 3/2*a*, 1/11*c*. R. T., double fare. From *Moorgate Street*, 3/6*a*, 2/1*c*. R. T., 7/0*a*, 4/2*c*. Pop. 2,063. *See* pp. 507, 508.
Map Square 23.

Red Lion Hotel. Telephone 98. Comfortable for Golf and Visitors to Aldenham Schools. Electric Light.
TRUST HOUSES, Ltd.

Aldenham Lodge. Residential Hotel. Inclusive terms. Licensed. 'Phone 105. Park 12 acres. Tennis. Golf. Electric Light. Verandah. Restaurant.
RESIDENT PROPRIETOR.

RADLEY (Berks) from *Paddington*, 58¼ miles. Fares, *via* Didcot, 12/3*a*, 7/4*c*. R. T. for two months, 24/6*a*. *Via* Oxford, 13/2*a*, 7/11*c*. R.T. for two months, 26/4*a*. Pop. 927.
Map Square 23.

Pad.	Radley	Radley	Pad.
AM 5.30	7. 7	AM 7.21	9. 0
6.30	8.24	8.43	9.50
7.30	9.56	8.56*r*	10.15
8.50	10.26	9.46	12. 0
9. 0	11.35	PM12.30	1.50
10.45	12.29	1.19	3.20
11.20	1.22	2.56	5. 6
PM 1.10*r*	3.22	5. 6	7.20
3.18	5.12	6.13	8.20
3.38	6.26	7. 6*r*	9.15
5.15	7. 1	8.33	10.45
6. 5*r*	7.53	9.50	2.45
6.55	9. 2	—	—
10. 0	11.32	—	—
—	—	—	—
—	—	—	—

Sunday Trains.

AM 9.10	10.56	AM 7.51	10.14
11.45	1.30	10. 5	2.40
PM 2. 0	4.55	PM 4.48	6.20
5.15	9.38	7.48	9.48
7.40	10. 8	8.52	11.38
10. 0	11.32	9.50	3.15
—	—	—	—
—	—	—	—

r Restaurant Car.

RADSTOCK (Somerset) from *Paddington*, *via* Frome, 109¼ miles. Fares, 22/9*a*, 13/8*c*. R. T. for two months, 45/6*a*. Pop. 3,661.
Map Square 22.

Pad.	Radsk.	Radsk.	Pad.
AM 1. 0*g*	8.45	AM 7.52	10.52
5.30	10.57	11.26	3.20
10.30	1. 5	PM 2. 2*t*	5.30
PM12.30*r*	3.46	3.40*r*	6.50
2. 0	5.16	5.58	10.45
3.30	6.40	8.34	2.45
5. 5	8.36	—	—
—	—	—	—
—	—	—	—

Sunday Trains.

PM 2.40	7. 9	AM10.25	3.35
—	—	—	—

g Mondays excepted.
r Restaurant Car.
t Tea Car.

ANOTHER ROUTE from *Paddington*, *via* Bristol, 134¼ miles. Fares, 25/5*a*, 15/3*c*. R. T. for two months, 50/10*a*.

Pad.	Radsk.	Radsk.	Pad.
AM 7.30	11.26	AM 7.53	11.30
9. 0	2. 2	10.57*r*	2. 0
11.15*dr*	2.54	PM 1. 5	6. 2
11.15*r*	3.40	3.46*r*	7. 0
PM 1.10*r*	5.58	5.16	10.25
2.45	7.10	8.36	2.45
4.15*r*	8.34	—	—
6.30*r*	10.21	—	—
12. 0*l*	7.52	—	—
12.30*v*	10.25	—	—

Sunday Trains.

PM12.30*r*	5.49	PM12.27	4. 5
10. 0	7.52	7. 9	3.15

h Thursdays and Saturdays only.
l Saturdays midnight excepted.
r Restaurant Car.
v Saturdays midnight only.

RADSTOCK—*continued.*

ANOTHER ROUTE from *Waterloo*, 138¾ miles. Fares, 24/0*a*, 14/5*c*. R.T. for two months, 48/0*a*.

W'loo.	Radsk.	Radsk.	W'loo.
AM 9. 0*r*	1. 7	AM 7.12*r*	11.10
10. 0*r*	3.17	8.57*r*	1.56
PM 1. 0*r*	5.36	10.45*r*	3. 8
3. 0*r*	7.30	11.56*r*	4.30
6. 0*r*	9.56	PM 1.32*r*	6. 0
—	—	3.10	7.40
—	—	5.14	10.50
—	—	6.42*h*	3.58
—	—	—	—

No Sunday Trains.
h *Via* Eastleigh.
r Restaurant Car.

RADWAY GREEN (Cheshire), 162 miles. No through fares. Departures *from* London as for Crewe. Departures *for* London about 4 times daily.
Map Square 12.

RADYR (Glamorgan), 157¾ miles. Fares, 32/11*a*, 19/9*c*. R. T. for two months, 65/10*a*, 39/6*c*. Departures *from* London as for Cardiff. Departures *for* London about 6 times daily. Pop. 1,238.
Map Square 21.

RAGLAN (Monmouth), 159¾ miles. Fares, 31/11*a*, 19/2*c*. R.T. for two months, 63/10*a*. Departures *from* London as for Monmouth. Departures *for* London about 4 times daily. Pop. 610.
Map Square 22.

RAINFORD VILLAGE (Lancs), 196½ miles. Fares, 40/8*a*, 24/5*c*. R.T. for two months, 81/4*a*. Departures *from* London as for St. Helens. Departures *for* London about 6 times daily. Pop. 3,496.
Map Square 12

RAINHAM (Essex), from *Fenchurch Street*, 12¾ miles. Fares, 1/10½*a*, 1/1½*c*. R.T. for six months, 3/9*a*, 2/3*c*. Pop. 2,196.
Map Square 24.

Fen. St.	Rainh'm	Rainh'm	Fen. St.
AM 5.37	6.23	AM 5.54	6.34
6.52	7.33	6.42	7.22
7.30	8.12	7.45	8.24
8.11	8.54	8.14	8.48
9. 5	9.36	9.22	10. 4*h*
9.39	10.21	10.13	10.49
11.35	12.16	11.36	12.16
PM12.25	1. 6	PM12.46*d*	1.27
1.35*d*	2.11	12.46*e*	1.33
1.48*e*	2.28	1.30*d*	2.10
2.40	3.20	1.58	2.34
4.16	4.50	3.32	4.10
4.46	5.18	4.32	5.18
5.32*d*	6.13	5. 8*e*	5.49
5.55*e*	6.30	5.50	6.33
6.38	7.15	6.16*e*	6.56
7.41*e*	8.16	6.45	7.24
8.13	8.55	7.28	8. 4
9.25	10. 2	8.36	9.15
10.45	11.20	9.40*h*	10.23
12. 0	12.31	10.45	11.23*h*
—	—	10.45	11.40
—	—	11.11	11.50
—	—	—	—
—	—	—	—
—	—	—	—
—	—	—	—

RAINHAM—continued.

Sunday Trains.

FEN. ST.	RAINH'M	RAINH'M	FEN. ST.
AM 8.40	9.25	AM 9.36	10.18
11.10	11.50	PM12.18	1. 1
PM 1. 6	1.44	1.55	2.33
2. 7	2.47	3.24	4. 4
4.30	5. 8	5.53	6.32
6.38	7.13	7. 3	7.45
7.22	8.37	8.31	9.11h
8.45	9.27	8.45	9.30
10.30	11. 3	10.21	11. 0

d Saturdays only.
e Saturdays excepted.
h Departs from or arrives at
Mark Lane Station.

RAINHAM (Kent) from
Victoria, Holborn Viaduct, and
St. Paul's, 39 miles. Fares, 8/4a,
6/8b, 4/11c. R. T. for two months,
16/8a, 13/4b. Pop. 4,335.
Map Square 24.

VICT.	Leave		Arr. at
(S.E.&C.)	HOL. V.	ST. PL.'s	RAINH'M
AM —	3.50h	—	5.18
5. 5	4.57	5. 0	7. 6
5.48f	5.40f	5.42f	7. 6
7.40f	7.30	7.33	9.14
9.20	—	—	10.42
11.40d	—	—	1. 3
11.40e	—	—	1.30
PM 1.25d	—	—	2.30
2. 5d	—	—	4.48
2. 8e	—	—	4.48
4.20	—	—	5.43
5.30e	—	—	6.43
5.30d	—	—	6.46
6.16	6.10e	6.13e	8.11
7. 5	7. 0	7. 3	8.47
7.50	—	—	11.14
9. 0e	8.57e	9. 0e	11.14

Sunday Trains.

AM 7.20	—	—	8.54
8.15	8. 0	—	9.33
10.30	10.25	—	2.13
PM 3.30	—	—	5.16
6.35	—	—	8.16

Trains from Rainham.

Leave		Arrive at	
RAINH'M	ST. PL.'s	HOL. V.	VICT.
AM 6.22	8. 8	8. 9	8.14
7. 9	9.16	9.18	—
7.53	9.37	9.39	—
9.25	—	—	11. 2
11.28e	12.59	1. 2	1.33
11.41d	—	—	1.22
PM 1.28	—	—	2.43
2.52e	4.46	—	4.39
2.59d	—	—	4.55
4.50	—	—	5.56
5.35e	—	—	8.33
6.39d	—	—	8.33
7.54	9.50	9.54	9.46
9.41	11.21	11.23	—

Sunday Trains.

AM 7.34	—	9.40	9.31
11. 5	—	1. 2	12.56
PM 4.14	—	—	5.31
9.33	—	12. 0	11.44
—	—	—	—
—	—	—	—
—	—	—	—

d Saturdays only.
e Saturdays excepted.
f Mondays only.
h Third Class only.

RAINHAM—continued.

ANOTHER ROUTE from
Charing Cross, Cannon Street, and
London Bridge, 38 miles. Fares
as above.

	Leave		Arr. at
CHAR. †	CAN. ST.	LON. B.	RAINH'M
AM —	—	3.57k	5.19
—	7.16	7.19	9.14
—	10.58h	11. 1h	12.43
—	10.58l	11. 1l	12.53
PM 2.45e	—	2.53e	4.48
3. 5d	—	3.12d	4.48
5.58d	—	6. 4d	7.31
6.22e	—	6.29e	8.11
6.55d	—	7..1d	8.47
—	7. 8e	7.11e	8.47
—	9.35	9.38	11.14

Sunday Trains.

PM 7. 0	—	7. 7	8.36

Trains from Rainham.

Leave		Arrive at	
RAINH'M	LON. B	CAN. ST.	CHAR. †
AM 7. 9	8.34	—	8.43
7.53	9. 0	9. 4	—
8.47	10.24	10.28	—
PM 5.55e	7.14	—	7.23
6.39d	8.15	8.20	—

Sunday Trains.

PM 9.33	11.15	—	11.24

d Saturdays only.
e Saturdays excepted.
h Wednesdays and Saturdays
excepted.
k Third Class only.
l Wednesdays only.

RAINHILL (Lancs), 193
miles. Fares, 40/2a, 24/1c. R.T.
for two months, 80/4a. Departures
from London as for Earlestown.
Departures *for* London about 5
times daily. Pop. 2,442.
Map Square 12.

RAMPSIDE (Lancs), 266
miles. No through fares. Departures *from* London as for Barrow-
in-Furness. Departures *for* London about 5 times daily. Pop. 439.
Map Square 6.

RAMSBOTTOM (Lancs),
200¼ miles. Fares, 41/5a, 24/10c.
R. T. for two months, 82/10a,
49/8c. Departures *from* London as
for Bury. Departures *for* London
about 4 times daily Pop. 15,370.
Map Square 12.

RAMSEY (Hunts) from
King's Cross, 75¾ miles. Fares,
14/10a, 8/11c. R.T. for two months,
29/8a, 17/10c. Pop. 5,136.
Map Square 18.

KING'S †	RAMSEY	RAMSEY	KING'S †
AM 5. 5	7.59	AM 6.55	9.56
—	7.45	10.33	9. 5	11.15
—	10.12	1.54	9.48	1.25
PM 1.55	4.29	PM12.45	3.50
5. 0	6.52	3.35	6.25
5.10	8. 3	7.15	10.20

No Sunday Trains.

ANOTHER ROUTE (HIGH
STREET) from *Liverpool Street,* 83
miles. Fares as above.

L'PL ST.	RAMSEY	RAMSEY	L'PL. ST.
AM 5.50	9.32	AM 7.36r	10.23
—	8.30r	11.34	10. 0f	2. 7
—	11.50fr	2.35	10.26g	2. 7
PM 2.34	5.20	PM12.54flr4.	2k
—	—	12.54f	5. 9
—	—	3. 5r	6.10
—	—	5.35r	8.33

No Sunday Trains.

f Mondays only.
g Mondays excepted.
k Arrives at St. Pancras Station.
l Commencing July 23.
r Restaurant Car.

RAMSEY (Isle of Man).
Fares, 53/9 First and Saloon, 37/3
Third and Saloon, 32/3 Third and
Steerage. R. T. for two months,
102/6 First and Saloon, 69/6 Third
and Saloon, 62/0 Third and Steerage. *See* trains to Liverpool,
thence by boat to Douglas.
Map Square 6.

RAMSGATE (HARBOUR)
(Kent) from *Victoria, Holborn
Viaduct,* and *St. Paul's,* 79 miles.
Fares, 15/5a, 12/4b, 9/3c. R. T.
for two months, 30/10a, 24/8b.
Pop. 36,560.
Map Square 24.

VICT.	Leave		Arr. at
(S.E.&C.)	HOL. V.	ST. PL.'s	RAMSG.
AM —	3.50k	—	7. 5
5. 5	4.57	5. 0	8.56
5.48f	5.40f	5.42f	8.56
8.25d	—	—	10.40
9. 0	—	—	10.55
9.20	—	—	11.55
10.10	—	—	12.10
10.25d	—	—	12.33
10.40	—	—	1. 8
11.30l	—	—	1.48
PM12.30d	—	—	2.29
12.40d	—	—	2.42
1. 5d	—	—	3.14
1.23d	—	—	4. 8
1.25e	—	—	3.23
2.20d	—	—	4.30
2. 8e	—	—	4.50
2.45d	—	—	4.58
3.15e	—	—	5. 6
3.15d	—	—	5.15
3.20e	—	—	5.45
3.2:d	—	—	5.54
4.15d	—	—	6.53
—	5. 5e	—	7. 0
5.10d	—	—	7.35
—	5.10e	5.12e	7.45
5.30e	—	—	8.35
5.30d	—	—	8.36
7. 0	—	—	9.16
8.30	—	—	10.49
12. 0h	—	—	2.22
12. 5d	—	—	2.12

Sunday Trains.

AM 7.20	—	—	10.17
9. 0	—	—	10.53
9.10	—	—	11.25
10.15v	—	—	12. 2
10.20	—	—	12.14
10.40	—	—	1. 0
PM 3.20	—	—	5.45
3.30	—	—	6.56
8.25	—	—	10.59

Trains from Ramsgate
(Harbour).

Leave		Arrive at	
RAMSG.	ST. PL.'s	HOL. V.	VICT.
AM 6.35	9.37	9.39	—
8.45	—	—	10.40
9. 0h	—	—	11.25
9.40	—	—	11.55
10. 0	—	—	12. 7
11. 0d	—	—	1.40
11.35d	—	—	2.15
11.35	—	—	2.43
PM 1. 0	—	—	3.23
1.25e	4.46	—	4.39
2. 0l	—	—	4. 5
l3. 0p	—	—	5. 3
3. 0s	—	—	5. 3
5. 0	—	—	6.58
5.50	—	—	7.54
6. 5	9.51	9.53	9.46
7.30	—	—	10.25

RAMSGATE (HARBOUR)— continued.

Sunday Trains.

Leave RAMSG.	ST. PL.'S	Arrive at HOL. V.	VICT.
AM 9.15	—	11.58	11.51
PM 2.15	—	—	4.42
2.30	—	—	5.32
4.15	—	—	6.24
5. 5	—	—	7. 7
5.40	—	—	7.40
6.20	—	—	8.30
7. 5v	—	—	8.50
7.20	—	—	9.27
8.55	—	—	11. 5

d Saturdays only.
e Saturdays excepted.
f Mondays only.
h Wednesdays only.
k Third Class only.
l Mondays, Fridays and Saturdays only.
p Pullman car attached.
s Mondays, Fridays, and Saturdays excepted.
v 1st Class Pullman cars only.

ANOTHER ROUTE (HAR-BOUR) from *Charing Cross, Cannon Street, London Bridge,* 78 miles. Fares as above.

CHAR. +	CAN. ST.	LON. B.	Arr. at RAMSG.
AM —	—	3.57h	7. 5
—	7.16	7.19	10.22
PM —	12.50d	12.53d	2.57
—	1.20d	1.23d	3.30
—	4.12e	4.15e	6.35
—	6.12e	—	8. 8

No Sunday Trains.

Trains from Ramsgate (Harbour).

Leave RAMSG.	LON. B.	Arrive at CAN. ST.	CHAR. +
AM 6.35	8.32	8.36	—
7. 5	9.15	9.19	—
7.40g	9.28	9.32	—
7.40f	9.32	9.36	—

No Sunday Trains.

d Saturdays only.
e Saturdays excepted.
f Mondays only.
g Mondays excepted.
h Third Class only.

RAMSGATE (TOWN)

from *Charing Cross, Cannon Street,* and *London Bridge,* 87 miles. Fares as above.

CHAR. +	CAN. ST.	LON. B.	Arr. at RAMSG.
AM —	5.20	5.25	9.36
—	—	7.50l	10.47
9.15	—	9.23	12. 1
—	—	k10.30l	12.40
11. 0	—	11. 7	2. 6
PM 1. 0d	—	—	2.58
1. 0	—	—	3.31
3. 0	—	3. 8	5.43
4.30	—	4.37	7.11
5.15e	5.12e	—	7.56
5.20d	—	5.26d	7.56
5.24d	—	5.34d	8.18
6. 0e	—	6. 5e	8.18
7.18	—	7.26	10.30

Sunday Trains.

Leave		Arr. at RAMSG.
AM 7.45	—	7.52	10.58
9.35h	—	—	12.29
PM 5.15h	—	—	8.46
7.35	—	7.45	10.31
9.25	—	9.31	12.36

RAMSGATE (TOWN)— continued.

Trains from Ramsgate (Town).

Leave RAMSG.	LON. B.	Arrive at CAN. ST.	CHAR. +
AM 6.21	9.32	9.36	—
7. 8	10. 0	10. 4	—
e7. 8h	—	—	10.16h
8.13	10.54	—	11. 3
8.55	11.43	—	11.57
10.28	1.36	—	1.50
PM12. 3	3.26	—	3.40
1.19k	4. 8	—	—
2.34h	—	—	5.42h
2.34	5.50	—	6. 3
4.28	7.25	7.30	7.49
7.25	10.22	—	10.35
10.13yl	—	1.20	—

Sunday Trains.

Leave		Arrive at
AM 6.29	10. 5	—	10.15
8.50	—	—	1. 5h
PM 4.20	7. 9	—	7.17
5.47	8.30	—	8.40
7.40	10.16	—	10.26
10.14y	—	1.23	—

d Saturdays only.
e Saturdays excepted.
h Departs from or arrives at Victoria (S.E. & C.R.).
k Mondays, Fridays and Saturdays only.
l Low Level platform.
y Third Class only.

ANOTHER ROUTE *via* Greenwich Pier and North Woolwich Pier, by Water ("Golden Eagle"). Fares from *Fenchurch Street,* 8/0*a,* 7/0*c.* R. T. for 15 days, 13/0*a,* 11/6*c.*

	Leave		Arr. at
G. PIER.	FEN. ST.	N. W. PIER.	RAMSG.
AM 8.55	9.25	9.25	2.10

SERVICE FROM RAMSGATE.

Leave			Arrive at
RAMSG.	N. W. PIER.	FEN. ST.	G. PIER.
PM 2.20	7.30	7.36	7.45

Sunday Service.

20 minutes later at each point.
See advt. back of Map.

Granville Hotel, overlooking Sea. Within easy distance of the classic Golf Links. Magnificent New Ballroom. Turkish and Electrical Baths and Treatment. Swimming Bath. Hard Tennis Courts (En-Tout-Cas). Garage. Terms on application to the Manager. Telephone, Ramsgate 12. Telegrams, "Granville, Ramsgate."
See advt. p. 283.

Royal Hotel. Old established Family Hotel, overlooking Harbour. Easy reach of Golf Links. Telephone 286 Ramsgate. And at Richmond. ARTHUR HOWITT.
See advt. p. 284.

Hotel Sanclu. First - class Hotel. Facing Sea. Excellent Cuisine. 'Phone, 80 Ramsgate.
See advt. p. 284.

Stroud's Royal Oak Hotel. Family and Commercial. Facing Harbour. Stock Rooms. Special Tariff for Anglers. Tel. 306.
A. WINKEL, Propr.
See advt. p. 282.

Westbourne Private Hotel and Boarding Establishment, West Cliff Promenade. En Pension. Commands magnificent Sea Views. Tariff on application.

RAMSGATE (TOWN)— continued.

"Kenmure" Boarding Establishment. Beautifully situated. Facing Sea in Wellington Crescent. Established 27 years. Separate Tables. Tariff on application. Miss LOCKITT.

Moore's Boarding Establishment, 31, Augusta Road. Excellent position on East Cliff. Good cooking. Home comforts. Separate tables. Tariff on application.

Aberdeen House. Private Boarding House. Large Rooms. Hard Tennis Court. Golf Links within easy reach. Apply—
CAPTAIN LANCHESTER.

Wellington House, Wellington Crescent. Superior Boarding Establishment. Charmingly situated; centre of Promenade, overlooking Sea. Bandstand. Separate tables. Tariff on application.
MRS. H. W. NEAVES.

House Agency and Auction Offices. SCARLETT & GOLDSACK, 36, High Street, and at Margate. Furnished or Unfurnished Houses to be Let or Sold.—Surveys.

RAMSGILL (Yorks), 219 miles. No through fares. Departures *from* London as for Pateley Bridge. Departures *for* London about 4 times daily. Pop. 324.
Map Square 7.

RANKINSTON (Ayr), 384½ miles. No through fares. Departures *from* London as for Ayr. Departures *for* London about 3 times daily.
Map Square 43.

RANNOCH (Perth), 490 miles. Fares, 97/3*a,* 58/4*c.* R. T. for two months, 194/6*a,* 116/8*c.* Departures *from* London as for Fort William. Departures *for* London about 3 times daily. Pop. 87.
Map Square 37.

RANSKILL (Notts) from *King's Cross,* 144 miles. Fares, 29/10*a,* 17/11*c.* R. T., double fare. Departures *from* London as for Retford. Departures *for* London about 4 times daily. Pop. 465.
Map Square 13.

RASKELF (Yorks), 201 miles. No through fares. Departures *from* London as for York. Departures *for* London about 4 times daily. Pop. 478.
Map Square 8.

RATBY (Leicester), 105½ miles. Fares, 22/3*a,* 13/4*c.* R. T., double fare. Departures *from* London as for Desford. Departures *for* London about 3 times daily. Pop. 2,112.
Map Square 18.

RATHEN (Aberdeen), 567½ miles. No through fares. Departures *from* London as for Fraserburgh. Departures *for* London about 3 times daily. Pop. 2,677.
Map Sq uare 35.

RATHO (Midlothian), 400½ miles. No through fares. Departures *from* London as for Edinburgh (Waverley). Departures *for* London about 4 times daily. Pop. 1,751.
Map Square 41.

RAUCEBY (Lincoln) from *King's Cross*, 118¼ miles. Fares, 23/2*a*, 13/11*c*. R. T., double fare. Departures *from* London as for Sleaford. Departures *for* London about 6 times daily. Pop. 683.
Map Square 13.

RAUNDS (Northampton) from *St. Pancras*, 81¾ miles. Fares, 14/9*a*, 8/10*c*. R. T., double fare. Pop. 3,762.
Map Square 18.

St. Pan.	Raunds	Raunds	St. Pan.
AM 4.25	9. 5	AM 8.42*r*	11. 0
8.25*r*	11. 6	PM12.56	3.25
11.35	2.50	4. 0	7. 3
PM 6.25*r*	8.34	6. 8	8.22

No Sunday Trains.
r Restaurant Car.

RAVENGLASS (Cumberland), 286¾ miles. Fares, 59/7*a*, 35/9*c*. R. T. for two months, 119/2*a*, 71/6*c*. Departures *from* London as for Millom. Departures *for* London about 5 times daily.
Map Square 6.

RAVENSBOURNE (London) from *Victoria, Holborn Viaduct, Ludgate Hill*, and *St. Paul's*, 10¾ miles. Fares, 1/6*a*, 1/2*b*, 0/10½*c*. R. T. for two days, 2/11*a*, 2/0*b*, 1/9*c*. *See* pp. 562-563.
Map Square 80.

RAVENSCAR (Yorks) from *King's Cross*, 239¾ miles. Fares, 50/2*a*, 30/1*c*. R. T. for two months, 100/4*a*, 60/2*c*.
Map Square 8.

King's +	R'scar.	R'scar.	King's +
AM 4.45	12.39	AM 9.10*r*	4.30
7.15*r*	3. 5	10.19*r*	4.45
10. 0*r*	4.29	11.34*r*	6.30
11.30	7.34	PM 3. 8*r*	10. 0
PM11.25*e*	8.37	6.54	3.25
—	—	8.54	5.40

Sunday Trains.

PM11.25	8.37	—	—

e Saturdays excepted.
r Restaurant Car.

RAVENSCOURT PARK from *Mansion House*, 7 miles. Also to and from Ealing, Hounslow, and Richmond. *See* p. 489.
Map Square 68.

RAVENSCRAIG (Renfrew), 425 miles. No through fares. Departures *from* London as for Wemyss Bay. Departures *for* London about 3 times daily.
Map Square 40.

RAVENSTHORPE (Yorks), 182¾ miles. Fares, 38/4*a*, 23/0*c*. R. T., double fares. Departures *from* London as for Thornhill (Yorks) or Huddersfield. Departures *for* London about 4 times daily. Pop. 6,376.

RAVENSTONEDALE (Westmorland), 268¾ miles. Fares, 52/3*a*, 31/4*c*. R. T., double fare. Departures *from* London as for Tebay. Departures *for* London about 4 times daily. Pop. 844.
Map Square 7.

RAWCLIFFE (Yorks), 177 miles. Fares, 35/7*a*, 21/4*c*. R. T., double fare. Departures *from* London as for Knottingley or Goole. Departures *for* London about 6 times daily. Pop. 2,300.
Map Square 13.

RAWTENSTALL (Lancs) from *Euston*, 202 miles. Fares, 41/10*a*, 25/1*c*. R.T. for two months, 83/8*a*, 50/2*c*. Departures *from* London as for Bacup. Departures *for* London about 4 times daily. Pop. 28,381.
Map Square 12.

RAWYARDS (Lanark), 424¾ miles. No through fares. Departures *from* London as for Edinburgh (Waverley). Departures *for* London about 4 times daily.

RAYDON WOOD (Suffolk) from *Liverpool Street*, 68¼ miles. Fares, 14/5*a*, 8/8*c*. R. T. for two months, 28/10*a*. Departures *from* London as for Hadleigh. Departures *for* London about 6 times daily. Pop. (Raydon) 492.
Map Square 19.

RAYLEIGH (Essex) from *Liverpool Street*, 33¼ miles. Fares, 5/5*a*, 3/3*c*. R. T. for two months, 10/10*a*. Pop. 3,125.
Map Square 24.

L'pl. St.	Rayl'gh	Rayl'gh	L'pl. St.
AM 5.26	6.58	AM 6.36	7.35
6.50	8.26	7.12	8.23
7.48	9.34	7.39	8.45
9. 6	10.38	8. 7	9.14
10.30	11.48	9. 2	9.50
11.56	1. 9	10. 8	11. 7
PM12.48*d*	1.50	10.30*h*	11.59
1.20*d*	2.10	10.39*k*	11.59
1.50*d*	2.52	11.55*e*	1.16
2. 0*e*	3.13	11.58*d*	1.16
2.20*e*	3.47	PM12.24*e*	1.25
2.30*d*	3.25	1.38	3. 5
2.58*d*	3.51	3.37*e*	4.51
3.26	4.44	3.41*d*	4.56
4.18	5.25	5. 4	6. 8
4.48*e*	5.43	5.47	6.52
5.39	6.38	7. 9	8.22
6. 5*e*	7. 4	7.51	9.10
6.26*e*	7.21	8.30	9.50
6.26*d*	7.38	8.50	9.56
7.10*e*	7.57	10.19	11.30
7.16*e*	8.19	—	—
8. 2*d*	9. 5	—	—
8. 2*e*	9. 8	—	—
8.45	9.45	—	—
9.45*d*	10.42	—	—
9.45*e*	10.51	—	—
11. 0	12.11	—	—
12. 0*m*	1. 6	—	—
—	—	—	—
—	—	—	—
—	—	—	—

Sunday Trains.

L'pl. St.	Rayl'gh	Rayl'gh	L'pl. St.
AM 8.30	9.38	AM 8.19	10.25
8.45	10.18	9.29	10.50
9.30	10.54	10.45	12.40
10.45	12.14	PM 1.47	3.15
PM 2.30	4. 4	4. 5	5.15
6. 0	7. 8	6.25	7.44
6.42	8. 5	6.52	7.58
8.46	10. 9	7.24	8.45
10.10	11.26	8.30	9.48
—	—	9. 1	10.45

d Saturdays only.
e Saturdays excepted.
h Fridays only.
k Fridays excepted.
m Midnight.

RAYNE (Essex) from *Liverpool Street*, 46¾ miles. Fares, 9/10*a*, 5/11*c*. R. T. for two months, 19/8*a*. Departures *from* London as for Felstead. Departures *for* London about 6 times daily. Pop. 361.
Map Square 19.

RAYNER'S LANE from *Baker Street*, 11 miles. Fares, 2/2½*a*, 1/4½*c*. R. T. for two days, 3/6*a*, 2/4*c*. Departures *from* London as for Uxbridge. Departures *for* London about 14 minutes later.
Map Square 48.

ANOTHER ROUTE from *Mansion House*, 16¾ miles, *via* Acton Town and South Harrow. *See* p. 489.

RAYNES PARK (Surrey) from *Waterloo*, 8¾ miles. Fares, 1/6*a*, 0/10½*c*. R. T. for two days, 3/0*a*, 1/9*c*. Pop. 5,812. *See* pp. 583-585, 591-594.
Map Squares 23 *and* 77.

RAYNHAM PARK (Norfolk) from *King's Cross*, 131¼ miles. Fares, 23/7*a*, 14/2*c*. R. T. for two months, 47/2*a*, 28/4*c*. Departures *from* London as for Massingham. Departures *for* London about 4 times daily.
Map Square 19.

READING (Berks) from *Paddington*, 36 miles. Fares, 7/6*a*, 4/6*c*. R. T. for two months, 15/0*a*. Pop. 92,274.
Map Square 23.

Pad.	Reading	Reading	Pad.
AM 1. 0*g*	1.45	AM 2. 0*g*	2.45
5.30	6.14	2.30*f*	3.15
6.30	7.35	2.48	3.30
7.30	8.15	6.20	7.10
7.35	9.23	7.14	8.20
8.45*r*	9.26	7.32	8.28
8.50	9.36	8. 0	8.56
9. 0	9.46	8.20	9. 0
9.30	10.12	8.47	9.30
9.45	10.31	9.19	10. 0
9.55	11.14	10. 0	10.45
10.45	11.33	10.12	10.57
11.20	12.11	10.20	11.35
11.25	12.52	11.15	12. 0
PM12.30	1.13	PM12.12	12.55
1.10*r*	1.55	12.20	1.46
1.35*r*	2.17	1. 6	1.50
1.50*d*	3. 0	1.48	2.30
2.45	3.27	2. 0	2.50
3.15	3.55	2.39	3.20
3.18	4.18	3. 5	3.50
3.38	4.53	3.53	4.35
4. 7	5.15	4.20	5. 6
5. 0	5.41	4.30	5.37
5. 5	5.48	5. 8	5.50
5.15	6. 5	5.22	6. 2
5.40	6.30	5.38	6.55
6. 5	6.47	6.33	7.20
6.30	7.10	7.40	8.20
6.55	7.42	8. 0	8.45
7.30	8.10	8.30	9.15
8. 0	8.40	9.36	10.25
8. 5	9.10	10. 3	10.45
8.35	9.56	10.20	12. 0
9.15	10. 5	—	—
10. 0	10.43	—	—
10.40	12. 5	—	—
11.20	12.16	—	—
12. 0*k*	12.45	—	—
12.15	1. 0	—	—
12.30*l*	1.17	—	—

Sunday Trains.

Pad.	Reading	Reading	Pad.
AM 1. 0	1.45	AM 2. 0	2.45
9.10	10. 3	2.48	3.30
10.35	11.17	6.20	7. 5
11. 0	12. 5	8.58	10.14
11.45	12.42	9.40	10.50
PM 1.45	2.57	11.30	1. 5
2. 0	3.34	PM 1.55	2.40
2.35	3.50	2.48	3.35
4.10	4.56	4.52	6. 0
4.45	6.15	5.35	6.20
5.15	6.25	6. 5	7.37
6. 5	7.37	7.12	8.20
7.40	9. 9	8.22	9.15
8.30	9.46	9. 5	9.48
9.15	10. 5	9.19	10. 0
10. 0	10.43	10.10	11.38
—	—	—	—

d Saturdays only.
f Mondays only.
g Mondays excepted.
k Saturdays midnight excepted.
l Saturday nights only.
r Restaurant Car.

READING—*continued.*

ANOTHER ROUTE from
Waterloo, 43½ miles. Fares, 7/6*a*, 4/6*c*. R. T. for two months, 15/0*a*, 9/0*c*.

W'LOO	READING	READING	W'LOO.
AM 5.10	7.20	AM 6.37	8.17
6.54	8.50	7.33	9.17
7.54	9.44	8.45	10.17
9.54	11.40	9.42	11.17
10.54	12.44	10.46	12.31
PM12.48	2.27	PM12.46	2.27
1.48	3.24	1.46	3.27
2.48	4.25	3.46	5.27
3.48*e*	5.24	4.46	6.27
3.48*d*	5.29	5.46	7.27
4.48*e*	6.17	6.46	8.27
4.48*d*	6.29	7.46	9.27
5.48	7.22	8.58	10.37
6.48	8.23	10.15*e*	12. 5
7.54	9.40	10.15*d*	12. 8
10.24	12. 6	—	—

Sunday Trains.

AM 8.18	10. 9	AM 8.20	10.30
PM12.18	2. 6	PM12.18	2. 3
4.18	6. 3	5.43	7.28
5.58	7.45	7.39	9.28
9.18	11. 7	8.47	10.28

d Saturdays only.
e Saturdays excepted.

Salter's Steamers (Caversham Lock, ten minutes from Station). Up Stream—10.50 a.m., 4.25 p.m. Down Stream—11.45 a.m., 5.25 p.m. *See advt.* facing first page of train service.

Great Western. Adjoining Stations. Three minutes from Thames. Refurnished and Redecorated. Electric light throughout. Telephone, 785 Reading. Garage 35 cars.

George Hotel. Central, quiet. Commercial. Good Stock-rooms. Hotel Porter meets trains. Covered yard, Garage, Stabling, Cycle House. Tel., 708. Managing Director, Miss E. NASH.

The Ship Hotel. Family and Commercial. Public Lounge, Spacious Lounge for Residents. Large Dining, Stock-rooms. Garage. Telephone 1029. Special Terms for Week-End.

Mansfield House Residential Hotel, Kendrick Road. Recently enlarged by acquisition of adjoining premises and spacious grounds, including Tennis, etc., Lawns. Station, Town, College and River readily accessible. Garage near by. Telephone 597.

READING WEST (Berks)
from *Paddington*, 37 miles. Fares, 7/9*a*, 4/8*c*. R. T. for two months, 15/6*a*. Departures *from* London as for Reading. Departures *for* London about 8 times daily.

REARSBY (Leicester),
107 miles. Fares, 1/8*a*, 13/0*c*. R.T., double fare. Departures *from* London as for Asfordby. Departures *for* London about 6 times daily. Pop. 409.
Map Square 18.

RECTORY ROAD (London) from *Liverpool Street*, 3¾ miles. Fares, 0/7½*a*, 0/6*b*, 0/4½*c*. R.T. for two days, 1/2*a*, 0/10½*b*, 0/7*c*. *See* pp. 534-536.
Map Square 52.

REDBOURN (Herts)
from *St. Pancras*, 28 miles. Fares, 5/8*a*, 3/5*c*. R. T. for two months, 11/4*a*, 6/10*c*. Departures as for Hemel Hempstead. Departures *for* London about 8 times daily. Pop. 1,987.
Map Square 22.

REDBRIDGE (Hants) from
Waterloo, 81½ miles. Fares, 17/1*a*, 10/3*c*. R. T. for two months, 34/2*a*, 20/6*c*.
Map Square 23.

W'LOO.	REDB'GE	REDB'GE	W'LOO.
AM 5.40	8.22	AM 7.58*r*	10. 6
5.50	9.18	9. 1*s*	11. 0
8.30*s*	10.57	9.55	12.22
10.30	12.28	10.28*r*	12.50
11.30	1.56	11.58*r*	2.20
PM12.30*r*	2.38	PM12.52	2.50
1.30*s*	3.46	1.51	4.20
2.30	4.35	3.48*s*	6.26
3.30*s*	5.57	4.55	6.58
4.30*r*	6.29	5.46*r*	8.20
6.30*r*	8.24	6.47*r*	8.50
7.30	9.47	8.10	10.50
8. 0	11. 1	8.33	11.28
—	—	10. 3	3.58
—	—	—	—
—	—	—	—
—	—	—	—
—	—	—	—
—	—	—	—
—	—	—	—

Sunday Trains.

AM11. 0*r*	1.27	AM 8.56	12.11
PM 2. 0*r*	4.31	10. 7*r*	2.27
—	—	PM 3.15*r*	6. 7
—	—	5.28	8. 3
—	—	7.20*r*	9.31
—	—	8.55	3.58
—	—	—	—
—	—	—	—
—	—	—	—
—	—	—	—
—	—	—	—
—	—	—	—
—	—	—	—

r Restaurant Car.
s Refreshments served.

REDBROOK (Monmouth)
from *Paddington*, 147¼ miles. Fares, 31/11*a*, 19/2*c*. R. T. for two months, 63/10*a*. Departures *from* London as for St. Briavels. Departures *for* London about 4 times daily.
Map Square 22.

REDCAR (Yorks) from
King's Cross, 246¼ miles. Fares, 51/5 , 30/10*c*. R. T. for two months, 102/10*a*, 61/8*c*. Pop. 16,399.
Map Square 8.

KING'S+	REDCAR	REDCAR	KING'S+
AM 4.45	12.18	AM 5.18	1. 5
7.15*r*	3. 4	7. 3*r*	1.15
10. 0*r*	3.57	8.42*g*	3.15
10.10*r*	5.14	9.26*r*	4.30
11.50*r*	5.29	PM12. 6*r*	6.15
PM 1.15*r*	7.17	2.24*r*	9.25
1.50*r*	8.32	4. 4*r*	10. 0
5.35*r*	11.17	7.55	3.25
11.25*e*	6.36	10.43*e*	5.40
11.25*d*	8. 5	10.43*d*	6. 0
—	—	—	—

Sunday Trains.

AM11.30*r*	9.38	AM 9.18	5.15
PM11.25	6.36	PM 9.15	5.40
—	—	—	—
—	—	—	—

d Saturdays only.
e Saturdays excepted.
g 1st and 3rd Class Pullman Cars only.
r Restaurant Car.

REDCASTLE (Ross), 584½
miles. Fares, 106/3*a*, 63/9*c*. R. T. for two months, 212/6*a*, 127/6*c*. Departures *from* London as for Inverness. Departures *for* London about twice daily.
Map Square 34.

REDDISH (Lancs) from
Euston, 179½ miles. Fares, 37/9*a*, 22/8*c*. R.T., double fare. Departures *from* London as for Stockport. Departures *for* London about 12 times daily. Pop. 14,252.
Map Square 12.

REDDITCH (Worcester)
from *Euston*, 128½ miles. Fares, 23/7*a*, 14/2*c*. R. T. for two months, 47/2*a*, 28/4*c*. Pop. 16,235.
Map Square 17.

EUSTON	R'DITCH	R'DITCH	EUSTON
AM 2.50	7.19	AM 7.25*r*	10.40
5. 0	9.16	8.48	12.40
8.30*dr*12. 2		10. 7*r*	1.25
9.10*cr*12. 2		11.33*s*	3. 0
9.15*r*	1. 5	PM 1.58*r*	5.35
11.30*r*	3.47	3.20*r*	6.50
PM 1.15*r*	5. 8	4.40*r*	8.20
2.20*t*	5.45	5.55*dr*10.45	
4.35*r*	8. 9	6.55*er*10.20	
6.55*er*	9.50	10. 2*e*	4. 0
7. 0*r*	10.46	10. 2*d*	5. 0
—	—	—	—
—	—	—	—
—	—	—	—
—	—	—	—

Sunday Trains.

PM 1. 0	6.37	AM10.49	5. 5
—	—	PM 8.24	5. 0
—	—	—	—

d Saturdays only.
e Saturdays excepted.
r Restaurant Car.
t Tea Car.

REDHILL (Surrey) from

London Bridge, Victoria, and *Clapham Junction,* 20¾ miles. Fares, 4/2*a*, 2/6*c*. R. T. for eight days, 8/4*a*, 4/10*c*. Pop. 17,998.
Map Square 23.

| | Leave | | Arr. at |
	Vict.	Clap. J.	Lon. B.	R'dhill
AM —	—	—	5.18	6.15
6.37	6.44	6.40	7.21
7.23	7.29	7.25	8.21
8.25	8.32	8. 7	9.13
9. 0	9. 8	9. 6	9.48
9.45	9.51	9.50	10.41
10.35	10.42	10.35	11.22
—	—	11.50	12.32
12. 0	12. 7	12.10	12.50
PM 2. 0	2. 7	2. 5	2.51
—	—	4. 0	4.34
5. 5	5.12	5.10	5.54
6. 6	6.12	6. 8	6.58
6.50	6.57	7. 0	7.42
7.15	7.22	7.20	8. 8
9. 3	9.10	9.12	9.54
10.30	10.38	10.35	11.22

Sunday Trains.

AM 6.55	7. 2	7. 2	8. 5
—	—	7.22	8.15
8.18	8.25	8.25	9.10
8.50	8.57	8.55	9.48
11.15	11.22	—	11.56
PM 1.14	1.21	1.10	2. 1
5.50	5.57	6. 0	6.51
6.33	6.40	6.33	7.26
8. 0	8. 8	8. 0	8.57
9. 5	9.13	9.10	10. 0

Trains from Redhill.

| Leave | Arrive at | | |
Redhill	Lon. B.	Clap. J.	Vict.
AM 7.25	8.15	8.15	8.24
8. 7	8.46	9. 0	9. 8
9. 4	9.42	—	9.58
10. 1	10.38	10.29	10.36
11.23	12.13	11.59	12. 7
11.40	12.19	—	12.17
PM12.55	1.42	1.39	1.49
1.40	2.22	2.13	2.22
3.37	—	4. 9	4.17
5. 5	5.54	5.47	5.55
5.56	6.36	6.26	6.34
7.56	8.46	8.39	8.48
9.38	10.25	10. 9	10.17
10. 4	10.58	11.10	11.17
12.14	12.59	12.50	1. 0

REDHILL—continued.

Sunday Trains.

| Leave | | Arrive at | |
Redhill	Lon. B.	Clap. J.	Vict.
AM 9.32	10.18	10.23	10.32
9.54	10.45	10.42	10.50
PM 4.15	5. 3	5. 1	5.11
7. 8	7.56	—	—
7.47	8.34	8.31	8.41
8.29	9.17	9. 4	9.13
8.43	9.32	9.24	9.34
10.49	11.34	11.34	11.42
11.43	12.27	—	—

ANOTHER ROUTE from

Charing Cross, Cannon Street, and *London Bridge* 22½ miles. Fares, 4/2*a*, 3/4*b*, 2/6*c*. R.T. for eight days, 8/4*a*, 6/8*b*, 4/10*c*.

| | Leave | | Arr. at |
Char. +	Can. St.	Lon. B.	R'dhill
AM —	4.44	5. 0	5.51
—	—	7.50*l*	8.37
—	—	9.33*l*	10.18
—	—	10. 31*h*	10.45
10.55	—	11. 3	11.58
PM —	12.55*d*	12.58*d*	1.37
12.55	—	1. 4	1.55
—	1.24*d*	1.27*d*	2.18
—	—	1.30*el*	2.18
2. 3*e*	2. 8*d*	2.10	3. 1
—	—	2.22*dl*	3.14
2.35*d*	—	2.41*d*	3.26
3.15	—	3.21	4.14
—	4.20*e*	4.23*e*	4.55
4.22*d*	—	4.28*d*	5.17
—	4.24*e*	4.28*e*	5.15
—	5.20*e*	5.23*e*	5.59
—	5.24*e*	5.27*e*	6. 7
5.42*d*	—	5.48*d*	6.32
—	6. 0*e*	6. 3*e*	6.43
6.27*e*	—	6.34*e*	7.15
—	6.36*e*	6.39*e*	7.27
6.34*d*	—	6.40*d*	7.30
7.24*d*	7.28*e*	7.30	8.20
8.28	—	8.36	9.26
9.25	—	9.31	10.23
10.17	—	10.23	11.12
11.27	—	—	12. 8
12. 0*k*	—	—	12.40

Sunday Trains.

AM 6.25	—	6.32	7.30
10. 5	—	10.11	10.55
10.20	—	10.28	11.18
PM 1.30	—	1.37	2.26
5.25	—	5.32	6.24
8.38	—	8.45	9.34
9.40	—	9.47	10.30

REDHILL—continued.

Trains from Redhill.

| Leave | | Arrive at | |
Redhill	Lon. B.	Can. St.	Char. +
AM 6.36	7.18	—	7.30
7.43	8.24	8.28	—
8.19	8.56	—	—
8.49	9.28	9.32	—
9.38	10.10	—	10.20
9.48	10.27	10.32	—
9.56*k*	10.31	—	10.43
10.22	11. 0	—	—
11. 1	11.46	—	11.59
12. 1	12.50	—	1. 0
PM 1.54	2.38	—	2.46 +
2.45	3.28*e*	—	3.42*d*
3.22*h*	4. 8	—	—
4. 9	5. 2	—	5.14
4.45*e*	5.28	—	—
5.14	5.56	—	—
6.37	7.20	—	7.29
8.19	9. 2	—	9.15
9.20	10. 3	—	10.13
11.14	11.57	—	12.10
12.43*s*	—		1.20	—

Sunday Trains.

AM 7.31	8.16	—	8.27
10.31	11.15	—	11.25
PM 3.50	4.33	—	4.42
6.29	7.13	—	7.25
9.15	9.52	—	—
9.25	10.11	—	10.23
12.46	—	1.23	—

d Saturdays only.
e Saturdays excepted.
h Mondays, Fridays and Saturdays only.
k Wednesdays only.
l Low Level Platform.
s Third class only.

Laker's Hotel. Family and Commercial. Opposite Station. Large garden; good stabling; carriages; motor car accommodation. Telephone 43. Luncheons and every accommodation.

Warwick Hotel. Family and Commercial. 3 minutes from Station. Stabling. Garage. A. A. & M. U. 'Phone, 381 Redhill. Proprietor, HARRY MIDDLETON.

South Eastern Hotel, close to Station. Lately re-built. Central Heating. Good Cuisine. Telephone 324.
CATERING HOUSES, LTD.

Rees, Leonard P., Auctioneer, Estate Agent and Surveyor, Station Road. Established 1852. Sanitary surveys personally conducted. Register of Properties. Telephone No. "Redhill 4."

REDLAND (Glo'ster) from

Paddington, 117¾ miles. Fares, 24/10*a*, 14/11*c*. R.T. for two months, 49/8*a*. Departures *from* London as for Avonmouth Docks. Departures *for* London about 9 times daily.

REDMILE (Leicester), 115¾

miles. Fares, 23/2*a*, 13/11*c*. R. T. for two months, 46/4*a*, 27/10*c*. Departures *from* London as for Hallaton or Bottesford. Departures *for* London about 4 times daily. Pop. 392.
Map Square 13.

REDMIRE (Yorks), 239¾

miles. Fares, 50/0*a*, 30/0*c*. R.T., double fare. Departures *from* London as for Leyburn. Departures *for* London about 5 times daily. Pop. 248.
Map Square 7.

REDNAL (Salop) from

Paddington, 166 miles. Fares, 34/7*a*, 20/9*c*. R.T. for two months, 69/2*a*. Departures *from* London as for Baschurch. Departures *for* London about 4 times daily.
Map Square 17.

RED ROCK (Lancs), 197

miles. Fares, 41/1*a*, 24/8*c*. R. T. for two months, 82/2*a*, 49/4*c*. Departures *from* London as for Wigan. Departures *for* London about 5 times daily.
Map Square 12.

REDRUTH (Cornwall) from

Paddington, 288¾ miles. Fares, 59/9*a*, 35/10*c*. R. T. for two months, 119/6*a*, 71/8*c*. Pop. 9,920.
Map Square 25.

Pad.	Redr.	Redr.	Pad.
AM 5.30	2.48	AM 8.54*r*	4.35
10.30*r*	4.51	9.59*r*	4.45
11.10*r*	5.43	11.43*r*	6.50
PM 2. 0*r*	9.33	PM 12.56*r*	9. 0
10. 0	6.47	9.29	7.10
12. 0*h*	10.36	—	—
12.30*k*	11. 0	—	—

Sunday Trains.

AM 10.30*r*	5. 7	AM 11.22	7. 5
PM 10. 0	6.47	1. 2*r*	7.55
—	—	PM 5.21	3.15

h Saturdays midnight excepted.
k Saturdays midnight only.
r Restaurant Car.

RED WHARF BAY

(Anglesey), 254¾ miles. Fares, 53/1*a*, 31/10*c*. R.T. for two months, 106/2*a*, 63/8*c*. Departures *from* London as for Gaerwen. Departures *for* London about 4 times daily.
Map Square 11.

REEDHAM (Norfolk) from

Liverpool Street, via Ipswich and Trowse, 126¼ miles. Fares 24/9*a*, 14/10*c*. R.T. for two months, 49/6*a*. Pop. 825.
Map Square 19.

L'pl. St.	Reedh'm	Reedh'm	L'pl. St.
AM 5. 0	9.32	AM 6.58*f*	10.36
8.15*r*	12. 7	8. 1*r*	11.22
9.50*r*	1. 9	9.20	1.20
10.12	2.49	PM 1.10*r*	4.58
PM 12.33*r*	4.20	2.19	6.32
3.10*r*	6.15	3. 6	7.51
5.18*r*	10.17	5.49*r*	9.22

Sunday Trains.

AM 9.20*r*	2.31	PM 1.41*r*	9.10
PM 4.40	9.49	—	—

f Mondays only.
r Restaurant Car.

REEDHAM—*continued.*

ANOTHER ROUTE from

Liverpool Street, via Cambridge, 135¼ miles. Fares as above.

L'pl St.	Reedh'm	Reedh'm	L'pl St.
AM 5. 5	9.32	AM 6.58	11.27
5.50	11.20	8. 1	12.40
8.30*r*	1. 9	9.20*r*	2.21
11.50*r*	4.20	PM 1.10*r*	5.17
PM 2.34	6.53	3. 6*r*	8.22
5.49*r*	10.17	4.17*r*	8.33
10.12	2.41	9.36	2.50

Sunday Trains.

AM 9.25	2.31	PM 1.41	6.40
PM 3.25	8.15	9.36	3. 0
9.12	2.41	—	—

r Restaurant Car.

ANOTHER ROUTE *via*

Ipswich and Beccles, 118¾ miles. Fares as above.

L'pl. St.	Reedh'm	Reedh'm	L'pl. St.
AM 5. 0	9.19	AM 7.27*r*	11.22
8.15*r*	1. 1	9.42	1.20
10. 0	2.18	11.21	3.42
PM 1. 0	5.45	PM 2. 2	5.55
3.18*r*	7.39	2.55	7.51
4.55*r*	9.26	5.10*r*	9.22
—	—	6.16*r*	10. 0

No Sunday Trains.
r Restaurant Car.

REEDNESS (Yorks), 174

miles. No through fares. Departures *from* London as for Goole. Departures *for* London about 4 times daily. Pop. 453.
Map Square 13.

REEDSMOUTH (Northumberland).

302¼ miles. No through fares. Departures *from* London as for Hexham or Carlisle. Departures *for* London about 3 times daily.
Map Square 3.

REEPHAM (Lincoln),

134¾ miles. Fares, 27/11*a*, 16/9*c*. R. T., double fare. Departures *from* London as for Lincoln. Departures *for* London about 5 times daily. Pop. 370.
Map Square 13.

Station closed on Sundays.

REEPHAM (Norfolk) from

Liverpool Street, 136¾ miles. Fares, 23/7*a*, 14/2*c*. R T. for two months, 47/2*a*. Departures *from* London as for Aylsham. Departures *for* London about 6 times daily. Pop. 414.
Map Square 19.

REGENT'S PARK

(Bakerloo Tube) *See* back of Map.

REIGATE (Surrey) from

Charing Cross, Cannon Street, and *London Bridge,* 25 miles. Fares, 4/7*a*, 3/8*b*, 2/9*c*. R. T. for two months, 9/2*a*, 7/0*b*, 4/10*c*. Pop. 28,913.
Map Square 23.

Leave Char. +	Can. St.	Lon. B.	Arr. at Reigate
AM —	4.44	5. 0	6. 3
—	—	7.50*l*	8.56
—	—	9.33*l*	10.33
10.55	—	11. 3	12.15
PM —	12.55*d*	12.58*d*	1.42
12.55	—	1. 4	2. 9
—	1.24*d*	1.27*d*	2.25
2. 3*e*	2. 8*d*	2.10	3.12
—	—	2.22*dl*	3.21
3.15	—	3.21	4.24
—	4.20*e*	4.23*e*	5. 1
4.22*d*	—	4.28*d*	5.25
—	4.44*e*	4.48*e*	5.28
—	5.20*e*	5.23*e*	6. 5
—	5.24*e*	5.27*e*	6.13
5.42*d*	—	5.48*d*	6.42
—	6. 0*e*	6. 3*e*	6.49
6.27*e*	—	6.34*e*	7.21
—	6.36*e*	6.39*e*	7.35
6.34*d*	—	6.40*d*	7.37
7.24*d*	7.28*e*	7.30	8.31
8.28	—	8.36	9.39
10.17	—	10.23	11.18
11.27	—	—	12.14
12. 0*h*	—	—	12.46

Sunday Trains.

AM 6.25	—	6.32	7.40
10. 5	—	10.11	11. 1
10.20	—	10.28	11.26
PM 1.30	—	1.37	2.32
5.25	—	5.32	6.34
8.38	—	8.45	9.47

Trains from Reigate.

Leave Reigate	Arrive at Lon. B.	Can. St.	Char. +
AM 6.30	7.18	—	7.30
7.35	8.24	8.28	—
8.10	8.56	—	—
8.41	9.28	9.32	—
9.10	9.48	9.52	—
9.30	10.10	—	10.20
9.41	10.27	10.32	—
9.49*h*	10.31	—	10.43
10. 9	11. 0	—	—
10.50	11.46	—	11.59
11.48	12.50	—	1. 0
PM 1.40	2.38	—	2.46
2.49*d*	4. 8	—	—
3.52	5. 2	—	5.14
5. 4	5.56	—	—
6.22	7.20	—	7.29
8. 9	9. 2	—	9.15
9.10	10. 3	—	10.13
11. 4	11.57	—	12.10

Sunday Trains.

AM 7.19	8.16	—	8.27
10.21	11.15	—	11.25
PM 3.42	4.33	—	4.42
6.16	7.13	—	7.25
9. 3	9.52	—	—
9.15	10.11	—	10.24

d Saturdays only.
e Saturdays excepted.
h Wednesdays only.
l Low Level Platform.

For Advertisement list, see over.

REIGATE—*continued.*

White Hart Hotel. First-class family. Grounds three acres. Remarkable caves. Electric light. Table d'hote, separate tables. Stabling and posting. Tennis, bowls, croquet. Telephone, 184.
A. THOMSON, Proprietor.

Swan Hotel. Quiet, comfortable Family. Centre Town. Electric Light throughout. Moderate Tariff. Excellent Cuisine. Garage. 'Phone, 107. Proprietor, GRAHAM BALL.

RENFREW, 417¼ miles. Fares, 82/6*a*, 49/6*c*. R. T. for two months, 165/0*a*, 99/0*c*. Departures *from* London as for Paisley or Glasgow (St. Enoch). Departures *for* London about 4 times daily. Pop. 14,137.
Map Square 40.

RENTON (Dumbarton), 417¼ miles. Fares, 84/7*a*, 50/9*c*. R.T. for two months, 169/2*a*, 101/6*c*. Departures *from* London as for Dumbarton. Departures *for* London about 4 times daily. Pop. 4,996.
Map Square 40.

REPTON (Derby) from *St. Pancras*, 132¼ miles. Fares, 26/6*a*, 15/11*c*. R.T. for two months, 53/0*a*, 31/10*c*. Pop. 1,858.
Map Square 17.

St. Pan.	Repton	Repton	St. Pan.
AM 2.25	6.49	AM 6.59	10.45*r*
4.25	9.16	8. 2*r*	11.35*l*
8.25*r*	12. 5	9.14*r*	1.30
10.25*r*	1.34	10.57*r*	1.45
PM12.25*r*	3.48	11.55*r*	4.10
1.25*r*	4.58	PM 1.12*r*	4.20
2.25*r*	6.12	2.47*r*	5.45
4.25*r*	7.57	4.15*r*	7.57
6.25*r*	9.36*l*	5.52*r*	9.15
12. 0*d*	6.48	6.34*r*	10. 5
—	—	10.16	4.20
—	—	—	—
—	—	—	—
—	—	—	—
—	—	—	—
—	—	—	—
—	—	—	—
—	—	—	—

Sunday Trains.

AM11.15*r*	5.28	AM 6.48*l*	11.53
PM 3.15	8. 1	11. 8*r*	5. 2
—	—	PM 5.28*r*	9.52*l*
—	—	—	—
—	—	—	—
—	—	—	—
—	—	—	—

d Saturdays only.
l Via Burton and Ashby.
r Restaurant Car.

RESOLVEN (Glamorgan), 197 miles. Fares (*via* Neath), 39/9*a*, 23/10*c*. R.T. for two months, 79/6*a*. *Via* Pontypool Road, 38/7*a*, 23/2*c*. R.T. for two months, 77/2*a*, 46/4*c*. Departures *from* London as for Neath or Aberdare (*via* Pontypool Road). Departures *for* London about 5 times daily. Pop. 3,831.
Map Square 21.

RESTON (Berwick), 346 miles. Fares, 72/9*a*, 43/8*c*. R. T. for two months, 145/6*a*, 87/4*c*. Departures *from* London as for Berwick-on-Tweed. Departures *for* London about 4 times daily. Pop. 1,271.
Map Square 41.

RETFORD (Notts) from *King's Cross*, 138¼ miles. Fares, 28/11*a*, 17/4*c*. R. T., double fare. Pop. 13,412.
Map Square 13.

King's +	Retfd.	Retfd.	King's +
AM 4.45	7.46	AM 8.30*r*	11.30
5. 5	9.45	10.13	1. 5
7.15*r*	10. 3	PM12.29	3.50
8.45	12. 4	2.42	6.25
10.10*r*	1.23	2.59*r*	6.30
11.30	3.17	4.27*r*	7.10
PM 1.50*r*	4.39	5.23	9. 0
4. 0*r*	6.52	12.10	3.25
5.45*r*	8.50	—	—
8.25	11.44	—	—
—	—	—	—
—	—	—	—
—	—	—	—
—	—	—	—
—	—	—	—
—	—	—	—
—	—	—	—

Sunday Trains.

AM 8.30	1.25	PM12.29*r*	3.45
12. 0*r*	3.11	2.37*r*	5.55
PM 5. 0*r*	8.10	3. 4	8. 8
8.25	11.44	7. 7*r*	10.20
—	—	—	—
—	—	—	—
—	—	—	—
—	—	—	—
—	—	—	—
—	—	—	—
—	—	—	—

r Restaurant Car.

White Hart Hotel. First-Class. Motor Garage. Telephone 22. Telegrams: "White Hart, Retford."
G. P. WOOD, Proprietor.

RHAYADER (Radnor), 212 miles. Fares, 41/5*a*, 24/10*c*. R. T. for two months, 82/10*a*. Departures *from* London as for Llanidloes. Departures *for* London about 4 times daily. Pop. 961.
Map Square 16.

RHEIDOL FALLS (Cardigan), 248¾ miles. No through fares. Departures *from* London as for Aberystwyth. Departures *for* London about 3 times daily.
Map Square 16.

RHEWL (Flint), 213¾ miles. Fares, 40/7*a*, 24/4*c*. R. T. for two months, 81/2*a*, 48/8*c*. Departures *from* London as for Denbigh. Departures *for* London about 5 times daily.
Map Square 11.

RHIWDERIN (Monmouth), 145¼ miles. Fares, 30/3*a*, 18/2*c*. R. T. for two months, 60/6*a*, 36/4*c*. Departures *from* London as for Bargoed. Departures *for* London about 8 times daily.

RHIWFRON (Cardigan), 250¼ miles. No through fares. Departures *from* London as for Aberystwyth. Departures *for* London about 4 times daily.

RHOOSE (Glamorgan), 164¾ miles. Fares, 34/5*a*, 20/8*c*. R. T. for two months, 68/10*a*, 41/4*c*. Departures *from* London as for Barry Docks. Departures *for* London about 4 times daily.

RHOS (Denbigh) from *Paddington*, 182¼ miles. Fares, 37/9*a*, 22/9*c*. R.T. for two months, 75/6*a*, 45/6*c*.
Map Square 12.

Pad.	Rhos	Rhos	Pad.
AM 9.10*r*	1.34	AM 8.40*r*	1.25
10.40*r*	3. 9	10. 0*r*	4.15
PM12.50*dr*	5.54	PM12.20*r*	5. 0
12.50*r*	6.40	1.37*r*	5.55
2.10*dt*	7.16	3.15*r*	8. 5
2.10*et*	7.29	5.16	10. 0
4.10*dt*	9.14	7.32*e*	3.30
6.10*r*	10.40	7.52*d*	3.30
12.15*h*	7.39	—	—
—	—	—	—
—	—	—	—
—	—	—	—
—	—	—	—

No Sunday Trains.

d Saturdays only
e Saturdays excepted.
h Saturdays midnight excepted.
r Restaurant Car.
t Tea Car.

RHOS-ON-SEA (Denbigh). Station at Colwyn Bay.

RHOSGOCH (Anglesey), 259¾ miles. Fares, 54/0*a*, 32/5*c*. R.T. for two months, 108/0*a*, 64/10*c*. Departures *from* London as for Gaerwen. Departures *for* London about 4 times daily.
Map Square 11.

RHOSNEIGR (Anglesey), 256 miles. Fares, 53/4*a*, 32/0*c*. R.T. for two months, 106/8*a*, 64/0*c*. Departures *from* London as for Gaerwen. Departures *for* London about 3 times daily.

RHOSTRYFAN (Carnarvon), 260 miles. No through fares. Departures *from* London as for Carnarvon. Departures *for* London about 4 times daily.
Map Square 11.

RHOSTYLLEN (Denbigh), 182¾ miles. Fares, 37/6*a*, 22/6*c*. R.T. for two months 75/0*a*, 45/0*c*. Departures *from* London as for Rhos. Departures *for* London about 4 times daily.

RHUDDLAN (Flint), 212¼ miles. Fares, 44/0*a*, 26/5*c*. R.T. for two months, 88/0*a*. Departures *from* London as for Rhyl. Departures *for* London about 6 times daily. Pop. 1,607.
Map Square 11.

RHYDOWEN (Pembroke), 251½ miles. Fares, 51/1*a*, 30/8*c*. R. T. for two months, 102/2*a*, 61/4*c*. Departures *from* London as for Cardigan. Departures *for* London about 4 times daily.
Map Square 16.

RHYDYMWYN (Flint) from *Euston*, 195¼ miles. Fares, 40/7*a*, 24/4*c*. R. T. for two months, 81/2*a*. Departures *from* London as for Mold. Departures *for* London about 7 times daily. Pop. 544.
Map Square 11.

RHYDYRONEN (Merioneth), 234½ miles. No through fares. Departures *from* London as for Machynlleth. Departures *for* London about twice daily.
Map Square 16.

RHYL (Flint) from *Euston*, 209¼ miles. Fares, 43/7*a*, 26/2*c*. R. T. for two months, 87/2*a*, 52/4*c*. Pop. 13,398.
Map Square 11.

Euston	Rhyl	Rhyl	Euston
AM 12.25	7. 0	AM 7.20*er*	12. 5
2.35	9.52	7.20*dr*	12.20
5. 0	10.49	8.19*dr*	1. 0
8.30*er*	1.46	8.39*er*	1. 0
8.30*dr*	2.12	8.59*r*	1.45
10.30*r*	3. 3	9.43*r*	2.20
11.10*r*	3.19	9.44*er*	3.10
11.50*e*	4.51	10.24*dr*	3.10
11.50*d*	5.17	10.49*r*	4.15
12. 0*nr*	6.32	PM 12.40*r*	5. 5
PM 2.35*t*	7.18	1. 6*r*	6.25
4. 5*r*	8.53	3. 5*r*	7.30
5.20*r*	10. 7	3.54*r*	9.20
6.30*er*	11.44	5. 5*r*	10.45
9.30*e*	3.22	10. 8	5. 0
11.50*d*	11.12	—	—
—	—	—	—

Sunday Trains.

PM 12.10*r*	6.53	AM 8.20	4. 0
9.15	3.22	PM 2.12*r*	7.10
—	—	10. 3	5. 0
—	—	—	—
—	—	—	—

d Saturdays only.
e Saturdays excepted.
n Noon.
r Restaurant Car.
t Tea Car.

Westminster Hotel. The Leading First-class Family Hotel. Facing Sea. Moderate Tariff. Omnibus. Telephone 188. *See* also Llandudno, Harlech, Dolgelley.

RHYMNEY (Monmouth) from *Paddington* (*via* Newport), 164¾ miles. Fares, 34/0*a*, 20/5*c*. R. T. for two months, 68/0*a*. Pop. 11,691.
Map Square 21.

Pad.	Rhymney	Rhymney	Pad.
AM 1. 0*g*	9.50	AM 8.29*r*	1. 0
8.45*r*	1.19	10. 5*r*	2.30
11.50*er*	5.11	11. 9*r*	4.20
PM 1.10*r*	6.11	PM 1.25*dr*	6.15
3.35*r*	8.13	2.45*r*	8.35
6. 0*r*	10.37	5.13*r*	9.25
—	—	6.40	3.30
—	—	—	—
—	—	—	—

Sunday Trains.

PM 9.15	9.50	—	—

d Saturdays only.
e Saturdays excepted.
g Mondays excepted.
r Restaurant Car.

RIBBLEHEAD (Yorks), 247¼ miles. Fares, 48/2*a*, 28/11*c*. R. T., double fare. Departures *from* London as for Settle. Departures *for* London about 5 times daily.
Map Square 7.

RIBBLETON (Lancs), 212¼ miles. Fares, 44/2*a*, 26/6*c*. Departures *from* London as for Preston. Departures *for* London about 6 times daily. Pop. 77.
Map Square 12.

RICCALL (Yorks), 178½ miles. Fares, 37/1*a*, 22/3*c*. R. T., double fare. Departures *from* London as for Selby. Departures *for* London about 3 times daily. Pop. 657.
Map Square 13.

RICCARTON (Roxburgh), 331½ miles. Fares, 67/4*a*, 40/5*c*. R.T. for two months, 134/8*a*, 80/10*c*. Departures *from* London as for Carlisle. Departures *for* London about 3 times daily.
Map Square 44.

RICHMOND (Surrey) from *Waterloo*, 9¾ miles. Fares, 1/3*a*, 0/9*c*. R. T. for two days, 2/6*a*, 1/6*c*. Pop. 35,639. *See* pp. 585, 587-591.
Map Squares 23 *and* 67.

From *Broad Street*, 16¼ miles. Fares, 1/4½*a*, 0/10½*c*. R. T., 2/9*a*, 1/9*c*. *See* pp. 501-505.

From *Mansion House*, 11¼ miles. *See* p. 489.

Roebuck Hotel, Richmond Hill. Established 1730. Unrivalled View. Excellent Cuisine. Finest wines. Charges moderate. Inclusive terms en pension. Annexe, Mount View, Richmond Hill. En pension.
T. W. MACNEE, Proprietor.

Pigeons Hotel. Facing River. Omnibuses pass door. Balcony overlooking river. Moderate inclusive weekly terms. Telephone 361.
W. G. EAST, Proprietor.

St. Helena House (Residential Hotel). Riverside. Near Station, Richmond Bridge, and Parks. Daily or Weekly Tariff. 'Phone 1139 Richmond.

RICHMOND (Yorks) from *King's Cross*, 236½ miles. Fares, 49/5*a*, 29/8*c*. R. T., double fare. Pop. 3,883.
Map Square 7.

King's +	Richm'd	Richm'd	King's +
AM 4.45	12.11	AM 7.45*r*	1.30
7.15*r*	2.44	9.39*r*	4.30
11.50*r*	5.46	PM 12.30*r*	6.15
PM 1.50*r*	9.49	3.42*r*	10. 0
5.35*dr*	11.25	6.10*e*	3.25
11.25*d*	9.27	10.10*d*	6. 0
11.25*e*	8.34	—	—
—	—	—	—
—	—	—	—
—	—	—	—
—	—	—	—
—	—	—	—
—	—	—	—
—	—	—	—

Sunday Trains.

AM 11.30*r*	9. 4	AM 7.20	5.15
PM 11.25	8.34	PM 6.48	5.40
—	—	—	—
—	—	—	—
—	—	—	—

d Saturdays only.
e Saturdays excepted.
r Restaurant Car.

RICKMANSWORTH (Herts) from *Euston*, 19¾ miles. Fares, 3/7*a*, 2/2*c*. R. T. for two months, 7/2*a*, 3/11½*c*. Pop. 7,510. *See* p. 500.
Map Square 23.

ANOTHER ROUTE from *Marylebone* and *Baker Street*, 17¼ miles. Fares, 3/7*a*, 2/2*c*. R. T. for two months, 7/2*a*, 3/11½*c*. *See* pp. 494, 495.

The Victoria Hotel. First-class Residential. Select parties catered for. Lovely Garden and surroundings, Golf Links, Fishing. Telephone, 24 Rickmansworth.

Ladywalk, Heronsgate, Rickmansworth. Midway between Chorley Wood and Rickmansworth. Private House in Grounds of 33 acres. Paying Guests received. Own Cows and Produce. Billiard Room. Central Heating. Electric Light. Telephone, 90 Chorley Wood

RIDDINGS (Cumberland), 313¼ miles. No through fares. Departures *from* London as for Carlisle. Departures *for* London about 3 times daily.
Map Square 3.

RIDGMONT (Bedford) from *Euston*, 53½ miles. Fares, 10/5*a*, 6/3*c*. R.T. for two months, 20/10*a*. Departures *from* London as for Woburn Sands. Departures *for* London about 8 times daily. Pop. 540.
Map Square 18.

RIDING MILL (Northumberland), 281¾ miles. Fares, 59/10*a*, 35/11*c*. R. T., double fare. Departures *from* London as for Newcastle-on-Tyne. Departures *for* London about 8 times daily. Pop. (Riding) 228.
Map Square 3.

RIGG (Dumfries), 310¾ miles. Fares, 62/11*a*, 37/9*c*. R. T. for two months, 125/10*a*, 75/6*c*. Departures *from* London as for Carlisle. Departures *for* London about 4 times daily.
Map Square 44.

RILLINGTON (Yorks), 213¾ miles. Fares, 44/5*a*, 26/8*c*. R. T., double fare. Departures *from* London as for Malton. Departures *for* London about 4 times daily. Pop. 661.
Map Square 8.

RIMINGTON (Yorks), 226½ miles. Fares, 43/9*a*, 26/3*c*. R. T. for two months, 87/6*a*, 52/6*c*. Departures *from* London as for Clitheroe. Departures *for* London about 4 times daily. Pop. 329.
Map Square 7.

RINGLEY ROAD (Lancs), 193¾ miles. No through fares. Departures *from* London as for Manchester. Departures *for* London about 6 times daily. Pop. (Ringley) 2,113.

RINGSTEAD (Northampton) from *Euston*, 84¾ miles. Fares, 13/9*a*, 8/3*c*. R. T. for six months, 27/6*a*, 16/6*c*. Departures *from* London as for Wellingborough. Departures *for* London about 4 times daily. Pop. 934.
Map Square 18.

RINGWOOD (Hants) from *Waterloo*, 103 miles. Fares, 21/8*a*, 13/0*c*. R. T. for two months, 43/4*a*, 26/0*c*. Pop. 5,055.
Map Square 27.

W'LOO.	RINGWD.	RINGWD	W'LOO.
AM 5.40	9.18	AM 7.27*r*	10. 6
5.50	10.24	9.16*s*	12.22
9.30	12.35	11. 4*r*	2.20
11.30*r*	2.25	PM 1.16	4.20
PM 12.30*r*	3.33	2.18	6.16
1.30*s*	4.31	3.15*s*	6.26
3.30*s*	6.35	5.19*r*	8.20
5.30*r*	8.27	7.41	11.28
6.30*r*	9.35	—	—
—	—	—	—
—	—	—	—

Sunday Trains.

AM 11. 0*r*	2.26	AM 9.12*r*	2.27
PM 2. 0*r*	5.34	PM 4.27	8. 3
—	—	—	—
—	—	—	—
—	—	—	—

r Restaurant Car.
s Refreshments served.

White Hart Hotel. Family and Commercial. Coarse fishing in River Avon. Billiards. Garage. "R. A. C." and "A. A." 'Phone No. 2.
F. J. WESTCOTT, Proprietor.

RIPLEY (Derby) from *St. Pancras*, 134 miles. Fares, 27/4*a*, 16/5*c*. R. T., double fare. Pop. 11,848.
Map Square 13.

ST. PAN.	RIPLEY	RIPLEY	ST. PAN.
AM 4.25	9.33	AM 7.54*r*	11.35
10.25*r*	1.58	9.42*r*	1.30
PM 12.25*r*	4.23	11.25*hr*	4.10
2.25*r*	6.30	PM 2. 8*r*	5.45
4.25*r*	8.19	4.48*r*	8.35
6.25*dr*	10.35	8.32*e*	4.20
—	—	9.47*d*	4.20

Sunday Trains.

AM 11.15*r*	6.14	PM 6.28	11. 7
—	—	—	—

d Saturdays only.
e Saturdays excepted.
h Tuesdays, Fridays and Saturdays only.
r Restaurant Car.

RIPLEY VALLEY (Yorks), 202½ miles. Fares, 41/11*a*, 25/2*c*. R. T., double fare. Departures *from* London as for Pateley Bridge. Departures *for* London about 4 times daily. Pop. (Ripley) 254.
Map Square 7.

RIPON (Yorks) from *King's Cross*, 217 miles, *via* Leeds. Fares, 43/7*a*, 26 2*c*. R. T. for two months, 87/2*a*, 52/4*c*. Pop. 8,389.
Map Square 7.

KING'S +	RIPON	RIPON	KING'S +
AM 4.45	12. 7	AM 7.20	1. 5
7.15*r*	1.47	9. 5	1.55
10.10*r*	4.43	10.47*gr*	3.15
11.15*gr*	3.35	11.42	5. 0
PM 1.40*lr*	6.38	PM 12. 7*kr*	6.15
1.50*kr*	8.26	1.47*r*	7.10
4. 0*r*	9.20	2.47*r*	9.25
5.45*fr*	11.22	9.18	3.25
10.45*e*	6.58	—	—
11.25*d*	8.36	—	—

Sunday Trains.

12. 0*nr*	5.48	AM 8.36*k*	5.15
PM 10.45	6.58	9.52	5.55
—	—	PM 7.30*k*	5.40
—	—	—	—

d Saturdays only.
e Saturdays excepted.
f Wednesdays and Saturdays only.
g 1st and 3rd Class Pullman Cars only.
k Via York.
l Via Church Fenton.
n Noon.
r Restaurant Car.

ANOTHER ROUTE from *St. Pancras*, 225½ miles. Fares as above.

ST. PAN.	RIPON	RIPON	ST. PAN.
AM 2.25*g*	10.35	AM 7.55*r*	2.10
4.25	12. 7	9. 5*r*	4.10
9. 0*r*	2.38	11. 3*r*	5.30
9.50*r*	4.43	11.42*r*	6.35
11.45*r*	5.22	PM 1.47*r*	7.57
PM 12.15*r*	6.38	2.47*r*	9.15
3.30*r*	9.20	8.26	4.20
5. 0*hr*	11.22	9.18	7.25
11.45*e*	6.58	—	—
11.50*d*	8.36	—	—

Sunday Trains.

AM 10.50*r*	6.33	AM 9.52	5.27
PM 11.45	6.58	PM 7.30	4.55

d Saturdays only.
e Saturdays excepted.
g Mondays excepted.
h Wednesdays and Saturdays only.
r Restaurant Car.

The Royal Spa Hotel. In own extensive grounds. Tennis. Croquet. Central Heating, Electric Light. Private Suites. Garage. R.A.C., A.A., A.C.A.

RIPON—*continued.*

Unicorn Hotel. The oldest established. Recommended by R.A.C. and A.A. Garage for 40 cars. Parties Catered for. Terms Moderate.

RIPPINGALE (Lincoln), 100¾ miles. Fares 21/0*a*, 12/7*c*. R. T., double fare. Departures *from* London as for Bourne. Departures *for* London about 5 times daily. Pop. 469.
Map Square 18.

RIPPLE (Worcester), from *Euston*, 156¾ miles. Fares, 24/5*a*, 14/8*c*. R.T. for two months, 48/10*a*, 29/4*c*. Departures *from* London as for Tewkesbury. Departures *for* London about 4 times daily. Pop. 705.
Map Square 17.

RIPPONDEN (Yorks), 197 miles. Fares, 40/8*a*, 24/5*c*. R. T. for two months, 81/4*a*, 48/10*c*. Departures *from* London as for Sowerby Bridge. Departures *for* London about 6 times daily. Pop. 3,831.
Map Square 12.

RISCA (Monmouth) from *Paddington*, 147¼ miles. Fares, 30/8*a*, 18/5*c*. R.T. for two months, 61/4*a*. Pop. 16,746.
Map Square 21.

PAD.	RISCA	RISCA	PAD.
AM 1. 0*g*	5.49	AM 6.59*r*	10.57
5.30	10.56	9.43*r*	1. 0
8.45*r*	12.11	11.13*r*	2.30
9. 0	2.19	PM 12.16*r*	4.20
11.50*r*	4. 2	2.55*r*	6.15
PM 1.10*r*	5.25	4.10*r*	8.35
3.35*r*	6.55	6. 7*r*	9.25
5. 0*r*	8.46	9.59	3.30
6. 0*r*	9.51	—	—
6.30*r*	10.52	—	—
8. 0*dr*	11.14	—	—
9.15*e*	5. 5	—	—
—	—	—	—
—	—	—	—
—	—	—	—
—	—	—	—

Sunday Trains.

AM 1. 0	9.38	AM 8.39	3.35
9.10	2. 9	PM 4.28*r*	8.25
PM 12.30*r*	5.49	8. 8	3.30
4.30	9. 9	—	—
9.15	5. 5	—	—

d Saturdays only.
e Saturdays excepted.
g Mondays excepted.
r Restaurant Car.

RISHTON (Lancs), 211½ miles. Fares, 43/7*a*, 26/2*c*. R. T. for two months, 87/2*a*, 52/4*c*. Departures *from* London as for Blackburn. Departures *for* London about 6 times daily. Pop. 7,016.
Map Square 12.

RISHWORTH (Yorks), 197¾ miles. Fares, 40/10*a*, 24/6*c*. R. T. for two months, 81/8*a*, 49/0*c*. Departures *from* London as for Sowerby Bridge. Departures *for* London about 6 times daily. Pop. 879.
Map Square 12.

ROADE (Northampton)

from *Euston*, 60 miles. Fares, 12/6a,
7/6c. R. T. for two months, 25/0a.
Pop. 660.
Map Square 18.

EUSTON	ROADE	ROADE	EUSTON
AM 6.45	8.27	AM 7.26	9.40
7.35	9.58	9.21	11.40
9.30	11.28	PM 2.34	4.15
12. 0nr	1.42	6. 2	7.55
PM12.15d	2.29	6.23	8.35
2. 0	4.27	8.28	10 50
4.15	5.54	9.42d	5. 0
5.32	7.20	—	—
6.10e	7.56	—	—
7.15d	9.45	—	—
7.50e	9.45	—	—

Sunday Trains.

AM 8.15	10.43	AM10.50	12.25
9.15	10.57	10.59	1.20
PM 6.45	8.37	PM 3.37	5. 5
—	—	3.49	5.50
—	—	8.18	10.10

d Saturdays only.
e Saturdays excepted.
n Noon.
r Restaurant Car.

ROBERTSBRIDGE

(Sussex) from *Charing Cross, Cannon Street,* and *London Bridge,*
50¼ miles. Fares, 10/7a, 8/50, 6/4c.
R.T. for two months, 21/2a, 16/10b.
Map Square 24.

	Leave		Arr. at
CHAR. +	CAN. ST.	LON. B.	ROB'DGE
AM —	3.40h	3.43h	5.31
—	5.20	5.25	8. 0
—	7.56	8. 0	10.15
9.25	—	9.33	11.22
10.40	—	10.46	12.29
PM12. 3	—	12.10	1.54
1. 5d	—	1.11d	2.37
2. 8	—	2.16	3.50
2.40d	—	2.46d	4.10
3.48e	—	—	5.28
5. 5d	—	—	6.44
—	5.12e	—	6.29
6. 5e	6.16e	6.19e	7.52
7.30	—	—	9.15
9.30	—	9.36	11. 0

Sunday Trains.

AM 8.45	—	—	10.21
9.50	—	9.56	11.24
PM 7.10	—	7.20	8.59
7.35	—	7.45	9.35

ROBERTSBRIDGE—

continued.

Trains from Robertsbridge.

Leave		Arrive at	
ROB'DGE	LON. B.	CAN. ST.	CHAR.+
AM 7.35	—	9.15	—
8.17	—	9.48	—
8.59d	10.29	—	10.59
9.30e	—	10.42	—
9.39e	11. 7	—	11.17
11.30	—	—	12.49
PM12.43	3. 6	—	3.19
2.14	4.15	—	4.25
3.58d	6.30	—	6.39
4. 9e	6.44	—	6.54
6. 6	8.26	—	8.35
8.11	10.15	—	10.23
9.21	11.35	—	11.44

Sunday Trains.

AM 7.39	10. 5	—	10.15
9.37	11.23	—	11.34
PM 6. 2	8.12	—	8.22
9.10	11. 4	—	11.15

d Saturdays only.
e Saturdays excepted.
h Third Class only.

ROBIN HOOD'S BAY

(Yorks), 244¾ miles. Fares, 50/10a,
30/6c. R. T. for two months,
101/8a, 61/0c. Departures *from*
London as for Ravenscar. Departures *for* London about 4 times
daily.
Map Square 8.

ROBROYSTON (Lanark),

399¾ miles. No through fares.
Departures *from* London as for
Coatbridge. Departures *for* London about 5 times daily.
Map Square 40.

ROBY (Lancs), 196¾ miles.

Fares, 41/0a, 24/7c. R. T. for
two months, 82/0a. Departures
from London as for Liverpool
(Lime Street), or Earlestown.
Departures *for* London about 5
times daily. Pop. 1,018.

ROCESTER (Stafford).

140 miles. Fares, 29/0a, 17/5c.
R. T. for two months, 58/0a.
Departures *from* London as for
Ashbourne. Departures *for* London about 3 times daily. Pop. 1,263.
Map Square 12.

ROCHDALE (Lancs) from

Euston, 195⅛ miles. Fares, 40/2a,
24/7c. R. T. for two months, 80/4a.
Pop. 90,807.
Map Square 12.

EUSTON	ROCHD'L.	ROCHD'L.	EUSTON
AM12.25	6.37	AM 5.27dr12.20	
2.35	9.30	7.15er12. 5	
5. 0	11. 0	7.25r 12.50	
8.45r	1.52	8.45r 1.15	
10.40r	3.40	9.14r 1.45	
11.50r	4.48	9.18r 2.20	
12. 0nr	6.20	9.25r 3.10	
PM 1.30er	7.11	11.11r 3.55	
2.50t	7.49	11.30dr 5.50	
4. 5r	8.57	12.15r 6. 0	
4.45r	10.26	12.55r 6.15	
6. 5r	10.43	1.20r 6.25	
9.30e	4.50	2. 0r 7.30	
11.50d	8.30	3. 6r 8.10	
—	—	3.48er 9. 5	
—	—	4.12er10. 0	
—	—	4.45dr10. 0	
—	—	5. 5er10.10	
—	—	9.20 5. 0	
—	—	10.33 5.40	

ROCHDALE—*continued.*

Sunday Trains.

EUSTON	ROCHD'L.	ROCHD'L.	EUSTON
PM12.30r	6. 5	AM 8.32	4. 0
12.50r	6.58	11.22r	5.45
9.15	4.50	PM 1. 4r	7.30
—	—	3. 9r	8.55
—	—	10.46	5. 0

d Saturdays only.
e Saturdays excepted.
n Noon.
r Restaurant Car.

ANOTHER ROUTE *via*

Horbury, 212½ miles. Fares as
above.

KING'S+	ROCHD'L.	ROCHD'L.	KING'S+
AM 4.45	11.28	AM 4.56	11.30
7.15r	1.37	7.19r	1. 5
10.10r	4.52	8.42r	1.55
PM 1.30r	7.14	9.32	3.50
1.50r	9. 9	10.30r	4.45
10.45e	9.33	11. 2	5. 0
—	—	PM 1.23r	7.10
—	—	4.15r	9.25
—	—	7.51e	3.25

Sunday Trains.

12. 0hn	8. 2	AM 9.11r	3.45
—	—	11. 5r	5.55
—	—	PM 2.30h	10.20

e Saturdays excepted.
h Passengers cross Wakefield at
own expense.
n Noon
r Restaurant Car.

ANOTHER ROUTE from

Marylebone, 213¾ miles. Fares as
above.

M'BONE.	ROCHDL	ROCHDL.	M'BONE.
AM 2.32e	10.26k	AM 7.25r	1.13
2 52d	11.0k	9.14kr	3. 0
8.45r	2.45k	PM 1.20kr	6.38
10. 0r	4. 2	2.50r	8.54
PM12.15r	6.20k	3.58dr	9.55
3.20r	8.57k	3.48ekr	9.55
5. 0r	10.43	9.20	3.57
10. 0d	8.30	—	—
10. 5e	4.50k	—	—

Sunday Trains.

AM11.15r	6. 5	AM11.22kr	5.40
—	—	PM 4.23kr10.24	

d Saturdays only.
e Saturdays excepted.
h Via Oldham (Clegg Street).
k Via Manchester (Victoria). Passengers cross Manchester at
own expense.
r Restaurant Car.

ROCHE (Cornwall) from

Paddington, 269 miles. Fares,
55/8a, 33/5c. R. T. for two
months, 111/4a. Departures *from*
London as for Newquay. Departures *for* London about 4 times
daily. Pop. 1,827.
Map Square 25.

ROCHESTER (Kent)

from *Victoria, Holborn Viaduct, and St. Paul's,* 33¼ miles. Fares, 6/8a, 5/4b, 4/0c. R. T. for two months, 13/4a, 10/8b. Pop. 31,261.

Vict. (S.E.&C.)	Leave Hol. V.	St. Pl.'s	Arr. at Rochst.
AM —	3.50	—	4.53
5.5	4.57	5.0	6.58
·	7.30	7.33	8.53
9.20	—	—	10.25
11.40*l*	—	—	12.45
11.40*e*	—	—	1.5
11.55*d*	—	—	1.15
PM —	1.24*d*	1.27*d*	2.33
2.8*e*	—	—	2.59
—	3.22	3.25	4.55
3.40*d*	3.33*d*	3.36*d*	5.29
4.20	—	—	5.11
4.25*e*	—	—	5 29
5.30*e*	—	—	6.26
5.30*d*	—	—	6.27
—	—	5.33*e*	6.48
6.16	6.10*e*	6.13*e*	7.58
7.5	7.0	7.5	8.12
9.0*e*	8.57*e*	9.0*e*	10.25
10.17	10.11	10.13	11.37

Sunday Trains.

AM 7.20	—	—	8.37
10.30	10.25	—	12.0
PM 3.30	—	—	4.54
6.35	—	—	7.54
—	10.12	—	11.45
10.25	—	—	11.23

Trains from Rochester.

Leave Rochst.	St. Pl.'s	Arrive at Hol. V.	Vict.
AM 6.42	8.8	8.9	8.14
7.0	8.25	8.27	8.29
7.34	9.16	9.18	—
8.19	9.37	9.39	—
9.53	—	—	11.2
11.35*d*	1.0	1.2	—
11.59*e*	—	—	1.33
PM 1.47	—	—	2.43
1.59	—	—	3.23
3.47*e*	5.32	5.34	5.21
5.19*e*	6.45	6.47	—
6.34*d*	8.0	8.2	—
8.18	9.50	9.54	9.46
10.1	11.21	11.23	—

Sunday Trains.

AM 7.54	—	9.40	9.31
9.48	—	11.27	11.23
10.55	—	11.58	11.51
11.30	—	1.2	12.56
PM 4.34	—	—	5.31
4.48	—	—	6.3
7.50	—	—	8.40
9.35	—	—	10.29
10.21	—	12.0	11.44

d Saturdays only.
e Saturdays excepted.
h Third class only.

ROCHESTER—*continued.*

ANOTHER ROUTE from

Charing Cross, Cannon Street, and London Bridge, 32¼ miles. Fares as above.

Leave Char.+	Can. St.	Lon. B.	Arr. at Rochst.
AM —	—	3.22*h*	4.43
—	—	3.57*h*	4.53
—	6.20	6.23	7.45
—	7.16	7.19	8.40
—	7.44	7.47	9.0
8.10	—	8.17	9.33
9.32	—	9.41	11.3
—	10.58	11.1	12.23
—	11.8*d*	11.11*d*	12.55
11.55	—	12.2	1.17
PM12.30*l*	—	12.37*d*	1.38
1.20*e*	—	1.27*e*	2.41
1.26*d*	—	1.34*d*	2.41
—	2.40*e*	2.43*e*	3.53
2.45*e*	—	2.55*e*	4.23
3.5*d*	—	3.12*d*	4.25
3.10*d*	—	3.17*d*	4.45
—	4.0*e*	4.5*e*	5.40
4.25*d*	—	4.31*d*	5.50
—	4.36*e*	4.39*e*	5.49
5.15*d*	—	5.22*d*	6.48
5.17*e*	—	5.25*e*	6.37
5.21*e*	—	5.29*e*	6.50
5.58*d*	—	6.4*d*	7.13
6.22*e*	—	6.29*e*	7.44
6.55*d*	—	7.1*d*	8.31
—	7.8*e*	7.11*e*	8.31
7.34	—	7.41	9.6
—	7.44*d*	7.47*d*	9.53
—	9.35	9.38	10.56
10.20	—	10.27	11.40
11.24	—	—	12.32

Sunday Trains.

AM 7.30	—	7.37	9.6
9.46	—	9.52	11.17
10.50	—	10.57	12.28
PM 1.15	—	1.22	2.53
3.15	—	3.22	4.48
4.50	—	4.57	6.21
7.0	—	7.7	8.18
8.42	—	8.49	10.3
10.30	—	10.38	12.19

Trains from Rochester.

Leave Rochst.	Lon. B.	Can. St.	Char.+
AM 6.29	8.13	8.17	—
7.9	8.31	8.35	—
7.24	8.34	—	8.41
7.37	8.51	8.55	—
8.32	9.34	—	9.43
9.2	10.24	10.28	—
9.29	10.38	—	10.45
10.0	11.20	11.24	—
10.47	12.3	—	12.14
PM12.14*d*	1.31	1.37	—
12.14*e*	1.36	—	1.45
h1.32*d*	3.21	3.26	—
1.38*e*	2.53	—	3.4
2.8*e*	3.26	—	3.36
2.26*d*	3.58	—	4.8
3.24*e*	4.48	4.52	—
3.29*d*	4.57	—	5.7
4.8*e*	5.36	5.40	—
4.8*d*	5.36	—	5.45
5.10*e*	6.35	6.39	—
5.42	7.10	—	7.19
5.57	7.27	7.32	—
6.58	8.15	8.20	—
8.29	9.36	—	9.46
9.34	10.51	—	10.59
10.52	12.35	—	12.45

ROCHESTER—*continued.*

Sunday Trains.

Leave Rochst.	Lon. B.	Can. St.	Char.+
AM 7.32	9.0	—	9.9
8.54	10.16	—	10.24
11.37	1.5	—	1.17
PM12.50	2.14	—	2.24
2.40	4.4	—	4.15
4.41	5.55	—	6.4
5.34	6.49	—	6.59
6.33	8.1	—	8.10
8.9	9.46	—	9.55
9.48	11.15	—	11.23

d Saturdays only.
e Saturdays excepted.
h Third Class only.

King's Head Hotel, facing Cathedral and Castle. Family and Commercial. Comfortable, inexpensive.
GEORGE LEES, Proprietor.

Bull Hotel. Immortalised by the late Charles Dickens. 'Phone 175. Resident Proprietors—Mr. and Mrs. W.H. OLIVER, formerly Hotel Metropole, Dublin, and Station Hotel, Newcastle-on-Tyne.

ROCHESTER BRIDGE

(Kent) from *Victoria, Holborn Viaduct,* and *St. Paul's,* 33 miles. Fares as above.

Station closed.
Nearest station at Rochester.

ROCHFORD (Essex) from

Liverpool Street, 38¼ miles. Fares, 5/5a, 3/3c. R. T. for two months, 10/10a. Pop. 2,077.
Map Square 24.

L'pl. St.	Rochf.	Rochf.	L'pl. St.
AM 5.10	6.19	AM 6.24	7.35
5.26	7.10	7.0	8.23
6.50	8.38	7.26	8.45
7.48	9.46	7.55	9.14
9.6	10.50	8.48	9.50
10.3	11.14	9.56	11.7
10.30	12.0	10 18*h*	11.59
11.56	1.2	10.27*k*	11.59
PM12.48*d*	2.2	11.43*e*	1.16
1.20*d*	2.22	11.46*d*	1.16
1.50*d*	3.4	PM12.12*e*	1.25
2.0*e*	3.7	1.26	3.5
2.20*e*	3.59	3.25*e*	4.51
2.30*d*	3.37	3.29*d*	4.53
2.58*d*	4.13	4.52	6.8
3.26	4.56	5.35	6.52
4.15	5.8	6.57	8.22
4.18	5.36	7.39	9.10
4.48*e*	5.55	8.18	9.50
5.39	6.50	8.38	9.56
6.5*e*	7.16	10.7	11.30
6.26*e*	7.46	—	—
6.26*d*	7.50	—	—
7.16*e*	8.31	—	—
8.2*d*	9.17	—	—
8.2*e*	9.20	—	—
8.45	9.57	—	—
9.45*d*	10.54	—	—
9.45*e*	11.3	—	—
11.0	12.23	—	—
12.0*m*	1.18	—	—

ROCHFORD—*continued.*

Sunday Trains.

L'pl. St.	Rochf.	Rochf.	L'pl. St.
AM 8.30	9.50	AM 8. 7	10.25
8.45	10.30	9.17	10.50
9.30	11. 6	10.33	12.40
10.30	11.47	PM 1.35	3.15
10.45	12.26	3.53	5.15
11.35	12.52	6.15	7.44
PM 2.30	4.16	6.40	7 58
6. 0	7.20	7.12	8.45
6.42	8.17	8.18	9.48
8.46	10.21	8.49	10.45
10.10	11.38	—	—
—	—	—	—
—	—	—	—
—	—	—	—
—	—	—	—

d Saturdays only.
e Saturdays excepted.
h Fridays only.
k Fridays excepted.
m Midnight.

ROCKCLIFFE (Cumberland), 303¼ miles. No through fares. Departures *from* London as for Carlisle. Departures *for* London about 3 times daily. Pop. 545.
Map Square 3.

ROCK FERRY (Cheshire), 192¾ miles. Fares, 40/2*a*, 24/1*c*. R.T. for two months, 80/4*a*. Departures *from* London as for Hooton. Departures *for* London about 6 times daily. Pop. 10,805.
Map Square 12.

ROCKINGHAM (Northampton) from *Euston*, 93¾ miles. Fares, 17/4*a*, 10/5*c*. R. T., double fare. Departures *from* London as for Market Harborough. Departures *for* London about 4 times daily. Pop. 154.
Map Square 18.

RODWELL (Dorset), 143 miles. Fares, 30/0*a*, 18/0*c*. R. T. for two months, 60/0*a*. Departures *from* London as for Portland. Departures *for* London about 4 times daily.
Map Square 27.

ROGART (Sutherland), 644½ miles. Fares, 115/8*a*, 69/5*c*. R.T. for two months, 231/4*a*. Departures *from* London as for Lairg. Departures *for* London about 3 times daily. Pop. 804.
Map Square 34.

ROGATE (Sussex) from *Waterloo*, 58¾ miles. Fares, 12/4*a*, 7/5*c*. R. T. for two months, 24/8*a*, 14/10*c*. Pop. 1,083.
Map Square 23.

W'loo.	Rogate	Rogate	W'loo
AM 5.50	8.16	AM 7.17*s*	9.44
6.50	9.30	8.15*r*	9.52
8.34*r*	10.42	9. 4	11.32
9.50	12. 8	11.26*r*	1.52
10.50	1.13	PM12.41	3. 6
PM12.20*d*	2.50	2. 3	4 16
12.50*er*	4. 8	3.31	5.52
2.34	5. 9	5. 8	7.46
4.50	6.39	6.11	9. 6
5.50	7.40	8.12	10.46
6.50*er*	8.58	—	—
6.50*dr*	9. 3	—	—
—	—	—	—

ROGATE—*continued.*

Sunday Trains.

W'loo.	Rogate	Rogate	W'loo.
AM 9.15*r*	11.33	AM 7.44	10.16
PM 1.50	4.23	PM 3.31	6.46
—	—	6.29	8.52
—	—	—	—
—	—	—	—
—	—	—	—
—	—	—	—
—	—	—	—
—	—	—	—
—	—	—	—
—	—	—	—

r Restaurant Car.
s Refreshments served.

ROGERSTONE (Monmouth) from *Paddington*, 145 miles. Fares, 30/3*a*, 18/2*c*. R. T. for two months, 60/6*a*. Departures *from* London as for Newport (Mon.). Departures *for* London about 7 times daily. Pop. 3,433.
Map Square 22.

ROLLESTON (Notts), from *St. Pancras*, 136½ miles. Fares, 25/0*a*, 15/0*c*. R. T., double fare. Departures *from* London as for Nottingham. Departures *for* London about 6 times daily. Pop. 181.
Map Square 13.

ROLLESTON-ON-DOVE (Stafford), 125½ miles. Fares, 26/1*a*, 15/8*c*. R. T. for two months, 52/2*a*, 31/4*c*. Departures *from* London as for Burton-on-Trent. Departures *for* London about 5 times daily. Pop. 872.
Map Square 17.

ROLVENDEN (Kent), 55½ miles. No through fares. Departures *from* London as for Tenterden. Departures *for* London about 4 times daily. Pop. 1,194.
Map Square 24.

ROMALDKIRK (Yorks), 254 miles. Fares, 53/1*a*, 31/10*c*. R. T., double fare. Departures *from* London as for Barnard Castle. Departures *for* London about 4 times daily. Pop. 240.
Map Square 7.

ROMAN BRIDGE (Carnarvon), 245¾ miles. Fares, 47/11*a*, 28/9*c*. R. T. for two months, 95/10*a*, 57/6*c*. Departures *from* London as for Bettws-y-Coed. Departures *for* London about 5 times daily.
Map Square 11.

ROMFORD (Essex) from *Liverpool Street*, 12¼ miles. Fares, 2/1*a*, 1/8*b*, 1/3*c*. R. T. for two months, 4/2*a*, 3/2½*b*, 2/2½*c*. Pop. 19,448. *See* pp. 528-534.
Map Square 24.

ROMILEY (Cheshire), 178½ miles. Fares, 36/11*a*, 22/2*c*. R. T., double fare. Departures *from* London as for Marple. Departures *for* London about 6 times daily. Pop. 2,898.
Map Square 12.

ROMSEY (Hants) from *Waterloo* (*via* Eastleigh), 80 miles. Fares, 16/11*a*, 10/2*c*. R. T. for two months, 33/10*a*, 20/4*c*. Pop. 4,826.
Map Square 22.

W'loo	Romsey	Romsey	W'loo
AM 5.40	8. 1	AM 7.45*hr*	10. 6
5.50	8.51	8.33*hs*	11. 0
8.30*s*	10.46	9.35	12. 0
9.30	12.31	PM12. 3*r*	2.20
11.30*r*	1.36	1.14	4. 6
PM12.30*hr*	3. 6	2. 0	4.20
1.30*s*	3.55	2.20*h*	4.50
3.30*s*	5.39	3. 5	6.16
3.40	6.43	4. 0*s*	6.26
4.30*hr*	6.59	5.11*r*	8.20
5.30*r*	7.38	6.35	9.52
6. 0	8.54	7.55	10.50
7.30	9.46	8.49	11.28
8. 0*k*	11.37	9.50	3.58
10. 0	1.58	11.45*k*	3.58
—	—	—	—

Sunday Trains.

AM11. 0*r*	1. 5	AM 9.45	12.11
PM 2. 0	6.24	PM 3. 5*h*	6. 7
6. 0	8 41	5.23	8. 3
7. 0*r*	9.21	7.34	10.53
—	—	—	—

h Via Southampton West.
k Wednesdays and Saturdays only.
r Restaurant Car.
s Refreshments served.

ANOTHER ROUTE (*via* Salisbury), 98 miles. Fares, 17/6*a*, 10/6*c*. R. T. for two months, 35/0*a*, 21/0*c*.

W'loo	Romsey	Romsey	W'loo
AM 7.30*h*	10. 4	AM 6.56*k*	9.56
10. 0	1.11	7.29	10.56
11. 0*r*	1.19	8. 5*h*	10.56
12. 0*r*	2.17	8.54*r*	11.10
PM 1. 0*r*	3.56	9.36*h*	12.22
3. 0*r*	5. 9	11.18*r*	1.56
5. 0	7.41	PM 1.21*r*	3.50
6. 0*hr*	8.46	2.15	4.30
—	—	3.42*r*	6. 0
—	—	4. 0*h*	7.40
—	—	5.31*r*	8.30
—	—	7.43	10.50
—	—	—	—

Sunday Trains.

12. 0*hnr*	3. 2	PM 6.26*r*	8.57
—	—	—	—
—	—	—	—

h Via Andover Junction.
k Via Whitchurch.
n Noon.
r Restaurant Car.

White Horse Hotel. Telephone 198. One of oldest hostelries of the County. Famous in local tradition. Comfortable Rooms and good modern Cuisine and Service. A good centre for the New Forest. Electric Light. Stabling and Garage.
TRUST HOUSES, Ltd.

ROOKERY (Lancs), 195¼ miles. No through fares. Departures *from* London as for St. Helens. Departures *for* London about 6 times daily.
Map Square 12.

ROOSE (Lancs), 263¼ miles. Fares, 54/10*a*, 32/11*c*. R. T. for two months, 109/8*a*, 65/10*c*. Departures *from* London as for Furness Abbey. Departures *for* London about 4 times daily.
Map Square 6.

ROPLEY (Hants) from

Waterloo, 54½ miles. Fares, 11/5a, 6/10c. R. T. for two months, 22/10x, 13/8c. Pop. 1,371.
Map Square 23.

W'LOO.	ROPLEY	ROPLEY	W'LOO.
AM 5.50	8. 1	AM 7.44	9.41
7. 0	9.22	8.39	10.26
9.20	11.22	10.42	12.40
PM 1.10	3. 4	PM 1.36	3.36
4. 0	5.52	5. 8	7. 7
6.34	8.24	7.45	9.52

Sunday Trains.

AM 8.45	11.13	AM 8.37	11.16
PM 6.20	8.27	PM 7.38	9.37

ROSEBUSH (Pembroke),

254¾ miles. Fares, 50/0a, 30/0c. R. T. for two months, 100/0x, 60/0c. Departures *from* London as for Clynderwen. Departures *for* London about twice daily.
Map Square 15.

ROSE GROVE (Lancs)

from *King's Cross, via* Horbury, 213½ miles. Fares, 41/10a, 25/1c. R. T. for two months, 83/8x, 50/2c. Departures *from* London as for Burnley. Departures *for* London about 6 times daily.
Map Square 12.

ROSEMOUNT (Perth),

469 miles. No through fares. Departures *from* London as for Blairgowrie. Departures *for* London about 4 times daily.

ROSHERVILLE (Kent)

from *Victoria, Holborn Viaduct,* and *St. Paul's*, 27 miles. Fares, 5/0x, 4/0b, 3/0c. R. T. for two months, 7/10x, 6/1b, 5/3c. Departures *from* London as for Southfleet. Departures *for* London about 8 times daily. Pop. 1,855.

ROSLIN (Midlothian), 434¾

miles. No through fares. Departures *from* London as for Edinburgh (Waverley). Departures *for* London about 4 times daily. Pop. 1,797.
Map Square 41.

ROSS (Hereford) from *Pad-*

dington, 13½ miles. Fares, 27/6a, 16/6c. R. T. for two months, 55/0x, 33/0c. Pop. 4,665.
Map Square 17.

PAD.	Ross	Ross	PAD.
AM 1. 0g	8. 0	M 8.15	12.20
5.30	10.24	10.50r	2.40
9. 0	1.16	M 1.41	5. 0
10.45	2.43	4.35r	8.45
PM 3.15t	6.59	9.30	3.30
6. 0r	9.28	—	—

Sunday Trains.

PM 9.15	8. 0	—	—

g Mondays excepted.
r Restaurant Car.
t Tea Car.

Swan Hotel. (Country

Hostels, Ltd.) Best appointed in Wye Valley. Every modern convenience. Telephone 44. Terms, apply MANAGERESS.

ROSSETT (Denbigh) from

Paddington, 188 miles. Fares, 37/4a, 22/5c. R. T. for two months, 74/8a. Pop.
Map Square 12.

PAD.	ROSSETT	ROSSETT	PAD.
AM 9.10r	2. 9	AM 7.28	12.25
10.40r	4.58	9.12r	2. 5
PM12.50r	5.47	11.32r	5. 0
2.10t	7. 3	PM 1.16r	5.55
4.10t	8.56	2.10r	8. 5
6.10r	10.40	4.35r	10. 0
12.15k	7.55	7.32	3.30
12.15k	8.58	—	—

Sunday Trains.

AM12.50r	6.45	AM10.17	6.20
—	—	PM 2.28r	9. 0

h Saturdays midnight excepted.
k Saturdays midnight only.
r Restaurant Car.
t Tea Car

ROSSINGTON (Yorks),

151½ miles. Fares, 31/6a, 18/11c. R. T., double fare. Departures *from* London as for Bawtry. Departures *for* London about 4 times daily. Pop. 371.
Map Square 13.

ROSSLARE HAR-

BOUR (Wexford) from *Paddington, via* Fishguard, 323 miles. Fares, 50/0 First and Saloon, 36/0 Third and Saloon, 30/0 Third and Steerage. R. T. for two months, 100/0 First and Saloon, 69/10 Third and Saloon, 58/7 Third and Steerage. Pop. 230.
Map Square 15.

PAD.	Ross.H.	Ross.H.	PAD.
PM 8. 0r	5.20h	PM11. 5r	9.10h

Service temporarily suspended.

h A.M.
r Restaurant Car.

ROSYTH (Fife). 407 miles.

Fares, 84/5a, 50/8c. R. T. for two months, 168/10a, 101/4c. Departures *from* London as for Inverkeithing. Departures *for* London about 4 times daily.

ROTHBURY (Northum-

berland), 309 miles. Fares, 65/0a, 39/0c. R. T. for two months, 130/0a, 78/0c. Departures *from* London as for Morpeth. Departures *for* London about 4 times daily. Pop. 1,682.
Map Square 3.

The County Hotel. The

finest Hotel in Northumberland. Overlooking Simonside and Vale of Coquet.
See advt. p. 285.

ROTHERFIELD (Sussex)

from *Victoria* and *London Bridge*, 38½ miles. Fares, 8/1a, 4/10c. R. T. for two months, 16/2a, 9/8c. Departures *from* London as for Heathfield. Departures *for* London about 8 times daily. Pop. 2,870.
Map Square 24.

ROTHERHAM (MAS-

BORO') (Yorks) from *St. Pancras,* 162¾ miles. Fares, 32/9a, 19/8c. R. T., double fare. Pop. 68,045.
Map Square 13.

ST PAN.	ROTH'M	ROTH'M	ST.PAN.
AM 2.25g	7.44	AM 4.30	7.50
2.25	8.56	8.30r	12.10
4.25	9.23	9.15r	1.30
9. 0r	1.17	9.55r	1.45
9.50r	2. 6	10. 8r	2.10
11.45r	4.18	11.50r	4.10
PM12.25r	4.58	PM 1.45r	5.30
1.50r	5.31	3. 2r	7.15
2.25r	6.36	4.18r	7.57
3.30r	7.39	4.48dr	9. 5
5. 0r	9. 7	10.52	4.20
6.15r	9.56	—	—
9.15	12.58	—	—
9.30e	1.18	—	—

Sunday Trains.

AM10.50r	3.40	AM 5. 8	8.57
PM 3.15	7.13	8.38r	5.10
9.15	1. 3	PM 1.16	5.27
9.30	1.18	5. 1r	9.43
—	—	10.52	4.55

d Saturdays only.
e Saturdays excepted.
g Mondays excepted.
r Restaurant Car.

ROTHERHAM AND

MASBORO' (Yorks) from *King's Cross*, 164¾ miles. Fares as above.

KING'S +	ROTH'M	ROTH'M	KING'S +
AM 4.45	9.54	AM 6. 1r	11.30
7.15r	11.40	7.57	1. 5
8.45	2.10	10.23	3.50
11.30r	5.21	12. 0	6.25
PM 1.50r	6.27	PM 1.25dr	6.30
4. 0r	9. 7	4. 1	9. 0
5.45r	10.57	8.56	3.25
—	—	—	—

Sunday Trains.

12. 0nr	7. 4	PM 1.29	5.55
—	—	5.25r	10.20

d Saturdays only.
n Noon.
r Restaurant Car.

ANOTHER ROUTE from

Marylebone, 167½ miles. Fares as above.

M'BONE	ROTH'M	ROTH'M	M'BONE
AM 2.32	7. 3	AM 6. 1r	11.10
8.45r	12.49	9.18r	1.13
10. 0r	2.10	10.23r	3. 0
PM12.15r	5.21	PM 2.32r	6.38
3.20r	6.40	4. 1r	8.55
5. 0r	9. 7	5.12r	9.55
6.20r	10.57	11.25	3.57
10. 0d	7.58	—	—
10. 5e	5.32	—	—

Sunday Trains.

AM11.15r	4. 9	PM 1.29r	5.40
—	—	5.25r	10.24

d Saturdays only.
e Saturdays excepted.
r Restaurant Car.

ROTHERHITHE from

Hammersmith, Paddington Bishop's Road), Baker Street, King's Cross and *Liverpool Street* (Met.), 10¾ miles. Fares from Hammersmith, 1/0a, 0/8c. R. T., 1/6 a, 1/4c. From Paddington. 0/11a, 0/7c. R.T., 1/10a, 1/2c. From Baker Street, 0/9a, 0/6c. R. T., 1/6 a, 1/0c. From King's Cross, 0/8a, 0/5c. R. T. 1/4a, 0/10c. From Liverpool Street, 0/5a, 0/3c, R. T. 0/10a, 0/6c. Pop. 35,449. *See back of Map.*
Map Square 61.

ROTHES (Elgin), 565

miles. Fares, 106/3a, 63/9c. R. T. for two months, 212/6a, 127/6c. Departures *from* London as for Aviemore or Keith (*via* Aberdeen). Departures *for* London about twice daily. Pop. 1,905.
Map Square 35.

ROTHESAY (Bute) from

Euston. Fares, 86/8a, 52/0c. R. T. for two months, 173/4a, 104/0c. Pop. 15,218.
Map Square 40.

EUSTON	R'THSAY	R'THSAY	EUSTON
AM 2.35e	6. 0	AM 8. 5r	6.25
5. 0	6.45	10.50r	10. 0
PM 9.20e	9.45	PM 2. 5er	5. 0
11.45e	10.50	2.50dr	5. 0
—	—	6.50e	6.55
—	—	7.30d	7.30

Sunday Trains.

PM 9.30	9.45	—	—
11.45	10.30	—	—
—	—	—	—

d Saturdays only.
e Saturdays excepted.
r Restaurant Car.

Rothesay (Bute). Glenburn

Hotel-Hydro.
See advt. p. **285.**

ROTHIEMAY (Banff),

565¼ miles. Fares, 106/3a, 63/9c. R. T. for two months, 212/6a, 127/6c. Departures *from* London as for Huntly. Departures *for* London about twice daily. Pop. 965.
Map Square 35.

ROTHIE NORMAN

(Aberdeen), 550½ miles. No through fares. Departures *from* London as for Inverurie. Departures *for* London about 3 times daily.
Map Square 35.

ROTHLEY (Leicester)

from *Marylebone,* 108 miles. Fares, 21/11a, 13/2c. R. T., double fare. Pop. 2,006.
Map Square 18.

M'BONE	R'THL'Y	R'THL'Y	M'BONE.
AM 2.32	6.51	AM 5.55	9.46
8.45r	11.34	7.50	10.36
10. 0r	12.43	8.51r	11.10
PM12.15r	2.56	10.15r	1.13
3.20r	5.30	11.41r	3. 0
5. 0r	7.29	PM 3.31r	6.38
6.20r	9. 1	6. 6r	8.55
6.25	10.51	6.55r	9.55
—	—	10.55	3.57

Sunday Trains.

AM 8.18	8.25	8.25	9.42
PM 6.33	6.40	6.33	8.42

ROTHLEY—*continued.*

Sunday Trains.

M'BONE.	R'THL'Y	R'THL'Y	M'BONE.
AM 9.30	1.16	AM10. 1	5.40
11.15r	2.56	PM 3.46	8.58
PM 5.30r	8.46	7.10r	10.24

r Restaurant Car.

ROUND OAK (Stafford),

123½ miles. Fares, 25/3a, 15/2c. R. T. for two months, 50/6a. Departures *from* London as for Stourbridge Junction. Departures *for* London about 5 times daily.

ROW (Dumbarton), 461¾

miles. Fares, 84/2a, 50/6c. R. T. for two months, 168/4a, 101/0c. Departures *from* London as for Arrochar and Tarbet. Departures *for* London about 4 times daily. Pop. 1,462.
Map Square 40.

ROWDEN MILL (Hereford), 137½ miles. Fares, 27/4a, 16/5c. R. T. for two months, 54/8a, 32/10c. Departures *from* London as for Bromyard. Departures *for* London about 4 times daily.
Map Square 17.

ROWFANT (Sussex) from

London Bridge, Victoria and *Clapham Junction,* 31¾ miles. Fares, 6/3a, 3/9c. R. T. for two months, 12/6a, 7/6c.
Map Square 23.

	Leave		Arr. at
VICT.	CLAP. J.	LON. B.	ROWFT.
AM —	—	5.18	7.12
7.23	7.29	7.25	9.11
9. 0	9. 8	9. 6	10.22
9.45	9.51	9.50	11.16
11.55	—	11.50	1. 9
PM 1.20e	1.27e	—	2.41
1.25d	—	1.10d	2.41
2. 0	2. 7	2. 5e	3.51
—	—	2. 8d	3.51
4. 0	4. 8	4. 5	5.12
—	—	5. 5	5.59
6. 6	6.12	6. 8	7.44
7.15	7.22	7.20	8.44

Sunday Trains.

AM 8.18	8.25	8.25	9.42
PM 6.33	6.40	6.33	8.42

ROWFANT—*continued.*

Trains from Rowfant.

Leave	Arrive at		
ROWFT.	LON. B.	CLAP. J	VICT.
AM 6.48	8.15	8.15	8.24
8. 9	9.10	—	9.19
9.48	10.55	10.40	10.48
10.52	12.13	11.59	12. 7
PM12.19	1.42	1.39	1.50
3.29	4.32	4.27	4.35
5.40	7.42	7.37	7.45
7.10	8.46	8.39	8.48
9.16	10.58	11.10	11.17

Sunday Trains.

AM 8. 4	10.18	10.23	10.32
PM 6.34	7.56	8.31	8.41

d Saturdays only.
e Saturdays excepted.

ROWLAND'S CASTLE

(Hants) from *Waterloo,* 63 miles. Fares, 13/4a 8/0c. R. T. for two months, 26/8a, 16/0c.
Map Square 28.

W'LOO.	Row. C.	Row. C.	W'LOO.
AM 5.50	8.12	AM 7. 6	9.12
6.50	9.16	7.36s	9.44
8.34r	10.36	8.37	10.50
9.50	12. 2	9.18	11.32
10.50	1.14	11.37r	1.52
PM 1.50e	4. 8	PM12.41	3. 6
2. 0d	4.15	2. 0	4.16
2.34	5. 3	3.32	5.52
3.50d	6. 5	5. 7	7.46
4.15e	6.21	6.38	9. 6
4.50	6.47	8. 6	10.46
5.50	7.48	9.31	12.16
6.50er	9. 0	—	—
6.50dr	9.12	—	—

Sunday Trains.

AM 8.20	10.55	PM12.53	3.15
9.15r	11.18	3.49r	6.17
PM 1.50	4.10	6.36	8.52
4.20	7.11	—	—

r Restaurant Car.
s Refreshments served.

ROWLANDS GILL (Durham), 273 miles. Fares, 56/11a, 34/2c. R. T., double fare. Departures *from* London as for Durham or Bishop Auckland. Departures *for* London about 6 times daily.
Map Square 3.

ROWLEY (Yorks), 263½

miles. No through fares. Departures *from* London as for Bishop Auckland. Departures *for* London about 3 times daily. Pop. 544.
Map Square 7.

ROWLEY REGIS

(Stafford), 117¾ miles. Fares, 24/5a, 14/8c. R. T. for two months, 48/10a. Departures *from* London as for Smethwick Junction. Departures *for* London about 5 times daily. Pop. 40,037.

ROWRAH (Cumberland),

305¾ miles. Fares, 63/4*a*, 38/0*c*.
R.T. for two months, 126/8*a*, 76/0*c*.
Departures *from* London as for
Moor Row. Departures *for* London about 3 times daily.
Map Square 6.

ROWSLEY (Derby) from

St. Pancras, 149½ miles. Fares,
31/0*a*, 18/7*c*. R.T., double fare.
Pop. 335.
Map Square 12.

ST. PAN.	ROWSL'Y		ROWSL'Y	ST. PAN.
AM 2.25	8.16	AM	7.33*r*	11.35
10.25*r*	2.17		9.17*r*	1.30
PM 12.25*r*	5.0		10.36	3.25
2.25*r*	6.25	PM	1.13*r*	5.45
4.25*r*	8.13		4.47*r*	8.35
12. 0*h*	8.14		6. 9*r*	10. 5
—	—		9. 9	4.20

Sunday Trains.

PM 3.15	7. 4	AM	11.26*r*	5. 2
—	—	PM	5.4*z*	9.52
—	—		8.35	4.55

h Saturdays midnight only.
r Restaurant Car.

ROWTHORN (Derby),

144½ miles. Fares, 29/5*a*, 17/8*c*.
R. T., double fare. Departures
from London as for Mansfield.
Departures *for* London about 4
times daily.
Map Square 13.

ROXBURGH, 353¼ miles.

No through fares. Departures
from London as for Kelso or
St. Boswells. Departures *for*
London about 4 times daily.
Map Square 41.

ROYAL ALBERT DOCKS.

See under CENTRAL,
CONNAUGHT ROAD or GALLIONS.

ROYAL OAK from Ald-

gate, 5½ miles. See back of Map.
Map Square 50.

ROY BRIDGE (Inverness),

513 miles. Fares, 101/11*a*, 61/2*c*.
R.T. for two months, 203/10*a*, 122/4*c*.
Departures *from* London as for
Fort William. Departures *for*
London about 3 times daily.
Map Square 37.

ROYDON (Essex) from

Liverpool Street, 20¼ miles. Fares,
4/5*a*, 2/8*c*. R. T. for two months,
8/10*a*. Pop. 1,182.
Map Square 23.

L'P'L ST.	ROYDON		ROYDON	L'P'L ST.
AM 5.50	6.36	AM	7.21	8.18
7.18	8.17		7.54	8.49
9.10	10.12		8. 9	8.57
10.34	12. 2		8.59	9.42
PM 12.40*d*	1.26		10.14	10.59
12.48*e*	1.49		11.17	12.15
1.19*d*	2. 2	PM	1.19	2. 7
2. 0*d*	2.45		2.38*d*	3.18
2.48	3.39		4. 5	5. 9
4.15	4.54		6. 9	7.19
5.10	5.54		7. 5	7.58
6. 0*e*	6.39		8.29	9.33
6.30	7. 9		10.24	11.12
7.41*d*	8.25		—	—
7.41*e*	8.28		—	—
9.17	10.14		—	—
11.50*k*	12.32		—	—

ROYDON—*continued.*

Sunday Trains.

L'P'L ST.	ROYDON		ROYDON	L'P'L ST.
AM 8.12	8.52	AM	8.14	9.33
9.25	10. 9		10.29	11.27
PM 1.50	3. 3	PM	8.18	9.10
4.50	5.54		9.43	10.40
7.15	8. 0		—	—
9.12	10. 8		—	—

d Saturdays only.
e Saturdays excepted.
k Wednesdays and Saturdays only.

ROYSTON (Herts) from

King's Cross, 45 miles. Fares,
9/5*a*, 5/8*c*. R. T., for two months,
18/10*a*, 11/4*c*. Pop. 3,826.
Map Square 18.

KING'S +	ROYST.		ROYST.	KING'S +
AM 5. 5	6.50	AM	7. 0	8.41
7. 0	9. 2		8. 7	9.34
8.45	10.13		8.46	9.56
11.30	1.14		9.51*h*	11.15
PM 12.40*d*	1.55		10.19	11.25
3. 0	4.15		11.32*k*	1.25
5. 0	6. 8		11.37*h*	1.25
6.15	7.38	PM	2. 8	3.50
7. 0	8.32		4.38	6. 0
8.30	10. 0		6.40	8. 5
—	—		8.26	10.20
—	—		9.25	11. 0

Sunday Trains.

AM 8.30	10.22	AM	7.50	9.53
PM 7.10	8.46	PM	6. 3	8. 8
—	—		9. 0	10.20

d Saturdays only.
h Tuesdays only.
k Tuesdays excepted.

Bull Hotel. Premier hotel.
Restaurant. Separate tables.
Masonic Room. Close Golf Links.
Garage. A.A., R.A.C., C.T.C.
Free House Tel. 42. Telegrams :
Harling.
Mr. F. E. HARLING, Proprietor.

Logsdon's Garage, Royston.
Well appointed Landaulettes and
Touring Cars. Weddings and
Funerals specially catered for
Lorries and Vans on hire. Taxis
meet all trains. Telephone 25.
E. LOGSDON.

ROYSTON (Yorks), 177½

miles. Fares, 36/6*a*, 21/8*c*. R. T.,
double fare. Departures *from*
London as for Cudworth. Departures *for* London about 4 times
daily. Pop. 6,455.
Map Square 12.

ROYTON (Lancs), 190½

miles. Fares, 39/2*a*, 23/6*c*. R.T.,
double fare. Departures *from*
London as for Manchester. Departures *for* London about 6
times daily. Pop. 17,207.
Map Square 12.

ROYTON JUNCT.

(Lancs), 189½ miles. Fares, 39/0*a*,
23/5*c*. R.T. for two months, 78/0*a*,
46/10*c*. Departures *from* London
as for Manchester. Departures
for London about 6 times daily.

RUABON (Denbigh) from

Paddington, 178½ miles. Fares,
37/1*a*, 22/3*c*. R. T. for two
months, 74/2*a*. Pop. 3,387.
Map Square 12.

PAD.	RUABON		RUABON	PAD.
AM 9.10*r*	1.32	AM	8.13	12.25
10.40*r*	2.33		9. 6*r*	1.25
PM 12.50*r*	5. 2		10.15*r*	2. 5
2.10*t*	6.17	PM	1. 4*r*	5. 0
4.10*t*	8.26		1.13*t*	5.55
6.10*kr* 10. 3			3.48*r*	8. 5
12.15*h*	5.55		5.46*r*	10. 0
12.15*kl*	5.54		8.33	3.30

Sunday Trains.

PM 12.50*r*	4.55	AM	10.50	6.20
—	—	PM	4.20*r*	9. 0

h Saturday midnight excepted.
k Calls to set down on notice to the
Guard at Shrewsbury.
l Saturdays midnight only.
r Restaurant Car.
t Tea Car.

RUBERY (Worcester), 124½

miles. Fares, 25/5*a*, 15/3*c*. R.T.
for two months, 50/10*a*, 30/6*c*. Departures *from* London as for
Smethwick Junction. Departures *for* London about 3 times
daily.
Map Square 17.

RUDDINGTON (Notts)

from Marylebone, 122½ miles.
Fares, 24/10*a*, 14/11*c*. R.T., double
fare. Pop. 2,771.
Map Square 13.

M'BONE	RUD'TON		RUD'TON	M'BONE
AM 2.32	7.19	AM	5.30	9.46
8.45*r*	12. 2		7.50*h*	10.36
10. 0*r*	1.11		8.20*r*	11.10
PM 12.15*r*	3.25		9.40*r*	1.13
3.20*r*	5.58		11.10*r*	3. 0
5. 0*r*	7.57	PM	3. 0*r*	6.38
6.20*r*	9.29		5.35*r*	8.55
—	—		6.24*r*	9.55
—	—		10.25	3.57

Sunday Trains.

AM 9.30	1.44	AM	9.30	5.40
11.15*r*	3.24	PM	3.15	8.58
PM 5.30*r*	9.14		6.37*r*	10.24

h Stops on notice being given at
the station.
r Restaurant Car.

RUDGWICK (Sussex) from

Victoria, Clapham Junction, and
London Bridge, 44½ miles. Fares,
8/1*a*, 4/10*c*. R.T. for two months,
16/2*a*. Pop. 1,246.
Map Square 23.

		Leave		Arr. at
	VICT.	CLAP. J.	LON. B.	R'WICK.
AM 6.18	6.25	6.35	8.14
8.55	7.56	7.35	10.36
10.35	10.42	10.35	1.22
PM 1.40	1.47*e*	1.50	3.53
3.55	4. 2	4. 0	5.38
5. 5	5.12	5.14	7. 2
7.20*d*	7.27*d*	7.20*d*	9.36

Sunday Trains.

AM 8.35	8.42	8.25	10.22
PM 4. 5	4.13	3.50	6.12

Trains from Rudgwick.

Leave		Arrive at	
R'WICK.	LON. B.	CLAP. J.	VICT.
AM 7.10*f*	9.10	9.31	9.19
8.45	10.45	10.40	10.48
9.46	11.50	11.35	11.42
11. 1	1.28	—	1.10
PM 12.13	2.22	2.13	2.22
2.51	4.27	4.27	4.55
5.49	7.48	7.31	7.39
8.17*d*	10. 8	9.53	10. 1
8.20*e*	10. 8	9.53	10. 1

RUDGWICK—*continued.*

Trains from Rudgwick.

Sunday Trains.

Leave	Arrive at		
R'WICK.	LON. B.	CLAP. J.	VICT.
AM 8.14	10.45	10.23	10.32
PM 7.29	9.32	9.24	9.34

d Saturdays only.
e Saturdays excepted.
f Mondays only.

RUDYARD (Stafford), 156¾ miles. Fares, 32/6*a*, 19/6*c*. R. T. for two months, 65/0*a*, 39/0*c*. Departures *from* London as for Leek. Departures *for* London about 4 times daily. Pop. 81.
Map Square 12.

RUFFORD (Lancs), 208 miles. No through fares. Departures *from* London as for Preston. Departures *for* London about 4 times daily. Pop. 794.
Map Square 12.

RUGBY (Warwick) from
Euston, 82½ miles. Fares, 17/3*a*, 10/4*c*. R. T. for two months, 34/6*a*. Pop. 23,098.
Map Square 18.

EUSTON	RUGBY	RUGBY	EUSTON
AM 2.35	4.13	AM 1.38*g*	4. 0
5. 0	6.48	2.55	5. 0
6.45	8.47	3.29*g*	5.40
8.30*r*	10. 7	5.39*g*	7.15
8.45*r*	10.16	5.55	7.30
9.15*h*	11.18	6. 5*g*	7.40
10. 0*r*	11.30	7.20*e*	9.32
10.40	12.49	8.21*r*	10. 0
11.35*r*	1. 6	9.32	11. 0
12. 0*nr*	2. 5	9.45	11.55
PM 1.30*r*	3. 5	9.55*d*	12.20
2.35*t*	4. 8	9.55*e*	12.32
2.59*t*	4.22	11.31*r*	1. 0
3. 5	5.27	PM12.45*r*	2.20
4. 5*t*	5.37	2.25	4.15
4.45*t*	6.17	3.12	5.35
5.20*t*	6.53	4.12*r*	5.50
5.32	7.47	4.30*t*	6. 0
6.30*er*	8.12	4.45*t*	6.15
7. 0*r*	8.45	5.35*t*	7.20
7.15*d*	10.45	5.56*r*	7.30
7.50*e*	9.36	7.16	9.20
8. 0*e*	9.49	9.15	10.45
9.20	10.54	—	—
9.30	11.11	—	—
11.45*e*	1.22	—	—
11.50	1.48	—	—
12.10*d*	2. 8	—	—

Sunday Trains.

AM 8.15	11.35	AM 2.55	5. 0
9.15	11.48	3.29	5.45
11.30*r*	1. 7	5.39	7.15
11.45*r*	1.22	5.55	7.30
PM12.10*r*	1.51	6. 5	7.40
12.30*r*	2.17	10. 4	12.25
1. 0*r*	2.32	10.15	1.20
3.50	6.27	11.43*r*	1.30
6. 0*r*	7.35	PM 1.55	4. 0
6.45	9.22	2.50	5. 5
7.50*r*	9.36	3. 5	5.50
9.15	11.23	5.57*r*	7.30
11.45	1.22	6.38*r*	8.20
11.50	1.52	7.14*r*	8.55
—	—	7.35	10.10

d Saturdays only.
e Saturdays excepted.
g Mondays excepted.
h Via Northampton.
n Noon.
r Restaurant Car.
t Tea Car.

RUGBY—*continued.*

ANOTHER ROUTE (CENTRAL) from *Marylebone*, 83½ miles.
Fares as above.

M'BONE	RUGBY	RUGBY	M'BONE
AM 2.32	4. 5	AM 6.49	9.46
6.45	9.45	8.45	10.38
8.45*r*	10.41	9.13	12. 2
10. 0*r*	11.47	11.24*r*	1.13
PM12.15*r*	2.11	PM 1.14*r*	3. 0
4.30	6.42	1.59	4.56
6.25*e*	9.12	7.12*r*	8.55
6.25*d*	9.21	8.10*r*	9.55
7.30*d*	11.14	—	—
10. 0*d*	11.49	—	—
10. 5*e*	11.54	—	—
—	—	—	—
—	—	—	—
—	—	—	—

Sunday Trains.

AM 9.30	12.23	AM 6.56	10.13
PM 5.30*r*	7.21	PM 5.41	8.58
6.30	9.51	8.41*r*	10.24
—	—	—	—

d Saturdays only.
e Saturdays excepted.
r Restaurant Car.

Royal George Hotel, Rugby. The leading First-class Family Hotel, nearest to the School. Electric Light. Excellent cuisine. Telephone No. 2.

RUGELEY (Stafford) from
Euston, 124½ miles. Fares, 26/0*a*, 15/7*c*. R.T. for two months, 52/0*a*. Pop. 4,607.
Map Square 17.

EUSTON	RUGEL'Y	RUGEL'Y	EUSTON
AM 5. 0	8. 5	AM 5.57*r*	10. 0
8.45*r*	11.53	7.50	11. 0
10.40*r*	2.22	10.40*r*	2.20
12. 0*nr*	4.15	PM12. 2	4.15
PM 2.50*r*	5.32	2.30*t*	6.15
4. 5*t*	7. 2	4.46*r*	8.10
5.20*dr*	9.35	6.37*r*	10.45
6.30*er*	9.35	9.15	5. 0
—	—	—	—

Sunday Trains.

AM 9.15	1.19	PM 1.16	5. 5
PM 3.50	7.44	—	—
—	—	—	—
—	—	—	—

d Saturdays only.
e Saturdays excepted.
n Noon.
r Restaurant Car.
t Tea Car.

RUISLIP (Middlesex) from
Baker Street, 13½ miles. Fares, 2/3*a*, 1/4½*c*. R.T. for two days, 3/8*a*, 2/6*c*. Departures *from* London as for Uxbridge. Departures *for* London about 6 minutes later. Pop. 9,112.
Map Squares 23 and 47.

ANOTHER ROUTE from
Mansion House, via Acton Town and South Harrow. 19 miles.
See p. 489.

RUISLIP&ICKENHAM
(Middlesex) from *Paddington*, 12½ miles. Fares, 2/3½*a*, 1/4½*c*. R.T. for two days, 4/7*a*, 2/6*c*. *See* pp. 490-491.

ANOTHER ROUTE from
Marylebone, 13½ miles. Fares as above. *See* pp. 495-496.

RUISLIP MANOR (Middlesex) from *Baker St.*, 13½ miles. Fares, 2/3½*a*, 1/4½*c*. R. T. for two days, 3/8*a*, 2/6*c*. Departures *from* London as for Uxbridge. Departures *for* London about 7 minutes later.
Map Square 47.

ANOTHER ROUTE from
Mansion House, via Acton Town and South Harrow, 18¾ miles.
See p. 489.

RUMBLING BRIDGE
(Kinross) 429½ miles. Fares, 87/1*a*, 52/3*c*. R. T. for two months, 174/2*a*, 104/6*c*. Departures *from* London as for Dunfermline or Stirling. Departures *for* London about 3 times daily.
Map Square 40.

RUMWORTH (Lancs), 196½ miles. Fares, 40/5*a*, 24/3*c*. R.T. for two months, 80/10*a*, 48/6*c*. Departures *from* London as for Kenyon. Departures *for* London about 6 times daily. Pop. 8,904.
Map Square 12.

RUNCORN (Cheshire)
from *Euston*, 180½ miles. Fares, 37/8*a*, 22/7*c*. R.T. for two months, 75/4*a*, 45/2*c*. Pop. 18,393.
Map Square 12.

EUSTON	RUNC'N	RUNC'N	EUSTON
AM 2.35	8.17	AM12.18	5.40
5. 0	9.53	8.24*er*12. 5	
6.45	12. 3	8.24*dr*12.20	
8.30*r*	1. 2	8.45*r*	1. 0
11.50*r*	3.53	9.35*r*	1.45
12. 0*nr*	4.50	10.53*r*	3.10
PM 1.30*r*	5.55	PM12.24*r*	5.35
2.35*t*	6.46	12.40*r*	5.50
4. 5*r*	8. 3	3. 5*r*	7.30
5.20*r*	9.20	4.54*er*	9. 5
11.50*d*	9.21	5.58*r*	10. 0
—	—	7.42	5. 0
—	—	—	—

Sunday Trains.

PM12.30*r*	5.22	AM12.18	5.45
3.50	9.30	9. 5	1.30
—	—	11. 4	4. 0

d Saturdays only.
e Saturdays excepted.
n Noon.
r Restaurant Car.
t Tea Car.

RUNEMEDE RANGE
(Middlesex) from *Paddington*, 18½ miles. Fares, 3/4*a*, 2/0*c*. R.T. for two months, 6/8*a*, 4/0*c*. Departures *from* London as for Colnbrook. Departures *for* London about 8 times daily.
Map Square 73.

RUSHBURY (Salop) 156¾ miles. Fares, 32/4*a*, 19/5*c*. R. T. for two months,64/8*a*. Departures *from* London as for Much Wenlock. Departures *for* London about 3 times daily. Pop. 576.
Map Square 17.

RUSHDEN (Northampton)

from *St. Pancras,* 66 miles. Fares, 13/2a, 7/11c. R. T., double fare. Pop. 13,511. *Map Square* 18.

ST. PAN.	R'DEN	R'DEN	ST. PAN.
AM 4.25	7.11	AM 7.27	9.30
7.50	10.30	8.27r	9.57
9.25	12.37	9.57	11.25
11.35	2..2	11.49r	1.30
PM 1.25r	3.46	PM 1.32	3.25
2.45	4.36	3.19	5.20
3.35	5.40	4.49	7.3
4.30r	6.35	5.57	8.22
6.30	8.31	7.34r	10.5
8.25	10.34	9.4	11.45
—	—	—	—

No Sunday Trains.
r Restaurant Car.

RUSHTON (Stafford), 159¾

miles. Fares, 33/.a, 19/11c. R.T. for two months, 66/4a, 39/10c. Departures *from London* as for Leek. Departures *for London* about 6 times daily. Pop. 919. *Map Square* 12.

RUSKINGTON (Lincoln),

114¼ miles. Fares, 23/9a, 14/3c. R.T., double fare. Departures *from* London as for Blankney. Departures *for London* about 4 times daily. Pop. 1,102. *Map Square* 13.

RUSSELL SQUARE

(Hammersmith and Finsbury Park Tube). *See* back of Map.

RUSWARP (Yorks), 242¾

miles. Fares, 50/7a, 30/4c. R.T., double fare. Departures *from London* as for Whitby. Departures *for London* about 4 times daily. Pop. 831. *Map Square* 8.

RUTHERFORD (Roxburgh), 356½ miles. No through fares. Departures *from London* as for Kelso or St. Boswells. Departures *for London* about 4 times daily. *Map Square* 41.

RUTHIN (Denbigh) from

Euston 215¼ miles. Fares, 40/7a, 24/4c. R.T. for two months, 81/2a, 48/8c. Pop. 2,767. *Map Square* 11.

EUSTON	RUTHIN	RUTHIN	EUSTON
AM 12.25	9.21	AM 7.15er	1.0
5.0	12.14	8.5r	1.45
8.30r	2.54	8.40r	2.20
10.30r	3.42	11.27hr	5.5
11.10¼r	5.30	PM 2.10r	8.10
11.50r	6.56	4.30r	10.45
PM 2.35t	8.13	7.30	5.0
4.5dr	10.4	—	—
—	—	—	—

No Sunday Trains.

d Saturdays only.
e Saturdays excepted.
h Via Rhyl.
r Restaurant Car.
t Tea Car.

RUTHIN—continued.

ANOTHER ROUTE from *Paddington,* 205¼ miles. Fares as above.

PAD	RUTHIN	RUTHIN	PAD.
AM 10.40r	5.30	AM 9.21r	5.0
PM 12.50r	7.30	PM 12.14r	8.5
AM 12.15h	11.27	3.42r	10.0
—	—	5.29	3.30

No Sunday Trains.

h Saturdays midnight excepted.
r Restaurant Car.

RUTHWELL (Dumfries),

323¾ miles. Fares, 65/7a, 39/4c. R.T. for two months, 131/2a, 78/8c. Departures *from London* for Annan. Departures *for London* about 4 times daily. Pop. 727. *Map Square* 44.

RYBURGH (Norfolk)

from *Liverpool Street,* 132 miles. Fares, 23/7a, 14/2c. R.T. for two months, 47/2a. Departures *from London* as for Dereham. Departures *for London* about 8 times daily. Pop. 781. *Map Square* 19.

RYDE PIER HEAD (Isle

of Wight) from *Victoria* and *London Bridge,* 91 miles. Fares, 17/6a, 10/9c. R.T. for two months, 35/0a, 21/6c. Pop. 11,295. *Map Square* 28.

Leave		Arr. at RYDE PIER HEAD
VICTORIA	LON. B.	
AM 6.18	6.35	10.40
8.55	—	12.0
10.15	10.22	1.40
11.35	—	2.25
PM 1.35	—	4.15
1.40	1.50	5.15
1.55	2.5	6.40
—	4.50	7.40

Sunday Trains.

AM 9.55		12.55
PM 1.14	1.10	6.20
—	—	—

Trains from Ryde Pier Head.

Leave RYDE (PIER HEAD).	Arrive at	
	LON. B.	VICTORIA
AM 6.45g	10.45	10.53
7.5f	10.45	10.52
8.0	10.55	—
10.5	—	1.10e
PM 1.5	4.27	4.34
2.5	—	5.12
4.5	7.48	6.50
5.45	—	8.33
6.15	10.8	10.1

Sunday Trains.

PM 5.0	8.50	7.56

f Mondays only.
g Mondays excepted.

RYDE PIER HEAD—continued.

ANOTHER ROUTE from *Waterloo,* 79 miles. Fares, Ryde (Esplanade) 17/8a, 10/10c. R.T. for two months, 35/4a, 21/8c.

W'LOO.	RYDE (PIER HEAD)	RYDE (PIER HEAD)	W'LOO.
AM 5.50	9.40	AM 6.45rg	9.52
8.34r	12.0	7.5fr	9.52
9.50	12.40	8.0	11.32
10.50	2.0	8.55	11.41
11.50d	3.15	11.5r	1.52
PM 12.50r	3.40	PM 12.5d	3.20
1.50d	4 40	12.30	4.16
2.34	6.15	3.5	5.56
3.50s	6.40	3.45	7.46
5.50	8.40	5.5r	7.56
—	—	6.15	10.46

Sunday Trains.

W'LOO.	RYDE	RYDE	W'LOO.
AM 8.0	11.10	AM 11.30	3.13
9.15r	12.55	PM 3.10r	6.16
PM 1.50	6.20	5.0	8.52
—	—	6.35	10.1

d Saturdays excepted.
f Mondays only.
g Mondays excepted.
r Restaurant Car.
s Refreshments served.

RYDE PIER HEAD—*continued.*

Crown Hotel, Family and Commercial. Under new management. Special week-end terms. Ordinary daily. Moderate tariff. Telephone 280.
E. BROWNING, Director.

Woodbine Private Hotel. Moderate terms, according to season, winter included. Comfort studied. Tel. No. 209. Motor side car. Proprietress,
J. CONSTANCE RICE.

RYE (Sussex) from *Charing Cross, Cannon Street,* and *London Bridge,* 72¼ miles. Fares, 15/0*a*, 12/0*b*, 9/0*c* R.T. for two months, 30/0*a*, 24/0*b*. Pop. 3,918.
Map Square 24.

Leave CHAR. +	CAN. ST.	LON. B.	Arr. at RYE
AM —	5.20	5.25	8.42
9.15	—	9.23	11.22
11. 0	—	11. 7	1.15
PM 1. 0	—	—	4.37
4.30*k*	—	4.37*k*	6.39
—	5. 0*l*	—	6.44
7.18	—	7.26	9.48
—	—	—	—
—	—	—	—
—	—	—	—
—	—	—	—

Sunday Trains.

AM 7.45	—	7.52	10.14
PM 7.35	—	7.45	9.52
—	—	—	—
—	—	—	—

Trains from Rye.

Leave RYE	Arrive at LON. B.	CAN. ST.	CHAR. +
AM 6.57	9.32	9.36	—
9.32	11.43	—	11.57
PM12.53	3.26	—	3.40
3.34	5.50	—	6. 3
5.50	8.54	9. 1	—
7.55	10.22	—	10.35
—	—	—	—
—	—	—	—
—	—	—	—
—	—	—	—

Sunday Trains.

AM 7. 4	10. 5	—	10.15
5. 9	7. 9	—	7.17
PM 8. 9	10.16	—	10.26
—	—	—	—

e Saturdays excepted.
k Fridays excepted.
l Fridays only.

ANOTHER ROUTE from *Victoria, Holborn Viaduct* and *St. Paul's* (*via* Ashford), 74¼ miles. Fares as above.

VICT. (S.E. & C.)	Leave HOL. V.	ST. PL's.	Arr. at RYE
AM —	6.40	6.42	11.22
9.45	—	—	1.15
PM 2.12*e*	1.24*d*	1.30*d*	4.37
2.40*d*	—	—	6.39
2.50*l*	—	—	6.39
2.50*h*	—	—	6.44
7.22	—	—	9.48
—	—	—	—
—	—	—	—
—	—	—	—
—	—	—	—

Sunday Trains.

AM 9.35	—	—	11.53
PM 5.15	—	—	8. 1
6.35	6.40	—	9.52
—	—	—	—
—	—	—	—
—	—	—	—

RYE—*continued.*

Trains from Rye.

Leave RYE.	Arrive at ST. PL's.	HOL. V.	VICT.
AM 6.57	9.53	9.55	—
9.32	12.59	1. 2	12.49
PM12.53	—	—	3.37
2.45	—	—	5.42
3.34	6.58	7. 0	—
7.55	11.43	11.45	—

Sunday Trains.

AM 7. 4	—	—	10.48
10.44	—	—	1. 5
PM 5. 9	—	9. 9	—
—	—	—	—

d Saturdays only.
e Saturdays excepted.
h Fridays only.
l Friday and Saturday excepted.

George Hotel. First-Class Family and Residential, recently redecorated, and every comfort studied. Three minutes from Station. Nearest to Golf Links. Special Terms to Golfers. Garage. M. A. C. M. U. Telephone 14. Proprietor, WALTER WOOD.

Mermaid Hotel. The famous Tudor Inn, XVth Century House, with every modern comfort. The only Hotel with Electric Light. Special Terms to Golfers and Families. Close to Station. Telegrams: "Mermaid," Rye. Telephone 22.
RESIDENT PROPRIETORS.

Royal William Hotel, Camber-Rye, Sussex. The only Hotel on the Links. Close to Golf Club House. Special Terms to Golfers. Excellent Cuisine. Moderate Terms. Telephone, Rye 94.
E. F. & R. J. TUNBRIDGE, Proprietors.

Flushing Inn and Fresco Club. Under New Management. Well Heated. Constant Hot Water. Excellent Cooking. Special Terms to Golfers. Near Station. Telephone 42. Resident Proprietor— S. WILSON.

RYE HILL (Yorks), 206¼ miles. No through fares. Departures *from* London as for Hull (Paragon). Departures *for* London about 5 times daily. Pop. 245.
Map Square 13.

RYEFORD (Gloucester), 123¾ miles. No through fares. Departures *from* London as for Gloucester. Departures *for* London about 6 times daily.
Map Square 22.

RYE HOUSE (Herts) from *Liverpool Street,* 19 miles. Fares, 4/2*a*, 3/4*b*, 2/6*c*. R. T. for two months, 8/4*a*, 6/7*b*, 4/11½*c*. *See* pp. 526-527.
Map Square 23.

RYELAND (Lanark), 402¾ miles. No through fares. Departures *from* London as for Hamilton. Departures *for* London about 3 times daily.
Map Square 40.

RYHALL (Rutland), 90¼ miles. Fares, 17/3*a*, 10/4*c*. R. T., double fare. Departures *from* London as for Stamford. Departures *for* London about 6 times daily. Pop. 701.
Map Square 18.

RYHILL (Yorks), 177¼ miles. Fares, 36/6*a*, 21/11*c*. R. T., double fare. Departures *from* London as for Barnsley. Departures *for* London about 6 times daily. Pop. 2,191.
Map Square 12.

RYHOPE (Durham), 258¼ miles. Fares, 54/0*a*, 32/5*c*. R.T., double fare. Departures *from* London as for Sunderland. Departures *for* London about 6 times daily Pop. 11,185.
Map Square 4.

RYLSTONE (Yorks), 226 miles. Fares, 44/0*a*, 26/5*c*. R.T., double fare. Departures *from* London as for Skipton. Departures *for* London about 4 times daily. Pop. 116.
Map Square 7.

RYSTON (Norfolk) from *Liverpool Street,* 85¾ miles. No through fares. Departures *from* London as for Stoke Ferry. Departures *for* London about 4 times daily. Pop. 27.
Map Square 19.

RYTON (Durham), 272¼ miles. Fares, 57/11*a*, 34/9*c*. R.T., double fare. Departures *from* London as for Newcastle-on-Tyne. Departures *for* London about 9 times daily. Pop. 14,263.
Map Square 3.

REFERENCE NOTES.

a signifies First Class. ·
b   ,,   Second Class.
c   ,,   Third Class.
d   ,,   On Saturdays only.
e   ,,   Saturdays excepted.
f   ,,   On Mondays only.
g   ,,   Mondays excepted.
r   ,,   Restaurant Car.
t   ,,   Tea Car.
x   ,,   Express.
R.T. ,,   Return Tickets.

All Trains in the Tables not
otherwise marked carry Third
Class Passengers.

S

SADDLEWORTH

(Yorks) from *Euston*, 191¼ miles.
Fares, 37/9a, 22/8c. R.T., double
fare. Pop. 12,565.
Map Square 12.

Euston	S'worth	S'worth	Euston
AM12.25	7.29	AM 6.49er	12. 5
2.35	9.41	7.21r	12.50
5. 0	11.29	8.34r	1.15
8.45r	1.33	9. 2r	1.45
10.40r	3.49	10. 1r	3.10
11.50r	4.49	10.59r	3.55
12. 0nr	6. 9	PM 1. 0r	6.15
PM 1.30r	7.34	1.55r	7.36
4. 5r	9. 4	3. 7r	8.10
6. 5r	10.49	5. 7er	10. 10
11.50d	8.34	9.37	5. 0
—	—	—	—
—	—	—	—
—	—	—	—

Sunday Trains.

PM12.10r	5.46	AM 8.16	4. 0
12.30r	9.18	11.51r	5.45
—	—	PM 1.41r	7.30
—	—	6.33	5. 0

d Saturdays only.
e Saturdays excepted
n Noon.
r Restaurant Car.

SAFFRON WALDEN

(Essex) from *Liverpool Street*, 43½
miles. Fares, 9/4a, 5/7c. R.T.
for two months, 18/8a. Pop. 5,876.
Map Square 19.

L'p'l St.	Saff. W.	Saff. W.	L'p'l. St.
AM 5.50	7.44	AM 7. 3	8.57
7.18	9.24	8. 0	9.27
8.30	9.48	8.50	10.17
10. 5	11.42	9.53	11.27
11.50	1. 8	PM12.14	2. 7
PM12.29d	1.58	1.34d	3.18
12.48eh	2.50	2.30	5. 9
12.48ek	3. 4	2.42dk	5. 9
1.19d	3. 4	3.35	5.17
2.34	3.49	4.16	6.10
2.48	4.41	5.55	7.58
4 15	5.43	6.46	8.22
4.45	6.16	9. 0	10.30
5.40	7.18	—	—
7.10	8.28	—	—
8.22	9.42	—	—
—	—	—	—
—	—	—	—

No Sunday Trains.

d Saturdays only.
e Saturdays excepted.
h Commencing July 23.
k Will cease to run after July 21.

ST. AGNES (Cornwall)

from *Paddington*, 288 miles.
Fares, 58/2 *a*, 34/11c. R.T. for two
months, 116/4 *a*, 69/10c. Departures
from London as for Perranporth.
Departures *for* London about 4
times daily. Pop. 3,835.
Map Square 25.

ST. ALBANS (Herts) from

St. Pancras, 19¼ miles. Fares, 4/2a,
2/6c. R.T., double fare. Pop.
25,888.
Map Square 23.

St. Pan.	St. Alb.	St. Alb.	St. Pan.
AM 4.25	4.58	AM 4.30f	4.55
6. 0	6.53	4.34g	5. 5
6.25	7.13	5.35	6. 0
7.50	8.22	6.42	7.37
8. 0	8.40	7.23	8.15
8.50	9.38	7.58	8.28
9.25	9.59	8.30	8.55
9.55	10.56	8.40	9.25
10.45	11.41	8.59	9.32g
11.35	12. 9	9.20	9.50c
11.48	12.43	9.38	10. 5
PM12.33	1.22	10. 2	10.31
12.42d	1.15	10.20	11.16
1. 8	1.41	11. 8	11.50
1.13	2. 2	11.39	12. 5
1.33d	2.11	PM12.20	1. 3
2. 0d	2.41	1. 2	1.55
2.15	2.53	1.55	2.52
2.35	3.31	2.38	3.10
3.35	4. 7	2.47	3.38
3.55	4.50	3.33	4.33
4.40	5.19	4.17	5.10
4.45	5.31	4.55	5.20
5. 5	5.40	5.11	6. 6
5.12	6. 0	5.56	6.30
5.20e	5.51	6. 2	6.50
5.45e	6.19	6.37	7. 3
6. 2e	6.45	7.20	8.12
6.35	7. 7	7.50	8.42
6.45e	7.23	8.28	8.58
6.50e	7.42	8.35	9.29
7.20	8. 8	9.55	10.48
7.50	8.23	10.47	11.35
8.25	8.58	11.12	11.45
9.18	10. 9	—	—
10. 5	10.38	—	—
10.35	11.23	—	—
11.35	12.23	—	—
12. 0	12.32	—	—
12. 7k	12.50	—	—
—	—	—	—
—	—	—	—

Sunday Trains.

AM 8. 0	8.55	AM 4.34	5. 5
10. 0	10.51	5.33	6. 0
PM12.50	1.42	9.17	10.15
1.35	2.15	11.17	12.10
2. 0	2.51	PM12.50	1.30
5. 0	3.53	3. 1	3.56
4.35	5.26	4.20	5.15
5.40	6.29	5.20	6.15
7. 0	7.48	5.53	6.27
8.25	8.58	7.25	8.20
8.38	9.27	7.56	8.30
9.35	10.25	8.10	9. 2
11.55	12.27	8.30	9.25
—	—	9.40	10.32
—	—	10.36	11. 7
—	—	—	—
—	—	—	—
—	—	—	—
—	—	—	—

d Saturdays only.
e Saturdays excepted.
f Mondays only.
g Mondays excepted.
h Arrives at King's + (Met.
Station).
k Monday mornings excepted.

ST. ALBANS—*contd.*

ANOTHER ROUTE from
King's Cross, 23¼ miles. Fares as above.

KING'S + (G.N.)	ST. ALB.	ST. ALB.	KING'S + (G.N.)
AM 7.45	·8.35	AM 7.52	8.41
9.20	10. 8	8.58	9.44
10.12	11.12	9.32	10.22
11.30	12.28	10.33	12. 3
PM 1. 8	2. 7	11.45	12.45
1.55*k*	3.22	PM 1.21	2.22
4.15	5.14	2.40*k*	4.23
5.50	6.43	4.27	5.45
7. 0	7.56	5.57	7. 5
10.55*k*	11.46	7.12	8. 5
—	—	8.30*d*	9.50

No Sunday Trains.

k Thursdays only.

ANOTHER ROUTE from
Euston, 24 miles. Fares, 4/5*a*, 2/8*c*. R.T. for two months, 8/10*a*, 5/4*c*.

EUSTON	ST. ALB.	ST. ALB.	EUSTON
AM 6. 5	7.20	AM 5.40	6.52
6.30	8. 2	6.38	7.52
7.15	8.24	7.24	8.24
8.30	9.33	8.28*e*	9.22
9.40	10.35	8.38	9.30
10.50	11.47	8.53*e*	9.52
11.30	12.47	9.38	10.30
PM12.15*d*	1.10	10.45	11.40
12.30*e*	1.45	PM12. 8	1.21
12.58*d*	1.45	12.53	1.50
1. 0*e*	2. 6	1.49*h*	2.45
1.10*d*	2. 6	2.13	3. 5
1.35*d*	2.30	2.45	3.50
2. 0	3. 2	3. ·8*d*	4.21
2. 7*d*	3.25	3.30	4.30
2.40*d*	3.47	3.55*d*	5.21
3. 5	4.12	4.20	5.35
3.30	4.37	4.55*e*	6.10
4.10	5.12	4.55*d*	6.15
4.55*d*	5.49	5.32*e*	6.40
5. 0*e*	5.49	5.32*d*	6.51
5.32	6.25	6.11	7. 5
6.10*d*	7. 0	6.44	7.51
6.15*e*	7. 0	7.22	8.35
6.35	7.39	8.20	9.20
7.15	8. 9	9.15	10.20
8. 5	9. 0	10. 9	11.20
9. 5	10. 2	—	—
9.55	10.52	—	—
11.40*h*	12.32	—	—

No Sunday Trains.

d Saturdays only.
e Saturdays excepted.
h Thursdays and Saturdays only.

Cedarhurst Private Hotel.
New Management. Spacious Grounds. Tennis. Near Midland Station and Golf Course. Separate Tables. 'Phone 391.
Resident PROPRIETOR.

The Peahen. Principal Hotel. Rebuilt. First-class accommodation. Moderate charges. Near Abbey. Telegrams: "Peahen, St. Albans." Telephone 0256. L. H. PRICE, Proprietor.

Red Lion Hotel. Under New Management. Hot Luncheon and Dinner daily. Moderate inclusive terms. E. L. Large Garage. Tariff on application. Telephone 265. Proprietress, C. LONG.

ST. ALBANS—*continued.*

St. Hilda's (Scruby's). Private Hotel. Boarding Establishment. Near Midland Station. Golf Links. Good cooking. Separate tables. Moderate terms. Established 1896. 'Phone 466.

ST. ANDREWS (Fife)

from *King's Cross*, 447¾ miles. Fares, 91/0*a*, 54/7*c*. R. T. for two months, 182/0*a*, 109/2*c*. Pop. 11,044.
Map Square 38.

KING'S+	ST. AND.	ST. AND.	KING'S+
AM 4.45	5.30	AM 8. 2	6.15
10. 0*r*	8.31	11.35	10. 0
PM 8.25*e*	8.40	PM 2.47	3.25
11.25*er*	9.22	5.33	6. 0
—	—	7.40*e*	6.50
—	—	7.40*d*	7. 5
—	—	—	—
—	—	—	—
—	—	—	—

Sunday Trains.

PM 8.25	8.40	—	—
11.25	9.22	—	—

e Saturdays excepted.
r Restaurant Car.

Seaton Court Hotel. Highest class. Adjoining station. Two minutes from links. Fine views. Table d'Hôte. Separate tables. Telegrams: "Quality, St. Andrews."

ST. ANN'S ROAD (Middlesex)

from *Moorgate Street* and *St. Pancras*, 5⅓ miles. Fares from St. Pancras, 0/10*a*, 0/6*c*. R. T. for two days, 1/7½*a*, 0/10½*c*. From Moorgate Street, 7¼ miles. Fares, 0/10*a*, 0/6*c*. R. T. for two days, 1/8*a*, 0/10½*c*. See pp. 506-507.
Map Square 52.

ST. ANNE'S (Lancs)

from *Euston*, 225¼ miles. Fares, 46/11*a*, 28/2*c*. R. T. for two months, 93/10*a* 56/4*c*. Pop. 15,041.
Map Square 12.

EUSTON	S. ANNE'S	S. ANNE'S	EUSTON
AM12.25	7.54	AM 7.59*r*	1.45
2.35	10.43	8.34*r*	3.10
5. 0	12. 3	10. 9*hr*	3.45
6.45	1.16	10.23*r*	4.15
11.35*r*	4.28	12. 0*dt*	6. 0
11.50*r*	5.46	PM12.21*et*	6. 0
PM 1.30*r*	6.57	2.18*r*	7.30
2.35*t*	7.59	4.46*r*	10.45
5.20*r*	10.28	9.56	5. 0
9.50*d*	9.43	—	—
11.50*d*	11.38	—	—
—	—	—	—
—	—	—	—

ST. ANNE'S—*continued.*

Sunday Trains.

EUSTON	S. ANNE'S	S. ANNE'S	EUSTON
AM11.45*r*	5.26	AM 6.46*r*	1.30
—	—	PM 1.17*r*	7.30
—	—	9. 3	5. 0
—	—	—	—
—	—	—	—

d Saturdays only.
e Saturdays excepted.
h Mondays and Saturdays only.
r Restaurant Car.
t Tea Car.

Hotel Majestic. The most modern and up-to-date Hotel in the Country. Elevator to all floors.
See advt. p. **287.**

ST. ANNE'S PARK

(Gloucester), 116½ miles. Fares, 24/4*a*, 14/7*c*. R. T. for two months 48/8*a*. Departures *from* London as for Keynsham. Departures *for* London about 6 times daily.
Map Square 22.

ST. ANTHONY'S

(Northumberland), 271 miles. No through fares. Departures *from* London as for Newcastle-on-Tyne. Departures *for* London about 6 times daily.

ST. ASAPH (Flint),

211½ miles. Fares, 44/0*a*, 26/5*c*. R. T. for two months 88/0*a*. Departures *from* London as for Rhyl. Departures *for* London about 6 times daily. Pop. 1,833.
Map Square 11.

ST. ATHAN ROAD

(Glamorgan), 178½ miles. No through fares. Departures *from* London as for Barry Docks. Departures *for* London about 4 times daily. Pop. 360.
Map Square 21.

ST. AUSTELL (Cornwall)

from *Paddington*, 265 miles. Fares, 54/10*a*, 32/11*c*. R. T. for two months, 109/8*a*, 65/10*c*. Pop. 3,247.
Map Square 25.

PAD.	ST. AUST.	ST. AUST.	PAD.
AM 5.30	1.55	AM10.16*r*	4.35
11.10*r*	4.54	10.35*lr*	4.45
12. 5*r*	7.48	PM12.33*r*	6.50
PM 2. 0*r*	8.45	1.59*r*	9. 0
10. 0	5.55	10.23	7.10
12. 0*k*	9.31	—	—
12.30*h*	10. 3	—	—

Sunday Trains.

PM10. 0	5.55	PM12.14	7. 5
—	—	1.50*r*	7.45
—	—	6.18	3.15

h Saturdays midnight only.
k Saturdays midnight excepted.
l Mondays and Fridays only.
r Restaurant Car.

ST. BEES (Cumberland),

298¾ miles. Fares, 62/3*a*, 37/4*c*. R.T. for two months, 124/6*a*, 74/8*c*. Departures *from* London as for Sellafield. Departures *for* London about 5 times daily. Pop. 1,436
Map Square 6.

ST. BLAZEY (Cornwall)

from *Paddington*, 260¾ miles. Fares, 54/0*a*, 32/5*c*. R. T. for two months, 108/0*a*, 64/10*c*. Departures *from* London as for Par. Departures *for* London about 5 times daily. Pop. 3,086.
Map Square 25.

ST. BOSWELLS (Roxburgh), from *St. Pancras*, 363¾ miles. Fares, 72/6*a*, 43/6*c*. R. T. for two months, 145/0*a*, 87/0*c*. Pop. 950.

St. Pan.	St. Bos.	St. Bos.	St. Pan.
AM 4.25	2.45	AM10.51*r*	7.15
9. 0*r*	5.48	PM 8.47	8. 3
PM 9.15	5.59	—	—
—	—	—	—

Sunday Trains.

PM 9.15	5.59	—	—

r Restaurant Car.

ST. BOTOLPH'S (Essex),

54 miles. Fares, 11/6*a*, 6/11*c*. R. T. for two months, 23/0*a*. Departures *from* London as for Colchester. Departures *for* London about 5 times daily.
Map Square 19.

ST. BRIAVELS (Glo'ster)

from *Paddington*, 147¾ miles. Fares, 30/8*a*, 18/5*c*. R. T. for two months, 61/4*a*. Pop. 1,128.
Map Square 22.

Pad.	St. Bria.	St. Bria.	Pad.
AM 1. 0*g*	8.24	AM 9.21*r*	2.40
5.30	11.38	PM12.31*r*	5. 0
10.45	3.36	4.11*r*	8.45
PM 1. 0*r*	5.26	8.51	3.30
3.15*t*	8. 3	—	—

Sunday Trains.

PM 9.15	8.24	—	—

g Mondays excepted.
r Restaurant Car.
t Tea Car.

ST. BUDEAUX (Devon)

from *Waterloo*, 227½ miles. Fares, 46/8*a*, 28/0*c*. R. T. for two months, 93/4*a*, 56/0*c*. Departures *from* London as for Tamerton Foliot. Departures *for* London about 6 times daily. Pop. 1,711.
Map Square 23.

ST. CLEARS (Carmarthen) from *Paddington*, 233½ miles. Fares, 47/9*a*, 28/8*c*. R. T. for two months, 95/6*a*, 57/4*c*. Departures *from* London as for Carmarthen. Departures *for* London about 4 times daily. Pop. 929.
Map Square 21.

ST. COLUMB ROAD

(Cornwall) from *Paddington*, 274¾ miles. Fares, 56/10*a*, 34/1*c*. R. T. for two months, 113/8*a*, 68/2*c*. Departures *from* London as for Newquay. Departures *for* London about 4 times daily. Pop. (St. Columb) 2,860.
Map Square 25.

ST. COMBS (Aberdeen),

574¾ miles. No through fares. Departures *from* London as for Fraserburgh. Departures *for* London about 4 times daily.
Map Square 35.

ST. CYRUS (Kincardine),

487½ miles. No through fares. Departures *from* London as for Montrose. Departures *for* London about 3 times daily Pop. 1,306.
Map Square 38.

ST. DENYS (Hants)

from *Waterloo*, 76½ miles. Fares, 16/3 *t*, 9/9*c*. R. T. for two months, 32/6*a*, 19/6*c*. Pop. 8,066.
Map Square 28.

W'loo.	St.Denys	St. Denys	W'loo
AM 5.40	8.34	AM 6.53	9.26
5.50	9. 0	7.54	10.20
7. 0	10.20	8. 5	11.16
8.30*s*	10.50	9.53	12. 0
9.30	12. 1	11.48*r*	2.20
11.30*r*	1.55	PM12.34	3.36
PM12.30	2.59	1.30	4. 6
1.30*s*	3.33	2.10	4.20
2.30	4. 9	3.13	6.16
3.30*s*	5.30	3.52*s*	6.26
3.40	6.33	4. 5	7. 7
4. 0	6.47	6. 5*r*	8.20
5. 0	7.12	6.44	9.52
5.30*r*	7.39	7.48	10.50
6. 0	8.42	9.12	11.28
7.30	9.26	11. 8	3.58
8. 0	10.38	—	—
—	—	—	—

Sunday Trains.

AM 8.43	12.13	AM 7.36	11.16
11. 0*r*	1. 6	9.57	12.11
12. 0*nr*	2.26	PM12. 2*r*	2.27
PM 2. 0*r*	4.11	3.37	6. 7
5. 5	7.51	5.49	8. 3
6. 0	8.31	6.31	9.37
7. 0*r*	9.52	7.39	10.52

n Noon.
r Restaurant Car.
s Refreshments served.

ST. DEVEREUX (Hereford), 151 miles. Fares, 31/10*a*, 19/1*c*. R. T. for two months, 63/8*a*. Departures *from* London as for Hereford. Departures *for* London about 5 times daily. Pop. 174.
Map Square 17.

ST. DUNSTANS (Yorks),

191¾ miles Fares, 39/5*a*, 23/8*c*. R. T., double fare. Departures *from* London as for Wakefield (Westgate) or Leeds. Departures *for* London about 6 times daily.

ST. ERTH (Cornwall), 299½ miles. Fares, 61/11*a*, 37/2*c*. R. T. for two months, 123/10*a*, 74/4*c*. Pop.1,210.
Map Square 25.

Pad.	St. Erth	St. Erth	Pad.
AM 5.30	3.18	AM10.16*r*	4.45
10.30*r*	4.49	11.16*r*	6.50
11.10*r*	6.15	PM12.18*r*	9. 0
PM 2. 0*r*	10. 0	8.56	7.10
10. 0*d*	7.14	—	—
10. 0*e*	7.23	—	—
12. 0*h*	11.16	—	—
12.30*k*	11.27	—	—

Sunday Trains.

AM10.30*r*	5.32	AM10.51	7. 5
PM10. 0	7.23	PM12.31	7.55
—	—	4.51	3.15

d Saturdays only.
e Saturdays excepted.
h Saturdays midnight excepted
k Saturdays midnight only.
r Restaurant Car.

ST. FAGANS (Glamorgan) from *Paddington*, 156¾ miles. Fares, 32/9*a*, 19/8*c*. R. T. for two months, 65/6*a*. Pop. 549.
Map Square 21.

Pad.	St. Fag.	St. Fag.	Pad.
AM 1. 0*g*	7.41	AM 9.30*r*	1. 0
5.30	10.41	10.24*r*	2.30
8.45*r*	1. 5	11.45*r*	4.20
11.50*r*	3.14	PM 2.13*r*	6.15
PM 1.10*r*	5.31	3.58*r*	8.35
3.35*r*	6.55	5.32*r*	9.25
5. 0*r*	8.55	10. 9	3.30
6. 0*r*	9.56	—	—
6.30*r*	10.54	—	—
—	—	—	—
—	—	—	—
—	—	—	—

Sunday Trains.

AM 1. 0	10. 6	PM 1.48*r*	8.25
9.10	2.41	9.18	3.30
PM 9.15	7.41	—	—

g Mondays excepted.
r Restaurant Car.

ST. FILLANS (Perth),

454 miles. Fares, 93/2*a*, 55/11*c*. R.T. for two months, 186/4*a*, 111/10*c*. Departures *from* London as for Comrie. Departures *for* London about 4 times daily. Pop. 591.
Map Square 37.

ST. FORT (Fife), 437 miles.

No through fares. Departures *from* London as for Leuchars. Departures *for* London about 3 times daily.

ST. GABRIEL'S (Glamorgan), 200¼ miles. No through fares. Departures *from* London as for Swansea (High Street). Departures *for* London about twice daily.

ST. GERMANS (Cornwall) from *Paddington*, 235 miles. Fares, 48/7*a*, 29/2*c*. R. T. for two months, 97/2*a*. Pop. 2,050.
Map Square 26.

Pad.	St. Ger.	St. Ger.	Pad.
AM 5.30	12.48	AM 7.48*r*	1.30
11.10*r*	4.11	11.9*r*	4.35
PM 2. 0*r*	7.37	PM12.55*r*	6.50
4.15*lr*11.37		5.14*r*	9. 0
10. 0*e*	6.34	9.15	7.10
10. 0*d*	7.53	—	—
12. 0*k*	8.15	—	—
12.30*h*	8.51	—	—
—	—	—	—
—	—	—	—
—	—	—	—

Sunday Trains.

AM10.30*r*	6.45	AM 9.13*r*	4. 5
PM 2.40*r*	9.10	PM 1.22*r*	7. 5
10. 0	6.34	7.31	3.15
—	—	9.56	7.10

d Saturdays only.
e Saturdays excepted.
h Saturdays midnight only.
k Saturdays midnight excepted.
l Thursdays and Saturdays only.
r Restaurant Car.

ST. HARMONS (Radnor), 206½ miles. No through fares. Departures *from* London as for Llanidloes. Departures *for* London about 3 times daily. Pop. 626.

Map Square 16.

ST. HELENS (Isle of Wight) from *Waterloo*, 85 miles. *Victoria* or *London Bridge*, 97¾ miles. Fares, 18/11*a*, 11/7*c*. R. T. for two months, 37/10*a*, 23/2*c* Departures *from* London as for Bembridge. Departures *for* London about 7 times daily. Pop. 5,706.

Map Square 28.

ST. HELENS (Lancs.) from *Euston*, 192 miles. Fares, 40/9*a*, 24/0*c*. R. T. for two months, 80/0*a*. Pop. 102,675.

Map Square 12.

Euston	S. H'lns.	S. H'lns.	Euston
AM 2.35	7.53	AM 6.50*er*	12. 5
5. 0	11. 2	6.50*dr*	12.20
6.45	12.38	9. 0*r*	1.45
8.30*dr*	1.43	10.55*kr*	3.45
8.30*er*	1.58	10.55*r*	4.15
10.45*r*	5. 2	PM12. 5*dt*	5.50
PM 1.30*r*	6.11	12 20*et*	5.50
2.35*t*	7.17	1. 0*t*	6. 0
5.20*r*	10.33	2.35*r*	7.30
11.50*d*	9.21	10.40	5. 0
—	—	—	—

Sunday Trains.

PM12.30*hr*	7.23	AM 7.45*r*	1.30
11.50	7.53	11 50*r*	7 30
—	—	PM 8.50	5. 0

d Saturdays only.
e Saturdays excepted.
h Via Edge Hill.
k Mondays and Saturdays only.
r Restaurant Car.
t Tea Car.

ANOTHER ROUTE (CENTRAL) from *Marylebone*, 230½ miles. Fares as above.

M'bone.	St. Hel	St. Hel.	M'bone.
AM 2.32	1.32	AM 8.13*r*	3. 0
8.45*r*	4.32	10. 0*r*	6.38
10. 0*r*	4.32	PM 2. 8*r*	8.55
PM12.15*r*	6.52	9. 0	3.57
5. 0*dr*	11.52	—	—
10. 5*e*	7.50	—	—

No Sunday Trains.

d Saturdays only.
e Saturdays excepted.
r Restaurant Car.

ST. IVES (Cornwall) from *Paddington*, 303¾ miles. Fares, 62/9*a*, 37/8*c*. R. T. for two months, 125/6*a*, 75/4*c*. Pop. 6,945.

Map Square 25.

Pad.	St. Ives	St. Ives	Pad.
AM 5.30	3.45	AM 9.40*r*	4.45
10.30*r*	5.10	10.25*r*	6.50
11.10*r*	6.50	11.50*r*	9. 0
PM 2. 0*r*	10.20	PM 8.35	7.10
10. 0*e*	7.44	—	—
10. 0*d*	10.15	—	—
12. 0*k*	11.40	—	—
12.30*h*	11.45	—	—

Sunday Trains.

AM10.30*r*	5.50	AM10 30	7. 5
PM10. 0	7.44	12. 0*r*	7 55
—	—	PM 2.50	3.15

d Saturdays only.
e Saturdays excepted.
h Saturdays midnight only.
k Saturdays midnight excepted.
r Restaurant Car.

ST. IVES—*continued.*

Tregenna Castle Hotel. Lounge, Billiards, Lawn Tennis, &c. Telephone: 33. *See* advt. p. **286**.

Porthminster Hotel. Close to and overlooking Sea and Bathing Beach. Easy distance from West Cornwall Golf Links. Terms of MANAGERESS.

York House Boarding Establishment. Extensive Sea Views. Near Station, Bathing Beach, Town, Tennis Courts. Moderate. Special Winter Terms.
Misses KNAPP.

Trevessa. Private and Residential Hotel. Moderate terms. En Pension. Unrivalled position, overlooking Bay. Three minutes Station and Beach.
Miss NEWTON.

James Lanham, Ltd., High Street, St. Ives, Cornwall, for Furnished Houses. St. Ives, Lelant, and Carbis Bay. Leading Artists' depôt in West.

ST. IVES (Hunts) from *Liverpool Street, via* Cambridge, 70½ miles. Fares, 12/3*a*, 7/4*c*. R. T., double fare. Pop. 2,797.

Map Square 18.

L'p'l. St.	St. Ives	St. Ives	L'p'l. St
AM 5. 5	7.21	AM 8.15*r*	10.23
5.50	8.50	9.52	12.40
8.30*r*	10.55	11. 6	2. 7
11.50*r*	2. 1	11.51*r*	2.21
PM12.29*d*	3.11	PM12.12*hr*	2.21
2.34	4.40	1.31*lr*	4. 2*k*
4.45	6.48	1.31	5. 9
5.49*r*	7.54	3.50*r*	6.10
7.10*lr*	9.20	6.15*r*	8.33
—	—	7.33	10.30
—	—	9.21	2.50

Sunday Trains.

PM 3.25	5.47	PM 4.15	6.40
—	—	—	—
—	—	—	—

d Saturdays only.
h Mondays and Saturdays only.
k Arrives at St. Pancras Station.
l Commencing July 23.
r Restaurant Car.

ANOTHER ROUTE from *King's Cross*, 64¼ miles. Fares as above.

King's +	St. Ives	St. Ives	King's +
AM 5. 5	7.19	AM 7.27	9.56
8.45	10.50	7.52	10.40
10.12	1.26	8.30*f*	10.40
11.30	2.59	9. 0*g*	11.15
PM 1.55	4.36	11. 6	1.25
5. 0	7.30	PM 2. 6	3.50
6.15*d*	8.42	3.55	6.25
6.15*e*	9.17	6.59	9. 0
—	—	—	—
—	—	—	—

No Sunday Trains.

f Mondays only.
g Mondays excepted.
h Mondays and Fridays only.

ST. JAMES DEEPING (Lincoln) from *King's Cross*, 83½ miles. Fares, 17/4*a*, 10/5*c*. R. T., double fare. Departures *from* London as for Peakirk. Departures *for* London about 5 times daily. Pop. 1,544.

Map Square 18.

ST. JAMES'S PARK to and from *Mansion House, Charing Cross, Victoria, South Kensington, High Street, Praed Street, Baker Street, King's Cross, Moorgate,* and all intermediate Stations every few minutes. Also to and from Ealing, Hounslow, Richmond and Wimbledon. *See* p. 489.

Map Square 69.

ST. JAMES'S STREET (Walthamstow) from *Liverpool Street*, 5¾ miles. Fares, 0/10*a*, 0/8*b*, 0/6*c*. R. T. for two days, 1/8*a*, 1/4*b*, 0/10½*c*. Pop. 24,936. *See* pp. 523-524.

Map Square 53.

ST. JOHN'S (New Cross) from *Charing Cross, Cannon Street,* and *London Bridge*, 6¼ miles. Fares from Charing Cross, 1/1*a*, 0/10*b*, 0/7½*c*. R. T. for two days, 2/2*a*, 1/8*b*, 1/3*c*. From Cannon Street, 0/10*a*, 0/8*b*, 0/6*c*. R. T. for two days, 1/8*a*, 1/4*b*, 1/0*c*. Pop. 14,677. *See* pp. 544-557.

Map Square 71.

ST. JOHN'S CHAPEL (Durham), 267¾ miles. No through fares. Departures *from* London as for Bishop Auckland. Departures *for* London about 4 times daily.

Map Square 7.

ST. JOHN'S WOOD ROAD from *Baker Street*, ¾ mile. Fares, 0/2½*a*, 0/1½*c*. R. T. for two days, 0/5*a*, 0/3*c*. *See* back of Map.

Map Square 60.

ST. KEW HIGHWAY (Cornwall) from *Waterloo*, 250 miles. Fares, 51/3*a*, 30/9*c*. R. T. for two months, 102/6*a*, 61/6*c*. Departures *from* London as for Port Isaac Road. Departures *for* London about 4 times daily. Pop. (St. Kew) 884.

Map Square 25.

ST. KEYNE (Cornwall), 247 miles. No through fares. Departures *from* London as for Looe. Departures *for* London about 4 times daily. Pop. 136.

Map Square 26.

ST. LAWRENCE (Isle of Wight), 95 miles. Fares, 20/3*a*, 12/5*c*. R. T for two months 40/6*a*, 24/10*c*. Departures *from* London as for Ventnor Town. Departures *for* London about 6 times daily. Pop. 366.

Map Square 28.

ST. IVES BAY, CORNWALL. **PORTHMINSTER HOTEL,** Facing and close to Sea. (See advt. above.)

ST. LEONARDS (WARRIOR SQUARE) (Sussex) from *Charing Cross, Cannon Street,* and *London Bridge,* 62¼ miles. Fares, 12/6a, 10/0b, 7/6c. R. T. for two months, 25/0a, 20/0b. Pop. 12,330. *Map Square* 29.

Leave CHAR.+	CAN. ST.	LON. B.	Arr. at ST. LEO.
AM			
—	3.40h	3.43h	5.53
—	5.20	5.25	8.36
—	7.56	8.0	10.45
8.30d	—	8.37d	10.15
9.25	—	9.33	11.24
10.40	—	10.46	12.31
PM12.3	—	12.10	2.22
12.40d	—	12.47d	2.35
1.5d	—	1.11d	3.5
2.0d	—	2.5d	3.51
2.8	—	2.16	4.1
2.40d	—	2.46d	4.33
3.40	—	—	5.7
3.48e	—	—	5.54
—	5.4e	—	6.36
5.5d	—	—	6.44
—	5.12e	—	7.13
6.5e	—	—	8.19
—	6.16e	6.19e	7.55
7.30	—	—	9.11
9.30	—	9.33	11.22
12.5y	—	—	1.44

Sunday Trains.

AM 7.5	—	7.11	9.40
8.45	—	—	10.24
9.50	—	9.56	11.50
11.20	—	—	12.56
PM 7.10	—	7.20	9.24
7.35	—	7.45	10.10

Trains from St. Leonards.

Leave ST. LEON.	Arrive at LON. B.	CAN. ST.	CHAR.+
AM 6.58e	8.48	8.52	—
7.39	—	9.15	—
8.13	—	9.48	—
8.32d	10.29	—	10.39
8.58e	10.29	—	10.39
9.5e	11.7	—	11.17
9.38y	11.31	—	11.38
9.48	11.43	—	11.57
11.3	—	—	12.49
PM12.12	3.6	—	3.19
1.33d	3.19	—	3.27
2.33	4.15	—	4.25
3.17d	5.0	—	5.8
3.27d	6.30	—	6.39
4.59	6.40	—	6.49
6.21	8.26	—	8.35
7.12	8.50	—	9.0
7.42	10.15	—	10.23
8.52	11.35	—	11.44

Sunday Trains.

AM 7.7	10.5	—	10.15
9.7	11.23	—	11.34
PM 5.23	—	—	7.3
5.32	8.12	—	8.22
7.12	9.4	—	9.14
8.27	10.8	—	10.16
8.42	11.4	—	11.15

d Saturdays only.
, Saturdays excepted.
h Third Class only.
y Wednesdays only.

ST. LEONARDS—*contd.*

ANOTHER ROUTE (WARRIOR SQUARE) from *London Bridge* and *Victoria,* 74½ miles. Fares, 12/6a, 7/6c. R. T. for two months, 25/0a, 15/0c.

Leave VICTORIA.	LON. B.	Arr. at ST. LEO.
AM		
—	6.15	8.27
6.37h	6.40h	10.8
9.0	—	11.16
10.5	9.50	12.39
11.55	—	1.58
12.0	12.10	2.41
PM 1.20e	—	3.46
1.25d	1.10d	3.46
—	2.0	4.9
3.20	—	5.16
3.40	4.5	6.22
5.20	5.5	7.19
5.45e	5.55e	8.26
6.40	—	9.0
6.50	7.0	9.30
10.30	10.35	1.23

Sunday Trains.

AM 6.55	7.22	10.16
9.30	9.30	11.56
11.15	—	2.17l
PM 12.15h	—	3.19
6.33	6.33	9.55
9.25h	—	12.15

Trains from St. Leonards.

Leave ST. LEON.	Arrive at LON. B.	VICTORIA.
AM 5.45	8.46	—
6.43	8.53	9.8
7.48	10.5	10.12
8.18	10.15	10.24
8.28	10.55	10.58
10.18	12.44	12.45
10.49	—	1.15
11.44	2.22	2.22
PM 1.3	4.0	4.2
2.14	4.32	4.35
2.58h	6.36	6.34
4.8h	—	7.30
5.16	7.42	7.48
6.8h	—	8.48
7.33	10.0	10.10
8.3	—	11.17
9.33h	12.59	1.0

Sunday Trains.

AM 6.48	10.18	10.32
9.18h	—	1.0
PM 4.48	7.56	7.37
5.53	8.34	8.41
7.18	—	10.19
8.11	10.50	10.45
9.18h	12.27	—

d Saturdays only.
e Saturdays excepted.
h Via Brighton.
l Departs from or arrives at West Marine Station.

ST. LEONARDS (WEST) from *Charing Cross, Cannon Street,* and *London Bridge,* 61½ miles. Fares as above. Departures *from* London as for St. Leonards (Warrior Square). Departures *for* London about 3 minutes later.

ST. LEONARDS (WEST MARINA) from *Victoria, Clapham Junction,* and *London Bridge,* 75½ miles. Fares, 12/6a, 10/0b, 7/6c. R. T. for two months, 25/0a, 20/0b, 15/0c. Departures *from* London as for St. Leonards. Departures *for* London about 4 minutes later.

Sussex Hotel. First-class. Nearest Links. Lift. Tennis. Garage. Telephone. Hastings 960. *See advt. p. 207.*

Royal Victoria Hotel. Leading Hotel. Facing Sea. Suites. Garage. Terms from 5½ guineas per week. Tel. 686 Hastings. Telegrams: "Victoria, St. Leonards." *See advt. p. 208.*

Yelton Private Hotel. Hastings. Facing New Bandstand. Telephone 614. *See advt. p. 209.*

Robertson House Hotel. Central. Lounge. Billiards. Garage on Premises. Personal Supervision. Telephone 543. Telegrams "Comfort." Proprietors, Mr. & Mrs. SHIRLEY (*née* Bruce). *See advt. p. 211.*

Queen's Hotel. Leading and best. Magnificent public rooms. Passenger Lift and Private Suites. En Pension terms by arrangement. Telephone 201. *See advt. p. 208.*

Medlow Private Hotel, 57, Eversfield Place. First Class. *See advt. p. 209.*

Wilton Hotel. Grosvenor Gardens. Sea front. Close Golf and Station. Reduced Winter Terms. *See advt. p. 210.*

Eversfield Hotel. First-class. Facing Sea. Telephone 57 Hastings. *See advt. p. 210.*

Alexandra Hotel. First class Family. Facing Sea. South. 100 Rooms. Private Suites. A.A. Inclusive Terms. Telephone: 608 Hastings. *See advt. p. 212.*

Cromwell Private Hotel. Opposite St. Leonards Pier. First-class Residential Hotel. Terms from 3 guineas. Personal supervision. Telephone 807 Hastings. Telegrams: "Cromwell, St Leonards-on-Sea." *See advt. p. 211.*

St. Leonards - Adelphi Hotel, Warrior Square. 50 Rooms. Ballroom, Billiards, Tennis. Garage. Inclusive from 3½ guineas. Telephone 622. Telegrams: Adelphi. *See advt. p. 212.*

Stafford Private Hotel, 50 and 51, Eversfield Place. Facing sea. Terms moderate. Tel.: 304. *See advt. p. 213.*

ST. LEONARDS.—ROYAL VICTORIA HOTEL.

ST. LEONARDS—*contd.*

Craig - y - Don. High Class Private Hotel. Facing Sea. Inclusive terms. Phone 448. *See advt.* p. **213**.

Berwyn Private Hotel, 7 and 8, Eversfield Place. Facing Sea. Centre of Promenade. Redecorated. Refurnished. Electric Light. Terms from £3 3s. Tel. 649. Resident Proprietors, Mr. and Mrs. G. F. STONE. *See advt.* p. **213**.

Maison Mascotte. Close St. Leonard's Pier. Separate tables. Moderate terms. *See advt.* p. **214**.

Regent House Private Hotel. Facing Sea. Terms from 2½ guineas. Liberal table. 'Phone 905. R. G. DIXON. *See advt.* p. **214**.

Drayton House Hotel. Centre of Promenade. Garage. Bridge Club. *See advt.* p. **214**.

Chatsworth Private Hotel, Carlisle Parade. Sea Front. Every comfort. Booklet.

Eversfield House Private Hotel. Eversfield Place. Facing Sea. Re-decorated and enlarged. Lounge. Separate tables. Five minutes Warrior Square Station. Telephone No. 689 Hastings. Resident Proprietress, Miss CLAYTON.

Lancaster House, Private Hotel. 65, Warrior Square. Cuisine excellent. Separate Tables. Billiards, Tennis. Near Golf Links. Garage. 'Phone 1124. Apply— PROPRIETOR.

Carlton Private Hotel (Pension), 10, Warrior Square Terrace. Best position between piers. Full sea views. Private Tennis Court. Sheltered. Electric light throughout. Excellent Cuisine. Modern comfort. From £3 3s. per week. MANAGERESS.

Edinburgh Hotel, Warrior Square. Facing South and Sea. Family Hotel. Electric Passenger Lift. Balconies. Licensed. Pension Terms. Telephone 428.

Warrior House Hotel. Family Hotel. Sunniest Position. South Aspect. Balconies facing Sea. Licensed. Telephone 300.

ST. LEONARDS—*contd.*

Riviera Private Hotel, Warrior Square. Electric Light. Excellent cuisine. Separate tables. Spacious lounges. Overlooking Sea and Gardens. From 56s. inclusive. Telephone 930 Hastings. Proprietors, Mr. and Mrs. J. G. TURNEY.

Charterhouse Private Hotel, Warrior Square. Finest Position. Overlooking Sea. Large Bedrooms. Lounges. Every comfort. Private Gardens. Tennis. Golf. Croquet. Expert Catering. Separate tables. Terms from 3 Gns. inclusive. Personal supervision. Resident Owners. 'Phone, 1137.

Melbourne House. Charming Home for Paying Guests in well-appointed sunny house near Warrior Square Station and Christ Church. Excellent cuisine. Separate tables. Drawing and Smoking Rooms. From 3 gns. single, 5 gns. double. Week-ends, 21s. 16, Dane Road. Telephone, Hastings 640.

Arnold House, 16, Stockleigh Road, Comfortable Board Residence. Close to Sea, Station, Shops. Good table. Terms moderate. Mrs. READING.

Beagley's (Established 1850), House Agents, Auctioneers, and Valuers. Illustrated List of Furnished and Unfurnished Houses in Hastings and St. Leonards sent free. Telephone No. 330. 27 Grand Parade. St. Leonards-on-Sea.

House Agents, JOHN BRAY & SONS, Fs.A.I. (Established 1864.) The Marina, St. Leonards. Telephone No. 313 Hastings.

ST. MARGARET'S

(Herts) from *Liverpool Street*, 20½ miles. Fares, 4/5a, 3/6b, 2/8c. R. T. for two months, 8/10a, 7/0b. Pop. 217. *See* pp. 526-527. *Map Square* 23.

ST. MARGARET'S

(Middlesex). from *Waterloo*, 10½ miles. Fares, 1/6a, 0/10½c. R. T. for two days, 3/0a, 1/9c. Pop. 4,089. *See* pp. 587-591. *Map Square* 67.

ST. MARGARET'S

BAY (Kent). Station at MARTIN MILL.

ST. MARGARET'S BAY—*continued.*

St. Margaret's Bay Hotel. Sheltered from north. Nearest Hotel to Sea. Patronised by Medical and Literary men. Telegrams Lanzarote, St. Margaret's at-Cliffe. Telephone 017 St. Margaret's-at-Cliffe.

Granville Hotel. Standing on the Cliffs, with unrivalled Sea View. Facing south. Telephone 12, St. Margaret's-at-Cliffe Station : Martin Mill. Under New Proprietorship.

ST. MARY CHURCH

ROAD (Glamorgan), 172 miles. No through fares. Departures from London as for Llantrissant. Departures for London about 3 times daily. *Map Square* 21.

ST. MARY CRAY (Kent)

from *Victoria*, *Holborn Viaduct*, and *St. Paul's*, 14¼ miles. Fares, 3/1d, 2/5b, 1/10c. R. T. for eight days, 6/2a, 4/10b. Pop. 2,178.

	VICT.	Leave		Arr. at
	S.E. & C.	HOL. V.	ST.PL.'s	S.MARYC
AM 5. 5	4.57	5. 0		5.57
—	6.40	6.42		7.23
8.32	8.20	8.23		9.16
10.15e	10. 9e		10.11e	11. 1
11. 4	10.58	11. 0		11.48
11.55d	—			12.33
PM —	12.33d	12.36d		1.13
—	1.27d	1.30d		2. 4
2. 9d	2.12d	2.14d		3. 4
2.12e	2.13e	2.16e		3. 1
2.40d	—		—	3.18
2.50e	—		—	3.28
—	3.22	3.25		4. 9
—	3.22d	3.25d		4.12
3.56e	—		—	4.33
4.45e	4.50e	4.53e		5.34
5. 3d	—		—	5.45
5. 8e	—		—	5.49
—	5.31e	5.34e		6.14
5.45d	—		—	6.19
6.16	6.10e	6.13e		6.55
6.40	6.34	6.37		7.19
7.22	7.22	7.24		8. 0
8.10	8. 5	8. 8		9. 3
9. 0	8.57	9. 0		9.39
10. 0	9.54	9.53		10.40
11.35	11.31	11.34		12.19
—	—	—		—
—	—	—		—
—	—	—		—
—	—	—		—

Sunday Trains.

AM 7.20	—	—		7.56
10.30	10.25			8.56
11.30	—			11.16
PM 1. 7	1. 5			12. 9
2. 5	2. 3			1.59
3.30	—			2.58
6. 7	—			4. 7
6.35	6.40			6.54
9. 5	9.33			7.18
—	—	—		10.19

ST. MARY CRAY—*contd.*

Trains from St. Mary Cray.

Leave S.MARY C	St. PL.'s	Arrive at Hol. V.	VICT.
AM 7.31	8. 8	8. 9	8.14
7.51	8.25	8.27	8.29
8. 8	8.40	8.42	8.50
8.35	9.16	9.18	9.36
9.44	—	—	10.10
10.25	11.22	11.29	11. 9
PM12.36	1.32	1.34	1.22
12.51	—	—	1.32
1.59*e*	—	—	2.40
2.43	3.38	—	3.23
3.54	—	—	4.33
4.33*e*	5.32	5.34	5.21
6.11*e*	6.45	6.47	—
7. 0*d*	7.54	—	—
7.24*d*	8. 0	8. 2	—
7.25*e*	8.17	8.20	8.10
8. 4	9.10	9.12	8.51
9. 1	9.50	9.54	9.46
9.41	10.29	10.31	10.22
10.18*d*	—	—	11.35
11. 4	11.44	11.46	12.10

Sunday Trains.

AM 8.42	—	9.40	9.31
10.37	—	11.27	11.23
PM12.19	—	1. 2	12.56
12.51	—	—	1.25
1.22	—	2.15	2.11
3.17	—	—	3.50
5.41	—	6.20	6.15
7.50	—	8.50	—
9.27	—	10.22	10. 5
11.10	—	12. 0	11.44

d Saturdays only.
e Saturdays excepted.
h Departs from Charing Cross (S.E. & C.R.).

ST. MARY'S (Hunts)

from *King's Cross,* 73¼ miles. Fares, 14/10*a*, 8/11*c*. R. T. for two months, 29/8*a*, 17/10*c*. Departures *from* London as for Ramsey. Departures *for* London about 7 times daily.
Map Square 18.

ST. MARY'S (White-

chapel) from *Ealing, Hounslow, Richmond* and *Wimbledon. See* p. 489.
Map Square 61. *No.* 13.

ST. MICHAEL'S (TEN-

TERDEN) (Kent), 55 miles. No through Fares. Departures *from* London as for Tenterden. Departures *for* London about 4 times daily.

ST. MICHAEL'S (Lancs),

214¾ miles. Fares, 41/1*a*, 24/8*c*. R. T., double fare. Departures *from* London as for Warrington (Central). Departures *for* London about 4 times daily.
Map Square 12.

ST. MONANS (Fife),

439 miles. Fares 88/11*a*, 53/4*c*. R. T. for two months, 177/10*a*, 106/8*c*. Departures *from* London as for St. Andrews. Departures *for* London about 3 times daily. Pop. 1,916.
Map Square 41.

ST. NEOTS (Hunts) from

King's Cross, 51¼ miles. Fares, 10/8*a*, 6/5*c*. R. T., double fare. Pop. 4,109.
Map Square 18.

KING's+	S. NEOTS	S. NEOTS	KING's+
AM 5. 5	6.46	AM 8. 9	9.56
7.45	9.28	9.56	11.15
10.12	12.19	11.40	1.25
11.30	1. 3	PM 2.39	3.50
PM 1.55	3.39	4.58	6.25
4.15	5.47	8.11	10.20
5.10	7.10	—	—
6.15	7.57	—	—
8.30	10. 9	—	—

Sunday Trains.

AM 8.30	10.28	PM 6. 1	8. 8
PM 7.10	9. 8	—	—

ST. OLAVE'S (Suffolk)

from *Liverpool Street,* 115¼ miles. Fares, 24/2*a*, 14/6*c*. R. T. for two months, 48/4*a*.
Map Square 19.

L'PL.ST.	ST. OLA.	ST. OLA.	L'PL.ST.
AM 5. 0	9. 5	AM 6.33*r*	10.30
8.15*r*	12.29	7.40*r*	11.22
10.20	2.17	9.47	1.20
PM 1. 0	4.46	11.45	3.42
3.18	7.11	PM 3.38	7.51
5.18*dr*	9. 1	5.38*r*	9.22
5.18*er*	9.10	6.21*r*	10. 9

Sunday Trains.

PM 4.40	8.30	AM 7.10	11.38
—	—	PM 5.25*r*	9.10

d Saturdays only.
e Saturdays excepted.
r Restaurant Car.

ST. PETER'S (Northum-

berland), 270½ miles. No through fares. Departures *from* London as for Newcastle-on-Tyne. Departures *for* London about 4 times daily.

ST. QUINTIN PARK

AND WORMWOOD SCRUBS from *Broad Street,* 11½ miles. Fares, 1/0½ *t*, 0/7½*c*. R. T. for two days, 2/1*a*, 1/2*c*. *See* pp. 501-505.
Map Square 59.

From *Earl's Court, via* Kensington (Addison Road), in connection with trains from Mansion House, Charing Cross, Victoria, &c., 2¾ miles. *See* pp. 501-505.

SALCOMBE (Devon)

from *Paddington.* No through fares. Station at Kingsbridge. Distance about 6½ miles. Pop. 2,291.
Map Square 26.

SALE (Cheshire), 189 miles.

Fares, *via* Manchester, 39/10*a*, 23/11*c*. R. T. for two months, 79/8*a*, 47/10*c*. Departures *from* London as for Manchester (London Road). Departures *for* London about 9 times daily. Pop. 16,337.
Map Square 12.

SALFORD (Lancs.), 187¼

miles. Fares, 38/7*a*, 23/2*c*. R. T., double fares. Departures *from* London as for Manchester. Departures *for* London about 6 times daily. Pop. 234,150.

SALFORD PRIORS

(Warwick), 112½ miles. No through fares. Departures *from* London as for Evesham. Departures *for* London about 4 times daily. Pop. 823.
Map Square 17.

SALHOUSE (Norfolk),

120 miles. Fares, 24/9*a*, 14/10*c*. R. T. for two months, 49/6*a*. Departures *from* London as for Wroxham. Departures *for* London about 4 times daily. Pop. 650.
Map Square 19.

SALISBURY (Wilts) from

Waterloo, 83¾ miles. Fares, 17/6a, 10/6c. R.T. 1or two months, 35/0a, 21/0c. Pop. 22,867.

Map Square 22.

W'LOO.	SALISB'Y.	SALISB'Y.	W'LOO.
AM 5.50	9.11	AM 7.18	9.56
7.30	9.37	8.48	10.56
9. 0r	10.49	9.37r	11.10
10. 0r	11.33	10. 7s	12.22
11. 0r	12.34	PM12.23r	1.56
12. 0r	1.33	12.32	2.36
PM 1. 0r	2.52	1.35r	3. 8
1.30	3.54	2.17r	3.50
3. 0r	4.33	2.57r	4.30
3.30s	5.57	4.27r	6. 0
5. 0	6.58	5.31	7.40
6. 0r	7.49	6.40r	8.30
7.30	9.57	8.39	10.50
8. 0	10.59	8.50	11.28
10. 0h	2.52	11. 0h	3.58
—	—	—	—
—	—	—	—
—	—	—	—

Sunday Trains.

AM 9. 0	12. 8	AM 9.35	12.11
12. 0r	2. 8	PM 7.15r	8.57
PM 6. 0	8.40	—	—
—	—	—	—
—	—	—	—
—	—	—	—
—	—	—	—

h Via Eastleigh.
r Restaurant Car.
s Refreshments served.

Taxi Cabs can be hired to meet any train at this Station. Telegrams : " Motors ;" telephone No. 170. Messrs. W. Rowland & Sons, Castle Street.

County Hotel. First-class Family. 50 Bedrooms. Patronized by Royalty. Cuisine a speciality. Finest Wines. Central Heating. Electric Light. Close Station and Cathedral. Appointed by all Motor Clubs. Garage. Fishing. Golf. Telephone 150.

The White Hart Hotel. Opposite the Cathedral. The principal Family Hotel. Patronised by Royalty and all Government Departments. Every accommodation for Motorists. Garage, 50 Cars; private Lock-ups, and Repair Shops on Premises. All Club appointments. Telephone 98.

Old George Hotel. First Class. (Unlicensed.) Formerly "Ye Greate Inn of Ye George." Well preserved Plantagenet house, built about 1320. Near Cathedral. Moderate Modern Sanitation. Garage adjacent Telephone 189.

Crown Hotel. First-class Family and Commercial. Established 1625. Fully Licensed. Moderate Tariff. Nearest Cathedral. Electric Light. Garage. Appointed A.A.M.U. and R.A.C. Hotel. Telephone 113.
Proprietors,
Mr. and Mrs. E. S. WHITBY.

SALISBURY—continued.

Red Lion Hotel. Old established Family and Commercial. Spacious Coffee and Commercial Rooms. Good Stock - rooms. Omnibus meets trains. Garage. Convenient for those visiting military camps. Telephone 73. Proprietor CHARLES THOMAS.

SALT (Stafford), 138 miles.

Fares, 28/2a, 16/11c. R. T. for two months, 56/4a. Departures from London as for Stafford. Departures for London about 6 times daily. Pop. 400.

Map Square 17.

SALTAIRE (Yorks), 206¾

miles. Fares, 40/0a, 24/0c. R. T., double fare. Departures from London as for Shipley. Departures for London about 6 times daily.

Map Square 12.

SALTASH (Cornwall) from

Paddington, 230 miles. Fares, 47/9a, 28/8c. R. T. for two months, 95/6a, 57/4c. Pop. 3,631.

Map Square 26.

PAD.	S'ASH.	S'ASH.	PAD.
AM 5.30	12.59	AM 8. 2r	1.30
11.10r	4. 1	11.18r	4.35
PM12. 5r	7. 0	11.40r	4.45
2. 0r	7.47	PM 1. 8r	6.50
3.30r	9. 2	3.25r	9. 0
4.15r	11.23	3.55e	2.45
10. 0e	6. 2	10.30	7.10
10. 0d	7.44	10.56l	7.10
12. 0k	8. 3	—	—
12.30h	8.40	—	—
—	—	—	—
—	—	—	—
—	—	—	—
—	—	—	—
—	—	—	—
—	—	—	—
—	—	—	—
—	—	—	—
—	—	—	—
—	—	—	—
—	—	—	—

Sunday Trains.

AM10.30r	4. 8	AM 9.25r	4. 5
PM 2.40r	8.43	PM 1.32	7. 5
10. 0	6. 2	7.42	3.15
—	—	10.30	7.10
—	—	—	—
—	—	—	—
—	—	—	—
—	—	—	—

d Saturdays only.
e Saturdays excepted.
h Saturdays midnight only.
k Saturdays midnight excepted.
l Fridays and Saturdays only.
r Restaurant Car.

SALTBURN (Yorks) from

King's Cross, 251¼ miles. Fares, 52/4a, 31/5c. R.T. for two months, 104/8a, 62/10c. Pop. 4,668.

Map Square 8.

KING'S +	SALTB'N.	SALTB'N.	KING'S +
AM 4.45	12.32	AM 5. 5r	1. 5
7.15r	3.13	6.50r	1.15
10. 0r	4.11	8.30g	3.15
10.10r	5.28	9.13r	4.30
11.50r	5.40	11.55r	6.15
PM 1.15r	7.28	PM 2.11r	9.25
1.50r	8.46	3.51r	10. 0
5.35r	11.31	7.44	3.25
11.25e	6.50	10.30e	5.40
11.25d	8.18	10.30d	6. 0
—	—	—	—
—	—	—	—
—	—	—	—

Sunday Trains.

AM11.30r	9.51	AM 9. 5	5.15
PM11.25	6.50	PM 9. 0	5.40

d Saturdays only.
e Saturdays excepted.
g 1st and 3rd Class Pullman Cars only.
r Restaurant Car.

Zetland Hotel. Charmingly situated, overlooking Bay and adjoining Station. Every Comfort. Thoroughly up-to-date. Owned and managed by London and North-Eastern Railway Company. See advt. p. 286.

SALTCOATS (Ayr), 403¾

miles. Fares, 82/6a, 49/6c. R. T. for two months, 165/0a, 99/0c. Departures from London as for Irvine. Departures for London about 4 times daily. Pop. 13,477.

Map Square 40.

SALTFLEETBY (Lincoln) from King's Cross, 142¼ miles.

Fares, 29/7a, 17/9c. R. T. for two months, 59/2a, 35/6c. Departures from London as for Mablethorpe. Departures for London about 5 times daily. Pop. 484.

Map Square 13.

SALTFORD (Somerset),

111¼ miles. Fares, 23/2a, 13/11c. R.T. for two months, 46/4a, 27/10c. Departures from London as for Bath. Departures for London about 6 times daily. Pop. 590.

Map Square 22.

SALTLEY (Warwick), 115

miles. Fares, 23/1a, 13/10c. R. T. for two months, 46/2a. Departures from London as for Birmingham (New Street). Departures for London about 6 times daily. Pop. 60,347.

Map Square 17.

SALTMARSHE (Yorks),

176 miles. Fares, 35/0a, 21/0c. R. T. for two months, 70/0a. Departures from London as for Goole. Departures for London about 6 times daily. Pop. 102.

Map Square 13.

SALTOUN (Eastlothian),

399¼ miles. No through fares. Departures *from* London as for Edinburgh (Waverley). Departures *for* London about 3 times daily.

SALWICK (Lancs), 214¼

miles. Fares, 44/7a, 26/9c. R. T. for two months, 89/2a, 53/6c. Departures *from* London as for Preston. Departures *for* London about 5 times daily. Pop. 425.

Map Square 12.

SAMPFORD COUR-

TENAY (Devon), 193¼ miles. Fares, 40/5 t, 24/3c. R. T. for two months, 80/10a, 48/6c. Departures *from* London as for Peodford. Departures *for* London about 5 times daily. Pop. 759.

Map Square 26.

SANDAL (Yorks), 174½ miles.

Fares, 36/1a, 21/8c. R. T., double fare. Departures *from* London as for Hemsworth. Departures *for* London about 5 times daily. Pop. 7,923.

Map Square 12.

SANDBACH (Cheshire)

from Euston, 162½ miles. Fares, 33/11a, 20/4c. R. T. for two months, 67/10a. Pop. 8,843.

Map Square 12.

Euston	Sandbh.	Sandbh.	Euston
AM 12 25	5.59	AM 8.31e	r12. 5
2.35	6.39	8.31d	r12.20
5. 0	9.18	9. 5r	1. 0
6.45	11.26	9.49r	1.45
8.30r	12.48	11.37er	3.10
10.40r	2.28	PM 12.24r	4.15
PM 1.30r	4.55	1.24er	5.50
2.35t	5.59	1.44dr	5.50
4. 5r	7.48	2.24er	6. 0
5.20r	8.44	2.38dr	6. 0
11.50d	8.30	3. 7	6.25
—	—	4.32r	8.10
—	—	6. 1er	9. 5
—	—	6. 1dr	9.15
—	—	7. 2r	10.45
—	—	10.40	5. 0

Sunday Trains.

PM 12.30r	8. 0	AM 12. 6	5. 0
—	—	10.27	4. 0
—	—	PM 3.50	7 .30
—	—	7.54	5. 0

d Saturdays only.
e Saturdays excepted.
r Restaurant Car.
t Tea Car.

SANDERSTEAD (Surrey)

from *Victoria, Cannon Street,* and *London Bridge,* 12¼ miles. Fares, 2/6a, 1/6c. R. T. for two days, 5/0a, 2/9c. Pop. 3,351

Map Square 23.

	Leave			Arr. at
	Vict.	Can. St.	Lon. B.	S'sthead.
AM 7.23	—	8. 7	8.40	
9.10	—	9. 6	9.45	
—	—	9.25	10.11	
10.35	—	10.35	11. 9	

SANDERSTEAD—*contd.*

	Leave			Arr. at
	Vict.	Can. St.	Lon. B.	S'stead.
12. 0	—	—	11.50	12.37
M —	12.16d	k12.20d	12.50	
—	—	12.50d	1.16	
1.20e	—	1.38e	2. 5	
1.25d	—	1.38d	2.10	
—	—	2. 5e	3. 7	
2.25	—	2.25d	3. 7	
—	—	2.57d	3.27	
4. 0	—	4.10	4.37	
—	4.16e	k4.20e	4.47	
4.50	—	4.44e	5.16	
5. 5	—	5.10	5.40	
—	—	5.21	5.49	
5.43	—	5.41e	6.13	
6. 6	—	6. 8	6.44	
6.50	—	7. 0	7.27	
7.15	—	7.38	8.10	
8. 5	—	8.10	8.40	
9. 3	—	9.12	9.37	
10.30	—	10.35	11. 5	
11.50h	—	—	12.17	
—	—	—	—	
—	—	—	—	
—	—	—	—	

Sunday Trains.

AM 8.18	—	8.30	9. 4
10.20	—	—	11. 6
PM 1.14	—	1.10	1.47
2.30	—	—	3. 8
6.33	—	6.46	7.19
9. 5	—	9.10	9.42

Trains from Sanderstead.

	Leave		Arr. at	
	S'stead.	Lon. B.	Can. St	Vict.
AM 7.36	8.15	—	8.24	
8.11	8.37	—	8.40	
8.37	9. 1k	9. 4	9. 8	
8.49	9.15	—	9.19	
9. 7	9.32	—	9.40	
9.26	9.55	—	9.58	
10.24	10.55	—	10.56	
11. 5	—	—	11.35	
11.45	12.13	—	12.17	
PM 12.53	1.42	—	1.26	
2.31	2.58	—	—	
3.13	4. 0	—	3.45	
4.24d	4.57	—	—	
4.52	5.21	—	5.55	
6. 2	6.36	—	6.29	
7.28	7.56	—	—	
7.46	8.46	—	8.27	
9.55	10.25	—	11.17	

Sunday Trains.

AM 9.37	10.18	—	10.20
10.42	11.15	—	—
PM 12. 4	—	—	12.47
1. 0	—	—	1.40
5.57	—	—	6.34
8.53	9.26	—	9.34
10.29	—	—	10.59

d Saturdays only.
e Saturdays excepted.
h Wednesdays and Saturdays only.
k Departs from or arrives at London Bridge, S.E. & C. Station.

SANDFORD (Somerset)

from *Paddington*, 138¾ miles. Fares, 27/11a, 16/9c. R. T. for two months, 55/10a. Departures *from* London as for Winscombe. Departures *for* London about 6 times daily.

Map Square 22.

SANDGATE (Kent) from

Charing Cross, Cannon Street, and *London Bridge,* 69 miles. Fares, 14/5a, 11/7b, 8/8c. R. T. for two months, 28/10a, 23/2b. Pop. 2,768.

Map Square 24.

	Leave			Arr. at
	Char. +	Can. St.	Lon. B.	S'gate
AM —	3.40s	3.43s	7.34	
—	5.20	5.25	9.24	
—	6.45	6.50	10. 4	
9.15	—	9.23	11.49	
—	—	k10.3l	12.19	
11. 0	—	11. 7	1.22	
11.15	—	—	12.54	
PM 1. 0	—	—	2.39	
2.25d	—	3. 1d	4.47	
3. 0	—	3. 8	5. 4	
4.30h	—	4.37h	6.28	
4.30j	—	4.37j	6.41	
—	5.12e	—	6.56	
5.15e	—	5.21e	7.22	
5.20d	—	5.26d	7.22	
5.24d	—	5.34d	8. 2	
6. 0e	—	6. 5e	7.55	
7.18	—	7.26	10. 4	

Sunday Trains.

AM 7.45	—	7.52	10.20
10.10	—	10.18	12.14

Trains from Sandgate.

	Leave		Arrive at	
	S'gate	Lon. B.	Can. St.	Char. +
AM 7. 3	9.32	9.36	—	
7.59e	9.36	9.40	—	
8. 9d	10. 0	10. 4	—	
8.55	10.54	—	11. 3	
9.35	11.43	—	11.57	
11.10	1.36	—	1.50	
PM 12.50	3.26	—	3.40	
3.20	5.50	—	6. 3	
5.10	7.25	7.30e	7.49	
8.10	10.22	—	10.35	

Sunday Trains.

PM 5. 8	7. 9	—	7.17
8. 0	10.16	—	10.26

d Saturdays only.
e Saturdays excepted.
h Fridays excepted.
j Fridays only.
k Mondays and Saturdays only.
l Low level platform.
s Third Class only.

ANOTHER ROUTE from

Victoria, Holborn, and *St. Paul's,* 71¼ miles. Fares as above.

		Leave		Arr. at
	Vict. S.E. & C.	Hol. V.	St. Pl.'s	S'gate.
AM —	6.40	6.42	10. 4	
9.45	—	—	11.49	
11. 4d	10.58d	11 0d	2.19	
11. 4	10.58	11. 0	2.39	
PM —	1.27d	1.30d	4.47	
2.12e	—	—	4.47	
2.40d	—	—	6.28	
2.50l	—	—	6.28	
2.50h	—	—	6.41	
4.25e	3.22e	3.25e	6.56	
7.22	—	—	10. 4	

Sunday Trains.

AM 9.35	—	—	12.14
PM 5.15	—	—	7.49

SANDGATE—*continued.*

Trains from Sandgate.

Leave S'GATE.	Arrive at ST. PL.'s	HOL. V.	VICT.
AM 7. 3	9.53	9.55	—
9.35	12.59	1. 2	12.49
11.10	—	—	2.40
PM 12.50	—	—	3.37
3.20	—	—	5.42
3.38	6.58	7. 0	—
5.10	—	—	8.51
8.10	11.43	11.45	—
—	—	—	—
—	—	—	—
—	—	—	—
—	—	—	—

Sunday Trains.

AM 10.40	—	—	.1. 5
PM 12.50	—	—	3.50
5. 8	—	9. 9	—

d Saturdays only.
e Saturdays excepted.
h Fridays only.
l Fridays and Saturdays excepted.

Royal Norfolk Hotel. Two minutes from sea and five from Hotel Metropole, Folkestone. Electric Light throughout. Billiards. Lounge. Near Links. Moderate terms. Bus meets trains. Telephone: 046. Resident Proprietor, G. P. KEELER.

Royal Kent Hotel. Facing Sea due South. Private Lawn reaching down to the Sea. Largest and best appointed. Winter Garden facing sea. Favourite resort of Ruskin. Garage adjoining. Telephone No. 47.
J. E. TANARE, Proprietor.

Sea View Hotel. Nearest Station. Ideal position, with 300 feet frontage. Illustrated tariff. Phone 29. E. B. HINTON. *See also under Hythe.*

"The Woodford" Private Hotel and Boarding Establishment. Facing sea. Electric light. Liberal catering. Separate tables. Garage. Moderate Terms.
A. WALLACE.

SANDHOLME (Yorks), 209 miles. Fares, 35/0*a*, 21/0*c*. R. T. for two months, 70/0*a*, 42/0*c*. Departures *from* London as for Cudworth. Departures *for* London about 5 times daily. *Map Square* 13.

SANDHURST HALT (Berks) from Charing Cross, Cannon Street, and London Bridge, 58½ miles. Fares, 7/1*a*, 5/8*b*, 4/3*c*. R.T. for two months, 14/2*a*, 11/4*b*, 8/6*c*. Departures *from* London as for Blackwater. Departures *for* London about 7 times daily.

SANDILANDS (Lanark), 379¾ miles. Fares, 77/4*a*, 46/5*c*. R.T. for two months,154/8*a*, 92/10*c*. Departures *from* London as for Carstairs. Departures *for* London about 4 times daily. *Map Square* 40.

SANDLING (Kent) from

Charing Cross, Cannon Street, and London Bridge, 66¼ *miles. Fares,* 13/9*a*, 11/0*b*, 8/3*c*. R. T. for two months, 27/6*a*, 22/0*b*. *Map Square* 24.

Leave CHAR. +	CAN. ST	LON. B	Arr. at SANDLG.
AM —	3.40*h*	3.45*h*	5.52
—	5.20	5.25	8.45
—	6.45	6.50	9.33
9.15	—	9.23	11.21
—	—	*k*10. 3*l*	11.57
11. 0	—	11. 7	1. 5
11.15	—	—	12.59
PM 1. 0	—	—	2.23
2.55*d*	—	3. 1*d*	4.22
3. 0	—	3. 8	4.48
4.30	—	4.57	6. 3
—	5.12*e*	—	6.46
5.15*e*	—	5.21*e*	7.12
5.20*d*	—	5.26*d*	7.15
5.24*d*	—	5.31*g*	7.49
6. 0*e*	—	6. 5*e*	7.39
7.18	—	7.26	9.51
9.30	—	9.36	11.10

Sunday Trains.

AM 7.45	—	7.52	9.56
10.10	—	10.18	11.53
PM 7.35	—	7.45	9.49
—	—	—	—

Trains from Sandling.

Leave SANDLG.	LON. B.	Arrive at CAN. ST.	CHAR. +
AM 7.14*e*	9.32	9.36	—
8.18*e*	9.36	9.40	—
8.21*d*	10. 0	10. 4	—
9. 7	10.54	—	11. 3
9.49	11.43	—	11.57
11.29	1.36	—	1.50
PM 1. 3	3.26	—	3.40
1.57*s*	4. 8	—	—
3.49	5.50	—	6. 3
5.21	7.25	7.30*e*	7.49
8.21	10.22	—	10.35
—	—	—	—
—	—	—	—

Sunday Trains.

AM 7.20	10. 5	—	10.15
PM 5.18	7. 9	—	7.17
8.12	10.16	—	10.26
10. 5*h*	—	1.23	—

d Saturdays only.
e Saturdays excepted.
h Third Class only.
k Mondays and Saturdays only.
s Mondays, Fridays and Saturdays only.

ANOTHER ROUTE from

Victoria, Holborn Viaduct, and St. Paul's, 68½ *miles.* Fares as above.

S.E. & C.	Leave HOL. V.	ST. PL.'s	Arr. at SANDLG.
AM —	6.40	6.42	9.33
9.45	—	—	11.38
11. 4*d*	10.58*l*	11. 0*d*	2. 1
11. 4	10.58	11. 0	2.23
PM —	1.27*d*	1.30*d*	4.36
2.12*e*	—	—	4.36
2.40*d*	—	—	6. 2
2.50*e*	—	—	6. 3
4 25*e*	3.22*e*	3.25*e*	6.46
7.22	—	—	9.51
—	7.22*d*	7.24*d*	11.10

Sunday Trains.

AM 9.35	—	—	12. 4
PM 5.15	—	—	7.36
6.35	6.40	—	9.49

SANDLING—*continued.*

Trains from Sandling.

Leave SANDLG.	ST. PL.'s	Arrive at HOL. V.	VICT.
AM 7.14	[9.53	9.55	—
9.49	12.59	1. 2	12.49
11.29	—	—	2.40
PM 1. 3	—	—	3.37
3.37	—	—	5.42
3.49	6.58	7 .0	—
5.21	—	—	8.51
8.21	11.43	11.45	—

Sunday Trains.

AM 7.20	—	—	10.48
10.53	—	—	1. 5
PM 1. 4	—	—	3.50
5.18	—	9. 9	—

d Saturdays only.
e Saturdays excepted.

SANDON (Stafford), 134¼ miles. Fares, 27/11*a*, 16/9*c*. R. T. for two months, 55/10*a*. Departures *from* London as for Colwich. Departures *for* London about 3 times daily. Pop. 508. *Map Square* 17.

SANDOWN (Isle of Wight) from *Victoria and London Bridge.* 97 miles. Fares, 19/0*a*, 11/7*c*. R. T. for two months, 38/0*a*, 23/2*c*. Pop. 7,664. *Map Square* 28.

Leave VICTORIA	LON. B.	Arr. at SANDWN.
AM 6.18	6.35	11.24
8.55	—	12.37
10.15	10.22	2.24
11.35	—	3.24
PM 1.35	—	4.51
1.40	1.50	5.51
1.55	2. 5	7.24
—	4.50	8.21

Sunday Trains.

AM 9.55	—	1.39
PM 1.14	1.10	6.52

Trains from Sandown.

Leave SANDWN.	LON. B.	Arrive at VICTORIA
AM 6.40*f*	10.45	10.52
7.28	10.55	—
9.24	—	1.10
PM 12.24	4.27	4.34
1.24	—	5.12
3.24	7.48	6.50
5.10	—	8.33
5.24	10. 8	10. 1

Sunday Trains.

PM 4.28	8 50	7.56
—	—	—

f Mondays only.
h Passengers cross Portsmouth at own expense.

ANOTHER ROUTE from

Waterloo, 85 miles. Fares, 19/0*a*, 11/7*c*. R. T. for two months, 38/0*a*, 23/2*c*.

W'LOO	SANDWN.	SANDWN.	W'LOO
AM 5.50	10.24	AM 6.40*f*	9.52
8.34*r*	12.37	7.28	11.42
9.50	1.24	8.24	11.41
10.50	2.51	10.24*r*	1.52
11.50*d*	3.51	11.24*d*	3.20
PM 12.50*r*	4.24	11.24*e*	4.16
1.50*d*	5.24	PM 1.24	5.56
2.34	6.51	3.10	7.46
3.50*s*	7.24	4.24*r*	7.56
5.50	9. 9	5.24	10.46
		8.57*hk*	3.58

SANDOWN—*continued.*

Sunday Trains.

W'LOO	SANDWN.	SANDWN.	W'LOO
AM 8. 0	11.47	PM 2.36*r*	6.16
9.15*r*	1.39	4.28	8.52
PM 1.50	6.52	5.56	10. 1

f Mondays only.
h Via Eastleigh.
k Passengers cross Portsmouth at own expense
r Restaurant Car.
s Refreshments served.

Royal Pier Hotel. Open all the year. First class Family. Best position facing Pier. Good Golf Links. Officially appointed R.A.C.& A.A. Garage. 'Phone 87.
E. E. BROWNING, Resident Director.
See advt. p. 288.

Sandringham Hotel (private), Esplanade. Terraced Gardens. Covered Balcony. Facing Sea. Excellent cuisine. Separate Tables. Spacious Lounge. Telephone 66. Proprietors,
Mr. & Mrs. THOMAS.
See advt. p. 288.

Ocean Hotel. Premier Hotel in the Island.
See advt. p. 289.

Burlington Hotel. (Private.) Half minute to beach. Excellent Cuisine. Terms on application.
G. E. THOMAS, Proprietor.
See advt. p. 289.

Seacroft Private Hotel. Facing Sea. Spacious Rooms. Terms moderate. Excellent Cuisine. Proprietresses,
L. & E. WOODFORD.
See advt. p. 289.

Savoy Hotel. High-class Residential and Family Hotel, with moderate terms.
G. H. SEWELL.

Seagrove Private Hotel and Boarding Establishment, Sandown. Finest position. Facing Sea. Excellent Cuisine. Moderate. Tel. No. 165. Electric light throughout.
H. CHILD, Proprietor.

South Cliffe. En Pension. Facing Sea and Pier. Separate Tables. Good Cuisine. Terms Moderate. Apply,
Mrs. McHUGH.

Balmoral Private Hotel, Esplanade. Facing Pier and Sea. Covered Balcony 80 feet long. Excellent Cuisine. Separate Tables. 'Phone 13. Terms apply,
Mrs. GOODFELLOW.

Sandown Hotel. Leading Hotel in Sandown. Finest position facing Sea. Fully licensed. Cuisine a special feature. Billiards. Garage (R.A.C. and A.A.). Entirely new and genial management. Moderate charges. Telephone 172 Sandown.

"St. Kilda." En pension. Close to Sea. Delightful Garden. Spacious Rooms. Excellent Cuisine. Separate Tables. Moderate Terms.
Mrs. BISHOP, Proprietress.

Holme Lea, Sandown. Comfortable Boarding House. Ideal position. Minute Sea. Excellent Cuisine. Separate Tables. Electric Light. Terms moderate. Under personal supervision. Apply—Proprietor.

SANDOWN—*continued.*

"Carlton' Boarding Establishment, Esplanade. Facing Sea and Pier. Good Bathing and Boating. Near Golf and Tennis. Separate Tables. Terms Moderate. Under personal supervision. 'Phone 39. Apply—
PROPRIETRESS.

"Radnor" Esplanade Boarding Establishment. Unrivalled position. Facing Sea. Late Dinner. Excellent Cuisine. Superior Accommodation. Comfortable, Congenial, Reasonable.
Mr. & Miss F. WILLIAMS, Proprietors.

Palestine House. Board Residence. Splendid position, facing Sea. Excellent bathing. Good table. Comfortable lounge. Terms moderate.
F. BROWN, Proprietor, Sandown.

Yarborough. Boarding Establishment. Ideal situation on Sea Front. Uninterrupted Views. Sands. Cliffs. Downs. Good Cuisine. Separate Tables.
F. ROE, Proprietor, Sandown.

Marine House Boarding Establishment. Esplanade. Bathing, Boating. Separate Tables. Delightful. Winter. Apartments full South. Moderate Terms.
FRED. BROWN, Proprietor.

Lucerne Mansions Hotel. Sandown Bay, Isle of Wight. Exclusive situation on Western Esplanade. Central for amusemen's, bathing and boating. Handsomely appointed. Replete with every modern comfort. Excellent cuisine. Wireless concerts in lounge. Terms on application.
MANAGERESS.

"The Bays" Private Boarding Hotel, Esplanade. Electric Light. Constant hot water. Separate Tables. Every comfort. Open all year.
Mrs. FISHWICK, Proprietress.

House Agency. Particulars of Furnished Houses and Properties for Sale, with Plan of Town.
W. G. Mitchell, 24, High Street, Sandown.

SANDPLACE (Cornwall).
24¾ miles. No through fares. Departures *from* London as for Looe. Departures *for* London about 4 times daily.
Map Square 26.

SANDSEND (Yorks)
from King's Cross, 247¼ miles. Fares, 51/8*a*, 31/0*c*. R. T. for two months, 103/4*a*, 62/0*c*.
Map Square 8.

KING'S +	S'SEND.	S'SEND.	KING'S +
AM 4.45	12.45	AM 11.44*r*	6.30
.0.10*r*	5.28	PM 2. 8*r*	10. 0
11.50*r*	9. 9	6.30	3.25
PM 1.25*e*	7.35	7. 4	5.40

Sunday Trains.

PM 11.25	7.35	—	—
—	—	—	—

e Saturdays excepted.
r Restaurant Car.

Sandsend Hotel. First-class. Facing Sea. Superb Scenery. Moderate. Garage. Telephone 3.
See advt. p. 344.

SANDSIDE (Westmorland), 244¼ miles. Fares, 50/10*a*, 30/6*c*. R. T. for two months, 101/8*a*. 61/0*c*. Departures *from* London as for Kendal. Departures *for* London about 4 times daily.
Map Square 7.

SANDWICH (Kent) from
Charing Cross, Cannon Street, and London Bridge, via Ashford and Minster Junction, 87¼ miles. Fares, 16/3*a*, 13/0*b*, 9/9*c*. R. T. for two months, 32/6*a*, 26/0*b*.
Pop 3,161.
Map Square 24.

	Leave			Arr. at
	CHAR. +	CAN. ST.	LON. B.	SANDW.
AM	—	5.20	5.25	9.42
	—	—	7.50*l*	10.51
	9.15	—	9.23	12.30
	11. 0	—	11. 7	2.18
PM 1. 0	—	—	—	3.33
	3. 0	—	3. 8	5.48
	5.15*e*	5.12*c*	5.21*e*	7.53
	5.20*d*	—	5.26*d*	7.53
	5.24*d*	—	5.34*d*	9. 7
	6. 0*e*	—	6. 5*e*	9. 7
	7.18	—	7.26	10.38

Sunday Trains.

AM	7.45	—	7.52	11.42
PM	7.35	—	7.45	10.40
	—	—	—	—

Trains from Sandwich.

	Leave	Arrive at		
	SANDW.	LON. B.	CAN. ST.	CHAR. +
AM	6.13	9.32	9.36	—
	8.22	10.54	—	11. 3
	8.51	11.43	—	11.57
	10.22	1.36	—	1.50
	11.56	3.26	—	3.40
PM	2.25	5.50	—	6. 3
	4.22	7.25	7.30	7.49
	7.12	10.22	—	10.35
	10. 7*y*	—	1.20	—

Sunday Trains.

AM	6.22	10. 5	—	10.15
PM	4.10	7. 9	—	7.17
	5.42	8.30	—	8.40
	7.37	10.16	—	10.26
	10. 7*y*	—	1.23	—

d Saturdays only.
e Saturdays excepted.
l Low level platform.
y Third Class only.

ANOTHER ROUTE from
Charing Cross, Cannon Street, and London Bridge, via Dover, 91 miles. Fares, 17/1*a*, 13/8*b*, 10/3*c*. R. T. for two months, 34/2*a*, 27/4*b*, £0/6*c*.

	Leave			Arr. at
	CHAR. +	CAN. ST.	LON. B.	SANDW.
AM	—	3.40*y*	3.43*y*	8. 2
	—	5.20	5.25	10. 3
	—	7.16*h*	7.19*h*	11.56
	9.15	—	9.23	12.43
	11.15	—	—	1.38
PM 1. 0*p*	—	—	3.35
	1.50*d*	—	1.56*d*	4.22
	4. 5	—	—	6.13
	4.30*j*	—	4.37*j*	7.12
	—	5.50*k*	—	7.12
	6. 0*e*	—	6. 5*e*	8.28
	—	6.12*e*	—	9. 8
	7. 0	—	—	9. 8

Sunday Trains.

AM	9.35	—	—	11.52
	10.15	—	10.18	1.14
PM	7.35	—	7.45	11.21
	—	—	—	—

e Sats. excepted ; f Mondays only ; g Mondays excepted ; r Restaurant. 377

SANDWICH—continued.

Trains from Sandwich.

Leave SANDW.	LON. B.	Arrive at CAN. ST	CHAR. +
AM 6.40d	10. 0	10. 4	—
7.15e	9.36	9.40	—
8.15	10.34	—	10.41
8.34	11.43	--	11.57
10. 5	—	—	12.20
PM12.30	3.26	—	3.40
d12.30p	3.26	—	3.40
1.23	4. 2	—	4.10
4.15	—	—	6.20
5.47	10.22	—	10.35
9. 7y	—	1.20	—

Sunday Trains.

PM 4.12	—	—	6.30
5.15	—	—	8.17
8.49y	—	1.23	—
--	—	—	—
--	—	—	—

d Saturdays only.
e Saturdays excepted.
h Via Chatham.
j Fridays excepted.
k Fridays only.
p Pullman Car attached.
y Third class only.

ANOTHER ROUTE from Victoria, Holborn Viaduct or St. Paul's (via Chatham), 88¼ miles. Fares as above.

VICT.	Leave HOL. V.	ST. PL.'s	Arr. at SANDW.
AM —	3.50l	—	8. 2
5. 5	4.57	5. 0	9.43
5.48f	5.40f	5.42f	9.42
—	7.30	7.33	11.57
9.45	—	—	12.47
10.40	—	—	2.25
11.40d	—	—	3.35
11.40e	--	—	4.22
PM 2. 5d	—	—	5.42
2. 8e	—	—	5.42
5.10d	5.10e	5.12e	8.28
5.30e	—	—	9. 8
5.30d	—	—	10. 7
7.22h	—	—	10.38

Sunday Trains.

AM 9.35	—	—	1.14
9.35	—	—	12.35
10.40	--	--	4.10
PM 3.30	—	—	7.58
5.15	—	—	8.49
8.25	—	--	11.20

Trains from Sandwich.

Leave SANDW.	ST. PL.'s	Arrive at HOL. V.	VICT.
AM 6.13h	9.53	9.55	—
6.40	—	—	11. 2
8.34	—	—	11.27
10.51	—	—	2.43
11.56h	—	—	3.36
PM12.30e	4.46	—	4.39
1.28d	—	—	4.55
1.28	—	—	5.26
2.18d	—	—	5.23
2.25h	—	—	5.42
4.55	—	—	8.33
6.46	—	—	10.25
7.12h	11.44	11.46	—
--	—	—	—

SANDWICH—continued.

Sunday Trains.

Leave SANDW.	ST. PL.'s	Arr. at HOL. V.	VICT.
AM 7.10	—	11.58	11.51
8.44	—	—	1. 5
11.42k	—	—	3.50
PM 5.15	—	—	8.40
—	—	—	—
—	—	—	—
—	—	—	—
—	—	—	—

d Saturdays only.
e Saturdays excepted.
f Mondays only.
h Via Minster Junction.
k Via Folkestone.
l Third class only.

Bell Hotel. First-class Golfing and Family Hotel. Special Terms to Golfers. Excellent Cuisine. Private Sitting Rooms. Officially appointed R. A. C. Tel. 26 Sandwich. Under new Resident Proprietress—
H. A. OSBORN.

SANDY (Beds) from King's Cross, 44½ miles. Fares, 9/2a, 5/6c. R. T., double fare. Pop. 3,377. Map Square 18.

KING'S +	SANDY	SANDY	KING'S +
AM 5. 5	6.31	AM 8.30	9.56
7.45	9.15	10. 8	11.15
8.45	9.52	11.55	1.25
10.12	11.55	PM 2.28	3.50
11.30	12.51	5. 9	6.25
PM 1.55	3.24	7.49	9. 0
3. 0	4.23	8.36	10.20
4.15	5.35	—	—
5.10	6.55	—	—
6.15	7.42	—	—
8.30	9.55	—	—
—	—	—	—

Sunday Trains.

AM 8.30	10.14	PM 6.18	8. 8
PM 7.10	8.53	—	—

SANDYCROFT (Flint), 185 miles. Fares, 38/6a, 23/1c. R. T. for two months, 77/0a. Departures from London as for Chester. Departures for London about 6 times daily. Map Square 12.

SANDY LODGE (Midx.) from Marylebone or Baker Street, 15½ miles. Fares, 3/2a, 1/11c. R. T. for two months, 6/4a, 3/8c. See pp. 494, 495.

SANKEY (Lancs), 201½ miles. Fares, 38/7a, 23/2c. R. T., double fares. Departures from London as for Warrington (Central). Departures for London about 4 times daily. Pop. 1,363. Map Square 12.

SANKEY BRIDGES (Lancs), 183½ miles. Fares, 38/2a, 22/11c. R. T., double fare. Departures from London as for Widnes. Departures for London about 6 times daily. Map Square 12.

SANQUHAR (Dumfries), 358¼ miles. Fares, 72/9a, 43/8c. R. T. for two months, 145/6a, 87/4c. Departures from London as for Thornhill (Dumfries). Departures for London about 4 times daily. Pop. 3,383. Map Square 43.

SARNAU (Carmarthen), 232 miles. Fares, 47/1a, 28/3c. R. T. for two months 94/2a, 56/6c. Departures from London as for Carmarthen. Departures for London about 4 times daily. Map Square 21.

SAUCHIE (Clackmannan), 421 miles. No through fares. Departures from London as for Stirling or Dunfermline. Departures for London about 4 times daily. Pop. 2,935. Map Square 40.

SAUGHALL (Cheshire), 199 miles. No through fares. Departures from London as for Wrexham. Departures for London about 5 times daily. Pop. 967. Map Square 12.

SAUGHTREE (Roxburgh), 333½ miles. No through fares. Departures from London as for Carlisle or Hexham. Departures for London about 3 times daily. Pop. 423. Map Square 44.

SAUNDERSFOOT (Pembroke), 252¾ miles. Fares, 51/5a, 30/10c. R. T. for two months, 102/10a, 61/8c. Departures from London as for Tenby. Departures for London about 4 times daily. Map Square 20.

SAUNDERTON (Bucks) from Paddington, 31½ miles. Fares, 6/3a, 3/9c. R. T. for two months, 12/6a, 7/6c. Pop. 443. Map Square 23.

PAD.	S'R'TON	S'R'TON	PAD.
AM 5.45	7.20	AM 7.33	8.34
7.53h	9. 8	8.13	9.20
8.12	9.32	8.55	10.40
9.10	10.25	11.14	12.52
PM12.18	1.35	PM12.14	1.18
1.25	2.28	2.31	3.50
2.23	3.40	3.39	4.40
3.40	5. 3	5.10	6.35
4.40	5.55	6.57	9. 5
5.23	6.23	7.47	9.18
6.25	7.28	8.58	11. 4
7.18	8.24	9.51d	11.41
9. 0	10.14	—	—

Sunday Trains.

AM 9.12	10.31	AM 8.24	10.14
9.35	11.33	9.28	11. 4
PM 2.35	4. 7	PM12.37	2.26
4. 0	5.20	7. 6	8.25
6. 5	7.45	7.46	9.35
—	—	8. 6	9.53

d Saturdays only.
h Not after July 27th.

SAUNDERTON—*contd.*

ANOTHER ROUTE from *Marylebone*, 32¾ miles. Fares as above.

M'bone.	S'r'ton	S'r'ton	M'bone.
AM 6.10	7.19	AM 7.33	8.49
7.10	9. 8	8.13	9.26
8. 4	9.32	8.55	9.55
9. 5	10.25	11.14*d*	12.43
PM12.15	1.35	11.14	1. 5
12.55	2.29	PM12.14*d*	3.10
2.10	3.40	12.14*e*	3.23
3. 5	5. 4	2.31*d*	3.53
4.55	5.55	2.31	4.28
5.38	6.32	3.39	5.48
5.43	7.28	4. 2	6. 3
6.35*d*	8.24	5.10	7. 5
6.45*e*	8.24	6.57	8. 6
8.30	10.14	7.47	9.27
—	—	8.58	9.55
—	—	9.51*d*	11.18
—	—	—	—

Sunday Trains.

AM 8.50	10. 3	AM 9.28	10.43
10.20	11.33	PM12.37	1.48
PM 2.15	4. 8	7.46	8.58
3.35	5.20	8. 6	10.38
6.30	7.45	—	—
—	—	—	—
—	—	—	—

d Saturdays only.
e Saturdays excepted.

SAVERNAKE (Wilts)

from *Paddington*, 70 miles. Fares, 14/7*a*, 8/9*c*. R. T. for two months, 29/2*a*. Pop. 194.

Map Square 22.

Pad.	S'nake	S'nake	Pad.
AM 7.30	9.31	AM 8.11	10. 0
8.45*r*	11.13	9.22	10.52
10.45	12.52	10.19	12.55
PM12.30*r*	2.29	PM 1. 4	2.50
2.45	5. 7	4.31	7.20
3.18	5.54	6.20	8.20
5. 5	6.51	8.24	10.45
5.55	7.39	—	—
6.30	8.21	—	—
—	—	—	—
—	—	—	—

Sunday Trains.

AM 9.10	11.29	AM 8.12	10.50
PM 5.15	7.50	PM 6.55	9.15
—	—	—	—
—	—	—	—
—	—	—	—

r Restaurant Car.

ANOTHER ROUTE from *Waterloo*, 82¾ miles. Fares, 15/3*a*, 9/2*c*. R. T. for two months, 30/6*a*.

W'loo	S'nake	S'nake	W'loo
PM 1. 0*r*	3.20	AM 9.41	12.22
3.30	6.15	PM12.21	2.36
6. 0*r*	8.31	5.22*r*	8.30
—	—	—	—
—	—	—	—
—	—	—	—
—	—	—	—

Sunday Trains.

PM 6. 0	9. 6	PM 5.28	8.57
—	—	—	—
—	—	—	—
—	—	—	—
—	—	—	—

r Restaurant Car.

SAWBRIDGEWORTH

(Herts) from *Liverpool Street*, 26¾ miles. Fares, 5/8*a*, 3/5*c*. R. T. for two months, 11/4*a*. Pop. 2,295.

Map Square 24.

L'pl. St.	Sawb'th	Sawb'th	L'pl. St.
AM 5.50	6.53	AM 1.48	2.50
7.18	8.35	7. 4	8.18
9.10	10.28	7.37	8.49
10.34	12.19	7.49	8.57
PM12.29*d*	1.14	8.28	9.42
12.40*d*	1.43	9. 2	9.47
12.48*e*	2. 6	9.35	10.17
1.19*d*	2.19	9.57	10.59
2. 0*d*	3. 1	10.59	12.15
2.48	3.55	PM 1. 2	2. 7
4.15	5.11	2.21*d*	3.18
5.10	6.11	3.48	5. 9
6. 0*e*	6.54	5.51	7.19
6.30	7.24	6.48	7.58
7.41*d*	8.42	8.12	9.33
7.41*e*	8.45	10. 7	11.12
9.17	10.32	—	—
11.50*k*	12.49	—	—
—	—	—	—
—	—	—	—
—	—	—	—

Sunday Trains.

AM 8.12	9.10	AM 1.48	3. 0
9.25	10.26	7.55	9.33
PM 1.50	3.20	10.11	11.27
4.50	6.11	PM 7.57	9.10
7.15	8.17	9.26	10.40
9.12	10.26	—	—
—	—	—	—
—	—	—	—
—	—	—	—

d Saturdays only.
e Saturdays excepted.
k Wednesdays and Saturdays only.

SAWDON (Yorks), 229½

miles. Fares, 47/11*a*, 28/9*c*. R.T. for two months, 95/10*a*, 57/6*c*. Departures *from* London as for Malton. Departures *for* London about 4 times daily.

Map Square 8.

SAWLEY (Derby) from

St. Pancras, 121½ miles. Fares, 24/10*a*, 14/11*c*. R. T., double fare. Departures *from* London as for Trent. Departures *for* London about 3 times daily. Pop. 3,288.

Map Square 18.

SAXBY (Leicester) from

St. Pancras, 101½ miles. Fares, 20/5*a*, 12/3*c*. R. T., double fare. Pop. 116.

Map Square 18.

St. Pan.	Saxby	Saxby	St. Pan.
AM 2.25	7.25	AM 7.48*r*	10.45
8.25*r*	11.44	9.14*r*	12.10
9.50*r*	12.44	9.52*r*	1.20
10.25*dr*	1.28	PM12.44*r*	4.10
10.25*er*	1.41	1.28*r*	4.20
PM12.25*r*	4. 3	4.58*r*	7.55
2.25*r*	5.37	5.37	8.22
3.30*r*	6. 8	6.26*r*	9.15
5.35*r*	8.35	6.57*r*	10. 5
6.25*r*	9.50	—	—
—	—	—	—
—	—	—	—
—	—	—	—
—	—	—	—
—	—	—	—

SAXBY—*continued.*

Sunday Trains.

St. Pan.	Saxby	Saxby	St. Pan.
PM 3.15	8.51	AM 7.45	11.53
—	—	PM 6.12*r*	9.52
—	—	—	—
—	—	—	—
—	—	—	—

d Saturdays only.
e Saturdays excepted.
r Restaurant Car.

SAXHAM (Suffolk) from

Liverpool Street, 81¾ miles. Fares, 16/11*a*, 10/2*c*. R. T. for two months, 33/10*a*, 20/4*c*. Departures *from* London as for Higham (Suffolk). Departures *for* London about 10 times daily. Pop. 386.

Map Square 19.

SAXILBY (Lincoln), 136¼

miles. Fares, 28/2*a*, 16/11*c*. R. T., double fare. Departures *from* London as for Lincoln. Departures *for* London about 5 times daily. Pop. 1,310.

Map Square 13.

SAXMUNDHAM (Suffolk)

from *Liverpool Street*, 91½ miles. Fares, 19/2*a*, 11/6*c*. R. T. for two months, 38/4*a*. Pop. 1,368.

Map Square 19.

L'pl. St.	Saxmdm.	Saxmdm.	L'pl. St.
AM 5. 0	8. 0	AM 7.40*r*	10.30
8.15*r*	11.27	8.45*r*	11.22
10. 0	12.20	9.25*r*	11.30
10.20	1.18	10.59	1.20
PM 1. 0	3.19	11.19*r*	2. 3
3.18*r*	6. 1	PM 1.29	3.42
4.55*r*	7.11	3.36	5.55
5.18*dr*	8. 0	4.44	7.51
5.18*er*	8. 4	6.47*r*	9.22
—	—	7.26*r*	10. 0
—	—	7.48	11.16
—	—	—	—

Sunday Trains.

AM10. 5*r*	12.45	AM 8.18	11.38
PM 4.40	7.27	PM 6.32*r*	9.10
—	—	7.59*r*	10.30
—	—	—	—
—	—	—	—
—	—	—	—
—	—	—	—
—	—	—	—
—	—	—	—
—	—	—	—
—	—	—	—

d Saturdays only.
e Saturdays excepted.
r Restaurant Car.

SCALBY (Yorks), 232¼ miles.

Fares, 48/6*a*, 29/1*c*. R. T. for two months, 97/0*a*, 58/2*c*. Departures *from* London as for Ravenscar. Departures *for* London about 5 times daily. Pop. 1,437.

Map Square 8.

SCALFORD (Leicester),

from *Euston* 110½ miles. Fares, 22/4*a*, 13/5*c*. R. T., double fare. Departures *from* London as for Melton Mowbray. Departures *for* London about 4 times daily. Pop. 688.

Map Square 18.

SCARBOROUGH (Yorks)

from *King's Cross*, 230¼ miles. Fares, 47/9*a*, 28/8*c*. R. T. for two months, 95/6*a*, 57/4*c*. Pop. 46,192.
Map Square 8.

King's +	Scarbr.	Scarbr.	King's +
AM 4.45	10.52	AM 8.20*r*	1.15
7.15*r*	1.23	8.30	3.50
10. 0*r*	2.55	10.50*r*	4.30
10.10*r*	3.48	11.30*r*	4.45
11.50*r*	4.20	PM 1.20*r*	6.30
PM 1.50*r*	7.19	3. 0*r*	7.30
5.35*e*	10.31	3.10*r*	9.25
5.35*d*	11.33	4.50*r*	10. 0
11 25*e*	5.55	8. 5*e*	3.25
11.25*d*	10. 7	10. 0*e*	5.40
—	—	10. 0*d*	6. 0

Sunday Trains.

PM11.25	5.55	PM 7.50	5.40
—	—	—	—
—	—	—	—

d Saturdays only.
e Saturdays excepted.
r Restaurant Car.

Pavilion Hotel. Central. Lounge. Lift. Garage. Private Suites. Hotel Porters meet trains. R.A.C., A.A. Telephone 70.
R. W. LAUGHTON, Proprietor.
See advt. p. **290**.

Prince of Wales Hotel. First-class. Overlooking Bay. Self-enclosed Suites. New Ball Room. Telegrams, "Princely, Scarborough." 'Phone 925-926.
See advt. p. **291**.

Royal Hotel. 200 Rooms. Centrally situated, overlooking South Bay. Extremely moderate tariff. Telephone No. 75.
See advt. p. **291**.

Crown Hotel. Esplanade. Finest position. Extensive sea views. Lounge and Billiard Room. Suites. Telephone No. 26.
See advt. p. **292**.

Esplanade Boarding Establishment. South Cliff. Sea views. Lounge. Tel. 186.
F. K. WHITE.
See advt. p. **292**.

Queen's Hotel. On Sea Front. Lounge. Terrace Gardens. Billiards. Near Links. Bowls, Bathing, Cricket, &c.
See advt. p. **293**.

Cambridge Hotel. South Cliff. Sheltered position. Lift. Near Spa. Golf. Tennis. Garage.
See advt. p. **293**.

Grand Hotel. Best. 350 rooms; 200 facing the sea. Orchestra. Apply for inclusive terms. Tel. Nos. 791 and 792.
See advt. p. **294**.

Swift's Boarding House. North Cliff. Spacious Lounge.
See advt. p. **294**.

Red-Lea Private Hotel, Prince of Wales' Terrace. Facing South. Open all year. Lounge. Accommodation for 100. Tel. 188.
MALCOLM ROWNTREE,
Resident Proprietor.
See advt. p. **294**.

The Balmoral Hotel. Family and Commercial. Most central. Moderate Tariff. Garage.
See advt. p. **295**.

SCARBOROUGH (Yorks) —*continued.*

Clarence Gardens Hotel. 100 Rooms. Excellent. Economical. Easily reached.
See advt. p. **295**.

Highly - recommended Select Boarding House. Absolute comfort. Excellent cuisine. Terms, 10s. to 15s. daily. Miss Palframan, "Kirkdale," Trinity Road.

Principal House Agents. Ward, Price and Co. 48, Westborough. Printed Registers of all Furnished and Unfurnished Properties free. Telephone 369.

SCARCLIFFE (Derby)

from *King's Cross*, 149 miles. Fares, 29/9*a*, 17/10*c*. R. T., double fare. Departures *from* London as for Edwinstowe. Departures *for* London about twice daily. Pop. 2,882.
Map Square 13.

SCAWBY (Lincoln), 162½

miles. Fares, 33/1*a*, 19/10*c*. R. T., double fare. Departures *from* London as for Gainsborough (*via* Retford). Departures *for* London about 5 times daily. Pop. 989.
Map Square 13.

SCHOLES (Yorks), 192¾

miles. No through fares. Departures *from* London as for Leeds or Wetherby. Departures *for* London about 6 times daily. Pop. 1,721.
Map Square 12.

SCILLY ISLANDS, 341

miles. No through fares. *See* trains to Penzance, and thence by steamer. From Penzance on Tuesdays and Fridays at 8.30 a.m. and on Wednesdays and Saturdays at 10.0 a.m. From St. Mary's on Mondays and Thursdays at 9.30 a.m. and on Tuesdays and Fridays at 4.0 p.m. Single Boat fare 10/0. Steam launch service from St. Mary's to outlying islands. Pop. 1,750.
Map Square 25.

Tregarthen's Hotel, St Mary's. Old Established Hotel, in own grounds. Commands panoramic views. Electric Light.
See advt. p. **295**.

Holgate's Hotel.—The largest First-class Hotel for Families and Gentlemen. On Sea Front. Omnibus and Porter meets the Steamer on arrival.
Mr. & Mrs. E. N. MUMFORD,
Resident Proprietors.

SCOPWICK (Lincoln), 119¼

miles. Fares, 24/10*a*, 14/11*c*. R. T., double fare. Departures *from* London as for Blankney. Departures *for* London about 4 times daily. Pop. 351.
Map Square 13.

SCORRIER (Cornwall),

286¼ miles. Fares, 59/2*a*, 35/6*c*. R. T. for two months, 118/4*a*, 71/0*c*. Departures *from* London as for Chacewater. Departures *for* London about 4 times daily.
Map Square 25.

SCORTON (Lancs), 221¾

miles. Fares, 46/3*a*, 27/9*c*. R. T. for two months, 92/6*a*, 55/6*c*. Departures *from* London as for Preston. Departures *for* London about 4 times daily. Pop. 478.
Map Square 7.

SCORTON (Yorks), 231¼

miles. Fares, 48/2*a*, 28/11*c*. R. T. for two months, 96/4*a*, 57/10*c*. Departures *from* London as for Richmond (Yorks). Departures *for* London about 4 times daily. Pop. 544.
Map Square 7.

SCOTBY (Cumberland),

301¼ miles. Fares, 60/3*a*, 36/2*c*. R. T., double fare. Departures *from* London as for Lazonby. Departures *for* London about 5 times daily. Pop. 757.
Map Square 3.

SCOTCH DYKE (Cumberland),

311 miles. Fares, 63/2*a* 37/11*c*. R. T. for two months, 126/4*a*, 75/10*c*. Departures *from* London as for Carlisle. Departures *for* London about 4 times daily.
Map Square 3.

SCOTSCALDER (Caithness),

710¾ miles. No through fares. Departures *from* London as for Helmsdale. Departures *for* London about 3 times daily.
Map Square 31.

SCOTSGAP (Northumberland),

296 miles. Fares, 62/4*a*, 37/5*c*. R. T. for two months, 124/8*a*. Departures *from* London as for Morpeth. Departures *for* London about 3 times daily.
Map Square 9.

SCOTSTOUNHILL

(Renfrew), 441½ miles. Fares, 82/6*a*, 49/6*c*. R.T. for two months, 165/0*a*, 99/0*c*. Departures *from* London as for Glasgow. Departures *for* London about 4 times daily.

SCOTSWOOD (Northumberland),

273¾ miles. Fares, 57/3*a*, 34/4*c*. R. T. for two months, 114/6*a*, 68/8*c*. Departures *from* London as for Newcastle-on-Tyne. Departures *for* London about 8 times daily.
Map Square 3.

SCREMERSTON (Northumberland),

331½ miles. No through fares. Departures *from* London as for Morpeth. Departures *for* London about 5 times daily. Pop. 879.
Map Square 3.

SCROOBY (Notts), 145¾

miles. Fares, 30/3*a*, 18/2*c*. R. T., double fare. Departures *from* London as for Retford. Departures *for* London about 5 times daily. Pop. 243.
Map Square 13.

SCRUTON (Yorks), 222

miles. Fares, 46/5*a*, 27/10*c*. R.T., double fare. Departures *from* London as for Leyburn. Departures *for* London about 6 times daily. Pop. 281.
Map Square 7.

SEACOMBE (Cheshire),

207¾ miles. No through fares. Departures *from* London as for Chester. Departures *for* London about 5 times daily. Pop. 14,815.

SEACROFT (Lincoln from

King's Cross, 130½ miles. Fares, 26/11*a*, 16/2*c*. R. T., double fare. Departures *from* London as for Skegness. Departures *for* London about 5 times daily
Map Square 14.

SEAFORD (Sussex) from

London Bridge and *Victoria*, 58¾ miles. Fares, 12/3a, 7/4c. R.T. for two months, 24/6a, 14/8c. Pop. 6,991.

Map Square 29.

	Leave		Arr. at
	VICT.	LON. B.	SEAF'D.
AM	—	6.15	8.15
	6.37l	6.40l	9.44
	7.23	7.25	10.18
	9. 0	—	11.10
	9.45	—	11.50
	10. 5	9.50	12.17
	11.15	—	1. 8
	11.55	—	1.42
	12. 0	12.10	2.18
PM	1.20e	2. 0e	3.44
	1.25d	2. 0d	3.44
	2. 0	2. 5	4.46
	3.20	—	5. 8
	3.40l	4. 5	5.53
	4.30	5. 5	6.33
	5.20	—	6.55
	5.35l	—	7.38
	5.45e	5.55e	7.38
	6.40	6. 0d	8.16
	6.50	7. 0	9.24
	8.35	—	10.15
	10. 0	—	12. 1

Sunday Trains.

AM	6.55	7.22	10.20
	9.30	9.30	11.38
	11.15	—	1.10
PM	12.15l	—	3. 0
	1.14l	1.10l	4. 8
	6.33	6.33	9.16

Trains from Seaford.

	Leave	Arrive at	
	SEAFORD	LON. B.	VICT.
AM	6.25	8.46	—
	7. 5	8.53	9. 8
	8.33	10.15	10.24
	8.47	10.55	10.56
	10.50	12.44	12.45
	11.15l	—	1.20
PM	12.10	2.22	2.22
	12.27l	3.40	3.45
	1.20	—	4.17
	2.30	4.32	4.35
	3.55l	6.36	6.34
	4.50l	—	7.30
	5.35	7.42	7.45
	6.12	7.56	7.50
	8.10	10.25	10.17
	8.58	—	11.17
	10. 3l	12.59	1. 0

Sunday Trains.

AM	7.40	10.18	10.32
	10.28l	—	1. 0
PM	1.50l	5. 3	5.11
	4.55	—	7.28
	5.50	7.56	7.37
	8.38	—	10.19
	9.30l	12.27	—
	—	—	—
	—	—	—

d Saturdays only.
e Saturdays excepted.
l Via Brighton.

Esplanade Hotel. The only licensed Hotel on the sea front. Facing and within forty yards of the sea. Spacious Dining and Public Rooms facing the sea. The hotel has recently been enlarged, re-furnished, and re-decorated. Telephone, No. 124 Seaford.
Apply, MANAGERESS.

SEAFORD—continued.

Eversley Hotel. Finest position. Facing Sea. Tennis. Own grounds. Recommended by Members Seaford Golf Clubs. 'Phone 15. Telegrams, "Eversley."

The Beach Hotel. On the Sea front. Moderate inclusive terms. Telephone 121 Seaford. Telegrams, "Beach Hotel, Seaford."

Ferndale (late HOLMWOOD) Boarding Establishment. Sunny position overlooking Sea. Three Minutes from Station. Golf Links easy distance. Terms Moderate.
Apply, PROPRIETRESS.

Bay Hotel. Fully licensed. First-class Family. Near Links. Hundred yards Sea and Station. Garage. Tel. 2 Seaford.
Apply, MANAGERESS.

The Carlton. Old Established. Comfortable Boarding House. Overlooking Sea. Near Golf Links and South Downs.
G. HERRING.

Battle Creek. Private Hotel. Board Residence. In own Grounds. Three minutes' Sea. Own Tennis Courts. Golf. Highly recommended. Telegrams: "Battle Creek." Apply, PROPRIETOR.

Sea Hotel (Private). Board Residence. Finest Position Sea Front. Bathing from Hotel. Golf Links ten minutes. Famous Downs five minutes.

Seaton House. Private Hotel. Centre of Esplanade. Bathing from house. Ten minutes from Golf Course. Inclusive Terms. Telephone, No. 37.

House Agents, Auctioneers, Surveyors. Best List Unfurnished and Furnished Houses, and Illustrated Register. 'Phone 185. Opposite Station.
STUART CALLF & Co.

SEAFORTH (Lancs), 205¼

miles. Fares, 41/6a, 24/11c. R.T. for two months, 83/0a. Departures *from* London as for Liverpool. Departures *for* London about 8 times daily. Pop.

Map Square 12.

SEAHAM (Durham), 259⅞

miles. Fares, 54/7a, 32/9c. R.T., double fare. Departures *from* London as for Sunderland or West Hartlepool. Departures *for* London about 6 times daily. Pop. 6,342.

Map Square 4.

SEAHOUSES (Northum-

berland), 321 miles. No through fares. Departures *from* London as for Morpeth. Departures *for* London about 4 times daily.

Map Square 3.

SEAMER (Yorks), 227½ miles.

Fares, 47/4a, 28/5c. R.T., double fare. Departures *from* London as for Malton Departures *for* London about 5 times daily. Pop. 660.

Map Square 8.

SEA MILLS (Gloucester),

123¼ miles. Fares, 25/7a, 15/4c. R.T. for two months, 51/2a, 30/8c. Departures *from* London as for Avonmouth Docks. Departures *for* London about 6 times daily.

Map Square 22.

SEASCALE (Cumberland),

290¾ miles. Fares, 60/7a, 36/4c. R.T. for two months, 121/2a, 72/8c. Departures *from* London as for Millom. Departures *for* London about 4 times daily. Pop. 699.

Map Square 6.

SEATON (Cumberland),

312¼ miles. No through fares. Departures *from* London as for Workington or Moor Row. Departures *for* London about 3 times daily. Pop. 1,801.

Map Square 6.

SEATON (Devon) from

Waterloo, 152⅝ miles. Fares, 31/10a, 19/1c. R.T. for two months, 63/8a, 38/2c. Pop. 2,294.

Map Square 27.

W'LOO	SEATON		SEATON	W'LOO
AM 7.30	12.20	AM	9.25r	1.56
	12. 0r	3.40		11.30r	3. 8
PM 1. 0kr	6. 2	PM	1.25r	6. 0
1. 0lr	6.30		2.45	7.40
3. 0r	8. 2		3.55r	8.30
6. 0r	10.10		4.55	10.50
—	—		8.12h	3.58

No Sunday Trains.

h Via Eastleigh.
k Fridays and Saturdays excepted.
l Fridays and Saturdays only.
n Noon.
r Restaurant Car.

Beach. Only First-class Hotel facing the Sea. Open for Visitors all the year round. Garage. Golf. Telephone No. 17.
E. A. SMITH, Proprietor.

Royal Clarence. First-class Hotel, overlooking sea. Hunting, Golf, Cricket, Tennis, Fishing, Posting. Garage. 'Bus. Telephone 15.
A. F. GODDARD, Proprietor.

Westleigh Private Hotel. On Sea Front. Half mile from 18-hole Links. Liberal Table (separate tables). Good fires and home comforts. Comfortable smoking-room. Good bathrooms. Terms *inclusive* per day or week. No Extras. Telephone No. 25.
Mrs. WALLACE.

Pole Arms. Oldest established Hotel. Extensive views. Old-fashioned garden. Near Sea. Posting. Cricket, Tennis, Golf. Moderate terms. Apply—
PROPRIETOR

Esplanade Hotel. Well-furnished. Hot and cold Water in Bedrooms. Electric Light. Telephone No. 6.
Miss BRYANT, Manageress.

The Cottage Hotel. Small, good class Private. Uninterrupted views, Sea and Valley. Convenient to Station and Golf Links.
W. S. STOKES, Proprietor.

SEAFORD.—THE ESPLANADE HOTEL. Only Hotel on the Sea Front. MODERATE TARIFF.

SEATON (Durham), 292 miles. No through fares. Departures *from* London as for West Hartlepool or Sunderland. Departures *for* London about 4 times daily. Pop. 388.
Map Square 3.

SEATON (Rutland) from *Euston* 97¾ miles. Fares, 17/3*a*, 10/4*c*. R. T., double fare. Pop. 198.
Map Square 18.

Euston	Seaton	Seaton	Euston
AM 2.35	8. 5	AM 7.58	11.55
5. 0	9.49	10 3	1. 0
10.40	2.31	PM 12.15	4.15
PM 1.30	4.22	2.41	5.50
2.50*t*	6.16	4.58*r*	9.20
7. 0	10. 4	7. 9	10.45
11.50*e*	4. 8	8.34*e*	4. 0
12.10*dm*	4. 8	8.34*d*	5. 0

No Sunday Trains.

d Saturdays only.
e Saturdays excepted.
m Midnight.
r Restaurant Car.
t Tea Car.

SEATON CAREW (Durham), 244¾ miles. Fares, 51/0*a*, 30/7*c*. R.T. for two months, 102/0*a*, 61/2*c*. Departures *from* London as for Stockton-on-Tees. Departures *for* London about 8 times daily. Pop. 2,265.
Map Square 8.

SEATON DELAVAL (Northumberland), 277¾ miles. Fares, 58/7*a*, 35/2*c*. R. T. for two months, 117/2*a*, 70/4*c*. Departures *from* London as for Newcastle-on-Tyne. Departures *for* London about 4 times daily. Pop. 7,859.
Map Square 3.

SEATON JUNCTION (Devon) from *Waterloo*, 148 miles. Fares, 30/10*a*, 18/6*c*. R. T. for two months, 61/8*a*, 37/0*c*.
Map Square 27.

W'loo	Seat. J.	Seat. J	W'loo
AM 7.30	11.50	AM 7.18*r*	11.10
12. 0*r*	3.10	9.53*r*	1.56
PM 1. 0*r*	5.21	11.59*r*	3. 8
3. 0*r*	7.10	PM 1.53*r*	6. 0
6. 0*r*	9.50	3.44	7.40
—	—	4.20*r*	8.30
—	—	6.33	10.50
—	—	8.40*h*	3.58

Sunday Trains.

AM 9. 0	2.49	PM 4.27*r*	8.57

h Via Eastleigh.
n Noon.
r Restaurant Car.

SEAVIEW (Isle of Wight). Station at Ryde, distance about 3 miles.

Seaview. Pier Hotel. Finest Bathing and Boating. Resident Proprietor. Station: Ryde Esplanade.
See advt. p. **295**.

SEDBERGH (Yorks) from *Euston*, 262½ miles. Fares, 51/11*a*, 31/2*c*. R.T. for two months, 103/10*a*, 62/4*c*. Departures *from* London as for Ingleton. Departures *for* London about 5 times daily. Pop. 2,405.
Map Square 7.

SEDGEBROOK (Lincs), 110 miles. Fares, 22/9*a*, 13/8*c*. R. T., double fare. Departures *from* London as for Bottesford. Departures *for* London about 3 times daily. Pop. 168.
Map Square 13.

SEDGEFIELD (Durham), 245 miles. Fares, 51/1*a*, 30/8*c*. R. T., double fare. Departures *from* London as for Ferryhill. Departures *for* London about 5 times daily. Pop. 3,327.
Map Square 7.

SEDGEFORD (Norfolk) from *Liverpool Street*, 112½ miles. Fares, 23/9*a*, 14/3*c*. R. T. for two months, 47/6*a*, 28/6*c*. Departures *from* London as for Burnham Market. Departures *for* London about 4 times daily. Pop. 694.
Map Square 14.

SEEDLEY (Lancs), 186¼ miles. Fares, 39/0*a*, 23/5*c*. R. T., double fare. Departures *from* London as for Manchester (London Road). Departures *for* London about 5 times daily.

SEEND (Wilts) from *Paddington*, 90¾ miles. Fares, *via* Theale, 18/9*a*, 11/3*c*. R. T. for two months, 37/6*a*. *Via* Chippenham, 19/10*a*, 11/11*c*. R.T. for two months, 39/8*a*. Departures *from* London as for Devizes. Departures *for* London about 8 times daily. Pop. 940.
Map Square 22.

SEER GREEN (Bucks) 21½ miles. Fares, 4/0*a*, 2/5*c*. R. T. for two months, 8/0*a*, 4/10*c*. Pop. 371. *See* pp. 490, 491, 495, 496.

SEFTON (Lancs), 221¼ miles. Fares, 41/11*a*, 25/2*c*. R.T. for two months, 83/10*a*, 50/4*c*. Departures *from* London as for Warrington (Central). Departures *for* London about 5 times daily. Pop. 340.
Map Square 12.

SEGHILL (Northumberland), 276¾ miles. No through fares. Departures *from* London as for Newcastle-on-Tyne. Departures *for* London about 6 times daily. Pop. 1,949.
Map Square 3.

SELBY (Yorks) from *King's Cross*, 174¼ miles. Fares, 35/0*a*, 21/0*c*. R. T., double fare. Pop. 9,990.
Map Square 13.

King's +	Selby	Selby	King's +
AM 4.45	8.54	AM 1.55	6. 0
7.15*r*	11. 0	8. 2*r*	11.30
8.45	1. 1	8.46	1. 5
10.10*r*	4. 8	10.46	3.50
11.30	4.23	PM 12.43*r*	4.30
PM 1.50*r*	5.39	1. 6*r*	4.45
4. 0*r*	7.50	3.43*r*	9. 0
5.45*r*	10.25	5.29*r*	9.25
10.45	2.27	10.40	3.25
—	—	—	—
—	—	—	—
—	—	—	—

Sunday Trains.

AM 8.30	2.40	AM 1.55	6. 0
11.30*r*	3.18	PM 1.12	5.15
PM 5. 0*r*	9.20	4.26*r*	8.15
10.45	2.27	—	—
—	—	—	—

r Restaurant Car.

SELBY—*continued.*

Another Route from *St. Pancras*, 195½ miles. Fares as above.

St. Pan.	Selby	Selby	St. Pan.
AM 2.25*g*	9.31	AM 6.55*r*	1.30
4.25	12.46	9.54*r*	4.10
9. 0*r*	3. 0	11.57*r*	5.30
9.50*r*	3.42	PM 2.48*r*	7.57
PM 1.50*r*	9.16	9.23	4.20
5. 0*r*	10.42	—	—
9.15	3.24	—	—

Sunday Trains.

—	—	PM 9.23	4.55

g Mondays excepted.
r Restaurant Car.

Londesborough Arms Hotel. Adjoining Selby Abbey. First-class Family, Commercial, and Posting House. Nineteen Bedrooms. Garage. 'Phone: 185 P.R.H.A. House.

SELHAM (Sussex) from *London Bridge*, *Victoria*, and *Clapham Junction*, 57¼ miles. Fares, 12/1*a*, 7/3*c*. R. T. for two months, 24/2*a*, 14/6*c*. Departures *from* London as for Petworth. Departures *for* London about 6 times daily. Pop. 83.
Map Square 23.

SELHURST (Surrey) from *London Bridge* and *Victoria*, 9¼ miles. Fares, from London Bridge, 1/11*a*, 1/2*c*. R. T. for two days, 3/10*a*, 2/0*c*. From Victoria, 1/11*a*, 1/2*c*. R. T. for two days, 3/8*a*, 2/0*c*. *See* pp. 567, 570–577.

SELKIRK, 368 miles. Fares, 75/5*a*, 45/3*c*. R.T. for two months, 150/10*a*, 90/6*c*. Departures *from* London as for Galashiels. Departures *for* London about 5 times daily. Pop. 7,069.
Map Square 41.

SELLAFIELD (Cumberland) from *Euston*, 292½ miles. Fares, 60/10*a*, 36/6*c*. R. T. for two months, 121/8*a*, 73/0*c*.
Map Square 6.

Euston	Self'ld	Self'ld	Euston
AM 2.35	12.36	AM 6.59*h*	3.45
5. 0	2.26	6.59*r*	4.15
6.45	4.11	12. 0*nr*	7.30
11.35*r*	6.50	PM 3.11*r*	10.45
PM 1.30*r*	9.13	7.29	5. 0
9.30*e*	7. 0	—	—
11. 0*d*	10.20	—	—

Sunday Trains.

AM 11.45	8.10	AM 10.26*r*	7.30
—	—	PM 6.38	5. 0

d Saturdays only.
e Saturdays excepted.
h Mondays and Saturdays only.
n Noon.
r Restaurant Car.

SELLING (Kent) from *Victoria*, *Holborn Viaduct*, and *St. Paul's*, 55¼ miles. Fares, 11/8*a*, 9/4*b*, 7/0*c*. R. T. for two months, 23/4*a*, 18/8*b*. Pop. 722.
Map Square 24.

Leave Vict. (S.E.& C.)	Leave Hol. V.	Leave St. Pl.'s	Arr. at Selling
AM —	3.50*l*	—	6. 5
5. 5	4.57	5. 0	7.59
5.48*f*	5.40*f*	5.42*f*	7.59
—	7.30	7.33	10. 9
7.40*f*	—	—	10. 9
10.40	—	—	12.14
PM 2. 5*d*	—	—	3.36
2. 8*e*	—	—	3.56
4.20	5.10	5.12	6.48
5.30*d*	—	—	7.36
8.30	—	—	9.59

Sunday Trains.

AM 8.15	8. 0	—	10.14
PM 3.30	—	—	6. 9
8.25	—	—	9.57

SELLING—continued.

Trains from Selling.

Leave SELLING	Arrive at St. PL.'s	HOL. V.	VICT.
AM 7.28k	—	—	9. 4k
7.28	9.37	9.39	—
8.31	—	—	11. 2
8.31k	—	—	9.52k
10.41e	1. 0	1. 2	1 33
10.53d	—	—	1.22
PM12.41	—	—	2.43
2.50e	4.46	—	4.39
3. 6d	—	—	4.55
3.46	—	—	5.26
d5.56k	—	—	8.20k
6.49	—	—	8.32
8.37	—	—	10.25

Sunday Trains.

AM 9.51	—	11.58	11.51
PM 2.59	—	—	5.31
8.44	—	—	10.29

d Saturdays only.
e Saturdays excepted.
f Mondays only.
k Departs from or arrives at Cannon Street.
l Third class only.

SELLY OAK (Worcester),
116¼ miles. Fares, 23/7a, 14/2c. R. T. for two months, 47/2a. Departures *from* London as for Birmingham (New Street). Departures *for* London about 6 times daily. Pop. 25,733.

SELSDON ROAD
(Surrey) from *London Bridge, Victoria,* and *Clapham Junction,* 11¼ miles. Fares, 2/6r, 1/6c. R. T. for two days, 5/0a, 2/7c. Departures *from* London as for Sanderstead. Departures *for* London about 15 times daily. No Sunday Trains.

SELSEY (Sussex) from
Victoria and *London Bridge,* 76¾ miles. Fares, 15/5a, 9/4c. R.T. for two months, 30/4a, 18/5c. Pop. 1,591.
Map Square 28.

Leave VICT.	LON. B.	Arr. at SELSEY.
AM 6.18	6.35	9.40
8.55	—	11.28
10.15	10.22	1.10
PM 1.40	1.50	4.50
3.55	4. 0	6.50
—	5. 5	8.35
5.45h	6. 0h	9. 0

Sunday Trains.

AM 9. 0	8.55	11.55
9.55	—	2.55
PM 1.14	1.10	6.55

Trains from Selsey.

Leave SELSEY.	Arrive at LON. B.	VICT.
AM 8.15	10.55	12. 0
9.45	—	1.10
PM 1.25	4.27	4.54
3. 5	7.48	6.50
5.30	—	8.33
7. 5	10. 8	10. 1

Sunday Trains.

PM 1.20	—	7. 0
5.30	8.50	7.56
7.15	11.34	10.53

d Saturdays only.
e Saturdays excepted.
h Wednesdays and Saturdays only.

SELSEY—continued.

Marine Hotel. Only Hotel on Sea Front. With grounds of two acres. Tennis and Croquet lawn. Garages. Near Golf Links. Telephone 15. Tariff, write—
MANAGERESS.

Selsey Hotel, near Station, Sea, Links. In own Grounds. Tennis Courts, Garage. Good English Catering. Moderate inclusive terms. Telephone No. 17.
Proprietor, G. ROWLAND.

SEMLEY (Wilts), from
Waterloo, 101¼ miles. Fares, 21/3a, 12/9c. R. T. for two months, 42/6a, 25/6c. Pop. 628.
Map Square 22.

W'LOO	SEMLEY	SEMLEY	W'LOO
AM 7.30	10.10	AM 8. 2	10.56
10. 0r	12.31	9.29	12.22
12. 0r	2.25	10.55r	1.56
PM 1. 0r	3.41	PM12.26r	3. 8
3. 0r	5.30	3.32r	6. 0
5. 0r	7.41	4.32	7.40
6. 0r	8.43	5.24r	8.30
—	—	7.34	10.50
—	—	10.24h	3.58

Sunday Trains.

AM 9. 0	1. 5	PM 6.21r	8.57
12. 0nr	3. 6	—	—
PM 6. 0	9.25	—	—

h Via Eastleigh.
n Noon.
r Restaurant Car.

SENGHENYDD (Glamorgan),
157 miles. Fares (via Cardiff) 34/2a, 20/6c. R. T. for two months, 68/4a, 41 0c. Departures *from* London as for Caerphilly or Cardiff. Departures *for* London about 4 times daily.
Map Square 21.

SESSAY (Yorks), 205¼ miles.
Fares, 42/11a, 25/9c. R.T., double fare. Departures *from* London as for York. Departures *for* London about 3 times daily. Pop. 268.
Map Square 8.

SETTLE (Yorks) from
St. Pancras 236¼ miles. Fares, 46/0a, 27/7c. R.T. for two months, 92/0a, 55/2c. Pop. 2,583.
Map Square 7.

ST. PAN.	SETTLE	SETTLE	ST. PAN.
AM 4.25	11.52	AM 7.11r	2.10
9.50r	3.13	8.37r	4.10
PM12.15r	5.32	10.51r	5.30
3.30dr	9.54	PM 1.20r	7.15
11.50e	8.20	2.30dr	7.55
—	—	6.52	4.20
—	—	10.42e	7.25

Sunday Trains.

PM11.45	8.20	—	—
—	—	—	—

d Saturdays only.
e Saturdays excepted.
r Restaurant Car.

SETTRINGTON (Yorks),
212¾ miles. Fares, 44/4a, 26/7c. R. T., double fare. Departures *from* London as for Malton. Departures *for* London about 3 times daily. Pop. 495.
Map Square 8.

SEVEN KINGS (Essex)
from *Liverpool Street,* 8¼ miles, or *Fenchurch Street,* 9 miles. Fares from Liverpool Street, 1/3a, 1/0b, 0/9c. R. T. for two days, 2/6a, 2/11b, 1/4c. Pop. 10,007. *See* pp. 528–534.

SEVENOAKS (TUBS HILL)
(Kent) from *Charing Cross, Cannon Street,* and *London Bridge,* 22¾ miles. Fares, 4/10a, 3/11b, 2/11c. R. T. for two months, 9/8a, 7/10b. Pop. 9,058.
Map Square 24.

Leave CHAR. +	CAN. ST.	LON. B.	Arr. at S'OAKS
AM	3.40h	3.43h	4.19
—	5.20	5.25	6.32
—	6.45	6.50	7.50
—	7.56	8. 0	8.59
9.38	—	9.45	10.40
11.15	—	11.23	12.20
—	11.56	12. 0	12.33
PM12. 3	—	12.10	1. 2
12.40d	—	12.47d	1.19
1. 5d	—	1.11d	1.45
—	1.12d	1.15d	2. 1
2. 8	—	2.16	2.50
2.17d	—	2.23d	3.14
2.40d	—	2.46d	3.20
3. 0e	—	3. 8e	3.40
3.50	—	3.57	4.51
—	4.36e	4.39e	5.12
4.55d	—	5. 1d	5.58
—	5. 4e	5. 7e	5.57
5.24d	—	5.34d	6. 5
5.26e	—	5.35e	6. 4
5.35d	—	5.41d	6.34
—	5.44e	5.47e	6.24
6. 3e	—	6. 9e	6.41
6.10e	—	6.17e	7. 8
6.34e	—	6.41e	7.17
7.18	—	7.26	8.15
8. 0	—	8. 8	8.54
9. 0	—	9. 6	9.57
10. 0	—	10. 6	10.52
10.45	—	10.51	11.40
11.45	—	—	12.23

Sunday Trains.

AM 7. 5	—	7.11	8.13
8. 5	—	8.12	9. 4
9.50	—	9.56	10.31
11.15	—	11.23	12.22
PM 3. 5	—	3.13	4.13
6. 0	—	6. 6	7. 8
6.55	—	6.43	7.15
7.10	—	7.20	8. 3
9.25	—	9.51	10.21
10.35	—	10.43	11.31

SEVENOAKS—*continued.*

Trains from Sevenoaks.

Leave S'OAKS	Arrive at		
	LON. B.	CAN. ST.	CHAR. +
AM 7.19	8.10	—	8.19
7.52	8.40	8.44	—
8.18	8.49	8.53	—
8.29	9.18	—	9.27
9. 2	9.32	9.36	—
9.34	10. 4	10. 8	—
9.53	10.28	10.52	—
10.52	11.32	—	11.44
PM 12.29	1.27	—	1.38
1. 0	1.36	—	1.50
2. 9	3. 7	—	3.19
4. 2	4.40	—	4.53
5.13	5.50	—	6. 3
5.24*d*	6.30	—	6.39
5.34*e*	6.44	—	6.54
6.48	7.25	7.30	—
7.35	8.26	—	8.35
7.59	8.54	*g*. 1	—
9.47	10.22	—	10.35
10.41	11.34	—	11.44
—	—	—	—
—	—	—	—
—	—	—	—
—	—	—	—
—	—	—	—

Sunday Trains.

AM 9. 6	10. 5		10.15
9.23	10.22	—	10.32
10.51	11.23	—	11.34
11. 2	11.49	—	12. 0
PM 1.57	2.50	—	3. 0
5.30	6.27	—	6.41
7.28	8.12	—	8.22
8.30	9. 4	—	9.14
8.45	9.38	—	—
10.20	11. 4	—	11.15
—	—	—	—.
—	—	—	—
—	—	—	—

d Saturdays only.
e Saturdays excepted.
h Third Class only.

Royal Crown Hotel. First Class; 500 feet above sea-level. Gravel Soil. Suites of apartments. Large dining-room overlooking delightful old-world garden with charming surroundings. Garage. Cars. Electric Light. Telephone 30.
G. MARSHALL, Proprietor.

Royal Oak Hotel. First-class. Opposite Knole Park. Beautiful scenery. Recommended. Suites of Apartments. Dining and Drawing Rooms overlooking Garden. Quiet and select. Central for Touring Kent. Golf Links. Hunting, etc. Stables, Garage. 161 'Phone.
Proprietor (late Chef Royal Artillery and Staff College),
F. ROBINSON.

Amherst Hotel, Riverhead. 10 minutes' walk Tubs Hill Station. Fully licensed. Excellent Cuisine. Home Comforts. Moderate Tariff. Garage. 'Phone, Riverhead 17. Under personal supervision of Proprietors—Mr. & Mrs. F. T. WHITTAKER PRICE.

SEVENOAKS—*continued.*

Bligh's Hotel. — First-class Residential XIIIth Century House, situated in its own grounds. 500 feet above sea level. Fully licensed. Moderate Tariff. Station, five minutes. Phone 331.
Proprietor, G. E. SMITH.

Lime Tree Hotel. Unlicensed. Every Comfort. Three acres Gardens in private estate. Café. Moderate Inclusive Terms. Parties Catered for. 'Phone 195.
Proprietor, E. WINDSOR.

House and Estate Agents. For available Residences and Estates apply Messrs. Cronk, High Street, Sevenoaks. Tele. : Sevenoaks 4.

SEVEN SISTERS

(Glamorgan), 200½ miles. No through fares. Departures *from* London as for Neath or Brecon. Departures *for* London about 3 times daily.
Map Square 21.

SEVEN SISTERS (Tottenham) from *Liverpool Street.* 5½ miles. Fares, 0/7½*a*, 0/6*b*, 0/4½*c*. R. T. for two days, 1/3*a*, 1/0*b*, 0/9*c*.
See pp. 534–536.
Map Square 21, No. 52.

SEVERN BRIDGE

(Gloucester), 135¾ miles. Fares, 28/4*a*, 17/0*c*. R. T. for two months, 56/8*a*, 34/0*c*. Departures *from* London as for Lydney. Departures *for* London about 5 times daily.
Map Square 22.

SEVERN TUNNEL

(Monmouth) from *Paddington*, 131¼ miles. Fares, *via* Gloucester or Severn Tunnel, 29/5*a*, 17/8*c*. R. T. for two months, 58/10*a*, 33/4*c*. *Via* Newport, 30/8*a*, 18/5*c*. R. T. for two months, 61/4*a*, 36/10*c*.
Map Square 22.

	PAD.	S. TUN.	S. TUN.	PAD.
AM 1. 0*g*	6.48	AM 6.34*r*	10.15	
	5.30	10. 0	6.50*kr*	10.57
	8.45	12. 5	7.39	11.30
	9. 0	1.26	8.41	12.20
	11.15*r*	2.19	10.48*r*	2. 0
	11.50*kr*	3.19	11.55*r*	2.30
PM 1. 0*r*	4.23	PM 12. 8*kr*	4.20	
	1.10*kr*	4.37	12.42	5. 0
	3.15*t*	7.11	1.34	6. 2
	3.35*kr*	7.18	3. 8*kr*	6.15
	5. 0*r*	9.40	5.14*r*	8.45
	6.30*r*	9.41	6.17*kr*	9.25
	—	—	6.35	10.25
	—	—	9.42	2.45
	—	—	10.22	3.30
	—	—	—	—
	—	—	—	—
	—	—	—	—

Sunday Trains.

AM 1. 0*k*	9.22	AM 9.27	3.35
9.10	1.17	10.15*k*	3.35
PM 12.30*k*	5.58	PM 5.40*r*	8.25
2. 0	9.38	9. 0	3.15
4.30	9.46	9.50*k*	3.30

g Mondays excepted.
k Via Newport.
r Restaurant Car.
t Tea Car.

SEXHOW (Yorks), 232¾ miles. No through fares. Departures *from* London as for Stockton-on-Tees. Departures *for* London about 5 times daily. Pop. 36.
Map Square 8.

SHACKERSTONE

(Leicester) from *Euston*, 107¾ miles. Fares, 22/3*a*, 13/4*c*. R. T., double fare. Pop. 229.
Map Square 18.

EUSTON	SHACKTN.	SHACKTN.	EUSTON
AM 5. 0	7.53	AM 7.54*r*	11. 0
10. 0	1.37	10.10	12.50
12. 0*nr*	3.48	PM 12.12*hr*	3.45
PM 4.45*t*	7.23	12.12*r*	4.15
5.20*r*	7.49	1.58	5.35
—	—	4.26*r*	8.10
—	—	7. 5*r*	10.45
—	—	—	—
—	—	—	—
—	—	—	—

No Sunday Trains.

h Mondays and Saturdays only.
n Noon
r Restaurant Car.
t Tea Car.

SHADWELL from *Fenchurch Street*, 1 mile. Fares, 0/2½*a*, 0/2*b*, 0/1½*c*. R. T. for two days, 0/5*a*, 0/4*b*, 0/2½*c*. Pop. 7,878. *See pp.* 524, 525.
Map Square 61.

ANOTHER ROUTE from *Hammersmith, Paddington (Bishop's Road), Baker Street, King's Cross,* and *Liverpool Street (Met.),* 10 miles. Fares from Hammersmith, 1/0*a*, 0/8*c*. R. T., 2/0*a*, 1/4*c*. From Paddington, 0/9*a*, 0/6*c*. R.T.,1/6*a*,1/0*c*. From Baker Street, 0/9*a*, 0/6*c*. R. T., 1/6*a*, 1/0*c*. From King's Cross, 0/8*a*, 0/5*c*. R.T., 1/4*a*, 0/10*c*. From Liverpool Street, 0/5*a*, 0/3*c*. R. T., 0/10*a*, 0/6*c*. *See back of* Map.

SHALFORD (Surrey) from *Charing Cross, Cannon Street,* and London Bridge, 41¾ miles. Fares, 6/3*a*, 5/0*b*, 3/9*c*. R. T. for two months, 12/6*a*, 8/9*b*. Pop. 3,077.
Map Square 23.

Leave			Arr. at
CHAR. +	CAN. ST.	LON. B.	SHALFD.
AM —	4.44	5. 0	6.45
—	—	7.50*l*	9.33
—	—	9.33*l*	11.12
10.55	—	11. 3	12.55
PM 12.55	—	1. 4	2.48
3.15	2. 3*s*	2.10	3.49
4.22*d*	—	3.21	5. 4
—	4.44*e*	4.28*d*	6. 6
—	5.24*e*	4.48*e*	6. 2
5.42*l*	—	5.48*d*	7.21
—	6. 0*e*	6. 3*e*	7.54
—	6.36*e*	6.39*e*	8.17
6 34*d*	—	6.40*d*	8.17
7.24*d*	—	7.30*d*	9.14
8.28	—	8.53	10.19
12. 0*h*	—	—	1.19
—	—	—	—
—	—	—	—

Sunday Trains.

AM 6.25	—	6.52	8.21
10.20	—	10.28	12. 5
PM 5.25	—	5.32	7.16
8.38	—	8.45	10.26
—	—	—	—
—	—	—	—

SHALFORD—*continued.*

Trains from Shalford.

| Leave SHALFD | Arrive at | | |
	LON. B.	CAN. ST.	CHAR. +
AM 7.27	8.56	—	—
8.23	9.49	9.53	—
8.56	10.10	—	10.20
9.12*h*	10.31	—	10.43
9.25	11. 0	—	—
11. 4	12 50	—	1. 0
PM12.58	2.38	—	2.46
3.11	5. 2	—	5.14
4.22	5.56	—	—
5.37	7.20	—	7.29
7.29	9. 2	—	9.15
8.30	10. 3	—	10.13
10.24	11.57	—	12.10
.—	.—	—	—
—	—	—	—
—	—	—	—

Sunday Trains.

AM 6.39	8.16	—	8.27
9.43	11.15	—	11.25
PM 5.33	7.13	—	7.25
8.35	10.11	—	10.24
—	—	—	.—
—	—	—	—
—	—	—	—
—	—	—	—
—	—	—	—

d Saturdays only.
e Saturdays excepted.
h Wednesdays only.
l Low Level Platform.

SHANDON (Dumbarton)

464½ miles. Fares 85/2*a*, 51/1*c*.
R.T. for two months,170/4*a*, 102/2*c*.
Departures *from* London as for
Arrochar and Tarbet. Departures
for London about 3 times daily.

SHANKEND (Roxburgh).

337½ miles. No through fares.
Departures *from* London as for
Carlisle. Departures *for* London
about 3 times daily.

Map Square 44.

SHANKLIN (Isle of Wight)

from *Victoria* and *London Bridge*,
99 miles. Fares,19/4*a*, 11/10*c*. R. T.
for two months, 38/8*a*, 23/8*c*. Pop.
7,374.

Map Square 28.

Leave VICTORIA	LON. B.	Arr. at SHANKLIN
AM 6.18	6.35	11.30
8.55	—	12.45
10.15	10.22	2.30
11.35	—	3.30
PM 1.35	—	4.55
1.40	1.50	5.55
1.55	2. 5	7.32
—	4.50	8.26

Sunday Trains.

AM 9.55	—	1.45
PM 1.14	1.10	6.58
—	—	—
—	—	—

SHANKLIN—*continued.*

Trains from Shanklin.

Leave SHANKLIN	LON. B.	Arrive at VICTORIA
AM 6.35*f*	10.45	10.52
7.22	10.55	—
9.18	—	1.10
PM 12.18	4.27	4.34
1.18	—	5.12
3.18	7.48	6.50
5. 3	—	8.33
5.18	10. 8	10. 1

Sunday Trains.

PM 4.21	8.50	7.56
—	—	—
—	—	—

f Mondays only.
h Passengers cross Portsmouth at
own expense.

ANOTHER ROUTE from

Waterloo, 87 miles. Fares 19/4*a*,
11/10*c*. R. T. for two months,
38/8*a*, 23/8*c*.

W'LOO.	SHANK.		SHANK.	W'LOO.
AM 5.50	10.30	AM 6.35*f*	9.52	
8.34*r*	12.45	7.22	11.32	
9.50	1.30	8.18	11.41	
10.50	2.55	10.18*r*	1.52	
11.50*l*	3.55	11.18*d*	3.20	
PM12.50*r*	4.30	11.18*e*	4.16	
1.50*d*	5.30	PM 2.18	5.56	
2.54	6.55	3. 3	7.46	
3.50*s*	7.32	4.18*r*	7.56	
5.50	9.15	5.18	10.46	
—	—	8.52*hk*	3.58	

Sunday Trains.

AM 8. 0	11.53	PM 2.29*r*	6.16
9.15*r*	1.45	4.21	8.52
PM 1.50	6.58	5.49	10. 1
—	—	—	—
—	—	—	—
—	—	—	—

f Mondays only.
k Passengers cross Portsmouth at
own expense.
r Restaurant Car.
s Refreshments served.

Channel View Private
Hotel. Finest position directly
facing Sea. Billiard Room (full-
sized table). Lounge. Sixty Bedrooms. Large Garden. Full-sized
Tennis Court and good Putting
Green. Under personal management of Proprietress. Telephone
72 Shanklin.
See advt. p. 296.

Shanklin Towers. New
Wing now Open. Tennis Courts,
grass and hard. Putting Green.
Billiards. Dancing. Central
Heating. Garage. Two acres
Grounds. 'Phone 29.
Mr. and Mrs. A. GOULD.
See advt. p 296.

Royal Spa. The largest and
only Hotel facing or near the Sea.
Lovely Winter Garden Lounge.
Moderate. Illustrated Tariff.
See advt. p. 297.

Daish's Hotel. First Class.
Finest Situation. Charming
grounds. Tennis. Croquet. Bil-
liards. Coaches from Hotel.
Finest cuisine. Terms moderate.
Omnibus meets trains. Illustrated
tariff on application to Manager.
Telephone, 481.
See advt. p. 297.

SHANKLIN—*continued.*

Wyecombe House Board-
ing Establishment. On Cliff.
Produce from own farm.
Mrs. K. OWEN.
See advt. p 298.

Holliers Hotel. The acme of
comfort. Oldest and most up-to-
date. Personal control of
PROPRIETOR
See advt. p. 298.

Milanese. Good class Boarding House. South aspect. Close
to Lift, Sea, Pier. Large Rooms.
Separate Tables. Tariff according
to season.
See advt. p. 298.

Medehamstede — En
pension. Facing South. Excellent Cuisine. Separate Tables.
Mr. and Mrs. C. G. CRAWLEY.
See advt. p. 298.

Monteagle Private Hotel.
Situated in old village. Tennis.
See advt. p. 299.

Cedars. Best position near
Chine. Billiards. Tennis. Re-
commended. Liberal Catering.
Moderate Tariff. Proprietress—
Mrs. E. J. ELLWOOD

Corda. High-class Boarding
Establishment. Extensive
grounds. Free Tennis. Covered
Verandah. Separate tables.
Good Cooking. Telephone 88.
Miss HOARE.

"The Clifton," on the Cliff.
First Class Boarding House, over-
looking Shanklin and Sandown
Bay. Home comforts, excellent
cuisine, highly recommended.
Near Esplanade. Tennis Courts.
Mrs. CLARK.

Chine Inn. This fine old
hostelry has a unique position.
Old English style. Every con-
venience. Excellent Cuisine.
Terms moderate.
SAMUEL J. CLARK, Proprietor.

Turret House. High-class
Board Residence. Good Position.
Splendid Views. Near Sea, Town,
and station. Home Comforts.
Excellent Table. Electric Light.
Moderate Terms. Highly recom-
mended.
Miss KING.

Napier Boarding Estab-
lishment. Centre of Esplanade.
Every attention and comfort.
First-class cuisine. Moderate
charges. Separate Tables.
Proprietress, Mrs. LANE.

Osborne House. Board
Residence. Ideal position facing
Pier. Two minutes from Tennis
Courts and Bowling Green. Tariff.
Mr. and Mrs. F. EDWARDS.

Coniscliffe, Palmerston Road.
Boarding Establishment. Near
Keat's Green, Pier, and Chine.
Terms moderate.
Proprietress, Miss HATCH.

SHANKLIN.—THE CEDARS. EN PENSION. See advt. above.

SHANKLIN—*continued.*

Norfolk House, Esplanade.
First-class Board Residence. Best Position on Sea Front. Separate Tables. Personal Supervision. Tariff on application to Miss GERMAN, Proprietress.

Esher House. Board Residence. Select Position on Sea Front. Lounge, Drawing and Dining Rooms face Sea. Minute Hard Courts. Separate Tables.
PROPRIETORS.

The House Agents for Shanklin are Bull & Porter, Regent Street (Phone 38). Particulars of Furnished and Unfurnished Houses and Properties for Sale on application.

SHAP (Westmorland), 269¾ miles. Fares, 54/0*a*, 32/5*c*. R. T. for two months, 108/0*a*. Departures *from* London as for Tebay. Departures *for* London about 3 times daily. Pop. 1,005.
Map Square 7.

SHAPWICK (Somerset), 138¼ miles. Fares, 28/7*a*, 17/2*c*. R. T. for two months, 57/2*a*. Departures *from* London as for Glastonbury. Departures *for* London about 4 times daily. Pop. 321.
Map Square 22.

SHARLSTON (Yorks) from *King's Cross*, 177¼ miles. Fares, 36/6*a*, 21/11*c*. R. T., double fare. Departures *from* London as for Featherstone. Departures *for* London about 7 times daily. Pop. 2,619.
Map Square 13.

SHARNAL STREET (Kent) from *Charing Cross, Cannon Street,* and *London Bridge,* 33½ miles. Fares, 7/1*a*, 5/8*b*, 4/3*c*. R. T. for two months, 14/2*a*, 11/4*b*. Departures *from* London as for Cliffe. Departures *for* London about 8 times daily.
Map Square 24.

SHARNBROOK (Beds) from *St. Pancras*, 57 miles. Fares 11/6*a*, 6/11*c*. R. T., double fare. Pop. 755.
Map Square 18.

St.Pan.	Sharnbk.		Sharnbk.	St.Pan.
AM 4.25	7. 6	AM	8. 1	9.30
6.25	8.54		8.27	10.31
9.25	11.38		10. 8	11.25
PM 12.30	1.57		11. 0	1. 3
3.35	5. 7	PM	12.55	3.25
4.30*r*	6.15		3.54	5.20
5.35*r*	6.58		5.27	7. 3
6.30	7.56		6.41	8.22
—	—		8.31*r*	10. 5

Sunday Trains.

AM 8. 0	10.26	AM 11. 9	1.50
PM 6.15*r*	7.48	PM 6.17	8.30

r Restaurant Car.

SHARPNESS (Glo'ster), 140 miles. Fares, 29/4*a*, 17/7*c*. R. T. for two months, 58/8*a*, 35/2*c*. Departures *from* London as for Lydney. Departures *for* London about 6 times daily.
Map Square 22.

SHAW (Lancs), 191¼ miles. Fares, 39/4*a*, 23/7*c*. R. T. for two months, 78/8*a*. Departures *from* London as for Manchester. Departures *for* London about 6 times daily. Pop. 5,067.
Map Square 12.

SHAWCLOUGH (Lancs), 197¾ miles. Fares, 40/8*a*, 24/5*c*. R. T. for two months, 81/4*a*, 48/10*c*. Departures *from* London as for Rochdale. Departures *for* London about 6 times daily.
Map Square 12.

SHAWFORD (Hants) from *Waterloo*, 69 miles. Fares, 14/7*a*, 8/9*c*. R. T. for two months, 29/2*a*, 17/6*c*.
Map Square 23.

W'loo	Shawfd.		Shawfd.	W'loo
AM 5.50	8.19	AM	7.15	9.26
7. 0	9.58		8.17*r*	10. 6
7.30	10. 6		8.28	10.55
9.30	11.28		10.19	12. 0
11.30*r*	1.30		10.31*s*	12.22
PM 1.30*s*	3.25	PM	12.30*r*	2.20
3.40	6.12		12.57	3.36
4. 0	6.26		1.51	4. 6
5. 0	6.52		2.31	4.20
6. 0	8.16		3.54	6.16
6.34	8.56		4.27*s*	6.26
7.30	9.14		5.56*r*	8.20
8. 0	10.17		7. 7	9.52
—	—		8.29	10.50
—	—		9.34	11.28
—	—		11.28	3.58

Sunday Trains.

AM 8.45	11.53	AM 7.56	11.16
9.45	12.11	10.22	12.11
11. 0*r*	1. 7	PM 12.25*r*	2.27
12. 0*r*	2. 3	4. 0	6. 7
PM 2. 0*r*	5.52	6.14	8. 3
4. 0	8. 6	6.56	9.37
7. 0*r*	9. 2	8.33	10.52

n Noon.
r Restaurant Car.
s Refreshments served.

SHAWFORTH (Lancs), 198 miles. No through fares. Departures *from* London as for Rochdale. Departures *for* London about 6 times daily. Pop. 1,368.
Map Square 12.

SHEEPBRIDGE (Derby), from *St. Pancras*, 148 miles. Fares, 30/7*a*, 18/4*c*. R. T., double fare. Departures *from* London as for Chesterfield. Departures *for* London about 6 times daily.
Map Square 12.

SHEERNESS (Kent) from *Charing Cross, Cannon Street, London Bridge, Victoria,* and *Holborn Viaduct,* 51 miles. Fares, 8/8*a*, 7/0*b*, 5/3*c*. R. T. for two months, 17/6*a*, 14/0*b*. Pop. 18,696.
Map Square 24.

	Leave			Arr. at
	Vict.	Hol. V.	St. Pl.'s	Sh'rn's.
AM —	3.50*h*	—	6.23
5. 5	4.57	5. 0	7.56
5.48*f*	5.40*f*	5.42*f*	7.56
7.40*f*	7.30	7.33	10.25
9.20	—	—	11.18
11.40*d*	—	—	1.58
11.40*e*	—	—	2.34
PM 1.23*d*	—	—	3.28
2. 8*e*	—	—	4.16
3.20*e*	—	—	4.57
3.29*d*	—	—	5. 7
4.20	—	—	6.41
5.30	—	—	7.43
7. 5	7. 0	7. 3	9.48
7.50	—	—	10.28

Sunday Trains.

AM 7.20	—	—	9.53
8.15	8. 0	—	11.28
10.30	10.25	—	3.13
PM 3.30	—	—	6.23
7.50	—	—	9.58

Trains from Sheerness.

Leave		Arr. at	
Sheerns.	St. Pl.'s	Hol. V.	Vict.
AM 5.25	8. 8	8. 9	8.14
7.10	9.37	9.39	—
8. 4	—	—	11. 2
8.55	—	—	11.27
9.47	—	—	12. 7
10.30*d*	—	—	1.22
10.30*e*	12.59	1. 2	1.33
PM 12.15*d*	—	—	2.15
12.15	—	—	2.43
1.55*e*	4.46	—	4.39
2. 5*d*	—	—	4.55
3.35	—	—	5.56
6. 5	—	—	8.33
6.55	9.50	9.54	9.46
8.15	—	—	10.25

Sunday Trains.

AM 6.30	—	9.40	9.35
9. 0	—	11.58	11.50
PM 1.45	—	—	4.42
3.20	—	—	5.31
8. 8	—	—	10.29

d Saturdays only.
e Saturdays excepted.
f Mondays only.
h Third Class only.

Royal Fountain Hotel. Telephone 24. Conveniently situated for Docks and Railway Station. Close to Pierhead and Pleasure Steamers. First-class accommodation. Central Heating. Electric Light.
TRUST HOUSES, Ltd.

Royal Hotel. Situated in healthiest and best part. Faces Sea. Splendid view. Three minutes from Station. Terms moderate. Telephone 26.
MILES & SON.

SHEFFIELD (Yorks) from

St. Pancras 158½ miles. Fares,
32/9a, 19/8c. R. T., double fare.
Pop. 490,724.

Map Square 12.

St. Pan.	Shef'ld.	Shef'ld.	St. Pan.
AM 2.25g	6.52	AM 3.46	7.25
2.25f	8.24	4.10	8. 3
4.25	9. 7	7. 7r	10.45
9. 0r	12.29	8.56r	12.10
9.50hr	1.27	9. 2r	1.20
9.50r	1.50	9.30r	1.30
11. 0r	2.53	9.52r	1.45
11.45r	3. 6	10.53r	2.10
PM12.25r	4.37	PM12.20r	4.10
1.50r	5.16	1.30r	5.30
2.25r	6.46	1.48r	5.45
3.30r	7. 6	3.48r	7.15
5. 0r	8.30	4.40r	7.55
6.15r	9.33	5.30r	9. 5
6.25r	11.17	11.40	4.20
9.15	1.46	—	—
11.50	4.22	—	—

Sunday Trains.

AM10.50r	3.13	AM 4.10	8. 5
PM 3.15	6.53	PM 1.38	5.27
6.15r	10.45	5.18r	9.43
9.15	1.47	11.40	4.55

f Mondays only.
g Mondays excepted.
h Mondays, Fridays and
Saturdays only.
r Restaurant Car.

ANOTHER ROUTE (Victoria) from *King's Cross*, 161½ miles. Fares as above.

King's+	Shef'ld.	Shef'ld.	King's+
AM 4.45	8.43	AM 7.35r	11.30
7.15r	10.45	8.35	1. 5
8.45	1.39	11.25	3.50
10.10r	3.59	PM12.50	6.25
11.30	4.57	1.58	6.30
PM 1.50r	6. 6	4.29	9. 0
4. 0r	8.13	11. 5	3.25
5.45r	9.41	—	—

Sunday Trains.

12. 0nr	4. 8	AM 9.30	3.45
PM 5. 0	8.58	PM 1.46	5.55
		6.10r	10.20

g Mondays excepted.
n Noon.
r Restaurant Car.

SHEFFIELD—*continued.*

ANOTHER ROUTE (Victoria) from *Marylebone*,164½ miles. Fares as above.

M'bone	Shef'ld.	Shef'ld.	M'bone
AM 2.32	5.50	AM12. 7g	3.57
8.45r	12.32	5. 5	10.36
10. 0r	1.32	7.50r	11.10
PM12.15r	4. 2	9.35r	1.13
3.20r	6.26	11.21r	3. 0
5. 0r	8.19	11.40r	4.56
6.20r	9.33	PM 3.26r	6.38
7.30d	1.16	5. 2r	8.55
10. 0d	1.40	6.21r	9.55
10. 5e	1.55	—	—

Sunday Trains.

AM11.15r	2.56	AM12. 7	3.57
PM 5.30r	9. 8	PM 1.55r	5.40
		6.43r	10.24

d Saturdays only.
e Saturdays excepted.
g Mondays excepted.
r Restaurant Car.

Royal Victoria Station

Hotel. Under the London and
North Eastern Railway's management. Covered way to Victoria
Station. Suites. Night porter.
High-class cuisine. Inclusive
terms. Headquarters of Automobile Club. Telegrams: "Hotel,
Sheffield." Telephone, National
4505.

LOUIS BONNET, Manager.

Grand Hotel. Most Central

position in City, containing upwards of 300 rooms.
See advt. p 299.

King's Head Hotel. Most

modern; and most central position. Lift. Elegant Sitting
Rooms. 100 Bedrooms; wellarranged Stock-rooms. FirstClass Restaurant. Telegrams:
"Nearest, Sheffield." Telephone,
3314.

SHEFFIELD PARK (Sussex) from *London Bridge*, *Victoria*, and *Cannon Street*, 40½ miles.

Fares, 8/7a, 5/2c. R. T. for two
months, 17/2a, 10/4c.

Map Square 23.

	Leave		Arr. at
	Vict.	Can. St.	Lon. B.	Shef. P.
---	---	---	---	---
AM 7.25	—	8. 7	10. 3
10.35	—	10.35	12.38
12. 0	—	11.50	1.54
PM —	—	2. 5e	4.33
2.25	—	2.25d	4.33
4. 0	—	4.10	6. 3
5.48	—	5.21f	7.36
		5.41c	7.36
6.50h	—	7. 0h	8.49

Sunday Trains.

AM 8.18	—	8.30	10.29
PM 6.33	—	6.46	8.45

SHEFFIELD PARK—*continued.*

Trains from Sheffield P'rk

Leave		Arrive at	
Shef. Pk.	Lon. B.	Can. St	Vict.
AM 7.10	9. 1k	9. 4	9. 8
8.37	10. 7	—	10.46
11.27	12.13	—	11.35
PM 2.13	1.42	—	1.26
6. 8	4.32	—	4.35
8.22	8.46	—	8.27
	10.25	—	11.17

Sunday Trains.

AM 9.18	11.15	—	—
PM 7.33	9.26	—	9.34

d Saturdays only.
e Saturdays excepted.
h Wednesdays and Saturdays only.
k Departs from or arrives at
London Bridge S.E. & C. Station.

SHEFFORD (Beds), from

King's Cross, 38¾ miles. Fares,
8/1a, 4/10c. R. T., double fare.
Pop. 842.

Map Square 18.

King's+	Shefrd.	Shefrd.	King's+
AM 5. 5	7.45	AM 6.46	8.41
8.45	10. 9	9.17k	11.15
10.12h	12.30	9.17	11.25
PM 1. 8	2.59	11.38h	1.25
3. 0k	4.40	PM 2. 3	3.50
5.50	7.18	6.15	8. 5
7. 0d	9.24	8. 5d	10.20

No Sunday Trains.
d Saturdays only.
h Tuesdays and Saturdays only.
k Tuesdays only.

SHEFFORD, GREAT

(Berks) from *Paddington*, 61½ miles.
Fares, 12/1a, 7/8c. R. T. for two
months, 24/2a, 15/4c. Departures
from London as for Lambourn.
Departures *for* London about 5
times daily. Pop. 478.

SHELFORD (Cambs) from

Liverpool Street 52½ miles. Fares,
11/1a, 6/8c. R. T. for two months,
22/2a. Pop. 1,931.

Map Square 18.

L'p'l. St.	Shelf'd.	Shelf'd.	L'p'l.St.
AM 5.50	7.54	AM 6.49	8.57
7.18	9.38	7.27	9.27
10. 5	11.57	8.42	10.17
11.50dr	1.39	9.55	11.27
PM12.29d	2.12	PM12. 1	2. 7
12.48e	3. 5	1.19d	3.18
1.19d	3.18	2.17h	5. 9
2.48	4.55	2.32k	5. 9
4.15	5.45	4. 7r	6.10
5.49r	7.31	5.45	7.58
6.30	8. 7	8.45	10.30
8.22d	10. 6	—	—
8.22e	10.18	—	—

Sunday Trains.

AM 8.12	10. 9	AM 9.12	11.27
PM 1.50	4.18	PM 5.37	7.26
9.12	11.15	—	—

d Saturdays only.
e Saturdays excepted.
h Commencing July 23.
k Will cease to run after July 21.
r Restaurant Car.

ROYAL VICTORIA STATION HOTEL, SHEFFIELD.

SHENFIELD (Essex) from

Liverpool Street, 20¼ miles. Fares,
4/2a, 2/6c. R. T. for two months.
8/4a, 5/0c. Pop. 2,604.
Map Square 24.

L'PL. ST.	SHENFD.	SHENFD.	L'PL. ST.
AM 5.10	5.55	AM 7. 1	7.35
5.26	6.28	7. 6	8. 8
6.50	7.50	7.43	8.23
7.28	8.30	8. 3	8.45
7.48	8.35	8.21	8.52
8.46	9.28	8.50	9.30
9. 1	9.47	9.13	9.46
10. 3	10.41	9.36	10.12
10.30	11.21	10.34	11. 7
10.47	11.35	11.23	11.59
11.26d	12.19	PM12.30	1.16
11.56e	12.36	12.52e	1.25
11.56d	12.40	2.20	3. 5
PM12.42e	1.49	2.36	3.12
12.48d	1.20	2.49	3.59
1. 3d	1.47	4. 5e	4.51
1.33d	2.17	4. 8d	4.56
1.38e	2.36	4.42e	5.51
1.50d	2.21	5.32	6. 8
2. 0e	2.41	5.44	6.40
2.20e	3.12	6.12	6.52
2.23d	3.13	6.25	7.29
2.40d	3.22	7.34	8.22
2.58d	3.30	7.55	8.42
3.26	4.14	8.20	9.10
4.18	4.56	8.27	9.17
4.48e	5.18	9. 0	9.50
5.39	6.10	9.19	9.56
5.42	6.23	9.48	10.32
5.45e	6.29	9.57	10.52
6. 5e	6.37	10.49	11.30
6. 8	6.51	—	—
6.26e	7. 2	—	—
6.26d	7.10	—	—
6.29e	7.26	—	—
6.33d	7.35	—	—
7.16	7.50	—	—
8. 2	8.36	—	—
8.45	9.17	—	—
8.54	9.43	—	—
9.45	10.18	—	—
11. 0	11.44	—	—
12. 0	12.34	—	—

Sunday Trains.

L'PL. ST.	SHENFD.	SHENFD.	L'PL. ST.
AM 7. 4	8.17	AM 7.48	8.52
8.15	9. 2	9.17	10.25
8.30	9.19	9.57	10.50
8.45	9.34	10.23	11.15
9.30	10.22	11.42	12.40
10.30	11.19	PM 2.23	3.15
10.45	11.38	4.31	5.15
11.35	12.24	4.55	5.45
PM 2.30	3.29	6.57	7.44
3.40	4.17	7.14	7.58
3.45	4.37	7.48	8.25
6. 0	6.48	8.18	8.58
6.15	7. 5	8.50	9.32
6.42	7.31	9. 0	9.48
7.40	8.15	9.13	10.22
8.46	9.38	10. 2	10.45
10.10	11. 1	—	—

d Saturdays only.
e Saturdays excepted.

SHENSTONE (Stafford),

121 miles. Fares, 24/4a, 14/7c.
R. T. for two months, 48/8a.
Departures *from* London as for
Lichfield. Departures *for* London
about 6 times daily. Pop. 2,296.
Map Square 17.

SHENTON (Leicester), 103¼

miles. Fares, 21/5a, 12/10c. R. T.,
double fare. Departures *from*
London as for Shackerstone. Departures *for* London about 5 times
daily. Pop. 181.
Map Square 18.

SHEPHERDS (Cornwall)

from *Paddington*, 287¾ miles.
Fares, 58/2a, 34/11c. R. T. for
two months, 116/4a, 69/10c. Departures *from* London as for Newquay or Perranporth. Departures
for London about 4 times daily.
Map Square 25.

SHEPHERD'S BUSH

from *Aldgate*, 7¼ miles. Trains
run about every 6 minutes
throughout the day. See back of
Map.
Map Square 59.

ANOTHER ROUTE (Central

London Tube). See back of Map.

SHEPHERD'S WELL

(Kent) from *Victoria, Holborn
Viaduct*, and *St. Paul's*, 71¾ miles.
Fares, 15/9a, 12/0b, 9/0c. R. T. for
two months, 30/0a, 24/0b.
Map Square 24.

VICT. (S.E.&C.)	Leave HOL. V	S. PL.'s	ARR at S RD's W.
AM	—	3.50s	—	6.53
5. 5	4.57	5. 0	8.43
5.48f	5.40f	5.42f	8.42
—	7.30	7.33	10.52
10.40	—	—	12.58
11.40d	—	—	2.14
11.40e	—	—	2.45
PM 2. 5d	—	—	4.12
2. 8e	—	—	4.38
4.20	—	—	6.42
5.10d	5.10e	5.12e	7.31
5.30e	—	—	8.33
5.30d	—	—	8.16
—	6.12el	—	8.33
8.30	—	—	10.42

Sunday Trains.

VICT.	HOL. V	S. PL.'s	S RD's W.
AM 8.15	8. 0	—	10.54
PM 3.30	—	—	6.51
8.25	—	—	10.56

Trains from Shepherd's Well.

Leave S'RD's W.	Arrive at S. PL.'s	HOL. V	VICT. S.E.&C
AM 6.56h	—	—	9. 4h
6.56	9.37	9.39	—
7.35h	—	—	9.52h
7.35	—	—	11. 2
9.38	—	—	11.28
10. 0e	1. 0	1. 2	1.33
10.12d	—	—	1.22
12. 0	—	—	2.43
PM 2.13e	4.46	—	4.39
2.31d	—	—	4.55
3. 7	—	—	5.26
d5.19h	—	—	8.20h
6.16	—	—	8.33
7.27d	—	—	10.25
7.53e	—	—	10.25

SHEPHERD'S WELL—

continued.

Sunday Trains.

Leave S'RD's W.	Arrive at S. PL.'s	HOL. V.	VICT. S.E.&C.
AM 9.12	—	11.58	11.51
PM 2.17	—	—	5.31
8. 4	—	—	10.29

d Saturdays only.
e Saturdays excepted.
h Departs from or arrives at
Cannon Street.
l Departs from Cannon Street.
s Third Class only.

SHEPLEY (Yorks), 180¼

miles. Fares, 36/6a, 21/11c. R. T.
for two months, 73/0a. Departures
from London as for Penistone.
Departures *for* London about 7
times daily. Pop. 1,738.
Map Square 12.

SHEPPERTON (Middle-

sex) from *Waterloo*, 19 miles.
Fares, 6/2a, 3/8c. R. T. for eight
days, 6/2a, 3/8c. Pop. 2,858. *See*
p. 585.
Map Square 23.

Salters' Steamers (Shep-

perton Lock, 20 minutes from
Station). Up-stream, 10.55 a.m.,
4.20 p.m. Down-stream, 11.50 a.m.,
5.23 p.m.
*See advt. facing first page of train
service.*

Anchor Hotel. Principal

and largest. Close to river.
Beautiful quiet old-world spot.
Moderate Tariff. Garage. Bil-
liards. 'Phone, 160 Weybridge.

SHEPRETH (Cambs) from

King's Cross, 49¾ miles. Fares,
10/5, 6.3c. R. T., double fare.
Pop. 426.
Map Square 18.

KING'S +	SH'R'TH	SH'R'TH.	KING'S +
AM 7. 0	9.13	AM 7.51	9.34
8.45	10.24	9.34k	11.15
11.30	1.25	9.34h	11.25
PM 3. 0	4.26	11.16	1.25
5. 0	6.30	PM 1.52	3.50
7. 0	8.43	4.22	6. 0
—	—	8.12	10.20

Sunday Trains.

KING'S +	SH'R'TH	SH'R'TH	KING'S +
AM 8.30	10.33	AM 7.36	9.53
—	—	PM 5.45	8. 8

h Tuesdays excepted.
k Tuesdays only.

SHEPSHED (Leicester)

190¼ miles. Fares, 22/11a, 13/9c.
R. T. for two months, 45/10a.
Departures *from* London as for
Shackerstone. Departures *for*
London about 4 times daily. Pop.
5,530.
Map Square 18.

SHEPTON MALLET

(Somerset) from *Paddington*, 115¼ miles. Fares *via* Witham, 24/0*a*, 14/5*c*. R. T. for two months, 48/0*a*. *Via* Yatton, 30/8*a*, 18/5*c*. R. T. for two months, 61/4*a*. Pop. 4,294.
Map Square 22.

Pad.	Sh. Mal.	Sh. Mal.	Pad.
AM 1. 0*g*	9. 5	AM 9.35	12.55
7.30	11.35	PM12.28	3.50
10.30	1.16	1.19*t*	5.30
PM12.30*r*	3.46	4.16	8.20
3.30	7.20	7.23	2.45
5. 5	9.20	—	—
—	—	—	—

Sunday Trains.

PM 2.40	5.49	PM 2.57*r*	7.55
—	—	5.55*k*	3.15
—	—	—	—

g Mondays excepted.
k Via Yatton.
r Restaurant Car.
t Tea Car.

ANOTHER ROUTE

from *Waterloo*, 127¼ miles. Fares, 24/0*a*, 14/5*c*. R. T. for two months, 48/0*a*.

W'loo.	Sh. Mal.	Sh. Mal.	W'loo.
AM 7.30	11.26	AM 7.48*r*	11.10
9. 0*r*	12.36	9.34*r*	1.56
10. 0*r*	2.46	11.11*r*	3. 8
PM 1. 0*r*	5. 1	PM12.25*r*	4.30
3. 0*r*	6.57	2. 9*r*	6. 0
6. 0*r*	9.31	3.40	7.40
—	—	4.44*r*	8.30
—	—	6. 2	10.50
—	—	7.30*eh*	3.58

No Sunday Trains.

e Saturdays excepted.
h Via Eastleigh.
r Restaurant Car.

SHERBORNE (Dorset)

from *Waterloo*, 118¼ miles. Fares, 24/9*a*, 14/10*c*. R.T. for two months, 49/6*a*, 29/8*c*. Pop. 6,394.
Map Square 22.

W'loo	Sherbn.	Sherbn.	W'loo
AM 7.30	10.47	AM 7.20	10.56
9. 0*r*	12. 6	8.26*r*	11.10
10. 0*r*	1. 6	10.56*r*	1.56
12. 0*r*	2.45	PM12.20*r*	3. 8
PM 1. 0*r*	4.18	3.18*r*	6. 0
3. 0*r*	5.36	4.33	7.40
5. 0	8.20	5.44*r*	8.30
6. 0*r*	8.46	6.45	10.50
10. 0*h*	3.59	9.42*h*	3.58
—	—	—	—

Sunday Trains.

AM 9. 0	1.43	PM 6.17*r*	8.57
12. 0*nr*	3.10	—	—
PM 6. 0	10. 2	—	—
—	—	—	—

h Via Eastleigh.
n Noon.
r Restaurant Car.

Digby Hotel. Stands in its own beautiful grounds. Loose boxes. Blackmore Vale and Cattistock Hounds. Excellent Garage. Headquarters R.A.C. and A.A.C. Golf. 'Phone No. 23.
Apply MANAGER.

SHERBURN COLLIERY

(Durham), 251¼ miles. Fares, 52/6*a*, 31/6*c*. R. T. for two months, 105/0*a*, 63/0*c*. Departures *from* London as for Ferryhill. Departures *for* London about 4 times daily. Pop. 2,918.
Map Square 7.

SHERBURN HOUSE

(Durham), 253¾ miles. No through fares. Departures *from* London as for Durham or West Hartlepool. Departures *for* London about 6 times daily. Pop. 217.

SHERBURN IN ELMET

(Yorks), 182¼ miles. Fares, 36/11*a*, 22/2*c*. R. T., double fare. Departures *from* London as for Ferrybridge. Departures *for* London about 4 times daily. Pop. 1,734.
Map Square 13.

SHERINGHAM (Norfolk)

from *Liverpool Street*, 142½ miles. Fares, 26/0*a*, 15/7*c*. R. T. for two months, 52/0*a*, 31/2*c*. Pop. 4,775.
Map Square 14.

L'pl.St.	Sherhm.	Sherhm.	L'pl.St.
AM 5. 5	10.38	AM 7.22*r*	11.22
8.15*r*	12.39	8.34	1.20
9.50*r*	1.49	PM12.23*r*	3.50
PM12.25*r*	3.39	3.14*r*	8.33
12.33*r*	4.36	5. 5*r*	9.22
3.10*r*	6.59	8.22	2.50
5.18*r*	9.34	—	—
—	—	—	—

No Sunday Trains.

r Restaurant Car.

ANOTHER ROUTE

from *King's Cross*, 155¾ miles. Fares as above.

King's +	Sherhm.	Sherhm.	King's +
AM 4.45	9.59	AM 8. 3	1. 5
7.15*r*	1.11	9.41*r*	3.50
10.10*r*	4.35	PM12.22*r*	4.30
PM 1.50*r*	6.59	3.16	9. 0
3. 0	7.18	—	—
—	—	—	—

No Sunday Trains.

r Restaurant Car.

Sheringham Hotel. Largest in Sheringham, situated in own grounds, several acres in extent. Sea and Land Views. Nearest Links. 'Phone 3.
P. CALDON, Manager.
See advt. p. **299.**

Grand Hotel. Only Hotel on the Sea Front. Redecorated throughout. Telephone No. 2. Telegrams, "Grand, Sheringham." Mr. and Mrs. HOLLINGS, Managers.
See advt. p. **300.**

Southlands Private Hotel. Own Grounds Close Sea and Links. Separate Tables.
See advt. p. **300.**

West Cliff Guest House, West Cliff. Very near Sea and Golf Links. Tel. 60. Terms, apply— PROPRIETRESS. (Late Manageress West Cliff, Cromer.)
See advt. p. **300.**

The Dormy House Private Hotel. Overlooking Golf Links and Sea. Close to Club House, Recreation Ground and Station. Suites of Rooms. Lounge, Sitting Rooms, Dance and Music Room. Billiards. Tennis. Telephone 6.
Apply Mrs. L. PLUMPTON.

Ye Homesteade, Cliff Road. Private Hotel. Well appointed, all home comforts. Own grounds. 3 minutes sea. High sunny position, commanding glorious views.
Mrs. F. SAGER, Manageress.

SHERINGHAM—*contd.*

House Agency. Furnished Houses. Register and map sent free on application. Apply Railway Road, Sheringham. Telephone No. 40. Offices of WALKERS.

House Agents, Auctioneers. Best selection of Furnished Houses to let in Sheringham and District. Telephone No. 53.
SIMONS & Co.

Furnished Houses and all classes of Property—Sheringham, Cromer, Overstrand, Mundesley and County. Register free. Limmers, Sheringham (Telephone 4); Cromer (Telephone 26).

SHETTLESTON (Lanark)

432¾ miles. Fares, 82/6*a*, 49/6*c*. R. T. for two months, 165/0*a*, 99/0*c*. Departures *from* London as for Edinburgh (Waverley). Departures *for* London about 4 times daily.

SHIDE (Isle of Wight)

from *London Bridge*, *Victoria*, or *Waterloo*, *via* Ryde, 89 miles. Fares, 19/10*a*, 12/2*c*. R. T. for two months, 39/8*a*, 24/4*c*. Departures *from* London as for Newport (I. of W.). Departures *for* London about 3 times daily.
Map Square 28.

SHIELDHILL (Dumfries)

332¾ miles. Fares, 67/4*a*, 40/5*c*. R.T. for two months, 134/8*a*, 80/10*c*. Departures *from* London as for Lockerbie. Departures *for* London about 4 times daily.
Map Square 44.

SHIELD ROW (Durham)

266½ miles. Fares, 56/1*a*, 33/8*c*. R. T., double fare. Departures *from* London as for Durham. Departures *for* London about 5 times daily.
Map Square 3.

SHIELDS (North) (Northumberland)

275½ miles. Fares, 57/9*a*, 34/8*c*. R.T., double fare. Departures *from* London as for Newcastle-on-Tyne. Departures *for* London about 8 times daily.
Map Square 3.

SHIELDS (South) (Durham)

from *King's Cross*, 268¼ miles. Fares, 56/1*a*, 33/8*c*. R. T. for two months, 112/2*a*, 67/4*c*. Pop. 116,667.
Map Square 3.

King's +	Shields	Shields	King's +
AM 4.45	11.54	AM 6.30*r*	1.15
7.15*r*	3.39	6.53*r*	1.30
9.50*r*	4.14	8.30*g*	3.15
11.15*g*	5.48	9.30*r*	4.30
11.50*r*	6.39	11. 6*r*	6.15
PM 1.15*r*	7.34	PM12.10*r*	6.30
1.50*r*	8.59	1.50*r*	9.25
5.30*r*	11.44	3.30*r*	10. 0
5.35*r*	12.19	7.10	3.25
11.25*d*	7.42	9.55*e*	5.40
11.40*e*	5.46	10.15	6. 0
—	—	10.50	7. 5
—	—	—	—

Sunday Trains.

AM11.30*r*	6.35	AM 9. 8	5.15
PM11.40	5.46	PM 1. 2*r*	8.15
—	—	10. 0	5.40
—	—	—	—
—	—	—	—

d Saturdays only.
e Saturdays excepted.
g 1st and 3rd Class Pullman Cars only.
r Restaurant Car.

SHIFNAL (Salop) from

Paddington, 135¾ miles. Fares, 28/2a, 16/11c. R.T. for two months, 56/4a. Pop. 3,436.
Map Square 17.

PAD.	SHIFNAL	SHIFNAL	PAD.
AM 9.10r	12.38	AM 7.55r	11. 0
10.40r	2.34	9. 5	12.25
10.45r	3.40	10.40r	2. 5
PM 2.10t	6.15	PM 1.23r	5. 0
4.10t	7. 5	2.50t	5.55
6.10r	9.48	4.23r	8. 5
7.10r	10.22	5.56	10. 0
12.15k	6.55	10.25	3.30
12.15h	8.13	—	—

Sunday Trains

PM12.50r	4. 2	AM 8.52r	1.40
6. 0r	9. 3	PM12.55	6.20

d Saturdays only.
h Saturdays midnight only.
k Saturdays midnight excepted.
r Restaurant Car.
t Tea Car.

SHILDON (Durham), 241

miles. Fares, 50/3a, 30/2c. R.T., double fare. Departures from London as for Bishop Auckland. Departures for London about 5 times daily. Pop. 14,166.
Map Square 7.

SHILLINGSTONE

(Dorset) 123½ miles. Fares, 25/8a, 15/5c. R.T. for two months, 51/4a. Departures from London as for Blandford (*via* Templecombe). Departures for London about 5 times daily. Pop. 565.
Map Square 27.

SHILTON (Warwick) from

Euston, 91¼ miles. Fares, 19/0a, 11 5c. R.T. for two months, 38/0a. Departures from London as for Brinklow. Departures for London about 5 times daily. Pop. 371.
Map Square 18.

SHINCLIFFE (Durham),

249¼ miles. No through fares. Departures from London as for Ferryhill. Departures for London about 6 times daily. Pop. 1,015.
Map Square 7.

SHIPLAKE (Oxford) from

Paddington, 33½ miles. Fares, 7/1a, 4/3c. R.T. for two months, 14/2a. Pop. 1,236.
Map Square 23.

PAD.	S'LAKE	S'LAKE	PAD.
AM 6.30	7.41	AM 7.12	8.20
7.35	9.28	7.31	8.28
9. 0	9.58	7.54	8.56
9.20	10.46	8.54	9.43
9.55	11. 1	9.19	10.24
11.20	12.16	10. 4	11. 6
11.25	12.53	11.14	12.15
PM12. 8	1.22	11.34	1.11

SHIPLAKE—*continued.*

PAD.	S'LAKE	S'LAKE	PAD.
PM12.33d	2.11	PM12.16	1.46
1.20d	2.25	1.18	2.35
1.50d	2.56	2.27d	3.38
2. 7e	3.13	2.27e	4.10
2.18d	3.21	3.34	5.17
3.38	4.36	4.26	5.37
4. 7	5.16	5.49	6.55
5.15	6. 8	6.49	8.10
5.18d	6.25	7.34d	9.12
5.40e	6.52	8. 9	9.33
5.40d	6.41	8.41	10.22
6.12e	7. 5	9.29	10.42
6.35	7.37	9.50	12. 0
6.55e	8. 3	—	—
6.55d	8.14	—	—
7.35	8.53	—	—
8. 5	9.16	—	—
9.15	10. 8	—	—
12. 3	1.10	—	—

Sunday Trains.

AM 9.10	10. 6	AM 8.54	10.14
10. 0	11. 1	9.39	10.50
10. 5	11.18	10.52	1. 5
10.45	11.42	PM 2.29	4.53
11. 0	12. 8	4.51	6. 0
PM 1.45	2.59	6.24	7.37
2. 0	3.41	7. 9	8.20
2.35	4.20	8.24	9.32
5.15	6.28	8.39	9.53
6. 5	7.38	9.19	10.33
7.40	9.11	10. 4	11. 6
8.30	9.53	—	—

d Saturdays only.
e Saturdays excepted.

SHIPLEY (Yorks) from

St. Pancras, 206 miles. Fares, 39/9a, 23/10c. R.T., double fare. Pop. 28,289.
Map Square 12.

ST. PAN.	SHIPLEY	SHIPLEY	ST. PAN.
AM 2.25g	9.55	AM 1.44	7.25
4.25	10.46	7.35r	12.10
9. 0r	2.10	7.48r	1.30
9.50r	2.35	8.24r	1.45
PM12.15r	4.38	9.35r	2.10
1.50r	7. 3	10.30r	4.10
3.30r	8.20	PM12.28r	5.30
5. 0r	9.45	2. 7r	6.35
6.15r	11.33	3.17r	7.55
9.15d	2.21	4.37r	9.15
9.30e	2.38	9. 6	4.20
11.45e	4.20	—	—
11.45d	4.50	—	—

Sunday Trains.

AM10.50r	6. 8	AM 1.34	8. 5
PM 3.15	11.13	10.55	6.25
11.45	4.20	PM 3.28r	9.43
—	—	9.35	4.55

d Saturdays only.
e Saturdays excepted.
g Mondays excepted.
r Restaurant Car.

SHIPLEY AND WINDHILL (Yorks), from King's Cross,

196 miles. Fares, 39/9a, 23/10c. R.T., double fare. Departures from London as for Bradford. Departures for London about 6 times daily.

SHIPLEY GATE (Derby)

from St. Pancras, 128½ miles. Fares, 26/1a, 15/8c. R.T., double fare. Departures from London as for Stapleford. Departures for London about 5 times daily. Pop. 662.

SHIPPEA HILL (Cambs.)

from Liverpool Street, and St. Pancras, 77½ miles. Fares, 16/3a, 9/9c. R.T. for two months, 32/6a. Departures from London as for Ely. Departures for London about 5 times daily.
Map Square 19.

SHIPSTON-ON-STOUR (Worcester) from Paddington,

100½ miles. Fares, 21/0a, 12/7c. R.T. for two months, 42/0a. Pop. 1,542.
Map Square 17.

PAD.	SHIPSTON	SHIPSTON	PAD.
AM 5.30	10.45	AM11.50r	2.55
9.45	2.45	PM 3.15	7.20
PM 1.35r	5.45	6.15	10.45

No Sunday Trains.
r Restaurant Car.

SHIPTON (Oxford) from

Paddington, 81½ miles. Fares, 16/11a, 10/2c. R.T. for two months, 33/10a. Pop. 654.
Map Square 22.

PAD.	SHIPTON	SHIPTON	PAD.
AM 5.30	8.23	AM 7.52	9.50
9.45	12.20	PM12. 1	2.12
11 20h	2.29	12.31hr	2.55
PM 1.35r	4.26	4.46	7.20
4.45t	6.44	8.26	10.45
6.55	9.14	—	—

Sunday Trains.

AM10.35	12.42	PM12. 6	2.40
PM 4.10	6.31	7.33r	9.48

h Thursdays and Saturdays only.
r Restaurant Car.
t Tea Car.

SHIRDLEY HILL (Lancs),

215¾ miles. Fares, 44/7a, 26/9c. R.T. for two months, 89/2a, 53/6c. Departures from London as for Southport. Departures for London about 8 times daily. Pop. 2,231.
Map Square 12.

SHIREBROOK (Derby)

from St. Pancras, 145 miles. Fares, 29/0a, 17/5c. R.T., double fare. Departures from London as for Mansfield. Departures for London about 8 times daily. Pop. 11,116.
Map Square 13.

SHIREHAMPTON

(Gloucester), 124¼ miles. Fares, 25/10a, 15/6c. R.T. for two months, 51/8a. Departures *from* London as for Avonmouth Docks. Departures *for* London about 6 times daily. Pop. 5,310. *Map Square 22.*

SHIREOAKS (Notts).

148¼ miles. Fares, 30/10 *a*, 18/6c. R.T., double fare. Departures *from* London as for Worksop or Shefield (Victoria). Departures *for* London about 5 times daily. Pop. 919. *Map Square 13.*

SHIRLEY (Warwick), 111

miles. Fares, 22/9a, 13/8a. R.T. for two months, 45/6a. Departures *from* London as for Henley-in-Arden. Departures *for* London about 3 times daily. Pop. 2,319.

SHOEBURYNESS

(Essex) from *Fenchurch Street*, 39¼ miles. Fares, 5/10a, 3/6c. R.T. for two months, 11/8a, 7/0c. Pop. 6,414. *Map Square 24.*

FEN. ST.	S'NESS	S'NESS	FEN. ST.
AM 5. 5	6.53	AM 5.10	6.45
5.37	8. 9	6. 5	7.54
6.52	9. 7	6.46	8.15
7.42	9.18	7.18	8.44
7.53	9.44	7.56	9.17
9.18	11.14	8.14	9.39
10.13h	11.48	8.48	10. 1
10.17	12. 9	9.12	10.35
10.45	12.25	9.52	10.57h
11.57d	1.16	10.10	11.40
PM12. 9	1.32	11. 8e	12.22
12.43d	2. 1	11. 8d	12.58
1. 0e	2.12	11.15h	1.11
1. 0d	2.18	PM12.35	1.56
1. 5d	2.26	2. 0d	3.29
1.48d	3. 6	2. 5e	3.29
2. 5ek	3.40	3. 0	4.54h
2. 6	3.22	4.10	5.49
2.26d	3.48	4.20	6.33
2.30	4.19	5.15	6.45
3. 8d	4.29	6. 6	7.51
3.45d	5. 6	6.52	8.30
4. 7	5.18	8.18	10. 8
4.27	5.48	9. 0	10.30
5. 6e	6.19	9.15	11.23h
5.16	6.28	10.10	11.40
5.25e	6.50	—	—
5.32	7.27	—	—
5.46e	7. 7	—	—
6.17e	7.35	—	—
6.25ek	8. 7	—	—
6.26	7.46	—	—
6.53e	8.15	—	—
7.20	8.40	—	—
8. 0e	9.19	—	—
8.45	10.12	—	—
9.19eh	10.56	—	—
9.20d	10.56	—	—
10.15	11.34	—	—
11.27eh	12.51	—	—
11.27dh	1. 0	—	—
12.20	1.39	—	—

SHOEBURYNESS—cont.

Sunday Trains.

FEN. ST.	S'NESS	S'NESS	FEN. ST.
AM 9.15	10.43	AM 7.35	9. 6
9.45	11.43	8. 0	10.18
10.40	12. 6	10. 0	11 35
11. 8h	12.40	11.40	1.10
11.45	1. 6	PM 2. 2	3.47
PM 2. 7	4.14	4. 5	6. 0
2.45	4.40	5.12	7.16
4.30	6.38	5.28	7.45
6.10	7.55	7.22	8.59h
7.22	8.52	8.52	10.25
8.28	9.57	9.25	10.48
8.45	10.56	—	—
9.45	11.32	—	—
10.36h	12. 2	—	—

d Saturdays only.
e Saturdays excepted.
h Departs from or arrives at Mark Lane Station.
k Departs from or arrives at Broad Street Station.

ANOTHER ROUTE from

St. Pancras, 45¾ miles. Fares, 5/10a, 3/6c. R.T. for two months. 11/8a, 7/0c.

ST. PAN.	S'NESS	S'NESS	ST. PAN.
AM 9.30	11.46	AM 7.56	10.10
PM12.20d	3.30	11.15	1.48
12.20e	4. 0	PM 3. 0	5.23
2.50d	5. 6	5.15	7.45
2.50	5.18	—	—
6.40	8.41	—	—

Sunday Trains.

ST. PAN.	S'NESS	S'NESS	ST. PAN.
AM10.10	12.40	PM 5.28	9.18

d Saturdays only.
e Saturdays excepted.

SHOLING (Hants) from

Waterloo, 79½ miles. Fares, 16/10a, 10/1c. R.T. for two months, 23/8a, 20/2c. Departures *from* London as for Netley. Departures *for* London about 8 times daily. Pop. 4,746. *Map Square 28.*

SHOOTERS HILL from

Charing Cross, Cannon Street, and *London Bridge*, 10¼ miles. Fares, 1/10a, 1/5b, 1/1c. R.T. for two days, 3/8a, 2/10b, 2/2c. See pp. 555, 556.

SHOOT HILL (Salop)

160 miles. No through fares. Departures *from* London as for Shrewsbury. Departures *for* London about 3 times daily.

SHOREDITCH from

Broad Street, ¼ mile. Fares, 0/2½a, 0/2b, 1½c. R.T. for two days, 0/5a, 0/4b. Pop. 104,248. See p. 499. *Map Square 61.*

SHOREHAM (Kent) from

Victoria, Holborn Viaduct, and *Ludgate Hill,* 22¼ miles. Fares, 4/9a, 3/9b, 2/10c. R.T. for two months, 9/6a, 7/6b. Pop. 1,509. *Map Square 24.*

VICT. (S.E.&C.)	Leave HOL. V.	ST. PL.'s	Arr. at SHREH'M
AM —	6.40	6.42	7.46
—	7.30	7.33	8.40
8.32	8.20	8.23	9.39
11. 4	10.58	11. 0	12. 9
PM —	12.33d	12.36d	1.31
—	1.27d	1.30d	2.26
2. 9d	2.11d	2.14d	3.22
2.40d	—	—	3.37
2.50e	—	—	3.51
4.25e	—	—	5.10
5.15eh	—	e5.21k	6. 7
5.20dh	—	d5.26k	6.13
5.30e	—	5.53e	6.23
—	—	6.16e	7. 0
6.40	6.34	6.37	7.37
7.22	7.22	7.24	8.19
8.55	—	—	9.44
10. 0	9.54	9.56	10.55

Sunday Trains.

VICT.	HOL. V.	ST. PL.'s	SHREH'M
AM —	8. 0	—	9.16
10.30	10.25	—	11.36
PM 2. 5	2. 3	—	3.17
6.35	6.40	—	7.39
10.15	10.12	—	11.17

Trains from Shoreham.

Leave SHOREH'M	Arrive at ST. PL.'s	HOL. V.	VICT.
AM 7.46	8.40	8.42	8.50
8.41	9.37	9.39	—
9.15	9.52	9.55	—
10.54	—	—	11.37
PM12. 4	12.59	1. 2	12.49
1.40	—	—	2.40
3.30	—	—	4.33
6. 5	6.58	7. 0	—
6.46d	8. 0	8. 2	—
6.46e	8.18	8.20	8.10
7.43	—	—	8.51
9. 8d	—	—	9.54
10.43	11.43	11.45	—

Sunday Trains.

SHOREH'M	ST. PL.'s	HOL. V.	VICT.
AM10. 1	—	—	10.48
PM12.30	—	—	1.25
2.58	—	—	3. 5
5.15	—	6.20	6. 3
9. 8	—	10.22	10. 5

d Saturdays only.
e Saturdays excepted,
h Departs from or arrives at Charing Cross (S.E. & C.R.).
k Departs from or arrives at London Bridge (S.E. & C.R.).

IDRIS LEMONADE.

SHOREHAM-BY-SEA

(Sussex) from *London Bridge* and *Victoria*, 55 miles. Fares, 11/6*a*, 6/11*c*. R. T. for two months, 23/0*a*, 13/10*c*. Pop. 7,272.
Map Square 28.

Leave		Arr. at
VICT.	LON. B.	SHOREH'H.
AM —	5.18	7.57
6.37	6.40	8.48
7.23	7.25	10.11
8.25	8. 7	10.29
9. 0	—	10.57
—	9. 6	11.17
10. 5	9.50	11.42
11. 0*l*	—	12.20
11.40	10.35	1.12
—	11.40*d*	1.24
11.55	11.50	1.43
PM12.45	—	2.37
—	1.20*d*	3. 7
1.55	—	3.21
—	2. 5	4. 2
2. 0*d*	—	4. 8
2. 0*e*	—	4.37
—	2. 8*d*	5. 7
3.10*l*	—	4.37
3.40	—	5.31
—	4. 0	5.38
4.30	—	5.57
—	5. 5*d*	6.59
—	5. 8*e*	6.31
5.45*e*	5.55*e*	7.16
5.45*d*	—	7.27
—	6. 0	7.48
—	6. 8	8.42
6.40	—	8.17
7.15	7.20	9. 7
8.35	—	10.18
9. 3*d*	9.12*d*	11.17
9. 3*e*	9.12*e*	11.27
10. 0	—	11.43
—	—	—
—	—	—
—	—	—
—	—	—

Sunday Trains.

AM 6.55	7. 2	9.47
8.50	8.55	11.28
9.45*k*	—	11.28
10.30*v*	—	11.52
11. 0*p*	—	12.17
11. 5	—	12.47
PM12.15	—	2. 2
1.10	—	2.57
1.14	1.10	3.42
4.55*k*	—	6.28
5.50	6. 0	8.58
6.30*p*	—	8.27
8. 0	8. 0	10.28
9.25	9.10	11.26
—	—	—
—	—	—

Trains from Shoreham-by-Sea.

Leave	Arrive at	
SHOREHAM.	LON. B.	VICT.
AM 5.51	8.15	8.24
6.28	8.19	—
7. 9	8.38	—
7.36	—	9.15
7.52*f*	—	9.22
7.52	9.25	—
8.22	9.50	—
8.28*e*	9.54	10.24
8.42*d*	10.33	—
8.53*e*	10.33	—

SHOREHAM-BY-SEA—
continued.

Leave	Arrive at	
SHOREHAM.	LON. B.	VICT.
AM 9.21	—	10.55
9.38	11.10	—
9.53*v*	11.20	11.17
10.30	12.19	12.17
10.43	1.42	—
11.48	—	1.20
PM12.39*l*	—	2.20
12.52*e*	2.23	—
1. 9	3.40	3.45
2.35*v*	—	4.17
2.46*d*	4.58	4.45
2.46	—	4.50
3.21	5.54	5.55
4.29	6.36	6.34
5.20*l*	—	6.45
5.35	7.42	7.30
6.57	—	8.48
7.16	10.25	10.17
8. 6*d*	10. 0	9.45
8.19	10.58	—
9.25	—	11.17
10.39	12.59	1. 0

Sunday Trains.

AM 7.37	10.45	—
9. 5	11.15	10.50
10.45	—	1. 0
PM12. 4	—	1.35
2.41	5. 3	5.11
4.31*p*	—	6. 0
5.13	7.56	7. 0
5.43	—	7.28
6.29*v*	—	7.50
6.57	9.17	9.13
9.11	—	10.55
9.13	11.34	11.42
10.14	12.27	—

d Saturdays only.
e Saturdays excepted.
f Mondays only.
k Third Class Pullman Cars only.
l First and Third Class Pullman Cars only.
p First Class Pullman Cars only.
v Pullman Car attached.

SHORNCLIFFE   (Kent)

from *Charing Cross, Cannon Street,* and *London Bridge*, 70 miles. Fares, 14/7*a*, 11/8*b*, 8/9*c*. R. T. for two months, 29/3*a*, 23/4*b*.
Map Square 24.

Leave			Arr. at
CHAR.+	CAN. ST.	LON. B.	SHRNCL'F
AM —	3.40*h*	3.43*h*	6. 4
—	5.20	5.25	8.54
—	6.45	6.50	9.41
9.15	—	9.23	11.21
11. 0	—	11. 7	1.15
PM 1. 0	—	—	2.30
3. 0	—	3. 8	4.56
4.30	—	4.37	6. 9
5.24*d*	—	5.34*d*	7.58
6. 0*e*	—	6. 5*e*	7.47
7.18	—	7.26	9.58
9.30	—	9.36	11.12
11.51*k*	—	—	1.44

Sunday Trains.

AM 7.45	—	7.52	10. 3
10.10	—	10.18	12. 0
PM 7.35	—	7.45	9.57
9.25	—	9.31	11.57

SHORNCLIFFE—contd.

Trains from Shorncliffe.

Leave		Arrive at	
SHORNCL'F	LON.B.	CAN. ST.	CHAR. +
AM 7. 5	9.32	9.36	—
8. 3*e*	10. 0	10. 4	—
8.12*d*	10. 0	10. 4	—
9.39	11.43	—	11.57
11.20	1.36	—	1.50
PM 1.38	3.26	—	3.40
3.19	5.50	—	6. 3
5.29	7.25	7.30*e*	7.49
8.12	10.22	—	10.35
—	—	—	—
—	—	—	—
—	—	—	—

Sunday Trains.

AM 7.10	10. 5	—	10.15
PM 5.27	7. 9	—	7.17
6.27	8.50	—	8.40
8.37	10.16	—	10.26
9.53*h*	—	1.23	—

d Saturdays only.
e Saturdays excepted.
h Third Class only.
k Wednesdays only.

ANOTHER ROUTE from

Victoria, Holborn Viaduct, and *St. Paul's,* 72¼ miles. Fares as above.

VICT.	Leave		Arr. at
S.E. & C.	HOL. V.	ST. PL.'s	SHRNCL'F
AM —	6.40	6.42	9.41
9.45	—	—	11.46
11. 4*d*	10.58*d*	11. 0*d*	2. 8
11. 4	10.58	11. 0	2.30
PM 2.12*e*	1.24*d*	1.30*d*	4.56
2.50*e*	—	—	6. 9
7.22	—	—	9.58
—	—	7.22*d*	7.24*d*	11.12

Sunday Trains.

AM 9.35	8. 0	—	12. 0
PM 5.15	—	*r*	7.45
6.35	6.40	—	9.57
—	—	—	*r*

Trains from Shorncliffe.

Leave	Arrive at		
SHORNCL'F	ST. PL.'s	HOL. V.	VICT.
AM 7. 5	9.53	9.55	—
9.39	12.59	1. 2	12.49
11.20	—	—	2.40
PM12.53	—	—	3.37
3.19	—	—	5.42
5.29	—	—	8.51
8.12	11.43	11.45	—
—	—	—	—
—	—	—	—

Sunday Trains.

AM 7.10	—	—	10.48
10.43	—	—	1. 5
PM12.55	—	—	3.50
6.27	—	9. 9	—

d Saturdays only.
e Saturdays excepted.

For Advertisement list, see over.

SHORNCLIFFE—contd.

Royal Kent Hotel, Sandgate. Largest and best appointed. Special Terms to Officers and Families. Nearest Hotel to Camp. Garage adjoining. Telephone 47 Sandgate.
J. E. TANARE, Proprietor.

Royal Norfolk Hotel, Sandgate, between Folkestone and Camp. Ten minutes' walk from each. Electric light throughout. Lounge. Telephone 46.
Proprietor, G. P. KEELER.

SHORT HEATH (Stafford), 123¾ miles. Fares, 25/2*a*, 15/1*c*. R. T. for two months, 50/4*a*, 30/2*c*. Departures *from* London as for Walsall. Departures *for* London about 6 times daily. Pop. 4,474.

SHORTLANDS (Kent) from *Victoria, Holborn Viaduct, Ludgate Hill,* and *St. Paul's,* 10 miles. Fares, 2/1*a*, 1/8*b*, 1/3*c*. R.T. for two days, 4/2*a*, 3/4*b*. Pop. 1,832. See pp. 558-561. Map Square 80.

ANOTHER ROUTE from *Charing Cross, Cannon Street,* and *London Bridge,* 12 miles. Fares as above. See pp. 544-547.

Shortlands House. Private Hotel. Extensive Grounds. Tennis, Billiards, Charming Country. See advt. p. **23**.

SHOTLEY BRIDGE (Durham), 267 miles. Fares, 59/5*a*, 35/8*c*. R. T., double fare. Departures *from* London as for Bishop Auckland or Durham. Departures *for* London about 6 times daily.
Map Square 3.

SHOTTLE (Derby), 136¼ miles. Fares, 28/2*a*, 16/11*c*. R. T., double fare. Departures *from* London as for Wirksworth. Departures *for* London about 6 times daily. Pop. 410.

SHOTTON (Flint), 187 miles. Fares, 38/7*a*, 23/2*c*. R. T. for two months, 77/2*a*, 46/4*c*. Departures *from* London as for Chester. Departures *for* London about 4 times daily.

SHOTTON BRIDGE (Durham), 250½ miles. Fares, 52/4*a*, 31/5*c*. R. T. for two months, 104/8*a*, 62/10*c*. Departures *from* London as for West Hartlepool. Departures *for* London about 6 times daily.
Map Square 7.

SHOTTS (Lanark). 394 miles. Fares, 79/9*a*, 47/10*c*. R. T. for two months, 159/6*a*, 95/8*c*. Departures *from* London as for Wishaw (Central). Departures *for* London about 4 times daily. Pop. 20,582.
Map Square 40.

SHRAWARDINE (Salop), 162¾ miles. No through fares. Departures *from* London as for Shrewsbury, or Oswestry, and thence about 2 times daily. Departures *for* London about 3 times daily. Pop. 179.
Map Square 17.

SHREWSBURY (Salop), from *Paddington,* 153 miles. Fares 31/11*a*, 19/2*c*. R. T. for two months, 63/10*a*, 38/4*c*. Pop. 31,013.
Map Square 17.

PAD.	SHREWS.	SHREWS.	PAD.
AM 9.10*r*	12.15	AM 7. 3*r*	11. 0
10.40*r*	1.50	9. 0	12.25
10.45*r*	3.37	9.43*r*	1.25
PM12.50*r*	4.19	10.56*r*	2. 5
2.10*t*	5.18	11.25*r*	4.15
4.10*t*	7.18	PM 1.42*r*	5. 0
6.10*r*	9.22	2.43*t*	5.55
7.10*r*	10.55	4.35*r*	8. 5
12.15	5. 7	6.28	10. 0
—	—	9.50	3.30

Sunday Trains.

PM12.50*r*	4. 7	AM 8.10*r*	1.40
6. 0*r*	9.50	PM12.15	6.20
—	—	5. 5*r*	9. 0

r Restaurant Car.
t Tea Car.

ANOTHER ROUTE from *Euston,* 162¾ miles. Fares *via* Stafford, 31/11*a*, 19/2*c*. R. T. for two months, 63/10*a*, 38/4*c*. *Via* Crewe, 34/7*a*, 20/9*c*. R. T. for two months, 69/2*a*. 41/6*c*.

EUSTON.	SHREWS.	SHREWS.	EUSTON.
AM 2.35	8.53	AM 7.55*er*12. 5	
5. 0	9.48	7.55*dr*12.20	
6.45*h*	11.37	10.12*r*	2.20
6.45	12.52	11.35*r*	3.10
8.45*r*	1.45	PM12. 5*t*	5.35
10.40*r*	2.13	2.25*t*	6.15
12. 0*nr*	4.45	2.48*r*	8.10
PM 1.15*r*	4.57	4.50*dr*	9.15
2.20*t*	7.35	4.50*er*	9.20
4.45*r*	8.48	5.42*r*	10. 0
5.20*dr*11.19		10.50	5. 0
6.30*er*11.19			
9.20*e*	2.59		

Sunday Trains.

AM 9.15	3.25	PM 4. 5*r*	8.55
PM 9.15	3. 5	9.45*y*	5. 0

d Saturdays only.
e Saturdays excepted.
h Mondays and Fridays only.
n Noon.
r Restaurant Car.
t Tea Car.
y Via Crewe.

Raven Hotel. 15th Century reconstructed building, retaining its picturesque charm. Excellent cuisine. Garage. Telephone 476 and 477.
Lady HONYWOOD, Managing Director.
See advt. p. **301**.

Lion Hotel. Telephone 236. Famous House. Spacious Public and Assembly Rooms. Leading Hotel in the town. Electric Light and large Garage.
TRUST HOUSES, Ltd.

Crown Hotel. First-class Family. Opposite General Post Office. Three minutes from Railway Station. Telephone 192.

George Hotel. First-class Family and Commercial Hotel. Under New Management since February, 1920. Fully Licensed. Centrally situated. Private Sitting Rooms. Fifty Bedrooms. Electric Light throughout. Garage. Official Hotel for A.A. and M.U. 'Phone 181.
H. PUGH, Manageress.

SHRIVENHAM (Berks) from *Paddington,* 71½ miles. Fares, 14/10*a*, 8/11*c*. R.T. for two months, 29/8*a*. Pop. 602.
Map Square 22.

PAD.	SHRIV.	SHRIV.	PAD.
AM 5.30	8.28	AM 6.57	9.30
7.30	10.22	7.54*r*	10.15
9. 0	11. 8	9.42	12. 0
10.45	1.20	PM12. 1	2.35
PM 1.35*r*	4. 3	2.17	5. 6
3.38	6.41	6.31	9.15
6.55	9. 2	7.32	10.45
—	—	—	—

Sunday Trains.

AM10.35	12.50	PM 3.16	6. 0
PM 2. 0	6.24	—	—
—	—	—	—
—	—	—	—
—	—	—	—

r Restaurant Car.

SHUSTOKE (Warwick), 119¾ miles. Fares, 21/10*a*, 13/1*c*. R. T., double fare. Departures *from* London as for Water Orton. Departures *for* London about 5 times daily. Pop. 432.
Map Square 17.

SIBLE AND CASTLE HEDINGHAM (Essex) from *Liverpool Street,* 59½ miles. Fares, 12/4*a*, 7/5*c*. R. T. for two months, 24/8*a*. Departures *from* London as for Halstead. Departures *for* London about 4 times daily. Pop. 1,762.
Map Square 19.

SIBLEYS (Essex) 38¼ miles. No through fares. Departures *from* London as for Thaxted. Departures *for* London about 4 times daily.
Map Square 19.

SIBSEY (Lincoln) from *King's Cross,* 112 miles. Fares, 23/2*a*, 13/11*c*. R. T., double fare. Pop. 1,004.
Map Square 13.

KING'S +	SIBSEY	SIBSEY	KING'S +
AM 4.45	8. 4	AM 7.20	10.40
8.45	12.24	11.30	3.50
11.30	3.39	PM 4.24	9. 0
PM 4. 0*r*	7. 4	6.38*r*	9.25
5.45*r*	8.41	—	—
—	—	—	—
—	—	—	—
—	—	—	—

Sunday Trains.

12. 0*nr*	3.25	AM11.36	3.45
—	—	—	—
—	—	—	—
—	—	—	—
—	—	—	—

n Noon.
r Restaurant Car.

SIDCUP (Kent) from
Charing Cross, 12½ miles. Fares, 2/4a, 1/11b, 1/5c. R. T. for two days, 4/8a, 3/10b, 2/10c. Fares from Cannon Street, 2/1a, 1/8b, 1/3c. R. T. for two days, 4/2a, 3/4b, 2/6c. Pop. 8,939. *See* pp. 552-554.
Map Square 23.

SIDDICK (Cumberland),
311½ miles. Fares, 64/2a, 38/6c. R. T. for two months, 128/4a, 77/0c. Departures *from* London as for Workington. Departures *for* London about 4 times daily.
Map Square 6.

SIDLESHAM (Sussex), 74½
miles. No through fares. Departures *from* London as for Selsey. Departures *for* London about 8 times daily. Pop. 884.
Map Square 28.

SIDLEY (Sussex) from
Charing Cross Cannon Street and *London Bridge*, 61¼ miles. Fares, 12/6a, 10/0b, 7/6c. R. T. for two months, 25/0a, 20/0b. Departures *from* London as for Crowhurst. Departures *for* London about 11 times daily.
Map Square 29.

SIDMOUTH (Devon) from
Waterloo, 168 miles. Fares, 35/0a, 21/0c. R. T. for two months, 70/0a, 42/0c. Pop. 5,669.
Map Square 26.

W'LOO	SIDM'TH	SIDM'TH	W'LOO
AM 9. 0r	1.10	AM10.10r	1.56
10. 0r	2. 2	10.55r	3. 8
12. 0nr	4. 0	PM12.32r	6. 0
PM 1. 0r	5.27	2.32	7.40
3. 0r	7.13	5.34	10.50
—	—	7.32h	3.58
—	—	—	—
—	—	—	—
—	—	—	—
—	—	—	—

No Sunday Trains.
h Via Eastleigh.
n Noon.
r Restaurant Car.

Knowle Hotel. First-class
hotel with amenities of a well-appointed country house. Beautiful gardens. Garage. Telephone 5.
See advt. p. **301.**

Victoria Hotel. South as-
pect. Splendid situation. Sea views. Excellent cuisine. Garage. English Manager and Waiters. French Chefs.
See advt. p. **302.**

Fortfield Hotel. First-class.
Overlooking Cricket-field and Sea, Handsome Suites. Telegrams, "Fortfield, Sidmouth." Telephone No. 39.
See advt. p. **302.**

Belmont Hotel. First Class.
Opened August, 1920. Splendid position, overlooking Sea. South aspect. Furnished by Maple & Co. Central Heating.
See advt. p. **303.**

SIDMOUTH—*continued.*

Bedford Hotel. Best
situated. Modern improvements. Magnificent lounge. Electric light.
See advt. p. **304.**

Royal York Hotel. Old
Established. Finest position in Sidmouth. Under New Management.
See advt. p. **304.**

Norton Garth, Private Hotel.
In best position, facing Sea. South Aspect. Excellent Cuisine. Sanitary Certificate. Electric Light. Miss HOGGETT, Proprietress.

Royal London Hotel. Family
and Principal Commercial Hotel, Close to Sea. Writing, Stock and Billiard Rooms. Telephone 27. Proprietor, H. GOODWIN.

Woodlands Private Hotel,
3 minutes from sea. Beautiful Gardens. Central Heating. Excellent Cuisine. Garage. Moderate terms. Telephone 120.
C. GILBERT, Proprietress.

Apartments. 1 Fortfield
Terrace. Elegantly furnished and re-decorated. Unrivalled position, overlooking Cricket Ground and facing Sea. Terms on application.
Mr. and Mrs. UPJOHN.

St. Helen's Hotel (private).
Highest class. Only hotel near 18-hole golf, 5 minutes; sea, 5; tennis, 5; south aspect, in own grounds, away from noisy traffic. Best quality food. Garage. From 3½ gns.; summer, 4, 4½; no extras.
Miss M. A. JONES.

House and Estate Agents.
PIDSLEY & SON have the best selection of Furnished and Unfurnished Houses for Sale or to Let. Map sent. Telegrams, Pidsley, Sidmouth. 'Phone No. 17.

House and Estate Agents.
—For Particulars of Houses Furnished and Unfurnished or for Sale, apply to POTBURY & SONS, Sidmouth.

SIDMOUTH JUNC.
(Devon) from *Waterloo*, 159½ miles. Fares, 33/4a, 20/0c. R. T. for two months, 66/8a, 40/0c.
Map Square 26.

W'LOO	SID. J.	SID. J.	W'LOO
AM 7.30	12.17	AM 6.55r	11.10
9. 0r	12.31	10.50r	1.56
10. 0r	1.30	11.34r	3. 8
12. 0nr	3.36	PM 1.30r	6. 0
PM 1. 0r	4.55	3.21	7.40
3. 0r	6.44	3.55r	8.30
6. 0r	10.17	6.10	10.50
—	—	8.16h	3.58

Sunday Trains.

AM 9. 0	3.17	PM 4. 0r	8.57
12. 0nr	5. 5	—	—

h Via Eastleigh.
n Noon.
r Restaurant Car.

SIGGLESTHORNE
(Yorks), 207½ miles. No through fares. Departures *from* London as for Hull (Paragon). Departures *for* London about 6 times daily. Pop. 216.
Map Square 8.

SILEBY (Leicester) from
St. Pancras, 106½ miles. Fares, 21/11a, 13/2c. R. T., double fare. Pop. 3,082.
Map Square 18.

ST. PAN.	SILEBY	SILEBY	ST. PAN.
AM 2.25	6.38	AM 6.49r	9.57
4.25	7.43	8.17r	11. 0
8.25r	11.12	9. 3r	11.35
10.25r	12.51	10.58r	1.30
PM12.25r	3. 6	11.53r	2.10
1.25r	4. 7	PM 1.25r	4.20
2.25r	4.43	3.15r	5.45
4.25r	6.53	5.27r	7.55
6.25r	8.46	6.41r	9.15
—	—	10.30	4.20
—	—	—	—
—	—	—	—
—	—	—	—
—	—	—	—

Sunday Trains.

PM 6.15r	8.59	AM 8.18	11.53
—	—	PM 6. 8r	9.52
—	—	9.48	4.55
—	—	—	—
—	—	—	—
—	—	—	—

r Restaurant Car.

SILECROFT (Cumber-
land), 276½ miles. Fares, 57/8a, 34/7c. R. T. for two months, 115/4a, 69/2c. Departures *from* London as for Millom. Departures *for* London about 4 times daily.
Map Square 6.

SILKSTONE (Yorks),
176½ miles. Fares, 35/8a, 21/5c. R. T., double fare. Departures *from* London as for Barnsley. Departures *for* London 4 times daily. Pop. 1,591.
Map Square 12.

SILLOTH (Cumberland),
321½ miles. Fares, 64/4a, 38/7c. R.T. for two months, 128/8a, 77/2c. Departures *from* London as for Carlisle. Departures *for* London about 3 times daily. Pop. 2,649.
Map Square 2.

SILVERDALE (Lancs),
239½ miles. Fares, 49/10a, 29/11c. R. T. for two months, 99/8a, 59/10c. Departures *from* London as for Carnforth. Departures *for* London about 6 times daily. Pop. 713.
Map Square 7.

SILVERDALE (Stafford),
150½ miles. Fares, 31/3a, 18/9c. R. T. for two months, 62/6a. Departures *from* London as for Newcastle-under-Lyme. Departures *for* London about 4 times daily. Pop. 7,795.
Map Square 12.

SILVER STREET (Ed-
monton) from *Liverpool Street*, 8 miles. Fares, 1/0½a, 0/10b, 0/7½c. R. T. for two days, 2/1a, 1/8b, 1/2c. *See* pp. 534-536.

SILVERTON (Devon), 166½ miles. Fares, *via* Taunton, 34/10*a*, 20/11*c*. R.T. for two months, 69/8*a*. *Via* Exeter, 36/11*a*, 22/2*c*. R.T. for two months, 73/10*a*, 44/4*c*. Departures *from* London as for Hele or Exeter (St. David's). Departures *for* London about 3 times daily. Pop. 1,141.

Map Square 26.

SILVERTOWN (Essex) from *Liverpool Street*, 8 miles, or *Fenchurch Street*, 8¼ miles. Fares, from Liverpool Street, 1/3*a*, 1/0*b*, 0/9*c*. R. T. for two days, 2/2½*a*, 1/7½*b*, 1/4*c*. Fenchurch Street, 1/0½*a*, 0/10*b*, 0/7½*c*. R. T. for two days, 2/0½*a*, 1/5½*b*, 1/2*c*. Pop. 32,030. *See* pp. 537–540.

SIMONSTONE (Lancs), 215½ miles. Fares, 44/5*a*, 26/8*c*. R. T. for two months, 88/10*a*, 53/4*c*. Departures *from* London as for Blackburn. Departures *for* London about 6 times daily.

Map Square 12.

SINCLAIRTOWN (Fife), 419½ miles Fares, 83/7*a*, 50/2*c*. R. T. for two months, 167/2*a*, 100/4*c*. Departures *from* London as for Kirkcaldy. Departures *for* London about 3 times daily.

SINDERBY (Yorks), 215¾ miles. Fares, 44/10*a*, 26/11*c*. R. T., double fare. Departures *from* London as for Ripon. Departures *for* London about 3 times daily. Pop. 92.

Map Square 7.

SINDLESHAM (Berks), 65½ miles. Fares, 7/6*a*, 6/0*b*, 4/6*c*. R.T. for two months, 15/0*a*, 11/4*b*. Departures *from* London as for Wellington College. Departures *for* London about 9 times daily.

SINGER (Dumbarton), 444½ miles. Fares 83/6*a*, 50/1*c*. R. T. for two months, 167/0*a*, 100/2*c*. Departures *from* London as for Dumbarton. Departures *for* London about 5 times daily.

SINGLETON (Lancs), 221½ miles. Fares, 46/1*a*, 27/8*c*. R. T. for two months, 92/2*a*, 55/4*c*. Departures *from* London as for Kirkham. Departures *for* London about 4 times daily. Pop. 355.

Map Square 12.

SINGLETON (Sussex) from *Victoria, Clapham Junction*, and *London Bridge*, *via* Midhurst, 66½ miles. Fares, 13/9*a*, 8/3*c*. R. T. for two months, 27/6*a*, 16/6*c*. *Via* Chichester, 75¾ miles. Fares, 14/7*a*, 8/9*c*. R. T. for two months, 29/2*a*, 17/6*c*. Pop. 518.

Map Square 28.

Vict.	Leave Clap. J.	Lon. B.	Arr. at Singlt'n
AM 6.18	6.25	6.35	9.10
8.55	7.56	7.35	11.31
10.15	10.22	10.30	1.11
PM 1.40	1.47*e*	1.50	4.36
1.55*h*	*e*2. 2*h*	2. 5*h*	6. 1
3.55	4. 2	4. 0	6.33
4.53*h*	5. 0*h*	4.50*h*	7.40
—	—	—	—
—	—	—	—
—	—	—	—

No Sunday Trains.

SINGLETON—*continued.*

Trains from Singleton.

Leave Singlet'n	Arrive at Lon. B.	Clap. J.	Vict.
AM 8.32	11.50	11.35	11.42
9.49	12. 8	—	12. 0
11. 0	3.32	3.22	3.32
PM12.32	3.40	3.37	3.45
1.10*h*	4.27	4.26	4.34
2.29	5.54	5. 4	5.12
4.35*h*	7.48	7.31	6.50
6.33*h*	—	—	8.33
7.40	10. 8	9.53	10. 1
—	—	—	—
—	—	—	—
—	—	—	—

No Sunday Trains.

e Saturdays excepted.

h *Via* Chichester.

SINNINGTON (Yorks), 223½ miles. Fares, 46/8*a*, 28/0*c*. R. T., double fare. Departures *from* London as for Ampleforth. Departures *for* London about 4 times daily. Pop. 321.

Map Square 8.

SIRHOWY (Monmouth), 164 miles. Fares, 34/0*a*, 20/5*c*. R.T. for two months, 68/0*a*, 40/10*c*. Departures *from* London as for Tredegar. Departures *for* London about 6 times daily. Pop. 5,939.

Map Square 21.

SITTINGBOURNE (Kent) from *Victoria, Holborn Viaduct*, and *St. Paul's*, 44¾ miles. Fares, 8/9*a*, 7/0*b*, 5/3*c*. R. T. for two months, 17/6*a*, 14/0*b*. Pop. 9,339.

Map Square 24.

Vict. (S.E.&C.)	Leave Hol. V.	St. Pl.'s	Arr. at Sitting.
AM —	3.50*h*		5.32
5. 5	4.57	5. 0	7.19
5.48*f*	5.40*f*	5.42*f*	7. 5
7.40*f*	—	—	9. 5
—	7.30	7.33	9.28
9.20	—	—	10.29
11.40*d*	—	—	1.16
11.40*e*	—	—	1.44
PM 1.23*d*	—	—	2.44
2. 8*e*	—	—	3.25
3.20*e*	—	—	4.22
3.29*d*	—	—	4.31
4.20	—	—	5.38
5.30*e*	—	—	6.57
5.30*d*	—	—	7. 0
6.16	6.10*e*	6.13*e*	8.25
7. 5	7. 0	7. 3	9. 0
7.50	—	—	9. 8
9.0*e*	8.57*e*	9. 0*e*	11.26
—	—	—	—
—	—	—	—
—	—	—	—

Sunday Trains.

AM 7.20	—	—	9. 7
8.15	8. 0	—	9.45
10.30	10.25	—	2.28
PM 3.30	—	—	5.31
6.35	—	—	8.30
7.50	—	—	9.11
—	—	—	—

SITTINGBOURNE—*continued.*

Trains from Sittingb'rne.

Leave Sitting.	Arrive at St. Pl.'s	Hol. V.	Vict.
AM 6. 6	8. 8	8. 9	8.14
6.55	9.16	9.18	—
7.52	9.37	9.39	—
9.12	—	—	11. 2
10. 5	—	—	11.27
11. 3	—	—	12. 7
11.12*e*	12.59	1. 2	1.33
11.25*d*	—	—	1.22
PM 1. 2*d*	—	—	2.15
1.13	—	—	2.43
3.14*e*	4.46	—	4.39
3.32*d*	—	—	4.55
3.38*l*	—	—	5.36
4.36	—	—	5.56
7.12	—	—	8.33
7.40	9.50	9.54	9.46
9. 3	—	—	10.25
9.27	11.21	11.23	—
—	—	—	—
—	—	—	—

Sunday Trains.

AM 7.20	—	9.40	9.31
10.28	—	11.58	11.51
10.48	—	1. 2	12.56
PM 3.25	—	—	4.42
4. 0	—	—	5.31
9.11	—	—	10.29
9.38	—	12. 0	11.44
—	—	—	—

d Saturdays only.
e Saturdays excepted.
f Mondays only.
h Third Class only.
l Fridays only.

ANOTHER ROUTE from *Charing Cross, Cannon Street*, and *London Bridge*, 43¾ miles. Fares as above.

Char. +	Leave Can. St.	Lon. B.	Arr. at Sitting.
AM —	—	3.57*h*	5.32
—	7.16	7.19	9. 5
—	10.58*k*	11. 1*k*	12.56
—	10.58*l*	11. 1*l*	1. 6
PM 2.45*e*	—	2.53*e*	5. 2
3. 5*d*	—	3.12*d*	5. 2
5.58*d*	—	6. 4*d*	7.45
6.22*e*	—	6.29*e*	8.25
6.55*d*	—	7. 1*d*	9. 0
—	7. 8*e*	7.11*e*	9. 0
—	9.35	9.38	11.26

Sunday Trains.

PM 7. 0	—	7. 7	8.50
—	—	—	—

Trains from Sittingb'rne.

Leave Sitting.	Lon. B.	Arrive at Can.St.	Char. +
AM 6.55	8.34	—	8.43
7.52	9. 0	9. 4	—
PM 5.19*e*	7.14	—	7.23
6.25*d*	8.15	8.20	—

Sunday Trains.

PM 9.20	11.15	—	11.24

d Saturdays only.
e Saturdays excepted.
h Third Class only.
k Wednesdays and Saturdays excepted.
l Wednesdays only.

Bull Family and Commercial Hotel. Up-to-date. Hot and Cold Luncheons daily. Garage. Stabling. Two hard Tennis Courts. Parties Catered for Tel. 46.
Proprietress, J. M. THORNE.

SIX-MILE BOTTOM (Cambridge) from *Liverpool Street*, 64¼ miles. Fares, 13/1*a*, 7/10*c*. R. T. for two months, 26/2*a*. Departures *from* London as for Fulbourne. Departures *for* London about 8 times daily.

Map Square 19.

SKARES (Ayr), 378¼ miles. No through fares. Departures *from* London as for Ayr. Departures *for* London about 4 times daily.

Map Square 43.

SKEGBY (Notts), from *King's Cross*, 142¾ miles. Fares, 28/2*a*, 16/11*c*. R. T., double fare. Departures *from* London as for Sutton-in-Ashfield. Departures *for* London about 6 times daily. Pop. 5,057.

Map Square 13.

SKEGNESS (Lincoln) from *King's Cross*, 131½ miles. Fares, 27/4*a*, 16/5*c*. R.T. for two months, 54/8*a*, 32/10*c*. Pop. 9,251.

Map Square 14.

King's +	Skegn's	Skegn's	King's +
AM 4.45	8.58	AM 6.35	10.40
7.15*r*	11.35	9.30	1. 5
8.45*l*	1.18	PM12.50*r*	4.30
8.45	1.50	3.20	9. 0
11.30*r*	4.40	5.40*r*	9.25
PM 4. 0*e*	7.47	8.20	3.25
4. 0	7.59	—	—
5.45*r*	9.27	—	—
10.45*e*	7.28	—	—

No Sunday Trains.

d Saturdays only.
e Saturdays excepted.
r Restaurant Car.

Seacroft Hotel. Facing Sea. Perfect Sanitation. Billiard Room. Electric Light. Choice Wines and Spirits. Five minutes from Golf Links. Garage. Telephone 52. Tel. address, "Nesscroft, Skegness." Special Week-end Terms.
Apply, Manageress.

SKELBO (Sutherland), 652 miles. No through fares. Departures *from* London as for Lairg. Departures *for* London about 3 times daily.

Map Square 34.

SKELLINGTHORPE (Lincoln), 133½ miles. Fares, 27/4*a*, 16/5*c*. R. T., double fare. Departures *from* London as for Lincoln. Departures *for* London about twice daily. Pop. 953.

Map Square 13.

SKELMANTHORPE (Yorks), 181¾ miles. Fares, 36/11*a*, 22/2*c*. R. T. for two months, 73/10*a*. Departures *from* London as for Penistone. Departures *for* London about 4 times daily. Pop. 3,900.

Map Square 12.

SKELMERSDALE (Lancs), 200 miles. No through fares. Departures *from* London as for St. Helens. Departures *for* London about 5 times daily. Pop. 6,687.

Map Square 12.

SKEWEN (Glamorgan), 192½ miles. Fares, 40/3*a*, 24/2*c*. R. T. for two months, 80/6*a*. Departures *from* London as for Neath. Departures *for* London about 6 times daily. Pop. 9,584.

SKINNINGROVE (Yorks), 257¾ miles. Fares, 53/9*a*, 32/3*c*. R. T. for two months, 107/6*a*, 64/6*c*. Departures *from* London as for Saltburn or Sandsend. Departures *for* London about 4 times daily. Pop. 2,620.

SKIPTON (Yorks) from *St. Pancras*, 221¼ miles. Fares, 42/6*a*, 25/6*c*. R. T., double fare. Pop. 12,013.

Map Square 7.

St. Pan.	Skipton	Skipton	St. Pan.
AM 4.25	10.55	AM 2.25	8. 3
9. 0*r*	2. 5	6.35*r*	12.10
9.50*r*	3. 5	8.58*r*	2.10
PM12.15*er*	5.45	9.53*r*	4.10
12.15*dr*	6.32	11.46*r*	5.30
3.30*r*	9. 6	PM 1.14*r*	6.35
5. 0*r*	10.10	2.42*r*	7.57
6.15*dr*	12.15	4. 0*r*	9.15
11.45*e*	5. 3	8.55	4.20
11.50*d*	7.45	—	—
—	—	—	—
—	—	—	—
—	—	—	—
—	—	—	—
—	—	—	—

Sunday Trains.

AM10.50*r*	6. 0	AM 2.25	8. 5
PM11.45	5. 3	10.40	6.25
—	—	PM12.25*r*	9.43
—	—	8.45	4.55
—	—	—	—
—	—	—	—
—	—	—	—

d Saturdays only.

e Saturdays excepted.

r Restaurant Car.

SKIRLAUGH (Yorks), 203¾ miles. Fares, 36/10*a*, 22/1*c*. R.T. for two months, 73/8*a*, 44/2*c*. Departures *from* London as for Hull (Paragon). Departures *for* London about 4 times daily. Pop. 281.

Map Square 13.

SLADE'S GREEN (Kent) from *Charing Cross, Cannon Street,* and *London Bridge,* 16 miles. Fares from Charing Cross, 3/2*a*, 2/7*b*, 1/11*c*. R. T. for eight days, 6/4*a*, 4/10*b*, 3/10*c*. Fares from Cannon Street, 2/9*a*, 2/3*b*, 1/8*c*. R. T. for eight days, 5/6*a*, 4/4*b*, 3/4*c*. Pop. 4,979. *See* pp. 547-551.

Map Square 24.

SLAGGYFORD (Northumberland), 312 miles. No through fares. Departures *from* London as for Hexham or Carlisle. Departures *for* London about 4 times daily.

Map Square 3.

SLAITHWAITE (Yorks), 198¾ miles. Fares, 37/9*a*, 22/8*c*. R. T., double fare. Departures *from* London as for Marsden. Departures *for* London about 6 times daily. Pop. 5,444.

SLAMANNAN (Stirling), 419¾ miles. No through fares. Departures *from* London as for Edinburgh (Waverley). Departures *for* London about 3 times daily. Pop. 3,409.

Map Square 40.

SLATEFORD (Midlothian), 397¼ miles. No through fares. Departures *from* London as for Carstairs. Departures *for* London about 6 times daily. Pop. 1,347.

Map Square 41.

SLEAFORD (Lincoln) from *King's Cross*, 112 miles. Fares, 23/2*a*, 13/11*c*. R. T., double fare. Pop. 6,680.

Map Square 13.

King's +	Sleaf'd	Sleaf'd	King's +
AM 4.45	8. 8	AM 8.17	11.30
5. 5*l*	9.40	8.20*l*	12.25
7.15*r*	11.23	9.50	1. 5
8.45	1.58	11.34	3.50
PM 1.15	4. 8	PM 1.48	4.45
3. 0*l*	6.30	2.16*f*	5. 0
4. 0*r*	7. 4	3.18*hr*	6.30
5.45*r*	9.51	4.22*l*	9. 0
—	—	6.46*r*	10. 0
—	—	10. 4	3.25
—	—	—	—
—	—	—	—
—	—	—	—
—	—	—	—
—	—	—	—

Sunday Trains.

—	—	PM 4. 6	10.20

f Mondays only.
h Wednesdays only.
l Via Essendine and Bourne.
r Restaurant Car.

ANOTHER ROUTE from *Liverpool Street*, 124¾ miles. Fares as above.

L'pl. St.	Sleaf'd	Sleaf'd	L'pl. St.
AM 5.50	11.20	AM 8.16	12.40
10. 5	1.58	10.48*lr*	4. 2*h*
11.50	4.44	10.48	5. 9
PM 2.34	7.42	PM12.43	5.17
4.45	9.51	1.49	6.10
—	—	5. 0	10.30
—	—	—	—
—	—	—	—

Sunday Trains.

AM 9.25	1. 1	PM 4. 6	7.40
—	—	—	—

h Arrives at St. Pancras Station.
l Commencing July 23.
r Restaurant Car.

SLEDMERE (Yorks), 213¼ miles. Fares, 40/10*a*, 24/6*c*. R. T. for two months, 81/8*a*, 49/0*c*. Departures *from* London as for Driffield. Departures *for* London about 3 times daily. Pop. 559.

Map Square 8.

SLEIGHTS (Yorks), 241¼ miles. Fares, 50/3*a*, 30/2*c*. R. T., double fare. Departures *from* London as for Whitby. Departures *for* London about 4 times daily.

Map Square 8.

SLINFOLD (Sussex) from *Victoria, Clapham Junction,* and *London Bridge,* 42¼ miles. Fares from London Bridge or Victoria, 8/1*a*, 4/10*c*. R.T. for two months, 16/2*a*. Departures *from* London as for Rudgwick. Departures *for* London about 8 times daily. Pop. 1,018.

Map Square 23.

SLINGSBY (Yorks), 216¼

miles. Fares, 44/5a, 26/8c. R. T., double fare. Departures *from* London as for Ampleforth. Departures *for* London about 4 times daily. Pop. 424.

Map Square 8.

SLOANE SQUARE to

and from *Mansion House, Charing Cross, Victoria, South Kensington, High Street, Praed Street, Baker Street, King's Cross, Moorgate,* and all intermediate stations every few minutes. Also to and from Ealing. Hounslow, Richmond and Wimbledon. *See* p. 489.

Map Square 69.

Royal Court Hotel, Sloane Square, S.W. 1. *See* advt. under London Hotels.

SLOUGH (Bucks) from

Paddington, 18¼ miles. Fares, 3/9a, 2/3c. R. T. for two months, 7/6a, 4/4½c. Pop. 16,392.

Map Squares 23 and 54.

	PAD.	SLOUGH		SLOUGH	PAD.
AM	5.45	6.38	AM	4.36	5.24
	6.30	7. 1		5.28	6.27
	6.35	7.33		6.31	7.25
	7.35	8.20		7. 0	7.55
	8. 5	8.49		7.55	8.20
	8.30	9. 2		8.19	8.49
	9.20	10. 0		8.44	9. 8
	9.32	10.23		8.55	9.25
	9.55	10.28		9.36	10. 6
	10.27h	11.20		9.55	10.55
	10.55	11.34		10.46	11.18
	11.25	11.54		11. 8	11.35
	11.35	12.25		11.19	11.55
PM	12. 8	12.40	PM	12.23	1.11
	12.33d	1. 9		12.41	1.32
	12.35e	1.30		1.17	1.46
	12.42d	1.30		2. 1	2.35
	1. 5d	1.34		2.15	3.10
	1.15	2. 9		2.49	3.40
	1.20d	1.52		3. 7d	3.58
	2. 7	2.35		3.45	4.10
	2.18d	2.45		4.23	5.17
	2.25	3.25		4.54	5.20
	2.33d	3.11		5.12	5.37
	3.18	3.49		5.54	6.25
	3.45	4.17		5.59	6.52
	4. 7	4.34		6.27	6.55
	4.30	4.58		6.38	7.29
	4.35	5.30		7.15	7.45
	5.18e	5.45		7.38	8.10
	5.18d	5.53		7.47	8.40
	5.35e	5.59		8.33d	9.12
	5.40d	6. 5		8.52	9.33
	6.12e	6.38		9. 3	9.52
	6.35	7. 1		9.34	10.22
	6.38d	7.26		10. 8	10.42
	7. 0	7.33		10.14	11. 4
	7. 5e	7.54		11. 3	12. 0
	7.37	8.13		—	—
	8. 5	8.30		—	—
	8.35	9. 5		—	—
	8.40	9.28		—	—
	9.30	10.19		—	—
	10. 5	10.37		—	—
	10.40	11.30		—	—
	11.30	12. 5		—	—
	11.33	12.21		—	—
	12. 3	12.35		—	—
	—	—		—	—
	—	—		—	—
	—	—		—	—
	—	—		—	—

SLOUGH—*continued.*

Sunday Trains.

	PAD.	SLOUGH		SLOUGH	PAD.
AM	6.30	7.20	AM	6.50	7.40
	8.20	9.13		8.18	9. 8
	9.45	10.15		9.38	10.14
	10. 5	10.38		9.47	10.42
	10.37	11.25		10.18	10 50
	11. 0	11.30	PM	12.15	1. 5
	11.45	12.12		2. 8	2.58
PM	12.55	1.45		2.51	3.42
	1.45	2.22		4. 2	4.53
	2. 0	2.54		5. 3	5.52
	2.35	3.10		5.28	6. 0
	3.35	4.25		5.45	6.23
	4.45	5.37		6.19	7.10
	5.15	5.48		7. 2	7.37
	6. 5	6.55		7.21	8.12
	7.40	8.33		8.10	8.45
	8.20	8.57		8.23	9.17
	8.30	9.13		9. 8	9.46
	9.25	10. 1		9.29	10.22
	10. 5	10.49		9.58	10.33
	11.15	11.56		10.48	11.38
	—	—		—	—
	—	—		—	—
	—	—		—	—
	—	—		—	—
	—	—		—	—

d Saturdays only.
e Saturdays excepted.
h Departs from or arrives at Bishops Road Station.

Royal Hotel. Telephone 61. Conveniently situated, close to Station. Quiet and comfortable. Electric Light. Garage, and cars for hire.
TRUST HOUSES, Ltd.

The Old Crown Hotel. Established 1315. Motoring, Commercial. Re-decorated and Refurnished. Luncheons. Teas, Dinners. Garage. Telephone 8. ALICE WADE, Proprietress.

SMALLFORD (Herts)

from *King's Cross*, 20¼ miles. Fares, 4/0a, 2/5c. R. T., double fare. Departures *from* London as for St. Albans. Departures *for* London about 11 times daily.

Map Square 23.

SMALLHEATH (Warwick),

108¼ miles. Fares, 22/8a, 13/7c. R. T. for two months, 45/4a. Departures *from* London as for Acock's Green. Departures *for* London 8 times daily. Pop. 28,693.

Map Square 17.

SMARDALE (Westmorland),

271¾ miles. No through fares. Departures *from* London as for Tebay. Departures *for* London about 4 times daily.

Map Square 7.

SMEATON (Midlothian),

387½ miles. No through fares. Departures *from* London as for Edinburgh (Waverley). Departures *for* London about 3 times daily.

SMEETH (Kent) from

Charing Cross, Cannon Street, and *London Bridge,* 61 miles. Fares, 12/9a, 10/3b, 7/8c. R. T. for two months, 25/6a, 20/6b. Pop. 445.

Map Square 24.

	Leave			Arr. at
CHAR. +	CAN. ST.	LON. B.		SMEETH
AM	—	5.20	5.25	8.33
9.15	—		9.23	11. 8
11. 0	—		11. 7	12.52
PM 4.30k	—		4.37k	6. 3
4.30h	—		4.37h	6.18
5.24d	—		5.34d	7.34
6. 0e	—		6. 5e	7.28
7.18	—		7.26	9.39

Sunday Trains.

AM 7.45	—	7.52	9.57
10.10	—	10.18	11.52
PM 7.35	—	7.45	9.35

Trains from Smeeth.

Leave		Arrive at	
SMEETH	LON. B.	CAN. ST.	CHAR. +
AM 7.28	9.32	9.36	—
10. 3	11.43	—	11.57
PM 1.16	3.26	—	3.40
4. 0	5.50	—	6. 3
5.32	7.25	7.30	7.49
8.35	10.22	—	10.35

Sunday Trains.

AM 7.33	10. 5	—	10.15
PM 5.31	7. 9	—	7.17
8.25	10.16	—	10.26
10.16s	—	1.23	—

d Saturdays only.
e Saturdays excepted.
h Fridays only.
k Fridays excepted.
s Third class only.

ANOTHER ROUTE from

Victoria, Holborn Viaduct, and *St. Paul's,* 63¾ miles. Fares as above.

	VICT.	Leave		Arr. at
S.E. & C.	HOL V.	ST. PL.'s		SMEETH
AM	—	6.40	6.42	11.18
9.45	—		—	12.52
11. 4d	10.58d	11. 0d		1.50
PM	—	1.27d	1.30d	6. 3
2.50h	—		—	6. 3
2.50l	—		—	6.18
4.25e	—		—	7.28
7.22	—		—	9.39

Sunday Trains.

AM 9.35	8. 0	—	11.53
PM 5.15	—	—	7.23
6.35	6.40	—	9.35
—	—	—	—

Trains from Smeeth.

Leave		Arrive at	
SMEETH	ST. PL. s	HOL. V.	VICT.
AM 7.28	9.53	9.55	—
10. 3	12.59	1. 2	12.49
PM 1.16	—	—	3.37
4. 0	6.58	7. 0	—
5.32	—	—	8.51
8.35	11.44	11.45	—

Sunday Trains.

AM 7.33	—	—	10.48
11. 6	—	—	1. 5
PM 1.16	—	—	3.50
5.31	—	9. 9	—

d Saturdays only.
e Saturdays excepted.
h Fridays and Saturdays excepted.
l Fridays only.

SMEETH ROAD (Norfolk), from *Liverpool Street*, 96¾ miles. Fares, 18/4*a*, 11/0*c*. R. T. for two months, 36/8*a*. Departures *from* London as for Wisbech. Departures *for* London about 4 times daily.

Map Square 19.

SMETHWICK (Stafford) from *Euston*, 116¼ miles. Fares, 23/9*a*, 14/3*c*. R. T. for two months, 47/6*a*. Pop. 75,757.

Map Square 17.

Euston	Smthw'k	Smthw'k	Euston
AM 2.30	5.43	AM 6.29	10. 0
5. 0	8.50	8. 3*r*	10.40
6.45	11.18	9.28	12.40
9.10*er*	11.33	10.28*r*	1.25
9.15*r*	12.38	11.45*e*	3. 0
11.30*r*	2.43	11.45*d*	4.15
PM 1.15*r*	4. 8	PM 1.43*t*	4.35
2.20*t*	5. 4	2.51*t*	5.35
4.35*t*	7. 8	4. 9*r*	6.50
5.50*r*	8.28	5.30*r*	8.20
6.55*r*	9.28	6. 4*dr*	10.45
7. 0	10.33	7.44*e*	10.20
11.50*d*	8.41	11.24*e*	4. 0
—	—	11.24*d*	5. 0
—	—	—	—
—	—	—	—
—	—	—	—
—	—	—	—
—	—	—	—

Sunday Trains.

AM 9.15	2.15	AM10. 0*r*	1.45
PM 1. 0*r*	7. 0	PM12.28	5. 5
5.10*r*	9.43	4.17*r*	8.20
—	—	10.14	5. 0
—	—	—	—
—	—	—	—
—	—	—	—

d Saturdays only.
e Saturdays excepted.
r Restaurant Car.
t Tea Car.

SMETHWICK JUNC. (Stafford), from *Paddington*, 114¾ miles. Fares, 23/11*a*, 14/4*c*. R. T. for two months, 47/10*a*.

Pad	Smthw'k.	Smthw'k.	Pad.
AM 6.30	10.51	AM 7. 5*r*	10. 0
9.10*r*	11.50	8.31*r*	11. 0
10.20*d*	12.43	9.49	12.25
10.40*r*	1.21	10.59*r*	1.25
PM12.50*r*	3.27	11.45*r*	2. 5
2.10*t*	4.46	PM 2.22*r*	5. 0
4.10*t*	6.52	3. 8*t*	5.55
6.10*r*	8.27	4.17*t*	6.40
7.10*r*	9.37	5.34*r*	8. 5
7.30	11.34	7. 9	10. 0
12.15*k*	5.58	10.48	3.30
12.15*l*	7.57	—	—

Sunday Trains.

PM12.50*r*	3.12	AM 9.48*r*	1.40
6. 0*r*	8.22	PM12.45	6.20
—	—	5.57*r*	9. 0
—	—	—	—

d Saturdays only.
k Saturday midnights excepted.
l Saturday midnight only.
r Restaurant Car.
t Tea Car.

SMITHAM (Surrey) from *Charing Cross, Cannon Street*, and *London Bridge*, 17¼ miles. Fares, 2/11*a*, 2/4*b*, 1/9*c*. R. T. for eight days, 5/10*a*, 4/8*b*, 3/6*c*. Departures *from* London as for Kingswood. Departures *for* London about 18 times daily.

SMITHY BRIDGE (Lancs), 197½ miles. Fares, 40/7*a*, 24/4*c*. R. T. for two months, 81/2*a*, 48/8*c*. Departures *from* London as for Rochdale. Departures *for* London about 6 times daily.

Map Square 12.

SNAINTON (Yorks), 227¾ miles. No through fares. Departures *from* London as for Malton. Departures *for* London about 4 times daily. Pop. 649.

Map Square 8.

SNAITH (Yorks) from *King's Cross*, 179¾ miles. Fares, 36/0*a*, 21/7*c*. R.T. for two months, 72/0*a*. Departures *from* London as for Knottingley or Goole. Departures *for* London about 7 times daily. Pop. 1,619.

Map Square 13.

SNARESBROOK (Essex) from *Liverpool Street* and *Fenchurch Street*, 7½ miles. Fares, from Liverpool Street, 1/3*a*, 1/0*b*, 0/9*c*. R. T. for two days, 2/6*a*, 1/11*b*, 1/4*c*. From Fenchurch Street, 1/3*a*, 1/0*b*, 0/9*c*. R. T. for two days, 2/6*a*, 1/11*b*, 1/4*c*. *See* pp. 541-544.

Map Squares 23 and 53.

SNARESTONE (Leicester) 110¾ miles. Fares, 22/9*a*, 13/8*c*. R. T. for two months, 45/6*a*. Departures *from* London as for Shackerstone. Departures *for* London about 6 times daily. Pop. 277.

Map Square 17

SNELLAND (Lincoln), 139¼ miles. Fares, 28/11*a*, 17/4*c*. R. T., double fare. Departures *from* London as for Lincoln. Departures *for* London about 4 times daily. Pop. 85.

Map Square 13.

Station closed on Sundays.

SNETTISHAM (Norfolk) from *Liverpool Street*, 106¼ miles. Fares, 22/6*a*, 13/6*c*. R. T. for two months, 45/0*a*. Departures *from* London as for Wolferton. Departures *for* London about 8 times daily. Pop. 1,440.

Map Square 14.

SNODLAND (Kent) from *Charing Cross, Cannon Street*, and *London Bridge*, 37¼ miles. Fares, 7/11*a*, 6/4*b*, 4/9*c*. R. T. for two months, 15/10*a*, 12/8*b*, 9/6*c*. Pop. 4,481.

Map Square 24.

Char. +	Leave Can.St.	Lon. B.	Arr. at Snodld.
AM —	—	3.22*h*	5.47
—	6.20	6.23	8. 0
—	7.16	7.19	8.41
—	7.44	7.47	9.14
8.10	—	8.17	9.47
9.32	—	9.41	11. 7
11.55	—	12. 2	1.21
PM12.30*d*	—	12.37*d*	1.49
1.20*e*	—	1.27*e*	2.55
1.26*d*	—	1.34*d*	2.55
—	1.48*d*	1.51*d*	3.23
2.45*e*	—	2.53*e*	4.28
3. 5*d*	—	3.12*d*	4.30
—	4.12*e*	4.15*e*	5.21
4.25*d*	—	4.31*d*	6. 4
—	4.36*e*	4.39*e*	6. 4
4.35*d*	—	4.43*d*	6.36

SNODLAND—*continued.*

Char. +	Leave Can. St.	Lon. B.	Arr. at Snodld.
PM —	5. 8*e*	5.11*e*	6.36
5.15*d*	—	5.22*d*	7. 2
—	5.56*e*	5.59*e*	7. 4
5.58*d*	—	6. 4*d*	7.27
—	6.20*e*	6.23*e*	7.32
6.22*e*	—	6.29*e*	8. 2
6.55*d*	—	7. 1*d*	8.48
—	7. 8*e*	7.11*e*	8.48
—	7.44	7.49	9.57
—	9.35	9.38	11.14

Sunday Trains.

AM 7.30	—	7.37	9.21
10.50	—	10.57	12.42
PM 1.15	—	1.22	3. 7
4.50	—	4.57	6.35
7. 0	—	7. 7	8.38
8.42	—	8.49	10.20

Trains from Snodland.

Leave Snodld.	Lon. B.	Arrive at Can. St.	Char. +
AM 5.11	7. 0	7. 4	—
7. 6	8.34	—	8.41
8.24	9.34	—	9.43
8.39	9.54	—	10. 1
9.39	10.38	—	10.45
10.35	12. 3	—	12.14
PM12. 1*d*	1.31	1.37	—
12. 1*e*	1.36	—	1.45
*d*1.20*h*	3.21	3.26	—
1.26*e*	2.54	—	3. 4
1.55*e*	3.26	—	3.36
2.12*d*	3.58	—	4. 8
3.13*e*	4.48	4.52	—
3.16*d*	4.57	—	5. 6
4.13*e*	5.36	5.40	—
4.13*d*	5.36	—	5.45
5.29	7.10	—	7.19
6. 0	7.14	—	7.23
6.46	8.15	8.20	—
8.10	9.36	—	9.46
9.22	10.51	—	10.59
10.31	12.35	—	12.45

Sunday Trains.

AM 7.19	9. 0	—	9. 9
8.38	10.16	—	10.24
11.24	1. 5	—	1.17
PM 2.27	4. 4	—	4.15
4.27	5.55	—	6. 4
7.53	9.46	—	9.55
9.34	11.15	—	11.23
—	—	—	—

d Saturdays only.
e Saturdays excepted.
h Third Class only.

SOHAM (Cambs) from *Liverpool Street*, 72½ miles. Fares, 15/0*a*, 9/0*c*. R.T. for two months, 30/0*c*. Pop. 4,682.

Map Square 19.

L'pool St.	Soham	Soham	L'pool St.
AM 5.50	8.54	AM 8.18*r*	10.23
8.30*r*	10.59	9.51	12.40
11.50*r*	2.45	PM12. 3*r*	2.21
PM 2.34	4.49	1.45*hr*	5.17
4.45	6.53	3.54*r*	6.10
—	—	5.55*r*	8.22

No Sunday Trains.

h Thursdays only.
r Restaurant Car.

SOHO (Stafford), 112¼ miles. Fares, 23/4*a*, 14/0*c*. R. T. for two months, 46/8*a*, 28/0*c*. Departures *from* London as for Birmingham (Snow Hill). Departures *for* London about 6 times daily. Pop. 13,244.

SOLE STREET (Kent)

from *Victoria, Holborn Viaduct,* and *St. Paul's*, 26¾ miles. Fares, 5/10*a*, 4/8*b*, 3/5*c*. R. T. for two months, 11/8*a*, 9/4*b*.

Map Square 24.

Vict. (S.E.& C.)	Leave Hol. V.	S. Pl.'s	Arr. at Sole St.
AM 5. 5	4.57	5. 0	6.27
—	7.30	7.33	8.38
9.20	—	—	10.14
11.40*e*	—	—	12.52
11.55*d*	—	—	1. 5
PM —	1.24*d*	1.27*d*	2.25
—	3.22	3.25	4.42
3.40*d*	3.33*d*	3.36*d*	5.17
4.25*e*	—	—	5.17
5.30*e*	—	5.33*e*	6.37
6.16	6.10*e*	6.13*e*	7.28
7. 5	7. 0	7. 3	8. 3
9. 0*e*	8.57*e*	9. 0*e*	10.11
10.17	10.11	10.13	11.25
—	—	—	—

Sunday Trains.

AM 7.20	—	—	8.27
10.30	10.25	—	11.49
PM 3.30	—	—	4.40
6.35	—	—	7.41
10.15	10.12	—	11.32
—	—	—	—

Trains from Sole Street.

Leave Sole St.	Arrive at S. Pl.'s	Hol. V.	Vict.
AM 7.16	8.25	8.27	8.29
8. 4	9.16	9.18	—
8.39	9.37	9.39	—
10.11	—	—	11. 2
11.52	1. 0	1. 2	—
PM12.14*e*	—	—	1.32
2.17	—	—	3.23
4. 2*e*	5.32	5.34	5.21
5.36*e*	6.45	6.47	—
6.52*d*	8. 0	8. 2	—
8.32	9.50	9.54	9.46
10.17	11.21	11.23	—

Sunday Trains.

AM 8. 9	—	9.40	9.31
10. 4	—	11.27	11.23
11.46	—	1. 2	12.56
PM 5. 7	—	—	6. 3
10.38	—	12. 0	11.44
—	—	—	—

d Saturdays only.
e Saturdays excepted.

SOLIHULL (Warwick)

from *Paddington*, 103¾ miles. Fares, 21/6*a*, 12/11*c*. R. T. for two months, 43/0*a*. Pop. 10,282.

Map Square 17.

Pad.	Solihull	Solihull	Pad.
AM 5.30	9.52	AM 7.25*r*	10. 0
6.30	10.47	8.32*r*	11. 0
10.40	1.35	10.38*r*	1.25
PM12.50*r*	4.17	11.42*r*	2. 5
2.10	5. 6	PM 2.22*r*	5. 0
4.10*t*	6.35	3.29*t*	5.55
6.10*r*	8.33	5.29*er*	8. 5
7.10*r*	9.31	5.33*dr*	8. 5
7.30	10.43	7.13	10. 0
12.15*k*	8.23	11.42	3.30
12.15*l*	9.46		

Sunday Trains.

AM10.35	2. 3	AM10.57*r*	1.40
PM 6. 0*r*	8.57	PM 2. 9	6.20
—	—	6.23*r*	9. 0

d Saturdays only.
e Saturdays excepted.
k Saturday midnights excepted.
l Saturdays midnight only.
r Restaurant Car.
t Tea Car.

SOMERFORD, GREAT

(Wilts) from *Paddington*, 90¾ miles. Fares, 18/11*a*, 11/4*c*. R.T. for two months, 37/10*a*. Departures *from* London as for Malmesbury. Departures *for* London about 6 times daily. Pop. 464.

Map Square 22.

SOMERFORD, LITTLE

(Wilts) from *Paddington*, 89¾ miles. Fares, 18/9*a*, 11/3*c*. R. T. for two months, 37/6*a*. Departures *from* London as for Chipping Sodbury. Departures *for* London about 5 times daily. Pop. 308.

Map Square 22.

SOMERLEYTON (Suffolk)

from *Liverpool Street*, 116½ miles. Fares, 24/9*a*, 14/10*c*. R. T. for two months, 49/6*a*. Departures *from* London as for Lowestoft (*via* Cambridge). Departures *for* London about 6 times daily. Pop. 526.

Map Square 19.

SOMERSHAM (Hunts)

from *Liverpool Street*, 76 miles. Fares, 13/4*a*, 8/0*c*. R. T. for two months, 26/8*a*. Pop. 1,404.

Map Square 18.

L'p'l St.	S'mrhm.	S'mrhm.	L'p'l St.
AM 5.50	9. 4	AM 7.59	10.23
8.30*r*	11. 8	10.53	2. 7
11.50*r*	2.14	PM 1.18*lr*	4. 2*k*
PM 2.34	4.54	1.18	5. 9
5.49*r*	8. 7	3.34*r*	6.10
7.10*dr*	9.34	6. 1*r*	8.33
—	—	8.40*d*	2.50

Sunday Trains.

PM 3.25	6. 0	PM 4. 3	6.40

d Saturdays only.
k Arrives at St. Pancras Station.
l Commencing July 23.
r Restaurant Car.

ANOTHER ROUTE from

King's Cross, 69¾ miles. Fares as above.

King's+	Somerm.	Somerm.	King's+
AM 5. 5	9. 3	AM 7.59	10.40
8.45	11. 7	10.53	1.25
10.12	2.13	PM 1.18	3.50
11.30*f*	3.50	3.34	6.25
PM 1.55	4.53	6. 1	9. 0
5. 0	8. 6	—	—
6.15*d*	9.33	—	—

No Sunday Trains.

d Saturdays only.
f Mondays only.

SOMERTON (Somerset)

from *Paddington*, 125¾ miles. Fares, 25/4*a*, 15/8*c*. R.T. for two months, 50/8*a*, 31/4*c*. Pop. 1,854.

Map Square 22.

Pad.	S'm'ton.	S'm'ton.	Pad.
AM 1. 0*g*	8.59	AM 9.19	12.55
5.30	10.45	PM12.26	3.50
PM12.30*r*	3.50	1.53*t*	5.30
3.30	6.42	4. 8	8.20
5. 5	8.42	5.30	2.45
—	—	8.33*h*	2.45

Sunday Trains.

AM 9.10	2.39	PM 4. 5*r*	7.55
PM10. 0	8.59	—	—

g Mondays excepted.
h Thursdays and Third class only.
r Restaurant Car.
t Tea Car.

SONNING-ON-THAMES (Berks).

Station at Twyford, 2½ miles, or Reading, 3 miles. Pop. 418.

White Hart Hotel. First-class. "The Rose Garden of the Stream." Electric light throughout. Meals served in Gardens weather permitting. Close to Sonning Golf Links. Tel. 17 Sonning. Garage.

French Horn Hotel. Delightfully Situated. River. Lawns. Tennis. Boating. Fishing. Private Bathing. Playing Fields. Near Golf Links. Telephone, Sonning 20.

SORBIE (Wigtown),

395¼ miles. Fares, 71/6*a*, 42/11*c*. R. T. for two months, 143/0*a*, 85/10*c*. Departures *from* London as for Wigtown. Departures *for* London about 3 times daily. Pop. 1,179.

Map Square 43.

SOUTH ACTON.

See Acton, South.

SOUTHALL (Middlesex)

from *Paddington*, 9 miles. Fares, 1/5½*a*, 0/10*c*. R.T. for two days, 2/11*a*, 1/6*c*. Pop. 30,287. *See* pp. 491-493.

Map Square 57.

SOUTHAM (Warwick)

from *Euston*, 85 miles. Fares, 16/11*a*, 10/2*c*. R.T. for two months, 33/10*a*. Departures *from* London as for Braunston. Departures *for* London about 4 times daily. Pop. 1,804.

SOUTHAMPTON

TOWN (Hants) from *Waterloo*, 78¾ miles. Fares, 16/6*a*, 9/11*c*. R.T. for two months, 33/0*a*, 19/10*c*. Pop. 160,997.

Map Square 28

W'loo	S'mpton	S'mpton	W'loo
AM 5.50	8.51	AM 1. 0	3.58
7. 0	10.28	6.45	9.26
8.30*s*	10.55	7.45	10.20
9.30	12.32	9.45	12. 0
11.30*r*	2.28	11.40*r*	2.20
PM 1.30*s*	3.41	PM12.25	3.36
3.30*s*	5.38	1.22	4. 6
3.40	6.41	1.50	4.20
4. 0	6.55	3. 5	6.16
5. 0	7.20	3.57*s*	6.26
5.30*r*	8.50	5.27*r*	8.20
7.30	9.43	6.35	9.52
8. 0	10.46	7.40	10.50
10. 0	12.30	8.17	11.28
—	—	—	—

Sunday Trains.

AM 8.45	12.18	AM 1. 0	3.58
11. 0*r*	1.33	7.30	11.16
12. 0*nr*	2.31	9.30	12.11
PM 2. 0*r*	6.20	11.55*r*	2.27
5. 5	7.56	PM 3.10	6. 7
6. 0	8.36	6.25	9.37
7. 0*r*	9.37	—	—
8.15	10.23	—	—
9.28	12.18	—	—

n Noon.
r Restaurant Car.
s Refreshments served.

SOUTH WESTERN HOTEL, SOUTHAMPTON.

SOUTHAMPTON

WEST from Waterloo, 78¾ miles.
Fares as above.
Map Square 28.

W'LOO	S'MPTON	S'MPTON	W'LOO
AM 5.40	7.50	AM 8.25r	10. 6
8.30s	10.33	9.28s	11. 0
9.30	11.32	9.35	12. 0
11.30r	1.17	10.24s	12.22
PM12.30r	2. 2	11.18r	12.50
1.30s	3.27	PM12.22r	2.20
2.30	4. 2	1.18	2.50
3.30s	5.27	2.22	4.20
4.30r	6. 2	3.18	4.50
5.30r	7.27	3.30	6.16
6.30r	8. 2	4.22s	6.26
7.30	9.32	5.26	6.58
8. 0	10.50	6.22r	8.20
—	—	7.18r	8.50
—	—	8. 3	10.50
—	—	9. 5	11.28

Sunday Trains.

AM11. 0r	12.57	AM 9.50	12.11
PM 2. 0r	3.47	PM12.33r	2.27
7. 0r	8.56	3.30	6. 7
—	—	4.47r	6.24
—	—	5.42	8. 3
—	—	7.51r	9.31
—	—	8. 7	10.52

r Restaurant Car.
s Refreshments served.

The South-Western Hotel.
Adjoining Station and opposite
the Dock Gates. The most convenient stopping place for
travellers between England and
the Continent. Porter in red
livery meets all trains at both
the Docks and the West Stations.
Garage, Motor 'bus. Telegrams:
"Welcome, Southampton." Telephone. Southampton 1906.
See advt. p. 305.

The Polygon, High-class
Residential Hotel. Inclusive
Tariff, by Day or Week. In best
and healthiest part of Southampton. Perfect quiet. Passenger
Lifts. Motor Garage, West Station.
See advt. p. 306.

Dolphin Hotel (Trust
Houses, Ltd.). Famous Hotel in
High Street. Telephone 1422.
See advt. p 306.

Hamtun House. Private and
Residential Hotel, Hulse Road.
Billiards. Tel 266.
Apply, MANAGERESS.
See advt. p. 307.

Scullard's Hotel, High
Street. Refurnished. Electric
Light. Splendid Grill Telephone
1120. Best position in Town. Proprietor, C. SCULLARD.
Manager, E. COOK.

Royal Pier Hotel. Near
Docks. Overlooking Southampton
Water. Minute from Isle of
Wight Boats. Telegrams : "Pier
Hotel." Telephone 1231.
J. B. ATKINS, Proprietor.

SOUTHAM ROAD

**(Warwick) from Paddington, 81¾
miles. Fares, 16/11a, 10/2c. R. T
for two months, 33/10a. Pop.
(Southam) 1,804.**
Map Square 18.

PAD	SOUTH. R.	SOUTH. R.	PAD.
AM 5.30	8.57	AM 6.43	9.50
9.10	11.32	10.20	12.25
9.45	1.22	PM12.16	3.50
10.45	2.57	2.32t	5. 0
PM 2.10	5 .7	5.26r	9.15
6.10	8.17	7.17	10.45
7.30d	10. 7	10.57d	3.30

Sunday Trains.

PM 4.10	7.54	PM 2.57	6.20
—	—	6.26r	9. 0

d Saturdays only.
r Restaurant Car.
t Tea Car.

SOUTH BANK (Yorks),

240¾ miles. Fares, 50/3a, 30/2c.
R. T., double fare. Departures
from London as for Middlesbrough.
Departures for London about 4
times daily. Pop. 14,977.
Map Square 8.

SOUTH BERMONDSEY. See BERMONDSEY, SOUTH.

SOUTHBOROUGH

**(Kent) from Charing Cross, Cannon Street, and London Bridge, 33¼
miles. Fares, 6/8a, 5/4b, 4/0c. R.T.
for two months, 13/4a, 10/8b, 8/0c.
Pop. 7,104.**
Map Square 24.

	Leave		Arr. at
CHAR. +	CAN. ST	LON. B.	S'BORO
AM —	3.40h	3.43h	5.54
—	5.20	5.25	7.14
—	6.45	6.50	8.34
—	7.56	8. 0	9.34
9.25	—	9.33	10.45
10.40	—	10 46	11.50
PM12. 3	—	12.10	1.27
1. 5d	—	1.11d	2.16
2. 8e	—	2.16e	3.35
3. 0d	—	3. 8d	4. 7
3.48e	—	—	4.46
3.50	—	3.57	5.23
—	5.12e	—	6.18
5.24d	—	5.34d	6.43
5.26e	—	5.33e	6.30
5.35d	—	5.41d	7.54
6. 3e	—	6. 9e	7.14
6.34e	—	6.41e	7.54
7.30	—	—	8.30
8. 0	—	8. 8	9.20
9.30	—	9.36	10.33
12. 5y	—	—	12.57

SOUTHBOROUGH—continued.

Sunday Trains.

	Leave		Arr. at
CHAR. +	CAN. ST.	LON. B.	S'BORO
AM 7. 5	—	7.11	8.44
8. 5	—	8.12	9.43
11.15	—	11.23	12.50
PM 3. 5	—	3.13	4.45
7.35	—	7.45	8.48
—	—	—	—
—	—	—	—
—	—	—	—

Trains from Southborough.

Leave	Arrive at		
S'BORO'	LON. B.	CAN. ST.	CHAR. +
AM 6.43	8.10	—	8.19
7.51	8.48	8.52	—
8.23	9.32	9.36	—
8.56	10. 0	10. 4	—
9.15	10.28	10.32	—
10.29y	11.31	—	11.38
10.38	11.43	—	11.57
11.32	1.28	—	1.38
PM 1.34	3. 7	—	3.19
1.49	3.26	—	3.40
2.59	4.40	—	4.54
3.50d	5.50	—	6. 3
4.21e	5.50	—	6. 3
4.49d	6.30	—	6.39
4.59e	6.44	—	6.54
6. 6	7.25	7.30e	—
6.53	8.26	—	8.37
8.55	10.15	—	10.23
9.13	10.22	—	10.35
10. 7	11.34	—	11.44

Sunday Trains.

	Leave		Arr. at
CHAR. +	CAN. ST	LON. B.	S'BORO
AM 8.27	10. 5	—	10.15
PM 1.28	2.50	⊠	3. 0
6.51	8 .12	—	8.22
7.53	9. 4	—	9.14
9.54	11. 4	—	11.15
10.35h	—	1.20	—

d Saturdays only.
e Saturdays excepted.
h Third Class only.
y Wednesdays only.

SOUTH BROMLEY.
See BROMLEY, SOUTH.

SOUTHBURN (Yorks),

202¼ miles. Fares, 39/0a, 23/5c.
R. T. for two months, 78/0a. 46/10c.
Departures from London as for
Market Weighton. Departures
for London about 6 times daily.
Pop. 95.
Map Square 8.

SOUTH CAVE (Yorks),

from St. Pancras, 214¼ miles.
Fares, 35/0a, 21/0c. R. T. for two
months, 70/0a. Departures from
London as for Cudworth. Departures for London about 4 times
daily. Pop. 956.
Map Square 13.

SOUTHCOATES

(Yorks), 198¾ miles. No through
fares. Departures from London
as for Hull (Paragon). Departures
for London about 5 times daily.

SOUTHAMPTON.—SCULLARD'S HOTEL. Central. Comfortable. Moderate.

SOUTH DOCK (London)

from *Fenchurch Street*, 3¼ miles. Fares, 0/6½*a*, 0/5*b*, 0/4*c*. R. T. for two days, 1/1*a*, 0/10*b*, 0/8*c*. See pp. 524, 525.

Map Square 71.

SOUTH EALING. *See* EALING, SOUTH.

SOUTH EASTRING-TON. *See* EASTRINGTON, SOUTH.

SOUTH ELMSALL

(Yorks), 164½ miles. Fares, 34/2*a*, 20/6*c*. R. T.,·double fare. Departures *from* London as for Hemsworth. Departures *for* London about twice daily. Pop. 4,359.

Map Square 13.

SOUTHEND (Essex) from

Fenchurch Street, 35½ miles. Fares, 5/5*a*, 3/3*c*. R. T. for two months. 10/10*a*, 6/6*c*. Pop. 106,021.

Map Square 24.

FEN. ST.	S'END	S'END	FEN. ST.
AM 5. 5	6.38	AM 4.25	5.35
5.37	7.55	5.25	6.43
6.52	8.53	6.20	7.34
7.42	9. 5	6.52	8. 6
7.55	9.51	7. 1	8.15
9.18	11. 1	7.15	8.22*h*
9.57*h*	11.25	7.33	8.44
10.15*h*	11.35	7.45	8.53
10.17	11.57	7.54	9. 4
10.45	12.11	8.11	9.17
11.57*d*	1. 4	8.16	9.34*h*
PM 12. 9	1.20	8.29	9.39
12.43*d*	1.49	8.37	9.54*k*
12.55*d*	1.57	8.53	9.52
1. 0*e*	2. 6	9. 4	10. 1
1. 0*d*	2. 6	9.15	10.18*h*
1. 5*d*	2.14	9.27	10.35
1.11*d*	2.27	9.47	10.57*h*
1.25*d*	2.35	10.26	11.40
1.48*d*	2.54	11.22*e*	12.22
1.56*d*	3. 1	11.22*d*	12.38
2. 5*dk*	3.28	11.50	1.11*h*
2. 6	3. 9	PM 12.50	1.56
2.26*d*	3.36	2.17	3.28
2.30	4. 6	2.50*d*	3.51
3. 8*d*	4.17	5.30	4.54*h*
3.16*h*	4.44	3.48*d*	5.12
3.45*d*	4.53	4.25	5.49
4. 7	5. 6	4.35	6.33
4.27	5.35	5.30	6.45
4.57*e*	5.56	6.12*e*	7.29*h*
5. 6*e*	6. 7	6.22	7.51
5.16	6.16	7. 7	8.31
5.25*e*	6 38	7.15	9.15
5. 32	7.15	8. 4	9.17*h*
5.38*e*	6.48	8.53	10. 8
5.46*e*	6.55	9. 0*d*	10.20
6. 7*e*	7. 8	9.15	10.30
6.17*e*	7.21	9.31	11.23*h*
6.23*ek*	7.52	10.25	11.40
6.26	7.34	—	—
6.53*e*	8. 3	—	—
6.53*d*	8.17	—	—
7.20	8.26	—	—
8. 0*e*	9. 7	—	—
8.45	10. 0	—	—
9.19*eh*	10.44	—	—
9.20*d*	10.44	—	—
10.15	11.22	—	—
11.27*eh*	12.39	—	—
11.27*dh*	12.48	—	—
12.20	1.27	—	—
—	—	—	—
—	—	—	—
—	—	—	—

SOUTHEND—*continued.*

Sunday Trains.

FEN. ST.	S'END.	S'END.	FEN. ST.
AM 9.15	10.31	AM 7.50	9. 6
9.45	11.31	8.15	10.18
10.4*c*	11.54	10.15	11.35
11. 8*h*	12.28	11.55	1.10
11.45	12.54	PM 2.17	3.47
PM 2. 7	4. 2	4.10	5.30
2.45	4.28	4.20	6. 0
4.50	6.24	5.20	6.47
5. 7*h*	6.43	5.28	7.16
6.10	7.43	5.42	7.45
7.22	8.40	7. 8	8.32
8.28	9.45	7.39	8.59*h*
8.45	10.44	8.39	10. 9
9.45	11.20	8.47	10.23
10.56*h*	11.50	9.40	10.48
—	—	9.50	11.22*h*

d Saturdays only.·
e Saturdays excepted.
h Departs from or arrives at Mark Lane Station.
k Departs from·or arrives at Broad Street Station.

ANOTHER ROUTE from

Liverpool Street, 41½ miles. Fares as above.

L'POOL ST.	S'END	S'END	L'POOL ST.
AM 5.10	6.27	AM 6.16	7.35
5.26	7.18	7.10	8.23
6.50	8.46	7.37	8.45
7.48	9.16	7.47	9.14
9. 1	10.27	8.11	9.17
9. 6	10.58	8.40	9.49
10. 3	11.23	9.16	10.16
10.30	12. 8	9.48	11. 7
11.56	1.10	10.42	11.59
PM 12.48*d*	1.55	11.35*e*	1.16
1.20*d*	2.32	11.38*d*	1.16
1.50*d*	2.53	PM 12. 4*e*	1.25
2. 0*e*	3.15	1.45	3. 5
2.20*e*	4. 7	3.17*e*	4.51
2.30*d*	3.33	3.21*d*	4.56
2.58*d*	4. 6	4.44	6. 8
3.26	5. 4	5.27	6.52
4.15	5.16	6.49	8.22
4.18	5.45	7.19	8.42
4.48*e*	6. 5	7.51	9.10
5.22*e*	6.24	8.10	9.50
5.39	6.58	8.30	9.56
6. 5*e*	7. 8	9.11	10.32
6.26*e*	7.38	10.19	11.30
6.26*d*	7.58	—	—
7.10*e*	8.11	—	—
7.16*e*	8.39	—	—
8. 2*e*	9. 8	—	—
8. 2*d*	9.25	—	—
8.45	10. 5	—	—
9.45*e*	10.47	—	—
9.45*d*	11. 2	—	—
11. 0	12.32	—	—
12. 0*m*	1. 9	—	—
—	—	—	—

Sunday Trains.

AM 8.30	9.58	AM 8. 0	10.25
8.45	10.58	9. 9	10.50
9.30	11.14	10.25	12.40
10.30	11.55	PM 1.27	3.15
10.45	12.34	3.45	5.15
11.35	1. 0	6. 5	7.44
PM 2.30	4.24	6.52	7.58
6. 0	7.28	7. 4	8.45
6.42	8.31	8.10	9.48
8.46	10.29	9.33	10.45
10.10	11.46	—	—

d Saturdays only.
e Saturdays excepted.
m Midnight.

SOUTHEND—*continued.*

ANOTHER ROUTE from

St. Pancras, 42 miles. Fares, 5/5*a*, 3/3*c*. R. T. for two months, 10·10*a*, 6/6*c*.

ST. PAN.	S'END	S'END	ST. PAN.
AM 9.30	11.25	AM 8.16	10.10
PM 12.20	2.20	11.50	1.48
2.50	4.44	PM 3.30	5.23
6.40	8.17	6. 5	7.45
—	—	—	—
—	—	—	—

Sunday Trains.

AM 10.10	12. 2	PM 7.15	9.18
—	—	—	—
—	—	—	—

ANOTHER ROUTE from

Charing Cross (District Rly.), 38 miles. Fares, 5/10*a*, 3/6*c*. R. T. for two months, 11/8*a*, 7/0*c*.

CHAR. +	S'END	S'END	CHAR. +
AM 9. 0	11. 1	AM 4.25	5.53
10. 3	11.33	7.15	8.51
10.18	12.11	9.15	10 27
PM 4.52*e*	6.52	PM 6.12*e*	7.39
9.10*e*	10.44	8. 4	9.26
11.18*e*	12.39	—	—
11.18*d*	12.49	—	—
12. 4*m*	1.27	—	—
—	—	—	—

Sunday Trains.

AM 10.59	12.28	PM 7.39	9. 9
PM 10.27	11.50	—	—

d Saturdays only.
e Saturdays excepted.
m Midnight.

ANOTHER ROUTE *via* Greenwich Pier and North Woolwich Pier by Water ("Golden Eagle.")

Leave — Arr. at

G. PIER.	FEN. ST.	N. W. PIER.	S'END.
AM 8.55	9.25	9.25	11.30

SERVICE FROM SOUTHEND.

Leave — Arrive at

S'END.	N. W. PIER.	FEN. ST.	G. PIER.
PM 4.55	7.30	7.36	7.45

Sunday Service.

20 minutes later at each point.
See advt. back of Map.

Palace Hotel. Choicest Site. Luxurious Winter Garden and Restaurant. Terrace facing Sea. Terms from 5 guineas.
See advt. p. **207.**

West Cliff Private Residen-tial Hotel. Finest position facing the Sea. Moderate tariff. Telephone No.598 (two lines Southend). Proprtr. W. J. HOCKLEY.
See advt. p. **339.**

Hotel Victoria. The Broadway, Southend-on-Sea. Firstclass Family and Commercial. Night Porter. Telephone No 12. Proprietor,
C. E. MORRIS.
See advt. p. **308.**

Queen's Hotel. The Leading and only Licensed Hotel in Westcliff. Facing South, in picturesque grounds. Lift. 'Phone 62 Southend.
J. H. KEEP, Proprietor.
See advt. p. **340.**

SOUTHEND—*continued.*

Grand Pier Hotel. Immediately facing Southend Pier. Telephone No. 216.

Proprietor, J. MOSS.

See advt. p. **307.**

Royal Hotel. Facing Sea. Overlooking Shrubbery and Pier. Oldest and Best Hotel. Telephone 32.

WEBSTER, Proprietor.

See advt. p. **308.**

Palmeira Towers. Finest Hotel. Balcony. Bedrooms facing sea. 'Phone 447. Telegrams: "Palton, Westcliff." Moderate Tariff.

House Agents, Rayner and Taplin. Opposite Post Office, Southend. Established 1887. Unfurnished Houses and Shops. List gratis.

SOUTHERNDOWN

ROAD (Glamorgan), 176¼ miles. Fares, 36/10a, 22/1c. R. T. for two months, 73/8a, 44/2c. Departures *from* London as for Barry Docks. Departures *for* London about 5 times daily.

Map Square 21.

SOUTHFIELDS (Wands-

worth) from *Mansion House,* 8¾ miles. Pop. 35,715. *See* p.489.

Map Square 77.

ANOTHER ROUTE from *Waterloo,* 6½ miles. Fares, 1/1a, 0/7½c. R. T. for two days, 2/2a, 1/3c. *See* p. 595.

SOUTHFLEET (Kent)

from *Victoria, Holborn Viaduct,* and *St. Paul's,* 25 miles. Fares, 4/10a, 3/11b, 2/11c. R. T. for two months, 7/9a, 6/0b, 5/3c. Pop. 1,331.

Map Square 24.

	Leave		Arr. at
Vict. (S.E. &C.)	Hol. V.	St. Pl.'s	S'fleet
AM —	5.59	5.59	7.18
—	6.40	6.42	7.52
—	7.30	7.33	8.41
9.20	—	—	10.19
11.40d	—	—	12.45
11.40e	—	—	12.52
PM —	1.24d	1.27d	2.25
2. 9d	2. 4d	2. 7d	3.34
2.12e	2.15e	2.16e	3.27
—	3.22d	3.25d	4.49
3.56e	—	—	4.56
5. 5d	—	—	6.11
5. 8e	—	—	6. 8
5.45e	5.31e	5.34e	6.46
5.45d	—	—	6.48
7.22	7.22	7.24	8.26
8.10d	8. 5d	8. 8d	9.30
—	—	—	—
—	—	—	—
—	—	—	—

Sunday Trains.

AM 7.20	—	—	8.42
8.25	—	—	9.35
11.30	—	—	12.36
PM 1. 7	1. 5	—	2.22
2. 5	2. 3	—	3.31
6.35	6.40	—	7.47

SOUTHFLEET—*contd.*

Trains from Southfleet.

	Leave	Arrive at	
	S'fleet	St. Pl.'s	Hol. V.	Vict.
AM 7.41	8.40	8.42	8.50
8.30	9.27	9.29	9.36
9.20	—	—	10.10
10. 1	11.22	11.29	11. 9
11.32	12.59	1. 2	12.48
PM 1.17d	—	—	2.40
2. 9e	3.38	—	3.23
2.53d	—	—	4.32
3.52e	5.32	5.34	5.20
5.22e	6.45	6.47	—
6.34d	7.54	—	—
6.51e	8.17	8.20	8.10
7.22	9.10	9.12	8.51
8.29	9.51	9.54	9.46
8.51	10.29	10.31	10.22
9.51d	11.21	11.23	11.35
—	—	—	—
—	—	—	—
—	—	—	—

Sunday Trains.

AM 9.57	—	11.27	11.23
PM12.58	—	2.15	2.11
2.43	—	—	3.50
4.57	—	—	6. 3
8.53	—	10.22	10. 5

d Saturdays only.
e Saturdays excepted.

SOUTHGATE, NEW

(Middlesex), 6¼ miles from *King's Cross, Moorgate Street,* and *Broad Street.* Fares, from King's Cross, 1/2a, 0/11b, 0/8½c. R. T. for two days, 2/4a, 1/10b, 1/5c. From Moorgate Street and Broad Street, 1/3a, 1/0b, 0/9c. R. T. for two days, 2/6a, 2/0b, 1/6c. Pop. 39,122. *See* pp. 511-517.

SOUTH GOSFORTH.

See Gosforth, South.

SOUTHHAMPSTEAD.

See Hampstead, South.

SOUTH HARROW.

See Harrow, South.

SOUTH HETTON (Dur-

ham), 253½ miles. Fares, 52/11a, 31/9c. R. T., double fare. Departures *from* London as for Sunderland or West Hartlepool. Departures *for* London about 3 times daily. Pop. 2,562.

Map Square 7.

SOUTH HOWDEN.

See Howden, South.

SOUTHILL (Beds) from

St. Pancras, 57 miles. Fares, 10/2a, 6/1c. R. T., double fare. Pop. 989.

Map Square 18.

St. Pan.	S'hill	S'hill	St. Pan.
AM 4.25	6.38	AM 7.52	9.30
6.25	9.11	10.15r	12. 5
9.25h	11.32	PM12.37h	3.25
gM12.30	1.58	3. 6	5.20
4.30r	6. 9	4.47k	7. 3
6.30d	7 59	7.26r	10. 5
—	—	—	—
—	—	—	—
—	—	—	—
—	—	—	—

No Sunday Trains.
d Saturdays only.
h Tuesdays and Saturdays only.
k Tuesdays only.
r Restaurant Car.

SOUTHILL—*continued.*

ANOTHER ROUTE from *King's Cross,* 41 miles. Fares, 8/7a, 5/2c. R. T., double fare.

King's +	S'hill	S'hill	King's +
AM 5. 5	7.52	AM 6.38	8.41
8.45	10.15	9.11k	11.15
10.12h	12.37	9.11	11.25
PM 1. 8	3. 6	11.32h	1.25
3. 0k	4.47	PM 1.58	3.50
5.50	7.26	6. 8	8. 5
—	—	7.59d	10.20

No Sunday Trains.

d Saturdays only.
h Tuesdays and Saturdays only.
k Tuesdays only.

SOUTH KENSING-

TON. *See* Kensington, South.

Hotel Wyndham, 73-4, Queen's Gate. Just opened. Central Heating. Terms from 4½ guineas. 'Phone, Kensington 748.

See advt. among London Hotels.

SOUTH KENTISH

TOWN (Hampstead Tube). *See* back of Map.

SOUTH LEIGH (Oxon)

72½ miles. Fares, 15/2a, 9/1c. R. T. for two months, 30/4a. Departures *from* London as for Witney. Departures *for* London about 5 times daily. Pop. 293.

Map Square 23.

SOUTH LYNN. *See*

Lynn, South.

SOUTH MILFORD. *See*

Milford, South.

SOUTHMINSTER

(Essex) from *Liverpool Street,* 45½ miles. Fares, 8/4a, 5/0c. R.T. for two months, 16/8a, 10/0c. Pop. 1,592.

Map Square 24.

L'pl St	S'minst.	S'minst.	L'pl St
AM 5.26	7.37	AM 7. 0	8.45
6.50	9. 6	8. 8	9.46
9. 1	10.56	9.25	11. 7
10.47d	12.59	11.15d	1.16
11.56	1.52	11.45e	1.25
PM 1.26d	2.49	PM 1. 0d	3. 5
2.20e	4.41	2.37d	4.56
2.40d	4.19	2.50e	4.51
4.15e	5.37	4.58	6.52
4.18d	5.58	6.17	8.22
5.39	7.12	7.58	9.56
6.26e	8.10	—	—
8. 2e	9.42	—	—
8.45d	10.18	—	—

Sunday Trains.

AM 8.45	10.32	AM 7.31	10.25
9.30	11.33	PM 6.31	8.45
PM 6.42	8.41	7.40	9.32

d Saturdays only.
e Saturdays excepted.

SOUTH MOLTON

(Devon), 177 miles. Fares, 36/11a, 22/2c. R. T. for two months, 73/10a. Departures *from* London as for Dulverton. Departures *for* London about 4 times daily. Pop. 2,818.

Map Square 21.

SOUTH MOLTON RD.

(Devon) from *Waterloo*, 197¾ miles. Fares, 36/11a, 22/2c. R. T. for two months, 73/10a, 44/4c. Departures *from London* as for Eggesford. Departures *for* London about 6 times daily.
Map Square 21.

SOUTHPORT (CHAPEL
STREET) (Lancs) from *Euston*, 212½ miles. Fares, 44/0a, 26/5c. R. T. for two months, 88/0a, 52/10c. Pop. 76,644.
Map Square 12.

EUSTON	S'PORT		S'PORT	EUSTON
AM 12.25	8.35	AM	8.33r	1.45
2. 35	9.38		8.45hr	1.45
5. 0	11.21		8.55r	3.10
6.45d	1. 4		10.38r	3.45
6.45e	1.14		10.38	4.15
8.30r	2.47		11. 0dt	5.50
10.30hr	3.18		11.58et	5.50
10.40d	3.56	PM	12.42ht	6. 0
10.40e	4. 3		1. 7t	6. 0
11.35r	4.15		2.35r	7.30
11.50r	5.44		4. 0er	9. 5
PM 1.30dr	6.39		4. 0dr	9.15
1.30er	6.53		9. 0	5. 0
2.35ht	7.41		—	—
5.20r	10.34		—	—
5.55hr	10.31		—	—
11.45e	7. 3		—	—
11.50d	11. 2		—	—

Sunday Trains.

AM 11.45	6.30	AM 8.15	4. 0
PM 11. 0	7. 3	PM 2. 0r	7.30
11.50	8.36	8.45	5. 0
—	—	—	—

d Saturdays only
e Saturdays excepted.
h *via* Edge Hill.
r Restaurant Car.
t Tea Car.
v Mondays and Saturdays only.

Palace Hotel. Facing Sea. 220 Rooms. 13 acres Grounds. Aeroplanes to and from Hotel. Telegrams: "Palace Birkdale." Phone, 521/524 Birkdale.
See advt. p. **309.**

Victoria Hotel. Opposite Pier. First-class Family. Cuisine and Wines unsurpassed. Charges strictly moderate. Telephone No. 8, Southport. Tele. Add.: "Victoria, Southport."
W. F. COLLINS, Manager.
See advt. p. **310.**

Avondale Hotel. Southport's Hotel-de-luxe. Unique position on Promenade. Tel. 27. Resident Proprietor,
FRED. T. PAMMENT.
See advt. p. **308.**

Prince of Wales Hotel. "The Leading Hotel." Excellent Cooking. Comfort. Moderate Terms. Home Farm. Great Golf Centre. Garage. Wires: "Prince, Southport." Telephone 1431.

Royal Hotel. Best position on Promenade. Home Farm. Great Golf Centre.

SOUTHPORT—*contd.*

Kenworthy's Hydropathic Establishment. Near Pier, Golf Links, Lord St., Entertainments. Lounge, Billiards, Lift. Visitor or Patients. Turkish, Radiant Heat (Dowsing) and all Electric Baths. From 12/- per day. Telephone 80. Telegrams, "Kenworthy's."
Apply—MANAGERESS.

Queen's Hotel, Promenade. Facing Sea. Family and Residential. Excellent Cuisine. Moderate Tariff. Telephone 1404 (two lines).
HERBERT E. TAYLOR,
Proprietor.

SOUTHREY (Lincoln)
from *King's Cross*, 126½ miles. Fares, 26/3a, 15/9c. R. T., double fare. Departures *from* London as for Kirkstead. Departures *for* London about 4 times daily.
Map Square 13.

SOUTHSEA, EAST
(Hants). Station at *FRATTON* or PORTSMOUTH.

Royal Beach Hotel, Southsea. Self-contained suites. Lift. Garage. Cuisine de première ordre. Telegrams, "Sunshine." 'Phone 2081.
Miss ARMSTRONG, Manageress.
See advt. p. **310.**

Queen's Hotel. Most Central. Magnificent Lounge. Own Garden. Telephone, 2037 Portsmouth.
Miss J. HOPE, Manageress.
See advt. p. **311.**

Royal Pier Hotel, Portsmouth. Most Comfortable. Telephone, 2051 Portsmouth.
Miss F M READING,
Manageress.
See advt. p. **312.**

Sandringham House Private Hotel and Pension. Facing Sea and New Pier. Book to Portsmouth Town Station.
See advt. p. **.311.**

Strathearn Mansions Hotel (Private). Full south. Sixty rooms, handsomely appointed. High-class cuisine. Separate Tables. Electric light throughout. Central heating.
PROPRIETOR.
See advt. p. **312.**

Grosvenor Hotel. Overlooking Solent. Near Piers. Every comfort. Excellent Cuisine. Phone 4797.
See advt. p. **313.**

SOUTHSEA, EAST—
continued.

Grand Central Hotel, one minute from Portsmouth Town Station; largest and best fitted. Large Grill Room and Table d'Hote open to non-residents; lift; night porter. Moderate Tariff.
Apply—MANAGER.
See advt. p. **281.**

Solent House Private Hotel, South Parade. Splendidly situated on Sea Front. Telegrams, "Soltros."
PROPRIETRESS.
See advt. p. **313.**

Gladstone House. First-class Residential. Finest position on Front.
See advt. p. **313.**

Cambrian Boarding Establishment, South Parade. Magnificent situation. Sea front. Home comforts. Excellent cuisine. Terms from 35/0; week ends, 12/0. Electric Light.

Eversfield Private Hotel, Clarence Parade. Facing south. Excellent views, Solent, etc. Separate Tables, Electric Light. Modern improvements. Ideal Winter residence.
PROPRIETRESS.

Portland Hotel, Kent Road. Family and Commercial. Near Common and Piers. Moderate charges, Week-ends a speciality. Tel. 5465.
W. WAINWRIGHT,
Proprietor.

Vermont Boarding Establishment, 21, South Parade. Facing Sea and Common. Good cooking. Moderate Terms.
Mrs. BUTLER, Proprietress.

Pendragon. Clarence Parade. Beautiful Views across Spithead to Isle of Wight. Best Cuisine. High-class Establishment. Garage. Tel. 5887.
PROPRIETORS.

SOUTH SHIELDS (Durham). *See* SHIELDS, SOUTH.
Map Square 3.

SOUTH TOTTENHAM. *See* TOTTENHAM, SOUTH.

SOUTHWAITE (Cumberland), 291¼ miles. Fares, 59/0a, 35/5c. R. T. for two months, 118/0a, 70/10c. Departures *from* London as for Penrith. Departures *for* London about 4 times daily.
Map Square 7.

SOUTHWATER (Sussex)

from *London Bridge, Victoria,* and *Clapham Junction,* 42 miles. Fares, 8/9a, 5/3c. R.T. for two months, 17/6a, 10/6c. Departures *from* London as for West Grinstead. Departures *for* London about 7 times daily. Pop. 850.
Map Square 23.

SOUTHWELL (Notts)

from *St. Pancras,* 139 miles. Fares, 25/0a, 15/0c. R. T., double fare. Pop. 3.349.
Map Square 13.

St.Pan.	S'hwell	S'hwell	St. Pan.
AM 2.25	9.21	AM 7.15r	10.45
4.25	9.50	8.55r	12.10
9. 0r	12.16	9.52r	1.20
11. 0hr	2.35	11.13	3.25
11. 0jr	2.53	PM12.46r	4.10
11.45dr	4.11	1.28r	5.30
PM 1.50r	4.56	2.45hr	6.35
3.30r	7.22	3.48r	7.15
6.15r	9.50	5.45r	9. 5
6.25lr	11.30	6.12r	10. 5
—	—	8.28	4.20
—	—	9.25l	4.20

No Sunday Trains.

h Wednesdays excepted.
j Wednesdays only.
l Thursdays and Saturdays only.
r Restaurant Car.

SOUTHWICK (Kirkcudbright), 344¾ miles.

Fares, 68/9a, 41/3c. R. T. for two months, 137/6a, 82/6c. Departures *from* London as for Dumfries. Departures *for* London about 4 times daily. Pop. 415.
Map Square 43.

SOUTHWICK (Sussex)

from *London Bridge* and *Victoria,* 53½ miles. Fares, 11/3a, 6/9c. R. T. for two months, 22/6, 13/6c. Pop. 4,849.
Map Square 28.

Vict.	Lon. B.	Arr. at S'wick.
AM —	5.18	7.52
6.37	6.40	8.44
7.23	7.25	10. 6
9. 0	—	10.53
—	9. 6	11.13
11.40	10.35	1. 8
—	11.40d	1.18
11.55	11.50	2.13
PM12.45	—	2.33
—	1.20d	3. 2
1.55	—	3.27
—	2. 5	3.56
2. 0d	—	4.13
2. 0e	—	4.32
—	2. 8d	5. 2
3.10l	—	4.32
3.40	—	5.25
4.30	4. 0	6. 3
—	5. 5d	6.55
—	5. 8e	6.27
5.45	5.55e	7.22
—	6. 0	7.44
—	6. 8	8.37
6.40	—	8.12
7.15	7.20	9. 3
8.35	—	10.12
9. 3d	9.12d	11.12
9. 3e	9.12e	11.22
10. 0	—	11.58

SOUTHWICK—*contd.*

Sunday Trains.

Leave Vict.	Lon. B.	Arr. at S'wick.
AM 6.55	7. 2	9.43
8.50	8.55	11.23
9.45k	—	11.23
11. 5	—	12.43
PM12.15	—	1.58
1.10	—	2.52
1.14	1.10	3.38
4.55k	—	6.22
5.50	6. 0	8.53
5.50p	—	8.22
8. 0	8. 0	10.25
9.25	9.10	11.21

Trains from Southwick.

Leave S'wick.	Lon. B.	Arrive at Vict.
AM 5.55	8.15	8.24
6.33	8.19	—
7. 1	8.38	—
7.41	9.25	9.15
8.25	9.50	—
8.32e	9.54	10.24
8.47d	10.33	—
8.57e	10.33	—
9.25	11.10	10.55
10.15	12.19	12.17
10.48	1.42	—
11.53	—	1.20
PM12.44l	—	2.20
12.58e	2.23	—
2.28	—	4.17
2.51d	4.58	4.45
2.51	—	4.50
3.25	5.54	5.55
4.35	6.36	6.34
5.24l	—	6.45
5.38	7.42	7.30
7. 1	—	8.48
7.21	10.25	10.17
7.50d	10. 0	9.45
8.23	10.58	—
9.30	—	11.17
10.44	12.59	1. 0

Sunday Trains.

AM 7.42	10.45	—
9. 9	11.15	10.50
10.50	—	1. 0
PM12. 9	—	1.35
2.45	5. 3	5.11
4.35p	—	6. 0
5. 5	7.56	7. 0
5.48	—	7.28
7. 2	9.17	9.13
9.15	—	10.55
9.18	11.34	11.42
10.19	12.27	—

d Saturdays only.
e Saturdays excepted.
k Third Class Pullman Cars only.
l First and Third Class Pullman Cars only.
p First-Class Pullman Cars only.

SOUTH WILLINGHAM (Lincoln), 139¾ miles.

Fares. 29/0a, 17/5c. R. T., double fare. Departures *from* London as for Wragby. Departures *for* London about 4 times daily. Pop. 252.
Map Square 13.

SOUTH WITHAM (Lincoln), from *St. Pancras,* 108½ miles.

Fares, 21/11a, 13/2c. R. T., double fare. Departures *from* London as for Bourne. Departures *for* London about 4 times daily. Pop. 410.
Map Square 18.

SOUTHWOLD (Suffolk)

from *Liverpool Street,* 109½ miles. Fares, 23/1a, 13/10c. R. T. for two months, 46/2a, 27/8c. Pop. 3,376.
Map Square 19.

L'pl. St.	S'wold	S'wold	L'pl. St.
AM 5. 0	9.21	AM 7.30r	11.22
10. 0	1.41	9.45	1.20
PM 1. 0	4.26	12. 0	3.42
3.18r	7.18	PM 2.20	5.55
4.55r	8.53	5.23r	9.22

Sunday Trains.

PM 4.40	8.41	PM 5.19r	9.10

r Restaurant Car.

SOWERBY BRIDGE

(Yorks) from *King's Cross, via* Horbury, 194½ miles. Fares, 40/2*a*, 24/1*c*. R. T. for two months, 80/4*a*. Pop. 11,452.

Map Square 12.

King's+	Sow. Br.	Sow. Br.	King's+
AM 4.45	11.25	AM 5.50	11.30
7.15*r*	12.48	8. 0	1. 5
10.10*r*	3.17	9.20*r*	1.55
PM 1.30*r*	6.37	10. 8	3.50
1.50*r*	8. 8	11. 3*r*	4.45
5.45*r*	11.11	11.55	5. 0
10.45*e*	8.55	PM 2.23*r*	7.10
—	—	4.41*r*	9.25
—	—	9.50*e*	3.25

Sunday Trains.

12. 0*hn*	7. 4	AM 9.50*r*	3.45
—	—	11.56*r*	5.55
—	—	PM 3.15*h*	10.20
—	—	—	—

e Saturdays excepted.
h Passengers cross Wakefield at own expense.
n Noon.
r Restaurant Car.

SPALDING (Lincoln) from

King's Cross, 93 miles. Fares, 19/4*a*, 11/7*c*. R. T., double fare. Pop. 10,702.

Map Square 18.

King's +	Spald.	Spald.	King's +
AM 4.45	7.16	AM 8.11	10.40
5. 5	8.26	8.30*v*	12.25
7.15*lr*	9.55	10.56	1. 5
7.15*rs*	10. 3	PM12.25	3.50
8.45	11.20	2.11*r*	4.30
11.30	2.42	2.50*slr*	5. 0
PM 1.50*dr*	3.57	3. 0*v*	6.25
3. 0	5.11	4. 5*v*	7.10
4. 0*r*	6.12	5.48	9. 0
5.45*r*	7.55	7.18*r*	9.25
10.45*e*	3.33	9.56	3.25
—	—	—	—
—	—	—	—

Sunday Trains.

12. 0*nr*	2.34	PM12.21	3.45
PM10.45	3.33	7.41	10.20
—	—	—	—

d Saturdays only.
e Saturdays excepted.
l Wednesdays only.
n Noon.
r Restaurant Car.
s Tuesdays only.
sl Tuesdays and Wednesdays only.
v Via Essendine and Bourne.

ANOTHER ROUTE from

Liverpool Street, 105¾ miles. Fares as above.

L'pl. St.	Spald.	Spald.	L'pl. St.
AM 5.50	10.40	AM 8.55	12.40
10. 5	1.32	11.31*lr*	4. 2*h*
11.50	4. 3	11.31	5. 9
PM 2.34	7.15	PM 1. 8	5.17
4.45	9. 9	2.45	6.10
—	—	6.43	10.30
—	—	—	—

Sunday Trains.

AM 9.25	12.29	PM 4.32	7.40

h Arrives at St. Pancras Station.
l Commencing July 23.
r Restaurant Car.

White Hart Hotel. Telephone 71. Central Heating. Electric Light. Garage and Stabling. Billiards and Stock rooms. TRUST HOUSES, Ltd.

SPARKFORD (Somerset)

from *Paddington*, 120½ miles. Fares, 25/0*a*, 15/0*c*. R. T. for two months, 50/0*a*. Departures *from* London as for Castle Cary. Departures *for* London about 4 times daily. Pop. 220.

Map Square 22.

SPARROWLEE (Stafford),

163¾ miles. No through fares. Departures *from* London as for Leek. Departures *for* London about 4 times daily.

Map Square 12.

SPEAN BRIDGE (Inverness),

516¼ miles. Fares, 102/8*a*, 61/7*c*. R. T. for two months, 205/4*a*, 123/2*c*. Departures *from* London as for Fort William. Departures *for* London about twice daily. Pop. 92.

Map Square 37.

SPEECH HOUSE

ROAD (Glos'ter), 140½ miles. Fares, 29/2*a*, 17/6*c*. R. T. for two months, 58/4*a*, 35/0*c*. Departures *from* London as for Lydney. Departures *for* London about 4 times daily.

Map Square 22.

SPEEN (Berks) from

Paddington, 54¾ miles. Fares, 11/4*a*, 6/10*c*. R. T. for two months, 22/8*a*, 13/8*c*. Departures *from* London as for Lambourn. Departures *for* London about 5 times daily. Pop. 1,125.

Map Square 23.

SPEETON (Yorks), 223¼

miles. No through fares. Departures *from* London as for Bridlington. Departures *for* London about 4 times daily. Pop. 150.

Map Square 8.

SPEKE (Lancs), 193¼ miles.

Fares, 40/3*a*, 24/2*c*. R. T. for two months, 80/6*a*. Departures *from* London as for Runcorn. Departures *for* London about 4 times daily. Pop. 449.

Map Square 12.

SPENNITHORNE

(Yorks), 233¾ miles. Fares, 48/9*a*, 29/3*c*. R. T., double fare. Departures *from* London as for Leyburn. Departures *for* London about 6 times daily. Pop. 174.

Map Square 7.

SPENNYMOOR (Durham),

248¾ miles. Fares, 51/11*a*, 31/2*c*. R. T., double fare. Departures *from* London as for Ferryhill. Departures *for* London about 6 times daily. Pop. 18,243.

Map Square 7.

SPETISBURY (Dorset),

20½ miles. Fares, 25/0*a*, 15/0*c*. R. T. for two months, 50/0*a*. Departures *from* London as for Wimborne or Broadstone. Departures *for* London about 5 times daily. Pop. 441.

Map Square 27.

SPEY BAY (Elgin), 581½

miles. Fares, 106/3*a*, 63/9*c*. R. T. for two months, 212/6*a*, 127/6*c*. Departures *from* London as for Huntly or Elgin (*via* Dunkeld). Departures *for* London about thrice daily.

Map Square 35.

SPILSBY (Lincoln), from

King's Cross, 126½ miles. Fares, 26/3*a*, 15/9*c*. R. T., double fare. Pop. 1,464.

Map Square 13.

King's +	Spilsby.	Spilsby.	King's+
AM 4.45	9. 1	AM 6.40	10.40
7.15*r*	11.30	9.50	1. 5
8.45	1.36	10.40	3.50
11.30	4.29	PM12.25	4.30
PM 4. 0*r*	7.34	3.30	9. 0
5.45*kr*	9.21	5.50*r*	9.25
10.45*e*	7.21	6.35	3.25
—	—	8.30*k*	3.25
—	—	—	—
—	—	—	—
—	—	—	—
—	—	—	—
—	—	—	—

No Sunday Trains.

e Saturdays excepted.
k Tuesdays, Thursdays, and Saturdays only.
r Restaurant Car.

SPINK HILL (Derby),

155¾ miles. Fares, 31/3*a*, 18/9*c*. R. T., double fare. Departures *from* London as for Edwinstowe. Departures *for* London about twice daily.

Map Square 13.

SPITAL (Cheshire), 190¼

miles. Fares, 39/9*a*, 23/10*c*. R. T. for two months, 79/6*a*. Departures *from* London as for Hooton. Departures *for* London about 8 times daily. Pop. 551.

Map Square 12.

SPOFFORTH (Yorks),

193¾ miles. Fares, 40/3*a*, 24/2*c*. R. T., double fare. Departures *from* London as for Wetherby. Departures *for* London about 8 times daily. Pop. 831.

Map Square 7.

SPONDON (Derby),

126 miles. Fares, 25/10*a*, 15/6*c*. R. T., double fare. Departures *from* London as for Trent. Departures *for* London about 8 times daily. Pop. 2,787.

Map Square 13.

SPON LANE (Stafford),

117¼ miles. Fares, 24/0*a*, 14/5*c*. R. T. for two months, 48/0*a*. Departures *from* London as for Smethwick. Departures *for* London about 6 times daily. Pop. 12,534.

SPOONER ROW (Norfolk),

111¼ miles. Fares, 22/9*a*, 13/8*c*. R. T. for two months, 45/6*a*, 27/4*c*. Departures *from* London as for Attleborough. Departures *for* London about 5 times daily.

Map Square 19.

IDRIS TONIC WATER.

SPRATTON (Northampton)

from *Euston*, 72½ miles. Fares, 14/7*a*, 8/9*c*. R. T. for two months, 29/2*a*. Departures *from* London as for Brixworth. Departures *for* London about 5 times daily. Pop. 718.

Map Square 18.

SPRINGFIELD (Fife),

434¼ miles. Fares, 88/2*a*, 52/11*c*. R. T. for two months, 176/4*a*, 105/10*c*. Departures *from* London as for Kirkcaldy. Departures *for* London about 3 times daily.

Map Square 41.

SPRINGSIDE (Ayr),

394¼ miles. Fares, 80/3*a*, 48/2*c*. R. T. for two months, 160/6*a*, 96/4*c*. Departures *from* London as for Irvine. Departures *for* London about 4 times daily.

Map Square 40.

SPRING VALE (Lancs),

206¼ miles. No through fares. Departures *from* London as for Bolton (*via* Manchester). Departures *for* London about 6 times daily.

Map Square 12.

SPROUSTON (Roxburgh),

348½ miles. No through fares. Departures *from* London as for Kelso. Departures *for* London about 4 times daily. Pop. 776.

Map Square 41.

STACKSTEADS (Lancs),

207¼ miles. Fares, 41/10*a*, 25/1*c*. R. T. for two months, 83/8*a*, 50/2*c*. Departures *from* London as for Bacup. Departures *for* London about 6 times daily.

Map Square 12.

STADDLETHORPE

(Yorks), 179¾ miles. Fares, 35/0*a*, 21/0*c*. R.T. for two months, 70/0*a*. Departures *from* London as for Goole. Departures *for* London about 6 times daily.

Map Square 13.

STAFFORD from *Euston*,

133½ miles. Fares, 27/9*a*, 16/8*c*. R. T. for two months, 55/6*a*. Pop. 28,632.

Map Square 17.

Euston	Staffrd.	Staffrd.	Euston
AM 2.35	5.20	AM 1.33	5. 0
5. 0	8.23	1.55*g*	5.40
6.45	10.22	5.32*r*	10. 0
8.45*r*	12.17	7.25	11. 0
10.40*r*	1. 6	9.39*er*	12. 5
12. 0*nr*	3.22	9.39*dr*	12.20
PM 2.50*t*	7. 5	9.46*e*	12.32
4. 5*t*	7.18	11.43*r*	2.20
4.45*r*	7.31	PM12.44*r*	3.10
5.20*dr*	9.57	1.42	5.35
6.30*er*	9.30	3.45*t*	6.15
9.20	12. 0	4.25*r*	8.10
11.50	4. 5	6. 8*r*	9.20
—	—	6.48*dr*	9.15
—	—	7.29*r*	10. 0
—	—	7.38*er*	10.10
—	—	—	—
—	—	—	—
—	—	—	—
—	—	—	—
—	—	—	—
—	—	—	—
—	—	—	—

STAFFORD—*continued.*

Sunday Trains.

Euston	Staffrd.	Staffrd.	Euston
AM 9.15	1.33	AM 1.33	5. 0
11.45*r*	2.26	1.55	5.45
PM12.10*r*	2.57	PM12.40	4. 0
3.50	8. 3	12.50	5. 5
9.15	12.50	6. 3*r*	8.55
11.50	4. 5	—	—

d Saturdays only.
e Saturdays excepted.
g Mondays excepted.
n Noon.
r Restaurant Car.
t Tea Car.

Station Hotel. Telephone 160. Close to Station. Comfortable headquarters. Excellent Restaurant. Electric Light. Billiards and Garage.
TRUST HOUSES, Ltd.

Swan Hotel. Oldest Established Family and Commercial. All modern conveniences. Stock Room. Garage. Tel. 26. Under new management.
A. H. TYACK, Proprietor.

STAINCLIFFE

(York), 212¼ miles. Fares, 37/9*a*, 22/8*c*. R. T., double fare. Departures *from* London as for Dewsbury. Departures *for* London about 6 times daily. Pop. 5,219.

STAINCROSS (Yorks),

173¼ miles. Fares, 36/1*a*, 21/8*c*. R. T., double fare. Departures *from* London as for Barnsley. Departures *for* London about 6 times daily.

STAINES (Middlesex)

from *Waterloo*, 19 miles. Fares, 3/4*a*, 2/0*c*. R. T. for eight days, 6/8*a*, 4/0*c*. Pop. 7,326.

Map Squares 23 *and* 73.

W'loo	Staines	Staines	W'loo
AM 5.10	6.13	AM 5.55	6.36
5.35	6.35	6.55	7.36
6.54	7.38	7.25	8. 6
7.24	8. 8	7.40	8.17
7.54	8.38	7.56	8.41
8.24	9. 9	8. 8	8.47
8.54	9.38	8.28	9. 6
9.24	10. 9	8.45	9.17
9.54	10.38	8.54	9.36
10.24	11. 8	9.25	10. 6
10.54	11.41	9.46	10.17
11.24	12. 8	10.25	11. 6
PM12.24	1. 8	10.42	11.17
12.48	1.19	11.16	11.57
12.54*d*	1.38	11.46	12.31
1.18*d*	1.49	PM12.16	12.57
1.24	2. 8	12.46	1.27
1.48	2.19	1.16	1.57
1.54*d*	2.38	1.46	2.27
2.18*d*	2.49	2.16	2.57
2.24	3. 8	2.46	3.27
2.48	3.19	3.16	3.57
3.24	4. 8	4.16	4.57
3.48*e*	4.19	4.46	5.27
3.48*d*	4.28	5.16	5.57
4.24	5. 8	5.46	6.27
4.48*d*	5.29	6.16	6.57
4.58*e*	5.38	6.46	7.27
5.18*e*	5.49	7.16	7.57
5.24	6. 8	7.46	8.27
5.48	6.19	8.16	8.57
5.54*e*	6.38	8.46	9.27
6.18*e*	6.49	9.55	10 37
6.24	7. 8	11.15*e*	12. 6
6.48	7.19	11.20*d*	12. 8
6.54*e*	7.38	—	—
7.24	8. 8	—	—
7.54	8.38	—	—
8.24	9. 8	—	—
9.24	10. 8	—	—
10.24	11. 8	—	—
11.44	12.27	—	—

STAINES—*continued.*

Sunday Trains.

W'loo	Staines	Staines	W'loo
AM 8.18	9. 4	AM 8.43	9.28
8.48	9.32	9.32	10.30
9.18	10. 6	10.58	11.43
10.18	11. 1	11.58	12.43
11.18	12. 1	PM12.58	1.43
PM12.18	1. 3	1.18	2. 3
1.18	2. 1	2.58	3.43
2.18	3. 4	4.47	5.28
3.18	4. 1	4.58	5.43
4.18	5. 2	5.58	6.43
5.18	6. 1	6.43	7.28
5.58	6.42	6.58	7.43
6.18	7. 1	7.58	8.43
7.18	8. 1	8.43	9.28
7.48	8.32	8.58	9.43
8.18	9. 1	9.34	10.18
8.58	9.41	9.48	10.28
9.18	10. 3	9 58	10.43
10.18	11. 1	10.58	11.51
—	—	—	—
—	—	—	—

d Saturdays only.
e Saturdays excepted.

ANOTHER ROUTE from

Paddington, 19½ miles. Fares, 3/4*a*, 2/0*c*. R. T. for eight days, 6/8*a*, 4/0*c*.

Pad.	Staines	Staines	Pad.
AM 6.35	7.38	AM 6.50	7.55
7.35	8.24	7.52	8.28
8. 5	9. 3	8.30*h*	9.24
9.20	10. 5	9.15	10. 6
9.55	10.35	10.40	11.18
10.55	11.50	11.12	11.55
PM12. 2*h*	12.55	PM12.15	1.11
12.35*e*	1.30	12.57	2. 2
12.42*d*	1.30	1.36	2.35
1.15*e*	2.17	2.43	3.40
1.50*d*	2.36	3.45	5.17
2. 5*d*	3. 0	4.40*d*	5.45
2.25	3.30	4.50*e*	5.52
2.33*d*	3.30	4.50	6. 3
3.45	4.24	5.45	6.52
4.50	5.33	6.58	7.52
5.45*e*	6.25	7.42	8.40
5.45*d*	6.31	8.35	9.33
7. 0	7.37	10. 5	11. 4
7.37	8.19	—	—
8.35	9.22	—	—
10. 5	10.42	—	—

Sunday Trains.

Pad.	Staines	Staines	Pad.
AM 9.25	10.21	AM 9.25	10.14
10.37	11.32	11.53	1. 5
11.35	12.45	PM 2. 3	2.58
PM12.55	1.53	2.40	3.42
1.45	2.37	3.50	4.53
2.35	3.20	5.35	6.23
3.35	4.35	6.10	7.10
4.45	6. 6	7.10	8.12
6. 5	7. 3	8.15	9.17
8.20	9. 3	9.22	10.22
9.25	10. 9	—	—

d Saturdays only
e Saturdays excepted.
h Departs from or arrives at Bishop's Road Station.

Salter's Steamers. Up stream, 12.5 p.m., 5.40 p.m ; down stream, 10.40 a.m., 4.10 p.m. Passengers ferry out from Pinchen's and Railway Bridge, 10 minutes from G.W.R. and L. & S.W.R. Stations respectively.
See advt. facing first page of train service.

For completion of Advertisements, see over.

STAINES—*continued.*

Bridge House Hotel. The Leading Hotel. Unrivalled position. Lawns to River. Launches, Boats. Garage. Telephone: No. 10 Staines.
Proprietress,
Mrs. G. A. MARSHALL.
See advt. p. **314.**

Pack Horse Hotel (Riverside). Refurnished and Redecorated. Spacious Lounge, Bowling Green, Tennis, Fishing, Garage. Cars for Hire. Five minutes Station. Telegrams, "Packhorse," Staines. Telephone 41.
T. S. HANSCOMB, Proprietor.

Angel Hotel. High Class. Excellent Cuisine. Stabling. Billiards. Large Tea Lawn. Garage. Telephone: 156 Staines.
ALFRED DE WINTER,
Proprietor.

John Tims and Sons, Boat Builders. Staines; and at "The Clappers" Boathouse, Reading. Skiffs, Punts, and Canoes for Sale or Hire. Boats housed, repaired, and varnished. Tents and tent-covered boats for camping. Good dressing-rooms. Ladies' Waiting Rooms. Telephone 93.

STAINFORTH (Yorks),

162¾ miles. Fares, 33/11*b*, 20/4*c*. R. T., double fare. Departures *from* London as for Doncaster. Departures *for* London about 4 times daily. Pop. 816.

Map Square 13.

STAINLAND (Yorks),

193¼ miles. Fares, 39/10*a*, 23/11*c*. R.T. for two months, 79/8*a*, 47/10*c*. Departures *from* London as for Brighouse. Departures *for* London about 6 times daily. Pop. 4,520.

Map Square 12.

STAINTON DALE

(Yorks), 237½ miles. Fares, 49/7*a*. 29/9*c*. R. T., double fare. Departures *from* London as for Ravenscar. Departures *for* London about 5 times daily. Pop. 281.

Map Square 8.

STAIRFOOT (Yorks),

169¾ miles. Fares, 35/3*a*, 21/2*c*. R. T., double fare. Departures *from* London as for Barnsley. Departures *for* London about 4 times daily.

Map Square 12.

STAITHES (Yorks), 255½

miles. Fares, 53/4*a*, 32/0*c*. R. T. for two months, 106/8*a*, 64/0*c*. Departures *from* London as for Sandsend. Departures *for* London about 5 times daily.

Map Square 8.

STALBRIDGE (Dorset),

116¼ miles. Fares, 24/2*a*, 14/6*c*. R. T. for two months, 48/4*a*. Departures *from* London as for Blandford (*via* Templecombe). Departures *for* London about 5 times daily. Pop. 1,383.

Map Square 22.

STALHAM (Norfolk)

from *King's Cross*, 168½ miles. Fares, 25/3*a*, 15/2*c*. R.T. for two months, 50/6*a*, 30/4*c*. Departures *from* London as for North Walsham. Departures *for* London about 3 times daily. Pop. 958.

Map Square 19.

STALLINGBORO (Lincoln),

159½ miles. Fares, 33/2*a*, 19/11*c*. R.T. for two months, 66/4*a*. Departures *from* London as for Grimsby or Brocklesby. Departures *for* London about 3 times daily. Pop. 469.

Map Square 13.

STALYBRIDGE (Cheshire)

from *Euston*, 185½ miles. Fares, 37/9*a*, 22/8*c*. R.T. for two months, 75/6*a*. Pop. 25,233.

Map Square 12.

Euston	S'bdge.	S'bdge.	Euston
AM 12.25	6.50	AM 6.20*dr*	12.20
2.35	9. 2	7.20*er*	12. 5
5. 0	10.55	7.55*r*	12.50
8.45*r*	12.57	8.57*r*	1.15
10.40*r*	2.59	9.28*r*	1.45
11.50*r*	4.37	10.30*r*	3.10
12. 0*nr*	5.39	PM 12.35*r*	6. 0
PM 1.30*r*	6.52	1.40*r*	6.15
2.50*t*	8. 1	2.28*r*	7.30
4. 5*r*	8.30	3.45*r*	8.10
4.45*r*	9.46	4.40*dr*	10. 0
6. 5*r*	10.15	4.40*er*	10.10
11.50*d*	7.58	10.15	5. 0
—	—	12. 0*m*	5.50
—	—	—	—
—	—	—	—
—	—	—	—
—	—	—	—
—	—	—	—

Sunday Trains.

PM 12.10*r*	5. 0	AM 8.50	4. 0
12.30*r*	6.48	PM 12.45*r*	5.45
—	—	2.18*r*	7.30
—	—	4. 7*r*	8.55
—	—	7.15	5. 0

d Saturdays only.
e Saturdays excepted.
m Midnight.
n Noon.
r Restaurant Car.

ANOTHER ROUTE from *Marylebone*, 203 miles. Fares as above.

M'bone	Stalybge.	Stalybge.	M'bone
AM 2.32	9.15	AM 8.10*r*	1.13
8.45*r*	1.48	9.25*r*	3. 0
10. 0*r*	3.41	PM 2.10*r*	6.38
PM 12.15*er*	5.30	4.10*r*	9.55
3.20*r*	8. 0	8.25	3.57
5. 0*dr*	10.28	—	—
10. 5*e*	6.40	—	—
—	—	—	—
—	—	—	—
—	—	—	—
—	—	—	—
—	—	—	—
—	—	—	—

No Sunday trains.

d Saturdays only.
e Saturdays excepted.
r Restaurant Car.

STAMFORD (Lincoln)

from *King's Cross*, 92¼ miles. Fares, 17/3*a*, 10/4*c*. R.T., double fare. Pop. 9,881.

Map Square 18.

King's +	Stamfd.	Stamfd.	King's +
AM 4.45	6.50	AM 8.35	10.40
5. 5	8.20	9.35	12.25
7.15*r*	10.27	PM 1. 5	3.50
8.45	11.20	3.32	6.25
11.30	2.25	4.50*r*	7.10
PM 1.50*lr*	4.15	6.25	9. 0
3. 0	5.30	7.25	3.25
4.15	7. 0	—	—
5.45*r*	7.55	—	—

No Sunday Trains.

l Tuesdays and Fridays only.
r Restaurant Car.

ANOTHER ROUTE from *St. Pancras*, 100½ miles. Fares as above.

St. Pan.	Stamfd.	Stamfd.	St. Pan.
AM 4.25	8.53	AM 8.20*r*	10.45
7.50	10.40	10.41*r*	1.20
8.25*r*	11.45	PM 12.33*r*	4.10
10.25*r*	2.30	4. 2*r*	7.55
PM 12.25*r*	5. 1	5.38	8.20
3.30*r*	6.31	8.45	4.20
4.30*r*	7.43	—	—
6.25*r*	10.40	—	—
—	—	—	—
—	—	—	—

Sunday Trains.

PM 3.15	9.46	AM 6.58	11.53
—	—	PM 5.14*r*	9.43
—	—	—	—
—	—	—	—
—	—	—	—

r Restaurant Car.

Stamford Hotel. Under New Management. Re-decorated throughout. Central heating. Every convenience for motorists. New Garage. Commercial room. Billiards. Telephone 301.

STAMFORD BRIDGE

(Yorks), 197¼ miles. Fares, 41/1*a*. 24/8*c*. R. T., double fare. Departures *from* London as for York. Departures *for* London about 4 times daily. Pop. 138.

Map Square 8.

STAMFORD BROOK

from *Mansion House*, 7½ miles. Also to and from *Ealing*, *Hounslow*, and *Richmond*. *See* p. 489.

STAMFORD HILL from

Liverpool Street, 5 miles. Fares, 0/7½*a*, 0/6*b*, 0/4½*c*. R.T. for two days, 1/2*a*, 0/10½*b*, 0/7*c*. Pop. 34,430. *See* pp. 534-536.

Map Square 52.

STANBRIDGEFORD

(Beds), from *Euston* 44½ miles. Fares, 7/11*a*, 4/9*c*. R.T. for two months, 15/10*a*, 9/6*c*. Departures *from* London as for Dunstable. Departures *for* London about 7 times daily.

Map Square 18.

STANDISH (Lancs), 197¼

miles. Fares, 41/1*a*, 24/8*c*. R.T. for two months, 82/2*a*. Departures *from* London as for Wigan. Departures *for* London about 5 times daily. Pop. 7,294.

Map Square 12.

STANDON (Herts) from

Liverpool Street, 29½ miles. Fares, 6/5*a*, 3/10*c*. R.T. for two months, 12/10*a*, 7/8*c*. Departures *from* London as for Buntingford. Departures *for* London about 9 times daily. Pop. 2,485.

Map Square 18.

STANDON BRIDGE

(Stafford), 143½ miles. Fares, 29/10*a*, 17/11*c*. R. T. for two months, 59/8*a*. Departures *from* London as for Norton Bridge. Departures *for* London about 5 times daily. Pop. (Standon) 438.

Map Square 12.

STANFORD-LE-HOPE

(Essex) from *Fenchurch Street*, 27½ miles. Fares, 4/0*a*, 2/5*c*. R. T. for two months, 8/0*a*, 4/10*c*. Pop. 3,379.

Map Square 24.

Fen. St.	S.-le-H.	S.-le-H.	Fen. St.
AM 5.37	7.14	AM 6. 2	7.22
6.52	8.16	7. 6	8.24
7.30	9. 2	7.31	8.48
9. 5	10.26	8.25	9.34
10.17	11.22	10. 9	11.20
11.13*d*	12.39	10.51	12.16
11.35	1. 0	PM12. 4*e*	1.22
11.42*e*	1. 0	12. 4*d*	1.27
PM 1.15*d*	2.30	1.14*d*	2.34
1.48*e*	3.13	2.47	4.10
2.15*d*	3.25	3.50	5.18
3.25	4.41	5. 8	6.33
4.16	5.49	5.55	7.24
5.32	6.36	7.51	9.15
5.55*e*	7.11	10. 5	11.23*h*
6.38	7.57	10. 5	11.40
7.41*e*	8.55	—	—
8.13	9.37	—	—
9.25	10.49	—	—
—	—	—	—
—	—	—	—

Sunday Trains.

AM 8.40	10.14	AM 8.50	10.18
11.10	12.36	11.35	1. 1
PM 2. 7	3.28	PM 2.40	4. 4
4.30	5.50	6.19	7.45
7.22	9.21	7.46	9.11*h*
8.45	10.10	8. 0	9.30
—	—	9.38	11. 0
—	—	—	—

d Saturdays only.
e Saturdays excepted.
h Arrives at Mark Lane Station.

STANHOE (Norfolk) from

Liverpool Street, 118 miles. Fares, 24/10*a*, 14/11*c*. R.T. for two months, 49/8*a*, 29/10*c*. Departures *from* London as for Burnham Market. Departures *for* London about 4 times daily. Pop. 367.

Map Square 14.

STANHOPE (Durham),

260½ miles. Fares, 54/2*a*, 32/6*c*. R. T., double fare. Departures *from* London as for Bishop Auckland. Departures *for* London about 6 times daily. Pop. 1,924.

Map Square 7.

STANLEY (Perth), 457

miles. Fares, 92/6*a*, 55/6*c*. R. T. for two months, 185/0*a*, 111/0*c*. Departures *from* London as for Perth. Departures *for* London about 3 times daily. Pop. 959.

Map Square 38.

STANLEY (Yorks), 180

miles. Fares, 37/4*a*, 22/5*c*. R. T., double fare. Departures *from* London as for Castleford. Departures *for* London about 8 times daily. Pop. 14,689.

STANMORE (Middlesex)

from *Euston* and *Broad Street*, 13½ miles. Fares from Euston, 2/6*a*, 1/6*a*. R. T. for two days, 4/8*a*, 2/7*c*. From Broad Street, 2/9*a*, 1/8*c*. R. T. for two days, 5/1½*a*, 2/11*c*. Pop. 3,864. *See* p. 500.

ANOTHER ROUTE (Bakerloo

Tube). Passengers change trains at Harrow and Wealdstone. *See* back of Map.

STANNER (Radnor), 164¼

miles. Fares, 33/6*a*, 20/1*c*. R. T. for two months, 67/0*a*. Departures *from* London as for Titley. Departures *for* London about 3 times daily.

Map Square 16.

STANNINGLEY (Yorks),

188½ miles. Fares, 39/2*a*, 23/6*c*. R. T., double fare. Departures *from* London as for Holbeck. Departures *for* London about 8 times daily. Pop. 3,056.

Map Square 12.

STANNINGTON (Northumberland),

281¾ miles. Fares, 59/5*a*, 35/8*c*. R. T., double fare. Departures *from* London as for Newcastle-on-Tyne. Departures *for* London about 5 times daily. Pop. 1,194.

Map Square 3.

STANSFIELD HALL

(Yorks), 203½ miles. No through fares. Departures *from* London as for Todmorden. Departures *for* London about 4 times daily.

STANSTED (Essex) from

Liverpool Street, 33½ miles. Fares, 7/1*a*, 4/3*c*. R. T. for two months, 14/2*a*. Pop. 2,344.

Map Square 19.

L'pl. St.	Stans'd.	Stans'd.	L'pl. St.
AM 5.50	7.12	AM 7.32	8.57
7.18	8.55	8.10	9.27
10. 5	11.14	8.46	9.46
PM12.29*d*	1.30	9.20	10.17
12.48*e*	2.22	10.22	11.27
1.19*d*	2.36	PM12.45	2. 7
2.48	4.13	2. 3*d*	3.18
4.15	5.20	3. 1*h*	5. 9
4.45	5.43	3.16*k*	5. 9
5.49*r*	6.50	4. 1*r*	5.17
6.30	7.26	4.51*r*	6.10
8.22*d*	9.25	6.30	7.58
8.22*e*	9.37	7.15*r*	8.22
10.12	11. 7	9.30	10.30
—	—	—	—
—	—	—	—

Sunday Trains.

AM 8.12	9.27	AM 9.55	11.27
PM 1.50	3.37	PM 6.23	7.26
9.12	10.47	—	—
—	—	—	—
—	—	—	—
—	—	—	—

d Saturdays only.
e Saturdays excepted.
h Commencing July 23.
k Ceases to run after July 21.
r Restaurant Car.

STANTON (Wilts), 79¼

miles. Fares, 16/11*a*, 10/2*c*. R. T. for two months, 33/10*a*, 20/4*c*. Departures *from* London as for Stratton. Departures *for* London about 6 times daily. Pop. 160.

Map Square 22.

STANTON GATE

(Notts) from *St. Pancras*, 124 miles. Fares, 25/3*a*, 15/2*c*. R. T., double fare. Departures *from* London as for Stapleford. Departures *for* London about 12 times daily.

STAPLE (Kent), 80¼ miles.

No through fares. Departures *from* London as for Wingham Colliery. Departures *for* London about 5 times daily. Pop. 447.

STAPLEFORD AND

SANDIACRE (Notts) from *St. Pancras*, 122½ miles. Fares 25/3*a*, 17/8*c*. R. T., double fare. Pop. 7,789.

Map Square 13.

St. Pan.	Stplefd	Stplefd.	St. Pan.
AM 2.25	7.56	AM 7.41*r*	10.45
4.25	8.56	8.10*r*	11.35
9. 0*r*	11.51	9.37*r*	1.20
10.25*r*	1.40	11.20*r*	4.10
PM12.25*r*	4.10	PM 1. 5*r*	4.20
1.50*er*	5.49	2.18*r*	5.30
1.50*dr*	6. 9	3.20*r*	7.15
3.30*r*	6.28	4.37	8.22
5. 0*r*	7.55	5.55*r*	9. 5
6.15*r*	8.47	9.48	4.20
12. 0*h*	10.14	*e* 10.17*d*	4.20
—	—	—	—
—	—	—	—
—	—	—	—
—	—	—	—

Sunday Trains.

PM 3.15	6.14	AM 7.13	11.53
—	—	11.20	5.27
—	—	PM 8.12	4.55
—	—	—	—
—	—	—	—
—	—	—	—

d Saturdays only.
e Saturdays excepted.
h Saturday midnight only.
r Restaurant Car

STAPLE HILL (Gloucester),

120¾ miles. No through fares. Departures *from* London as for Bristol. Departures *for* London about 4 times daily.

STAPLEHURST (Kent)

from *Charing Cross*, *Cannon Street*, and *London Bridge*, 42½ miles. Fares, 8/11*a*, 7/1*b*, 5/4*c*. R. T. for two months 17/10*a*, 14/2*b*. Pop. 1,897.

Map Square 24.

Char. +	Leave Can. St.	Lon. B.	Arr. at Stplhst.
AM —	5.20	5.25	7.31
—	6.45	6.50	8.39
9.25	—	9.33	10.51
—	11.56	12. 0	1.20
PM12.40*d*	—	12.47*d*	2. 4
3. 0	—	3. 8	4.27
3.50*d*	—	3.57*d*	5.53
—	4.36*e*	4.39*e*	5.53
5.24*d*	—	5.34*d*	6.53
6. 0*e*	—	6. 5*e*	7.16
7.30	—	7.26	9.21
9.30	—	9.36	10.53
—	—	—	—
—	—	—	—
—	—	—	—

STAPLEHURST—*contd.*

Sunday Trains.

Char. +	Leave Can.St.	Lon. B.	Arr. at Stplhst
AM 7.45	—	7.52	9. 9
PM 6.35	—	6.43	8.16
9.25	—	9.31	10.56
—	—	—	—
—	—	—	—

Trains from Staplehurst.

Leave Stplhst	Lon. B.	Arrive at Can. St.	Char. +
AM 7. 5	8.40	8.44	—
8.11	9.32	9.36	—
9. 8	10.28	10.32	—
10. 3	11.33	—	11.45
11.51	1.36	—	1.50
PM 2. 2	3.26	—	3.40
4.36*f*	5.50	—	6. 3
5. 7	7.25	7.30	—
6.58	8.54	9. 1	—
9.27	11.34	—	11.43
—	—	—	—
—	—	—	—
—	—	—	—

Sunday Trains.

AM 8.15	10. 5	—	10.15
PM 6.52	8.20	—	8.28
—	—	—	—
—	—	—	—

d Saturdays only.
e Saturdays excepted.
f Mondays only.

STAPLETON ROAD

(Gloucester) from *Paddington*, 116 miles. Fares, 24/7*a*, 14/9*c*. R. T. for two months, 49/2*a*. Departures *from* London as for Bristol. Departures *for* London about 6 times daily. Pop. 26,157.
Map Square 22.

STARBECK (Yorks),

200 miles. Fares, 41/3*a*, 24/9*c*. R. T., double fare. Departures *from* London as for York or Harrogate. Departures *for* London about 5 times daily. Pop. 217.
Map Square 7.

STARCROSS (Devon)

from *Paddington*, 182½ miles. Fares, 37/6*a*, 22/6*c*. R. T. for two months, 75/0*a*, 45/0*c*. Pop. 978.
Map Square 26.

Pad.	Starcrs.	Starcrs.	Pad.
AM 5.30	11.33	AM 9.14*r*	1.30
9.15*r*	1.26	PM12.56*r*	4.35
PM12. 5*r*	4.13	1.48*r*	6.50
2. 0*r*	6.31	4.40*r*	9. 0
3.30*r*	8. 6	6.31	2.45
4.15*r*	10. 0	10.42	7.10
12. 0*l*	7.14	—	—
12.30*h*	9.34	—	—
—	—	—	—
—	—	—	—
—	—	—	—

Sunday Trains.

AM10.30*r*	2.34	AM 8.52*r*	3.35
PM 2.40	7.48	11. 6*r*	4. 5
4.30*r*	9.16	PM12.16	7. 5
10. 0	7.14	3.45*r*	7.55
—	—	8.57	3.15

h Saturdays midnight only.
l Saturdays midnight excepted.
r Restaurant Car.

STAVELEY (Westmorland),

255¾ miles. Fares, 53/2*a*, 31/11*c*. R.T. for two months, 106/4*a*. Departures *from* London as for Kendal. Departures *for* London about 6 times daily. Pop. 271.
Map Square 7.

STAVELEY TOWN

(Derby), 152¾ miles. Fares 31/3*a*, 18/9*c*. R. T., double fare. Departures *from* London as for Chesterfield (Central). Departures *for* London about 6 times daily. Pop. 12,018.
Map Square 13.

STAVERTON (Devon),

205½ miles. Fares, 42/4*a*, 25/5*c*. R.T. for two months, 84/8*a*. Departures *from* London as for Ashburton. Departures *for* London about 6 times daily. Pop. 668.
Map Square 26.

STAWARD (Northumberland),

297¾ miles. No through fares. Departures *from* London as for Hexham. Departures *for* London about 3 times daily.
Map Square 3.

STECHFORD (Worcester)

from *Euston*, 109½ miles. Fares, 22/9*a*, 13/8*c*. R.T. for two months, 45/6*a*.
Map Square 17.

Euston	Stechfd.	Stechfd.	Euston
AM 2.30	6.49	AM 7.37*r*	10. 0
5. 0	7.50	7.43*r*	11. 0
6.45	9.48	8.52	11.55
9.15*r*	12.43	9. 4	12.40
10. 0*d*	12.57	10.34*r*	2.20
10. 0*e*	1. 4	PM 1.12*et*	4.35
11.30*r*	2.31	1.30*dt*	4.35
PM 1.15*r*	3.49	2.44*t*	5.35
2.20*t*	5. 5	4.14*t*	7.20
2.50*t*	5.57	5.51*r*	8.20
4.45*r*	7.26	7.12*dr*	10.45
5.50*r*	8.21	7.30*er*	10.45
7. 0*r*	9.25	10.54*e*	4. 0
*d*12.10*m*	10. 7	10.59*d*	5. 0
—	—	—	—
—	—	—	—
—	—	—	—
—	—	—	—

Sunday Trains.

AM 9.15	1.13	AM 8.49	12.25
PM 1. 0*r*	5.51	PM 1.15	5. 5
5.10*r*	7.54	5.22*r*	8.20
—	—	9.47	5. 0
—	—	—	—
—	—	—	—
—	—	—	—

d Saturdays only.
e Saturdays excepted.
m Midnight.
r Restaurant Car.
t Tea Car.

STEELE ROAD (Roxburgh),

328 miles. No through fares. Departures *from* London as for Carlisle. Departures *for* London about 3 times daily.
Map Square 44.

STEENS BRIDGE (Hereford),

144 miles. Fares, 28/7*a*, 17/2*c*. R.T. for two months, 57/2*a*, 34/4*c*. Departures *from* London as for Bromyard. Departures *for* London about 4 times daily.
Map Square 17.

STEER POINT (Devon)

from *Paddington*, 229 miles. Fares, 47/4*a*, 28/8*c*. R. T. for two months, 94/8*a*, 57/4*c*. Departures *from* London as for Yealmpton. Departures *for* London about 5 times daily.
Map Square 26

STEETON (Yorks) from

St. Pancras, 215 miles. Fares, 41/3*a*, 24/9*c*. R. T., double fare. Departures *from* London as for Keighley. Departures *for* London about 5 times daily. Pop. 2,307.
Map Square 7.

STEPFORD (Dumfries),

341 miles. No through fares. Departures *from* London as for Dumfries. Departures *for* London about twice daily.

STEPNEY from *Fenchurch*

Street, 1½ miles. Fares, 0/2½*a*. 0/2*b*, 0/1½. R. T. for two days, 0/5*a*, 0/4*b*, 0/3*c*. Pop. 249,657. *See* pp. 510, 524, 525, 528-534, 537-544.
Map Square 61.

STEPNEY GREEN from

Ealing, Hounslow, Richmond, and *Wimbledon*. *See* p. 497.
Map Square 61. *No.* 14.

STEPS ROAD (Lanark),

398¾ miles. No through fares. Departures *from* London as for Coatbridge. Departures *for* London about 5 times daily.
Map Square 40.

STEVENAGE (Herts) from

King's Cross, 28½ miles. Fares, 6/0*a*, 3/7*c*. R. T., double fare. Pop. 5,039.
Map Square 18.

King's +	Stvnage.	Stvnage.	King's +
AM 5. 5	5.56	AM 6.23	7.30
7. 0	8.28	7.43	8.41
8. 5	9.12	8.10	8.55
9.20*d*	10.15	8.46	9.34
10.12	11.15	9.24	10.22
PM12.40*d*	1.24	11. 8	12. 3
1. 8	2.17	PM 1. 8	2.22
1.55	2.47	3.20	4.23
2.30*d*	3.25	4.38	5.45
4.15	5.21	6. 2	7. 5
5.10	5.55	7.15	8. 5
5.50	6.44	9.12	10.20
6.30	7.22	10. 8	11. 0
7. 0	7.57	—	—
8.30	9.22	—	—
9.10	10. 9	—	—
10.55	11.47	—	—
11.45*h*	12.46	—	—
—	—	—	—
—	—	—	—
—	—	—	—
—	—	—	—
—	—	—	—
—	—	—	—

Sunday Trains.

AM 8.30	9.39	AM 8.30	9.53
10.30	11.24	PM 5.28	6.17
PM 7.10	8. 9	7. 0	8. 8
9.30	10.26	—	—
—	—	—	—
—	—	—	—
—	—	—	—

d Saturdays only.
h Wednesdays only.

STEVENSTON (Ayr),

402¼ miles. Fares, 81/11a, 49/2c. R. T. for two months, 163/10a, 98/4c. Departures *from* London as for Irvine. Departures *for* London about 4 times daily. Pop. 13,190.

Map Square 40.

STEVENTON (Berks)

from *Paddington*, 56½ miles. Fares, 11/10a, 7/1c. R.T. for two months, 23/8a. Pop. 811.

Map Square 23.

PAD.	STEVNTN.	STEVNTN.	PAD.
AM 5.30	7.51	AM 7.40	9.30
7.30	9.38	8.43r	10.15
9. 0	10.35	10.18	12. 0
10.45	12.35	PM12.33	2.35
PM 1.35r	3.28	2.51	5. 6
3.38	5.53	7. 3	9.15
6.55	8.28	8. 8	10.45
—	—	—	—
—	—	—	—
—	—	—	—
—	—	—	—
—	—	—	—
—	—	—	—

Sunday Trains.

AM10.35	12.16	PM 3.52	6. 0
PM 2. 0	5.43	—	—
—	—	—	—
—	—	—	—

r Restaurant Car.

STEWARTON (Ayr),

395¾ miles. Fares, 80/7a, 48/4c. R. T. for two months, 161/2a, 96/8c. Departures *from* London as for Kilmarnock. Departures *for* London about 4 times daily. Pop. 3,937.

Map Square 40.

STEYNING (Sussex) from

London Bridge, Victoria, and *Clapham Junction,* 52¾ miles. Fares, 11/1a, 6/8c. R.T. for two months, 22/2a, 13/4c. Departures *from* London as for Henfield. Departures *for* London about 9 times daily. Pop. 1,729.

Map Square 28.

STICKNEY (Lincoln) 127

miles. Fares, 25/10a, 15/6c. R.T. for two months, 51/8a, 31/0c. Departures *from* London as for Midville. Departures *for* London about 5 times daily. Pop. 596.

Map Square 13.

STILLINGTON(Durham),

240½ miles. No through fares. Departures *from* London as for Stockton-on-Tees. Departures *for* London about 5 times daily. Pop. 87.

Map Square 7.

STIRCHLEY (Salop), 155½

miles. Fares, 29/9a, 17/10c. R. T. for two months, 59/6a, 35/8c. Departures *from* London as for Wellington (Salop). Departures *for* London about 4 times daily. Pop. 177.

Map Square 17.

STIRLING from *Euston,*

416½ miles. Fares, 85/0a, 51/0c. R.T. for two months 170/0a, 102/0c. Pop. 21,345.

Map Square 40.

EUSTON	STIRLING	STIRLING	EUSTON
AM 5. 0	4.33	AM 9.57r	7.30
10. 0r	7. 5	PM 1.14r	10.45
PM 1.30r	11.45	4.22r	5. 0h
7.50er	4.47	10.10	7.40
11. 0d	8.45	10.54	8. 0
11.35e	8.23	—	—
—	—	—	—
—	—	—	—

Sunday Trains.

PM 7.50r	4.47	PM 4.47r	5. 0h
11.35	8.23	—	—
—	—	—	—
—	—	—	—
—	—	—	—

d Saturdays only.
e Saturdays excepted.
h A.M.
r Restaurant Car.

ANOTHER ROUTE from

King's Cross, 432 miles. Fares as above.

KING'S+	STIRLING	STIRLING	KING'S+
AM 4.45	5.23	AM 8.30r	6.15
10. 0r	8. 4	PM12.17r	10. 0
PM 7.45er	7.38	3.15	3.25
8.25e	7.45	5.50	6. 0
11.40e	9.40	7.45	6.50f
—	—	—	—
—	—	—	—
—	—	—	—

Sunday Trains.

PM 7.45r	7.38	PM 4.47	6. 0
8.25	7.45	—	—
11.40	9.40	—	—

e Saturdays excepted.
f Arrives 7.5 a.m. Sundays.
r Restaurant Car.

STIXWOULD (Lincoln)

from *King's Cross,* 125 miles. Fares, 26/0a, 15/7c. R. T., double fare. Departures *from* London as for Kirkstead. Departures *for* London about 4 times daily. Pop. 170.

Map Square 13.

STOBO (Peebles) from

Euston. 378½ miles. Fares, 76/11a, 46/2c. R. T. for two months, 153/10a, 92/4c. Departures *from* London as for Peebles. Departures *for* London about 4 times daily. Pop. 362.

Map Square 41.

STOBS (Roxburgh), 340½

miles. Fares, 69/4a, 41/7c. R. T. for two months, 138/8a, 83/2c. Departures *from* London as for Carlisle. Departures *for* London about twice daily.

Map Square 44.

STOCKBRIDGE (Hants)

from *Waterloo,* 71½ miles. Fares, 15/0a, 9/0c. R. T. for two months, 30/0a, 18/0c. Departures *from* London as for Longparish or Andover Junction. Departures *for* London about 6 times daily. Pop. 915.

Map Square 22.

STOCKCROSS (Berks)

from *Paddington,* 55¾ miles. Fares, 11/6a, 7/0c. R. T. for two months, 23/0a, 14/0c. Departures *from* London as for Lambourn. Departures *for* London about 5 times daily. Pop. 641.

Map Square 23.

STOCKINGFORD (Warwick), 113 miles. Fares, 20/3a, 12/0c. R.T., double fare. Departures *from* London as for Water Orton. Departures *for* London about 5 times daily. Pop. 9,709.

Map Square 17.

STOCKPORT (Cheshire)

from *Euston,* 177½ miles. Fares, 37/9a, 22/8c. R. T., double fare. Pop. 123,315.

Map Square 12.

EUSTON	ST'PORT	ST'PORT	EUSTON
AM12.25	4.15	AM12.16g	5.40
2.35	8. 7	7.36dr12.20
5. 0	9.48	8.10er12. 5
6.45	12.11	8.40r	12.50
8.45r	12.26	9.45r	1.15
10. 0r	1.50	10. 9r	1.45
10.40r	2. 9	10.25r	2.20
10.45r	3.11	10.50r	3.10
11.50r	3.26	PM12.15r	3.55
12. 0nr	5. 5	12.51dr	5.50
PM 1.30r	5.47	1.27er	6. 0
2.50t	6.31	1.43lr	6. 0
4. 5r	7.42	2.20r	6.15
4.45r	8.54	2.27r	6.25
6. 5r	9.35	3. 0r	7.30
8. 0e	1.15	4.20r	8.10
8.45d	1.15	4.50dr	9.15
9.30	2.56	5. 0er	9. 5
11. 0dr	3.26	5.41er10. 0
11.50d	5.41	6.15dr10. 0
—	—	6.15er10.10
—	—	10.45	5. 0
—	—	11.11d	5. 0

Sunday Trains.

AM 9.15	3.26	AM12.16	5.45
PM12.10r	4.26	P0.55	4. 0
12.30r	5.19	PM 1.10r	5.45
6. 0r	9.51	2.53r	7.30
7.50r	1. 3	4.30r	8.55
—	—	11.51	5. 0
—	—	—	—
—	—	—	—
—	—	—	—
—	—	—	—
—	—	—	—

d Saturdays only.
e Saturdays excepted.
g Mondays excepted.
n Noon.
r Restaurant Car.
t Tea Car.

ANOTHER ROUTE (Tiviot

Dale) from *St. Pancras,* 182 miles. Fares as above.

ST. PAN.	ST'PORT	ST'PORT.	ST.PAN.
AM 4.25	10.38	AM12.23g	6. 0
8.25r	1.26	6.32r	11.35
10.25r	3.42	8.58r	1.30
PM 1.25r	6.24	PM 1. 0r	5.45
4.25r	8.46	3.15r	8.35
12. 0	5.22	4.43r	10. 5
—	—	7. 8	4.20
—	—	—	—
—	—	—	—
—	—	—	—
—	—	—	—
—	—	—	—

STOCKPORT—contd.

Sunday Trains.

St. Pan.	St'port.	St'port.	St. Pan.
AM11.15r	3.58	AM12.23	6. 0
PM 3.15	8.17	PM12.18r	5. 2
6.15r	10.28	4.35r	9.52
11.55	5.22	11. 0	4.55
—	—	—	—
—	—	—	—
—	—	—	—

g Mondays excepted.
r Restaurant Car.

ANOTHER ROUTE (Tiviot
Dale) from *Marylebone*, 203¼ miles.
Fares as above.

M'bone.	St'port.	St'port.	M'bone.
AM 2.32	11.33	AM 6.39r	1.13
10. 0r	5.19	PM 1.27r	6.38
PM12.15r	6. 9	2.58r	8.55
3.20r	8.58	6.25	3.57
10. 0d	3.22	—	—
10. 5e	3.42	—	—
—	—	—	—

Sunday Trains.

AM11.15r	9. 4	PM 4.20r	10.24
—	—	—	—
—	—	—	—
—	—	—	—

d Saturdays only.
e Saturdays excepted.
r Restaurant Car.

STOCKSFIELD (North-
umberland), 279½ miles. Fares,
59/4*a*, 35/9*c*. R. T., double fare.
Departures *from* London as for
Newcastle-on-Tyne. Departures
for London about 6 times daily.
Map Square 3.

STOCKSMOOR (Yorks),
181¾ miles. Fares, 37/9*a*, 22/8*c*.
R. T., double fare. Departures
from London as for Penistone.
Departures *for* London about 8
times daily.
Map Square 12.

STOCKTON BROOK
(Stafford),151¾ miles. Fares,31/8*a*,
19/0*c*. R. T. for two months, 63/4*a*,
38/0*c*. Departures *from* London
as for Stoke-on-Trent. Departures
for London about 5 times daily.
Map Square 12.

STOCKTON-ON-
TEES (Durham) from *King's
Cross*, 235½ miles. Fares, 49/0*a*,
29/5*c*. R. T. double fare. Pop.
64,150.
Map Square 8.

King's +	S'kton.	S'kton.	King's +
AM 4.45	11.39	AM 5.57	1. 5
7.15r	2.26	7.59	1.15
10. 0r	3.21t	9.19gt	3.15
10.10r	4.28	9.58r	4.30
11.50r	5.37	PM 1. 2rt	6.15
PM 1.15r	7.17	3. 0r	9.25
1.50r	8. 1	4.15r	10. 0
5.35r	10.35	7.25e	3.25
11.25	5. 8	8. 8d	3.25
—	—	10.49e	5.40
—	—	10.49d	6. 0
—	—	—	—

STOCKTON-ON-
TEES—continued.

Sunday Trains.

King's +	S'kton.	S'kton.	King's +
AM 8.30	5. 7t	AM10. 3t	5.15
11.30r	8.59	PM 2.22t	8.15
PM11.25	6.28	9.47t	5.40
—	—	—	—
—	—	—	—
—	—	—	—

d Saturdays only.
e Saturdays excepted.
g 1st and 3rd Pullman Cars only.
r Restaurant Car.
t Thornaby Station.

STOCKWELL (City and
South London Tube). Pop. 32,841.
See back of Map.

STOGUMBER (Somerset).
154¾ miles. Fares, 32/4*a*, 19/5*c*.
R. T. for two months, 64/8*a*.
Departures *from* London as for
Bishop's Lydeard. Departures *for*
London about 4 times daily. Pop.
790.
Map Square 21.

STOKE (Suffolk) from
Liverpool Street, 60¾ miles. Fares,
12/9*a*, 7/8*c*. R. T. for two months,
25/6*a*. Departures *from* London as
for Clare. Departures *for* London
about 6 times daily. Pop. 538.
Map Square 19.

STOKE CANON (Devon).
170½ miles. Fares, *via* Taunton,
35/7*a*, 21/4*c*. R. T. for two months,
71/2*a*. *Via* Exeter, 36/6*a*, 21/11*c*.
R.T. for two months,73/0*a*, 43/10*c*.
Departures *from* London as for
Hele or Exeter (St. David's).
Departures *for* London about 4
times daily. Pop. 380.
Map Square 26.

STOKE EDITH (Here-
ford),139½ miles. Fares, 28/2*a*,16/11*c*.
R. T. for two months, 56/4*a*, 33/10*c*.
Departures *from* London as for
Malvern. Departures *for* London
about 5 times daily. Pop. 162.
Map Square 17.

STOKE FERRY (Norfolk)
from *Liverpool Street*, 91½ miles.
No through fares. Pop. 652.
Map Square 19.

L'p'l. St.	Stoke F.	Stoke F.	L'p'l. St.
AM 5.50	9.52	AM 8.25	11.27
8.30r	11.32	10.15	2. 7
11.50r	2.48	PM 1.34r	6.10
PM 2.34h	6.22	5.15r	8.22
2.34k	6.27	—	—
—	—	—	—
—	—	—	—
—	—	—	—
—	—	—	—
—	—	—	—

No Sunday Trains.

h Tuesdays excepted.
k Tuesdays only.
r Restaurant Car.

STOKE-GOLDING
(Leicester),101¾ miles. Fares,20/10*a*,
12/6*c*. R. T., double fare. Departures *from* London as for Shackerstone. Departures *for* London
about 6 times daily. Pop. 613.
Map Square 18.

STOKE MANDEVILLE
(Bucks) from *Marylebone*, 35½ miles.
Fares, 7/5*a*, 4/5*c*. R. T. for two
months, 14/10*a*, 8/10*c*. Pop. 309.
Map Square 23.

M'bone.	S.Mvle.	S.Mvle.	M'bone.
AM 6.45	7.51	AM 6.30	7.50
7.20	8.43	7.11	8.22
7.50	9.11	7.37e	8.42
8.50	10. 7	7.37d	8.46
10. 5	11.20	8.32	9.46
11.15	12.28	10. 4	11.36
PM 1. 5d	2.13	11.51	12.59
1.10e	2.21	PM12.48	2. 2
1.41d	2.54	1.43e	3.28
1.55e	3.33	2.51	3.59
2.15d	3.53	4.21e	6.22
2.45d	4.27	5.25d	7.15
3.25	4.39	6.49	8.11
5. 4	6.16	7.23	8.31
5.24e	6.31	9.15	10.41
6.25e	7.23	9.55	11. 0
6.25d	7.31	—	—
6.31e	7.46	—	—
6.55e	8.32	—	—
7.30	8.45	—	—
9. 0	10.12	—	—
10.30	11.42	—	—
11.35d	1. 5	—	—

Sunday Trains.

AM 9.30	10.43	AM 9. 0	10.13
11. 0	12.15	11.36	12.46
PM 1. 0	2.13	PM 1. 6	2.16
2.30	3.43	4.11	5.20
3.15	4.50	5.30	6.55
4.30	5.43	6.26	7.35
5.30	6.53	6.58	8.16
7.45	9.15	8.20	9.44
8.50	10.43	8.49	9.55
—	—	—	—
—	—	—	—
—	—	—	—

d Saturdays only.
e Saturdays excepted.

ANOTHER ROUTE from
Baker Street, 36 miles. Fares as
above.

Baker S.	S.Mvle.	S.Mvle.	Baker S.
AM 6. 5	7.20	AM 6.30	7.41
6.30	7.51	7.11	8.35
7. 3	8.43	7.27	8.42
7.50	9.11	7.37d	8.51
8.34	10. 7	7.37e	8.57
9.51	11.20	8.32	9.39
10.11d	11.27	9.11	10.25
10.18e	11.30	10. 4	11. 5
11. 0	12.28	11.51e	1.22
PM12. 8	1.27	11.51d	1.24
12.50e	2.21	PM12.48d	2.17
12.54d	2.13	12.48e	2.22
1.17d	2.35	1.43	2.58
1.21d	2.54	2.39d	3.55
2.17e	3.33	2.51	4.22
2.19d	3.35	4.21	5.41
3.10	4.39	5. 7e	6.33
3.18d	4.27	5.25d	6.39
4.10d	5.25	6.49	8. 8
4.16e	5.57	7.23	8.47
4.40d	6.16	8.16	9.37
4.42e	6.16	9.15d	10.28
5. 7e	6.30	9.13e	10.43
5.45e	6.54	9.55	11.18
5.46d	7. 0	10.30	11.40
5.49e	7.23	—	—
6.30	7.46	—	—
7.15e	8.32	—	—
7.15d	8.44	—	—
7.19e	8.44	—	—
8.40	10.13	—	—
10.10	11.42	—	—
11.50d	1. 2	—	—

STOKE MANDEVILLE
—continued.

Sunday Trains.

BAKER S.	S. M'VLE.	S. M'VLE.	BAKER S.
AM 8.47	10. 3	AM 8.22	9.48
9.10	10.43	9. 0	10.27
9.47	11. 4	10.34	11.48
10.33	11.51	11.36	1. 5
10.45	12.13	PM 1. 6	2.35
11.11	12.32	1.56	3. 9
12. 0	1.15	2.39	3.52
PM12.45	2.13	4.11	5.42
2. 0	3.15	4.41	5.54
2.15	3.43	5.30	6.45
3.35	4.50	6.26	7.57
4.15	5.43	6.58	8.12
5.37	6.53	7.36	8.51
7.59	9.15	7.59	9.12
9.29	10.43	8.20	9.31
—	—	8.49	10.20
—	—	10. 0	11.14

d Saturdays only.
e Saturdays excepted.

STOKE NEWINGTON
from Liverpool Street, 4¼ miles. Fares, 0/7½a, 0/6b, 0/4½c. R. T., 1/2a, 0/10½b, 0/7c. Pop. 52,172. See pp. 534-536.
Map Square 52.

STOKE - ON - TRENT
(Stafford) from Euston, 146 miles. Fares, 30/3a, 18/2c. R. T. for two months, 60/6a. Pop. 240,440.
Map Square 12.

EUSTON	STOKE	STOKE	EUSTON
AM 2.35	7.57	AM 1.20g	5.40
5. 0	9.27	6.38	11. 0
8.45r	11.32	8.46er	12. 5
10.40r	2.20	8.46dr	12.20
12. 0nr	4.18	9.45r	12.50
PM 2.50t	5.39	10.55r	2.20
4.45r	8. 0	11.48d	3.10
6.30er	10.15	PM 1.13r	3.55
6.55r	10.56	3.16r	6.15
d12.10m	11. 0	5.17	9.20
—	—	6.39r	10. 0
—	—	9.14	5. 0

Sunday Trains.

PM12.10r	4. 6	AM 1.20	5.45
3.50	10.16	11.35	4. 0
—	—	PM 5. 5r	8.55
—	—	8.35	5. 0

d Saturdays only.
e Saturdays excepted.
g Mondays excepted.
m Midnight.
n Noon.
r Restaurant Car
t Tea Car.

STOKE-ON-TRENT—
continued.

North Stafford Hotel.
Telephone 1561. Finest Hotel in Potteries. Central Heating. Electric Light.
TRUST HOUSES, Ltd.

STOKESLEY (Yorks), 236
miles. Fares, 49/2a, 29/6c. R. T., double fare. Departures from London as for Stockton-on-Tees, times daily. Pop. 1,624.
Map Square 8.

STOKE WORKS (Worcester), 129½ miles. Fares, 23/9a, 14/3c. R. T. for two months, 47/6a, 28/6c. Departures from London as for Bromsgrove or Droitwich. Departures for London about 5 times daily. Pop. (Stoke Prior) 3,042.
Map Square 17.

STONE (Stafford) from
Euston, 138¾ miles. Fares, 28/11a, 17/4c. R. T. for two months, 57/10a. Pop. 5,552.
Map Square 12.

EUSTON	STONE	STONE	EUSTON
AM 2.35	7.59	AM 7.10	11. 0
5. 0	9.11	9. 4er	12. 5
8.45r	11. 8	9. 4dr	12.20
10.40r	2. 1	11.13r	2.20
12. 0nr	4. 0	PM12. 0dr	3.10
PM 4. 5er	7.52	12.58t	5.35
4. 5dr	8. 1	2.54r	8.10
6.30er	9.57	5.37	9.20
6.55r	10.36	6.57r	10. 0
d12.10m	10.40	9.33	5. 0

Sunday Trains.

PM12.10r	3.46	AM11.53	4. 6
3.50	9.56	PM 5.23r	8.55
—	—	9. 0	5. 0

d Saturdays only.
e Saturdays excepted.
m Midnight.
n Noon.
r Restaurant Car.

STONEA (Cambs), 82 miles.
Fares, 15/10a, 9/6c. R. T., for two months, 31/8a, 19/0c. Departures from London as for March. Departures for London about 5 times daily.
Map Square 17.

STONEBRIDGE PARK
(Middlesex) from Euston or Broad Street, 7 miles. Fares from Euston, 1/4½a, 0/10c. R. T. for two days, 2/2½a, 1/5½c. From Broad Street, 1/4½a, 0/10c. R. T. for two days, 2/7½a, 1/7½c. Pop. 17,749. See pp. 496-499.

ANOTHER ROUTE (Bakerloo
Tube). See back of Map.

STONEHAVEN (Kincardine) from King's Cross, 506½ miles. Fares, 100/0a, 60/0c. R. T. for two months, 200/0a, 120/0c. Pop. 4,856.
Map Square 38.

KING'S+	S'HAVN.	S'HAVN.	KING'S+
AM 4.45	5. 3	AM 6.41r	6.30
10. 0r	9.43	10.17r	10. 0
PM 8.25er	7. 7	PM 1.17	3.25
11.25dr	10.48	4. 6	6. 0
11.25er	10.56	6.13	7. 5
—	—	8. 1	7.25

Sunday Trains.

PM 7.45	7. 7	PM 3.37	6. 0
11.25	10.56	—	—

d Saturdays only.
e Saturdays excepted.
r Restaurant Car.

ANOTHER ROUTE from
Euston, 523½ miles. Fares as above.

EUSTON	S'HAVN	S'HAVN.	EUSTON
AM 5. 0	8.39	AM 7.15	7.30l
10. 0r	9.51	10.30r	10.45l
PM 1.30r	2.35	PM12.55r	5. 0h
7.50er	7.15	8.14	5. 0h
11. 0d	11.24h	—	—
11.35e	11.13h	—	—

Sunday Trains.

PM 7.50r	7.15h	PM 1.35	5. 0
11.35	11.13h	—	—

d Saturdays only.
e Saturdays excepted.
h A.M. l P.M.
r Restaurant Car.

Bay Hotel.
High-class, every comfort. Sea view. Garage. Moderate Terms.
See advt. p. 315.

STONEHOUSE (Gloucester) from Paddington, 105 miles. Fares, 21/11a, 13/2c. R. T. for two months, 43/10a. Pop. 2,304.
Map Square 22.

PAD.	STONEHSE.	STONEHSE.	PAD.
AM 5.30	8.50	AM 7.55r	10.45
7.30	10.19	9.30	12.20
9. 0	11.52	11.30r	2.40
10.45	2.25	PM12.25	3.20
PM 1.10r	4.15	2.20	5. 0
3.15dt	5.55	5.30r	8.45
3.15t	6.11	7.21	10.25
6. 0r	8.35	9.40	3.30
—	—	11.16h	3.30

Sunday Trains.

PM12.30r	3.47	PM 7. 1	10. 0
2. 0	7.59	9.30	3.30

d Saturdays only.
h Thursdays and Saturdays only.
r Restaurant Car.
t Tea Car.

STONEHOUSE (Lanark),
395½ miles. Fares, 80/0a, 48/0c. R. T. for two months, 160/0a, 96/0c. Departures from London as for Hamilton. Departures for London about 4 times daily. Pop. 4,204.
Map Square 40.

STONEYWOOD (Aberdeen), 528 miles. No through fares. Departures *from* London as for Aberdeen. Departures *for* London about 4 times daily.

Map Square 35.

STORETON (Cheshire), 206¼ miles. No through fares. Departures *from* London as for Wrexham. Departures *for* London about 6 times daily. Pop. 280.

Map Square 11.

STORNOWAY(Cromarty). Fares, 141/7a, 82/9c. R. T. for two months, 276/10a, 161/4c. Departures *from* London as for Kyle of Lochalsh. Departures *for* London about once a day.

Map Square 30.

STOTTESDON (Salop), 146¼ miles. No through fares. Departures *from* London as for Cleobury Mortimer. Departures *for* London about twice daily. Pop. 1,006.

STOULTON (Worcester) from *Paddington*, 114¼ miles. Fares, 23/9a, 14/3c. R.T. for two months, 47/6a. Departures *from* London as for Pershore. Departures *for* London about 5 times daily. Pop. 329.

Map Square 17.

STOURBRIDGE (Worcester) from *Paddington, via* Birmingham, 124 miles. Fares, 25/3a, 15/2c. R.T. for two months, 50/6a. Pop. 18,023.

Map Square 17.

PAD.	S'BRIDGE.	S'BRIDGE.	PAD.
AM 6.30	11.30	AM 6.27r	10. 0
9.10r	12.13	8. 0r	11. 0
10.20d	1.19	9.33	12.25
10.40r	1.33	10.35r	1.25
PM12.50r	3.32	11. 8r	2. 5
1.30hr	4.50	PM12.45hr	4.15
2.10t	5.33	1.45r	5. 0
4.10t	7.16	2.30t	5.55
4.45ht	8.18	3.55t	6.40
6.10r	8.53	4.51r	8. 5
7.10r	10.17	6.28	10. 0
7.30l	12.10	10. 8	3.30
12.15k	6.37	—	—

No Sunday Trains.

d Saturdays only.
h Via Worcester.
k Saturdays midnight excepted.
l Thursdays and Saturdays only.
r Restaurant Car.
t Tea Car.

STOURBRIDGE JUNC. (Worcester) from *Paddington* (*via* Birmingham), 122¾ miles. Fares, 25/3a, 15/2c. R.T. for two months, 50/6a.

Map Square 17.

PAD.	STOUR.J.	STOUR. J.	PAD.
AM 6.30	11.18	AM 6.35r	10. 0
9.10r	12. 5	8. 5r	11. 0
10.20d	1.11	9.38	12.25
10.40dr	1.15	10.40r	1.25
10.40er	1.25	11.13r	2. 5
PM12.50r	3.25	PM12.52hr	4.15
1.30hr	4.42	1.50r	5. 0
2.10t	5.27	2.40et	5.55
4.10t	7. 8	2.45dt	5.55
4.45ht	8. 2	4. 1t	6.40
6.10r	8.42	5. 0r	8. 5
7.10r	10. 5	6.40	10. 0
7.30	12. 2	10.20	3.30
12.15k	6.26	—	—
12.15l	8.25	—	—

STOURBRIDGE JUNC. —continued.

Sunday Trains.

PAD.	STOUR. J.	STOUR.J.	PAD.
AM12.50r	3.40	AM 9.20r	1.40
PM 6. 0r	8.50	PM12.12	6.20
—	—	5.25r	9. 0
—	—	—	—
—	—	—	—

d Saturdays only.
e Saturdays excepted.
h Via Worcester.
k Saturdays midnight excepted.
l Saturdays midnight only.
r Restaurant Car.
t Tea Car.

STOURPORT(Worcester) from *Paddington*, 134½ miles. Fares, 25/10a, 15/6c. R. T. for two months, 51/8a, 31/0c. Departures *from* London as for Bewdley. Departures *for* London about 6 times daily. Pop. 4,778.

STOW (Midlothian), 370¾ miles. Fares, 75/7a, 45/4c. R.T. for two months, 151/2a, 90/8c. Departures *from* London as for Galashiels. Departures *for* London about 3 times daily. Pop. 1,325.

Map Square 41.

STOW (Norfolk) from *Liverpool Street*, 88½ miles. Fares, 18/7a, 11/2c. R.T. for two months, 37/2a. Departures *from* London as for Downham. Departures *for* London about 3 times daily. Pop. 1,347.

Map Square 12.

STOW BEDON (Norfolk) from *Liverpool Street*, 103½ miles. Fares, 21/3a, 12/9c. R.T. for two months, 42/6a. Departures *from* London as for Watton. Departures *for* London about 4 times daily. Pop. 302.

Map Square 19.

STOWMARKET (Suffolk) from *Liverpool Street*, 80½ miles. Fares, 16/11a, 10/2c. R.T. for two months, 33/10a. Pop. 4,245.

Map Square 19.

L'PL.ST.	STOWMKT.	STOWMKT.	L'PL.ST.
AM 5. 0	7.16	AM 8.10r	10.30
8.15r	10.25	8.36f	10.36
9.50r	11.39	9. 3r	11.22
10.12	12.36	10. 3	12.39
10.20	12.47	11.47r	2. 3
PM12.33r	2.50	PM12.42	3.36
1. 0	3. 2	2.39r	4.58
1.33d	4.49	3.26	5.55
3.10r	5. 3	4.28	6.32
3.26	6.43	5.14	7.51
5.18r	7.16	7.29r	9.22
5.42	8.42	7.40r	10. 0
7.45r	10.20	8.23	11.16
—	—	—	—

Sunday Trains.

AM 9.20r	11.58	AM 8.40	11.38
11.30r	2.52	PM 2.32	7.10
PM 4.40	6.53	7.18r	9.10
—	—	7.44	10.15

d Saturdays only.
f Mondays only.
r Restaurant Car.

STOW-ON-THE-WOLD (Gloucester) from *Paddington*, 89 miles. Fares, 18/6a, 11/1c. R.T. for two months, 37/0a. Pop. 1,204.

Map Square 17.

PAD.	STOW.	STOW.	PAD.
AM 5.30	8.49	AM 7.21	9.50
9.45	1.23	11.27	2.12
PM 1.30k	3.19	PM12.50hr	2.55
1.35r	5.14	4. 2	7.20
6. 5r	8.59	7.53	10.45
—	—	—	—
—	—	—	—

No Sunday Trains.

h Calls to pick up passengers. Notice to be given at station.
k Sets down passengers on notice to guard.
r Restaurant Car.

STOW PARK (Lincoln), 140½ miles. Fares, 29/0a, 17/5c. R. T., double fare. Departures *from* London as for Lincoln. Departures *for* London about 4 times daily. Pop. (Stow) 309.

Map Square 13.

STRACATHRO (Forfar), 499½ miles. Fares, 98/6a, 59/1c. R. T. for two months, 197/0a, 118/2c. Departures *from* London as for Brechin. Departures *for* London about 4 times daily. Pop. 444.

Map Square 38.

STRADBROKE (Suffolk), 98½ miles. Fares, 20/8a, 12/5c. R.T. for two months, 41/4a, 24/10c. Pop. 1,012.

Map Square 19.

L'POL.ST.	S'BROKE.	S'BROKE.	L'POL.ST.
AM 5. 0	10.32	AM 7.48h	11.22
10.12	1.53	8.23k	12.40
PM 3.10e	6.32	11.18	3.36
3.10d	6.57	PM 3.38	7.51
—	—	—	—
—	—	—	—
—	—	—	—

No Sunday Trains.

d Saturdays only.
e Saturdays excepted.
h Tuesdays excepted.
k Tuesdays only.

STRAND(Hampstead Tube)
See back of Map.

STRANRAER (Wigtown) from *Euston*, 405½ miles. Fares, 68/9a, 41/3c. R.T. for two months, 137/6a, 82/6c. Pop. 6,138.

Map Square 43.

EUSTON	STRANR.	STRANR.	EUSTON
AM 5. 0	5.43l	AM 7.35r	6.25
10. 0r	7.44k	PM12.15r	10. 0
PM 8. 0e	5.42k	3.40	5. 0h
11.45e	11.25h	9.42	7.15
—	—	—	—
—	—	—	—
—	—	—	—

Sunday Trains.

PM 7.50r	5.42k	—	—
8.30	6.10k	—	—
11.45	11.25h	—	—

e Saturdays excepted.
h A.M.
k Harbour Station.
l P.M.
r Restaurant Car.

STRANRAER—*continued.*

ANOTHER ROUTE from *St. Pancras,* 414 miles. Fares as above.

St. Pan.	Stranr.	Stranr.	St. Pan.
AM 4.25	5.43	AM 7.35*r*	6.35
9.50*r*	7.44*h*	9.30*r*	9.15
9.50*r*	8.20	PM 9.42*eh*	7.50
PM 12.15*r*	10.13*h*	9.42*dh*	8.57
11.45*e*	11.25	—	—
—	—	—	—
—	—	—	—
—	—	—	—
—	—	—	—

Sunday Trains.

PM 11.45	11.25	—	—
—	—	—	—
—	—	—	—
—	—	—	—

d Saturdays only.
e Saturdays excepted.
h Stranraer Harbour Station.
r Restaurant Car.

STRATA-FLORIDA

(Cardigan) from *Paddington,* 270½ miles. Fares, 48/9*a*, 29/3*c*. R.T. for two months, 97/6*a*. Departures *from* London as for Lampeter. Departures *for* London about 4 times daily. Pop. 498.

Map Square 16.

STRATFORD (Essex)

from *Liverpool Street,* 4 miles, or from *Fenchurch Street,* 4½ miles. Fares from Liverpool Street, 0/7½*a*, 0/6*b*, 0/4½*c*. R.T. for two days, 1/3*a*, 1/0*b*, 0/9*c*. Fares from Fenchurch Street, 0/7½*a*, 0/6*b*, 0/4½*c*. R.T. for two days, 1/2*a*, 0/10½*b*, 0/7*c*. Pop. 50,729. *See* pp. 528–534, 541–544.

Map Square 62.

STRATFORD MARKET,

West Ham (Essex) from *Fenchurch Street,* 4½ miles, or from *Liverpool Street,* 4¾ miles. Fares from Fenchurch Street, 0/7½*a*, 0/6*b*, 0/4½*c*. R.T. for two days, 1/2*a*, 0/10½*b*, 0/7*c*. From Liverpool Street, 0/7½*a*, 0/6*b*, 0/4½*c*. R. T. for two days, 1/3*a*, 1/0*b*, 0/9*c*. *See* pp. 528–534, 537–540.

Map Square 62.

STRATFORD-ON-AVON

(Warwick) from *Paddington,* 103 miles. Fares, 21/1*a*, 12/8*c*. R.T. for two months, 42/2*a*, 25/4*c*. Pop. 9,391.

Map Square 17.

Pad.	Stratfd.	Stratfd.	Pad.
6.30	10.25	AM 7. 5*r*	10. 0
AM 9.10	11.25	8.43*r*	11. 0
10.40	12.50	11.15*r*	1.25
PM 12.50*r*	3. 9	11.45*r*	2. 5
2.10	4.20	PM 2.26*r*	5. 0
4.10*t*	6.20	3.25*t*	5.55
6.10*r*	8.27	5.40*r*	8. 5
7.30	10.50	6.45	10. 0
12.15*k*	8.52	9.50	3.30
12.15*l*	11.50	—	—
—	—	—	—
—	—	—	—

Sunday Trains.

AM 10.35	3. 0	AM 10.20*r*	1.40
PM 6. 0*r*	8.57	PM 2. 5	6.20

k Saturdays midnight excepted.
l Saturdays, midnight only.
r Restaurant Car.
t Tea Car.

STRATFORD-ON-AVON—*continued.*

ANOTHER ROUTE from *Marylebone,* 93 miles. Fares as above.

M'bone	Stratfd.	Stratfd.	M'bone
AM 6.45	10.24	AM 7.55	10.36
PM 12.15*r*	3. 5	PM 12.20*r*	3. 0
6.20	8.40	6.10*r*	8.55
—	—	—	—
—	—	—	—
—	—	—	—
—	—	—	—

No Sunday Trains.

r Restaurant Car.

The Shakespeare. Under entirely new management. 14th century building, with every modern improvement. First-class Chef; American Bar; Garage. All trains met. Close River, Golf Links, Theatre. Telephone 188. Address Secretary. *See* advt. p. **315**.

Red Horse Hotel (known to Americans as "Washington Irving's Inn"). First-class Accommodation, Baths. Billiards, Bowling Green, Garage. Telephone 197.

Golden Lion Hotel. Known in Shakespeare's time as "Ye Peacocke Inne." Same management. terms, &c., as "Red Horse." Telephone 197.

STRATHAVEN (Lanark),

399 miles. Fares, 80/8*a*, 48/5*c*. R. T. for two months, 161/4*a*, 96/10*c*. Departures *from* London as for Hamilton. Departures *for* London about 4 times daily. Pop. 4,207.

Map Square 40.

STRATHBLANE (Stirling),

442¾ miles. No through fares. Departures *from* London as for Glasgow. Departures *for* London about 4 times daily. Pop. 1,275.

Map Square 40.

STRATHCARRON

(Ross), 632¼ miles. Fares, 115/8*a*, 69/5*c*. R. T. for two months, 231/4*a*, 138/10*c*. Departures *from* London as for Kyle of Lochalsh. Departures *for* London about 3 times daily.

Map Square 34.

STRATHMIGLO (Fife),

431½ miles. Fares, 88/9*a*, 53/3*c*. R.T. for two months, 177/6*a*, 106/6*c*. Departures *from* London as for Cupar. Departures *for* London about 3 times daily. Pop. 1,609.

Map Square 41

STRATHORD (Perth),

455 miles. Fares, 92/1*a* 55/3*c*. R.T. for two months, 184/2*a*, 110/6*c*. Departures *from* London as for Perth. Departures *for* London about 3 times daily.

Map Square 38.

STRATHPEFFER

(Ross) from *Euston,* 591 miles. Fares, 107/3*a*, 64/4*c*. R.T. for two months, 214/6*a*, 128/8*c*. Pop. 875.

Map Square 34.

Euston	S'peffer	S'peffer	Euston
PM 1.30*er*	8.40*h*	AM 9. 0*r*	5. 0*h*
7.40*er*	11.10	PM 1.10	7.40*h*
11.35*v*	4.25*l*	6.35*er*	7.30*l*
11.35*k*	6.25*l*	—	—

Sunday Trains.

PM 7.50*r*	11.10*h*	—	—
11.35	6.25*l*	—	—

e Saturdays excepted.
h A.M.
k Thursdays and Saturdays excepted.
l P.M.
r Restaurant Car.
v Thursday night.

ANOTHER ROUTE from *King's Cross,* 581¼ miles. Fares as above.

King's +	S'pefr.	S'pefr.	King's +
AM 11.50*er*	8.40*k*	AM 9. 0	3.25*k*
PM 7.45*er*	11.10*k*	PM 1.10	7. 5*k*
11.25*l*	4.25*h*	6.35*er*	6.30*h*
11.25*v*	6.25*h*	—	—

Sunday Trains.

PM 7.45*r*	11.10	—	—
11.25*e*	6.25*h*	—	—

e Saturdays excepted.
h P.M. *k* A.M.
l Thursdays only.
r Restaurant Car.
v Thursdays and Saturdays excepted.

Highland Hotel. Modern Comfort. Private Suites. Hard Tennis Courts. Own Grounds. Owned and Managed by London, Midland and Scottish Railway. *See* advt. p. **315**.

The Ben Wyvis. Principal Hotel in the Spa. *See* advt. p. **316**.

STRATHYRE (Perth),

441½ miles. Fares, 90/3*a*, 54/2*c*. R. T. for two months, 180/6*a*, 108/4*c*. Departures *from* London as for Callander. Departures *for* London about 4 times daily.

Map Square 37.

STRATTON (Wilts) from

Paddington, 77¾ miles. Fares, 16/6*a*, 9/11*c*. R.T. for two months, 33/0*a*. Pop. 3,689.

Map Square 22.

Pad.	Stratton	Stratton	Pad.
AM 1. 0*d*	5.51	AM 6.57*dr*	10.15
1. 0*l*	6.11	8.33	10.45
5.30	7.29	10.17*h*	12.20
7.30*h*	9.30	PM 1.47	5. 0
9. 0*d*	12.38	5.54*r*	8.35
10.45*e*	12.59	7.10	10.25
PM 3.15*t*	5. 8	9. 7	2.45
4.15*t*	6. 6	—	—
6. 0*r*	8. 3	—	—

Sunday Trains.

AM 1. 0	6.40	AM 7.50	3.35
PM 12.30*r*	6. 1	PM 7.20	10. 0

d Saturdays only.
e Saturdays excepted.
h Mondays and Saturdays only.
l Mondays and Saturdays excepted.
r Restaurant Car.
t Tea Car.

STRAVITHIE (Fife), 452¼

miles. Fares, 91/0*a*, 54/7*c*. R.T. for two months, 182/0*a*, 109/2*c*. Departures *from* London as for St. Andrews. Departures *for* London about 3 times daily.

Map Square 41.

STRAWBERRY HILL (Middlesex) from *Waterloo*, 12½ miles. Fares, *via* Richmond, 1/8*a*, 1/0*c*. R. T. for two days 3/4*a*, 2/0*c*. *Via* Kingston, 2/1*a*, 1/3*c*. R. T. for two days, 4/2*a*, 2/6*c*. *See* pp. 585, 587-591.
Map Square 75.

STREATHAM (London) from *London Bridge*, 7¾ miles. Fares, 1/3*a*, 0/9*c*. R. T. for two days, 2/6*a*, 1/5*c*. Pop 49,191. *See* pp. 565, 566, 570.
Map Square 78.

STREATHAM COMMON from *London Bridge* and *Victoria*, 12½ miles. Fares from London Bridge, 1/11*a*, 1/2*c*. R. T. for eight days, 3/10*a*, 2/0*c*. *Via* Tulse Hill, 1/6*a*, 0/10½*c*. R. T. for two days, 2/11*a*, 1/7*c*. From Victoria, 1/3*a*, 0/9*c*. R.T. for two days, 2/6*a*, 1/5*c*. *See* pp. 567. 570-577.
Map Square 78.

STREATHAM HILL from *London Bridge* and *Victoria*, 10½ miles. Fares, 1/6*a*, 0/10½*c*. R.T. for two days, 3/0*a*, 1/9*c*. *Via* Tulse Hill, 7¾ miles. Fares, 1/1*a*, 0/7½*c*. R. T. for two days, 2/2*a*, 1/2*c*. From Victoria, 0/10*a*, 0/6*c*. R. T. for two days, 1/8*a*, 0/10½*c*. *See* pp. 567, 568, 578, 579.
Map Square 78.

STREETLY (Warwick), 132 miles. Fares, 24/4*a*, 14/7*c*. R.T. for two months, 48/8*a*, 29/2*c*. Departures *from* London as for Water Orton. Departures *for* London about 8 times daily.
Map Square 17.

STRENSALL (Yorks), 194¾ miles. Fares, 40/7*a*, 24/4*c*. R. T., double fare. Departures *from* London as for York. Departures *for* London about 6 times daily. Pop. 710.
Map Square 8.

STRETFORD (Lancashire) from *Euston*, 187¾ miles. Fares, 39/5*a*, 23/8*c*. R.T. for two months, 78/10*a*, 47/4*c*. Departures *from* London as for Manchester. Departures *for* London about 9 times daily. Pop. 46,535.

STRETHAM (Cambs) from *Liverpool Street*, 71½ miles. Fares, 15/5*a*, 9/3*c*. R.T. for two months, 30/10*a*. Departures *from* London as for Haddenham (*via* Ely). Departures *for* London about 4 times daily. Pop. 1,170.
Map Square 19

STRETTON (Derby), 145½ miles. Fares, 30/2*a*, 18/1*c*. R. T. for two months, 60/4*a*, 36/2*c*. Departures *from* London as for Ambergate. Departures *for* London about 5 times daily. Pop. 640.
Map Square 12.

STRETTON (Stafford), 124¾ miles. Fares, 25/10*a*, 15/6*c*. R. T. for two months, 51/8*a*, 31/0*c*. Departures *from* London as for Burton-on-Trent. Departures *for* London about 5 times daily. Pop. 804.
Map Square 17.

STRETTON-ON-FOSSE (Warwick), 95¾ miles. Fares, 19/10*a*, 11/11*c*. R. T. for two months, 39/8*a*. Departures *from* London as for Shipston-on-Stour. Departures *for* London about twice daily. Pop. 286.
Map Square 17.

STRICHEN (Aberdeen), 560 miles. Fares, 107/9*a*, 64/8*c*. R. T. for two months, 215/6*a*, 129/4*c*. Departures *from* London as for Fraserburgh. Departures *for* London about 3 times daily. Pop. 2,243.
Map Square 35.

STRINES (Derby), 174¾ miles. Fares, 36/1*a*, 21/8*c*. R. T. double fare. Departures *from* London as for Bugsworth. Departures *for* London about 4 times daily.

STROME FERRY (Ross), 639½ miles. Fares, 117/4*a*, 70/5*c*. R. T. for two months, 234/8*a*, 140/10*c*. Departures *from* London as for Kyle of Lochalsh. Departures *for* London about 3 times daily.
Map Square 34.

STROOD (Kent) from *Charing Cross*, *Cannon Street*, and *London Bridge*, 31¾ miles. Fares, 6/8*a*, 5/4*b*, 4/0*c*. R. T. for two months, 13/4*a*, 10/8*b*. Pop. 10,283.
Map Square 24.

Leave Char. +	Leave Can. St.	Leave Lon. B.	Arr at Strood
AM —	—	3.22*h*	4.35
—	6.20	6.23	7.38
—	7.16	7.19	8.23
—	7.44	7.47	8.53
8.10	—	8.17	9.28
9.32	—	9.41	10.50
—	10.58	11. 1	12.14
—	11. 8*d*	11.11*d*	12.50
11.55	—	12. 2	1. 7
PM12.30*d*	—	12.37*d*	1.31
—	1. 2*d*	1. 5*d*	2.21
1.20*e*	—	1.27*e*	2.33
1.26*d*	—	1.34*d*	2.33
—	1.48*d*	1.51*d*	3. 8
2.10*d*	—	2.17*d*	3.33
—	2.40	2.43	3.43
2.45*e*	—	2.53*e*	4.12
3. 5*d*	—	3.12*d*	4.13
3.10*d*	—	3.17*d*	4.38
—	4.12*e*	4.15*e*	5. 1
4.25*d*	—	4.31*d*	5.45
—	4.36*e*	4.39*e*	5.44
4.35*d*	—	4.43*d*	6.20
—	5. 8*e*	5.11*e*	6.15
5.15*d*	—	5.22*d*	6.43
5.17*e*	—	5.25*e*	6.32
5.21*e*	—	5.29*e*	6.42
—	5.56*e*	5.59*e*	6.53
5.58*d*	—	6. 4*d*	7. 7
—	6.20*e*	6.23*e*	7.16
6.22*e*	—	6.29*e*	7.37
6.55*d*	—	7. 1*d*	8.19
—	7. 8*e*	7.11*e*	8.22
7.34	—	7.41	9. 1
—	7.44	7.47	9.22
—	9.35	9.38	10.46
10.20	—	10.27	11.32
11.24	—	—	12.27
11.33	—	—	12.45
—	—	—	—
—	—	—	—

Sunday Trains.

AM 7.30	—	7.37	9. 0
9.46	—	9.52	11.11
10.50	—	10.57	12.22
PM 1.15	—	1.22	2.48
3.15	—	3.22	4.41
4.50	—	4.57	6.16
7. 0	—	7. 7	8.13
8.42	—	8.49	9.55
10.30	—	10.38	12.13
—	—	—	—

STROOD—*continued.*

Trains from Strood.

Leave Strood	Arrive at Lon. B.	Arrive at Can St.	Arrive at Char. +
AM 4.25	5.47	5.51	—
5.34	7. 0	7. 4	—
6.39	8.13	8.17	—
7.13	8.31	8.35	—
7.29	8.34	—	8.41
7.41	8.51	8.55	—
8.37	9.34	—	9.43
8.59	9.54	—	10. 1
9.12	10.24	10.28l	—
9.49	10.38	—	10.45
10. 6	11.20	11.24	—
10.56	12. 3	—	12.14
11.55	12.57	—	1. 7
PM12.23*d*	1.31	1.37	—
12.23*e*	1.36	—	1.45
1.23*d*	2.44	—	2.54
*h*1.44*d*	3.21	3.26	—
1.46*e*	2.53	—	3. 4
2.16*e*	3.26	—	3.36
2.36*d*	3.58	—	4. 8
3.34*e*	4.48	4.52	—
3.37*d*	4.57	—	5. 7
4.29*e*	5.36	5.40	—
4.29*d*	5.36	—	5.45
5.16*e*	6.36	6.40	—
5.50	7.10	—	7 19
6.25	7.14	—	7.23
7. 7	8.15	8.20	—
7.48	9. 6	9.11	—
8.38	9.38	—	9.47
9.40	10.51	—	11. 0
11. 3	12.35	—	12.45
—	—	—	—
—	—	—	—

Sunday Trains.

AM 7.41	9. 0	—	9. 9
9. 2	10.16	—	10.24
11.42	1. 5	—	1.17
PM12.56	2.14	—	2.24
2.45	4. 4	—	4.15
4.47	5.55	—	6. 4
5.39	6.49	—	6.59
6.40	8. 1	—	8.10
8.14	9.46	—	9.55
9.57	11.15	—	11.23
10. 4	11.20	—	—
—	—	—	—
—	—	—	—

d Saturdays only.
e Saturdays excepted.
h Third Class only.

STROUD (Gloucester) from *Paddington*, 102 miles. Fares, 21/3*a*, 12/9*c*. R. T. for two months, 42/6*a*. Pop. 8,561.
Map Square 22.

Pad.	Stroud	Stroud	Pad.
AM 1. 0*g*	3.38	AM12.48	3.30
5.30	8.43	8. 5*r*	10.45
7.30	10.12	10. 5	12.20
9. 0	11.46	PM12.27*r*	2.40
10.45	1.34	12.34	3.20
PM 1.10*r*	4. 7	3. 7	5. 0
3.15*t*	5.39	6.20*r*	8.45
6. 0*r*	8.16	7.31	10.25
9.15	12. 7	—	—
—	—	—	—
—	—	—	—

Sunday Trains.

AM 1. 0	3.38	AM12.48	3.30
PM12.30*r*	3.39	PM 1.45	4. 5
2. 0	7.31	7.11	10. 0
9.15	12. 7	—	—
—	—	—	—

g Mondays excepted.
r Restaurant Car.
t Tea Car.

STROUD GREEN (Middlesex) from *King's Cross*, *Moorgate Street*, and *Broad Street*, 3¼ miles. Fares from King's Cross, 0/7½*b*, 0/6*b*, 0/4½*c*. R. T. for two days, 1/3*a*, 1/0*b*, 0/9*c*. From Moorgate Street and Broad Street, 0/9*a*, 0/7*b*, 0/5½*c*. R. T. for two days, 1/6*a*, 1/2*b*, 0/11*c*. Pop. 8,589. *See* pp. 518–522.
Map Square 51.

STRUAN (Perth), 489¼ miles. Fares, 99/5*a*, 59/8*c*. R. T. for two months, 198/10*a*, 119/4*c*. Departures *from* London as for Blair Atholl. Departures *for* London about 3 times daily.
Map Square 37.

STUBBINS (Lancs), 201¼ miles. Fares, 41/6*a*, 24/11*c*. R. T. for two months, 83/0*a*, 49/10*c*. Departures *from* London as for Bury. Departures *for* London about 4 times daily.
Map Square 12.

STUDLEY (Warwick), from *Euston* (*via* Birmingham), 131¾ miles. Fares, 23/7*a*, 14/2*c*. R. T. for two months, 47/2*a*, 28/4*c*. Pop. 3,019.
Map Square 17.

Euston	Studley	Studley	Euston
AM 2.35	7.34	AM 7.15*r*	10.40
5. 0	9.37	8.23	12.40
9.15*dr*	1.55	9.57*r*	1.25
9.15*er*	2.20	11.25*er*	3. 0
PM 1.15*r*	5.18	PM 12.59*dt*	5.35
2.20*t*	6. 2	3.11*r*	6.50
4.35*r*	8.22	4.31*r*	8.20
—	—	5.44*er*	10.20
—	—	5.44*dr*	10.45
—	—	8.43*e*	4. 0
—	—	9.13*d*	5. 0

Sunday Trains.

PM 1. 0	6.47	AM 10.39	5. 5
—	—	PM 8.14	5. 0
—	—	—	—
—	—	—	—

d Saturdays only.
e Saturdays excepted.
r Restaurant Car.
t Tea Car.

STURMER (Essex) from *Liverpool Street* and *St. Pancras*, 57¼ miles. Fares, 12/1*a*, 7/3*c*. R.T. for two months, 24/2*a*, 14/6*c*. Departures *from* London as for Clare. Departures *for* London about 4 times daily. Pop. 285.
Map Square 19.

STURMINSTER NEWTON (Dorset), 120½ miles. Fares, 25/0*a*, 15/0*c*. R. T. for two months, 50/0*a*. Departures *from* London as for Blandford (*via* Templecombe). Departures *for* London about 5 times daily. Pop. 1,787.
Map Square 27.

STURRY (Kent) from *Charing Cross*, *Cannon Street*, and *London Bridge*, 73½ miles. Fares, 13/6*a*, 10/9*b*, 8/1*c*. R. T. for two months, 27/0*a*, 21/6*b*. Pop. 1,386.
Map Square 24.

Char. +	Leave Can. St	Lon. B.	Arr. at Sturry
AM —	5.20	5.25	9. 2
9.15	—	9.23	11.30
11. 0	—	11. 7	1.32
PM 1. 0	—	—	2.58
3. 0	—	3. 8	5.14
4.30	—	4.37	6.40
5.24*d*	—	5.34*d*	8.26
6. 0*e*	—	6. 5*e*	8.26
7.18	—	7.26	10. 3

STURRY—*continued.*

Sunday Trains.

Char. +	Leave Can. St.	Lon. B.	Arr. at Sturry
AM 7.45	—	7.52	10.25
9.35*k*	—	—	11.58
PM 7.35	—	7.45	10. 0
—	—	—	—
—	—	—	—
—	—	—	—
—	—	—	—
—	—	—	—
—	—	—	—

Trains from Sturry.

Leave Sturry	Arrive at Lon. B.	Can. St.	Char. +
AM 6.49	9.32	9.36	—
7.35	10. 0	10. 4	—
*e*7.35*k*	—	—	10.16*k*
9.27	11.43	—	11.57
10.58	1.36	—	1.50
PM 12.33	3.26	—	3.40
3. 4*k*	—	—	5.42*k*
3. 4	5.50	—	6. 3
5. 0	7.25	7.30	7.49
7.37	10.22	—	10.35
10.42*y*	—	1.20	—
—	—	—	—
—	—	—	—
—	—	—	—
—	—	—	—
—	—	—	—
—	—	—	—
—	—	—	—
—	—	—	—

Sunday Trains.

AM 6.56	10. 5	—	10.15
PM 4.49	7. 9	—	7.17
8. 5	10.16	—	10.26
9.40*y*	—	1.23	—
—	—	—	—
—	—	—	—

d Saturdays only.
e Saturdays excepted.
k Departs from or arrives at Victoria (S.E. & C.R.).
y Third Class only.

STURTON (Notts), 144¾ miles. Fares, 30/0*a*, 18/0*c*. R. T., double fare. Departures *from* London as for Retford. Departures *for* London about 4 times daily. Pop. 497.
Map Square 13.

STYAL (Cheshire), 178¾ miles. Fares, 37/3*a*, 22/4*c*. R. T. for two months, 74/6*a*, 44/8*c*. Departures *from* London as for Wilmslow. Departures *for* London about 6 times daily. Pop. 1,309.

SUCKLEY (Worcester), 130½ miles. Fares, 25/10*a*, 15/6*c*. R. T. for two months, 51/8*a*, 31/0*c*. Departures *from* London as for Bromyard. Departures *for* London about 4 times daily.
Map Square 17.

SUDBURY (Derby), 131½ miles. Fares, 27/4*a*, 16/5*c*. R.T. for two months, 54/8*a*, 32/10*c*. Departures *from* London as for Tutbury. Departures *for* London about 5 times daily. Pop. 547.
Map Square 17.

SUDBURY (Suffolk) from *Liverpool Street*, 58½ miles. Fares, 12/4*a*, 7/5*c*. R. T for two months 24/8*a*. Pop. 7,046.
Map Square 19.

L'pl. St.	Sudbury	Sudbury	L'pl. St.
AM 6.50	9.39	AM 8.15	9.53
10. 0	11.47	10. 5	11.42
PM 12.36	2.21	PM 12. 4*h*	2. 3
2.15	4.20	2.37*h*	5. 5
4.58	6.41	4.26*h*	6.32
5.42	7.29	6.47	9.17
—	—	—	—
—	—	—	—
—	—	—	—
—	—	—	—
—	—	—	—
—	—	—	—

Sunday Trains.

AM 9.20	11.13	AM 9.20	12.40
PM 3.40	5.46	PM 4.40*h*	7.10
4.40*h*	8.33	6.38	8.58
—	—	—	—
—	—	—	—
—	—	—	—
—	—	—	—

h Via Colchester.

SUDBURY AND HARROW ROAD (Middlesex) from *Marylebone*, 7¾ miles. Fares, 1/7½*a*, 1/0*c*. R. T. for two days, 2/6*a*, 1/9*c*. *See* pp. 495, 496.
Map Square 49.

SUDBURY HILL (Middlesex) from *Mansion House*, 14½ miles. *See* p. 489.
Map Square 48.

SUDBURY TOWN from *Mansion House*, 13½ miles. *See* p. 489.
Map Square 48.

SULLY (Glamorgan), 160¼ miles. No through fares. Departures *from* London as for Penarth. Departures *for* London about 4 times daily.
Map Square 21.

SUMMER LANE (Yorks), 178 miles. Fares, 35/8*a*, 21/5*c*. R. T., double fare. Departures *from* London as for Barnsley (Court House). Departures *for* London about 4 times daily.
Map Square 12.

SUMMERSEAT (Lancs), 199 miles. Fares, 41/1*a*, 24/8*c*. R. T. for two months, 82/2*a*, 49/4*c*. D[illegible]rtures *from* London as for B[illegible]. Departures *for* London about 4 times daily.
Map Square 12.

SUMMERSTON (Dumbarton), 441¼ miles. No through fares. Departures *from* London as for Glasgow. Departures *for* London about 4 times daily.
Map Square 40.

SUNBURY (Middlesex) from *Waterloo*, 16¾ miles. Fares, 2/8*a*, 1/7*c*. R. T. for eight days, 5/3*a*, 3/2*c*. Pop. 5,350. *See* p. 585.
Map Square 23.

Magpie Hotel. Charming position on River. Excellent Cuisine. Boating. Fishing. Terms moderate. Telephone: 24 Sunbury. Proprietress—
Mrs. BEATRICE GRAHAM.

SUNDERLAND (Durham)

from *King's Cross*, 261¼ miles.
Fares, 54/7*a*, 32/9*c*. R. T. for two
months, 109/2*a*, 65/6*c*. Pop.
159,100.
Map Square 3.

King's + Sunder.		Sunder. King's +	
AM 4.45	11.39	AM 7. 5*r*	1.15
7.15*r*	3. 9	7.20*r*	1.30
9.50*r*	4.19	8.30*g*	3.15
11.15*g*	5.39	9.54*r*	4.30
11.50*r*	6. 5	11.35*r*	6.15
PM 1.15*r*	7.39	12. 0*r*	6.30
1.50*r*	8.27	PM 1.48*r*	9.25
5.35*r*	11.29	3.30*r*	10. 0
11.25*d*	6.11	7.30	3.25
11.40*e*	5.26	10.26*e*	5.40
—	—	10.26*d*	6. 0
—	—	10.35	7. 5

Sunday Trains.

AM 11.30*r*	6.52	AM 9.10	5.15
PM 11.40	5.26	PM 1.15*r*	8.15
—	—	9.40	5.40

d Saturdays only.
e Saturdays excepted.
g 1st and 3rd Class Pullman Cars
only.
r Restaurant Car

Grand Hotel. One minute
from Station. Good Stock Rooms.
Every comfort for families and
·Commercial gentlemen. Tariff
on application.

Park Hotel. Entirely new.
Three minutes station. Family,
Commercial. Quiet. Comfortable.
Moderate Charges. Telephone, 665.
JOSEPH ROBERTS, Proprietor.

SUNDRIDGE PARK

(Kent) from *Charing Cross, Cannon
Street*, and *London Bridge*, 11
miles. Fares from Charing Cross,
2/4*a*, 1/11*b*, 1/5*c*. R. T. for two
days, 4/8*a*, 3/10*b*, 2/10*c*. From
Cannon Street, 2/4*a*, 1/11*b*, 1/2*c*.
R. T. for two days, 4/8*a*, 3/10*b*,
2/4*c*. Pop. 4,604. *See* pp. 556, 557.
Map Square 80.

SUNILAWS (Berwick), 344
miles. Fares, 73/6*a*, 44/1*c*. R. T.,
double fare. Departures *from*
London as for Kelso. Departures
for London about 4 times daily.
Map Square 3.

SUNNINGDALE (Berks)

from *Waterloo*, 27 miles. Fares,
5/0*a*, 3/0*c*. R.T. for two months,
10/0*a*, 6/0*c*. Pop. 1,537.
Map Square 23.

W'loo Sunning.		Sunning.	W'loo.
AM 5.10	6.37	AM 7.21	8 J7
6.54	8. 1	7.48	8 17
7.54	9 5	8.24	9.17
8.54	10. 1	9. 1	9.47
9.54	11. 2	9.26	10.17
10.54	12. 5	10.23	11.17
PM 12.48	1.45	11.27	12.31
1.18*d*	2.12	PM 12.27	1.27
1.48	2.43	1.27	2.27
2.18*d*	3.14	2.27	3.27
2.48	3.43	4.27	5.27
3.48*e*	4.43	5.27	6.27
3.48*d*	4.51	6.27	7.27
4.48*e*	5.38	7.27	8.27
4.48*d*	5.51	8.27	9.27
5.18*e*	6.12	9.34	10.37
5.48	6.42	10.56*e*	12. 5
6.18*c*	7.12	10.56*d*	12. 8
6.48	7.42	—	—
7.54	9. 1	—	—
9.24	10.31	—	—
10.24	11.31	—	—

SUNNINGDALE—contd.

Sunday Trains.

W'loo Sunning.		Sunning.	W'loo
AM 8.18	9.31	AM 9.12	10.30
9.18	10.13	11.23	12.43
PM 12.18	1.28	PM 12.58	2. 3
2.18	3.29	4.29	5.28
4.18	5.25	6.23	7.28
5.58	7. 7	8.23	9.28
7.48	8.54	9.15	10.18
9.18	10.29	9.28	10.28

d Saturdays only.
e Saturdays excepted.

Sunningdale Hotel.
Old-established Family Hotel.
Close to Station and Golf Links.
Open to non-residents. Moderate
inclusive terms. Telephone—
Ascot, 208.
TOM A. BROOKS, Proprietor.

SURBITON (Surrey) from

Waterloo, 12 miles. Fares, 2/1*a*,
1/3*c*. R. T. for two days, 4/2*a*,
2/6*c*. Pop. 19,547. *See* pp. 591-594.
Map Square 23.

Southampton Hotel. Adjoining Station. Ten minutes
from River. All home comforts.
Moderate inclusive charges. Large
ornamental grounds. Garage.
Cars for hire. Telephone—Kingston, 1897. Proprietors,
SPIERS & POND, Ltd.

Maple House, Surbiton.
Private Residential Hotel. Near
Station and River. Excellent
Cuisine. Separate Tables. Terms
moderate. Telephone—Kingston
1558.

Fox and Hounds Hotel.
Family and Commercial. Facing
River. Fully Licensed. Lun-
cheons, Teas, Dinners. Garage.
Telephone, Kingston 827.
Proprietor, WALTER LE GROS.

House and Estate Agents,
Facing Surbiton Station. Lists
of Residences Furnished and Un-
furnished. Map and Illustrated
Guide Free. NIGHTINGALE,
PAGE & BENNETT.

SURFLEET (Lincoln) from

King's Cross, 97 miles. Fares,
20/2*a*, 12/1*c*. R. T., double fare.
Pop. 1,010.
Map Square 18.

King's+ Surflt.		Surflt. King's+	
AM 4.45	7.26	AM 7.58	10.40
5. 5	8.38	10.11	1. 5
7.15*lr*	10. 5	PM 12.13	3.50
8.45	11.38	2.41*lr*	5. 0
11.30	2.56	5.36	9. 0
PM 1.50*dr*	4.18	7.36	3.25
3. 0	5.29	—	—
5.45*r*	8. 6	—	—

Sunday Trains.

12. 0*nr*	2.44	PM 12.11*r*	3.45
—	—	7.31*r*	10.20

d Saturdays only.
l Wednesdays only.
n Noon.
r Restaurant Car.

SURREY DOCKS from

*Hammersmith, Paddington (Bis-
hop's Road), Baker Street, King's
Cross*, and *Liverpool Street* (Met.),
11½ miles. Fares from Hammersmith, 1/0*a*, 0/8*c*. R. T., 2/0*a*,
1/4*c*. From Paddington, 0/11*a*,
0/7*c*. R. T., 1/10*a*, 1/2*c*. From
Baker Street, 0/11*a*, 0/7*c*. R. T.,
1/10*a*, 1/2*c*. From King's Cross,
0/9*a*, 0/6*c*. R. T., 1/6*a*, 1/0*c*.
From Liverpool Street, 0/6*a*·0/4*c*.
R. T., 1/0*a*, 0/8*c*. *See* back of Map.
Map Square 70.

SUTTON(Cambridge)from

Liverpool Street and *St. Pancras*,
76 miles. Fares, 14/2*a*, 8/6*c*.
R. T. for two months, 28/4*a*. Departures *from* London as for Haddenham. Departures *for* London
about 4 times daily. Pop. 1,531.
Map Square 18.

SUTTON (Surrey) from

London Bridge, 13¼ miles. Fares,
2/4*a*, 1/5*c*. R. T. for two days,
4/4*a*, 2/10*c*. Pop. 21,063. *See* pp.
564-566.
Map Square 23.

ANOTHER ROUTE from

Victoria and *Clapham Junction*,
12 miles. Fares as above. *See*
pp. 571-574.

Cock Hotel. Family and
Commercial. Near Station.
Every modern convenience.
Billiards, Garage, Stabling. Ordin-
ary daily. Excellent cuisine.
Coffee, Smoking, Private Sitting-
rooms. Highly recommended.
Tel. 103, Sutton. Proprietor,
CHARLES H. BADCOCK.

SUTTON BINGHAM

(Somerset), 125½ miles. Fares, 26/1*a*,
15/8*c*. R. T. for two months,
52/2*a*, 31/4*c*. Departures *from* London as for Yeovil Junction. Departures *for* London about 5 times
daily. Pop. 59.
Map Square 27.

SUTTON BRIDGE (Lin-

coln), from *King's Cross*, 103¾
miles. Fares, 19/0*a*, 11/5*c*. R. T.
for two months, 38/0*a*. Pop. 2,342.
Map Square 18.

King's+ Sut.Bge.		Sut.Bge. King's+	
AM 4.45	7.38	AM 7.17	10.40
5. 5*e*	9.19	8.47	12.25
5. 5*d*	9.46	10.22	1. 5
7.15*r*	10.57	PM 12.22	3.50
8.45	12.21	1.57*r*	4.30
10.10*r*	1.57	2.41	6.25
11.30	4. 6	5.23	9. 0
PM 1.50*r*	4.23	6.31*r*	9.25
3. 0	5.37	—	—
5.45*r*	8.24	—	—

No Sunday Trains.

d Saturdays only.
e Saturdays excepted.
r Restaurant Car.

SUTTON COLDFIELD

(Warwick), 117¼ miles. Fares,
24/0*a*, 14/5*c*. R. T. for two
months, 48/0*a*. Departures *from*
London as for Birmingham (New
Street). Departures *for* London
about 8 times daily. Pop. 23,028.
Map Square 17.

SUTTON-IN-ASHFIELD

(Notts) from *King's Cross*, 141½ miles. Fares, 28/2*a*, 16/11*c*. R. T., double fare. Pop. 23,852.

Map Square 13.

King's +	Sutton	Sutton	King's +
AM 7.15*h*	12.43	AM 7.27*r*	11.30
10.10*r*	1.51	9.32*h*	1.30
11.30*h*	4.25	PM 1. 8	6.25
11.30	5.54	2.17*h*	6.30
PM 1.50*er*	7.25	4.12	9. 0
4. 0*d*	8.38	5.26*h*	9.25
5.35*er*	10. 3	6.41	3.25
5.45*dr*	10.40	—	—

No Sunday Trains.
d Saturdays only.
e Saturdays excepted.
h Wednesdays and Saturdays only.
r Restaurant Car.

ANOTHER ROUTE

from *Marylebone*, 140 miles. Fares as above.

M'bone.	Sutton	Sutton	M'bone.
AM 2.32	6.21	AM 7.12	10.36
8.45*r*	12.24	8. 7*r*	11.10
10. 0*dr*	1.45	9.41*r*	1.13
10. 0*r*	2.12	11.31*r*	3. 0
PM12.15*r*	4. 0	PM 3.35*r*	6.38
3.20*r*	6.16	4.33*r*	8.55
5. 0*r*	8. 3	5.54*r*	9.55
6.20*r*	9.24	10.18*e*	3.57
—	—	10.26*d*	3.57
—	—	—	—
—	—	—	—

Sunday Trains.

AM11.15*r*	3.40	PM 1.18*r*	5.40
PM 5.30*r*	8.58	6.53*r*	10.24

d Saturdays only.
e Saturdays excepted.
r Restaurant Car.

SUTTON, LITTLE

(Cheshire), 188¾ miles. Fares, 39/0*a*, 23/5*c*. R. T. for two months, 78/0*a*. Departures *from* London as for Hooton. Departures *for* London about 8 times daily. Pop. 1,327.

SUTTON-ON-HULL

(Yorks), 200 miles. Fares, 36/0*a*, 21/7*c*. R. T. for two months, 72/0*a*, 43/2*c*. Departures *from* London as for Hull (Paragon). Departures *for* London about 6 times daily. Pop. 1,825.

Map Square 13.

SUTTON-ON-SEA

(Lincoln) from *King's Cross*, 135 miles. Fares, 27/11*a*, 16/9*c*. R. T. for two months, 55/10*a*, 33/6*c*. Pop. (Sutton-le-Marsh) 835.

Map Square 14.

King's +	Sutton	Sutton	King's +
AM 4.45	9. 2	AM 9.33	1. 5
7.15*r*	11.25	PM12.12*r*	4.30
8.45	1.23	3.17	9. 0
11.30	4.59	4.27*r*	9.25
PM 4. 0*r*	7.33	7.35	3.25
10.45*e*	8.17	—	—
—	—	—	—
—	—	—	—

Sunday Trains.

PM10.45	8.17	—	—
—	—	—	—

e Saturdays excepted.
r Restaurant Car.

The Grange and Links Hotel. Pleasantly situated. Near Sea and Golf Links. Tennis Court. Garage. Under personal supervision of Proprietor.
A. POWELL.

SUTTON PARK

(Stafford) from *St. Pancras*. 129½ miles. Fares, 24/0*a*, 14/5*c*. R. T. for two months, 48/0*a*, 28/10*c*. Departures *from* London as for Water Orton. Departures *for* London about 8 times daily.

Map Square 17.

SUTTON SCOTNEY

(Hants), from *Paddington*, 72½ miles. Fares, 12/8*a*, 7/7*c*. R. T. for two months, 25/4*a*, 15/2*c*. Departures *from* London as for Whitchurch (Hants). Departures *for* London about 7 times daily.

Map Square 23.

SUTTON WEAVER

(Cheshire), 177½ miles. Fares, 36/11*a*, 22/2*c*. R. T. for two months, 73/10*a*. Departures *from* London as for Acton Bridge. Departures *for* London about 5 times daily. Pop. 409.

SWADLINCOTE

(Derby) from *St. Pancras*, 126 miles. Fares, 25/0*a*, 15/0*c*. R. T., double fare. Pop. 4,107.

Map Square 17.

St. Pan.	Swadcte.	Swadcte.	St. Pan.
AM 2.25	8.36	AM 6.59*r*	11. 0
10.25*r*	1.50	11.15	3.25
—	—	PM 5.25*r*	9.15
—	—	—	—
—	—	—	—
—	—	—	—
—	—	—	—

No Sunday Trains.
r Restaurant Car.

SWAFFHAM

(Norfolk) from *Liverpool Street, via* Thetford, 116¼ miles. Fares, 23/1*a*, 13/10*c*. R. T. for two months, 46/2*a*. Pop. 2,913.

Map Square 19.

L'pool St.	Sw'f'm.	Sw'f'm.	L'pool St.
AM 5. 5	9.34	AM 7.30	11.27
8.30*r*	12.33	10. 5*r*	2.21
11.50*r*	3.48	PM 1.14*hr*	5.17
PM 2.34*k*	6.25	1.22*kr*	5.17
2.34*h*	6.30	4.10*r*	8.22
5.49*r*	9.41	7.20	2.50
—	—	—	—
—	—	—	—
—	—	—	—

No Sunday Trains.
h Wednesdays only.
k Wednesdays excepted.
r Restaurant Car.

ANOTHER ROUTE

from *Liverpool Street, via* King's Lynn, 110¾ miles. Fares as above.

L'pool St.	Sw'f'm.	Sw'f'm.	L'pool St.
AM 5.50*d*	10.49	AM 7.51	11.27
8.30*r*	1. 5	9.41	2. 7
11.50*r*	3.42	PM12.1*lr*	4. 2*k*
PM 2.34	6. 4	2.25*r*	6.10
5.49*r*	9.27	4.46*r*	8.22
—	—	5.19*d*	10.30
—	—	8. 4	2.50
—	—	—	—
—	—	—	—

No Sunday Trains.
d Saturdays only.
k Arrives at St. Pancras Station.
l Commencing July 23.
r Restaurant Car.

SWAFFHAM PRIOR

(Cambs) from *Liverpool Street*, 63¾ miles. Fares, 13/2*a*, 7/11*c*. R. T. for two months, 26/4*a*. Departures *from* London as for Mildenhall. Departures *for* London about 5 times daily. Pop. 934.

Map Square 19.

SWAINSTHORPE

(Norfolk) from *Liverpool Street*, 109¾ miles. Fares, 23/1*a*, 13/10*c*. R. T. for two months, 46/2*a*. Departures *from* London as for Forncett. Departures *for* London about 6 times daily. Pop. 284.

Map Square 19.

SWALWELL

(Durham), 270¾ miles. Fares, 57/8*a*, 34/7*c*. R. T. for two months, 115/4*a*, 69/2*c*. Departures *from* London as for Durham or Bishop Auckland. Departures *for* London about 6 times daily. Pop. 3,889.

Map Square 3.

SWANAGE

(Dorset) from *Waterloo*, 131½ miles. Fares, 27/6*a*, 16/6*c*. R. T. for two months, 55/0*a*, 33/0*c*. Pop. 7,112.

Map Square 27.

W'loo.	Swanage	Swanage	W'loo.
AM 5.40	10.12	AM 7.40*s*	11. 0
8.30*s*	12.29	9.15*r*	12.50
10.30	1.50	9.50*r*	2.20
11.30	3.15	11.20	2.50
PM12.30*r*	3.50	PM 1.25	4.50
2.30*s*	5.50	2.15	6.26
4.30*r*	7.55	3.25*r*	6.58
6.30*r*	9.47	5.25*r*	8.50
—	—	6.27	11.28
—	—	8.40	3.58
—	—	—	—

Sunday Trains.

AM11. 0*r*	3.36	AM10.15*r*	2.27
PM 2. 0*r*	6.37	PM 2.10*r*	6.24
—	—	5.15*r*	9.31
—	—	—	—

r Restaurant Car.
s Refreshments served.

Taxi Cabs can be hired to meet any train at this Station by telegram or Telephone No. 93. Grosvenor Hotel Garage, Swanage.

Hotel Grosvenor. The Largest and admittedly best situated, overlooking Bay. Beautiful grounds sloping to the sea. New Management. Electric Lift. Garage. Tennis, etc. Moderate. Illustrated Tariff. Tel. 93.
EXTON HOTELS, LTD.
See advt. p. **316**.

Grand Hotel. Leading Hotel. Due South. Facing Sea. Nearest to Links. Fully licensed. Excellent Cuisine. Garage. Telephone 98.
See advt. p. **317**.

Magnolia Boarding Establishment. Centrally situated. Magnificent Views. Charming Old World Garden. Phone 123.
See advt. p. **317**.

Osborne House, Boarding Establishment, facing Sea and Pier Gates. Large Garden. South aspect. Moderate. Personal management. Tel. 41.
Mrs. BURT.

Highcliffe Pension. Unrivalled position on sea front. Near Golf Links. Excellent Cuisine. Inclusive Terms. Large New Wing, 1911. Telephone—47 Swanage.
Mrs. HOOKE, Proprietress.

For completion of Advertisements, see over.

P

SUTTON-ON-SEA.—GRANGE & LINKS HOTEL. FIRST CLASS. Pleasantly Situated.

SWANAGE—continued.

Beecholme Boarding House. Best position on Sea Front, with private steps to sands. Minute Tennis Courts. Liberal table. Terms moderate.
Mrs. HUNTLEY.

Craigside Private Hotel. Open all year. Excellent position. Close Sands, Station, and Town. Smoking Lounge.— Over 40 Rooms. Telephone 6. PROPRIETOR.

Westbury. En Pension. Close to Station, Shops and Sands. Overlooking Recreation Ground and Sea on the level. Good cuisine unlimited. Separate tables. Mrs. JOHNSON.

Craig-y-don. En Pension. Highly recommended. Excellent Liberal Table. Facing Sea. Tennis and Croquet Lawns. Own Garden Produce, Eggs, etc. Moderate Tariff.
Mrs. BATTYE MILLS.

Penlu Board Residence. Fine Sea views. Two minutes Beach. Good reception rooms. Excellent Table. Garden. New Management. Moderate.
Misses WILEY & STOVOLD.

Woodstock Park Road. Superior Board Residence. Near Sea, Shops and Downs. Sunny position. Comfortable and homely. Moderate Terms.
Mrs. BESWICK.

Danes' Fort. Highcliffe Road. Board Residence. Facing South. Balcony. Steps to bathing tents. Near Golf Links. Moderate terms. Misses CLARK.

HouseAgents, Auctioneers. For particulars of Houses for Sale and To Let Furnished. PLUMMERS, 1, Station Road. Established 1896. Telephone 12.

Eardley Brooke, Auctioneers. Furnished Houses a speciality. Freehold and other Properties for Sale in Dorset and neighbouring Counties. Particulars Gratis. Telephone 59.

SWANBOURNE (Bucks)

from *Euston*, 51¼ miles. Fares, 10/3a, 6/2c.   R. T., double fare. Pop. 427.
Map Square 18.

Euston	Swanbne.	Swanbne.	Euston
AM 6.45	8.25	AM 8.39	10. 0
7.35	10.20	10.19	11.55
10.40	12.20	PM12.34h	2.45
12. 0nr	1.35	2.59	4.15
PM 3. 5	4.40	3.33	5.35
4.15	5.35	6. 3	7.55
5.32	7. 0	7.56	9.20
6.10e	7.42	8.25e	10.10
7.15d	9.20	8.25d	10.50
8. 0e	9.20	—	—
—	—	—	—
—	—	—	—

Sunday Trains.

AM 8.15	10.30	PM 1. 7	5. 5
9.15	11.55	4.58	7.10
PM12.30	1.15	7.50	9.45
2.15	5. 0	8.29	10.10
3.50	5.50	—	—

d Saturdays only.
e Saturdays excepted.
h Thursdays and Saturdays only.
n Noon.

SWANLEY (Kent) from

Victoria, Holborn Viaduct, and *St. Paul's,* 17¼ miles. Fares, 3/9a, 3/0b, 2/3c. R. T. for eight days, 7/6a, 6/0b. Pop. 3,759.
Map Square 24.

	Leave		Arr. at
(S.E.&C.)	Hol. V.	St. Pl.'s	Swanly.
AM 5. 5	4.57	5. 0	6. 2
—	5.57	5.59	6.58
—	6.40|	6.42	7.28
—	7.30	7.33	8.11
8.32	8.20	8.23	9.21
9.20	—	—	9.47
10.15e	10. 9e	10.11e	11. 6
11. 4	10.58	11. 0	11.53
11.40d	—	—	12.19
11.40e	—	—	12.23
11.55d	—	—	12.38
PM —	12.33d	12.36d	1.18
—	1.24d	1.27d	1.59
—	1.27d	1.30d	2. 9
2. 9d	2. 4d	2. 7d	2.44
—	2.11d	2.14d	3. 9
2.12e	2.13e	2.16e	3. 7
2.40d	—	—	3.23
2.50e	—	—	3.34
—	3.22	3.25	4.15
3.40d	3.35d	3.36d	4.54
3.56e	—	—	4.38
4.25e	—	—	4.54
4.45e	4.50e	4.53e	5.40
5. 3d	—	—	5.50
5. 8e	—	—	5.55
5.15h	—	5.21k	5.48
d5.20h	—	d5.26k	5.54
5.30e	—	—	6. 2
—	—	5.33e	6.10
—	5.31e	5.34e	6.19
5.45	—	—	6.24
—	—	6.16e	6.48
6.16	6.10e	6.13e	7. 1
6.40	6.34	6.37	7.24
7.22	7.22	7.24	8. 5
8.10	8. 5	8. 8	9. 8
8.55	—	—	9.52
9. 0	8.57	9. 0	9.45
10. 0	9.54	9.56	10.44
10.17	10.11	10.13	10.55
11.35	11.31	11.34	12.24
12. 0l	—	—	12.32

Sunday Trains.

AM 7.20	—	—	8. 1
—	8. 0	—	9. 2
8.25	—	—	9.18
10.30	10.25	—	11.21
11.30	—	—	12.15
PM 1. 7	1. 5	—	2. 5
2. 5	2. 3	—	3. 3
3.30	—	—	4.13
6. 7	—	—	7. 0
6.35	—	—	7.14
—	6.40	—	7.24
9. 5	9.33	—	10.27
10.15	10.12	—	11. 4

Trains from Swanley.

Leave		Arrive at	
Swanley	St. Pl.'s	Hol. V.	Vict.
AM 7.24	8. 8	8. 9	8.14
7.44	8.25	8.27	8.29
8. 1	8.40	8.42	—
8.18	—	—	8.50
8.28	9.16	9.18	—
8.52	9.27	9.29	9.36
9. 1	9.37	9.39	—
9.38	—	—	10.10
10.19	11.22	11.29	11. 9
11. 6	—	—	11.37
PM12.16	12.59e	1. 2e	12.49
12.20d	1. 0	1. 2	—
12.30d	—	—	1.21
12.45e	—	—	1.32
1.52	—	—	2.40
2.41	—	—	3.23

SWANLEY—continued.

	Leave		Arrive at
	Swanley	St. Pl.'s	Hol. V.	Vict.
PM 3.47	—	—	4.33
4.26e	5.32	5.34	5.21
5. 7d	—	—	5.42
6. 3	6.45	6.47	—
6.18	6.58	7. 0	—
6.53d	7.54	—	—
7.18d	8. 0	8. 2	—
7.18e	8.17	8.20	8.10
7.57	—	—	8.51
8.55	9.50	9.54	9.46
9.21d	—	—	9.54
10.45	11.21	11.23	—
10.57	11.44	11.46	—

Sunday Trains.

AM 8.35	—	9.40	9.31
10.14	—	—	10.48
10.30	—	11.27	11.23
PM12.12	—	1. 2	12.56
12.45|	—	—	1.25
1.16	—	2.15	2.11
3.10	—	—	3.50
5.30	—	—	6. 3
5.34	—	6.20	6.15
7.43	—	8.50	—
9.20	—	10.22	10. 5
9.55	—	10.59	10.54
11. 3	—	12. 0	11.44

d Saturdays only.
e Saturdays excepted.
h Departs from Charing Cross (S.E. & C.R.).
k Departs from London Bridge (S.E. & C.R.).
l Wednesdays only.

SWANNINGTON (Leicester) from *St. Pancras*, 114 miles.

Fares, 23/2a, 13/11c. R. T., double fare. Pop. 2,050.
Map Square 18.

St. Pan.	Swanton.	Swanton.	St. Pan.
AM 2.25	8. 0	AM 7.45r	11. 0
4.25	10. 1	11.57	3.25
10.25r	1.16	PM 1.56r	5.45
PM12.25r	3.33	4. 1r	6.35
2.25r	5.26	6.23r	9.15
4.25r	7.27	9.32	4.20
6.25r	10. 4	—	—

Sunday Trains.

PM 6.15r	9.29	AM 7.54	11.53
—	—	PM 6.24r	9.52

r Restaurant Car.

SWANSEA (High Street) (Glamorgan) from *Paddington*, 198¼ miles. Fares, 41/5a, 24/10c. R. T. for two months, 82/10a, 49/8c. Pop. 157,561.

Map Square 21.

Pad.	Swansea	Swansea	Pad.
AM 1. 0g	7.30	AM 6.30r	10.57
5.30	11.47	8.35r	1. 0
8.45r	12.55	9.40r	2.30
11.50r	4.25	12. 0r	4.20
PM 1.10r	5.50	PM 1.30r	6.15
3.35r	7.55	3.35r	8.35
5. 0r	9.50	5.30r	9.25
6. 0r	10.40	8.55	3.30
8. 0r	12.10	—	—
9.15	4.25	—	—

SWANSEA—*continued.*

Sunday Trains.

Pad.	Swansea	Swansea	Pad.
AM 1. 0	8.10	AM 9. 0	3.35
PM12.30*r*	6. 0	10.30	4. 5
4.30	10.14	PM 3. 5*r*	8.25
9.15	4.25	8.55	3.50

g Mondays excepted.

r Restaurant Car.

Hotel Metropole, Swansea. One of the finest Hotels in provinces. Electric Light throughout. Lift. Terms moderate.
E. T. TUCK, Manager.

Mumbles Pier, Swansea. Open Daily. Great Attractions during Summer Season. Concerts daily. Bands—frequent Musical Contests. Refreshments of all kinds.

Bank.—The National Bank, Ltd.

SWAN VILLAGE (Stafford) from *Paddington* 116½ miles. Fares, 24/4*a*, 14/7*c*. R. T. for two months, 48/8*a*. Departures *from* London as for West Bromwich. Departures *for* London about 6 times daily.

SWANWICK (Hants), 76½ miles. Fares, *via* Fareham, 16/0*a*, 9/7*c*. R. T. for two months, 32/0*a*, 19/2*c*. *Via* St. Denys, 17/11*a*, 10/9*c*. R. T. for two months, 35/10*a*, 21/6*c*. Departures *from* London as for Burlsedon. Departures *for* London about 8 times daily.
Map Square 23.

SWAVESEY (Cambs) from *Liverpool Street*, 67½ miles. Fares, 12/3*a*, 7/4*c*. R. T., double fare. Departures *from* London as for St. Ives (Hunts). Departures *for* London about 10 times daily. Pop. 904.
Map Square 18.

SWAY (Hants), 95 miles. Fares, 20/0*a*, 12/0*c*. R. T. for two months, 40/0*a*, 24/0*c*. Departures *from* London as for Brockenhurst. Departures *for* London about 6 times daily. Pop. 1,010.
Map Square 27.

SWAYTHLING (Hants), 75½ miles. Fares, 15/10*a*, 9/6*c*. R.T. for two months, 31/8*a*, 19/0*c*. Departures *from* London as for Eastleigh. Departures *for* London about 12 times daily.
Map Square 23.

SWIMBRIDGE (Devon), 183½ miles. Fares, 38/4*a*, 23/0*c*. R. T. for two months, 76/8*a*. Departures *from* London as for Dulverton. Departures *for* London about 4 times daily. Pop. 1,089.
Map Square 21.

SWINDERBY(Lincoln),148 miles from *St. Pancras*. Fares, 26/6*a*, 15/11*c*. R. T., double fare. Departures *from* London as for Collingham. Departures *for* London about 5 times daily. Pop. 484.
Map Square 13.

SWINDON (Wilts) from *Paddington*, 77¼ miles. Fares, 16/1*a*, 9/8*c*. R. T. for two months, 32/2*a*. Pop. 54,920.
Map Square 22.

Pad.	Swindon	Swindon	Pad.
AM 1. 0*g*	2.42	AM 1.27*f*	3.15
5.30	7.14	1.42	3.30
7.30	9. 7	5.13	7.10
9. 0	10.50	6.45	9.30
10.45	12.42	7.30*r*	10.15
PM 1.10*r*	2.56	9. 0*r*	10.45
1.35*r*	4.13	9.30	12. 0
3.15*t*	4.46	10.54	12.20
4.15*t*	5.34	PM 1.15*r*	2.40
5.15	7.10	1.44	3.20
6. 0*r*	7.28	3.45	5. 0
8.55	9.12	4.17	6. 2
9.15	11.10	6.55*r*	8.35
10. 0	11.48	7.10*r*	8.45
12. 0*h*	1.52	8.50	10.25
12.30*k*	2.22	12.37	2.45

Sunday Trains.

AM 1. 0	2.42	AM 1.42	3.30
9.10	11. 6	5.13	7. 5
10.35	1. 0	PM 1.45	3.35
PM12.30*r*	2.12	2.40	4. 5
2. 0	6.35	3. 5	3. 0
9.15	11.13	6.57*r*	8.25
10. 0	11.48	8.18	10. 0

f Mondays only.

g Mondays excepted.

h Saturdays midnight excepted.

k Saturdays midnight only.

r Restaurant Car.

t Tea Car.

SWINDON TOWN (Wilts) from *Waterloo*, 99¼ miles. Fares as above.
Map Square 22.

W'loo.	Swindon	Swindon	W'loo.
AM 7.30	12.12	AM 9. 0	12.22
PM 1. 0*r*	3.57	11.45	2.36
3.30	6.49	PM 2.45	6.26
6. 0*r*	9.12	4.35*r*	8.30

Sunday Trains.

PM 6. 0	9.46	PM 4.50	8.57

r Restaurant Car.

SWINE (Yorks), 202¼ miles. No through fares. Departures *from* London as for Hull (Paragon). Departures *for* London about 6 times daily. Pop. 218.
Map Square 13.

SWINESHEAD (Lincoln) 113½ miles. Fares, 23/2*a*, 13/11*c*. R. T., double fare. Departures *from* London as for Boston. Departures *for* London about 5 times daily. Pop. 1,899.
Map Square 13.

SWINTON (Lancs), 191¾ miles. Fares, 39/7*a*, 23/9*c*. R. T. for two months, 79/2*a*, 47/6*c*. Departures *from* London as for Manchester. Departures *for* London about 8 times daily. Pop. 30,924.

SWINTON (Yorks) from *St. Pancras*, 167 miles. Fares, 33/9*a*, 20/3*c*. R. T., double fare. Pop. 13,925.
Map Square 13.

St. Pan.	Swinton	Swinton	St. Pan.
AM 2.25*g*	7.41	AM 7.48*r*	12.10
2.25	9.11	8.47*r*	1.30
4.25	9.46	9.53*r*	2.10
9. 0*r*	1.33	PM12. 6*r*	7.15
9.50d*r*	2.32	2.25*r*	7.15
9.50e*r*	2.43	3.51*r*	7.57
11.45*r*	4.35	4.15e*r*	9. 5
PM12.25*r*	5. 7	4.37d*r*	9. 5
1.50*r*	5.54	9.58	4.20
3.30*r*	7.55	—	—
5. 0*r*	9.24	—	—
6.15*r*	10.31	—	—

Sunday Trains.

PM 3.15	7.41	AM 8.21*r*	5. 2
—	—	PM 3.22*r*	9.43
—	—	8.22	4.55

d Saturdays only.

e Saturdays excepted.

g Mondays excepted.

r Restaurant Car.

SWANSEA.—HOTEL METROPOLE. See advt. above.

SWISS COTTAGE from
Baker Street, 1¾ miles. Fares,
0/3a, 0/2c.   R. T. for two days,
0/6a, 0/4c. *See* back of Map.
Map Square 60.

SYDENHAM (London)
from *London Bridge*, 6½ miles.
Fares, 1/3a, 0/9c. R. T. for two
days, 2/6a, 1/5c.   Pop. 32,132.
See pp. 568, 570, 580, 581.
Map Square 79.

SYDENHAM HILL from
Victoria, Holborn Viaduct, and
Ludgate Hill, 5½ miles. Fares,
1/2a, 2/11½b, 0/8½c. R. T. for two
days, 2/2a, 1/9b, 1/4c. *See* pp. 558-
561.
Map Square 79.

SYDENHAM, LOWER
from *Charing Cross* and *Cannon
Street*, 9½ miles. Fares, 1/6a, 1/2b,
0/10½c. R. T. for two days, 2/7a,
1/9b, 1/5c. *See* pp. 544-547.
Map Square 80.

SYDENHAM, UPPER
from *Victoria, Holborn Viaduct,*
and *Ludgate Hill*, 9 miles. Fares,
from Victoria, 1/6a, 1/2b, 0/10½c.
R. T. for two days, 2/7a, 2/0b,
1/7c. *See* pp. 562, 563.
Map Square 79.

SYMINGTON (Lanark)
366 miles. Fares, 74/5a, 44/8c.
R. T. for two months, 148/10d,
89/4c. Departures *from* London
as for Lockerbie. Departures
for London about 4 times daily.
Pop. 608.
Map Square 40.

SYMOND'S YAT
(Hereford) from *Paddington*, 139¾
miles. Fares 29/0a, 17/5c.   R. T.
for two months, 58/0a, 34/10c. De-
partures *from* London as for
Kerne Bridge. Departures *for*
London about 4 times daily.
Map Square 22.

SYSTON (Leicester) from
St. Pancras, 104 miles. Fares,
21/3a, 12/9c. R. T., double
fare. Pop. 3,087.
Map Square 18.

St. Pan	Syston	Syston	St. Pan.
AM 2.25	6.31	AM 7.28r	9.57
4.25	7.37	8.24r	11. 0
8.25r	10.55	9.10r	11.35
9.50r	12. 4	9.53r	12.10
10.25r	12.44	11. 5r	1.30
PM12.25r	3. 0	12. 0r	2.10
1.25r	4. 0	PM 1.32r	4.20
2.25r	4.36	3.24r	5.45
3.30r	6.21	5.34r	7.57
4.25r	6.48	6.17r	8.35
6.25r	8.40	7. 5r	9.15
—	—	7.22r	10. 5
—	—	10.36	4.20

Sunday Trains.

PM 3.15	8.11	AM 8.33	11.53
6.15r	8.53	PM 6.58r	9.52
—	—	9.55	4.55
—	—	—	—
—	—	—	—
—	—	—	—

e Saturdays excepted.
r Restaurant Car.

T

TADCASTER (Yorks),
184½ miles. Fares, 38/4a, 23/0c.
R. T., double fare. Departures
from London as for Wetherby.
Departures *for* London about 6
times daily. Pop. 3,399.
Map Square 8.

TADWORTH (Surrey) from
Charing Cross, Cannon Street, and
London Bridge, 23 miles. Fares,
2/11a, 2/4b, 1/9c. R. T. for eight
days, 5/10a, 4/8b, 3/6c. Pop.   .
Map Square 23.

	Leave		Arr. at
Char. +	Can. St.	Lon. B.	Tadwh.
AM —	4.44	5. 0	5.59
—	—	7.50l	8.48
—	—	9.13l	10. 6
—	10.12	10.15	11.10
10.55	—	11. 3	12. 3
—	11.40d	11.45d	12.34
11.48e	—	11.54e	12.49
PM —	—	12.45el	1.36
12.44d	—	12.51d	1.40
12.55d	—	1. 4d	2. 0
—	1.20d	1.23d	2.16
--	—	1.50dl	2.36
2.46d	—	2.52d	3.40
3.15	—	3.21	4.22
—	—	4.20dl	5.12
—	4.44e	4.48e	5.42
—	—	4.50dl	5.42
5. 6e	—	5.14e	6. 9
—	—	5.35el	6.20
5.30d	—	5.36d	6.28
—	—	5.48el	6.40
—	6.20e	6.23e	7.13
6.17d	—	6.23d	7.14
6.46e	—	6.53e	7.43
7.24d	7.23e	7.50	8.27
8.28	—	8.36	9.33
9.25	—	9.31	10.20
10.17	—	10.23	11.18
11.42	—	—	12.34

TADWORTH—continued.

Sunday Trains.

	Leave		Arr. at.
CHAR. +	CAN. ST.	LON. B.	TADWH.
AM 9. 8	—	9.14	9.58
10.20	—	10.28	11.31
PM 1.30	—	1.37	2.34
6.50	—	6.56	7.44
7.45	—	7.52	8.44
9.40	—	9.47	10.44
—	—	—	—
—	—	—	—
—	—	—	—
—	,	—	—
—	—	—	—

Trains from Tadworth.

Leave		Arrive at	
TADWTH	LON. B.	CAN. ST.	CHAR. +
AM 7. 6	7.58	—	8. 7
7.49	8.40	8.44	—
8.12	9. 5	9. 9	—
8.33	9.22	—	9.30
8.54	9.45	—	—
9.26	10.19	10.22	—
10.39	11.24	—	11.33
11.35	12.26	—	—
PM 1. 5	1.58	—	2. 5
2.12	3. 4	3. 8e	—
3. 2	3.52	—	—
4. 2	5. 2	—	5.14
5.15	6.10	—	6.18
6.11	6.58	—	7. 5
7.36	8.23	—	8.31
8.10	9. 2	—	9.15
9.16	10. 3	—	10.13
11. 9	11.57	—	12 10
—	.	—	—

Sunday Trains.

AM10.20	11.15	—	11.25
PM 3.35	4.33	—	4.42
5.39	6.25	—	6.34
8.15	9. 1	—	9. 9
9.18	10.11	—	10.24
—	.	—	—

d Saturdays only.
e Saturdays excepted.
l Low Level platform.

TAFFS WELL (Glamorgan), 159 miles. Fares, 33/2*a*, 19/11*c*. R.T. for two months, 66/4*a*, 39/10*c*. Departures from London as for Cardiff. Departures for London about 8 times daily. Pop. 2,866.

TAIN (Ross), from *Euston*, 612 miles. Fares, 108/9*a*, 65/3*c*. R. T. for two months, 217/6*a*, 130/6*c*. Pop. 2,394.

Map Square 34.

EUSTON	TAIN	TAIN	EUSTON
PM 1.30*er*	8.30*h*	AM 8.10*r*	5. 0*h*
7.40*er*11.53*h*		PM 1.18	7.40*h*
11.35*e*	7.30*l*	7. 8*er*	7.30*l*
—	—	—	—
—	—	—	—
—	—	—	—

Sunday Trains.

PM 7.50*r*	11.53*h*	—	—
11.35	7.30*l*	—	—

e Saturdays excepted.
h A.M.
l P.M.
r Restaurant Car.

TAIN—continued.

ANOTHER ROUTE from *King's Cross*, 602 miles. Fares as above.

KING's +	TAIN	TAIN	KING's +
AM11.50*er*	8.30*h*	AM8.10	5.25*k*
PM 7.45*er*11.53*k*		PM1.18	7. 5*k*
11.25*e*	7.30*h*	7.8*er*	6.30*h*

Sunday Trains.

PM 7.45*r*	11.53	—	—
11.25	7.30*k*	—	—

e Saturdays excepted.
h P.M.
k A.M.
r Restaurant Car.

TAKELEY (Essex) from Liverpool Street, 35½ miles. Fares, 7/8*a*, 4/7*c*. R. T. for two months, 15/4*a*. Departures from London as for Dunmow. Departures for London about 6 times daily. Pop. 849.

Map Square 24.

TALACRE (Flint), 202½ miles. Fares, 42/1*a*, 25/3*c*. R. T. for two months, 84/2*a*, 50/6*c*. Departures from London as for Chester. Departures for London about 5 times daily.

Map Square 11.

TALERDDIG (Montgomery), 199½ miles. No through fares. Departures from London as for Newtown. Departures for London about 3 times daily.

Map Square 16.

TALGARTH (Brecon), 173¼ miles. Fares from Paddington (via Hay), 36/0*a*, 21/7*c*. R. T. for two months, 72/0*a*, 43/2*c*. From Euston (via Builth Wells), 37/6*a*, 22/6*c*. R. T. for two months, 75/0*a*. Departures from London as for Hay or Builth Wells. Departures for London about 4 times daily. Pop. 1,761.

Map Square 16.

TALLEY ROAD (Carmarthen), from *Paddington*. 219 miles. Fares, 43/2*a*, 25/11*c*. R. T. for two months, 86/4*a*. Departures from London as for Llandilo. Departures for London about 4 times daily. Pop. (Talley) 562.

Map Square 21.

TALLINGTON (Lincoln), 84½ miles. Fares, 17/6*a*, 10/5*c*. R. T., double fare. Departures from London as for Peterboro'. Departures for London about 6 times daily. Pop. 210.

Map Square 18.

TALSARNAU (Merioneth), 248 miles. Fares, 51/6*a*, 30/11*c*. R. T. for two months, 103/0*a*. Departures from London as for Harlech. Departures for London about 5 times daily. Pop. 626.

Map Square 11.

TALYBONT (Brecon), 192½ miles. Fares, 37/4*a*, 22/5*c*. R. T. for two months, 74/8*a*. Departures from London as for Bargoed or Brecon. Departures for London about 4 times daily.

Map Square 21.

TALY-CAFN (Denbigh), 228¼ miles. Fares, 47/8*a*, 28/7*c*. R. T. for two months, 95/4*a*, 57/2*c*. Departures from London as for Llanrwst and Trefriw. Departures for London about 4 times daily.

Map Square 11.

TALYLLYN (Brecon), 178¾ miles. Fares (via Hay), 36/11*a*, 22/2*c*. R. T. for two months, 73/10*a*, 44/4*c*. Via Bargoed, 37/4*a*, 22/5*c*. R. T. for two months, 74/8*a*, 44/10*c*. Departures from London as for Bargoed or Hay. Departures for London about 6 times daily. Pop. 268.

Map Square 16.

TAMERTON FOLIOT (Devon) from *Waterloo*, 225 miles. Fares, 46/8*a*, 28/0*c*. R. T. for two months, 93/4*a*, 56/0*c*. Pop. 1,076.

Map Square 26.

W'LOO.	T. FOL.	T. FOL.	W'LOO.
AM11. 0*r*	4.59	AM 8.12*r*	1.56
PM 3. 0*r*	8.36	11.33*r*	6. 0
—	—	PM 1.49*r*	8.30
—	—	3.19	10.50
—	—	4.44*h*	3.58

Sunday Trains.

12. 0*nr*	8.20	PM 2. 5*r*	8.57
—	—	—	—

h Via Eastleigh.
n Noon.
r Restaurant Car.

TAMWORTH (Stafford) from *Euston*, 110 miles. Fares, 22/9*a*, 13/8*c*. R. T. double fare. Pop. 8,032.

Map Square 17.

EUSTON	TAMWTH	TAMWTH	EUSTON
AM 5. 0	8.34	AM 2.27*g*	5.40
6.45	9.41	6.28*r*	10. 0
8.45*r*	11.23	8.22	11. 0
10.40*r*	1.53	10.20*e*	12.32
12. 0*nr*	3.26	11.16*r*	2.20
PM 2.50*t*	5. 8	PM12.28*r*	4.15
4. 5*r*	6.35	2.18	5.35
5.20*r*	9. 3	3.14*t*	6.15
9.30	12. 2	5.29*r*	8.10
—	—	7.27*r*	10.45
—	—	9.50	5. 0

Sunday Trains.

AM 9.15	12.48	AM 2.27	5.45
PM 3.50	7.21	PM 1.42	5. 5
9.30	11.52	—	—

e Saturdays excepted.
g Mondays excepted.
n Noon.
r Restaurant Car.
t Tea Car.

TANFIELD (Yorks), 217½ miles. Fares, 45/3*a*, 27/2*c*. R. T., double fare. Departures from London as for Ripon. Departures for London about 4 times daily. Pop. 526.

Map Square 7.

TANNADICE (Forfar), 487½ miles. Fares, 97/6*a*, 58/6*c*. R. T. for two months, 195/0*a*, 117/0*c*. Departures from London as for Brechin. Departures for London about 3 times daily. Pop. 918.

Map Square 38.

TANSHELF (Yorks) from *King's Cross*, 173½ miles. Fares, 36/0*a*, 21/7*c*. R. T., double fare. Departures from London as for Pontefract (Monkhill). Departures for London about 7 times daily. Pop. 7,002.

TAN-Y-BWLCH (Merioneth), 235 miles. No through fares. Departures from London as for Blaenau Festiniog. Departures for London about 4 times daily.

Map Square 11.

TAN-Y-GRISIAU (Merioneth), 230½ miles. No through fares. Departures from London as for Blaenau Festiniog. Departures for London about 4 times daily.

Map Square 11.

TAPLOW (Bucks) from

Paddington, 22½ miles. Fares, 4/7a, 2/8c. R. T. for two months, 9/2a, 5/6c. Pop. 1,127.
Map Square 23.

PAD.	TAPLOW	TAPLOW	PAD.
AM 5.45	6.56	AM 6. 8	7.25
6.30	7.20	7.43	8.20
6.35	7.47	8. 5	8.49
7.35	8.30	8.28	8.56
8.30	9.13	8.35	9.25
9.20	10. 9	9. 2e	9.34
9.55	10.42	9. 6d	9.37
10.55	11.44	9.17	10. 6
11.25	12. 4	9.53	10.24
PM12. 8	12.49	10.35	11. 6
12.33d	1.32	10.54	11.35
12.35e	1.40	11.44	12.15
1. 5d	1.43	PM12.10	1.11
1.20d	2. 6	12.48	1.46
2. 7	2.46	1.48	2.35
2.18d	2.54	2. 2	3.10
3.38	4. 9	2.55d	3.38
4. 7	4.44	3.31	4.10
4.30	5.10	4.10	5.17
5. 5	5.33	4.59	5.37
5.18e	5.59	6.16	6.55
5.18d	6. 6	7. 4	7.45
5.35e	6.29	7.23	8.10
5.40d	6.29	8.21d	9.12
6. 5	6.33	8.40	9.33
6.12e	7. 2	8.50	9.52
6.35	7.11	9.23	10.22
7. 0	7.53	9.56	10.42
7.35	8. 5	10. 2	11. 4
8. 5	8.43	10.50	12. 0
8.35	9.14	—	—
10. 5	10.45	—	—
10.40	11.39	—	—
11.20	11.50	—	—
12. 3	12.44	—	—

Sunday Trains.

AM 8.20	9.23	AM 9.27	10.14
9.45	10.24	10. 8	10.50
10. 0	10.35	PM12. 4	1. 5
10. 5	10.48	3.50	4.53
10.25	11. 0	5.34	6.23
10.45	11.19	6.51	7.37
11. 0	11.39	7.39	8.20
PM 1.45	2.31	7.59	8.45
2. 0	3. 5	8.10	9.17
2.35	3.19	8.52	9.32
4.45	5.47	9.12	9.53
5.15	5.57	9.18	10.22
6. 5	7.10	9.48	10.33
7.40	8.42	10.27	11. 6
8.20	9. 6	10.36	11.38
10. 5	10.58	—	—
11.15	12. 5	—	—

d Saturdays only.
e Saturdays excepted.

Brazil House. Private Residential Hotel. Ten minutes Station and River. Nice Grounds. Tennis Courts. Terms moderate, inclusive. 'Phone, Maidenhead 718.

TARBOLTON (Ayr), 385¼

miles. Fares, 78/6a, 47/1c. R.T. for two months, 157/0a, 94/2c. Departures *from London* as for Ayr. Departures *for London* about 4 times daily. Pop. 4,981.
Map Square 40.

TARFF (Kirkcudbright),

358¾ miles. Fares, 68/9a, 41/3c. R. T. for two months, 137/6a, 82/6c. Departures *from London* as for Kirkcudbright. Departures *for London* about 4 times daily.
Map Square 43.

TARSET (Northumberland), 307¼ miles. Fares, 65/3a, 39/2c. R. T. for two months, 130/6a, 78/4c. Departures *from London* as for Hexham. Departures *for London* about 3 times daily. Pop. 98.
Map Square 3.

TATTENHALL ROAD

(Cheshire) from *Euston*, 172½ miles. Fares, 36/0a, 21/7c. R. T. for two months, 72/0a. Pop. (Tattenhall) 1,043.
Map Square 12.

EUSTON	T'HALLRD	T'HALLRD	EUSTON
AM 2.35	8.38	AM 6.55er12. 5	
8.30r	12.25	6.55dr12.20	
11.50r	3.38	8.47r	1. 0
12. 0nr	4.56	11.55r	4.15
PM 2.35t	7.17	PM 2.43r	6.25
5.20r	9.16	5.27er	9. 5
11.50d	9. 6	5.27dr	9.15
—	—	6.33r	10.45
—	—	10.15	5. 0

Sunday Trains.

PM12.10r	4.34	AM10. 8	4. 0
—	—	PM 8. 0	5. 0

d Saturdays only.
e Saturdays excepted.
n Noon.
r Restaurant Car.
t Tea Car.

TATTERSHALL (Lincoln) from *King's Cross*, 119½ miles. Fares, 24/10a, 14/11c. R. T., double fare. Departures *from London* as for Kirkstead. Departures *for London* about 6 times daily. Pop. 415.
Map Square 13.

TAUNTON (Somerset)

from *Paddington*, 143 miles. Fares, *via* Bristol, 31/3a, 18/9c. R. T. for two months, 62/6a. *Via* Westbury, 29/10a, 17/11c. R. T. for two months, 59/8a. Pop. 23,219.
Map Square 21.

PAD	TAUNTON	TAUNTON	PAD
AM 5.30	9.49	AM 2.46	7.10
7.30	11.42	7.20	11.30
9.15r	12.10	11. 0r	1.30
11.15r	2.36	PM12.40	4. 5
PM12. 5r	2.55	2.44r	5.30
2. 0r	4.44	4.12r	6.50
3.30	5.58	6.28r	9. 0
4.15r	7.32	8.50	2.45
6.30r	9.52	—	—
10. 0	2. 0	—	—
12. 0h	4.27	—	—
12.30k	4.57	—	—

Sunday Trains.

AM 9.10r	1.58	AM 2.46	7. 5
PM12.30r	5.10	10.23	3.35
2.40	5.29	PM 4.20	7. 5
10. 0	2. 0	10.57	3.15

h Saturdays midnight excepted.
k Saturdays midnight only.
r Restaurant Car.

County Hotel. Telephone 134. The leading Hotel. Public Restaurant. Electric Light. Garage.
TRUST HOUSES, Ltd.

TAVISTOCK (Devon)

from *Waterloo*, 213½ miles. Fares, 44/5a, 26/8c. R. T. for two months, 88/10a, 53/4c. Pop. 4,317.
Map Square 26.

W'LOO	TAVISTK.	TAVISTK.	W'LOO
AM 9. 0r	2.12	AM 9.11r	1.56
10. 0r	3. 9	10.55r	3.50
11. 0r	4. 6	PM12.45r	6. 0
PM 1. 0r	6.43	2.59r	8.30
3. 0r	7.45	4.43	10.50
6. 0r	11.20	5.15h	3.58

Sunday Trains.

12. 0rn	5.54	PM 3.44r	8.57

h Via Eastleigh.
n Noon.
r Restaurant Car.

TAVISTOCK—continued.

ANOTHER ROUTE from *Paddington*, (via Plymouth), 235¼ miles. Fares, 46/11a, 28/2c. R.T. for two months, 93/10a, 56/4c.

PAD.	TAVISTK.	TAVISTK.	PAD.
AM 5.50k	2.40	AM 7.32r	1.30
5.30	3. 0	10.40r	4.35
10.30r	4. 9	PM12.50r	6.50
11.10r	6. 6	3. 2r	9. 0
PM12. 5r	7.18	11. 5	7.10
2. 0r	8.11	—	—
3.30r	9.14	—	—
4.15r	10.55	—	—
10. 0e	7.12	—	—
12. 0h	8.34	—	—
12.30l	11.28	—	—

Sunday Trains.

PM 2.40r	9.10	AM11.55	7. 5
10. 0	7.12	PM 4.35	3.15
—	—	9.20	7.10

d Saturdays only.
e Saturdays excepted.
h Saturdays midnight excepted.
k Wednesdays and Saturdays only.
l Saturdays midnight only.
r Restaurant Car.

Bedford Hotel. First-class Family. Close Moors, Golf Links (18 holes). Excellent Hunting. Fishing centre. Tennis, Croquet, Hunters. Cars on hire. Garden (two acres). All fast trains stop at Tavistock. Moderate tariff. Telephone 37.
W. I. LAKE, Proprietor.

Queen's Head Hotel. Centre of Town. Has been thoroughly renovated and refurnished. Electric light. Modern Sanitation. Ample accommodation. P.R H.A. House.

TAYNUILT (Argyll), 480½

miles. Fares, 100/5a, 60/3c. R. T. for two months, 200/10a, 120/6c. Departures *from London* as for Crianlarich. Departures *for London* about 3 times daily.
Map Square 37.

TAYPORT (Fife), 448¾

miles. Fares, 91/1a, 54/8c. R. T. for two months, 182/2a, 109/4c. Departures *from London* as for Leuchars. Departures *for London* about twice daily. Pop. 3,296.
Map Square 38.

TEAN (Stafford), 153¾ miles.

Fares, 31/1a, 18/8c. R. T. for two months, 62/2a, 37/4c. Departures *from London* as for Longton. Departures *for London* about 4 times daily.
Map Square 12.

TEBAY (Westmorland)

from *Euston*, 262½ miles. Fares, 52/4a, 31/5c. R. T., double fare. Pop. 966.
Map Square 7.

EUSTON	TEBAY	TEBAY	EUSTON
AM12.25	8.55	AM 7.48r	3.10
2.35	10.41	9.37hr	3.45
5. 0	1.44	9.45hr	4.15
6.45	4.19	11.38r	6. 0
10.40r	4.55	11.55r	5.13
PM 1.30r	7.59	2.39er	9. 5
—	—	2.39dr	9.15
—	—	2.50r	10.45
—	—	8.25	5. 0

Sunday Trains.

AM11.45r	7.32	PM 5.23	5. 0

d Saturdays only.
e Saturdays excepted.
h Mondays and Saturdays only.
k Mondays and Saturdays excepted.
r Restaurant Car.

TEDDINGTON (Midd'x)

from *Waterloo*, 13¾ miles. Fares, 1/11a, 1/2c. R. T. for two days, 3/10a, 2/4c. Pcp. 21,213. *See* pp. 584, 585, 587-591.

Map Square 75.

Anglers' Hotel, Teddington Lock. Facing River. Newly decorated and Furnished. Excellent Catering. Garage. Telephone: 517 Kingston. Tariff.
Mrs. ROGERS, Proprietress.

Clarence Hotel, First Class Family. Modern Sanitation, Redecorated. Comfortable Reception Rooms. Beautiful Grounds. Lawn Tennis. Garage. Billiards. Table d'Hote, 7.15. Close to Station. Moderate Tariff. Telephone 645 Kingston.
Mr. and Mrs. C. F. GLANFIELD.

TEIGNGRACE (Devon),

192¼ miles. Fares (*via* Newton Abbot), 40/5a, 24/3c. R. T. for two months, 80/10a, 48/6c. (*Via* Ide), 39/7a, 23/9c. R. T. for two months, 79/2a, 47/6c. Departures *from* London as for Moretonhampstead. Departures *for* London about 6 times daily. Pop. 165.

Map Square 26.

TEIGNMOUTH (Devon)

from *Paddington*, 188¾ miles. Fares, 38/11a, 23/4c. R. T. for two months, 77/10a, 46/8c. Pop. 10,976.

Map Square 26.

PAD. TEIGNTH.		TEIGNTH.	PAD.
AM 5.30	11.52	AM 9.43*r*	1.30
7.30*d*	12.45	10.12	4. 5
7.30	1. 4	PM12.38*r*	4.35
9.15*r*	1.29	2.20*r*	6.50
PM12. 5*r*	4.11	4.22*r*	9. 0
2. 0*r*	6. 2	6.12	2.45
3 30*r*	7. 6	10.24	7.10
4.15*r*	8.49	—	—
6.30*r*	11. 8	—	—
12. 0*h*	5.52	—	—
12.30*k*	6.22	—	—

Sunday Trains.

AM 10.30*r*	12.55	AM 8.33*r*	3.35
PM 2.40	8. 7	10.49*r*	4. 5
4.50*r*	9.32	PM 2.21	7. 5
10. 0	7.35	3.23*r*	7.55
—	—	9.32	3.15

d Saturdays only.
h Saturdays midnight excepted.
k Saturdays midnight only.
r Restaurant Car.

Marina Residential Hotel. Finest position. Sea Front. Uninterrupted Views. S.W. aspect. Ideal Home. Electric light. Easily accessible for Dartmoor excursions. Appointed A.A. and M.U. Illustrated Tariff. Telephone 55.
ERNEST W. PARSONS, Proprietor.

"The Portland" Private Hotel. Sea front, facing Pier. Tennis Courts. Bowling Green. Electric Light. Central Heating. Separate Tables. Lounge, etc. Moderate Tariff. Proprietors—
Mr. and Mrs. A. BUCKNELL.

TEIGNMOUTH—cont.

Barnpark Private Hotel, Charmingly situated in own beautiful Lawns and Gardens (3 acres), South Aspect. Garage. Tennis and Badminton. Telephone Teignmouth 15.
Mr. and Mrs. H. E. STEVENS, Resident Proprietors.

TEMPLE. To and from

Mansion House, Charing Cross, Victoria, South Kensington, High Street, Praed Street, Baker Street, King's Cross, Moorgate, and all intermediate stations every few minutes ; also to and from *Ealing, Hounslow, Richmond,* and *Wimbledon. See* p. 489.

Map Square 61, *No.* 12.

TEMPLECOMBE

(Somerset), from *Waterloo*, 112¼ miles. Fares, 23/4a, 14/0c. R. T. for two months, 46/8a, 28/0c. Pop. 705.

Map Square 22.

W'LOO. TPLCMBE.		TPLCMBE. W'LOO.	
AM 7.30	10.37	AM 7.37	10.56
9. 0*r*	11.43	8.52*r*	11.10
10. 0*r*	12.30	9. 6	12.22
12. 0*r*	2.19	11.23*r*	1.56
PM 1. 0*r*	3.39	PM12.54*r*	3. 8
3. 0*r*	5.24	1. 7*r*	3.50
5. 0	8. 5	2.16*r*	4.30
6. 0*r*	8.34	3.46*r*	6. 0
10. 0*h*	3.44	4.50	7.40
—	—	6. 0*r*	8.30
—	—	7.58	10.50
—	—	10. 1*h*	3.58

Sunday Trains.

AM 9. 0	1.28	PM 5.55*r*	8.57
PM 6. 0	9.49	—	—

h Via Eastleigh.
n Noon.
r Restaurant Car.

TEMPLE HIRST (Yorks),

169¾ miles. Fares, 35/0a, 21/0c. R. T., double fare. Departures *from* London as for Doncaster. Departures *for* London about 4 times daily. Pop. 103.

Map Square 13.

TEMPLE SOWERBY

(Westmorland), 288½ miles. Fares, 55/10a, 33/6c. R. T., double fare. Departures *from* London as for Tebay. Departures *for* London about 4 times daily. Pop. 352.

Map Square 7.

TEMPLETON(Pembroke),

249¼ miles. Fares, 50/8a, 30/5c. R. T. for two months, 101/4a. Departures *from* London as for Tenby. Departures *for* London about 4 times daily. Pop. 403.

Map Square 15.

TEMPSFORD (Beds)

from *King's Cross*, 47½ miles. Fares, 9/10a, 5/11c. R. T. double fare. Pop. 431.

Map Square 18.

KING'S + TMPSFD.		TMPSFD. KING'S +	
AM 5. 5	6.38	AM 8.18	9.56
7.45	9.20	11.48	1.25
10.12	12.10	PM 2. 9	3.50
PM 1.55	3.31	4.41	6.25
5.10	7. 2	8.18	10.20
6.15	7.49	—	—
8.30	10. 2	—	—

Sunday Trains.

AM 8.30	10.20	PM 6.10	8. 8

TENBURY WELLS

(Worcester) from *Paddington* 148½ miles. Fares, 29/7a, 17/9c. R. T. for two months, 59/2a. Pop. 2,016.

Map Square 17.

PAD. TENBURY		TENBURY PAD.	
AM 1. 0*g*	10.32	AM 7.15*h*	11.15
5.30	1.28	8.45*kr*	1.25
10.40*k*	2.52	PM12.13*hr*	4.15
10.45*r*	5.26	3. 0*r*	8.45
PM 1.30*hr*	5.30	4. 0*hr*	9.15
2.10*kt*	6.58	7. 0	3.30
4.45*lt*	8.44	8.55*kl*	3.30

No Sunday Trains.

g Mondays excepted.
h Via Kidderminster.
k Via Birmingham.
l Thursdays only.
r Restaurant Car.
t Tea Car.

TENBY (Pembroke) from

Paddington, 257 miles. Fares, 52/4c, 31/5c. R. T. for two months, 104/8a, 62/10c. Pop. 4,830.

Map Square 20.

PAD. TENBY		TENBY PAD.	
AM 1. 0*g*	11.37	AM10. 0*r*	4.20
8.45*r*	2.57	10.51*r*	6.15
11.50*r*	6.55	11.40*r*	8.35
PM 1.10*r*	2. 6	PM 2.37*r*	9.25
9.15*e*	6.39	6.35	3.30
—	—	—	—
—	—	—	—
—	—	—	—

Sunday Trains.

PM 9.15	6.39	—	—

e Saturdays excepted.
g Mondays excepted.
r Restaurant Car.

Royal Gate House Hotel. Under new management. Fully licensed 'Phone 12.
See advt. p. **318.**

Cobourg Hotel. First class. Picturesque view of Cliffs and Bay. Private Garage. Tel. 9.
HUGHES, Proprietress.

W. Bill, Irish Cloth Merchant. London Address : 29 and 31, Great Portland Street, W., where all communications should now be addressed, and where a call from his old Customers when in town will be appreciated.
See advt. p. **1.**

TENTERDEN TOWN

(Kent) from *Charing Cross, Cannon Street* and *London Bridge, via* Headcorn. 54 miles. No through fares. Pop. 3,438.

Map Square 24.

	Leave		Arr. at
CHAR. +	CAN. ST.	LON. B.	TENTDN.
AM —	—	7.50*l*	10.28
9.25	—	9.33	12.35
PM —	11.56	12. 0	2.32
3. 0*e*	—	3. 8*e*	5. 5
4.30*d*	—	4.37*d*	6. 4
—	4.36*e*	4.39*e*	6.40
7.30*h*	—	7.26*h*	10. 2
—	—	—	—

No Sunday Trains.

TENTERDEN—continued.
Trains from Tenterden Town.

TENT'DEN	LON. B.	CAN. ST.	CHAR.+
Leave	Arrive at		
AM 8.57	11.33	—	11.45
11.11	1.36	—	1.50
PM12.40	3.26	—	3.40
3.50e	5.50	—	6. 3
4.51d	8.54	—	—
5. 8e	8.54	9. 1	—
8.40h	11.34	—	11.43
—	—	—	—
—	—	—	—

No Sunday Trains.
d Saturdays only.
e Saturdays excepted.
h Wednesdays only.
l Low Level Platform.

ANOTHER ROUTE from
Charing Cross, Cannon Street and
London Bridge, via Robertsbridge.
64 miles. No through fares.

CHAR. +	CAN. ST	LON. B	TENTDN.
Leave			Arr. at
AM —	5.20	5.25	8.57
—	7.56	8. 0	11.10
9.25	—	9.33	12.25
PM12. 3e	—	12.10e	3.12
1. 5d	—	1.11d	3.46
2. 8e	—	2.16e	4.55
2.40d	—	2.46d	4.56
—	5.12e	—	7.15
5. 5d	—	—	7.44
7.30d	—	—	10.15

No Sunday Trains.

Trains from Tenterden Town.

TENT'DEN	LON. B.	CAN. ST.	CHAR. +
Leave	Arrive at		
AM 7 6	—	9.48	—
10.29	—	—	12.49
PM 1.20	4.15	—	4.25
3. 0	6.30	—	6.39
5.15e	8.26	—	8.57
6. 5d	10.22	—	10.35
8.20d	11.35	—	11.44
—	—	—	—
—	—	—	—

No Sunday Trains.
d Saturdays only.
e Saturdays excepted.

TERN HILL (Salop), 156½
miles. Fares, 32/8d, 19/7c. R.T.
for two months, 65/4a, 39/2c. Departures *from* London as for
Market Drayton. Departures *for*
London about 4 times daily.
Map Square 17.

TERRINGTON (Norfolk)
from *King's Cross*, 108½ miles.
Fares, 19/10a, 11/1c. R. T. for two
months, 39/8a. Pop. 3,044.
Map Square 19.

KING'S +TERRTN.		TERRTN. KING'S +	
AM 4.45	7.48	AM.7. 9	10.40
5. 5e	9.32	8.37	12.25
5. 5d	9.58	10.12	1. 5
7.15r	10.48	PM12.10	3.50
8.45	12.33	2.29	6.25
10.10r	2. 8	4.10	9. 0
PM 1.50r	4.35	6.10r	9.25
5.45r	8.36	—	—
—	—	—	—
—	—	—	—
—	—	—	—

No Sunday Trains.
d Saturdays only.
e Saturdays excepted.
r Restaurant Car.

TETBURY (Gloucester)
from *Paddington*, 98½ miles. Fares,
20/5a, 12/3c. R. T. for two months,
40/10a. Pop. 1,593.
Map Square 22.

PAD.	TETB'Y.	TETB'Y	PAD.
AM 5.30	9. 7	AM 7.40r	10.45
7.30	10.57	9.20	12.20
10.45	1.42	PM12.15r	2.40
PM 3.15t	5.44	6. 5r	8.45
4.15t	7.14	7.33	10.25
6. 0r	8.44	—	—

Sunday Trains.

PM 2. 0	8.34	PM 5.55	10. 0
—	—	—	—
—	—	—	—

r Restaurant Car.
t Tea Car.

TEVERSALL (Notts), 147¾
miles. Fares, 28/2a, 16/11c. R. T.,
double fare. Departures *from*
London as for Mansfield or Alfreton. Departures *for* London
about 3 times daily. Pop. 465.
Map Square 13.

TEWKESBURY (Glou-
cester) from *Euston*, 153 miles.
Fares, 23/9a, 14/3c. R. T. for two
months, 47/6a, 28/6c. Pop. 4,704.
Map Square 17.

EUSTON	TEWKBY.	TEWKBY.	EUSTON
AM 2.30	8.44	AM 9. 0r	1.25
5. 0-	11.17	11.45t	4.35
9.15r	2.15	PM 1.45r	6.50
11.30d	3.34	4.50dr10.45	
11.30e	4.40	5.18er10.20	
12. 0nr	5.40	7. 7e	4. 0
PM 2.20t	7.31	7. 7d	5. 0

No Sunday Trains.
d Saturdays only.
e Saturdays excepted.
n Noon.
r Restaurant Car.
t Tea Car.

ANOTHER ROUTE from
Paddington, via Gloucester, 128¾
miles. No through fares.

PAD.	TEWKBY.	TEWKBY.	PAD.
AM 1. 0g	8.44	AM 8.19	12.20
7.30	12. 5	9. 0r	2.40
9. 0	2.15	11.24	5. 0
10.45	4.40	PM 4.16r	8.45
PM 3.15t	7.31	5.15	10.25
—	—	7. 7	3.30

Sunday Trains.

PM 9.15	8.44	—	—

g Mondays excepted.
r Restaurant Car.
t Tea Car.

TEYNHAM (Kent) from
Victoria, Holborn Viaduct, and
St. Paul's, 48 miles. Fares, 10/2a,
8/1b, 6/0c. R. T. for two months,
20/4a, 16/2b. Pop. 1,734.
Map Square 24.

VICT. (S.E.&C.)	Leave HOL. V.	ST. PL.'s	Arr. at TEYNH.
AM 5. 5	4.57	5. 0	7.29
5.48f	5.40f	5.42f	7.29
7.40f	7.30	7.33	9.38
9.20	—	—	11. 5
11.40d	—	—	1.25
PM 1.23d	—	—	2.53
4.20	—	6. 1	4.44
5.30e	—	7. 9	—
5.30d	—	—	7.12
6.16	6.10e	6.13e	8.37
7.50h	—	—	9.16
7.50	—	—	11.37
9. 0e	8.57e	9. 0e	11.37

TEYNHAM—continued.
Sunday Trains.

VICT. (S.E.&C.)	Leave HOL. V.	ST.PL.'s	Arr. at TEYNH.
AM 8.15	8. 0	—	9.55
10.30	10.25	—	2.38
PM 3.30	—	—	5.42
6.35	—	—	8 40
7.50	—	—	9.23

Trains from Teynham.

TEYNH.	ST. PL.'s	Arrive at HOL. V.	VICT.
AM 5.58	8. 8	8. 9	8.14
7.13	9.37	9.39	—
9. 4	—	—	11. 2
11. 3e	12.58	1. 2	1.33
11.16d	—	—	1.22
PM 1. 2	—	—	2.43
2.27e	4.46	—	4.39
2.38d	—	—	4.55
4.28	—	—	5.56
5. 9e	—	—	8.33
6.16d	—	—	8.33
9.19	11.21	11.23	—

Sunday Trains.

AM10.39	—	1. 2	12.56
PM 3.49	—	—	5.31
9.12	—	12. 0	11.44

d Saturdays only.
e Saturdays excepted.
f Wednesdays only.

ANOTHER ROUTE from
Charing Cross, Cannon Street and
London Bridge, 47 miles. Fares
as above.

CHAR. +	CAN. ST.	LON. B	Arr. at TEYNH.
AM —	7.16	7.19	9.38
—	10.58h	11. 1h	1. 5
—	10.58l	11. 1l	1.15
PM 5.58d	—	6. 4d	7.55
6.22e	—	6.29e	8.37
—	9.35	9.38	11.37

Sunday Trains.

PM 7. 0	—	7. 7	9. 0

Trains from Teynham.

TEYNH.	LON. B.	CAN. ST.	Arr. at CHAR. +
AM 5.58	8.34	—	8.41
PM 5. 9e	7.14	—	7.23
6.16d	8.15	8.20	—

Sunday Trains.

PM 9.12	11.15	—	11.24

d Saturdays only.
e Saturdays excepted
h Wednesdays and Saturdays
excepted.
l Wednesdays only.

THACKLEY (Yorks), from
King's Cross, 194½ miles. Fares,
39/9a, 23/10c. R. T., double fare.
Departures *from* London as for
Bradford. Departures *for* London
about 6 times daily.

THAME (Oxon) from
Paddington,
via High Wycombe, 8/2a, 4/11c.
9/10c. R. T. for two months, 16/4a,
9/10c. *Via* Oxford, 13/4a, 8/0c.
R.T. for two months, 26/8a, 16/0c.
Pop. 2,918.
Map Square 23.

PAD.	THAME	THAME	PAD.
AM 5.30k	9. 7	AM 7.36	9.20
8.12	10. 3	9. 8	10.40
9.20h	11.30	10. 3k	12. 5
9.45k	11.49	11.49	*1.18
PM12.18	2. 3	PM 2. 3k	4.15
2.23	4. 8	3.13	4.40
4.40	6. 2	4. 8k	7.20
4.45h	7.15	5.22h	7.32
6.25	7.55	7.15	9.18
7.10	8.15	7.55h	10.45
7.30dk	9.29	8.25	11 4
9. 0d	10.53	9.29d	11.41
—	—	10.53d	3.30

THAME—*continued.*

Sunday Trains.

Pad.	Thame	Thame	Pad.
AM 9.12	10.59	AM 7.56	10.14
PM 4. 0	5.50	10.59*k*	2.40
4.10*k*	6.40	PM 6.40	8.25
—	—	—	—
—	—	—	—

d Saturdays only.
h Tuesdays only.
k Via Oxford.

THAMES DITTON

(Surrey) from *Waterloo*, 14 miles. Fares, 2/6*a*, 1/6*c*. R. T. for two days, 4/8*a*, 3/0*c*. Pop. 5,588. *See* pp. 594, 595.

THANKERTON (Lanark),

367½ miles. No through fares. Departures *from* London as for Lockerbie. Departures *for* London about 4 times daily. Pop. 290.
Map Square 40.

THATCHAM (Berks) from

Paddington, 49½ miles. Fares, 10/3*a*, 6/2*c*. R. T. for two months, 20/6*a*. Pop. 2,416.
Map Square 23.

Pad.	Thatch.	Thatch.	Pad.
AM 6.30	8.24	AM 8. 4	9.30
8.45*r*	10. 3	9.18	10.45
9.30	10.51	11. 7	12.55
10.45	12.28	PM12. 8	1.50
11.20	1.23	1. 8	2.30
PM 1.10*r*	2.39	2.10	3.50
1.35*r*	3.34	3. 8	4.35
3.18	5. 9	4.17	5.50
4. 7	5.57	5.17	7.20
5. 5	6.31	7.39	9.15
5.40	7. 9	8.23	10.25
8. 0	9.16	9.11	10.45
10. 0*f*	11.29	10.30	2.45
—	—	—	—
—	—	—	—
—	—	—	—

Sunday Trains.

AM 9.10	10.45	AM 9. 0	10.50
PM 5.15	7. 4	PM 7.46	9.15

f Wednesdays and Saturdays only.
r Restaurant Car.

THATTO HEATH

(Lancs), 193¼ miles. Fares, 40/3*a*, 24/2*c*. R. T. for two months, 80/6*a*, 48/4*c*. Departures *from* London as for Earlestown. Departures *for* London about 6 times daily.

THAXTED (Essex) from

Liverpool Street, 41½ miles. No through fares. Pop. 1,596.
Map Square 19.

L'pool St.	Thx'd.	Thx'd.	L'pool St.
AM 7.18	9.32	AM 8.10	9.46
10. 5	11.46	PM12.10	2. 7
PM12.48*e*	2.53	1.50*e*	5. 9
1.19*d*	3.20	2. 5*d*	5. 9
2.48	4.46	3.47	6.10
4.45	6.17	5.20	7.56
6.30	8. 0	6.27	8.22
—	—	—	—
—	—	—	—
—	—	—	—
—	—	—	—

No Sunday Trains.

d Saturdays only.
e Saturdays excepted.

THEALE (Berks) from

Paddington, 41¾ miles. Fares, 8/7*a*, 5/2*c*. R. T. for two months, 17/2*a*. Pop. 1,047.
Map Square 23.

Pad.	Theale	Theale	Pad.
AM 6.30	8. 5	AM 8.26	9.30
8.45*r*	9.44	9.37	10.45
9.30	10.32	11.28	12.55
10.45	12. 8	PM12.27	1.50
11.20	1. 4	1.27	2.30
PM 1.10*r*	2.20	2.29	3.50
1.35*r*	3.15	3.28	4.35
3.18	4.50	4.33	5.50
4. 7	5.38	5.36	7.20
5. 5	6.12	7.59	9.15
5.40	6.50	8.42	10.25
8. 0	8.57	9.30	10.45
10. 0*f*	11.10	10.43*h*	2.45
—	—	—	—
—	—	—	—
—	—	—	—
—	—	—	—
—	—	—	—

Sunday Trains.

AM 9.10	10.27	AM 9.23	10.50
PM 5.15	6.45	PM 8. 6	9.15
—	—	—	—
—	—	—	—
—	—	—	—

f Wednesdays and Saturdays only.
h Wednesdays only.
r Restaurant Car.

THEDDINGWORTH

(Leicester) from *Euston*, 88½ miles. Fares, 17/6*a*, 10/6*c*. R. T. for two months, 35/0*a*. Departures *from* London as for Welford. Departures *for* London about 4 times daily. Pop. 228.
Map Square 18.

THEDDLETHORPE

(Lincoln), 140¾ miles. Fares, 29/0*a*, 17/5*c*. R. T. for two months, 58/0*a*, 34/10*c*. Departures *from* London as for Mablethorpe. Departures *for* London about 3 times daily. Pop. 491.
Map Square 13.

THE HALE (Middlesex)

from *King's Cross* and *Moorgate Street*, 10 miles. Fares, 1/9½*a*, 1/5*b*, 1/1*c*. R. T. for two days, 3/7*a*, 2/10*b*, 2/2*c*. From Broad Street, and Moorgate Street, 2/0*a*, 1/7*b*, 1/2½*c*. R. T. for two days, 4/0*a*, 3/2*b*, 2/4½*c*. *See* pp. 518–522.

THELWALL (Cheshire),

185½ miles. Fares, 37/9*a*, 22/8*c*. R. T., double fare. Departures *from* London as for Lymm. Departures *for* London about twice daily. Pop. 517.
Map Square 12.

THE MOUND (Sutherland),

648¾ miles. Fares, 116/6*a*, 69/11*c*. R. T. for two months, 233/0*a*, 139/10*c*. Departures *from* London as for Lairg. Departures *for* London about twice daily.
Map Square 34.

THE OAKS (Lancs), 199¾

miles. No through fares. Departures *from* London as for Bolton (*via* Manchester). Departures *for* London about 6 times daily.

THETFORD (Norfolk)

from *Liverpool Street*, 93¾ miles. Fares, 18/11*a*, 11/4*c*. R. T. for two months, 37/10*a*. Pop. 4,704.
Map Square 19.

L'p'l St.	Thetf'd	Thetf'd	L'p'l St.
AM 5. 5	7.44	AM 7.40*r*	10.23
5.50	9.32	8.39	11.27
7.18*d*	10.55	9.55	12.40
8.30*r*	11.26	11.35*r*	2.21
11.50*r*	2.30	PM 2.45*r*	5.17
PM 2.34	5. 7	5.29*r*	8.22
5.49*r*	8.34	5.55*r*	8.33
7.10*r*	9.40	11.36	2.50
10.12	1. 2	—	—
—	—	—	—

Sunday Trains.

AM 9.25	12.39	PM 3.36	6.40
PM 3.25	6.29	7.11	9.40
9.12	12.59	11.36	3. 0
—	—	—	—

d Saturdays only.
r Restaurant Car.

THETFORD BRIDGE

(Norfolk), 94¾ miles. Fares, 18/11*a*, 11/4*c*. R.T. for two months, 37/10*a*, 22/8*c*. Departures *from* London as for Thetford or Ingham. Departures *for* London about 3 times daily.
Map Square 19.

THEYDON BOIS

(Essex) from *Fenchurch Street* or *Liverpool Street*, 15 miles. Fares, 3/2*a*, 2/7*b*, 1/11*c*. R. T. for two months, 6/4*a*, 5/1½*b*, 3/4½*c*. From Fenchurch Street, 3/2*a*, 2/6*b*, 1/11*c*. R. T. for two months, 6/1½*a*, 4/10*b*, 3/2½*c*. Pop. 1,267. *See* pp. 541–544.
Map Square 23.

THIRSK (Yorks) from

King's Cross, 210 miles. Fares, 43/9*a*, 26/3*c*. R. T., double fare. Pop. 2,937.
Map Square 8.

King's+	Thirsk	Thirsk	King's+
AM 7.15*r*	12.47	AM 7.22	1. 5
10. 0*r*	3.12	8.54	1.15
11.30	6. 2	10. 3*dr*	4.30
PM 1.50*r*	7.42	PM 1. 6*r*	6.15
5.35*r*	10. 5	4.19*r*	9.25
10.45	4.25	9. 7	3.25
—	—	—	—
—	—	—	—
—	—	—	—
—	—	—	—

Sunday Trains.

AM11.30*r*	6.24	AM 9.14	5.15
PM11.25	7.55	PM 8.14	5.40

d Saturdays only.
r Restaurant Car.

THONGSBRIDGE

(Yorks), 184½ miles. Fares (*via* Penistone), 37/4*a*, 22/5*c*. R. T. for two months, 74/8*a*, 44/10*c*. Departures *from* London as for Holmfirth. Departures *for* London about 6 times daily.
Map Square 12.

THORINGTON (Essex)

from *Liverpool Street*, 59½ miles. Fares, 12/9*a*, 7/8*c*. R. T. for two months, 25/6*a*. Departures *from* London as for Alresford (Essex). Departures *for* London about 8 times daily. Pop. 397.
Map Square 24.

THORNABY (Yorks) from

King's Cross, 235¼ miles. Fares, 49/0*a*, 29/5*c*. R. T. double fare. Pop. 19,831.
Map Square 8.

King's+	Thorb'y	Thorb'y	King's+
AM 4.45	11.38	AM 7.58*r*	1.15
7.15*r*	2.30	9.19*g*	3.15
10. 0*r*	3.21	9.55*r*	4.30
10.10*r*	4.29	PM 1. 2*r*	6.15
11.30	7.49	3. 0*r*	9.25
11.50	5. 4	4.40*r*	10. 0
PM 1.15*r*	6.29	8.20	3.25
1.50*r*	7.59	11. 9*e*	5.40
5.45*r*	10.43	11. 9*d*	6. 0
11.25	5.36	—	—
—	—	—	—

Sunday Trains.

AM 8.30	5. 7	AM10. 3	5.15
11.30*r*	8.51	PM 2.22	8.15
PM11.25	5.50	6.32	5.40

d Saturdays only.
e Saturdays excepted.
g Mondays excepted.
r Restaurant Car.

THORNBURY (Glo'ster),

135 miles. No through fares. Departures *from* London as for Bristol. Departures *for* London about 4 times daily. Pop. 2,646.
Map Square 22.

THORNE (Yorks), from

King's Cross, *via* Doncaster. 165¾ miles. Fares, 34/5*a*, 20/8*c*. R. T., double fare. Pop. 5,290.
Map Square 13.

King's +	Thorne	Thorne	King's +
AM 4.45	9. 7	AM 6.46*r*	11.30
7.15*r*	10.44	9.24	1. 5
10.10*r*	1.32	10.42	3.50
11.30*d*	4.34	PM12.30*r*	4.30
PM 1.40*r*	5.22	2.30*r*	6.15
4. 0*r*	8.22	5.13*r*	9.25
—	—	7.40*e*	3.25
—	—	9. 1*d*	3.25
—	—	—	—

Sunday Trains.

12. 0*nr*	8.25	AM10.35*r*	3.45
—	—	—	—
—	—	—	—

d Saturdays only.
e Saturdays excepted.
n Noon.
r Restaurant Car.

THORNER (Yorks), 191¼

miles. No through fares. Departures *from* London as for Leeds or Wetherby. Departures *for* London about 6 times daily. Pop. 1,096.
Map Square 12.

THORNEY (Cambs), 84¾

miles. Fares, 17/4*a*, 10/5*c*. R. T., double fare. Departures *from* London as for Wisbech St. Mary. Departures *for* London about 5 times daily. Pop. 1,871.
Map Square 18.

THORNFALCON (Somerset)

from *Paddington*, 141¾ miles. Fares, 29/10*a*, 17/11*c*. R. T. for two months, 59/8*a*. Departures *from* London as for Ilminster. Departures *for* London about 6 times daily. Pop. 161.
Map Square 22.

THORNHILL (Dumfries),

from *St. Pancras*, 355¼ miles. Fares, 70/3*a*, 42/2*c*. R. T. for two months, 140/6*a*, 84/4*c*. Pop. 1,577.
Map Square 43.

St. Pan.	Th'hill	Th'hill	St. Pan.
AM 4.25	3.10	AM 9.41*r*	6.35
9.50*r*	6.14	PM12. 3*r*	9.15
PM12.15*dr*	8.17	10.27*e*	7.25
9.30*e*	6.52	10.27*d*	8.57
11.45*e*	8.48	—	—
—	—	—	—
—	—	—	—
—	—	—	—
—	—	—	—
—	—	—	—

Sunday Trains.

PM 9.30	6.52	PM10.57	7.25
11.45	8.48	—	—
—	—	—	—
—	—	—	—

d Saturdays only.
e Saturdays excepted.
r Restaurant Car.

THORNHILL (Yorks)

from *King's Cross*, *via* Horbury, 182 miles. Fares, 37/9*a*, 22/8*c*. R. T., double fare. Pop. 11,303.

King's +	Th'hill	Th'hill	King's +
AM 4.45	10.52	AM 6.32*r*	11.30
7.15*r*	12.16	8.26	1. 5
10.10*dr*	2.40	9.56*r*	1.55
10.10*er*	3.14	10.36*r*	3.50
PM 1.30*r*	5.47	PM12.26	5. 0
1.50*r*	7.36	3. 0*r*	7.10
5.45*r*	10.32	4.43	9.25
—	—	8.57*e*	3.25
—	—	—	—
—	—	—	—
—	—	—	—

Sunday Trains.

12. 0*hn*	6.24	AM10.35*r*	3.45
—	—	PM 3.51*h*	10.20
—	—	—	—
—	—	—	—

d Saturdays only.
e Saturdays excepted.
h Passengers cross Wakefield at own expense.
n Noon.
r Restaurant Car.

THORNIELEE (Selkirk),

370½ miles. No through fares. Departures *from* London as for Galashiels. Departures *for* London about 5 times daily.
Map Square 41.

THORNLEY (Durham),

249½ miles. No through fares. Departures *from* London as for West Hartlepool. Departures *for* London about 5 times daily. Pop. 3,380.
Map Square 7.

THORNLIEBANK (Renfrew),

404½ miles. No through fares. Departures *from* London as for Hamilton. Departures *for* London about 5 times daily. Pop. 2,289.

THORNTON (Fife),

423 miles. Fares, 85/8*a*, 51/5*c*. R. T. for two months, 171/4*a*, 102/10*c*. Departures *from* London as for Kirkcaldy. Departures *for* London about 4 times daily. Pop. 1,728.
Map Square 41.

THORNTON (Lancs), 225¼

miles. Fares, 46/11*a*, 28/2*c*. R. T. for two months, 93/10*a*, 56/4*c*. Departures *from* London as for Kirkham. Departures *for* London about 8 times daily. Pop. 6,179.
Map Square 7.

THORNTON (Yorks),

from *King's Cross*, 197½ miles. Fares, 39/9*a*, 23/10*c*. R. T. for two months, 79/6*a*. Departures *from* London as for Keighley. Departures *for* London about 6 times daily. Pop. 304.

THORNTON ABBEY

(Lincoln), 167½ miles. Fares, 34/10*a*, 20/11*c*. R. T. for two months, 69/8*a*, 41/10*c*. Departures *from* London as for Brocklesby. Departures *for* London about 5 times daily. Pop. (Thornton Curtis) 452.
Map Square 13.

THORNTON DALE

(Yorks), 222½ miles. Fares, 46/6*a*, 27/11*c*. R. T., double fare. Departures *from* London as for Malton. Departures *for* London about 4 times daily. Pop. 1,181.
Map Square 8.

THORNTONHALL

(Lanark), 402 miles. No through fares. Departures *from* London as for Hamilton. Departures *for* London about 5 times daily.

THORNTON HEATH

(Surrey) from *Victoria* and *London Bridge*, 8¾ miles. Fares from Victoria, 1/8*a*, 1/0*c*. R. T. for two days, 3/1*a*, 2/0*c*. From London Bridge, *via* Tulse Hill, 1/8*a*, 1/0*c*. R. T. for two days, 3/4*a*, 1/9*c*. Pop. 20,819. *See* pp. 567, 570-577.

THORNTON IN CRAVEN

(Yorks), from *St. Pancras*, 226½ miles. Fares, 42/6*a*, 25/6*c*. R. T., double fare. Departures *from* London as for Colne. Departures *for* London about 6 times daily. Pop. 310.
Map Square 7.

THORP ARCH (Yorks),

188 miles. Fares, 39/0*a*, 23/5*c*. R. T., double fare. Departures *from* London as for Wetherby. Departures *for* London about 6 times daily. Pop. 409.
Map Square 8.

THORPE (Northampton)

from *Euston*, 90½ miles. Fares, 14/9*a*, 8/10*c*. R. T. for two months, 29/6*a*, 17/8*c*. Departures *from* London as for Thrapston. Departures *for* London about 6 times daily. Pop. 177.
Map Square 18.

THORPE BAY (Essex)

from *Fenchurch Street* or *St. Pancras*, 38 miles. Fares from Fenchurch Street, 5/8*a*, 3/5*c*. R. T. for two months, 11/4*a*, 6/10*c*. From St. Pancras, 5/8*a*, 3/5*c*. R. T. for two months, 11/4*a*, 6/10*c*. Departures *from* London as for Shoeburyness. Departures *for* London about 20 times daily. Pop. (Thorpe) 10,342.
Map Square 24.

THORPE-CLOUD

(Derby), 149¾ miles. Fares, 31/0*a*, 18/7*c*. R. T. for two months, 62/0*a*. Departures *from* London as for Ashbourne. Departures *for* London about 5 times daily. Pop. (Thorpe) 178.
Map Square 12.

THORPE CULVERT

(Lincoln),124¾ miles. Fares, 25/10a, 15/6c. R. T., double fare. Departures *from London* as for Skegness. Departures *for* London about 5 times daily.
Map Square 13.

THORPE - LE - SOKEN

(Essex) from *Liverpool Street*, 65¼ miles. Fares, 14/0a, 8/5c. R. T. for two months, 28/0a. Pop. 1,130.
Map Square 24.

L'PL. ST.	THORPE	THORPE	L'PL. ST.
AM 5. 0	7.11	AM 7.13r	8.52
6.50	9.57	7.55	9.36
8.18	10.22	8.23r	9.53
8.46	11.48	10. 8	11.43
10.23	12.25	11.54r	2. 3
11.26d	1.30	PM12.45d	2.23
11.30e	1.57	1.51	3.36
PM12.36	2.24	3.29	5. 5
1.30dr	3. 7	4.36	6.32
2. 3d	3.52	5.57	7.40
2.15	4.46	6. 9	9.17
3.23	5.10	7.55	9.36
3.26	6.13	8.10	11.16
4.58r	6.47	—	—
5.30r	6.58	—	—
5.42	8. 5	—	—
6.39	8.21	—	—
7.45r	9.55	—	—
8.45	10.39	—	—
12. 0d	1.44	—	—

Sunday Trains.

AM 9. 8	10.47	AM 9.10	11.38
9.20r	11.50	PM 6. 7	8.25
PM 4.40	6.38	8.15	10. 9

d Saturdays only.
e Saturdays excepted.
r Restaurant Car.

THORPENESS (Suffolk)

97¾ miles. Fares, 20/5a, 12/3c. R. T. for two months, 40/10a, 24/6c. Departures *from* London as for Aldeburgh. Departures *for* London about 8 times daily.
Map Square 19.

THORPE - ON - THE-

HILL (Lincoln), 150¼ miles. Fares, 26/11a, 16/2c. R. T. for two months, 53/10a, 32/4c. Departures *from* London as for Collingham. Departures *for* London about 5 times daily. Pop. 291.
Map Square 13.

THORPE THEWLES

(Durham), 239¼ miles. Fares, 50/0a, 30/0c. R. T. for two months, 100/0a, 60/0c. Departures *from* London as for Stockton-on-Tees. Departures *for* London about 4 times daily.
Map Square 8.

THORVERTON (Devon),

173 miles. Fares, 36/11a, 22/2c. R. T. for two months, 73/10a. Departures *from* London as for Exeter (St. David's). Departures *for* London about 6 times daily. Pop. 734.
Map Square 26.

THRAPSTON (North-

ampton) from *Euston*, 87¾ miles. Fares, 14/9a, 8/10c. R. T., double fare. Pop. 1,836.
Map Square 18.

EUSTON.	THRAPS.	THRAPS.	EUSTON.
AM 5. 0	8. 5	AM 7.37	10.15
6.45	10.28	8.57	11.55
9.30d	12.10	10.25	12.40
10.40	1.15	11.23h	2.45
PM12.15e	3.38	11.23k	4.15
12.15d	3.43	PM12.35d	3.45
3. 5	5.44	2.31	5.35
4.15	7.18	4.34	7.20
7. 0	9.33	6.58	9.20
—	—	8. 2	11.35

No Sunday Trains.

d Saturdays only.
e Saturdays excepted.
h Thursdays and Saturdays only.
k Thursdays and Saturdays excepted.

ANOTHER ROUTE from

St. Pancras, 78¾ miles. Fares as above.

ST.PAN.	THRAPSTN.	THRAPSTN.	ST.PAN.
AM 4.25	8.55	AM 8.52r	11. 0
8.25r	10.57	PM 1. 3	3.25
11.35	2.40	4. 8	7. 3
PM 3.30r	5.27	6.15	8.22
6.25r	8.23	—	—

No Sunday Trains.

r Restaurant Car.

THREE BRIDGES

(Sussex) from *London Bridge, Victoria*, and *Clapham Junction*, 29½ miles. Fares, 6/1a, 3/8c. R. T. for two months, 12/2a, 7/4c.
Map Square 23.

	Leave		Arr. at
VICT.	CLAP. J.	LON. B.	THR.BR.
AM —	—	5.18	6.35
7.23	7.29	7.25	8.42
8.25	8.32	8. 7	9.31
9. 0	9. 8	9. 6	10. 1
9.45	9.51	9.50	11. 3
10.35	10.42	10.35	11.40
11.55	—	—	12.40
—	—	11.50	12.45
12. 0	12. 7	12.10	1. 8
PM 1.20e	1.27e	—	2.18
1.25d	—	1.10d	2.18
2. 0d	2. 7d	2. 5d	3. 8
2. 0e	2. 7e	2. 5e	3.10
—	—	2. 8d	3.19
*4. 0	4 8	4. 5	5. 2
4.30	—	—	5.11
—	—	5. 5	5.50
5. 5	5.12	5.10	6.13
5.27	—	5.21	6.31
—	—	6. 0	6.50
6. 6	6.12	6. 8	7.20
7.15	7.22	7.20	8.28
9. 3	9.10	9.12	10.11
10.30	10.38	10.55	11.45

Sunday Trains.

AM 6.55	7. 2	7. 2	8.24
8.18	8.25	8.25	9.27
8.50	8.57	8.55	10. 9
PM 1.14	1.21	1.10	2.21
5.50	5.57	6. 0	7.11
6.35	6.40	6.33	7.41
8. 0	8. 8	8. 0	9.16
—	—	—	—

THREE BRIDGES—*cont.*

Trains from Three Bridges.

	Leave	Arrive at	
THR. BR.	LON. B.	CLAP. J.	VICT.
AM 7. 0	8.15	8.15	8.24
8.20	9.10	—	9.19
8.36	—	9.37	9.44
8.41	9.42	—	9.58
9. 7	9.58	—	—
9.58	10.55	10.40	10.48
11. 2	12.13	11.59	12. 7
PM12.31	1.42	1.39	1.50
1.26	2.22	2.13	2.22
2.31	3.40	3.37	3.45
3.10	—	4. 9	4.17
3.40	4.32	4.27	4.35
4.38	5.54	5.47	5.55
5.42	6.36	6.26	6.34
6.50	7.42	7.37	7.45
7.31	8.46	8.39	8.48
9.43	10.58	11.10	11.17
11.59	12.59	12.50	1. 0
—	—	—	—
—	—	—	—
—	—	—	—

Sunday Trains.

AM 9.18	10.18	—	—
9.34	10.45	10.25	10.32
PM 5. 3	5. 3	5. 1	5.11
6.49	7.56	—	—
7.33	8.34	8.31	8.41
8.15	9.17	9. 4	9.13
8.22	9.32	9.24	9.34
10.29	11.34	11.34	11.42
—	—	—	—
—	—	—	—

d Saturdays only.
e Saturdays excepted.

THREE COCKS (Brecon)

171 miles. Fares, from *Paddington*, 35/5a, 21/3c. R. T. for two months, 70/10a. From *Euston*, 37/6a, 22/6c. R. T. for two months, 75/0a. Departures *from* London as for Hay or Builth Wells. Departures *for* London about 3 times daily.
Map Square 16.

THREE COUNTIES

(Beds) from *King's Cross*. 35¾ miles. Fares, 7/4a, 4/5c. R. T., double fare. Departures *from* London as for Arlesey. Departures *for* London about 5 times daily.
Map Square 18.

THRELKELD (Cumber-

land), 295½ miles. No through fares. Departures *from* London as for Keswick. Departures *for* London about 6 times daily. Pop. 521.
Map Square 7.

THRUMSTER (Caith-

ness), 733 miles. No through fares. Departures *from* London as for Wick. Departures *for* London about 3 times daily.
Map Square 32.

THURGARTON (Notts)

from *St. Pancras*, 132¼ miles. Fares, 26/1a, 15/8c. R. T., double fare. Departures *from* London as for Nottingham. Departures *for* London about 6 times daily. Pop. 288.
Map Square 13.

THURLBY (Lincoln), from *King's Cross*, 93¾ miles. Fares, 19/4*a*, 11/7*c*. R. T., double fare. Departures *from* London as for Bourne. Departures *for* London about 6 times daily. Pop. 756. *Map Square* 18.

THURLESTONE. *See* KINGSBRIDGE.

THURNBY (Leicester), 105½ miles. Fares, 20/2*a*, 12/1*c*. R. T., double fare. Departures *from* London as for Bottesford. Departures *for* London about 3 times daily. Pop. 226. *Map Square* 18.

THURSFORD (Norfolk) from *King's Cross*, 141½ miles. Fares, 23/7*a*, 14/2*c*. R. T. for two months, 47/2*a*. Departures *from* London as for Fakenham Town. Departures *for* London about 4 times daily. Pop. 228. *Map Square* 14.

THURSO (Caithness) from *Euston*, 721½ miles. Fares, 131/8*a*, 79/0*c*. R. T. for two months, 263/4*a*. Pop. 4,278. *Map Square* 31.

EUSTON	THURSO	THURSO	EUSTON
PM 1.30*er*	1.10*l*	AM 8.15	7.40*h*
7.40*er*	4.20*l*	PM 2.30*er*	7.30*l*
11.35*v*	9. 5*h*	—	—

Sunday Trains.

PM 7.50*r*	4.20	—	—

e Saturdays excepted.
h A.M.
l P.M.
r Restaurant Car.
v Thursdays only.

ANOTHER ROUTE from *King's Cross*, 711½ miles. Fares as above.

KING'S+	THURSO	THURSO	KING'S+
AM11.53*er*	1.10*h*	AM 8.15	7.15*h*
PM 7.45*er*	4.20*h*	PM 2.30*er*	6.30*h*
11.25*es*	9. 5	—	—

Sunday Trains.

AM 7.45*r*	4.20	—	—

e Saturdays excepted.
h P.M.
k A.M.
r Restaurant Car.
s Fridays only.

THURSTASTON (Cheshire), 196¼ miles. Fares, 41/0*a*, 24/7*c*. R. T. for two months, 82/0*a*. Departures *from* London as for Hooton. Departures *for* London about 6 times daily. Pop. 138. *Map Square* 11.

THURSTON (Suffolk) from *Liverpool Street*, 89 miles. Fares, 17/1*a*, 10/3*c*. R. T. for two months, 34/2*a*. Departures *from* London as for Elmswell. Departures *for* London about 6 times daily. Pop. 628. *Map Square* 19.

THUXTON (Norfolk) from *Liverpool Street*, 117¾ miles. Fares, 23/7*a*, 14/2*c*. R. T. for two months, 47/2*a*. Departures *from* London as for Dereham. Departures *for* London about 5 times daily. Pop. 78. *Map Square* 19.

TIBSHELF (Derby), 143 miles. Fares, 28/2*a*, 16/11*c*. R. T., double fare. Departures *from* London as for Kirkby and Pinxton. Departures *for* London about 4 times daily. Pop. 3,926. *Map Square* 13.

TIBSHELF AND NEWTON (Derby), 138¾ miles. Fares, 28/2*a*, 16/11*c*. R. T., double fare. Departures *from* London as for Alfreton. Departures *for* London about 3 times daily. Pop. (Tibshelf) 3,926.

TICEHURST ROAD (Sussex) from *Charing Cross*, *Cannon Street*, and *London Bridge*, 44½ miles. Fares, 9/4*a*, 7/5*b*, 5/7*c*. R.T. for two months, 18/8*a*, 14/10*b*. Pop. (Ticehurst) 2,853. *Map Square* 24.

	Leave		Arr. at
CHAR. +	CAN. ST.	LON. B.	TICE. R.
AM —	5.20	5.25	7.44
—	7.56	8. 0	10. 1
9.25	—	9.33	11. 5
10.40	—	10.46	12.15
PM12. 3*e*	—	12.10*e*	2. 4
12.40*d*	—	12.47*d*	2. 5
1. 5*d*	—	1.11*d*	2.41
3.48*e*	—	—	5.15
5. 5*d*	—	—	6.29
—	5.12*e*	—	6.33
6. 3*e*	6.16*e*	6.19*e*	7.39
7.30	—	—	8.58

Sunday Trains.

AM 8.45	—	—	10. 8
PM 7.35	—	7.45	9.19

Trains from Ticehurst Road.

	Leave		Arrive at	
	TICE. RD.	LON. B.	CAN. ST.	CHAR. +
AM 7.51	—	9.15	—	—
8.30	—	9.48	—	—
9.15*d*	10.29	—	—	10.39
9.54*e*	11. 7	—	—	11.17
10.58	—	—	—	12.49
PM 1. 1	3. 6	—	—	3.19
2.29	4.15	—	—	4.25
3.23*d*	5. 0	—	—	5. 8
4.15*d*	6.30	—	—	6.39
4.25*e*	6.44	—	—	6.54
6.22	8.26	—	—	8.35
8.26	10.15	—	—	10.23
9.36	11.34	—	—	11.44

Sunday Trains.

AM 7.55	10. 5	—	—	10.15
9.55	11.23	—	—	11.34
PM 6.20	8.12	—	—	8.22
9.27	11. 4	—	—	11.15

d Saturdays only.
e Saturdays excepted.

TICKHILL (Yorks), 158⅔ miles. Fares, 33/7*a*, 20/2*c*. R. T., double fare. Departures *from* London as for Doncaster. Departures *for* London about 4 times daily. Pop. 2,106. *Map Square* 13.

TIDAL BASIN (Victoria Docks) from *Liverpool Street* or *Fenchurch Street*, 6½ miles. Fares from Liverpool Street, 0/10*a*, 0/8*b*, 0/6*c*. R. T. for two days, 1/8*a*, 1/4*b*, 0/9*c*. From Fenchurch Street, 0/7½*a*, 0/6*b*, 0/4½*c*. R. T. for two days, 1/3*a*, 1/0*b*, 0/9*c*. Pop. 33,923. *See* pp. 537-540. *Map Square* 62.

TIDDINGTON (Oxon) from *Paddington*, 44½ miles. Fares, 9/4*a*, 5/7*c*. R. T. for two months, 18/8*a*. Departures *from* London as for Wheatley. Departures *for* London about 4 times daily. Pop. 156. *Map Square* 23.

TIDENHAM (Glo'ster) from *Paddington*, 140½ miles. Fares, 29/10*a*, 17/11*c*. R. T. for two months, 59/8*a*. Departures *from* London as for Tintern. Departures *for* London about 3 times daily. Pop. 1,710. *Map Square* 22.

TIDWORTH (Hants) from *Waterloo*, 76½ miles. Fares, 16/0*a*, 9/7*c*. R. T. for two months, 32/0*a*. Pop. 4,840. *Map Square* 22.

W'LOO	T'DW'TH	T'DW'TH	W'LOO
AM 7.30	10.22	AM 8.45	10.56
9.30*d*	1.45	PM12.20	2.36
PM 1. 0*r*	3. 9	3.20	6.26
3.30	6.12	5.30*e*	7.40
6. 0*r*	8.19	5.30*r*	8.30
—	—	—	—

Sunday Trains.

PM 6. 0	8.35	—	—

d Saturdays only.
e Saturdays excepted.
r Restaurant Car.

TIGHNABRUAICH (Argyll). *See* trains to and from Greenock and thence by steamer about twice daily each way. Pop. 1,009.

TILBURY (Essex) from *Fenchurch Street*, 22½ miles. Fares, 2/6*a*, 1/6*c*. R. T. for two months, 4/4½*a*, 2/7½*c*. Pop. 9,582. *Map Square* 24.

FEN. ST.	TILBURY	TILBURY	FEN. ST.
AM 5.37	6.51	AM 5.28	6.34
6.15	7.34	6.18	7.22
6.52	7.59	7.22	8.24
7.30	8.37	7.47	8.48
7.42	8.53	8.44	9.34
8.11	9.22	8.55	10. 4*h*
9. 5	10. 4	9.20	10.22
9.39	10.47	9.48	10.49
10.17	11. 2	10.25	11.20
11.13	12. 2	11.10	12.16
11.35	12.42	PM12.10*dk*	1.10
11.42*e*	12.21	12.20*d*	1.27
PM12.21	1.31	12.36*e*	1.22
1.15*d*	2. 8	1. 0*d*	2.10
1.35*d*	2.35	1.32	2.34
1.48*e*	2.54	2.33	3.18
2.15*d*	3. 7	3. 5	4.10
2.26*d*	3.21	3.42	5. 4*h*
2.40	3.48	4. 8	5.18
3.25	4.20	4.40*e*	5.42
4.16	5.18	4.52*ek*	5.49
4.46	5.41	5. 5*e*	6.10
5.32	6.17	5.24	6.33
5.46*e*	6.42	5.50*e*	6.56
5.55*e*	6.54	6.20	7.24
6.17*e*	7.13	6.55*e*	7.51
6.38	7.40	7. 4	8. 4
6.53	7.52	8.10	9.15
7.41*e*	8.41	9.14*d*	10.20
8.13	9.20	9.14	10.23*h*
9.25	10.26	10.20	11.23*h*
10.45	11.44	10.20	11.40
12. 0	12.57	10.50	11.50
—	—	—	—
—	—	—	—

TILBURY—*continued.*
Sunday Trains.

Fen. St.	Tilbury	Tilbury	Fen. St.
AM 8.40	9.51	AM 8.42	9.36
9.45	11. 5	9. 8	10.18
11.10	12.13	11.54	1. 1
PM 1. 6	2. 6	PM12.12	2. 2*h*
2. 7	3.11	1.30	2.33
4.30	5.32	2.58	4. 4
6.10	7.25	5.28	6.32
6.38	7.35	6.38	7.45
7.22	9. 0	8. 5	9.11*h*
8.45	9.51	8.18	9.30
10.30	11.27	9.55	11. 0
—	—	10.10	11.22*h*

d Saturdays only.
e Saturdays excepted.
h Departs from or arrives at Mark Lane Station.
k Arrives at or departs from Docks Station.

TILBURY DOCKS
(Essex) from *Fenchurch Street,* 21½ miles. Fares, 2/6*a*, 1/6*c*. R.T. for two months, 4/4½*a*, 2/7½*c*. Departures *from* London as for Tilbury. Departures *for* London about 3 minutes later.
Map Square 24.

TILE HILL (Warwick),
9¾ miles. Fares, 20/3*a*, 12/2*c*. R. T. for two months, 40/6*a*. Departures *from* London as for Coventry. Departures *for* London about 3 times daily.
Map Square 17.

TILEHURST (Berks) from
Paddington, 38½ miles. Fares, 8/1*a*, 4/10*c*. R. T. for two months, 16/2*a*. Pop. 3,175.
Map Square 23.

Pad.	Tilh'st	Tilh'st	Pad.
AM 5.30	6.58	AM 8.12	9. 0
6.30	8. 8	8.36	9.30
7.30	8.49	9. 6	10. 0
9. 0	10. 5	9.41	10.45
9.45	10.51	10.46	12. 0
11.20	12.23	PM12.45	1.50
PM12.30	1.34	2.13	3.20
1.10*dr*	2.13	3.16	4.35
1.35*r*	2.32	4. 4	5. 6
1.50*d*	3.17	5. 5	6. 2
3.18	4.38	5.58	7.20
3.38	5. 1	7.17	8.20
5. 0	6.55	8.23	9.15
5.40	6.40	9.29	10.45
6. 5	7. 2	10.25*h*	2.45
6.55	7.58	—	—
7.30	8.26	—	—
8. 5	9.24	—	—
10. 0*h*	11.11	—	—
—	—	—	—
—	—	—	—

Sunday Trains.

AM 9.10	10.21	AM 8.43	10.14
10.35	11.28	PM12.12	2.40
11. 0	12.14	4.40	6. 0
PM 1.45	3. 6	7. 2	8.20
2. 0	3.48	8. 2	9.15
4.10	5.36	8.41	9.48
5.15	6.39	9.52	11.38
7.40	9.20	—	—
—	—	—	—

d Saturdays only.
h Wednesdays and Saturdays only.
r Restaurant Car.

TILLICOULTRY (Clackmannan), 422¾ miles. Fares, 85/8*a*, 51/5*c*. R. T. for two months, 171/4*a*, 102/10*c*. Departures *from* London as for Stirling or Dunfermline. Departures *for* London about 4 times daily. Pop. 4,645.
Map Square 40.

TILLIETUDLEM
(Lanark), 392½ miles. Fares, 80/3*a*, 48/2*c*. R. T. for two months, 160/6*a*, 96/4*c*. Departures *from* London as for Hamilton. Departures *for* London about 4 times daily.
Map Square 40.

TILLYFOURIE (Aberdeen), 546¾ miles. No through fares. Departures *from* London as for Aberdeen. Departures *for* London about 3 times daily.
Map Square 35.

TILLYNAUGHT (Banff), 581½ miles. No through fares. Departures *from* London as for Huntly. Departures *for* London about 3 times daily.
Map Square 35.

TILMANSTONE
COLLIERY (Kent), 74 miles. No through fares. Departures *from* London as for Eastry. Departures *for* London about 5 times daily. Pop. 347.

TILTON (Leicester) from
Euston, 97 miles. Fares, 19/7*a*, 11/9*c*. R. T. for two months, 39/2*a*. Departures *from* London as for Hallaton. Departures *for* London about 4 times daily. Pop. 130.
Map Square 18.

TIMPERLEY (Cheshire), 190½ miles. Fares, 40/2*a*, 24/1*c*. R. T. for two months, 80/4*a*, 48/2*c*. Departures *from* London as for Manchester (London Road). Departures *for* London about twice daily. Pop. 4,090.
Map Square 12.

TIMPERLEY, WEST
(Cheshire) from *St. Pancras,* 188½ miles. Fares, 37/9*a*, 22/8*c*. R. T. for two months, 75/6*a*, 45/4*c*.
Map Square 12.

St. Pan.	W. T'f'ly	W. T'f'ly	St. Pan.
AM 8.25*r*	1.57	AM 8.50*r*	1.30
10.25*r*	6.31	PM12. 6*r*	4.20
PM 4.25*r*	8.50	2.43*r*	8.35
12. 0*h*	6. 3	6. 2	4.20
—	—	9.47	6. 0
—	—	—	—
—	—	—	—
—	—	—	—
—	—	—	—
—	—	—	—

Sunday Trains.

PM11.55	6. 3	—	—
—	—	—	—

h Saturdays midnight excepted.
r Restaurant Car.

TINGLEY (Yorks), 181½ miles. Fares, 37/9*a*, 22/8*c*. R. T., double fare. Departures *from* London as for Wakefield (Westgate). Departures *for* London about 8 times daily.

TINSLEY (Yorks), 162¼ miles. Fares, 32/9*a*, 19/8*c*. R. T., double fare. Departures *from* London as for Rotherham. Departures *for* London about 5 times daily. Pop. 5,284.
Map Square 3.

TINTERN (Monmouth)
from *Paddington,* 144¼ miles. Fares, 61/2*a*, 36/8*c*. R. T. for two months, 61/2*a*, 36/8*c*. *Via* Newport, 31/11*a*, 19/2*c*. R. T. for two months, 63/10*a*, 38/4*c*. Pop. 325.
Map Square 22.

Pad.	Tintern	Tintern	Pad.
AM 1. 0*g*	8.17	AM 9.29*r*	2. 0
5.30	11.31	PM12.39*r*	5. 0
10.45	3.29	4.18*r*	8.45
PM 1. 0*r*	5.19	9. 0	3.30
3.15*t*	7.56	—	—
—	—	—	—
—	—	—	—

Sunday Trains.

PM 9.15	8.17	—	—
—	—	—	—
—	—	—	—

g Mondays excepted.
r Restaurant Car.
t Tea Car.

TIPTON (Stafford), 123½ miles. Fares, 25/2*a*, 15/1*c*. R. T. for two months, 50/4*a*. Departures *from* London as for Dudley. Departures *for* London about 5 times daily. Pop. 34,131.
Map Square 17.

TIPTON ST. JOHN'S
(Devon) from *Waterloo,* 164½ miles. Fares, 34/4*a*, 20/7*c*. R. T. for two months, 68/8*a*, 41/2*c*.
Map Square 26.

W'loo.	Tip.St.J.	Tip.St.J.	W'loo.
AM 9. 0*r*	12.52	AM10.23*r*	1.56
10. 0*r*	1.48	11.10*r*	3. 8
12. 0*r*	4. 4	PM 1. 0*r*	6. 0
PM 1. 0*r*	5.15	2.53	7.40
3. 0*r*	7. 1	5.52	10.50
—	—	7.55*h*	3.58

No Sunday Trains.

h *Via* Eastleigh.
r Restaurant Car.

TIPTREE (Essex), 45¾ miles. No through fares. Departures *from* London as for Tollesbury. Departures *for* London about 4 times daily. Pop. (Tiptree Heath) 1,272.
Map Square 24.

TIR PHIL (Glamorgan) 165 Miles. Fares (*via* Bassaleg) 33/7*a*, 20/2*c*. R. T. for two months, 67/2*a*, 40/4*c*. *Via* Cardiff, 35/10*a*, 21/6*c*. R.T. for two months, 71/8*a*, 43/0*c*. Departures *from* London as for Bargoed or Cardiff. Departures *for* London about 4 times daily.

TIRYDAIL (Carmarthen)
from *Paddington,* 210 miles. Fares, 43/2*a*, 25/11*c*. R. T. for two months, 86/4*a*. Departures *from* London as for Llandilo. Departures *for* London about 4 times daily.
Map Square 21.

TISBURY (Wilts) from

Waterloo, 96½ miles. Fares, 20/2*a*, 12/1*c*. R. T. for two months, 40/4*a*, 24/2*c*. Pop. 1,525.
Map Square 22.

W'LOO	TISBURY	TISBURY	W'LOO.
AM 7.30	10.43	AM 8.12	10.56
10. 0*r*	12.21	9.37	12.22
12. 0*r*	2.12	11. 4*r*	1.56
PM 1. 0*r*	3.32	PM12.34*r*	3. 8
3. 0*r*	5.19	3.41*r*	6. 0
5. 0	7.30	4.41	7.40
6. 0*r*	8.32	5.34*r*	8.30
10. 0*h*	3.11	7.44	10.50
—	—	10.33*h*	3.58
—	—	—	—
—	—	—	—

Sunday Trains.

AM 9. 0	12.51	PM 6.31*r*	8.57
12. 0*nr*	2.55	—	—
PM 6. 0	9.14	—	—
—	—	—	—
—	—	—	—

h Via Eastleigh.
n Noon.
r Restaurant Car.

TISSINGTON (Derby),

151¼ miles. Fares, 31/1*a*, 18/8*c*. R. T. for two months, 62/2*a*, 37/4*c*. Departures *from* London as for Ashbourne. Departures *for* London about 5 times daily. Pop. 266.
Map Square 12.

TISTED (Hants) from

Waterloo, 52¾ miles. Fares, 11/0*a*, 6/7*c*. R. T. for two months, 22/0*a*, 13/2*c*. Pop. (East Tisted) 246.
Map Square 23.

W'LOO.	TISTED	TISTED	W'LOO.
AM 4.50	7.22	AM 8.42	10.26
7. 0	9.17	10.29	12.11
9.20	11.21	11.57	1.40
11.20	1.28	PM 3.40	5.46
PM 3.15	5. 2	5. 4	7. 7
6.34	8.21	8.57	11.10
—	—	—	—
—	—	—	—
—	—	—	—
—	—	—	—

Sunday Trains.

PM 6.20	8.26	PM 7.40	9.37

TITLEY (Hereford) from

Paddington, 159¾ miles. Fares, 32/6*a*, 19/6*c*. R. T. for two months, 65/0*a*. Pop. 296.
Map Square 17.

PAD.	TITLEY	TITLEY	PAD.
AM 1. 0*g*	10.22	AM 7.25*r*	2.12
5.30*k*	1.16	11.17*kr*	4.15
10.45	5.25	PM 3. 2*kr*	8.45
PM 1.30*r*	6.34	7.45	3.30
4.45*kt*	9.23	—	—
—	—	—	—

No Sunday Trains.

g Mondays excepted.
k Via Bromyard and Worcester.
r Restaurant Car.
t Tea Car.

TIVERTON (Devon) from

Paddington, 163¾ miles. Fares, *via* Tiverton Junction, 34/2*a*, 20/6*c*. R. T. for two months, 68/4*a*. *Via* Dulverton, 35/0*a*, 21/0*c*. R. T. for two months, 70/0*a*. *Via* Exeter, 36/11*a*, 22/2*c*. R. T. for two months, 73/10*a*. Pop. 9,715.
Map Square 26.

PAD.	TIVERTON	TIVERTON	PAD.
AM 5.30	11.10	AM 9.20*r*	1.30
7.30*r*	1.47	11.20	4. 5
PM12. 5*r*	4.35	PM 1. 5*r*	5.30
2. 0*rv*	6.39	4. 3	9. 0

TIVERTON—*continued.*

PAD.	TIVERTON	TIVERTON	PAD.
PM 3.30	7.20	PM 7.35	2.45
4.15*r*	9.10	8.35*h*	7.10
12. 0*kv*	7.40	9.35*l*	7.10
12. 0*k*	9. 0	—	—
—	—	—	—
—	—	—	—
—	—	—	—
—	—	—	—

Sunday Trains.

PM10. 0	9. 0	—	—
—	—	—	—

h Thursdays, Fridays, and Saturdays excepted.
k Saturdays midnight excepted.
l Thursdays, Fridays, and Saturdays only.
r Restaurant Car.
v Via Exeter.

Palmerston. First-class accommodation for Visitors. Hunting Stag and Fox. Fishing. Garage. Stables. 'Bus meets trains. Telephone, 45. Proprietor, F. P. LANGFORD.

TIVERTON JUNC.

(Devon) from *Paddington*, 158¾ miles. Fares, *via* Somerton, 33/2*a*, 19/11*c*. R. T. for two months, 66/4*a*. *Via* Exeter, 36/11*a*, 22/2*c*. R. T. for two months, 73/10*a*.
Map Square 26.

PAD.	TIV. J.	TIV. J.	PAD.
AM 5.30	10.55	AM 6.47	11.30
7.30*h*	1.24	9.48*r*	1.30
PM12. 5*r*	3.44	11.38	4. 5
2. 0*hr*	6.25	PM 1.24*r*	5.30
3.30*h*	7. 3	4.20*e*	9. 0
4.15*r*	8.56	4.47*d*	9. 0
6.30*r*	11.20	7.59	2.45
12. 0*hk*	6.47	9.56	7.10
12. 0*k*	7.46	—	—
12.30*l*	9. 4	—	—
—	—	—	—

Sunday Trains.

PM10. 0	7.46	AM 9.47	3.35
—	—	—	—
—	—	—	—
—	—	—	—

d Saturdays only.
e Saturdays excepted.
h Via Exeter.
k Saturdays midnight excepted.
l Saturdays midnight only.
r Restaurant Car.

TIVETSHALL (Norfolk)

from *Liverpool Street*, 100 miles. Fares, 21/1*a*, 12/8*c*. R. T. for two months, 42/2*a*. Pop. 647.
Map Square 19.

L'PL. ST.	TIVSHL.	TIVSHL.	L'PL. ST.
AM 5. 0	8. 5	AM 7.21*r*	10.30
10.12	1.26	8. 6*f*	10.36
PM12.33	3.39	9.21	12.39
3.10*r*	6. 7	11. 0*r*	2. 3
5.18*dr*	8.24	PM 1.33*r*	4.58
5.18*er*	8.28	4.23	7.51
—	—	7.39	11.16
—	—	—	—
—	—	—	—
—	—	—	—

Sunday Trains.

AM 9.20*r*	12.47	AM 7.50	11.38
PM 4.40	7.40	PM 6.33	10.15
—	—	—	—

d Saturdays only.
e Saturdays excepted.
f Mondays only.
r Restaurant Car.

TOCHIENEAL (Banff),

588½ miles. No through fares. Departures *from* London as for Huntly. Departures *for* London about 3 times daily.
Map Square 35.

TODDINGTON (Gloucester)

from *Paddington*, 111¼ miles. Fares, 23/2*a*, 13/11*c*. R. T. for two months, 46/4*a*. Departures *from* London as for Broadway. Departures *for* London about 7 times daily. Pop. 333.
Map Square 17.

TODMORDEN (Yorks)

from *King's Cross*, *via* Horbury, 203½ miles. Fares, 40/0*a*, 24/0*c*. R. T. for two months, 80/0*a*. Pop. 23,888.
Map Square 12.

KING'S +	TODMOR.	TODMOR.	KING'S +
AM 4.45	11.11	AM 5.21	11.30
7.15*r*	1.15	7.39*r*	1. 5
10.10*r*	4. 9	8.59*r*	1.55
PM 1.30*r*	6.58	9.49	3.50
1.50*r*	8.28	10.48*r*	4.45
10.45*e*	9.24	11.26	5. 0
—	—	PM 1.47*r*	7.10
—	—	4. 1*r*	9.25
—	—	8. 7*e*	3.25
—	—	—	—

Sunday Trains.

12. 0*hn*	7.36	AM 9.31*r*	3.45
—	—	11.32*r*	5.55
—	—	PM 2.51*h*	10.20
—	—	—	—

e Saturdays excepted.
h Passengers cross Wakefield at own expense.
n Noon.
r Restaurant Car.

ANOTHER ROUTE from

Euston, 203½ miles. Fares as above.

EUSTON	TODMOR.	TODMOR	EUSTON
AM12.25	7. 7	AM 4.43*er*	12. 5
2.35	9.47	4.43*dr*	12.20
5. 0	11.23	8. 4*r*	1.15
8.45*r*	2.16	8.41*r*	2.20
10. 0	3.32	9.27	3.10
10.40*r*	3.59	10.46*r*	3.55
11.50*r*	5. 2	11.15*dr*	5.50
12. 0*nr*	6.39	11.55*r*	6. 0
PM 2.50*t*	8. 5	PM12.22*r*	6.15
4. 5*r*	9.22	1.19*r*	7.30
6. 5*hr*	11.40	2.27*r*	8.10
9.30*e*	5.16	3.22*dr*	10. 0
11.50*d*	9. 1	4.30*er*	10.10
—	—	8.55	5. 0
—	—	10. 7*e*	5.40
—	—	10. 7*d*	5.45
—	—	—	—

Sunday Trains.

PM12.30*r*	7.26	AM 8. 4	4. 0
9.15	5.16	10.55*r*	5.45
—	—	PM12.46*r*	7.30
—	—	2.51*r*	8.55
—	—	10.21	5. 0
—	—	—	—
—	—	—	—
—	—	—	—
—	—	—	—

d Saturdays only.
e Saturdays excepted.
h Tuesdays and Saturdays only.
n Noon.
r Restaurant Car.
t Tea Car.

TOLLER (Dorset) from

Paddington, 142½ miles. Fares, 28/11a, 17/4c. R.T. for two months, 57/10a. Departures *from* London as for Powerstock. Departures *for* London about 5 times daily. Pop. (Toller Fratrum) 50.
Map Square 27.

TOLLERTON (Yorks),

197½ miles. Fares, 41/1a, 24/8c. R. T., double fare. Departures *from* London as for York. Departures *for* London about 6 times daily Pop. 487.
Map Square 8.

TOLLESBURY (Essex)

from *Liverpool Street*, 50¾ miles. No through fares. Pop. 1,721.
Map Square 24.

L'pool St.	Tolles.	Tolles.	L'pool St.
AM 8.18	10.26	AM 8.24	10.22
10.47	1.10	10.36	12.39
PM 4.18	6.27	PM 3.15	5.47
—	—	6.42	9.17
—	—	—	—
—	—	—	—
—	—	—	—
—	—	—	—

No Sunday Trains.

TOLLESHUNT

D'ARCY (Essex), 49 miles. No through fares. Departures *from* London as for Tollesbury. Departures *for* London about 4 times daily. Pop. 861.
Map Square 24.

TOMATIN (Inverness), 549

miles. Fares, 106/3a, 63/9c. R. T. for two months, 212/6a, 127/6c. Departures *from* London as for Aviemore. Departures *for* London about twice daily.
Map Square 34.

TONBRIDGE (Kent) from

Charing Cross, Cannon Street and *London Bridge*, 30¼ miles. Fares, 6/5a, 5/1b, 3/10c. R. T. for two months, 12/10a, 10/2b. Pop. 15,929.
Map Square 24.

Leave Char. +	Can. St.	Lon. B.	Arr. at Tonbge.
AM —	3.40s	3.43s	4.34
—	4.44c	5. 0k	6.52
—	5.20	5.25	6.50
—	6.45	6.50	8. 8
—	7.56	k7.50l	9. 5
—	—	9.15	10.20
9.25	—	9.33	10.20
9.38	—	9.45	10.55
—	—	j k10. 3l	11.13
10.40	—	10.46	11.28
10.55k	—	11. 3k	12.43
—	11.56	12. 0	12.50
PM12. 3	—	12.10	1.15
12.40d	—	12.47d	1.31
12.55k	—	1. 4k	2.42
1. 5d	—	1.11d	1.56
—	1.12d	1.15d	2.17
2. 8	—	2.16	3. 2
2.17d	—	2.23d	3.28
2.40d	—	2.46d	3.34
3. 0	—	3. 8	3.52
3.15k	—	3.21k	4.46
3.48e	—	—	4.53
3.50	—	3.57	5. 7
—	4.36e	4.39e	5.28
—	5.12e	—	5.54
5.24d	—	5.34d	6.20
5.26e	—	5.35e	6.20

TONBRIDGE—*continued.*

Leave Char. +	Can. St.	Lon. B.	Arr. at Tonbge.
PM 5.35d	—	5.41d	6.50
—	5.44e	5.47e	6.37
6. 0e	—	6. 5e	6.45
6. 3e	—	6. 9e	6.54
6.34e	—	6.41e	7.32
—	—	7.26	8.28
7.30	—	—	8.14
8. 0	—	8. 8	9.10
9.30	—	9.36	10.18
10. 0	—	10. 6	11. 8
10.45	—	10.51	11.52
11.45	—	—	12.36
—	—	—	—
—	—	—	—
—	—	—	—
—	—	—	—

Sunday Trains.

Char. +	Can. St.	Lon. B.	Tonbge.
AM 6.25k	—	6.32k	8.23
7. 5	—	7.11	8.30
7.45	—	7.52	8.42
8. 5	—	8.12	9.20
9.50	—	9.56	10.44
11.15	—	11.23	12.38
PM 3. 5	—	3.13	4.30
5.25k	—	5.32k	7.14
6.35	—	6.43	7.35
7.10	—	7.20	8.17
7.35	—	7.45	8.29
8.58k	—	8.45k	10.14
9.25	—	9.31	10.35
10.35	—	10.43	11.45
—	—	—	—
—	—	—	—
—	—	—	—

Trains from Tonbridge.

Leave Tonbge.	Lon. B.	Can. St.	Arrive at Char. +
AM 7. 0	8. 9	—	8.19
7.37	8.40	8.44	—
8. 3	8.49	8.53	—
8.10	9.18	—	9.27
8.43	9.32	9.36	—
9.12	10. 0	10. 4	—
9.17	10. 4	10. 8	—
9.37	10.28	10.32	—
9.55k	11. 0	—	—
10. 9	10.58	11. 2	—
10.35	11.32	—	11.44
10.42v	11.31	—	11.38
10.58	11.43	—	11.57
11.18k	12.50	—	1. 0
PM12.11	1.27	—	1.38
12.40	1.36	—	1.50
1. 7k	2.38k	—	2.46
1.49	3. 1	—	3.19
2.41	3.26	—	3.40
2.51j	—	—	4. 8
3.45	4.40	—	4.53
4.58	5.50	—	6. 3
5. 6d	6.30	—	6.39
5.15e	6.44	—	6.55
6.33	7.25	7.30	—
7.20	8.26	—	8.35
7.41	8.55	9. 1	—
8.35	10. 3	—	10.13
9. 8	10.15	—	10.23
9.32	10.22	—	10.55
10.25	11.34	—	11.43
10.30k	12. 1	—	12.10
k12.11s	—	1.20	—

TONBRIDGE—*continued.*

Sunday Trains.

Leave Tonbge.	Lon. B.	Can. St.	Arrive at Char. +
AM 8.47	10. 5	—	10.15
9. 5	10.22	—	10.32
10.36	11.23	—	11.34
10.45	11.50	—	12. 0
PM12. 5h	—	1. 5h	—
1.40	2.50	—	3. 0
5.10	6.27	—	6.41
6.28	7. 9	—	7.17
7.13	8.12	—	8.22
7.25	8.20	—	8.28
8.15	9. 4	—	9.14
9.35	10.16	—	10.26
10. 5	11. 4	—	11.15
12.11s	—	1.23	—
—	—	—	—

d Saturdays only.
e Saturdays excepted.
h Arrives at Victoria (S.E. & C).
j Fridays only.
k Via Redhill.
l Low level platform.
s Third Class only.
v Wednesdays only.

Taxi Cabs can be hired to meet any train at this Station. Telegrams, "Baker Motors, Tonbridge." Telephone No. 105. Messrs. Chas. Baker & Co., 150 High Street.

Rose and Crown Hotel. Telephone 128. An excellent centre. Garage and Stabling. TRUST HOUSES, Ltd.

TONDU (Glamorgan), from

Paddington, 176 miles. Fares, 36/8a, 22/0c. R. T. for two months, 73/4a, 44/0c.
Map Square 21.

Pad.	Tondu	Tondu	Pad.
AM 1. 0g	9. 7	AM 9. 2r	1. 0
5.30	11.44	10.29r	2.30
8.45dr	1.14	10.40r	4.20
8.45r	2.22	PM 1.18r	6.15
11.50r	5. 8	4. 1r	8.35
PM 1.10r	6.26	9.19	3.30
3.35r	7.44	9.44h	3.30
6. 0r	10.11	—	—
—	—	—	—

Sunday Trains.

Pad.	Tondu	Tondu	Pad.
PM 9.15	9. 7	—	—

d Saturdays only.
g Mondays excepted.
h Wednesdays and Saturdays only.
r Restaurant Car.

TONFANAU (Merioneth),

234¾ miles. Fares, 47/9a, 28/8c. R. T. for two months, 95/6a. Departures *from* London as for Machynlleth. Departures *for* London about 4 times daily.
Map Square 16.

TONGE (Leicester), 125¼

miles. Fares, 26/1a, 15/8c. R. T. doublefare. Departures *from* London as for Melbourne (*via* Ashby). Departures *for* London about 4 times daily.
Map Square 18.

TONGHAM (Surrey) from

Waterloo, 37¼ miles. Fares, 7/9*a*, 4/8*c*. R. T. for two months, 15/6*a*, 9/4*c*. Pop. 1,612. *Map Square* 23.

W'LOO	TONGHAM	TONGHAM	W'LOO
AM 6.50	8.17	AM 8. 7	9.12
7. 5	8.57	9. 6	10.15
9. 0	10.23	10.57	12.46
11. 5	12.40	PM 1.17	3. 0
PM 12.50	2. 9	2.35	4.16
2. 5	3.52	4.35	5.52
3.50	4.57	5.20	6.52
5.24	6.26	6.45	7.56
5.50	7.23	7.56	9.46
7. 5	8.40	8.58	10.46
—	—	—	—
—	—	—	—
—	—	—	—

No Sunday Trains.

TONYPANDY (Gla-

morgan), 170½ miles. Fares, 34/4*a*, 20/7*c*. R. T. for two months, 68/8*a*, 41/2*c*. Departures *from* London as for Treherbert. Departures *for* London about 5 times daily.

TONYREFAIL (Glamor-

gan) from *Paddington*, 169 miles. Fares, 34/5*a*, 20/8*c*. R. T. for two months, 68/10*a*, 41/4*c*. Departures *from* London as for Llantrisant. Departures *for* London about 5 times daily.

TOOTING UPPER.

See BALHAM.

TOPCLIFFE (Yorks),

212½ miles. No through fares. Departures *from* London as for Thirsk or Ripon. Departures *for* London about 5 times daily. Pop. 542. *Map Square* 7.

TOPSHAM (Devon) from

Waterloo, 175 miles. Fares, 36/11*a*, 22/2*c*. R. T. for two months, 73/10*a*, 44/4*c*. Departures *from* London as for Exmouth (*via* Exeter). Departures *for* London about 7 times daily. Pop. 2,874. *Map Square* 26.

TORKSEY (Lincoln),

140 miles. Fares, 29/0*a*, 17/5*c*. R. T., double fare. Departures *from* London as for Lincoln or Retford. Departures *for* London about 4 times daily. Pop. 183. *Map Square* 13.

TORPANTAU (Brecon),

178½ miles. Fares, 36/3*a*, 21/9*c*. R. T. for two months, 72/6*a*, 43/6*c*. Departures *from* London as for Bargoed. Departures *for* London about 4 times daily. *Map Square* 21.

TORPHINS (Aberdeen),

545½ miles. Fares, 105/0*a*, 63/0*c*. R. T. for two months, 210/0*a*, 126/0*c*. Departures *from* London as for Ballater. Departures *for* London about twice daily. Pop. 555. *Map Square* 38.

TORQUAY (Devon) from

Paddington, 199½ miles. Fares, 41/1*a*, 24/8*c*. R. T. for two months, 82/2*c*, 49/4*c*. Pop. 39,432. *Map Square.*

PAD	TORQUAY	TORQUAY	PAD.
AM 5.30	11.44	AM 12.53*g*	7.10
7.50*d*	1.16	9. 1*r*	1.30
7.30*e*	1.42	PM 12.10*r*	3.45
9.15*r*	2. 5	12.18*r*	4.35
11.10*r*	3.14	2.25*er*	6.50
12. 0*r*	3.35	2.55*dr*	7. 5
PM 12. 5*r*	4.48	4.23*r*	9. 0
2. 0*r*	6.44	5.25	2.45
3.30*r*	7.45	—	—
4.15*r*	9. 7	—	—
6.30*r*	11.41	—	—
10. 0*e*	4.10*h*	—	—
12. 0*s*	7.12	—	—
12.30*k*	7.17	—	—

Sunday Trains.

AM 10.30*r*	2.47	AM 12.53	7. 5
PM 2.40	7.27	7.55*r*	3.35
4.30*r*	9.42	10.49*r*	4. 5
10. 0	4.10*h*	PM 2.25	7. 5
—	—	8.50	5.15
—	—	10.36	7.10

d Saturdays only.
e Saturdays excepted.
g Mondays excepted.
h Torre Station.
k Saturdays midnight only.
r Restaurant Car.
s Saturdays midnight excepted.

Grand Hotel. The Leading Hotel. Best Position. Sea Front. Unequalled View. Nearest Station. Garage Telephone 134. *See advt.* p. 319.

Imperial Hotel. Patronised by Royalty. Standing in own sheltered grounds. Facing south. Self-contained Suites. Garage. *See advt.* p. 320.

Palace Hotel. Largest and most palatial in Devonshire. Beautifully situated in 25 acres, magnificent woodland scenery, with superb sea views. Ball room. Tennis. Golf. Garage. Motor Bus meets all trains. Orchestra. Telephone 971.
  F. MONTAGUÉ HAYDEN,
        Manager.
See advt. p. 321.

Victoria and Albert Hotel. South aspect. Sea view. Comfortable Lounge. Separate Smoking and Billiard Lounge. Lift. Garage. Tel. Address: "Vanda, Torquay."
  E. T. PARSONS, Manager.
See advt. p. 322.

Torbay Hotel, Ltd. First class only. Due South. Perfect position. Newly - constructed. Dining-room. Ball-room. Fine Lounge. Billiard - rooms. Orchestra. Excellent Cuisine. New Management. Telephone 318.
      Apply MANAGERESS.
See advt. p. 323.

Templestowe Boarding Establishment. First Class. Electric light throughout. *See advt.* p. 323.

Elfordleigh Private Hotel, Belgrave Crescent. Tennis. Croquet. Garage. Facing Sea. 'Phone, 468. *See advt.* p. 324.

TORQUAY—*continued.*

Torquay Hydro Hotel. 200 feet above sea level. Magnificent views. *See advt.* p. 324.

Edenhurst, Private Hotel. Commanding finest panoramic views. Owner's personal superintendence. *See advt.* p. 325.

Osborne Hotel. Extensively enlarged and modernised. Private Grounds. Superb Views. Suites on Ground Floor. Lift. Entirely New Management. Telegrams: "Osbonotel." *See advt.* p. 325.

Sandringham Private Hotel. South aspect. Over 60 Bedrooms. Electric Light. Billiards. Lounge. Convenient for Pavilion, Golf Links, etc. Tel. 485. Resident Proprietors—
        Mr. & Mrs.
  L. HAMILTON MONTAGUE.
See advt. p. 326.

Lincombe Hall. First Class Residential Hotel. Beautiful Situation. Four acres charming Grounds. *See advt.* p. 326.

The Bungalow Hotel. Picturesquely situated in extensive grounds, facing Torbay. Luxuriously appointed. Central heating. Accessible and Sheltered. Tel. 822. *See advt.* p. 327.

Touraine Private Hotel. Magnificent Position. Unrivalled Cuisine. Telephone No. 188. *See advt.* p. 327.

Nepaul. First-class Private Hotel. Under entirely new management. Ideal position. *See advt.* p. 328.

Links Hotel, St. Marychurch. Ideal Golfers Resort. Billiards. Ball-room. Hard Tennis Court. Garage. 2 minutes Golf Course. Terms from 5 Guineas. Tel. 913. *See advt.* p. 328.

Rosetor Private Hotel. Magnificent situation. Excellent Cuisine. Telephone 355. *See advt.* p. 329.

Bute Court. High - class Private Hotel and Boarding Establishment. Facing Sea. Sands. *See advt.* p. 329.

Roslin Hall Hotel occupies ideal position. Comfortably furnished. Cuisine of the best. *See advt.* p. 329.

San Remo. Private Hotel. Standing in own grounds, about one acre. Facing sea. *See advt.* p. 330.

Inglewood. First-class Private Hotel, Belgrave Road. Charmingly situated. South Aspect.
  Miss REDFERN, Manageress.
See advt. p. 330.

TORQUAY'S PALACE HOTEL.

TORQUAY—*continued.*

Allerdale. Facing Sea. Central Heating, Electric Light. Separate Tables. Phone 667. *See* advt. p. **330.**

Belgrave Hotel. Splendidly situated. Extensive pleasure grounds. Excellent cuisine. Telephone 62. *See* advt. p. **330.**

Argyll Hall. Private and Residential Hotel. Magnificent Views. South Aspect. Tel. 625. Proprietresses, The Misses MORRIS. *See* advt. p. **331.**

Vernon Court, Private Hotel. South aspect. Finest position. Most comfortable. *See* advt. p. **331.**

Villa Belza. High Class. Illustrated Tariff. From 3 guineas per week. *See* advt. p. **331.**

Sea Lawn Private Hotel. Unrivalled views over Tor Bay. Excellent Cuisine. Moderate tariff. Apply PROPRIETORS. *See* advt. p. **331.**

Conway Court Private Hotel. Finest position Sea Front. Ideal winter and summer. *See* advt. p. **332.**

South Hill House. Ideal situation. Moderate terms. Garage. Personal supervision. *See* advt. p. **332.**

Savernake Private Hotel. Old Established. Facing South. Billiards. Garage. *See* advt. p. **332.**

Ebbor House Private Hotel. Ideal central position, facing Bathing Beach. Reasonable Charges. English Food. Tel. 942. *See* advt. p. **318.**

White House Private Hotel. Magnificent sea views. Modern improvements. ;Mrs. WRIGHT. *See* advt. p **332.**

Marsworth Private Hotel. Magnificent Views. Separate Tables. Winter Terms from £3 3s. Telephone 78. Mrs. G. BUSON.

Rosetor. Torquay's leading Private Hotel, combining two of Torquay's splendid mansions arranged on modern lines. High-class Private Hotel in own grounds of 3 acres. Beautifully situated on Sea Front, due South. Private walk direct to Tor Abbey Sands. Near three Golf Courses. Tennis, Billiards, &c. Garage. Illustrated tariff. Telephone 355. Mr. and Mrs. W. S. BROCKMAN.

TORQUAY—*continued.*

Chillingworth. First-class Private Hotel. In own grounds. Sea View, South aspect. Near Promenade. Garage. Miss K. COLE and Mrs. PIKE, Proprietresses.

"Kistor." Private Hotel, Belgrave Road. Unrivalled situation. One minute from Sea. Central Heating. Electric Light. Excellent cuisine. Tel. 325. Mrs. A. BAKER.

The Withens, Belgrave Road. Superior Boarding Establishment. Near Sea and Gardens. Excellent cuisine. Most comfortable. Moderate terms. PROPRIETRESS.

Lorna-Doone, Torwood Gardens. First - class Private Hotel. Ideal situation. Sheltered. Most central. Electric light. Central heating. Mr. and Mrs. T. C. JONES.

Toorak Private Hotel (and Pendreath Annexe). In own grounds. Best position. Close sea, &c. Excellent cuisine. No accommodation for children. PROPRIETRESSES.

Belfield, Croft Road. High Class Private Hotel, facing South in own grounds and Park. Premier position.

Falkland Lodge. Private Hotel. Beautifully situated, near Sea. Charming Views. Every Comfort. Excellent Cuisine. Separate Tables. Garage. Personal supervision. Telephone 576. Tariff— PROPRIETRESS.

Howden Court, Croft Road. Comfortable, excellently appointed and well managed Hotel. Extensive South and Sea Views. A.A. Hotel. Moderate Tariff. Tel. 600. K. R. KAY.

Royal Hotel. Family and Commercial. Facing Sea and Strand. Central for everything. Electric Light. Speciality, good food. 'Phone 313. Apply MANAGERESS.

House Agents. T. OLIVER & SONS, Ltd., 16, Strand, Torquay. Established 1805. List of all the best Properties to be Let or Sold in Torquay and neighbourhood, post free on application.

House Agents. SMITH & SON, F.A.I., 9, Strand, Torquay. Illustrated Register of all available houses in Torquay free. Established 1867.

Cox & Son, House and Estate Agents, Auctioneers, &c. Established 1805. Monthly list of Houses and Estates for disposal, post free.

TORRANCE (Stirling), 439

miles. No through fares. Departures *from* London as for Glasgow. Departures *for* London about 5 times daily. Pop. 1,210.

TORRE (Devon) from

Paddington, 198¾ miles. Fares, 41/0*a*, 24/7*c*. R. T. for two months, 82/0*a*. Departures *from* London as for Plymouth. Departures *for* London about 9 times daily. Pop. 4,199.
Map Square 26.

TORRINGTON (Devon)

from *Waterloo,* 225¾ miles. Fares, 42/1*a*, 25/3*c*. R. T. for two months, 84/2*a*, 50/6*c*. Pop. 2,931.
Map Square 21.

W'LOO	TOR'TON	TOR'TON	W'LOO
AM 9. 0*r*	3.19	AM 8.15*r*	1.56
11. 0*r*	4.28	10.39*r*	3.50
PM 1. 0*r*	7.12	PM12.25*r*	6. 0
3. 0	8.14	1.45*r*	8.20
—	—	3.20	10.50
—	—	4.45*h*	3.58
—	—	—	—

No Sunday Trains.

h Via Eastleigh.
r Restaurant Car.

TORRYBURN (Fife),

413¾ miles. No through fares. Departures *from* London as for Dunfermline. Departures *for* London about 3 times daily. Pop. 2,224.
Map Square 41.

TORVER (Lancs) 276½ miles.

Fares, 57/6*a*, 34/6*c*. R. T. for two months, 115/0*a*, 69/0*c*. Departures *from* London as for Coniston. Departures *for* London about 4 times daily. Pop. 776.
Map Square 6.

TOTLAND BAY (Isle of

Wight) from *Waterloo, via* Lymington and Yarmouth, 106½ miles. Fares, 22/10*a*, 14/2*c*. R. T. for two months, 45/1*a*, 27/7*c*. Pop. 1,441.
Map Square 27.

W'LOO	T. BAY	T. BAY	W'LOO
AM 5.40	10. 0	AM10.25*r*	2.20
8.30*s*	12.10	PM12.15	4.20
11.30*r*	3. 5	3.25	6.58
PM 1.30*s*	5.10	5.25	10.50
3.30	7.35	—	—

No Sunday Service.

r Restaurant Car.
s Refreshments served.

"Clevedon." Comfortable Board-residence. Close to Sea and Downs. Separate Tables. Good Cooking. Hot Baths. Moderate charges.

TOTNES (Devon) from

Paddington, 202¼ miles. Fares, 41/8*a*, 25/0*c*. R. T. for two months, 83/4*a*, 50/0*c*. Pop. 3,982.
Map Square 26.

PAD.	TOTNES	TOTNES	PAD
AM 5.30	12.38	AM 8.37*r*	1.30
7.30	1.38	PM12.17*r*	4.35
9.15*r*	3. 8	1.50*r*	6.50
11.10*r*	3.29	3.48*r*	9. 0
12. 5*r*	4.43	5.31	2.45
PM 3.50*r*	7.57	10.19	7.10
4.15*r*	9.22	—	—
6.30*r*	11.40	—	—
12. 0*k*	6.32	—	—
12.30*h*	7. 2	—	—

TORQUAY.—MARSWORTH PRIVATE HOTEL. Convenient Situation *Telephone:* **78.**

TOTNES—*continued.*

Sunday Trains.

Pad.	Totnes.	Totnes.	Pad.
AM10.30*r*	4.10	AM 7.55*r*	3.35
PM 2.40	8.42	PM 8.57	3.15
10. 0	7.49	—	—
—	—	—	—
—	—	—	—
—	—	—	—
—	—	—	—
—	—	—	—
—	—	—	—
—	—	—	—
—	—	—	—

h Saturdays midnight only.
k Saturdays midnight excepted.
r Restaurant Car.

TOTTENHAM (Middlesex)

from *Liverpool Street*, 6 miles. Fares, 0/10*a*, 0/8*b*, 0/6*c*. R. T. for two days, 1/8*a*, 1/4*b*, 0/10½*c*. Pop. 146,711. *See* pp. 526–527.
Map Square 52.

TOTTENHAM (SOUTH)

from *St. Pancras* and *Moorgate Street*, 5¾ miles. Fares, 0/10*a*, 0/6*c*. R. T. for two days, 1/7½*a*, 0/10½*c*. *See* pp. 506–507.
Map Square 52.

TOTTENHAM COURT

ROAD (Central London and Hampstead Tubes). *See* back of Map.

TOTTERIDGE (Herts)

from *King's Cross, Moorgate Street* and *Broad Street*, 9¼ miles. Fares from King's Cross, 1/9½*a*, 1/5*b*, 1/1*c*. R. T. for two days, 3/7*a*, 2/10*b*, 2/2*c*. From Moorgate Street and Broad Street, 1/10½*a*, 1/6*b*, 1/1½*c*. R. T. for two days, 3/9*a*, 3/0*b*, 2/3*c*. Pop. 961. *See* pp. 518–522.

TOTTINGTON (Lancs),

199 miles. No through fares. Departures *from* London as for Bury. Departures *for* London about 6 times daily. Pop. 6,762.

TOTTON (Hants)

from *Waterloo*, 82 miles. Fares, 17/3*a*, 10/4*c*. R. T. for two months, 34/6*a*, 20/8*c*.
Map Square 27.

W'loo	Totton	Totton	W'loo
AM 5.40	8.27	AM 7.43*r*	10. 6
5.50	9.22	8.58*s*	11. 0
8.30*s*	11. 0	10.25*r*	12.50
10.30	12.32	11.55*r*	2.20
PM12.30*r*	2.42	PM 1.47	4.20
1.30*s*	3.49	3.19	6.16
2.30	4.38	3.45*s*	6.26
3.30*s*	5.48	4.52	6.58
4.30*r*	6.35	5.43*r*	8.20
6.30*r*	8.27	6.44*r*	8.50
7.30	9.51	8. 7	10.50
8. 0	11. 3	8.30	11.28
—	—	10. 0	3.58
—	—	—	—
—	—	—	—
—	—	—	—
—	—	—	—
—	—	—	—

TOTTON—*continued.*

Sunday Trains.

W'loo	Totton	Totton	W'loo
AM11. 0*r*	1.31	AM10. 4*r*	2.27
PM 2. 0*r*	4.34	PM 3 .2*r*	6. 7
7. 0*r*	9.38	5.25	8. 3
—	—	7.17*r*	9.31
—	—	8.52	3.58
—	—	—	—

r Restaurant Car.
s Refreshments served.

TOVIL (Kent)

from *Charing Cross, Cannon Street*, and *London Bridge*, 45 miles. Fares, 8/6*a*, 6/9*b*, 5/1*c*. R. T. for two months, 17/0*a*, 13/6*b*. Departures *from* London as for East Farleigh. Departures *for* London about 7 times daily. Pop. 1,324.
Map Square 24.

TOWCESTER (Northampton)

from *Euston*, 67 miles. Fares, 14/0*a*, 8/5*c*. R. T. for two months, 28/0*a*. Pop. 2,349.
Map Square 18.

Euston	T'cester	T'cester	Euston
AM 6.45	9. 4	AM 8.10	10.15
10.40	1.29	9.30	11.55
12. 0*nr*	2.41	11.17	12.50
PM 3. 5	5.32	PM 1.37*h*	3.45
4.15	6.27	1.37	4.15
7. 0	8.49	4.57	6.25
—	—	5.35	7.55
—	—	7.36*e*	10.10
—	—	7.36*d*	10.50
—	—	—	—
—	—	—	—

No Sunday Trains.

d Saturdays only.
e Saturdays excepted.
h Mondays and Saturdays only.
n Noon.
r Restaurant Car.

TOWER HILL (Devon)

from *Waterloo*, 218¾ miles. Fares, 45/7*a*, 27/4*c*. R. T. for two months, 91/2*a*, 54/8*c*. Departures *from* London as for Halwill Junction. Departures *for* London about 4 times daily.
Map Square 26.

TOW LAW (Durham), 254¾

miles. Fares, 53/2*a*, 31/11*c*. R. T., double fare. Departures *from* London as for Bishop Auckland. Departures *for* London about 5 times daily. Pop. 4,073.
Map Square 7.

TOWNELEY (Lancs), 211¾

miles. Fares, 41/10*a*, 25/1*c*. R.T. for two months, 83/8*a*, 50/2*c*. Departures *from* London as for Burnley (Manchester Road). Departures *for* London about 6 times daily.
Map Square 12.

TOWN GREEN (Lancs),

210¾ miles. Fares, 43/2*a*, 25/11*c*. R. T. for two months, 86/4*a*. Departures *from* London as for Liverpool (Lime Street). Departures *for* London about 4 times daily.
Map Square 12.

TOWYN (Merioneth), 232¼

miles. Fares, 47/4*a*, 28/5*c*. R. T. for two months, 94/8*a*. Departures *from* London as for Machynlleth. Departures *for* London about 4 times daily. Pop. 4,411.
Map Square 16.

TRABBOCH (Ayr), 386

miles. No through fares. Departures *from* London as for Ayr. Departures *for* London about 4 times daily.
Map Square 40.

TRAFALGAR SQUARE

(Bakerloo Tube). *See* back of Map.

TRAFFORD PARK

(Lancs), 192¾ miles. Fares, 39/2*a*, 23/6*c*. R. T. for two months, 78/4*a*, 47/0*c*. Departures *from* London as for Glazebrook. Departures *for* London about 8 times daily.
Map Square 12.

TRAM INN (Hereford),

148¾ miles. Fares, 31/1*a*, 18/8*c*. R. T. for two months, 62/2*a*. Departures *from* London as for Hereford. Departures *for* London about 5 times daily.
Map Square 17.

TRAVELLER'S REST

(Glamorgan), 168½ miles. No through fares. Departures *from* London as for Pontypridd. Departures *for* London about twice daily.
Map Square 21.

TRAWSCOED (Cardigan)

from *Paddington*, 275¾ miles. Fares, 48/9*a*, 29/3*c*. R. T. for two months, 97/6*a*. Departures *from* London as for Lampeter. Departures *for* London about 4 times daily.
Map Square 16.

TRAWSFYNYDD (Merioneth),

from *Paddington*, 221¼ miles. Fares, 46/3*a*, 27/9*c*. R. T. for two months, 92/6*a*, 55/6*c*. Departures *from* London as for Blaenau Festiniog. Departures *for* London about 3 times daily. Pop. 1,708.
Map Square 11.

TREBORTH (Carnarvon),

241¼ miles. Fares, 50/3*a*, 30/2*c*. R. T. for two months, 100/6*a*, 60/4*c*. Departures *from* London as for Bangor. Departures *for* London about 5 times daily.
Map Square 11.

TREDEGAR (Monmouth)

from *Paddington* (*via* Newport), 163 miles. Fares, 34/0*a*, 20/5*c*. R. T. for two months, 68/0*a*, 40/10*c*. Pop. 25,105.
Map Square 21.

Pad.	Tredegar	Tredegar	Pad.
AM 1. 0*g*	8.47	AM 5.50*r*	10.57
5.30	11.50	8.41*r*	1. 0
8.45*r*	1.24	9.35*r*	2.30
11.50*r*	5.20	11.30*r*	4.20
PM 1.10*r*	6.37	PM 2.13*r*	6.15
3.35*r*	8.44	4.57*r*	9.25
6. 0*dr*	10.25	7.50*e*	3.30
6. 0*er*	10.34	9.25*d*	3.30
8. 0*dr*	12.34	—	—
9.15*e*	5.39	—	—
—	—	—	—
—	—	—	—

Sunday Trains.

PM 9.15	5.39	—	—

d Saturdays only.
e Saturdays excepted.
g Mondays excepted.
r Restaurant Car.

TREETON (Yorks), from
St. Pancras, 158¾ miles. Fares, 32/9a, 19/8c. R. T., double fare. Departures from London as for Chesterfield. Departures for London about 6 times daily. Pop. 1,839.
Map Square 13.

TREFNANT (Denbigh),
209 miles. Fares, 44/0a, 26/5c. R. T. for two months, 88/0a. Departures from London as for Rhyl. Departures for London about 6 times daily. Pop. 508.
Map Square 11.

TREFOREST (Glamorgan),
164¼ miles. Fares, 33/2a, 19/11c. R. T. for two months, 66/4a, 39/10c. Departures from London as for Cardiff. Departures for London about 6 times daily. Pop. 10,355.

TREFRIW (Denbigh).
Station at Llanrwst.

Hotel Belle Vue (Trefriw).
Overlooking River Conway and beautiful Trefriw Valley. First Class.
See advt. p. 333.

TREGARON (Cardigan)
from Paddington, 265¼ miles. Fares, 48/9a, 29/3c. R. T. for two months, 97/6a. Departures from London as for Lampeter. Departures for London about 4 times daily. Pop. 7,521.
Map Square 16.

TREGARTH (Carnarvon),
241 miles. Fares, 50/5a, 30/2c. R.T. for two months, 100/10a, 60/5c. Departures from London as for Bangor. Departures for London about 6 times daily.
Map Square 11.

TREHAFOD (Glamorgan),
167¼ miles. Fares, 33/7a, 20/2c. R. T. for two months, 67/2a, 40/4c. Departures from London as for Treherbert. Departures for London about 4 times daily.

TREHARRIS (Glamorgan),
164½ miles. Fares, 34/0a, 20/5c. R. T. for two months, 68/0a, 40/10c. Departures from London as for Nelson and Llancaiach. Departures for London about 5 times daily. Pop. 8,818.

TREHERBERT (Glamorgan), from Paddington (via Cardiff),
176 miles. Fares, 35/5a, 21/3c. R.T. for two months, 70/10a, 42/6c.
Map Square 21.

PAD.	TREHBT.	TREHBT.	PAD.
AM 1. 0gh	7.49	AM 6.22hr	10.57
5.30	12. 7	8.15r	1. 0
8.45r	1.14	9.10r	2.30
11.50r	4.28	11.47r	4.20
PM 1.10r	7.14	PM 1. 0hr	6.15
5.35r	8.47	5.32r	8.35
6. 0r	10.54	4.15r	9.25
6.30kr	12. 0	8.52	3.30
9.15eh	6.24	—	—

TREHERBERT—contd.
Sunday Trains.

PAD.	TREHBT.	TREHBT.	PAD.
AM 1. 0	9.38	AM 7.54	3.35
PM12.30r	5.59	11.20r	8.25
4.30	10.16	PM 8.10	3.30
9.15h	6.24	—	—

e Saturdays excepted.
g Mondays excepted.
h Passengers cross Cardiff at own expense.
k Thursdays and Saturdays only.
r Restaurant Car.

TRENCH CROSSING
(Salop), 150¼ miles. Fares, 29/9a, 17/10c. R. T. for two months, 59/6a, 35/8c. Departures from London as for Newport (Salop). Departures for London about 3 times daily.
Map Square 17.

TRENHOLME BAR
(Yorks), 229¾ miles. No through fares. Departures from London as for Stockton-on-Tees. Departures for London about 5 times daily.
Map Square 8.

TRENT (Derby) from St.
Pancras, 119¾ miles, via Leicester. Fares, 24/9a, 14/10c. R. T., double fare.
Map Square 18.

ST. PAN.	TRENT	TRENT	ST. PAN.
AM 2.25	7.15	AM 1. 3g	4.20
4.25	8.30	4.58	7.25
8.25r	11.45	5.40	7.50
10.25r	1.22	7.17r	9.57
PM12.25r	3.38	7.42r	11. 0
2.25r	5.17	8.46r	11.35
4.25r	7.28	10.25r	1.30
5.35r	8.18	11. 7r	2.10
6.15r	8.26	PM 1.41r	4.20
11.45	2. 2	2.45r	5.45
—	—	5.20r	7.55
—	—	6.58r	9.15
—	—	7. 6r	10. 5

Sunday Trains.

AM10.50r	1.45	AM 1. 3	4.20
PM 1.35	5.32	6.18	8.57
3.15	5.47	8.35	11.53
6.15r	9.33	PM 3. 2	5.27
11.45	2. 2	5.20r	9.52
—	—	7.30	11. 7
—	—	9.14	4.55

g Monday mornings excepted.
r Restaurant Car.

TRENTHAM (Stafford)
from Euston, 143 miles. Fares, 29/10a, 17/11c. R. T. for two months, 59/8a. Pop. 3,059.
Map Square 12.

EUSTON	TRENT.	TRENT.	EUSTON
AM 2.35	7.50	AM 6.45	11. 0
5. 0	9.16	8.54er	12. 5
10.40r	2.15	8.54dr	12.20
12. 0nr	4. 6	11. 3r	2.20
PM 4. 5r	8. 7	11.48d	3.10
6.30er	10. 8	PM12.48t	5.55
6.55r	10.46	2.45r	8.10
d12.10m	10.55	5.25r	9.20
—	—	6.19r	10. 0
—	—	9.22-	5. 0

TRENTHAM—contd.
Sunday Trains.

EUSTON	TRENT.	TRENT.	EUSTON
PM12.10r	3.59	AM11.43	4. 0
3.50	10. 9	PM 5.13r	8.55
—	—	8.43	5. 0

d Saturdays only.
e Saturdays excepted.
m Midnight.
n Noon.
r Restaurant Car.
t Tea Car.

TREORCHY (Glamorgan),
174¼ miles. Fares, 35/2a, 21/1c. R. T. for two months, 70/4a, 42/2c. Departures from London as for Treherbert. Departures for London about 4 times daily.
Map Square 21.

TRESMEER (Devon),
231¼ miles. Fares, 47/6a, 28/6c. R. T. for two months, 95/0a, 57/0c. Departures from London as for Launceston. Departures for London about 4 times daily. Pop. 191.
Map Square 26.

TRETHOMAS (Monmouth),
150¾ miles. Fares, 31/5a, 18/10c. R.T. for two months, 62/10a, 37/8c. Departures from London as for Bargoed. Departures for London about 4 times daily.

TREVIL (Monmouth),
172¾ miles. Fares, 34/0a, 20/5c. R. T. for two months, 68/0a, 40/10c. Departures from London as for Abergavenny. Departures for London about 5 times daily.
Map Square 21.

TREVOR (Denbigh),
179¼ miles. Fares, 37/9a, 22/8c. R. T. for two months, 75/6a. Departures from London as for Llangollen. Departures for London about 5 times daily.
Map Square 11.

TRIANGLE (Yorks),
195¼ miles. No through fares. Departures from London as for Sowerby Bridge. Departures for London about 6 times daily. Pop. 932.
Map Square 12.

TRIMDON (Durham),
249 miles. Fares, 52/4a, 31/5c. R. T., double fare. Departures from London as for Ferryhill. Departures for London about 5 times daily. Pop. 5,259.
Map Square 7.

TRIMINGHAM (Norfolk),
137½ miles. Fares, 26/3a, 15/9c. R. T. for two months, 52/6a, 31/6c. Departures from London as for Mundesley. Departures for London about 7 times daily. Pop. 250.
Map Square 14.

TRIMLEY (Suffolk), 82¾
miles. Fares, 17/4a, 10/5c. R. T. for two months, 34/8a. Departures from London as for Felixstowe. Departures for London about 6 times daily. Pop. 1,539.
Map Square 19.

TRIMSARAN ROAD
(Carmarthen), 216½ miles. Fares, 45/2a, 27/1c. R. T. for two months, 90/4a, 54/2c. Departures from London as for Pembrey. Departures for London about 3 times daily.

TRING (Herts) from *Euston*

and Broad Street, 31¼ miles. Fares
from *Euston*, 6/6a, 3/11c. R. T. for
two months, 13/0a, 7/10c. From
Broad Street, 6/11a, 4/2c. R. T. for
two months, 13/10a, 8/4c. Pop. 4,352.
Map Square 23.

Leave		Arrive at
EUSTON	BROAD ST.	TRING
AM 5.25	—	6.56
7.15	6.45	8.25
7.35	7.10	8.45
8.35	8.15	9.49
9.40	9. 6	10.53
10.50	10.17	11.58
PM12.15	11.47	1.21
12.50d	12.20d	1.49
1. 3d	12.43d	2.11
1.10d	1.15d	2.33
1.35d	1.18d	2.45
2. 0	1.36e	3.13
—	1.35d	3.13
2.40d	2. 6d	3.48
4.10	3.47	5.18
4.55e	—	5.46
4.55d	—	5.54
5. 0e	4.20e	5.54
—	4.50e	6. 1
5.20d	4.47d	6.32
5.25e	—	6.23
—	5.24e	6.54
5.45e	5.28e	6.51
6.10d	5. 6d	7. 6
—	6. 0e	7.10
6.15e	—	7. 5
6.35	6.15e	7.33
—	6.40e	7.53
—	6.47d	8.22
7.15	6.52e	8.22
8. 5	7.36	9. 8
9. 5	8.17	10.10
9.55e	9.17e	11. 3
9.55d	9.17d	11.10
11.40	10.47	12.37

Sunday Trains.

AM 8.15	—	9.31
9.23	8.55	10.45
10.23	9.55	12. 0
PM12.53	12.25	2.30
2.15	1.25	3.18
2.53	2.25	4.13
4.53	4.25	6.15
6.10	5.25	7.15
6.53	6.25	8.13
9.40	9.10	10.46

Trains from Tring.

Leave	Arrive at	
TRING	BROAD ST.	EUSTON
AM 5.45	7.15	7 18
7.14	8.40	8.24
7.40	—	8.58
7.50	9. 0	8.58
8. 1	9.28d	9. 6
8.12e	9.21	—
8.21e	9.40	9.22
8.41	—	9.40
8.45	9.54	9.52e
9.28	10.50	10.30
10.32	12. 8	11.40
PM12.38	2. 8	1.50
1.55	3.38	3. 5
3.14	4.44	4.30
4. 5d	5.38	5.21
5. 2	6.36	6.15
6. 0	7.38	7. 5
6.40	8.15	7.55
7.31	9. 8	8.35
8.50	10.37	10.10
9.56	1M 5	10.50

TRING—*continued*.

Sunday Trains.

Leave	Arrive at	
TRING	BROAD ST	EUSTON
AM 8. 4	10. 5	9.22
10.53	12.35	12.15
PM12. 7	2. 5	1.20
1.25	3. 5	2.44
2.40	4.20	4.14
4.51	6.20	6.15
5.10	6.50	6.44
6.25	8. 5	7.44
7. 9	8.50	8.15
8.25	10. 5	—
8.59	10.20	9.45
9.34	11. 2	10.40

d Saturdays only.

e Saturdays excepted.

Rose and Crown Hotel.

Telephone 26. On Rothschild
estate. Tennis, Croquet, Racquets.
'Bus from Station.
TRUST HOUSES, Ltd.

TROEDYRHIEW (Glamorgan), 174 miles. Fares, 35/2a,
21/1c. R. T. for two months, 70/4a,
42/2c. Departures *from* London as
for Pontypridd or Merthyr (*via*
Pontypool Road). Departures *for*
London about 6 times daily.

TROEDYRHIEW
GARTH (Glamorgan), 180¼ miles.
Fares, 37/6a, 22/6c. R.T. for two
months, 75/0a, 45/0c. Departures
from London as for Tondu. Departures *for* London about 4 times
daily.

TROON (Ayr), 394 miles.
Fares, 81/5a, 48/10c. R. T. for two
months, 162/10a, 97/8c. Departures
from London as for Ayr or Kilmarnock. Departures *for* London
about 4 times daily. Pop. 9,420.
Map Square 40.

TROUTBECK (Cumber-
land), 290¼ miles. Fares, 58/7a,
35/2c. R. T. for two months,
117/2a, 70/4c. Departures *from*
London as for Keswick. Departures *for* London about 6 times
daily.
Map Square 7.

TROWBRIDGE (Wilts)
from *Paddington*, 97¼ miles. Fares,
via Theale, 19/10a, 11/11c. R. T. for
two months, 39/8a. *Via* Bath,
22/6a, 13/6c. R. T. for two months,
45/0a, 27/0c. Pop. 12,133.
Map Square 22.

PAD.	TROWBR.	TROWBR.	PAD.
AM 1. 0g	6.33	AM 7.18	10. 0
5.30	8.54	7.30r	10.15
7.30	10.29	8.15k	10.52
9.30k	11.59	9. 8	12.20
10.30k	12.25	10.23k	12.55
10.45	1.47	11.12r	2.40
PM12. 5k	2.19	11.25	2.50
12.30kr	3.29	PM12.29	3.20
2. 0k	4.22	2.30	6. 2
2.45	5.15	4.50kr	6.50
3.30k	5.58	5.18k	8.20
4.15t	6.51	7.28	10.25
5. 5k	8.10	10. 0	2.45
5.55	8.28	—	—
6.30	8.55	—	—

TROWBRIDGE—*contd.*

Sunday Trains.

PAD.	TROWBR.	TROWBR.	PAD.
AM 9.10	12.46	AM 7. 5	10.50
PM12.30	3.58	PM12.13	3.35
2.40k	6.17	4.30kr	7.55
5.15	8.44	5.45	9.15
10. 0	6.58	6.28	10. 0
—	—	—	—

g Mondays excepted.
h Tuesdays, Thursdays and
Saturdays only.
k *Via* Westbury.
r Restaurant Car.
t Tea Car.

TROWELL (Notts) from
St. Pancras, 125¼ miles. Fares,
25/8a, 15/5c. R. T., double fare.
Departures *from* London as for
Stapleford. Departures *for* Lon-
don about 10 times daily. Pop. 404.
Map Square 13.

TROWSE (Norfolk). See
under NORWICH.

TRURO (Cornwall) from
Paddington, 279¼ miles. Fares,
57/9a, 34/8c. R. T. for two
months, 115/6a, 69/4c. Pop. 10,833.
Map Square 25.

PAD.	TRURO	TRURO	PAD.
AM 5.30	2.18	AM 9.50r	4.35
10.30r	4. 4	11. 2r	4.45
11.10r	5.17	PM12. 6r	6.50
PM12. 5r	8.11	1.26r	9. 0
2. 0r	9. 8	9.56	7.10
10. 0	6.18	—	—
12. 0k	10. 5	—	—
12.30h	10.29	—	—

Sunday Trains.

AM10.30r	4.43	AM11.45	7. 5
PM10. 0	6.18	PM 1.24r	7.55
—	—	5.47	3.15
—	—	—	—

h Saturdays midnight only.
k Saturdays midnight excepted.
r Restaurant Car.

Taxi Cabs can be hired to
meet any train at this Station.
By telegram or telephone No. 174.
Taylor's Transport Co., Ltd.

Red Lion. First-class Family
Hotel. Over 200 years old. Close
to Cathedral. Most central for
tourists visiting Cornwall. Moderate tariff.　PROPRIETRESS.

TRUSHAM (Devon),
186½ miles. Fares (*via* Idel, 38/6a,
23/1c. R.T. for two months, 77/0a,
Via Newton Abbot, 41/6a, 24/11c.
R. T. for two months, 83/0a, 49/9c.
Departures *from* London as for
Exeter (St. David's). Departures
for London about 4 times daily.
Pop. 175.
Map Square 26.

TRYFAN (Carnarvon), 252¾
miles. No through fares. Departures *from* London as for Carnarvon. Departures *for* London about
3 times daily.
Map Square 11.

TUE BROOK (Lancs),
200½ miles. Fares, 41/3a, 24/9c.
R. T. for two months, 82/6a, 49/6c.
Departures *from* London as for
Liverpool (Lime Street). Departures *for* London about 8 times
daily.

TUFNELL PARK
(Hampstead Tube). See back of Map.

TULLIBARDINE (Perth),
436½ miles. Fares, 88/9a, 53/3c. R.T. for two months, 177/6a, 106/6c. Departures from London as for Crieff. Departures for London 4 times daily. Map Square 40.

TULLOCH (Inverness), 507¼
miles. Fares, 100/8a, 60/5c. R.T. for two months, 201/4a, 120/10c. Departures from London as for Fort William. Departures for London about twice daily. Map Square 37.

TULSE HILL (Surrey)
from London Bridge, 6 miles. Fares, 1/1a, 0/7½c. R.T. for two days, 1/9a, 1/0c. Pop. 32,235. See pp. 565-568, 570, 581, 582. Map Square 79.

TUMBY WOODSIDE
(Lincoln), 129¾ miles. Fares, 26/3a, 15/9c. R.T., double fare. Departures from London as for Midville. Departures for London about 4 times daily. Pop. 295. Map Square 13.

TUNBRIDGE WELLS
(CENTRAL) (Kent) from Charing Cross, Cannon Street, and London Bridge, 35 miles. Fares, 6/10a, 5.5b, 4/1c. R.T. for two months, 13/8a, 10/10b. Pop. 35,568 Map Square 24.

Char.+	Can. St.	Lon. B.	Arr. at Tun. W.
AM —	3.40s	3.43s	4.58
—	5.20	5.25	7.19
—	6.45	6.50	8.38
—	7.56	8.0	9.39
8.30d	—	8.37d	9.31
9.25	—	9.33	10.35
10.40	—	10.46	11.42
PM12.3	—	12.10	1.31
12.40d	—	12.47d	1.45
1.5d	—	1.11d	2.11
2.0d	—	2.5d	3.3
2.8	—	2.16	3.15
2.40d	—	2.46d	3.47
3.0d	—	3.8d	4.10
3.40d	—	—	4.29
5.48e	—	—	4.50
3.50	—	3.57	5.28
—	5.4e	—	5.56
5.5d	—	—	5.58
—	5.12e	—	6.7
5.24d	—	5.34d	6.47
5.26e	—	5.53e	6.34
5.35d	—	5.41d	7.59
6.3e	—	—	7.17
—	6.16e	6.19e	7.7
6.54e	—	6.41e	7.59
7.30	—	—	8.25
8.0	—	8.8	9.25
9.30	—	9.36	10.37
11.45h	—	—	12.47
12.5y	—	—	1.1

Sunday Trains.

Char.+	Can. St.	Lon. B.	Arr. at Tun. W.
AM 7.5	—	7.11	8.49
8.45	—	—	9.39
9.50	—	9.56	10.57
11.20	—	—	12.14
PM 3.5	—	3.13	4.50
7.10	—	7.20	8.32
7.35	—	7.45	8.53

TUNBRIDGE WELLS
(CENTRAL)—continued.

Trains from Tunbridge Wells (Central).

Leave Tun. W.	Lon. B.	Can. St.	Char.+ (Arrive at)
AM 6.40	8.10	—	8.19
7.48	8.48	8.52	—
8.28	—	9.15	—
9.0	—	9.48	—
9.12	10.28	10.32	—
9.45d	10.29	—	10.39
9.56e	—	10.40	—
10.21e	11.7	—	11.17
10.26y	11.31	—	11.38
10.35	11.43	—	11.57
11.57	—	—	12.49
PM 1.30	3.7	—	3.19
2.22d	3.19	—	3.27
3.25	4.15	—	4.25
3.47d	5.50	—	6.3
4.5d	5.0	—	5.8
4.18e	5.50	—	6.3
4.46d	6.30	—	6.39
5.49	6.40	—	6.49
6.3	7.25	7.30e	—
7.8	8.26	—	8.35
8.1	8.50	—	9.0
8.52	10.15	—	10.23
9.10	10.22	—	10.35
10.4	11.34	—	11.44

Sunday Trains.

Leave Tun. W.	Lon. B.	Can. St.	Char.+ (Arrive at)
AM 8.24	10.5	—	10.15
10.24	11.23	—	11.54
PM 1.25	2.50	—	3.0
6.13	—	—	7.3
6.48	8.12	—	8.22
8.3	9.4	—	9.14
9.20	10.8	—	10.16
9.51	11.4	—	11.15
10.32s	—	1.23	—

d Saturdays only.
e Saturdays excepted.
h Wednesdays and Saturdays only. s Third Class only.
y Wednesdays only.

ANOTHER ROUTE from
London Bridge, Victoria, Cannon Street, 37½ miles. Fares (First and Third) as above.

Leave Vict.	Can. St.	Lon. B.	Arr. at Tun. W.
AM 5.30	—	5.18	7.9
6.37	—	6.40	8.22
7.23	—	8.7	9.45
9.10	—	9.6	10.50
11.5h	—	10.35h	12.35
12.0	—	11.50	2.0
12.0d	12.16d	d12.20k	1.51
PM —	—	12.50d	2.32
1.20e	—	1.38e	3.7
1.25d	—	1.38d	3.11
—	—	2.5e	4.8
2.25	—	2.25d	4.8
3.45	—	—	4.51
4.0	—	4.0	6.1
4.0e	4.16e	e4.20k	5.46
4.50	—	4.44e	6.16
5.5	—	5.21	6.48
5.48	—	5.41e	7.31
6.6	—	6.8	7.41
6.50	—	7.0	8.42
7.15	—	7.38	9.32
8.5	—	8.10	9.38
9.3l	—	9.12l	11.2

TUNBRIDGE WELLS—
continued.

Sunday Trains.

Leave Vict.	Can. St.	Lon. B.	Arr. at Tun. W.
AM 8.50	—	8.30	10.25
PM 1.14	—	1.10	2.48
2.30	—	—	4.8
7.5	—	6.46	8.54

Trains from Tunbridge Wells.

Leave Tun. W.	Lon. B.	Can. St.	Arrive at Vict.
AM 6.36	8.15	—	8.24
7.10	8.37	—	8.40
7.15	9.1k	9.4	9.8
7.45	9.15	—	9.19
8.36	10.4	—	10.12
8.56	10.38	—	—
9.28	10.55	—	10.46
9.55	—	—	11.54
10.45	12.13	—	12.17
11.5h	12.44	—	12.35
11.38	1.42	—	1.26
PM 1.20	2.58	—	—
2.7	4.0	—	3.45
2.20	4.32	—	4.35
3.20	5.21	—	5.55
4.48	6.36	—	6.29
6.20	7.56	—	8.27
8.48	10.25	—	10.10

Sunday Trains.

Leave Tun. W.	Lon. B.	Can. St.	Arrive at Vict.
AM 8.27	10.18	—	10.20
12.0	—	—	1.40
PM 4.55	—	—	6.34
5.45	7.56	—	8.41
7.32	9.17	—	9.0

d Saturdays only.
e Saturdays excepted.
h Via Eridge.
k Departs from or arrives at London London Bridge S. E. & C. Station.
l Fridays only.

TUNBRIDGE WELLS— *continued.*

Marlborough. Private Hotel. Finest position. Mount Ephraim facing South. Noted for Comfort and Cuisine. Central heating. Redecorated throughout. Near Links and Stations. Phone 61.   Terms, Manageress.

Norfolk Hotel (Private). Quiet and High-class. Facing South. Central for all places of amusement and interest. Moderate Terms. Garage. Telephone 809. Tariff on application. Proprietress Miss A. A. BATES.

Castle Hotel. Facing Common. Established 1700. Family and Commercial. Telephone 94. Near Stations. Hunting, Coursing, Golf, Opera House, County Cricket. A.A. * * * W. E. URQUHART, Proprietor.

Harewood Private Hotel and Pension. Centrally situated, facing Common. Separate tables. Electric Light. Excellent cuisine. Telephone 574. Miss K. BRIANT.

St. Andrew's, Molyneux Park, Mount Ephraim. Superior Board - Residence in a gentlewoman's beautifully situated House. South aspect. Perfect sanitation. Near Links. Terms moderate. Telephone, 690.

Vale Royal Private Hotel. Facing Common. South aspect. Central position. Perfect sanitation. Every comfort. Separate Tables. Excellent cuisine. Telephone, 580. Apply, Manageress.

Lonsdale Mansions Private Hotel. South aspect. Central position. Dining Room (separate tables). Smoking Room, Lounge, etc. Heated throughout. Every comfort. Terms upon application. Telephone, 886. Apply Manageress.

Romanoff Private Hotel and Pension. Superb position on Common, near Mount Ephraim. Every comfort. Terms from 9/- per day.

Thurlstane Private Hotel and Pension, Mount Ephraim. Handsome lounge. Garden. Facing south and Common. New Management. Redecorated. Catering unsurpassed. 'Phone 1008.

Hotel Russell (Private). 79, London Road. Facing Common. Elevated Position. High-class. Separate Tables. Terms Moderate. Telephone 659.

Tweeddale Private Hotel. Facing Common. S.W. aspect. Separate Tables. Electric light. Moderate Terms. Apply— Mrs. G. CHANE-COX.

Caxton House. Private Hotel. Under new management. South aspect, central position, near Links. Good Cooking. Separate Tables. Every comfort. Garage. Special Winter Terms. 2½ to 4 guineas. Telephone 762.

TUNBRIDGE WELLS— *continued.*

Carlton Hotel. Family and Residential. Facing Common. Near Stations. Excellent cooking. Fully licensed. Large parties catered for. Garage. 'Phone 669.

Pembury, Tunbridge Wells 2¾ miles. Camden Hotel. Beautiful gardens. Tennis. R.A.C., A.A. Write or 'phone, 12 Pembury, for Illustrated Tariff. EDWARD SIMMS, Proprietor.

St. Ermin's Private Hotel Madeira Park. Centrally heated, elevated position. Southern aspect. Large rooms. Electric light. Separate tables. Tennis. Billiards. Recreation room. Garage. Moderate terms. Phone 1123. Tariff. Proprietors— Mr. & Mrs. A. ASHFORD KING.

Rockmount Private Hotel. Adjoining Mount Ephraim. Sunniest house in Tunbridge Wells. High position, facing South. Magnificent views over Common. Large rooms. Electric light. Good food. Good fires. Bedroom gas fires. Wireless. Constant hot water. Separate tables. Tel. 313. From 3 guineas.

Gibraltar Cottage, The Common. Paying Guests in Gentlewoman's Private House. Central Heating. Electric Light. Garden. Garage. Telephone 141. References exchanged.

Mount Edgecumbe House. Private Hotel. Situated on highest part of Common, and considered finest position in Tunbridge Wells. Central heating and all modern conveniences. Terms moderate. Apply Raiswell. Telephone 197.

House and Estate Agents. Furnished and Unfurnished Houses. Estates, Business Premises in District. Established 1840. Telephone 157. RICHARDSON AND PIERCE.

TUNSTALL (Stafford),

150½ miles. Fares, 31/5a, 18/10c. R. T. for two months, 62/10a. Departures *from* London as for Burslem. Departures *for* London about 6 times daily. Pop. 22,494. *Map Square 12.*

TURNBERRY (Ayr) from

St. Pancras, 417½ miles. Fares, 83/6a, 50/1c. R. T. for two months, 167/0a, 100/2c. *Map Square 43.*

St. Pan.	Turnb'y.	Turnb'y.	St. Pan.
AM 4.25	4.47	AM 7.47r	6.35
9.50r	8.48	9.57r	9.15
PM 3.06	9.17	PM 7. 2c	7.25
11.45c	10.46	7. 2d	8.57
—	—	—	—
—	—	—	—
—	—	—	—

Sunday Trains.

PM 9.30	9.17	—	—
11.45	10.46	—	—

d Saturdays only. *e* Saturdays excepted. *r* Restaurant Car.

Station Hotel. Most modern hotel in Scotland. Sea water baths. Fine centre for holidays. Tel. "Souwestern."

TURNCHAPEL (Devon),

from *Waterloo,* 235¼ miles. Fares, 47/3a, 28/4c. R. T. for two months, 94/6a, 56/8c. Departures *from* London as for Plymouth. Departures *for* London about 4 times daily. *Map Square 26.*

TURNHAM GREEN

from *Mansion House,* 7¼ miles. Also from Ealing, Hounslow and Richmond. *See* p. 489. *Map Square 68.*

TURNHOUSE (Midlothian), 398¾ miles. No through

fares. Departures *from* London as for Edinburgh (Waverley). Departures *for* London about 6 times daily.

TURRIFF (Aberdeen),

561 miles. Fares, 106/3a, 63/9c. R.T. for two months, 212/6a, 127/6c. Departures *from* London as for Inverurie. Departures *for* London about twice daily. Pop. 3,911. *Map Square 35.*

TURTON (Lancs), 202

miles. Fares, 41/10a, 25/1c. R. T. for two months, 83/8a, 50/2c. Departures *from* London as for Bolton (*via* Manchester). Departures *for* London about 6 times daily. Pop. 12,157. *Map Square 12.*

TURVEY (Beds), 56 miles.

Fares, 11/1a, 6/8c. R. T., double fare. Departures *from* London as for Olney. Departures *for* London about 5 times daily. Pop. 841. *Map Square 18.*

TUTBURY (Stafford) from

St. Pancras, via Derby, 139½ miles. Fares, 26/6a, 15/11c. R. T. for two months, 53/0a, 31/10c. Pop. 2,186. *Map Square 17.*

St. Pan.	Tutbury	Tutbury	St. Pan.
AM 2.25	7.52	AM 7.15r	11. 0
4.25	9.32	10.14r	1.30
10.25r	1.53	PM12.53r	4.20
PM12.25r	3.21	1.36dr	5.45
1.25r	4.53	2.53r	6.15
2.25r	5.55	5.49r	9.15
4.25r	7.36	6.37dr	10. 5
6.25r	9.51	10.29	4.20
—	—	—	—

Sunday Trains.

PM 3.15	6.45	AM11.14r	5. 2
—	—	PM 7.31	4.55

d Saturdays only. *r* Restaurant Car

TUXFORD (Notts) from

King's Cross, 132 miles. Fares, 27/4a, 16/5c. R. T., double fare. Pop. 1,154. *Map Square 13.*

King's +	Tuxfd.	Tuxfd.	King's +
AM 5. 5	9.35	AM 8.40r	11.30
10.10	1.23	9.46	1. 5
PM 1.50r	5. 3	PM12. 9	3.50
4. 0	7.15	3.10r	6.50
—	—	5.34	9. 0
—	—	7.32r	10. 0

Sunday Trains.

AM 8.30	1.15	PM 3.15	8. 3
—	—	—	—
—	—	—	—

r Restaurant Car.

TWEEDMOUTH (North-umberland), 333¾ miles. Fares, 70/3a, 42/2c. R. T., double fare. Departures *from* London as for Morpeth. Departures *for* London about 5 times daily. Pop. 4,965.
Map Square 3.

TWENTY (Lincoln), 99 miles. Fares, 20/5a, 12/3c. R. T., double fare. Departures *from* London as for Bourne or Spalding. Departures *for* London about 5 times daily.
Map Square 18.

TWICKENHAM (Middle-sex) from *Waterloo*, 11½ miles. Fares, 1/8a, 1/0c. R. T. for two days, 3/4a, 2/0c. Pop. 34,790. *See* pp. 585 587-591.
Map Square 76.

TWIZELL (Northumber-land), 343¾ miles. Fares, 72/4a, 43/5c. R. T., double fare. Departures *from* London as for Berwick-on-Tweed. Departures *for* London about 4 times daily. Pop. 186.
Map Square 3.

TWYFORD (Berks) from *Paddington*, 31 miles. Fares, 6/6a, 3/11c. R. T. for two months, 13/0a. Pop. 1,157.
Map Square 23.

PAD.	TWYFD.	TWYFD.	PAD.
AM 6.50	7.26	AM 7.25	8.20
6.35	8. 5	7.42	8.28
7.35	9.14	8.11	8.56
8.50	9.58	9. 5	9.43
9. 0	9.43	9.28	10.24
9.20	10.34	10.14	11. 6
9.55	11. 3	10.51	11.35
11.20	12. 2	11.24	12.15
11.25	12.41	11.51	1.11
PM12. 8	1. 7	PM12.30	1.46
1.20d	2.10	1.31	2.35
1.50d	2.47	2.38d	3.58
2. 7e	3. 4	2.38e	4.10
2.18d	3.12	3.52	5.17
3.58	4.27	4.41	5.57
4. 7	5. 4	5.59	6.55
5.15	5.55	7. 6	8.10
5.40	6.21	8. 4d	9.12
6.12e	6.56	8.21	9.33
6.35	7.28	9. 6	10.22
6.55	7.55	9.30	10.42
7.35	8.24	10.31	12. 0
8. 5	9. 1	—	—
8.35	9.47	—	—
9.15	9.55	—	—
10.40	11.56	—	—
11.20	12. 7	—	—
12. 3	1. 2	—	—
—	—	—	—

Sunday Trains.

AM 9.10	9.54	AM 9. 9	10.14
10. 0	10.52	9.51	10.50
10. 5	11. 6	11.40	1. 5
11. 0	11.56	PM 2.40	4.53
PM 1.45	2.48	5. 3	6. 0
2. 0	3.25	6.34	7.37
2.35	3.41	7.22	8.20
4.45	6. 5	8.34	9.32
5.15	6.15	8.54	9.53
6. 5	7.28	9.28	10.53
7.40	9. 0	—	—
8.30	9.57	—	—
—	—	—	—

d Saturdays only.
Saturdays excepted.

TWYWELL (Northampton), from *St. Pancras*, 76¼ miles. Fares, 14/9a, 8/10c. R.T., double fare. Departures *from* London as for Thrapston. Departures *for* London about 5 times daily. Pop. 460.
Map Square 18.

TY-CROES (Anglesey), 254¼ miles. Fares, 52/11a, 31/9c. R. T. for two months, 105/10a, 63/6c. Departures *from* London as for Gaerwen. Departures *for* London about 4 times daily.
Map Square 1.

TYDD (Lincoln) from *King's Cross*, 101½ miles. Fares, 18/7a, 11/2c. R. T. for two months, 37/2a. Departures *from* London as for Ferry. Departures *for* London about 4 times daily. Pop. (Tydd St. Mary) 854.
Map Square 18.

TYLDESLEY (Lancs) from *Euston*, 194½ miles. Fares, 39/7a, 23/9c. R. T., double fare. Departures *from* London as for Leigh (Lancs). Departures *for* London about 6 times daily. Pop. 15,651.;
Map Square 12.

TYLORSTOWN (Glamorgan), 171 miles. Fares, 34/5a, 20/8c. R.T. for two months, 68/10a, 41/4c. Departures *from* London as for Pontypridd. Departures *for* London about 4 times daily.
Map Square 21.

TYLWCH (Montgomery), 201¼ miles. Fares, 41/5a, 24/10c. R. T. for two months, 83/10a. Departures *from* London as for Llanidloes. Departures *for* London about 4 times daily.
Map Square 16.

TYNDRUM (Perth), 467 miles. Fares, 92/4a, 55/5c. R. T. for two months, 184/8a, 110/10c. Departures *from* London as for Crianlarich. Departures *for* London about 4 times daily.
Map Square 37.

TYNEHEAD (Midlothian), 381½ miles. Fares, 77/9a, 46/8c. R. T. for two months, 155/6a, 93/4c. Departures *from* London as for Galashiels. Departures *for* London about 3 times daily.
Map Square 41.

TYNEMOUTH (Northumberland), 276¼ miles. Fares, 58/4a, 35/0c. R.T., double fare. Departures *from* London as for Newcastle-on-Tyne. Departures *for* London about 8 times daily. Pop. 63,786.
Map Square 3.

TYSELEY (Warwick), 107½ miles. Fares, 22/4a, 13/5c. R. T. for two months, 44/8a. Departures *from* London as for Acock's Green. Departures *for* London about 6 times daily.

TYTHERINGTON (Glo'ster), 132½ miles. No through fares. Departures *from* London as for Bristol. Departures *for* London about 4 times daily. Pop. 541.
Map Square 22.

UCKFIELD—*continued.*

Trains from Uckfield.

Leave UCKFLD.	Arrive at LON. B.	VICT.
AM 7.44*k*	9.50	—
8.27	10.15	10.24
10.37	12.44	12.45
PM 12. 3	2.22	2.22
2.41*k*	—	4.50
3.50*k*	6.36	6.34
5.11	7.42	7.45
7.17	10. 0	10.10
8.13	10.25	10.17
9.20*e*	—	11.17
10.12*k*	12.59	1. 0
—	—	—

Sunday Trains.

AM 7.44	10.18	10.32
10.49*k*	—	1. 0
PM 1.56*k*	5. 3	5.11
5.27	7.56	7.37
8. 3	10.50	10.19
—	—	—

e Saturdays excepted.
k Via Brighton.

ANOTHER ROUTE *via* Groombridge, 46 miles. Fares, 9/7*a*, 5/9*c*. R. T. for two months, 19/2*a*, 11/6*c*.

Leave VICT.	LON. B.	Arr. at UCKFLD.
AM 5.30	5.18	7.44
6.37	6.40	9.54
7.23	8. 7	10.37
9.10	9. 6	11. 4
11. 5	10.35	12.39
12. 0	11.50	2.41
12. 0*d*	*d*12.20*k*	2.41
PM 1.20*e*	1.38*e*	3.39
1.25*d*	1.38*d*	3.39
3.45	—	5.10
—	4.44*e*	6. 9
4.50	—	6.37
5. 5	5.21	7.17
6. 6*e*	6. 8*e*	7.37
6. 6	6. 8	8.12
8. 5	8.10	9.35
—	—	—

Sunday Trains.

AM 8.50	8.30	10.39
PM 1.14	1.10	4.19
2.30	—	5.27
7. 5	6.46	9.30
—	—	—

Trains from Uckfield.

Leave UCKFLD.	Arrive at LON. B.	VICT.
AM 7.58	9.32	9.40
8.32	10. 4	10.12
8.49	10.55	10.20
10. 4	12.13	12.17
10.53	12.44	12.35
PM 12.44	2.58	—
1.33	—	3.45
2.22	5.21	5.55
4.35	6.36	6.29
5.50	7.56	8.27
8. 5	10.25	10.10

U

UCKFIELD (Sussex) from

London Bridge and *Victoria*, via Lewes, 58½ miles. Fares, 10/7*a*, 6/4*c*. R. T. for two months, 21/2*a*, 12/8*c*. Pop. 3,384.
Map Square 24.

Leave VICT.	LON. B.	Arr. at UCKFLD.
AM —	6.15	8.49
9. 0	—	10.54
9.45	—	11.46
—	9.50	12.44
11.15	—	1.23
11.55	12.10	2.22
PM —	2. 0	3.45
3.20	—	5.11
4.30	4. 5	6.23
5.20	5. 5	7.11
5.45*e*	5.55*e*	8. 5
6.50	7. 0	9.10
8.20	8.10	9.58
10. 0	—	12. 0
—	—	—

Sunday Trains.

AM 6.55	7.22	10.25
PM 12.15*k*	—	2.55
6.33	6.33	9.10
8.20	8. 0	10. 2
—	—	—

UCKFIELD—*continued.*

Sunday Trains.

Leave UCKFLD.	Arr. at LON. B.	VICT.
AM 10.25	—	1.40
PM 4.27	—	6.54
7.59	—	9.47
—	—	—

d Saturdays only.
e Saturdays excepted.
k Departs from London Bridge S. E. & C. Station.

Maiden's Head Hotel.

Family and Commercial. Four minutes from Station. Good Bed, Sitting, Billiard, and Assembly Rooms. Posting, Stabling and Garage. Tariff on application. Tel. 19.
A. WEBBER, Proprietor.

UDDINGSTON (Lanark),

393 miles. Fares, 80/0*a*, 48/0*c*. R.T. for two months, 160/0*a*, 96/0*c*. Departures *from* London as for Motherwell. Departures *for* London about 4 times daily. Pop. 8,414.

UDNY (Aberdeen), 537½ miles.

No through fares. Departures *from* London as for Fraserburgh or Peterhead. Departures *for* London about 3 times daily. Pop. 1,547.
Map Square 35.

UFFCULME (Devon),

from *Paddington*, 161½ miles. Fares, 33/9*a*, 20/3*c*. R. T. for two months, 67/6*a*. Pop. 1,595.
Map Square 26.

PAD.	UF'C'LME.	UF'C'LME.	PAD.
AM 5.30	12.12	AM 8.10*r*	1.30
PM 12. 5*er* 4.38		11.10	4. 5
12. 5*dr* 4.53		PM 3.30	9. 0
3.30*r* 7.18		6. 7	2.45
12. 0*h* 9.12		—	—

Sunday Trains.

PM 10. 0	9.12	—	—

d Saturdays only.
e Saturdays excepted.
h Saturdays midnight excepted.
r Restaurant Car.

UFFINGTON (Berks) from

Paddington, 66½ miles. Fares, 13/11*a*, 8/4*c*. R. T. for two months, 27/10*a*. Pop. 523.
Map Square 22.

PAD.	UFFINGTON	UFFINGTON	PAD.
AM 5.30	8.18	AM 7. 9	9.30
7.30	10.12	8.12*r*	10.15
9. 0	10.58	9.54	12. 0
10.45	1.10	PM 12.12	2.35
PM 1.35*r*	3.52	2.29	5. 6
3.58	6.31	6.42	9.15
6.55	8.52	7.44	10.45

Sunday Trains.

AM 10.35	12.40	PM 3.26	6. 0
PM 2. 0	6.11	—	—

r Restaurant Car.

UFFINGTON (Lincoln),

85½ miles. Fares, 17/3*a*, 10/4*c*. R.T. for two months, 34/6*a*, 20/8*c*. Departures *from* London as for Peterborough. Departures *for* London about 4 times daily. Pop. 419.

Map Square 18.

ULBSTER (Caithness),

736¾ miles. No through fares. Departures *from* London as for Wick. Departures *for* London about twice daily.

Map Square 32.

ULCEBY (Lincoln) from

King's Cross 164¾ miles. Fares, 34/4*a*, 20/7*c*. R.T. for two months, 68/8*a*, 41/2*c*. Departures *from* London as for Brocklesby. Departures *for* London about 6 times daily. Pop. 947.

Map Square 13.

ULLESKELF (Yorks),

197 miles. Fares, 41/1*a*, 24/8*c*. R.T. for two months, 82/2*a*, 49/4*c*. Departures *from* London as for York. Departures *for* London about 5 times daily. Pop. 393.

Map Square 13.

ULLESTHORPE (Leicester)

from *Euston*, 90½ miles. Fares, 18/9*a*, 11/3*c*. R. T., double fare. Departures *from* London as for Broughton Astley. Departures *for* London about 5 times daily. Pop. 395.

Map Square 18.

ULLOCK (Cumberland),

308¾ miles. No through fares. Departures *from* London as for Moor Row or Cockermouth. Departures *for* London about 5 times daily.

Map Square 6.

ULVERSTON (Lancs)

from *Euston*, 255¼ miles. Fares, 53/2*a*, 31/11*c*. R. T. for two months, 106/4*a*, 63/10*c*. Pop. 10,121.

Map Square 6.

Euston	Ulverst'n	Ulverst'n	Euston
AM 12.25	9. 4	AM 7.23*r*	3.10
2.35	10.36	9. 6*h*	3.45
5. 0	12.38	9.40*r*	4.15
6.45	2.13	11.11*r*	6. 0
11.35*r*	5. 5	PM 1.26*r*	7.30
11.50*r*	7. 8	2.21*er*	9. 5
PM 1.30*r*	7.30	2.21*dr*	9.15
2.35*t*	9.38	4.51*r*	10.45
5.20*r*	11.40	8.57	5. 0
9.30*e*	5.38	—	—
11. 0*d*	8 21	—	—
—	—	—	—
—	—	—	—

Sunday Trains.

AM 11.45*r*	6.18	PM 12.27*r*	7.30
—	—	8.37	5. 0
—	—	—	—
—	—	—	—
—	—	—	—
—	—	—	—
—	—	—	—
—	—	—	—

d Saturdays only.
e Saturdays excepted.
h Mondays and Saturdays only.
r Restaurant Car.
t Tea Car.

ULVERSTON—*contd.*

ANOTHER ROUTE from

St. Pancras, 277¾ miles. Fares as above.

St. Pan.	Ulverstn.	Ulverstn.	St. Pan.
AM 4.25	2.13	AM 7.20*r*	4.10
9.50*r*	5. 5	9.40*r*	5.30
PM 12.15*r*	7. 8	11.11*hr*	6.35
11.50*e*	10.36	PM 1.26*r*	9.15
11.50*d*	10.43	5.20*e*	4.20
—	—	6. 6*d*	4.20
—	—	—	—
—	—	—	—

Sunday Trains.

AM 10.50*r*	8.53	AM 7.27	5.27
PM 11.45	10.36	PM 5.17	4.55
—	—	—	—
—	—	—	—
—	—	—	—

d Saturdays only.
e Saturdays excepted.
h Wednesdays and Thursdays excepted.
r Restaurant Car.

UMBERLEIGH (Devon),

204¾ miles. Fares, 38/4*a*, 23/0*c*. R.T. for two months, 76/8*a*, 46/0*c*. Departures *from* London as for Eggesford. Departures *for* London about 5 times daily.

Map Square 21.

UNSTONE (Derby), from

St. Pancras, 150¼ miles. Fares, 31/0*a*, 18/7*c*. R. T., double fare. Departures *from* London as for Chesterfield. Departures *for* London about 6 times daily. Pop. 2,117.

Map Square 12.

UP-EXE (Devon), 173¾ miles.

Fares, 36/11*a*, 22/2*c*. R. T. for two months, 73/10*a*. Departures *from* London as for Exeter (St. David's). Departures *for* London about 6 times daily.

Map Square 26.

UPHALL (Linlithgow),

405¼ miles. No through fares. Departures *from* London as for Edinburgh (Waverley). Departures *for* London about 4 times daily. Pop. 12,497.

Map Square 41.

UPHOLLAND (Lancs), 200¾

miles. No through fares. Departures *from* London as for Wigan. Departures *for* London about 6 times daily. Pop. 5,532.

Map Square 12.

UPLAWMOOR (Ayr),

410¾ miles. Fares, 82/6*a*, 49/6*c*. R.T. for two months, 165/0*a*, 99/0*c*. Departures *from* London as for Glasgow (Central). Departures *for* London about 5 times daily.

Map Square 40.

UPMINSTER (Essex) from

Fenchurch Street, 15¼ miles. Fares, 2/11*a*, 1/9*c*. R. T. for two months, 5/10*a*, 2/11*c*. Pop. 3,559. *See* p. 509.

Map Square 24.

ANOTHER ROUTE from

Moorgate Street and *St. Pancras*, 21½ miles. Fares from St. Pancras, 2/6*a*, 1/6*c*. R. T. for two months, 5/0*a*, 3/0*c*. *See* p. 508.

UPPER BANK (Glamorgan),

222 miles. Fares, 41/5*a*, 24/10*c*. R. T. for two months, 82/10*a*, 49/8*c*. Departures *from* London as for Brecon (*via* Hereford). Departures *for* London about 3 times daily.

UPPER HOLLOWAY.

See HOLLOWAY, UPPER.

UPPER LYDBROOK

(Glo'ster), 144½ miles. Fares, 30/5*a*, 18/3*c*. R.T. for two months, 60/10*a*, 36/6*c*. Departures *from* London as for Lydney. Departures *for* London about 4 times daily.

Map Square 21.

UPPER NORWOOD.

See CRYSTAL PALACE or GIPSY HILL

UPPER PONTNEWYDD (Monmouth),

147½ miles. Fares, 30/5*a*, 18/3*c*. R. T. for two months 60/10*a*, 36/6*c*. Departures *from* London as for Newport (Mon.). Departures *for* London about 5 times daily.

Map Square 22.

UPPER SYDENHAM.

See SYDENHAM, UPPER.

UPPER TOOTING. *See*

BALHAM.

UPPER WARLINGHAM

See WARLINGHAM, UPPER.

UPPINGHAM (Rutland)

from *Euston*, 101½ miles. Fares, 18/1*a*, 10/10*c*. R. T., double fare. *Via* Rugby, 18/4*a*, 11/0*c*. R. T. for two months, 36/8*a*. Pop. 2,573.

Map Square 18.

Euston	Up'ham.	Up'ham.	Euston
AM 2.35	8.30	AM 7.40	11.55
5. 0	10.15	9.32	1. 0
10.40	2.58	11.55	4.15
PM 1.30	4.35	PM 2.15	5.50
2.50*t*	6.32	4.40*r*	9.20
—	—	6.50	10.45
—	—	—	—

No Sunday Trains.

r Restaurant Car.
t Tea Car.

UPTON (Berks), 55¾ miles.

Fares, 11/8*a*, 7/0*c*. R. T. for two months, 23/4*a*, 14/0*c*. Departures *from* London as for Hampstead Norris. Departures *for* London about 6 times daily. Pop. 209.

Map Square 23.

UPTON (Cheshire), 209¼

miles. No through fares. Departures *from* London as for Wrexham. Departures *for* London about 5 times daily. Pop. 1,006.

Map Square 11.

UPTON (Yorks), 183¼ miles.

Fares, 34/2*a*, 20/6*c*. R. T., double fare. Departures *from* London as for Cudworth. Departures *for* London about 3 times daily. Pop. 266.

Map Square 13.

UPTON MAGNA (Salop),

149 miles. Fares, 31/1*a*, 18/8*c*. R. T. for two months, 62/2*a*. Departures *from* London as for Wellington (Salop). Departures *for* London about 3 times daily. Pop. 441.

Map Square 17.

UPTON-ON-SEVERN

(Worcester), from *Euston*, 158½ miles. Fares, 24/10a, 14/11c. R. T. for two months, 49/8a, 29/10c. Departures *from* London as for Tewkesbury. Departures *for* London about 4 times daily. Pop. 2,222.

Map Square 17.

UPTON PARK (Essex)

from *Fenchurch Street*, 5¼ miles. Fares, 1/0½a, 0/7½c. R. T. for two days, 1/9a, 1/0¾c. Pop. 18,244. *See* p. 510.

ANOTHER ROUTE from

Ealing, Hounslow, Richmond, and *Wimbledon, via* District Railway. *See* p. 489.

UPWEY (Dorset), 159¾ miles.

Fares, 27/4a, 17/7c. R. T. for two months, 58/8a, 35/2c. Departures *from* London as for Dorchester. Departures *for* London about 4 times daily. Pop. 871.

Map Square 27.

URMSTON (Lancs),

194¼ miles. Fares, 39/7a, 23/9c. R. T. for two months 79/2?, 47/6c. Departures *from* London as for G'azebrook. Departures *for* London about 4 times daily. Pop. 8,297.

Map Square 12.

URQUHART (Elgin), 577½ miles.

Fares, 106/3a, 63/9c. R. T. for two months, 212/6a, 127/6c. Departures *from* London as for Huntly or Elgin (*via* Dunkeld). Departures *for* London about 3 times daily. Pop. 1,563.

Map Square 35.

USHAW MOOR

(Durham), 255 miles. Fares, 53/7a, 32/2c. R. T. for two months, 107/2a, 64/4c. Departures *from* London as for Durham. Departures *for* London about 6 times daily.

Map Square 7.

USK (Monmouth), 155¾ miles.

Fares, 31/11a, 19/2c. R. T. for two months, 63/10a, 38/4c. Departures *from* London as for Monmouth or Pontypool Road. Departures *for* London about 6 times daily. Pop. 1,496.

Map Square 22.

USWORTH (Durham),

261½ miles. Fares, 54/7a, 32/9c. R. T., double fare. Departures *from* London as for Ferryhill or Durham. Departures *for* London about 8 times daily. Pop. 7,986.

Map Square 3.

UTTOXETER (Stafford)

from *Euston*, 136 miles. Fares, 28/2a, 16/11c. R. T. for two months, 56/4a. Pop. 5,361.

Map Square 12.

EUSTON	UTTOX.	UTTOX.	EUSTON
AM 5. 0	9.47	AM 7	2dr12.20
6.45	11.26	7. 2er	12.32
8.45r	2.10	8.38r	2.20
10.40dr	5. 9	11.40	5.35
12. 0nr	5. 9	PM 2.43r	8.10
PM 2.50t	7.55	5.38r	10.45
4. 5t	10.10	6.20d	5. 0

No Sunday Trains.
d Saturdays only.
e Saturdays excepted.
n Noon.
r Restaurant Car.
t Tea Car.

UTTOXETER—*contd.*

ANOTHER ROUTE from

St. Pancras, 140¾ miles. Fares as above.

ST.PAN.	UTTOXTR.	UTTOXTR.	ST.PAN.
AM 2.25	8.14	AM 7. 2r	11. 0
4.25	9.47	10. 1r	1.30
10.25r	2.10	PM12.40r	4.20
PM12.25r	3.38	1.25dr	5.45
1.25r	5. 9	2.43r	6.15
2.25r	6.16	5.18r	8.35
4.25r	7.53	5.38r	9.15
6.25r	10.10	6.20dr	10. 5
—	—	10.16	4.20
—	—	—	—
—	—	—	—
—	—	—	—

Sunday Trains.

PM 3.15	7. 6	AM10.55r	5. 2
—	—	PM 7.12	4.55

d Saturdays only.
r Restaurant Car.

ANOTHER ROUTE from

King's Cross, 164 miles. Fares as above.

KING's+	UTTOXTR.	UTTOXTR.	KING's+
AM 5. 5	11.52	AM 7. 2	1. 5
8.45	2.29	10. 1	3.50
10.10r	3.38	PM 2.50	9. 0
11.30	5. 9	8. 9	3.25
PM 1.50r	7.53	—	—
5.35dr	10.10	—	—
11.25e	9.47	—	—
—	—	—	—
—	—	—	—
—	—	—	—
—	—	—	—

No Sunday Trains.
d Saturdays only.
e Saturdays excepted.
r Restaurant Car.

UXBRIDGE (Vine Street)

(Middlesex) from *Paddington,* 15¼ miles. Fares, 2/9a, 1/8c. R. T. for two months, 5/6a, 2/11c. Pop. 12,919.

Map Squares 23 and 55.

PAD.	UXBRIDGE	UXBRIDGE	PAD.
AM 4.12	5.19	AM 5.40	6.27
5. 5	5.55	6.10	6 55
5.45	6.50	6.32	7.25
6.30	7. 7	7. 2	7.55
6.35	7.38	7.40	8.25h
7.10	8. 5	7.57	8.28
7.35	8.20	8.18	8.49
8. 5	8.47	8.27h	9.24
8.20	9.10	8.53	9.25
9.20	9.57	9. 5	9.52
9.55	10.30	9.35	10. 6
10.27h	11.19	10. 0	10.55
10.55	11.40	10.45	11.18
11.35	12.25	11.10	11.55
PM12. 2h	12.51	11.30	12.32
12.33d	1. 3	PM12. 2	1.11
12.35e	1.25	12.42	1.32
12.42d	1.25	1.18	2. 2
1. 8d	1.44	1.45	2.35
1.15	2. 7	2. 0k	2.35
1.50d	2.27	2.15	3.10
1.49h	2.37	2.45	3.40
2. 5d	3. 9	3.32	4.19h
2.25	3.25	4.20	5.17
2.53d	3. 9	4.53d	5.45

UXBRIDGE—*continued.*

PAD.	UXBDGE	UXBDGE	PAD.
PM 2.55	3.40	PM 5. 2e	5.52
3.45	4.15	5. 2	6. 3
3.55	4.48	5.27e	6.20
4.18	5. 4	5.42	6.32
4.50	5.22	6.27	6.55
5. 3h	5.46	6.38	7.29
5.18d	5.52	7. 3	7.52
5.45e	6.15	7.45	8.40
5.45d	6.22	8.30d	9.12
6. 7d	7. 0	8.53	9.33
6.20e	7. 0	9.25	10.22
7. 0	7.29	9.57	11. 4
7.37	8.11	11. 5	12. 0
7.42e	8.32	—	—
8.35	9. 4	—	—
8.40e	9.27	—	—
10. 5	10.36	—	—
10.40	11.29	—	—
11.30	12. 3	—	—
12. 3	12.35	—	—

Sunday Trains.

PAD.	UXBDGE	UXBDGE	PAD.
AM 6.30	7.21	AM 8.20	9. 8
8.20	9.12	9.35	10.14
9.25	10.12	PM12. 2	1. 5
10.37	11.22	2. 0	2.58
11.35	12.35	2.46	3.42
PM12.55	1.43	3.28	4.22
1.45	2.32	4. 0	4.53
2.35	3.15	5. 5	5.52
2.55	3.47	5.40	6.23
3.35	4.25	6.20	7.10
4.45	5.34	7.20	8.12
6. 5	6.52	8. 5	9.17
8.20	8.54	9. 8	9.46
9.25	9.59	9.32	10.22
10. 5	10.46	10.50	11.38
11.15	11.54	—	—

d Saturdays only.
e Saturdays excepted.
h Departs from or arrives at Bishop's Road Station.
k Wednesdays and Saturdays only.

ANOTHER ROUTE from

Baker Street, 16¼ miles. Fares 2/9a, 1/8c. R. T. for two months, 4/3a, 2/11c.

B. ST.	UXBDGE	UXBDGE.	B. ST.
AM 5.22	6. 6	AM 5.30	6.19
6. 6	6.51	6.15	7. 1
6.30	7.19	6.59	7.37
7. 0	7.53	7.27	8. 6
7. 3	7.47	7.45	8.28
7.23	8. 8	7.58	8.35
7.33	8.17	8.13	8.48
7.52	8.36	8.28	8.59
8.20	9. 5	8.53	9.27
8.43	9.28	9.14	9.49
9.11	9.55	9.32	10. 5
9.32	10.18	10. 1	10.38
9.59	10.41	10.30	11.13
10.31	11.14	10.48	11.30
11. 0	11.44	11. 0	11.35
11.11d	11.58	11.19	12. 2
11.30e	12.14	11.47e	12.30
11.35d	12.19	11.48d	12.50
11.40d	12.24	PM12.18e	1. 0
PM12. 1e	12.45	12.26d	1. 2
12.18d	12.55	12.45d	1.25

UXBRIDGE—*continued.*

B. St. Uxbdge.	Uxbdge. B. St.
PM12.30*e* 1.14	PM12.48*e* 1.30
12.45*d* 1.24	1. 0*d* 1.40
1. 0*e* 1.44	1.18*e* 2. 0
1. 4*d* 1.45	1.33*d* 2.17
1.20*d* 2. 3	1.48*e* 2.30
1.30*d* 2.10	1.59*d* 2.43
1.30*e* 2.14	2.17*e* 2.59
1.46*d* 2.20	2.18*d* 3. 3
2. 0*e* 2.44	2.33*d* 3.17
2. 3*d* 2.41	2.48 3.36
2.23*d* 3. 6	3.20*e* 4. 2
2.30*e* 3.14	3.28*d* 4.10
2.53*d* 3.31	3.48*d* 4.30
3. 0*e* 3.44	3.52*e* 4.35
3. 4*d* 3.49	4.17*e* 5. 2
3.30*e* 4.14	4.22*d* 5. 5
3.37*d* 4.22	4.48*e* 5.26
4. 0 4.44	4.48*d* 5.30
4.17*e* 5. 1	5.12*e* 5.45
4.31*d* 5.16	5.13*d* 5.57
4.42*e* 5.16	5.32*e* 6. 8
5. 4*d* 5.50	5.33*d* 6.15
5.17*e* 5.51	5.52*d* 6.37
5.29*d* 6.14	5.59*e* 6.29
5.30*e* 6.13	6.18*d* 7. 0
5.53*e* 6.28	6.25*e* 7. 2
6. 1*d* 6.48	6.32*e* 7.14
6.21*e* 6.58	6.53*d* 7.35
6.31*d* 7.14	6.54*e* 7.39
6.41*e* 7.17	7. 5*e* 7.50
7. 0*d* 7.44	7.18*d* 8. 0
7. 3*e* 7.36	7.27*e* 8.12
7.19*e* 7.57	7.48 8.31
7.25*d* 8.10	8. 1*e* 8.47
7.34*e* 8.14	8.18 9. 0
7.45*d* 8.29	8.43 9.27
7.49*e* 8.33	9. 3*d* 9.48
8. 7*d* 8.51	9.18 10. 0
8.30 9.14	9.48 10.30
9. 0 9.44	10.18 11. 2
9.31 10.14	10.48 11.32
9.59 10.43	11.22 12. 6
10.37 11.11	11.46 12.30
11. 0 11.44	— —
11.40 12.15	— —
12. 9*h* 12.38	

Sunday Trains.

AM 7.34 8.20	AM 8.24 9. 8
8.29 9.13	9.43 10.27
9.10 9.54	10.11 10.55
9.29 10.13	10.41 11.27
9.59 10.44	11.11 11.57
10.29 11.13	11.41 12.27
10.59 11.44	PM12.13 12.57
11.30 12.15	12.43 1.27
PM12. 1 12.44	1.13 1.57
12.31 1.15	1.43 2.27
1. I 1.44	2.12 2.57
1.31 2.15	2.43 3.27
2. 1 2.44	3.13 3.57
2.31 3.15	3.43 4.27
3. 0 3.44	4.12 4.57
3.30 4.13	4.43 5.27
4. 3 4.47	5.13 5.57
4.31 5.15	5.43 6.27
5. 0 5.44	6.13 6.57
5.30 6.15	6.43 7.27
6. 0 6.44	7.13 7.57
6.30 7.13	7.42 8.27
7. 0 7.44	8.13 8.57
7.30 8.13	8.43 9.27
8. 0 8.44	9.13 9.57
8.30 9.13	9.43 10.27
9. 0 9.44	10.13 10.57
9.31 10.15	10.40 11.27
10.30 11.14	— —
11. 3 11.35	— —

d Saturdays only.
e Saturdays excepted.
h Wednesdays and Saturdays only.

UXBRIDGE—*continued.*

ANOTHER ROUTE from *Mansion House,* 21¾ miles, *via* Acton Town and South Harrow. *See* p. 489.

ANOTHER ROUTE from *Paddington,* (*via* Ruislip) 15¾ miles. Fares, 2/9*a*, 1/8*c*. R.T. for two months, 5/6*a*, 2/11*c*. *See* pp. 490–491.

UXBRIDGE ROAD from *Broad Street,* 13 miles. Fares, 1/0½*a*, 0/7½*c*. R. T. for two days, 2/1*a*, 1/2*c*. *See* pp. 501–505. *Map Square* 59.

From *Earl's Court,* 1½ miles, *via Kensington* (Addison Road) in connection with trains from Mansion House, Charing Cross, Victoria, etc. *See* pp. 501–505.

From *Aldgate,* 7¾ miles. Trains run about every 12 minutes throughout the day. *See* back of Map.

REFERENCE NOTES.

a signifies First Class.
b   „   Second Class.
c   „   Third Class.
d   „   On Saturdays only.
e   „   Saturdays excepted.
f   „   On Mondays only.
g   „   Mondays excepted.
r   „   Restaurant Car.
t   „   Tea Car.
x   „   Express.
R.T. „   Return Tickets.

All Trains in the Tables not otherwise marked carry Third Class Passengers.

V

VALLEY (Anglesey), 260¼ miles. Fares, 54/2*a*, 32/6*c*. R. T. for two months, 108/4*a*, 65/0*c*. Departures *from* London as for Holyhead. Departures *for* London about 3 times daily. *Map Square* 11.

VARTEG (Monmouth), 156 miles. Fares, 31/11*a*, 19/2*c*. R. T. for two months, 63/10*a*, 38/4*c*. Departures *from* London as for Abersychan. Departures *for* London about 4 times daily. *Map Square* 22.

VAUXHALL (London) from *Waterloo*, by R. T. Fares, 0/2½*a*, 0/1½*c*. R. T. for two days, 0/5*a*, 0/3*c*. Pop. 30,665. *See* pp. 507-512, 583-595. *Map Square* 69.

VAUXHALL (Warwick), 112¾ miles. Fares, 23/2*a*, 13/11*c*. R. T. for two months, 46/4*a*, 27/10*c*. Departures *from* London as for Birmingham (New Street). Departures *for* London about 15 times daily.

VELVET HALL (Northumberland), 337¾ miles. Fares, 71/1*a*, 42/8*c*. R. T., double fare. Departures *from* London as for Berwick-on-Tweed. Departures *for* London about 5 times daily. *Map Square* 3.

VENN CROSS (Devon) from *Paddington*, 157 miles. Fares, 32/9*a*, 19/8*c*. R. T. for two months, 65/6*a*. Departures *from* London as for Dulverton. Departures *for* London about 4 times daily. *Map Square* 21.

VENTNOR (Isle of Wight)

from *Waterloo, via Ryde*, 91¼ miles. Fares, 20/3*a*, 12/5*c*. R. T. for two months, 40/6*a*, 24/10*c*. Pop. 6,063. *Map Square* 28.

W'LOO	VENTNOR	VENTNOR	W'LOO.
AM 5.50	10.44	AM 6.25*fr*	9.52
8.34*r*	12.59	7.10	11.32
9.50	1.44	8. 5	11.41
10.50	3.44	10. 5*r*	1.52
PM 12.50*r*	4.44	11. 5*d*	3.20
1.50	5.44	11. 5*e*	4.16
3.50*s*	7.45	PM 2. 5	5.56
5.50	9.27	4. 5*r*	7.56
—	—	5. 5	10.46
—	—	8.40*hk*	3.58

Sunday Trains.

AM 8. 0	12. 7	PM 2.15*r*	6.16
9.15*r*	1.59	4. 7	8.52
PM 1.50	7.12	5.35	10. 1

d Saturdays only.
e Saturdays excepted.
f Mondays only.
h Via Eastleigh.
k Passengers cross Portsmouth at own expense.
r Restaurant Car.
s Refreshments served.

ANOTHER ROUTE from

Victoria and *London Bridge*, 103 miles. Fares as above.

Leave		Arr. at
VICT.	LON. B.	VENTNOR
AM 6.18	6.35	11.44
8.55	—	12.59
10.15	10.22	2.44
11.35	—	3.44
PM 1.35	—	5.44
1.40	1.50	6.44
1.55	2. 5	7.45
—	4.50	8.39

Sunday Trains.

AM 9.55	—	1.59
PM 1.14	1.10	7.12
—	—	—

Trains from Ventnor.

Leave	Arrive at	
VENTNOR	LON. B.	VICT.
AM 6.25*f*	10.45	10.52
7.10	. 10.55	—
9. 5	—	1.10
12. 5	4.27	4.34
PM 1. 5	—	5.12
3. 5	7.48	6.50
4. 5	—	8.33
5. 5	10. 8	10. 1

Sunday Trains.

PM 4. 7	8.50	7.56
—	—	—

f Mondays only.

ANOTHER ROUTE from

Waterloo, via Southampton, 112 miles. No through fares. *Map Square* 28.

W'LOO	VENTNOR	VENTNOR	W'LOO
AM 5.40	10.44	AM 8.45*h*r	12.50
8.50*s*	1.44	PM 12. 5	4.50
PM 12.30*r*	4.44	2.45*h*	6.58
1.50*s*	6.44	5. 5	10.50
4.50*r*	9.27	—	—

Sunday Trains.

AM 11. 0*r*	5.27	PM 2.15	8. 3
PM 2. 0*r*	8. 2	4. 7	10.52

h Ventnor West Station.
r Restaurant Car.
s Refreshments served.
Passengers cross Southampton at own expense.

VENTNOR (WEST)—contd.

ANOTHER ROUTE from

Victoria and *London Bridge, via* Newport, 109 miles. Fares, 20/3*a*, 12/5*c*. R. T. for two months, 40/6*a*, 24/10*c*.

Leave		Arr. at
VICT.	LON. B.	VEN. W.
AM 6.18	6.35	12.55
8.55	—	2.25
11.35	—	3.55
PM 1.40	1.50	6.55
—	4.50*d*	9.25

No Sunday Trains.

Trains from Ventnor W.

Leave	Arrive at	
VEN. W.	LON. B.	VICT.
AM 8.45	—	1.10
11.45	4.27	4.34
PM 2.45	7.48	6.50
4.20	10. 8	10. 1

No Sunday Trains.

d Saturdays only.

VENTNOR—continued.

Pension, St. Vincent Esplan- ade. Close to Sea and Pier. Separate Tables. Private Apart- ments during Winter Months. Miss MAUD LAMBERT, Proprietress.

Alma Boarding House. Facing Sea. Minute from Beach. Established 23 years. Removed to own house nearer sea. Winter Apartments. Misses SCOTT.

St. Catherine's Boarding House, Bellevue Road. Ideal position. South Aspect. Draw- ing room with balcony facing sea. Every comfort with good food. Mr. and Mrs. EELES.

Caws' Crab and Lobster Hotel. Charming grounds. Ideal position. From 10/6 day. Daily motor excursions, Land and Sea. Programme from proprietor. Telephone 161.

Craigdarroch. Alpine Road. First Class Board Residence. Facing South. Balcony. Good Views Sea and Downs. Terms Moderate.

Wellington House Boarding Establishment. Overlooking Sea. Terrace Garden to Esplanade. Drawing-room and lounge opening on to Balconies. Separate tables. Good cuisine. The Misses HUGHES & NORMAN.

Palmerston Boarding Establishment. Finest position in the Town. Overlooking Cas- cade and Pier. On Town level. Electric Light. Separate Tables. Spacious Lounge. Billiards. Per- fect Cuisine. Proprietors— Mr. and Mrs. ALLISTONE.

Bonchurch, Ventnor. Pen- sion "Umballa." Modern. De- lightfully situated on shore, facing South. Bathing from house. Sep- arate tables. Excellent cuisine. R. JOHNSON.

House Agency. Furnished and Unfurnished Houses. Proper- ties for Sale. Telephone 63x. Address. Church Street, Ventnor. ALBERT BULL and PORTER.

VERNEY JUNCTION

(Bucks) from *Baker Street*, 50½ miles. Fares, 10/6*a*, 6/4*c*. R. T. for two months, 21/0*a*, 12/6½*c*. *Map Square* 18.

Baker St.	Verney	Verney	Baker St.
AM 6. 5	8.19	AM 7.27	9.39
8.29	10.21	8.50	11. 5
10.11*d*	12.16	10.50*e*	1.22
10.18*e*	12.16	10.50*d*	1.24
PM12. 8	2.16	PM12.50	2.58
2.17*e*	4.11	3.30	5.41
2.19*d*	4.16	6. 7	8. 8
4.10*d*	6.40	7. 8	9.18
4.16*e*	6.40	9.50	11.40
6.30	8.21	—	—
—	—	—	—

Sunday Trains.

PM 3.35	5.40	AM 7.36	9.48
—	—	PM 6.17	8.12

d Saturdays only. *e* Saturdays excepted.

VERNEY JUNCTION —continued.

ANOTHER ROUTE from *Marylebone*, 50½ miles. Fares as above.

M'bone	Verney	Verney	M'bone
AM 8.45	10.21	AM 7.27	9.46
10. 5	12.16	8.50	10.56
11.15	2.16	10.50	12.59
PM 1.55*e*	4.11	PM12.50	3. 0
2.15*d*	4.11	3.30*e*	6.22
5. 0	6.40	3.30	7.15
6.25*d*	8.20	6. 7	8.11
6.31*e*	8.21	7. 8	8.55

Sunday Trains.

PM 3.15	5.40	AM 7.36	10.13
—	—	PM 6.17	8.16

d Saturdays only. *e* Saturdays excepted.

ANOTHER ROUTE from *Euston*, 55¾ miles. Fares, 10/3*a*, 6/2*c*. R. T., double fare.

Euston	Verney	Verney	Euston
AM 6.45	8.37	AM 8.18*e*	9.52
7.35	10.35	8.27	10. 0
10.40*d*	12. 2	10. 6	11.55
10.40*e*	12.35	PM12.21*h*	2.45
12. 0*nr*	1.47	2.46	4.15
PM 3. 5	4.55	3.18	5.35
4.15	5.47	5.45	7.55
5.32	7.12	7.42	9.20
6.10*e*	7.57	8.10*e*	10.10
—	—	8.10*d*	10.50

Sunday Trains.

AM 8.15	10.42	PM12.55	5. 5
9.15	12. 7	3.49	5.50
PM12.30	2.10	4.40	7.10
2.15	5.12	7.38	9.45
3.50	6. 2	8.17	10.10

d Saturdays only. *e* Saturdays excepted. *h* Thursdays and Saturdays only. *n* Noon. *r* Restaurant Car.

VERWOOD (Dorset) from *Waterloo*, 101 miles. Fares, 21/6*a*, 12/11*c*. R. T. for two months, 40/0*a*, 25/10*c*. Departures *from* London as for Fordingbridge. Departures *for* London about 6 times daily. Pop. 1,146. *Map Square* 27.

VICTORIA(L. B. & S. C. Rly.) from *London Bridge*, 8⅓ miles. Fares, 0/9*d*, 0/5½*c*. R. T. for two days, 1/2*a*, 0/7*c*. See p. 570. *Map Squares* 23 and 69.

VICTORIA (District Rly.) from *Mansion House, Charing Cross, South Kensington, High Street, Praed Street, Baker Street, King's Cross, Moorgate,* and all intermediate stations, every few minutes. Also to and from Eal- ing, Hounslow, Richmond and Wimbledon. See p. 489. *Map Squares* 23 and 69.

Royal Court Hotel, Sloane Square, S.W. 1. *See advt.* under London Hotels.

For Messengers & Theatre Tickets, apply 195 Victoria Street, S.W. Telephone No., Victoria 5019.

VICTORIA (Monmouth), 160½ miles. Fares, 33/4*a*, 20/0*c*. R. T. for two months, 66/8*a*, 40/0*c*. Departures *from* London as for Ebbw Vale. Departures *for* London about 6 times daily.

VICTORIA DOCKS, See Custom House (Victoria Docks).

VICTORIA PARK from *Broad Street*, 4 miles. Fares, 0/6½*a*, 0/5*b*, 0/4*c*. R. T. for two days, 1/1*a*, 0/10*b*, 0/7*c*. See p. 500. *Map Square* 62.

VIRGINIA WATER

(Surrey) from *Waterloo, via* Staines, 23¼ miles. Fares, 4/2*a*, 2/6*c*. R. T. for eight days, 8/4*a*, 5/0*c*. Pop. 1,821. *Map Squares* 23 and 72.

W'loo.	Virg. W.	Virg. W.	W'loo.
AM 5.10	6.28	AM 7.28	8.17
6.54	7.52	7.55	8.47
7.54	8.56	8.32	9.17
8.54	9.52	9. 8	9.47
9.54	10.53	9.33	10.17
10.54	11.56	10.30	11.17
PM12.48	1.56	11.34	12.31
1.18*d*	2. 3	PM12.34	1.27
1.48	2.34	1.34	2.27
2.18*d*	3. 5	2.34	3.27
2.48	3.53	4.34	5.27
3.48*e*	4.34	5.34	6.27
3.48*d*	4.42	6.34	7.27
4.48*e*	5.29	7.34	8.27
4.48*d*	5.42	8.34	9.27
5.18*e*	6. 3	9.42	10.37
5.48	6.34	11. 3*e*	12. 5
6.18*e*	7. 3	11. 3*d*	12. 8
6.48	7.33	—	—
7.54	8.52	—	—
9.24	10.22	—	—
10.24	11.22	—	—

Sunday Trains.

AM 8.18	9.22	AM 9.19	10.30
9.18	10.16	9.32	11.43
PM12.18	1.19	11.30	12.43
2.18	3.20	PM 1. 5	2. 3
4.18	5.16	4.56	5.28
5.58	6.58	6.30	7.28
7.48	8.45	8.31	9.28
9.18	10.20	9.22	10.18
—	—	9.35	10.28

d Saturdays only. *e* Saturdays excepted.

ANOTHER ROUTE from *Waterloo, via* Weybridge, 25 miles. Fares, 4/19*a*, 2/11*c*. R. T. for two months, 9/8*a*, 5/10*c*.

W'loo.	Virg. W.	Virg. W.	W'loo.
AM 4.50	6.15	AM 6.35	7.41
6.10	7.19	7.33	8.36
7. 0	8.26	8.30	9.31
8.15	9.22	8.40	9.36
9.15	10.26	9.39	10.45
10.20	11.26	10.41	11.46
11.20	12.26	11.40	12.46
PM12.15	1.26	PM12.38	1.46
1.20	2.26	1.40	2.46
2.20	3.26	2.40	3.46
3.15	4.26	3.58	4.46
4.20	5.26	4.40*e*	5.46
5.20	6.26	4.42*d*	5.46
6.20	7.26	5.40*e*	6.46
7.20	8.26	5.45*d*	6.46
8.20	9.26	6.40	7.46
9.20	10.21	7.40	8.46
—	—	8.40	9.46
—	—	9.43	10.46
—	—	10.40	12.16

Sunday Trains.

AM 8.20	9.20	AM 8.20	9.45
10.20	11.26	10.17	11.16
11.20	12.51	11.33	12.41
PM 1.50	2.51	PM 3.22	5.41
3.20	4.51	5.25	6.46
5.20	6.21	6.52	7.41
6.30	7.28	7.32	8.41
7.20	8.27	8.32	9.44
8.20	9.25	9.36	10.41

d Saturdays only. *e* Saturdays excepted.

For Advertisement list, see over.

VIRGINIA WATER—*con.*

Wheatsheaf Hotel. Beautifully situated in Windsor Park. Garden adjoins Lake. Most convenient for Ascot Races. Fully Licensed. Old-established. Excellent Cuisine. Garage. Telephone, 10 Egham.
L. M. UPCRAFT, Proprietress.

VOWCHURCH(Hereford),

160¼ miles. Fares, 33/7*a*, 20/2*c*. R. T. for two months, 67/2*a*,40/4*c*. Departures *from* London as for Abbeydore. Departures *for* London about 3 times daily. Pop.277. *Map Square* 17.

IDRIS

SODA WATER
LEMONADE
DRY GINGER ALE
BREWED GINGER
BEER
GINGER ALE

To be obtained at all Clubs, Hotels, Restaurants, Grocers, Wine Merchants, and Chemists.

REFERENCE NOTES.

a signifies First Class.
b   „   Second Class.
c   „   Third Class.
d   „   On Saturdays only.
e   „   Saturdays excepted.
f   „   On Mondays only.
g   „   Mondays excepted.
r   „   Restaurant Car.
t   „   Tea Car.
x   „   Express.
R.T. „   Return Tickets.

All Trains in the Tables not otherwise marked carry Third Class Passengers.

W

WADBOROUGH (Worcester), 119 miles. No through fares. Departures *from* London as for Worcester. Departures *for* London about 5 times daily. *Map Square* 17.

WADDESDON (Bucks)

from *Marylebone*, 42¼ miles. Fares, 9/0*a*, 5/5*c*. R. T. for two months, 18/0*a*, 10/8*c*. *Map Square* 23.

M'BONE.	WAD'SDON	WAD'SDON	M'BONE
AM 6.45	8.11	AM 6. 4	7.50
7.50	9.32	8.27	9.46
8.45	10. 0	9.15	10.36
10. 5	11.55	10.52	12. 2
11.15	12.47	11.14	12.59
PM 1.55*e*	3.49	PM 1.10	3. 0
2.15*d*	3.49	3.25	4.56
3.25	4.55	3.52*e*	6.22
5. 0	6.15	6.11	7.15
6.25*e*	7.46	6.29	8.11
6.25*d*	7.53	7.28	8.55
6·31*e*	8. 0	9.39	11. 0
7.30	9. 5	—	—
—	—	—	—
—	—	—	—

Sunday Trains.

AM 9.30	10.58	AM 8.41	10.13
PM 3.15	5.11	11.21	12.46
5.30	7. 6	PM 6.39	8.16
6.45	8. 8	7.44	9.44
—	—	8.33	9.55

d Saturdays only.
e Saturdays excepted.

WADDESDON—*contd.*

ANOTHER ROUTE from *Baker Street*, 43 miles. Fares as above.

BAKER S.	WD'SDON	WD'SDON	BAKER S.
AM 6. 5	7.40	AM 6. 4	7.41
6.30	8.11	8.12	9.39
7.50	9.32	8.27	9.49
8.29	10. 0	8.45	10.24
10.11*d*	11.55	9.15	11. 5
10.18*e*	11.55	10.52	12.22
11. 0	12.47·	11.12*e*	1.22
PM12. 8	1.55	11.12*d*	1.24
2.17*e*	3.49	PM 1.10	2.58
2.19*d*	3.53	3.25	5.14
3.10	4.55	3.52	5.41
3.18*d*	4.55	6.11	7.32
4.10*d*	6.15	6.29	8. 8
4.16*e*	6.15	7.28	9.18
5.46*d*	7.53	9.39	11.18
5.49*e*	7.46	9.50	11.40
6.30	8. 0	—	—
7.15*d*	9. 5	—	—
7.19*e*	9. 5	—	—
—	—	—	—
—	—	—	—

Sunday Trains.

AM 9.10	10.58	AM 8. 3	9.48
PM 3.35	5.11	8.41	10.27
5.37	7. 7	11.21	1. 5
6.30	8. 8	PM 6.39	8.12
—	—	7.44	9.12
—	—	8.33	10.20

d Saturdays only.
e Saturdays excepted.

WADDESDON ROAD

(Bucks) from *Baker Street*, 45½ miles. Fares, 9/6*a*, 5/8*c*. R. T. for two months, 19/0*a*, 11/4*c*.
Pop. 1,569.
Map Square 23.

BAKER S.	W.ROAD	W.ROAD	BAKERS.
AM 7.50	9.56	AM 8.27	10.24
10.11	12.15	11. 0	1.22
PM 2.17	4.14	PM 3.33	5.41
4.10	6.40	6. 6	8. 8
7.15*d*	9.30	9. 3*d*	11.18
—	—	—	—
—	—	—	—

No Sunday Trains.
d Saturdays only.

ANOTHER ROUTE from *Marylebone*, 45½ miles. Fares as above.

M'BONE.	W.ROAD	W. ROAD	M'BONE
AM 7.50	9.56	AM 8.27	10.36
10. 5	12.15	11. 0	12.59
PM 1.55*e*	4.14	PM 3.33*e*	6.22
2.15*d*	4.14	3.33	7.15
5. 0	6.40	6. 6	8.11
7.30*d*	9.30	—	—
—	—	—	—

No Sunday Trains.
d Saturdays only.
e Saturdays excepted.

WADDINGTON(Lincoln), 126 miles. Fares, 26/1*a*, 15/8*c*. R. T., double fare. Departures *from* London as for Lincoln. Departures *for* London about 6 times daily. Pop. 864. *Map Square* 13.

WADDON (Surrey) from *London Bridge*, 11¼ miles. Fares, 2/4*a*, 1/3*c*. R. T. for two days, 4/4*a*, 2/6*c*. *See* pp. 564–565.

ANOTHER ROUTE from *Victoria*, 11¾ miles. Fares as above. *See* pp. 571–574.

WADEBRIDGE (Cornwall)

from *Waterloo*, 254 miles. Fares, 52/1*a*, 31/3*c*. R. T. for two months, 104/2*a*, 62/6*c*. Pop. 2,319.

W'LOO.	W'BDGE.	W'BDGE.	W'LOO.
AM 10. 0*r*	4. 9	AM 8.35*r*	3.50
11. 0*r*	6.19	9.51*r*	4.30
PM 3. 0*r*	9.26	PM 12.49*r*	8.30
—	—	2.58	10.50
—	—	—	—

No Sunday Trains.

r Restaurant Car.

ANOTHER ROUTE

from *Paddington*, 263½ miles. Fares as above.

Map Square 25.

PAD.	W'BDGE.	W'BDGE.	PAD.
AM 5.30	3.13	AM 9.50*r*	4.35
11.10*r*	5.37	11.50*r*	6.50
PM 2. 0*r*	9.17	PM 1.40*r*	9. 0
12. 0*h*	9.34	7. 0	7.10
—	—	—	—

Sunday Trains.

PM 10. 0	9.34	—	—

h Saturdays midnight excepted.
r Restaurant Car.

WADHURST (Sussex)

from *Charing Cross*, *Cannon Street* and *London Bridge*, 40 miles. Fares, 8/4*a*, 6/8*b*, 5/0*c*. R. T. for two months, 16/8*a*, 13/4*b*. Pop. 3,647.

Map Square 24.

CHAR +	Leave CAN. ST.	LON. B.	Arr. at WADH'ST
AM —	3.40*h*	3.43*h*	6.12
—	5.20	5.25	7.37
—	7.56	8. 0	9.54
9.25	—	9.33	11. 1
10.40	—	10.46	12. 7
PM 12. 3*e*	—	12.10*e*	1.56
12.40*d*	—	12.47*d*	1.57
1. 5*d*	—	1.11*d*	2.33
2. 8	—	2.16	3.33
3. 0*d*	—	3. 8*d*	4.22
3.48*e*	—	—	5. 6
3.50	—	3.57	5.40
5. 5*d*	—	—	6.21
—	5.12*e*	—	6.24
5.26*e*	—	5.33*e*	6.47
5.24*d*	—	5.34*d*	7. 0
6. 3*e*	—	—	7.30
—	6.16*c*	6.19*c*	7.19
7.30	—	—	8.49
8. 0	—	8. 8	9.40

Sunday Trains.

AM 7. 5	—	7.11	8.59
8.45	—	—	10. 1
9.50	—	9.56	11. 6
11.15	—	11.23	1. 4
PM 3. 5	—	3.13	5. 3
7.35	—	7.45	9.10

Trains from Wadhurst.

Leave WADH'RST	Arrive at LON. B.	CAN. ST.	CHAR. +
AM 6.22	8.10	—	8.19
8. 4	—	9.15	—
8.40	—	9.48	—
9.26*d*	10.29	—	10.39
9.35*e*	10.29	—	10.39
10. 5*e*	11. 7	—	11.17
11.10	—	—	12.49
PM 1.12	3. 7	—	3.19

WADHURST—*continued.*

Leave WADH'RST	Arrive at LON. B.	CAN. ST.	CHAR. +
PM 2.41	4.15	—	4.25
3.34*d*	5. 0	—	5. 8
4. 5*e*	5.50	—	6. 3
4.27*d*	6.30	—	6.39
4.37*e*	6.44	—	6.54
4.55*d*	6.40	—	6.49
5.50	7.25	7.30	—
6.34	8.26	—	8.35
8.37	10.15	—	10.23
9.47	11.34	—	11.44
—	—	—	—

Sunday Trains.

AM 8. 7	10. 5	—	10.15
10. 7	11.23	—	11.34
PM 1.15	2.50	—	3. 0
6.32	8.12	—	8.22
7.35	9. 4	—	9.14
9. 8	10. 8	—	10.16
9.38	11. 4	—	11.15
10.20*h*	—	1.23	—
—	—	—	—

d Saturdays only.
e Saturdays excepted.
h Third class only.

WADSLEY BRIDGE

(Yorks), 164½ miles. Fares, 33/4*a*, 20/0*c*. R. T., double fare. Departures *from* London as for Sheffield (Victoria). Departures *for* London about 4 times daily.

Map Square 12.

WAEN AVON (Monmouth)

160¾ miles. Fares, 33/2*a*, 19/11*c*. R. T. for two months, 66/4*a*, 39/10*c*. Departures *from* London as for Abersychan. Departures *for* London about 4 times daily.

Map Square 21.

WAENFAWR (Carnarvon),

254½ miles. No through fares. Departures *from* London as for Carnarvon. Departures *for* London about 4 times daily Pop. 1,531.

Map Square 11.

WAINFLEET (Lincoln)

from *King's Cross*, 126½ miles. Fares, 26/3*a*, 15/9*c*. R. T., double fare. Departures *from* London as for Skegness. Departures *for* London about 6 times daily. Pop. 1,944.

Map Square 13.

WAKEFIELD (WESTGATE)

(Yorks) from *King's Cross*, 175¾ miles. Fares, 36/6*a*, 21/11*c*. R.T., double fare. Pop. 52.892.

Map Square 12.

KING'S +	WAKEF'D	WAKEF'D	KING'S +
AM 4.45	8.56	AM 8.11	11.30
7.15*r*	10.56	9.22	1. 5
10.10*r*	1.35	10.36*r*	1.55
PM 1.30*r*	4.51	11.20	3.50
1.50*r*	5.54	PM 12.33*r*	4.45
4. 0*r*	7.43	1.31*r*	5. 0
5.45*r*	9.14	1.43	6.25
10.45*e*	2.35	3.37*r*	7.10
—	—	5.53*r*	9.25
—	—	10.52	3.25
—	—	—	—

Sunday Trains.

12. 0*nr*	4. 5	AM 11.25*r*	3.45
PM 5. 0*r*	9. 8	PM 1.35	5.55
10.45	2.35	6. 5*r*	10.20
—	—	—	—

e Saturdays excepted.
n Noon.
r Restaurant Car.

WAKEFIELD—*continued.*

ANOTHER ROUTE (KIRKGATE)

from *King's Cross*, 175 miles. Fares as above.

KING'S +	WAKEF'D (K'gate)	WAKEF'D (K'gate)	KING'S +
AM 4.45	9. 8	AM 7. 2*r*	11.30
7.15*r*	11.23	9.10	1. 5
10.10*r*	1.58	10.19*r*	1.55
PM 1.30*r*	5.15	11.26	3.50
1.50*r*	6.20	11.45*r*	4.45
4. 0*r*	8.54	PM 1. 3	5. 0
5.45*r*	9.25	3.25*r*	7.10
—	—	5.35*r*	9.25
—	—	11. 0	3.25
—	—	—	—

Sunday Trains.

—	—	AM 11.33*r*	3.45
—	—	PM 1.10*r*	5.55
—	—	—	—
—	—	—	—

r Restaurant Car.

WAKERLEY (Northampton)

from *King's Cross*, 91½ miles. Fares, 17/4*a*, 10/5*c*. R. T. for two months, 34/8*a*. Departures *from* London as for Peterborough. Departures *for* London about 4 times daily. Pop. 156.

Map Square 18.

WALBERSWICK (Suffolk)

from *Liverpool Street*, 108½ miles. Fares, 22/9*a*, 13/8*c*. R.T. for two months, 45/6*a*. Departures *from* London as for Southwold. Departures *for* London about 4 times daily. Pop 372.

Map Square 19.

WALCOT (Salop), 146½

miles. Fares, 30/7*a*, 18/4*c*. R. T. for two months, 61/2*a*. Departures *from* London as for Wellington (Salop). Departures *for* London about 6 times daily.

Map Square 17.

WALDRON (Sussex) from

Victoria and *London Bridge*, 47½ miles. Fares, 10/0*a*, 6/0*c*. R. T. for two months, 20/0*a*, 12/0*c*. Departures *from* London as for Heathfield (*via* Groombridge). Departures *for* London about 8 times daily. Pop. 2,178.

Map Square 24.

WALESWOOD (Yorks),

154½ miles. Fares 33/1*a*, 19/10*c*. R. T., double fare. Departures *from* London as for Worksop or Beighton. Departures *for* London about 3 times daily.

WALHAM GREEN

From *Mansion House*, 6 miles. *See* p. 489.

Map Square 68.

WALKDEN (Lancs), 194½

miles. Fares, 40/0*a*, 24/0*c*. R. T. for two months, 80/0*a*, 48/0*c* Departures *from* London as for Manchester (London Road). Departures *for* London about 6 times daily.

Map Square 12.

WALKER (Northumberland),

272½ miles. No through fares. Departures *from* London as for Newcastle-on-Tyne. Departures *for* London about 6 times daily. Pop. 15.786.

WALKERBURN(Peebles),
374 miles.   Fares,   76/1a,   45/8c.
R.T.for two months, 152/2a, 91/4c.
Departures *from* London as for
Galashiels.   Departures *for* London about 4 times daily. Pop. 1,169.
Map Square 41.

WALKERGATE (Northumberland), 27¾ miles. Fares,
57/3a, 34/4c.   R. T., double fare.
Departures *from* London as for
Newcastle-on-Tyne.   Departures
for London about 9 times daily.

WALKERINGHAM
(Notts), 150¾ miles. Fares, 31/1a,
18/8c. R.T., double fare. Departures *from* London as for Gainsborough. Departures *for* London
about 5 times daily. Pop. 829.
Map Square 13

WALL (Northumberland),
290¼ miles.   No through fares.
Departures *from* London as for
Carlisle or Hexham.   Departures
for London about 3 times daily.
Pop: 369.
Map Square 3.

WALLASEY (Cheshire),
206¼ miles.   No through fares.
Departures *from* London as for
Birkenhead or Hooton.   Departures *for* London about 4 times
daily. Pop. 90,721.
Map Square 12.

WALL GRANGE (Stafford), 154½ miles.   Fares, 32/4a,
19/5c. R. T. for two months, 64/8a,
38/10c. Departures *from* London
as for Stoke-on-Trent.   Departures *for* London about 6 times
daily.
Map Square 12.

WALLINGFORD (Berks)
from *Paddington*, 51 miles. Fares,
10/8a, 6/5b.   R. T for two
months, 21/4a. Pop. 2,724.
Map Square 23.

Pad.	Wallingf'd	Wallingf'd Pad.	
AM 5.30	8.14	AM 7.12	9. 0
6.30	8.48	7.52	9.30
7.30	9.39	8.25	10. 0
9. 0	10.45	9. 2	10.45
9.45	12.12	10.10	12. 0
11.20	1. 0	11.45	1.50
PM12.30	2.12	PM 1.37	3.20
1.35r	3. 9	2.40	4.35
1.50d	3.50	3.28	5. 6
3.38	5.37	4.53	7.20
5. 0	6.36	6.45	8.20
6. 5	7.38	7.15	9.15
7.30	9.15	8.40	10.45
10. 0h	11.43	9.55h	2.45

No Sunday Trains.

d Saturdays only.
h Wednesdays and Saturdays only.
r Restaurant Car.

Salter's Steamers (Wallingford Bridge). 10 minutes from
Station.   Up-stream, 9.0 a.m.,
2.45 p.m. ; down-stream, 9.0 a.m.,
2.45 p.m.
See advt. facing first page of train
service.

Hotel Beau Regard, Shillingford Hill. Ideal River Hotel.
Fully Licensed.   Ball - room.
Garage.
See advt. p. **338.**

George Hotel. Family and
Commercial. Old Established.
Two minutes river; near Station.
Every accommodation for Boating.
Good stabling. Billiards. Tel. 36.
Proprietor, CHAS. A. EVANS.

WALLINGTON (Surrey)
from *London Bridge*, 13 miles.
Fares, 2/4a. 1/5c.   R. T. for two
days, 4/4a. 2/10c.   Pop. 9,223.
See pp. 564-565.

ANOTHER ROUTE from
Victoria, 13¾ miles.   Fares as
above. *See* pp. 571-574.

WALLSEND(Northumberland) 271¾ miles. Fares, 57/4a,
34/5c. R. T., double fare. Departures *from* London as for
Newcastle-on-Tyne.   Departures
for London about 9 times daily.
Pop. 43,013.
Map Square 3.

WALMER (Kent) from
Victoria, *Holborn Viaduct*, and
St. Paul's (*via* Chatham), 824 miles.
Fares, 17/1a, 13/8b, 10/3c.   R. T.
for two months, 34/2a, 27/4b, 20/6c.
Pop. 5,354.
Map Square 24.

Vict. (S.E.&C.)	Leave Hol. V.	St. Pl.'s	Arr. at Walmer
AM —	3.50l	—	7.43
5. 5	4.57	5. 0	9.20
5.48f	5.40f	5.42f	9.19
—	7.30	7.33	11.38
9.20	—	—	11.52
9.45	—	—	12.30
10.40	—	—	2. 8
11.40d	—	—	3. 1
11.40e	—	—	4. 3
PM 2. 5d	—	—	4.45
2. 8e	—	—	5.20
5.10d	5.10e	5.12e	8.13
5.30e	—	—	8.51
5.30d	—	—	9.50
7.22k	—	—	11. 5
8.30	—	—	11.17
—	—	—	—

Sunday Trains.

AM 8.15	8. 0	—	12.19
10.40	—	—	3.52
PM 3.30	—	—	7.42
5.15	—	—	8.43
8.25	—	—	11. 6

Trains from Walmer.

Leave Walmer	St. Pl.'s	Arrive at Hol. V.	Vict.
AM 6. 5f	9.37	9.39	—
6.57	—	—	11. 2
8.56	—	—	11.27
9.15d	—	—	1.22
9.15e	1. 0	1. 2	1.33
11. 7	—	—	2.43
11.38k	—	—	3.36
PM 1.20e	4.46	—	4.39
1.58d	—	—	4.55
2. 8k	—	—	5.42
2.25	—	—	5.26
5.25	—	—	8.33
7. 4	—	—	10.25

Sunday Trains.

AM 8.25	—	11.58	11.51
9.50h	—	—	1. 5
12. 0h	—	—	3.50
PM 6. 5	—	—	8.40

d Saturdays only.
e Saturdays excepted.
f Mondays only.
h Via Folkestone.
k Via Minster Junction.
l Third Class only.

WALMER—*continued.*

ANOTHER ROUTE from
Charing Cross, Cannon Street, and
London Bridge, via Ashford and
Minster Junction, 93 miles. Fares
as above.

Char. +	Leave Can. St.	Lon. B.	Arr. at Walmer
AM —	5.20	5.25	10. 2
—	—	7.50l	11. 7
9.15	—	9.23	12.46
11. 0d	—	11. 7d	2.35
PM 1. 0	—	—	3.53
3. 0	—	3. 8	6.19
5.15e	5.12e	5.21e	8. 9
5.20d	—	5.26d	8. 9
5.24d	—	5.34d	9.25
6. 0e	—	6. 5e	9.25
7.18	—	7.26	11. 5
—	—	—	—
—	—	—	—

Sunday Trains.

AM 7.45	—	7.52	12. 0
—	—	—	—

Trains from Walmer.

Leave Walmer	Lon. B.	Arrive at Can. St.	Char.+
AM 7.43	10.54	—	11. 3
8.38	11.43	—	11.57
9.48	1.56	—	1.50
11.38	3.26	—	3.40
PM 2. 8	5.50	—	6. 3
4. 3	7.25	7.30	7.49
6.49	10.22	—	10.35
9.50y	—	1.20	—

Sunday Trains.

PM 3.52	7. 9	—	7.17
—	—	—	—

d Saturdays only.
e Saturdays excepted.
l Low level platform.
y Third Class only.

ANOTHER ROUTE from
Charing Cross, Cannon Street, and
London Bridge, via Dover, 85
miles. Fares as above.

Char. +	Leave Can. St.	Lon. B.	Arr. at Walmer
AM —	3.40y	3.43y	7.42
—	5.20	5.25	9.47
—	7.16h	7.19h	11.38
—	—	l10. 3k	12.46
11.15	—	—	1.23
PM1. 0p	—	—	3. 1
1.50d	—	1.56d	3.48
4. 5	—	—	5.56
4.30j	—	4.37j	6.49
—	5. 0l	—	6.54
—	5.12e	—	8. 2
6. 0e	—	6. 5e	8. 2
—	6.12e	—	8.55
7. 0	—	—	8.55
7.18	—	7.26	11.17
11.51s	—	—	2.27

Sunday Trains.

AM 9.35	—	—	11.30
10.15	—	—	12.19
PM 7.35	—	7.45	11. 7

WALMER—*continued.*

Trains from Walmer.

Leave Walmer	Lon. B.	Arrive at Can. St.	Char. +
AM *f*6. 5*h*	9. 4	9. 8	—
7.34*e*	9.36	9.40	—
7.30*d*	10. 0	10. 4	—
8.35	10.34	—	10.41
8.56	11.43	—	11.57
10.21	—	—	12.20
PM12.46	3.26	—	3.40
*d*12.46*p*	3.26	—	3.40
1.58	4. 2	—	4.10
2.25	5.50	—	6. 3
4.31	—	—	6.30
6.19	10.22	—	10.33
9.25*y*	—	1.20	—

Sunday Trains.

PM 4.30	—	—	6.30
6. 5	—	—	8.17
7.40	10.16	—	10.26
9. 5*y*	—	1.23	—

d Saturdays only.
e Saturdays excepted.
h *Via* Chatham.
j Fridays excepted.
k Mondays, Fridays and Saturdays only.
l Fridays only.
p Pullman Car attached.
s Wednesdays only.
y Third Class only

WALPOLE (Norfolk) from

King's Cross, 106½ miles. Fares, 19/5*a*, 11/8*c*. R. T. for two months, 38/10*a*. Departures *from* London as for Sutton Bridge. Departures *for* London about 7 times daily. Pop. 1,847.
Map Square 19.

WALSALL (Stafford) from

Euston, 120½ miles. Fares, 24/5*a*, 14/8*c*. R. T. for two months, 48/10*a*. Pop. 96,964.
Map Square 17.

Euston	W'sall	W'sall	Euston
AM 2.30	6.37	AM 6.46*r*	10. 0
5. 0	8.46	7.55*r*	10.40
9.10*er*	11.47	9.19	12.40
9.15	12.55	10.40*r*	1.25
11.30*er*	2.10	PM12.10*er*	3. 0
11.30*dr*	2.28	1.34*t*	4.35
PM 1.15*r*	4. 5	2.10*t*	5.35
2.20*t*	5.11	3.39*dt*	6.50
4.35*t*	7.13	4.10*et*	6.50
5.50*er*	8.20	5.35*r*	8.20
5.50*dr*	9.13	7.38*er*	10.20
6.55*r*	9.25	10.30*e*	4. 0
7. 0*r*	10.24	10.30*d*	5. 0
—	—	—	—

Sunday Trains.

PM 1. 0*r*	4.22*h*	AM10.10*hr*	1.45
5.10*r*	9.26	PM12.10	5 .5
—	—	4.30*r*	8.20
—	—	5. 0*hr*	8.35
—	—	9.40	5. 0

d Saturdays only.
e Saturdays excepted.
h *Via* Dudley Port.
r Restaurant Car.
t Tea Car.

WALSDEN (Yorks), 202¼

miles. Fares, 40/0*a*, 24/0*c*. R. T. for two months, 80/0*a*. Departures *from* London as for Rochdale. Departures *for* London about 9 times daily. Pop. 4,478.
Map Square 12.

WALSINGHAM (Norfolk)

from *Liverpool Street*, 132½ miles. Fares, 25/8*a*, 15/5*c*. R. T. for two months, 51/4*a*. Departures *from* London as for Fakenham. Departures *for* London about 8 times daily. Pop. 1,168.
Map Square 14.

WALTHAM (Lincoln),

152 miles. Fares, 31/6*a*, 18/11*c*. R. T., double fare. Departures *from* London as for Louth. Departures *for* London about 5 times daily. Pop. 821.
Map Square 13.

WALTHAM CROSS

(Herts) from *Liverpool Street*, 12¾ miles. Fares, 2/1*a*, 1/8*b*, 1/3*c*. R. T. for two months, 4/2*a*, 3/4*b*, 2/4*c*. Pop. 6,847. *See* pp. 526–527.
Map Square 23.

WALTHAMSTOW

(Essex). *See* St. James's Street, Hoe Street, and Wood Street. Pop. 129,395.
Map Square 53.

ANOTHER ROUTE from

St. Pancras and *Moorgate Street*, 8¼ miles. Fares, 1/3*a*, 0/9*c*. R. T. for two days, 2/2½*a*, 1/2*c*. *See* pp. 506–507.

WALTON (Northampton),

78¾ miles. No through fares. Departures *from* London as for Peterboro'. Departures *for* London about 4 times daily. Pop. 864.
Map Square 18.

WALTON (Surrey) from

Waterloo, 17¼ miles. Fares, 3/7*a*, 2/2*c*. R. T. for eight days, 7/0*a*, 4/4*c*. Pop. 14,647.
Map Square 23.

W'loo.	Walton	Walton	W'loo.
AM 4.50	5.36	AM 3.18	3.58
6.10	6.57	5.26	6.13
7. 0	7.34	7. 0	7.41
7.50	8.24	7.45	8.20
8.15	8.47	7.59	8.36
9.15	9.53	8.29	9. 5
10.20	10.55	8.41	9. 8
11.20	11.53	8.56	9.31
PM12.14*d*	12.41	9. 9	9.36
12.15	12.53	9.41	10.11
12.40*d*	1.10	10.10	10.45
12.54*d*	1.28	11.10	11.46
1.15*d*	1.41	PM12.10	12.46
1.20	1.55	1.10	1.46
1.44*d*	2.12	2.10	2.46
2.20	2.55	3.10	3.46
3.15	3.53	4.11	4.46
4.20	4.55	5.10	5.46
4.40	5.11	5.44	6.16
4.54*e*	5.26	6.10	6.46
5.15*e*	5.41	7.10	7.46
5.20	5.55	8.10	8.46
5.44*e*	6.12	9.10	9.46
5.54*e*	6.26	10.10	10.46
6.15*e*	6.41	10.35	11.10
6.20	6.55	11.34	12.16
7. 0*e*	7.33	—	—
7.20	7.55	—	—
8.20	8.55	—	—
8.55	9.34	—	—
9.20	9.55	—	—
10.20	10.55	—	—
11.15*e*	11.49	—	—
11.40	12.13	—	—

Sunday Trains.

AM 8.20	8.58	AM 3.18	3.58
9.20	10. 1	9. 4	9.45
9.45	10.18	10.41	11.16
10.20	11. 1	11.59	12.41
11.20	12. 1	PM12.59	1.41
PM12.20	1. 1	2. 2	2.44
1.20	2. 1	3. 2	3.44
3.20	4. 1	4.59	5.41
4.20	4.54	6. 5	6.46
5.20	5.54	6.59	7.41
6.30	7. 4	7.59	8.41
7.20	7.54	9. 1	9.44
8.20	9. 1	9.58	10.41
9.28	10. 8	10. 9	10.47
9.45	10.20	11. 0	11.43
10.15	10.54	—	—
—	—	—	—

d Saturdays only.
e Saturdays excepted.

WALTON—*continued.*

Ashley Park Hotel, opposite station. Beautifully situated. Pleasant Garden and Surroundings. Billiards, Garage, Late Dinner. Open to Non-Residents. Tel. 196. Apply Manageress.

Oatlands Park Hotel. Largest and most important Hotel in Walton and Weybridge district. Grounds, 36 acres. Accommodation, 150 guests. Newly appointed, decorated throughout. First-class cuisine. Garage, Tennis, Boating. Close Burhill and St. George's Hill Golf Clubs. Telephone: Weybridge 666.

Estate Agents.—Waring & Co., Agents for all available Residences. Offices adjoining Railway Station, Walton-on-Thames. Telephone, 151 Walton-on-Thames.

WALTON JUNCTION

(Lancs), 202½ miles. Fares, 41/11*a*, 25/2*c*. R. T. for six months, 83/10*a*, 50/4*c*. Departures *from* London as for Liverpool (Lime Street). Departures *for* London about 12 times daily. Pop. 12,153.

WALTON-IN-GORDANO

(Somerset), 133 miles. No through fares. Departures *from* London as for Portishead. Departures *for* London about 3 times daily. Pop. 697.

WALTON-ON-THE-NAZE

(Essex) from *Liverpool Street*, 70½ miles. Fares, 15/2*a*, 9/1*c*. R. T. for two months, 30/4*a*, 18/2*c*. Pop. 3,666.
Map Square 24.

L'pl.St.	Walton	Walton	L'pl.St.
AM 5. 0	8.20	AM 6.52*r*	8.52
6.50	10.23	7.35	9.36
8.18	10.43	8. 1*r*	9.53
8.46	12. 9	9.48	11.42
10.23	12.47	11.33*r*	2. 3
11.26*d*	2.19	PM12.22*d*	2.23
11.30*e*	2.19	1.27	3.36
PM12.36	2.46	3. 8	5. 5
1.30*dr*	3.27	4.15	6.32
2. 3*d*	4.13	5.33	7.40
2.15	5. 7	7.34	9.36
3.23	5.30	7.52	11.16
3.26	6.32	—	—
4.58*r*	7. 7	—	—
5.30*r*	7.17	—	—
5.42	8.26	—	—
6.39	8.40	—	—
7.45*r*	10.15	—	—
8.45	10.58	—	—
12. 0*d*	2. 2	—	—

Sunday Trains.

AM 9. 8	11. 8	AM 8.50	11.38
9.20*r*	12.10	PM 5.44	8.25
PM 4.40	7.13	7.50	10. 9

d Saturdays only.
e Saturdays excepted.
r Restaurant Car.

For Advertisement list, see over.

WALTON-ON-THE-NAZE—*continued.*

Marine Hotel ('Barker's'). The leading Hotel. 30 Bedrooms, facing Sea. Central Heating. Week-end terms. Illus. Tariff. Telephone No. 6.
Prop., CHAS. F. J. BARKER.

Eastcliffe Private Hotel. High-class. Unrivalled position, facing Sea. Highly recommended. Excellent cuisine. Adjoining Tennis, 6 Hard Courts. 'Phone 31.

Royal Albion Hotel. Premier position, overlooking Sea. Remodelled. Newly furnished. Electric Light. Garage. Billiards. Magnificent Dining and Ball Room. Lounge. 3 minutes' Station and Tennis Courts. 'Phone 15.
Apply, PROPRIETOR.

Tomkins, Homer & Ley, House and Estate Agents, 29 The Parade. Furnished and Unfurnished Houses. Apartments. Land. Telephone No. 21.

WAMPHRAY (Dumfries), 333½ miles. No through fares. Departures *from* London as for Lockerbie. Departures *for* London about 3 times daily. Pop. 390.
Map Square 44.

WANBOROUGH (Surrey) from *Waterloo*, 34¼ miles. Fares, 7/1*a*, 4/3*c*. R. T. for two months, 14/2*a*, 8/6*c*. Pop. 303.
Map Square 23.

W'LOO.	W'BORO.	W'BORO.	W'LOO.
AM 6.50	8. 8	AM 8.16	9.12
7. 5	8.48	9.15	10.15
9. 0	10.14	11. 6	12.46
11. 5	12.31	PM 1.26	3. 0
PM 12.50	2. 0	2.44	4.16
2. 5	3.43	4.44	5.52
3.50	4.48	5.29	6.52
5.24	6.17	6.54	7.56
5.50	7.14	8. 5	9.46
7. 5	8.31	9. 7	10.46
—	—	—	—

Sunday Trains.

AM 8. 0	9.34	AM 11.22	12.55
9.15	10.29	PM 1.44	3.13
10.20	11.59	5. 7	6.17
PM 2. 8	4. 9	7.41	9.44
4.20	5.44	9. 7	10.41
6.20	8.14	—	—

WANDSWORTH from *Waterloo*, 4¾ miles. Fares, 0/7½*a*, 0/4½*c*. R. T. for two days, 1/3*a*, 0/9*c*. Pop. 328,307. *See* pp. 586-591, 595.
Map Square 68.

WANDSWORTH COMMON from *London Bridge, via* Crystal Palace, 12¼ miles. Fares, 1/6*a*, 0/10½*c*. R. T. for eight days, 3/0*a*, 1/9*c*. From Victoria, 4 miles. Fares, 0/7½*a*, 0/4½*c*. R. T. for two days, 1/3*a*, 0/9*c*. *See* pp. 567, 568, 571-580.
Map Square 78.

WANDSWORTH ROAD from *London Bridge*, 6¾ miles, or *Victoria*, 2 miles. Fares from London Bridge, 0/7*a*, 0/4½*c*. R.T. for two days, 1/0*a*, 0/9*c*. From Victoria, 0/5*a*, 0/3*c*. R. T. for two days, 0/10*a*, 0/6*c*. *See* p. 570.
Map Square 69.

WANLOCKHEAD (Dumfries), 359½ miles. No through fares. Departures *from* London as for Lockerbie. Departures *for* London about 3 times daily. Pop. 590.
Map Square 43.

WANSFORD (Northampton), from King's Cross, 81¾ miles. Fares, 15/10*a*, 9/6*c*. R. T., double fare. Departures *from* London as for Peterboro'. Departures *for* London about 5 times daily. Pop. 82.
Map Square 18.

WANSTEAD PARK from *St. Pancras* and *Moorgate Street*, 11¼ miles. Fares, 1/3*a*, 0/9*c*. R. T. for two days, 2/4*a*, 1/4*c*. Pop. (Wanstead) 15,298. *See* pp. 506, 507.
Map Square 53.

WANSTROW (Somerset) from *Paddington*, 109 miles. Fares, 22/9*a*, 13/8*c*. R. T. for two months, 45/6*a*. Departures *from* London as for Cranmore. Departures *for* London about 4 times daily. Pop. 317
Map Square 22.

WANTAGE ROAD (Berks) from *Paddington*, 60½ miles. Fares, 12/8*a*, 7/7*c*. R. T. for two months, 25/4*a*.
Pop. (Wantage) 3,886.
Map Square 23.

PAD.	WANT. R.	WANT. R.	PAD.
AM 5.30	8. 2	AM 7.30	9.30
7.30	9.47	8.34*r*	10.15
9. 0	10.44	10. 9	12. 0
10.45	12.43	PM 12.25	2.35
PM 1.35*r*	3.37	2.43	5. 6
3.38	6. 2	6.55	9.15
6.55	8.37	7.59	10.45
—	—	—	—
—	—	—	—
—	—	—	—
—	—	—	—
—	—	—	—
—	—	—	—

Sunday Trains.

AM 10.35	12.25	PM 3.43	6. 0
PM 2. 0	5.53	—	—
—	—	—	—
—	—	—	—
—	—	—	—
—	—	—	—
—	—	—	—

r Restaurant Car.

Bear Hotel (Country Hostels Ltd.) A quiet comfortable hotel close to the famous Berkshire Downs. Good cuisine Moderate tariff. Electric light. Garage. Telephone 39.
Apply MANAGERESS.

WAPPENHAM (Northampton), 71 miles. Fares, 14/0*a*, 8/5*c*. R. T. for two months, 28/0*a*. Departures *from* London as for Towcester. Departures *for* London about 3 times daily. Pop. 354.
Map Square 18.

WAPPING from *Hammersmith, Paddington (Bishop's Road), Baker Street, King's Cross* and *Liverpool Street* (Met.), 10½ miles. Fares from *Hammersmith*, 1/0*a*, 0/8*c*. R. T., 2/0*a*, 1/4*c*. From *Paddington* (*Bishop's Road*), 0/11*a*, 0/7*c*. R. T, 1/10*a*, 1/2*c*. From *Baker Street*, 0/9*a*, 0/6*c*. R.T., 1/6*a*, 1/0*c*. From *King's Cross*, 0/8*a*, 0/5*c*. R.T., 1/4*a*, 0/10*c*. From *Liverpool Street*, 0/5*a*, 0/3*c*. R. T., 0/10*a*, 0/6*c*. Pop. 3,217. *See* back of Map.
Map Square 61.

WARBOYS (Hunts), from *Liverpool Street*, 80¼ miles. Fares, 14/4*a*, 8/7*c*. R. T. for two months, 28/8*a*. Departures *from* London as for Ramsey. Departures *for* London about 6 times daily. Pop. 1,790.
Map Square 18.

WARCOP (Westmorland), 277¼ miles. Fares, 54/7*a*, 32/9*c*. R. T. double fare. Departures *from* London as for Barnard Castle. Departures *for* London about 4 times daily. Pop. 604.
Map Square 7.

WARDHOUSE (Aberdeen), 554 miles. No through fares. Departures *from* London as for Inverurie. Departures *for* London about 4 times daily.
Map Square 35.

WARDLEWORTH (Lancs), 196½ miles. Fares 40/2*a* 24/1*c*. R. T. for two months, 80/4*a*, 48/2*c*. Departures *from* London as for Rochdale. Departures *for* London about 8 times daily. Pop. 16,554.

WARE (Herts) from *Liverpool Street*, 22¼ miles. Fares, 4/10*a*, 3/10*b*, 2/11*c*. R. T. for two months, 9/8*a*, 7/8*b*. Pop. 5,949. *See* pp. 526-527.
Map Square 23.

Saracen's Head, High St. Good Food and Garages.
Mrs. L. E. LLOYD.
See advt. p. 338.

WAREHAM (Dorset) from *Waterloo*, 120 miles. Fares, 25/3*a*, 15/2*c*. R. T. for two months, 50/6*a*, 30/4*c*. Pop. 1,994.
Map Square 27.

W'LOO.	WAREH'M	WAREH'M	W'LOO
AM 5.40	9.24	AM 8.14*s*	11. 0
5.50	11.24	8.29*s*	12.22
8.30*s*	11.53	10. 2*r*	12.50
10.30	1.15	10.18*r*	2.20
11 30	2.48	PM 12. 2	2.50
PM 12.30*r*	3.15	12.28	4.20
2.30*s*	5.15	2. 2	4.50
4.30*r*	7.15	2.41	6.26
6.30*r*	9.15	4. 2*r*	6.58
10. 0	2.49	6. 1*r*	8.50
—	—	7.21	11.28
—	—	10.47	3.58
—	—	—	—
—	—	—	—
—	—	—	—
—	—	—	—
—	—	—	—

IDRIS GREEN GINGER WINE.

WAREHAM—*continued.*

Sunday Trains.

W'LOO.	WAREH'M	WAREH'M	W'LOO.
AM11.0r	2.43	AM 8. 0	12.11
PM 2. 0r	5.40	10.46r	2.27
7. 0r	10.40	PM 3.10r	6.24
9.28	2.49	6.13r	9.31
—	—	10.47	3.58
—	—	—	—
—	—	—	—
—	—	—	—
—	—	—	—
—	—	—	—

r Restaurant Car.
s Refreshments served.

WARGRAVE (Berks) from
Paddington, 32¾ miles. Fares,
6/10a, 4/1c. R. T. for two months,
13/8a, 8/2c. Pop. 2,112.
Map Square 23.

PAD.	WARGR'VE	WARGR'VE	PAD.
AM 6.30	7.37	AM 7.16	8.29
7.35	9.24	7.35	8.28
9. 0	9.54	7.58	8.56
9.20	10.42	8.58	9.43
9.55	10.56	9.23	10.24
11.20	12.11	10. 8	11. 6
11.25	12.49	11.18	12.15
PM12. 8	1.18	11.38	1.11
12.33d	2. 7	PM12.20	1.46
1.20d	2.20	1.22	2.35
1.50d	2.52	2.31d	3.38
2. 7e	3. 8	2.31e	4.10
2.18d	3.16	3.38	5.17
3.38	4.31	4.30	5.37
4. 7	5.12	5.53	6.55
5.15	6. 3	6.53	8.10
5.18d	6.20	7.38d	9.12
5.40e	6.27	8.13	9.33
5.40d	6.37	8.47	10.22
6.12e	7. 0	9.33	10.42
6.35	7.32	10. 3	12. 0
6.55e	7.59	—	—
6.55d	8.10	—	—
7.35	8.28	—	—
8. 5	9.12	—	—
9.15	10. 4	—	—
12. 3	1. 6	—	—

Sunday Trains.

AM 9.10	10. 2	AM 8.58	10.14
10. 0	10.56	9.43	10.50
10. 5	11.14	10.56	1. 5
10.45	11.37	PM 2.33	4.53
11. 0	12. 4	4.55	6. 0
PM 1.45	2.55	6.28	7.37
2. 0	3.37	7.13	8.20
2.35	4.16	8.28	9.32
5.15	6.24	8.43	9.53
6. 5	7.34	9.23	10.33
7.40	9. 7	10. 8	11. 6
8.30	9.49	—	—

d Saturdays only.
e Saturdays excepted

Chiltern Towers Hotel,
Wargrave-on-Thames. Extensive
grounds. Newly furnished. Ten
minutes station, river. Billiards.
Garage. Tennis. Phone, 48
Wargrave.
Miss HOLMES, Proprietress.

WARGRAVE—*continued.*

St. George & Dragon Hotel.
Only Hotel facing River.
Moderate Terms Boats to Let.
Phone 15. Open May to October.
Proprietor, V. F. WYATT.

WARK (Northumberland),
298¾ miles. Fares, 63/4a, 38/0c.
R. T. for two months, 126/8a,
76/0c. Departures *from* London as
for Hexham or Carlisle. Departures *for* London about 3 times
daily. Pop. 634.
Map Square 3.

WARKWORTH (North-
umberland), 299¾ miles. Fares.
63/2a, 37/11c. R.T. for two months,
126/4a, 75/10c. Departures *from*
London as for Morpeth. Departures *for* London about 3
times daily. Pop. 710.
Map Square 3.

WARLINGHAM (Surrey),
from *Charing Cross, Cannon Street,*
and *London Bridge,* 19 miles.
Fares, 3/2a, 2/7b, 1/11c. R. T. for
eight days, 6/4a, 5/2b, 3/8c. Departures *from* London as for Caterham. Departures *for* London
about 18 times daily. Pop. 3,897.

WARLINGHAM,
UPPER (Surrey) from *Victoria,*
Cannon Street and *London Bridge,*
15¼ miles. Fares, 3/2a, 1/11c. R. T.
for eight days, 6/4a, 3/8c.
Map Square 23.

Leave		Arr. at
VICT.	CAN. ST.	LON. B.	WARL'M
AM 5.30	—	5.18	6.11
6.37	—	6.40	7.15
7.25	—	8. 7	8.48
9.10	—	9. 6	9.53
10.35	—	10.35	11.17
12. 0	—	11.50	12.45
PM —	12.13d	d12.20k	12.57
—	—	12.50d	1.22
1.20e	—	1.3Se	2.12
1.25d	—	1.38d	2.16
—	—	2. 5e	3.15
2.25	—	2.25d	3.15
—	—	2.57d	3.35
4. 0	—	4.10	4.45
—	4.16e	e4.20k	4.55
4.50	—	4.44e	5.22
5. 5	—	5.10	5.49
—	—	5.21	5.57
5.48	—	5.41e	6.22
6. 6	—	6. 8	6.51
6.50	—	7. 0	7.34
7.15	—	7.38	8.17
8. 5	—	8.10	8.46
9. 3	—	9.12	9.44
10.30	—	10.35	11.13
11.50h	—	—	12.25

Sunday Trains.

AM 8.18	—	8.30	9.11
8.50	—	—	9.27
10.20	—	—	11.13
PM 1.14	—	1.10	1.54
2.30	—	—	3.16
6.33	—	6.46	7.27
7. 5	—	—	7.43
9. 5	—	9.10	9.50

WARLINGHAM—*contd.*

Trains from Warlingham, Upper.

Leave	Arrive at		
WARL'M	LON. B	CAN. ST.	VICT.
AM 7.29	8.15	—	8.24
8. 5	8.37	—	8.40
8.30	9. 1/c	9. 4	9. 8
8.42	9.15	—	9.19
9. 0	9.32	—	9.40
9.20	9.55	—	9.58
10. 9	10.38	—	10.46
10.59	—	—	11.35
11.39	12.13	—	12.17
PM12.46	1.42	—	1.26
2.24	2.58	—	—
3. 6	4. 0	—	3.45
4.17d	4.57	—	—
4.45	5.21	—	5.55
5.54	6.36	—	6.29
7.20	7.56	—	—
7.39	8.46	—	8.27
9.48	10.25	—	11.17

Sunday Trains.

AM 9.30	10.18	—	10.20
10.34	11.15	—	—
11.57	—	—	12.47
PM12.53	—	—	1.40
5.50	—	—	6.34
8.45	9.26	—	9.34
9.15	—	—	9.47
10.22	—	—	10.59

d Saturdays only.
e Saturdays excepted.
h Wednesdays only.
k Departs from or arrives at
London Bridge (S.E. & C. Station).

WARMINSTER (Wilts)
from *Paddington,* 100½ miles. Fares,
via Westbury, 20/0a, 12/0c. R. T.
for two months, 40/0a. *Via* Bath,
22/6a, 13/6c. R. T. for two months,
45/0a, 27/0c. Pop. 5,389.
Map Square 22.

PAD.	WARMINST'R	WARMINST'R	PAD.
AM 1. 0g	7.36	AM 8.19	10.52
5.30	9.49	10.23	12.55
7.30	11.42	11.17	2.50
10.30	12.32	PM 1.31	3.50
PM12. 5r	2.20	3. 9t	5.30
12.30r	3. 0	4.53r	6.50
2. 0	4.21	5.38	8.20
3.30	5.44	8.36	2.45
5. 5	7.50	—	—
6.30	10. 5	—	—

Sunday Trains.

PM 2.40	5. 8	PM12.43r	7.55
10. 0	7.36	—	—

g Mondays excepted.
r Restaurant Car.
t Tea Car.

WARMLEY (Gloucester),
123¼ miles. No through fares. Departures *from* London as for
Bristol. Departures *for* London
about 4 times daily. Pop. 17,188.
Map Square 21.

WARNHAM (Sussex) from

London Bridge, Victoria, and *Clapham Junction*, 35½ miles. Fares, 7/6*a*, 4/6*c*. R. T. for two months, 15/0*a*, 9/0*c*. Pop. 1,140.
Map Square 23.

	Leave		Arr. at
Vict	Clap. J.	Lon. B	W'nhm.
AM 5.18	5.28	5.28	7.12
7.45	7.56	7.35	9.37
8.58	—	9.22	11. 8
10.30	10.38	10.35	12.17
PM12.35	12.42	12.24	2.17
4. 5	4.12	—	5.30
—	—	5.14	6.37
6. 0	—	5.59	7.44
—	—	—	—
—	—	—	—

Sunday Trains.

AM —	—	6.55	8.37
PM 5.40	5.47	5.40	7.40
—	—	—	—
—	—	—	—

Trains from Warnham.

Leave	Arrive at		
W'nhm.	Lon. B.	Clap. J.	Vict.
AM 7.45	9.17	—	9.34
8.59	10.22	—	10.28
11.14	—	12.33	12.42
11.39	1.28	1.48	1.57
PM 1.53	3.32	3.22	3.32
4.24	—	5.59	6. 8
6.53	8.41	8.46	8.55
9.25	11.11	11.12	11.20
—	—	—	—

Sunday Trains.

AM 8. 8	10.11	10. 6	10.13
9.14	11. 8	10.59	11. 6
PM 8.31	10.25	10.32	10.42
—	—	—	—
—	—	—	—

WARREN STREET

(Hampstead Tube). *See* back of Map.

WARRINGTON (Bank Quay)

(Lancs) from *Euston*, 182¼ miles. Fares, 37/9*a*, 22/8*c*. R. T. double fare. Pop. 76,811.
Map Square 12.

Euston	Warrtn.	Warrtn.	Euston
AM12.25*f*	5.36	AM 8.10*er*	12. 5
12.25*g*	5.59	8.10*dr*	12.20
2.35	7. 7	9.45*r*	1.45
5. 0	10. 3	10.17*r*	3.10
6.45	11.38	11.45*hr*	3.45
8.30*r*	12.55	PM12. 7*r*	4.15
10.40*r*	2.41	1.30*r*	5.50
11.50*r*	4.20	2. 5*t*	6. 0
PM 1.30*r*	5.21	3.28*dr*	7.30
2.35*t*	6.29	3.36*er*	7.30
5.20*r*	8.59	3.59*dr*	8.10
9.30	2.10	5. 8*er*	9. 5
11. 0*d*	2.31	5. 8*dr*	9.15
11.45*e*	3.41	11.33	5. 0
11.50*d*	5.36	—	—

Sunday Trains.

AM11.45*r*	3.52	AM 9.28*r*	1.30
PM 6. 0*r*	10. 6	10.30	4. 0
9.15	2.29	PM 3.21*r*	7.30
11.45	3.40	11.36	5. 0
—	—	—	—
—	—	—	—
—	—	—	—

d Saturdays only.
e Saturdays excepted.
f Mondays only.
g Mondays excepted.
h Mondays and Saturdays only.
r Restaurant Car.
t Tea Car.

WARRINGTON—*contd.*

ANOTHER ROUTE (CENTRAL) from *St. Pancras*, 199½ miles.

Fares as above.

St. Pan.	Warrtn.	Warrtn.	St. Pan.
AM 2.25	7.49	AM 5.34*r*	11.35
4.25	10.49	8.35*r*	1.30
8.25*r*	1.49	8.55*r*	1.45
10.25*r*	2.59	11.50*r*	4.20
PM12.25*r*	4.38	PM 1.20*r*	6.15
2.25*r*	6.49	3.55*r*	8.35
4.25*r*	9. 5	5.30*r*	10. 5
12. 0*h*	6.24	6.55	4.20
12. 0*k*	8.52	11.24	6. 0
—	—	—	—

Sunday Trains.

AM11.15*r*	4.59	AM11.16*r*	5. 2
PM 3.15	9.40	PM 4.25*r*	9.52
11.55	6.24	9.43	4.55
—	—	—	—
—	—	—	—

h Saturdays midnight excepted.
k Saturdays midnight only.
r Restaurant Car.

ANOTHER ROUTE (CENTRAL) from *Marylebone*, 222¼ miles.

Fares as above.

M'bone.	Warrtn.	Warrtn.	M'bone.
AM 2.32	10.49	AM 6.35*rk*	1.13
8.45*r*	2.59	8.55*r*	3. 0
10. 0*r*	3.55	PM12.55*kr*	6.38
PM12.15*r*	6.59	2.25*r*	8.55
3.20*r*	8.19	3.55*r*	9.55
5. 0*r*	10.45	9.55	3.57
10. 0*d*	4. 3	—	—
10. 5*e*	4.30	—	—

Sunday Trains.

AM11.15*r*	4.59	AM11.16*r*	5.40
—	—	PM 4.25*r*	10.24

d Saturdays only.
e Saturdays excepted.
k Passengers cross Manchester at own expense.
r Restaurant Car.

WARSOP (Notts) from

King's Cross, 144¾ miles. Fares, 29/0*a*, 17/5*c*. R. T., double fare. Departures *from* London as for Edwinstowe. Departures *for* London about twice daily. Pop. 7,237.
Map Square 13.

ANOTHER ROUTE from *St. Pancras*, 147½ miles.

Fares as above. Departures *from* London as for Edwinstowe. Departures *for* London about 3 times daily.

WARTHILL (Yorks), 194¼

miles. No through fares. Departures *from* London as for York. Departures *for* London about 6 times daily. Pop. 188.
Map Square 8.

WARTLE (Aberdeen), 546¾

miles. No through fares. Departures *from* London as for Inverurie. Departures *for* London about 3 times daily.
Map Square 35.

WARWICK from *Paddington*,

89½ miles. Fares, 18/7*a*, 11/2*c*. R. T. for two months, 37/2*a*, 22/4*c*. Pop. 12,862.
Map Square 17.

Pad.	Warwick	Warwick	Pad.
AM 5.30	9.20	AM12. 8*g*	3.30
6.30	9.53	8. 0*r*	10. 0
9.10	10.55	9.16*r*	11. 0
10.40	12.25	11.38*r*	1.25
PM12.50*r*	2.37	PM12.20*r*	2. 5
2.10	3.55	12.52	3.50

WARWICK—*continued.*

Pad.	Warwick	Warwick	Pad.
PM 4.10*t*	5.55	PM 3. 0*r*	5. 0
6.10*r*	7.55	4. 5*t*	5.55
7.10*r*	8.55	4.33	7.20
7.30	10. 0	6. 7*r*	8. 5
12.15*k*	7.21	7.46	10. 0
12.15*l*	9. 0	—	—

Sunday Trains.

AM10.35	1.30	AM12. 8	3.30
PM 4.10	6.55	11.32*r*	1.40
6. 0*r*	8.21	PM 2.40	6.20
—	—	7. 0*r*	9. 0

g Mondays excepted.
k Saturdays midnight excepted.
l Saturdays midnight only.
r Restaurant Car.
t Tea Car

ANOTHER ROUTE (MILVERTON) from *Euston*, 98¼ miles.

Fares as above.

Euston	Warwick	Warwick	Euston
AM 2.30	6.58	AM 7.20*k*	10. 0
5. 0*h*	8.55	8.45*kr*	11. 0
6.45*h*	9.51	*e*8.55*kr*	12.32
9.15*r*	11.46	8.55*dr*	12.20
10. 0*k*	12.59	9.12*d*	12.40
11.30*dh*	1.40	10.41*kr*	1. 0
11.30*eh*	1.56	11.32	2.20
12. 0*hnr*	3. 6	PM 1.10*k*	4.15
PM 2.20*ht*	4.20	1.53*hr*	4.35
2.50*t*	5. 0	3.20*kr*	5.50
4. 5*hr*	6.28	4.45	7.20
4.45*t*	6.55	5.43*er*	8.20
5.50*r*	8.12	6.48*dr*	10.45
7. 0*hr*	9.41	7.50*er*	10.20
11.50*eh*	3.42	10.22*e*	4. 0
—	—	10.22*d*	5. 0
—	—	—	—
—	—	—	—
—	—	—	—

Sunday Trains.

AM 9.15*h*	2.38	AM 8.43*h*	12.25
PM 1. 0*hr*	3.26	11.32*hr*	1.45
5.10*h*	7.51	11.58	5. 5
11.50*h*	3.42	PM 5.33*hr*	8.20
—	—	8.23*h*	5. 0

d Saturdays only.
e Saturdays excepted.
h *Via* Coventry.
k *Via* Leamington.
n Noon.
r Restaurant Car.
t Tea Car.

The "Woolpack." First-class Family Hotel. Heated throughout. Garage (Inspection Pit). Stabling. Central for visiting Shakespeare's country. Moderate. Telegrams, "Woolpack, Warwick."

Warwick Arms. Adjoining the Castle grounds. Electric light. Central heating. Garage. Stabling. Officially appointed R.A.C. and A.A. Telephone 193.
A. H. TYACK, Proprietor.

WARWICK AVENUE

(Bakerloo Tube) *See* back of Map.

WASHFORD (Somerset),

162 miles. Fares, 33/9*a*, 20/3*c*. R. T. for two months, 67/6*a*, 40/6*c*. Departures *from* London as for Watchet. Departures *for* London about 5 times daily.
Map Square 21.

WASHINGBORO' (Lincoln)

from *King's Cross*, 131¼ miles. Fares, 27/8*a*, 16/7*c*. R. T., double fare. Departures *from* London as for Lincoln or Bardney. Departures *for* London about 5 times daily. Pop. 674.
Map Square 13.

WASHINGTON (Durham), 260¼ miles. Fares, 54/4a, 32/7c. R. T., double fare. Departures *from* London as for Ferryhill or Durham. Departures *for* London about 6 times daily. Pop. 7,821.
Map Square 3.

WATCHET (Somerset) from *Paddington*, 159½ miles. Fares, 33/4a, 20/0c. R. T. for two months, 66/8a, 40/0c. Pop, 1,884.
Map Square 21.

PAD.	WATCH.	WATCH.	PAD.
AM 5.30	11.55	AM 9.55r	1.30
9.15	1.11	11.38	4. 5
PM12. 5	3.44	PM 1.40t	5.30
3.30	7. 0	2.58r	6.50
4.15r	8.33	4.51r	9. 0
12. 0h	8. 8	7.27	2.45
—	—	9.45	7.10
—	—	—	—
Sunday Trains.			
PM10. 0	8. 8	—	—
—	—	—	—
—	—	—	—

h Saturday midnight excepted.
r Restaurant Car.
t Tea Car.

WATERBEACH (Cambridge) from *Liverpool Street*, 61 miles. Fares, 12/11a, 7/9c. R. T. for two months, 25/10c. Pop. 1,430.
Map Square 19.

L'PL. ST.	WATER-BEACH	WATER-BEACH.	L'PL. ST.
AM 5. 5	6.44	AM 7.31	9.27
5.50	8.22	9. 7	11.27
8.30r	10.28	10.56	12.40
10. 5	11.55	PM 1.51rl	4. 2k
11.50hr	1.56	1.51	5. 9
PM 2.34	4.23	5.15	7.58
4.15	6. 5	8. 3	10.30
5.49r	7.42	9.53	2.50
10.12d	12. 0	—	—
Sunday Trains.			
AM 8.12	10.32	AM 8.50	11.27
PM 1.50	4.48	PM 4.48	6.40
3.25	5.10	—	—
—	—	—	—
—	—	—	—

d Saturdays only.
h Thursdays only.
k Arrives at St. Pancras Station.
l Commencing July 23.
r Restaurant Car.

WATERFOOT (Lancs), 206¼ miles. Fares, 41/10a, 25/1c. R. T. for two months, 83/8a, 50/2c. Departures *from* London as for Bacup. Departures *for* London about 8 times daily. Pop. 3,150.
Map Square 12.

WATERFORD from *Paddington, via* Fishguard and Rosslare, 253½ miles. Fares, First and Saloon, Third and Saloon, Third and Steerage. R. T. for two months, First and Saloon, Third and Saloon, Third and Steerage. Pop. 27,464.

PAD.	WTFORD	WTFORD.	PAD.
PM 8. 0r	7. 0h	PM10. 5r	9.10h
—	—	—	—
—	—	—	—

Service temporarily suspended.
h A.M.
r Restaurant Car.

WATERFORD—*contd.*

ANOTHER ROUTE from *Paddington, via* Fishguard and Boat direct, 356 miles. Fares, 50/0 First and Saloon, 37/6 Third and Saloon, 30/0 Third and Steerage. R. T. for two months, 100/0 First and Saloon, 69/10 Third and Saloon, 58/7 Third and Steerage.

PAD	W'T'FORD	W'T'FORD.	PAD.
PM 5. 0r	8.30l	PM 5.25er	10.57l
—	—	5.25dr	3.35

d Saturdays only.
e Saturdays excepted.
l A.M.
r Restaurant Car.

Bank.—The National Bank, Ltd.

WATERHOUSES (Durham), 257½ miles. Fares, 54/2a, 32/6c. R.T. for two months, 108/4a, 65/0c. Departures *from* London as for Durham. Departures *for* London about 6 times daily. Pop. 3,295.
Map Square 7.

WATERHOUSES (Stafford), 162½ miles. Fares, 34/10a, 20/11c. R. T. for two months, 69/8a, 41/0c. Departures *from* London as for Leek. Departures *for* London about 4 times daily

WATERINGBURY (Kent), from *Charing Cross, Cannon Street,* and *London Bridge,* 40¾ miles. Fares, 8/6a, 6/9b, 5/1c. R. T. for two months, 17/0a, 13/6b. Pop. 1,143.
Map Square 24.

CHAR. +	Leave CAN. ST.	LON. B.	Arr. at W'RBY.
AM —	5.20	5.25	7.36
—	6.45	6.50	8.48
—	7.56	8. 0	9.56
9.25	—	9.33	11.26
10.40d	—	10.46d	12.28
—	11.56	12. 0	1.22
PM 2. 8	—	2.16	3.40
3. 0	—	3. 8	4.32
3.15	—	3.21	5.11
3.48e	—	—	5.11
3.50	—	3.57	6. 5
—	4.36e	4.39e	6. 5
5.35d	—	5.41d	7.36
6. 3e	—	6. 9e	7.31
8. 0	—	8. 8	9.43
Sunday Trains.			
AM 8. 5	—	8.12	9.47
9.50	—	9.56	11.34
PM 7.10	—	7.20	8.49

Trains from Wateringbury.

Leave W'RBY.	LON. B	Arrive CAN. ST.	CHAR. +
AM 6.20	8. 9	—	8.19
8. 7	9.32	9.36	—
9.43	10.59	11. 2	—
10.19	11.43	—	11.57
11.59	1.36	—	1.50
PM 1.57	3.26	—	3.40
3.56	5.50	—	6. 3
5. 5	7.25	7.30	—
6.46	8.26	—	8.35
8.25	10.22	—	10.35
d11.14s	—	1.20	—
Sunday Trains.			
AM 8.30	10.22	—	10.32
PM 6.45	8.12	—	8.22
7.23	9. 7	—	9.17

d Saturdays only.
e Saturdays excepted.
s Third Class only.

WATERLOO (LONDON) from *Charing Cross*, ¾ mile, or *Cannon Street*, 1¼ mile. Fares from Charing Cross, 0/2½a, 0/2b, 0/1½c. R. T. for two days, 0/5a, 0/4b, 0/3c. From Cannon Street, 0/4½a, 0/3½b, 0/2½c. R. T. for two days, 0/9a, 0/6b, 0/4c. *See* pp. 544-557.
Map Squares 23 *and* 61.

ANOTHER ROUTE (Bakerloo and Waterloo and City Tubes.) *See* back of Map.

WATERLOO (Lancs), 206¾ miles. Fares, 41/8a, 25/0c. R. T. for two months, 83/4a, 50/0c. Departures *from* London as for Liverpool. Departures *for* London about 10 times daily. Pop. 12,845.
Map Square 12.

WATER ORTON (Warwick) from *St. Pancras*, 124¾ miles. Fares, 22/9a, 13/8c. R. T., double fare. Pop. 631.
Map Square 17.

ST. PAN.	W. ORTON	W. ORTON	ST. PAN.
AM 2.25	7.54	AM 9.16r	1.20
4.25	9.49	10.54	3.25
8.25r	12.24	PM 1.24r	5.45
PM12.15r	3.19	3.33r	7.57
1.25r	5.34	5.29r	9. 5
4.25r	8.56	6.24er	10. 5
—	—	10.53d	4.20
Sunday Trains.			
PM 3.15	9.21	AM 7.11	11.53
—	—	PM 6. 1r	9.52

d Saturdays only.
e Saturdays excepted.
r Restaurant Car.

WATERSIDE (Ayr), 391¼ miles. Fares, 82/4a, 49/5c. R. T. for two months, 164/8a, 98/10c. Departures *from* London as for Ayr. Departures *for* London about 4 times daily. Pop. 2,609.
Map Square 43.

WATFORD (High St.) from *Euston*, 16¾ miles. Fares, 3/4a, 2/0c. R.T. for two months, 6/8a, 3/9½c. *See* p. 500.

ANOTHER ROUTE (Bakerloo Tube). *See* back of Map.

WATFORD JUNCTION (HERTS) from *Euston* and *Broad Street*, 17½ miles. Fares from Euston, 3/4a, 2/0c. R. T. for two months, 6/8a, 3/9½c. From Broad Street, 3/7a, 2/2c. R.T. for two months, 7/2a, 4/1c. Pop. 45,922. *See* pp. 496-499.
Map Square 23.

ANOTHER ROUTE (Bakerloo Tube). *See* back of Map.

WATFORD WEST (Herts) from *Euston*, 17¾ miles. Fares from Euston, 3/4a, 2/0c. R. T. for six months, 6/8a, 3/9½c. From Broad Street, 3/9a, 2/3c. R.T. for two months, 7/6a, 4/4½c. *See* p. 500.

For completion of Advertisements, see over.

WATFORD WEST—continued.

Malden Hotel. Residential Commercial. Opposite Station. Fully Licensed. Special Week End Terms to Golfers and others. 'Phone 242.

WATH - IN - NIDDER-

DALE (Yorks), 214¼ miles. No through fares. Departures *from* London as for Pateley Bridge. Departures *for* London about 4 times daily.
Map Square 7.

WATH - ON - DEARNE

(Yorks) from *King's Cross*, 164½ miles. Fares, 34/2*a*, 20/6*c*. R. T., double fare. Departures *from* London as for Doncaster. Departures *for* London about 3 times daily. Pop. 12,866.
Map Square 13.

ANOTHER ROUTE from *St. Pancras*, 169 miles. Fares as above. Departures *from* London as for Swinton. Departures *for* London about 6 times daily.

WATLINGTON (Oxon)

from *Paddington*, 43¾ miles. Fares, 8/0*a*, 5/2*c*. R. T. for two months, 16/0*a*, 10/4*c*. Pop. 1,548.
Map Square 23.

PAD.	WATLING	WATLING	PAD.
AM 9.10	10.27	AM 8.40*r*	10. 0
PM12.18	2.14	11.30	1.18
2.23	4.23	PM 3. 0	4.40
4.40	6.10	4.33	6.33
7.10	8.22	6.50	9.18
—	—	—	—
—	—	—	—

No Sunday Trains.
r Restaurant Car.

WATTEN (Caithness), 721¼

miles. No through fares. Departures *from* London as for Wick. Departures *for* London about twice daily. Pop. 934.
Map Square 32.

WATTON (Norfolk) from

Liverpool Street, 106½ miles. Fares, 21/10*a*, 13/1*c*. R. T. for two months, 43/8*a*. Pop. 1,436.
Map Square 19.

L'F'L. ST.	WATTON	WATTON	L'F'L. ST.
AM 5. 5	9.16	AM 7.51	11.27
8.30*r*	12.15	10.26*r*	2.21
11.50*r*	3.30	PM 1.43*r*	5.17
PM 2.54	6. 7	4.31	8.22
5.49*r*	9.23	7.46	2.50
—	—	—	—
—	—	—	—

No Sunday Trains.
r Restaurant Car.

WAVERTON (Cheshire)

from *Euston*, 176 miles. Fares, 36/8*a*, 22/0*c*. R. T. for two months, 73/4*a*. Departures *from* London as for Tattenhall Road. Departures *for* London about 5 times daily. Pop. 538.
Map Square 12.

WAVERTREE (Lancs), 198

miles. Fares, 41/3*a*, 24/9*c*. R. T. for two months, 82/6*a*. Departures *from* London as for Runcorn. Departures *for* London about 5 times daily. Pop. 21,139.
Map Square 12.

WEARHEAD (Durham),

269¾ miles. Fares, 56/1*a*, 33/8*c*. R.T., double fare. Departures *from* London as for Bishop Auckland. Departures *for* London about 6 times daily.
Map Square 7.

WEAR VALLEY

(Durham), 247¾ miles. No through fares. Departures *from* London as for Bishop Auckland. Departures *for* London about 6 times daily.
Map Square 7.

WEASTE (Lancs), 186¾

miles. Fares, 39/0*a*, 23/5*c*. R. T., double fare. Departures *from* London as for Manchester (London Road) Departures *for* London about twice daily. Pop. 19,674.
Map Square 12.

WEAVERTHORPE

(Yorks), 221 miles. Fares, 46/0*a*, 27/7*c*. R. T., double fare. Departures *from* London as for Malton. Departures *for* London about 6 times daily. Pop. 380.
Map Square 8.

WEDNESBURY (Stafford)

from *Paddington*, 118 miles. Fares, 24/5*a*, 14/8*c*. R. T. for two months, 48/10*a*. Pop. 30,407.
Map Square 17.

PAD.	WEDNESBY	WEDNESBY	PAD.
AM 5.30	10.35	AM 7. 3*r*	10. 0
9.10*er*	11.48	8.22*r*	11. 0
9.10*d*	12.19	9.26	12.25
10.40*r*	1.44	10.48*r*	1.25
PM12.50*r*	3.12	11.27*r*	2. 5
2.10*t*	4.45	PM 1.57*r*	5. 0
4.10*t*	6.41	2.50*t*	5.55
6.10*r*	9. 0	3.44*t*	6.40
7.10*r*	9.32	5. 5*r*	8. 5
7.30	10.57	6.48	10. 0
12.15*k*	5.59	11.19	3.30
12.15*h*	7.25	—	—
—	—	—	—

Sunday Trains.

AM10.35	2.46	AM11.13*r*	1.40
PM12.50*r*	5. 6	PM 1.51	6.20
4.10	7.55	5.55*r*	9. 0
6. 0*r*	8.56	—	—

d Saturdays only.
e Saturdays excepted.
h Saturdays midnight only.
k Saturdays midnight excepted.
r Restaurant Car.
t Tea Car.

WEDNESFIELD (Stafford), 126 miles. Fares, 25/7*a*, 15/4*c*. R. T. for two months, 51/2*a*, 30/8*c*. Departures *from* London as for Walsall. Departures *for* London about 6 times daily. Pop. 7,492.
Map Square 17.

WEEDON (Northampton)

from *Euston*, 69¾ miles. Fares, 14/5*a*, 8/8*c*. R.T. for two months, 28/10*d*. Pop. 1,593.
Map Square 18.

EUSTON	WEEDON	WEEDON	EUSTON
AM 6.45	8.50	AM 8. 7*h*	10.15
9.15*r*	10.56	8.58	11.40
9.30*h*	12.23	10.30*d*	12.20
12. 0*nr*	2. 1	10.30*e*	12.32
PM 1.35*dy*	4.40	PM 2.12	4.15
2. 0	4.52	2.56*h*	5.35
4.15*h*	6.30	4. 0*h*	6.25
5.32	7.37	5.40	7.55
7. 0*h*	8.45	8. 6	10.50
—	—	—	—
—	—	—	—

WEEDON—continued.

Sunday Trains.

EUSTON	WEEDON	WEEDON	EUSTON
AM 8.15	11. 5	AM10.37	1.20
		PM 3.28	5.50
—	—	—	—

d Saturdays only.
e Saturdays excepted.
h Via Northampton.
n Noon.
r Restaurant Car.
y Change at Willesden.

WEELEY (Essex) from

Liverpool Street, 63 miles. Fares, 13/7*a*, 8/2*c*. R. T. for two months, 27/2*a*. Pop. 648.
Map Square 24.

L'F'L. ST.	WEELEY	WEELEY	L'F'L. ST.
AM 5. 0	7. 6	AM 7.43	9.36
6.50	9.52	9.47	11.42
8.46	11.43	12. 0	2. 3
11.26*d*	1.52	PM 2.48	5. 5
11.30*e*	1.52	4.42	6.32
PM 2.15	4.41	6.15	9.17
3.26	6. 8	8.16	11.16
5.42	8. 0	—	—
7.45*r*	9.50	—	—
8.45	10.33	—	—

Sunday Trains.

AM 9.20*r*	11.45	AM 9.16	11.38
PM 4.40	6.33	PM 6.13	8.25
—	—	7. 2	10. 9

d Saturdays only.
e Saturdays excepted.
r Restaurant Car.

WEETON (Yorks), 196

miles. Fares, 40/10*a*, 24/6*c*. R.T. for two months, 81/8*a*, 49/0*c*. Departures *from* London as for Leeds. Departures *for* London about 6 times daily. Pop. 461.
Map Square 7.

WELBURY (Yorks), 223½

miles. Fares, 46/6*a*, 27/11*c*. R. T., double fare. Departures *from* London as for Stockton-on-Tees. Departures *for* London about 6 times daily. Pop. 208.
Map Square 8.

WELDON (Northampton)

from *St. Pancras*, 79¾ miles. Fares, 16/3½*a*, 9/9*c*. R. T., double fare. Pop. 837.
Map Square 18.

ST. PAN.	WELDON	WELDON	ST. PAN.
AM 2.25	6.32	AM 8.46*r*	11. 0
8.25*r*	10.52	9.36	1. 3
11.35	2.20	PM 1.40*r*	4.10
PM 3.30*r*	5.14	6.50*r*	9. 5
5.35*r*	7.40	—	—

No Sunday Trains.
r Restaurant Car.

WELFORD (Northampton)

from *Euston*, 91¼ miles. Fares, 17/6*a*, 10/6*c*. R. T. for two months, 35/0*a*. Pop. 849.
Map Square 18.

EUSTON	WELFORD	WELFORD	EUSTON
AM 2.35	7. 8	AM 6.44*e*	9.52
5. 0	8.54	7.34	10. 0
10.40	1.26	9. 9	11.55
PM 1.30	3.38	10.56	1. 0
2.50*dt*	5.20	PM 1. 9	4.15
2.50*e*	5.39	3.29	5.50
4.45*t*	6.52	5.51	9.20
7. 0	9.14	8. 3	10.45
—	—	9.11*d*	9.17

Sunday Trains.

PM 6. 0	8.10	PM 5.48	8.20
—	—	—	—

d Saturdays only.
e Saturdays excepted.
t Tea Car.

WELFORD PARK (Berks)

from *Paddington*, 59¼ miles. Fares, 11/10*a*, 7/5*c*. R. T. for two months, 23/8*a*, 14/10*c*. Departures *from* London as for Lambourne. Departures *for* London about 5 times daily. Pop. (Welford) 722.
Map Square 23.

WELLFIELD (Durham),

248¼ miles. Fares, 51/11*a*, 31/2*c*. R. T., double fare. Departures *from* London as for West Hartlepool. Departures *for* London about 4 times daily.
Map Square 7.

WELL HALL (London)

from *Charing Cross, Cannon Street,* and *London Bridge*, 9¼ miles. Fares from Charing Cross, 1/8*a*, 1/4*b*, 1/0*c*. R. T. for two days, 3/4*a*, 2/8*b*.
From Cannon Street, 1/6*a*, 1/2*b*, 0/10½*c*. R. T. for two days, 3/0*a*, 2/4*b*. See pp. 555-556.

WELLING (Kent) from

Charing Cross, Cannon Street, and *London Bridge*, 12 miles. Fares from Charing Cross, 2/4*a*, 1/11*b*, 1/3*c*. R. T. for two days, 4/8*a*, 3/10*b*. From Cannon Street, 2/1*a*, 1/8*b*, 1/3*c*. R. T. for two days, 4/2*a*, 3/4*b*. See pp. 555-556.

WELLINGBOROUGH

(Northampton) from *St. Pancras*, 65 miles. Fares, 13/2*a*, 7/11*c*. R. T., double fare. Pop. 20,365.
Map Square 18.

St. Pan.	Welbo.	Welbo.	St. Pan.
AM 4.25	6.14	AM 3.11*g*	5. 5
6.25	9.14	4.10*g*	6. 0
7.50	9.34	7.40	9.30
9.25	11.14	8.40*r*	9.57
11.35	1.47	9.50	11.25
PM12.30	2.19	10.40	1. 3
1.25*r*	2.47	PM12.13*r*	1.30
2.45	4.23	1.48	3.25
3.35	5.26	3.34	5.20
4.30*r*	5.58	5.11	7. 3
6.30	8.17	6.53	8.22
8.25	10.15	8.12*r*	10. 5
12. 0	1.43	9 33	11.45
—	—	—	—
—	—	—	—

Sunday Trains.

AM 8. 0	10.45	AM 3.11	5. 5
PM 1.35	3.36	4.10	6. 0
6.15*r*	8. 8	10.15	11.53
8.25	10.15	10.45	1.30
11.55	1.43	PM 5.55	8.30
—	—	9.16	11. 7
—	—	—	—
—	—	—	—

g Mondays excepted.
r Restaurant Car.

ANOTHER ROUTE from

Euston, 77¾ miles. Fares, 13/2*a*, 7/11*c*. R. T., double fare.

Euston	Welbo.	Welbo.	Euston
AM 5. 0	7.40	AM 8. 5	10.15
6.45	10. 2	9.25	11.55
9.30*d*	11.48	10.43	12.40
10.40	12.50	11.48*h*	2.45
PM12.15*c*	3.12	11.48*k*	4.15
12.15*d*	3.17	PM 1. 0*d*	3.45
3. 5	5.20	2.57	5.35
4.15	6.52	4.59	7.20
7. 0	9. 7	7.17	9.20
—	—	8.26	11.35

No Sunday Trains.

d Saturdays only.
e Saturdays excepted.
h Thursdays and Saturdays only.
k Thursdays and Saturdays excepted.

WELLINGTON (Salop)

from *Paddington*, 142½ miles. Fares, 29/9*a*, 17/10*c*. R. T. for two months. 59/6*a*. Pop. 8,148.
Map Square 17.

Pad.	Wellton.	Wellton.	Pad.
AM 6.30	11.37	AM 7.33*r*	11. 0
9.10*f*r12. 3		9.17	12.25
9.10*r*	12.53	9.59*r*	1.25
10.40*r*	2.18	11. 0*r*	2. 5
10.45*r*	3.17	11.42*r*	4.15
PM12.50*r*	4. 5	PM 1.10*r*	5. 0
2.10*t*	5. 4	2.29*t*	5.55
4.10*t*	7.25	3. 5*t*	6.40*l*
6.10*r*	9. 7	4.54*r*	8. 5
7.10*r*	10.41	6.47	10. 0
12.15*k*	7.20	10.10	3.30
12.15*h*	4.43	—	—

Sunday Trains.

PM12.50*f*	3.53	AM 8.36*r*	1.40
6. 0*r*	9.19	PM12.35	6.20
—	—	5.24*r*	9. 0

f Mondays only.
h Saturdays midnight only.
k Saturdays midnight excepted.
r Restaurant Car.
t Tea Car.

ANOTHER ROUTE from

Euston, 152½ miles. Fares as above.

Euston	Welngtn.	Welngtn.	Euston
AM 2.35	8.25	AM 8.20*er*12. 5	
5. 0	9.31	8.20*dr*12.20	
6.45*h*	11. 0	10.29*r*	2.20
6.45	12.35	11.54*r*	3.10
8.45*r*	1.29	PM12.35*t*	5.35
10.40*r*	2.57	2.46*t*	6.15
12. 0*nr*	4.25	3.16*r*	8.10
PM 1.15*r*	6. 5	5.10*dr*	9.15
2.20*t*	6.58	5.10*er*	9.20
4.45*r*	8.30	6.11*r*	10. 0
5.50*dr*10.57		11. 7	5. 0
6.30*er*10.57		—	—
9.20*c*	2.41	—	—

Sunday Trains.

AM 9.15	3. 7	PM 4.22*r*	8.55
—	—	—	—

d Saturdays only.
e Saturdays excepted.
h Mondays and Fridays only.
n Noon.
r Restaurant Car.
t Tea Car.

WELLINGTON (Somerset) from *Paddington*, 150 miles.

Fares, 31/5*a*, 18/10*c*. R. T. for two months, 62/10*a*. Pop. 7,221.
Map Square 21.

Pad.	Wellton.	Wellton.	Pad.
AM 5.30*n*	10.38	AM 7. 4	11.30
PM12. 5*r*	3.27	10. 9*r*	1.30
3.30*r*	6.37	11.59	4. 5
4.15*r*	8.36	PM 1.57*r*	5.30
6.30*r*	11. 5	4 59	9. 0
12. 0*h*	7.23	8.23	2.45
12.30*k*	8.45	10.11	7.10

Sunday Trains.

PM10. 0	7.23	AM10. 4	3.35
—	—	—	—

h Saturdays midnight excepted.
k Saturdays midnight only.
n Mondays and Thursdays only.
r Restaurant Car.

WELLINGTON COLLEGE (Berks)

from *Charing Cross, Cannon Street* and *London Bridge*, 59 miles. Fares, 7/1*a*, 5/8*b*, 4/3*c*. R. T. for two months, 14/2*a*, 11/4*b*.

Char. +	Can.St.	Lon. B.	Well.C.
AM —	4.44	5. 0	7.57
—	—	7.50*l*	10.26
—	—	9.33*l*	12. 4
10.55	—	11. 3	1.45

WELLINGTON COLLEGE—continued.

Char. +	Can. St.	Lon. B.	Arr. at Well.C
PM12.55	—	1. 4	3.46
2. 3*h*	—	2.10*h*	4.39
2. 3*k*	—	2.10*k*	4.54
—	2. 8*d*	—	4.54
—	—	2.22*dl*	4.43
3.15*d*	—	3.21*d*	5.55
3.15*e*	—	3.21*e*	6. 1
4.22*d*	—	4.28*d*	6.55
—	4.44*e*	4.48*e*	6.54
—	5.24*e*	5.27*e*	7.40
5.42*d*	—	5.48*d*	8. 9
—	6. 0*e*	6. 3*e*	8.28
—	6.36*e*	6.39*e*	9. 7
6.34*d*	—	6.40*d*	9. 8
7.24*d*	—	7.30*d*	10. 3
8.28	—	8.36	11.11

Sunday Trains.

AM 6.25	—	6.32	9.15
10.20	—	10.28	12.54
PM 5.25	—	5.32	8. 7
8.38	—	8.45	11. 9

Trains from Wellington College.

Well. C.	Lon. B.	Can.St.	Char. +
AM 6.42	8.56	—	—
8.10	10.10	—	10.20
8.24*y*	10.31	—	10.43
8.35	11. 0	—	—
9.39	11.46	—	11.59
10.14	12.50	—	1. 0
PM12. 8	2.38	—	2.46
2.23	5. 2	—	5.14
3.39	5.56	—	—
4.47	7.20	—	7.29
6.38	9. 2	—	9.15
7.41	10. 3	—	10.13
9.38	11.57	—	12.10

Sunday Trains.

AM 5.54	8.16	—	8.27
8.56	11.15	—	11.25
PM 4.43	7.13	—	7.23
7.46	10.11	—	10.24

d Saturdays only.
e Saturdays excepted.
h Mondays, Fridays, and Saturdays excepted.
k Mondays, Fridays, and Saturdays only.
l Low Level Platform.
y Wednesdays only.

Taxi Cabs can be hired to meet any train at this station by letter, or telephone No. 37 Crowthorne. S. C. James, Proprietor, Wellington Hotel.

WELLOW (Somerset),

132½ miles. Fares, 24/0*a*, 14/5*c*. R.T. for two months, 48/0*a*. Departures *from* London as for Radstock. Departures *for* London about 4 times daily. Pop. 2,033.
Map Square 22.

WELLS (Norfolk) from

Liverpool Street, via Wymondham, 146¾ miles. Fares, 26/6*a*, 15/1*c*. R. T. for two months, 53/0*a*. Pop. 2,647.
Map Square 14.

L'pl. St.	Wells	Wells	L'pl. St.
AM 5. 5	9.58	AM 5.55*f*	10.36
5.50	12.23	7.30	12.40
9.50*r*	2.45	9. 9*r*	2.21
11.50*er*	5. 8	PM12.50*r*	5.17
PM12.33*dr*	5.33	3.20*r*	8.22
3.10*r*	8.21	5.45*e*	2.50
5.18*fr*	9.37	5.55*d*	2.50

Sunday Trains.

PM 3.25	8.50	PM 4.45	9.40

d Saturdays only.
e Saturdays excepted.
f Mondays only.
r Restaurant Car.

WELLS—*continued.*

ANOTHER ROUTE from *Liverpool Street, via* King's Lynn, 127¾ miles. Fares as above.

L'pl. St.	Wells	Wells	L'pl. St.
AM 8.30*r*	12.43	AM 7. 3	11.27
11.50*kr*	4. 6	10. 7*r*	2.21
11.50*hr*	4.42	PM12.58*r*	6.10
PM 2.34*e*	7. 1	5.15*e*	10.30
2.34*d*	7.26	5.40*d*	10.30

No Sunday Trains.
d Saturdays only.
e Saturdays excepted.
h Tuesdays only.
k Tuesdays excepted.
r Restaurant Car.

WELLS (Somerset)

from *Paddington, via* Witham, 120¼ miles. Fares, 25/2*a*, 15/1*c*. R. T. for two months, 50/4*a*, 30/2*c*. Pop. 4,372.
Map Square 22.

Pad.	Wells	Wells	Pad.
AM 1. 0*g*	9.17	AM 9.20	12.55
7.30	11.45	PM12.15	3.50
10.30	1.28	1. 2*t*	5.30
PM12.30*r*	3.58	4. 2	8.20
3.30	7.35	7. 9	2.45
5. 5	9.50	—	—
Sunday Trains.			
PM 2.40	6. 5	PM 2.30*r*	7.55

g Mondays excepted.
r Restaurant Car.
t Tea Car.

ANOTHER ROUTE from *Paddington, via* Yatton, 147½ miles. Fares, 30/8*a*, 18/5*c*. R. T. for two months, 61/4*a*, 36/10*c*.

Pad.	Wells	Wells	Pad.
AM 5.30	10.44	AM 7.15	11.30
7.30	12.19	9.50*r*	2. 0
11.15*r*	3.31	PM12.35	6. 2
PM 1. 0*r*	4.28	2. 2*r*	7. 0
1.10*r*	6.46	4.55	10.25
4.15*r*	8.55	8.10	2.45
12. 0*l*	8.49	—	—
12.30*s*	1.30	—	—
Sunday Trains.			
PM10. 0	8.49	PM 6.23	3.15

l Saturdays midnight excepted.
r Restaurant Car.
s Saturdays midnight only.

ANOTHER ROUTE from *Waterloo*, 139 miles. Fares, 25/2*a*, 15/1*c*. R. T. for two months, 50/4*a*, 30/2*c*.

W'loo	Wells	Wells	W'loo
AM 9. 0*r*	1.33	AM 6.55*r*	11.10
12. 0*r*	4.18	10. 5*r*	1.56
PM 1. 0*r*	6. 8	12. 0*r*	4.30
3. 0*r*	7.28	PM 3.40*r*	8.30
6. 0*r*	9.55	4.50	10.50
—	—	6.40*h*	3.58

No Sunday Trains.
h Via Eastleigh.
r Restaurant Car.

Swan Hotel. Facing the Cathedral, and the only Hotel from which a view of it can be obtained. Telephone 21.

WELNETHAM (Suffolk)

from *Liverpool Street*, 73 miles. Fares, 15/5*a*, 9/3*c*. R. T. for two months, 30/10*a*. Pop. 484.
Map Square 19.

L'pl.St.	Welnhm.	Welnhm.	L'pl.St.
AM 6.50	10.27	AM 7.36	9.53
10. 0	12.29	9.24	11.42
PM12.36	3. 5	11.22*h*	2. 3
2.15	5. 0	PM 1.50*h*	5. 5
5.42	8. 7	3.50*h*	6.32
—	—	6. 0	9.17

No Sunday Trains.
h Via Colchester.

WELSHAMPTON

(Salop), 178¾ miles. Fares, 35/3*a*, 21/2*c*. R. T. for two months, 70/6*a*. Departures *from* London as for Whitchurch (Salop). Departures *for* London about 4 times daily. Pop. 500.
Map Square 12.

WELSHPOOL (Montgomery)

from *Paddington*, 172½ miles. Fares, 36/0*a*, 21/7*c*. R. T. for two months, 72/0*a*, 43/2*c*. Pop. 5,677.
Map Square 16.

Pad.	W'pool	W'pool	Pad.
AM 6.30	12.50	AM 8.55*r*	2. 5
10.20*r*	2. 8	10.37*r*	4.15
10.40*r*	3. 0	PM12.40*r*	5. 0
PM 2.10*t*	6. 5	2.20*r*	6.40
4.10*t*	8.25	3.23*r*	8. 5
6.10*r*	10.25	4.31	10. 0
12.15*h*	7.10	5.10*d*	10. 0
12.15*k*	8.35	8.50	3.30

No Sunday Trains.
d Saturdays only.
h Saturdays midnight only.
k Saturdays midnight excepted.
r Restaurant Car.
t Tea Car.

ANOTHER ROUTE from *Euston*, 182 miles. Fares as above.

Euston	W'pool	W'pool	Euston
AM 5. 0	11.22	AM 7.35*ry*	1.45
10.40*r*	3. 0	8.55*r*	2.20
11.50*ry*	5.45	10.37*r*	3.10
PM 1.15*r*	6. 5	PM12.18*ty*	5.50
1.15*r*	7.25	1.32*t*	6.15
2.20*t*	8.25	3.18*ry*	9. 5
4.45*r*	10.25	3.28*dr*	9.15
9.20*e*	4. 5	3.28*er*	9.20
11. 0*dy*	7.10	4.30*ry*	10.45
—	—	8.50	5. 0
Sunday Trains.			
PM 9.15	4. 0	PM 8.35	5. 0

d Sats. only. *e* Sats. excepted.
r Restaurant Car.
t Tea Car.
y Via Crewe.

WELTON (Northampton)

from *Euston*, 75¼ miles. Fares, 15/8*a*, 9/5*c*. R. T. for two months, 31/4*a*. Pop. 380.
Map Square 18.

Euston	Welton	Welton	Euston
AM 6.45	9. 3	AM 8.47	11.40
9.15*r*	11. 6	9.56*d*	12.20
12. 0*nr*	2.13	9.56*e*	12.32
PM 2. 0	5. 5	PM 2. 2	4.15
5.32	7.49	5. 6	7.55
—	—	7.56	10.50
Sunday Trains.			
AM 8.15	11.19	AM10.26	1.20
—	—	PM 3.17	5.50

d Saturdays only.
e Saturdays excepted.
n Noon.
r Restaurant Car.

WELWYN (Herts)

from *King's Cross*, 22 miles. Fares, 4/7*a*, 2/9*c*. R. T. for two months, 9/2*a*, 5/6*c*. Pop. 1,762.
Map Square 23.

King's+	Welwyn	Welwyn	King's+
AM 7. 0	8.16	AM 6.43	7.30
8. 5	8.59	8. 1	8.41
9.20*d*	10. 2	8.22	8.55
10.12	11. 1	9. 1	9.34
PM12.40*d*	1.11	9.33	10.22
1. 8	2. 1	11.21	12. 3
1.55	2.33	PM 1.21	2.22
2.30*d*	3.13	3.34	4.23
4.15	5. 7	4.51	5.45
5.10	5.43	6.16	7. 5
5.50	6.32	7.29	8. 5
6.30	7. 8	9.26	10.20
7. 0	7.43	10.22	11. 0
8.30	9. 8	—	—
9.10	9.55	—	—
10.55	11.33	—	—
11.45*h*	12.32	—	—

WELWYN—*continued.*

Sunday Trains.

King's+	Welwyn	Welwyn	King's+
AM 8.30	9.26	AM 8.48	9.53
10.30	11.11	PM 5.41	6.17
PM 7.10	7.55	7.18	8. 8
9.30	10.12	—	—

d Saturdays only.
h Wednesdays only.

WELWYN GARDEN CITY

from *King's Cross*, 20¾ miles. Fares, 4/5*a*, 2/8*c*. R.T. for two months, 8/10*a*, 5/4*c*.

King's+	W.G.C.	W.G.C.	King's+
AM 7. 0	8.16	AM 7.56	8.41
7.45	8.31	8.42	9.29
9.20	9.57	9. 3	9.44
11.30	12.21	11.48	12.45
PM 1. 8	2. 6	PM 1.32	2.22
1.55*d*	2.34	3.28*d*	4.23
2.30*d*	3.14	4.34	5.45
4.15	5. 6	6.10	7. 5
5.10	5.46	7.13	8. 5
5.50	6.39	8.48	9.50
6.15	6.56	9.27	10.20
7. 0	7.51	10.14*e*	11. 0
8.30	9.11	—	—
9.10	9.59	—	—
10.45	11.36	—	—
11.45*l*	12.33	—	—
Sunday Trains.			
AM 8.30	9.26	AM 8.47	9.53
10.30	11.12	PM 6.33	7.40
PM 7.10	7.54	8.51	9.48

d Saturdays only.
e Saturdays excepted.
l Wednesdays only.

WEM (Salop), 173½ miles.

from Euston. Fares, 34/7*a*, 20/9*c*. R. T. for two months, 69/2*a*. Departures *from* London as for Shrewsbury or Whitchurch (Salop). Departures *for* London about 6 times daily. Pop. 2,176.
Map Square 17.

WEMBLEY (Middlesex)

from *Euston* and *Broad Street*, 8 miles. Fares from Euston, 1/4½*a*, 0/10*c*. R. T. for two days, 2/2½*a*, 1/5½*c*. From Broad Street, 1/7*a*, 0/11½*c*. R. T. for two days, 2/7½*a*, 1/9*c*. Pop. 16,187. *See* pp. 496-499.
Map Square 49.

ANOTHER ROUTE (Bakerloo Tube). *See* back of Map.

WEMBLEY HILL

(Middlesex) from *Marylebone*, 6¾ miles. Fares, 1/4½*a*, 0/10*c*. R. T. for two days, 2/2½*a*, 1/5½*c*. *See* pp. 495-496.
Map Square 49.

WEMBLEY NORTH

(Middlesex) from *Euston*, 8¾ miles. Fares, 1/7*a*, 0/11½*c*. R.T. for two days, 2/7½*a*, 1/8½*c*. From Broad Street, 1/9½*a*, 1/1*c*. R. T. for two days, 3/0½*a*, 2/0*c*. *See* pp. 496-499.

ANOTHER ROUTE (Bakerloo Tube). *See* back of Map.

WEMBLEY PARK (Middlesex)

from *Baker Street*, 6¾ miles. Fares, 1/4½*a*, 0/10*c*. R. T. for two days, 2/2½*a*, 1/5½*c*. *See* back of Map.
Map Squares 23 *and* 49.

WEMYSS BAY (Renfrew)

from *Euston*, 430½ miles. Fares, 85/3*a*, 51/2*c*. R. T. for two months, 170/6*a*, 102/4*c*. Pop. 360.
Map Square 40.

Euston	W. Bay	W. Bay	Euston
AM 2.35*e*	5.12	AM 8.42*r*	6.25
5. 0*d*	5.35	11.30*r*	10. 0
5. 0*e*	5.24	PM 3. 5*er*	5. 0
10. 0*dr*	8. 4	3.30*dr*	5. 0
10. 0*er*	9.54	7.30*e*	6.55
PM 9.20*e*	8.52	8.15*dr*	7.30
11.45*e*	11.20	—	—

WEMYSS BAY—*contd.*

Sunday Trains.

Euston	W. Bay	W. Bay	Euston
PM 9.30	8.52	—	—
11.45	11.20	—	—

d Saturdays only.
e Saturdays excepted.
r Restaurant Car.

Wemyss Bay Hydro. Fifty minutes from Glasgow. Finest Scenery on Clyde. Russian, Turkish, Sea-Water Baths. Garage, Golf Course. Telegrams, "Hydro, Skelmorlie."
See advt. p. 338.

WEMYSS CASTLE

(Fife), 425½ miles. No through fares. Departures *from* London as for Kirkcaldy. Departures *for* London about 4 times daily. Pop. (Wemyss) 24,530.
Map Square 41.

WENDLING (Norfolk)

from *Liverpool Street*, 118¾ miles. Fares, 23/7*a*, 14/2*c*. R. T. for two months, 47/2*a*. Departures *from* London as for Swaffham or Dereham. Departures *for* London about 7 times daily. Pop. 272.
Map Square 19.

WENDOVER (Bucks)

from *Marylebone*, 33¼ miles. Fares, 7/0*a*, 4/2*c*. R. T. for two months, 14/0*a*, 8/4*c*. Pop. 1,856.
Map Square 23.

M'bone	Wendor.	Wendor.	M'bone
AM 6.25	7.30	AM 6.36	7.50
6.45	7.46	7.17	8.22
7.20	8.36	7.44*e*	8.42
7.50	9. 6	7.44*d*	8.46
8.50	10. 2	8.10	9. 9
9.14*e*	10.54	8.52	9.46
9.14*d*	10.58	10.10	11.36
10. 5	11.15	11.56	12.59
11.15	12.23	PM12.55	2. 2
PM 1. 5*d*	2. 8	1.49*e*	3.28
1.10*e*	2.15	2.57	3.59
1.41*d*	2.49	3.48	4.56
1.55*e*	3.28	4.27*e*	6.22
2.15*d*	3.28	5.31*d*	7.15
2.45*d*	4.22	6.40	7.43
3.25	4.34	6.56	8.11
5. 4	6.11	7.29	8.31
5.24*e*	6.26	9.19	10.41
6.25*e*	7.18	10. 0	11. 0
6.25*d*	7.26	—	—
6.31*e*	7.41	—	—
6.53*e*	8.27	—	—
7.30	8.40	—	—
9. 0	10. 7	—	—
10.30	11.37	—	—
11.35	1. 0	—	—

Sunday Trains.

AM 9.30	10.38	AM 9. 6	10.13
11. 0	12. 8	11.42	12.46
PM 1. 0	2. 8	PM 1.12	2.16
2.30	3.38	4.17	5.20
3.15	4.46	5.36	6.55
4.30	5.38	6.32	7.35
5.30	6.49	7. 4	8.16
6.10	7.33	8.26	9.44
6.45	7.50	8.55	9.55
7.45	9. 9	—	—
8.50	10.39	—	—

d Saturdays only.
e Saturdays excepted.

ANOTHER ROUTE from *Baker Street*, 33½ miles. Fares as above.

BakerS.	Wendor.	Wendor.	BakerS.
AM 6. 5	7.15	AM 6.36	7.41
6. 6	7.31	7.17	8.35
6.30	7.46	7.33	8.42
7. 3	8.36	7.44*d*	8.51
7.50	9. 6	7.44*e*	8.57
8.34	10. 2	8.10	9.28
9.51*e*	10.54	8.38	9.38
9.51*d*	10.58	8.52	9.49

WENDOVER—*continued.*

BakerS.	Wendor.	Wendor.	BakerS.
AM10.11*d*	11.22	AM 9.17	10.25
10.18*e*	11.25	10.10	11. 5
11. 0	12.23	11.25	12.35
PM12. 8	1.22	11.56*e*	1.22
12.50*e*	2.16	11.56*d*	1.24
12.54*d*	2. 8	PM12.55*d*	2.17
1.17*d*	2.30	12.55*e*	2.22
1.21*d*	2.49	1.49	2.58
2.17*e*	3.28	2.45*d*	3.54
2.19*d*	3.30	2.57	4.22
3.10	4.34	3.48	5.14
3.18*d*	4.22	4.27	5.41
4.10*d*	5.20	5.15*e*	6.33
4.16*e*	5.52	5.31*d*	6.39
*4.40*d*	6.11	6.40	8. 0
4.42*e*	6.11	6.56	8. 8
5. 7*e*	6.25	7.29	8.47
5.45*e*	6.49	8.22	9.36
5.46*d*	6.55	9.19*d*	10.28
5.49*e*	7.18	9.19*e*	10.43
6.30	7.41	10. 0	11.18
7.15*e*	8.27	10.35	11.40
7.15*d*	8.39	—	—
7.19*e*	8.39	—	—
8.40	10. 8	—	—
9.25	10.34	—	—
10.10	11.37	—	—
11.50	1. 0	—	—

Sunday Trains.

AM 8.47	9.59	AM 8.29	9.48
9.10	10.38	9. 6	10.27
9.47	11. 0	10.40	11.48
10.33	11.48	11.42	1. 5
10 45	12. 8	PM 1.12	2.35
11.11	12.27	2. 2	3. 9
12. 0	1.11	2.45	3.52
PM12.45	2. 8	4.17	5.42
2. 0	3.11	4.47	5.54
2.15	3.38	5.36	6.45
3.35	4.46	6.32	7.57
4.15	5.38	7. 4	8.12
5.37	6.49	7.42	8.51
6.24	7.33	8. 5	9.12
6.30	7.50	8.26	9.31
7.59	9.10	8.55	10.20
9.29	10.39	10. 6	11.14

d Saturdays only.
e Saturdays excepted.

Ye Olde Red Lion Hotel, Wendover. Established 1620. High-class Family, etc. Moderate charges. Special Luncheon, Sundays, 1.0. Tennis, Golf, etc. 'Phone, 5 P.O. Tariff, apply—Proprietors, J. E. CHAMBERS & H. W. STRATTON.

WENHASTON (Suffolk)

from *Liverpool Street*, 103¼ miles. Fares, 21/8*a*, 13/0*c*. R. T. for two months, 43/4*a*. Departures *from* London as for Southwold. Departures *for* London about 4 times daily. Pop. 831.
Map Square 19.

WENNINGTON (Lancs),

249½ miles. Fares, 47/11*a*, 28/9*c*. R.T., double fare. Departures *from* London as for Giggleswick. Departures *for* London about 6 times daily. Pop. 133.
Map Square 7.

WENSLEY (Yorks), 237¼

miles. Fares, 49/7*a*, 29/9*c*. R. T., double fare. Departures *from* London as for Leyburn. Departures *for* London about 4 times daily. Pop. 246.
Map Square 7.

WENTWORTH (Yorks),

167¼ miles. Fares, 34/7*a*, 20/9*c*. R.T., double fare. Departures *from* London as for Chapeltown. Departures *for* London about 8 times daily. Pop. 1,949.
Map Square 12.

WENVOE (Glamorgan),

161 miles. Fares, 33/11*a*, 20/4*c*. R.T. for two months, 67/10*a*, 40/8*c*. Departures *from* London as for Cardiff. Departures *for* London about 5 times daily. Pop. 505.
Map Square 21.

WEIN LAS (Salop), 168¼

miles. No through fares. Departures *from* London as for Shrewsbury or Oswestry. Departures *for* London about 3 times daily.

WEST AUCKLAND

(Durham), 245¼ miles. Fares, 51/6*a*, 30/11*c*. R. T. for two months, 103/0*a*, 61/10*c*. Departures *from* London as for Bishop Auckland. Departures *for* London about 5 times daily. Pop. 4,471.
Map Square 7.

WESTBOURNE PARK

from *Aldgate* and *Paddington*, 1½ miles. From Paddington, 0/2½*a*, 0/1½*c*. R. T. for two days, 0/5*a*.
See pp. 490-493, and back of Map.
Map Square 52.

WEST BROMPTON

(London). *See* Brompton West.

WEST BROMWICH

(Stafford), from *Paddington*, 115½ miles. Fares, 24/0*a*, 14/5*c*. R. T. for two months, 48/0*a*. Pop. 73,761.
Map Square 17.

Pad.	W. Brom	W. Brom.	Pad.
AM 5.30	10.27	AM 7.10*r*	10. 0
9.10*er*	11.38	8.32*r*	11. 0
9.10*dr*	12.10	9.53	12.25
10.40*er*	1. 7	10.56*r*	1.25
10.40*d*	1.17	11.38*r*	2. 5
PM12.50*r*	3. 5	PM 2.11*r*	5. 0
2.10*t*	4.37	3.25*t*	5.55
4.10*t*	6.33	3.51*t*	6.40
6.10*r*	8.49	5.30*r*	8. 5
7.10*r*	9.25	7. 3	10. 0
7.30	10.50	11.27	3.30
12.15*k*	5.50	—	—
12.15*h*	7.18	—	—

Sunday Trains.

AM11.10*r*	2.57	AM11.20*r*	1.40
PM 4.10	7.47	PM 2. 1	6.20
6. 0*r*	8.47	6. 5*r*	9. 0
—	—	—	—

d Saturdays only.
e Saturdays excepted.
h Saturdays midnight only.
k Saturdays midnight excepted.
r Restaurant Car.
t Tea Car.

WESTBROOK (Hereford),

167½ miles. Fares, 34/10*a*, 20/11*c*. R. T. for two months, 69/8*a*, 41/10*c*. Departures *from* London as for Abbeydore. Departures *for* London about 3 times daily.
Map Square 17.

WESTBURY (Salop),

163¾ miles. Fares, 34/2*a*, 20/6*c*. R. T. for two months, 68/4*a*. Departures *from* London as for Buttington. Departures *for* London about 4 times daily. Pop. 1,115.
Map Square 17.

WESTBURY (Wilts) from

Paddington, 95½ miles. Fares *via* Theale, 19/10*a*, 11/11*c*. R.T. for two months, 39/8*a*. *Via* Bath, 22/6*a*, 13/6*c*. R.T. for two months, 45/0*a*. Pop. 3,712.
Map Square 22.

Pad.	Westby.	Westby.	Pad.
AM 1. 0*g*	6.52	AM 6.52	10. 0
5.30	9.24	8.43	10.52
7.30	10.37	8.48	12.20
9.30	11.20	10.43	12.55
10.30	12. 8	11.58	2.50
PM12. 5*r*	1.55	PM12.18	3.20
12.30*r*	2.37	1.49	3.50
2. 0	3.51	2.12	6. 2

WESTBURY—*continued.*

PAD.	WESTBY.	WESTBY.	PAD.
PM 3.50	5. 7	PM 3.44*t*	5.30
5. 5	7.26	5.10*r*	6.50
6.50	9. 8	5.34*r*	7.35
—	—	6.16	8.20
—	—	6.30	10.25
—	—	6.55	10.45
—	—	9.27	2.45
—	—	10.26*h*	2.45

Sunday Trains.

AM 9.10	1.20	PM12. 3	3.35
PM12.30*r*	4. 8	6. 5*r*	7.55
2.40	4.27	6.10	10. 0
10. 0	6.52	—	—

g Mondays excepted.
h Thursdays only.
r Restaurant Car.
t Tea Car.

WEST CALDER (Mid-
lothian), 393 miles. Fares, 80/2*a*,
48/1*c*. R.T. for two months, 160/4*a*,
96/2*c*. Departures *from* London as
for Edinburgh (Waverley) or
Wishaw (Central). Departures *for*
London about 4 times daily.
Pop. 7,874.
Map Square 40.

WESTCLIFF (Essex) from
Fenchurch Street, 35 miles. Fares,
5/5*a*, 3/3*c*. R. T. for two months,
10/10*a*, 6/6*c*.
Map Square 24.

FEN.ST.	W.CLIFF	W.CLIFF	FEN ST.
AM 5. 5	6.31	AM 4.28	5.35
5.37	7.48	5.28	6.43
6.52	8.47	6.23	7.34
7.42	8.58	6.55	8. 6
7.53	9.25	7. 4	8.15
9.18	10.55	7.18*h*	8.22
9.57*h*	11.20	7.30	8.33
10.13*h*	11.30	7.49	8.53
10.17	11.52	7.57	9. 4
10.45	12. 4	8.15	9.17
11.57*d*	12.58	8.26	9.30
PM12. 9	1.15	8.33	9.39
12.43*d*	1.44	8.40	9.54*k*
12.55*d*	1.52	8.50	9.50
1. 0*e*	1.55	9. 1	9.52
1. 0*d*	2. 1	9. 7	10. 2
1. 5*d*	2. 9	9.18	10.18*h*
1.11*d*	2.22	9.30	10.35
1.25*d*	2.30	9.50	10.57*h*
1.48*d*	2.49	10.31	11.40
1.56*d*	2.57	11.25*e*	12.22
2. 5*dk*	3.24	11.25*d*	12.38
2. 6	3. 4	11.55	1.11*h*
2.26*d*	3.31	PM12.53	1.56
2.30	4. 1	2.21	3.28
3. 8*d*	4.12	2.35*d*	3.51
3.16*h*	4.38	3.35	4.54*h*
3.45*d*	4.47	3.53*d*	5.12
4. 7	5. 1	4.30	5.49
4.27	5.30	4.38	6.33
4.57*e*	5.51	5.34	6.45
5. 6*e*	6. 2	6.16*e*	7.29*h*
5.16	6.11	6.26	7.51
5.25*e*	6.33	7.11	8.30
5.32	7.10	7.19	9.15
5.38*e*	6.43	8. 7	9.17*h*
5.46*e*	6.50	8.38	10. 8
6. 7*e*	7. 3	9. 4*d*	10.20
6.17*e*	7.16	9.18	10.30
6.23*ek*	7.48	9.35	11.23*h*
6.26	7.29	10.28	11.40
6.53*e*	7.58	—	—
6.53*d*	8.12	—	—
7.20	8.21	—	—
8. 0*e*	9. 2	—	—
8.45	9.55	—	—
9.19*eh*	10.39	—	—
9.20*d*	10.39	—	—
10.15	11.17	—	—
11.27*eh*	12.35	—	—
11.27*dh*	12.44	—	—
12.20	1.23	—	—

WESTCLIFF—*continued.*

Sunday Trains.

FEN.ST.	W.CLIFF	W.CLIFF	FEN ST.
AM 9.15	10.26	AM 7.54	9. 6
9.45	11.26	8.18	10.18
10.40	11.50	10.19	11.35
11. 8*h*	12.23	11.59	1.10
11.45	12.49	PM 2.21	3.47
PM 2. 7	3.57	4.14	5.30
2.45	4.23	4.23	6. 0
4.30	6.19	5.31	7.16
5. 7*h*	6.38	5.46	7.45
6.10	7.38	7.12	8.32
7.22	8.36	7.43	8.59*h*
8.28	9.40	8.44	10. 9
8.45	10.39	8.51	10.*25*
9.45	11.15	9.44	10.48
10.36*h*	11.45	9.54	11.22*h*

d Saturdays only.
e Saturdays excepted.
h Departs from or arrives at Mark
Lane Station.
k Departs from or arrives at Broad
Street Station.

ANOTHER ROUTE from
St. Pancras, 41 miles. Fares, 5/5*a*,
3/3*c*. R. T. for two months, 10/10*a*,
6/6*c*.

ST.PAN.	W.CLIFF	W.CLIFF	ST.PAN.
AM 9.30	11.20	AM 8.19	10.10
PM12.20	2.14	11.55	1.48
2.50	4.38	PM 3.35	5.23
6.40	8.12	6. 9	7.45
—	—	—	—

Sunday Trains.

AM10.10	11.57	PM 7.20	9.18
—	—	—	—

ANOTHER ROUTE from
Charing Cross (District Railway),
37 miles. Fares, 5/10*a*, 7/0*c*. R. T.
for two months, 11/8*a*, 7/0*c*.

CHAR.+	W.CLIFF	W.CLIFF	CHAR.+
AM 9. 0	10.55	AM 4.28	5.53
10. 3	11.28	7.18	8.31
10.18	12. 4	9.18	10.27
PM 4.52*e*	6.27	PM 6.16*e*	7.59
9.10*e*	10.39	8. 7	9.26
11.18*e*	12.35	—	—
11.18*d*	12.45	—	—
12. 4*m*	1.23	—	—

Sunday Trains.

AM10.59	12.23	PM 7.43	9. 9
PM10.27	11.45	—	—

d Saturdays only.
e Saturdays excepted.
m Midnight.

Court Hotel, en pension,
Holland Road and The Leas, 3
minutes Station. Tel. : 144
Southend.
G. SHAPLAND, Proprietor.
See advt. p. 339.

West Cliff Private Resi-
dential Hotel. Finest position ;
facing Sea. Moderate tariff.
Tel. No. 598 (2 lines). Southend.
W. J. HOCKLEY, Proprietor.
See advt. p. 339.

Palace Hotel. Choicest site.
Luxurious Winter Garden and
Restaurant. Terrace facing Sea.
Terms from Five Guineas.
See advt. p. 307.

WESTCLIFF—*continued.*

Hotel Victoria, Southend.
The Broadway. First-Class Family
and Commercial.
See advt. p. 308.

Overcliff Hotel. Finest
Position opposite Sea, one minute
from Station. Moderate inclusive
tariff. Separate tables. Special
Winter terms. Telephone 192.
See advt. p. 340.

Queen's Hotel. The leading
and only licensed Hotel in Westcliff. Facing South, in picturesque
grounds. Lift. 'Phone, 62
Southend.
J. H. KEEP, Proprietor.
See advt. p 340.

Grand Pier Hotel, Southend.
Immediately facing Southend
Pier. Telephone No. 216.
Proprietor, J. MOSS.
See advt. p. 307.

Royal Hotel, Southend.
Facing Sea, overlooking Shrubbery
and Pier. Oldest and Best Hotel.
Telephone 32.
WEBSTER, Proprietor.
See advt. p. 308.

Palmeira Towers. Finest
Hotel and position. Balcony
bedrooms. Facing Sea. 'Phone
447. Moderate Tariff.

Boston Hall Hotel. The
Leas. Finest position on Sea
Front. Special inclusive terms
for Permanent Residents. Cuisine
a special feature. Billiards.
Tennis. Garage. 'Phone 568.
Misses ALLARDYCE &
FRANKLIN.

Hasleham's (Roseneath),
Palmerston Road, one minute
Westcliff Station and Sea. Estab-
lished 1898. Saturday to Monday
21s.
Mr. & Mrs. GALE-HASLEHAM.

Palmeira House, Palmeira
Gardens. High-class Boarding
Establishment. Sea-view. Minute
from Station. Electric light.
Late dinner.

Holmhurst. High-class
Boarding Establishment, Palmerston Road. Minute Sea and
Station. Electric light throughout. Separate tables. Smoking
lounge. Croquet. Moderate terms.

"Eversley," Palmerston
Road. Private Boarding Establish-
ment. Minute Sea and Station.
Excellent Cuisine. Electric light.
Separate tables. Smoking lounge.
Moderate Tariff.
Miss WILLIAMS.

Winton Hall. En Pension.
Ideal position on highest ground
between Station and Bandstand.
Dining-room seats 60. Spacious
Lounge. Full-sized Billiard Table.
Garage. Perfect cuisine. Terms
Moderate. Special for perma-
nency. 'Phone 239 Southend. Tele-
grams : "Winton Hall, Westcliff."
Mrs. E. K. HIPKIN.

The Warwick Hotel, West-
cliff Avenue. Finest position.
Facing Sea. Billiards (full size),
tennis court. Excellent cuisine.
Moderate terms. Telephone, 296,
Southend. PROPRIETRESS.

Greenway Court, Palmers-
ton Road. High Class Board Residence. One minute Sea and
Station. Separate Tables. Moderate Tariff.
PROPRIETRESS.

WESTCLIFF'S FINEST HOTEL, "PALMEIRA TOWERS."

WESTCLIFF—continued.

Grosvenor Hotel. Best position Westcliff Promenade. All rooms face sea. Stands in own picturesque grounds. Tennis. Croquet. Garage. Superior cuisine. Under new and personal supervision of Proprietress. Telephone 437 Southend.

Carlton Private Hotel, Winton Avenue—Close Station. Band, and Sea. Full sized Billiard Table. Accommodation for 50. Well recommended. Terms from 3 gns. per week—10/6 per day. 'Phone 135 Southend.
Mrs. and Miss PARSONS.

Sandringham Hotel, Westcliff Avenue. Central. Perfect Cuisine. Lounge, Billiards. Special terms permanencies. Write for illustrated Tariff. Telephone 395. Telegrams: "Sandringham, Westcliff."

Whitehall Hotel, Manor Road. Facing Sea. Three Minutes Station. Inclusive £3 3s., or 10s. 6d. per day. Weekends 21/-. Special arrangements for City gentlemen. Full-sized Billiard Table. Extension and Sports Room now opened. 'Phone 161 Southend. Garage.
Mr. and Mrs. H. CLINCH.

Queen Anne's, The Cliffs. Facing Sea close to Bandstand. Electric light. Separate tables. Moderate terms. Telephone 691 Southend. Resident Proprietress.

Mount Liell Private Hotel. Facing Sea. Finest position in Westcliff. Gas Fires. Excellent Cuisine. Terms from 10/6 per day. Phone 471 Southend.

Leas Hotel, Westcliff. Parade. Eight minutes Station. Excellent Cuisine. Palm Court Smoking Lounge Terms Moderate. Telephone 638 Southend. Proprietress, Mrs. FOX.

Glenariff, Second Avenue, Westcliff. Board Residence £3 3s. Week-ends 21s. inclusive. Gas fires; bedrooms; separate tables. Ten minutes Station. ½ minute Front. Bookings July onwards. 'Phone Southend 702.

Shorefield Gardens and Welcome Club. Lovely Wooded Grounds on Cliffs. Facing Sea. Residential Club for Gentlemen. 3½ guineas. Write to Secretary for Brochure. Public Café adjoining. Luncheons. Teas, Parties Catered for. Wilson James Gaieties perform here during Summer. 'Phone Southend 363.

Station Private Hotel, Station Road. High Class Boarding Establishment. Minute Sea and Station. Separate Tables. From 3 guineas.
Apply MANAGERESS.

House Agent, WILBER L. BULLIVANT, 40, Hamlet Court Road. Furnished and unfurnished houses. Land Property Auctions. Valuations. Surveys. Map of town free. Offices opposite Station and at Leigh-on-Sea. 'Phone, 47Y Southend.

House Agents. Oldest established. W. G. KIMPTON & Son, F.A.I., 194, Hamlet Court Road. Property List on application. Auctioneers, Surveyors, Valuers, Arbitrators. City offices, 34. Coleman Street. 'Phone Bank 897.

WESTCOMBE PARK

(Kent) from *Charing Cross, Cannon Street,* and *London Bridge,* 7¾ miles. Fares from Charing Cross, 1/7a, 1/3b, 0/11½c. R. T. for two days, 3/2a, 2/6b, 1/9c. From Cannon Street, 1/3a, 1/0b, 0/9c. R.T. for two days, 2/6a, 2/0b, 1/6c. See pp. 547-551.
Map Square 71.

WEST CORNFORTH.
See CORNFORTH, WEST.

WESTCOTT (Bucks),
45¾ miles. Fares, 9/7a, 5/9c. R. T. for two months, 19/2a, 11/6c. Departures *from* London as for Waddesdon. Departures *for* London about 4 times daily.
Map Square 23.

WESTCRAIGS (Lanark),
416¾ miles. No through fares. Departures *from* London as for Edinburgh (Waverley). Departures *for* London about 5 times daily.
Map Square 40.

WEST CULTS (Aberdeen)
525¾ miles. No through fares. Departures *from* London as for Aberdeen. Departures *for* London about twice daily.
Map Square 38.

WEST DERBY (Lancs),
215 miles. Fares, 41/3a, 24/9c. R.T., double fare. Departures *from* London as for Warrington (Central). Departures *for* London about 5 times daily. Pop. 19,571.
Map Square 12.

WEST DRAYTON
(Middlesex) from *Paddington,* 13¼ miles. Fares, 2/3a, 1/4½c. R.T. for two months, 4/7a, 2/6c. Pop. 2,060.
See pp. 491-493.
Map Squares 23 and 56.

WEST EALING. See
EALING, WEST.

WEST END LANE from
Broad Street, 8 miles. Fares, 0/10a, 0/6c. R. T. for two days, 1/5½a, 0/10½c. See pp. 501-505.
Map Square 59, No. 1.

WESTENHANGER
(Kent) from *Charing Cross, Cannon Street,* and *London Bridge,* 64¾ miles. R. T. for two months, 27/2a, 21/10b.
Map Square 24.

	Leave		Arr. at
	CHAR.+	CAN. ST.	LON. B.	WEST'R.

	CHAR.+	CAN. ST.	LON. B.	WEST'R.
AM	—	5.20	5.25	8.41
	9.15	—	9.23	11.17
	11. 0	—	11. 7	1. 1
PM	3. 0	—	3. 8	4.44
	4.30*k*	—	4.37*k*	6.12
	4.30*h*	—	4.37*h*	6.26
	5.24*d*	—	5.34*d*	7.44
	6. 0*e*	—	6. 5*e*	7.35
	7.18	—	7.26	9.47

Sunday Trains.

	CHAR.+	CAN. ST.	LON. B.	WEST'R.
AM	7.45	—	7.52	10. 5
	10.10	—	10.18	12. 0
PM	7.35	—	7.45	9.44

Trains from Westenhanger.

	Leave	Arrive at		
	WEST'R.	LON. B.	CAN. ST.	CHAR. +
AM	7.19	9.32	9.36	—
	9.55	11.43	—	11.57
PM	1. 8	3.26	—	3.40
	3.52	5.50	—	6. 3
	5.24	7.25	7.30*e*	7.49
	8.26	10.22	—	10.35

WESTENHANGER—
continued.

Sunday Trains.

	Leave		Arrive at	
	WEST'R.	LON. B.	CAN. ST.	CHAR. +
AM	7.24	10. 5	—	10.15
PM	5.23	7. 9	—	7.17
	8.17	10.16	—	10.26
	10. 8*s*	—	1.23	—

d Saturdays only.
e Saturdays excepted.
h Fridays only.
k Fridays excepted.
s Third Class only.

ANOTHER ROUTE from
Victoria, Holborn Viaduct, and *St. Paul's,* 67¾ miles. Fares as above.

	Leave		Arr. at
(S.E.& C.)	VICT.	HOL. V.	ST. PL.'s	WEST'R.

	VICT.	HOL. V.	ST. PL.'s	WEST'R.
AM	—	6.40	6.42	11.17
	9.45	—	—	1. 1
	11. 4*d*	10.58*d*	11. 0*d*	1.57
PM	2.12*e*	1.24*d*	1.30*d*	4.44
	2.50*h*	—	—	6.12
	2.50*l*	—	—	6.26
	4.25*e*	—	—	7.35
	7.22	—	—	9.47

Sunday Trains.

	VICT.	HOL. V.	ST. PL.'s	WEST'R.
AM	9.35	—	—	12. 0
PM	5.15	—	—	7.52
	6.35	6.40	—	9.44

Trains from Westenhanger.

	Leave	Arrive at		
	WEST'R.	ST. PL.'s	HOL. V.	VICT.
AM	7.19	9.53	9.55	—
	9.55	12.59	1. 2	12.49
PM	1. 8	—	—	3.37
	3.52	6.58	7. 0	—
	5.24	—	—	8.51
	8.26	11.43	11.45	—

Sunday Trains.

	WEST'R.	ST. PL.'s	HOL. V.	VICT.
AM	7.24	—	—	10.48
	10.58	—	—	1. 5
PM	1. 8	—	—	3.50
	5.23	—	9. 9	—

d Saturdays only.
e Saturdays excepted.
h Fridays and Saturdays excepted.
l Fridays only.

WESTERFIELD (Suffolk)
from *Liverpool Street,* 72¾ miles. Fares, 15/3a, 9/2c. R. T. for two months, 30/6a. Pop. 108.
Map Square 19.

	L'PL.ST.	WESTRFD	WESTRFD	L'PL.ST.
AM	5. 0	7.16	AM 7.37*r*	9.53
	8.15*r*	10.35	8.29*r*	10.30
	8.46	11 23	9.51*r*	11.22
	10.20	12.33	9.39*gr*	11.22
PM 1. 0	2.52	11.23	1.20
	1.33*d*	4.33	PM 1. 3	3.36
	3.18*r*	5.15	1.42	3.42
	5.18*r*	7.11	2.52*r*	4.58
	5.42*d*	8.54	4.33	6.32
	6.39*e*	8.54	5.35	7.51
	7.45*r*	10. 4	7.33*r*	9.22˙
	—	—	7.44*r*	10. 0
	—	—	8.33	11.16

Sunday Trains.

	L'PL.ST.	WESTRFD	WESTRFD	L'PL.ST.
AM	10. 5*r*	12.19	AM 9. 8	11.38
	11.30*r*	2.29	PM 5.50	8.58
PM	3.40	6.21	7.19*r*	9.10
	4.40	6.45	8. 5	10.15

d Saturdays only.
e Saturdays excepted.
g Mondays excepted.
r Restaurant Car.

WESTERHAM (Kent) from

Charing Cross, Cannon Street, and London Bridge, 26 miles. Fares, 5/0a, 4/0b, 3/0c.   R. T. for two months, 10/0a, 8/0b. Pop. 3,162.
Map Square 23.

CHAR. +	Leave CAN. ST.	LON. B.	Arr. at WEST'M.
AM —	5.20	5.25	6.51
—	6.45	6.50	8.29
—	7.56	8. 0	9.11
9.38	—	9.45	11.11
11.15	—	11.23	12.51
PM —	1.12d	1.15d	2.11
2.17d	—	2.23d	3.26
3.50	—	3.57	5. 3
4.55d	—	5. 1d	6. 9
—	5. 4e	5. 7e	6. 9
5.35d	—	5.41d	6.43
—	5.44e	5.47e	6.36
6.34e	—	6.41e	7.27
7.18	—	7.26	8.27
9. 0	—	9. 6	10. 6
10.45l	—	10.51l	11.49
11.45h	—	—	12.41
—	—	—	—

Sunday Trains.

AM 7. 5	—	7.11	8.28
8. 5	—	8.12	9.35
11.15	—	11.23	12.33
—	1. 7k	—	2.31
PM 3. 5	—	·3.13	4.21
6. 0	—	6. 6	7.21

Trains from Westerham.

WEST'M.	LON. B.	Arrive at CAN. ST.	CHAR. +
AM 7. 7	8.10	—	8.19
7.42	8.40	8.44	—
8.40	9.40	9.44	—
9.40	10.28	10.32	—
10.40	11.32	—	11.44
12. 0	1.27	—	1.38
KM 1.40	3. 7	—	3.19
3.50	4.40	—	4.53
5.12d	6.30	—	6.39
5.25e	6.44	—	6.54
7.45	8.54	9. 1	—
9.15	10.15	—	10.23
10.34l	11.34	—	11.44
—	—	—	—

Sunday Trains.

AM 8.48	10. 5	—	10.15
10.50	11.49	—	12. 0
PM 12.47k	—	2.11k	—
5.20	6.27	—	6.41
7.50	9. 7	—	9.18
8.30	9.38	—	—
9.20k	—	10.54k	—

d Saturdays only.
e Saturdays excepted.
h Mondays and Thursdays only.
k Departs from or arrives at Victoria (S. E. & C. R.).
l Wednesdays only.

F. J. Meadows, Motor Car Proprietor. London Road, Garage, King's Arms Hotel. Trains met by Appointment. 'Phone. Westerham 29.

WESTERTON (Dumbarton) 441½ miles. No through fares. Departures *from* London as for Dumbarton. Departures *for* London about 8 times daily.

WESTFIELD (Linlithgow),
441½ miles. No through fares. Departures *from* London as for Edinburgh (Waverley). Departures *for* London about 4 times daily.
Map Square 40.

WESTGATE (Kent) from

Victoria, Holborn Viaduct, and St. Paul's, 72¼ miles. Fares, 15/3a, 12/3b, 9/1c.   R.T. for two months, 30/6a, 24/6b. Pop. 5,096.
Map Square 24.

(VICT.) S. E.&C.)	Leave HOL. V.	ST. PL.'s	Arr. at W'GATE
AM —	3.50k	—	6.34
5. 5	4.57	5. 0	8.29
5.48f	5.40f	5.42f	8.19
9. 0	—	—	10.56
9.20	—	—	11.51
10.40	—	—	12.41
11.30l	—	—	1.23
11.40e	—	—	2.52
PM 1.23d	—	—	3.44
1.25e	—	—	3. 0
2. 8e	—	—	4.27
2.45d	—	—	4.35
3.20e	—	—	5.20
3.29d	—	—	5.29
4.15d	—	—	6.28
—	5.10e	5.12e	7. 6
5.10d	—	—	7.11
5.30d	—	—	8. 9
5.30e	—	—	8.11
7. 0	—	—	8.52
8.50	—	—	10.26
12. 0h	—	—	2. 0
12. 5d	—	—	1.51

Sunday Trains.

AM 7.20	—	—	9.54
9.10	—	—	11. 3
10.25	—	—	12.16
10.40	—	—	12.39
PM 3.30	—	—	6.33
8.25	—	—	10.34

Trains from Westgate.

W'GATE	Leave ST. PL.'s	Arrive at HOL. V.	VICT.
AM 7. 1	9.37	9.39	—
8. 7	—	—	11. 2
9. 9	—	—	11.27
9.21h	—	—	11.23
10.26	—	—	12. 7
11.26d	—	—	1.40
PM 12. 1d	—	—	2.15
12. 1	—	—	2.43
1.28	—	—	3.23
1.51l	—	—	4. 5
1.51e	4.46	—	4.39
2.45	—	—	5. 3
3.29	—	—	5.23
5.46	—	—	7.54
6.28	9.51	9.53	9.46
7.56	—	—	10.25

Sunday Trains.

AM 9. 8	—	11 58	11.51
PM 2.55	—	—	5.32
6.15	—	—	8.20
7.56	—	—	10. 8
9.17	—	—	11. 5

d Saturdays only.
e Saturdays excepted.
f Mondays only.
h Wednesdays only.
k Third Class only
l Mondays, Fridays, and Saturdays only.

ANOTHER ROUTE from

Charing Cross, Cannon Street, and London Bridge, via Strood, 71¼ miles. Fares as above.

CHAR. +	Leave CAN. ST.	LON. B.	Arr. at W'GATE
AM —	—	3.57h	6.34
PM —	1.20d	1.23d	3. 8
—	4.12e	4.15e	6.12
—	6.12e	—	8.11

No Sunday Trains.

WESTGATE—continued.

Trains from Westgate.

W'GATE	Leave	LON. B	Arrive at CAN. ST.	CHAR. +
AM 7. 1	9. 0	9. 4	—
7.25	9.15	9.19	—
8. 7ep	9.48	9.52	—
8. 7d	9.48	9.52	—

No Sunday Trains.

d Saturdays only.
e Saturdays excepted.
h Third Class only.
p Pullman Car attached.

WESTGATE-IN-WEAR-
DALE (Durham), 266¼ miles. No through fares. Departures *from* London as for Bishop Auckland. Departures *for* London about 4 times daily.
Map Square 7.

WEST GOSFORTH.
See GOSFORTH, WEST.

WEST GREEN (Middle-
sex) from *Liverpool Street*, 6¼ miles. Fares, 0/10*a*, 0/8*b*, 0/6*c*. R. T. for two days, 1/8*a*, 1/4*b*, 0/10½*c*. Pop. 18,446. *See* pp. 534-536.
Map Square 52.

WEST GRINSTEAD
(Sussex) from *Victoria, Clapham Junction*, and *London Bridge*, 45 miles. Fares from London Bridge or Victoria, 9/5*a*, 5/8*c*. R.T. for two months, 18/10*a*, 11/4*c*. Pop. 1,623.
Map Square 23.

	Leave		Arr. at
VICT.	CLAP. J.	LON. B.	W.GRIN.
AM 5.18	5.28	5.28	7.38
6.18	6.25	6.35	8.27
8.55	7.56	7.35	10.32
10.15	10.22	10.22	11.55
11.55	—	11.50	1.53
PM 1.40	1.47*e*	1.50	3.36
2. 0	2. 7	2. 5	4.38
—	—	2. 8*d*	4.38
4. 5	4.12	4. 0	5.56
5. 5	5.12	5.14	7. 7
6.15	—	6. 0	7.43
7.20	7.27	7.15	9. 5

Sunday Trains.

AM 6.55	7. 2	7. 2	9.22
PM 7. 0	7. 7	6.38	8.39

Trains from West Grinstead.

Leave	Arrive at		
W. GRIN.	LON. B	CLAP. J.	VICT.
AM 7.17	9.10	9.31	9.19
8.53	10.45	10.40	10.48
10.30	12. 8	12.33	12. 0
PM12.37	3.32	3.22	3.52
2.48	4.27	4.27	4.35
4.33	6.36	6.26	6.34
6. 2	7.48	7.31	7.39
7.55	10. 8	9.53	10. 1
8.50	10.58	11.10	11.17

Sunday Trains.

AM 8.19	10.45	10.23	10.32
PM 3. 6	5. 3	5. 1	5.11
7. 4	8.50	8.33	8.42
—	—	—	—

d Saturdays only.
e Saturdays excepted.

WEST HALLAM (Derby),
139½ miles. Fares, 26/6*a*, 15/11*c*. R. T., double fare. Departures *from* London as for Ilkeston. Departures *for* London about 5 times daily. Pop. 728.
Map Square 13.

WEST HALTON. *See*
HALTON, WEST.

WEST HAM *from*
Ealing, Hounslow, Richmond, and *Wimbledon, via* District Railway. Pop. 300,860. *See v.* 489.

WEST HAMPSTEAD.
See HAMPSTEAD, WEST.

WEST HARROW. *See*
HARROW, WEST.

WEST HARTLEPOOL
(Durham) from *King's Cross*, 247 miles. Fares, 51/6*a*, 30/11*c*. R. T. for two months, 103/0*a*, 61/10*c*. Pop. 68,689.
Map Square 8.

KING's+	W.HART.	W.HART.	KING's+
AM 4.45	12. 8	AM 5.28*r*	1. 5
7.15*r*	2.53	7.38*r*	1.15
10.10*r*	4.53	8. 8*g*	3.15
11.50*r*	6. 9	9.25*r*	4.30
PM 1.15*r*	7.48	PM12. 5*r*	6.15
1.50*r*	8.27	2.25*r*	9.25
5.35*r*	10.58	3.25*r*	10. 0
11.25	5.35	6.50	3.25
—	—	10.15*e*	5.40
—	—	10.15*d*	6. 0

Sunday Trains.

AM11.30*r*	9.35	AM 8.10	5.15
PM11.25	6.27	PM 5.43	5.40
—	—	—	—
—	—	—	—

d Saturdays only.
e Saturdays excepted.
g First and Third Class Pullman Cars only.
r Restaurant Car.

Grand Hotel. The premier Hotel on Tees-side. Close to Station. Every Comfort. Thoroughly Up-to-date. Owned and managed by London and North Eastern Railway Company.
See advt. p. 342.

WEST HOATHLY
(Sussex) from *London Bridge, Victoria*, and *Cannon Street*, 34 miles. Fares *via* East Grinstead, 7/1*a*, 4/3*c*. R. T. for two months, 14/2*a*, 8/6*c*. *Via* Hayward's Heath, 8/9*a*, 5/3*c*. R. T. for two months, 17/6*a*. Pop. 1,522.
Map Square 23.

Leave		Arr. at	
VICT.	CAN. ST.	LON. B.	W.HOAT
AM 6.37	—	6.40	8.29
7.23	—	8. 7	9.47
9.10	—	9. 6	10.53
10.35	—	10.35	12.22
12. 0	—	11.50	1.40
PM 1.20*e*	—	1.38*e*	3.11
1.25*d*	—	1.38*d*	3.18
—	—	2. 5*e*	4.15
2.25	—	2.25*d*	4.15
4. 0	—	4.10	5.46
5.48	—	5.21	7.18
—	—	5.41*e*	7.18
6.50	—	7. 0	8.31
7.15	—	7.38	9.16

Sunday Trains.

AM 8.18	—	8.30	10.12
PM 6.33	—	6.46	8.27
—	—	—	—
—	—	—	—
—	—	—	—

Trains from W. Hoathly.

Leave		Arrive at	
W.HOAT.	LON. B.	CAN.ST.	VICT.
AM 7. 2	8.37	—	8.40
7.30	9. 1*k*	9. 4	9. 8
8.48*h*	10. 5	—	10.12
8.58	10. 7	—	10.46
10. 4	12.13	—	11.35
11.51	1.42	—	1.26
PM 2.32	4.32	—	4.35
3.54	5.21	—	5.55
6.30	8.46	—	8.27
8.42	10.25	—	11.17

WEST HOATHLY—
continued.
Sunday Trains.

Leave	Arrive at		
W.HOAT	LON. B.	CAN.ST.	VICT.
AM 9.40	11.15	—	—
PM 7.53	9.26	—	9.34
—	—	—	—
—	—	—	—

d Saturdays only.
e Saturdays excepted.
h *Via* Hayward's Heath.
k Departs *from* or arr.ves at London Bridge (N.E. & C.) Station.

WESTHOUGHTON
(Lancs), 202 miles. Fares, 41/6*a*, 24/11*c*. R. T. for two months, 83/0*a*, 49/10*c*. Departures *from* London as for Bolton (*via* Manchester). Departures *for* London about 4 times daily. Pop.15,593.

WESTHOUSES (Derby),
137½ miles. Fares, 27/11*a*, 16/9*c*. R.T., double fare. Departures *from* London as for Alfreton. Departures *for* London about 4 times daily.
Map Square 13.

WEST INDIA DOCKS
from *Fenchurch Street*, 2¼ miles. Fares, 0/4*a*, 0/3*b*, 0/2½*c*. R. T. for two days, 0/8*a*, 0/6*b*, 0/5*c*. *See* pp. 524, 525.
Map Square 62.

WEST JESMOND (Nor-
thumberland), 270 miles. Fares, 56/11*a*, 34/2*c*. R.T. for two months, 113/10*a*, 68/4*c*. Departures *from* London as for Newcastle-on-Tyne. Departures *for* London about 6 times daily.

WEST KENSINGTON.
See KENSINGTON, WEST

WEST KILBRIDE (Ayr),
409½ miles. Fares, 83/4*a*, 50/0*c*. R. T. for two months, 166/8*a*, 100/0*c*. Departures *from* London as for Ardrossan. Departures *for* London about 4 times daily. Pop. 4,628.
Map Square 40.

WEST KIRBY (Cheshire),
199 miles. Fares, 41/1*a*, 24/8*c*. R. T. for two months, 82/2*a*. Departures *from* London as for Hooton. Departures *for* London about 8 times daily. Pop. 6,511.
Map Square 11.

WEST LEIGH (Lancs),
193½ miles. Fares, 39/7*a*, 23/9*c*. R. T. for two months, 79/2*a*. Departures *from* London as for Kenyon. Departures *for* London about 5 times daily.
Map Square 12.

WEST MEON (Hants)
from *Waterloo*, 59½ miles. Fares, 12/6*a*, 7/6*c*. R. T. for two months, 25/0*a*, 15/0*c*. Departures *from* London as for Tisted. Departures *for* London about 6 times daily. Pop. 799.
Map Square 23.

WEST MILL (Herts), 32¾
miles. Fares, 6/11*a*, 4/2*c*. R.T. for two months, 13/10*a*, 8/4*c*. Departures *from* London as for Buntingford. Departures *for* London about 9 times daily. Pop. 332.
Map Square 18.

WESTMINSTER
to and from *Mansion House, Charing Cross, Victoria, South Kensington, Praed Street, Baker Street, King's Cross, Moorgate*, and all intermediate stations every few minutes, also to and from *Ealing, Hounslow, Richmond* and *Wimbledon*. Pop.141,578. *See p.* 489.
Map Square 69.

WEST MOORS (Dorset)

from *Waterloo, via* Southampton, 108 miles. Fares, 22/3s, 13/4c. R. T. for two months, 44/6a, 26/8c.
Map Square 27.

W'LOO.	W. MRS.	W. MRS.	W'LOO.
AM 5.40	9.28	AM 7.14r	10. 6
9.30	12.44	9. 4s	12.22
11.30r	2.34	10.53r	2.20
PM12.30r	3.42	PM 1. 5	4.20
.1.30s	4.40	2. 5	6.16
3.30s	6.44	3. 2s	6.26
5.30r	8.36	5. 6r	8.20
6.30r	9.44	7.25	11.28
—	—	—	—

Sunday Trains.

AM11. 0r	2.35	AM 8.59r	2.27
PM 2. 0r	5.43	PM 4.14	8. 3
—	—	—	—

r Restaurant Car.
s Refreshments served.

ANOTHER ROUTE from

Waterloo, via Salisbury, 105 miles.
Fares as above.

W'LOO.	W. MRS.	W. MRS.	W'LOO.
AM 7.30	10.37	AM 7.34	10.56
11. 0r	1.58	8.15r	11.10
PM 1. 0r	4.11	11. 9r	1.56
3. 0r	5.53	PM 3.11r	6. 0
6. 0r	9.32	4.55r	8.30
—	—	—	—

Sunday Trains

12. 0nr	4. 4	PM 4.40	8.57
—	—	—	—

n Noon.
r Restaurant Car.

WEST NORWOOD. See

NORWOOD, WEST.

WESTON (Lincoln) from

King's Cross, 95½ miles. Fares, 19/10 f, 11/11c. R. T., double fare. Departures *from* London as for Holbeach. Departures *for* London about 5 times daily. Pop. 817.
Map Square 18.

WESTON (Somerset), 131

miles. No through fares. Departures *from* London as for Bristol. Departures *for* London about 4 times daily Pop. 6,235.
Map Square 22.

WESTON (Stafford),

132 miles. Fares, 27/4a, 16/5c. R. T. for two months, 54/8a, 32/10c. Departures *from* London as for Colwich. Departures *for* London about 4 times daily. Pop. 361.
Map Square 17.

WESTON-ON-TRENT

(Derby), 126½ miles. Fares, 25/8a, 15/5c. R. T., double fare. Departures *from* London as for Trent. Departures *for* London about 5 times daily. Pop. 330.
Map Square 18.

WESTON-SUB-EDGE

(Worcester), 104 miles. Fares, 21/6a, 12/11c. R. T. for two months, 43/0a, 25/10c. Departures *from* London as for Broadway. Departures *for* London about 8 times daily. Pop. 330.
Map Square 17.

WESTON-SUPER-MARE (Somerset) from *Paddington*, 136⅜ miles. Fares, 28/6a, 17/1c. R. T. for two months, 57/0a, 34/2c. Pop. 31,653.
Map Square 22.

PAD.	WESTON	WESTON	PAD.
AM 5.30	9.37	AM 6.50r	10.15
7.30	11. 0	8.23	11.30
8.45	11.57	8.43	12.20
9. 0d	12.55	11.15r	2. 0
9. 0	1.14	PM12.35	4. 5
11.15r	1.52	2.25	6. 2
PM 1. 0r	3.49	4.15r	7. 0
1.10r	4.52	5. 0r	8.45
2.45	6.50	6.49	10.25
4.15r	7.32	10. 6	2.45
5.15	9.23	—	—
6.30r	9.41	—	—
8. 0	11.49	—	—
12. 0l	7.39	—	—
12.30h	7.24	—	—

Sunday Trains.

AM 9.10r	1.12	AM11.30	3.35
PM12.30r	6.28	PM 4.50	8.10
10. 0	6.47	9. 0	3.15
—	—	—	—

d Saturdays only.
h Saturdays midnight only.
l Saturdays midnight excepted.
r Restaurant Car.

Royal Hotel. Old established Family. Facing the sea, and standing in its own grounds of 8 acres. Finest wines. Cuisine personally supervised. Billiards, garage, and tennis courts. Telephone, No. 277.
Address, PROPRIETORS.

The York. Central. Facing Grand Pier and Bay. Uninterrupted View. Near Golf Links. Excellent Cuisine. Telephone 132. Manageress, Miss ASHMAN.

Madeira Private Hotel. Overlooking Cove and Beach. Electric Light throughout. Every comfort. Moderate terms. Tel. 291. Telegrams, "Sea."

The Sandringham. Splendid Sea View. Central, convenient for Rail and Steamer. Every comfort.
Write Proprietors,
The Misses NICHOLLS & Miss COE.

Crosby Hall Private Hotel. Tel. No. 320. Telegrams, Crosbyhall. First class cuisine. Every comfort. Gas fires in bedrooms. Terms moderate. Illustrated Tariff on application. Special week-end terms.
RESIDENT PROPRIETORS.

WEST PENNARD

(Somerset), 128¼ miles. Fares, 25/3a, 15/2c. R. T. for two months, 50/6a. Departures *from* London as for Glastonbury. Departures *for* London about 4 times daily Pop. 638.
Map Square 22.

WEST RUNTON (Norfolk) from *Liverpool Street*, 140½ miles. Fares, 26/0a, 15/7c. R. T. for two months, 52/0a, 31/2c. Pop. 907.
Map Square 14.

L'PLST	W.RUNT	W.RUNT.	L'PL.ST
AM 5. 5	10.35	AM 7.26r	11.22
8.15r	12.36	8.38	1.20
9.50r	1.46	PM12.30r	3.50
PM12.25r	3.33	3.18r	8.33
12.33r	4.33	5. 9r	9.22
3.10r	6.56	8.26	2.50
5.18r	9.31	—	—

No Sunday Trains.

r Restaurant Car.

ANOTHER ROUTE from

King's Cross, 157¼ miles. Fares as above.

KING's+	W.RUNT.	W.RUNT.	King's+
AM 4.45	10. 3	AM 7.59	1. 5
7.15r	1.15	9.34	3.50
10.10r	4.40	PM12.14r	4.30
PM 1.50r	7. 3	3. 9	9. 0
3. 0	7.22	—	—

No Sunday Trains.

r Restaurant Car.

West Runton Estate Agency. Best selection Furnished Houses and Apartments, West Runton and District. HENRY BRETT & CO., West Runton.

WEST TINSLEY (Yorks),

from St. Pancras 161¾ miles. Fares, 31/3a, 18/10c. R. T., double fare. Departures *from* London as for Sheffield. Departures *for* London about 4 times daily.

WEST VALE (Yorks), 192¼

miles. No through fares. Departures *from* London as for Brighouse. Departures *for* London about 6 times daily.
Map Square 12.

WESTWARD HO!

(Devon). Station at Bideford.

Golden Bay Hotel. Overlooking Sea and Links. Apply MANAGERESS. Telegrams, "Royal," Westward Ho! 'Phone, 14, Westward Ho! Garage, cars for hire.
See advt. p. **342.**

WEST WICKHAM

(Kent) from *Charing Cross, Cannon Street,* and *London Bridge,* 13¾ miles. Fares, 2/6a, ;2/0b, 1/6c. R. T. for two days, 5/0a, 3/6b, 2/11c. Pop. 1,301. *See* pp. 544-547.

WESTWOOD (Yorks),

168¾ miles. Fares, 34/4a, 20/7c. R. T., double fare. Departures *from* London as for Sheffield (Victoria). Departures *for* London about 6 times daily.
Map Square 12.

WESTWOOD, HIGH

(Durham), 269 miles. No through fares. Departures *from* London as for Durham or Bishop Auckland. Departures *for* London about 6 times daily.

WEST WORTHING. See

WORTHING, WEST.

WEST WYCOMBE. See

WYCOMBE, WEST.

WETHERAL (Cumberland)

WETHERAL (Cumberland), 303¼ miles. Fares, 60/10a, 36/6c. R. T. for two months, 121/8a, 73/0c. Departures *from* London as for Carlisle. Departures *for* London about 6 times daily. Pop. 3,328.
Map Square 3

WETHERBY (Yorks)

WETHERBY (Yorks) from *King's Cross*, 191¼ miles. Fares, *Via* Selby or Holbeek 39/7a, 23/9c. R. T. for two months, 79/2a, 47/6c. *Via* York, 41/3a, 24/9c. R. T. for two months, 82/6a, 49/6c. Pop. 2,284.
Map Square 7.

King's+	W'erby	W'erby	King's+
AM 4.45h	10.45	AM 7.13r	1. 5
4.45	10.45	8.41r	1.30
7.15r	12.22	8.41hr	3.50
8.45	3.55	10.27r	4.30
10.10hr	3.55	PM 2.13r	9.25
11.30hr	6. 3	4. 2kr	9.25
PM 1.40r	6. 3	7.26	3.25
1.50r	7. 9	9.13	6. 0
4. 0r	9.16	—	—
10.45e	8.16	—	—

Sunday Trains.

AM10.45	8.16	—	—

e Saturdays excepted.
h Via York.
k Via Harroga*e.*
r Restaurant Car.

WETTON MILL (Stafford)

WETTON MILL (Stafford), 167¾ miles. No through fares. Departures *from* London as for Leek. Departures *for* London about 4 times daily. Pop. (Wetton) 284.

WETWANG (Yorks)

WETWANG (Yorks), 211¾ miles. No through fares. Departures *from* London as for Driffield. Departures *for* London about 3 times daily. Pop. 540.
Map Square 8.

WEYBOURNE (Norfolk)

WEYBOURNE (Norfolk) from *King's Cross*, 153 miles. Fares, 25/5a, 15/3c. R. T. for two months, 50/10a, 30/6c. Departures *from* London as for Holt. Departures *for* London about 4 times daily. Pop. 330.
Map Square 14.

Weybourne Court Hotel.
Open all the year round. R.A.C. listed.
See advt. p. 341.

WEYBRIDGE (Surrey)

WEYBRIDGE (Surrey) from *Waterloo*, 19½ miles. Fares, 4/0a, 2/5c. R. T. for eight days, 8/0a, 4/10c. Pop.6,688.
Map Square 23.

W'loo	Weybr	Weybr	W'loo
AM 4.50	5.41	AM 3.12	3.58
6.10	7. 2	5.20	6.13
6.50	7.24	6.54	7.41
7. 0	7.39	7.58	8.21
7.50	8.29	7.53	8.36
8.15	8.52	8.23	9. 5
9.15	9.58	8.35	9. 8
10.20	11. 0	8.50	9.31
10.34	11.11	9. 3	9.36
11.20	11.58	9.35	10.11
PM12.14d	12.46	10. 4	10.45
12.15	12.58	11. 4	11.46
12.40e	1.12	PM12. 4	12.46
12.40d	1.15	12.41	1.20
12.54d	1.33	1. 4	1.46
1.15d	1.46	2. 4	2.46
1.20	2. 0	2.31	3. 6
1.44d	2.17	3. 4	3.46
2.20	3. 0	4. 5	4.46
2.34	3.11	4.41	5.20
3.15	3.58	5. 4	5.46
3.40	4.13	5.38	6.16

WEYBRIDGE—continued.

W'loo.	Weybr.	Weybr.	W'loo.
PM 4.20	5. 0	PM 6. 4	6.46
4.40	5.16	7. 4	7.46
4.54e	5.31	8. 4	8.46
5.15e	5.46	8.31	9. 6
5.20	6. 0	8.48	9.26
5.44e	6.17	9. 4	9.46
5.54e	6.31	10. 4	10.46
6.15e	6.46	10.29	11.10
6.20	7. 0	11.26	12.16
6.40d	7.13	—	—
7. 0e	7.38	—	—
7.20	8. 0	—	—
8.20	9. 0	—	—
8.55	9.39	—	—
9.20	10. 0	—	—
10.20	11. 0	—	—
11.15e	11.54	—	—
11.40	12.18	—	—

Sunday Trains.

AM 8. 0	8.37	AM 3.12	3.58
8.20	9. 3	8.58	9.45
9.20	10. 7	10.35	11.16
9.45	10.23	11.53	12.41
10.20	11. 6	PM12.53	1.41
11.20	12. 6	1.56	2.44
PM12.20	1. 6	2.56	3.44
1.20	2. 6	4.53	5.41
1.50	2.23	5.59	6.46
3.20	4. 6	6.53	7.41
4.20	4.59	7.53	8.41
5.20	5.59	8.10	8.52
6.30	7. 9	8.55	9.44
7.20	7.59	9.22	10. 1
8.20	9. 6	9.52	10.41
9.28	10.13	10. 3	10.47
9.45	10.26	10.54	11.43
10.15	10.59	—	—

d Saturdays only.
e Saturdays excepted.

Hand and Spear Hotel.
For Families and Gentlemen. High ground. Among pines. Close to Station and near Thames, the Wey and Brooklands. Excellent cuisine. Table d'Hote daily. Telephone No 9. Garage. Under the personal supervision of Mrs. ALFRED UNWIN.

Lincoln Arms Hotel, Weybridge Overlooking river. Fine gardens. Electric light. Large and small parties catered for. Telephone, 109.

Oatlands Park Hotel. Largest and most important Hotel in Weybridge and Walton District Grounds 36 acres. Accommodation, 150 guests. Newly appointed decorated throughout. First Class cuisine. Garage, Tennis, Eoating. Close Burhill and St Georges Hill Golf Clubs. Telephone, Weybridge 666.

Estate Agents, Auctioneers and Valuers, Ewbank & Co. (H. B. Ewbank, F.A.I.) Offices: Weybridge. Phone 61 and 62; and at London.

Estate Agents, Alex. H. Turner & Co. (incorporated with Alfred Savill & Sons), Station Approach. Telephone 12; and at Guildford, Woking, and London.

WEYHILL (Hants)

WEYHILL (Hants), 70 miles. Fares, 14/5a, 8/8c. R. T. for two months, 28/10a, 17/4c. Departures *from* London as for Andover Junction. Departures *for* London about 5 times daily. Pop. 377.
Map Square 22.

WEYMOUTH (Dorset)

WEYMOUTH (Dorset) from *Waterloo*, 142 miles. Fares, 29/10a, 17/11c. R. T. for two months, 59/8a, 35/10c. Pop. 24,570.
Map Square 27.

W'loo.	Weymth.	Weymth.	W'loo
AM 5.40	10.13	AM 7.35s	11. 0
5.50	12.17	9.20r	12.50
8.30s	12.37	11.15	2.50
10.30	1.58	11.55	4.20
PM12.30r	3.56	PM 1.18	4.50
2.30s	5.56	3.17	6.58
4.30r	7.56	5.20r	8.50
6.30r	9.54	6.40	11.28
—	—	9.50	3.58

Sunday Trains.

AM11. 0r	3.34	AM10. 0	2.27
PM 2. 0r	6.33	PM 2.20r	6.24
—	—	5.20r	9.31
—	—	9.50	3.58

r Restaurant Car.
s Refreshments served.

ANOTHER ROUTE from *Paddington*, 154½ miles. Fares as above.

Pad.	Weymth	Weymth	Pad.
AM 1. 0g	10.35	AM 6.55	10.52
5.30	11.31	8.55	12.55
9.30	12.50	10.30	3.20
10.30	1.50	11.50	3.50
PM12.30r	4.20	PM 1.50t	5.30
2. 0	5.40	3.10r	6.50
3.30	6.40	3.45hr	7.35
5. 5	9.15	4.30	8.20
—	—	7.25	2.45
—	—	8.35k	2.45

Sunday Trains.

PM 2.40	6.52	AM 9.35	3.35
—	—	PM 3.35r	7.55

g Mondays excepted.
h Weymouth Landing Stage.
k Thursdays and Third Class only.
r Restaurant Car.
t Tea Car.

Gloucester Hotel.
Characteristic Georgian Architecture. Situated on the Marine Front with sea views from almost every window. Telegrams, "Gloucester, Weymouth"; Telephone No. 170.
See advt. p. 343.

Wyke House Residential Hotel. Superb Old Residence Modernly equipped. In own extensive grounds, 500 feet above sea level. Tennis. Croquet. Golf. Irreproachable service and catering. Telephone 160. Telegrams, "Wyrek." *See advt. p.* 343.

Hotel Burdon. Facing Sea. All Public Rooms Sea Front. 'Bus meets trains. Golf. Fishing. Special Winter Terms. Tariff. Phone 144.
SEFTON SMITH.
See advt. p. 343.

The Royal Hotel, Limited. Leading and only modern Hotel, facing Sea. Electric light. Lift. All Public Rooms, and most Bedrooms face the Sea. Hotel 'Bus meets all trains. Accommodation for 30 cars. Pic. Telephone No. 262.

For completion of Advertisements, see over.

WEYMOUTH—*continued.*

Gilchrist's Private Hotel, Esplanade. An ideal winter residence. One minute Station. Home-like, comfortable, every convenience. Suitable business visitors. Moderate charges.

Clarence House Private Hotel. Established 1877. Telephone: Weymouth 392. Facing Bay, Alexandra Gardens and Pier. Moderate Tariff. Miss TUCKER, Proprietress.

Hotel Edward, Alexandra Gardens. Facing Bay and Landing Stage of Channel Island Steamers. Fine Rooms. Excellent Cuisine. Home Comforts. Electric Light throughout. Moderate Terms. Telephone 199. JAMES STIRTON, Resident Proprietor.

Your Weymouth holiday will be incomplete without visiting the **Rambler Restaurant,** Old Castle Road. Tennis, hard courts and grass. Tents. Day Bungalows for hire. Private Bathing. Unrivalled situation and every convenience.

WHALEY BRIDGE (Cheshire), 178½ miles. Fares, *via* Macclesfield, 35/3 *a*, 21/2*c*. R. T., double fare. *Via* Stockport, 37/9*a*, 22/8*c*. R. T., double fare. Departures *from* London as for Macclesfield or Stockport. Departures *for* London about 4 times daily. *Map square 12.*

WHALLEY (Lancs), 213½ miles. Fares, 43/9*a*, 26/3*c*. R. T. for two months, 87/6*a*, 52/6*c*. Departures *from* London as for Blackburn. Departures *for* London about 8 times daily. Pop. 1,327. *Map Square 12.*

WHAPLODE (Lincoln) from *King's Cross*, 98½ miles. Fares, 20/7*a*, 12/4*c*. R. T., double fare. Departures *from* London as for Holbeach. Departures *for* London about 5 times daily. Pop. 2,270. *Map Square 18*

WHARRAM (Yorks), 215½ miles. Fares 45/0*a*, 27/0*c*. R. T., double fare. Departures *from* London as for Malton. Departures *for* London about 4 times daily. Pop. 181. *Map Square 8.*

WHATSTANDWELL (Derby), 140½ miles. Fares, 29/0*a*, 17/5*c*. R. T., double fare. Departures *from* London as for Ambergate. Departures *for* London about 4 times daily. *Map Square 12.*

WHAUPHILL (Wigtown), 392½ miles. Fares, 71/0*a*, 42/7*c*. R. T. for two months, 142/0*a*, 85/2*c*. Departures *from* London as for Wigtown. Departures *for* London about 4 times daily. *Map Square 43.*

WHEATHAMPSTEAD

(Herts) from *King's Cross*, 25 miles. Fares, 5/2 *t*, 3/1*c*. R. T. for two months, 10/4*a*. Pop. 2,870. *Map Square 23.*

KING's +	WHSTD.	WHSTD.	KING's +
AM 7.45	8.43	AM 7.46	8.41
9.20	10. 9	8.53	9.44
11.30	12.33	11.33	12.45
PM 1. 8	2.18	PM 1.22	2.22
4.15	5.18	4.24	5.45
5.50	6.51	7. 2	8. 5
7. 0	8. 3	8.38	9.50
9.10*d*	10.10	—	—

WHEATHAMPSTEAD

—*continued.*

Sunday Trains.

KING's+	WHSTD.	WHSTD.	KING's+
AM 8.30	9.33	AM 8.37	9.53
PM 7.10	8. 5	PM 6.23	7.40
—	—	8.41	9.48

d Saturdays only.

WHEATLEY (Oxon) from *Paddington*, 48 miles. Fares, *via* Thame, 10/0*a*, 6/0*c*. R. T. for two months, 20/0*a*. *Via* Oxford, 26/8*a*, 16/0*c*. Pop. 918. *Map Square 23.*

PAD.	WH'TL'Y	WH'TL'Y	PAD.
AM 5.30*h*	8.40	AM 7.19	9.20
	8.12	10.22	8.40	10.40
9.45*h*	11.31	8.42*h*	10.45
PM12.18	2.23	10.22*h*	12. 5
2.23	4.23	11.31	1.18
4.45*h*	6.50	PM 2.23*h*	4.15
6.25	8.13	2.55	4.40
7.30*dh*	9.13	4.28*h*	7.20
9. 0*d*	11. 8	6.50	9.18
—	—	8.13*h*	10.45
—	—	9.13*d*	11.41
—	—	11. 8*d*	3.50

Sunday Trains.

AM 9.12	11.19	AM 7.23	10.14
PM 4. 0	6.14	11.19*h*	2.40
4.10*h*	6.17	PM 6.17	8.25

d Saturdays only.
h Via Oxford.

WHEELOCK (Cheshire), 158½ miles. Fares, 32/11*a*, 19/9*c*. R. T. for two months, 65/10*a*. Departures *from* London as for Stoke-on-Trent. Departures *for* London about 4 times daily. Pop. 672. *Map Square 12.*

WHERWELL (Hants) from *Waterloo*, 67½ miles. Fares, 14/2*a*, 8/6*c*. R. T. for two months, 28/4*a*, 17/0*c*. Departures *from* London as for Longparish. Departures *for* London about 4 times daily. Pop. 529. *Map Square 23.*

WHETSTONE (Leicester), from *Marylebone*, 98½ miles. Fares, 20/2*a*, 12/1*c*. R. T., double fare. Pop. 1,386. *Map Square 18.*

M'BONE	WHETS'N.	WHETS'N.	M'BONE.
AM 2.32	7. 8	AM 6.19	9.46
6.45	10.12	7.30	10.36
10. 0*kr*	1.23	8.39	12. 2
PM12.15*r*	3. 5	11.24*hr*	3. 0
4.30	7. 0	PM12. 7*dr*	3. 0
6.25*e*	9.44	1.28	4.56
6.25*d*	9.51	5.24*r*	8.55
—	—	6.59*r*	9.55

Sunday Trains.

AM 9.30	12.50	AM 6.24	10.13
PM 6.30	10.25	PM 5. 9	8.58

d Saturdays only.
e Saturdays excepted.
h Wednesdays only.
k Wednesdays and Saturdays only.
r Restaurant Car.

WHIMPLE (Devon) from *Waterloo*, 163½ miles. Fares, 34/2*a*, 20/6*c*. R. T. for two months, 68/4*a*, 41/0*c*. Departures *from* London as for Sidmouth Junction. Departures *for* London about 6 times daily. Pop. 730. *Map Square 26.*

WHIPPINGHAM (Isle of Wight), 85½ miles. Fares, 19/2*a*, 11/9*c*. R. T. for two months, 38/4*a*, 23.6*c*. Departures *from* London as for Ryde. Departures *for* London about 4 times daily. Pop. 2,545. *Map Square 28.*

WHISSENDINE (Rutland), 99½ miles. Fares, 19/10*a*, 11/11*c*. R. T., double fare. Departures *from* London as for Ashwell. Departures *for* London about 4 times daily. Pop. 673. *Map Square 18.*

WHISTLEFIELD (Dumbarton), 468½ miles. Fares, 86/3*a*, 51/9*c*. R. T. for two months, 172/6*a*, 103/6*c*. Departures *from* London as for Arrochar and Tarbet. Departures *for* London about 4 times daily. *Map Square 40.*

WHITACRE (Warwick), 121½ miles. Fares, 22/1*a*, 13/3*c*. R. T. double fare. Departures *from* London as for Water Orton. Departures *for* London about 4 times daily. Pop. 606. *Map Square 17.*

WHITBURN (Linlithgow), 413½ miles. No through fares. Departures *from* London as for Edinburgh (Waverley). Departures *for* London about twice daily. Pop 1,971.

WHITBY (Yorks) from *King's Cross*, 244½ miles. Fares, 50/10*a*, 30/6*c*. R.T. for two months, 101/8*a*, 61/0*c*. Pop. 12,512. *Map Square 8.*

KING's +	WHITBY	WHITBY	KING's+
AM 4.45	11.57	AM 7.10*r*	1.15
7.15*r*	3.50	7.52	3.50
10. 0*r*	3.55	8.31*rt*	4.30
10.10*r*	4.37	10.40*r*	4.45
11.50*r*	6.59	PM12.15*r*	6.30
PM 1.50*r*	8.20	1.25*r*	7.30
11.25*e*	6.50	3.55*r*	10. 0
11.25*d*	12.14	7. 0	3.25
—	—	8. 4*e*	5.40
—	—	8. 4*d*	6. 0

Sunday Trains.

PM11.25	6.50	PM 6. 0	5.40

d Saturdays only.
e Saturdays excepted.
r Restaurant Car.
t West Cliff Station.

Hotel Metropole. Principal Hotel facing Sea. Magnificent Lounge. Telegrams : " Metropole, Whitby." Telephone : 62 Whitby. FREDERICK HOTELS, Ltd. *See advt. p. 344.*

Crown Hotel. Near station, Beach, and Golf Links. Modern Tariff. *See advt. p 344.*

Royal Hotel, Whitby. Facing Sea. Self-contained Suites of Rooms. Hotel re-furnished throughout. Terms, apply— Phone 125. Manager.

Sandsend Hotel. Two miles from Whitby. First - class. Superb Scenery. Facing Sea. Bracing. Garage. 'Phone, Sandsend " 3." *See advt. p. 344.*

WHITBY.—ROYAL HOTEL. Private Suites Moderate Tariff.

WHITCHURCH (Hants) from *Waterloo*, 59¼ miles. Fares, 12/4*a*, 7/5*c*. R.T. for two months, 24/8*a*, 14/10*c*. Pop. 2,370.
Map Square 23.

W'LOO	WHITCH.	WHITCH.	W'LOO.
AM 5.50	8.13	AM 8.13	9.56
7.30	9.37	9.30	10.56
9.30	11.23	10.49*s*	12.22
11.30*r*	1.24	PM12.33*r*	2.20
PM 1.30*r*	3. 4	2.20	4.20
3.30*s*	5. 5	4.26*s*	6.26
5. 0	6.40	5.47	7.40
6. 0*r*	7.51	8.19	10.50
7.30	9. 5	9.42	11.28
8. 0	10.10	—	—

Sunday Trains.

AM 9. 0	11.12	AM10.28	12.11
PM 6. 0	7.45	PM 6.57	9.12

r Restaurant Car.
s Refreshments served.

ANOTHER ROUTE from *Paddington*, 67 miles. Fares as above.

PAD.	WHITCH.	WHITCH.	PAD.
AM 7.30	9.45	AM 7.42	10. 0
9.30	12.27	8.45	10.52
PM12.30*r*	2.36	10.56	12.55
2.45	4.45	PM12.28	2.50
5.55	7.44	3. 2	5.50
8. 0*d*	10.46	5.58*r*	8.20

No Sunday Trains.
d Saturdays only.
r Restaurant Car.

WHITCHURCH (Salop), from *Euston*, 170¾ miles. Fares, 34/7*a*, 20/9*c*. R.T. for two months, 69/2*a*. Pop. 5,656.
Map Square 12.

EUSTON	WCHURCH.	WCHURCH.	EUSTON
AM 2.35	8. 3	AM 8.10*er*	12. 5
5. 0	9.45	8.10*dr*	12.20
8.30*r*	12.46	9.50*r*	1.45
10. 0*r*	1.46	11.32*h*	3.45
11.50*r*	3.50	11.32*r*	4.15
12. 0*nr*	5. 3	PM12.22*t*	5.35
PM 1.30*er*	5.49	1.45*t*	5.50
2.35*t*	6.30	3.10*r*	7.30
4. 5*r*	8. 8	5.10*er*	9. 5
5.20*r*	9.44	5.10*dr*	9.15
9.30	2.15	6.30*r*	10.45
11. 0*d*	2.29	10.30	5. 0

Sunday Trains.

PM 9.15	2.35	AM 7. 5*r*	1.30
—	—	PM 1.10*r*	5.45
—	—	10.22	5. 0

d Saturdays only.
e Saturdays excepted.
h Mondays and Saturdays only.
n Noon.
r Restaurant Car.
t Tea Car.

WHITEBEAR (Lancs), 199¼ miles. Fares, 41/6*a*, 24/11*c*. R. T. for two months, 83/0*a*. Departures *from* London as for Wigan. Departures *for* London about 6 times daily.

WHITEBOROUGH (Notts), 140¼ miles. Fares, 28/2*a*, 16/11*c*. R. T., double fare. Departures *from* London as for Alfreton. Departures *for* London about 4 times daily.

WHITECHAPEL from *Ealing, Hounslow, Richmond, Wimbledon* and *Mansion House*, *See* p. 489.
Map Square 61.

WHITECRAIGS (Renfrew), 403 miles. Fares, 82/6*a*, 49/6*c*. R. T. for two months, 165/0*a*. Departures *from* London as for Glasgow (Central). Departures *for* London about 4 times daily.
Map Square 40.

WHITECROFT (Glo'ster), 136¾ miles. Fares, 28/6*a*, 17/1*c*. R. T. for two months, 57/0*a*, 34/2*c*. Departures *from* London as for Lydney. Departures *for* London about 4 times daily.
Map Square 22.

WHITEDALE (Yorks), 206¼ miles. No through fares. Departures *from* London as for Hull (Paragon). Departures *for* London about twice daily.
Map Square 8.

WHITEFIELD (Lancs), 192¾ miles. Fares, 39/10*a*, 23/11*c*. R. T. for two months, 79/8*a*, 47/10*c*. Departures *from* London as for Manchester. Departures *for* London about 6 times daily. Pop. 6,902.

WHITEGATE (Cheshire), 179¾ miles. No through fares. Departures *from* London as for Northwich. Departures *for* London about 5 times daily. Pop. 1,503.
Map Square 12.

WHITE HART LANE (Tottenham) from *Liverpool Street*, 7¼ miles. Fares, 0/10*a*, 0/8*b*, 0/6*c*. R. T. for two days, 1/8*a*, 1/4*b*, 0/10½*c*. *See* pp. 534-536.

WHITEHAVEN (Cumberland) from *Euston*, 303¼ miles. Fares, *via* Carnforth, 63/2*a*, 37/11*c*. R. T. for two months, 126/4*a*. Pop. 19,536.
Map Square 6.

EUSTON.	WHTHVN.	WHTHVN.	EUSTON.
AM12.25*k*	11.25	AM 6.33*h*	3.45
2.35	1. 5	6.35*r*	4.15
5. 0	2.58	9.25*t*	6. 0
6.45	4.40	11.35*r*	7.30
11.35*r*	7.18	PM 2.45*r*	10.45
PM 1.30*r*	9.35	7. 5	5. 0
9.30*e*	7.25	—	—
11. 0*d*	10.50	—	—

Sunday Trains.

AM11.45	8.40	AM10. 0*r*	7.30
—	—	PM 6.10	5. 0
—	—	—	—
—	—	—	—

d Saturdays only.
e Saturdays excepted.
h Mondays and Saturdays only.
k Thursdays only.
r Restaurant Car.
t Tea Car

ANOTHER ROUTE from *St. Pancras*, 325¾ miles. Fares as above.

ST. PAN.	WHTHVN.	WHTHVN.	ST. PAN.
AM 4.25	4.40	AM 6.35*r*	5.30
9.50*r*	7.18	9.25*hr*	6.35
PM12.15*r*	9.35	11.35*r*	9.15
11.50*e*	1. 5	PM 2.45	4.20
11.50*d*	8.40	—	—

Sunday Trains.

PM11.45	1. 5	AM10. 0	4.55*v*
—	—	—	—

d Saturdays only.
e Saturdays excepted.
h Wednesdays and Thurdays excepted.
l Corkickle Station.
r Restaurant Car.
v A.M.

WHITEHOUSE (Aberdeen), 549½ miles. Fares, 105/7*a*, 63/4*c*. R. T. for two months, 211/2*a*, 126/8*c*. Departures *from* London as for Aberdeen. Departures *for* London about 3 times daily.
Map Square 35.

WHITE NOTLEY (Essex) from *Liverpool Street*, 41¾ miles. Fares, 8/11*a*, 5/4*c*. R. T. for two months, 17/10*a*. Departures *from* London as for Braintree. (*via* Witham). Departures *for* London about 6 times daily. Pop. 389.
Map Square 24.

WHITERIGG (Lanark), 425½ miles. No through fares. Departures *from* London as for Edinburgh (Waverley). Departures *for* London about 4 times daily.

WHITHORN (Wigtown), 401 miles. Fares, 72/9*a*, 43/8*c*. R. T. for two months, 145/6*a*, 87/4*c*. Departures *from* London as for Wigtown. Departures *for* London about 4 times daily. Pop. 1,033.
Map Square 43.

WHITLAND (Carmarthen) from *Paddington*, 241½ miles. Fares, 49/0*a*, 29/5*c*. R. T. for two months, 98/0*a*. Pop. 1,332.
Map Square 21.

PAD.	WHITLD.	WHITLD.	PAD.
AM 1. 0*g*	10.32	AM 8.40*r*	2.30
8.45*r*	1.58	10.42*r*	4.20
11.50*r*	5.43	PM12. 2*r*	6.15
PM 1.10*r*	8. 9	1.39*r*	8.35
9.15	5.43	3.30*r*	9.25
—	—	7.33	3.30
—	—	—	—
—	—	—	—

Sunday Trains.

PM 9.15	5.43	AM 7. 7	3.35
—	—	PM 7.33	3.30
—	—	—	—

g Mondays excepted.
r Restaurant Car.

WHITLEY BAY (Northumberland), 277¾ miles. Fares, 58/4*a*, 35/0*c*. R. T. for two months, 116/8*a*, 70/0*c*. Departures *from* London as for Newcastle-on-Tyne. Departures *for* London about 8 times daily. Pop. (Whitley) 11,436.
Map Square 3.

WHITLEY BRIDGE (Yorks), 175¼ miles. Fares, 36/0*a*, 21/7*c*. R. T. for two months, 72/0*a*, 43/2*c*. Departures *from* London as for Knottingley. Departures *for* London about 6 times daily. Pop. (Whitley) 386.
Map Square 13.

WHITLINGHAM (Norfolk), 116 miles. Fares, 24/0*a*, 14/5*c*. R.T. for two months, 48/0*a*. Departures *from* London as for Wroxham. Departures *for* London about twice daily. Pop. 67.
Map Square 19.

WHITMORE (Stafford), from *Euston*, 147¼ miles. Fares, 30/8*a*, 18/5*c* R. T. for two months, 61/4*a*. Departures *from* London as for Norton Bridge. Departures *for* London about 4 times daily. Pop. 326.
Map Square 12.

WHITNEY-ON-WYE (Hereford), 161½ miles. Fares, 33/6*a*, 20/1*c*. R. T. for two months, 67/0*a*, 40/2*c*. Departures *from* London as for Hay. Departures *for* London about 3 times daily. Pop. 214.
Map Square 16.

WHITSTABLE (Kent)

from *Victoria, Holborn Viaduct,* and *St. Paul's,* 59 miles. Fares, 12/4*a*, 9/11*b*, 7/4*c*. R. T. for two months, 24/8*a*, 19/10*b*. Pop. 9,842.
Map Square 24.

VICT. (S.E.& C.)	Leave HOL. V.	ST. PL.'s	Arr. at W'STBLE
AM —	3.50*k*	—	6. 3
5. 5	4.57	5. 0	8. 1
5.48*f*	5.40*f*	5.42*f*	7.45
8.25*d*	—	—	9.53
9. 0	—	—	10.28
9.20	—	—	11. 1
10.40	—	—	12.12
11.30*l*	—	—	12.52
11.40*c*	—	—	2.23
PM 1. 5*d*	—	—	2.32
1.23*d*	—	—	3.15
2. 8*e*	—	—	3.57
2.45*d*	—	—	4.10
3.20	—	—	4.51
3.29*d*	—	—	5. 0
4.15*d*	—	—	5.57
—	5.10*e*	5.12*e*	6.39
5.10*d*	—	—	6.42
5.30*c*	—	—	7.43
5.30*d*	—	—	7.37
7. 0	—	—	8.24
8.30	—	—	9.58
12. 0*h*	—	—	1.33
12. 5*d*	—	—	1.29

Sunday Trains.

AM 7.20	—	—	9.27
9.10	—	—	10.36
10.25	—	—	11.49
10.40	—	—	12.11
PM 3.20	—	—	4.57
3.50	—	—	6. 6
8.25	—	—	10. 6

Trains from Whitstable.

Leave WHIT'BLE	Arrive at ST.PL.'s.	HOL. V.	VICT.
AM 7.27	9.37	9.39	—
8.31	—	—	11. 2
9.37	—	—	11.27
9.47*h*	—	—	11.23
10.30	—	—	11.55
11.56*d*	—	—	1.40
PM 12.32*d*	—	—	2.15
12.52	—	—	2.43
1.59	—	—	3.23
2.23*l*	—	—	4. 5
2.23*e*	4 46	—	4.39
3.58	—	—	5.26
6.17	—	—	7.54
6.58	9.51	9.53	9.46
8.29	—	—	10.25

Sunday Trains.

AM 9.44	—	11.58	11.50
PM 3. 4	—	—	4.42
3.24	—	—	5.32
6. 7	—	—	7.30
6.47	—	—	8.20
8.26	—	—	10. 8
9.43	—	—	11. 5

d Saturdays only.
e Saturdays excepted.
f Mondays only.
h Wednesdays only.
k Third Class only.
l Mondays, Fridays and Saturdays only.
p Pullman Car attached.

ANOTHER ROUTE from

Charing Cross, Cannon Street, and *London Bridge, via Chatham,* 58 miles. Fares as above.

CHAR. +	Leave CAN. ST.	LON. B.	Arr. at WHITBL
AM —	—	3.57*h*	6. 3
—	7.16	7.19	9.37
PM —	1.20*d*	1.23*d*	2.40
—	4.12*c*	4.15*c*	5.45
—	6.12*c*	—	7.43

No Sunday Trains.

WHITSTABLE—*contd.*

Trains from Whitstable.

Leave WHITBL.	Arrive at LON. B.	CAN. ST.	CHAR. +
AM 7.15	8.32	8.36	—
7.27	9. 0	9. 4	—
7.53	9.15	9.19	—
*e*8.31*p*	9.48	9.52	—
8.31*d*	9.48	9.52	—

No Sunday Trains.

d Saturdays only.
e Saturdays excepted.
h Third Class only.
p Pullman Car attached.

Bear and Key Hotel.

Family, Commercial. Fully Licensed, entirely free. Stabling. Motor Garage. Inspection Pit. Billiards. Moderate tariff. Telephone 25. For terms apply Manager.
See advt. p. **345.**

Tankerton Hotel. In Oyster

Land. First class. Fully Licensed. Standing high in own grounds facing Sea. Special Week-end Terms. Telephone 24.
Proprietor, JOHN STRANG.

Cliff Hotel. Private,

Residential. Highest Point facing Sea. Moderate and inclusive terms. Own grounds and Poultry. Golf, fishing.
MRS. PENN, Proprietress.

Arran House, Joy Lane.

Board Residence. Hard Tennis Court. Five minutes Sea and Golf Links. Moderate Tariff.
A. & M. DINE.

WHITSTONE (Cornwall)

from *Waterloo,* 222¾ miles. Fares, 46/6*a*, 27/11*c*. R. T. for two months, 93/0*a*, 55/10*c*. Departures *from* London as for Holsworthy. Departures *for* London about 4 times daily. Pop. 364.
Map Square 26.

WHITTINGHAM (North-

umberland), 315¼ miles. Fares, 66/6*a*, 39/11*c*. R. T., double fare. Departures *from* London as for Alnwick. Departures *for* London about 3 times daily. Pop. 1,304.
Map Square 3.

WHITTINGTON (Derby),

from *St. Pancras,* 148¾ miles. Fares, 30/8*a*, 18/5*c*. R. T., double fare. Departures *from* London as for Chesterfield. Departures *for* London about 6 times daily. Pop. 10,344.
Map Square 13.

WHITTINGTON (Salop)

from *Paddington,* 169 miles. Fares, 35/3*a*, 21/2*c*. R. T. for two months, 70/6*a*. Pop. 2,354.
Map Square 17.

	PAD.	WHITTN.		WHITTN.	PAD.
AM	10.40*r*	2.46	AM	8.47*r*	1.25
PM	12.50*r*	5.27	PM	12.59*r*	5. 0
	2.10*t*	7.16		3.22*r*	8. 5
	12.15*h*	8.21		7.24	3.30
	12.15*k*	9.52		—	—

Sunday Trains.

PM	12.50*r*	5.46	AM	11.21	6.20

h Saturdays midnight excepted.
k Saturdays midnight only.
r Restaurant Car.

WHITTLESEA (Cambs),

from *Liverpool Street,* 94⅓ miles. Fares, 15/10*a*, 9/6*c*. R. T., double fare. Departures *from* London as for Peterborough. Departures *for* London about 6 times daily. Pop. 4,208.
Map Square 18.

WHITTLESFORD (Cam-

bridge) from *Liverpool Street,* 49 miles. Fares, 10/5*a*, 6/3*c*. R. T. for two months, 20/10*a*. Pop. 720.
Map Square 18.

L'F'L ST.	WHITLFD.	WHITLFD.	L'F'LST.
AM 5.50	7.47	AM 6.56	8.57
7.18	9.31	7.34	9.27
10. 5	11.50	8. 9	9.47
11.50*r*	1.30	9.42	11.27
PM 12.29*d*	2. 5	PM 12. 8	2. 7
12.48*e*	2.57	1.26*d*	3.18
1.19*d*	3.11	2.24*h*	5. 9
2.48	4.48	2.39*k*	5. 9
4.15	5.36	4.14*r*	6.10
5.49*r*	7.24	5.52	7.58
6.30	8. 0	8.52	10.30
8.22*d*	9.59	—	—
8.22*e*	10.11	—	—

Sunday Trains.

AM 8.12	10. 1	AM 9.19	11.27
PM 1.50	4.11	PM 5.44	7.26
9.12	11.10	—	—

d Saturdays only.
e Saturdays excepted.
h Commencing July 23.
k Ceases to run after July 21.
r Restaurant Car.

WHITTON (Lincoln), 180¼

miles. Fares, 22/5*c*. R. T. for two months, 44/10*c*. Departures *from* London as for Thorne or Barnetby. Departures for London about twice daily. Pop. 167.
Map Square 13.

WHITWELL (Derby), from

St. Pancras 150¾ miles. Fares, 30/3*a*, 18/2*c*. R. T., double fare. Departures *from* London as for Mansfield. Departures *for* London about 5 times daily. Pop. 4,366.
Map Square 13.

WHITWELL (Isle of

Wight). 94½ miles. Fares, 20/3*a*, 12/5*c*. R. T. for two months, 40/6*a*, 24/10*c*. Departures *from* London as for Ventnor Town. Departures *for* London about 4 times daily. Pop. 681.
Map Square 28.

WHITWELL (Norfolk), 153

miles. Fares, 23/7*a*, 14/2*c*. R. T. for two months, 47/2*a*. Departures *from* London as for Guestwick. Departures *for* London about 3 times daily. Pop. 405.
Map Square 19.

WHITWICK (Leicester)

from *Euston,* 115 miles. Fares, 22/11*a*, 13/9*c*. R. T., double fare. Departures *from* London as for Shackerstone. Departures *for* London about 6 times daily. Pop. 1,650.

WHITWORTH (Lancs)

199¾ miles. Fares, 41/1*a*, 24/8*c*. R.T. for two months, 82/2*a*, 49/4*c*. Departures *from* London as for Rochdale. Departures *for* London about 6 times daily. Pop. 8,782.
Map Square 12.

WHYTELEAFE (Surrey),
from *Charing Cross, Cannon Street* and *London Bridge*, 18¼ miles. Fares, 3/1*a*, 2/5*b*, 1/10*c*. R. T. for eight days, 6/3*a*, 4/10*b*, 3/6*c*.

	Leave		Arr. at
CHAR.+	CAN. ST.	LON. B.	W'LEAFE
AM —	4.44	5. 0	5.53
—	—	7.50*l*	8.53
—	—	9.13*l*	9.50
—	10.12	10.15	10.54
10.55	—	11. 3	11.49
—	11.40*d*	11.43*d*	12.24
11.48*e*	—	11.54*e*	12.35
PM —	12.40*d*	12.43*d*	1.19
—	—	*e*12.45*l*	1.19
12.55*d*	—	1. 4*d*	1.46
—	1.20	1.23	2. 0
—	—	*d*1.50*l*	2.28
2. 3*s*	2. 8*d*	2.10	2.54
—	—	*d*2.22*l*	3. 5
2.46*d*	—	2.52*d*	3.32
3.15	—	3.21	4. 5
—	—	*d*4.20*l*	4.56
—	4.24*e*	4.28*e*	5. 9
—	4.44*e*	4.48*e*	5.26
—	—	*d*4.50*l*	5.26
5. 6*e*	—	5.14*s*	5.53
5.30*e*	—	5.37*e*	6.13
5.30*d*	—	5.36*d*	6.12
—	—	*e*5.48*s*	6.28
—	6.20*e*	6.23*s*	6.57
6.17*d*	—	6.23*d*	6.58
6.46*e*	—	6.53*s*	7.32
7.24*s*	7.28*e*	7.30	8.13
8.28	—	8.36	9.19
9.25	—	9.31	10.11
10.17	—	10.23	11. 6
11.42	—	—	12.21

Sunday Trains.

AM 6.25	—	6.32	7.19
9. 8	—	9.14	9.50
10.20	—	10.28	11.17
PM 1.30	—	1.37	2.19
5.25	—	5.32	6.14
6.50	—	6.56	7.35
7.45	—	7.52	8.29
8.38	—	8.45	9.27
9.40	—	9.47	10.29

Trains from Whyteleafe.

Leave	Arrive at		
W'LEAFE	LON. B.	CAN.ST.	CHAR.+
AM 7.24	7.58	—	8. 7
7.49	8.24	8.28	—
8. 7	8.40	8.44	—
8.30	9. 5	9. 9	—
8.41	9.22	—	9.30
9. 3	9.40	9.44	—
9.44	10.19	10.22	—
10.24	11. 0	—	—
10.46	11.24	—	11.33
11.52	12.26	—	—
PM 1.22	1.58	—	2. 5
2. 0*e*	2.37*e*	—	2.45
2.29	3. 4	3. 8*e*	—
3.19	3.52	—	—
4.18	5. 2	—	5.14
5.33	6.10	—	6.18
6.18	6.58	—	7. 5
7.42	8.23	—	8.31
8.26	9. 2	—	9.15
9.22	10. 3	—	10.13
11.14	11.57	—	12.10

Sunday Trains.

AM 7.38	8.16	—	8.27
10.36	11.15	—	11.25
PM 3.52	4.33	—	4.42
5.46	6.25	—	6.34
6.35	7.13	—	7.25
8.21	9. 1	—	9. 9
9.52	10.32	—	10.32

d Saturdays only.
e Saturdays excepted.
l Low Level platform.

WICK (Caithness), from
Euston, 729 miles. Fares, 133/2*a*, 79/11*c*. R. T. for two months. 266/4*a*, 159/10*c*. Pop. 11,322.
Map Square 32.

	EUSTON	WICK	WICK	EUSTON
	PM 1.30*er*	1.30*l*	AM 8.10	7.40*h*
	7.40*er*	4.30*l*	PM 2.30*er*	7.30*l*
	11.35*v*	9.15*h*		

Sunday Trains.

	PM 7.50*r*	4.30*l*		—
	e Saturdays excepted.			
	l P.M.			
	r Restaurant Car.			
	v Thursdays only.			

ANOTHER ROUTE from
Kings Cross, 719¼ miles. Fares as above.

	KING'S+	WICK	WICK	KING'S+
	AM11.50*er*	1.30*l*	AM 8.10	7 .5*k*
	PM 7.45*er*	4.30*l*	PM 2.30*er*	6.30*h*
	11.35*s*	9.15*h*		

Sunday Trains.

	PM 7.45*r*	4.30		—
	e Saturdays excepted.			
	h P.M.	*k* A.M.		
	r Restaurant Car.			
	s Thursdays only.			

WICKENBY (Lincoln), 140¾
miles. Fares, 29/2*a*, 17/6*c*. R. T., double fare. Departures *from* London as for Lincoln. Departures *for* London about 4 times daily. Pop. 204.
Map Square 13. Station closed on Sundays.

WICKFORD (Essex) from
Liverpool Street, 29¼ miles. Fares, 5/5*a*, 3/3*c*. R. T. for two months, 10/10*a*, 6/6*c*. POD. 1,473.
Map Square 24.

L'PL. ST.	WICKFD	WICKFD.	L'PL. ST.
AM 5.26	6.45	AM 6.43	7.35
6.50	8.12	7.19	8.23
7.48	8.54	7.46	8.45
9. 1	10. 5	8.14	9.14
9. 6	10.27	8.54	9.46
10. 3	10.58	10.16	11. 7
10.30	11.37	11. 4	11.59
10.47*d*	11.57	PM12. 3*e*	1.16
11.56	12.57	12. 6*d*	1.16
PM12.48*d*	1.35	12.32*e*	1.25
1.50*d*	2.41	3.46*e*	4.51
2. 0*e*	3. 2	3.50*d*	4.56
2.20*e*	3.33	5.12	6. 8
2.30*d*	3.10	5.55	6.52
2.40*d*	3.39	7.16	8.22
2.58*d*	3.49	8. 2	9.10
3.26	4.32	8.38	9.50
4.15	4.54	9. 1	9.56
4.18	5.13	9.32	10.32
4.48*e*	5.34	10.26	11.30
5.39	6.27	—	—
6. 5*e*	6.55	—	—
6.26*e*	7.25	—	—
6.26*d*	7.27	—	—
7.16*e*	8. 9	—	—
8. 2*d*	8.54	—	—
8. 2*e*	8.57	—	—
8.45	9.35	—	—
9.45*d*	10.32	—	—
9.45*e*	10.41	—	—
11. 0	12. 3	—	—
12. 0*m*12.49	—	—

Sunday Trains.

AM 8.45	9.51	AM 8.31	10.25
9.30	10.41	9.37	10.50
10.45	12. 2	10.54	12.40
PM 2.30	3.53	PM 1.56	3.15
6.42	7.52	4.14	5.15
8.46	9.59	6 35	7.44
10.10	11.16	7.37	8.45
—	—	8.29	9.32
—	—	8.40	9.48
—	—	9. 9	10.45

d Saturdays only.
e Saturdays excepted.
m Midnight.

WICKHAM (Hants) from
Waterloo, 68½ miles. Fares, 14/4*a*, 8/7*c*. R. T. for two months, 28/8*a*, 17/2*c*. Pop. 1,198.
Map Square 28.

W'LOO	WICKHM.	WICKHM.	W'LOO
AM 4.50	8. 0	AM 7.59	10.26
7. 0	9.50	9.51	12.11
9.20	11.57	11.18	1.40
11.20	2. 3	PM 3. 1	5.46
PM 3.15	5.38	4.25	7. 7
6.34	8.53	8.16	11.10

Sunday Trains.

PM 6.20	9. 1	PM 7. 1	9.37

WICKHAM BISHOPS
(Essex) from *Liverpool Street,* 41½ miles. Fares, 8/2*a*, 4/11*c*. R.T. for two months, 16/4*a*. Departures *from* London as for Maldon East (*via* Witham). Departures *for* London about 8 times daily.
Map Square 24.

WICKHAM MARKET
(Suffolk) from *Liverpool Street,* 84½ miles. Fares, 17/9*a*, 10/8*c*. R. T. for two months, 35/6*a*. Pop. 1,343.
Map Square 19.

L'PL. ST.	WICKM.	WICKM.	L'PL. ST.
AM 5. 0	7.46	AM 7.54*r*	10.30
8.15*r*	11.15	8.58*r*	11.22
10.20	1. 6	10. 9*h*	1.20
PM 1. 0	3.28	11.34*r*	2. 3
3.18*r*	5.44	PM 1. 9	3.42
4.55*r*	6.58	3.49	5.56
5.18*dr*	7.48	4.57	7.51
5.18*er*	7.51	7. 1*r*	9.22
—	—	8. 1	11.16

Sunday Trains.

AM10. 5*r*	12.32	AM 8.33	11.38
PM 4.40	7.14	PM 6.45*r*	9.10

d Saturdays only.
e Saturdays excepted.
h Tuesdays only.
r Restaurant Car.

WICK ST. LAWRENCE
(Somerset), 139½ miles. No through fares. Departures *from* London as for Clevedon. Departures *for* London about 3 times daily.
Map Square 22.

WICKWAR (Gloucester),
132 miles. No through fares. Departures *from* London as for Bristol. Departures *for* London about 4 times daily. Pop. 860.
Map Square 22.

WIDDRINGTON (Northumberland), 291¾ miles. Fares, 61/5*a*, 36/10*c*. R. T., double fare. Departures *from* London as for Morpeth. Departures *for* London about 6 times daily. Pop. 843.
Map Square 3.

WIDFORD (Herts) from
Liverpool Street, 24¼ miles. Fares, 5/3*a*, 3/2*c*. R. T. for two months, 10/6*a*, 6/4*c*. Departures *from* London as for Buntingford. Departures *for* London about 9 times daily. Pop. 436.
Map Square 23.

WIDMERPOOL (Notts),
from *St. Pancras*, 115¼ miles. Fares, 23/7*a*, 14/2*c*. R. T., double fare. Departures *from* London as for Melton Mowbray. Departures *for* London about 6 times daily. Pop. 175.
Map Square 18.

WIDNES (Lancs),
from *Euston*, *via* Warrington, 188½ miles. Fares, 39/0*a*, 23/5*c*. R.T. for two months, 78/0*a*, 46/10*c*. Pop. 38,879.
Map Square 12.

Euston	Widnes	Widnes	Euston
AM 2.35	7.42	AM 7.42*eh*	12. 5*r*
5. 0*h*	10.12	7.42*dh*	12.20*r*
6.45	12.30	8.48*r*	1.45
8.30*dhr*	1.36	9.37*r*	3.10
8.30*r*	2. 0	10.49*dr*	3.45
10.40*dr*	3.22	10.49*er*	4.15
10.40*er*	4.10	PM12.47*r*	5.50
11.50*er*	5. 8	2. 0*hr*	7.30
11.50*dr*	5.27	3.34*dr*	9.15
PM 1.30*hr*	6.50	3.49*er*	9. 5
2.35*t*	8.22	5.27*hr*	10. 0
5.20*dr*	9.35	9.33	5. 0
5.20*er*	10.25	10.25*h*	5.40
—	—	—	—
—	—	—	—

Sunday Trains.

AM11.45*r*	8. 9	AM10.10	4. 0
—	—	PM 2.37*r*	7.30
—	—	8. 6	5. 0

d Saturdays only.
e Saturdays excepted.
h *Via* Runcorn.
r Restaurant Car.
t Tea Car.

WIDNEY MANOR (Warwick)
from *Paddington*, 102¾ miles. Fares, 21/3*a*, 12/9*c*. R. T. for two months, 42/6*a*. Departures *from* London as for Knowle. Departures *for* London about 4 times daily.
Map Square 17.

WIGAN (Lancs)
from *Euston*, 194 miles. Fares, 40/5*a*, 24/3*c*. R. T. for two months, 80/10*a*. Pop. 89,447.
Map Square 12.

Euston	Wigan	Wigan	Euston
AM12.25	6.23	AM 6.30*er*	12. 5
2.35	8. 0	6.30*dr*	12.20
5. 0	10.26	9.25*r*	1.45
6.45	12. 0	9.56	3.10
8.30*r*	2. 9	11.25*hr*	3.45
10.40*r*	2.47	11.45*r*	4.15
11.35*r*	3.18	PM12.45*t*	5.50
11.50*r*	4.40	1.43*t*	6. 0
PM 1.30*r*	5.38	2.45*r*	7.30
2.35*t*	6.50	4.43*er*	9. 5
5.20*r*	9.20	4.43*dr*	9.15
7.50*e*	12. 2	10.30	5. 0
8. 0*er*	12.18	—	—
9.30	2. 4	—	—
11. 0	2.48	—	—
11.45*e*	5.59	—	—
11.50*d*	9.23	—	—

Sunday Trains.

AM11.45*r*	4.32	AM 9. 7*r*	1.30
PM 6. 0*r*	10.36	9.50	4. 0
7.50*r*	12.2	PM 3.22*r*	7.30
9.30	1.55	11.15	5. 0
—	—	—	—
—	—	—	—
—	—	—	—

d Saturdays only.
e Saturdays excepted.
h Mondays and Saturdays only.
r Restaurant Car.
t Tea Car.

WIGAN—*continued.*

ANOTHER ROUTE (Central)
from *Marylebone*, 228¼ miles. Fares as above.

M'bone	Wigan	Wigan	M'bone
AM 2.32	1.33	AM 6.40*kr*	1.13
8.45*r*	4.33	8. 5*r*	3. 0
10. 0*r*	4.33	9.50*e*	6.38
PM12.15*r*	6.57	11.35*dr*	6.38
5. 0*dr*	11.44	PM 2. 0*r*	8.55
10. 5*e*	7.58	8.55	3.57
—	—	—	—
—	—	—	—
—	—	—	—

No Sunday Trains.

d Saturdays only.
e Saturdays excepted.
k Passengers cross Manchester at own expense.
r Restaurant Car.

WIGSTON (Leicester)
from *St. Pancras*, 95½ miles. Fares, 19/5*a*, 11/8*c*. R. T., double fare. Pop. 8,590.
Map Square 18.

St. Pan.	Wigstn.	Wigstn.	St. Pan.
AM 4.25	8. 8	AM 6.44*r*	9.57
8.25*r*	11.24	8.14*r*	11. 0
11. 0*r*	1.51	10.37*r*	1.20
11.35	3. 8	PM12.37	3.25
PM 3.30*r*	5.55	1.14*r*	4.10
4.30*r*	7.23	3.19	7. 3
6.30	9.44	5. 4	8.22
—	—	6.23*r*	9. 5
—	—	7.44*e*	11.45
—	—	9.14*e*	5. 5
—	—	11. 0*d*	5. 5

Sunday Trains.

AM 8. 0	12.12	AM 8.24	11.53
PM 6.15*r*	9.32	PM 4.30	8.30
—	—	—	—
—	—	—	—
—	—	—	—

d Saturdays only.
e Saturdays excepted.
r Restaurant Car.

WIGSTON (Glen Parva)
(Leicester) from *Euston*, 111½ miles. Fares, 20/2*a*, 12/1*c*. R. T., double fare. Departures *from* London as for Hinckley. Departures *for* London about 8 times daily. Pop. (Glen Parva) 620.

WIGTON (Cumberland),
310¾ miles. Fares, 62/11*a*, 37/9*c*. R. T., double fare. Departures *from* London as for Maryport. Departures *for* London about 5 times daily Pop. 3,659.
Map Square 6.

WIGTOWN from *Euston*,
388¾ miles. Fares, 70/3*a*, 42/2*c*. R. T. for two months, 140/6*a*, 84/4*c*. Pop. 1,299.
Map Square 43.

Euston	Wigtown	Wigtown	Euston
AM 5. 0	5.11	AM 8. 5*r*	6.25
10. 0*r*	8.15	10. 1*r*	10. 0
PM 8. 0*e*	6.45	PM12.35*rv*	10. 0
11.45*e*	11. 5	4. 5	5. 0*h*
—	—	7.40	7.15
—	—	—	—

Sunday Trains.

PM 8.30	6.45	—	—
11.45	11. 5	—	—
—	—	—	—

e Saturdays excepted.
h A.M.
r Restaurant Car.
v Fridays only.

WIGTOWN—*continued.*

ANOTHER ROUTE
from *St. Pancras*, 394 miles. Fares as above.

St. Pan.	Wigtown	Wigtown	St. Pan.
AM 4.25	5.11	AM 8. 5*r*	6.35
9.50*r*	8.15	10. 1*r*	9.15
PM11.45*e*	11. 5	PM 4. 5	7.25
—	—	6.40*e*	7.50
—	—	6.40*d*	8.57
—	—	—	—

Sunday Trains.

PM11.45	11. 5	—	—
—	—	—	—

d Saturdays only.
e Saturdays excepted.
r Restaurant Car.

WILBURTON (Cambs),
from *Liverpool Street*, 73¾ miles. Fares, 14/10*a*, 8/11*c*. R. T. for two months, 29/8*a*. Departures *from* London as for Haddenham, *via* Ely. Departures *for* London about 4 times daily. Pop. 475.
Map Square 19.

WILBY (Suffolk), 99½ miles.
Fares, 21/0*a*, 12/7*c*. R. T. for two months, 42/0*a*, 25/2*c*. Departures *from* London as for Stradbroke. Departures *for* London about twice daily. Pop. 343.
Map Square 19.

WILLASTON (Cheshire),
159¾ miles. Fares, 32/11*a*, 19/9*c*. R. T. for two months, 65/10*a*. Departures *from* London as for Crewe. Departures *for* London about 6 times daily. Pop. 2,715.
Map Square 12.

WILLENHALL (Stafford)
from *Euston*, 122 miles. Fares, 25/3*a*, 15/2*c*. R. T. for two months, 50/6*a*. Pop. 19,671.
Map Square 17.

Euston	W'hall.	W'hall	Euston.
AM 2.30*h*	7.22	AM 6. 3*hr*	10. 0
5. 0	8.46	7.39*r*	10.40
*e*9.10*hr*	12.22	8.59	12.40
9.15*r*	1. 1	10.26*r*	1.25
11.30*hr*	3.56	11.22*dh*	4.15
PM 1.15*r*	5. 5	11.22*eh*	3. 0
2.20*ht*	5.37	PM 1.17*r*	4.35
4.35*r*	7.24	2.53*dhr*	6.50
5.50*r*	9.24	3.52*ehr*	6.50
6.55*hr*	10. 8	4.59*hr*	8.20
—	—	6. 4*er*	10.20
—	—	9.42*eh*	4. 0
—	—	9.42*dh*	5. 0

No Sunday Trains.

d Saturdays only.
e Saturdays excepted.
h *Via* Walsall.
r Restaurant Car.
t Tea Car.

WILLERBY (Yorks), 222¼
miles. Fares, 35/0*a*, 21/0*c*. R. T. for two months, 70/0*a*. Departures *from* London as for Cudworth. Departures *for* London about 5 times daily. Pop. 1,247.
Map Square 13.

WILLESDEN (Middlesex)
from *Euston*, 5½ miles. Fares, 1/0½*a*, 0/7½*c*. R. T. for two days, 1/9*a*, 1/2*c*. Pop. 165,674. *See* pp. 496-499.
Map Squares 23 *and* 59.

From *Broad Street*, 9¾ miles. Fares, 0/11½*a*, 0/7*c*. R. T. for two days, 1/11*a*, 1/2*c*. *See* pp. 496-499.

IDRIS LEMONADE.

WILLESDEN—*continued.*

From *Earl's Court, via Kensington* (Addison Road), in connection with trains from *Mansion House, Charing Cross*, and *Victoria*, 4 miles. *See* pp. 501-505.

From *Elephant and Castle* (Bakerloo Tube). *See* p. 498.

WILLESDEN GREEN and CRICKLEWOOD from *Baker Street*, 4 miles. Fares, 0/9*a*, 0/5*c*. R. T. for two days, 1/6*a*, 0/10*c*. Pop. 16,565. *See* back of Map. *Map Square* 59.

WILLINGTON (Bedford), from *Euston*, 66½ miles. Fares, 10/5*a*, 6/3*c*. R.T. for two months, 20/10*a*. Departures *from* London as for Bedford. Departures *for* London about 5 times daily. Pop. 370. *Map Square* 18.

WILLINGTON (Durham), 248½ miles. Fares, 51/10*a*, 31/1*c*. R.T. for two months, 103/8*a*, 62/2*c*. Departures *from* London as for Bishop Auckland. Departures *for* London about 5 times daily. Pop. 9,197. *Map Square* 7.

WILLINGTON QUAY (Northumberland), 274¾ miles. No through fares. Departures *from* London as for Newcastle-on-Tyne. Departures *for* London about 6 times daily. Pop. 4,204

WILLITON (Somerset), 157¾ miles. Fares, 32/11*a*, 19/9*c*. R. T. for two months, 65/10*a*. Departures *from* London as for Bishop's Lydeard. Departures *for* London about 5 times daily. Pop. 1,269. *Map Square* 21.

WILLOUGHBY (Lincoln) from *King's Cross*, 128 miles. Fares, 26/6*a*, 15/11*c*. R. T., double fare. Pop. 519. *Map Square* 13.

King's+	Willo'by	Willo'by	King's+
AM 4.45	8.41	AM 6.44	10.40
7.15*r*	11.10	9.55	1. 5
8.45	1. 2	10.50	3.50
11.30	4.17	PM 1. 7*r*	4.30
PM 4. 0*r*	7.10	3.42	9. 0
—	—	5.58*r*	9.25
—	—	—	—

Sunday Trains.

12.0*nr*	4. 1	AM11. 0*r*	3.45
—	—	—	—

n Noon.
r Restaurant Car.

WILMCOTE (Warwick) from *Paddington*, 100 miles. Fares, 20/10*a*, 12/6*c*. R. T. for two months, 41/8*a*. Departures *from* London as for Bearley. Departures *for* London about 6 times daily. Pop. 493. *Map Square* 17.

WILMINGTON (Yorks), 198 miles. No through fares. Departures *from* London as for Hull (Paragon). Departures *for* London about 5 times daily. Pop. 5,425. *Map Square* 13.

WILMSLOW (Cheshire) from *Euston* 177 miles. Fares, 36/11*a*, 22/2*c*. R. T. for two months, 73/10*a*. Pop. 8,266. *Map Square* 12.

Euston	Wil'slow	Wil'slow	Euston
AM12.25	7. 4	AM 8.28*er*	12. 5
2.35	7.29	7.55*dr*	12.20
5. 0	10.37	8.28*er*	1. 0
6.45	12.29	10. 2*r*	1.15
8.30*r*	1.29	11.42*r*	4.15
10.30*r*	2.41	PM12.22*t*	5.35
10.40*r*	3. 0	1. 7*dr*	5.50
11.50*r*	3.14	1.46*er*	6. 0
12. 0*nr*	4.53	2. 1*dr*	6. 0
PM 1.30*r*	5.29	2.43*r*	6.25
2.35*t*	6.47	3.58*r*	8.10
4. 5*r*	7.43	5.10*dr*	9.15
5.20*r*	9. 6	5.18*er*	9. 5
6. 5*r*	9.16	6.32*er*	10. 0
11.50*d*	9.13	10. 2	5. 0
—	—	11.29*d*	5. 0
—	—	—	—
—	—	—	—

Sunday Trains.

AM 9.15	3.12	AM 9.50	4. 0
PM12.10*r*	4.34	PM 1.26*r*	5.45
12.30*r*	8.42	3.10	7.30
6. 0*r*	9.59	4.46*r*	8.55
—	—	7.12	5. 0

d Saturdays only.
e Saturdays excepted.
n Noon.
r Restaurant Car.
t Tea Car.

WILNECOTE (Warwick), 127¾ miles. Fares, 23/2*a*, 13/11*c*. R. T., double fare. Departures *from* London as for Water Orton. Departures *for* London about 5 times daily. Pop. 4,196. *Map Square* 17.

WILPSHIRE (Lancs), 215 miles. Fares, 43/9*a*, 26/3*c*. R. T. for two months, 87/6*a*, 52/6*c*. Departures *from* London as for Blackburn. Departures *for* London about 4 times daily. Pop. 1,068. *Map Square* 12.

WILSDEN (Yorks), from *King's Cross*, 200 miles. Fares, 40/3*a*, 24/2*c*. R. T., double fare. Departures *from* London as for Keighley. Departures *for* London about 6 times daily. Pop. 2,958. *Map Square* 12.

WILSONTOWN (Lanark), 381¾ miles. No through fares. Departures *from* London as for Carstairs. Departures *for* London about 5 times daily *Map Square* 40.

WILTON (Wilts) from *Waterloo*, 86½ miles. Fares, 18/1*a*, 10/10*c*. R. T. for two months, 36/2*a*, 21/8*c*. Pop. 2,024. *Map Square* 22.

W'loo	Wilton	Wilton	W'loo
AM 7.30	10.24	AM 8.35	10.56
10. 0*r*	11. 2	9.56	12.22
12. 0*r*	1.52	11.23*r*	1.56
PM 1. 0*r*	3.13	PM12.52*r*	3. 8
3. 0*r*	5. 1	4. 0*r*	6. 0
5. 0	7.11	5. 1	7.40
6. 0*r*	8.12	5.53*r*	8.30
—	—	8. 3	10.50

Sunday Trains.

AM 9. 0	12.27	PM 6.51*r*	8.57
12. 0*nr*	2.37	—	—
PM 6. 0	8.54	—	—

n Noon.
r Restaurant Car.

WIMBLEDON (Surrey) from *Waterloo, via* Main Line, 7¼ miles. Fares, 1/3*a*, 0/9*c*. R. T. for two days, 2/6*a*, 1/6*c*. Pop. 61,418. *See* pp. 583-585, 591-594. *Map Square* 77.

ANOTHER ROUTE from *Waterloo, via* East Putney, 8½ miles. Fares, 1/3*a*, 0/9*c*. R. T. for two days, 2/6*a*, 1/6*c*. *See* p. 595.

From *London Bridge*, 11¼ miles. Fares, *via* Tooting Junc. or *via* West Croydon, 2/1*a*, 1/3*c*. R. T. for two days, 4/2*a*, 2/2*c*. *See* p. 577.

From *Mansion House*, 10½ miles. *See* p. 489.

From *Victoria*. 9¾ miles. Fares, *via* Tooting Junc. or *via* West Croydon, 2/1*a*, 1/3*c*. R. T. for two days, 4/2*a*, 2/2*c*. *See* p. 577.

WIMBLEDON PARK from *Mansion House*, 9¾ miles. *See* p. 489. *Map Square* 77.

ANOTHER ROUTE from *Waterloo*, 7¾ miles. Fares 1/3*a*, 0/9*c*. R. T. for two days, 2/6*a*, 1/6*c*. *See* p. 595.

WIMBLINGTON (Cambs), from *Liverpool Street*, 85 miles. Fares, 15/3*a*, 9/2*c*. R. T. for two months, 30/6*a*. Pop. 1,238. *Map Square* 18.

L'pool St.	W'gton	W'gton.	L'pool St.
AM 5.50	9.21	AM 7.42*r*	10.23
8.30*r*	11.25	10.36	2. 7
11.50*r*	2.31	PM 1.31*lr*	4. 2*k*
PM 2.34	5.12	1.31	5. 9
5.49*r*	8.24	3.14*r*	6.10
7.10*dr*	9.51	5.42*r*	8.33
—	—	8.23*d*	2.50
—	—	—	—
—	—	—	—
—	—	—	—

Sunday Trains.

PM 3.25	6.17	PM 3.45	6.40
—	—	—	—
—	—	—	—

d Saturdays only.
k Arrives at St. Pancras Station.
l Commencing July 23.
r Restaurant Car.

WIMBORNE (Dorset) from *Waterloo, via* Southampton. 112½ miles. Fares, 23/7*a*, 14/2*c*. R. T. for two months, 47/2*a*, 28/4*c*. Pop. 3,742. *Map Square* 27.

W'loo	Wimbne.	Wimbne.	W'loo
AM 5.40	9.36	AM 7. 5*r*	10. 6
9.30	12.52	8.55*s*	12.22
11.30*r*	2.42	10.44*r*	2.20
PM12.30*r*	3.50	PM12.55	4.20
1.30*s*	4.48	1.56	6.16
3.30*s*	6.52	2.53*s*	6.26
5.30*r*	8.44	4.57*r*	8.20
6.30*r*	9.52	7.15	11.28
—	—	—	—
—	—	—	—
—	—	—	—
—	—	—	—

WIMBORNE—*continued.*

Sunday Trains.

W'LOO	WIMBNE	WIMBNE.	W'LOO
AM 11.0*r*	2.43	AM 8.49*r*	2.27
PM 2. 0*r*	5.51	PM 4. 5	8. 3

r Restaurant Car.
s Refreshments served

ANOTHER ROUTE from
Waterloo, via Salisbury, 109¾ miles. Fares as above.

W'LOO	WIMBNE.	WIMBNE.	W'LOO
AM 7.30	10.45	AM 7.25	10.56
11. 0*r*	2. 7	8. 5*r*	11.10
PM 1. 0*r*	4.19	11. 0*r*	1.56
3. 0*r*	6. 1	PM 3. 2*r*	6. 0
6. 0*r*	9.40	4.44*r*	8.30
—	—	—	—
—	—	—	—

Sunday Trains.

12. 0*nr*	4.13	PM 4.29	8.57
—	—	—	—
—	—	—	—

n Noon.
r Restaurant Car

WINCANTON (Somerset)
from *Waterloo,* 115¾ miles. Fares, 23/4*a*, 14/0*c*. R. T. for two months, 46/8*a*. Pop. 1,976.
Map Square 22.

W'LOO	WINCAN.	WINCAN.	W'LOO
AM 9. 0*r*	12. 1	AM 8.30*r*	11.10
10. 0*r*	2. 9	11. 3*r*	1.56
PM 1. 0*	4.19	11.48*r*	3. 8
3. 0*r*	6.19	PM 1.52*r*	4.30
6. 0*r*	8.56	2.51*r*	6. 0
—	—	4.11	7.40
—	—	5.23*r*	8.30
—	—	6.47	10.50
—	—	8. 7*h*	3.58
—	—	—	—
—	—	—	—

No Sunday Trains.
h Via Eastleigh.
r Restaurant Car.

WINCHBURGH (Linlithgow), 404¾ miles. No through fares. Departures *from* London as for Edinburgh (Waverley). Departures *for* London about 5 times daily.
Map Square 41.

WINCHCOMBE (Gloucester) from *Paddington,* 113¾ miles. Fares, 23/7*a*, 14/2*c*. R. T. for two months, 47/2*a*. Pop. 9,647.
Map Square 17.

PAD.	W'COMBE	W'COMBE	PAD.
AM 5.30	10.28	AM 7.56	12. 5
6.30*k*	11.47	10.20	2.12
9.45	1.57	11.42*r*	2.55
PM 2.10*k*	6.22	PM 4.15*kr*	8. 5
4.45	7.48	5.31*r*	9.15
—	—	6.39	10.45
—	—	—	—
—	—	—	—

Sunday Trains.

PM 4.10	8. 5	AM 8.13	2.40
—	—	PM 5.33*r*	9.48

k Via Stratford-on-Avon.
r Restaurant Car.

WINCHELSEA (Sussex)
from *Charing Cross, Cannon Street* and *London Bridge,* 74 miles. Fares, 15/0*a*, 12/0*b*, 9/0*c*. R. T. for two months, 30/0*a*, 24/0*b*. Pop. 101.
Map Square 24.

	Leave			Arr. at
CHAR. +	CAN. ST.	LON. B		WINCHL.
AM —	5.20	5.25		8.51
9.15	—	9.23		11.28
11. 0	—	11. 7		1.20
PM 1. 0	—	—		4.43
4.30*l*	—	4.37*l*		6.46
—	5. 0*k*	—		6.51
7.18	—	7.26		9.55

Sunday Trains.

AM 7.45	—	7.52		10.19
PM 7.35	—	7.45		9.58

Trains from Winchelsea.

Leave			Arrive at	
WINCHEL.	LON. B.	CAN. ST.	CHAR. +	
AM 6.50	9.32	9.36	—	
9.24	11.43	—	11.57	
PM12.47	3.26	—	3.40	
3.29	5.50	—	6. 3	
5.45	8.54	9. 1	—	
7.49	10.22	—	10.35	

Sunday Trains.

AM 6.59	10. 5	—	10.15	
PM 5. 4	7. 9	—	7.17	
8. 4	10.16	—	10.26	
—	—	—	—	

k Fridays only.
l Fridays excepted.

ANOTHER ROUTE from
Victoria, Holborn Viaduct, and *St. Paul's (via* Ashford), 72¼ miles. Fares as above.

VICT.	Leave		Arr. at
(S.E.&C.)	HOL. V.	ST. PL.'s	WINCHL.
AM —	6.40	6.42	11.28
9.45	—	—	1.20
PM 2.12*e*	1.24*d*	1.30*d*	4.43
2.40*d*	—	—	6.46
2.50*l*	—	—	6.46
2.50*h*	—	—	6.51
7.22	—	—	9.55

Sunday Trains.

AM 9.35	—	—	12. 0
PM 5.15	—	—	8. 7
6.35	6.40	—	9.58

Trains from Winchelsea.

Leave		Arrive at	
WINCHEL.	ST. PL.'s	HOL. V.	VICT.
AM 6.50	9.53	9.55	—
9.24	12.59	1. 2	12.49
PM12.47	—	—	3.37
2. 2	—	—	5.42
3.29	6.58	7. 0	—
7.49	11.43	11.45	—

Sunday Trains.

AM 6.59	—	—	10.48
10.39	—	—	1. 5
PM 5. 4	—	9. 9	—

d Saturdays only.
e Saturdays excepted.
h Fridays only.
l Fridays and Saturdays excepted.

The "New Inn" Hotel.
Family and Commercial. Beautiful situation. Lock-up Garage. Carriages meet train upon request.
A. G. BEADELL, Proprietor.

WINCHESTER (Hants)
from *Waterloo,* 66 miles. Fares, 13/11*a*, 8/4*c*. R. T. for two months, 27/10*a*, 16/8*c*. Pop. 23,791.
Map Square 23.

W'LOO	WINCHTR.	WINCHTR.	W'LOO
AM 5.40	7.25	AM 1.39	3.58
5.50	8.12	7.26	9.26
7. 0	9.51	8.48*r*	10. 6
7.30	9.59	8.57	10.56
8.30*s*	10. 9	10.29	12. 0
9.30	11.14	10.56*s*	12.22
11.30*r*	12.59	PM12.54*r*	2.20
PM 1.30*s*	3. 1	1. 8	3.36
3.30*s*	5. 1	2. 1	4. 6
3.40	6. 5	2.54	4.20
4. 0	6.19	4. 3	6.16
5. 0	6.45	4.54*s*	6.26
5.30*r*	7. 4	6.54*r*	8.20
6. 0	8. 9	7.17	9.52
6.34	8.49	8.39	10.50
7.30	9. 1	9.44	11.28
8. 0	10. 9	--	—
8.55	11.25	—	—
10. 0	11.54	—	—
—	—	—	—
—	—	—	—
—	—	—	—

Sunday Trains.

AM 8.45	11.46	AM 1.39	3.58
9.45	12. 4	8. 6	11.16
11. 0*r*	12.29	10.32	12.11
12. 0*nr*	1.56	PM 1. 6*r*	2.27
PM 2. 0*r*	3.23	4.10	6. 7
5. 5	7.14	6.24	8. 3
6. 0	7.59	7. 6	9.37
7. 0*r*	8.28	8.44	10.52
8.15	9.57	—	—
9.28	11.52	—	—
—	—	—	—

n Noon.
r Restaurant Car.
s Refreshments served.

ANOTHER ROUTE from
Paddington, 79½ miles. Fares as above.

PAD.	WINCHTR.	WINCHTR.	PAD.
AM 7.30	10.11	AM 7.12	10. 0
9.30	12.52	8.16	10.52
PM12.30*r*	3. 4	10.28	12.55
2.45	5.10	11.58	2.50
5.55	8. 9	PM 2.33	5.50
8. 0*d*	11.11	5.30*r*	8.20
—	—	—	—
—	—	—	—
—	—	—	—

No Sunday Trains.

d Saturdays only.
r Restaurant Car.

George Hotel.
First-class Old-established. Near Cathedral and College. Table d'Hôte, separate tables. Winter Garden. Hotel 'Phone 491. Garage 'Phone 368. Cars for hire. Tariff.
THE MANAGERESS.

Black Swan Hotel.
First-class Family and Commercial. Near Cathedral. Coffee, Drawing and Private Sitting Rooms. Billiards. Motor Garage. Posting. Omnibus meets trains. Telephone 450.
H. T. ANSTISS, Proprietor.

WINCHESTER—contd.

R o y a l H o t e l. Leading Family Hotel. Nearest College and Cathedral. Overlooks own attractive Garden. Centre of City but very quiet. Table d'hôte, separate tables. Electric light. Garage. Telephone 31.
GEORGE JAMES, Proprietor.

Eagle Hotel. Facing Station. Under new management. Moderate Tariff and every comfort. Newly furnished and redecorated. Electric Light. Stabling and Garage. 'Phone : 446.
CHARLES BAKER,
Late Chief Steward Royal Mail Co.

Carfax Hotel, Station Hill. Commercial, Comfortable, Unlicensed. Recommended by every Commercial Traveller on the Road. Telephone 269.
E. H. THOMPSON Proprietor.

Apply to **William Tanner,** Auctioneer, Winchester, for Furnished and Unfurnished Residences and other Properties in Winchester and surrounding district.

WINCHFIELD (Hants)

from *Waterloo,* 40 miles. Fares, 8/4a, 5/0c. R. T. for two months, 16/8a, 10/0c. Pop. 466.
Map Square 23.

W'LOO	WINCHFD.	WINCHFD.	W'LOO
AM 5.50	7.21	AM 7.26	8.41
7.30	8.51	8.19	9.26
8.34	9.55	9. 0	9.56
9.20	10.38	9.50	10.56
10.34	11.59	10.56	12.11
PM12.40	2. 1	11.56	1.20
1.15d	2.39	PM 2. 2	3.16
2.34	4. 3	2.53	4. 6
3.40	5. 2	3.56	5.20
4.40	6. 9	4.56	6.16
5.10e	6.19	5.52	7. 7
6. 0	7. 3	7.59	9.26
6.40d	8. 1	10.25	12.16
6.54e	7.59	—	—
8. 0	9.18	—	—
8.55	10.32	—	—

Sunday Trains.

AM 9. 0	10.20	AM 8. 3	9.45
9.45	11.14	10.25	12.41
11.15	12.32	11.31	12.52
PM 5. 5	6.23	PM 5. 0	6. 7
6. 0	7.18	7.54	9.12
7.20	8.48	9.34	10.52
9.28	11. 0	—	—

d Saturdays only.
e Saturdays excepted.

WINCHMORE HILL

(Middlesex) from *King's Cross, Moorgate Street,* and *Broad Street,* 7¼ miles. Fares from King's Cross, 1/5½a, 1/2b, 0/10½c. R. T. for two days, 2/11a, 2/4b, 1/9c. From Moorgate Street and Broad Street, 1/7a, 1/3b, 0/11½c. R. T. for two days, 3/2a, 2/6b, 1/9½c. Pop. 7,493. *See* pp. 511-517.

WINCOBANK (Yorks)

from *St. Pancras,* 162 miles. Fares, 32/9a, 19/8c. R. T., double fare. Departures *from* London as for Sheffield. Departures *for* London about 6 times daily. Pop. 8,095.

WINDER (Cumberland),

304½ miles. Fares, 63/2a, 37/11c. R. T. for two months, 126/4a, 75/10c. Departures *from* London as for Moor Row. Departures *for* London about 4 times daily.
Map Square 6.

WINDERMERE (Westmorland) from *Euston,* 259½ miles. Fares, 53/9a, 32/3c. R. T. for two months, 107/6a, 64/6c. Pop. 6,496.
Map Square 7.

EUSTON	WINDER.	WINDER.	EUSTON
AM12.25	8.53	AM 7.20r	3.10
2.35	10.53	8.30hr	3.45
5. 0	1. 0	9.10kr	4.15
6.45	2.21	9.25hr	4.15
10.40dr	5.13	11.25r	6. 0
11.35r	5.30	PM 2.15er	9. 5
11.50r	7. 5	2.15dr	9.15
PM 1.30er	7.19	4.35r	10.45
1.30dr	7.50	8.35	5. 0
2.35t	9.35	—	—
9.30e	5.43	—	—
11. 0d	5.30	—	—
11.45e	8.28	—	—

Sunday Trains.

AM11.45r	7.42	PM 5.10	5. 0
PM 9.30	5.43	—	—
11.45	8.28	—	—

d Saturdays only.
e Saturdays excepted.
h Mondays and Saturdays only.
k Mondays and Saturdays excepted.
r Restaurant Car.
t Tea Car.

ANOTHER ROUTE (LAKE SIDE) from *Euston,* 261 miles. Fares as above.

EUSTON	WINDER. LAKE S.	WINDER. LAKE S.	EUSTON
AM12.25	9.40	AM 8.30h	3.45
2.35	11.10	8.30r	4.15
5. 0	1.30	10. 0t	6. 0
6.45	2.50	PM12.25r	7.30
11.35r	5.35	1.40er	9. 5
PM 1.30r	8. 0	1.40dr	9.15
11. 0d	11.15	4.20r	10.45
—	—	8.20	5. 0

Sunday Trains.

AM11.45r	7.25	AM11.55r	7.30
—	—	PM 8. 5	5. 0

d Saturdays only.
e Saturdays excepted.
h Mondays and Saturdays only.
r Restaurant Car.
t Tea Car.

ANOTHER ROUTE from *St. Pancras.* 283½ miles. Fares as above.

ST. PAN.	WINDER. LAKE S.	WINDER. LAKE S.	ST. PAN.
AM 4.25	2.50	AM 8.30r	5.30
9.50r	5.35	10. 0hr	6.35
PM12.15r	8. 0	PM12.25r	9.15
11.50e	11.10	4.20e	4.20
11.50d	11 15	—	—

Sunday Trains.

PM11.45	11.10	—	—

d Saturdays only.
e Saturdays excepted.
h Mondays, Tuesdays, Fridays and Saturdays only.
r Restaurant Car.

Windermere Hydro. Stands in own grounds. Magnificent view of Lake and Mountains. Turkish Baths. Large Ballroom. Ladies' Orchestra.
THE MANAGER.
See advt. p. 345.

Beautiful Buttermere. Victoria Family Hotel. Private and comfortable.
See advt. p. 119.

WINDMILL END (Worcester), 120¼ miles. Fares, 25/0a, 15/0c. R. T. for two months, 50/0a. Departures *from* London as for Smethwick Junction. Departures *for* London about 6 times daily.

WINDSOR (Berks) from *Paddington.* 21¼ miles. Fares, 4/5a, 2/8c. R. T. for two months, 8/10a, 5/3c. Pop. 20,115.
Map Square 23 *and* 63.

PAD.	WINDSOR	WINDSOR	PAD.
AM 6.30	7.15	AM 6.22	7.25
6.35	8.10	7.45	8.20
7.35	8.35	8.12	8.49
8. 5	8.58	8.36	9. 8
8.30	9.12	8.47	9.25
9.20	10. 7	9.27	10. 6
9.55	10.42	10.37	11.18
10.55	11.46	11. 7	11.55
11.25	12. 4	PM12.10	1.11
11.35	12.37	12.28	1.32
PM12. 8	12.51	1. 7	1.46
12.33d	1.15	1.40	2.35
12.35e	1.38	2. 2	3.10
12.42d	1.37	2.40	3.40
1. 5d	1.46	3.27	4.10
1.15	2.15	4.43	5.20
1.20d	2. 2	5.43	6.25
2. 7e	2.45	6.12	6.55
2.18d	2 55	7. 2	7.45
2.33d	3.17	7.25	8.10
3.18	4. 0	8.18d	9.12
3.45	4.24	8.35	9.33
4. 7	4.48	9.18	10.22
4.30	5. 5	9.50	10.42
5.18e	5.57	10.45	12. 0
5.18d	6. 5	—	—
5.35e	6. 5	—	—
5.40d	6.16	—	—
6.12e	6.50	—	—
6.35	7.14	—	—
7. 0	7.40	—	—
7.37	8.20	—	—
8. 5	8.43	—	—
8.35	9.17	—	—
8.40	9.50	—	—
10. 5	10.48	—	—
10.40	11.40	—	—
11.30	12.12	—	—
12. 3	12.45	—	—

Sunday Trains.

AM 8.20	9.45	AM 8.10	9. 8
9.45	10.25	9.20	10.14
10. 5	10.47	10. 5	10.50
11. 0	11.40	11.55	1. 5
11.45	12.23	PM 2. 0	2.58
PM12.55	1.52	2.43	3.42
1.45	2.32	3.47	4.53
2.35	3.20	4.55	5.52
3.35	4.32	5.15	6. 0
4.45	5.47	6.10	7.10
5.15	6. 2	6.50	7.37
6. 5	7. 2	7.12	8.12
7.40	8.47	7.58	8.45
8.20	9. 7	9. 0	9.46
8.50	9.24	9.40	10.33
9.25	10. 8	10.33	11.38
10. 5	11. 0	—	—
11.15	12. 5	—	—

d Saturdays only.
e Saturdays excepted.

Salter's Steamers. (Bridge Landing Stage, ten minutes from Station.) Up-stream, 9.30 a.m., 2.45 p.m.; down-stream, 9.20 a.m., 2.45 p.m. *See* advt. facing first page of train service.

ETON.—THE BRIDGE HOUSE HOTEL. Unequalled position on whole of River.

WINDSOR—continued.

ANOTHER ROUTE from

Waterloo, 25¾ miles. Fares, 4/5a, 2/8c. R. T. for two months, 8/10a, 5/3c.

W'LOO	WINDSOR	WINDSOR	W'LOO
AM 5.35	6.53	AM 5.36	6.36
7.24	8.26	6.36	7.36
8.24	9.27	7. 6	8. 6
9.24	10.27	7.37	8.41
10.24	11.26	8. 9	9. 6
11.24	12.26	8.54	9.36
PM12.24	1.26	9. 6	10. 6
12.54d	1.56	10. 6	11. 6
1.24	2.26	10.57	11.57
1.54d	2.56	11.57	12.57
2.24	3.26	PM12.57	1.57
3.24	4.26	1.57	2.57
4.24	5.26	2.57	3.57
4.58e	5.56	3.57	4.57
5.24	6.26	4.57	5.57
5.54e	6.56	5.57	6.57
6.24	7.26	6.57	7.57
6.54e	7.56	7.57	8.57
7.24	8.26	9.20	10.37
8.24	9.26	10.45e	12. 5
9.24	10.31	10.45d	12. 8
10.24	11.31	—	—
11.44	12.45	—	—
—	—	—	—
—	—	—	—
—	—	—	—
—	—	—	—

Sunday Trains.

AM 8.48	9.49	AM 8.25	9.28
10.18	11.17	10.59	11.43
11.18	12.17	11.59	12.43
PM12.18	1.35	PM12.59	1.43
1.18	2.17	2.59	3.43
2.18	3.26	3.59	5.28
3.18	4.17	4.59	5.43
4.18	5.26	5.59	6.43
5.18	6.17	6.59	7.43
6.18	7.17	7.59	8.43
7.18	8.17	8.59	9.43
8.18	9.21	9.59	10.43
8.58	9.57	10.59	11.51
10.18	11.17	—	—

d Saturdays only.
e Saturdays excepted.

White Hart (Ye Harte and Garter), facing Castle. Principal Hotel. 100 Rooms. Moderate Tariff. Telephone 309. Telegrams, White Hart.

The Bridge House Hotel. The only fully licensed Residential Hotel on River. Unequalled position. Catering, Boating. Telephone, 289.
JOSEPH T. HALLIGAN.

Castle Hotel. Telephone 191. First-class. Excellent Ballroom. Banqueting Hall. Central Heating. Electric Light. Garage.
TRUST HOUSES, Ltd.

The Star and Garter. The Commercial Hotel. Parties catered for. Billiards. Horses and Carriages of every description. Loose Boxes. Riding lessons given. Close both Stations. Telephone No. 327.
F. GODFREY, Proprietor.

WINDSOR—continued.

Riverholme Hotel. Adjoining Bridge. Landing-stage from River. Garden. Terms moderate. Telephone 418. Also Riverholme Annexe. Telephone 33. Telegrams: "Outlaw, Windsor."
Miss OUTLAW, Proprietress.

Tower House Private Hotel, Thames Street. Facing Castle, near River, close both stations, adjacent Theatre. Comfortable, old fashioned, well furnished, excellent cooking. Teas served in Garden, Telephone, 456.
Proprietresses—
The Misses STUDD & GRAYDON.

Launches and Boats of every description on hire. Catering, large or small parties, Dining-rooms and Verandah facing river. Marquee to seat 200. Launches from £3 3s. per day.
A. JACOBS, Thames Hotel.
Telephone No. 199.

A. T. Barber & Co., Auctioneers, Valuers, Agents for principal Residences, Furniture Warehousemen, Expert Removers with Motor Pantechnicons. Offices, 51, High Street. Auction Galleries, 54, Peascod Street, Windsor. 'Phone 144.

WINGATE (Durham), 247½

miles. Fares, 52/9a, 31/8c. R. T., double fare. Departures *from* London as for Ferryhill. Departures *for* London about 6 times daily. Pop. 10,890.
Map Square 7.

WINGFIELD (Derby), 141¾

miles. Fares, 29/5a, 17/8c. R. T., double fare. Departures *from* London as for Ambergate. Departures *for* London about 6 times daily. Pop.
Map Square 12.

WINGHAM COLLIERY

(Kent), from *Victoria*, *Holborn Viaduct*, and *St. Paul's*, 81¾ miles. No through fares. Pop. 1,240.

	VICT.	Leave	Arr. at
	(S.E.&C.)	HOL. V.	ST. PL'S.	W'GHAM
AM	—	3.50h	—	7.49
	10.40	—	—	1.58
PM	2. 5d	—	—	6. 5
	2. 8e	—	—	5.50
	5.10d	—	—	8.20
	—	—	—	—
	—	—	—	—
	—	—	—	—

No Sunday Trains.

Trains from Wingham.

Leave			Arr. at	VICT.
W'GHAM	ST. PL'S.	HOL. V.		(S.E.&C)
AM 8.35	—	—	11.35
PM 2. 2d	—	—	5.56
5.57e	—	—	10.25
6.12d	—	—	10.25
—	—	—	—
—	—	—	—

No Sunday Trains.

d Saturdays only.
e Saturdays excepted.
h Third Class only.

WINSCOMBE (Somerset)

from *Paddington*, via Yatton, 132¼ miles. Fares, via Witham, 27/8a, 16/7c. R. T. for two months, 55/4a, 33/2c. Via Yatton, 28/2a, 16/11c. R. T. for two months, 56/4a. Pop. 1,542.
Map Square 22.

PAD.	WINSC'MBE	WINSC'MBE	PAD.
AM 5.30	10.11	AM 7.48	11.30
7.30	11.46	8.11h	12.55
10.30h	2.35	10.23r	2. 0
11.15r	2.58	PM 1. 6	6. 2
PM12.30hr	5.29	2.35r	7. 0
1. 0r	3.55	5.29	10.25
1.10r	6.11	8.45	2.45
4.15r	8.19	—	—
12. 0k	8.11	—	—
12.30l	12.38	—	—

Sunday Trains.

PM 2.40h	7.39	PM12.38hr	7.55
10. 0	8.11	7.39	3.15

h Via Witham.
k Saturdays midnight excepted.
l Saturdays midnight only.
r Restaurant Car.

WINSFORD (Cheshire)

from *Euston*, 165¼ miles. Fares, 34/5a, 20/8c. R. T. for two months, 68/10a. Pop. 10,957.
Map Square 12.

EUSTON	WINSFD.	WINSFD.	EUSTON
AM 2.35	6.25	AM 7.40er	12. 5
6.45	11.30	7.40dr	12.20
8.30r	12.14	9.17r	1. 0
11.50r	3.21	11.53r	3.10
PM 1.30r	5.28	PM 2. 8r	5.50
2.35t	6. 0	3.39er	7.30
5.20r	9.13	5.42er	9. 5
11.50d	7.36	5.42dr	9.15
—	—	6.22r	10. 0
—	—	8.18er	5. 0
—	—	10.59d	5. 0

Sunday Trains.

PM 3.50	9. 3	AM11.12	4. 0
6. 0	9.40	PM 3.49r	7.30

d Saturdays only.
e Saturdays excepted.
r Restaurant Car.
t Tea Car.

WINSLOW (Bucks) from

Euston, 53½ miles. Fares, 10/3a, 6/2c. R. T., double fare. Pop. 1,698.
Map Square 18.

EUSTON	WINSLOW	WINSLOW	EUSTON
AM 6.45	8.30	AM 8.23e	9.52
7.35	10.25	8.33	10. 0
10.40	12.25	10.13	11.55
12. 0n	1.40	PM12.27h	2.45
PM 3. 5	4.32	2.52	4.15
4.15	5.41	3.51	5.35
5.32	7. 5	5.54	7.55
6.10e	7.48	7.50	9.20
7.15d	9.25	8.16e	10.10
8. 0e	9.25	8.16d	10.50
—	—	11.53h	5. 0

Sunday Trains.

AM 8.15	10.35	PM1. 1	5. 5
9.15	12. 0	3.55	5.50
PM12.30	2. 0	4.48	7.10
2.15	5. 5	7.44	9.45
3.50	5.55	8.22	10.10

d Saturdays only.
e Saturdays excepted.
h Thursdays and Saturdays only.
n Noon.
r Restaurant Car.

WINSLOW ROAD

(Bucks) from *Baker Street* or *Marylebone*, 49¼ miles. Fares, 10/3a, 6/2c. R. T. for two months, 20/6a, 12/3c. Departures *from* London as for Verney. Departures *for* London about 9 times daily.
Map Square 18.

WINSON GREEN (Warwick), 114¾ miles. Fares, 23/4a, 14/0c. R. T. for two months, 46/8a, 28/0c. Departures *from* London as for Birmingham (New Street). Departures *for* London about 8 times daily.

WINSTON (Durham), 243 miles. Fares, 50/8a, 30/5c. R. T., double fare. Departures *from* London as for Barnard Castle. Departures *for* London about 4 times daily. Pop. 312.
Map Square 7.

WINTERBOURNE (Glo's-ter) from *Paddington*, 109¾ miles. Fares, 22/11a, 13/9c. R. T. for two months, 45/10a. Departures *from* London as for Chipping Sodbury. Departures *for* London about 5 times daily. Pop. 3,191.
Map Square 22.
Station closed on Sundays.

WINTERINGHAM (Lincoln), 186¾ miles. Fares, 22/2c. R. T., double fare. Departures *from* London as for Thorne or Barnetby. Departures *for* London about 3 times daily. Pop. 606.
Map Square 13.

WINTERTON (Lincoln), 183½ miles. Fares 21/8c. Departures *from* London as for Thorne or Barnetby. Departures *for* London about 3 times daily. Pop. 1,693.
Map Square 13.

WINTON (East Lothian), 393¾ miles. No through fares. Departures *from* London as for Edinburgh (Waverley). Departures *for* London about twice daily.
Map Square 41.

WIRKSWORTH (Derby), from *St. Pancras*, 141½ miles. Fares, 29/4a, 17/7c. R. T., double fare. Pop. 3,615.
Map Square 12.

St.Pan.	Wkswth.	Wkswth.	St.Pan.
AM 2.25	7.40	AM 7.55r	11.35
4.25	8.55	9. 3r	1.30
8.25r	12.49	PM 1. 0r	4.20
10.25r	2.54	3. 5r	7.15
PM 2.25r	5 45	5.55r	10. 5
4.25r	8.36	8.50	4.20

Sunday Trains.

AM11.15r	5.12	PM 5.30r	9.52
—	—	—	—

r Restaurant Car.

WISBECH (Cambridge) from *Liverpool Street*, via March, 93¾ miles. Fares, 17/6a, 10/6c. R. T. for two months, 35/0a. Pop. 11,316.
Map Square 18.

L'pool St.	W'bech	W'bech	L'pool St.
AM 5.50h	10.11	AM 6.19	9.27
5.50	10.15	7.51r	10.23
8.30r	11.51	9.20	12.40
10 5h	1.50	10.13	2. 7
10. 5	2. 9	10.19hr	2.21
11.50r	3. 0	PM12.27	5. 9
PM 2.34	5.47	3. 6r	6.10
4.45	7.14	3. 6r	6.10
5.49r	8.55	5. 7r	8.22
10.12	1.16	7.47	10.30
—	—	11. 1	2.50

Sunday Trains.

AM 9.25	12.27	PM 3.10	6 40
PM 3.25	6.50	—	—

h Via King's Lynn.
k Arrives at St. Pancras Station.
l Commencing July 23.
r Restaurant Car.

WISBECH—*continued.*

ANOTHER ROUTE from *King's Cross*, 96½ miles, via Peterboro'. Fares as above.

King's +	Wisbch.	Wisbch.	King's +
AM 4.45	7.24	AM 9. 8	12.25
7.15r	10.19	10.41	1. 5
10.10r	1.39	PM12.42	3.50
PM 1.50r	4. 5	2.10r	4.30
3. 0	5.19	3. 1	6.25
5.45r	8. 7	5.38	9. 0
—	—	6.52r	9.25
—	—	—	—
—	—	—	—

No Sunday Trains.

r Restaurant Car.

WISBECH ST. MARY (Cambs) from *King's Cross*, 94 miles, via Peterboro'. Fares, 17/6a, 10/6c. R. T. for two months, 35/0a, 21/0c. Pop. 2,099.
Map Square 18.

King's +	Wisbch.	Wisbch.	King's +
AM 7.15r	10.12	AM 9.14	12.25
10.10r	1.33	PM12 43	3.50
PM 1.50r	3.58	3. 7	6.25
5.45r	8. 0	6.58r	9.25
—	—	—	—
—	—	—	—

No Sunday Trains.

r Restaurant Car.

WISHAW CENTRAL (Lanark), from *Euston*, 385½ miles. Fares, 78/6a, 47/1c. R. T. for two months, 157/0a, 94/2c. Pop. 68,869.
Map Square 40.

Euston.	Wishaw.	Wishaw.	Euston
AM 5. 0v	4.23	AM 8.48r	6.25
10. 0r	6.16	PM 4.31	5. 0
PM 9.20ev	7. 1	6.54v	7.40
11.35e	8.34	—	—
—	—	—	—

Sunday Trains.

PM11.35	8.34	—	—

e Saturdays excepted.
r Restaurant Car.
v Via Motherwell.

WISHAW SOUTH (Lanark), 385½ miles. No through fares. Departures *from* London as for Carstairs. Departures *for* London about 5 times daily.

WISHFORD (Wilts) from *Paddington*, 11b miles. Fares, via Westbury, 20/0a, 12/0c. R. T. for two months, 40/0a. Via Bath, 22/6a, 13/6c. R. T. for two months, 45/0a. Departures *from* London as for Warminster. Departures *for* London about 5 times daily. Pop. 249.
Map Square 22.

WISTOW (Yorks), 177¾ miles. Fares, 35/8a, 21/5c. R. T., double fare. Departures *from* London as for Selby. Departures *for* London about 4 times daily. Pop. 650.
Map Square 13.

WITHAM (Essex) from *Liverpool Street*, 38¾ miles. Fares, 8/2a, 4/1c. R. T. for two months, 16/4a. Pop. 3,719
Map Square 24.

L'pl.St.	Witham	Witham	L'pl.St.
AM 5. 0	6.10	AM 2.11	3.50
6.50	8.30	7.39	8.52
8.15r	9.18	8.10	9.30
8.18	9.27	8.24	9.36
8.46	10. 7	9.20	10.22
10.47	12.14	9.38r	10.30
11.30	12.31	10.13	11.16
PM 1.33d	2.50	11.38	12.40
1.38e	3. 7	11.51	1.16
2.15	3.22	PM 1.50	3.13
3.26	4.50	2.35	3.36
4.18	5.31	4.44	5.47
4.58r	5.57	6. 3	7.40
5.42d	6.57	7.46	9.17
5.42e	7. 1	10. 0	11.16
6.39	7.51	—	—
7.16	8.22	—	—
7.45r	8.44	—	—
8.54	10.22	—	—
—	—	—	—
—	—	—	—
—	—	—	—

Sunday Trains.

AM 7. 4	8.55	AM 2.11	3.50
8.15	9.37	8. 2	10.25
9.20r	10.29	9.44	11.15
10. 5r	11.10	10.58	12.40
10.45	12.14	PM 1.44	3.15
PM 3.40	4.54	6. 8	7.10
3.45	5.10	6.36	8.39
6.15	7.38	7.14	8.25
7.40	8.50	7.44	8.58
8.46	10.19	8.32	10.22

d Saturdays only.
e Saturdays excepted.
r Restaurant Car.

White Hart Hotel. Family and Commercial. A.A., R.A.C., etc. Stabling. Garage.
ERNIE MOSS, Proprietor.

WITHAM (Somerset) from *Paddington*, 106½ miles. Fares, via Westbury, 22/3a, 13/4c. R. T. for two months, 44/6a. Via Bath, 22/6a, 13/6c. R. T. for two months, 45/0a. Pop. 376.
Map Square 22.

Pad.	Witham	Witham	Pad.
AM 1. 0g	7.50	AM 9.59	12.55
5.30	9.58	PM12.51	3.50
7.30	11.10	1.41t	5.30
10.30	12.51	3.42r	6.50
PM12.30r	3.13	5.37	8.20
3.30	5.56	8.33	2.45
5. 5	8.33	9.20h	2.45
—	—	—	—

Sunday Trains.

AM 9.10	1.48	AM11.35	3.35
PM 2.40	5.11	PM 4. 6r	7.55

g Monday excepted.
h Thursdays and 3rd Class only.
r Restaurant Car.
t Tea Car.

WITHCALL (Lincoln), 145 miles. Fares, 29/4a, 17/7c. R. T., double fare. Departures *from* London as for Wragby. Departures *for* London about 4 times daily. Pop. 208.
Map Square 13.

WITHERNSEA (Yorks),
216¼ miles. Fares, 37/6a, 22/6c. R. T. for two months, 75/0a, 45/0c. Departures *from* London as for Hull (Paragon). Departures *for* London about 6 times daily. Pop. 4,702.
Map Square 13.

WITHINGTON (Glo'ster)
from *Waterloo*, 125 miles. Fares, 21/1a, 12/8c. R. T. for two months, 42/2a. Departures *from* London as for Cirencester. Departures *for* London about 5 times daily. Pop. 522.
Map Square 22.

WITHINGTON (Hereford),
142½ miles. Fares, 29/0a, 17/5c. R. T. for two months, 58/0a. Departures *from* London as for Malvern. Departures *for* London about 4 times daily. Pop. 797.
Map Square 17.

WITHINGTON (Lancs)
from *St. Pancras*, 184½ miles. Fares, 38/2a, 22/11c. R. T., double fare. Pop. 7,730.

St. Pan.	W'th'ton	W'th'ton	St.Pan.
AM 4.25	10.59	AM 7. 2r	11.35
8.25r	1.49	8.41r	1.30
10.25r	3. 1	9.42	3.25
PM12.25r	4.32	11.56dr	4.20
1.25r	6.54	PM12.21r	5.45
4.25r	8.46	1.29dr	6.15
6.25r	10.31	2.56r	8.35
12. 0k	6.59	4.21r	10. 5
12. 0l	7.54	5.44er10. 5	
—	—	11. 9	6. 0

Sunday Trains.
AM11.15r	4.15	AM 9.24r	5. 2
PM 3.15r	9.14	PM 5.25hr	9.52
6.15r	10.40	9.59	4.55
11.55	6.59	—	—

d Saturdays only.
e Saturdays excepted.
h Takes up when required.
k Saturdays midnight excepted.
l Saturdays midnight only.
r Restaurant Car

WITHNELL (Lancs), 207½
miles. Fares, 43/2a, 25/11c. R. T. for two months, 86/4a. Departures *from* London as for Chorley. Departures *for* London about 5 times daily. Pop. 3,391.
Map Square 12.

WITHYHAM (Sussex) from
London Bridge, Victoria, and *Cannon Street,* 38½ miles. Fares, 6/8a, 4/0c. R. T. for two months, 13/4a, 8/0c. Pop. 2,479.
Map Square 24.

Vict.	Leave Can. St.	Lon. B.	Arr. at W'thym.
AM 5.30h	—	5.18h	7.27
6.37	—	6.40	8.35
7.23	—	8. 7	9.51
9.10	—	9. 6	10.59
12. 0	—	11.50	1.46
PM	—	12.50d	2.19
1.20e	—	—	3.17
1.25d	—	1.10d	3.17
—	—	d1.38h	3.33
3.45h	—	—	5. 5
4. 0	—	4.10	5.48
4.50h	—	e4.44h	6.24
5.48	—	5.41e	7.17
6. 6	—	6. 8	8.19
7.15	—	7.38	9.19

Sunday Trains.
AM 8.18	—	8.30	10.17
PM 2.30h	—	—	5.58
6.33	—	6.46	9.20

WITHYHAM—*continued.*

Trains from Withyham.

Leave Withym	Lon. B.	Arrive at Can. St.	Vict.
AM 7.27	9. 1k	9. 4	9. 8
7.52	9.32	—	9.40
8.46	10. 7	—	—
9. 8	10.55	—	10.48
10. 2	—	—	11.35
10.59h	12.44	—	12.35
11.33	1.42	—	1.26
PM 1.46h	4. 0	—	3.45
2.32	4.32	—	4.35
3.33	5.21	—	5.55
5. 5	7.42	—	7.45
5.48h	7.56	—	—
6.24	8.46	—	8.27
8.19h	—	—	10.10
8.37	10.25	—	11.17

Sunday Trains.
AM 7.28	10.18	—	10.32
10.17h	—	—	1.40
PM 5.58	7.56	—	8.41

d Saturdays only.
e Saturdays excepted.
h Via Groombridge.
k Departs from or arrives at London Bridge, S.E. & C. Station.

WITLEY (Surrey) from
Waterloo, 38½ miles. Fares, 8/1a, 4/10c. R. T. for two months, 16/2a, 9/8c. Pop. 4,289.
Map Square 23.

W'loo.	Witley	Witley	W'loo.
AM 5.50	7.15	AM 6.41	8.20
6.50	8.22	7.24	8.41
7.50	9.29	8. 2	9.12
9.50	11. 8	8.37	9.44
10.50	12.15	9.41	10.50
11.50d	1. 7	10.16	11.52
PM12.20d	1.27	PM12.35r	1.52
12.50er	2. 3	1.40	3. 6
1.50e	3.14	2.58	4.16
2. 0d	3.23	4.32	5.52
2.34	4.10	6. 8	7.46
3.50d	5. 7	7.38	9. 6
4.15e	5.23	9. 6	10.46
5.24	6.30	10.28	12.16
5.40	7.10	—	—
6.50er	8. 6	—	—
6.50dr	8.16	—	—
8. 0	9.33	—	—
9.50	11.14	—	—

Sunday Trains.
AM 8.20	10. 0	AM 8.58	10.16
PM 1.50	3.16	PM 1.52	3.13
4.20	5.55	4.52	6.17
6.20	7.47	9. 2	10.41
8.20	10. 3	9.59	11.43

d Saturdays only.
e Saturdays excepted.
r Restaurant Car.

WITNEY (Oxon) from
Paddington, 75¼ miles. Fares, 15/8a, 9/5c. R. T. for two months, 31/4a. Pop. 3,364.
Map Square 22.

Pad.	Witney	Witney	Pad.
AM 5.30	8.34	AM 7.40	9.50
6.30	9.48	8.55	11.15
9.45	12.14	9.51	12. 5
PM 1.35r	3.49	11.31	1.50
4.45t	6.49	PM12.52dr	2.55
7.30	9.34	3. 7	5.50
		5. 3	7.20
		7.19	10.45

Sunday Trains.
AM11.45	5. 9	PM 7.13r	9.48

d Saturdays only.
r Restaurant Car.
t Tea Car.

WITNEY—*continued.*

Marlborough Arms Hotel.
Family and Commercial, A.A. and M.U. Electric Light throughout. Tourists specially catered for. Telephone, 25.
S. H. CRULEY, Proprietor.

WITTERSHAM ROAD
(Kent) from *Charing Cross, Cannon Street,* and *London Bridge,* 58¼ miles. No through fares. Departures *from* London as for Tenterden. Departures *for* London about 6 times daily. Pop. (Wittersham) 643.
Map Square 24.

WITTON (Warwick), 112¼
miles. Fares, 23/6a, 14/1c. R. T. for two months, 47/0a. Departures *from* London as for Birmingham (New Street). Departures *for* London about 8 times daily.
Map Square 17.

WITTON GILBERT
(Durham), 256 miles. No through fares. Departures *from* London as for Durham. Departures *for* London about 6 times daily. Pop. 7,098.
Map Square 7.

WITTON - LE - WEAR
(Durham),248¾ miles. Fares,51/10a, 31/1c. R. T., double fare. Departures *from* London as for Bishop Auckland. Departures *for* London about 4 times daily. Pop. 2,271.
Map Square 7.

WIVELISCOMBE (Somerset), 152¾ miles. Fares, 31/10a, 19/1c. R. T. for two months, 63/8a. Departures *from* London as for Dulverton. Departures *for* London about 4 times daily. Pop. 1,255.
Map Square 21.

WIVELSFIELD (Sussex)
from *London Bridge, Victoria,* and *Clapham Junction,* 40½ miles. Fares, 8/6a, 5/1c. R. T. for two months, 17/0a, 10/2c. Pop. 2,241.
Map Square 25.

Vict.	Leave Clap. J.	Lon. B.	Arr. at Wivlfd
AM	—	6.15	7.25
6.37	6.44	6.40	7.52
7.23	7.29	7.25	9.25
9. 0	9. 8	—	10.22
—	—	9. 6	10.29
10. 5	10.11	9.50	11.23
10.35	10.42	10.35	12. 9
PM12.45	—	12.10	1.51
—	—	1.20d	2.30
2. 0e	2. 7e	2. 5e	3.37
2. 0	2. 7	2. 5	3.50
—	—	2. 8d	4. 5
3.40	—	4. 5	5.16
4.30	—	5. 5d	6. 6
—	—	5. 8e	6. 6
5.45	—	5.55e	7.14
—	—	6. 0d	7.14
6. 6	6.12	6. 8	7.51
6.50	6.57	7. 0	8.17
7.15	7.22	7.20	9.10
8.35	—	—	9.41
9. 3	9.10	9.12	10.40

Sunday Trains.
AM 6.55	7. 2	7. 2	8.52
—	—	7.22	8.59
8.50	8.57	8.55	10.54
PM 1.14	1.21	1.10	3.20
5.50	5.57	6. 0	7.36
6.33	6.40	6.33	8. 2

WIVELSFIELD—*contd.*

Trains from Wivelsfield.

Leave WIVELFD.	LON. B.	Arrive at CLAP J.	VICT.
AM 6.17	8.15	8.15	8.24
7.23	8.46	9. 0	9. 8
9.22	—	—	10.24
10.34	12.13	11.59	12. 7
11.23	12.44	12.36	12.45
11.58	1.42	1.39	1.50
PM12.52	2.22	2.13	2.22
1.51	3.40	3.37	3.45
2.52	4.32	4. 9	4.17
3.30	5.54	5.47	5.55
4.55	6.36	6.26	6.34
6.12	7.42	7.21	7.30
6.58	8.46½	8.39	8.48
8.52	10. 0	10.′ 2	10.10
9.15	10.58	—	—
9.58	—	11.10	11.17
10.38	12.59	12.50	1. 0
—	—	—	—
—	—	—	—
—	—	—	—
—	—	—	—

Sunday Trains.

AM 8.51	10.18	10.23	10.32
8.58	10.45	10.42	10.50
PM 3.19	5. 3	5. 1	5.11
6.11	7.56	—	—
7. 0	8.34	8.31	8.41
—	—	—	—
—	—	—	—
—	—	—	—
—	—	—	—

d Saturdays only.
e Saturdays excepted.

WIVENHOE (Essex) from

Liverpool Street, 56 miles. Fares, 12/3a, 7/4c. R. T. for two months, 24/6a. Pop. 2,330.
Map Square 19.

L'PL. ST.	WIVENH.	WIVENH.	L'PL. ST.
AM 5. 0	6.47	AM 8.10	9.36
6.50	9.31	8.15r	9.53
8.18	10. 6	8.51r	10.30
8.46	11.13	10. 5	11.42
10.23	12. 8	10.26	12.40
11.26d	1.30	PM12.21r	2. 3
11.30e	1.30	1.30	3.36
PM12.36	2. 7	3. 8	5. 5
2.15	4.20	5. 0	6.32
3.23	4.53	5.52	7.40
3.26	5.47	6.33	9.17
4.58r	6.31	8.11	9.36
5.42	7.40	8.34	11.16
6.39	8. 5	—	—
7.45r	9.30	—	—
8.45	10.14	—	—
—	—	—	—
—	—	—	—
—	—	—	—
—	—	—	—

Sunday Trains.

AM 9.20r	11.24	AM 9.34	11.38
PM 4.40	6.12	PM 6.32	8.25
—	—	8.31	10. 9
—	—	—	—
—	—	—	—

d Saturdays only.
e Saturdays excepted.
r Restaurant Car.

WIXFORD (Warwick)

from *Marylebone*, 101¼ miles. No through fares. Departures *from* London as for Stratford-on-Avon. Departures *for* London about 4 times daily. Pop. 93.
Map Square 17.

WOBURN SANDS

(Bucks) from *Euston* 50½ miles. Fares, 10/5a, 6/3c. R. T. for two months, 20/10a, 12/6c. Pop. 1,086.
Map Square 18.

EUSTON	W. SANDS	W. SANDS	EUSTON
AM 6.45	8.24	AM 7. 9	9. 5
7.35	9.43	8.45	10. 0
9.30	11.54	9.18	11.40
10.40	12.11	10.20	11.55
12. 0nr	1.47	11.10d	12.20
PM12.15e	3.43	11.10e	12.32
1.35d	3.43	11.42	1.50
2. 0	4. 7	PM 1.15h	2.45
3. 5	4.39	1.15k	4.15
5.32e	7. 0	3.33	5. 5
5.32d	7.14	6. 1	7.55
6.10e	7.42	6.22	8.35
7.15d	9.35	7. 5e	9.20
8. 0e	9.35	8.23e	10.10
—	—	8.23d	10.50
—	—	9.12	11.35

Sunday Trains.

AM 9.15	11.52	PM 1. 8	5. 5
PM12.30	2.12	7.34	9.45

d Saturdays only.
e Saturdays excepted.
h Thursdays and Saturdays only.
k Thursdays and Saturdays excepted.
n Noon.
r Restaurant car.

WOKING (Surrey) from

Waterloo, 24½ miles. Fares, 5/2a, 3/1c. R. T. for two months, 10/4a, 6/2c. Pop. 26,430.
Map Square 23.

W'LOO.	WOKING	WOKING	W'LOO.
AM 4.50	5.58	AM 3. 1	3.58
5.40	6.17	7. 1	7.46
5.50	6.28	7.24	8.20
6.50	7.35	7.40	8.36
7. 0	7.55	8. 6	8.41
7.30	8. 8	8.13	8.56
7.50	8.43	8.22	9. 8
8.15	9. 5	8.52	9.26
8.30	9. 9	9. 6	9.41
8.34	9.13	9.21	10.11
9. 0	9.38	9.47	10.21
9.20	9.54	9.50	10.46
9.30	10. 7	10.42	11.16
10.20	11.15	10.59	11.32
10.34	11.21	11.37	12.11
11.20	12.12	PM12. 6	12.40
PM12.14d	1. 0	12.31	1.20
12.15	1.12	1. 6	1.40
12.40e	1.22	1.50	2.46
12.40d	1.25	2.21	3. 6
1.10	1.43	2.33	3.16
1.15d	2. 0	3. 1	3.36
1.20	2.15	3.27	4. 6
1.44d	2.31	3.37	4.16
1.50e	2.28	3.52	4.46
2. 0d	2.38	4.31	5.20
2.20	3.15	4.50	5.46
2.34	3.21	5.28	6.16
3.15	3.48	5.50	6.46
3.40	4.23	6.33	7. 7
4. 0	4.33	7. 0	7.40
4.20	5.14	7.50	8.46
4.40	5.30	8.21	9. 6
5. 0	5.32	8.38	9.26
5.10	5.44	8.50	9.46
5.30	6. 1	9.11	9.52
5.50	6.24	9.50	10.46
6.10e	6.44	10. 9	10.50
6.15e	7. 0	10.16	11.10

WOKING—*continued.*

W'LOO.	WOKING	WOKING	W'LOO.
PM 6.34	7. 6	PM10.48	11.28
6.40d	7.23	11.11	12.16
6.54e	7.26	—	—
7.20	8.15	—	—
8. 0	8.41	—	—
8.20	9.15	—	—
8.55	9.50	—	—
9.20	10.15	—	—
9.50	10.24	—	—
10. 0	10.34	—	—
10.20	11.15	—	—
11.15e	12. 8	—	—
11.40	12.34	—	—
12. 5m12.39	—	—	—

Sunday Trains.

AM 8. 0	8.47	AM 3. 1	3.58
8.20	9.17	8.45	9.45
8.45	9.28	9.42	10.16
9. 0	9.39	10.21	11.16
9.20	10.20	11.40	12.41
9.45	10.38	PM12. 7	12.52
10.20	11.21	12.40	1.41
11.15	11.54	1.42	2.44
11.20	12.20	2.31	3.13
12. 0	12.38	2.42	3.44
PM12.20	1.21	4.40	5.41
1.20	2.20	5.33	6. 7
1.50	2.33	5.46	6.46
3.20	4.20	6.40	7.41
4.20	5.13	7.40	8.41
5. 0	5.45	8. 0	8.52
5.20	6.13	8.32	9.12
6. 0	6.34	9. 4	9.37
6.20	6.54	9.12	10. 1
6.30	7.23	9.40	10.41
7.20	8.13	9.52	10.47
8.15	8.53	10. 7	10.52
8.20	9.20	10.40	11.43
9.30	10. 6	—	—
9.45	10.40	—	—
10.15	11. 9	—	—
10.45	11.21	—	—

d Saturdays only.
e Saturdays excepted.
m Midnight.

Cotteridge Private Hotel.
Near Station. Excellent Cuisine. Separate Tables. Constant Hot Water. Tennis, Ball Room. Garage. Magnificent Golf Centre, 5 Courses. Telegrams : Cotteridge, Woking. Telephone 240, Woking.

Albion Hotel. Close to
Station. High-class Family and Commercial. Central for several Golf Links. Fully Licensed. Tel. 233.
CATERING HOUSES, LTD.

Wheatsheaf Hotel. Facing
Horsell Common, lately rebuilt and refurnished. About ten minutes from Station. Special Week End Terms to Golfers. 'Phone Woking 173.
CATERING HOUSES, LTD.

House Agents. Atherton
& Co. Particulars of Furnished and Unfurnished Houses or Building Sites. Telephone No. 9. Woking.

Estate Agents. Alex. H.
Turner and Co., incorporated with Alfred Savill & Sons. Opposite Station. Telephone 54. And at Guildford, Weybridge and London.

WOKINGHAM (Berks).

from Waterloo, 36¼ miles. Fares, 7/6a, 4/6c. R. T. for two months, 15/0a, 9/0c. Pop. 4,473.
Map Square 23.

W'LOO	WOK'HAM	WOK'HAM	W'LOO
AM 5.10	7. 5	AM 6.54	8.17
6.54	8.36	7.53	9.17
7.54	9.30	8.35	9.47
9.54	11.26	9. 2	10.17
10.54	12.30	9.59	11.17
PM12.48	2.13	11. 3	12.31
1.48	3.10	PM 1. 3	2.27
2.48	4.11	2. 3	3.27
3.48e	5.10	4. 3	5.27
3.48d	5.15	5. 3	6.27
4.48e	6. 2	6. 3	7.27
4.48d	6.15	7. 3	8.27
5.48	7. 8	8. 3	9.27
6.48	8. 9	9.11	10.37
7.54	9.25	10.32e	12. 5
10.24	11.55	10.32	12. 8

Sunday Trains.

W'LOO	WOK'HAM	WOK'HAM	W'LOO
AM 8.18	9.55	AM 8.40	10.30
PM12.18	1.52	PM12.35	2. 3
4.18	5.49	6. 0	7.28
5.58	7.31	7.58	9.28
9.18	10.53	9. 4	10.28

d Saturdays only.
e Saturdays excepted.

WOLDINGHAM (Surrey)

from Victoria, Cannon Street and London Bridge, 17 miles. Fares, 3/7a, 2/2c. R. T. for eight days, 7/2a, 4/3c. Pop. 646.
Map Square 23.

VICT.	CAN. ST.	LON. B.	Arr. at W'D'HM
AM 5.30	—	5.18	6.17
6.37	—	6.40	7.20
7.23	—	8. 7	8.53
9.10	—	9. 6	9.58
10.35	—	10.35	11.22
12. 0	—	11.50	12.49
PM —	12.16d	d12.20k	1. 4
—	—	12.50d	1.26
1.20e	—	1.38e	2.17
1.25d	—	1.38d	2.21
—	—	2. 5e	3.20
2.25	—	2.25d	3.20
—	—	2.57d	3.40
4. 0	—	4.10	4.50
—	4.16e	e4.20k	5. 0
4.50	—	4.44e	5.27
5. 5	—	5.10	5.53
—	—	5.21	6. 3
5.48	—	5.41e	6.26
6. 6	—	6. 8	6.56
6.50	—	7. 0	7.39
7.15	—	7.38	8.23
8. 5	—	8.10	8.51
9. 3	—	9.12	9.49
10.30	—	10.35	11.18
11.50h	—	—	12.30

Sunday Trains.

VICT.	CAN. ST.	LON. B.	Arr. at W'D'HM
AM 8.18	—	8.30	9.16
10.20	—	—	11.18
PM 1.14	—	1.10	1.59
2.30	—	—	3.21
6.33	—	6.46	7.32
7. 5	—	—	7.48
9. 5	—	9.10	9.55

WOLDINGHAM—contd.
Trains from Woldingham.

Leave W'LD'HM	LON. B.	CAN. ST.	Arrive at VICT.
AM 7.24	8.15	—	8.24
8. 0	8.37	—	8.40
8.25	9. 1k	9. 4	9. 8
8.37	9.15	—	9.19
8.55	9.32	—	9.40
9.15	9.55	—	9.58
10. 3	10.33	—	10.46
10.54	—	—	11.35
11.34	12.13	—	12.17
PM12.41	1.42	—	1.26
2.19	2.58	—	—
3. 1	4. 0	—	3.45
4.11d	4.57	—	—
4.40	5.21	—	5.55
5.49	6.36	—	6.29
7.15	7.56	—	—
7.34	8.46	—	8.27
9.43	10.25	—	11.17

Sunday Trains.

Leave W'LD'HM	LON. B.	CAN. ST.	Arrive at VICT.
AM 9.25	10.18	—	10.20
10.29	11.15	—	—
11.52	—	—	12.47
PM12.48	—	—	1.40
5.45	—	—	6.34
8.40	9.26	—	9.34
10.17	—	—	10.59

d Saturdays only.
e Saturdays excepted.
h Wednesdays only.
k Departs from, or arrives at London Bridge, S.E. & C. Station.

WOLFERTON (Norfolk)

(for SANDRINGHAM) from Liverpool Street, 102½ miles. Fares, 21/8a, 13/0c. R. T. for two months, 43/4a, 26/0c. Pop. 194.
Map Square 19.

L'POOL ST.	WOLF	WOLF.	L'POOL ST.
AM 5.50	10.29	AM 7.24r	10.23
8.30r	11.35	8.13	11.27
10. 5	2. 3	9.24	2. 7
11.20klr	2. 3	11.26r	2.21
11.50r	3. 2	PM 1. 8lr	4. 2k
PM 2.34	5.29	2.54r	6.10
4.45	7.33	5. 7r	8.22
5.49r	8.58	7.28	10.30
—	—	10. 2	2.50

Sunday Trains.

L'POOL ST.	WOLF	WOLF.	L'POOL ST.
AM 9.25	1.13	PM 6.43	9.40

k Departs from or arrives at St. Pancras Station.
l Commencing July 23.
r Restaurant Car.

WOLSINGHAM (Durham),

255¾ miles. Fares, 53/2a, 31/11c. R. T., double fare. Departures from London as for Bishop Auckland. Departures for London about 4 times daily. Pop. 3,414.
Map Square 7.

WOLVERHAMPTON

(HIGH LEVEL) (Stafford) from Euston, 125 miles. Fares, 25/8a, 15/5c. R. T. for two months, 51/4a. Pop. 102,373.
Map Square 17.

EUSTON	W'LV'H'TN	W'LV'H'TN	EUSTON
AM 2.30	6.11	AM 6.50r	10. 0
5. 0e	8.5C	8. 3r	10.40
5. 0d	8.57	9.34	12.40
8.30r	11.28	10.50r	1.25
9.10er	11.45	11. 0r	2.20
9.15r	12.10	PM12.25er	3. 0
11.30r	2.10	1.55t	4.35
PM 1.15r	3.50	2.34t	5.35
2.20t	4.55	4.15t	6.50
4.35t	7. 0	5.40r	8.20
5.50r	8.25	6. 9dr	10.45
6.55r	9.30	7.27er	10.20
7. 0r	10.35	10.53e	4. 0
11.50	3.37	10.53d	5. 0

WOLVERHAMPTON—continued.
Sunday Trains.

EUSTON	W'LV'H'TN	W'LV'H'TN	EUSTON
AM 9.15	2.17	AM 6.37	12.25
PM 1. 0r	4. 0	11. 0r	1.45
5.10r	8. 0	11.50	5. 5
11.50	3.32	PM 3.40r	8.20
—	—	5.40r	8.35
—	—	9.40	5. 0

d Saturdays only.
e Saturdays excepted.
r Restaurant Car.
t Tea Car.

ANOTHER ROUTE (LOW LEVEL) from Paddington, 123 miles. Fares as above.

PAD.	WOLVHTN.	WOLVHTN.	PAD.
AM 6.30	10.55	AM 6.50r	10. 0
9.10r	11.34	8.35r	11. 0
10.20	12.49	9.50	12.25
10.40r	1. 6	11. 0r	1.25
10.45r	2.47	11.42r	2. 5
PM12.50r	3.25	PM12.21r	4.15
2.10t	4.34	2.27r	5. 0
4.10t	6.34	3.29t	5.55
6.10r	8.34	3.55t	6.40
7.10r	9.45	5.28r	8. 5
7.30	11.10	7.20	10. 0
12.15k	4.20	11. 5	3.30
12.15t	4. 9	—	—

Sunday Trains.

PAD.	WOLVHTN.	WOLVHTN.	PAD.
AM10.15	3. 2	AM11. 0r	1.40
PM12.50r	3.20	PM 2.10	6.20
4.10	8. 8	6. 5r	9. 0
6. 0r	8.25	—	—

k Saturdays midnight excepted.
l Saturdays midnight only.
r Restaurant Car.
t Tea Car.

WOLVERTON (Bucks)

from Euston 52¼ miles. Fares, 11/0a, 6/7c. R. T. for two months, 22/0a. Pop. 14,052.
Map Square 18.

EUSTON	WOLV'TON	WOLV'TON	EUSTON
AM 6.45	8. 9	AM 7.43	9.40
7.35	9.45	8.29e	9.52
9.30	11.10	9. 4	10.15
12. 0nr	1.25	9.43	11.40
PM12.15	2.10	10.59d	12.20
2. 0	4. 9	10.59e	12.32
4.15	5.36	PM 1.20k	2.45
5.32	6.54	2.52	4.15
6.10e	7.38	6.18	7.55
7.15d	9.28	6.40	8.35
9.50r	9.28	8.44	10.50
11.50h	1. 6	9.41d	11.30
12.10d	1.30	9.58d	5. 0

WOLVERTON—*contd.*

Sunday Trains.

Euston	Wolv'ton	Wolv'ton	Euston
AM 8.15	10.25	AM11.19	1.20
PM 6.45	8.20	PM 4. 4	5.50
9.15	10.27	8.35	10.10
—	—	—	—
—	—	—	—
—	—	—	—

d Saturdays only.
e Saturdays excepted.
h Wednesday nights only.
k Thursdays and Saturdays only.
n Noon.
r Restaurant Car.

Crauford Arms Hotel.
Recently built. Every modern convenience. Ample accommodation for large parties. Good bedrooms. Tea-lawn. Near Trams. P.R.H.A. House.

WOMBWELL (Yorks),
170½ miles. Fares, 34/7a, 20/9c. R. T., double fare. Departures *from* London as for Chapeltown. Departures *for* London about 8 times daily. Pop. 19,035
Map Square 12.

WOMERSLEY (Yorks)
from *King's Cross*, 166½ miles. Fares, 34/9a, 20/10c. R. T. for two months, 69/6a, 41/8c. Departures *from* London as for Knottingley. Departures *for* London about 7 times daily. Pop. 413.
Map Square 13.

WOOBURN GREEN
(Bucks) from *Paddington*, 30 miles. Fares, 5/3a, 3/2c. R. T. for two months, 10/6a, 6/4c. Pop. (Wooburn) 4,047.
Map Square 23.

Pad.	Woo.Gr.	Woo.Gr.	Pad.
AM 5.45	7.21	AM 8. 1	8.56
6.30	8.12	8.36	9.37
7.35	9. 4	9.41	11. 6
8.30	9.57	10.25	11.35
9.20	10.38	11. 8	12.15
11.25	12.31	PM 1.14	2.35
PM12.35*e*	2. 7	3. 3	4.10
1. 5*d*	2. 9	4.16	5.37
2. 7	3.12	5.40	6.55
3.38	4.39	6.33	7.45
4.50	5.50	8.14	9.33
5.45	6.44	9.26	10.42
6.55	7.49	10.15	12. 0
8.35	9.39	—	—
10. 5*h*	11. 9	—	—
—	—	—	—
—	—	—	—
—	—	—	—

Sunday Trains.

AM 8.20	9.49	AM 8.52	10.14
9.45	10.48	11.37	1. 5
11.45	12.45	PM 2.51	4.53
PM 2.35	3.43	5. 7	6.23
5.15	6.23	7.40	9.17
8.20	9.30	8.47	9.53
—	—	—	—
—	—	—	—
—	—	—	—

d Saturdays only.
e Saturdays excepted.
h Wednesdays and Saturdays only.

WOODBOROUGH
(Wilts) from *Paddington*, 78½ miles. Fares, 16/6a, 9/11c. R. T. for two months, 33/0a. Pop. 367.
Map Square 22.

Pad.	W'dboro	W'dboro'	Pad.
AM 7.30	9.47	AM 7.53	10. 0
8.45*r*	11.29	9.57	12.55
10.45	1. 8	PM12.18	2.50
PM12.30*r*	2.46	4.12	7.20
2.45	5.23	4.48	8.20
3.18	6.35	7.59	10.45
6.30	8.37	—	—

Sunday Trains.

AM 9.10	12.11	AM 7.49	10.50
PM 5.15	8. 6	PM 6.54	9.15
—	—	—	—
—	—	—	—

r Restaurant Car.

WOODBRIDGE (Suffolk)
from *Liverpool Street*, 79 miles. Fares, 16/8a, 10/0c. R. T. for two months, 33/4a. Pop. 4,598.
Map Square 19.

L'PL. ST.	W'D'GE	W'DB'GE	L'PL. ST.
AM 5. 0	7.30	AM 8. 9*r*	10.30
8.15*r*	11. 0	9.12*r*	11.22
10.20	12.51	11.18	1.20
PM 1. 0	2.56	11.49*r*	2. 3
3.18	5.29	PM 1.25	3.42
4.55*r*	6.46	4. 0	5.56
5.18*r*	7.34	5.11	7.51
—	—	7.16*r*	9.22
—	—	8.16	11.16

Sunday Trains.

AM10. 5*r*	12.20	AM 8.48	11.38
PM 4.40	6.58	PM 6.59*r*	9.10
—	—	—	—
—	—	—	—

r Restaurant Car.

Taxi Cabs can be hired to
meet any train at this Station by telegram or Telephone No. 96. A. J. GARNHAM, Jobmaster and Motor Proprietor.

Crown Hotel. Telephone 34.
Comfortable Hotel. Billiards. Garden with Tennis Court. Garage. Stabling.
TRUST HOUSES, Ltd.

Bull Hotel. Old established
Free House, close to station and river. Own motors can meet trains, moderate tariff. Noted Golf course. Billiards, Yachting, Fishing, Motor - boats, Wildfowling. Motor trips. Telegrams "Bull," Woodbridge, Telephone 89.
J. CECIL PAGET, Proprietor.

WOODBURN (Northumberland), 306½ miles. Fares, 64/5a, 38/8c. R. T. for two months, 128/10a, 77/4c. Departures *from* London as for Morpeth or Hexham. Departures *for* London about twice daily.
Map Square 3.

WOODBURY ROAD
(Devon) from *Waterloo*, 176½ miles. Fares, 37/3a, 22/4c. R. T. for two months, 74/6a, 44/8c. Departures *from* London as for Exmouth (*via* Exeter). Departures *for* London about 7 times daily. Pop. 1,603.
Map Square 26.

WOODCHESTER (Gloucester), 124½ miles. No through fares. Departures *from* London as for Stroud. Departures *for* London about 6 times daily Pop. 831.
Map Square 22.

WOODEND (Cumberland),
298¼ miles. Fares, 62/1a, 37/3c. R. T. for two months, 124/2a, 74/6c. Departures *from* London as for Sellafield. Departures *for* London 6 times daily.
Map Square 6.

WOODFORD (Essex)
from *Liverpool Street*, 9 miles, or from *Fenchurch Street*, 9½ miles. Fares from Liverpool Street, 1/8a, 1/4b, 1/0c. R. T. for two days, 3/4a, 2/7½b, 1/9c. From Fenchurch Street 1/8a, 1/4b, 1/0c. R. T. for two days, 3/4a, 2/7½b, 1/9c. Pop. 21,236. *See* pp 53b, 541-544.
Map Square 23.

Wilfrid Lawson Hotel, Ltd.
Family and Commercial. Exceedingly comfortable. Near Epping Forest's charming scenery. Moderate inclusive terms. Write Manager for Tariff.

WOODFORD (Northampton) from *Marylebone*, 69 miles. Fares, 14/5a, 8/8c. R. T., double fare. Pop. 1,505.
Map Square 18.

M'bone	W'ford	W'ford	M'bone
AM 6.45	9.10	AM 7.18	9.46
8.45*r*	10.21	9. 7	10.36
10. 0*r*	11.29	10. 8	12. 2
11.15	2. 5	11.45*r*	1.13
PM12.15*r*	1.50	PM 1.34*r*	3. 0
4.30	6. 6	2.30	4.56
4.55	7 7	7.31*r*	8.55
6.20	7.42	8.30*r*	9.55
6.25*e*	8.36	8.40	11.0
6.25*d*	8.46	—	—
7.30	10. 6	—	—

Sunday Trains.

AM 9.30	11.53	AM 7.26	10.13
PM 5.30*r*	7. 4	PM 6.11	8.58
6.30	9.15	—	—

d Saturdays only
e Saturdays excepted.
r Restaurant Car.

WOODGRANGE PARK
from *St. Pancras* or *Moorgate Street*, 12 miles. Fares from *St. Pancras*, 1/5½a,0/10½c. R.T. for two days, 2/11a, 1/9c. Pop. (Woodgrange) 13,559. *See* pp. 506, 507.

WOOD GREEN (Middlesex) from *King's Cross, Broad Street*, and *Moorgate Street*, 5 miles. Fares from King's Cross, 0/11½a, 0/9b, 0/7c. R. T. for two days, 1/11a, 1/6b, 1/2c. From Moorgate Street and Broad Street, 1/0½a, 0/10b, 0/7½c. R.T. for two days, 2/1a, 1/8b, 1/2½c. Pop. 50,707. *See* pp. 511-517.

WOODHALL JUNCTION (Lincoln) from *King's Cross*, 122½ miles. Fares, 25/7a, 15/4c. R. T., double fare.
Map Square 13.

King's+	Wood.J.	Wood.J.	King's+
AM 4.45	8.22	AM 9.46	1. 5
5. 5*s*	10.10	11.15	3.50
7.15*r*	11.12	PM 1. 5*r*	4.30
8.45	12.50	4.33	9. 0
11.30	3.55	7.10	3.25
PM 3. 0	6.28	—	—
4. 0	7. 7	—	—

Sunday Trains.

—	—	—	—
12. 0*nr*	3.42	PM 6.31*r*	10.20
—	—	—	—
—	—	—	—

n Noon.
r Restaurant Car.
s Fridays only.

WOODHALL SPA (Lincoln) from *King's Cross*, 124 miles. Fares, 25/8*a*, 15/5*c*. R. T. for two months, 51/4*a*, 30/10*c*. Pop. 1,635.
Map Square 13.

King's +	W'hall.	W'hall.	King's +
AM 4.45	8.45	AM 9.27	1. 5
7.15*r*	11.25	11. 2	3.50
8.45	1.15	PM12.40	4.30
11.30	4.10	4.11	9. 0
PM 3. 0	6.50	6.15	3.25
4. 0	7.22	—	—
—	—	—	—

No Sunday Trains.
r Restaurant Car.

Eagle Lodge Hotel. First class. Fully licensed. Open throughout year. Near Golf Links and Baths. Convenient for Lincoln. Telegrams: "Eagle, Woodhall Spa." Telephone No. 32. Tariff from— Miss LAMB.
See advt. p. **346**.

Spa Hotel. Centrally Situated. Excellent Public Rooms. Large Grounds. Fully Licensed. Best English Cooking. Telephone No. 9.
Miss K. SPRING, Manageress.
See advt. p. **345**.

"Woodlands" (Private Hotel). Central. Ground floor suite. Smoke Room. Comfort studied. Good Cuisine. Highly recommended. Garage. Personally supervised.
Mr. and Mrs. HUNTER.

Golf Hotel (late Clevedon). Standing in its own grounds, close to 18-hole Golf Course and Spa. Baths. Fully licensed. Billiards. Smoking Room. Telephone 8. Apply—
MANAGERESS.

WOODHAM FERRERS (Essex) from *Liverpool Street*, 34 miles. Fares, 6/6*a*, 3/11*c*. R. T. for two months, 13/0*a*, 7/10*c*. Pop. 1,168.
Map Square 24.

L'pl. St.	W. Fer.	W. Fer.	L'pl. St.
AM 5.26	7. 5	AM 7.26	8.45
6.50	8.34	8.38	9.46
9. 1	10.28	9.49	11. 7
10.47*d*	12.11	11.40*d*	1.16
11.56	1.21	PM12.10*e*	1.25
PM 1.26*d*	2.22	1.25*d*	3. 5
2.20*e*	4. 7	3. 6*d*	4.56
2.40*d*	3.52	3.16*e*	4.51
4.15*e*	5.10	5.32	6.52
4.18*d*	5.31	6.50	8.23
5.39	6.44	8.28	9.56
6.26*e*	7.41	—	—
8. 2*e*	9.15	—	—
8.45*d*	9.51	—	—
—	—	—	—

Sunday Trains.

AM 8.45	10. 4	AM 8. 0	10.25
9.30	11. 5	PM 7. 8	8.45
PM 6.42	8.11	8.13	9.32
—	—	—	—

d Saturdays only.
e Saturdays excepted.

WOODHAY (Hants) from *Paddington*, 56½ miles. Fares, 11/10*a*, 7/1*c*. R. T. for two months, 23/8*a*, 14/2*c*. Pop. 1,642.
Map Square 23.

Pad.	Woodhay	Woodhay	Pad.
AM 7.30	9.16	AM 8.12	10. 0
9.30	11.56	9.15	10.52
PM12.30*r*	2. 6	11.22	12.55
2.45	4.18	PM12.55	2.50
5.55	7.15	3.27	5.50
8. 0*d*	10.18	6.27*r*	8.20
—	—	—	—
—	—	—	—
—	—	—	—
—	—	—	—

No Sunday Trains.
d Saturdays only.
r Restaurant Car.

WOODHEAD (Yorks), 183¾ miles. Fares, 37/4*a*, 22/5*c*. R. T., double fare. Departures *from* London as for Penistone. Departures *for* London about 4 times daily. Pop. 3,882.
Map Square 12.
Station closed on Sundays.

WOODHOUSE (Yorks), 156¾ miles. Fares, 32/6*a*, 19/6*c*. R.T., double fare. Departures *from* London as for Worksop or Beighton. Departures *for* London about 5 times daily. Pop. 5,305.
Map Square 13.

WOODHOUSE MILL (Yorks), from *St. Pancras*, 157½ miles. Fares, 32/6*a*, 19/6*c*. R. T., double fare. Departures *from* London as for Chesterfield. Departures *for* London about 6 times daily.
Map Square 13.

WOODKIRK (Yorks), 182¾ miles. Fares, 38/1*a*, 22/10*c*. R. T., double fares. Departures *from* London as for Wakefield (Westgate). Departures *for* London about 4 times daily.

WOODLAND (Lancs), 272¾ miles. Fares, 56/10*a*, 34/1*c*. R. T. for two months, 113/8*a*, 68/2*c*. Departures *from* London as for Coniston. Departures *for* London about 3 times daily. Pop. 297.
Map Square 6.

WOODLAND PARK (Flint), 206½ miles. No through fares. Departures *from* London as for Prestatyn. Departures *for* London about 6 times daily.
Map Square 11.

WOODLANDS ROAD (Lancs), 188½ miles. Fares, 39/0*a*, 23/5*c*. R. T. for two months, 78/0*a*, 46/10*c*. Departures *from* London as for Manchester. Departures *for* London about 5 times daily.

WOOD LANE (Central London Tube). *See* back of Map.

WOODLESFORD (Yorks) from *St. Pancras*, 190 miles. Fares, 37/6*a*, 22/6*c*. R. T., double fare. Pop. 3,205.
Map Square 12.

St. Pan.	Woodfd.	Woodfd.	St. Pan.
AM 2.25*g*	8.49	AM 6.45*r*	12.10
9. 0*r*	2. 6	8.45*r*	2.10
PM 1.50*r*	6.33	PM12.23*r*	5.45
3.30*r*	8.59	3.17*r*	8.35
—	—	9.25	4.20
—	—	10.42*e*	7.50
—	—	11.13*d*	8. 5
—	—	—	—
—	—	—	—
—	—	—	—

WOODLESFORD—*contd*

Sunday Trains.

St. Pan.	Woodfd.	Woodfd.	St. Pan.
AM11.15*r*	8.24	AM 7.18*r*	5. 2
PM 3.15	8.43	PM 2.12*r*	9.43
—	—	9.22	4.55

d Saturdays only.
e Saturdays excepted.
g Mondays excepted.
r Restaurant Car.

WOODLEY (Cheshire), 179½ miles. Fares, 37/1*a*, 22/3*c*. R. T., double fare. Departures *from* London as for Marple. Departures *for* London about 4 times daily.
Map Square 12.

WOODNESBOROUGH COLLIERY (Kent), 78½ miles. No through fares. Departures *from* London as for Wingham Colliery. Departures *for* London about 5 times daily. Pop. 965.

WOODSIDE (Perth), 463½ miles. Fares, 93/11*a*, 56/4*c*. R. T. for two months, 187/10*a*, 112/8*c*. Departures *from* London as for Perth. Departures *for* London about 3 times daily. Pop. 529.
Map Square 38.

WOODSIDE (Surrey) from *Charing Cross, Cannon Street*, and *London Bridge*, 12¾ miles. Fares, 2/1*a*, 1/8*b*, 1/3*c*. R. T. for two days, 4/2*a*, 3/1*b*, 2/2*c*. *See* pp. 544-547.

WOODSIDE PARK (Herts) from *King's Cross, Moorgate Street*, and *Broad Street*, 8¾ miles. Fares from King's Cross, 1/7*a*, 1/3*b*, 0/11½*c*. R. T. for two days, 3/2*a*, 2/6*b*, 1/11*c*. From Moorgate Street and Broad Street, 1/8*a*, 1/4*b*, 1/0*c*. R. T. for two days, 3/4*a*, 2/8*b*, 1/11½*c*. *See* pp. 518-522.

WOOD STREET (Walthamstow) from *Liverpool Street*, 7 miles. Fares, 1/0½*a*, 0/10*b*, 0/7½*c*. R. T. for two days, 2/0½*a*, 1/5½*b*, 1/0½*c*. Pop. 17,589. *See* pp. 523, 524.
Map Square 53.

WOODVALE (Lancs), 228 miles. Fares, 43/4*a*, 26/0*c*. R. T. for two months, 86/8*a*, 52/0*c*. Departures *from* London as for Warrington (Central). Departures *for* London about 6 times daily.
Map Square 12.

WOODVILLE (Derby) from *St. Pancras*, 124½ miles. Fares, 24/9*a*, 14/10*c*. R. T., double fare. Departures *from* London as for Swadlincote. Departures *for* London about 4 times daily. Pop. 2,871.
Map Square 17.

WOODY BAY (Devon), 205½ miles. Fares, 42/6*a*, 25/6*c*. R. T. for two months, 85/0*a*, 51/0*c*. Departures *from* London as for Lynton. Departures *for* London about twice daily.
Map Square 21.

Woody Bay Hotel. Most perfect spot in Devon. 700 ft above sea. Modern sanitation. Baths. High Class Cooking.
STANLEY HOLMAN, Proprietor.

WOOFFERTON (Salop), 156 miles. Fares, *via* Leominster, 30/0*a*, 18/0*c*. R. T. for two months, 60/0*a*, 36/0*c*. *Via* Shrewsbury, 31/11*a*, 19/2*c*. R. T. for two months, 63/10*a*, 38/4*c*. Departures *from* London as for Leominster. Departures *for* London about 6 times daily.
Map Square 17.

WOODY BAY HOTEL. All Rooms Face Sea.

WOOKEY (Somerset), from *Paddington*, 122 miles. Fares, *via* Witham, 25/3*a*, 15/2*c*. R. T. for two months, 50/6*a*. *Via* Yatton, 30/9*a*, 18/3*c*. R. T. for two months 60/10*a*. Departures *from* London as for Wells (Somerset). Departures *for* London about 4 times daily. Pop. 933.
Map Square 22.

WOOL (Dorset) from *Waterloo*, 125¼ miles. Fares, 26/3*a*, 15/9*c*. R. T. for two months, 52/6*a*. 31/6*a*. Pop. 463.
Map Square 27.

W'loo.	Wool	Wool	W'loo.
AM 5.40	9.39	AM 7.22*s*	11. 0
5.50	11.37	9.20*r*	12.50
10.30	1.51	11.23	2.50
PM12.30*r*	3.51	PM12.17	4.20
2.30*s*	5.51	1.14	4.50
4.30*r*	7.58	3.21	6.58
6.30*r*	9.51	5.21*r*	8.50
—	—	10.34	3.58
—	—	—	—
—	—	—	—

Sunday Trains.

AM11. 0*r*	2.57	AM 7.49	12.11
PM 2. 0*r*	5.55	10.36*r*	2.27
7. 0*r*	10.58	PM 3. 0*r*	6.24
—	—	6. 0*r*	9.31
—	—	10.34	3.58
—	—	—	—

r Restaurant Car.
s Refreshments served.

Cove Hotel, Lulworth, facing English Channel. Magnificent Dorset scenery. Fishing, Sailing, Bathing. Apply for Tariff.
P W. ENNIS, Proprietor.
See advt. p. **64**.

WOOLASTON (Glo'ster) from *Paddington*,136¼ miles. Fares (*via* Gloucester), 28/4*a*, 17/0*c*. R. T. for two months, 56/8*a*. *Via* Severn Tunnel, 30/0*a*, 18/0*c*. R.T. for two months, 60/0*a*, 36/0*c*. Departures *from* London as for Lydney. Departures *for* London about 6 times daily. Pop. 779.
Map Square 22.

WOOLER (Northumberland), 327½ miles. Fares, 69/0*a*, 41/5*c*. R. T. for two months, 138/0*a*, 82/10*c*. Departures *from* London as for Alnwick. Departures *for* London about 4 times daily. Pop. 1,382.
Map Square 3.

WOOLFOLD (Lancs), 198 miles. No through fares. Departures *from* London as for Bury. Departures *for* London about 10 times daily.
Map Square 12.

WOOLSTON (Hants) from *Waterloo*, 79¼ miles. Fares, 16/8*a*, 10/0*c*. R. T. for two months, 33/4*a*, 20/0*c*. Departures *from* London as for Netley. Departures *for* London about 8 times daily. Pop. 6,030.
Map Square 28.

WOOLWICH AR-SENAL (London) from *Charing Cross, Cannon Street*, and *London Bridge*, 10 miles. Fares from Charing Cross, 1/11*a*, 1/7*b*, 1/2*c*. R. T. for two days, 3/10*a*, 2/11*b*, 2/0*c*. From Cannon Street, 1/8*a*, 1/4*b*, 1/0*c*. R. T. for two days, 3/4*a*, 2/8*b*, 2/0*c*. *See* pp. 547-551.
Pop. (Woolwich) 140,389.
Map Square 23.

WOOLWICH DOCK-YARD from *Charing Cross, Cannon Street*, and *London Bridge*, 9½ miles. Fares from Charing Cross, 1/11*a*, 1/7*b*, 1/2*c*. R. T for two days, 3/10*a*, 2/11*b*, 2/0*c*. From Cannon Street, 1/7*a*, 1/3*b*, 0/11½*c*. R. T. for two days, 3/2*a*, 2/6*b*, 1/11*c*. *See* pp. 547-551.
Map Square 23.

WOOLWICH, NORTH (London) from *Fenchurch Street*, 7¾ miles, or from *Liverpool Street*, 8¼ miles. Fares from Fenchurch Street, 1/0½*a*,0/10*b*, 0/7½*c*. R. T. for two days, 2/0*a*, 1/8*b*, 1/2*c*. From Liverpool Street, 1/3*a*, 1/0*b*, 0/9*c*. R. T. for two days, 2/6*a*, 1/11*b*, 1/4*c*.
Pop. 8,842. *See* pp. 537-540.
Map Square 23.

WOOPERTON (Northumberland), 321 miles. Fares, 67/9*a*, 40/8*c*. R. T., double fare. Departures *from* London as for Alnwick. Departures *for* London about 3 times daily. Pop. 54.
Map Square 3.

WOOTTON (Isle of Wight), 85 miles. Fares, 19/1*a*, 11/8*c*. R.T. for two months, 38/2*a*, 23/4*c*. Departures *from* London as for Ryde. Departures *for* London about 4 times daily. Pop. 143.
Map Square 28.

WOOTTON BASSETT (Wilts) from *Paddington*,83 miles. Fares, 17/4*a*, 10/5*c*. R. T. for two months, 34/8*a*. Pop. 1,991.
Map Square 22.

	Pad.	Woot. B.	Woot. B.	Pad.
AM 1. 0*g*	5.45	AM 8.27	10.45	
5.30	7.40		10.23	12.20
7.30	9.30	PM12.47*r*	2.40	
9. 0	11.19		3.39	6. 2
10.45	1. 4		6.31*r*	8.35
PM 3.15*t*	5.13		7.26	10.25
4.15*et*	6. 3		9.49	2.45
5.15	7.26		—	—
6. 0*r*	8.19		—	—
6.55	9.41		—	—

Sunday Trains.

AM10.35	1.20	PM 2.40	6. 0
PM12.30*r*	3.10		7.39	10. 0
2. 0	6.59		—	—
10. 0	5.45		—	—

e Saturdays excepted.
g Mondays excepted.
r Restaurant Car.
t Tea Car.

WOOTTON, NORTH (Norfolk) from *Liverpool Street*, 99½ miles. Fares, 20/10*a*,12/6*c*. R. T. for two months, 41/8*a*, 25/0*c*. Departures *from* London as for King's Lynn. Departures *for* London about 7 times daily. Pop. 317.
Map Square 19.

WORCESTER (SHRUB HILL) from *Paddington*,120½ miles. Fares, 23/9*a*, 14/3*c*. R. T. for two months, 47/6*a*. *Via* Gloucester, 27/11*a*, 16/9*c*. R T. for two months, 55/10*a*. Pop. 48,848.
Map Square 17.

	Pad.	Worces.	Worces.	Pad.
AM 5.30	10.10	AM 6.30	9.50	
8.50	11.39		8.55	11.15
9.45	12.43		9. 2	12. 5
10.40*h*	3.12		10.20	2.12
PM 1.30*r*	3.40		12. 0*r*	2.55
1.35*r*	4.32	PM 2. 0*r*	4.15	
4.45*t*	7. 7		3. 0	5.50
6. 5*r*	8.45		3.10	7.20
6.10*h*	9.54		4. 5*hr*	8. 5
6.55	10.42		6. 0*r*	9.15
—	—		6.40	10.45

Sunday Trains.

AM10.35*r*	2.15	AM10.35	2.40
PM 4.10	8. 0	PM 5.50*r*	9.48
—	—	—	—
—	—	—	—
—	—	—	—
—	—	—	—

h Via Stratford-on-Avon.
r Restaurant Car.
t Tea Car.

ANOTHER ROUTE (SHRUB HILL) from *Euston*, 138¾ miles, *via* Birmingham. Fares, 23/9*a*, 14/3*c*. R. T. for two months, 47/6*a*, 28/6*c*.

	Euston	Worces.	Worces.	Euston
AM 2.30	8.15	AM 7.12	10.40	
· 5. 0	9.52		8.23	12.40
6.45	11.25		10. 2*r*	1.25
9.15*r*	1.24	PM12.33*t*	4.35	
11.30*r*	3.30		3.15*r*	6.50
12. 0*nr*	4.21		4.28*r*	8.20
PM 2.20*t*	5.37		5.53*dr*10.45	
2.50*t*	7.31		6.45*er*10.20	
4.35*r*	8. 7		9.15*e*	4. 0
6.55*r* 10.13			9.15*d*	5. 0
9.30	3.40	—	—	
*d*12.10*m*10. 0			—	—

Sunday Trains.

AM 9.15	3.45	AM 8.42*r*	1.45
PM 1. 0*r*	6. 0	11. 4	5. 5
5.10	9.48	PM 9.10	5. 0
9.15	3.40	—	—
—	—	—	—

d Saturdays only.
e Saturdays excepted.
m Midnight.
n Noon.
r Restaurant Car.
t Tea Car.

Star Hotel. County and Family. Every Comfort. Electric Lift. Lounge. Grill, Drawing, Reading, Writing and Assembly Rooms. Garage. Telephone 203-204.
G. E. SPURR, Proprietor.

Crown Hotel. Established 200 years. Family and Commercial. Renowned for good cooking. Garage. Telephone 338.
Miss GODFREY, Manageress.

WORCESTER.—STAR HOTEL. GARAGE for 100 Cars. OPEN and CLOSED CARS for HIRE.

WORCESTER PARK

(Surrey) from *Waterloo*, 10¼ miles.
Fares, 2/0a, 1/3c. R. T. for two
days, 3/6a, 2/4c. *See* pp. 583, 584.

WORKINGTON (Cumberland)

from *Euston, via Penrith*,
320½ miles. Fares, *via* Penrith or
Barrow, 63/11a, 38/4c. R. T. for two
months, 127/10a, 76/8c. *Via* Carlisle. 65/0a, 39/0c. R. T. for two
months, 130/0a, 78/0c. Pop. 26,480.
Map Square 6.

EUSTON WORK'TON		WORK'TON EUSTON	
AM12.25	11.45	AM 6.40'r	3.45
5. 0	3. 7	6.40kr	4.15
5. 0v	3.11	9.10r	6. 0
10. 0rv	5.33	10.32rv	6.25
11.35ry	8 15	11. 0ry	7.30
11.35ry	9. 5	PM 1.52rvl0. 0	
PM 1.30ry	9.55	2.15ryl0.45	
11. 0dv	9.30	7. 5v	5. 0
11 35v	6.43	10. 0ev	6.55
—	—	10. 0dv	7.15

Sunday Trains.

PM11.35v	6.43	AM11.15rv	7.30
11.45	9.16	PM 5.37v	5. 0

d Saturdays only.
e Saturdays excepted.
h Mondays and Saturdays only.
k Mondays and Saturdays excepted.
r Restaurant Car.
v Via Carlisle.
y Via Whitehaven.

WORKINGTON

BRIDGE (Cumberland),310½ miles.
Fares, 63/11a, 38/4c. R. T. for two
months, 127/10a, 76/8c. Departures
from London as for Workington.
Departures *for* London about 4
times daily.
Map Square 6.

WORKSOP (Notts) from

King's Cross, 146½ miles. Fares,
30/7a, 18/4c. R. T., double fare.
Pop. 23,193.
Map Square 13.

KING'S+ WORKSP.		WORKSP. KING'S+	
AM 4.45	8. 4	AM 3. 5r	11.30
7.15r	10.22	9.13	1. 5
8.45	1.15	PM12. 2	3.50
10.10r	3. 3	1.34	6.25
11.30	4.31	2.31	6.30
PM 1.50r	5.42	4.52	9. 0
4. 0r	7.43	11.38	3.25
5.45r	9.17	—	—

Sunday Trains.

12. 0nr	3.41	AM10. 7	3.45
PM 5. 0r	8.33	PM 2.12	5.55
—	—	6.35r	10.20

n Noon.
r Restaurant Car.

WORKSOP—*continued.*

ANOTHER ROUTE from
Marylebone, 167 miles. Fares as
above.

M'BONE. WORKSP.		WORKSP. M'BONE.	
AM 2.52	7.10	AM 6. 9r	11.10
8.45r	1.28	8.48r	1.13
10. 0r	2.29	10.22r	3. 0
PM12.15r	4.52	PM 2.31r	6.38
3.20r	7.14	4.31r	8.55
6.20r	10.30	5.43r	9 55
10. 0d	2. 9	9.40	3.57
10. 5e	3.26	—	—

Sunday Trains.

AM11.15r	7.45	AM11. 1r	5.40
—	—	PM 5.53r	10.24

d Saturdays only.
e Saturdays excepted.
r Restaurant Car.

WORLESTON (Cheshire)

161¼ miles. Fares, 33/9a, 20/3c.
R. T. for two months, 67/6a. Departures *from* London as for
Crewe. Departures *for* London
about 3 times daily. Pop. 540.
Map Square 12.

WORLINGWORTH

(Suffolk), 95¼ miles. Fares, 20/0a,
12/0c. R. T. for two months,
40/0a, 24/0c. Departures *from*
London as for Stradbroke. Departures *for* London about twice
daily. Pop. 575.
Map Square 19.

WORMALD GREEN

(Yorks), 205 miles. Fares, 42/8a,
25/7c. R. T., double fare. Departures *from* London as for Harrogate. Departures *for* London about
twice daily.
Map Square 7.

WORMIT (Fife, 449 miles.

No through fares. Departures
from London as for Leuchars.
Departures *for* London about twice
daily.

WORMW'D SCRUBS.

See ST. QUINTIN PARK.

WORPLESDON (Surrey)

from *Waterloo*, 26¼ miles. Fares,
5/8a, 3/5c. R. T. for two
months, 11/4a, 6/10c. Pop. 2,593.
Map Square 23.

W'LOO WPLESDN.		WPLESDN. W'LOO.	
AM 5.50	6.37	AM 7.14	8.20
6.50	7.45	7.32	8.36
7.50	8.52	7.56	8.41
9. 0	9.52	8.36	9.12
9.15	10.22	8.51	9.41
10.20	11.25	9.28	10.20
11.20	12.27	9.58	11.16
PM12.15	1.22	10.50	11.32
12.40d	1.54	11.38	12.46
1.50e	2.38	PM 1.38	2.46
2. 0d	2.48	2.12	3. 6
2.34	3.31	3.42	4.46
3.15	4.22	4.29	5.46
4.20	5.24	5. 7	6.16
5. 0	5.46	5.41	6.46

WORPLESDON—*contd.*

W'LOO WPLESDN.		WPLESDN. W'LOO.	
PM 5.50	6.37	PM 6.42	7.46
6.10e	6.54	8.12	9. 6
6.40d	7.42	8.42	9.46
6.54e	7.42	9.40	10.46
8. 0	8.57	11. 1	12.16
8.20	9.27	—	—
9.50	10.34	—	—

Sunday Trains.

AM 8.20	9.26	AM 9.32	10.16
9.20	10.28	11.33	12.41
10.20	11.30	PM 2.33	3.44
PM 1.50	2.43	5.21	6.46
5.20	6.30	6.32	7.41
6.20	7.12	7.32	8.41
7.20	8.28	8.32	9.44
8.20	9.29	9.32	10.41
—	—	10.31	11.43

d Saturdays only.
e Saturdays excepted.

WORSLEY (Lancs) from

Euston, 189¼ miles. Fares, 39/7a,
23/9c. R. T. for two months,
79/2a. Departures *from* London
as for Manchester (London Road).
Departures *for* London about 6
times daily. Pop. 13,929.
Map Square 19.

WORSTEAD (Norfolk)

from *Liverpool Street*, 127¼ miles.
Fares, 25/3a, 15/2c. R. T. for two
months, 50/6a. Departures *from*
London as for Wroxham. Departures *for* London about 8 times
daily. Pop. 747.
Map Square 19.

WORTHING (Sussex)

from *London Bridge* and *Victoria*,
59½ miles. Fares, 12/6a, 7/6c.
R. T. for two months, 25/0a,
15/0c. Pop. 35,224.
Map Square 28.

Leave		Arr. at
VICT.	LON. B.	W'THING.
AM —	5.18	8. 9
6.37	6 40	9. 0
7.23	7.25	10.23
8.25	8. 7	10.39
9. 0	—	11.11
—	9. 6	11.29
10. 5	9.50	11.54
11. 0l	—	12.29
—	10.35	1.26
11.40	—	1. 5
—	11.40d	1.36
11.55	11.50	1.55
PM12.45	—	2.16
—	1.20d	2.57
1.55	—	3.30
2. 0d	2. 5	4.18
2. 0e	—	4.49
—	2. 8d	5.19
3.10l	—	4.49
3.40p	—	5.25
—	4. 0	5.50
4.30	—	6. 6
—	5. 5d	6.27
—	5. 8ep	6.26
5.45p	—	7.16
—	5.55e	7.27
—	6. 0	7.43
—	6. 8	8.54
6.40	—	8.13
7.15	7.20	9.19
8.35	—	10. 0
9. 3d	9.12d	11.40
10. 0	9.12e	11.56

WORTHING—*continued.*

Sunday Trains.

	Leave	Arr. at
Vict.	Lon. B.	Wthing.
AM 6.55	7. 2	10. 1
8.50	8.55	11.40
9.45*k*	—	11.40
10.30*p*	—	12. 0
11. 0*h*	—	12.26
11. 5	—	1. 1
PM 12.15	—	2.16
1.10	—	3. 9
1.14	1.10	3.56
5.50	6. 0	9.10
6.30*p*	—	8.39
8. 0	8. 0	10.40
9.25	9.10	11.36
—	—	—
—	—	—

Trains from Worthing.

Leave	Arrive at	
Wthing.	Lon. B.	Vict.
AM 5.40	8.15	8.24
6.15	8.19	—
7. 0	8.38	—
7.25	—	9.15
7.43*f*	—	9.22
*g*7.55*p*	—	9.22
8. 2*e*	9.50	—
8.16*e*	—	10.24
8.24*d*	9.50	—
8.30*d*	10.53	—
*e*8.58*p*	9.55	—
8.41*e*	10.53	—
9.10	—	10.55
9.29	11.10	—
9.43*p*	11.20	11.17
10.20	12.19	12.17
10.52	1.42	—
11.34	—	1.20
PM 12.26*l*	—	2.20
12.35*e*	2.23	—
12.57	3.40	3.45
2.25*p*	—	4.17
2.55*d*	4.58	4.45
2.55	—	4.50
3. 9	5.54	5.55
4.16	6.36	6.34
5. 8*l*	—	6.45
5.33	7.42	7.30
6.45	—	8.48
7. 2	10. 9	10.17
7.57*d*	10. 0	9.45
8. 8	10.58	—
9.14	—	11.17
10.28	12.59	1. 0

Sunday Trains.

AM 7.23	10.45	—
8.55	11.15	10.50
10.32	—	1. 0
11.55	—	1.35
PM 2.30	5. 3	5.11
4.20*h*	—	6. 0
5. 3	7.56	7. 0
5.30	—	7.28
6.20*p*	—	7.50
6.45	9.17	9.13
9. 0	—	10.55
10. 2	12.27	—

d Saturdays only.
e Saturdays excepted.
f Mondays only.
g Mondays excepted.
h First-class Pullman Cars only.
k Third-class Pullman Cars only.
l First and Third-class Pullman Cars only.
p Pullman Car attached.

WORTHING—*continued.*

Warnes Hotel, Marine Parade. Elegantly furnished. Choicest cuisine and wines. Telegrams, "Warne, Worthing." Moderate tariff. Entirely new Proprietorship and Management. *See advt. p. 347.*

Burlington Hotel. Worthing's most up-to-date Hotel. Facing Sea. Private Suites. R.A.C. and A.A. Telephones, 80 and 81. Tariff on application. R. SCHNEIDER, Proprietor. *See advt. p. 348.*

Beach Hotel. This first-class Private Residential Hotel will appeal to people of refinement. Situated on front, luxuriously furnished. Moderate charges. Telephone, 509. *See advt. p. 349.*

Percival's Hotel (unlicensed). Finest position. Sea Front. Passenger Lift. Central heating. Hot and Cold water in Bedrooms. Balcony suites South. Private Bathrooms. Extreme comfort. Choice cuisine. Best English provisions. Garage. For tariff and testimonials apply "A.B.C." Percival's Hotel. 'Phone 161. *See advt. p. 350.*

Marine Hotel. Most central position, facing sea and pier. Under entirely new management. Re-decorated. Excellent Cuisine. Fully licensed. Large Garage attached. 'Phone, 274. *See advt. p. 351.*

Steyne Hotel, facing Steyne Gardens and Sea. Reconstructed and refurnished. Tel. 151. Proprietor, J. O. KORDINA. *See advt. p. 351.*

South View Private Hotel. Marine Parade. Facing Sea and Pier. Highly recommended. High-class Cuisine. Tel. 326. *See advt. p. 352.*

Stanhoe Hotel. Finest position Sea front. Under new management. Moderate inclusive terms from 15/0 a day. Telephone, 173. Telegrams, "Stanhoe." Proprietors—
F. BIRD & P. FRANKHAM. For particulars apply ditto. *See advt. p. 352.*

Cavendish Hotel, 115-116 Marine Parade. Private Residential. Moderate inclusive. *See advt. p. 353.*

Brunswick Hotel, fully Licensed. Finest position Sea Front. Terms moderate. S. T. WAYMENT. *See advt. p. 353.*

The Little Hotel, Marine Parade (Private and Residential). Facing Sea. Old-fashioned, Comfortable. Electric Light. Moderate Charges.
Proprietress, Mrs. ROLFS (late Manageress, Marine Hotel, Worthing.)

WORTHING—*continued.*

Eardley House. High-class Boarding Establishment, Marine Parade. 36 Bedrooms, many facing the Sea. Large Dining, Drawing, Billiard, Smoking, and Recreation Rooms. Private Sitting Rooms, with Separate Board if required. Established 1881. Telephone : 490. Conducted by the Proprietress, Miss BUTLER.

Sea Crest Boarding Establishment. 11, Bedford Row. Best position. Close to Sea. Near Pier. Baths, and Golf Links. Home Comforts. Terms moderate Proprietress, Mrs. JOHNSON.

Marlborough Hotel. Opposite bandstand. Thirty rooms. Facing Sea. Redecorated. Large new lounge. Excellent cuisine. Lawn. Bathing from Hotel. 'Phone 591.
PROPRIETRESS.

Gardner's Hotel, Private and Residential, 7. Heene Terrace. Finest position on Sea Front. Private Lawns front and rear. Liberal Cuisine. Home Comfort. Electric Lighting throughout. Latest approved sanitation. Garage. Telephone, 111. Mrs. GARDNER,
Proprietress.

Whitehall Private Hotel, 95, Marine Parade. Uninterrupted Sea Views. Redecorated. Luxuriously Furnished. Modern Improvements. Excellent Cuisine. Separate Tables. Personal Supervision.

Heene Road (15). One minute from Sea. Paying guests received. Every comfort. Excellent cuisine and attendance. Electric light. Separate Tables. Bridge. From 3½ guineas.
Mrs. E. M. HEAD.

Railway Hotel. Family and Commercial. One minute from Station. Luncheons, Teas, Suppers daily. Garage. A.A. New Wing fitted with Central Heating, &c. Telephone 170.
Proprietors, HOWELL & SONS.

Winchilsea, Windsor Road. Board Residence. Good position adjoining Sea Front. Comfortable. Good Cuisine. Personal Supervision. Electric light. Terms moderate. PROPRIETRESS.

Avenue Lodge, Grand Avenue. Small Select Private Hotel, charmingly situated by Sea. Detached. Well appointed. Electric Light. Excellent Cuisine. Separate Tables. Large Gardens. Tennis Lawn. From 3½ guineas. Tel phone 349.

House Agents, Auctioneers, Write, Phone, or call for complete List. Postage, 2d. Tel. 244. Wire, Normans, Worthing.
NORMAN & SPENCER, Chapel Road, Worthing.

For completion of Advertisements, see over.   **R**

WORTHING—*continued.*

House and Estate Agents,

JORDAN and COOK, 79, South Street. Best selection of Furnished and Unfurnished Residences. Telegrams, "Auctioneer, Worthing." 'Phone 142.

Auction, House and Estate

Agency Offices, Chapel Road. Messrs. A. PATCHING & Co.'s register forwarded free. Telephone No. 2. Telegrams, "Agency" Worthing.

WORTHING WEST

from *London Bridge* and *Victoria*, 60½ miles. Fares, 12/8a, 7/7c. R.T. for two months, 25/4a, 15/2c.
Map Square 28.

	Leave	Arr. at
	VICT.	LON. B.	WOR. W.
AM	—	5.18	3.12
	6.37	6.40	9.19
	8.25	8. 7	10.44
	9. 0	—	11.17
	—	9. 6	11.32
	10. 5	9.50	11.58
	—	10.35	1.29
	11. 0*l*	—	12.33
	11.40	—	1.10
	11.55	11.50	1.59
PM	12.45	—	2.21
	—	1.20*d*	3. 1
	1.55	—	3.34
	2. 0*d*	2. 5	4.23
	2. 0*e*	—	4.52
	—	2. 8*d*	5.23
	3.10*l*	—	4.52
	3.40*v*	—	5.30
	—	4. 0	5.54
	4.30	—	6.11
	—	5. 5*d*	6.31
	—	5. 8*e*	6.30
	5.45	—	7.21
	—	5.55*e*	7.31
	6.40	—	8.17
	7.15	7.20	9.21
	10. 0	9.12	12. 0
	—	—	—
	—	—	—

Sunday Trains.

AM	6.55	7. 2	10. 6
PM	1.14	1.10	4. 9
	—	—	—

Trains from Worthing West.

	Leave	Arrive at	
	WOR. W.	LON. B.	VICT.
AM	6.11	8.19	—
	6.54	8.38	—
	7.22	9.25	9.15
	7.39*f*	—	9.22
	7.48*g*	—	9.22
	7.57*e*	9.50	—
	8.20*d*	9.50	—
	8.29*e*	9.55	—
	8.37*e*	10.33	—
	9.25	11.10	—
	9.38	11.20	11.17
	10.16	12.19	12.17
	11.28	—	1.20
PM	12.15*e*	2.23	—
	12.23*l*	—	2.20
	12.53	3.40	3.45
	2.16	—	4.17
	2.50*d*	4.58	4.45
	2.50	—	4.50
	3. 5	5.54	5.55

WORTHING WEST—*continued.*

	Leave	Arrive at	
	WOR. W.	LON. B.	VICT.
PM	4.10	6.36	6.54
	5. 5*l*	—	6.45
	5.30	7.42	7.30
	6.40	—	8.48
	6.56	10.25	10.17
	7.53*d*	10. 0	9.45
	7.55*e*	10.58	—
	8.45	—	11.17
	10.15	12.59	1. 0

Sunday Trains.

AM	7.19	10.45	10.50
	10.28	—	1. 0
	11.28	—	1.35
PM	4.58	7.56	7. 0
	8.45	—	10.55

d Saturdays only.
e Saturdays excepted.
f Mondays only.
g Mondays excepted.
l First and Third-class Pullman Cars only.
v Pullman Car attached.

WORTHINGTON (Leicester), 123½ miles. Fares, 25/8a, 15/5c. R. T., double fare. Departures *from* London as for Melbourne (*via* Ashby). Departures *for* London about 4 times daily. Pop. 1,016.
Map Square 18.

WORTLEY (Yorks), 170½ miles. Fares, 34/5a, 20/8c. R. T., double fare. Departures *from* London as for Sheffield (Victoria). Departures *for* London about 5 times daily. Pop. 891.
Map Square 12.

WOTTON (Bucks), from *Marylebone*, 46½ miles. Fares, 9/10a, 5/11c. R. T. for two months, 19/8a, 11/6½c. Pop. 223.
Map Square 23.

M'BONE.	WOTTON	WOTTON	M'BONE.
AM 6.10	7.47*h*	AM 8.11	10.36
7.50	10. 9	8.26*h*	9.55
10. 5	12.28	10.46	12.59
PM 1.55*e*	4.27	PM 3.19*e*	6.22
2.15*d*	4.27	3.19	7.15
4.55	6.22*h*	5.52	8.10
5. 0	6.53	8.30*h*	9.55
7.30*d*	9.43	—	—

Sunday Trains:

AM 8.50	10.31*h*	AM 8.54*h*	10.43
PM 6.30	8.15*h*	PM 7.11*h*	8.58
—	—	—	—

d Saturdays only.
e Saturdays excepted.
h L. & N.E. Station.

ANOTHER ROUTE from *Baker Street*, 48 miles. Fares as above.

BAKERST.	WOTTON	WOTTON	BAKERST.
AM 7.50	10. 9	AM 8.11	10.24
10.11	12.28	10.46	1.22
PM 2.17	4 27	PM 3.19	5.41
4.10	6.53	5.52	8. 8
7.15*d*	9.43	8.49*d*	11.18

No Sunday Trains.
d Saturdays only.

WRABNESS (Essex) from *Liverpool Street*, 65 miles. Fares, 13/9a, 8/3c. R. T. for two months, 27/6a. Departures *from* London as for Mistley. Departures *for* London about 6 times daily. Pop. 338.
Map Square 21.

WRAFTON (Devon), 216¼ miles. Fares, 40/2a, 24/1c. R. T for two months, 80/4a, 48/2c. Departures *from* London as for Barnstaple. Departures *for* London about 6 times daily.
Map Square 21.

WRAGBY (Lincoln) from *King's Cross*, 135 miles. Fares, 27/11a, 16/9c. R. T., double fare Pop. 454.
Map Square 13.

KING'S+	WRAGBY	WRAGBY	KING'S+
AM 4.45	9. 3	AM 8.23*r*	1.30
7.15*r*	11.38	10.38	3.50
8.45	1.38	11.38*r*	4.30
11.30	4.33	PM 3.43	9. 0
PM 3. 0	7.10	4.33*r*	9.25
10.45*e*	8.23	7.10	3.25
—	—	—	—
—	—	—	—
—	—	—	—
—	—	—	—

Sunday Trains.

PM 10.45	8.23	—	—

e Saturdays excepted.
r Restaurant Car.

WRANGATON (Devon) from *Paddington*, 211½ miles. Fares, 43/7a, 26/2c. R. T. for two months, 87/2a. Departures *from* London about 5 times daily. Departures *for* London as for Brent.
Map Square 26.

WRAYSBURY (Bucks) from *Waterloo*, 21½ miles. Fares, 3/9a, 2/3c. R. T. for eight days, 7/6a, 4/6c. Pop. 956.
Map Squares 23 and 64.

W'LOO	WRAYSBY.	WRAYSBY.	W'LOO
AM 5.35	6.43	AM 5.48	6.36
7.24	8.16	6.48	7.36
8.24	9.17	7.18	8. 6
9.24	10.17	7.49	8.41
10.24	11.16	8.21	9. 6
11.24	12.16	8.46	9.36
PM 12.24	1.16	9.18	10. 6
12.54*d*	1.46	10.18	11. 6
1.24	2.16	11. 9	11.57
1.54*d*	2.46	PM 12. 9	12.57
2.24	3.16	1. 9	1.57
3.24	4.16	2. 9	2.57
4.24	5.16	3. 9	3.57
4.58*e*	5.46	4. 9	4.57
5.24	6.16	5. 9	5.57
5.54*e*	6.46	6. 9	6.57
6.24	7.16	7. 9	7.57
6.54*e*	7.46	8. 9	8.57
7.24	8.16	9.32	10.37
8.24	9.16	10.57*e*	12. 5
9.24	10.21	10.57*d*	12. 8
10.24	11.21	—	—
11.44	12.35	—	—
—	—	—	—
—	—	—	—
—	—	—	—

MARINE HOTEL, WORTHING.

WRAYSBURY—*contd.*
Sunday Trains.

W'LOO WRAYSBY.	WRAYSBY. WLOO		
AM 8.48	9.40	AM 8.37	9.28
10.18	11. 8	10.51	11.43
11.18	12. 8	11.51	12.43
PM12.18	1.26	PM12.51	1.43
1.18	2. 8	2.51	3.43
2.18	3.17	3.51	5.28
3.18	4. 8	4.51	5.43
4.18	5.17	5.51	6.43
5 18	6. 8	6.51	7.43
6.18	7. 8	7.51	8.43
7.18	8. 8	8.51	9.43
8.18	9.12	9.51	10.43
8.58	9.48	10.51	11.51
10.18	11. 8	—	—

d Saturdays only.
e Saturdays excepted.

WREA GREEN (Lancs),
218¾ miles. Fares, 45/7a, 27/4c. R. T. for two months, 91/2d, 54/8c. Departures *from* London as for Kirkham. Departures *for* London about 6 times daily. *Map Square 12.*

WREAY (Cumberland), 294¼
miles. Fares, 59/5a, 35/8c. R. T. for two months,118/10a, 71/4c. Departures *from* London as for Penrith. Departures *for* London about 5 times daily. Pop. 167. *Map Square 7.*

WRENBURY (Cheshire),
165½ miles. Fares, 33/11a, 20/4c. R. T. for two months, 67/10a. Departures *from* London as for Nantwich. Departures *for* London about 4 times daily. Pop. 494. *Map Square 12.*

WRESSLE (Yorks), 180¾
miles. Fares, 35/0a, 21/0c. R. T. for two months, 70/0a, 42/0c. Departures *from* London as for Howden. Departures *for* London about twice daily. Pop. 264. *Map Square 13.*

WRETHAM (Norfolk)
from *Liverpool Street,* 100 miles. Fares, 20/5a, 12/3c. R. T. for two months, 40/10a. Departures *from* London as for Watton. Departures *for* London about 4 times daily. Pop. 281. *Map Square 19.*

WREXHAM (Denbigh)
from *Paddington,* 183miles. Fares, 37/4a, 22/5c. R. T. for two months, 74/8a. Pop. 19,002. *Map Square 12.*

PAD.	WREXM.	WREXM.	PAD.
AM 9.10r	1. 0	AM 8. 2	12.25
10.40r	2.42	8.56r	1.25
PM12.50r	5.15	10. 3r	2. 5
2.10t	6.27	10.37r	4.15
4.10t	8.35	PM12.48r	5. 0
6.10r	10.14	1.59r	5.55
12.15	6.12	3.55r	8. 5
—	—	5.32	10. 0
—	—	8.23r	3.30

Sunday Trains.

PM 12.50r	5. 5	AM10.35	6.20
—	—	PM 4. 8r	9. 0
—	—	—	—

r Restaurant Car.
t Tea Car.

WREXHAM—*continued.*
ANOTHER ROUTE (CENTRAL) from *Euston,* 194¼ miles. Fares as above.

EUSTON	WREXM.	WREXM.	EUSTON
AM 2.35	9.25	AM 7.45r	1.45
5. 0	11. 2	9.45	5.35
10. 0r	3.12	11.15r	5.50
11.50r	7. 7	PM 1.20r	7.30
PM 2.35t	8.10	3.30er	9. 5
4. 5d	10.15	3.30dr	9.15
—	—	7.55e	5. 0
—	—	3.50d	5. 0

No Sunday Trains.
d Sats. only.   *e* Sats. excepted.
r Restaurant Car.   *t* Tea Car.

Wynnstay Arms Hotel.
Family and Commercial. 100 Rooms. Central Heating. Stabling. Lock-up Garages. Telephone 165.
R. M. HOWARD, Manager.

WRINGTON (Somerset)
from *Paddington,* 134 miles. Fares, 27/11a, 16/9c. R. T. for two months, 55/10a. Pop. 1,367. *Map Square 22.*

PAD.	WRING.	WRING.	PAD.
AM 5.30	10.28	AM 8.57r	2. 0
8.45	1.13	PM12.25	4. 5
11.15r	3.30	1.51	6. 2
PM 2.45	6.58	6. 9	10.25
12.30h	8.53	—	—

Sunday Trains.

—	—	AM 7.57	3.35

h Saturdays midnight only.
r Restaurant Car.

WROTHAM (Kent) from
Victoria, Holborn Viaduct, and *St. Paul's,* 29½ miles. Fares, 6/5a, 5/1b, 3/9c. R. T. for two months, 12/10a, 10/2b. Pop. 1,898. *Map Square 24.*

VICT. (S.E.&C.J.)	Leave HOL. V.	ST. PL.'s	ARr. at WROTM.
AM —	6.40	6.42	8. 6
8.32	8.20	8.23	10. 0
11. 4	10.58	11. 0	12.29
PM —	12.33d	12.36d	1.43
—	1.27d	1.30d	2.43
2. 9d	2. 4d	2. 7d	3. 8
2.40d	—	—	3.55
2.50e	—	—	4. 9
4.25c	—	—	5.28
e5.15h	—	5.21ek	6 .8
d5.20h	—	5.26dk	6.13
5.30e	—	5.53e	6.39
—	—	6.16e	7.18
6.40	6.34	6.37	7.53
7.22	7.22	7.24	8.38
8.55	—	—	9.59
9 55	—	—	10.44
10. 0	9.54	9.56	11.13

Sunday Trains.

AM —	8. 0	—	9.33
PM 2. 5	2. 3	—	3.36
6.35	6.40	—	7.58
10.15	10.12	—	11.34

Trains from Wrotham.

Leave WROTH.	ST. PL.'s	Arrive at HOL. V.	VICT.
AM 7.29	8.40	8.42	8.50
8.20	9.37	9.39	—
8.58	9.52	9.55	—
9.44d	10.41	—	—
9.44	—	10.43	—
10.37	—	—	11.37
11.47	12.59	1. 2	12.49
PM 1.22	—	—	2.40
3.11	—	—	4.33
5.44	6.58	7. 0	—
6.30	7.36k	—	7.49h
6.30d	8. 0	8. 2	—
6.30e	8.18	8.20	8.10
7.25	—	—	8.51
8.51d	—	—	9.54
10.25	11.43	11.45	—

WROTHAM—*continued.*
Sunday Trains.

Leave WROTH.	ST. PL.'s	Arrive at HOL. V.	VICT.
AM 3.41	—	—	10.48
PM 2.40	—	—	3.50
4.55	—	6.20	6. 3
8.49	—	10.22	10. 5

d Saturdays only.
e Saturdays excepted.
h Departs from or arrives at Charing + (S.E. & C.R.).
k Departs from or arrives at London Bridge (S.E. & C.R.).

WROXALL (Isle of
Wight), 89¼ miles, from *Waterloo,* or from *Victoria* and *London Bridge.* Fares 20/0a, 12/3c, 24/6c. Departures *from* London as for Shanklin. Departures *for* London about 6 times daily. Pop. 828. *Map Square 28.*

WROXHAM (Norfolk) from
Liverpool Street, 122¾ miles. Fares, 25/3a, 15/2c. R. T. for two months, 50/6a, 30/4c. Pop. 729. *Map Square 19.*

L'POOL. ST.	WROX.	WROX.	L'POOL. ST.
AM 5. 5	9.48	AM 7. 5f	10.56
8.15r	11.42	8.21r	11.22
9.50r	1. 2	9.47	1.20
10.12	2.33	PM 1.34r	4.58
PM12.33r	3.46	2.56	6.32
5.10r	6.11	3.45d	8. 2
5.18r	8.44	4.18r	8.33
—	—	6. 6r	9.22
—	—	9.20	2.50

Sunday Trains.

AM 9.20r	2.32	PM 1.32	6.40
PM 4.40	9.33	6.10r	9.10
—	—	8.34	3. 0

d Saturdays only.
f Mondays only.
r Restaurant Car.

WRYDE (Cambs) from
King's Cross, 87 miles. Fares, 17/4a, 10/3c. R. T., double fare. Departures *from* London as for Wisbech St. Mary. Departures *for* London about 5 times daily. *Map Square 18.*

WYCOMBE, HIGH
(Bucks) from *Paddington, via* Beaconsfield, 26¼ miles. Fares, 5/3a, 3/2c. R. T. for two months, 10/6a, 6/4c. Pop. 21,952. *Map Square 23.*

PAD.	WYCMB.	WYCMB.	PAD.
AM 5.45	7. 6	AM 6.38	8.14
6.10	7.45	7.44	8.34
6.35	8.10	8. 3	9.14
7.33h	8.53	8.30	9.20
8.12	9.15	9.50	10.40
9.10	9.41	11.27	12.32
9.44k	11.35	PM12.26	1.18
PM12.18	1.12	2.44	3.50
12.35	1.53	2.57d	4.19k
1.25	2.15	3.52	4.40
2.23	3.25	5.35	6.35
3.40	4.30	6.30	7.32
4.40	5.24	7. 9	9. 5
5.25	6.11	8.14	9.18
6.25	7.14	8.30	9.52
7.18	8.11	9.40	11. 4
7.42	9.26	10.23	11.41
7.55e	9.26	—	—
9. 0	10. 1	—	—
10.10	11.31	—	—

WYCOMBE, HIGH —continued.

Sunday Trains.

PAD.	WYCMB.	WYCMB.	PAD.
AM 9.12	10.16	AM 9.42	11. 4
9.35	11.20	PM12.50	2.26
11.15	12.20	2.20	3.27
PM 1.45	3.13	3.25	4.45
2.28	3.31	6.40	7.47
3.15	4.33	7.19	8.25
4. 0	5. 5	7.59	9.35
6. 5	7.30	9. 5	10. 7
7.20	8.20	10. 0	11. 0
8. 5	9.25	—	—
9.25	10.54	—	—

d Saturdays only.

e Saturdays excepted.

h No: after July 27th.

k Departs from Bishops Road Station.

ANOTHER ROUTE from
Paddington, *via* Maidenhead, 34 miles. Fares as above.

PAD.	WYCMB.	WYCMB.	PAD.
AM 5.45	7.52	AM 7.50	8.56
6 30	8.23	8.25	9.37
7.35	9.15	9.30	11. 6
8.30	10. 8	10.14	11.35
9.20	10.54	10.57	12.15
11.25	12.43	PM 1. 3	2.35
PM.2.35e	2.20	2.52	4.10
1. 5d	2.20	4. 5	5.37
2. 7	3.23	5.29	6.55
3.38	4.50	6.23	7.45
4.50	6. 1	8. 3	9.33
5.45	6.55	9.15	10.42
6.55	8. 0	10. 5	12. .0
8.35	9.50	—	—
10. 5h	11.20	—	—

Sunday Trains.

AM 8.20	10. 0	AM 8.41	10.14
9.45	11. 0	11.25	1. 5
11.45	12.57	PM 2.40	4.53
PM 2.35	3.54	4.55	6.22
5.15	6.34	7.28	9.17
8.20	9.42	8.35	9.53
—	—	—	—

d Saturdays only.

e Saturdays excepted.

h Wednesdays and Saturdays only.

ANOTHER ROUTE from
Marylebone, 28 miles. Fares as above.

M'BONE.	WYCMB.	WYCMB.	M'BONE.
AM 5.15	6. 8	AM 6.38	7.35
6.10	7. 6	7.33	8.32
6.50	7.43	8. 3	8.49
7.10	8.10	8.44	9.26
8. 4	9.15	9. 9	9.55
9. 5	10.10	11.27d	12.43
10. 0	10.36	PM12. 7	1. 5
10.35	11.35	12.26d	3.10
PM12.15	12.51	2.25d	3.15
12.55	1.53	2.25e	3.23
1.37d	2.26	2.57d	3.53
2.10	3. 8	3.30	4.28
3. 5	4. 3	3.52	5.48
4.30	5. 6	5. 3	6. 3
4.55	5.42	5.35	7. 5
5.38	6.19	7. 9	8. 6
5.43	7.14	8.30	9.27
6.35d	7.31	9.21	9.55
6.41e	7.25	9.40	10.31
6.45e	8.11	10.23	11.18
8.30	9.25	—	—
10.35	11.31	—	—
11.50	12.45	—	—

WYCOMBE, HIGH —continued.

Sunday Trains.

M'BONE.	WYCMB.	WYCMB.	M'BONE.
AM 8.50	9.49	AM 9.42	10.43
10.20	11.20	PM12.50	1.48
11.15	11.55	1.45	2.43
11.50	12.48	3.25	4.23
PM 2.15	3.12	5.' 2	5.40
3.35	4.33	5.25	6.23
6.30	7.31	7.59	8.58
8.30	9.25	9.40	10.38
10. 0	10.54	—	—

d Saturdays only.

e Saturdays excepted.

Red Lion Hotel. Telephone
152. Famous House from which Disraeli made his speech to the electors. Electric Light. Garden. Garage.

TRUST HOUSES, Ltd.

WYCOMBE, WEST
(Bucks) from *Paddington*, 28¾ miles. Fares, 5/8a, 3/5c. R. T. for two months, 11/4a, 6/10c. Pop. 2,931.

Map Square 23.

PAD.	WYC. W.	WYC. W.	PAD.
AM 5.45	7.14	AM 7.38	8.34
7.35h	9. 2	8.18	9.20
8.12	9.26	9.41	10.40
9.10	10.19	11.19	12.32
9.20	11. 0	PM12.19	1.18
PM12.18	1.29	2.36	3.50
1.25	2.22	3.44	4.40
2.23	3.34	5.15	6.35
3.40	4.57	6.13	7.32
4.40	5.49	7. 3	9. 5
5.23	6.18	7.53	9.18
6.25	7.22	9. 4	11. 4
7.18	8.18	9.56d	11.41
9. 0	10. 8	—	—
—	—	—	—

Sunday Trains.

AM 9.12	10.26	AM 8.32	10.14
9.35	11.27	9.34	11. 4
PM 2.35	4. 1	PM12.43	2.26
4. 0	5.14	7.12	8.25
6. 5	7.39	7.51	9.35
—	—	8.11	9.53

d Saturdays only.
h Not after July 27th.

ANOTHER ROUTE from
Marylebone, 30¼ miles. Fares as above.

M'BONE.	WYC.W.	WYC. W.	M'BONE.
AM 6.10	7.13	AM 7.38	8.49
7.10	9. 2	8.30	9.26
8. 4	9.26	9. 1	9.55
9. 5	10.19	11.19d	12.43
10. 0	11. 0	11.19	1. 5
PM12.15	1.30	PM12.19d	3.10
12.55	2.23	12.19e	3.23
2.10	3.34	2.36d	3.53
3. 5	4.58	2.36	4.28
4.55	5.49	3.44	5.48
5.38	6.26	4. 7	6. 3
5.43	7.22	5.15	7. 5
6.35d	8.18	7. 3	8. 6
6.45e	8.18	7.53	9.27
8.30	10. 8	9. 4	9.55
—	—	9.56d	11.18

WYCOMBE, WEST —continued.

Sunday Trains.

M'LONF.	WYC.W.	WYC. W.	M'BONE.
AM 8.50	9.57	AM 9.34	10.43
10.20	11.27	PM12.43	1.48
PM 2.15	4. 2	7.51	8.58
3.35	5.14	8.11	10 38
6.30	7.39	—	—
—	—	—	—

d Saturdays only.
e Saturdays excepted.

WYE (Kent) from *Charing Cross, Cannon Stree*, and *London Bridge*, 61 miles. Fares, 12/9a, 10/3b, 7/8c. R. T. for two months, 25/6 c, 20/6b, 15,4c. Pop. 1,390.
Map Square 24.

	Leave		Arr. at
CHAR. +	CAN. ST.	LON. B.	WYE
AM —	5.20	5.25	8.28
9.15	—	—	9.23	10.58
11. 0	—	11. 7	1. 3
PM 1. 0	—	—	2.28
3. 0	—	3. 8	4.43
4.30	—	4.37	6.11
5.24d	—	5.34d	7.58
6. 0e	—	6 5e	7.58
7.18	—	7.26	9.32

Sunday Trains.

AM 7.45	—	7.52	9.58
9.35k	—	—	11.32
PM 5.15k	—	—	7.28
7.35	—	7.45	9.29
—	—	—	—

Trains from Wye.

Leave		Arrive at	
WYE	LON. B.	CAN. ST.	CHAR. +
AM 7.18	9.32	9.36	—
8. 5	10. 0	10. 4	—
e8. 5h	—	—	10.16k
9. 5	16.54	—	11. 3
9.56	11.43	—	11.57
11.29	1.36	—	1.50
PM 1. 2	3.26	—	3 40
3.36k	—	—	5.42k
3.36	5.50	—	6. 3
5.32	7.25	7.30	7.49
8.21	10.22	—	10.35

Sunday Trains.

AM 7.26	10. 5	—	10.15
PM 5.21	7. 9	—	7.17
8.34	10.16	—	10.26
10. 6	—	12. 3h	—
—	—	—	—

d Saturdays only.
e Saturdays excepted.
h Third Class only.
k Departs from, or arrives at, Victoria (S.E. & C.R.).

WYKE (Yorks), 190½ miles.
Fares, 39/9a, 23/10c. R. T., double fare. Departures *from* London as for Lowmoor. Departures *for* London about 5 times daily. Pop. 6,145.

Map Square 12.

WYKEHAM (Yorks), 231¼

miles. No through fares. Departures *from* London as for Malton. Departures *for* London about 5 times daily. Pop. 437.

Map Square 8.

WYLAM (Northumberland),

274¼ miles. Fares, 58/3*a*, 34/11*c*. R. T., double fare. Departures *from* London as for Newcastle-on-Tyne. Departures *for* London about 9 times daily. Pop. 1,312.

Map Square 3.

WYLAM NORTH (Northumberland),

276¼ miles. Fares, 58/3*a* 34/11*c*. R. T., double fare. Departures *from* London as for Newcastle-on-Tyne. Departures *for* London about 4 times daily.

Map Square 3.

WYLDE GREEN (Warwick),

115¾ miles. Fares, 24 0*a*, 14/5*c*. R. T. for two months, 48/0*a*. Departures *from* London as for Birmingham (New Street). Departures *for* London about 6 times daily. Pop. 2,829.

WYLYE (Wilts) from

Paddington, 110 miles. Fares, *via* Westbury, 20/0*a*, 12/0*c*. R. T. for two months, 40/0*a*. *Via* Bath 22/6*a*, 13/6*c*. R. T. for two months, 45/0*a*. Departures *from* London as for Warminster. Departures *for* London about 5 times daily. Pop. 392.

Map Square 22.

WYMONDHAM (Norfolk)

from *Liverpool Street*, *via* Cambridge, 113¾ miles. Fares, 23/4*a*, 14/0*c*. R. T. for two months, 46/8*a*. Pop. 4,794.

Map Square 19.

L'PL. ST.	WYHM.	WYHM.	L'PL. ST.
AM 5. 5	8.23	AM 6.58*r*	10.23
5.50	10.12	7.56	11.27
7.18*d*	11.28	9.13	12.40
8.30*r*	12. 1	10.54*r*	2.21
11.50*r*	2.58	PM 2.18*r*	5.17
PM 2.34	5.39	4.47*r*	8.22
5.49*r*	9.14	5.21*r*	8.33
7.10*r*	10.12	10.51	2.50
10.12	1.34	—	—
—	—	—	—
—	—	—	—
—	—	—	—
—	—	—	—
—	—	—	—
—	—	—	—
—	—	—	—
—	—	—	—

Sunday Trains.

AM 9.25	1.17	PM 2.52	6.40
PM 3.25	7.14	6.37	9.40
9.12	1.31	10.52	3. 0
—	—	—	—
—	—	—	—
—	—	—	—
—	—	—	—
—	—	—	—
—	—	—	—
—	—	—	—
—	—	—	—

d Saturdays only.
r Restaurant Car.

WYMONDHAM—*contd.*

ANOTHER ROUTE from

Liverpool Street, *via* Forncett, 111 miles. Fares as above.

L'PL. ST.	WYMON.	WYMON.	L'PL. ST.
AM 5. 0	8.33	AM 7.34*f*	10.36
9.50*r*	12.53	7.56*g*	12.40
10.12	1.55	9.14*r*	1.20
PM 12.33*r*	4. 6	PM 12.15*r*	4.58
3.10*r*	6.36	3. 8	6.32
5.18*r*	8.16	4.50*dr*	9.22
.—	—	7. 5	11.16
—	—	—	—
—	—	—	—

No Sunday Trains.

d Saturdays only.
f Mondays only.
g Mondays excepted.
r Restaurant Car.

WYNYARD (Durham),

242 miles. No through fares. Departures *from* London as for Stockton-on-Tees. Departures *for* London about 4 times daily.

Map Square 8.

WYRE DOCK (Lancs),

229 miles. Fares, 47/9*a*, 28/8*c*. R. T. for two months, 94/6*a*, 56/8*c*. Departures *from* London as for Kirkham. Departures *for* London about 8 times daily.

Map Square 7.

WYRE FOREST (Worcester),

137¾ miles. Fares, 27/3*a*, 16/4*c*. R. T. for two months, 54/6*a*, 32/8*c*. Departures *from* London as for Cleobury Mortimer. Departures *for* London about 5 times daily.

Map Square 17.

WYRLEY (Stafford), 127

miles. Fares, 26/3*a*, 15/9*c*. R. T. for two months. 52/6*a*. Departures *from* London as for Walsall. Departures *for* London about 6 times daily. Pop. 1,017.

Map Square 17.

REFERENCE NOTES.

a	signifies	First Class.
b	,,	Second Class.
c	,,	Third Class.
d	,,	On Saturdays only.
e	,,	Saturdays excepted.
f	,,	On Mondays only.
g	,,	Mondays excepted.
r	,,	Restaurant Car.
t	,,	Tea Car.
x	,,	Express.
R.T.	,,	Return Tickets.

All Trains in the Tables not otherwise marked carry Third Class Passengers.

Y

YALDING (Kent) from

Charing Cross, Cannon Street, and *London Bridge*, 39 miles. Fares, 8/2*a*, 6/7*b*, 4/11*c*. R. T. for two months, 16/4*a*, 13/2*b*. Pop. 2,535.

Map Square 24.

		Leave		Arr. at
	CHAR. +	CAN. ST.	LON. B.	YALD'G
AM	—	5.20	5.25	7.31
	—	6.45	6.50	8.43
	—	7.56	8. 9	9.51
	9.25	—	9.33	11.21
	10.40*d*	—	10.46*d*	12.23
	—	11.56	12. 0	1.18
PM	2. 8	—	2.16	3.36
	3. 0	—	3. 8	4.28
	3.15	—	3.21	5. 6
	3.48*e*	—	—	5. 6
	3.50	—	3.57	6. 0
	—	4.36*e*	4.39*e*	6. 0
	5.35*d*	—	5.41*d*	7.31
	6. 3*e*	—	6. 9*e*	7.26
	8. 0	—	8. 8	9.38
	—	—	—	—

Sunday Trains.

AM 8. 5	—	8.12	9.42
9.50	—	9.56	11.29
PM 7.10	—	7.20	8.44
—	—	—	—
—	—	—	—

YALDING—*continued.*

Trains from Yalding.

Leave Yalding	Arrive at Lon. B.	Can. St	Char. +
AM 6.24	8. 9	—	8.19
8.12	9.32	9.36	—
9.23	10.58	11. 2	—
10.24	11.43	—	11.57
PM12. 4	1.36	—	1.50
2. 1	3.26	—	3.40
4. 0	5.50	—	6. 3
5.10	7.25	7.30	—
6.51	8.26	—	8.35
8.30	10.22	—	10.35
*d*11.19*s*	—	1.20	—
—	—	—	—
—	—	—	—

Sunday Trains.

AM 8.35	10.22	—	10.32
PM 6.50	8.12	—	8.22
7.28	9. 7	—	9.17
—	—	—	—
—	—	—	—

d Saturdays only.
e Saturdays excepted.
s Third Class only.

YARM (Yorks), 231¼ miles.

Fares, 48/2*a*, 28/11*c*. R. T., double fare. Departures *from* London as for Stockton-on-Tees. Departures *for* London about 4 times daily. Pop. 1,617.

Map Square 8.

YARMOUTH (Norfolk)

(South Town) from *Liverpool Street, via* Ipswich, 121¾ miles. Fares, 25/3*a*, 15/2*c*. R. T. for two months, 50/6*a*, 30/4*c*. Pop. 60,710.

Map Square 19.

L'pl. St.	Yarmth.	Yarmth.	L'pl. St.
AM 5. 0	9.20	AM 6.18*r*	10.30
8.15*r*	12.38	7.25*r*	11.22
9.55	12.54	8.24*r*	11.30
10. 0	1.30	9.50	1.20
10.20	2.32	PM12.20	3.42
PM12.30*r*	3. 3	1.35*r*	4. 5
1. 0	4.22	2.24	5.55
3.15	6.22	3.23	7.51
3.18*r*	7.26	4.25*r*	7.23
4.55*r*	8.15	5.22*r*	9.22
5.18*dr*	9.16	6.24*r*	10. 0
5.18*er*	9.25	—	—

Sunday Trains.

AM10.5*r*	1.53	AM 6.55	11.38
11.30*r*	2.30	PM 3.40*r*	6.35
PM 4.40	8.46	5.10*r*	9.10
—	—	7. 0*r*	10.30
—	—	—	—
—	—	—	—

d Saturdays only.
e Saturdays excepted.
r Restaurant Car.

Another Route (Vauxhall) from *Liverpool Street, via* Cambridge, 141¼ miles. Fares as above.

L'pl. St.	Yarmth.	Yarmth.	L'pl. St.
AM 5. 5	9.49	AM 6.38	11.27
5.50	12. 0	7.42	12.40
7.18*d*	12.30	9.34*r*	2.21
8.30*r*	1.12	PM12.50*r*	5.17
11.50*r*	4.32	2.10*er*	8.22
PM 2.34	7.18	3.30*dr*	8.22
5.49*r*	10.35	4. 0*r*	8.33
7.10*r*	11.27	9.15	2.50
10.12	3. 0	—	—
—	—	—	—
—	—	—	—

YARMOUTH—*continued.*

Sunday Trains.

L'pl. St.	Yarmth.	Yarmth.	L'pl. St.
AM 9.25	2.33	PM 1.21	6.40
PM 3.25	8.37	5.10	9.40
9.12	3. 0	9.18	3. 0
—	—	—	—

d Saturdays only.
e Saturdays excepted.
r Restaurant Car.

YARMOUTH (BEACH)

from *King's Cross*, 186 miles. Fares as above.

King's+	Yarmth.	Yarmth.	King's+
AM 4.45	10.55	AM 7. 0	1. 5
7.15*r*	2. 5	8.55	3.50
10.10*r*	5.14	11.25*r*	4.30
PM 1.50*r*	7.45	PM 2.45*r*	9. 0
3. 0	8.55	—	—
—	—	—	—

No Sunday Trains.

r Restaurant Car.

Queen's Hotel. The Popular Hotel in Great Yarmouth. Fine New Lounge. New Garage. Sea View Unrivalled. Excellent Cuisine. 'Phone 28.
W. NIGHTINGALE.
See advt. p. **353.**

Hotel Victoria. First-class Family. Ideal position facing Sea. R.A.C. and A.A. Garage. 'Phone No. 205.
G. H. A. VICK, Proprietor.
See advt. p. **354.**

Royal Hotel. Facing Sea. Close to all amusements. Moderate Terms.
See advt. p. **354.**

The Kimberley Private Hotel, Marine Parade. Premier position.
See advt. p. **355.**

Tregarron Private Hotel, Wellesley Road. Facing Sea. Moderate and Inclusive Terms.
See advt. p. **355.**

Manor House Hotel, Caister-on-Sea. Close Golf Links. Yarmouth Station 20 minutes.
See advt. p. **120.**

Powell's Garibaldi Hotel, Great Yarmouth. Boarding House for Gentlemen. Greatly enlarged. 150 Bedrooms, and Dining Room seating 300. Near the Front. Liberal Table at Moderate Inclusive Charges. National Telephone No.116.

Angel Hotel. Old established Commercial and Family Hotel, centrally situated. Well appointed Stock Rooms, Billiard Room (2 tables), Stabling. Hotel Bus meets trains. Telephone No. 99. MANAGERESS.

Cromwell Hotel. Central situation for business or pleasure. Special week-end terms. Stockrooms on application. Resident Proprietor, FRANK WOLSEY. 'Phone 343.

Royal Hotel. Unrivalled Position. Facing sea, Winter Gardens, 100 Bedrooms. Extensive Lounges. Palm Court. Excellent Cuisine. Phone, 26. Proprietors, E. & C. TAYLOR.

YARMOUTH (Isle of W.)

from *Waterloo, via* Lymington, 102 miles. Fares, 21/8*a*, 13/3*c*. R. T. for two months, 42/9*a*, 26/3*c*. Pop. 847.

Map Square 27.

W'loo	Yarmth.	Yarmth	W'loo.
AM 5.40	9.25	AM 7.35*fs*	11. 0
9.30	1. 0	9.15	12.50
11.30*r*	3. 0	10.35*r*	2.20
PM 1.30*s*	5.50	PM12.50	4.20
3.30	7. 0	1.15	6.16
4.30*s*	7.55	3.30	6.58
—	—	4.50*r*	8.20
—	—	6. 0	10.50
—	—	—	—
—	—	—	—

No Sunday Trains.

f Mondays only.
r Restaurant Car.
s Refreshments served.

Another Route from *Waterloo, via* Ryde, 97¾ miles. Fares, 21/8*a*, 13/3*c*. R. T. for two months, 42/9*a*, 26/3*c*.

W'loo.	Yarmth.	Yarmth.	W'loo
AM 5.50	12. 7	AM 9.45	1.52
9.50*d*	3.47	PM 2.25*r*	7.56
PM12.50*e*	5. 9	5.30*e*	10.46
12.50*d*	5.41	5.57*d*	10.46
1.50*l*	7.17	7.45*hl*	3.58
3.50*ds*	9.12	—	—
—	—	—	—
—	—	—	—

No Sunday Trains.

d Saturdays only.
e Saturdays excepted.
h *Via* Eastleigh.
l Passengers cross Portsmouth at own expense.
r Restaurant Car.
s Refreshments served.

Another Route from *Victoria* and *London Bridge*, 109¾ miles. Fares as above.

Leave Vict.	Leave Lon. B.	Arr. at Yar'th
AM 6.18	6.35	12. 7
8.55	—	1.42
11.35*d*	—	3.47
11.35*e*	—	5. 9
PM 1.40	1.50	7.17
—	4.50*d*	9.12
—	—	—
—	—	—

No Sunday Trains.

Trains from Yarmouth.

Leave Yar'th.	Arrive at Lon. B.	Vict.
AM 8.10	—	1.10
9.45	4.27	4.34
PM12.26	—	5.12
2.25	7.48	6.50
4. 5*d*	10. 8	10. 1
—	—	—

No Sunday Trains.

d Saturdays only.
e Saturdays excepted.

Pier Hotel, Yarmouth. Charming old Family House. Modern improvements. Electric Light. Garden to Sea. Boating, Bathing, Fishing, Billiards. Golf, Yachting. Best Motor Route to Island. Phone No. 14.

GT. YARMOUTH. *The Leading Family Hotel.* **QUEEN'S HOTEL.** *Golf (Sunday Play). River and Sea Angling. Yachting (Norfolk Broads).*

YARNTON (Oxon), 67
miles. Fares, 14/0a, 8/5c. R. T.
for two months, 28/0a. Departures
from London as for Oxford. Departures *for* London about 5 times
daily. Pop. 312.
Map Square 23.

YATE (Glo'ster), 127¼ miles.
No through fares. Departures
from London as for Bristol. Departures *for* London about 3 times
daily. Pop. 1,309.
Map Square 22.

YATTON (Somerset) from
Paddington, 129½ miles. Fares,
26/11a, 16/2c. R T. for two months,
53/10a. Pop. 1,962.
Map Square 22.

PAD.	YATTON	YATTON	PAD.
AM 5.30	9.50	AM 7. 5r	10.15
7.30	10.47	8.10	11.30
8.45	11.45	9. 2	12.20
9. 0	1. 0	11.30r	2. 0
11.15r	2.10	PM12.52	4. 5
PM 1. 0r	3.37	2.42	6. 2
1.10r	5.11	4.32r	7. 0
2.45	6.39	5.19r	8.45
4.15r	7.21	7. 4	10.25
5.15	9. 9	10.22	2.45
6.30r	9.29	—	—
8. 0	11.37	—	—
12. 0k	7.24	—	—
12.30h	7. 8	—	—

Sunday Trains.

PM12.30r	6. 8	AM 8.32	3.35
10. 0	7.24	PM 8.24	3.15
—	—	—	—
—	—	—	—

h Saturdays midnight only.
k Saturdays midnight excepted.
r Restaurant Car.

YAXHAM (Norfolk) from
Liverpool Street, 120½ miles. Fares,
23/7a, 14/2c. R. T. for two months,
47/2a. Departures *from* London
as for Dereham. Departures *for*
London about 5 times daily.
Pop. 404.
Map Square 19.

YAXLEY (Hunts), 72½ miles.
Fares, 15/2a, 9/1c. R. T., double
fare. Departures *from* London
as for Holme. Departures *for*
London about 6 times daily. Pop.
1,697.
Map Square 18.

YEALMPTON (Devon)
from *Paddington*, 232 miles. Fares,
47/6a, 28/11c. R.T. for two months,
95/0a, 57/10c. Pop. 901.
Map Square 26.

PAD.	Y'MPTON	Y'MPTON	PAD.
AM 5.30	1.47	AM 9.45r	4.35
10.30r	3.49	11.20r	4.45
11.10r	5.54	PM 2.57r	9. 0
PM 3.30r	9.39	9.45	7.10
4.15r	11.27	11.33l	7.10
12. 0k	8. 0	—	—
12.30h	10.34	—	—

Sunday Trains.

PM 2.40r	8.59	AM10.40	7. 5
10. 0	8.. 0	PM 3. 0	3.15
—	—	9.10	7.10

h Saturdays midnight only.
k Saturdays midnight excepted.
l Wednesdays, Thursdays and
  Saturdays only.
r Restaurant Car.

YEATHOUSE (Cumber-
land), 303½ miles. Fares, 63/1a,
37/10c. R.T. for two months,126/2a,
75/8c. Departures *from* London as
for Moor Row. Departures *for*
London about 3 times daily.
Map Square 6

YELDHAM (Essex), 62¼
miles. Fares, 13/1a, 7/10c. R. T.
for two months, 26/2a. Departures *from* London as for Halstead.
Departures *for* London 4 times
daily. Pop. 879.
Map Square 19.

YELVERTOFT (North-
ampton) from *Euston*, 87¾ miles.
Fares, 17/6a, 10/6c. R. T. for two
months, 35/0a. Pop. 360.
Map Square 18.

EUSTON	YELV.	YELV.	EUSTON
AM 2.35	7. 0	AM 6.55e	9.52
5. 0	8.45	7.45	10. 0
10.40	1.15	9.20	11.55
PM 2.50e	5.30	11. 5	1. 0
4.45r	6.42	PM 1.20	4.15
7. 0½	9. 7	3.37	5.50
—	—	6. 1	9.20
—	—	8.11	10.45
—	—	—	—
—	—	—	—

Sunday Trains.

PM 6. 0	7.59	PM 6. 2r	8.20
—	—	—	—
—	—	—	—

e Saturdays excepted.
r Restaurant Car.

YELVERTON (Devon)
from *Paddington*, 230 miles.
Fares, 46/11a, 28/2c. R.T. for two
months, 93/10a. Departures *from*
London as for Tavistock. Departures *for* London 6 times daily.
Map Square 26.

Devon Tors Hotel. Alti-
tude 620 feet. Magnificent posi-
tion South. Central heating.
Electric Light. Listed R.A.C.,
A.A. and M.U. Garage. Private
Grounds. Golf. Five minutes
Station NORMAN WILSON,
  Resident Owner.

YEOFORD (Devon) from
Waterloo, 183 miles. Fares, 36/11a,
22/2c. R. T. for two months,
73/10a, 44/4c.
Map Square 26.

W'LOO	Y'FORD	Y'FORD	W'LOO
AM 9. 0r	1.43	AM 9. 0r	1.56
11. 0r	3.24	12. 0r	3.50
PM 1. 0r	6.12	PM 1.59r	6. 0
3. 0r	6.48	3.54r	8.30
6. 0r	10.26	5.54	10.50
—	—	6.43h	3.58
—	—	—	—
—	—	—	—
—	—	—	—
—	—	—	—

Sunday Trains.

12. 0nr	6.28	PM 1. 6r	8.57
—	—	—	—

h Via Eastleigh.
n Noon.
r Restaurant Car.

YEOVIL (Somerset) from
Waterloo, 124½ miles. Fares, 26/0a,
15/7c. R. T. for two months,
52/0a, 31/2c. Pop. 14,987.
Map Square 22.

W'LOO	YEOVIL	YEOVIL	W'LOO
AM 7.30	11.10	AM 7. 0	10.56
9. 0r	11.53	8.10r	11.10
10. 0r	1.39	10.35r	1.56
12. 0r	3. 7	PM12. 0r	3. 8
PM 1. 0r	4.10	3. 0r	6. 0
3. 0r	5.57	4.12	7.40
5. 0	8.40	5.23r	8.30
6. 0r	9. 7	7.20	10.50
10. 0h	4.23	9.18h	3.58
—	—	—	—
—	—	—	—
—	—	—	—
—	—	—	—

Sunday Trains.

AM 9. 0	2. 5	PM 5.55r	8.57
12. 0nr	3.32	—	—
PM 6. 0	10.26	—	—
—	—	—	—

h Via Eastleigh.
n Noon.
r Restaurant Car.

ANOTHER ROUTE (Pen
Mill) from *Paddington*, 127 miles.
Fares as above.

PAD.	YEOVIL	YEOVIL	PAD.
AM 1. 0g	8.33	AM 7.43	10.52
5.30	10.38	9.47	12.55
10.30	12.56	11.25	3.20
PM12.30r	3.29	PM12.51	3.50
2. 0	4.45	2.43t	5.30
3.30	5.58	4. 2r	6.50
5. 5	8.18	5.24	8.20
—	—	8.31	2.45
—	—	9.30h	2.45
—	—	—	—
—	—	—	—
—	—	—	—

Sunday Trains.

PM 2.40	5.51	AM10.36	3.35
10. 0	8.33	PM 4.50r	7.55
—	—	—	—
—	—	—	—

g Mondays excepted.
h Thursdays and Third Class only.
r Restaurant Car.
t Tea Car.

YEOVIL JUNCTION
(Somerset) from *Waterloo*, 123
miles. Fares, 25/8a, 15/5c. R. T.
for two months, 51/4a, 30/10c.

W'LOO	Y. JUNC.	Y. JUNC.	W'LOO
AM 7.30	10.57	AM 7.10	10.56
9. 0r	11.41	8.18r	11.10
10. 0r	1.16	10.48r	1.56
12. 0r	2.53	PM12.10r	3. 8
PM 1. 0r	3.54	3. 0r	6. 0
3.10r	5.44	4.23	7.40
5.50	8.28	5.34r	8.30
6. 0r	8.54	7.33	10.50
10. 0h	4.11	9.32h	3.58
—	—	—	—
—	—	—	—

YEOVIL JUNCTION—*continued.*

Sunday Trains.

W'LOO.	Y. JUNC.	Y. JUNC.	W'LOO.
AM 9. 0	1.51	PM 6. 7*r*	8.57
12. 0*nr*	3.18	—	—
PM 6. 0	10.11	—	—
—	—	—	—
—	—	—	—

h Via Eastleigh.
n Noon.
r Restaurant Car.

YETMINSTER (Dorset)

from *Paddington,* 131¼ miles. Fares, 26/8*a*, 16/0*c*. R. T. for two months, 53/4*a*. Pop. 620.
Map Square 27.

PAD.	YETMSTR.	YETMSTR.	PAD.
AM 1. 0*g*	9. 5	AM 8.26	12.55
5.30	11.27	10.31	3.20
10.30	2.14	PM12.39	3.50
PM12.30*r*	4.21	2. 0*t*	5.30
3.30	7.22	4.31	8.20
5. 5	8.31	8.17	2.45
—	—	—	—
—	—	—	—
—	—	—	—

Sunday Trains.

PM 2.40	6. 6	AM10.22	3.35
10. 0	9. 5	PM 4.37*r*	7.55
—	—	—	—

g Mondays excepted.
r Restaurant Car.
t Tea Car.

YNISHIR (Glamorgan), 169½

miles. Fares, 34/0*a*, 20/5*c*. R. T. for two months, 68/0*a*, 40/10*c*. Departures *from* London as for Pontypridd. Departures *for* London about 6 times daily. Pop. 11,141.
Map Square 21.

YNYS (Carnarvon), 261¾

miles. Fares, 54/5*a*, 32/8*c*. R. T. for two months, 108/10*a*, 65/4*c*. Departures *from* London as for Carnarvon. Departures *for* London about 5 times daily.
Map Square 11.

YNYSDDU (Monmouth),

152 miles. Fares, 31/8*a*, 19/0*c*. R. T. for two months, 63/4*a*, 38/0*c*. Departures *from* London as for Tredegar. Departures *for* London about 3 times daily Pop. 4,881.

YNYSLAS (Cardigan), 229

miles. Fares, 46/6*a*, 27/11*c*. R. T. for two months, 93/0*a*. Departures *from* London as for Machynlleth. Departures *for* London about 5 times daily.
Map Square 16.

YNYSYBWL (Glamorgan),

169 miles. Fares, 20/5*c*. R. T. for two months, 40/10*c*. Departures *from* London as for Pontypridd. Departures *for* London about 8 times daily. Pop. 5,149.

YOCKLETON (Salop),

160 miles. Fares, 33/6*a*, 20/1*c*. R. T. for two months, 67/0*a*. Departures *from* London as for Buttington. Departures *for* London about 4 times daily. Pop. 293.
Map Square 17.

YOKER (Renfrew), 406½

miles. Fares, 82/6*a*, 49/6*c*. R. T. for two months, 165/0*a*, 99/0*c*. Departures *from* London as for Glasgow (Central). Departures *for* London about 6 times daily. Pop. 4,361.

YORK from *King's Cross,*

188¼ miles. Fares, 39/2*a*, 23/6*c*. R. T., double fare. Pop. 82,282.
Map Square 8.

KING'S +	YORK	YORK	KING'S +
AM 4.45	9.18	AM 1. 0	5.40
7.15*r*	11.25	1.28	6. 0
8.45	1.24	3. 2*g*	6.50
10. 0*r*	1.45	3.17	7. 5
10.10*r*	2. 7	3.30*g*	7.25
11.30	4.48	7.40*r*	11.30
11.50*r*	3.20	8.17	1. 5
PM 1.50*r*	6. 5	9.28*r*	1.15
4. 0*r*	8.15	10.25	3.50
5.35*r*	9.22	PM12.20*r*	4.30
5.45*r*	10.50	12.40*r*	4.45
7.45*er*	11.25	2.27*r*	6.15
8.20*er*	11.55	2.42*r*	6.30
8.25	12.59	4. 0*r*	7.30
10.45	2.50	5. 5*r*	9.25
11.25	3. 4	6.13*r*	10. 0
—	—	10.10*r*	3.25
—	—	—	—
—	—	—	—
—	—	—	—
—	—	—	—
—	—	—	—

Sunday Trains.

AM 8.30	3. 5	AM 1.28	6. 0
11.30*r*	3.45	3.17	7. 5
PM 5. 0*r*	9 .50	3.30	7.25
7.35	11.25	PM12.40	5.15
8.25	12.59	4. 1*r*	8.15
10.45	2.50	—	—
11.25	3. 4	—	—
—	—	—	—
—	—	—	—
—	—	—	—

e Saturdays excepted.
g Mondays excepted.
r Restaurant Car.

ANOTHER ROUTE from *St. Pancras,* 202¾ miles. Fares as above.

ST. PAN.	YORK	YORK	ST. PAN.
AM 4.25	12.35	AM 1.40*h*	7.50
9. 0*r*	3.10	7.25*r*	1.30
9.50*r*	3.15	10.10*r*	4.10
10.25*r*	4. 0	PM12. 8*r*	5.30
PM12.25*r*	6.10	1. 0*r*	7.15
2.25*r*	7.31	2.30*r*	7.55
5. 0*r*	10.39	3.10*r*	8.35
6.15*r*	12.17*h*	4. 8*r*	9.15
9.15	3.18	9.30	4.20
11.50*e*	8.17*h*	—	—
11.50*d*	9. 8*h*	—	—
—	—	—	—
—	—	—	—
—	—	—	—
—	—	—	—

Sunday Trains.

AM10.50*r*	8. 3*h*	AM 1.40*h*	8.57
PM 9.15	3.18	10.35*h*	5.27
—	—	PM 1. 0*hr*	9.43
—	—	9.30	4.55
—	—	—	—
—	—	—	—

d Saturdays only.
e Saturdays excepted.
h Via Normanton.
r Restaurant Car.

Royal Station Hotel
Central situation adjoining Station. Thoroughly up-to-date. Every Comfort. Owned and managed by the London and North Eastern Railway Company.
See advt. p. **355.**

YORK ROAD (Battersea).

See BATTERSEA PARK.

YORK ROAD (King's

Cross). Hammersmith and Finsbury Park Tube. *See* back of Map.
Station closed on Sundays.

YORTON (Salop), 170

miles. Fares, 33/4*a*, 20/0*c*. R. T. for two months, 66/8*a*. Departures *from* London as for Shrewsbury Departures *for* London about 4 times daily.
Map Square 17.

YSTALYFERA (Glamorgan), 211¾ miles.

No through fares. Departures *from* London as for Swansea (High Street). Departures *for* London about 3 times daily. Pop. 7,185.
Map Square 21.

YSTRAD (Glamorgan), 173

miles. Fares, 34/10*a*, 20/11*c*. R. T. for two months, 69/8*a*. Departures *from* London as for Treherbert. Departures *for* London about 5 times daily. Pop. 5,483.

YSTRADGYNLAIS

(Brecon), 209¼ miles. Fares, 41/5*a*, 24/10*c*. R.T. for two months, 82/10*a*, 49/8*c*. Departures *from* London as for Neath or Brecon. Departures *for* London about 4 times daily. Pop. 10,471.
Map Square 21.

YSTRAD MYNACH

(Glamorgan), 158¼ miles. Fares (*via* Cardiff), 34/5*a*, 20/8*c*. R. T. for two months, 68/10*a*, 41/4*c*. Departures *from* London as for Caerphilly or Cardiff. Departures *for* London about 5 times daily. Pop. 2,081.

YSTRADOWEN (Glamorgan), 169¼ miles.

No through fares. Departures *from* London as for Llantrisant. Departures *for* London about 8 times daily. Pop. 228.
Map Square 21.

Z

ZEEBRUGGE, *via* Harwich,

from Liverpool Street. Every week day.
See advt. p. **3**.

IDRIS

SODA WATER
LEMONADE
DRY GINGER ALE
BREWED GINGER BEER
GINGER ALE

To be obtained at all Clubs, Hotels, Restaurants, Grocers, Wine Merchants, and Chemists.

ACTON TOWN, EALING AND HOUNSLOW.

Trains run about every half hour from Barking, about every 15 minutes from East Ham, Upton Park, Plaistow, West Ham, Bromley, and about every 10 minutes from Bow Road to Mile End, Stepney Green, Whitechapel, New Cross, Surrey Docks, Rotherhithe, Wapping, Shadwell, St. Mary's, Aldgate East, Mark Lane, Monument, Cannon Street (closed on Sundays), Mansion House, Blackfriars, Temple, Charing Cross, Westminster, St. James's Park, Victoria, Sloane Square, South Kensington, Gloucester Road, Earl's Court, West Kensington, Baron's Court, Hammersmith, Ravenscourt Park, Stamford Brook, Turnham Green, Chiswick Park, Acton Town, Ealing Common, and Ealing Broadway.

TO EALING BROADWAY.

STATIONS.	Weekdays First train	Weekdays Last train	Sundays First train	Sundays Last train	STATIONS.	Weekdays First train	Weekdays Last train	Sundays First train	Sundays Last train
	AM	PM	AM	PM		AM	PM	AM	PM
Barking ....dep	5 20	12 3	8 12	10 58	Shadwell ....dep.	5 15	1150	7 54	11 19
East Ham	5 23	12 7	8 0	11 14	Mansion House	5 48	AM1230	8 25	11 38
Bow Road	5 24	12 17	8 12	11 25	Charing Cross	5 52	1234	8 26	11 43
Whitechapel............	5 39	12 22	8 17	11 30	Victoria	5 57	1240	8 31	11 48
New Cross (S.E. & C.R.) ..	5 7	11 42	7 50	11 9	South Kensington	6 2	1244	8 35	11 52
New Cross (L.B. & S.C.R.) ..	5 18	11 48	7 54	11 3	Earl's Court	6 6	1248	8 39	11 56
Surrey Docks	5 10	11 45	7 47	11 12	Hammersmith.............	6 17	1253	8 44	12 1
Rotherhithe.............	5 12	11 47	7 49	11 14	Turnham Green	6 22	1258	8 49	12 6
Wapping.................	5 13	11 48	7 50	11 15	Acton Town	6 26	1 2	8 53	12 10

TO BARKING.

	AM	PM	AM	PM		AM	PM	AM	PM
Ealing Broadway ......dep.	5 13	11 53	7 55	10 25	Victoria ....dep.	5 32	12 20	8 22	10 53
Acton Town	4 40	11 58	8 0	10 30	Charing Cross	5 37	12 25	8 28	10 58
Turnham Green	4 46	12 2	8 4	10 34	Mansion House...........	5 42	12*30	8 33	11*3
Hammersmith..............	4 50	12 7	8 9	10 39	East Ham	6 7	12 52	9 1	11 28
Earl's Court...............	4 54	12 12	8 14	10 45	Barking...............arr.	6 10	12 55	9 4	11 31
South Kensington..........	5 28	12 16	8 18	10 49					

k Not to West Ham or Bromley.   l Last train for East Ham leaves Mansion House 11.33 P.M

MANSION HOUSE TO PUTNEY BRIDGE AND WIMBLEDON.

Trains run about every 5 or 10 minutes from Mansion House to Earl's Court, West Brompton, Walham Green, Parson's Green, Putney Bridge, East Putney, Southfields, Wimbledon Park, and Wimbledon.

TO WIMBLEDON.

STATIONS.	Weekdays First train	Weekdays Last train	Sundays First train	Sundays Last train
	AM	AM	AM	PM
Mansion House..........dep.	5 48	12 30	8 25	11 26
Earl's Court	5 39	12 49	8 27	11 44
Walham Green	5 42	12 52	8 30	11 47
Parsons Green	5 45	12 54	8 32	11 49
Putney Bridge..............	5 47	12 56	8 34	11 51
Southfields................	5 52	1 1	8 39	11 56

TO MANSION HOUSE.

STATIONS.	Weekdays First train	Weekdays Last train	Sundays First train	Sundays Last train
	AM	PM	AM	PM
Wimbledon..............dep.	5 15	11 39	8 11	10 56
Southfields................	5 20	11 44	8 16	11 1
Putney Bridge	5 25	12 5	8 3	11 5
Parsons Green	4 48	12 7	8 5	11 7
Walham Green	4 50	12 8	8 6	11 8

MANSION HOUSE TO KEW GARDENS AND RICHMOND.

Trains run about every 15 minutes from Mansion House to Turnham Green, Gunnersbury, Kew Gardens, and Richmond.

TO RICHMOND.

STATIONS.	Weekdays First train	Weekdays Last train	Sundays First train	Sundays Last train
	AM	AM	AM	PM
Mansion House..........dep.	5 48	12 21	8 25	10 46
Earl's Court......t.......	5 49	12*19	8 45	11 4
Turnham Green	5 53	12 31	8 0	11 14
Kew Gardens	6 6	12 36	8 6	11 20

TO MANSION HOUSE.

STATIONS.	Weekdays First train	Weekdays Last train	Sundays First train	Sundays Last train
	AM	AM	AM	PM
Richmond...............dep.	6 14	11 44	8 12	10 57
Kew Gardens	6 17	11 47	8 15	11 0
Gunnersbury	6 20	11 50	8 18	11 3

* Change at Turnham Green.

MANSION HOUSE TO OSTERLEY AND HOUNSLOW.

Trains run about every 10 minutes from Acton Town to South Ealing, Northfields, and Little Ealing, Boston Manor, Osterley, Hounslow Town, Heston-Hounslow, and Hounslow Barracks.

STATIONS.	TO HOUNSLOW TOWN AND HOUNSLOW BARRACKS. Weekdays First train	Weekdays Last train	Sundays First train	Sundays Last train	TO HESTON-HOUNSLOW. Weekdays First train	Weekdays Last train	Sundays First train	Sundays Last train	STATIONS.	TO MANSION HOUSE. Weekdays First train	Weekdays Last train	Sundays First train	Sundays Last train
dep.	AM	AM	AM	PM	AM	AM	PM	dep.	AM	PM	AM	PM
Mansion House	5 48	12 21	8 25	5 43	8 25	11 6	Hounslow Barracks	5 18	11 37	7 48	10 43
Acton Town ..	5 22	12 53	8 10	11 42	6 33	1 4	8 10	11 42	Heston-Hounslow	5 20	11 39	7 50	10 45
Northfields	5 25	12 57	8 14	11 46	6 37	12 57	8 14	11 46	Hounslow Town ..	5 22	11 41	7 52	10 47
Boston Manor	5 27	12 59	8 16	11 48	6 39	12 59	8 16	11 48	Osterley........	5 23	11 43	7 54	10 49
Osterley	5 30	1 2	8 19	11 51	6 42	1 2	8 19	11 51	Boston Manor	5 25	11 45	7 56	10 51
Hounslow Town	5 32	1 4	8 22	11 54	6 45	1 4	8 22	11 54	Northfields....	5 27	11 46	7 58	10 53

MANSION HOUSE TO SOUTH HARROW AND UXBRIDGE.

Trains run about every 10 or 20 minutes from Mansion House to North Ealing, Park Royal, Alperton, Sudbury Town, Sudbury Hill and South Harrow, and about every 30 minutes to Rayner's Lane, Eastcote, Ruislip Manor, Ruislip, Ickenham, and Uxbridge.

TO UXBRIDGE (MET.).

STATIONS.	Weekdays First train	Weekdays Last train	Sundays First train	Sundays Last train		STATIONS.	Weekdays First train	Weekdays Last train	Sundays First train	Sundays Last train
	AM	PM	AM	PM	PM		AM	AM	AM	PM	PM
Mansion House ....dep.	6 4	12 27	8 7	10*15		Alperton ....dep.	5 56	12 3	8 13	10 26	11*0
Acton Town............	5 48	11 57	8 6	10 18	10*51	South Harrow	6 4	12 11	9 12	10 35	11*7

TO MANSION HOUSE.

STATIONS.	AM	PM	AM	PM		STATIONS.	AM	PM	AM	PM
Uxbridge (Met.) ....dep.	6 38	11 10	9 29	10 6		Alperton ....dep.	5 43	11 41	7 54	10 51
South Harrow	5 37	11 35	7 48	10 45		* To Ruislip and Uxbridge only.				

METROPOLITAN RAILWAY (INNER CIRCLE TRAINS).

Calling at Mansion House, Blackfriars, Temple, Charing Cross, Westminster, St. James's Park, Victoria, Sloane Square, South Kensington, Gloucester Road, Kensington (High Street), Notting Hill Gate, Queen's Road, Paddington (Praed Street) (for G.W. Rly.), Edgware Road, Baker Street, Great Portland Street, Euston Square, King's Cross, Farringdon Street, Aldersgate Street, Moorgate Street, Liverpool Street, Aldgate, Mark Lane, Monument, and Cannon Street every few minutes.

WEEK DAYS.

	AM	AM	AM	AM	AM	AM	AM	AM	AM	AM	AM	AM	AM	AM	AM	AM	AM
Paddington ....dep.	5·45	6 10	6 35	—	7 10	7 33	—	7 48	8 12	8 20	—	9 5	9 32	—	—	—	10 51
Bishops Road															9 44	—	
Westbourne Park ...	5 49	6 14	6 39	7 12	7 14	7 37	7 40	7 52	—	8 24	8 42	9 9	9 36	9 40	9 52	10 24	11 0
Old Oak Lane Halt ..	—	—	—	7 17	—	—	7 45	—	—	—	—	—	—	9 45	—	—	—
Park Royal	—	—	—	7 20	—	—	7 48	—	—	8 50	—	—	—	9 48	—	—	—
Brentham	—	—	—	7 23	—	—	7 51	—	—	8 53	—	—	—	9 51	—	10 34	—
Perivale	—	—	—	7 27	—	—	7 55	—	—	8 57	—	—	—	9 55	—	10 38	—
Greenford	6 13	6 39	7 14	7 32	7 44	8 0	8 3	8 17	8 37	8 52	9 2	9 29	10 0	10 2	10 37	10 42	11 26
Northolt Halt (W.E.)	6 16	6 43	—	—	—	8 2	—	—	—	8 54	—	—	10 3	—	10 40	—	11 28
Northolt Junction .	6 20	6 47	7 22	—	7 51	8 7	—	—	—	8 58	—	—	10 7	—	10 44	—	11 32
Ruislip & Ickenham	6 24	6 51	7 26	—	7 55	8 11	—	—	8 45	9 2	—	9 38	10 11	—	10 48	—	11 36
Denham	6 30	—	7 44	—	—	8q25	—	—	8 51	—	—	9 43	—	—	11 10	—	11 42
Denham Golf Club ..	7 13	—	7 47	—	—	8?28	—	—	9 35	—	—	9 46	—	—	11 13	—	12 28
Uxbridge High St. ...	6 58	—	—	—	—	—	—	—	9 21	—	—	—	—	—	—	—	12 11
Gerrards Cross ...	6 37	7 23	7 52	—	—	8?34	—	—	8 57	—	—	9 51	—	—	11 18	—	12 33
Seer Green ....arr.	—	7 34	7 58	—	—	8 40	—	—	9 3	—	—	9 57	—	—	11 24	—	—

WEEK DAYS.

	AM	AM	PM	PM	e	PM	d	PM	PM	PM		PM	e	d	PM	d	d
Paddington ....dep.	11 35	—	12 18	12 35	—	12 55	—	1 15	1 25	1 38	—	—	2 5	2 23	—	—	
Bishops Road	—	—	—	—	—	—	—	—	—	—	1 49	—	—	—	—		
Westbourne Park..	11 39	11 50	12 7	12 39	12 57	12 59	1 12	1 19	—	1 42	1 50	1 54	2 9	—	2 15	2 42	
Old Oak Lane Halt .	—	11 55	—	—	1 2	—	—	—	—	—	1 55	—	—	—	—	2 47	
Park Royal	—	11 58	—	—	1 5	—	—	—	—	—	1 58	—	—	—	—	2 50	
Brentham	—	12 1	—	—	1 8	—	1 22	—	—	—	2 0	—	—	—	2 27	2 53	
Perivale	—	12 5	—	—	1 12	—	1 26	—	—	—	2 5	—	—	—	2 32	2 57	
Greenford	12 9	12 12	12 37	1 2	1 17	1 23	1 29	1 55	1 39	2 9	2 10	2 24	2 33	2 43	2 36	3 2	
Northolt Halt (W.E.)	12d13	—	—	1 6	—	—	—	—	—	—	—	—	—	2 55	3 0	—	
Northolt Junction .	12d17	—	—	1 10	—	—	—	1 44	—	—	—	—	—	2 59	3 4	—	
Ruislip & Ickenham	12d25	—	—	1 14	—	—	—	1 48	—	—	—	—	—	2 53	3 8	—	
Denham	12d31	—	12 49	1 28	—	—	—	1 53	—	—	—	—	—	3 1	3 38	—	
Denham Golf Club ..	—	—	—	1 31	—	—	—	—	—	—	—	—	—	3 41	3 41	—	
Uxbridge High St. ..	—	—	1 6	—	—	—	—	—	—	—	—	—	—	—	—	—	
Gerrards Cross	—	—	12 55	1 36	—	—	—	1 59	—	—	—	—	—	3 8	3 46	—	
Seer Green ....arr.	—	—	—	1 42	—	—	—	2d15	—	—	—	—	—	3 52	3 52	—	

WEEK DAYS.

	e	PM	d	PM	PM	PM	PM	d	PM		e	PM	PM	PM	PM	PM
Paddington ....dep.	—	2 55	—	3 40	3 55	4 35	4 40	—	5* 8	—	5 23	—	5 32	5 53	6 25	—
Bishops Road	—	—	—	—	—	—	—	—	5d 3	—	—	—	—	—	—	—
Westbourne Park ..	2 50	2 59	3 5	3 52	—	3 59	4 39	—	4 54	5d 7	5 12	—	5 35	—	5 47	—	6 25
Old Oak Lane Halt .	2 55	—	3 10	3 57	—	—	—	—	4 59	—	—	—	—	—	—	—
Park Royal.........	2 58	—	3 13	4 0	—	—	—	—	5 2	—	—	—	—	—	—	—
Brentham	3 1	—	3 16	4 3	—	—	—	—	5 5	—	5 22	—	5 45	—	—	6 38
Perivale	3 5	—	3 20	4 7	—	—	—	—	5 9	—	5 26	—	5 49	—	—	6 42
Greenford	3 10	3 24	3 29	4 12	3 53	4 26	5 7	—	5 14	5 38	5 30	—	5 54	6 4	6 28	6 38	6 45
Northolt Halt (W.E.)	—	3 29	—	—	—	4 29	5 24	—	5 24	—	—	—	—	—	—	6 46
Northolt Junction .	—	3 34	—	—	—	—	5 28	—	5 23	—	—	—	—	—	—	6 50
Ruislip & Ickenham	—	3 38	—	—	4 2	4 36	5 32	—	5 32	—	—	5 42	—	—	—	6 53
Denham	—	—	—	4 7	4 42	—	—	5 2	—	—	—	5 47	—	—	—	6 56
Denham Golf Club ..	—	—	—	—	—	—	—	5 30	—	—	—	—	—	—	—	6 53
Uxbridge High St. ..	—	—	—	4 31	—	—	—	—	—	—	—	—	—	—	—	7 16
Gerrards Cross	—	—	—	4 13	—	—	—	5 8	—	—	—	5 53	—	—	—	6 5?
Seer Green ....arr.	—	—	—	4 19	—	—	—	5 31	—	—	—	5 59	—	—	—	7 14

WEEK DAYS.

	PM	d	e	PM		PM	e	PM	PM		PM			PM	PM	
Paddington ....dep.	—	6 38	6 48	7 18	—	7 42	7 55	8 10	—	9 0	—	—	10 10	11 33	
Bishops Road......	—	—	—	—	—	—	—	—	—	—	—	—	—	—	
Westbourne Park ..	6 55	6 42	6 52	—	7 50	7 46	—	8 14	8 52	—	9 45	10 14	11 37	
Old Oak Lane Halt ..	7 0	—	—	—	7 55	—	—	—	8 57	—	—	—	—	
Park Royal.........	7 3	—	—	—	7 58	—	—	—	9 0	—	—	—	—	
Brentham	7 6	—	—	—	8 1	—	—	—	9 55	—	—	—	—	
Perivale	7 10	—	—	—	8 5	—	—	—	10 0	—	—	—	—	
Greenford	7 15	7 22	7 22	7 32	8 10	8 22	8 22	8 45	9 12	9 22	10 5	10 39	12 2	
Northolt Halt (W.E.)	—	7 26	7 23	—	—	8 25	8 25	—	—	9 29	—	10 42	—	
Northolt Junction..	—	7 30	7 30	—	—	8 29	8 29	—	—	9 33	—	10 46	—	
Ruislip & Ickenham	—	7 34	7 34	7 40	—	8 33	8 33	—	—	9 30	—	10 50	—	
Denham	—	—	—	7 45	—	9 3	9 3	—	—	9 35	—	11 8	—	Sats. only.
Denham Golf Club ..	—	—	—	C R	—	9 28	9 28	—	—	p	—	—	—	
Uxbridge High St. ..	—	—	—	—	—	—	—	—	—	10 21	—	—	—	
Gerrards Cross	—	—	—	7 53	—	9 9	9 9	—	—	9 43	—	11 14	—	
Seer Green ....arr.	—	—	—	7 59	—	9 15	9 15	—	—	9 49	—	11 20	—	

WEEK DAYS.

	AM	AM	AM	AM	AM	AM	AM	AM	AM	AM	AM	AM	AM	AM	AM	AM	AM
Seer Green ....dep	—	6 50	—	7 56	—	8 15	8 42	—	—	—	—	—	—	—	—	—	—
Gerrards Cross ...	—	6 56	—	8 2	—	8 21	8 48	—	—	10 9	—	—	—	—	—	—	—
Uxbridge High St...	—	—	—	—	—	8 37	—	—	—	—	—	—	—	—	—	—	—
Denham Golf Club ..	—	—	—	—	—	8 52	—	—	—	—	—	—	—	—	—	—	—
Denham	—	7 2	—	8 7	—	8 55	—	—	—	10 14	—	—	—	—	—	—	—
Ruislip & Ickenham	—	7 12	—	7 38 8 12	—	8 35	9 0	—	9 10	10 22	—	10 28	11 3	—	—	—	—
Northolt Junction..	—	7 16	—	7 42	—	8 39	—	—	9 14	—	—	10 32	11 7	—	—	—	—
Northolt Halt (W.E.)	—	7 20	—	—	—	8 43	—	—	9 18	—	—	10 36	11 11	—	—	—	—
Greenford	6 47	7 8	7 23	7 30	7 51	8 21	8 23	8 26	8 48	9 17	9 22	10 2	—	10 5	10 39	11 15	11 27
Perivale	6 50	—	7 26	—	—	—	—	—	—	9 20	—	10 5	—	—	—	—	11 30
Brentham	6 53	—	7 29	—	—	—	—	8 32	—	9 23	—	10 8	—	—	—	—	11 33
Park Royal	6 56	—	—	—	—	—	—	—	—	9 26	—	10 11	—	—	—	—	11 36
Old Oak Lane Halt..	7 2	—	—	—	—	—	—	—	—	9 32	—	10 17	—	—	—	—	11 42
Westbourne Park ..	7 9	7 33	7 39	8 10	—	—	8 42	—	—	9 39	9 48	10 23	—	10 51	11 4	—	11 49
Bishops Road......	—	—	—	—	8 19	—	—	—	—	—	—	—	—	—	11 9	—	—
Paddington .....arr.	—	7 37	—	8 14	—	8 34	8 50	—	9 14	9 20	—	9 52	—	10 40	10 55	—	11 55

WEEK DAYS.

	AM	e	e	d	d	PM	PM	PM	PM	PM	d	PM	e	PM	d	d	PM
Seer Green ....dep.	11 40	—	—	—	—	12 19	—	—	—	—	—	—	—	—	—	—	—
Gerrards Cross....	11 46	—	—	—	—	12 25	12 43	—	—	—	—	—	—	—	—	—	—
Uxbridge High St. ..	—	—	—	—	—	12 20	12 20	—	—	—	—	—	—	—	—	—	—
Denham Golf Club ..	11 50	—	—	—	—	12 29	—	—	—	—	—	—	—	—	—	—	—
Denham	11 53	—	—	—	—	12 38	12 48	—	—	—	—	—	—	—	—	—	—
Ruislip & Ickenham	11 59	—	—	12 22	—	12 44	12 54	—	—	1 38	—	—	—	—	—	—	—
Northolt Junction .	—	—	—	12 26	—	12 48	—	—	—	1 42	—	—	—	—	—	—	—
Northolt Halt (W.E.)	—	—	—	12 30	—	12 52	—	—	—	1 46	—	—	—	—	—	—	—
Greenford	—	12 25	12 30	12 35	12 47	12 55	1 5	1 27	1 30	1 50	2 17	2 20	2 27	2 37	2 42	3 5	3 30
Perivale	—	—	12 38	—	12 50	—	—	1 33	—	—	2 20	—	2 30	—	2 45	—	3 33
Brentham	—	—	12 41	—	12 53	—	—	1 36	—	—	2 23	—	2 33	—	2 48	—	3 36
Park Royal	—	—	12 44	—	12 56	—	—	1 39	—	—	2 26	—	2 36	—	2 51	—	3 45
Old Oak Lane Halt .	—	—	12 48	—	—	—	—	1 42	—	—	2 32	—	2 42	—	2 57	—	3 45
Westbourne Park ..	12 28	12 53	12 56	1 7	1 11	1 28	—	1 49	1 58	2 23	2 32	48 2 50	3 5	3 4	3 36	3 51
Bishops Road	—	—	—	—	—	—	—	—	2 27	—	—	—	—	—	—	—	—
Paddington ..... arr.	12 32	12 57	—	1 11	—	1 32	1 18	—	2 2	—	2 52	—	3 10	—	3 40	—

WEEK DAYS.	PM	PM	PM	PM	PM	PM	d	PM	PM	PM	PM	PM	PM	PM	PM	PM
SEER GREEN ....dep.	2 57	—	3 42	—	—	—	—	—	—	—	5 15	5 48	—	—	—	6 43
GERRARDS CROSS	3 3	3d13	4 9	—	—	—	—	—	4 18	—	5 21	5 54	—	—	—	6 49
Uxbridge High St. ..	2 45	—	—	—	—	—	—	—	—	—	—	—	—	—	—	6 23
Denham Golf Club ..	3 7	3d17	3 52	—	—	—	—	—	4 22	—	5 25	5 58	—	—	—	6 53
Denham	3 10	3d20	4 14	—	—	—	—	—	5 8	—	5 28	6 1	—	—	—	6 56
Ruislip & Ickenham.	3 16	3 35	4 22	—	—	4 30	—	—	5 14	—	5 45	6 7	—	—	—	7 2
NORTHOLT JUNCTION..	3 20	3 39	—	—	—	—	—	—	5 18	—	5 49	—	—	—	—	7 6
Northolt Halt (W.E.)	—	3 43	—	—	—	—	—	—	5 22	—	5 53	—	—	—	—	—
Greenford	3 26	3 48	—	4 15	4 33	4 40	5 4	5 10	5 27	5 52	5 57	6 15	6 22	6 32	6 46	7 12
Perivale	—	—	—	—	4 36	—	—	5 15	—	5 55	—	—	—	6 35	—	7d14
Brentham	—	—	—	—	4 39	—	—	5 18	—	5 58	—	—	—	6 38	—	—
Park Royal	—	—	—	—	4 42	—	—	5 21	—	6 1	—	—	—	6 41	—	—
Old Oak Lane Halt..	—	—	—	—	4 45	—	—	5 27	—	6 7	—	—	—	6 47	—	—
Westbourne Park ..	3 46	4 14	—	4 44	4 52	5 13	5 41	5 34	5 58	6 16	6 28	6 31	6 48	6 54	7 18	7 28
Bishops Road	—	4 19	—	4 49	—	—	—	—	—	—	—	—	—	—	—	—
PADDINGTON ....arr.	3 50	—	4 40	—	—	5 17	5 45	—	6 3	—	6 32	6 35	6 52	—	7 22	7 32

WEEK DAYS.	PM	PM	PM	PM	PM	PM	PM	PM	PM	PM
SEER GREEN .. . dep.	—	—	7 21	—	—	8 42	—	9d52	—	—
GERRARDS CROSS	—	—	7 27	—	8 32	8 48	—	9 57	10 39	11 8
Uxbridge High St. ..	—	—	—	—	—	—	—	—	—	10 50
Denham Golf Club ..	—	—	7 31	—	—	—	—	—	—	—
Denham	—	—	7 34	—	8 37	8 54	—	10 3	10 45	11 14
Ruislip & Ickenham	7 8	—	8 8	—	8 43	9 8	—	10 11	10 55	11 20
NORTHOLT JUNCTION..	7 12	—	8 12	—	—	9 12	—	10 15	10 59	—
Northolt Halt (W.E.)	7 16	—	8 16	—	—	9 16	—	10 19	11 3	—
Greenford	7 20	7 27	8 20	8 28	8 52	9 20	9 27	10 22	11 7	11 29
Perivale	—	7 30	—	8 31	—	—	9 30	—	—	—
Brentham	—	7 33	—	8 34	—	—	9 34	—	—	—
Park Royal	—	7 36	—	8 37	—	—	—	—	—	—
Old Oak Lane Halt..	—	7 42	—	8 43	—	—	—	—	—	—
Westbourne Park....	7 48	7 49	9 1	8 51	9 14	9 47	9 44	11 0	11 37	11 55
Bishops Road........	—	—	—	—	—	—	—	—	—	—
PADDINGTON......arr.	7 52	—	9 5	—	9 18	9 52	—	11 4	11 41	12 0

d Saturdays only.
e Saturdays excepted.
f Mondays excepted.
h Change at Ealing Broadway.
k Change at Ruislip.
l Not after July 27th.
p Sets down by request from London only; give notice to Guard.
q After July 27th arrive 8.36 a.m.
r After July 27th arrive 16 mins. later.
s Change at Denham.
‡ Change at Greenford.
C R Call to set down only.

SUNDAYS.	AM	AM	AM	AM	AM	AM	AM	AM	AM	noon	PM	PM	PM	PM	PM	PM	PM	PM	PM	PM	PM	PM
PADDINGTON .....dep.	820	850	912	925	935	1010	1042	1115	1120	12 0	12 2	1255	140	145	210	228	245	255	315	340	4 0	445
Bishops Road........	—	—	—	—	—	—	—	—	—	—	—	—	144	—	—	—	—	—	—	—	—	—
Westbourne Park ...	825	854	—	929	939	1014	1046	1119	1124	12 4	12 6	1259	149	—	214	232	249	259	319	344	4 4	449
Old Oak Lane Halt..	—	—	—	—	944	—	1051	—	1129	—	1211	—	152	—	219	—	254	—	324	349	—	—
Park Royal	—	—	—	—	947	—	1054	—	1132	—	1214	—	155	—	222	—	257	—	327	352	—	—
Brentham	—	—	—	—	950	—	1057	—	1135	—	1217	—	159	—	225	—	3 0	—	330	355	—	—
Perivale	—	—	—	—	954	—	11 1	—	1139	—	1221	—	2 2	—	229	—	3 4	—	334	359	—	—
Greenford	849	917	934	10 0	10 2	1050	11 4	1137	1142	1228	1224	1 22	—	217	232	251	3 7	331	337	4 2	4 23	518
Northolt Halt(W.E.).	—	—	—	—	10 5	—	11 8	—	—	—	—	1 26	—	221	—	—	—	—	341	4 8	—	—
NORTHOLT JUNCTION ..	—	—	939	—	10 9	—	1112	1143	—	—	—	1 30	—	225	—	—	—	—	345	412	—	—
Ruislip & Ickenham.	—	—	944	—	1013	—	1116	1148	—	—	—	1 34	—	229	—	3 0	—	—	349	416	4 32	—
Denham	—	—	950	—	1055	—	1122	1154	—	—	—	—	—	248	—	3 6	—	—	4 8	422	4 37	—
Denham Golf Club...	—	—	953	—	1058	—	—	1157	—	—	—	—	—	251	—	—	—	—	411	—	4 40	—
Uxbridge High St....	—	—	—	—	—	—	—	—	—	—	—	—	—	—	—	—	—	—	—	—	—	—
GERRARDS CROSS.....	—	—	958	—	11 3	—	—	12 2	—	—	—	—	—	253	—	313	—	—	416	—	4 47	—
SEER GREEN......arr.	—	—	10 4	—	11 9	—	—	12 8	—	—	—	—	—	3 2	—	319	—	—	422	—	4 53	—

SUNDAYS.	PM	PM	PM	PM	PM	PM	PM	PM	PM	PM
PADDINGTON ....dep	452	6 2	6 5	650	7 20	730	8 5	—	9 10	925
Bishops Road	—	—	—	—	—	—	—	—	—	—
Westbourne Park....	456	6 6	6 9	654	—	734	8 9	830	9 14	935
Old Oak Lane Halt ..	5 1	6 11	—	659	—	739	—	835	—	—
Park Royal..........	5 4	6 14	—	7 2	—	742	—	838	—	—
Brentham	5 7	6 17	—	7 5	—	745	—	841	—	—
Perivale	511	6 21	—	7 9	—	749	—	845	—	—
Greenford	514	6 24	6 33	712	7 41	752	8 33	848	9 37	955
Northolt Halt (W E.)	—	—	6 36	—	—	—	8 38	—	—	959
NORTHOLT JUNCTION..	—	—	6 40	—	7 46	—	8 42	—	—	10 3
Ruislip & Ickenham	—	—	6 44	—	7 50	—	8 46	—	—	10 7
Denham	—	—	6 50	—	7 56	—	9 3	—	—	1032
Denham Golf Club ..	—	—	—	—	7 59	—	—	—	—	—
Uxbridge High St. ..	—	—	—	—	—	—	—	—	—	—
GERRARDS CROSS	—	—	7 11	—	8 4	—	9 10	—	—	1039
SEER GREEN .. arr.	—	—	7 18	—	—	—	—	—	—	—

SUNDAYS.	AM	AM	AM	AM	AM	PM
SEER GREEN ....dep.	—	—	—	954	—	—
GERRARDS CROSS	—	—	—	10 0	—	—
Uxbridge High St. ..	—	—	—	—	—	—
Denham Golf Club ..	—	—	—	10 4	—	—
Denham	—	—	—	10 7	—	1212
Ruislip & Ickenham.	—	—	—	1025	—	1218
NORTHOLT JUNCTION..	—	—	—	1029	—	1222
Northolt Halt (W.E.)	—	—	—	1033	—	1226
Greenford	850	925	10 4	1037	1052	1232
Perivale	853	—	10 7	—	1055	1235
Brentham	857	—	1011	—	1059	1239
Park Royal.........	9 0	—	1014	—	11 2	1242
Old Oak Lane Halt..	9 6	—	1020	—	11 8	1248
Westbourne Park ..	912	952	1027	11 0	1115	1255
Bishops Road........	—	—	—	—	—	—
PADDINGTON......arr.	916	956	1031	11 4	1119	1259

SUNDAYS.	PM	PM	PM	PM	PM	PM	PM	PM	PM	PM	PM	PM	PM	PM	PM	PM	PM	PM	PM	PM	PM	PM	PM
SEER GREEN ....dep.	—	1 2	—	—	157	2 33	—	337	—	—	—	—	—	—	653	—	7 33	—	—	—	—	—	—
GERRARDS CROSS	—	1 8	—	—	2 3	2 39	—	343	—	—	—	—	—	—	659	—	7 39	—	8 15	—	922	—	10 17
Uxbridge High St. ..	—	—	—	—	—	—	—	—	—	—	—	—	—	—	—	—	—	—	—	—	—	—	—
Denham Golf Club .	—	112	—	—	2 7	2 43	—	347	—	—	—	—	—	—	7 3	—	7 43	—	8 19	—	—	—	—
Denham	—	115	—	—	210	2 47	—	350	—	5 0	—	—	—	—	7 7	7 20	7 46	—	8 22	—	927	—	10 22
Ruislip & Ickenham.	—	140	—	—	242	2 53	—	4 6	—	5 6	—	—	—	—	713	7 26	7 52	—	8 50	—	935	—	10 27
NORTHOLT JUNCTION..	—	144	—	—	246	—	—	410	—	510	—	—	—	—	—	7 30	—	—	8 54	—	937	—	10 16
Northolt Halt (W.E.)	—	148	—	—	250	—	—	414	—	514	—	—	—	—	—	7 34	—	—	8 58	—	—	—	10 20
Greenford	110	151	2 5	240	255	3 1	3 8	418	422	518	520	610	626	655	722	7 38	8 0	8 5	9 3	9 9	943	10 5	10 35
Perivale	113	—	2 8	243	258	—	—	421	—	—	523	615	—	7 0	—	—	—	810	—	914	—	1010	—
Brentham	117	—	212	247	3 2	—	—	425	—	—	527	619	—	7 4	—	—	—	814	—	918	—	1014	—
Park Royal....... ..	120	—	215	250	3 5	—	—	428	—	—	530	622	—	7 7	—	—	—	817	—	921	—	—	—
Old Oak Lane Halt..	126	—	221	256	311	—	—	434	—	—	536	628	—	713	—	—	—	823	—	927	—	—	—
Westbourne Park ..	133	222	228	3 3	318	3 23	338	441	449	548	543	636	7 [illegible]	721	742	8 8	8 21	829	9 31	933	10 3	1026	10 56
Bishops Road	—	—	—	—	—	—	—	—	—	—	—	—	—	—	—	—	—	—	—	—	—	—	—
PADDINGTON......arr.	137	226	232	3 7	322	3 27	342	445	453	552	547	640	710	725	747	8 12	8 25	—	9 35	—	10 7	1030	11 0

PADDINGTON TO SOUTHALL AND WEST DRAYTON.

WEEK DAYS.	AM	AM	AM	AM	AM	AM	AM	AM	AM	AM	AM	AM	AM	AM	AM	AM	AM	AM
PADDINGTON ....dep.	4 12	5 5	5 45	6 10	6 30	6 35	7 10	7 30	7 33	7 35	7 48	8 5	8 12	8 20	8 30	8 50	8 52	9 5
Bishop's Road	—	—	—	—	—	—	—	—	—	—	—	—	—	—	—	—	—	—
Westbourne Park .	4 16	5 10	5 49	6 14	—	6 39	7 14	—	7 37	—	7 52	—	—	8 24	—	—	8 56	9 9
Acton...............	4 22	5 16	5 55	6 21	—	6 47	7 22	—	7 43	—	7 58	—	8 21	8 30	—	—	9 2	9 16
Ealing Broadway....	4 26	5 20	6 0	6 25	—	6 52	7 27	7 40	7 47	7 46	8 2	8 16	8 26	8 35	8 40	9 0	9 6	9 20
West Ealing	4 29	5 23	6 3	6 29	—	6 56	7 31	—	7 50	—	8 5	8 19	8 29	8 38	—	—	9 9	9 23
Hanwell & Elthorne	4 32	5 26	6 6	6 32	—	7 0	7 34	—	7 53	—	8 8	8 22	—	8 41	—	—	9 12	—
SOUTHALL...........	4 36	5 35	6 12	6 38	—	7 7	7 41	—	8 0	—	8 14	8 27	—	8 47	—	—	9 18	—
Brentford	5 39	—	6 24	6 54	—	7 24	7 54	—	—	—	8 24	8 54	—	—	—	—	9 27	—
Hayes	5 6	5 40	6 17	6 43	—	7 14	7 48	—	8 5	7 57	8 19	8 32	—	8 53	—	—	9 22	—
WEST DRAYTON ..arr.	5 12	5 48	6 24	6 58	6 50	7 20	7 54	—	—	8 2	8 25	8 37	—	8 58	—	—	—	—

WEEK DAYS.

	AM	AM	AM	AM	AM	AM	AM	AM	AM	PM	PM	PM	d	d	e	d
Paddington ....dep.	—	9 2)	9 32	—	9 55	—	10 55	—	11 35	—	12 8	12 18	12 33	12 35	12 35	12 42
Bishop's Road	9 3	—	—	9 44	—	10 27	—	10 51	—	12 2	—	—	—	—	—	—
Westbourne Park....	9 12	—	9 36	9 52	—	10 35	—	11 0	11 39	12 7	—	—	—	12 39	12 39	—
Acton	9 21	—	9 42	9 58	—	10 41	—	11 7	11 46	12 13	—	—	—	12 45	12 45	—
Ealing Broadway....	9 25	9 30	9 46	10 2	—	10 45	11 7	11 11	11 50	12 17	12 19	12 29	—	12 49	12 49	12 53
West Ealing	9 28	—	9 49	10 5	—	10 48	—	11 14	11 53	12 20	—	12 32	—	12 52	12 52	—
Hanwell & Elthorne	9 31	—	9 52	10 8	—	10 51	—	11 17	11 56	12 23	—	—	—	12 55	12 55	—
Southall	9 36	—	9 59	10 13	—	10 58	—	11 21	12 2	12 30	—	—	—	12 59	1 2	1 2
Brentford	10 9	—	10 9	10 34	—	11 24	—	—	12 24	12 54	—	—	—	—	1 24	1 24
Hayes	—	9 43	10 5	—	10 13	11 3	—	—	12 8	12 36	—	—	—	—	1 8	1 8
West Drayton ..arr.	—	9 48	10 11	—	10 19	11 9	11 20	—	12 14	12 40	—	—	12 5	—	1 15	1 15

WEEK DAYS.

	d	PM	d	PM	d	d	d	d	PM	d	PM	d	PM	PM	PM
Paddington ..dep.	—	12 55	1 8	1 15	1 20	1 33	1 38	1 50	—	2 5	2 25	2 33	2 55	3 18	3 45
Bishop's Road	12 46	—	—	—	—	—	—	—	1 49	—	—	—	—	3 20	—
Westbourne Park.	—	12 59	—	1 19	—	1 42	—	1 54	2 9	2 29	—	2 59	3 25	—	
Acton	12 55	1 5	—	1 25	—	1 48	—	2 0	2 15	2 38	—	3 5	3 31	—	
Ealing Broadway.	12 59	1 9	1·20	1 29	1 31	1 52	2 1	2 4	2 19	2 43	2·44	3 9	3 29	3 35	—
West Ealing	1 2	1 12	1 23	1 32	—	1 46	1 56	—	2 7	2 23	2 47	—	3 12	3 38	—
Hanw'll&Elthorne	1 5	1 15	—	1 35	—	1 49	1 59	—	2 10	2 26	2 50	—	3 15	3 41	—
Southall	1 9	1 19	—	1 41	—	1 53	2 5	—	2 16	2 32	2 59	—	3 21	3 47	—
Brentford	1 24	—	—	1 54	—	—	2 24	—	—	—	3 24	—	—	4 24	—
Hayes	—	—	1 37	1 47	—	2 0	2 11	—	2 21	2 38	3 6	—	3 26	3 51	—
West Drayton arr.	—	—	1 37	1 54	—	—	2 20	2·14	2 30	2 45	3 13	2 57	3 33	—	4 5

WEEK DAYS.

	PM	PM	PM	PM	PM	e	PM	PM	PM	d	e	PM	PM	PM
Paddington...dep.	3 55	4 18	4 35	4 50	—	5 8	5 18	5 20	5 32	5 32	—	5 42	5 45	5 53	5 53
Bishop's Road	—	—	—	—	5 3	—	—	—	—	5 36	—	—	—	—
Westbourne Park.	3 59	4 22	4 39	—	5d 7	—	5 24	—	5 36	—	5 46	—	5 57	
Acton	4 5	4 28	4 47	—	5 12	5 17	—	5 30	—	5 42	5 45	5 46	—	6 3
Ealing Broadway.	4 9	4 32	4 51	—	5 16	5 21	5 28	5 34	5 43	5 46	5 49	5 58	—	6 4	6 7
West Ealing	4 12	4 35	4 55	—	5 19	5 24	—	5 37	5·47	5 49	5 52	6 2	—	6 7	6 10
Hanw'll&Elthorne	4 15	4 38	4 58	—	5 22	5 27	—	5 40	—	5 52	5 55	6 5	—	6 10	6 13
Southall	4 21	4 44	5 5	—	5 27	5 33	—	5 46	5 51	5 58	6 2	6 14	—	6 16	6 17
Brentford......	—	—	5 28	—	5·54	6 0	—	6° 0	—	—	6 24	6 24	—	—	
Hayes	4 26	4 50	5 11	—	5 32	5 40	—	5 50	6 59	6 3	6 8	6 21	—	—	
West Drayton arr.	4 33	4 57	5 18	5 10	5 39	5 46	5 42	—	6 8	6 9	6 14	6 29	6 5	—	

WEEK DAYS.

	e	d	e		PM	e	d	PM	PM	PM	d	e	PM	PM	PM
Paddington ..dep.	6 7	6 7	—	6 20	6 27	—	6 38	6 48	7 0	7 5	7 12	7 25	7 37	7 42	7 55	8 10
Bishop's Road ·....	—	—	6 15	—	—	6 38	—	—	—	—	—	—	—	—	—	—
Westbourne Park	6 11	6 11	—	—	6 31	—	6 42	6 52	—	7 9	7 16	7 29	—	7 46	—	8 14
Acton	6 17	6 17	6 25	—	6 37	—	6 48	6 58	—	7 15	7 22	7 35	—	7 52	8 3	8 20
Ealing Broadway..	6 21	6 21	6 29	6 31	6 41	6 50	6 52	7 2	—	7 19	7 26	7 29	7 48	7 56	8 7	8 24
West Ealing	6 24	6 24	6 32	—	6 44	6 53	6 55	7 5	—	7 22	7 29	7 42	—	7 59	8 10	8 27
Hanw'll&Elthorne	6 27	6 27	6 35	—	6 47	6 56	6 58	7 8	—	7 25	7 32	7 45	—	8 2	8 13	8 30
Southall	6 31	—	6 35	6 42	6 39	6 51	7 3	7 4	7 15	—	7 32	7 36	7 50	—	8 8	8 19	8 36
Brentford	—	—	6 54	6 54	6 54	—	7 26	7 26	7 26	—	—	—	—	8 24	—	8 54
Hayes	—	6 40	—	6 44	·—	7 8	7 9	7 21	—	7 37	—	—	—	—	8 12	8 23	8 41
West Drayton arr.	—	6 46	—	6 50	—	7 12	7 15	7 28	7 19	7 43	-·-	—	8 0	8 19	—	8 45

WEEK DAYS

	PM	PM	PM	PM	PM	PM	PM	PM	PM	PM	PM	PM	PM	PM	PM
Paddington ..dep.	8 35	8 40	9 10	9 30	10 5	10 10	10 40	11 5	11 30	11 53	12 3	12 5	12 40		
Bishop's Road	—	—	—	—	—	—	—	—	—	—	—	—	—		
Westbourne Park	—	8 44	9 14	9 34	—	10 14	10 44	11 9	—	11 37	—	12 9	12 44		
Acton	—	8 50	9 20	9 40	—	10 20	10 50	11 16	—	11 43	—	12 15	12 50		
Ealing Broadway.	—	8 54	9 24	9 44	—	10 24	10 54	11 20	11 41	11 47	—	12 19	12 54		
West Ealing	—	8 57	9 27	9 47	—	10 27	10 57	11 23	—	11 50	—	12 22	12 57		
Hanw'll&Elthorne	—	9 0	9 30	9 50	—	10 30	11 0	11 26	—	11 53	—	12 25	1 0		
Southall	—	9 6	9 34	9 56	—	10 36	11 6	11 30	—	11 59	—	12 30	1 4		
Brentford	—	—	—	—	—	—	—	—	—	—	—	—	—		
Hayes	—	9 11	—	10 1	—	10 40	11 11	—	—	12 4	—	12 34	—		
West Drayton arr.	8 54	9 17	—	10 8	10·25	—	11 17	—	11 52	12 10	12 22	—	—		

SUNDAYS.

	AM	AM	AM	AM	AM	AM	AM	AM	AM	AM	AM	AM	AM	AM	AM
Paddington ..dep.	6 30	8 20	8 50	9 12	9 25	9 45	10 0	10 5	10 10	10 25	10 37	10 45	11 0	11 15	11 35
Bishop's Road	—	—	—	—	—	—	—	—	—	—	—	—	—	—	—
Westbourne Park	6 34	8 25	8 54	—	9 29	—	—	—	10 14	—	10 40	—	—	11 19	11 39
Acton	6 40	8 31	9 0	—	9 35	—	—	—	10 20	—	10 47	—	—	11 25	11 45
Ealing Broadway.	6 44	8 35	9 4	9 24	9 39	9 55	10 10	10 15	10 24	10 36	10 51	10 55	11 11	11 29	11 49
West Ealing	6 47	8 38	9 7	9 27	9 42	—	—	—	10 27	10 43	10 54	—	—	11 32	11 52
Hanw'll&Elthorne	6 50	8 41	9 10	—	9 45	—	—	—	10 30	—	10 57	—	—	—	11 55
Southall	6 56	8 47	9 14	—	9 51	—	—	—	10 35	—	11 2	—	—	—	12 1
Brentford	—	—	—	—	—	—	—	—	—	—	—	—	—	—	—
Hayes	7 2	8 52	—	—	9 56	—	—	—	—	—	11 7	—	—	—	12 6
West Drayton arr.	7 8	8 59	—	—	10 2	—	—	—	—	—	11 2	—	—	—	12 12

SUNDAYS.

	noon	PM	PM	PM	PM	PM	PM	PM	PM	PM	PM	PM	PM	PM	PM	PM
Paddington ..dep.	12 0	12 55	1 45	2 0	2 28	2 35	2 55	3 35	4 0	4 10	4 45	5 15	5 30	6 5	645	7 20
Bishop's Road...	—	—	—	—	—	—	—	—	—	—	—	—	—	—	—	—
Westbourne Park.	12 4	12 59	—	2 4	2 32	2 39	2 59	3 39	4 4	—	4 49	—	5 34	6 9	649	—
Acton	12 10	1 5	—	2 10	2 38	—	3 5	3 45	4 10	—	4 55	—	5 40	6 15	655	—
Ealing Broadway .	12 14	1 9	1 56	2 14	2 42	2 47	3 9	3 49	4 14	4 20	4 59	5 26	5 44	6 19	639	7 31
West Ealing	12 17	1 12	1 59	2 17	2 45	—	3 12	3 52	4 17	—	5 2	5 29	5 47	6 22	7 7	7 34
Hanw'll&Elthorne	12 20	1 15	—	2 20	—	—	3 15	3 55	—	—	5 5	5 38	5 50	6 25	7 5	—
Southall	12 24	1 21	—	2 27	—	—	3 21	4 1	—	—	5 12	5 42	5 54	6 31	7 9	—
Brentford	—	2 24	—	2 54	—	—	—	4 24	—	—	5 24	5 54	6 24	6 56	724	—
Hayes	—	1 26	—	2 32	—	—	3 26	4 6	—	—	5 17	—	—	6 36	—	—
West Drayton arr.	—	1 32	2 11	2 39	—	2 59	3 30	4 12	—	—	5 23	—	—	6 42	—	—

SUNDAYS.

	PM	PM	PM	PM	PM	PM	PM	PM	PM	PM	PM	PM	PM
Paddington ..dep.	7 40	8 5	8 20	8 30	9 10	9 25	—	9 55	10 5	10 30	11 5	11 15	
Bishop's Road	—	—	—	—	—	—	—	—	—	—	—	—	
Westbourne Park.	7 44	8 9	—	8 34	9 14	—	9 35	9 59	—	10 34	11 9	—	
Acton	7 50	8 15	—	8 40	9 20	—	9 41	10 5	—	10 40	11 15	—	
Ealing Broadway.	7 54	8 19	8 31	8 44	9 24	9 45	10 9	10 16	10 44	11 19	11 26		
West Ealing	7 57	8 22	—	8 47	9 27	—	9 48	10 12	—	10 47	11 22	—	
Hanw'll&Elthorne	8 0	8 25	—	8 50	9 30	—	—	10 15	—	10 50	11 25	—	
Southall	8 6	8 31	—	8 56	9 36	—	—	10 19	10 24	10 54	11 29	11 34	
Brentford	8 24	8 59	—	—	—	—	—	—	—	—	—	—	
Hayes	8 11	8 35	—	—	9 41	—	—	10 29	—	—	11 39	—	
West Drayton arr.	8 17	—	8 43	—	9 45	9 50	—	10 35	—	—	11 45	—	

WEEK DAYS

	AM	AM	AM	AM	AM	AM	AM	AM	AM	AM	AM	AM	AM	AM	AM	AM
W. Drayton.. dep.	—	—	4 48	—	5 49	6 18	—	6 44	—	—	7 12	—	—	7 51	8 10	—
Hayes	—	—	4 53	—	5 55	6 24	—	6 51	7 5	7 17	7 22	—	—	7 56	—	—
Brentford	—	—	—	—	5 45	—	6 30	—	—	6 56	—	—	7 28	—	—	—
Southall	3 20	4 15	5 0	5 30	6 2	6 31	6 50	6 58	7 12	7 25	7 30	7 50	7 57	8 3	—	8 8
Hanw'll & Elth'rne	3 24	4 19	5 4	5 34	6 6	6 35	6 54	7 2	7 16	7 29	7 34	7 54	8 1	8 7	—	8 12
West Ealing	3 27	4 22	5 7	5 37	6 10	6 38	6 57	7 6	7 20	7 33	7 38	7 57	8 4	8 10	—	8 15
Ealing Broadway	3 30	4 25	5 10	5 40	6 13	6 41	7 0	7 10	7 23	7 36	7 41	8 0	8 7	8 13	—	8 18
Acton	3 34	4 29	5 14	5 44	6 17	6 45	7 4	7 14	7 27	7 40	7 45	8 4	8 11	8 17	—	8 22
Westbourne Park	3 40	4 35	5 20	5 50	6 23	6 51	7 10	7 21	7 33	7 46	7 51	8 10	—	—	—	8 28
Bishop's Road	—	—	—	—	—	—	—	—	—	—	—	—	8 19	8 25	—	—
Paddington ..arr.	3 44	4 39	5 24	5 54	6 27	6 55	7 14	7 25	7 37	7 50	7 55	8 14	—	—	8 28	8 32

WEEK DAYS

	AM	AM	AM	AM	AM	AM	AM	AM	AM	AM	AM	AM	AM	AM	AM	AM
W. Drayton..dep.	—	8 15	—	—	8 27	8 31	—	—	8 48	9 7	—	9 4	9 17	9 33	9 48	—
Hayes	—	8 15	—	—	8 32	—	—	—	8 52	—	—	9 10	9 22	9 38	—	9 50
Brentford	8 0	—	—	—	—	—	8 30	—	—	—	—	9 0	—	9 30	—	—
Southall	8 16	8 21	8 26	8 33	8 38	—	8 45	8 55	8 59	—	9 6	9 16	9 28	9 44	—	9 56
Hanw'll & Elthorne	8 20	8 25	8 32	8 37	8 42	—	8 49	8 59	9 3	—	9 10	9 20	9 32	9 48	—	10 0
West Ealing	8 23	8 28	8 35	8 40	8 45	—	8 52	9 1	9 6	—	9 13	9 23	9 35	9 51	—	10 3
Ealing Broadway	8 26	8 31	8 38	8 43	8 48	—	8 55	9 4	9 9	—	9 16	9 26	9 38	9 54	—	10 6
Acton	8 30	8 35	8 42	8 47	8 52	—	8 59	—	9 13	—	9 20	9 30	9 42	9 58	—	10 10
Westbourne Park	—	8 41	—	8 53	—	—	9 5	—	9 20	—	9 26	—	9 48	10 4	—	10 16
Bishop's Road	8 38	—	—	—	9 0	—	—	—	9 24	—	—	9 38	—	10 8	—	
Paddington...arr.	—	8 45	8 50	8 57	—	8 49	9 9	9 14	—	9 25	9 30	—	9 52	—	10 6	10 20

WEEK DAYS

	AM	AM	AM	AM	AM	AM	PM	PM	PM	PM	PM	PM	PM	PM	PM	PM
W. Drayton.. dep.	10 —	—	10 59	—	11 33	11 38	—	12 34	12 54	1 27	—	2 11	—	2 28	3 2	
Hayes	10 15	—	—	11 7	—	11 44	12 25	12 40	1 0	1 32	—	—	2 20	2 34	3 7	
Brentford	10 12	—	—	10 35	—	11 9	—	12 30	—	—	1 30	—	2 0	2 30	—	
Southall	10 25	10 44	—	11 12	—	11 52	12 31	12 47	1 6	1 38	2 3	—	2 26	2 42	3 14	
Hanw'll & Elth'rne	10 30	10 48	—	11 16	—	11 56	12 35	—	1 10	1 42	2 7	—	2 30	2 46	3 18	
West Ealing	10 35	10 51	—	11 19	—	12 13	12 38	—	1 13	1 45	2 10	—	2 33	2 49	3 21	
Ealing Broadway	10 38	10 54	—	11 22	11 44	12 16	12 41	12 53	1 16	1 48	2 13	—	2 36	2 52	3 24	
Acton	10 42	10 58	—	11 26	—	12 20	12 45	—	1 20	1 52	2 17	—	2 40	2 57	3 28	
Westbourne Park	10 51	11 4	—	11 34	—	12 28	12 53	1 7	1 28	1 58	2 23	2 31	2 48	3 5	3 36	
Bishop's Road	—	11 9	—	—	—	—	—	—	—	—	2 27	—	—	—	—	
Paddington .. arr.	10 55	—	11 18	11 38	11 55	12 32	12 57	1 11	1 32	2 2	—	2 35	2 52	3 10	3 40	

WEEK DAYS

	d PM	PM	PM	PM	PM	PM	e PM	PM	e PM	PM	PM	PM	PM	PM	PM	PM
W. Drayton.. dep.	3 17	—	3 42	—	4 36	5 2	5 10	5 16	5 37	5 50	6 10	637	—	6 51	7 14	7 35
Hayes	—	—	3 47	4 18	4 43	5 9	5 17	5 23	5 44	5 57	6 10	—	6⁹ 47	6 57	7 20	7 41
Brentford	—	—	3 30	—	—	—	—	5 30	—	—	6 27	—	—	7 0	7 30	
Southall	—	—	3 54	4 24	4 49	5 16	5 23	5 32	5 52	6 4	6 25	—	6 42	6 53	7 3	7 26 7 47
Hanw'll & Elth'rne	—	—	3 58	4 28	4 53	5 20	5 28	5 37	5 57	6 8	6 19	—	6 46	6 57	7 7	7 30
West Ealing	—	3 31	4 1	4 31	4 58	5 24	5 32	5 41	6 1	6 12	6 33	—	6 49	7 1	7 10	7 33 7 53
Ealing Broadway	—	3 34	4 4	4 34	5 1	5 27	5 36	5 44	6 4	6 15	6 36	—	6 52	7 4	7 13	7 36 7 56
Acton	—	3 38	4 8	4 38	5 5	5 31	5 40	5 48	6 8	6 19	6 40	—	7 10	7 17	7 40	
Westbourne Park	—	3 46	4 14	4 44	5 15	5 41	5 47	5 58	6 16	6 28	6 48	7 3	7 18	7 25	7 48	8 7
Bishop's Road	—	—	4 19	4 49	—	—	—	—	—	—	—	—	—	—	—	
Paddington .. arr.	3 38	3 50	—	5 17	5 45	5 52	6 3	6 20	6 32	6 52	655	7	7 22	7 29	7 52	8 11

WEEK DAYS

	PM	PM	PM	d PM	PM	PM	PM	PM	PM	PM	PM	PM	PM	PM
West Drayton dep.	—	8 0	—	8 44	9 3	9 16	9 22	9 46	—	10 23	—	—	11 17	
Hayes	—	8 7	8 33	—	—	9 28	9 51	—	10 32	11 0	—	11 24		
Brentford	—	—	—	—	9 0	—	—	—	—	—	—			
Southall	7 57	8 13	8 39	—	9 0	9 26	9 35	9 56	—	10 36	11 5	—	11 32	
Hanw'll & Elth'rne	8 1	8 17	8 43	—	9 4	—	9 42	10 0	—	10 42	11 9	—	11 36	
West Ealing	8 4	8 21	8 46	8 58	9 15	9 32	9 42	10 3	—	10 45	11 12	11 20	11 39	
Ealing Broadway	8 7	8 24	8 49	8 56	9 1	9 18	9 35	9 45	10 6	1026	10 48	11 15	11 23	11 42
Acton	8 11	8 28	8 53	—	9 5	—	—	9 49	10 10	—	10 52	11 19	11 27	11 47
Westbourne Park	8 20	8 36	9 1	9 8	9 14	9 29	9 47	9 57	10 18	1038	11 0	11 27	11 37	11 55
Bishop's Road	—	—	—	—	—	—	—	—	—	—	—			
Paddington .. arr.	8 24	8 40	9 5	9 12	9 18	9 33	9 52	10 2	10 22	1042	11 4	11 31	11 41	12 0

SUNDAYS

	AM	AM	AM	AM	AM	AM	AM	AM	AM	PM	PM	PM	PM	PM	PM	PM
West Drayton dep.	—	7 2	8 30	—	9 46	—	10 0	—	—	12 27	—	2 21	—	3 3	3 45	4 15
Hayes	—	7 8	8 36	—	—	—	9 6	—	—	12 33	—	2 27	—	3 0	3 50	4 21
Brentford	—	—	—	—	—	—	—	—	—	—	—	—	3 0	—	4 0	
Southall	5 30	7 16	8 42	9 30	—	10 0	10 14	—	11 0	12 39	2 0	2 32	—	3 16	3 56	4 27
Hanw'll & Elth'rne	5 34	7 20	8 46	9 34	—	10 4	10 18	—	11 4	12 43	2 4	2 36	—	3 20	4 0	4 31
West Ealing	5 37	7 23	8 49	9 37	—	10 7	10 22	10 45	11 7	12 46	2 7	2 39	3 7	3 23	4 3	4 34
Ealing Broadway	5 40	7 26	8 52	9 40	—	10 10	10 25	10 48	11 10	12 49	2 10	2 42	3 10	3 26	4 6	4 37
Acton	5 44	7 30	8 56	9 44	—	10 14	10 30	10 52	11 14	12 53	2 14	2 46	3 14	3 30	4 10	4 41
Westbourne Park	5 50	7 36	9 4	9 52	10 10	10 22	10 38	11 0	11 22	1 1	2 22	2 54	3 23	3 38	4 18	4 49
Bishop's Road	—	—	—	—	—	—	—	—	—	—	—					
Paddington .. arr.	5 54	7 40	9 8	9 56	10 14	10 26	10 42	11 4	11 26	1 2	2 26	2 58	3 27	3 42	4 22	4 53

SUNDAYS

	PM	PM	PM	PM	PM	PM	PM	PM	PM	PM	PM	PM	PM	PM	PM	PM	PM	PM
West Drayton dep.	5 15	5 55	—	6 32	—	7 34	—	—	8 36	—	9 18	—						
Hayes	5 21	—	6 38	—	7 40	—	—	8 42	—	9 3	—							
Brentford	5 0	—	5 30	6 30	—	7 30	—	8 0	—	9 0	—							
Southall	5 26	—	6 6	6 44	—	7 46	—	8 16	—	8 48	9 9	—						
Hanw'll & Elth'rne	5 30	—	6 10	6 48	—	7 50	—	8 20	—	8 53	9 13	—						
West Ealing	5 33	—	6 13	6 51	—	7 53	—	8 23	—	8 57	9 16	—	9 49					
Ealing Broadway	5 36	8 6	6 16	6 54	7 22	7 30	7 56	8 4	8 26	8 30	9 0	9 17	9 19	9 31	9 38	9 52		
Acton	5 40	—	6 20	6 58	—	7 34	8 0	—	9 5	—	9 23	—						
Westbourne Park	5 48	6 19	6 28	7 6	7 33	7 42	8 8	8 15	8 21	8 38	8 41	9 11	9 13	9 28	9 31	9 42	9 49	10 3
Bishop's Road	—	—	—	—	—	—	—	—	—	—								
Paddington .. arr.	5 52	6 23	6 32	7 10	7 37	7 47	8 12	8 20	8 25	8 42	8 45	9 15	9 17	9 32	9 35	9 46	9 53	10 7

SUNDAYS

	PM	PM	PM	PM	PM	PM
West Drayton dep.	9 42	—	10 0	—	11 0	—
Hayes	9 48	—	10 5	—	11 6	—
Brentford	—	—	—	—		
Southall	9 54	—	1010	—	11 12	—
Hanwell & Elth'rne	9 58	—	1014	—	11 16	—
West Ealing	10 2	—	1017	10 41	11 19	—
Ealing Broadway	10 5	10 18	1020	10 44	10 51	11 22
Acton	10 9	—	1024	10 48	11 26	—
Westbourne Park	10 18	10 29	1032	10 56	11 2	11 34
Bishop's Road	—	—	—	—		
Paddington ..arr	10 22	10 33	1036	11 0	11 6	11 38

d Saturdays only. e Saturdays excepted.
f Mondays only. g Mondays excepted.
h Runs into Paddington Station on Saturdays.

WEEK DAYS.

WEEK DAYS	AM	AM	AM	AM	AM	AM	e	AM	AM	AM	AM	AM	AM	AM	AM	AM	d
MARYLEBONE... dep.	—	6 25	—	6 45	—	7 20	7 40	7 50	—	—	8 45	8 50	9 14	—	—	10 5	—
Baker Street	6 5	6 6	6 12	6 30	6 35	7 3	7 23	7 23	7 50	7 57	8 29	8 34	9 1	9 17	9 51	—	10 11
Harrow	6 24	6 40	6 38	7 7	7 3	7 35	7 53	8 5	8 12	8 30	9 0	9 6	9 29	9 36	10 9	10 20	10 30
Harrow, North	—	6 43	6 33	—	7 6	7 38	—	—	8 15	—	—	9 9	9 32	9 39	—	10 23	10 33
Pinner	6 28	6 46	6 56	—	7 9	7 41	7 59	8 9	8 18	8 35	—	9 12	9 35	9 43	—	10 26	10 36
Northwood	6 33	—	7 1	7 9	7 13	7 46	8 3	8 14	8 23	8 40	9 8	9 18	9 40	9 48	10 17	10 32	10 41
Sandy Lodge	—	—	—	—	—	—	—	—	8 26	—	—	9 21	9 43	9 51	10 20	10 35	10 44
Rickmansworth	6 40	6 57	7 6	7 17	7 22	7 54	—	8 22	8 31	8 47	—	9 28	9 48	9 55	10 21	10 41	10 50
Chorley Wood	6 46	7 3	7 12	—	8 0	—	8 28	8 37	—	—	9 34	9 54	10 2	10 27	10 47	10 56
Chalfont & Latimer	6 53	—	7 19	—	8 5	—	8 34	8 44	—	—	9 40	10 0	—	10 33	10 53	11 1
Chesham	—	—	7 28	—	7 41	—	8 42	—	—	—	9 51	—	—	10 44	11 20	11 20

WEEK DAYS.

WEEK DAYS	e	AM	PM	PM	d	d	PM	d	d	d	d	d	PM	d	d	d
MARYLEBONE... dep.	—	11 15	—	12 35	—	1 5	1 10	—	—	1 41	—	2 15	—	—	2 45	—
Baker Street	10 18	11 1	12 8	12 18	12 54	—	12 50	1 12	1 17	1 21	1 52	2 3	2 17	2 35	—	3 18
Harrow	10 37	11 31	12 27	12 50	—	—	1 25	—	—	1 56	2 10	2 31	2 35	2 53	3 0	3 36
Harrow, North	—	—	12 30	12 53	—	—	1ʰ28	—	1 40	1 59	2 13	—	2 38	2 56	3 3	—
Pinner	—	11 35	12 33	12 56	—	—	1 29	1 36	1 43	2 2	2 16	2 35	2 41	2 59	3 6	—
Northwood	—	11 40	12 38	1 1	—	1 26	1 34	1 41	1 48	2 7	2 22	2 41	2 46	3 4	3 11	—
Sandy Lodge	10 46	11 43	12 41	1 4	—	1 29	1ʰ37	—	1 51	2 10	2 26	2 45	2 49	—	3 14	—
Rickmansworth	10 52	11 48	12 46	1 9	1 25	1 34	1ʰ42	1 48	1 55	2 15	2 30	2 50	2 54	3 11	3 18	3 48
Chorley Wood	10 58	11 54	12 52	1 15	1 31	1 40	1ʰ48	1 54	2 1	2 21	2 36	2 56	3 0	3 17	—	3 54
Chalfont & Latimer	11 4	12 1	1 0	1 21	1 37	1 46	1ʰ54	2 0	2 7	2 27	2 42	3 3	3 6	3 23	—	4 0
Chesham	11 20	12 33	1 13	1 29	—	—	—	—	2 20	—	2 51	3 12	3ʰ28	3 32	—	—

WEEK DAYS.

WEEK DAYS	PM	e	d	d	e	PM	PM	e	PM	e	PM	e	d	e
MARYLEBONE... dep.	3 25	—	—	—	—	4 59	—	5 24	5 29	—	—	—	6 25	6 31
Baker Street	3 10	3 45	3 45	4 10	4 16	4 40	5 7	—	5 17	5 35	5 45	5 46	5ʰ49	6 3	—
Harrow	3 42	4 4	4 4	4 27	4 34	5 19	5ʰ25	—	5 44	5 52	—	6 4	6 15	6 22	—
Harrow, North	—	4 7	4 7	4 30	—	5 22	—	—	5 47	5ʰ56	—	—	6 18	6 25	—
Pinner	3 46	4 10	4 10	4 33	4 38	5 25	5 30	—	5 50	5 57	—	6 9	6 21	6 28	—
Northwood	3 52	4 15	4 15	4 39	4 43	5 30	5 35	5 44	5 54	6 2	—	6 14	6 26	6 33	6 45	6 52
Sandy Lodge	3 55	4 18	4 18	4 42	—	5 33	5 39	—	—	—	—	—	6 29	—	6 55
Rickmansworth	4 0	4 23	4 23	4 47	4 49	5 37	5 42	5 51	—	6 9	6 16	6 21	6 34	6 40	6 52	7 0
Chorley Wood	4 6	4 29	—	4 53	4 56	5 43	5 48	5 57	—	—	6 22	6 27	6 40	6 46	6 58	7 6
Chalfont & Latimer	4 12	4 35	—	4 59	5 2	5 48	5 54	6 3	—	6 18	6 28	6 33	6 46	6 51	7 4	7 12
Chesham	4 24	—	—	5 24	5 15	—	6 4	—	—	6ʰ27	6 38	6 54	—	7 0	7 21	7 20

WEEK DAYS.

WEEK DAYS	PM	PM	e	PM	PM	PM	PM	e	PM	PM	PM	PM	PM
MARYLEBONE... dep	—	6 53	—	7 30	—	8 20	9 0	—	10 30	—	11 35	—	—
Baker Street	6 30	6 34	7 15	7 15	8 5	—	8 40	9 25	10 3	10 10	11 12	11 20	11 50
Harrow	6ʰ48	7 8	7 33	7 46	8 23	8 35	9 15	9 43	10 22	10 45	11 30	11 50	12 8
Harrow, North	6 52	7 11	7 36	7 49	8 26	8 38	9 18	9 46	—	10 48	11 33	11 53	12 11
Pinner	6 55	7 14	7 39	7 52	8 29	8 41	9 21	9 49	10 27	10 51	11 36	11 56	12 14
Northwood	7 0	7 19	7 44	7 57	8 34	8 46	9 26	9 54	10 32	10 56	11 41	12 1	12 19
Sandy Lodge	—	—	7 47	—	8 37	—	9 29	—	—	—	—	—	—
Rickmansworth	7 7	7 26	7 52	8 4	8 42	8 53	9 33	10 1	10 39	11 3	11 47	12 8	12 26
Chorley Wood	7 13	7 32	7 58	8 10	8 48	8 59	9 39	10 7	10 45	11 9	11 53	12 14	12 32
Chalfont & Latimer	7 19	7 38	8 5	8 17	8 54	9 5	9 45	10 13	—	11 15	—	12 20	12 38
Chesham	7ʰ31	7 46	8 14	—	9 3	—	9 55	10 24	—	11 25	—	12 28	12 49

SUNDAYS.

SUNDAYS	PM	AM	AM	AM	AM	AM	AM	AM	AM	AM	PM	PM	PM	PM	PM
MARYLEBONE... dep	—	—	9 30	—	—	—	11 0	—	—	—	1 0	—	2 30	—	3 15
Baker Street	7 34	8 47	9 10	9 47	10 15	10 33	10 44	11 11	12 0	12 31	1245	2 0	2 15	2 57	3 0
Harrow	8 4	9 6	9 45	10 6	10 33	10 54	11 15	11 32	12 18	1 0	1 15	2 19	2 45	3 16	3 30
Harrow, North	8 7	9 9	9 48	10 9	10 36	10 57	11 18	11 35	12 21	1 3	1 18	2 22	2 48	3 19	3 33
Pinner	8 10	9 12	9 51	10 12	10 39	11 0	11 21	11 38	12 24	1 6	1 21	2 25	2 51	3 23	3 36
Northwood	8 15	9 17	9 56	10 18	10 45	11 5	11 26	11 44	12 29	1 11	1 26	2 30	2 56	3 28	3 41
Sandy Lodge	8 18	9 20	9 59	10 21	10 48	11 8	11 29	11 47	12 32	1 14	1 29	2 33	2 59	3 31	3 44
Rickmansworth	8 23	9 25	10 4	10 26	10 53	11 13	11 34	11 52	12 37	1 19	1 34	2 38	3 4	3 36	3 49
Chorley Wood	8 29	9 31	10 10	10 32	10 59	11 19	11 40	11 57	12 43	1 25	1 40	2 44	3 10	3 40	3 55
Chalfont & Latimer	8 35	9 37	10 16	10 38	11 5	11 25	11 46	12 5	12 49	1 31	1 46	2 50	3 16	3 46	4 1
Chesham	8 44	9 47	—	—	11 14	—	12 16	12 16	—	1 40	2 6	—	3 29	—	4 9

SUNDAYS.

SUNDAYS	PM	PM	PM	PM	PM	PM	PM	PM	PM	PM	PM	PM	PM	PM
MARYLEBONE... dep.	—	—	4 30	5 30	—	6 10	—	6 45	7 45	—	8 50	—	10 15	—
Baker Street	3 35	4 2	4 15	5 15	5 37	5 52	6 24	6 30	7 30	7 59	8 27	8 30	9 29	10 0	10 38
Harrow	3 54	4 21	4 45	5 45	5 56	6 25	6 43	7 0	8 0	8 17	8 46	9 5	9 47	10 36	10 59
Harrow, North	3 57	—	4 48	—	5 59	6 28	6 46	—	8 3	8 20	8 49	9 8	9 50	10 33	11 2
Pinner	4 0	4 25	4 51	—	6 2	6 31	6 49	7 4	8 6	8 23	8 52	9 11	9 53	10 36	11 5
Northwood	4 5	4 30	4 56	—	6 7	6 36	6 54	7 9	8 11	8 28	8 57	9 16	9 58	10 41	11 10
Sandy Lodge	—	4 33	4 59	—	6 10	6 39	—	—	—	—	—	—	—	—	—
Rickmansworth	4 12	4 38	5 4	—	6 15	6 44	7 1	7 16	8 18	8 35	9 4	9 23	10 5	10 47	11 17
Chorley Wood	4 18	4 44	5 10	—	6 21	6 50	—	7 22	8 24	8 41	9 10	—	10 11	—	11 23
Chalfont & Latimer	4 24	4 50	5 16	—	6 27	6 56	7 11	7 28	8 50	8 47	9 16	—	10 17	—	11 28
Chesham	—	5 1	—	—	6 38	7 4	—	7 41	8 38	—	9 25	—	10 37	—	—

WEEK DAYS.

WEEK DAYS	AM	AM	AM	AM	AM	e	AM	AM	AM	AM	AM	AM	AM
CHESHAM... dep.	5 45	6 36	7 0	—	7 43	7 54	—	8 17	—	—	8 48	—	9 15	—
Chalfont & Latimer	5 54	6 58	7 9	7 40	7 56	8 6	—	8 26	8 34	8 40	—	8 58	—	9 24	9 39
Chorley Wood	5 58	7 2	7 13	7 44	8 0	8 10	—	8 30	8 38	8 44	—	9 2	—	9 28	9 43	10 19
Rickmansworth	6 3	7 6	7 18	7 50	8 5	8 15	—	8 35	8 43	8 49	8 58	—	9 33	9 48	10 24
Sandy Lodge	—	—	7 22	7 54	8 9	—	8 39	—	—	—	—	—	—	9 52	10 28
Northwood	6 10	7 13	7 25	7 57	8 13	8 22	8 27	8 43	8 50	8 56	9 5	9 12	—	9 40	9 56	10 32
Pinner	6 15	7 17	7 29	8 2	8 17	8ʰ26	8 31	8 48	—	9 0	9 9	—	9 44	10 1	10 36
Harrow, North	—	7 20	7 31	8 4	8 20	8ʰ28	8 33	—	—	9 2	—	9 46	10 3	10 38
Harrow	6 20	—	7 36	8 9	—	8ʰ33	8 38	—	—	9 5	9 18	—	9 33	9 51	10 10	10 45
Baker Street	6 52	7 41	7 56	8 35	8 42	8ʰ51	8 57	9 10	—	9 28	9 35	9 39	9 49	10 23	10 25	10 59
MARYLEBONE	6 33	—	7 49	8 22	—	8 42	8 51	—	9 9	9 21	—	—	10 3	—

WEEK DAYS.

WEEK DAYS	AM	AM	AM	AM	AM	PM	d	PM	d	d	PM	d	d	PM	d	d
CHESHAM... dep.	10 21	—	—	11 32	—	12 17	12 47	—	1 44	1ʰ59	—	2 54	2 54	3 37	3ʰ59	4 15	—
Chalfont & Latimer	10 32	1055	11 43	12 18	1ʰ19	—	1 55	2 12	2 42	3 3	3 19	3 46	4 10	4 24	—
Chorley Wood	—	1059	—	11 53	12 22	1 24	—	1 59	2 16	2 46	3 12	3 23	3 50	4 15	4 28	—
Rickmansworth	—	11 4	11 33	11 58	12 27	1 29	—	2 4	2 21	2 51	3 17	3 28	3 55	4 21	4 33	4 43
Sandy Lodge	—	11 8	—	12 2	12 31	—	—	2 8	2 25	2 55	3 21	—	—	4 26	4 38	—
Northwood	—	1112	11 40	12 6	12 35	1 36	1 50	2 11	2 29	2 59	3 25	3 35	4 2	4 30	4 42	4 50
Pinner	—	1116	—	12 11	12 39	1 41	1 55	2 15	2 33	3 3	3 29	3 39	4 6	4 35	4 46	4 55
Harrow, North	—	1118	—	12 13	12 41	1 44	1 58	2 18	2 35	3 5	3 31	—	4 8	4 37	4 48	4 57
Harrow	10 51	1123	11 49	12 20	12 46	1 48	2 2	2 22	2 42	3 12	3 38	3 46	4 15	4 43	4 53	5 4
Baker Street	11 5	1150	12 22	12 35	1 22	2 22	2 35	2 53	2 58	3 28	3 54	4 22	4 31	5 14	—	5 20
MARYLEBONE	—	1136	12 2	—	12 59	2 2	2 16	2 36	—	—	3 59	—	4 56	5 6	—

WEEK DAYS (down/up — Chesham to Marylebone)

WEEK DAYS	d	PM	e	d	PM	e	d	d	e	PM	d	e	PM	PM	PM	PM	PM	PM
Chesham...dep.	—	4 40	—	5 5	—	5 28	—	—	6 8	—	6 35	6 41	—	6 58	6 58	—	—	8 20
Chalfont & Latimer	—	4 51	5 14	5 14	—	5 50	5 54	—	6 24	—	6 51	6 53	7 2	7 19	7 30	751	—	8 29
Chorley Wood	—	4 55	5 18	5 18	—	5 54	5 58	—	6 28	—	6 56	6 57	7 6	7 23	7 34	755	—	8 33
Rickmansworth	4 54	5 1	5 23	5 23	—	5 57	6 3	6 31	6 33	6 52	7 1	7 2	7 12	7 30	7 38	8 0	—	8 38
Sandy Lodge	4 59	5 5	—	5 27	—	6 2	6 7	6 35	6 37	—	—	7 17	7 34	—	8 5	—	—	—
Northwood	5 3	5 9	5 30	5 31	5 58	6 6	6 11	6 39	6 41	—	7 8	7 9	7 21	7 38	7 46	8 9	8 36	8 47
Pinner	5 7	5 14	5 34	5 35	6 2	6 10	6 15	6 43	6 45	—	7 13	7 13	—	7 43	7 50	813	—	8 51
Harrow, North	5 9	5 16	5 36	5 37	6 4	—	6 17	6 45	6 47	—	7 15	—	—	7 45	7 52	—	—	—
Harrow	5 14	5 24	5 43	5 44	6 9	6 18	6 23	6 49	6 50	7 4	7 21	7 21	7 30	7 52	7 57	818	8 43	8 59
Baker Street	5 40	5 41	5 58	6 0	—	6 33	6 39	7 9	7 14	7 33	7 37	7 36	8 1	8 8	8 32	847	9 18	9 27
Marylebone	5 27	—	—	—	6 22	—	—	—	—	7 13	—	—	7 43	—	8 11	831	8 55	9 12

WEEK DAYS	e	PM	PM	d	PM	PM	PM	
Chesham...dep.	8 31	8d37	9 15	9 31	—	—	10 44	
Chalfont & Latimer	8 40	8 50	9 24	9 42	10. 1	—	10 56	
Chorley Wood	8 44	8 54	9 29	9 47	947	10 5	10 25	11 0
Rickmansworth	8 49	8 59	9 34	9 52	952	10 10	10 30	11 5
Sandy Lodge	—	9 3	—	—	—	—	—	
Northwood	8 58	9 7	9 41	9 59	959	10 17	10 37	11 12
Pinner	9 2	9 11	9 45	10 3	10 3	10 21	10 41	11 16
Harrow, North	9 4	9 13	9 47	10 5	10 5	10 23	—	11 18
Harrow	9 8	9 20	9 54	10 9	1012	10 28	10 47	11 25
Baker Street	9 39	9 36	10 10	10 42	1028	11 2	11 18	11 40
Marylebone	—	—	—	—	—	10 41	11 0	—

d Saturdays only.
e Saturdays excepted.
h Stops on notice being given to Guard.

SUNDAYS

SUNDAYS	AM	AM	AM	AM	AM	AM	PM	PM	PM	PM	PM	PM	PM	PM	PM	PM
Chesham...dep.	7 49	—	9 17	10 2	—	11 52	12 56	—	2 11	2 54	—	4 14	—	—	5 45	6 5
Chalfont & Latimer	7 59	8 55	9 30	10 11	11 1	12 4	1 5	1 34	2 23	3 6	4 5	4 39	5 8	5 34	5 58	6 14
Chorley Wood	8 3	8 59	9 34	10 15	11 5	12 8	1 9	1 38	2 27	3 10	4 10	4 43	5 12	5 38	6 2	6 18
Rickmansworth	8 9	9 5	9 39	10 20	11 11	12 13	1 14	1 43	2 32	3 15	4 15	4 48	5 17	5 44	6 7	6 23
Sandy Lodge	—	—	9 43	10 24	11 15	12 18	1 18	1 47	2 35	3 19	4 19	4 52	5 21	5 48	6 11	6 27
Northwood	8 16	9 12	9 47	10 28	11 19	12 22	1 22	1 51	2 39	3 23	4 23	4 56	5 25	5 52	6 15	6 31
Pinner	8 21	9 17	9 51	10 32	11 23	12 26	1 26	1 56	2 43	3 27	4 27	5 0	5 29	5 36	6 19	6 35
Harrow, North	8 23	9 19	9 54	10 34	11 25	12 28	1 28	1 58	2 45	3 29	4 29	5 2	5 31	5 58	6 21	6 37
Harrow	8 30	9 26	10 0	10 41	11 32	12 33	1 35	2 3	2 52	3 36	4 36	5 7	5 38	6 5	6 28	3 42
Baker Street	8 49	9 48	10 27	11 1	11 48	1 5	1 51	2 35	3 9	3 52	4 54	5 42	5 54	6 21	6 44	7 20
Marylebone	—	—	10 13	—	—	12 46	—	2 16	—	—	—	5 20	—	—	—	6 55

SUNDAYS	PM	d	PM	PM	PM	PM	PM	PM	PM	PM	PM	PM
Chesham...dep.	—	7 11	7 24	—	8 6	—	8 55	9 5	—	—	9 51	10 5
Chalfont & Latimer	6 54	7 25	7 34	8 2	8 26	—	9 4	9 17	—	—	10 1	10 28
Chorley Wood	6 58	7 29	7 38	8 7	8 31	8 50	9 8	9 21	—	—	10 6	10 32
Rickmansworth	7 3	7 34	7 44	8 12	8 36	8 55	9 13	9 26	9 40	—	10 11	10 37
Sandy Lodge	7 7	7 38	7 48	8 16	—	8 59	—	—	—	—	—	—
Northwood	7 11	7 42	7 52	8 20	8 43	9 3	9 20	9 33	9 47	—	10 18	10 44
Pinner	7 15	7 46	7 56	8 24	8 47	9 7	9 24	9 37	9 52	—	10 23	10 48
Harrow, North	7 17	7 48	7 58	8 28	8 49	—	9 26	—	—	—	10 25	10 50
Harrow	7 22	7 55	8 3	8 35	8 56	9 15	9 31	9 42	9 57	10 11	10 32	10 54
Baker Street	7 57	8 12	8 35	8 51	9 12	9 31	9 51	10 5	10 20	10 27	10 42	10 48	11 14
Marylebone	7 35	—	8 16	—	—	—	9 44	9 55	10 10	10 24	—	—

MARYLEBONE TO WEMBLEY, SOUTH HARROW, & SEER GREEN.

WEEK DAYS (Marylebone to Seer Green)

WEEK DAYS	AM	AM	AM	AM	AM	AM	AM	AM	AM	d	d	PM	d	e	d	PM
Marylebone...dep.	5 15	6 10	6 50	7 10	8	4 8	5 5 9	5	10 35	11 5	11 35	12	5 12	25	12 55	1 15	1 30	1 37	1 45
Wembley Hill	5 27	6 22	7	2 7	22	8 16	9	7 9	18	10 47	1117	11 47	12 17	12 37	1	7	1 27	1 42	—	1 57
Sudbury & Harrow Road	5 34	6 29	7 9	7	29 8	23 9	13 9	25	10 56	1123	11 54	12 23	12 43	1	14 1	33	1 48	—	2 4
South Harrow	—	6 34	7 14	7 34	8 28	—	9 30	11 1	—	11 59	—	—	1 19	—	—	2 9	
Northolt Junction	5 42	6 38	7 18	7 39	8 32	—	9 34	11 5	—	12 2	—	1 23	—	1 58	2 12	
Ruislip and Ickenham	5 47	6 43	—	7 44	8 36	—	9 43	11 10	—	12 31	—	1 28	—	2 3	—	
Denham	—	7 13	—	7 47	8 45	—	9 46	11 13	—	—	—	1 31	—	—	—	
Denham Golf Club	5 53	6 51	7 28	7 52	8 50	—	9 51	11 18	—	—	—	1 36	—	2 9	—	
Gerrards Cross	—	—	—	7 58	—	—	9 57	11 24	—	—	—	1 42	—	2 15	—	
Seer Green...arr.																

WEEK DAYS

WEEK DAYS	PM	d	PM	PM	PM	e	d	PM	PM	e	PM	e	PM	PM	PM	PM
Marylebone...dep.	2 10	2 35	3	5 4	15 4	55 5	19 5	38 5	43	6 6	6 35	6 41	6 45	7 25	8 30	9 25	10 35	11 50
Wembley Hill	2 22	2 47	3	17 4	27 5	7	5 31	—	5 55	6 18	6 47	—	6 56	7 36	8 43	9 37	10 47	12 2
Sudbury & Harrow Road	2 26	2 51	3	21 4	31	—	5 35	—	5 59	6 22	6 51	—	7 0	7 40	8 45	9 41	10 51	12 6
South Harrow	2 34	3	0	3	29 4	39	—	—	6	8	6 30	—	—	7 9	7 49	8 53	9 49	10 59	12 14
Northolt Junction	2 38	3	3	3	33 4	42 5	15 5	47	—	6 12	6 33	7 2	—	7 14	7 52	8 57	9 52	11 2	12 18
Ruislip and Ickenham	2 43	—	3	38	—	—	—	6 16	—	7	7	—	7 19	7 56	9 2	—	11 8	12 23
Denham	2 46	—	3	41	—	—	—	—	—	7	9	—	7 38	—	9 28	—	—	—
Denham Golf Club	2 51	—	3	46	—	5 25	—	6	6 37	—	7 14	7 7	7 26	—	9 8	—	11 15	12 30
Gerrards Cross	2 57	—	3	52	—	5 31	—	—	—	—	7 21	7 13	—	—	9 15	—	—	—
Seer Green...arr.																

WEEK DAYS (Seer Green to Marylebone)

WEEK DAYS	AM	AM	AM	AM	AM	e	d	PM	PM	d	e	d	PM
Seer Green...dep.	6 50	—	7 45	8 15	—	—	—	—	—	—	12 19	—	—
Gerrards Cross	6 56	—	7 51	8 21	—	9 1	—	9 25	—	—	12 25	—	—
Denham Golf Club	—	—	—	—	—	—	—	—	—	—	12 29	—	—
Denham	7 2	—	7 57	—	8 44	—	—	9 30	9 54	—	12 32	—	—
Ruislip and Ickenham	7 7	—	8 2	8 30	8 49	—	9 36	9 59	—	12 35	—	—	2 42
Northolt Junction	7 11	—	8 6	—	8 53	—	—	10 3	—	12 19	12 41	—	2 46
South Harrow	7 167	36 8	13	—	838	8	58	9 23	—	10 10	11 31	12 22	1 4	4 11	5 1	50 1	57 2	51
Sudbury & Harrow Road	7 19	7 39	8 16	—	841	9 1	—	9 26	—	10 13	11 34	12 27	12 49	1 4	1 4 1	8	1 53	2 54
Wembley Hill	7 27	7 43	8 20	—	845	9 5	—	9 30	—	10 17	11 38	12 31	12 53	1 8	1 57	2 2	58
Marylebone...arr.	7 35	7 54	8 31	8 49	857	9 16	9 26	9 42	9 55	10 30	11 50	12 43	1	5 120	1 24 2	9 2	16 3	10

WEEK DAYS

WEEK DAYS	d	PM	d	PM	PM	PM	e	d	PM	PM	d	e	PM	PM	PM
Seer Green...dep.	2 37	2 37	—	3 42	—	—	—	—	8 42	—	—	—	—	—
Gerrards Cross	2 43	2 43	3 13	3 43	5 21	—	—	7 26	7 50	—	8 48	9 57	—	10 39
Denham Golf Club	2 47	2 47	3 17	3 52	5 25	—	—	7 30	—	—	—	—	—	—
Denham	2 50	2 50	3 20	3 55	—	5 28	—	6 33	—	7 33	8 10	8 17	8 54	10 3	—
Ruislip and Ickenham	2 55	2 55	3 10	3 25	4 4	5 20	5 33	5 58	6 38	6 55	7 38	8 18	8 22	8 59	10 8	10 17	10 50
Northolt Junction	—	—	3	14 3	29 4	4	5 24	5 37	6	2 6 41	6 59	7 42	—	8 26	9 3	—	10 21	10 54
South Harrow	—	—	3	18 3	34 4	9	5 29	5 45	6	10 6	48 7	4 7	47	—	8 30	9 11	—	10 27	11 1
Sudbury & Harrow Road	3 7	3 22	3 37	4 12	5 32	5 45	6 10	6 48	7 7	7 50	—	8 34	9 11	—	10 31	11 3
Wembley Hill	3 11	3 26	3 41	4 16	5	36 5	51 6	14 6	52	7 11	7 54	—	8 38	9 15	—	10 35	11 5
Marylebone...arr.	3 15	3 22	3 38	5 53	4 28	5 40	3 36	26	7	4 7 23	8	6 8	36 8	50 9	27 10	31 10 45	11 17

SUNDAYS.	AM	AM	AM	PM	PM	PM	PM	PM
MARYLEBONE.....dep.	8 50	10 20	11 50	2 15	3 35	6 30	8 30	10 0
Wembley Hill	9 1	10 32	12 2	2 27	3 47	6 43	8 42	10 12
Sudbury & Harrow Rd.	9 7	10 38	12 6	2 31	3 51	6 47	8 46	10 16
South Harrow	9 10	10 41	12 9	2 34	3 54	6 50	8 49	10 19
Northolt Junction....	9 15	10 46	12 14	2 39	3 59	—	8 54	k
Ruislip and Ickenham	9 19	10 50	12 18	2 43	4 3	6 59	8 58	10 27
Denham	9 25	10 55	12 23	2 48	4 8	7 5	9 3	10 32
Denham Golf Club....	9 28	10 58	12 26	2 50	4 11	—	—	—
GERRARDS CROSS	9 33	11 3	12 31	2 55	4 16	7 11	9 10	10 39
SEER GREEN ......arr.	9 39	11 9	12 37	3 2	4 22	7 18	—	—

SUNDAYS.	AM	PM	PM	PM	PM	PM	PM
SEER GREEN ......dep.	9 54	1 2	1 57	3 37	5 37	—	—
GERRARDS CROSS	10 0	1 8	2 3	3 43	5 43	8 15	9 56
Denham Golf Club ...	10 4	1 12	2 7	3 47	5 47	8 19	—
Denham	10 7	1 15	2 10	3 50	5 50	8 22	10 2
Ruislip and Ickenham	10 13	1 20	2 15	3 55	5 55	8 27	10 7
Northolt Junction	10 17	1 24	2 19	3 59	5 59	8 31	10 11
South Harrow	10 22	1 29	2 24	4 4	6 4	8 38	10 18
Sudbury & Harrow Rd.	10 27	1 32	2 27	4 7	6 7	8 42	10 22
Wembley Hill	10 31	1 36	2 31	4 11	6 11	8 46	10 26
MARYLEBONE ......arr.	10 43	1 48	2 43	4 23	6 23	8 58	10 38

d Saturdays only.   *e* Saturdays excepted.   *k* Stops on notice being given to guard.

EUSTON, WILLESDEN, HARROW AND WATFORD.

WEEK DAYS.	AM	AM	AM	AM	AM	AM	AM	AM	AM	AM	AM	AM	AM	AM	AM	AM	AM	AM	AM	AM	AM	AM	AM	AM
EUSTON ....dep.	525	6 5	—	630	—	7 0	715	—	735	730	—	754	8 0	815	—	830	835	845	—	9 0	915	—	930	930	940
BUSTON STREET../......	—	530	6 6	—	637	640	645	7 6	710	—	736	—	—	810	815	--	820	838	—	—	9 6	—	—	917
Chalk Farm...........	—	—	619	—	650	—	—	719	—	749	—	—	—	822	—	—	851	—	919	—	—	—	—
South Hampstead ..	—	6 9	621	634	653	7 4	—	722	—	734	752	759	8 4	—	824	834	—	853	9 4	—	922	—	934	—
Kilburn	—	610	623	635	654	7 5	—	723	—	735	753	8 0	8 5	—	825	835	—	854	9 5	—	923	—	935	—
Queens Pk.(W.Kilb'n)	—	612	625	637	656	7 7	—	725	—	731	755	8 2	8 7	—	827	837	—	856	9 7	—	925	—	937	—
Kensal Green	—	614	627	639	658	7 9	—	727	—	739	757	8 4	8 9	—	—	839	—	858	9 9	—	927	—	939	—
WILLESDEN J. Main L.	536	—	—	—	—	—	725	—	745	—	—	—	—	—	845	—	—	—	—	942	—	—	950
WILLESDEN J.NewStn.	—	617	630	642	7 1	712	—	730	—	742	8 0	8 7	812	824	831	842	—	854	9 1	912	924	930	—	942	—
Harlesden	—	619	632	644	7 3	714	—	732	—	744	8 2	—	814	826	—	844	—	856	—	914	926	—	—	944	—
Stonebridge Park	—	621	—	646	7 5	716	—	734	—	746	—	811	816	—	—	—	858	—	916	—	—	946	—
Wembley	549	624	636	649	7 8	719	—	737	—	749	8 6	814	819	831	837	848	—	9 1	9 6	919	931	—	—	949	—
North Wembley......	—	626	638	651	710	721	—	739	—	751	—	816	821	833	—	850	—	9 3	—	921	933	—	—	951	—
Kenton	—	629	—	654	713	724	—	754	—	—	824	—	853	—	924	—	—	954	—
HARROW	558	631	642	656	715	726	—	743	—	756	812	821	826	838	843	855	9 0	9 8	912	926	938	—	—	956	—
Headstone Lane	—	634	—	659	718	729	—	—	759	—	829	—	929	—	—	955	—
Hatch End forPinner)	—	636	646	7 1	720	731	—	747	—	8 1	816	825	831	843	848	859	—	912	916	931	943	—	10 1	—
CARPENDER'S PARK ..	—	—	—	—	—	—	—	—	—	—	—	—	—	—	—	—	—	914	—	934	—	—
Bushey and Oxhey ..	611	642	651	7 7	726	737	—	752	8 5	8 7	822	830	837	848	853	9 4	—	917	921	937	949	—	10 7	—
WATFORD JUNCTION ..	620	648	658	713	734	746	747	758	810	816	823	—	845	354	859	910	912	923	927	945	955	—	102	103	013

WEEK DAYS.	*e* AM	AM	AM	AM	AM	AM	AM	AM	AM	AM	AM	*d* PM	*d*	*d*	PM	*d*	*e*	*d*
EUSTON ....dep.	9 45	—	10 0	—	1030	1040	1050	—	11 0	—	1130	—	—	12 0	12 5	12 7	1215	—	1226
BROAD STREET........	—	934	—	10 6	—	—	—	1036	—	11 6	—	1136	—	—	—	—	—	12 6	12 6	—
Chalk Farm..........	—	947	—	1021	—	—	—	1049	—	1119	—	1149	—	—	—	—	1219	1219	—
South Hampstead ..	—	950	10 4	1024	1034	—	—	1052	11 4	1122	1134	1152	—	12 4	—	1211	—	1222	1222	—
Kilburn	—	951	10 5	1025	1035	—	—	1053	11 5	1123	1135	1153	—	J2 5	—	1212	—	1223	1223	—
QueensPk.(W.Kilb'n)	—	953	10 7	1027	1037	—	—	1055	11 7	1125	1137	1155	—	12 7	—	1214	—	1225	1225	—
Kensal Green	—	955	10 9	1029	1039	—	—	1057	11 9	1127	1139	1157	—	12 9	—	1216	—	1227	1227	—
WILLESDEN J. Main L.	—	—	—	—	—	1050	11 1	—	—	—	—	—	—	—	—	1226	—	—
WILLESDEN J.NewStn.	954	958	1012	1032	1042	—	—	11 0	1112	1130	1142	12 0	12 0	1212	—	1219	—	1230	1230	1234
Harle den	956	—	1014	—	1044	—	—	—	1114	—	1144	—	12 2	1214	—	1221	—	1232	—	1236
Stonebridge Park	—	—	1016	—	1046	—	—	—	1116	—	1146	—	12 4	1216	—	1223	—	—	—
Wembley	10 1	—	1019	—	104	--	—	—	1119	—	1149	—	12 7	1219	—	1226	—	1236	—	1240
North Wembley	10 3	—	1021	—	1051	—	—	—	1121	—	1151	—	12 9	1221	—	1228	—	1238	—	1242
Kenton	—	—	1024	—	1054	—	—	—	1124	—	1154	—	1212	1224	—	1231	—	—	—	1245
HARROW	10 8	—	1026	—	1056	—	—	—	1126	—	1156	—	1214	1226	1224	1233	—	1242	—	1247
Headstone Lane	—	—	1029	—	1059	—	—	—	1129	—	1159	—	—	1229	—	1236	—	1245	—	1250
Hatch End	1013	—	1031	—	11 1	—	—	—	1131	—	12 1	—	1219	1231	—	1238	—	1247	—	1252
CARPENDER'S PARK ..	1016	—	1034	—	11 4	—	—	—	1134	—	12 4	—	—	1234	—	—	—	—	—	1255
Bushey and Oxhey ..	1019	—	1038	—	11 7	—	—	—	1137	—	12 7	—	1225	1237	—	1244	—	1253	—	1258
WATFORD JUNCTION ..	1025	—	1043	—	1113	1111	1121	—	1143	—	1213	—	—	1243	1235	1250	1245	125	—	1 4

WEEK DAYS.	*d*	*e*	*d*	*d*	*d*	*e*	*d*	*d*	*d*	*d*	*d*	*d*	*d*	*e*	*d*	*d*	*e*	*d*	*d*	*d*	*d*	*d*
EUSTON ....dep.	*d*	—	1230	1237	—	—	1250	—	1256	1258	1 3	1 0	—	1 7	110	—	—	126	130	—	135	137
BROAD STREET	1220	—	—	—	1235	1236	—	1243	—	—	—	—	1250	—	—	1 6	110	115	—	120	—	135
Chalk Farm	1233	—	—	—	1248	1249	—	—	—	—	—	—	—	—	1219	121	—	—	148
South Hampstead ..	1237	1234	1241	1230	1251	1252	—	—	—	—	1 4	1 6	111	—	122	123	—	134	136	—	141	150
Kilburn	1233	1235	1242	1251	1252	—	—	—	—	1 5	1 7	112	—	123	124	—	135	137	—	142	151
Queens Pk.(W.Kilb'n)	1239	1237	1244	1253	1255	—	—	—	—	1 7	1 9	114	—	125	126	—	137	139	—	144	153
Kensal Green	1241	1239	1246	—	1257	—	—	—	—	1 9	111	116	—	127	—	—	135	—	145	—
WILLESDEN J. Main L.	—	—	—	—	—	—	—	—	—	—	—	—	—	—	—	145	—
WILLESDEN J.NewStn.	1244	1242	1249	1258	1 1	—	—	1 4	—	112	114	119	—	130	—	134	142	144	—	149	158
Harlesden	1246	1244	1251	—	—	—	1 6	—	114	116	121	—	—	136	144	146	—	151	—
Stonebridge Park	—	—	1246	1253	—	—	1 3	—	—	116	—	123	—	—	146	—	153	—
Wembley	1250	1249	1256	—	—	1 6	110	—	119	120	126	125	—	134	—	140	149	150	—	156	—
North Wembley	—	—	1251	1258	—	—	1 8	112	—	121	—	128	—	—	142	151	—	158	—
Kenton	1254	1254	1 1	—	—	—	115	—	124	124	131	—	—	145	154	154	—	2 1	—
HARROW	1256	1256	1 3	—	—	112	117	—	122	126	128	133	132	—	140	—	147	156	156	157	2 3	—
Headstone Lane	1259	1259	—	—	—	115	120	—	129	129	—	—	143	—	150	159	—	—
Hatch End forPinner)	1 1	1 1	1 7	—	1 11	117	122	—	—	131	131	137	136	—	145	—	152	2 1	2 1	—	2 7	—
CARPENDER'S PARK ..	—	1 4	—	—	1120	120	125	—	—	134	—	—	148	—	155	2 4	—	—
Bushey and Oxhey ..	1 6	1 7	112	—	—	—	123	128	—	131	137	136	142	141	—	151	152	158	2 7	2 6	—	212	—
WATFORD JUNCTION ..	112	1 13	118	—	—	—	129	134	1 24	136	143	—	142	148	146	—	159	157	—	213	212	218	—

WEEK DAYS.	e	d	d	PM	d	e	d	d	e	PM	d	e	d	PM	PM	PM	PM	e	d	e	d	PM	e	e	d
Euston ....dep.	—	—	156	2 0	—	2 0	2 7	—	—	230	240	—	—	3 0	3 5	—	330	—	—	357	4 0	410	412	—	—
Broad Street	136	143	—	—	150	—	—	2 6	2 6	—	—	236	236	—	—	3 6	—	336	336	—	—	347	—	4 6	4 6
Chalk Farm..........	149	—	—	—	2 3	—	—	219	219	—	—	249	249	—	—	319	—	349	349	—	—	—	—	419	419
South Hampstead ..	152	—	—	—	2 6	2 4	211	222	222	234	—	252	252	3 4	—	322	334	352	352	4 1	4 4	—	416	422	422
Kilburn..............	153	—	—	—	2 7	2 5	212	223	223	235	—	253	253	3 5	—	323	336	353	353	4 2	4 5	—	417	423	423
QueensPk. (W.Kilb'n)	155	—	—	—	2 9	2 7	214	225	225	237	—	255	255	3 7	—	325	337	355	355	4 4	4 7	—	419	425	425
Kensal Green	157	—	—	—	211	2 9	216	227	227	239	—	257	257	3 9	—	327	339	357	357	4 6	4 9	—	421	427	427
Willesden J.Main L.	—	—	—	211	—	—	—	—	—	—	—	—	—	—	316	—	—	—	—	—	—	421	—	—	—
Willesden J.NewStn.	2 0	—	2 4	—	214	212	219	230	230	242	—	3 0	3 0	312	—	330	342	4 0	4 0	4 9	412	—	424	430	430
Harlesden	—	—	2 6	—	216	214	221	232	—	244	—	—	3 2	314	—	—	344	4 2	—	411	414	—	426	432	—
Stonebridge Park	—	2 3	—	—	—	216	223	234	—	246	—	—	3 4	316	—	—	346	4 4	—	413	417	—	428	—	—
Wembley	—	2 6	210	—	220	219	226	237	—	249	—	—	3 7	319	—	—	349	4 7	—	416	420	—	431	436	—
North Wembley......	—	2 8	212	—	—	221	228	239	—	251	—	—	3 9	321	—	—	351	4 9	—	418	422	—	—	438	—
Kenton	—	—	215	—	224	224	231	242	—	254	—	—	312	324	—	—	354	412	—	421	425	—	435	—	—
Harrow	—	212	217	—	226	226	233	244	—	256	259	—	314	326	—	—	356	414	—	423	428	435	437	442	—
Headstone Lane	—	215	220	—	229	229	—	247	—	259	—	—	317	329	—	—	359	417	—	426	431	—	440	—	—
HatchEnd(forPinner)	—	217	222	—	231	231	237	249	—	3 1	—	—	319	331	—	—	4 1	419	—	428	433	—	442	446	—
Carpender's Park ..	—	220	225	—	—	234	—	252	—	3 4	—	—	—	334	—	—	4 4	—	—	431	436	—	—	449	—
Bushey and Oxhey ..	—	223	228	—	236	237	242	255	—	3 7	3 8	—	325	337	—	—	4 7	424	—	436	439	—	447	452	—
Watford Junction ..	—	—	234	230	242	243	248	3 1	—	313	313	—	331	343	335	—	413	430	—	—	447	445	453	458	—

WEEK DAYS.	e	d	e	e	e	d	e	d	e	e	e	d	e	e	e	e	d	e	PM	e	e	e	d	PM	e
Euston ....dep.	430	430	—	442	—	—	—	455	5 0	—	5 0	5 0	5 5	—	5 7	—	—	—	520	526	—	—	530	532	537
Broad Street	—	—	420	—	435	436	443	—	—	450	—	—	—	452	—	5 5	5 6	512	—	—	520	524	—	—	—
Chalk Farm..........	—	—	433	—	448	449	—	—	—	—	—	—	—	5 5	—	518	519	—	—	—	532	—	—	—	—
South Hampstead ...	—	434	436	446	450	452	—	—	—	—	—	5 4	—	5 8	511	520	522	—	—	—	535	—	534	—	541
Kilburn..............	—	435	437	447	451	453	—	—	—	—	—	5 5	—	5 9	512	521	523	—	—	—	536	—	535	—	542
Queens Pk.(W.Kilb'n)	—	437	439	449	453	455	—	—	—	—	—	5 7	—	511	514	523	525	—	—	—	538	—	537	—	544
Kensal Green	—	439	441	451	—	457	—	—	—	—	—	5 9	—	513	516	—	527	—	—	—	540	—	539	—	546
Willesden J.Main L.	—	—	—	—	—	—	—	—	—	—	—	—	—	—	—	—	—	—	—	—	—	—	—	—	—
Willesden J.NewStn.	438	442	444	454	458	5 0	—	—	—	—	5 8	512	—	516	519	528	530	—	—	534	543	—	542	—	549
Harlesden	440	444	446	456	—	—	—	—	—	—	510	514	—	518	521	—	—	—	—	536	545	—	544	—	551
Stonebridge Park....	—	446	—	458	—	—	5 3	—	—	—	—	516	—	—	523	—	—	533	—	—	—	—	546	—	553
Wembley	444	449	450	5 1	—	—	5 6	—	—	—	514	519	—	522	526	—	—	536	535	540	549	—	549	—	556
North Wembley......	446	451	—	—	—	—	5 8	—	—	—	516	521	—	—	528	—	—	538	—	542	551	—	551	—	558
Kenton..	449	454	454	5 5	—	—	—	—	—	—	519	524	—	526	531	—	—	—	—	545	554	—	554	—	6 1
Harrow	451	456	456	5 7	—	—	512	—	—	—	521	526	524	528	533	—	—	542	542	547	556	—	556	—	6 3
Headstone Lane	454	459	459	—	—	—	515	—	—	—	524	529	—	531	—	—	—	545	—	550	559	—	559	—	—
HatchEnd(forPinner)	456	5 1	5 1	511	—	—	517	—	—	—	526	531	529	533	537	—	—	547	—	552	6 1	—	6 1	—	6 7
Carpender's Park...	459	5 4	—	—	—	—	520	—	—	—	529	534	—	—	—	—	—	550	—	555	—	—	6 4	—	—
Bushey and Oxhey ..	5 2	5 7	5 6	516	—	—	523	—	—	524	532	537	535	538	542	—	—	553	551	558	6 6	558	6 7	—	612
Watford Junction ..	5 8	513	512	524	—	—	529	520	526	529	—	544	540	544	548	—	—	559	556	6 4	612	6 3	613	557	—

WEEK DAYS.	e	PM	e	e	e	e	d	e	d	e	e	d	e	e	d	PM	e	e	e	d	e	e	d	e	e
Euston ....dep.	545	—	—	556	—	—	6 0	6 7	610	615	—	—	—	626	630	635	—	637	—	—	—	656	7 0	—	7 7
Broad Street	—	535	544	—	549	6 0	—	—	—	—	6 5	6 6	615	—	—	—	620	—	640	636	643	—	—	650	—
Chalk Farm	—	548	—	—	6 2	—	—	—	—	—	618	619	—	—	—	—	633	—	—	649	—	—	—	7 3	—
South Hampstead ...	—	550	—	—	6 5	—	6 4	611	—	—	620	621	—	—	634	—	636	641	—	652	—	—	7 4	7 6	711
Kilburn..............	—	551	—	—	6 6	—	6 5	612	—	—	621	623	—	—	635	—	637	642	—	653	—	—	7 5	7 7	712
Queens Pk.(W.Kilb'n)	—	553	—	—	6 8	—	6 7	614	—	—	623	625	—	—	637	—	639	644	—	655	—	—	7 7	7 9	714
Kensal Green	—	—	—	—	610	—	6 9	616	—	—	—	627	—	—	639	—	641	646	—	657	—	—	7 9	711	716
Willesden J.Main L.	555	—	—	—	—	—	—	—	—	—	—	—	—	—	—	—	—	—	—	—	—	—	—	—	—
Willesden J.NewStn.	—	558	—	6 4	613	—	612	619	—	—	628	630	—	634	642	—	644	649	—	7 0	7 0	7 4	712	714	719
Harlesden............	—	—	—	6 6	615	—	614	621	—	—	—	—	—	636	644	—	646	651	—	—	—	7 6	714	—	721
Stonebridge Park	—	—	6 3	—	—	—	616	623	—	—	—	—	—	—	646	—	—	653	—	—	—	7 8	716	—	723
Wembley	—	—	6 6	610	619	—	619	626	—	—	—	—	635	640	649	—	650	656	—	—	7 5	711	719	—	726
North Wembley......	—	—	6 8	612	621	—	621	628	—	—	—	—	637	642	651	—	—	658	—	—	7 7	713	721	—	728
Kenton	—	—	—	615	624	—	624	631	—	—	—	—	—	645	654	—	654	7 1	—	—	710	716	724	—	731
Harrow..............	6 8	—	612	617	626	—	626	633	—	—	—	—	641	647	656	—	656	7 3	—	—	712	718	726	—	733
Headstone Lane	—	—	615	620	629	—	629	—	—	—	—	—	644	650	659	—	659	—	—	—	715	721	729	—	736
HatchEnd(forPinner)	—	—	617	622	631	—	631	637	—	—	—	—	646	652	7 1	—	7 1	7 7	—	—	717	723	731	—	738
Carpender's Park ...	—	—	620	625	—	—	634	—	—	—	—	—	648	654	7 4	—	—	—	—	—	—	725	734	—	—
Bushey and Oxhey ..	—	—	623	628	636	634	637	642	—	—	—	—	651	657	7 7	—	7 6	712	714	—	723	728	737	—	743
Watford Junction ..	619	—	629	634		639	643	648	635	640	—	—	657	7 3	714	7 0	714	718	719	—	—	734	743	—	749

WEEK DAYS.	PM	PM	PM	PM	PM	PM	PM	PM	PM	PM	PM	PM	PM	PM	PM	PM	PM	PM	PM	PM	PM	mid
Euston.......... dep.	715	—	730	—	8 5	8 0	—	830	—	9 0	9 5	—	930	—	955	10 0	1030	11 0	1120	1140	1150	1210
Broad Street	—	7 6	—	736	—	—	8 6	—	836	—	—	9 6	—	936	—	—	—	—	—	—	—	—
Chalk Farm..........	—	719	—	749	—	—	819	—	849	—	—	919	—	949	—	—	—	—	—	—	—	—
South Hampstead....	—	722	734	751	—	8 4	822	834	852	9 4	—	922	934	952	—	—	—	—	—	—	—	—
Kilburn..............	—	723	735	753	—	8 5	823	835	853	9 5	—	923	935	953	—	—	—	—	—	—	—	—
Queens Pk.(W.Kilb'n)	—	725	737	755	—	8 7	825	837	855	9 7	—	925	937	955	—	10 7	1037	11 7	1127	—	1157	1217
Kensal Green	—	727	739	757	—	8 9	827	839	857	9 9	—	927	939	957	—	10 9	1039	11 9	1129	—	1159	1219
Willesden J. Main L.	726	—	—	—	815	—	—	—	—	—	—	—	—	—	10 6	—	—	—	—	—	—	—
Willesden J.NewStn.	—	730	742	8 0	—	812	830	842	9 0	912	—	930	942	100	—	1012	1042	1112	1132	—	12 2	1222
Harlesden	—	—	744	—	—	814	—	844	—	914	—	—	944	—	—	1014	1044	1114	—	—	12 4	1224
Stonebridge Park	—	—	746	—	—	816	—	846	—	916	—	—	946	—	—	1016	1046	1116	—	—	12 6	1226
Wembley	—	—	749	—	—	819	—	849	—	919	—	—	949	—	—	1019	1049	1119	—	—	12 9	1229
North Wembley	—	—	751	—	—	821	—	851	—	921	—	—	951	—	—	1021	1051	1121	—	—	1211	1231
Kenton	—	—	754	—	—	824	—	854	—	924	—	—	954	—	—	1024	1054	1124	—	—	1214	1234
Harrow..............	—	—	756	—	—	826	—	856	—	926	923	—	956	—	1018	1026	1056	1126	—	—	1216	1236
Headstone Lane......	—	—	759	—	—	829	—	859	—	929	—	—	959	—	—	1029	1059	1129	—	—	1219	1239
HatchEnd(forPinner)	—	—	8 1	—	—	831	—	9 1	—	931	—	—	10 1	—	—	1031	11 1	1131	—	—	1221	1241
Carpender's Park ..	—	—	8 4	—	—	—	—	—	—	—	—	—	—	—	—	—	—	—	—	—	—	—
Bushey and Oxhey ..	—	—	8 7	—	—	837	—	9 7	—	937	—	—	10 7	—	—	1036	11 6	1136	—	—	1226	1246
Watford Junction ..	746	—	813	—	834	843	—	915	—	943	935	—	1013	—	1029	1043	1113	1143	—	12 5	1232	1253

SUNDAYS.	AM	AM	AM	AM	AM	AM	AM	AM	PM	PM	PM	PM	PM	PM	PM	PM	PM
Euston ....dep.	8 15	9 15	9 23	9 53	10 23	10 53	11 23	11 53	12 23	12 53	1 23	1 53	2 15	2 23	2 53	3 23	3 50
Broad Street	—	8 55	8 55	9 25	9 55	10 25	10 55	11 25	11 55	12 25	12 55	1 25	—	1 55	2 25	2 55	3 25
Chalk Farm	—	—	—	—	—	—	—	—	—	—	—	—	—	—	—	—	—
South Hampstead ..	—	—	9 27	9 57	10 27	10 57	11 27	11 57	12 27	12 57	1 27	1 57	—	2 27	2 57	3 27	—
Kilburn..............	—	—	9 28	9 58	10 28	10 58	11 28	11 58	12 28	12 58	1 28	1 59	—	2 28	2 58	3 28	—
Queens Pk.(W.Kilbn.)	—	—	9 30	10 0	10 30	11 0	11 30	12 0	12 30	1 0	1 30	2 0	—	2 30	3 0	3 30	—
Kensal Green	—	—	9 32	10 2	10 32	11 2	11 32	12 2	12 32	1 2	1 32	2 2	—	2 32	3 2	3 32	—
Willesden J. Main L.	8 26	9 26	—	—	—	—	—	—	—	—	—	—	2 25	—	—	—	4 0
Willesden J.NewStn.	—	—	9 35	10 5	10 35	11 5	11 35	12 5	12 35	1 5	1 35	2 5	—	2 35	3 5	3 35	—
Harlesden............	—	—	9 37	10 7	10 37	11 7	11 37	12 7	12 37	1 7	1 37	2 7	—	2 37	3 7	3 37	—
Stonebridge Park	—	—	9 39	10 9	10 39	11 9	11 39	12 9	12 39	1 9	1 39	2 9	—	2 39	3 9	3 39	—
Wembley............	—	—	9 42	10 12	10 42	11 12	11 42	12 12	12 42	1 12	1 42	2 12	—	2 42	3 12	3 42	—
North Wembley......	—	—	9 44	10 14	10 44	11 14	11 44	12 14	12 44	1 14	1 44	2 14	—	2 44	3 14	3 44	—
Kenton................	—	—	9 47	10 17	10 47	11 17	11 47	12 17	12 47	1 17	1 47	2 17	—	2 47	3 17	3 47	—
Harrow..............	8 42	—	9 50	10 20	10 50	11 20	11 50	12 20	12 50	1 20	1 50	2 20	—	2 50	3 20	3 50	—
Headstone Lane.....	—	—	9 53	10 23	10 53	11 23	11 53	12 23	12 53	1 23	1 53	2 23	—	2 53	3 23	3 53	—
HatchEnd(forPinner)	—	—	9 55	10 25	10 55	11 25	11 55	12 25	12 55	1 25	1 55	2 25	—	2 55	3 25	3 55	—
Carpender's Park ..	9‡13	9‡58	9 58	10 28	10 58	11 28	11 58	12 28	12 58	—	—	2 28	—	2 58	3 28	3 58	—
Bushey and Oxhey ..	—	—	10 1	10 31	11 1	11 31	12 1	12 31	1 1	1 31	2 1	2 31	—	3 1	3 31	4 1	—
Watford Junction ..	8 54	9 50	10 8	10 38	11 8	11 38	12 8	12 38	1 8	1 38	2 8	2 38	2 44	3 8	3 38	4 8	4 28

e Sats. excepted. *d* Sats. only.

SUNDAYS.	PM	PM	PM	PM	PM	PM	PM	PM	PM	PM	PM	PM	PM	PM	PM	PM	PM	PM
Euston ....dep.	3 53	4 23	4 53	5 23	5 53	6 10	6 23	6 45	6 53	7 23	7 53	8 23	8 53	9 23	9 40	9 53	10 23	10 53
Broad Street........	3 25	3 55	4 25	4 55	5 25	—	5 55	6 10	6 25	6 55	7 25	7 55	8 25	8 55	—	9 25	9 55	10 20
Chalk Farm...........	—	—	—	—	—	—	—	—	—	—	—	—	—	—	—	—	—	—
South Hampstead ..	3 57	4 27	4 57	5 27	5 57	—	6 27	—	6 57	7 27	7 57	8 27	8 57	9 27	—	9 57	10 27	10 57
Kilburn.............	3 58	4 28	4 58	5 28	5 58	—	6 28	—	6 58	7 28	7 58	8 28	8 58	9 28	—	9 58	10 28	10 58
QueensPk.(W.Kilbn.)	4 0	4 30	5 0	5 30	6 0	—	6 30	—	7 0	7 30	8 0	8 30	9 0	9 30	—	10 0	10 30	11 0
Kensal Green	4 2	4 32	5 2	5 32	6 2	—	6 32	—	7 2	7 32	8 2	8 32	9 2	9 32	—	10 2	10 32	11 2
Willesden J. Main L.	—	—	—	—	—	—	—	6 56	—	—	—	—	—	—	9 51	—	—	—
Willesden J. NewStn.	4 5	4 35	5 5	5 35	6 5	—	6 35	—	7 5	7 35	8 5	8 35	9 5	9 35	—	10 5	10 35	11 5
Harlesden	4 7	4 37	5 7	5 37	6 7	—	6 37	—	7 7	7 37	8 7	8 37	9 7	9 37	—	10 7	10 37	11 7
Stonebridge Park....	4 9	4 39	5 9	5 39	6 9	—	6 39	—	7 9	7 39	8 9	8 39	9 9	9 39	—	10 9	10 39	11 9
Wembley	4 12	4 42	5 12	5 42	6 12	—	6 42	—	7 12	7 42	8 12	8 42	9 12	9 42	—	10 12	10 42	11 12
North Wembley......	4 14	4 44	5 14	5 44	6 14	—	6 44	—	7 14	7 44	8 14	8 44	9 14	9 44	—	10 14	10 44	11 14
Kenton	4 17	4 47	5 17	5 47	6 17	—	6 47	—	7 17	7 47	8 17	8 47	9 17	9 47	—	10 17	10 47	11 17
Harrow..............	4 20	4 50	5 20	5 50	6 20	6 30	6 50	—	7 20	7 50	8 20	8 50	9 20	9 50	—	10 20	10 50	11 20
Headstone Lane	4 23	4 53	5 23	5 53	6 23	—	6 53	—	7 23	7 53	8 23	8 53	9 23	9 53	—	10 23	10 53	11 23
HatchEnd(forPinner)	4 25	4 55	5 25	5 55	6 25	—	6 55	—	7 25	7 55	8 25	8 55	9 25	9 55	—	10 25	10 55	11 25
Carpender's Park ..	4 28	4 58	5 28	5 58	6 28	—	6 58	—	7 28	7 58	—	—	—	—	—	—	—	—
Bushey and Oxhey ..	4 31	5 1	5 31	6 1	6 31	—	7 1	—	7 31	8 1	8 31	9 1	9 31	10 1	—	10 31	11 1	11 31
Watford Junction ..	4 38	5 8	5 38	6 8	6 38	6 41	7 8	7 18	7 38	8 8	8 38	9 8	9 38	10 8	10 10	10 38	11 8	11 38

WATFORD JUNCT. HARROW, WILLESDEN AND EUSTON.

WEEK DAYS.	AM	AM	AM	AM	AM	AM	AM	AM	AM	AM	AM	AM	AM	AM	AM	AM	AM	AM	AM	AM	AM
Watford Junct. dep.	4 55	—	5 41	—	—	6 9	6 26	6 39	—	6 56	7 0	7 9	7 15	725	7 26	7 30	—	740	745	750	757
Bushey and Oxhey ...	4 59	—	5 45	—	—	6 13	6 30	6 43	—	7 0	7 4	7 13	7 19	730	7 30	7 34	7 43	743	749	753	8 1
Carpender's Park ..	—	—	—	—	—	—	—	—	—	—	—	—	—	—	—	—	—	—	—	—	—
HatchEnd(forPinner)	5 3	—	5 49	—	—	6 17	—	6 47	—	—	7 8	7 18	7 23	—	7 34	7 38	7 48	—	753	—	8 5
Headstone Lane.......	—	—	—	—	—	—	—	—	—	—	—	7 20	—	—	—	—	7 50	—	—	—	—
Harrow	5 7	—	5 53	—	—	6 21	6 37	6 51	—	7 7	7 12	7 23	7 27	739	7 38	7 42	7 53	752	757	—	8 9
Kenton	—	—	5 55	—	—	6 23	—	6 53	—	—	7 14	7 25	7 29	—	—	7 44	7 55	—	759	—	—
North Wembley	—	—	5 58	—	—	6 26	—	6 56	—	—	7 17	—	7 32	—	7 42	—	—	—	8 2	—	813
Wembley	5 12	—	6 0	—	—	6 29	6 43	6 58	—	7 13	7 19	7 29	7 34	—	7 44	7 48	7 59	759	8 4	—	815
Stonebridge Park	—	—	6 3	—	—	6 32	—	—	—	—	7 22	—	7 37	—	—	7 51	—	—	8 7	—	818
Harlesden	—	—	6 5	—	—	6 34	6 47	7 2	7 5	7 17	7 24	7 33	7 39	—	—	7 53	8 3	—	—	—	—
Willesden J. NewStn.	5 17	6 5	6 7	6 20	6 34	6 37	6 49	7 4	7 8	7 19	7 26	7 35	7 41	—	7 50	7 55	8 5	—	810	—	—
Willesden J. Main L.	—	—	—	—	—	—	—	—	—	—	—	—	—	—	—	—	—	—	—	812	—
Kensal Green	5 19	6 6	6 9	6 21	6 35	6 39	6 51	7 6	7 9	7 21	7 28	7 37	—	—	7 52	7 57	8 7	—	—	—	—
Queens Pk.(W.Kilb'n)	5 21	6 8	6 11	6 23	6 37	6 42	6 53	7 8	7 11	7 23	7 30	7 39	—	—	7 54	7 59	8 9	—	814	—	—
Kilburn..............	—	6 10	6 13	6 25	6 39	6 44	6 55	7 10	7 13	7 25	7 32	7 41	—	—	7 56	8 1	8 11	—	—	—	—
South Hampstead....	—	6 12	6 15	6 27	6 41	6 46	6 57	7 12	7 15	7 27	7 34	7 43	—	—	7 58	8 3	8 13	—	—	—	—
Chalk Farm..........	—	6 15	—	6 30	6 44	—	7 0	—	7 18	7 30	—	7 46	—	—	8 1	—	8 16	—	—	—	—
Broad Street	6 2	6 34	—	6 45	6 58	—	7 15	—	7 32	7 45	7 57	8 0	—	—	8 15	8 25	8 30	—	—	—	842
Euston	5 29	—	6 21	—	—	6 52	—	7 18	—	—	7 40	—	7 52	758	—	8 9	—	815	822	824	—

WEEK DAYS.	AM	AM	AM	AM	AM	AM	AM	AM	AM	AM	AM	AM	AM	e	AM	e	AM	AM	AM	AM
Watford Junct. dep.	—	—	8 10	—	8 15	8 14	8 21	8 23	8 27	—	8 30	8 34	8 39	8 43	—	8 52	8 57	8 57	—	9 0
Bushey and Oxhey ..	—	8 4	—	8 14	8 18	8 18	8 24	8 26	8 31	—	8 34	—	8 43	8 47	8 49	—	9 1	9 0	—	9 4
Carpender's Park...	—	—	—	—	—	—	—	—	—	—	—	—	—	—	—	—	—	—	—	—
HatchEnd(forPinner)	—	8 9	—	8 18	—	8 22	—	—	8 35	—	8 39	—	8 47	—	8 53	—	9 5	9 6	—	9 9
Headstone Lane......	—	—	—	8 20	—	8 24	—	—	—	—	—	—	8 49	—	8 55	—	—	—	—	—
Harrow..............	—	8 13	8 19	8 23	—	8 27	—	8 34	8 39	—	8 43	—	8 52	—	8 58	—	9 9	9 11	—	9 13
Kenton	—	8 15	—	8 25	—	8 29	—	—	—	—	8 45	—	8 54	—	9 0	—	—	—	—	9 15
North Wembley......	—	8 17	—	8 28	—	—	—	—	8 43	—	—	—	—	—	9 3	—	9 13	—	—	—
Wembley............	—	8 20	—	—	8 30	8 33	—	—	8 45	—	8 49	—	8 59	—	9 5	—	9 15	—	—	9 19
Stonebridge Park	—	8 23	—	—	—	—	—	—	8 48	—	8 52	—	—	—	—	—	9 18	—	—	9 22
Harlesden...........	—	8 25	—	—	—	8 37	—	—	—	—	8 54	—	9 3	—	—	—	—	—	—	9 24
Willesden J. NewStn.	8 23	8 27	—	—	—	8 39	—	—	—	8 53	8 56	—	9 5	—	9 10	—	—	—	9 23	9 26
Willesden J. Main L.	—	—	—	—	8 36	—	—	8 47	—	—	—	8 51	—	—	—	9 11	—	—	—	—
Kensal Green	8 25	8 29	—	—	—	8 41	—	—	—	8 54	8 58	—	—	—	—	—	—	—	—	9 28
Queens Pk.(W.Kilb'n)	8 27	8 31	—	—	—	8 43	—	—	—	8 56	9 0	—	9 8	—	—	—	—	—	9 25	9 30
Kilburn.............	8 29	8 33	—	—	—	8 45	—	—	—	8 58	9 2	—	9 10	—	—	—	—	—	9 27	9 32
South Hampstead....	8 31	8 35	—	—	—	8 46	—	—	—	9 0	9 4	—	9 12	—	—	—	—	—	9 29	9 34
Chalk Farm..........	8 34	—	—	—	—	8 49	—	—	—	9 4	—	—	9 14	—	—	—	—	—	9 32	—
Broad Street.......	8 49	8 57	—	—	—	9 4	9 0	—	9 10	9 18	—	—	9 28	9 22	—	—	9 40	—	9 46	—
Euston..............	—	8 41	8 38	8 45	8 48	—	—	8 58	—	—	9 10	9 5	—	—	9 20	9 22	—	9 30	—	9 40

WEEK DAYS.	AM	AM	AM	AM	AM	e	AM	AM	AM	AM	AM	AM	AM	AM	AM	AM	AM	AM
Watford Junct. .dep.	—	9 9	9 15	9 16	9 29	9 30	9 39	—	9 42	959	—	10 8	—	10 38	—	11 8	11 8	—
Bushey and Oxhey ...	—	9 13	9 18	9 20	9 33	—	9 43	—	9 46	10 2	—	10 12	—	10 42	—	—	11 12	—
Carpender's Park..	—	—	—	—	—	—	—	—	—	—	—	10 14	—	10 44	—	—	11 14	—
HatchEnd(forPinner)	—	9 18	—	9 24	9 37	—	9 47	—	9 51	—	—	10 17	—	10 47	—	—	11 17	—
Headstone Lane......	—	9 20	—	—	—	—	—	—	9 53	—	—	10 19	—	10 49	—	—	11 19	—
Harrow	—	9 23	—	9 28	9 41	—	9 51	—	9 56	—	—	10 22	—	10 52	—	—	11 22	—
Kenton	—	9 25	—	9 30	9 43	—	9 53	—	9 58	—	—	10 24	—	10 54	—	—	11 24	—
North Wembley......	—	—	—	9 33	9 46	—	9 56	—	10 1	—	—	10 27	—	10 57	—	—	11 27	—
Wembley......	—	9 29	—	9 35	9 48	—	9 58	—	10 3	—	—	10 29	—	10 59	—	—	11 29	—
Stonebridge Park	—	—	—	9 38	9 51	—	10 1	—	—	—	—	10 32	—	11 2	—	—	11 32	—
Harlesden	—	9 33	—	—	9 53	—	—	—	—	—	—	10 34	—	11 4	—	—	11 34	—
Willesden J. NewStn.	—	9 35	—	9 41	9 55	—	10 4	10 6	10 8	—	10 20	10 36	1050	11 6	1120	—	11 36	—
Willesden J. Main L.	9 29	—	—	—	—	—	—	—	—	1019	—	—	—	—	—	1130	—	11 42
Kensal Green	—	9 37	—	—	9 57	—	—	10 7	10 10	—	10 21	10 38	1051	11 8	1121	—	11 38	—
Queens Pk.(W.Kilb'n)	—	9 39	—	—	9 59	—	—	10 9	10 12	—	10 23	10 40	1053	11 10	1123	—	11 40	—
Kilburn.............	—	9 41	—	—	10 1	—	—	10 11	10 14	—	10 25	10 42	1055	11 12	1125	—	11 42	—
South Hampstead....	—	9 43	—	—	10 3	—	—	10 13	10 16	—	10 27	10 44	1057	11 14	1127	—	11 44	—
Chalk Farm..........	—	9 46	—	—	—	—	—	10 16	—	—	10 30	—	11 0	—	1130	—	—	—
Broad Street........	—	10 0	9 53	1020	—	—	10 24	10 30	—	1050	10 44	—	1114	—	1144	—	—	—
Euston	9 40	—	—	9 52	10 9	9 52	—	—	10 22	1030	—	10 50	—	11 20	—	1140	11 50	11 55

WEEK DAYS.	AM	AM	PM	PM	d	PM	PM	d	d	PM	d	e	d	PM	d	d	PM	PM	d	PM	d	PM
Watford Junct. dep.	—	1138	—	12 8	—	—	1238	—	1251	—	1257	1 8	1 8	115	112	120	—	138	1 50	—	214	2 8
Bushey and Oxhey ..	—	1142	—	1212	1226	—	1242	1246	1255	—	1 1	112	112	—	116	124	—	142	1 54	—	—	212
Carpender's Park ...	—	1144	—	1214	—	—	1244	—	—	—	1 4	114	114	—	—	—	—	144	—	—	—	214
HatchEnd(forPinner)	—	1147	—	1217	1230	—	1247	1251	1 0	—	1 7	117	117	—	121	129	—	147	1 59	—	—	217
Headstone Lane	—	1149	—	1219	1232	—	1249	—	1 2	—	1 9	119	119	—	123	131	—	149	2 1	—	—	219
Harrow..............	—	1152	—	1222	1235	—	1252	1256	1 5	—	112	122	122	—	126	134	—	152	2 4	—	—	222
Kenton	—	1154	—	1224	1237	—	1254	1258	1 7	—	114	124	124	—	129	137	—	154	2 7	—	—	224
North Wembley......	—	1157	—	1227	1240	—	1257	1 1	110	—	117	127	127	—	132	140	—	157	2 10	—	—	227
Wembley	—	1159	—	1229	1242	—	1259	1 4	112	—	119	129	129	—	134	142	—	159	2 12	—	—	229
Stonebridge Park	—	12 2	—	1232	1245	—	1 2	—	115	—	122	132	132	—	137	145	—	2 2	2 15	—	—	232
Harlesden........	—	12 4	12d17	1234	1247	—	1 4	1 8	117	—	124	134	134	—	139	147	—	2 4	2 17	—	—	234
Willesden J. NewStn.	1150	12 6	12 20	1236	1250	1250	1 6	110	119	119	126	136	136	—	141	149	149	2 6	2 19	219	—	237
Willesden J. Main L.	—	—	—	—	—	—	—	—	—	—	—	—	—	136	—	—	—	—	—	—	233	—
Kensal Green	1151	12 8	12 21	1238	—	1251	1 8	112	—	121	128	138	138	—	143	—	151	2 8	—	221	—	238
Queens Pk.(W.Kilb'n)	1153	1210	12 23	1240	—	1253	110	114	—	123	130	140	140	—	145	—	153	210	—	223	—	240
Kilburn	1155	1212	12 25	1242	—	1255	112	116	—	125	132	142	142	—	147	—	155	212	—	225	—	242
South Hampstead ...	1157	1214	12 27	1244	—	1257	114	118	—	127	134	144	144	—	149	—	157	214	—	227	—	244
Chalk Farm..........	12 0	—	12 30	—	—	1 0	—	—	—	130	—	—	147	—	—	—	2 0	—	—	230	—	—
Broad Street	1214	—	12 44	—	—	114	—	—	—	144	—	—	2 1	2 8	—	—	214	—	—	244	—	—
Euston	—	1220	—	1250	—	—	120	124	—	—	140	150	—	150	155	—	—	220	—	—	245	250

WEEK DAYS.	d	PM	PM	PM	PM	PM	e	PM	PM	PM	PM	e	PM	PM	PM	e	e	PM	e	PM	e	PM	e	PM
Watford Junct. dep.	2 20	—	234	238	—	3 8	—	—	338	357	—	—	4 8	—	—	425	—	4 38	—	—	457	5 0	—	5 8
Bushey and Oxhey ..	2 24	—	—	242	—	312	316	—	342	—	—	4 0	412	—	—	429	—	4 42	4 55	—	5 1	—	—	512
Carpender's Park ..	—	—	—	244	—	314	—	—	344	—	—	—	414	—	—	—	—	4 44	—	—	—	—	—	514
Hatch End (for Pinner)	2 29	—	—	247	—	317	321	—	347	—	—	4 5	417	—	—	434	—	4 47	5 0	—	5 5	—	—	517
Headstone Lane	2 31	—	—	249	—	319	—	—	349	—	—	4 7	419	—	—	436	—	4 49	5 2	—	—	—	—	519
Harrow..............	2 34	—	—	252	—	322	326	—	352	—	—	410	422	—	—	439	—	4 52	5 5	—	5 9	—	—	522
Kenton..............	2 37	—	—	254	—	324	328	—	354	—	—	413	424	—	—	441	—	4 54	5 7	—	512	—	—	524
North Wembley......	2 40	—	—	257	—	327	332	—	357	—	—	416	427	—	—	444	—	4 57	5 10	—	515	—	—	527
Wembley	2 42	—	—	259	—	329	333	—	359	—	—	419	429	—	—	446	—	4 59	5 12	—	517	—	—	529
Stonebridge Park....	2 45	—	—	3 2	—	332	336	—	4 2	—	—	422	432	—	—	449	—	5 2	5 15	—	520	—	—	532
Harlesden	2 47	—	—	3 4	—	334	338	—	4 4	—	—	424	434	—	—	451	—	5 4	5 17	—	522	—	—	534
Willesden J. New Stn.	2 49	249	—	3 6	320	336	341	350	4 6	—	420	426	436	450	455	454	5 3	5 6	5 19	519	524	—	533	536
Willesden J. Main L.	—	—	253	—	—	—	—	—	—	419	—	—	—	—	—	—	—	—	—	—	—	520	—	—
Kensal Green	—	251	—	3 8	321	338	343	351	4 8	—	421	428	438	451	—	457	—	5 8	—	521	526	—	—	538
Queens Pk. (W. Kilb'n)	—	253	—	310	323	340	346	353	410	—	423	431	440	453	—	459	5 6	5 10	—	523	528	—	536	540
Kilburn..............	—	255	—	312	325	342	348	355	412	—	425	433	442	455	—	5 1	5 8	5 12	—	525	530	—	538	542
South Hampstead ..	—	257	—	314	327	344	350	357	414	—	427	435	444	457	—	5 3	510	5 14	—	527	532	—	540	544
Chalk Farm	—	3 0	—	—	330	—	—	4 0	—	—	430	—	—	5 0	—	—	513	—	—	530	—	—	543	--
Broad Street........	—	314	338	—	344	—	—	414	—	—	444	—	—	514	—	—	527	—	—	544	—	—	557	--
Euston	—	—	3 5	320	—	350	358	—	420	430	—	443	450	—	5 5	510	—	5 20	—	—	540	535	--	550

WEEK DAYS.	PM	e	PM	e	PM	PM	e	e	PM	e	PM	e	PM	PM	PM	e	PM	PM	PM	PM	PM	PM	PM
Watford Junct. .dep.	512	5 22	—	525	538	541	541	—	—	5 56	6 8	6 25	633	—	638	6 50	—	657	7 8	720	—	7 38	—
Bushey and Oxhey ..	—	5 26	—	529	542	544	545	5 53	—	6 0	612	6 29	—	—	642	6 54	—	—	712	—	—	7 42	—
Carpender's Park...	—	—	—	—	544	—	—	—	—	—	614	—	—	—	644	—	—	—	714	—	—	7 44	—
Hatch End (for Pinner)	—	—	—	534	547	—	551	5 59	—	6 5	617	6 34	—	—	647	6 59	—	—	717	—	—	7 47	—
Headstone Lane......	—	—	—	536	549	—	553	6 1	—	—	619	—	—	—	649	7 1	—	—	719	—	—	7 49	—
Harrow	—	5 34	—	539	552	—	556	6 4	—	6 9	622	6 38	—	—	652	7 4	—	—	722	—	—	7 52	—
Kenton	—	5 36	—	542	554	—	558	6 7	—	6 12	624	6 41	—	—	654	7 7	—	—	724	—	—	7 54	—
North Wembley	—	5 39	—	545	557	—	6 1	6 10	—	6 15	627	—	—	—	657	7 10	—	—	727	—	—	7 57	—
Wembley	—	5 42	—	548	559	—	6 3	6 12	—	6 17	629	6 47	—	—	659	7 12	—	—	729	—	—	7 59	—
Stonebridge Park	—	—	—	551	6 2	—	6 6	6 15	—	6 20	632	—	—	—	7 2	7 15	—	—	732	—	—	8 2	—
Harlesden............	—	5 47	—	553	6 4	—	6 8	6 17	—	6 22	634	—	—	—	7 4	7 17	—	—	734	—	—	8 4	—
Willesden J. New Stn.	—	5 49	5 49	555	6 6	—	610	6 19	619	6 24	636	6 53	—	653	7 6	7 19	719	—	736	—	750	8 6	8 20
Willesden J. Main L.	—	—	—	—	—	6 3	—	—	—	—	—	—	655	—	—	—	—	—	—	741	—	—	—
Kensal Green	—	—	5 51	557	6 8	—	612	—	621	6 26	638	—	--	654	7 8	—	721	—	738	—	751	8 8	8 21
Queens Pk. (W. Kilb'n)	—	—	5 53	559	610	—	615	—	623	6 28	640	—	—	656	710	—	723	—	740	—	753	8 10	8 23
Kilburn..............	—	—	5 55	6 1	612	—	617	—	625	6 30	642	—	—	658	712	—	725	—	742	—	755	8 12	8 25
South Hampstead....	—	—	5 57	6 3	614	—	619	—	627	6 32	644	—	—	7 0	714	—	727	—	744	—	757	8 14	8 27
Chalk Farm	—	—	6 1	—	—	—	622	—	630	—	—	—	—	7 3	—	—	730	—	—	—	8 0	—	8 30
Broad Street........	—	—	6 16	632	—	636	636	—	644	—	—	—	—	717	—	—	744	—	—	—	814	—	8 44
Euston	535	—	—	610	620	615	—	—	—	6 40	652	—	7 5	—	722	—	—	720	750	755	—	8 20	—

WEEK DAYS.	PM	PM	PM	PM	PM	PM	PM	PM	PM	PM	PM	PM	PM	PM	PM	PM
Watford Junct. dep.	8 3	8 8	—	8 38	8 56	—	9 8	—	9 24	9 38	10 8	10 11	—	10 38	10 58	11 8
Bushey and Oxhey ..	—	8 12	—	8 42	—	—	9 12	—	9 30	9 42	10 12	—	—	10 42	--	11 12
Carpender's Park ..	—	8 14	—	8 44	—	—	9 14	—	—	—	—	—	—	—	—	—
Hatch End (for Pinner)	—	8 17	—	8 47	—	—	9 17	—	9 36	9 47	10 17	—	—	10 47	—	11 17
Headstone Lane	—	8 19	—	8 49	—	—	9 19	—	—	9 49	10 19	—	—	10 49	—	11 19
Harrow	—	8 22	—	8 52	—	—	9 22	—	9 42	9 52	10 22	—	—	10 52	—	11 22
Kenton	—	8 24	—	8 54	—	—	9 24	—	—	9 54	10 25	—	—	10 54	—	11 24
North Wembley......	—	8 27	—	8 57	—	—	9 27	—	—	9 57	10 27	—	—	10 57	—	11 27
Wembley	—	8 29	—	8 59	—	—	9 29	—	9 49	9 59	10 29	—	—	10 59	—	11 29
Stonebridge Park....	—	8 32	—	9 2	—	—	9 32	—	—	10 2	10 32	—	—	11 2	—	11 32
Harlesden	—	8 34	—	9 4	—	—	9 34	—	—	10 4	10 34	—	—	11 4	—	11 34
Willesden J. New Stn.	—	8 36	8 50	9 6	—	9 20	9 36	9 44	—	10 6	10 36	—	10 56	11 6	—	11 33
Willesden J. Main L.	8 24	—	—	—	—	—	—	—	9 56	—	—	10 29	—	—	11 20	—
Kensal Green........	—	8 38	8 51	9 8	—	9 21	9 38	9 45	—	10 8	10 38	—	10 58	11 8	—	11 38
Queens Pk. (W. Kilb'n)	—	8 40	8 53	9 10	—	9 23	9 40	9 47	—	10 11	10 41	—	11 1	11 11	—	11 41
Kilburn..............	—	8 42	8 55	9 12	—	9 25	9 42	9 49	—	—	—	—	—	—	—	—
South Hampstead ..	—	8 44	8 57	9 14	—	9 27	9 44	9 51	—	—	—	—	—	—	—	—
Chalk Farm	—	—	9 0	—	—	9 30	—	9 54	—	—	—	—	—	—	—	—
Broad Street	9 8	—	9 14	—	—	9 44	—	10 10	—	—	—	—	—	—	—	—
Euston	8 35	8 50	—	9 20	9 20	—	9 50	—	10 10	10 20	10 50	10 50	11 10	11 20	11 35	11 50

d Saturdays only. *e* Saturdays excepted. *g* Mondays excepted.

SUNDAYS.	AM	AM	AM	AM	AM	AM	AM	AM	AM	noon	PM	PM	PM	PM	PM	PM	PM	PM
Watford Junct. dep.	5 7	830	8 44	9 0	9 30	10 0	10 30	11 0	11 30	12 0	12 30	12 41	1 0	1 30	2 0	2 30	3 0	3 30
Bushey and Oxhey ..	—	834	--	9 4	9 34	10 4	10 34	11 4	11 34	12 4	12 34	—	1 4	1 34	2 4	2 34	3 4	3 34
Carpender's Park ..	—	—	—	9 7	9 37	10 7	10 37	11 7	11 37	12 7	12 37	—	1 7	—	—	2 37	3 7	3 37
Hatch End (for Pinner)	—	840	—	9 10	9 40	10 10	10 40	11 10	11 40	12 10	12 40	—	1 10	1 40	2 10	2 40	3 10	3 40
Headstone Lane......	—	842	—	9 12	9 42	10 12	10 42	11 12	11 42	12 12	12 42	—	1 12	1 42	2 12	2 42	3 12	3 42
Harrow	—	845	8 56	9 15	9 45	10 15	10 45	11 15	11 45	12 15	12 45	12 52	1 15	1 45	2 15	2 45	3 15	3 45
Kenton	—	848	—	9 18	9 48	10 18	10 48	11 18	11 48	12 18	12 48	—	1 18	1 48	2 18	2 48	3 18	3 48
North Wembley	—	851	—	9 21	9 51	10 21	10 51	11 21	11 51	12 21	12 51	—	1 21	1 51	2 21	2 51	3 21	3 51
Wembley	—	854	—	9 24	9 54	10 24	10 54	11 24	11 54	12 24	12 54	—	1 24	1 54	2 24	2 54	3 24	3 54
Stonebridge Park	—	857	—	9 27	9 57	10 27	10 57	11 27	11 57	12 27	12 57	—	1 27	1 57	2 27	2 57	3 27	3 57
Harlesden	—	859	—	9 29	9 59	10 29	10 59	11 29	11 59	12 29	12 59	—	1 29	1 59	2 29	2 59	3 29	3 59
Willesden J. New Stn.	—	9 1	—	9 31	10 1	10 31	11 1	11 31	12 1	12 31	1 1	—	1 31	2 1	2 31	3 1	3 31	4 1
Willesden J. Main L.	534	—	9 10	—	—	—	—	—	—	—	—	1 5	—	—	—	—	—	—
Kensal Green	—	9 3	—	9 33	10 3	10 33	11 3	11 33	12 3	12 33	1 3	—	1 33	2 3	2 33	3 3	3 33	4 3
Queens Pk. (W. Kilb'n)	—	9 5	—	9 35	10 5	10 35	11 5	11 35	12 5	12 35	1 5	—	1 35	2 5	2 35	3 5	3 35	4 5
Kilburn..	—	9 7	—	9 37	10 7	10 37	11 7	11 37	12 7	12 37	1 7	—	1 37	2 7	2 37	3 7	3 37	4 7
South Hampstead....	—	9 9	—	9 39	10 9	10 39	11 9	11 39	12 9	12 39	1 9	—	1 39	2 9	2 39	3 9	3 39	4 9
Chalk Farm..	—	—	—	—	—	—	--	—	—	—	—	—	—	—	—	—	—	—
Broad Street	—	—	—	10‡ 5	10‡35	11‡ 5	11‡35	12‡ 5	12‡35	1‡ 5	1‡35	--	2‡ 5	2‡35	3‡ 5	3‡35	4‡ 5	4‡35
Euston	545	915	9 22	9 44	10 15	10 45	11 15	11 45	12 15	12 45	1 15	1 20	1 45	2 15	2 45	3 15	3 45	4 14

SUNDAYS.	PM	PM	PM	PM	PM	PM	PM	PM	PM	PM	PM	PM	PM	PM	PM	PM	PM	PM	PM
Watford Junct. dep.	4 0	4 30	5 0	511	5 30	6 0	6 30	7 0	7 30	743	8 0	8 30	9 0	9 12	9 30	935	10 0	10 7	10 30
Bushey and Oxhey ..	4 4	4 34	5 4	—	5 34	6 4	6 34	7 4	7 34	—	8 4	8 34	9 4	—	9 34	—	10 4	—	10 34
Carpender's Park ..	4 7	4 37	5 7	—	5 37	6 7	6 37	7 7	7 37	—	8 7	—	—	—	—	—	—	—	—
Hatch End (for Pinner)	4 10	4 40	5 10	—	5 40	610	6 40	710	7 40	—	810	8 40	910	—	9 40	—	10 10	—	10 40
Headstone Lane......	4 12	4 42	5 12	—	5 42	612	6 42	712	7 42	—	812	8 42	912	—	9 42	—	10 12	—	10 42
Harrow	4 15	4 45	5 15	522	5 45	615	6 45	715	7 45	—	815	8 45	915	—	9 45	—	10 15	—	10 45
Kenton	4 18	4 48	5 18	—	5 48	618	6 48	718	7 48	—	818	8 48	918	—	9 48	—	10 18	—	10 48
North Wembley	4 21	4 51	5 21	—	5 51	621	6 51	721	7 51	--	821	8 51	921	—	9 51	—	10 21	—	10 51
Wembley	4 24	4 54	5 24	—	5 54	624	6 54	724	7 54	—	824	8 54	924	--	9 54	—	10 24	—	10 54
Stonebridge Park	4 27	4 57	5 27	—	5 57	627	6 57	727	7 57	—	827	8 57	927	—	9 57	—	10 27	—	10 57
Harlesden	4 29	4 59	5 29	—	5 59	629	6 59	729	7 59	—	829	8 59	929	—	9 59	—	10 29	—	10 59
Willesden J. New Stn.	4 31	5 1	5 31	—	6 1	631	7 1	731	8 1	—	831	9 1	931	—	10 1	—	10 31	—	11 1
Willesden J. Main L.	—	—	—	535	—	—	—	—	--	8 3	—	--	—	9 33	—	956	—	1028	—
Kensal Green	4 33	5 3	5 33	—	6 3	633	7 3	733	8 3	—	833	9 3	933	—	10 3	—	10 33	—	11 3
Queens Pk. (W. Kilb'n)	4 35	5 5	5 35	—	6 5	635	7 5	735	8 5	—	835	9 5	935	—	10 6	—	10 35	—	11 5
Kilburn..............	4 37	5 7	5 37	—	6 7	637	7 7	737	8 7	—	837	9 7	937	—	10 7	—	10 37	—	11 7
South Hampstead....	4 39	5 9	5 39	—	6 9	639	7 9	739	8 9	—	839	9 9	939	—	10 9	—	10 39	—	11 9
Chalk Farm..........	—	—	—	—	—	—	—	—	—	—	—	—	—	—	—	—	—	—	—
Broad Street	5‡ 5	5‡35	6‡ 5	—	6‡35	7‡5	7‡35	8‡5	8‡35	—	9‡5	9‡35	10‡5	10‡20	10‡35	1035	11‡ 2	11‡2	11‡32
Euston	4 45	5 15	5 45	550	6 15	645	7 15	745	8 15	815	845	9 15	945	9 45	10 15	1010	10 45	1040	11 15

‡ Passengers for Broad Street change at Willesden.

(Week days only).

WEEK DAYS.	AM	AM	AM	AM	AM	AM	AM	AM	AM	AM	AM	d	d	AM	d	d	e	d
Euston ....dep.	5 25	5 25	6	5 6	30	7	0	715	7 54	815	8 30	8 45	9 0	9 15	9 40	945	10 50	11 30	12 15	12 30	1256
Watford High St. arr.	6 34	6 42	7	7 7	25	7 43	755	—	852	9	8 9	23	952	10 5	10 27	1027	11 28	—	12 56	1 34	134
Watford West	6 37	—	7 10	7 28	7 46	758	8 33	855	—	9 26	955	—	10 30	1030	11 31	12 30	12 59	1 37	137
Croxley Green........	6 40	—	7 13	7 31	7 49	8 1	8 38	858	—	9 29	958	—	10 33	1033	11 34	12 33	1 2	1 40	140
Rickmansworth.....	—	6 52	—	—	—	811	—	9 18	—	—	10 15	—	—	11 44	—	1 16	1 51	151

WEEK DAYS.	e	d	e	d	PM	PM	d	PM	—	e	PM	e	—	d	d	PM	PM	PM	d
Euston ....dep.	1 0	126	130	137	2 0	230	240	336	357	410	430	5 0	5 0	5 7	537	532	556	610	635	715	8 0	8 59	9 5	955
Watford High St. arr.	142	—	223	223	241	312	320	421	—	462	518	—	551	551	—	621	—	642	7 5	754	9 6	834	943	1035
Watford West	—	2 3	—	228	244	323	323	424	440	458	521	538	554	554	617	624	642	—	7 8	8 2	—	837	954	—
Croxley Green........	—	2 6	—	231	247	326	326	427	443	5 1	524	541	557	557	620	627	645	—	711	8 5	—	840	957	—
Rickmansworth.....	151	—	233	233	—	321	—	—	—	5 2	—	—	6 4	6 4	—	—	—	652	—	8 4	915	—	952	1044

RICKMANSWORTH & CROXLEY GREEN TO EUSTON
(Week days only).

WEEK DAYS.	AM	AM	AM	AM	AM	AM	AM	AM	AM	AM	AM	AM	d	d	d	PM	d	PM	PM
Rickmansworth dep.	—	—	—	—	7 31	—	829	—	9 23	—	1036	11 58	—	—	—	1 20	1 54	—	2 36	—
Croxley Green	6 20	648	7 20	7 37	752	8 7	843	9 6	9 36	10 5	1051	—	12 25	1240	1 9	—	1 48	2 18	2 52	3 33
Watford West	6 21	649	7 21	7 38	753	8 9	844	9 7	9 38	10 6	1052	—	12 26	1241	1 10	—	1 49	2 19	2 53	3 34
Watford High St. ...	6 25	653	7 25	7 40	757	—	839	9 11	9 41	1010	1056	12 8	12 30	—	1 14	1 30	2 2	2 23	2 57	3 38
Euston ....arr.	7 18	740	8	9 8	22	838	845	920	9 52	10 23	1121	1140	12 51	1 20	1 24	2 20	2 20	2 51	3 53	50	4 20

WEEK DAYS.	PM	PM	e	e	PM	e	PM	e	d	e	PM	d	PM	e	d	PM	PM	d	e	PM	PM
Rickmansworth dep.	4 21	—	—	5 12	5 12	—	6 14	—	—	7 0	—	—	8 7	—	9 426	10 0	—	10 52			
Croxley Green......	—	4 34	4 49	5	7 5	30	5 46	6	8 6	28	629	6 50	—	7 22	7 50	8 55	9 27	—	10 10	—	10
Watford West......	—	4 35	4 50	5	8 5	31	5 48	6	9 6	29	640	6 51	—	7 23	7 51	8 21	8 56	9 28	—	10 12	—
Watford High St. ...	4 30	4 39	—	5	22	5 35	—	6 24	6	33	644	6 55	7	9 7	27	7 55	8 25	9 0	9 32	10 9	10 16	11
Euston ....arr.	5 21	5 20	5 40	6	10 6	20	6 40	7	5 7	22	720	7 50	7 50	8 21	8 35	9 21	9 51	10 20	1050	11 10	11 50

d Saturdays only.   *e Saturdays excepted.*

BROAD STREET TO POPLAR.

WEEK DAYS.	AM	AM	AM		PM	PM		AM	AM	PM	PM
Broad Street ...	5 24	5 54	6 7	Then (Saturdays excepted) every 15 min-	10 9	1039		8 5	—	—	1110
Shoreditch	—	—	6 9	utes until 10.7 a.m. ; from that hour							
Haggerston	—	—	6 12	until 4.35 p.m. every 30 minutes ; also at			ᵟᵁᴺᴰᴬʸˢ.				
Dalston Junction	5 30	6 0	6 15	12.22 p.m. and 12.52 p.m., after 4.35 p.m.	1015	1045		8 10	9	5	1035	1115
Hackney........	5 33	6 3	6 18	each 15 minutes until 7.37 p.m., then	1018	1048		8 13	9 8	1038	1118
Homerton	5 35	6 5	6 20	every 30 minutes until 10.39 p.m., also at	1020	1050		8 15	9 10	1040	1120
Victoria Park ...	5 38	6 8	6 23	11.9 and 11.39 p.m. to Bow.	1023	1053		8 28	9 13	1043	1123
Old Ford.........	5 40	6 10	6 25	On Saturdays only every 15 minutes until	1025	1055		8 29	9 15	1045	1125
Bow...........	5 42	6 12	6 27	10.7 a.m. ; then every 30 minutes until	1027	1057		8 22	9 17	1047	1127
South Bromley ..	5 45	6 15	6 30	12.7 p.m. ; thence every 15 minutes until	1030	11 0		8 25	9 20	1050	1130
Poplar.........	5 47	6 17	6 32	5.35 p.m. ; every 30 minutes afterwards until 10.39 p.m. Also at 11.9 p.m. and 11.39 p.m. to Bow.	1032	11 2		8 27	9 22	1052	1132

On Sundays at 8.5, from Broad Street and from Dalston Junction at 9.5 a.m., and every half hour to 10.35 a.m. and at 11.10 p.m. from Broad Street.

POPLAR TO BROAD STREET.

WEEK DAYS.	AM	AM	AM	AM	AM		PM		AM	PM
Poplar.........	—	—	—	—	6 0		11 0		7 25	10 30
South Bromley	—	—	—	—	6 2		11 2	ᵟᵁᴺᴰᴬʸˢ.	7 27	10 32
Bow	5 6	5 20	5 35	5 50	6 5	Then every 15 minutes until 9.30	11 5		7 30	10 35
Old Ford.........	5 8	5 22	5 37	5 52	6 7	a.m. ; from that hour every 30	11 7		7 32	10 37
Victoria Park	5 11	5 25	5 40	5 55	6 10	minutes until 12.30 p.m.; also at	11 10		7 35	10 40
Homerton	5 13	5 27	5 42	5 57	6 12	12.28, 12.43, and 1.0 p.m. on Saturdays	11 12		7 37	10 42
Hackney.........	5 16	5 30	5 45	6	0 6	15	from Bow, and after that every 15		7 40	10 45
Dalston Junction ...	5 19	5 34	5 49	6	2 6	17	minutes until 7.0 p.m., then every	11 19		7 43	10 48
Haggerston	—	—	—	6	6 6	21	30 minutes until 11.0 p.m.			
Shoreditch	—	—	—	6	8 6	23				
Broad Street.........	5 25	5 40	5 55	6 11	6 26		11 25		7 59	10 54

On Sundays at 7.25 a.m., and 10.30 p.m., to Broad Street and to Dalston Junction at 8.35, 9.35 a.m., and every 30 minutes to 10.0 p.m.

EUSTON TO STANMORE. (Week days only.)

Week days.	AM	AM	AM	AM	AM	AM	AM	AM	AM	AM	AM	AM	AM	d	d	e	d	d
Euston....dep.	6 30	7 0	7 15	7 30	7 35	8 0	8 15	8 35	8 45	9 15	9 30	9 45	11 0	12 0	12 15	1230	1	3 1	0	1 10	1 30
Stanmore..arr.	7 15	7 40	7 57	8 10	8 25	8 39	8 57	9 13	9 31	9 46	10	4 10	2 11	35	1235	12 52	1 51	301	351	50	2 7

Week days.	d	PM	d	e	d	PM	d	e	PM	d	e	PM	d	e	d	PM	e	s	PM
Euston....dep.	1	35	2 0	2 7	230	240	3 0	333	410	412	442	5 0	5 5	520	526	530	5 45	5 56	6	0 6	76	26	6 56	7	7 7	30
Stanmore..arr.	2	7	238	256	3	9 3	9	335	4	3	450	450	519	519	533	533	550	6	4	620	6	206	356	356	51	7	5 7	27	7 42	8	5

Week days.	d	PM	PM	PM	PM	PM	PM
Euston....dep.	8 0	8 30	9	5	5 10	30	10	0	11	20
Stanmore..arr.	8 35	9 5	9 35	10 27	11	5 11	35	12 15

d Saturdays only.   *e Saturdays excepted.*

STANMORE TO EUSTON. (Week days only.)

Week days.	AM	AM	AM	AM	AM	AM	AM	AM	AM	AM	d	PM	PM	PM	d	PM	e	PM	PM	PM
Stanmore..dep	6 44	7 25	7 44	7 59	8 13	8 27	8 41	9 0	9 16	9 48	10	8 10	43	1213	1240	1254	1 131	32	1 43	210	224	243
Euston ....arr.	7 18	7 53	8 15	8 41	8 45	8 56	9 21	9	309	5210	23	10 5	11	21	1251	1 21	1.01	502	20	2 20	250	3 5	320

Week days.	d	e	PM	e	PM	e	PM	e	PM	d	e	PM	e	PM	d	e	PM	PM	PM
Stanmore..dep.	3 13	3 50	3504	4 35	452	4	525	5	15	536	5526	6	6 22	637	7	7 23	7 44	8	13 8	43	9	13	943	1035	1113
Euston ....arr.	3 51	4 42	450	5 20	540	5	50 6	10	5 21	640	6 51	7	5 7	227	51	7 51	8 20	8 21	8 51	9	21 9	51	1020	1120	1150

d Saturdays only.   *e Saturdays excepted.*

WEEK DAYS.	AM	AM	AM	AM	AM	AM	AM	AM	AM	AM	AM	AM	AM	AM	AM	AM	AM	AM	AM	AM	AM	AM
BROAD STREET dep.	—	5 30	—	6 0	6 6	6 15	—	6 30	6 34	637	6 40	6 45	6 55	7 0	7 6	7 10	7 20	727	7 30	736	740	745
Dalston Junction ..	—	5 34	—	6 4	6 10	6 19	—	6 34	6 38	641	6 44	6 49	6 59	7 4	710	7 14	7 24	731	7 34	740	744	749
Canonbury	—	—	—	6 7	—	6 22	—	6 37	—	—	—	6 52	7 2	7 7	—	7 17	7 27	—	7 37	—	747	—
Highbury	—	5 37	—	6 9	6 13	6 24	—	6 39	6 41	644	6 47	6 54	7 4	7 9	713	7 19	7 29	734	7 39	743	749	752
Caledonian Road ..	—	—	—	6 11	—	6 26	—	6 41	6 43	—	—	6 56	7 6	7 11	—	7 21	7 31	736	7 41	—	751	—
CAMDEN TOWN	—	5 41	—	6 14	6 17	6 29	—	6 44	6 46	648	6 51	6 59	7 9	7 14	717	7 24	7 34	739	7 44	747	754	757
Chalk Farm	—	—	—	—	6 19	—	—	—	—	650	—	—	—	—	719	—	—	—	—	749	—	—
Kentish Town	—	5 43	—	—	—	6 31	—	6 46	6 49	—	6 53	7 1	7 11	7 16	—	7 26	7 36	741	7 46	—	756	759
Gospel Oak..........	—	5 45	—	6 17	—	6 33	—	6 48	6 51	—	6 55	7 3	7 13	7 18	—	7 28	7 38	743	7 48	—	758	8 1
Hampstead Heath ..	—	5 47	—	6 19	—	6 35	—	6 50	6 53	—	6 57	7 5	7 15	7 20	—	7 30	7 40	745	7 50	—	8 0	8 3
Finchley Road	—	5 49	—	6 21	—	6 37	—	6 52	6 55	—	—	7 7	7 17	7 22	—	7 32	7 42	—	7 52	—	8 2	8 5
West End Lane	—	—	—	—	—	6 38	—	6 53	6 56	—	—	7 8	7 18	7 23	—	7 33	7 43	—	7 53	—	8 3	8 6
Brondesbury	—	5 52	—	6 24	—	6 40	—	6 55	6 58	—	7 1	7 10	7 20	7 25	—	7 35	7 45	749	7 55	—	8 5	8 8
Brondesbury Park ..	—	—	—	—	—	6 41	—	6 56	—	—	—	7 11	7 21	7 26	—	7 36	7 46	—	7 56	—	8 6	8 9
Kensal Rise	—	5 55	—	6 27	—	6 43	—	6 58	7 1	—	7 4	7 13	7 23	7 28	—	7 38	7 48	753	7 58	—	8 8	811
WILLESDEN JN.	558	6 0	625	6 30	6 30	6 46	650	7 1	7 4	717	7 7	7 16	7 27	7 31	730	7 41	7 51	755	8 1	8 0	811	814
St. Quintin Park....	6 1	—	—	—	6 42	6 57	—	—	—	—	—	7 22	—	—	—	7 46	—	—	—	8 8	—	827
Uxbridge Road	6 4	—	630	—	6 45	7 0	—	—	—	—	—	7 25	7 35	—	—	7 49	—	—	—	811	—	830
Kensington (A. R.)..	6 9	—	633	—	6 49	7 4	—	—	—	—	—	7 29	7 38	—	—	7 53	—	—	—	816	—	835
EARL'S COURT	613	—	—	—	6 53	7 9	—	—	—	—	—	7 34	—	—	—	7 57	—	—	—	820	—	839
Acton	—	6 9	—	6 34	—	6 50	653	7 5	7 8	—	7 11	7 20	7 31	7 35	—	7 45	7 55	—	8 5	—	815	818
South Acton	—	6 13	—	6 36	—	6 52	655	7 7	7 11	—	7 14	7 22	7 33	7 37	—	7 47	7 57	—	8 7	—	817	820
KEW BRIDGE	—	6 17	—	6 40	—	6 56	—	—	7 15	—	—	7 26	—	—	—	7 51	—	—	—	—	—	824
Gunnersbury	—	—	—	—	—	—	658	7 9	—	—	7 16	—	7 35	7 39	—	—	8 3	—	8 13	—	820	—
Kew Gardens........	—	—	—	—	—	—	7 1	7 12	—	—	7 19	—	7 38	7 42	—	—	8 6	—	8 16	—	823	—
RICHMOND	—	—	—	—	—	—	7 5	7 16	—	—	7 23	—	7 42	7 46	—	—	8 10	—	8 20	—	827	—

WEEK DAYS.	AM	AM	AM	AM	AM	AM	AM	AM	AM	AM	AM	AM	AM	AM	AM	AM	AM	AM	AM
BROAD STREET ..dep.	7 55	8 2	8 6	8 10	8 15	8 20	8 30	8 38	—	8 45	8 55	9 0	9 6	9 17	—	9 30	9 34	9 47	10 0
Dalston Junction ..	7 59	8 6	8 10	8 14	8 19	8 24	8 34	8 42	—	8 49	8 59	9 4	9 10	9 21	—	9 34	9 38	9 51	10 4
Canonbury	8 2	—	—	—	—	—	8 36	—	—	8 51	9 1	9 6	—	—	—	9 36	—	—	10 6
Highbury	8 4	8 9	8 13	—	—	8 27	8 38	8 45	—	8 53	9 3	9 8	9 13	9 24	—	9 38	9 41	9 54	10 8
Caledonian Road ..	8 6	—	—	—	—	—	—	—	—	8 55	9 5	9 10	—	—	—	9 40	—	—	10 10
CAMDEN TOWN	8 9	8 13	8 17	8 20	—	8 31	8 42	8 49	—	8 58	9 9	9 13	9 17	9 23	—	9 43	9 45	9 58	10 13
Chalk Farm	—	—	—	8 22	—	—	—	8 51	—	—	—	—	9 19	—	—	—	9 47	—	—
Kentish Town	8 11	—	8 20	—	—	8 33	8 44	—	—	9 0	9 11	9 15	—	9 30	—	9 45	—	10 0	10 15
Gospel Oak..........	8 13	8 16	8 22	—	—	8 35	8 46	—	—	9 2	9 13	9 17	—	9 32	—	9 47	—	10 2	10 17
Hampstead Heath ..	8 15	8 18	8 24	—	—	8 37	8 48	—	—	9 4	9 15	9 19	—	9 34	—	9 49	—	10 4	10 19
Finchley Road	8 17	8 20	8 26	—	—	8 39	8 50	—	—	9 6	9 17	9 21	—	9 36	—	9 51	—	10 6	10 21
West End Lane	8 18	8 21	—	—	8 29	8 40	8 51	—	—	9 7	9 18	9 22	—	9 37	—	9 52	—	10 7	10 22
Brondesbury	8 20	8 23	8 28	—	8 30	8 42	8 53	—	—	9 9	9 20	9 24	—	9 39	—	9 54	—	10 9	10 24
Brondesbury Park ..	8 21	8 24	8 29	—	—	8 43	8 54	—	—	9 10	9 21	9 25	—	9 40	—	9 55	—	10 10	10 25
Kensal Rise	8 23	8 26	—	—	8 33	8 45	8 56	—	—	9 12	9 23	9 27	—	9 42	—	9 57	—	10 12	10 27
WILLESDEN JN.	8 26	8 29	8 32	8 31	8 36	8 48	8 59	9 1	9†13	9 15	9 26	9 30	9 30	9 45	9 49	10 0	9 58	10 15	10 30
St. Quintin Park....	—	—	—	—	8 42	8 54	9 6	9 6	—	9 24	—	—	9 42	—	—	—	—	—	—
Uxbridge Road	—	8 40	—	—	8 44	8 56	9 9	9 9	9 20	9 26	—	—	9 45	—	—	—	—	—	—
Kensington (A. R.)..	—	8 43	—	—	8 47	9 0	9 13	9 13	9 24	9 30	—	—	9 49	—	—	—	—	—	—
EARL'S COURT	—	—	—	—	8 54	9 7	9 20	9 20	—	9 34	—	—	9 54	—	—	—	—	—	—
Acton	8 30	8 33	8 37	—	8 40	8 52	9 3	—	—	9 19	9 31	9 34	—	9 49	9 54	10 4	—	10 19	10 34
South Acton	8 32	8 35	8 39	—	8 43	8 54	9 5	—	—	9 21	9 33	9 36	—	9 51	9 56	10 6	—	10 21	10 36
KEW BRIDGE	—	8 39	—	—	—	8 58	—	—	—	9 25	—	9 40	—	—	10 0	—	—	10 28	—
Gunnersbury........	8 34	—	8 41	—	8 46	—	9 8	—	—	—	9 37	—	—	9 53	—	10 8	—	10 23	10 38
Kew Gardens........	8 37	—	8 44	—	8 49	—	9 11	—	—	—	9 40	—	—	9 56	—	10 11	—	10 26	10 41
RICHMOND	8 41	—	8 48	—	8 56	—	9 15	—	—	—	9 44	—	—	10 0	—	10 15	—	10 30	10 45

WEEK DAYS.	AM	AM	AM	AM	AM	AM	AM	AM	AM	AM	AM	PM	noon	PM	d	PM	d
BROAD STREET..dep.	10 6	10 17	10 30	10 36	10 47	11 0	11 6	11 17	11 30	11 36	11 47	—	12 0	12 6	12 10	12 17	12 20
Dalston Junction ..	1010	10 21	10 34	10 40	10 51	11 4	11 10	11 21	11 34	11 40	11 51	—	12 4	12 10	—	12 21	12 24
Canonbury	—	—	10 36	—	—	11 6	—	—	11 36	—	—		12 6	—	—	—	—
Highbury	1013	10 24	10 38	10 43	10 54	11 8	11 13	11 24	11 38	11 43	11 54	Saturdays only.	12 8	12 13	—	12 24	12 27
Caledonian Road ..	—	—	10 40	—	—	11 10	—	—	11 40	—	—		12 10	—	—	—	—
CAMDEN TOWN	1017	10 28	10 43	10 47	10 58	11 13	11 17	11 28	11 43	11 47	11 58		12 13	12 17	—	12 28	12 31
Chalk Farm	1021	—	—	10 49	—	—	11 19	—	—	11 49	—		—	12 19	—	—	12 33
Kentish Town	—	10 30	10 45	—	11 0	11 15	—	11 30	11 45	—	12 0		12 15	—	—	12 30	—
Gospel Oak	—	10 32	10 47	—	11 2	11 17	—	11 32	11 47	—	12 2		12 17	—	12 22	12 32	—
Hampstead Heath..	—	10 34	10 49	—	11 4	11 19	—	11 34	11 49	—	12 4		12 19	—	12 24	12 34	—
Finchley Road......	—	10 36	10 51	—	11 6	11 21	—	11 36	11 51	—	12 6		12 21	—	12 26	12 36	—
West End Lane	—	10 37	10 52	—	11 7	11 22	—	11 37	11 52	—	12 7		12 22	—	12 27	12 37	—
Brondesbury........	—	10 39	10 54	—	11 9	11 24	—	11 39	11 54	—	12 9		12 24	—	—	12 39	—
Brondesbury Park..	—	10 40	10 55	—	11 10	11 25	—	11 40	11 55	—	12 10		12 25	—	—	12 40	—
Kensal Rise	—	10 42	10 57	—	11 12	11 27	—	11 42	11 57	—	12 12	—	12 27	—	12 32	12 42	—
WILLESDEN JN.	1032	10 45	11 0	11 0	11 15	11 30	11 30	11 45	12 0	12 0	12 15	12 19	12 30	12 30	12 35	12 45	12 44
St. Quintin Park ..	1041	—	—	—	—	—	11 40	—	—	12[d]12	—	—	—	12 40	12 40	—	—
Uxbridge Road	1044	—	—	—	11 35	—	11 43	—	—	12[d]17	—	—	—	12 43	12 43	—	—
Kensington (A. R.) .	1048	—	—	—	11 38	—	11 47	—	—	12[d]21	—	—	—	12 49	12 49	—	—
EARL'S COURT	1051	—	—	—	—	—	11 51	—	—	12[d]25	—	—	—	12 53	12 53	—	—
Acton	—	10 49	11 4	—	11 19	11 34	—	11 49	12 4	—	12 19	12 23	12 34	—	12 39	12 49	—
South Acton........	—	10 51	11 6	—	11 21	11 36	—	11 51	12 6	—	12 21	12 25	12 36	—	—	12 51	—
KEW BRIDGE	—	10 58	—	—	11 28	—	—	11 58	—	—	12 28	12 29	—	—	—	12 58	—
Gunnersbury	—	10 53	11 8	—	11 23	11 38	—	11 53	12 8	—	12 23	—	12 38	—	12 42	12 53	—
Kew Gardens..	—	10 56	11 11	—	11 26	11 41	—	11 56	12 11	—	12 26	—	12 41	—	12 45	12 56	—
RICHMOND	—	11 0	11 15	—	11 30	11 45	—	12 0	12 15	—	12 30	—	12 45	—	12 49	1 0	—

WEEK DAYS.	PM	PM	d	PM	d	d	e	d	e	d	d	e	d	d	PM	PM	d	PM	d
BROAD STREET ..dep.	12 30	12 35	12 45	12 47	12 50	1 0	1 0	1 2	1 6	1 13	1 18	1 17	1 20	1 22	1 30	1 35	1 45	1 47	1 50
Dalston Junction ..	12 34	12 39	12 49	12 51	12 54	1 4	1 4	1 6	1 10	—	—	1 21	1 24	1 26	1 34	1 39	1 49	1 51	1 54
Canonbury..........	12 36	—	—	—	—	—	1 6	1 8	—	—	—	—	—	—	1 36	—	—	—	—
Highbury	12 38	12 42	—	12 54	12 57	—	1 8	1 10	1 13	—	—	1 24	1 27	1 29	1 38	1 42	—	1 54	1 57
Caledonian Road ..	12 40	—	—	—	—	—	1 10	1 12	—	—	—	—	—	—	1 40	—	—	—	—
CAMDEN TOWN	12 43	12 46	—	12 58	1 1	—	1 13	1 15	1 17	—	—	1 28	1 31	1 33	1 43	1 46	—	1 58	2 1
Chalk Farm	—	12 48	—	—	1 3	—	—	—	1 19	—	—	—	1 33	—	—	1 48	—	—	2 3
Kentish Town	12 45	—	—	1 0	—	—	1 15	1 17	—	1 26	—	1 30	—	1 35	1 45	—	—	2 0	—
Gospel Oak	12 47	—	12 57	1 2	—	1 13	1 17	1 19	—	1 28	1 30	1 32	—	1 37	1 47	—	1 58	2 2	—
Hampstead Heath..	12 49	—	12 59	1 4	—	1 15	1 19	1 21	—	1 29	1 32	1 34	—	1 39	1 49	—	2 0	2 4	—
Finchley Road......	12 51	—	1 1	1 6	—	1 17	1 21	1 23	—	—	1 34	1 36	—	1 41	1 51	—	2 2	2 6	—
West End Lane	12 52	—	—	1 7	—	1 18	1 22	1 24	—	—	—	1 37	—	1 42	1 52	—	2 3	2 7	—
Brondesbury........	12 54	—	—	1 9	—	1 20	1 24	1 26	—	—	—	1 39	—	1 44	1 54	—	—	2 9	—
Brondesbury Park..	12 55	—	—	1 10	—	1 21	1 25	1 27	—	—	—	1 40	—	1 45	1 55	—	—	2 10	—
Kensal Rise	12 57	—	1 5	1 12	—	1 23	1 27	1 29	—	—	1 38	1 42	—	1 47	1 57	—	2 7	2 12	—
WILLESDEN JN.	1 0	12 58	1 8	1 15	1 14	1 26	1 30	1 32	1 30	1 35	1 41	1 45	1 44	1 50	2 0	1 58	2 10	2 15	2 14
St. Quintin Park....	1[d] 7	—	—	—	1 28	—	—	—	1 40	—	—	—	—	—	2[d] 7	—	—	2[e]22	—
Uxbridge Road	1[d] 10	—	—	—	1 30	—	—	—	1 43	—	—	—	—	—	2[d]10	—	—	2[e]25	—
Kensington (A. R.)	1[d] 14	—	—	—	1 33	—	—	—	1 47	—	—	—	—	—	2[d]13	—	—	2[e]28	—
EARL'S COURT	1[d] 18	—	—	—	—	—	—	—	1 51	—	—	—	—	—	2[d]18	—	—	2[e]32	—
Acton	1 4	—	1 12	1 19	—	1 30	1 34	1 36	—	—	1 45	1 49	—	1 54	2 4	—	—	2 19	—
South Acton........	1 6	—	—	1 21	—	—	1 36	1 38	—	—	—	1 51	—	1 56	2 6	—	—	2 21	—
KEW BRIDGE........	—	—	—	1 32	—	—	—	1 42	—	—	—	2 1	—	2 3	—	—	—	2 28	—
Gunnersbury	1 8	—	1 15	1 23	—	1 34	1 38	—	—	—	1 48	1 53	—	1 58	2 8	—	—	2 23	—
Kew Gardens	1 11	—	1 18	1 26	—	1 37	1 41	—	—	—	1 51	1 56	—	2 1	2 11	—	—	2 26	—
RICHMOND	1 15	—	1 22	1 30	—	1 41	1 45	—	—	—	1 55	2 0	—	2 5	2 15	—	—	2 30	—

WEEK DAYS.	PM	PM	PM	PM	PM	PM	PM	PM	PM	PM	PM	PM	PM	PM	PM	e	PM	PM	e
Broad Street dep.	2 0	2 6	2 17	2 30	2 36	2 47	3 0	3 6	3 17	3 30	3 36	3 47	4 0	4 6	4 17	4 20	4 30	4 35	4 45
Dalston Junction ..	2 4	2 10	2 21	2 34	2 40	2 51	3 4	3 10	3 21	3 34	3 40	3 51	4 4	4 10	4 21	4 24	4 34	4 39	4 49
Canonbury..........	2 6	—	—	2 36	—	—	3 6	—	—	3 36	—	—	4 6	—	—	—	4 36	—	—
Highbury	2 8	2 13	2 24	2 38	2 43	2 54	3 8	3 13	3 24	3 38	3 43	3 54	4 8	4 13	4 24	4 27	4 38	4 42	—
Caledonian Road ..	2 10	—	—	2 40	—	—	3 10	—	—	3 40	—	—	4 10	—	—	—	4 40	—	—
Camden Town	2 13	2 17	2 28	2 43	2 47	2 58	3 13	3 17	3 28	3 43	3 47	3 58	4 13	4 17	4 28	4 31	4 43	4 46	—
Chalk Farm	—	2 19	—	—	2 49	—	—	3 19	—	—	3 49	—	—	4 19	—	4 33	—	4 48	—
Kentish Town	2 15	—	2 30	2 45	—	3 0	3 15	—	3 30	3 45	—	4 0	4 15	—	4 30	—	4 45	—	—
Gospel Oak	2 17	—	2 32	2 47	—	3 2	3 17	—	3 32	3 47	—	4 2	4 17	—	4 32	—	4 47	—	4 58
Hampstead Heath..	2 19	—	2 34	2 49	—	3 4	3 19	—	3 34	3 49	—	4 4	4 19	—	4 34	—	4 49	—	5 0
Finchley Road	2 21	—	2 36	2 51	—	3 6	3 21	—	3 36	3 51	—	4 6	4 21	—	4 36	—	4 51	—	5 2
West End Lane	2 22	—	2 37	2 52	—	3 7	3 22	—	3 37	3 52	—	4 7	4 22	—	4 37	—	4 52	—	5 3
Brondesbury........	2 24	—	2 39	2 54	—	3 9	3 24	—	3 39	3 54	—	4 9	4 24	—	4 39	—	4 54	—	5 5
Brondesbury Park..	2 25	—	2 40	2 55	—	3 10	3 25	—	3 40	3 55	—	4 10	4 25	—	4 40	—	4 55	—	5 6
Kensal Rise	2 27	—	2 42	2 57	—	3 12	3 27	—	3 42	3 58	—	4 12	4 27	—	4 42	—	4 57	—	5 8
Willesden Junct.	2 30	2 30	2 45	3 0	3 0	3 15	3 30	3 30	3 45	4 0	4 0	4 15	4 30	4 30	4 45	4 45	5 0	4 58	5 11
St. Quentin Park ..	—	2d38	2e58	—	3d 9	—	—	3d40	—	—	4 10	4e23	—	4 40	4 57	4 57	—	5 12	—
Uxbridge Road	—	2d41	3e 1	—	3d12	—	—	3d43	—	—	4 13	4e26	—	4 43	5 0	5 0	—	5 14	—
Kensington (A.R†)..	—	2d45	3e 4	—	3d16	—	—	3d47	—	—	4 17	4e29	—	4 47	5 3	5 3	—	5 17	—
Earl's Court	—	2d49	3e10	—	3d20	—	—	3d54	—	—	4 21	4e36	—	4 53	5 10	5 10	—	—	—
Acton	2 34	—	2 49	3 4	—	3 19	3 34	—	3 49	4 4	—	4 19	4 34	—	4 49	5 1	5 4	—	5 15
South Acton........	2 36	—	2 51	3 6	—	3 21	3 36	—	3 51	4 6	—	4 21	4 36	—	4 51	5 3	5 6	—	5 18
Kew Bridge........	—	—	2 58	—	—	3 28	—	—	3 58	—	—	4 28	—	—	4 58	—	5 10	—	—
Gunnersbury	2 38	—	2 53	3 8	—	3 23	3 38	—	3 53	4 8	—	4 23	4 38	—	4 52	5 7	5d 8	—	5 20
Kew Gardens	2 41	—	2 56	3 11	—	3 26	3 41	—	3 56	4 11	—	4 26	4 41	—	4 56	5 10	5d11	—	5 23
Richmond	2 45	—	3 0	3 15	—	3 30	3 45	—	4 0	4 15	—	4 30	4 45	—	5 0	5 14	5d15	—	5 27

WEEK DAYS.	d	e	e	e	d	PM	e	PM	e	e	d	e	PM	e	e	d	e	e	d	e
Broad Street ....dep.	4 47	4 52	4 54	5 0	5 0	5 5	514	517	5 20	528	5 30	5 30	5 35	5 40	5 47	5 47	549	5 54	6 0	6 2
Dalston Junction	4 51	4 56	4 58	5 4	5 4	5 9	518	521	5 24	—	5 34	5 34	5 39	5 44	—	5 51	553	5 58	6 4	6 6
Canonbury............	—	—	5 0	—	5 6	—	—	—	—	—	5 36	5 36	—	—	—	—	—	6 0	6 6	—
Highbury	4 54	4 59	5 2	5 7	5 8	5 12	—	524	—	—	5 38	5 39	5 42	—	—	5 54	556	6 2	6 8	6 9
Caledonian Road	—	—	5 4	—	5 10	—	—	—	—	—	5 40	5 40	—	—	—	—	—	6 3	6 10	—
Camden Town	4 58	5 3	5 7	5 11	5 13	5 16	—	526	5 30	—	5 43	5 43	5 46	—	—	5 58	6 0	6 7	6 13	6 13
Chalk Farm	—	5 5	—	—	—	5 18	—	—	5 32	—	—	—	5 48	—	—	—	6 2	—	—	—
Kentish Town	5 0	—	5 9	5 13	5 15	—	—	530	—	—	5 45	5 45	—	—	—	6 0	—	6 9	6 15	—
Gospel Oak............	5 2	—	5 11	5 15	5 17	—	526	532	—	540	5 47	5 47	—	5 53	5 59	6 2	—	6 11	6 17	6 16
Hampstead Heath	5 4	—	5 13	5 17	5 19	—	528	534	—	542	5 49	5 49	—	5 55	6 1	6 4	—	6 13	6 19	6 18
Finchley Road........	5 6	—	5 15	5 19	5 21	—	530	536	—	544	5 51	5 51	—	5 57	6 3	6 6	—	6 15	6 21	6 20
West End Lane	5 7	—	5 16	5 20	5 22	—	—	537	—	545	5 52	—	—	5 58	—	6 7	—	6 16	6 22	6 21
Brondesbury	5 9	—	5 18	5 22	5 24	—	—	539	—	547	5 54	—	—	6 0	—	6 9	—	6 18	6 24	6 23
Brondesbury Park	5 10	—	5 19	5 23	5 25	—	—	540	—	548	5 55	5 55	—	6 1	—	6 10	—	6 19	6 25	6 24
Kensal Rise	5 12	—	5 21	5 25	5 27	—	534	542	—	550	5 57	5 57	—	6 3	6 7	6 12	—	6 21	6 27	6 26
Willesden Junction..	5 15	5 15	5 24	5 28	5 30	5 29	537	545	5 43	553	6 0	6 0	5 58	6 6	6 10	6 15	613	6 24	6 30	6 29
St. Quintin Park......	—	—	5 33	5 33	—	5d35	—	552	5 52	—	—	6 7	—	—	6 17	6 20	—	—	—	—
Uxbridge Road	—	—	5 36	5 36	—	5d38	—	555	5 55	—	—	6 10	—	—	6 20	6 23	—	6 30	—	—
Kensington (A. R.)....	—	—	5 39	5 39	—	5d42	—	6 0	6 0	—	—	6 15	—	—	6 24	6 27	—	6 33	—	—
Earl's Court	—	—	5 43	5 43	—	5d46	—	6 4	6 4	—	—	6 22	—	—	6 31	6 31	—	—	—	—
Acton	5 19	—	5 28	5 32	5 34	—	541	549	—	557	6 4	6 4	—	6 10	6 14	6 19	—	6 28	6 34	6 33
South Acton	5 21	—	5 30	5 34	5 36	—	—	551	—	559	6 6	6 6	—	6 12	—	6 21	—	6 30	6 36	6 35
Kew Bridge	5 28	—	5 34	—	—	—	—	558	—	—	—	6 10	—	6 16	—	6 28	—	6 34	—	—
Gunnersbury..........	5 23	—	5 36	5 36	5d38	—	544	553	—	6 3	6 8	—	—	—	6 17	6 23	—	—	6 38	6 37
Kew Gardens	5 26	—	5 39	5 39	5d41	—	547	556	—	6 6	6 11	—	—	—	6 20	6 26	—	—	6 41	6 40
Richmond	5 30	—	5 43	5 43	5d45	—	551	6 0	—	610	6 15	—	—	—	6 24	6 30	—	—	6 45	6 44

WEEK DAYS.	PM	e	e	d	e	e	e	d	d	e	d	e	e	e	PM	PM	PM	PM	PM	PM
Broad Street ....dep.	6 5	612	617	6 17	6 20	6 22	6 30	630	6 36	6 43	6 47	6 48	6 50	6 52	7 0	7 6	7 17	7 30	7 36	7 47
Dalston Junction	6 9	—	—	6 21	6 24	6 26	6 34	634	6 40	—	6 51	6 52	6 54	6 56	7 4	7 10	7 21	7 34	7 40	7 51
Canonbury	—	—	—	—	—	6 28	—	636	—	—	—	—	—	—	7 6	—	—	7 36	—	—
Highbury	6 12	—	—	6 24	6 27	6 30	6 37	638	6 43	—	6 54	—	6 57	6 59	7 8	7 13	7 24	7 38	7 43	7 54
Caledonian Road	—	—	—	—	—	6 31	—	640	—	—	—	—	—	—	7 10	—	—	7 40	—	—
Camden Town	6 16	—	—	6 28	6 31	6 35	6 41	643	6 47	—	6 58	—	7 1	7 3	7 13	7 17	7 28	7 43	7 47	7 58
Chalk Farm	6 18	—	—	—	6 33	—	—	—	6 49	—	—	—	7 3	—	—	7 19	—	—	7 49	—
Kentish Town	—	—	—	6 30	—	6 37	6 43	645	—	—	7 0	—	—	7 5	7 15	—	7 30	7 45	—	8 0
Gospel Oak............	—	—	629	6 32	—	6 39	6 45	647	—	—	7 2	7 0	—	7 7	7 17	—	7 32	7 47	—	8 2
Hampstead Heath	—	—	631	6 34	—	6 41	6 47	649	—	—	7 4	7 2	—	7 9	7 19	—	7 34	7 49	—	8 4
Finchley Road	—	—	633	6 36	—	6 43	6 49	651	—	—	7 6	7 4	—	7 11	7 21	—	7 36	7 51	—	8 6
West End Lane	—	—	—	6 37	—	6 44	6 50	652	—	—	7 7	7 5	—	7 12	7 22	—	7 37	7 52	—	8 7
Brondesbury	—	—	635	6 39	—	6 46	6 52	654	—	—	7 9	7 7	—	7 14	7 24	—	7 39	7 54	—	8 9
Brondesbury Park	—	—	—	6 40	—	6 47	6 53	655	—	—	7 10	7 8	—	7 15	7 25	—	7 40	7 55	—	8 10
Kensal Rise	—	—	638	6 42	—	6 49	6 55	657	—	—	7 12	7 10	—	7 17	7 27	—	7 42	7 57	—	8 12
Willesden Junction..	6 28	634	640	6 45	6 44	6 52	6 58	7 0	7 0	7 0	7 15	7 13	7 14	7 20	7 30	7 31	7 45	8 0	8 1	8 15
St. Quintin Park......	6 36	639	—	—	—	—	—	—	7 10	7 10	7 25	—	—	7 25	—	—	—	—	8 10	—
Uxbridge Road	6 39	642	—	—	—	—	—	—	7 13	7 13	7 28	—	—	7 28	—	—	—	—	8 13	—
Kensington (A. R.)....	6 43	646	—	—	—	—	—	—	7 17	7 17	7 32	—	—	7 32	—	—	—	—	8 17	—
Earl's Court	6 48	651	—	—	—	—	—	—	7 21	7 21	7 36	—	—	7 36	—	—	—	—	8 21	—
Acton	—	—	644	6 49	—	6 56	7 2	7 4	—	—	7 19	7 17	—	7 24	7 34	—	7 49	8 4	—	8 19
South Acton	—	—	—	6 51	—	6 58	7 4	7 6	—	—	7 21	—	—	7 26	7 36	—	7 51	8 6	—	8 21
Kew Bridge	—	—	—	6 58	—	7 2	—	—	—	—	7 31	—	—	7 33	—	—	7 58	—	—	8 28
Gunnersbury..........	—	—	647	6 53	—	—	7 8	7 8	—	—	7 23	7 20	—	7 28	7 38	—	7 53	8 8	—	8 23
Kew Gardens..........	—	—	650	6 56	—	—	7 11	711	—	—	7 26	7 23	—	7 31	7 41	—	7 56	8 11	—	8 26
Richmond	—	—	654	7 0	—	—	7 15	715	—	—	7 30	7 27	—	7 35	7 45	—	8 0	8 15	—	8 30

WEEK DAYS.	PM	PM	PM	PM	PM	PM	PM	PM	PM	PM	PM	PM	PM	PM
Broad Street ....dep.	8 0	8 6	8 17	8 30	8 36	8 47	9 0	9 6	9 17	9 30	9 36	9 50	10 17	10 47
Dalston Junction	8 4	8 10	8 21	8 34	8 40	8 51	9 4	9 10	9 21	9 34	9 40	9 54	10 21	10 51
Canonbury............	8 6	—	—	8 36	—	—	9 6	—	—	9 36	—	9 56	—	—
Highbury	8 8	8 13	8 24	8 38	8 43	8 54	9 8	9 13	9 24	9 38	9 43	9 58	10 24	10 54
Caledonian Road	8 10	—	—	8 40	—	—	9 10	—	—	9 40	—	—	—	—
Camden Road	8 13	8 17	8 28	8 43	8 47	8 58	9 13	9 17	9 28	9 43	9 47	10 2	10 28	10 58
Chalk Farm	—	8 19	—	—	8 49	—	—	9 19	—	—	9 49	—	—	—
Kentish Town........	8 15	—	8 30	8 45	—	9 0	9 15	—	9 30	9 45	—	10 4	10 30	11 0
Gospel Oak............	8 17	—	8 32	8 47	—	9 2	9 17	—	9 32	9 47	—	10 6	10 32	11 2
Hampstead Heath....	8 19	—	8 34	8 49	—	9 4	9 19	—	9 34	9 49	—	10 8	10 34	11 4
Finchley Road........	8 21	—	8 36	8 51	—	9 6	9 21	—	9 36	9 51	—	10 10	10 36	11 6
West End Lane	8 22	—	8 37	8 52	—	9 7	9 22	—	9 37	9 52	—	10 11	10 37	11 7
Brondesbury..........	8 24	—	8 39	8 54	—	9 9	9 24	—	9 39	9 54	—	10 13	10 39	11 9
Brondesbury Park	8 25	—	8 40	8 55	—	9 10	9 25	—	9 40	9 55	—	10 14	10 40	11 10
Kensal Rise	8 27	—	8 42	8 57	—	9 12	9 27	—	9 42	9 57	—	10 16	10 42	11 12
Willesden Junction..	8 30	8 30	8 45	9 0	9 0	9 15	9 30	9 30	9 45	10 0	10 0	10 19	10 45	11 15
St. Quintin Park......	—	8 43	—	—	9 10	—	—	—	—	—	10 10	—	—	—
Uxbridge Road........	—	8 46	—	—	9 13	—	—	—	—	—	10 13	—	—	—
Kensington (A.R.)....	—	8 50	—	—	9 17	—	—	—	—	—	10 17	—	—	—
Earl's Court	—	—	—	—	9 21	—	—	—	—	—	10 21	—	—	—
Acton	8 34	—	8 49	9 4	—	9 19	9 34	—	9 49	10 4	—	10 26	10 49	11 19
South Acton..........	8 36	—	8 51	9 6	—	9 21	9 36	—	9 51	10 6	—	10 30	10 51	11 21
Kew Bridge..........	—	—	8 58	—	—	9 28	—	—	9 58	10 17	—	—	—	—
Gunnersbury..........	8 38	—	8 53	9 8	—	9 23	9 38	—	9 53	10 8	—	10 32	10 53	11 23
Kew Gardens	8 41	—	8 56	9 11	—	9 26	9 41	—	9 56	10 11	—	10 35	10 56	11 26
Richmond	8 45	—	9 0	9 15	—	9 30	9 45	—	10 0	10 15	—	10 39	11 0	11 30

d Saturdays only. *e* Saturdays excepted
† Low Level platform.

SUNDAYS

SUNDAYS	AM	AM	AM	AM	AM	AM	AM	AM	PM	PM	PM	PM	PM	PM	PM	PM	PM	PM
Broad Street .. dep.	825	855	925	955	1025	1055	1125	1155	1225	1255	125	1 40	155	2 10	225	—	2 40	2 55
Dalston Junction	829	859	929	959	1029	1059	1129	1159	1229	1259	129	1 44	159	2 14	229	—	2 44	2 59
Canonbury	831	9 1	931	10 1	1031	11 1	1131	12 1	1231	1 1	131	1 46	2 1	2 16	231	—	2 46	3 1
Highbury	833	9 3	933	10 3	1033	11 3	1133	12 3	1233	1 3	133	1 48	2 3	2 18	233	—	2 48	3 3
Caledonian Road	835	9 5	935	10 5	1035	11 5	1135	12 5	1235	1 5	135	1 50	2 5	2 20	235	—	2 50	3 5
Camden Town	838	9 8	938	10 8	1038	11 8	1138	12 8	1238	1 8	138	1 53	2 8	2 23	238	—	2 53	3 8
Chalk Farm	—	—	—	—	—	—	—	—	—	—	—	—	—	—	—	—	—	—
Kentish Town	840	910	940	1010	1040	1110	1140	1210	1240	110	140	1 55	210	2 25	240	—	2 55	3 10
Gospel Oak...........	842	912	942	1012	1042	1112	1142	1212	1242	112	142	1 57	212	2 27	242	—	2 57	3 12
Hampstead Heath	844	914	944	1014	1044	1114	1144	1214	1244	114	144	1 59	214	2 29	244	—	2 59	3 14
Finchley Road	846	916	946	1016	1046	1116	1146	1216	1246	116	146	2 1	216	2 31	246	—	3 1	3 16
West End Lane	847	917	947	1017	1047	1117	1147	1217	1247	117	147	2 2	217	2 32	247	—	3 2	3 17
Brondesbury	849	919	949	1019	1049	1119	1149	1219	1249	119	149	2 4	219	2 34	249	—	3 4	3 19
Brondesbury Park	850	920	950	1020	1050	1120	1150	1220	1250	120	150	2 5	220	2 35	250	—	3 5	3 20
Kensal Rise	852	922	952	1022	1052	1122	1152	1222	1252	122	152	2 7	222	2 37	252	—	3 7	3 22
Willesden Junction..	855	925	955	1025	1055	1125	1155	1225	1255	·125	155	2 10	225	2 40	255	3 3	3 10	3 25
St. Quintin Park ...	—	—	—	—	—	—	—	—	—	—	—	—	—	—	—	—	—	—
Uxbridge Road	—	—	—	—	—	—	—	—	—	—	—	—	—	—	—	—	—	—
Kensington (A. R.)..	—	—	—	—	—	—	—	—	—	—	—	—	—	—	—	—	—	—
Earl's Court	—	—	—	—	—	—	—	—	—	—	—	—	—	—	—	—	—	—
Acton	859	929	959	1029	1059	1129	1159	1229	1259	129	159	2 14	229	2 44	259	3 6	3 14	3 29
South Acton	9 1	931	10 1	1031	11 1	1131	12 1	1231	1 1	131	2 1	2 16	231	2 46	3 1	3 8	3 16	3 31
Kew Bridge	—	—	—	—	—	—	—	—	—	—	—	—	—	—	—	312	—	—
Gunnersbury........	9 3	933	10 3	1033	11 3	1133	12 3	1233	1 3	133	2 3	2 18	233	2 48	3 3	—	3 18	3 33
Kew Gardens........	9 6	936	10 6	1036	11 6	1136	12 6	1236	1 6	136	2 6	2 21	239	2 51	3 6	—	3 21	3 36
Richmond	910	940	1010	1040	1110	1140	1210	1240	110	140	210	2 2	240	2 55	310	—	3 25	3 40

SUNDAYS.

SUNDAYS.	PM	PM			PM	PM	PM	PM	PM	PM		
Broad Street ....dep	3 10	325			855	9 10	9 25	940	9 55	1020		
Dalston Junction ...	3 14	329			859	9 14	9 29	944	9 59	1024		
Canonbury	3 16	331			9 1	9 16	9 31	946	10 1	—		
Highbury	3 18	333			9 3	9 18	9 33	948	10 3	1027		
Caledonian Road....	3 20	335			9 5	9 20	9 35	950	10 5	—		
Camden Town	3 23	338			9 8	9 23	9 38	953	10 8	1031		
Chalk Farm	—	—			—	—	—	—	—	—		
Kentish Town	3 25	340			910	9 25	9 40	955	1010	1033		
Gospel Oak........	3 27	342			912	9 27	9 42	957	1012	1035		
Hampstead Heath ...	3 29	344			914	9 29	9 44	959	1014	1037		
Finchley Road	3 31	346			916	9 31	9 46	10 1	1016	1039		
West End Lane	3 32	347	Then at same minutes		917	9 32	9 47	10 2	1017	1040		
Brondesbury	3 34	349	past each hour until		919	9 34	9 49	10 4	1019	1042		
Brondesbury Park ...	3 35	350			920	9 35	9 50	10 5	1020	1043		
Kensal Rise	3 37	352			922	9 37	9 52	10 7	1022	1045		
Willesden Junction..	3 40	355			925	9 40	9 55	1010	1025	1048		
St. Quintin Park ...	—	—			—	—	—	—	—	—		
Uxbridge Road	—	—			—	—	—	—	—	—		
Kensington (A. R.) ..	—	—			—	—	—	—	—	—		
Earl's Court	—	—			—	—	—	—	—	—		
Acton	3 44	359			929	9 44	9 59	1014	1029	1052		
South Acton	3 46	4 1			931	9 46	10 1	1016	1031	1054		
Kew Bridge	—	410			940	—	—	—	—	—		
Gunnersbury........	3 48	4 3			933	9 48	10 3	1018	1033	1056		
Kew Gardens........	3 51	4 6			936	9 51	10 6	1021	1036	1059		
Richmond	3 55	410			940	9 55	1010	1025	1040	11 3		

(right margin, vertical text: d Saturdays only.   e Saturdays excepted.   † Low Level platform.)

WEEK DAYS.   RETURN TRAINS.

WEEK DAYS.	AM	AM	AM	AM	AM	AM	AM	AM	AM	AM	AM	AM	AM	AM	AM	AM	AM	AM	AM	AM	AM	AM	AM	AM	AM
Richmond ......dep.	—	—	—	—	—	—	—	—	6 54	—	—	—	—	7 25	—	—	—	—							
Kew Gardens........	—	—	—	—	—	—	—	—	6 56	—	—	—	—	7 27	—	—	—	—							
Gunnersbury........	—	—	—	—	—	—	—	—	6 59	—	—	—	—	7 30	—	—	—	—							
Kew Bridge	—	—	—	—	6 30	—	6 50	—	—	—	7 8	7 22	—	—	7 40	—	—	—							
South Acton	—	—	—	—	6 32	—	6 52	7 1	—	7 10	7 24	—	—	7 32	7 42	—									
Acton	—	—	—	—	6 34	—	6 54	7 3	—	7 12	7 26	—	—	7 34	7 44	—									
Earl's Court.......	—	—	6 18	—	—	—	—	—	6 58	—	—	—	—	—	—	—									
Kensington (A. R.)..	—	—	6 23	—	—	—	—	7 2	—	—	—	7 30	—	—	—										
Uxbridge Road.....	—	—	6 25	—	—	—	—	7 3	—	—	—	7 31	—	—	—										
St. Quintin Park.....	—	—	6 27	—	—	—	—	7 6	—	—	—	7 34	—	—	—										
Willesden Jn.......	5 35	6	5 56	20	6 20	634	6 35	6 39	6 49	6 55	6 59	7 8	7 8	719	7 17	7 31	7 35	7 39	7 49	750					
Kensal Rise	5 36			6 21	—	6 36	6 41	6 57	7 1	7 10	—	719	7 33	—	7 41	7 51	—								
Brondesbury Park ..	—		—	6 43	—	—	—	7 3	7 12	7 21	—	—	7 43	7 53	—										
Brondesbury	5 39		6 24	6 38	6 44	6 59	7 4	7 13	7 22	7 35	7 44	7 54	—												
West End Lane	5 41		6 26	6 40	6 46	7 1	7 6	7 15	7 24	7 46	7 56	—													
Finchley Road	5 42		6 27	—	6 47	—	7 7	7 16	7 25	7 38	7 47	7 57	—												
Hampstead Heath ..	5 44		6 29	—	6 49	—	7 9	7 18	7 27	7 40	7 49	7 59	—												
Gospel Oak........	5 46		6 31	6 44	6 51	7 5	7 11	7 20	7 29	7 42	7 51	8 1	—												
Kentish Town	5 48		6 33	6 46	6 53	—	7 13	—	7 31	7 44	7 53	8 3	—												
Chalk Farm	—	6 15	6 30	644	—	7 0	—	718	—	730	—	7 46	—	8 1											
Camden Town	5 35	5 50	6	2	6 19	6 33	6 35	646	6 49	6 55	7	3 7	7	8 7	15	720	7 23	732	7 33	7 46	7 48	7 55	8	6 8	3
Caledonian Road....	—	6	4	6 22	—	6 38	—	6 58	—	7 18	—	735	7 36	—	7 58	—									
Highbury	5 37	5 53	6	5 6	23	6 36	6 39	649	6 52	6 59	7	6 7	11	7 19	723	7 26	736	7 37	7 49	7 51	7 59	8	9 8	6
Canonbury	—	6	7	6 25	—	6 41	—	7 1	—	7 21	—	—	—	—	—	—									
Dalston Junction ..	5 40	5 56	6	11	6 28	6 39	6 44	652	6 55	7	4 7	9 7	14	7 24	726	7 29	739	7 41	7 52	7 54	8	4 8	12 8	9	
Broad Street	5 46	6	2	6 18	6 34	6 45	6 50	658	7	1 7	10	7 15	7 20	7 30	732	7 35	745	7 47	7 58	8	0 8	10	8 18	815	

WEEK DAYS.

WEEK DAYS.	AM	AM	AM	AM	AM	AM	AM	AM	AM	AM	AM	AM	AM	AM	AM	AM	AM	AM	AM	AM	AM	AM	AM	AM	AM	AM	AM
Richmond ......dep.	747	—	8	3	8	8	—	8 20	—	8	3 8	36	—	—	8	55	9	3	—								
Kew Gardens........	749	—	8	5	8 10	—	8 22	—	8	32	8 38	—	—	8	57	9	5	—									
Gunnersbury........	752	—	8	8	8 13	—	8 25	—	8	35	8 41	—	—	9	0	9	8	—									
Kew Bridge	—	—	—	—	8 16	—	8 30	—	—	—	8 48	—	—	—	—	—	—	9 10									
South Acton	755	—	8	11	8 17	8 20	—	8 27	—	8	32	8 37	—	8	50	—	9	2	—	9 12							
Acton	—	—	8	8 18	—	8 29	—	8	34	8 39	8 44	—	8	52	—	9	4	9 11	9 14								
Earl's Court.......	743	—	8	1	—	—	—	—	—	—	—	847	—	—	9	6	—									
Kensington (A. R.)..	748	—	8	1	—	8 16	—	—	8	29	—	—	851	—	—	8	59	—									
Uxbridge Road.....	750	—	8	7	—	8 17	—	—	8	33	—	—	852	—	—	9	0	—									
St. Quintin Park.....	753	—	8	10	—	—	—	—	8	36	—	—	856	—	—	9	10	—									
Willesden Jn.......	8 08	58	58	16	8 22	8 23	8 25	8 29	8 34	839	8 39	8 44	8 49	8 53	8	57	9	59	5	9	9 16	9 23	9 19				
Kensal Rise	8 28	6	—	8 18	—	8 27	—	8 36	—	8 41	8 46	—	8	59	—	9	11	—	9 21								
Brondesbury Park ..	—	8	8	—	—	—	8 31	—	8	43	8 48	—	9	1	—	9	13	—	9 23								
Brondesbury	—	8	8 21	—	8 29	8 32	—	8	44	8 49	8 53	9	2	—	9	9	9 14	9 24									
West End Lane	—	8 11	—	8 27	—	8 34	—	8	46	8 51	8 55	—	9	4	—	9 11	9 16	9 21	9 25								
Finchley Road	8 68	12	—	8 28	—	8 35	8 40	8	47	8 53	8 56	—	9	5	—	9 12	9 17	9 22	9 27								
Hampstead Heath ..	8 88	14	—	8 30	—	8 37	8 42	8	49	—	8 58	—	9	7	—	9 14	9 19	9 24	9 29								
Gospel Oak........	810 8	16	—	8 25	8 32	—	8 39	8 44	8	51	8 55	9	0	—	9	9	9 16	9 21	9 26	9 31							
Kentish Town	—	8 18	—	—	8 37	—	—	—	8	57	—	9	18	—	—	9 33										
Chalk Farm	—	8 16	—	8 34	—	—	849	—	—	—	9	18	—	—	—											
Camden Town	813 8	21	8 18	—	8 37	8 39	8 42	—	851	—	9	0	9	4	9	7	914	9	32	—						
Caledonian Road ..	—	8 24	—	—	—	—	—	—	—	9	3	—	—	916	9	20	9 24	—	9	34	9 26					
Highbury	8 16 8	23	8 21	—	8 42	8 45	—	854	—	9	4	—	—	—	9	24	—	9	37	9	40					
Canonbury	—	8 27	—	—	—	—	—	—	—	9	6	—	—	—	9	26	—	9	41							
Dalston Junction ..	819 8	30 8	24 8	34 8	41 8	45 8	48	—	858 9	0	9	9	9	9	14 9	19	9 22 9	29 9	31 9	36 9	40	9	44				
Broad Street	825 8	36 8	30 8	40 8	47 8	49 8	51 8	54 8	57 9	4 9	6 9	14 9	16 9	18 9	24 928	9	29 9	31 9	36 9	40 9	46 9	50				

WEEK DAYS.	AM	AM	AM	AM	AM	AM	AM	AM	AM	AM	AM	AM	AM	AM	AM	AM	AM	AM
Richmond ......dep.	9 17	—	—	9 28	—	—	—	9 53	—	10 8	10 23	—	10 38	10 52	—	11 8	11 23	—
Kew Gardens	9 19	—	—	9 30	—	—	—	9 55	—	10 10	10 25	—	10 40	10 54	—	11 10	11 25	—
Gunnersbury........	9 22	—	—	9 33	—	—	—	9 58	—	10 13	10 28	—	10 43	10 57	—	11 13	11 28	—
Kew Bridge	—	—	—	—	9 40	—	—	—	—	10 8	—	—	10 38	—	—	11 8	—	—
South Acton	—	—	—	—	9 42	—	—	10 0	—	10 15	10 30	—	10 45	11 0	—	11 15	11 30	—
Acton	9 25	9 30	—	9 36	9 44	—	—	10 2	—	10 17	10 32	—	10 47	11 2	—	11 17	11 32	—
Earl's Court	—	9 13	—	9 26	—	9 46	—	—	—	—	10 22	—	—	—	—	—	11 18	—
Kensington (A.R.) ..	—	9 18	—	9 31	—	9 51	—	—	—	—	10 26	—	—	—	—	—	11 22	—
Uxbridge Road	—	9 19	—	9 33	—	9 52	—	—	—	—	10 27	—	—	—	—	—	11 23	—
St. Quintin Park....	—	9 22	—	9 35	—	9 54	—	—	—	—	10 30	—	—	—	—	—	11 26	—
Willesden Jn.	—	9 34	9 35	9 41	9 49	10 4	10 6	10 7	1020	10 22	10 37	1050	10 52	11 7	1120	11 22	11 37	1150
Kensal Rise..........	9 31	9 36	—	—	9 51	—	—	10 9	—	10 24	10 39	—	10 54	11 9	—	11 24	11 39	—
Brondesbury Park ..	—	—	—	9 44	9 53	—	—	10 11	—	10 26	10 41	—	10 56	11 11	—	11 26	11 41	—
Brondesbury	—	9 38	—	—	9 54	—	—	10 12	—	10 27	10 42	—	10 57	11 12	—	11 27	11 42	—
West End Lane	9 35	9 40	—	—	9 56	—	—	10 14	—	10 29	10 44	—	10 59	11 14	—	11 29	11 44	—
Finchley Road......	9 36	9 41	—	9 47	9 57	—	—	10 15	—	10 30	10 45	—	11 0	11 15	—	11 30	11 45	—
Hampstead Heath..	9 38	—	—	9 49	9 59	—	—	10 17	—	10 32	10 47	—	11 2	11 17	—	11 32	11 47	—
Gospel Oak..........	9 40	—	—	9 51	10 1	—	—	10 19	—	10 34	10 49	—	11 4	11 19	—	11 34	11 49	—
Kentish Town	—	—	—	—	10 3	—	—	10 21	—	10 36	10 51	—	11 6	11 21	—	11 36	11 51	—
Chalk Farm	—	—	9 46	—	—	—	1016	—	1030	—	—	11 0	—	—	1130	—	—	12 0
Camden Town	—	9 46	9 48	—	10 5	—	1018	10 23	1032	10 38	10 53	11 2	11 8	11 23	1132	11 38	11 53	12 2
Caledonian Road....	—	—	—	—	10 8	—	—	10 26	—	—	10 56	—	—	11 26	—	—	11 56	—
Highbury	—	—	9 51	9 56	10 9	—	1021	10 27	1035	10 41	10 57	11 5	11 11	11 27	1135	11 41	11 57	12 5
Canonbury..........	—	—	—	—	10 11	—	—	10 29	—	—	10 59	—	—	11 29	—	—	11 59	—
Dalston Junction ...	—	—	9 54	9 59	10 14	—	1024	10 32	1038	10 44	11 2	11 8	11 14	11 32	1138	11 44	12 2	12 8
Broad Street.......	9 55	9 58	10 0	10 5	10 20	10 24	1030	10 38	1044	10 50	11 8	1114	11 20	11 38	1144	11 50	12 8	1214

WEEK DAYS.	AM	d	e	PM	d	PM	e	d	d	PM	d	d	PM	PM	d	e	d	PM
Richmond ......dep.	11 38	1150	11 53	d	—	—	12 8	1210	12 17	12 23	—	—	—	12 38	12 50	12 53	12 56	—
Kew Gardens........	11 40	1152	11 55	—	—	—	12 10	1212	12 19	12 25	—	—	—	12 40	12 52	12 56	12 58	—
Gunnersbury........	11 43	1155	11 58	—	—	—	12 13	1215	12 22	12 28	—	—	—	12 43	12 55	12 58	1 1	—
Kew Bridge	11 38	—	—	—	12 8	—	12 8	—	12 17	—	—	12 38	—	12 38	—	—	—	—
South Acton	11 45	1157	12 0	—	12 13	—	12 15	1217	12 24	12 30	—	12 40	—	12 45	12 57	1 0	1 3	—
Acton	11 47	1159	12 2	12 8	12 15	—	12 17	1219	12 26	12 32	1238	12 42	—	12 47	12 59	1 2	1 5	—
Earl's Court	—	—	—	—	—	12 4	—	—	—	12e13	—	12 31	—	—	—	—	—	1d 2
Kensington (A. R.)..	—	—	11 56	—	—	12 8	—	—	—	12 17	—	12 36	1236	—	—	—	—	1d 6
Uxbridge Road	—	—	—	—	—	12 9	—	—	—	12 18	—	12 37	1237	—	—	—	—	1d 7
St. Quintin Park....	—	—	—	—	—	1212	—	—	—	12e21	—	12 40	1240	—	—	—	—	1d10
Willesden Jn.	11 52	12 4	12 7	12 12	12 21	1220	12 22	1224	12 31	12 37	1242	12 47	1250	12 52	1 4	1 7	1 10	1 19
Kensal Rise	11 54	12 6	12 9	12 14	12 23	—	12 24	1226	12 34	12 39	1244	12 49	—	12 54	1 6	1 9	1 12	—
Brondesbury Park ..	11 56	12 8	12 11	—	—	—	12 26	1228	—	12 41	1246	—	—	12 56	1 8	1 11	—	—
Brondesbury	11 57	12 9	12 12	12 16	12 26	—	12 27	1229	12 36	12 42	1247	12 52	—	12 57	1 9	1 12	1 14	—
West End Lane	11 59	1211	12 14	—	12 28	—	12 29	1231	—	12 43	1249	12 54	—	12 59	1 11	1 14	—	—
Finchley Road	12 0	1212	12 15	12 19	—	—	12 30	1232	12 39	12 45	1250	12 55	—	1 0	1 12	1 15	1 16	—
Hampstead Heath ..	12 2	1214	12 17	12 21	—	—	12 32	1234	12 42	12 47	1252	12 57	—	1 2	1 14	1 17	1 18	—
Gospel Oak	12 4	1216	12 19	12 23	12 33	—	12 34	1236	12 46	12 49	1254	12 59	—	1 4	1 16	1 19	1 20	—
Kentish Town	12 6	1218	12 21	—	12 35	—	12 36	1238	—	12 51	1256	1 1	—	1 6	1 18	1 21	—	—
Chalk Farm	—	—	—	—	—	1230	—	—	—	—	—	—	1 0	—	—	—	—	1 30
Camden Town	12 8	1220	12 23	12 26	12 37	1232	12 38	1240	12 49	12 53	1258	1 4	1 2	1 8	1 20	1 23	1 23	1 32
Caledonian Road....	—	1223	12 26	—	12 40	—	—	—	—	12 56	—	1 7	—	—	—	1 26	1 26	—
Highbury	12 11	1224	12 27	12 29	12 41	1235	12 41	1244	12 52	12 57	1 1	1 8	1 5	1 11	1 23	1 27	1 27	1 35
Canonbury..........	—	1226	12 29	—	12 43	—	—	—	—	12 59	—	1 10	—	—	—	1 29	1 29	—
Dalston Junction ..	12 14	1229	12 32	12 32	12 46	1238	12 44	1248	12 56	1 2	1 4	1 13	1 8	1 15	1 26	1 32	1 32	1 38
Broad Street	12 20	1235	12 38	12 38	12 52	1244	12 50	1254	1 2	1 8	110	1 19	1 14	1 21	1 32	1 38	1 38	1 44

WEEK DAYS.	PM	d	PM	d	PM	PM	d	PM	PM	PM	PM	PM	PM	PM	PM	PM	PM	PM	PM	PM
Richmond ......dep.	1 8	—	1 23	1 30	—	1 38	—	1 53	—	2 8	2 23	—	2 38	2 53	—	3 8	3 23	—	3 38	3 53
Kew Gardens	1 10	—	1 25	1 32	—	1 40	—	1 55	—	2 10	2 25	—	2 40	2 55	—	3 10	3 25	—	3 40	3 55
Gunnersbury	1 13	—	1 28	1 35	—	1 43	—	1 58	—	2 13	2 28	—	2 43	2 58	—	3 13	3 28	—	3 43	3 58
Kew Bridge	1 8	—	—	—	—	1 38	1 50	—	—	2 8	—	—	2 38	—	—	3 8	—	—	3 38	—
South Acton	1 15	—	1 30	—	—	1 45	1 52	2 0	—	2 15	2 30	—	2 45	3 0	—	3 15	3 30	—	3 45	4 0
Acton	1 17	—	1 32	1 38	—	1 47	1 54	2 2	—	2 17	2 32	—	2 47	3 2	—	3 17	3 32	—	3 47	4 2
Earl's Court	—	—	1e17	1 26	—	—	—	—	1 58	—	—	2d25	2e37	—	3d 3	—	3e13	3d30	—	—
Kensington (A. R.)..	—	—	1e21	1 31	—	—	—	1 56	2 2	—	—	2d30	2e42	—	3d 8	—	3 26	3d35	—	—
Uxbridge Road	—	—	1e22	1 32	—	—	—	—	2 3	—	—	2d31	2e43	—	3d 9	—	3 27	3d36	—	—
St. Quintin Park ...	—	—	1e25	1 35	—	—	—	—	2 6	—	—	2d34	2e46	—	3d12	—	3 30	3d39	—	—
Willesden Jn........	1 22	1 36	1 37	1 43	1 49	1 52	1 59	2 7	2 19	2 22	2 37	2 49	2 52	3 7	3 20	3 22	3 37	3 50	3 52	4 7
Kensal Rise..........	1 24	—	1 39	1 45	—	1 54	—	2 9	—	2 24	2 39	—	2 54	3 9	—	3 24	3 39	—	3 54	4 9
Brondesbury Park ..	1 26	—	1 41	—	—	1 56	—	2 11	—	2 26	2 41	—	2 56	3 11	—	3 26	3 41	—	3 56	4 11
Brondesbury.........	1 27	—	1 42	1 48	—	1 57	—	2 12	—	2 27	2 42	—	2 57	3 12	—	3 27	3 42	—	3 57	4 12
West End Lane.....	1 29	—	1 44	1 50	—	1 59	—	2 14	—	2 29	2 44	—	2 59	3 14	—	3 29	3 44	—	3 59	4 14
Finchley Road	1 30	—	1 45	1 51	—	2 0	—	2 15	—	2 30	2 45	—	3 0	3 15	—	3 30	3 45	—	4 0	4 15
Hampstead Heath..	1 32	—	1 47	1 53	—	2 2	—	2 17	—	2 32	2 47	—	3 2	3 17	—	3 32	3 47	—	4 2	4 17
Gospel Oak	1 34	—	1 49	1 55	—	2 4	—	2 19	—	2 34	2 49	—	3 4	3 19	—	3 34	3 49	—	4 4	4 19
Kentish Town	1 36	—	1 51	—	—	2 6	—	2 21	—	2 36	2 51	—	3 6	3 21	—	3 36	3 51	—	4 6	4 21
Chalk Farm	—	1 47	—	—	2 0	—	—	—	2 30	—	—	3 0	—	—	3 30	—	—	4 0	—	—
Camden Town	1 38	1 49	1 53	1 58	2 2	2 8	—	2 23	2 32	2 38	2 53	3 2	3 8	3 23	3 32	3 38	3 53	4 2	4 8	4 23
Caledonian Road ...	—	—	1e56	2 0	—	—	—	2 26	—	—	2 56	—	—	3 26	—	—	3 56	—	—	4 26
Highbury	1 41	1 52	1 57	2 1	2 5	2 11	—	2 27	2 35	2 41	2 57	3 5	3 11	3 27	3 35	3 41	3 57	4 5	4 11	4 27
Canonbury..........	—	—	1e59	2 3	—	—	—	2 29	—	—	2 59	—	—	3 29	—	—	3 59	—	—	4 29
Dalston Junction ...	1 44	1 55	2 2	2 6	2 8	2 14	—	2 32	2 38	2 44	3 2	3 8	3 14	3 32	3 38	3 44	4 2	4 8	4 14	4 32
Broad Street.......	1 50	2 1	2 8	2 12	2 14	2 20	—	2 38	2 44	2 50	3 8	3 14	3 20	3 38	3 44	3 50	4 8	4 14	4 20	4 38

WEEK DAYS.	PM	e	PM	PM	PM	PM	e	d	e	e	PM	e	d	e	e	e	d	e	e	PM
Richmond ......dep.	—	—	4 10	4 23	—	4 38	4 50	4 53	4 56	—	—	—	5 8	—	5 12	5 20	5 23	—	5 33	—
Kew Gardens	—	—	4 12	4 25	—	4 40	4 52	4 55	4 58	—	—	—	5 10	—	5 14	5 22	5 25	—	5 35	—
Gunnersbury........	—	—	4 15	4 28	—	4 43	4 55	4 58	5 1	—	—	—	5 13	—	5 17	5 25	5 28	—	5 38	—
Kew Bridge	4e 8	—	4 8	—	—	4 38	—	—	—	5 5	—	—	5 8	5 12	—	—	—	5 32	—	—
South Acton	4e10	—	4 17	4 30	—	4 45	4 57	5 0	5 7	5 9	—	—	5 15	5 16	5 19	5 27	5 30	5 34	5 40	—
Acton	4e12	—	4 19	4 32	—	4 47	4 59	5 2	5 8	—	—	5 15	5 17	5 18	5 21	5 29	5 32	5 36	5 42	—
Earl's Court	4 3	—	—	—	4 33	—	4 46	—	—	—	—	—	5 2	5 2	—	—	—	5 26	—	—
Kensington (A.R.)..	4 7	—	—	—	4 38	—	4 52	—	—	—	—	—	5 8	5 8	—	5 17	5 17	5 31	—	—
Uxbridge Road......	4 8	—	—	—	4 39	—	4 53	—	—	—	—	—	5 9	5 9	—	5 18	5 18	5 32	—	—
St. Quentin Park ..	4 11	—	—	—	4 42	—	4 56	—	—	—	—	—	5 12	5 12	—	—	—	5 35	—	—
Willesden Junction	4 20	4 22	4 26	4 37	4 50	4 52	5 4	5 7	5 13	5 15	5 19	—	5 22	5 23	5 26	5 34	5 37	5 41	5 47	5 49
Kensal Rise	—	4 23	4 28	4 39	—	4 54	5 6	5 9	—	5 17	—	5 20	5 24	—	5 28	5 36	5 39	5 43	5 49	—
Brondesbury Park ..	—	4 25	4 30	4 41	—	4 56	5 8	5 11	—	—	—	—	5 26	—	5 30	5 38	5 41	5 45	—	—
Brondesbury	—	4 26	4 31	4 42	—	4 57	5 9	5 12	—	5 19	—	5 22	5 27	5 27	5 31	5 39	5 42	5 46	5 51	—
West End Lane	—	4 28	4 33	4 44	—	4 59	5 11	5 14	—	—	—	5 24	5 29	—	5 33	5 41	5 44	5 48	5 53	—
Finchley Road	—	4 29	4 34	4 45	—	5 0	5 12	5 15	—	—	—	5 26	5 30	—	5 34	5 42	5 45	5 49	5 54	—
Hampstead Heath..	—	4 31	4 36	4 47	—	5 2	5 14	5 17	—	—	—	5 28	5 32	—	5 36	5 44	5 47	5 51	5 56	—
Gospel Oak..........	—	4 33	4 38	4 49	—	5 4	5 16	5 19	—	5 24	—	5 30	5 34	—	5 38	5 46	5 49	5 53	5 58	—
Kentish Town	—	4 35	4 40	4 51	—	5 6	5 18	5 21	—	—	—	5 32	5 36	5 35	5 40	5 48	5 51	5 55	—	—
Chalk Farm	4 30	—	—	—	5 0	—	—	—	—	—	5 30	—	—	—	—	—	—	—	—	6 1
Camden Town	4 32	4 37	4 42	4 53	5 2	5 8	5 20	5 24	5 22	5 27	5 32	5 34	5 38	5 37	5 42	5 50	5 53	5 57	6 1	6 4
Caledonian Road....	—	—	—	4 56	—	—	—	5 26	5 25	—	—	—	—	5 40	—	5 53	5 56	—	—	—
Highbury	4 35	4 40	4 45	4 57	5 5	5 11	5 23	5 27	5 27	5 30	5 35	5 37	5 41	5 41	5 45	5 54	5 57	6 0	6 4	6 7
Canonbury	—	—	—	4 59	—	—	5 25	5 29	—	—	—	—	—	5 43	—	5 56	5 59	—	—	—
Dalston Junction ..	4 38	4 46	4 49	5 4	5 8	5 14	5 28	5 32	5 31	5 34	5 38	5 40	5 44	5 46	5 48	5 59	6 2	6 3	6 7	6 10
Broad Street	4 44	4 54	4 57	5 10	5 14	5 20	5 34	5 38	5 37	5 40	5 44	5 46	5 50	5 52	5 54	6 7	6 8	6 9	6 13	6 16

WEEK DAYS.	*d*	*e*	*e*	*d*	*e*	*e*	PM	PM	PM	PM	PM	PM	PM	PM	PM	PM	PM	PM	PM
Richmond ......dep.	5 38	—	5 50	553	—	5 58	—	6 8	6 23	—	6 38	6 53	—	7 8	7 23	—	7 38	7 53	—
Kew Gardens........	5 40	—	5 52	555	—	6 0	—	6 10	6 25	—	6 40	6 55	—	7 10	7 25	—	7 40	7 55	—
Gunnersbury........	5 43	—	5 55	558	—	6 3	—	6 13	6 28	—	6 43	6 58	—	7 13	7 28	—	7 43	7 58	—
Kew Bridge	5 38	5 45	—	—	—	—	—	6 8	6*20	—	6 38	—	—	7 8	—	—	7 38	—	—
South Acton	5 45	5 47	5 57	6 0	—	6 5	—	6 15	6 30	—	6 45	7 0	—	7 15	7 30	—	7 45	8 0	—
Acton	5 47	5 49	5 59	6 2	—	6 7	—	6 17	6 32	—	6 47	7 2	—	7 17	7 32	—	7 47	8 2	—
Earl's Court	5 26	—	5 48	548	—	—	—	—	6 10	—	6*29	6 46	7 0	—	—	7 27	—	7 49	—
Kensington (A. R.)..	5 31	—	5 53	553	—	5 59	5 59	—	6 14	—	6*33	6 49	7 6	—	—	7 32	—	7 52	—
Uxbridge Road......	5 32	—	5 54	554	—	6 0	6 0	—	6 15	—	6*35	6 51	7 7	—	—	7 33	—	7 54	—
St. Quintin Park....	5 35	—	5 57	557	—	—	—	—	6 18	—	6*38	6 54	7 10	—	—	7 36	—	7 57	—
Willesden Junction	5 52	5 54	6 4	6 7	6 10	6 12	6 19	6 22	6 37	6 53	6 52	7 7	7 19	7 22	7 37	7 50	7 52	8 7	8 20
Kensal Rise	5 54	5 56	6 6	6 9	—	6 14	—	6 24	6 39	—	6 54	7 9	—	7 24	7 39	—	7 54	8 9	—
Brondesbury Park ..	5 56	—	6 8	611	—	—	—	6 26	6 41	—	6 56	7 11	—	7 26	7 41	—	7 56	8 11	—
Brondesbury	5 57	5 58	6 9	612	—	6 17	—	6 27	6 42	—	6 57	7 12	—	7 27	7 42	—	7 57	8 12	—
West End Lane	5 59	—	6 11	614	—	—	—	6 29	6 44	—	6 59	7 14	—	7 29	7 44	—	7 59	8 14	—
Finchley Road	6 0	6 1	6 12	615	—	6 19	—	6 30	6 45	—	7 0	7 15	—	7 30	7 45	—	8 0	8 15	—
Hampstead Heath ..	6 2	6 3	6 14	617	—	6 21	—	6 32	6 47	—	7 2	7 17	—	7 32	7 47	—	8 2	8 17	—
Gospel Oak..........	6 4	6 5	6 16	619	—	6 23	—	6 34	6 49	—	7 4	7 19	—	7 34	7 49	—	8 4	8 19	—
Kentish Town	6 6	—	6 18	621	—	—	—	6 36	6 51	—	7 6	7 21	—	7 36	7 51	—	8 6	8 21	—
Chalk Farm	—	—	—	—	6 22	—	6 30	—	—	7 3	—	—	7 30	—	—	8 0	—	—	8 30
Camden Town	6 8	6 8	6 20	623	6 24	6 26	6 32	6 38	6 53	7 5	7 8	7 23	7 32	7 38	7 53	8 2	8 8	8 23	8 32
Caledonian Road ...	—	6 11	—	626	—	6 29	—	—	6 56	—	—	7 26	—	—	7 56	—	—	8 26	—
Highbury	6 11	6 12	6 23	627	6 27	6 30	6 35	6 41	6 57	7 8	7 11	7 27	7 35	7 41	7 57	8 5	8 11	8 27	8 35
Canonbury..........	—	6 14	—	629	—	6 32	—	—	6 59	—	—	7 29	—	—	7 59	—	—	8 29	—
Dalston Junction ..	6 14	6 17	6 26	632	6 30	6 35	6 38	6 44	7 2	7 11	7 14	7 32	7 38	7 44	8 2	8 8	8 14	8 32	8 38
Broad Street	6 20	6 23	6 32	638	6 36	6 41	6 44	6 50	7 8	7 17	7 20	7 38	7 44	7 50	8 8	8 14	8 20	8 38	8 44

WEEK DAYS.	PM	PM	PM	PM	PM	PM	PM	PM	PM	PM	PM	PM	PM	PM	PM	PM
Richmond ......dep.	8 8	8 23	—	8 38	8 53	—	9 8	9 23	—	9 38	9 53	10 8	—	10 23	10 53	11 6
Kew Gardens........	8 10	8 25	—	8 40	8 55	—	9 10	9 25	—	9 40	9 55	10 10	—	10 25	10 55	11 8
Gunnersbury........	8 13	8 28	—	8 43	8 58	—	9 13	9 28	—	9 43	9 58	10 13	—	10 28	10 58	11 11
Kew Bridge	8 8	—	—	8 38	—	—	9 8	—	—	9 38	—	10 3	10 23	—	—	—
South Acton	8 15	8 30	—	8 45	9 0	—	9 15	9 30	—	9 45	10 0	10 15	10 25	10 30	11 0	11 13
Acton	8 17	8 32	—	8 47	9 2	—	9 17	9 32	—	9 47	10 2	10 17	10 27	10 32	11 2	11 15
Earl's Court........	—	—	—	—	8 46	—	—	—	—	—	9 47	—	—	—	10 47	—
Kensington (A. R.)..	8 12	—	—	—	8 50	9 7	—	—	—	—	9 51	—	—	—	10 51	—
Uxbridge Road......	8 13	—	—	—	8 51	9 8	—	—	—	—	9 52	—	—	—	10 52	—
St. Quintin Park. ..	—	—	—	—	8 54	9 11	—	—	—	—	9 55	—	—	—	10 55	—
Willesden Junction	8 22	8 37	8 50	8 52	9 7	9 20	9 22	9 37	9 44	9 52	10 7	10 23	10 33	10 37	11 7	11 20
Kensal Rise	8 24	8 39	—	8 54	9 9	—	9 24	9 39	—	9 54	10 9	—	—	10 39	11 9	11 22
Brondesbury Park ..	8 26	8 41	—	8 56	9 11	—	9 26	9 41	—	9 56	10 11	—	—	10 41	11 11	11 24
Brondesbury	8 27	8 42	—	8 57	9 12	—	9 27	9 42	—	9 57	10 12	—	—	10 42	11 12	11 25
West End Lane	8 29	8 44	—	8 59	9 14	—	9 29	9 44	—	9 59	10 14	—	—	10 44	11 14	11 27
Finchley Road	8 30	8 45	—	9 0	9 15	—	9 30	9 45	—	10 0	10 15	—	—	10 45	11 15	11 28
Hampstead Heath ..	8 32	8 47	—	9 2	9 17	—	9 32	9 47	—	10 2	10 17	—	—	10 47	11 17	11 30
Gospel Oak..........	8 34	8 49	—	9 4	9 19	—	9 34	9 49	—	10 4	10 19	—	—	10 49	11 19	11 32
Kentish Town	8 36	8 51	—	9 6	9 21	—	9 36	9 51	—	10 6	10 21	—	—	10 51	11 21	11 34
Chalk Farm	—	—	9 0	—	—	9 30	—	—	9 54	—	—	—	—	—	—	—
Camden Town	8 38	8 53	9 2	9 8	9 23	9 32	9 38	9 53	9 57	10 8	10 23	—	—	10 53	11 23	11 36
Caledonian Road ..	—	8 56	—	—	9 26	—	—	9 56	—	—	—	—	—	—	—	—
Highbury	8 41	8 57	9 5	9 11	9 27	9 35	9 41	9 57	10 0	10 11	10 26	—	—	10 56	11 26	11 39
Canonbury..........	—	8 59	—	—	9 29	—	—	9 59	—	—	10 28	—	—	—	—	—
Dalston Junction ..	8 44	9 2	9 8	9 14	9 32	9 38	9 44	10 2	10 4	10 14	10 31	—	—	10 59	11 29	11 42
Broad Street	8 50	9 8	9 14	9 20	9 38	9 44	9 50	10 8	1010	10 20	10 37	—	—	11 5	11 35	11 48

d Saturdays only.
e Saturdays excepted.
* High Level Station.

SUNDAYS.	AM	AM	AM	AM	AM	AM	AM	AM	PM	PM	PM	PM	PM	PM	PM	PM	PM
Richmond ....dep	—	8 20	9 20	9 50	10 20	10 50	11 20	11 50	12 20	1250	1 20	150	2 20	2 35	2 50	3 5	320
Kew Gardens..........	—	8 22	9 22	9 52	10 22	10 52	11 22	11 52	12 22	1252	1 22	152	2 22	2 37	2 52	3 7	322
Gunnersbury	—	8 25	9 25	9 55	10 25	10 55	11 25	11 55	12 25	1255	1 25	155	2 25	2 40	2 55	3 10	325
Kew Bridge	—	—	—	—	—	—	—	—	—	—	—	—	—	—	—	—	320
South Acton	—	8 27	9 27	9 57	10 27	10 57	11 27	11 57	12 27	1257	1 27	157	2 27	2 42	2 57	3 12	327
Acton	—	8 29	9 29	9 59	10 29	10 59	11 29	11 59	12 29	1259	1 29	159	2 29	2 44	2 59	3 14	329
Earl's Court	—	—	—	—	—	—	—	—	—	—	—	—	—	—	—	—	—
Kensington (A. R.) ..	—	—	—	—	—	—	—	—	—	—	—	—	—	—	—	—	—
Uxbridge Road........	—	—	—	—	—	—	—	—	—	—	—	—	—	—	—	—	—
St. Quintin Park	—	—	—	—	—	—	—	—	—	—	—	—	—	—	—	—	—
Willesden Junction*	—	8 34	9 34	10 4	10 34	11 4	11 34	12 4	12 34	1 4	1 34	2 4	2 34	2 49	3 4	3 19	334
Kensal Rise	—	8 36	9 36	10 6	10 36	11 6	11 36	12 6	12 36	1 6	1 36	2 6	2 36	2 51	3 6	3 21	336
Brondesbury Park	—	8 38	9 38	10 8	10 38	11 8	11 38	12 8	12 38	1 8	1 38	2 8	2 38	2 53	3 8	3 23	338
Brondesbury	—	8 39	9 39	10 9	10 39	11 9	11 39	12 9	12 39	1 9	1 39	2 9	2 39	2 54	3 9	3 24	339
West End Lane	—	8 41	9 41	10 11	10 41	11 11	11 41	12 11	12 41	1 11	1 41	211	2 41	2 56	3 11	3 26	341
Finchley Road........	—	8 42	9 42	10 12	10 42	11 12	11 42	12 12	12 42	1 12	1 42	212	2 42	2 57	3 12	3 27	342
Hampstead Heath	—	8 44	9 44	10 14	10 44	11 14	11 44	12 14	12 44	1 14	1 44	214	2 44	2 59	3 14	3 29	344
Gospel Oak	—	8 46	9 46	10 16	10 46	11 16	11 46	12 16	12 46	1 16	1 46	216	2 46	3 1	3 16	3 31	346
Kentish Town	—	8 48	9 48	10 18	10 48	11 18	11 48	12 18	12 48	1 18	1 48	218	2 48	3 3	3 18	3 33	348
Chalk Farm	—	—	—	—	—	—	—	—	—	—	—	—	—	—	—	—	—
Camden Town	8 0	8 50	9 50	10 20	10 50	11 20	11 50	12 20	12 50	1 20	1 50	220	2 50	3 5	3 20	3 35	350
Caledonian Road	8 2	8 53	9 53	10 23	10 53	11 23	11 53	12 23	12 53	1 23	1 53	223	2 53	3 8	3 23	3 38	353
Highbury	8 3	8 54	9 54	10 24	10 54	11 24	11 54	12 24	12 54	1 24	1 54	224	2 54	3 9	3 24	3 39	354
Canonbury............	8 5	8 56	9 56	10 26	10 56	11 26	11 56	12 26	12 56	1 26	1 56	226	2 56	3 11	3 26	3 41	356
Dalston Junction	8 8	8 59	9 59	10 29	10 59	11 29	11 59	12 29	12 59	1 29	1 59	229	2 59	3 14	3 29	3 44	359
Broad Street	814	9 5	10 5	10 35	11 5	11 35	12 5	12 35	1 5	1 35	2 5	235	3 5	3 20	3 35	3 50	4 5

SUNDAYS.	PM		PM	PM	PM	PM	PM	PM	PM	PM	PM
Richmond ....dep.	3 35		9 5	920	935	—	950	10 5	1020	1035	1050
Kew Gardens..........	3 37		9 7	922	937	—	952	10 7	1022	1037	1052
Gunnersbury	3 40		9 10	925	940	—	955	1010	1025	1040	1055
Kew Bridge	—		—	920	—	950	—	—	—	—	—
South Acton	3 42		9 12	927	942	952	957	1012	1027	1042	1057
Acton	3 44		9 14	929	944	954	959	1014	1029	1044	1059
Earl's Court	—		—	—	—	—	—	—	—	—	—
Kensington (A. R.)....	—		—	—	—	—	—	—	—	—	—
Uxbridge Road........	—		—	—	—	—	—	—	—	—	—
St. Quintin Park......	—		—	—	—	—	—	—	—	—	—
Willesden Junction*	3 49		9 19	934	949	10 0	10 4	1019	1034	1049	11 4
Kensal Rise	3 51	Then at same minutes past each hour until	9 21	936	951	—	10 6	1021	1036	1051	11 6
Brondesbury Park	3 53		9 23	938	953	—	10 8	1023	1038	1053	11 8
Brondesbury	3 54		9 24	939	954	—	10 9	1024	1039	1054	11 9
West End Lane	3 56		9 26	941	956	—	1011	1026	1041	1056	1111
Finchley Road	3 57		9 27	942	957	—	1012	1027	1042	1057	1112
Hampstead Heath	3 59		9 29	944	959	—	1014	1029	1044	1059	1114
Gospel Oak............	4 1		9 31	946	10 1	—	1016	1031	1046	11 1	1116
Kentish Town	4 3		9 33	948	10 3	—	1018	1033	1048	11 3	1118
Chalk Farm	—		—	—	—	—	—	—	—	—	—
Camden Town	4 5		9 35	950	10 5	—	1020	1035	1050	11 5	1120
Caledonian Road......	4 8		9 38	953	10 8	—	1023	—	—	—	—
Highbury	4 9		9 39	954	10 9	—	1024	1038	1053	11 8	1123
Canonbury	4 11		9 41	956	1011	—	1026	—	—	—	—
Dalston Junction	4 14		9 44	959	1014	—	1029	1041	1056	1111	1126
Broad Street	4 20		9 50	10 5	1020	—	1035	1047	11 2	1117	11 [illegible]

WEEK DAYS.	g	AM	AM	AM	AM	AM	AM	AM	AM	AM	AM	AM	AM	d	AM	d
Moorgate Street dep.	—	—	—	—	—	—	—	—	7 54	8 43	9 18	9 47	10 13	—	—	—
King's + (Met.)	—	—	—	—	—	—	—	—	8 2	8 51	9 26	9 55	10 21	—	—	—
St. Pancras	12 25	2 35	4 15	5 0	5 53	6 48	—	—	7 53	—	8 50	9 30	—	—	11 48	—
Kentish Town	12 32	2 41	4 22	5 7	5 59	6 55	—	7 38	7 59	8 15	9 0	9 39	10 4	10 40 11 30	11 57	12 20
Junction Road	—	—	—	6 2	7 1	7 18	7 43	8 6	8 21	9 5	9 44	10 8	10 44 11 35	12 2	12 25
Upper Holloway	12 38	2 45	—	5 13	6 4	7 3	7 20	7 45	8 8	8 23	9 7	9 46	10 10 10 46	11 38	12 4	12 27
Hornsey Road	—	—	—	6 6	6 7	5 7	22	—	8 10	8 25	9 9	—	10 12 10 48	—	12 6	12 29
Crouch Hill	—	—	—	6 8	8 7	7 7	24	7 48	8 12	8 27	9 11	9 50	10 14 10 50 11 42	12 8	12 31
Harringay Park	12 46	2 53	4 35	5 19	6 12	7 11	7 27	7 51	8 15	8 30	9 14	9 53	10 17 10 53 11 46	12 12	12 35
St. Ann's Road	12 49	2 56	4 38	5 22	6 15	7 14	7 30	—	8 18	8 33	9 17	—	10 21 10 56	—	12 15	12 38
South Tottenham	12 52	2 59	4 41	5 25	6 18	7 17	7 34	7 55	8 21	8 36	9 20	9 57	10 24 10 59 11 53	12 18	12 41
Black Horse Road	12 56	3 3	4 45	5 31	6 22	7 21	7 38	7 59	8 25	8 40	9 24	10 1	10 28 11 3 11 57	12 22	12 45
Walthamstow	12 59	3 6	4 48	5 34	6 25	7 24	7 41	8 2	8 28	8 43	9 27	10 4	10 31 11 6 12 0	12 25	12 48
Leyton	1 2	3 9	4 51	5 37	6 28	7 27	7 44	8 5	8 31	8 46	9 30	10 8	10 34 11 9 12 3	12 28	12 51
Leytonstone	1 5	3 12	5 55	5 40	6 31	7 30	7 47	8 8	8 34	8 49	9 33	10 11	10 37 11 12 12 6	12 31	12 54
Wanstead Park	1 9	3 16	5 0	5 45	6 36	7 35	7 52	8 12	8 38	8 53	9 37	10 16	10 41 11 16 12 11	12 36	12 59
Woodgrange Park	1 12	—	5 49	6 41	7 40	7 56	8 16	8 41	8 57	9 41	10 22	10 46 11 20 12 15	12 40	1 4
East Ham	—	—	5 11	5 53	6 46	—	8 0	8 20	—	9 1	—	10 50 11 25	—	12 45	—
Barking	—	—	—	—	7 45	—	8 0	8 20	—	9 45	10 23	—	—	—	1 9

WEEK DAYS.	PM	d	PM	d	PM	d	PM	d	PM	e	PM	e	PM	e	PM	e
Moorgate Street dep.	—		12 50	12 58	1 47	1 50	2 11		—		—		4 50	5 4	5 17	5 27	5 43
King's + (Met.)	—		12 58		1 6	1 25	1 58	2 19		—		—		4 58	5 12	5 25	5 35	5 52
St. Pancras	12 20	—	1 4	1 13	—	2 15	—	2 50	3 25	3 55	4 35	—	5 12	—	—	5 45
Kentish Town	12 29	1 0	1 10	1 20	1 34	2 6	2 30	2 47	2 56	3 33	4 5	4 41	5 5	5 21	5 34	5 43	6 0
Junction Road	12 36	—	1 15	1 30	1 39	2 13	2 37	—	3 39	4 10	4 46	5 10	—	5 39	5 48
Upper Holloway	12 38	1 5	1 17	1 32	1 41	2 15	2 39	2 52	3 3	3 41	4 12	4 48	5 12	5 27	5 41	5 50
Hornsey Road	—		1 19	1 34	1 43	2 17	2 41	—	3 43	4 14	4 50	5 14	—	5 43	5 52
Crouch Hill	12 43	1 9	1 21	1 36	1 45	2 19	2 43	2 56	3 7	3 45	4 16	4 52	5 16	—	5 45	5 54
Harringay Park	12 47	1 13	1 25	1 40	1 49	2 23	2 47	2 59	3 12	3 48	4 20	4 56	5 19	5 33	5 49	5 58
St. Ann's Road	—		1 28	1 43	1 52	2 26	2 50	—	3 51	4 23	4 59	5 22	—	5 52	6 1
South Tottenham	12 52	1 17	1 32	1 46	1 56	2 30	2 54	3 5	3 17	3 54	4 26	5 2	5 25	5 37	5 55	6 4	6 12
Black Horse Road	12 56	1 22	1 36	1 51	2 0	2 34	2 58	3 9	3 21	3 58	4 30	5 7	5 29	5 41	5 59	6 8	6 16
Walthamstow	12 59	1 26	1 39	1 54	2 3	2 37	3 1	3 12	3 24	4 1	4 35	5 10	5 32	5 44	6 2	6 11	6 19
Leyton	1 2	1 29	1 42	1 57	6 2	4 13	5 3	3 15	3 27	4 4	4 36	5 13	5 35	5 47	6 5	6 14	6 22
Leytonstone	1 6	1 34	1 45	—	2 9	2 44	3 8	3 18	3 30	4 7	4 39	5 16	5 38	5 50	6 8	6 17	6 25
Wanstead Park	1 11	1 39	1 50	—	2 14	2 49	3 13	3 22	3 35	4 11	4 44	5 20	5 42	5 54	6 13	6 21	6 30
Woodgrange Park	1 17	1 45	1 54	—	2 18	2 52	3 17	3 26	3 39	4 14	4 48	5 25	5 46	6 0	6 17	6 26	6 35
East Ham	—		—		2 23	—	3 22	—	—	4 20	4 53	—	—	6 22	—	6 43
Barking	1 25	—	2 0	—	—	—	3 45	—	—	5 31	5 51	6 5	—	6 31	—

WEEK DAYS.	PM	e	PM	PM	PM	PM	PM
Moorgate Street dep.	—	6 15	—	—	—	—	—
King's + (Met.)	—	6 23	—	—	—	—	—
St. Pancras	6ᵈ 0	—	6 40	7 37	8 33	9 25	10 30 11 25
Kentish Town	6 6	6 30	6 46	7 44	8 40	9 31	10 40 11 32
Junction Road	6 11	6 35	—	7 49	8 46	9 35	10 47 —
Upper Holloway	6 13	6 37	6 50	7 51	8 48	9 37	10 49 11 37
Hornsey Road	6 15	6 39	—	7 53	8 50	9 39	10 51 11 39
Crouch Hill	6 17	6 41	—	7 55	8 52	9 41	10 53 11 41
Harringay Park	6 21	6 45	6 54	7 58	8 55	9 44	10 56 11 45
St. Ann's Road	6 24	6 48	—	8 1	8 58	9 47	10 59 11 48
South Tottenham	6 27	6 49	6 58	8 4	9 1	9 50	11 3 11 52
Black Horse Road	6 31	6 53	7 2	8 9	9 5	9 54	11 7 11 56
Walthamstow	6 34	6 56	7 5	8 11	9 8	9 57	11 10 12 0
Leyton	6 37	7 0	7 8	8 14	9 11	10 0	11 13 12 3
Leytonstone	6 40	—	7 11	8 17	9 15	10 3	11 17 12 6
Wanstead Park	6 44	—	7 15	8 22	9 20	10 7	11 22 12 10
Woodgrange Park	6 47	—	7 20	8 26	9 25	10 11	11 26 12 13
East Ham	6 53	—	—	8 30	—	10 15	— —
Barking	—	—	7 27	—	9 30	—	11 31 —

d Saturdays only.
e Saturdays excepted.
g Mondays excepted.
h Mondays and Saturdays only.

SUNDAYS	AM	AM	AM	AM	AM	PM
Moorgate Street dep.	—	—	—	—	—	—
King's + (Met.)	—	—	—	—	—	—
St. Pancras	12 25	6 10	8 6	9 10	10 10	10 20
Kentish Town	12 32	6 17	8 12	9 17	10 17	10 27
Junction Road	—	6 22	8 17	9 22	10 22	10 32
Upper Holloway	12 38	6 24	8 19	9 24	10 24	10 34
Hornsey Road	—	6 26	8 21	9 26	—	10 36
Crouch Hill	—	6 28	8 23	9 28	10 28	10 38
Harringay Park	12 46	6 32	8 27	9 32	10 32	10 42
St. Ann's Road	12 49	6 35	8 30	9 35	—	10 45
South Tottenham	12 52	6 39	8 33	9 38	10 39	10 48
Black Horse Road	12 56	6 43	8 37	9 42	10 43	10 52
Walthamstow	12 59	6 46	8 40	9 45	10 46	10 55
Leyton	1 2	6 49	8 43	9 48	10 49	10 58
Leytonstone	1 5	6 52	8 46	9 51	10 52	11 1
Wanstead Park	1 9	6 56	8 51	9 56	10 57	11 6
Woodgrange Park	1 12	7 1	8 55	10 0	11 3	11 10
East Ham	—	7 6	9 0	—	—	11 15
Barking	—	7 27	—	10 5	11 8	—

Extra trains leave St. Pancras, 10.40, 11.40 A.M., 1.10, 2.10, 3.10, 3.40, 5.10, 6.10, 6.40, 7.40, 8.38 and 9.40 P.M. stopping all stations to East Ham.

BARKING & EAST HAM TO ST. PANCRAS & MOORGATE ST.

WEEK DAYS	AM	AM	AM	AM	AM	AM	AM	AM	AM	AM	AM	AM	AM	AM	AM	AM
Barking dep.	—	—	—	—	—	—	—	—	7 58	—	—	—	—	—	—	9 7
East Ham	—	—	5 43	6 16	—	—	7 0	7 30	—	—	8 13	8 30	—	—	—
Woodgrange Park	—	—	5 49	6 23	6 45	—	7 5	7 37	—	7 57	8 6	8 20	8 36	8 47	9 13
Wanstead Park	2 45	3 39	4 55	5 52	6 27	6 49	—	7 10	7 41	—	8 1	8 11	8 24	8 40	8 52	9 18
Leytonstone	2 49	3 43	4 58	5 56	6 31	6 53	—	7 14	7 45	—	8 5	8 15	8 28	8 44	8 56	9 22
Leyton	2 52	3 46	5 1	5 59	6 34	6 56	7 3	7 17	7 48	8 3	8 8	8 18	8 31	8 47	8 59	9 26
Walthamstow	2 56	3 50	5 5	6 3	6 38	7 1	7 8	7 22	7 52	8 7	8 12	8 22	8 35	8 51	9 3	9 30
Black Horse Road	2 59	3 53	5 8	6 6	6 41	7 5	7 12	7 25	7 55	8 10	8 15	8 25	8 38	8 54	9 6	9 34
South Tottenham	3 5	3 59	5 13	6 11	6 47	7 10	7 16	7 30	8 1	8 15	8 21	—	8 44	8 59	9 11	9 39
St. Ann's Road	—	4 1	5 15	6 13	6 49	7 12	7 19	7 32	8 3	—	—	—	8 48	9 1	9 13	9 41
Harringay Park	3 10	4 4	5 18	6 16	6 52	7 15	7 23	7 35	8 6	8 19	8 26	—	8 51	9 3	9 16	9 44
Crouch Hill	—	—	5 20	6 19	6 55	7 18	7 25	7 38	8 9	—	—	—	8 54	9 6	9 18	9 46
Hornsey Road	—	—	—	6 21	6 57	7 20	7 27	7 40	8 11	—	—	—	8 56	9 8	9 20	9 48
Upper Holloway	3 16	4 11	5 25	6 23	7 0	7 22	7 29	7 42	8 14	8 24	—	8 35	8 59	9 10	9 22	9 50
Junction Road	—	—	5 27	6 26	7 2	—	7 31	7 44	8 16	—	—	—	9 1	9 12	9 24	9 52
Kentish Town	3 24	4 19	5 32	6 30	7 10	7 30	7 38	7 49	8 22	8 30	8 33	8 41	9 7	9 16	9 30	10 0
St. Pancras	3 30	4 25	5 40	6 37	7 15	7 37	7 45	—	8 35	8 40	—	8 47	9 25	—	9 38	10 10
King's + (Met.)	—	—	—	—	—	7 38	—	7 56	8 30	8 37	—	8 55	9 14	9 32	9 48	—
Moorgate Street	—	—	—	—	—	7 48	—	8 4	8 38	8 45	—	—	9 22	9 40	9 56	—

WEEK DAYS.	AM	AM	AM	AM	PM	PM	d	d	PM	PM	PM	d	PM	d	PM	e	PM	PM	PM
Barking.........dep.	—	10 20	—	—	12 48	—	1 30	2 0	2 15	—	—	—	4 20	4 36	—	—	5 43	—	657
East Ham	938	—	11	3 11	48	—	1 12	—	—	2	58	3 33	—	—	—	4	50	5 4	—	632	—
Woodgrange Park....	943	10 26	11	9 11	55	12 55	1 18	1 36	2 6	2 20	3	4 3	40	4 20	4 25	4 43	4 57	5 10	5 50	639	—
Wanstead Park	946	10 29	11	12 12	0	1 0	1 22	1 39	2 9	2 24	3	9 3	44	4 25	4 30	4 47	5	1 5	14 5	54	643	—
Leytonstone	950	10 33	11	16 12	5	1 4	1 26	1 43	2 13	2 28	3	13 3	48	4 28	4 34	4 51	5	5 5	18 5	58	647	7 7
Leyton	953	10 36	11	19 12	8	1 7	1 29	1 46	2 16	2 31	3	16 3	51	4 31	4 37	4 54	5	8 5	21 6	1	650	712
Walthamstow	957	10 40	11	23 12	12	1 11	1 32	1 50	2 20	2 35	3	20 3	55	4 34	4 41	4 57	5	12 5	25 6	5	654	—
Black Horse Road....	10 0	10 43	11	26 12	15	1 15	1 36	1 53	2 23	2 38	3	23 3	58	4 37	4 45	5 0	5	16 5	29 6	—	657	—
South Tottenham	10 5	10 48	11	31 12	20	1 21	1 43	1 59	2 29	2 44	3	28 4	3	4 44	4 51	5 5	5	22 5	34 6	14	7 2	720
St. Ann's Road:......	10 7	10 50	11	33 12	22	—	1 44	2 1	2 31	2 46	3	30 4	5	4 46	—	5 8	5	23 5	36 6	16	7 4	—
Harringay Park	10 9	10 53	11	36 12	25	1 26	1 47	2 4	2 34	2 49	3	34 4	8	4 49	4 55	5 11	5	26 5	39 6	19	7 7	—
Crouch Hill	1012	10 56	11	39 12	28	1 29	1 50	2 7	2 37	2 52	3	37 4	11	4 51	4 58	5 14	5	29 5	42 6	22	710	—
Hornsey Road	1014	10 58	11	41 12	30	—	1 52	2 9	2 39	2 54	3	39 4	13	4 53	—	5 16	5	31 5	44 6	24	712	—
Upper Holloway	1016	11	1 11	44 12	33	1 34	1 55	2 12	2 42	2 57	3	42 4	16	4 56	5	2 5	19 5	34 5	47 6	27	714	730
Junction Road	1018	11	3 11	46 12	35	—	1 57	2 14	2 44	2 59	3	44 4	18	4 58	5	4 5	22 5	36 5	49 6	29	716	—
Kentish Town	1022	11	8 11	50 12	44	1 42	2	2 20	2 50	3	6 3	51	4 23	5 4	5	18 5	27 5	45 5	53 6	32	723	738
St. Pancras	1031	11 16	—	12 51	1 48	2 15	—	3	14 3	58	4 33	—	5	23	—	5 50	6	5 6	50	728	745
King's + (Met.)	—	—	12 35	1 0	—	—	—	—	—	—	—	—	—	538	—	—	—	—	—
Moorgate Street	—	—	12 43	1 8	—	—	—	—	—	—	—	—	—	546	—	—	—	—	—

WEEK DAYS.	d	PM	e	PM	PM	PM	PM
Barking ....dep.	7 6	—	8 13	—	9 48	—	11 38
East Ham	—	7 20	—	8 48	—	10 30	—
Woodgrange Park	715	7 27	8 20	8 55	9 56	10 35	11 46
Wanstead Park.......	719	7 31	8 24	8 59	10 1	10 39	11 49
Leytonstone	723	7 35	8 28	9 3	10 5	10 43	11 52
Leyton	726	7 38	8 31	9 6	10 8	10 46	11 55
Walthamstow	730	7 42	8 35	9 10	10 12	10 50	11 58
Black Horse Road	733	7 47	8 38	9 15	10 15	10 53	12 1
South Tottenham	739	7 52	8 43	9 21	10 20	10 59	12 5
St. Ann's Road	741	7 55	8 45	9 23	10 22	11 1	12 7
Harringay Park	745	7 57	8 48	9 26	10 25	11 4	12 11
Crouch Hill............	748	8 0	8 51	9 29	10 28	11 7	—
Hornsey Road	750	8 2	8 53	9 31	10 30	11 9	—
Upper Holloway	753	8 7	8 56	9 35	10 33	11 12	12 18
Junction Road	755	8 9	8 58	9 38	10 35	11 14	—
Kentish Town	8 0	8 17	9 2	9 45	10 45	11 22	12 23
St. Pancras	—	8 25	—	9 50	10 53	11 29	—
King's + (Met.)	—	—	—	—	—	—	—
Moorgate Street.....	—	—	—	—	—	—	—

MILNERS' SAFES.

SUNDAYS.	AM	AM	AM	AM	PM
Barking ....dep.	—	7 44	9 20	10 20	10 50
East Ham	—	7 55	9 25	10 25	10 55
Woodgrange Park	4 59	7 59	9 29	10 29	10 59
Wanstead Park	5 2	8 3	9 33	10 33	11 3
Leytonstone	5 7	8 6	9 36	10 36	11 6
Leyton	5 11	8 10	9 40	10 40	11 10
Walthamstow	5 14	8 13	9 43	10 43	11 13
Black Horse Road.....	5 20	8 19	9 48	10 49	11 19
South Tottenham	5 22	8 21	9 50	10 51	11 21
St. Ann's Road.......	5 25	8 24	9 53	10 54	11 24
Harringay Park	5 28	8 27	9 56	10 57	11 27
Crouch Hill	5 30	8 29	9 58	10 59	11 29
Hornsey Road	5 33	8 32	10 1	11 2	11 32
Upper Holloway	5 35	8 35	10 4	11 5	11 35
Junction Road	5 42	8 42	10 12	11 12	11 40
Kentish Town	5 48	8 48	10 19	11 18	—
St. Pancras	—	—	—	—	—
King's + (Met.)	—	—	—	—	—
Moorgate Street.....	—	—	—	—	—

And 11.50 A.M., 12.50, 2.20, 3.50,
4.20, 5.8, 5.20, 6.20, 7.20, 7.50, 9.20,
10.20 P.M., from East Ham to
St. Pancras, stopping all Stations, and at 8.15 P.M. from
Barking. Not stopping at St.
Ann's Road or Hornsey Road.

MOORGATE ST. & ST. PANCRAS TO RADLETT & NAPSBURY.

WEEK DAYS.	AM	AM	AM	AM	AM	AM	AM	AM	AM	AM	AM	AM	PM	d	PM	d	PM	d
Moorgate Street dep.	—	—	—	—	—	8 10	—	9 33	—	—	—	—	—	1230	12 58	—
King's + (Met.)	—	—	—	—	—	8 18	—	9 41	—	—	—	—	—	1258	1 6	—
St. Pancras	5 30	6 0	6 25	7 15	7 30	8 0	8 30	8 50	925	9 55	10 45	11 48	12 33	1242	1 8	—	1 13	1 33
Kentish Town ....dep.	5 37	6 6	6 31	7 2	7 56	—	8 36	8 56	—	10	2 10	51 11	54 12	39	—	—	1 6	1 19	—
Finchley Road	5 43	6 11	—	7 27	—	8 43	—	—	10	11 11	2 12	2	—	—	—	—	—
West Hampstead	5 47	6 14	—	7 31	7 42	—	8 47	—	—	10	14 11	5 12	6	—	—	1 24	—
Cricklewood	5 52	6 19	6 39	7 36	7 49	—	8 52	—	—	10	18 11	7 12	7 12	48	—	—	1 30	—
Hendon	5 56	6 24	6 44	7 41	7 55	—	8 57	—	—	10	24 11	12 12	14 12	54	—	—	1 35	—
Mill Hill	—	6 31	6 49	7 46	8 1	8 17	9 2	9 11	—	10	30 11	17 12	19 1	0	—	1 24	1 40	1 50
Elstree	—	6 38	6 56	7 53	8 8	8 24	9 9	9 18	—	10	37 11	24 12	26 1	7	1 3	—	1 31	1 47	1 58
Radlett	—	6 44	7	2 7	58 8	14 8	30 9	14 9	24	950	10 45	11	30 12	32	1 13	—	1 32	1 37	1 53	—
Napsbury	—	—	—	8 20	—	—	9 30	—	—	11	36 12	38	—	—	1 43	1 59	—

WEEK DAYS.	AM	PM	PM	PM	PM	e	PM	e	e	PM	PM	PM	PM	PM	AM
Moorgate Street dep.	130	—	2 11	—	—	4 50	511	537	—	6 2	—	6 15	—	—	—
King's + (Met.)	138	—	2 19	—	—	4 58	519	545	—	6 10	—	6 23	—	—	—
St. Pancras	145	2 0	2 35	355	440	445	5 12	—	6 2	—	6 10	645	6 50	720	8 8	918	1015	1035	1135	12 7
Kentish Town ....dep.	—	2 4	4 1	—	451	5 18	526	555	—	6 18	6 18	—	6 56	727	8 15	924	1022	—	1142	—
Finchley Road	—	2 46	4	—	—	—	—	—	—	—	—	7	0	—	8 21	929	—	—	—
West Hampstead	—	2 50	410	—	5	5	5 24	—	—	—	—	7	4 732	8 24	933	1030	—	—	—
Cricklewood	157	2 56	415	—	5	0 5	29	537	—	6 29	6 30	—	7 9 737	8 30	938	1035	1048	1152	—
Hendon	2 2	215	3	2 420	—	5	5 5	34	542	—	6 34	6 36	—	7 15 743	8 35	943	1039	1053	1157	1222
Mill Hill	2 7	220	3	7 425	—	510	5	39 547	610	620	6 40	6 40	7 1	7 20 747	8 40	948	—	1059	12 2	1227
Elstree	214	227	3	14 432	—	517	5	46 554	617	627	6 43	6 47	—	7 28 754	8 47	955	—	11 6	12 9	1234
Radlett	221	233	3	20 433	5	523	5	52 6	0	—	634	6 47	6 53	715	7 34 8 0	8 53	10 1	—	1112	1215	1240
Napsbury	—	—	3	26 444	—	—	6	6	—	—	6	59 6	59	—	—	8 59	—	—	—	—

d Saturdays only. *e* Saturdays excepted. *g* Monday mornings excepted. *k* Wednesdays only.

WEEK DAYS.	AM	AM	AM	AM	AM	AM	AM	AM	AM	AM	AM	AM	AM	AM	AM
Napsbury ....dep.	—	—	—	—	—	—	—	—	8 22	8 45	—	—	—	10 25	—
Radlett	—	—	6 52	7 33	—	7 49	8 5	8-27	8 40	9 51	9 0	9 29	9 40	10 31	11 17
Elstree	—	—	7 1	7 41	—	7 57	8 13	8 35	8 48	8 59	9 8	—	9 48	10 39	11 25
Mill Hill...............	—	—	7 7	7 47	—	8 4	8 19	8 42	8 54	9 5	9 14	—	9 54	10 45	11 31
Hendon	5 25	6 28	7 14	7 54	—	8 11	8 27	8 48	9 0	—	9 20	—	10 1	10 51	—
Cricklewood	5 30	6 33	7 19	7 59	—	8 16	—	—	9 5	—	9 25	—	10 6	10 56	—
West Hampstead.....	5 34	6 37	—	—	—	8 20	—	—	—	—	9 29	—	—	11 0	—
Finchley Road	5 37	6 40	—	—	—	8 23	—	—	—	—	9 32	—	—	11 3	—
Kentish Town	5 44	6 47	7 32	8 9	8 22	8 30	—	9 0	9 14	9 20	9 40	—	10 15	11 11	11 45
St. Pancras	5 46	6 52	7 37	8 15	8 28	8 35	8 40	—	—	9 25	—	9 50	10 22	11 16	11 50
King's + (Met.)	—	—	—	—	8 30	8 37	8 47	9 6	9 22	—	9 48	—	—	—	—
Moorgate Street.....	—	—	—	—	8 38	8 45	8 55	9 14	9 30	—	9 56	—	—	—	—

WEEK DAYS.	PM	PM	PM	PM	PM	PM	PM	PM	PM	PM	PM	PM	PM	PM	PM	PM
Napsbury ....dep.	—	—	—	2 1	—	—	—	4 22	5 16	—	—	6 45	—	8 40	—	—
Radlett	—	12 26	1 10	2 7	2 50	2 55	3 48	4 28	5 22	6 8 6	10 6	51 7	23 7 58	3 46	10 6	10 55
Elstree	—	12 34	1 18	2 15	—	3 3	3 56	4 36	5 30	—	6 18	6 59	7 36 8	t	54	10 14	11
Mill Hill...............	—	12 40	1 24	2 21	—	3 9	4 2	4 42	5 36	—	6 24	7 5	7 42 8	12	9 0	10 20	11 9
Hendon	12 46	1 30	2 27	—	3 15	4 8	4 48	5 42	—	6 30	7 11	7 49 8	18	9 5	10 25	11 15
Cricklewood	1241	12 52	1 35	2 32	—	3 20	4 13	4 54	5 47	—	6 35	7 16	7 54 8	23	9 10	10 30	11 20
West Hampstead......	—	12 57	1 39	2 36	—	3 24	4 17	—	5 51	—	—	7 20	7 58 8	28	9 14	10 34	—
Finchley Road	—	1 0	1 42	2 39	—	—	4 20	—	—	—	—	7 23	—	9 17	—	—
Kentish Town	1255	1 9	1 49	2 47	—	3 53	4 28	5 4	6 0	—	6 45	7 30	8 7 8	37	9 24	10 43	11 30
St. Pancras	1 3	1 15	1 55	2 52	3 10	3 38	4 33	5 10	6	5 6	30	6 50	7 35	8 12 8	42	9 29	10 48	11 35
King's + (Met.)	—	—	—	—	—	—	—	—	—	—	—	—	—	—	—	—
Moorgate Street......	—	—	—	—	—	—	—	—	—	—	—	—	—	—	—	—

d Saturdays only.   **e** Saturdays excepted

SUNDAYS.	AM	AM	AM	PM	PM	PM	PM	PM	PM	PM	PM
Moorgate Street dep.	12 7	—	—	—	—	—	—	—	—	—	—
King's + (Met.)	—	—	—	—	—	—	—	—	—	—	—
St. Pancras	—	8 0	10 0	1250	2 0	3 0	4 35	5 40	7 0	8 38	9 35
Kentish Town ....dep.	—	8 6	10 6	1256	2 6	3 6	4 42	5 46	7 7	8 45	9 42
Finchley Road	—	—	—	—	—	—	—	—	—	—	—
West Hampstead........	—	8 11	10 12	1 2	2 12	3 12	4 47	5 52	7 12	8 51	9 47
Cricklewood	—	8 17	10 17	1 7	2 17	3 17	4 52	5 57	7 17	8 56	9 52
Hendon	—	8 24	10 22	1 12	2 22	3 22	4 57	6 2	7 22	9 1	9 57
Mill Hill..............	1224	8 29	10 27	1 17	2 28	3 27	5 2	6 7	7 27	9 6	10 2
Elstree	1231	8 36	10 34	1 24	2 34	3 34	5 9	6 14	7 34	9 13	10 9
Radlett	1237	8 42	10 40	1 30	2 40	3 40	5 15	6 21	7 40	9 19	10 15
Napsbury	—	—	10 46	1 36	2 46	3 46	—	—	—	—	—

SUNDAYS.	AM	AM	PM	PM	PM	PM	PM	PM	PM	PM♣
Napsbury ....dep.	9 22	11 22	12 34	3 6	4 25	5 25	—	—	—	—
Radlett	9 28	11 28	12 41	3 12	4 31	5 31	7 34	8 18	8 39	9 48
Elstree	9 36	11 36	12 49	3 20	4 39	5 39	7 42	8 26	8 47	9 56
Mill Hill	9 42	11 42	12 56	3 26	4 45	5 45	7 49	8 32	8 54	10 2
Hendon	9 49	11 48	1 2	3 32	4 51	5 51	7 55	8 37	9 0	10 8
Cricklewood	9 55	11 53	1 7	3 37	4 56	5 56	8 0	8 42	9 5	10 13
West Hampstead......	9 59	—	1 11	3 41	5 0	6 0	8 5	8 46	9 9	10 17
Finchley Road	—	—	—	—	—	—	—	—	—	—
Kentish Town	10 9	12 5	1 23	3 51	5 8	6 8	8 14	8 56	9 19	10 26
St. Pancras	10 15	12 10	1 30	3 56	5 15	6 15	8 20	9 2	9 25	10 32
King's + (Met.)	—	—	—	—	—	—	—	—	—	—
Moorgate Street.. ...	—	—	—	—	—	—	—	—	—	—

ST. PANCRAS AND MOORGATE STREET TO DAGENHAM AND UPMINSTER.

WEEK DAYS.	AM·	PM	PM	e	PM		AM
St. Pancras ......dep.	9 30	12 20	2 50	—	6 40	SUNDAY TRAINS.	10 10
Moorgate Street.......	5*18			5 4	—		
Kentish Town	9 39	12 29	2 56	5 21	6 46		10 17
Dagenham	—	1*38	3 55	6 18	7 51		1 42
Hornchurch	—	1*43	4 1	6 23	7 57		1 47
Upminster	10 43	1*38	4 6	6 27	8 5		1 51

WEEK DAYS.	AM	PM	PM	PM	e		PM
Upminster ....dep.	8 54	12 27	2 42	6 44	7 53	SUNDAY TRAINS.	7 59
Hornchurch	—	12 32	2 47	—	7 58		6 32
Dagenham	—	12 37	2 52	—	8 3		6 37
Kentish Town	10 3	1 42	5 18	7 38	9 2		9 12
Moorgate Street......	—		5*33	—	—		—
St. Pancras	10 10	1 48	5 34	7 45	—		9 18

d Saturdays only.   **e** Saturdays excepted.   **h** On Saturdays arrive 1.46 p.m.
k Change at Kentish Town.

WEEK DAYS.	AM	AM	AM	AM	AM	AM	AM	AM	PM	d	e	e	d	d	d	d	d	d	d	PM	d
Fenchurch St. dep.	5 5	615	652	742	753	918	939	10 45	12 9	1233	1ʰ 01	01	5 111	1 25	1 48	1 56	215	2 26	2 30	3 8	
East Ham	522	—	713	759	816	942	10 4 11	1	—	1251	—	—	—	—	—	—	235	—	2 54	—	
Barking	529	640	720	—	821	950	10 8 11	5	12 28	—	1 25	—	—	130	—	—	239	—	3 0	—	
Dagenham	537	647	743	—	829	958	—	11 13	12 41	—	—	—	—	138	—	—	—	—	3 7	—	
Hornchurch	543	653	748	—	835	10 4	—	11 19	12 46	—	—	—	—	143	—	—	2 22	—	3 13	—	
Upminster	547	7 1	751	815	841	1011	1043	11 26	12 41	1 6	1 38	1 26	1 33	147	1 55	2 16	—	3 4	2 54	3 17	338
East Horndon	555	710	—	831	849	1019	—	—	12 53	—	—	—	—	2 7	—	—	312	—	3 25	—	
Laindon	6 4	719	—	831	853	1028	—	—	1 9	—	1 51	—	—	2 1	2 17	—	—	321	—	3 34	—

WEEK DAYS.	PM	PM	PM	e	e	e	e	PM	e	a	e	e	e	PM	d	PM	PM	h	PM
Fenchurch St. dep.	325	427	5ᴬ2	5 6	5 25	5 46	6 17	6 26	6 53	6 53	7 20	7⋅46	8	0	8 45	920	10 15	10 45	11 27 12 20
East Ham	341	—	523	—	—	—	—	—	7 9	—	8 21	8 15	—	—	—	—	11 1	—	
Barking	346	445	535	—	5 42	—	—	6 44	—	7 13	—	8 25	—	9 3	941	10 33	11 7	11 52 12 35
Dagenham	355	457	—	—	5 50	—	—	6 57	—	—	7 43	8 33	—	9 11	—	10 46	—	12 42
Hornchurch	4 1	5 2	—	—	5 55	—	—	7 2	—	—	7 57	8 38	—	9 17	—	10 51	—	12 47
Upminster	4 6	453	—	531	5 59	6 13	6 43	7 6	7 23	7 27	8	5 8	42.8	30	9 23	954	10 55	—	12 4 12 51
East Horndon	—	512	—	—	6 21	—	7 13	—	—	8 12	8 50	—	10⋅	2 10	2 11	2	—	12ᵈ12	—
Laindon	—	521	559	—	6 30	—	7 21	7 37	—	8 21	8 59	—	10⋅	12	1012	11 10	—	12 21	—

SUNDAYS.	AM	AM	AM	h	PM	PM	PM	PM	PM	PM	PM
Fenchurch St. dep.	9 15	9 45	11 10	1 9	2 45	4 30	6 10	7 22	8 28	9 45	10 30
East Ham	9 33	10 14	11 33	—	3 12	4 51	6 33	7 41	8 45	10 8	10 46
Barking	9 38	10 20	11 37	1 35	3 19	4 55	6 37	7 46	8 49	10 12	10 50
Dagenham	—	10 28	—	1 42	3 27	5 48	6 44	—	8 57	10 20	—
Hornchurch	—	10 34	—	1 47	3 33	5 54	6 50	—	9 3	10 26	11 11
Upminster	—	10 40	—	1 51	3 39	5 59	6 54	8 0	9 8	10 31	11 16
East Horndon	—	10 48	—	—	3 47	—	7 2	—	—	10 39	—
Laindon	10 3	10 58	—	—	3 56	6 13	7 11	—	—	10 48	—

WEEK DAYS.	AM	AM	AM	AM	AM	AM	AM	AM	AM	AM	AM	AM	AM	AM	AM	AM
Laindon dep.	—	5 58	—	6 30	6 54	—	7 31	—	8 13	—	—	—	9 3	—	—	9 56
East Horndon	—	—	—	6 37	7 3	—	—	—	—	—	—	—	—	—	—	—
Upminster	4 58	—	6 15	6 57	7 11	7 32	—	7 52	8 13	—	8 31	—	8 54	9 14	9 21	9 49
Hornchurch	—	—	6 20	6 49	7 16	—	—	7 56	8 16	—	—	8 42	—	9 17	—	9 53
Dagenham	5 6	—	6 25	6 54	7 21	—	—	8 1	8 21	—	—	8 47	—	9 22	—	9 58
Barking	5 13	6 21	6 33	7 13	7 29	7 47	—	8 13	8 27	—	—	—	9 7	9 28	—	10 5 10 18
East Ham	—	6 25	6 37	—	7 34	—	—	—	—	—	—	—	—	—	—	—
Fenchurch Street	5 35	6 43	7 0	7 34	7 58	8 6	8 15	8ᵃ34	8ᵃ53	8 53	9 4	9 10	9ᵃ34	9ᵃ53	9 49	10 22 10 35

WEEK DAYS	AM	AM	e	d	PM	PM	PM	PM	PM	PM	PM	e	PM	PM	PM	PM	PM
Laindon dep.	—	10 33	—	—	1 3	—	2 26	—	—	5 40	—	6 55	—	9 8	—	10 51
East Horndon	—	10 41	—	—	1 10	—	2 34	—	—	5 50	—	7 3	—	9 16	—	—
Upminster	10 23	10 53	115⋅	1156	12 27	1 27	1 33	2 42	4	10 5	5 6	8 6	44 6	52 7	11 7	48 9	25 9 51 11
Hornchurch	—	10 57	—	—	12 32	—	1 38	2 47	4	14 5	10 6	3	—	7 16	—	9 30	9 56 11 5
Dagenham	—	11 1	—	—	12 37	—	1 43	2 52	4	19 5	15 6	8	—	7 21	—	9 35	10 1 11 10
Barking	10 34	11 18	—	1210	12 49	—	1 51	2 59	4	25 5	23 6	23 6	58 7	8 7	29 8	29 43 10 9 11 17
East Ham	—	11 22	—	1215	—	—	1 55	—	—	5 28	6 28	7	2	—	7 34 8	7 9 47 10 13 11 21
Fenchurch Street	10ᴬ57	11 40	1222	1238	1ᴬ11	1 53	2 18	3ᴬ28	5ᴬ 4	5 49	6 45	7 24	7ᴬ29	7 51	8 30	10 8 10 30 11 40

SUNDAYS.	AM	AM	PM	PM	PM	PM	PM	PM	PM	PM	PM	PM	PM	PM
Laindon dep.	9 7	—	—	2 51	4 53	—	6 2	7 5	—	8 36	9 21	—	—	
East Hornden	9 15	—	—	2 59	5 2	—	6 11	—	—	8 43	9 29	—	—	
Upminster	8 30	9 23	10 58	12 37	1 10 3	8 5	10 5	58 6	20 7	18 7	59 8	20 8	51 9	37 — 10 37
Hornchurch	8 35	9 28	—	—	1 15 3	13 5	15 6	3 6	25 7	23	—	8 56	9 42	— 10 42
Dagenham	8 40	9 33	—	—	1 20 3	18 5	20 6	6 6	30 7	28	—	9 1	9 47	— 10 47
Barking	8 48	9 49	11 12	12 49	1 27 3	26 5	28 6	18 6	41 8	38 43 8	38 9	9	9 55	10 28 10 54
East Ham	—	9 54	11 17	12 54	—	3 31	5 33	6 23	6 47	8 8	—	9 13	10 0	—
Fenchurch Street	9 6	10 18	11 35	1 10	2ᴬ 2	3 47	6 0	6 47	7 15	8 32	9ᴬ11	8ᴬ59	9 38	10 23 10 48 11ᴬ22

d Saturdays only. e Saturdays excepted. h Depart from Mark Lane. k Arr. Mark Lane.

FENCHURCH STREET TO BARKING & DAGENHAM DOCK

WEEK DAYS

	AM	AM	AM	AM	AM	AM	AM	AM	AM	AM	AM	AM	AM	PM	PM	p
Fenchurch St......dep.	5 5	5 37	6 52	7 30	7 53	8 11	9 5	9 18	9 39	10 17	10 45	11 13	11 35	12 9	12 21	1 11
Stepney	5 11	5 43	6 58	7 37	7 59	8 17	9 10	9 23	9 48	10 22	10 50	11 19	11 40	12 16	12 27	1 17
Burdett Road	5 13	5 45	7 0	7 40	8 1	8 19	—	—	9 50	10 24	10 52	11 21	11 42	12 18	12 29	1 19
Bromley	—	5 49	—	—	—	—	—	—	—	—	—	—	—	—	—	—
Plaistow	—	5 54	—	7 46	8 9	8 27	—	9 33	9 57	—	—	11 27	11 49	—	12 39	—
Upton Park	—	5 57	—	7 49	8 12	8 31	—	9 37	10 0	—	—	—	11 52	—	12 42	—
East Ham	5 23	6 2	7 13	7 53	8 16	8 35	9 20	9 42	10 4	—	11 1	11 32	11 56	—	12 46	—
Barking	5 29	6 10	7 20	7 57	8 21	8 41	9 25	9 50	10 8	10 34	11 5	—	12 3	12 23	12 51	1 30
Dagenham Dock	—	6 17	7 27	8 4	—	8 48	9 31	—	10 15	—	—	—	12 10	—	12 59	—

WEEK DAYS

	d	d	e	e	d	PM	PM	PM	d	PM	PM	PM	e	PM	e	PM
Fenchurch St......dep.	1 15	1 35	1 48	2 6	2 15	2 30	2 40	3 25	4 7	4 16	4 27	4 46	5 25	5 32	5 46	5 55
Stepney	1 21	1 40	1 54	2 12	2 21	2 35	2 46	3 31	4 13	4 22	4 33	4 51	5 31	5 40	—	—
Burdett Road	1 23	—	1 56	—	2 23	2 37	2 48	3 33	—	4 24	4 35	4 53	—	—	5 53	6 1
Bromley	—	—	2 0	—	—	—	—	—	—	—	—	—	—	—	—	—
Plaistow	—	1 48	2 4	—	—	2 47	2 55	—	—	—	—	4 59	—	—	—	6 8
Upton Park	1 30	—	2 7	—	2 31	2 50	2 58	—	—	—	—	—	—	—	—	—
East Ham	1 33	1 54	2 11	—	2 35	2 54	3 2	3 41	4 24	4 32	—	5 4	—	5 49	—	6 13
Barking	—	1 58	2 15	2 25	2 39	3 0	3 7	3 46	—	4 37	4 45	5 8	5 42	6 4 0	—	6 17
Dagenham Dock	—	2 5	2 22	—	—	—	3 14	—	—	4 44	—	—	—	6 4 7	—	6 24

WEEK DAYS

	PM	PM	PM	e	PM	e	PM	PM	PM	PM	PM	PM	PM	PM
Fenchurch St......dep	6 26	6 38	6 53	7 4	7 20	7 41	8 13	8 45	9 25	10 15	10 45	12 0	12 20	
Stepney	6 32	6 44	6 59	7 10	7 26	7 46	8 19	8 51	9 30	10 21	10 51	12 6	—	
Burdett Road	—	6 46	7 1	7 12	7 28	7 48	8 21	8 53	9 32	—	10 53	12 8	—	
Bromley	—	—	—	—	—	—	—	—	—	—	—	—	—	
Plaistow	—	6 53	—	7 20	—	7 54	8 28	—	9 38	—	—	—	—	
Upton Park	—	—	7 4 9	7 23	—	7 57	8 31	—	9 41	—	—	—	—	
East Ham	—	6 58	7 4 12	7 27	7 4 37	8 1	8 35	—	9 45	—	11 1	12 16	—	
Barking	6 44	7 2	—	—	—	8 5	8 42	9 3	9 49	10 33	11 7	12 21	12 35	
Dagenham Dock	—	7 9	—	—	—	—	8 49	—	9 56	—	11 14	—	—	

SUNDAYS

	AM	AM	AM	AM	AM	AM	PM	PM	PM	PM	PM	PM	PM	PM	PM	PM	PM
Fenchurch St......dep.	8 40	915	945	1040	11 10	11 45	1 6	2 7	2 45	4 30	6 10	638	728	8 28	8 45	9 45	1030	1055	1110
Stepney	846	921	951	1047	11 16	11 51	—	2 13	2 51	4 36	6 16	644	—	8 34	8 51	9 51	1036	11 2	1116
Burdett Road	848	923	953	1049	11 18	11 53	—	2 15	2 53	4 38	6 18	—	8 36	8 53	9 53	1038	11 4	1118
Bromley	852	—	957	—	11 22	—	—	2 19	—	—	—	—	—	—	—	—	1122
Plaistow	858	—	10 3	—	11 26	—	1 21	2 23	3 4	4 46	6 25	—	—	9 1	10 0	—	1112	1126
Upton Park	9 2	—	10 7	—	11 29	—	—	2 26	3 7	4 47	6 28	—	—	9 5	10 4	—	1115	1129
East Ham	9 7	933	1012	1058	11 33	12 2	1 26	2 30	3 12	4 51	6 32	654	741	8 45	9 10	10 8	1048	1119	1133
Barking	912	938	1018	11 2	11 37	12 6	1 31	2 34	3 19	4 55	6 36	7 0	746	8 49	9 14	10 12	1050	1123	1137
Dagenham Dock	919	—	—	11 44	—	1 38	2 41	—	5 2	—	7 7	831	—	9 21	—	1057	—	—

d Saturdays only.   **e** Saturdays excepted.

DAGENHAM DOCK & BARKING TO FENCHURCH STREET.

WEEK DAYS

	AM	AM	AM	AM	AM	AM	AM	AM	AM	AM	AM	AM	AM	AM	AM	AM
Dagenham Dock....dep.	—	—	—	5 59	—	6 47	—	—	—	—	7 50	8 19	—	—	9 28
Barking	4 12	4 47	5 13	6 7	6 21	6 33	6 55	7 13	—	7 23	7 29	7 47	8 0	8 27	9 14	9 35
East Ham	4 17	4 52	—	6 11	6 25	6 37	6 59	—	7 22	7 28	7 34	—	8 4	8 31	9 18	—
Upton Park	4 21	4 56	—	6 15	—	6 41	7 3	—	—	7 32	7 38	—	—	—	—	—
Plaistow	4 24	4 59	5 20	6 18	—	6 44	7 6	—	7 28	7 35	7 41	—	—	—	—	—
Bromley	—	—	—	—	—	—	—	—	—	—	—	—	—	—	—	—
Burdett Road	4 32	5 7	—	6 26	6 35	6 52	7 14	7 26	7 36	—	7 48	7 57	8 14	—	—	—
Stepney	4 35	5 10	—	6 29	6 38	6 55	7 17	7 29	7 39	7 48	7 51	8 0	8 17	8 43	9 29	—
Fenchurch Street	4 40	5 15	5 35	6 34	6 43	7 0	7 22	7 34	7 46	7 53	7 58	8 6	8 24	8 48	9 34	10 4

WEEK DAYS

	AM	AM	AM	AM	AM	d	AM	d	AM	AM	AM	PM	PM	PM
Dagenham Dock....dep.	—	10 18	—	—	11 41	12 16	12 51	1 36	—	2 3	2 40	—	3 37	4 37	5 4
Barking	—	10 25	10 53	11 18	11 49	12 40	1 0	1 44	1 51	2 11	2 48	3 7	3 47	4 46	5 12
East Ham	10 18	10 27	10 57	11 22	11 53	12 45	1 4	1 49	1 55	2 15	3 3	—	3 51	4 52	5 17
Upton Park	—	10 31	11 1	—	11 57	12 49	1 8	—	1 59	—	—	—	—	5 21
Plaistow	—	10 34	11 4	—	12 0	12 53	1 11	—	2 2	—	—	—	4 58	5 24
Bromley	—	—	11 8	—	—	—	—	—	—	—	—	—	—	—
Burdett Road	—	10 41	11 12	11 32	12 8	—	1 19	1 59	—	2 25	—	4 2	—	—
Stepney	10 30	10 44	11 15	11 35	12 11	—	1 22	2 2	2 13	2 28	3 13	3 21	4 5	5 10	—
Fenchurch Street	10 35	10 49	11 20	11 40	12 16	1 10	1 28	2 10	2 18	2 34	3 18	3 28	4 10	5 18	5 42

WEEK DAYS

	PM	e	PM	PM	e	PM	PM	PM	PM	PM	PM	d	PM	PM	PM
Dagenham Dock....dep.	5 16	—	5 55	—	—	6 50	7 29	7 40	8 2	8 41	—	9 45	—	11 1	11 6
Barking	5 23	5 32	6 2	6 23	6 28	6 58	7 37	7 48	8 8	8 49	9 43	9 52	9 59	10 9	11 17	11 23
East Ham	5 28	5 37	6 6	6 28	6 33	7 2	7 34	7 44	7 8	8 53	9 47	—	10 3	10 13	11 21	11 28
Upton Park	—	5 41	6 10	—	6 37	—	—	8 11	8 57	—	—	—	11 32
Plaistow	—	5 48	6 14	—	6 40	7 7	—	7 49	8 14	9 0	9 52	—	—	11 35
Bromley	—	—	—	—	—	—	—	—	—	—	—	—	—	—
Burdett Road	5 40	6 1	6 23	6 37	6 47	7 15	—	—	8 22	9 7	10 0	—	10 12	10 22	11 32	11 42
Stepney	—	6 4	6 26	6 40	6 51	7 18	7 46	7 59	8 25	9 10	10 3	—	10 15	10 25	11 35	11 45
Fenchurch Street	5 49	6 10	6 33	6 45	6 56	7 24	7 51	8 4	8 30	9 15	10 8	10 4 23	10 20	10 30	11 40	11 50

SUNDAYS

	AM	AM	AM	AM	PM	PM	PM	PM	PM	PM	PM	PM	PM	PM	PM	PM
Dagenham Dock....dep.	—	—	—	9 41	12 23	—	2 1	—	3 29	—	5 58	—	7 8	—	3 38
Barking	—	8 48	9 12	9 49	12 31	12 49	2 8	3 26	3 37	4 59	5 28	6 6	18 6	41	7 16	8	3 43
East Ham	7 52	—	9 18	9 54	12 35	12 54	2 12	3 13	3 41	5 16	6 23	6 47	7 21	8
Upton Park	7 56	—	—	9 58	12 39	—	—	3 45	5 9	5 37	6 14	6 27	6 32	7 25	8 12
Plaistow	7 59	—	—	10 2	12 42	—	2 17	—	3 48	5 12	5 40	6 17	6 31	6 57	7 29	8 16
Bromley	—	—	—	—	12 46	—	—	—	—	—	—	—	—
Burdett Road	8 7	—	9 28	10 10	12 53	—	—	3 56	5 22	5 52	6 24	6 39	7 7	7 37	8 24	—
Stepney	8 10	9 1	9 31	10 13	12 56	1 5	2 27	—	3 59	5 25	5 55	6 27	6 42	7 10	7 40	8 27	—
Fenchurch St.	8 15	9 6	9 36	10 18	1 1	1 1	1 10	2 33	3 47	4	4 5	30 6	0 6	32 6	47 7	15 7	45 8	32 9	4 11

SUNDAYS

	PM	PM	PM	PM	PM
Dagenham Dock....dep.	8 50	—	—	—	10 26
Barking	8 59	9 37	9 55	10 28	10 34
East Ham	9 4	9 42	10 0	—	10 38
Upton Park	9 8	9 46	10 4	—	10 42
Plaistow	9 13	9 49	10 8	—	10 45
Bromley	—	—	—	—	—
Burdett Road	9 22	10 0	10 15	—	10 52
Stepney	9 25	10 3	10 18	10 43	10 55
Fenchurch St.	9 30	10 9	10 23	10 48	11 0

d Saturdays only.   **e** Saturdays excepted.   **k** Arr. Mark Lane.

WEEK DAYS.

	AM	AM	AM	AM	AM	AM	AM	AM	AM	AM	AM	AM	AM	AM	AM	AM
Moorgate Street ......dep.	—	—	—	—	—	5 25	—	—	6 23	—	—	—	—	7 10	—	—
Farringdon Street	—	—	—	—	—	5 29	—	—	6 27	—	—	—	—	7 14	—	—
King's + (Met.)	—	—	—	—	—	5 33	—	—	6 31	—	—	—	—	7 18	—	—
King's Cross	2 5	4 25	—	5	5 5	5 22	5 36	—	6 15	6 34	6 40	—	7 0	—	7 21	—	7 18
Broad Street	—	—	—	—	—	—	—	—	—	6 5	6 42	6 48	—	7 3	—	7 3
Dalston Junction	—	—	—	—	—	—	—	—	—	6 12	6 49	6 55	—	7 10	—	7 10
Finsbury Park	2 10	4 32	5 0	5 12	5 29	5 42	6 11	6 21	6 40	6 58	7 4	7 7	9 7	19 7	26 7 33	7 25
Harringay	2 14	4 35	—	5	32 5 45	6 14	6 24	6 43	7 1	7 7	12 7	24	—	—	7 28
Hornsey	2 16	4 38	—	5	34 5 47	6 16	6 27	6 45	7 3	7 9	18 7	26	—	—	7 30
Wood Green	2 19	4 41 5 5	—	5	37 5 50	6 19	6 30	6 48	7 6	7 12	7 23	7 29	—	—	7 33
Bowes Park	2 22	—	5 9	—	—	5 53	6 22	—	6 51	—	7 15	—	7 32	—	—	7 37
Palmer's Green	2 25	—	5 12	—	—	5 56	6 25	—	6 54	—	7 18	—	7 35	—	—	7 42
Winchmore Hill	2 28	—	5 15	—	—	5 59	6 28	—	6 57	—	7 21	—	7 38	—	—	7 47
Grange Park	—	—	5 17	—	—	6 1	6 30	—	6 59	—	7 23	—	—	—	—	7 49
Enfield	2 31	—	5 20	—	—	6 4	6 33	—	7 2	—	7 26	—	7 41	—	—	7 52
Gordon Hill	2 34	—	5 23	—	—	6 8	6 38	—	7 5	—	7 29	—	7 44	—	—	7 58
Crews Hill	—	—	—	—	—	—	—	—	—	—	—	—	—	—	—	8 3
Cuffley	—	—	—	—	—	—	6 48	—	—	—	—	—	—	—	—	8 7
Southgate, New	—	4 45	—	5 41	—	—	6 34	—	7 11	—	7 28	—	7 42	—
Oakleigh Park	—	4 50	—	5 46	—	—	6 39	—	7 17	—	7 33	—	—
New Barnet	—	4 52	—	5 48	—	—	6 41	—	7 19	—	7 38	—	7 48	—
Hadley Wood	—	—	—	—	—	—	—	—	—	—	7 43	—	—
Potter's Bar	—	—	5 28	—	—	—	—	—	—	—	7 49	—	—
Hatfield	—	—	5 35	—	—	—	—	—	—	—	7 58	—	—

WEEK DAYS.

	AM	AM	AM	AM	AM	AM	AM	AM	AM	AM	AM	AM	AM	AM	AM	AM	AM
Moorgate Street ......dep.	7 27	—	—	—	7 40	7 48	—	—	—	—	8 16	8 28	—	8 33	—	8 40	8 51
Farringdon Street	7 31	—	—	—	7 44	7 52	—	—	—	—	8 20	8 32	—	8 37	—	8 44	8 55
King's + (Met.)	7 35	—	—	—	7 48	7 56	—	—	—	—	8 24	8 36	—	8 41	—	8 48	8 59
King's Cross	7 38	—	7 45	—	7 52	7 58	8 5	—	—	—	8 27	8 39	—	8 44	8 45	8 51	9 2
Broad Street	—	7 38	—	7 50	—	—	—	8 0	—	8 20	8 27	—	—	8 34	—	—
Dalston Junction	—	7 44	—	7 57	—	—	—	8 5	—	8 27	8 32	—	—	8 40	—	—
Finsbury Park	7 44	7 53	7 53	8 6	7 58	—	8 13	8 11	8 34	8 39	8 34	8 45	8 54	8 50	8 51	8 56	9 7
Harringay	—	7 56	—	8 1	—	—	8 14	—	8 41	—	—	8 57	8 53	—	—
Hornsey	—	7 58	—	8 3	—	—	8 16	—	8 43	—	—	8 59	8 55	—	—
Wood Green	7 49	8 1	—	8 6	—	8 19	8 19	8 39	8 46	—	8 50	9 2	8 58	—	—
Bowes Park	—	8 4	—	—	—	—	8 22	8 42	—	—	—	—	9 1	—	—
Palmer's Green	—	8 7	—	—	—	—	8 25	8 45	—	—	8 55	—	9 4	—	—
Winchmore Hill	—	8 10	—	—	—	—	8 28	8 48	—	—	8 58	—	9 7	—	—
Grange Park	—	8 12	—	—	—	—	8 30	8 50	—	—	—	—	—	—	—
Enfield	—	8 15	—	—	—	—	8 33	8 53	—	—	9 1	—	9 10	—	—
Gordon Hill	—	8 18	—	—	—	—	8 36	8 56	—	—	9 10	—	9 13	—	—
Crews Hill	—	—	—	—	—	—	—	—	—	—	9 10	—	—
Cuffley	—	—	—	—	—	—	—	—	—	—	9 14	—	—
Southgate, New	7 53	—	—	8 10	—	8 24	—	—	8 50	—	—	9 6	—	—
Oakleigh Park	7 58	—	—	8 15	—	8 29	—	—	8 55	—	—	9 11	—	—
New Barnet	8 0	—	—	8 18	—	8 32	—	—	8 57	—	—	9 14	—	—
Hadley Wood	—	—	—	—	—	8 36	—	—	—	—	—	9 18	—	—
Potter's Bar	—	—	—	—	—	8 41	—	—	—	—	—	9 23	—	—
Hatfield	—	—	8 16	—	—	8 50	—	—	—	—	—	9 33	—	9 15	—

WEEK DAYS.

	AM	AM	AM	AM	AM	AM	AM	AM	AM	AM	AM	AM	AM	AM
Moorgate Street ......dep.	—	8 57	9 2	—	9 15	9 23	—	9 52	—	10 6	—	—	10 24	10 42
Farringdon Street	—	9 1	9 4	—	9 19	9 27	—	9 56	—	10 10	—	—	10 28	10 46
King's + (Met.)	—	9 5	9 10	—	9 23	9 31	—	10 0	—	10 14	—	—	10 32	10 50
King's Cross	9 2	9 8	9 13	9 20	9 26	9 34	—	10 4	10 12	10 17	—	—	10 50	10 52	11 5
Broad Street	8 50	—	—	—	9 10	—	9 35	9 55	—	—	10 11	10 27	—
Dalston Junction	8 56	—	—	—	9 16	—	9 42	10 2	—	—	10 18	10 34	—
Finsbury Park	9 7	9 15	9 20	9 26	9 32	9 40	9 53	10 11	10 19	10 23	10 30	10 44	10 56	—	11 12
Harringay	9 12	9 18	9 23	—	9 35	9 43	9 56	10 14	—	10 26	10 33	10 47	10 59	—	11 15
Hornsey	9 14	9 20	9 23	—	9 37	9 45	9 58	10 16	—	10 28	10 36	10 49	11 1	—	11 17
Wood Green	9 17	9 23	9 28	—	9 40	9 48	10 1	10 19	—	10 31	10 39	10 52	11 4	—	11 21
Bowes Park	9 20	—	9 31	—	9 43	—	10 4	—	—	10 34	10 42	—	11 7	—
Palmer's Green	9 23	—	9 34	—	9 46	—	10 7	—	—	10 37	10 45	—	11 10	—
Winchmore Hill	9 26	—	9 37	—	9 49	—	10 10	—	—	10 40	10 48	—	11 13	—
Grange Park	9 28	—	9 39	—	9 51	—	10 12	—	—	10 42	10 50	—	11 15	—
Enfield	9 31	—	9 42	—	9 54	—	10 15	—	—	10 45	10 53	—	11 18	—
Gordon Hill	9 34	—	9 45	—	9 59	—	—	—	—	10 50	10 58	—	11 21	—
Crews Hill	—	—	—	—	10 4	—	—	—	—	10 55	—	—
Cuffley	—	—	—	—	10 8	—	—	—	—	10 59	—	—
Southgate, New	—	9 27	—	—	9 52	—	10 23	—	—	—	10 56	—	11 25
Oakleigh Park	—	9 32	—	—	9 57	—	10 29	—	—	—	11 1	—	11 30
New Barnet	—	9 35	—	—	9 59	—	10 31	10 34	—	—	11 4	—	11 36
Hadley Wood	—	9 39	—	—	—	—	—	10 38	—	—	11 8	—	11 40
Potter's Bar	—	9 44	—	—	—	—	—	10 44	—	—	11 13	—	11 45
Hatfield	—	—	—	9 46	—	—	—	10 52	—	—	—	—	11 54

WEEK DAYS.

	AM	AM	e	d	PM	d	PM	d	e	d	d	d	d	d	PM	d
Moorgate Street ......dep.	—	8 57	—	11 43	—	0 12d 6	—	—	12 16	12 26	—	12 35	12 40	—	1247
Farringdon Street	—	9 1	—	11 47	—	12 4	12d40	—	12 20	12 30	—	12 39	12 44	—	1251
King's + (Met.)	—	9 5	—	11 51	—	12 8	12d14	—	12 24	12 34	—	12 43	12 48	—	1255
King's Cross	1130	1137	11 45	11d55	12 4	1211	12 17	—	12 25	12 28	12 37	12 37	12 46	12 52	1245	1259
Broad Street	—	—	11 27	11 52	—	11 52	—	—	—	12 20	—	—	1234	1240
Dalston Junction	—	—	11 34	11 59	—	11 59	—	—	—	12 25	—	—	1241	1247
Finsbury Park	1137	1143	11 52	12 1	12 12	1217	12 23	1229	12 31	12 35	12 43	12 43	12 52	12 59	1251	1 6
Harringay	—	1146	11 54	12 4	12 15	1220	12 26	1232	12 34	12 38	12 46	—	12 55	1 2	1254	1 9
Hornsey	—	1148	11 56	12 6	12 17	1222	12 28	1234	12 36	12 40	12 48	—	12 57	—	1256	112
Wood Green	—	1151	11 59	12 9	12 20	1225	12 31	1237	12 39	12 43	12 51	—	1 0	1 7	1259	116
Bowes Park	—	1154	—	12 23	—	—	—	1240	12 42	12 46	—	12 50	1 3	1 10	—	119
Palmer's Green	—	1157	—	12 26	—	—	—	1243	12 45	12 49	—	12 53	1 6	1 13	—	122
Winchmore Hill	—	12 0	—	12 29	—	—	—	1246	12 48	12 52	—	12 56	1 9	1 16	—	125
Grange Park	—	12 2	—	12 31	—	—	—	—	12 50	12 54	—	12 58	1 11	1 18	—	127
Enfield	—	12 5	—	12 34	—	—	1249	12 53	12 57	—	1 1	1 14	1 21	—	130
Gordon Hill	—	12 7	—	12 39	—	—	1252	12 56	1 0	—	1 17	1 25	—	133
Crews Hill	—	—	—	12 44	—	—	—	—	—	—	1 30	—
Cuffley	—	—	—	12 48	—	—	—	—	—	—	1 34	—
Southgate, New	—	—	12 3	12 13	—	12 35	—	—	12 55	—	—	1 3	—
Oakleigh Park	—	—	12 8	12 17	—	12 40	—	—	1 0	—	—	1 8	—
New Barnet	—	—	12 12	12 19	—	12 43	—	—	1 2	—	—	111	—
Hadley Wood	—	—	12 16	12 23	—	12 47	—	—	—	—	—	115	—
Potter's Bar	—	—	12 20	12 28	—	12 52	—	—	—	—	—	119	—
Hatfield	12 1	—	—	—	—	—	—	—	—	—	—	—

WEEK DAYS.

	d	d	e	d	d	d	PM	d	d	PM	d	d	d	PM	d	d	d	d
MOORGATE STREET ....dep	—	—	—	12 55	1 1	4	—	—	1ᵈ 9	—	—	—	—	1 27	—	1 33	1 38	
Farringdon Street	—	—	—	12 59	1 5	8	—	—	1ᵈ11	—	—	—	—	1 31	—	1 37	1 42	
King's + (Met.)	—	—	—	1ᵈ 3	1 9	12	—	—	1ᵈ17	—	—	—	—	1 35	—	1 41	1 46	
KING'S CROSS	12 58	1 2	1 6	—	—	—	1 8	1 11	1 16	—	1 23	—	1ᵈ27	—	1 33	—	—	
BROAD STREET	—	—	—	1 3	—	—	—	—	—	—	—	1ᵈ18	1 25	—	—	—	—	
Dalston Junction	—	—	—	1 9	—	—	—	—	—	—	—	1·25	1 31	—	—	—	—	
FINSBURY PARK	1 4	—	1 12	1 13	1 19	1 21	1 14	1 18	1 23	1 26	—	1 31	1 35	1 39	—	1 40	1 49	1 55
Harringay	—	1 9	1 15	1 16	—	1 24	—	—	1 26	1 29	1 30	1 34	1 38	1 42	—	—	1 52	1 58
Hornsey	—	1 11	1 18	1 19	—	1 26	—	—	1 28	1 31	1 32	1 36	1 41	1 45	—	—	1 54	2 1
WOOD GREEN	—	1 14	1 21	1 21	—	1 29	—	—	1 31	1 34	1 35	1 39	1 44	1 48	—	1 45	1 57	2 5
Bowes Park	—	1 17	1 24	1 26	—	1 32	—	—	1 34	1 37	—	—	1 47	—	—	—	—	2 8
Palmer's Green	—	—	1 27	1 29	—	—	—	—	1 26	1 37	1 40	—	1 50	—	—	—	—	2 11
Winchmore Hill	—	—	1 30	1 32	—	—	—	—	1 29	1 40	1 43	—	1 53	—	—	—	—	2 14
Grange Park	—	—	1 32	1 34	—	—	—	—	1 31	—	1 45	—	1 55	—	—	—	—	2 16
ENFIELD	—	—	1 35	1 37	—	—	—	—	1 33	1 43	1 48	—	1 58	—	—	—	—	2 19
Gordon Hill	—	—	1 38	1 40	—	—	—	—	1 53	—	—	—	—	—	—	—	—	2 22
Crews Hill	—	—	—	—	—	—	—	—	1 57	—	—	—	—	—	—	—	—	—
Cuffley	—	—	—	—	—	—	—	—	2 1	—	—	—	—	—	—	—	—	—
Southgate, New	1 12	—	—	—	1 27	—	—	—	—	1 39	—	—	1 53	—	1 49	—	—	
Oakleigh Park	1 17	—	—	—	1 32	—	—	—	—	1 44	—	—	1 59	—	1 54	—	—	
NEW BARNET	1 19	—	—	—	1 35	—	—	—	—	1 46	—	—	2 5	—	1 56	—	—	
Hadley Wood	—	—	—	—	—	1 35	—	—	—	—	—	—	2 9	—	—	—	—	
Potter's Bar	—	—	—	—	—	1 40	—	—	—	—	—	—	2 14	—	—	—	—	
HATFIELD	—	—	—	—	—	1 47	—	—	—	—	—	—	—	—	—	—	—	

WEEK DAYS.

	d	d	PM	e	d	d	d	d	d	e	PM	d	a	d	d	PM	e	d
MOORGATE STREET ....dep	—	—	—	—	—	—	—	1 54	—	—	2 6	—	—	—	2ᵈ27	—	—	
Farringdon Street	—	—	—	—	—	—	—	1 58	—	—	2 10	—	—	—	2ᵈ31	—	—	
King's + (Met.)	—	—	—	—	—	—	—	2 2	—	—	2 14	—	—	—	2ᵈ35	—	—	
KING'S CROSS	1 43	—	1 55	—	1 50	—	2 0	2 3	2 11	—	—	2 27	—	2 30	2 39	2 48	—	
BROAD STREET	—	—	—	—	—	1 50	—	1 58	1 55	2 0	—	—	2 17	—	—	—	2 41	
Dalston Junction	—	—	—	—	—	1 55	—	2 3	2 2	—	—	—	2 23	—	—	—	2 46	
FINSBURY PARK	—	1 45	2 1	2 1	2 1	56	2 4	—	2 11	2 16	2 16	2 20	2 25	2 34	2 35	2 37	2 46	2·54 2 55
Harringay	1 51	1 48	—	2 5	—	2 9	2 7	14	2 19	2 19	2 23	2 28	2 37	2 38	—	2 49	2 57	2 58
Hornsey	1 54	1 50	—	2 7	—	2 9	9	17	2 21	2 21	2 25	2 30	2 39	2 40	—	2 51	2 59	3 1
WOOD GREEN	1 58	1 53	—	2 10	2 1	2 12	2 12	2 21	2 24	2 24	2 28	2 33	2 42	2 43	—	2 54	3 23	4
Bowes Park	2 1	1 56	—	2 13	—	—	2 15	2 24	—	—	2 31	—	2 45	—	—	2 57	—	3 7
Palmer's Green	2 4	1 59	—	2 16	—	—	2 18	2 27	—	—	2 34	—	2 49	—	—	3 0	—	3 10
Winchmore Hill	2 7	2 2	—	2 19	—	—	2 21	2 30	—	—	2 37	—	2 51	—	—	3 3	—	3 13
Grange Park	2 9	2 4	—	2 21	—	—	2 23	2 33	—	—	2 39	—	2 53	—	—	3 5	—	3 15
ENFIELD	2 12	2 7	—	2 24	—	—	2 26	2 36	—	—	2 42	—	2 56	—	—	3 8	—	3 18
Gordon Hill	2 15	2 10	—	2 27	—	—	2 31	2 39	—	—	2 47	—	2 59	—	—	3 13	—	3 21
Crews Hill	—	—	—	—	—	—	2 36	—	—	—	2 52	—	—	—	—	3 18	—	—
Cuffley	—	—	—	—	—	—	2 40	—	—	—	2 56	—	—	—	—	3 22	—	—
Southgate, New	—	—	—	2 5	2 16	—	—	2 29	2 28	—	2 39	—	2 47	—	—	3 6	—	—
Oakleigh Park	—	—	—	2 10	2 22	—	—	2 34	2 33	—	2 44	—	2 53	—	—	3 11	—	—
NEW BARNET	—	—	—	2 12	2 25	—	—	2 37	2 33	—	2 46	—	2 55	—	—	3 14	—	—
Hadley Wood	—	—	—	—	—	—	—	2 41	2 40	—	—	—	2 59	—	—	—	—	—
Potter's Bar	—	—	—	—	—	—	—	2 46	2 45	—	—	—	3 4	2 55	—	—	—	—
HATFIELD	—	—	2 24	—	—	—	—	2 53	—	—	—	—	—	—	3 3	—	—	

WEEK DAYS.

	d	e	d	e	d	PM	PM	PM	PM	PM	e	PM	e	e	d	e
MOORGATE STREET ....dep	—	—	2 59	—	3 13	—	—	4 ⁰0	—	—	—	—	4ᵈ23	—	4 36	—
Farringdon Street	—	—	3 3	—	3 17	—	—	4 ⁴4	—	—	—	—	4ᵈ27	—	4 40	—
King's + (Met.)	—	—	3 7	—	3 21	—	—	4 ⁸8	—	—	—	—	4ᵈ31	—	4 44 4 48	—
KING'S CROSS	2 53	3 5	3 10	3 21	3 24	2 9	3 30	3 45	4 0	4 12	4 15	—	4 26 4 35	—	4 48	—
BROAD STREET	—	—	—	3 35	—	—	4 3	—	4 20	4 20	—	4 40	—			
Dalston Junction	—	—	—	3 41	—	—	4 10	—	4 27	4 27	—	4 46	—			
FINSBURY PARK	2 59	3 11	3 16	3 27	3 30	3 35	3 38	3 51	6 4	19	4 24	4 27	36	4 42	4 48	4 56	4 56	4 57
Harringay	—	3 14	3 19	3 30	3 33	3 51	—	3 54	9	4 22	—	4 30	4 39	4 45	4 51	—	5 0
Hornsey	—	3 16	3 21	3 32	3 35	3 41	—	3 56	4 11	4 24	—	4 32	4 41	4 47	4 53	—	5 1 5 3
WOOD GREEN	3 4	3 19	3 24	3 35	3 38	3 43	4 33	3 59	4 14	4 27	—	4 35	4 44	4 50	4 56	—	5 4 5 6
Bowes Park	—	3 22	3 27	—	3 47	—	4 2	—	4 30	—	—	4 53	—	5 3 5 7	—	
Palmer's Green	—	3 25	3 30	—	3 50	—	4 5	—	4 33	—	—	4 56	—	5 6 5 10	—	
Winchmore Hill	—	3 28	3 33	—	3 53	—	4 8	—	4 36	—	—	4 59	—	5 9 5 13	—	
Grange Park	—	3 30	3 35	—	3 55	—	4 10	—	4 38	—	—	5 1	—	5 11 5 15	—	
ENFIELD	—	3 33	3 38	—	3 58	—	4 13	—	4 41	—	—	5 4	—	5 14 5 18	—	
Gordon Hill	—	3 36	3 43	—	—	—	4 16	—	4 46	—	—	5 7	—	5 17 5 21	—	
Crews Hill	—	3 42	3 48	—	—	—	—	4 51	—	—	—	—	—	—		
Cuffley	—	3 46	3 52	—	—	—	—	4 55	—	—	—	—	—	—		
Southgate, New	3 8	—	3 39	3 42	—	3 47	—	4 18	—	4 39	4 48	—	—	5 10		
Oakleigh Park	3 13	—	3 44	3 47	—	3 52	—	4 23	—	4 44	4 53	—	—	5 15		
NEW BARNET	3 15	—	3 46	3 50	—	3 58	—	4 26	—	4 46	4 56	—	—	5 17		
Hadley Wood	—	—	—	—	4 2	—	4ᵈ30	—	5 0	—	—	—				
Potter's Bar	—	—	—	—	4 7	—	4ᵈ34	—	4 41	5 5	—	—				
HATFIELD	—	—	—	—	4 15	—	—	4 49	—	—	—	—				

WEEK DAYS.

	PM	PM	e	e	PM	d	e	PM	PM	e	e	e	e	d	e	d
MOORGATE STREET ....dep	4ᵈ46	—	4 55	5 1	—	—	—	—	—	5 20	—	5 24	—	—		
Farringdon Street	4ᵈ50	—	4 59	5 5	—	—	—	—	—	5 24	—	5 28	—	—		
King's + (Met.)	4ᵈ54	—	5 3	5 9	—	—	—	—	—	5 28	—	5 32	—	—		
KING'S CROSS	4 57	5	5 7	—	5 10	5 11	5 13	—	5 18	5 25	—	5 34	—	5 34	5 40	
BROAD STREET	—	4 54	—	5 0	—	—	—	—	—	—	—	5 25	—	—		
Dalston Junction	—	5 1	—	5 6	—	—	512	—	—	—	—	5 30	—	—		
FINSBURY PARK	5 3	5 11	5 13	5 20	5 20	5 19	522	526	5 26	5 31	5 35	5 36	5 40	5 42	5 41	—
Harringay	5 6	—	5 16	5 23	—	5 25	—	—	529	—	5 39	5 43	5 45	—	5 41	5 49
Hornsey	5 8	—	5 18	5 25	—	5 28	—	—	531	—	5 41	5 45	5 47	—	5 43	5 51
WOOD GREEN	5 11	5ᵈ16	5 24	5 28	—	5 28	—	—	534	—	5 38	5 42	—	5 48	5 50	5 47 5 46 5 54
Bowes Park	5 14	—	5 27	—	5 31	—	—	5 33	5 41	—	5 51	5 53	5 50	—		
Palmer's Green	5 17	—	—	—	5 34	5 27	—	5 36	—	5 46	5 54	—	5 53	—		
Winchmore Hill	5 20	—	—	—	5 37	5 30	—	5 39	—	5 49	5 57	—	5 56	—		
Grange Park	5 22	—	—	—	5 39	—	—	5 41	—	5 51	5 59	—	5 58	—		
ENFIELD	5 25	—	—	—	5 42	5 33	—	5 44	—	5 54	6 2	—	6 1	—		
Gordon Hill	5 30	—	—	—	5 45	5 36	—	5 47	—	5 59	6 4	—	6 4	—		
Crews Hill	5 35	—	—	—	5 53	—	—	—	—	—	6 12	—	—	—		
Cuffley	5 39	—	—	—	5 57	—	—	—	—	—	6 16	—	—	—		
Southgate, New	—	5 20	—	5 22	—	—	538	—	—	—	—	5 50	5 58	—		
Oakleigh Park	—	5 25	—	5 27	—	—	543	—	—	—	—	5 55	6 3	—		
NEW BARNET	—	5 28	—	5 39	—	—	534 546	—	—	—	—	5 57	6 5	—		
Hadley Wood	—	5 32	—	—	—	—	538	—	—	—	—	—	—	—		
Potter's Bar	—	5 37	—	—	—	—	543	—	—	—	—	—	—	—		
HATFIELD	—	—	—	5 35	—	—	—	—	—	—	—	—	—	—		

WEEK DAYS.

	e	e	e	PM	e	e	PM	PM	e	e	d	e	e	d	e
Moorgate Street ..dep.	—	—	—	—	5 40	—	5°47	—	5 53	—	—	5 59	—	—	—
Farringdon Street	—	—	—	—	5 44	—	5°51	—	5 57	—	—	6 3	—	—	—
King's + (Met.)	—	—	—	—	5 48	—	5°55	—	6 1	—	—	6 7	—	—	—
King's Cross	—	£ 43	—	5 50	5 53	—	5°56	5 59	—	—	—	—	—	—	—
Broad Street	5 32	—	—	—	5 41	—	—	—	—	—	—	—	6 3	6 3	—
Dalston Junction	5 39	—	—	—	5 46	—	—	—	—	—	—	—	6 10	6 10	—
Finsbury Park	5 49	5 50	5 52	5 57	5 59	5 59	5 59	6 4	6 6	6 10	6 10	6 10	6 17	6 21	6 21
Harringay	—	—	5 55	—	—	—	6 2	—	—	—	6 13	6 13	—	6 24	6 24
Hornsey	5 53	—	5 57	—	—	6 5	—	6 10	—	6 15	6 15	6 21	6 25	6 26	6 26
Wood Green	5 56	—	6 0	—	—	6 5	6 9	6 9	6 13	6 16	6 18	6 18	6 24	6 29	6 30
Bowes Park	—	—	—	—	6 8	6 12	—	6 16	6 19	6 21	—	6 27	—	6 33
Palmer's Green	—	5 58	—	6 7	—	6 15	—	6 22	6 24	—	6 30	—	—
Winchmore Hill	—	6 1	—	6 10	—	6 18	—	6 25	6 27	—	6 33	—	—
Grange Park	—	—	—	6 12	—	6 20	—	6 27	6 29	—	6 35	—	—
Enfield	—	6 4	—	6 15	—	6 23	—	6 30	6 32	—	6 37	—	—
Gordon Hill	—	6 7	—	6 18	—	6 26	—	6 35	6 37	—	—	—
Crews Hill	—	—	—	—	—	6 40	6 42	—	—	—
Cuffley	—	—	—	—	—	6 44	6 46	—	—	—
Southgate, New	6 0	—	—	—	6 13	—	—	6 22	—	6 31	6 33	—
Oakleigh Park	6 5	—	—	—	6 18	—	—	6 27	—	6 36	6 38	—
New Barnet	6 7	—	—	—	6 21	—	—	6 29	—	6 38	6 40	—
Hadley Wood	—	—	6 10	—	6ᵈ25	—	—	—	—	—
Potter's Bar	—	—	6 15	—	6ᵈ30	—	—	—	—	—
Hatfield	—	—	6 23	—	—	—	—	—	—

WEEK DAYS.

	PM	PM	e	e	d	e	e	PM	e	e	d	PM	e	e
Moorgate Street ..dep.	—	6° 5	—	6 12	—	—	6 18	—	—	6 23	—	—	—
Farringdon Street	—	6° 9	—	6 16	—	—	6 22	—	—	6 27	—	—	—
King's + (Met.)	—	6°13	—	6 20	—	—	6 26	—	—	6 31	—	—	—
King's Cross	6 15	—	6 19	6 23	6 27	6 28	—	—	6 30	6 34	—	6 42	6 42	—	6 47	—
Broad Street	—	6 10	—	—	—	—	6 20	—	—	6 27	—	—	—	6 41
Dalston Junction	—	6 15	—	—	—	—	6 25	—	—	6 33	—	—	—	6 46
Finsbury Park	6 22	6 25	6 25	6 30	—	6 33	6 34	6 36	6 37	6 40	6 43	6 48	6 48	6 50	—	6 57
Harringay	—	6 28	—	—	6 34	6 37	—	—	6 43	6 46	—	—	6 53	6 54	—
Hornsey	—	6 31	—	—	6 36	6 39	6 39	—	6 45	6 49	—	—	6 55	6 56	—
Wood Green	—	6 36	6 30	—	6 39	6 42	6 42	6 41	—	6 49	6 52	—	6 53	6 59	6 59	7 3
Bowes Park	—	6 39	—	—	—	6 45	—	—	6 52	—	—	7 5	—	7 6
Palmer's Green	—	6 42	—	6 38	—	—	—	—	6 55	—	—	7 8	—	7 9
Winchmore Hill	—	6 45	—	6 41	—	—	—	—	6 58	—	—	7 8	—	7 12
Grange Park	—	6 47	—	—	—	—	—	—	7 0	—	—	7 10	—	7 14
Enfield	—	6 50	—	6 44	—	—	—	—	7 3	—	—	7 13	—	7 16
Gordon Hill	—	6 53	—	6 47	—	—	—	—	7 6	—	—	7 18	—
Crews Hill	—	—	—	—	—	—	—	—	—	—	—	7 23	—
Cuffley	—	—	—	—	—	—	—	—	—	—	—	7 27	—
Southgate, New	—	—	—	—	6 46	—	6 45	—	—	6 56	—	6 57	—	7 3	—
Oakleigh Park	—	—	—	—	6 51	—	6 50	—	—	7 1	—	7 2	—	7 8	—
New Barnet	—	—	6 39	—	6 54	—	6 52	—	—	7 3	7 0	7 4	—	7 10	—
Hadley Wood	—	—	6 43	—	6 58	—	—	—	—	—	7 4	—
Potter's Bar	—	—	6 48	—	7 3	—	—	—	—	—	7 9	—
Hatfield	6 48	—	—	—	7 11	—	—	7 0	—	—	7 18	—

WEEK DAYS.

	d	e	e	PM	e	e	e	e	d	e	PM	PM	e	PM	PM
Moorgate Street ..dep.	—	—	—	6 52	—	7 0	—	—	—	7 14	—	—	—	—	7°48
Farringdon Street	—	—	—	6 56	—	7 4	—	—	—	7 17	—	—	—	—	7°52
King's + (Met.)	—	—	—	7 0	—	7 8	—	—	—	7 21	—	—	—	—	7°56
King's Cross	6 41	6 57	—	7 0 7	3 7	4	7 11	—	—	7 21	7 21	7 25	7 35	7 58 7 52	—	8 0
Broad Street	6 41	—	—	6 55	—	—	—	—	7 11	—	7 21	—	—	7 41	7 41
Dalston Junction	6 46	—	—	7 0	—	—	—	—	7 16	—	7 27	—	—	7 46	7 46
Finsbury Park	6 59	—	7 1	7 7	7 10	7 15	7 18	7 12	7 27	7 27	7 27	7 31	7 42	8 4	—	7 55	8 6
Harringay	7 2	7 4	7 4	—	—	7 18	7 21	7 14	7 30	7 30	—	7 34	7 45	8 7	7 59	7 58	8 9
Hornsey	7 4	7 7	7 6	—	—	7 21	7 23	7 16	7 32	7 32	—	7 36	7 47	8 9	8 1	8 12
Wood Green	7 7	7 10	7 9	7 15	7 24	7 26	7 19	7 35	7 35	7 32	7 39	7 50	8 12	8 4	8 15
Bowes Park	7 10	7 13	—	—	—	—	7 22	—	7 38	7 35	7 42	—	—	8 7	8 18
Palmer's Green	7 13	7 16	—	—	—	—	7 25	—	7 41	7 38	7 45	—	—	8 10	8 21
Winchmore Hill	7 16	7 19	—	—	—	—	7 28	—	7 44	7 41	7 48	—	—	8 13	8 24
Grange Park	7 18	7 21	—	—	—	—	7 31	—	7 46	7 43	7 50	—	—	8 15	8 26
Enfield	7 21	7 24	—	—	—	—	7 34	—	7 49	7 46	7 53	—	—	8 18	8 29
Gordon Hill	7 24	7 29	—	—	—	—	7 37	—	7 52	7 49	7 56	—	—	8 21	8 34
Crews Hill	—	7 34	—	—	—	—	—	—	—	—	—	8 39
Cuffley	—	7 38	—	—	—	—	—	—	—	—	—	8 43
Southgate, New	—	—	—	7 19	7 28	7 30	—	—	—	7 54	8 16	8 8	—
Oakleigh Park	—	—	—	7 24	7 33	7 35	—	—	—	7 59	8 21	8 18	—
New Barnet	—	—	7 27	7 37	7 38	—	—	—	8 2	8 24	8 15	—
Hadley Wood	—	—	—	7 31	7 41	—	—	—	8 6	8 28	—
Potter's Bar	—	—	—	7 36	7 46	—	—	—	8 11	8 33	—
Hatfield	—	—	7 32	—	—	—	—	—	—	—

WEEK DAYS.

	e	PM	PM	PM	PM	PM	PM	PM	PM·	PM	PM	PM	PM	PM	PM
Moorgate Street ..dep.	—	8° 8													
Farringdon Street	—	8°12													
King's + (Met.)	—	8°16													
King's Cross	8 11	8 20	8 26	8 30	—	9 0	9 10	9 12	9 23	9 45	10 0	10 2	10 20	10 23	10 45	10 55
Broad Street	8 10	8 10	—	8 34	—	8 57	9 20	—	9 20	—	10 20	—
Dalston Junction	8 17	8 17	—	8 41	—	9 2	9 27	—	9 27	—	10 25	—
Finsbury Park	8 17	8 26	8 32	8 37	8 51	9 0	9 19	9 39	9 51	10 0	8 10	10 26	10 34	10 51	11 1
Harringay	8 20	8 29	8 35	—	8 54	9 22	9 42	9 54	—	10 11	10 29	10 37	10 54	—
Hornsey	8 22	8 31	8 37	—	8 57	9 11	9 24	9 44	9 56	—	10 13	10 31	10 39	10 56	—
Wood Green	8 25	8 34	8 40	—	9 0	9 14	—	9 27	9 47	9 59	—	10 16	10 34	10 42	10 59	—
Bowes Park	8 28	8 37	—	—	9 3	—	9 30	—	10 2	—	10 19	—	10 45	—
Palmer's Green	8 31	8 40	—	—	9 6	—	9 33	—	10 5	—	10 22	—	10 48	—
Winchmore Hill	8 34	8 43	—	—	9 9	—	9 36	—	10 8	—	10 25	—	10 51	—
Grange Park	8 36	8 45	—	9 11	—	9 38	—	10 10	—	10 27	—	10 53	—
Enfield	8 39	8 48	—	9 14	—	9 41	—	10 13	—	10 30	—	10 56	—
Gordon Hill	8 42	8 51	—	9 17	—	9 44	—	10 16	—	10 33	—	10 59	—
Crews Hill	—	—	—	—	—	9 49	—	—	10ᵈ39	—	—
Cuffley	—	—	—	—	—	9 53	—	—	10ᵈ43	—	—
Southgate, New	—	—	8 44	—	9 18	—	9 51	—	10 13	—	10 38	—	11 3	—
Oakleigh Park	—	—	8 49	—	9 23	—	9 56	—	10 18	—	10 43	—	11 8	—
New Barnet	—	—	8 51	—	9 26 9 28	—	9 59	—	10 21	—	10 45	—	11 10	—
Hadley Wood	—	—	—	—	9 32	—	10 3	—	10 25	—	—	—
Potter's Bar	—	—	—	—	9 38	—	10 8	—	10 30	—	—	—
Hatfield	—	—	9 0	—	9 46	—	—	—	—	—	—	11 25

July, 1923.   S

WEEK DAYS.	PM	PM	PM	PM	PM	PM
MOORGATE STREET ..dep.	—	—	—	—	—	—
Farringdon Street	—	—	—	—	—	—
King's + (Met.)	—	—	—	—	—	—
KING'S CROSS	11 0	11 15	11 35	11 45	11 55	12 20
BROAD STREET	—	—	—	—	—	—
Dalston Junction	—	—	—	—	—	—
FINSBURY PARK	11 6	11 21	11 40	11 51	12 1	12 26
HARRINGAY	11 9	11 24	11 44	—	12 4	12 29
HORNSEY	11 11	11 26	11 47	—	12 6	12 31
WOOD GREEN	11 14	11 29	11 50	—	12 9	12 34
BOWES PARK	11 17	—	11 53	—	12 12	12 37
Palmer's Green	11 20	—	11 56	—	12 15	12 40
Winchmore Hill	11 23	—	11 59	—	12 18	12 43
Grange Park	11 25	—	12 1	—	12 20	12 45
ENFIELD	11 28	—	12 4	—	12 23	12 48
Gordon Hill	11 31	—	12 7	—	12 26	12 51
Crews Hill	—	—	—	—	—	—
Cuffley	—	—	—	—	—	—
Southgate, New	—	11 34	—	11 58	—	—
Oakleigh Park	—	11 39	—	12 3	—	—
New Barnet	—	11 42	—	12 6	—	—
Hadley Wood	—	11 46	—	12 10	—	—
Potter's Bar	—	11 51	—	12 15	—	—
HATFIELD	—	—	—	12 24	—	—

d Saturdays only.
e Saturdays excepted.
h Wednesdays only.

SUNDAYS.	PM	AM	AM	AM	AM	AM	AM	AM	PM	PM	PM	PM	PM	PM	PM	PM	PM	PM
MOORGATE STREET ..dep.	—	—	—	—	—	—	—	—	—	—	—	—	—	—	—	—	—	—
Farringdon Street	—	—	—	—	—	—	—	—	—	—	—	—	—	—	—	—	—	—
King's + (Met.)	—	—	—	—	—	—	—	—	—	—	—	—	—	—	—	—	—	—
KING'S CROSS	8 15	8 30	8 40	9 15	10 15	10 30	11 5	1140	1 6	1 10	1 40	2 40	3 10	3 20	4 15	4 35	5 0	5 42
BROAD STREET	—	—	—	—	—	—	—	—	—	—	—	—	—	—	—	—	—	—
Dalston Junction	—	—	—	—	—	—	—	—	—	—	—	—	—	—	—	—	—	—
FINSBURY PARK	8 21	8 39	8 45	9 21	10 21	10 37	1111	1146	1 12	1 16	1 46	2 46	3 17	3 26	4 21	4 41	5 6	5 48
HARRINGAY	8 24	—	8 49	9 24	10 24	—	1114	1149	1 15	1 19	1 49	2 49	3 20	3 29	4 24	4 44	5 9	5 51
HORNSEY	8 27	—	8 52	9 26	10 26	—	1116	1151	1 17	1 21	1 51	2 51	3 22	3 31	4 26	4 46	5 11	5 53
WOOD GREEN	8 34	—	8 55	9 29	10 32	—	1119	1154	1 20	1 24	1 54	2 54	3 25	3 34	4 29	4 49	5 14	5 56
BOWES PARK	—	—	8 58	—	10 32	—	—	1157	—	1 27	—	2 57	—	3 0	—	3 37	4 32	—
Palmer's Green	—	—	9 1	—	10 35	—	—	12 0	—	1 30	—	3 0	—	3 40	4 35	—	5 20	—
Winchmore Hill	—	—	9 4	—	10 38	—	—	12 3	—	1 33	—	3 3	—	3 43	4 38	—	5 23	—
Grange Park	—	—	9 6	—	10 40	—	—	12 5	—	1 35	—	3 5	—	3 45	4 40	—	5 25	—
ENFIELD	—	—	9 9	—	10 43	—	—	12 8	—	1 38	—	3 8	—	3 48	4 43	—	5 28	—
Gordon Hill	—	—	9 13	—	10 47	—	—	1213	—	1 41	—	3 13	—	3 52	4 46	—	5 33	—
Crews Hill	—	—	9 19	—	10 52	—	—	1218	—	1 48	—	3 18	—	3 57	4 50	—	5 38	—
Cuffley	—	—	9 22	—	10 56	—	—	1222	—	1 52	—	3 22	—	4 1	4 55	—	5 42	—
Southgate, New	8 38	—	—	9 33	—	—	1123	—	1 24	—	1 58	—	3 29	—	—	4 53	—	6 0
Oakleigh Park	8 42	—	—	9 38	—	—	1128	—	1 29	—	2 3	—	3 34	—	—	4 58	—	6 5
New Barnet	8 45	8 54	—	9 41	—	—	1131	—	1 32	—	2 6	—	3 37	—	—	5 1	—	6 8
Hadley Wood	—	9 0	—	9 45	—	10 50	1135	—	1 36	—	2 10	—	3 41	—	—	5 5	—	6 12
Potter's Bar	—	9 6	—	9 50	—	—	1140	—	1 41	—	2 14	—	3 46	—	—	5 10	—	6 17
HATFIELD	—	9 14	—	—	—	11 3	—	—	—	—	2 24	—	3 56	—	—	—	—	6 26

SUNDAYS.	PM	PM	PM	PM	PM	PM	PM	PM	PM	PM	PM	PM	PM	PM	PM
MOORGATE STREET ..dep.	—	—	—	—	—	—	—	—	—	—	—	—	—	—	—
Farringdon Street	—	—	—	—	—	—	—	—	—	—	—	—	—	—	—
King's + (Met.)	—	—	—	—	—	—	—	—	—	—	—	—	—	—	—
KING'S CROSS	5 50	6 25	6 50	7 10	7 22	8 0	8 10	8 30	8 35	9 0	9 30	9 45	10 0	10 34	10 52
BROAD STREET	—	—	—	—	—	—	—	—	—	—	—	—	—	—	—
Dalston Junction	—	—	—	—	—	—	—	—	—	—	—	—	—	—	—
FINSBURY PARK	5 56	6 31	6 56	7 18	7 28	8 6	8 16	8 36	8 41	9 6	—	9 51	10 7	10 41	10 58
HARRINGAY	5 59	6 34	6 59	—	7 31	—	8 19	8 39	8 44	9 9	—	9 54	10 10	10 44	11 1
HORNSEY	6 1	6 36	7 1	—	7 33	—	8 21	8 41	8 47	9 11	—	9 56	10 13	10 46	11 3
WOOD GREEN	6 4	6 39	7 4	—	7 36	—	8 24	8 44	8 50	9 14	—	9 59	10 16	10 49	11 6
BOWES PARK	6 7	6 42	—	—	7 39	—	8 27	8 47	—	9 17	—	—	10 19	10 52	—
Palmer's Green	6 10	6 45	—	—	7 42	—	8 30	8 50	—	9 20	—	—	10 22	10 55	—
Winchmore Hill	6 13	6 48	—	—	7 45	—	8 33	8 53	—	9 23	—	—	10 25	10 58	—
Grange Park	6 15	6 50	—	—	7 47	—	8 35	8 56	—	9 25	—	—	10 27	11 0	—
ENFIELD	6 18	6 53	—	—	7 50	—	8 38	8 58	—	9 28	—	—	10 30	11 3	—
Gordon Hill	6 22	6 58	—	—	7 53	—	8 42	9 3	—	9 33	—	—	10 33	11 6	—
Crews Hill	6 27	7 3	—	—	—	—	8 47	9 8	—	9 38	—	—	—	—	—
Cuffley	6 31	7 7	—	—	—	—	8 51	9 12	—	9 42	—	—	—	—	—
Southgate, New	—	—	7 8	—	—	—	—	8 54	—	—	—	10 3	—	—	11 10
Oakleigh Park	—	—	7 13	—	—	—	—	8 59	—	—	—	10 8	—	—	11 15
New Barnet	—	—	7 15	7 30	—	8 18	—	9 2	—	—	—	10 11	—	—	11 17
Hadley Wood	—	—	—	—	—	8 22	—	9 6	—	—	—	10 15	—	—	—
Potter's Bar	—	—	—	—	—	8 27	—	9 11	—	—	—	10 20	—	—	—
HATFIELD	—	—	—	7 44	—	8 36	—	—	—	—	—	10 3	10 30	—	—

HATFIELD TO KING'S CROSS, BROAD ST., & MOORGATE ST.

WEEK DAYS.	AM	AM	AM	AM	AM	AM	AM	AM	AM	AM	AM	AM	AM	AM	AM	AM
HATFIELD ..dep.	—	—	—	—	—	—	—	—	—	—	—	—	—	6 52	—
Potter's Bar	—	—	—	—	—	—	—	—	—	—	—	—	—	7 0	—
Hadley Wood	—	—	—	—	—	—	—	—	—	—	—	—	—	7 4	—
New Barnet	—	—	5 0	—	5 42	—	6 12	—	—	—	6 58	—	7 9	—
Oakleigh Park	—	—	5 2	—	5 44	—	6 14	—	—	—	7 0	—	7 12	—
Southgate, New	—	—	5 7	—	5 49	—	6 19	—	—	—	7 5	—	7 17	—
Cuffley	—	—	—	—	—	—	—	—	—	—	—	—	—	—
Crews Hill	—	—	—	—	—	—	—	—	—	—	—	—	—	—
Gordon Hill	2 50	4 27	—	5 6	—	5 55	—	6 22	—	6 46	—	—	—	—
ENFIELD	2 53	4 29	—	5 9	—	5 58	—	6 25	—	6 44	6 49	—	7 8	—
Grange Park	—	4 31	—	5 12	—	6 0	—	6 27	6 36	6 46	6 51	—	7 10	—
Winchmore Hill	2 56	4 33	—	5 14	—	6 3	—	6 30	6 39	6 49	6 54	—	7 13	—
Palmer's Green	2 59	4 36	—	5 17	—	6 6	—	6 33	6 42	6 52	6 57	—	7 16	—
Bowes Park	3 2	4 39	—	5 20	—	6 9	—	6 36	6 45	6 55	7 0	—	7 20	7 24	7 32
WOOD GREEN	3 5	4 42	5 11	5 23	5 53	5 56	5 12	6 23	6 39	6 48	6 58	7 3	7 9	7 17	7 23	7 27	7 35
HORNSEY	3 8	4 45	5 14	5 26	5 56	5 59	6 16	6 29	6 42	6 51	7 1	7 6	7 12	7 20	7 26	7 30	7 38
HARRINGAY	3 11	4 48	5 17	5 29	5 59	6 18	6 29	6 45	6 54	7 4	7 9	7 15	7 23	7 29	7 33	7 41
FINSBURY PARK	3 14	4 51	5 19	5 31	6 2	6 20	6 32	6 48	6 58	7 7	7 12	7 18	7 25	7 33	—	7 25	7 44
Dalston Junction	—	—	—	—	—	—	—	—	—	—	—	—	—	7 41	7 46
BROAD STREET	—	—	—	—	—	—	—	—	—	—	—	—	—	—
KING'S CROSS	3 19	—	5 26	5 37	6 7	6 27	6 37	—	7 3	7 13	7 18	7 24	7 32	7 39	7 30	7 49
King's + (Met.)	—	5 6	—	—	6 30	—	6 57	—	7 16	7 21	7 27	7 35	—	—	7 52
Farringdon Street	—	5 6	—	—	6 34	—	7 1	—	7 20	7 25	7 31	7 39	—	—	7 56
MOORGATE STREET	—	5 10	—	—	6 38	—	7 5	—	7 24	7 29	7 35	7 43	—	—	8 0

WEEK DAYS.	AM	AM	AM	AM	AM	AM	AM	AM	AM	AM	AM	AM	AM	AM	AM
Hatfield ....dep.	—	—	—	—	—	7 43	—	—	—	—	—	—	—	—	—
Potter's Bar	—	—	—	—	—	7 52	—	—	—	—	—	—	—	—	—
Hadley Wood	—	—	—	—	—	7 56	—	—	—	—	—	—	—	—	—
New Barnet............	—	—	7 32	7 45	—	8 0	—	—	—	—	—	—	8 8	—	—
Oakleigh Park	—	—	7 34	7 47	—	8 2	—	—	—	—	—	—	8 10	—	—
Southgate, New	7 5	—	7 39	7 52	—	8 7	—	—	—	—	—	—	8 15	—	—
Cuffley................	7 5	—	—	—	—	—	—	—	—	—	—	—	—	—	—
Crews Hill............	—	—	—	—	—	—	—	—	—	—	—	—	—	—	—
Gordon Hill	7 15	7 26	—	—	—	—	7 44	—	7 53	—	8 3	8 6	—	—	—
Enfield	7 18	7 29	—	—	—	—	7 47	—	7 56	—	8 6	8 9	—	—	—
Grange Park...........	7 20	7 31	—	—	—	—	7 49	—	7 58	—	—	8 11	—	—	—
Winchmore Hill	7 23	7 34	—	—	—	—	7 52	—	8 1	—	8 9	8 14	—	—	—
Palmer's Green	7 26	7 37	—	—	—	—	7 55	—	8 4	—	8 13	8 17	—	—	—
Bowes Park	7 29	7 40	—	—	—	—	7 58	—	8 7	8 12	—	—	—	—	8 23
Wood Green............	7 32	7 44	7 43	7 56	8 3	—	8 2	8 11	—	—	—	8 22	8 19	8 19	8 27
Hornsey	7 35	—	7 46	8 59	8 6	—	8 5	8 14	—	—	—	—	—	8 22	—
Harringay	7 38	—	7 49	8 2	8 9	—	8 8	8 17	—	—	8 21	—	—	8 25	—
Finsbury Park	7 41	—	7 52	8 6	—	8 14	8 12	8 20	8 17	8 20	8 25	8 23	—	8 28	—
Dalston Junction	—	—	—	—	—	—	8 21	8 36	—	—	8 32	—	—	—	—
Broad Street	—	—	—	—	—	—	8 28	8 43	—	—	8 39	—	—	—	—
King's Cross..........	7 46	7 53	7 57	8 14	8 15	8 19	—	8 26	8 24	—	—	8 33	—	8 37	8 37
King's + (Met.)	—	—	—	8 17	—	—	—	—	8 27	—	—	—	8 34	8 40	—
Farringdon Street	—	—	—	8 21	—	—	—	—	8 31	—	—	—	8 38	8 44	—
Moorgate Street	—	—	—	8 25	—	—	—	—	8 35	—	—	—	8 42	8 48	—

WEEK DAYS.	AM	AM	AM	AM	AM	AM	AM	AM	AM	AM	AM	AM	AM	AM	AM
Hatfield ....dep.	—	8 10	—	—	—	—	—	—	8 18	—	—	—	—	—	—
Potter's Bar	—	8 19	—	—	—	—	—	—	8 28	—	—	—	—	—	—
Hadley Wood	—	8 23	—	—	—	—	—	—	8 32	—	—	—	—	—	—
New Barnet............	—	—	8 15	—	—	—	8 21	—	8 36	—	—	—	—	—	8 49
Oakleigh Park	—	—	8 17	—	—	—	8 23	—	8 39	—	—	—	—	—	8 51
Southgate, New	—	—	8 22	—	—	8 10	8 28	—	8 44	—	—	—	—	—	8 56
Cuffley................	—	—	—	—	—	8 10	—	—	—	—	—	—	—	—	—
Crews Hill............	—	—	—	—	—	8 14	—	—	—	—	—	—	—	—	—
Gordon Hill	—	—	—	—	—	8 19	—	8 24	—	—	—	8 30	—	—	8 43
Enfield	—	—	—	8 18	—	8 22	—	8 27	—	—	—	8 33	—	—	8 46
Grange Park...........	—	—	—	8 22	—	8 24	—	8 29	—	—	—	8 25	8 40	—	—
Winchmore Hill	—	—	—	8 22	—	8 27	—	8 32	—	—	—	8 38	8 43	—	8 49
Palmer's Green........	—	—	—	8 26	—	8 31	—	8 35	—	—	—	8 42	8 47	—	8 53
Bowes Park...........	—	—	—	8 30	—	—	—	8 38	—	—	8 46	—	8 50	—	—
Wood Green............	—	—	8 26	8 34	—	8 32	—	—	—	8 43	8 49	—	8 53	8 59	—
Hornsey	8 26	—	8 29	—	8 38	8 38	—	8 43	—	8 46	8 52	8 49	—	9 2	—
Harringay	8 29	—	8 32	—	8 41	—	8 37	8 46	—	8 49	8 55	8 52	—	—	—
Finsbury Park	—	8 35	8 37	—	8 45	8 43	8 39	8 48	8 54	8 51	8 59	8 56	—	9 6	9 3
Dalston Junction	—	—	8 45	—	8 52	—	8 52	—	—	—	—	9 7	—	—	9 11
Broad Street	—	—	8 51	—	8 58	—	8 58	—	—	—	—	9 13	—	—	9 16
King's Cross..........	8 35	8 40	—	8 44	8 53	8 48	8 47	8 57	8 59	—	9 5	—	9 3	—	9 8
King's + (Met.)	—	—	—	—	8 56	—	—	—	—	—	—	—	—	—	—
Farringdon Street	—	—	—	—	9 0	—	—	—	—	—	—	—	—	—	—
Moorgate Street	—	—	—	—	9 4	—	—	—	—	—	—	—	—	—	—

WEEK DAYS.	AM	AM	AM	AM	AM	AM	AM	AM	AM	AM	AM	AM	AM	AM	AM
Hatfield ....dep.	—	—	—	—	—	8 53	—	9 9	—	—	9 15	—	—	—	—
Potter's Bar	—	—	—	—	—	9 3	—	—	—	—	9 24	—	—	—	—
Hadley Wood	—	—	—	—	—	9 8	—	—	—	—	—	—	—	—	—
New Barnet............	—	—	—	9 0	—	9 12	—	—	—	9 15	—	9 31	—	—	—
Oakleigh Park	—	—	—	9 2	—	—	—	—	—	9 17	—	9 33	—	—	—
Southgate, New	8 39	—	—	9 7	—	—	—	—	—	9 22	—	9 38	—	—	9 28
Cuffley................	8 43	—	—	—	—	—	—	—	—	—	—	—	—	—	9 32
Crews Hill............	8 48	—	—	8 55	—	—	9 0	—	9 11	—	—	—	—	9 24	9 37
Gordon Hill	8 51	—	—	8 58	—	—	9 3	—	9 14	—	—	—	—	9 27	9 40
Enfield	—	—	8 56	9 0	—	—	9 5	—	—	9 17	—	9 23	—	9 29	9 42
Grange Park...........	8 55	—	8 59	9 3	—	—	9 8	—	—	9 20	—	9 26	—	9 32	9 45
Winchmore Hill	8 59	—	9 2	9 6	—	—	9 11	—	—	9 23	—	9 29	—	9 35	9 48
Palmer's Green........	—	8 58	9 5	9 9	—	—	9 14	—	9 19	9 23	—	9 32	9 38	9 41	9 51
Bowes Park	—	9 3	—	—	9 10	—	—	—	9 22	9 26	9 38	9 35	9 41	9 54	—
Wood Green............	—	9 6	—	—	9 13	—	—	—	9 25	9 29	—	9 38	9 44	9 57	—
Hornsey	—	—	—	—	9 16	—	—	—	9 28	9 32	—	9 41	9 47	10 0	—
Harringay	9 10	9 10	9 12	9 17	9 14	9 19	9 24	9 23	9 29	9 31	9 34	9 38	9 45	9 43	9 50	10 4
Dalston Junction	—	—	—	—	—	—	9 32	—	9 42	—	9 47	—	—	—	—
Broad Street	—	—	—	—	—	—	9 38	—	9 52	—	—	—	—	—	—
King's Cross..........	9 16	9 15	9 20	9 23	9 19	9 24	—	9 34	9 37	9 40	—	9 44	9 50	9 50	9 56	10 10
King's + (Met.)	9 19	—	9 26	—	—	9 39	—	—	—	—	—	—	—	9 59	10 13
Farringdon Street	9 23	—	9 30	—	—	9 41	—	—	—	—	—	—	—	10 3	10 17
Moorgate Street	9 27	—	9 34	—	—	9 43	—	—	—	—	—	—	—	10 7	10 21

WEEK DAYS.	AM	AM	AM	AM	AM	AM	AM	AM	AM	AM	d	AM	AM	d	AM
Hatfield ....dep.	9 30	9 50	—	—	10 5	—	—	—	—	—	11 30	—	—	11 43
Potter's Bar	9 39	10 0	—	—	10 14	—	—	—	—	—	11 38	—	—	11 48
Hadley Wood	9 43	—	—	—	10 19	—	—	—	—	—	—	—	—	11 48
New Barnet............	9 47	—	10 8	10 24	—	10 40	—	—	11 10	—	—	—	—	11 52
Oakleigh Park	9 49	—	10 10	10 26	—	10 42	—	—	11 12	—	—	—	—	11 54
Southgate, New	9 54	—	10 15	10 31	—	10 47	—	—	11 17	—	—	—	—	11 59
Cuffley................	—	—	—	—	10 34	—	—	—	—	—	11 26	—	—	—
Crews Hill............	—	—	—	—	10 38	—	—	—	—	—	11 30	—	—	—
Gordon Hill	—	—	9 58	10 1	—	—	10 43	11 10	—	—	11 35	—	—	—
Enfield	—	—	9 55	10 4	—	10 27	10 46	11 13	—	—	11 37	—	—	—
Grange Park...........	—	—	9 57	10 6	—	10 29	10 48	11 15	—	—	11 40	—	—	—
Winchmore Hill	—	—	10 0	10 9	—	10 32	10 51	11 18	—	—	11 43	—	—	—
Palmer's Green........	—	—	10 3	10 12	—	10 35	10 54	11 21	—	—	11 46	—	—	—
Bowes Park...........	—	—	10 6	10 15	—	10 38	10 57	11 24	—	—	11 49	—	—	—
Wood Green............	—	—	10 9	10 19	10 36	—	10 51	11 0	11 27	11 21	—	11 52	—	12 3
Hornsey	—	—	10 12	10 22	10 39	—	10 54	11 3	11 30	11 24	—	11 55	—	12 6
Harringay	—	—	10 15	10 25	10 42	—	10 57	11 6	11 33	11 27	—	11 58	—	12 9
Finsbury Park	10 3	10 17	10 19	10 28	10 47	10 47	10 59	11 8	11 33	11 31	11 43	11 53	12 1	12 12	9 12	12 12
Dalston Junction	10 11	—	10 27	—	10 55	—	—	—	11 46	11 39	—	—	—	12 20
Broad Street	10 18	—	10 33	—	11 3	—	—	—	11 54	11 46	—	—	—	12 27
King's Cross..........	10 8	10 22	—	10 33	10 52	—	11 18	—	—	11 51	12 3	12 6	12 17	—
King's + (Met.)	—	—	—	—	—	—	11 21	—	11 54	—	12 6	12 20	—
Farringdon Street	—	—	—	—	—	—	11 23	—	11 58	—	12 10	12 24	—
Moorgate Street	—	—	—	—	—	—	11 26	—	12 2	—	12 14	12 28	—

WEEK DAYS.	d	d	e	d	PM	d	e	d	PM	e	d	d	PM	PM	PM	PM	PM
Hatfield ...... dep.	—	—	—	—	12 5	—	—	—	—	—	—	—	—	—	—	—	1 45
Potter's Bar	—	—	—	—	12 14	—	—	—	—	12 42	1242	—	—	1 24	—	1 54	
Hadley Wood	—	—	—	—	12 19	—	—	—	—	12 47	1247	—	—	1 2)	—	1 55	
New Barnet	—	—	—	—	12 23	—	—	—	—	12 53	1253	—	—	1 33	—	2 02	4
Oakleigh Park	—	—	—	—	12 25	—	—	—	—	12 56	1256	—	—	1 35	—	2 2	—
Southgate, New	—	—	—	—	12 30	—	—	—	—	1 1	1 1	—	—	1 40	—	2 7	—
Cuffley	—	—	—	—	—	—	—	—	—	—	—	1 2	—	—	—	—	
Crews Hill	—	—	—	—	—	—	—	—	—	—	—	1 6	—	—	—	—	
Gordon Hill	12 5	—	12 15	12 20	—	12 36	—	—	—	1 0	1 10	—	1 40	—			
Enfield	12 8	—	12 18	12 23	—	12 39	—	—	—	1 5	1 13	—	1 43	—			
Grange Park	12 10	—	12 20	12 25	—	12 41	—	—	—	1 8	1 15	—	1 45	—			
Winchmore Hill	12 13	—	12 23	12 28	—	12 44	—	—	—	1 8	1 18	—	1 48	—			
Palmer's Green	12 16	—	12 26	12 31	—	12 47	—	—	—	111	1 21	—	1 51	—			
Bowes Park	12 19	—	12 29	12 34	—	12 50	—	—	—	114	1 24	—	1 54	—			
Wood Green	12 22	—	12 32	12 37	12 34	—	12 53	—	1 51	5	117	1 27	1 44	1 57	2 11	—	
Hornsey	12 25	—	12 35	12 40	—	12 56	—	1 81	8	120	1 30	1 47	2 0	2 14	—		
Harringay	12 28	—	12 38	12 43	—	12 59	—	1 11	1 11	123	1 33	1 50	2 3	2 17	—		
Finsbury Park	12 30	1238	12 40	12 47	12 40	12 58	1 1	12	1 20	1 15	15	126	1 37	1 53	2 6	2 20	2 17
Dalston Junction																	
Broad Street																	
King's Cross	—	1245	—	12 54	12 45	1 4	—	1 18	1 25	1 20	1	20	133	1 45	1 59	2'12 2 25	2 22
King's + (Met.)	12 40	1248	—	12 57	1 7	—	1 21	—	1	26	1361448	2'24 2415	2432				
Farringdon Street	12 44	1252	—	1 1	—	1 11	—	1 25	—	1	30	140 1d52	2'4 6 2419	2,36			
Moorgate Street	12 48	1256	—	1 5	—	1 15	—	1 29	—	1	34	144 1d56	2'10 2'23	2'40	—		

WEEK DAYS.	d	e	d	PM	PM	d	e	d	d	d	d	PM	e	PM	PM	e	d
Hatfield .... dep.														3 45			
Potter's Bar	—	—	—	2 20	—	2 33	—	—	—	—	—	3 10	—	3 53	—		
Hadley Wood	—	—	—	2 25	—	2 38	—	—	—	—	—	3 15	—	3 58	—		
New Barnet	—	—	—	2 29	—	2 42 2 58	—	—	—	—	—	3 20	3 39	—	4 3	—	
Oakleigh Park	—	—	—	2 31	—	2 44 3 0	—	—	—	—	—	3 23	3 41	—			
Southgate, New	—	—	—	2 36	—	2 49 3 5	—	—	—	—	—	3 29	3 46	—			
Cuffley	—	—	—	—	2 24	—	—	—	2 52	—	3 9	—	3 43	—			
Crews Hill	—	—	—	—	2 28	—	—	—	2 56	—	3 13	—	3 47	—			
Gordon Hill	—	2 8	2 8	—	2 33	—	2 51	2 51	3 0	—	3 17	—	3 52	—	4 6		
Enfield	—	2 11	2 11	—	2 36	—	2 54	2 54	3 2	—	3 20	—	3 55	—	4 8		
Grange Park	—	2 13	2 13	—	2 38	—	2 56	2 56	3 4	—	3 22	—	3 57	—	4 10		
Winchmore Hill	—	2 16	2 16	—	2 41	—	2 59	2 59	3 7	—	3 25	—	4 0	—	4 13		
Palmer's Green	—	2 19	2 19	—	2 44	—	3 2	3 2	3 10	—	3 28	—	4 3	—	4 16		
Bowes Park	—	2 22	2 22	—	2 47	—	3 53	3 53	3 13	—	3 31	—	4 6	—	4 19		
Wood Green	—	2 25	2 25	2 40	2 50	2 55 3	9 3	83	83	3 16	—	3 43	3 43	3 50	4 9	—	4 22
Hornsey	—	2 28	2 28	2 43	2 53	2 58 3	12 3	11	—	3 19	—	3 56	4 13	3 53	4 12	—	4 25
Harringay	—	2 31	2 31	2 46	2 56	3	1 3	15	3 14	—	3 22	—	3 40	3 44	2 56	4 15	—	4 28
Finsbury Park	227	3	34	2 34	2 49	2 59	3	63	183	183	183	3 24	343 343	3'43 3	463	59 4	20 4 18 432	4 32
Dalston Junction	236	2	42	—	—	3	163	26	—	3	26	—	351	—	4d 1	—	—	440	4 40
Broad Street	243	2	49	—	—	3	233	34	—	3	34	—	258	—	4d 7	—	—	445	4 45
King's Cross	—	2	42	2 44	2 54	3"	4	—	3	23	—	—	348	3'50	—	4	5 4 27	4 23	—
King's + (Met.)	—	—	2	47	—	—	—	—	—	—	3'53	—	4 8	4'30	—		
Farringdon Street	—	—	2	53	—	—	—	—	—	—	3'57	—	4 12	4'34	—		
Moorgate Street	—	—	2	55	—	—	—	—	—	—	4' 1	—	4 16	4'38	—		

WEEK DAYS.	e	PM	e	PM	e	PM	e	PM	PM	PM	e	PM	PM	e	PM	d	e	PM
Hatfield .... dep.					5 0	—												
Potter's Bar	—	—	—	—	5 9	—	—	—	5 19	—								
Hadley Wood	—	—	—	—	5 14	—	—	—	5 23	—								
New Barnet	4 30	—	—	4 45	5 19 5 8	—	—	5 29	—	—	5 53	—	6 23					
Oakleigh Park	4 32	—	—	4 58	5 21 5 10	—	—	5 31	—	—	5 55	—	6 25					
Southgate, New	4 37	—	—	'5 3	5 27 5 15	—	—	5 36	—	—	6 0	—	6 30					
Cuffley	—	—	—	—	—	4 50	—	—	—	—	5 26	—	—	5 58 5 58	—			
Crews Hill	—	—	—	—	—	4 54	—	—	—	—	5 30	—	—	6 2 6 2	—			
Gordon Hill	—	—	—	4 32	—	5 0 5 20	—	—	—	5 35	—	—	6 6 6 6	—				
Enfield	—	—	—	4 35	—	5 5 5 23	—	—	—	5 38 5 44	—	—	6 9 6 9	—				
Grange Park	—	—	—	4 37	—	5 8 5 28	—	—	—	5 40 5 46	—	—	6 11 6 12	—				
Winchmore Hill	—	—	—	4 43	—	5 9 5 28	—	—	—	5 43 5 49	—	—	6 15 6 15	—				
Palmer's Green	—	—	—	4 43	—	5 13 5 31	—	—	—	5 46 5 52	—	—	6 18 6 18	—				
Bowes Park	—	—	—	4 46	—	5 17 5 34	—	—	—	5 49 5 55	—	—	6 21 6 21	—				
Wood Green	4 41	—	—	4 49 5	7 5 31 5 19 5 21 5 37 5 40	—	—	5 52 5 58 6	4 6 24 6 24 6 34								
Hornsey	4 44	—	—	4 52 5 10	—	5 24 5 40 5 43	—	—	5 55 6	1 6 7 6 27 6 27 6 37								
Harringay	4 47	—	—	4 55 5 13	—	5 27 5 43 5 46	—	—	5 58 6	4 6 10 6 30 6 30 6 40								
Finsbury Park	4 45 4 49 4 58 5	2 5 18 5 40 5 25 5 31 5 46 5 49 5 52 5 55 6	36 7 6 13 6 33 6 33 6 42															
Dalston Junction	—	—	—	5 10	—	—	—	—	5 56	—								
Broad Street	—	—	—	5 15	—	—	—	—	6 4	—								
King's Cross	4 52 4 59 5 5	—	5 25 5 45 5 31 5'38 5'52	—	6 06 6 6 13	—	6 40 6 43 6'50											
King's + (Met.)	4 55 5' 2 5 8	—	5 28	—	5 34 5'41 5'55	—	6 1	—	6'13 6 16 6'22	—	6 46 6'53							
Farringdon Street	4 59 5' 6 5 12	—	5 32	—	5 38 5'45 5'59	—	6 5	—	6'17 6 20 6'26	—	6 50 6'57							
Moorgate Street	5 3 5'10 5 16	—	5 36	—	5 42 5'49 6' 3	—	6 9	—	6'21 6 24 6'30	—	6 54 7' 1							

WEEK DAYS.	PM	d	e	d	e	d	PM	PM	PM	e	PM	PM	e	PM	PM	PM
Hatfield .... dep.	6 27							7 38			7 55	—				
Potter's Bar	6 36	—	—	—	—	—	7 30	—	—	7 47	—					
Hadley Wood	6 40	—	—	—	—	—	7 35	—	—	8 8	—					
New Barnet	6 46	—	6 38	—	6 47	7 17	—	7 40	—	—	8 12	—				
Oakleigh Park	—	—	6 40	—	6 49	7 19	—	7 42	—	—	8 14	—				
Southgate, New	—	—	6 45	—	6 54	7 24	—	7 47	—	—	8 19	—				
Cuffley	—	6 15 6 22	—	6 58	—	—	—	—	—	7 40	—	7 54	—			
Crews Hill	—	6 19 6 26	—	6 42	—	—	—	—	—	7 44	—	7 58	—			
Gordon Hill	—	6 20 6 29 6 30	—	6 43 6 47	7 3 7 9	—	7 37	—	7 49	—	8 8 18				
Enfield	—	6 23 6 26 6 33	—	6 46 6 50	7 5 7 12 7 25 7 40	—	7 52	—	8 6 8 21					
Grange Park	—	6 25 6 29 6 35	—	6 48 6 52	7 7 7 14 7 27 7 42	—	7 54	—	8 8 8 23					
Winchmore Hill	—	6 28 6 31 6 38	—	6 51 6 55	7 9 7 17 7 30 7 45	—	7 57	—	8 11 8 26					
Palmer's Green	—	6 31 6 34 6 41	—	6 54 6 58	7 12 7 20 7 33 7 48	—	8 0	—	8 14 8 29					
Bowes Park	—	6 34 6 37 6 44	—	6 58 7 2	7 15 7 23 7 36 7 51	—	8 3	—	8 17 8 32					
Wood Green	—	6 37 6 40 6 47 6 49 7	6 58 7 18 7 28 7 39 7 56 7 51	6	8 6	—	8 20 8 35							
Hornsey	—	6 40 6 43 6 50	—	7 57 7 87	7 21 7 27 7 42 7 59 7 54	—	8 9	8 27 8 23 8 38						
Harringay	—	6 43 6 46 6 53	—	7 55 7 7 11 7	7 24 7 34 7 45 8 2 7 57	—	8 12	8 30 8 26 8 41						
Finsbury Park	7 06 6 46 6 49 6 53 7	7 16 7 14 7	37 7 39 7 49 8 8	8 18 8 33 8 28 8 43										
Dalston Junction	—	6 55	—	7 8	—	7 16 7 38	—	7 57 8 16 8	9 8	8'47	—				
Broad Street	—	7 3	—	7 13	—	7 24 7 44	—	8 4 8 23 8 16	8 16	—					
King's Cross	7 5	—	6 54 6 59	—	7 21 7 19	—	7 44	—	—	8 5	—	8 38 8 40				
King's + (Met.)	—	—	7 2	—	7 24	—	7'47	—	—							
Farringdon Street	—	—	7 6	—	7 29	—	7'53	—	—							
Moorgate Street	—	—	7 10	—	7 33	—	7'55	—	—							

WEEK DAYS

	PM	PM	PM	PM	PM	PM	PM	PM	PM	PM	PM	PM	PM	PM
Hatfield ...dep.	—	—	—	—	9 15	—	—	—	9 43	—	10 30	—	—	—
Potter's Bar	8 27	—	—	—	9 24	—	—	—	9 52	—	10 39	—	10 50	—
Hadley Wood	8 32	—	—	—	9 29	—	—	—	9 56	—	—	—	10 55	—
New Barnet	8 37	—	—	9 15	9 34	—	9 55	—	10 1	—	—	—	10 59	—
Oakleigh Park	8 39	—	—	9 17	—	—	9 57	—	—	—	—	—	11 1	—
Southgate, New	8 44	—	—	9 22	—	—	10 2	—	—	—	—	—	11 6	—
Cuffley	—	—	8 54	—	—	—	—	—	—	10 6	—	10 50	—	—
Crews Hill	—	—	8 57	—	—	—	—	—	—	10 10	—	10 54	—	—
Gordon Hill	—	8 42	9 2	—	—	9 29	—	9 55	—	10 15	—	10 59	—	11 19
Enfield	—	8 45	9 5	—	—	9 32	—	9 58	—	10 18	—	11 2	—	11 22
Grange Park	—	8 47	9 7	—	—	9 34	—	10 0	—	10 20	—	11 4	—	11 24
Winchmore Hill	—	8 50	9 10	—	—	9 37	—	16 3	—	10 23	—	11 7	—	11 27
Palmer's Green	—	8 53	9 13	—	—	9 40	—	10 6	—	10 26	—	11 10	—	11 30
Bowes Park	—	8 56	9 16	—	—	9 43	—	10 9	—	10 29	—	11 13	—	11 33
Wood Green	8 47	8 59	9 19	9 26	—	9 46	10 6	10 12	—	10 32	—	11 16	11 10	11 36
Hornsey	8 51	9 2	9 22	9 29	—	9 49	10 9	10 15	—	10 35	—	11 19	11 13	11 39
Harringay	8 54	9 5	9 25	9 32	—	9 52	10 12	10 18	—	10 38	—	11 22	11 15	11 42
Finsbury Park	8 57	9 9	9 28	9 35	9 45	9 54	10 14	10 21	10 15	10 42	10 55	11 24	11 19	11 44
Dalston Junction	—	9 17	—	—	—	10 2	—	—	—	—	—	—	—	—
Broad Street	—	9 24	—	—	—	10 7	—	—	—	—	—	—	—	—
King's Cross	9 2	—	9 33	9 41	9 50	—	—	10 26	10 20	10 47	11 0	11 50	—	11 50
King's + (Met.)	—	—	—	—	—	—	—	—	—	—	—	—	—	—
Farringdon Street	—	—	—	—	—	—	—	—	—	—	—	—	—	—
Moorgate Street	—	—	—	—	—	—	—	—	—	—	—	—	—	—

SUNDAYS.

	AM	AM	AM	AM	AM	AM	AM	PM	PM	PM	PM	PM	PM	PM	PM	PM	PM
Hatfield ...dep.	—	—	9 0	—	—	—	—	2 40	—	—	4 20	—	5 50	—			
Potter's Bar	—	—	9 11	—	10 3	—	12 10	1 54	—	2 49	—	4 29	—	5 35			
Hadley Wood	—	—	9 16	—	10 8	—	12 15	1 58	—	2 54	—	4 34	—	5 40			
New Barnet	—	7 58	9 15	9 20	—	10 12	—	12 19	2 2	—	2 57	—	4 38	—	5 44		
Oakleigh Park	—	8 0	9 17	9 23	—	10 14	—	12 21	2 4	—	2 59	—	4 41	—	5 46		
Southgate, New	—	8 5	9 22	9 29	—	10 19	—	12 26	2 9	—	3 4	—	4 46	—	5 51		
Cuffley	—	—	—	9 35	—	11 40	1 4	—	2 4	—	3 30	4 40	—	5 5	—		
Crews Hill	—	—	—	9 43	—	11 44	1 8	—	2 8	—	3 34	4 44	—	5 9	—		
Gordon Hill	7 30	—	—	9 44	—	11 49	1 13	—	2 12	—	3 38	4 49	—	5 14	—		
Enfield	7 32	—	—	9 47	—	11 52	1 16	—	2 15	—	3 41	4 52	—	5 17	—		
Grange Park	7 34	—	—	9 49	—	11 54	1 18	—	2 17	—	3 43	4 54	—	5 19	—		
Winchmore Hill	7 36	—	—	9 52	—	11 57	1 21	—	2 20	—	3 46	4 57	—	5 22	—		
Palmer's Green	7 39	—	—	9 55	—	12 0	1 24	—	2 23	—	3 49	5 0	—	5 25	—		
Bowes Park	7 42	—	—	9 58	—	12 3	1 27	—	2 26	—	3 52	5 3	—	5 28	—		
Wood Green	7 45	8 9	9 26	9 34	10	1 10 23	12 6	1 30	2 13	2 29	3 8	3 55	5 6	4 50	5 31	—	5 55
Hornsey	7 48	8 12	9 29	9 38	10	4 10 26	12 9	1 33	2 16	2 32	3 11	3 58	5 9	4 53	5 34	—	5 58
Harringay	7 51	8 15	9 32	9 42	10	7 10 29	12 12	1 36	2 19	2 35	3 14	4 1	5 12	4 56	5 37	—	6 1
Finsbury Park	7 53	8 18	9 35	9 48	10 10	10 32	12 15	1 39	2 22	2 37	3 17	4 4	4 15	5 0	5 40	6 12	6 3
Dalston Junction	—	—	—	—	—	—	—	—	—	—	—	—	—	—	—		
Broad Street	—	—	—	—	—	—	—	—	—	—	—	—	—	—	—		
King's Cross	8 0	8 25	9 40	9 53	10 15	10 38	12 20	1 44	2 27	2 43	3 23	4 9	5 20	5 5	5 45	6 17	6 9
King's + (Met.)	—	—	—	—	—	—	—	—	—	—	—	—	—	—	—		
Farringdon Street	—	—	—	—	—	—	—	—	—	—	—	—	—	—	—		
Moorgate Street	—	—	—	—	—	—	—	—	—	—	—	—	—	—	—		

SUNDAYS.

	PM	PM	PM	PM	PM	PM	PM	PM	PM	PM	PM			
Hatfield ...dep.	—	6 55	—	—	7 30	—	—	9 0	—	—	—			
Potter's Bar	—	7 5	—	—	7 40	—	—	9 10	—	9 48	—			
Hadley Wood	—	7 10	—	—	7 45	—	—	9 15	—	9 52	—			
New Barnet	—	7 14	—	—	7 50 8 10	—	—	9 19	—	9 57	—			
Oakleigh Park	—	7 16	—	—	—	8 12	—	9 22	—	9 59	—			
Southgate, New	—	7 21	—	—	—	8 17	—	9 27	—	10 4	—			
Cuffley	5 51	—	7 5 7 35	—	—	—	9 1	—	9 30 9 52	—				
Crews Hill	5 55	—	7 9 7 39	—	—	—	9 5	—	9 34 9 56	—				
Gordon Hill	6 0	—	7 15 7 44	—	—	8 19	9 9	—	9 39 10 0	—	10 45			
Enfield	6 3	—	7 17 7 47	—	—	8 22	9 12	—	9 42 10 3	—	10 48			
Grange Park	6 5	—	7 20 7 49	—	—	8 24	9 14	—	9 44 10 5	—	10 50			
Winchmore Hill	6 8	—	7 23 7 52	—	—	8 27	9 17	—	9 47 10 8	—	10 53			
Palmer's Green	6 11	—	7 26 7 55	—	—	8 30	9 20	—	9 50 10 11	—	10 56			
Bowes Park	6 14	—	7 29 7 58	—	—	8 33	9 23	—	9 53 10 14	—	10 59			
Wood Green	6 17	7 25 7 33 8 1	—	8 21	8 36	9 26 9 32	9 56 10 17 10 8	11 2						
Hornsey	6 20	7 28 7 36 8 4	—	8 24	8 40	9 29 9 36	9 59 10 20 10 11	11 5						
Harringay	6 23	7 31 7 39 8 7	—	8 27	8 43	9 32 9 39	10 2 10 23 10 14	11 8						
Finsbury Park	6 27	7 35 7 41 8 10	8 38 30	8 46	9 35 9 43	10 5 10 26 10 16	11 11							
Dalston Junction	—	—	—	—	—	—	—	—	—	—	—			
Broad Street	—	—	—	—	—	—	—	—	—	—	—			
King's Cross	6 32	7 40	—	8 15	8 8 35	8 51	9 40	9 48	10 10 10 31	—	11 16			
King's + (Met.)	—	—	—	—	—	—	—	—	—	—	—			
Farringdon Street	—	—	—	—	—	—	—	—	—	—	—			
Moorgate Street	—	—	—	—	—	—	—	—	—	—	—			

d Saturdays only. e Saturdays excepted. o Mondays excepted. n Noon.

WEEK DAYS. (Section 1)

	AM	AM	AM	AM	AM	AM	AM	AM	AM	AM	AM	AM	AM	AM	AM	AM	AM	AM	AM
Moorgate Street .... dep.	—	—	—	—	6 45	—	7 10	—	—	—	—	—	7 48	7 57	8 16	—	—		
Farringdon Street	—	—	—	—	6 49	—	7 14	—	—	—	—	—	7 52	8 1	8 20	—	—		
King's Cross	5 32	—	6 15	6 40	6 53	—	7 21	—	7 38	7 52	—	—	7 56	8 5	8 27	—	—		
Broad Street	—	—	6 5	—	6 48	—	7 10	—	—	7 43	7 50	8 0	—	—	—	8 20	8 27		
Haggerston	—	—	6 10	—	6 53	—	7 8	—	—	—	7 57	—	—	—	—	8 25	—		
Dalston Junction	—	—	6 12	—	6 55	—	7 16	—	—	7 48	7 59	8 5	—	—	—	8 27	8 32		
Mildmay Park	—	—	6 14	—	6 57	—	7 19	—	—	7 50	8 1	8 7	—	—	—	8 30	8 34		
Canonbury	—	—	6 16	—	6 59	—	7 21	—	—	7 52	8 6	8 9	—	—	—	8 32	8 36		
Finsbury Park	5 39	5 35	6 21	6 46	7 6	7 1	7 27	28	7 40	7 57	7 57	—	8 14	—	8 20	8 33	8 37	8 40	
Stroud Green	5 42	5 38	6 24	6 49	—	7 15	7 32	7 43	7 40	8	—	—	8 17	—	8 23	8 36	—	8 44	
Crouch End	5 43	5 41	6 27	6 52	—	7 18	7 35	7 46	7 43	8 5	—	—	8 20	—	8 26	8 39	—	8 47	
Highgate	5 49	5 45	6 31	6 56	7 13	—	7 22	7 39	7 50	7 47	8 9	—	8 24	—	8 30	8 43	—	8 51	
Cranley Gardens	—	—	—	—	—	—	—	7 50	—	—	—	—	8 27	—	—	8 46	—		
Muswell Hill	—	5 49	—	—	—	—	—	7 52	—	—	—	—	8 30	—	—	8 48	—		
Alexandra Palace	—	—	—	—	—	—	—	7 54	—	—	—	—	8 33	—	—	8 50	—		
East Finchley	5 53	—	6 37	6 59	7 17	—	7 26	7 43	7 54	—	8 13	—	—	—	8 34	—	—	8 55	
Finchley	5 57	—	6 41	7 4	7 21	—	7 31	7 48	8 5	—	8 17	—	—	—	8 39	—	—	8 59	
Mill Hill	—	—	6 53	—	—	—	7 40	—	8 8	—	8 40	—	—	—	—	—	—	9 11	
The Hale	—	—	6 57	—	—	—	7 44	—	8 12	—	8 44	—	—	—	—	—	—	9 15	
Edgware	—	—	7 0	—	—	—	7 47	—	8 15	—	8 47	—	—	—	—	—	—	9 18	
Woodside Park	6 1	—	6 45	7 8	—	—	7 35	7 51	—	—	8 21	—	—	—	8 43	—	—	9 3	
Totteridge and Whetstone	6 4	—	6 48	7 11	—	—	7 38	7 55	—	—	8 24	—	—	—	8 46	—	—	9 6	
High Barnet	6 9	—	6 52	7 15	—	—	7 42	7 59	—	—	8 29	—	—	—	8 50	—	—	9 10	

WEEK DAYS. (Section 2)

	AM	AM	AM	AM	AM	AM	AM	AM	AM	AM	AM	AM	AM	AM	AM	AM	AM
Moorgate Street ......dep.	—	—	8 45	8 51	—	8 57	9 2 9	7	9 30	9 52	10	010	6	10 24	—	—	—
Farringdon Street	—	—	8 49	8 55	—	9 1	9 6	9 11	9 34	9 56	10	4	10	10 28	—	—	—
King's Cross	—	—	8 53	8 59	—	9 5	9 10	9 15	9 43	10	4	10	8	10 20	10 36	—	—	11 25
Broad Street	8 34	8 42	—	9 0	—	9 10	—	—	—	—	9 55	—	—	—	—	—	10 27
Haggerston	—	8 42	—	8 57	—	9 12	—	—	—	—	10 0	—	—	—	—	—	10 32
Dalston Junction	8 40	8 47	—	9 5	—	9 16	—	—	—	—	10 2	—	—	—	—	—	10 34
Mildmay Park	8 42	8 49	—	8 58	—	9 18	—	—	—	—	10 4	—	—	—	—	—	10 26
Canonbury	8 44	8 51	—	9 0	—	9 21	—	—	—	—	10 6	—	—	—	—	—	10 38
Finsbury Park	8 48	8 59	9	3 9	12 9	15 9	19 9	27 9	30	9 54	10	11 10	19 10	29 10	43 10	53 11	12	11 32
Stroud Green	—	8 59	9 6	—	9 18	9 22	9 30	9 32	9 57	10	14 10	22 10	32 10	46 11	1 11	15	11 35	
Crouch End	—	9	9 9	—	9 21	9 25	9 33	9 37	10	0 10	17 10	25 10	35 10	49 11	4 11	18	11 38	
Highgate	8 56	—	9 13	—	9 26	9 29	9 37	9 41	10	4 10	21 10	29 10	39 10	53 11	8 11	22	11 42	
Cranley Gardens	—	—	—	—	9 32	—	9 44	—	10	24 10	32	—	10 56	—	11 25	—	
Muswell Hill	9	1 9	10	—	9 22	—	9 34	—	9 46	—	10	26 10	34	—	10 58	—	11 27	—
Alexandra Palace	9	3 9	12	—	9 25	—	9 36	—	9 49	—	10	28 10	36	—	11 0	—	11 29	—
East Finchley	—	—	9 17	—	9 29	—	9 41	—	10	8	—	—	10 43	—	11 12	—	11 48
Finchley	—	—	9 21	—	9 34	—	9 45	—	10	12	—	—	10 47	—	11 17	—	11 53
Mill Hill	—	—	9 30	—	9 38	—	—	—	10	16	—	—	10 51	—	11 25	—	—
The Hale	—	—	9 42	—	—	—	—	—	10	20	—	—	10 55	—	11 29	—	—
Edgware	—	—	9 45	—	—	—	—	—	10	23	—	—	10 53	—	11 32	—	—
Woodside Park	—	9 25	—	9 38	—	9 49	—	10	16	—	—	10 51	—	11 21	—	11 57	
Totteridge and Whetstone	—	9 28	—	9 41	—	9 52	—	10	19	—	—	10 54	—	11 24	—	12 0	
High Barnet	—	9 32	—	9 45	—	9 57	—	10	23	—	—	10 58	—	11 28	—	12 4	

WEEK DAYS. (Section 3)

	AM	d	d	e	AM	PM	e	e	e	d	d	PM	d	e	d
Moorgate Street ......dep.	—	—	11 43	—	—	12 11	—	—	12 16	12 21	12 31	—	—	—	—
Farringdon Street	—	—	11 47	—	—	12 15	—	—	12 20	12 25	12 35	—	—	—	—
King's Cross	11 37	11 45	11 55	—	—	12 10	12 19	—	12 28	12 32	12 39	12 45	—	—	—
Broad Street	11 27	—	—	11 52	—	—	—	12 20	—	12 20	—	12 34	—	—	—
Haggerston	11 32	—	—	11 57	—	—	—	12 12	—	12 12	—	12 39	—	—	—
Dalston Junction	11 34	—	—	11 59	—	—	—	12 25	—	12 25	—	12 41	—	—	—
Mildmay Park	11 36	—	—	12 1	—	—	—	12 27	—	12 27	—	12 43	—	—	—
Canonbury	11 38	—	—	12 3	—	—	—	12 29	—	12 29	—	12 45	—	—	—
Finsbury Park	11 44	11 51	12	6 12	10	—	12 16	12 29	12 34	12 35	12 38	12 38	12 48	12 54	—	1 2	1 6
Stroud Green	11 47	11 54	12	9 12	13	—	12 19	12 32	12 37	—	—	12 41	12 5	12 58	—	1 5	1 9
Crouch End	11 50	11 57	12	12 12	16	—	12 22	12 35	12 40	12 40	—	12 44	12 54	1 1	—	1 8	1 12
Highgate	11 54	12	1 12	16 12	20	—	12 26	12 39	12 44	—	—	12 48	12 58	1 6	—	1 12	1 16
Cranley Gardens	11 57	—	12 19	—	—	12 29	12 42	—	—	—	—	1 1	—	—	1 15	1 19
Muswell Hill	11 59	—	12 21	—	—	12 31	12 44	—	—	—	—	1 3	—	—	1 17	1 21
Alexandra Palace	12 1	—	12 23	—	—	12 33	12 46	—	—	—	—	1 5	—	—	1 19	1 23
East Finchley	—	12 5	—	12 23	—	—	—	12 48	12 46	—	12 52	—	1 10	—	—
Finchley	—	12 10	—	12 23	12 15	—	—	12 53	12 51	—	12 56	—	1 15	1 25	—
Mill Hill	—	—	—	—	12 18	—	—	12 58	12 58	—	—	—	—	1 28	—
The Hale	—	—	—	—	12 22	—	1 2	1 2	—	—	—	—	—	1 22	—
Edgware	—	—	—	—	12 25	—	1 5	1 5	—	—	—	—	—	1 35	—
Woodside Park	—	12 14	—	12 32	—	—	—	12 57	12 55	—	1 0	—	1 19	—	—
Totteridge and Whetstone	—	12 17	—	12 35	—	—	—	1 0	12 58	—	1 3	—	1 22	—	—
High Barnet	—	12 21	—	12 40	—	—	—	1 4	1 1	—	1 7	—	1 26	—	—

WEEK DAYS. (Section 4)

	PM	PM	d	e	d	PM	d	PM	e	PM	d	d	d	d	d	e	PM	d
Moorgate Street ......dep.	Sats. only.	Sats only	—	—	—	1 13	—	1 19	—	—	1 27	—	1 47	—	1 54	—	1 59	2 6
Farringdon Street			—	—	—	1 17	—	1 23	—	—	1 31	—	1 51	—	1 58	—	2 3	2 10
King's Cross			—	—	—	1 21	1 27	1 27	1 34	—	1 35	—	1 55	2 2	2 2	2 10	2 7	2 14
Broad Street		1 3	1 11	1 10	—	—	1 18	—	—	1 25	—	1 41	1 50	—	—	—	—	2 11
Haggerston		12 57	1 12	1 15	—	—	—	—	—	1 27	—	1 37	1 43	—	—	—	—	2 12
Dalston Junction		1 9	1 16	1 17	—	—	1 25	—	—	1 31	—	1 46	1 55	—	—	—	—	2 16
Mildmay Park		1 11	—	1 19	—	—	1 27	—	—	—	—	—	1 58	—	—	—	—	—
Canonbury		1 13	—	1 21	—	—	1 29	—	—	1 34	—	—	1 59	—	—	—	—	—
Finsbury Park	1 12	1 18	1 23	1 26	1 26	1 30	1 34	1 39	1 41	1 39	1 44	1 54	2 2	2 10	2 13	2 16	2 18	2 25
Stroud Green	1 15	1 21	—	1 29	1 29	1 33	1 37	1 42	1 44	—	1 47	1 57	2 7	2 13	2 19	2 2	2 21	2 28
Crouch End	1 18	1 24	—	1 32	1 32	1 36	1 40	1 45	1 47	—	1 50	2	2 10	2 16	2 19	2 22	2 24	2 31
Highgate	1 22	1 28	1 32	1 36	1 36	1 40	1 44	1 49	1 51	—	1 54	2 4	2 14	2 20	2 23	2 26	2 28	2 35
Cranley Gardens	—	1 31	—	—	—	1 43	—	1 52	1 54	—	—	2 7	—	2 23	—	—	2 31	—
Muswell Hill	—	1 33	—	—	—	1 45	—	1 54	1 56	—	—	2 9	—	2 25	—	—	2 33	—
Alexandra Palace	—	1 36	—	—	—	1 47	—	1 56	1 58	—	—	2 11	—	2 28	—	—	2 35	—
East Finchley	1 23	—	1 36	1 40	—	—	1 48	—	—	1 58	—	2 18	—	2 26	2 30	—	2 39	
Finchley	1 31	—	1 41	1 45	—	—	1 52	—	—	2 2	—	2 23	—	2 31	2 35	—	2 43	
Mill Hill	—	—	—	—	—	—	1 54	—	—	2 6	—	2 26	—	—	2 38	—	—	
The Hale	—	—	—	—	—	—	2	—	—	2 10	—	2 30	—	—	2 42	—	—	
Edgware	1 35	—	1 45	1 49	—	—	2 5	—	—	2	—	2 33	—	—	2 45	—	—	
Woodside Park	—	1 38	—	—	—	—	1 56	—	—	2 6	—	—	—	2 35	2 39	—	2 47	
Totteridge and Whetstone	1 38	—	1 48	1 52	—	—	1 59	—	—	2 9	—	—	—	2 38	2 42	—	2 50	
High Barnet	1 42	—	1 52	1 56	—	—	2 3	—	—	2 13	—	—	—	2 42	2 46	—	2 55	

d Saturdays only.   e Saturdays excepted.

WEEK DAYS.

WEEK DAYS.	d	PM	PM	PM	d	d	e	d	d	e	PM	PM	e	d	PM	PM	e	PM
Moorgate Street ....dep.	2 17	—	—	—	2 44	2 50	—	3 13	—	d	—	—	—	—	4·14	—	—	—
Farringdon Street	2 19	—	—	—	2 48	2 54	—	3 15	—	—	—	—	—	—	4·18	—	—	—
King's Cross	2 23	2 33	2 39	2 48	2 55	2 58	—	3 10	3 21	—	3 29	3 45	—	—	4 22	—	—	4 25
Broad Street	—	—	2 27	2·41	—	—	—	—	—	—	—	3 35	—	4 3	—	—	4 20
Haggerston	—	—	2 32	—	—	—	—	—	—	—	—	3 40	—	4 8	—	—	4 25
Dalston Junction	—	—	2 34	—	—	—	—	—	—	d	—	3 42	—	4 10	—	—	4 27
Mildmay Park	—	—	2 36	—	—	—	—	—	—	—	—	2 44	—	4 12	—	—	4 29
Canonbury	—	—	2 38	—	—	—	—	—	—	—	—	3 46	—	4 14	—	—	4 31
Finsbury Park	2 35	2 40	2 47	2 54	3 4	3 9	3 11	3 16	3 30	3 31	3 39	3 51	4 6	4 14	4 19	4 32	4 41	4 33
Stroud Green	2 38	2 43	2 50	2 57	3 7	3 12	3 14	3 19	3 33	3 34	3 42	3 54	4 9	4 17	4 22	4 35	4 44	4 39
Crouch End	2 41	2 46	2 53	3 0	3 10	3 15	3 17	3 22	3 36	3 37	3 45	3 57	4 12	4 20	4 25	4 38	4 47	4 42
Highgate	2 45	2 50	2 57	3 4	3 14	3 19	3 21	3 26	3 40	3 41	3 49	4 1	4 16	4 24	4 29	4 42	4 51	4 45
Cranley Gardens	—	2 53	—	3 7	3 17	—	3 29	—	3 44	3 52	—	4 19	4 27	—	4 45	4 54	—
Muswell Hill	—	2 55	—	3 9	3 19	—	3 31	—	3 46	3 54	—	4 21	4 29	—	4 47	4 56	—
Alexandra Palace	—	2 57	—	3 11	3 22	—	3 33	—	3 48	3 56	—	4 23	4 31	—	4 49	4 58	—
East Finchley	2 49	—	3 1	—	3 22	3 24	—	3 44	—	—	4 5	—	—	4 33	—	4 49
Finchley	2 53	—	3 5	—	3 27	3 29	—	3 49	—	—	4 9	—	—	4 37	—	4 53
Mill Hill	2 56	—	—	—	3 32	3 32	—	—	—	—	4 19	—	—	—	—	4 58
The Hale	3 0	—	—	—	3 36	3 36	—	—	—	d	—	4 23	—	—	—	—	5 2
Edgware	3 3	—	—	—	3 39	3 39	—	—	—	—	4 26	—	—	—	—	5 5
Woodside Park	2 57	3 9	—	3 31	3 33	—	3 53	—	—	4 13	—	4 41	—	4 57
Totteridge and Whetstone	3 0	3 12	—	3 34	3 36	—	3 56	—	—	4 16	—	4 44	—	5 0
High Barnet	3 5	3 16	—	3 38	3 40	—	4 0	—	—	4 20	—	4 49	—	5 4

(Sats. only.)

WEEK DAYS.

WEEK DAYS.	PM	PM	PM	PM	d	e	e	d	e	e	PM	PM	e	d	d	e	e	PM
Moorgate Street ....dep.	4·36	4·46	—	5· 1	—	5 8	5 14	—	5 19	5 30	—	5 34	—	—	—	—	5 47
Farringdon Street	4·40	4·50	—	5· 5	—	5 12	5 18	—	5 23	5 34	—	5 38	—	—	—	—	5 51
King's Cross	4 48	4 57	—	5·d 5	—	5 16	5 22	—	5 33	5 38	—	5 42	5 47	5 49	—	—	5 55
Broad Street	4 40	—	4 54	5 2	—	5 10	—	5 25	5 32	—	5 32	—	—	5 41	5 41	5 50
Haggerston	4 40	—	4 59	—	—	5 10	—	5 25	5 37	—	5 37	—	—	—
Dalston Junction	4 46	—	5 1	5 7	—	5 15	—	5 30	5 39	—	5 39	—	5 46	5 46	5 55
Mildmay Park	4 48	—	5 3	5 9	—	5 17	—	5 25	5 42	—	5 41	—	5 48	5 48
Canonbury	4 50	—	5 5	5 11	—	5 19	—	5 34	—	—	5 43	—	5 50	5 50
Finsbury Park	4 56	5 3	5 11	5 18	—	5 26	5 31	5 37	5 40	5 49	5 52	5 53	5 58	5 58	5 6	5 6	6
Stroud Green	4 59	5 6	5 14	5 21	—	5 34	—	5 43	—	5 52	5 56	6 1	6 1	—
Crouch End	5 2	5 9	5 17	5 24	—	5 37	5 42	5 46	—	5 55	5 59	6 4	6 4	6 1	—
Highgate	5 7	5 13	5 21	5 28	—	5 41	—	5 50	—	5 59	—	6 36	8 6	9	6 14
Cranley Gardens	—	5 16	—	5 31	—	5 44	—	5 53	—	6 1	6 66 11	—
Muswell Hill	—	5 18	—	5 33	—	5 46	—	5 55	—	6 36	6 8 6 13	—
Alexandra Palace	—	5 20	—	5 35	—	5 48	—	5 57	—	6 5 6 10 6 15	—
East Finchley	5 10	—	5 26	—	5 35	—	5 48	—	5 57	6 3	—	6 13 6 8 6 18
Finchley	5 15	—	5 30	—	5 30	5 40	—	5 52	—	6 1 6 8	—	6 18 6 13 6 23
Mill Hill	—	—	5 33 5 43	—	—	6 17	—	6 17
The Hale	—	—	5 37 5 47	—	—	6 21	—	6 21
Edgware	—	—	5 40 5 50	—	—	6 24	—	6 24
Woodside Park	5 19	—	5 34	—	5 44	—	5 56	—	6 6 6 12	—	6 22 6 17 6 27
Totteridge and Whetstone	5 22	—	5 37	—	5 47	—	5 59	—	6 9 6 15	—	6 25 6 20 6 30
High Barnet	5 26	—	5 41	—	5 51	—	6 3	—	6 13 6 19	—	6 29 6 24 6 34

WEEK DAYS.

WEEK DAYS.	e	e	PM	e	e	d	d	PM	PM	e	d	PM
Moorgate Street ....dep.	—	—	6 5	—	6 12	—	—	6·29	6 40	—	—
Farringdon Street	—	—	6 9	—	6 16	—	—	6·33	6 44	—	6 57
King's Cross	6 7	—	6 11	6 13	6 17	6 20	—	6·37	6 51	—	6 57
Broad Street	—	—	—	—	6 20	—	6 28	—	6 42	6 55
Haggerston	—	—	—	—	6 10	—	6 26	—	6 45	6 55
Dalston Junction	—	—	—	—	6 25	—	6 34	—	6 47	7 0
Mildmay Park	—	—	—	—	6 27	—	6 36	—	6 49	7 2
Canonbury	—	—	—	—	6 29	—	6 37	—	6 51	7 4
Finsbury Park	6 13	6 17	6 22	6 24	6 30	6 35	6 34	6 40	6 43	6 48	6 57	7 2 7 10
Stroud Green	6 16	6 20	6 25	6 27	6 33	—	6 37	6 43	6 46	6 51	7 0	7 5
Crouch End	6 16	6 19	6 23	6 28	6 30	—	6 40	6 40	6 46	6 49	6 54	7 3	7 8
Highgate	6 20	6 23	6 27	6 32	6 34	—	6 45	6 44	6 50	6 54	6 58	7 7	7 12 7 18
Cranley Gardens	6 23	6 26	—	6 35	6 37	—	6 48	—	6 53	7 1	7 15 7 21
Muswell Hill	6 25	6 28	—	6 37	6 39	—	6 50	—	6 55	7 3	7 17 7 23
Alexandra Palace	6 27	6 30	—	6 39	6 41	—	6·52	—	6 57	7 5	7 19 7 25
East Finchley	—	6 31	—	6 40	—	6 47	—	6 58	7 11	7 —
Finchley	—	6 36	—	6 44	—	6 51	—	7 2	7 15 7 21
Mill Hill	—	—	6 47	—	6 54	—	7 18 7 24
The Hale	—	—	6 51	—	6 58	—	7 22 7 28
Edgware	—	—	6 54	—	7 1	—	7 25 7 31
Woodside Park	—	6 40	—	6 48	—	6 55	—	7 6	7 19
Totteridge and Whetstone	—	6 43	—	6 51	—	6 58	—	7 9	7 22
High Barnet	—	6 47	—	6 55	—	7 2	—	7 13	7 26

WEEK DAYS.

WEEK DAYS.	PM	PM	d	d	PM	e	e	e	PM	PM	PM	PM	PM	d	PM	PM
Moorgate Street ....dep.	—	7 0	—	7 8	—	—	7·32	—	—	—	—	—	—	—
Farringdon Street	—	7 4	—	7 12	—	—	7·35	—	—	—	—	—	—	—
King's Cross	7 6	7 8	—	7 19	—	7 40	7 49	—	8 11	—	8 26	8 40	—	8 45	—
Broad Street	—	—	7 11	—	7 21	—	7 41	8 10	—	—	8 34	8 51
Haggerston	—	—	7 11	—	7 11	—	7 42	8 15	—	—	8 39	8 42
Dalston Junction	—	—	7 16	—	7 27	—	7 46	8 17	—	—	8 41	8 55
Mildmay Park	—	—	7 18	—	7 29	—	7 48	8 19	—	—	8 43	8 57
Canonbury	—	—	7 21	—	7 31	—	7 50	8 21	—	—	8 45	8 59
Finsbury Park	7 12	7 18	7 27	7 27	7 31	7 41	7 49	7 55	8 12	8 17	8 26	8 32	8 46	8 51	9 6
Stroud Green	7 15	7 21	7 30	—	7 34	—	7 57	7 59	8 15	8 20	8 29	8 35	8 49	8 54	9 9
Crouch End	7 18	7 24	7 33	—	7 37	7 46	7 55	8 2	8 18	8 23	8 32	8 38	8 52	8 57	9 12
Highgate	7 22	7 28	7 37	—	7 41	7 50	7 59	8 6	8 22	8 27	8 36	8 42	8 56	9 1	9 16
Cranley Gardens	—	7 31	7 40	—	7 44	7 53	—	8 9	8 25	—	—	8 45	9 4
Muswell Hill	—	7 33	7 42	—	7 46	7 55	—	8 11	8 27	—	—	8 47	9 6
Alexandra Palace	7 26	7 35	7 44	—	7 48	7 57	—	8 13	8 29	—	—	8 49	9 8
East Finchley	7 26	—	7 35	7·45	—	8 3	—	8 30	8 40	—	9 0	—	9 20
Finchley	7 31	—	7 47	7·52	—	8 8	—	8 35	8 45	—	9 5 9 7	—	9 25
Mill Hill	—	—	7 50	7·55	—	—	8·d28	8 47	—	9 10	—
The Hale	—	—	7 54	7·59	—	—	8·d42	8 51	—	9 14	—
Edgware	—	—	7 57	8·d 2	—	—	8·d45	8 54	—	9 17	—
Woodside Park	7 35	—	7 44	7·54	—	8 12	—	8 39	8 51	—	9 9	—	9 29
Totteridge and Whetstone	7 38	—	7 47	7·57	—	8 15	—	8 42	8 51	—	9 12	—	9 32
High Barnet	7 42	—	7 51	8·d 1	—	8 19	—	8 46	8 55	—	9 16	—	9 36

(Sats. excepted. / Sats. only.)

d Saturdays only.   *e* Saturdays excepted.

WEEK DAYS.

	PM	PM	PM	PM	PM	PM	PM	PM	PM	PM	PM	PM
Moorgate Street ......dep.	—	—	—	—	—	—	—	—	—	—	—	—
Farringdon Street	—	—	—	—	—	—	—	—	—	—	—	—
King's Cross	9 23	9 33	—	10 0	—	10 26	11 0	11 20	—	11 42	11 45	12 20
Broad Street	—	9 33	—	—	—	10 20	—	—	—	—	—	—
Shoreditch	—	9 22	—	—	—	—	—	—	—	—	—	—
Haggerston	—	9 25	—	—	—	—	—	—	—	—	—	—
Dalston Junction	—	9 27	—	—	—	10 25	—	—	—	—	—	—
Mildmay Park	—	9 29	—	—	—	—	—	—	—	—	—	—
Canonbury	—	9 31	—	—	—	10 28	—	—	—	—	—	—
Finsbury Park	9 29	9 39	9 52	10 8	10 26	10 34	11 6	11 27	11 32	11 49	11 51	12 26
Stroud Green	9 32	9 42	9 55	10 11	10 29	10 37	11 9	11 30	11 35	—	11 54	12 29
Crouch End	9 35	9 45	9 58	10 14	10 32	10 40	11 12	11 33	11 38	—	11 57	12 32
Highgate	9 39	9 49	10 2	10 18	10 36	10 44	11 16	11 37	11 42	—	12 1	12 36
Cranley Gardens	9 42	—	10 5	—	10 39	—	—	—	11 45	—	12 4	—
Muswell Hill	9 44	—	10 7	—	10 41	—	—	—	11 57	—	12 6	—
Alexandra Palace	9 46	—	10 9	—	10 43	—	—	—	11 49	—	12 8	—
East Finchley	—	9 53	—	10 22	—	10 47	11 20	11 41	—	11 57	—	12 40
Finchley	—	9 58	—	10 26	—	10 51	11 25	11 45	—	12 2	—	12 45
Mill Hill	—	10 1	—	10 33	—	—	11 28	—	—	12 5	—	—
The Hale	—	10 5	—	10 37	—	—	11 32	—	—	12 9	—	—
Edgware	—	10 8	—	10 40	—	—	11 35	—	—	12 12	—	—
Woodside Park	—	10 2	—	10 30	—	10 55	11 28	11 49	—	12 6	—	12 49
Totteridge and Whetstone ..	—	10 5	—	10 33	—	10 58	11 31	11 52	—	12 9	—	12 52
High Barnet	—	10 9	—	10 33	—	11 2	11 35	11 57	—	12 13	—	12 56

SUNDAYS.

	AM	AM	AM	PM	PM	PM	PM	PM	PM	PM	PM	PM	PM	PM	PM	PM
Moorgate Street ......dep.	—	—	—	—	—	—	—	—	—	—	—	—	—	—	—	—
Farringdon Street	—	—	—	—	—	—	—	—	—	—	—	—	—	—	—	—
King's Cross	8 50	9 20	1125	1 0	1 33	2 20	3 5	4 30	5 10	6 20	7 15	8 15	8 52	9 38	10 6	10 56
Broad Street	—	—	—	—	—	—	—	—	—	—	—	—	—	—	—	—
Shoreditch	—	—	—	—	—	—	—	—	—	—	—	—	—	—	—	—
Haggerston	—	—	—	—	—	—	—	—	—	—	—	—	—	—	—	—
Dalston Junction	—	—	—	—	—	—	—	—	—	—	—	—	—	—	—	—
Mildmay Park	—	—	—	—	—	—	—	—	—	—	—	—	—	—	—	—
Canonbury	—	—	—	—	—	—	—	—	—	—	—	—	—	—	—	—
Finsbury Park	8 56	9 26	1131	1 6	1 40	2 26	3 11	4 36	5 16	6 25	7 21	8 21	8 58	9 47	10 12	11 2
Stroud Green	8 59	9 29	1134	1 9	1 43	2 29	3 14	4 39	5 19	6 29	7 24	8 24	9 1	9 50	10 15	11 5
Crouch End	9 2	9 32	1137	1 12	1 46	2 32	3 17	4 42	5 22	6 32	7 27	8 27	9 4	9 53	10 18	11 8
Highgate	9 6	9 36	1141	1 16	1 50	2 36	3 21	4 46	5 26	6 36	7 31	8 31	9 8	9 57	10 22	11 12
Cranley Gardens	—	—	—	—	—	—	—	—	—	—	—	—	—	—	—	—
Muswell Hill	—	—	—	—	—	—	—	—	—	—	—	—	—	—	—	—
Alexandra Palace	—	—	—	—	—	—	—	—	—	—	—	—	—	—	—	—
East Finchley	9 10	9 40	1145	1 19	1 54	2 40	3 25	4 50	5 30	6 40	7 35	8 35	9 12	10 1	10 26	11 17
Finchley	9 15	9 45	1150	1 23	1 58	2 44	3 30	4 54	5 35	6 44	7 40	8 39	9 16	10 5	10 31	11 22
Mill Hill	9 18	9 53	—	—	2 3	2 53	3 36	4 58	5 46	6 49	7 46	8 45	—	10 8	—	11 25
The Hale	9 22	9 57	—	—	2 7	2 57	3 40	5 2	5 50	6 53	7 50	8 49	—	10 12	—	11 29
Edgware	9 25	10 0	—	—	2 10	3 0	3 43	5 5	5 53	6 56	7 53	8 52	—	10 15	—	11 32
Woodside Park	9 19	9 49	1154	1 27	—	2 48	3 34	4 54	5 39	6 48	7 44	8 43	9 20	10 9	10 36	11 28
Totteridge and Whetstone	9 22	9 52	1157	1 30	—	2 51	3 37	5 1	5 42	6 51	7 47	8 46	9 23	10 12	10 39	11 31
High Barnet	9 26	9 56	12 1	1 34	—	2 55	3 41	5 5	5 45	6 55	7 51	8 50	9 27	10 17	10 44	11 35

WEEK DAYS.

	AM	AM	AM	AM	AM	AM	AM	AM	AM	AM	AM	AM	AM	AM	AM	AM
High Barnet ....dep.	5 15	6 30	—	7 6	—	7 37	7 44	—	—	7 58	—	8 7	—	8 18	—	—
Totteridge and Whetstone ..	5 19	6 34	—	7 10	—	7 41	7 48	—	—	8 2	—	8 11	—	8 22	—	—
Woodside Park	5 22	6 37	—	7 13	—	7 44	7 51	—	—	8 5	—	8 14	—	8 25	—	—
Edgware	—	6 25	—	—	—	7 22	—	—	7 53	—	—	—	—	—	—	8 26
The Hale	—	6 28	—	—	—	7 25	—	—	7 56	—	—	—	—	—	—	8 29
Mill Hill	—	6 32	—	—	—	7 29	—	—	8 0	—	—	—	—	—	—	8 33
Finchley	5 26	6 41	—	7 17	—	7 49	7 55	—	8 4	—	8 18	—	8 31	8 40		
East Finchley	5 30	6 46	—	7 21	—	7 53	7 59	—	8 8	8 14	—	8 23	—	—		
Alexandra Palace	—	—	—	—	—	—	—	8 0	—	—	8 12	—	8 25	—		
Muswell Hill	—	—	7 12	—	7 27	—	—	8 2	—	—	8 14	—	8 23	8 27	—	
Cranley Gardens	—	—	7 15	—	7 30	—	—	8 5	—	—	8 17	—	8 26	8 30	—	
Highgate	5 34	6 50	7 18	7 25	7 33	7 57	8 3	8 8	8 12	—	8 20	—	8 29	8 33	—	8 47
Crouch End	5 37	6 53	7 21	7 28	7 36	8 0	8 6	8 11	8 15	8 19	8 23	8 28	8 32	8 36	—	8 50
Stroud Green	5 39	6 55	7 23	7 30	7 38	8 2	8 8	8 13	8 17	8 21	8 25	—	8 34	8 38	8 41	8 52
Finsbury Park	5 42	6 57	7 25	7 32	7 41	8 6	8 11	8 17	—	8 24	8 29	8 33	8 36	—	8 44	8 55
Canonbury	—	—	—	—	—	8 10	—	8 21	—	—	8 34	—	—	8 48	—	
Mildmay Park	—	—	—	—	—	8 12	—	8 23	—	—	8 36	—	—	8 50	—	
Dalston Junction	—	—	—	—	—	8 14	—	8 25	—	—	8 38	—	—	8 52	—	
Haggerston	—	—	—	—	—	—	—	—	—	—	—	—	—	—	—	
Broad Street	—	—	—	—	8 19	—	8 32	—	—	8 44	—	—	8 58	—		
King's Cross	5 48	—	7 39	7 42	7 46	—	8 22	—	8 24	8 30	—	8 41	—	8 51	—	9 0
Farringdon Street	5 55	—	—	7 46	8 3	—	8 26	—	—	—	—	8 48	—	8 55	—	9 7
Moorgate Street	5 59	—	—	7 50	8 7	—	8 30	—	—	—	—	8 52	—	8 59	—	9 11

WEEK DAYS.

	AM	AM	AM	AM	AM	AM	AM	AM	AM	AM	AM	AM	AM	AM
High Barnet ....dep.	—	—	8 34	—	8 44	—	—	9 0	—	—	—	9 8	—	9 25
Totteridge and Whetstone..	—	—	8 38	—	8 48	—	—	9 4	—	—	—	9 12	—	9 29
Woodside Park	—	—	8 41	—	8 51	—	—	9 7	—	—	—	9 15	—	9 32
Edgware	—	—	—	—	—	—	—	8 54	—	—	—	—	—	9 22
The Hale	—	—	—	—	—	—	—	8 57	—	—	—	—	—	9 25
Mill Hill	—	—	—	—	—	—	—	9 1	—	—	—	—	—	9 29
Finchley	—	—	8 45	—	8 56	—	—	9 11	—	—	9 19	—	9 28	9 37
East Finchley	—	8 40	8 50	—	—	9 4	9 16	—	—	9 24	—	9 33	—	
Alexandra Palace	8 32	—	8 42	—	8 49	8 57	—	9 5	9 16	—	9 25	—	—	
Muswell Hill	8 34	—	8 44	—	8 51	8 59	—	9 7	9 18	—	9 27	—	—	
Cranley Gardens	8 37	—	8 47	—	8 54	9 2	—	9 10	9 21	—	9 30	—	—	
Highgate	8 40	8 44	8 50	8 54	8 57	9 5	9 8	9 12	9 21	9 24	9 28	9 33	9 37	—
Crouch End	8 43	8 47	8 53	8 57	9 0	9 8	9 11	9 16	9 24	9 27	9 31	9 36	9 44	
Stroud Green	8 45	8 49	8 55	—	9 2	9 6	9 10	9 13	9 18	9 26	9 33	9 38	9 42	9 46	9 50
Finsbury Park	—	8 57	9 1	—	9 10	—	9 17	9 23	9 20	9 28	9 33	9 36	9 41	9 46	9 50
Canonbury	—	—	—	—	—	9 17	—	—	9 37	—	9 46	—	—	
Mildmay Park	—	—	—	—	—	9 19	—	—	9 39	—	9 48	—	—	
Dalston Junction	—	8 59	—	—	9 17	9 21	9 24	—	9 41	—	9 51	—	9 56	
Haggerston	—	9 6	—	—	—	—	—	—	9 47	—	9 57	—	10 2	
Broad Street	—	9 6	—	9 23	9 26	9 30	—	9 47	—	9 57	—	10 2		
King's Cross	8 52	—	9 8	9 10	—	—	9 29	9 26	—	9 42	—	9 54	—	
Farringdon Street	—	—	9 15	—	—	—	9 39	—	9 49	—	9 58	—		
Moorgate Street	—	—	9 19	—	—	—	9 43	—	9 53	—	10 2	—		

WEEK DAYS.	AM	AM	AM	AM	AM	AM	AM	AM	AM	AM	e	d	AM	d	d
High Barnet ....dep.	—	9 41	9 51	—	—	—	10 21	10 41	—	11 10	—	—	11 50	—	—
Totteridge and Whetstone	—	9 45	9 55	—	—	—	10 25	10 45	—	11 14	—	—	11 54	—	—
Woodside Park............	—	9 48	9 58	—	—	—	10 28	10 48	—	11 17	—	—	11 57	—	—
Edgware.................	—	—	9 49	—	—	—	—	10 33	—	11 6	—	—	11 48	—	—
The Hale.................	—	—	9 52	—	—	—	—	10 36	—	11 9	—	—	11 51	—	—
Mill Hill.................	—	—	9 56	—	—	—	—	10 40	—	11 13	—	—	11 55	—	—
Finchley	—	9 52	10 2	—	—	—	10 32	10 52	—	11 21	—	—	12 1	—	—
East Finchley	—	9 57	10 7	—	—	—	10 37	10 57	—	11 25	—	—	12 5	—	—
Alexandra Palace	9 46	—	—	10 10	10 26	10 44	—	—	11 12	—	11 36	11 39	—	—	12 7
Muswell Hill.............	9 48	—	—	10 12	10 28	10 46	—	—	11 14	—	11 38	11 40	—	—	12 9
Cranley Gardens	9 51	—	—	10 15	10 31	10 49	—	—	11 17	—	11 41	11 43	—	—	12 12
Highgate.................	9 54	10 1	10 11	10 18	10 34	10 52	—	11 1	11 20	11 29	11 44	11 46	12 8	—	12 15
Crouch End	9 57	10 4	10 14	10 21	10 37	10 55	—	11 4	11 23	11 32	11 47	11 49	12 11	—	12 18
Stroud Green.............	9 59	10 6	10 16	10 23	10 39	10 57	—	11 6	11 25	11 34	11 49	11 51	12 13	—	12 20
Finsbury Park	10 3	10 8	10 19	10 25	10 42	11 0	10 45	11 10	11 30	11 37	11 51	11 55	12 16	1214	12 24
Canonbury	10 7	—	10 23	—	—	—	—	11 14	—	—	—	—	—	—	—
Mildmay Park	10 9	—	10 25	—	—	—	—	11 16	—	—	—	—	—	—	—
Dalston Junction	10 11	10 17	10 27	—	—	—	—	11 18	—	—	—	—	—	—	—
Haggerston...............	10 13	—	—	—	—	—	—	11 20	—	—	—	—	—	—	—
Broad Street	10 18	10 23	10 33	—	—	—	—	11 25	—	—	—	—	—	—	—
King's Cross	—	—	10 25	—	10 47	11 5	—	—	11 35	11 42	—	12 2	12 21	1224	12 30
Farringdon Street	—	—	10 32	—	—	—	—	—	—	11ᵈ50	—	12 9	12ᵈ32	1228	12 37
Moorgate Street	—	—	10 36	—	—	—	—	—	—	11ᵈ54	—	12 13	12ᵈ36	1232	12 41

WEEK DAYS.	e	d	e	d	PM	d	PM	PM	PM	PM	e	d	PM	PM	PM	d	d
High Barnet ....dep.	12 10	12 15	—	—	12 36	12 43	—	1 0	—	1 20	—	—	—	1 40	—	—	
Totteridge and Whetstone	12 14	12 19	—	—	12 40	12 47	—	1 4	—	1 24	—	—	—	1 44	—	—	
Woodside Park, ...	12 17	12 22	—	—	12 43	12 50	—	1 7	—	1 27	—	—	—	1 47	—	—	
Edgware.................	—	—	—	—	12 32	—	—	—	—	1 4 9	—	—	—	1 39	—	—	
The Hale.................	—	—	—	—	12 35	—	—	—	—	1ᵈ12	—	—	—	1 43	—	—	
Mill Hill.................	—	—	—	—	12 39	—	—	—	—	1ᵈ16	—	—	—	1 47	—	—	
Finchley	12 21	12 26	—	—	12 47	12 54	—	1 11	—	1 31	—	—	—	1 51	—	—	
East Finchley	12 25	12 31	—	—	12 51	12 59	—	1 16	—	1 36	—	—	—	1 55	—	—	
Alexandra Palace	—	—	12 25	12 35	—	—	1 1	—	1 15	—	1 21	1 26	1 36	—	—	2 12	
Muswell Hill.............	—	—	12 27	12 37	—	—	1 3	—	1 17	—	1 23	1 28	1 38	—	—	2 14	
Cranley Gardens	—	—	12 30	12 40	—	—	1 6	—	1 20	—	1 26	1 31	1 41	—	—	2 17	
Highgate.................	12 29	12 35	12 33	12 43	12 55	1 3	1 9	1 20	1 23	1 40	1 29	1 34	1 44	—	1 59	—	2 20
Crouch End	—	12 38	12 36	12 46	12 58	1 6	1 12	1 23	1 26	1 43	1 32	1 37	1 47	—	2 2	—	2 23
Stroud Green.............	—	12 40	12 38	12 48	1 0	1 8	1 14	1 25	1 28	1 45	1 34	1 39	1 49	—	2 4	—	2 25
Finsbury Park	12 34	12 44	12 42	12 50	1 3	1 12	1 18	1 28	1 30	1ᵈ48	1 36	1 42	1 51	2 3	2 9	2 27	2 27
Canonbury	—	—	—	—	—	—	1 22	1 32	—	1ᵈ52	—	—	—	2 8	2 13	2 31	—
Mildmay Park	—	—	—	—	—	—	1 24	1 34	—	1ᵈ54	—	—	—	2 10	2 15	2 33	—
Dalston Junction	—	—	—	—	—	—	1 26	1 36	Sats.	1ᵈ56	—	—	—	2 12	2 18	2 36	—
Haggerston...............	—	—	—	—	—	—	1 28	1 38	only	1ᵈ58	—	—	—	2 14	2 20	2 38	—
Broad Street	—	—	—	—	—	—	1 33	1 43	—	2ᵈ 3	—	—	—	2 19	2 25	2 43	—
King's Cross	—	—	12 51	12 47	12 59	1 8	1 18	—	Sats.	1 39	—	1 52	—	—	—	—	2 35
Farringdon Street	—	—	12 58	—	1 6	1ᵈ17	1 25	—	only	1 46	—	1 56	—	—	—	—	2 42
Moorgate Street	—	—	1 2	—	1 10	1ᵈ21	1 29	—	—	1 50	—	2 0	—	—	—	—	2 46

WEEK DAYS.	e	e	e	PM	d	PM	d	PM	d	PM	PM	PM	PM	PM	d	e	e	d
High Barnet ....dep.	—	2 5	—	2 22	2 31	—	2 40	—	3 10	—	3 30	—	—	4 4	—	—	—	
Totteridge and Whetstone	—	2 9	—	2 26	2 35	—	2 44	—	3 14	—	3 34	—	—	4 8	—	—	—	
Woodside Park............	—	2 12	—	2 29	2 38	—	2 47	—	3 17	—	3 37	—	—	4 11	—	—	—	
Edgware.................	—	—	—	2 9	—	239	—	—	3 7	—	—	—	—	3 55	—	—	—	
The Hale.................	—	—	—	2 12	—	242	—	—	3 10	—	—	—	—	3 58	—	—	—	
Mill Hill.................	—	—	—	2 16	—	246	—	—	3 14	—	—	—	—	4 2	—	—	—	
Finchley	—	2 16	—	2 33	2 42	249	2 51	—	3 21	—	3 41	—	—	4 15	—	—	—	
East Finchley	—	2 21	—	2 38	2 47	—	2 55	—	3 25	—	3 46	—	—	4 19	—	—	—	
Alexandra Palace	2 21	—	2 30	—	—	—	—	3	2 3 10	—	3 38	—	3 51	—	4 23	4 29	—	4 46
Muswell Hill.............	2 23	—	2 32	—	—	—	—	3	4 3 12	—	3 40	—	3 53	—	4 25	4 31	—	4 48
Cranley Gardens	2 26	—	2 35	—	—	—	—	3	7 3 15	—	3 43	—	3 56	—	4 28	4 34	—	4 51
Highgate.................	2 29	2 25	2 38	2 42	2 51	—	2 59	3 10	3 18	3 29	3 46	3 50	3 59	4 23	4 34	4 37	—	4 54
Crouch End	2 32	2 28	2 41	2 45	2 54	—	3 2	3 13	3 21	3 32	3 49	3 53	—	4 2	4 26	4 34	4 40	—	4 57
Stroud Green.............	2 34	2 30	2 43	2 47	2 56	—	3 4	3 15	3 23	3 34	3 51	3 55	—	4 4	4 28	4 36	4 42	—	4 59
Finsbury Park	2 36	2 34	2 45	2 51	3 1	—	3 8	3 19	3 26	3 36	3 54	3 58	3ᵈ59	4 8	4 30	4 40	4 45	439	5 2
Canonbury	—	2 38	2 52	—	3 5	—	—	—	—	—	—	4 6	—	—	—	—	—	
Mildmay Park	—	2 40	2 54	—	3 7	—	—	—	—	—	—	4 8	—	—	—	—	—	
Dalston Junction..........	—	2 43	2 56	—	3 9	—	—	—	—	—	—	4 11	—	—	—	—	—	
Haggerston...............	—	2 45	2 58	—	3 11	—	—	—	—	—	—	4 13	—	—	—	—	—	
Broad Street	—	2 49	3 3	—	3 16	—	—	—	—	—	—	—	—	—	—	—	5 15	
King's Cross	2 42	—	2 59	—	—	3 13	—	3 13	3 42	—	—	—	—	4' 5 4	14 4'39	4 45	4 52	446
Farringdon Street	—	—	3 6	—	—	—	—	—	3ᵈ50	—	—	—	4'12	4'21	4' 46	—	4 59	453
Moorgate Street	—	—	3 10	—	—	—	—	—	3ᵈ54	—	—	—	4'16	4'25	4'50	—	5 3	457

WEEK DAYS.	e	PM	d	PM	d	PM	d	d	e	PM	e	PM	d
High Barnet ....dep.	—	4 43	—	5 12	—	—	—	5 19	5 36	5 40	—	5 51	—
Totteridge and Whetstone	—	4 47	—	5 16	—	—	—	5 23	5 40	5 44	—	5 55	—
Woodside Park............	—	4 50	—	5 19	—	—	—	5 26	5 43	5 47	—	5 58	—
Edgware.................	—	4 55	—	—	5 11	5 16	—	—	—	—	—	—	5 47
The Hale.................	—	4 38	—	—	5 14	5 19	—	—	—	—	—	—	5 50
Mill Hill.................	—	4 42	—	—	5 18	5 23	—	—	—	—	—	—	5 54
Finchley	—	4 54	—	5 23	—	5 28	—	5 30	5 47	5 51	—	6 2	—
East Finchley	—	4 59	—	5 28	—	5 33	—	5 35	5 51	5 55	—	6 6	—
Alexandra Palace	4 46	—	5 21	—	5 21	—	—	5 40	—	—	5 56	—	—
Muswell Hill.............	4 48	—	5 23	—	5 23	—	5 40	5 42	—	—	5 58	—	—
Cranley Gardens	4 51	—	5 26	—	5 26	—	5 43	5 45	—	—	6 1	—	—
Highgate.................	4 54	5 5	5 29	5 29	5 32	5 37	5 46	5 48	5 39	5 55	6 4	6 10	—
Crouch End	4 57	5 8	5 32	5 32	5 35	5 40	5 49	5 51	5 53	5 46	6 6	9 6	13	—
Stroud Green........	4 59	5 8	5 34	5 34	5 37	5 42	5 51	5 53	5 46	6 6	2 6	11 6	19	—
Finsbury Park	5 3	5 48	5 18	5 37	5 37	5 40	5 44	5 52	5 54	5 57	5 49	6 2	6 11	6 19
Canonbury	—	—	—	—	5 46	—	—	—	—	6 6	6 16	—	—
Mildmay Park	—	—	—	—	5 48	—	—	—	—	6 13	6 13	6 18	—
Dalston Junction..........	—	—	—	—	5 50	—	—	—	—	—	—	—	—
Haggerston...............	—	—	—	—	5 53	—	—	—	—	—	—	—	—
Broad Street	—	—	—	—	5 58	—	—	—	6 18	6 18	6 18	6 34	—
King's Cross	5 10	5 15	5'21	5 25	5 44	5 42	—	5 51	5 58	5 59	6 7	—	—
Farringdon Street	5 17	5 22	5'28	5 32	5 51	—	—	—	6 5	—	6 11	—	—
Moorgate Street	5 21	5 26	5'32	5 36	5 55	—	—	—	6 9	—	6 15	—	—

WEEK DAYS.	e	d	e	PM	d	e	e	d	e	PM	e	PM	PM	e	d	PM	e	PM
High Barnet ....dep.	—	6 15	6 15	—	6 35	6 41	—	—	6 48	6 59	—	7 8	—	7 35	7 40	7 51	—	8 16
Totteridge and Whetstone	—	6 19	6 19	—	6 39	6 45	—	—	6 52	7 3	—	7 12	—	7 39	7 44	7 55	—	8 20
Woodside Park............	—	6 22	6 22	—	6 42	6 48	—	—	6 55	7 6	—	7 15	—	7 42	7 47	7 58	—	8 23
Edgware.................	—	—	5 54	—	6 28	6 28	—	—	—	6 57	—	7 4	—	7 30	7 35	—	—	8 13
The Hale................	—	—	5 57	—	6 31	6 31	—	—	—	7 0	—	7 7	—	7 33	7 38	—	—	8 16
Mill Hill...............	—	—	6 1	—	6 35	6 35	—	—	—	7 4	—	7 11	—	7 37	7 42	—	—	8 20
Finchley...............	6 11	6 26	6 26	—	6 46	6 52	—	—	6 59	7 10	—	7 19	—	7 46	7 51	8 2	—	8 27
East Finchley	6 16	6 31	6 31	—	6 51	6 56	—	—	7 4	7 15	—	7 24	—	7 51	7 56	8 7	—	8 32
Alexandra Palace	—	—	—	6 17	—	—	6 46	6 56	—	—	7 17	—	7 36	—	—	—	9 12	—
Muswell Hill............	—	—	—	6 20	—	—	6 48	6 58	—	—	7 19	—	7 38	—	—	—	8 14	—
Cranley Gardens	—	—	—	6 22	—	—	6 51	7 1	—	—	7 22	—	7 41	—	—	—	8 17	—
Highgate...............	6 20	6 35	6 35	6 25	6 55	7 0	6 54	7 4	7 7	7 19	7 25	7 28	7 44	7 55	8	0 8	11 8	8 36
Crouch End.............	—	6 38	6 38	6 28	6 58	7 3	6 57	7 7	7 11	7 22	7 28	7 31	7 47	7 58	8	3 8	14 8	8 39
Stroud Green............	—	6 40	6 40	6 30	7 0	7 5	6 59	7 9	7 13	7 24	7 30	7 33	7 49	8	0 8	5 8	16 8	8 41
Finsbury Park	6 25	6 43	6 42	6 33	7 2	7 7	7 1	7 11	7 16	7 26	7 33	7 40	7 51	8	5 8	9 8	19 8	8 44
Canonbury	—	—	—	6 37	—	—	—	—	7 22	—	7 37	7 44	—	—	—	8 23	8 32	—
Mildmay Park	—	—	—	6 39	—	—	—	—	7 24	—	7 39	7 46	—	—	—	8 25	8 34	—
Dalston Junction........	—	—	—	6 42	—	—	—	—	7 26	—	—	7 48	—	—	—	8 27	8 36	—
Haggerston.............	—	—	—	—	—	—	—	—	7 28	—	—	7 50	—	—	—	8 29	8 38	—
Broad Street	—	—	—	6 47	—	—	—	—	7 33	—	—	7 55	—	—	—	8 34	8 43	—
King's Cross	6 31	6 48	—	—	—	—	7 9	—	—	—	—	—	7 57	8 10	8 14	—	—	8 49
Farringdon Street	6 38	—	—	—	—	—	7 16	—	—	—	—	—	—	—	—	—	—	—
Moorgate Street	6 42	—	—	—	—	—	7 20	—	—	—	—	—	—	—	—	—	—	—

WEEK DAYS.	d	PM	PM	d	e	PM	PM	PM	PM	PM	PM	PM	PM	PM	PM	PM	PM
High Barnet ....dep.	—	8 40	—	9 0	—	9 28	—	9 40	—	10 15	—	10 50	—	11 15	—	12 10	
Totteridge and Whetstone	—	8 44	—	9 4	—	9 32	—	9 44	—	10 19	—	10 54	—	11 19	—	12 14	
Woodside Park............	—	8 47	—	9 7	—	9 35	—	9 47	—	10 22	—	10 57	—	11 22	—	12 17	
Edgware.................	—	—	8 55	—	—	9 25	—	—	—	10 13	—	—	—	11 5	1140		
The Hale................	—	—	8 58	—	—	9 28	—	—	—	10 16	—	—	—	11 8	1143		
Mill Hill...............	—	—	9 2	—	—	9 32	—	—	—	10 20	—	—	—	11 12	1147		
Finchley...............	—	8 51	9 6	9 11	—	9 39	—	9 51	—	10 26	—	11 1	—	11 15	1150	12 21	
East Finchley	—	8 56	9 11	9 16	—	9 43	—	9 56	—	10 30	—	11 6	—	11 31	—	12 25	
Alexandra Palace	8 22	8 40	—	—	9 20	—	9 47	—	10 19	—	1050	—	1110	—	—	—	
Muswell Hill............	8 24	8 42	—	—	9 23	—	9 49	—	10 22	—	1052	—	1112	—	—	—	
Cranley Gardens	8 27	8 45	—	—	9 25	—	9 52	—	10 24	—	1055	—	1115	—	—	—	
Highgate...............	8 30	8 48	9 0	9 15	9 20	9 28	9 47	9 55	10	0 10	27 10	34 1058	11 10	1118	11 35	—	12 29
Crouch End	8 32	8 51	9 3	9 18	9 23	9 31	9 50	9 58	10	3 10	30 10	37 11	1 11	13 1121	11 38	—	12 32
Stroud Green............	8 35	8 53	9 5	9 20	9 25	9 33	9 52	10	0 10	5 10	32 10	39 11	3 11	15 1123	11 40	—	12 34
Finsbury Park	8 39	8 55	9 7	9 22	9 27	9 36	9 55	10	3 10	10 10	34 10	42 11	5 11	19 1126	11 45	—	12 37
Canonbury	8 43	—	9 13	—	—	—	—	10 13	—	—	—	—	—	—	—	—	
Mildmay Park	8 45	—	9 15	—	—	—	—	—	—	—	—	—	—	—	—	—	
Dalston Junction........	8 47	—	9 17	—	—	—	—	10 16	—	—	—	—	—	—	—	—	
Haggerston.............	8 49	—	9 19	—	—	—	—	10 24	—	—	—	—	—	—	—	—	
Broad Street	8 54	—	9 24	—	—	—	10 2	—	—	—	—	—	—	11 24	1131	11 50	12 42
King's Cross	—	—	—	—	—	—	—	—	—	—	—	—	11 24	1131	11 50	12 42	
Farringdon Street	—	—	—	—	—	—	—	—	—	—	—	—	—	—	—	—	
Moorgate Street	—	—	—	—	—	—	—	—	—	—	—	—	—	—	—	—	

SUNDAYS.	AM	AM	AM	PM	PM	PM	PM	PM	PM	PM	PM	PM	PM	PM	PM	PM	PM
High Barnet ....dep.	7 54	9 38	10 9	1215	1250	2 27	3 10	4 10	5 30	5 58	7 15	8 20	9 18	9 49	10 30		
Totteridge and Whetstone	7 58	9 42	10 13	1219	1254	2 31	3 14	4 14	5 34	6 2	7 19	8 24	9 22	9 53	10 34		
Woodside Park............	8 1	9 45	10 16	1222	1257	2 34	3 17	4 17	5 37	6 5	7 22	8 27	9 25	9 56	10 37		
Edgware.................	—	9 34	10 8	—	2 25	3 9	4 8	5 24	5 57	7 15	8 16	9 5	—	10 28			
The Hale................	—	9 37	10 11	—	2 28	3 12	4 11	5 27	6 0	7 18	8 19	9 8	—	10 31			
Mill Hill...............	—	9 41	10 15	—	2 32	3 16	4 15	5 31	6 4	7 22	8 23	9 12	—	10 35			
Finchley...............	8 5	9 49	10 20	1226	1	2 38	3 21	4 21	5 41	6 9	7 26	8 31	9 29	10	0 10	41	
East Finchley	8 10	9 54	10 25	1231	5	2 43	3 26	4 26	5 46	6 14	7 30	8 36	9 34	10	5 10	46	
Alexandra Palace	—	—	—	—	—	—	—	—	—	—	—	—	—	—	—		
Muswell Hill............	—	—	—	—	—	—	—	—	—	—	—	—	—	—	—		
Cranley Gardens	—	—	—	—	—	—	—	—	—	—	—	—	—	—	—		
Highgate...............	8 14	9 58	10 29	1235	1	9 2	47 3	30 4	30 5	50 6	18 7	34 8	40 9	38 1C	9 10	50	
Crouch End	8 17	10 1	10 32	1238	1	12 2	50 3	33 4	33 5	53 6	21 7	37 8	43 9	41 10	12 10	53	
Stroud Green............	8 19	10 3	10 34	1240	1	14 2	52 3	35 4	35 5	55 6	23 7	39 8	45 9	43 10	14 10	55	
Finsbury Park	8 22	10 6	10 37	1243	1	17 2	54 3	39 4	38 5	57 6	25 7	42 8	49 9	46 10	16 10	59	
Canonbury	—	—	—	—	—	—	—	—	—	—	—	—	—	—	—		
Mildmay Park	—	—	—	—	—	—	—	—	—	—	—	—	—	—	—		
Dalston Junction........	—	—	—	—	—	—	—	—	—	—	—	—	—	—	—		
Haggerston.............	—	—	—	—	—	—	—	—	—	—	—	—	—	—	—		
Shoreditch.............	—	—	—	—	—	—	—	—	—	—	—	—	—	—	—		
Broad Street	—	—	—	—	—	—	—	—	—	—	—	—	—	—	—		
King's Cross	8 27	10 11	10 42	1248	1	22 3	0 3	44 4	43	—	7 47	8 54	9 51	10 23	11 4		
Farringdon Street	—	—	—	—	—	—	—	—	—	—	—	—	—	—	—		
Moorgate Street	—	—	—	—	—	—	—	—	—	—	—	—	—	—	—		

d Saturdays only.

e Saturdays excepted.

WEEK DAYS.	AM	AM	AM	AM	AM	AM	AM	AM	AM	AM	AM	AM	AM	AM	AM	AM
Liverpool St. ......dep.	1 32	2 32	3 32	4 37	5 10	5 30 6	1 6 19	6 38	6 50	7	6 7 18	7 22	7 26	7 30	7 34
Bethnal Green	1 35	2 36	3 35	4 41	5 14	5 34 6	5 6 23	6 42	6 54	—	7 23	—	7 31	—	7 39
Cambridge Heath.........	1 39	2 39	3 39	4 44	—	—	—	—	—	—	—	—	—	—	7 39
London Fields	1 41	2 41	3 41	4 46	—	—	—	—	—	—	—	—	—	—	—
Hackney Downs	1 44	2 44	3 44	4 49	5 19	5 39 6	10 6 28	6 47	6 59	—	7 32	—	7 39	—	7 48
Clapton	1 47	2 47	3 47	4 52	5 23	5 43 6	14 6 32	6 51	7	3	7 35	—	—	—	7 51
St. James's Street.........	1 51	2 51	3 51	4 56	5 27	5 47 6	18 6 36	6 55	7	7	7 19 7 39	7 35	7 46	—	—
Hoe Street	1 54	2 54	3 54	4 59	5 30	5 50 6	21 6 39	6 58	7	10	7 22 7 42	—	7 49	7 44	7 56
Wood Street	1 57	2 57	3 57	5	2	5 33 5	53 6 24	6 42	7	2	7 13 7 25	7 45	7 39	—	7 47	8 0
Higham's Park	—	—	—	5	7	—	5 58	—	6 47	7	6	7 18 7 30	7 50	—	7 56	—	8 4
Chingford	—	—	—	5 12	—	6	3	—	6 53	7 15	7 24	7 35 7 55	—	8 1	—	8 10

WEEK DAYS.	AM	AM	AM	AM	AM	AM		PM	PM
Liverpool St..........dep.	7 38	7 42	7 46	7 50	7 54	7 58		9 5	9 20
Bethnal Green	—	7 47	—	7 55	—	—		9 9	9 24
Cambridge Heath............	—	—	—	—	—	—		—	—
London Fields	—	—	—	—	—	—		—	—
Hackney Downs	—	7 55	—	—	—	—	Thence every few minutes to	9 14	9 29
Clapton	—	—	—	—	—	—		9 18	9 33
St. James's Street.........	7 51	8 1	—	8 5	8 9	—	most stations until	9 22	9 37
Hoe Street	—	8 4	8 0	—	—	8 15		9 25	9 40
Wood Street	7 55	—	8 3	8 9	8 13	8 19		9 28	9 43
Higham's Park	—	8 11	—	—	—	8 23		9 32	9 47
Chingford	—	8 17	—	—	—	8 29		9 38	9 53

WEEK DAYS.	PM	PM	PM	PM	PM	PM	PM	PM	PM	PM	Mid.	Mid.
Liverpool St..........dep.	9 35	9 50	10 5	10 20	10 35	10 50	11 5	11 20	11 35	11 52	12 5	12 35
Bethnal Green	9 39	9 54	10 9	10 24	10 39	10 54	11 9	11 24	11 39	11 56	12 9	12 39
Cambridge Heath.........	—	—	—	—	—	—	—	—	—	—	—	12 41
London Fields	—	—	—	—	—	—	—	—	—	—	—	12 44
Hackney Downs	9 44	9 59	10 14	10 29	10 44	10 59	11 14	11 29	11 44	12 1	12 14	12 46
Clapton	9 48	10 3	10 18	10 33	10 48	11 3	11 18	11 33	11 48	12 5	12 18	12 50
St. James's Street.........	9 52	10 7	10 22	10 37	10 52	11 7	11 22	11 37	11 52	12 9	12 22	12 54
Hoe Street	9 55	10 10	10 25	10 40	10 55	11 10	11 25	11 40	11 55	12 12	12 25	12 57
Wood Street	9 58	10 13	10 28	10 43	10 58	11 13	11 28	11 43	11 58	12 15	12 28	1 0
Higham's Park	10 2	10 17	10 32	10 47	11 2	11 17	11 32	11 47	12 2	12 19	12 32	1 5
Chingford	10 8	10 23	10 38	10 53	11 8	11 23	11 33	11 53	12 8	12 25	12 38	1 10

WEEK DAYS.	AM	AM	AM	AM	AM	AM	AM	AM	AM	AM	AM	AM	AM	AM	AM
Chingford ....dep.	1255	—	—	—	—	4 48	5 18	5 40	6 0	6 12	—	6 31	6 37	—	6 49
Higham's Park	1259	—	—	—	—	4 53	5 23	5 45	6 5	6 17	—	6 35	6 41	—	6 53
Wood Street	1 4	2 4	3 4	4	4 4 31	4 57	5 27	5 49	6 9	6 21	6 32	6 41	6 45	6 54	6 58
Hoe Street	1 7	2 7	3 7	4 7	4 34	5 0	5 30	5 52	6 12	6 24	6 35	—	6 49	6 57	—
St. James's Street.........	1 9	2 9	3 9	4 9	4 36	5 3	5 33	5 55	6 15	6 27	—	6 41	6 51	—	7 2
Clapton....................	1 13	2 13	3 13	4 13	4 40	5 7	5 37	5 59	6 19	6 31	6 40	6 50	6 55	—	7 6
Hackney Downs	1 16	2 16	3 16	4 16	4 44	5 11	5 41	6 3	6 23	6 35	6 44	—	6 59	7 6	—
London Fields	1 18	2 18	3 18	4 18	—	—	—	—	—	—	—	—	—	—	—
Cambridge Heath.........	1 21	2 21	3 21	4 21	—	—	—	—	—	—	—	—	—	—	—
Bethnal Green	1 24	2 24	3 24	4 24	4 49	5 16	5 46	6 8	6 28	6 40	6 49	—	7 4	7 11	—
Liverpool Street............	1 27	2 27	3 27	4 27	4 53	5 20	5 50	6 12	6 32	6 44	6 53	7 2	7 8	7 14	7 18

WEEK DAYS.	AM	AM	AM	AM	AM	AM	AM	AM	AM	AM	AM	AM	AM	AM
Chingford ....dep.	—	6 56	—	—	7 5	—	7 12	—	7 21	—	7 23	—	7 35	—
Higham's Park	—	7 0	—	—	7 9	—	7 18	—	7 25	—	7 32	—	—	—
Wood Street	7 1	—	—	7 10	7 14	7 18	—	7 26	7 30	7 33	—	—	—	7 46
Hoe Street	—	7 7	7 10	—	—	—	7 25	7 29	—	—	7 39	7 42	7 46	—
St. James's Street.........	7 5	—	—	7 14	7 18	7 22	—	—	7 34	7 37	—	7 44	—	7 50
Clapton....................	—	7 12	—	—	7 22	—	7 30	—	—	—	7 44	—	—	—
Hackney Downs	7 13	7 16	—	7 22	—	7 30	7 34	7 38	7 42	7 45	7 43	—	7 54	7 58
London Fields	—	—	—	—	—	—	—	—	—	—	—	—	—	—
Cambridge Heath.........	—	—	—	—	—	—	—	—	—	—	—	—	—	—
Bethnal Green	7 18	—	—	7 27	—	7 35	—	7 43	—	7 50	—	—	7 59	—
Liverpool Street............	7 21	7 24	7 26	7 30	7 34	7 38	7 42	7 46	7 50	7 53	7 56	7 53	8 2	8 6

WEEK DAYS.	AM	AM	AM	AM		PM	PM	PM
Chingford ....dep.	7 41	7 50	—	8 2		8 8	8 22	8 37
Higham's Park	7 45	7 54	—	8 6		8 12	8 27	8 41
Wood Street	7 49	7 59	8 5	8 11		8 16	8 31	8 45
Hoe Street	7 53	8 2	8 8	—	Thence every few minutes to	8 20	8 35	8 50
St. James's Street.........	7 55	8 4	8 10	8 15		8 22	8 37	8 52
Clapton	7 59	8 9	—	8 19	most stations until	8 26	8 41	8 55
Hackney Downs............	—	8 13	8 17	—		8 30	8 45	9 0
London Fields............	—	—	—	—		—	8 48	—
Cambridge Heath.........	—	—	—	—		—	8 50	—
Bethnal Green	8 8	8 18	—	8 28		8 35	8 52	9 5
Liverpool Street............	8 12	8 22	8 26	8 32		8 39	8 56	9 9

WEEK DAYS.	AM	AM	AM	AM	AM	AM	AM	AM	AM	AM	AM	AM	AM	AM	AM	AM	AM
Chingford ....dep.	8 53	9 8	9 22	9 37	9 53	10 8	10 23	10 33	10 53	11 8	11 22	11 50
Higham's Park	8 58	9 12	9 27	9 41	9 58	10 12	10 28	10 42	10 58	11 12	11 27	11 54
Wood Street	9 2	9 16	9 31	9 45	10 2	10 16	10 32	10 46	11 2	11 16	11 31	11 59
Hoe Street	9 6	9 20	9 35	9 49	10 6	10 20	10 36	10 50	11 6	11 20	11 35	12 2
St. James's Street.........	9 8	9 22	9 37	9 51	10 8	10 22	10 38	10 52	11 8	11 22	11 37	12 4
Clapton....................	9 12	9 26	9 41	9 55	10 12	10 26	10 42	10 56	11 12	11 26	11 41	12 8
Hackney Downs	9 16	9 30	9 45	9 59	10 16	10 30	10 43	11 0	11 16	11 30	11 45	12 12
London Fields	—	—	—	—	—	—	—	—	—	—	—	12 15
Cambridge Heath.........	—	—	—	—	—	—	—	—	—	—	—	12 18
Bethnal Green	—	9 35	9 50	10 5	10 20	10 35	10 51	11 5	11 20	11 35	11 50	12 20
Liverpool Street............	9 24	9 39	9 54	10 9	10 24	10 39	10 55	11 9	11 24	11 39	11 54	12 24

SUNDAYS.

	AM	AM	AM	AM	AM	AM	AM	AM	AM	AM		PM	PM	AM
LIVERPOOL ST. dep.	8 5	8 35	9 5	9 35	10 5	10 35	11 5	11 20	11 35	11 50		11 35	11 50	12 35
Bethnal Green ..	8 9	8 39	9 9	9 39	10 9	10 39	11 9	11 24	11 39	11 54	Then every 15 minutes	11 39	11 54	12 39
Cambridge Heath....	8 11	8 41	9 11	9 41	10 11	10 41	11 11	—	11 41	—	from 12.5 p.m. to	11 41	—	12 41
London Fields....	8 14	8 44	9 14	9 44	10 14	10 44	11 14	—	11 44	—	11.35 p.m.	11 44	—	12 44
Hackney Downs ..	8 16	8 46	9 16	9 46	10 16	10 46	11 16	11 29	11 46	11 59		11 46	11 59	12 46
CLAPTON	8 20	8 50	9 20	9 50	10 20	10 50	11 20	11 33	11 50	12 3	Train starting 20 and	11 50	12 3	12 50
St. James's Street	8 24	8 54	9 24	9 54	10 24	10 54	11 24	11 37	11 54	12 7	50 minutes after each	11 54	12 7	12 54
Hoe Street	8 27	8 57	9 27	9 57	10 27	10 57	11 27	11 40	11 57	12 10	hour not stopping at	11 57	12 10	12 57
Wood Street......	8 30	9 0	9 30	10 0	10 30	11 0	11 30	11 43	12 0	12 13	Cambridge Heath and	12 0	12 13	1 0
Higham's Park ..	8 35	9 5	9 35	10 5	10 35	11 5	11 35	11 47	12 5	12 17	London Fields.	12 5	12 17	1 5
CHINGFORD	8 40	9 10	9 40	10 10	10 40	11 10	11 40	11 53	12 10	12 23		12 10	12 23	1 10

CHINGFORD AND WOOD STREET TO LIVERPOOL STREET.

SUNDAYS.

	AM	AM	AM	AM	AM	AM	AM	AM	AM	AM		PM	PM
CHINGFORD ..dep.	7 8	7 48	8 18	8 48	9 18	9 48	10 0	10 18	10 33	10 48	Then every 15 minutes	10 48	11 48
Higham's Park ..	7 12	7 52	8 22	8 52	9 22	9 52	10 5	10 22	10 37	10 52	from 11.3 a.m. to	10 52	11 52
Wood Street......	7 17	7 57	8 27	8 57	9 27	9 57	10 10	10 27	10 42	10 57	10.48 p.m.	10 57	11 57
Hoe Street.......	7 20	8 0	8 30	9 0	9 30	10 0	10 13	10 30	10 45	11 0		11 0	12 0
St. James's Street	7 22	8 2	8 32	9 2	9 32	10 2	10 17	10 32	10 47	11 2		11 2	12 2
CLAPTON	7 26	8 6	8 36	9 6	9 36	10 6	10 21	10 36	10 51	11 6	Train starting 33 and	11 6	12 6
Hackney Downs	7 30	8 10	8 40	9 10	9 40	10 10	10 25	10 40	10 55	11 10	3 minutes after each	11 10	12 10
London Fields ..	7 33	8 13	8 43	9 13	9 43	10 13	—	10 43	—	11 13	hour not stopping at	11 13	12 13
Cambridge Heath	7 36	8 16	8 46	9 16	9 46	10 16	—	10 46	—	11 16	London Fields and	11 16	12 16
Bethnal Green ..	7 38	8 18	8 48	9 18	9 48	10 18	10 30	10 48	11 0	11 18	Cambridge Heath.	11 18	12 18
LIVERPOOL STREET	7 42	8 22	8 52	9 22	9 52	10 22	10 34	10 52	11 4	11 22		11 22	12 22

FENCHURCH STREET TO MILLWALL DOCKS & BLACKWALL.

WEEK DAYS.

	AM	AM	AM	AM	AM	AM	AM	AM	AM	AM	AM	AM	AM
FENCHURCH STREET .....dep.	6 42	7 10	7 26	7 41	7 55	8 13	8 32	8 53	9 11	9 25	9 43	9 55	10 11
Leman Street	6 44	7 12	7 28	7 43	7 57	8 15	8 34	8 55	9 13	9 27	9 45	9 57	10 13
Shadwell and St. George's, East	6 46	7 14	7 30	7 45	7 59	8 17	8 36	8 57	9 15	9 29	9 47	9 59	10 15
Stepney	6 49	7 18	7 33	7 48	8 2	8 21	8 40	9 1	9 18	9 32	9 52	10 2	10 19
Limehouse	6 51	7 20	7 35	7 50	8 4	8 23	8 42	9 3	9 20	9 34	9 54	10 4	10 21
West India Docks	6 52	7 21	7 36	7 51	8 5	8 24	8 43	9 4	9 21	9 35	9 55	10 5	10 22
MILLWALL JUNCTION { arr.	6 54	7 23	7 38	7 53	8 7	8 26	8 45	9 6	9 23	9 37	9 57	10 7	10 24
{ dep.	6 57	7 26	—	7 54	8 14	8 27	8 47	9 15	—	9 42	—	10 12	—
South Dock	7 0	7 29	—	7 57	—	8 30	8 50	9 18	—	9 45	—	10 15	—
Millwall Docks.......	7 3	7 32	—	8 0	—	8 33	8 53	9 21	—	9 48	—	10 18	—
North Greenwich (Cubitt Town) ..arr.	7 6	7 35	—	8 3	—	8 36	8 55	9 24	—	9 51	—	10 21	—
Poplar	6 56	7 25	7 40	7 55	8 9	8 27	8 47	9 8	9 25	9 39	9 59	10 9	10 26
BLACKWALL	6 58	7 27	7 42	7 57	8 11	8 29	8 49	9 10	9 27	9 41	10 1	10 11	10 29

WEEK DAYS.

	AM	AM	AM	AM	AM	AM	AM	AM	AM	e	d	e	PM
FENCHURCH STREET .....dep.	10 26	10 40	10 55	11 10	11 25	11 40	11 54	12 10	12 25	12 52	12 44		12 52
Leman Street	10 28	10 42	10 57	11 12	11 27	11 42	11 56	12 12	12 27	12 34	12 44		12 54
Shadwell and St. George's, East ..	10 30	10 44	10 59	11 14	11 29	11 44	11 59	12 14	12 29	12 36	12 46		12 56
Stepney	10 33	10 47	11 ·2	11 17	11 32	11 47	12 2	12 17	12 32	12 39	12 49		12 59
Limehouse	10 35	10 49	11 4	11 19	11 34	11 49	12 5	12 19	12 34	12 41	12 51		1 1
West India Docks	10 36	10 50	11 5	11 20	11 35	11 50	12 6	12 20	12 35	12 42	12 52		1 2
MILLWALL JUNCTION { arr.	10 39	10 52	11 7	11 22	11 37	11 52	12 8	12 22	12 37	12 44	12 54		1 4
{ dep.	10 40		11 18		11 42		12 12	12 42	12 42				1 12
South Dock	10 43		11 21		11 45		12 15	12 45	12 45				1 15
Millwall Docks.......	10 46		11 24		11 48		12 18	12 48	12 48				1 18
North Greenwich (Cubitt Town) ..arr.	10 49		11 27		11 51		12 21	12 51	12 51				1 21
Poplar	10 40	10 55	11 9	11 24	11 39	11 54	12 10	12 24	12 39	12 46	12 56		1 8
BLACKWALL	10 42	10 57	11 11	11 26	11 41	11 56	12 12	12 26	12 41	12 48	12 58		1 10

WEEK DAYS.

	PM	PM	PM	PM	PM	PM	PM	PM	PM	PM	PM	e	e
FENCHURCH STREET .....dep.	1 10	1 25	1 40	1 55	2 12	2 25	2 39	2 55	3 12	3 25	3 40	3 55	4 9
Leman Street	1 12	1 27	1 42	1 57	2 14	2 27	2 41	2 57	3 14	3 27	3 42	3 57	4 11
Shadwell and St. George's, East	1 14	1 29	1 44	1 59	2 16	2 29	2 43	2 59	3 16	3 29	3 44	3 59	4 13
Stepney	1 17	1 32	1 47	2 2	2 19	2 32	2 46	3 1	3 19	3 32	3 47	4 2	4 16
Limehouse	1 19	1 34	1 49	2 4	2 21	2 34	2 48	3 3	3 21	3 34	3 49	4 4	4 18
West India Docks	1 20	1 35	1 50	2 5	2 22	2 35	2 49	3 4	3 22	3 35	3 50	4 6	4 19
MILLWALL JUNCTION { arr.	1 22	1 37	1 52	2 7	2 24	2 37	2 51	3 7	3 24	3 37	3 52	4 8	4 21
{ dep.	1 42		2 12		2 42			3 8	3 48			4 12	
South Dock	1 45		2 15		2 45			3 11	3 51			4 15	
Millwall Docks.......	1 48		2 18		2 48			3 14	3 54			4 18	
North Greenwich (Cubitt Town)..arr.	1 51		2 21		2 51			3 17	3 57			4 21	
Poplar	1 24	1 39	1 54	2 9	2 26	2 39	2 55	3 8	3 26	3 39	3 54	4 10	4 23
BLACKWALL	1 26	1 41	1 56	2 11	2 28	2 41	2 57	3 10	3 28	3 41	3 56	4 12	4 25

WEEK DAYS.

	PM	e	PM	PM	PM	PM	PM	PM	PM	PM	PM	PM	PM
FENCHURCH STREET ....dep.	4 25	4 38	4 55	5 7	5 25	5 38	5 54	6 10	6 25	6 40	6 55	7 23	7 56
Leman Street	4 27	4 40	4 57	5 9	5 27	5 40	5 56	6 12	6 27	6 42	6 57	7 25	7 58
Shadwell and St. George's, East......	4 29	4 42	4 59	5 11	5 29	5 42	5 58	6 14	6 29	6 44	6 59	7 27	8 0
Stepney	4 32	4 45	5 2	5 14	5 32	5 45	6 0	6 17	6 31	6 47	7 2	7 30	8 3
Limehouse	4 34	4 47	5 4	5 16	5 34	5 47	6 2	6 19	6 33	6 49	7 4	7 32	8 5
West India Docks.....	4 35	4 48	5 5	5 17	5 35	5 48	6 3	6 20	6 34	6 50	7 5	7 33	8 6
MILLWALL JUNCTION { dep.	4 37	4 50	5 7	5 19	5 37	5 50	6 5	6 22	6 36	6 52	7 7	7 35	8 8
{ dep.	4 42	5 0			5 42		6 12		6 42		7 12	7 42	8 12
South Dock..........	4 45	5 3			5 45		6 15		6 45				
Millwall Docks.......	4 48	5 6		5 25	5 48		6 18		6 47		7 17	7 47	8 17
North Greenwich (Cubitt Town)..arr.	4 51	5 9		5 28	5 51		6 21		6 50		7 20	7 50	8 20
Poplar	4 39	4 52	5 9	5 21	5 39	5 52	2 55	6 8	6 24	6 38	6 54	7 37	8 10
BLACKWALL	4 41	4 54	5 11	5 23	5 41	5 54	6 10	6 26	6 40	6 56	7 11	7 39	8 12

d Saturdays only.   e Saturdays excepted.

No Sunday Trains.

WEEK DAYS	AM	AM	AM	AM	AM	AM	AM	AM	AM	AM	AM	AM	AM	AM
Blackwall ....dep.	6 50	7 5	7 20	7 32	7 50	8 2	8 20	8 43	9 2	9 20	9 35	9 50	10 7	10 20
Poplar	6 51	7 6	7 21	7 33	7 51	8 3	8 21	8 44	9 3	9 21	9 36	9 51	10 8	10 21
North Greenwich (Cubitt Tn.)	6 40	—	7 9	—	7 39	—	8 9	8 37	8 56	—	9 27	—	9 54	—
Millwall Docks	6 43	—	7 12	—	7 42	e	8 12	8 49	8 59	—	9 30	—	9 57	—
South Dock	—	—	7 15	—	7 45	—	8 15	8 43	9 2	—	9 33	—	10 0	—
Millwall Junction .. { arr.	6 48	—	7 18	—	7 48	—	8 15	8 46	9 4	—	9 36	—	10 3	—
Millwall Junction .. { dep.	6 53	7 8	7 23	7 35	7 53	8 5	8 23	8 47	9 5	9 23	9 38	9 53	10 8	10 23
West India Docks	6 55	7 10	7 25	7 37	7 55	8 7	8 25	8 49	9 7	9 25	9 40	9 55	10 10	10 25
Limehouse..................	6 57	7 12	7 27	7 39	7 57	8 9	8 27	8 51	9 9	9 27	9 42	9 57	10 12	10 27
Stepney	6 59	7 14	7 29	7 41	7 59	8 11	8 29	8 53	9 12	9 29	9 44	9 59	10 14	10 29
Shadwell and St. George's, E.	7 2	7 17	7 32	7 44	8 2	8 14	8 32	8 56	9 15	9 32	9 48	10 2	10 18	10 32
Leman Street	7 4	7 19	7 34	7 46	8 4	8 16	8 34	8 58	9 17	9 34	9 50	10 4	10 20	10 34
Fenchurch Street............	7 6	7 21	7 36	7 48	8 6	8 18	8 36	9 1	9 19	9 36	9 52	10 6	10 22	10 36

WEEK DAYS	AM	AM	AM	AM	AM	AM	PM	PM	PM	e	d	e
Blackwall ....dep.	10 35	10 50	11 5	11 20	11 35	11 47	12 5	12 18	12 35	12 50	12 59	1 5
Poplar	10 36	10 51	11 6	11 21	11 36	11 48	12 6	12 19	12 36	12 51	1 0	1 6
North Greenwich (Cubitt Tn.)	10 24	—	10 50	—	11 28	—	11 54	—	12 24	—	12 52	12 54
Millwall Docks	10 27	—	10 53	—	11 31	—	11 57	—	12 27	—	12 55	12 57
South Dock	10 30	—	10 56	—	11 34	—	12 0	—	12 30	—	12 58	1 0
Millwall Junction .. { arr.	10 33	—	10 59	—	11 37	—	12 3	—	12 33	—	1 1	1 3
Millwall Junction .. { dep.	10 38	10 53	11 8	11 23	11 38	11 50	12 8	12 21	12 38	12 53	1 2	1 8
West India Docks	10 40	10 55	11 10	11 25	11 40	11 52	12 10	12 23	12 40	12 55	1 4	1 10
Limehouse..................	10 42	10 57	11 12	11 27	11 42	11 54	12 12	12 25	12 42	12 57	1 6	1 12
Stepney	10 44	10 59	11 14	11 29	11 44	11 56	12 14	12 27	12 44	12 59	1 8	1 14
Shadwell and St. George's, E.	10 47	11 2	11 17	11 32	11 47	11 59	12 17	12 30	12 47	1 2	1 11	1 17
Leman Street	10 49	11 4	11 19	11 34	11 49	12 1	12 19	12 32	12 49	1 4	1 13	1 19
Fenchurch Street............	10 51	11 6	11 21	11 36	11 51	12 3	12 21	12 34	12 51	1 6	1 15	1 21

WEEK DAYS.	PM	PM	PM	PM	e	PM	e	PM	e	e	e	e	e	e
Blackwall ....dep.	1 20	1 35	1 50	2 5	2 20	2 35	2 50	3 5	3 20	3 35	3 49	4 5	4 18	4 35
Poplar	1 21	1 36	1 51	2 6	2 21	2 36	2 51	3 6	3 21	3 36	3 50	4 6	4 19	4 36
North Greenwich (Cubitt Tn.)	—	1 22	—	1 54	—	2 24	—	2 54	—	3 18	—	3 58	—	4 22
Millwall Docks	—	1 25	—	1 57	—	2 27	—	2 57	—	3 21	—	—	4 1	4 25
South Dock	—	1 28	—	2 0	—	2 30	—	3 0	—	3 24	—	—	4 4	4 28
Millwall Junction .. { arr.	—	1 31	—	2 3	—	2 33	—	3 3	—	3 27	—	—	4 7	4 31
Millwall Junction .. { dep.	1 23	1 38	1 53	2 8	2 23	2 38	2 53	3 8	3 23	3 38	3 52	4 8	4 21	4 38
West India Docks	1 25	1 40	1 55	2 10	2 25	2 40	2 55	3 10	3 25	3 40	3 54	4 10	4 23	4 40
Limehouse..................	1 27	1 42	1 57	2 12	2 27	2 42	2 57	3 12	3 27	3 42	3 56	4 12	4 25	4 42
Stepney	1 29	1 44	1 59	2 14	2 29	2 44	2 59	3 14	3 29	3 44	3 58	4 14	4 27	4 44
Shadwell and St. George's, E.	1 32	1 47	2 2	2 17	2 32	2 47	3 2	3 17	3 32	3 47	4 1	4 17	4 30	4 47
Leman Street	1 34	1 49	2 4	2 19	2 34	2 49	3 4	3 19	3 34	3 49	4 3	4 19	4 32	4 49
Fenchurch Street............	1 36	1 51	2 6	2 21	2 36	2 51	3 6	3 21	3 36	3 51	4 5	4 21	4 34	4 51

WEEK DAYS.	e	e	e	e	e	e	e	e	e	e	e
Blackwall ....dep.	4 48	5 5	5 18	5 35	5 50	6 5	6 20	6 35	7 4	7 35	8 5
Poplar	4 49	5 6	5 19	5 36	5 51	6 6	6 21	6 36	7 5	7 36	8 6
North Greenwich (Cubitt Tn.)	—	4 51	5 10	5 29	—	5 55	—	6 24	6 55	7 25	7 55
Millwall Docks.............	—	4 54	5 13	5 32	—	5 55	—	6 27	6 58	7 28	7 58
South Dock	—	4 57	5 16	5 35	—	5 58	—	6 30	—	—	—
Millwall Junction .. { arr.	—	4 59	5 19	5 37	—	6 1	—	6 33	7 3	7 33	8 3
Millwall Junction .. { dep.	4 51	5 8	5 21	5 38	5 53	6 8	6 23	6 38	7 7	7 38	8 8
West India Docks	4 53	5 10	5 23	5 40	5 55	6 10	6 25	6 40	7 9	7 40	8 10
Limehouse..................	4 55	5 12	5 25	5 42	5 57	6 12	6 27	6 42	7 11	7 42	8 12
Stepney	4 57	5 14	5 27	5 44	5 59	6 14	6 29	6 44	7 13	7 44	8 14
Shadwell and St. George's, E.	5 0	5 17	5 30	5 47	6 2	6 17	6 32	6 47	7 16	7 47	8 17
Leman Street	5 2	5 19	5 32	5 49	6 4	6 19	6 34	6 49	7 18	7 49	8 19
Fenchurch Street............	5 4	5 21	5 34	5 51	6 6	6 21	6 36	6 51	7 20	7 51	8 21

d Saturdays only.   e Saturdays excepted.

No Sunday Trains.

WEEK DAYS.

	AM	AM	l	AM	AM	AM	AM				AM	AM	l	AM	AM	AM	AM	AM
LIVERPOOL ST. dep.	4 20	5 20	5 50	5 26	6 10	6 30	7 6	7 18	7 31	7 55	8 30	8 48	9 10	10 5	10 34	11 29		
Bethnal Green	4 26	5 24	—	5 30	6 14	6 34	7 11	—	7 25	7 59	—	—	—	—	10 38	—		
Hackney Downs	—	5 31	5 59	—	—	—	7 17	—	7 42	8 4	—	—	—	—	—	11 30		
Clapton	—	5 34	—	—	—	—	—	—	7 45	8 7	—	9 1	9 21	—	—	—		
Lea Bridge	4 52	—	—	6 12	6 33	6 50	—	—	—	—	—	—	—	10 56	—	—		
TOTTENHAM	4 56	5 42	—	6 18	6 38	6 55	7 26	7 42	7 51	8 13	—	9 6	9 23	—	11 0	11 39		
Park	5 0	5 45	—	6 21	6 42	6 59	7 29	7 45	7 54	8 17	—	9 9	9 31	—	11 6	11 42		
Angel Road	5 3	5 48	—	6 24	6 45	7 3	7 32	7 48	7 57	8 20	—	9 12	9 34	—	11 9	11 45		
EDMONTON, Lower	—	—	—	—	—	—	—	—	—	—	—	—	—	—	—	—		
Ponder's End	5 9	5 53	6 12	6 30	6 50	7 8	7 37	—	8 2	8 26	—	9 18	9 41	—	11 15	11 50		
Brimsdown	5 12	5 56	—	6 33	6 53	7 11	7 40	—	8 5	8 29	—	9 21	9 44	—	11 18	11 53		
Enfield Lock	5 15	5 59	6 18	6 38	6 56	7 14	7 43	—	8 8	8 32	—	9 24	9 47	10 27	11 21	11 57		
Waltham, C. & A.	5 19	6 3	—	6 43	7 0	7 18	7 46	7 59	8 12	8 37	—	9 28	9 51	—	11 25	12 16		
Cheshunt	5 23	6 7	—	6 47	7 3	7 22	—	8 7	8 17	8 41	—	9 32	9 56	—	11 29	12 20		
BROXBOURNE	—	6 12	6 27	6 53	—	7 28	—	8 16	8 23	8 50	8 58	9 39	10 2	10 36	11 35	12 26		
Rye House	—	—	—	7 1	—	7 36	—	8 21	—	8 57	9 16	—	10 14	10 49	11 43	12 33		
St. Margarets	—	—	—	7 8	—	7 43	—	8 30	—	9 1	9 20	—	10 18	10 54	11 47	12 38		
WARE	—	—	—	7 14	—	7 46	—	8 36	—	9 6	9 23	—	10 23	11 0	11 52	12 43		

WEEK DAYS.

	d	d	e	d	d	d	e	d	e	d	PM	PM	e	PM	e	e
LIVERPOOL ST. dep.	12 20	1240	12 48	12 48	1 14	1 19	1 20	1 39	2 0	2 0	2 48	3 5	3 50	4 15	4 30	4 37
Bethnal Green	—	—	—	12 53	1 18	—	1 24	—	—	—	—	3 9	—	—	—	4 41
Hackney Downs	—	—	12 56	—	—	—	—	—	—	—	2 58	—	3 59	—	—	—
Clapton	—	—	1 0	1 1	—	—	—	—	—	—	—	—	4 2	—	—	—
Lea Bridge	12 51	—	—	—	1 40	—	1 50	—	—	—	—	3 36	—	—	—	5 1
TOTTENHAM	12 57	—	1 8	1 8	1 45	—	1 54	—	2 15	—	3 6	3 42	4 8	—	—	5 5
Park	1 1	—	1 11	1 11	1 48	—	1 58	1 55	—	—	3 9	3 45	4 11	—	—	5 9
Angel Road	1 4	—	1 14	1 14	1 51	—	2 1	1 58	—	—	—	3 48	—	—	—	5 12
EDMONTON, Lower	—	—	—	—	—	—	—	—	—	—	—	—	—	—	—	—
Ponder's End	1 10	—	1 18	1 19	1 56	—	2 8	2 4	—	—	—	3 53	4 17	—	—	5 16
Brimsdown	1 13	—	1 21	1 22	1 59	—	2 11	2 7	—	—	—	3 56	—	—	—	5 19
Enfield Lock	1 16	—	1 24	1 25	2 2	—	2 14	2 10	2 25	2 24	—	3 59	4 23	—	—	5 22
Waltham, C. & A.	1 20	1 2	1 28	1 29	2 6	1 45	2 18	2 15	2 29	2 28	3 20	4 4	4 27	—	4 53	5 26
Cheshunt	1 24	1 7	1 32	1 33	2 9	—	2 22	2 19	—	—	3 24	4 8	4 30	—	4 57	5 30
BROXBOURNE	—	1 13	1 36	1 39	—	1 53	2 28	2 25	2 37	2 36	3 30	4 14	—	4 43	5 3	5 36
Rye House	—	1 21	1 51	—	—	2 5	—	—	2 45	2 47	3 43	4 24	—	—	5 9	—
St. Margarets	—	1 25	1 56	—	—	2 10	—	—	2 49	2 51	3 49	4 27	—	—	5 14	—
WARE	—	1 30	2 1	—	—	2 15	—	—	2 54	2 56	3 56	4 34	—	—	5 19	—

WEEK DAYS.

	PM	e	PM	e	d	PM	e	PM	e	PM	PM	PM	PM	PM	PM	h	PM
LIVERPOOL ST. dep.	5 10	5 17	5 20	6 0	6 0	6 7	6 27	6 30	6 38	7 18	7 41	7 48	8 24	8 22	9 17	10 40	11 50	12 0
Bethnal Green	—	5 21	—	—	—	6 31	—	—	—	—	8 29	—	—	10 44	—	—	
Hackney Downs	—	—	—	—	6 18	—	—	7 28	—	7 58	—	—	9 26	10 49	—	12 9	
Clapton	—	—	—	—	6 52	—	—	—	—	8 50	—	—	—	10 52	—	—	
Lea Bridge	—	—	—	—	—	—	—	—	—	—	—	—	—	—	—	—	
TOTTENHAM	—	5 46	5 34	—	6 25	6 57	6 54	7 35	—	8 4	8 55	—	9 34	10 53	—	12 17	
Park	—	5 49	5 37	—	6 28	7 4	—	7 38	—	8 7	8 59	—	9 37	11 1	—	12 20	
Angel Road	—	5 52	5 40	—	6 31	7 7	—	7 41	—	8 10	9 2	—	9 40	11 4	—	12 23	
EDMONTON, Lower	—	5 56	—	—	—	—	—	—	—	—	—	—	—	—	—	—	
Ponder's End	—	5 45	—	—	6 36	7 14	—	7 46	—	8 15	9 7	—	9 45	11 9	—	12 28	
Brimsdown	—	5 48	—	—	6 39	7 18	—	7 49	—	8 18	9 10	—	9 48	11 12	—	12 31	
Enfield Lock	5 33	5 51	—	—	6 43	7 21	—	7 52	—	8 22	9 13	—	9 51	11 15	—	12 34	
Waltham, C. & A.	5 37	5 55	6 22	6 23	6 45	7 24	—	7 56	7 56	8 8	8 29	9 20	9 55	11 19	12 14	12 38	
Cheshunt	—	5 59	6 29	6 27	7 3	7 41	—	7 12	8 0	8 29	—	9 59	11 23	12 18	12 42		
BROXBOURNE	5 45	6 5	6 27	6 33	7 4	8 7	8 47	6 58	7 18	8 6	8 16	8 50	10 5	11 29	12 25	12 48	
Rye House	5 56	6 11	6 34	6 39	7 15	7 15	7 24	—	8 28	8 42	9 1	10 16	11 37	12 54			
St. Margarets	6 0	6 16	6 37	6 44	7 19	7 19	7 28	—	8 32	8 48	9 6	10 20	11 41	12 58			
WARE	6 5	6 20	6 49	6 49	7 24	7 24	7 33	—	8 37	8 53	9 11	10 25	11 46	1 3			

SUNDAYS.

	AM	l	AM	l	l	AM	l	PM	l	PM	PM	PM	l	PM
LIVERPOOL ST. dep.	7 25	8 12	8 50	9 25	10 12	10 42	1 50	3 42	4 50	6 25	7 15	8 25	9 12	10 25
Bethnal Green	7 30	—	8 54	—	10 16	10 46	1 54	3 46	4 54	6 29	—	—	—	10 29
Hackney Downs	—	8 22	9 0	—	—	10 53	—	3 52	—	6 35	—	—	—	10 35
Clapton	—	—	9 3	—	—	10 56	—	3 55	—	6 39	—	—	—	—
Lea Bridge	7 44	—	—	—	—	—	2 11	—	5 8	—	—	8 40	—	—
TOTTENHAM	7 49	—	9 9	—	10 36	11 3	2 17	4 1	5 12	6 45	7 30	8 45	9 29	10 44
Park	7 53	—	9 12	—	10 39	11 6	2 22	4 4	5 16	6 48	—	8 50	—	10 48
Angel Road	7 56	—	9 17	—	—	11 10	2 25	4 7	5 19	6 53	—	8 53	—	10 51
EDMONTON, Lower	—	—	—	—	—	—	—	—	—	—	—	—	—	—
Ponder's End	8 1	—	9 22	—	10 45	11 16	2 33	4 12	5 24	6 59	—	8 59	9 38	10 57
Brimsdown	8 4	—	9 25	—	—	11 19	2 36	4 15	5 27	7 2	—	9 2	9 41	11 0
Enfield Lock	8 7	—	9 28	—	—	11 22	2 39	4 18	5 31	7 5	—	9 5	9 44	11 3
Waltham, C. & A.	8 11	—	9 32	—	10 50	11 26	2 43	4 22	5 35	7 9	7 43	9 9	9 48	11 7
Cheshunt	8 15	—	9 36	—	10 54	11 30	2 47	4 26	5 39	7 14	—	9 13	9 53	11 11
BROXBOURNE	8 22	8 42	9 41	9 53	10 59	11 36	2 53	4 33	5 45	7 20	7 51	9 19	9 59	11 17
Rye House	—	8 55	9 48	—	11 7	11 43	3 5	4 40	—	7 27	—	9 26	—	11 24
St. Margarets	—	9 0	9 53	—	11 10	11 48	3 9	4 44	—	7 34	—	9 30	—	11 28
WARE	—	9 5	9 58	—	11 26	11 53	3 14	4 49	—	7 40	—	9 35	—	11 33

d Saturdays only. e Saturdays excepted. h Wednesdays and Saturdays only.

l 1st and 3rd Class only.

WEEK DAYS.	l	AM	AM	AM	AM	AM	AM	AM	AM	l	AM	AM	l	AM	AM	AM
Ware ....dep.	—	—	6 4	—	—	7 9	—	7 41	7 54	—	8 33	8 43	—	—	9 22	—
St. Margarets	—	—	6 9	—	—	7 14	—	7 47	7 59	—	8 38	8 51	—	—	9 28	—
Rye House	—	—	6 13	—	—	7 17	—	7 51	8 3	—	—	8 55	--	—	—	—
Broxbourne	2 11	—	6 18	6 38	—	7 31	—	8 4	8 16	8 30	8 56	9 8	—	9 18	9 36	10 2
Cheshunt.........	—	5 54	6 24	6 44	—	7 38	7 54	8 11	—	8 36	—	—	—	9 24	--	10 8
Waltham C. & A...	2 20	5 58	6 28	6 48	—	7 42	7 58	8 15	8 25	8 40	—	—	9 21	9 28	9 44	10 12
Enfield Lock	—	6 .1	6 32	6 52	—	7 46	8 2	8 20	—	8 43	—	—	—	9 31	—	10 15
Brimsdown.......	—	6 4	6 35	6 55	—	—	8 5	—	—	8 46	—	—	—	9 34	—	10 18
Ponder's End	—	6 7	6 38	6 58	—	7 51	8 8	8 25	8 32	8 49	—	—	—	9 38	—	10 21
Edmonton, Lower	—	—	—	—	7 18	—	—	—	—	—	—	—	—	—	—	—
Angel Road	—	6 13	6 44	7 4	—	—	8 13	—	—	8 54	—	—	—	—	—	10 26
Park	—	6 16	6 47	7 7	—	7 57	8 16	8 32	—	8 57	—	—	—	9 45	—	10 29
Tottenham	—	6 19	6 50	7 11	—	8 2	8 20	—	8 42	9 2	—	9 26	—	9 48	—	10 34
Lea Bridge	—	6 24	6 55	7 16	—	—	8 26	—	—	—	—	—	—	—	—	—
Clapton	—	—	—	—	—	—	—	—	—	—	—	—	—	—	—	—
Hackney Downs ..	—	—	—	—	—	8 9	—	—	—	—	—	—	—	9 55	—	10 40
Bethnal Green	—	6 39	7 21	7 30	—	—	—	—	—	—	—	—	—	—	—	10 46
Liverpool Street	2 50	6 43	7 25	7 34	7 44	8 18	8 46	8 49	8 57	9 18	9 27	9 40	9 46	10 3	10 9	10 49

WEEK DAYS.	AM	l	AM	d	d	PM	d	PM	l	d	e	l	d	h	k	m	d	PM
Ware ....dep.	9 59	10 56	11 34	—	—	12 11	—	12 52	—	2 6	2 11	—	—	2 £1	3 4	—	—	3 51
St. Margarets	10 5	11	11 39	—	—	12 16	—	12 58	—	2 12	2 16	—	—	2 57	3 9	—	—	3 57
Rye House	10 9	11	7 11 43	—	—	12 20	—	1 2	—	2 16	2 20	—	—	3 1	3 13	--	—	4 1
Broxbourne	10 24	11 25	11 47	—	—	12 26	—	1. 9	1 30	2 23	2 26	2 47	3 0	3 3	3 20	—	—	4 19
Cheshunt.........	10 30	11 31	11 54	—	12 17	12 32	12 55	1 15	—	2 29	2 32	—	3 6	3 15	3 27	4 2	—	4 26
Waltham C. & A...	10 34	11 35	11 58	—	12 21	12 36	12 59	1 19	1 38	2 33	2 36	—	3 10	3 19	3 31	4 7	—	4 30
Enfield Lock	—	11 39	—	—	12 25	12 40	1 2	1 22	1 41	2 36	2 39	—	3 13	3 22	3 34	4 10	—	4 34
Brimsdown.......	—	11 42	—	—	12 28	12 43	1 5	1 25	—	2 39	2 42	—	3 16	3 26	3 38	4 14	—	—
Ponder's End.....	—	11 45	—	—	12 31	12 46	1 8	1 28	—	2 42	2 45	—	3 19	3 42	3 41	4 17	—	4 40
Edmonton, Lower	—	—	—	—	—	—	—	—	—	—	—	—	—	—	—	—	—	—
Angel Road	—	11 50	—	12 10	12 36	12 52	1 14	1 33	—	2 47	2 50	—	3 24	3 47	3 46	4 22	—	—
Park	—	11 53	—	12 13	12 39	12 55	1 17	1 36	—	2 50	2 53	—	3 27	3 50	3 49	4 25	—	—
Tottenham	—	12 0	12 12	12 16	12 42	12 59	1 20	1.42	1 52	2 55	2 57	—	3 33	3 54	3 53	4 29	—	4 52
Lea Bridge	—	—	—	—	12 47	1 4	—	—	—	3 0	—	—	3 28	—	—	4 34	—	—
Clapton	—	—	—	12 22	—	—	1 26	—	—	—	3 3	—	—	—	—	—	—	—
Hackney Downs ..	—	—	—	—	—	—	1 49	—	—	3 6	—	—	4 14 1	—	—	—	—	—
Bethnal Green	—	—	—	—	1 20	1 35	—	—	—	3 18	—	—	—	—	—	5 20	—	—
Liverpool Street	10 59	12 1F	12 28	12 35	1 6	1 24	1 39	1 58	2 7	3 21	3 16	3 18 4	7 4	11 4	11	5 24	5 9

WEEK DAYS.	PM	PM	e	e	PM	PM	PM	e	PM	PM	PM	PM	l	PM
Ware ....dep.	—	4 41	—	—	5 54	—	6 54	—	7 58	—	8 49	—	9 41	10 32
St. Margarets	—	4 47	—	—	6 3	—	6 59	—	8 3	—	8 57	—	9 46	10 37
Rye House	—	4 51	—	—	6 7	—	7 3	—	8 7	—	9 1	--	9 50	10 41
Broxbourne	—	4 58	—	5 52	6 12	6 21	7 16	—	7 22	8 16	8 39	9 8	10 32	10 46
Cheshunt.........	4 56	5	5 14	—	5 58	—	6 29	—	7 28	8 25	8 46	9 14	9 35	10 53
Waltham C. & A...	5 0	5 8	5 18	5 26	6 2	6 21	6 34	7 24	7 32	8 29	8 50	9 19	9 39	10 <0	10 57
Enfield Lock	5 3	5 11	5 24	5 30	6 6	—	6 37	—	7 35	8 32	8 53	9 22	9 42	—	11 0
Brimsdown.......	5 6	5 14	5 27	5 33	6 9	—	—	—	7 38	8 35	8 57	9 25	9 45	—	11 3
Ponder's End.....	5 9	5 17	5 30	5 36	6 13	6 27	6 43	—	7 41	8 38	9 0	9 28	9 48	—	11 6
Edmonton, Lower	—	—	—	—	—	—	—	7 48	—	—	—	—	—	—
Angel Road	5 14	5 22	5 36	5 42	6 18	—	6 49	—	7 51	7 46	8 44	9 5	9 33	9 53	11 11
Park	5 17	5 25	5 39	5 44	6 21	—	6 52	—	7 57	8 47	9 8	9 36	9 56	—	11 14
Tottenham	5 22	5 29	5 43	5 48	6 24	6 36	7 1	7 42	7 59	7 55	8 52	9 14	9 41	9 59	10 54	11 18
Lea Bridge	5 27	—	—	5 54	6 29	--	7 7	—	8 4	—	8 57	—	10 4	—
Clapton	—	5 35	—	—	—	—	—	—	—	—	9 20	9 48	11 0	11 24
Hackney Downs ..	—	5 38	5 49	—	—	—	7 11	—	8 2	—	9 24	9 51	11 4	11 27
Bethnal Green	5 47	—	—	—	—	—	—	—	—	9 29	9 56	—	11 32
Liverpool Street	5 53	5 47	5 59	6 26	6 47	7 0	7 19	7 56	8 33	8 10	9 24	9 33	10 0	10 32	11 12	11 ⅖

SUNDAYS.	l	AM	l	AM	PM	PM	PM	e	PM	PM	PM	PM	PM
Ware ....dep.	—	—	8 10	10 15	11 45	2 5	5 5	6 10	—	—	7 48	—	9 18	—
St. Margarets	—	—	8 20	10 20	11 50	2 10	5 10	6 15	—	7 38	7 54	—	9 23	—
Rye House	—	—	8 24	10 24	11 55	2 15	5 15	6 20	—	7 43	7 59	—	9 28	—
Broxbourne	2 11	7 9	8 33	10 38	12 1	2 21	5 20	6 26	6 51	7 49	8 4	8 25	9 35	9 51
Cheshunt	—	7 15	8 40	—	12 7	2 27	5 27	6 32	—	7 55	8 10	8 31	9 41	9 57
Waltham, C. & A......	2 20	7 19	8 45	10 46	12 11	2 31	5 31	6 36	6 59	7 59	8 14	8 36	9 45	10 1
Enfield Lock ,.......	—	7 23	8 49	—	12 15	2 35	5 35	6 40	—	8 3	8 18	—	9 49	10 5
Brimsdown.,.........	—	7 26	8 52	—	12 18	2 38	5 38	—	—	8 6	8 21	—	9 52	—
Ponder's End	—	7 29	8 56	10 53	12 21	2 41	5 41	6 45	—	8 10	8 25	8 43	9 55	10 10
Edmonton, Lower.....	—	—	—	—	—	—	—	—	—	—	—	—	—	—
Angel Road	—	7 35	9 3	—	12 27	2 47	5 47	—	—	8 16	8 31	—	10 1	—
Park	—	7 38	9 6	—	12 30	2 50	5 50	—	—	8 19	8 34	—	10 4	10 17
Tottenham	—	7 42	9 11	11 4	12 34	2 54	5 54	6 54	7 12	8 23	8 38	8 54	10 9	10 22
Lea Bridge	—	7 47	—	—	12 40	—	—	—	—	—	—	—	10 15	—
Clapton	—	—	9 18	—	—	2 59	5 59	6 59	—	8 29	8 44	—	—	—
Hackney Downs	—	—	9 23	—	—	3 2	6 2	7 2	—	8 32	8 47	9 2	—	10 32
Bethnal Green	—	8 2	9 28	—	—	3 7	6 7	7 7	—	8 37	8 52	9 7	10 32	10 37
Liverpool Street	2 50	8 5	9 31	11 27	12 57	3 10	6 10	7 10	7 26	8 46	8 55	9 10	10 35	10 40

d Saturdays only.   e Saturdays excepted.   h 14th and 21st July only.
k Commence running July 23rd.   l 1st and 3rd class only.   m Cease running 21st July.

WEEK DAYS	AM	AM	h	AM	h	AM	AM	h	AM	AM	AM	AM	AM	AM	AM	h	AM
LIVERPOOL ST. ....dep.	2 0	4 20	5 10	5 14	5 26	6 10	—	6 50	6 58	—	7 14	7 28	7 32	7 36	7 39	7 48	7 53
Bethnal Green	—	4 26	—	5 19	5 30	6 14	—	—	—	—	—	—	—	—	7 44	—	—
Coborn Road	—	4 30	—	5 23	—	6 18	—	—	—	—	—	—	—	—	7 48	—	—
FENCHURCH STREET	—	—	—	—	—	—	6 20	—	—	7 6	—	—	—	—	—	—	—
Stepney	—	—	—	—	—	—	6 27	—	—	7 13	—	—	—	—	—	—	—
Burdett Road	—	—	—	—	—	—	6 29	—	—	7 15	—	—	—	—	—	—	—
Bow Road	—	—	—	—	—	—	6 32	—	—	7 18	—	—	—	—	—	—	—
STRATFORD MARKET	—	—	—	—	—	—	—	—	—	—	—	—	—	—	—	—	—
STRATFORD (W. Ham.)	2 12	4 33	5 19	5 31	5 39	6 23	6 38	7 2	7 10	7 25	7 27	7 41	7 45	7 43	7 53	7 59	—
Maryland Point	2 14	4 40	—	5 33	—	6 25	6 40	—	7 12	7 27	—	—	—	7 50	7 55	—	8 5
Forest Gate	2 17	4 45	—	5 37	5 45	6 28	6 43	—	7 15	7 30	—	—	—	7 53	7 58	—	8 8
Manor Park	2 20	4 48	—	5 40	5 49	6 31	6 46	—	7 18	7 33	—	—	7 51	7 56	8 1	—	8 11
ILFORD	2 24	4 50	5 26	5 45	5 55	6 35	6 49	7 10	7 22	7 36	7 35	7 50	7 55	8 0	8	4 8	9 8 16
Seven Kings	2 27	—	—	5 49	5 58	—	6 39	—	—	7 25	—	7 38	7 53	7 58	—	—	—
Goodmayes	2 30	—	—	5 52	—	—	6 42	—	—	7 28	—	7 41	7 56	8 0	—	—	—
CHADWELL HEATH	2 33	—	—	5 56	6 3	6 46	—	—	—	7 31	—	7 44	8 0	—	—	—	—
ROMFORD	—	—	5 35	6 2	6 9	6 52	—	7 21	—	—	—	8 6	—	—	—	8 19	—
GIDEA PARK	—	—	5 51	6 5	—	6 55	—	7 25	—	—	—	8 10	—	—	—	—	—
Harold Wood	—	—	5 55	—	—	—	—	7 30	—	—	—	8 14	—	—	—	—	—
BRENTWOOD	—	—	5 48	—	6 23	—	—	7 42	—	—	—	8 24	—	—	—	8 30	—

WEEK DAYS.	AM	AM	h	AM	AM	AM	AM	AM	AM	h	AM	AM	AM	AM	AM	AM
LIVERPOOL ST. ....dep.	8 0	8 3	—	8 18	8 33	8 35	8 38	8 33	8 46	—	9 1	9 6	9 24	—	—	9 41
Bethnal Green	—	8 22	8 37	—	—	8 42	—	—	—	—	9 10	9 29	—	—	—	—
Coborn Road	—	—	—	8 41	—	8 47	—	—	—	—	9 15	9 33	—	—	—	—
FENCHURCH STREET	—	7 58	—	—	—	—	—	8 46	—	—	—	—	9 21	9 33	—	—
Stepney	—	8 6	—	—	—	—	—	8 52	—	—	—	—	9 28	9 38	—	—
Burdett Road	—	8 8	—	—	—	—	—	8 54	—	—	—	—	9 30	9 40	—	—
Bow Road	—	8 11	—	—	—	—	—	8 57	—	—	—	—	9 33	9 43	—	—
STRATFORD MARKET	—	—	—	—	—	—	—	—	—	—	—	—	—	—	—	—
STRATFORD (W. Ham.)	8 12	8 15	8 18	8 30	8 47	8 45	—	8 55	8 57	9 4	9 14	9 22	9 38	9 42	9 48	9 52
Maryland Point	—	8 18	8 21	8 32	—	—	8 52	8 57	—	9 6	—	9 24	9 40	9 44	9 50	9 54
Forest Gate	—	8 21	8 24	8 35	8 51	—	8 55	9 3	—	9 9	—	9 27	9 43	9 47	9 53	9 57
Manor Park	—	8 24	8 27	8 38	8 54	—	8 58	9 7	—	9 12	—	9 30	9 46	9 50	—	10 1
ILFORD	8 20	8 29	8 34	8 43	8 57	8 55	9 2	9 12	—	9 15	9 21	9 34	9 50	9 53	9 58	10 5
Seven Kings	8 23	8 32	—	8 47	—	8 58	9 6	9 15	—	—	—	9 37	—	—	—	—
Goodmayes	8 26	8 36	—	8 50	—	9 1	9 6	9 18	—	—	—	9 40	—	—	—	—
CHADWELL HEATH	8 30	8 42	—	8 53	—	9 5	9 12	—	—	—	—	9 44	—	—	—	—
ROMFORD	—	8 51	—	—	—	9 15	—	—	—	—	—	9 50	—	—	—	—
GIDEA PARK	—	8 55	—	—	—	9 18	—	—	—	—	—	9 54	—	—	—	—
Harold Wood	—	8 59	—	—	—	—	—	—	—	—	—	9 58	—	—	—	—
BRENTWOOD	—	9 6	—	—	—	—	—	—	9 21	—	9 42	10 5	—	—	—	—

WEEK DAYS	AM	AM	AM	AM	AM	AM	AM	AM	AM	h	AM	AM	AM	AM	AM
LIVERPOOL ST. ......dep.	9 46	—	10 8	—	10 23	10 30	—	10 47	10 50	—	11 13	11 25	11 45	—
Bethnal Green	—	—	—	—	10 27	—	—	—	—	—	—	—	—	—
Coborn Road	—	—	—	—	10 31	—	—	—	—	—	—	—	—	—
FENCHURCH STREET	—	9 52	—	10 8	—	—	10 30	—	—	11 8	—	—	—	11 51
Stepney	—	10 0	—	10 13	—	—	10 37	—	—	11 15	—	—	—	11 58
Burdett Road	—	10 4	—	10 15	—	—	10 39	—	—	11 17	—	—	—	12 0
Bow Road	—	10 7	—	10 19	—	—	10 43	—	—	11 21	—	—	—	12 3
STRATFORD MARKET	—	—	—	—	—	—	—	—	—	—	—	—	—	—
STRATFORD (W. Ham.)	9 56	10 16	10 19	10 25	10 36	10 40	10 50	—	11 1	11 23	11 23	11 58	12 10	—
Maryland Point	9 58	10 27	10 21	—	10 38	—	10 52	—	11 8	11 30	11 26	11 39	12 12	—
Forest Gate	10 2	10 20	10 25	—	10 41	—	10 55	—	11 6	11 35	11 29	11 44	12 6	12 15
Manor Park	10 6	10 24	10 29	—	10 44	—	10 59	—	11 9	11 40	11 32	11 48	12 10	12 19
ILFORD	10 10	10 27	10 34	—	10 48	10 48	11 3	—	11 14	11 43	11 36	11 54	12 16	12 23
Seven Kings	10 14	—	—	—	10 51	—	11 6	—	11 17	—	11 40	11 57	12 19	—
Goodmayes	10 18	—	—	—	10 54	—	11 9	—	11 20	—	11 43	12 0	12 22	—
CHADWELL HEATH	10 23	—	—	—	10 58	10 54	11 12	—	11 25	—	11 47	12 4	12 27	—
ROMFORD	10 31	—	—	—	11 4	11 0	—	11 13	11 32	—	11 53	—	12 34	—
GIDEA PARK	10 34	—	—	—	11 8	11 4	—	11 17	11 36	—	11 56	—	12 37	—
Harold Wood	—	—	—	—	—	11 8	—	11 21	11 40	—	—	—	—	—
BRENTWOOD	—	—	—	—	—	11 16	—	11 28	11 47	—	—	—	—	—

WEEK DAYS	e h	d h	e	d	d	d	d	d	d	d	PM	d	d
LIVERPOOL ST. ......dep.	11 55	11 56	12	3	12 13	12 15	12 18	12 20	—	12 39	12 42	12 42	1251	—	12 54	—	1 3
Bethnal Green	—	—	—	—	12 19	12 22	—	—	—	12 46	—	—	—	—
Coborn Road	—	—	—	—	12 23	12 26	—	—	—	—	—	—	—	—
FENCHURCH STREET	—	—	—	—	—	—	12 17	—	—	12 46	—	12 56	—
Stepney	—	—	—	—	—	—	12 24	—	—	12 53	—	1 3	—
Burdett Road	—	—	—	—	—	—	12 26	—	—	12 55	—	1 5	—
Bow Road	—	—	—	—	—	—	12 29	—	—	12 58	—	1 8	—
STRATFORD MARKET	—	—	—	—	—	—	—	—	—	—	—	—	—
STRATFORD (W. Ham.)	—	—	12 14	12 23	12 27	12 31	12 31	12 37	—	—	12 54	—	1 3	1 6	1 13
Maryland Point	—	—	12 16	12 25	—	12 33	—	12 40	—	12 54	12 56	—	1 5	1 8	1 15
Forest Gate	—	—	12 20	12 28	—	12 36	—	12 44	—	12 57	12 59	—	1 8	1 11	1 18
Manor Park	—	—	12 23	12 31	—	12 40	—	12 47	—	1 0	1 3	—	1 11	1 14	1 21
ILFORD	12 13	—	12 27	12 35	—	12 44	12 40	12 52	12 57	1 4	1 8	1 8	1 15	1 20	1 24
Seven Kings	—	—	12 30	12 38	—	12 47	12 44	12 55	1 9	—	1 11	1 11	1*18	1 23	—
Goodmayes	—	—	12 32	12 41	—	12 51	12 48	12 58	1 4	—	1 14	1 13	1*21	1 25	—
CHADWELL HEATH	—	—	12*39	12 44	—	12 55	12 52	1 2	1 7	—	1 18	—	1*24	—	—
ROMFORD	—	—	—	—	—	1 1	—	1 12	—	—	1 24	—	—	1 24
GIDEA PARK	—	—	—	—	4	1 4	—	—	—	—	1 28	—	—	1 28
Harold Wood	—	—	—	—	1 9	—	—	—	—	1 32	—	—	1 32
BRENTWOOD	12 31	12 34	—	—	1 16	—	—	—	—	1 43	—	—	1 41

WEEK DAYS.	e	d	d	d	d	PM	d	e	d	d	e	d	d	d	d	d
LIVERPOOL ST. ....dep.	1 5	1 6	1 9	1 9	1 13	1 17	—	1 23	1 20	1 33	1 36	1 33	1 39	1 43	1 46	—	1 55
Bethnal Green	—	—	1 13	—	—	—	—	1 24	—	—	—	—	—	—	—	1 59
Coborn Road	—	—	—	—	—	—	—	1 28	—	—	—	—	—	—	2 3
FENCHURCH STREET	—	—	—	—	—	1 17	—	—	—	—	—	—	—	1 44	—
Stepney	—	—	—	—	—	1 24	—	—	—	—	—	—	—	1 51	—
Burdett Road	—	—	—	—	—	1 26	—	—	—	—	—	—	—	1 53	—
Bow Road	—	—	—	—	—	1 29	—	—	—	—	—	—	—	1 56	—
STRATFORD MARKET	—	—	—	—	—	—	—	—	—	—	—	—	—	—	—
STRATFORD (W. Ham.)	1 16	—	—	1 21	—	1 37	—	1 33	—	—	1 46	1 49	—	—	2 3	2 8
Maryland Point	1 18	—	1 21	1 24	—	1 28	1 40	—	1 35	—	—	—	1 58	2	2 5	2 10
Forest Gate	1 23	—	—	1 27	—	1 31	1 43	—	1 38	—	—	—	—	2	2 8	2 13
Manor Park	1 25	—	1 26	1 31	—	—	1 46	1 38	1 41	—	—	—	2	2 6	2 11	2 16
ILFORD	1 30	1 21	1 29	1 35	1 30	—	1 50	1 42	1 45	—	1 52	1 57	1 57	2	2 9	2 15	2 19
Seven Kings	1 34	—	—	1 38	1 33	—	1*54	1 45	1 48	—	1 55	—	2 0	2 9	—
Goodmayes	1 37	—	—	1 40	1 36	—	1*56	1 48	1 51	—	1 58	—	2 3	2 13	—
CHADWELL HEATH	1 41	1 37	—	—	1 40	—	—	1 52	1 54	—	2 1	2 4	—	2 16	—
ROMFORD	1 47	1 43	—	—	—	—	—	—	1 55	—	—	2 24	—	—
GIDEA PARK	1 50	1 36	—	—	—	—	—	2 3	1 59	—	2 15	—	—
Harold Wood	—	—	—	—	—	—	—	2 19	—	—
BRENTWOOD	—	—	—	—	—	—	—	2 11	—	2 28	—	—

WEEK DAYS.	e	eh	d	e	d	e	d	e	d	e	d	d	dh	e	d	PM	e	d
LIVERPOOL STREET ..dep.	154	2 0	2 0	2 6	2 9	—	2 19	220	223	2 23	—	2 33	2 40	2 50	2 51	—	2 58	258
Bethnal Green	158	—	—	—	—	—	—	—	2 27	—	—	—	—	—	2 55	—	3 2	—
Coborn Road	2 2	—	—	—	—	—	—	—	2 31	—	—	—	—	—	2 59	—	3 6	—
FENCHURCH STREET.	—	—	—	—	2 9	—	—	—	—	2 18	—	—	—	—	—	2 50	—	—
Stepney	—	—	—	—	2 16	—	—	—	—	2 25	—	—	—	—	—	2 57	—	—
Burdett Road	—	—	—	—	2 19	—	—	—	—	2 28	—	—	—	—	—	2 59	—	—
Bow Road	—	—	—	—	2 22	—	—	—	—	2 31	—	—	—	—	—	3 2	—	—
STRATFORD MARKET	—	—	—	—	—	—	—	—	—	—	—	—	—	—	—	—	—	—
STRATFORD (W. Ham)	2 7	—	—	216	—	2 29	2 30	231	233	2 36	2 37	—	—	3 0	3 5	3 8	3 12	—
Maryland Point	2 9	—	—	218	—	2 31	2 33	—	—	2 38	2 39	2 44	—	—	3 8	3 10	3 14	—
Forest Gate	212	—	—	221	222	2 34	2 37	—	—	2 41	2 42	2 47	—	—	3 11	3 13	3 17	—
Manor Park	215	—	—	224	—	2 38	2 40	—	—	2 44	2 45	2 50	—	—	3 14	3 16	3 20	—
ILFORD	219	214	216	227	228	2 43	2 46	240	242	2 49	2 49	2 53	—	3 8	3 18	3 20	3 24	—
Seven Kings	222	—	—	231	—	2 49	—	—	—	2 52	—	2 57	—	—	3 21	—	3 29	—
Goodmayes	225	—	—	233	—	2 53	—	—	—	2 55	—	3 0	—	—	3 24	—	3 32	—
CHADWELL HEATH	226	—	—	237	—	2 58	—	—	—	2 59	—	3 3	—	—	3 27	—	3 35	—
ROMFORD	—	224	225	—	—	3 5	250	252	3 5	—	—	—	3 1	3 18	—	—	—	—
GIDEA PARK	—	—	228	—	—	3 8	254	255	3 8	—	—	—	3 5	3 21	—	—	—	—
Harold Wood	—	—	—	—	—	—	258	3 0	—	—	—	—	3 9	—	—	—	—	—
BRENTWOOD	—	236	—	—	—	—	3 7	3 8	—	—	—	—	3 17	—	—	—	—	325

WEEK DAYS.	d	d	h	PM	PM	PM	PM	h	e	e	e'	e	d	e	PM	PM
LIVERPOOL STREET ..dep.	3 5	—	3 26	3 39	—	4 2	4 5	4 18	4 22	4 25	—	4 37	4 38	4 51	—	5 1
Bethnal Green	—	—	—	3 34	—	—	4 9	—	—	—	—	4 41	4 42	—	—	—
Coborn Road	—	—	3 38	—	—	4 13	—	—	—	—	—	4 45	4 46	—	—	—
FENCHURCH STREET	—	3 20	—	3 47	—	—	—	—	—	4 28	—	—	—	4 58	—
Stepney	—	3 27	—	3 54	—	—	—	—	—	4 35	—	—	—	5 5	—
Burdett Road	—	3 29	—	3 56	—	—	—	—	—	4 37	—	—	—	5 7	—
Bow Road	—	3 32	—	3 59	—	—	—	—	—	4 40	—	—	—	5 10	—
STRATFORD MARKET	—	—	—	—	—	—	—	—	—	—	—	—	—	—	—
STRATFORD (W. Ham)	3 16	3 38	—	3 44	4 6	4 14	4 19	—	4 32	4 36	4 46	4 52	4 53	—	5 16	—
Maryland Point	3 18	3 40	—	3 46	4 8	—	4 21	—	—	4 38	4 48	4 54	4 55	5 3	5 18	—
Forest Gate	3 21	3 43	—	3 49	4 11	4 18	4 24	—	—	4 41	4 51	4 57	4 58	5 6	5 21	—
Manor Park	3 24	3 46	—	3 52	4 14	—	4 28	—	—	4 44	4 54	5 0	5 1	5 9	5 24	—
ILFORD	3 28	3 51	—	3 56	4 19	4 25	4 32	—	4 41	4 49	4 57	5 4	5 13	5 28	5'17
Seven Kings	3 31	—	—	3 59	4'21	4 29	4 35	—	4 44	—	5 1	5 7	5 8	5 16	—	—
Goodmayes	3 33	—	—	4 2	4'24	4 33	4 38	—	4 47	—	5 4	5 9	5 11	5 19	—	—
CHADWELL HEATH	3 37	—	—	4 6	4'27	4 37	4 42	—	4 51	—	5 7	—	5 14	5 23	—	—
ROMFORD	—	—	3 50	4 12	—	4 43	4 46	—	4 57	—	—	—	—	5 29	5 23
GIDEA PARK	—	—	3 54	4 15	—	4 47	4 51	—	5 0	—	—	—	—	5 32	5 27
Harold Wood	—	—	3 58	—	—	4 51	—	—	—	—	—	—	—	—	5 31
BRENTWOOD	—	—	4 7	—	—	5 1	—	4 48	—	—	—	—	—	—	5 38

WEEK DAYS.	e	d	e	d	e	d	e	e	—	e	PM	h	e	e	e	e	e	d
LIVERPOOL STREET ..dep.	5 0	5 4	5 8	5 9	5 13	5 23	5 26	—	5 33	5 36	5 42	5 45	5 48	—	5 52	5 52
Bethnal Green	—	—	—	—	—	—	—	—	—	—	—	—	—	—	—	—
Coborn Road	—	—	—	—	—	—	—	—	—	—	—	—	—	—	—	—
FENCHURCH STREET	—	—	—	—	—	5 18	—	—	—	—	—	5 46	—	—
Stepney	—	—	—	—	—	5 24	—	—	—	—	—	5 53	—	—
Burdett Road	—	—	—	—	—	5 26	—	—	—	—	—	5 56	—	—
Bow Road	—	—	—	—	—	5 29	—	—	—	—	—	5 59	—	—
STRATFORD MARKET	—	—	—	—	—	—	—	—	—	—	—	—	—	—
STRATFORD (W. Ham)	—	5 20	—	5 23	—	5 37	—	5'46	—	—	—	6 5	—	—
Maryland Point	—	5 16	5 23	—	5 25	5 36	—	5 40	—	5 48	—	—	6 7	—	6 3
Forest Gate	5 13	5 19	5 26	—	5 28	5 39	—	5 43	—	5 51	—	—	6 10	—	6 6
Manor Park	—	5 22	5 29	—	5 31	5 42	—	5 46	—	5 54	—	—	6 13	—	6 9
ILFORD	5 18	5 25	5 33	5 25	5 35	5 46	5 41	5 50	5 48	5 59	—	6 4	6 16	6 8	6 12
Seven Kings	5 21	—	5 36	5 28	5 38	—	5 44	—	5 51	6 2	—	6 7	—	6 11	—
Goodmayes	5 24	—	5 39	5 32	5 41	—	5 47	—	5 53	6 5	—	6 10	—	6 13	—
CHADWELL HEATH	—	—	5 42	5 35	—	5 50	—	—	6 8	—	6 13	—	—
ROMFORD	—	—	—	—	—	—	—	—	6 15	6 8	—	—
GIDEA PARK	—	—	—	—	—	—	—	—	6 18	6 12	—	—
Harold Wood	—	—	—	—	—	—	—	—	—	6 16	—	—
BRENTWOOD	—	—	—	—	—	—	—	—	—	6 12	6 24	—	—

WEEK DAYS.	e	e	e	PM	e	—	e	d	e	e	e	d	eh	dh	e	e	PM	e
LIVERPOOL STREET ..dep.	5 54	5 56	—	6 8	6 11	—	6 14	6 15	6 17	6 20	6 23	6 26	6 29	—	6 32	—
Bethnal Green	5 59	—	—	—	—	—	—	—	—	—	—	—	—	—	6'37	—
Coborn Road	6 3	—	—	—	—	—	—	—	—	—	—	—	—	—	—	—
FENCHURCH STREET	—	—	5 57	—	6 4	—	—	—	—	—	—	—	6 31	6 33
Stepney	—	—	6 4	—	6 11	—	—	—	—	—	—	—	6 24	6 40
Burdett Road	—	—	6 6	—	6 13	—	—	—	—	—	—	—	6 26	6 43
Bow Road	—	—	6 9	—	6 16	—	—	—	—	—	—	—	6 30	6 46
STRATFORD MARKET	—	—	—	—	—	—	—	—	—	—	—	—	—	—
STRATFORD (W. Ham)	6 8	—	6 14	—	6 22	—	6 25	—	—	—	—	—	6 38	6'45	6 52
Maryland Point	6 10	6 11	6 16	—	6 24	—	6 27	6 29	—	6 36	—	—	6 41	6'47	6 55
Forest Gate	6 13	6 14	6 19	—	6 22	6 27	—	6 30	6 32	—	6 40	—	—	6 44	6 48	6 59
Manor Park	6 16	6 17	6 22	—	6 25	6 30	—	6 34	6 35	—	6 43	—	—	6 48	6 51	7 2
ILFORD	6 20	6 22	6 26	—	6 28	6 34	6 31	6 38	6 38	6 36	6 49	—	—	6 46	6 51	6 55	7 5
Seven Kings	6 23	6 25	—	—	—	6 34	6 41	—	6 39	—	—	6 49	—	6 58	—
Goodmayes	6 26	6 28	—	—	—	6 37	6 44	—	6 42	—	—	6 52	—	7 1	—
CHADWELL HEATH	6 30	6 32	—	—	—	6 40	6 47	—	6 45	—	—	6 57	—	7 5	—
ROMFORD	6 36	6 38	—	6 29	—	—	—	—	6 52	—	6 49	7 3	—	7 11	—
GIDEA PARK	6 33	6 41	—	6 33	—	—	—	—	6 55	—	6 53	7 6	—	7 15	—
Harold Wood	—	—	—	6 39	—	—	—	—	—	—	7 10	—	7'22	—
BRENTWOOD	—	—	—	6 45	—	—	—	—	—	6 56	7 5	7 21	—	7'30	—

WEEK DAYS.	e	e	e	PM	d	PM	e	e	e	e	d	e	e	e	PM	h	d
LIVERPOOL STREET ..dep.	6 36	6 45	6 48	6 50	—	6 59	7 3	7 10	7 13	7 20	7 23	7 30	7 30	—	7 48	8 2	—
Bethnal Green	—	—	—	—	—	—	—	—	—	—	—	—	—	—	—	—
Coborn Road	—	—	—	—	—	—	—	—	—	—	—	—	—	—	—	—
FENCHURCH STREET.	—	—	6 47	—	—	—	—	—	—	—	7 26	—	7 49
Stepney	—	—	6 54	—	—	—	—	—	—	—	7 33	—	7 56
Burdett Road	—	—	6 56	—	—	—	—	—	—	—	7 35	—	7 58
Bow Road	—	—	6 59	—	—	—	—	—	—	—	7 38	—	8 1
STRATFORD MARKET	—	—	—	—	—	—	—	—	—	—	—	—	—
STRATFORD (W. Ham)	6 46	7 1	7 5	—	7 19	7 23	—	7 40	7 44	7 58	—	8 6
Maryland Point	6 49	7 3	7 7	7 1	—	7 14	7 21	7 25	—	7 42	7 41	7 47	7 48	8 0	—	8 8
Forest Gate	6 52	7 6	7 10	—	7 17	7 24	7 28	—	7 45	7 44	7 51	7 52	8 3	—	8 11
Manor Park	6 55	7 9	7 13	—	7 20	7 27	7 31	—	7 48	7 47	7 54	8 6	—	8 14
ILFORD	7 1	7 12	7 13	7 17	7 24	7 31	7 34	7 40	7 52	7 50	7 59	8 10	—	8 18
Seven Kings	7 4	—	7 16	—	7 34	7 38	—	7 43	7 55	—	8 13	—
Goodmayes	7 6	—	7 19	—	7 37	7 41	—	7 46	7 58	—	8 17	—
CHADWELL HEATH	7 11	—	7 22	—	7 41	—	7 39	7 50	8 1	—	8 21	—
ROMFORD	7 17	—	—	—	7 47	—	7 43	7 59	—	8 28	—
GIDEA PARK	7 20	—	—	7 50	—	7 48	—	8 31	—
Harold Wood	—	—	—	—	—	—	8 36	—
BRENTWOOD	—	—	—	7 59	—	—	8 43	8 32	—

WEEK DAYS

WEEK DAYS.	e	d	e	e	e	PM	e	d	PM	PM	PM	PM	d	h	PM	PM	PM
Liverpool Street ..dep.	7 56	8 5	8 6	8 17	—	8 24	8 42	8 50	8 54	—	9 10	9 30	9 40	9 45	9 54	—	10 20
Bethnal Green	8 0	—	—	—	—	8 28	—	—	—	—	9 14	—	—	—	9 58	—	10 24
Coborn Road	8 4	—	—	—	—	8 32	—	—	—	—	9 18	—	—	—	10 .2	—	10 28
Fenchurch Street	—	—	—	—	8 15	—	—	—	8 54	—	—	—	—	—	9 53	—	
Stepney	—	—	—	—	8 22	—	—	—	9 2	—	—	—	—	—	10 1	—	
Burdett Road	—	—	—	—	8 24	—	—	—	9 4	—	—	—	—	—	10 4	—	
Bow Road	—	—	—	—	8 27	—	—	—	9 7	—	—	—	—	—	10 7	—	
Stratford Market	—	—	—	—	—	—	—	—	—	—	—	—	—	—	—	—	
Stratford (W.Ham)	8 8	8 16	8 17	—	8 32	8 37	—	9 1	—	9 12	9 23	9 41	9 50	—	10 7	10 12	10 34
Maryland Point	8 10	8 18	—	8 28	8 34	8 39	—	9 4	—	9 14	9 25	9 43	9 52	—	10 9	10 14	10 36
Forest Gate	8 13	8 21	—	8 31	8 38	8 43	—	9 7	—	9 17	9 30	9 46	9 55	—	10 12	10 17	10 39
Manor Park	8 16	8 24	—	8 35	8 41	8 46	—	9 10	—	9 20	9 33	9 49	9 58	—	10 15	10 20	10 42
Ilford	8 20	8 28	8 24	8 38	8 45	8 50	8 59	9 14	—	9 24	9 39	9 52	10 1	—	10 19	10 23	10 47
Seven Kings	8 23	8 31	8 27	—	8 54	9 2	9*17	—	9 28	9 42	9 57	—	—	10 22	10 27	10 50	
Goodmayes	8 26	8 34	8 30	—	8 57	9 5	9*20	—	9 31	9 45	10 1	—	—	10 25	10 30	10 53	
Chadwell Heath	8 29	8 37	8 34	—	9 1	5 8	9*24	—	9 35	9 49	10 4	—	—	10 29	10 33	10 57	
Romford	—	—	8 40	—	9 9	—	9 30	9 16	9 41	9 55	—	—	—	10 35	—	11 4	
Gidea Park	—	—	8 43	—	9 12	—	9*33	9 22	9 45	9 58	—	—	—	10 38	—	11 7	
Harold Wood	—	—	—	—	—	—	—	9 26	9 49	—	—	—	—	10 43	—	—	
Brentwood	—	—	—	—	—	—	—	9 36	9 56	—	—	—	—	10 12	10 50	—	—

WEEK DAYS.	PM	h	PM	PM	PM	PM	h	mid.	mid.
Liverpool Street ..dep.	10 50	11 0	11 10	11 25	1145	11 55	12 0	12 12	12 25
Bethnal Green	10 54	—	11 14	11 29	—	—	—	—	12 39
Coborn Road	10 58	—	—	11 33	—	—	—	—	12 43
Fenchurch Street	—	—	—	—	—	—	—	—	—
Stepney	—	—	—	—	—	—	—	—	—
Burdett Road	—	—	—	—	—	—	—	—	—
Bow Road	—	—	—	—	—	—	—	—	—
Stratford Market	—	—	—	—	—	—	—	—	—
Stratford (W. Ham)	11 3	—	11 22	11 38	—	12 5	—	12 22	12 46
Maryland Point	11 5	—	11 24	11 40	—	—	—	12 24	12 50
Forest Gate	11 8	—	11 27	11 43	—	12 9	—	12 27	12 53
Manor Park	11 11	—	11 30	11 46	—	—	—	12 30	12 56
Ilford	11 17	—	11 34	11 50	12 0	12 15	—	12 34	1 0
Seven Kings	11 20	—	11 37	11 53	—	12 18	—	12 37	1 3
Goodmayes	11 23	—	11 40	11 56	—	12 21	—	12 40	1 6
Chadwell Heath	11 27	—	11 44	11 59	12 6	12 24	—	12 44	1 10
Romford	11 33	11 22	11 50	—	12 12	—	—	12 50	1 16
Gidea Park	11 36	11 25	11 53	—	12 15	—	—	12 54	1 19
Harold Wood	—	11 30	—	—	—	—	—	12 58	—
Brentwood	—	11 38	—	—	—	12 29	1 5	—	

d Saturdays only.

e Saturdays excepted.

h No 2nd Class carriages are run on this train.

SUNDAYS

SUNDAYS.	AM	AM	AM	AM	AM	AM	AM	AM	AM	AM	AM	AM	AM	AM	AM	AM	AM	AM
Liverpool Street ..dep.	4 20	7 4	8 7	8 15	—	8 20	8 37	8 45	—	9 7	—	9 30	—	9 37	10 7	—	10 30	10 37
Bethnal Green	4 25	7 8	8 11	—	—	—	8 41	—	—	9 11	—	—	—	9 41	10 11	—	—	10 41
Coborn Road	—	—	8 15	—	—	—	8 45	—	—	9 15	—	—	—	9 45	10 15	—	—	10 45
Fenchurch Street	—	—	—	3 19	—	—	—	8 51	—	9 19	—	—	—	10 19	—	—	
Stepney	—	—	—	8 25	—	—	—	8 56	—	9 24	—	—	—	10 24	—	—	
Burdett Road	—	—	—	8 27	—	—	—	8 58	—	9 26	—	—	—	10 26	—	—	
Bow Road	—	—	—	8 30	—	—	—	9 1	—	9 29	—	—	—	10 29	—	—	
Stratford Market	—	—	—	—	—	—	—	—	—	—	—	—	—	—	—	—	
Stratford (W. Ham)	4 36	7 18	8 21	—	8 35	8 40	8 51	8 55	9 7	9 21	9 35	9 41	9 51	10 21	10 35	10 41	10 51
Maryland Point	4 39	7 20	8 23	—	8 37	—	8 53	—	9 9	9 23	9 37	—	9 53	10 23	10 37	—	10 53
Forest Gate	4 41	7 25	8 26	—	8 40	—	3 56	—	9 12	9 26	9 40	—	9 56	10 26	10 40	—	10 56
Manor Park	4 44	7 29	8 29	—	8 43	—	8 59	—	9 15	9 29	9 43	—	9 59	10 29	10 43	—	10 59
Ilford	4 47	7 35	8 34	—	8 46	8 50	9 29	5 9	18 9	34 9	46 9	50	10 4	10 24	10 46	10 50	11 4
Seven Kings	—	7 38	8 37	—	—	—	—	—	9 37	—	—	10 7	10 37	—	—	11 7	
Goodmayes	—	7 41	8 40	—	—	—	—	—	9 40	—	—	10 10	10 40	—	—	11 10	
Chadwell Heath	—	7 44	8 44	—	—	—	—	—	9 44	—	—	10 14	10 44	—	—	11 14	
Romford	—	7 50	8 50	8 45	—	8 59	—	9 14	—	9 50	—	9 59	10 23	10 50	—	10 59	11 20
Gidea Park	—	7 54	8 53	—	9 4	—	9 19	—	9 53	—	10 4	10 26	11 53	—	11 4	11 23	
Harold Wood	—	7 59	—	—	—	—	—	—	—	—	10 8	—	—	—	—	—	
Brentwood	—	8 8	—	8 56	—	9 14	—	9 29	—	—	1017	—	—	—	11 14	—	

SUNDAYS.	AM	AM	AM	h	AM	AM	AM	AM	PM	PM	PM	PM	PM	PM	PM	PM	PM	PM
Liverpool Street ..dep	10 45	—	—	11 35	11 37	12 7	—	12 37	1 7	—	2 7	—	2 30	2 37	—	3 7	—	
Bethnal Green	—	—	—	11 41	12 11	—	12 41	1 11	—	2 11	—	—	2 41	—	3 11	—	
Coborn Road	—	—	—	11 45	12 15	—	12 45	1 15	—	2 15	—	—	2 45	—	3 15	—	
Fenchurch Street	—	10 49	11 20	—	—	12 19	—	1 49	—	2 19	—	2 52	—	3 19			
Stepney	—	10 54	11 25	—	—	12 24	—	1 54	—	2 26	—	2 57	—	3 24			
Burdett Road	—	10 56	11 27	—	—	12 26	—	1 56	—	2 28	—	2 59	—	3 26			
Bow Road	—	10 59	11 30	—	—	12 29	—	1 59	—	2 31	—	3 2	—	3 29			
Stratford Market	—	—	—	—	—	—	—	—	—	—	—	—	—	—			
Stratford (W. Ham)	10 56	11 36	11 46	11 51	12 23	12 35	12 51	1 23	5 5	2 21	2 37	2 41	2 51	3 23	3 35	
Maryland Point	—	11 7	11 38	—	11 53	12 23	12 37	12 53	1 23 2	7 2	23	2 39	—	2 53	3 10	3 23	3 37
Forest Gate	—	11 10	11 41	—	11 56	12 26	12 40	12 56	1 26	2 10	2 26	2 42	—	2 56	3 13	3 26	3 40
Manor Park	—	11 13	11 44	—	11 59	12 29	12 43	12 59	1 29	2 13	2 29	2 45	—	2 59	3 16	3 29	3 43
Ilford	11 5	11 16	11 47	11 55	12 4	12 34	12 46	1 4	1 34	2 34	2 48	2 50	3 4	3 19	3 34	3 46
Seven Kings	—	—	—	12 7	12 37	—	1 7	1 37	—	2 37	—	2 53	3 7	—	3 37	
Goodmayes	—	—	—	12 10	12 40	—	1 10	1 40	—	2 40	—	2 56	3 10	—	3 40	
Chadwell Heath	—	—	—	12 14	12 44	—	1 14	1 44	—	2 44	—	3 3	3 14	—	3 44	
Romford	11 14	—	12 4	12 20	12 50	—	1 20	1 50	—	2 50	—	3 6	3 20	—	3 50	
Gidea Park	11 19	—	12 9	12 23	12 53	—	1 24	1 53	—	2 53	—	3 11	3 24	—	3 53	
Harold Wood	11 23	—	—	—	—	—	1 28	—	—	—	—	3 15	3 28	—	—	
Brentwood	11 32	—	12 19	—	—	—	1 36	—	—	—	—	3 24	3 36	—	—	

SUNDAYS.	PM	PM	PM	PM	PM	PM	PM	PM	PM	PM	PM	PM	PM	PM	h	h	PM	h
Liverpool Street ..dep	3 37	3 45	—	4 7	—	4 37	—	5 7	—	5 37	—	6 0	6 7	6 15	—	6 42	
Bethnal Green	3 41	—	—	4 11	—	4 41	—	5 11	—	5 41	—	6 11	—	—			
Coborn Road	3 45	—	—	4 15	—	4 45	—	5 15	—	5 45	—	6 15	—	—			
Fenchurch Street	—	3 49	—	4 19	—	4 49	—	5 19	—	5 49	—	6 19	—				
Stepney	—	3 54	—	4 24	—	4 54	—	5 24	—	5 54	—	6 26	—				
Burdett Road	—	3 56	—	4 26	—	4 56	—	5 26	—	5 56	—	6 26	—				
Bow Road	—	3 59	—	4 29	—	4 59	—	5 29	—	5 59	—	6 29	—				
Stratford Market	—	—	—	—	—	—	—	—	—	—	—	—	—				
Stratford (W. Ham)	3 51	3 56	4 5	4 21	4 35	4 51	5 5	5 21	5 35	5 51	6 5	6 11	6 21	6 26	6 34	6 52
Maryland Point	3 53	—	4 7	4 23	4 37	4 53	5 7	5 23	5 37	5 53	6 7	—	6 23	—	6 36	
Forest Gate	3 56	—	4 10	4 26	4 40	4 56	5 10	5 26	5 40	5 56	6 10	—	6 26	—	6 39	
Manor Park	3 59	—	4 13	4 29	4 43	4 59	5 13	5 29	5 43	5 59	6 13	—	6 29	—	6 42	
Ilford	4 4	4 5	4 16	4 34	4 46	5 4	5 16	5 34	5 47	6 4	6 16	6 20	6 36	6 35	6 46	7 1
Seven Kings	4 7	—	—	4 37	—	5 7	—	5 37	—	6 7	—	6 40	—	—	
Goodmayes	4 10	—	—	4 40	—	5 10	—	5 40	—	6 10	—	6 40	—	—	
Chadwell Heath	4 14	—	—	4 44	—	5 14	—	5 44	—	6 14	—	6 44	—	—	
Romford	4 21	4 14	—	4 50	—	5 20	—	5 50	—	6 20	—	6 29	6 50	6 44	7 10
Gidea Park	4 23	4 16	—	4 53	—	5 23	—	5 53	—	6 23	—	6 33	6 52	6 48	7 14
Harold Wood	—	4 22	—	—	—	—	—	5 58	—	—	—	—	—	—	7 20
Brentwood	—	4 31	—	—	—	—	—	6 5	—	—	—	6 43	6 58	—	7 26

SUNDAYS

Station	PM	PM	PM	PM	PM	PM	PM	PM	PM	PM	PM	PM	PM	PM
LIVERPOOL STREET..dep.	6 37	—	7 7	—	7 37	—	8 7	—	8 37	8 46	9 7	—	9 37	—
Bethnal Green	6 41	—	7 11	—	7 41	—	8 11	—	8 41	—	9 11	—	9 41	—
Coborn Road	6 45	—	7 15	—	7 45	—	8 15	—	8 45	—	9 15	—	9 45	—
FENCHURCH STREET	—	6 49	—	7 19	—	7 49	—	8 19	—	—	—	9 19	—	9 52
Stepney	—	6 54	•	7 24	—	7 54	—	8 24	—	—	—	9 25	—	9 57
Burdett Road	—	6 56	—	7 26	—	7 56	—	8 26	—	—	—	9 27	—	9 59
Bow Road	—	6 59	—	7 29	—	7 59	—	8 29	—	—	—	9 30	—	10 2
STRATFORD MARKET	—	—	—	—	—	—	—	—	—	—	—	—	—	—
STRATFORD (W. Ham)	6 51	7 5	7 21	7 35	7 51	8 5	8 21	8 35	8 51	—	9 21	9 35	9 51	10 8
Maryland Point	6 53	7 7	7 23	7 37	7 53	8 7	8 23	8 37	8 53	—	9 23	9 37	9 53	10 10
Forest Gate	6 58	7 10	7 26	7 40	7 56	8 10	8 26	8 40	8 56	—	9 26	9 40	9 56	10 12
Manor Park	6 59	7 13	7 29	7 43	7 59	8 13	8 29	8 43	8 59	—	9 29	9 43	9 59	10 16
ILFORD	7 4	7 16	7 34	7 46	8 4	8 16	8 34	8 46	9 4	—	9 34	9 46	10 4	10 19
Seven Kings	7 7	—	7 37	—	8 7	—	8 37	—	9 7	—	9 37	—	10 7	—
Goodmayes	7 10	—	7 40	—	8 10	—	8 40	—	9 10	—	9 40	—	10 10	—
CHADWELL HEATH	7 14	—	7 44	—	8 14	—	8 44	—	9 14	—	9 44	—	10 14	—
ROMFORD	7 20	—	7 50	—	8 20	—	8 53	—	9 20	9 14	9 50	—	10 20	—
GIDEA PARK	7 23	—	7 53	—	8 23	—	8 57	—	9 23	9 18	9 53	—	10 24	—
Harold Wood	—	—	—	—	—	—	9 1	—	—	9 22	—	—	10 26	—
BRENTWOOD	—	—	—	—	—	—	9 8	—	—	9 32	—	—	10 36	—

SUNDAYS

Station	PM	h	PM	PM	PM	PM	PM
LIVERPOOL STREET..dep.	10 7	10 10	—	10 37	—	—	11 7
Bethnal Green	10 11	—	—	10 41	—	—	11 11
Coborn Road	10 15	—	—	10 45	—	—	11 15
FENCHURCH STREET	—	—	10 19	—	10 52	11 2	—
Stepney	—	—	10 26	—	10 58	11 7	—
Burdett Road	—	—	10 28	—	11 0	11 9	—
Bow Road	—	—	10 31	—	11 3	11 12	—
STRATFORD MARKET	—	—	—	—	—	11 17	—
STRATFORD (W. Ham)	10 21	10 21	10 37	10 51	11 9	—	11 21
Maryland Point	10 23	—	10 39	10 53	11 11	—	11 23
Forest Gate	10 26	—	10 42	10 56	11 14	—	11 26
Manor Park	10 29	—	10 45	10 59	11 17	—	11 29
ILFORD	10 32	10 30	10 48	11 4	11 20	—	11 34
Seven Kings	10 36	—	—	11 7	—	—	11 37
Goodmayes	10 39	—	—	11 10	—	—	11 40
CHADWELL HEATH	10 42	—	—	11 14	—	—	11 44
ROMFORD	—	10 40	—	11 20	—	—	11 50
GIDEA PARK	—	10 44	—	11 23	—	—	11 54
Harold Wood	—	10 48	—	—	—	—	11 58
BRENTWOOD	—	10 56	—	—	—	—	12 6

A No 2nd Class carriages are run on this train.

WEEK DAYS

Station	AM	AM	AM	AM	AM	AM	AM	AM	AM	AM	AM	AM	AM	h	AM	AM
BRENTWOOD..dep.	—	2 52	—	4 19	—	—	—	5 36	—	—	—	—	—	6 36	—	—
Harold Wood	—	—	—	4 25	—	—	—	5 42	—	—	—	—	—	6 43	—	—
GIDEA PARK	—	—	2 59	3 42	4 29	—	4 52	5 46	—	6 20	—	—	—	6 47	712	—
ROMFORD	—	—	3 3	3 46	4 33	—	4 56	5 50	—	6 24	—	—	—	6 51	—	—
CHADWELL HEATH	2 42	—	3 10	3 52	4 39	—	5 2	5 56	6 15	6 30	6 45	—	—	6 57	—	7 4
Goodmayes	2 45	—	3 13	3 55	4 42	—	5 5	5 59	6 18	6 33	6 48	—	7 0	—	—	7 7
Seven Kings	2 48	—	3 16	3 58	4 45	—	5 8	6 2	6 21	6 36	6 51	—	7 3	—	—	7 11
ILFORD	2 52	—	3 24	4 2	4 49	—	5 12	5 23	6 6	6 25	6 40	6 56	7	7 7	7 10	7 16
Manor Park	2 56	—	3 27	4 5	4 52	—	5 15	5 26	6 9	6 28	6 44	7 0	7 5	7 10	7 14	7 19
Forest Gate	3 0	—	3 31	4 9	4 56	—	5 19	5 30	6 13	6 32	6 48	7 4	7 9	7 14	7 18	7 23
Maryland Point	3 3	—	—	4 12	4 59	—	5 22	5 33	6 16	6 35	6 51	7 7	7 12	7 17	7 21	7 26
STRATFORD (W. Ham)	3 6	3 41	4 15	5 2	5 6	5 25	5 36	6 19	6 38	6 55	7 10	—	7 20	—	7 24	7 29
STRATFORD MARKET	—	—	—	—	—	—	—	—	—	—	—	—	—	—	—	—
Bow Road	—	—	—	—	5 10	—	5 40	—	6 42	—	—	—	—	—	7 30	—
Burdett Road	—	—	—	—	5 13	—	5 43	—	6 45	—	—	—	—	—	7 33	—
Stepney	—	—	—	—	5 17	—	5 47	—	6 48	—	—	—	—	—	7 36	—
FENCHURCH STREET	—	—	—	—	5 24	—	5 51	—	6 55	—	—	—	—	—	7 44	—
Coborn Road	3 11	—	4 20	5 7	—	5 30	—	—	—	—	7 16	—	—	—	—	—
Bethnal Green	3 15	—	4 24	5 11	—	5 34	—	6 28	—	—	7 21	—	—	—	—	—
LIVERPOOL STREET	3 18	3 50	4 28	5 15	—	5 37	—	6 32	—	7 5	7 25	7 26	7 30	735	—	7 39

WEEK DAYS

Station	AM	AM	AM	AM	AM	AM	AM	AM	AM	h	AM	AM
BRENTWOOD..dep.	—	—	—	—	7 16	—	—	—	—	7 49	—	7 55
Harold Wood	—	—	—	—	7 22	—	—	—	—	—	—	8 1
GIDEA PARK	6 59	—	—	—	—	7 18	—	7 34	—	7 49	7 57	8 5
ROMFORD	7 4	—	—	—	—	7 22	—	7 38	—	7 53	—	8 9
CHADWELL HEATH	7 10	—	—	—	7 34	7 25	—	7 46	7 52	—	—	8 15
Goodmayes	7 13	—	—	—	7 37	7 31	—	7 49	7 55	—	8 2	—
Seven Kings	7 16	—	—	—	7 40	7 34	—	7 52	—	—	8 5	—
ILFORD	7 20	7 23	7 30	—	7 45	7 33	7 53	7 57	8 1	8 5	8 9	8 11
Manor Park	7 24	7 28	—	7 33	7 48	7 42	7 56	—	8 4	8 8	8 12	8 15
Forest Gate	7 28	7 32	—	—	7 52	7 46	8 0	8 3	8 8	8 12	8 16	8 20
Maryland Point	7 31	7 35	—	—	7 55	7 49	8 3	8 7	8 10	8 15	8 19	8 23
STRATFORD (W. Ham)	7 34	7 38	—	7 41	7 58	7 52	—	8 10	8 14	8 18	8 22	—
STRATFORD MARKET	—	—	—	—	—	—	—	—	—	—	—	8 22
Bow Road	7 38	—	—	—	—	—	—	—	8 25	—	—	8 29
Burdett Road	7 41	—	—	—	—	—	—	—	8 28	—	—	8 32
Stepney	7 44	—	—	—	—	—	—	—	8 32	—	—	8 35
FENCHURCH STREET	7 52	—	—	—	—	—	—	—	8 39	—	—	8 42
Coborn Road	—	7 43	—	—	—	7 57	—	—	8 19	—	—	—
Bethnal Green	—	7 47	—	—	—	8 2	—	—	8 23	—	—	—
LIVERPOOL STREET	—	7 50	7 48	7 54	7 57	8 8	8 6	8 14	8 20	8 27	—	8 32	8 23	8 34	—	8 38

WEEK DAYS

Station	AM	AM	AM	AM	AM	AM	AM	AM	AM	h	AM	AM
BRENTWOOD..dep.	—	—	—	8 17	—	—	—	8 32	—	8 39	—	8 39	8 49
Harold Wood	—	—	—	—	—	—	—	—	—	8 45	—	8 45
GIDEA PARK	—	—	—	—	—	8 16	—	8 39	—	8 49	—	8 49
ROMFORD	—	—	—	—	—	8 20	—	8 43	—	—	—	—
CHADWELL HEATH	—	—	—	—	—	—	8 38	—	—	8 34	—	—
Goodmayes	—	8 16	—	—	—	8 25	8 32	—	—	8 37	—	—
Seven Kings	—	—	—	—	—	8 28	8 37	—	—	8 40	—	—
ILFORD	8 19	8 22	8 27	—	8 31	8 35	—	8 44	—	8 44	—	8 52	8 56
Manor Park	8 23	8 28	—	—	8 36	8 39	—	8 48	—	8 48	—	8 56
Forest Gate	8 26	—	—	—	—	8 42	—	8 52	8 50	9 0	—	—
Maryland Point	—	—	—	—	—	8 45	—	8 55	8 55	8 59	9 3	—
STRATFORD (W. Ham)	—	—	—	—	—	—	—	8 55	—	8 58	—	—
STRATFORD MARKET	—	—	—	—	—	—	—	—	—	—	—	—
Bow Road	—	—	—	—	—	8 50	—	—	—	9 3	—	—
Burdett Road	—	—	—	—	—	8 52	—	—	—	9 6	—	—
Stepney	—	—	—	—	—	8 56	—	—	—	9 9	—	—
FENCHURCH STREET	—	—	—	—	—	9 4	—	—	—	9 15	—	—
Coborn Road	—	—	—	—	—	—	—	—	—	—	—	—
Bethnal Green	8 37	—	—	—	—	—	—	—	—	—	—	—
LIVERPOOL STREET	8 40	8 43	8 42	8 45	6 49	—	8 57	9 0	4 9	7 9	14	—	9 10	9 13	9 14	9 17

WEEK DAYS (first block)

Station	AM	AM	AM	AM	AM	AM	AM	AM	h	AM	AM	AM	AM	h	AM	AM	AM
BRENTWOOD ...... dep.	—	—	—	—	—	—	—	—	9 19	—	—	—	—	—	9 42	—	10 18
Harold Wood	—	—	—	—	9 0	—	—	—	—	—	—	—	—	9 48	—	—	10 24
GIDEA PARK	—	8 44	—	—	—	—	9 14	—	—	—	—	9 38	—	—	—	—	10 29
ROMFORD	—	8 48	—	—	9 6	—	9 17	—	—	—	—	9 42	9 53	—	—	—	10 33
CHADWELL HEATH	8 47	8 54	—	—	—	9 9	—	—	—	9 36	9 48	—	—	—	10 16	10 4?
Goodmayes	8 50	—	9 2	—	—	9 12	—	—	—	9 39	9 5?	—	—	—	10 19	10 43
Seven Kings	8 53	8 58	9 5	—	—	—	9 24	—	—	9 42	9 54	—	—	—	10 22	10 46
ILFORD	8 57	9 2?	9 9	8 9	13 9	14 9	18 9	28	—	9 35	9 42	9 46	9 58	—	10 2?	10 26	10 5?
Manor Park	9 0	9 5	—	9 11	9 16	—	9 21	—	—	9 38	9 45	—	10 1	—	10 24	10 29	10 53
Forest Gate	9 4	9 10	—	9 15	9 20	—	9 25	—	—	9 42	9 49	—	10 5	—	10 28	10 33	10 57
Maryland Point	9 7	—	—	9 18	9 23	—	9 28	—	—	9 45	9 52	—	10 8	—	10 31	10 36	11 0
STRATFORD (W. Ham)	9 10	—	9 17	9 21	9 28	—	—	—	—	9 48	9 56	—	10 11	—	10 36	10 41	11 2
STRATFORD MARKET	—	—	—	—	—	—	—	—	—	—	—	—	—	—	—	—	—
Bow Road	9 17	—	—	9 32	—	—	—	—	—	10 1	—	—	—	—	10 45	—	—
Burdett Road	9 20	—	—	9 35	—	—	—	—	—	10 4	—	—	—	—	10 4?	—	—
Stepney	9 23	—	—	9 38	—	—	—	—	—	10 7	—	—	—	—	10 52	—	—
FENCHURCH STREET	9 30	—	—	9 46	—	—	—	—	—	10 14	—	—	—	—	11 1	—	—
Coborn Road	—	—	9 26	—	—	—	—	—	—	—	—	—	—	—	10 46	—
Bethnal Green	—	—	9 30	—	—	—	9 56	—	—	—	—	—	—	10 51	—
LIVERPOOL STREET	—	9 24	27	9 33	—	9 30	9 39	9 43	9 46	9 59	—	10 2	10 20	10 1	—	10 55	11 12

WEEK DAYS (second block)

Station	AM	d	AM	AM	d	e	h	d	d	AM	PM	AM	d	d
BRENTWOOD ...... dep.	10 39	—	—	—	—	—	11 23	—	—	—	—	—	—	—
Harold Wood	—	—	—	—	—	—	—	—	—	—	—	—	—	—
GIDEA PARK	—	—	10 48	—	—	—	—	—	—	11 40	—	11 58	—	—
ROMFORD	10 49	—	10 52	—	—	—	—	—	—	11 44	—	12 2	—	—
CHADWELL HEATH	—	—	11 0	—	11 17	—	—	11 37	11 59	—	12 8	—	12 24
Goodmayes	—	—	11 3	—	11 20	—	—	11 40	11 53	—	12 11	—	12 27
Seven Kings	—	—	11 6	—	11 23	—	—	11 43	11 56	—	12 14	—	12 30
ILFORD	—	11 0	11 10	11 16	11 28	11 28	—	11 33	11 47	12	1 12 10	12 18	12 21 12 26	12 34
Manor Park	—	11 3	11 13	11 18	11 31	11 31	—	11 36	11 50	12	5 12 13	12 21	12 25 12 29	12 37
Forest Gate	—	11 7	11 17	11 22	11 35	11 35	—	11 40	11 54	12	9 12 17	12 25	12 29 12 33	12 41
Maryland Point	—	11 10	11 20	11 25	11 38	11 38	—	11 43	11 57	12 12	12 20	12 28	12 32 12 36	12 44
STRATFORD (W. Ham)	—	11 13	11 23	11 29	11 41	11 41	11 49	11 47	12 0	12 16	12 23	12 32	12 35	—	12 47
STRATFORD MARKET	—	—	—	—	—	—	—	—	—	—	—	—	—	—
Bow Road	—	—	—	11 33	—	—	11 55	—	—	12 27	—	12 40	—
Burdett Road	—	—	—	11 36	—	—	11 59	—	—	12 30	—	12 43	—
Stepney	—	—	—	11 39	—	—	12 2	—	—	12 33	—	12 46	—
FENCHURCH STREET	—	—	—	11 46	—	—	12 9	—	—	12 40	—	12 51	—
Coborn Road	—	—	11 29	—	11 46	—	—	—	—	—
Bethnal Green	—	11 21	11 33	—	11 51	—	—	—	—	—
LIVERPOOL STREET	11 7	11 25	11 37	—	11 51	11 55	11 57	—	12 10	12 27	—	12 44	—	12 51	1 1

WEEK DAYS (third block)

Station	e	d	d	PM	h	PM	e	PM	d	e	d	d	d	d	PM
BRENTWOOD ...... dep.	—	—	—	12 17	12 33	—	12 56	—	—	—	1 0	1 12	—	—	—
Harold Wood	—	—	—	12 23	—	—	—	—	—	—	1 6	1 18	—	—	—
GIDEA PARK	—	—	—	12 27	—	12d48	—	12 57	—	—	1 10	1 22	—	1 28	—
ROMFORD	—	—	—	12 31	12 45	12d52	—	—	—	—	1 14	1 27	—	1 32	—
CHADWELL HEATH	12 22	—	12 35	12 37	—	12d58	—	1 7	—	1 16	1 20	1 33	—	1 40	1d47
Goodmayes	12 25	—	12 39	12 40	—	1d1	—	1 10	—	1 19	1 23	1 36	1 33	1 43	1 49
Seven Kings	12 28	—	12 42	12 43	—	1d4	—	1 13	—	1 22	1 26	1 40	1 36	1 46	1 52
ILFORD	12 32	12 37	12 46	12 47	12 58	1 8	—	1 17	1 11	1 17	1 26	1 30	1 45	1 41	1 51	1 57
Manor Park	12 35	12 41	—	12 50	—	1 11	—	1*20	1 15	1 20	1 29	—	1 48	1 45	1 55	2 0
Forest Gate	12 39	12 45	—	12 54	—	1 15	—	1*24	1 19	1 24	1 33	—	1 52	1 49	1 59	2-4
Maryland Point	12 42	12 48	—	12 57	—	1 18	—	1*27	1 22	1 27	1 36	—	1 54	1 52	2 2	2 7
STRATFORD (W. Ham)	12 45	12 52	12 55	1 0	—	1 21	—	1*30	1 26	1 30	1 39	1 38	1 58	1 55	2 5	2 10
STRATFORD MARKET	—	—	—	—	—	—	—	—	—	—	—	—	—	—	—
Bow Road	12 50	12 57	—	—	—	1 26	—	—	—	—	—	—	1 59	—	2 15
Burdett Road	12 53	1 0	—	—	—	1 29	—	—	—	—	—	—	2 2	—	2 18
Stepney	12 56	1 3	—	—	—	1 32	—	—	—	—	—	—	2 5	—	2 21
FENCHURCH STREET	1 3	1 10	—	—	—	1 39	—	—	—	—	—	—	2 12	—	2 28
Coborn Road	—	—	—	—	—	—	—	—	—	—
Bethnal Green	—	—	—	—	—	—	—	—	—	—
LIVERPOOL STREET	—	—	1 6	1 10	1 16	—	1 23	1 41	1 37	1 42	1 49	1 49	2 7	—	2 16	—

WEEK DAYS (fourth block)

Station	PM	PM	e	d	PM	e	d	e	d	e	PM	PM	d	e	PM
BRENTWOOD ...... dep.	—	1d42	2 6	—	2 26	—	—	—	—	—	2 57	—	—	—	—
Harold Wood	—	1d48	2 12	—	2 32	—	—	—	—	—	3 3	—	—	—	—
GIDEA PARK	—	2 0	2 16	2 16	2 36	—	—	—	—	—	3 7	—	—	—	—
ROMFORD	—	2 4	2 20	2 20	2 40	—	—	—	—	—	3 11	—	—	—	—
CHADWELL HEATH	1d51	2 10	2 25	2 25	—	2 44	2 59	2 55	—	—	3 17	3 36	—	3 55	—
Goodmayes	1d54	2 13	2 28	2 28	—	2 48	3 3	2 58	2 58	—	3 20	3 39	—	3 58	—
Seven Kings	1d57	2 16	2 31	2 31	—	2 51	3 6	3 3	3 1	—	3 23	3 42	—	4 1	—
ILFORD	2 2	2 20	2 36	2 36	2 48	2 55	3 10	3 5	5 3	3 11	3 23	3 27	3 46	3 40	3 58	4 4	4 3
Manor Park	2 5	2 23	2 39	2 39	—	2 58	3 13	3 8	8 8	3 13	3 25	3 30	3 49	3 43	4 2	—	4 6
Forest Gate	2 9	2 27	2 42	2 43	—	3 2	3 17	3 12	3 12	3 17	3 29	3 34	3 53	3 47	4 6	—	4 11
Maryland Point	2 12	2 30	2 46	2 46	—	3 5	3 20	3 15	3 15	3 20	3 32	3 37	3 56	3 50	4 9	—	4 14
STRATFORD (W. Ham)	2 15	2 33	2 49	2 50	—	3 9	3 23	3 18	3 18	3 23	3 25	3 30	3 40	3 59	3 54	4 13	4 18
STRATFORD MARKET	—	—	—	—	—	—	—	—	—	—	—	—	—	—
Bow Road	—	—	2 57	—	—	—	3 25	3 29	—	4 1	—
Burdett Road	—	—	3 1	—	—	—	3 28	3 32	—	4 5	—
Stepney	—	—	3 4	—	—	—	3 31	3 35	—	4 8	—
FENCHURCH STREET	—	—	3 11	—	—	—	3 37	3 42	—	4 15	—
Coborn Road	—	2 39	2 54	—	—	—	—	—	—	—
Bethnal Green	—	2 44	2 58	—	—	—	—	—	—	—
LIVERPOOL STREET	2 25	2 48	3 2	—	3 5	3 18	3 33	3 28	—	3 45	3 50	4 9	—	4 22	4 25	4 28

WEEK DAYS (fifth block)

Station	d	PM	e	PM	e	d	e	PM	e	e	PM	e	d	h
BRENTWOOD ...... dep.	—	PM	—	4 12	—	—	—	—	—	4 48	—	—	—	5 38
Harold Wood	—	—	—	4 18	—	—	—	—	—	4 54	—	—	—	—
GIDEA PARK	3 50	—	4 14	4 22	—	4 29	—	—	4 53	—	5 2	—	5 14	—
ROMFORD	3 54	—	4 18	4 26	—	4 33	—	—	4 57	—	5 6	—	5 18	—
CHADWELL HEATH	4 0	—	4 24	—	—	4 40	4 55	—	5 0	5 11	5 17	—	5 25	—
Goodmayes	4 3	—	4 16	—	—	4 43	4 58	—	5 10	5 15	5 20	—	5 29	—
Seven Kings	4 6	—	4 31	—	—	4 46	—	5 1	—	5 13	—	5 23	—
ILFORD	4 10	4 10	4 16	4 23	4 34	4 39	4 51	4 54	5 5	5 9	5 15	5 27	5 32	5 36	5 40
Manor Park	—	4 14	4 19	4 26	—	4 43	4 55	—	5 5	5 20	5 24	5 30	5 35	5 40	5 43
Forest Gate	—	4 18	4 23	4 30	—	4 47	4 59	—	5 13	5 17	—	5 24	5 28	5 34	5 39	5 44	5 47
Maryland Point	—	4 21	4 26	4 33	—	5 0	5 2	—	5 16	5 20	—	5 27	5 32	5 37	5 42	5 47	5 50
STRATFORD (W. Ham)	4 18	4 25	4 29	4 36	4d46	4 53	5 7	5 3	5 19	5 23	5 25	5 30	5 36	5 41	—	5 15	5 53
STRATFORD MARKET	—	—	—	—	—	—	—	—	—	5 47	—
Bow Road	—	4 30	—	—	4 57	—	—	5 27	—	5 43	—	5 53	—
Burdett Road	—	4 33	—	—	5 0	—	—	5 30	—	5 47	—	5 56	—
Stepney	—	4 36	—	—	5 3	—	—	5 33	—	5 50	—	5 59	—
FENCHURCH STREET	4 44	—	—	5 2	—	—	5 40	—	—	5 56	—	6 5	—
Coborn Road	—	4 34	—	—	—	—	—	5 35	—	5d45	—
Bethnal Green	—	4 38	—	—	—	—	—	5 40	—	5d48	—
LIVERPOOL STREET	4 27	—	4 43	4 45	4 51	—	5 17	5 14	5 29	—	5 36	5 44	—	5 51	—	6 1	6 6	6 8

WEEK DAYS.

	e	e	e	d	e	PM	*e	e	PM	e	h	PM	e	e	PM	e	PM	d
BRENTWOOD ....dep.	—	—	—	—	—	—	—	5 50	—	6 18	--	—	—	—	—	—	6 3¼	—
Harold Wood	—	—	—	—	—	—	—	5 50	5 56	—	—	—	—	—	—	—	6 38	—
GIDEA PARK	—	—	—	5 33	—	—	5 49	5 54	6 0	—	—	—	—	—	6 35	—	6 42	—
ROMFORD	—	—	—	5 42	—	—	5 53	5 59	6 4	—	6 27	—	—	—	6 39	—	6 48	—
CHADWELL HEATH	—	5 49	5 48	—	—	—	5 59	6 4	6 10	—	—	6 17	—	6 30	6 45	—	6 54	—
Goodmayes	—	5 53	5 51	5 48	5*59	6	2 6	7	—	—	—	6 20	6 29	6 33	6 48	7 10	6 57	—
Seven Kings	—	5 56	5 54	5 51	6*	2 6	5 6	10	—	—	—	6 23	6 32	6 36	6 51	7 13	7 0	—
ILFORD	5 49	5 53	6	1 5	58	5 57	6	6	6 10	6 15	6 18	6 24	6 35	6 28	6 38	6 43	6 55	7 17	7 5	7 10
Manor Park	5 52	5 56	—	6	2	6	1	6	9	—	—	6 27	—	6 32	6 42	6 46	6 58	7 21	7	8	7 13
Forest Gate	5 56	6	0	—	6	6	5	6	13	—	—	6 31	—	6 36	6 46	6 50	7	2	7 25	7 12	7 17
Maryland Point	5 59	6	3	—	6	9	6	9	6	16	—	6 21	—	6 34	—	6 39	6 49	6 53	7	5	7 28	7 15	7 20
STRATFORD (W. Ham)	6	2	6	6	—	6	13	6	13	6	19	—	6 25	6 27	6 37	—	6 43	6 52	6 56	7	8	7 33	7 20	7 23
STRATFORD MARKET	—	—	—	—	—	—	—	—	—	—	—	—	—	—	—	—	—	—
Bow Road	—	6 12	—	—	—	6 24	—	—	—	—	—	—	6 58	—	—	—	7 28	—
Burdett Road	⌐	6 15	—	—	—	6 28	—	—	—	—	—	—	7 ·1	—	—	—	7 31	—
Stepney	—	6 18	—	—	—	6 32	—	—	—	—	—	—	7 ·4	—	—	—	7 34	—
FENCHURCH STREET	—	6 25	—	—	—	6 39	—	—	—	—	—	—	7 12	—	—	—	7 41	—
Coborn Road	6 8	—	—	6 18	—	—	—	—	—	—	—	—	—	—	—	—	—	—
Bethnal Green	6 12	—	—	6 22	—	—	—	—	—	—	—	—	—	—	—	—	—	—
LIVERPOOL STREET	6 16	—	6 20	6 26	6 26	—	6 29	6	36	6	36	6	47	6	52	6	54	—	7	5	7 18	7 43	7 29	—

WEEK DAYS.

	e	PM	e	PM	e	PM	PM	h	PM	PM	h	PM	h	PM	PM	PM	h
BRENTWOOD ....dep.	—	—	—	—	⌐	7 41	—	—	8 1	—	—	—	—	—	8 33	—	—	9 6	—
Harold Wood	—	—	—	—	—	7 47	—	—	—	—	—	—	—	8 39	—	—	—
GIDEA PARK	—	7 7	—	—	—	—	—	8 8	—	8 23	—	—	8 43	8 50	—	—
ROMFORD	—	7 11	—	—	—	7 54	—	8 13	—	8 27	8 34	—	8 43	8 54	—	—
CHADWELL HEATH	—	7 18	—	7*33	—	—	8*4	0	—	8 19	8 33	8 40	8 49	—	9 2	—	9 18	—
Goodmayes	—	7 22	—	7*36	—	—	8	3	—	8 22	8 36	8 43	8 52	—	9 5	—	9 21	—
Seven Kings	—	7 26	—	7*39	—	--	8	6	—	8 25	8 39	8 46	8 55	—	9 8	—	9 24	—
ILFORD	7 27	7 32	7 37	7 43	7 52	8	3	8 14	8 10	8 22	8 30	8 43	8 51	9	0	8 57	9 20	9 28	9 38
Manor Park	7 31	7 35	7 40	7 46	7 56	—	8	17	8 13	—	8 34	8 46	—	9	4	—	9 15	9 23	—
Forest Gate	7 35	7 39	7 44	7 50	8	0	—	8	21	8 17	—	8 38	8 50	—	9	8	—	9 19	9 27	9 34
Maryland Point	7 38	7 42	7 47	7 53	8	3	—	8	24	8 20	—	8 41	8 53	—	9	11	—	9 22	9 30	—
STRATFORD (W. Ham)	7 41	7 45	7 50	7 57	8	6	8	12	8	27	8 23	8 30	8 45	8 56	9	1	9	14	9	8	9 25	9 33	9 40	9 48
STRATFORD MARKET	—	—	—	—	—	—	—	—	—	—	—	—	—	—	—	—	—
Bow Road	7 46	—	—	—	—	8 32	—	—	—	—	—	—	—	9 31	—	—
Burdett Road	7 49	—	—	—	—	8 35	—	—	—	—	—	—	—	9 34	—	—
Stepney	7 52	—	—	—	—	8 38	—	—	—	—	—	—	—	9 37	—	—
FENCHURCH STREET	7 59	—	—	—	—	8 45	—	—	—	—	—	—	—	9 44	—	—
Coborn Road	—	—	—	—	—	—	—	—	8 50	—	—	—	—	—	—	—
Bethnal Green	—	—	—	—	—	—	—	—	8 54	—	—	—	—	—	—	—
LIVERPOOL STREET	—	7 55	8	3 8	7 8	16	8	22	—	8 33	8	40	8 53	9	5	9 10	9 24	9 17	—	9 43	9 50	9 58

WEEK DAYS.

	PM		PM		PM	PM	h	PM		PM	
BRENTWOOD ....dep.	—	9 53	—	10 4	—	10 36	—	10 55	—	
Harold Wood	—	—	—	10 10	—	—	—	—	—	
GIDEA PARK	9 31	—	10	10 15	—	—	—	11 7		
ROMFORD	9 35	10	3	10	8	10 19	—	11	4	11	11	
CHADWELL HEATH	9 41	—	10	14	10	25	10 35	—	10 57	—	11 17	
Goodmayes	9 45	—	10	17	—	10 38	—	11	0	—	11 20	
Seven Kings	9 48	—	10	20	—	10 41	—	11	3	—	11 23	
ILFORD	9 53	10 12	10	24	10	32	10	45	10	56	11	7	11	12	11	27	
Manor Park	9 57	—	10	27	—	10	48	—	11	10	—	11	30	
Forest Gate	10	1	—	10	31	—	10	52	—	11	14	—	11	34	
Maryland Point	10	4	—	10	34	—	10	55	—	11	17	—	11	37	
STRATFORD (W. Ham)	10	7	10	22	10	37	10	42	10	58	11	6	11	20	11	20	11	40	
STRATFORD MARKET	—	—	—	—	—	—	—	—	—	
Bow Road	—	—	—	—	—	—	—	—	—	
Burdett Road	—	—	—	—	—	—	—	—	—	
Stepney	—	—	—	—	—	—	—	—	—	
FENCHURCH STREET	—	—	—	—	—	—	—	—	—	
Coborn Road	10 12	—	—	—	11	3	—	11 25	—	11 45	
Bethnal Green	10 16	—	—	—	11	7	—	11 29	—	11 49	
LIVERPOOL STREET	10	20	10 32	10	47	10	52	11	11	11	16	11	33	11	29	11	52	

SUNDAYS.

	AM	AM	AM	AM	AM	AM		h	PM		AM	AM	AM	AM	AM	h	AM
BRENTWOOD ....dep.	2 54	—	—	—	—	—	7 55	—	—	—	—	—	9 26	—	10 4	—
Harold Wood	—	—	—	—	—	—	8	1	—	—	—	—	9 32	—	—	—
GIDEA PARK	—	3	5	5	12	6 11	6 58	—	—	8	5	—	8 36	—	9	5	—	9 37	—	10 11	—
ROMFORD	—	3	11	5	18	6	17	7	2	—	—	8	10	—	8 40	—	9	9	—	9 41	—	10 15	—
CHADWELL HEATH	—	3	15	5	21	6	20	7	11	—	—	8	15	—	8 46	—	9	15	—	9 47	—	10 21	—
Goodmayes	—	3	14	5	21	6	20	7	11	—	—	8	18	—	8 49	—	9	18	—	9 50	—	10 24	—
Seven Kings	—	3	17	5	24	6	23	7	14	—	—	8	21	—	8 52	—	9	21	—	9 53	—	10 27	—
ILFORD	—	3	25	5	29	6	27	7	19	7 42	7	56	8	12	8	26	8	42	8	56	9	12	9	26	9 42	9	58	10	15	10 32	10 42
Manor Park	—	3	29	5	32	6	30	7	22	7	45	7	59	8	15	8	29	8	45	8	59	9	15	9	29	9 45	10	1	—	—	10 45
Forest Gate	3 33	5	36	6	34	7	26	7	49	8	3	8	19	8	33	8	49	9	3	9	19	9 33	9	49	10	5	—	—	10 49
Maryland Point	—	5	39	6	37	7	29	7	52	8	6	8	22	8	36	8	52	9	6	9	22	9 36	9	52	10	8	—	—	10 52
STRATFORD (W. Ham)	3 41	5	42	6	40	7	33	7	57	8	10	8	25	8	40	8	56	9	10	9	25	9 40	9	56	10	13	10	23	10 41	10 55
STRATFORD MARKET	—	—	—	—	—	—	—	—	—	—	—	—	—	—	—	—	—
Bow Road	—	—	—	8	1	—	8 29	—	9	1	—	9 31	—	9 59	—	—	11 2
Burdett Road	—	—	—	8	4	—	8 32	—	9	4	—	9 34	—	10	2	—	—	11 6
Stepney	—	—	—	8	7	—	8 35	—	9	7	—	9 37	—	10	5	—	—	11 10
FENCHURCH STREET	—	—	—	8	13	—	8 40	—	9	12	—	9 42	—	10	10	—	—	11 15
Coborn Road	—	—	—	7	38	—	8	15	—	8	45	—	9	15	—	9	45	—	10	18	—	—
Bethnal Green	—	—	—	7	42	—	8	19	—	8	49	—	9	19	—	9	49	—	10	22	—	—
LIVERPOOL STREET	3 50	6	0	6	50	7	45	—	8	22	—	8	52	—	9	22	—	9	52	—	10	25	10	33	10	50	—

SUNDAYS.

	AM	AM	AM	AM	AM	AM	h	PM		PM		PM	PM	
BRENTWOOD ....dep.	10 32	—	—	—	11 50	—	—	—	—	—	—	1 54	—
Harold Wood	10 39	—	—	—	11 57	—	—	—	—	—	—	2 0	—
GIDEA PARK	10 43	10	35	11	5	11	35	12	1	—	12 35	—	1	5	—	1	35	—	2	5	2 35
ROMFORD	10 47	10	39	11	9	11	39	12	6	—	12 39	—	1	9	—	1	39	—	2	9	2 39
CHADWELL HEATH	—	10	45	11	15	11	45	—	—	12 45	—	1	15	—	1	45	—	2	15	2 45
Goodmayes	—	10	48	11	18	—	11	48	—	12 48	—	1	18	—	1	48	—	2	18	2 48
Seven Kings	—	10	51	11	21	—	11	51	—	12 51	—	1	21	—	1	51	—	2	21	2 51
ILFORD	10 56	10	56	11	25	11	42	11	56	—	12 26	12	56	1	21	1	26	1	42	1	56	2	12	2	26	2 42	2 56
Manor Park	—	10	59	11	29	11	45	11	59	—	12 29	12	59	1	15	1	29	1	45	1	59	2	15	2	29	2 45	2 59
Forest Gate	—	11	3	11	33	11	49	12	3	—	12 33	1	3	1	19	1	33	1	49	2	3	2	19	2	33	2 49	3 4
Maryland Point	—	11	6	11	36	11	52	12	6	—	12 36	1	6	1	22	1	36	1	52	2	6	2	22	2	36	2 52	3 6
STRATFORD (W. Ham)	11 5	11	10	11	40	11	55	12	10	—	12 40	1	10	1	25	1	40	1	55	2	10	2	25	2 40	2 55	3 10
STRATFORD MARKET	—	—	—	—	—	—	—	—	—	—	—	—	—	—
Bow Road	—	—	—	—	1 29	—	1 59	—	2 29	—	2 59	—	
Burdett Road	—	12	2	—	—	1 32	—	10	2	—	2 32	—	3 2	—	
Stepney	—	12	5	—	—	1 35	—	10	5	—	2 35	—	3 5	—	
FENCHURCH STREET	—	12	10	—	—	1 40	—	2	10	—	2 40	—	3 10	—	
Coborn Road	11 15	11	45	—	12	15	—	12 45	—	1	15	1	45	—	2	15	—	2 45	—	3 15
Bethnal Green	11 19	11	49	—	12	19	—	12 49	—	1	19	1	49	—	2	19	—	2 49	—	3 19
LIVERPOOL STREET	11 15	11	22	11	52	—	12	22	12	40	12	52	1	22	—	1	52	—	2	22	—	2 52	—	3 22

d Saturdays only.

e Saturdays excepted.

h No 2nd class carriages are run on this train.

k Wednesdays only.

SUNDAYS.

	PM	PM	PM	PM	PM	PM	PM	PM	PM	h	PM	PM	PM	PM	PM	PM
Brentwood ......dep.	2 32	—	—	—	—	—	—	—	4 24	4 38	—	5 2	—	—	—	—
Harold Wood	2 39	—	—	—	—	—	—	—	4 31	—	—	5 9	—	—	—	—
Gidea Park	2 43	—	3 5	—	3 35	—	4 5	—	4 35	—	—	5 13	5 5	—	5 35	—
Romford	2 47	—	3 9	—	3 39	—	4 9	—	4 39	4 47	—	5 17	5 9	—	5 39	—
Chadwell Heath	—	—	3 15	—	3 45	—	4 15	—	4 45	—	—	—	5 15	—	5 45	—
Goodmayes..........	—	—	3 18	—	3 48	—	4 18	—	4 48	—	—	—	5 18	—	5 48	—
Seven Kings..........	—	—	3 21	—	3 51	—	4 21	—	4 51	—	—	—	5 21	—	5 51	—
Ilford	2 56	3 12	3 25	3 42	3 56	4 12	4 25	4 42	4 56	4 56	5 12	5 26	5 26	5 42	5 56	6 15
Manor Park..........	—	3 15	3 29	3 45	3 59	4 15	4 29	4 45	4 59	—	5 15	—	5 29	5 45	5 59	6 18
Forest Gate..........	—	3 19	3 32	3 49	4 3	4 19	4 33	4 49	5 3	—	5 19	—	5 33	5 49	6 3	6 22
Maryland Point......	—	3 22	3 33	3 52	4 6	4 22	4 36	4 52	5 6	—	5 22	—	5 36	5 52	6 6	6 25
Stratford (W. Ham)..	3 5	3 25	3 40	3 55	4 10	4 25	4 40	4 55	5 10	5 5	5 25	5 35	5 40	5 55	6 10	6 28
Stratford Market																
Bow Road............	—	3 29	—	3 59	—	4 29	—	4 59	—	—	5 29	—	—	5 59	—	6 32
Burdett Road	—	3 32	—	4 2	—	4 32	—	5 2	—	—	5 32	—	—	6 2	—	6 35
Stepney	—	3 35	—	4 5	—	4 35	—	5 5	—	—	5 35	—	—	6 5	—	6 38
Fenchurch Street....	—	3 40	—	4 10	—	4 40	—	5 10	—	—	5 40	—	—	6 10	—	6 43
Coborn Road........	—	—	3 45	—	4 15	—	4 45	—	5 15	—	—	—	5 45	—	6 15	—
Bethnal Green	—	—	3 49	—	4 19	—	4 49	—	5 19	—	—	—	5 49	—	6 19	—
Liverpool Street	3 15	—	3 52	—	4 22	—	4 52	—	5 22	5 15	—	5 45	5 52	—	6 22	—

SUNDAYS.

	PM	PM	PM	PM	PM	PM	PM	PM	PM	h	PM	PM	h	PM	PM	h
Brentwood ......dep.	—	—	—	6 50	7 3	7 21	—	—	7 34	—	8 2	—	—	8 56	—	9 7
Harold Wood	—	—	—	6 57	—	—	—	—	7 42	—	8 9	—	—	—	—	—
Gidea Park	6 5	—	6 35	—	7 11	—	—	7 35	7 46	8 5	8 13	—	8 41	9 3	—	9 16
Romford	6 9	—	6 39	—	7 16	7 15	7 30	7 39	7 50	8 9	8 17	—	8 45	—	—	9 20
Chadwell Heath	6 15	—	6 45	—	7 13	—	—	7 45	7 56	8 15	—	—	8 51	—	—	—
Goodmayes	6 18	—	6 48	—	7 16	—	—	7 48	7 59	8 18	—	—	8 54	—	—	—
Seven Kings	6 21	—	6 51	—	7 19	—	—	7 51	8 2	8 21	—	—	8 57	—	—	—
Ilford	6 26	6 42	6 56	7 12	7 25	7 24	7 39	7 42	7 56	8 10	8 26	8 26	8 39	8 42	9 1	9 14 9 12 9 29
Manor Park..........	6 29	6 45	6 59	7 15	7 29	—	7 45	7 54	8 14	8 29	—	8 45	9 4	—	9 15	—
Forest Gate..........	6 33	6 49	7 3	7 19	7 33	—	7 49	8 3	8 20	8 33	—	8 49	9 8	—	9 19	—
Maryland Point......	6 36	6 52	7 6	7 22	7 36	—	7 52	8 6	—	8 36	—	8 52	9 11	—	9 22	—
Stratford (W. Ham)..	6 40	6 55	7 10	7 25	7 40	7 33	7 48	7 55	8 10	8 29	8 40	8 35	8 55	9 14	9 23	9 25 9 36
Stratford Market																
Bow Road	—	6 59	—	7 29	—	—	7 59	—	—	—	—	8 59	—	—	9 29	—
Burdett Road	—	7 2	—	7 32	—	—	8 2	—	—	—	—	9 2	—	—	9 32	—
Stepney	—	7 5	—	7 35	—	—	8 5	—	—	—	—	9 5	—	—	9 35	—
Fenchurch Street....	—	7 10	—	7 40	—	—	8 10	—	—	—	—	9 10	—	—	9 40	—
Coborn Road........	6 45	—	7 15	—	7 45	—	—	8 15	—	8 45	—	—	9 19	—	—	—
Bethnal Green	6 49	—	7 19	—	7 49	—	—	8 19	—	8 49	—	—	9 23	—	—	—
Liverpool Street	6 52	—	7 22	—	7 52	7 44	7 58	—	8 22	8 39	8 52	8 45	8 58	—	9 26	9 32 9 48

SUNDAYS.

	PM	PM	PM	PM	PM	PM	PM	PM			PM	PM
Brentwood ......dep.	—	—	9 22	10 8	—	—	—	10 25				
Harold Wood	—	—	9 28	—	—	—	—	10 33				
Gidea Park	9 8	—	9 32	—	—	—	10 5	10 37				
Romford	9 12	—	9 36	—	—	—	10 9	10 41				
Chadwell Heath....	9 18	—	9 43	—	—	—	10 15	10 48				
Goodmayes	9 21	—	9 46	—	—	—	10 18	10 51				
Seven Kings	9 24	—	9 49	—	—	—	10 21	10 54				
Ilford	9 29	9 42	9 56	10 26	10 15	—	10 25	10 59			*h* No 2nd Class carriages	
Manor Park..........	9 32	9 45	9 59	—	10 18	—	10 29	11 2			are run on this train.	
Forest Gate..........	9 36	9 49	10 3	—	10 22	—	10 33	11 6				
Maryland Point......	9 39	9 52	10 6	—	10 25	—	10 36	11 9				
Stratford (W. Ham)	9 43	9 55	10 10	10 35	10 28	—	10 40	11 13				
Stratford Market						10 39	—	—				
Bow Road..........	—	10 1	—	—	10 34	10 44	—	—				
Burdett Road........	—	10 6	—	—	10 37	10 47	—	—				
Stepney	—	10 9	—	—	10 40	10 50	—	—				
Fenchurch Street....	—	10 14	—	—	10 45	10 55	—	—				
Coborn Road	9 48	—	10 15	—	—	—	10 45	11 18				
Bethnal Green	9 52	—	10 19	—	—	—	10 49	11 22				
Liverpool Street....	9 55	—	10 22	10 45	—	—	10 52	11 25				

LIVERPOOL STREET TO PALACE GATES & ENFIELD.

WEEK DAYS.	AM	AM	AM	AM	AM	AM	AM	AM	AM	AM	AM	AM	AM	AM	AM	AM	AM	AM
Liverpool St.....dep.	4 50	5 35	6 5	6 22	6 34	6 55	7 4	7 8	7 12	7 16	7 20	7 24	7 28	7 32	7 35	7 40	7 44	7 52
Bethnal Green	4 54	5 39	6 9	6 26	6 38	6 59	—	—	—	7 20	—	—	7 36	—	—	—	—	—
Cambridge Heath....	4 57	5 41	6 11	6 28	6 40	7 1	—	—	—	—	—	—	—	—	—	—	—	—
London Fields........	4 59	5 44	6 14	6 31	6 43	7 4	—	—	—	—	—	—	—	—	7 48	—	—	—
Hackney Downs......	5 2	5 47	6 17	6 34	6 46	7 6	—	7 15	—	—	7 32	—	—	—	—	—	—	—
Rectory Road	5 5	5 50	6 20	6 37	6 49	7 9	—	—	7 22	—	—	7 38	—	—	7 54	—	—	—
Stoke Newington	5 8	5 52	6 22	6 39	6 51	7 11	7 15	7 20	—	7 31	7 36	—	7 47	7 52	—	8 3	—	—
Stamford Hill........	5 11	5 55	6 25	6 42	6 54	—	7 23	7 26	7 30	—	7 39	7 42	7 46	—	7 55	7 58	—	—
Seven Sisters........	5 14	5 57	6 27	6 44	6 56	7 15	7 19	7 18	7 27	7 25	7 28	—	7 35	7 41	7 43	—	7 51	7 57 7 59 8 7
West Green	—	—	6 33	—	7 11	7 18	7 27	—	7 32	—	7 47	—	7 57	—	—	8 3	—	—
Noel Park	—	—	6 37	—	7 15	7 22	7 31	—	7 36	—	7 51	—	8 1	—	—	8 7	—	—
Palace Gates........	—	—	6 40	—	7 18	7 25	7 34	—	7 39	—	7 54	—	8 4	—	—	8 10	—	—
Bruce Grove..........	5 16	6 0	6 30	6 47	7 1	—	7 28	—	7 33	—	7 44	—	7 49	—	8 0	—	—	—
White Hart Lane	5 18	6 3	6 33	6 50	7 4	—	7 23	7 31	—	7 39	7 47	—	7 55	8 3	—	—	8 11	—
Silver Street........	5 21	6 6	6 36	6 53	7 7	—	7 28	7 31	—	7 38	—	7 50	—	7 54	—	8 6	—	—
Lower Edmonton	5 24	6 9	6 39	6 56	7 10	—	7 28	7 37	—	7 44	7 49	7 53	—	8 0	8 9	—	8 16	—
Bush Hill Park	5 27	6 12	6 42	6 59	7 13	—	—	7 40	—	7 44	7 49	7 56	—	8 0	—	8 12	—	—
Enfield Town........	5 30	6 15	6 46	7 3	7 19	—	7 34	7 43	—	7 47	7 47	7 59	—	8 3	8 6	8 15	—	8 23

WEEK DAYS.	AM	AM	AM	AM	AM						PM	PM	PM	PM
Liverpool St.....dep.	7 56	8 0	8 4	8 10							10 30	10 45	11 0	11 15
Bethnal Green........	—	8 8	—	8 8							10 34	—	11 4	—
Cambridge Heath	—	—	—	8 15							10 36	—	11 6	—
London Fields........	—	—	—	8 18							10 39	—	11 9	—
Hackney Downs......	8 4	—	8 14	8 20							10 41	10 53	11 11	11 23
Rectory Road	—	8 10	—	8 23							10 44	10 56	11 14	11 26
Stoke Newington	8 8	—	—	8 25							10 46	10 57	11 16	11 27
Stamford Hill........	8 11	8 14	8 21	8 28							10 50	11 0	11 20	11 30
Seven Sisters........	8 13	8 15	—	8 30		Thence every few minutes to					10 52	11 2	11 22	11 32
West Green	—	8 19	—	—		most Stations until					10 55	—	11 31	—
Noel Park	—	8 23	—	—							10 59	—	11 35	—
Palace Gates........	—	8 26	—	—							11 2	—	11 34	—
Bruce Grove........	8 16	—	8 25	8 33							10 53	11 5	11 23	11 35
White Hart Lane	8 19	—	—	8 36							10 56	11 7	11 26	11 38
Silver Street	8 22	—	8 29	8 39							10 58	11 10	11 28	11 41
Lower Edmonton	8 25	—	—	8 41							11 1	11 12	11 31	11 44
Bush Hill Park	8 28	—	8 34	8 45							11 4	11 15	11 34	11 47
Enfield Town........	8 33	—	8 38	8 48							11 6	11 18	11 36	11 51

WEEK DAYS.	PM	PM	d	e
Liverpool St...dep.	11 30	11 45	12 15	12 15
Bethnal Green	11 34	—	12 19	12 19
Cambridge Heath..	11 36	—	12 21	12 21
London Fields......	11 39	--	12 24	12 24
Hackney Downs....	11 41	11 53	12 26	12 26
Rectory Road	11 44	11 56	12 29	12 29
Stoke Newington ..	11 46	11 57	12 31	12 32
Stamford Hill......	11 50	12 1	12 33	12 35
Seven Sisters......	11 52	12 4	12 36	12 37
West Green	11 57	—	12 40	12 43
Noel Park	12 1	—	12 44	12 47
Palace Gates.	12 4	—	12 47	12 50
Bruce Grove........	11 53	12 7	12 38	12 40
White Hart Lane ..	11 56	12 9	12 41	12 43
Silver Street	11 58	12 12	12 43	12 46
Lower Edmonton ..	12 1	12 14	12 46	12 48
Bush Hill Park ...	12 4	12 17	12 49	12 52
Enfield Town	12 6	12 20	12 51	12 55

SUNDAYS.	h	AM	AM		PM
Liverpool St...dep.	6 10	8 25	8 55		11 25
Bethnal Green	6 15	8 29	8 59		11 29
Cambridge Heath..	6 18	8 31	9 1		11 31
London Fields.....	6 20	8 34	9 4		11 34
Hackney Downs....	6 23	8 36	9 6		11 36
Rectory Road	6 26	8 39	9 9	Then at the same minutes	11 39
Stoke Newington ..	6 28	8 41	9 11	past each hour until	11 41
Stamford Hill......	6 33	8 45	9 15		11 4
Seven Sisters......	6 38	8 47	9 17	h Calls to set down	11 47
West Green	7 52	8 52	9 22	passengers only.	11 52
Noel Park	7 56	8 56	9 26		11 5(
Palace Gates	7 59	8 59	9 29		11 55
Bruce Grove.......	6 40	8 50	9 20		11 50
White Hart Lane ..	6 42	8 53	9 23		11 53
Silver Street	6 45	8 56	9 26		11 5(
Lower Edmonton ..	6 51	8 58	9 28		11 5(
Bush Hill Park	6 54	9 2	9 32		12 2
Enfield Town......	6 57	9 5	9 35		12 5

d Saturdays only. *e* Saturdays excepted. *h* Sets down passengers only.

WEEK DAYS.	AM	AM	AM	AM	AM	AM	AM	AM	AM	AM	AM	AM	AM	AM	AM	AM
Enfield Town dep.	3 56	4 46	5 16	5 34	5 47	6 8	6 26	6 29	6 33	6 43	6 46	6 50	6 59	7 2	—	—
Bush Hill Park	3 59	4 48	5 19	5 37	5 51	6 11	—	6 32	6 36	—	6 49	6 53	—	7 5	—	—
Lower Edmonton ..	4 3	4 52	5 23	5 41	5 55	6 16	6 32	—	6 40	6 49	—	6 57	7 4	—	7 12	7 18
Silver Street	4 5	4 55	5 25	5 43	5 57	6 18	—	6 37	6 43	—	6 54	7 0	—	7 10	—	—
White Hart Lane ..	4 8	4 58	5 28	5 46	6 0	6 21	6 36	—	6 45	6 53	—	7 2	7 8	—	—	—
Bruce Grove........	4 11	5 1	5 31	5 49	6 3	6 24	—	6 41	6 48	—	6 58	7 5	—	7 14	—	—
Palace Gates......	—	—	5 20	—	—	6 15	—	—	—	6 46	—	6 57	—	—	—	—
Noel Park	—	—	5 22	—	—	6 17	—	—	—	6 48	—	6 59	—	—	—	—
West Green	—	—	5 25	—	—	6 20	—	—	—	6 51	—	7 2	—	—	—	—
Seven Sisters	4 14	5 4	5 34	5 52	6 6	6 27	6 40	—	6 51	6 57	—	7 t	7 13	—	—	—
Stamford Hill......	4 17	5 17	5 37	5 55	6 9	6 30	—	6 45	6 54	—	7 2	7 11	—	7 18	—	—
Stoke Newington ..	4 20	5 10	5 40	5 58	6 12	6 33	6 45	—	6 57	7 2	—	7 14	7 17	—	—	—
Rectory Road	4 22	5 12	5 42	6 0	6 14	6 35	—	6 50	—	—	7 6	—	—	—	7 22	—
Hackney Downs ..	4 25	5 16	5 45	6 3	6 17	6 38	6 50	6 54	7 3	7 6	7 10	7 19	7 22	7 26	7 30	—
London Fields	4 28	5 18	5 48	6 6	6 20	6 41	—	6 56	7 5	—	7 12	7 21	—	7 28	—	—
Bethnal Green	4 31	5 21	5 51	6 9	6 23	6 44	6 54	—	7 10	—	—	7 26	—	—	7 34	—
Cambridge Heath..	4 32	5 24	5 53	6 11	6 25	6 46	6 56	—	7 12	—	—	7 28	—	—	7 35	—
Liverpool Street..	4 37	5 27	5 57	6 15	6 29	6 50	7 0	7 4	7 12	7 16	7 20	7 28	7 32	7 35	7 40	7 45

WEEK DAYS.	AM	AM	AM	AM	AM	AM	AM	AM			e	d	PM
Enfield Town dep.	7 12	7 16	7 21	7 30	7 37	7 47	8 0				9 53	9 57	10 12
Bush Hill Park	—	7 19	7 24	7 32	7 40	7 50	—	8 3			9 56	10 0	10 15
Lower Edmonton ..	7 18	—	7 28	7 36	7 44	7 54	—	8 7			10 0	10 3	10 19
Silver Street	—	7 24	7 31	—	7 46	7 56	—	8 9			10 2	10 5	10 22
White Hart Lane ..	7 22	—	7 33	7 40	7 49	7 59	—	8 12			10 5	10 8	10 24
Bruce Grove........	—	7 28	7 36	—	7 52	8 2	—	8 15			10 8	10 10	10 27
Palace Gates	7 14	—	7 27	—	7 44	7 52	8 4	—			10 0	10 1	—
Noel Park	7 16	—	7 29	—	7 46	7 54	8 6	—			10 2	10 3	—
West Green	7 19	—	7 32	—	7 49	7 57	8 9	—			10 5	10 6	—
Seven Sisters......	7 26	7 31	7 39	7 45	7 55	8 5	8 12	8 18			10 11	10 13	10 30
Stamford Hill......	7 29	7 34	7 42	—	7 58	8 8	8 15	8 21			10 14	10 15	10 33
Stoke Newington ..	7 32	—	7 45	7 49	8 1	8 11	8 18	8 24			10 17	10 18	10 36
Rectory Road	—	7 38	7 47	—	8 3	8 13	8 20	—			10 19	10 19	10 38
Hackney Downs ...	7 37	7 42	7 51	7 54	8 6	8 16	8 24	8 28			10 22	10 22	10 41
London Fields ...	7 39	7 44	7 53	—	8 9	8 19	8 26	—			10 25	10 25	—
Cambridge Heath..	7 42	—	—	7 58	8 12	8 22	—	8 32			10 28	10 28	—
Bethnal Green	7 44	—	—	8 0	8 14	8 24	—	8 34			10 30	10 30	—
Liverpool Street..	7 48	7 52	8 0	8 4	8 18	8 28	8 34	8 38			10 34	10 34	10 49

Thence every few minutes to most Stations until

WEEK DAYS.	PM	e	d	e	d	e	d
Enfield Town dep.	10 23	10 42	10 46	10 53	10 57	11 23	11 26
Bush Hill Park	10 26	10 45	10 48	10 56	11 0	11 26	11 29
Lower Edmonton ..	10 30	10 49	10 52	11 0	11 3	11 30	11 32
Silver Street	10 32	10 51	10 54	11 2	11 5	11 32	11 35
White Hart Lane ..	10 35	10 54	10 56	11 5	11 8	11 35	11 38
Bruce Grove........	10 38	10 57	10 59	11 8	11 10	11 38	11 40
Palace Gates	10 30	—	—	11 2	11 1	11 30	11 31
Noel Park	10 32	—	—	11 2	11 1	11 32	11 33
West Green	10 35	—	—	11 5	11 6	11 35	11 36
Seven Sisters......	10 41	11 0	11 1	11 11	11 13	11 41	11 43
Stamford Hill......	10 44	11 3	11 4	11 14	11 16	11 44	11 45
Stoke Newington ..	10 47	11 6	11 6	11 17	11 18	11 47	11 48
Rectory Road	10 49	11 8	11 8	11 19	11 19	11 49	11 49
Hackney Downs....	10 52	11 11	11 11	11 22	11 22	11 52	11 52
London Fields.....	10 55	—	—	11 25	11 25	11 55	11 55
Cambridge Heath..	10 58	—	—	11 28	11 28	11 58	11 58
Bethnal Green	11 0	—	—	11 30	11 30	12 0	12 0
Liverpool Street..	11 4	11 19	11 19	11 34	11 34	12 4	12 4

SUNDAYS	AM	AM		PM		
Enfield Town dep.	7 30	8 0		10 30		
Bush Hill Park	7 33	8 3		10 33		
Lower Edmonton ..	7 37	8 7		10 37		
Silver Street........	7 39	8 9		10 39		
White Hart Lane ..	7 42	8 12		10 42		
Bruce Grove........	7 45	8 15		10 35		
Palace Gates	7 36	8 6	Then at the same minutes	10 36		
Noel Park	7 38	8 8	past each hour until	10 38		
West Green	7 41	8 11		10 41		
Seven Sisters......	7 48	8 18		10 48		
Stamford Hill......	7 51	8 21		10 51		
Stoke Newington ..	7 54	8 24		10 54		
Rectory Road	7 56	8 26		10 56		
Hackney Downs....	7 59	8 29		10 59		
London Fields	8 2	8 32		11 2		
Cambridge Heath ..	8 5	8 35		11 5		
Bethnal Green	8 7	8 37		11 7		
Liverpool Street..	8 11	8 41		11 11		

MILNERS SAFES.

LIVERPOOL STREET TO CHIGWELL, VIA WOODFORD.

WEEK DAYS.	AM	AM	AM	AM	AM	AM	AM	AM	AM	AM	d	e	d	e	d	d	e	d	d
Liverpool St...dep.	—	5 56	6 30	7 10	—	7 47	8 27	—	8 38	9 28	10 30	10 30	—	11 40	1140	12 3	1233	1243	1 6
Fenchurch St. ,,	—	—	6 20	—	—	7 39	8 6	—	8 35	9 0	10 8	10 8	—	11 6	11 6	11 51	1151	1223	12 46
Woodford ..... ,,	—	6 30	7 16	7 43	—	8 20	9 1	—	9 27	10 14	11 8	11 7	—	12 16	1216	12 39	112	120	1 35
Chigwell ......arr.	—	7 9	7 27	7 59	—	8 28	9 7	—	9 33	10 20	11 12	11 12	—	12 22	1222	12 45	118	128	1 41
Grange Hill ... ,,	—	7 12	7 29	8 2	—	8 30	9 9	—	9 36	10 22	11 15	11 15	1210	12 24	1224	12 47	120	128	1 43
Fairlop ...... ,,	—	7 18	7 43	8 7	—	8 40	—	930	9 41	10 28	11 21	1216	12 30	—	1 1	129	135	—
Barkingside ... ,,	—	7 22	7 46	8 10	—	8 43	—	933	9 44	10 31	11 25	1219	12 33	—	1 4	132	138	—
Newbury Park . ,,	6 55	7 24	7 48	—	8 20	8 46	—	935	9 46	10 33	11 27	1221	12 35	—	1 6	134	140	—
Ilford .... ,,	6 59	7 28	7 52	—	8 26	8 50	—	939	9 50	10 37	11 31	1225	12 39	—	1 10	138	—	—
Fenchurch Street.	7 44	—	8 39	—	—	9 30	—	1014	11 11	46	12	2	11 41	110	1 39	—	1 53	228	—
Liverpool Street .	7 25	7 48	8 14	8 40	8 42	9 14	—	10 2	1020	11 12	11 59	12 10	1251	1 10	—	1 36	2 8	—	—

WEEK DAYS.	d	d	AM	AM	d	e	d	e	d			d	e	d	d	e	d	e	d	d
Liverpool St. dep.	1 33	1 35	2 10	242	3	8 3	3 54	8 42	5 4	4 25	—	5	5 5	17	5 35	5 39	556	6	36	6 36	27	6 37	6 55	—
Fenchurch St... ,,	1 17	1 18	2	0 2	9 2	5	02	5 03	47	413	—	435	—	5	14	—	5	18	543	5	58	5	57	6	18	—	6 42	—
Woodford ..... ,,	2	5	2	12	2	47	322	3	46	4	15	4	46	45	7	5 16	518	5	42	5	52	6	7	6	15	625	6	36	6	42	7	0	7	14	7	23	—
Chigwell ......arr.	2	11	2	18	2	53	328	3	52	4	23	4	52	5	4	5	22	524	5	48	5	53	6	13	6	21	631	6	42	6	48	7	7	7	19	7	29	7	56
Grange Hill ... ,,	2	13	2	20	2	56	340	3	54	4	25	4	54	5	6	5	24	533	5	51	6	5	20	6	25	633	6	44	6	50	7	9	7	22	7	38	7	59
Fairlop ...... ,,	2	19	2	31	3	1	345	4	0	4	59	5	0	520	5	30	538	5	56	6	10	6	30	6	30	639	6	50	7	0	7	33	7	33	7	43	8	4
Barkingside ... ,,	2	22	2	34	3	4	348	4	3	5	2	5	3	523	5	33	541	5	59	6	13	6	33	6	33	—	7	3	7	37	3	67	7	46	8	7
Newbury Park . ,,	2	24	2	36	3	6	350	4	5	5	5	5	5	525	5	35	543	6	1	6	15	6	42	6	42	—	7	5	7	39	3	69	7	48	8	9
Ilford .... ,,	2	28	2	38	3	10	354	4	9	5	10	5	9	530	5	40	547	6	5	6	20	6	48	6	48	—	7	9	7	42	—	3	2	98	2	98	8	13
Fenchurch Street.	3	11	3	37	3	42	445	4	45	535	5	416	5	—	626	6	33	7	12	—	7	59	—	7	42	—	3	298	298	8	45
Liverpool Street	3	5	3	5	3	50	422	4	45	5	36	5	436	6	0	6	26	176	366	45	7	18	7	18	—	7	39	8	3	8	78	7	18	8	41

WEEK DAYS.	PM	PM	PM	PM	d	PM	PM	PM	h	AM			AM	PM	PM
Liverpool St...dep.	7 5	7 38	8	5	8	45	9 20	946	1046	1145		836			830	945
Fenchurch St. ,,	6 47	7 26	7 49	8	15	8	54	854	953			819	Then at the same	819	919
Woodford ..... ,,	7 42	8	14	8	42	9	22	9	56	1026	1127	1222		9 7	minute past each	9 7	10 7
Chigwell ......arr.	7 48	8	20	8	48	9	28	10	1	1032	1133	1227		913	hour until 8.30 p.m.	913	1013
Grange Hill.... ,,	7 51	8	23	8	50	9	31	10	4	1035	1135	1230		915		915	1021
Fairlop ...... ,,	8	3	8	28	9	4	9	36	10	10	1040	—	—	926	1.30 p.m. does not	926	1026
Barkingside ... ,,	8	6	8	31	9	7	9	39	10	13	1043	—	—	929	start from	929	1029
Newbury Park ,,	8	8	8	33	9	9	9	41	10	15	1045	—	—	931	Fenchurch Street.	931	1031
Ilford	8	12	8	37	9	13	9	45	10	19	1049	1148	—	935		935	1059
Fenchurch Street	8	45	9	44	—	—	—	—	—	—	—	1010		1014	—
Liverpool Street..	8	41	9	5	9	43	10	20	10	47	1116	—	—	1015		1015	1125

SUNDAY TRAINS.

d Saturdays only. *e* Saturdays excepted. *h* Wednesdays and Saturdays only.

LIVERPOOL STREET TO CHIGWELL, VIA ILFORD.

WEEK DAYS.	AM	AM	AM	AM	AM	AM	AM	AM	AM	e	d	d	d	d	d	d	d	e
Liverpool St. dep.	6 10	—	6 58	7 36	7 53	8 3	8 33	—	9 41	1034	1034	1113	1145	12 5	1242	1251	1242	1 23	1 46	2 6
Fenchurch St. ,,	—	—	7 6	—	7 53	8 6	—	9 33	1030	1030	—	1151	1151	1217	1246	1246	17	1 44	—
Ilford .... ,,	6 36	—	7 28	8 0	8 16	8 34	8 57	—	10 6	11 8	11 8	1136	1223	1230	1 4	116	125	1 50	2 15	2 36
Newbury Park arr.	6 45	7 15	7 33	8 8	8 18	8 39	9 2	—	10 11	1113	1113	1145	1228	1240	1 9	121	130	1 52	2 20	2 41
Barkingside ,,	6 47	7 17	7 35	8 7	—	8 41	9 4	—	10 13	1115	1115	1147	1230	1242	—	123	132	1 57	2 22	2 43
Fairlop ,,	6 50	7 20	7 38	8 10	—	8 54	9 7	—	10 16	1118	1118	1150	1233	1245	—	126	135	2 0	2 25	2 46
Grange Hill ,,	7 2	7 27	7 43	8 26	—	8 59	—	925	10 31	1129	1131	1154	1246	1249	—	137	139	2 5	2 29	2 51
Chigwell ,,	7 5	7 30	7 45	8 29	—	9 2	—	929	10 34	1131	1134	—	1248	1252	—	140	144	2 18	2 41	2 54
Woodford ,,	7 12	7 36	8 0	8 36	—	9 10	—	936	10 50	1149	12 4	—	1255	118	—	147	220	2 36	2 48	3 20
Fenchurch Street	7 52	8 26	8 42	9 21	—	9 57	—	1014	11 46	1241	1251	—	139	228	—	228	310	3 42	3 42	4 24
Liverpool Street	7 43	8 14	8 30	9 3	—	9 39	—	10 5	11 20	1218	1235	—	127	148	—	216	250	3 3	3 24	3 50

WEEK DAYS.	d	d	d	d	d	d	d	e	d	e	d	d	e	d	d	e	d	e
Liverpool St. dep.	2 19	2 50	3 0	3	8	335	4	224	4	5	5	15	4	5	235	546	11	614	6	296	366	50	7	3	7	10	7	30	748	7	48
Fenchurch St. ,,	2 18	2 50	2	50	3	0	347	4	13	—	4	84	4	83	585	571	66	46	—	6	47	647	—	—	726	7	49
Ilford .... ,,	2 50	3 21	3	3	3	51	418	4	45	4	32	5	295	26	5	46	626	30	635	6	52	7	1	7	17	724	7	40	7	51	818	8	19
Newbury Park arr.	2 55	3 26	3	36	3	56	423	4	50	5	2	5	35	5	31	5	51	631	6	40	640	6	57	7	6	7	22	728	7	45	7	56	820	8	24
Barkingside ,,	2 57	3 28	3	33	3	58	425	4	52	5	4	5	35	5	33	5	53	633	6	37	—	7	0	7	9	7	24	730	7	47	7	58	822	8	26
Fairlop ,,	3 2	3 31	3	41	4	1	428	4	55	5	7	5	39	5	36	5	56	636	6	40	—	7	3	7	12	7	27	741	7	50	8	1	825	8	29
Grange Hill ,,	3 7	3 36	3	46	4	12	432	5	0	5	11	5	50	5	41	6	16	4	16	6	46	4	7	7	18	0	7	507	4	8	7	829	8	33
Chigwell ,,	3 24	3 54	3	48	4	14	435	5	16	5	15	5	54	5	46	6	6	476	53	—	7	10	7	20	8	4	743	8	10	8	23	839	8	43
Woodford ,,	3 34	4 0	4	5	4	21	442	5	22	6	10	6	3	6	8	57	—	7	29	7	42	7	55	8	10	8	23	839	8	43
Fenchurch Street	4 45	—	4	54	—	541	6	256	256	39	—	7	297	49	—	8	29	—	8	45	845	—	—	944	—
Liverpool Street	4 7	4 48	4	37	—	526	6	6	406	36	39	—	7	297	297	34	—	7	53	—	8	16	833	8	40	8	54	936	—

WEEK DAYS.	e		PM	PM	PM	PM	e	d			AM	AM	AM			PM	PM
Liverpool St. dep.	8 5	8 17	8 42	930	10	20	2	—			AM	945	937			6	427	537	837
Fenchurch St. ,,	8	15	—	934	9	59		—			819	919			7	29	7	19	819
Ilford .... ,,	8	34	8	44	9	10	1010	10	52	—		8	8	9	5	10	8		7	18	8	8
Newbury Park arr.	8	39	8	51	9	15	1015	10	57			813	914	1013			7	148	13	913
Barkingside ,,	8	41	8	53	9	17	1017	10	59			815	916	1015	Then at the same	7	168	15	915
Fairlop ,,	8	44	8	56	9	20	1020	11	2			818	919	1018	minute past each	7	198	18	918
Grange Hill ,,	8	49	9	0	9	24	1024	11	6			822	923	1022	hour until 5.37 p.m.	7	238	22	922
Chigwell ,,	8	52	9	4	9	27	1027	11	12			829	929	1029		7	298	29	925
Woodford ,,	8	58	9	11	9	34	1034	11	18			835	935	1035		7	358	35	935
Fenchurch Street	9	44	—	—	—	—	—			942	1115	—			9	40	1040
Liverpool Street	9	37	9	50	10	15	1121	11	57			915	1015	1115		8	159	15	1015

SUNDAY TRAINS.

d Saturdays only. *e* Saturdays excepted.

WEEK DAYS.

	AM	AM	AM	AM	AM	AM	AM	AM	AM	AM	AM	AM	AM	AM	AM	AM	AM
Liverpool St. dep.	4 20	—	—	5 26	—	6 10	—	—	6 30	—	6 50	6 58	7 3	—	7 10	—	7 18
Bethnal Green	4 26	—	—	5 30	—	6 14	—	—	6 34	—	—	—	7 8	—	7 14	—	—
Fenchurch Street	—	—	5 14	—	6 8	—	—	6 20	6 48	—	—	—	7 13	—	7 21	—	—
Stepney	—	—	5 21	—	6 15	—	—	6 27	6 54	—	—	—	7 18	—	7 27	—	—
Burdett Road	—	—	5 24	—	6 18	—	—	6 29	6 57	—	—	—	7 21	—	7 29	—	—
Bromley	—	—	—	—	—	—	—	—	—	—	—	—	—	—	7 34	—	—
Bow Road	—	—	5 27	—	6 21	—	—	6 32	7 0	—	—	—	—	—	—	—	—
Stratford Market..	4 55	5 17	5 32	5 49	6 26	6 30	6 37	6 42	6 48	7 7	7 12	7 18	7 23	—	7 32	—	7 39
Canning Town	5 0	5 22	5 37	5 54	6 31	6 35	6 43	6 48	6 53	7 12	7 17	7 23	7 28	7 30	7 36	7 40	7 44
Victoria {T. B.	5 3	5 25	5 40	5 57	6 33	6 37	6 47	6 51	6 56	7 14	7 19	7 25	7 30	7 32	—	7 42	7 46
Docks {C. H.	5 6	5 31	5 43	6 1	6 36	6 41	6 49	6 53	7 0	7 16	7 22	7 28	7 34	7 36	—	7 45	7 48
Royal {Con. Rd..	—	—	—	—	6 40	—	6 52	—	—	7 22	—	—	—	7 40	—	—	7 50
Albert {Central..	—	—	—	—	6 43	—	6 55	—	—	7 26	—	—	—	7 43	—	—	7 53
Docks {Manor W.	—	—	—	—	6 45	—	6 58	—	—	7 29	—	—	—	7 45	—	—	7 56
{Gallions .	—	—	—	—	6 47	—	7 0	—	—	7 31	—	—	—	7 47	—	—	7 58
Beckton	—	5 37	—	—	—	—	7 2	—	—	—	—	—	—	—	—	—	—
Silvertown	5 10	—	5 47	6 5	6 40	6 45	—	—	7 3	—	7 26	7 32	7 38	7 40	—	7 49	—
North Woolwich..	5 13	—	5 50	6 9	6 42	6 48	—	—	7 6	—	7 29	7 35	7 41	7 43	—	7 52	—

WEEK DAYS.

	AM	AM	AM	AM	AM	AM	AM	AM	AM	AM	AM	AM	AM	AM	AM	AM	AM	AM
Liverpool St. dep.	7 22	7 36	—	7 57	8 5	—	—	8 18	8 38	—	9 0	9 6	—	9 28	—	—	10 8
Bethnal Green	7 27	—	—	—	—	—	—	8 22	8 42	—	9 5	9 10	—	9 32	—	—	10 19
Fenchurch Street	—	—	7 46	—	—	8 6	8 17	—	8 35	8 53	—	9 0	9 20	9 21	9 40	10 4	—
Stepney	—	—	7 52	—	—	8 11	8 23	—	8 41	8 59	—	9 7	9 25	9 28	9 45	10 10	—
Burdett Road	—	—	7 55	—	—	8 14	8 26	—	8 43	9 1	—	9 9	9 27	9 31	9 47	10 12	—
Bromley	—	—	—	—	—	—	—	—	—	—	—	—	—	—	—	—	—
Bow Road	7 31	—	7 58	—	—	8 17	8 29	—	8 50	9 4	—	9 12	9 30	9 34	9 50	10 15	—
Stratford Market..	7 44	7 58	8 3	8 19	8 23	8 27	8 38	8 44	9 3	9 12	9 21	9 31	9 37	9 52	9 57	10 20	10 35
Canning Town	7 49	8 3	8 8	8 24	8 28	8 32	8 43	8 49	9 8	9 17	9 26	9 36	9 42	9 57	10 2	10 25	10 39
Victoria {T. B.	7 51	8 5	8 10	8 26	8 30	8 34	8 45	8 51	9 10	9 19	9 28	9 38	9 44	9 59	10 5	10 27	—
Docks {C. H.	7 53	8 8	8 13	8 29	8 33	8 36	8 48	8 54	9 13	9 22	9 31	9 41	9 46	10 2	10 8	10 30	—
Royal {Con. Rd..	7 56	8 10	—	—	—	8 39	8 52	—	9 17	—	9 35	—	9 50	—	10 12	—	—
Albert {Central..	7 59	8 13	—	—	—	8 42	8 55	—	9 20	—	9 38	—	9 53	—	10 15	—··	—
Docks {Manor W.	8 2	8 17	—	—	—	8 45	8 57	—	9 22	—	9 40	—	9 56	—	10 17	—	—
{Gallions .	8 4	8 20	—	—	—	8 47	8 59	—	9 24	—	9 42	—	9 58	—	10 19	—	—
Beckton	—	—	—	—	—	—	—	—	—	—	—	—	—	—	—	—	—
Silvertown	—	8 12	8 17	8 33	8 37	—	8 52	8 58	9 17	9 26	9 35	9 45	—	10 6	10 12	10 34	—
North Woolwich.	—	8 15	8 20	8 37	8 41	—	8 56	9 2	9 20	9 29	9 33	9 48	—	10 9	10 15	10 37	—

WEEK DAYS

	AM	AM	AM	AM	AM	AM	AM	AM	AM	AM	AM	AM	d	PM	d	PM
Liverpool St. dep.	—	—	10 34	—	—	10 50	—	11 13	11 25	—	—	11 45	—	12 13	—	—
Bethnal Green	—	—	10 38	—	—	—	—	—	—	—	—	—	—	12 23	—	—
Fenchurch Street	10 23	10 36	—	10 51	11 5	—	11 21	—	—	11 38	11 50	—	12 5	—	—	12 17
Stepney	—	10 41	—	10 56	11 10	—	—	—	—	11 43	11 55	—	12 10	—	—	—
Burdett Road	—	10 43	—	10 58	11 12	—	—	—	—	11 45	11 57	—	12 12	—	—	—
Bromley	—	—	—	11 3	—	—	—	—	—	—	12 1	—	—	—	—	—
Bow Road	—	—	—	—	11 15	—	—	—	—	11 48	—	—	12 15	—	—	—
Stratford Market .	—	—	10 55	—	11 21	11 26	—	11 36	11 50	11 53	—	12 6	12 20	12 30	—	—
Canning Town	10 35	10 51	11 0	11 7	11 26	11 31	11 33	11 42	11 55	11 58	12 6	12 11	12 25	12 35	12 29	—
Victoria {T. B.	10 37	10 53	11 2	11 9	11 28	11 33	11 35	11 45	11 58	12 0	12 8	12 13	12 27	12 37	12 31	—
Docks {C. H.	10 39	10 56	11 5	11 11	11 31	11 36	11 37	11 48	12 2	12 3	12 11	12 16	12 30	12 40	12 33	—
Royal {Con. Rd..	10 43	—	—	11 14	—	—	11 41	—	—	12 10	—	12 28	—	—	12 37	—
Albert {Central..	10 46	—	—	11 17	—	—	11 44	—	—	12 13	—	12 31	—	—	12 40	—
Docks {Manor W.	10 49	—	—	11 20	—	—	11 47	—	—	12 15	—	12 34	—	—	12 43	—
{Gallions .	10 51	—	—	11 22	—	—	11 49	—	—	12 17	—	12 36	—	—	12 45	—
Beckton	—	—	—	—	—	—	—	—	—	—	—	—	—	—	—	—
Silvertown	—	11 0	11 9	—	11 35	11 41	—	11 52	12 5	—	12 15	12 20	12 34	12 44	—	—
North Woolwich.	—	11 3	11 12	—	11 38	11 46	—··	11 55	12 8	—	12 18	12 23	12 37	12 47	—	—

WEEK DAYS.

	d	PM	e	PM	d	PM	PM	e	PM	e	PM	e	PM	PM	PM	e	PM
Liverpool St. dep.	12 20	12 24	—	12 32	12 42	—	—	1 5	1 6	1 29	—	1 38	—	—	—	2 10	—
Bethnal Green	—	12 28	—	—	12 46	—	—	—	—	1 33	—	—	—	—	—	2 14	—
Fenchurch Street	—	—	12 35	—	—	12 52	1 3	—	1 23	—	1 35	—	1 53	2 3	2 20	—	2 35
Stepney	—	—	12 40	—	—	12 57	1 8	—	—	—	1 40	—	1 58	2 9	—	—	2 40
Burdett Road	—	—	12 42	—	—	12 59	1 10	—	—	—	1 42	—	2 0	2 11	—	—	2 42
Bromley	—	—	—	—	—	—	—	—	—	—	1 47	—	—	—	—	—	—
Bow Road	—	—	—	—	—	—	1 14	—	—	—	—	—	2 14	—	—	—	—
Stratford Market..	12 38	12 37	12 50	1 6	1 15	—	1 20	1 33	1 25	1 42	—	1 59	—	2 19	—	2 33	—
Canning Town	12 43	12 42	12 55	1 11	1 20	1 6	1 25	1 39	1 41	1 47	1 52	2 4	2 8	2 24	2 33	2 40	2 50
Victoria {T. B.	12 45	12 44	12 58	1 7	1 22	1 8	1 27	1 41	1 32	1 49	1 54	2 6	2 10	2 26	2 35	2 40	2 52
Docks {C. H.	12 48	12 47	1 1	1 10	1 24	—	1 30	1 44	1 35	1 52	1 57	2 9	2 12	2 29	2 37	2 43	2 55
Royal {Con. Rd..	—	1 14	—	—	—	1 14	1 43	—	1 43	1 d57	2 16	—	2 16	2 34	2 41	—	—
Albert {Central..	—	1 17	—	—	—	1 17	1 46	—	1 46	2 d 0	2 19	—	2 19	2 37	2 44	—	—
Docks {Manor W.	—	1 20	—	—	—	1 20	1 49	—	1 49	2 d 2	2 22	—	2 22	2 39	2 47	—	—
{Gallions .	—	1 22	—	—	—	1 22	1 51	—	1 51	2 d 4	2 24	—	2 24	2 42	2 49	—	—
Beckton	—	—	—	—	1 33	—	—	—	—	—	—	—	—	—	—	—	—
Silvertown	12 52	12 50	—	1 14	—	—	1 34	1 48	1 39	1 56	2 1	2 13	—	2 33	—	2 d 47	2 59
North Woolwich..	12 55	12 57	1 8	1 17	—	—	1 37	1 51	1 42	1 59	2 4	2 16	—	2 36	—	2 d 50	3 2

WEEK DAYS.

	PM	e	PM	e	d	PM	e	PM	e	e	PM	e	PM	PM	e	PM
Liverpool St. dep.	2 23	—	—	—	3 8	—	3 20	3 35	—	3 35	—	4 5	4 18	4 25	4 37	4 57
Bethnal Green	2 27	—	—	—	3 12	—	3 34	3 39	—	3 39	—	4 9	4 12	4 29	4 41	—
Fenchurch Street	—	2 49	3 5	3 20	—	3 35	—	—	—	3 52	4 5	—	4 31	4 38	—	4 55
Stepney	—	2 54	3 10	—	—	3 40	—	—	—	3 58	4 10	—	4 29	4 44	—	5 2
Burdett Road	—	2 56	3 12	—	—	3 42	—	—	—	4 0	4 12	—	4 31	4 46	—	—
Bromley	—	3 1	—	—	—	—	—	—	—	4 4	—	—	—	4 49	—	—
Bow Road	—	—	3 15	—	—	—	—	—	—	4 15	—	—	—	4 d49	—	5 5
Stratford Market .	2 48	—	3 20	—	3 33	—	3 51	3 55	3 59	—	4 20	4 25	4 38	4 d54	5 6	5 16
Canning Town	2 54	3 6	3 25	3 33	3 38	3 50	3 56	4 4	4 6	4 25	4 30	4 43	4 40	4 55	5 11	5 21
Victoria {T. B.	2 57	3 8	3 27	3 35	3 40	3 53	3 58	4 2	4 6	4 10	4 32	4 45	4 42	4 57	5 16	5 24
Docks {C. H.	3 0	3 10	3 30	3 37	3 43	3 55	4 1	4 4	4 9	4 30	4 34	4 48	4 44	4 59	5 21	5 27
Royal {Con. Rd..	—	3 14	3 34	—	—	—	—	4 6	—	—	4 37	—	4 48	5 12	—	5 33
Albert {Central..	—	3 17	3 37	3 44	—	—	—	4 19	4 19	—	4 40	—	4 51	5 d15	—	5 36
Docks {Manor W.	—	3 19	3 39	3 46	—	—	—	4 21	4 22	—	4 42	—	4 53	5 17	—	5 38
{Gallions .	—	3 22	3 41	3 49	—	—	—	4 24	4 24	—	4 45	—	4 56	5 d19	—	5 40
Beckton	—	—	—	—	—	4 11	—	—	—	—	—	—	—	—	—	—
Silvertown	3 4	—	3 34	—	3 47	3 59	4 5	—	4 13	—	4 34	—	4 52	—	5 4	5 31
North Woolwich..	3 7	—	3 37	—	3 50	4 2	4 8	—	4 16	—	4 37	—	4 55	—	5 7	5 35

d Saturdays only.   *e Saturdays excepted.*

538 LIVERP'L ST. & VICT. & ALBERT DOCKS TO N. WOOLWICH.

WEEK DAYS.

	PM	e	PM	d	e	PM	e	PM	e	d	e	e	d	PM	d	PM
Liverpool St. dep.	—	5 17	—	5 35	5 39	—	6 3	—	6 36	6 42	6 42	—	6 50	7 5	7 10	—
Bethnal Green	—	5 21	—	5 39	5 43	—	6 7	—	—	6 46	6 46	—	—	7 9	—	—
Fenchurch Street	5 9	5 14	5 28	—	5 43	6 2	6 4	6 30	—	—	6 42	6 57	6 47	—	—	7 25
Stepney	5 14	5 19	5 34	—	5 48	6 7	6 11	6 36	—	—	6 47	7 3	6 54	—	—	7 30
Burdett Road ...	5 17	—	5 36	—	5·50	6 9	6 13	6 38	—	—	6 49	7 5	6 56	—	—	7 32
Bromley	—	—	—	—	—	—	—	—	—	—	—	—	—	—	—	—
Bow Road	5 20	5 23	5 39	—	5 53	6 12	6 17	6 41	—	—	6 52	7 8	6 59	—	—	7 35
Stratford Market..	5 25	5 38	5 44	5 58	6 7	6 17	6 31	6 46	6 66	6 56	7 5	7 12	7 13	7 29	7 33	7 41
Canning Town ...	5 30	5 43	5 49	6 3	6 12	6 22	6 35	6 51	7 1	7 1	7 10	7 17	7 18	7 34	7 39	7 46
Victoria { T. B.	5 32	5 45	5 51	6 5	6 14	6 24	6 38	6 53	7 3	7 3	—	7 19	7 20	7 36	7 41	7 48
Docks { C. H.	5 35	5 48	5 54	6 8	6 17	6 27	6 41	6 56	7 6	7 6	—	7 22	7 23	7 39	7 44	7 51
Royal Albert Docks { Con. Rd..	—	—	5·57	—	—	6·33	—	—	7 11	—	—	—	—	—	—	—
{ Central..	—	—	6· 0	—	—	6·36	—	—	7 14	—	—	—	—	—	—	—
{ Manor W.	—	—	6· 2	—	—	6·38	—	—	7 16	—	—	—	—	—	—	—
{ Gallions .	—	—	6· 4	—	—	6·40	—	—	7 18	—	—	—	—	—	—	—
Beckton	—	—	—	—	—	—	—	—	—	—	—	—	—	—	—	—
Silvertown	5 39	5 53	5 58	6 12	6 21	6 31	6 45	7 0	7 10	7 10	—	7 26	7 27	7 43	7 48	7 55
North Woolwich..	5 42	5 57	6 4	6 15	6 24	6 34	6 48	7 3	7 13	7 13	—	7 29	7 30	7 46	7 51	7 58

WEEK DAYS.

	d	e	e	PM	d	e	PM	PM	PM	PM	PM	PM	PM	PM
Liverpool St. dep.	7 48	7 51	—	7·56	8 5	8 5	—	8 50	9·0	—	9 48	10 20	—	11 30
Bethnal Green	—	—	—	8· 0	8 9	8 9	—	—	9·4 3	—	9 52	10 24	—	11 34
Fenchurch Street	—	7 55	7·49	7 49	—	8 33	—	8 54	9 30	—	9 53	10 50	—	
Stepney	—	8 0	7·53	7 56	—	8 39	—	9 1	9 35	—	10 0	10 55	—	
Burdett Road	—	8 2	7·58	7 58	—	8 41	—	9 4	9 37	—	10 3	10 57	—	
Bromley	—	—	—	—	—	—	—	—	—	—	—	—	—	
Bow Road	—	8 5	8·1	8 1	—	8 44	—	9 7	9 40	—	10 6	11 0	—	
Stratford Market.	8 10	8 4	8 10	8 20	8 28	8 33	8 49	9 9	9 27	9 45	10 10	10 40	11 5	11 44
Canning Town ...	8 15	8 9	8 15	8 25	8 33	8 38	8 54	9 14	9 32	9 50	10 15	10 45	11 10	11 49
Victoria { T. B.	8 17	8 11	8 17	8 23	8 35	8 40	8 56	9 16	9 35	9 52	10 17	10 47	11 12	11 51
Docks { C. H.	8 20	8 14	8 20	8 31	8 38	8 43	8 59	9 19	9 33	9 55	10 20	10 50	11 15	11 54
Royal Albert Docks { Con. Rd.. / Central.. / Manor W. / Gallions .	—	—	—	—	—	—	—	—	—	—	—	—	—	
Beckton	—	—	—	—	—	—	9 33	—	—	—	—	—	—	
Silvertown	8 24	8 18	8 24	8 35	8 42	8 47	9 3	9 23	9 42	9 59	10 24	10 54	11 19	11 58
North Woolwich..	8 27	8 21	8 27	8 38	8 48	8 50	9 6	9 28	9 45	10 2	10 27	10 57	11 22	12 1

N. WOOLWICH, VICTORIA & ALBERT DOCKS TO LIVERP'L ST.

WEEK DAYS. (AM)

	AM	AM	AM	AM	AM	AM	AM	AM	AM	AM	AM	AM	AM	AM	AM	AM
N. Woolwich dep.	5 28	5 50	6 0	6 14	—	6 31	6 45	7 3	7 7	7 15	7 22	7 30	—	7 48	7 55	8 7
Silvertown	5 31	5 53	6 4	6 17	—	6 34	6 48	7 6	7 11	7 18	7 25	7 33	—	7 51	7 58	8 9
Beckton	—	—	—	—	6 20	—	—	—	—	—	—	—	—	—	—	—
Royal Albert Docks { Gallions	—	—	—	—	—	—	6 52	—	—	7 22	7 32	7 41	—	7 50	—	
{ Manor W.	—	—	—	—	—	—	6 54	—	—	7 24	7 34	—	—	7 52	—	
{ Central..	—	—	—	—	—	—	6 56	—	—	7 26	7 36	—	—	7 54	—	
{ Con. Rd.	—	—	—	—	—	—	6 59	—	—	7 29	7 39	—	—	7 57	—	
Victoria { C. H.	5 35	5 57	6 8	6 21	6 26	6 33	6 52	7 10	7 14	—	7 29	7 37	7 42	7 49	7 55	8 2 / 8 14
Docks { T. B.	5 37	5 59	6 11	6 24	6 30	6 40	6 54	7 13	7 16	—	7 31	7 39	7 44	7 52	7 57	8 4 / 8 16
Canning Town	5 40	6 3	6 15	6 27	6 33	6 43	6 57	7 16	7 19	7 26	7 34	7 42	7 47	7 53	8 0	8 7 / 8 19
Stratford Market..	5 45	6 8	6 20	6 32	6 37	6 48	7 2	7 21	7 24	7 31	7 39	7 47	7 52	8 0	8 5	8 12 / 8 24
Bow Road	5 49	6 13	—	6 38	—	—	7 7	7 27	—	7 38	7 47	—	—	7 57	8 14	8 16 / 8 43
Bromley	—	—	—	—	—	—	—	—	—	—	—	—	—	—	—	—
Burdett Road	5 52	6 17	—	6 41	—	—	7 10	7 30	7 41	7 50	—	—	8 0	8 17	—	8 20 / 8 46
Stepney	5 55	6 20	—	6 44	—	—	7 13	7 33	7 44	7 54	—	—	8 3	8 20	—	8 23 / 8 49
Fenchurch Street	6 3	6 25	—	6 51	—	—	7 18	7 38	7 52	8 1	—	—	8 9	8 26	—	8 28 / 8 56
Bethnal Green	—	—	6 39	—	7 1	—	—	—	7 40	7 47	7 50	8 2	—	—	—	—
Liverpool Street .	—	—	6 43	—	7 5	7 0	7 30	—	7 43	7 50	8 6	7 59	—	—	8 20	8 46

WEEK DAYS. (AM)

	AM	AM	AM	AM	AM	AM	AM	AM	AM	AM	AM	AM	AM	AM	AM
N. Woolwich dep.	8 24	8 34	8 51	8 59	9 9	9 15	9 42	9 46	—	10 1	10 14	—	10 39	10 47	—
Silvertown	8 27	8 37	8 54	9 2	9 12	9 18	9 45	9 49	—	10 4	10 17	—	10 42	10 50	—
Beckton	—	—	—	—	—	—	—	—	—	—	—	—	—	—	—
Royal Albert Docks { Gallions	—	8 24	—	8 52	—	9 7	9 35	—	9 55	—	10 7	10 30	10 30	—	10 58
{ Manor W.	—	8 26	—	8 54	—	9 9	9 37	—	9 57	—	10 9	10 32	10 32	—	11 0
{ Central..	—	8 25	—	8 56	—	9 11	9 39	—	9 59	—	10 11	10 34	10 34	◄	11 2
{ Con. Rd.	—	8 31	—	8 59	—	9 14	9 42	—	10 2	—	10 14	10 37	10 37	—	11 5
Victoria { C. H.	8 31	8 41	8 58	9 6	9 16	9 22	9 49	9 53	10 5	10 8	10 21	10 46	10 46	10 54	11 8
Docks { T. B.	8 33	8 43	9 0	9 8	9 18	9 24	9 51	9 55	10 7	10 10	10 23	10 42	10 48	10 56	11 10
Canning Town	8 36	8 46	9 3	9 11	9 21	9 27	·54	9 58	10 10	10 13	10 26	10 45	10 51	10 59	11 13
Stratford Market.	8 41	8 51	9 8	9 16	9 26	—	9 59	—	—	—	10 18	10 31	—	10 56	—
Bow Road	8 46	9 3	9 13	—	—	—	—	—	—	—	—	10 35	—	—	—
Bromley	—	—	—	—	—	9 32	—	10 4	10 15	—	—	—	—	—	11 18
Burdett Road	8 50	9 6	9 16	—	—	9 36	—	10 8	10 19	—	—	10 38	—	11 8	11 22
Stepney	8 53	9 9	9 19	—	—	9 39	—	10 11	10 22	—	—	10 41	—	11 11	11 25
Fenchurch Street	8 58	9 16	9 25	—	—	9 44	—	10 17	10·27	—	—	10 45	11 0	11 16	11 30
Bethnal Green	—	9 17	—	9 56	—	—	—	—	—	—	—	—	—	—	—
Liverpool Street .	—	9 21	—	9 36	9 59	—	10 20	—	—	10 42	—	—	11 12	—	

WEEK DAYS.

	d	AM	AM	AM		AM	d	AM	e	PM	d	PM	PM	PM
N. Woolwich dep.	11 0	11 14	11 25	—	11 38	11 43	11 47	11 59	12·4	—	12 14	12 23	—	12 34
Silvertown	11 3	11 17	11 28	—	11 42	11 46	11 50	12·2	12·4	—	12 13	12 17	12 27	12 38
Beckton	—	—	—	—	—	—	—	—	—	—	—	12 20	—	—
Royal Albert Docks { Gallions	—	—	11 31	11 31	11 31	—	12·4	0 12 3	—	12 10	—	12 10	—	12 27
{ Manor W.	—	—	11 33	11 33	11 33	—	12·4	0 12 5	—	12 12	—	12 12	—	12 29
{ Central..	—	—	11 35	11 35	11 35	—	12·4	12 7	—	12 14	—	12 14	—	12 31
{ Con. Rd.	—	—	11 38	11 38	11 38	—	12·7	12 10	—	12 17	—	12 17	—	12 34
Victoria { C. H.	11 7	11 21	11 32	11 32	11 41	11 46	11 50 11 54 12 6	12 12	12 13	12 17	12 21	12 32	12 36	12 43
Docks { T. B.	11 9	11 23	11 34	11 43	11 48	11 52	11 56	12 8	12 13	12 15	12 19	12 23	12 34	12 45
Canning Town	11 12	11 26	11 37	11 46	11 51	11 55	11 59	12 11	12 15	12 18	12 22	12 26	12 37	12 48
Stratford Market..	11 17	11 31	11 42	—	11 56	—	—	12 17	12 20	12 28	12 27	12 31	12 42	12 53
Bow Road	11 33	11 35	11 59	—	—	—	—	—	—	12 35	12 57	—	—	—
Bromley	—	—	—	—	—	—	12 20	—	—	—	—	—	—	—
Burdett Road	11 36	11 48	—	—	12 3	12 7	—	12 24	—	—	12 38	1 0	—	—
Stepney	11 39	11 41	—	11 55	—	12 6	12 10	—	12 27	—	12 41	1 3	12 50	—
Fenchurch Street	11 46	11 46	—	12 0	—	12 11	12 15	—	12 32	—	12 46	1 0	12 53	—
Bethnal Green	—	—	11 51	—	12 6	—	—	12 41	—	12 48	—	—	—	—
Liverpool Street .	11 38	—	11 58	—	12 10	—	12 43	—	12 43	12 52	—	1 6	—	1 10

d Saturdays only.   *e Saturdays excepted.*

WEEK DAYS.	d	PM	e	d	PM	PM	d	PM	d	e	PM	PM	PM	PM	e	d	PM	e	e
N. Woolwich dep.	12 39	12 46	12 51	12 56	1 5	1 14	1 28	1 46	1 51	1 56	—	2 6	2 13	—	—	—	2 47	2 56	—
Silvertown	12 42	12 49	12 54	12 59	1 8	1 17	1 31	1 49	1 54	1 59	—	2 9	2 16	—	—	—	2 50	2 59	—
Beckton	—	—	—	—	—	—	—	—	—	—	—	2 30	—	—	—	—	—	—	—
Royal Albert Docks ⎰ Gallions	—	—	—	—	12 57	1´10	—	1 31	1 31	—	1 58	—	1 58	—	2 32	2 40	2´40	—	2 58
⎱ Manor W.	—	—	—	—	12 59	1´12	—	1 33	1 33	—	2 0	—	2 0	—	2 34	2 42	2´42	—	3 0
Central..	—	—	—	—	1 1	1´14	—	1 35	1 35	—	2 2	—	2 2	—	2 36	2 44	2´44	—	3 2
Con. Rd.	—	—	—	—	1 4	1´17	—	1 38	1 38	—	2 5	—	2 5	—	2 39	2 47	2´47	—	3 5
Victoria ⎰ C. H.	12 46	12 53	12 56	1 3	1 12	1 21	1 35	1 53	1 58	2 3	2 8	213	2 20	2 36	2 42	2 49	2 54	3 3	3 8
Docks ⎱ T. B.	12 48	12 55	1 0	1 5	1 14	1 23	1 37	1 55	2 0	2 5	2 10	215	2 22	2 40	2 44	2 51	2 56	3 5	3 10
Canning Town	12 51	12 58	1 3	1 8	1 17	1 26	1 40	1 58	2 3	2 8	2 13	218	2 25	2 43	2 47	2 54	2 59	3 8	3 13
Stratford Market..	12 56	—	1 8	1 13	1 22	1 31	1 45	—	2 8	2 13	2´18	223	2 20	2 47	—	2 59	—	3 13	—
Bow Road	—	—	—	—	1 35	—	—	—	—	—	—	2 34	—	—	—	—	—	—	—
Bromley	—	—	—	—	1 18	—	—	—	—	—	2´18	—	—	—	—	—	—	—	3 18
Burdett Road	—	1 6	—	—	1 22	1 38	—	2 6	—	—	2´22	—	2 37	—	—	—	3 7	—	3 22
Stepney	—	1 9	—	—	1 25	1 41	—	2 9	—	—	2´25	—	2 40	—	—	—	3 10	—	3 25
Fenchurch Street	—	1 14	—	—	1 30	1 45	—	2 15	—	—	2´30	—	2 44	—	2 59	—	3 15	—	3 31
Bethnal Green	1 20	—	1 16	1 32	1´41	—	2 13	—	—	2 41	2´41	241	—	—	—	3 18	—	3 18	—
Liverpool Street.	1 23	—	1 19	1 35	1 38	—	2 16	—	2 26	2 45	2´45	245	—	3 18	—	3 21	—	3 33	—

WEEK DAYS.	PM	PM	e	d	PM	e	d	PM	PM	d	e	e	PM	e	d	e	PM
N. Woolwich dep.	3 10	3 31	—	3 42	—	4 11	—	4 28	—	4 43	4 50	—	5 2	5 13	—	—	5 24
Silvertown	3 13	3 34	—	3 45	—	4 14	—	4 31	—	4 46	4 53	—	5 7	5 16	5 12	—	5 27
Beckton	—	—	—	—	—	4 18	—	—	—	—	—	—	—	—	—	—	—
Royal Albert Docks ⎰ Gallions	3´4 3	—	3 32	—	4 0	4´ 0	4 5	4´20	4 32	—	—	4 56	—	—	5 3	5´ 9	—
⎱ Manor W.	3´4 5	—	3 34	—	4 2	4´ 2	4 7	4´22	4 34	—	—	4 58	—	—	5 5	5´11	—
Central..	3´4 7	—	3 36	—	4 4	4´ 4	4 9	4´24	4 36	—	—	5 0	—	—	5 7	5´13	—
Con. Rd..	3´4 10	—	3 39	—	4 7	4´ 7	4 12	4´27	4 39	—	—	5 3	—	—	5 10	5´16	—
Victoria ⎰ C. H.	3 17	3 38	3 42	3 49	4 10	4 18	4 24	4 35	4 42	4 50	4 57	5 6	5 11	5 20	5 16	5 20	5 30
Docks ⎱ T. B.	3 19	3 40	3 44	3 51	4 12	4 20	4 26	4 37	4 44	4 53	4 59	5 8	5 13	5 22	5 18	5 22	5 32
Canning Town	3 22	3 43	3 47	3 54	4 15	4 23	4 29	4 40	4 47	4 56	5 2	5 11	5 16	5 25	5 21	5 25	5 35
Stratford Market..	3 27	3 48	—	3 59	—	4 29	4 33	4 45	—	5 3	5 7	5 16	5 21	5 30	5 26	5 30	5 40
Bow Road	3 32	—	—	4 5	—	4 35	—	4´54	—	—	5 12	5 28	—	5 35	—	5 34	5 53
Bromley	—	—	—	—	4 20	—	—	—	—	—	—	—	—	—	—	—	—
Burdett Road	3 35	—	—	4 8	4 24	4 38	—	4´57	4 56	—	5 15	5 31	—	5 38	—	5 37	5 56
Stepney	3 38	—	—	4 11	4´27	4 41	—	5´ 0	4 59	—	5 18	5 34	—	5 41	—	5 40	5 59
Fenchurch Street	3 43	—	3 59	4 16	4 32	4 46	—	5´ 6	5 4	—	5 23	5 41	—	5 46	—	5 45	6 5
Bethnal Green	—	4 4	—	—	—	—	—	5 2	—	5 20	—	5 35	5 39	—	5 47	—	—
Liverpool Street.	—	4 7	—	—	—	—	—	5 6	—	5 24	—	5 39	5 45	—	5 52	—	6 0

WEEK DAYS.	PM	PM	e	e	e	PM	PM	PM	d	e	d	e	PM	e	d	e	PM	e	PM
N. Woolwich dep.	—	530	—	5 38	5 44	5 49	5 54	6 10	6 12	6 20	6 25	6 28	6 33	6 40	6 56	—	7 15	7 37	
Silvertown	—	533	5 35	5 41	5 47	5 53	5 58	6 13	6 15	6 23	6 28	6 31	6 41	6 43	7 0	—	7 18	7 40	
Beckton	5 17	—	—	—	—	—	—	—	—	—	—	—	—	—	—	—	—	—	
Royal Albert Docks ⎰ Gallions	—	—	—	5 33	5´33	—	5´50	—	6 12	—	—	6 30	6´30	—	7 6	—	7´30		
⎱ Manor W.	—	—	—	5 35	5´35	—	5´52	—	6 14	—	—	6 32	6´32	—	7 8	—	7´32		
Central..	—	—	—	5 37	5´37	—	5´54	—	6 16	—	—	6 34	6´34	—	7 10	—	7´34		
Con. Rd..	—	—	—	5 40	5´40	—	5´57	—	6 19	—	—	6 37	6´37	—	7 13	—	7´37		
Victoria ⎰ C. H.	5 23	537	5 39	5 46	5 51	5 58	6 2	6 17	6 19	6 27	6 32	—	6 46	6 47	7 5	7 16	7 22	7 44	
Docks ⎱ T. B.	5 26	539	5 26	5 48	5 53	6 0	6 4	6 19	6 21	6 29	6 34	—	6 48	6 50	7 7	7 18	7 24	7 46	
Canning Town	5 29	542	5 29	5 51	5 56	6 3	6 7	6 22	6 24	6 32	6 37	6 40	6 51	6 53	7 11	7 21	7 27	7 49	
Stratford Market..	5 33	547	5 33	5 57	6 1	6 7	6 12	6 27	6 29	6 37	6 42	6 46	6 56	6 58	7 17	7 26	7 32	7 54	
Bow Road	—	—	—	6 5	—	6 24	—	6 42	—	6 58	—	7 3	—	—	7 37	7 59			
Bromley	—	—	—	—	—	—	—	—	—	—	—	—	—	—	—	—		
Burdett Road	—	—	—	6 9	—	6 28	—	6 45	—	7 1	—	7 6	—	—	7´40	8 2		
Stepney	—	—	—	6 12	—	6 32	—	6 48	—	7 4	—	7 8	—	—	7´43	8 5		
Fenchurch Street	—	—	—	6 17	—	6 39	—	6 53	—	7 12	—	7 16	—	—	7´48	8 10		
Bethnal Green	—	6 6	9	6 12	—	6´17	6´29	6 39	—	—	7 6	—	—	7 27	—	—		
Liverpool Street.	—	6 2	6 13	6 17	—	6 21	6´33	6 44	6 47	—	7 0	7 9	7 18	—	7 31	7 43	7´55	—	

WEEK DAYS.	PM	PM	e	e	PM	e	d	PM	d	PM	PM	e	e	PM	PM	PM	PM
N. Woolwich dep.	7 41	7´58	8 6	8 23	8 45	8 50	9´ 0	9 6	9 20	9 35	10 0	10 8	—	10 30	10 45	11 15	
Silvertown	7 44	8´4 1	8 10	8 26	8 48	8 53	9´ 2	9 9	9 23	9 38	10 3	10 11	—	10 33	10 48	11 18	
Beckton	—	—	—	—	—	—	—	—	—	—	—	10 15	—	—	—	—	
Royal Albert Docks ⎰ Gallions	7´30	—	—	—	—	—	—	—	—	—	—	—	—	—	—	—	
⎱ Manor W.	7´32	—	—	—	—	—	—	—	—	—	—	—	—	—	—	—	
Central..	7´34	—	—	—	—	—	—	—	—	—	—	—	—	—	—	—	
Con. Rd..	7´37	—	—	—	—	—	—	—	—	—	—	—	—	—	—	—	
Victoria ⎰ C. H.	7 48	8´4 5	8 14	8 30	8 52	8 57	9´ 7	9 13	9 27	9 42	10 7	10 15	10 21	10 37	10 52	11 23	
Docks ⎱ T. B.	7 50	8´4 7	8 16	8 32	8 54	8 59	9´ 9	9 15	9 29	9 44	10 9	10 17	10 24	10 39	10 54	11 24	
Canning Town	7 53	8 10	8 19	8 35	8 57	9 2	9 12	9 18	9 32	9 48	10 12	10 20	10 27	10 42	10 57	11 27	
Stratford Market..	7 58	8 16	8 24	8 40	9 2	9 7	9 17	9 24	9 37	9 53	10 17	10 25	10 32	10 47	11 2	11 32	
Bow Road	8 15	8 32	—	—	9 7	—	9 31	—	—	—	—	—	—	—	—	—	
Bromley	—	—	—	—	—	—	—	—	—	—	—	—	—	—	—	—	
Burdett Road	8 18	8 35	—	—	9 10	—	9 34	—	—	—	—	10 33	—	—	—	—	
Stepney	8 22	8 41	—	—	9 13	—	9 37	—	—	—	—	10 36	—	—	—	—	
Fenchurch Street	8 23	8 45	—	—	9 18	—	9 44	—	—	—	—	10 41	—	—	—	—	
Bethnal Green	8 13	—	8´54	—	—	9 34	9 47	—	10 12	—	—	10 49	11 7	11 11	11 49		
Liverpool Street.	8 16	8 33	8 41	8 53	—	9 24	9 37	9 50	9 54	10 15	10 32	—	10 53	11 11	11 14	11 53	

d Saturdays only. *e Saturdays excepted.*

SUNDAYS.	AM	AM	AM	AM	AM	AM	AM	AM	AM	AM	AM	AM	PM	PM	PM	PM	PM	PM	PM
Liverpool St. dep.	5 12	7 26	—	8 30	—	9 7	9 30	—	10 30	—	—	—	1135	—	12 7	—	1 30	—	2 30	237
Bethnal Green	—	7 30	—	8 40	—	911	9 34	—	—	—	—	—	1146	—	12 11	—	1 34	—	—	241
Fenchurch Street	—	—	—	8 19	9 5	—	9 19	10	2 10	19	11	2 11	20	—	12	2	12 19	1	2	—	2 2	2 19	—
Stepney	—	—	—	8 24	9 10	—	9 24	10	7 10	24	11	7 11	25	—	12	7	12 24	1	7	—	2 7	2 26	—
Burdett Road	—	—	—	8 26	9 12	—	9 26	10	9 10	26	11	9 11	27	—	12	9	12 26	1	9	—	2 9	2 28	—
Bow Road	—	—	—	8 29	9 15	—	9 29	—	10 29	11	12 11	30	—	12	12	12 29	1	12	—	2 12	2 31	—
Stratford Market.	7 10	7 47	8 17	8 47	9 20	932	9 47	10	17 10	47	11	17 11	47	1155	12	17	12 47	1	17	1 52	2 17	2 47	257
Canning Town	7 15	7 52	8 22	8 52	9 25	937	9 52	10	22 10	52	11	22 11	52	12 0	12	22	12 52	1	22	1 57	2 22	2 52	3 2
Victoria { T. B.	7 17	7 54	8 24	8 54	9 27	939	9 54	10	24 10	54	11	24 11	54	12 2	12	24	12 54	1	24	1 59	2 24	2 54	3 4
Docks { C. H.	7 20	7 57	8 27	8 57	9 30	942	9 57	10	27 10	57	11	27 11	57	12 5	12	27	12 57	1	27	2	2 2	2 27	2 57	3 7
Royal	Con. Rd.	—	—	—	—	—	—	—	—	—	—	—	—	—	—	—	—	—	—	—	—
Albert	Central ..	—	—	—	—	—	—	—	—	—	—	—	—	—	—	—	—	—	—	—	—
Docks	ManorW.	—	—	—	—	—	—	—	—	—	—	—	—	—	—	—	—	—	—	--	—
	Gallions .	—	—	—	—	—	—	—	—	—	—	—	—	—	—	—	—	—	—	—	—
Beckton ...•......	—	—	—	—	—	—	—	—	—	—	—	—	—	—	—	—	—	—	—	—
Silvertown	—	8	1	8 31	9 1	9 34	946	10	1	10 31	1	1	1 31	12	1	12 9	12 31	1	1	1 31	2	6 2	31	3	1 311
North Woolwich ..	7 27	8	4	8 34	9	4	9 37	949	10	4	10 34	11	4 11	34	12	4	1212 12	34	1	4	1 34	2	9 2	34	3	4 314

SUNDAYS.	PM	PM	PM	PM	PM	PM	PM	PM	PM	PM	PM	PM	PM	PM	PM	PM	PM	PM	PM	PM	PM	PM
Liverpool St. dep.	—	3 7	—	4 7	43	—	5 7	—	6	7	537	—	7	7	730	—	8 25	837	8 45	—	9 15	—	1015	—
Bethnal Green	—	311	—	411	43	—	5 11	—	6	11	641	—	7	11	734	—	—	841	8 49	—	9 19	—	1019	—
Fenchurch Street	3 2	319	4	5 419	—	5 2	519	6	2 6	19	—	7	5 7	19	—	8	2 8	19	—	—	9	5	9 19	10 2	1019	11 2
Stepney	3 7	324	410	424	—	5	7 5	24	6	7 6	24	—	7	10 7	24	—	8	7 8	24	—	—	9	10	9 24	10 7	1026	11 7
Burdett Road	3 9	326	412	426	—	5	9 5	26	6	9 6	26	—	7	12 7	26	—	8	9 8	26	—	—	9	12	9 26	10 9	1028	11 9
Bow Road	312	329	415	429	—	512	5 29	6	12 6	29	—	7	15 7	29	—	8	12 8	29	—	—	9	15	9 29	1012	1031	1112
Stratford Market.	317	347	420	447	455	517	547	6	17 6	47	657	7	20 7	47	755	8	17 8	47	857	9	6 9	20	9 47	1017	1047	1117
Canning Town	322	523	425	452	5	0	522	552	6	22 6	52	7	2 7	25	7	52	8	0 8	22	8 52	9	2 9	11	9 25	9 52	1022	1052	1122
Victoria { T. B.	324	543	427	454	5	2	524	554	6	24 6	54	7	4 7	27	7	54	8	2 8	24	8 54	9	4 9	13	9 27	9 54	1024	1054	1124
Docks { C. H.	327	573	430	457	5	5	527	557	6	27 6	57	7	7 7	30	7	57	8	6 8	27	8 57	9	7 9	15	9 30	9 57	1027	1057	1127
Royal	Con. Rd.	—	—	—	—	—	—	—	—	—	—	—	—	—	—	—	—	—	—	—	—	—
Albert	Central ..	—	—	—	—	—	—	—	—	—	—	—	—	—	—	—	—	—	—	—	—	—
Docks	Manor W	—	—	—	—	—	—	—	—	—	—	—	—	—	—	—	—	—	—	—	—	—
	Gallions	—	—	—	—	—	—	—	—	—	—	—	—	—	—	—	—	—	—	—	—	—
Beckton	—	—	—	—	—	—	—	—	—	—	—	—	—	—	—	—	9 25	—	—	—	—	—
Silvertown	331	4	1	434	5	1 5	9	531	6	1 6	31	7	1	711	7	34	8	1	810	8 31	9	1	911	—	9	34	10	1	1031	11	1	1131
North Woolwich	334	4	4	437	5	4	512	534	6	4 6	34	7	4	714	7	37	8	4	813	8	34 9	4	914	—	9	37	10	4	1034	11	4	1134

N. WOOLWICH VICTORIA & ALBERT DOCKS TO LIVERPOOL ST.

SUNDAYS.	AM	AM	AM	AM	AM	AM	AM	AM	AM	AM	PM	AM	PM	PM	PM	PM	PM	PM
North Woolwich dep.	7 52	8 22	8 52	9 22	952	10 22	1030	1052	11 22	1152	12 22	1230	12 52	1 22	1 52	2 22	2 52	3 22
Silvertown	7.55	8 25	8 55	9 25	955	10 25	1033	1055	11 25	1155	12 25	1233	12 55	1 25	1 55	2 25	2 55	3 25
Beckton	—	—	—	—	—	—	—	—	—	—	—	—	—	—	—	—	—	—
Royal	Gallions	—	—	—	—	—	—	—	—	—	—	—	—	—	—	—	—	—
Albert	ManorW.	—	—	—	—	—	—	—	—	—	—	—	—	—	—	—	—	—
Docks	Central	—	—	—	—	—	—	—	—	—	—	—	—	—	—	—	—	—
	Con. Rd.	—	—	—	—	—	—	—	—	—	—	—	—	—	—	—	—	—
Victoria { C. H.	7 59	8 29	8 59	9 29	959	10 29	1037	1059	11 29	1159	12 29	1237	12 59	1 29	1 59	2 29	2 59	3 29
Docks { T. B.	8 1	8 31	9 1	9 31	10 1	10 31	1039	11 1	11 31	12 1	12 31	1239	1 1	1 31	2 1	2 31	3 1	3 31
Canning Town	8 4	8 34	9 4	9 34	10 4	10 34	1042	11 4	11 34	12 4	12 34	1242	1 4	1 34	2 4	2 34	3 4	3 34
Stratford Market ...	8 9	8 40	9 9	9 39	10 9	10 39	1047	11 9	11 39	12 9	12 39	1247	1 9	1 39	2 9	2 39	3 9	3 39
Bow Road	8 29	8 46	9 31	9 44	—	10 44	11 2	—	11 44	—	12 44	—	1 29	1 44	2 29	2 44	3 29	3 44
Burdett Road	8 32	8 49	9 34	9 47	—	10 47	11 6	—	11 47	—	12 47	—	1 32	1 47	2 32	2 47	3 32	3 47
Stepney	8 35	8 52	9 37	9 50	—	10 50	1110	—	11 50	—	12 50	—	1 35	1 50	2 35	2 50	3 35	3 50
Fenchurch Street	8 40	8 57	9 42	9 55	—	10 55	1115	—	11 55	—	12 55	—	1 40	1 55	2 40	2 55	3 40	3 55
Bethnal Green	8 42	—	9 42	—	—	—	1112	—	—	1242	—	1 12	1 42	—	2 42	—	3 42	—
Liverpool Street.....	8 45	—	9 45	—	1033	—	1115	1127	—	1245	—	1.15	1 45	—	2 45	—	3 45	—

SUNDAYS.	PM	PM	PM	PM	PM	PM	PM	PM	PM	PM	PM	PM	PM	PM	PM	PM	PM	PM	PM	PM	PM	PM
North Woolwich dep.	332	3 52	4 22	4 52	5 22	530.5	52	6 22	6 52	7 22	732	7 52	8 22	832	8 52	9 22	932	952	1022	1052
Silvertown	335	3 55	4 25	4 55	5 25	533.5	55	6 25	6 55	7 25	735.7	55.8	25	835.8	55	9 25	935	955	1025	1055
Beckton	—	—	—	—	—	—	—	—	—	—	—	—	—	—	—	—	—	—	—	—
Royal	Gallions	—	—	—	—	—	—	—	—	—	—	—	—	—	—	—	—	—	—	—
Albert	ManorW.	—	—	—	—	—	—	—	—	—	—	—	—	—	—	—	—	—	—	—
Docks	Central	—	—	—	—	—	—	—	—	—	—	—	—	—	—	—	—	—	—	—
	Con. Rd.	—	—	—	—	—	—	—	—	—	—	—	—	—	—	—	—	—	—	—
Victoria { C. H.	339	3 59	4 29	4 59	5 29	537.5	59	6 29	6 59	7 29	739.7	59.8	29	839.8	59	9 29	939	959	1029	1059
Docks { T. B.	341	4 1	4 31	5 1	5 31	539.6	1	6 31	7 1	7 31	741.8	1	8 31	841.9	1	9 31	941	10 1	1031	11 1
Canning Town	344	4 4	4 34	5 4	5 34	542.6	4	6 34	7 4	7 34	744.8	4	8 34	844.9	4	9 34	944	10 4	1034	11 4
Stratford Market ...	349	4 9	4 39	5 9	5 39	547.6	9	6 39	7 9	7 39	749.8	8	40	849.9	9	9 39	949	10 9	1039	11 9
Bow Road	359	4 29	4 44	5 29	5 44	559.6	29	6 44	7 29	7 44	759	—	8 46	9 19	2 9	44	—	1029	1044	—
Burdett Road	4 2	4 32	4 47	5 32	5 47	6 2	6 32	6 47	7 32	7 47	8 2	—	8 49	9 49	3 29	47	10 6	1032	1047	—
Stepney	4 5	4 35	4 50	5 35	5 50	6 5	6 35	6 50	7 35	7 50	8 5	—	8 52	9 7	9 35	9 50	10 9	1035	1050	—
Fenchurch Street	410	4 40	4 55	5 40	5 55	610.6	40	6 55	7 40	7 55	810	—	8 57	912	9 40	9 55	1014	1040	1055	—
Bethnal Green	412	4 42	—	5 42	—	612	6 42	—	7 27	—	812	—	—	912	9 23	—	—	1027	—	1124
Liverpool Street.....	415	4 45	—	5 45	—	615	6 45	—	7 30	—	815	8 39	—	915	9 26	—	—	1030	—	1127

WEEK DAYS

	AM	AM	AM	AM	AM	AM	AM	AM	AM	AM	AM	AM	AM	AM	AM	AM
LIVERPOOL ST...	5 56	6 30	7 3	7 10	7 35	7 47	8 2	--	8 27	8 38	9 0	—	9 28	10 0	10 8	10 30
Bethnal Green	6 0	6 34	7 8	7 14	—	7 52	8 7	—	—	8 42	9 4	—	9 32	10 5	—	10 34
Coborn Road .	6 4	6 38	7 12	7 18	—	7 56	8 11	—	8 35	8 47		—	9 36	10 9	—	10 38
FENCHURCH ST.	—	6 20	—	—	7 39	—	—	8 6	—	8 35	8 46	9 0	—	9 33	10 8	—
Stepney	—	6 27	—	—	7 45	—	—	8 11	—	8 41	8 52	9 6	—	9 38	10 13	—
Burdett Road	—	6 29	—	—	7 47	—	—	8 14	—	8 43	8 54	9 8	—	9 40	10 15	—
Bow Road	--	6 32	—	—	7 50	—	—	8 17	—	8 50	8 57	9 11	—	9 43	10 19	—
STRATFORD	6 11	6 38	7 18	7 23	7 56	8 2	8 17	8 22	8 40	8 57	9 11	9 16	9 42	10 14	10 26	10 41
Leyton	6 15	7 1	7 22	7 27	7 59	8 5	8 20	8 28	8 44	9 0	9 17	9 21	9 45	10 18	10 30	10 47
Leytonstone	6 19	7 5	7 26	7 32	8 3	8 9	8 24	8 32	8 48	9 4	9 21	9 25	9 49	10 22	10 34	10 51
Snaresbrook	6 23	7 9	7 30	7 36	8 7	8 13	8 28	8 37	8 52	9 8	9 25	9 29	9 53	10 26	10 38	10 55
George Lane	6 26	7 12	7 36	7 40	8 10	8 16	8 31	8 41	8 55	9 11	9 28	9 33	9 56	10 29	10 41	10 58
WOODFORD	6 30	7 16	7 40	7 45	8 14	8 20	8 35	8 45	9 1	9 15	9 32	9 37	10 0	10 33	10 45	11 2
Buckhurst Hill	6 34	7 20	7 44	—	8 18	—	8 39	8 49	—	9 19	9 36	9 41	10 4	10 37	10 49	11 6
LOUGHTON	6 37	7 23	7 51	—	8 21	—	8 42	8 59	—	9 22	9 42	9 48	10 7	10 41	10 52	11 13
Chigwell Lane..	—	—	7 55	—	—	—	—	9 3	—	—	9 46	9 52	10 13	10 45	—	11 17
Theydon Bois ..	—	—	7 59	—	—	—	—	9 7	—	—	9 51	9 57	10 18	10 50	—	11 22
EPPING	—	—	8 9	—	—	—	—	9 13	—	—	9 56	—	10 22	10 54	—	11 28
North Weald ..	—	—	8 15	—	—	—	—	9 19	—	—	10 2	—	—	—	—	11 34
Blake Hall	—	—	8 19	—	—	—	—	9 24	—	—	10 7	—	—	—	—	11 39
ONGAR	—	--	8 23	—	—	—	—	9 28	—	—	10 11	—	—	—	—	11 43

WEEK DAYS.

	AM	AM	AM	PM	d	d	d	d	e	d	d	d	d	d	d	d	d
LIVERPOOL ST...	10 45	11 10	11 40	12 3	—	12 22	12 32	—	12 33	12 43	12 46	1 0	1 2	1 6	—	1 14	1 21
Bethnal Green	10 49	11 14	11 44	12 7	12 19	—	—	12 37	—	12 50	—	1 6	—	—	1 18	—
Coborn Road ..	10 53	11 18	11 48	12 11	12 23	—	—	12 41	—	12 54	—	1 10	—	—	1 22	—
FENCHURCH ST.	10 30	11 6	—	11 51	—	—	12 17	12 28	—	—	—	—	12 46	12 46	1 7	—
Stepney	10 37	11 13	—	11 58	—	—	12 24	12 34	—	—	—	—	12 53	12 53	1 12	—
Burdett Road ..	10 39	11 15	—	12 0	—	—	12 26	12 37	—	—	—	—	12 55	12 55	1 14	—
Bow Road	10 43	11 18	—	12 3	—	—	12 29	12 41	—	—	—	—	12 58	12 58	1 17	—
STRATFORD	10 58	11 24	11 53	12 8	12 35	—	12 43	12 47	12 47	—	1 0	—	1 15	1 16	1 22	1 27	1 32
Leyton	11 2	11 28	11 56	12 17	12 39	—	12 46	12 51	12 51	12 57	1 4	1 12	1 18	1 18	1 25	1 31	1 36
Leytonstone	11 6	11 32	12 0	12 21	12 43	12 37	12 50	12 55	12 56	1 2	1 8	1 16	1 22	1 22	1 29	1 35	1 40
Snaresbrook	11 10	11 36	12 4	12 25	12 47	12 41	12 54	12 58	1 0	1 6	1 12	1 20	1 26	1 26	1 33	1 39	1 44
George Lane	11 13	11 39	12 7	12 28	—	12 44	12 58	1 3	1 3	1 9	—	1 23	1 29	1 29	1 35	1 42	—
WOODFORD	11 17	11 43	12 11	12 32	—	12 48	1 0	1 7	1 7	1 14	—	1 27	1 33	1 33	1 40	1 46	—
Buckhurst Hill	11 21	11 47	12 15	12 38	—	12 52	—	1 11	1 11	1 19	—	1 31	1 37	—	1 44	1 50	—
LOUGHTON	11 24	11 55	12 18	12 41	—	12 56	—	1 16	1 18	1 23	—	1 35	1 40	—	1 48	1 54	—
Chigwell Lane..	—	11ᵈ59	12 26	—	—	1 1	—	1 22	1 22	—	—	1 42	—	—	1 54	—	—
Theydon Bois ..	—	12ᵈ4	12 31	—	—	1 7	—	1 27	1 27	—	—	1 48	—	—	2 0	—	—
EPPING	—	12ᵈ10	12ᵗ35	—	—	1 12	—	1 33	1 34	—	—	1 53	—	—	2 5	—	—
North Weald ..	—	12ᵈ16	—	—	—	—	—	1 38	1 40	—	—	—	—	—	—	—	—
Blake Hall	—	12ᵈ21	—	—	—	—	—	1 42	1 44	—	—	—	—	—	—	—	—
ONGAR	—	12ᵈ25	—	—	—	—	—	1 46	1 48	—	—	—	—	—	—	—	—

WEEK DAYS.

	d	d	e	PM	d	PM	d	PM	PM	PM	PM	PM	e	PM	e	PM
LIVERPOOL ST...	1 30	1 33	1 35	1 42	1 46	1 55	2 3	2 10	2 23	2 42	3 5	3 35	4 —	4 25	—	4 48
Bethnal Green	1 37	1 39	—	1 50	1 59	—	2 14	2 27	2 46	3 9	3 39	4 12	—	4 29	—	4 52
Coborn Road ..	1 41	1 43	—	1 54	2 3	—	2 18	2 31	2 50	3 13	3 43	4 16	—	4 33	—	4 56
FENCHURCH ST.	1 17	1 18	—	—	2 0	—	—	2 9	2 50	3ᵈ20	3 47	4 13	—	4 35	—	—
Stepney	1 24	1 24	—	—	2 6	—	—	2 16	2 57	3ᵈ27	3 54	4 19	—	4 40	—	—
Burdett Road ..	1 26	1 27	—	—	2 8	—	—	2 19	2 59	3ᵈ29	3 56	4 21	—	4 42	—	—
Bow Road	1 29	1 31	—	—	2 11	—	—	2 23	3 2	3ᵈ32	3 59	4 23	—	4 45	—	—
STRATFORD	1 45	1 48	—	1 59	2 8	—	2 21	2 35	2 28	3 19	3 48	4 22	4 29	4 38	4 51	5 1
Leyton	1 50	1 51	1 54	2 2	2 21	2 15	2 25	2 40	2 58	3 22	3 52	4 25	4 32	4 41	4 58	5 5
Leytonstone	1 46	1 54	1 55	1 58	2 6	2 25	2 18	2 29	2 44	3 3	3 26	3 56	4 29	4 35	4 45	5 2	5 9
Snaresbrook	1 58	1 59	2 2	2 10	2 29	2 23	2 33	2 48	3 6	3 30	4 0	4 33	4 39	4 49	5 6	5 12
George Lane	2 1	2 2	2 5	2 13	2 32	2 26	2 36	2 51	3 9	3 33	4 3	4 36	4 42	4 52	5 9	—
WOODFORD	1 55	2 5	2 6	2 9	2 17	2 36	2 30	2 40	2 54	3 13	3 37	4 7	4 40	4 46	4 56	5 13
Buckhurst Hill	1 59	2 10	2 12	2 21	2 40	2 34	2 46	2 58	3 17	3 42	4 11	4 44	4 50	5ᵈ4	5 17	—
LOUGHTON	2 6	2 17	2 17	2 24	2 43	2 37	2 54	3 20	3 45	4 17	4 48	4 56	5ᵈ4	5 23	—
Chigwell Lane..	2 10	2 21	2 21	2 31	—	—	2 58	3ᵈ28	—	4 21	4 54	5ᵈ0	5 29	—
Theydon Bois ..	2 15	2 26	2 29	2 36	—	—	3 2	3ᵈ34	—	4 26	5ᵈ0	5ᵈ15	5 32	—
EPPING	2 20	2 30	2 33	—	—	—	3 9	3ᵈ39	—	4 32	5ᵈ5	5ᵈ20	5 37	—
North Weald ..	2 25	—	—	—	—	—	3 13	—	—	4 38	—	—	5 43	—
Blake Hall	2 29	—	—	—	—	—	3 18	—	—	4 43	—	—	5 48	—
ONGAR	2 33	—	—	—	—	—	3 22	—	—	4 47	—	—	5 52	—

WEEK DAYS.

	e	PM	e									PM				PM
LIVERPOOL ST...	4 57	5 5	5 13	—	5 17	5 33	5 35	5 36	5 39	5 46	—	5 56	—	6 3	6 10	6 16	6 19
Bethnal Green	—	5 9	—	—	5 21	—	5 39	—	5 43	—	—	—	—	6 7	—	—
Coborn Road ..	—	5 13	—	—	5 26	—	5 48	—	5 47	—	—	—	—	6 11	—	—
FENCHURCH ST.	—	—	5 13	—	—	—	—	5 18	—	5 43	—	5 58	5ᵈ57	—	—	6 4
Stepney	—	—	5 18	—	—	—	—	5 25	—	5 48	—	6 5	6ᵈ4	—	—	6 10
Burdett Road ..	—	—	—	—	5 23	—	—	5 27	—	5 50	—	6 6ᵈ4	—	—	6 13
Bow Road	—	—	—	—	—	—	—	5 30	—	5 53	—	6 7	6ᵈ9	—	—	6 17
STRATFORD	5 7	5 18	—	5 28	5 32	—	5 47	—	5 52	—	6 6	6 10	6 17	—	6 26	6 30
Leyton	5 10	5 22	5 26	5 31	5 37	—	5 51	5 55	5 59	6 4	6 9	6 13	6 20	—	6 29	6 33	6 38
Leytonstone	5 14	5 26	5 30	5 34	5 41	—	5 55	5 51	6 0	6 8	6 13	6 16	6 25	6 29	6 33	6 38
Snaresbrook	5 18	5 30	5 34	5 38	5 45	5 50	5 59	5 55	6 4	6 12	6 16	6 22	6 29	6 32	6 36	6 41	6 47
George Lane	5 21	5 33	5 37	5 41	5 48	—	6 2	5 58	6 7	—	6 19	—	6 32	6 36	6 41	6 47
WOODFORD	5 25	5 37	5 40	5 45	5 52	5 57	6 6	6 1	6 11	6 19	6 23	6 30	6 37	6ᵈ40	6 45	6 51
Buckhurst Hill	5 29	5 41	—	5 49	5 56	—	6 10	6 5	6 15	—	6 28	—	6ᵈ44	6 48	6 55
LOUGHTON	5 33	5 47	—	5 53	—	6 7	6 15	—	6 19	—	6 37	6ᵈ44	6 48	6 58
Chigwell Lane..	5 39	5ᵈ51	—	—	6 15	—	6 30	—	6 49	6ᵈ54	—
Theydon Bois ..	5 45	5ᵈ57	—	6 15	6 24	—	6 30	—	6 49	6ᵈ54	7 0	—
EPPING	5 50	6ᵈ4	—	6 20	6 28	—	6 35	—	6 54	6ᵈ59	7 5	—
North Weald ..	—	6ᵈ8	—	6 25	—	—	—	—	—	—	—
Blake Hall	—	6ᵈ13	—	6 29	—	—	—	—	—	—	—
ONGAR	—	6ᵈ17	—	6 34	—	—	—	—	—	—	—

d Saturdays only.   e Saturdays excepted.

WEEK DAYS.	e		e	d	e		e	e	PM	e	d	PM	PM	e	PM	d	PM		e
LIVERPOOL ST. dep.	6 27	6 35	6 37	6 41	—	6 55	7 5	7 25	7 25	7 38	8 5	8 23	8 45	9 0	9 20	9 48
Bethnal Green	6 31	—	6 41	6 45	—		7 9		7 29	7 42	8 9	8 32	8 49	9 8	9 24	9 52
Coborn Road ...	6 35	—	6 49	6 49	—		7 13		7 33	7 46	8 12	8 36	8 53	9 7	9 28	9 56
FENCHURCH ST. ..	6 18	—	—	6 33	6 42	—	6 47	—		7 26	7 49	8 15	—	—	8 54	—
Stepney	6 24	—	—	6 40	6 47	—	6 54	—		7 33	7 56	8 22	—	—	9 1	—
Burdett Road	6 26	—	—	6 43	6 49	—	6 56	—		7 35	7 58	8 24	—	—	9 3	—
Bow Road	6 30	—	—	6 46	6 52	—	6 59	—		7 38	8 1	8 27	—	—	9 7	—
STRATFORD........	6 41	—	6 50	6 53	6 58	—	7 18	7 34	7 37	7 50	8 18	8 32	8 58	9 12	9 33	10 1
Leyton	6 44	—	6 54	6 58	7 2	7 8	7 21	7 39	7 42	7 55	8 22	8 45	9 1	9 16	9 36	10 5
Leytonstone......	6 49	6 52	6 58	7 2	7 7	7 12	7 25	7 43	7 46	7 59	8 26	8 49	9 5	9 20	9 40	10 9
Snaresbrook....	6 52	6 56	7 2	7 6	7 11	7 16	7 29	7 47	7 50	8 3	8 30	8 53	9 9	9 24	9 44	10 13
George Lane	6 56	7 1	7 8	—	7 14	7 19	7 32	7 50	7 53	8 6	8 33	8 56	9 12	9 27	9 47	10 16
WOODFORD	7 0	7 5	7 9	—	7 18	7 23	7 36	7 53	7 57	8 10	8 37	9 0	9 16	9 31	9 51	10 20
Buckhurst Hill ..	—	7 9	7 13	—	7 22	—	7 40	7 58	8 1	8 14	8 41	9 4	9 20	9 35	9 54	10 24
LOUGHTON	—	7 20	7 20	—	7 25	—	7 43	8 1	8 4	8 19	8 46	9 7	9 27	9 38	10 1	10 31
Chigwell Lane..	—	7 24	7 25	—	—	—	7 51			8 24	8 50	—	9 31	—	10 5	10 35
Theydon Bois	—	7 29	7 31	—	—	—	7 57			8 30	8 55	—	9 36	—	10 10	10 40
EPPING	—	7 35	7 38	—	—	—	8 3			8 37	9 0	—	9 41	—	10 14	10 46
North Weald	—	7 41	7 46	—	—	—	—			8 43	—	—	9 46	—	—	10 52
Blake Hall	—	7 46	7 51	—	—	—	—			8 48	—	—	9 51	—	—	10 57
ONGAR............	—	7 50	7 55	—	—	—	—			8 52	—	—	9 56	—	—	11 1

WEEK DAYS.	d	PM	PM	PM	PM	PM	PM			AM	AM	AM	AM	AM	AM	PM
LIVERPOOL ST. dep.	9 48	10 15	10 46	11 15	11 45	12 15				8 30	9 0	9 30	10 30	11 0	11 30	12 0
Bethnal Green ..	9 52	10 19	10 49	11 19	11 49	12 19				8 34	9 4	9 34	10 34	11 4	11 34	12 4
Coborn Road ...	9 56	10 23	10 54	11 23	11 53	12 23				8 38	9 8	9 38	10 38	11 8	11 38	12 8
FENCHURCH ST. ..	—	9 53	—	—	—	—				8 19	8 51	9 19	10 19	10 49	11 20	—
Stepney	—	10 0	—	—	—	—				8 24	8 56	9 24	10 24	10 54	11 25	—
Burdett Road ...	—	10 3	—	—	—	—				8 26	8 58	9 26	10 26	10 56	11 27	—
Bow Road	—	10 6	—	—	—	—				8 29	9 1	9 29	10 29	10 59	11 30	—
STRATFORD........	10 5	10 28	11 0	11 27	11 58	12 28				8 43	9 13	9 42	10 42	11 13	11 36	12 13
Leyton	10 10	10 31	11 4	11 31	12 3	12 32				8 47	9 17	9 47	10 46	11 16	11 47	12 16
Leytonstone......	10 14	10 35	11 8	11 35	12 7	12 36				8 51	9 21	9 51	10 50	11 20	11 51	12 20
Snaresbrook....	10 18	10 39	11 12	11 39	12 11	12 40				8 55	9 25	9 55	10 54	11 24	11 55	12 24
George Lane	10 21	10 42	11 15	11 42	12 14	12 43				8 58	9 28	9 58	10 57	11 27	11 58	12 27
WOODFORD	10 25	10 46	11 19	11 46	12 18	12 47				9 2	9 32	10 2	11 1	11 31	12 2	12 31
Buckhurst Hill ..	10 29	10 50	11 23	11 50	12 22	12 51				9 6	9 36	10 6	11 5	11 35	12 6	12 35
LOUGHTON	10 35	10 53	11 27	11 53	12 26	12 54				9 9	9 39	10 13	11 10	11 38	12 11	12 39
Chigwell Lane..	10 40	—	11 32	—	12 30	—				9 46	10 18	11 16	—	12 16	—
Theydon Bois	10 46	—	11 38	—	12 35	—				9 52	10 24	11 22	—	12 22	—
EPPING	10 53	—	11 43	—	12 41	—				9 57	10 31	11 27	—	12 27	—
North Weald	10 59	—	—	—	—	—				—	10 39	—	—	—	—
Blake Hall	11 5	—	—	—	—	—				—	10 44	—	—	—	—
ONGAR............	11 10	—	—	—	—	—				—	10 48	—	—	—	—

SUNDAY TRAINS.

SUNDAYS.	PM	PM	PM	PM	PM	PM	PM	PM	PM	PM	PM	PM	PM	PM	PM	PM	PM	PM	PM
LIVERPOOL ST.dep.	12 30	1 0	1 30	2 0	2 30	3 30	4 30	5 30	6 30	7 30	7 45	8 30	9 0	9 15	9 30	11 0	11 30
Bethnal Green ..	12 34	1 4	1 34	2 4	2 34	3 34	4 34	5 34	6 34	7 34	7 49	8 34	9 4	9 19	9 34	11 4	11 34
Coborn Road ...	12 38	1 8	1 38	2 8	2 38	3 38	4 38	5 38	6 38	7 38	7 53	8 38	9 8	9 23	9 38	11 8	11 38
FENCHURCH ST. ..	12 19	—	—	1 49	2 19	3 19	4 19	5 19	6 19	7 19	—	8 19	—	—	9 19	10 52	—
Stepney	12 24	—	—	1 54	2 26	3 24	4 24	5 24	6 24	7 24	—	8 24	—	—	9 24	10 58	—
Burdett Road...	12 26	—	—	1 56	2 28	3 26	4 26	5 26	6 26	7 26	—	8 26	—	—	9 26	11 0	—
Bow Road	12 29	—	—	1 59	2 31	3 29	4 29	5 29	6 29	7 29	—	8 29	—	—	9 29	11 3	—
STRATFORD........	12 35	1 13	1 43	2 13	2 37	3 42	4 35	4 3	6 13	6 43	7 43	7 58	8 42	9 13	9 28	9 42	11 11	11 43
Leyton	12 47	1 17	1 47	2 17	2 47	3 47	4 46	5 46	6 17	6 47	7 47	8 2	8 46	9 17	9 32	9 46	11 14	11 47
Leytonstone......	12 51	1 21	1 51	2 21	2 51	3 51	4 50	5 50	6 21	6 51	7 51	8 6	8 50	9 21	9 36	9 50	11 18	11 51
Snaresbrook....	12 55	1 25	1 55	2 25	2 55	3 55	4 54	5 54	6 25	6 55	7 55	8 10	8 54	9 25	9 40	9 54	11 22	11 55
George Lane	12 58	1 28	1 58	2 28	2 58	3 58	4 57	5 57	6 28	6 58	7 58	8 13	8 57	9 28	9 43	9 57	11 25	11 58
WOODFORD..........	1 2	1 32	2 2	2 32	3 2	4 2	4 5	5 16	1 6	6 27	2 8	2 8	8 17	9 1	9 32	9 47	10 1	11 29	12 2
Buckhurst Hill ..	1 6	1 36	2 6	2 36	3 6	4 6	4 55	5 56	3 6	6 36	7 6	8 8	8 21	9 5	9 36	9 50	10 5	11 33	12 6
LOUGHTON	1 11	1 41	2 11	2 43	3 11	4 11	5 10	6 10	6 41	7 8	8 26	9 10	9 39	9 56	10 1	11 0	12 36	12 9
Chigwell Lane..	1 16	1 46	2 16	2 48	3 16	4 16	5 16	6 16	6 46	7 16	8 26	—	10	1 10	18 11	46	—
Theydon Bois	1 22	1 52	2 22	2 54	3 22	4 22	5 22	6 22	6 52	7 22	8 32	—	10	1 10	18 11	46	—
EPPING	1 27	1 57	2 27	3 1	3 27	4 27	5 27	6 27	6 57	7 27	8 29	8 42	9 27	—	10 14	10 31	11 57
North Weald	—	—	—	3 9	—	—	—	—	—	—	8 37	—	—	10 39	—
Blake Hall	—	—	—	3 14	—	—	—	—	—	—	8 42	—	—	10 44	—
ONGAR............	—	—	—	3 18	—	—	—	—	—	—	8 47	—	—	10 48	—

Extra trains Sundays Liverpool St. to Loughton at 10.0 a.m., 3.0, 4.0, 5.0, 7.0, 8.0, 8.15, 8.45, 9.45, 10.0, 10.15, 10.30, 10.45 p.m.

d Saturdays only.   *e* Saturdays excepted.

ONGAR & LOUGHTON TO FENCHURCH ST. & LIVERPOOL ST.

WEEK DAYS.	AM	AM	AM	AM	AM	AM	AM	AM	AM	AM	AM	AM	AM	AM	AM
ONGAR........dep.	—	—	—	—	—	—	—	—	7 7	—	—	—	—	—	—
Blake Hall	—	—	—	—	—	—	—	—	7 12	—	—	—	—	—	—
North Weald ...	—	—	—	—	—	—	—	—	7 16	—	—	—	—	—	—
EPPING	—	—	—	6 30	—	—	—	—	7 23	—	—	—	—	—	—
Theydon Bois	—	—	—	6 34	—	—	—	—	7 27	—	—	—	—	—	8 3
Chigwell Lane....	—	—	—	6 39	—	—	—	—	7 32	—	—	—	—	—	—
LOUGHTON	—	5 5	5 59	6 47	—	7 14	—	7 33	7 41	7 47	—	7 57	—	8 10	—
Buckhurst Hill ..	—	5 9	6 3	6 51	—	7 18	—	7 40	7 45	7 51	—	8 1	—	8 14	8 22
WOODFORD	—	5 13	6 7	6 35	6 55	7 12	7 22	7 28	7 44	7 49	7 55	8 0	8 5	—	8 18	—
George Lane	—	5 16	6 10	6 38	6 58	7 15	7 26	7 31	7 47	7 52	7 58	8 3	8 8	—	8 22	—
Snaresbrook....	—	5 19	6 13	6 41	7 1	7 18	7 29	7 34	7 50	7 55	8 1	8 6	8 11	—	8 25	—
Leytonstone......	—	5 23	6 16	6 45	7 5	7 22	7 33	7 38	7 54	7 59	8 6	8 10	8 15	—	8 29	8 34
Leyton	4 10	5 26	6 19	6 48	7 8	7 26	7 36	7 41	7 57	8 2	—	8 16	—	8 22	8 32	8 37
STRATFORD........	4 15	5 29	6 23	6 51	7 11	7 29	7 41	—	8 0	8 5	—	8 18	—	8 35	—
Bow Road	—	5 36	6 42	—	7 20	7 38	7 47	—	8 14	—	8 26	—	8 43	—
Burdett Road ...	—	5 43	6 45	—	7 23	7 41	7 50	—	8 17	—	8 32	—	8 46	—
Stepney	—	5 47	6 48	—	7 26	7 44	7 54	—	8 20	—	8 35	—	8 49	—
FENCHURCH ST. ..	4 34	5 54	6 55	—	7 32	7 52	8 0	—	8 26	—	8 42	—	8 54	—
Coborn Road ...	4 20	5 35	6 29	6 57	—	7 31	7 57	—	8 6	8 15	—	8 27	—	—
Bethnal Green ..	4 24	5 39	6 33	7 1	—	7 40	8 2	—	8 10	—	8 26	8 31	8 34	—	8 48
LIVERPOOL STREET	4 28	5 42	6 37	7 5	7 30	7 43	8 6	7 57	8 14	8 20	8 23	8 28	8 34	8 37	—	8 52

WEEK DAYS.	AM	AM	AM	AM	AM	AM	AM	AM	AM	AM	AM	AM	AM	AM	AM
Ongar..........dep.	7 49	—	—	—	—	—	—	—	—	—	8 50	—	—	9 36	—
Blake Hall	7 54	—	—	—	—	—	—	—	—	—	8 55	—	—	9 41	—
North Weald	7 58	—	—	—	—	—	—	—	—	—	8 59	—	—	9 45	—
Epping	8 5	—	—	—	—	8 39	—	—	—	9 0	9 6	—	—	9 52	—
Theydon Bois	8 9	—	—	—	—	8 43	—	—	—	9 4	9 10	—	—	9 56	—
Chigwell Lane.....	8 14	—	—	—	—	—	—	—	—	9 9	9 14	—	—	10 1	—
Loughton	8 23	—	—	8 37	8 43	8 50	—	—	—	9 14	9 22	—	9 49	10 9	10 42
Buckhurst Hill	—	—	—	8 41	8 47	8 54	—	—	—	9 19	9 26	—	9 53	10 13	10 46
Woodford..........	8 30	—	8 36	—	8 45	8 51	8 59	9 3	9 9	9 23	9 30	9 35	9 57	10 17	10 50
George Lane.......	8 33	—	8 39	—	8 49	8 54	9 2	—	9 12	9 26	9 33	9 38	10 0	10 20	10 53
Snaresbrook.......	8 36	8 38	8 43	8 46	8 52	8 57	9 5	9 8	9 15	9 29	9 36	9 42	10 3	10 23	10 56
Leytonstone.......	—	8 42	8 46	8 50	8 55	9 1	—	9 12	9 19	9 33	9 40	9 45	10 7	10 27	11 0
Leyton	—	8 45	8 49	8 53	8 58	9 4	—	9 15	9 22	9 36	—	9 48	10 10	10 30	11 3
Stratford..........	—	—	—	8 56	9 2	9 8	—	—	9 27	9 39	—	9 52	10 13	10 33	11 8
Bow Road..........	—	—	—	—	9 9	9 17	—	—	—	9 48	—	10 1	10 45	—	11 33
Burdett Road	—	—	—	—	9 12	9 20	—	—	—	9 48	—	10 4	10 49	—	11 36
Stepney	—	—	—	—	9 15	9 23	—	—	—	9 51	—	10 7	10 52	—	11 39
Fenchurch Street	—	—	—	—	9 21	9 30	—	—	—	9 57	—	10 14	11 1	—	11 46
Coborn Road	—	—	—	9 2	—	9 13	—	—	—	—	—	9 58	10 19	—	11 13
Bethnal Green	—	—	—	9 6	—	9 17	—	—	—	9 56	—	10 2	10 23	—	11 17
Liverpool Street..	8 54	8 59	9 1	9 9	—	9 20	9 21	9 28	9 36	9 59	9 54	10 5	10 27	10 45	11 20

WEEK DAYS.	AM	d	e	d	e	d	e	PM	d	d	d	e	d	e	e
Ongar..........dep.	10 37	—	—	—	—	—	—	—	—	—	—	12 35	12 35	—	—
Blake Hall	10 42	—	—	—	—	—	—	—	—	—	—	12 40	12 40	—	—
North Weald	10 46	—	—	—	—	—	—	—	—	—	—	12 44	12 44	—	—
Epping	10 53	11 13	11 27	—	—	11 55	12 22	—	—	—	—	12 52	12 52	—	11 17
Theydon Bois	10 57	11 17	11 31	—	—	11 59	12 26	—	—	—	—	12 56	12 56	—	11 21
Chigwell Lane.....	11 2	11 22	11 36	—	—	12 4	12 31	—	—	—	—	1 1	1 1	—	11 26
Loughton	11 10	11 27	11 41	11 55	12 3	12 10	12 37	12 57	—	1 14	1 10	1 32	—	—	—
Buckhurst Hill	11 14	11 31	11 45	11 59	12 7	12 14	12 41	1 1	—	1 18	1 13	1 36	—	—	—
Woodford..........	11 18	11 35	11 49	12 4	12 11	12 19	12 45	12 57	1 5	1 10	1 17	1 22	1 17	1 39	—
George Lane.......	11 21	11 38	11 52	12 7	12 15	12 22	12 48	1 0	1 8	1 14	1 21	1 26	1 20	1 42	—
Snaresbrook.......	11 24	11 41	11 55	12 10	12 18	12 25	12 51	1 3	1 11	1 17	1 24	1 29	1 23	1 45	—
Leytonstone.......	11 28	11 45	11 59	12 0	12 14	12 22	12 29	12 55	1 7	1 15	1 21	1 28	1 33	1 27	1 49
Leyton	11 31	11 48	12 2	12 3	12 17	12 26	12 32	12 58	1 10	1 18	1 25	1 31	1 36	1 30	1 52
Stratford..........	11 35	11 52	12 5	12 6	12 21	12 32	12 36	1 2	1 14	1 21	1 28	1 34	1 40	1 34	1 55
Bow Road..........	11 59	12 2	12 5	12 31	12 40	12 50	12 57	1 26	1 26	—	1 41	1 59	—	2 15	—
Burdett Road	11 59	12 2	12 31	12 31	12 43	12 53	1 0	1 29	1 29	—	1 44	2 2	—	2 18	—
Stepney	12 2	12 5	12 34	12 34	12 46	12 56	1 3	1 32	1 32	—	1 47	2 5	—	2 21	—
Fenchurch Street	12 9	12 10	12 41	12 41	12 51	1 3	1 10	1 39	1 39	—	1 53	2 12	—	2 25	—
Coborn Road	—	—	12 11	12 12	12 27	12 37	12 43	1 7	1 20	1 28	1 35	—	1 41	2 1	—
Bethnal Green	—	—	12 15	12 16	12 31	12 41	12 48	1 11	1 24	1 32	1 39	—	1 45	2 7	—
Liverpool Street..	11 44	12 10	12 18	12 20	12 35	12 44	12 51	1 14	1 27	1 35	1 45	—	1 52	1 48	2 10

WEEK DAYS.	d	e	PM	d	e	PM	d	e	PM	e	e	d	PM	e	e	d
Ongar..........dep.	—	1 17	—	—	2 14	—	—	2 55	—	—	3 56	—	—	—	—	—
Blake Hall	—	1 22	—	—	2 19	—	—	3 0	—	—	4 0	—	—	—	—	—
North Weald	—	1 26	—	—	2 23	—	—	3 4	—	—	4 5	—	—	—	—	—
Epping	—	1 35	—	2 14	2 30	2 30	—	3 15	3 12	—	4 23	—	—	—	—	—
Theydon Bois	—	1 39	—	2 18	2 34	2 34	—	3 19	3 16	—	4 27	—	—	—	—	—
Chigwell Lane.....	—	1 44	—	2 23	2 39	2 39	—	3 24	3 21	—	4 32	—	—	—	—	—
Loughton	—	1 53	2 11	2 27	2 47	2 47	3 12	3 30	3 30	3 43	3 57	4 7	4 27	4 40	—	5 5
Buckhurst Hill	—	1 57	2 15	2 31	2 51	2 51	3 16	3 34	3 34	3 46	4 1	4 11	4 31	4 50	4 53	5 9
Woodford..........	1 47	2 1	2 19	2 35	2 55	2 55	3 20	3 38	3 38	3 50	4 5	4 15	4 35	4 54	4 57	5 13
George Lane.......	1 50	2 5	2 22	2 38	2 58	2 58	3 23	3 41	3 41	3 54	4 18	4 38	4 57	5 0	—	5 16
Snaresbrook.......	1 53	2 9	2 26	2 41	3 1	3 1	3 26	3 44	3 44	3 57	4 21	4 41	5 0	5 3	5 15	5 19
Leytonstone.......	1 57	2 13	2 30	2 45	3 5	3 5	3 30	3 48	3 48	4 16	4 25	4 45	5 6	5 17	5 23	5 23
Leyton	2 0	2 16	2 33	2 48	3 8	3 8	3 33	3 51	3 51	4 4	4 19	4 28	4 48	5 6	5 19	5 26
Stratford..........	2 4	2 20	2 38	2 51	3 11	3 11	3 36	3 54	3 54	4 10	4 24	4 31	4 52	5 9	5 15	5 31
Bow Road..........	2 15	—	2 57	2 59	—	3 25	—	4 1	4 34	—	4 43	5 28	5 22	—	—	—
Burdett Road	2 18	3 1	—	3 2	3 28	3 32	4 4	—	4 37	4 46	—	5 31	5 26	—	—	—
Stepney	2 21	3 4	—	3 5	3 31	3 35	4 8	—	4 40	4 49	—	5 34	5 29	—	—	—
Fenchurch Street	2 28	3 11	—	3 11	3 37	3 42	4 15	—	4 46	4 56	—	5 41	5 35	—	—	—
Coborn Road	2 9	2 25	2 43	—	3 17	3 17	3 42	4 0	—	—	4 38	4 58	5 16	—	5 30	5 36
Bethnal Green	2 13	2 29	2 47	—	3 21	3 21	3 46	4 4	—	4 32	4 42	5 2	5 20	—	5 33	5 40
Liverpool Street..	2 16	2 32	2 50	3 18	3 24	3 24	3 50	4 4	7 4	4 25	4 37	4 46	5 6	5 24	5 36	5 43

WEEK DAYS.	e	e	PM	e	e	d	e	e	PM
Ongar..........dep	—	—	4 56	—	5 15	—	—	6 2	—	—	7 0	—
Blake Hall	—	—	5 0	—	5 20	—	—	6 6	—	—	7 4	—
North Weald	—	—	5 6	—	5 24	—	—	6 11	—	—	7 9	—
Epping	—	5 15	5 12	—	5 31	5 47	—	6 15	26 6 35	—	6 55	7 16
Theydon Bois	—	5 19	5 17	—	5 36	5 51	—	6 20	6 31 6 40	—	6 59	7 21
Chigwell Lane.....	—	5 24	5 22	—	5 40	5 56	—	6 25	6 36 6 45	—	7 4	7 25
Loughton	5 7	5 29	5 32	—	5 50	6 6	6 15	6 31	6 46 6 56	7 11	7 38	—
Buckhurst Hill	5 11	5 33	5 35	—	5 54	6 6	6 18	6 35	6 50 6 56	7 15	7 42	—
Woodford..........	5 15	5 35 5 37	5 40 5 52	6 6	6 10 6 16	6 22 6 39	6 54 7	7 2 7 20	7 24 7 46	7 57	—	—
George Lane.......	5 18 5 35	5 41 5 43	5 55 5 56	1 6	6 6 6 18	6 26 6 43	6 57 7	7 2 7 23	7 27 7 49	8 0	—	—
Snaresbrook.......	5 21 5 38	5 44 5 46	5 58 5 6	2 6	6 13 6 20	6 25 6 32	6 50 7	7 4 7 17	7 30 7 52	8 3	—	—
Leytonstone.......	5 25 5 42	5 48 5 50	6 2 6	6 8	6 13 6 20	6 25 6 32	6 50 7	7 47 10	7 13 7 34	7 56 8 7	—	—
Leyton	5 28 5 45	5 51 5 53	6 5 6	6 11	6 16 6 23	6 30 6 37	6 56 7	7 17	7 36 7 51	7 53 8 16	8 33	—
Stratford..........	5 33 5 50	5 57 5 57	6 13 6 14	6 19 6 28	6 33 6 40	6 56 7 11	7 16 7 27	7 36 7 40	8 4 8 13	—	—	—
Bow Road..........	5 40	6 12 6 24	6 18 6 32	—	—	7 5 7 42	—	7 31 7 49	—	8 18	—	—
Burdett Road	5 43	6 15 6 26	6 18 6 35	—	—	7 1 7 31	—	7 34 7 52	—	8 35	—	—
Stepney	5 46	6 18 6 32	6 29 6 22	—	—	7 12 7 42	—	7 34 7 57	7 59	8 45	—	—
Fenchurch Street	5 52	6 25 6 39	6 29 6 39	—	—	7 12 7 48	—	7 41 8 4	—	—	—	—
Coborn Road	5 43 5 55	6 2 6	—	—	6 25 6 33	6 46 7	7 17 7 22	7 27 7 46	8 9	5 30 5 36	—	—
Bethnal Green	5 47 6 1	6 9 6	—	—	6 29 6 37	6 39 6 50 7	6 7 17 26	7 31 7 47	7 50 8 13	5 35 5 40	—	—
Liverpool Street..	5 52 6 6	6 13 6 13	6 26 6 33	6 40 6 42	6 53 7	7 24 7 29	7 34 7 51	7 53 8 16	8 33	5 36 5 43	—	—

d Saturdays only. e Saturdays excepted.

WEEK DAYS.	PM	d	PM	PM	PM	PM	PM	PM	PM			AM	AM	AM	AM	AM
ONGAR.........dep.	—	—	—	8 17	—	—	—	10 10	—			—	—	7 53	—	—
Blake Hall	—	—	—	8 24	—	—	—	10 15	—			—	—	7 59	—	—
North Weald	—	—	—	8 30	—	—	—	10 19	—			—	—	8 5	—	—
EPPING	—	7 45	8 0	8 40	—	9 22	—	10 26	11 2			—	—	8 13	9 22	10 22
Theydon Bois	7 34	7 51	8 4	8 44	—	9 26	—	10 30	11 6			—	—	8 19	9 26	10 26
Chigwell Lane.....	7 39	7 56	8 9	8 49	—	9 31	—	10 35	11 11			—	—	8 25	9 31	10 31
LOUGHTON	7 44	8 3	8 15	8 58	9 12	9 37	10 15	10 44	11 17			7 36	8 7	8 34	9 37	10 37
Buckhurst Hill ...	7 48	8 7	8 19	9 2	9 16	9 41	10 19	10 48	11 21			7 40	8 11	8 38	9 41	10 41
WOODFORD.........	7 52	8 11	8 23	9 6	9 20	9 45	10 23	10 52	11 25			7 44	8 15	8 45	9 45	10 45
George Lane.....	7 55	8 14	8 26	9 10	9 24	9 49	10 26	10 55	11 29			7 47	8 18	8 48	9 48	10 48
Snaresbrook.....	7 58	8 17	8 30	9 13	9 27	9 52	10 29	10 58	11 32			7 50	8 21	8 51	9 51	10 51
Leytonstone........	8 2	8 21	8 34	9 17	9 31	9 56	10 33	11 2	11 36			7 54	8 25	8 55	9 55	10 55
Leyton	8 5	8 24	8 37	9 20	9 34	9 59	10 36	11 5	11 39			7 57	8 28	8 58	9 58	10 58
STRATFORD.........	8 8	8 27	8 41	9 24	9 37	10 2	10 39	11 8	11 45			8 0	8 31	9 1	10 1	11 1
Bow Road..........	8 15	—	—	9 31	—	—	—	—	—			8 29	9	9 31	—	—
Burdett Road......	8 18	—	—	9 34	—	—	—	—	—			8 32	9	9 34	—	—
Stepney	8 22	—	—	9 37	—	—	—	—	—			8 35	9	9 37	—	—
FENCHURCH ST.	8 29	—	—	9 44	—	—	—	—	—			8 40	9	9 42	—	—
Coborn Road	—	8 33	8 47	9 30	9 43	10 8	10 45	11 14	11 50			8 7	8 38	9 8	10 8	11 8
Bethnal Green	—	8 37	8 51	9 34	9 47	10 12	10 49	11 18	11 54			8 11	8 42	9 12	10 12	11 12
LIVERPOOL ST. ...	8 23	8 40	8 54	9 37	9 50	10 15	10 53	11 21	11 57			8 14	8 45	9 15	10 15	11 15

SUNDAYS.	AM	PM	PM	PM	PM	PM	PM	PM	PM	PM	PM	PM	PM	PM
ONGAR.........dep.	—	12 29	—	—	—	—	—	—	—	7 59	—	9 15	—	—
Blake Hall	—	12 35	—	—	—	—	—	—	—	8 5	—	9 22	—	—
North Weald	—	12 41	—	—	—	—	—	—	—	8 11	—	9 28	—	—
EPPING	11 52	12 50	1 22	1 52	2 22	2 52	3 52	4 52	5 52	8 20	8 52	9 37	9 52	10 25
Theydon Bois	11 56	12 54	1 26	1 56	2 26	2 56	3 56	4 56	5 56	8 24	8 56	9 41	9 56	10 29
Chigwell Lane.....	12 1	12 59	1 31	2 1	2 31	3 1	4 1	5 1	6 1	8 29	9 1	9 46	10 1	10 34
LOUGHTON	12 7	1 7	1 37	2 7	2 37	3 7	4 7	5 7	6 7	8 37	9 7	9 52	10 7	10 40
Buckhurst Hill ...	12 11	1 11	1 41	2 11	2 41	3 11	4 11	5 11	6 11	8 41	9 11	9 56	10 11	10 44
WOODFORD.........	12 15	1 15	1 45	2 15	2 45	3 15	4 15	5 15	6 15	8 45	9 15	10 0	10 15	10 48
George Lane.....	12 18	1 18	1 48	2 18	2 48	3 18	4 18	5 18	6 18	8 48	9 18	10 3	10 18	10 51
Snaresbrook.....	12 21	1 21	1 51	2 21	2 51	3 21	4 21	5 21	6 21	8 51	9 21	10 6	10 21	10 54
Leytonstone........	12 25	1 25	1 55	2 25	2 55	3 25	4 25	5 25	6 25	8 55	9 25	10 10	10 25	10 58
Leyton	12 28	1 28	1 58	2 28	2 58	3 28	4 28	5 28	6 28	8 58	9 28	10 13	10 28	11 1
STRATFORD.........	12 31	1 31	2	2 31	3 1	3 31	4 31	5 31	6 31	8 31	9 1	9 31	10 16	10 31	11 4
Bow Road	—	1 59	2 29	2 59	3 29	3 59	4 59	5 59	6 59	—	8 59	—	10 34	—
Burdett Road	—	2 2	2 32	3 2	3 32	4 2	5 2	6 2	7 2	—	9 2	—	10 37	—
Stepney	—	2 5	2 35	3 5	3 35	4 5	5 5	6 5	7 5	—	9 5	—	10 40	—
FENCHURCH ST. ...	—	2 12	2 40	3 10	3 40	4 10	5 10	6 10	7 10	—	9 10	—	10 45	—
Coborn Road	12 38	1 38	2 8	2 38	3 8	3 38	4 38	5 38	6 38	7 38	8 8	8 33	9 3	9 38	10 23	10 35	11 10
Bethnal Green	12 42	1 42	2 12	2 42	3 12	3 42	4 42	5 42	6 42	7 42	8 12	8 42	9 12	9 42	10 27	10 42	11 14
LIVERPOOL ST....	12 45	1 45	2 15	2 45	3 15	3 45	4 45	5 45	6 45	7 45	8 15	8 45	9 15	9 45	10 30	10 45	11 17

Extra trains Sundays Loughton to Liverpool St. will leave at 9.9, 10.7, 11.7, 11.37 a.m.; 12.37, 3.37, 4.37, 5.37, 6.37, 6.52, 7.23, 7.52, 8.22, 8.52, 9.22, and 9.37 p.m.

CHARING X & CANNON ST. TO ADDISCOMBE RD. & BICKLEY.

WEEK DAYS.	AM	AM	AM	AM	AM	AM	AM	AM	AM	e	AM	d		PM	d	e	d	d
CHARING CROSS ....dep.	—	—	—	—	—	—	—	10 22	—	11 10	—	—	12 3	1218	—	—
Waterloo	—	—	—	—	—	—	—	10 24	—	11 12	—	—		1220	—	—
CANNON STREET	5 30	6 32	7 12	7 32	7 56	8 12	8 26	9 24	—	10 56	—	11 52	12 5	—	1230	1232	1236
LONDON BRIDGE........	5 33	6 35	7 15	7 36	7 59	8 15	8 30	9 27	10 29	11 0	11 17	11 55	12 8	1210	1225	1233	1235	1239
New Cross	5 41	6 42	—	7 44	—	8 25	8 38	9 37	10 36	11 7	—	—	12 15	—	1240	—	—
St. John's......	—	6 44	6 45	—	7 47	8 8	—	—	—	—	—	—	—	—	—	—
LEWISHAM JUNCTION ..	—	6 48	7 25	7 50	8 11	8 30	8 42	9 41	10 40	—	11 28	—	12 19	—	—	—	1248
Lady Well	5 47	6 52	7 28	7 53	8 14	8 33	8 45	9 45	10 43	11 13	11 31	12 6	12 22	—	1235	1246	—	1251
Catford Bridge	5 51	6 55	7 31	7 56	8 17	8 36	8 49	9 48	10 45	11 16	11 34	12 9	12 25	—	1238	1249	1248	1254
Lower Sydenham.....	5 56	7 0	7 36	—	8 22	8 41	8 54	9 54	10 50	11 21	11 38	12 13	12 29	—	1242	1253	—	—
New Beckenham	5 58	7 3	7 39	8 2	8 25	8 44	8 57	9 57	10 53	11 23	11 40	12 16	12 32	—	1245	1253	1253	1259
Clock House	6 4	7 6	7 42	8 5	—	8 47	9 0	9 59	10 56	11 26	11 43	12 19	—	—	1246	1256	1256	—
Elmer's End	6 9	7 9	7 46	8 9	—	8 50	9 4	10 3	10 59	11 29	11 46	12 22	—	—	—	—	1 1	1 0
Eden Park	—	7	7 56	8 14	—	9	9 23	10 23	11 4	—	11d52	12d25	—	—	—	1 5	—
West Wickham......	—	7 16	7 59	8 17	—	9	9 26	10 26	11 7	—	11d55	12d29	—	—	—	110	—
Hayes	—	7 20	8 3	8 20	—	9	9 30	10 29	11 11	—	11d58	12d32	—	—	—	114	—
Woodside........	6 13	7 14	7 52	—	—	8 54	9	9 59	10 56	11 31	11 50	12 26	—	—	1252	1 5	1 4	—
ADDISCOMBE ROAD ...	6 17	7 18	7 56	8 31	—	8 58	9	12 10	11 11	11 37	11 54	12 30	—	—	1256	1 9	1 9	—
BECKENHAM JUNCTION.	6 10	—	—	8 29	—	—	—	—	—	—	—	—	1230	—	—	1 3
Shortlands	6 33	—	—	8 53	—	—	—	—	—	—	—	—	—	—	110
Bromley, South......	6 36	—	—	8 56	—	—	—	—	—	—	—	—	1238	—	—	113
BICKLEY	6 39	—	—	9 0	—	—	—	—	—	—	—	—	—	—	118

WEEK DAYS.	d	d		d		d	d	e	d		e		d		d	e	d	d
CHARING CROSS ....dep.	—	1252	—	1 8	—	1 14	—	130	—	1 52	—	—	2 15	—	—	3 10
Waterloo	—	1254	—	1 10	—	1 16	—	132	—	—	—	—	2 17	—	—	3 12
CANNON STREET	1240	1244	—	1258	1 5	—	1 16	—	124	—	140	142	—	152	158	210	—	2 20	2 42	3 14
LONDON BRIDGE........	1243	1247	1 0	1 1	1 8	1 61	1 19	1 21	127	138	143	145	1 58	155	2	1 213	2 23	2 23	2 45	3 17
New Cross	—	—	—	1 8	—	1 28	—	—	—	2	5	2 3	—	2 29	—	2 52	—	3 24
St. John's	—	1255	—	—	—	—	—	—	—	2 6	—	2 33	—	—	—	3 28
LEWISHAM JUNCTION ..	1251	1256	—	1 18	—	1 29	1 32	—	—	2 9	211	—	2 35	—	2 56	3 27	3 30
Lady Well	—	1 2	1 9	115	121	1 27	1 33	135	—	147	—	156	212	214	—	2 38	2 35	2 59	3 30	3 33
Catford Bridge	—	1 5	1 13	—	125	1 30	1 37	138	141	150	155	2 0	—	215	217	225	2 41	2 38	3 2	3 33	3 37
Lower Sydenham......	1 3	1 9	—	122	—	1 34	—	146	—	1 55	2 5	—	218	—	229	2 45	2 42	3 6	3 37	3 41
New Beckenham	1 6	112	—	125	131	—	142	143	149	156	2 3	2 8	216	221	—	232	2 47	2 46	3 9	3 40	3 44
Clock House	1 9	—	121	128	—	1 38	145	146	152	—	2 4	—	219	224	—	2 50	2 48	3 12	3 43	3 47
Elmer's End	113	—	125	—	1 42	1 50	156	—	2 8	—	2 23	227	—	2 52	2 53	3 16	3 46	3 50
Eden Park	—	—	131	—	1 49	—	—	—	2 28	—	2	2 59	3	—	3 51	—
West Wickham......	119	—	134	—	1 52	—	—	—	2 35	—	3 2	3 4	—	3 54	—
Hayes	123	—	138	—	1 56	—	—	—	2 35	—	3 6	3 8	—	3 57	—
Woodside..........	117	—	—	135	—	1 511	542	0	—	212	—	2 27	230	—	2 57	2 56	3 19	3 50	3 54
ADDISCOMBE ROAD ..	122	—	—	140	—	1 561	582	5	—	217	—	2 31	234	—	3 1	3 0	3 23	3 54	3 58
BECKENHAM JUNCTION..	—	116	—	—	135	—	—	2 0	210	—	—	236	—	2 53	—	—
Shortlands	—	128	—	—	140	—	—	2 4	224	—	—	254	—	3 8	—	—
Bromley, South	—	131	—	—	143	—	—	2 7	227	—	—	257	—	3 12	—	—
BICKLEY	—	135	—	—	147	—	—	211	231	—	—	3 1	—	3 16	—	—

d Saturdays only.   e Saturdays excepted.
Passengers to and from Shortlands, Bromley and Bickley change carriages at Beckenham.

WEEK DAYS.	e	d	e	d	e	e	e	e	e	e	d	e	e	d	e
Charing Cross ....dep.	3 30	—	—	4 12	—	4 26	—	4 46	—	510	5 12	—	—	—
Waterloo	3 32	—	—	4 14	—	4 28	—	4 48	—	512	5 14	—	—	—
Cannon Street	—	3 48	4 4	—	4 16	—	4 40	—	5 0	—	—	5 20	5 23	5 30	5 34
London Bridge........	3 37	3 51	4 7	4 19	4 19	4 33	4 43	4 53	5 3	517	5 19	5 23	5 25	5 33	5 37
New Cross	—	3 58	4 13	4 26	—	—	4 50	5 1	—	—	5 26	—	—	—	5 40
St. John's...........	—	—	—	—	4 27	—	—	—	—	—	—	—	—	—
Lewisham Junction .	—	4 2	—	4 30	4 30	—	4 53	5 5	5 13	—	5 30	—	5 36	5 44
Lady Well	—	4 5	4 18	4 33	4 33	—	4 57	5 8	5 16	527	5 33	—	5 39	5 47
Catford Bridge	3 48	4 8	4 21	4 36	4 36	4 44	5 1	5 11	5 19	530	5 36	5 36	5 42	5 50
Lower Sydenham.....	—	4 12	4 26	4 40	4 40	—	5 6	—	5 23	—	5 40	5 40	—	5 54
New Beckenham	—	4 15	4 28	4 42	4 42	—	5 9	5 17	5 26	—	5 43	5 42	5 47	5 57	5 53
Clock House	—	—	4 30	4 45	4 46	—	5 12	5 20	—	538	5 46	5 45	—	5 59
Elmer's End	—	—	4 35	4 48	4 49	—	5 15	5 22	—	—	5 49	5 49	—	—
Eden Park	—	—	4 40	4 52	—	—	5 23	—	—	—	5 53	5 55	—	—
West Wickham.......	—	—	4 43	4 55	—	—	5 26	—	—	—	5 56	5 58	—	—
Hayes	—	—	4 46	4 58	—	—	5 29	—	—	—	5 59	6 2	—	—
Woodside...	—	—	4 39	4 52	4 53	—	5 19	5 26	—	544	5 53	5 53	—	6 5
Addiscombe Road	—	—	4 43	4 56	4 57	—	5 23	5 30	—	549	5 57	5 58	—	6 9
Beckenham Junction.	3 56	4 19	—	—	—	4 60	—	—	5 30	—	—	—	5 51	6 1
Shortlands..........	4 0	—	—	—	—	5 2	—	—	5 34	—	—	—	6 14	6 13
Bromley, South	4 3	—	—	—	4 58	—	—	5 37	—	—	—	6 10	6 16
Bickley	4 6	—	—	—	5 2	—	—	5 42	—	—	—	6 15	6 20

WEEK DAYS.	e	d	e	e	e	e	e	d	e	e	d	e	e	e	d
Charing Cross....dep.	5 34	545	—	545	—	5 54	5 55	—	—	—	6 30	—	—	6 50	7 12
Waterloo.............	5 36	—	—	547	—	5 56	—	—	—	—	6 32	—	—	6 52	7 14
Cannon Street........	—	—	5 48	—	5 56	—	—	6 12	6 16	6 24	6 28	—	6 35	644	—
London Bridge.......	5 41	551	5 51	553	5 59	6 1	6 1	6 15	6 19	6 27	6 31	6 37	6 39	647	6 57	7 19
New Cross............	—	—	—	—	—	—	—	—	—	—	6 38	6 44	—	—	7 26
St. John's	—	—	6 1	—	—	—	—	—	—	—	—	6 47	—	—	—
Lewisham Junction...	—	—	6 4	—	6 11	—	—	6 29	—	6 41	6 50	—	657	—	7 30
Lady Well	5 53	6 0	—	6 11	6 15	6 10	—	6 32	—	6 44	6 53	6 51	7 0	—	7 33
Catford Bridge.......	5 56	6 3	6 8	—	6 19	6 13	6 28	—	6 40	6 47	6 56	—	7 3	7 8	7 36
Lower Sydenham......	—	—	612	6 18	—	6 17	6 32	—	—	—	7 0	6 56	—	7 12	7 40
New Beckenham	6 26	6 9	615	—	6 26	6 20	—	6 39	—	6 53	7 3	6 59	7 9	7 15	7 42
Clock House	—	—	—	6 22	6 29	6 23	6 36	6 42	6 47	—	7 6	7 1	—	7 18	7 45
Elmer's End	—	6 14	—	—	6 33	6 26	6 40	—	6 51	—	7 9	7 5	—	7 22	7 48
Eden Park	—	6 19	—	—	—	6 32	6 45	—	7 1	—	—	—	—	—	7 52
West Wickham	—	6 22	—	—	—	6 38	6 48	—	7 4	—	7 2½	—	—	7 33	7 55
Hayes	—	6 26	—	—	—	6 39	6 52	—	7 7	—	7 28	—	—	7 37	7 58
Woodside	—	—	—	6 28	6 37	6 30	—	6 48	6 55	—	7 13	7 9	—	7 27	7 52
Addiscombe Road.....	—	—	—	6 33	6 42	6 34	—	6 53	6 59	—	7 17	7 13	—	7 31	7 56
Beckenham Junction..	6	6 6	6 8	—	619	—	—	—	—	—	6 57	—	713	—
Shortlands..........	6 14	613	—	630	—	—	—	—	—	7 18	—	738	—
Bromley, South	6 17	616	—	633	—	—	—	—	—	7 7	—	747	—
Bickley	6 20	620	—	633	—	—	—	—	7 11	—	750	—

WEEK DAYS.	e	e	e	d	PM	e	PM	PM	PM	PM	PM	PM	mid
Charing Cross ....dep.	—	—	7 44	—	8 15	8 55	9 20	9 55	1032	11 5	1130	11 48	12 15
Waterloo.............	—	—	7 46	—	8 17	8 57	9 23	9 57	1034	11 7	—	—	—
Cannon Street........	7 12	7 24	—	7 52	—	—	—	—	—	—	—	—	—
London Bridge........	7 15	7 27	7 51	7 55	8 22	9 2	9 28	10 2	1039	11 12	—	—	12 21
New Cross	7 22	—	—	8 2	8 29	9 10	9 35	10 12	1046	11 19	—	—	—
St. John's	7 25	—	—	—	—	—	—	10 15	—	11 22	—	—	—
Lewisham Junction...	—	7 36	8 1	8. 6	8 33	9 13	9 39	10 18	1050	11 25	—	—	12 31
Lady Well	7 30	7 39	8 4	8 9	8 36	9 16	9 42	10 21	1053	11 28	—	12 3	12 34
Catford Bridge........	7 33	7 42	8 7	8 12	8 39	9 20	9 45	10 24	1056	11 31	—	12 6	12 37
Lower Sydenham......	7 37	—	8 12	8 16	8 43	9 25	9 49	10 28	11 0	11 35	—	12 10	—
New Beckenham	7 ,40	7 48	8 15	8 19	8 46	9 28	9 52	10 31	11 3	11 38	—	12 12	12 42
Clock House	—	7 50	8 18	8 23	8 49	9 31	9 55	10 34	11 6	11 41	—	12 15	12 45
Elmer's End	—	7 55	8 22	8 25	8 52	9 35	9 58	10 38	11 9	11 44	—	12 18	12 48
Eden Park	—	8 3	—	—	—	—	—	—	—	—	—	—	—
West Wickham...	—	8 6	—	9 0	9 42	—	10 46	—	—	—	12½46	—	—
Hayes	—	8 10	—	9 4	9 46	—	10 50	—	—	—	12½30	—	—
Woodside	—	7 59	8 26	8 29	8 56	9 37	10 2	10 42	1113	11 48	—	12 22	12 52
Addiscombe Road.....	—	8 4	8 31	8 33	9 0	9 41	10 6	10 46	1117	11 52	—	12 26	12 56
Beckenham Junction..	7 43	—	—	—	—	—	—	—	—	—	1150	—	—
Shortlands..........	8 2	—	—	—	—	—	—	—	—	—	1156	—	—
Bromley, South	8 5	—	—	—	—	—	—	—	—	—	1159	—	—
Bickley	8 8	—	—	—	—	—	—	—	—	—	12 3	—	—

SUNDAYS.	AM	AM	AM	AM		PM	PM	PM	PM	PM	PM	PM
Charing Cross ...dep	7 55	8 35	9 55	10 25		6 40	7 25	7 50	8 20	8 50	9 28	10 20
Waterloo.............	7 57	8 37	9 57	10 27		6 42	7 27	7 52	—	8 52	9 30	10 22
Cannon Street........	—	—	—	—		—	—	—	—	—	—	—
London Bridge	8 2	8 42	10 2	10 32		6 47	7 32	7 57	8 27	8 57	9 36	10 27
New Cross	8 9	8 49	10 9	10 39		6 54	7 39	8 4	8 34	9 4	9 44	—
St. John's	—	—	—	—		—	—	—	—	—	—	—
Lewisham Junction ..	8 12	8 53	10 12	10 42		6 58	7 42	8 7	8 37	9 7	9 47	10 34
Lady Well	8 15	8 56	10 15	10 45		7 1	7 45	8 10	8 40	9 10	9 50	10 37
Catford Bridge.......	8 18	8 59	10 18	10 48		7 4	7 48	8 13	8 43	9 13	9 53	10 40
Lower Sydenham......	8 23	9 3	10 22	10 52		7 8	7 52	8 17	8 47	9 17	9 59	10 43
New Beckenham	8 25	9 5	10 24	10 54		7 10	7 54	8 19	8 49	9 19	10 1	10 46
Clock House	8 28	9 8	10 27	10 57		7 13	7 57	8 22	8 52	9 22	10 4	10 50
Elmer's End	8 31	9 11	10 30	11 2		7 16	8 0	8 25	8 55	10 7	10 53
Eden Park	—	—	—	—		7 21	—	—	9 30	—	—
West Wickham	—	—	10 36	—		7 24	—	8 31	—	9 33	—
Hayes..............	—	—	10 40	—		7 27	—	8 35	—	9 36	—
Woodside	8 34	9 14	—	11 4		—	8 4	—	8 58	—	10 10	10 56
Addiscombe Road.....	8 38	9 18	—	11 8		—	8 8	—	9 2	—	10 13	11 0
Beckenham Junction..	—	—	—	—		—	—	—	—	—	—	—
Shortlands	—	—	—	—		—	—	—	—	—	—	—
Bromley, South	—	—	—	—		—	—	—	—	—	—	—
Bickley	—	—	—	—		—	—	—	—	—	—	—

Vertical text in center of Sundays table: Then at the same minutes past each hour until 1.55, 2.55, 3.55, 4.55, 5.55, stops at Eden Park.

Passengers to and from Shortlands, Bromley and Bickley change carriages at Beckenham.
d Saturdays only.   e Saturdays excepted.   h Wednesdays only.

July, 1923.   T

WEEK DAYS (Section 1)

	AM	AM	AM	AM	AM	AM	AM	AM	AM	AM	AM	AM	AM	AM	AM	AM	AM
BICKLEY ....dep.	—	—	—	—	—	—	—	—	—	—	7 20	—	7 42	—	—	—	8 5
Bromley, South	—	—	—	—	—	—	—	—	—	—	7 24	—	7 46	—	—	—	8 9
Shortlands............	—	—	—	—	—	—	—	—	—	—	7 28	—	7 49	—	—	—	8 12
BECKENHAM JUNCTION..	—	—	—	—	—	—	—	—	—	—	7 44	—	7 55	—	—	—	8 22
ADDISCOMBE ROAD	3 55	5 15	6	6 39	6 59	—	—	—	7 28	7 35	—	7 42	—	7 55	—	8 9	—
Woodside	3 57	5 17	6 2	6 41	7 1	7 6	—	—	7 30	—	—	7 44	—	7 57	—	8 11	—
Hayes	—	—	6 31	—	—	—	—	—	7 26	—	7 34	—	7 53	—	—	—
West Wickham	—	—	6 34	—	—	—	—	—	7 29	—	7 37	—	7 56	—	—	—
Eden Park	—	—	—	—	—	—	—	—	7 32	—	7 40	—	7 59	—	—	—
Elmer's End	4 0	5 20	6 6	6 45	—	7 9	—	—	7 39	—	7 47	—	—	8 4	—	—
Clock House	4 2	5 23	6 9	6 48	7 6	7 12	—	7 28	—	—	7 50	—	—	8 6	8 16	—
New Beckenham......	—	5 26	6 12	6 52	—	—	—	—	—	7 46	—	7 58	—	8 9	—	8 25
Lower Sydenham	—	5 28	6 14	6 54	—	7 16	—	—	7 44	—	7 54	—	8 6	8 11	—	8 27
Catford Bridge.......	4 9	5 32	6 18	6 58	7 13	—	7 30	7 34	—	7 51	7 58	8 3	8 10	8 15	8 23	8 31
Lady Well	4 12	5 35	6 21	7 1	—	7 22	—	—	—	7 54	8 1	8 6	8 13	8 18	8 26	8 35
LEWISHAM JUNCTION ..	4 15	5 38	6 24	7 4	—	—	—	—	—	—	8 4	—	—	—	—	8 38
St. John's	4 18	5 41	6 27	—	—	—	—	—	—	7 58	—	—	—	—	—	—
New Cross	4 21	5 44	6 30	7 8	—	—	—	—	—	8 0	—	8 11	—	—	8 31	—
LONDON BRIDGE.......	4 30	5 50	6 37	7 16	7 26	7 34	7 44	7 46	7 54	7 58	8 8	8 16	8 18	8 26	8 28	8 38	8 48
CANNON STREET.......	4 34	—	7 20	—	7 33	7 43	—	—	8 0	8 13	8 20	—	—	8 32	—	8 52
Waterloo	—	5 55	6 42	—	7 31	—	—	7 51	7 58	—	—	8 23	8 31	—	8 43	—
CHARING CROSS.......	—	5 59	6 46	—	7 35	—	—	7 55	8 0	—	—	8 27	8 35	—	8 47	—

WEEK DAYS (Section 2)

	AM	AM	AM	AM	AM	AM	AM	AM	AM	AM	e	e	d	e	PM	a
BICKLEY ....dep.	—	8 14	—	—	8 52	—	9 7	—	—	—	—	—	—	—	—	—
Bromley, South	—	8 17	—	—	9 1	—	9 12	—	—	—	—	—	—	—	—	—
Shortlands............	—	8 21	—	—	9 4	—	9 1	—	—	—	—	—	—	—	—	—
BECKENHAM JUNCTION..	—	8 38	—	—	9 12	—	9 31	—	—	—	—	—	—	—	—	—
ADDISCOMBE ROAD	8 23	—	8 41	8 54	—	9 12	—	9 51	10 10	10 45	11 7	11 23	11 45	12 36	12 50
Woodside	8 25	—	8 43	8 56	—	9 14	—	9 33	10 12	10 47	11 9	11 25	11 48	12 38	12 52
Hayes	8 15	8 39	—	—	—	9 3	—	—	10 2	10 37	—	11 13	—	12*28	—
West Wickham	8 18	8 42	—	—	—	9 6	—	—	10 5	10 40	—	11 16	—	12*31	—
Eden Park	8 21	8 45	—	—	—	9 9	—	—	10 9	10 43	—	11 19	—	—	—
Elmer's End	8 30	8 48	—	—	—	9 18	—	9 37	10 15	10 50	11 13	11 29	11 51	12 41	12 56
Clock House	8 33	8 51	—	9 1	—	9 21	—	9 40	10 18	10 53	11 16	11 32	11 54	12 44	12 58
New Beckenham......	8 37	—	8 43	—	9 4	9 14	9 25	—	9 44	10 21	10 56	11 19	11 34	11 57	12 46	1 2
Lower Sydenham	—	8 44	—	—	9 15	—	—	9 46	10 23	10 58	11 21	11 37	11 59	12 48	—
Catford Bridge.......	—	8 57	8 48	8 53	9 9	9 19	—	9 37	9 50	10 27	11 2	11 25	11 41	12 3	12 52	1 6
Lady Well	—	9 0	9 51	8 56	—	9 22	—	9 40	9 53	10 30	11 5	11 28	11 44	12 6	12 56	1 9
LEWISHAM JUNCTION ..	—	—	—	—	—	—	—	—	10 33	—	—	—	12 9	—	—
St. John's	—	9 4	—	—	—	—	—	—	10 36	11 9	—	11 48	—	1 0	—
New Cross	—	9 6	—	—	—	9 45	—	—	—	11 12	—	11 51	—	1 3	—
LONDON BRIDGE......	8 52	9 14	9 3	9 8	9 20	9 34	9 38	9 52	10 4	10 44	11 9	11 38	11 58	12 18	1 10	1 21
CANNON STREET.......	8 56	—	9 12	9 24	9 38	—	9 56	—	11 23	11 42	—	—	—	1 26
Waterloo	—	9 19	9 8	—	—	9 42	—	10 9	10 49	—	—	12 3	12 23	1 15	—
CHARING CROSS.......	—	9 23	9 12	—	—	9 45	—	10 13	10 53	—	—	12 7	12 27	1 19	—

WEEK DAYS (Section 3)

	e	d	d	PM	e	d	e	d	e	d	e	d	e	e	e	d
BICKLEY ....dep.	—	12 43	1 31	—	—	—	—	—	—	—	3 52	—	—	—	—
Bromley, South	—	12 47	1 34	—	—	—	—	—	—	—	3 56	—	—	—	—
Shortlands............	—	12 51	1 37	—	—	—	—	—	—	—	3 59	—	—	—	—
BECKENHAM JUNCTION..	—	1 9	1 42	—	—	—	—	—	—	—	4 12	—	4 45	4 41	—
ADDISCOMBE ROAD	1 0	1 13	—	—	1 35	1 57	2 10	2 25	2 43	2 55	3 8	3 31	4 8	4 12	—	5 12
Woodside	1 2	1 15	—	—	1 37	1 59	2 12	2 27	2 45	2 58	3 10	3 33	4 10	4 14	—	5 14
Hayes	—	12 57	—	—	—	1 47	—	—	2 35	2 42	—	—	4 0	4 4	—	5 4
West Wickham	—	1 0	—	—	—	1 50	—	—	2 38	2 45	—	—	4 3	4 7	—	5 7
Eden Park	—	1 3	—	—	—	1 52	—	—	2 41	2 48	—	—	4 6	4 10	—	5 10
Elmer's End	1 5	1 17	—	—	1 40	2 2	2 16	2 31	2 48	3 2	3 14	3 37	4 14	4 17	—	5 17
Clock House	1 8	1 20	—	—	1 43	2 5	2 19	2 34	2 51	3 6	3 17	3 40	4 17	4 20	—	5 20
New Beckenham......	1 11	1 24	1 13	—	1 47	2 8	2 22	2 37	2 54	3 9	3 21	3 43	4 20	4 23	4 48	4 44	5 23
Lower Sydenham	1 13	—	1 15	—	1 49	2 12	2 24	2 39	2 56	3 11	3 23	3 45	4 22	4 25	—	4 46	5 25
Catford Bridge.......	1 17	1 30	1 19	—	1 53	2 16	2 28	2 43	3 0	3 15	3 27	3 49	4 26	4 29	4 53	4 50	5 29
Lady Well	1 20	1 34	1 22	—	1 56	2 19	2 31	2 46	3 3	3 18	3 30	3 52	4 29	4 32	4 56	4 54	5 32
LEWISHAM JUNCTION ..	1 24	1 37	1 25	—	—	2 22	2 34	—	3 6	3 21	3 33	3 55	4 32	4 35	4 59	4 57	5 35
St. John's	1 27	1 40	—	—	2 0	—	—	—	3 9	—	3 58	—	—	—	—
New Cross	1 30	1 43	1 29	—	—	2 25	—	—	3 12	3 25	3 37	4 2	4 36	4 39	—	5 1	5 38
LONDON BRIDGE.......	1 38	1 52	1 36	—	2 9	2 32	2 44	2 57	3 20	3 32	3 44	4 10	4 44	4 46	5 3	5 9	5 45
CANNON STREET.......	1 43	1 57	1 40	—	—	2 37	2 43	3 1	3 24	3 35	—	4 16	4 48	—	5 12	5 13	—
Waterloo	—	—	—	2 14	—	—	—	—	3 50	—	—	4 51	—	5 50
CHARING CROSS.......	—	—	—	2 2	2 18	—	—	—	—	3 54	—	—	4 55	—	5 54

WEEK DAYS (Section 4)

	e	e	d	e	PM	e	e	e	d	e	d	e	PM	d	e	e	PM
BICKLEY ....dep	4 42	—	—	—	5 17	—	—	—	5 52	—	6 55	—	6 55	—	—
Bromley, South	4 46	—	—	—	5 28	—	—	—	6 15	—	6 58	—	6 58	—	8 1
Shortlands..........	4 49	—	—	—	—	—	—	—	5 59	—	7 1	—	7 1	—	7 40
BECKENHAM JUNCTION..	5 15	—	—	5 36	5 57	—	—	—	6 29	—	7 6	—	7 25	—	8 9
ADDISCOMBE ROAD	—	5 18	5 30	5 35	—	—	5 56	6 4	6 16	—	6 30	—	6 59	7 14	—	7 26	—
Woodside	—	5 21	5 32	5 37	—	5 52	5 59	6 6	6 18	—	6 22	—	7 2	7 16	—	7 28	—
Hayes	—	5 3	—	—	—	5 38	—	6 8	—	6 20	—	7 5	—	7 11	—
West Wickham	—	5 6	—	—	—	5 41	—	6 11	—	6 23	—	7 8	—	7 14	—
Eden Park	—	5 9	—	—	—	5 41	—	6 14	—	6 26	—	7 11	—	7 17	—
Elmer's End	—	5 22	5 36	5 41	—	—	5 56	6 6	6 21	—	6 36	—	7 20	—	7 32	—
Clock House	—	5 25	5 39	5 44	—	—	5 59	6 4	6 12	6 24	—	6 39	—	7 7	7 23	—	7 35	—
New Beckenham......	5 18	5 29	5 42	5 47	5 38	—	6 2	—	—	6 27	6 31	6 42	—	7 10	7 27	7 28	7 38	—
Lower Sydenham	5 20	5 31	5 44	5 50	5 40	—	—	6 8	—	6 29	6 33	6 44	—	—	7 29	7 30	7 40	—
Catford Bridge.......	5 24	5 35	5 48	5 54	5 44	—	6 7	6 12	6 18	6 33	6 38	6 48	—	7 15	7 33	7 34	7 44	—
Lady Well	5 28	5 38	5 51	5 57	5 47	6 4	—	6 15	—	6 36	6 41	6 51	—	7 18	7 36	—	7 47	—
LEWISHAM JUNCTION ..	—	5 54	—	6 6	—	6 17	6 24	6 39	—	6 54	—	7 39	7 39	—
St. John's	5 32	—	—	6 1	—	—	6 20	6 28	—	—	—	—	—	—
New Cross	5 35	5 44	5 58	6 4	5 52	6 11	6 13	6 23	6 31	6 43	6 47	6 57	7 23	7 42	7 43	7 52	8 22
LONDON BRIDGE.......	5 42	5 51	6 5	6 12	6 0	6 18	6 20	6 30	6 40	6 50	6 54	7 4	7 30	7 49	7 49	7 59	8 29
CANNON STREET.......	5 57	—	6 16	6 4	—	6 24	6 36	6 44	—	7 0	7 8	—	—
Waterloo............	5 47	—	6 11	—	6 23	—	—	6 55	—	—	7 54	8 4	—
CHARING CROSS.......	5 51	—	6 14	—	6 27	—	—	6 58	—	7 25	7 37	7 59	7 58	8 37

Passengers to and from Shortlands, Bromley and Bickley change carriages at Beckenham.

d Saturdays only.   e Saturdays excepted.

WEEK DAYS.	e	d	e	e	e	PM	PM	PM	PM
BICKLEY ....dep.	—	—	—	—	—	—	—	—	—
Bromley, South	—	—	—	—	—	—	—	—	—
Shortlands...........	—	—	—	—	—	—	—	—	—
BECKENHAM JUNCTION..	—	—	—	—	—	—	—	—	—
ADDISCOMBE ROAD	8 3	8 11	9 23	8 35	9 0	9 30	10 2	10 31	11 23
Woodside	8 6	8 13	8 26	8 37	9 5	9 32	10 4	10 33	11 25
Hayes	7 46	8 4	—	8 25	—	9 20	—	10 18	—
West Wickham	—	8 7	—	8 28	—	9 23	—	10 21	—
Eden Park	—	8 10	—	8 31	—	—	—	—	—
Elmer's End	8 10	8 16	8 30	8 42	9 7	9 36	10 7	10 33	11 26
Clock House	8 13	8 19	8 33	8 44	9 10	9 39	10 10	10 36	11 29
New Beckenham	8 17	8 22	8 36	8 48	9 14	9 42	10 13	10 40	11 33
Lower Sydenham	8 19	8 24	8 38	8 50	—	9 44	10 15	10 42	11 35
Catford Bridge.......	8 23	8 28	8 42	8 54	9 18	9 48	10 19	10 46	11 39
Lady Well	8 26	8 31	8 45	8 57	9 22	9 51	10 22	10 49	11 42
LEWISHAM JUNCTION ..	8 29	8 34	8 48	9 0	9 26	9 54	10 25	10 52	11 45
St. John's	—	—	—	9 3	—	9 57	—	10 55	—
New Cross	8 31	8 39	8 52	9 5	9 31	10 0	10 29	10 58	11 50
LONDON BRIDGE.......	8 38	8 45	8 59	9 13	9 38	10 7	10 36	11 9	11 56
CANNON STREET.......	—	—	—	—	—	—	—	—	—
Waterloo	8 44	8 50	9 4	9 19	—	10 12	10 41	11 15	—
CHARING CROSS	8 48	8 54	9 9	9 23	—	10 16	10 45	11 19	12 2

SUNDAYS.	AM	AM	AM	AM	AM	PM	PM		PM	PM	PM	PM	PM	PM	PM
BICKLEY dep.........	—	—	—	—	—	—	—		—	—	—	—	—	—	—
Bromley, South	—	—	—	—	—	—	—		—	—	—	—	—	—	—
Shortlands...........	—	—	—	—	—	—	—		—	—	—	—	—	—	—
BECKENHAM JUNCTION..	—	—	—	—	—	—	—		—	—	—	—	—	—	—
ADDISCOMBE ROAD ...	7 27	8 55	10 24	—	11 23	12 24	—		—	—	—	9 24	—	10 25	
Woodside	7 29	8 57	10 26	—	11 26	12 26	—		—	—	—	9 26	—	10 27	
Hayes	—	—	—	10 52	—	—	12 50		5 54	6 50	7 50	8 46	—	9 55	—
West Wickham	—	—	—	10 55	—	—	12 53		5 57	6 53	7 53	8 49	—	9 58	—
Eden Park	—	—	—	—	—	—	—		6 0	6 56	7 56	8 52	—	10 1	—
Elmer's End	7 32	9 0	10 29	11 1	11 29	12 29	12 59		6 6	7 0	8 1	8 57	9 29	10 6	10 30
Clock House	7 35	9 3	10 32	11 3	11 32	12 31	1 1		6 9	7 2	8 3	8 59	9 32	10 8	10 33
New Beckenham......	7 38	9 6	10 35	11 6	11 35	12 34	1 4		6 12	7 5	8 5	9 2	9 35	10 10	10 37
Lower Sydenham	7 40	9 8	10 37	11 8	11 37	12 36	1 6		6 15	7 7	8 8	9 4	9 37	10 13	10 40
Catford Bridge.......	7 44	9 12	10 41	11 12	11 41	12 40	1 10		6 19	7 11	8 11	9 8	9 41	10 17	10 44
Lady Well	7 47	9 15	10 44	11 16	11 44	12 43	1 13		6 23	7 14	8 15	9 11	9 44	10 20	10 47
LEWISHAM JUNCTION ..	7 50	9 18	10 47	11 19	11 47	12 46	1 16		6 26	7 17	8 18	9 14	9 47	10 23	10 50
St. John's	—	—	—	—	—	—	—		—	—	—	—	—	—	—
New Cross	7 54	9 21	10 50	11 23	11 51	12 52	1 19		6 30	7 21	8 21	9 17	9 50	10 26	10 53
LONDON BRIDGE.......	8 1	9 28	10 57	11 31	11 57	12 59	1 26		6 37	7 28	8 28	9 23	9 57	10 33	11 0
CANNON STREET.......	—	—	—	—	—	—	—		—	—	—	—	—	—	—
Waterloo............	8 5	9 33	11 2	11 36	12 2	1 4	1 31		6 42	7 33	8 33	—	10 2	10 38	11 5
CHARING CROSS........	8 9	9 37	11 6	11 40	12 6	1 8	1 35		6 45	7 37	8 37	9 30	10 5	10 42	11 8

Then at the same minutes past each hour until 2.50, 3.50, 4.50 from Hayes stops at Eden Park.

CHARING X & CANNON ST. TO WOOLWICH & SLADE'S GREEN.

WEEK DAYS.	AM	AM	AM	AM	AM	AM	AM	AM	AM	AM	AM	AM	AM	AM	AM	AM
CHARING CROSS ....dep.	—	—	5 18	—	5 57	6 15	—	6 40	—	7 2	—	—	—	—	—	8 10
Waterloo	—	—	5 20	—	5 59	6 17	—	6 42	—	7 4	—	—	—	—	—	8 12
CANNON STREET	—	4 43	—	5 53	—	—	6 28	—	6 50	—	—	7 32	7 40	7 44	7 48	8 8
LONDON BRIDGE	3 22	4 46	5 25	5 56	6 4	6 22	6 33	6 47	6 53	7 9	—	7 35	7 43	7 47	7 51	8 11
GREENWICH	—	4 56	—	6 7	—	6 30	—	6 55	—	7 20	—	7 43	—	—	—	—
MazeHill(E.Greenwich)	—	4 59	—	6 10	—	6 33	—	6 58	—	7 23	—	7 46	—	—	—	—
Westcombe Park	—	5 3	—	6 14	—	6 36	—	7 1	—	7 26	—	7 49	—	—	—	—
New Cross	—	—	5 34	—	6 11	—	6 38	—	7 0	—	7 27	—	7 50	—	7 58	8 18
St. John's	—	—	5 37	—	6 14	—	6 41	—	7 3	—	7 29	—	—	—	8 1	8 21
LEWISHAM JUNCTION....	—	—	5 40	—	6 17	—	6 44	—	7 6	—	7 30	—	7 54	—	8 4	8 25
Blackheath	—	—	5 44	—	6 21	—	6 48	—	7 10	—	7 34	—	7 58	—	8 8	8 30
Charlton Junction	—	5 7	5 48	6 17	6 27	6 39	6 54	7 4	7 16	7 29	—	7 52	8 4	—	8 14	8 38
WOOLWICH (D.	—	5 11	5 52	6 21	6 31	6 43	6 57	7 8	7 19	7 33	7 42	7 56	8 8	—	8 17	8 41
WOOLWICH {A.	3 40	5 14	5 55	6 24	6 34	6 46	7 0	7 11	7 22	7 36	7 45	7 59	8 11	8 4	8 24	8 44 8 36
Plumstead	—	5 20	5 59	6 28	6 37	6 49	7 3	7 15	7 25	7 39	7 48	8 0	8 14	—	8 24	8 47
Abbey Wood	—	5 26	6 5	6 34	6 43	6 55	7 9	7 21	7 30	7 45	7 54	—	8 20	—	8 30	—
Belvedere	—	5 30	6 9	6 38	6 47	6 59	7 13	7 25	7 34	7 49	7 58	—	8 24	—	8 34	—
ERITH	—	5 35	6 13	6 42	6 51	7 3	7 17	7 30	7 38	7 53	8 2	—	8 28	8 14	8 38	8 46
SLADE'S GREEN	—	5 42	6 17	6 49	6 55	7 7	7 21	—	7 42	8 0	—	—	—	—	—	—

WEEK DAYS.	AM	AM	AM	AM	AM	AM	AM	AM	AM	AM	AM	AM	AM	AM	AM	AM
CHARING CROSS ....dep.	—	—	8 34	8 38	8 50	—	—	9 18	9 32	—	10 2	—	10 10	—	—	—
Waterloo	—	—	8 36	8 40	8 52	—	—	9 20	9 35	—	10 4	—	10 12	—	—	—
CANNON STREET	8 24	8 30	—	—	—	9 4	9 12	—	—	9 56	—	10 16	—	10 58	10 50	11 6
LONDON BRIDGE	8 27	8 33	8 41	8 43	8 57	9 7	9 15	9 25	9 41	9 59	10 9	10 19	10 17	11 1	10 53	11 9
GREENWICH	8 35	—	—	8 53	—	—	—	—	—	10 10	—	10 28	—	—	—	11 17
MazeHill(E.Greenwich)	8 38	—	—	8 56	9 6	—	—	—	—	10 13	—	10 31	—	—	—	11 20
Westcombe Park	8 41	—	—	9 0	—	—	—	—	—	10 16	—	10 34	—	—	—	11 23
New Cross	—	8 41	—	—	9 15	—	9 32	—	—	—	10 17	—	10 25	—	11 1	—
St. John's	—	8 44	—	—	9 18	—	—	—	—	—	—	10 20	—	10 28	—	11 4
LEWISHAM JUNCTION....	—	8 47	—	9 21	9 23	9 36	—	—	—	—	10 21	—	10 31	—	11 7	—
Blackheath	—	8 51	—	9 25	9 27	9 40	—	—	—	—	10 25	—	10 35	—	11 11	—
Charlton Junction	8 44	8 57	—	9 3 9 11	9 31	—	9 46	—	9 49	—	10 19	—	10 37 10 40 10 42	—	11 19 11 26	—
WOOLWICH (D.	—	9 1	—	9 7	9 14	9 34	—	9 49	—	—	10 22	—	10 40 10 43 10 45	—	11 22 11 30	—
WOOLWICH {A.	8 50	9 5	—	9 11	9 17	9 37	—	9 52	10 0	—	10 23	—	10 37 10 43 10 50	10 46 10 52	11 19 11 25	11 33
Plumstead	8 54	9 10	9 0	9 15	9 20	9 40	—	9 56	—	—	10 29	10 41	10 46 10 43	—	11 28	11 37
Abbey Wood	9 0	9 16	—	9 21	9 25	9 46	—	—	—	—	10 35	—	10 58	—	11 34	—
Belvedere	9 4	9 20	—	9 29	9 50	—	—	—	—	—	10 39	—	11 2	—	11 38	—
ERITH	8 9	9 25	—	9 33	9 54	—	—	10 10	10 13	10 50	—	11 6	—	11 42	—	—
SLADE'S GREEN	9 12	9 32	—	9 58	—	—	—	—	—	10 47	10 59	—	11 10	—	11 53	—

WEEK DAYS.	AM	AM	AM	PM	d	e	d	d	d	e	e	d	d	d
CHARING CROSS ...dep.	—	—	11 55	—	12 15	—	—	—	—	—	—	—	—	—
Waterloo	—	—	11 57	—	12 17	—	—	—	—	—	—	—	—	—
CANNON STREET	11 8	11 50	—	12 8	—	12 12	12 24	12 33	12 46	12 50	1 2	1 2	1 7	1 10
LONDON BRIDGE	11 11	11 53	12 2	12 11	12 22	12 15	12 27	12 36	12 49	12 53	1 5	1 5	1 11	1 13
GREENWICH	—	—	—	12 19	12 30	—	—	12 46	12 57	—	1 13	—	—	1 21
MazeHill(E.Greenwich)	—	—.	—	12 22	12 33	—	—	12 50	1 0	—	1 16	—	—	1 24
Westcombe Park	—	—	—	12 25	12 36	—	—	12 53	1 3	—	1 19	1 16	—	1 27
New Cross..............	11 19	12 3	—	—	—	12 22	12 35	—	—	1 2	—	1 18	—
St. John's	11 22	12 6	—	—	—	12 22	12 38	—	—	1 6	—	1 21	—
LEWISHAM JUNCTION....	11 25	12 9	—	—	—	12 28	12 41	—	—	1 9	—	1 24	—
Blackheath	11 29	12 14	—	—	—	12 32	12 45	—	—	1 12	—	1 28	—
Charlton Junction	11 35	12 20	—	12 28	12 39	12 38	12 51	12 56	—	1 18	1 23	—	1 35	1 30
Woolwich {D.	11 39	12 23	—	12 31	12 42	12 42	12 54	1 0	—	1 21	1 27	—	1 39	1 33
{A.	11 42	12 26	12 21	12 35	12 45	12 45	12 57	1 4	1 9	1 24	1 31	1 23	1 42	1 36
Plumstead	11 46	12 29	—	12 37	12 48	12 49	1 1	1 8	1 12	1 27	1 34	1 26	1 46	1 39
Abbey Wood	11 52	12 35	—	—	12 54	12 55	—	1 14	—	1 33	—	1 32	1 52	1 45
Belvedere	11 56	12 39	—	—	12 58	12 59	—	1 19	—	1 37	—	1 36	1 56	1 49
ERITH	12 0	12 43	12 30	—	1 2	1.3	—	1 23	—	1 42	—	1 40	2 0	1 53
SLADE'S GREEN	12 7	12 51	12 51	—	—	1 7	—	1 28	—	1 51	—	—	—	1 57

WEEK DAYS.	e	d	d	d	e	d	e	d	d	d	PM	PM	d	e	e	d
CHARING CROSS ....dep.	—	—	1 42	—	—	1 46	—	—	—	2 20	—	—	—	—	—
Waterloo	—	—	1 44	—	—	1 48	—	—	—	2 22	—	—	—	—	—
CANNON STREET	1 23	1 32	—	1 50	1 44	—	2 0	2 8	2 12	—	2 40	2 50	3 0	3 16	3 24
LONDON BRIDGE	1 26	1 35	1 49	1 53	1 47	1 53	2 3	2 11	2 15	2 27	2 43	2 53	3 3	3 19	3 27
GREENWICH	—	1 43	—	2 1	—	—	—	—	2 23	2 35	—	—	3 15	—	3 35
MazeHill(E.Greenwich)	—	1 46	—	2 4	—	—	—	—	2 26	2 38	—	—	3 18	—	3 38
Westcombe Park	—	1 49	—	2 7	—	—	—	—	2 29	2 41	—	—	3 21	—	3 42
New Cross.............	1 33	—	—	—	1 55	—	2 11	2 20	—	—	2 58	3 10	—	3 30	—
St. John's	1 36	—	—	—	1 58	2 2	2 14	2 23	—	—	3 1	3 13	—	3 33	—
LEWISHAM JUNCTION....	1 39	—	—	—	2 1	2 5	2 17	2 26	—	—	3 4	3 16	—	3 37	—
Blackheath	1 43	—	—	—	2 5	2 9	2 21	2 30	—	—	3 8	3 20	—	3 41	—
Charlton Junction	1 49	1 52	—	2 10	2 11	2 15	2 27	2 35	2 32	2 44	—	3 14	3 26	3 24	3 48	3 45
Woolwich {D.	1 53	1 55	—	2 13	2 15	2 19	2 30	2 39	2 35	2 48	—	3 18	3 30	3 28	3 52	3 49
{A.	1 57	1 58	2 5	2 16	2 18	2 22	2 33	2 42	2 38	2 51	2 59	3 21	3 33	3 31	3 55	3 52
Plumstead	2 3	2 1	—	2 19	2 21	2 26	2 36	2 46	2 41	2 54	—	3 25	3 37	3 35	3 59	3 57
Abbey Wood	2 10	—	—	—	2 27	2 32	—	2 52	2 47	—	—	3 31	3 43	—	4 5	—
Belvedere	2 14	—	—	—	2 31	2 36	—	2 56	2 51	—	—	3 35	3 47	—	4 9	—
ERITH	2 19	—	2 14	—	2 35	2 40	—	3 0	2 55	—	—	3 39	3 51	—	4 13	—
SLADE'S GREEN	2 24	—	—	—	2 43	2 44	—	3 4	2 59	—	—	3 45	—	—	4 16	—

WEEK DAYS.	d	e	e	e	d	e	e	d	d	d	e	e	e	d	e	d
CHARING CROSS ....dep.	3 35	—	—	—	4 0	—	—	—	4 35	—	5 0	—	—	5 17	—	—
Waterloo	3 37	—	—	—	4 2	—	—	—	4 37	—	—	—	—	5 19	—	—
CANNON STREET	—	3 40	3 52	4 0	—	4 20	4 32	4 36	—	4 52	—	5 8	5 16	—	5 23	5 28
LONDON BRIDGE	3 42	3 43	3 55	4 4	4 7	4 23	4 35	4 39	4 42	4 55	5 6	5 11	5 19	5 25	5 26	5 31
GREENWICH	—	4 3	—	4 31	—	—	—	5 3	—	5 19	—	—	5 34	5 39
MazeHill(E.Greenwich)	—	4 6	—	4 34	—	—	—	5 6	—	5 22	—	—	5 37	5 42
Westcombe Park	—	4 9	—	4 37	—	—	—	5 9	—	5 25	—	—	5 40	5 45
New Cross.............	3 50	3 50	—	4 10	4 17	—	4 45	—	4 51	—	5 13	—	5 27	—
St. John's	3 53	3 54	—	4 12	4 20	—	—	4 58	—	5 16	—	—
LEWISHAM JUNCTION....	3 56	3 57	—	4 15	4 23	—	4 49	—	4 58	—	5 19	—	5 31	—
Blackheath	4 0	4 1	—	4 19	4 27	—	4 53	—	5 2	—	5 23	—	5 35	—
Charlton Junction	4 6	4 9	4 12	4 25	4 33	4 40	4 59	—	5 8	5 12	5 29	5 23	5 41	—	5 43	5 48
Woolwich {D.	4 10	4 13	4 16	4 29	4 36	4 44	5 3	—	5 12	5 16	5 32	5 32	—	—	5 47	5 52
{A.	4 13	4 16	4 19	4 32	4 39	4 46	5 6	—	5 16	5 19	5 34	5 35	5 47	5 41	5 50	5 55
Plumstead	4 18	4 19	4 23	4 36	4 43	4 50	5 10	—	5 20	5 22	5 38	5 38	5 50	5 44	5 54	5 58
Abbey Wood	4 24	—	4 29	4 42	4 49	—	—	5 26	5 28	5 43	—	5 56	—	—	6 4	—
Belvedere	4 28	—	4 33	4 47	4 53	—	—	5 31	5 32	5 47	—	6 0	—	—	6 8	—
ERITH	4 32	4 28	4 37	4 51	4 57	—	5 6	5 36	5 36	5 51	—	6 4	5 50	—	6 12	—
SLADE'S GREEN	4 36	—	—	4 55	5 1	—	5 26	5 41	5 40	—	6 9	—	—	6 16	—

WEEK DAYS.	e	e	e	d	e	e	d	d	d	d	e	d
CHARING CROSS ....dep.	—	5 38	—	5 58	—	6 5	6 18	—	—	6 37	—	7 15
Waterloo	—	5 40	—	—	—	6 7	6 20	—	—	6 39	—	7 17
CANNON STREET	5 36	—	5 48	5 54	6 3	6 8	—	6 28	6 40	—	6 48	7 8	7 8	7 22
LONDON BRIDGE	5 39	5 45	5 51	5 57	6 4	6 6	6 11	6 12	6 25	6 27	6 31	6 44	6 51	7 11	7 11	7 25
GREENWICH	—	—	5 59	—	—	6 22	—	6 36	6 39	6 51	—	6 59	7 19	7 31
MazeHill(E.Greenwich)	—	—	6 2	—	—	6 22	—	6 39	6 41	6 54	—	7 2	7 22	7 34
Westcombe Park	—	5 36	6 5	—	—	6 25	—	6 36	6 43	6 44	6 57	—	7 5	7 25	—	7 37
New Cross.............	5 46	—	—	—	6 21	—	—	6 50	—	7 17	—
St. John's	—	—	—	—	6 24	—	—	6 54	—	7 21	—
LEWISHAM JUNCTION...	5 50	—	—	—	6 27	—	—	6 58	—	7 24	—
Blackheath	5 54	—	—	—	6 31	—	—	7 2	—	7 28	—
Charlton Junction	6 2	—	6 8	—	6 19	6 28	6 37	—	6 46	6 48	7 0	7 7	7 8	7 28	7 34	7 40
Woolwich {D.	6 6	—	—	—	6 23	6 32	6 41	—	6 50	6 50	—	7 11	7 12	7 32	7 38	7 44
{A.	6 9	6 2	—	6 14	6 20	6 26	6 35	6 44	6 43	6 54	6 57	7 7	7 14	7 15	7 37	7 42	7 48
Plumstead	6 12	6 5	—	—	6 29	6 38	6 48	6 47	6 58	6 58	7 7	7 17	7 18	7 38	7 46	7 52
Abbey Wood	—	—	—	6 35	—	6 54	6 53	7 4	—	7 11	—	7 44	7 52	—
Belvedere	—	—	—	6 35	—	6 59	6 57	7 9	—	7 19	—	7 48	7 56	—
ERITH	—	—	—	6 30	6 43	—	7 4	7 7	7 14	—	7 23	—	7 52	8 0	—
SLADE'S GREEN	—	—	—	—	6 47	—	7 5	7 19	—	7 27	—	7 56	8 4	—

WEEK DAYS.	e	PM	e	d	e	e	e	PM	PM	PM	e	PM	PM
CHARING CROSS ....dep.	—	—	—	—	8 30	—	8 45	—	9 36	10 20	—	10 25	1040	11 20
Waterloo	—	—	—	—	8 32	—	8 47	—	9 39	10 22	—	10 27	10 43	—
CANNON STREET	7 28	7 44	8 18	8 24	—	8 40	—	9 23	9 35	—	10 30	—	—
LONDON BRIDGE	7 31	7 47	8 21	8 27	8 37	8 43	8 52	9 26	9 38	9 44	10 27	10 33	10 33	10 48	11 26
GREENWICH	7 39	—	8 29	8 35	—	8 52	—	9 34	—	—	10 41	10 41	—	11 36
MazeHill(E.Greenwich)	7 42	—	8 32	8 38	—	8 55	—	9 37	—	—	10 44	10 44	—	11 40
Westcombe Park	7 45	—	8 35	8 41	—	8 58	—	9 40	—	—	10 47	10 47	—	11 44
New Cross.............	—	7 54	—	—	8 44	—	9 3	—	9 52	—	—	10 55	—
St. John's	—	7 57	—	—	8 47	—	9 6	—	9 55	—	—	10 58	—
LEWISHAM JUNCTION....	—	8 0	—	—	8 50	—	9 9	—	9 58	—	—	11 1	—
Blackheath	—	8 4	—	—	8 54	—	9 13	—	10 2	—	—	11 5	—
Charlton Junction	—	8 10	8 38	8 44	9 1	9 1	9 19	9 43	—	10 8	—	10 50	10 50	11 11	11 47
Woolwich {D.	7 52	8 14	8 41	8 48	9 5	9 5	9 23	9 47	—	10 11	—	10 54	10 54	11 14	11 50
{A.	7 55	8 17	8 44	8 51	9 8	9 8	9 26	9 50	9 56	10 14	10 45	10 57	10 57	11 17	11 53
Plumstead	7 58	8 21	8 47	8 55	9 13	9 13	9 33	9 53	—	10 17	—	11 0	11 0	11 20	11 56
Abbey Wood	8 4	8 27	8 53	—	9 19	9 19	9 39	—	—	10 23	—	—	11 26	—
Belvedere	8 8	8 31	8 67	—	9 24	9 24	9 43	—	—	10 27	—	—	11 30	—
ERITH	8 12	8 35	9 1	—	9 28	9 28	9 47	—	10 5	10 31	10 55	—	11 34	—
SLADE'S GREEN	8 16	8 39	9 5	—	9 32	9 32	—	—	10 41	10 35	—	—	11 38	—

WEEK DAYS.	PM	PM	mid.	mid.
Charing Cross ....dep.	11 24	11 54	12 6	12 30
Waterloo Junction	—	—	12 8	12 32
Cannon Street	—	—	—	—
London Bridge	—	12 0	12 13	12 41
Greenwich	—	—	12 21	—
MazeHill(E.Greenwich)	—	—	12 24	—
Westcombe Park	—	—	12 27	—
New Cross	—	12 7	—	12 49
St. John's	—	12 10	—	12 52
Lewisham Junction ..	—	12 13	—	12 55
Blackheath	—	12 17	—	12 59
Charlton Junction	—	12 23	12 30	1 4
Woolwich { D.	—	12 27	12 34	1 8
Woolwich { A.	11 44	12 30	12 37	1 11
Plumstead	—	12 33	12 40	1 16
Abbey Wood.	—	12 39	12[d]42	—
Belvedere	—	12 43	12[d]46	—
Erith	11 53	12 47	12[d]50	—
Slade's Green	—	12 51	12[d]54	—

SUNDAYS.	AM	AM	AM	AM	AM	AM	AM	AM	AM	AM	PM	PM	PM	PM	PM	PM	PM
Charing Cross ....dep.	6 20	7 0	—	8 15	8 27	9 12	9 20	10 30	10 40	11 35	12 33	1 3	1 35	2 10	2 33	3 20	3 35
Waterloo Junction	6 22	7 2	—	8 17	8 29	9 14	9 22	10 32	10 42	11 37	12 35	1 5	1 37	2 12	2 35	3 22	3 37
Cannon Street	—	—	—	—	—	—	—	—	—	—	—	—	—	—	—	—	—
London Bridge	6 27	7 7	7 30	8 22	8 34	9 19	9 27	10 38	10 47	11 42	12 40	1 10	1 43	2 17	2 40	3 27	3 42
Greenwich	—	—	8 30	—	9 27	—	10 45	—	—	—	1 18	—	2 25	—	3 35	—	—
MazeHill(E.Greenwich)	—	—	8 33	—	9 30	—	10 48	—	—	—	1 21	—	2 28	—	3 38	—	—
Westcombe Park	—	—	8 36	—	9 33	—	10 52	—	—	—	1 24	—	2 31	—	3 41	—	—
New Cross	6 34	7 15	7 36	—	8 43	—	9 34	—	10 56	11 49	12 49	—	1 50	—	2 49	—	3 49
St. John's	6 37	7 18	—	—	8 46	—	9 37	—	10 59	11 52	12 52	—	1 53	—	2 52	—	3 52
Lewisham Junction ..	6 40	7 21	7 40	—	8 49	—	9 40	—	11 2	11 55	12 55	—	1 56	—	2 55	—	3 55
Blackheath	6 45	7 25	7 44	—	8 53	—	9 44	—	11 6	11 59	12 59	—	2 0	—	2 59	—	3 59
Charlton Junction	6 52	7 31	7 50	8 39	8 59	9 36	9 50	10 56	11 12	12 5	1 5	1 27	2 5	2 34	3 5	3 44	4 5
Woolwich { D.	6 55	7 35	—	8 42	9 3	9 39	9 54	11 0	11 15	12 9	1 9	1 31	2 9	2 38	3 9	3 48	4 9
Woolwich { A.	6 58	7 38	7 56	8 45	9 6	9 42	9 57	11 3	11 18	12 12	1 12	1 34	2 12	2 41	3 12	3 51	4 12
Plumstead	7 2	7 41	—	8 48	9 10	9 45	10 0	11 7	11 21	12 16	1 16	1 38	2 16	2 45	3 15	3 55	4 16
Abbey Wood	7 7	7 47	—	8 54	9 16	—	10 6	—	11 27	12 22	1 22	—	2 22	—	3 22	—	4 22
Belvedere	7 11	7 51	—	8 58	9 20	—	10 10	—	11 31	12 26	1 26	—	2 26	—	3 26	—	4 26
Erith	7 15	7 55	8 6	9 2	9 24	—	10 14	—	11 35	12 30	1 30	—	2 30	—	3 30	—	4 30
Slade's Green	7 25	7 59	—	9 6	9 28	—	10 18	—	11 39	12 34	1 34	—	2 34	—	3 34	—	4 34

SUNDAYS.	PM	PM	PM	PM	PM	PM	PM	PM	PM	PM	PM	PM	PM	PM	PM
Charing Cross ....dep.	4 10	4 28	5 10	5 40	6 10	6 20	6 55	7 0	7 18	7 30	8 15	8 32	8 40	9 10	9 35
Waterloo Junction	4 12	4 30	5 12	5 42	6 12	6 22	6 57	7 2	7 20	7 32	8 17	8 35	8 42	9 12	9 37
Cannon Street	—	—	—	—	—	—	—	—	—	—	—	—	—	—	—
London Bridge	4 17	4 35	5 17	5 47	6 17	6 27	7 2	7 7	7 26	7 37	8 22	8 40	8 47	9 17	9 42
Greenwich	4 25	—	5 25	—	6 25	—	—	—	7 34	—	8 30	—	—	9 25	—
MazeHill(E.Greenwich)	4 28	—	5 28	—	6 28	—	—	—	7 37	—	8 33	—	—	9 28	—
Westcombe Park	4 31	—	5 31	—	6 31	—	—	—	7 40	—	8 36	—	—	9 31	—
New Cross	—	4 44	—	5 54	—	6 34	7 11	—	—	7 44	—	8 49	—	—	9 51
St. John's	—	4 47	—	5 57	—	6 37	7 14	—	—	7 47	—	8 52	—	—	9 54
Lewisham Junction ..	—	4 50	—	6 0	—	6 40	7 17	—,	—	7 50	—	8 55	—	—	9 57
Blackheath	—	4 54	—	6 4	—	6 44	7 21	—	—	7 54	—	8 59	—	—	10 1
Charlton Junction	4 34	5 0	5 34	6 10	6 34	6 50	7 27	—	7 43	8 0	8 39	9 5	—	9 34	10 7
Woolwich { D.	4 38	5 4	5 38	6 14	6 38	6 54	7 30	—	7 43	8 4	8 43	9 9	—	9 38	10 11
Woolwich { A.	4 41	5 7	5 41	6 17	6 41	6 57	7 33	7 24	7 46	8 7	8 46	9 12	9 4	9 41	10 14
Plumstead	4 45	5 11	5 45	6 21	6 45	7 1	7 37	—	7 49	8 11	8 50	9 16	—	9 45	10 18
Abbey Wood	—	5 17	—	6 27	—	7 7	7 43	—	7 52	8 17	—	9 22	—	9 50	10 24
Belvedere	—	5 21	—	6 31	—	7 11	7 47	—	—	8 21	—	9 26	—	9 54	10 28
Erith	—	5 25	—	6 35	—	7 15	7 51	—	—	8 25	—	9 30	—	9 58	10 32
Slade's Green	—	5 29	—	6 39	—	7 19	7 55	—	—	8 29	—	9 34	—	—	10 36

SUNDAYS.	PM	PM	PM
Charing Cross ....dep.	10 5	10 30	11 0
Waterloo Junction	10 7	10 33	11 2
Cannon Street	—	—	—
London Bridge	10 12	10 38	11 7
Greenwich	10 20	—	—
MazeHill(E.Greenwich)	10 23	—	—
Westcombe Park	10 26	—	—
New Cross	—	10 45	11 17
St. John's	—	10 49	11 20
Lewisham Junction ..	—	10 52	11 23
Blackheath	—	10 56	11 27
Charlton Junction	10 29	11 2	11 33
Woolwich { D.	10 33	11 5	11 37
Woolwich { A.	10 36	11 8	11 40
Plumstead	10 40	11 11	11 44
Abbey Wood	—	11 17	—
Belvedere	—	11 21	—
Erith	—	11 25	—
Slade's Green	—	11 29	—

d Saturdays only.   e Saturdays excepted.

WEEK DAYS.	AM	AM	AM	AM	AM	AM	AM	AM	AM	AM	AM	AM	AM	AM	AM	AM	AM
Slade's Green dep.	—	4 24	5 3	5 52	6 15	6 34	6 46	6 54	—	—	7 5	—	—	—	7 21	—	—
Erith	—	4 28	5 7	5 56	6 19	6 38	6 50	6 57	—	—	7 10	—	—	—	7 26	—	7 46
Belvedere	—	4 32	5 11	6 0	6 23	6 42	6 54	7 4	—	—	7 14	—	—	—	7 30	—	7 50
Abbey Wood	—	4 36	5 15	6 4	6 27	6 46	—	7 8	—	—	7 18	—	—	—	7 34	—	7 54
Plumstead	3 53	4 42	5 21	6 10	6 33	6 52	7 0	7 14	7 7	—	—	7 27	7 33	—	7 40	7 50	8 0
Woolwich {A.	3 55	4 45	5 24	6 13	6 36	6 55	7 3	—	7 9	—	—	7 31	—	7 39	7 43	7 52	—
{D.	3 58	4 49	5 27	6 16	6 39	6 59	—	—	7 13	—	7 27	—	—	—	7 48	7 56	8 6
Charlton Junction	4 2	4 53	5 30	6 20	6 42	7 3	—	—	7 17	7 24	7 31	—	—	—	7 52	8 0	8 10
Blackheath	4 8	5 0	—	6 26	—	7 9	—	—	7 21	—	—	—	—	—	7 58	—	—
Lewisham Junction	4 15	5 9	—	6 29	—	7 12	7 16	—	7 28	—	—	—	—	—	8 1	—	—
St. John's	4 18	5 12	—	6 32	—	—	—	—	—	—	—	—	—	—	—	—	—
New Cross	4 21	5 15	—	6 35	—	7 16	7 20	—	—	—	—	—	—	—	8 5	—	—
Westcombe Park	—	—	5 33	—	6 45	—	—	—	—	—	7 26	—	—	—	—	8 3	8 13
Maze Hill	—	—	5 36	—	6 48	—	—	—	—	—	7 29	—	—	—	—	8 6	—
Greenwich	—	—	5 39	—	6 51	—	—	—	—	—	7 32	—	—	—	—	8 9	8 18
London Bridge	4 30	5 24	—	6 42	7 0	7 24	7 28	7 33	7 39	7 42	7 48	7 50	7 52	7 56	8 12	8 19	8 28
Cannon Street	4 34	5 28	5 51	6 46	7 4	7 28	7 32	—	7 43	7 45	7 52	—	7 56	8 0	8 16	8 23	8 32
Waterloo	—	—	—	—	—	—	7 39	—	—	—	7 55	—	—	—	—	—	—
Charing Cross	—	—	—	—	—	—	7 43	—	—	—	7 59	—	—	—	—	—	—

WEEK DAYS.	AM	AM	AM	AM	AM	AM	AM	AM	AM	AM	AM	d	AM	AM	AM	AM
Slade's Green dep.	—	8 7	8 12	8 23	—	8 56	—	9 46	—	—	—	—	10 29	10 46	10 53	—
Erith	—	8 11	8 22	8 32	—	9 5	—	9 52	—	10 10	—	—	10 33	10 50	11 2	—
Belvedere	—	8 15	8 25	8 36	—	9 8	—	9 56	—	10 13	—	—	10 37	—	11 5	—
Abbey Wood	—	8 19	8 29	8 40	—	9 12	—	10 0	—	10 17	—	—	10 41	—	11 9	—
Plumstead	—	8 15	8 24	8 35	—	9 4	9 18	9 28	—	10 18	10 23	10 36	10 46	10 58	11 15	11 28
Woolwich {A.	8 10	8 17	8 27	8 38	8 47	9 6	9 21	9 30	10 7	10 20	10 26	10 38	10 49	11 1	11 18	11 30
{D.	—	8 20	—	8 42	—	9 24	9 24	—	10 24	10 31	10 42	10 52	—	11 23	11 35	
Charlton Junction	—	8 24	8 33	8 46	8 54	9 12	9 28	9 38	—	10 28	10 35	10 46	10 55	—	11 27	11 39
Blackheath	—	8 30	—	8 52	—	9 34	—	—	10 34	—	11 1	—	11 32	—		
Lewisham Junction	—	8 33	—	8 55	—	9 37	—	—	10 37	—	11 4	—	11 35	—		
St. John's	—	8 36	—	—	—	—	—	—	—	—	11 7	—	11 38	—		
New Cross	—	—	—	8 59	—	—	—	—	—	10 41	—	11 10	—	11 41	—	
Westcombe Park	8 19	—	8 37	—	8 57	9 15	—	9 41	—	—	10 39	10 49	—	—	—	11 42
Maze Hill	8 22	—	8 40	—	9 0	9 18	—	9 44	—	—	10 42	10 52	—	—	—	11 45
Greenwich	—	—	8 43	—	9 3	9 21	—	9 47	—	—	10 45	10 55	—	—	—	11 48
London Bridge	8 34	8 46	8 52	9 6	9 12	9 30	9 46	9 56	10 24	10 48	10 53	11 4	11 17	11 19	11 49	11 59
Cannon Street	—	—	—	—	9 16	—	—	10 0	10 23	10 52	10 57	11 8	11 21	11 19	11 53	12 3
Waterloo	8 39	8 51	8 58	9 11	—	9 35	9 51	—	—	—	—	—	—	—	—	—
Charing Cross	8 43	8 55	9 1	9 14	—	9 39	9 55	—	—	—	—	—	—	—	—	—

WEEK DAYS.	e	AM	d	d	AM	e	e	d	d	d	d	e	d	e
Slade's Green dep.	—	11 8	—	—	11 52	—	12 16	—	12 19	12 28	—	—	12 37	—	12 49
Erith	—	11 21	—	—	11 57	—	12 30	12 15	12 23	12 32	—	—	12 40	1 6	1 5	12 53
Belvedere	—	11 24	—	—	12 2	—	—	12 18	12 27	12 36	—	—	12 44	—	1 8	12 58
Abbey Wood	—	11 28	—	—	12 6	—	—	12 23	12 31	12 40	—	—	12 48	—	1 12	1 2
Plumstead	—	11 34	11 43	11 50	12 12	12 22	—	12 29	12 37	12 46	—	1 0	12 54	—	1 18	1 8
Woolwich {A.	11 43	11 37	11 47	11 53	12 15	12 24	12 39	12 32	12 40	12 51	12 45	1 2	12 57	16	1 21	1 13
{D	—	11 41	11 49	11 55	12 20	12 29	—	12 37	12 43	12 53	12 47	1 5	—	—	1 25	1 15
Charlton Junction	—	11 45	11 53	11 59	12 24	12 33	—	12 41	12 47	12 57	12 51	1 8	1 3	—	—	1 19
Blackheath	—	11 51	11 59	—	12 30	—	—	12 47	—	—	12 57	1 11	1 9	—	—	1 26
Lewisham Junction	—	11 54	12 2	—	12 34	—	—	12 50	—	1 0	1 14	1 15	—	—	1 29	
St. John's	—	11 57	—	—	12 37	—	—	12 53	—	1 3	1 17	1 18	—	—	1 32	
New Cross	—	12 0	12 6	—	12 40	—	—	12 56	—	1 8	1 6	1 20	1 21	—	—	1 35
Westcombe Park	—	—	—	12 2	—	12 36	—	—	—	12 51	—	—	—	—	—	
Maze Hill	—	—	—	12 6	—	12 39	—	—	—	12 54	—	—	—	—	—	
Greenwich	—	—	—	12 8	—	12 42	—	—	—	12 57	—	—	—	—	—	
London Bridge	12 4	12 7	12 13	12 18	12 49	12 51	12 57	1 3	1 15	1 13	1 25	1 28	1 36	1 40	1 44
Cannon Street	—	12 11	—	12 25	12 53	12 56	—	1 11	1 19	1 17	1 29	1 32	—	—	1 52
Waterloo	12 10	—	12 21	—	—	—	—	1 8	—	—	—	—	1 40	1 47	—
Charing Cross	12 14	—	12 25	—	—	1 5	1 12	—	—	—	—	—	1 44	1 51	—

WEEK DAYS.	d	d	d	e	d	d	e	d	d	d	e	e
Slade's Green..dep.	—	—	—	1 18	1 9	1 34	1 40	1 49	—	2 8	2 16	2 29	—	2 41	—	—
Erith	—	1 11	—	1 27	1 32	1 38	1 56	1 54	—	2 28	2 28	2 34	—	2 45	—	3 12
Belvedere	—	1 15	—	1 30	1 35	1 42	2 0	1 58	—	2 31	2 31	2 39	—	2 49	—	3 15
Abbey Wood	—	1 19	—	1 34	1 39	1 46	2 4	2 2	—	2 35	2 35	2 44	—	2 53	—	3 19
Plumstead	—	1 24	1 33	1 32	1 40	1 45	1 52	2 10	2 8	2 29	2 40	2 41	2 50	—	2 59	3 17	3 24
Woolwich {A	1 15	1 27	1 35	1 34	1 43	1 48	1 55	2 13	2 11	2 27	2 43	2 44	2 53	3 7	3 2	3 19	3 27
{D.	1 18	—	1 39	1 38	1 46	1 52	1 59	2 16	2 15	2 30	2 49	2 48	2 59	—	3 6	3 22	3 30
Charlton Junction..	1 21	1 33	1 43	1 41	1 50	1 56	2 3	2 20	2 19	2 34	2 52	2 52	3 3	—	3 10	3 26	3 34
Blackheath	1 28	1 39	1 49	—	2 2	2 9	—	2 25	—	2 59	2 58	—	—	3 16	—	
Lewisham Junction	1 32	1 43	1 52	—	2 5	2 13	—	2 28	—	3 2	3 1	—	—	3 19	—	
St. John's	1 35	—	—	—	2 8	2 16	—	2 31	—	3 5	3 4	—	—	3 22	—	
New Cross	1 38	1 47	1 56	—	2 11	2 19	—	2 34	—	3 8	3 7	—	—	3 25	—	
Westcombe Park...	—	—	1 44	1 53	—	2 23	—	2 37	—	3 6	—	3 29	3 37			
Maze Hill	—	—	1 47	1 56	—	2 26	—	2 40	—	3 9	—	3 32	3 40			
Greenwich	—	—	1 51	1 59	—	2 29	—	2 43	—	3 12	—	3 35	3 43			
London Bridge	1 46	1 54	2 3	2 2	7	2 18	2 26	2 39	2 41	2 52	3 17	3 16	3 21	3 26	3 32	3 44	3 53
Cannon Street	1 50	1 58	—	2 5	—	2 22	2 30	2 41	2 45	2 56	—	3 20	3 26	3 36	3 48	3 58
Waterloo	—	—	—	2 12	—	2 16	—	—	—	—	3 32	—	—	
Charing Cross	—	—	2 10	—	2 16	—	—	—	3 24	—	3 36	—	

WEEK DAYS.	e	PM	e	e	d	e	d	e	e	d
Slade's Green dep.	—	3 29	—	4 4	—	4 22	4 24	—	—	—	—	5 8	5 9	5 0
Erith	—	3 34	4 19	4 7	—	4 26	4 28	4 37	—	4 57	—	5 14	5 10	
Belvedere	—	3 38	—	4 11	—	4 30	4 32	4 40	—	5 1	—	5 17	5 13	
Abbey Wood	—	3 42	—	4 15	—	4 34	4 37	4 44	—	5 5	—	5 21	5 18	
Plumstead	3 28	3 48	—	4 21	4 20	4 36	4 40	4 42	4 46	4 50	4 55	5 0	5 6	5 11	5 20	5 27	5 24
Woolwich {A.	3 30	3 51	4 28	4 24	4 22	4 38	4 43	4 45	4 48	4 53	4 57	5 1	5 6	5 13	5 16	5 22	5 30	5 27
{D.	3 34	3 55	—	4 27	4 25	4 41	4 47	4 49	—	4 57	5 1	5 5	5 10	5 17	5 25	5 29	5 37	5 32
Charlton Junction..	3 37	3 59	—	4 31	4 29	4 45	4 51	4 51	—	5 10	5 17	5 22	5 29	5 37	5 37	
Blackheath	3 44	4 5	—	4 38	4 35	—	4 58	4 59	—	5 28	—	5 44	5 44	
Lewisham Junction	3 47	4 8	—	4 42	4 39	—	5 3	5 2	—	5 19	—	5 32	5 47	5 47	
St. John's	3 50	4 11	—	4 45	4 42	—	—	—	—	5 34	—	—	5 50	
New Cross	3 53	4 14	—	4 48	4 45	—	5 8	5 6	—	5 24	—	5 36	5 51	5 53	
Westcombe Park ..	—	—	—	4 49	—	4 57	5 5	5 9	—	—	5 33	—		
Maze Hill	—	—	—	4 52	—	5 0	5 8	5 12	—	—	5 36	—		
Greenwich	—	—	—	4 55	—	5 3	5 11	5 15	—	—	5 39	—		
London Bridge	4 0	4 22	4 48	4 52	4 54	5 5	5 16	5 16	5 19	5 25	5 30	5 35	5 40	5 49	5 52	5 58	6 0
Cannon Street	4 4	—	4 52	5 0	5 8	—	5 16	5 24	—	5 36	—	5 43	5 52	—	
Waterloo	—	4 27	—	—	4 59	—	5 22	5 21	—	—	6 3	—	
Charing Cross	—	4 31	—	—	5 3	—	5 26	5 25	—	—	6 7	6 9	

WEEK DAYS.	d	e	d	e	d	e	e	e	e	d	e	d	e	d	PM	e
SLADE'S GREEN..dep.	—	5 23	5 25	—	5 32	5 40	5 46	5 58	—	5 58	6 1	6 7	—	—	6 42	—
ERITH	—	5 27	5 29	—	5 36	5 44	5 51	6 2	—	6 2	6 7	6 10	—	6 36	6 46	—
Belvedere	—	5 31	5 32	—	5 40	5 48	5 55	6 6	—	6 6	6 11	6 14	—	6 40	6 50	—
Abbey Wood	—	5 36	5 37	—	5 44	5 52	5 59	6 10	—	6 10	6 15	6 18	—	6 44	6 54	—
Plumstead	5 35	5 44	5 44	5 48	5 50	5 57	6 5	6 15	6 10	6 16	6 20	6 24	—	6 50	7 0	7 14
WOOLWICH ⟨A.	5 37	5 47	5 47	5 50	5 53	6 0	6 8	6 18	6 12	6 19	6 23	6 28	—	6 54	7 3	7 16
WOOLWICH ⟨D.	—	5 49	5 52	5 53	5 58	6 3	6 11	—	6 16	6 23	6 27	6 31	—	—	7 6	7 19
Charlton Junction	5 44	5 51	5 56	5 57	6 2	—	6 14	—	6 20	6 27	—	6 35	6 55	6 58	7 10	7 23
Blackheath	—	5 57	6 1	—	6 8	6 11	—	—	6 26	—	6 36	6 41	—	7 2	—	7 29
LEWISHAM JUNCTION	—	6 0	6 4	—	6 12	6 14	—	—	6 31	—	6 39	6 44	—	7 5	—	7 32
St. John's	—	6 3	—	—	6 15	—	—	—	6 34	—	6 41	6 47	—	7 8	—	—
New Cross	—	6 6	6 8	—	6 18	6 19	—	—	6 37	—	6 44	6 50	—	7 11	—	7 36
Westcombe Park	5 48	—	—	6 2	—	—	6 17	—	—	6 30	—	—	6 57	—	7 13	—
Maze Hill	5 51	—	—	6 6	—	—	6 20	—	—	6 33	—	—	7 0	—	7 16	—
GREENWICH	5 55	—	—	6 10	—	—	6 23	—	—	6 36	—	—	7 3	—	7 19	—
LONDON BRIDGE	6 4	6 14	6 15	6 20	6 25	6 28	6 32	6 36	6 44	6 47	6 52	6 59	7 12	7 19	7 28	7 44
CANNON STREET	—	—	6 19	6 24	—	6 32	—	—	6 48	—	6 56	7 0	7 16	—	7 32	7 43
Waterloo	—	6 19	—	—	6 31	—	6 39	6 43	—	6 51	—	—	—	7 29	—	—
CHARING CROSS	—	6 23	—	—	6 35	—	6 43	6 47	—	6 56	—	—	—	7 33	—	—

WEEK DAYS.	d	e	PM	e	e	d	PM	e	PM	PM	PM	PM	PM	PM
SLADE'S GREEN..dep.	7 10	7 5	7 18	—	7 37	7 40	8 2	—	8e 9	—	9 26	9 30	10 31	11 42
ERITH	7 14	7 12	7 22	—	7 48	7 50	8 6	—	8 35	—	9 30	10 22	10 35	11 46
Belvedere	7 18	7 15	7 27	—	7 51	7 53	8 10	—	8 38	—	9 34	—	10 39	11 50
Abbey Wood	7 22	7 19	7 32	—	7 55	7 57	8 14	—	8 42	—	9 38	—	10 43	11 54
Plumstead	7 28	7 25	7 38	8	8 1	8 3	8 19	8 35	8 48	9 22	9 44	10 29	10 49	12 0
WOOLWICH ⟨A.	7 31	7 28	7 41	7 52	8 4	8 6	8 22	8 37	8 51	9 24	9 48	10 32	10 52	12 3
WOOLWICH ⟨D.	7 34	7 33	7 45	7 56	8 8	8 10	8 25	8 40	8 56	9 28	9 52	—	10 55	12 7
Charlton Junction	7 38	7 37	7 49	8 0	8 12	8 14	8 28	8 44	9 0	9 32	9 56	—	10 59	12 11
Blackheath	7 44	7 43	—	8 6	—	—	8 34	8 50	9 6	—	10 2	—	—	12 17
LEWISHAM JUNCTION	7 47	7 46	—	8 10	—	—	8 37	8 53	9 9	—	10 5	—	—	12 20
St. John's	7 50	7 49	—	8 13	—	—	8 40	8 56	9 12	—	10 8	—	—	12 23
New Cross	7 53	7 52	—	8 16	—	—	8 43	8 59	9 15	—	10 11	—	—	12 26
Westcombe Park	—	—	7 53	—	8 15	8 17	—	—	—	9 38	—	—	11 2	—
Maze Hill	—	—	7 56	—	8 18	8 20	—	—	—	9 41	—	—	11 5	—
GREENWICH	—	—	7 59	—	8 21	8 23	—	—	—	9 45	—	—	11 8	—
LONDON BRIDGE	8 0	8 0	8 9	8 23	8 30	8 32	8 50	9 6	9 22	9 54	10 20	10 51	11 17	12 35
CANNON STREET	8 5	8 5	8 13	8 28	—	—	—	9 11	—	—	—	—	—	—
Waterloo	—	—	8d14	—	8 38	8 54	—	9 30	10 0	10 27	—	11 22	12 41	
CHARING CROSS	—	—	8d19	—	8 42	8 58	—	9 35	10 4	10 31	10 59	11 26	12 45	

d Saturdays only.   e Saturdays excepted.

SUNDAYS.	AM	AM	AM	AM	AM	AM	AM	AM	AM	PM	PM	PM	PM	PM	PM
SLADE'S GREEN dep.	6 34	—	—	—	8 43	—	9 51	10 49	11 49	—	12 54	—	1 54	—	2 51
ERITH	6 38	—	—	—	8 47	—	9 53	10 53	11 53	—	12 58	—	1 58	—	2 55
Belvedere	6 42	—	—	—	8 51	—	9 58	10 58	11 58	—	1 2	—	2 2	—	2 59
Abbey Wood	6 46	—	—	—	8 55	—	10 3	11 3	12 2	—	1 6	—	2 6	—	3 3
Plumstead	6 52	7 11	8 10	8 22	9 1	9 22	10 9	11 9	12 8	12 21	1 12	1 26	2 12	2 25	3 9
WOOLWICH ⟨A	6 56	7 14	8 13	8 24	9 5	9 24	10 12	11 12	12 11	12 23	1 15	1 28	2 15	2 27	3 12
WOOLWICH ⟨D	6 59	7 19	8 17	8 28	9 9	9 28	10 16	11 16	12 15	12 27	1 18	1 31	2 19	2 31	3 16
Charlton Junction	7 3	7 24	8 21	8 32	9 13	9 32	10 20	11 20	12 19	12 31	1 24	1 35	2 22	2 35	3 20
Blackheath	—	7 31	—	8 38	9 19	—	10 26	11 26	12 25	—	1 30	—	2 29	—	3 26
LEWISHAM JUNCTION	—	7 34	—	8 41	9 22	—	10 29	11 29	12 28	—	1 34	—	2 32	—	3 29
St. John's	—	7 37	—	8 44	9 25	—	10 32	11 32	12 31	—	1 38	—	2 35	—	3 32
New Cross	—	7 40	—	8 47	9 28	—	10 35	11 35	12 34	—	1 41	—	2 39	—	3 35
Westcombe Park	7 6	—	8 24	—	—	9 33	—	—	—	12 34	—	1 38	—	2 38	—
MazeHill (E.Greenwich)	7 9	—	8 27	—	—	9 36	—	—	—	12 37	—	1 41	—	2 41	—
GREENWICH	7 12	—	8 30	—	—	9 40	—	—	—	12 40	—	1 45	—	2 45	—
LONDON BRIDGE	7 20	7 49	8 38	8 56	9 35	9 49	10 46	11 42	12 43	12 48	1 49	1 53	2 48	2 51	3 44
CANNON STREET												2 53			
Waterloo	7 25	7 55	8 44	9 1	9 40	9 54	10 51	11 47	12 48	12 54	1 54	1 58	—	2 58	3 49
CHARING CROSS	7 29	7 59	8 48	9 5	9 44	9 59	10 55	11 51	12 52	12 58	1 59	2 2	2 57	3	3 53

SUNDAYS.	PM	PM	PM	PM	PM	PM	PM	PM	PM	PM	PM	PM	PM	PM	PM	PM	PM
SLADE'S GREEN dep.	—	3 51	—	4 50	—	—	5 56	—	6 54	—	7 50	—	8 47	—	9 47	—	10 49
ERITH	—	3 55	—	4 54	—	5 28	6 0	6 21	6 58	—	7 55	—	8 52	—	9 51	10 43	10 53
Belvedere	—	3 59	—	4 58	—	—	6 4	—	7 2	—	8 0	—	8 57	—	9 55	—	10 57
Abbey Wood	—	4 3	—	—	—	—	6 8	—	7 6	—	8 4	—	9 2	—	9 59	—	11 1
Plumstead	3 22	4 9	4 24	5 8	5 18	—	6 14	—	6 45	7 12	7 23	8 10	8 49	9 8	9 40	10 5	11 7
WOOLWICH ⟨A	3 24	4 12	4 26	5 11	5 20	5 37	6 17	6 30	6 47	7 15	7 25	8 13	8 51	9 11	9 42	10 8	11 10
WOOLWICH ⟨D	3 28	4 16	4 29	5 14	5 23	—	6 21	—	6 51	7 19	7 28	8 16	8 54	9 15	9 46	10 12	11 16
Charlton Junction	3 32	4 20	4 33	5 18	5 27	—	6 25	—	6 55	7 23	7 32	8 20	8 58	9 19	9 50	10 15	11 20
Blackheath	—	4 26	—	5 24	—	—	6 31	—	7 29	—	8 26	—	9 26	—	10 22	11 5	11 26
LEWISHAM JUNCTION	—	4 29	—	5 27	—	—	6 34	—	7 32	—	8 29	—	9 30	—	10 25	11 8	11 29
St. John's	—	4 32	—	5 30	—	—	6 37	—	7 35	—	8 32	—	9 34	—	10 28	11 11	11 32
New Cross	—	4 35	—	5 33	—	—	6 40	—	7 38	—	8 35	—	9 37	—	10 31	11 12	11 35
Westcombe Park	3 35	—	4 36	—	5 20	—	6 58	—	7 36	—	7 39	—	9 4	—	9 56	—	
MazeHill (E.Greenwich)	3 38	—	4 39	—	5 33	—	7 1	—	7 39	—	9 4	—	9 56	—			
GREENWICH	3 41	—	4 42	—	5 36	—	7 5	—	7 43	—	9 9	—	9 59	—			
LONDON BRIDGE	3 49	4 43	4 50	5 40	5 44	5 54	6 49	6 49	7 13	7 45	7 52	8 44	9 14	9 46	10 7	10 38	11 20	11 44
Waterloo	3 55	4 49	4 55	5 45	5 50	6 0	6 52	6 55	7 18	7 50	7 57	8 50	9 19	9 51	10 11	10 43	11 50
CHARING CROSS	3 59	4 54	4 59	5 49	5 54	6 4	6 56	6 59	7 22	7 54	8 1	8 54	9 23	9 55	10 15	10 47	11 54

WEEK DAYS.

	AM	AM	AM	AM	AM	AM	AM	AM	AM	AM	AM	AM	AM	AM	AM	AM	AM
Charing Cross..dep.	—	—	4 50	5 18	5 45	5 57	6 15	—	6 30	—	—		7 38	—	8 2	8 10	8 16
Waterloo	—		4 52	5 20	5 47	5 59	6 17	—	6 32				7 40	—	8 4	8 12	8 19
Cannon Street	—	4 43	—					6 20		6 28	6 50	7 15	—	7 44	—		
London Bridge	3 22	4 46	4 58	5 25	5 53	6 4	6 22	6 23	6 37	6 31	6 53	7 18	7 45	7 47	8 9	8 17	8 25
New Cross	—		5 8	5 34	6 4	6 11	-~		6 44	6 38	7 0		7 53		8 17	—	8 32
St. John's	—		5 11	5 37	6 7	6 14	—		6 47	6 41	7 3		7 56		—	—	8 35
Hither Green	—		5 16		6 12	—			6 52	—			8 1		8 23	—	—
Lee	—		5 21		6 16	—			6 55	—			8 4		8 26	—	—
Eltham	—		5 24		6 21	—			7 0	—			8 10		8 31	—	—
New Eltham	—		5 29		6 25	—			7 3	—			8 13		8 34	—	—
Sidcup	—		5 35		6 29	—			7 7	—			8 17		8 38	—	—
Bexley	—		5 41		6 35	—			7 11	—			8 22		8 42	—	—
Crayford	—		5 47		6 40	—	6 54		7 15	—			8 26		8 46	—	—
Dartford	4 0	5 48	5 54	6 22	6 50	7 0	7 13	6 58	7 24	7 27	7 47	7 48	8 31	8 21	8 55	8 53	9 14
Greenhithe	5 34			6 41				7 8		7 35		8 8		8 29		9 2	—
Northfleet	5 41			6 49				7 14		7 40		8 15		8 34		9 7	—

WEEK DAYS.

	AM	AM	AM	AM	AM	AM	AM	AM	AM	AM	AM	AM	AM	AM	d	e
Charing Cross dep.					9 32		10 10	10 26				11 33	11 55		—	—
Waterloo					9 35		10 12	10 28				11 35	11 57		—	—
Cannon Street	8 24	8 44	9 4	9 12		9 56			10 58	11 8				12 10	12 12
London Bridge	8 27	8 47	9 7	9 15	9 41	9 59	10 17	10 33	11 1	11 11	11 40	12 3	12 13	12 15
New Cross		8 57	9 15	9 25			10 25	10 42		11 19	11 47		12 20	12 22
St. John's		9 0	9 18	9 29			10 28	10 45		11 22				12 25
Hither Green		9 5		9 34				10 50			11 53		12 26
Lee		9 8		9 37				10 53			11 55		12 29
Eltham		9 14		9 42				10 58			12 1		12 34
New Eltham		9 18		9 45				11 1			12 4		12 37
Sidcup		9 22		9 49				11 5			12 8		12 41
Bexley		9 27		9 53				11 10			12 12		12 45
Crayford		9 32		9 58				11 15			12 16		12 50
Dartford	9 17	9 38	10 3	10 6	10 17	10 53	11 15	11 20	11 33	12"13	12 23	12 38	12 56	1 12
Greenhithe					10 24				11 42	12"25		12 54	—
Northfleet					10 30				11 48	12"30		1 1	—

WEEK DAYS.

	e	d	e		d		d	d	d	d	e		d	d	d
Charing Cross dep.	12 7	12 30	12 35	—		12 48	1 0	—	1 5	—		1 20	1 25	1 40
Waterloo	12 9	12 32	12 37	—		12 50	1 2	—	—	—		1 22	1 27	1 42
Cannon Street				12 38	12 34		1 2		1 10	1 10	1 23	—			1 48
London Bridge	12 14	12 37	12 43	—	12 37	12 55	1 7	1 7	1 5	1 11	1 13	1 13	1 26	1 27	1 31	1 47	1 51
New Cross			12 50	12 48	—				1 18	—		1 33			1 58
St. John's											1 36	—
Hither Green	12 27	12 48	12 56	12 55	—	1 6	1 18	—	1 24	1 25	—	—	2 5
Lee	12 30	—	12 59	12 53	—	1 9	1 21	--	1 27	1 29	—	—	2 8
Eltham	12 36	—	1 4	1 4	—	1 15	1 26	—	1 32	1 34	—	—	2 14
New Eltham	12 39	—	1 7	1 7	—	1 18	1 2?	—	1 35	1 38	—	1 49	2 17
Sidcup	12 44	—	1 11	1 11	—	1 22	1 34	—	1 39	1 42	—	—	2 21
Bexley	12 49	—	1 15	1 15	—	1 26	1 38	—	1 44	1 46	—	1 56	2 25
Crayford	12 53	—	1 19	1 19	—	1 31	1 43	—	1 48	1 51	—	—	2 29
Dartford	12 58	1 5	1 24	1 24	1 33	1 37	1 51	1 47	1 53	—	2 1	2 30	1 58	2 6	2 20	2 34
Greenhithe	—	1 36					1 54			2 40	2 5	—	—	2 41
Northfleet	—	1 44					1 59			2 46	2 10	—	—	2 46

WEEK DAYS.

	d	d	d	d	PM	PM	d	d	e	d	d	e	d	d	d
Charing Cross dep.	1 46	—	2 10	—	—	—	—	2 45	3 5	3 10	—	3 35	—	4 0	4 14
Waterloo	1 48	—	2 12	—	—	—	—	2 47	3 7	3 12	—	3 37	—	4 2	4 16
Cannon Street	—	2 2	—	2 10	2 12	2 28	2 40	2 45	2 50	—	—	3 16	—	3 48	4 0	—
London Bridge	1 53	2 5	2 17	2 13	2 15	2 31	2 43	2 48	2 53	2 53	3 12	3 17	3 19	3 42	3 51	4 3	4 7	4 20
New Cross	—	2 24	2 20	—		2 56	3 0	3 1	-	3 26	3 50	3 58	4 10	4 17	4 27
St. John's	2 2	—	2 23	—		2 59	3 4	—		3 53	4 1	4 12	4 20
Hither Green	—	2 16	2 30	—	2 43	3 4	3 9	—	3 32	—	4 6	—	4 33
Lee	—	2 19	2 33	—	2 46	3 7	3 12	—	3 35	—	4 9	—	4 37
Eltham	—	2 24	2 39	—	2 51	3 12	3 18	—	3 40	—	4 14	—	4 43
New Eltham	—	2 27	2 42	—	2 54	3 16	3 21	—	3 43	—	4 17	—	4 47
Sidcup	—	2 31	2 46	—	2 58	3 20	3 25	—	3 47	—	4 21	—	4 51
Bexley	—	2 35	2 50	—	3 2	3 24	3 29	—	3 51	—	4 25	—	4 56
Crayford	—		2 54	—	3 5	3 28	3 33		3 55		4 29		5 0
Dartford	2 50	2 43	2 59	3 8	3 4	3 10	3 13	3 33	3 50	3 33	3 40	4 3	4 22	4 41	4 34	5 1	5 5 14
Greenhithe			3 6	—		3 20			3 45	3 47		4 49	5 9	—
Northfleet			3 11	—		3 25			3 50	3 52		4 54	5 15	—

WEEK DAYS.

	d	e	d	d	e	d	e	d	e	d	e	e	d	d	e
Charing Cross dep.	4 25	—	4 35	4 42	—	—	5 0	—	5 17	5 15	5 23	—	5 37	5 42	5 58	—
Waterloo		—	4 37	4 44	—		5 19	5 17	5 23	—	5 39
Cannon Street	—	4 36	—	—	4 52	5 8	—	5 16	—	—	5 28	5 32	—	—	6 0	6 4
London Bridge	4 31	4 39	4 42	4 49	4 55	5 11	5 6	5 19	5 25	5 22	5 29	5 31	5 35	5 44	5 49	6 4	6 3	6 7
New Cross	4 39		4 53	4 56	—	5 13	—	—	5 30	—	5 39	5 42	—	5 56	—
St. John's			4 57		—	5 16	—		5 42	—
Hither Green	4 45	—	5 2		—		5 37	—	5 45	5 48	—	6 2	6 15
Lee	4 48	—	5 5	5 23	—		5 40	—	5 51	5 56	6 6	—	6 18
Eltham	4 53	—	5 11	5 28	—		5 46	5 45	—	5 57	6 11	—	6 24
New Eltham	4 57	—	5 19		—	5 34	5 49	5 48	—	6 0	6 4	6 15	—	6 27
Sidcup	5 1	—	5 23	5 34	—		5 53	5 52	—	6 4	6 8	6 19	—	6 31
Bexley	5 5	—	5 28	5 39	—		5 58	5 57	—	6 9	6 13	6 24	—	6 35
Crayford	5 9	—	5 32	5 43	—		6 2	6 1	—	6 14	6 16	6 28	—	6 49
Dartford	5 15	5 13	5 46	5 33	5 45	5 49	6 1	6 13	6 6	6 22	—	6 22	6 33	6 37	6 46	6 55
Greenhithe		5 28	5 55	—	—	6 5	6 15	6 13	—	6 40	6 44	—
Northfleet		5 35	6 0	—	—	6 10	6 20	6 18	—	6 45	6 49	—

WEEK DAYS.

	d	e	d	e	d	e	d	e	d	e	d	e	d	PM	e	PM
Charing Cross dep.	6 10	—	6 18	6 22	—	6 30	—	6 55	7 2	—	—	7 3:	—	8 6
Waterloo	6 12	—	6 20	6 24	—	6 32	—		—		7 3:	—	8 8
Cannon Street	—	6 20	—	—	6 32	—	6 40	6 52	—	—	7 8	7 23	—	8 2
London Bridge	6 17	6 2.	6 25	6 29	6 35	6 27	6 28	6 43	6 55	7 7	7 8	7 11	7 17	7 31	7 41	7 47	8 13
New Cross	6 24	—	—		7 2	—		7 18	7 50	8 20
St. John's								7 21		7 54
Hither Green	6 31	—	6 48	—	7 8	7 17	—	7 56	7 57	8 26
Lee	6 34	—	6 49	—	7 11	7 20	—	7 59	8 29
Eltham	6 39	—	6 55	—	7 16	7 25	—	8 5	8 34
New Eltham	6 42	—	6 48	6 58	—	7 20	7 28	—	8 8	8 37
Sidcup	6 46	6 43	6 53	7	—	7 24	7 32	7 36	8 12	8 41
Bexley	6 50	—	6 57	7 7	—	7 28	7 36	7 41	8 17	8 46
Crayford	6 54	—		7 12	—	7 33	7 40		8 21	8 50
Dartford	7 0	—	7 10	7 4	7 20	7 23	7 25	7 32	7 39	7 45	7 53	7 49	8 18	9 8	8 22	8 28	8 55
Greenhithe	—	7 11	—	7 40	7 53	—	8 21	8 21	8 33	8 52
Northfleet	—	7 16	—	7 45	7 58	—	8 28	8 28	8 38	8 57

WEEK DAYS.

	e	d	e	PM	PM	PM	PM	PM	PM	PM	PM	PM	PM	PM	PM	PM
Charing Cross dep.	—	8 30	—	8 40	9 8	—	9 36	9 52	10 23	10 40	10 50	10 55	11 23	11 33	11 54	11 55
Waterloo	—	8 32	—	8 42	9 10	—	9 39	9 54	10 22	10 43	—	10 57	—	—	—	11 57
Cannon Street	8 18	—	8 40	—	—	9 35	—	—	—	—	—	—	—	—	—	—
London Bridge	8 21	8 37	8 43	8 48	9 15	9 33	9 44	9 59	10 27	10 48	10 56	11 2	—	—	12 0	12 2
New Cross	—	8 44	—	8 55	9 21	—	9 52	10 6	—	10 55	11 5	—	—	—	12 7	12 9
St. John's	—	8 47	—	8 58	—	—	9 55	10 9	—	10 58	—	—	—	—	12 10	—
Hither Green	—	—	—	9 3	9 28	—	—	10 14	—	—	—	11 13	—	—	—	12 16
Lee	—	—	—	9 6	9 31	—	—	10 17	—	—	—	11 16	—	11 48	—	12 19
Eltham	—	—	—	9 11	9 36	—	—	10 23	—	—	—	11 21	—	11 53	—	12 24
New Eltham	—	—	—	9 14	9 39	—	—	10 27	—	—	—	11 25	—	11 56	—	12 27
Sidcup	—	—	—	9 18	9 43	—	—	10 32	—	—	—	11 30	—	12 0	—	12 31
Bexley	—	—	—	9 22	9 48	—	—	10 37	—	—	—	11 35	—	12 4	—	12 35
Crayford	—	—	—	9 27	9 52	—	—	10 41	—	—	—	11 39	—	12 ?	—	h
Dartford	9 10	9 37	9 36	9 33	9 57	10 10	10 40	10 47	11 2	11 43	11 43	11 45	12 1	12 13	12 56	12 44
Greenhithe	—	—	—	9 48	—	10 18	—	—	11 9	—	—	—	—	12 2?	—	—
Northfleet	—	—	—	9 55	—	10 23	—	—	11 14	—	—	—	—	12 26	—	—

SUNDAYS.

	AM	AM	AM	AM	AM	AM	AM	AM	AM	AM	PM	PM	PM	PM	PM	PM	PM
Charing Cross dep.	7 0	—	7 30	8 15	8 27	9 0	9 20	9 46	10 40	10 50	11 35	12 5	12 33	1 15	1 35	2 33	3 15	3 35
Waterloo	7 2	—	7 32	8 17	8 23	9 2	9 22	—	10 42	10 52	11 37	12 7	12 35	1 17	1 37	2 35	3 17	3 37
Cannon Street	—	—	—	—	—	—	—	—	—	—	—	—	—	—	—	—	—
London Bridge	7 7	7 30	7 37	8 22	8 31	9 7	9 27	9 52	10 47	10 57	11 42	12 12	12 40	1 22	1 42	2 40	3 22	3 42
New Cross	7 15	7 36	7 45	—	8 43	9 14	9 34	9 59	10 56	11 6	11 49	12 19	12 49	1 31	1 49	2 49	3 29	3 49
St. John's	7 18	—	7 48	—	8 46	—	9 37	10 2	10 59	11 9	11 52	—	12 52	1 34	1 52	2 52	3 32	3 52
Hither Green	—	—	7 53	—	—	9 20	—	10 7	—	11 14	—	12 25	—	1 40	—	—	3 36	—
Lee	—	—	7 55	—	—	9 23	—	10 10	—	11 17	—	12 28	—	1 43	—	—	3 39	—
Eltham	—	—	8 2	—	—	9 28	—	10 16	—	11 23	—	12 33	—	1 49	—	—	3 44	—
New Eltham	—	—	8 5	—	—	9 31	—	10 19	—	11 26	—	12 36	—	1 52	—	—	3 47	—
Sidcup	—	—	8 9	—	—	9 35	—	10 23	—	11 31	—	12 40	—	1 57	—	—	3 51	—
Bexley	—	—	8 14	—	—	9 39	—	10 27	—	11 36	—	12 45	—	2 1	—	—	3 55	—
Crayford	—	—	8 18	—	—	9 43	—	10 31	—	11 40	—	12 49	—	2 6	—	—	3 58	—
Dartford	8 48	8 12	8 23	9 11	9 33	8 48	10 23	10 36	11 44	11 49	12 39	12 55	1 39	2 22	2 39	3 39	4 4	4 39
Greenhithe	—	—	8 32	—	—	—	—	10 44	—	11 55	—	—	—	2 20	—	—	4 13	—
Northfleet	—	—	8 37	—	—	—	—	10 49	—	12 0	—	—	—	2 25	—	—	4 18	—

SUNDAYS.

	PM	PM	PM	PM	PM	PM	PM	PM	PM	PM	PM	PM	PM	PM	PM	PM	PM
Charing Cross dep.	1 23	4 50	5 40	6 20	6 30	6 55	7 0	7 30	7 38	8 25	8 32	8 40	—	9 35	9 55	10 30	10 50
Waterloo	1 30	4 52	5 42	6 22	6 32	6 57	7 2	7 32	7 40	8 27	8 35	8 42	—	9 37	9 57	10 33	10 52
Cannon Street	—	—	—	—	—	—	—	—	—	—	—	—	—	—	—	—	—
London Bridge	1 35	4 57	5 47	6 27	6 37	7 2	7 7	7 37	7 45	8 32	8 40	8 47	9 20	9 42	10 2	10 38	10 57
New Cross	1 44	5 5	5 46	3 46	6 44	7 11	—	7 44	7 52	8 39	8 49	—	9 26	9 51	10 10	10 45	—
St. John's	1 47	5 8	5 57	6 37	6 47	7 14	—	7 47	—	8 42	8 52	—	9 28	9 54	10 13	10 49	—
Hither Green	—	5 13	—	—	6 52	—	—	—	7 58	8 46	—	—	9 33	—	10 18	—	11 8
Lee	—	5 16	—	—	6 55	—	—	—	8 1	8 49	—	—	9 36	—	10 21	—	11 11
Eltham	—	5 21	—	—	7 1	—	—	—	8 6	8 54	—	—	9 41	—	10 26	—	11 16
New Eltham	—	5 25	—	—	7 4	—	—	—	8 9	8 57	—	—	9 44	—	10 29	—	11 20
Sidcup	—	5 28	—	—	7 8	—	—	—	8 13	9 1	—	—	9 48	—	10 33	—	11 24
Bexley	—	5 32	—	—	7 12	—	—	—	8 18	9 5	—	—	9 52	—	10 37	—	11 28
Crayford	—	5 36	—	—	7 16	—	—	—	8 22	9 9	—	—	9 56	—	10 41	—	11 32
Dartford	5 34	5 42	6 44	7 23	7 21	8 0	7 38	8 35	8 27	9 14	9 39	9 18	10	10 41	10 46	11 37	11 37
Greenhithe	—	5 49	—	—	—	7 45	—	—	—	—	9 25	—	—	—	—	11 45	—
Northfleet	—	5 55	—	—	—	7 50	—	—	—	—	9 30	—	—	—	—	11 49	—

d Saturdays only.   e Saturdays excepted.

h Calls at Crayford on Wednesdays and Saturdays only.

NORTHFLEET TO CANNON STREET AND CHARING CROSS.

WEEK DAYS.

	AM	AM	AM	AM	AM	AM	AM	AM	AM	AM	AM	AM	AM	AM	AM	AM
Northfleet dep.	—	—	4 46	—	—	5 53	—	6 8	—	6 46	—	7 3	—	7 31	—	7 58
Greenhithe	—	—	4 51	—	—	5 58	—	6 16	—	6 51	—	7 8	—	7 36	—	8 3
Dartford	4 8	4 38	4 59	5 10	5 48	6 11	6 22	6 30	6 42	7 1	7 7	7 17	7 30	7 47	7 52	7 57	8 0	8 3
Crayford	—	—	—	5 14	—	—	6 26	—	—	—	7 11	—	7 34	7 51	—	8 3	15
Bexley	—	—	—	5 19	—	—	6 31	—	—	—	7 17	—	7 40	7 56	8 10	—	8 20
Sidcup	—	—	—	5 24	—	—	6 37	—	—	—	7 23	—	7 46	8 4	8 15	—	8 26
New Eltham	4 23	—	—	5 28	—	—	6 41	—	—	—	7 27	—	7 50	8 8	8 19	—	8 30
Eltham	4 26	—	—	5 31	—	—	6 44	—	—	—	7 30	—	7 53	8 12	8 23	—	8 34
Lee	4 30	—	—	5 35	—	—	6 48	—	—	—	7 34	—	7 57	8 16	8 27	—	8 38
Hither Green	4 33	—	—	5 38	—	—	6 51	—	—	—	—	—	8 0	8 19	8 30	—	—
St. John's	—	5 12	—	—	6 32	—	6 56	—	—	—	—	—	—	—	—	—
New Cross	4 38	5 15	—	5 43	6 35	—	6 59	7 16	7 21	—	7 41	8 8	7 8	8 24	—	—
London Bridge	4 44	5 24	5 47	5 50	6 42	7 7	6 7	7 23	7 29	7 43	7 48	8 12	8 14	8 31	8 42	8 34	8 52	8 52
Cannon Street	4 48	5 28	5 51	5 55	6 46	7 7	4 —	7 27	7 33	7 52	7 52	8 16	—	8 35	—	8 55	—
Waterloo	—	—	—	—	—	7 11	—	—	—	—	—	—	8 19	—	8 46	8 39	8 58
Charing Cross	—	—	—	—	—	7 15	—	—	—	—	—	—	8 22	—	8 50	8 43	9 2

WEEK DAYS.

	AM	AM	AM	AM	AM	AM	AM	AM	AM	AM	AM	AM	e	AM	AM
Northfleet dep.	—	8 26	—	9 14	—	—	—	—	—	—	10 26	—	—	11 16	—
Greenhithe	—	8 31	—	9 21	—	—	—	—	—	—	10 31	—	—	11 21	—
Dartford	8 24	8 39	—	9 9	9 28	9 43	10 15	10 20	10 25	10 42	10 48	11 18	11 30	11 43	11 43
Crayford	8 31	8 43	—	9 13	—	9 44	—	10 24	—	—	10 52	11 22	—	11 47	11 48
Bexley	8 36	8 48	—	9 19	—	9 50	—	10 29	—	—	10 58	11 27	—	11 52	11 53
Sidcup	8 42	8 54	9 13	9 25	—	9 56	—	10 35	—	—	11 3	11 33	—	11 58	12 3
New Eltham	8 46	8 58	—	9 29	—	10 0	—	10 39	—	—	11 7	11 37	—	12 2	12 6
Eltham	8 50	9 2	—	9 33	—	10 4	—	10 43	—	—	11 11	11 41	—	12 6	12 6
Lee	8 54	9 6	—	9 37	—	10 8	—	10 47	—	—	11 15	11 45	—	12 10	12 10
Hither Green	8 57	—	—	—	—	10 11	—	10 50	—	—	—	—	—	12 14	12 14
St. John's	—	—	—	—	—	—	—	—	11 6	—	—	—	—	12 19
New Cross	—	—	9 26	—	—	—	—	11 11	—	—	—	11 24	—	12 22
London Bridge	9 10	9 12	9 29	9 34	9 50	9 54	10 22	10 24	10 38	11 2	11 17	11 19	11 31	12 0	12 29
Cannon Street	9 9	9 16	9 24	—	—	—	10 28	—	11 11	11 21	11 24	12 4	—	—
Waterloo	9 15	—	—	9 39	9 55	—	10 27	—	—	11 7	—	—	11 36	—	12 10	12 34
Charing Cross	9 19	—	—	9 43	9 59	10 1	10 31	—	—	10 45	11 11	—	—	11 40	—	12 14	12 38

WEEK DAYS.

Station	AM	d	AM	d		e		d	e	d	e		e	d	PM	d	e	PM
NORTHFLEET ....dep.	—	11 49	11 55	—	—	—	—	—	12 46	12 46	—	—	—	—	—	12 53	1 25	1 46
Greenhithe	—	11 54	12* 2	—	—	—	—	—	12 51	12 51	—	—	—	—	—	1 0	1 32	1 52
DARTFORD	11 48	12 5	12 24	12 15	12 24	12 30	12 38	1 0	1 0	12 45	1	5	1 5	1 37	1 32	1 44	2 2
Crayford	—	12 17	—	—	—	12 34	12 42	—	1 4	—	1	9	—	1 41	—	—	2 6
Bexley	—	—	—	—	—	12 39	12 47	—	—	—	1	14	—	1 46	—	—	2 11
Sidcup	—	12 25	—	—	—	12 45	12 53	—	—	—	1	20	—	1 51	—	—	2 17
New Eltham	—	12 29	—	—	—	12 49	12 58	—	—	—	1	24	—	1 55	—	—	2 22
Eltham	—	—	—	—	—	12 52	1 1	—	—	—	1 27	—	1 58	—	—	2 23
LEE	—	12 37	—	—	—	12 33	1 5	—	—	—	1 31	—	2 2	—	—	2 28
Hither Green	—	12 41	—	—	—	12 59	1 8	—	1 19	—	1 34	—	2 5	—	—	2 31
St. John's	12 37	12 44	—	—	—	1 4	—	—	—	1 32	—	—	—	—	—	
New Cross	12 40	12 51	12 57	1 7	1 8	1 15	1 7	1 13	—	1 35	—	1 47	2 11	2 20	—	2 37
LONDON BRIDGE ...	12 49	12 56		1 11	1 14	1 20	1 35	1 33	1 43	1 47	1 54	2 18	2 27	2 41	2 44
CANNON STREET ...	12 53		1 11	1 19	1 18	—	—	1 37	1 49	—	1 58	2*22	2 31	2 45	
Waterloo.........	—	1d 3	—	—	—	1 26	1 40	—	—	—	—	—	—	—	2 50
CHARING CROSS ...	—	1 5	—	—	1 30	1 44	—	1 55	—	2d25	—	—	2 54

WEEK DAYS.

Station	e	d	e	d		e	d	PM		e	e	d	d	e	PM	d	d	e
NORTHFLEET ....dep.	2 9	2 9	2 40	—	—	3 0	—	3 34	3 58	3 58	—	—	—	4 49	—	—	—
Greenhithe	2 14	2 15	2 45	—	—	3 6	—	3 39	4 3	4 2	—	—	—	4 55	—	—	—
DARTFORD	2 23	2 24	2 54	2 37	3 0	3 15	3 25	3 48	4 12	4 12	4 20	4 23	4 18	5 4	4 50	5 12	5 17	5 20
Crayford	—	—	—	—	3 4	3 19	—	3 52	—	4 16	—	4 28	—	5 12	—	5 16	5 22	—
Bexley	—	—	—	—	3 9	3 24	—	3 57	—	4 22	—	4 33	—	—	—	5 21	5 28	—
Sidcup	—	—	—	—	3 15	3 30	—	4 5	—	4 28	—	4 39	—	—	—	5 27	5 34	—
New Eltham	—	—	—	—	3 19	3 34	—	4 7	—	4 32	—	4 43	—	—	—	5 32	5 38	—
Eltham	—	—	—	—	3 22	3 37	—	4 10	—	4 35	—	4 46	—	—	—	5 36	5 41	—
LEE	—	—	—	—	3 26	3 41	—	4 14	—	4 40	—	4 50	—	—	—	5 40	5 45	—
Hither Green	—	—	—	—	3 29	3 44	—	4 17	—	4 43	—	4 53	—	—	—	5 43	5 48	—
St. John's	—	—	—	3 22	—	—	4 11	4 21	—	4 58	—	—	—	—	—	5 53	6 3
New Cross	2 45	—	—	3 25	3 34	3 51	4 14	—	4 50	5 8	5 1	5 6	5 36	—	5 50	5 56	6 6
LONDON BRIDGE.....	2 53	3 21	3 26	3 32	3 42	3 58	4 22	4 30	4 48	4 57	5 16	5 10	5 14	5 40	5 44	5 57	6 5	6 14
CANNON STREET.....	—	3 23	—	3 36	—	—	—	4 36	4 52	—	—	—	—	5 49	—	—	—
Waterloo.........	3 0	—	3 32	—	3 47	4 4	4 27	—	5 3	5 21	5 15	5 20	—	6 2	6 10	6 19
CHARING CROSS ...	3 4	—	3 36	—	3 52	4 8	4 31	—	5 7	5 25	5 19	5 25	5d44	—	6 6	6 15	6 23

WEEK DAYS.

Station	d	e	e	e	PM		PM		d	e	PM	PM	d	PM	PM	PM	PM	PM
NORTHFLEET ....dep.	—	5 19	—	5 34	—	—	6 11	—	—	6 25	—	—	6 59	7 30	—	7 37	—	8 59
Greenhithe	—	5 25	—	5 39	—	—	6 16	—	—	6 30	—	—	7 4	7 35	—	7 44	—	9 4
DARTFORD	5 28	5 36	5 54	5 49	5 54	6 10	6 24	6 30	6 32	6 38	7 1	7 6	7 12	7 43	7 48	7 53	8 26	9 12
Crayford	—	—	—	5 53	—	—	6 28	—	—	—	7 6	—	—	7 47	7 53	—	8 30	—
Bexley	—	—	—	5 59	—	—	6 33	—	—	—	7 11	—	—	—	7 58	—	8 35	—
Sidcup	—	—	—	6 5	—	—	6 39	—	—	—	7 17	—	—	—	8 4	—	8 41	—
New Eltham	—	—	—	6 9	—	—	6 43	—	—	—	7 21	—	—	—	8 8	—	8 45	—
Eltham	—	—	—	6 13	—	—	6 46	—	—	—	7 24	—	—	—	8 11	—	8 48	—
LEE	—	—	—	6 16	—	—	6 50	—	—	—	7 28	—	—	—	8 15	—	8 52	—
Hither Green	—	—	—	6 19	—	—	6 53	—	—	—	7 31	—	—	8 2	8 18	—	8 55	—
St. John's	—	—	—	—	6*34	6 49	6 59	7 10	7 13	—	7 36	7 49	—	—	—	8 40	9 0	—
New Cross	6 14	6 19	—	6 26	6*37	6 52	7 2	7 13	7 16	—	7 39	7 52	—	8 7	8 23	8 43	9 3	—
LONDON BRIDGE.....	6 23	6 28	6 36	6 36	6 44	7 0	7 10	7 21	7 23	7 27	7 46	8 0	8 8	8 15	8 30	8 50	9 10	9 36
CANNON STREET.....	—	6 32	—	6 40	6 48	7 4	—	—	7 28	7 31	—	—	8*14	8 20	8 34	—	—	—
Waterloo.........	6 31	—	6 43	—	6d51	—	7 15	7 29	—	—	7 51	—	8d14	—	—	8 54	—	6 43
CHARING CROSS ...	6 35	—	6 47	—	6d55	—	7 19	7 33	—	—	7 55	—	8d19	—	—	8 58	9 18	9 47

WEEK DAYS.

Station	PM	PM	PM	PM	PM	PM	PM	PM								
NORTHFLEET ....dep.	—	—	9 12	10 2	—	10 32	11 24									
Greenhithe	—	—	9 19	10 7	—	10 39	11 29									
DARTFORD	9 15	9 20	10 0	10 16	10 21	10 26	11 45	11 38								
Crayford	9 20	—	—	—	10 25	—	11 49	—								
Bexley	9 26	—	—	—	10 29	—	11 54	—								
Sidcup	9 32	—	—	—	10 35	—	12 0	—								
New Eltham	9 36	—	—	—	10 39	—	12 4	—								
Eltham	9 40	—	—	—	10 42	—	12 7	—					*d* Saturdays only.			
LEE	9 44	—	—	—	10 46	—	12 11	—					*e* Saturdays excepted.			
Hither Green	9 47	—	—	—	10 49	—	12 14	—								
St. John's	9 52	10 8	—	—	—	—	12 23									
New Cross	9 55	10 11	10 40	—	10 56	—	12 19	12 26								
LONDON BRIDGE	10 2	10 20	10 47	10 51	11 3	11 17	12 26	12 35								
CANNON STREET.....	—	—	10 51	—	—	—	—	—								
Waterloo...........	—	10 30	—	—	11 10	11 22	—	12 41								
CHARING CROSS ...	10 9	10 34	—	10 59	11 14	11 26	12 33	12 45								

SUNDAYS.

Station	AM	AM	AM	AM	AM	AM	AM	AM	AM	PM		PM	PM	PM	PM	PM	PM	PM
NORTHFLEET ....dep.	—	8 4	—	9 22	—	—	—	—	12 3	—	1 16	—	—	—	3 7	—	—
Greenhithe	—	8 9	—	9 27	—	—	—	—	12 8	—	1 21	—	—	—	3 12	—	—
DARTFORD	6 30	7 27	8 18	6 41	9 35	9 47	10 45	10 55	11 45	12 17	12 50	1 30	1 50	2 47	3 21	3 47	4 53
Crayford	—	7 31	8 22	—	9 39	—	10 59	—	12 21	—	1 34	—	—	—	3 25	—	4 57
Bexley	—	7 36	8 27	—	9 44	—	11 4	—	12 26	—	1 39	—	—	—	3 30	—	5 2
Sidcup	—	7 42	8 33	—	9 49	—	11 10	—	12 32	—	1 45	—	—	—	3 35	—	5 8
New Eltham	—	7 46	8 37	—	9 53	—	11 13	—	12 36	—	1 49	—	—	—	3 39	—	5 11
Eltham	—	7 49	8 40	—	9 56	—	11 16	—	12 40	—	1 52	—	—	—	3 42	—	5 14
LEE	—	7 53	8 44	—	10 0	—	11 20	—	12 44	—	1 56	—	—	—	3 45	—	5 18
Hither Green	—	7 56	8 47	—	10 3	—	11 23	—	12 47	—	1 59	—	—	—	3 48	—	5 21
St. John's	—	8 0	—	9 26	—	10 33	11 32	11 28	12 32	—	1 37	2	4 2	3 53	4 32	5 25
New Cross	—	8 3	8 52	9 29	10 8	10 36	11 35	11 31	12 35	—	1 40	2 7	2 39	3 33	3 56	4 35	5 28
LONDON BRIDGE	7 20	8 10	9 0	9 36	10 16	10 46	11 42	11 38	12 44	1 5	1 49	2 14	2 46	3 43	4 3	4 43	5 35
CANNON STREET.....	—	—	—	—	—	—	—	—	—	—	—	—	—	—	—	—	—
Waterloo...........	7 25	8 15	9 5	9 41	10 20	10 51	11 47	11 43	12 49	1 12	1 54	2 20	2 53	3 49	4 11	4 49	5 40
CHARING CROSS ...	7 28	8 19	9 9	9 45	10 24	10 55	11 51	11 47	12 53	1 17	1 59	2 24	2 57	3 53	4 15	4 54	5 44

SUNDAYS.

Station	PM	PM	PM	PM	PM	PM	PM	PM	PM	PM		PM	PM	PM	PM
NORTHFLEET ....dep.	5 7	—	5 59	—	—	7 1	—	—	8 56	—	10 18	—		
Greenhithe	5 11	—	6 4	—	—	7 6	—	—	—	—	10 23	—		
DARTFORD	5 22	5 28	5 52	6 15	6 26	6 50	7 15	7 46	8 10	8 43	9 43	10 32	10 45		
Crayford	—	5 32	—	—	6 30	—	7 19	—	8 14	—	9 13	—	10 36	—	
Bexley	—	5 37	—	—	6 35	—	7 24	—	8 20	—	9 18	—	10 41	—	
Sidcup	—	5 43	—	—	6 41	—	7 31	—	8 26	—	9 24	—	10 46	—	
New Eltham	—	5 46	—	—	6 45	—	7 35	—	8 30	—	9 28	—	10 50	—	
Eltham	—	5 49	—	—	6 48	—	7 39	—	8 33	—	9 31	—	10 54	—	
LEE	—	5 53	—	—	6 52	—	7 43	—	8 37	—	9 35	—	10 58	—	
Hither Green	—	5 56	—	—	6 55	—	7 47	—	8 40	—	9 38	—	11 1	—	
St. John's	—	6 0	6 37	—	—	7 35	7 51	8 32	—	9 32	—	10 28	11 5	11 32	
New Cross	—	6 3	6 40	—	7 0	7 38	7 54	8 35	8 45	9 35	9 43	10 31	11 8	11 35	
LONDON BRIDGE	5 54	6 10	6 49	6 49	7 7	7 45	8 1	8 44	8 52	9 44	9 50	10 38	11 15	11 44	
CANNON STREET.....	—	—	—	—	—	—	—	—	—	—	—	—	—	—	
Waterloo...........	6 0	6 16	6 52	6 55	7 12	7 50	8 6	8 50	—	9 51	9 55	10 43	11 20	11 50	
CHARING CROSS ...	6 4	6 20	6 56	6 59	7 16	7 54	8 10	8 54	—	9 55	9 59	10 47	11 24	11 54	

WEEK DAYS.

WEEK DAYS.	AM	AM	AM	AM	AM	AM	AM	AM	AM	d	e	d	d	PM	e	d	d
Charing Cross ...dep	5 18	—	—	—	8 16	—	9 45	10 10	—	—	—	—	—	1 18	—	—	—
Waterloo	5 20	—	—	—	8 19	—	9 47	10 12	—	—	—	—	—	1 20	—	—	—
Cannon Street	—	6 55	7 24	8	0	—	8 48	—	—	8	12	0	12	12 12	22 12 54	—	1 23	1 32	1 44
London Bridge	5 25	6 58	7 27	8	3	8 25	8 52	9 53	10 18	11	11	12	3	12 15 12 25	12 57	1 25	1 26	1 35	1 47
New Cross	5 34	7	5	7 35	8 11	8 32	9	1	10	1	10 25	11	19	12 10	12 22	—	—	1 34	1 44	1 54
St. John's	5 37	7	8	—	—	8 35	9	4	10	4	10 28	11	22	12 13	12 25	—	—	1 37	1 47	1 57
Lewisham Junction	5 40	7 11	7 39	8 15	8 38	9	7	10	7	10 31	11 25	12 16	12 28	12 35	—	1 34	1 40	1 50	2 0
Blackheath	5 44	7 15	7 43	8 19	8 42	9 11	10	11	10 35	11 37	12 20	12 32	12 39	1	9	1 38	1 44	1 54	2 4
Kidbrooke	5 53	7 19	7 47	8 23	8 46	9 15	10 15	10 44	11 40	12 24	12 42	12 43	1 13	1 42	1 52	1 58	2 9
Well Hall	5 57	7 23	7 51	8 27	8 50	9 19	10 18	10 48	11 44	12 28	12 46	12 47	1 16	1 46	1 56	2 2	2 13
Shooter's Hill	6 0	7 26	7 54	8 30	8 53	9 22	10 21	10 51	11 47	12 31	12 49	12 50	1 19	1 49	1 59	2 5	2 16
Welling	6 5	7 31	7 59	8 35	8 58	9 27	10 26	10 56	11 52	12 36	12 54	12 55	1 24	1 54	2 4	2 10	2 21
Bexley Heath	6 9	7 36	8	3	8 40	9	2	9 32	10 31	11	0	11 56	12 40	12 53	1 0	1 28	1 58	2 8	2 14	2 25
Barnehurst	6 13	7 40	8	7	8 44	9	6	9 49	10 39	11	3	11 59	12 44	1 1	1 13	1 32	2 2	2 11	2 18	2 29
Erith	—	—	8	16	9 0	—	10 0	10 57	11 12	12	8	12 55	1 13	1 22	1 45	2 13	2 20	2 27	2 40

WEEK DAYS.	d	e	d	d	e	d	PM	e	d	e	e	e	d	e	e	e	d
Charing Cross ...dep	2 0	—	—	3 18	—	3 35	—	4 21	4 35	4 58	—	—	5 49	—	—	—	6 30	6 37
Waterloo	2 2	—	—	—	—	3 37	—	4 24	4 37	5 0	—	—	—	—	—	—	6 32	6 39
Cannon Street	—	2 0	2 45	—	3 16	—	4 0	—	—	—	5 26	5 44	—	6 46	8	6 24	—	—
London Bridge	2 7	2	3	2 48	3 24	3 19	3 42	4	3 4	29	4 42	5	5 29	5 47	5 54	6	7 6	11	6 27	6 37	6 44
New Cross	—	2 11	—	—	3 30	3 50	4 10	4 37	4 51	—	—	—	6 18	—	—	6 52
St. John's	—	2 14	—	—	3 33	3 53	4 12	4 39	4 55	5 14	5 38	5 55	—	—	6 21	6 36	—	6 55
Lewisham Junction	2 16	2 17	2 57	3 33	3 36	3 56	4 15	4 42	4 58	5 17	5 41	—	6	3 6	16	6 24	—	6 46	6 58
Blackheath	2 20	2 21	3	1	3 37	3 40	4	0	4 19	4 46	5	2 5	21	5 45	6	0 6	7 6	20	6 28	6 40	6 50	7 2
Kidbrooke	2 24	2 31	3	5	3 41	3 50	4 10	4 28	4 50	5 13	5 25	5 49	6	4 6	11	—	6 32	—	6 54	—
Well Hall	2 28	2 36	3	9	3 45	3 54	4 15	4 32	4 55	5 17	5 29	5 53	6	8 6	15	6 27	6 37	6 48	6 59
Shooter's Hill	2 31	2 39	3 12	3 48	3 57	4 18	4 35	4 58	5 20	5 32	5 56	6 11	6 18	6 30	6 40	6 51	7 2
Welling	2 36	2 44	3 17	3 53	4	2	4 24	4 40	5	3 5	25	5 37	6	1 6	16	6 23	6 35	6 46	6 57	7 8
Bexley Heath	2 40	2 48	3 22	3 57	4	6	4 29	4 44	5	8 5	29	5 41	6	5 6	20	6 28	6 39	6 50	7	1	7 12
Barnehurst	2 44	3	3	3 26	4	1	4 10	4 33	4 48	5 13	5 33	5 45	6	9 6	24	6 48	6 43	6 54	7	5	7 16
Erith	2 55	—	3 40	4 10	4 31	—	—	—	—	6 5	—	—	—	—	—	—

WEEK DAYS.	e	e	d	e	e	d	e	PM	PM	PM	PM	PM
Charing Cross ...dep	6 42	6 54	7 2	—	—	8*30	—	9 48	10 28	10 50	11 39	
Waterloo	6 44	6 56	—	—	—	8*32	—	10 30	—	—	
Cannon Street	—	—	—	7 20	7 44	7 56	8*35	9 20	—	—	—	
London Bridge	6 49	7	1	7	8	7 23	7 47	7 59	8*39	9 23	9 54	10 36	10 56	—
New Cross	6 57	—	—	—	7 54	8	8	8 45	—	—	11	5	—
St. John's	7 0	7	9	—	—	7 57	8	10	8 48	—	—	—	—
Lewisham Junction	7 3	7 12	7 17	7 32	8	0	8 13	8 51	9 32	10	3	—	11	9	11 51
Blackheath	7 7	7 16	7 21	7 36	8	4	8 17	8 55	9 36	10	7	—	11 13	11 55
Kidbrooke	—	7 20	7 25	7 40	8 13	8 21	9	0	9 40	—	—	11 59
Well Hall	7 14	7 24	7 29	7 44	8 17	8 25	9	4	9 43	10 15	—	11 20	12 2
Shooter's Hill	7 17	7 27	7 32	7 47	8 20	8 28	9	7	9 46	10 18	—	11 23	12 5
Welling	7 22	7 32	7 37	7 52	8 25	8 33	9 12	9 51	10 23	—	11 28	12 10
Bexley Heath	7 26	7 36	7 41	7 56	8 29	8 37	9 16	9 55	10 28	—	11 32	12 15
Barnehurst	7 30	7 40	7 45	8	0	8 33	8 42	9 20	10	0	—	—	—
Erith	7 41	—	—	8 13	8 42	8 54	9 35	—	—	—	—	—

d Saturdays only.
e Saturdays excepted.

SUNDAYS.

SUNDAYS.	AM	AM	AM	AM	AM	AM	AM	AM	PM	PM	PM	PM	PM	PM	PM
Charing Cross ...dep	7	0	8 27	9 20	10 40	11 35	12 33	1 35	2 33	3 35	4 28	5 40	6 20	7	30	8 34	9 47	10 30	11 0
Waterloo	7	2	8 29	9 22	10 42	11 37	12 35	1 37	2 35	3 37	4 30	5 42	6 22	7	32	8 37	—	10 33	11 2
Cannon Street	—	—	—	—	—	—	—	—	—	—	—	—	—	—	—	—
London Bridge	7	7	8 34	9 27	10 47	11 42	12 40	1 42	2 40	3 42	4 36	5 47	6 27	7	37	8 42	9 53	10 38	11 7
New Cross	7 15	8 43	9 34	10 56	11 49	12 49	1 49	2 49	3 49	4 44	5 54	6 34	7	44	8 51	—	10 45	11 17
St. John's	7 18	8 46	9 37	10 59	11 52	12 52	1 52	2 52	3 52	4 47	5 57	6 37	7	47	8 54	—	10 48	11 20
Lewisham Junction	7 21	8 49	9 40	11	2	11 55	12 55	1 55	2 55	3 55	4 50	6	0	6 40	7	50	8 57	10	0	10 51	11 23
Blackheath	7 25	8 53	9 44	11	6	11 59	12 59	1 59	2 59	3 59	4 54	6	4	6 44	7	54	9	1	10	6	10 56	11 27
Kidbrooke	—	—	—	—	—	—	—	—	—	—	—	—	—	—	—	—
Well Hall	7 37	9	6	9 56	11 18	12	1	1 1	2	1	3	1	4 11	5	5	6	6	6 56	8	6	9 13	10	8	11	8	11 39
Shooter's Hill	7 40	9	9	9 59	11 21	12	4	1	4	2	4	3	4	4 14	5	8	6	9	6 59	8	9	9 16	10	11	11	11	11 49
Welling	7 45	9 14	10	4	11 26	12	9	1	9	2	9	3	9	4 19	5 14	6 14	7	4	8 14	9 19	10 16	11	16	11 55
Bexley Heath	7 49	9 18	10	8	11 30	12 23	1 23	2 23	3 23	4 23	5 18	6 27	6 58	8	18	9 23	10 20	11 20	—
Barnehurst	7 53	9 21	10 11	11 33	12 26	1 26	2 26	3 26	4 26	5 23	6 31	7	0	8 23	9 28	10 25	11 25	—
Erith	—	9 30	10 20	11 42	12 35	1 35	2 35	3 35	4 35	5 34	6 40	7	20	8 30	9 37	10 35	11 30	—*

ERITH TO CANNON STREET AND CHARING CROSS.

WEEK DAYS.

WEEK DAYS.	AM	AM	AM	AM	AM	AM	AM	AM	AM	AM	AM	e	d
Erith ....dep	—	—	—	—	—	—	—	—	—	—	—	10 15	10 15
Barnehurst	—	5 45	6 32	6 55	7 22	7 46	7 57	8 18	8 39	8 50	9 5	—	9 54	10 30	10 30
Bexley Heath	4 48	5 49	6 36	6 59	7 26	7 50	8	1	8 22	8 43	8 54	9 9	—	9 58	10 33	10 33
Welling	4 53	5 54	6 40	7	3	7 30	7 54	8	5	8 26	8 47	8 58	9 13	—	10	2	10 39	10 39
Shooter's Hill	4 59	6	0	6 46	7	7	7 36	8	0	8 11	8 32	8 53	9	4	—	10	8	10 45	10 45
Well Hall	5	1	6	2	6 48	7 11	7 38	8	2	8 13	8 34	8 56	9	6	9 21	9 50	10	10 47	10 47
Kidbrooke	—	6	5	6 51	7 14	7 41	8	8	8 16	8 37	8 59	9	9	9 24	9 53	10	10 50	10 50
Blackheath	5	6	6	9	6 55	7 18	7 45	8	9	8 20	8 41	9	2	9 13	9 28	9 56	10 17	10 54	10 54
Lewisham Junction	5	9	6 12	6 58	7 21	—	8 13	8	9 24	9	9 17	9 31	9 59	10	10 58	10 58
St. John's	5 12	6 15	7	1	7 24	—	8 26	—	—	—	9 34	10	2	10 11	11	1	—
New Cross	5 15	6 18	7	4	7 27	—	8 17	8 29	8 48	—	9 37	10	5	10 17	11	4	—
London Bridge	5 24	6 27	7 12	7 36	7 56	8 24	8 38	8 57	9 16	9 26	9 44	10 14	10 25	11	11	—
Cannon Street	5 28	—	7 16	7 40	8	0	8 28	—	—	9 16	9	10 17	10 28	11	11	—
Waterloo	—	6 32	—	—	—	—	—	—	9·31	—	—	—	—
Charing Cross	—	6 36	—	—	—	—	—	—	9 35	—	—	—	—

WEEK DAYS.	AM	AM	AM	AM	PM	PM	PM	PM	PM	PM	PM	PM	PM	PM	PM	PM
Erith ....dep	10 56	11 50	12	7	12 47	12 47	1 18	1 48	2 20	2 40	3 27	3 50	4 23	4 33	5 15
Barnehurst	11	4	11 59	12	17	12 56	12 56	1 34	1 56	2 28	2 48	3 36	3 58	4 31	4 45	5 24
Bexley Heath	11	8	12	3	12 20	12 59	1	4	1 38	2	0	2 32	2 52	3 40	4	2	4 35	4 49	5 30
Welling	11 12	12	8	12 24	1	4	1	4	1 42	2	5	2 36	2 56	3 44	4	4	4 39	4 53	5 34
Shooter's Hill	11 18	12 14	12 30	1 10	1 10	1 48	2 10	2 42	3	1	3 50	4 14	4 45	4 59	5 40
Well Hall	11 20	12 17	12 33	1 12	1 12	1 50	2 13	2 43	3	4	3 52	4 16	4 48	5	1	5 42
Kidbrooke	11 23	12 20	12 36	1 15	1 15	1 53	2 16	2 46	3	7	3 55	4 19	4 51	5	4	5 45
Blackheath	11 32	12 30	12 39	1 18	1 18	1 26	1 56	2 22	2 50	3 10	3 16	4	4	4 23	4 59	5	7	5 49
Lewisham Junction	11 35	12 34	12 42	12 45	—	1 32	—	2	31	—	2 53	3 19	4	8	4 26	5	3	5 10	5 55
St. John's	11 38	12 37	12 45	—	—	1 32	—	2	34	—	—	3 22	4 11	—	—	5 13	5 56
New Cross	11 41	12 40	12 48	—	—	1 35	—	2	37	—	—	3 25	4 ·15	—	—	5 16	5 59
London Bridge	11 50	12 49	12 57	1	2	—	1 44	2	11	2 46	3	3	3	3 34	4 24	4 40	5	3	5 23	6	8
Cannon Street	11 52	12 53	1	0	1	—	1 48	2 16	2 46	—	3 36	—	4 43	—	5 26	6 12
Waterloo	—	—	—	—	—	—	—	4 29	—	5 21	—	—
Charing Cross	—	—	—	—	3 10	—	4 33	—	5 25	—	—

WEEK DAYS.	d	d	e	e	d	e	d	PM	PM	PM	PM
ERITH ....dep.	—	5 58	—	—	—	7 25	—	9 24	—	—	10 38
Barnehurst	5 32	6 6	6 16	6 43	7 14	7 32	7 33	8 36	9 33	10 9	—
BEXLEY HEATH	5 36	6 10	6 22	6 49	7 18	7 37	7 37	8 41	9 38	10 14	10 49
Welling	5 41	6 14	6 26	6 53	7 23	7 41	7 41	8 46	9 42	10 19	10 53
Shooter's Hill	5 47	6 19	6 32	6 59	7 29	7 47	7 47	8 52	9 48	10 25	10 59
Well Hall	5 49	6 21	6 35	7 1	7 31	7 49	7 49	8 54	9 50	10 27	11 1
Kidbrooke .....—....	5 52	6 24	6 38	7 4	7 34	7 52	7 52	8 57	9 53	—	—
BLACKHEATH	6 1	6 28	6 41	7 8	7 44	7 57	7 57	9 0	9 57	10 33	11 8
Lewisham Junction ..	6 4	6 31	6 44	7 11	7 47	8 0	9 4	10 1	10 36	11 12
St. John's	—	—	6 47	7 14	7 50	8 3	8 3	7	—	—	11 15
New Cross	6 8	—	6 50	7 17	7 53	8 6	8 6	9 11	10 5	10 40	11 18
LONDON BRIDGE	6 15	6 40	6 59	7 24	8 0	8 14	8 14	9 18	10 12	10 47	11 25
CANNON STREET......	6 19	—	7 4	7 28	8 5	8 18	8 18	9 22	10ᵈ17	10 51	—
Waterloo	—	—	—	—	—	—	—	—	10ᵈ18	—	11 31
CHARING CROSS.......	—	6 47	—	—	—	—	—	—	10ᵈ22	—	11 36

SUNDAYS	AM	AM	AM	AM	AM	AM	PM	PM	PM	PM	PM	PM	PM	PM	PM	PM	PM	PM
ERITH ....dep.	7 22	8 0	—	9 50	10 48	11 49	12 54	1 53	2 50	3 50	4 48	5 54	6 53	7 48	8 45	9 48	10 50
Barnehurst	7 30	8 10	8 53	9 58	10 56	11 57	1 2	2 1	2 58	3 58	4 56	6 2	7 1	7 58	8 53	9 56	10 58
BEXLEY HEATH	7 34	8 14	8 57	10 2	11 0	12 1	1 6	2 5	3 3	4 2	5 0	6 6	7 5	8 2	8 57	10 0	11 2
Welling	7 38	8 18	9 1	10 6	11 4	12 5	1 10	2 9	3 5	4 6	5 4	6 10	7 9	8 6	9 1	10 4	11 6
Shooter's Hill	7 43	8 24	9 6	10 12	11 12	12 11	1 16	2 15	3 11	4 12	5 10	6 16	7 15	8 12	9 7	10 10	11 12
Well Hall	7 45	8 26	9 8	10 14	11 14	12 13	1 18	2 17	3 13	4 14	5 12	6 18	7 17	8 14	9 9	10 12	11 14
Kidbrooke	—	—	—	—	—	—	—	—	—	—	—	—	—	—	—	—	—
BLACKHEATH	7 51	8 38	9 19	10 26	11 26	12 25	1 24	2 29	3 26	4 26	5 25	6 30	7 29	8 26	9 14	10 24	11 26
Lewisham Junction .	7 54	8 41	9 22	10 30	11 29	12 28	1 34	2 32	3 29	4 29	5 28	6 33	7 32	8 29	9 17	10 27	11 29
St. John's	—	8 44	9 25	10 33	11 32	12 31	1 38	2 35	3 32	4 32	5 31	6 36	7 35	8 32	—	10 30	11 32
New Cross	7 58	8 47	9 28	10 36	11 35	12 34	1 41	2 39	3 35	4 35	5 34	6 39	7 38	8 35	9 21	10 33	11 35
LONDON BRIDGE	8 5	8 57	9 36	10 46	11 42	12 43	1 49	2 48	3 44	4 43	5 43	6 47	7 45	8 40	9 29	10 40	11 44
CANNON STREET	—	—	—	—	—	—	—	—	—	—	—	—	—	—	—	—	—
Waterloo	8 10	9 1	9 40	10 51	11 47	12 48	1 54	2 54	3 49	4 49	5 48	6 51	7 50	8 50	9 34	10 45	11 50
CHARING CROSS	8 14	9 5	9 44	10 55	11 51	12 52	1 59	2 59	3 53	4 54	5 52	6 55	7 54	8 54	9 38	10 49	11 54

d Saturdays only. *e* Saturdays excepted.

CHARING CROSS AND CANNON STREET TO BROMLEY, NORTH.

WEEK DAYS.	AM	AM	AM	AM	AM	AM	AM	AM	AM	AM	d	e	d	e	d
CHARING CROSS ..dep.	—	—	7 26	—	—	—	—	—	11 15	11 42	12 10	12 20	12 26	—
Waterloo	—	—	7 28	—	—	—	—	—	11 17	11 44	12 12	12 22	12 28	—
CANNON STREET	5 20	6 45	—	7 52	7 56	8 40	9 36	10 28	—	—	—	—	—	12 48
London Bridge	5 25	6 50	7 33	7 55	8 0	8 43	9 39	10 31	11 23	11 49	12 17	12 27	12 33	12 51
New Cross	5 35	6 58	7 40	—	8 8	8 52	—	10 39	11 31	11 56	12 24	12 34	—	—
St. John's	—	—	—	—	—	—	—	11 34	—	—	—	—	—	—
Hither Green	5 42	7 4	7 46	8 8	8 15	8 58	9 52	10 45	11 39	12 2	12 30	12 40	12 44	1 3
Grove Park	5 50	7 9	7 51	8 13	8 20	9 3	9 57	10 50	11 44	12 7	12 35	12 45	12 49	1 8
Sundridge Park	6 0	7 19	—	8 18	—	9 9	10 9	10 56	11 55	12 12	12 40	12 49	12 54	1 14
BROMLEY, NORTH	6 3	7 22	—	8 20	—	9 12	10 12	10 59	11 58	12 15	12 43	12 52	12 57	1 17

WEEK DAYS.	e	d	d	e	d	e	d	e	d	e	d	PM	e	d
CHARING CROSS ..dep.	12 50	—	1 33	—	1 50	—	—	2 30	2 50	—	3 20	—	4 6	4 55
Waterloo	12 53	—	1 36	—	1 53	—	—	2 32	2 52	—	—	—	4 8	—
CANNON STREET	—	1 18	—	1 28	—	2 4	2 32	—	—	3 8	—	3 28	—	4 43
London Bridge	12 58	1 21	1 41	1 32	1 58	2 7	2 35	2 37	2 57	3 11	3 25	3 31	4 13	4 46	5 1
New Cross	1 5	—	—	1 39	—	2 15	2 42	2 44	3 4	—	3 32	—	4 20	4 53	5 9
St. John's...........	1 8	—	—	—	—	—	—	—	—	—	—	—	4 23	—
Hither Green	1 13	1 32	1 52	1 45	2 10	—	2 48	2 50	3 10	3 22	3 38	3 41	4 28	4 59	—
Grove Park	1 18	1 37	1 57	1 50	2 15	2 24	2 53	2 55	3 15	3 27	3 43	3 46	4 33	5 4	5 18
Sundridge Park	1 23	1 42	—	1 55	2 22	2 32	2 58	3 2	3 22	3 32	3 48	3 51	4 39	5 10	5 25
BROMLEY, NORTH ...	1 26	1 45	—	1 58	2 25	2 35	3 1	3 4	3 25	3 35	3 51	3 54	4 42	5 13	5 27

WEEK DAYS.	e	e	PM	e	—	PM	e	—	—	—	PM	e	—	PM	e	PM
CHARING CROSS. dep.	—	—	5 35	—	5 51	6 5	6 15	—	6 40	7 5	7 26	—	—	8 10	8 38
Waterloo	—	—	—	—	—	6 8	—	—	6 43	7 7	7 28	—	—	8 13	8 40
CANNON STREET	5 10	5 32	5˙38	5 52	—	—	6 44	—	—	—	—	7 52	8 13	—	—
London Bridge	5 13	5 35	5 41	5 55	5 57	6 13	6 20	6 47	6 48	7 12	7 33	7 55	8 16	8 19	8 45
New Cross	5 20	—	—	—	—	—	6 27	6 54	6 55	—	7 40	—	8 23	8 27	8 52
St. John's...........	—	—	—	—	—	—	—	—	—	—	7 43	—	—	—	—
Hither Green	5 26	5 45	5 52	6 5	6 7	—	6 33	7 1	7 7	7 23	7 48	8 5	8 29	8 33	8 57
Grove Park	5 31	5 50	—	6 10	6 12	6 25	6 39	7 6	7 7	7 29	7 53	8 10	8 34	8 39	9 4
Sundridge Park	5 37	5 55	—	6 16	6 17	6 32	6 46	7 11	7 11	7 35	7 58	8 15	8 39	8 45	9 8
BROMLEY, NORTH	5 40	5 58	—	6 19	6 19	6 35	6 48	7 14	7 14	7 37	8 1	8 18	8 42	8 48	9 11

WEEK DAYS.	PM	PM	PM	PM	PM	PM	AM
CHARING CROSS ..dep.	9 14	9 50	10 0	10 35	11 15	11 36	—
Waterloo	9 16	9 52	—	10 37	11 17	—	—
CANNON STREET	—	—	—	—	—	—	—
London Bridge	9 21	9 57	10 6	10 43	11 22	—	12ʰ42
New Cross	9 28	10 4	—	10 51	11 29	—	12 48
St. John's...........	—	—	—	—	—	—	12 51
Hither Green	9 34	10 10	—	10 57	11 35	11 50	12 56
Grove Park	9 39	10 15	10 20	11 2	11 40	11 55	1 0
Sundridge Park	9 44	10 20	—	11 7	11 45	12 0	1 6
BROMLEY, NORTH	9 47	10 22	—	11 10	11 48	12 3	1 9

d Saturdays only. *e* Saturdays excepted. *h* Also leave Holborn Viaduct 12.33, St. Paul's 12.34.

SUNDAYS.	AM	AM	AM	AM	AM	AM	n	PM	PM	PM	PM	PM	PM	PM	PM
CHARING CROSS ..dep.	8.10	8 55	9 35	10 0	11 0	11 15	12 0	1 0	2 0	3 0	3 54	4 0	5 0	6 0	6 5
Waterloo	8 12	8 57	—	10 2	11 2	11 17	12 2	1 2	2 2	3 2	3 54	4 2	5 2	—	6 7
CANNON STREET	—	—	—	—	—	—	—	—	—	—	—	—	—	—	—
London Bridge	8 17	9 2	9 36	10 7	11 7	11 23	12 7	1 7	2 7	3 7	3 13	4 7	5 7	6 6	6 12
New Cross............	8 24	9 9	9 43	10 14	11 14	11 31	12 14	1 14	2 14	3 14	3 21	4 14	5 14	6 14	6 19
St. John's............	—	—	—	10 17	—	—	12 17	—	2 17	—	—	4 17	—	—	6 22
Hither Green	8 30	9 15	9 49	10 22	11 20	11 37	12 22	1 20	2 22	3 20	3 27	4 22	5 20	6 20	6 27
Grove Park	8 31	9 20	9 54	10 27	11 25	11 43	12 27	1 25	2 26	3 25	3 32	4 27	5 29	6 25	6 32
Sundridge Park......	8 39	9 24	—	10 31	11 29	—	12 31	1 29	2 31	3 29	—	4 31	5 29	6 34	6 36
BROMLEY, NORTH	8 42	9 27	—	10 34	11 32	—	12 34	1 32	2 34	3 32	—	4 34	5 32	6 42	6 39

SUNDAYS.	PM	PM	PM	PM	PM	PM	PM	PM	PM	PM
CHARING CROSS ..dep.	6 52	7 10	8 0	8 55	9 25	10 0	10 35	11 5
Waterloo	6 54	7 13	8 2	8 57	—	10 2	10 38	11 7
CANNON STREET	—	—	—	—	—	—	—	—
London Bridge......	6 59	7 20	8 7	9 2	9 31	10 7	10 43	11 12
New Cross............	7 6	7 28	8 14	9 9	9 38	10 14	10 51	11 19
St. John's............	—	—	8 17	—	—	10 17	—	—
Hither Green........	7 11	7 34	8 21	9 15	9 43	10 22	10 56	11 25
Grove Park	7 16	—	8 26	9 20	9 48	10 28	11 1	11 30
Sundridge Park....	7 20	—	8 30	9 25	—	10 31	—	11 34
BROMLEY, NORTH	7 23	—	8 33	9 28	—	10 34	—	11 37

MILNERS' SAFES.

BROMLEY, NORTH, TO CANNON STREET AND CHARING CROSS.

WEEK DAYS.	AM	AM	AM	AM	AM	AM	AM	AM	AM	AM	AM	AM	AM	AM	AM	AM
BROMLEY, NORTH dep.	3 20	4 20	5 18	6 13	6 40	7 7	—	7 42	—	8 0	—	8 23	—	8 38	—
Sundridge Park....	—	—	5 19	6 14	6 41	7 8	—	7 43	—	8 1	—	8 24	—	8 39	—
Grove Park	3 26	4 25	5 24	6 18	6 46	7 14	7 25	—	7 49	7 55	8 6	8 24	—	8 37	8 44	—
Hither Green........	3 30	4 29	5 27	6 23	6 50	7 18	—	7 25	7 53	—	8 9	—	8 33	8 42	8 47	9 7
St. John's............	3 34	4 33	5 31	—	6 54	—	7 32	—	—	—	8 13	—	8 46	—	—
New Cross............	3 37	4 36	5 34	—	6 57	7 23	7 35	—	7 59	8 3	—	m	8 37	8 48	—
London Bridge	3 46	4 42	5 40	6 33	7 4	7 30	7 42	7 38	8 6	8 10	8 20	8 40	8 44	8 56	8 58	9 18
CANNON STREET	—	—	—	—	7 8	—	—	—	—	—	8 24	8 44	8 48	9 0	9 3	—
Waterloo	3 50	—	5 45	6 38	—	7 35	—	7 43	8 11	8 15	—	—	—	—	—	9 23
CHARING CROSS	3 54	—	5 49	6 42	—	7 39	7 49	7 47	8 15	8 19	—	—	—	—	9 7	9 27

WEEK DAYS.	AM	AM	AM	AM	AM	AM	AM	AM	AM	d	e	d	e	PM	PM	d
BROMLEY, NORTH dep.	9 5	9 20	9 33	9 55	10 28	11 5	11 28	11 55	12 14	12 31	12 55	—	1 25	—	1 45
Sundridge Park....	9 6	9 21	9 34	9 56	10 29	11 6	11 29	11 57	12 15	12 34	12 56	—	1 26	—	1 46
Grove Park	9 11	9 26	9 40	10 1	10 34	11 11	11 34	12 1	12 20	12 37	1 2	1 8	1 31	1 55	1 55
Hither Green........	—	9 29	9 43	10 4	10 37	11 15	11 38	12 4	12 23	12 41	1 6	1 14	1 34	1 59	1 59
St. John's............	—	—	—	—	—	—	11 43	—	—	—	—	—	—	—	—
New Cross............	—	—	m	10 9	10 43	11 21	11 46	12 12	12 28	12 46	1 12	1 19	—	2 5	2 5
London Bridge......	9 25	9 40	9 56	10 16	10 50	11 28	11 53	12 19	12 35	12 53	1 19	1 28	1 44	2 12	2 12
CANNON STREET	9 29	—	10 0	10 20	—	11 32	12¹ 1	12 25	12 40	12 57	·1 23	—	—	—	—
Waterloo..............	—	9 45	—	—	10 55	—	11ˀ58	—	—	—	—	1 34	1 49	—	—
CHARING CROSS......	—	9 49	—	—	10 59	—	12ˀ 2	—	—	—	1 38	1 53	2 19	2 20

WEEK DAYS.	PM	e	PM	d	PM	d	e	PM	e	d	e	e	e	e	d
BROMLEY, NORTH dep.	2 10	2 35	—	2 57	3 29	4 7	4 8	—	4 56	—	5 7	—	5 40	5 50	—	6 0
Sundridge Park.... .	2 11	2 36	—	2 58	3 30	4 8	4 9	—	4 59	—	5 8	—	5 42	5 51	—	6 1
Grove Park	2 17	2 41	2 49	3 3	3 35	4 16	4 14	4 16	5 4	5 10	5 14	5 28	5 47	5 57	6	3 6 6
Hither Green	2 21	2 44	2 53	3 6	3 39	4 22	4 18	4 22	5	5 15	5 17	5 32	5 51	6	1 6 8
St. John's............	2 25	—	—	—	3 44	—	—	—	5 14	—	—	5 36	—	6 5	6 12	—
New Cross............	2 28	2 50	2 59	—	3 47	4 27	4 23	4 27	5 17	5 21	·5 22	5 39	5 57	6	8 6 15	6 13
London Bridge	2 35	2 56	3 6	3 16	3 54	4 36	4 30	4 36	5 24	5 28	5 29	5 46	6	4 6 16	6 22	6 20
CANNON STREET	2 40	—	3 0	—	3 20	—	—	4 40	5 28	—	—	—	6	8 6 20	6 28	—
Waterloo	2 40	—	3 15	—	3 59	4 41	4 35	—	—	5 33	5 35	5 51	—	—	—
CHARING CROSS......	2 44	—	3 19	—	4 3	4 45	4 39	—	—	5 37	5 39	5 54	—	—	6 28

WEEK DAYS.	d	PM	e	PM	d	PM	d	PM	PM	PM	PM	PM	PM	PM	PM	PM
BROMLEY, NORTH dep.	—	6 13	6 43	7 10	7 35	8 12	—	8 47	9 5	—	9 55	10 27	10 57	—
Sundridge Park......	—	6 15	6 44	7 11	7 36	8 13	—	8 48	9 6	—	9 56	10 28	10 58	—
Grove Park	6 7	6 21	6 52	7 16	7 41	8 18	8 34	8 53	9 10	—	10 1	10 33	11 3	11 15
Hither Green	6 13	6 27	6 56	7 20	7 44	8 21	8 40	8 56	9 15	10 2	10 4	10 36	11 7	11 19
St. John's	6 19	—	—	—	—	8 25	—	—	—	—	10 8	—	—	—
New Cross............	6 22	6 35	7 1	7 25	7 49	8 28	8 47	9 1	9 21	10 8	10 11	10 41	11 13	11 25
London Bridge	6 30	6 44	7 8	7 32	7 56	8 35	8 54	9 8	9 28	10 15	10 18	10 48	11 20	11 34
CANNON STREET	—	—	7 12	—	8 0	—	9 1	9 12	—	—	—	—	—	—
Waterloo	—	6 50	—	7 37	—	8 41	—	—	9 34	10 20	10 23	10 53	11 25	—
CHARING CROSS	6 39	6 54	—	7 41	—	8 45	—	—	9 39	10 23	10 27	10 57	11 29	11 44

SUNDAYS.	AM	AM	AM	AM	AM	AM	AM	AM	PM	PM	PM	PM	PM	PM	PM
BROMLEY, NORTH dep.	—	7 55	9 3	—	9 58	—	—	10 55	—	11 58	12 57	1 58	—	2 57
Sundridge Park......	—	7 56	9 4	—	9 59	—	—	10 56	—	11 59	12 58	1 59	—	2 58
Grove Park	—	8 1	9 9	9 45	10 4	10 1	10 48	11 1	11 32	12 4	1 3	2 4	2 33	3 3
Hither Green	7 15	8 4	9 13	9 50	10 8	10 4	10 53	11 5	11 36	12 8	1 6	2 6	2 37	3 6
St. John's............	7 19	—	—	—	—	—	—	11 9	—	—	1 10	—	—	3 10
New Cross............	7 22	—	9 18	9 57	10 13	10 13	10 59	11 12	11 42	12 13	1 13	2 13	2 43	3 13
London Bridge......	7 29	8 14	9 25	10 5	10 20	10 22	11 6	11 19	11 49	12 20	1 20	2 20	2 50	3 20
CANNON STREET......	—	—	—	—	—	—	—	—	—	—	—	—	—	—
Waterloo............	7 34	8 19	9 30	10 10	10 25	—	11 11	11 13	11 25	11 56	12 25	1 26	2 25	2 56	3 25
CHARING CROSS......	7 38	8 23	9 34	10 15	10 29	10 32	11 13	11 29	12 0	12 29	1 29	2 29	3 0	3 29

SUNDAYS.	PM	PM	PM	PM	PM	PM	PM	PM	PM	PM	PM	PM	PM	PM
BROMLEY, NORTH dep.	4 0	4 55	5 53	6 55	—	8 0	—	8 53	—	10 5	—	10 58	—
Sundridge Park......	4 1	4 56	5 54	6 57	—	8 1	—	8 54	—	10 6	—	10 59	—
Grove Park	4 6	5 1	5 59	7 2	—	8 6	—	8 59	9 20	10 12	10 47	11 4	—
Hither Green	4 9	5 4	6 2	7 5	7 59	8 7	8 10	8 18	8 54	9 3	9 24	10 16	10 51	11 7
St. John's............	—	5 8	—	7 9	—	—	—	9 7	—	—	—	11 11	—
New Cross............	4 15	5 11	6 8	7 12	8 4	8 12	8 16	8 23	9 0	9 10	9 30	10 21	10 57	11 14
London Bridge......	4 22	5 18	6 15	7 19	8 12	—	8 23	8 30	9 7	9 17	9 38	10 28	11 4	11 20
CANNON STREET......	—	—	—	—	—	—	—	—	—	—	—	—	—	—
Waterloo............	4 27	5 23	—	7 24	8 18	8 20	8 29	8 36	9 13	9 22	—	10 33	11 11	11 25
CHARING CROSS......	4 31	5 27	6 24	7 29	8 22	8 25	8 33	8 40	9 18	9 24	—	10 37	11 15	11 29

d Saturdays only. e Saturdays excepted. k Arrive Holborn Viaduct 4.28.

l Arrive St. Paul's 4.48, Holborn Viaduct 4.51. m Call at New Cross to set down Passengers only.

WEEK DAYS.	AM	AM	AM	AM	AM	AM	AM	AM	AM	AM	AM	AM	AM	AM	AM	AM	AM
VICTORIA (S.E. & C.R.) dep.	—	—	5 4	—	—	—	—	—	—	—	—	—	8 30	—	9 25	9 45	—
Brixton	—	—	5 12	—	—	—	—	—	—	—	—	—	8 39	—	9 33	—	—
HOLBORN VIADUCT	—	—	4 57	5 15	5 56	—	6 40	7 13	7 30	—	—	8 20	—	—	—	—	—
LUDGATE HILL																	
ST. PAUL'S	1 15	3 15	5 0	5 18	5 57	6 27	6 42	7 16	7 33	7 44	7 54	8 23	—	9 10	9 19	—	10 2
Elephant and Castle	—	3 19	5 4	5 22	6 2	6 31	6 47	7 20	—	7 49	7 58	8 27	—	9 14	9 25	—	10 7
Loughborough Junction	1 23	3 23	5 10	5 27	6 8	6 36	—	7 23	—	7 54	8 3	—	—	9 19	9 30	—	10 12
HERNE HILL	1 26	3 26	5 20	5 30	6 12	—	6 53	7 30	—	—	8 7	8 35	8 43	—	9 36	—	—
Dulwich	1 30	3 30	5 24	5 34	6 16	—	—	7 34	—	—	8 11	8 38	8 47	—	9 40	—	—
Sydenham Hill	—	—	5 27	5 37	6 19	—	—	7 37	—	—	8 14	—	—	—	9 43	—	—
Penge East	1 36	3 36	5 31	5 42	6 23	—	7 2	7 41	—	—	8 18	8 44	—	—	9 47	—	—
Kent House	1 39	3 39	5 34	5 45	6 26	—	—	7 44	—	—	8 21	8 46	—	—	9 50	—	—
Beckenham Junction	1 40	3 43	5 38	5 48	6 29	—	7 6	7 47	—	—	8 24	8 48	8 55	—	9 53	—	—
Shortlands	1 46	3 46	5 42	—	6 34	7 4	—	7 52	—	8 22	8 28	8 53	—	9 48	9 57	—	10 40
Bromley, South	1 48	3 50	5 46	—	6 37	7 7	7 12	7 55	7 58	8 25	8 31	8 56	9	2	9 51	10 0	10 0	6	10 43
BICKLEY	—	—	5 50	—	6 40	7 11	7 16	8 2	—	8 30	8 35	9 0	9	8	9 55	10 4	—	10 47
ORPINGTON	—	—	6 2	—	7 13	—	8 10	—	8 35	8 44	—	—	10 11	10 11	—	10 5

WEEK DAYS.	AM	AM	AM	AM	AM	AM	AM	d	e	d	e	d	d	d	d
VICTORIA (S.E. & C.R.) dep.	10 15	—	11 4	11 4	—	11 40	—	—	12 13	—	—	12 34	—	—	—
Brixton	10 23	—	11 12	11 12	—	—	—	—	12 21	—	—	12 42	—	—	—
HOLBORN VIADUCT	10 9	—	10 57	11 5	11 18	—	—	12 5	12 7	12 17	12 33	12 37	12 42	12 56	—
LUDGATE HILL															
ST. PAUL'S	10 11	10 40	10 59	11 8	11 21	—	11 48	12 8	12 10	12 20	12 36	12 40	12 45	12 59	1 3
Elephant and Castle	10 16	10 44	11 4	11 13	11 25	—	11 52	12 12	12 13	12 24	12 40	12 44	—	1 3	1 6
Loughborough Junction	10 21	10 49	—	11 18	11 30	—	11 57	12 18	12 18	—	—	—	—	—	—
HERNE HILL	10 26	—	11 17	11 22	11 32	11 53	—	12 21	12 24	12 31	—	12 51	—	1 10	1 13
Dulwich	10 30	—	—	11 26	—	—	—	12 25	12 28	12 35	—	12 55	12 59	—	—
Sydenham Hill	10 33	—	—	11 29	—	—	—	12 28	12 30	—	—	—	1 2	—	—
Penge East	10 37	—	—	11 34	—	—	—	12 32	12 35	12 41	—	1 1	1 6	1 18	1 21
Kent House	10 40	—	—	11 37	—	—	—	12 35	12 37	12 44	—	1 4	1 9	1 21	1 24
Beckenham Junction	10 43	—	11 29	11 39	—	12 5	—	12 38	12 42	12 47	—	—	1 12	1 24	1 26
Shortlands	10 47	11 17	—	11 44	—	—	12 25	12 43	12 46	12 51	—	1 9	1 16	1 28	1 31
Bromley South	10 50	11 20	11 36	11 47	—	12 12	12 28	12 46	12 49	12 54	1 3	1 12	1 19	1 31	1 34
BICKLEY	10 54	11 26	11 41	11 51	—	—	12 32	12 51	12 53	12 59	—	1 16	1 23	1 35	1 38
ORPINGTON	—	11 33	—	—	—	—	12 39	12 58	1 1	1 6	—	1 23	1 44	1 44	1 46

WEEK DAYS.	d	e	d	d	d	d	e	PM	e	d	d	e	d	e	PM	PM
VICTORIA (S.E. & C.R.) dep.	1 2	1 7	—	—	1 37	1 30	—	1 43	—	—	—	2 12	—	2 24	2 35	—
Brixton	1 10	1 15	—	—	—	1 39	—	1 51	—	—	—	—	—	2 32	2 43	—
HOLBORN VIADUCT	1	1	1 6	1 24	—	1 25	1 24	1 40	—	2 11	—	2 12	2 20	2 28	—
LUDGATE HILL																
ST. PAUL'S	1	1 4	1 9	1 30	1 32	—	1 28	1 30	1 43	1 52	1 57	2 14	—	2 15	2 23	2 31	2 47	3 5
Elephant and Castle	1	1 8	—	1 36	—	1 32	—	1 47	1 56	2 1	2 18	—	2 19	2 27	2 35	2 51	3 9
Loughborough Junction	1	1 13	—	—	1 37	—	—	2 1	2 6	2 24	—	2 24	—	2 40	2 56	—
HERNE HILL	1 13	1 18	—	1 43	1 48	1 42	—	1 55	—	—	2 27	—	2 28	2 35	2 46	—
Dulwich	1 17	1 23	1 21	—	1 47	1 52	1 46	—	1 59	—	2 31	—	—	2 39	2 50	—
Sydenham Hill	1	1 26	1 24	—	1 55	1 49	—	2 2	—	—	—	—	2 42	2 53	—
Penge East	1 23	1 30	1 29	—	1 53	1 59	1 53	—	2 6	—	2 37	—	2 36	2 46	2 57	—
Kent House	1 26	1 33	1 32	—	1 56	—	1 56	—	2 9	—	2 40	—	—	2 49	3 0	—
Beckenham Junction	1 29	1 36	1 34	—	1 59	2 3	1 59	—	2 26	—	2 43	—	2 40	2 52	3 3	—
Shortlands	—	1 40	1 39	—	2 3	2 7	2 4	—	2 24	2 29	2 32	2 47	—	2 44	2 56	3 8	3 22	3 39
Bromley, South	1 35	1 43	1 43	1 54	2 6	2 11	2 8	1 54	2 27	2 32	2 35	2 51	2 35	2 49	3 0	3 12	3 24	3 43
BICKLEY	1 39	1 47	1 47	—	2 10	2 15	2 14	—	2 31	2 36	2 43	2 57	—	2 54	3 4	3 16	—	4 9
ORPINGTON	—	1 55	—	—	2 22	2 22	—	—	2 50	—	—	3 11	3 24	—	4 18

WEEK DAYS	le	e	d	PM	PM	e	e	PM	PM	PM	PM	d	d	e	e	e	e	d
VICTORIA (S.E.& C.R.) dep	2 50	—	2 55	—	3 40	3 56	4 7	—	4 23	4 45	—	5 3	5	3 5	7 5	8	—	5 20	5 30
Brixton	—	—	3 3	—	3 48	—	—	—	4 35	—	—	—	—	—	—	—	5 28	—
HOLBORN VIADUCT	—	2 50	2 56	3 22	3 33	—	4 3	—	4 25	4 39	4 50	—	5 13	—	—	—	5 19	—
LUDGATE HILL																		
ST. PAUL'S	—	2 53	2 59	3 25	3 36	—	4 6	4 17	4 27	4 41	4 52	—	5 16	—	5 8	5 18	5 22	—
Elephant and Castle	—	2 57	3 3	3 30	3 40	—	4 10	4 21	4 31	4 45	—	—	5 20	—	5 12	5 22	5 26	—
Loughborough Junction	—	3 2	3 9	—	3 45	—	4 27	—	—	—	—	—	5 16	—	—	—
HERNE HILL	2 59	3 4	3 12	3 38	3 51	—	4 17	—	4 38	4 54	—	5 13	5 26	5 16	5 20	—	5 33	—
Dulwich	3 8	3 16	—	3 55	—	4 21	—	4 43	4 58	—	—	5 30	—	5 24	5 31	5 36	—
Sydenham Hill	3 11	3 19	—	3 58	—	—	—	4 46	—	—	—	5 33	—	—	5 33	—	—
Penge East	3 16	3 23	—	4 3	—	4 26	—	4 51	5 4	—	5 21	5 38	—	5 29	—	5 42	—
Kent House	3 19	3 26	—	4 6	—	—	—	4 54	—	—	5 24	5 41	5 26	—	5 38	—	—
Beckenham Junction	3 22	3 29	3 48	4 10	4 15	4 30	—	4 57	5 8	—	5 27	5 44	5 29	5 33	—	—	5 45	6 50
Shortlands	3 12	3 28	3 33	—	4 14	—	4 34	4 56	5 1	5 11	5 14	5 31	5 49	5 33	—	5 43	5 50	—
Bromley, South	3 17	3 33	3 36	3 55	4 17	4 21	4 38	4 59	5 4	—	5 17	5 34	5 52	5 36	5 38	5 47	5 55	5 56
BICKLEY	3 21	3 37	3 40	4 1	4 22	4 26	4 47	5 2	5 8	—	5 25	5 38	5 56	5 42	—	5 51	6 2	—
ORPINGTON	—	—	3 48	4 18	4 31	—	4 54	5 9	5 10	—	—	—	—	5 58	6 10	—

WEEK DAYS	e	e	e	e	e	PM	e	e	e	e	PM	e	e	d	e	e
VICTORIA (S.E. & C.R.) dep	—	—	—	—	5 50	—	—	6 0	6	2 6	7 6	16	—	6 16	—	—	6 25
Brixton	—	—	—	—	5 58	—	—	6 8	6 10	6 16	—	—	—	—	—	—
HOLBORN VIADUCT	—	—	5 31	—	5 41	5 41	5 52	5 59	5 55	6	26	5 6	6 10	6 18	6 15	6 17	6 29	—
LUDGATE HILL																
ST. PAUL'S	5 33	—	5 34	5 36	5 44	5 44	5 55	6 2	5 57	6	4 6	6 13	6 21	6 18	6 20	6 32	6 25	—
Elephant and Castle	—	—	5 38	5 41	5 48	5 49	5 59	6 6	—	6 2	6	8 6	17	6 25	6 22	6 24	—	6 29
Loughborough Junction	—	—	—	—	—	—	—	—	—	6 7	—	—	—	—	—	6 34	—
HERNE HILL	—	—	—	5 56	6 2	6 6	—	6 12	6 15	6 20	6 26	—	6 30	—	6 42	—	6 35
Dulwich	—	5 48	—	6 0	6 7	6 11	—	6 16	6 19	6 24	—	6 35	6 34	6 34	6 46	—	6 40
Sydenham Hill	—	—	—	6 10	—	—	6 19	—	—	6 32	—	6 37	—	—	—	—
Penge East	—	5 54	—	6 7	6 17	6 24	6 23	6 25	6 30	—	6 41	6 41	6 40	6 52	—	6 49
Kent House	—	5 56	—	—	6 14	6 20	6 25	—	6 28	6 32	6 38	—	6 44	—	—	—	6 51
Beckenham Junction	5 51	—	—	6 27	6 27	6 27	6 31	6 35	—	6 48	6 46	4 46	6 51	—	6 54
Shortlands	5 55	—	6 12	6 14	6 21	6 26	—	6 33	6 35	6 40	—	6 48	6 51	6 48	7 0	7 2	6 56
Bromley, South	5 57	6	6 16	6 20	6 29	6 33	6 38	6 39	6 47	6 50	6 52	5 54	6 52	7 4	7 5	6 59
BICKLEY	—	6	7 6	19	6 20	6 29	—	6 50	6 46	—	6 57	6 59	6 56	7 7	7	16	7 3
ORPINGTON	—	—	6 27	—	6 37	—	6 50	6 46	—	—	7 4	7	6 7	—	7 23	7 11

d Saturdays only. *e Saturdays excepted.* *h Wednesdays only.* *k Not from Holborn on Mondays.*

WEEK DAYS.	e	PM	e	e	e	d	e	PM	e	PM	PM	PM	PM	PM	e	PM	PM
VICTORIA (S.E. & C.R.) dep.	—	6 40	—	—	6 50	6 50	6 53	7 3	—	—	7 20	—	7 35	7 35	—	8 10	8 10
Brixton	—	—	—	—	—	—	7 11	—	—	—	—	7 43	7 43	—	8 18	8 18
HOLBORN VIADUCT	—	6 34	6 38	6 43	—	6 45	—	6 58	7 5	—	—	7 22	7 31	7 31	7 44	8 4	8 4
LUDGATE HILL	—	—	—	—	—	—	—	—	—	—	—	—	—	—	—	—
ST. PAUL'S	6 39	6 37	6 41	6 46	—	6 48	—	7 0	7 8	7 12	—	7 24	7 34	7 34	7 47	8 7	8 8
Elephant and Castle	6 37	6 41	6 45	6 50	—	6 52	—	—	7 12	7 16	—	—	7 38	7 38	7 51	8 11	8 12
Loughborough Junction	—	6 50	—	—	—	—	—	7 9	—	7 91	—	—	—	—	7 56	8 16	8 17
HERNE HILL	—	6 50	6 53	6 57	7 0	7 0	7 3	7 14	7 19	—	—	7 46	7 49	7 59	8 21	8 24
Dulwich	—	—	—	7 2	7 4	7 4	7 7	—	7 23	—	—	7 37	7 53	—	—	8 28
Sydenham Hill	—	6 59	—	7 7	7 7	7 7	7 10	—	—	—	—	—	7 56	—	—	8 31
Penge East	—	—	7 8	7 11	7 12	7 14	—	7 29	—	—	—	7 54	8 1	—	8 29	8 35
Kent House	—	7 4	7 11	7 13	7 15	7 17	—	7 31	—	—	—	8 3	—	—	8 38
Beckenham Junction	7 1	—	7 14	7 16	7 19	7 19	—	7 34	—	7 45	7 57	8 6	—	8 33	8 41
Shortlands	7 8	—	7 11	7 18	—	7 23	—	7 39	7 49	—	8 2	8 11	—	8 37	8 45
Bromley, South	7 12	7 7	7 13	7 22	—	7 32	—	7 27	7 47	7 52	7 43	7 51	8 5	8 14	—	8 40	8 48
BICKLEY	7 17	7 11	—	7 26	—	7 35	—	—	7 50	7 57	—	8 9	8 18	—	8 44	8 54
ORPINGTON	7 24	—	—	7 33	—	7 43	—	—	8 4	—	—	8 18	—	—	8 51	—

WEEK DAYS.	e	PM	PM	PM	PM	PM	PM	PM	PM	PM	PM	PM	PM	PM	PM	PM
VICTORIA (S.E. & C.R.) dep.	—	8 35	8 35	8 55	9 0	9 0	—	9 30	9 30	9 55	10 0	10 0	10 17	10 17	—	10 30
Brixton	—	8 43	8 43	—	9 8	9 8	—	9 38	9 38	—	—	—	—	—	—	10 38
HOLBORN VIADUCT	—	8 28	8 32	—	8 57	8 57	—	9 25	9 25	—	9 54	9 54	10 11	10 11	—	10 27
LUDGATE HILL	—	—	—	—	—	—	—	—	—	—	—	—	—	—	—	—
ST. PAUL'S	8 15	8 31	8 35	—	9 0	9 0	9 10	9 27	9 27	—	9 56	9 56	10 13	10 13	10 20	10 30
Elephant and Castle	8 19	8 35	8 39	—	9 4	9 4	9 14	9 32	9 32	—	10 1	10 1	10 18	10 18	10 24	10 34
Loughborough Junction	8 24	—	—	—	—	—	9 19	9 37	9 37	—	10 6	10 6	10 23	10 23	10 29	—
HERNE HILL	—	8 46	8 49	—	9 12	9 15	—	9 41	9 44	—	10 10	10 13	10 27	10 30	—	10 41
Dulwich	—	—	8 53	—	9 19	—	—	9 49	—	—	10 17	—	10 34	—	—	—
Sydenham Hill	—	—	8 56	—	9 23	—	—	9 52	—	—	10 20	—	10 37	—	—	—
Penge East	—	8 54	9 0	—	9 20	9 26	—	9 49	9 57	—	10 18	10 24	—	10 41	—	10 49
Kent House	—	—	9 3	—	9 29	—	—	10 0	—	—	—	10 27	—	10 44	—	—
Beckenham Junction	8 58	8 58	9 6	9 14	9 24	9 32	—	9 53	10 3	—	10 22	10 30	—	10 47	—	10 53
Shortlands	8 53	8 9	9 10	—	9 36	9 47	9 57	10 6	—	—	10 34	—	10 52	10 58	10 57
Bromley, South	8 57	6 9	9 14	—	9 30	9 39	9 50	10 0	10 9	10 16	10 29	10 37	10 42	10 55	11 2	11 0
BICKLEY	9 1	9 10	9 18	—	9 43	9 54	10 4	10 13	—	10 33	10 40	—	10 59	11 6	11 4
ORPINGTON	9 10	9 18	9 25	—	10 2	—	10 20	—	—	—	—	—	11 6	11 15	—

WEEK DAYS.	PM	PM	PM	PM	mid	mid		AM	AM	AM	AM	AM	AM	AM	AM
VICTORIA (S.E. & C.R.) dep.	10 30	—	11 0	11 35	11 48	—	12 30		7 20	—	—	8 15	8 25	—	9 35	9 53
Brixton	10 38	—	11 8	—	11 56	—	12 38		—	—	—	8 32	—	—	10 1
HOLBORN VIADUCT	10 27	—	10 57	11 31	11 43	—	12 25		7 50	8 0	—	—	8 53	—	9 50
LUDGATE HILL	—	—	—	—	—	—	—		—	—	—	—	—	—	—
ST. PAUL'S	10 30	10 42	11 0	11 34	11 46	12 20	12 28		—	—	—	—	—	—	—
Elephant and Castle	10 34	10 46	11 4	11 38	11 50	12 24	12 32		7 55	—	—	6 58	—	9 55
Loughborough Junction	10 51	—	—	—	12 29	12 37		8 0	—	—	9 3	—	10 0
HERNE HILL	10 44	—	11 11	11 45	11 56	—	12 41		7 31	—	8 11	8 27	8 36	—	10 4
Dulwich	10 48	—	11 15	11 49	12 0	—	12 45		—	8 17	—	8 40	—	10 8
Sydenham Hill	10 51	—	11 18	11 52	12 3	—	12 48		—	8 20	—	8 43	—	10 11
Penge East	10 55	—	11 22	11 56	12 8	—	12 52		—	8 24	—	8 48	—	10 16
Kent House	10 58	—	11 25	11 59	12 11	—	12 55		—	8 27	—	8 51	—	10 19
Beckenham Junction	11 1	—	11 28	12 2	12 14	—	12 58		—	8 29	—	8 54	—	9 53	10 22
Shortlands	10 34	—	11 20	11 39	—	12 44	1 31		8 28	8 35	—	8 59	9 31	—	10 27
Bromley, South	10 37	1058	11 3	11 33	11 43	11 58	12 48	1 6		7 46	8 31	8 43	8 43	9 3	9 34	9 59	10 30
BICKLEY	10 41	11 8	—	11 37	11 48	12 2	12 56	1 1		8 34	8 49	—	9 7	9 37	—	10 33
ORPINGTON	10 49	—	—	11 55	—	1 2	—		—	—	—	—	—	—	—

SUNDAYS.	AM	AM	AM	AM	AM	AM	PM	PM	PM	PM	PM	PM	PM	PM	PM	PM
VICTORIA (S.E. & C.R.) dep.	—	1030	1040	—	11 5	11 30	12 10	—	1 5	—	2 5	—	3 0	3 30	—	4 25
Brixton	—	—	—	—	11 13	—	12 18	—	1 13	—	2 13	—	3 8	3 38	—	4 33
HOLBORN VIADUCT	9 55	1025	—	10 52	11 3	—	12 7	12 52	1 0	1 50	2 2	2 43	2 57	—	3 50	4 20	4 50
LUDGATE HILL	—	—	—	—	—	—	—	—	—	—	—	—	—	—	—	—
ST. PAUL'S	—	—	—	—	—	—	—	—	—	—	—	—	—	—	—	—
Elephant and Castle	10 1	1030	—	10 57	11 8	—	12 12	12 58	1 5	1 56	2 7	2 48	3 2	—	3 55	4 26	4 55
Loughborough Junction	10 6	—	—	11 2	11 13	—	12 17	1 3	1 10	2 1	2 12	2 53	3 7	—	4 0	4 31	5 0
HERNE HILL	—	1039	—	—	11 11	11 40	12 22	—	1 17	—	2 16	—	3 11	3 42	—	4 36
Dulwich	—	—	—	—	11 20	—	12 26	—	1 21	—	2 20	—	3 15	—	—	4 40
Sydenham Hill	—	—	—	—	11 23	—	12 29	—	1 24	—	2 23	—	3 18	—	—	4 43
Penge East	—	—	—	—	11 28	11 47	12 34	—	1 28	—	2 28	—	3 22	—	—	4 47
Kent House	—	—	1051	—	11 31	—	12 37	—	1 34	—	2 31	—	3 25	—	—	4 50
Beckenham Junction	10 34	—	—	11 34	11 52	12 40	—	1 34	—	2 35	—	3 28	—	—	4 53
Shortlands	10 34	—	—	11 30	11 39	—	12 44	1 31	1 39	2 30	2 40	3 23	3 32	—	4 28	4 57	5 28
Bromley, South	10 37	1058	11 3	11 33	11 43	11 58	12 48	1 94	42	2 33	2 45	3 31	3 53	56	4 31	5 0	5 32
BICKLEY	10 41	11 8	—	11 37	11 48	12 2	12 56	1 37	42	2 37	2 50	3 34	3 39	4 0	4 34	5 6	5 35
ORPINGTON	10 49	—	—	11 55	—	1 2	—	1 55	—	—	—	—	3 46	—	—	5 13

SUNDAYS.	PM	PM	PM	PM	PM	PM	PM	PM	PM	PM	PM	PM	PM	PM	PM	PM
VICTORIA (S.E. & C.R.) dep.	5 15	5 20	—	5 56	35	6 43	—	7 30	—	8 5	—	9 5	—	10 15	10 55
Brixton	—	5 28	—	6 13	6 43	6 43	—	7 38	—	8 13	—	9 13	—	10 23	11 3
HOLBORN VIADUCT	—	5 15	5 50	—	6 40	6 50	7 0	—	7 52	8 0	8 52	9 0	9 30	9 57	10 12	10 50
LUDGATE HILL	—	—	—	—	—	—	—	—	—	—	—	—	—	—	—
ST. PAUL'S	—	—	—	—	—	—	—	—	—	—	—	—	—	—	—
Elephant and Castle	—	5 20	5 55	—	6 55	7 5	—	7 57	8 5	8 57	9 5	9 35	10 2	10 17	10 55
Loughborough Junction	—	5 25	6 0	—	—	8 2	8 10	9 2	9 10	9 40	10 7	10 22	11 0
HERNE HILL	—	5 31	—	6 17	6 47	6 52	—	7 12	7 41	—	8 14	—	9 14	9 44	—	10 26	11 7
Dulwich	—	5 35	—	6 21	—	—	7 16	7 45	—	8 18	—	9 18	9 48	—	10 30	11 11
Sydenham Hill	—	5 38	—	6 24	—	—	7 19	7 48	—	8 21	—	9 21	9 51	—	11 14
Penge East	—	5 43	—	6 28	—	—	7 24	7 53	—	8 26	—	9 25	9 55	—	10 36	11 18
Kent House	—	5 46	—	6 31	—	—	7 27	7 55	—	8 28	—	9 28	9 58	—	11 20
Beckenham Junction	5 32	5 49	—	6 34	7 3	—	7 30	7 57	—	8 31	—	9 31	10 1	—	10 40	11 23
Shortlands	—	5 54	6 28	6 38	—	7 7	28	7 34	—	8 30	8 39	9 9	9 30	10 5	10 34	10 44	11 27
Bromley, South	—	5 58	6 32	6 41	7 2	7 9	33	7 41	—	8 33	8 43	9 33	9 39	10 10	10 37	10 47	11 30
BICKLEY	5 38	6 4	6 35	6 45	—	7 7	7 34	41	—	8 36	8 49	8 49	9 47	10 12	10 41	10 52	11 33
ORPINGTON	—	6 11	—	—	—	7 49	—	—	9 54	—	10 49	—	11 41

d Saturdays only.   e Saturdays excepted.

WEEK DAYS.

	AM	AM	AM	AM	AM	AM	AM	AM	AM	AM	AM	AM	AM	AM	AM
ORPINGTON ....dep.	—	—	4 50	5 50	6·20	6 41	—	6 48	—	—	—	7 10	—	7 28	—
BICKLEY	—	—	4 57	5 57	6 28	6 49	—	6 56	7 4	—	7 15	7 20	—	7 37	7 42
Bromley, South	3 3	4 5	5 0	6 0	6 31	6 53	—	7 0	7 8	—	7 19	7 24	7 39	7 41	7 46
Shortlands	3 7	4 9	5 4	6 4	6 35	6 56	—	7 3	7 11	—	7 22	7 28	—	7 44	7 49
Beckenham Junction	3 11	4 11	5 8	6 8	6 39	7 1	—	—	—	—	—	7 33	—	7 48	7 53
Kent House	3 14	4 14	5 11	6 12	6 42	7 4	—	—	—	—	—	7 36	—	7 51	7 56
Penge East	3 17	4 17	5 14	6 15	6 45	7 7	7 13	—	—	—	—	7 39	7 46	7 54	7 59
Sydenham Hill	—	4 22	5 19	6 20	6 50	—	7 18	—	—	—	—	7 44	—	—	8 3
Dulwich	3 23	4 25	5 22	6 23	6 53	—	7 21	—	—	—	—	7 47	—	8 0	8 6
HERNE HILL	3 26	4 29	5 26	6 27	6 57	7 15	7 25	—	—	7 35	—	7 52	7 54	8 4	8 10
Loughborough Junction	3 29	4 32	5 29	6 30	7 0	7 18	—	—	—	7 38	—	—	—	—	—
Elephant and Castle	3 34	4 37	5 34	6 35	7 5	7 20	—	7 33	7 39	7 43	—	7 59	8 1	—	8 17
ST. PAUL'S	3 37	4 40	5 37	6 39	7 8	7 27	7 35	7 37	7 43	7 47	—	8 2	8 7	—	8 21
LUDGATE HILL	—	—	—	—	—	—	—	—	—	—	—	—	—	—	—
HOLBORN VIADUCT	3 40	4 43	5 40	6 42	7 11	7 30	7 38	—	—	7 50	—	8 6	8 9	—	8 23
Brixton	—	4 35	5 31	6 33	7 3	—	7 33	—	—	—	—	—	—	8 7	—
VICTORIA (S.E. & C.R.)	—	4 42	5 38	6 40	7 10	—	7 40	—	—	—	7 42	—	—	8 14	—

WEEK DAYS.

	AM	AM	AM	AM	AM	AM	AM	AM	AM	AM	AM	AM	AM	AM	AM
ORPINGTON ....dep.	—	—	7 30	7 53	—	8 7	—	8 3	8 15	—	8 23	—	—	—	8 45
BICKLEY	—	—	8 2	8 0	8 5	8 14	—	8 17	8 23	—	8 34	8 41	—	8 43	8 54
Bromley, South	—	—	8 5	8 4	8 9	8 17	8 28	8 20	8 34	—	8 41	8 45	—	8 47	9 5 8 58
Shortlands	—	—	8 8	8·8	8 12	8 21	—	8 24	8 37	—	8 45	—	—	8 50	9 8 9 1
Beckenham Junction	8 2	7 56	—	8 12	—	8 25	—	—	8 41	—	8 49	8 51	8 59	—	9 12
Kent House	—	8 9	—	8 15	—	8 28	—	—	8 44	8 28	8 52	8 54	—	—	9 15
Penge East	8 6	8 12	—	8 18	—	—	—	—	8 47	8 41	—	8 58	9 3	—	9 18
Sydenham Hill	—	8 16	—	—	—	—	—	—	8 46	—	—	9 7	—	—	—
Dulwich	—	8 19	—	8 24	—	8 36	—	—	8 53	8 49	9 0	9 4	9 10	—	9 24
HERNE HILL	8 15	8 23	—	8 28	—	—	8 45	—	8 57	8 53	9 3	9 8	—	—	9 28
Loughborough Junction	—	—	—	—	—	—	—	—	—	—	—	—	—	—	—
Elephant and Castle	—	—	8 40	—	8 42	—	8 52	8 54	—	9 0	9 11	—	9 19	9 11	9 29
ST. PAUL'S	8 25	8 30	8 44	—	8 46	8 48	8 57	8 58	9 8	9 4	—	9 24	9 16	—	9 33
LUDGATE HILL	—	8 35	—	—	—	—	—	—	—	9 14	—	—	—	—	—
HOLBORN VIADUCT	8 27	8 37	—	—	8 51	8 59	—	—	9 10	9 7	9 17	—	9 26	9 18	—
Brixton	8 22	—	—	—	—	—	—	—	—	—	—	—	—	—	—
VICTORIA (S.E. & C.R.)	8 29	—	8 37	—	—	—	—	—	—	9 15	9 16	—	—	9 36	—

WEEK DAYS.

	AM	AM	AM	AM	AM	AM	AM	AM	AM	AM	AM	AM	AM	AM
ORPINGTON ....dep.	—	—	—	9 8	—	—	—	—	—	—	10 29	—	—	10 55
BICKLEY	—	9 7	—	9 20	—	9 32	—	9 52	—	—	10 34	10 39	10 45	11 3
Bromley, South	9 13	9 12	9 16	9 24	—	9 35	9 57	10 4	10 15	10 38	10 38	10 43	10 49	11 7
Shortlands	—	9 16	—	9 28	—	9 39	—	10 8	—	—	10 42	10 46	10 53	11 10
Beckenham Junction	—	9 20	9 33	—	9 43	—	10 12	10 21	—	10 47	—	—	—	—
Kent House	—	—	9 31	—	—	9 46	—	10 15	—	—	—	11 0	—	—
Penge East	—	—	9 34	—	—	9 49	—	10 18	—	—	10 51	11 3	—	—
Sydenham Hill	—	—	9 38	—	—	9 53	—	—	—	—	—	11 8	—	—
Dulwich	—	9 28	9 41	—	—	9 56	—	10 24	—	10 50	—	11 11	—	—
HERNE HILL	—	9 32	9 45	9 44	9 49	10 0	10 9	10 28	10 32	10 54	10 58	11 15	—	—
Loughborough Junction	—	—	—	—	—	—	—	—	—	—	11 13	11 18	11 37	—
Elephant and Castle	9 33	9 38	9 52	—	9 57	—	—	—	—	—	11 18	11 23	11 42	—
ST. PAUL'S	9 37	9 41	9 57	—	10 2	10 9	10 21	—	10·41	—	11 22	11 26	11 46	—
LUDGATE HILL	—	—	—	—	—	—	—	—	—	—	—	—	—	—
HOLBORN VIADUCT	9 39	9·44	9 59	—	10 4	10 12	10 23	—	10 43	—	11 29	—	—	—
Brixton	—	—	—	9 53	9 57	—	—	—	—	—	11 2	—	—	—
VICTORIA (S.E. & C.R.)	—	—	9 53	9 57	—	10 16	10 36	—	—	11 2	11 9	—	—	—

WEEK DAYS.

	e AM	AM	AM	AM	AM	PM	PM	PM	PM	PM	PM	PM	e	d	PM
ORPINGTON ....dep.	—	—	—	11 30	11 45	—	11 45	—	—	—	—	1 23	1 37	1 43	—
BICKLEY	—	11 19	—	11 37	11 53	—	12 27	—	12 43	—	—	1 31	1 46	1 53	2 5
Bromley, South	11 19	11 22	—	11 41	11 57	—	12 34	12 32	12 47	—	1 4 1 12	1 34	1 51	1 56	2 10
Shortlands	—	11 26	—	11 44	12 0	—	12 38	—	12 50	—	—	1 37	1 55	1 59	—
Beckenham Junction	—	11 30	—	—	12 4	—	—	—	12 55	—	1 12	1 46	—	—	2 17
Kent House	—	11 33	—	—	12 7	—	—	—	12 58	—	—	1 49	—	—	—
Penge East	—	11 36	—	—	12 10	—	—	—	1 1	—	—	1 52	—	—	—
Sydenham Hill	—	11 41	—	—	12 15	—	—	—	1 6	—	—	1 57	—	—	—
Dulwich	—	11 44	—	—	12 18	—	—	—	2 9	—	—	2 0	—	—	—
HERNE HILL	—	11 48	11 50	—	12 21	12 40	—	12 48	1 13	1 18 1 23	—	2 4	—	2 27	
Loughborough Junction	—	—	—	12 11	—	1 4	—	—	1 22	—	1 39	2 13	2 22	—	
Elephant and Castle	—	—	11 57	12 15	—	1 9	—	—	1 27	—	1 44	2 18	2 28 2 30	—	
ST. PAUL'S	—	—	12 2	12 19	—	1 14	12 58	—	1 32	—	1 49	2 21	2 32 2 34	—	
LUDGATE HILL	—	—	12 4	—	—	—	1 0	—	1 34	—	—	2 24	—	—	
HOLBORN VIADUCT	—	11 52	—	—	—	—	—	1 26	—	—	—	2 32			
Brixton	—	—	—	—	12 31	12 49	—	1 22	—	1 33	—	2 12	—	2 40	
VICTORIA (S.E. & C.R.)	11 37	11 59	—	12 31	12 49	—	1 22	—	1 33	—	2 12	—	2 40		

WEEK DAYS.

	e	d'	PM	PM	PM	PM	PM	PM	PM	PM	PM	PM	e	PM	PM	PM	PM	PM	PM
ORPINGTON ....dep.	—	2 23	—	—	—	3 3	3 47	—	—	4 25	—	5 45	—						
BICKLEY	2 18	2 20	2 31	—	—	3 11 3 25	3 54	4 2	—	4 31	4 42	5 25	5 52	—					
Bromley, South	2 21	2 23	2 35	2 59	3 9 3 17	3 19 3 29	3 58	4 4	13	4 34	4 46	5 29 5 19	5 56	5 55					
Shortlands	2 24	2 27	2 38	—	3 23	3 33	4 1	—	4 38	4 49	5 33	6 0	5 59						
Beckenham Junction	2 30	2 32	3 4	—	3 27	—	4 5 4 14	4 20	4 54	5 26	6 5	6 4							
Kent House	2 33	2 35	—	3 30	—	4 8	—	4 57	—	5 26	6 8	6 7							
Penge East	2 36	2 38	—	3 33	4 11	—	5 0	—	6 11	6 10									
Sydenham Hill	2 41	2 43	—	3 37	—	5 5	6 15	6 15											
Dulwich	2 44	2 46	—	3 43	—	5 8	6 18	6 18											
HERNE HILL	2 48	2 50	3 14	3 43	4 21 4 25	4 31 4 51	5 12	6 22	6 22										
Loughborough Junction	2 53	3 5	3 49	4 14	24 4 46	4 55													
Elephant and Castle	2 57	2 58	3 10	3 56	4 29	4 51 5 0	5 19	6 2											
ST. PAUL'S	3 0	3 13	12	—	4 24	10 4 33	4 54 5 4	5 16	6 5										
LUDGATE HILL	3 3	3 4	—	4 5	—	5 8													
HOLBORN VIADUCT	—	—	—	—	6 23	6 25													
Brixton	2 51	2 55	—	—	—	6 23	6 25												
VICTORIA (S.E. & C.R.)	2 58	3 2	3 23 3 31	3 37	4 33 4 39	5 21	5 42	6 30	6 32										

d Saturdays only. *e Saturdays excepted.* *l Wednesdays only.*

WEEK DAYS.		e	PM	PM	PM	PM	PM	PM	e	d	PM	PM	PM	PM	PM	PM	PM	PM
ORPINGTON	dep.	—	—	—	—	—	7 4	—	—	—	7 33	—	—	—	8 55	9 27	9 35	—	10 7
BICKLEY		6 17	—	—	—	6 48	7 11	—	7 31	7 37	7 42	8 12	8 20	9 7	9 34	9 43	—	10 14
Bromley, South		6 20	—	6 13	6 29	6 51	7 15	7 32	7 36	7 41	7 45	8 18	8 23	9 11	9 37	9 46	10 3	10 21
Shortlands		—	—	6 16	—	6 55	7 18	—	7 40	7 44	7 48	8 24	8 27	9 14	9 40	9 50	—	—
Beckenham Junction		—	—	—	—	6 59	—	—	7 45	7 49	—	8 30	8 31	9 18	—	9 54	—	10 25
Kent House		—	—	—	—	7 2	—	—	7 48	7 52	—	—	8 34	9 21	—	9 57	—	10 27
Penge East		—	—	—	—	7 5	—	—	7 51	7 55	—	—	8 37	9 24	—	10 0	—	10 30
Sydenham Hill		—	—	—	—	7 10	—	—	7 55	7 59	—	—	8 42	9 28	—	10 5	—	—
Dulwich		—	—	—	6 41	7 13	—	—	7 58	8 2	—	—	8 45	9 31	—	10 8	—	10 35
HERNE HILL		—	6 37	—	6 45	7 17	—	—	8 1	8 5	—	8 41	8 46	9 35	—	10 12	—	10 38
Loughborough Junction		—	6 40	6 43	—	7 21	7 45	—	8 9	8 10	8 14	—	8 53	9 41	10 8	10 19	—	—
Elephant and Castle		6 40	6 45	6 48	6 53	7 26	7 50	7 55	8 14	8 15	8 20	—	8 58	9 47	10 13	1C 24	—	—
ST. PAUL'S		6 45	6 48	6 52	6 58	7 30	7 54	8 0	8 17	8 20	8 24	—	9 2	9 50	10 16	10 28	—	—
LUDGATE HILL																		
HOLBORN VIADUCT		6 47	6 51	—	7 0	7 33	—	8 2	8 20	8 22	—	—	9	9 54	—	10 31	—	—
Brixton		—	—	—	—	—	—	—	—	—	—	8 44	—	9 38	—	10 15	—	10 41
VICTORIA (S.E. & C.R.)		—	—	—	—	—	—	—	8 10	8 13	—	8 51	8 56	9 46	—	10 22	10 25	10 48

WEEK DAYS.		PM	PM	PM	PM	PM			AM	AM	AM	AM	AM	AM	AM	AM
ORPINGTON	dep.	—	—	—	—	11 22			6 55	7 38	7 46	—	—	9 37	—	—
BICKLEY		—	10 40	11	0	11	11 30			7	37	46	7 53	8 49	8 52	9 45	9 52	—
Bromley, South		10 56	10 56	11	4	11 33			7	6	7 50	7 57	8 53	8 56	9 49	9 56	10 25
Shortlands		—	11	0	11 8	—	11 37			7	9	7 53	8 0	8 56	8 59	9 52	9 59	—
Beckenham Junction		—	11 4	—	—	11 42			7 13	7 57	—	9 2	—	9 56	—	10 31
Kent House		—	11 7	—	—	11 45			7 16	8 0	—	9 5	—	9 59	—	—
Penge East		—	11 9	—	—	11 48			7 19	8 3	—	9 8	—	10 2	—	—
Sydenham Hill		—	11 14	—	—	11 53			7 23	8 8	—	9 13	—	10 7	—	—
Dulwich		—	11 17	—	—	11 56			7 26	8 11	—	9 16	—	10 10	—	—
HERNE HILL		11 10	11 20	—	11 29	12 0			7 30	8 15	—	9 21	—	10 14	—	—
Loughborough Junction		—	11 23	11 37	—	—			—	8 21	8 27	9 29	—	10 19	10 27	—
Elephant and Castle		11 16	11 28	11 42	11 36	—			7 39	8 26	8 32	9 34	9 30	10 24	10 32	—
ST. PAUL'S		11 21	11 33	11 46	11 42	—										
LUDGATE HILL																
HOLBORN VIADUCT		11 23	11 35	—	11 44	—			—	8 31	8 37	9 39	9 35	10 29	10 37	—
Brixton		—	11 28	—	—	12 3			7 33	—	—	9 24	—	10 17	—	—
VICTORIA (S.E. & C.R.)		—	11 35	—	—	12 10			7 40	—	—	9 31	—	10 24	—	10 48

SUNDAY TRAINS.

SUNDAYS		AM	AM	AM	PM	PM	PM	PM	PM	PM	PM	PM	PM	PM	PM	PM	PM	PM	PM
ORPINGTON	dep.	—	—	11 37	—	—	—	—	1 25	—	2 25	—	—	3 12	—	4 45	—	—
BICKLEY		10 42	10 47	11 45	—	12 26	12 52	—	1 32	1 52	2 32	2 52	—	3 19	3 53	4 53	—	5 25
Bromley, South		10 47	10 51	11 50	12 14	12 29	12 56	1 0	1 36	1 56	2 36	2 56	3 24	3 23	3 56	4 57	5 11	5 29
Shortlands		10 50	10 54	11 53	—	—	12 59	—	1 39	1 59	2 39	2 59	—	3 31	3 59	5 0	—	5 32
Beckenham Junction		10 55	—	11 58	12 20	12 35	—	1 6	1 43	—	2 43	—	3 31	3 36	—	—	—	5 36
Kent House		10 58	—	12 1	—	—	—	—	1 46	—	2 46	—	—	3 39	—	—	—	5 39
Penge East		11 1	—	12 4	—	—	—	—	1 49	—	2 49	—	—	3 42	—	—	—	5 42
Sydenham Hill		11 6	—	12 9	—	—	—	—	1 54	—	2 54	—	—	3 47	—	—	—	5 47
Dulwich		11 9	—	12 12	—	—	—	—	1 57	—	2 57	—	—	3 50	—	—	—	5 50
HERNE HILL		11 14	—	12 17	—	12 47	—	1 16	2 1	—	3 1	—	3 42	3 54	—	—	5 24	5 54
Loughborough Junction		—	11 22	—	—	12 52	1 26	—	2 6	2 26	3 6	3 26	—	3 59	4 26	5 27	—	5 57
Elephant and Castle		11 23	11 27	—	—	12 57	1 31	—	2 11	2 31	3 11	3 31	—	4 4	4 31	5 32	—	6 2
ST. PAUL'S																		
LUDGATE HILL																		
HOLBORN VIADUCT		11 27	11 32	—	1 2	1 36	—	2 15	2 36	3 15	3 36	—	4 8	4 36	5 36	—	6 7
Brixton		—	12 20	—	—	—	—	2 4	—	3 4	—	—	3 57	—	—	—	—
VICTORIA (S.E & C.R.)		11 23	—	12 27	12 39	12 56	—	1 25	2 11	—	3 11	—	3 50	4 4	—	—	5 32	—

SUNDAYS		PM	PM	PM	PM	PM	PM	PM	PM	PM	PM	PM	PM	PM	PM	PM	PM	PM
ORPINGTON	dep.	—	—	6 3	—	—	—	—	8 57	—	9 25	—	10 5	—	11 5
BICKLEY		—	5 54	6 11	6 52	7 45	—	7 56	—	9 5	—	9 40	9 52	10 15	11 17	11 13
Bromley, South		5 42	5 49	5 57	6 15	6 56	7 49	8	2 8 10	8 46	9 9	9 36	9 44	9 56	10 19	11 21	11 22
Shortlands		—	6 1	6 19	6 59	7 52	—	8 13	—	9 12	9 41	9 47	9 59	10 22	—	11 26
Beckenham Junction		—	5 55	6 23	—	7 56	—	8 44	—	9 45	9 51	—	10 26	—	11 30
Kent House		—	—	6 26	—	—	—	—	—	9 54	—	10 29	—	11 33
Penge East		—	—	6 29	8 0	—	8 48	—	9 57	—	10 32	—	11 36
Sydenham Hill		—	—	6 34	—	—	8 53	—	—	—	10 37	—	11 41
Dulwich		—	—	6 37	8 6	—	8 56	—	—	10 5	—	10 40	—	11 44
HERNE HILL		—	6 5	6 41	8 10	—	9 0	—	9 56	10 9	—	10 44	11 35	11 48
Loughborough Junction		—	6 10	6 27	—	7 26	8 12	—	8 40	—	9 39	10 12	10 12	10 26	10 49	11 51	11 51
Elephant and Castle		—	6 15	6 32	6 48	7 31	8 17	—	8 45	—	9 5	9 44	10 17	10 17	10 31	10 54	11 56	11 56
ST. PAUL'S																		
LUDGATE HILL																		
HOLBORN VIADUCT		—	6 20	6 37	6 52	7 36	8 21	—	8 50	—	9 9	9 49	10 22	10 22	10 36	10 59	12 0	12 0
Brixton		—	6 8	—	—	—	—	—	—	—	—	—	—	—	—	10 47	—	—
VICTORIA (S.E. & C.R.)		6 3	6 15	—	—	—	8 20	—	9 9	—	—	10 5	—	10 54	11 44	—

KENT—BROMLEY, BECKENHAM, BICKLEY, CHISLEHURST, and District.

BAXTER, PAYNE & LEPPER,

Auctioneers, Land and Estate Agents and Valuers,

Established over a Century and a Half,

Have in their hands to LET or SELL the principal Residences in the market.

Full particulars at Offices:—Bromley and Beckenham, Kent; and 28-30, Lime Street, E.C. 3.

WEEK DAYS.

	AM	AM	AM	AM	AM	AM	AM	AM	AM	AM	AM	AM	AM	AM	AM	AM	AM	AM	AM
LUDGATE HILL ... dep.	—	—	—	—	—	—	—	—	—	—	—	—	—	—	—	—	—	—	—
ST. PAUL'S	1250	1 53	2 50	4 17	4 55	5 59	6 27	—	7 19	7 37	—	7 44	8 7	8 50	9 3	9 10	9 25	10 2	10 40
Elephant and Castle	1253	1 57	2 54	4 21	4 59	6 3	6 31	—	7 23	—	—	7 49	8 11	8 54	9 8	9 14	9 29	10 7	10 44
Loughborough Junctn.	1258	2 2	—	4 26	5 4	6 11	6 36	—	7 28	7 45	—	7 54	8 16	8 59	9 13	9 19	—	10 12	10 49
Denmark Hill	—	—	—	—	—	6 14	6 39	—	7 30	—	—	7 57	—	9 2	9 16	9 22	9 36	10 15	10 52
Peckham Rye	1 2	2 6	3	2 4	3 0	5	8	6 17	6 42	—	7 33	7 49	—	8	0 8	20	9 5	9 20	9 26 9 39 10 18 10 55
NUNHEAD { arr.	1 5 2	9 3	5 4	3 35	11 6	20 6	45	—	7 36	7 52	—	8	3 8	22 9	8 22	9 29	9 41	10 21	10 58
{ dep.	1 6 2	10 3	6 4	34 5	12 6	21 6	46 7	5 7	37 7	53 7	55 8	4 8	23 9	9 9	23 9	30 9	42 10	22 10 59
Crofton Park	1 9 2	13 3	9 4	37 5	15 6	24 6	49	—	—	7 56	—	8	7 8	27 9	9 12	—	9 33	9 46 10 25 11 2
CATFORD	1 12 2	16 3	12 4	40 5	18 6	27 6	52	—	—	7 59	—	8	10 8	30 9	15	—	9 36	9 49 10 28 11 5
Bellingham	1 15 2	18 3	14 4	43 5	21 6	30 6	55	—	7 43	8	0	—	8	13 8	33 9	18	—	9 39	9 52 10 31 11 8
Beckenham Hill	—	—	—	—	—	6 58	—	—	—	—	—	8 16	—	—	—	9 42	—	10 34 11 11
Ravensbourne	—	—	—	—	—	7 1	—	—	—	—	8 18	8 37	—	—	—	9 45	9 55 10 37 11 14
Honor Oak	—	—	—	—	—	—	7 11	—	8 1	—	—	—	9 29	—	—	—	—	—
Lordship Lane	—	—	—	—	—	—	7 15	—	8 5	—	—	—	9 33	—	—	—	—	—
Upper Sydenham	—	—	—	—	—	—	7 18	—	8 8	—	—	—	9 36	—	—	—	—	—
CRYSTAL PALACE ... arr.	—	—	—	—	—	—	7 20	—	8 11	—	—	—	9 39	—	—	—	—	—

WEEK DAYS.

	AM	AM	AM	PM	e	d	e	d	e	d	d	d	e	d	d	d	d	d	d
LUDGATE HILL ... dep.	—	—	—	—	—	12 15	—	—	—	—	—	—	—	—	—	1 13	—	1 22
ST. PAUL'S	10 53	11 31	11 48	12 12	12 14	—	12 23	12 30	12 38	12 42	12 51	12 53	1 3	1 12	—	1 21	—	1 26
Elephant and Castle	10 57	11 35	11 52	12 16	12 18	12 19	12 27	12 34	12 42	12 46	12 55	12 57	1 7	—	1 18	—	1 26
Loughborough Junctn.	11 2	11 41	11 57	—	12 23	12 24	12 32	12 40	12 47	—	—	1 3	1 12	—	1 24	—	1 31
Denmark Hill	11 5	11 45	12 0	12 23	12 26	12 27	12 35	—	12 50	12 52	1 2	1 6	1 15	—	1 27	—	1 34
Peckham Rye	11 8	11 48	12 3	12 26	12 29	12 30	12 38	12 43	12 53	12 55	1 5	1 9	1 18	1 23	—	1 31	1 37
NUNHEAD { arr.	12 12	11 51	12 6	12 29	12 32	12 33	12 41	12 47	12 56	12 58	—	1 12	1 21	—	1 31	1 34	1 40
{ dep.	11 13	11 52	12 7	12 30	12 33	12 34	12 42	12 48	12 57	12 59	—	1 13	1 22	—	1 32	1 35	1 41
Crofton Park	—	11 55	12 10	12 33	—	—	12 45	—	—	—	1 2	1 11	—	1 25	1 30	—	1 38	—
CATFORD	—	11 58	12 13	12 36	—	—	12 48	—	—	—	1 5	1 14	—	1 28	1 33	—	1 41	—
Bellingham	—	12 1	12 16	12 39	—	—	12 51	—	—	—	1 8	1 16	—	1 31	1 37	—	1 43	—
Beckenham Hill	—	—	12 19	—	—	—	—	—	—	—	1 11	—	—	—	1 40	—	—
Ravensbourne	—	—	12 22	—	—	—	—	—	—	—	1 14	—	—	—	1 43	—	—
Honor Oak	11 18	—	—	12 38	12 40	—	12 54	1 2	—	—	—	1 19	—	—	1 38	—	1 48
Lordship Lane	11 21	—	—	12 41	12 44	—	12 58	1 5	—	—	—	1 23	—	—	1 42	—	1 52
Upper Sydenham	11 24	—	—	12 44	12 47	—	1 1	1 8	—	—	—	1 26	—	—	1 45	—	1 55
CRYSTAL PALACE ... arr.	11 26	—	—	12 46	12 50	—	1 4	1 10	—	—	—	1 29	—	—	1 48	—	1 58

WEEK DAYS.

	d	e	d	d	d	d	PM	PM	PM	d	PM	e	d	PM	d	e	e
LUDGATE HILL ... dep.	—	—	—	—	—	2 19	—	—	—	—	—	—	4 35	—	—	5 1
ST. PAUL'S	1 35	1 36	1 37	1 52	1 57	2 3	—	2 37	2 47	3 16	3 22	3 38	4 10	4 18	4 30	—	4 37 4 56
Elephant and Castle	1 39	1 40	1 41	1 56	2 1	2 7	2 24	2 41	2 51	3 20	3 26	3 43	4 14	4 22	4 35	4 39	4 41 5 0
Loughborough Junctn.	—	1 45	1 47	2 1	2 6	—	2 30	2 46	—	3 25	3 32	3 48	4 19	4 27	4 39	4 44	4 46 5 5 9
Denmark Hill	—	1 48	1 50	2 4	—	2 14	—	2 49	2 58	3 28	3 36	3 51	4 22	4 30	4 42	4 47	— 5 12
Peckham Rye	—	1 51	1 53	2 7	2 10	2 17	2 35	2 52	3 1	3 31	3 39	3 54	4 26	4 33	4 45	4 50	4 51 5 15
NUNHEAD { arr.	1 48	1 54	—	2 10	2 13	2 20	2 37	2 55	3 4	3 34	3 41	3 57	4 29	4 36	4 48	4 53	4 53 5 10 5 17
{ dep.	1 49	1 55	—	2 11	2 14	2 21	2 38	2 57	3 5	3 35	3 42	3 58	4 30	4 37	4 49	4 54	4 54 5 15 5 18
Crofton Park	1 52	—	—	2 14	2 17	2 24	—	3	8 3	38	—	4 1	—	4 41	—	—	4 57 5 14 —
CATFORD	1 55	—	—	2 17	2 20	2 27	—	3	11 3	41	—	4 4	—	4 44	—	—	5 0 5 17 —
Bellingham	1 57	—	—	2 20	2 23	2 29	—	3	14 3	43	—	4 6	—	4 47	—	—	5 2 5 19 —
Beckenham Hill	—	—	—	2 23	2 26	—	—	3 16	—	—	—	4 50	—	—	—	—
Ravensbourne	—	—	—	2 26	2 29	—	—	3 19	—	—	—	4 53	—	—	—	—
Honor Oak	—	2 0	2 1	—	—	2 44	3 2	—	—	3 48	—	4 35	—	4 54	4 59	—	5 25
Lordship Lane	—	2 3	2 5	—	—	2 48	3 6	—	—	3 51	—	4 38	—	4 57	5 2	—	5 29
Upper Sydenham	—	2 6	2 8	—	—	2 51	3 9	—	—	3 54	—	4 41	—	5 0	5 5	—	5 32
CRYSTAL PALACE ... arr.	—	2 8	2 11	—	—	2 54	3 11	—	—	3 56	—	4 43	—	5 2	5 7	—	5 35

WEEK DAYS.

	e	d	d	d	e	d	e	d	e	e	d	e	PM	PM
LUDGATE HILL ... dep.	5 19	—	—	5 38	—	5 51	—	6 6	—	6 27	—	—	—	—
ST. PAUL'S	5 23	5 25	5 37	5 36	5 48	5 50	6 0	6 18	6 25	6 32	6 41	6 46	6 47	12 7 7 37
Elephant and Castle	5 23	5 24	5 41	5 41	5 43	5 52	5 54	5 55	6 4	6 10	6 22	6 29	6 31	6 37 6 46 6 46 6 51 7 16 7 41
Loughborough Junctn.	5 29	5 47	—	5 49	—	6 1	—	6 15	6 27	6 34	—	6 51	—	6 56 7 21 7 46
Denmark Hill	5 32	5 32	5 50	—	5 52	5 59	6 1	—	6 11	—	6 31	6 37	6 38	— 6 54 — 6 59 7 24 7 49
Peckham Rye	5 35	5 35	5 53	5 49	5 55	—	6 4	6 6	—	6 19	—	6 40	6 41	6 45 6 45 6 57 6 54 7 2 7 27 7 52
NUNHEAD { arr.	5 37	5 38	5 55	5 52	—	6 4	6 7	6 9	6 15	6 23	6 34	6 43	6 43	6 48 7 0 6 57 7 5 7 30 7 54
{ dep.	5 38	5 39	5 56	5 53	—	6 5	6 8	6 10	6 16	6 24	6 35	6 44	6 44	6 49 7 1 6 58 7 6 7 31 7 55
Crofton Park	—	5 42	—	5 56	—	6 8	6 11	—	6 20	—	6 39	6 47	—	6 53 — 7 1 — 7 35 —
CATFORD	—	5 45	—	5 59	—	6 11	6 14	—	6 23	—	6 42	6 50	—	6 56 — 7 4 — 7 38 —
Bellingham	—	5 47	—	6 3	—	6 15	6 17	—	6 25	—	6 45	6 53	—	6 59 — 7 6 — 7 41 —
Beckenham Hill	—	—	—	6 6	—	6 18	6 20	—	—	—	6 48	6 56	—	— — — — 7 43 —
Ravensbourne	—	—	—	6 9	—	6 20	6 22	—	—	6 51	6 59	7 5	—	— — — 7 46 —
Honor Oak	5 43	6 1	—	6 3	—	6 17	—	6 30	—	—	6 51	—	7 6	— 7 12 — 8 1
Lordship Lane	5 47	6 4	—	6 7	—	6 20	—	6 34	—	—	6 55	—	7 9	— 7 16 — 8 4
Upper Sydenham	5 51	6 7	—	6 10	—	6 23	—	6 37	—	—	6 58	—	7 12	— 7 19 — 8 7
CRYSTAL PALACE ... arr	5 54	6 9	—	6 13	—	6 26	—	6 40	—	—	7 1	—	7 14	— 7 22 — 8 9

WEEK DAYS.

	PM	e	d	e	PM	PM	PM	PM	PM	PM	PM	PM	PM	mdt.	h
LUDGATE HILL ... dep.	—	—	—	—	—	—	—	—	—	—	—	—	—	—	—
ST. PAUL'S	f 31	8 17	8 20	8 39	8 42	9 8	9 37	9 42	10 20	10 42	10 52	11 15	11 43	11 50	12 20 12 50
Elephant & Castle	7 35	8 21	8 24	8 43	8 46	9 12	9 41	9 47	10 24	10 46	10 56	11 19	—	11 54	12 24 12 53
Loughborough Junct.	—	8 26	8 29	8 48	8 51	9 17	—	9 52	10 29	10 51	11	1 11 24	11 50	11 59	12 29 12 58
Denmark Hill	7 43	8 29	8 32	8 51	8 54	9 20	9 48	9 55	10 32	10 54	11 5	11 27	—	12 2	—
Peckham Rye	7 46	8 32	8 35	8 54	8 57	9 23	9 51	9 58	10 36	10 57	11 8	11 30	—	12 5	12 34 1 2
NUNHEAD { arr.	7 49	8 35	8 38	8 57	9 0	9 25	9 54	10	1 10 39	11 0	11 11	11 33	11 55	12 9	12 37 1 5
{ dep.	7 50	8 36	8 39	8 58	9 1	9 26	9 55	10 2	10 40	11 1	11 12	11 34	11 56	12 10	12 38 1 6
Crofton Park	7 54	8 40	8 42	9 1	—	9 29	9 58	—	10 43	11 5	—	11 37	11 59	—	12 41 1 9
CATFORD	7 57	8 43	8 45	9 4	—	9 32	10 1	—	10 46	11 8	—	11 40	12 2	—	12 44 1 12
Bellingham	7 59	8 46	8 48	9 7	—	9 35	10 4	—	10 49	11 11	—	11 43	12 4	—	12 47 1 15
Beckenham Hill	—	8 49	8 54	9 11	—	9 38	—	—	10 53	11 14	—	—	—	—	—
Ravensbourne	—	8 52	8 56	—	—	9 41	—	—	10 55	11 17	—	—	—	—	—
Honor Oak	—	—	—	9 6	—	—	10 7	—	—	—	11 17	—	12 15	—	—
Lordship Lane	—	—	—	9 9	—	—	10 10	—	—	—	11 20	—	12 18	—	—
Upper Sydenham	—	—	—	9 12	—	—	10 13	—	—	—	11 23	—	12 21	—	—
CRYSTAL PALACE ... arr.	—	—	—	9 14	—	—	10 15	—	—	—	11 25	—	12 23	—	—

d Saturdays only.   *e* Saturdays excepted.   *h* Sunday mornings only.

No Sunday Trains.

WEEK DAYS.	AM	AM	AM	AM	AM	AM	AM	AM	AM	AM	AM	AM	AM	AM	AM	AM	AM	AM	AM
CRYSTAL PALACE ..dep.	—	—	—	—	—	6 43	—	—	—	7 20	—	7 45	—	8 2	—	—	8 24	—	—
Upper Sydenham	—	—	—	—	6 45	—	—	—	7 23	—	7 47	—	8 4	—	—	8 26	—	—
Lordship Lane	—	—	—	—	6 48	—	—	—	7 26	—	7 50	—	8 7	—	—	8 29	—	—
Honor Oak	—	—	—	—	6 51	—	—	—	7 29	—	7 53	—	8 10	—	—	8 32	—	—
Ravensbourne........	—	—	—	6 8	—	—	—	7 13	—	—	—	—	—	8 15	—	8 26	8 36
Beckenham Hill	—	—	—	—	—	7 7	7 16	—	—	—	—	—	—	8 18	—	8 29	—
Bellingham	2 25	3 22	4 10	4 55	6 13	—	6 45	7 10	7 19	—	7 33	—	7 56	—	8 12	8 21	—	8 32	8 40
CATFORD	2 28	3 25	4 13	4 58	6 16	—	6 48	7 13	7 22	—	7 37	—	7 59	—	8 15	8 24	—	8 35	8 43
Crofton Park	2 31	3 28	4 16	5 1	6 19	—	6 51	7 16	—	—	7 40	—	8 2	—	8 18	8 27	—	8 38	8 46
NUNHEAD { arr.	2 34	3 31	4 19	5 4	6 22	6 54	6 54	7 19	7 27	7 32	—	7 56	8 5	8 13	8 21	—	8 39	8 41	—
NUNHEAD (dep.	2 35	3 32	4 20	5 5	6 23	6 55	6 55	7 20	7 28	7 33	—	7 57	8 6	8 14	8 22	—	8 36	8 42	—
Peckham Rye	2 38	3 35	4 24	5 8	6 26	6 58	6 58	7 23	—	7 36	—	8 9	—	8 17	8 25	—	8 39	8 45	—
Denmark Hill	—	—	—	5 11	6 29	7 1	7 1	7 26	—	7 39	—	8 3	—	8 10	8 28	8 35	8 42	—	8 54
Loughborough Junct..	2 42	3 39	4 28	5 14	6 32	7 4	7 4	—	—	—	—	8 6	8 11	8 23	—	—	8 45	—	8 58
Elephant and Castle..	2 47	3 44	4 33	5 19	6 37	7 9	7 9	7 33	7 39	7 46	7 54	8 11	8 17	8 28	—	8 42	8 50	8 53	9 3
ST. PAUL'S	2 50	3 47	4 37	5 23	6 40	7 13	7 13	7 37	7 43	—	7 58	—	8 20	—	8 38	8 46	—	8 57	9 6
LUDGATE HILL ....arr.	—	—	—	—	—	—	—	—	—	7 49	—	8 15	—	8 32	—	—	8 54	—	—

WEEK DAYS.	AM	AM	AM	AM	AM	AM	AM	AM	AM	AM	AM	AM	AM	PM	PM
CRYSTAL PALACE .. dep.	8 42	—	9 0	—	9 33	—	10 2	—	10 46	—	—	—	11 56	—	—
Upper Sydenham	8 45	—	9 3	—	9 36	—	10 4	—	10 48	—	—	—	11 58	—	—
Lordship Lane	8 48	—	9 6	—	9 39	—	10 7	—	10 51	—	—	—	12 1	—	—
Honor Oak	8 51	—	9 9	—	9 42	—	10 11	—	10 54	—	—	—	12 4	—	—
Ravensbourne	—	8 56	—	9 2	9 21	—	—	10 7	—	10 48	11 12	11 46	—	—	12 40
Beckenham Hill	—	—	—	9 5	—	—	—	10 10	—	10 51	11 15	11 48	—	—	12 43
Bellingham	—	8 58	—	9 8	9 25	—	9 40	—	10 12	—	10 54	11 18	11 50	—	12 17	12 46
CATFORD	—	9 1	—	9 11	9 28	—	9 43	—	10 15	—	10 57	11 21	11 53	—	12 20	12 49
Crofton Park	—	9 4	—	9 14	9 31	—	9 46	—	10 18	—	11 0	11 24	11 56	—	12 23	12 52
NUNHEAD { arr.	8 54	—	9 12	—	9 33	—	9 49	10 14	10 20	10 57	11 3	11 27	11 59	12 7	12 26	12 55
NUNHEAD (dep.	8 55	—	9 13	—	9 34	—	9 50	10 15	10 21	10 58	11 4	11 28	12 0	12 8	12 27	12 56
Peckham Rye	8 58	9 9	9 16	9 20	9 36	—	+9 53	10 18	10 24	11 1	11 7	11 31	12 3	12 11	12 30	12 59
Denmark Hill	9 2	—	9 21	—	9 41	9 48	9 56	10 21	10 27	11 4	11 10	11 34	—	12 14	12 33	1 2
Loughborough Junctn.	9 2	—	9 21	—	9 41	—	9 59	10 24	10 30	11 7	11 13	11 37	12 8	12 17	12 36	1 5
Elephant and Castle ..	9 7	—	9 26	9 29	9 47	—	10 4	10 29	10 33	11 12	11 18	11 42	12 13	12 22	12 41	1 10
ST. PAUL'S	—	9 21	—	9 33	9 52	—	10 8	10 33	10 39	11 16	11 22	11 46	12 17	12 27	12 45	1 14
LUDGATE HILL.... arr.	9 11	—	9 30	—	9 57	—	—	—	—	—	—	—	—	—	—	—

WEEK DAYS.	e	d	e	d	e	d	PM	e	d	PM	PM	PM	PM	PM	d	e	e	d
CRYSTAL PALACE .. dep.	12 57	1 12	—	1 43	1 57	—	—	—	2 50	—	3 32	—	4 3	4 10	—
Upper Sydenham......	12 59	1 14	—	1 45	1 59	—	—	—	2 52	—	3 34	—	4 6	4 12	—
Lordship Lane	1 2	1 17	—	1 48	2 2	—	—	—	2 55	—	3 37	—	4 9	4 15	—
Honor Oak	1 5	1 20	—	1 51	2 5	—	—	—	2 59	—	3 40	—	4 12	4 18	—
Ravensbourne........	—	—	—	—	—	1 57	2 18	2 41	—	—	3 37	—	—	—
Beckenham Hill.......	—	—	—	—	—	2 0	2 21	2 44	—	—	3 40	—	—	—
Bellingham	—	—	1 20	1 30	—	2 3	2 24	2 35	2 47	—	3 20	—	3 44	—	4 20	4 23
CATFORD	—	—	1 23	1 33	—	2 6	2 27	2 39	2 50	—	3 23	—	3 47	—	4 23	4 26
Crofton Park	—	—	1 26	1 36	—	2 9	2 30	2 42	2 53	—	3 26	—	3 50	—	4 26	4 29
NUNHEAD { arr.	1 8	1 23	1 29	1 39	1 54	2 8	2 12	2 33	2 45	2 56	3 2	3 29	3 43	3 52	4 15	4 21	4 28	4 32
NUNHEAD (dep.	1 9	1 24	1 30	1 40	1 55	2 9	2 13	2 34	2 46	2 57	3 3	3 30	3 44	3 53	4 16	4 22	4 29	4 33
Peckham Rye	1 12	1 27	1 33	1 43	1 58	2 12	2 16	2 37	—	1 49	3 0	3 6	3 33	3 47	3 56	4 19	4 25	4 33	4 36
Denmark Hill	1 15	1 30	1 36	1 46	2 1	2 15	2 19	2 40	ℓ 52	—	3 6	3 33	3 47	3 59	4 22	4 28	4 37	4 39
Loughborough Junctn.	1 18	—	1 39	1 48	2 4	2 18	2*18	2 44	2 56	3 5	3 12	3 39	3 53	4 3	4 25	4 31	4 41	4 42
Elephant and Castle ..	1 23	1 36	1 44	1 53	2 10	2 23	2 28	2 49	3 1	3 10	3 17	3 44	3 58	4 9	4 30	4 36	4 46	4 47
ST. PAUL'S	1 26	1 40	1 49	1 57	2 13	2 27	2 33	2 52	3 5	5 13	3 14	3 21	3 48	4 2	4 13	4 34	—	4 50	4 50
LUDGATE HILL..... arr.	—	—	—	—	—	—	—	—	—	—	—	4 2	—	4 40	—	—

WEEK DAYS.	PM	PM	PM	PM	PM	PM	PM	PM	PM	PM	PM	PM	PM	e	e	e
CRYSTAL PALACE .. dep.	—	4 53	4 56	—	5 17	—	—	6 56	3	—	6 30	—	6 52	—	7 37	7 43	—
Upper Sydenham......	—	4 55	4 58	—	5 19	—	—	6 7	6 6	—	6 32	—	6 54	—	7 39	7 45	—
Lordship Lane	—	4 58	5 1	—	5 22	—	—	6 10	6 9	—	6 35	—	6 57	—	7 42	7 48	—
Honor Oak	—	5 1	5 4	—	5 25	—	—	6 13	6 12	—	6 40	—	7 0	—	7 45	7 51	—
Ravensbourne........	4 43	—	—	—	5 35	—	5 55	—	6 19	—	6 42	—	7 7	—	—	7 50
Beckenham Hill.......	4 46	—	—	—	5 38	—	5 58	—	6 21	—	6 45	—	7 23	—	—	7 53
Bellingham	4 49	—	5 14	—	5 41	5 55	6 1	—	6 24	—	6 48	—	7 26	—	—	7 56
CATFORD	4 53	—	5 16	—	5 44	5 58	6 4	—	6 27	—	6 51	—	7 29	—	—	7 59
Crofton Park	4 56	—	5 19	—	5 47	6 1	6 7	—	6 30	—	6 54	—	7 32	—	—	8 2
NUNHEAD { arr.	4 59	5 4	5 5	5 23	5 28	5 49	6 4	6 10	6 16	6 33	6 41	6 57	3 7	7 34	7 48	7 54	8 4
NUNHEAD (dep.	5 0	5 5	6 5	5 24	5 29	5 50	6 5	6 11	6 17	6 34	6 42	6 58	7 4	7 35	7 49	7 55	8 5
Peckham Rye	5 3	5 8	5 11	5 27	5 32	5 53	6 8	6 14	6 20	6 37	6 45	7 1	7 7	7 38	7 52	7 58	8 8
Denmark Hill	5 6	5 12	5 14	5 30	5 35	—	6 11	6 17	6 23	—	6 40	6 48	7 4	7 10	7 41	7 57	8 1	8 11
Loughborough Junctn.	5 —	5 14	5 17	5 33	—	—	6 20	6 26	6 24	6 43	—	7 7	7 13	7 45	7 58	8 1	8 14
Elephant and Castle ..	5 14	5 20	5 22	5 39	5 43	6 2	6 18	6 25	6 31	—	6 48	6 55	7 12	7 18	7 50	8 3	8 10	8 20
ST. PAUL'S	5 18	5 24	5 25	5 43	5 46	6 5	6 22	6 29	6 35	6 31	6 52	6 58	7 16	7 22	7 54	8 6	8 14	8 24
LUDGATE HILL .... arr.	—	—	—	—	—	—	—	—	—	—	—	—	—	—	—	—

WEEK DAYS.	PM	PM	PM	PM	PM	PM	PM	PM		
CRYSTAL PALACE .. dep.	—	8 35	—	9 35	—	10 30	—		
Upper Sydenham......	—	8 37	—	9 37	—	10 32	—		
Lordship Lane	—	8 40	—	9 40	—	10 35	—		
Honor Oak	—	8 43	—	9 43	—	10 35	—		
Ravensbourne........	8 26	—	9 24	—	9 44	—	11 11	**No Sunday Trains.**	
Beckenham Hill.......	8 29	—	9 24	—	9 47	—	11 14		
Bellingham	8 32	—	9 27	—	9 50	10 25	—	11 17	
CATFORD	8 35	—	9 30	—	9 53	10 28	—	11 20	
Crofton Park	8 38	—	9 33	—	9 56	10 31	—	11 23	*d* Saturdays only.
NUNHEAD { arr. / (dep.	8 41	8 46	9 36	9 39	9 59	10 34	10 41	11 26	*e* Saturdays excepted.
NUNHEAD (dep.	8 42	8 47	9 37	9 40	10 0	10 35	10 42	11 27	
Peckham Rye	8 45	8 50	9 40	9 50	10 3	10 38	10 45	11 30	
Denmark Hill	8 48	8 53	9 43	9 53	10 6	10 41	10 48	11 33	
Loughborough Junctn.	—	8 56	9 46	9 56	10 9	10 44	10 52	11 37	
Elephant and Castle ..	8 53	9 1	9 51	10 1	10 14	10 49	10 57	11 42	
ST. PAUL'S	8 58	9 5	9 54	10 5	10 18	10 53	11 1	11 46	
LUDGATE HILL .... arr.	—	—	—	—	—	—	—	—	

WEEK DAYS.	AM	AM	AM	AM	AM	AM	AM	AM	AM	AM	AM	AM	AM	AM	AM
LONDON BRIDGE (L.B.R.) dep.	5 15	5 35	5 50	6 35	6 55	7	7	7 35	8 17	8 24	8 57	9 8	9 36	10 20	10 47
Penge West	5 33	6 0	6 15	—	7 18	—	8 0	8 40	8 52	9 21	9 37	9 58	10 43	11 12
Anerley	5 35	6 2	6 17	—	7 20	—	8 2	8 42	8 54	9 23	9 39	10 0	10 45	11 14
NORWOOD JUNCTION	5 39	6 6	6 21	—	7 25	7 36	8 7	8 46	8 58	9 27	9 45	10 5	10 50	11 20
West Croydon	5 44	6 11	6 27	—	7 31	7 47	8 14	8 51	—	9 33	—	10 10	10 55	11 25
Waddon	5 48	—	6 33	—	7 35	7 50	8 20	8 57	—	9 38	—	10 16	10 59	11 29
Wallington	5 53	—	6 89	—	7 41	7 54	8 25	9 2	—	9 45	—	10 22	11 5	11 34
Beeches Halt	—	—	—	—	7 57	—	9 24	—	—	—	11ʰ22	—
Sutton	5 58	—	6 44	6 58	7 46	8 1	8 34	9 7	—	9 50	—	10 27	11 10	11 39
Cheam	—	—	6 48	—	7 57	—	8 38	—	—	9 55	—	11 12	11 15	11 43
Ewell East	—	—	6 52	—	8 1	—	8 42	—	—	—	—	11 16	—	11 47
Epsom	—	—	6 56	—	7 54	—	8 48	9 37	—	—	—	10 36	—	11 51

WEEK DAYS.	AM	AM	PM	d	d	e	d	PM	d	d	d	PM	d
LONDON BRIDGE dep.	11 14	11 58	12 24	12 25	1257	1 0	1 3	1 17	1 25	1 32	1 40	2 10	2 38
Penge West	11 40	12 23	—	—	1 15	1 25	1 28	1 43	—	1 50	2 3	—	2 41
Anerley	11 42	12 25	—	—	—	1 27	1 30	1 45	—	1 52	2 6	—	2 43
NORWOOD JUNCTION	11 46	12 30	—	12 44	1 21	1 31	1 34	1 49	—	1 56	2 10	2 31	2 48	2 53
West Croydon	12 12	12 36	—	12 50	1 26	1 36	1 39	—	1 47	—	2 16	2 36	2 53	2 59
Waddon	12 17	12 41	—	1 7	1 29	1 39	1 52	—	1 52	—	2 20	2 40	2ˢ57	3 2
Wallington	12 21	12 48	—	12 57	1 34	1 44	1 58	—	1 58	—	2 25	2 45	3ˢ 2	3 7
Beeches Halt	12 24	—	—	1ʰ14	—	—	—	—	2 19	—	—	—	—
Sutton	12 28	12 53	1 7	1 2	—	1 50	2 4	—	2 4	—	—	2 50	3ˢ 7	3 12
Cheam	—	12 57	1 12	1 6	—	—	—	—	—	—	—	2 54	3ˢ11	3 15
Ewell East	—	—	1 16	1 16	—	—	—	—	—	—	—	—	3ˢ15	3 19
Epsom	—	1 3	1 20	1 20	—	—	—	—	—	—	—	—	3ˢ19	3 23

WEEK DAYS.	d	e	d	d	e	PM	e	PM	e	PM	e	e	d	PM	PM
LONDON BRIDGE dep.	2 53	3 10	3 15	3 52	4 2	4 12	4 15	4 38	5 10	5 13	5 45	5 51	5 13	6 16	6 45
Penge West	3 11	—	—	—	—	4 38	—	—	—	5 36	—	6 12	6 18	—	—
Anerley	3 13	—	—	—	—	4 40	—	—	—	5 39	—	6 14	6 20	—	—
NORWOOD JUNCTION	3 17	3 35	3 35	4 11	4 36	4 44	4 31	4 57	—	5 45	6 1	6 18	6 24	6ˢ35	7ᵈ 2
West Croydon	3 22	3 40	3 40	4 17	4 40	4 49	4 40	5 2	5 34	—	6 5	6 23	6 29	6 38	7 7
Waddon	3 26	3 44	3 44	4 20	—	—	—	5 6	5 38	—	6 9	—	6 32	6 43	7 12
Wallington	3 31	3 49	3 49	4 25	4 45	4ˢ55	4 45	5 11	5 43	—	6 14	6 33	6 37	6 48	7 17
Beeches Halt	—	4ʰ10	—	4ʰ36	4 48	—	4 48	—	6ʰ 7	—	—	—	—	—
Sutton	3 36	3 54	3 54	4ʰ40	4 52	5ˢ 5	4 52	5 16	5 48	—	6 19	—	6 42	6 54	7 24
Cheam	—	3 57	3 57	—	—	5ˢ 9	—	5 37	5 51	—	—	—	—	—	7 28
Ewell East	—	4 1	4 1	—	—	—	—	5 7	5 55	—	—	—	—	—	7 32
Epsom	—	4 5	4 5	—	—	—	—	5 11	5 58	—	—	—	—	—	7 36

WEEK DAYS.	e	PM	PM	PM	PM	PM	PM	PM	PM	PM	PM	PM	PM	Mid.
LONDON BRIDGE dep.	7 5	7 25	7 40	8 22	8 50	9 40	10 12	10 27	11 15	11 43	12 30
Penge West	—	7 50	—	—	—	—	10 37	10 52	11 40	12 8	12 55
Anerley	—	7 52	8 3	8 42	—	—	10 39	10 54	11 42	12 10	12 57
NORWOOD JUNCTION	7 23	7 56	8 7	8 46	9 7	10 3	10 43	10 57	11 46	12 14	1 1
West Croydon	7 29	8 2	8 12	8 51	9 19	10 8	10 48	11 8	11 51	12 19	1 6
Waddon	7 32	—	8 14	8 54	9 23	10 12	10 52	—	11 54	—	—
Wallington	7 37	—	8 19	8 59	9 28	10 17	10 57	—	11 59	—	—
Beeches Halt	7 55	—	—	—	9 31	—	—	—	—	—	—
Sutton	7 59	—	8 24	9 4	9 35	10 22	11 2	—	12 4	—	—
Cheam	—	—	8 27	9 14	10 5	10 25	11 32	—	12 18	—	—
Ewell East	—	—	8 31	9 18	—	10 29	11ᴬ36	—	12ᴬ22	—	—
Epsom	—	—	8 35	9 22	10 11	10 33	11 39	—	12 11	—	—

SUNDAYS.	AM	AM	AM	PM	PM	PM	PM	PM	PM	PM	PM
LONDON BRIDGE dep.	9 10	9 35	9 50	12 45	1 13	2 40	3 48	4 43	6 15	6 38	8 10	9 35
Penge West	9 35	10 1	10 15	—	1 38	3 8	4 13	5 8	6 40	—	8 35	10 2
Anerley	9 37	10 3	10 17	—	1 40	3 10	4 15	5 10	6 42	—	8 37	10 2
NORWOOD JUNCTION	9 41	10 7	10 21	1 9	1 45	3 14	4 19	5 14	6 46	7 1	8 41	10 7
West Croydon	9 46	—	11 17	1 14	1 50	3 19	4 24	5 19	6 51	7 7	8 46	10 12
Waddon	9 50	—	11 20	1 17	1 54	3 42	4 27	5 24	6 55	7ˢ27	8 49	10 15
Wallington	9 55	—	11 24	1 22	2 2	3 46	4 32	5 29	7 0	7ˢ31	8 54	10 20
Beeches Halt	—	—	—	—	—	5 23	—	—	—	7ˢ34	—	—
Sutton	10 0	—	11 29	1 27	2 7	3 51	4 37	5 35	7 5	7 38	8 59	10 25
Cheam	—	—	11 39	1 31	2 20	—	4 42	5 38	—	—	9 13	10 28
Ewell East	—	—	11 43	1 35	2 24	—	4 46	5 42	—	—	9 18	10 46
Epsom	—	—	11 48	1 39	2 29	—	4 50	5 46	—	7 26	9 24	10 34

SUNDAYS.	PM	PM
LONDON BRIDGE dep.	10 30	11 20
Penge West	10 55	11 45
Anerley	10 57	11 47
NORWOOD JUNCTION	11 1	11 51
West Croydon	11 7	11 56
Waddon	11 11	—
Wallington	11 16	—
Beeches Halt	—	—
Sutton	11 21	—
Cheam	—	—
Ewell East	—	—
Epsom	—	—

h Wednesdays only.

EPSOM, SUTTON & WEST CROYDON TO LONDON BRIDGE.

WEEK DAYS.	AM	AM	AM	AM	AM	AM	AM	AM	AM	AM	AM	AM	AM	AM	AM
Epsom dep.	—	—	5 32	—	7 21	7 54	—	8 35	—	—	—	9 37	—
Ewell, East	—	—	5 35	—	7 25	7 58	—	8 39	—	—	—	9 40	—
Cheam	4 12	—	5 39	6 32	—	7 35	8 11	—	8 44	—	—	9 44	10 37
Sutton	4 16	5 5	5 43	6 38	—	7 39	8 15	—	8 44	8ˢ56	—	9 15	9 42	9 49	10 41
Beeches Halt	—	—	—	—	—	—	—	—	8ˢ58	—	9 44	—
Wallington	4 20	5 9	5 49	6 43	6 50	7 44	8 19	8 27	8 50	9 8	—	9 19	9 47	9 53	10 46
Waddon	—	—	5 53	6 47	—	7 48	8 24	—	8 54	—	—	9 23	9 51	9 57	10 50
West Croydon	4 26	5 16	5 59	6 52	6 56	7 53	8 30	8 49	8 59	—	9 20	9 28	9 55	10 2	10 54
NORWOOD JUNCTION	4 31	5 20	6 4	6 56	7 0	7 57	—	—	—	—	9 33	—	10 7	11 0
Anerley	4 35	5 24	—	—	7 4	8 1	—	—	—	9 26	—	—	11 4
Penge West	4 37	5 26	—	—	7 6	8	—	—	—	9 28	—	—	11 6
LONDON BRIDGE (L.B.R.)	4 55	5 48	6 25	7 13	7 24	8 22	8 50	9 16	9 20	9 32	9 47	9 51	—	10 26	11 30

d Saturdays only.   e Saturdays excepted.
u Motor, third class only; change at West Croydon.

WEEK DAYS.	AM	AM	PM	d	d	PM	d	PM	PM	d	PM	e	e	PM
Epsom ....dep.	10 53	11 57	12 56	—	—	1 45	—	2 57	3 42	—	4^{d}48	—	5 15	—
Ewell East	11 1	12 1	12 59	—	—	1 48	—	3 2	3 45	—	4^{d}51	—	5 20	—
Cheam	11 5	12 26	1 3	—	—	1 52	—	3 6	3 49	—	4^{d}55	—	5 32	5 58
Sutton	11 8	12 34	1 8	1 25	—	1 56	2 10	3 11	3 53	4 28	5 4	—	5 37	6 2
Beeches Halt........	10 57	11^{m}55	—	—	—	—	—	—	3^{m}47	—	—	4 58	5 28	—
Wallington.........	11 14	12 40	1 12	1 29	1 45	2 2	2 14	3 16	3 58	4 55	5 9	5 4	5 42	6 18
Waddon	11 18	12 44	1 16	1 33	1 48	2 6	—	3 20	4 2	4 58	5 13	5 8	5 46	6 21
West Croydon	11 23	12 49	1 22	1 37	1 53	2 12	2 40	3 25	4 10	5 3	5 18	5 13	5 50	6 25
Norwood Junction ..	11 28	12 55	1 27	1 55	1 59	2 17	2 44	3 30	4 14	5 8	5 23	5 17	5 56	6 30
Anerley	11 32	12 59	1 31	1 58	2 3	2 22	2 48	3 34	4 18	5 11	5 28	—	6 0	6 34
Penge West	11 34	1 2	1*33	2 0	2 5	2 24	2 50	3 37	4 20	5 14	5 30	—	6 2	6 36
London Bridge......	11 57	1 23	1 50	2 22	2 28	2 46	3 13	3 55	4 43	5 36	5 51	6 4	6 25	6 58

WEEK DAYS.	PM	PM	PM	PM	PM	PM	PM	PM
Epsom ....dep.	6 30	7 15	7 47	8 15	8 52	9 40	10 46	—
Ewell East	6 32	7 18	7^{d}36	8 19	8 55	9 43	10^{k}49	—
Cheam	6 36	7 22	7^{d}41	8 24	8 59	9 47	—	—
Sutton	7 2	7 29	8 5	8 30	9 4	9 52	10 57	11 30
Beeches Halt........	—	7 31	8 7	—	8^{m}38	—	10^{m}12	—
Wallington.........	7 6	7 34	8 10	8 36	9 9	9 57	11 2	11 34
Waddon	7 10	7 38	8 14	8 40	9 13	10 1	11 6	—
West Croydon	7 15	7 42	8 30	8 45	9 21	10 6	11 11	11 42
Norwood Junction..	7 20	8 10	8 34	8 52	9 26	10 11	11 16	11 47
Anerley	7 24	8 14	8 38	8 56	9 30	10 15	11 20	11 51
Penge West	7 26	8 16	8 40	8 59	9 32	10 17	11 22	11 53
London Bridge (L.B.R.) ..	7 49	8 32	9 3	9 25	9 57	10 40	11 45	12 15

SUNDAYS.	AM	AM	AM	PM	PM	PM	PM	PM	PM	PM	PM	PM	PM	PM	PM	PM	PM	PM	PM
Epsom ....dep.	6 40	8 32	10 8	1 51	2 56	4 49	—	5 55	7 5	7 48	8 57	9 28	•9 50	10 21
Ewell East	—	8 35	10 13	1 55	3 0	4 53	—	5 58	7 8	7 52	9 1	—	9 53	10 25
Cheam	—	8 39	10 17	1 59	3 4	4 57	—	6 2	7 12	7 56	9 5	9 35	•9 58	10 29
Sutton	6 48	8 44	10 30	2 4	3 9	5 14	—	6 5	7 17	8 32	9 10	9 48	10 15	10 34
Beeches Halt..........	—	—	—	—	2^{m}49	—	—	5^{m}49	7^n 7	—	8 52	8^{m}52	10 2	—
Wallington.........	6 52	8 49	10 35	—	3 14	—	—	6 9	7 21	8 37	9 16	9 53	10 20	—
Waddon	—	8 53	10 39	—	3 18	—	—	6 13	7 25	8 41	9 20	9 57	10 24	—
West Croydon	6 59	8 58	10 48	—	3 30	—	5 30	6 20	7 30	8 45	9 26	10 1	10 28	—
Norwood Junction.........	7 3	9 2	10 54	—	3 35	—	5 35	6 24	7 39	8 50	9 33	10 9	10 34	—
Anerley	7 8	9 6	10 58	—	3 39	—	5 39	6 28	7 43	8 54	9 37	10 13	10 38	—
Penge West	7 9	9 8	11 0	—	3 41	—	5 41	6 30	7 45	8 55	9 39	10 15	10 40	—
London Bridge	7 33	9 31	11 26	2 44	4 3	5 54	6 5	6 52	8 8	9 21	10 1	10 40	11 2	11 15

d Saturdays only.   e Saturdays excepted.   k Wednesdays only.
n Motor, third class only ; change at West Croydon.

LONDON BRIDGE TO SUTTON, EPSOM & LEATHERHEAD.

WEEK DAYS.	AM	AM	AM	AM	AM	AM	d	PM	d	d	d
London Bridge (L.B.R.) dep.	5 23	7 5	7 30	7 35	8 24	9 22	10 35	12 0	12 24	12 52	1 5	1 33	1 50	1 53
Peckham Rye	5 35	7 12	7 39	—	8 32	9 29	10 42	—	12^{k}30	—	—	—	—	—
East Dulwich	5 38	7 15	—	—	8 35	—	—	—	12 33	—	—	—	—	—
North Dulwich..........	5 40	7 17	—	—	—	—	—	—	—	—	—	—	—	—
Tulse Hill	5 44	7 20	7 46	—	8 42	9 36	10 49	12 12	12 39	1 4	1 18	1 46	—	—
Streatham	5 49	—	7 51	—	8 47	9 42	10 55	12 17	12 47	1 9	1 23	1 51	—	—
Mitcham Junction.......	5 55	—	7 58	—	—	9 50	11 2	12 23	12 55	—	1 29	—	—	—
Hackbridge	5 59	—	—	—	8 57	9 54	11 7	—	—	—	—	—	—	2 15
Carshalton	6 2	—	8 5	—	—	9 58	11 10	12 28	1 1	1 19	1 34	—	—	2 19
Sutton	6 7	8 1	8 10	8 31	9 3	10 2	11 13	—	1 6	1 24	1 39	2 2	2 15	2 25
Cheam	6 13	—	8 15	8 38	—	10 7	11 20	12 57	1 12	1 28	1 50	2 5	—	—
Ewell East	6 17	—	8 19	8 42	—	1 (11	11 24	—	1 16	1 32	—	2 9	—	—
Epsom	6 23	—	8 23	8 48	9 37	10 17	11 31	1 3	1 20	1 37	1 55	2 13	—	2 32
Ashtead	6 30	—	—	8 55	—	10 23	11 37	—	1 35	1 43	—	—	—	2 38
Leatherhead	6 35	—	9 0	—	10 28	11 41	—	1 39	1 47	—	—	2 43

WEEK DAYS.	PM	d	PM	e	PM	d	PM	PM	PM	e	d
London Bridge (L.B.R.) dep.	2 0	2 17	2 50	3 10	3 15	4 0	4 2	4 40	5 0	5 14	5 29	5 38	5 44
Peckham Rye	—	2 26	—	—	—	4 9	—	4 49	—	—	5 36	5 45	—
East Dulwich	—	—	—	—	—	4 14	—	4 54	—	—	—	—	—
North Dulwich..........	—	—	—	—	—	4 14	—	4 52	—	—	—	—	—
Tulse Hill	2 12	2 32	3 2	—	—	4 17	4 20	4 55	—	—	5 43	5 51	—
Streatham	2 17	2 37	3 7	—	—	—	4 25	—	—	—	5 48	5 56	5 59
Mitcham Junction	2 23	2 43	3 13	—	—	—	4 31	—	—	5 33	5 54	6 3	—
Hackbridge	2 27	2 47	3 17	—	—	—	4 35	—	—	—	5 58	6 6	—
Carshalton	2 30	2 50	3 20	—	—	—	4 39	—	—	5 38	6 1	6 9	—
Sutton	2 35	2 55	3^{d}25	3 54	3 54	4 24	4 52	4 44	5 34	5 24	5 43	6 6	6 13	6 11
Cheam	2 38	3 4	3^{d}38	3 57	3 57	—	—	4 48	5 37	5 27	5 47	6 10	6 17	—
Ewell East	2 42	3 8	3^{d}42	4 1	4 0	—	—	4 52	—	—	5 49	—	—	—
Epsom	2 46	3 12	3^{d}36	4 5	4 4	4 45	—	4 57	—	5 34	5 55	—	—	6 19
Ashtead	2 53	—	—	4 11	4 10	4 51	—	5 3	—	5 40	6 1	—	—	6 26
Leatherhead	2 58	—	—	4 16	4 15	4 55	—	5 7	—	5 45	6 5	—	—	6 30

WEEK DAYS.	PM	e	PM	e	PM	PM	PM	PM	PM	e	d
London Bridge (L.B.R.) dep.	5 58	6 29	6 45	7 15	7 30	8 40	8 52	10 30	—	—	—
Peckham Rye	—	—	—	—	7 37	8 47	8 59	10 37	—	—	—
East Dulwich	—	—	—	—	—	8 50	9 2	10 40	—	—	—
North Dulwich.........	—	—	—	—	—	8 52	—	10 42	—	—	—
Tulse Hill	6 12	—	—	—	7 44	8 55	9 8	10 46	—	—	—
Streatham	6 17	6^{k}45	—	—	7 50	—	9 13	10 51	—	—	—
Mitcham Junction........	6 25	6 51	—	—	7 57	—	9 19	10 57	—	—	—
Hackbridge	—	—	—	—	—	—	9 23	—	—	—	—
Carshalton	6 30	6 55	—	—	—	—	9 26	11 3	—	—	—
Sutton	6 36	7 0	7 24	7 40	8 8	9 34	9 30	11 8	—	—	—
Cheam	6 41	7 4	7 28	—	8 12	—	9 33	11 11	—	—	—
Ewell East	6 45	7 7	7 32	—	8 15	—	9 39	^{h}	—	—	—
Epsom	6 49	7 13	7 36	—	8 20	—	9 43	11 39	—	—	—
Ashtead	6 55	7 18	7^{d}43	—	8 26	—	9 50	1. 46	—	—	—
Leatherhead	7 0	7 24	7^{d}48	—	8 31	—	9 55	11 51	—	—	—

d Saturdays only.   e Saturdays excepted.   h Wednesdays only.   k Calls to take up only.

SUNDAYS.	AM	AM	AM	AM	PM	PM	PM	PM	PM	PM
London Bridge (L.B.R.) dep.	6 55	8 55	9 30	10 35	1 25	3 50	5 40	8 27	9 35	11 0
Peckham Rye	7 4	9k 2	9 37	10 44	1 35	3 56	5 47	8 37	—	11 9
East Dulwich	7 8	—	9 40	10 47	1 38	3 59	5 52	8 40	—	11 12
North Dulwich	—	—	—	—	—	—	—	—	—	—
Tulse Hill	7 13	—	9 47	10 52	1 45	4 5	5 58	8 46	—	11 19
Streatham	7 18	—	9 52	—	1 54	4 10	6 6	8 51	—	11 24
Mitcham Junction	7 21	—	9 58	—	2 0	4 16	6 15	8 57	—	11 29
Hackbridge	—	—	10 2	—	2 4	4 20	6 19	9 1	—	11 33
Carshalton	7 29	—	10 5	—	2 7	4 23	6 23	9 4	—	11 36
Sutton	7 34	9 22	10 9	11 29	2 11	4 27	6 29	9 8	10 25	11 40
Cheam	7 43	—	10 14	11 39	2 20	4 42	6 36	9 12	10 28	--
Ewell East	7 44	—	10 18	11 43	2 24	4 46	6 40	9 17	10 46	—
Epsom	7 49	9 41	10 23	11 48	2 29	4 50	6 46	9 22	10 34	11 49
Ashtead	7 55	—	10 30	11 55	2 36	4 56	6 54	9 29	10 58	—
Leatherhead	8 0	9 49	10 35	12 0	2 41	5 1	6 59	9 35	11 3	—

k Calls to take up passengers only.

LEATHERHEAD, EPSOM & SUTTON TO LONDON BRIDGE.

WEEK DAYS.	AM	AM	AM	AM	AM	AM	AM	AM	AM	AM	AM	AM	AM	AM
Leatherhead dep.	—	—	—	7 9	7 41	8 6	8 22	—	8 43	—	9 1	—	9 41	10 4
Ashtead	—	—	—	7 14	7 46	8 11	8 27	—	—	—	9 6	—	—	—
Epsom	—	—	—	7 21	7 54	8 19	8 35	—	8 53	—	9 13	9 20	9 38	10 14
Ewell East	—	—	—	7 25	7 58	8 23	8 39	—	8 57	—	—	9 23	9 41	10 0
Cheam	—	—	—	7 29	8 2	8 27	8 44	—	—	9 3	—	—	9 45	10 4
Sutton	6 3	7 8	—	7 34	8 6	8 32	8 48	—	9 2	9 6	—	9 29	9 57	10 23
Carshalton	6 7	7 11	—	7 38	8 10	8 36	8 52	8 57	—	—	—	9 33	—	—
Hackbridge	6 10	7 15	7 21	7 41	—	—	—	—	—	—	—	—	—	—
Mitcham Junction	6 15	7 19	7 25	7 45	8 15	8 41	8 57	—	—	—	—	9 38	10 4	—
Streatham	6 20	—	7 32	7 51	—	8 47	—	9 7	—	9 18	—	9 45	—	—
Tulse Hill	6 25	—	7 37	7 56	8 26	—	—	9 12	—	9 23	—	—	—	—
North Dulwich	6 29	—	7 41	—	—	—	—	—	—	—	—	—	—	—
East Dulwich	6 31	—	7 43	8 1	—	—	—	9 17	—	—	—	—	—	—
Peckham Rye	6 34	—	7 46	8 4	8 32	—	—	—	—	—	—	—	—	—
London Bridge	6 46	7 41	7 58	8 12	8 40	9 5	9 17	9 27	9 30	9 36	9 47	10 1	10 22	10 45

WEEK DAYS.	AM	AM	AM	AM	d	PM	PM	PM	PM	PM	PM	PM	PM
Leatherhead dep.	—	—	—	11 46	—	12 23	2 30	2 44	—	4 11	5 2	5 46	—
Ashtead	—	—	—	11 51	—	12 28	—	2 49	--	4 16	5 7	5 51	—
Epsom	—	—	—	11 57	—	12 36	2 40	2 57	—	4 24	5 14	6 13	6 30
Ewell East	—	—	—	12 1	—	12 40	—	3 2	—	4 28	5 18	6 15	6 32
Cheam	—	—	—	12 26	—	12 44	—	3 6	—	4 32	5 58	6 30	6 36
Sutton	10 37	11 20	—	12 34	12 42	12 49	2 51	3 35	4 2	4 37	6 2	6 34	7 19
Carshalton	10 50	11 24	11 42	—	—	12 53	2 56	3 38	—	4 40	—	6 38	—
Hackbridge	10 56	—	—	—	—	12 56	2 59	3 41	—	4 43	—	6 41	—
Mitcham Junction	11 0	11 31	11 49	—	12 48	1 0	3 3	3 45	—	4 47	—	6 45	7 26
Streatham	11 8	—	—	—	12 55	1 7	3 11	3 52	—	4 54	—	6 51	7 33
Tulse Hill	11 14	—	—	—	—	1 12	3 17	3 57	—	5 0	—	6 56	—
North Dulwich	11 18	—	—	—	—	1 15	—	—	—	5 4	—	7 0	—
East Dulwich	11 21	—	—	—	—	1 17	—	4 2	—	5 6	—	7 2	—
Peckham Rye	11 24	--	—	—	—	1 20	3 24	4 5	—	5 9	—	7 5	—
London Bridge	11 32	11 50	12 8	1 28	1 12	1 28	3 32	4 13	4 27	5 16	6 58	7 13	7 48

WEEK DAYS.	PM	PM	PM	PM	PM
Leatherhead dep	7 33	8 2	8 29	—	10 1
Ashtead	7 38	8 7	8 34	—	16 6
Epsom	7 47	8 15	8 43	9 26	10 15
Ewell East	—	8 19	8 47	9 1	10 19
Cheam	—	8 24	8 52	9 5	10 24
Sutton	7 58	8 30	8 58	9 40	10 28
Carshalton	8 2	—	9 2	—	10 33
Hackbridge	8 5	—	9 5	—	10 36
Mitcham Junction	8 9	—	9 9	9 47	10 40
Streatham	8 18	—	9 15	—	10 47
Tulse Hill	8 24	—	9 20	—	10 53
North Dulwich	—	—	—	—	10 57
East Dulwich	8 29	—	—	—	11 0
Peckham Rye	8 33	—	9 27	—	11 3
London Bridge	8 41	9 25	9 35	10 8	11 11

d Saturdays only.

e Saturdays excepted.

SUNDAYS.	AM	AM	PM	PM	PM	PM	PM	PM	PM	PM
Leatherhead dep.	8 50	9 54	1 39	—	4 36	6 41	7 36	—	9 14	10 9
Ashtead	8 55	9 59	1 44	—	4 41	6 46	7 41	—	9 20	10 14
Epsom	9 4	10 8	1 51	—	4 49	7 5	7 48	—	9 28	10 21
Ewell East	9 8	10 13	1 55	—	4 53	7 8	7 52	—	—	10 25
Cheam	9 13	10 17	1 59	—	4 57	7 12	7 56	—	9 35	10 29
Sutton	9 30	10 22	2 4	3 15	5 14	7 17	8 1	8 20	9 43	10 34
Carshalton	9 34	10 26	2 8	3 18	5 17	—	8 5	—	9 47	10 38
Hackbridge	9 37	10 29	—	3 21	5 20	—	8 8	—	9 51	10 41
Mitcham Junction	9 42	10 33	2 12	3 25	5 24	—	8 12	8 27	9 55	10 45
Streatham	9 50	10 43	2 18	3 32	5 30	—	8 18	—	10 1	10 52
Tulse Hill	9 55	10 50	2 23	3 37	5 35	—	8 23	—	10 10	10 57
North Dulwich	—	—	—	—	—	—	—	—	—	—
East Dulwich	10 0	10 55	2 29	3 43	5 41	—	8 29	--	10 15	11 3
Peckham Rye	10 3	10 58	2 32	3 46	5 44	—	8 32	8h42	10 18	11 6
London Bridge	10 11	11 8	2 44	3 54	5 54	8 8	8 46	8 50	10 25	11 15

h Calls to set down only.

WEEK DAYS.	AM	AM	AM	AM	AM	AM	AM	AM	AM	AM	AM	AM	AM	AM	AM	AM
London Bridge ..	5 15	5 35	—	—	—	—	—	7 7	—	—	—	8 7	—	—	—	—
Selhurst	5 48	6 11	6 28	6 48	7 3	7 8	7 17	7 42	8 1	8 6	8 11	8 40	8 46	8 55	9 7	9 18
Thornton Heath..	5 51	6 21	6 31	6 52	7 6	7 11	7 20	7 46	8 4	8 9	8 14	8 43	8 49	8 58	9 10	9 21
Norbury	5 55	6 25	6 35	6 56	7 10	—	7 32	7 50	8 8	8 13	8 18	8 47	—	9 3	9 14	9 25
Streatham Com. ..	5 58	6 28	6 38	6 59	7 13	7 17	7 28	7 53	8 11	8 17	8 21	8 50	8 54	9 6	9 17	9 28

WEEK DAYS.	AM	AM	AM	AM	AM	AM	AM	PM	d	PM	PM	d	d	PM	PM	
London Bridge....	—	—	9 8	—	—	—	—	12 15	12 38	—	1 27	1 38	1 57	2 2	—	
Selhurst	9 25	9 43	9 50	10 33	10 53	11 19	11 23	12 33	12 40	1 8	1 33	1 50	2 8	2 21	2 24	3 33
Thornton Heath..	9 28	9 45	9 53	10 36	10 56	11 22	11 27	12 36	12 43	1 11	1 36	1 54	2 11	2 24	2 27	3 36
Norbury	9 32	9 49	9 58	10 40	11 0	11 26	11 31	12 40	12 47	1 15	1 40	1 58	2 15	2 28	2 31	3 40
Streatham Com...	9 35	9 52	10 2	10 43	11 3	11 29	11 34	12 43	12 50	1 18	1 43	2 3	2 19	2 31	2 34	3 43

WEEK DAYS.	d	PM	PM	PM	PM	e	PM	e	e	PM	e	PM	e	PM	PM	
London Bridge....	3 0	4 15	4 47	—	5 28	5 36	—	6 5	6 13	6 30	6 48	7 9	7 28	—	8 4	—
Selhurst	3 38	4 36	5 24	—	5 52	6 12	6 23	6 31	6 44	6 59	7 20	7 34	7 48	—	8 41	8 58
Thornton Heath.	3 42	4 39	5 27	5 37	5 55	6 16	6 26	6 34	6 47	7 2	7 23	7 37	7 51	8 3	8 44	9 1
Norbury	3 47	4 43	5 31	5 41	5 59	6 20	6 30	6 38	6 51	7 6	7 27	7 41	7 55	—	8 48	9 5
Streatham Com. ..	3 51	4 46	5 35	5 45	6 2	6 24	6 33	6 41	6 54	7 10	7 30	7 44	7 59	8 10	8 51	9 0

WEEK DAYS.	PM	PM	PM	PM	PM	PM	PM
London Bridge ...	—	8 50	—	9 22	—	10 27	—
Selhurst	9 29	9 11	9 38	9 57	10 50	11 2	11 23
Thornton Heath..	9 7	9 14	9 41	10 0	10 53	11 5	11 26
Norbury	9 12	9 18	9 45	10 4	10 57	11 9	11 30
Streatham Com. ..	9 16	9 21	9 48	10 7	11 0	11 13	11 33

WEEK DAYS	AM	AM	AM	AM	AM	AM	AM	AM	AM	AM	AM	AM	AM	AM	AM	AM	AM
Streatham Com. ..	4 50	5 51	6 55	7 9	7 16	7 21	7 30	7 51	8 41	8 53	9 5	9 20	9 25	—	10 26	11 7	11 47
Norbury	4 53	5 54	6 57	7 12	7 18	7 24	—	7 54	8 44	8 56	9 9	9 23	9 28	—	10 29	11 10	11 50
Thornton Heath ..	4 57	5 59	7 1	7 16	7 23	7 29	7 35	7 58	8 49	9 0	9 14	9 27	9 32	9 50	10 34	11 14	11 54
Selhurst	5 0	6 2	7 5	7 19	7 26	—	7 38	8 1	8 53	9 3	9 18	—	9 35	9 53	10 37	11 17	11 57
London Bridge....	5 32	6 38	7 36	—	7 45	7 56	8 6	8 28	9 24	9 30	—	—	—	10 24	—	—	—

WEEK DAYS	PM	PM	PM	d	PM	d	d	PM	PM	d	PM	PM	d	PM	PM	d	e
Streatham Com. ..	12 17	1 8	1 13	1 22	1 34	1 39	1 45	2 6	2 17	2 32	2 43	2 51	2 56	3 7	3 19	4 1	4 7
Norbury	12 20	1 11	1 16	1 25	1 37	1 42	1 48	2 10	2 20	2 35	—	2 54	2 59	3 10	3 22	4 4	4 10
Thornton Heath ..	12 24	1 15	1 21	1 31	1 41	1 46	1 52	2 15	2 24	2 39	2 48	2 58	3 4	3 14	3 26	4 8	4 14
Selhurst	12 27	1 18	1 24	1 34	—	1 50	1 55	2 17	2 27	2 42	—	3 1	3 7	3 17	3 29	4 11	4 17
London Bridge....	—	—	—	2 8	—	2 22	—	—	—	—	—	—	3 56	—	—	—	—

WEEK DAYS	PM	PM	PM	PM	e	PM	e	PM	PM	e	PM	PM	PM	PM	PM	PM
Streatham Com. ..	452	4 56	5 9	5 22	5 39	5 44	6 2	6 8	6 33	6 38	7 4	7 20	7 35	7 58	8 10	8 27
Norbury	455	4 59	5 12	5 25	5 42	5 47	6 5	6 11	—	6 40	7 7	7 23	7 38	8 1	8 13	8 30
Thornton Heath..	5 0	5 3	5 16	5 29	5 45	6 2	6 9	6 15	6 38	6 44	7 11	7 27	7 42	8 5	8 18	8 34
Selhurst	5 3	5 6	5 19	5 32	—	6 4	6 12	—	6 41	6 47	7 14	7 30	7 45	8 8	8 21	8 37
London Bridge....	—	5 40	—	—	6 37	—	—	—	7 14	—	7 38	8 3	—	—		

WEEK DAYS.	PM	PM	PM	PM	PM	PM	PM	PM
Streatham Com. ..	8 48	8 57	9 32	10 14	10 24	10 57	11 32	11 53
Norbury	8 51	9 0	9 35	10 17	10 28	11 0	11 35	11 56
Thornton Heath..	8 55	9 4	9 39	10 21	10 33	11 4	11 39	12 0
Selhurst	—	9 7	9 42	10 24	10 37	11 7	—	12 3
London Bridge ..	—	—	10 14	—	11 11	—	—	

SUNDAYS	AM	AM	PM	PM	PM	PM	PM
London Bridge....	7 50	9 35	1 45	3 10	5 40	7 20	9 20
Selhurst	8 27	10 11	2 20	3 45	6 15	7 55	9 57
Thornton Heath ..	8 31	10 14	2 23	3 48	6 18	7 58	10 1
Norbury	8 35	10 18	2 27	3 52	6 22	8 2	10 6
Streatham Com. ..	8 38	10 21	2 30	3 55	6 25	8 5	10 9

SUNDAYS.	AM	PM	PM	PM	PM	PM	PM	PM	PM
Streatham Com. ..	8 26	10 4	12 57	1 49	4 31	6 24	7 31	3 59	10 2
Norbury	8 29	10 7	1 0	1 53	4 34	6 27	7 34	9 2	10 6
Thornton Heath ..	8 33	10 11	1 4	1 58	4 38	6 31	7 38	9 6	10 11
Selhurst	8 36	10 14	1 8	2 1	4 41	6 34	7 41	9 9	10 14
London Bridge ..	9 9	10 46	1 41	2 34	5 14	7 7	8 15	9 43	10 52

d Saturdays only.   e Saturdays excepted.

LONDON BRIDGE TO CLAPHAM JUNCTION.

WEEK DAYS.	AM	AM	AM	AM	AM	AM	AM	AM	AM	PM	PM	d	e	d	d
London Bridge ..	6 38	7 30	8 1	8 22	841	8 52	9 13	9 38	10 28	11 29	12 20	12 40	12 52	1 7	1 10
Queen's Road	6 43	—	—	8 27	—	—	—	—	—	11 35	12 25	—	12 57	—	1 15
Peckham Rye	6 45	7 39	8 10	8 29	—	8 59	9 21	9 45	10 35	11 37	12 27	12 47	12 59	1 14	1 17
East Dulwich	6 48	—	—	8 32	—	9 2	9 24	9 48	10 38	11 40	12 30	12 50	1 2	1 17	1 20
North Dulwich....	6 50	—	—	8 35	—	9 4	9 26	—	10 40	11 42	12 32	12 52	1 4	1 19	1 22
Tulse Hill	6 54	7 46	8 17	8 39	855	9 7	9 31	9 53	10 44	11 46	12 36	12 55	1 7	1 23	1 26
Streatham Hill ..	6 57	—	8 21	8 42	9 0	9 11	9 36	9 56	10 47	11 57	12 39	—	1 10	1 26	1 29
Balham	7 3	—	—	8 45	9 3	9 14	9 39	9 59	10 50	12 8	12d42	1 2	1 20	1 29	1 36
Wandsworth Com.	7 5	—	8 25	8 47	9 5	9 16	9 41	10 1	10 52	12 10	12d44	1 4	1 22	1 31	1 38
Clapham Junction	7 8	—	8 28	8 50	9 8	9 19	9 44	10 4	10 55	12 13	12d47	—	1 25	1 34	1 41

WEEK DAYS.	PM	PM	d	PM	PM	PM	PM	PM	e	PM	e	PM	PM	PM	PM	PM
London Bridge....	1 25	1 42	2 10	2 13	2 40	3 13	4 13	4 27	4 52	5 25	5 46	5 53	6 7	6 32	6 38	
Queen's Road	1 30	—	2 15	2 18	2 45	3 18	—	4 32	4 57	—	5 52	—	6 12	—	6 43	
Peckham Rye	1 32	1 48	2 17	2 20	2 47	3 20	4 20	4 34	4 59	5 32	5 52	6 0	6 14	6 39	6 45	
East Dulwich	1 35	1 51	2 20	2 23	2 50	3 23	4 23	4 37	5 2	5 35	5 55	5 7	6 17	6 42	6 48	
North Dulwich....	1 37	1 53	2 22	2 25	2 53	3 28	4 28	4 42	5 7	5 37	5 57	5 59	6 19	6 44	6 49	
Tulse Hill	1 40	1 57	2 25	2 28	2 55	3 28	4 28	4 42	5 7	5 41	5 41	6 2	6 22	6 47	6 52	
Streatham Hill ..	1 44	2 0	2 28	2 31	2 59	3 31	4 31	4 46	5 10	5 44	5 44	6 6	6 13	6 26	6 53	6 59
Balham	1 47	2 3	2 38	2 34	3 2	3 34	4 34	4 45	5 13	5 47	5 56	6 9	6 16	6 29	6 53	6 59
Wandsworth Com.	1 49	2 5	2 40	2 36	3 4	3 36	4 36	4 51	5 15	5 49	5 58	6 11	6 18	6 31	6 56	7 1
Clapham Junction	1 52	2 8	2 43	2 39	3 7	3 39	4 39	4 54	5 18	5 52	6 1	6 14	6 21	6 34	6 58	7 4

WEEK DAYS	PM	PM	PM	PM	PM	PM
London Bridge...	6 50	7 8	7 25	7 53	8 10	8 58
Queen's Road	6 55	7 13	7 30	7 58	8 15	9 3
Peckham Rye	6 57	7 15	7 32	8 0	8 17	9 5
East Dulwich....	7 0	7 18	7 35	8 3	8 20	9 8
North Dulwich....	7 2	7 20	7 37	8 5	8 22	9 10
Tulse Hill	7 6	7 23	7 40	8 8	8 25	9 13
Streatham Hill ..	7 9	7 27	7 44	8 23	8 29	9 16
Balham	7 12	7 30	7 47	8 26	8 32	9 25
Wandsworth Com.	7 14	7 32	7 49	8 28	8 34	—
Clapham Junction	7 17	7 35	7 52	8 31	8 38	9 30

No Sunday Trains.

WEEK DAYS	AM	AM	AM	AM	AM	AM	AM	AM	AM	AM	AM	PM	e	d	d	e
Clapham Junction	6 51	7 26	7 49	8 11	8 27	8 55	9 20	9 45	9 55	1052	11 18	12 1	12 30	—	1258	1 18
Wandsworth Com.	6 54	7 29	7 53	8 14	8 31	8 59	9 23	9 48	9 58	1055	11 21	12 4	12 33	1257	1 15	1 21
Balham	6 56	7 31	7 55	8 16	8 35	9 1	9 25	9 50	10 0	1057	11 23	12 6	12 35	1259	1 17	1 23
Streatham Hill	6 59	7 40	7 58	8 19	8 39	9 5	9 28	9 53	10 3	11 0	11 26	12 18	12 38	1 2	1 20	1 35
Tulse Hill	7 2	7 43	8 2	8 23	8 43	9 9	9 31	9 56	10 7	11 3	11 30	12 21	12 48	1 5	1 23	1 38
North Dulwich	7 5	7 46	8 5	8 26	—	9 12	9 34	9 59	10 10	11 6	11 33	12 24	12 51	1 8	1 26	1 41
East Dulwich	7 7	7 48	8 7	8 28	8 48	—	9 35	10 1	10 12	11 8	11 35	12 26	12 53	1 10	1 28	1 43
Peckham Rye	7 10	7 50	8 10	8 31	—	—	9 37	10 3	—	1110	11 37	12 28	12 55	1 12	—	1 45
Queen's Road	7 12	—	8 12	8 33	—	—	—	—	—	—	—	—	—	—	—	1 47
London Bridge	7 17	7 58	8 17	8 38	8 57	9 21	9 43	10 11	10 20	1118	11 45	12 36	1 3	1 20	1 37	1 54

WEEK DAYS.	d	d	d	e	d	PM	e	PM	PM	d	d	d	d	e	d	e
Clapham Junction	1 32	—	1 55	2 16	2 27	3²⁷27	3 46	4 20	4 42	5 5	5 17	5 49	5 59	6 7	6 25	6 36
Wandsworth Com.	1 35	—	1 58	2 19	2 30	3ᵈ39	3 49	4 23	4 45	5 8	5 20	5 52	6 2	6 10	6 28	6 39
Balham	1 37	—	2 0	2 21	2 32	3ᵈ32	3 50	4 25	4 47	5 10	5 22	5 54	6 4	6 12	6 30	6 41
Streatham Hill	1 40	1 51	2 3	2 37	2 37	3 35	3 54	4 35	4 55	5 19	5 25	5 57	6 15	6 15	6 33	6 44
Tulse Hill	1 43	1 55	2 6	2 40	2 40	3 38	4 7	4 38	4 58	5 22	5 29	6 0	6 19	6 19	6 37	6 47
North Dulwich	1 46	1 58	2 9	2 43	2 43	3 41	4 10	4 41	5 .1	5 25	5 32	6 3	6 22	6 22	6 40	6 50
East Dulwich	1 48	2 0	2 11	2 45	2 45	3 43	4 12	4 43	5 3	5 27	5 34	6 5	6 24	6 24	6 42	6 52
Peckham Rye	1 50	2 2	2 13	2 47	2 47	3 45	4 15	4 45	5 6	5 30	5 36	—	6 26	6 26	6 45	6 54
Queen's Road	1 52	—	—	—	—	—	—	—	5 ª8	—	—	—	—	—	—	—
London Bridge	1 58	2 9	2 20	2 55	2 55	3 53	4 22	4 53	5 14	5 37	5 43	6 14	6 34	6 34	6 52	7 1

WEEK DAYS.	e	d	d	e	d	PM	e	PM	
Clapham Junction	6 42	7 2	7 21	7 29	7 53	8 7	8 52	9 2	9 57
Wandsworth Com.	6 45	7 5	7 24	7 32	7 56	8 10	8 55	9 5	10 0
Balham	6· 47	7 7	7 26	7 34	7 58	8 12	8 57	9 7	10 2
Streatham Hill	6 50	7 13	7 29	7 37	8 1	8 20	9 0	9 10	10 12
Tulse Hill	6 54	7 17	7 32	7 41	8 4	8 23	9 3	9 13	10 15
North Dulwich	6 57	7 20	7 35	7 44	8 7	8 26	9 6	9 16	10 18
East Dulwich	6 59	7 22	7 37	7 46	8 9	8 28	9 8	9 18	10 20
Peckham Rye	7 1	7 24	7 39	7 48	8 11	8 30	9 11	9 20	10 22
Queen's Road	—	—	7 41	—	—	—	9 13	—	10 24
London Bridge	7 8	7 31	7 47	7 56	8 18	8 37	9 20	9 27	10 32

No Sunday Trains.

d Saturdays only.   e Saturdays excepted.

LONDON BRIDGE TO NORWOOD JCN. AND CROYDON (LOCAL).

WEEK DAYS.	AM	AM	AM	AM	AM	AM	AM	AM	AM	AM	AM	AM	AM	AM	AM	AM	AM	AM	AM	AM	AM
London B.(L.B.R.)dep	5 15	5 18	5 35	5 50	6 40	6 43	6 55	7	7 7	25	7 35	8	7 8	17	8 24	8 58	9 6	9 8	9 3	9 36	950
New Cross Gate	—	5ᴬ26	5 41	5 56	—	6 50	7	2 7	18	7ᴬ31	7 44	—	8 23	8 30	—	—	9 15	9 32	9 42	—
Brockley	—	—	5 45	6 0	—	6 54	—	7 17	—	—	—	8 27	8 34	—	—	—	9 21	9 36	—	—
Honor Oak Park	—	—	5 50	6 5	—	6 59	—	7 22	—	—	—	—	8 39	—	—	—	9 24	9 41	—	—
Forest Hill	5 27	—	5 54	6 9	—	7 4	7 12	7 26	—	7 53	—	8 35	8 44	9 14	—	9 30	9 46	9 51	—
Sydenham	5 31	—	5 57	6 12	—	7 8	—	7 30	—	7 57	—	9 38	8 48	9 17	—	9 33	9 50	9 54	—
Penge West	5 34	—	6 0	6 15	—	7 12	7 18	—	—	8 0	—	8 41	8 52	9 21	—	9 37	9 53	9 58	—
Anerley	5 36	—	6 2	6 17	—	7 14	7 20	—	—	8 2	—	8 43	8 54	9 23	—	9 45	10 0	—
Norwood Junction	5 40	5 43	6	6 6	21	—	7 18	7 25	7 36	7 45	8	7 8	25	9 46	8 59	9 27	—	9 45	10 1	10 5	—
Croydon East (Local)	—	6 1	—	7 10	7 29	—	7 26	—	7 47	—	—	8 59	9 5	—	—	10 1	10 7	—
Croydon South	—	—	—	—	—	—	—	—	—	8 35	9 19	8	—	9 41	10 4	—	1017

WEEK DAYS.	AM	AM	AM	AM	AM	AM	AM	AM	AM	AM	AM	AM	AM	AM	d	d	d	d
London B.(L.B.R.)dep	9 57	10 20	10 35	10 47	11	11 15	11 23	11 52	11 58	12 20	12 25	12 30	1243	12 50	12 57	1 0	1	3 1 10
New Cross Gate	—	10 26	—	10 53	11 21	—	12 4	—	—	—	—	—	—	—	—	1 6	1 9	—
Brockley	—	—	—	10 57	11 25	—	—	12 8	—	—	—	—	—	—	—	1 10	1 13	—
Honor Oak Park	—	10 33	—	11 1	11 30	—	—	12 13	—	—	—	—	—	1	7 1	15 1	18	—
Forest Hill	—	10 37	—	11 6	11 34	—	—	12 17	—	—	—	—	—	1	11 1	19 1	22	—
Sydenham	—	10 40	—	11 9	11 37	—	—	12 20	—	—	—	—	—	—	1	22 1	25	—
Penge West	—	10 43	—	11 12	11 40	—	—	12 23	—	—	—	—	1	15 1	25 1	28	—
Anerley	—	10 45	—	11 14	11 42	—	—	12 25	—	—	—	—	—	1	27 1	30	—
Norwood Junction	10 28	10 50	10 56	11 20	11 46	—	1227	12 30	—	12 44	1	1 1	27	—	1	21 1	31 1	34 1 28
Croydon East (Local)	10 33	11 1	—	—	11 52	12 2	1231	—	—	—	1	6 1	32	—	—	—	1 35
Croydon South	10 36	11	4 11	9	—	11 56	—	1234	—	12 45	—	1	9 1	35	1 12	—	—	1 39

WEEK DAYS.	AM	d	d	PM	d	PM	d	d	PM	d	d	d	d	d	d	d	PM	d
London B.(L.B.R.)dep	117	1 32	1 38	1 38	1 40	2 2	2	8 2	10	2 15	2 25	2 38	2 53	2 57	3	0 3	0 3	10 3 15	3 30 3 52
New Cross Gate	124	—	—	—	—	—	—	—	2 25	2ᴬ31	—	—	—	3	3 16	3 21	3 36	—
Brockley	128	—	—	—	—	—	—	—	—	2 28	—	—	—	3 10	—	—	3 40	—
Honor Oak Park	133	—	—	—	1 51	—	—	—	—	2 31	—	—	—	3 15	—	—	3 45	—
Forest Hill	137	1 45	—	—	1 55	—	—	—	—	2 38	—	3	8	—	3	19 3	25	—	3 49 4 4
Sydenham	140	—	1 53	—	1 59	—	—	—	—	2 41	—	3 11	—	3 25	—	—	3 53	—
Penge West	143	1 50	—	—	2 3	—	—	—	—	2 43	—	3 13	—	3 27	—	—	3 57	—
Anerley	145	1 52	1 58	—	2 6	—	—	—	—	2 45	—	—	—	—	—	—	—	—
Norwood Junction	149	1 56	2	2	—	2 10	2 42	—	2 32	2 47	2 43	2 43	2 53	3 17	3 13	3 18	3 32	3 35 3 35 4	1 4 11
Croydon East (Local)	156	2	2	—	2	21 2	47 2	34 2	47	—	3	6	—	3 22	—	—	4	7	—
Croydon South	2 0	2	6	—	2	1 2	24 2	50 2	38 2	50	—	2 54	3 10	—	3	21 3	26	—	4 11	—

WEEK DAYS.	PM	PM	e	PM	d	PM	d	PM	d	PM	d	d	d	d	d	d	PM	d
London B.(L.B.R.)dep	4 10	4 12	4 20	4 23	4 35	4 38	5	4 5	13	5 21	5 30	5 37	5 41	5 45	5 51	5 53	6 8	6 16
New Cross Gate	—	4 19	—	4 51	4 42	—	5 19	—	—	—	—	—	5 59	—	—	—
Brockley	—	4 23	—	—	4 46	—	■	—	—	—	—	—	6 3	—	—	—
Honor Oak Park	—	4 28	—	—	4 50	—	—	—	—	—	—	—	6 6	—	—	—
Forest Hill	—	4 32	—	—	4 54	—	5 30	—	—	—	—	—	6 6	6 12	—	6 28
Sydenham	—	4 35	—	—	4 57	—	5 33	—	—	—	—	—	6 9	6 15	—	—
Penge West	—	4 38	—	—	5	—	5 36	—	—	—	—	—	6 12	6 18	—	—
Anerley	—	4 40	—	—	5 2	—	5 39	—	—	5 45	—	—	6 14	6 20	—	—
Norwood Junction	4 33	4 44	—	4 51	5 6	4 57	5 57	5 45	—	5 49	6 15	5 57	6	6 18	6 24	—	6 34
Croydon East (Local)	—	4 55	—	4 55	5 11	—	5 41	5 52	—	6 19	6 19	6 19	—	—	—	—
Croydon South	4 33	4 58	4 42	4 58	5 15	—	5 44	5 56	5 45	6	6 21	6 6	—	—	—	6 36	—

d Saturdays only.   e Saturdays excepted.   h Calls to take up passengers only.

For Trains Croydon East (Main Line), see Alphabetical Section.

WEEK DAYS.	e	PM	PM	PM	PM	PM	PM	PM	PM	PM	PM	PM	PM	PM	PM
LONDON B. (L B.R.) dep.	6 30	6 55	7 0	7 20	7 25	7 38	7 40	8 10	9 22	8 55	9 12	9 22	9 42	10 12	10 27
New Cross Gate	—	7 1	—	—	7 31	—	7 46	—	8 28	9 0	—	9 28	9 48	10 18	10 33
Brockley	—	7 5	—	—	7 35	—	7 50	—	—	9 4	—	9 32	—	10 22	10 37
Honor Oak Park	—	7 10	—	—	7 40	—	7 54	—	—	9 9	—	9 37	—	10 27	10 42
Forest Hill	—	7 14	—	—	7 44	—	7 58	—	8 37	9 3	—	9 41	9 57	10 31	10 46
Sydenham	—	7 17	—	—	7 47	—	—	—	—	9 16	—	9 44	—	10 34	10 47
Penge West	—	7 20	—	—	7 50	—	—	—	—	9 19	—	9 47	—	10 37	10 52
Anerley	—	7 22	—	—	7 52	—	8 3	—	8 42	9 21	—	9 49	...	10 39	10 54
NORWOOD JUNCTION	6 47	7 26	—	—	7 56	—	8 7	—	8 46	9 25	—	9 53	10 4	10 43	10 57
Croydon East (Local)	6 53	7 32	—	—	—	—	8 16	—	—	9 34	—	10 4¹	—	—	—
CROYDON SOUTH	6 57	7 36	7 25	7 48	—	8 4	8 18	8 35	—	9 33	9 34	10 6	—	—	—

WEEK DAYS	PM	e		PM	PM	PM	AM								
LONDON B. (L.B.R.) dep.	1035	10 50	11 15	11 43	12 30										
New Cross Gate	—	10 57	11 21	11 49	12 36										
Brockley	—	11 1	11 25	11 53	12 40										
Honor Oak Park	—	11 6	11 30	11 58	12 45										
Forest Hill	—	11 10	11 34	12 2	12 49				For Trains Croydon East (Main Line),					
Sydenham	—	11 13	11 37	12 5	12 52				see Alphabetical Section.					
Penge West	—	—	11 40	12 8	12 55										
Anerley	—	11 17	11 42	12 10	12 57										
NORWOOD JUNCTION	—	11 21	11 46	12 14	1 1										
Croydon East (Local)	—	—													
CROYDON SOUTH	1059	11 30													

WEEK DAYS.	AM	AM	AM	AM	AM	AM	AM	AM	AM	AM	AM	AM	AM	AM	AM	AM	AM	AM
CROYDON SOUTH dep.	—	5 41	—	6 30	—	—	—	7 30	7 45	—	—	8 10	8 25	8 39	8 32	8 48	8 54	—
Croydon East(Local)	—	5 46	—	6 35	—	—	—	7 35	—	—	—	8 13	—	—	8 36	—	—	—
NORWOOD JUNCTION	4 31	5 20	5 51	6 46	40	6 56	7 0	7 6	—	7 56	7 57	8 12	8 19	—	8 44	—	—	—
Anerley	4 35	5 24	5 56	—	6 44	—	7 3	—	—	—	8 1	—	—	—	8 48	—	—	—
Penge West	4 37	5 26	5 59	—	6 46	—	7 5	—	—	—	—	—	—	—	8 50	—	—	—
Sydenham	4 40	5 29	6 2	—	6 49	—	7 8	—	—	8 4	—	—	—	—	—	—	—	—
Forest Hill	4 43	5 32	6 5	—	6 52	—	—	—	—	—	—	—	—	—	—	—	—	8 59
Honor Oak Park	—	5 35	6 8	—	6 55	—	—	—	—	—	8 8	—	—	—	—	—	—	9 2
Brockley	—	5 33	6 11	—	6 58	—	—	—	—	—	8 11	—	—	—	8 56	—	—	—
New Cross Gate	—	5 41	6 14	6 17	7 1	—	7 16	—	—	8 6	8 14	—	—	—	8 59	—	—	9 7
LONDON BRIDGE	4 55	5 48	6 23	6 25	7 8	7 13	7 23	7 34	7 55	8 15	8 22	8 31	8 34	8 46	9 1	9 7	9 10 9 15	9 15

WEEK DAYS.	AM	AM	AM	AM	AM	AM	AM	AM	AM	AM	AM	AM	AM	AM	PM	PM
CROYDON SOUTH dep.	9 8	—	—	933	—	—	9 32	—	10	6	10 17	10 27	10 31	11	5	11 49	12 16	12 16
Croydon East (Local)	9 12	—	—	—	945	958	9 36	—	10	—	10 32	10 38	11	5	—	—	12 26	—
NORWOOD JUNCTION	9 19	—	933	—	—	—	9 57	10 8	10 15	—	—	11	0	11 23	—	—	12 34	1255
Anerley	—	9 26	—	—	—	—	10 1	—	10 19	—	—	11	4	11 32	—	—	12 38	1259
Penge West	—	9 28	—	—	—	—	10 3	—	10 21	—	—	11	6	11 34	—	—	12 40	1 2
Sydenham	—	9 31	—	—	—	—	10 6	—	10 24	—	—	11	9	11 37	—	—	12 44	1 5
Forest Hill	—	9 34	—	—	—	—	10 9	—	10 27	—	—	11 12	11 40	—	—	12 47	1 9
Honor Oak Park	—	9 37	—	—	—	—	10 12	—	10 30	—	—	11 15	11 43	—	—	12 50	113
Brockley	—	—	—	—	—	—	—	—	10 33	—	—	11 18	11 46	—	—	12 53	116
New Cross Gate	—	—	—	—	—	—	10 17	—	10 36	—	—	11 22	11 49	12⁴ 0	—	12 57	120
LONDON BRIDGE	9 35	9 48	951	10 0	10 4	1015	10 24	1027	10 43	10 38	11 13	11 30	11 57	12 13	12 44	1 5	128

WEEK DAYS.	PM	d	e	PM	PM	PM	e	d	PM	e	d	d	PM	PM	PM	PM	PM
CROYDON SOUTH dep.	1 14	1 3	1 3	1 27	1 40	1 55	—	2	3 2	36	—	2 38	2 53	2 53	—	3 13	3 28	—	4 25
Croydon East (Local)	—	1 6	1 6	1 32	1 45	—	2 3	—	2 7	—	—	2 41	2 56	2 56	—	3 16	3 31	—	—
NORWOOD JUNCTION	1 24	1 27	1 27	1 40	1 55	—	—	1 59	2 17	—	2 44	3 0	3 0	3 0	3 20	3 3	3 35	3 54	4 14	4 37
Anerley	—	1 31	1 31	1 44	1 58	—	—	2 3	2 22	—	2 48	—	—	—	—	3 35	—	4 18	—
Penge West	—	—	1 33	1 46	2 0	—	—	2 5	2 24	—	2 50	—	—	—	—	3 37	—	4 20	—
Sydenham	—	1 36	1 49	2 3	—	—	2 8	2 27	—	2 53	—	3 17	—	—	3 40	—	4 23	—
Forest Hill	—	1 36	1 39	1 52	2 6	—	—	2 11	2 30	—	2 56	—	3 20	—	—	3 43	—	4 26	—
Honor Oak Park	—	—	1 42	1 55	2 9	—	—	2 14	2 33	—	2 59	—	3 23	—	—	—	—	4 29	—
Brockley	—	—	1 45	1 58	—	—	—	2 17	—	—	3 2	—	3 26	—	—	—	—	4 32	—
New Cross Gate	1⁴35	1 43	1 48	2 1	2 15	2⁴13	—	2 20	2 38	—	3 5	—	3 29	—	3⁴31	3 49	—	4 35	—
LONDON BRIDGE	1 42	1 50	1 55	2 8	2 22	2 20	2 23	2 28	2 46	2 58	3 13	3 27	3 37	3 42	3 40	3 56	4 7	4 43	4 57

WEEK DAYS.	PM	PM	d	PM	PM	PM	PM	e	d	e	PM	PM	PM	PM	PM	PM	PM
CROYDON SOUTH dep.	4 46	4 57	—	5 37	5 43	—	—	6 30	6 50	—	—	7 33	7 48	8 0	—	—
Croydon East (Local)	4 50	—	—	5 42	5 46	—	—	6 34	6 53	—	—	—	7 52	8 5	—	—
NORWOOD JUNCTION	4 53	—	5 7	5 35	5 47	5 51	5 56	6 6	30	6 46	6 39	7 18	7 20	7 24	—	7 57	8 10	8 26	8 34
Anerley	5 0	—	5 11	5 39	5 51	—	6 0	—	6 34	6 49	—	7 24	—	—	—	3 14	—	8 38
Penge West	5 5	—	5 13	5 42	5 53	—	6 2	—	6 36	6 51	—	7 23	—	—	—	8 16	—	8 40
Sydenham	5 5	—	5 16	5 45	5 56	—	6 5	—	6 39	6 55	—	7 29	—	—	—	8 19	—	8 43
Forest Hill	5 8	—	5 19	5 49	5 59	—	6 8	—	6 42	6 57	—	7 32	—	—	—	8 22	—	8 46
Honor Oak Park	5 11	—	5 22	—	6 2	—	6 11	—	6 45	7 0	—	7 35	—	—	—	8 25	—	8 49
Brockley	5 14	—	5 25	—	6 5	—	6 14	—	6 48	7 3	—	7 38	—	—	—	8 28	—	8 52
New Cross Gate	5 17	—	5 28	5 56	6 8	—	6 17	—	6 51	7 6	—	7 41	7⁴35	—	—	8 31	8⁴38	8 55
LONDON BRIDGE	5 25	5 21	5 35	6 4	6 15	6 20	6 25	645	6 58	7 14	7 16	7 38	7 49	7 42	7 55	8 31	8 38	8 46	9 3

WEEK DAYS.	PM	PM	PM	d	PM	PM	PM	e	PM	PM	PM	PM	PM	PM	PM	PM
CROYDON SOUTH dep.	—	8 52	8 59	—	9 31	10 0	—	10 23	10 30							
Croydon East (Local)	—	—	9 4	—	9 24	—	—	10 33								
NORWOOD JUNCTION	8 52	—	9 26	944	9 45	10	9 10	11	10 30	10 43	11	15 11	47	12 40		
Anerley	8 56	—	9 30	—	9 49	10	15	—	10 47	11	20 11	51				
Penge West	8 59	—	9 32	—	9 51	10	17	—	10 49	11	22 11	53	—			
Sydenham	9 3	—	9 35	—	9 54	10	20	—	10 52	11	25 11	56	—			
Forest Hill	9 6	—	9 38	—	9 57	10	23	—	10 55	11	28 11	59	—			
Honor Oak Park	9 9	—	9 41	—	10	0	10	26	—	10 58	11	31 12	2	—		
Brockley	9 13	—	9 44	—	10	3	10	29	...	11	1 11	34 12	5	—		
New Cross Gate	9 17	—	9 47	—	10	6	—	10	32 10⁴49	11	4 11	37 12	8 12⁴51			
LONDON BRIDGE	9 25	9 42	9 55	10 0	10 14	10 14	10 25	10 40	10 58	11	11 11	45 12	15 12	59		

d Saturdays only.   *e Saturdays excepted.*   *h Calls to take up passengers only.*

k Calls to set down only.

SUNDAYS.	AM	AM	AM	AM	AM	AM	AM	AM	AM	AM	PM	P M	PM	PM	PM	PM	PM	PM	PM	PM
LONDON B. (L.B.R.) dep.	7 27	9 27	7 50	8 25	8 35	8 55	9 10	9 35	9 50	12 45	12 50	1 21	1 21	1 52	2 50	3 35	3 43	4 43	
New Cross Gate	7⁴10	7⁴30	7 56	8⁴31	8⁴38	9¹	1 9	16	9 42	9 56	12 51	12 58	14 17	1 29	1 51	2 56	—	3 54	4 49	
Brockley	—	8 0	—	—	9 20	9 46	10	0	—	1 2	—	1 23	1 55	3 1	—	3 58	4 53			
Honor Oak Park	—	8 5	—	—	9 25	3 51	10	5	—	1 7	—	1 28	2 0	3 6	—	4 3	4 58			
Forest Hill	—	8 9	—	—	9 29	8 55	10	9	1 1	1 11	—	1 32	2 4	3 11	—	4 7	5 2			
Sydenham	—	8 12	—	—	9 32	9 58	10	12	—	1 14	—	1 35	2 7	3 14	—	4 10	5 5			
Penge West	—	8 15	—	—	9 35	10	1	10	15	—	1 17	—	1 38	2 10	3 18	—	4 13	5 8			
Anerley	—	8 17	—	—	9 37	10	3	10	17	—	1 19	—	1 40	2 12	3 20	—	4 15	5 10			
NORWOOD JUNCTION	7 26	7 45	8 22	8 44	8 50	9 15	9 41	10	7	10 21	1 9	1 21	1 32	1 45	2 16	3 24	4 14	4 13	4 19	5 14	
Croydon East (Local)	—	—	8 42	—	—	9 21	—	—	10	13	10 29	—	1 29	—	2 40	1 42	—	4 40	5 40		
CROYDON SOUTH	7 43	—	8 45	—	9 0	9 27	—	10	20	10 29	1	1 33	—	2 43	3 45	—	4 43	5 43		

SUNDAYS.	PM	PM	PM	PM	PM	PM	PM	PM	PM	PM
LONDON BRIDGE (L.B.R.) dep.	5 40	6 0	6 15	6 46	8 0	9 10	9 35	9 55	10 30	11 20
New Cross Gate	5 46	6 h 6	6 21	6h52	8h 8	—	9 41	10 1	10 36	11 26
Brockley	5 50	—	6 25	—	—	—	9 45	—	10 40	11 30
Honor Oak Park	5 55	—	6 30	—	—	—	9 50	—	10 44	11 33
Forest Hill	5 59	—	6 34	—	—	—	9 54	10 10	10 48	11 39
Sydenham	6 5	—	6 37	—	—	—	9 57	10 13	10 51	11 42
Penge West	6 5	—	6 40	—	—	—	10 0	—	10 55	11 45
Anerley	6 7	—	6 42	—	—	—	10 2	—	10 57	11 47
NORWOOD JUNCTION	6 11	6 20	6 46	7 5	8 23	9 28	10 7	10 20	11 1	11 51
Croydon East (Local)	6 40	6 40	—	—	—	—	—	10 42	—	—
CROYDON SOUTH	6 43	6 43	—	7 15	8 38	9 39	—	10 45	—	—

SUNDAYS	AM	AM	AM	AM	AM	AM	AM	AM	AM	AM	PM	PM	PM	PM	PM
CROYDON SOUTH dep.	—	8 11	8 50	9 {	—	—	9 50	—	10 45	—	10 48	3 13	—	4 59	5 13
Croydon East (Local)	—	8 15	8 53	9 12	—	—	9 53	—	—	—	10 52	3 16	—	5 5	5 16
NORWOOD JUNCTION	7 3	8 40	9 2	9 17	9 57	10 18	10 24	10 54	10 54	10 57	3 29	4 44	5 10	5 35	6 24
Anerley	7 8	8 44	9 6	9 21	—	10 22	--	—	10 58	—	3 33	—	5 14	5 39	6 28
Penge West	7 9	8 46	9 8	9 23	—	10 24	—	—	11 0	—	3 35	—	5 16	5 41	6 30
Sydenham	7 12	8 49	9 11	9 26	—	10 27	—	—	11 3	—	3 38	—	5 19	5 44	6 33
Forest Hill	7 16	8 52	9 14	9 29	—	10 30	—	—	11 7	—	3 41	—	5 22	5 47	6 36
Honor Oak Park	7 19	8 55	9 17	9 32	—	10 33	—	—	11 11	—	3 44	—	5 25	5 50	6 39
Brockley	7 22	8 58	9 20	9 35	—	10 36	—	—	11 14	—	3 47	—	5 28	5 53	6 42
New Cross Gate	7 25	9 1	9 23	9 38	10 k 9	10 39	10h36	11h 6	11 18	—	3 50	4h55	5 31	5 57	6 45
LONDON BRIDGE (L.B.R.)	7 33	9 9	9 31	9 45	10 18	10 46	10 45	11 15	11 26	11 29	3 57	5	3 5	39	6 52

SUNDAYS.	PM	PM	PM	PM	PM	PM	PM	PM	PM	PM	PM	PM	PM	PM
CROYDON SOUTH dep.	7 10	—	8 5	8 13	8 46	8 57	9 3	9 10	—	—	10 53	—
Croydon East (Local)	7 13	—	8 16	—	—	—	9 12	—	—	10 8	—	10 56	—
NORWOOD JUNCTION	7 39	7 36	8 14	8 50	8 59	9 6	9 13	9 33	9 54	10 9	10 18	10 32	10 34	11 14	12 8
Anerley	7 43	—	—	8 54	—	—	—	9 37	9 58	10 13	10 22	—	10 38	—
Penge West	7 45	—	—	8 55	—	—	—	9 39	10 0	10 15	10 24	—	10 40	—
Sydenham	7 48	—	—	8 58	—	—	—	9 42	10 3	10 18	10 27	—	10 43	—
Forest Hill	7 51	—	—	9 2	—	—	—	9 45	10 6	10 22	10 30	—	10 46	—
Honor Oak Park	7 54	—	—	9 6	—	—	—	9 48	10 9	10 25	10 33	—	10 49	—
Brockley	7 57	—	—	9 9	—	—	—	9 51	10 12	10 28	10 33	—	10 52	—
New Cross Gate	8 0	7h48	8h25	9 13	9h10	9h17	9h24	9 54	10 15	10 32	10 39	10h42	10 55	11h25	12h19
LONDON BRIDGE (L.B.R.)	8 8	7 56	8 34	9 21	9 17	9 26	9 32	10 1	10 22	10 40	10 46	10 50	11 2	11 34	12 27

h Calls to take up passengers only.   *k* Calls to set down only.

For Trains Croydon East (Main Line), see Alphabetical Section.

LONDON BRIDGE, STREATHAM AND NORWOOD JUNCTION.

WEEK DAYS.	AM	AM	AM	*d*	*d*	PM	*e*	PM	*e*	*e*	PM	PM	PM
LONDON BRIDGE (L.B.R.) dep.	8 18	8 55	11 23	1 13	2 30	2 52	4 37	5 2	5 16	5 46	6 25	8 23	10 0	—
South Bermondsey	—	—	—	—	—	—	—	—	—	—	—	—	—	—
Queen's Road	—	—	—	—	—	2 57	—	—	—	—	—	—	—	—
Peckham Rye	—	9 2	11 30	—	—	2 59	—	—	—	—	—	8 30	10 7	—
East Dulwich	—	9 5	11 33	—	—	3 2	—	5 24	—	—	8 33	—	—	—
North Dulwich	—	9 7	11 35	—	—	3 4	—	5`26	—	—	8 35	—	—	—
Tulse Hill	8 30	9 11	11 39	1 26	2 42	3 7	4 49	5 14	5 30	5 59	—	8 39	10 14	—
Streatham	8 37	9 16	11 44	1 31	2 47	—	4 54	5 19	5 35	6 4	6 41	8 44	10 19	—
STREATHAM COMMON	8 41	9 20	11 47	1 34	2 51	—	4 58	5 22	5 39	6 8	6 44	8 48	10 24	11 53
Norbury	8 44	9 23	11 50	1 37	2 54	—	5 1	5 25	5 42	6 11	6 47	8 51	10 28	11 56
Thornton Heath	8 49	9 27	11 54	1 41	2 58	—	5 5	5 29	5 46	6 15	6 51	8 55	10 32	12 0
Selhurst	8 53	9d35	11 57	1 50	3 1	—	5 8	5 32	—	—	6 54	9 7	10 35	12 3
NORWOOD JUNCTION	8 58	—	—	1 55	3 5	—	5 13	—	—	6 21	—	—	10 43	—

WEEK DAYS.	AM	AM	AM	AM	AM	AM	AM	AM		*e*	PM	PM	*e*	PM	PM
NORWOOD JUNCTION dep.	6 13	7 0	—	—	8 36	—	—	—	1 45	2 20	5 49	6 6	6 40	7 44	—
Selhurst	6 28	7 3	8 18	10 8	8 40	9 25	9 43	10 33	11 23	1 50	2 25	5 53	6 12	6 44	7 48	8 3
Thornton Heath	6 30	7 6	8 48	12 8	8 43	9 28	9 46	10 36	11 27	1 54	2 28	5 56	6 16	6 47	7 51	9 7
Norbury	6 34	7 10	8 8	8 16	8 47	9 32	9 49	10 40	11 31	1 57	2 32	6 0	6 20	6 51	7 55	9 12
STREATHAM COMMON	6 37	7 13	8 11	8 20	8 50	9 35	9 52	10 43	11 36	2 3	2 35	6 4	6 24	6 54	7 59	9 16
Streatham	6 41	7 18	8 15	8 25	8 55	9 39	9 56	10 49	11 40	2 10	2 39	—	6 28	6 59	8 4	9 20
Tulse Hill	6 46	7 23	—	—	9 44	10 1	10 54	11 48	2 17	2 44	—	6 33	7 5	8 10	9 25
North Dulwich	6 50	—	—	—	—	10 58	11 52	2 21	2`48	—	7 9	—	—
East Dulwich	6 52	7 28	8 24	—	—	11 0	11 54	2 24	2 50	—	7 11	—	9 31
Peckham Rye	6 55	7 31	8 27	—	—	10	8 11	3 11	11 57	2 27	2 53	—	7 15	8 16	9 34
Queen's Road	—	7 34	—	—	—	—	—	—	—	—	—	—
South Bermondsey	—	7 38	—	—	—	—	—	—	—	—	—	—
LONDON BRIDGE (L.B.R.)	7 3	7 42	8 35	8 43	9 12	9 57	10 16	11 13	12 5	2 37	3 0	—	6 48	7 23	8 24	9 42

d Saturdays only.   *e* Saturdays excepted.

SOUTH LONDON LINE.

WEEK DAYS.	AM	AM	AM	AM	AM		PM	PM			AM	AM	AM		PM	PM
LONDON BRIDGE	4 58	—	5 40	5 55	6 7		10 34	11 0			—	7 15	7 45		10 15	10 45
South Bermondsey	5 1	—	5 43	5 58	6 10	Thence at frequent intervals until	10 37	11 3	SUNDAYS.		—	7 18	7 48	Thence about every half-hour until	10 18	10 48
Queen's Road, Peckham	5 5	—	5 47	6 2	6 14		10 41	11 7			—	7 22	7 52		10 22	10 52
Peckham Rye	5 8	5 29	5 49	6 4	6 16		10 43	11 9		6 50	7 24	7 54		10 24	10 54
Denmark Hill	5 10	5 31	5 51	6 6	6 18		10 45	—		6 52	7 26	7 56		10 26	—
°East Brixton	5 12	5 33	5 53	6 8	6 20		10 47	—		—	—	—		—	—
Clapham	5 15	5 36	5 56	6 11	6 23		10 50	—		6 57	7 31	8 1		10 31	—
Wandsworth Road	5 16	5 37	5 57	6 12	6 24		10 51	—		6 58	7 32	8 2		10 32	—
Battersea Park	5 19	5 40	6 0	6 15	6 27		10 54	—		7 1	7 35	8 5		10 35	—
VICTORIA	5 23	5 44	6 4	6 19	6 31		10 58	—		7 5	7 39	8 9		10 39	—

WEEK DAYS.	AM	AM	AM	AM	AM		PM	PM			AM	AM	AM		PM	PM
VICTORIA	—	—	5 30	5 50			10 33	11 13			—	7 15	7 45		10 15	10 45
Battersea Park	—	—	5 33	5 53		Thence at frequent intervals until	10 36	11 16	SUNDAYS.		—	7 18	7 48	Thence about every half-hour until	10 18	10 48
Wandsworth Road	—	—	5 35	5 55			10 38	11 18			—	7 20	7 50		10 20	10 50
Clapham	—	—	5 38	5 56			10 39	11 19			—	7 21	7 51		10 21	10 51
°East Brixton	—	—	5 39	5 59			10 42	11 22			—	—	—		—	—
Denmark Hill	—	—	5 41	6 1			10 44	11 24			—	7 26	7 56		10 26	10 56
Peckham Rye	4 40	5 14	5 30	5 44	6 4		10 47	11 27		7 0	7 29	7 59		10 29	10 59
Queen's Road, Peckham	4 42	5 16	5 32	5 46	6 6		10 49	—		7 2	7 31	8 1		10 31	—
South Bermondsey	4 46	5 20	5 36	—	6 10		10 54	—		7 7	7 36	8 6		10 36	—
LONDON BRIDGE	4 50	5 24	5 40	5 54	6 14		10 57	—		7 10	7 39	8 9		10 39	—

* East Brixton Station closed on Sundays.

WEEK DAYS (Block 1)

	AM	AM	AM	AM	AM	AM	AM	AM	AM	d	AM	AM	AM	AM	AM	AM	AM
VICTORIA (L.B.R.)dep.	5 18	5 57	6 18	6 48	7 0	7 18	7 45	8 48	8 58	9 6	9 25	9 50	10 8	10 30	10 50	11 37	11 40
Battersea Park	5 22	6 1	—	6 52	7 3	—	7 49	—	—	—	—	—	—	—	—	11 40	—
Clapham Junction	5 23	6 8	6*25	6 57	7 7	7 25	7 56	—	—	9 14	9 31	9 57	10 15	10 38	10 57	11 44	11 47
Wandsworth Common	5 32	6 13	—	7 1	7 10	—	—	—	—	—	9 34	—	—	—	—	11 47	—
Balham	5 35	6 17	—	7 4	7 12	7 31	8 2	8 59	9 8	9 19	9 35	—	10 21	10 44	11 2	11 49	11 52
Streatham Common	—	6 23	—	7 9	—	—	9 5	—	9 25	—	—	10 26	—	11 7	—	—
Norbury	—	6 27	—	7 12	—	—	9 9	—	9 28	—	—	10 29	—	11 10	—	—
Thornton Heath	—	6 32	—	7 16	—	—	9 14	—	9 32	—	—	10 34	—	11 14	—	—
Selhurst	—	6 36	—	7 19	—	—	9 18	—	9 35	—	—	10 37	—	11 17	—	—
Mitcham Junction	5 44	—	6 41	—	—	7 41	8 12	—	9 17	—	—	10 9	—	10 55	—	—	12 2
Hackbridge	5 59	—	—	—	—	7 45	8 16	—	9 21	—	—	10 13	—	10 59	—	—	12 6
Carshalton	6 2	—	—	—	—	7 49	8 20	—	9 25	—	—	10 16	—	11 3	—	—	12 10
West Croydon	—	6 41	—	7 23	7 47	—	—	9 22	—	9 39	10 10	—	10 42	—	11 21	12 12	—
Waddon	—	6 45	—	7 28	7 50	—	—	9 38	—	—	10 16	—	10 59	—	11 29	12 17	—
Wallington	—	6 49	—	7 34	7 54	—	—	9 45	—	—	10 22	—	10 48	—	11 34	12 21	—
Beeches Halt	—	—	—	7 57	—	—	—	—	—	—	—	—	—	12 24	—
Sutton	6 7	—	6 50	7 46	8 1	7 53	8 26	9 50	9 30	—	10 27	10 21	11 10	11 8	11 39	12 26	12 15
Cheam	6 13	—	—	—	—	7 57	8 38	9 55	9 53	—	—	10 25	11 15	11 12	11 43	—	12 20
Ewell East	6 17	—	—	—	8 1	8 42	—	10 11	—	—	—	11 16	11 47	—	12 24
Epsom	6 23	—	—	7 54	8 5	8 48	—	9 35	—	10 36	—	—	11 20	11 51	—	12 30
Ashtead	6 30	—	—	—	—	8 55	—	10 23	—	—	—	11 39	—	—	12 36
Leatherhead	6 35	—	—	—	—	9 0	—	10 28	—	—	—	11 43	—	—	12 40

WEEK DAYS (Block 2)

	AM	PM	PM	PM	PM	d	d	d	d	PM	d	d	d	e	d	e	PM
VICTORIA (L.B.R.) dep.	12 0	12 24	12 35	12 47	12 53	12 1	1 22	1 23	1 32	1 40	1 50	1 53	2 12	2 12	2 17	2 45	3 0
Battersea Park	—	—	—	12 51	—	—	—	—	—	—	—	—	—	—
Clapham Junction	12 7	12 30	12 42	12 56	12 59	—	1 35	—	1*47	—	1 59	2 20	2 20	—	3 7
Wandsworth Common	—	12 33	—	1 0	1 2	—	1 38	—	—	2 2	2 24	2 24	—	3 11
Balham	12 12	12 36	—	1 3	1 4	1 33	1 40	—	2k 1 2	4 2	2 27	2 27	2 55	3 14
Streatham Common	12 17	—	—	1 8	—	1 39	—	1 45	—	2 6	—	2 32	2 32	—	3 19
Norbury	12 20	—	—	1 11	—	1 43	—	1 48	—	2 10	—	2 35	2 35	—	3 22
Thornton Heath	12 24	—	—	1 15	—	1 47	—	1 52	—	2 15	—	2 39	2 39	—	3 26
Selhurst	12 27	—	—	1 18	—	1 50	—	1 55	—	2 19	—	2 42	2 42	—	3 29
Mitcham Junction	—	—	12 59	—	1 32	—	—	2 1	—	—	2 35	3 4	—
Hackbridge	—	—	1 3	—	—	—	—	—	—	2 39	3 8	—
Carshalton	—	—	1 7	—	1 39	—	—	—	—	2 42	3 12	—
West Croydon	12 32	—	—	1 22	1d 36	—	—	1 59	—	2 24	2 36	2 46	2 46	—	3 33
Waddon	12 43	—	—	1*29	—	—	2 12	—	2 29	2 4	2 50	2 57	—	3 36
Wallington	12 48	—	—	1d34	—	—	2 5	—	2 34	2 45	2 53	3 2	—	3 41
Beeches Halt	1"14	—	—	—	—	—	2 19	—	—	—
Sutton	12 53	—	1 12	—	1 45	—	2 20	2 9	—	2 50	3 0	3 7	2 47	3 18	3 46
Cheam	12 57	—	1 17	—	1 50	—	—	2 38	—	2 55	3 4	3 11	2 55	—	3 57
Ewell East	—	—	1 22	—	2 9	—	—	2 42	—	3 8	3 15	—	4 1
Epsom	1 4	—	1 28	—	1 55	—	2 32	2 46	—	3 12	3 19	—	4 5
Ashtead	—	—	1 35	—	—	—	2 38	2 53	—	—	4 11
Leatherhead	—	—	1 39	—	—	—	2 43	2 58	—	—	4 16

WEEK DAYS (Block 3)

	d	d	d	PM	PM	PM	PM	PM	e	e	PM	e	PM	e
VICTORIA (L.B.R.) dep.	3 0	3 42	3 48	3 55	4 5	4 13	4 30	4 46	4 53	5 15	5 21	5 22	5 23	5 32	6 0	6 3
Battersea Park	—	—	—	—	4*16	—	—	—	—	—
Clapham Junction	—	3 49	3 55	4*2	4*12	4 20	4 37	—	5 0	5 21	—
Wandsworth Common	—	3 53	3 59	—	4 23	—	4 55	—
Balham	3 11	3 56	4 2	—	4 25	—	4 58	—	5 26	—	5 34	5 39	5 42	—
Streatham Common	—	4 1	4 7	—	—	—	—	5 45	5 47	—
Norbury	—	4 4	4 10	—	—	—	—	5 47	5 50	—
Thornton Heath	—	4 8	4 14	—	—	—	5 40	—	5 51	5 54	—	6 19
Selhurst	—	4 11	4 17	—	—	—	5 43	—	5 54	5 57	—
Mitcham Junction	3 21	—	—	4 26	—	4 50	—	—	5 44	—
Hackbridge	3 25	—	—	—	4 54	—	5 48	—
Carshalton	3 29	—	—	4 31	—	4 57	—	5 52	—
West Croydon	—	4 15	4 21	—	5 2	5 22	—	5 58	5 47	—	5 59	6 1	—	6 27
Waddon	—	4 20	—	—	5 6	5 24	—	6 0	—	6 16	6 12	—
Wallington	—	4 25	4 26	—	5 11	—	5 29	—	6 4	5 54	—	6 16	6 7	—	6 33
Beeches Halt	—	—	—	—	—	6 7	—	6 19	—
Sutton	3 35	—	4 32	4 20	4 36	5 16	5 1	5 34	5 19	6 11	—	5 58	6 21	6 24	6 22	—
Cheam	3 39	—	—	—	4 48	—	5 37	5 27	—	6 27	—
Ewell East	3 43	—	—	4 43	—	5 6	—	5 49	—	6 7	—	6 45	—
Epsom	3 48	—	—	4 43	—	5 10	—	5 34	—	6 11	—	6 34	—
Ashtead	3 54	—	—	4 50	—	—	—	6 55	—
Leatherhead	3 58	—	—	4 55	—	—	5 34	—	6 42	—

WEEK DAYS (Block 4)

	PM	PM	PM	PM	PM	PM	PM	PM	PM	e	e	PM	PM	d	PM
VICTORIA (L.B.R.) dep.	6 10	6 21	6 23	6 30	6 58	7 7	7 20	7 20	7 30	7 38	7 55	8 10	8 15	8 38	8 40	8 55	9 22
Battersea Park	—	—	—	—	—	—	8*18	—	8 58	9 25
Clapham Junction	—	6 29	—	7 6	7*14	—	7*26	7 36	7 44	8*	2 8 17	8 22	8 45	8 47	9 2	9 29
Wandsworth Common	—	6 32	—	—	7 17	—	7 39	7 47	—	8 25	—	9 5	9 32
Balham	6 21	6 32	6 34	—	7 11	7 19	7 30	—	7 41	7 53	—	8 22	8 27	8 50	8 52	9 7	9 34
Streatham Common	—	d	—	—	7 35	—	7 58	—	8 27	—	8 57	—
Norbury	—	6 40	—	—	7 38	—	8 1	—	8 30	—	9 0	—
Thornton Heath	—	6 44	—	—	7 42	—	8 5	—	8 34	—	9 4	—
Selhurst	—	6 47	—	—	7 45	—	8 8	—	8 37	—	9 7	—
Mitcham Junction	6 31	—	—	7 20	—	7 44	—	8 16	—	8 59	—
Hackbridge	6 35	—	—	7 24	—	7"52	—	8 20	—
Carshalton	6 38	—	—	7 28	—	7"55	—	8 24	—	9 5	—
West Croydon	—	6 52	7 1	—	7 45	7 48	—	8 5	8 14	—	8 41	8 55	—	9 11	9 18	10 8
Waddon	—	6 55	—	—	7 48	7 53	—	8 14	8"21	—	8*53	—	9 15	9 23	10 12
Wallington	—	7 0	7 7	—	7 52	7 58	—	8 19	8"26	—	8*59	—	9 20	9 28	10 17
Beeches Halt	—	—	7 10	—	7 55	—	—	—
Sutton	6 43	7 5	7 13	6 53	7 33	7 59	—	7 49	8 24	—	8 30	9c 4	—	10 9	10 25	9 35	10 22
Cheam	6 46	7 8	—	6 57	—	7 38	—	8 8	—	8*40	—	9 18	9 34	10 25
Ewell East	6 50	—	—	7 1	7 41	—	8 16	8 31	—	8*45	—	9 18	9 38	10 29
Epsom	6 54	—	—	7 5	7 45	—	8 20	8 35	—	9 22	9 42	10 33
Ashtead	—	—	7 11	—	8 26	—	9 49	—
Leatherhead	—	—	7 17	—	8 31	—	9 54	—

d Saturdays only. e Saturdays excepted. h To set down Passengers only. k To take up Passengers only.

n Motor Third Class only ; change at West Croydon.

WEEK DAYS.	PM	PM	PM	PM	PM	PM	PM
VICTORIA (L.B.R.) ..dep.	9 30	10 38	10 58	11 25	11 40	11 43	11 45
Battersea Park	—	10 42	—	11 28	—	11 46	—
CLAPHAM JUNCTION	9*36	10 47	11 5	11 32	—	11 50	—
Wandsworth Common..	—	—	—	11 35	—	11 53	—
Balham	9*41	10 52	11 10	11 37	—	11 55	—
Streatham Common..	—	10 57	—	—	11 53	—	—
Norbury	—	11 0	—	—	11 56	—	—
Thornton Heath	—	11 4	—	—	12 0	—	—
Selhurst	—	11 7	—	—	12 3	—	—
MITCHAM JUNCTION	9 49	—	11 18	—	—	12 3	—
Hackbridge	9 55	—	11*22	—	—	12*4d 7	—
Carshalton	9 58	—	11 24	—	—	12 9	—
WEST CROYDON	—	11 11	—	11 52	12 7	12 19	—
Waddon	—	11 15	—	11 51	12 10	—	—
Wallington	—	11 20	—	11 59	12 15	—	—
Beeches Halt	—	—	—	—	—	—	—
SUTTON	10 2	11 25	11 28	12 4	—	12 15	—
Cheam	10 5	—	11 32	—	—	12 18	—
Ewell East	—	—	l	—	—	l	—
EPSOM	10 11	—	11 37	12 11	—	12 25	—
Ashtead	—	—	11 46	—	—	—	—
LEATHERHEAD	—	—	11 51	—	—	—	—

SUNDAYS.	AM	AM	AM	AM	AM	AM	PM	PM	PM	PM	PM	PM	PM	PM	PM
VICTORIA (L.B.R.) ..dep.	8*35	9 0	9 5	9 10	10 40	11 3	12 20	1 0	1 5	1 10	1 40	2 3	3 30	4 5
Battersea Park	—	9 9	9 14	10 43	—	12 23	1 3	—	1 14	1 43	—	3 3	3 43	—
CLAPHAM JUNCTION	8*42	9* 7	9 14	9 19	10 47	11 10	12 27	1 7	1 12	1 19	1 47	2 12	3 7	3 47	4 13
Wandsworth Common..	—	—	9 18	9 23	10 50	—	12 30	1 10	1 16	1 23	1 50	—	3 10	3 50	—
Balham	—	—	9 21	9 26	10 52	11 15	12 32	1 12	1 19	1 26	1 52	2 17	3 12	3 52	4 18
Streatham Common..	—	—	9 27	—	—	—	—	—	1 24	—	—	2 22	—	—	—
Norbury	—	—	9 30	—	—	—	—	—	1 27	—	—	2 25	—	—	—
Thornton Heath	—	—	9 35	—	—	—	—	—	1 31	—	—	2 29	—	—	—
Selhurst	—	—	9 38	—	—	—	—	—	1 34	—	—	2 32	—	—	—
MITCHAM JUNCTION	—	9 20	—	9 35	—	11 24	—	—	—	1 34	—	—	—	—	4 27
Hackbridge	—	—	—	—	—	11 28	—	—	—	1 38	—	—	—	—	4 31
Carshalton..	—	—	9 40	—	11 31	—	—	—	1 41	—	—	—	—	4 34
WEST CROYDON	—	—	9 42	—	11 17	—	1 15	1 50	1 33	—	2 17	2 36	3 39	4 18	—
Waddon	—	—	9 50	—	11 20	—	1 17	1 54	1 41	—	—	3 42	4 27	—
Wallington	—	—	9 55	—	11 24	—	1 22	2 2	1 46	—	—	2 41	3 46	4 32	—
Beeches Halt	—	—	—	—	—	—	—	—	—	—	—	—	—	—
SUTTON	9 1	9 28	10 0	9 44	11 29	11 36	1 27	2 7	1 51	1 46	—	2 46	3 51	4 37	4 38
Cheam	—	—	10 14	10 14	—	11 39	1 31	2 20	1 49	—	—	—	—	4 42
Ewell East	—	—	10 18	10 18	—	11 43	1 35	2 24	2 24	1 53	—	—	—	—	4 46
E:SOM	—	9 41	10 10	10 23	—	11 48	1 39	2 29	2 29	1 57	—	—	—	—	4 50
Ashtead	—	—	10 17	10 30	—	11 55	—	2 36	2 36	2 5	—	—	—	—	4 56
LEATHERHEAD	—	9 49	10 22	10 35	—	12 0	—	2 41	2 41	2 10	—	—	—	—	5 1

SUNDAYS.	PM	PM	PM	PM	PM	PM	PM	PM	PM	PM	PM	PM	PM	PM	PM	PM
VICTORIA (L.B.R.) ..dep.	5 28	5 40	6 0	6 40	6 45	7 0	7 0	8 4	8 10	9 5	9 25	10 5	10 28	11 0	11 20
Battersea Park	5 32	—	6 3	6 43	—	7 3	—	8*14	—	—	—	—	10*42	11 3	11 23
CLAPHAM JUNCTION	5 38	5 47	6 7	6 47	6 53	7* 7	7 7	7 8	8 11	8 19	9 12	9 32	10 12	10 37	11 7	11 27
Wandsworth Common..	5 42	—	6 10	6 50	—	7 10	—	8 23	—	—	—	10 41	11 10	11 30
Balham	5 45	5 52	6 12	6 52	6 57	—	7 12	8 16	8 26	9 17	9 39	10 17	10 44	11 12	11 32
Streatham Common....	5 51	—	—	—	7 2	—	—	8 21	—	9 22	—	—	10 49	—	—
Norbury	5 54	—	—	—	7 5	—	—	8 24	—	9 25	—	—	10 52	—	—
Thornton Heath	5 58	—	—	—	7 9	—	—	8 28	—	9 29	—	—	10 56	—	—
Selhurst	6 61	—	—	—	7 12	—	—	8 31	—	9 32	—	—	10 59	—	—
MITCHAM JUNCTION	—	6 2	—	—	—	—	—	—	8 35	—	9 48	10 26	—	—	—
Hackbridge	—	6 6	—	—	—	—	—	—	8 39	—	9 52	10 30	—	—	—
Carshalton	—	6 10	—	—	—	—	—	—	8 42	—	9 55	10 33	—	—	—
WEST CROYDON	6 5	—	6 51	7 19	7 16	—	7 51	8 35	—	9 36	—	—	11 3	11 43	11 56
Waddon	6 20	—	6 55	7 22	7 22	—	7 53	8 49	—	9 46	—	—	11 11	—	—
Wallington	6 24	—	7 0	7 26	7 26	—	7 57	8 54	—	9 50	—	—	11 16	—	—
Beeches Halt	6 27	—	—	7 29	7 29	—	8 0	—	—	9 53	—	—	—	—	—
SUTTON	6 31	6 15	7 5	7 33	7 33	7 25	8 4	8 59	8 46	9 57	10 0	10 38	11 21	—	—
Cheam	—	6 37	—	—	—	—	—	—	8 50	—	—	10 42	—	—	—
Ewell East	—	6 41	—	—	—	—	—	—	8 54	—	—	10 46	—	—	—
EPSOM	—	6 47	7 26	—	—	—	—	—	8 58	—	—	10 51	11 49	—	—
Ashtead	—	6 55	—	—	—	—	—	—	9 29	—	—	10 58	—	—	—
LEATHERHEAD	—	7 0	—	—	—	—	—	—	9 35	—	—	11 3	—	—	—

LEATHERHEAD, EPSOM, WEST CROYDON TO VICTORIA.

WEEK DAYS.	AM	AM	AM	AM	AM	AM	AM	AM	AM	AM	AM	AM	AM	AM	AM
LEATHERHEAD ......dep.	—	—	—	—	—	—	7 9	—	—	7 41	—	8 6	8 43	—
Ashtead	—	—	—	—	—	—	7 14	—	—	7 46	—	8 11	8 4,	—
EPSOM	—	—	5 32	—	—	—	7 21	7 46	—	7 54	8 12	8 19	9 0	—
Ewell East	—	—	5 35	—	—	—	7 25	7 51	—	7 58	8 15	8 23	9 8	—
Cheam	4 12	5 39	6 32	—	6 32	—	7 35	7 55	—	8 11	8 19	8 27	9 7	—
Cheam	5 5	5 44	6 39	—	6 38	—	7 20	7 39	7 59	—	8 15	8 24	8 41	9 10	—
Beeches Halt	—	—	—	—	—	—	—	—	—	—	—	—	—	—
Wallington	5 9	5 49	—	—	7 5	—	7 55	—	—	8 27	—	—	8 55	—
Waddon	—	5 53	—	—	7 8	—	7 58	—	—	—	—	—	8 58	—
WEST CROYDON	5 16	6 15	—	6 45	7 13	—	8 2	—	—	8 32	—	—	9 3	—
Carshalton	—	—	6 43	—	—	—	7 24	—	8 3	—	—	8 28	8 44	—
Hackbridge	—	—	6 46	—	—	—	7 27	—	8 6	—	—	—	8 47	—
MITCHAM JUNCTION .. :	—	—	6 50	—	—	—	7 31	—	8 10	—	—	—	8 51	—
Selhurst	—	—	—	6 48	7 18	—	—	8 6	—	8 6	—	—	—	9 7
Thornton Heath	—	—	—	6 52	7 21	7 26	—	8 9	—	8 9	—	—	—	9 11
Norbury	—	—	—	6 56	7 30	—	—	8 13	8 40	—	—	—	9 15
Streatham Common....	—	—	—	6 59	7 26	—	—	8 17	—	—	—	—	9 18
Balham	5 41	6 41	6 59	7 4	7 31	—	—	8 19	—	—	9 0	9 23
Wandsworth Common..	5 43	6 43	—	7 34	—	—	—	—	8 42	—	—
CLAPHAM JUNCTION ..	5 46	6 46	7 4	7 38	7 40	8 22	3 24	—	—	3 5	—
Battersea Park	5 49	6 49	—	—	—	—	—	—	—
VICTORIA (L.B.R.)..	5 53	6 53	7 12	7 15	7 45	7 47	7 50	8 30	8 32	8 33	8 56	8 53	9 12	9 34	9 34

d Saturdays only.   e Saturdays excepted.   h To set down Passengers only.   k To take up Passengers only.

n Motor Third Class only ; change at West Croydon.   l Wednesdays to set down only.

WEEK DAYS.

	AM	AM	AM	AM	AM	AM	AM	AM	AM	AM	AM	AM	PM	PM
LEATHERHEAD ...... dep.	—	9 17	9 41	—	10 4	—	—	—	—	—	11 46	—	—	12 23
Ashtead	—	9 22	—	—	—	—	—	—	—	—	11 51	—	—	12 28
Epsom	—	9 23	—	9 57	10 14	—	11 7	10 58	—	11 57	—	—	—	11 10
Ewell East	—	9 23	—	10 0	—	—	—	11 1	—	12 1	—	—	—	1 13
Cheam	—	9 34	—	10 4	—	—	—	11 5	—	12 5	—	—	—	1 18
Sutton	9 21	9 38	10 2	10 9	10 27	10 35	—	11 16	11 10	—	12 9	11 53	—	1 23
Beeches Halt	—	—	—	—	—	—	—	—	—	—	—	11 55	—	—
Wallington	—	—	—	—	—	10 40	11 8	—	11 15	—	—	11 58	—	—
Waddon	—	—	—	—	—	10 44	11 11	—	11 19	—	—	12 2	—	—
WEST CROYDON	—	—	—	—	—	10 49	11 15	—	11 23	—	—	12 16	12 30	—
Carshalton	9 25	—	—	10 13	—	—	—	—	—	—	12 14	—	—	1 27
Hackbridge	9 28	—	—	10 16	—	—	—	—	—	—	12 17	—	—	1 30
MITCHAM JUNCTION	9 32	9 46	10 9	10 20	—	—	11 23	—	—	—	12 21	—	—	1 34
Selhurst	—	—	—	—	10 53	11 19	—	—	—	—	—	—	12 33	—
Thornton Heath	—	—	—	—	10 56	11 22	—	—	—	—	—	—	12 36	—
Norbury	—	—	—	—	11 0	11 26	—	—	—	—	—	—	12 40	—
Streatham Common	—	—	—	—	11 3	11 29	—	—	—	—	—	—	12 43	—
Balham	9 40	—	—	—	11 8	11 34	—	—	—	12 23	—	12 39	12 48	1 43
Wandsworth Common ..	9 42	—	—	—	—	—	—	—	—	12 25	—	—	12 41	—
CLAPHAM JUNCTION	9 46	—	—	10 32	10 45	11 13	11 39	11 34	—	12 28	12 33	12 44	12 53	1 48
Battersea Park	—	—	—	—	—	—	—	—	—	—	—	—	—	—
VICTORIA (L.B.R.)	9 54	10 4	10 26	10 40	10 53	11 20	11 46	11 42	—	12 35	12 42	12 50	1 0	1 57

WEEK DAYS.

	PM	d	PM	e	e	PM	PM	PM	d	PM	PM	e	PM	PM	e	e
LEATHERHEAD ...... dep.	—	—	—	—	—	—	2 30	—	—	—	—	—	—	—	—	—
Ashtead	—	—	—	—	—	—	—	2 49	—	—	—	—	4 16	5 7	—	—
Epsom	12 56	—	1 45	—	1 45	—	2 40	2 57	—	3 42	—	—	4 24	5 14	—	5 40
Ewell East	12 59	—	1 48	—	1 49	—	—	3 2	—	3 45	—	—	4 28	5 18	—	5 43
Cheam	1 3	—	1 52	—	1 53	—	—	3 6	—	3 49	—	—	4 32	5 22	5 32	5 47
Sutton	1 8	1 25	2 10	1 38	2 10	2 40	2 58	3 11	3 17	4 6	4 28	—	5 4	5 31	5 37	5 52
Beeches Halt	—	—	—	1 40	—	2 43	—	—	—	—	4 58	—	—	—	5 28	—
Wallington	1 12	1 29	2 14	1 43	2 14	2 46	—	3 16	3 21	—	4 33	5 4	5 9	—	5 42	5 57
Waddon	1 16	1 33	2 6	1 47	—	2 50	—	3 20	3 25	—	4 37	5 8	5 13	—	5 46	6 1
WEST CROYDON	1 30	1 37	2 21	1 56	2 21	2 57	—	3 30	3 30	—	4 42	5 13	5 17	—	5 56	6 6
Carshalton	—	—	—	—	—	—	3 3	—	—	—	—	—	5 35	—	—	—
Hackbridge	—	—	—	—	—	—	—	—	—	—	—	—	5 38	—	—	—
MITCHAM JUNCTION ...	—	—	—	—	—	—	3 8	—	—	4 14	—	—	5 42	—	—	—
Selhurst	1 33	—	2 24	—	2 24	3 1	—	3 33	3 33	—	—	—	—	—	—	—
Thornton Heath	1 36	—	2 27	—	2 27	3 4	—	3 36	3 36	—	4 48	—	5 37	—	—	6 10
Norbury	1 40	—	2 31	—	2 31	3 8	—	3 40	3 40	—	4 52	—	5 41	—	—	6 14
Streatham Common ...	1 43	—	2 34	—	2 34	3 11	—	3 43	3 43	—	4 55	—	5 45	—	—	—
Balham	1 48	2 6	2 39	2 23	2 39	3 16	3 17	3 48	3 48	—	4 58	5 37	5 51	5 51	6 19	6 22
Wandsworth Common ..	—	2 8	2 42	2 25	2 42	3 19	—	—	—	—	—	5 39	—	—	6 21	—
CLAPHAM JUNCTION	1 53	2 11	2 46	2 28	2 46	3 23	3 22	3 53	3 53	4 26	5 3	5 42	5 56	5 57	6 24	6 27
Battersea Park	—	—	—	2 31	—	—	—	—	—	—	—	—	—	—	—	—
VICTORIA (L.B.R.)	2 0	2 17	2 54	2 35	2 54	3 30	3 32	4 0	4 34	5 11	5 49	5 6	5 6	5 31	6 31	6 35

WEEK DAYS.

	PM	d	PM	PM	PM	PM	PM	PM	PM	PM	PM	PM	PM	d
LEATHERHEAD ...... dep.	—	5 46	—	—	—	—	7 19	—	—	7 33	8 2	—	8 29	8 59
Ashtead	—	5 51	—	—	—	—	7 24	—	—	7 38	8 7	—	8 34	9 4
Epsom	—	5 59	6 30	—	7 15	7 32	—	—	—	8 7	8 15	8 52	8 57	9 11	9 26
Ewell East	—	6 3	6 32	—	7 18	7 36	—	—	8 10	8 19	8 55	9 15	—
Cheam	5 58	6 7	6 36	6 51	7 14	7 22	7 41	7 29	—	8 15	8 24	8 59	9 5	9 20
Sutton	6 2	6 11	6 39	6 51	7 14	7 27	7 47	7 29	8 5	8 20	8 37	9 9	9 25	9 35
Beeches Halt	—	—	—	—	—	—	7 31	—	8 7	—	8 40	—	—
Wallington	6 9	—	—	—	—	7 34	7 55	8 10	8 43	9 10	—
Waddon	6 14	—	—	—	—	7 38	—	8 14	8 47	9 14	—
WEST CROYDON	6 18	—	—	—	—	7 42	8 2	8 17	8 52	9 18	—
Carshalton	6 15	6 43	—	7 30	—	—	—	8 25	—	9 14	9 29
Hackbridge	6 18	6 45	—	7 33	—	—	—	8 28	—	9 17	9 32
MITCHAM JUNCTION	6 22	6 50	—	7 37	—	—	—	8 32	—	9 21	9 36	9 42
Selhurst	6 23	—	—	—	—	8 6	—	8 58	—
Thornton Heath	6 26	—	—	—	—	8 9	—	9 1	—
Norbury	6 30	—	—	—	—	8 13	—	9 5	—
Streatham Common ...	6 33	—	—	—	—	8 16	—	9 8	—
Balham	6 39	6 31	6 58	—	7 46	8 8	8 11	8 21	8 41	8 41	9 13	9 30	9 45
Wandsworth Common ..	—	—	—	—	—	8 13	—	8 43	9 16	—
CLAPHAM JUNCTION	6 44	6 37	7 3	7 7	7 51	7 51	8 8	8 16	8 26	8 46	8 46	9 20	9 36	9 50	9 53
Battersea Park	—	—	—	—	—	—	—	8 49	9 25	—
VICTORIA (L.B.R.)	6 52	6 45	7 10	7 15	7 39	7 58	8 15	8 22	8 33	8 53	8 55	9 30	9 42	9 57	10 0

WEEK DAYS.

	PM	PM	PM
LEATHERHEAD ...... dep.	10 1	—	—
Ashtead	10 6	—	—
Epsom	10 26	10 46	—
Ewell East	10 19	10^49	—
Cheam	10 24	—	—
Sutton	10 34	10 57	11 36
Beeches Halt	—	—	—
Wallington	10 39	11 2	—
Waddon	—	11 6	—
WEST CROYDON	10 46	11 20	—
Carshalton	—	—	11 40
Hackbridge	—	—	—
MITCHAM JUNCTION	—	—	11 45
Selhurst	10 50	11 23	—
Thornton Heath	10 53	11 26	—
Norbury	10 57	11 30	—
Streatham Common ...	11 0	11 33	—
Balham	11 5	11 38	11 54
Wandsworth Common ..	11 8	11 41	—
CLAPHAM JUNCTION	11 12	11 45	11 59
Battersea Park	—	11 50	—
VICTORIA (L.B.R.)	11 20	11 55	12 8

d Saturdays only.

e Saturdays excepted.

h Wednesdays only.

k Passengers are not booked from Clapham Junction by these trains.

n Motor, Third Class only; change at West Croydon.

SUNDAYS.	AM	AM	AM	AM	PM	PM	PM	PM	PM	PM	PM	PM	PM	PM	PM
Leatherhead..dep.	—	8 50	9 54	9 54	—	1 39	—	2 44	—	4 36	—	6 41	—	7 36	—
Ashtead	—	8 55	10 59	10 59	—	1 44	—	2 49	—	4 41	—	6 46	—	7 41	—
Epsom	6 40	9 3	10 8	10 8	—	1 51	2 10	2 56	—	4 49	5 55	6 52	7 5	7 48	—
Ewell East	—	9 7	10 13	10 13	—	1 55	—	3 0	—	4 53	5 58	—	7 8	7 52	—
Cheam	—	9 11	10 17	10 17	—	1 59	2 15	3 4	—	4 57	6 2	—	7 12	7 56	—
Sutton	6 48	9 18	10 35	10 30	12 5	2 23	2 19	3 9	4 3	5 2	6 25	7 1	7 5	8 5	8 16
Beeches Halt	—	—	—	—	—	—	—	2 49	—	—	6 27	—	7 7	—	—
Wallington	6 52	9 24	—	10 35	12 9	2 27	—	3 14	4 7	—	6 31	—	7 10	—	—
Waddon	—	9 28	—	10 39	12 13	—	—	3 18	4 11	—	6 35	—	7 14	—	—
West Croydon	6 59	9 32	—	10 46	12 17	2 34	—	3 22	4 15	—	6 39	—	7 18	—	—
Carshalton	—	—	10 38	—	—	—	2 23	—	—	5 6	—	7 5	—	8 9	—
Hackbridge	—	—	10 41	—	—	—	2 26	—	—	5 9	—	—	—	8 12	—
Mitcham Junction	—	—	10 45	—	—	—	2 30	—	—	5 11	—	7 10	—	8 16	—
Selhurst	—	—	—	10 49	—	2 37	—	—	4 19	—	—	—	—	—	—
Thornton Heath	—	—	—	10 52	—	2 40	—	—	4 21	—	—	—	—	—	—
Norbury	—	—	—	10 56	—	2 44	—	—	4 25	—	—	—	—	—	—
Streatham Common	—	—	—	11 0	—	2 47	—	—	4 28	—	—	—	—	—	—
Balham	7 41	10 0	10 54	11 6	12 41	2 52	2 39	3 44	4 33	5 21	7 1	7 19	7 41	8 24	—
Wandsworth Com.	7 43	10 3	—	11 9	12 43	—	2 42	—	—	—	7 3	—	7 43	—	—
Clapham Junction	7 46	10 8	10 59	11 13	12 46	2 57	2 46	3 49	4 39	5 26	7 6	7 25	7 46	8 29	8ᵏ33
Battersea Park	7 49	—	—	11 18	12 49	—	—	—	—	—	7 9	—	7 49	—	—
Victoria (L.B.R.)	7 53	10 16	11 6	11 24	12 53	3 5	2 53	3 57	4 48	5 33	7 13	7 33	7 53	8 37	8 42

SUNDAYS.	PM	PM	PM	PM	PM	PM
Leatherhead..dep.	—	—	8 57	9 14	—	10 9
Ashtead	—	—	9 2	9 20	—	10 14
Epsom	—	—	9 9	9 50	—	10 54
Ewell East	—	—	—	9 53	—	10 25
Cheam	—	—	—	9 58	—	10 29
Sutton	8 32	8 48	9 18	10 3	10 15	11 2
Beeches Halt	—	8 50	—	—	—	—
Wallington	8 37	8 53	—	—	—	11 7
Waddon	8 41	—	—	—	10 19	11 11
West Croydon	8 50	9 6	—	—	10 23	11 16
Carshalton	—	—	—	10 8	10 25	—
Hackbridge	—	—	—	10 11	—	—
Mitcham Junction	—	—	9 26	10 15	—	—
Selhurst	8 53	9 9	—	—	10 38	11 20
Thornton Heath	8 56	9 12	—	—	10 41	11 23
Norbury	—	9 16	—	—	10 45	11 27
Streatham Common	9 1	9 19	—	—	10 48	11 30
Balham	9 6	9 24	9 35	10 25	10 53	11 35
Wandsworth Com.	—	9 27	9 38	10 28	10 56	11 38
Clapham Junction	9 11	9 32	9 42	10 32	11 0	11 42
Battersea Park	—	9 37	—	10 37	11 5	11 47
Victoria (L.B.R.)	9 18	9 42	9 50	10 42	11 10	11 52

k Passengers are not booked from Clapham Junction by these trains.

VICTORIA TO CROYDON EAST (LOCAL) AND SOUTH.

WEEK DAYS.	AM	AM	AM	AM	AM	AM	AM	AM	AM	AM	AM	d AM	AM	AM	AM	AM
Victoria(L.B.R.)	5 30	5 32	6 37	6 35	6 48	7 0	7 0	7 30	8 18	8 40	8 48	9 6	9 10	9 25	9 45	9 52
Battersea Park	—	5 36	—	6 38	6 52	7 3	7 4	—	—	—	—	—	—	—	—	—
Clapham Junction	5ᵏ37	5 41	6ᵏ44	6 42	6 57	7 7	7 7	7 38	8ᵏ24	—	—	9 14	9ᵏ17	9 31	5ᵏ52	9 58
Wandsworth Comm.	—	—	—	6 45	7 7	7 10	7 13	—	8 27	—	—	—	9 34	—	—	10 1
Balham	—	5 46	—	6 47	7 4	7 12	7 16	7 44	8 29	8 50	8 59	9 19	—	9 36	—	10 3
Streatham Common	—	5 51	—	—	7 9	—	7 21	7 51	—	8 55	9 5	9 25	—	—	—	—
Norbury	—	5 54	—	—	7 13	—	7 24	7 54	—	8 59	9 9	9 28	—	—	—	—
Thornton Heath	—	5 59	—	—	7 16	—	7 29	7 58	—	9 3	9 14	9 32	9 30	—	—	—
Selhurst	—	6 2	—	—	7 19	—	—	8 1	—	9 6	9 18	9 35	—	—	—	—
Norwood Junction	—	6 9	—	7 18	—	7 39	—	—	8 52	—	—	—	—	9 58	—	—
Croydon East (Local)	—	—	—	7 26	—	7 44	—	—	8 58	9 13	—	—	—	10 2	—	10 33
Croydon South	6 1	—	7	6 7	7 29	—	7 47	—	—	9 1	9 16	—	9 41	10 5	10 17	10 36

WEEK DAYS.	AM	AM	AM	AM	AM	AM	AM	AM	AM	AM	PM	PM	PM	PM	PM	PM
Victoria (L.B.R.)dep.	10 8	10 20	10 31	10 35	10 50	11 7	11 54	12 6	12 0	12 24	12 41	12 47	12 53	12 57		
Battersea Park	—	—	10ᵏ34	—	—	—	11ᵏ57	—	—	12ᵏ27	12ᵏ46	12ᵏ51	—	—		
Clapham Junction	10 15	10 26	10 38	10ᵏ42	10 57	11 13	12 1	12 7	12ᵏ4	12 30	12 52	12 56	12 59	—		
Wandsworth Comm.	—	10 29	10 42	—	—	—	12 4	—	—	12 33	—	1 0	1 2	—		
Balham	10 21	10 31	10 44	—	11 2	11 17	12 6	12 12	—	12 35	12 59	1 3	1 4	—		
Streatham Common	10 26	—	—	—	11 7	—	—	12 17	—	—	—	1 8	—	1 13		
Norbury	10 29	—	—	—	11 10	—	—	12 20	—	—	—	1 11	—	1 16		
Thornton Heath	10 34	—	—	—	11 14	—	—	12 24	—	1 7	—	1 15	—	1 20		
Selhurst	10 37	—	—	—	11 17	—	—	12 27	—	—	—	1 18	—	1 24		
Norwood Junction	—	10 56	11 15	—	—	11 46	12 28	—	12 56	—	—	1 27				
Croydon East (Local)	—	11 1	11 19	—	—	11 52	12 32	—	1 1	1 14	—	1 32				
Croydon South	—	11 4	11 22	11 5	—	11 56	12 35	—	12 32	1ᵏ 4	1 18	—	1 35			

WEEK DAYS.	PM	PM	d	PM	PM	d	d	d	PM	d	PM	PM	PM	PM	d	d
Victoria(L.B.R.)dep.	1 5	1 15	1 22	1 25	1 32	1 32	1 40	1 41	1 53	2 0	2 8	2 12	2 25	2 28	2 37	2 50
Battersea Park	—	—	1ᵏ28	—	—	—	1 43	—	—	—	—	—	—	—	—	—
Clapham Junction	1 12	1ᵏ22	—	1 32	—	1 38	1 47	1 47	1 59	2 6	2 14	2 20	2ᵏ33	—	2 44	2 57
Wandsworth Comm.	1ᵏ15	—	—	1 35	—	1 41	1 50	1 50	2 2	—	2 17	2 24	—	—	2 48	—
Balham	1ᵏ17	—	1 33	1 37	—	1 43	1 52	1 52	2 4	2 12	2 19	2 27	—	2 38	2 51	3 2
Streatham Common	1 22	—	1 39	—	1 45	—	—	—	—	2 17	—	2 32	2 43	—	2 56	3 7
Norbury	1 25	—	1 43	—	1 48	—	—	—	—	2 20	—	2 35	—	—	2 59	3 10
Thornton Heath	1 29	—	1 47	—	1 52	—	—	—	—	2 24	—	2 39	2 48	—	3 4	3 14
Selhurst	1 32	—	1 50	—	1 55	—	—	—	—	2 27	—	2 42	—	—	3 7	3 17
Norwood Junction	1 38	—	1 55	2 2	—	2 1	—	2 13	2 24	2 32	2 42	—	—	3 0	—	3 21
Croydon East (Local)	—	1 40	—	2 7	—	—	2 16	2 21	—	2 47	—	—	3 6	3 13		
Croydon South	—	1 44	—	2 10	—	—	—	2 24	—	2 50	—	3 2	3 10	3 16		

WEEK DAYS	PM	PM	d	PM	PM	PM	PM	PM	PM	PM	PM	PM	e	PM	d	PM
Victoria (L.B.R.)dep.	3 0	3 10	—	3 40	3 42	3 48	4 0	4 13	4 15	4 36	4 53	5 5	5 10	5 15	5 21	5 27
Battersea Park	—	—	—	—	—	—	—	4ᵏ16	—	4ᵏ40	—	—	5ᵏ13	—	—	—
Clapham Junction	3 7	3 16	3 40	3 46	3 49	3 55	4 8	4 20	4ᵏ22	4 45	5ᵏ0	5ᵏ12	5 17	5 21	—	—
Wandsworth Comm.	3 11	3 19	—	3 49	3 53	3 59	—	4 23	—	—	4 51	—	5 20	—	—	—
Balham	3 14	3 21	—	3 51	3 56	4 2	—	4 25	—	4 51	—	5 22	5 26	—	—	—
Streatham Common	3 19	—	—	4 1	4 7	—	—	—	4 56	5 9	—	—	—	—	—	—
Norbury	3 22	—	—	4 4	4 10	—	—	4 32	4 59	5 12	—	5 40	—	—	—	—
Thornton Heath	3 26	—	—	4 8	4 14	—	—	4 36	5 3	5 16	—	—	—	—	—	—
Selhurst	3 29	—	—	4 11	4 17	—	—	—	5 6	5 19	—	5 43	—	—	—	—
Norwood Junction	—	3 53	4 10	—	—	—	4 51	5 12	—	5 57	—					
Croydon East (Local)	—	3 57	4 7	4 16	—	—	4 55	4 41	5 24	—	5 4)					
Croydon South	—	4 0	4 11	4 16	—	4 33	4 58	4 45	5 28	5 34	—	6 6	5 53			

WEEK DAYS.

	e	d	e	d	e	PM	PM	e	PM	e	PM	PM	PM	PM	e	e
VICTORIA (L.B.R.)dep.	5 28	5 32	5 38	5 43	5 45	5 52	6 6	6 12	6 12	6 18	6 21	6 27	6 40	6 46	7 6	7 10
Battersea Park	—	—	—	—	—	—	6^15	6^15	—	—	—	—	6^45	—	—	—
CLAPHAM JUNCTION	—	—	5 45	5 49	5 53	—	6^12	6 19	6 19	—	—	—	6^49	6 53	—	7 18
Wandsworth Comm.	—	—	—	5 52	—	—	6 22	6 22	—	—	—	6^52	—	—	—	7 20
Balham	5 38	5 42	5 50	5 54	—	—	6 24	6 24	—	6 33	—	6^54	6 58	—	7 4	7 20
Streatham Common	5 44	5 47	—	6 ·2	—	—	—	—	6 ·33	A	—	—	—	7 7	7 23	
Norbury	5 48	5 50	—	6 5	6 8	—	—	—	—	6 38	—	—	—	7 11	7 27	
Thornton Heath	5 52	5 54	—	6 9	—	—	—	6 38	6 44	—	—	—	7 14	7 30		
Selhurst	5 55	5 57	—	6 12	—	—	—	6 41	6 47	—	—	7 14	7 18	7 35	7 38	
NORWOOD JUNCTION	—	—	6 15	6 15	6 18	—	6 47	6 42	6 45	—	—	6 48	7 21	—	—	
Croydon East (Local)	—	—	6 19	6 19	—	6 14	—	6 53	—	—	—	6 51	7 24	—	—	
CROYDON SOUTH	—	—	6 21	6 21	—	6 17	6 33	6 57	—	—	—	—	—	—	—	

WEEK DAYS.

	PM	PM	PM	PM	PM	e	PM	e	PM	PM	PM	PM	PM	PM	PM	PM
VICTORIA (L.B.R.)dep.	7 14	7 15	7 20	7 33	7 38	7 52	8 5	8 7	8 10	8 30	8 40	8 55	9 3	9 5	9 15	9 20
Battersea Park	7^17	—	—	—	—	—	—	—	8^33	—	8 58	—	9 8	—	9 23	
CLAPHAM JUNCTION	7 21	7^22	—	7 44	7 45	7 59	8^12	8 14	8 17	8 37	8 47	9 2	9^10	9 12	9 22	9 27
Wandsworth Comm.	7 24	—	—	7 47	7 50	—	—	8 17	—	8 40	—	9 5	—	9 15	—	9 30
Balham	7 26	—	7 30	7 49	7 53	8 5	—	8 19	8 22	8 42	8 52	9 7	—	9 17	9 27	9 32
Streatham Common	—	—	7 35	—	7 58	8 10	—	8 22	8 27	—	8 57	—	—	—	9 32	
Norbury	—	—	7 38	—	8 1	8 13	—	8 25	8 30	—	9 0	—	—	—	9 35	
Thornton Heath	—	—	7 42	—	8 5	8 18	—	8 29	8 34	—	9 4	—	—	—	9 39	
Selhurst	—	—	7 45	—	8 8	8 21	—	8 32	8 37	—	9 7	—	—	—	9 42	
NORWOOD JUNCTION	—	—	—	8 12	—	—	8 37	—	9 1	—	—	—	9 34	9 46	10 0	
Croydon East (Local)	—	—	—	8 16	—	8 32	—	—	9 5	—	—	—	—	—	10 4	
CROYDON SOUTH	—	7 48	—	8 18	—	8 36	8 35	—	—	9 3	—	9 34	—	—	10 7	

WEEK DAYS.

	PM	PM	PM	PM	PM	PM	PM	PM	PM	PM	PM	l	PM
VICTORIA (L.B.R.)dep.	9 50	9 55	10 15	10 30	10 38	10 45	11 5	11 15	11 25	11 35	11 40	11 43	11 50
Battersea Park	9 53	9^59	10 18	—	10 42	10 48	11 8	—	—	—	—	11 46	—
CLAPHAM JUNCTION	9 57	10 4	10 22	10^37	10 47	10 52	11 12	11 22	11 31	11 41	—	11 50	—
Wandsworth Comm.	10 0	—	10 25	—	—	10 55	11 15	—	11 34	11 44	—	11 53	—
Balham	10 2	10 9	10 27	—	10 52	10 57	11 17	11 25	11 36	11 46	—	11 55	—
Streatham Common	—	10 14	—	—	10 57	—	—	—	—	—	11 53	—	—
Norbury	—	10 17	—	—	11 0	—	—	11 32	—	—	11 56	—	—
Thornton Heath	—	10 21	—	—	11 4	—	—	11 36	—	—	12 0	—	—
Selhurst	—	10 24	—	—	11 7	—	—	—	—	—	12 3	—	—
NORWOOD JUNCTION	10 19	—	10 45	—	—	11 14	11 37	—	11 53	12 4	—	12 12	—
Croydon East (Local)	—	10 28	—	—	—	—	—	—	—	—	—	—	—
CROYDON SOUTH	—	10 31	—	10 59	—	—	11 47	—	—	—	—	—	12 13

WEEK DAYS.

	d	PM
VICTORIA (L.B.R.)dep.	12 0	12 10
Battersea Park	12 3	12 13
CLAPHAM JUNCTION	12 7	12 17
Wandsworth Comm.	12 10	12 20
Balham	12 12	12 22
Streatham Common	—	—
Norbury	—	—
Thornton Heath	—	—
Selhurst	—	—
NORWOOD JUNCTION	12 30	12 39
Croydon East (Local)	—	—
CROYDON SOUTH	—	—

d Saturdays only.

e Saturdays excepted.

h Passengers are not booked to Clapham Junction by these trains.

k Calls to take up passengers only

l Mondays, Wednesdays, Thursdays and Saturdays only.

SUNDAYS.

	AM	AM	AM	AM	AM	AM	AM	AM	AM	AM	AM	AM	AM	AM
VICTORIA (L.B.R.)dep	6 55	7 40	8 0	8 5	8 18	8 40	9 5	9 40	9 47	10 0	10 20	10 30	10 35	12 0
Battersea Park	—	7 43	8 3	8 9	—	8 43	9 9	9 43	—	10 3	—	—	—	12 3
CLAPHAM JUNCTION	7^2	7 47	8 7	8 14	8^25	8 47	9 14	9 47	9 54	10 7	10^27	—	10 42	12 7
Wandsworth Comm.	—	7 50	8 10	8 18	—	8 50	9 18	9 50	—	10 10	—	—	—	12 10
Balham	7 8	7 52	8 12	8 21	8 31	8 52	9 21	9 52	9 59	10 12	10 33	—	10 47	12 12
Streatham Common	7 15	—	—	8 26	—	—	9 27	—	10 4	—	10 39	—	10 52	—
Norbury	—	—	—	8 29	—	—	9 30	—	10 7	—	10 43	—	10 55	—
Thornton Heath	7 22	—	8 33	8 39	—	—	9 35	—	10 11	—	10 48	—	10 59	—
Selhurst	—	—	8 36	—	—	—	9 38	—	10 14	—	—	—	11 2	—
NORWOOD JUNCTION	—	8 13	8 38	8 40	—	9 13	—	10 13	10 18	—	—	—	—	12 36
Croydon East (Local)	—	8 17	8 42	—	—	9 17	—	10 17	—	—	10 48	—	—	12 40
CROYDON SOUTH	7 43	8 20	8 45	—	—	9 20	—	10 20	—	—	11 2	—	—	12 43

SUNDAYS.

	PM	PM	PM	PM	PM	PM	PM	PM	PM	PM	PM	PM	PM	PM	PM
VICTORIA (L.B.R.)dep.	12 40	0 1	0 5	1 13	1 28	2 0	2 5	2 30	3 0	4 0	4 0	4 10	5 0	5 20	5 48
Battersea Park	—	1 3	—	—	1 32	2 3	—	—	3 3	—	4 3	—	—	5 24	—
CLAPHAM JUNCTION	12 47	1 7	1 12	1^20	1 38	2 7	2 12	2^37	3 7	4^7	4 7	4 19	5 7	5 29	5^56
Wandsworth Comm.	—	1 10	1 16	—	1 41	2 10	—	—	3 10	—	4 10	4 23	5 10	5 33	—
Balham	12 52	1 12	1 19	—	1 44	2 12	2 17	—	3 12	—	4 12	4 26	5 12	5 36	6 4
Streatham Common	12 57	—	1 24	—	1 49	—	2 22	—	—	—	4 31	—	5 41	6 9	
Norbury	1 0	—	1 27	—	1 53	—	2 25	—	—	—	4 34	—	5 44	—	
Thornton Heath	1 4	—	1 31	—	1 58	—	2 29	2 52	—	—	4 38	—	5 48	6 14	
Selhurst	1 8	—	1 34	—	2 1	—	2 32	—	—	—	4 41	—	5 51	—	
NORWOOD JUNCTION	1 12	1 30	—	—	2 5	2 35	—	3 39	—	4 35	4 45	5 36	—	—	
Croydon East (Local)	—	1 40	—	—	—	2 40	—	3 42	—	4 40	—	5 40	—	—	
CROYDON SOUTH	—	1 43	—	1 43	—	2 43	—	3 5	3 45	4 24	4 43	—	5 43	—	

SUNDAYS.

	PM	PM	PM	PM	PM	PM	PM	PM	PM	PM	PM	PM	PM	PM	PM
VICTORIA (L.B.R.)dep.	6 0	6 5	6 45	7 5	7 3	7 14	8 0	8 4	8 42	9 0	9 5	9 5	9 42	10 5	
Battersea Park	6 3	—	—	7 3	—	7 14	—	8 3	—	9 3	—	9^46	10 3		
CLAPHAM JUNCTION	6 7	6 12	6 53	7 7	7^12	7 19	8^4	8 7	8 11	8 49	9 7	9^13	9 12	9 52	10 12
Wandsworth Comm	6 10	6 16	—	7 10	—	7 23	—	8 10	8 13	—	9 10	—	—	—	10 10
Balham	6 12	6 19	6 57	7 12	—	7 26	8 16	8 12	8 16	8 54	9 12	—	9 17	9 58	10 12
Streatham Common	—	6 24	7 2	—	—	7 31	—	8 21	8 59	9 2	—	—	9 22	10 3	
Norbury	—	6 27	7 5	—	—	7 34	—	8 24	9 2	—	—	9 25	10 6		
Thornton Heath	—	6 31	7 9	—	—	7 38	—	8 28	9 6	—	—	9 29	10 11		
Selhurst	—	6 34	7 12	—	—	7 41	—	8 31	9 9	—	—	9 32	10 14		
NORWOOD JUNCTION	—	6 39	—	7 36	—	7 47	—	8 38	9 14	9 37	—	10 18	10 43		
Croydon East (Local)	6 40	—	7 40	—	—	8 42	9 42	—	—	10 42					
CROYDON SOUTH	6 43	—	7 43	7 33	—	8 38	8 45	—	9 45	9 39	—	10 45			

SUNDAYS.

	PM	PM	PM	PM	PM	PM
VICTORIA (L.B.R.)dep.	10 15	10 28	10 50	11 5	11 20	11 40
Battersea Park	—	10^32	—	11 3	11 23	11 46
CLAPHAM JUNCTION	10 22	10 37	10 57	11 7	11 27	11 50
Wandsworth Comm.	—	10 41	—	11 10	11 30	11 53
Balham	10 27	10 44	—	11 12	11 32	11 55
Streatham Common	10 32	10 49	11 5	—	—	—
Norbury	10 35	10 52	11 8	—	—	—
Thornton Heath	10 39	10 56	11 12	—	—	—
Selhurst	10 42	10 59	—	—	—	—
NORWOOD JUNCTION	—	—	—	11 29	11 49	12 12
Croydon East (Local)	10 46	—	11 18	—	—	—
CROYDON SOUTH	10 50	—	11 21	—	—	—

h Passengers are not booked to Clapham Junction by these trains.

k Calls to take up passengers only.

For Trains Croydon East (Main Line), see Alphabetical Section.

WEEK DAYS.	AM	AM	AM	AM	AM	AM	AM	AM	AM	AM	AM	AM	AM	AM	AM
CROYDON SOUTH ..dep.	—	—	—	—	—	6 30	—	7 3	—	—	—	—	—	—	—
Croydon East (Local) ..	—	—	5 41	—	—	6 33	—	7 8	—	—	—	—	—	—	—
NORWOOD JUNCTION	5 25	5 44	5 46	6 13	—	6 51	7 5	7 13	—	7 19	—	—	7 33	7 36	7 48
Selhurst	—	5 48	5 55	6 18	6 48	—	7 8	—	7 17	—	—	—	—	7 42	—
Thornton Heath	—	5 51	—	6 21	6 52	—	7 11	—	7 20	—	7 26	7 33	—	7 46	—
Norbury	—	5 55	—	6 25	6 56	—	—	—	—	—	7 30	—	—	7 50	—
Streatham Common	—	5 58	—	6 28	6 59	—	7 17	—	7 25	—	—	—	—	7 53	—
Balham	5 41	6 3	6 11	6 33	7 4	7 13	7 22	7 31	7 30	7 34	—	—	7 51	7 58	8 4
Wandsworth Common	5 43	—	6 13	—	—	7 15	—	7 33	7 33	7 38	—	—	7 53	8	8 6
CLAPHAM JUNCTION	5 46	6 8	6 16	6 38	—	7 18	7 27	7 36	7 37	7 41	7 40	—	7 56	8 5	8 9
Battersea Park	5 49	—	6 19	—	—	7 21	7 32	—	—	7⁴44	—	—	—	—	—
VICTORIA (L.B.R.)	5 53	6 15	6 23	6 45	7 18	7 25	7 37	7 42	7 44	7 47	7 48	7 52	8 2	8 13	8 15

WEEK DAYS.	AM	AM	AM	AM	AM	AM	AM	AM	AM	AM	AM	AM	AM	AM	AM
CROYDON SOUTH ..dep.	7 41	—	8 5	8 0	8 13	8 18	8 38	—	—	8 46	8 53	—	9 8	—	—
Croydon East (Local) ..	—	—	8 8	8 4	—	8 22	—	—	—	8 50	—	—	9 12	—	9 16
NORWOOD JUNCTION	—	—	8 8	8	—	8 27	—	—	8 42	—	—	—	—	9 10	—
Selhurst	7 59	8 6	—	—	—	—	—	8 39	8 46	8 55	—	9 7	—	—	—
Thornton Heath	8 2	8 9	8 13	—	—	—	—	8 42	8 49	8 58	—	9 11	—	—	9 21
Norbury	—	—	8 17	—	—	—	—	8 46	—	9 3	—	9 15	—	—	9 25
Streatham Common ..	—	—	8 20	—	—	—	—	8 49	8 54	9 6	—	9 18	—	—	9 28
Balham	—	—	—	8 27	—	8 51	—	8 54	—	—	9 23	—	9 29	—	—
Wandsworth Common	—	—	8 26	8 39	—	8 53	—	—	—	—	—	—	9 32	—	—
CLAPHAM JUNCTION	8⁴15	8 22	—	8 33	8⁴32	8 56	9⁴ 0	8 59	9 3	—	—	—	9⁴31	9 36	9 36
Battersea Park	—	—	—	—	—	—	—	—	—	—	—	—	—	—	—
VICTORIA (L.B.R.)	8 24	8 30	8 35	8 40	8 40	9 2	9 8	9 6	9 11	9 22	9 19	9 31	9 38	9 44	9 44

WEEK DAYS.	AM	AM	AM	AM	AM	AM	AM	AM	AM	AM	AM	AM	PM	PM	d
CROYDON SOUTH ..dep.	9 32	9 44	—	10 17	—	10 31	—	11 5	11 5	—	11 39	12 16	—	—	—
Croydon East (Local) ..	9 36	—	—	—	—	10 38	—	11 5	11 8	—	11 43	—	—	—	—
NORWOOD JUNCTION	9 41	—	9 45	—	—	10 42	—	—	11 12	—	11 48	—	—	—	12 36
Selhurst	—	—	9 50	—	10 13	—	10 53	—	—	11 19	—	—	—	12 33	12 40
Thornton Heath	—	—	9 53	—	10 16	—	10 56	—	—	11 22	—	—	—	12 36	12 43
Norbury	—	—	9 57	—	10 20	—	11 0	—	—	11 26	—	—	—	12 40	12 47
Streatham Common ..	—	—	10 2	—	10 23	—	11 3	—	—	11 29	—	—	—	12 43	12 50
Balham	10 5	—	10 8	—	10 28	11 3	11 8	—	11 36	11 34	12 8	—	12 48	—	—
Wandsworth Common	10 7	—	10 11	—	—	11 5	—	—	11 39	—	12 10	—	—	—	—
CLAPHAM JUNCTION	10 10	10⁴ 5	10 15	10⁴39	10 33	11 8	11 13	11⁴26	11 41	11 39	12 13	12⁴36	12 53	—	—
Battersea Park	—	—	—	—	—	—	—	—	—	—	—	—	—	—	—
VICTORIA (L.B.R.)	10 16	10 12	10 24	10 46	10 41	11 14	11 20	11 34	11 47	11 46	12 19	12 45	1 0	1 5

WEEK DAYS.	PM	PM	PM	PM	PM	d	e	PM	d	d	PM	PM	e	d	d	e
CROYDON SOUTH ..dep.	12 53	—	1 2	1 14	—	1 27	1 40	1 55	—	2 3	2 6	—	2 37	2 53	8 3 13
Croydon East (Local) ..	—	—	1 6	—	—	1 32	1 45	—	—	2 7	2 9	—	2 41	2 56	3 12 3 16
NORWOOD JUNCTION	—	1 4	1 10	—	—	1 57	1 49	—	2 3	2 12	2 13	—	2 45	3 0	3 17 3 20
Selhurst	—	1 8	—	—	1 23	—	—	—	2 8	—	—	2 24	—	—	—
Thornton Heath	—	1 10	—	—	1 36	—	—	—	2 11	—	—	2 27	—	—	—
Norbury	—	1 14	—	—	1 40	—	—	—	2 15	—	—	2 31	—	—	—
Streatham Common .	—	1 17	—	—	1 43	—	—	—	2 19	—	—	2 34	—	—	—
Balham	—	1 22	1 36	—	1 48	2 6	2 23	—	2 25	2 41	2 38	2 39	3 9	3 24 3 39 3 39
Wandsworth Common	—	—	1 38	—	—	2 8	2 25	—	—	2 40	2 42	3 11	3 26	3 41 3 41
CLAPHAM JUNCTION ...	1⁴19	1 27	1 41	1⁴39	1 53	2 11	2 28	2⁴13	2 30	2 45	2 43	2 46	3 14	3 29 3 44 3 44
Battersea Park	—	—	1 44	—	—	—	2⁴31	—	—	—	—	—	—	3⁴47 3⁴47
VICTORIA (L.B.R.) ...	1 26	1 34	1 48	1 49	2 0	2 17	2 35	2 22	2 39	2 51	2 49	2 54	3 20	3 53 3 51 3 51

WEEK DAYS.	PM	PM	d	e	PM	PM	d	PM	PM	PM	PM	e
CROYDON SOUTH....dep.	3 16	—	3 28	—	—	4 30	4 51	—	5 18	—	5 43	—
Croydon East (Local) ..	—	—	3 31	—	—	4 34	4 53	—	—	—	—	—
NORWOOD JUNCTION	—	—	3 35	3 32	3 58	4 31	4 39	4 59	5 18	—	5 49	5 51	6 27
Selhurst	—	3 33	—	3 38	—	4 36	—	—	5 23	—	5 53	—	6 23 3 31
Thornton Heath	—	3 36	—	3 42	—	4 39	4 48	—	5 25	—	5 35 5 56	—	6 26 6 34
Norbury	—	3 40	—	3 47	—	4 43	4 52	—	5 30	—	5 39 6 0	—	6 30 6 38
Streatham Common ..	—	3 43	—	3 51	—	4 46	4⁴53	—	5 33	—	5 43 6 4	—	6 33 6 41
Balham	—	3 48	3 53	3 56	4 14	4 51	4 58	5 9	5 22	5 38	5 49 6 10	6 19 6 39	6 46
Wandsworth Common	—	—	3 55	3 59	4 16	—	—	5 11	5 24	—	—	6 21	6 49
CLAPHAM JUNCTION	3⁴37	3 53	3 58	4 3	4 19	4 57	5 3	5 14	5 27	5 43	5 47 5 54	6 16 6 24	6 44 6 53
Battersea Park	—	—	4 1	4 8	—	—	—	—	5 48	—	—	—	—
VICTORIA (L.B.R.)	3 45	4 0	4 5	4 13	4 25	5 4	5 11	5 20	5 33	5 53	5 57 6 3	6 23 6 31	6 52 7 1

WEEK DAYS.	PM	PM	PM	PM	PM	PM	PM	PM	PM	PM	PM	PM	PM
CROYDON SOUTH....dep.	—	6 50	—	7 30	7 51	7 48	8 23	—	8 59	—	9 31	—	10 30
Croydon East (Local) ..	—	6 53	—	7 34	—	7 52	8 26	—	9 4	—	9 34	—	10 33
NORWOOD JUNCTION	6⁴54	6 57	7 29	7 38	—	7 57	8 36	8 37	9 9	—	9 39	9 53	10 37
Selhurst	6 59	—	7 34	—	—	—	8 41	8 53	—	9 38	—	9 57	—	10 50
Thornton Heath	7 3	—	7 37	—	8 3	—	8 44	9 1	—	9 41	—	10 0	—	10 53
Norbury	7 7	—	7 41	—	—	—	8 48	9 5	—	9 45	—	10 4	—	10 57
Streatham Common ..	7 11	—	7 44	—	8 8	—	8 51	9 8	—	9 48	—	10 7	—	11 0
Balham	7 16	7 21	7 49	7 59	—	8 25	8 56	8 56	9 13	9 25	9 53	10 6	10 12	11 1	11 5
Wandsworth Common	—	7 23	7 52	8 1	—	8 27	8 58	—	9 16	—	9 56	10 8	—	11 2	11 6
CLAPHAM JUNCTION	7 21	7 23	7 56	8 4	8⁴19	8 30	9 1	9 1	9 20	9 30	10 0	10 9	10 11	10 19	11 6	11 12
Battersea Park	—	7⁴29	8 1	—	—	8 33	—	—	9 25	—	—	10 14	—	11 9	—
VICTORIA (L.B.R.)	7 29	7 33	8 6	8 10	8 27	8 37	9 7	9 8	9 29	9 38	10 7	10 18	10 25	11 13	11 20

WEEK DAYS.	PM	PM
CROYDON SOUTH....dep.	—	—
Croydon East (Local)..	—	—
NORWOOD JUNCTION	10 58	—
Selhurst	11 2	11 23
Thornton Heath	11 5	11 26
Norbury	11 9	11 30
Streatham Common ..	11 13	11 33
Balham	11 18	11 38
Wandsworth Common	11 21	11 41
CLAPHAM JUNCTION	11 25	11 45
Battersea Park	—	11 50
VICTORIA (L.B.R.)	11 33	11 55

d Saturdays only.
e Saturdays excepted.
f Mondays only.
g Mondays excepted.
h Passengers between Clapham Junction and Victoria are not conveyed by these trains.
k Calls to set down passengers only.

For Trains Croydon East (Main Line), see Alphabetical Section.

SUNDAYS.	AM	AM	AM	AM	AM	AM	AM	AM	AM	AM	AM	AM	AM	AM	AM	AM
CROYDON SOUTH....dep.	—	—	—	—	8 50	9 4	9 41	9 50	—	—	—	—	—	—	10 48	12 8
Croydon East (Local) ..	—	—	7 39	8 15	8 53	9 12	—	9 53	—	—	—	—	—	10 52	—
NORWOOD JUNCTION	6 50	7 6 7 25	—	8 20	8 28	8 57	9 38	—	9 58	10 7	—	—	—	—	10 57	—
Selhurst	—	—	7 42	—	8 23	—	—	—	—	10 7	—	10 23	10 49	—	—
Thornton Heath	—	—	7 45	—	8 31	—	9 51	—	10 14	—	10 31	10 52	—	12 17
Norbury	—	—	7 49	—	8 35	—	—	—	10 18	—	10 35	10 56	—	12 21
Streatham Common ..	—	—	7 52	—	8 38	—	10 1	—	10 21	—	10 39	11 0	—	12 25
Balham	7 57	21 7 41	—	8 43	8 43 8 46	9 21 10	1 10 8	10 21 10 26	10 41	10 44	11 6	11 21	12 33
Wandsworth Common	7 77	23 7 43	—	8 43 8 46	9 23 10	3 —	10 23 10 29	10 43	—	11 8	11 23	12 34
CLAPHAM JUNCTION	7 10 7 26	7 46 8	8 46 8	50 9 26	10 6 10 16	10 33 10	40 10 50	11 13	11 26	12 38
Battersea Park	7 13 7 29	7 49	—	8 49 8	53 9 21	10 9 —	10 29 10 38	10 44	—	11 18	11 29	—
VICTORIA (L.B.R.)	7 17 7 33	7 53 8	7 8 53 9	0 9 33	10 13 10 20	10 33 10 43	10 52 11 0	11 24	11 33	12 47

SUNDAYS.

	PM	PM	PM	PM	PM	PM	PM	PM	PM	PM	PM	PM	PM	PM
Croydon South....dep.	1 4	1 13	—	2 13	2 39	—	3 13	—	—	4 13	—	5 13	6 1	—
Croydon East (Local) ..	—	1 16	—	2 16	—	—	3 16	—	—	4 16	—	5 16	—	—
Norwood Junction	—	1 20	2 16	2 20	—	—	3 20	3 41	—	4 20	—	5 20	—	6 11
Selhurst	—	—	2 29	—	—	2 37	—	3 45	4 19	—	—	—	—	6 15
Thornton Heath	1 13	—	2 23	—	—	2 40	—	3 48	4 22	—	4 49	—	6 10	6 18
Norbury	1 17	—	2 27	—	—	2 44	—	3 52	4 26	—	—	—	—	6 22
Streatham Common ..	1 21	—	2 30	—	—	2 47	—	3 55	4 29	—	—	—	6 15	6 25
Balham	1 26	1 41	2 35	2 41	—	2 52	3 41	4 0	4 34	4 41	—	5 41	6 20	6 31
Wandsworth Common	—	1 43	2 38	2 43	—	—	3 43	—	—	4 43	—	5 43	—	6 34
Clapham Junction	1 32	1 46	2 42	2 46	2⁴56	2 57	3 45	4 6	4 40	4 46	5ᵏ 1	5 46	6⁴25	6 39
Battersea Park	—	1 49	—	2 49	—	—	3 49	—	—	4 49	—	5 49	—	6 43
Victoria	1 40	1 53	2 49	2 53	3 5	3 5	3 53	4 13	4 43	4 53	5 11	5 53	6 31	6 45

SUNDAYS.

	PM	PM	PM	PM	PM	PM	PM	PM	PM	PM	PM	PM	PM	PM
Croydon South....dep.	6 13	—	7 10	—	3 5	8 13	8 46	—	9 3	—	9 10	9 21	—	10 4
Croydon East (Local) ..	6 16	—	7 13	—	—	8 16	—	—	—	—	9 12	—	—	10 8
Norwood Junction	6 20	—	7 17	7 51	—	8 20	—	—	—	—	9 17	—	9 52	10 14
Selhurst	—	7 10	—	7 55	—	—	—	8 53	—	9 9	—	—	9 57	—
Thornton Heath	—	7 13	—	7 58	8 19	—	—	8 56	—	9 12	—	9 33	10 1	—
Norbury	—	7 17	—	8 2	—	—	—	—	—	9 16	—	9 37	10 6	—
Streatham Common ...	—	7 20	—	8 5	—	—	—	9 1	—	9 19	—	9 41	10 9	—
Balham	6 41	7 23	7 41	8 10	—	8 41	—	9 6	—	9 24	9 41	—	10 14	10 41
Wandsworth Common	6 43	7 28	7 43	—	—	8 43	—	—	—	9 27	9 43	—	—	10 43
Clapham Junction	6 46	7 33	7 46	8 15	8⁴31	8 46	9ᵏ 4	9 11	9ᵏ21	9 32	9 45	9 49	10 19	10 46
Battersea Park	6 49	7 38	7 49	—	—	8 49	—	—	—	9 37	9 49	—	—	10 49
Victoria	6 53	7 43	7 53	8 22	8 41	8 53	9 13	9 18	9 34	9 42	9 53	10 0	10 27	10 53

SUNDAYS.

	PM	PM	PM
Croydon South....dep.	—	—	—
Croydon East (Local) ..	—	—	—
Norwood Junction	—	—	—
Selhurst	10 38	—	11 20
Thornton Heath	10 41	11 20	11 23
Norbury	10 45	—	11 27
Streatham Common ..	10 48	—	11 30
Balham	10 53	11 30	11 35
Wandsworth Common.	11 56	—	11 38
Clapham Junction	11 0	11⁴35	11 42
Battersea Park	11 5	—	11 47
Victoria	11 10	11 45	11 52

d Saturdays only.   e Saturdays excepted.   h Passengers between Clapham Junction and
Victoria are not conveyed by these trains.   k Calls to set down passengers only.

VICTORIA AND LONDON BRIDGE TO WIMBLEDON.

WEEK DAYS.

	AM	AM	AM	AM	AM	AM	d	AM	AM	AM	d	d	e	PM	PM	d	e
Victoria....dep.	5 57	6 18	7 0	7 13	—	8 43	9 6	9 50	10 8	10 30	11 35	12 0	12 8	12 35	—	1 50	1 54
London Bridge..	5 50	—	7 7	7 30	8 17	8 57	—	9 22	10 35	10 35	12 0	12 25	11 58	12 25	2 0	1 40	1 52
Beddington Lane	7 2	—	8 2	—	9 2	10 10	10 10	—	11 10	—	12 26	1 9	1 9	—	—	2 38	2 39
Mitcham Junc...	7 4	7 48	4 9	3 9	4	10 12	10 12	10 12	11 14	11 13	12 28	1 11	1 11	1 11	2 40	2 40	2 40
Mitcham	7 7	7 8	7 8	8 3	7 10	10 15	10 15	11 15	11 17	11 16	12 31	1 12	1 14	1 14	2 43	2 42	2 43
Morden	7 9	7 9	9 8	11 8	10 9	10 18	10 18	11 18	11 18	11 21	11 20	12 35	1 18	1 18	2 47	2 47	2 47
Merton Park....	7 13	7 13	13 8	12 9	10 20	10 20	10 20	11 21	11 22	11 35	1 20	1 20	2 49	2 49	2 49
Wimbledon	7 16	7 16	8 16	8 15	9 15	10 23	10 23	11 26	11 25	12 40	1 23	1 23	2 52	2 52	2 52

WEEK DAYS.

	d	PM	PM	PM	e	e	PM	PM	d	e	PM	d	e	PM	PM	PM	PM	PM	PM
Victoria....dep.	2 13	3 10	4 46	—	—	5 22	5 43	6	3 6	10	6 0	6 22	6 42	6 53	8 10	8 33	8 40	9 35	9 30
London Bridge..	—	3 10	4 33	5	10 5	14 5	14 6	16 6	—	6ᵏ30	6 45	6 45	—	7 27	7 28	—	9 1	9 51	10 41
Beddington Lane	3 58	5 50	5 50	—	6 56	6 56	—	—	7 27	7 28	—	9 1	9 51	10 41
Mitcham Junc...	2 40	4 0	5 52	5 52	5 38	5 57	1 7	1 7	7 4	7 29	7 30	7 29	9 39	9 53	10 43
Mitcham	2 43	4 3	5 55	5 55	5 38	5 57	1 7	7 10	7 32	7 33	7 32	9 69	9 56	10 46
Morden	2 47	4 7	5 59	5 59	43 6	1	—	—	7 10	7 35	7 37	7 35	9 10	9 10	10 10	10 50
Merton Park ...	2 49	4 9	6 1	6 1	43 6	1	—	—	7 12	7 37	7 39	7 37	9 12	9 12	10 10	10 52
Wimbledon	2 52	4 12	6 4	6 4	46 6	4	—	—	7 15	7 40	7 42	7 40	9 15	9 15	10 10	10 55

SUNDAYS.

	AM	AM	AM	PM	PM	PM	PM	PM	PM	PM
Victoria....dep.	—	9 5	—	1 40	—	—	—	—	—	—
London Bridge..	—	9 10	9 30	1 35	1 25	4 43	6 15	6 38	—	8 45	8 27
Beddington Lane	9 11	10 38	—	2 31	—	5 26	7	9 38	—
Mitcham Junc...	9 13	10 40	10 40	2 33	2 34	5 28	7 11	8 38	8 38	9 38	9 38
Mitcham	9 16	10 43	10 43	2 36	2 37	5 31	7 14	8 41	8 41	9 41	9 41
Morden	9 20	10 47	10 47	2 41	2 41	5 35	7 18	8 45	8 45	9 45	9 45
Merton Park	9 22	10 49	10 49	2 43	2 43	5 37	7 20	8 47	8 47	9 47	9 47
Wimbledon	9 25	10 52	10 52	2 46	2 46	5 40	7 23	8 50	8 50	9 50	9 50

WEEK DAYS.

	AM	AM	AM	AM	AM	AM	AM	AM	AM	d	AM	AM	AM	PM	PM	PM	PM	PM	PM
Wimbledon dep.	7	7 27	7 29	7 32	—	—	8 20	9 20	10 35	10 35	11 30	11 33	1 6	1 36	3 54	4 50	6 9
Merton Park....	7 27	7 27	8 26	8 27	9 22	9 22	10 37	11 32	11 33	1 6	1 38	2 59	4 51	6 11
Morden	7 29	7 29	8 28	8 29	9 24	9 24	10 39	11 34	11 37	1 10	1 40	3 4	4 53	6 13
Mitcham	7 32	7 32	8 32	8 32	9 27	9 27	10 42	11 37	11 37	1 14	1 43	3 5	4 57	6 16
Mitcham Junc..	—	7 35	—	8 35	9 30	9 30	10 45	—	11 40	1 17	1 46	3 8	5 0	6 19
Beddington Lane	7 37	7 37	8 37	9 32	10 47	11 42	1 19	1 48	3 10	5 2
London Bridge..	8 13	8 13	8 26	8 27	9 15	10 7	11 10	11 32	12 42	12 35	2 22	2 45	3 55	5 51	7 13
Victoria	8 32	8 32	8 30	9 12	9 34	9 55	10 41	11 32	12 42	12 35	2 36	4 2	6 44

SUNDAYS.

	AM	AM	AM	AM	AM	AM	AM	PM	PM	PM	PM	PM	PM	PM
Wimbledon dep.	9 36	11 4	11 4	5 48	8 0	8 0	8 0	9 4	—	—
Merton Park....	9 37	11 4	3	5 50	8 1	8 1	8 1	9 4	10 7	10 7
Morden	9 40	11 4	3	5 52	8 4	8 4	8 4	9 4	10 7	10 7
Mitcham	9 43	11 7	3	5 55	8 7	8 7	8 7	10 10	10 10
Mitcham Junc. .	9 46	11 10	3 10	5 58	—	8 10	9 10	10 13
Beddington Lane	9 48	11 10	5	—	7 12	—	9 32	10 15
London Bridge..	12 29	3 54	6 52	8 46	9 21	11 32	10 1	11 5
Victoria	12 13	3 57	8 37	9 18	9 50	10 42	11 15

d Saturdays only.
e Saturdays excepted.

WEEK DAYS	AM	AM	AM	AM	AM	AM	AM	AM	AM	AM	AM	AM	AM	e	AM
Victoria (L.B.R.)..dep.	6 20	6 35	6 43	7 0	7 19	7 50	7 59	8 18	8 32	8 40	8 57	9 3	9 25	9 42	9 52
Battersea Park	6 23	6 38	—	7 3	7 22	7 53	—	h	—	8^A43	9 0	9^A 6	—	—	—
Clapham Junction	6 27	6 42	6 51	7 7	7 26	7 57	8 6	8 24	8 36	8 47	9 4	9 10	9 31	9 48	9 58
Wandsworth Common	6 30	6 45	6 54	7 10	7 29	8 0	8 9	8 27	—	8 50	—	9 14	9 34	9 51	10 1
Balham	6 32	6 47	6 56	7 12	7 31	8 2	8 11	8 29	8 42	8 52	9 9	9 16	9 35	9 53	10 3
Streatham Hill	6 35	6 50	6 59	7 15	7 34	8 5	8 14	8 32	8 45	8 55	9 12	9 19	9 38	9 56	10 6
West Norwood	6 39	6 54	—	7 19	7 38	8 9	8 18	8 36	8 49	8 59	—	9 23	9 42	10 0	10 10
Gipsy Hill	6 42	6 57	⊥	7 22	7 41	8 12	8 21	8 40	—	9 2	—	9 26	9 45	10 3	10 13
Crystal Palace	6 46	7 0	—	7 25	7 44	8 15	8 24	8 44	8 53	9 5	9 18	9 29	9 43	10 6	10 16

WEEK DAYS	AM	AM	AM	AM	AM	AM	AM	AM	PM	PM	d	PM	d
Victoria (L.B.R.)..dep.	10 2	10 18	10 31	10 54	11 7	11 23	11 35	11 53	12 8	12 24	12 33	12 40	12 48
Battersea Park	10 5	—	10 34	10 57	—	11 26	11 38	11 56	12 11	12^c27	—	12^h43	—
Clapham Junction	10 9	10 24	10 38	11 3	11 13	11 30	11 42	12 0	12 15	12 30	12 39	12 47	—
Wandsworth Common	10 12	10 27	10 42	11 6	—	11 23	11 45	12 3	12 18	12 33	12 42	12 50	12 57
Balham	10 14	10 29	10 44	11 8	11 17	11 35	11 47	12 5	12 20	12 35	12 44	12 52	12 59
Streatham Hill	10 17	10 32	10 47	11 11	11 20	11 38	11 50	12 8	12 23	12 38	12 47	12 55	1 2
West Norwood	10^c21	10 36	10 51	11 15	11 24	11 42	11 54	12 12	12 27	12 42	—	12 59	—
Gipsy Hill	10^c24	10 39	10 54	11 18	11 27	11 45	11 57	12 15	12 30	12 45	—	1 2	—
Crystal Palace	10^c27	10 42	10 57	11 21	11 30	11 48	12 0	12 18	12 33	12 48	—	1 5	—

WEEK DAYS	PM	PM	d	PM	d	d	PM	d	d	d	PM	e	d	PM
Victoria (L.B.R.)..dep.	12 52	1 10	1 16	1 24	1 29	1 32	1 39	1 41	1 53	1 53	2 2	2 8	2 25	2 28	2 43
Battersea Park	—	1^d13	—	1^c27	—	1 42	—	—	1 56	—	—	2 28	—
Clapham Junction	12 58	1 17	1 22	1 31	1 35	1 38	1 46	1 47	1 59	2 0	2 10	2 14	2 32	—	2 49
Wandsworth Common	1 1	1 20	1 25	1 34	1 38	1 41	1 49	1 50	2 2	2 2	2 14	2 17	2 35	—	2 52
Balham	1 3	1 22	1 27	1 36	1 40	1 43	1 51	1 52	2 4	2 5	2 16	2 19	2 37	2 38	2 54
Streatham Hill	1 6	1 25	1 30	1 39	1 43	1 46	1 54	1 55	2 7	2 8	2 19	2 22	2 40	2 41	2 57
West Norwood	1 10	1 29	2 34	1 44	4 47	1 50	1 58	1 59	2 11	2 12	2 19	2 23	2 26	2 44	2 45	3 1
Gipsy Hill	1 13	1 32	1 37	1 47	—	1 53	2 1	2 2	—	2 15	2 26	2 29	2 47	2 48	3 4
Crystal Palace	1 16	1 36	1 40	1 50	1 51	1 56	2 4	2 5	2 15	2 18	2 29	2 32	2 50	2 52	3 7

WEEK DAYS	PM	PM	PM	PM	PM	PM	PM	PM	PM	PM	PM	e	PM	e	e
Victoria (L.B.R.)..dep.	2 57	3 10	3 25	3 40	3 55	4 13	4 26	4 36	4 46	4 58	5 10	5 15	5 24	5 32	5 38
Battersea Park	3 0	—	3 28	—	3 58	4^A16	—	—	—	5^A 1	5^A13	—	—	5^A35	—
Clapham Junction	3 4	3 16	3 32	3 46	4 2	4 20	4 32	4 42	—	5 5	5 17	5 21	5^c30	5 39	5 45
Wandsworth Common	3 7	3 19	3 35	3 49	4 5	4 23	4 36	4 45	4 55	5 8	5 20	—	5 32	5 42	—
Balham	3 9	3 21	3 37	3 50	4 7	4 26	4 38	4 47	4 58	5 10	5 22	5 26	5 34	—	5 49
Streatham Hill	3 12	3 24	3 40	3 53	4 10	4 28	4 41	4 50	5 2	5 13	5 25	5 30	5 38	5 46	5 53
West Norwood	3 16	3 28	3 44	3 57	4 14	4 32	4 45	4 54	—	5 17	5^d29	5 34	5 42	5 50	5 59
Gipsy Hill	3 19	3 31	3 47	4 0	4 17	4 35	4 48	4 57	—	5 20	5^d32	5 37	5 45	5 53	6 3
Crystal Palace	3 22	3 34	3 51	4 3	4 20	4 38	4 51	5 0	5 10	5 23	5^d35	5 40	5 48	5 56	6 7

WEEK DAYS	d	e	PM	e	e	e	PM	e	PM	e	PM	PM	d	e	PM
Victoria (L.B.R.)..dep.	5 42	5 52	5 53	6 0	6 5	6 12	6 18	6 22	6 27	6 35	6 40	6 54	7 0	7 14	7 30
Battersea Park	—	—	6^A 3	—	6^A15	—	—	—	6^A38	6^d43	—	—	7^A17	—
Clapham Junction	5 48	—	5 59	6 6	6 11	6 19	6 24	6 29	6 33	6 42	6 d49	7 0	7 14	7 21	7 36
Wandsworth Common	5 51	—	6 2	6 9	6 14	6 22	6 27	6 32	6 36	6 45	6 52	7 2	7 17	18 7 24	7 39
Balham	5 53	6 2	6 4	6 11	6 15	6 24	6 29	6 34	6 38	6 47	6 50	7 4	7 19	20 7 26	7 41
Streatham Hill	5 56	6 5	6 7	6 14	6 18	6 27	6 32	6 38	6 41	6 50	6 53	7 8	22 7 23	7 29	7 44
West Norwood	6 0	6 9	6 11	—	6 23	6 31	—	6 42	6 45	—	6 57	7 12	26 7 27	7 33	7 51
Gipsy Hill	6 3	6 12	6 14	—	6 26	6 34	—	6 45	6 48	—	7 0	7 15	29 7 30	7 36	7 51
Crystal Palace	6 7	6 15	6 17	—	6 29	6 37	—	6 48	6 51	—	7 6	7 18	7 33	7 39	7 54

WEEK DAYS	PM	PM	PM	e	PM	d	PM	PM	PM	PM	PM	PM
Victoria (L.B.R.)..d p.	7 37	7 46	8 0	8 7	8 14	8 30	8 45	8 55	9 3	9 20	9 35	9 50	10 15	10 30	10 43
Battersea Park	—	7^A49	8^A 3	8 10	8^A17	8^A33	8 48	8 58	9 6	9 23	9 38	9 53	10 18	10 33	10 46
Clapham Junction	7 43	7 53	8 7	8 14	8 21	8 37	8 52	9 2	9 10	9 27	9 41	9 57	10 22	10 36	10 50
Wandsworth Common	7 46	7 56	8 10	8 17	8 24	8 40	8 55	9 5	9 13	9 30	9 44	10 0	10 25	10 39	10 53
Balham	7 48	7 58	8 13	8 19	8 26	8 42	8 57	9 7	9 15	9 32	9 46	10 2	10 27	10 41	10 55
Streatham Hill	7 51	8 1	8 15	8 22	8 29	8 45	9 0	9 10	9 18	9 35	9 49	10 5	10 30	10 44	10 58
West Norwood	7 55	8 5	8 19	8 26	8 34	8 49	9 4	9 14	9 22	9 39	9 53	10 9	10 34	10 48	11 2
Gipsy Hill	7 58	8 8	8 22	8 29	8 37	8 52	9 7	9 17	9 25	9 42	9 56	10 12	10 37	10 51	11 5
Crystal Palace	8 2	8 11	8 25	8 32	8 41	8 55	9 11	9 20	9 28	9 45	9 59	10 15	10 40	10 55	11 8

WEEK DAYS	PM	PM	PM	PM	d	mdt.		
Victoria (L.B.R.)..dep.	11 5	11 25	11 35	11 43	12 0	12 10		
Battersea Park	11 8	11 28	—	11 46	12 3	12 13		
Clapham Junction	11 12	11 31	11 41	11 50	12 7	12 17		
Wandsworth Common	11 15	11 34	11 44	11 53	12 10	12 20		
Balham	11 17	11 36	11 46	11 55	12 12	12 22		
Streatham Hill	11 20	11 39	11 49	11 57	12 15	12 25		
West Norwood	11 24	11 43	11 53	12 1	12 19	12 29		
Gipsy Hill	11 27	11 46	11 56	12 5	12 22	12 32		
Crystal Palace	11 30	11 49	11 59	12 8	12 25	12 35		

d Saturdays only.
e Saturdays excepted.
h Calls to take up passengers only.

SUNDAYS.	AM	AM	AM		PM	PM	PM	PM	PM	PM
Victoria ....dep.	7 20	7 40	8 0		9 20	9 40 10 0	10 20 10 40	11 0 11 20	11 40
Battersea Park	7 23	7 43	8 3	Then at	9 23	9 43 10 3	10 23 10 43	11 3 11 23	11 43
Clapham Junction	7 27	7 47	8 7	the same	9 27	9 47 10 7	10 27 10 47	11 7 11 27	11 47
Wandsworth Common	7 30	7 50	8 10	minutes	9 30	9 50 10 10	10 30 10 50	11 10 11 30	11 50
Balham	7 32	7 52	8 12	past each	9 32	9 52 10 12	10 32 10 52	11 12 11 32	11 52
Streatham Hill	7 35	7 55	8 15	hour until	9 35	9 55 10 15	10 35 10 55	11 15 11 35	11 55
West Norwood	7 39	7 59	8 19		9 39	9 59 10 19	10 39 10 59	11 19 11 39	12 2
Gipsy Hill	7 42	8 2	8 22		9 42	10 2 10 22	10 42 11 2	11 22 11 42	12 5
Crystal Palace	7 45	8 5	8 25		9 45	10 5 10 25	10 45 11 5	11 25 11 45	12 8

WEEK DAYS	AM	AM	AM	AM	AM	AM	AM	AM	AM	AM	AM	AM	AM	AM	AM	AM
Crystal Palace dep.	5 30	6 0	6 15	6 29	6 44	—	7 2	7 20	7 25	7 29	—	7 40	7 53	8 2	—	8 16
Gipsy Hill	5 32	6 2	6 17	6 32	6 47	—	7 4	7 22	7 27	7 32	—	7 42	7 55	8 5	—	
West Norwood	5 34	6 4	6 19	6 34	6 49	—	7 6	7 24	7 29	7 34	—	7 44	7 57	8 7	—	
Streatham Hill	5 38	6 8	6 23	6 38	6 53	6 57	7 10	7 28	7 33	7 38	—	7 43	8 1	8 11	8 21	—
Balham	5 41	6 11	6 26	6 41	6 56	7 3	7 13	7 31	7 36	7 41	7 45	7 51	8 4	8 14	—	8 27
Wandsworth Common	5 43	6 13	6 28	6 43	6 58	7 5	7 15	7 33	7 38	7 43	—	7 53	8 6	8 16	8 25	8 30
Clapham Junction	5 46	6 16	6 31	6 46	7 1	7 8	7 18	7 35	7 41	7 46	7 51	7 56	8 9	8 19	8 28	8 34
Battersea Park	5 49	6 19	6 34	6 49	7 4	—	7 21	—	7ᴴ44	—	—	—	—	8 22	8 31	—
Victoria	5 53	6 23	6 38	6 53	7 8	7 14	7 25	7 43	7 48	7 52	7 59	8 3	8 15	8 25	8 35	8 41

WEEK DAYS.	AM	AM	AM	AM	AM	AM	AM	AM	AM	AM	AM	AM	AM	AM	AM	AM
Crystal Palace..dep.	8 21	—	8 30	—	8 39	—	8 57	—	9 8	9 18	9 24	—	9 35	—	9 53	10 7
Gipsy Hill	8 23	—	8 31	—	8 42	—	8 59	—	9 10	—	9 26	—	9 38	—	9 55	10 9
West Norwood	8 25	—	8 34	—	8 44	—	9 1	—	9 12	9 21	9 28	—	9 40	—	9 57	10 12
Streatham Hill	8 29	8 33	8 38	3 42	8 48	9 1	9 5	9 11	9 16	9 25	9 32	9 36	9 44	9 56	10 1	10 16
Balham	—	8 36	8 41	8 45	8 51	9 4	9 8	9 14	9 19	9 29	9 35	9 39	9 47	9 59	10 4	10 19
Wandsworth Common	8 34	8 38	—	8 47	8 53	9 6	9 10	9 16	9 21	9 32	9 37	9 41	9 49	10 1	10 6	10 21
Clapham Junction	8 37	9 41	8 46	8 50	8 56	9 9	9 13	9 19	9 24	9 36	9 40	9 44	9 52	10 4	10 9	10 24
Battersea Park	—	8ᴬ44	—	8 53	—	9 13	—	9 22	—	—	—	9ᴬ47	—	10 7	—	10 27
Victoria	8 43	8 48	8 52	8 57	9 2	9 17	9 19	9 26	9 31	9 44	9 47	9 51	9 58	10 11	10 15	10 30

WEEK DAYS.	AM	AM	AM	AM	AM	AM	AM	AM	AM	AM	PM	PM	PM	d	PM	PM
Crystal Palace dep.	10 20	10 35	—	10 52	11 10	11 25	11 39	11 57	12 11	12 27	12 41	—	12 53	1 8		
Gipsy Hill	10 22	10 37	—	10 54	11 12	11 27	11 42	11 59	12 14	12 29	12 44	—	12 56	1 11		
West Norwood	10 24	10 39	—	10 57	11 14	11 29	11 44	12 1	12 16	12 31	12 46	—	12 58	1 13		
Streatham Hill	10 28	10 43	10 47	11 0	11 18	11 33	11 48	12 5	12 20	12 35	12 50	12 59	1 2	1 17		
Balham	10 31	10 46	10 50	11 3	11 21	11 36	11 50	12 8	12 23	12ᴹ38	12 53	1 2	1 5	1 20		
Wandsworth Common	10 33	10 48	10 52	11 8	11 23	11 39	11 53	12 10	12 25	12ᴹ40	12 55	1 4	1 7	1 22		
Clapham Junction	10 36	10 51	10 55	11 8	11 26	11 41	11 56	12 13	12 29	12ᴹ43	12 58	—	1 10	1 25		
Battersea Park	10 39	10 55	10 58	—	—	11 59	—	—	12 31	—	1 1	—	1 13	1 28		
Victoria	10 43	10 59	11 2	11·14	11 32	11 47	12 3	12 19	12 35	12 49	1 5	1 13	1 16	1 32		

WEEK DAYS.	d	PM	PM	PM	d	PM	PM	PM	PM	PM	d	e	PM	PM	PM	PM
Crystal Palace..dep.	1 24	—	1 40	1 54	2 10	—	2 27	2 41	2 58	3 12	—	3 23	3 41	4 3	—	4 27
Gipsy Hill	1 27	—	1 42	1 56	2 14	—	2 29	2 44	3 0	3 15	—	3 30	3 44	4 5	—	4 29
West Norwood	1 29	—	1 44	1 58	2 16	—	2 31	2 46	3 2	3 17	—	3 32	3 46	4 7	—	4 31
Streatham Hill	1 33	1 44	1 48	2 2	2 20	2 31	2 35	2 50	3 6	3 21	3 31	3 36	3 50	4 11	4 33	4 35
Balham	1 36	1 47	1 51	2 5	2 23	2 34	2 38	2 53	3 9	3 24	3 34	3 39	3 53	4 14	4 33	4 38
Wandsworth Common	1 38	1 49	1 53	2 7	2 25	2 36	2ᴹ40	2 55	3 11	3 26	3 36	3 41	3 55	4 16	4 35	4 40
Clapham Junction	1 41	1 52	1 56	2 10	2 28	2 39	2 43	2 58	3 14	3 29	3 39	3 44	3 58	4 19	4 38	4 43
Battersea Park	1 44	—	1 58	—	2 31	—	—	3 1	—	3 32	3 42	3 47	4 1	—	—	4ᴬ46
Victoria	1 48	1 53	2 3	2 16	2 35	2 45	2 49	3 5	3 20	3 35	3 46	3 51	4 5	4 25	4 44	4 50

WEEK DAYS.	d	e	PM	PM	PM	e	PM	PM	d	e	e '	d	e	PM	PM	PM
Crystal Palace..dep.	4 38	—	4 58	5 10	5 26	—	5 45	5 54	—	—	6 8	6 12	—	6 25	6 42	6 47
Gipsy Hill	4 40	—	5 0	5 12	5 28	—	5 47	5 57	—	—	6 10	6 14	—	6 27	6 44	6 49
West Norwood	4 42	—	5 2	5 13	5 30	—	5 49	5 59	—	—	6 12	6 16	—	6 29	6 46	6 51
Streatham Hill	4 46	4 46	5 6	5 17	5 34	5 44	5 53	6 3	6 6	6 13	6 16	6 20	6 26	6 33	6 50	6 55
Balham	4 49	4 49	5 9	5 20	5 37	5 47	5 56	6 6	6 9	6 16	6 19	6 23	6 29	6 36	6 53	6 58
Wandsworth Common	4 51	4 51	5 11	5 22	5 39	5 49	5 58	6 8	6 11	6 18	6 21	6 25	6 31	6 38	6 55	7 0
Clapham Junction	4 54	4 54	5 14	5 25	5 42	5 52	6 1	6 11	6 14	6 22	6 24	6 28	6 34	6 41	6 57	7 3
Battersea Park	—	—	—	—	—	5ᴴ55	—	—	—	6ᴬ17	6ᴬ25	—	—	—	6ᴬ45	7ᴬ 8
Victoria	5 0	5 1	5 20	5 31	5 49	5 59	6 7	6 18	6 21	6 29	6 31	5 34	6 40	6 48	7 4	7 12

WEEK DAYS.	e	PM	d	PM	PM	PM	PM	PM	PM	PM	PM	PM	PM	PM	PM	PM
Crystal Palace..dep.	6 58	6 59	7 9	—	7 30	7 47	7 59	8 14	—	8 30	8 45	9 0	9 14	9 22	9 39	
Gipsy Hill	7 0	7 2	7 12	—	7 32	7 50	8 2	8 17	—	8 33	8 47	9 2	—	9 25	9 41	
West Norwood	7 0	7 4	7 14	—	7 34	7 52	8 4	8 18	—	8 34	8 49	9 4	—	9 27	9 43	
Streatham Hill	7 4	7 8	7 18	7 27	7 88	7 55	8 8	8 22	8 29	8 38	8 53	9 8	9 21	9 31	9 47	
Balham	—	7 11	7 21	7 30	7 41	7 59	8 11	8 25	8 32	8 41	8 56	9 11	9 29	9 34	9 50	
Wandsworth Common	—	7 13	7 23	7 32	7 43	8 1	8 13	8 27	8 34	8 43	8 58	9 13	—	9 36	—	
Clapham Junction	7 12	7 16	7 26	7 35	7 46	8 4	8 16	8 30	8 38	8 46	9 1	9 16	9 30	9 39	9 54	
Battersea Park	—	7ᴬ19	7ᴬ29	—	7ᴴ49	—	—	—	8 33	8 41	8 49	—	—	9 42	—	
Victoria	7 17	7 23	7 33	7 41	7 53	8 10	8 22	8 37	8 45	8 53	9 7	9 22	9 38	9 45	10 0	

WEEK DAYS.	PM	PM	PM	PM	PM	PM	PM	PM								
Crystal Palace..dep.	9 55	10 15	10 32	10 50	11 10											
Gipsy Hill	9 57	10 17	10 35	10 52	11 12	11 42										
West Norwood	9 59	10 19	10 37	10 54	11 14	11 44										
Streatham Hill	10 3	10 23	10 41	10 55	11 15	11 48										
Balham	10 6	10 26	10 44	11 1	11 21	11 51										
Wandsworth Common	10 8	10 28	10 46	11 3	11 23											
Clapham Junction	10 11	10 31	10 49	11 6	11 26	11 55										
Battersea Park	10 14	10 34	—	11 9	11 29	11 58										
Victoria	10 18	10 38	10 55	11 13	11 33	12 2										

d Saturdays only.

e Saturdays excepted.

h Calls to set down passengers only

SUNDAYS.	AM	AM	AM	AM	AM	AM	AM	AM	AM	AM	AM	AM	AM	AM		PM
Crystal Palace..dep.	6 54	7 10	7 29	7 50	8 10	8 30	8 50	9 10	9 29	9 50	10 10	10 30	10 50		Then at	10 10
Gipsy Hill	6 56	7 12	7 32	7 52	8 12	8 31	8 52	9 12	9 32	9 52	10 12	10 32	10 52		the same	10 12
West Norwood	6 58	7 14	7 34	7 54	8 14	8 34	8 54	9 14	9 34	9 54	10 14	10 34	10 54		minutes	10 14
Streatham Hill	7 2	7 18	7 38	7 58	8 18	8 38	8 59	9 18	9 38	9 58	10 18	10 38	10 58		past each	10 18
Balham	7 5	7 21	7 41	8 1	8 21	8 41	9 1	9 21	9 41	10 1	10 21	10 41	11 1		hour until	10 21
Wandsworth Common	7 7	7 23	7 43	8 3	8 23	8 43	9 3	9 23	9 43	10 3	10 23	10 43	11 3			10 23
Clapham Junction	7 10	7 26	7 46	8 6	8 26	8 46	9 6	9 26	9 46	10 6	10 26	10 46	11 6			10 26
Battersea Park	7 13	7 29	7 49	9 8	8 29	8 49	9 9	9 29	9 49	10 9	10 29	10 49	11 9			10 29
Victoria	7 17	7 33	7 53	8 13	8 33	8 53	9 13	9 33	9 53	10 13	10 33	10 53	11 13			10 33

SUNDAYS.	PM	PM	PM	PM												
Crystal Palace..dep.	10 30	10 50	11 10													
Gipsy Hill	10 32	10 52	11 12													
West Norwood	10 34	10 54	11 14													
Streatham Hill	10 38	10 58	11 18													
Balham	10 41	11 1	11 21													
Wandsworth Common	10 43	11 3	11 23													
Clapham Junction	10 46	11 6	11 26													
Battersea Park	10 49	11 9	11 29													
Victoria	10 53	11 13	11 33													

WEEK DAYS.	AM	AM	AM	d	PM	d	d	d	PM	e	d	e	PM
Victoria .....dep.	5 32	7 0	7 32	9 6	1 5	1 22	2 0	2 50	4 33	5 28	5 32	6 18	6 46
Battersea	5 36	7 4	—	—	—	—	—	—	4h37	—	—	—	—
Clapham Junction ..	5 41	7 9	7 40	9 14	1 12	—	2 6	2 57	4 42	—	—	—	6 53
Wandsworth Com...	—	7 10	—	—	1'15	—	2 2	—	—	—	—	—	—
Balham	5 46	7 16	7 46	9 19	1'17	-1 33	2 12	3 2	4 47	5 39	5 42	—	6 59
Anerley	6 13	7 46	8 8	10 1	1 43	1 58	2 48	3 25	5 17	6 13	6 13	6 49	7 25
Penge	6 15	7 48	8 11	10 3	1 46	2 0	2 50	3 27	5 19	6 15	6 15	6 51	7 27

WEEK DAYS.	e	PM	PM
Victoria ....dep.	7 6	9 15	9 55
Battersea	—	9 6	9h59
Clapham Junction ..	—	9 22	10 4
Wandsworth Com...	—	—	—
Balham	—	9 27	10 9
Anerley	7 39	9 50	10 47
Penge	7 41	9 52	10 49

WEEK DAYS.	AM	AM	AM	d	PM	d	d	d	PM	PM	e	e	d	e	PM
Penge ....dep.	5 33	7 18	9 37	12 23	—	1 50	2 3	3 25	5 10	5 33	—	6 33	6 49	—	7 20
Anerley	5 35	7 20	9 39	12 25	1 0	1 58	2 6	3 27	5 13	5 39	5 45	6 51	6 51	—	7 22
Balham	6 3	7 58	10 8	—	1 23	2 25	2 39	3 56	5 40	6 10	6 10	7 16	7 16	7 21	7 49
Wandsworth Com...	6 6	8 1	10 11	—	—	—	2 42	3 59	—	—	—	—	—	7 23	7 52
Clapham Junction ..	6 8	8 5	10 15	—	—	2 30	2 46	4 3	5 45	6 15	6 15	7 21	7 21	7 26	7 56
Battersea	6 9	—	—	—	—	—	3 1	4 8	—	—	6 23	—	—	—	8 1
Victoria	6 15	8 13	10 24	1 5	1 35	2 39	2 54	4 13	5 52	6 23	6 23	7 29	7 29	7 33	8 6

WEEK DAYS.	PM	PM	PM
Penge ....dep.	8 30	9 47	10 52
Anerley	8 32	9 49	10 54
Balham	8 56	10 12	11 18
Wandsworth Com...	—	10 28	11 21
Clapham Junction ..	9 1	10 17	11 25
Battersea	—	10 34	—
Victoria	9 8	10 25	11 33

SUNDAYS.	AM	AM	PM	PM	PM	PM	PM	PM	PM
Victoria .....dep.	8 5	9 47	12 40	1 28	4 10	6 5	7 10	8 42	9 42
Battersea	8 9	9 43	—	1 32	4 14	6 3	7 14	8 43	9h46
Clapham Junction ..	8 14	9 54	12 47	1 38	4 19	6 12	7 19	8 49	9 52
Wandsworth Com...	8 18	9 50	—	1 41	4 23	6 16	7 23	8 50	9 50
Balham	8 21	9 59	12 52	1 44	4 26	6 19	7 26	8 54	9 58
Anerley	8 44	10 22	1 16	2 9	4 49	6 43	7 51	9 18	10 22
Penge	8 46	10 24	1 18	2 11	4 51	6 45	7 53	9 20	10 24

SUNDAYS.	AM	AM	PM	PM	PM	PM	PM	PM
Penge ....dep.	8 15	10 1	2 10	3 35	6 5	7 45	9 45	
Anerley	8 17	10 3	2 12	3 37	6 7	7 47	9 47	
Balham	8 43	10 26	2 35	4 0	6 31	8 10	10 14	
Wandsworth Com...	8 46	10 29	2 38	—	6 34	8 23	10 23	
Clapham Junction ..	8 50	10 33	2 42	4 6	6 38	8 15	10 19	
Battersea	8 55	10 38	—	—	6 43	8 29	10 29	
Victoria	9 0	10 43	2 49	4 13	6 48	8 22	10 27	

d Saturdays only.   *e Saturdays excepted.*   *h Calls to take up Passengers only.*

LONDON BRIDGE TO CRYSTAL PALACE.

WEEK DAYS.	AM	AM	AM	AM	AM	AM	AM	AM	d	PM	e	d	PM	e	d
London Bridge dep.	6 12	—	7 45	8 8	8 36	8 50	9 55	10 30	12 12	12 28	1 11	1 12	1 17	1 40	1 42	1 48
New Cross Gate	6 18	7 24	7 51	8 14	8 43	8 56	10	10 36	12 18	12 34	1 17	1 19	1 24	1 46	1 48	—
Brockley	6 22	7 28	7 55	8 18	8 46	9	3 10	10 40	12 22	12 38	—	1 23	1 28	1 50	1 52	—
Honor Oak Park.....	6 27	7 33	8 0	8 23	8 52	9	5 10 11	10 45	12 27	12 42	1 23	1 28	1 33	1 55	1 57	1 59
Forest Hill	6 31	7 37	8 4	8 27	8 55	9	9 10 15	10 48	12 31	12 46	1 27	1 32	1 37	1 58	2 0	2 4
Sydenham..........	6 34	7 40	8 7	8 30	8 58	9	12 10 18	10 51	12 34	12 49	1 30	1 35	1 40	2 1	2 3	2 7
Crystal Palace.....	6 39	7 45	8 12	8 35	9 3	9	17 10 23	10 57	12 39	12 55	1 35	1 41	—	2 7	2 8	2 13

WEEK DAYS.	d	PM		PM	PM				PM				PM	PM			PM	PM
London Bridge dep.	2 5	2 40	3 10	3 20	4 26	4 53	5 18	5 33	5 53	6 10	6 20	6 48	7 12	7 48
New Cross Gate	—	2 46	—	3 26	4 32	5 0	5 24	5 26	5 39	5 59	—	6 26	6 45	6 54	7 18	7 54
Brockley	—	2 50	—	3 30	4 36	5 4	5 28	5 30	5 43	6 3	—	6 30	—	6 58	7 22	7 58
Honor Oak Park....	—	2 55	3 20	3 35	4 41	5 9	5 33	5 35	5 48	6 8	6 23	6 35	6 51	7 3	7 26	8 2
Forest Hill	2 16	2 58	3 24	3 39	4 44	5 12	5 37	—	5 52	6 12	6 27	6 39	6 55	7 7	7 30	8 6
Sydenham	—	3 1	3 27	3 42	4 47	5 15	5 40	—	5 55	6 15	6 30	6 42	6 58	7 10	7 33	8 9
Crystal Palace.....	2 22	3 6	3 32	3 47	4 52	5 20	5 45	5 42	6 0	6 20	6 35	6 48	7 3	7 15	7 38	8 14

WEEK DAYS.	PM	PM	PM	PM
London Bridge dep.	8 46	9 50	10 38	10 50
New Cross Gate	8 52	9 56	10 45	10 57
Brockley	8 56	10 0	10 49	11 1
Honor Oak Park....	9 0	10 4	10 54	11 6
Forest Hill.........	9 4	10 8	10 57	11 10
Sydenham	9 7	10 11	11 0	11 13
Crystal Palace.....	9 12	10 16	11 5	—

SUNDAYS.	AM	AM	AM	AM		PM	PM	PM	PM	PM	PM
London Bridge dep.	8 0	9 0	10 0	10 0	Then at the same minutes past each hour until	5 0	7 0	8 0	9 0	10 40	11 0
New Cross Gate	8 6	9 6	10 0	10 6		5 6	7 6	8 6	9 6	10 46	11 6
Brockley	8 10	9 10	10 10	10 10		5 10	7 10	8 10	9 10	10 50	11 10
Honor Oak Park.....	8 15	9 15	10 15	10 15		5 14	7 14	8 14	9 14	10 54	11 14
Forest Hill	8 19	9 19	10 19	10 19		5 18	7 18	8 18	9 18	10 58	11 18
Sydenham	8 22	9 22	10 22	10 22		5 21	7 21	8 21	9.21	11 1	11 21
Crystal Palace.....	8 26	9 26	10 26	10 26		5 26	7 26	8 26	9 26	11 6	11 26

d Saturdays only.   *e Saturdays excepted.*

WEEK DAYS.	AM	AM	AM	AM	AM	AM	AM	AM	AM	AM	AM	PM
CRYSTAL PALACE dep.	7 10	7 3)	7 52	8 19	—	8 38	8 42	8 58	9 20	9 55	10 55	12 10
Sydenham	7 13	7 53	7 55	8 22	8 26	8 41	—	9 1	9 24	9 58	10 58	12 13
Forest Hill	7 16	7 35	7 58	—	8 29	—	8 47	9 4	9 27	10 1	11 1	12 16
Honor Oak Park	7 19	7 38	8 1	8 26	8 32	8 46	8 50	—	9 30	—	11 4	12 19
Brockley	7 22	—	8 4	8 29	8 35	8 49	—	9 10	9 33	10 6	11 7	12 22
New Cross Gate	7 25	7 44	8 7	8 32	8 38	—	—	9 13	9 36	—	11 10	12 25
LONDON BRIDGE	7 33	7 52	8 14	8 39	8 45	8 58	9 1	9 2)	9 44	10 14	11 17	12 32

WEEK DAYS.	d	d	PM	d	PM	PM	PM	e	PM	PM	e	PM	e	d	e
CRYSTAL PALACE dep.	12 55	1 13	1 42	2 10	2 38	3 14	3 42	4 0	4 26	5 7	5 26	5 46	6 7	6 10	6 27
Sydenham	12 58	1 16	1 45	2 13	2 41	3 17	3 45	4 3	4 29	5 10	5 29	5 51	6 10	6 13	6 30
Forest Hill	1 1	1 19	1 47	2 16	2 44	3 20	3 48	4 6	4 32	5 13	5 32	5 54	6 13	6 16	6 33
Honor Oak Park	1 4	1 22	1 51	2 19	2 47	3 23	3 51	4 9	4 35	5 16	5 35	5 57	6 16	—	6 36
Brockley	1 7	1 25	1 54	2 22	2 50	3 26	3 54	4 12	—	5 19	5 38	6 0	6 19	—	6 39
New Cross Gate	1 10	1 28	1 57	2 25	2 53	3 29	3 57	4 15	—	5 22	5 41	6 3	6 22	6 22	6 42
LONDON BRIDGE	1 18	1 35	2 5	2 32	3 0	3 37	4 4	4 23	4 47	5 29	5 49	6 10	6 29	6 29	--

WEEK DAYS.	PM	PM	PM	PM	PM	PM	PM	PM	PM	PM	PM
CRYSTAL PALACE dep.	6 42	7 12	7 37	7 58	8 30	9 28	—	10 35	11 15		
Sydenham	6 45	7 15	7 40	8 1	8 33	9 31	955	10 38	11 18		
Forest Hill	6 48	7 18	7 43	8 4	8 36	9 34	958	10 41	11 21		
Honor Oak Park	6 51	7 21	7 46	8 7	8 39	9 37	10 1	10 44	11 24		
Brockley	6 54	7 24	7 49	8 10	8 42	9 40	10 4	10 47	11 27		
New Cross Gate	6 57	7 27	7 52	8 13	8 45	9 43	10 7	10 50	11 30		
LONDON BRIDGE	7 5	7 34	7 59	8 20	8 52	9 50	1014	10 57	11 37		

SUNDAYS.	AM	AM	AM	AM	AM	PM	PM	PM	PM	PM	PM	PM	PM	PM	PM
CRYSTAL PALACE dep.	7 32	8 32	9 32	10 32	11 32	12 32	1 32	2 32	3 32	4 32	6 2	7 32	8 32	9 32	10 32	11 32
Sydenham	7 35	8 35	9 35	10 35	11 35	12 35	1 35	2 35	3 35	4 35	6 5	7 35	8 35	9 35	10 35	11 35
Forest Hill	7 38	8 38	9 38	10 38	11 38	12 38	1 38	2 38	3 38	4 38	6 8	7 38	8 38	9 38	10 38	11 38
Honor Oak Park	7 41	8 41	9 41	10 41	11 41	12 41	1 41	2 41	3 41	4 41	6 11	7 41	8 41	9 41	10 41	11 41
Brockley	7 44	8 44	9 44	10 44	11 44	12 44	1 44	2 44	3 44	4 44	6 14	7 44	8 44	9 44	10 44	11 44
New Cross Gate	7 47	8 47	9 47	10 47	11 47	12 47	1 47	2 47	3 47	4 47	6 17	7 47	8 47	9 47	10 47	11 47
LONDON BRIDGE	7 52	8 54	9 54	10 54	11 54	12 54	1 54	2 54	3 54	4 54	6 24	7 51	8 54	9 54	10 54	11 54

d Saturdays only.   e Saturdays excepted.

LONDON BRIDGE TO CRYSTAL PALACE, VIA TULSE HILL.

WEEK DAYS.	AM	AM	AM	AM	AM	AM	AM	AM	AM	AM	d	e	d
LONDON BR. ...dep.	7 5	7 25	7 40	8 10	8 35	9 25	9 57	10 40	11 15	11 52	12 30	12 43	12 56
Queen's Road	7 10	7 30	7 45	8 15	8 46	—	—	10 45	11 20	11 57	—	12 48	—
Peckham Rye	7 12	7 32	7 47	8 17	8 42	9 33	10 4	10 47	11 22	11 59	12 37	12 50	1 3
East Dulwich	7 15	7 35	7 50	8 20	8 45	9 36	10 7	10 50	11 25	12 2	12 40	12 53	1 6
North Dulwich	7 17	7 37	7 52	8 22	8 47	9 38	10 9	10 52	11 27	12 4	12 42	12 55	1 8
Tulse Hill	7 20	7 40	7 56	8 25	8 50	9 42	10 12	10 56	11 30	12 7	12 45	12 59	1 12
West Norwood	7 23	7 43	7 59	8 28	8 53	9 46	10 15	10 59	11 33	12 10	12 48	1 2	1 15
Gipsy Hill	7 26	7 46	8 2	8 31	8 56	9 49	10 18	11 2	11 36	12 13	12 51	1 5	1 18
CRYSTAL PALACE	7 29	7 49	8 5	8 34	8 59	9 52	10 21	11 5	11 39	12 16	12 54	1 8	1 21

WEEK DAYS.	PM	d	e	PM	PM	PM	PM	PM	PM	PM	PM	e	PM
LONDON BR. ...dep.	1 20	1 35	1 52	2 2	2 22	2 52	3 21	3 36	4 2	4 23	4 40	5 4	5 23	5 37
Queen's Road	1 25	1 40	1 57	—	2 27	2 57	3 26	3 41	4 7	—	4 45	—	—	5 42
Peckham Rye	1 27	1 42	1 59	2 9	2 29	2 59	3 28	3 43	4 9	—	4 47	5 11	—	5 45
East Dulwich	1 30	1 45	2 2	2 12	2 32	3 2	3 31	3 46	4 12	4 31	50	5 14	5 31	5 48
North Dulwich	1 32	1 47	2 4	2 14	2 34	3 4	3 33	3 48	4 14	4 33	4 52	5 16	5 33	5 50
Tulse Hill	1 36	1 50	2 7	2 17	2 37	3 7	3 36	3 51	4 17	4 36	4 55	5 19	5 37	5 53
West Norwood	1 39	1 53	2 10	2 20	2 40	3 10	3 39	3 54	4 20	4 39	4 58	5 22	5 40	5 56
Gipsy Hill	1 42	1 56	—	2 23	2 43	3 13	3 42	3 57	4 23	4 42	5 1	5 25	5 43	5 59
CRYSTAL PALACE	1 45	1 59	2 14	2 26	2 46	3 16	3 45	4 0	4 26	4 45	5 4	5 28	5 45	6 2

WEEK DAYS.	PM	e	e	PM	e	PM	PM	PM	PM	PM	d	PM	e	PM
LONDON BR. ...dep.	6 0	6 20	6 27	6 37	7 0	7 18	7 25	7 40	8 13	8 23	8 40	9 17	9 39	9 55
Queen's Road	—	—	6 32	6 42	7 5	7 23	7 30	7 45	8 18	—	8 45	9 24	9 35	10 0
Peckham Rye	6 8	—	6 34	6 44	7 7	7 25	7 22	7 47	8 20	8 29	8 47	9 26	9 37	10 2
East Dulwich	6 11	6 28	6 37	—	7 10	7 28	7 35	7 50	8 23	8 32	8 50	9 29	9 40	10 5
North Dulwich	6 14	6 30	6 39	6 49	7 12	7 30	7 37	7 52	8 25	—	8 52	9 31	9 42	10 7
Tulse Hill	6 16	6 33	6 42	6 52	7 15	7 34	7 40	7 55	8 28	8 36	8 55	9 34	9 45	10 10
West Norwood	6 18	6 36	6 45	6 54	7 18	7 37	7 43	7 58	8 31	8 39	8 58	9 37	9 48	10 13
Gipsy Hill	6 22	6 39	6 48	6 57	7 21	7 40	7 46	8 3	8 34	8 42	9 1	9 40	9 51	10 16
CRYSTAL PALACE.	6 26	6 42	6 51	7 0	7 24	7 43	7 49	8 6	8 37	8 45	9 4	9 43	9 54	10 19

WEEK DAYS.	PM	PM
LONDON BR. ...dep.	10 22	10 55
Queen's Road	10 27	—
Peckham Rye	10 29	11 2
East Dulwich	10 32	11 5
North Dulwich	10 34	11 7
Tulse Hill	10 37	11 10
West Norwood	10 40	11 13
Gipsy Hill	10 43	11 16
CRYSTAL PALACE	10 46	11 19

SUNDAYS	AM		PM	PM
LONDON BR. dep.	8 35		9 35	10 52
Queen's Road ..	8 42	Then at	9 42	10 59
Peckham Rye ..	8 44	the same	9 44	11 1
East Dulwich ..	8 47	minutes	9 47	11 4
North Dulwich..	—	past each		
Tulse Hill	8 52	hour until	9 52	11 9
West Norwood ..	8 55		9 55	11 12
Gipsy Hill	8 58		9 58	11 15
CRYSTAL PALACE	9 1		10 1	11 18

d Saturdays only.   e Saturdays excepted.

WEEK DAYS.	AM	AM	AM	AM	AM	AM	AM	AM	AM	AM	AM	AM	AM	PM
Crystal Palace ....dep.	6 4	6 35	7 12	7 45	8 6	8 27	—	8 47	9 12	9 30	10 11	10 42	11 15	12 4
Gipsy Hill	6 7	6 37	7 14	7 47	8 9	8 23	—	8 49	9 14	9 32	10 13	10 44	11 17	12 7
West Norwood	6 9	6 39	7 16	7 49	8 11	8 31	—	8 51	9 16	9 34	10 15	10 46	11 19	12 9
Tulse Hill	6 12	6 42	7 19	7 52	8 13	8 32	—	—	9 19	9 37	10 18	10 49	11 22	12 12
North Dulwich	6 15	6 45	7 22	7 55	8 16	8 35	8 50	8 57	9 22	9 40	10 21	10 52	11 25	12 15
East Dulwich	6 17	6 47	7 24	7 57	8 18	8 37	—	—	9 24	9 42	10 23	10 54	11 27	12 17
Peckham Rye	6 19	6 49	7 27	7 59	8 21	—	—	9 1⅓	9 27	9 44	10 25	10 56	11 29	12 20
Queen's Road	6 21	6 51	7 29	8 1	h	—	—	9 1⅓	—	—	10 27	10 58	—	—
London Bridge	6 27	6 57	7 34	8 7	8 28	8 47	9 1	9 8	9 34	9 51	10 33	11 4	11 37	12 25

WEEK DAYS.	d	PM	e	PM	d	PM	PM	d	PM	d
Crystal Palace ....dep.	12 34	12 46	1 21	1 50	2 21	2 45	3 5	3 20	3 45	4 0	4 13	4 42
Gipsy Hill	12 36	12 48	1 23	1 52	2 23	2 47	3 7	3 22	3 47	4 2	4 15	4 44
West Norwood	12 38	12 50	1 25	1 54	2 25	2 49	3 9	3 24	3 49	4 4	4 17	4 46
Tulse Hill	12 41	12 53	1 28	1 58	2 28	2 52	3 12	3 27	3 52	4 7	4 20	4 49
North Dulwich	12 44	12 56	1 31	2 1	2 31	2 55	3 15	3 30	3 55	4 10	4 23	4 52
East Dulwich	12 46	12 58	1 33	2 3	2 33	2 57	3 17	3 32	3 57	4 12	4 25	4 54
Peckham Rye	12 49	1 1	1 36	2 6	2 35	2 59	3 19	3 34	3 59	4 15	4 27	4 56
Queen's Road	—	—	—	2 8	2 37	—	—	—	—	—	4 29	—
London Bridge	12 56	1 8	1 43	2 16	2 43	3 7	3 27	3 42	4 7	4 22	4 35	5 4

WEEK DAYS.	e	e	d	e	PM	e	PM	e	PM	PM	e
Crystal Palace ....dep.	4 45	5 6	5 20	5 39	5 59	6 22	6 30	6 40	6 55	7 15	7 40	8 10	8 22
Gipsy Hill	4 47	5 9	5 22	5 41	6 1	6 25	6 32	6 42	6 57	7 17	7 42	8 12	8 24
West Norwood	4 49	5 11	5 24	5 43	6 3	6 27	6 34	6 44	6 59	7 19	7 44	8 14	8 26
Tulse Hill	4 52	5 14	5 27	5 46	6 6	6 30	6 37	6 47	7 2	7 22	7 47	8 17	8 29
North Dulwich	4 55	5 17	5 30	5 49	6 9	6 33	6 40	6 50	7 5	7 25	7 50	8 20	8 32
East Dulwich	4 57	5 19	5 32	5 51	6 11	6 35	6 42	6 52	7 7	7 27	7 52	8 22	8 34
Peckham Rye	4 59	5 22	5 35	5 54	6 13	6 38	6 45	6 54	7 9	7 29	7 55	8 24	8 37
Queen's Road	—	5 24	—	5 56	—	6 40	—	—	—	—	—	—	—
London Bridge	5 6	5 32	5 45	6 4	6 20	6 46	6 51	7 1	7 16	7 36	8 1	8 31	8 44

WEEK DAYS.	PM	PM
Crystal Palace ....dep.	8 48	9 52
Gipsy Hill	8 50	9 54
West Norwood	8 52	9 56
Tulse Hill	8 55	9 59
North Dulwich	8 58	10 2
East Dulwich	9 0	10 4
Peckham Rye	9 3	10 6
Queen's Road	—	10 8
London Bridge	9 9	10 14

SUNDAYS.	AM		PM	PM
Crystal Palace ....dep.	8 5		9 5	10 25
Gipsy Hill	8 7	Then at	9 7	10 27
West Norwood	8 9	the same	9 9	10 29
Tulse Hill	8 12	minutes	9 12	10 32
North Dulwich		past each		
East Dulwich	8 17	hour until	9 17	10 37
Peckham Rye	8 19		9 19	10 39
Queen's Road	8 21		9 21	10 41
London Bridge	8 29		9 29	10 49

d Saturdays only.   *e* Saturdays excepted.   *h* Sets down passengers only.

VICTORIA AND LONDON BRIDGE TO EPSOM DOWNS.

WEEK DAYS.	AM	AM	AM	AM	AM	AM	AM	AM	AM	AM	AM	AM	AM	AM
Victoria (L.B.R.) dep.	6 18	7 18	—	7 45	—	—	8 58	8 53	9 53	10 8	10 33	—	10 50	11·40
London Bridge	6 35	7 7	7 30	7 35	—	8 24	—	8 53	9 35	1030	10 35	—	10 47	—
Sutton	7 35	8 2	8 22	8 32	8 41	9 16	9 31	10 0	10 25	11 4	11 18	10 37	11 40	12 17
Belmont	7 37	8 6	8 26	—	8 44	9 19	9 19	9 35	10 3	10 32	11 7	11 21	10 40	11 51	12 20
Banstead	7 42	8 10	8 29	8 41	8 48	9 23	9 39	10 7	10 36	—	11 25	10 44	11 55	12 24
Epsom Downs	—	—	—	8 46	9 15	—	9 44	—	10 42	—	11 31	—	—	12 30

WEEK DAYS.	AM	e	d	PM	e	d	PM	d	e	d	e	d	d₁
Victoria (L.B.R.) dep.	11 14	11 58	12 25	12 35	12 35	—	12 35	1 12	1 40	1 45	2 12	2 17	2 18
London Bridge	11 29	2	12 24	12 24	1 5	1 0	1 25	1 50	1 33	1 53	2 15	2 0	2 38
Sutton	11 32	1 5	1 7	1 20	1 36	1 40	2 0	2 6	2 24	2 17	2 27	3 10	2 47	3 15
Belmont	—	1 5	1 7	1 23	1 39	1 44	2 3	2 11	2 27	2 20	2 30	3 15	2 51	3 18
Banstead	—	1 9	1 11	1ᵈ 33	1 44	1 49	2 7	2 17	2 31	2 25	2 34	3 17	2 56	3 22
Epsom Downs	—	—	—	—	—	—	2 13	2 22	—	—	2 40	3 23	—	3 28

WEEK DAYS.	PM	PM	PM	PM	PM	PM	e	PM	PM	PM	PM	PM	PM
Victoria (L.B.R.) dep.	2·45	3 0	3 55	4 5	4 53	—	5 22	—	6 0	—	6 30	6 53	7 20	—	7·55
London Bridge	2·38	3 10	4 0	4 9	5 0	5 14	5e29	5 44	6 28	6 k30	6 47	7 15	7 30	7 40
Sutton	3 26	3 57	4 35	4 50	5 28	5 50	6 9	6 18	6 40	7 5	7 36	7 55	8 10	8 32
Belmont	3 30	4 0	4 38	4 53	5 31	5 54	6 12	6 18	6 31	6 43	7 8	7 39	7 58	8 13	8 36
Banstead	3 34	4 4	4 42	4 58	5 35	5 58	6 16	—	6 35	6 47	7 12	7 43	8 2	8 17	8 39
Epsom Downs	—	4 10	—	5 3	—	—	6 22	—	—	—	7 17	—	—	8 22	—

WEEK DAYS.	PM	PM	PM	h
Victoria (L.B.R.) dep.	8 38	8 40	9 30	—
London Bridge	8 22	8 52	—	9 40
Sutton	9 13	9 40	10 30	10 30
Belmont	9 16	9 43	10 8	10 33
Banstead	9 20	9 47	10 11	10 37
Epsom Downs	—	—	—	—

SUNDAYS.	AM	AM	AM	PM	PM	PM	PM	PM	PM	PM	PM	PM	PM	PM	PM
Victoria (L.B.R.) dep.	9 0	9 10	11	12 45	1 10	—	2 5	—	3 0	—	4 5	—	6 30	7 40	8 0	10	9 25
London Bridge	8 55	9 30	10 35	12·45	—	1 25	—	2 40	—	3 50	—	4 43	5 40	6 38	—	8 27	8 45
Sutton	9 35	10 11	11 19	1 30	1 55	2 20	2 47	3 24	3 53	4 24	4 42	5 28	6 26	2 6	3 27	3 56	9 0	9 11	10 9
Belmont	9 38	10 14	11 43	1 33	1 58	2 23	2 51	3 27	3 56	4 28	4 46	5 32	6 5	36 7	38 8	53 9	14 10 6
Banstead	9 42	10 18	11 46	1 37	2 1	2·27	2 56	3 31	4 0	4 32	4 51	5 36	6 9	6 40	7 41	8 57	9 18	1010
Epsom Downs	—	—	—	—	—	—	—	—	—	—	—	—	—	—	—	—	—

d Saturdays only.   *e* Saturdays excepted.   *h* Wednesdays and Saturdays only.
k On Saturdays leave at 6.16.

EPSOM DOWNS TO LONDON BRIDGE AND VICTORIA.

WEEK DAYS.	AM	AM	AM	AM	AM	AM	AM	AM	AM	AM	AM	AM	AM	AM	AM
Epsom Downs ....dep	—	8	8	—	—	—	—	—	9 10	—	9 42	—	10 22	10 43	—
Banstead	7 45	8 12	8 20	8 32	8 40	8 52	9 1	9 14	9 28	9 46	10 11	10 26	10 52	—	—
Belmont ......·....	7 47	8 15	8 22	8 34	8 42	8 54	9 3	9 18	9 30	9 49	10 13	10 28	10 55	11 10	11 33
Sutton.............	7 51	8 19	8 26	8 38	8 46	8 58	9 7	9 22	9 34	9 53	1C 17	10 33	10 59	11 15	11 36
London Bridge	8 41	9 5	9 5	—	9 17	9 30	9 51	10 1	—	10 22	10 45	11 30	11 51	11 50	12 8
Victoria (L.B.R.) ...	8 32	8 53	—	9 12	—	—	9 34	9 55	10 4	10 26	10 53	—	11 42	11 44	—

WEEK DAYS.	AM	AM	AM	PM	PM	PM	e	e	d	e	d	e	d	e	PM	d	PM
Epsom Downs ....dep.	11 32	—	—	12 32	12 50	—	—	—	—	—	—	—	—	2 17	—	2 50	3 38
Banstead	11 36	11 52	—	12 36	12 54	1 12	1 14	—	1 37	1 47	2 0	2 21	2 34	2 55	3 42
Belmont	11 39	11 54	12 35	12 40	12 58	1 14	1 16	1 27	1 40	1 49	2 4	2 24	2 36	3 0	3 45
Sutton.............	11 43	11 58	12 38	12 44	1 2	1 18	1 20	1 30	1 43	1 53	2 8	2 26	2 40	3 4	3 49
London Bridge	—	1 28	1 12	1 23	1 55	—	2 49	—	2 46	2 46	3 13	3 32	3 32	3 55	4 27
Victoria (L.B.R.) ...	12 42	12 42	—	1 57	1 57	1 57	1 57	2 35	—	2 54	2 54	3 30	3 30	4 0	4 34

WEEK DAYS.	PM	PM	PM	PM	PM	e	PM	PM	PM	PM	PM	PM	PM	PM	PM	PM
Epsom Downs ....dep.	4 15	—	5 10	—	—	6 25	—	—	7 22	—	8 26	—	—	—
Banstead	4 19	4 52	5 14	5 38	6 1	—	6 29	6 53	—	7 26	7 46	8 10	8 30	8 42	9 1	9 23
Belmont	4 22	4 54	5 17	5 40	6 3	6 20	6 32	6 55	7 20	7 29	7 48	8 12	8 33	8 44	9 3	9 25
Sutton.............	4 26	4 58	5 21	5 44	6 7	6 23	6 36	6 59	7 24	7 33	7 52	8 16	8 37	8 48	9 7	9 29
London Bridge	5 15	5 51	6 25	6 58	7 13	7 13	7 49	7 49	7 51	8 41	8 41	9 26	—	9 35	—	10 8
Victoria (L.B.R.) ...	5 12	6 8	6 35	6 44	—	7 12	7 39	7 58	8 15	—	8 55	9 38	—	9 42	10 1

WEEK DAYS	PM	h
Epsom Downs ....dep.	—	—
Banstead	10 20	10 42
Belmont	10 22	10 44
Sutton.............	10 26	10 48
London Bridge	11 11	11 45
Victoria (L.B.R.) ...	11 20	11 55

d Saturdays only.   *e* Saturdays excepted.
h Wednesdays and Saturdays only.

SUNDAYS.	AM	AM	AM	PM	PM	PM	PM	PM	PM	PM	PM	PM	PM	PM	PM	PM	PM	PM	PM	PM
Epsom Downs ....dep.																			
Banstead	10 0	1026	1152	145	2 8	240	335	355	437	5 5	540	615	650	751	811	822	842	9 1	927	947	1015
Belmont	10 2	1028	1154	147	210	242	337	358	439	5 8	542	617	652	753	813	824	844	9 3	929	949	1017
Sutton.............	10 6	1032	1158	151	214	246	341	4 1	443	513	546	621	656	757	817	828	848	9 7	933	953	1021
London Bridge	11 8	—	1 29	245	—	354	—	—	554	652	729	8 8	846	850	921	—	10 1	1025	11 2	1115
Victoria (L.B.R.)	..| —	11 6	1253	—	253	353	—	448	532	—	—	713	732	837	—	920	942	950	—	1042	1152

CLAPHAM JUNCTION TO KENSINGTON.

First and Third Class only.

WEEK DAYS.	S AM	B AM	S AM	AM	B AM	AM	B AM	B AM	B AM	S AM	B AM	B AM	S AM	AM	B AM	d AM	d AM	d AM	d AM
Clapham Junction....	6 5	6 45	7 10	—	7 33	7 46	8	4 8	15	8 30	8 50	9 35	10 10	10 11	38	11 58	12	5 12	25	1243
Battersea	6 7	6 47	7 13	7 24	7 35	7 49	8	6 8	17	8 32	8 53	9 17	9 38	10 12	—	12	1 12	7 12	27	1246
Chelsea and Fulham	6 10	6 50	7 16	7 27	7 37	7 52	8	9 8	20	8 35	8 56	9 20	9 41	10 15	11 14	4 12	4 12	10 12	30	1249
West Brompton	6 12	6 52	7 18	7 29	7 40	7 54	8	11 8	22	8 37	8 58	9 22	9 43	10 17	—	6 12	6 12	12 12	32	1251
Kensington	6 16	6 55	7 21	7 33	7 44	7 57	8	15 8	26	8 41	9 1	9 26	9 46	10 21	11 50	12	9 12	16 12	36	1254

WEEK DAYS	B PM	d PM	B PM	e PM	S PM	B PM	B PM	B PM	S PM	B PM	B PM	B PM	B PM	S PM	B PM	B PM	S PM	B PM
Clapham Junction....	1 5	1 30	1 58	—	3 34	3 43	4 22	4 46	5	5 5	15	5 35	5 45	6	5 6	34	7 21	—	7 50	8 15
Battersea	1 7	1 33	2 0	3 14	3 37	3 46	4 24	4 49	5	7 5	17	5 38	5 47	6	7 6	37	7 23	7 46	7 53	8 17
Chelsea and Fulham.	1 10	1 36	2	3 17	3 40	3 49	4	27	4 52	5	10	5 20	5	41	5 50	6	10	6	40	7	51	7	56	8 20
West Brompton	1 12	1 38	2	3 19	3 42	3 50	4	29	4 54	5	12	5 22	5	43	5 52	6	12	6	43	7	54	7	58	8 22
Kensington	1 16	1 47	2	9	3 23	3 45	3 54	4 33	4 57	5	16	5 26	5	46	5 56	6	16	6	45	7	32	7	58	8	1 8 26

WEEK DAYS.	AM	AM	AM	AM	AM	AM	AM	AM	AM	AM	AM	d AM	d AM	d AM	d	d
Kensington	6 40	6 52	7 15	7 26	7 39	8	0 8	25	8 40	8 50	9	10 9	37	9	43	9 53	10	5	11	41	12	24	12 45	1 8
West Brompton	6 42	6 55	7 17	7 29	7 41	8	2 8	28	8 42	8 52	9	13 9	40	9	45	9 55	10	8	11	43	12	27	12 47	1 10
Chelsea and Fulham	6 44	6 57	7 19	7 31	7 43	8	4 8	30	8 44	8 54	9	15 9	42	9	47	9 57	10	10	11	45	12	29	—	1 12
Battersea	6 47	7	0 7	22	7 34	7 46	8	7 8	33	8 47	8 57	9	18 9	45	9	50	10	0	10	13	11	48	12	32	—	1 15
Clapham Junction....	—	7	3 7	26	7 37	7 50	8	11 8	36	8 51	9	1 9	21	9	49	9	54	10	4	10	16	11	52	12	35	12	54	1 18

WEEK DAYS.	d PM	PM	e PM	PM	PM	PM	PM	PM	PM	PM	PM	PM	PM	PM	e	e	e	e
Kensington	1 27	1 37	2	2	20	4	6	4	23	4	40	4	50	5	5	520	5	44	6	5	6	32	6	40	7	22	7	45	6	0	0
West Brompton	1 30	1 39	2	2	22	—	4	26	4	42	4	52	5	8	522	5	46	6	7	6	34	6	42	7	25	7	47	8	9	2
Chelsea and Fulham.	1 32	1 41	2	2	24	4	9	4	28	4	44	4	54	5	10	524	5	48	6	10	6	36	6	44	7	27	7	49	8	11	9	4
Battersea	1 35	1 44	2	2	27	—	4	31	4	47	4	57	5	13	527	5	51	6	13	6	39	6	47	7	30	7	52	8	14	9	7
Clapham Junction....	1 38	1 48	2	3	—	4	14	4	34	4	51	5	1 5	15	531	5	55	6	16	6	43	—	7	33	7	56	8	17	9	11

d Saturdays only.   *e* Saturdays excepted.
S Departs from No. 1 Platform, Clapham Junction.
B Departs from No. 12 Platform, Clapham Junction.

No Sunday Trains.

WATERLOO TO EPSOM, LEATHERHEAD AND BOOKHAM.

WEEK DAYS.	AM	AM	AM	AM	AM	AM	AM	AM	AM	AM	AM	d	PM	d	PM	PM	PM	e
Waterloo ....dep.	6 10	6 45	7 45	7 55	8 45	9 45	10 45	11 45	12 45	1 14	1 45	2 14	2 45	3 45	4 45	5 14
Vauxhall.............	6 13	—	—	7 58	—	—	—	—	—	—	—	—	—	—	—	—
Clapham Junction	6 18	—	—	8 3	—	—	—	—	—	—	—	—	—	—	—	—
Earlsfield	6 22	—	—	8 7	—	—	—	—	1 25	—	2 25	—	—	—	5 25
Wimbledon	6 25	7 18	8 0	8 11	9 0	10 0	11 0	12 0	1 0	1 30	2 1	2 30	3 0	4 0	5 0	5 30
Raynes Park	6 29	7 5	8 4	8 14	9 4	10 4	11 4	12 4	1 4	1 34	2 5	2 34	3 4	4 4	5 4	5 34
Worcester Park	6 38	7 10	8 9	8 21	9 9	10 9	11 9	12 9	1 9	1 39	2 10	2 39	3 9	4 9	5 9	5 39
Ewell, West	6 45	7 15	8 15	8 27	9 14	10 14	11 15	12 15	1 15	1 45	2 16	2 45	3 15	4 15	5 15	5 45
Epsom	6 49	7 22	8 20	8 32	9 19	10 23	11 22	12 20	1 20	1 50	2 21	2 51	3 20	4 20	5 21	5 50
Ashtead	7 0	7 28	8 26	—	9 25	10 29	11 28	12 26	1 26	1 56	2 27	2 59	3 26	4 26	5 27	5 56
Leatherhead ....·..	7 7	7 33	8 31	8 45	9 30	10 33	11 33	12 31	1 31	2 0	2 31	3 4	3 31	4 31	5 33	6 0
Bookham.............	7 12	7 40	8 37	8 50	9 37	10 41	11 39	12 37	1 37	2 6	2 39	3 10	3 37	4 37	5 3 6	6 6

WEEK DAYS.	d	e	e	PM	PM	PM	PM	PM	PM	e
Waterloo ....dep.	5 45	5 45	6 14	6 45	7 15	7 45	8 45	9 45	10 45	11 50
Vauxhall.............	—	—	—	—	—	—	9 50	10 50	11 50
Clapham Junction	—	—	—	—	—	—	—	11 56	—
Earlsfield	—	—	—	—	—	—	2 26	—
Wimbledon	6 06	—	6 35	0	7 3	8	9 0	10 0	2	11 2	12 6
Raynes Park	6 46	4 46	34 7	4 7	4 8	4 10	9 4	10 4	6	11 6	12 10
Worcester Park	6 9 6	9 6	39 7	9 7	40 8	10 9	9 10	11 10	11	11 11	12 15
Ewell, West	6 15 6	15 6	44 7	14 7	46 8	15 9	15 10	17	11 17	12 20
Epsom	6 20 6	23 6	53 7	19 7	51 8	24 9	20 10	22	11 22	12 26
Ashtead	6 26 6	30 7	2 7	26 7	57 8	30 9	26 10	28	11 28	12 36
Leatherhead	6 31 6	36 7	7 7	31 8	1 8	36 9	31 10	33	11 32	12 36
Bookham.............	6 37 6	53 7	13 7	3	—	8 44 9	37 10	3	—	12·42

SUNDAYS.	AM	AM	AM	PM	PM	PM	PM	PM	PM	PM	PM
WATERLOO ....dep.	8 18	10 38	11 38	12 38	2 33	4 33	5 38	6 33	7 38	8 33	10 33
Vauxhall	—	—	—	—	—	—	—	—	—	—	—
Clapham Junction	8 28	10 47	11 48	12 47	2 47	4 47	5 48	6 47	7 48	8 47	10 47
Earlsfield	—	—	—	—	—	—	—	—	—	—	—
WIMBLEDON	8 36	10 55	11 56	12 55	2 55	4 55	5 56	6 55	7 56	8 55	10 55
Raynes Park	8 40	10 59	12 0	1 2	2 59	4 59	6 0	6 59	8 0	8 59	10 59
Worcester Park........	8 45	11 4	12 5	1 7	3 4	5 4	6 5	7 4	8 5	9 5	11 4
Ewell, West..........	8 51	11 10	12 11	1 13	3 10	5 10	6 11	7 10	8 10	9 11	11 10
Epsom	8 56	11 15	12 16	1 18	3 15	5 15	6 16	7 15	8 17	9 18	11 15
Ashtead	9 2	11 21	12 22	1 24	3 21	5 21	6 22	7 21	8 23	9 24	11 21
LEATHERHEAD	9 9	11 26	12 29	1 28	3 26	5 23	6 23	7 26	8 31	9 29	11 26
BOOKHAM	9 15	11 35	12 35	1 37	3 35	5 35	6 35	7 35	8 37	9 38	

BOOKHAM, LEATHERHEAD AND EPSOM TO WATERLOO.

WEEK DAYS.	AM	AM	AM	AM	AM	AM.	AM	AM	AM	AM	AM	AM	AM	PM	PM
BOOKHAM ....dep.	—	—	—	—	7 23	7 45	8 6	—	8 47	9 2	9 41	10 41	11 41	12 41	1 41
LEATHERHEAD	5 22	6 22	6 52	—	7 32	7 51	8 13	—	8 53	9 8	9 53	10 51	11 52	12 53	1 53
Ashtead	5 27	6 27	6 57	—	7 37	7 56	8 19	—	8 58	9 13	9 58	10 56	11 57	12 58	1 58
Epsom	5 33	6 33	7 3	7 28	7 43	8 3	8 25	8 39	9 4	9 19	10 4	11 4	12 4	1 4	2 4
Ewell, West..........	5 37	6 37	7 7	7 33	7 47	8 7	—	8 34	9 8	9 23	10 8	11 8	12 8	1 8	2 8
Worcester Park	5 43	6 43	7 13	7 39	7 53	8 13	8 33	8 40	9 14	9 29	10 14	11 14	12 14	1 14	2 14
Raynes Park	5 43	6 48	7 18	7 46	7 58	8 18	—	8 45	9 19	—	10 19	11 19	12 19	1 19	2 19
WIMBLEDON	5 52	6 52	7 22	7 50	8 2	8 22	—	8 49	9 23	—	10 23	11 23	12 23	1 23	2 23
Earlsfield ..., ...	5 56	6 56	7 26	7 56	8 7	8 26	—	—	—	—	—	—	—	—	—
Clapham Junction. arr.	—	—	—	—	—	—	—	—	—	—	—	—	—	—	—
Vauxhall	—	—	7 4	—	—	—	—	9 0	—	—	—	—	—	—	—
WATERLOO	6 8	7 10	7 38	8 10	8 19	8 38	8 52	9 6	9 38	9 48	10 38	11 38	12 38	1 38	2 38

WEEK DAYS.	PM	PM	PM	PM	PM	PM	PM	PM	PM	PM	PM
BOOKHAM ....dep.	2 41	3 41	4 34	5 41	6 41	7 41	8 41	9 41	10 41		
LEATHERHEAD	2 53	3 50	4 45	5 53	6 53	7 53	8 53	9 53	10 53		
Ashtead	2 58	3 55	4 50	5 58	6 58	7 58	8 58	9 58	10 58		
Epsom	3 4	4 4	5 4	6 4	7 4	8 4	9 4	10 4	11 4		
Ewell, West..........	3, 8	4 8	5 8	6 8	7 8	8 8	9 8	10 8	11 8		
Worcester Park	3 14	4 14	5 14	6 14	7 14	8 14	9 14	10 14	11 14		
Raynes Park	3 19	4 19	5 19	6 19	7 19	8 19	9 19	10 19	11 19		
WIMBLEDON	3 23	4 23	5 23	6 23	7 23	8 23	9 23	10 23	11 23		
Earlsfield	—	—	—	—	—	—	—	—	—		
Clapham Junction, arr.	—	—	—	—	—	—	—	—	—		
Vauxhall	—	—	—	—	—	—	—	—	—		
WATERLOO	3 33	4 33	5 38	6 38	7 38	8 38	9 38	10 38	11 38		

d Saturdays only.　　　　*e* Saturdays excepted.　　　　*k* Wednesdays only.

SUNDAYS.	AM	AM	PM	PM	PM	PM	PM	PM	PM	PM		PM
BOOKHAM..........dep.	—	10 24	12 24	1 24	2 24	4 24	6 24	7 24	8 27	9 24		
LEATHERHEAD	8 37	10 37	12 37	1 33	2 37	4 30	6 30	7 33	8 37	9 33		10 33
Ashtead	8 42	10 42	12 42	1 38	2 42	4 35	6 35	7 38	8 42	9 38		10 38
Epsom	8 48	10 48	12 48	1 45	2 48	4 48	6 48	7 48	8 45	9 48		10 48
Ewell, West	8 52	10 52	12 52	1 52	2 52	4 52	6 52	7 52	8 52	9 52		10 52
Worcester Park.......	8 58	10 58	12 58	1 58	2 58	4 58	6 58	7 58	8 58	9 58		10 58
Raynes Park	9 3	11 3	1 3	2 3	3 3	5 3	7 3	8 3	9 3	10 3		11 3
WIMBLEDON	9 6	11 7	1 7	2 7	3 7	5 7	7 7	8 7	9 7	10 7		11 7
Earlsfield	—	—	—	—	—	—	—	—	—	—		—
Clapham Junction, arr.	9 14	11 14	1 14	2 15	3 14	5 15	7 15	8 15	9 15	10 15		11 17
Vauxhall	—	—	—	—	—	—	—	—	—	—		—
WATERLOO	9 24	11 24	1 24	2 24	3 24	5 24	7 24	8 24	9 24	11 24		11 24

WATERLOO TO NORBITON, KINGSTON AND TEDDINGTON.

WEEK DAYS.	AM	AM	AM	AM	AM	AM	AM	AM	AM	AM	AM	AM
WATERLOO ....dep.	1 0	2 15	3 35	4 50	5 30	6 0	6 10	6 20	6 30	6 40	6 55	7 0
Vauxhall	1 5	2 20	3 40	—	5 34	6 3	6 13	6 23	6 33	6 43	6 58	7 3
Clapham Junction.............	1 14	2 26	3.47	—	5 41	6 8	6 18	6 28	6 38	6 48	7 3	7 8
Earlsfield	1 19	2 31	3 52	—	5 45	6 12	6 22	6 32	6 42	6 52	7 7	7 12
WIMBLEDON	1 24	2 36	4 1	5 7	5 51	6 16	6 26	6 36	6 46	6 56	7 11	7 16
Raynes Park	1 28	2 40	4 5	5 19	5 56	6 19	6 29	6 39	6 49	6 59	—	7 19
Malden	1 32	2 44	4 9	5 22	5 59	6 22	6 32	6 42	6 52	7 2	7 16	7 22
Norbiton........................	1 36	2 48	4 13	5 25	6 3	6 25	6 35	6 50	6 55	7 5	7 19	7 25
KINGSTON........................	1 39	2 51	4 18	5 28	6 6	6 28	6 38	6 53	6 58	7 8	7 22	7 28
Hampton Wick...................	—	—	—	—	—	6 30	6 40	6 55	7 0	7 10	7 24	7 30
TEDDINGTON	1 45	2 56	4 22	5 33	6 12	6 33	6 43	7 0	7 3	7 13	7 27	7 33

WEEK DAYS.	AM	AM	AM	AM	AM		AM
WATERLOO ....dep.	7 10	7 25	7 30	7 40	7 55		11 55
Vauxhall	7 13	7 28	7 33	7 43	7 58		11 58
Clapham Junction.............	7 18	7 33	7 38	7 48	8 3	Then at	12 3
Earlsfield	7 22	7 37	7 42	7 52	8 7	the same	12 7
WIMBLEDON	7 26	7 41	7 46	7 56	8 11	minutes	12 11
Raynes Park....................	7 29	—	7 49	7 59	—	past each	12 14
Malden	7 32	7 46	7 52	8 2	8 16	hour until	12 16
Norbiton........................	7 35	7 49	7 55	8 5	8 19		12 19
KINGSTON........................	7 33	7 52	7 58	8 8	8 22		12 22
Hampton Wick..................	7 40	7 54	8 0	8 10	8 24		12 24
TEDDINGTON	7 43	7 58	8 3	8 13	8 28		12 27

SUNDAYS.	AM	AM	AM	AM	AM	AM	AM		PM	PM	PM	PM	PM	PM
WATERLOO...............dep.	1 15	6 25	7 25	7 45	750	8	8 25		9:0	10 5	1025	10 45	11 5	11 25
Vauxhall	1 20	6 28	7 28	7 48	753	8	8 28	Then at	953	10 8	1028	10 48	11 8	11 28
Clapham Junction.............	1 29	6 33	7 33	7 53	758	8	8 33	the same	958	1013	1033	10 53	11 13	11 33
Earlsfield	1 34	6 37	7 37	57 8	2 8	18	8 37	minutes	10 2	1017	1037	10 57	11 17	11 37
WIMBLEDON	1 39	6 41	7 41	418	1 8	618	21 8	41	past each	10 6	1021	1041	11 1	11 21	11 41
Raynes Park....................	1 43	6 44	7 44	8	4 8	9 8	24 8	44	hour until	10 9	1024	1044	11 4	11 24	11 44
Malden	1 47	6 47	7 47	7 47	8	7 812	8	27 8	47	1012	1027	1047	11 7	11 27	11 47
Norbiton........................	1 51	6 50	7 50	8 10	815	8	30 8	50	1015	1030	1050	11 10	11 30	11 50
KINGSTON........................	1 54	6 53	7 53	8 13	818	8	33 8	53	1018	1033	1053	11 13	11 33	11 53
Hampton Wick...................	—	6 55	7 55	8 15	820	8	35 8	55	1020	1035	1055	11 15	11 35	11 55
TEDDINGTON	1 59	6 58	7 58	8 18	823	8	38 8	58	1023	1038	1058	11 18	11 38	11 58

WEEK DAYS.

WEEK DAYS.	AM	AM	AM	AM	AM	AM	AM	AM	AM	AM	AM	AM	AM	AM	AM
Teddington ....dep.	2 4	3 33	4 8	5 15	5 31	5 46	6 1	6 16	6 21	6 31	6 46	7 1	7 16	7 21
Hampton Wick	—	—	—	—	—	—	—	6 19	6 24	6 34	6 49	7 4	7 19	7 24
Kingston............	2 45	3 41	4 15	5 19	5 36	5 51	6 6	6 21	6 26	6 36	6 51	7 6	7 21	7 26
Norbiton	2 48	3 45	4 19	5 21	5 38	5 53	6 8	6 23	6 28	6 38	6 53	7 8	7 23	7 28
Malden........	2 52	3 49	4 23	5 25	5 42	5 57	6 12	6 27	6 32	6 42	6 57	7 12	7 27	7 32
Raynes Park........	2 56	3 53	4 27	5 28	5 45	—	6 15	—	6 35	6 45	—	7 15	—	7 35
Wimbledon..........	3 0	3 58	4 31	5 31	5 48	6 2	6 16	6 32	6 38	6 49	7 2	7 18	7 32	7 36
Earlsfield...........	3 5	4 3	4 36	5 35	5 51	6 5	6 21	6 35	6 41	6 51	7 5	7 21	7 35	7 41
Clapham Junction ..	3 10	4 7	4 41	5 39	5 55	6 9	6 25	6 39	6 45	6 55	7 9	7 25	7 39	7 45
Vauxhall...........	3 17	4 13	4 46	5 44	6 0	6 14	6 30	6 44	6 50	7 0	7 14	7 30	7 44	7 50
Waterloo	3 24	4 20	4 52	5 48	6 4	6 18	6 24	6 48	6 54	7 4	7 18	7 34	7 48	7 54

WEEK DAYS.	AM	AM	AM		PM	PM	PM
Teddington ....dep.	7 31	7 46	7 51		11 1	11 16	11 51
Hampton Wick......	7 34	7 49	7 54	Then at	11 4	11 19	11 54
Kingston	7 33	7 51	7 56	the same	11 6	11 21	11 56
Norbiton	7 38	7 53	7 58	minutes	11 8	11 23	12 4
Malden.............	7 42	7 57	8 2	past each	11 12	11 27	12 7
Raynes Park........	—	—	8 5	hour until	11 15	—	12 10
Wimbledon	7 48	8 2	8 8		11 18	11 32	12 13
Earlsfield	7 51	8 5	8 11		11 21	11 35	—
Clapham Junction ..	7 55	8 9	8 15		11 25	11 39	—
Vauxhall...........	8 0	8 14	8 20		11 30	11 44	—
Waterloo	8 4	8 18	8 24		11 34	11 48	—

SUNDAYS.

SUNDAYS.	AM	AM	AM	AM	AM	AM	AM	AM	AM		AM	PM	PM	PM
Teddington ....dep.	—	6 45	7 25	7 45	—	8 5	8 25	8 45	9 0		10 0	10 5	10 25	10 45 11 4
HamptonWick......	—	6 48	7 28	7 48	—	8 8	8 28	8 48	9 3	Then at	10 3	10 8	10 28	10 48 11 7
Kingston............	5 20	6 50	7 30	7 50	8 5	8 10	8 30	8 50	9 5	the same	10 5	10 10	10 30	10 50 11 9
Norbiton............	5 23	6 52	7 32	7 52	8 8	8 12	8 32	8 52	9 8	minutes	10 8	10 12	10 32	10 52 1112
Malden.............	5 28	6 56	7 36	7 56	8 11	8 16	8 36	8 56	9 11	past each	1011	10 16	10 36	10 56 1115
Raynes Park........	5 32	6 59	7 39	7 59	8 14	8 19	8 39	8 59	9 14	hour until	1014	10 19	10 39	10 59 1118
Wimbledon	5 36	7 2	7 42	8 2	8 17	8 22	8 42	9 2	9 17		1017	10 22	10 42	11 2 1121
Earlsfield	5 41	7 6	7 46	8 6	8 21	8 26	8 46	9 6	9 21		1021	10 26	10 46	11 6 1125
Clapham Junction ..	5 46	7 10	7 50	8 10	8 25	8 30	8 50	9 10	9 25		1025	10 30	10 50	11 10 1129
Vauxhall...........	5 53	7 15	7 55	8 15	8 30	8 35	8 55	9 15	9 30		1020	10 35	10 55	11 15 1134
Waterloo	5 59	7 19	7 59	8 19	8 34	8 39	8 59	9 19	9 34		1034	10 39	10 59	11 19 1138

WATERLOO TO SHEPPERTON.

WEEK DAYS	AM	AM	AM	AM	AM	AM	AM	AM		PM	e	d	e	d	e	d
Waterloo ......dep.	4 50	6 0	6 30	6 55	7 18	7 25	7 43	7 55	8 25		12 25	12 55	1 9	1 25	1 39	1 55	2 9
Clapham Junction ..	—	6 8	6 38	7 3	—	7 33	—	8 3	8 33		12 28	1 3	—	1 33	—	2 3	—
Richmond	—	—	—	—	7 35	—	8 2	—	—	Then at	—	—	1 25	—	1 55	—	2 25
Twickenham	—	—	—	—	7 40	—	8 8	—	—	the same	—	—	1 30	—	2 0	—	2 30
Strawberry Hill	—	—	—	—	7 43	—	8 13	—	—	minutes	—	—	1 33	—	2 3	—	2 33
Fulwell	5 43	6 37	7 7	8 17	7 48	3 8	17 8	33 9 1		past each	1 1	1 31	1 36	2 12	2 6	2 31	2 36
Hampton	5 47	6 41	7 11	7 35	7 52	8 8	8 22	8 38	9 5	hour until	1 5	1 35	1 40	2 5	2 10	2 35	2 40
Sunbury	5 51	6 45	7 16	7 39	7 57	8 13	8 27	8 45	9 9		1 9	1 39	1 44	2 9	2 14	2 39	2 44
Shepperton	5 55	6 49	7 20	7 43	8 2	8 18	8 32	8 50	9 13		1 13	1 43	1 48	2 13	2 18	2 43	2 48

WEEK DAYS.	e	d	PM	PM	e	PM	e	d	e	d	e	PM	e	PM	PM		PM
Waterloo ......dep.	225	233	325	355	425	455	5 9	525	539	555	6 9	624	625	639	655	7 9	725 755
Clapham Junction..	233	—	333	4 3	433	5 3	—	533	—	6 3	—	633	—	7 3	—	733	8 3
Richmond	—	255	—	—	—	525	—	555	—	625	—	655	—	725	—	—
Twickenham	—	3 0	—	—	—	530	—	6 0	—	630	—	7 0	—	730	—	—
Strawberry Hill	—	3 3	—	—	—	533	—	6 3	—	633	—	7 3	—	733	—	—
Fulwell	3 1	3 6	4 1	431	5 1	531	536	6 1	6 6	631	636	655	7 1	7 6	731	736	8 1 831
Hampton	3 5	310	4 5	435	5 5	535	540	6 5	610	635	640	659	7 5	710	735	740	8 5 835
Sunbury	3 9	314	4 9	439	5 9	539	544	6 9	614	639	644	7 3	7 9	714	739	744	8 9 839
Shepperton	313	319	413	443	513	543	548	613	618	643	648	7 7	713	718	743	748	813 843

SUNDAYS.	AM	AM	AM	AM		PM
Waterloo ......dep.	7 50	8 50	9 25	9 50	Then at the same	9 50
Clapham Junction..	7 58	8 58	—	9 58	minutes past each	9 58
Richmond	—	—	—	—	hour until	—
Twickenham	—	—	—	—		—
Strawberry Hill	—	—	—	—	Extra Trains.	—
Fulwell	8 27	9 27	10 0	10 27	9 25, 10 25, 11 25 A.M.,	10 27
Hampton	8 31	9 31	10 4	10 31	12 25, 6 25, 7 25,	10 31
Sunbury	8 35	9 35	10 8	10 35	8 25, 9 25.	10 35
Shepperton	8 39	9 39	10 12	10 39		10 39

d Saturdays only.
e Saturdays excepted.

SHEPPERTON TO WATERLOO.

WEEK DAYS.... dep.	AM	AM	AM	AM	AM	AM	AM	AM	AM		PM
Shepperton.... dep.	5 30	6 0	6 30	6 46	7 0	7 16	7 30	7 46	9 0	8 16	8 30	8 46	9 0	9 30	11 0
Sunbury	5 34	6 4	6 36	6 50	7 4	7 20	7 34	7 50	8 4	8 20	8 34	8 50	9 4	9 34	Then at	11 4
Hampton	5 38	6 8	6 38	6 54	7 8	7 24	7 38	7 54	8 8	8 24	8 38	8 54	9 8	9 38	the same	11 8
Fulwell	5 41	6 11	6 41	6 57	7 11	7 27	7 41	7 57	8 11	8 27	8 41	8 57	9 11	9 41	minutes	11 12
Strawberry Hill	—	—	—	7 0	—	7 30	—	8 0	—	8 30	—	9 0	—		past each	
Twickenham	—	—	—	7 4	—	7 34	—	8 4	—	8 34	—	9 4	—		hour until	
Richmond	—	—	—	7 9	—	7 39	—	8 9	—	8 39	—	9 9	—			
Clapham Junction ..	6 9	6 39	7 9	7 39	—	8 9	—	9 9	—	9 39	10 0		11 39
Waterloo	6 18	6 48	7 18	7 27	7 48	7 57	8 18	8 27	8 45	8 57	9 18	9 27	9 48	10 18		11 48

SUNDAYS.	AM	AM		PM	PM
Shepperton .... dep.	8 44	9 44	Then at the same	9 44	10 48
Sunbury	8 48	9 48	minutes past each	9 48	10 52
Hampton	8 52	9 52	hour until	9 52	10 56
Fulwell	8 56	9 56		9 56	11 0
Strawberry Hill	—	—	Extra Trains.	—	—
Twickenham	—	—	10 19, 11 19, 12 19,	—	—
Richmond	—	—	1 19, 5 19, 6 19,	—	—
Clapham Junction ..	9 25	10 25	7 19, 8 19, 9 19,	10 25	—
Waterloo	9 34	10 34	10 19.	10 34	11 38

WEEK DAYS.	AM	AM	AM	AM	AM	AM	AM	AM	AM	AM	AM	AM
WATERLOO ......dep.	5 10	5 51	6 21	6 51	7 21	7 48	7 51	8 13	8 21	8 43	8 51	9 21
Vauxhall............	—	5 54	6 24	6 54	7 24	—	7 54	—	8 24	—	8 54	9 24
Queen's Road.......	—	5 57	6 27	6 57	7 27	—	7 57	—	8 27	—	8 57	9 27
Clapham Junction ..	—	6 0	6 30	7 0	7 30	—	8 0	8 20	8 31	—	9 0	9 30
Wandsworth	—	—	—	—	—	—	—	—	—	—	—	—
Putney..............	—	6 4	6 34	7 4	7 34	—	8 4	8 22	8 35	8 52	9 4	9 34
BARNES.............	5 25	6 7	6 37	7 7	7 37	8 1	8 7	8 25	8 38	8 55	9 7	9 37
Barnes Bridge	—	6 9	6 39	7 9	7 39	8 3	8 9	8 27	8 40	8 57	9 9	9 39
Chiswick	—	6 12	6 42	7 12	7 42	8 6	8 12	8 30	8 43	9 0	9 12	9 42
KEW BRIDGE	5 34	6 15	6 45	7 15	7 45	8 9	8 15	8 33	8 46	9 3	9 15	9 45
Brentford	5 40	6 18	6 48	7 18	7 48	8 12	8 18	8 36	8 49	9 6	9 18	9 48
Isleworth	5 46	6 21	6 51	7 21	7 51	8 15	8 21	8 39	8 52	9 9	9 21	9 51
HOUNSLOW	5 54	6 25	6 55	7 25	7 55	8 18	8 25	8 42	8 55	9 12	9 25	9 55

WEEK DAYS.	AM			PM	
WATERLOO ......dep.	9 51			11 51	
Vauxhall............	9 54	Then at the same		11 54	
Queen's Road	9 57	minutes past each		11 57	
Clapham Junction..	10 0	hour until		12 1	
Wandsworth........	—				
Putney.............	10 4	**Extra Trains.**		12 5	*d* Saturdays only.
BARNES............	10 7			12 8	*e* Saturdays excepted.
Barnes Bridge	10 9	12*d*43, 1*d*43, 1*d*43,		12 10	
Chiswick	10 12	2*d*13, 2*d*43, 4*e*43,		12 13	
KEW BRIDGE	10 15	5*e*13, 5*e*43, 6*e*13,		12 16	
Brentford	10 18	6*e*43, 7*e*13.		12 19	
Isleworth	10 21			12 22	
HOUNSLOW	10 25			12 25	

SUNDAYS.	AM	AM	AM	AM		PM	PM	PM	PM
WATERLOO ......dep.	7 45	8 0	8 15	8 45		10 0	10 15	10 45	11 15
Vauxhall............	7 48	8 3	8 18	8 48		10 3	10 18	10 48	11 18
Queen's Road	7 51	8 6	8 21	8 51		10 6	10 21	10 51	11 21
Clapham Junction..	7 54	8 9	8 24	8 54	Then at	10 9	10 24	10 54	11 24
Wandsworth	7 56	8 11	8 26	8 56	the same	10 11	10 26	10 56	11 26
Putney.............	7 59	8 14	8 29	8 59	minutes	10 14	10 29	10 59	11 29
BARNES............	8 2	8 17	8 32	9 2	past each	10 17	10 32	11 2	11 32
Barnes Bridge	8 4	8 19	8 34	9 4	hour until	10 19	10 34	11 4	11 34
Chiswick	8 7	8 22	8 37	9 7		10 22	10 37	11 7	11 37
KEW BRIDGE	8 10	8 25	8 40	9 10		10 25	10 40	11 10	11 40
Brentford	8 13	8 28	8 43	9 13		10 28	10 43	11 13	11 43
Isleworth	8 16	8 31	8 46	9 16		10 31	10 46	11 16	11 46
HOUNSLOW	8 20	8 35	8 50	9 20		10 35	10 50	11 19	11 49

HOUNSLOW AND KEW TO WATERLOO.

WEEK DAYS.	AM	AM	AM	AM	AM	AM	AM	AM	AM	AM	AM	AM	AM	AM
HOUNSLOW ...... dep.	5 11	5 41	6 11	6 41	7 0	7 11	7 30	7 41	8 0	8 11	8 30	8 41	9 0	9 11
Isleworth	5 14	5 44	6 14	6 44	7 3	7 14	7 33	7 44	8 3	8 14	8 33	8 44	9 3	9 14
Brentford	5 17	5 47	6 17	6 47	7 6	7 17	7 36	7 47	8 6	8 17	8 36	8 47	9 6	9 17
KEW BRIDGE	5 20	5 50	6 20	6 50	7 9	7 20	7 39	7 50	8 9	8 20	8 39	8 50	9 9	9 20
Chiswick	5 23	5 53	6 23	6 53	7 12	7 23	7 42	7 53	8 12	8 23	8 42	8 53	9 12	9 23
Barnes Bridge	—	—	6 25	6 55	7 14	7 25	7 44	7 55	8 14	8 25	8 44	8 55	9 14	9 25
BARNES	5 28	5 57	6 28	6 58	7 17	7 28	7 47	7 58	8 17	8 28	8 47	8 58	9 17	9 28
Putney.............	5 31	6 0	6 31	7 1	7 20	7 31	7 50	8 1	8 20	8 31	8 50	9 1	9 20	9 31
Wandsworth	5 33	6 3	—	7 4	7 22	7 33	7 52	8 3	8 22	8 33	8 52	—	—	—
Clapham Junction..	5 35	6 5	6 35	—	—	—	—	8 5	—	8 35	—	9 5	—	9 35
Queen's Road......	5 38	6 8	6 38	—	—	—	—	8 8	—	8 38	—	9 8	—	9 38
Vauxhall	5 41	6 11	6 41	—	7 28	—	7 58	8 11	8 28	8 41	8 58	9 11	9 28	9 41
WATERLOO	5 45	6 15	6 45	7 12	7 32	7 42	8 2	8 15	8 32	8 45	9 2	9 15	9 32	9 45

WEEK DAYS.	AM	AM	AM	AM		PM	PM
HOUNSLOW ......dep.	9 30	9 41	10 11	10 41		10 41	11 11
Isleworth	9 33	9 44	10 14	10 44	Then at	10 44	11 14
Brentford	9 36	9 47	10 17	10 47	the same	10 47	11 17
KEW BRIDGE	9 39	9 50	10 20	10 50	minutes	10 50	11 20
Chiswick	9 42	9 53	10 23	10 53	past each	10 53	11 23
Barnes Bridge	9 44	9 55	10 25	10 55	hour until	10 55	11 25
BARNES............	9 47	9 58	10 28	10 58		10 58	11 28
Putney.............	9 50	10 1	10 31	11 1	**Extra Trains.**	11 1	11 31
Wandsworth	—	—	—	—		—	11 34
Clapham Junction..	—	10 5	10 35	11 5	1*d*30, 2*d*0, 5*e*30,	11 5	11 37
Queen's Road	—	10 8	10 38	11 8	6*e*0, 6*e*30.	11 8	11 40
Vauxhall...........	—	10 11	10 41	11 11		11 11	11 43
WATERLOO	10 1	10 15	10 45	11 15		11 15	11 47

SUNDAYS.	AM	AM	AM	AM		PM	PM	PM
HOUNSLOW ......dep.	8 0	8 15	8 45			10 0	10 15	11 0
Isleworth	8 3	8 18	8 48			10 3	10 18	11 3
Brentford	8 6	8 21	8 51			10 6	10 21	11 6
KEW BRIDGE	8 9	8 24	8 54		Then at	10 9	10 24	11 9
Chiswick	8 12	8 27	8 57		the same	10 12	10 27	11 12
Barnes Bridge......	8 14	8 29	8 59		minutes	10 14	10 29	11 14
BARNES............	8 17	8 32	9 2		past each	10 17	10 32	11 17
Putney	8 20	8 35	9 5		hour until	10 20	10 35	11 20
Wandsworth	8 23	8 38	9 8			10 23	10 38	11 23
Clapham Junction..	8 25	8 40	9 10			10 25	10 43	11 25
Queen's Road......	8 28	8 42	9 12			10 28	10 43	11 28
Vauxhall	8 31	8 46	9 16		*d* Saturdays only.	10 31	10 46	11 31
WATERLOO	8 35	8 49	9 19		*e* Saturdays excepted.	10 35	10 50	11 35

WEEK DAYS.

	AM	AM	AM	AM	AM	AM	AM	AM	AM	AM	AM	AM	AM	AM	AM	AM	AM	AM	AM
WATERLOO ....dep.	1 15	2 30	5 35	5 56	6 26	6 46	6 54	6 56	7 6	7 16	7 18	7 24	7 26	7 36	7 43	7 46	7 54	7 56	
Vauxhall	1 20	2 35	5 40	5 59	6 29	6 49	—	6 59	7 9	7 19	—	—	7 29	7 39	—	7 49	—	7 59	
Queen's Road	1 24	—	—	—	—	—	—	7 12	—	—	—	—	7 42	—	—	—	—	—	
Clapham J.	1 29	2 42	5 49	6 4	6 34	6 54	—	7 4	7 15	7 24	—	—	7 34	7 45	—	7 54	—	8 4	
Wandsworth	1 33	2 45	5 53	6 7	6 37	6 57	—	7 7	—	7 27	—	—	7 37	—	—	7 57	—	8 7	
Putney	1 37	2 49	5 57	6 11	6 40	7 0	—	7 10	7 19	7 30	—	—	7 40	7 49	7 52	8 0	—	8 10	
Barnes	1 41	2 53	6 1	6 13	6 42	7 3	—	7 13	7 22	7 33	—	—	7 43	7 52	7 55	8 3	—	8 13	
Mortlake	1 45	2 57	6 5	6 16	6 46	7 6	—	7 16	7 25	7 36	—	—	7 46	7 55	7 58	8 6	—	8 16	
RICHMOND	1 50	3 3	6 11	6 20	6 50	7 10	7 14	7 20	7 28	7 40	7 35	7 44	7 50	7 59	8 2	8 10	8 14	8 20	
St. Margarets	—	—	—	6 22	6 52	7 12	—	7 22	7 31	7 42	7 38	—	7 52	8 1	8 5	8 12	—	8 23	
Twickenham	1 56	3 9	6 17	6 25	6 55	7 15	7 20	7 25	7 34	7 45	7 40	7 50	7 55	8 4	8 8	8 15	8 20	8 25	
Strawberry Hill	1 59	3 13	—	6 28	6 58	7 18	—	7 28	—	7 48	7 43	—	7 58	—	8 13	8 18	—	8 28	
TEDDINGTON	2 3	3 16	—	6 31	7 1	7 21	—	7 31	—	7 51	—	—	8 1	—	8 21	—	8 31		

WEEK DAYS.

	AM	AM	AM	AM	AM	AM	AM	AM	AM	AM	AM	AM	AM	AM	AM
WATERLOO ...dep.	8 6	8 16	8 24	8 26	8 36	8 46	8 54	8 56	9 6	9 16	9 24	9 26	9 36	9 43	9 54	9 56
Vauxhall	8 9	8 19	—	8 29	8 39	8 49	—	8 59	9 9	9 19	—	9 29	9 39	9 49	—	9 59
Queen's Road	8 12	—	—	8 42	—	—	—	9 12	—	—	—	—	9 42	—	—	—
Clapham J.	8 15	8 24	—	8 34	8 45	8 54	—	9 4	9 15	9 24	—	9 34	9 45	9 54	—	10 4
Wandsworth	—	8 27	—	8 37	—	8 57	—	9 7	—	9 27	—	9 37	—	9 57	—	10 7
Putney	8 19	8 30	—	8 40	8 49	9 0	—	9 10	9 19	9 30	—	9 40	9 49	10 0	—	10 10
Barnes	8 22	8 33	—	8 43	8 52	9 3	—	9 13	9 22	9 33	—	9 43	9 52	10 3	—	10 13
Mortlake	8 25	8 36	—	8 46	8 55	9 6	—	9 16	9 25	9 36	—	9 46	9 55	10 6	—	10 16
RICHMOND	8 28	8 40	8 45	8 50	8 58	9 10	9 14	9 20	9 29	9 40	9 45	9 50	9 59	10 10	10 14	10 20
St. Margarets	8 31	8 42	—	8 52	9 1	9 12	—	9 22	9 31	9 42	—	9 52	10 1	10 12	—	10 22
Twickenham	8 34	8 45	8 51	8 55	9 4	9 15	9 20	9 25	9 34	9 45	9 51	9 55	10 4	10 15	10 20	10 25
Strawberry Hill	—	8 48	—	8 58	—	9 18	—	9 28	—	9 48	—	9 58	—	10 18	—	10 28
TEDDINGTON	—	8 51	—	9 1	—	9 21	—	9 31	—	9 51	—	10 1	—	10 21	—	10 31

WEEK DAYS.

	AM	AM	AM	AM	AM	AM	AM	AM	AM	AM	AM	AM	AM	AM
WATERLOO....dep.	10 6	10 16	10 24	10 26	10 36	10 46	10 54	10 56	11 6	11 16	11 24	11 26	11 36	11 46
Vauxhall	10 9	10 19	—	10 29	10 39	10 49	—	10 59	11 9	11 19	—	11 29	11 39	11 49
Queen's Road	10 12	—	—	10 42	—	—	—	11 12	—	—	—	—	11 42	—
Clapham J.	10 15	10 24	—	10 34	10 45	10 54	—	11 4	11 15	11 24	—	11 34	11 45	11 54
Wandsworth	—	10 27	—	10 37	—	10 57	—	11 7	—	11 27	—	11 37	—	11 57
Putney	10 19	10 30	—	10 40	10 49	11 0	—	11 10	11 19	11 30	—	11 40	11 49	12 0
Barnes	10 22	10 33	—	10 43	10 52	11 3	—	11 13	11 22	11 33	—	11 43	11 52	12 3
Mortlake	10 25	10 36	—	10 46	10 55	11 6	—	11 16	11 25	11 36	—	11 46	11 55	12 6
RICHMOND	10 29	10 40	10 44	10 50	10 58	11 10	11 14	11 20	11 29	11 40	11 44	11 50	11 59	12 10
St. Margarets	10 31	10 42	—	10 52	11 1	11 12	—	11 22	11 31	11 42	—	11 52	12 1	12 12
Twickenham	10 34	10 45	10 50	10 55	11 4	11 15	11 20	11 25	11 34	11 45	11 49	11 55	12 4	12 15
Strawberry Hill	—	10 48	—	10 58	—	11 18	—	11 28	—	11 48	—	11 58	—	12 18
TEDDINGTON	—	10 51	—	11 1	—	11 21	—	11 31	—	11 51	—	12 1	—	12 21

WEEK DAYS.

	AM	PM	PM	PM	PM	PM	PM	d	PM	PM	PM	PM	PM	d	PM
WATERLOO....dep.	11 56	12 6	12 16	12 24	12 26	12 36	12 46	12 54	12 56	1 6	1 9	1 16	1 24	1 26	1 36
Vauxhall	11 59	12 9	12 19	—	12 29	12 39	12 49	—	12 59	1 9	—	1 19	—	1 29	1 39
Queen's Road	—	12 12	—	—	12 42	—	—	—	1 12	—	—	—	—	1 42	—
Clapham J.	12 4	12 15	12 24	—	12 34	12 45	12 54	—	1 4	1 15	—	1 24	—	1 34	1 45
Wandsworth	12 7	—	12 27	—	12 37	—	12 57	—	1 7	—	—	1 27	—	1 37	—
Putney	12 10	12 19	12 30	—	12 40	12 49	1 0	—	1 10	1 19	—	1 30	—	1 40	1 49
Barnes	12 13	12 22	12 33	—	12 43	12 52	1 3	—	1 13	1 22	—	1 33	—	1 43	1 52
Mortlake	12 16	12 25	12 36	—	12 46	12 55	1 6	—	1 16	1 25	—	1 36	—	1 46	1 55
RICHMOND	12 20	12 28	12 40	12 44	12 50	12 59	1 10	1 14	1 20	1 29	1 25	1 40	1 44	1 50	1 59
St. Margarets	12 22	12 31	12 42	—	12 52	1 1	1 12	—	1 22	1 31	1 28	1 42	—	1 52	2 1
Twickenham	12 25	12 34	12 45	12 50	12 55	1 4	1 15	1 20	1 25	1 34	1 30	1 45	1 50	1 55	2 4
Strawberry Hill	12 28	—	12 48	—	12 58	—	1 18	—	1 28	—	1 33	1 48	—	1 58	—
TEDDINGTON	12 31	—	12 51	—	1 1	—	1 21	—	1 31	—	1 51	—	2 1		

WEEK DAYS.

	d	PM	PM	d	PM	PM	PM	d	PM	PM	d	PM	PM	d	PM
WATERLOO ....dep.	1 54	1 56	2 6	2 9	2 16	2 24	2 26	2 36	2 39	2 46	2 54	2 56	3 6	3 9	3 56
Vauxhall	—	1 59	2 9	—	2 19	—	2 29	2 39	—	2 49	2 59	3 9	—	3 39	3 59
Queen's Road	—	2 12	—	—	2 42	—	—	—	—	3 12	—	—	—	—	—
Clapham J.	—	2 4	2 15	—	2 24	—	2 34	2 45	—	2 54	3 4	—	3 34	3 45	3 54
Wandsworth	—	2 7	—	—	2 27	—	2 37	—	—	2 57	3 7	—	3 37	—	3 57
Putney	—	2 10	2 19	—	2 30	—	2 40	2 49	—	3 0	3 10	—	3 40	3 49	4 0
Barnes	—	2 13	2 22	—	2 33	—	2 43	2 52	—	3 3	3 13	—	3 43	3 52	4 3
Mortlake	—	2 16	2 25	—	2 36	—	2 46	2 55	—	3 6	3 16	—	3 46	3 55	4 6
RICHMOND	2 14	2 20	2 29	2 25	2 40	2 44	2 50	2 59	2 55	3 10	3 20	3 25	3 50	3 54	4 10
St. Margarets	—	2 22	2 31	2 28	2 42	—	2 52	3 1	2 58	3 12	3 22	3 28	3 52	4 1	4 13
Twickenham	2 20	2 25	2 34	2 30	2 45	2 50	2 55	3 4	3 0	3 15	3 25	3 30	3 55	4 4	4 15
Strawberry Hill	—	2 28	—	2 33	2 48	—	2 58	—	3 3	3 18	3 28	—	3 58	—	4 18
TEDDINGTON	—	2 31	—	2 51	—	3 1	—	3 21	3 31	—	3 51	—	4 1	—	4 21

WEEK DAYS.

	PM	PM	PM	PM	PM	PM	PM	PM	e	PM	e	PM	PM	PM	PM
WATERLOO ....dep.	4 6	4 16	4 24	4 26	4 36	4 46	4 48	4 54	4 58	5 6	5 16	5 24	5 26	5 36	5 39	5 46
Vauxhall	4 9	4 19	—	4 29	4 39	4 49	—	4 59	—	5 9	—	5 19	—	5 29	5 39	—
Queen's Road	4 12	—	—	4 42	—	—	—	5 12	—	—	—	—	5 42	—	—	—
Clapham J.	4 15	4 24	—	4 34	4 45	4 54	—	5 4	—	5 15	—	5 24	—	5 34	5 46	—
Wandsworth	—	4 27	—	4 37	—	4 57	—	5 7	—	—	—	5 27	—	5 37	—	—
Putney	4 19	4 30	—	4 40	4 49	5 0	—	5 10	—	5 19	—	5 30	—	5 40	5 50	—
Barnes	4 22	4 33	—	4 43	4 52	5 3	—	5 13	—	5 22	—	5 33	—	5 43	5 53	—
Mortlake	4 25	4 36	—	4 46	4 55	5 6	—	5 16	—	5 25	—	5 36	—	5 46	5 56	—
RICHMOND	4 29	4 40	4 44	4 50	4 59	5 10	—	5 20	5 25	5 29	5 35	5 40	5 44	5 50	5 55	6 0
St. Margarets	4 31	4 42	—	4 52 5	5 1	5 12	—	5 25	—	5 31	5 38	5 42	—	5 52	5 58	6 12
Twickenham	4 34	4 45	4 50	4 55	5 4	5 15	5 20	5 25	5 30	5 40	5 45	5 49	5 55	6 0	6 15
Strawberry Hill	—	4 48	—	4 58	—	5 18	—	5 28	—	5 48	—	5 58	—	6 18	—	6 18
TEDDINGTON	—	4 51	—	5 1	—	5 21	—	5 31	—	5 51	—	6 1	—	6 21		

WEEK DAYS.

	e	PM	PM	PM	PM	PM	PM	PM	PM	PM	PM	PM	PM	PM	PM
WATERLOO ...dep.	5 54	5 56	6 6	6 16	6 19	6 26	6 29	6 39	6 46	6 54	6 56	7 6	7 16	7 24	7 26
Vauxhall	—	5 59	6 9	—	6 19	—	6 29	6 39	—	6 49	6 59	7 9	—	7 51	7 29
Queen's Road	—	—	6 12	—	—	—	6 42	—	—	—	7 12	—	—	—	—
Clapham J.	—	6 4	6 15	—	6 24	—	6 34	6 45	—	6 54	7 4	—	7 34	—	7 34
Wandsworth	—	6 7	—	—	6 27	—	6 37	—	—	6 57	7 7	—	7 37	—	7 37
Putney	6 10	6 19	—	6 30	—	6 40	6 49	—	7 10	7 19	—	7 40	—	7 40	
Barnes	6 13	6 22	—	6 33	—	6 43	6 52	—	7 13	7 22	—	7 43	—	7 43	
Mortlake	6 16	6 25	—	6 36	—	6 46	6 55	—	7 16	7 25	—	7 46	—	7 46	
RICHMOND	6 14	6 20	6 29	6 40	6 44	6 50	6 59	6 55	7 10	7 20	7 14	7 29	7 40	7 44	7 50
St. Margarets	—	6 22	6 31	6 42	—	6 52	7 1	6 58	7 12	7 22	—	7 42	—	7 52	
Twickenham	6 20	6 25	6 34	6 33	6 45	6 55	7 4	7 0	7 15	7 25	7 20	7 45	7 50	7 55	
Strawberry Hill	—	6 28	—	6 33	6 48	—	6 58	—	7 18	7 28	—	7 48	—	7 58	
TEDDINGTON	—	6 31	—	6 51	—	7 1	—	7 21	—	7 31	—	7 51	—	8 1	

WEEK DAYS

	PM	PM	PM	PM	PM	PM	PM	PM	PM	PM	PM	PM	PM	PM	PM
WATERLOO....dep.	7 36	7 46	7 54	7 56	8 6	8 16	8 24	8 26	8 36	8 46	8 56	9 6	9 16	9 24	9 26
Vauxhall.........	7 39	7 49	—	7 59	8 9	8 19	—	8 29	8 39	8 49	8 59	9 9	9 19	—	9 29
Queen's Road....	7 42	—	—	—	8 12	—	—	—	8 42	—	—	9 12	—	—	—
Clapham J.......	7 45	7 54	—	8 4	8 15	8 24	—	8 34	8 45	8 54	9 4	9 15	9 24	—	9 34
Wandsworth	—	7 57	—	8 7	—	8 27	—	8 37	—	8 57	9 7	—	9 27	—	9 37
Putney...........	7 49	8 0	—	8 10	8 19	8 30	—	8 40	8 49	9 0	9 10	9 19	9 30	—	9 40
BARNES	7 52	8 3	—	8 13	8 22	8 33	—	8 43	8 52	9 3	9 13	9 22	9 33	—	9 43
Mortlake.........	7 55	8 6	—	8 16	8 25	8 36	—	8 46	8 55	9 6	9 16	9 25	9 36	—	9 46
RICHMOND	7 59	8 10	8 14	8 20	8 29	8 40	8 44	8 50	8 59	9 10	9 20	9 29	9 29	9 40	9 44	9 50
St. Margaret's...	8 1	8 13	—	8 22	8 31	8 42	—	8 52	9 1	9 12	9 22	9 31	9 42	—	9 52
Twickenham	8 4	8 15	8 20	8 25	8 34	8 45	8 50	8 55	9 4	9 15	9 25	9 34	9 45	9 50	9 55
Strawberry Hill...	—	8 18	—	8 28	—	8 48	—	8 58	—	9 18	9 28	—	9 48	—	9 58
TEDDINGTON	—	8 21	—	8 31	—	8 51	—	9 1	—	9 21	9 31	—	9 51	—	10 1

WEEK DAYS

	PM	PM	PM	PM	PM	PM	PM	PM	PM	PM	PM	PM	PM	PM
WATERLOO ....dep.	9 36	9 46	9 56	10 6	10 16	10 24	10 26	10 36	10 46	10 56	11 6	11 16		
Vauxhall..........	9 39	9 49	9 59	10 9	10 19	—	10 29	10 39	10 49	10 59	11 9	11 19		
Queen's Road......	9 42	—	—	10 12	—	—	—	10 42	—	—	11 12	—		
Clapham J.......	9 45	9 54	10 4	10 15	10 24	—	10 34	10 46	10 54	11 4	11 15	11 24		
Wandsworth	—	9 57	10 7	—	10 27	—	10 37	—	10 57	11 7	—	11 27		
Putney...........	9 49	10 0	10 10	10 19	10 30	—	10 40	10 50	11 0	11 10	11 19	11 30		
BARNES	9 52	10 3	10 13	10 22	10 33	—	10 43	10 53	11 3	11 13	11 22	11 33		
Mortlake	9 55	10 6	10 16	10 25	10 36	—	10 46	10 56	11 6	11 16	11 25	11 36		
RICHMOND	9 59	10 10	10 20	10 29	10 40	10 44	10 50	11 0	11 10	11 20	11 29	11 40		
St. Margarets	10 1	10 12	10 22	10 31	10 42	—	10 52	11 2	11 12	11 21	11 31	11 42		
Twickenham	10 4	10 15	10 25	10 34	10 45	10 50	10 55	11 5	11 15	11 26	11 34	11 45		
Strawberry Hill ..	—	10 18	10 28	—	10 48	—	10 58	—	11 18	11 28	—	11 49		
TEDDINGTON.......	—	10 21	10 31	—	10 51	—	11 1	—	11 21	—	—	11 51		

WEEK DAYS

	PM	PM	PM	PM
WATERLOO.....dep.	11 26	11 36	11 44	11 56
Vauxhall..........	11 29	11 39	—	11 59
Queen's Road......	—	11 42	—	—
Clapham J.........	11 34	11 45	—	12 4
Wandsworth	11 37	—	—	12 7
Putney...........	11 40	11 49	—	12 10
BARNES	11 43	11 52	—	12 13
Mortlake	11 46	11 55	—	12 16
RICHMOND.. ...	11 50	11 59	12 4	12 20
St. Margarets	11 52	12 1	—	12 22
Twickenham	11 55	12 4	12 9	12 25
Strawberry Hill...	11 58	12 7	—	12 28
TEDDINGTON	12 1	12 10	—	—

TEDDINGTON AND RICHMOND TO WATERLOO.

WEEK DAYS

	AM	AM	AM	AM	AM	AM	AM	AM	AM	AM	AM	AM	AM	AM	AM	AM
TEDDINGTON ..dep.	1 45	2 57	4 23	—	5 33	6 3	—	6 13	—	6 43	—	7 0	—	7 13	—
Strawberry Hill ..	—	3 1	4 27	5 17	5 37	6 7	—	6 17	—	6 37	6 47	—	7 2	7 7	—	7 17
Twickenham	1 53	3 51	4 31	5 20	5 40	6 10	6 14	6 20	6 31	6 40	6 52	7 1	7 5	7 10	7 14	7 20	7 31
St. Margarets ...	—	3 55	4 35	5 22	5 43	6 12	—	6 22	6 33	6 42	6 52	7 3	7 7	7 12	—	7 22	7 33
RICHMOND	1 58	4	0	4 40	5 25	5 45	6 15	6 19	6 25	6 36	6 45	6 55	7 5	7 10	7 15	7 19	7 25	7 36
Mortlake.........	—	4 4	4 45	5 28	5 48	6 18	—	6 28	6 39	6 48	6 58	7 7	—	7 18	—	7 28	7 39
BARNES...........	—	4 9	4 50	5 31	5 51	6 21	—	6 31	6 42	6 51	7 1	7 12	—	7 21	—	7 31	7 42
Putney...........	2 6	4 13	4 54	5 34	5 54	6 24	—	6 34	6 45	6 54	7 4	7 15	—	7 24	—	7 34	7 45
Wandsworth......	—	—	—	5 37	5 57	6 27	—	6 37	—	6 57	7 7	—	—	7 27	—	7 37	—
Clapham Junc arr.	2 12	4 19	5 0	5 40	6 0	6 30	—	6 40	6 49	7 0	7 10	7 19	—	7 30	—	7 40	7 49
Queen's Road ...	—	4 23	5 4	5 43	6 3	—	—	—	6 52	—	—	7 22	—	—	—	—	7 52
Vauxhall.........	2 18	4 27	5 8	5 46	6 6	6 35	—	6 45	6 55	7 5	7 15	7 25	—	7 35	—	7 45	7 55
WATERLOO	2 23	4 32	5 13	5 50	6	9 6	39	6 36	6 49	6 59	7 7	7 19	7 29	7 27	7 39	7 36	7 49	7 59

WEEK DAYS

	AM	AM	AM	AM	AM	AM	AM	AM	AM	AM	AM	AM	AM	AM	AM	AM
TEDDINGTON ..dep.	—	7 33	—	7 43	—	3	—	8 13	—	—	8 33	—	8 43	—	9 3	—
Strawberry Hill ..	7 32	7 37	—	7 47	8	2	8 7	8 17	—	8 32	8 37	—	8 47	—	9 2	9 7	—
Twickenham	7 35	7 40	7 44	7 50	8	1 8	5	8 10	8 15	8 20	—	8 31	8 35	8 40	8 46	8 50	9	1 9	5	9 10	9 15
St. Margarets ...	7 37	7 43	—	7 52	8	3 8	7	8 12	—	8 22	—	8 33	8 37	8 42	—	8 52	9	3 9	7	9 12	—
RICHMOND	7 40	7 45	7 49	7 55	8	6 8	10	8 15	8 20	8 25	8 30	8 36	8 40	8 45	—	8 55	9	6 9	10	9 15	—
Mortlake,.........	—	7 43	—	7 58	8	9	—	8 18	—	8 28	—	8 39	—	8 48	—	9 58	9	—	9 18	—
BARNES	—	7 51	—	8 1	8 12	—	8 21	—	8 31	—	8 42	—	8 51	—	9 1	9 12	—	9 21	—
Putney...........	—	7 54	—	8 4	8 15	—	8 24	—	8 34	—	8 45	—	8 54	—	9 4	9 15	—	9 24	—
Wandsworth	—	7 57	—	8 7	—	—	8 27	—	8 37	—	—	8 57	—	9 7	—	—	9 27	—
Clapham Junc· arr.	—	8 0	—	8 10	8 19	—	8 30	—	8 40	—	8 49	—	9 0	—	9 10	9 19	—	9 30	—
Queen's Road ...	—	—	—	—	8 22	—	—	—	—	—	8 52	—	—	—	9 22	—	—	—	—
Vauxhall.........	—	8 5	—	8 15	8 25	—	8 35	8 36	8 45	—	8 55	—	9 5	—	9 15	9 25	—	9 35	—
WATERLOO	7 57	8 9	8 6	8 19	8 29	8 27	8 39	8 41	8 49	8 47	8 59	8 57	9 9	9 6	9 19	9 29	9 27	9 39	9 36

WEEK DAYS

	AM	AM	AM	AM	AM	AM	AM	AM	AM	AM	AM	AM	AM	AM	AM	AM
TEDDINGTON dep...	9 13	—	9 33	—	9 43	—	10 3	10 13	—	10 33	—	10 43	—	11 3	
Strawberry Hill ..	4 17	—	9 37	—	9 47	—	10 7	10 17	—	10 37	—	10 47	—	11 7	
Twickenham	9 20	9 31	9 40	9 44	9 50	10 1	10 10	10 20	10 31	10 40	10 44	10 50	11 1	11 10	
St. Margarets	9 22	9 33	9 42	—	9 52	10 3	10 12	10 22	10 33	10 42	—	10 52	11 3	11 12	
RICHMOND	9 25	9 36	9 45	9 49	9 55	10 6	10 15	10 25	10 36	10 45	10 49	10 55	11 6	11 15	
Mortlake	9 28	9 39	9 48	—	9 58	10 9	10 18	10 28	10 39	10 48	—	10 58	11 9	11 18	
BARNES	9 31	9 42	9 51	—	10 1	10 12	10 21	10 31	10 42	10 51	—	11 1	11 12	11 21	
Putney...........	9 34	9 45	9 54	—	10 4	10 15	10 24	10 34	10 45	10 54	—	11 4	11 15	11 24	
Wandsworth	9 37	—	9 57	—	10 7	—	10 27	10 37	—	10 57	—	11 7	—	11 27	
Clapham Junc. arr.	9 40	9 49	10 0	—	10 10	10 19	10 30	10 40	10 49	11 0	—	11 10	11 19	11 30	
Queen's Road.....	—	9 52	—	—	—	10 22	—	—	10 52	—	—	—	11 22	—	
Vauxhall.........	9 45	9 53	10 5	—	10 15	10 25	10 33	10 45	10 53	11 5	—	11 15	11 25	11 35	
WATERLOO	9 49	9 59	10 9	10 6	10 19	10 29	10 39	10 49	10 59	11 5	11 6	11 19	11 29	11 39	

WEEK DAYS

	AM	AM	AM	AM	AM	PM	PM	PM	PM	PM	PM	PM	PM	PM	PM	PM
TEDDINGTON ...dep.	11 13	—	—	11 33	11 43	—	—	12 3	12 13	—	—	12 33	12 43	—	—	1 3
Strawberry Hill ..	11 17	—	—	11 37	11 47	—	—	12 7	12 17	—	—	12 37	12 47	—	—	1 7
Twickenham	11 20	11 31	11 35	11 40	11 50	12 1	12 5	12 10	12 20	12 26	12 31	12 35	12 40	12 50	1 1	1 5	1 10	1 15
St. Margarets	11 22	11 33	—	11 42	11 52	12 3	—	12 12	12 22	—	12 33	—	12 42	12 52	1 3	—	1 12
RICHMOND	11 25	11 36	11 40	11 45	11 55	12 6	12 10	12 15	12 25	12 36	12 40	12 45	12 55	1 6	1 10	1 15
Mortlake	11 28	11 39	—	11 48	11 58	12 9	—	12 18	12 28	—	12 39	—	12 48	12 58	1 9	—	1 18
BARNES	11 31	11 42	—	11 51	12 1	12 12	—	12 21	12 31	12 42	—	12 51	1 1	1 12	—	1 21
Putney...........	11 34	11 45	—	11 54	12 4	12 15	—	12 24	12 34	12 45	—	12 57	1 7	1 4	1 15	—	1 24
Wandsworth	11 37	—	—	11 57	12 7	—	—	12 27	12 37	—	—	12 57	1 7	—	—	1 27
Clapham Junc. arr.	11 40	11 49	—	12 0	12 10	12 19	—	12 30	12 40	12 49	—	1 0	1 10	1 19	—	1 30
Queen's Road.....	—	11 52	—	—	—	12 22	—	—	12 52	—	—	—	1 22	—	—	—
Vauxhall.........	11 45	11 55	—	12 5	12 15	12 25	12 26	12 35	12 45	12 55	—	1 5	1 15	1 25	1 35	
WATERLOO	11 49	11 59	11 57	12 9	12 19	12 29	12 31	12 39	12 49	12 59	12 57	1 9	1 19	1 29	1 27	1 39

d Saturdays only.   e Saturdays excepted.   g Monday mornings excepted.

WEEK DAYS.

	PM	PM	PM	PM	PM	PM	PM	PM	PM	PM	PM	PM	PM	PM	PM	PM
Teddington ....dep.	1 13	—	—	1 33	1 43	—	—	2 3	2 13	—	—	2 33	2 43	—	—	3 3
Strawberry Hill	1 17	—	—	1 37	1 47	—	—	2 7	2 17	—	—	2 37	2 47	—	—	3 7
Twickenham	1 20	1 31	1 35	1 40	1 50	2 1	2 5	2 10	2 20	2 35	2 31	2 40	2 50	3 1	3 5	3 16
St. Margarets	1 22	1 33	—	1 42	1 52	2 3	—	2 12	2 22	—	2 33	2 42	2 52	3 3	—	3 12
Richmond	1 25	1 36	1 40	1 45	1 55	2 6	2 10	2 15	2 25	2 40	2 36	2 45	2 55	3 6	3 10	3 15
Mortlake	1 28	1 39	—	1 48	1 58	2 9	—	2 18	2 28	—	2 39	2 48	2 58	3 9	—	3 18
Barnes	1 31	1 42	—	1 51	2 1	2 12	—	2 21	2 31	—	2 42	2 51	3 1	3 12	—	3 21
Putney	1 34	1 45	—	1 54	2 4	2 15	—	2 24	2 34	—	2 45	2 54	3 4	3 15	—	3 24
Wandsworth	1 37	—	—	1 57	2 7	—	—	2 27	2 37	—	—	2 57	3 7	—	—	3 27
Clapham Junc...arr.	1 40	1 49	—	2 0	2 10	2 19	—	2 30	2 40	—	2 49	3 0	3 10	3 19	—	3 30
Queen's Road	—	1 52	—	—	—	2 22	—	—	—	—	2 52	—	—	3 22	—	—
Vauxhall	1 45	1 55	—	2 5	2 15	2 25	—	2 35	2 45	—	2 55	3 5	3 15	3 25	—	3 35
Waterloo	1 49	1 59	1 57	2 9	2 19	2 29	2 27	2 39	2 49	2 57	2 59	3 9	3 19	3 29	3 27	3 39

WEEK DAYS.

	PM	PM	PM	PM	PM	PM	PM	PM	PM	PM	PM	PM	PM	PM	PM	PM
Teddington ....dep.	3 13	—	—	3 33	3 43	—	4 3	4 13	—	—	4 33	4 43	—	—	5 3	5 13
Strawberry Hill	3 17	—	—	3 37	3 47	—	4 7	4 17	—	—	4 37	4 47	—	—	5 7	5 17
Twickenham	3 20	3 31	3 25	3 40	3 56	4 1	4 10	4 20	4 35	4 31	4 40	4 52	5 1	5 5	5 12	5 20
St. Margarets	3 22	3 33	—	3 42	3 52	4 3	4 12	4 22	—	4 33	4 42	4 52	5 3	3	—	5 22
Richmond	3 25	3 36	3 40	3 45	3 55	4 6	4 15	4 25	4 40	4 36	4 45	4 55	5 6	5 10	5 15	5 25
Mortlake	3 28	3 39	—	3 48	3 58	4 9	4 18	4 28	—	4 39	4 48	4 58	5 9	—	5 18	5 28
Barnes	3 31	3 42	—	3 51	4 1	4 12	4 21	4 31	—	4 42	4 51	5 1	5 12	—	5 21	5 31
Putney	3 34	3 45	—	3 54	4 4	4 15	4 24	4 34	—	4 45	4 54	5 4	5 15	—	5 24	5 37
Wandsworth	3 37	—	—	3 57	4 7	—	4 27	4 37	—	—	4 57	5 7	—	—	5 27	5 37
Clapham Junc...arr.	3 40	3 49	—	4 0	4 10	4 19	4 30	4 40	—	4 49	5 0	5 10	5 19	—	5 30	5 40
Queen's Road	—	3 52	—	—	—	4 22	—	—	—	4 52	—	—	5 23	—	—	—
Vauxhall	3 45	3 55	—	4 5	4 15	4 25	4 35	4 45	—	4 55	5 5	5 15	5 25	—	5 35	5 45
Waterloo	3 49	3 59	3 57	4 9	4 19	4 29	4 39	4 49	4 57	4 59	5 9	5 19	5 29	5 27	5 39	5 49

WEEK DAYS.

	PM	PM	PM	PM	PM	PM	PM	PM	PM	PM	PM	PM	PM	PM	PM
Teddington ....dep.	—	—	5 33	5 43	—	—	6 3	6 13	—	—	6 33	6 43	—	—	7 3
Strawberry Hill	—	—	5 37	5 47	—	—	6 7	6 17	—	—	6 37	6 47	—	—	7 7
Twickenham	5 35	5 31	5 40	5 50	6 1	6 5	6 10	6 20	6 35	6 31	6 40	6 50	7 1	7 5	7 10
St. Margarets	—	5 33	5 42	5 52	6 3	—	6 12	6 22	—	6 33	6 42	6 52	7 3	—	7 12
Richmond	5 40	5 36	5 45	5 55	6 6	6 10	6 15	6 25	6 40	6 36	6 45	6 55	7 6	7 10	7 15
Mortlake	—	5 39	5 48	5 58	6 9	—	6 18	6 28	—	6 39	6 48	6 58	7 9	—	7 18
Barnes	—	5 42	5 51	6 1	6 12	—	6 21	6 31	—	6 42	6 51	7 1	7 12	—	7 21
Putney	—	5 45	5 54	6 4	6 15	—	6 24	6 34	—	6 45	6 54	7 4	7 15	—	7 24
Wandsworth	—	—	5 57	6 7	—	—	6 27	6 37	—	—	6 57	7 7	—	—	7 27
Clapham Junc...arr.	5 49	6 0	6 10	6 19	—	6 30	6 40	—	6 49	7 0	7 10	7 19	—	7 30	
Queen's Road	5 52	—	—	6 22	—	—	—	6 52	—	—	7 22	—			
Vauxhall	5 55	6 5	6 15	6 25	—	6 35	6 45	—	6 55	7 5	7 15	7 25	—	7 35	
Waterloo	5 57	5 59	6 9	6 19	6 29	6 27	6 39	6 49	6 55	6 59	7 9	7 19	7 29	7 27	7 39

WEEK DAYS.

	PM	PM	PM	PM	PM	PM	PM	PM	PM	PM	PM	PM	PM	PM	PM
Teddington ....dep.	7 13	—	—	7 33	7 43	—	—	8 3	8 13	—	—	8 33	8 43	—	—
Strawberry Hill	7 17	—	—	7 37	7 47	—	—	8 7	8 17	—	—	8 37	8 47	—	—
Twickenham	7 20	7 31	7 35	7 40	7 50	8 1	8 5	8 10	8 20	8 31	8 35	8 40	8 50	9 1	9 5
St. Margarets	7 22	7 33	—	7 42	7 52	8 3	—	8 12	8 22	8 33	—	8 42	8 52	9 3	—
Richmond	7 25	7 36	7 40	7 45	7 55	8 6	8 10	8 15	8 25	8 36	8 40	8 45	8 55	9 6	9 10
Mortlake	7 28	7 39	—	7 48	7 58	8 9	—	8 18	8 28	8 39	—	8 48	8 58	9 9	—
Barnes	7 31	7 42	—	7 51	8 1	8 12	—	8 21	8 31	8 42	—	8 51	9 1	9 12	—
Putney	7 34	7 45	—	7 54	8 4	8 15	—	8 24	8 34	8 45	—	8 54	9 4	9 15	—
Wandsworth	7 37	—	—	7 57	8 7	—	—	8 27	8 37	—	—	8 57	9 7	—	—
Clapham Junc...arr.	7 40	7 49	—	8 0	8 10	8 19	—	8 30	8 40	8 49	—	9 0	9 10	9 19	—
Queen's Road	—	7 52	—	—	—	8 22	—	—	8 52	—	—	9 22	—		
Vauxhall	7 45	7 55	—	8 5	8 15	8 25	—	8 35	8 45	8 55	—	9 5	9 15	9 25	—
Waterloo	7 49	7 59	7 57	8 9	8 19	8 29	8 27	8 39	8 49	8 59	8 57	9 9	9 19	9 29	9 27

WEEK DAYS.

	PM	PM	PM	PM	PM	PM	PM	PM	PM	PM	PM	PM	PM	PM
Teddington ....dep.	9 3	9 13	—	9 33	9 43	—	10 7	—	10 13	—	10 33	10 43		
Strawberry Hill	9 7	9 17	—	9 37	9 47	—	10 7	—	10 17	—	10 37	10 47		
Twickenham	9 10	9 20	9 31	9 40	9 50	10 1	10 10	10 14	10 21	10 33	10 40	10 50	11 1	
St. Margarets	9 12	9 22	9 33	9 42	9 52	10 3	10 12	—	10 22	10 33	10 42	10 52	11 3	
Richmond	9 15	9 25	9 36	9 45	9 55	10 6	10 15	10 20	10 25	10 36	10 45	10 55	11 6	
Mortlake	9 18	9 28	9 39	9 48	9 58	10 9	10 18	—	10 28	10 39	10 48	10 58	11 9	
Barnes	9 21	9 31	9 42	9 51	10 1	10 12	10 21	—	10 31	10 42	10 51	11 1	11 12	
Putney	9 24	9 34	9 45	9 54	10 4	10 15	10 24	—	10 34	10 45	10 54	11 4	11 15	
Wandsworth	9 27	9 37	—	9 57	10 7	—	10 27	—	10 37	—	10 57	11 7	—	
Clapham Junc...arr.	9 30	9 40	9 49	10 0	10 10	10 19	10 30	—	10 40	10 49	11 0	11 10	11 19	
Queen's Road	—	9 52	—	—	10 22	—	—	10 52	—	—	11 22			
Vauxhall	9 35	9 45	9 55	10 5	10 15	10 25	10 35	—	10 45	10 55	11 5	11 15	11 25	
Waterloo	9 39	9 49	9 59	10 9	10 19	10 29	10 37	10 49	10 59	11 9	11 19	11 29		

WEEK DAYS.

	PM	PM
Teddington ....dep.	11 15	—
Strawberry Hill	11 19	—
Twickenham	11 22	11 34
St. Margarets	11 24	—
Richmond	11 27	11 39
Mortlake	11 30	—
Barnes	11 33	11 45
Putney	11 36	11 50
Wandsworth	11 39	—
Clapham Junc...arr.	11 40	11 56
Queen's Road	—	—
Vauxhall	11 45	12d 3
Waterloo	11 49	12 5

SUNDAYS.

	AM	AM	AM	AM	AM	AM	AM	AM	AM	AM	AM	AM	AM	AM	AM	AM	AM	AM	AM
Waterloo.......dep.	7 30	7 50	8 10	818	8	848	8	50	9 5	9 13	918	920	923	9 30	9 35	9 50	10	10 10	1018
Vauxhall	7 33	7 53	8 13	—	8 33	8 38	—	8 53	9 13	—	923	928	9 33	9 38	9 41	9 56	10 10	10 16	—
Queen's Road	7 36	7 56	8 16	—	8 36	8 41	—	9 0	9 14	19 16	—	929	934	9 40	9 44	10 0	10 14	10 20	—
Clapham Junc.	7 40	8 0	8 20	—	8 40	8 44	—	9 0	9 14	9 20	—	929	934	9 40	9 44	10 0	10 16	10 22	—
Wandsworth	7 42	8 2	8 22	—	8 42	8 46	—	9 2	9 16	9 23	—	931	936	9 42	9 46	10 2	10 16	10 22	—
Putney	7 45	8 5	8 25	—	8 45	8 49	—	9 5	9 19	9 25	—	934	939	9 45	9 49	10 5	10 19	10 25	—
Barnes	7 48	8 8	8 28	—	8 48	8 52	—	9 8	9 22	9 29	—	937	942	9 48	9 52	10 8	10 22	10 28	—
Mortlake	7 51	8 11	8 31	—	8 51	8 55	—	9 11	9 25	9 31	—	940	945	9 51	10 0	10 11	10 25	10 31	—
Richmond	7 54	8 14	8 34	839	8 54	8 58	8 59	9 14	9 34	9 38	944	948	954	9 53	10 10	10 34	1033		
St. Margarets	7 57	8 17	8 37	—	8 57	9 0	—	9 17	9 31	9 37	—	946	951	957	10 1	10 17	10 31	10 37	—
Twickenham	8 0	8 20	8 40	845	9 0	7	914	9 20	9 35	9 37	—	949	954	10 0	10 7	10 10	10 30	10 34	1043
Strawberry Hill	8 2	8 22	8 42	—	9 5	—	9 22	—	9 42	—	957	10 2	—	10 22	—	10 42	—		
Teddington	8 5	8 25	8 45	—	9 5	—	9 25	—	9 45	—	10 5	—	10 5	—	10 45	—			

SUNDAYS.	AM	AM	AM	AM	AM	AM	AM	AM	AM	AM	PM	PM	PM	PM	PM	PM
WATERLOO ......dep.	10 20	10 30	10 35	10 50	11 10	1118	11 20	11 30	11 35	11 50	12 5	12 10	12 18	12 20	12 30	12 35
Vauxhall..........	10 23	10 33	10 38	10 53	11 13	—	11 23	11 33	11 38	11 53	12 8	12 13	—	12 23	12 33	12 38
Queen s Road	10 26	10 36	10 41	10 56	11 16	—	11 26	11 36	11 41	11 56	12 11	12 16	—	12 26	12 36	12 41
Clapham Junc.......	10 29	10 40	10 44	11 0	11 20	—	11 29	11 40	11 44	12 0	12 14	12 20	—	12 29	12 40	12 44
Wandsworth	10 31	10 42	10 46	11 2	11 22	—	11 31	11 42	11 46	12 2	12 16	12 22	—	12 31	12 42	12 46
Putney	10 34	10 45	10 49	11 5	11 25	—	11 34	11 45	11 49	12 5	12 19	12 25	—	12 34	12 45	12 49
BARNES	10 37	10 48	10 52	11 8	11 28	—	11 37	11 48	11 52	12 8	12 22	12 28	—	12 37	12 48	12 52
Mortlake	10 40	10 51	10 55	11 11	11 31	—	11 40	11 51	11 55	12 11	12 25	12 31	—	12 40	12 51	12 55
RICHMOND	10 43	10 54	10 58	11 14	11 34	1138	11 43	11 54	11 58	12 14	12 28	12 34	12 39	12 43	12 54	12 58
St. Margarets	10 46	10 57	11 1	11 17	11 37	—	11 46	11 57	12 1	12 17	12 31	12 37	—	12 46	12 57	1 1
Twickenham	10 50	11 0	11 7	11 20	11 40	1143	11 50	12 0	12 7	12 20	12 35	12 40	12 45	12 50	1 0	1 7
Strawberry Hill	—	11 2	—	11 22	11 42	—	—	12 2	—	12 22	—	12 42	—	—	1 2	—
TEDDINGTON	—	11 5	—	11 25	11 45	—	—	12 5	—	12 25	—	12 45	—	—	1 5	—

SUNDAYS.	PM	PM	PM	PM	PM	PM	PM	PM	PM	PM	PM	PM	PM	PM	PM	PM	PM	PM	PM	PM
WATERLOO ......dep.	12 50	1 5	1 10	1 18	1 20	1 30	1 35	1 50	2 5	2 10	218	2 20	2 30	2 35	2 50	3 5	3 10	3 18	320	3 30
Vauxhall	12 53	1 8	1 13	—	1 23	1 33	1 38	1 53	2 8	2 13	—	2 23	2 33	2 38	2 53	3 8	3 13	—	323	3 33
Queen's Road.......	12 56	1 11	1 16	—	1 26	1 36	1 41	1 56	211	2 16	—	2 26	2 36	2 41	2 56	311	3 16	—	326	3 36
Clapham Junc.	1 0	1 14	1 20	—	1 29	1 40	1 44	2 0	214	2 20	—	2 29	2 40	2 44	3 0	314	3 20	—	329	3 40
Wandsworth	1 2	1 16	1 22	—	1 31	1 42	1 46	2 2	216	2 22	—	2 31	2 42	2 46	3 2	316	3 22	—	331	3 42
Putney	1 5	1 19	1 25	—	1 34	1 45	1 49	2 5	219	2 25	—	2 34	2 45	2 49	3 5	319	3 25	—	334	3 45
BARNES............	1 8	1 22	1 28	—	1 37	1 48	1 52	2 8	222	2 28	—	2 37	2 48	2 52	3 8	322	3 28	—	337	3 48
Mortlake	1 11	1 25	1 31	—	1 40	1 51	1 55	2 11	225	2 31	—	2 40	2 51	2 55	3 11	325	3 31	—	340	3 51
RICHMOND	1 14	1 28	1 34	1 38	1 43	1 54	1 58	2 14	228	2 34	239	2 43	2 54	2 58	3 14	328	3 34	3 38	343	3 54
St. Margarets.......	1 17	1 31	1 37	—	1 46	1 57	2 1	2 17	231	2 37	—	2 46	2 57	3 1	3 17	331	3 37	—	346	3 57
Twickenham	1 20	1 35	1 40	1 43	1 50	2 0	2 7	2 20	235	2 40	245	2 50	3 0	3 7	3 20	335	3 40	3 43	350	4 0
Strawberry Hill	1 22	—	1 42	—	—	2 2	—	2 22	—	2 42	—	—	3 2	—	3 22	—	3 42	—	—	4 2
TEDDINGTON	1 25	—	1 45	—	—	2 5	—	2 25	—	2 45	—	—	3 5	—	3 25	—	3 45	—	—	4 5

SUNDAYS.	PM	PM	PM	PM	PM	PM	PM	PM	PM	PM	PM	PM	PM	PM	PM	PM	PM	PM	PM	PM
WATERLOO ......dep.	3 35	3 50	4 5	4 10	4 18	4 20	4 30	4 35	4 50	5 5	5 10	518	5 20	5 30	5 35	5 50	558	6 5	6 10	618
Vauxhall...........	3 38	3 53	4 8	4 13	—	4 23	4 33	4 38	4 53	5 8	5 13	—	5 23	5 33	5 38	5 53	—	6 8	6 13	—
Queen's Road	3 41	3 56	4 11	4 16	—	4 26	4 36	4 41	4 56	5 11	5 16	—	5 26	5 36	5 41	5 56	—	6 11	6 16	—
Clapham J.	3 44	4 0	4 14	4 20	—	4 29	4 40	4 44	5 0	5 14	5 20	—	5 29	5 40	5 44	6 0	—	6 14	6 20	—
Wandsworth	3 46	4 2	4 16	4 22	—	4 31	4 42	4 46	5 2	5 16	5 22	—	5 31	5 42	5 46	6 2	—	6 16	6 22	—
Putney	3 49	4 5	4 19	4 25	—	4 34	4 45	4 49	5 5	5 19	5 25	—	5 34	5 45	5 49	6 5	—	6 19	6 25	—
BARNES............	3 52	4 8	4 22	4 28	—	4 37	4 48	4 52	5 8	5 22	5 28	—	5 37	5 48	5 52	6 8	—	6 22	6 28	—
Mortlake...........	3 55	4 11	4 25	4 31	—	4 40	4 51	4 55	5 11	5 25	5 31	—	5 40	5 51	5 55	6 11	—	6 25	6 31	—
RICHMOND	3 58	4 14	4 28	4 34	4 39	4 43	4 54	4 58	5 14	5 28	5 34	538	5 43	5 54	5 58	6 14	618	6 28	6 34	638
St. Margarets	4 1	4 17	4 31	4 37	—	4 46	4 57	5 1	5 17	5 31	5 37	—	5 46	5 57	6 1	6 17	—	6 31	6 37	—
Twickenham	4 7	4 20	4 35	4 40	4 45	4 50	5 0	5 7	5 20	5 35	5 40	543	5 50	6 0	6 7	6 20	624	6 35	6 40	643
Strawberry Hill	—	4 22	—	4 42	—	—	5 2	—	5 22	—	5 42	—	—	6 2	—	6 22	—	—	6 42	—
TEDDINGTON.........	—	4 25	—	4 45	—	—	5 5	—	5 25	—	5 45	—	—	6 5	—	6 25	—	—	6 45	—

SUNDAYS.	PM	PM	PM	PM	PM	PM	PM	PM	PM	PM	PM	PM	PM	PM	PM	PM	PM	PM	PM	PM	PM
WATERLOO ......dep.	6 20	6 25	6 30	6 35	6 50	7 5	7 10	718	7 20	7 25	7 30	7 35	7 48	7 50	8 5	810	818	820	825	830	835
Vauxhall...........	6 23	6 28	6 33	6 38	6 53	7 8	7 13	—	7 23	7 28	7 33	7 38	—	7 53	8 8	813	—	823	828	833	838
Queen's Road	6 26	6 31	6 36	6 41	6 56	7 11	7 16	—	7 26	7 31	7 36	7 41	—	7 56	811	816	—	826	831	836	841
Clapham J.	6 29	6 34	6 40	6 44	7 0	7 14	7 20	—	7 29	7 34	7 40	7 44	—	8 0	814	820	—	829	834	840	844
Wandsworth	6 31	6 36	6 42	6 46	7 2	7 16	7 22	—	7 31	7 36	7 42	7 46	—	8 2	816	822	—	831	836	842	846
Putney.............	6 34	6 39	6 45	6 49	7 5	7 19	7 25	—	7 34	7 39	7 45	7 49	—	8 5	819	825	—	834	839	845	849
BARNES............	6 37	6 42	6 48	6 52	7 8	7 22	7 28	—	7 37	7 42	7 48	7 52	—	8 8	822	828	—	837	842	848	852
Mortlake...........	6 40	6 45	6 51	6 55	7 11	7 25	7 31	—	7 40	7 45	7 51	7 55	—	8 11	825	831	—	840	845	851	855
RICHMOND	6 43	6 48	6 54	6 58	7 14	7 28	7 34	738	7 43	7 48	7 54	7 58	8 8	8 14	828	834	838	843	848	854	858
St. Margarets	6 46	6 51	6 57	7 1	7 17	7 31	7 37	—	7 46	7 51	7 57	8 1	—	8 17	831	837	—	846	851	857	9 1
Twickenham........	6 50	6 54	7 0	7 7	7 20	7 35	7 40	743	7 50	7 54	8 0	8 7	8 13	8 20	835	840	844	850	854	9 0	9 7
Strawberry Hill	—	6 57	7 2	—	7 22	—	7 42	—	—	7 57	8 2	—	—	8 22	—	842	—	—	857	9 2	—
TEDDINGTON.........	—	—	7 5	—	7 25	—	7 45	—	—	—	8 5	—	—	8 25	—	845	—	—	—	9 5	—

SUNDAYS.	PM	PM	PM	PM	PM	PM	PM	PM	PM	PM	PM	PM	PM	PM	PM	PM	PM	PM	PM	PM	PM
WATERLOO ......dep.	850	858	9 5	910	918	920	925	930	935	950	10 5	1010	1018	1020	1025	1030	1035	1050	1110	1125	1130
Vauxhall...........	853	—	9 8	913	—	923	928	933	938	953	10 8	1013	—	1023	1028	1033	1038	1053	1113	1128	1133
Queen's Road	856	—	911	916	—	926	931	936	941	956	1011	1016	—	1026	1031	1036	1041	1056	1116	1131	1136
Clapham J.	9 0	—	914	920	—	929	934	940	944	10 0	1014	1020	—	1029	1034	1040	1044	11 0	1120	1134	1140
Wandsworth	9 2	—	916	922	—	931	936	942	946	10 2	1016	1022	—	1031	1036	1042	1046	11 2	1122	1136	1142
Putney	9 5	—	919	925	—	934	939	945	949	10 5	1019	1025	—	1034	1039	1045	1049	11 5	1125	1139	1145
BARNES............	9 8	—	922	928	—	937	942	948	952	10 8	1022	1028	—	1037	1042	1048	1052	11 8	1128	1142	1148
Mortlake...........	911	—	925	931	—	940	945	951	955	1011	1025	1031	—	1040	1045	1051	1055	1111	1131	1145	1151
RICHMOND	914	918	928	934	939	943	948	954	958	1014	1028	1034	1038	1043	1048	1054	1058	1114	1134	1148	1154
St. Margarets	917	—	931	937	—	946	951	957	10 1	1017	1031	1037	—	1046	1051	1057	11 1	1117	1137	1151	1157
Twickenham........	920	923	935	940	945	950	954	10 0	10 7	1020	1035	1040	1043	1050	1054	11 0	11 4	1120	1140	1154	12 0
Strawberry Hill	922	—	—	942	—	—	957	10 2	—	1022	—	1042	—	—	1057	11 2	—	1122	1142	1157	12 2
TEDDINGTON	925	—	—	945	—	—	—	10 5	—	1025	—	1045	—	—	—	11 5	—	—	1145	—	—

SUNDAYS	AM	AM	AM	AM	AM	AM	AM	AM	AM	AM	AM	AM	AM	AM	AM	AM	AM	AM	AM	AM
TEDDINGTON ....dep.	—	6 58	—	—	—	7 58	8 18	—	—	—	8 38	—	—	9 1	9 18	—	—	—	9 38	—
Strawberry Hill	6 46	7 1	7 21	7 41	—	8 1	8 21	—	833	—	8 41	—	—	9 4	9 21	—	933	—	9 41	—
Twickenham	6 49	7 9	7 26	7 46	7 56	8 11	8 26	831	836	841	8 46	856	9 2	911	9 26	931	936	941	9 46	956
St. Margarets..	6 51	7 11	7 28	7 48	7 58	8 13	8 28	833	838	843	8 48	859	—	913	9 28	933	938	943	9 48	958
RICHMOND	6 54	7 14	7 31	7 51	8 1	8 16	8 31	836	841	846	8 51	9 1	9 8	916	9 31	936	941	946	9 51	10 1
Mortlake	6 57	7 17	7 34	7 54	8 4	8 19	8 34	839	844	849	8 54	9 4	—	919	9 34	939	944	949	9 54	10 4
BARNES	7 0	7 20	7 37	7 57	8 7	8 22	8 37	842	847	852	8 57	9 7	—	922	9 37	942	947	952	9 57	10 7
Putney	7 3	7 23	7 40	8 0	8 10	8 25	8 40	845	850	855	9 0	910	—	925	9 40	945	950	955	10 0	1010
Wandsworth	7 6	7 26	7 43	8 3	8 13	8 28	8 43	848	853	858	9 3	913	—	928	9 43	948	953	958	10 3	1013
Clapham Junc. ..arr	7 8	7 28	7 45	8 5	8 15	8 30	8 45	850	855	9 0	9 5	915	—	930	9 45	950	955	10 0	10 5	1015
Queen's Road.......	7 11	7 31	7 48	8 8	8 18	8 33	8 48	853	858	9 3	9 8	918	—	933	9 48	953	958	10 3	10 8	1018
Vauxhall	7 14	7 34	7 51	8 11	8 21	8 36	8 51	856	9 1	9 6	9 11	921	—	936	9 51	956	10 1	10 6	10 11	1021
WATERLOO	7 18	7 38	7 55	8 15	8 25	8 40	8 55	9 0	9 5	910	9 15	925	928	940	9 55	10 0	10 5	1010	10 15	1025

SUNDAYS.	AM	AM	AM	AM	AM	AM	AM	AM	AM	AM	AM	AM	AM	AM	AM	AM	PM	PM
TEDDINGTON ....dep.	—	10 1	1018	—	—	—	10 38	—	11 1	—	11 18	—	—	—	11 38	—	12 1	—
Strawberry Hill	—	10 4	1021	—	1033	—	10 41	—	11 4	—	11 21	—	1133	—	11 41	—	12 4	—
Twickenham	10 3	10 11	1026	1031	1036	1041	10 46	1056	11 11	1117	11 26	1131	1136	1141	11 46	1156	12 11	1217
St. Margarets.......	—	10 13	1028	1033	1038	1043	10 48	1058	11 13	—	11 28	1133	1138	1143	11 48	1158	12 13	—
RICHMOND	10 9	10 16	1031	1036	1041	1046	10 51	11 1	11 16	1123	11 31	1136	1141	1146	11 51	12 1	12 16	1223
Mortlake	—	10 19	1034	1039	1044	1049	10 54	11 4	11 19	—	11 34	1139	1144	1149	11 54	12 4	12 19	—
BARNES	—	10 22	1037	1042	1047	1052	10 57	11 7	11 22	—	11 37	1142	1147	1152	11 57	12 7	12 22	—
Putney	—	10 25	1040	1045	1050	1055	11 0	1110	11 25	—	11 40	1145	1150	1155	12 0	1210	12 25	—
Wandsworth	—	10 28	1043	1048	1053	1058	11 3	1113	11 28	—	11 43	1148	1153	1158	12 3	1213	12 28	—
Clapham Junc. arr.	—	10 30	1045	1050	1055	11 0	11 5	1115	11 30	—	11 45	1150	1155	12 0	12 5	1215	12 30	—
Queen's Road.......	—	10 33	1048	1053	1058	11 3	11 8	1118	11 33	—	11 48	1153	1158	12 3	12 8	1218	12 33	—
Vauxhall	1025	10 36	1051	1056	11 1	11 6	11 11	1121	11 36	—	11 51	1156	12 1	12 6	12 11	1221	12 36	—
WATERLOO	1030	10 40	1055	11 0	11 5	1110	11 15	1125	11 40	1143	11 55	12 0	12 5	1210	12 15	1225	12 40	1243

SUNDAYS.	PM	PM	PM	PM	PM	PM	PM	PM	PM	PM	PM	PM	PM	PM	PM	PM	PM	PM	PM	PM
Teddington ....dep.	12 18	—	—	12 38	—	1 1	—	1 18	—	—	—	1 38	—	2 1	2 18	—	—	2 38	—	3 1
Strawberry Hill....	12 21	—	—	12 41	—	1 4	—	1 21	—	—	—	1 41	—	2 4	2 21	—	—	2 41	—	3 4
Twickenham	12 26	1231	1241	12 47	1256	1 11	117	1 26	131	1 37	141	1 46	156	2 11	2 26	231	241	2 46	256	3 11
St. Margarets	12 28	1233	1243	12 49	1258	1 13	—	1 28	133	—	143	1 48	158	2 13	2 28	233	243	2 48	258	3 13
Richmond	12 31	1236	1246	12 52	1 1	1 16	123	1 34	136	1 43	146	1 51	2 1	2 16	2 31	236	246	2 51	3 1	3 16
Mortlake	12 34	1239	1249	12 55	1 4	1 19	—	1 37	139	—	149	1 54	2 4	2 19	2 34	239	249	2 54	3 4	3 19
Barnes	12 37	1242	1252	12 58	1 7	1 22	—	1 40	142	—	152	1 57	2 7	2 22	2 37	242	252	2 57	3 7	3 22
Putney	12 40	1245	1255	1 1	110	1 25	—	1 43	145	—	155	2 0	210	2 25	2 40	245	255	3 0	310	3 25
Wandsworth	12 43	1248	1258	1 4	113	1 28	—	1 45	148	—	158	2 3	213	2 28	2 43	248	258	3 3	313	3 28
Clapham Junc. arr.	12 45	1250	1 0	1 7	115	1 30	—	1 48	150	—	2 0	2 5	215	2 30	2 45	250	3 0	3 5	315	3 30
Queen's Road	12 48	1253	1 3	1 10	118	1 33	—	1 51	153	—	2 3	2 8	218	2 33	2 48	253	3 3	3 8	318	3 33
Vauxhall	12 51	1256	1 6	1 13	121	1 36	—	1 55	156	—	2 6	2 11	221	2 36	2 51	256	3 6	3 11	321	3 36
Waterloo	12 55	1 0	110	1 17	125	1 40	143	1 58	2 0	2 3	210	2 15	225	2 40	2 55	3 1	310	3 15	325	3 40

SUNDAYS	PM	PM	PM	PM	PM	PM	PM	PM	PM	PM	PM	PM	PM	PM	PM	PM	PM	PM	PM	PM	PM	PM
Teddington	—	3 18	—	—	3 38	—	4 1	4 18	—	—	4 38	—	5 1	—	—	5 18	—	—	—	5 38	—	6 1
Strawberry Hill....	—	3 21	—	—	3 41	—	4 4	4 21	—	—	4 41	—	5 4	—	—	5 21	—	533	—	5 41	—	6 4
Twickenham	3 17	3 26	331	341	3 46	356	4 11	4 26	431	441	4 46	456	5 11	—	5 17	5 26	531	536	541	5 46	556	6 11
St. Margarets	—	3 28	333	343	3 48	358	4 13	4 28	433	443	4 48	458	5 13	—	—	5 28	533	538	543	5 48	558	6 13
Richmond	3 23	3 31	336	346	3 51	4 1	4 16	4 31	436	446	4 51	5 1	5 16	5 8	5 23	5 31	536	541	546	5 51	6 1	6 16
Mortlake	—	3 34	339	349	3 54	4 4	4 19	4 34	439	449	4 54	5 4	5 19	—	—	5 34	539	544	549	5 54	6 4	6 19
Barnes	—	3 37	342	352	3 57	4 7	4 22	4 37	442	452	4 57	5 7	5 22	—	—	5 37	542	547	552	5 57	6 7	6 22
Putney	—	3 40	345	355	4 0	410	4 25	4 40	445	455	5 0	510	5 25	—	—	5 40	545	550	555	6 0	610	6 25
Wandsworth........	—	3 43	348	358	4 3	413	4 28	4 43	448	458	5 3	513	5 28	—	—	5 43	548	553	558	6 3	613	6 28
Clapham Junc. arr.	—	3 45	350	4 0	4 5	415	4 30	4 45	450	5 0	5 5	515	5 30	—	—	5 45	550	555	6 0	6 5	615	6 30
Queen's Road	—	3 48	353	4 3	4 8	418	4 33	4 48	453	5 3	5 8	518	5 33	—	—	5 48	553	558	6 3	6 8	618	6 33
Vauxhall	—	3 51	356	4 6	4 11	421	4 36	4 51	456	5 6	5 11	521	5 36	—	—	5 51	556	6 1	6 6	6 11	621	6 36
Waterloo	3 43	3 55	4 1	410	4 15	425	4 40	4 55	5 0	510	5 15	525	5 40	528	5 43	5 55	6 0	6 5	610	6 15	625	6 40

SUNDAYS.	PM	PM	PM	PM	PM	PM	PM	PM	PM	PM	PM	PM	PM	PM	PM	PM	PM	PM	PM	PM	PM	PM	PM
Teddington ....dep.	—	6 18	—	—	—	6 38	—	—	7 1	—	7 18	—	—	—	7 38	—	8 1	—	8 18	—	—	—	8 38
Strawberry Hill....	—	6 21	—	633	—	6 41	—	—	7 4	—	7 21	—	733	—	7 41	—	8 4	—	8 21	—	833	—	8 41
Twickenham	617	6 26	631	636	641	6 46	656	7 2	711	717	7 26	731	736	741	7 46	756	8 11	817	8 26	831	836	841	8 46
St. Margarets	—	6 28	633	638	643	6 48	658	—	713	—	7 28	733	738	743	7 48	758	8 13	—	8 28	833	838	843	8 48
Richmond	623	6 31	636	641	646	6 51	7 1	7 8	716	723	7 31	736	741	746	7 51	8 1	8 16	823	8 31	836	841	846	8 51
Mortlake	—	6 34	639	644	649	6 54	7 4	—	719	—	7 34	739	744	749	7 54	8 4	8 19	—	8 34	839	844	849	8 54
Barnes	—	6 37	642	647	652	6 57	7 7	—	722	—	7 37	742	747	752	7 57	8 7	8 22	—	8 37	842	847	852	8 57
Putney	—	6 40	645	650	655	7 0	710	—	725	—	7 40	745	750	755	8 0	810	8 25	—	8 40	845	850	855	9 0
Wandsworth	—	6 43	648	653	658	7 3	713	—	728	—	7 43	748	753	758	8 3	813	8 28	—	8 43	848	853	858	9 3
Clapham Junc. arr.	—	6 45	650	655	7 0	7 5	715	—	730	—	7 45	750	755	8 0	8 5	815	8 30	—	8 46	850	855	9 0	9 5
Queen's Road	—	6 48	653	658	7 3	7 8	718	—	733	—	7 48	753	758	8 3	8 8	818	8 33	—	8 48	853	858	9 3	9 8
Vauxhall	—	6 51	656	7 1	7 6	7 11	721	—	736	—	7 51	756	8 1	8 6	8 11	821	8 36	—	8 51	856	9 1	9 6	9 11
Waterloo	643	6 55	7 0	7 5	710	7 15	725	728	740	743	7 55	8 0	8 5	810	8 15	825	8 40	843	8 55	9 0	9 5	910	9 15

SUNDAYS.	PM	PM	PM	PM	PM	PM	—	PM	PM	PM	PM	PM	PM	PM	PM	PM	PM	PM	PM	PM
Teddington ....dep.	—	—	9 1	—	9 18	—	—	—	938	—	—	—	10 1	—	1018	—	—	1038	—	—
Strawberry Hill....	—	—	9 4	—	9 21	—	933	—	941	—	—	—	10 4	—	1021	—	1033	1041	—	—
Twickenham	856	9 2	9 11	9 17	9 26	931	936	941	946	952	956	10 2	1011	1017	1026	1031	1036	1046	1056	1117
St. Margarets	858	—	9 13	—	9 28	933	938	943	948	—	958	—	1013	—	1028	1033	1038	1048	1058	—
Richmond	9 1	9 8	9 16	9 23	9 31	936	941	946	951	958	10 1	10 8	1016	1023	1031	1036	1041	1051	11 1	1123
Mortlake	9 4	—	9 19	—	9 34	939	944	949	954	—	10 4	—	1019	—	1034	1039	1044	1054	11 4	—
Barnes	9 7	—	9 22	—	9 37	942	947	952	957	—	10 7	—	1022	—	1037	1042	1047	1057	11 7	1130
Putney	910	—	9 25	—	9 40	945	950	955	10 0	—	1010	—	1025	—	1040	1045	1050	11 0	1110	1134
Wandsworth........	913	—	9 28	—	9 43	948	953	958	10 3	—	1013	—	1028	—	1043	1048	1053	11 3	1113	—
Clapham Junc. arr.	915	—	9 30	—	9 45	950	955	10 0	10 5	—	1015	—	1030	—	1045	1050	1055	11 5	1115	1140
Queen's Road	918	—	9 33	—	9 48	953	958	10 3	10 8	—	1018	—	1033	—	1048	1053	1058	11 8	1118	—
Vauxhall	921	—	9 36	—	9 51	956	101	10 6	1011	—	1021	—	1036	—	1051	1056	11 1	1111	1121	1146
Waterloo	925	928	9 40	9 43	9 55	10 0	105	1010	1015	1018	1025	1028	1040	1043	1055	11 0	11 5	1115	1125	1151

WATERLOO TO WIMBLEDON AND SURBITON.

WEEK DAYS	AM	AM	AM	AM	AM	AM	AM	AM	AM	AM	AM	AM	PM	AM	AM	AM	AM	AM
Waterloo ......dep.	4 50	5 40	5 50	6 0	6 5	6 10	6 20	6 30	6 40	6 50	6 50	7 0	7 0	7 5	7 5	7 20	7 30	7 33
Vauxhall	—	—	—	6 3	—	6 13	6 23	6 33	6 43	—	6 53	—	7 3	—	7 8	7 23	—	7 38
Clapham Junction.	—	—	—	6 8	—	6 18	6 28	6 38	6 48	—	6 58	—	7 8	—	7 13	7 28	—	7 43
Earlsfield	—	—	—	6 12	—	6 22	6 32	6 42	6 52	—	7 2	—	7 12	—	7 17	7 32	—	7 47
Wimbledon	5 7	—	—	6 16	—	6 26	6 36	6 46	6 56	—	7 6	—	7 16	—	7 21	7 36	—	7 51
Raynes Park..	—	—	—	6 19	—	6 29	6 39	6 49	6 59	—	7 9	—	7 19	—	7 24	7 38	—	7 54
Malden	5 13	—	—	6 22	—	6 32	6 42	6 52	7 2	—	7 12	—	7 22	—	7 27	7 42	—	7 57
Surbiton	5 18	5 59	6 10	—	6 26	—	6 47	—	—	7 11	7 17	7 21	—	7 26	7 32	7 47	7 51	8 2

WEEK DAYS.	AM	AM	AM	AM	AM	AM	AM	AM	AM	AM	AM	AM	AM	AM	AM	AM	AM	AM
Waterloo ......dep.	7 50	7 50	8 5	8 5	8 15	8 20	8 30	8 31	8 35	8 50	9 0	9 4	9 5	9 15	9 20	9 30	9 35	9 50
Vauxhall	—	7 53	—	8 8	—	8 23	—	—	8 38	8 53	—	—	9 8	—	9 23	—	9 38	9 53
Clapham Junction..	—	7 58	—	8 13	—	8 28	—	—	8 43	8 58	—	—	9 13	—	9 28	—	9 43	9 58
Earlsfield	—	8 2	—	8 17	—	8 32	—	—	8 47	9 2	—	—	9 17	—	9 32	—	9 47	10 2
Wimbledon	—	8 6	—	1 21	—	8 36	—	—	8 51	9 6	—	—	9 21	9 30	9 36	—	9 51	10 6
Raynes Park........	—	8 9	—	8 24	—	8 39	—	—	8 54	9 9	—	—	9 24	—	9 39	—	9 54	10 9
Malden	—	8 12	—	8 27	—	8 42	—	—	8 57	9 12	—	—	9 27	—	9 42	—	9 57	10 12
Surbiton	8 9	8 17	8 26	8 32	8 35	8 47	8 52	8 56	9 2	9 17	9 21	9 24	9 32	9 40	9 47	9 51	10 2	10 17

WEEK DAYS.	AM	AM	AM	AM	AM	AM	AM	AM	AM	AM	AM	AM	AM	AM	PM	PM
Waterloo	10 5	10 5	10 20	10 20	10 34	10 35	10 50	10 50	11 5	11 5	11 20	11 20	11 35	11 50	12 5	12 5
Vauxhall	—	10 8	—	10 23	—	10 38	—	10 53	—	11 8	—	11 23	11 38	11 53	—	12 8
Clapham Junction..	—	10 13	—	10 28	—	10 43	—	10 58	—	11 13	—	11 28	11 43	11 58	—	12 13
Earlsfield	—	10 17	—	10 32	—	10 47	—	11 2	—	11 17	—	11 32	11 47	12 2	—	12 17
Wimbledon	—	10 21	—	10 36	10 50	10 51	—	11 6	—	11 21	—	11 36	11 51	12 6	—	12 21
Raynes Park........	—	10 24	—	10 39	—	10 54	—	11 9	—	11 24	—	11 39	11 54	12 9	—	12 24
Malden	—	10 27	—	10 42	—	10 57	—	11 12	—	11 27	—	11 42	11 57	12 12	—	12 27
Surbiton............	10 23	10 32	10 40	10 47	10 59	11 2	11 12	11 17	11 26	11 32	11 40	11 47	12 2	12 17	12 26	12 32

WEEK DAYS.	PM	PM	PM	PM	PM	*d*	PM	PM	PM	PM	*d*	PM	PM	*d*	*d*	PM
Waterloo ......dep.	12 15	12 20	12 40	12 35	12 50	12 54	1 5	1 5	1 20	1 20	1 35	1 35	1 50	1 54	2 0	2 5
Vauxhall	—	12 23	—	12 38	12 53	—	—	1 8	—	1 23	—	1 38	1 53	—	—	2 8
Clapham Junction..	—	12 28	—	12 43	12 58	—	—	1 13	—	1 28	—	1 43	1 58	—	—	2 13
Earlsfield	—	12 32	—	12 47	1 2	—	—	1 17	—	1 32	—	1 47	2 2	—	—	2 17
Wimbledon	12 30	12 36	—	12 51	1 6	—	—	1 21	—	1 36	—	1 51	2 6	—	—	2 21
Raynes Park........	—	12 39	—	12 54	1 9	—	—	1 24	—	1 39	—	1 54	2 9	—	—	2 24
Malden	—	12 42	—	12 57	1 12	—	—	1 27	—	1 42	—	1 57	2 12	—	—	2 27
Surbiton	12 40	12 47	1 0	1 2	1 17	1 14	1 26	1 32	1 40	1 47	1 56	2 2	2 17	2 14	2 21	2 32

d Saturdays only. *e* Saturdays excepted.

WATERLOO TO WIMBLEDON AND SURBITON.

WEEK DAYS.	PM	PM	PM	PM	PM	PM	PM	PM	AM	PM	PM	PM	PM	PM
Waterloo	2 5	2 20	2 20	2 34	2 35	2 50	3 5	3 5	3 20	3 20	3 40	3 35	3 50	4 5
Vauxhall	—	—	2 23	—	2 38	2 53	—	3 8	—	3 23	—	3 38	3 53	—
Clapham Junction..	—	—	2 28	—	2 43	2 58	—	3 13	—	3 28	—	3 43	3 58	—
Earlsfield	—	—	2 32	—	2 47	3 2	—	3 17	—	3 32	—	3 47	4 2	—
Wimbledon	—	—	2 36	2 50	2 51	3 6	—	3 21	—	3 36	—	3 51	4 6	—
Raynes Park	—	—	2 39	—	2 54	3 9	—	3 24	—	3 39	—	3 54	4 9	—
Malden	—	—	2 42	—	2 57	3 12	—	3 27	—	3 42	—	3 57	4 12	—
Surbiton	2 26	2 42	2 47	2 59	3 2	3 17	3 26	3 32	3 40	3 47	4 1	4 2	4 17	4 26

WEEK DAYS.	PM	PM	PM	PM	PM	PM	e	PM	PM	PM	PM	PM	PM	PM	PM	e	e
Waterloo....dep.	4 5	4 20	4 20	4 35	4 40	4 50	4 54	5 4	5 5	5 20	5 20	5 37	5 35	5 50	5 54	6 4
Vauxhall	4 8	—	4 23	4 38	—	4 53	—	—	5 8	—	5 23	—	5 38	5 53	—	—
Clapham Junction..	4 13	—	4 28	4 43	—	4 58	—	—	5 13	—	5 28	—	5 43	5 58	—	—
Earlsfield	4 17	—	4 32	4 47	—	5 2	—	—	5 17	—	5 32	—	5 47	6 2	—	—
Wimbledon	4 21	—	4 36	4 51	—	5 6	—	—	5 21	—	5 36	—	5 51	6 6	—	—
Raynes Park	4 24	—	4 39	4 54	—	5 9	—	—	5 24	—	5 39	—	5 54	6 9	—	—
Malden	4 27	—	4 42	4 57	—	5 12	—	—	5 27	—	5 42	—	5 57	6 12	—	—
Surbiton	4 32	4 40	4 47	5 2	4 59	5 17	5 14	5 25	5 32	5 40	5 47	5 58	6 2	6 17	6 14	6 26

WEEK DAYS	PM	PM	PM	PM	PM	e	d	PM	e	PM	PM	PM	PM	PM	PM	PM
Waterloo....dep	6 5	6 20	6 20	6 30	6 35	6 38	6 40	6 50	7 0	7 5	7 5	7 20	7 20	7 35	7 50	8 0
Vauxhall	6 8	—	6 23	—	6 38	—	—	6 53	—	—	7 8	—	7 23	7 38	7 53	—
Clapham Junction.	6 13	—	6 28	—	6 43	—	—	6 58	—	—	7 13	—	7 28	7 43	7 58	—
Earlsfield	6 17	—	6 32	—	6 47	—	—	7 2	—	—	7 17	—	7 32	7 47	8 2	—
Wimbledon	6 21	—	6 36	—	6 51	—	—	7 6	—	—	7 21	—	7 36	7 51	8 6	—
Raynes Park	6 24	—	6 39	—	6 54	—	—	7 9	—	—	7 24	—	7 39	7 54	8 9	—
Malden	6 27	—	6 42	—	6 57	—	—	7 12	—	—	7 27	—	7 42	7 57	8 12	—
Surbiton	6 32	6 40	6 47	6 51	7 2	6 57	6 59	7 17	7 19	7 26	7 32	7 40	7 47	8 2	8 17	8 20

WEEK DAYS.	PM	PM	PM	PM	PM	PM	PM	PM	PM	PM	PM	PM	PM	PM	PM	PM
Waterloo....dep.	8 5	8 5	8 20	8 20	8 35	8 50	8 55	9 5	9 5	9 20	9 20	9 35	9 50	10 5	10 5	10 20
Vauxhall	—	8 8	—	8 23	8 38	8 53	—	—	9 8	—	9 23	9 38	9 53	—	10 8	—
Clapham Junction..	—	8 13	—	8 28	8 43	8 58	9 6	—	9 13	—	9 28	9 43	9 58	—	10 13	—
Earlsfield	—	8 17	—	8 32	8 47	9 2	—	—	9 17	—	9 32	9 47	10 2	—	10 17	—
Wimbledon	—	8 21	—	8 36	8 51	9 6	—	—	9 21	—	9 36	9 51	10 6	—	10 21	—
Raynes Park	—	8 24	—	8 39	8 54	9 9	—	—	9 24	—	9 33	9 54	10 9	—	10 24	—
Malden	—	8 27	—	8 42	8 57	9 12	—	—	9 27	—	9 42	9 57	10 12	—	10 27	—
Surbiton	8 26	8 32	8 40	8 47	9 2	9 17	9 20	9 26	9 32	9 40	9 47	10 2	10 17	10 26	10 32	10 40

WEEK DAYS.	PM	PM	PM	PM	PM	PM	PM	g
Waterloo ......dep.	10 20	10 50	11 15	11 20	11 34	11 40	12 5	
Vauxhall	10 23	10 53	—	11 23	—	—	12 8	
Clapham Junction..	10 28	10 58	—	11 28	—	—	12 13	
Earlsfield	10 32	11 2	—	11 32	—	—	12 17	
Wimbledon	10 36	11 6	—	11 36	—	—	12 21	
Raynes Park	10 39	11 9	—	11 39	—	—	12 24	
Malden	10 42	11 12	—	11 42	—	—	12 27	
Surbiton	10 47	11 17	11 36	11 47	11 54	12 0	12 32	

SURBITON AND WIMBLEDON TO WATERLOO.

WEEK DAYS.	g	AM	AM	AM	AM	AM	AM	AM	AM	AM	AM	AM	AM	AM
Surbiton ......dep.	3 34	4 35	5 47	6 17	6 32	6 47	6 55	7 2	7 14	7 17	7 20	7 32	7 42	7 47
Malden	—	4 41	5 53	6 20	6 36	6 51	—	7 6	7 21	7 21	7 25	7 36	7 49	7 51
Raynes Park	—	4 45	5 53	6 23	6 39	6 54	—	7 9	—	7 24	—	7 39	—	—
Wimbledon	—	4 49	5 56	6 26	6 42	6 57	—	7 12	7 27	7 27	7 31	7 42	7 57	7 57
Earlsfield	—	4 54	6 0	6 30	6 45	7 0	—	7 15	—	7 30	—	7 45	—	8 0
Clapham Junction..	—	4 59	6 4	6 34	6 49	7 4	—	7 19	—	7 34	—	7 49	—	8 6
Vauxhall	—	5 4	6 9	6 39	6 54	7 9	—	7 24	—	7 39	—	7 54	—	8 1
Waterloo	3 55	5 10	6 13	6 43	6 58	7 13	7 17	7 29	7 41	7 43	7 46	7 58	8 14	8 13

WEEK DAYS.	AM	AM	AM	e	AM	AM	AM	AM	AM	AM	AM	AM	AM	AM	AM
Surbiton ......dep.	7 59	8 2	8 5	8 14	8 17	8 25	8 32	8 32	8 43	8 46	8 59	9 4	9 10	9 16	9 32	9 35
Malden	—	8 6	8 12	—	8 20	8 31	8 38	8 36	—	8 50	—	9 8	—	9 20	9 36	—
Raynes Park	—	8 9	—	—	8 23	—	—	8 39	—	8 53	—	—	—	9 23	9 39	—
Wimbledon	—	8 12	—	—	8 26	—	—	8 42	—	8 56	—	9 13	—	9 26	9 42	—
Earlsfield	—	8 15	—	—	8 30	—	—	8 45	—	9 0	—	—	—	9 29	9 45	—
Clapham Junction..	—	8 19	—	—	8 34	—	—	8 49	—	9 4	—	9 19	—	9 33	9 49	—
Vauxhall	—	8 24	—	—	8 39	—	—	8 54	—	9 9	—	9 24	—	9 38	9 54	—
Waterloo	8 20	8 28	8 30	8 36	8 43	8 48	8 56	8 58	9 4	9 13	9 21	9 28	9 31	9 42	9 58	10 0

WEEK DAYS.	AM	AM	e	AM	AM	AM	AM	AM	AM	AM	AM	AM	AM	AM	AM	AM
Surbiton ......dep.	9 47	10 2	10 14	10 17	10 24	10 32	10 45	10 49	11 2	11 17	11 25	11 32	11 35	11 47
Malden	9 50	10 6	—	10 21	—	10 36	—	10 53	11 6	11 22	—	11 36	—	11 50
Raynes Park	9 53	10 9	—	10 24	—	10 39	—	10 56	11 9	11 25	—	11 39	—	11 53
Wimbledon	9 56	10 12	—	10 27	—	10 42	—	10 59	11 12	11 26	—	11 42	—	11 56
Earlsfield	10 0	10 15	—	10 30	—	10 45	—	11 2	11 15	11 30	—	11 45	—	12 0
Clapham Junction..	10 4	10 19	—	10 34	—	10 49	—	11 6	11 19	11 34	—	11 49	—	12 4
Vauxhall	10 9	10 24	—	10 39	—	10 54	—	11 11	11 24	11 39	—	11 54	—	12 9
Waterloo	10 13	10 28	10 36	10 43	10 46	10 58	11 6	11 15	11 28	11 43	11 45	11 58	11 56	12 13

WEEK DAYS.	PM	PM	PM	PM	PM	PM	PM	PM	PM	PM	PM	PM	PM	PM	PM
Surbiton ......dep	12 2	12 17	12 25	12 32	12 39	12 47	12 55	1 2	1 17	1 25	1 32	1 39	1 47	2 2	2 17
Malden	12 6	12 21	—	12 36	—	12 50	—	1 6	1 21	—	1 36	—	1 50	2 6	2 21
Raynes Park	12 9	12 24	—	12 39	—	12 53	—	1 9	1 24	—	1 39	—	1 53	2 9	2 23
Wimbledon	12 12	12 27	—	12 42	—	12 56	1 6	1 12	1 27	—	1 42	—	1 56	2 12	2 26
Earlsfield	12 15	12 30	—	12 45	—	1 0	—	1 15	1 30	—	1 45	—	2 0	2 15	2 30
Clapham Junction..	12 19	12 34	—	12 49	—	1 4	—	1 19	1 34	—	1 49	—	2 4	2 19	2 34
Vauxhall	12 24	12 39	—	12 54	—	1 9	—	1 24	1 39	—	1 54	—	2 9	2 24	2 39
Waterloo	12 28	12 43	12 46	12 58	1 0	1 13	1 20	1 28	1 43	1 46	1 58	2 0	2 13	2 28	2 43

WEEK DAYS.	PM	PM	PM	PM	PM	PM	PM	PM	PM	PM	PM	PM	PM	PM	PM	PM
Surbiton ......dep.	2 25	2 32	2 39	2 44	2 46	2 52	3 2	3 17	3 25	3 32	3 39	3 45	3 47	3 53	4 2	4 17	4 25
Malden	—	2 36	—	—	2 50	—	3 6	—	3 36	—	3 39	—	3 50	—	4 6	—
Raynes Park	—	2 39	—	—	2 53	—	3 9	3 24	—	3 39	—	3 53	—	4 9	4 24	—
Wimbledon	—	2 42	—	2 56	3 2	3 12	3 27	—	3 42	—	3 57	—	4 12	4 27	—
Earlsfield	—	2 45	—	3 0	—	3 15	3 30	—	3 45	—	4 0	—	4 15	4 30	—
Clapham Junction..	—	2 49	—	3 4	—	3 19	3 34	—	3 49	—	4 4	—	4 19	4 34	—
Vauxhall	—	2 54	—	3 9	—	3 24	3 39	—	3 54	—	4 9	—	4 24	4 39	—
Waterloo	2 46	2 58	3 1	3 6	3 13	3 16	3 28	3 43	3 46	3 58	4 0	4 6	4 13	4 15	4 28	4 43	4 46

d Saturdays only.   e Saturdays excepted.   g Monday mornings excepted.

WEEK DAYS.	PM	PM	PM	PM	PM	PM	PM	PM	PM	PM	PM	PM	PM	PM
Surbiton ......dep.	4 32	4 33	4 47	4 55	5 2	5 17	5 25	5 32	5 42	5 47	5 55	6 2	6 6	6 17
Malden	4 36	—	4 50	—	5 6	5 21	—	5 36	—	5 50	—	6 6	—	6 20
Raynes Park......	4 39	—	4 53	—	5 9	5 24	—	5 39	—	5 53	—	6 9	—	6 23
Wimbledon	4 42	—	4 56	5 6	5 12	5 27	—	5 42	—	5 56	—	6 12	—	6 23
Earlsfield	4 45	—	5 0	—	5 15	5 30	—	5 45	—	6 0	—	6 15	—	6 30
Clapham Junction.	4 49	—	5 4	—	5 19	5 34	—	5 49	—	6 4	—	6 19	—	6 34
Vauxhall	4 54	—	5 9	—	5 24	5 39	—	5 54	—	6 9	—	6 24	—	6 39
Waterloo	4 58	5 0	5 13	5 20	5 28	5 43	5 46	5 58	6 10	6 13	6 16	6 28	6 23	6 43

WEEK DAYS.	PM	PM	PM	PM	PM	PM	PM	PM	PM	PM	PM	PM	PM	PM	PM
Surbiton ......dep.	6 25	6 31	6 32	6 47	7 2	7 17	7 19	7 25	7 32	7 39	7 47	8 2	8 17	8 25	8 32	8 49
Malden	—	—	6 36	6 50	7 6	7 20	—	—	7 33	—	7 50	8 6	8 21	—	8 36	—
Raynes Park......	—	—	6 39	6 53	7 9	7 24	—	—	7 39	—	7 53	8 9	8 24	—	8 39	—
Wimbledon	—	—	6 42	6 56	7 12	7 26	—	—	7 42	—	7 56	8 12	8 27	—	8 42	—
Earlsfield	—	—	6 45	7 0	7 15	7 30	—	—	7 45	—	8 0	8 15	8 30	—	8 45	—
Clapham Junction..	—	—	6 49	7 4	7 19	7 34	—	—	7 49	—	8 4	8 19	8 34	—	8 49	—
Vauxhall	—	—	6 54	7 9	7 24	7 39	—	—	7 54	—	8 9	8 24	8 31	—	8 54	—
Waterloo	6 46	6 52	6 58	7 13	7 28	7 43	7 40	7 46	7 58	8 0	8 13	8 23	8 43	8 46	8 53	9 0

WEEK DAYS	PM	PM	PM	PM	PM	PM	PM	PM	PM	PM	PM	PM	PM	PM	PM
Surbiton ......dep.	8 45	8 47	9 1	9 2	9 17	9 25	9 31	9 32	9 39	9 47	10 17	10 25	10 29	10 35	10 49
Malden	—	8 50	—	9 6	9 20	—	—	9 36	—	9 50	10 20	—	—	—	—
Raynes Park......	—	8 53	—	9 9	9 23	—	—	9 39	—	9 53	10 23	—	—	—	—
Wimbledon	—	8 56	9 12	9 12	9 26	—	—	9 42	—	9 56	10 26	—	—	—	—
Earlsfield	—	9 0	—	9 15	9 30	—	—	9 45	—	10 0	10 30	—	—	—	—
Clapham Junction..	—	9 4	—	9 19	9 34	—	—	9 49	—	10 4	10 34	—	—	—	—
Vauxhall	—	9 9	—	9 24	9 39	—	—	9 54	—	10 9	10 39	—	—	—	—
Waterloo	9 6	9 13	9 26	9 28	9 43	9 45	9 52	9 58	10 0	10 13	10 43	10 46	10 50	11 56	11 10

WEEK DAYS.	PM	PM	PM	d	PM
Surbiton ......dep.	10 47	11 7	11 17	11 38	11 49
Malden	10 50	—	11 20	11 42	—
Raynes Park	10 53	—	11 23	11 45	—
Wimbledon	10 56	—	11 26	11 48	11 59
Earlsfield	11 0	—	11 30	11 51	—
Clapham Junction..	11 4	—	11 34	11 55	12 7
Vauxhall	11 9	—	11 39	12 0	—
Waterloo	11 13	11 28	11 43	12 4	12 16

SUNDAYS.	AM	AM	AM	AM	AM	AM	AM	AM	AM	AM	AM	AM	AM	AM	AM	AM	AM	AM
Waterloo ......dep.	7 35	8 0	8 15	8 20	8 38	8 45	8 55	9 0	9 15	9 15	9 20	9 35	9 45	9 55	10	8 10	15	10 20	10 35
Vauxhall	7 38	—	8 18	—	—	—	8 58	—	—	9 18	—	—	9 38	—	9 58	—	10 18	10 38
Clapham Junction..	7 43	—	8 23	8 30	8 48	8 55	9 3	—	—	9 23	9 30	9 43	—	10 3	10 18	10 23	10 29	10 43
Earlsfield	7 47	—	8 27	—	—	—	9 7	—	—	9 27	—	9 47	—	10 7	—	10 27	—	10 47
Wimbledon	7 51	8 15	8 31	—	8 56	—	9 11	—	—	9 31	9 38	9 51	—	10 11	10 26	10 31	10 37	10 51
Raynes Park......	7 54	—	8 34	—	—	—	9 14	—	—	9 34	—	9 54	—	10 14	—	10 34	—	10 54
Malden	7 57	—	8 37	—	9 2	—	9 17	—	--	9 37	—	9 57	—	10 17	—	10 37	—	10 57
Surbiton	8 1	8 25	8 41	8 45	5 9	11	9 21	9 21	9 23	9 41	9 48	10 1	10 7	10 21	10 33	10 41	10 47	11 1

SUNDAYS.	AM	AM	AM	AM	AM	AM	PM	PM	PM	PM	PM	PM	PM	PM	PM
Waterloo ....dep.	10 55	11 8	11 15	11 15	11 20	11 35	11 53	12 0	12 8	12 15	12 20	12 35	12 55	1 8	1 15	1 20	1 35
Vauxhall	10 58	—	—	11 18	—	11 38	11 58	—	—	12 18	—	12 38	12 58	—	1 18	—	1 38
Clapham Junction..	11 3	11 18	—	11 23	11 30	11 43	12 3	—	12 18	12 23	12 29	12 43	1 3	1 18	1 23	1 30	1 43
Earlsfield	11 7	—	—	11 27	—	11 47	12 7	—	—	12 27	—	12 47	1 7	—	1 27	—	1 47
Wimbledon	11 11	11 26	—	11 31	11 38	11 51	12 11	—	12 26	12 31	12 37	12 51	1 11	1 26	1 31	1 38	1 51
Raynes Park......	11 14	—	—	11 34	—	11 54	12 14	—	—	12 34	—	12 54	1 14	—	1 34	—	1 54
Malden	11 17	—	—	11 37	—	11 57	12 17	—	—	12 37	—	12 57	1 17	—	1 37	—	1 57
Surbiton	11 21	11 35	11 37	11 41	11 47	12 1	12 21	12 21	12 36	12 41	12 47	1 1	1 21	1 35	1 41	1 47	2 1

SUNDAYS	PM	PM	PM	PM	PM	PM	PM	PM	PM	PM	PM	PM	PM	PM	PM	PM
Waterloo ......dep.	1 50	1 55	2 8	2 15	2 35	2 55	3 8	3 15	3 20	3 35	3 55	4 15	4 20	4 35	4 55	5 8	5 15	5 20	5 35
Vauxhall	—	1 58	—	2 18	2 38	2 58	—	3 18	—	3 38	3 58	—	4 38	4 58	—	5 18	—	5 38
Clapham Junction..	—	2 3	2 18	2 23	2 43	3 3	3 18	3 23	3 30	3 43	4 3	4 23	4 43	5 3	5 17	5 23	—	5 43
Earlsfield	—	2 7	—	2 27	2 47	3 7	—	3 27	—	3 47	4 7	4 27	4 47	5 7	—	5 27	—	5 47
Wimbledon	—	2 11	2 26	2 31	2 51	3 11	3 26	3 31	3 38	3 51	4 11	4 31	4 51	5 11	5 25	5 31	—	5 51
Raynes Park......	—	2 14	—	2 34	2 54	3 14	—	3 34	—	3 54	4 14	4 34	4 54	5 14	—	5 34	—	5 54
Malden	—	2 17	—	2 37	2 57	3 17	—	3 37	—	3 57	4 17	4 37	4 57	5 17	—	5 37	—	5 57
Surbiton	2 10	2 21	2 36	2 41	3 1	3 21	3 35	3 41	3 48	4 1	4 21	4 41	4 41	5 1	5 21	5 35	5 41	5 40	6 1

SUNDAYS.	PM	PM	PM	PM	PM	PM	PM	PM	PM	PM	PM	PM	PM	PM	PM	PM
Waterloo ......dep.	5 55	6 8	6 15	6 20	6 35	6 55	7 8	7 15	7 20	7 35	7 55	8 8	8 15	8 20	8 35	8 55	9 8	9 15
Vauxhall	5 58	—	6 18	—	6 38	6 58	—	7 18	—	7 38	7 58	—	8 18	—	8 38	8 58	—	9 18
Clapham Junction..	6 3	6 18	6 23	—	6 43	7 3	7 17	7 23	—	7 43	8 3	8 18	—	8 23	8 30	8 43	9 3	9 18	9 23
Earlsfield	6 7	—	6 27	—	6 47	7 7	—	7 27	—	7 47	8 7	—	8 27	—	8 47	9 7	—	9 27
Wimbledon	6 11	6 26	6 31	—	6 51	7 11	7 25	7 31	—	7 51	8 11	8 26	—	8 31	8 38	8 51	9 11	9 26	9 31
Raynes Park......	6 14	—	6 34	—	6 54	7 14	—	7 34	—	7 54	8 14	—	8 34	—	8 54	9 14	—	9 34
Malden	6 17	—	6 37	—	6 57	7 17	—	7 37	—	7 57	8 17	—	8 37	—	8 57	9 17	—	9 37
Surbiton	6 21	6 36	6 41	6 51	7 1	7 21	7 35	7 41	7 40	8 1	8 21	8 36	8 36	8 41	8 48	9 1	9 21	9 35	9 41

SUNDAYS.	PM	PM	PM	PM	PM	PM	PM	PM	PM	PM	PM
Waterloo ....dep.	9 35	9 28	9 45	9 55	10 15	10 15	10 30	11 10	11 35
Vauxhall	9 38	—	—	9 58	10 18	—	10 38	11 13	11 38
Clapham Junction..	9 43	9 39	—	10 7	10 23	10 25	10 43	11 18	11 43
Earlsfield	9 47	—	—	10 7	10 27	—	10 47	11 22	11 47
Wimbledon	9 51	—	—	10 11	10 31	—	10 51	11 26	11 51
Raynes Park......	9 54	—	—	10 14	10 34	—	10 54	11 29	11 54
Malden	9 57	—	—	10 17	10 37	—	10 57	11 32	11 57
Surbiton	10 1	9 56	10 6	10 21	10 41	10 40	11 1	11 36	12 1

SUNDAYS.	AM	AM	AM	AM	AM	AM	AM	AM	AM	AM	AM	AM	AM	AM	AM
Surbiton ......dep.	3 34	7 2	7 42	8 22	8 42	9 2	9 18	9 22	9 42	10 2	10 22	10 26	10 29	10 42	10 55	11 2	11 22	11 23
Malden	—	7 6	7 46	8 26	8 46	9 6	—	9 26	9 46	10 6	10 26	—	10 46	—	11 6	11 26	—
Raynes Park	—	7 9	7 49	8 29	8 49	9 9	—	9 29	9 49	10 9	10 29	—	10 49	—	11 9	11 29	—
Wimbledon	—	7 12	7 52	8 32	8 52	9 12	—	9 32	9 52	10 12	10 32	10 39	10 52	—	11 12	11 32	11 38
Earlsfield	—	7 16	7 56	8 36	8 56	9 16	—	9 36	9 56	10 16	10 36	—	10 56	—	11 16	11 36	—
Clapham Junction..	—	7 20	8 0	8 40	9 0	9 20	9 29	9 40	10 0	10 20	10 40	10 47	11 0	—	11 20	11 40	11 46
Vauxhall	—	7 25	8 5	8 45	9 5	9 25	9 38	9 45	10 5	10 25	10 45	—	11 5	—	11 25	11 45	—
Waterloo	3 55	7 29	8 9	8 49	9 9	9 29	9 45	9 49	10 9	10 29	10 49	10 55	11 9	11 16	11 29	11 49	11 55

d Saturdays only. e Saturdays excepted. f Mondays only. g Mondays excepted. h Wednesday nights only.

SUNDAYS	AM	AM	PM	PM	PM	PM	PM	PM	PM	PM	PM	PM	PM	PM	PM	PM	PM	PM
Surbiton ......dep.	11 42	11 50	12 2	12 14	12 22	12 27	12 28	12 42	1 2	1 14	1 22	1 28	1 42	2 2	2 17	2 22
Malden	11 46	—	12 6	—	12 26	—	—	12 46	1 6	—	1 26	—	1 46	2 6	—	2 26
Raynes Park........	11 49	—	12 9	—	12 29	—	12 33	12 49	1 9	—	1 29	—	1 49	2 9	—	2 29
Wimbledon	11 52	—	12 12	12 24	12 32	—	—	12 52	1 12	1 24	1 32	1 38	1 52	2 12	2 27	2 32
Earlsfield	11 56	—	12 16	—	12 36	—	—	12 56	1 16	—	1 36	—	1 56	2 16	—	2 36
Clapham Junction..	12 0	—	12 20	12 32	12 40	12 43	12 45	1 0	1 20	1 32	1 40	1 46	2 0	2 20	2 35	2 40
Vauxhall	12 5	—	12 25	—	12 45	—	—	1 5	1 25	—	1 45	—	2 5	2 25	—	2 45
WATERLOO..........	12 9	12 11	12 29	12 41	12 49	12 52	12 55	1 9	1 29	1 41	1 49	1 55	2 9	2 29	2 44	2 49

SUNDAYS.	PM	PM	PM	PM	PM	PM	PM	PM	PM	PM	PM	PM	PM	PM	PM	PM	PM	PM	PM	PM
Surbiton ......dep.	2 28	2 42	2 51	3 2	3 15	3 22	3 42	4 2	4 22	4 28	4 42	5 2	5 14	5 22	5 42	5 56	6 2	6 19	6 22
Malden	—	2 46	—	3 6	—	3 26	3 46	4 6	4 26	—	4 46	5 6	—	5 26	5 46	—	6 6	—	6 26
Raynes Park	—	2 49	—	3 9	—	3 29	3 49	4 9	4 29	—	4 49	5 9	—	5 29	5 49	—	6 9	—	6 29
Wimbledon	2 38	2 52	—	3 12	3 27	3 32	3 52	4 12	4 32	4 38	4 52	5 12	5 24	5 32	5 52	—	6 12	6 29	6 32
Earlsfield	—	2 56	—	3 16	—	3 36	3 56	4 16	4 36	—	4 56	5 16	—	5 36	5 56	—	6 16	—	6 36
Clapham Junction..	2 46	3 0	—	3 20	3 35	3 40	4 0	4 20	4 40	4 46	5 0	5 20	5 32	5 40	6 0	—	6 20	6 37	6 40
Vauxhall	—	3 5	—	3 25	—	3 45	4 5	4 25	4 45	—	5 5	5 25	—	5 45	6 5	—	6 25	—	6 45
WATERLOO..........	2 55	3 9	3 13	3 29	3 44	3 49	4 9	4 29	4 49	4 55	5 9	5 29	5 41	5 49	6 9	6 17	6 29	6 46	6 49

SUNDAYS.	PM	PM	PM	PM	PM	PM	PM	PM	PM	PM	PM	PM	PM	PM	PM	PM	PM	PM
Surbiton ......dep.	6 28	6 42	7 2	7 14	7 22	7 23	7 42	7 42	8 2	8 14	8 22	8 25	8 38	8 42	8 51	9 2	9 16	9 22
Malden	—	6 46	7 6	—	7 26	—	7 46	8 6	—	8 26	—	—	8 46	—	9 6	—	9 26
Raynes Park	—	6 49	7 9	—	7 29	—	7 49	8 9	—	8 29	—	—	8 49	—	9 9	—	9 29
Wimbledon	6 38	6 52	7 12	7 24	7 32	7 38	—	7 52	8 12	8 24	8 32	8 35	8 48	8 52	—	9 12	9 27	9 32
Earlsfield	—	6 56	7 16	—	7 36	—	—	7 56	8 16	—	8 36	—	—	8 56	—	9 16	—	9 36
Clapham Junction..	6 46	7 0	7 20	7 32	7 40	7 46	—	8 0	8 20	8 32	8 40	8 43	8 56	9 0	—	9 20	9 35	9 40
Vauxhall	—	7 5	7 25	—	7 45	—	—	8 5	8 25	—	8 45	—	—	9 5	—	9 25	—	9 45
WATERLOO..........	6 55	7 9	7 29	7 41	7 49	7 55	8 3	8 9	8 29	8 41	8 49	8 52	9 5	9 9	9 12	9 29	9 44	9 49

SUNDAYS.	PM	PM	PM	PM	PM	PM	PM	PM	PM	PM	PM
Surbiton ......dep.	9 28	9 37	9 42	10 2	10 11	10 20	10 27	10 28	10 37	11 2	11 14
Malden	—	—	9 46	10 6	10 17	—	—	—	10 41	11 6	—
Raynes Park	—	—	9 49	10 9	—	—	—	—	10 44	11 9	—
Wimbledon	9 38	9 47	9 52	10 12	10 24	10 30	—	10 37	10 38	10 47	11 12	11 24
Earlsfield	—	—	9 56	10 16	—	—	—	—	10 51	11 16	—
Clapham Junction..	9 43	—	10 0	10 20	10 32	10 38	—	10 46	10 55	11 20	11 32
Vauxhall	—	—	10 5	10 25	—	—	—	—	11 0	11 25	11 37
WATERLOO..........	9 55	10 1	10 9	10 29	10 41	10 47	10 52	10 56	11 4	11 29	11 43

WATERLOO TO THAMES DITTON AND HAMPTON COURT.

WEEK DAYS.	AM	AM	AM	AM	AM	AM	AM	AM	AM	AM	AM	AM	AM	AM	AM	AM	AM	AM	AM
WATERLOO ......dep.	4 50	5 30	6 20	6 50	7 5	7 20	7 35	7 50	8 5	8 20	8 35	8 50	9 5	9 20	9 35	9 50	10 5
Thames Ditton......	5 51	6 21	6 51	7 21	7 36	7 51	8 6	8 21	8 36	8 51	9 6	9 21	9 36	9 51	10 6	10 21	10 36
HAMPTON COURT ...	5 54	6 24	6 54	7 24	7 39	7 54	8 9	8 24	8 39	8 54	9 9	9 24	9 39	9 54	10 9	10 24	10 39

WEEK DAYS.	AM	AM	AM	AM	AM	AM	AM	AM	AM	PM	PM	PM	PM	PM	PM	PM	PM
WATERLOO ......dep.	10 20	10 35	10 50	11 5	11 20	11 35	11 50	12 5	12 20	12 35	12 50	1 5	1 20	1 35
Thames Ditton......	10 51	11 6	11 21	11 36	11 51	12 6	12 21	12 36	12 51	1 6	1 21	1 36	1 51	2 6
HAMPTON COURT ...	10 54	11 9	11 24	11 39	11 54	12 9	12 24	12 39	12 54	1 9	1 24	1 39	1 54	2 9

WEEK DAYS.	PM	PM	PM	PM	PM	PM	PM	PM	PM	PM	PM	PM	PM	PM	PM	PM	PM
WATERLOO ......dep.	1 50	2 5	2 20	2 35	2 50	3 5	3 20	3 35	3 50	4 5	4 20	4 35	4 50	5 5	5 20	5 35
Thames Ditton	2 21	2 36	2 51	3 6	3 21	3 36	3 51	4 6	4 21	4 36	4 51	5 6	5 21	5 36	5 51	6 6
HAMPTON COURT	2 24	2 39	2 54	3 9	3 24	3 39	3 54	4 9	4 24	4 39	4 54	5 9	5 24	5 39	5 54	6 9

WEEK DAYS.	PM	PM	PM	PM	PM	PM	PM	PM	PM	PM	PM	PM	PM	PM
WATERLOO ......dep.	5 50	6 5	6 20	6 35	6 50	7 5	7 20	7 35	7 50	8 5	8 20	8 35	8 50	9 5	9 20
Thames Ditton......	6 21	6 36	6 51	7 6	7 21	7 36	7 51	8 6	8 21	8 36	8 51	9 6	9 21	9 36	9 51
HAMPTON COURT	6 24	6 39	6 54	7 9	7 24	7 39	7 54	8 9	8 24	8 39	8 54	9 9	9 24	9 39	9 54

WEEK DAYS.	PM	PM	PM	PM	PM	PM	PM	PM
WATERLOO ......dep.	9 35	9 50	10 5	10 20	10 50	11 20	12 5
Thames Ditton......	10 6	10 21	10 36	10 51	11 21	11 51	12 36
HAMPTON COURT	10 9	10 24	10 39	10 54	11 24	11 54	12 39

SUNDAYS.	AM	AM	AM	AM	AM	AM	AM	AM	AM	AM	AM	AM	AM	AM	PM
WATERLOO ......dep.	7 35	8 15	8 55	9 15	9 35	9 55	10 15	10 35	10 55	11 15	11 35	11 55	12 15	12 35
Thames Ditton....	8 5	8 45	9 25	9 45	10 5	10 25	10 45	11 5	11 25	11 45	12 5	12 25	12 45	1 5
HAMPTON COURT	8 8	8 48	9 28	9 48	10 8	10 28	10 48	11 8	11 28	11 48	12 8	12 28	12 48	1 8

SUNDAYS.	PM	PM	PM	PM	PM	PM	PM	PM	PM	PM	PM	PM	PM	PM	PM	PM	PM	PM
WATERLOO ......dep.	12 55	1 15	1 35	1 55	2 15	2 35	2 55	3 15	3 35	3 55	4 15	4 35	4 55	5 15	5 35	5 56	6 15
Thames Ditton	1 25	1 45	2 5	2 25	2 45	3 5	3 25	3 45	4 5	4 25	4 45	5 5	5 25	5 45	6 5	6 25	6 45
HAMPTON COURT	1 28	1 48	2 8	2 28	2 48	3 8	3 28	3 48	4 8	4 28	4 48	5 8	5 28	5 48	6 8	6 28	6 48

SUNDAYS.	PM	PM	PM	PM	PM	PM	PM	PM	PM	PM	PM	PM	PM	PM	PM	PM
WATERLOO ......dep.	6 35	6 55	7 15	7 35	7 55	8 15	8 35	8 55	9 15	9 35	9 55	10 15	10 35	11 10	11 35
Thames Ditton......	7 5	7 25	7 45	8 5	8 25	8 45	9 5	9 25	9 45	10 5	10 25	10 45	11 5	11 40	12 5
HAMPTON COURT	7 8	7 28	7 48	8 8	8 28	8 48	9 8	9 28	9 48	10 8	10 28	10 48	11 8	11 43	12 8

WEEK DAYS.	AM	AM	AM	AM	AM	AM	AM	AM	AM	AM	AM	AM	AM	AM	AM
Hampton Court, dep.	5 39	6 9	6 24	6 39	6 54	7 9	7 24	7 39	7 54	8 9	8 24	8 39	8 56	9 9	9 24
Thames Ditton	5 42	6 12	6 27	6 42	6 57	7 12	7 27	7 42	7 57	8 12	8 27	8 42	8 59	9 11	9 27
Waterloo	6 13	6 43	6 58	7 13	7 23	7 43	7 58	8 13	8 28	8 43	8 58	9 13	9 28	9 42	9 58

WEEK DAYS.	AM	AM	AM	AM	AM	AM	AM	AM	AM	AM	AM	PM	PM	PM	PM
Hampton Court, dep.	9 39	9 54	10 9	10 24	10 41	10 54	11 9	11 24	11 39	11 54	12 9	12 24	12 39
Thames Ditton	9 42	9 57	10 12	10 27	10 44	10 57	11 12	11 27	11 42	11 57	12 12	12 27	12 42
Waterloo	10 13	10 28	10 43	10 58	11 15	11 28	11 43	11 53	12 13	12 28	12 43	12 58	1 13

WEEK DAYS.	PM	PM	PM	PM	PM	PM	PM	PM	PM	PM	PM	PM	PM	PM	PM
Hampton Court, dep.	12 54	1 9	1 24	1 39	1 54	2 9	2 24	2 39	2 54	3 9	3 24	3 39	3 54	4 9	4 24
Thames Ditton	12 57	1 12	1 27	1 42	1 57	2 12	2 27	2 42	2 57	3 12	3 27	3 42	3 57	4 12	4 27
Waterloo	1 28	1 43	1 58	2 13	2 28	2 43	2 58	3 13	3 28	3 43	3 58	4 13	4 28	4 43	4 58

WEEK DAYS.	PM	PM	PM	PM	PM	PM	PM	PM	PM	PM	PM	PM	PM	PM
Hampton Court, dep.	4 39	4 54	5 9	5 24	5 39	5 54	6 9	6 24	6 39	6 54	7 9	7 24	7 39	7 54
Thames Ditton	4 42	4 57	5 12	5 27	5 42	5 57	6 12	6 27	6 42	6 57	7 12	7 27	7 42	7 57
Waterloo	5 13	5 28	5 43	5 58	6 13	6 28	6 43	6 33	7 13	7 28	7 43	7 58	8 13	8 28

WEEK DAYS.	PM	PM	PM	PM	PM	PM	PM	PM	PM	PM	d
Hampton Court, dep.	8 9	8 24	8 39	8 54	9 9	9 24	9 39	10 9	10 39	11 9	11 30
Thames Ditton	8 12	8 27	8 42	8 57	9 12	9 27	9 42	10 12	10 42	11 12	11 33
Waterloo	8 43	8 58	9 13	9 28	9 43	9 58	10 13	10 43	11 13	11 43	12 4

SUNDAYS.	AM	AM	AM	AM	AM	AM	AM	AM	AM	AM	AM	AM	AM	AM	AM
Hampton Court, dep.	6 55	7 35	8 15	8 35	8 55	9 15	9 35	9 55	10 15	10 35	10 55	11 15	11 35	11 55	12 15
Thames Ditton	6 58	7 38	8 18	8 38	8 58	9 18	9 38	9 58	10 18	10 38	10 58	11 18	11 38	11 58	12 18
Waterloo	7 29	3 9	8 49	9 9	9 29	9 49	10 9	10 29	10 49	11 9	11 29	11 49	12 9	12 29	12 49

SUNDAYS.	PM	PM	PM	PM	PM	PM	PM	PM	PM	PM	PM	PM	PM	PM	PM
Hampton Court, dep.	12 25	12 55	1 15	1 35	1 55	2 15	2 35	2 55	3 15	3 35	3 55	4 15	4 35	4 55	5 15 5 35
Thames Ditton	12 58	12 58	1 18	1 38	1 58	2 18	2 38	2 58	3 18	3 38	3 58	4 18	4 38	4 58	5 18 5 38
Waterloo	1 5	1 29	1 49	2 9	2 29	2 49	3 9	3 29	3 49	4 9	4 29	4 49	5 9	5 29	5 49 6 9

SUNDAYS.	PM	PM	PM	PM	PM	PM	PM	PM	PM	PM	PM	PM	PM	PM	PM
Hampton Court, dep.	5 55	6 15	6 35	6 55	7 15	7 35	7 55	8 15	8 35	8 55	9 15	9 35	9 55	10 30	10 55
Thames Ditton	5 58	6 18	6 38	6 58	7 18	7 38	7 58	8 18	8 38	8 58	9 18	9 38	9 58	10 33	10 58
Waterloo	6 29	6 49	7 9	7 29	7 49	8 9	8 29	8 49	9 9	9 29	9 49	10 9	10 29	11 4	11 29

WATERLOO TO SOUTHFIELDS AND WIMBLEDON.

WEEK DAYS.	AM	AM	AM	AM	AM	AM	AM	AM	d	e	d	d	e
Waterloo dep.	7 33	8 3	8 33	9 3	9 33	10 3	11 3	12 3	12 33	1 3	1 3	1 33	2 3
Vauxhall	7 36	8 6	8 36	9 6	9 36	10 6	11 6	12 6	—	1 6	—	—	2 6
Queen's Road	7 39	8 9	8 39	9 9	9 39	10 9	11 9	12 9	—	1 9	—	—	2 9
Clapham Junction..	7 42	8 12	8 42	9 12	9 42	10 12	11 12	12 12	—	1 12	—	—	2 12
Wandsworth	7 45	8 15	8 45	9 15	9 45	10 15	11 15	12 15	12 41	1 15	1 11	1 41	2 15
East Putney	7 48	8 18	8 48	9 18	9 48	10 18	11 18	12 18	12 44	1 18	1 15	1 44	2 18
Southfields	7 51	8 21	8 51	9 21	9 51	10 21	11 21	12 21	12 47	1 21	1 18	1 47	2 21
Wimbledon Park..	7 54	8 24	8 54	9 24	9 54	10 24	11 24	12 24	12 50	1 24	1 21	1 50	2 24
Wimbledon	7 56	8 26	8 56	9 26	—	10 26	11 26	12 26	12 52	1 26	1 23	1 52	2 26

WEEK DAYS.	d	d	PM	PM	e	d	PM	e	PM	PM	PM
Waterloo dep.	2 3	2 33	3 3	4 3	4 33	5 3	5 3	5 33	6 3	6 3	6 33
Vauxhall	—	2 36	3 6	4 6	—	5 6	—	—	6 6	—	—
Queen's Road	—	2 39	3 9	4 9	—	5 9	—	—	6 9	—	—
Clapham Junction..	—	2 42	3 12	4 12	—	5 12	—	—	6 12	—	—
Wandsworth	2 11	2 45	3 15	4 15	4 41	5 15	5 41	6 15	6 15	6 41	7 15
East Putney	2 14	2 48	3 18	4 18	4 44	5 18	5 44	6 18	6 18	6 44	7 18
Southfields	2 17	2 51	3 21	4 21	4 47	5 21	5 47	6 21	6 21	6 47	7 21
Wimbledon Park	2 20	2 54	3 24	4 24	4 50	5 24	5 50	6 24	6 24	6 50	7 24
Wimbledon	2 22	2 56	3 26	4 26	4 52	5 26	5 52	6 26	6 26	6 52	—

WEEK DAYS.	PM	PM
Waterloo dep.	10 3	11 3
Vauxhall	10 6	11 6
Queen's Road	10 9	11 9
Clapham Junction..	10 12	11 12
Wandsworth	10 15	11 15
East Putney	10 18	11 18
Southfields	10 21	11 21
Wimbledon Park ..	10 24	11 24
Wimbledon		

WEEK DAYS.	AM	AM	AM	AM	AM	AM	AM	AM	AM	PM	PM	PM	PM
Wimbledon dep.	—	7/20	8 5	8 35	9 5	9 35	10 33	11 31	—	12 31	1 3	1 33	2 3
Wimbledon Park ..	6 42	7 23	8 7	8 37	9 7	9 37	10 35	11 33	12 3	12 33	1 5	1 35	2 5
Southfields	6 45	7 26	8 10	8 40	9 10	9 40	10 38	11 36	12 6	12 36	1 8	1 38	2 8
East Putney	6 48	7 29	8 13	8 43	9 13	9 43	10 41	11 39	12 9	12 39	1 11	1 41	2 11
Wandsworth	6 51	7 32	8 16	8 46	9 16	9 46	10 44	11 42	12 12	12 42	1 14	1 44	2 14
Clapham Junction..	6 54	7 35	—	—	—	—	10 47	11 45	12 15	12 45	1 17	1 47	2 17
Queen's Road	6 57	7 38	—	—	—	—	10 50	11 48	12 18	12 48	—	—	—
Vauxhall	7 0	7 41	—	—	—	—	10 53	11 51	12 21	12 51	—	—	—
Waterloo	7 4	7 45	8 25	8 55	9 25	9 55	10 57	11 55	12 25	12 55	1 25	1 55	2 25

WEEK DAYS.	e	e	PM	PM	e	PM	PM	PM
Wimbledon	4 33	5 3	5 33	6 3	6 33			
Wimbledon Park	4 5	4 35	5 5	5 35	6 6	6 38	7 35	8 33
Southfields	4 8	4 33	5 8	5 38	6 8	6 38	7 39	8 36
East Putney	4 11	4 41	5 11	5 41	6 11	6 41	7 41	8 39
Wandsworth	4 14	4 44	5 14	5 44	6 14	6 44	7 44	8 42
Clapham Junction..	4 17	4 47	5 17	5 47	6 17	6 47	7 47	8 45
Queen's Road	4 20	—						8 48
Vauxhall	4 23	—						8 51
Waterloo	4 27	4 55	5 25	5 55	6 25	6 55	7 55	8 55

d Saturdays only.   e Saturdays excepted.   f Mondays only.

WALKING TOURS
in
LOVELY WEST HERTS

Cheap Walking Tour Tickets are issued on weekdays, available by any ordinary train in either direction, on day of issue only, as under :—

FROM

Euston, Broad Street, Dalston, Camden Town, Kensington (Addison Road), Willesden,

TO			RETURNING FROM			FARES FROM EUSTON 3rd Class
Kenton	...	...	Stanmore	...	...	**1/6**
Stanmore	...	...	Bushey	...	...	**1/10**
Watford	...	...	Bricket Wood		...	**2/5**
Watford	...	...	St. Albans	...	...	**2/6**
Watford	...	...	Boxmoor	...	...	**3/-**
Watford	...	...	Croxley Green		...	**2/3**
Boxmoor	...	...	Berkhamsted		...	**3/5**
King's Langley	...		Croxley Green		...	**2/5**
King's Langley	...		Rickmansworth		...	**2/5**

The tickets are available for use in the reverse direction if desired.

SUNDAY EXCURSIONS.

Cheap Tickets are also issued every Sunday from Euston, Broad Street, etc., to Watford, King's Langley, Boxmoor, Berkhamsted, and Tring, and are available by any ordinary train after 10 a.m., returning by any ordinary train on day of issue only.

Further particulars may be obtained from the Stations, Town Offices, and Ticket Agencies of the Company.

ARTHUR WATSON, *General Manager.*

LONDON & NORTH EASTERN RAILWAY·

THROUGH RESTAURANT CAR EXPRESSES
COMMENCING 9th JULY

BETWEEN LONDON (KING'S CROSS)
AND
YORKSHIRE COAST

	WEEK-DAYS.	
	A.M.	P.M.
LONDON (King's Cross) dep.	11.50	1.50
	P.M.	
BRIDLINGTON ... arr.	6. 2	7. 9
SCARBOROUGH ... ,,	4.20	7.19
WHITBY ... ... ,,	6.59	8.20
	A.M.	P.M.
WHITBY ... ... dep.	10.40	1.25
SCARBOROUGH ... ,,	11.30	3. 0
BRIDLINGTON ... ,,	11.50	1.45so
LONDON (King's Cross) arr.	4.45	7.30

S.O. Saturdays only.

HARROGATE

	WEEK-DAYS.				
	A.M.	A.M.	A.M.	P.M.	P.M.
LONDON (King's Cross) dep.	7.15	10.10	11P15	1.40	5.45
	NOON.				
HARROGATE ... arr.	12. 5	2.43	3.15	6.10	10.20
	A.M.	A.M.	P.M.	P.M.	P.M.
HARROGATE ... dep.	9.35	11P15	12.30	2.30	4.45
LONDON (King's Cross) arr.	1.55	3.15	5. 0	7.10	9.25

P "Pullman" Car Express 1st & 3rd Class.

YORKSHIRE TOWNS

	WEEK-DAYS.						SUNDAYS	
	A.M.	A.M.	A.M.	P.M.	P.M.	P.M.	A.M.	P.M.
LONDON (King's Cross) dep.	7.15	10.10	11P15	1.30	4. 0	5.45	12. 0	5. 0
WAKEFIELD (Westgate) arr.	10.56	1.35	—	4.51	7.43	9.14	4. 5	9. 8
LEEDS (Central) ... ,,	11.20	1.56	2 40	5.12	8. 5	9.35	4.30	9.32
BRADFORD (Exchange) ,,	11.45	2.12	3. 9	5.26	8.25	9.55	4.52	9.50

	WEEK-DAYS.					SUNDAYS.	
	A.M.	A.M.	A.M.	P.M.	P.M.	A.M.	P.M.
BRADFORD (Exchange) dep.	7.25	9.50	11P10	3. 0	5.10	10.35	5.20
LEEDS (Central) .. ,,	7.50	10.15	11.50	3.15	5.30	11. 0	5.40
WAKEFIELD (Westgate) ,,	8.11	10.36	—	3.37	5.53	11.25	6. 5
LONDON (King's Cross) arr.	11.30	1.55	3.15	7.10	9.25	3.45	10.20

P "Pullman" Car Express 1st & 3rd Class.
For Full Service see respective pages within.